Department of Economic and Social Affairs
Département des affaires économiques et sociales

2002

Demographic Yearbook
Annuaire démographique

Fifty-fourth issue/Cinquante-quatrième édition

United Nations/Nations Unies
New York, 2005

The Department of Economic and Social Affairs of the United Nations Secretariat is a vital interface between global policies in the economic, social and environmental spheres and national action. The Department works in three main interlinked areas: (i) it compiles, generates and analyses a wide range of economic, social and environmental data and information on which States Members of the United Nations draw to review common problems and to take stock of policy options; (ii) it facilitates the negotiations of Member States in many intergovernmental bodies on joint courses of action to address ongoing or emerging global challenges; and (iii) it advises interested Governments on the ways and means of translating policy frameworks developed in United Nations conferences and summits into programmes at the country level and, through technical assistance, helps build national capacities.

Le Département des affaires économiques et sociales du Secrétariat de l'Organisation des Nations Unies sert de relais entre les orientations arrêtées au niveau international dans les domaines économiques, sociaux et environnementaux et les politiques exécutées à l'échelon national. Il intervient dans trois grands domaines liés les uns aux autres : i) il compile, produit et analyse une vaste gamme de données et d'éléments d'information sur des questions économiques, sociales et environnementales dont les Etats Membres de l'Organisation se servent pour examiner des problèmes communs et évaluer les options qui s'offrent à eux; ii) il facilite les négociations entre les Etats Membres dans de nombreux organes intergouvernementaux sur les orientations à suivre de façon collective afin de faire face aux problèmes mondiaux existants ou en voie d'apparition; iii) il conseille les gouvernements intéressés sur la façon de transposer les orientations politiques arrêtées à l'occasion des conférences et sommets des Nations Unies en programmes exécutables au niveau national et aide à renforcer les capacités nationales au moyen de programmes d'assistance technique.

NOTE

Symbols of United Nations documents are composed of capital letters combined with figures. Mention of such a symbol indicates a reference to a United Nations document.

The designations used in this publication have been provided by the competent authorities. Those designations and the presentation of material in this publication do not imply the expression of any opinion whatsoever on the part of the Secretariat of the United Nations concerning the legal status of any country, territory, city or area or of its authorities, or concerning the delimitation of its frontiers or boundaries.

Where the designation "country or area" appears in the headings of tables, it covers countries, territories, cities or areas.

NOTE

Les cotes des documents de l'Organisation des Nations Unies se composent de lettres majuscules et de chiffres. La simple mention d'une cote dans un texte signifie qu'il s'agit d'un document de l'Organisation.

Les appellations employées dans cette publication ont été fournies par les autorités compétentes. Ces appellations et la présentation des données qui figurent dans cette publication n'impliquent, de la part du Secrétariat de l'Organisation des Nations Unies, aucune prise de position quant au statut juridique des pays, territoires, villes ou zones, ou de leurs autorités, ni quant au tracé de leurs frontières ou limites.

L'appellation « pays ou zone » figurant dans les titres des rubriques des tableaux désigne des pays, des territoires, des villes ou des zones.

ST/ESA/STAT/SER.R/33

UNITED NATIONS PUBLICATION
Sales No. E/F.05.XIII.1

PUBLICATION DES NATIONS UNIES
Numéro de vente : E/F.05.XIII.1

ISBN 92-1-051096-8

Topics of the Demographic Yearbook series: 1948 - 2002

Sujets des diverses éditions de l'Annuaire démographique: 1948 - 2002

Year Année	Sales No. - Numéro de vente	Issue - Edition	Special topic - Sujet spécial
1948	49.XIII.1	First-Première	General demography-Démographie générale
1949-50	51.XIII.1	Second-Deuxième	Natality statistics-Statistiques de la natalité
1951	52.XIII.1	Third-Trosième	Mortality statistics-Statistiques de la mortalité
1952	53.XIII.1	Fourth-Quatrième	Population distribution-Répartition de la population
1953	54.XIII.1	Fifth-Cinquième	General demography-Démographie générale
1954	55.XIII.1	Sixth-Sixième	Natality statistics -Statistiques de la natalité
1955	56.XIII.1	Seventh-Septième	Population censuses-Recensement de population
1956	57.XIII.1	Eighth-Huitième	Ethnic and economic characteristics of population-Caractéristiques ethniques et économiques de la population
1957	58.XIII.1	Ninth-Neuvième	Mortality statistics- Statistiques de la mortalité
1958	59.XIII.1	Tenth-Dixième	Marriage and divorce statistics- Statistiques de la nuptialité et de la divortialitè
1959	60.XIII.1	Eleventh-Onzième	Natality statistics- Statistiques de la natalité
1960	61.XIII.1	Twelfth-Douzième	Population trends- l' évolution de la population
1961	62.XIII.1	Thirteenth-Treizième	Mortality Statistics- Statistiques de la mortalité
1962	63.XIII.1	Fourteenth-Quatorzième	Population census statistics I - Statistiques des recensements de population I
1963	64.XIII.1	Fifteenth-Quinzième	Population census statistics II- Statistiques des recensements de population II
1964	65.XIII.1	Sixteenth-Seizième	Population census statistics III- Statistiques des recensements de population III
1965	66.XIII.1	Seventeenth-Dix-septième	Natality statistics- Statistiques de la natalité
1966	67.XIII.1	Eighteenth-Dix-huitième	Mortality statistics I- Statistiques de la mortalité I
1967	E/F.68.XIII.1	Nineteenth-Dix-neuvième	Mortality statistics II - Statistiques de la mortalité II
1968	E/F.69.XIII.1	Twentieth-Vingtième	Marriage and divorce statistics-Statistiques de la nuptialité et de la divortialité
1969	E/F.70.XIII.1	Twenty-first-Vingt et unième	Natality statistics-Statistiques de la natalité
1970	E/F.71.XIII.1	Twenty-second-Vingt-deuxième	Population trends-l' évolution de la population
1971	E/F.72.XIII.1	Twenty-third-Vingh-troisième	Population census statistics I- Statistiques de recensements de population I
1972	E/F.73.XIII.1	Twenty-fourth-Vingt-quatrième	Population census statistics II- Statistiques des recensements de population II
1973	E/F.74.XIII.1	Twenty-fifth-Vingt-cinquième	Population census statistics III- Statistiques des recensements de population III
1974	E/F.75.XIII.1	Twenty-sixth-Vingt-sixième	Mortality statistics - Statistiques de la mortalité
1975	E/F.76.XIII.1	Twenty-seventh-Vingt-septième	Natality statistics- Statistiques de la natalité
1976	E/F.77.XIII.1	Twenty-eighth-Vingt-huitième	Marriage and divorce statistics- Statistiques de la nuptialité et de la divortialité
1977	E/F.78.XIII.1	Twenty-ninth-Vingt-neuvième	International Migration Statistics- internationales
1978	E/F.79.XIII.1	Thirtieth-Trentième	General tables- Tableaux de caractère général
1978	E/F.79.XIII.8	Special issue-Edition spéciale	Historical supplement-Supplément rétrospectif
1979	E/F.80.XIII.1	Thirty-first-Trente et unième	Population census statistics-Statistiques des recensements de population

Topics of the Demographic Yearbook series: 1948 - 2002

Sujets des diverses éditions de l'Annuaire démographique: 1948 - 2002

Year Année	Sales No. - Numéro de vente	Issue - Edition	Special topic - Sujet spécial
1980	E/F.81.XIII.1	Thirty-second- Trente-deuxième	Mortality statistics- Statistiques de la mortalité
1981	E/F.82.XIII.1	Thirty-third- Trente-troisième	Natality statistics- Statistiques de la natalité
1982	E/F.83.XIII.1	Thirty-fourth- Trente-quatrième	Marriage and divorce statistics- Statistiques de la nuptialité et de la divortialité
1983	E/F.84.XIII.1	Thirty fifth- Trente-cinquième	Population census statistics I- Statistiques des recensements de population I
1984	E/F.85.XIII.1	Thirty-sixth- Trente-sixième	Population census statistics II- Statistiques des recensements de population II
1985	E/F.86.XIII.1	Thirty-seventh- Trente-septième	Mortality statistics- Statistiques de la mortalité
1986	E/F.87.XIII.1	Thirty-eightth- Trente-Hiutième	Natality statistics- Statistiques de la natalité
1987	E/F.88.XIII.1	Thirty-ninth- Trente-neuvième	Household composition- Les éléments du ménage
1988	E/F.89.XIII.1	Fortieth- Quarantième	Population census statistics- Statistiques des recensements de population
1989	E/F.90.XIII.1	Forty-first- Quarante-et-unième	International Migration Statistics- Statistiques des migration internationales
1990	E/F.91.XIII.1	Forty-second- Quarante-deuxième	Marriage and divorce statistics- Statistiques de la nuptialité et de la divortialité
1991	E/F.92.XIII.1	Forty-third- Quarante-troisième	General tables- Tableaux de caractère général
1991	E/F.92.XIII.8	Special issue- Edition spéciale	Population ageing and the situation of elderly persons- Vieillissement de la population et situation des personnes agées
1992	E/F.94.XIII.1	Forty-forth- Quarante-quatrième	Fertility and mortality statistics- Statistiques de la fecondité et de la mortalité
1993	E/F.95.XIII.1	Forty-fifth- Quarante-cinquième	Population census statistics I- Statistiques des recensements de population I
1994	E/F.96.XIII.1	Forty-sixth- Quarante-sixième	Population census statistics II- Statistiques des recensements de population II
1995	E/F.97.XIII.1	Forty-seventh- Quarante-septième	Household composition-Les éléments du ménage
1996	E/F.98.XIII.1	Forty-eighth- Quarante-hutième	Mortality statistics- Statistiques de la mortalité
1997	E/F.99.XIII.1	Forty-ninth- Quarante-neuvième	General tables- Tableaux de caractère général
1997	E/F.99.XIII.12	Special issue- Edition spéciale (CD)	Historical supplement- Supplément rétrospectif
1998	E/F.00.XIII.1	Fiftieth- Cinquantième	General tables- Tableaux de caractère général
1999	E/F.01.XIII.1	Fifty-first- Cinquante-et-unième	General tables- Tableaux de caractère général
1999	E/F.02.XIII.6	Special issue- Edition spéciale (CD)	Natality Statistics- Statistiques de la natalité
2000	E/F.02.XIII.1	Fifty-second- Cinquante-deuxième	General tables- Tableaux de caractère général
2001	E/F.03.XIII.1	Fifty-third- Cinquante- troisième	General tables- Tableaux de caractère général
2002	E/F.05.XIII.1	Fifty-fourth- Cinquante-quatrième	General tables- Tableaux de caractère général

CONTENTS - TABLE DES MATIERES

EXPLANATIONS OF SYMBOLS

Category not applicable	..
Data not available..	...
Magnitude zero	-
Magnitude not zero, but less than half of unit employed	0 and/or 0.0
Provisional	*
Data tabulated by year of registration rather than occurrence	+
Based on less than specified minimum	◆
Relatively reliable data	Roman type
Data of lesser reliability	*Italics*

EXPLICATION DES SIGNES

Sans objet	..
Données non disponibles	...
Néant	-
Chiffre inférieur à la moitié de l'unité employée	0 et/ou 0.0
Données provisoires	*
Donnée exploitées selon l'année de l'enregistrement et non l'année de l'événement	+
Rapport fondé sur un nombre inférieur à celui spécifié	◆
Données relativement sûres...	Charactères romains
Données dont l'exactitude est moindre	*Italiques*

INTRODUCTION

The *Demographic Yearbook* is an international collection of national demographic statistics, provided by national statistical authorities to the Statistics Division of the United Nations Department of Economic and Social Affairs. The *Yearbook* is part of the set of coordinated and interrelated publications issued by the United Nations and its specialized agencies,[1] designed to supply basic statistical data for such users as demographers, economists, public-health workers and sociologists.. Through the co-operation of national statistical services, official demographic statistics are compiled in the *Yearbook*, as available, for over 230 countries or areas throughout the world.

The *Demographic Yearbook 2002* is the fifty-fourth in a series published by the United Nations since 1948. It contains general tables including a world summary of selected demographic statistics, statistics on the size, distribution and trends in national populations, natality, foetal mortality, infant and maternal mortality, general mortality, nuptiality and divorce. Data are shown by urban/rural residence, as available. In addition, the volume provides Technical Notes, a synoptic table, a subject-matter index, a historical index and a listing of the issues of the *Yearbook* published to date.

The Technical Notes on the Statistical Tables are provided to assist the reader in using the tables. Table A, the synoptic table, provides a glance of the completeness of data coverage of the current *Yearbook*. The subject-matter index is a detailed guide to the current Yearbook. The cumulative historical index, located at the end of the *Yearbook*, is a guide on content and coverage of all fifty-four issues, and indicates for each of the topics that have been published, the issues in which they are presented and the years covered. A list of the *Demographic Yearbook* issues, with their corresponding sales number and the special topics featured in each issue are shown on pages iv and v.

Until the 48th issue (1996), each Issue consisted of two parts, the general tables and special topic tables, published in the same volume with the regular topics.[2] Beginning with the 49th issue (1997), the special topic tables were being disseminated on CD-ROMs as supplements to the regular issues. Two CD-ROMs have so far been issued: the *Demographic Yearbook Historical Supplement*, which presents a wide panorama of basic demographic statistics for the period 1948 to 1997, and the *Demographic Yearbook: Natality Statistics*, which contains a series of detailed tables dedicated to natality and covering the period from 1980 to 1998. Three volumes of a new Demographic Yearbook Special Census Topics are now being prepared and are presented at: http://unstats.un.org/unsd/demographic/products/dyb/default.htm

Population statistics are not available for all countries or areas, for a variety of reasons. In an effort to provide estimates of mid-year population and of selected vital statistics for all countries and areas, two annexes have been introduced since the 53rd issue of the *Demographic Yearbook*. Annex 1 presents United Nations population estimates for the period 1993-2002 and the second presents the medium variant estimates of crude birth and death rates, infant mortality and total fertility rates, as well as expectation of life at birth over the period 2000-2005. These data are produced by the United Nations Population Division and published in the *World Population Prospects - The 2004 Revision*.[3]

Demographic statistics shown in this issue of the *Yearbook* are available online at the *Demographic Yearbook* website http://unstats.un.org/unsd/demographic/products/dyb/default.htm. Information about the Statistics Division's data collection and dissemination programme is also available on the same website. Additional information can be made available by contacting the Statistics Division of the United Nations Secretariat, at demostat@un.org.

TECHNICAL NOTES ON THE STATISTICAL TABLES

1. GENERAL REMARKS

1.1 Arrangement of Technical Notes

These Technical Notes are designed to provide the reader with relevant information for using the statistical tables. Information pertaining to the *Yearbook* in general is presented in the sections dealing with geographical aspects, population and vital statistics. In addition, preceding each table are notes describing the variables, remarks on the reliability and limitation of the data, countries and areas covered, and information on the presentation of earlier data. When appropriate, details on computation of rates, ratios or percentages are presented.

1.2 Arrangement of tables

This issue contains general tables only. Since the numbering of the tables does not correspond exactly to those in previous issues, the reader is advised to use the historical index that appears at the end of this book to find the reference to data in earlier issues.

1.3 Source of data

The statistics presented in the *Demographic Yearbook* are national data provided by official statistical authorities unless otherwise indicated. The primary source of data for the *Yearbook* is a set of questionnaires sent annually by the United Nations Statistics Division to over 230 national statistical services and other appropriate government offices. Data reported on these questionnaires are supplemented, to the extent possible, with data taken from official national publications, official websites and through correspondence with national statistical services. In the interest of comparability, rates, ratios and percentages have been calculated by the Statistics Division of the United Nations, except for the life table functions, and total fertility rate, and also crude birth rate and crude death rate for some countries or areas, in table 4, as appropriately noted. The methods used by the Statistics Division to calculate these rates and ratios are described in the Technical Notes for each table. The population figures used for these computations are those pertaining to the corresponding years published in this or previous issues of the *Yearbook* .

In cases when data in this issue of the *Demographic Yearbook* differ from those published in earlier issues or related publications, statistics in this issue may be assumed to reflect revisions to these data received by October 2004, or in some cases, by May 2005. In particular, data shown as provisional are generally subject to further revision by national offices.

2. GEOGRAPHICAL ASPECTS

2.1 Coverage

Data are shown for all individual countries or areas that provided the information. Table 3 is the most comprehensive in geographical coverage, presenting data on population and surface area for all countries and areas with a population of at least 50 persons. Not all of these countries or areas appear in subsequent tables. In many cases the data required for a particular table are not available. In general, the more detailed the data required for a table, the fewer the number of countries or areas that can provide them.

In addition, with one exception, rates and ratios are presented only for countries or areas reporting at least a minimum number of relevant events. The minimums are stated in the Technical Notes to individual tables. The exception, in which rates for countries or areas are shown regardless of the number of events on which they were based, is table 4, presenting a summary of vital statistics rates, crude birth rates and crude death rates respectively.

Except for summary data shown for the world and by major areas and regions in tables 1 and 2 and data shown for capital city and cities with a population of 100 000 or more in table 8, all data are presented at the national level. The number of countries shown in each table is provided in table A, the *Demographic Yearbook* 2002 synoptic table.

2.2 Territorial composition

To the extent possible, all data, including time series data, relate to the territory within 2002 boundaries, when the data were requested from the countries or areas. Exceptions to this are footnoted in individual tables. Additionally, in table 3, recent changes and other relevant clarifications are specified.

Data relating to the People's Republic of China generally do not include those for Taiwan Province except in tables 1 and 2.

Through accession of the German Democratic Republic to the Federal Republic of Germany, as of 3 October 1990, the two German States have united to form one sovereign State — Germany. Data pertaining to Germany prior to 3 October 1990 are indicated separately for the Federal Republic of Germany and the former German Democratic Republic based on their respective boundaries at the time indicated; they are otherwise presented jointly under "Germany".

In 1991, the Union of Soviet Socialist Republics formally dissolved into fifteen individual countries (Armenia, Azerbaijan, Belarus, Estonia, Georgia, Kazakhstan, Kyrgyzstan, Latvia, Lithuania, Republic of Moldova, Russian Federation, Tajikistan, Turkmenistan, Ukraine and Uzbekistan). Data for the period after 1991 are shown for each of these individual countries.

2.3 Nomenclature

Because of space limitations, the country or area names listed in the tables are generally the commonly employed short titles in use in the United Nations as of October 2004[4], the full titles being used only when a short form is not available. The latest version of the *Standard Country or Area Codes for Statistics Use* can be accessed at http://unstats.un.org/unsd/methods/m49/m49.htm.

2.3.1 Order of presentation

Countries or areas are listed in English alphabetical order within the following continents: Africa, North America, South America, Asia, Europe and Oceania.

The designations and presentation of the material in this publication were adopted solely for the purpose of providing a convenient geographical basis for the accompanying statistical series. The same qualification applies to all notes and explanations concerning the geographical units for which data are presented.

2.4 Surface area data

Surface area data, shown in tables 1 and 3, represent the total surface area, comprising land area and inland waters (assumed to consist of major rivers and lakes) and excluding only Polar Regions and uninhabited islands. The surface area given is the most recent estimate available. They are presented in square kilometres, a conversion factor of 2.589988 having been applied to surface areas originally reported in square miles.

2.4.1 Comparability over time

Comparability over time in surface area estimates for any given country or area may be affected by changes in the surface area estimation procedures, increases in actual land surface by reclamation, boundary changes, changes in the concept of "land surface area" used or a change in the unit of measurement used. In most cases it was possible to ascertain the reason for a revision; otherwise, the latest figures have generally been accepted as correct and substituted for those previously on file.

2.4.2 International comparability

Lack of international comparability between surface area estimates arises primarily from differences in definition. In particular, there is considerable variation in the treatment of coastal bays, inlets and gulfs, rivers and lakes. International comparability is also impaired by the variation in methods employed to estimate surface area. These range from surveys based on modern scientific methods to conjectures based on diverse types of information. Some estimates are recent while others may not be. Since neither the exact method of determining the surface area nor the precise definition of its composition and time reference is known for all countries or areas, the estimates in table 3 should not be considered strictly comparable from one country or area to another.

3. POPULATION

Population statistics, that is, those pertaining to the size, geographical distribution and demographic characteristics of the population, are presented in a number of tables of the *Demographic Yearbook*.

Data for countries or areas include population census figures, estimates based on results of sample surveys (in the absence of a census), postcensal or intercensal estimates and those derived from continuous population registers. In the present issue of the *Yearbook*, the latest available census figure of the total population of each country or area and mid-year estimates for 1995 and 2002 are presented in table 3. Mid-year estimates of total population for 10 years (1993-2002) are shown in table 5 and mid-year estimates of urban and total population by sex for 10 years (1993-2002) are shown in table 6. The latest available data on population by age, sex and urban/rural residence are given in table 7. The latest available figures on the population of capital cities and of cities or urban agglomerations of 100,000 or more inhabitants are presented in table 8.

Summary estimates of the mid-year population of the world, major areas and regions for selected years and of its age and sex distribution in 2002 are set forth in tables 1 and 2, respectively.

The statistics on total population, population by age, sex and urban/rural distribution are used in the calculation of rates in the *Yearbook*. Vital rates by age and sex were calculated using data that appear in table 7 in this issue or the corresponding tables of previous issues of the *Demographic Yearbook*.

3.1 Sources of variation of data

The comparability of data is affected by several factors, including (1) the definition of total population; (2) the definition used to classify the population into its urban/rural components; (3) the accuracy of age reporting; (4) the extent of over-enumeration or under-enumeration in the most recent census or other source of bench-mark population statistics; and (5) the quality of population estimates. These five factors will be discussed in some detail in sections 3.1.1 to 3.2.2 below. Other relevant problems are discussed in the technical notes to the individual tables. Readers interested in more detail, relating in particular to the basic concepts of population size, distribution and characteristics as elaborated by the United Nations, should consult the *Principles and Recommendations for Population and Housing Censuses, Revision 1.*[5]

3.1.1 Total population

The most important impediment to comparability of total populations is the difference between the concept of a de facto and de jure population. A de facto population should include all persons physically present in the country or area at the reference date. The de jure population, by contrast, should include all usual residents of the given country or area, whether or not they were physically present in the area at the reference date. By definition, therefore, a de facto total and a de jure total are not entirely comparable.

Comparability of even two de facto or de jure totals is often affected by the fact that strict conformity to either of these concepts is rare. For example, some so-called de facto counts do not include foreign military, naval and diplomatic personnel present in the country or area on official duty, and their accompanying family members and servants; some do not include foreign visitors in transit through the country or area or transients on ships in the harbour. On the other hand, they may include such persons as merchant seamen and fishermen who are temporarily out of the country or area working at their trade.

The de jure population figure presents even greater variations in comparability, in part because it depends in the first place on the concept of "usual residence", which varies from one country or area to another and is difficult to apply consistently in a census or survey enumeration. For example, non-national civilian temporarily in a country or area as short-term workers may officially be considered residents after a stay of a specified period of time or they may be considered as non-residents throughout the duration of their stay; at the same time, these individuals may be officially considered as residents or non-residents of the country or area from which they came, depending on the duration and/or purpose of their absence. Furthermore, regardless of the official treatment, individual respondents may apply their own interpretation of residence in responding to the inquiry. In addition, there may be considerable differences in the accuracy with which countries or areas are informed about the number of their residents temporarily out of the country or area.

As far as possible, the population statistics presented in the tables of the *Yearbook* refer to the de facto population. Those reported to have been based on the de jure concept are identified as such. Figures not otherwise qualified may, therefore, be assumed to have been reported by countries or areas as being based on a de facto definition of the population. In an effort to overcome, to the extent possible, the effect of the lack of strict conformity to either the de facto or the de jure concept given above, significant exceptions with respect to inclusions and exclusions of specific population groups, are footnoted when they are known.

It should be remembered, however, that the necessary detailed information has not been available in many cases. It cannot, therefore, be assumed that figures not thus qualified reflect strict de facto or de jure definitions.

A possible source of variation within the statistics of a single country or area may arise from the fact that some countries or areas collect information on both the de facto and the de jure population in, for example, a census, but prepare detailed tabulations for only the de jure population. Hence, even though the total population shown in table 3 is de facto, the figures shown in the tables presenting various characteristics of the population, for example, urban/rural distribution, age and sex distribution, may be de jure. These de jure figures are footnoted when known.

3.1.2 Urban/rural classification

International comparability of urban/rural distributions is seriously impaired by the wide variation among national definitions of the concept of "urban". The definitions used by individual countries or areas and their implications are shown at the end of technical notes for table 6.

3.1.3 Age distribution

The classification of population by age is a core element of most analyses, estimation and projection of population statistics. Unfortunately, age data are subject to a number of sources of error and non-comparability. Accordingly, the reliability of age data should be of concern to users of these statistics.

3.1.3.1 Collection and compilation of age data

Age is the estimated or calculated interval of time between the date of birth and the date of the census or survey, expressed in completed solar years.[2] There are two methods of collecting information on age. The first is to obtain the date of birth for each member of the population in a census or survey and then to calculate the completed age of the individual by subtracting the date of birth from the date of enumeration.[6] The second method is to record the individual's completed age at the time of the census or survey, that is to say, age at last birthday.

The recommended method is to calculate age at last birthday by subtracting the exact date of birth from the date of the census. Some practices, however, do not use this method but instead calculate the difference between the year of birth and the year of the census. Classifications of this type are footnoted whenever possible. They can be identified to a certain extent by a smaller than expected population under one year of age. However, an irregular number of births from one year to the next or age selective omission of infants may also obscure the expected population under one year of age.

3.1.3.2 Errors in age data

Errors in age data may be due to a variety of causes, including ignorance of the correct age; reporting years of age in terms of a calendar concept other than completed solar years since birth,[7] carelessness in reporting and recording age; a general tendency to state age in figures ending in certain digits (such as zero, two, five and eight); a tendency to exaggerate length of life at advanced ages; a subconscious aversion to certain numbers; and wilful misrepresentations.

These reasons for errors in reported age data are common to most investigations of age and to most countries or areas, and they may significantly impair comparability of the data.

As a result of the above-mentioned difficulties, the age-sex distribution of population in many countries or areas shows irregularities which may be summarized as follows: (1) a deficiency in the number of infants and young children; (2) a concentration at ages ending with zero and five (that is, 5, 10, 15, 20...); (3) heaping at even ages (for example, 10, 12, 14...) relative to odd ages (for example, 11, 13, 15...); (4) unexpectedly large differences between the frequency of males and females at certain ages; and (5) unaccountably large differences between the frequencies in adjacent age groups. Comparing of identical age-sex cohorts from successive censuses, as well as studying the age-sex composition of each census, may reveal these and other inconsistencies, some of which in varying degree are characteristic of even the most modern censuses.

3.1.3.3 Evaluation of accuracy

To measure the accuracy of data by age, based on the evidence of irregularities in 5-year groups, an index was devised for presentation in the *Demographic Yearbook 1949-1950*[8]. Although this index was sensitive to various sources of inaccuracy in the data, it could also be affected considerably by real fluctuations in past demographic processes. It could not, therefore, be applied indiscriminately to all types of statistics, unless certain adjustments were made and caution used in the interpretation of results.

The publication of population statistics by single years of age in the *Demographic Yearbook 1955* made it possible to apply a simple, yet highly sensitive, index known as Whipple's Index, or the Index of Concentration,[9] the interpretation of which is relatively free from consideration of factors not connected with the accuracy of age reporting. More refined methods for the measurement of accuracy of distributions by single year of age have been devised, but this particular index was selected for presentation in the *Demographic Yearbook* for its simplicity and the wide use it has already found in other sources.

Whipple's Index is obtained by summing the age returns between 23 and 62 years inclusive and finding what percentage is borne by the sum of the returns of years ending with 5 and 0 to one-fifth of the total sum.

The results would vary between a minimum of 100, representing no concentration at all, and a maximum of 500, if no returns were recorded with any digits other than the two mentioned.[10]

The index is applicable to all age distributions for which single years are given at least to the age of 62, with the following exceptions: (1) where the data presented are the result of graduation, no irregularity is scored by Whipple's Index, even though the graduated data may still be affected by inaccuracies of a different type; and (2) where statistics on age have been derived by reference to the year of birth, and tendencies to round off the birth year would result in an excessive number of ages ending in odd numbers, the frequency of age reporting with terminal digits 5 and 0 is not an adequate measure of their accuracy.

Using statistics for both sexes combined, the index has now been computed for all the single-year age distributions in table 26 of the 1993 *Yearbook* from censuses held between 1985 and 1993, with the exception of those excluded on the criteria set forth above. The ratings achieved by such distributions can be found on pages 19 to 20 of the *Demographic Yearbook 1993*.[11] The present issue of the *Demographic Yearbook* does not display the population by single years of age; the Index and the ratings are planned to be included in the next special issue of the *Demographic Yearbook* focusing on population censuses. For future data dissemination plans, please refer to the *Demographic Yearbook* website at http://unstats.un.org/unsd/demographic/products/dyb/default.htm.

Although Whipple's Index measures only the effects of preferences for ages ending in 5 and 0, it can be assumed that such digit preference is usually connected with other sources of inaccuracy in age statements and the index can be accepted as a fair measure of the general reliability of the age distribution.

3.2 Methods used to indicate quality of published statistics

To the extent possible, efforts have been made to give the reader an indication of eliability of the statistics published in the *Demographic Yearbook*. This has been approached in several ways. Any information regarding a possible under-enumeration or over-enumeration, coming from a postcensal survey, for example, has been noted in the footnotes to table 3. Any deviation from full national coverage, as explained in section 2.1 under Geographical Aspects, has also been noted. In addition, national statistical offices have been asked to evaluate the estimates of total population they submit to the Statistics Division of the United Nations.

3.2.1 Treatment of time series of population estimates

When a series of mid-year population estimates are presented, the same indication of quality is shown for the entire series as was determined for the latest estimate. The quality is indicated by the type face employed.

No attempt has been made to split the series even though it is evident that in cases where the data are now considered reliable, in earlier years, many may have been considerably less reliable than the current classification implies. Thus it will be evident that this method overstates the probable reliability of the time series in many cases. It may also understate the reliability of estimates for years immediately preceding or following a census enumeration.

3.2.2 Treatment of estimated distributions by age and other demographic characteristics

Estimates of the age-sex distribution of population may be constructed by two major methods: (1) by applying the specific components of population change to each age-sex group of the population as enumerated at the time of the census, and (2) by distributing the total estimated for a postcensal year proportionately according to the age-sex structure at the time of the census. Estimates constructed by the latter method are not published in the *Demographic Yearbook*.

Estimated age-sex distributions are categorized as "reliable" or otherwise, according to the method of construction established for the latest estimate of total mid-year population. Hence, the quality designation of the total figure, as indicated by the code, is considered to apply also to the whole distribution by age and sex, and the data are set in *italic* or roman type, as appropriate, on this basis alone. Further evaluation of detailed age structure data has not been undertaken to date.

4. VITAL STATISTICS

For purposes of the *Demographic Yearbook*, vital statistics have been defined as statistics of live birth, death, foetal death, marriage and divorce.

This volume of the *Yearbook* presents general tables on natality, nuptiality and divorce as well as tables on mortality referring to: foetal mortality, infant and maternal mortality and general mortality, including tables on deaths by cause.

4.1 Sources of variation of data

Most of the vital statistics data published in this *Yearbook* come from national civil registration systems. The completeness and the accuracy of the data which these systems produce vary from one country or area to another.

The provision for a national civil registration system is not universal, and in some cases, the registration system covers only certain vital events. For example, in some countries or areas only births and deaths are registered. There are also differences in the effectiveness with which national laws pertaining to civil registration operate in the various countries or areas. The manner in which the law is implemented and the degree to which the public complies with the legislation determine the reliability of the vital statistics obtained from the civil registers.

It should be noted that some statistics on marriage and divorce are obtained from sources other than civil registers. For example, in some countries or areas, the only source for data on marriages is church registers. Divorce statistics, on the other hand, are obtained from court records and/or civil registers according to national practice. The actual compilation of these statistics may be the responsibility of the civil registrar, the national statistical office or other government offices.

Other factors affecting international comparability of vital statistics are much the same as those that must be considered in evaluating the variations in other population statistics. Differences in statistical definitions of vital events, differences in geographical and ethnic coverage of the data and diverse tabulation procedures may also influence comparability.

In addition to vital statistics from civil registers, some vital statistics published in the *Yearbook* are official estimates. These estimates are frequently from sample surveys. As such, their comparability may be affected by the national completeness of reporting in household surveys, non-sampling and sampling errors and other sources of bias.

Readers interested in more detailed information on standards for vital statistics should consult the *Principles and Recommendations for a Vital Statistics System Revision 2*[12] *Handbook of vital statistics systems and Methods Volume 1, Legal, Organizational and Technical Aspects;*[13] *Handbook of Vital Statistics Systems and Methods, Volume 2, Review of national practices;*[13] *Handbook on Civil Registration and Vital Statistics Systems: Management, Operation and Maintenance;*[14] *Handbook on Civil Registration and Vital Statistics Systems: Preparation of a Legal Framework;*[15] *Handbook on Civil Registration and Vital Statistics Systems: Developing Information, Education and Communication;*[16] *Handbook on Civil Registration and Vital Statistics Systems: Policies and Protocols for the Release and Archiving of Individual Records;*[17] and *Handbook on Civil Registration and Vital Statistics Systems: Computerization*[18]. The *Handbook of Household Surveys*[19] provides information in collection and evaluation of data on fertility, mortality and other vital events collected in household surveys. These publications are also available on the website at http://unstats.un.org/unsd/demographic/sources/civilreg/default.htm .

4.1.1 Statistical definition of events

An important source of variation lies in the statistical definition of each vital event. The *Demographic Yearbook* attempts to collect data on vital events, using the standard definitions put forth in paragraph 57 of *Principles and Recommendations for a Vital Statistics System Revision 2.*[14] These are as follows:

LIVE BIRTH is the complete expulsion or extraction from its mother of a product of conception, irrespective of the duration of pregnancy, which after such separation breathes or shows any other evidence of life such as beating of the heart, pulsation of the umbilical cord, or definite movement of voluntary muscles, whether or not the umbilical cord has been cut or the placenta is attached; each product of such a birth is considered live-born regardless of gestational age.

DEATH is the permanent disappearance of all evidence of life at any time after live birth has taken place (postnatal cessation of vital functions without capability of resuscitation). This definition therefore excludes foetal deaths.

FOETAL DEATH is death prior to the complete expulsion or extraction from its mother of a product of conception, irrespective of the duration of pregnancy; the death is indicated by the fact that after such separation the foetus does not breathe or show any other evidence of life, such as beating of the heart, pulsation of the umbilical cord, or definite movement of voluntary muscles. Late foetal deaths are those of twenty-eight or more completed weeks of gestation. These are synonymous with the events reported under the pre-1950 term stillbirth[20]*.*

MARRIAGE is an act, ceremony or process by which the legal relationship of husband and wife is constituted. The legality of the union may be established by civil, religious or other means as recognized by the laws of each country or area.

DIVORCE is a final legal dissolution of a marriage, that is, that separation of husband and wife which confers on the parties the right to remarriage under civil, religious and/or other provisions, according to the laws of each country.

In addition to these recommended definitions, the *Demographic Yearbook* collects and presents data on abortions, defined as:

ABORTION is defined, with reference to the woman, as any interruption of pregnancy before 28 weeks of gestation with a dead foetus. There are two major categories of abortion: spontaneous and induced. Induced abortions are those initiated by deliberate action undertaken with the intention of terminating pregnancy; all other abortions are considered as spontaneous.

4.1.2 Problems relating to standard definitions

A basic problem affecting international comparability of vital statistics is deviations from the standard definitions of vital events. An example of this can be seen in the cases of live births and foetal deaths.[21] In some countries or areas, an infant must survive for at least 24 hours, to be inscribed in the live-birth register. Infants who die before the expiration of the 24-hour period are classified as late foetal deaths and, barring special tabulation procedures, they would not be counted either as live births or as deaths. Similarly, in several other countries or areas, those infants who are born alive but who die before registration of their birth, are also considered as late foetal deaths.

Unless special tabulation procedures are adopted in such cases, the live-birth and death statistics will both be deficient by the number of these infants, while the incidence of late foetal deaths will be increased by the same amount. Hence the infant mortality rate is underestimated. Although both components (infant deaths and live births) are deficient by the same absolute amount, the deficiency is proportionately greater in relation to the infant deaths, causing greater errors in the infant mortality rate than in the birth rate.

Moreover, the practice exaggerates the late foetal death ratios. Some countries or areas make provision for correcting this deficiency (at least in the total frequencies) at the tabulation stage. Data for which the correction has not been made are indicated by footnote whenever possible.

The definitions used for marriage and divorce also present problems for international comparability. Unlike birth and death, which are biological events, marriage and divorce are defined only in terms of law and custom and as such are less amenable to universally applicable statistical definitions. They have therefore been defined for statistical purposes in general terms referring to the laws of individual countries or areas. Laws pertaining to marriage and particularly to divorce, vary from one country or area to another. With respect to marriage, the most widespread requirement relates to the minimum age at which persons may marry but frequently other requirements are specified.

When known the minimum legal age of men and women at which marriage can occur with (or in some cases without) parental consent is presented in table 24 showing marriages by age of groom and age of bride. Laws and regulations relating to the dissolution of marriage by divorce range from total prohibition, through a wide range of grounds upon which divorces may be granted, to the granting of divorce in response to a simple statement of desire or intention by husbands.

4.1.3 Fragmentary geographical or ethnic coverage

Ideally, vital statistics for any given country or area should cover the entire geographical area and include all ethnic groups. Fragmentary coverage is, however, not uncommon. In some countries or areas, registration is compulsory for only a small part of the population, limited to certain ethnic groups, for example. In other places there is no national provision for compulsory registration, but only municipal or state ordinances that do not cover the entire geographical area. Still others have developed a registration area that comprises only a part of the country or area, the remainder being excluded because of inaccessibility or for economic and cultural considerations that make regular registration practically impossible.

4.1.4 Tabulation procedures

4.1.4.1 By place of occurrence

Vital statistics presented on the national level relate to the de facto, that is, the present-in-area population. Thus, unless otherwise noted, vital statistics for a given country or area cover all the events which occur within its present boundaries and among all segments of the population therein. They may be presumed to include events among nomadic tribes and indigenous peoples, and among nationals and foreigners. When known, deviations from the de facto concept are footnoted.

Urban/rural differentials in vital rates for some countries may vary considerably depending on whether the relevant vital events were tabulated on the basis of place of occurrence or place of usual residence. For example, if a substantial number of women residing in rural areas near major urban centres travel to hospitals or maternity homes located in a city to give birth, urban fertility and neo-natal and infant mortality rates will usually be higher (and the corresponding rural rates will usually be lower) if the events are tabulated on the basis of place of occurrence rather than on the basis of place of usual residence. A similar process will affect general mortality differentials if substantial numbers of persons residing in rural areas use urban health facilities when seriously ill.

4.1.4.2 By date of occurrence versus by date of registration

To the extent possible, the vital statistics presented in the *Demographic Yearbook* refer to events that occurred during the specified year, rather than to those that were registered during that period. However, a considerable number of countries or areas tabulate their vital statistics not by date of occurrence, but by date of registration. Because such statistics can be very misleading, the countries or areas known to tabulate vital statistics by date of registration are identified in the tables by a plus sign (+). Since information on the method of tabulating vital statistics is not available for all countries and areas, tabulation by date of registration may be more prevalent than the symbols on the vital statistics tables would indicate.

Because quality of data is inextricably related to the timeliness of registration, this must always be considered in conjunction with the quality code description in section 4.2.1 below. If registration of births is complete and timely (code C), the ill effects of tabulating by date of registration, are, for all practical purposes, nullified. Similarly, with respect to death statistics, the effect of tabulating events by date of registration may be minimized in many countries or areas in which the sanitary code requires that a death must be registered before a burial permit can be issued, and this regulation tends to make registration prompt. With respect to foetal death, registration is usually done right away or not at all. Therefore, if registration is prompt, the difference between statistics tabulated by date of occurrence and those tabulated by date of registration may be negligible. In many cases, the length of the statutory time period allowed for registering various vital events plays an important part in determining the effects of tabulation by date of registration on comparability of data.

With respect to marriage and divorce, the practice of tabulating data by date of registration does not generally pose serious problems. In many countries or areas marriage is a civil legal contract which, to establish its legality, must be celebrated before a civil officer. It follows that for these countries or areas registration would tend to be almost automatic at the time of, or immediately following, the marriage ceremony. Because the registration of a divorce in many countries or areas is the responsibility solely of the court or the authority which granted it, and since the registration record in such cases is part of the records of the court proceedings, it follows that divorces are likely to be registered soon after the decree is granted.

On the other hand, if registration is not prompt, vital statistics by date of registration will not produce internationally comparable data. Under the best circumstances, statistics by date of registration will include primarily events that occurred in the immediately preceding year; in countries or areas with less developed systems, tabulations will include some events that occurred many years in the past. Examination of available information reveals that delays of many years are not uncommon for birth registration, though the majority is recorded between two to four years after birth.

As long as registration is not prompt, statistics by date of registration will not be internationally comparable either among themselves or with statistics by date of occurrence.

It should also be mentioned that lack of international comparability is not the only limitation introduced by date-of-registration tabulation. Even within the same country or area, comparability over time may be lost by the practice of counting registrations rather than occurrences. If the number of events registered from year to year fluctuates because of ad hoc incentives to stimulate registration, or to the sudden need, for example, for proof of (unregistered) birth or death to meet certain requirements, vital statistics tabulated by date of registration are not useful in measuring and analyzing demographic levels and trends. All they can give is an indication of the fluctuations in the need for a birth, death or marriage certificate and the work-load of the registrars. Therefore statistics tabulated by date of registration may be of very limited use for either national or international studies.

4.2 Methods used to indicate quality of published vital statistics

The quality of vital statistics can be assessed in terms of a number of factors. Most fundamental is the completeness of the civil registration system on which the statistics are based. In some cases, the incompleteness of the data obtained from civil registration systems is revealed when these events are used to compute rates. However, this technique applies only where the data are markedly deficient, where they are tabulated by date of occurrence and where the population base is correctly estimated. Tabulation by date of registration will often produce rates which appear correct, simply because the numerator is artificially inflated by the inclusion of delayed registrations and, conversely, rates may be of credible magnitude because the population at risk has been underestimated. Moreover, it should be remembered that knowledge of what is credible in regard to levels of fertility, mortality and nuptiality is extremely scanty for many parts of the world, and borderline cases, which are the most difficult to appraise, are frequent.

4.2.1 Quality code for vital statistics from registers.

In the *Demographic Yearbook* annual "Questionnaire on vital statistics" national statistical offices are asked to provide their own estimates of the completeness of the births, deaths, late foetal deaths, marriages and divorces recorded in their civil registers.

On the basis of information from the questionnaires, from direct correspondence and from relevant official publications, it has been possible to classify current national statistics from civil registers of birth, death, infant death, late foetal death, marriage and divorce into three broad quality categories, as follows:

C: Data estimated to be virtually complete, that is, representing at least 90 per cent of the events occurring each year.

U: Data estimated to be incomplete, that is representing less than 90 per cent of the events occurring each year.

|: Data not derived from civil registration systems but considered reliable, such as estimates derived from projections, other estimation techniques or population and housing census.

...: Data for which no specific information is available regarding completeness.

These quality codes appear in the first column of the tables which show total frequencies and crude rates (or ratios) over a period of years for live births (table 9), late foetal deaths (table 12), infant deaths (table 15), deaths (table 18), marriages (table 23), and divorces (table 25).

The classification of countries and areas in terms of these quality codes may not be uniform. Nevertheless, it was felt that national statistical offices were in the best position to judge the quality of their data. It was considered that even the very broad categories that could be established on the basis of the available information would provide useful indicators of the quality of the vital statistics presented in this *Yearbook*.

In the past, the bases of the national estimates of completeness were usually not available. In connection with the *Demographic Yearbook 1977*, countries were asked, for the first time, to provide some indication of the basis of their completeness estimates. They were requested to indicate whether the completeness estimates reported for registered live births, deaths, and infant deaths were prepared on the basis of demographic analysis, dual record checks or some other specified method. Relatively few countries or areas have responded to this new question; therefore, no attempt has been made to revise the system of quality codes used in connection with the vital statistics data presented in the *Yearbook*. It is hoped that, in the future, more countries will be able to provide this information so that the system of quality codes used in connection with the vital statistics data presented in the *Yearbook* may be revised.

Among the countries or areas indicating that the registration of live births was estimated to be 90 per cent or more complete (and hence classified as C in table 9), the following countries or areas provided information on the basis of this completeness estimate:

(a) Demographic analysis -- Argentina, Australia, Canada, Chile, Croatia, Cuba, Czech Republic, Egypt, French Guiana, Guadeloupe, Guernsey, Iceland, Ireland, Israel, Republic of Korea, Kuwait, Latvia, Mauritius, Puerto Rico, Romania, San Marino, Singapore, Sweden, Switzerland and United States.

(b) Dual record check -- Bahamas, Barbados, Belgium, Bulgaria, Cook Islands, Cuba, Cyprus, Denmark, Estonia, Fiji, Finland, France, French Guiana, Greece, Guam, Guadeloupe, Guernsey, Hungary, Iceland, Isle of Man, Japan, Kyrgyzstan, Lithuania, Maldives, New Zealand, Peninsular Malaysia, Romania, Saint Kitts and Nevis, Saint Lucia, Singapore, Sri Lanka, Sweden, Switzerland, Tokelau, Uruguay and Venezuela.

(c) Other specified methods -- Belgium, Bermuda, Cayman Islands, China Hong Kong SAR, China Macao SAR, Germany, Greenland, Iceland, Japan, Luxembourg, Netherlands, Norway, Poland, Singapore and Slovenia.

Among the countries or areas indicating that the registration of deaths was estimated to be 90 per cent or more complete (and hence classified as C in table 18), the following countries or areas provided information on the basis of this completeness estimate:

(a) Demographic analysis -- Argentina, Australia, Canada, Chile, Cuba, Egypt, French Guiana, Guadeloupe, Guernsey, Iceland, Ireland, Israel, Kuwait, Latvia, Mauritius, Puerto Rico, Romania, San Marino, Singapore, Switzerland and United States.

(b) Dual record check -- Bahamas, Bulgaria, Cook Islands, Cuba, Denmark, Fiji, Finland, France, Greece, Greenland, Guam, Guernsey, Iceland, Isle of Man, Maldives, New Zealand, Romania, Saint Kitts and Nevis, Saint Lucia, Singapore, Sri Lanka, Sweden, Switzerland, Tokelau and Uruguay.

(c) Other specified methods -- Belgium, Bermuda, Cayman Islands, Germany, Hong Kong SAR, Iceland, Ireland, Japan, Luxembourg, Netherlands, Norway, Poland, Singapore and Slovenia.

Among the countries or areas indicating that the registration of infant deaths was estimated to be 90 per cent or more complete (and hence classified as C in table 15), the following countries or areas provided information on the basis of this completeness estimate:

(a) Demographic analysis -- Argentina, Australia, Canada, Chile, Cuba, Egypt, Iceland, Ireland, Israel, Kuwait, Latvia, Mauritius, Puerto Rico, Romania, San Marino, Singapore, Sri Lanka, Switzerland and United States.

(b) Dual record check -- Bahamas, Bulgaria, Cook Islands, Cuba, Denmark, Fiji, Finland, France, Greece, Greenland, Guam, Guernsey, Iceland, Isle of Man, Japan, Maldives, New Zealand, Romania, Saint Kitts and Nevis, Saint Lucia, Singapore, Sweden, Switzerland, Tokelau and Uruguay.

(c) Other specified methods -- Belgium, Bermuda, Cayman Islands, Germany, Hong Kong SAR, Iceland, Japan, Luxembourg, Netherlands, Norway, Poland, Singapore and Slovenia.

4.2.2 Treatment of vital statistics from registers

On the basis of the quality code described above, the vital statistics shown in all tables of the *Yearbook* are treated as either reliable or unreliable. Data coded C are considered reliable and appear in roman type. Data coded U or ... are considered unreliable and appear in *italics*. Although the quality code itself appears only in certain tables, the indication of reliability (that is, the use of *italics* to indicate unreliable data) is shown in all tables presenting vital statistics data.

In general, the quality code for deaths shown in table 18 is used to determine whether data on deaths in other tables appear in roman or *italic* type. However, for some of the maternal deaths data shown in *italics* in table 17, the known quality code differs from that ascribed on the basis of the completeness of registration of the total number of deaths. In cases where the quality code in table 18 does not correspond with the quality level implied by the typeface used in table 17, relevant information regarding the completeness of maternal mortality is given in a footnote.

The same indication of reliability used in connection with tables showing the frequencies of vital events is also used in connection with tables showing the corresponding vital rates. For example, death rates computed using deaths from a register that is incomplete or of unknown completeness are considered unreliable and appear in *italics*. Strictly speaking, to evaluate vital rates more precisely, one would have to also take into account the accuracy of population data used in the denominator of these rates. The quality of population data is discussed in section 3.2 of the Technical Notes.

It should be noted that the indications of reliability used for infant mortality rates, maternal mortality rates and late foetal death ratios (all of which are calculated using the number of live births in the denominator) are determined on the basis of the quality codes for infant deaths, deaths and late foetal deaths respectively. To evaluate these rates and ratios more precisely, one would have to take into account the quality of the live-birth data used in the denominator of these rates and ratios. The quality codes for live births are shown in table 9 and described more fully in the text of the technical notes for that table.

4.2.3 Treatment of time series of vital statistics from registers

The quality of a time series of vital statistics is more difficult to determine than the quality of data for a single year. Since a time series of vital statistics is usually generated only by a system of continuous civil registration, it was assumed that the quality of the entire series was the same as that for the latest year's data obtained from the civil register. The entire series is treated as described in section 4.2.2 above. That is, if the quality code for the latest registered data is C, the frequencies and rates for earlier years are also considered reliable and appear in roman type. Conversely, if the latest registered data are coded as U or ... then data for earlier years are considered unreliable and appear in *italics*. It is recognized that this method is not entirely satisfactory because it is known that data from earlier years in many of the series were considerably less reliable than the current code implies.

4.2.4 Treatment of estimated vital statistics

In addition to data from vital registration systems, estimated frequencies and rates of the events, usually ad hoc official estimates which have been derived either from the results of a sample survey or by demographic analyses, also appear in the *Demographic Yearbook*. Estimated frequencies and rates have been included in the tables because it is assumed that they provide information which is more accurate than that from existing civil registration systems. By implication, therefore, they are also assumed to be reliable and as such they are not set in italics. Estimated frequencies and rates continue to be treated in this manner even when they are interspersed in a time series with data from civil registers.

In tables showing the quality code, the code applies only to data from civil registers. If a series of data for a country or area contains both data from a civil register and estimated data, the code applies only to the registered data; if only estimated data are shown, the symbol (|) is shown.

4.3 Cause of death

World Health Organization (WHO) Member States are bound by the International Nomenclature Regulations to provide the Organization with cause of death data coded in accordance with the current revision of the International Statistical Classification of Diseases and Related Health Problems (ICD) as adopted from time to time by the World Health Assembly[22]. The data are collected by the WHO using the ICD. In order to promote international comparability of cause of death statistics, the World Health Organization organizes and conducts an international Conference for the revision of the ICD on a regular basis in order to insure that the Classification is kept current with the most recent clinical and statistical concepts. The data are now usually submitted to WHO at the full four-character level of detail provided by the ICD and are stored in the WHO Mortality Database at the level of detail as provided by the country. For earlier versions, however, the data are only available according to the ICD's list of 150 causes. Data from the WHO Mortality Database are available in electronic format at http://www3.who.int/whosis/menu.cfm.

Although revisions provide an up-to-date version of the ICD, such revisions create several problems related to the comparability of cause of death statistics. The first is the lack of comparability over time that inevitably accompanies the use of a new classification. The second problem affects comparability between countries and areas because they may adopt the new classification at different times. The more refined the classification becomes the greater is the need for expert clinical diagnosis of cause of death. In many countries or areas, few of the deaths occur in the presence of an attendant, who is medically trained, i.e., most deaths are certified by a lay attendant. Because the ICD contains many diagnoses that cannot be identified by a non-medical person, the ICD does not always promote international comparability particularly between countries and areas where the level of medical services differ widely.

The chapters of the tenth revision[23], the latest revision of the ICD, consist of an alphanumeric coding scheme of one letter followed by three numbers at the four-character level. Chapter one contains infectious and parasitic diseases, chapter two refers to all neoplasms, chapter three to disorders of the immune mechanism including diseases of the blood and blood-forming organs; and chapter four to endocrine, nutritional and metabolic diseases. The remaining chapters group diseases according to the anatomical site affected, except for chapters that refer to mental disorders; complications of pregnancy, childbirth and the puerperium; congenital malformations; and conditions originating in the perinatal period. Finally, an entire chapter is devoted to symptoms, signs, and abnormal findings.

4.3.1 Maternal mortality

According to the tenth revision of the ICD, "Maternal death" is defined as the death of a woman while pregnant or within 42 days of termination of pregnancy, irrespective of the duration and the site of the pregnancy, from any cause related to or aggravated by the pregnancy or its management but not from accidental or incidental causes.

"Maternal deaths should be subdivided into direct and indirect obstetric deaths. Direct obstetric deaths are those resulting from obstetric complications of the pregnant state (pregnancy, labour and puerperium), from interventions, omissions, incorrect treatment, or from a chain of events resulting from any of the above.

Indirect obstetric deaths are those resulting from previous existing disease or disease that developed during pregnancy and which was not due to direct obstetric causes, but which was aggravated by physiologic effects of pregnancy".

While the denominator maternal rate should be the number of pregnant women, it is impossible to determine the number of pregnant women. A further recommendation by the tenth revision conference is therefore that maternal mortality rates be expressed per 100,000 live births or per 100,000 total births (live births and foetal deaths).[24] The maternal mortality rate calculated here is expressed per 100,000 live births. Although live births do not represent an unbiased estimate of pregnant women, this figure is more reliable than other estimates in particular, live births are more accurately registered than live births plus foetal deaths.

4.3.2 Perinatal mortality

The definition of perinatal death was recommended by the Study Group on Perinatal Mortality set up by the World Health Organization. The International Conference for the Eighth Revision of the International Classification of Diseases adopted the recommendation that the perinatal period be defined "as extending from the 28th week of gestation to the seventh day of life". Noting that several countries considered as late foetal deaths any foetal death of 20 weeks or longer gestation, the Conference agreed to accept a broader definition of perinatal death that extends from the 20th week of gestation to the 28th day of life. This alternative definition was believed to promote more complete registration of events between 28 weeks of gestation and the end of the first 6 days of life. In 1975, the Ninth Revision Conference recommended the collection of perinatal mortality statistics by use of a standard perinatal death certificate according to a definition which not only includes a minimum length of gestation but also minimum weight and length criteria.

In table 19 of the *Demographic Yearbook 1996* and previous issues of the Yearbook that included perinatal mortality statistics, the definition of perinatal deaths used is the sum of late foetal deaths (foetal deaths of 28 or more weeks of gestation) and infant deaths within the first week of life. In addition, in order to standardize the definition and eliminate differences due to national practice, the figures on perinatal death are calculated by the Statistics Division for inclusion in the *Demographic Yearbook*. Following the recommendations of the Tenth Revision Conference, the perinatal mortality rate is calculated per 1,000 live births in order to minimize the effect of limited foetal death registration on the magnitude of the denominator.[25]

NOTES

[1] The data on maternal mortality are from the World Health Organization, and are available at http://www3.who.int/whosis/menu.cfm, as on cause of death.

[2] There are two exceptions – the 1978 and 1991 issues, which were disseminated in separate volumes from the respective regular issues.

[3] *World Population Prospects: The 2004 Revision*, United Nations, New York, forthcoming. Until this is published, highlights and selected output are available by following links at www.unpopulation.org, and information about methodology and data are available in *World Population Prospects: The 2002 Revision*, Sales No. E.03.XIII.6, United Nations, New York, 2003.

[4] ST/ESA/STAT/SER.M/49/Rev.4/WWW ; http://unstats.un.org/unsd/methods/m49/m49.htm; see also Standard Country or Area Codes for Statistical Use, Sales No. M.98.XVII.9, United Nations, New York, 1999.

[5] Sales No. E.98.XVII.8, United Nations, New York, 1998.

[6] Alternatively, if a population register is used, completed ages are calculated by subtracting the date of birth of individuals listed in the register from a reference date to which the age data pertain.

[7] A source of non-comparability may result from differences in the method of reckoning age, is for example, the Western versus the Eastern or, as it is usually known, the English versus the Chinese system. By the latter, a child is considered one year old at birth and advances an additional year at each Chinese New Year. The effect of this system is most obvious at the beginning of the age span, where the frequencies in the under-one-year category are markedly understated. The effect on higher age groups is not so apparent. Distributions constructed on this basis are often adjusted before publication, but the possibility of such aberrations should not be excluded when census data by age are compared.

[8] In this index, differences were scored f rom expected values oi ratios between numbers of either sex in the same age group, and numbers of the same sex in adjoining age group. In compounding the score, allowance had to be made for

certain factors such as the effects of past fluctuations in birth rates, of heavy war casualties, and of the smallness of the population itself. A detailed description of the index, with results from its application to the data presented in the 1949-1950 and 1951 issues of the *Demographic Yearbook*, is furnished in *Population Bulletin, No. 2* (United Nations publication, Sales No. 52.XIII.4), pp. 59-79. The scores obtained from statistics presented in *Demographic Yearbook 1952* are presented in that issue, and the index has also been briefly explained in that issue, as well as those of 1953 and 1954.

[9] United States, Bureau of the Census, Thirteenth Census, Vol. I (Washington, D.C., U.S. Government Printing Office), pp. 291-292.

[10] J. T. Marten, Census of India, 1921, vol. I, part I (Calcutta, 1924), pp. 126-127.

[11] *Demographic Yearbook 1993*, Sales No. E/F.95.XIII.1, United Nations, New York, 1995.

[12] Sales No. E 01.XVII.10, United Nations, New York, 2001; http://unstats.un.org/unsd/demographic/vital_statistics/index.htm.

[13] Sales No. E.84.XVII.11, United Nations, New York, 1985; http://unstats.un.org/unsd/demographic/vital_statistics/index.htm.

[14] *Handbook on Civil Registration and Vital Statistics Systems: Management, Operation and Maintenance*, Sales No. E.98.XVII.11, United Nations, New York, 1998. http://unstats.un.org/unsd/demographic/vital_statistics/index.htm.

[15] Sales No. E. 98.XVII.7, United Nations, New York, 1998; http://unstats.un.org/unsd/demographic/vital_statistics/index.htm.

[16] Sales No. E.98.XVII.4, United Nations, New York, 1998; http://unstats.un.org/unsd/demographic/vital_statistics/index.htm.

[17] Sales No. E.98.XVII.6, United Nations, New York, 1998; http://unstats.un.org/unsd/demographic/vital_statistics/index.htm.

[18] Sales No. E.98.XVII.10, United Nations, New York, 1998; http://unstats.un.org/unsd/demographic/vital_statistics/index.htm.

[19] *Handbook of Household Surveys*, Sales No. E.83.XVII.13, United Nations, New York, 1984.

[20] For more detailed discussion on this issue, refer to *Principles and Recommendations for a Vital Statistics System Revision 2*, Sales No. E 01.XVII.10, United Nations, New York, 2001, para 57.

[23] For more information on historical and legal background on the use of differing definitions of live births and foetal deaths, comparisons of definitions used as of 1 January 1950, and evaluation of the effects of these differences on the calculation of various rates, see *Handbook of Vital Statistics Systems and Methods Volume 2, Review of National Practices*, Sales No. E.84.XVII.11, United Nations, New York, 1985, Chapter IV.

[22] The World Health Assembly is the annual meeting of the Member States of the World Health Organization and its highest governing body.

[23] *International Statistical Classification of Diseases and Related Health Problems*, Tenth Revision, Volume 2, World Health Organization, Geneva, 1992.

[24] *International Statistical Classification of Diseases and Related Health Problems*, Tenth Revision, Volume 2, World Health Organization, Geneva, 1992, pp. 129-136.

INTRODUCTION

L'Annuaire démographique est un recueil de statistiques démographiques internationales qui est établi par la Division de statistique du Département des affaires économiques et sociales de l'Organisation des Nations Unies. Il fait partie d'un ensemble de publications complémentaires publiées par l'Organisation des Nations Unies et les institutions spécialisées[1], qui ont pour objet de fournir des statistiques de base aux démographes, aux économistes, aux spécialistes de la santé publique et aux sociologues. Grâce à la coopération des services nationaux de statistique, il a été possible de faire figurer dans la présente édition des statistiques démographiques officielles pour plus de 230 pays ou zones du monde entier.

L'Annuaire démographique 2002 est le cinquante-quatrième d'une série que publie l'ONU depuis 1948. Le présent volume contient des tableaux à caractère général, y compris un aperçu mondial des statistiques démographiques de base et des tableaux qui regroupent des statistiques sur la dimension, la répartition et les tendances de la population, la natalité, la mortalité fœtale, la mortalité infantile et la mortalité liée à la maternité, la mortalité générale, la nuptialité et la divortialité. Des donnée classées selon le lieu de résidence (zone urbaine ou rurale) sont présentées dans un grand nombre de tableaux. En outre, l'Annuaire contient des notes techniques, un tableau synoptique, un index thématique, un index historique et une liste des éditions de l'Annuaire publiées jusqu'à présent.

Les notes techniques sur les tableaux statistiques sont destinées à aider le lecteur. Le tableau A, qui correspond au tableau synoptique, permet de se rendre compte en un coup d'oeil du niveau d'exhaustivité des données publiées dans le présent Annuaire et l'index thématique facilite le repérage des sujets abordés. À la fin de l'Annuaire, un index cumulatif donne des renseignements sur les matières traitées dans chacune des 54 éditions et sur les années sur lesquelles portent les données. Les numéros de vente des éditions antérieures et une liste des sujets spéciaux traités dans les différentes éditions sont indiqués aux pages iv et v.

Jusqu'à la 48ème édition (1996), chaque édition se composait de deux parties : les tableaux de caractère général et ceux sur des sujets spéciaux[2]. À partir de 49ème édition (1997), les tableaux sur les sujets spéciaux ont été publiés sur CD-ROM sous forme de suppléments à l'Annuaire. Deux CD-ROM ont été produits jusqu'à présent : l'Annuaire démographique : Supplément historique, qui présente un grand nombre de statistiques démographiques pour la période allant de 1948 à 1997, et l'Annuaire démographique : Statistiques de la natalité, qui contient des tableaux détaillés sur la natalité pour la période allant de 1980 à 1998. Trois volumes concernant un nouvel Annuaire démographique consacré à des thèmes de recensement spéciaux sont en cours d'établissement et sont présentés à l'adresse suivante : http://unstats.un.org/unsd/demographic/products/dyb/default.htm.

Les statistiques sur la population ne sont pas disponibles pour tous les pays et zones pour plusieurs raisons. Deux annexes ont été ajoutées à partir de la 53ème édition afin d'offrir des estimations sur la population en milieu d'année et un aperçu des statistiques de l'état civil. La première porte sur des estimations concernant la population pour chaque pays ou zone pour la période 1993-2002. La seconde présente les estimations des variantes moyennes concernant les taux bruts de natalité et de mortalité, la mortalité infantile, les indicateurs synthétiques de fécondité et l'espérance de vie à la naissance pour la période 2000-2005. Ces données ont été établies par la Division de la population de l'ONU et publiées dans World Population Prospects - The 2004 Revision[3].

Les statistiques démographiques figurant dans la présente édition de l'Annuaire sont disponibles en ligne sur les pages Web consacrées à l'Annuaire :
http://unstats.un.org/unsd/demographic/products/dyb/default.htm.
On trouvera également des renseignements sur le programme de collecte et de diffusion des données de la Division de statistique sur le même site. Il est possible de se procurer d'autres données en contactant la Division de statistique de l'Organisation des Nations Unies à l'adresse suivante : demostat@un.org.

NOTES TECHNIQUES SUR LES TABLEAUX STATISTIQUES

1. REMARQUES D'ORDRE GÉNÉRAL

1.1 Notes techniques

Les notes techniques ont pour but de donner au lecteur tous les renseignements dont il a besoin pour se servir des tableaux statistiques. Les renseignements qui concernent l'*Annuaire* en général sont présentés dans des sections portant sur diverses considérations géographiques, sur la population et sur les statistiques de natalité et de mortalité. Les tableaux sont ensuite commentés séparément et l'on trouvera pour chacun une description des variables et des observations sur la fiabilité et les lacunes des données ainsi que sur les pays et zones visés et sur les données publiées antérieurement. Des détails sont également donnés, le cas échéant, sur le mode de calcul des taux, quotients et pourcentages.

1.2 Tableaux

La présente édition contient seulement des tableaux de caractère général. Comme la numérotation des tableaux ne correspond pas exactement à celle des éditions précédentes, il est recommandé de se reporter à l'index qui figure à la fin du présent ouvrage pour trouver les données publiées dans les précédentes éditions.

1.3 Origine des données

Sauf indication contraire, les statistiques présentées dans l'*Annuaire démographique* sont des données nationales fournies par les organismes de statistique officiels. Elles sont recueillies essentiellement au moyen de questionnaires qui sont envoyés tous les ans à plus de 230 services nationaux de statistique et autres services gouvernementaux compétents. Les données communiquées en réponse à ces questionnaires sont complétées, dans toute la mesure possible, par des données tirées de publications nationales officielles et des sites Web d'organismes officiels et des renseignements communiqués par les services nationaux de statistique à la demande de l'ONU. Pour que les données soient comparables, les taux, rapports et pourcentages ont été calculés par la Division de statistique de l'ONU, à l'exception des paramètres des tables de mortalité et des indicateurs synthétiques de fécondité ainsi que des taux bruts de natalité et de mortalité pour certains pays et zones dans le tableau 4, qui ont été dûment signalés en note. Les méthodes suivies par la Division pour le calcul des taux et rapports sont décrites dans les notes techniques relatives à chaque tableau. Les chiffres de population utilisés pour ces calculs sont ceux qui figurent dans la présente édition de l'*Annuaire* ou qui ont paru dans des éditions antérieures.

Chaque fois que l'on constatera des différences entre les données du présent volume et celles des éditions antérieures de l'*Annuaire démographique*, ou de certaines publications apparentées, on pourra en conclure que les statistiques publiées cette année sont des chiffres révisés communiqués à la Division de statistique avant octobre 2004 et dans certains cas avant mai 2005. On notera en particulier que les chiffres présentés comme provisoires pourront être révisés eux aussi.

2. CONSIDÉRATIONS GÉOGRAPHIQUES

2.1 Portée

La portée géographique des tableaux du présent *Annuaire* est aussi complète que possible. Des données sont présentées sur tous les pays ou zones qui en ont communiquées. Le tableau 3, le plus complet, contient des données sur la population et la superficie de chaque pays ou zone ayant une population d'au moins 50 habitants. Ces pays ou zones ne figurent pas tous dans les tableaux qui suivent. Dans bien des cas, les données requises pour un tableau particulier n'étaient pas disponibles. En général, les pays ou zones qui peuvent fournir des données sont d'autant moins nombreux que les données demandées sont plus détaillées.

De plus, sauf dans un cas, les taux et rapports ne sont présentés que pour les pays ou zones ayant communiqué des chiffres correspondant à un nombre minimal de faits considérés. Les minimums sont indiqués dans les notes techniques relatives à chacun des tableaux. Le tableau faisant exception, c'est-à-dire celui où les taux pour les pays ou zones sont présentés quel que soit le nombre de faits sur lequel ils se fondent, est le tableau 4, où figurent des données récapitulatives sur les taux démographiques, les taux bruts de natalité et les taux bruts de mortalité.

À l'exception des données récapitulatives présentées dans les tableaux 1 et 2 pour l'ensemble du monde et les grandes zones et régions et des données relatives aux capitales et aux villes de 100 000 habitants ou plus dans le tableau 8, toutes les données se rapportent aux pays. Le nombre de pays sur lequel porte chacun des tableaux est indiqué dans le tableau A.

2.2 Composition territoriale

Autant que possible, toutes les données, y compris les séries chronologiques, se rapportent au territoire de 2002. Les exceptions à cette règle sont signalées en note à la fin des tableaux. On trouve dans le tableau 3 des renseignements concernant les changements intervenus récemment et d'autres précisions intéressantes.

Les données relatives à la République populaire de Chine ne comprennent généralement pas celles de la province de Taiwan ; à l'exception de celles des tableaux 1 et 2.

En vertu de l'adhésion de la République démocratique allemande à la République fédérale d'Allemagne, qui a pris effet le 3 octobre 1990, les deux États allemands se sont unis pour former un seul État souverain. À compter de la date de l'unification, la République fédérale d'Allemagne est désignée à l'ONU sous le nom d'Allemagne. Toutes les données se rapportant à l'Allemagne avant le 3 octobre figurent dans deux rubriques distinctes fondées sur les territoires respectifs de la République fédérale d'Allemagne et de l'ancienne République démocratique allemande selon la période indiquée.

En 1991, l'Union des républiques socialistes soviétiques s'est séparée en 15 pays distincts (Arménie, Azerbaïdjan, Bélarus, Estonie, Fédération de Russie, Géorgie, Kazakhstan, Kirghizstan, Lettonie, Lituanie, Ouzbékistan, République de Moldova, Tadjikistan, Turkménistan et Ukraine). Les données pour la période qui a suivi 1991 sont présentées pour ces pays pris séparément.

2.3 Nomenclature

En règle générale, pour gagner de la place, on a jugé commode de désigner dans les tableaux les pays ou zones par les noms abrégés couramment utilisés par l'Organisation des Nations Unies en octobre 2004[4], les désignations complètes n'étant utilisées que lorsqu'il n'existait pas de forme abrégée. La liste des désignations des pays ou zones est disponible à l'adresse suivante :
http://unstats.un.org/unsd/methods/m49/m49alphaf.htm.

2.3.1 Ordre de présentation

Les pays ou zones sont classés dans l'ordre alphabétique anglais et regroupés par continent comme ci-après : Afrique, Amérique du Nord, Amérique du Sud, Asie, Europe et Océanie.

Les appellations employées dans la présente édition et la présentation des données qui y figurent n'ont d'autre objet que de donner un cadre géographique commode aux séries statistiques. La même observation vaut pour toutes les notes et précisions concernant les unités géographiques pour lesquelles des données sont présentées.

2.4 Superficie

Les données relatives à la superficie qui figurent dans les tableaux 1 et 3 représentent la superficie totale, c'est-à-dire qu'elles englobent les terres émergées et les eaux intérieures (qui sont censées comprendre les principaux lacs et cours d'eau) mais excluent les régions polaires et les îles inhabitées. Les données relatives à la superficie correspondent aux chiffres estimatifs les plus récents. Les superficies sont toutes exprimées en kilomètres carrés ; les chiffres qui avaient été communiqués en miles carrés ont été convertis au moyen d'un coefficient de 2,589988.

2.4.1 Comparabilité dans le temps

La révision des estimations antérieures de la superficie, des augmentations effectives de la superficie terrestre due par exemple à des travaux d'assèchement, à des rectifications de frontières, à des changements d'interprétation du concept de « terres émergées » ou à l'utilisation de nouvelles unités de mesure peut avoir des incidences sur à comparabilité dans le temps des estimations relatives à la superficie d'un pays ou d'une zone donnés. Dans la plupart des cas, il a été possible de déterminer la raison de ces révisions; toutefois, même lorsque la raison n'était pas connue, on a remplacé les anciens chiffres par les nouveaux et on a généralement admis que ce sont ces derniers qui sont exacts.

2.4.2 Comparabilité internationale

Le manque de comparabilité internationale entre les données relatives à la superficie est dû principalement à des différences de définition. En particulier, la définition des golfes, baies et criques, lacs et cours d'eau varie sensiblement d'un pays à l'autre. La diversité des méthodes employées pour estimer les superficies nuit elle aussi à la comparabilité internationale. Certaines données proviennent de levés effectués selon des méthodes scientifiques modernes ; d'autres ne représentent que des conjectures reposant sur diverses catégories de renseignements. Certains chiffres sont récents, d'autres pas. Étant donné que ni la méthode de calcul de la superficie ni la composition du territoire et la date à laquelle se rapportent les données ne sont connues avec précision pour tous les pays ou zones, les estimations figurant dans le tableau 3 ne doivent pas être considérées comme rigoureusement comparables d'un pays ou d'une zone à une autre.

3. POPULATION

Les statistiques de la population, c'est-à-dire celles qui se rapportent à la dimension, à la répartition géographique et aux caractéristiques démographiques de la population, sont présentées dans un certain nombre de tableaux de *l'Annuaire démographique*.

Les données concernant les pays ou les zones représentent les résultats de recensements de population, des estimations fondées sur les résultats d'enquêtes par sondage (s'il n'y a pas eu recensement), des estimations postcensitaires ou intercensitaires, ou des estimations établies à partir de données provenant des registres permanents de population. Dans la présente édition, le tableau 3 indique pour chaque pays ou zone le chiffre le plus récent de la population totale issu du dernier recensement et des estimations établies au milieu de l'année 1995 et de l'année 2002. Le tableau 5 contient des estimations de la population totale au milieu de chaque année pendant 10 ans (1993-2002), et le tableau 6 des estimations de la population urbaine et de la population totale, par sexe, au milieu de chaque année pendant 10 ans (1993-2002). Les dernières données disponibles sur la répartition de la population selon l'âge, le sexe et le lieu de résidence (zone urbaine ou rurale) sont présentées dans le tableau 7. Les derniers chiffres disponibles sur la population des capitales et des villes de 100 000 habitants ou plus sont regroupés dans le tableau 8.

Les tableaux 1 et 2 présentent respectivement des estimations récapitulatives de la population du monde, des grandes zones et des régions en milieu d'année, pour certaines années, ainsi que des estimations récapitulatives, pour 2002, concernant la population répartie selon l'âge et le sexe.

On a utilisé pour le calcul des taux les statistiques de la population totale et de la population répartie selon l'âge, le sexe et le lieu de résidence (zone urbaine ou rurale). Les taux démographiques selon l'âge et le sexe ont été calculés à partir des données qui figurent dans le tableau 7 de la présente édition ou dans les tableaux correspondants d'éditions précédentes de *l'Annuaire démographique*.

3.1 Sources de variation des données

Plusieurs facteurs influent sur la comparabilité des données : 1) la définition de la population totale ; 2) les définitions utilisées pour faire la distinction entre population urbaine et population rurale ; 3) les difficultés liées aux déclarations d'âge ; 4) l'étendue du sur-dénombrement ou du sous-dénombrement dans le recensement le plus récent ou dans une autre source de statistiques de référence sur la population ; 5) la qualité des estimations relatives à la population. Ces cinq facteurs sont analysés en détail aux sections 3.1.1 à 3.2.2 ci-après. D'autres questions seront traitées dans les notes techniques relatives à chaque tableau. Pour plus de précisions concernant, notamment, les notions fondamentales de dimension, de répartition et de caractéristiques de la population qui ont été élaborées par l'Organisation des Nations Unies, le lecteur est invité à se reporter aux *Principes et recommandations concernant les recensements de la population et de l'habitat*.

3.1.1 Population totale

Le principal obstacle à la comparabilité des données relatives à la population totale est la différence qui existe entre population de fait et population de droit. La population de fait comprend toutes les personnes présentes dans le pays ou la zone à la date de référence, tandis que la population de droit comprend toutes celles qui résident habituellement dans le pays ou la zone, qu'elles y aient été ou non présentes à la date de référence. Par définition, la population totale de fait et la population totale de droit ne sont donc pas rigoureusement comparables entre elles.

Même lorsque l'on veut comparer deux totaux qui se rapportent à des populations de fait ou deux totaux qui se rapportent à des populations de droit, on risque souvent de faire des erreurs pour cette raison qu'il est rare que l'une et l'autre notions soient appliquées strictement. Pour citer quelques exemples, certains chiffres qui sont censés porter sur la population de fait ne tiennent pas compte du personnel militaire, naval et diplomatique étranger en fonction dans le pays ou la zone, ni des membres de leurs familles et de leurs domestiques les accompagnant; d'autres ne comprennent pas les visiteurs étrangers de passage dans le pays ou la zone ni les personnes à bord de navires ancrés dans les ports. En revanche, il arrive que l'on compte des personnes, inscrits maritimes et marins pêcheurs par exemple, qui, en raison de leur activité professionnelle, se trouvent hors du pays ou de la zone de recensement.

Les risques de disparités sont encore plus grands quand il s'agit de comparer des populations de droit, car les comparaisons dépendent au premier chef de la définition que l'on donne à l'expression « lieu de résidence habituel », qui varie d'un pays ou d'une zone à l'autre et qu'il est, de toute façon, difficile d'appliquer uniformément pour le dénombrement lors d'un recensement ou d'une enquête. Par exemple, les civils étrangers qui se trouvent temporairement dans un pays ou une zone comme travailleurs à court terme peuvent officiellement être considérés comme résidents après un séjour d'une durée déterminée, mais ils peuvent aussi être considérés comme non-résidents pendant toute la durée de leur séjour ; ailleurs, ces mêmes personnes peuvent être considérées officiellement comme résidents ou comme non-résidents du pays ou de la zone d'où elles viennent, selon la durée et, éventuellement, la raison de leur absence. Qui plus est, quel que soit son statut officiel, chacun des recensés peut, au moment de l'enquête, interpréter à sa façon la notion de résidence. De plus, les autorités nationales ou les entités responsables des zones ne savent pas toutes avec la même précision combien de leurs résidents se trouvent temporairement à l'étranger.

Les chiffres de population présentés dans les tableaux de l'*Annuaire* représentent, autant qu'il a été possible, la population de fait. Sauf indication contraire, on peut supposer que les chiffres présentés ont été communiqués par les pays ou les zones comme se rapportant à la population de fait. Les chiffres qui ont été communiqués comme se rapportant à la population de droit sont indiqués comme tels. Lorsque l'on savait que les données avaient été recueillies selon une définition de la population de fait ou de la population de droit qui s'écartait sensiblement de celle exposée plus haut, on l'a signalé en note, de manière à compenser dans toute la mesure possible les conséquences des divergences.

Il ne faut pas oublier néanmoins que l'on ne disposait pas toujours de renseignements détaillés à ce sujet. On ne peut donc partir du principe que les chiffres qui ne sont pas accompagnés d'une note signalant une divergence correspondent exactement aux définitions de la population de fait ou de la population de droit.

Il peut y avoir hétérogénéité dans les statistiques d'un même pays ou d'une même zone dans le cas des pays ou zones qui ne font une exploitation statistique détaillée des données que pour la population de droit alors qu'ils recueillent des données sur la population de droit et sur la population de fait à l'occasion d'un recensement, par exemple. Ainsi, tandis que les chiffres relatifs à la population totale qui figurent au tableau 3 se rapportent à la population de fait, ceux des tableaux qui présentent des données sur diverses caractéristiques de la population, par exemple le lieu de résidence (zone urbaine ou rurale), l'âge et le sexe, peuvent n'avoir trait qu'à la population de droit. Lorsque l'on savait que les chiffres se rapportaient à la population de droit, on l'a signalé en note.

3.1.2 Lieu de résidence (zone urbaine ou rurale)

L'hétérogénéité des définitions nationales du terme « urbain » nuit considérablement à la comparabilité internationale des données concernant la répartition selon le lieu de résidence. Les définitions utilisées par les différents pays ou zones et leurs implications sont exposées à la fin des notes techniques correspondant au tableau 6.

3.1.3 Répartition par âge

La répartition de la population selon l'âge est un paramètre fondamental de la plupart des analyses, estimations et projections relatives aux statistiques de la population. Malheureusement, ces données sont sujettes à un certain nombre d'erreurs et difficilement comparables. C'est pourquoi pratiquement tous les utilisateurs de ces statistiques doivent considérer ces répartitions avec la plus grande circonspection.

3.1.3.1 Collecte et exploitation des données sur l'âge

L'âge est l'intervalle de temps déterminé par calcul ou par estimation qui sépare la date de naissance de la date du recensement et qui est exprimé en années solaires révolues [3]. Les données sur l'âge peuvent être recueillies selon deux méthodes : la première consiste à obtenir la date de naissance de chaque personne à l'occasion d'un recensement ou d'un sondage, puis à calculer l'âge en années révolues en soustrayant la date de naissance de celle du dénombrement [6]. La seconde consiste à enregistrer l'âge en années révolues au moment du recensement, c'est-à-dire l'âge au dernier anniversaire.

La méthode recommandée consiste à calculer l'âge au dernier anniversaire en soustrayant la date exacte de la naissance de la date du recensement. Toutefois, on n'a pas toujours recours à cette méthode ; certains pays ou zones calculent l'âge en faisant la différence entre l'année du recensement et l'année de la naissance. Lorsque les données sur l'âge ont été établies de cette façon, on l'a signalé chaque fois que possible par une note. On peut d'ailleurs s'en rendre compte dans une certaine mesure, car les chiffres dans la catégorie des moins d'un an sont plus faibles qu'ils ne devraient l'être. Cependant, un nombre irrégulier de naissances d'une année à l'autre ou l'omission de certains âges parmi les moins d'un an peut aussi fausser les chiffres de la population de moins d'un an.

3.1.3.2 Erreurs dans les données sur l'âge

Les causes d'erreurs dans les données sur l'âge sont diverses : on peut citer notamment l'ignorance de l'âge exact, la déclaration d'années d'âge correspondant à un calendrier différent de celui des années solaires révolues depuis la naissance [7], la négligence dans les déclarations et dans la façon dont elles sont consignées, la tendance générale à déclarer des âges se terminant par certains chiffres tels que 0, 2, 5 ou 8, la tendance pour les personnes âgées à exagérer leur âge, une aversion subconsciente pour certains nombres, et les fausses déclarations faites délibérément.

Les causes d'erreurs mentionnées ci-dessus, communes à la plupart des enquêtes sur l'âge et à la plupart des pays ou zones, peuvent nuire sensiblement à la comparabilité.

À cause des difficultés indiquées ci-dessus, les répartitions par âge et par sexe de la population d'un grand nombre de pays ou de zones font apparaître les irrégularités suivantes : 1) sous-estimation des groupes d'âge correspondant aux enfants de moins d'un an et aux jeunes enfants ; 2) polarisation des déclarations sur les âges se terminant par les chiffres 0 ou 5 (c'est-à-dire 5, 10, 15, 20...) ; 3) prépondérance des âges pairs (par exemple 10, 12, 14...) au détriment des âges impairs (par exemple 11, 13, 15...) ; 4) écart considérable et surprenant entre le rapport masculin/féminin à certains âges ; 5) différences importantes et difficilement explicables entre les données concernant des groupes d'âge voisins. En comparant les statistiques provenant de recensements successifs pour des cohortes identiques sur le plan de l'âge et de la répartition par sexe et en étudiant la répartition par âge et par sexe de la population à chaque recensement, on peut déceler l'existence de ces incohérences et de quelques autres, un certain nombre d'entre elles se retrouvant à des degrés divers même dans les recensements les plus modernes.

3.1.3.3 Évaluation de l'exactitude

Pour déterminer, sur la base des anomalies relevées dans les groupes d'âge quinquennaux, le degré d'exactitude des statistiques par âge, on avait mis au point un indice spécial [8] pour l'Annuaire démographique 1949-1950. Cet indice était sensible à l'influence des différents facteurs qui limitent l'exactitude des données et il n'échappait pas non plus à celle des véritables fluctuations démographiques du passé. On ne pouvait donc l'appliquer indistinctement à tous les types de données à moins d'effectuer les ajustements nécessaires et de faire preuve de prudence dans l'interprétation des résultats.

La publication dans l'Annuaire démographique 1955 de statistiques de la population par année d'âge a permis d'utiliser un indice simple, mais très sensible, connu sous le nom d'indice de Whipple ou indice de concentration [9], dont l'interprétation échappe pratiquement à l'influence des facteurs sans rapport avec l'exactitude des déclarations d'âge. Il existe des méthodes plus perfectionnées pour évaluer l'exactitude des répartitions de population par année d'âge, mais on a décidé de se servir ici de l'indice de Whipple à cause de sa simplicité et de la large utilisation dont il a déjà fait l'objet dans d'autres publications.

L'indice de Whipple s'obtient en additionnant les déclarations d'âge comprises entre 23 et 62 ans inclusivement et en calculant le pourcentage des âges déclarés se terminant par 0 ou 5 par rapport au cinquième du nombre total de déclarations .

Les résultats varient entre un minimum de 100, s'il n'y a aucune concentration, et un maximum de 500, si aucun âge déclaré ne se termine par un chiffre autre que 0 et 5[10].

Cet indice est applicable à toutes les répartitions par âge pour lesquelles les années d'âge sont données au moins jusqu'à 62 ans, sauf dans les cas suivants : 1) lorsque les données présentées ont déjà fait l'objet d'un ajustement, l'indice de Whipple ne révèle aucune irrégularité bien que des inexactitudes d'un type différent puissent fausser ces données ; 2) lorsque les statistiques relatives à l'âge sont établies sur la base de l'année de naissance et que la tendance à arrondir l'année de naissance se traduit par une fréquence excessive des âges impairs, on ne peut utiliser la méthode reposant sur les déclarations d'âge se terminant par 5 et 0 pour évaluer l'exactitude des données recueillies.

À partir de chiffres relatifs à l'ensemble des deux sexes, on a calculé l'indice de Whipple pour toutes les répartitions par année d'âge du tableau 26 de l'édition de 1993 de *l'Annuaire démographique* en se fondant sur les recensements effectués entre 1985 et 1993, à l'exception de celles que l'on a écartées pour les motifs indiqués plus haut. L'édition de 1993 de *l'Annuaire démographique* (p. 19 à 20) donne une évaluation de l'exactitude des déclarations d'âge pour les répartitions données[11]. La présente édition de l'*Annuaire* ne fait pas apparaître la répartition par année d'âge ; les évaluations de l'exactitude des déclarations d'âge obtenues par application de l'indice de Whipple seront présentées dans l'édition de l'*Annuaire démographique* consacrée aux recensements de population. Pour les futurs plans de diffusion des données, se reporter aux pages Web consacrées à l'*Annuaire démographique* (http://unstats.un.org/unsd/demographic/products/dyb/default.htm).

Bien que l'indice de Whipple ne mesure que les effets de la préférence pour les âges se terminant par 5 et 0, il semble que l'on puisse admettre qu'il existe généralement certains liens entre cette préférence et d'autres sources d'inexactitudes dans les déclarations d'âge, de telle sorte que l'on peut dire qu'il donne une assez bonne idée de l'exactitude de la répartition par âge en général.

3.2 Méthodes utilisées pour indiquer la qualité des statistiques publiées

On a cherché dans toute la mesure possible à donner au lecteur une indication du degré de fiabilité des statistiques publiées dans *l'Annuaire démographique*. Pour ce faire, on a procédé de diverses façons . Chaque fois que l'on savait, grâce par exemple à une enquête post censitaire, qu'il y avait eu sous-dénombrement ou surdénombrement, on l'a signalé dans les notes qui accompagnent le tableau 3. Comme on l'a indiqué à la section 2.1 sous la rubrique « Considérations géographiques », chaque fois que les données ne portaient pas sur la totalité du pays, on l'a également signalé en note. De plus, les services nationaux de statistique ont été invités à fournir une évaluation des estimations de la population totale qu'ils communiquaient à la Division de statistique de l'ONU.

3.2.1 Traitement des séries chronologiques d'estimations de la population

En ce qui concerne les séries d'estimations de la population en milieu d'année, on considère que la qualité de la série tout entière est la même que celle de la dernière estimation. La qualité de la série est indiquée par le caractère d'imprimerie utilisé.

On n'a pas cherché à subdiviser les séries, mais il est évident que les données qui sont jugées sûres actuellement n'ont pas toutes le même degré de fiabilité et que, pour les premières années, nombre d'entre elles étaient peut-être bien moins sûres que la classification actuelle ne le laisse supposer. Ainsi, il apparaît clairement que cette méthode tend, dans bien des cas, à surestimer la fiabilité probable des séries chronologiques. Elle peut aussi inciter à sous-estimer la fiabilité des estimations pour les années qui précèdent ou qui suivent immédiatement un recensement.

3.2.2 Traitement des séries estimatives selon l'âge et d'autres caractéristiques démographiques

Des estimations de la répartition de la population par âge et par sexe peuvent être obtenues selon deux grandes méthodes : 1) en appliquant les composantes spécifiques du mouvement de la population, pour chaque groupe d'âge et pour chaque sexe, à la population dénombrée lors du recensement ; 2) en répartissant proportionnellement le chiffre total estimé pour une année postcensitaire d'après la composition par âge et par sexe au moment du recensement. Les estimations obtenues par la seconde méthode ne sont pas publiées dans l'*Annuaire démographique*.

Les séries estimatives selon l'âge et le sexe qui sont publiées sont classées en deux catégories, « sûres » ou « moins sûres », selon la méthode retenue pour le plus récent calcul estimatif de la population totale en milieu d'année. Ainsi, l'appréciation de la qualité du chiffre total, telle qu'elle ressort des signes de code, est censée s'appliquer aussi à l'ensemble de la répartition par âge et par sexe, et c'est sur cette seule base que l'on décide si les données figureront en caractères italiques ou romains. On n'a pas encore procédé à une évaluation plus poussée des données détaillées concernant la composition par âge.

4. STATISTIQUES DE L'ÉTAT CIVIL

Aux fins de l'*Annuaire démographique*, on entend par statistiques de l'état civil les statistiques des naissances vivantes, des décès, des morts fœtales, des mariages et des divorces.

Dans le présent volume de l'*Annuaire*, on n'a présenté que les tableaux de caractère général sur la natalité, la mortalité, la nuptialité et la divortialité. Les tableaux consacrés à la mortalité sont groupés sous les rubriques suivantes : mortalité fœtale, mortalité infantile, mortalité liée à la maternité et mortalité générale, y compris des tableaux portant sur la cause des décès.

4.1 Sources de variations des données

La plupart des statistiques de l'état civil publiées dans le présent *Annuaire* émanent des systèmes nationaux d'enregistrement des faits d'état civil. Le degré d'exhaustivité et d'exactitude de ces données varie d'un pays ou d'une zone à l'autre.

Il n'existe pas partout de système national d'enregistrement des faits d'état civil et, dans quelques cas, seuls certains faits sont enregistrés. Par exemple, dans certains pays ou zones, seuls les naissances et les décès sont enregistrés. Il existe également des différences quant au degré d'efficacité avec lequel les lois relatives à l'enregistrement des faits d'état civil sont appliquées dans les divers pays ou zones. La fiabilité des statistiques provenant des registres d'état civil dépend des modalités d'application de la loi et de la mesure dans laquelle le public s'y soumet.

Il est à signaler que dans certains cas les statistiques de la nuptialité et de la divortialité sont tirées d'autres sources que les registres d'état civil. Dans certains pays ou zones, par exemple, les seules données disponibles sur la nuptialité proviennent des registres des églises. Selon la pratique suivie par chaque pays, les statistiques de la divortialité sont tirées des actes des tribunaux et/ou des registres d'état civil. L'officier de l'état civil, le service national de statistique ou d'autres services administratifs peuvent être chargés d'établir ces statistiques.

Les autres facteurs qui influent sur la comparabilité internationale des statistiques de l'état civil sont à peu près les mêmes que ceux qu'il convient de prendre en considération pour interpréter les variations observées dans les statistiques de la population. La définition des faits d'état civil aux fins de statistique, la portée des données du point de vue géographique et ethnique ainsi que les méthodes d'exploitation des données sont autant d'éléments qui peuvent influer sur la comparabilité.

En plus des statistiques tirées des registres d'état civil, l'*Annuaire* présente des statistiques de l'état civil qui sont des estimations officielles nationales, fondées souvent sur les résultats de sondages. Aussi leur comparabilité varie-t-elle en fonction du degré d'exhaustivité des déclarations recueillies lors d'enquêtes sur les ménages, des erreurs d'échantillonnage ou autres, et des distorsions d'origines diverses.

Pour plus de détails au sujet des pratiques nationales relatives au rassemblement des statistiques d'état civil, le lecteur pourra se reporter aux : *Principes et recommandations pour un système de statistiques de l'état civil, deuxième révision*[12] ; *Manuel de statistiques de l'état civil, Volume I: aspects juridiques, organisationnels et techniques*[13] ; *Manuel des systèmes d'enregistrement des faits d'état civil et de statistiques de l'état civil : Gestion, fonctionnement et tenue*[14]; *Manuel des systèmes d'enregistrement des faits d'état civil et de statistiques de l'état civil : Élaboration d'un cadre juridique*[15] ; *Manuel des systèmes d'enregistrement des faits d'état civil et de statistiques de l'état civil : Élaboration de programmes d'information, d'éducation et de communication[16] ; Manuel des systèmes d'enregistrement des faits d'état civil et de statistiques de l'état civil : Principes et protocoles concernant la communication et l'archivage des documents individuels[17]; Manuel des systèmes d'enregistrement des faits d'état civil et de statistiques de l'état civil : Informatisation[18].* Le *Manuel des méthodes d'enquêtes sur les ménages[19]* fournit des informations ayant trait à la collecte et à l'évaluation des données sur la fécondité, sur la mortalité et sur d'autres faits d'état civil, qui ont été recueillies au cours des enquêtes sur les ménages. Ces publications sont également disponibles sur le Web à partir de l'adresse suivante : http://unstats.un.org/unsd/demographic/sources/civilreg/default.htm.

4.1.1 Définition des faits d'état civil aux fins de la statistique

Une cause importante d'hétérogénéité dans les données est le manque d'uniformité des définitions des différents faits d'état civil. Aux fins de *l'Annuaire démographique*, il est recommandé de recueillir les données relatives aux faits d'état civil en utilisant les définitions établies au paragraphe 57 des *Principes et recommandations pour un système de statistiques de l'état civil, deuxième révision[14]*. Ces définitions sont les suivantes :

La *NAISSANCE VIVANTE est l'expulsion ou l'extraction complète du corps de la mère, indépendamment de la durée de la gestation, d'un produit de la conception qui, après cette séparation, respire ou manifeste tout autre signe de vie, tel que battement de cœur, pulsation du cordon ombilical ou contraction effective d'un muscle soumis à l'action de la volonté, que le cordon ombilical ait été coupé ou non et que le placenta soit ou non demeuré attaché; tout produit d'une telle naissance est considéré comme « enfant né vivant ».*

Le *DÉCÈS est la disparition permanente de tout signe de vie à un moment quelconque postérieur à la naissance vivante (cessation des fonctions vitales après la naissance sans possibilité de réanimation). Cette définition ne comprend donc pas les morts fœtales.*

La *MORT FŒTALE est le décès d'un produit de la conception lorsque ce décès est survenu avant l'expulsion ou l'extraction complète du corps de la mère, indépendamment de la durée de la gestation; le décès est indiqué par le fait qu'après cette séparation le fœtus ne respire ni ne manifeste aucun signe de vie, tel que battement de cœur, pulsation du cordon ombilical ou contraction effective d'un muscle soumis à l'action de la volonté. Les morts fœtales tardives sont celles qui sont survenues après 28 semaines de gestation ou plus. Il n'y a aucune différence entre ces « morts fœtales tardives » et les faits désignés, avant 1950, par le terme « mortinatalité[20] ».*

Le *MARIAGE est l'acte, la cérémonie ou la procédure qui établit un rapport légal entre mari et femme. L'union peut être rendue légale par une procédure civile ou religieuse, ou par toute autre procédure, conformément à la législation du pays.*

Le *DIVORCE est la dissolution légale et définitive des liens du mariage, c'est-à-dire la séparation de l'époux et de l'épouse qui confère aux parties le droit de se remarier civilement ou religieusement, ou selon toute autre procédure, conformément à la législation du pays.*

Des données concernant les avortements sont également recueillies et présentées dans *l'Annuaire démographique*, la définition retenue étant la suivante :

Par référence à la femme, *l'AVORTEMENT se définit comme toute interruption de grossesse qui est survenue avant 28 semaines de gestation et dont le produit est un fœtus mort. Il existe deux grandes catégories d'avortement: l'avortement spontané et l'avortement provoqué. L'avortement provoqué a pour origine une action délibérée entreprise en vue d'interrompre une grossesse. Tout autre avortement est considéré comme spontané.*

4.1.2 Problèmes posés par les définitions établies

Les variations par rapport aux définitions établies des faits d'état civil sont le principal obstacle à la comparabilité internationale des statistiques de l'état civil. Un exemple en est fourni par le cas des naissances vivantes et celui des morts fœtales[21]. Dans certains pays ou zones, il faut que le nouveau-né ait vécu 24 heures pour pouvoir être inscrit sur le registre des naissances vivantes. Les décès d'enfants qui surviennent avant l'expiration du délai de 24 heures sont classés parmi les morts fœtales tardives et, en l'absence de méthodes spéciales d'exploitation des données, ne sont comptés ni dans les naissances vivantes ni dans les décès. De même, dans plusieurs autres pays ou zones, les décès d'enfants nés vivants et décédés avant l'enregistrement de leur naissance sont également comptés parmi les morts fœtales tardives.

À moins que des méthodes spéciales n'aient été adoptées pour l'exploitation de ces données, les statistiques des naissances vivantes et des décès ne tiendront pas compte de ces cas, qui viendront en revanche accroître d'autant le nombre des morts fœtales tardives. Le taux de mortalité infantile sera donc sous-estimé. Bien que les éléments constitutifs du taux (décès d'enfants de moins d'un an et naissances vivantes) accusent exactement la même insuffisance en valeur absolue, les lacunes sont proportionnellement plus fortes pour les décès de moins d'un an, ce qui cause des erreurs plus importantes dans les taux de mortalité infantile.

De plus, cette pratique augmente les rapports de mortinatalité. Quelques pays ou zones effectuent les ajustements nécessaires pour corriger cette anomalie (du moins dans les fréquences totales) au moment de l'établissement des tableaux. Si aucun ajustement n'a été effectué, cela est indiqué dans les notes chaque fois que possible.

Les définitions du mariage et du divorce posent aussi un problème du point de vue de la comparabilité internationale. Contrairement à la naissance et au décès, qui sont des faits biologiques, le mariage et le divorce sont uniquement déterminés par la législation et la coutume et, de ce fait, il est moins facile d'en donner une définition statistique qui ait une application universelle. À des fins statistiques, ces notions ont donc été définies de manière générale par référence à la législation de chaque pays ou zone. La législation relative au mariage et plus particulièrement au divorce varie d'un pays ou d'une zone à l'autre. En ce qui concerne le mariage, l'âge de nubilité est la condition la plus fréquemment requise mais il arrive souvent que d'autres conditions soient exigées.

Lorsqu'il est connu, l'âge minimum auquel le mariage peut avoir lieu avec le consentement des parents (et dans certains cas sans le consentement des parents) est indiqué au tableau 24, lequel est consacré aux mariages selon l'âge de l'époux et de l'épouse. Les lois et règlements relatifs à la dissolution du mariage par le divorce vont de l'interdiction absolue, en passant par diverses conditions requises pour l'obtention du divorce, jusqu'à la simple déclaration, par l'époux, de son désir ou de son intention de divorcer.

4.1.3 Portée géographique ou ethnique restreinte

En principe, les statistiques de l'état civil devraient s'étendre à l'ensemble du pays ou de la zone auxquels elles se rapportent et englober tous les groupes ethniques. En fait, il n'est pas rare que les données soient fragmentaires. Dans certains pays ou zones, l'enregistrement n'est obligatoire que pour une petite partie de la population, par exemple pour certains groupes ethniques. Dans d'autres, il n'existe pas de disposition qui prescrive l'enregistrement obligatoire sur le plan national, mais seulement des règlements ou décrets des municipalités ou des États, qui ne s'appliquent pas à l'ensemble du territoire. Il en est encore autrement dans d'autres pays ou zones où les autorités ont institué une zone d'enregistrement comprenant seulement une partie du territoire, le reste étant exclu en raison des difficultés d'accès ou parce qu'il est pratiquement impossible, pour des raisons d'ordre économique ou culturel, d'y procéder à un enregistrement régulier.

4.1.4 Exploitation des données

4.1.4.1 Selon le lieu de l'événement

Les statistiques de l'état civil qui sont présentées pour l'ensemble du territoire national se rapportent à la population de fait ou population présente. En conséquence, sauf indication contraire, les statistiques de l'état civil relatives à une zone ou à un pays donné portent sur tous les faits survenus dans l'ensemble de la population, à l'intérieur des frontières actuelles de la zone ou du pays considéré. On peut donc estimer qu'elles englobent les faits d'état civil survenus dans les tribus nomades et parmi les populations autochtones ainsi que parmi les ressortissants du pays et les étrangers. Des notes signalent les exceptions lorsque celles-ci sont connues.

Pour certains pays, les écarts entre les taux démographiques pour les zones urbaines et pour les zones rurales peuvent varier notablement selon que les faits d'état civil ont été exploités sur la base du lieu de l'événement ou du lieu de résidence habituel. Par exemple, si un nombre appréciable de femmes résidant dans des zones rurales proches de grands centres urbains accouchent dans les hôpitaux ou maternités d'une ville, les taux de fécondité ainsi que les taux de mortalité néo-natale et infantile seront généralement plus élevés dans les zones urbaines (et par conséquent plus faibles dans les zones rurales) si les faits sont exploités en se fondant sur le lieu de l'événement et non sur le lieu de résidence habituel. Le phénomène sera le même dans le cas de la mortalité générale si un bon nombre de personnes résidant dans des zones rurales font appel aux services de santé des villes lorsqu'elles sont gravement malades.

4.1.4.2 Selon la date de l'événement ou la date de l'enregistrement

Autant que possible, les statistiques de l'état civil figurant dans *l'Annuaire démographique* se rapportent aux faits survenus pendant l'année considérée et non aux faits enregistrés au cours de ladite année. Bon nombre de pays ou zones, toutefois, exploitent leurs statistiques de l'état civil selon la date de l'enregistrement et non selon la date de l'événement. Comme ces statistiques risquent d'induire gravement en erreur, les pays ou zones dont on sait qu'ils établissent leurs statistiques d'après la date de l'enregistrement sont signalés dans les tableaux par un signe plus (+). On ne dispose toutefois pas pour tous les pays ou zones de renseignements complets sur la méthode d'exploitation des statistiques de l'état civil et les données sont peut-être exploitées selon la date de l'enregistrement plus souvent que ne le laisserait supposer l'emploi des signes.

Étant donné que la qualité des données est inextricablement liée aux retards dans l'enregistrement, il faudra toujours considérer en même temps le code de qualité qui est décrit à la section 4.2.1 ci-après. Évidemment, si l'enregistrement des naissances est complet et effectué en temps voulu (code 'C'), les effets perturbateurs de la méthode consistant à exploiter les données selon la date de l'enregistrement seront pratiquement annulés. De même, s'agissant des statistiques des décès, les effets pourront bien souvent être réduits au minimum dans les pays ou zones où le code sanitaire subordonne la délivrance du permis d'inhumer à l'enregistrement du décès, ce qui tend à hâter l'enregistrement. Quant aux morts fœtales, elles sont généralement déclarées immédiatement ou ne sont pas déclarées du tout. En conséquence, si l'enregistrement se fait dans un délai très court, la différence entre les statistiques établies selon la date de l'événement et celles qui sont établies selon la date de l'enregistrement peut être négligeable. Dans bien des cas, la durée des délais légaux accordés pour l'enregistrement des faits d'état civil est un facteur dont dépend dans une large mesure l'incidence sur la comparabilité de l'exploitation des données selon la date de l'enregistrement.

En ce qui concerne le mariage et le divorce, la pratique consistant à exploiter les statistiques selon la date de l'enregistrement ne pose généralement pas de graves problèmes. Le mariage étant, dans de nombreux pays ou zones, un contrat juridique civil qui, pour être légal, doit être conclu devant un officier de l'état civil, il s'ensuit que dans ces pays ou zones l'enregistrement a lieu presque systématiquement au moment de la cérémonie ou immédiatement après. De même, dans de nombreux pays ou zones, le tribunal ou l'autorité qui a prononcé le divorce est seul habilité à enregistrer cet acte, et comme l'acte d'enregistrement figure alors sur les registres du tribunal l'enregistrement suit généralement de peu le jugement.

En revanche, si l'enregistrement n'a lieu qu'avec un certain retard, les statistiques de l'état civil établies selon la date de l'enregistrement ne sont pas comparables sur le plan international. Au mieux, les statistiques par date de l'enregistrement prendront surtout en considération des faits survenus au cours de l'année précédente ; dans les pays ou zones où le système d'enregistrement n'est pas très développé, il y entrera des faits datant de plusieurs années. Il ressort des documents dont on dispose que des retards de plusieurs années dans l'enregistrement des naissances ne sont pas rares, encore que, dans la majorité des cas, les retards ne dépassent pas deux à quatre ans.

Tant que l'enregistrement se fera avec retard, les statistiques fondées sur la date d'enregistrement ne seront comparables sur le plan international ni entre elles ni avec les statistiques établies selon la date de fait d'état civil.

Il convient également de noter que l'exploitation des données selon la date de l'enregistrement ne nuit pas seulement à la comparabilité internationale des statistiques. Même à l'intérieur d'un pays ou d'une zone, le procédé qui consiste à compter les enregistrements et non les faits peut compromettre la comparabilité des chiffres sur une longue période. Si le nombre des faits d'état civil enregistrés varie d'une année à l'autre (par suite de l'application de mesures visant tout particulièrement à encourager l'enregistrement ou parce qu'il est subitement devenu nécessaire de produire le certificat d'une naissance ou d'un décès non enregistré pour l'accomplissement de certaines formalités), les statistiques de l'état civil établies d'après la date de l'enregistrement ne permettent pas de quantifier ni d'analyser l'état et l'évolution de la population. Tout au plus peuvent-elles révéler l'évolution des conditions d'exigibilité du certificat de naissance, de décès ou de mariage et les fluctuations du volume de travail des bureaux d'état civil. Les statistiques établies selon la date de l'enregistrement peuvent donc ne présenter qu'une utilité très réduite pour des études nationales ou internationales.

4.2 Méthodes utilisées pour indiquer la qualité des statistiques de l'état civil qui sont publiées

La qualité des statistiques de l'état civil peut être évaluée en se fondant sur plusieurs facteurs. Le facteur essentiel est la complétude du système d'enregistrement des faits d'état civil d'après lequel les statistiques sont établies. Dans certains cas, on constate que les données tirées de l'enregistrement ne sont pas complètes lorsque l'on les utilise pour le calcul des taux. Toutefois, cette observation est valable uniquement lorsque les statistiques présentent des lacunes évidentes, qu'elles sont exploitées d'après la date de l'événement et que l'estimation du chiffre de population pris pour base est exacte. L'exploitation des données d'après la date de l'enregistrement donne souvent des taux qui paraissent exacts, tout simplement parce que le numérateur est artificiellement gonflé par suite de l'inclusion d'un grand nombre d'enregistrements tardifs ; inversement, il arrive que des taux paraissent vraisemblables parce que l'on a sous-évalué la population étudiée. Il ne faut pas non plus oublier que les renseignements dont on dispose sur les taux de fécondité, de mortalité et de nuptialité considérés comme normaux sont extrêmement sommaires dans un grand nombre de régions du monde et que les cas limites, qui sont les plus difficiles à évaluer, sont fréquents.

4.2.1 Codage qualitatif des statistiques provenant des registres de l'état civil

Dans le questionnaire relatif au mouvement de la population qui leur est envoyé chaque année dans le cadre de l'établissement de l'*Annuaire démographique*, les services nationaux de statistique sont invités à donner leur propre évaluation du degré de complétude des données sur les naissances, les décès, les décès d'enfants de moins d'un an, les morts fœtales tardives, les mariages et les divorces figurant dans leurs registres d'état civil.

D'après les renseignements directement communiqués par les gouvernements ou extraits des questionnaires ou de publications officielles pertinentes, il a été possible de classer les statistiques de l'enregistrement des faits d'état civil (naissances, décès, décès d'enfants de moins d'un an, morts fœtales tardives, mariages et divorces) en trois grandes catégories, selon leur qualité :

C : Données jugées pratiquement complètes, c'est-à-dire représentant au moins 90 p. 100 des faits d'état civil survenant chaque année.

U : Données jugées incomplètes, c'est-à-dire représentant moins de 90 p. 100 des faits survenant chaque année.

| : Données ne provenant pas des systèmes nationaux d'enregistrement des faits d'état civil mais jugées fiables, telles que les estimations dérivées des projections, d'autres techniques d'estimation ou recensements de population ou du logement.

... : Données dont le degré de complétude ne fait pas l'objet de renseignements précis.

Ces codes de qualité figurent dans la deuxième colonne des tableaux qui présentent, pour un nombre d'années déterminé les chiffres absolus et les taux (ou rapports) bruts concernant les naissances vivantes (tableau 9), les morts fœtales tardives (tableau 12), les décès d'enfants de moins d'un an (tableau 15), les décès (tableau 18), les mariages (tableau 23) et les divorces (tableau 25).

La classification des pays ou zones selon ces codes de qualité peut ne pas être uniforme. On a estimé néanmoins que les services nationaux de statistique étaient les mieux placés pour juger de la qualité de leurs données. On a pensé que les catégories que l'on pouvait distinguer sur la base des renseignements disponibles, bien que très larges, permettaient cependant de se faire une idée de la qualité des statistiques de l'état civil publiées dans l'*Annuaire*.

Par le passé, les bases sur lesquelles les pays évaluaient l'exhaustivité de leurs données n'étaient généralement pas connues. À l'occasion de l'établissement de l'*Annuaire démographique 1977*, les pays ont été invités, pour la première fois, à donner des indications à ce sujet. On leur a demandé de préciser si leurs estimations du degré d'exhaustivité des données d'enregistrement des naissances vivantes, des décès et de la mortalité infantile reposaient sur une analyse démographique, un double contrôle des registres ou d'autres méthodes qu'ils devaient spécifier. Relativement peu de pays ou zones ont jusqu'à présent répondu à cette nouvelle question ; on n'a donc pas cherché à réviser le système de codage qualitatif utilisé pour les statistiques de l'état civil présentées dans l'*Annuaire*. Il faut espérer qu'à l'avenir davantage de pays pourront fournir ces renseignements afin que l'on puisse adapter le système de codage qualitatif.

Sur les pays ou zones qui ont estimé à 90 p. 100 ou plus le degré d'exhaustivité de leur enregistrement des naissances vivantes (classé 'C' dans le tableau 9), les pays ou zones suivants ont communiqué des renseignements concernant les bases sur lesquelles leur estimation reposait :

a) Analyse démographique : Argentine, Australie, Canada, Chili, Croatie, Cuba, Égypte, États-Unis, Guadeloupe, Guernesey, Guyane française, Irlande, Islande, Israël, Koweït, Lettonie, Maurice, Porto Rico, République de Corée, République tchèque, Roumanie, Saint-Marin, Singapour, Suède et Suisse.

b) Double contrôle des registres : Bahamas, Barbade, Belgique, Bulgarie, Chypre, Cuba, Danemark, Estonie, Fidji, Finlande, France, Guadeloupe, Guam, Guyane française, Grèce, Guernesey, Hongrie, Île de Man, Îles Cook, Islande, Kirghizistan, Lituanie, Japon, Malaisie péninsulaire, Maldives, Nouvelle-Zélande, Saint-Kitts-et-Nevis, Sainte-Lucie, Roumanie, Singapour, Sri Lanka, Suède, Suisse, Tokélaou, Uruguay et Venezuela.

c) Autre méthode : Allemagne, Belgique, Bermudes, Chine, Groenland, région administrative spéciale de Hong Kong (Chine), région administrative spéciale de Macao (Chine), Îles Caïmanes, Islande, Japon, Luxembourg, Norvège, Pays-Bas, Pologne, Singapour et Slovénie.

Sur les pays ou zones qui ont estimé à 90 p. 100 ou plus le degré d'exhaustivité de leur enregistrement des décès (classé 'C' dans le tableau 18), les pays ou zones suivants ont donné des indications touchant la base de cette estimation :

a) Analyse démographique : Argentine, Australie, Canada, Chili, Cuba, Égypte, États-Unis, Guadeloupe, Guernesey, Guyane française, Irlande, Islande, Israël, Koweït, Lettonie, Maurice, Porto Rico, Roumanie, Saint-Marin, Singapour et Suisse.

b) Double contrôle des registres : Bahamas, Bulgarie, Cuba, Danemark, Fidji, Finlande, France, Grèce, Groenland, Guam, Guernesey, Îles Cook, Île de Man, Islande, Maldives, Nouvelle-Zélande, Roumanie, Saint-Kitts-et-Nevis, Sainte-Lucie, Singapour, Sri Lanka, Suède, Suisse, Tokélaou et Uruguay.

c) Autre méthode : Allemagne, Belgique, Bermudes, région administrative spéciale de Hong Kong, Îles Caïmanes, Irlande, Islande, Japon, Luxembourg, Norvège, Pays-Bas, Pologne, Singapour et Slovénie.

Sur les pays ou zones qui ont estimé à 90 p. 100 ou plus le degré d'exhaustivité de leur enregistrement des décès à moins d'un an (classé 'C' dans le tableau 15), les pays ou zones suivants ont donné des indications touchant la base de cette estimation :

a) Analyse démographique : Argentine, Australie, Canada, Chili, Cuba, Égypte, États-Unis, Irlande, Islande, Israël, Koweït, Lettonie, Maurice, Porto Rico, Roumanie, Saint-Marin, Singapour, Sri Lanka et Suisse.

b) Double contrôle des registres : Bahamas, Bulgarie, Cuba, Danemark, Fidji, Finlande, France, Grèce, Groenland, Guam, Guernesey, Île de Man, Îles Cook, Islande, Japon, Maldives, Nouvelle-Zélande, Roumanie, Saint-Kitts-et-Nevis, Sainte-Lucie, Singapour, Suède, Suisse, Tokélaou et Uruguay.

c) Autre méthode : Allemagne, Belgique, Bermudes, région administrative spéciale de Hong Kong, Îles Caïmanes, Islande, Japon, Luxembourg, Norvège, Pays-Bas, Pologne, Singapour et Slovénie.

4.2.2 Traitement des statistiques tirées des registres d'état civil

Dans tous les tableaux de l'*Annuaire*, on a indiqué le degré de fiabilité des statistiques de l'état civil en se fondant sur le codage qualitatif décrit ci-dessus. Les statistiques codées 'C', jugées sûres, sont imprimées en caractères romains. Celles qui sont codées 'U' ou '...', jugées douteuses, sont reproduites en *italique*. Bien que le codage qualitatif proprement dit n'apparaisse que dans certains tableaux, l'indication du degré de fiabilité (c'est-à-dire l'emploi des caractères italiques pour désigner les données douteuses) se retrouve dans tous les tableaux présentant des statistiques de l'état civil.

En général, le code de qualité pour les décès utilisé au tableau 18 sert à déterminer si, dans les autres tableaux, les données relatives aux décès apparaissent en caractères romains ou en italique. Toutefois, le code associé à certaines données sur les décès liés à la maternité dans le tableau 17 diffère de celui employé dans le tableau 18 lorsque l'on sait que le degré d'exhaustivité des données diffère grandement de celui du nombre total des décès. Dans les cas où le code de qualité du tableau 18 ne correspond pas aux caractères utilisés dans le tableau 17, les renseignements concernant l'exhaustivité des statistiques des décès selon la cause sont indiqués en note à la fin du tableau.

On a utilisé la même indication de fiabilité dans les tableaux des taux démographiques et dans ceux des fréquences correspondantes. Par exemple, les taux de mortalité calculés d'après les décès figurant sur un registre incomplet ou d'exhaustivité indéterminée sont jugés douteux et apparaissent en italique. Au sens strict, pour évaluer de façon plus précise les taux démographiques, il faudrait tenir compte de la précision des données sur la population figurant au dénominateur dans les taux. La qualité des données sur la population est étudiée à la section 3.2 des notes techniques.

Il convient de noter que, pour les taux de mortalité infantile, les taux de mortalité liée à la maternité et les rapports de morts fœtales tardives (calculées en utilisant au dénominateur le nombre de naissances vivantes), les indications relatives à la fiabilité sont déterminées sur la base des codes de qualité utilisés pour les décès d'enfants de moins d'un an, les décès totaux et les morts fœtales tardives, respectivement. Pour évaluer ces taux et rapports de façon plus précise, il faudrait tenir compte de la qualité des données relatives aux naissances vivantes, utilisées au dénominateur dans leur calcul. Les codes de qualité pour les naissances vivantes figurent au tableau 9 et sont décrits plus en détail dans les notes techniques se rapportant à ce tableau.

4.2.3 Traitement des séries chronologiques de statistiques tirées des registres d'état civil

Il est plus difficile de déterminer la qualité des séries chronologiques de statistiques de l'état civil que celle des données pour une seule année. Étant donné qu'une série chronologique de statistiques de l'état civil ne peut généralement avoir pour source qu'un système permanent d'enregistrement des faits d'état civil, on a arbitrairement supposé que le degré d'exactitude de la série tout entière était le même que celui de la dernière tranche annuelle de données tirées du registre d'état civil. La série tout entière est traitée de la manière décrite à la section 4.2.2 ci-dessus : lorsque le code de qualité relatif aux données d'enregistrement les plus récentes est 'C', les fréquences et les taux relatifs aux années antérieures sont eux aussi considérés comme sûrs et figurent en caractères romains. Inversement, si les données d'enregistrement les plus récentes sont codées 'U' ou '...', les données des années antérieures sont jugées douteuses et figurent en italique. Cette méthode n'est certes pas entièrement satisfaisante, car les données des premières années de la série sont souvent beaucoup moins sûres que le code actuel ne le laisse supposer.

4.2.4 Traitement des estimations fondées sur les statistiques de l'état civil

En plus des données provenant des systèmes d'enregistrement des faits d'état civil, l'Annuaire démographique contient aussi des estimations relatives aux fréquences et aux taux. Il s'agit d'estimations officielles, généralement calculées à partir des résultats d'un sondage ou par analyse démographique. Si des estimations concernant les fréquences et les taux figurent dans les tableaux, c'est parce que l'on considère qu'elles fournissent des renseignements plus exacts que les systèmes existants d'enregistrement des faits d'état civil. En conséquence, elles sont également jugées sûres et ne sont donc pas indiquées en italique, même si elles sont entrecoupées dans une série chronologique de données tirées des registres d'état civil.

Dans les tableaux qui indiquent le code de qualité, ce code ne s'applique qu'aux données tirées des registres d'état civil. Si une série pour un pays ou une zone comprend à la fois des données tirées d'un registre d'état civil et des données estimatives, le code ne s'applique qu'aux données d'enregistrement. Si seules des données estimatives apparaissent, le symbole '|' est utilisé.

4.3 Causes de décès

Les États membres de l'Organisation mondiale de la santé (OMS) sont tenus de communiquer à celle-ci les données sur les causes de décès codifiées selon la révision en vigueur de la Classification internationale des maladies et des problèmes de santé connexes (CIM) adoptée par l'Assemblé mondiale de la santé[22]. Les données sont collectées par l'OMS sur la base de la CIM. Pour assurer la comparabilité internationale des statistiques des causes de décès, l'OMS organise régulièrement des conférences internationales de révision de la Classification internationale des maladies afin de suivre, au fur et à mesure, les progrès les plus récents de la médecine clinique et de la statistique. Les données sont généralement envoyées à l'OMS selon la classification à 4 caractères prévue par la CIM et sont archivées dans la base de données sur la mortalité de l'OMS telles qu'elles ont été présentées par le pays. Pour les versions antérieures, par contre, les données sont disponibles seulement selon la liste A de 150 causes de la CIM. Les données de l'OMS sont disponibles sur le site Internet suivant: http://www3.who.int/whosis/menu.cfm.

Les révisions de la CIM permettent certes de disposer d'une version actualisée, mais elles posent plusieurs problèmes de comparabilité des statistiques des causes de décès. Le premier tient au manque de comparabilité dans le temps, qui accompagne inévitablement la mise en oeuvre d'une classification nouvelle. Le deuxième est celui de la comparabilité entre pays ou zones, car les différents pays peuvent adopter la nouvelle classification à des époques différentes. Établir la cause des décès exige des compétences de plus en plus poussées à mesure que la classification devient plus précise. Or, dans beaucoup de pays ou zones, il est rare que les décès se produisent en présence d'un témoin possédant une formation médicale et le certificat de décès est le plus souvent établi par quelqu'un qui n'est pas qualifié sur le plan médical. Étant donné que la CIM répertorie de nombreux diagnostics qu'il est impossible d'établir si l'on n'a pas de formation en médecine, elle ne favorise pas toujours la comparabilité internationale, notamment entre pays ou zones où la qualité des services médicaux est très disparate.

La dixième révision[23] est la dernière qu'ait connue la CIM. Les chapitres de la dixième révision se fondent sur un système de codification alphanumérique à une lettre suivie de trois chiffres pour les catégories à quatre caractères. Le chapitre 1 concerne les maladies infectieuses et parasitaires et le chapitre 2 l'ensemble des néoplasmes. Le chapitre 3 a trait aux troubles du système immunitaire, aux maladies du sang et aux organes hématopoïétiques. Le chapitre 4 porte sur les maladies du système endocrinien, de la nutrition et du métabolisme. Les autres chapitres groupent les maladies selon leur site anatomique, à l'exception de ceux qui concernent les affections mentales, les complications de la grossesse, de l'accouchement et des suites de couches, les malformations congénitales et les affections de la période périnatale. Enfin, un chapitre entier est consacré aux symptômes, manifestations et résultats anormaux.

4.3.1 Mortalité liée à la maternité

D'après la dixième révision de la CIM, la « mortalité liée à la maternité » est définie comme le décès d'une femme survenu au cours de la grossesse ou dans un délai de 42 jours après sa terminaison, quelle qu'en soit la durée et la localisation, pour une cause quelconque déterminée ou aggravée par la grossesse ou les soins qu'elle a motivés, mais ni accidentelle ni fortuite.

Les décès liés à la maternité se répartissent en deux groupes :

1) Décès par cause obstétricale directe qui résultent de complications obstétricales (grossesse, travail et suites de couches), d'interventions, d'omissions, d'un traitement incorrect ou d'un enchaînement d'événements de l'un quelconque des facteurs ci-dessus ;
2) Décès par cause obstétricale indirecte qui résultent d'une maladie préexistante ou d'une affection apparue au cours de la grossesse, sans qu'elle soit due à des causes obstétricales directes, mais qui a été aggravée par les effets physiologiques de la grossesse.

Il est recommandé dans la dixième révision d'exprimer les taux de mortalité liée à la maternité sur la base de 100 000 naissances vivantes ou 100 000 naissances totales (naissances vivantes et morts fœtales)[24]. Le nombre de femmes enceintes aurait dû être pris comme dénominateur, mais étant donné qu'il est impossible de le déterminer, le taux de mortalité liée à la maternité est ici calculé par 100 000 naissances vivantes. Bien que les naissances vivantes ne permettent pas d'évaluer sans distorsion le nombre des femmes enceintes, leur nombre est plus fiable que d'autres estimations car le nombre des naissances vivantes est plus exactement enregistré que celui des naissances vivantes et des morts fœtales.

4.3.2 Mortalité périnatale

La définition de la mortalité périnatale a été recommandée par le Groupe d'étude sur la mortalité périnatale, constitué par l'Organisation mondiale de la santé. La Conférence internationale pour la huitième révision de la Classification internationale des maladies a adopté la recommandation selon laquelle la période périnatale devait être définie comme suit: « période comprise entre la vingt-huitième semaine de gestation et la septième journée de vie ». Considérant que plusieurs pays comptaient comme mort fœtale tardive toute mort fœtale intervenue 20 semaines ou plus après le début de la gestation, la Conférence a décidé d'accepter aussi une définition plus large de la mortalité périnatale qui s'étend de la vingtième semaine de la gestation à la vingt-huitième journée de vie. Cette deuxième définition devait en principe permettre un enregistrement plus complet des morts fœtales intervenues entre la vingt-huitième semaine de gestation et la fin des six premières journées de la vie. En 1975, la Conférence chargée de la neuvième révision a recommandé que les statistiques de la mortalité périnatale s'appuient sur un certificat de décès périnatal normalisé, fondé sur une définition qui prévoit non seulement une durée minimale de gestation, mais également une taille et un poids minimaux.

Dans le tableau 19 de l'*Annuaire démographique 1996* et dans les éditions antérieures de l'*Annuaire* où figuraient des statistiques sur la mortalité périnatale, la définition de mortalité périnatale s'appuie sur la somme des morts fœtales tardives (mortalité fœtale au terme de 28 semaines de gestation ou plus) et de la mortalité infantile dans la première semaine de vie. De plus, afin de normaliser la définition et d'éliminer les différences dues aux pratiques nationales, les chiffres de la mortalité périnatale cités dans l'*Annuaire démographique* sont calculés par la Division de statistique. Conformément aux recommandations de la dixième conférence de révision, le taux de mortalité périnatale a été calculé sur 1 000 naissances vivantes, afin de réduire l'effet des insuffisances d'enregistrement des morts fœtales sur le dénominateur de la fraction[25].

NOTES

[1] Les données relatives à la mortalité liée à la maternité et aux taux de mortalité selon la cause émanent de l'Organisation mondiale de la santé et sont disponibles à l'adresse suivante : http://www3.who.int/whosis/menu.cfm.

[2] Les éditions de 1978 et de 1991 font exception à la règle, puisque les tableaux sur des sujets spéciaux ont été publiés séparément.

[3] *World Population Prospects: The 2004 Revision*. Nations Unies, New York, à paraître. Dans l'intervalle, on peut consulter des extraits et certaines données sur le site www.unpopulation.org. On trouve également des éléments d'information sur les méthodes et les données dans *World Population Prospects: The 2002 Revision*, publication des Nations Unies, numéro de vente : E.03.XIII.6, New York, 2003.

[4] ST/ESA/STAT/SER.M/49/Rev.4/WWW ; http://unstats.un.org/unsd/methods/m49/m49.htm; voir également *Code standard des pays et des zones à usage statistique*, numéro de vente : M.98.XVII.9, Nations Unies, New York, 1999.

5 Publication des Nations Unies, numéro de vente : F.98.XVII.8, 1998.

[6] Lorsque l'on utilise un registre de la population, on peut également calculer l'âge en années révolues en soustrayant la date de naissance de chaque personne inscrite sur le registre de la date de référence à laquelle se rapportent les données sur l'âge.

[7] L'emploi de méthodes différentes de calcul de l'âge, par exemple la méthode occidentale et la méthode orientale, ou, comme on les désigne plus communément, la méthode anglaise et la méthode chinoise, représente une cause de non-comparabilité. Selon la méthode chinoise, on considère que l'enfant est âgé d'un an à sa naissance et qu'il avance d'un an à chaque nouvelle année chinoise. Les répercussions de cette méthode sont particulièrement apparentes dans les données pour le premier âge : les données concernant les enfants de moins d'un an sont nettement inférieures à la réalité. Les effets sur les chiffres relatifs aux groupes d'âge suivants sont moins visibles. Les séries ainsi établies sont souvent ajustées avant d'être publiées, mais il ne faut pas exclure la possibilité d'aberrations de ce genre lorsque l'on compare des données censitaires sur l'âge.

[8] Dans cet indice, on déterminait les différences à partir des rapports prévus de masculinité dans un groupe d'âge et dans les groupes d'âge adjacents. Il fallait pour cela tenir compte de l'influence de facteurs tels que les mouvements passés des taux de natalité, les pertes de guerre élevées et, le cas échéant, le faible effectif de la population. On trouvera dans le *Bulletin démographique*, no 2 (publication des Nations Unies, numéro de vente : 52.XIII.4), p. 64 à 87, un exposé détaillé sur cet indice ainsi que les résultats de son application aux données présentées dans les éditions de 1949-1950 et de 1951 de l'*Annuaire démographique*. On a fait les mêmes calculs sur les statistiques publiées dans l'*Annuaire démographique 1952* et les résultats obtenus sont indiqués dans l'édition correspondante de l'*Annuaire*, qui, comme celles de 1953 et de 1954, donne de brèves explications sur l'indice en question.

[9] United States Bureau of the Census, Thirteenth Census, vol. I (Washington, D.C., U.S. Government Printing Office), p. 291 et 292.

[10] J.T. Marten, Census of India, 1921, vol. I, partie I (Calcutta, 1924), p. 126 et 127.

[11] *Annuaire démographique 1993*, numéro de vente : E/F.95.XIII.1. Publication des Nations Unies, New York, 1995.

[12] Numéro de vente : F.01.XVII.10, publication des Nations Unies, New York, 2003 ; http://unstats.un.org/unsd/demographic/sources/civilreg/default.htm.

[13] Numéro de vente : *E.84*.XVII.11, publication des Nations Unies, New York, 1985 ; http://unstats.un.org/unsd/demographic/sources/civilreg/default.htm.

[14] Numéro de vente : F.98.XVII.11, publication des Nations Unies, New York, 1998 ; http://unstats.un.org/unsd/demographic/sources/civilreg/default.htm.

[15] Numéro de vente : F. 98.XVII.7, publication des Nations Unies, New York, 1998 ; http://unstats.un.org/unsd/demographic/sources/civilreg/default.htm.

[16] Numéro de vente : F.98.XVII.4, publication des Nations Unies, New York, 1998 ; http://unstats.un.org/unsd/demographic/sources/civilreg/default.htm.

[17] Numéro de vente : F.98.XVII.6, publication des Nations Unies, New York, 1998 ; http://unstats.un.org/unsd/demographic/sources/civilreg/default.htm.

[18] Numéro de vente : F.98.XVII.10, publication des Nations Unies, New York, 1998 ; http://unstats.un.org/unsd/demographic/sources/civilreg/default.htm.

[19] Numéro de vente : F.83.XVII.13, publication des Nation Unis, New York, 1984.

[20] Pour plus de précisions, voir *Principes et recommandations pour un système de statistiques de l'état civil, deuxième révision,* numéro de vente : F.01.XVII.10, publication des Nations Unies, New York, 2001, par. 57.

[21] Pour plus de précisions au sujet des considérations historiques et juridiques auxquelles se rattachent les différentes définitions correspondant aux naissances vivantes et aux morts fœtales, pour une comparaison des définitions utilisées depuis le 1er janvier 1950 et pour une évaluation des effets de ces différences de définition sur le calcul de divers taux, voir le *Manuel de statistique de l'état civil, Volume II, Étude des pratiques nationales,* numéro de vente : F.84.XVII.11, publication des Nations Unies, New York, 1985, chap. IV.

[22] Les États membres de l'Organisation mondiale de la santé se réunissent annuellement dans le cadre de l'Assemblée mondiale de la santé, qui est l'organe directeur de l'Organisation.

[23] Organisation mondiale de la santé, *Classification statistique internationale des maladies et problèmes de santé connexes,* dixième révision, vol. 2, Genève, 1992.

[24] Ibid., p. 129 à 136.

Table A. *Demographic Yearbook 2002* synoptic table: Availability of data by country/area, table and sex, where applicable
Tableau A. Tableau synoptique de l'*Annuaire démographique 2002:* Disponibilité des données par pays ou zone, tableau et le sexe , si disponible

(See notes at end of table. — Voir notes à la fin du tableau.)

		General topic and table number- Suject général et numéro de tableau													
Continent, country or area Continent, pays ou zone	Table totals	Summary - Apercu				Population							Natality - Natalité			
		3		4	5	6		7		8		9	10		11	11a
		Total	M/F			Total	M/F	Total	M/F	Total	M/F		Total	M/F		
Total number of countries or areas - Total des pays ou zones	..	233	215	169	204	127	122	177	176	228	112	157	127	84	90	144
AFRICA — AFRIQUE																
Algeria - Algérie	16	•	•	...	•	...	•	...	...	•	...	•	...	...	...	•
Angola	4	•	...	...	...	...	...	...	...	•	•	...	...	...	...	...
Benin - Bénin	12	•	...	•	•	•	•	•	•	•	...	•	...	...	...	...
Botswana	17	•	•	•	•	•	•	•	•	•	...	•	...	...	...	...
Burkina Faso	9	•	•	...	•	...	•	...	•	•	...	•	...	...	...	...
Burundi	13	•	•	•	•	...	•	•	•	•	•	•	...	...	...	...
Cameroon - Cameroun	4	•	•	...	•	...	...	...	...	•	...	...	...	...	...	...
Cape Verde - Cap-Vert	11	•	•	•	•	•	•	•	•	•	...	•	...	...	...	•
Central African Republic - République centrafricaine	4	•	•	...	...	...	...	...	...	•	...	...	...	...	...	...
Chad - Tchad	8	•	•	...	•	•	...	...	...	•	...	•	...	...	...	...
Comoros - Comores	3	•	•	...	...	...	...	...	...	•	...	...	...	...	...	...
Congo	2	•	...	...	...	...	...	...	...	•	...	...	...	...	...	...
Côte d'Ivoire	11	•	•	•	•	•	...	...	...	•	...	•	...	...	...	...
Democratic Republic of the Congo - République démocratique du Congo	3	•	•	...	...	...	...	...	...	•	...	...	...	...	...	...
Djibouti	4	•	•	...	...	...	...	...	...	•	...	...	...	...	...	...
Egypt - Égypte	30	•	•	•	•	•	•	•	•	•	•	•	•	•	•	•
Equatorial Guinea - Guinée équatoriale	2	•	...	...	...	...	...	...	...	•	...	...	...	...	...	...
Eritrea - Érythrée	3	•	...	...	...	...	...	...	...	•	...	...	...	...	...	...
Ethiopia - Éthiopie	16	•	•	•	•	•	•	•	•	•	•	•	...	...	...	...
Gabon	10	•	•	•	•	•	•	•	•	•	•	...	...	...	...	...
Gambia - Gambie	7	•	•	...	•	...	...	•	•	•	•	...	...	...	...	...
Ghana	8	•	•	•	•	•	•	•	•	•	...	...	...	...	...	...
Guinea - Guinée	2	•	...	...	...	...	...	...	...	•	...	...	...	...	...	...
Guinea-Bissau - Guinée-Bissau	3	•	•	...	...	...	...	...	...	•	...	...	...	...	...	...
Kenya	6	•	•	...	...	...	...	...	...	•	...	...	...	...	...	...
Lesotho	10	•	•	•	•	•	...	...	...	•	...	...	...	...	...	...
Liberia - Libéria	5	•	•	...	•	•	...	...	...	•	...	...	...	...	...	...
Libyan Arab Jamahiriya - Jamahiriya arabe libyenne	14	•	•	•	•	...	...	...	...	•	...	•	•	•	...	...
Madagascar	10	•	•	...	•	...	...	...	...	•	...	•	...	...	...	...
Malawi	18	•	•	•	•	•	•	•	•	•	...	•	...	...	...	•
Mali	8	•	•	...	•	...	...	•	•	•	...	•	...	...	...	•
Mauritania - Mauritanie	6	•	•	...	...	...	...	...	•	•	...	•	...	...	...	...
Mauritius - Maurice	30	•	•	•	•	•	•	•	•	•	...	•	•	•	•	...
Morocco - Maroc	19	•	•	•	•	•	•	•	•	•	...	•	•	•	•	...
Mozambique	16	•	•	•	•	•	•	•	•	•	...	...	...	...	...	...
Namibia - Namibie	6	•	•	...	...	...	...	...	...	•	...	...	...	...	...	...
Niger	4	•	...	...	...	...	...	...	...	•	•	...	...	...	...	...
Nigeria - Nigéria	6	•	•	...	•	...	...	...	•	•	...	...	...	...	...	...
Réunion	23	•	•	•	•	•	•	•	•	•	...	•	•	•	...	•
Rwanda	4	•	•	...	...	...	...	...	...	•	...	...	...	...	...	•
Saint Helena ex. dep. - Sainte-Hélène sans dép.	22	•	•	•	•	•	•	•	•	•	...	•	•	•	...	•
Saint Helena: Ascension - Sainte-Hélène: Ascension	3	•	•	...	...	...	...	...	...	...	...	...	...	...	...	•
Saint Helena: Tristan da Cunha - Sainte-Hélène: Tristan da Cunha	4	•	•	...	...	...	•	•	•	...	...	...	...	...	...	...
Sao Tome and Principe - Sao Tomé-et-Principe	4	•	•	...	•	...	...	...	•	...	...	...	...	...	...	...
Senegal - Sénégal	7	•	•	...	•	•	...	•	•	•	...	...	...	...	...	...

33

Table A. *Demographic Yearbook 2002* synoptic table: Availability of data by country/area, table and sex, where applicable

Tableau A. Tableau synoptique de l'*Annuaire démographique 2002:* **Disponibilité des données par pays ou zone, tableau et le sexe , si disponible (continued — suite)**

(See notes at end of table. — Voir notes à la fin du tableau.)

Continent, country or area / Continent, pays ou zone	Foetal mortality - Mortalité foetale			Infant and maternal mortality - Mortalité infantile et mortalité liée à la maternité				General mortality - Mortalité générale							Nuptiality and divorces - Nuptialité et divortialité		
	12	13	14	15	16 Total	16 M/F	17	18	19 Total	19 M/F	20 Total	20 M/F	21	22	23	24	25
Total number of countries or areas - Total des pays ou zones	83	54	37	144	106	101	100	159	135	133	84	84	100	104	135	91	116
AFRICA — AFRIQUE																	
Algeria - Algérie	•	...	...	•	...	...	...	•	•	•	...	...	...	•	•	...	...
Angola	...	...	...	...	...	...	...	...	...	...	...	...	...	...	...	...	...
Benin - Bénin	...	...	...	•	...	...	...	•	...	...	...	...	...	...	...	...	...
Botswana	...	...	...	•	...	...	...	•	•	•	•	•	...	...	...	...	...
Burkina Faso	...	...	...	...	...	...	...	...	...	...	...	...	...	...	...	...	...
Burundi	...	...	...	•	...	...	...	•	...	...	...	...	...	...	...	...	...
Cameroon - Cameroun	...	...	...	...	...	...	...	...	...	...	...	...	...	...	...	...	...
Cape Verde - Cap-Vert	...	...	...	...	...	...	...	...	...	...	...	...	...	...	...	...	...
Central African Republic - République centrafricaine	...	...	...	...	...	...	...	•	...	...	...	...	...	...	...	...	...
Chad - Tchad	...	...	...	...	...	...	...	•	...	...	...	...	...	...	...	...	...
Comoros - Comores	...	...	...	...	...	...	...	...	...	...	...	...	...	...	...	...	...
Congo	...	...	...	...	...	...	...	...	...	...	...	...	...	...	...	...	...
Côte d'Ivoire	...	...	...	•	...	...	...	•	...	...	...	...	...	...	...	...	•
Democratic Republic of the Congo - République démocratique du Congo	...	...	...	...	...	...	...	...	...	...	...	...	...	...	...	...	...
Djibouti	...	...	...	...	...	...	...	...	...	...	...	...	...	...	•	...	•
Egypt - Égypte	•	...	...	•	•	•	•	•	•	•	•	•	•	•	•	...	...
Equatorial Guinea - Guinée équatoriale	...	...	...	...	...	...	...	...	...	...	...	...	...	...	...	...	...
Eritrea - Érythrée	...	...	...	...	...	...	...	...	...	...	...	...	...	...	...	...	...
Ethiopia - Éthiopie	...	...	...	•	...	...	...	•	...	...	...	...	...	...	•	...	•
Gabon	...	...	...	...	...	...	...	...	...	...	...	...	...	...	...	...	...
Gambia - Gambie	...	...	...	...	...	...	...	...	...	...	...	...	...	...	...	...	...
Ghana	...	...	...	...	...	...	...	...	...	...	...	...	...	...	...	...	...
Guinea - Guinée	...	...	...	...	...	...	...	...	...	...	...	...	...	...	...	...	...
Guinea-Bissau - Guinée-Bissau	...	...	...	...	...	...	...	...	...	...	...	...	...	...	...	...	...
Kenya	...	...	...	...	...	...	...	...	...	...	...	...	...	...	...	...	...
Lesotho	...	...	...	...	...	...	...	...	...	...	...	...	...	...	...	...	...
Liberia - Libéria	...	...	...	...	...	...	...	...	...	...	...	...	...	...	...	...	...
Libyan Arab Jamahiriya - Jamahiriya arabe libyenne	...	...	...	•	...	...	...	•	•	•	...	...	...	...	•	...	•
Madagascar	...	...	...	...	...	...	...	...	•	•	•	•	...	...	...	...	...
Malawi	...	...	...	•	...	...	...	...	•	•	•	•	...	•	...	...	...
Mali	...	...	...	...	...	...	...	...	...	...	...	...	...	...	...	...	...
Mauritania - Mauritanie	...	...	...	...	...	...	...	...	...	...	...	...	...	...	...	...	...
Mauritius - Maurice	•	...	...	•	•	•	•	•	•	•	•	•	•	•	•	•	•
Morocco - Maroc	...	...	...	•	•	•	...	•	•	•	...	...	...	...	...	...	...
Mozambique	...	...	...	•	...	...	...	•	•	•	•	•	...	...	...	...	...
Namibia - Namibie	...	...	...	...	...	...	...	...	...	...	...	...	...	...	...	...	...
Niger	...	...	...	...	...	...	...	...	...	...	...	...	...	...	...	...	...
Nigeria - Nigéria	...	...	...	...	...	...	...	...	...	...	...	...	...	...	...	...	...
Réunion	...	•	...	•	...	...	...	•	•	•	•	•	...	...	•	•	•
Rwanda	...	...	...	...	...	...	...	...	...	...	...	...	...	...	...	...	...
Saint Helena ex. dep. - Sainte-Hélène sans dép.	...	...	...	•	•	•	...	...	...	...	...	...	...	...	•	...	•
Saint Helena: Ascension - Sainte-Hélène: Ascension	...	...	...	...	...	...	...	...	...	...	...	...	...	...	...	...	...
Saint Helena: Tristan da Cunha - Sainte-Hélène: Tristan da Cunha	...	...	...	...	...	...	...	...	...	...	...	...	...	...	...	...	...
Sao Tome and Principe - Sao Tomé-et-Principe	...	...	...	...	...	...	...	...	...	...	...	...	...	...	...	...	...
Senegal - Sénégal	...	...	...	...	...	...	...	...	...	...	...	...	...	...	...	...	...

Table A. *Demographic Yearbook 2002* synoptic table: Availability of data by country/area, table and sex, where applicable
Tableau A. Tableau synoptique de l'*Annuaire démographique 2002:* Disponibilité des données par pays ou zone, tableau et le sexe , si disponible (continued — suite)

(See notes at end of table. — Voir notes à la fin du tableau.)

Continent, country or area / Continent, pays ou zone	Table totals	3 Total	3 M/F	4	5	6 Total	6 M/F	7 Total	7 M/F	8 Total	8 M/F	9	10 Total	10 M/F	11	11a
AFRICA — AFRIQUE																
Seychelles	19	•	•	•	•	...	...	•	•	•	...	•	•	•	•	•
Sierra Leone	5	•	•	...	•	•	...	•	...	•	...	•	...	...	...	...
Somalia - Somalie	7	•	•	...	...	•	•	•	...	•	...	•	...	...	...	...
South Africa - Afrique du Sud	22	•	•	•	•	•	•	•	•	•	•	•	•	...	...	...
Sudan - Soudan	8	•	•	...	•	•	•	•	...	•	...	•	•	...	...	...
Swaziland	15	•	•	•	•	•	•	•	•	•	•	...	•	...	•	...
Togo	3	•	...	...	...	•	...	...	...	...	...	...	...	...	...	...
Tunisia - Tunisie	23	•	•	•	•	•	•	•	•	•	•	•	•	•	...	•
Uganda - Ouganda	7	•	•	...	•	•	•	...	...	•	...	•	•	...	...	...
United Republic of Tanzania - République Unie de Tanzanie	5	•	•	...	•	...	...	...	...	•	•	...	...	...	...	...
Western Sahara - Sahara occidental	3	•	•	...	...	...	...	...	...	•	...	...	...	...	...	...
Zambia - Zambie	9	•	•	...	•	•	•	•	•	•	•	•	...	...	...	...
Zimbabwe	8	•	...	...	•	•	•	•	•	•	•	...	...	...	...	...
AMERICA, NORTH — AMERIQUE DU NORD																
Anguilla	18	•	•	•	•	...	...	•	•	•	...	⊚	⊚	...	•	...
Antigua and Barbuda - Antigua-et-Barbuda	17	•	•	•	•	...	...	•	•	•	...	•	⊚	...	...	•
Aruba	15	•	•	•	•	...	...	•	•	•	...	•	•	...	...	...
Bahamas	22	•	•	•	•	...	...	•	•	•	•	•	•	•	...	•
Barbados - Barbade	12	•	•	•	•	...	...	...	...	•	...	⊚	•	...	...	⊚
Belize	24	•	•	•	•	•	•	•	•	•	•	•	•	•	...	•
Bermuda - Bermudes	24	•	•	•	•	...	...	•	•	•	•	•	•	•	•	•
British Virgin Islands - Iles Vierges britanniques	13	•	•	•	...	...	•	•	•	...	...	•	...	...	...	•
Canada	32	•	•	•	•	•	•	•	•	•	•	•	•	•	•	•
Cayman Islands - Îles Caïmanes	17	•	...	•	•	...	...	•	•	•	•	•	•	...	...	•
Costa Rica	28	•	•	•	•	•	•	•	•	•	•	•	•	•	...	•
Cuba	30	•	•	•	•	•	•	•	•	•	•	•	•	•	...	•
Dominica - Dominique	14	•	•	•	•	...	...	•	•	•	...	•	•	...	...	•
Dominican Republic - République dominicaine	23	•	•	•	•	•	...	•	•	•	...	•	•	•	...	•
El Salvador	29	•	•	•	•	•	•	•	•	•	•	•	•	•	...	•
Greenland - Groenland	26	•	•	•	•	•	•	•	•	•	•	•	•	•	...	•
Grenada - Grenade	17	•	•	•	•	...	...	•	•	•	...	⊚	•	...	...	•
Guadeloupe	21	•	•	•	•	...	...	•	•	•	•	•	⊚	•	...	•
Guatemala	27	•	...	•	•	•	•	•	•	•	•	•	•	•	...	•
Haiti - Haïti	8	•	•	•	•	...	...	•	•	•	...	•	•	...	...	•
Honduras	8	•	•	•	•	...	...	•	•	•	...	•	•	...	...	•
Jamaica - Jamaïque	17	•	•	•	•	...	...	•	•	•	...	•	•	•	•	•
Martinique	21	•	•	•	•	...	...	•	•	•	•	•	•	•	•	•
Mexico - Mexique	28	•	•	•	•	•	•	•	•	•	•	•	•	•	•	•
Montserrat	5	•	•	•	...	...	...	•	•	•	...	...	...	...	...	•
Netherlands Antilles - Antilles néerlandaises	11	•	•	•	•	...	...	•	•	•	...	•	...	...	...	...
Nicaragua	25	•	•	•	•	•	•	•	•	•	•	•	•	•	...	•
Panama	30	•	•	•	•	•	•	•	•	•	•	•	•	•	•	•
Puerto Rico - Porto Rico	30	•	•	•	•	•	•	•	•	•	•	•	•	•	•	•
Saint Kitts and Nevis - Saint-Kitts-et-Nevis	20	•	•	•	•	...	...	•	•	•	...	•	•	•	...	•
Saint Lucia - Sainte-Lucie	27	•	•	•	•	...	•	•	•	•	•	•	•	•	...	•
Saint Pierre and Miquelon - Saint Pierre-et-Miquelon	5	•	•	•	...	...	...	•	•	•	...	•	...	...	...	...
Saint Vincent and the Grenadines - Saint Vincent-et-les Grenadines	24	•	•	•	•	•	•	•	•	•	•	•	•	•	...	•
Trinidad and Tobago - Trinité-et-Tobago	22	•	•	•	•	...	...	•	•	•	•	•	•	•	•	•

Table A. *Demographic Yearbook 2002* synoptic table: Availability of data by country/area, table and sex, where applicable

Tableau A. Tableau synoptique de l'*Annuaire démographique 2002:* Disponibilité des données par pays ou zone, tableau et le sexe , si disponible (continued — suite)

(See notes at end of table. — Voir notes à la fin du tableau.)

Continent, country or area / Continent, pays ou zone	Foetal mortality - Mortalité foetale 12	13	14	Infant and maternal mortality - Mortalité infantile et mortalité liée à la maternité 15	16 Total	16 M/F	17	General mortality - Mortalité générale 18	19 Total	19 M/F	20 Total	20 M/F	21	22	Nuptiality and divorces - Nuptialité et divortialité 23	24	25
AFRICA — AFRIQUE																	
Seychelles	...	...	...	●	...	...	...	●	●	●	...	...	...	...	●	●	●
Sierra Leone	...	...	...	...	...	...	...	...	...	...	...	...	...	...	...	...	...
Somalia - Somalie	...	...	...	...	...	...	...	●	...	...	...	...	...	...	...	...	...
South Africa - Afrique du Sud	...	●	...	●	...	●	...	●	●	●	...	...	...	...	...	...	...
Sudan - Soudan	...	...	...	...	...	...	...	●	●	●	●	●	...	●	...	...	...
Swaziland	...	...	...	...	...	...	...	...	...	...	...	...	...	...	●	●	...
Togo	...	...	...	●	●	...	...	●	●	●	...	...	...	...	●	...	...
Tunisia - Tunisie	...	...	...	●	●	...	...	●	●	●	...	...	...	...	●	...	●
Uganda - Ouganda	...	...	...	...	...	...	...	...	...	...	...	...	...	...	...	...	...
United Republic of Tanzania - République Unie de Tanzanie	...	...	...	...	...	...	...	...	...	...	...	...	...	...	...	...	...
Western Sahara - Sahara occidental	...	...	...	...	...	...	...	...	...	...	...	...	...	...	...	...	...
Zambia - Zambie	...	...	...	...	...	...	...	...	...	...	...	...	...	...	...	...	...
Zimbabwe	...	...	...	...	...	...	...	...	...	...	...	...	...	...	...	...	...
AMERICA, NORTH — AMERIQUE DU NORD																	
Anguilla	...	...	...	●	...	●	...	●	●	...	...	...	●	...	●	...	●
Antigua and Barbuda - Antigua-et-Barbuda	...	...	...	●	●	●	...	●	●	...	...	...	●	...	●	...	●
Aruba	...	...	...	●	●	●	...	●	●	...	...	...	●	...	●	...	●
Bahamas	...	...	...	●	●	●	...	●	●	...	...	...	●	...	●	...	●
Barbados - Barbade	...	...	...	●	●	●	...	●	●	...	...	...	●	...	●	...	●
Belize	...	...	...	●	●	●	...	●	●	...	...	...	●	...	●	...	●
Bermuda - Bermudes	●	...	...	●	●	●	...	●	●	...	...	...	●	...	...	...	...
British Virgin Islands - Îles Vierges britanniques	...	...	...	●	...	...	...	●	●	...	...	...	●	...	...	...	...
Canada	●	●	●	●	●	●	...	●	●	●	...	...	●	...	●	●	●
Cayman Islands - Îles Caïmanes	...	...	...	●	●	...	...	●	●	...	...	...	●	...	●	...	●
Costa Rica	●	...	...	●	●	●	...	●	●	●	...	...	●	...	●	...	●
Cuba	●	...	...	●	●	●	...	●	●	●	...	...	●	...	●	...	●
Dominica - Dominique	...	...	...	●	...	...	...	●	●	...	...	...	●	...	●	...	●
Dominican Republic - République dominicaine	●	●	...	●	●	●	...	●	●	●	...	...	●	...	...	...	●
El Salvador	●	...	...	●	●	●	...	●	●	●	...	...	●	...	...	...	...
Greenland - Groenland	●	●	...	●	●	●	...	●	●	...	...	...	●	...	...	...	...
Grenada - Grenade	...	...	...	●	●	...	...	●	●	...	...	...	...	...	●	...	●
Guadeloupe	●	...	...	●	●	●	...	●	●	●	...	...	●	...	●	...	●
Guatemala	●	...	...	●	●	●	...	●	●	●	...	...	●	...	●	...	●
Haiti - Haïti	...	...	...	●	...	...	...	●	...	...	...	...	...	...	●	...	●
Honduras	...	...	...	●	...	...	...	●	...	...	...	...	...	...	●	...	●
Jamaica - Jamaïque	...	...	...	●	...	...	...	●	...	...	...	...	...	...	●	...	●
Martinique	●	...	...	●	●	●	...	●	●	●	...	...	●	...	●	...	●
Mexico - Mexique	●	...	...	●	●	●	...	●	●	●	●	●	●	...	●	...	●
Montserrat	...	...	...	...	...	...	...	●	...	...	...	...	...	...	●	...	●
Netherlands Antilles - Antilles néerlandaises	...	...	...	...	...	...	...	●	...	...	...	...	...	...	●	...	●
Nicaragua	...	...	...	...	...	...	...	...	...	...	...	...	●	...	●	●	●
Panama	●	●	●	●	●	●	...	●	●	●	...	...	...	...	●	●	●
Puerto Rico - Porto Rico	●	●	...	●	●	●	...	●	●	●	●	●	●	...	●	●	●
Saint Kitts and Nevis - Saint-Kitts-et-Nevis	...	...	...	●	...	...	...	●	●	...	...	...	●	...	●	...	●
Saint Lucia - Sainte-Lucie	●	...	...	●	●	...	...	●	●	...	...	...	●	...	●	...	●
Saint Pierre and Miquelon - Saint Pierre-et-Miquelon	...	...	...	...	...	...	...	...	...	...	...	...	...	...	...	...	...
Saint Vincent and the Grenadines - Saint Vincent-et-les Grenadines	●	...	...	●	●	●	...	●	●	●	...	...	●	...	●	...	●
Trinidad and Tobago - Trinité-et-Tobago	...	...	...	...	●	●	...	●	●	●	●	●	●	...	...	...	...

Table A. *Demographic Yearbook 2002* synoptic table: Availability of data by country/area, table and sex, where applicable
Tableau A. Tableau synoptique de l'*Annuaire démographique 2002:* Disponibilité des données par pays ou zone, tableau et le sexe , si disponible (continued — suite)

(See notes at end of table. — Voir notes à la fin du tableau.)

Continent, country or area / Continent, pays ou zone	Table totals	Summary - Apercu 3 Total	3 M/F	4	5	Population 6 Total	6 M/F	7 Total	7 M/F	8 Total	8 M/F	9	Natality 10 Total	10 M/F	11	11a
AMERICA, NORTH — AMERIQUE DU NORD																
Turks Caicos Islands - Îles Turques et Caïques	10	•	•	•	...	•	...	...	•	•	...	•	...	...	...	•
United States - États-Unis	27	•	•	•	•	•	...	•	•	•	•	•	•	•	...	•	•
United States Virgin Islands - Îles Vierges américaines	15	•	•	...	•	...	...	•	•	•	•	...	•	•	...	•
AMERICA, SOUTH — AMERIQUE DU SUD																
Argentina - Argentine	25	•	•	•	•	•	•	•	•	...	•	•	•	•	•
Bolivia - Bolivie	14	•	•	•	•	•	•	•	•	...	•	•	•	•	...
Brazil - Brésil	26	•	•	•	•	•	•	•	•	...	•	•	•	•	...
Chile - Chili	30	•	•	•	•	•	•	•	•	•	•	•	•	•	•
Colombia - Colombie	23	•	•	•	•	•	•	•	•	...	•	•	•	•	•
Ecuador - Équateur	26	•	•	•	•	•	•	•	•	...	•	•	•	•	...
Falkland Islands (Malvinas) - Îles Falkland (Malvinas)	9	•	•	•	...	•	...	•	•	...	...	...	...	...	...
French Guiana - Guyane française	24	•	•	•	•	•	...	•	•	...	•	•	...	•	...
Guyana	8	•	•	•	•	...	...	...	•	...	...	...	...	•	...
Paraguay	13	•	•	•	•	•	...	•	•	...	...	...	...	...	•
Peru - Pérou	23	•	•	•	•	•	•	•	•	...	•	•	•	•	•
Suriname	22	•	•	•	•	...	•	•	•	...	•	•	•	•	•
Uruguay	29	•	•	•	•	•	•	•	•	...	•	•	•	•	•
Venezuela	29	•	•	•	•	•	•	•	•	...	•	•	•	•	•
ASIA — ASIE																
Afghanistan	6	•	•	...	•	•	...	•	•	...	•	...	...	...	...
Armenia - Arménie	30	•	•	...	•	•	•	•	•	•	•	•	•	...	...
Azerbaijan - Azerbaïdjan	32	•	•	•	•	•	•	•	•	•	•	•	•	•	•
Bahrain - Bahreïn	25	•	•	•	•	•	•	•	•	•	•	•	•	...	•
Bangladesh	6	•	•	...	•	•	•	•	•	...	•	...	...	...	•
Bhutan - Bhoutan	6	•	...	...	•	•	...	•	•	...	•	...	...	...	...
Brunei Darussalam - Brunéi Darussalam	22	•	•	...	•	•	•	•	•	•	•	•	•	•	•
Cambodia - Cambodge	9	•	•	...	•	•	•	•	•	•	•	...	...	...	...
China - Chine[1]	17	•	•	•	•	•	•	•	•	•	...	...	...	...	...
China: Hong Kong SAR - Chine: Hong Kong RAS	30	•	•	•	•	•	•	•	•	•	•	•	•	•	...
China: Macao SAR - Chine: Macao RAS	26	•	•	•	•	•	•	•	•	•	•	•	•	•	•
Cyprus - Chypre	25	•	•	•	•	•	•	•	•	•	•	•	•	•	...
Georgia - Géorgie	30	•	•	•	•	•	•	•	•	...	•	•	•	•	•
India - Inde[2]	12	•	•	•	•	•	•	•	•	...	•	...	...	...	...
Indonesia - Indonésie	10	•	•	•	•	•	•	•	•	...	...	...	...	...	...
Iran (Islamic Republic of) - Iran (République islamique d')	17	•	•	•	•	•	•	•	•	...	•	•	•	...	•
Iraq	13	•	•	•	•	•	•	•	•	...	•	•	...	...	•
Israel - Israël[3]	32	•	•	•	•	•	•	•	•	•	•	•	•	•	•
Japan - Japon	32	•	•	•	•	•	•	•	•	•	•	•	•	•	•
Jordan - Jordanie	15	•	•	•	•	•	•	•	•	...	•	...	...	...	•
Kazakhstan	31	•	•	•	•	•	•	•	•	...	•	•	•	•	•
Korea (Dem. People's Republic of) - Corée (Rép. populaire dém. de)	12	•	•	...	...	•	•	•	•	...	•	...	...	...	...
Korea (Republic of) - Corée (République de)	27	•	•	•	•	•	•	•	•	...	•	•	•	•	•
Kuwait - Koweït	25	•	•	•	•	•	•	•	•	...	•	...	...	...	•
Kyrgyzstan - Kirghizistan	31	•	•	•	•	•	•	•	•	...	•	•	•	•	•

37

Table A. *Demographic Yearbook 2002* synoptic table: Availability of data by country/area, table and sex, where applicable
Tableau A. Tableau synoptique de l'*Annuaire démographique 2002:* Disponibilité des données par pays ou zone, tableau et le sexe , si disponible (continued — suite)

(See notes at end of table. — Voir notes à la fin du tableau.)

Continent, country or area / Continent, pays ou zone	Foetal mortality - Mortalité foetale			Infant and maternal mortality - Mortalité infantile et mortalité liée à la maternité				General mortality - Mortalité générale							Nuptiality and divorces - Nuptialité et divortialité		
	12	13	14	15	16 Total	16 M/F	17	18	19 Total	19 M/F	20 Total	20 M/F	21	22	23	24	25
AMERICA, NORTH — AMERIQUE DU NORD																	
Turks Caicos Islands - Îles Turques et Caïques	...	...	...	...	•	•	•	...	...	...	...	...	•	...	•	...	...
United States - États-Unis	•	...	...	•	•	•	•	•	•	...	...	...	•	•	•	•	•
United States Virgin Islands - Îles Vierges américaines	...	...	...	...	•	•	•	•	•	...	...	...	•	...	•	...	...
AMERICA, SOUTH — AMERIQUE DU SUD																	
Argentina - Argentine	•	...	...	•	•	•	•	•	•	•	•	•	•	...	•	...	...
Bolivia - Bolivie	...	...	...	•	...	...	...	...	...	...	...	...	•	...	•	...	...
Brazil - Brésil	•	...	...	•	•	•	...	•	•	•	•	•	•	...	•	•	•
Chile - Chili	•	...	...	•	•	•	•	•	•	•	•	•	•	•	•	•	•
Colombia - Colombie	•	...	...	•	•	•	•	•	•	•	•	•	•	...	•	•	•
Ecuador - Équateur	•	...	...	•	•	•	•	•	•	•	•	•	•	...	•	•	•
Falkland Islands (Malvinas) - Îles Falkland (Malvinas)	...	...	...	...	...	...	...	•	•	...	...	...	•	...	...	...	...
French Guiana - Guyane française	•	...	...	•	•	•	•	•	•	•	...	...	•	...	•	...	•
Guyana	...	...	...	...	...	...	...	•	•	...	...	...	•	...	•	...	...
Paraguay	...	...	...	•	•	•	...	•	•	•	•	•	•	...	•	•	•
Peru - Pérou	•	...	...	•	•	•	•	•	•	•	•	•	•	...	•	•	•
Suriname	•	...	...	•	•	•	•	•	•	•	•	•	•	...	•	•	•
Uruguay	•	...	...	•	•	•	•	•	•	•	•	•	•	...	•	•	•
Venezuela	•	...	...	•	...	...	...	•	•	•	•	•	•	...	•	•	•
ASIA — ASIE																	
Afghanistan	...	...	...	•	...	...	...	•	•	...	...	...	•	...	...	...	...
Armenia - Arménie	•	•	...	•	•	•	...	•	•	•	•	•	•	...	•	•	•
Azerbaijan - Azerbaïdjan	•	•	•	•	•	•	•	•	•	•	•	•	•	...	•	•	•
Bahrain - Bahreïn	•	•	...	•	•	•	•	•	•	•	•	•	•	...	•	•	•
Bangladesh	...	...	...	...	...	...	...	...	...	...	...	...	...	...	...	...	...
Bhutan - Bhoutan	...	...	...	...	...	...	...	...	...	...	...	...	...	...	•	•	•
Brunei Darussalam - Brunéi Darussalam	...	...	...	•	...	...	...	•	•	...	...	...	•	...	•	•	•
Cambodia - Cambodge	...	...	...	...	...	...	...	•	•	...	...	...	•	...	•	...	...
China - Chine[1]	...	...	...	...	...	...	...	•	•	•	•	•	•	...	•	...	...
China: Hong Kong SAR - Chine: Hong Kong RAS	•	•	•	•	•	•	•	•	•	•	•	•	•	...	•	•	•
China: Macao SAR - Chine: Macao RAS	•	...	...	•	•	•	...	•	•	•	•	•	•	...	•	•	•
Cyprus - Chypre	...	...	...	•	•	•	...	•	•	•	•	•	•	...	•	•	•
Georgia - Géorgie	•	...	...	•	•	•	...	•	•	•	•	•	•	...	•	•	•
India - Inde[2]	...	...	...	...	...	...	...	...	...	...	...	...	...	...	...	...	...
Indonesia - Indonésie	...	...	...	...	...	...	...	...	...	...	...	...	...	...	...	...	...
Iran (Islamic Republic of) - Iran (République islamique d')	...	...	...	•	...	...	...	•	•	...	...	...	•	...	•	...	•
Iraq	...	...	...	...	...	...	...	•	...	...	...	...	...	...	•	...	...
Israel - Israël[3]	•	•	•	•	•	•	•	•	•	•	•	•	•	...	•	•	•
Japan - Japon	•	•	•	•	•	•	•	•	•	•	•	•	•	...	•	•	•
Jordan - Jordanie	...	...	...	...	...	...	...	...	...	...	...	...	...	...	•	...	...
Kazakhstan	•	•	•	•	•	•	•	•	•	•	•	•	•	...	•	•	•
Korea (Dem. People's Republic of) - Corée (Rép. populaire dém. de)	...	...	...	...	...	...	...	•	•	...	...	...	•	...	...	...	...
Korea (Republic of) - Corée (République de)	...	...	...	•	...	...	...	•	•	...	...	...	•	...	•	•	•
Kuwait - Koweït	•	...	...	•	•	•	...	•	•	•	•	•	•	...	•	•	•
Kyrgyzstan - Kirghizistan	•	•	...	•	•	•	•	•	•	•	•	•	•	...	•	•	•

Table A. *Demographic Yearbook 2002* synoptic table: Availability of data by country/area, table and sex, where applicable
Tableau A. Tableau synoptique de l'*Annuaire démographique 2002*: Disponibilité des données par pays ou zone, tableau et le sexe , si disponible (continued — suite)

(See notes at end of table. — Voir notes à la fin du tableau.)

Continent, country or area / Continent, pays ou zone	Table totals	Summary - Apercu 3 Total	3 M/F	4	5	Population 6 Total	6 M/F	7 Total	7 M/F	8 Total	8 M/F	9	Natality - Natalité 10 Total	10 M/F	11	11a
ASIA — ASIE																
Lao People's Democratic Republic - République démocratique populaire lao	9	•	•	•	•	•	•	•	•	•	•		...	...	...	...
Lebanon - Liban	9	•	•	•	•	•	•	•	•	•	•		...	...	...	...
Malaysia - Malaisie	23	•	•	•	•	•	•	•	•	•	•		•	•	...	•
Maldives	24	•	•	•	•	•	•	•	•	•	•		•	•	•	•
Mongolia - Mongolie	25	•	•	•	•	•	•	•	•	•	•		•	•	•	•
Myanmar	11	•	•	...	•	•	•	•	•	•	•		...	...	...	...
Nepal - Népal	15	•	•	•	•	•	•	•	•	•	•		...	...	...	...
Occupied Palestinian Territory - Territoire palestinien occupé	22	•	•	•	•	•	•	•	•	•	•		...	...	...	•
Oman	14	•	•	•	...	...	•	•	•	•	•		...	...	...	...
Pakistan[4]	24	•	•	•	•	•	•	...	...	•	•		•	•	•	•
Philippines	26	•	•	•	•	•	•	...	...	•	•		•	•	•	•
Qatar	24	•	•	•	•	•	...	...	...	•	•		•	•	•	•
Saudi Arabia - Arabie saoudite	17	•	•	•	•	•	•	•	•	•	•		•	•	•	•
Singapore - Singapour	29	•	•	•	•	•	•	•	•	...	•		•	•	•	•
Sri Lanka	25	•	•	•	•	•	•	•	•	•	•		•	•	•	•
Syrian Arab Republic - République arabe syrienne	15	•	•	•	•	•	•	•	•	•	•		...	...	...	...
Tajikistan - Tadjikistan	25	•	•	•	•	•	•	•	•	•	•		•	•	...	•
Thailand - Thaïlande	23	•	•	•	•	•	•	•	•	•	•		•	•	•	...
Timor-Leste	3	•	•	...	...	...	...	...	...	...	...	...	...	...	...	...
Turkey - Turquie	20	•	•	•	•	•	•	•	•	•	•		•	•	•	...
Turkmenistan - Turkménistan	14	•	•	•	•	•	•	•	•	•	•		...	...	...	...
United Arab Emirates - Émirats arabes unis	10	•	•	•	•	•	•	•	•	•	•		...	...	...	...
Uzbekistan - Ouzbékistan	29	•	•	•	•	•	•	•	•	•	•		•	•	•	•
Viet Nam	8	•	•	...	•	•	...	...	...	•	•		...	...	...	...
Yemen - Yémen	8	•	•	•	•	•	...	...	...	•	•		...	...	...	...
EUROPE																
Albania - Albanie	14	•	•	•	•	...	...	...	...	•	•		•	•	...	...
Andorra - Andorre	14	•	...	•	•	...	...	•	•	•	•		...	...	...	...
Austria - Autriche	29	•	•	•	•	•	•	•	•	•	•		•	•	•	•
Belarus - Bélarus	31	•	•	•	•	•	•	•	•	•	•		•	•	•	•
Belgium - Belgique	27	•	•	•	•	...	...	•	•	•	•		•	•	...	...
Bosnia and Herzegovina - Bosnie-Herzégovine	14	•	•	•	•	...	...	...	...	•	•		...	...	...	...
Bulgaria - Bulgarie	32	•	•	•	•	•	•	•	•	•	•		•	•	•	•
Channel Islands: Guernsey - Îles Anglo-Normandes: Guernesey	21	•	•	•	•	•	•	•	•	•	•		•	•	...	•
Channel Islands: Jersey - Îles Anglo-Normandes: Jersey	15	•	•	...	...	...	•	•	•	•	•		•	•	...	•
Croatia - Croatie	31	•	•	•	•	•	•	•	•	•	•		•	•	•	•
Czech Republic - République tchèque	32	•	•	•	•	•	•	•	•	•	•		•	•	•	•
Denmark - Danemark	29	•	•	•	•	•	•	•	•	•	•		•	•	•	•
Estonia - Estonie	32	•	•	•	•	•	•	•	•	•	•		•	•	•	•
Faeroe Islands - Îles Féroé	4	•	•	...	...	•	•	•	•	•	•		...	...	...	...
Finland - Finlande	32	•	•	•	•	•	•	•	•	•	•		•	•	•	•
France	30	•	•	•	•	•	•	•	•	•	•		•	•	•	•
Germany - Allemagne	29	•	•	•	•	•	•	•	•	•	•		•	•	...	•
Gibraltar	10	•	•	...	•	•	•	•	•	•	•		...	...	...	...
Greece - Grèce	27	•	•	•	•	•	•	•	•	•	•		•	•	...	...
Holy See - Saint-Siège	7	•	•	•	•	•	•	•	•	•	•		...	...	...	...
Hungary - Hongrie	32	•	•	•	•	•	•	•	•	•	•		•	•	•	•

39

Table A. *Demographic Yearbook 2002* synoptic table: Availability of data by country/area, table and sex, where applicable

Tableau A. Tableau synoptique de l'*Annuaire démographique 2002*: Disponibilité des données par pays ou zone, tableau et le sexe , si disponible (continued — suite)

(See notes at end of table. — Voir notes à la fin du tableau.)

Continent, country or area / Continent, pays ou zone	Foetal mortality - Mortalité foetale			Infant and maternal mortality - Mortalité infantile et mortalité liée à la maternité				General mortality - Mortalité générale							Nuptiality and divorces - Nuptialité et divortialité		
					16				19		20						
	12	13	14	15	Total	M/F	17	18	Total	M/F	Total	M/F	21	22	23	24	25

ASIA — ASIE

Continent, country or area	12	13	14	15	16 Total	16 M/F	17	18	19 Total	19 M/F	20 Total	20 M/F	21	22	23	24	25
Lao People's Democratic Republic - République démocratique populaire lao	...	...	...	...	...	...	...	...	...	...	...	...	...	...	...	...	...
Lebanon - Liban	...	...	...	...	...	...	...	•	...	...	...	...	...	•	•	...	•
Malaysia - Malaisie	•	...	...	•	•	•	...	•	•	•	•	•	...	•	•	...	•
Maldives	...	...	...	•	•	...	...	•	•	•	•	•	...	•	•	•	•
Mongolia - Mongolie	...	•	...	•	•	...	...	•	•	•	•	•	...	•	•	•	•
Myanmar	...	...	...	•	•	...	...	•	•	...	•	...	...	...	...	...	...
Nepal - Népal	...	...	...	•	•	...	...	•	•	...	•	...	...	...	...	...	...
Occupied Palestinian Territory - Territoire palestinien occupé	...	...	...	•	•	•	...	•	...	...	...	...	...	•	•	•	•
Oman	•	...	...	•	•	...	...	•	•	•	•	•	...	•	...	...	...
Pakistan[4]	...	...	...	...	...	...	...	...	...	...	...	...	...	...	...	...	...
Philippines	•	...	...	•	•	•	...	•	•	•	•	•	...	•	•	...	•
Qatar	...	...	...	•	•	•	...	•	•	•	•	•	...	•	•	...	•
Saudi Arabia - Arabie saoudite	...	...	...	•	•	•	...	•	•	•	•	•	...	•	...	...	...
Singapore - Singapour	•	•	•	•	•	•	...	•	•	•	•	•	...	•	•	...	•
Sri Lanka	...	...	...	•	•	...	...	•	•	•	•	•	...	...	...	...	•
Syrian Arab Republic - République arabe syrienne	...	...	...	...	...	...	...	•	•	•	•	•	...	•	•	...	•
Tajikistan - Tadjikistan	...	•	...	•	•	•	...	•	•	•	•	•	...	•	•	...	•
Thailand - Thaïlande	...	...	...	•	•	...	...	•	•	•	•	•	...	•	•	...	•
Timor-Leste	...	...	...	...	...	...	...	...	...	...	...	...	...	...	...	...	...
Turkey - Turquie	...	...	...	•	•	...	...	•	•	•	•	•	...	•	•	...	•
Turkmenistan - Turkménistan	...	...	...	•	•	...	...	•	•	•	•	•	...	•	•	...	•
United Arab Emirates - Émirats arabes unis	...	...	...	•	•	•	...	•	•	•	•	•	...	•	•	...	•
Uzbekistan - Ouzbékistan	•	•	•	•	•	•	...	•	•	•	•	•	...	•	•	...	•
Viet Nam	...	...	...	...	...	•	...	...	...	...	...	...	...	...	•	...	•
Yemen - Yémen	...	...	...	...	...	...	...	...	...	...	...	...	...	...	...	...	...

EUROPE

Continent, country or area	12	13	14	15	16 Total	16 M/F	17	18	19 Total	19 M/F	20 Total	20 M/F	21	22	23	24	25
Albania - Albanie	...	...	...	•	•	...	...	•	...	...	...	...	...	•	•	...	...
Andorra - Andorre	•	...	...	•	•	...	...	•	•	•	...	...	...	•	•	...	...
Austria - Autriche	•	...	...	•	•	•	...	•	•	•	•	•	•	•	•	•	•
Belarus - Bélarus	...	•	•	•	•	•	...	•	•	•	•	•	•	•	•	•	•
Belgium - Belgique	•	•	•	•	•	•	...	•	•	•	•	•	•	•	•	•	•
Bosnia and Herzegovina - Bosnie-Herzégovine	...	...	...	...	...	...	...	•	•	•	•	•	•	•	•	•	•
Bulgaria - Bulgarie	•	•	•	•	•	•	...	•	•	•	•	•	•	•	•	•	•
Channel Islands: Guernsey - Îles Anglo-Normandes: Guernesey	•	•	•	•	•	...	...	•	•	•	...	...	...	•	•	•	•
Channel Islands: Jersey - Îles Anglo-Normandes: Jersey	...	...	...	...	...	...	...	...	...	...	...	...	...	...	...	...	...
Croatia - Croatie	•	•	•	•	•	•	...	•	•	•	•	•	•	•	•	•	•
Czech Republic - République tchèque	•	•	•	•	•	•	...	•	•	•	•	•	•	•	•	•	•
Denmark - Danemark	•	•	•	•	•	•	...	•	•	•	•	•	•	•	•	•	•
Estonia - Estonie	•	•	•	•	•	•	...	•	•	•	•	•	•	•	...	...	...
Faeroe Islands - Îles Féroé	...	...	...	•	•	...	...	•	•	...	...	...	...	...	...	...	...
Finland - Finlande	•	•	•	•	•	•	...	•	•	•	•	•	•	•	•	...	•
France	•	•	•	•	•	•	...	•	•	•	•	•	•	•	•	...	•
Germany - Allemagne	•	•	•	•	•	•	...	•	•	•	...	...	...	•	•	...	•
Gibraltar	...	...	...	...	...	...	...	•	•	•	...	...	...	...	•	...	•
Greece - Grèce	•	•	•	•	•	•	...	•	•	•	...	...	...	•	•	...	•
Holy See - Saint-Siège	...	...	...	...	...	...	...	...	...	...	...	...	...	...	...	...	...
Hungary - Hongrie	•	•	•	•	•	•	...	•	•	•	•	•	•	•	•	•	•

Table A. *Demographic Yearbook 2002* synoptic table: Availability of data by country/area, table and sex, where applicable
Tableau A. Tableau synoptique de l'*Annuaire démographique 2002:* Disponibilité des données par pays ou zone, tableau et le sexe , si disponible (continued — suite)

(See notes at end of table. — Voir notes à la fin du tableau.)

Continent, country or area / Continent, pays ou zone	Table totals	Summary - Apercu 3 Total	M/F	4	5	Population 6 Total	M/F	7 Total	M/F	8 Total	M/F	9	Natality 10 Total	M/F	11	11a
EUROPE																
Iceland - Islande	32	•	•	•	•	•	•	•	•	•	•	•	•	•	•	•
Ireland - Irlande	27	•	•	•	•	•	•	•	•	•	•	•	•	...	•	•
Isle of Man - Îles de Man	21	•	•	•	•	•	•	•	•	•	•	...	•	...	•	•
Italy - Italie	31	•	•	•	•	•	•	•	•	•	•	•	•	...	•	•
Latvia - Lettonie	32	•	•	•	•	•	•	•	•	•	•	•	•	•	•	•
Liechtenstein	17	•	•	•	...	•	...	•	...	•	•	•	•	...	•	•
Lithuania - Lituanie	32	•	•	•	•	•	•	•	•	•	•	•	•	•	•	•
Luxembourg	27	•	•	•	•	•	•	•	•	•	...	•	•	•	•	•
Malta - Malte	25	•	•	•	•	•	•	•	•	•	•	•	•	...	•	•
Monaco	11	•	•	•	•	•	•	•	•	•	•	•	•	...	...	...
Netherlands - Pays-Bas	31	•	•	•	•	•	•	•	•	•	•	•	•	...	•	•
Norway - Norvège	31	•	•	•	•	•	•	•	•	•	•	•	•	...	•	•
Poland - Pologne	29	•	•	•	•	•	•	•	•	•	•	•	•	...	•	•
Portugal	27	•	•	•	...	...	•	•	•	•	•	•	•	...	•	•
Republic of Moldova - République de Moldova	31	•	•	•	•	•	•	•	•	•	•	•	•	•	•	•
Romania - Roumanie	32	•	•	•	•	•	•	•	•	•	•	•	•	•	•	•
Russian Federation - Fédération de Russie	31	•	•	•	•	•	•	•	•	•	•	•	•	...	•	•
San Marino - Saint-Marin	28	•	•	•	•	•	•	•	•	•	•	•	•	•	•	•
Serbia and Montenegro - Serbie-et-Montenegro	32	•	•	•	•	•	•	•	•	•	•	•	•	•	•	•
Slovakia - Slovaquie	32	•	•	•	•	•	•	•	•	•	•	•	•	•	•	•
Slovenia - Slovénie	32	•	•	•	•	•	•	•	•	•	•	•	•	•	•	•
Spain - Espagne	30	•	•	•	•	...	...	•	•	•	•	•	•	•	•	•
Sweden - Suède	29	•	•	•	•	...	•	•	•	•	•	•	•	...	•	•
Switzerland - Suisse	30	•	•	•	•	•	•	•	•	•	•	•	•	•	•	•
The Former Yugoslav Rep. of Macedonia - L'ex-République yougoslave de Macédoine	31	•	•	•	•	•	•	•	•	•	•	•	•	•	•	•
Ukraine	29	•	•	•	•	•	•	•	•	•	•	•	•	•	•	•
United Kingdom - Royaume-Uni	29	•	•	•	•	...	•	•	•	•	•	•	•	...	•	•
OCEANIA — OCEANIE																
American Samoa - Samoas américaines	14	•	•	•	•	...	...	•	•	•	...	•	•	...	...	•
Australia - Australie	28	•	•	•	•	...	...	•	•	•	•	•	•	•	•	•
Cook Islands - Îles Cook	13	•	•	•	•	•	...	•	...	•	...	•	...	...	...	•
Fiji - Fidji	17	•	•	•	•	•	•	•	•	•	•	•	•	...	...	•
French Polynesia - Polynésie française	10	•	...	•	•	•	...	•	...	•	...	•	...	...	...	•
Guam	17	•	•	•	•	•	•	•	•	•	•	•	•	...	...	•
Kiribati	4	•	•	...	•	...	...	•	...	•	...	...	...	...	...	...
Marshall Islands - Îles Marshall	14	•	•	•	•	•	...	•	...	•	...	•	...	...	...	•
Micronesia, Federated States of - Micronésie (États fédérés de)	6	•	•	...	•	•	...	•	...	•	...	...	...	...	...	...
Nauru	4	•	•	...	•	•	...	•	...	•	...	...	...	...	...	...
New Caledonia - Nouvelle-Calédonie	28	•	•	•	•	•	•	•	•	•	•	•	•	•	•	•
New Zealand - Nouvelle-Zélande	32	•	•	•	•	•	•	•	•	•	•	•	•	•	•	•
Niue - Nioué	12	•	•	•	•	•	•	•	•	•	...	•	...	...	...	•
Norfolk Island - Île Norfolk	4	•	•	...	•	...	...	•	...	•	...	...	...	...	...	...
Northern Mariana Islands - Îles Mariannes septentrionales	13	•	•	•	•	•	...	•	...	•	...	•	...	...	...	•
Palau - Palaos	14	•	...	•	•	•	...	•	...	•	...	•	...	...	...	•
Papua New Guinea - Papouasie-Nouvelle-Guinée	7	•	•	•	•	...	...	•	...	•	...	•	...	...	...	•
Pitcairn	4	•	...	...	...	•	...	•	...	•	...	...	...	...	...	...
Samoa	9	•	•	...	•	...	...	•	...	•	...	...	...	...	...	•
Solomon Islands - Îles Salomon	3	•	•	...	...	...	...	•	...	...	...	...	...	...	...	...

Table A. *Demographic Yearbook 2002* synoptic table: Availability of data by country/area, table and sex, where applicable
Tableau A. Tableau synoptique de l'*Annuaire démographique 2002:* Disponibilité des données par pays ou zone, tableau et le sexe , si disponible (continued — suite)

(See notes at end of table. — Voir notes à la fin du tableau.)

Continent, country or area / Continent, pays ou zone	Foetal mortality - Mortalité foetale			Infant and maternal mortality - Mortalité infantile et mortalité liée à la maternité				General mortality - Mortalité générale							Nuptiality and divorces - Nuptialité et divortialité		
	12	13	14	15	16 Total	16 M/F	17	18	19 Total	19 M/F	20 Total	20 M/F	21	22	23	24	25
EUROPE																	
Iceland - Islande	•	•	•	•	•	•	•	•	•	•	•	•	•	•	•	•	•
Ireland - Irlande	•	...	...	•	•	...	•	•	•	•	•	•	•	•	•	...	•
Isle of Man - Îles de Man	•	...	...	•	•	•	•	•	•	...	...	...	•	•	•	•	•
Italy - Italie	...	•	•	•	•	•	•	•	•	•	•	•	•	•	•	•	•
Latvia - Lettonie	•	•	•	•	•	•	•	•	•	•	•	•	•	•	•	•	•
Liechtenstein	...	...	...	•	•	...	•	•	•	...	...	...	•	•	•	•	•
Lithuania - Lituanie	•	•	•	•	•	•	•	•	•	•	•	•	•	•	•	•	•
Luxembourg	•	...	...	•	•	•	•	•	•	•	•	•	•	•	•	•	...
Malta - Malte	...	...	...	•	•	•	•	•	•	...	...	...	•	•	•	•	•
Monaco	...	...	...	•	•	...	•	•	•	...	...	...	•	•	•	•	•
Netherlands - Pays-Bas	•	•	•	•	•	•	•	•	•	•	•	•	•	•	•	•	•
Norway - Norvège	•	•	•	•	•	•	...	•	•	•	•	•	•	•	•	•	•
Poland - Pologne	•	•	•	•	•	•	...	•	•	•	•	•	•	•	•	•	•
Portugal	•	...	...	•	•	•	•	•	•	•	•	•	•	•	•	•	•
Republic of Moldova - République de Moldova	...	•	•	•	•	•	•	•	•	•	•	•	•	•	•	•	•
Romania - Roumanie	•	•	•	•	•	•	•	•	•	•	•	•	•	•	•	•	•
Russian Federation - Fédération de Russie	•	•	•	•	•	•	•	•	•	•	•	•	•	•	•	•	•
San Marino - Saint-Marin	•	...	...	•	•	•	•	•	•	...	...	...	•	•	•	•	•
Serbia and Montenegro - Serbie-et-Montenegro	•	•	•	•	•	•	•	•	•	•	•	•	•	•	•	•	•
Slovakia - Slovaquie	•	•	•	•	•	•	•	•	•	•	•	•	•	•	•	•	•
Slovenia - Slovénie	•	•	•	•	•	•	•	•	•	•	•	•	•	•	•	•	•
Spain - Espagne	•	•	•	•	•	•	•	•	•	•	•	•	•	•	•	•	•
Sweden - Suède	•	•	•	•	•	•	•	•	•	•	•	•	•	•	•	•	•
Switzerland - Suisse	•	...	...	•	•	•	•	•	•	•	•	•	•	•	•	•	•
The Former Yugoslav Rep. of Macedonia - L'ex-République yougoslave de Macédoine	•	•	•	•	•	•	•	•	•	•	•	•	•	•	•	•	•
Ukraine	•	...	...	•	•	•	•	•	•	•	•	•	•	•	•	•	•
United Kingdom - Royaume-Uni	•	•	•	•	•	•	•	•	•	•	•	•	•	•	•	•	•
OCEANIA — OCEANIE																	
American Samoa - Samoas américaines	...	...	...	•	...	...	...	•	•	•	...	...	...	...	...	...	...
Australia - Australie	•	...	...	•	•	•	•	•	•	•	•	•	•	•	•	•	•
Cook Islands - Îles Cook	...	...	...	•	...	...	...	•	...	...	...	...	...	...	•	...	...
Fiji - Fidji	...	...	...	•	...	...	...	•	...	...	...	...	...	...	•	...	...
French Polynesia - Polynésie française	...	...	...	•	...	...	...	•	...	...	...	...	...	...	•	...	...
Guam	...	...	...	•	...	...	...	•	...	...	...	...	...	...	•	...	...
Kiribati	...	...	...	...	...	...	...	...	...	...	...	...	...	...	...	...	...
Marshall Islands - Îles Marshall	...	...	...	•	...	...	...	•	•	...	...	...	...	...	...	...	...
Micronesia, Federated States of - Micronésie (États fédérés de)	...	...	...	...	...	...	...	...	...	...	...	...	...	...	...	...	...
Nauru	...	...	...	...	...	...	...	...	...	...	...	...	...	...	...	...	...
New Caledonia - Nouvelle-Calédonie	•	•	...	•	•	•	•	•	•	...	•	•	•	•	•	•	•
New Zealand - Nouvelle-Zélande	•	•	•	•	•	•	•	•	...	...	•	•	•	•	•	•	•
Niue - Nioué	...	...	...	...	...	...	...	•	...	...	...	...	...	...	•	...	•
Norfolk Island - Île Norfolk	...	...	...	...	...	...	...	...	...	...	...	...	...	...	...	...	...
Northern Mariana Islands - Îles Mariannes septentrionales	...	...	...	•	...	...	...	•	•	•	•	...	...	...	...	...	...
Palau - Palaos	...	...	...	•	...	...	...	•	•	•	•	...	...	...	...	...	...
Papua New Guinea - Papouasie-Nouvelle-Guinée	...	...	...	•	...	...	...	...	...	...	...	...	...	...	...	...	...
Pitcairn	...	...	...	...	...	...	...	...	...	...	...	...	...	...	...	...	...
Samoa	...	...	...	•	...	...	...	•	...	...	...	...	...	...	•	...	...
Solomon Islands - Îles Salomon	...	...	...	...	...	...	...	...	...	...	...	...	...	...	...	...	...

Table A. *Demographic Yearbook 2002* synoptic table: Availability of data by country/area, table and sex, where applicable
Tableau A. Tableau synoptique de l'*Annuaire démographique 2002*: Disponibilité des données par pays ou zone, tableau et le sexe , si disponible (continued — suite)

(See notes at end of table. — Voir notes à la fin du tableau.)

Continent, country or area Continent, pays ou zone	Table totals	Summary - Apercu				Population							Natality - Natalité			
		3 Total	3 M/F	4	5	6 Total	6 M/F	7 Total	7 M/F	8 Total	8 M/F	9	10 Total	10 M/F	11	11a
OCEANIA — OCEANIE																
Tokelau - Tokélaou	2	•	...	...	...	...	...	...	...	...	...	...	...	...	...	•
Tonga	23	•	•	•	•	•	•	•	•	•	•	...	•	...	•	•
Tuvalu	3	•	•	...	...	...	...	...	...	•	...	...	...	...	...	...
Vanuatu	6	•	•	...	•	•	•	...	...	•	...	...	...	...	...	...
Wallis and Futuna Islands - Îles Wallis et Futuna	3	•	•	...	...	...	...	...	...	•	...	...	...	...	...	...

Table A. *Demographic Yearbook 2002* synoptic table: Availability of data by country/area, table and sex, where applicable
Tableau A. Tableau synoptique de l'*Annuaire démographique 2002:* Disponibilité des données par pays ou zone, tableau et le sexe , si disponible (continued — suite)

(See notes at end of table. — Voir notes à la fin du tableau.)

Continent, country or area Continent, pays ou zone	general topic																	

General topic and table number- Suject général et numéro de tableau

Continent, country or area Continent, pays ou zone	Foetal mortality - Mortalité foetale			Infant and maternal mortality - Mortalité infantile et mortalité liée à la maternité				General mortality - Mortalité générale						Nuptiality and divorces - Nuptialité et divortialité		
					16				19		20						
	12	13	14	15	Total	M/F	17	18	Total	M/F	Total	M/F	21	22	23	24	25

OCEANIA — OCEANIE

Continent, country or area	12	13	14	15	16 Total	16 M/F	17	18	19 Total	19 M/F	20 Total	20 M/F	21	22	23	24	25
Tokelau - Tokélaou	...	...	...	...	...	...	...	...	...	...	...	...	...	...	...	...	...
Tonga	...	...	...	•	•	•	•	•	•	•	...	...	...	...	•	•	•
Tuvalu	...	...	...	...	...	...	...	...	...	...	...	...	...	...	...	...	...
Vanuatu	...	...	...	...	...	...	...	...	...	...	...	...	...	...	...	...	...
Wallis and Futuna Islands - Îles Wallis et Futuna	...	...	...	...	...	...	...	...	...	...	...	...	...	...	...	...	...

FOOTNOTES - NOTES

• Data presented in the table - Les données présentées dans le tableau.

... Data not available - Données pas disponibles.

[1] For statistical purposes, the data for China do not include those for the Hong Kong Special Administrative Region (Hong Kong SAR), Macao special Administrative Region (Macao SAR) and Taiwan province of China. - Pour la présentation des statistiques, les données pour Chine ne comprend pas la Région Administrative Spéciale de Hong Kong (Hong Kong RAS), la Région Administrative Spéciale de Macao (Macao RAS) et Taïwan province de Chine.

[2] Including data for the Indian-held part of Jammu and Kashmir, the final status of which has not yet been determined. - Y compris les données pour la partie du Jammu et du Cachemire occupée par l'Inde dont le statut définitif n'a pas encore été déterminé.

[3] Including data for East Jerusalem and Israeli residents in certain other territories under occupation by Israeli military forces since June 1967. - Y compris les données pour Jérusalem-Est et les résidents israéliens dans certains autres territoires occupés depuis 1967 par les forces armées israéliennes.

[4] Excluding data for the Pakistan-held part of Jammu and Kashmir, the final status of which has not yet been determined. - Non compris les données concernant la partie du Jammu et Cachemire occupée par le Pakistan dont le statut définitif n'a pas été déterminé.

Table 1

Table 1 presents for the world, major areas and regions estimates of the order of magnitude of population size, rates of population increase, crude birth and death rates, surface area as well as population density.

Description of variables: Estimates of world population by major areas and by regions are presented for 1950, 1960, 1970, 1980, 1990, 2000 and 2002. The average annual percentage rates of population growth, the crude birth and crude death rates are shown for the period 2000 to 2005. Surface area in square kilometers and population density estimates relate to 2002.

All population estimates and rates presented in this table were prepared by the Population Division of the United Nations, Department of Economic and Social Affairs, and have been published in *World Population Prospects: The 2002 Revision. Volume 1: Comprehensive Tables*[1].

The scheme of regionalization used for these estimates is described below. Although some continental totals are given, and all can be derived, the basic scheme presents six major areas that are so drawn as to obtain greater homogeneity in sizes of population, types of demographic circumstances and accuracy of demographic statistics. Five of the major areas are subdivided into a total of 20 regions, which are arranged within the major areas; these regions together with Northern America, which is not subdivided, make a total of 21 regions.

The major areas of Northern America and Latin America were distinguished, rather than the conventional continents of North America and South America, because population trends in the middle American mainland and the Caribbean region more closely resemble those of South America than those of America north of Mexico. Data for the traditional continents of North and South America can be obtained by adding Central America and Caribbean region to Northern America and deducting from Latin America. Latin America, as defined here, has somewhat wider limits than it would be if defined only to include the Spanish-speaking, French-speaking and Portuguese-speaking countries.

The average annual percentage rates of population growth were calculated by the Population Division, United Nations Department of Economic and Social Affairs, using an exponential rate of increase.

Crude birth and crude death rates are expressed in terms of the average annual number of births and deaths, respectively, per 1 000 mid-year population. These rates are estimated.

Surface area totals were obtained by summing the figures for individual countries or areas shown in table 3.

Computation: Density, calculated by the Statistics Division of the United Nations Department of Social and Economic Affairs, is the number of persons in the 2002 total population per square kilometer of total surface area.

Reliability of data: With the exception of surface area, all data are set in *italic* type to indicate their conjectural quality.

Limitations: The estimated orders of magnitude of population and surface area are subject to all the basic limitations set forth in connection with table 3, and to the same qualifications set forth for population and surface area statistics in sections 3 and 2.4 of the Technical Notes, respectively.

Likewise, the rates of population increase and the density index are affected by the limitations of the original figures. However, it may be noted that, in compiling data for regional and major areas totals, errors in the components may tend to compensate each other and the resulting aggregates may be more reliable than the quality of the individual components would imply.

Because of their estimated character, many of the birth and death rates shown should also be considered only as orders of magnitude, and not as measures of the true level of natality or mortality. Rates for 2002-2005 published in this Demographic Yearbook were estimated on the basis of the data available in 2002 and are, therefore, based on newer information than previously published estimates for the same years. As a result they may be different from the rates published in previous issues of the Demographic Yearbook.

45

Because surface area totals were obtained by summing the figures for individual countries or areas shown in table 3, they exclude places with a population of less than 50, for example, uninhabited polar areas.

In interpreting the population densities, one should consider that some of the regions include large segments of land that are uninhabitable or barely habitable, and density values calculated as described make no allowance for this, nor for differences in patterns of land settlement.

Composition of macro geographical regions and sub-regions

AFRICA

Eastern Africa
Burundi
Comoros
Djibouti
Eritrea
Ethiopia
Kenya
Madagascar
Malawi
Mauritius
Mozambique
Réunion
Rwanda
Seychelles
Somalia
Uganda
United Republic of Tanzania
Zambia
Zimbabwe

Middle Africa
Angola
Cameroon
Central African Republic
Chad
Congo
Democratic Republic of the Congo
Equatorial Guinea
Gabon
Sao Tome and Principe

Northern Africa
Algeria
Egypt
Libyan Arab Jamahiriya
Morocco
Sudan
Tunisia
Western Sahara
Southern Africa
Botswana
Lesotho
Namibia
South Africa
Swaziland

Western Africa

Benin
Burkina Faso
Cape Verde
Côte d'Ivoire
Gambia
Ghana
Guinea
Guinea-Bissau
Liberia
Mali
Mauritania
Niger
Nigeria
Saint Helena
Senegal
Sierra Leone
Togo

ASIA

Eastern Asia
China
China - Hong Kong SAR
China - Macao SAR
Japan
Korea, Democratic People's Republic of
Korea, Republic of
Mongolia

South-central Asia
Afghanistan
Bangladesh
Bhutan
India
Iran (Islamic Republic of)
Kazakhstan
Kyrgyzstan
Maldives
Nepal
Pakistan
Sri Lanka
Tajikistan
Turkmenistan
Uzbekistan

South-eastern Asia
Brunei Darussalam
Cambodia
Indonesia

Lao People's Democratic Republic
Malaysia
Myanmar
Philippines
Singapore
Thailand
Timor Leste
Viet Nam

Western Asia
Armenia
Azerbaijan
Bahrain
Cyprus
Georgia
Iraq
Israel
Jordan
Kuwait
Lebanon
Occupied Palestinian Territory
Oman
Qatar
Saudi Arabia
Syrian Arab Republic
Turkey
United Arab Emirates
Yemen

EUROPE

Eastern Europe
Belarus
Bulgaria
Czech Republic
Hungary
Poland
Republic of Moldova
Romania
Russian Federation
Slovakia
Ukraine

Northern Europe
Åland Island
Channel Islands
Denmark
Estonia

Faeroe Islands
Finland
Iceland
Ireland
Isle of Man
Latvia
Lithuania
Norway
Sweden
United Kingdom of Great Britain
 and Northern Ireland

Southern Europe
Albania
Andorra
Bosnia and Herzegovina
Croatia
Gibraltar
Greece
Holy See
Italy
Malta
Portugal
San Marino
Serbia and Montenegro
Slovenia
Spain
The Former Yugoslav Republic
 of Macedonia

Western Europe
Austria
Belgium
France
Germany
Liechtenstein
Luxembourg
Monaco
Netherlands
Switzerland

**LATIN AMERICA
 + the CARIBBEAN**

Caribbean
Anguilla
Antigua and Barbuda
Aruba

Bahamas
Barbados
British Virgin Islands
Cayman Islands
Cuba
Dominica
Dominican Republic
Grenada
Guadaloupe
Haiti
Jamaica
Martinique
Montserrat
Netherlands Antilles
Puerto Rico
Saint Kitts and Nevis
Saint Lucia
Saint Vincent and the
 Grenadines
Trinidad and Tobago
Turks and Caicos Islands
United States Virgin
 Islands

Central America
Belize
Costa Rica
El Salvador
Guatemala
Honduras
Mexico
Nicaragua
Panama

South America
Argentina
Bolivia
Brazil
Chile
Colombia
Ecuador
Falkland Islands (Malvinas)
French Guiana
Guyana
Paraguay
Peru
Suriname
Uruguay

Venezuela

NORTHERN AMERICA

Bermuda
Canada
Greenland
Saint Pierre and Miquelon
United States of America

OCEANIA

Australia and New Zealand
Australia
New Zealand
Norfolk Island

Melanesia
Fiji
New Caledonia
Papua New Guinea
Solomon Islands
Vanuatu

Micronesia
Guam
Kiribati
Marshall Islands
Micronesia (Federated States of)
Nauru
Northern Mariana Islands
Palau

Polynesia
American Samoa
Cook Islands
French Polynesia
Niue
Pitcairn
Samoa
Tokelau
Tonga
Tuvalu
Wallis and Futuna Islands

NOTES

[1] *World Population Prospects, the 2002 Revision, Volume 1: Comprehensive Tables,* United Nations publication Sales No. E.03.XIII.6, United Nations, New York, 2003.

Tableau 1

Le tableau 1 présente, pour l'ensemble du monde et les grandes zones et régions, des estimations concernant l'ordre de grandeur de la population, les taux d'accroissement démographique, les taux bruts de natalité et de mortalité, la superficie et la densité de peuplement.

Description des variables : Des estimations de la population mondiale par grandes zones et régions sont présentées pour 1950, 1960, 1970, 1980, 1990 et 2000 ainsi que pour 2002. Les taux annuels moyens d'accroissement de la population et les taux bruts de natalité et de mortalité portent sur la période allant de 2000 à 2005. Les indications concernant la superficie exprimée en kilomètres carrés et les estimations de la densité de population se rapportent à 2002.

Toutes les estimations de population et les taux de natalité, taux de mortalité et taux annuels d'accroissement de la population qui sont présentés dans le tableau 1 ont été établis par la Division de la population du Département des affaires économiques et sociales (Secrétariat de l'Organisation des Nations Unies), et ont été publiés dans *World Population Prospects: The 2002 Revision, Volume 1: Comprehensive Tables*[1].

Bien que l'on ait donné certains totaux pour les continents (tous les autres pouvant être calculés), on a réparti le monde en huit grandes zones qui ont été découpées de manière à obtenir une plus grande homogénéité du point de vue des dimensions de population, des types de situations démographiques et de l'exactitude des statistiques démographiques.

Cinq de ces huit grandes zones ont été subdivisées en 20 régions. Avec l'Amérique septentrionale, qui n'est pas subdivisée, on arrive à un total de 21 régions.

Au lieu de faire la distinction classique entre l'Amérique du Nord et l'Amérique du Sud, on a choisi d'opérer une comparaison entre l'Amérique septentrionale et l'Amérique latine, parce que les tendances démographiques dans la partie continentale de l'Amérique centrale et dans la région des Caraïbes se rapprochent davantage de celles de l'Amérique du Sud que de celles de l'Amérique au nord du Mexique. On obtient les données pour les continents traditionnels de l'Amérique du Nord et de l'Amérique du Sud en extrayant les données concernant l'Amérique centrale et les Caraïbes de celles relatives à l'Amérique latine et en les regroupant avec celles relatives à l'Amérique septentrionale. L'Amérique latine ainsi définie a par conséquent des limites plus larges que celles des pays ou zones de langues espagnole, portugaise et française qui constituent l'Amérique latine au sens le plus strict du terme.

La Division de la population a calculé les taux annuels moyens d'accroissement de la population en appliquant un taux d'accroissement exponentiel.

Les taux bruts de natalité et de mortalité représentent respectivement le nombre annuel moyen de naissances et de décès par millier d'habitants en milieu d'année. Ces taux sont estimatifs.

La superficie totale a été obtenue en faisant la somme des superficies des pays ou zones du tableau 3.

Calculs : La densité, calculée par la Division de statistique du Département des affaires économiques et sociales, est égale au rapport entre l'effectif total de la population en 2001 et la superficie totale exprimée en kilomètres carrés.

Fiabilité des données : À l'exception des données concernant la superficie, toutes les données sont reproduites en *italique* pour en faire ressortir le caractère conjectural.

Insuffisance des données : Les estimations concernant l'ordre de grandeur de la population et la superficie reposent en partie sur les données du tableau 3; elles appellent donc toutes les réserves fondamentales formulées à propos de ce tableau, et celles qui ont été respectivement formulées aux sections 3 et 2.4 des Notes techniques en ce qui concerne les statistiques relatives à la population et à la superficie.

Les taux d'accroissement et les indices de densité de la population se ressentent eux aussi des insuffisances inhérentes aux données de base. Toutefois, il est à noter que, lorsque l'on additionne des données par territoire pour obtenir des totaux régionaux et par grandes zones, les erreurs qu'elles comportent arrivent parfois à s'équilibrer, de sorte que les agrégats obtenus peuvent être un peu plus exacts que chacun des éléments dont on est parti.

Vu leur caractère estimatif, nombre des taux de natalité et de mortalité du tableau 1 doivent être considérés uniquement comme des ordres de grandeur et ne sont pas censés mesurer exactement le niveau de la natalité ou de la mortalité. On s'est fondé pour établir les taux de la période 2000-2005 sur les données dont on disposait en 2002, date à laquelle les nouvelles estimations ont été établies, et beaucoup d'éléments nouveaux sont alors intervenus dans le calcul de celles-ci. C'est pourquoi il se peut qu'elles s'écartent d'estimations antérieures publiées dans d'autres éditions de l'*Annuaire* pour ces mêmes années.

Parce que les totaux des superficies ont été obtenus en additionnant les chiffres pour chaque pays ou zones, qui apparaissent dans le tableau 3, ils ne comprennent pas les lieux où la population est inférieure à 50 personnes, tels que les régions polaires inhabitées.

Pour interpréter les valeurs de la densité de population, on se souviendra qu'il existe dans certaines des régions de vastes étendues de terres inhabitables ou à peine habitables et que les chiffres calculés selon la méthode indiquée ne tiennent compte ni de ce fait ni des différences de dispersion de la population selon le mode d'habitat.

Composition des grandes zones et régions

AFRIQUE

Afrique orientale
Burundi
Comores
Djibouti
Érythrée
Éthiopie
Kenya
Madagascar
Malawi
Maurice
Mozambique
Ouganda
République-Unie de Tanzanie
Réunion
Rwanda
Seychelles
Somalie
Zambie
Zimbabwe

Afrique centrale
Angola
Cameroun
Congo
Gabon
Guinée équatoriale
République centrafricaine
République démocratique du Congo
Sao Tomé-et-Principe
Tchad

Afrique septentrionale
Algérie
Égypte
Jamahiriya arabe libyenne
Maroc
Sahara occidental
Soudan

Tunisie

Afrique australe
Afrique du Sud
Botswana
Lesotho
Namibie
Swaziland

Afrique occidentale
Bénin
Burkina Faso
Cap-Vert
Côte d'Ivoire
Gambie
Ghana
Guinée
Guinée-Bissau
Libéria
Mali
Mauritanie
Niger
Nigéria
Sainte-Hélène
Sénégal
Sierra Leone
Togo

AMÉRIQUE LATINE

Caraïbes
Anguilla
Antigua-et-Barbuda
Antilles néerlandaises
Aruba
Bahamas
Barbade
Cuba
Dominique
Grenade

Guadeloupe
Haïti
Îles Caïmanes
Îles Turques et Caïques
Îles Vierges américaines
Îles Vierges britanniques
Jamaïque
Martinique
Montserrat
Porto Rico
République dominicaine
Saint-Kitts-et-Nevis
Sainte-Lucie
Saint-Vincent-et-les Grenadines
Trinité et Tobago

Amérique centrale
Belize
Costa Rica
El Salvador
Guatemala
Honduras
Mexique
Nicaragua
Panama

Amérique du Sud
Argentine
Bolivie
Brésil
Chili
Colombie
Équateur
Guyana
Guyane française
Îles Falkland (Malvinas)
Paraguay
Pérou
Suriname
Uruguay

Venezuela

AMÉRIQUE SEPTENTRIONALE

Bermudes
Canada
États-Unis d'Amérique
Groenland
Saint-Pierre-et-Miquelon

ASIE

Asie orientale
Chine
Chine - Région administrative spéciale de Hong Kong
Chine - Région administrative spéciale de Macao
Japon
Mongolie
République de Corée
République populaire démocratique de Corée
-

Asie centrale et Asie du Sud
Afghanistan
Bangladesh
Bhoutan
Inde
Iran (République Islamique d')
Kazakhstan
Kirghizistan
Maldives
Népal
Ouzbékistan
Pakistan
Sri Lanka
Tadjikistan
Turkménistan

Asie du Sud-Est
Brunéi Darussalam
Cambodge
Indonésie
Malaisie
Myanmar
Philippines
République démocratique populaire lao
Singapour
Thaïlande
Timor-Leste
Viet Nam

Asie occidentale
Arabie saoudite
Arménie

Azerbaïdjan
Bahreïn
Chypre
Émirats arabes unis
Géorgie
Iraq
Israël
Jordanie
Koweït
Liban
Oman
Qatar
République arabe syrienne
Territoire palestinien occupé
Turquie
Yémen

EUROPE

Europe orientale
Bélarus
Bulgarie
Fédération de Russie
Hongrie
Pologne
République de Moldova
République tchèque
Roumanie
Slovaquie
Ukraine

Europe septentrionale
Danemark
Estonie
Finlande
Île de Man
Îles Anglo-Normandes
Îles Féroé
Îles Svalbard et Jan Mayen
Irlande
Islande
Lettonie
Lituanie
Norvège
Royaume-Uni de Grande-Bretagne et d'Irlande du Nord
Suède

Europe méridionale
Albanie
Andorre
Bosnie-Herzégovine
Croatie
Espagne
Ex-République yougoslave de Macédoine

Gibraltar
Grèce
Italie
Malte
Portugal
Saint-Marin
Saint-Siège
Serbie-et-Monténégro
Slovénie

Europe occidentale
Allemagne
Autriche
Belgique
France
Liechtenstein
Luxembourg
Monaco
Pays-Bas
Suisse

OCÉANIE

Australie et Nouvelle-Zélande
Australie
Île Norfolk
Nouvelle-Zélande

Mélanésie
Fidji
Îles Salomon
Nouvelle-Calédonie
Papouasie-Nouvelle-Guinée
Vanuatu

Micronésie
Guam
Îles Mariannes septentrionales
Îles Marshall
Kiribati
Micronésie (États fédérés de)
Nauru
Palaos

Polynésie
Îles Cook
Îles Wallis et Futuna
Nioué
Pitcairn
Polynésie française
Samoa
Samoa américaines
Tokélaou
Tonga
Tuvalu

---

[1] *World Population Prospects, The 2002 Revision, Volume 1: Comprehensive Tables*, numéro de vente: E.03.XIII.6, publication des Nations Unies, New York, 2003.

1. Population, rate of increase, birth and death rates, surface area and density for the world, major areas and regions: selected years
Population, taux d'accroissement, taux de natalité et taux de mortalité, superficie et densité pour l'ensemble du monde, les régions macro géographiques et les composantes géographiques: diverses années

(See notes at end of table. — Voir notes à la fin du tableau.)

Major areas and regions / Régions macro géographiques et composantes	Mid-year population estimates - Estimations de population au milieu de l'année (millions)							Annual rate of increase - Taux d'accroissement annuel (%)	Crude birth rate - Taux bruts de natalité	Crude death rate - Taux bruts de mortalité	Surface area (km2) - Superficie (km2) (000s)	Density - Densité[1]
	1950	1960	1970	1980	1990	2000	2002	2000 - 2005			2002	2002
WORLD TOTAL - ENSEMBLE DU MONDE	2 519	3 021	3 692	4 435	5 264	6 071	6 225	1.2	21	9	136 056	46
AFRICA - AFRIQUE	221	277	357	470	622	796	832	2.2	37	15	30 250	28
Eastern Africa - Afrique orientale	66	83	108	144	195	253	264	2.2	41	19	6 300	42
Middle Africa - Afrique centrale	26	32	41	53	71	93	98	2.7	47	20	6 613	15
Northern Africa - Afrique septentrionale	53	67	86	111	143	174	180	1.9	26	7	8 525	21
Southern Africa - Afrique méridionale	16	20	26	33	42	50	51	0.6	24	18	2 675	19
Western Africa - Afrique occidentale	60	76	97	128	172	226	238	2.6	41	15	6 138	39
LATIN AMERICA AND CARIBBEAN - AMERIQUE LATINE ET CARAIBES	167	218	285	361	442	520	535	1.4	22	6	20 546	26
Caribbean - Caraïbes	17	20	25	29	34	38	38	0.9	20	9	234	162
Central America - Amérique centrale	37	49	68	90	111	135	140	1.7	24	5	2 480	56
South America - Amérique du Sud	112	148	192	242	296	347	355	1.4	21	7	17 832	20
NORTHERN AMERICA - AMERIQUE SEPTENTRIONALE[2]	172	204	232	256	284	316	322	1.0	14	8	21 776	15
ASIA - ASIE[3]	1 398	1 701	2 143	2 632	3 168	3 680	3 776	1.3	20	8	31 870	118
Eastern Asia - Asie orientale	671	792	987	1 178	1 350	1 481	1 502	0.7	14	7	11 763	128
South Central Asia - Asie centrale méridionale	499	620	783	981	1 225	1 486	1 538	1.7	26	9	10 791	143
South Eastern Asia - Asie méridionale orientale	178	223	286	358	440	520	536	1.4	22	7	4 495	119
Western Asia - Asie occidentale[3]	51	67	87	115	153	192	201	2.1	27	6	4 822	42
EUROPE[3]	547	604	656	692	721	728	727	-0.1	10	12	22 050	33
Eastern Europe - Europe orientale	220	253	276	295	311	305	302	-0.5	11	13	18 814	16
Northern Europe - Europe septentrionale	77	81	87	89	92	94	95	0.2	11	10	1 748	54
Southern Europe - Europe méridionale	109	118	127	138	143	146	146	0.1	10	10	1 317	111
Western Europe - Europe occidentale	141	152	166	170	176	184	184	0.2	10	10	1 108	166
OCEANIA - OCEANIE[2]	12.8	16.0	10.4	22.0	20.7	31.0	31.8	1.2	17	8	8 564	4
Australia and New Zealand - Australie et Nouvelle-Zélande	10.1	12.6	15.4	17.7	20.2	22.9	23.4	0.9	13	7	8 012	3
Melanesia - Melanésie	2.3	2.7	3.4	4.4	5.5	7.0	7.3	2.1	30	8	541	13
Micronesia - Micronésie	0.2	0.2	0.2	0.3	0.4	0.5	0.5	1.7	25	5	3	167
Polynesia - Polynésie	0.2	0.3	0.4	0.5	0.5	0.6	0.6	1.3	24	6	8	75

GENERAL NOTES - NOTES GENERALES

Unless otherwise specified all figures are estimates of the order of magnitude and are subject to substantial margin of error; all data except for surface area are therefore set in italics. For composition of major areas and regions and for method of construction of estimates, see Technical Notes for this table. — Sauf indication contraire, tous les chiffres sont des estimations de l'ordre de grandeur comportant une assez grande marge d'erreur; toutes les données à l' exception de celles relatives à la 'superficie', sont de ce fait en italique. Pour la composition des régions macro géographiques et la méthode utilisée afin d'établir les estimations, voir Notes tecniques pour ce tableau.

FOOTNOTES - NOTES

[1] Population per square kilometre of surface area. Figures are estimates of population divided by surface area and are not to be considered as either reflecting density in the urban sense or as indicating the supporting power of a territory's land and resources. — Habitants per kilomèter corré. Il s'agit simplement du quotient calculé en divisant la population par la superficie et n'est par considéré comme indiquant la densité au sens urbain du mot ni l'effectif de population que les terres et les ressources du territoire sont capables de nourrir.

[2] Hawaii, a state of the United States of America, is included in Northern America rather than in Oceania. — Hawaii, un Etat des Etats-Unis d'Amérique, est compris en Amérique septentrionale plutôt qu'en Océanie.

[3] The European part of Turkey is included in Western Asia rather than Europe. — La partie européenne de la Turquie est comprise en Asie Occidentale plutôt qu'en Europe.

Table 2

Table 2 presents estimates of population and the percentage distribution by age and sex as well as the sex ratio for all ages; data are presented for the world, the six major areas and the 20 regions for 2002.

Description of variables: All population estimates presented in this table were prepared by the Population Division of the United Nations Department of Economic and Social Affairs. These estimates have been published (using more detailed age groups) in the *World Population Prospects: The 2002 Revision, Volume II, Sex and Age Distribution of Populations*[1].

The scheme of regionalization used for these estimates is discussed in detail in the technical notes for table 1. Age groups presented in this table are: under 15 years, 15-64 years and 65 years and over. Sex ratio refers to the number of males per 100 females of all ages.

The percentage distributions and the sex ratios that appear in this table have been calculated by the Statistics Division of the United Nations, Department of Economic and Social Affairs using the Population Division estimates.

Reliability of data: All data are set in *italic* type to indicate their conjectural quality.

Limitations: The data presented in this table are from the same series of estimates, prepared by the Population Division, presented in table 1. The estimated orders of magnitude of population are subject to all the basic limitations set forth for population statistics in section 3 of the Technical Notes. In brief, because they are estimates, these distributions by broad age groups and sex should be considered only as orders of magnitude. However, it may be noted that, in compiling data for regional and macro region totals, errors in the components may tend to compensate each other and the resulting aggregates may be somewhat more reliable than the quality of the individual components would imply.

In addition, data in this table are limited by factors affecting data by age. These factors are described in the technical notes for table 7. Because the age groups presented in this table are so broad, these problems are minimized.

NOTES

[1] *World Population Prospects, the 2002 Revision, Volume 1: Comprehensive Tables,* United Nations publication Sales No. E.03.XIII.6, United Nations, New York, 2003.

Tableau 2

Le tableau 2 présente, pour l'ensemble du monde, les six grandes zones et les 20 régions, des estimations concernant la population en 2002 ainsi que sa répartition en pourcentage selon l'âge et le sexe, et le rapport de masculinité pour tous les âges.

Description des variables : Toutes les données figurant dans le tableau 2 ont été établies par la Division de la population du Département des affaires économiques et sociales (Secrétariat de l'Organisation des Nations Unies) et ont été publiées dans l'ouvrage intitulé *World Population Prospects: The 2002 Revision, Volume II: Sex and Age Distribution of Populations*[1].

La classification géographique utilisée pour établir ces estimations est exposée en détail dans les notes techniques relatives au tableau 1. Les groupes d'âge présentés dans ce tableau sont définis comme suit : moins de 15 ans, de 15 à 64 ans et 65 ans et plus. Le rapport de masculinité correspond au nombre d'individus de sexe masculin pour 100 individus de sexe féminin sans considération d'âge.

Les pourcentages et les rapports de masculinité qui sont présentés dans le tableau 2 ont été calculés par la Division de statistique de l'ONU à partir des estimations établies par la Division de la population.

Fiabilité des données : Toutes les données figurant dans ce tableau sont reproduites en *italique* pour en faire ressortir le caractère conjectural.

Insuffisance des données : Les données de ce tableau appartiennent à la même série d'estimations, établie par la Division de la population, que celles qui figurent au tableau 1. Les estimations concernant l'ordre de grandeur de la population appellent donc toutes les réserves fondamentales qui ont été formulées à la section 3 des Notes techniques à propos des statistiques relatives à la population. Sans entrer dans le détail, il convient de préciser que les données relatives à la répartition par grand groupe d'âge et par sexe doivent être considérées uniquement comme des ordres de grandeur en raison de leur caractère estimatif. Toutefois, il est à noter que, lorsque l'on additionne des données par territoire pour obtenir des totaux régionaux et par grandes zones, les erreurs qu'elles comportent arrivent parfois à s'équilibrer, de sorte que les agrégats obtenus peuvent être un peu plus exacts que chacun des éléments dont on est parti.

En outre, les donnés figurant dans le tableau 2 comportent certaines imprécisions en raison des facteurs influant sur les données par âge (voir à ce propos les notes techniques relatives au tableau 7). Ces imprécisions sont cependant atténuées du fait de l'étendue des groupes d'âge présentés dans le tableau 2.

NOTE

[1] *World Population Prospects, the 2002 Revision, Volume 1: Comprehensive Tables*, publication des Nations Unies, numéro de vente E.03.XIII.6, New York, 2003.

2. Estimates of population and its percentage distribution, by age and sex and sex ratio for all ages for the world, major areas and regions: 2002
Estimations de la population et pourcentage de répartition selon l'âge et le sexe et rapport de masculinité pour l'ensemble du monde, les grandes régions et les régions géographiques: 2002

(See notes at end of table. — Voir notes à la fin du tableau.)

Major areas and regions Grandes régions et régions	Population (millions)											
	Both sexes - Les deux sexes				Male - Masculin				Female - Féminin			
	All ages - Tous âges	-15	15-64	65+	All ages - Tous âges	-15	15-64	65+	All ages - Tous âges	-15	15-64	65+
WORLD TOTAL - ENSEMBLE DU MONDE	6 225	1 830	3 954	440	3 131	940	2 000	191	3 094	890	1 954	249
AFRICA - AFRIQUE	832	351	454	27	414	177	224	12	418	174	229	15
Eastern Africa - Afrique orientale	264	120	137	8	131	60	67	3	134	60	70	4
Middle Africa - Afrique centrale	98	45	50	3	48	23	25	1	49	22	25	2
Northern Africa - Afrique septentrionale	180	62	110	8	90	32	55	4	90	31	55	4
Southern Africa - Afrique méridionale	51	18	32	2	25	9	15	1	26	9	16	1
Western Africa - Afrique occidentale	238	106	125	7	119	54	62	3	119	53	63	4
LATIN AMERICA AND CARIBBEAN - AMERIQUE LATINE ET CARAIBES	536	166	339	30	265	85	167	13	271	82	172	17
Caribbean - Caraïbes	38	11	25	3	19	6	12	1	19	5	12	2
Central America - Amérique centrale	140	48	85	7	69	25	42	3	71	24	44	4
South America - Amérique du Sud	357	107	229	21	177	54	113	9	181	53	116	12
NORTHERN AMERICA - AMERIQUE SEPTENTRIONALE[1]	322	69	214	40	158	35	107	17	164	33	108	23
ASIA - ASIE[2]	3 776	1 114	2 432	230	1 927	576	1 246	105	1 849	538	1 186	125
Eastern Asia - Asie orientale	1 502	342	1 039	122	768	180	533	55	735	162	505	67
South Central Asia - Asie centrale méridionale	1 538	533	932	73	790	275	480	34	748	258	451	38
South Eastern Asia - Asie méridionale orientale	536	168	341	26	267	86	170	12	268	83	171	14
Western Asia - Asie occidentale	201	70	121	9	103	36	63	4	98	35	58	5
EUROPE[2]	727	122	495	111	350	62	245	43	377	59	249	68
Eastern Europe - Europe orientale	302	51	210	41	143	26	103	14	159	25	108	27
Northern Europe - Europe septentrionale	95	18	62	15	46	9	31	6	49	9	31	9
Southern Europe - Europe méridionale	146	22	99	25	71	12	50	10	75	11	49	14
Western Europe - Europe occidentale	184	31	123	30	90	16	62	12	94	15	61	18
OCEANIA - OCEANIE[1]	31.84	8.12	20.58	3.14	15.98	4.18	10.40	1.41	15.86	3.94	10.19	1.74
Australia and New Zealand - Australie et Nouvelle Zélande	23.39	4.79	15.70	2.89	11.63	2.46	7.89	1.28	11.76	2.33	7.81	1.61
Melanesia - Melanésie	7.31	2.92	4.19	0.20	3.76	1.51	2.15	0.10	3.55	1.41	2.04	0.09
Micronesia - Micronésie	0.52	0.18	0.31	0.02	0.27	0.09	0.16	0.01	0.25	0.09	0.15	0.01
Polynesia - Polynésie	0.63	0.22	0.38	0.03	0.32	0.11	0.20	0.01	0.30	0.11	0.18	0.02

2. Estimates of population and its percentage distribution, by age and sex and sex ratio for all ages for the world, major areas and regions: 2002
Estimations de la population et pourcentage de répartition selon l'âge et le sexe et rapport de masculinité pour l'ensemble du monde, les grandes regions et les régions géographiques: 2002 (continued — suite)

(See notes at end of table. — Voir notes à la fin du tableau.)

Major areas and regions / Grandes régions et régions	Percent - Pourcentage												Sex ratio (Males per 100 females of all ages) - Rapport de masculinité (Hommes pour 100 femmes de tous âges)
	Both sexes - Les deux sexes				Male - Masculin				Female - Féminin				
	All ages - Tous âges	-15	15-64	65+	All ages - Tous âges	-15	15-64	65+	All ages - Tous âges	-15	15-64	65+	
WORLD TOTAL - ENSEMBLE DU MONDE	100.0	29.4	63.5	7.1	100.0	30.0	63.9	6.1	100.0	28.8	63.2	8.1	101
AFRICA - AFRIQUE	100.0	42.2	54.5	3.3	100.0	42.8	54.2	2.9	100.0	41.6	54.8	3.6	99
Eastern Africa - Afrique orientale	100.0	45.3	51.8	2.9	100.0	46.0	51.4	2.6	100.0	44.6	52.3	3.1	98
Middle Africa - Afrique centrale	100.0	46.0	51.1	2.9	100.0	46.5	50.9	2.6	100.0	45.4	51.3	3.3	98
Northern Africa - Afrique septentrionale	100.0	34.7	61.0	4.3	100.0	35.3	60.8	3.9	100.0	34.1	61.2	4.7	101
Southern Africa - Afrique méridionale	100.0	34.3	61.8	3.9	100.0	35.3	61.6	3.0	100.0	33.3	62.0	4.6	95
Western Africa - Afrique occidentale	100.0	44.7	52.4	2.9	100.0	45.2	52.1	2.7	100.0	44.2	52.6	3.2	100
LATIN AMERICA AND CARIBBEAN - AMERIQUE LATINE ET CARAIBES	100.0	31.0	63.3	5.7	100.0	31.9	63.1	5.0	100.0	30.1	63.6	6.3	98
Caribbean - Caraïbes	100.0	28.5	64.2	7.3	100.0	29.3	64.0	6.7	100.0	27.8	64.3	7.9	99
Central America - Amérique centrale	100.0	34.4	60.8	4.8	100.0	35.6	60.1	4.4	100.0	33.3	61.5	5.2	98
South America - Amérique du Sud	100.0	30.0	64.2	5.8	100.0	30.8	64.1	5.1	100.0	29.1	64.3	6.6	98
NORTHERN AMERICA - AMERIQUE SEPTENTRIONALE[1]	100.0	21.3	66.4	12.3	100.0	22.2	67.2	10.6	100.0	20.4	65.6	14.0	97
ASIA - ASIE[2]	100.0	29.5	64.4	6.1	100.0	29.9	64.7	5.4	100.0	29.1	64.2	6.7	104
Eastern Asia - Asie orientale	100.0	22.8	69.1	8.1	100.0	23.4	69.5	7.1	100.0	22.1	68.8	9.1	105
South Central Asia - Asie centrale méridionale	100.0	34.7	60.6	4.7	100.0	34.8	60.8	4.4	100.0	34.5	60.3	5.1	106
South Eastern Asia - Asie méridionale orientale	100.0	31.4	63.7	4.9	100.0	32.0	63.6	4.4	100.0	30.8	63.8	5.4	100
Western Asia - Asie occidentale	100.0	35.2	60.3	4.6	100.0	35.0	60.9	4.0	100.0	35.3	59.6	5.1	105
EUROPE[2]	100.0	16.7	68.1	15.2	100.0	17.8	70.0	12.2	100.0	15.7	66.2	18.0	93
Eastern Europe - Europe orientale	100.0	16.8	69.7	13.5	100.0	18.2	72.0	9.9	100.0	15.5	67.7	16.8	90
Northern Europe - Europe septentrionale	100.0	18.6	65.7	15.6	100.0	19.6	67.1	13.2	100.0	17.7	64.4	17.9	95
Southern Europe - Europe méridionale	100.0	15.4	67.7	16.9	100.0	16.2	69.4	14.4	100.0	14.6	66.1	19.2	96
Western Europe - Europe occidentale	100.0	16.8	66.8	16.4	100.0	17.6	69.0	13.5	100.0	16.0	64.7	19.3	96
OCEANIA - OCEANIE[1]	100.0	25.5	64.6	9.9	100.0	26.2	65.0	8.8	100.0	24.8	64.2	10.9	101
Australia and New Zealand - Australie et Nouvelle Zélande	100.0	20.5	67.1	12.4	100.0	21.1	67.8	11.0	100.0	19.8	66.4	13.7	99
Melanesia - Mélanésie	100.0	40.0	57.3	2.7	100.0	40.2	57.1	2.7	100.0	39.7	57.6	2.6	106
Micronesia - Micronésie	100.0	35.7	59.5	4.8	100.0	35.5	60.1	4.4	100.0	36.0	58.8	5.2	107
Polynesia - Polynésie	100.0	34.7	60.6	4.7	100.0	34.7	61.1	4.2	100.0	34.7	60.1	5.2	107

GENERAL NOTES - NOTES GENERALES

All figures are estimates of the order of magnitude and are subject to a substantial margin of error; all data are therefore set in italics. For composition of major areas and regions and for method of construction of estimates, see Technical Notes for this table. — Tous les chiffres sont des estimations de grandeur comportant une assez grande marge d'erreur, toutes les données sont de ce fait en italique. Pour le composition des grandes régions et la méthode utilisée afin d'établir les estimations, voir

Notes techniques pour ce tableau.

FOOTNOTES - NOTES

[1] Hawaii, a state of the United States of America, is included in Northern America rather than in Oceania. — Hawaii, un Etat des Etats-Unis d'Amérique, est compris en Amérique septentrionale plutôt qu'en Océanie.

[2] The European part of Turkey is included in Western Asia rather than Europe. — La partie européenne de la Turquie est comprise en Asie Occidentale plutôt qu'en Europe.

Table 3

Table 3 presents for each country or area of the world the total, male and female population enumerated at the latest population census, estimates of the mid-year total population for 1995 and 2002, the average annual exponential rate of increase (or decrease) for the period 1995 to 2002 the surface area and the population density for 2002.

Description of variables: The total, male and female population is, unless otherwise indicated, the de facto (present-in-area) population enumerated at the most recent census for which data are available. The date of this census is given. Population census data are usually the results of a nation-wide enumeration. If, however, a nation-wide enumeration has not taken place, the results of a sample survey, essentially national in character, may be presented. Results of surveys referring to less than 50 percent of the total territory or population are not included.

Mid-year population estimates refer to the population on 1 July. Otherwise, a footnote is appended. Mid-year estimates of the total population are those provided by national statistical offices, unless otherwise indicated.

Surface area, expressed in square kilometres, refers to the total surface area, comprising land area and inland waters (assumed to consist of major rivers and lakes) and excluding Polar Regions as well as uninhabited islands. Exceptions to this are noted. Surface areas, originally reported in square miles by the country or area, have been converted to square kilometres using a conversion factor of 2.589988.

Computation: The annual rate of increase is the average annual percentage rate of population growth between 1995 and 2002, computed by the Statistics Division of the United Nations Department of Economic and Social Affairs using the unrounded mid-year estimates as presented in this table applying an exponential rate of increase.

Density is the number of persons in the 2002 total population per square kilometre of total surface area.

Reliability of data: Reliable mid-year population estimates are those that are based on a complete census (or a sample survey) and have been adjusted by a continuous population register or on the basis of the calculated balance of births, deaths and migration. Mid-year estimates of this type are considered reliable and appear in roman type. Mid-year estimates not calculated on this basis are considered less reliable and are shown in italics. Estimates for years prior to 2002 are considered reliable or less reliable on the basis of the 2002 quality code and appear in roman type or in *italics*, accordingly.

Census data and sample survey results are considered reliable and, therefore, appear in roman type.

Rates of population increase that were calculated using population estimates considered less reliable, as described above, are set in italics rather than roman type.

All surface area data are assumed to be reliable and therefore appear in roman type.

Population density data, however, are considered reliable or less reliable on the basis of the reliability of the 2002 population estimates used as the numerator.

Limitations: Statistics on the total population enumerated at the time of the census, estimates of the mid-year total population and surface area data are subject to the same qualifications as have been set forth for population and surface area statistics in sections 3 and 2.4 of the Technical Notes, respectively.

Regarding the limitations of census data, it should be noted that although census data are considered reliable, and therefore appear in roman type, the actual quality of census data varies widely from one country or area to another. When known, an estimate of the extent of over-enumeration or under-enumeration is given in footnotes. In the case of sample surveys, a description of the population covered is provided.

Because the reliability of the population estimates for any given country or area is based on the quality of the 2002 estimate, the reliability of estimates prior to 2002 may be overstated.

Rates of population increase are subject to all the qualifications of the population estimates mentioned above. In some cases, they simply reflect the rate calculated or assumed in constructing the estimates themselves when adequate measures of natural increase and net migration were not available.   Despite their shortcomings, these rates provide a useful index for studying population change and can be useful also in evaluating the accuracy of vital and migration statistics.

Population density data as shown in this table give only an indication of actual population density as they do not take account of the dispersion or concentration of population within countries or areas nor the proportion of habitable land. They should not be interpreted as reflecting density in the urban sense nor as indicating the supporting power of a territory's land and resources.

Tableau 3

Le tableau 3 indique pour chaque pays ou zone du monde la population totale selon le sexe d'après les derniers recensements effectués, les estimations concernant la population totale au milieu de l'année 1995 et de l'année 2002, le taux moyen d'accroissement annuel exponentiel positif ou négatif pour la période allant de 1995 à 2002, ainsi que la superficie et la densité de population en 2002.

Description des variables : Sauf indication contraire, la population masculine et féminine totale est la population de fait ou population présente dénombrée à l'occasion du dernier recensement dont les résultats sont disponibles. La date de ce recensement est précisée. Les données de recensement résultent généralement d'un dénombrement de population nationale. S'il n'y a jamais eu de dénombrement général, ce sont les résultats d'une enquête par sondage à caractère essentiellement national qui sont indiqués. Il n'est pas présenté de résultats d'enquêtes portant sur moins de 50 p. 100 de l'ensemble du territoire ou de la population.

Les estimations de la population en milieu d'année sont celles de la population au 1er juillet. Lorsque la date est différente, cela est signalé par une note. Les estimations de la population totale en milieu d'année sont celles qui ont été communiquées par les services nationaux de statistique.

La superficie - exprimée en kilomètres carrés - représente la superficie totale, c'est-à-dire qu'elle englobe les terres émergées et les eaux intérieures (qui sont censées comprendre les principaux lacs et cours d'eau) mais exclut les régions polaires et certaines îles inhabitées. Les exceptions à cette règle sont signalées en note. Les superficies initialement exprimées en miles carrés par les pays ou les zones ont été transformées en kilomètres carrés au moyen d'un coefficient de conversion de 2,589988.

Calculs : Le taux d'accroissement annuel est le taux annuel moyen de variation (en pourcentage) de la population entre 1995 et 2002, calculé par la Division de statistique du Département des affaires économiques et sociales (Secrétariat de l'Organisation des Nations Unies) à partir des estimations en milieu d'année non arrondies qui figurent dans le tableau après application d'un taux exponentiel d'accroissement.

La densité est égale au rapport de l'effectif total de la population en 2002 à la superficie totale, exprimée en kilomètres carrés.

Fiabilité des données : Les estimations en milieu d'année qui sont considérées sûres sont fondées sur un recensement complet (ou sur une enquête par sondage) et ont été ajustées en fonction des données provenant d'un registre permanent de population ou en fonction de la balance établie par le calcul des naissances, des décès et des migrations. Les estimations de ce type sont considérées comme sûres et apparaissent en caractères romains. Les estimations en milieu d'année dont le calcul n'a pas été effectué sur cette base sont considérées comme moins sûres et apparaissent en italique. Les estimations relatives aux années antérieures à 2002 sont jugées plus ou moins sûres en fonction du codage qualitatif de 2002 et indiquées, selon le cas, en caractères romains ou en italique.

Les données de recensements ou les résultats d'enquêtes par sondage sont considérés comme sûrs et apparaissent par conséquent en caractères romains.

Les taux d'accroissement de la population, calculés à partir d'estimations jugées moins sûres d'après les normes décrites ci-dessus, sont indiqués en italique plutôt qu'en caractères romains.

Toutes les données de superficie sont présumées sûres et apparaissent par conséquent en caractères romains. En revanche, les données relatives à la densité de la population sont considérées plus ou moins sûres en fonction de la fiabilité des estimations de la population en 2002 ayant servi de numérateur.

Insuffisance des données : Les statistiques portant sur la population totale dénombrée lors d'un recensement, les estimations de la population totale en milieu d'année et les données de superficie appellent les mêmes réserves que celles formulées aux sections 3 et 2.4 des Notes techniques à propos des statistiques relatives à la population et à la superficie.

S'agissant de l'insuffisance des données obtenues par recensement, il convient d'indiquer que, bien que ces données soient considérées comme sûres et apparaissent par conséquent en caractères romains, leur qualité réelle varie considérablement d'un pays ou d'une région à l'autre. Lorsque l'on possédait les renseignements voulus, on a donné une estimation du degré de sur-dénombrement ou de sous-dénombrement. Dans le cas des enquêtes par sondage, une description de la population considérée est fournie.

La fiabilité des estimations de la population d'un pays ou zone quelconque reposant sur la qualité des estimations de 2002, il se peut que la fiabilité des estimations antérieures à 2002 soit surévaluée.

Les taux d'accroissement appellent toutes les réserves formulées plus haut à propos des estimations concernant la population. Dans certains cas, ils représentent seulement le taux qu'il a fallu calculer ou que l'on a pris pour base pour établir les estimations elles-mêmes lorsque l'on ne disposait pas de mesures appropriées de l'accroissement naturel et des migrations nettes. Malgré leurs imperfections, ces taux fournissent des indications intéressantes pour l'étude du mouvement de la population et, utilisés avec les précautions nécessaires, ils peuvent également servir à évaluer l'exactitude des statistiques de l'état civil et des migrations.

Les données relatives à la densité de population figurant dans le tableau 3 n'ont qu'une valeur indicative en ce qui concerne la densité de population effective, car elles ne tiennent compte ni de la dispersion ou de la concentration de la population à l'intérieur des pays ou zones, ni de la proportion du territoire qui est habitable. Il ne faut donc y voir d'indication ni de la densité au sens urbain du terme ni du nombre d'habitants qui pourraient vivre sur les terres et avec les ressources naturelles du territoire considéré.

3. Population by sex, rate of population increase, surface area and density
Population selon le sexe, taux d'accroissement de la population, superficie et densité

(See notes at end of table. — Voir notes à la fin du tableau.)

Continent, country or area and census date / Continent, pays ou zone et date du recensement	Census type[a]	Latest available census — Dernier recensement disponible (in units — en unités)			Mid-year estimates - Estimations au milieu de l'année (in thousands — en milliers)		Estimate type	Annual rate of increase Taux d' accroissement annuel 1995-2002	Surface area Superficie (km²) 2002	Density Densité 2002[1]
		Both sexes Les deux sexes	Male Masculin	Female Feminin	1995	2002				
AFRICA — AFRIQUE										
Algeria - Algérie 25 VI 1998	DJ	29 100 867	14 698 589	14 402 278	28 060	31 357	DJ	1.6	2 381 741	13
Angola[2] 15 XII 1970	DF	5 646 166	2 943 974	2 702 192	...	...	...	...	1 246 700	...
Benin - Bénin 11 II 2002	DJ	*6 752 569	...	...	...	...	...	...	112 622	...
Botswana 17 VIII 2001	DF	*1 680 863	*813 488	*867 375	...	...	...	...	581 730	...
Burkina Faso 10 XII 1996	DF	10 312 609	4 970 882	5 341 727	...	...	...	...	274 000	...
Burundi 16 VIII 1990	DF	5 139 073	2 473 599	2 665 474	...	...	...	...	27 834	...
Cameroon - Cameroun 10 IV 1987	DF	10 493 655	...	...	...	...	...	...	475 442	...
Cape Verde - Cap-Vert 16 VI 2000	DF	436 863	211 479	225 384	386	453	DF	2.3	4 033	112
Central African Republic - République centrafricaine 8 XII 1988	DF	2 463 616	1 210 734	1 252 882	...	...	...	...	622 984	...
Chad - Tchad[3] 8 IV 1993	DF	6 279 931	...	...	...	...	...	...	1 284 000	...
Comoros - Comores[4] 15 IX 1991	DF	446 817	221 152	225 665	...	...	...	...	2 235	...
Congo 22 XII 1984	DF	1 843 421	...	...	...	...	...	...	342 000	...
Côte d'Ivoire 1 III 1988	DF	10 815 694	5 527 343	5 288 351	...	...	...	...	322 463	...
Democratic Republic of the Congo - République démocratique du Congo 1 VII 1984	DF	29 916 800	14 543 800	15 373 000	...	...	...	...	2 344 858	...
Djibouti 11 XII 1960	DF	81 200	...	...	...	...	...	...	23 200	...
Egypt - Égypte 19 XI 1996	DF	59 312 914	30 351 390	28 961 524	57 510	66 628	DF	2.1	1 001 449	67
Equatorial Guinea - Guinée équatoriale[5] 4 VII 1994	DF	406 151	...	...	...	...	...	...	28 051	...
Eritrea - Érythrée 9 V 1984	DF	2 748 304	1 374 452	1 373 852	...	...	...	...	117 600	...
Ethiopia - Éthiopie 11 X 1994	DF	53 477 265	26 910 698	26 566 567	54 649	67 220	DF	3.0	1 104 300	61
Gabon 31 VII 1993	DF	1 014 976	501 784	513 192	...	...	...	...	267 668	...
Gambia - Gambie 15 IV 2003	DF	*1 364 507	*676 726	*687 781	...	...	...	...	11 295	...
Ghana 26 III 2000	DF	18 912 079	9 357 382	9 554 697	...	...	...	...	238 533	...
Guinea - Guinée 1 XII 1996	DF	*7 156 406	...	...	...	...	...	...	245 857	...
Guinea-Bissau - Guinée-Bissau 1 XII 1991	DF	983 367	476 210	507 157	...	...	...	...	36 125	...

3. Population by sex, rate of population increase, surface area and density
Population selon le sexe, taux d'accroissement de la population, superficie et densité
(continued — suite)

(See notes at end of table. — Voir notes à la fin du tableau.)

Continent, country or area and census date / Continent, pays ou zone et date du recensement	Census type[a]	Latest available census — Dernier recensement disponible (in units — en unités)			Mid-year estimates - Estimations au milieu de l'année (in thousands — en milliers)		Estimate type	Annual rate of increase Taux d' accroissement annuel 1995-2002	Surface area Superficie (km²) 2002	Density Densité 2002[1]
		Both sexes Les deux sexes	Male Masculin	Female Feminin	1995	2002				
AFRICA — AFRIQUE										
Kenya										
24 VIII 1999	DF	28 686 607	14 205 589	14 481 018	...	...	...	...	580 367	...
Lesotho										
14 IV 1996	DJ	1 960 069	964 346	995 723	...	...	...	...	30 355	...
Liberia - Libéria										
1 II 1984	DF	2 101 628	1 063 127	1 038 501	...	...	...	...	111 369	...
Libyan Arab Jamahiriya - Jamahiriya arabe libyenne[6]										
11 VIII 1995	DF	4 404 986	2 236 943	2 168 043	*4 395*	*5 484*	DF	3.2	1 759 540	*3*
Madagascar										
1 VIII 1993	DF	12 092 157	5 991 171	6 100 986	...	...	...	...	587 041	...
Malawi[7]										
1 IX 1998	DF	9 933 868	4 867 563	5 066 305	*9 788*	*11 175	DF	1.9	118 484	94
Mali										
1 IV 1998	DJ	9 790 492	4 847 436	4 943 056	...	...	...	...	1 240 192	...
Mauritania - Mauritanie										
1 XI 2000	DF	2 548 157	1 240 414	1 307 743	...	...	...	...	1 025 520	...
Mauritius - Maurice										
2 VII 2000	DJ	1 178 848	583 756	595 092	1 122	1 210	DJ	1.1	2 040	593
Morocco - Maroc										
2 IX 1994	DF	26 019 280	12 944 517	13 074 763	*26 386*	*29 631*	DF	1.7	446 550	*66*
Mozambique[8]										
1 VIII 1997	DF	16 099 246	7 714 306	8 384 940	...	...	...	...	801 590	...
Namibia - Namibie										
27 VIII 2001	DF	1 826 854	936 718	890 136	...	...	...	...	824 292	...
Niger										
20 V 1988	DF	7 248 100	3 590 070	3 658 030	...	...	...	...	1 267 000	...
Nigeria - Nigéria[7]										
26 XI 1991	DF	88 992 220	44 529 608	44 462 612	99 210	122 444	DF	3.0	923 768	133
Réunion										
8 III 1999	DJ	706 180	347 076	359 104	...	...	...	...	2 510	...
Rwanda										
16 VIII 2002	DF	*8 128 553	*3 879 448	*4 249 105	...	...	...	...	26 338	...
Saint Helena ex. dep. - Sainte-Hélène sans dép.										
8 III 1998	DF	5 157	2 612	2 545	...	...	...	...	122	...
Saint Helena: Ascension - Sainte-Hélène: Ascension										
31 XII 1978	DF	849	608	241	...	...	...	...	88	...
Saint Helena: Tristan da Cunha - Sainte-Hélène: Tristan da Cunha										
31 XII 1988	DF	296	139	157	...	...	...	...	...	...
Sao Tome and Principe - Sao Tomé-et-Principe										
4 VIII 1991	DF	116 998	57 837	59 161	...	...	...	...	964	...
Senegal - Sénégal										
27 V 1988	DJ	6 896 808	3 353 599	3 543 209	...	...	...	...	196 722	...
Seychelles										
29 VIII 1997	DF	75 876	37 589	38 287	75	*81	DF	1.0	455	178

3. Population by sex, rate of population increase, surface area and density
Population selon le sexe, taux d'accroissement de la population, superficie et densité
(continued — suite)

(See notes at end of table. — Voir notes à la fin du tableau.)

| Continent, country or area and census date / Continent, pays ou zone et date du recensement | Census type[a] | Latest available census — Dernier recensement disponible (in units — en unités) | | | Mid-year estimates - Estimations au milieu de l'année (in thousands — en milliers) | | Estimate type | Annual rate of increase Taux d' accrois sement annuel 1995-2002 | Surface area Superficie (km²) 2002 | Density Densité 2002[1] |
		Both sexes Les deux sexes	Male Masculin	Female Feminin	1995	2002				
AFRICA — AFRIQUE										
Sierra Leone[9] 15 XII 1985	DF	3 515 812	1 746 055	1 769 757	*4 421*	*5 167*	DF	2.2	71 740	*72*
Somalia - Somalie 15 II 1987	DF	7 114 431	3 741 664	3 372 767	...	...	...	...	637 657	...
South Africa - Afrique du Sud 10 X 2001	DF	*44 819 778	*21 434 041	*23 385 737	*39 477*	*45 454*	DF	2.0	1 221 037	*37*
Sudan - Soudan 15 IV 1993	DF	24 940 683	12 518 638	12 422 045	*27 008*	*32 468*	DF	2.6	2 505 813	*13*
Swaziland 11 V 1997	DF	929 718	440 154	489 564	...	...	...	...	17 364	...
Togo 22 XI 1981	DF	2 703 250	...	...	...	...	...	...	56 785	...
Tunisia - Tunisie 20 IV 1994	DF	8 785 711	4 439 289	4 346 422	*8 958*	*9 782	DF	1.3	163 610	60
Uganda - Ouganda 12 IX 2002	DF	*24 748 977	*12 124 761	*12 624 216	...	...	...	...	241 038	...
United Republic of Tanzania - République Unie de Tanzanie 24 VIII 2002	DF	*34 569 232	*16 910 321	*17 658 911	...	...	...	...	883 749	...
Western Sahara - Sahara occidental[10] 31 XII 1970	DF	76 425	43 981	32 444	...	...	...	...	266 000	...
Zambia - Zambie 25 X 2000	DF	9 885 591	4 946 298	4 939 293	*9 112*	*10 409*	DF	1.9	752 618	*14*
Zimbabwe 17 VIII 2002	DF	*11 634 663	...	...	...	...	...	...	390 757	...
AMERICA, NORTH — AMERIQUE DU NORD										
Anguilla 9 V 2001	DF	11 430	5 628	5 802	10	12	DF	2.8	91	131
Antigua and Barbuda - Antigua-et-Barbuda 28 V 2001	DF	77 426	37 002	40 424	...	...	...	...	442	...
Aruba 14 X 2000	DJ	90 508	43 435	47 073	80	*94	DJ	2.3	180	520
Bahamas 1 V 2000	DF	303 611	147 715	155 896	...	...	...	...	13 878	...
Barbados - Barbade 1 V 2000	DF	250 010	119 926	130 084	...	...	...	...	430	...
Belize 12 V 2000	DF	240 204	121 278	118 926	*216*	*265*	DF	2.9	22 966	12
Bermuda - Bermudes[11] 20 V 2000	DJ	62 059	29 802	32 257	...	...	...	...	53	...
British Virgin Islands - Îles Vierges britanniques 21 V 2001	DF	*20 647	*10 627	*10 020	...	...	...	...	151	...
Canada[12] 15 V 2001	DJ	30 007 095	14 706 850	15 300 245	29 302	31 373	DJ	1.0	9 970 610	3
Cayman Islands - Îles Caïmanes 10 X 1999	DF	39 410	...	...	33	*40	DJ	2.9	264	152

3. Population by sex, rate of population increase, surface area and density
Population selon le sexe, taux d'accroissement de la population, superficie et densité
(continued — suite)

(See notes at end of table. — Voir notes à la fin du tableau.)

Continent, country or area and census date / Continent, pays ou zone et date du recensement	Census type[a]	Latest available census — Dernier recensement disponible (in units — en unités)			Mid-year estimates - Estimations au milieu de l'année (in thousands — en milliers)		Estimate type	Annual rate of increase Taux d' accrois sement annuel 1995-2002	Surface area Superficie (km²) 2002	Density Densité 2002[1]
		Both sexes Les deux sexes	Male Masculin	Female Feminin	1995	2002				
AMERICA, NORTH — AMERIQUE DU NORD										
Costa Rica										
26 VI 2000	DJ	3 810 179	1 902 614	1 907 565	3 136	3 998	DJ	3.5	51 100	78
Cuba										
6 IX 2002	DJ	11 177 743	5 597 233	5 580 510	10 978	11 251	DF	0.4	110 861	101
Dominica - Dominique										
12 V 2001	DF	*71 239	*36 313	*34 926	73	70	DF	-0.4	751	94
Dominican Republic - République dominicaine										
18 X 2002	DF	*8 230 722	*4 102 880	*4 127 842	...	...	...	...	48 511	...
El Salvador										
27 IX 1992	DF	5 118 599	2 485 613	2 632 986	5 669	6 518	DF	2.0	21 041	310
Greenland - Groenland[13]										
1 VII 2000	DJ	56 124	29 989	26 135	...	...	...	...	2 175 600	...
Grenada - Grenade[14]										
25 V 2001	DF	102 632	50 481	52 151	...	...	...	...	344	...
Guadeloupe[15]										
8 III 1999	DJ	422 222	203 146	219 076	405	437	DJ	1.1	1 705	256
Guatemala[16]										
24 XI 2002	DJ	*11 237 196	...	...	9 976	*11 987	DF	2.6	108 889	110
Haiti - Haïti										
30 VIII 1982	DJ	5 053 792	2 448 370	2 605 422	...	...	...	...	27 750	...
Honduras										
28 VII 2001	DF	*6 071 200	*3 000 530	*3 070 070	5 808	6 695	DF	2.5	112 088	60
Jamaica - Jamaïque										
10 IX 2001	DF	*2 607 633	*1 283 547	*1 324 085	...	...	...	...	10 991	...
Martinique										
8 III 1999	DJ	381 325	180 910	200 415	369	*389	DJ	0.8	1 102	353
Mexico - Mexique										
14 II 2000	DJ	97 483 412	47 592 253	49 891 159	91 992	103 229	DJ	1.6	1 958 201	53
Montserrat										
12 V 1991	DF	10 639	5 290	5 349	...	...	...	...	102	...
Netherlands Antilles - Antilles néerlandaises[17]										
29 I 2001	DJ	175 653	82 521	93 132	...	...	...	...	800	...
Nicaragua										
25 IV 1995	DJ	4 357 099	2 147 105	2 209 994	4 427	5 162	DJ	2.2	130 000	40
Panama										
14 V 2000	DF	2 839 177	1 432 566	1 406 611	2 631	*3 060	DF	2.2	75 517	41
Puerto Rico - Porto Rico[18]										
1 IV 2000	DJ	3 808 610	1 833 577	1 975 033	3 655	3 859	DJ	0.8	8 875	435
Saint Kitts and Nevis - Saint-Kitts-et-Nevis										
14 V 2001	DF	45 841	22 784	23 057	...	...	...	...	261	...
Saint Lucia - Sainte-Lucie[19]										
22 V 2001	DF	157 164	76 741	80 423	145	159	DF	1.3	539	295
Saint Pierre and Miquelon - Saint Pierre-et-Miquelon										
8 III 1999	DF	6 316	3 147	3 169	...	...	...	...	242	...

63

3. Population by sex, rate of population increase, surface area and density
Population selon le sexe, taux d'accroissement de la population, superficie et densité
(continued — suite)

(See notes at end of table. — Voir notes à la fin du tableau.)

| Continent, country or area and census date — Continent, pays ou zone et date du recensement | Census type[a] — Census type[a] | Latest available census — Dernier recensement disponible (in units — en unités) | | | Mid-year estimates - Estimations au milieu de l'année (in thousands — en milliers) | | Estima-te type | Annual rate of increase Taux d' accrois sement annuel 1995-2002 | Surface area Superficie (km²) 2002 | Density Densité 2002[1] |
		Both sexes Les deux sexes	Male Masculin	Female Feminin	1995	2002				
AMERICA, NORTH — AMERIQUE DU NORD										
Saint Vincent and the Grenadines - Saint Vincent-et-les Grenadines[20] 14 V 2001	DF	*109 202	...	...	111	108	DF	-0.4	388	278
Trinidad and Tobago - Trinité-et-Tobago 15 V 2000	DF	1 262 366	633 051	629 315	1 260	*1 276	DF	0.2	5 130	249
Turks Caicos Islands - Îles Turques et Caïques 31 V 1990	DF	12 350	6 289	6 061	...	...	...	...	430	...
United States - États-Unis[21,22] 1 IV 2000	DJ	*281 421 906	*138 053 563	*143 368 343	263 044	288 369	DJ	1.3	9 629 091	30
United States Virgin Islands - Îles Vierges américaines[18] 1 IV 2000	DJ	108 612	51 864	56 748	108	109	DJ	0.1	347	314
AMERICA, SOUTH — AMERIQUE DU SUD										
Argentina - Argentine 18 XI 2001	DF	36 260 130	17 659 072	18 601 058	*34 768*	*37 944*	DF	1.2	2 780 400	*14*
Bolivia - Bolivie 5 IX 2001	DF	8 280 184	4 130 342	4 149 842	...	...	...	...	1 098 581	...
Brazil - Brésil[23] 1 VIII 2000	DJ	169 799 170	83 576 015	86 223 155	*155 822*	*174 633*	DF	1.6	8 514 047	21
Chile - Chili 24 IV 2002	DF	15 116 435	7 447 695	7 668 740	14 210	15 589	DF	1.3	756 626	21
Colombia - Colombie 24 X 1993	DF	33 109 840	16 296 539	16 813 301	*38 542*	*43 834*	DF	1.8	1 138 914	*38*
Ecuador - Équateur[24] 25 XI 2001	DF	12 156 608	6 018 353	6 138 255	*11 460*	*12 661*	DF	1.4	283 561	*45*
Falkland Islands (Malvinas) - Îles Falkland (Malvinas)[25,26] 8 IV 2001	DF	2 913	1 598	1 315	...	...	...	...	12 173	...
French Guiana - Guyane française 8 III 1999	DJ	156 790	78 963	77 827	137	175	DJ	3.5	90 000	2
Guyana 12 V 1991	DF	701 704	344 928	356 776	...	...	...	...	214 969	...
Paraguay 28 VIII 2002	DF	*5 206 101	*2 640 068	*2 566 033	...	...	...	...	406 752	...
Peru - Pérou[16,27] 11 VII 1993	DF	22 048 356	10 956 375	11 091 981	*23 837*	*26 749*	DF	1.6	1 285 216	*21*
Suriname[28] 31 III 2003	DJ	*481 146	*241 837	*239 292	434	476	DF	1.3	163 820	3
Uruguay[16] 22 V 1996	DF	3 163 763	1 532 288	1 631 475	3 217	3 361	DF	0.6	175 016	19
Venezuela[27] 30 X 2001	DF	23 054 210	11 402 869	11 651 341	21 844	25 220	DF	2.1	912 050	28

3. Population by sex, rate of population increase, surface area and density
Population selon le sexe, taux d'accroissement de la population, superficie et densité
(continued — suite)

(See notes at end of table. — Voir notes à la fin du tableau.)

Continent, country or area and census date / Continent, pays ou zone et date du recensement	Census type[a]	Latest available census — Dernier recensement disponible (in units — en unités)			Mid-year estimates - Estimations au milieu de l'année (in thousands — en milliers)		Estima-te type	Annual rate of increase Taux d' accrois sement annuel 1995-2002	Surface area Superficie (km²) 2002	Density Densité 2002[1]
		Both sexes Les deux sexes	Male Masculin	Female Feminin	1995	2002				
ASIA — ASIE										
Afghanistan[29]										
23 VI 1979	DF	13 051 358	6 712 377	6 338 981	...	...	...	...	652 090	...
Armenia - Arménie[30,31]										
10 X 2001	DF	3 002 594	1 407 220	1 595 374	3 760	<3 213	...	...	29 800	108
Azerbaijan - Azerbaïdjan										
27 I 1999	DJ	7 953 438	3 883 155	4 070 283	7 685	8 172	DF	0.9	86 600	94
Bahrain - Bahreïn										
7 IV 2001	DF	650 604	373 649	276 955	559	672	DF	2.6	694	968
Bangladesh										
22 I 2001	DF	*123 151 246	*62 735 988	*60 415 258	...	...	...	...	143 998	...
Bhutan - Bhoutan										
11 XI 1969	DF	1 034 774	...	...	582	*716	DF	3.0	47 000	15
Brunei Darussalam - Brunéi Darussalam										
21 VIII 2001	DF	*332 844	*168 974	*163 870	287	341	DF	2.4	5 765	59
Cambodia - Cambodge[32]										
3 III 1998	DF	11 437 656	5 511 408	5 926 248	10 200	<13 041	DF	3.5	181 035	72
China - Chine[33,34]										
1 XI 2000	DJ	1242612226	640 275 969	602 336 257	...	...	...	...	9 596 961	...
China: Hong Kong SAR - Chine: Hong Kong RAS[31,35]										
14 III 2001	DJ	6 708 389	3 285 344	3 423 045	6 156	6 787	...	...	1 099	G 176
China: Macao SAR - Chine: Macao RAS										
23 VIII 2001	DJ	435 235	208 865	226 370	409	*439	DJ	1.0	26	16 891
Cyprus - Chypre[36,37,38]										
1 X 2001	DJ	689 565	338 497	351 068	742	797	DJ	1.0	9 251	86
Georgia - Géorgie										
17 I 2002	DJ	4 371 535	2 061 753	2 309 782	...	...	...	...	69 700	...
India - Inde[39,40]										
1 III 2001	DF	1028610328	532 156 772	496 453 556	923 459	1 050 640	DF	1.8	3 287 263	320
Indonesia - Indonésie[41]										
30 VI 2000	DF	206 264 595	103 417 180	102 847 415	...	...	...	...	1 904 569	...
Iran (Islamic Republic of) - Iran (République islamique d')										
23 X 1996	DJ	60 055 488	30 515 159	29 540 329	59 187	65 540	DJ	1.5	1 648 195	40
Iraq[42]										
16 X 1997	DF	19 184 543	9 536 570	9 647 973	...	...	...	...	438 317	...
Israel - Israël[16,43]										
4 XI 1995	DJ	5 548 523	2 738 175	2 810 348	5 545	6 570	DJ	2.4	22 145	297
Japan - Japon[44]										
1 X 2000	DF	126 925 843	62 110 764	64 815 079	125 472	127 401	DF	0.2	377 873	337
Jordan - Jordanie[45]										
10 XII 1994	DF	4 139 458	2 160 725	1 978 733	>4 291	>5 329	DF	3.1	89 342	60
Kazakhstan										
26 II 1999	DJ	14 953 126	7 201 785	7 751 341	15 816	14 859	DF	-0.9	2 724 900	5
Korea (Dem. People's Republic of) - Corée (Rép. populaire dém. de)										
31 XII 1993	DF	21 213 378	10 329 699	10 883 679	...	...	...	...	120 538	...

3. Population by sex, rate of population increase, surface area and density
Population selon le sexe, taux d'accroissement de la population, superficie et densité
(continued — suite)

(See notes at end of table. — Voir notes à la fin du tableau.)

Continent, country or area and census date / Continent, pays ou zone et date du recensement	Census type[a]	Latest available census — Dernier recensement disponible (in units — en unités)			Mid-year estimates - Estimations au milieu de l'année (in thousands — en milliers)		Estima-te type	Annual rate of increase Taux d' accrois sement annuel 1995-2002	Surface area Superficie (km²) 2002	Density Densité 2002[1]
		Both sexes Les deux sexes	Male Masculin	Female Feminin	1995	2002				
ASIA — ASIE										
Korea (Republic of) - Corée (République de)[46]										
1 XI 2000	DF	46 136 101	23 158 582	22 977 519	45 093	47 640	DF	0.8	99 538	479
Kuwait - Koweït										
20 IV 1995	DF	1 575 570	913 402	662 168	1 802	2 262	DF	3.2	17 818	127
Kyrgyzstan - Kirghizistan										
24 III 1999	DJ	4 822 938	2 380 465	2 442 473	4 590	4 993	DF	1.2	199 900	25
Lao People's Democratic Republic - République démocratique populaire lao										
1 III 1995	DF	4 574 848	2 260 986	2 313 862	4 536	*5 500	DF	2.8	236 800	23
Lebanon - Liban[47]										
15 XI 1970	SDF	2 126 325	1 080 015	1 046 310	...	...	...	...	10 400	...
Malaysia - Malaisie[48,49]										
5 VII 2000	DJ	23 274 690	11 853 432	11 421 258	...	...	...	...	329 847	...
Maldives										
31 III 2000	DF	270 101	137 200	132 901	...	...	...	...	298	...
Mongolia - Mongolie										
5 I 2000	DF	2 373 493	1 177 981	1 195 512	2 243	2 475	DF	1.4	1 566 500	2
Myanmar										
31 III 1983	DF	35 307 913	17 518 255	17 789 658	...	...	...	...	676 578	...
Nepal - Népal[50]										
22 VI 2001	DJ	23 151 423	11 563 921	11 587 502	...	...	...	...	147 181	...
Occupied Palestinian Territory - Territoire palestinien occupé[51]										
9 XII 1997	DF	2 601 669	1 322 264	1 279 405	2 483	3 465	DF	4.8	6 020	576
Oman										
7 XII 2003	DF	2 340 815	1 313 239	1 027 576	...	...	...	...	309 500	...
Pakistan[52]										
2 III 1998	DF	130 579 571	67 840 137	62 739 434	122 360	144 852	DF	2.4	796 095	182
Philippines										
1 V 2000	DJ	76 504 077	38 524 267	37 979 810	70 267	79 504	DJ	1.8	300 000	265
Qatar										
1 III 1997	DF	522 023	342 459	179 564	...	...	...	...	11 000	...
Saudi Arabia - Arabie saoudite										
27 IX 1992	DF	16 948 388	9 479 973	7 468 415	18 123	*22 000	DF	2.8	2 149 690	10
Singapore - Singapour[53]										
30 VI 2000	DF	4 017 700	2 061 800	1 955 900	3 526	4 171	DF	2.4	683	6 107
Sri Lanka[54]										
17 VII 2001	DF	*16 864 544	*8 343 964	*8 520 580	18 136	*19 007	DF	0.7	65 610	290
Syrian Arab Republic - République arabe syrienne[55]										
3 IX 1994	DF	13 782 315	7 048 906	6 733 409	14 153	17 130	DF	2.7	185 180	93
Tajikistan - Tadjikistan										
20 I 2000	DF	*6 127 000	*3 082 000	*3 045 000	5 836	*6 433	DF	1.4	143 100	45
Thailand - Thaïlande										
1 IV 2000	DJ	60 617 200	29 850 100	30 767 100	59 401	*63 482	DJ	0.9	513 115	124

3. Population by sex, rate of population increase, surface area and density
Population selon le sexe, taux d'accroissement de la population, superficie et densité
(continued — suite)

(See notes at end of table. — Voir notes à la fin du tableau.)

Continent, country or area and census date Continent, pays ou zone et date du recensement	Census type[a]	Latest available census — Dernier recensement disponible (in units — en unités)			Mid-year estimates - Estimations au milieu de l'année (in thousands — en milliers)		Estima-te type	Annual rate of increase Taux d' accrois sement annuel 1995-2002	Surface area Superficie (km²) 2002	Density Densité 2002[1]
		Both sexes Les deux sexes	Male Masculin	Female Feminin	1995	2002				
ASIA — ASIE										
Timor-Leste										
31 X 1990	DF	747 750	386 939	360 811	...	...	...	...	14 874	...
Turkey - Turquie										
22 X 2000	DF	67 803 927	34 346 735	33 457 192	61 737	69 626	DF	1.7	783 562	89
Turkmenistan - Turkménistan										
10 I 1995	DF	4 483 251	2 225 331	2 257 920	...	...	...	...	488 100	...
United Arab Emirates - Émirats arabes unis[56]										
17 XII 1995	DF	2 411 041	1 606 804	804 237	...	...	...	...	83 600	...
Uzbekistan - Ouzbékistan										
12 I 1989	DJ	19 810 077	9 784 156	10 025 921	22 690	*25 368	DF	1.6	447 400	57
Viet Nam										
1 IV 1999	DF	76 324 753	37 519 754	38 804 999	73 962	79 727	DF	1.1	331 689	240
Yemen - Yémen										
16 XII 1994	DF	14 587 807	7 473 540	7 114 267	15 369	*19 495	DF	3.4	527 968	37
EUROPE										
Albania - Albanie										
1 IV 2001	DF	*3 069 275	*1 530 443	*1 538 832	...	...	...	...	28 748	...
Andorra - Andorre										
12 VII 1989	DF	46 166	...	...	...	...	...	...	468	...
Austria - Autriche										
15 V 2001	DJ	8 032 926	3 889 189	4 143 737	8 047	8 053	DJ	-	83 858	96
Belarus - Bélarus										
16 II 1999	DJ	10 045 237	4 717 621	5 327 616	10 281	9 925	DF	-0.5	207 600	48
Belgium - Belgique										
1 X 2001	DJ	10 296 350	5 035 446	5 260 904	10 137	10 333	DJ	0.3	30 528	338
Bosnia and Herzegovina - Bosnie-Herzégovine										
31 III 1991	DJ	4 377 033	2 183 795	2 193 238	4 180	*3 828	DJ	-1.3	51 197	75
Bulgaria - Bulgarie										
1 III 2001	DF	*7 928 901	*3 862 465	*4 066 436	8 406	7 869	DF	-0.9	110 912	71
Channel Islands: Guernsey - Îles Anglo-Normandes: Guernesey										
29 IV 2001	DJ	59 807	29 138	30 669	...	...	...	...	78	...
Channel Islands: Jersey - Îles Anglo-Normandes: Jersey										
11 III 2001	DJ	87 186	42 485	44 701	...	...	...	...	116	...
Croatia - Croatie										
31 III 2001	DJ	4 437 460	2 135 900	2 301 560	4 669	4 443	DJ	-0.7	56 538	79
Czech Republic - République tchèque										
1 III 2001	DJ	10 230 060	4 982 071	5 247 989	10 331	10 201	DJ	-0.2	78 866	129
Denmark - Danemark[57]										
1 I 1991	DJ	5 146 469	2 536 391	2 610 078	5 228	5 376	DJ	0.4	43 094	125
Estonia - Estonie										
31 III 2000	DJ	*1 370 052	*631 851	*738 201	1 484	1 359	DF	-1.3	45 100	30

3. Population by sex, rate of population increase, surface area and density
Population selon le sexe, taux d'accroissement de la population, superficie et densité
(continued — suite)

(See notes at end of table. — Voir notes à la fin du tableau.)

Continent, country or area and census date Continent, pays ou zone et date du recensement	Census type[a]	Latest available census — Dernier recensement disponible (in units — en unités)			Mid-year estimates - Estimations au milieu de l'année (in thousands — en milliers)		Estimate type	Annual rate of increase Taux d'accrois sement annuel 1995-2002	Surface area Superficie (km²) 2002	Density Densité 2002[1]
		Both sexes Les deux sexes	Male Masculin	Female Feminin	1995	2002				
EUROPE										
Faeroe Islands - Îles Féroé										
22 IX 1977	DJ	41 969	21 997	19 972	...	...	...	...	1 399	...
Finland - Finlande										
31 XII 2000	DJ	5 181 115	2 529 341	2 651 774	5 108	5 201	DJ	0.3	338 145	15
France[58]										
8 III 1999	DJ	58 520 688	28 419 419	30 101 269	57 844	59 486	DJ	0.4	551 500	108
Germany - Allemagne										
....	...	...	...	...	81 661	82 488	DJ	0.1	357 022	231
Germany: Fed. Rep. of Germany - Allemagne: République fédérale d'Allemagne[59]										
25 V 1987	DJ	61 077 042	29 322 923	31 754 119	...	...	...	...	248 647	...
Germany: Former German Dem. Rep. - Allemagne: Ancienne république démocratique allema[59]										
31 XII 1981	DJ	16 705 635	7 849 112	8 856 523	...	...	...	...	108 333	...
Gibraltar[60]										
12 XI 2001	DF	27 486	13 639	13 847	27	29	DF	0.7	6	4 753
Greece - Grèce[61,62]										
18 III 2001	DF	10 964 020	5 431 816	5 532 204	10 454	<10 969	DF	0.7	131 957	83
Holy See - Saint-Siège[13,63]										
1 VII 2000	DF	*798	*529	*269	...	...	...	...	-	...
Hungary - Hongrie										
1 II 2001	DF	10 198 315	4 850 650	5 347 665	10 229	10 159	DF	-0.1	93 032	109
Iceland - Islande										
1 XII 1970	DJ	204 930	103 621	101 309	267	288	DJ	1.0	103 000	3
Ireland - Irlande										
28 IV 2002	DF	3 917 203	1 946 164	1 971 039	3 601	3 917	DF	1.2	70 273	56
Isle of Man - Îles de Man										
29 IV 2001	DJ	76 315	37 372	38 943	72	77	DJ	1.0	572	135
Italy - Italie										
21 X 2001	DF	57 110 144	27 617 335	29 492 809	57 301	*57 482	DJ	-	301 318	191
Latvia - Lettonie										
31 III 2000	DJ	2 377 383	1 094 964	1 282 419	2 485	2 339	DF	-0.9	64 600	36
Liechtenstein										
2 XII 1980	DF	25 215	12 519	12 696	31	34	DF	1.3	160	211
Lithuania - Lituanie										
6 IV 2001	DJ	3 483 972	1 629 148	1 854 824	3 629	3 469	DJ	-0.6	65 300	53
Luxembourg										
15 II 2001	DJ	439 539	216 541	222 998	409	446	DJ	1.3	2 586	173
Malta - Malte[64,65]										
26 XI 1995	DJ	378 132	186 836	191 296	>378	397	DJ	0.7	316	1 257
Monaco										
23 VII 1990	DJ	29 972	14 237	15 735	...	...	...	...	1	...
Netherlands - Pays-Bas[66]										
1 I 2002	DJ	16 105 285	7 971 967	8 133 318	15 459	16 149	DJ	0.6	41 528	389
Norway - Norvège[67]										
3 XI 2001	DJ	4 520 947	2 240 281	2 280 666	4 359	4 538	DJ	0.6	385 155	12

3. Population by sex, rate of population increase, surface area and density
Population selon le sexe, taux d'accroissement de la population, superficie et densité
(continued — suite)

(See notes at end of table. — Voir notes à la fin du tableau.)

Continent, country or area and census date / Continent, pays ou zone et date du recensement	Census type[a]	Latest available census — Dernier recensement disponible (in units — en unités)			Mid-year estimates - Estimations au milieu de l'année (in thousands — en milliers)		Estimate type	Annual rate of increase Taux d'accroissement annuel 1995-2002	Surface area Superficie (km²) 2002	Density Densité 2002[1]
		Both sexes Les deux sexes	Male Masculin	Female Feminin	1995	2002				
EUROPE										
Poland - Pologne[68] 20 V 2002	DF	*38 230 000	*18 516 000	*19 714 000	38 588	38 425	DF	-0.1	323 250	119
Portugal[69] 12 III 2001	DF	*10 355 824	*4 999 964	*5 355 860	9 916	*10 368	DF	0.6	91 982	113
Republic of Moldova - République de Moldova[70] 12 I 1989	DF	4 337 592	2 058 160	2 279 432	4 348	3 623	DJ	-2.6	33 851	107
Romania - Roumanie 18 III 2002	DJ	*21 680 974	*10 568 741	*11 112 233	22 681	21 795	DJ	-0.6	238 391	91
Russian Federation - Fédération de Russie 9 X 2002	DF	*145 537 200	*67 805 700	*77 731 500	...	...	...	...	17 075 400	...
San Marino - Saint-Marin 30 XI 1976	DF	19 149	9 654	9 495	...	...	...	...	61	...
Serbia and Montenegro - Serbie-et-Montenegro[71] 31 III 2002	DJ	8 134 617	3 960 684	4 173 933	10 547	<10 662	DJ	0.2	102 173	104
Slovakia - Slovaquie 25 V 2001	DJ	5 379 455	2 612 515	2 766 940	5 364	5 379	DJ	-	49 033	110
Slovenia - Slovénie 31 III 2002	DJ	*1 948 250	*943 994	*1 004 256	1 988	1 996	DJ	0.1	20 256	99
Spain - Espagne[72] 1 XI 2001	DF	40 847 371	20 012 882	20 834 489	39 223	<40 851	DJ	0.6	505 992	81
Svalbard and Jan Mayen Islands - Îles Svalbard et Jan Mayen[73] 1 XI 1960	DF	3 431	2 545	886	...	...	...	...	62 422	...
Sweden - Suède 1 XI 1990	DJ	8 587 353	4 242 351	4 345 002	8 827	8 925	DJ	0.2	449 964	20
Switzerland - Suisse 5 XII 2000	DJ	7 204 055	3 519 698	3 684 357	7 041	7 290	DJ	0.5	41 284	177
The Former Yugoslav Rep. of Macedonia - L'ex-République yougoslave de Macédoine 1 XI 2002	DJ	2 022 547	1 015 377	1 007 170	1 963	<2 039	DF	0.5	25 713	79
Ukraine 5 XII 2001	DJ	48 457 102	22 441 344	26 015 758	51 728	48 402	DF	-0.9	603 700	80
United Kingdom - Royaume-Uni[74] 29 IV 2001	DF	58 789 187	28 579 867	30 209 320	58 612	*59 232	DF	0.2	242 900	244
OCEANIA — OCEANIE										
American Samoa - Samoas américaines[18] 1 IV 2000	DJ	57 291	29 264	28 027	...	...	...	...	199	...
Australia - Australie 7 VIII 2001	DF	18 972 350	9 362 021	9 610 329	18 072	19 641	DJ	1.2	7 741 220	3

3. Population by sex, rate of population increase, surface area and density
Population selon le sexe, taux d'accroissement de la population, superficie et densité
(continued — suite)

(See notes at end of table. — Voir notes à la fin du tableau.)

Continent, country or area and census date / Continent, pays ou zone et date du recensement	Census type[a]	Latest available census — Dernier recensement disponible (in units — en unités)			Mid-year estimates - Estimations au milieu de l'année (in thousands — en milliers)		Estimate type	Annual rate of increase Taux d' accrois sement annuel 1995-2002	Surface area Superficie (km²) 2002	Density Densité 2002[1]
		Both sexes Les deux sexes	Male Masculin	Female Feminin	1995	2002				
OCEANIA — OCEANIE										
Cook Islands - Îles Cook[75,76]										
1 XII 2001	DF	18 027	9 303	8 724	19	18	DF	-0.8	236	78
Fiji - Fidji										
25 VIII 1996	DF	775 077	393 931	381 146	...	...	...	...	18 274	...
French Polynesia - Polynésie française[77]										
7 XI 2002	DF	245 516	...	...	...	...	...	...	4 000	...
Guam[18]										
1 IV 2000	DJ	154 805	79 181	75 624	144	161	DJ	1.6	549	293
Kiribati[78]										
7 XI 1995	DF	*77 658	*38 478	*39 180	...	...	...	...	726	...
Marshall Islands - Îles Marshall										
1 VI 1999	DF	50 848	26 034	24 814	56	57	DF	0.3	181	313
Micronesia, Federated States of - Micronésie, États Fédérés de La										
1 IV 2000	DJ	107 008	54 191	52 817	107	120	DJ	1.6	702	170
Nauru										
17 IV 1992	DF	9 919	5 079	4 840	...	...	...	...	21	...
New Caledonia - Nouvelle-Calédonie[79]										
16 IV 1996	DF	196 836	100 762	96 074	194	217	DF	1.6	18 575	12
New Zealand - Nouvelle-Zélande[80]										
6 III 2001	DJ	3 820 749	1 863 309	1 957 440	3 673	3 939	DJ	1.0	270 534	15
Niue - Nioué										
7 IX 2001	DF	1 788	897	891	...	...	...	...	260	...
Norfolk Island - Île Norfolk										
7 VIII 2001	DF	2 601	1 257	1 344	...	...	...	...	36	...
Northern Mariana Islands - Îles Mariannes septentrionales										
1 IV 2000	DF	69 221	31 984	37 237	...	...	...	...	464	...
Palau - Palaos										
15 IV 2000	DF	19 129	...	...	17	20	DF	2.2	459	44
Papua New Guinea - Papouasie-Nouvelle-Guinée[81]										
9 VII 2000	DF	5 190 786	2 691 744	2 499 042	4 074	5 462	DF	4.2	462 840	12
Pitcairn										
31 XII 1991	DF	66	...	...	...	...	...	...	5	...
Samoa										
5 XI 2001	DF	176 710	92 050	84 660	...	...	...	...	2 831	...
Solomon Islands - Îles Salomon[82]										
21 XI 1999	DF	409 042	211 381	197 661	...	...	...	...	28 896	...
Tokelau - Tokélaou										
11 XII 1991	DF	1 577	...	...	...	...	...	...	12	...
Tonga										
30 XI 1996	DF	97 784	49 615	48 169	>98	>101	DF	0.5	650	155
Tuvalu										
1 XI 2002	DF	9 561	4 729	4 832	...	...	...	...	26	...

3. Population by sex, rate of population increase, surface area and density
Population selon le sexe, taux d'accroissement de la population, superficie et densité
(continued — suite)

Continent, country or area and census date / Continent, pays ou zone et date du recensement	Census type[a]	Latest available census — Dernier recensement disponible (in units — en unités)			Mid-year estimates - Estimations au milieu de l'année (in thousands — en milliers)		Estima-te type	Annual rate of increase Taux d' accrois sement annuel 1995-2002	Surface area Superficie (km²) 2002	Density Densité 2002[1]
		Both sexes Les deux sexes	Male Masculin	Female Feminin	1995	2002				
OCEANIA — OCEANIE										
Vanuatu										
16 XI 1999	DJ	186 678	95 682	90 996	...	...	...	...	12 189	...
Wallis and Futuna Islands - Îles Wallis et Futuna										
3 X 1996	DF	14 166	6 984	7 182	...	...	...	...	200	...

GENERAL NOTES - NOTES GENERALES

Surface area estimates include inland waters. For method of evaluation and limitation of data, see Technical Notes for this table. — Pour le méthode d'évaluation et les insuffisances des données, voireNotes techniques, pour ce tableau.

FOOTNOTES - NOTES

* Provisional. — Données provisoires.

< Data refer to 1 January — Données se raportent au 1 Janvier.

\> Data refer to 31 December — Données se raportent au 31 Décembre.

[a] 'Code' indicates the source of data, as follows:
DF - De facto
DJ - De jure
SDF - Sample survey, de facto
Le 'Code' indique la source des données, comme suit:
DF - Population de fait
DJ - Population de droit
SDF - Enquête par sondage, population de fait

[1] Population per square kilometre of surface area in 2002. Figures are estimates of population divided by surface area and are not to be considered either as reflecting density in the urban sense or as indicating the supporting power of a territory's land and resources. — Nombre d'habitants au kilomètre carré en 2002. Il s'agit simplement d'éstimations de la population divisé par celui de la superficie: il ne faut pas y voir d'indication de la densité au sens urbain du terme ni de l'effectif de population que les terres et les ressources du territoire sont capables de nourrir.
[2] Including the enclave of Cabinda. - Y compris l'enclave de Cabinda.
[3] Census results have been adjusted for underenumeration, estimated at 1.4 per cent. - Les résultat du recensement ont été ajustées pour compenser les lacunes du dénombrement, estimées à 1,4 p. 100.
[4] Census result, excluding Mayotte. - Les résultat du recensement, non compris Mayotte.
[5] Comprising Bioko (which includes Pagalu) and Rio Muni (which includes Corisco and Elobeys). - Comprend Bioko (qui comprend Pagalu) et Rio Muni (qui comprend Corisco et Elobeys).
[6] Data refer to Libyan nationals only. - Les données se raportent aux nationaux libyens seulement.
[7] Data for estimates refer to national projections. - Les données se referent aux projections nationales.
[8] Census results have been adjusted for underenumeration, estimated at 5.1 per cent. - Les résultats du recensement ont été ajustées pour compenser les lacunes du dénombrement, estimées à 5,1 p. 100.
[9] Census results have been adjusted for underenumeration, estimated

at 9 per cent. - Les résultats du recensement ont été ajustées pour compenser les lacunes du dénombrement, estimées à 9 p. 100.
[10] Comprising the Northern Region (former Saguia el Hamra) and Southern Region (former Rio de Oro). - Comprend la région septentrionale (ancien Saguia-el-Hamra) et la région méridionale (ancien Rio de Oro).
[11] Excluding the institutional population. - Non compris la population dans les institutions.
[12] Revised intercensal estimates adjusted for net undercoverage. - - Estimations inter censitaires corrigées pour tenir en compte du sous dénombrement net.
[13] Population statistics are based on administrative records. - La source de la statistique de la population sont des fichiers administratifs.
[14] Including Carriacou and other dependencies in the Grenadines. - Y compris Carriacou et les autres dépendances du groupe des îles Grenadines.
[15] Including dependencies: Marie-Galante, la Désirade, les Saintes, Petite-Terre, St. Barthélemy and French part of St. Martin. - Y compris les dépendances: Marie-Galante, la Désirade, les Saintes, Petite-Terre, Saint-Barthélemy et la partie française de Saint-Martin.
[16] Mid-year estimates have been adjusted for underenumeration, at latest census. - Les estimations au milieu de l'année tiennent compte d'une ajustement destiné à compenser les lacunes du dénombrement lors du dernier recensement.
[17] Comprising Bonaire, Curaçao, Saba, St. Eustatius and Dutch part of St. Martin. - Comprend Bonaire, Curaçao, Saba, Saint-Eustache et la partie néederlandaise de Saint-Martin.
[18] Including armed forces stationed in the area. - Y compris les militaires en garnison sur le territoire.
[19] Census data refer to the total enumerated household population plus institutional population. - Les données de recensement se rapportent à la population totale recensée au sein des ménages et des institutions.
[20] Including Bequia and other islands in the Grenadines. - Y compris Bequia et des autres îles dans les Grenadines.
[21] Excluding armed forces overseas and civilian citizens absent from country for an extended period of time. - Non compris les militaires à l'étranger, et les civils hors du pays pendant une période prolongée.
[22] Excluding civilian citizens absent from country for extended periods of time. - Non compris les civils hors du pays pendant une période prolongée.
[23] Data include persons in remote areas, military personel outside the country, merchant seamen at sea, civilian seasonal workers outside the country, and other civilians outside the country, and exclude nomads, foreign military, civilian aliens temporarily in the country, transients on ships and Indian jungle population. - Y compris les personnes dans des régions éloignées, le personel militaire en dehors du pays, les marins marchands, les ouvriers saisonniers civils de couture en dehors du pays, et autres civils en dehors du pays, et non compris les nomades, les militaires étrangers, les étrangers civils temporairement dans le pays, les transiteurs sur des bateaux et les Indiens de la jungle.
[24] Excluding nomadic Indian tribes. - Non compris les tribus d'Indiens nomades.
[25] Excluding dependencies, of which South Georgia (area 3 755 km2) had an estimated population of 499 in 1964 (494 males, 5 females). The other dependencies namely, the South Sandwich group (surface area 337

km2) and a number of smaller islands, are presumed to be uninhabited. - -
Non compris les dépendances, parmi lesquelles figure la Georgie du Sud
(3 755 km2) avec une population estimée à 499 personnes en 1964 (494
du sexe masculin et 5 du sexe féminin). Les autres dépendances,
c'est-à-dire le groupe des Sandwich de Sud (superficie: 337 km2) et
certaines petites-îles, sont présumées inhabitées.

[26] A dispute exists between the governments of Argentina and the
United Kingdom of Great Britain and Northern Ireland concerning
sovereignty over the Falkland Islands (Malvinas). - La souveraineté sur les
îles Falkland (Malvinas) fait l'objet d'un différend entre le Gouvernement
argentin et le Gouvernement du Royaume-Uni de Grande-Bretagne et
d'Irlande du Nord.

[27] Excluding Indian jungle population. - Non compris les Indiens de la
jungle.

[28] Data for the total population include 17 diplomats. - La population
totale indiquée comprend 17 diplomates.

[29] Census result, excluding nomad population. - Les résultat du
recensement, non compris les nomades.

[30] The methodology used for calculating the number of the de facto and
de jure population in the 2001 census data differs as follows from the
methodology used in previous censuses: the duration that defines a
person as being ' temporary present ' or ' temporary absent ' is now ' under
one year '. The previously applied definition was for ' 6 months '. - La
méthode utilisée pour dénombrer la population présente et la population
légale dans le contexte du recensement de 2001 diffère de celle qui a été
appliquée lors des recensements antérieurs en ce que la durée considérée
pour définir la ' présence temporaire ' ou ' l'absence temporaire ' était
dorénavant fixée à ' moins d'un an ' alors qu'elle était de ' 6 mois '
auparavant.

[31] Annual growth rate not computed, since the source of estimates for
1995 differs from the source for 2002, and therefore comparibility could
not be assumed. - Le taux d'accroissement de la population n'a pas été
calculé à cause des différences entre les sources et les estimations de
1995 et du 2002. En conséquence la comparabilité des donnés n'est pas
assurée complément.

[32] Excluding foreign diplomatic personnel and their dependants. - Non
compris le personnel diplomatique étranger et les membres de leur famille
les accompagnant.

[33] For statistical purposes, the data for China do not include those for
the Hong Kong Special Administrative Region (Hong Kong SAR), Macao
Special Administrative Region (Macao SAR) and Taiwan province of
China. - Pour la présentation des statistiques, les données pour Chine ne
comprend pas la Région Administrative Spéciale de Hong Kong (Hong
Kong RAS), la Région Administrative Spéciale de Macao (Macao RAS) et
Taïwan province de Chine.

[34] For the civilian population of 31 provinces, municipalities and
autonomous regions. - Pour la population civile seulement de 31
provinces, municipalités et régions autonomes.

[35] Data refer to Hong Kong resident population at the census moment,
which covers usual residents and mobile residents. Usual residents refer to
two categories of people: (1) Hong Kong permanent residents who had
stayed in Hong Kong for at least three months during the six months
before or for at least three months during the six months after the census
moment, regardless of whether they were in Hong Kong or not at the
census moment; and (2) Hong Kong non-permanent residents who were in
Hong Kong at the census moment. Mobile Residents, they are Hong Kong
permanent residents who had stayed in Hong Kong for at least one month
but less than three months during the six months before or for at least one
month but less than three months during the six months after the census
moment, regardless of whether they were in Hong Kong or not at the
census moment. - Les données se rapportent à la population résidente à
Hong Kong au moment du recensement. Cette population est composée
des résidants habituels et des résidants mobiles. La population résidente
est partagée en deux catégories: (1) les résidents permanents qui ont
habité à Hong Kong au moins trois mois pendant les six mois précédents
ou les six mois suivants le recensement; (2) les habitants non-permanents
de Hong Kong qui étaient à Hong Kong au moment du recensement. La
population mobile se rapporte aux résidents permanents de Hong Kong
qui ont habité à Hong Kong pendant les six mois après le recensement
pour une période comprise entre un mois et trois mois, indépendamment
du fait qu'ils étaient à Hong Kong au moment du recensement au pays.

[36] Estimates of the number of Turkish Cypriots from 1974 onwards are
the result of population projections based on the age and sex structure of
the Turkish Cypriot community as at Census 1960 and with assumptions of
fertility and mortality similar to the rest of the Cyprus population. With
regard to the migration of Turkish Cypriots after 1974, migration
assumptions are based on figures obtained from Turkish Cypriot sources.
Settlers from Turkey are not included. - Les estimations du nombre de
Chypriotes turcs depuis 1974 résultent des projections de population
préparées sur la base de la structure par sexe et age de la communauté
chypriote turque au recensement de 1960, et avec des hypothèses de
fécondité et de mortalité similaires à celles du reste de la population de

Chypre. En ce qui concerne la migration des Chypriotes turcs après 1974,
les hypothèses sont basées sur les données obtenues de sources
chypriotes turques. Les occupants venus de Turquie ne sont pas inclus.

[37] Data for the period 1993-2002 have been revised on the basis of the
Population Census of 2001. - Les données pour 1993 à 2002 ont été
calculées sur la base du recensement de population de 2001.

[38] Data include all population irrespective of citizenship, who at the time
of the census have resided in the country or intended to reside for a period
of at least one year. It does not distinguish between those present or
absent at the time of census. Data refer to government controlled areas. - -
Les chiffres comprennent toute la population, quelle que soit la nationalité,
qui à l'époque de recensement avait résidé dans le pays, ou avait
l'intention de résider, pendant une période de au moins un an. Il n'y a pas
de distinction entre les personnes présentes ou absentes au moment du
recensement. Les données se raportent aux zones contrôlées par le
Gouvernement.

[39] Including data for the Indian-held part of Jammu and Kashmir, the
final status of which has not yet been determined. - Y compris les données
pour la partie du Jammu et du Cachemire occupée par l'Inde dont le statut
définitif n'a pas encore été déterminé.

[40] Census data exclude Mao-Maram, Paomata and Purul sub-divisions
of Senapati districtof Manipur. The population of Manipur including the
estimated population of the three sub-divisions of Senapati district is
2,291,125 (Males 1,161,173 and females 1,129,952). - Les données de
recensement non compris les subdivisions Mao-Maram Paomata et Purul
du district de Senapati dans l'État du Manipur. Cet État compte 2 291 125
habitants (1 161 173 hommes et 1 129 952 femmes), y compris la
population estimative des trois subdivisions du district de Senapati.

[41] The figure includes an estimated population of 459 557 persons in
urban and 1 857 659 persons in rural areas that were not directly
enumerated, and a population of 566 403 persons in urban and 1 717 578
persons in rural areas that decline the participation. Also included are 421
399 non permanent residents (the homeless, the crew of ships carrying
national flag, boat/floating house people, remote tribesmen and
refugees.) - Y compris la population estimée a 459 557 personnes dans
les zones urbaines et de 1 857 659 personnes dans les zones rurales qui
n'ont pas été énumérées directement, aussi que 566 403 personnes qui
non pas répondu dans les zones urbaines et de 1 717 578 personnes dans
les zones rurales. Y compris 421 399 résidants non permanents (les sans
abri, l'équipage des bateaux portant le drapeau national, les habitants des
embarcations ou des maisons flottantes, les habitants des tribus isolées et
les réfugies.)

[42] For the 1997 population census, data exclude population in three
autonomous provinces in the north of the country. - Pour le recensement
de 1997, la population des trois provinces autonomes dans le nord du
pays est exclue.

[43] Including data for East Jerusalem and Israeli residents in certain other
territories under occupation by Israeli military forces since June 1967. - Y
compris les données pour Jérusalem-Est et les résidents israéliens dans
certains autres territoires occupés depuis 1967 par les forces armées
israéliennes.

[44] Excluding diplomatic personnel outside the country and foreign
military and civilian personnel and their dependants stationed in the area. -
Non compris le personnel diplomatique hors du pays ni les militaires et
agents civils étrangers en poste sur le territoire et les membres de leur
famille les accompagnant.

[45] Excluding data for Jordanian territory under occupation since June
1967 by Israeli military forces. Excluding foreigners, including registered
Palestinian refugees. - Non compris les données pour le territoire jordanien
occupé depuis juin 1967 par les forces armées israéliennes. Non compris
les étrangers, mais y compris les réfugiés de Palestine enregistrés.

[46] Including diplomats and their families abroad, but excluding foreign
diplomats, foreign military personnal, and their families in the country. - Y
compris le personnel diplomatique et les membres de leurs familles à
l'étranger, mais sans tenir compte du personnel diplomatique et militaire
étranger et des membres de leurs familles.

[47] Excluding Palestinian refugees in camps. - Non compris les réfugiés
de Palestine dans les camps.

[48] Excluding Malaysian citizens and permanent residents who were
away or intended to be away from the country for more than six months.
Excluding Malaysian military, naval and diplomatic personnel and their
families outside the country, and tourists, businessman who intended to be
in Malaysia for less than six months. - Non compris les citoyens malaisiens
et les résidents permanents qui étaient ou qui ont prévu d'être hors du
pays pour six mois ou plus. Non compris le personnel militaire Malaisien,
le personnel naval ou diplomatique et leurs familles hors du pays, et les
touristes et les hommes d'affaires qui avaient l'intention de rester en
Malaisie moins de six mois.

[49] Census results have been adjusted for underenumeration. - Les
résultats du recensement ont été ajustées pour compenser les lacunes du
dénombrement

[50] Data including estimated population from household listing from Village Development Committees and Wards which could not be enumerated at the time of census. - Les données incluent la population estimée par les listes des ménages des comités de développement des villages et des circonscriptions qui n'ont pas pu être énumérée au moment du recensement.

[51] Total population does not include Palestinian population living in those parts of Jerusalem governorate which were annexed by Israel in 1967, amounting to 210 209 persons. Likewise, the results does not include the estimates of not enumerated population based on the findings of the post enumeration study, i.e 83 805 persons. - Les données relatives à la population totale ne comprennent pas la population palestinienne -équivalent à 210 209 personnes - habitant dans les territoires du gouvernorat de Jérusalem qui ont été annexés par Israël en 1967. Egalement, les données ne tiennent pas compte des estimations de la population calculée sur la base des résultats de l'enquête postcensitaire, équivalent à 83 805 personnes.

[52] Excluding data for the Pakistan-held part of Jammu and Kashmir, the final status of which has not yet been determined. - Non compris les données concernant la partie du Jammu et Cachemire occupée par le Pakistan dont le statut définitif n'a pas été déterminé.

[53] Census result, excluding transients afloat and non-locally domiciled military and civilian services personnel and their dependants and visitors. - Les résultat du recensment, non compris les personnes de passage à bord de navires ni les militaires et agents civils non-résidents et les membres de leur famille les accompagnant et visiteurs.

[54] The Population and Housing Census 2001 did not cover the whole area of the country due to the security problems; the Census was complete in 18 districts only; in three districts it was not possible to conduct it; and in four districts it was partially conducted. - Le recensement de la population et de l'habitat en 2001 n'a pas couvert la totalité du pays pour des problèmes de sécurité ; le recensement a été complété seulement en 18 districts ; dans 3 districts ça n'a pas été possible de conduire le recensement et dans 4 districts il a été partiellement conduit.

[55] Including Palestinian refugees. - Y compris les réfugiés de Palestine.

[56] Comprising 7 sheikdoms of Abu Dhabi, Dubai, Sharjah, Ajaman, Umm al Qaiwain, Ras al Khaimah and Fujairah, and the area lying within the modified Riyadh line as announced in October 1955. - Comprend les sept cheikhats de Abou Dhabi, Dabai, Ghârdja, Adjmân, Oumm-al-Quiwaïn, Ras al Khaïma et Foudjaïra, ainsi que la zone délimitée par la ligne de Riad modifiée comme il a été annoncé en octobre 1955.

[57] Excluding Faeroe Islands and Greenland. - Non compris les Iles Féroé et Gröenland.

[58] Excluding Overseas Departments, namely French Guiana, Guadeloupe, Martinique and Reunion, shown separately. De jure population but excluding diplomatic personnel outside the country and including members of alien armed forces not living in military camps and foreign diplomatic personnel not living in embassies or consulates. - Non compris les départements d'outre-mer, c'est-à-dire la Guyane française, la Guadeloupe, la Martinique et la Réunion, qui font l'objet de rubriques distinctes. Population de droit, non compris le personnel diplomatique hors du pays et y compris les militaires étrangers ne vivant pas dans des camps militaires et le personnel diplomatique étranger ne vivant pas dans les ambassades ou les consulats.

[59] All data shown pertaining to Germany prior to 3 October 1990 are indicated separately for the Federal Republic of Germany and the former German Democratic Republic based on their respective territories at the time indicated. - Toutes les données se rapportant à l'Allemagne avant le 3 octobre 1990 figurent dans deux rubriques séparées basées sur les territoires respectifs de la République fédérale de l'Allemagne et l'ancienne République démocratique allemande selon la période.

[60] Excluding armed forces. - Non compris les militaires en garnison.

[61] Census data including armed forces stationed outside the country, but excluding alien armed forces stationed in the area. - Les données de recensement y compris les militaires hors du pays, mais non compris les militaires étrangers en garnison sur le territoire.

[62] Mid-year population excludes armed forces stationed outside the country, but includes alien armed forces stationed in the area. - Les estimations au millieu de l'année non compris les militaires en garnison hors du pays, mais y compris les militaires étrangers en garnison sur le territoire.

[63] Data refer to the Vatican City State. - Les données se rapportent aux Etat du Saint-Siè-ge.

[64] Including foreigners residing in Malta for 12 months before the census date and excluding foreign diplomatic personnel. - Y compris les les étrangers habitant à Malte pour 12 mois avant le recensement et le personnel diplomatique étrangers.

[65] Data for estimates including work and resident permit holders and foreigners residing in Malta. - Les estimations y compris les titulaires de permis de travail et de permis de séjour et les ét rangers résidant à Malte.

[66] Census result, based on compilation of continuous accounting and sample surveys. - Les résultat du recensement, d'après les résultats des dénombrements et enquêtes par sondage continue.

[67] Including residents temporarily outside the country. - Y compris les résidents se trouvant temporairement hors du pays.

[68] Excluding civilian aliens within country, but including civilian nationals temporarily outside country. - Non compris les civils étrangers dans le pays, mais y compris les civils nationaux temporairement hors du pays.

[69] Including the Azores and Madeira Islands. - Y compris les Açores et Madère.

[70] Data do not include information for Transnistria and the municipality of Bender. - Les données ne tiennent pas compte de l'information sur la Transnistria et la municipalité de Bender.

[71] The census figure for Serbia and Montenegro consists of the results of the population census held in Serbia in 2002 and population estimates for Montenegro for the same year (7,498,001 and 636,616 respectively). - - Le total pour la Serbie-et-Montenegro se consiste des résultats de recensement da la population de Serbie du 31 Mars 2002 et des estimations de la population pour le Montenegro (7.498.001 et 636.616 respectivement).

[72] Including the Balearic and Canary Islands, and Alhucemas, Ceuta, Chafarinas, Melilla and Penon de Vélez de la Gomera. - Y compris les Baléares et les Canaries, Al Hoceima, Ceuta, les îles Zaffarines, Melilla et Penon de Vélez de la Gomera.

[73] Inhabited only during the winter season. Census data are for total population while estimates refer to Norwegian population only. Included also in the de jure population of Norway. - N'est habitée pendant la saison d'hiver. Les données de recensement se rapportent à la population totale, mais les estimations ne concernent que la population norvégienne, comprise également dans la population de droit de la Norvège.

[74] Excluding Channel Islands and Isle of Man, shown separately. - Non compris les îles Anglo-Normandes et l'île de Man, qui font l'objet de rubriques distinctes.

[75] Excluding Niue, shown separately, which is part of Cook Islands, but because of remoteness is administered separately. - Non compris Nioué, qui fait l'objet d'une rubrique distincte et qui fait partie des îles Cook, mais qui, en raison de son éloignement, est administrée séparément.

[76] For 2001, the resident population consisted of 14,990 (7,738 males and 7,252 females). - Pour 2001, population résidente de 14 990 (7 738 hommes et 7 252 femmes).

[77] Comprising Austral, Gambier, Marquesas, Rapa, Society and Tuamotu Islands. - Comprend les îles Australes, Gambier, Marquises, Rapa, de la Societé et Tuamotou.

[78] Including Christmas, Fanning, Ocean and Washington Islands. - Y compris les îles Christmas, Fanning, Océan et Washington.

[79] Including the islands of Huon, Chesterfield, Loyalty, Walpole and Belep Archipelago. - Y compris les îles Huon, Chesterfield, Loyauté et Walpole, et l'archipel Belep.

[80] Including Campbell and Kermadec Islands (population 20 in 1961, surface area 148 km2) as well as Antipodes, Auckland, Bounty, Snares, Solander and Three Kings island, all of which are uninhabited. - Y compris les îles Campbell et Kermadec (20 habitants en 1961, superficie : 148 km2) ainsi que les îles Antipodes, Auckland, Bounty, Snares, Solander et Three Kings, qui sont toutes inhabitées.

[81] Comprising eastern part of New Guinea, the Bismarck Archipelago, Bougainville and Buka of Solomon Islands group and about 600 smaller islands. - Comprend l'est de la Nouvelle-Guinée, l'archipel Bismarck, Bougainville et Buka (ces deux dernières du groupe des Salomon) et environ 600 îlots.

[82] Comprising the Solomon Islands group (except Bougainville and Buka which are included with Papua New Guinea shown separately), Ontong, Java, Rennel and Santa Cruz Islands. - Comprend les îles Salomon(à l'exception de Bougainville et de Buka dont la population est comprise dans celle de Papouasie-Nouvelle Guinée qui font l'objet d'une rubrique distincte), ainsi que les îles Ontong, Java, Rennel et Santa Cruz.

Table 4

Table 4 presents, for each country or area of the world, basic vital statistics including: live births, crude birth rate, deaths, crude death rate and rate of natural increase, infant deaths, infant mortality rate, the expectation of life at birth by sex and the total fertility rate.

Description of variables: The vital events and rates shown in this table are defined as follows[1]:

Live birth is the complete expulsion or extraction from its mother of a product of conception, irrespective of the duration of pregnancy, which after such separation breathes or shows any other evidence of life such as beating of the heart, pulsation of the umbilical cord, of definite movement of voluntary muscles, whether or not the umbilical cord has been cut or the placenta is attached; each product of such a birth is considered live-born regardless of gestational age.

Death is the permanent disappearance of all evidence of life at any time after live birth has taken place (post-natal cessation of vital functions without capability of resuscitation).

Infant deaths are deaths of live-born infants under one year of age.

Expectation of life at birth is defined as the average number of years of life for males and females if they continued to be subject to the same mortality experienced in the year(s) to which these life expectancies refer.

The total fertility rate is the average number of children that would be born alive to a hypothetical cohort of women if, throughout their reproductive years, the age-specific fertility rates for the specified year remained unchanged. The standard method of calculating the total fertility rate is the sum of the age-specific fertility rates.

Crude birth rates and crude death rates presented in this table are calculated using the number of live births and the number of deaths obtained from civil registers. These civil registration data are used only if they are considered reliable (estimated completeness of 90 per cent or more).

Similarly, infant mortality rates presented in this table are calculated using the number of live births and the number of infant deaths obtained from civil registers. If, however, the registration of births or infant deaths for any given country or area is estimated to be less than 90 per cent complete, the rates are not calculated.

The expectation-of-life values are those provided by national statistical offices.

Rate computation: The crude birth and death rates are the annual number of each of these vital events per 1 000 mid-year population.

Infant mortality rate is the annual number of deaths of infants under one year of age per 1 000 live births in the same year.

Rates of natural increase are the difference between the crude birth rate and the crude death rate. It should be noted that the rates of natural increase presented here may differ from the population growth rates presented in table 3 as rates of natural increase do not take net international migration into account while the population growth rates do.

Rates that appear in this table have been calculated by the Statistics Division of the United Nations Department of Economic and Social Affairs, unless otherwise noted. Exceptions include official estimated rates, many of which were based on sample surveys.

Rates calculated by the Statistics Division of the United Nations presented in this table have been limited to those countries or areas having a minimum number of 30 events in a given year.

Reliability of data: Rates calculated on the basis of registered vital statistics which are considered unreliable (estimated to be less than 90 per cent complete) are not calculated. Estimated rates, prepared by the individual countries or areas, have been presented whenever applicable.

The designation of vital statistics as being either reliable or unreliable is discussed in general in section 4.2 of the Technical Notes. The technical notes for tables 9, 15 and 18 provide specific information on reliability of statistics on live births, infant deaths and deaths, respectively.

The values shown for life expectancy in this table come from official life tables. It is assumed that, if necessary, the basic data (population and deaths classified by age and sex) have been adjusted for deficiencies before their use in constructing the life tables.

Limitations: Statistics on births, deaths and infant deaths are subject to the same qualifications as have been set forth for vital statistics in general in section 4 of the Technical Notes and in the technical notes for individual tables presenting detailed data on these events (table 9, live births; table 15, infant deaths; table 18, deaths).

In assessing comparability it is important to take into account the reliability of the data used to calculate the rates, as discussed above.

It should be noted that crude rates are particularly affected by the age-sex structure of the population. Infant mortality rates, and to a much lesser extent crude birth rates and crude death rates, are affected by the variation in the definition of a live birth and tabulation procedures.

NOTES

[1] *Principles and Recommendations for a Vital Statistics System, Revision 2,* United Nations publication, Sales No. E.01.XVII.10, United Nations, New York, 2001.

Tableau 4

Le tableau 4 présente, pour chaque pays ou zone du monde, des statistiques de base de l'état civil comprenant, dans l'ordre, les naissances vivantes, le taux brut de natalité, les décès, le taux brut de mortalité et le taux d'accroissement naturel de la population, les décès d'enfants de moins d'un an et le taux de mortalité infantile, l'espérance de vie à la naissance par sexe et l'indice synthétique de fécondité.

Description des variables : Les faits d'état civil utilisés aux fins du calcul des taux présentés dans le tableau 4 sont définis comme suit[1] :

La naissance vivante est l'expulsion ou l'extraction complète du corps de la mère, indépendamment de la duré de la gestation, d'un produit de la conception qui après cette séparation, respire ou manifeste tout autre signe de vie, tel que battement de cœur, pulsation du cordon ombilical ou contraction effective d'un muscle soumis à l'action de la volonté, que le cordon ombilical ait été coupé ou non et que le placenta soit ou non demeuré attaché ; tout produit d'une telle naissance est considéré comme « enfant né vivant ».

Le décès est la disparition permanente de tout signe de vie à un moment quelconque postérieur à la naissance vivante (cessation des fonctions vitales après la naissance sans possibilité de réanimation).

Il convient de préciser que les chiffres relatifs aux décès d'enfants de moins d'un an se rapportent aux naissances vivantes.

L'espérance de vie à la naissance est le nombre moyen d'années que vivraient les individus de sexe masculin et de sexe féminin s'ils continuaient d'être soumis aux mêmes conditions de mortalité que celles qui existaient pendant les années auxquelles se rapportent les valeurs indiquées.

L'indice synthétique de fécondité représente le nombre moyen d'enfants que mettrait au monde une cohorte hypothétique de femmes qui seraient soumises, tout au long de leur vie, aux mêmes conditions de fécondité par âge que celles auxquelles sont soumises les femmes, dans chaque groupe d'âge, au cours d'une année ou d'une période donnée. La méthode standard pour calculer l'indice synthétique de fécondité consiste à additionner les taux de fécondité par âge simple.

Les taux bruts de natalité et de mortalité ont été établis sur la base du nombre de naissances vivantes et du nombre de décès inscrits sur les registres de l'état civil. Ces données n'ont été utilisées que lorsqu'elles étaient considérées comme sûres (degré estimatif de complétude égal ou supérieur à 90 p. 100).

De même, les taux de mortalité infantile présentés dans le tableau 4 ont été établis à partir du nombre de naissances vivantes et du nombre de décès d'enfants de moins d'un an inscrits sur les registres de l'état civil. Toutefois, lorsque les données relatives aux naissances ou aux décès d'enfants de moins d'un an pour un pays ou zone quelconque n'étaient pas considérées complètes à 90 p. 100 au moins, les indices n'ont pas été calculés.

Les chiffres concernant l'espérance de vie émanent des services nationaux de statistique.

Calcul des taux : Les taux bruts de natalité et de mortalité, représentent le nombre annuel de chacun de ces faits d'état civil pour 1 000 habitants au milieu de l'année considérée.

Les taux de mortalité infantile correspondent au nombre annuel de décès d'enfants de moins d'un an pour 1 000 naissances vivantes survenues pendant la même année.

Le taux d'accroissement naturel est égal à la différence entre le taux brut de natalité et le taux brut de mortalité. Il y a lieu de noter que les taux d'accroissement naturel indiqués dans le tableau 4 peuvent différer des taux d'accroissement de la population figurant dans le tableau 3, les taux d'accroissement naturel ne tenant pas compte des taux nets de migration internationale, alors que ceux-ci sont inclus dans les taux d'accroissement de la population.

Sauf indication contraire, les taux figurant dans le tableau 4 ont été calculés par la Division de statistique du Département des affaires économiques et sociales (Secrétariat de l'Organisation des Nations Unies). Les exceptions comprennent les taux estimatifs officiels, dont bon nombre ont été établis sur la base d'enquêtes par sondage.

Les taux calculés par la Division de statistique de l'ONU qui sont présentés dans le tableau 4 se rapportent aux seuls pays ou zones où l'on a enregistré au moins 30 événements au cours d'une année donnée.

Fiabilité des données : Les taux n'ont pas été calculés lorsque les statistiques de l'état civil issues de systèmes d'enregistrement d'état civil étaient jugées douteuses (degré estimatif de complétude inférieur à 90 p.100) et des taux estimatifs, calculés par les pays ou zones, ont été présentés lorsqu'ils étaient disponibles.

On trouve à la section 4.2 des Notes techniques des explications générales concernant la façon dont les statistiques de l'état civil ont été classées selon leur degré de fiabilité. Les notes techniques relatives aux tableaux 9, 15 et 18 ont trait respectivement à la fiabilité des statistiques des naissances vivantes, des décès d'enfants de moins d'un an et des décès.

Étant donné que les valeurs relatives à l'espérance de vie figurant dans le tableau 4 proviennent de tables officielles de mortalité, elles sont toutes présumées sûres.

Insuffisance des données : Les statistiques des naissances, décès et décès d'enfants de moins d'un an appellent toutes les réserves qui ont été formulées à propos des statistiques de l'état civil en général à la section 4 des Notes techniques et dans les notes techniques relatives aux différents tableaux présentant des données détaillées sur ces événements [tableau 9 (naissances vivantes), tableau 15 (décès d'enfants de moins d'un an) et tableau 18 (décès)].

Pour évaluer la comparabilité des divers taux, il importe de tenir compte de la fiabilité des données utilisées pour calculer ces taux, comme il a été indiqué précédemment.

Il y a lieu de noter que la structure par âge et par sexe de la population influe de façon particulière sur les taux bruts. Le manque d'uniformité dans la définition des naissances vivantes et dans les procédures de mise en tableaux a une incidence sur les taux de mortalité infantile et, à un moindre degré, sur les taux bruts de natalité et les taux bruts de mortalité.

NOTE

[1] *Principes et recommandations pour un système de statistiques de l'état civil, deuxième révision*, numéro de vente : F.01.XVII.10, publication des Nations Unies, New York, 2001.

4. Vital statistics summary and expectation of life at birth: 1998-2002
Aperçu des statistiques de l'état civil et espérance de vie à la naissance: 1998-2002

(See notes at end of table. — Voir notes à la fin du tableau.)

Continent, country or area and year / Continent, pays ou zone et année	Live births - Naissances vivantes			Deaths - Décès			Rate of natural increase / Taux d'accroiss-ement naturel	Infant deaths - Décès d'enfants de moins d'un an			Expectation of life at birth / Espérance de vie à la naissance		Total fertility rate / L'indice synthétique de fécondité
	Code[a]	Number Nombre	Crude birth rate Taux bruts de natalité	Code[a]	Number Nombre	Crude death rate Taux bruts de mortalité	Taux d'accroiss-ement naturel	Code[a]	Number Nombre	Rate (per 1000 births) Taux (par 1000 naiss-ances)	Male Masculin	Female Féminin	
AFRICA — AFRIQUE													
Algeria - Algérie[1,2]													
1998	C	620 322	21.0	U	171 775	...	...	U	33 093	...	...	...	2.670
1999	C	593 643	19.8	U	129 686	...	...	U	21 798	...	...	...	2.640
2000	C	588 628	19.4	U	127 951	...	...	U	20 291	...	72.5	74.2	2.630
2001	C	618 380	20.0	U	129 092	...	...	U	21 622	...	...	...	2.570
2002	C	616 963	19.7	U	126 557	...	...	U	19 850	...	...	...	...
Benin - Bénin[3]													
1998	I	260 610	44.8	I	72 130	12.4	32.4	I	24 422	93.7	...	...	...
1999	I	265 980	44.4	I	71 680	12.0	32.4	...	...	...	...	...	...
2000	I	272 640	44.2	I	71 540	11.6	32.6	...	...	...	...	...	...
2001	I	263 726	41.1	I	83 417	13.0	28.1	I	25 001	94.8	...	...	...
Botswana[3]													
1998	I	50 606	32.2	I	16 244	10.3	21.9	...	...	...	65.4	68.8	...
1999	I	53 407	33.2	I	16 352	10.2	23.0	...	...	...	65.7	69.0	...
2001	I	53 735	32.0	I	16 570	9.9	22.1	I	1 576	29.3	...	...	...
Burundi[3]													
1998	I	290 982	46.2	I	115 693	18.4	27.8	I	45 684	157.0	...	...	...
Cape Verde - Cap-Vert													
1998	C	15 460	37.1	...	...	...	...	...	...	...	...	...	...
2000	C	12 746	29.3	...	...	...	...	...	...	...	...	...	...
2001	C	12 926	29.1	...	...	...	...	...	...	...	...	...	...
2002	C	13 123	29.0	...	...	...	...	...	...	...	...	...	...
Chad - Tchad													
2001	...	397 896	...	...	138 025	...	...	...	...	...	...	...	...
Côte d'Ivoire[3]													
1998	I	614 667	40.0	I	189 010	12.3	27.7	I	44 045	71.7	...	...	...
2000	I	655 904	40.0	I	201 690	12.3	27.7	I	47 000	71.7	...	...	...
Egypt - Égypte													
1998	C	1 687 252	27.5	C	399 772	6.5	21.0	C	49 168	29.1	...	...	...
1999	C	1 693 025	27.0	C	401 433	6.4	20.6	C	49 765	29.4	...	...	...
2001	...	...	...	...	...	...	...	...	...	...	65.6	67.4	...
Ethiopia - Éthiopie													
1999	...	2 186 023	...	...	1 062 114	...	...	...	232 660	...	...	...	...
Gabon													
2000	...	...	...	...	...	...	...	...	...	...	...	...	4.300
Lesotho													
2001	...	...	...	...	...	...	...	...	...	...	48.7	56.3	...
Libyan Arab Jamahiriya - Jamahiriya arabe libyenne													
2000	C	98 752	19.3	U	17 367	...	...	U	2 155	...	...	...	...
2001	C	99 187	18.7	U	18 334	...	...	U	2 568	...	...	...	...
2002	C	111 053	20.2	U	19 362	...	...	...	...	...	...	...	...
Malawi[4,5]													
1998	I	496 524	50.0	I	208 040	20.9	29.0	I	44 928	90.5	...	...	...
1999	I	531 160	52.3	I	234 641	23.1	29.2	...	...	...	41.1	43.8	...
2000	I	543 654	51.9	I	228 245	21.8	30.1	...	...	...	41.7	44.3	...
2001	I	555 558	51.4	I	221 963	20.5	30.8	...	...	...	42.2	44.9	...
2002	I	567 241	50.8	I	217 205	19.4	31.3	...	...	...	42.8	45.5	...
Mali													
2001	U	525 685	...	...	...	...	...	...	...	...	...	...	...
Mauritius - Maurice													
1998	+C	19 434	16.7	+C	7 839	6.8	10.0	+C	376	19.3	66.6	74.4	1.960
1999	+C	20 311	17.3	+C	7 944	6.8	10.5	+C	396	19.5	^68.2	^75.3	2.050
2000	+C	20 205	17.0	+C	7 982	6.7	10.3	+C	322	15.9	...	...	1.990
2001	+C	19 696	16.4	+C	7 983	6.7	9.8	+C	282	14.3	...	...	1.911
2002	+C	19 983	16.5	+C	8 310	6.9	9.6	+C	297	14.9	^68.4	^75.3	1.938

(See notes at end of table. — Voir notes à la fin du tableau.)

Continent, country or area and year — Continent, pays ou zone et année	Live births — Naissances vivantes			Deaths — Décès			Rate of natural increase — Taux d'accroiss-ement naturel	Infant deaths — Décès d'enfants de moins d'un an			Expectation of life at birth — Espérance de vie à la naissance		Total fertility rate — L'indice synthétiq-ue de fécondité
	Code[a]	Number Nombre	Crude birth rate Taux bruts de natalité	Code[a]	Number Nombre	Crude death rate Taux bruts de mortalité		Code[a]	Number Nombre	Rate (per 1000 births) Taux (par 1000 naiss-ances)	Male Masculin	Female Féminin	
AFRICA — AFRIQUE													
Morocco - Maroc													
1998	C	540 907	19.5	U	95 111	...	...	U	9 061	...	...	...	3.000
1999	C	529 383	18.7	U	98 304	...	...	U	8 885	...	...	...	...
Mozambique[3]													
2000		...	...		...	...	...		...	...	...	...	5.800
2001	i	753 252	42.7	i	331 162	18.8	23.9	i	99 164	131.6	...	...	5.700
2002	...	...	...	...	...	...	...		...	...	...	...	5.500
Réunion[1]													
1998	C	13 538	19.4	C	3 731	5.3	14.1	C	111	8.2	...	...	2.310
1999	C	14 153	19.9	C	3 825	5.4	14.5	C	84	5.9	...	...	2.400
2000	C	14 842	20.6	C	3 781	5.2	15.3	C	88	5.9	...	...	2.470
2001	C	14 541	19.8	C	3 740	5.1	14.7	C	89	6.1	71.0	79.4	2.500
Saint Helena ex. dep. - Sainte-Hélène sans dép.													
1998	C	59	11.4	C	39	7.6	3.9	C	1	...	...	...	...
1999	C	52	...	C	45	...	...	C	-	...	...	...	...
2000	C	56	...	C	53	...	...	C	-	...	...	...	...
2001	C	36	...	C	41	...	...	C	-	...	...	...	...
Seychelles													
1998	+C	1 412	17.9	+C	570	7.2	10.7	+C	12	...	...	...	2.040
1999	+C	1 460	18.2	+C	560	7.0	11.2	+C	15	...	...	...	2.040
2000	+C	1 512	18.6	+C	553	6.8	11.8	+C	15	...	...	...	2.080
2001	+C	1 440	17.7	+C	554	6.8	10.9	+C	19	...	...	...	1.980
2002	+C	1 481	18.3	+C	647	8.0	10.3	+C	26	...	...	...	...
South Africa - Afrique du Sud													
1998	U	1 216 337	...	...	...	...	...	...	...	...	...	...	...
1999	U	1 363 800	...	...	...	...	...	...	...	...	...	...	...
2000	U	1 407 833	...	...	...	...	...	...	...	...	...	...	...
Tunisia - Tunisie													
1998	C	166 718	17.9	U	42 571	...	...	U	3 098	...	...	...	2.230
1999	C	160 169	16.9	U	54 400	...	...	U	4 200	...	...	...	...
2001	C	163 300	16.9	U	53 300	...	...	...	...	...	...	...	...
AMERICA, NORTH — AMERIQUE DU NORD													
Anguilla													
1998	+C	155	14.5	+C	62	5.8	8.7	+C	-	...	...	...	...
1999	+C	176	16.1	+C	58	5.3	10.8	+C	1	...	...	...	...
2000	+C	193	17.1	+C	73	6.5	10.7	+C	1	...	...	...	...
2001	+C	183	15.8	+C	50	4.3	11.5	+C	-	...	...	...	...
2002	+C	169	14.2	+C	52	4.4	9.8	+C	2	...	...	...	...
Antigua and Barbuda - Antigua-et-Barbuda													
1998	+C	1 366	...	+C	456	...	...	...	...	...	...	...	...
1999	+C	1 329	...	+C	508	...	...	...	...	...	...	...	...
2000	+C	1 528	...	+C	451	...	...	...	...	...	...	...	...
Aruba[6]													
1998	+U	1 315	...	+U	505	...	...	...	...	...	...	...	...
1999	+U	1 225	...	+U	554	...	...	...	...	...	...	...	...
2000	+U	1 294	...	+U	531	...	...	...	...	...	70.0	76.0	...
2001	+U	1 266	...	+U	477	...	...	+U	4	...	...	...	...
2002	+U	1 374	...	+U	489	...	...	...	...	...	...	...	...
Bahamas[6]													
1998	U	5 880	...	C	1 725	5.9	...	C	59	10.0	...	...	2.264
1999	U	5 367	...	C	1 567	5.3	...	C	48	8.9	...	...	2.057

4. Vital statistics summary and expectation of life at birth: 1998-2002
Aperçu des statistiques de l'état civil et espérance de vie à la naissance: 1998-2002 (continued — suite)

(See notes at end of table. — Voir notes à la fin du tableau.)

Continent, country or area and year / Continent, pays ou zone et année	Code[a]	Live births — Naissances vivantes: Number Nombre	Live births: Crude birth rate Taux bruts de natalité	Code[a]	Deaths — Décès: Number Nombre	Deaths: Crude death rate Taux bruts de mortalité	Rate of natural increase Taux d'accroissement naturel	Code[a]	Infant deaths — Décès d'enfants de moins d'un an: Number Nombre	Infant deaths: Rate (per 1000 births) Taux (par 1000 naissances)	Expectation of life at birth — Espérance de vie à la naissance: Male Masculin	Expectation of life at birth: Female Féminin	Total fertility rate L'indice synthétique de fécondité
AMERICA, NORTH — AMERIQUE DU NORD													
Bahamas[6]													
2000	U	*5 287*	...	C	1 625	5.4	...	C	52	9.8	...	...	1.985
2001	U	*5 353*	...	C	1 609	5.2	...	C	37	6.9	...	...	1.995
Barbados - Barbade													
2000	+C	3 762	14.1	+C	2 367	8.8	5.2	+C	63	16.7	...	...	...
Belize													
1998	U	*5 986*	...	U	*1 350*	...	...	U	*144*	...	...	...	...
1999	U	*6 218*	...	U	*1 190*	...	...	U	*123*	...	...	...	...
2000	U	*7 313*	...	U	*1 534*	...	...	U	*155*	...	...	...	...
2001	U	*7 082*	...	U	*1 261*	...	...	U	*120*	...	...	...	...
2002	U	*7 356*	...	U	*1 284*	...	...	U	*145*	...	...	...	...
Bermuda - Bermudes													
1998	C	825	13.2	C	505	8.1	5.1	C	-	...	...	...	...
1999	C	828	13.2	C	427	6.8	6.4	C	2	...	...	...	...
2000	C	838	13.3	C	473	7.5	5.8	C	-	...	...	...	1.646
2001	C	831	13.4	C	442	7.1	6.3	C	3	...	...	...	...
2002	C	830	...	C	404	...	...	C	-	...	...	...	...
British Virgin Islands - Îles Vierges britanniques								+C	1	...	...	...	...
2000	...	...	...	...	...	...	...	...	...	...	...	...	...
2001	+C	318	15.4	+C	101	4.9	10.5	...	...	...	...	...	...
Canada[7]													
1998	C	342 418	11.4	C	218 091	7.2	4.1	C	1 811	5.3	76.1	78.8	...
1999	C	337 249	11.1	C	219 530	7.2	3.9	C	1 776	5.3	76.3	81.7	...
2000	C	327 882	10.7	C	218 062	7.1	3.6	C	1 737	5.3	77.0	82.2	...
2001	C	333 744	10.8	C	219 538	7.1	3.7	C	1 739	5.2	...	...	1.510
2002	C	328 802	10.5	C	223 603	7.1	3.4	C	1 762	5.4	...	...	...
Cayman Islands - Îles Caïmanes													
1998	C	545	14.5	C	117	3.1	11.4	...	...	...	...	...	...
1999	C	604	15.5	C	128	3.3	12.2	...	...	...	...	...	...
2000	C	619	15.4	C	137	3.4	12.0	...	...	...	...	...	...
2001	C	622	15.0	C	132	3.2	11.9	...	...	...	...	...	...
Costa Rica													
1998	C	76 982	23.0	C	14 708	4.4	18.6	C	970	12.6	...	...	2.600
1999	C	78 526	23.0	C	15 052	4.4	18.6	C	925	11.8	...	...	2.600
2000	C	78 178	22.4	C	14 944	4.3	18.1	C	798	10.2	...	...	...
2001	C	76 401	19.6	C	15 609	4.0	15.6	C	827	10.8	...	...	...
2002	C	71 144	17.8	C	15 004	3.8	14.0	C	793	11.1	...	...	...
Cuba													
1998	C	151 080	13.6	C	77 565	7.0	6.6	C	1 070	7.1	74.2	78.2	...
1999	C	150 785	13.5	C	79 499	7.1	6.4	C	977	6.5	...	...	...
2000	C	143 528	12.8	C	76 463	6.8	6.0	C	1 039	7.2	...	...	...
2001	C	138 718	12.4	C	79 395	7.1	5.3	C	861	6.2	...	...	...
2002	C	141 276	12.6	C	73 882	6.6	6.0	C	922	6.5	...	...	...
Dominica - Dominique													
1998	+C	1 230	17.1	+C	595	8.3	8.8	...	...	...	...	...	...
1999	+C	1 291	18.0	+C	631	8.8	9.2	...	...	...	...	...	...
2000	+C	1 199	16.8	+C	503	7.0	9.7	...	...	...	...	...	...
2001	+C	1 213	17.1	+C	510	7.2	9.9	C	24	...	...	...	...
2002	+C	1 081	15.4	...	...	...	...	...	...	...	...	...	...
Dominican Republic - République dominicaine													
1998	+U	*179 372*	...	+U	*25 278*	...	...	+U	*1 972*	...	...	...	...
1999	+U	*193 418*	...	+U	*26 956*	...	...	+U	*1 966*	...	...	...	...

4. Vital statistics summary and expectation of life at birth: 1998-2002
Aperçu des statistiques de l'état civil et espérance de vie à la naissance: 1998-2002 (continued — suite)

(See notes at end of table. — Voir notes à la fin du tableau.)

Continent, country or area and year / Continent, pays ou zone et année	Code[a]	Number Nombre	Crude birth rate Taux bruts de natalité	Code[a]	Number Nombre	Crude death rate Taux bruts de mortalité	Rate of natural increase Taux d'accroiss-ement naturel	Code[a]	Number Nombre	Rate (per 1000 births) Taux (par 1000 naiss-ances)	Male Masculin	Female Féminin	Total fertility rate L'indice synthétiq-ue de fécondité
AMERICA, NORTH — AMERIQUE DU NORD													
Dominican Republic - République dominicaine													
2000	+U	189 332	...	+U	23 776	...	...	+U	2 116	...	...	...	...
El Salvador													
1998	C	158 350	26.3	C	29 919	5.0	21.3	C	2 380	15.0	^66.5	^72.5	...
1999	C	153 636	25.0	C	28 056	4.6	20.4	C	1 768	11.5	...	...	...
2000	C	150 176	23.9	C	28 154	4.5	19.4	C	1 678	11.2	^67.7	^73.7	...
2001	C	138 354	21.6	C	29 559	4.6	17.0	C	1 682	12.2	...	...	...
2002	C	129 363	19.8	C	27 458	4.2	15.6	C	1 284	9.9	...	...	...
Greenland - Groenland													
1998	C	986	17.6	C	468	8.3	9.2	C	25	...	^62.7	^68.0	2.393
1999	C	947	16.9	C	482	8.6	8.3	C	16	...	...	...	2.340
Grenada - Grenade													
1998	+C	1 938	19.4	+C	819	8.2	11.2	+C	37	19.1	...	...	...
1999	+C	1 791	17.8	+C	794	7.9	9.9	+C	29	...	...	...	...
2000	+C	1 883	18.6	+C	716	7.1	11.5	+C	27	...	...	...	...
2001	+C	1 899	18.8	+C	727	7.2	11.6	+C	33	17.4	...	...	...
Guadeloupe[1]													
1998	C	7 141	17.0	C	2 564	6.1	10.9	C	65	9.1	...	...	2.100
1999	C	7 341	17.3	C	2 670	6.3	11.0	C	55	7.5	...	...	2.200
2000	C	7 653	17.9	C	2 698	6.3	11.6	C	57	7.4	...	...	2.300
2001	C	7 503	17.3	C	2 765	6.4	11.0	C	49	6.5	...	...	2.300
2002	C	6 995	16.0	C	2 584	5.9	10.1	C	45	6.4	74.6	81.5	2.200
Guatemala													
1998	C	409 829	45.4	C	70 504	6.6	38.8	C	15 414	31.5	^61.4	^67.2	...
1999	C	360 759	32.5	C	64 563	5.8	26.7	C	13 161	36.5	...	...	...
2000	C	426 346	37.4	C	66 831	5.9	31.6	C	13 247	31.1	...	...	...
2001	C	403 532	34.5	C	69 934	6.0	28.6	...	...	...	...	...	...
Jamaica - Jamaïque													
1998	+C	56 937	22.1	+C	18 110	7.0	15.1	+C	480	8.4	...	...	...
1999	+C	56 911	22.0	+C	17 353	6.7	15.3	...	...	...	...	...	...
2000	+C	54 035	20.7	+C	16 338	6.3	14.5	...	...	...	...	...	...
2001	+C	55 270	21.1	+C	17 205	6.6	14.5	...	...	...	...	...	...
Martinique[1]													
1998	C	5 816	15.3	C	2 548	6.7	8.6	C	52	8.9	...	...	1.900
1999	C	5 789	15.2	C	2 581	6.8	8.4	C	41	7.1	...	...	1.900
2000	C	6 059	15.8	C	2 692	7.0	8.8	C	40	6.6	...	...	2.000
2001	C	5 908	15.3	C	2 754	7.1	8.1	C	43	7.3	...	...	2.000
2002	C	5 446	14.0	C	2 681	6.9	7.1	C	33	6.1	75.4	82.2	1.900
Mexico - Mexique													
1998	+U	2 668 428	...	C	444 665	4.6	...	C	42 183	15.8	...	...	...
1999	+U	2 769 089	...	C	443 950	4.5	...	C	40 283	14.5	...	...	...
2000	+U	2 798 339	...	C	437 667	4.4	...	C	38 621	13.8	...	...	...
2001	+U	2 767 610	...	C	443 127	4.4	...	C	35 911	13.0	...	...	...
2002	+U	2 527 732	...	...	...	...	...	...	...	...	...	...	...
Netherlands Antilles - Antilles néerlandaises													
1998	C	3 111	15.0	C	1 282	6.2	8.8	...	...	...	...	...	...
1999	C	2 803	13.7	C	1 321	6.4	7.2	...	...	...	...	...	...
Nicaragua													
1998	+U	111 154	...	+U	14 804	...	...	+U	2 552	...	...	...	...
1999	+U	123 446	...	+U	10 818	...	...	+U	1 768	...	...	...	...
2000	+U	126 873	...	+U	13 602	...	...	+U	2 075	...	...	...	...
2001	+U	108 299	...	+U	12 789	...	...	+U	1 933	...	^67.2	^71.9	3.299
2002	+U	120 846	...	+U	15 061	...	...	+U	2 217	...	...	...	...

(See notes at end of table. — Voir notes à la fin du tableau.)

Continent, country or area and year / Continent, pays ou zone et année	Code[a]	Live births Naissances vivantes — Number Nombre	Crude birth rate Taux bruts de natalité	Code[a]	Deaths - Décès — Number Nombre	Crude death rate Taux bruts de mortalité	Rate of natural increase Taux d'accroiss-ement naturel	Code[a]	Infant deaths Décès d'enfants de moins d'un an — Number Nombre	Rate (per 1000 births) Taux (par 1000 naiss-ances)	Expectation of life at birth Espérance de vie à la naissance — Male Masculin	Female Féminin	Total fertility rate L'indice synthétiq-ue de fécondité
AMERICA, NORTH — AMERIQUE DU NORD													
Panama													
1998	C	62 351	22.6	U	11 824	...	...	U	1 047	...	...	...	...
1999	C	64 248	22.9	U	11 938	...	...	U	1 005	...	...	...	...
2000	C	64 839	22.7	U	11 841	...	...	U	1 081	...	72.2	76.8	...
2001	C	63 900	22.1	U	12 442	...	...	U	1 053	...	...	...	2.495
2002	C	61 671	20.2	...	...	...	...	...	...	...	...	...	...
Puerto Rico - Porto Rico													
1998	C	60 518	16.1	C	29 990	8.0	8.1	C	637	10.5	^71.4	^79.3	1.902
1999	C	59 684	15.8	C	29 145	7.7	8.1	C	632	10.6	...	...	1.858
2000	C	59 460	15.6	C	28 550	7.5	8.1	C	589	9.9	...	...	2.034
2001	C	55 982	14.6	C	28 794	7.5	7.1	C	515	9.2	...	...	1.916
2002	C	52 871	13.7	C	28 098	7.3	6.4	C	516	9.8	...	...	1.817
Saint Kitts and Nevis - Saint-Kitts-et-Nevis													
1998	+C	865	21.6	+C	390	9.7	11.8	+C	24	...	68.2	70.7	2.600
1999	+C	864	20.3	+C	418	9.8	10.5	...	...	...	...	...	...
2000	+C	838	20.7	+C	357	8.8	11.9	...	...	...	...	...	...
2001	+C	803	17.4	+C	352	7.6	9.8	...	...	...	...	...	...
Saint Lucia - Sainte-Lucie													
1998	C	2 950	19.4	C	976	6.4	13.0	C	48	16.3	70.4	72.4	2.141
1999	C	2 997	19.5	C	981	6.4	13.1	C	42	14.0	69.5	73.2	2.118
2000	C	2 840	18.2	C	941	6.0	12.2	C	38	13.4	68.7	73.6	2.035
2001	C	2 788	17.7	C	998	6.3	11.3	C	37	13.3	...	...	...
2002	C	2 529	15.9	C	957	6.0	9.9	C	36	14.2	72.0	76.7	...
Saint Vincent and the Grenadines - Saint Vincent-et-les Grenadines													
1998	+C	2 112	19.0	+C	830	7.5	11.5	+C	47	22.3	...	...	...
1999	+C	2 171	19.5	+C	833	7.5	12.0	+C	47	21.6	...	...	...
2000	+C	2 149	19.2	+C	700	6.3	13.0	+C	35	16.3	...	...	...
2001	+C	2 109	19.3	+C	765	7.0	12.3	+C	39	18.5	...	...	...
2002	+C	1 985	18.4	+C	770	7.1	11.3	+C	36	18.1	...	...	...
Trinidad and Tobago - Trinité-et-Tobago													
2002	C	18 026	14.1	C	9 670	7.6	6.6	...	...	...	...	...	...
Turks Caicos Islands - Îles Turques et Caïques													
1998	+C	272	...	+C	22	...	...	...	...	...	...	...	...
1999	+C	292	...	+C	39	...	...	...	...	...	...	...	...
2000	+C	290	...	+C	67	...	...	...	...	...	...	...	...
United States - États-Unis													
1998	C	3 941 553	14.6	C	2 337 256	8.6	5.9	C	28 371	7.2	73.8	79.5	...
1999	C	3 959 417	14.5	C	2 391 399	8.8	5.8	C	27 937	7.1	73.9	79.4	...
2000	C	4 058 814	14.7	C	2 403 351	8.7	6.0	C	28 035	6.9	74.3	79.7	...
2001	C	4 025 933	14.1	C	2 416 425	8.5	5.7	C	27 568	6.8	74.4	79.8	...
2002	C	4 021 726	13.9	C	2 447 864	8.5	5.5	C	27 977	7.0	...	...	...
AMERICA, SOUTH — AMERIQUE DU SUD													
Argentina - Argentine													
1998	C	683 301	18.9	C	280 180	7.8	11.2	C	13 082	19.1	...	...	...
1999	C	686 748	18.8	C	289 543	7.9	10.9	C	12 120	17.6	...	...	...
2000	C	701 878	19.0	C	277 148	7.5	11.5	C	11 649	16.6	...	...	...
2001	C	683 495	18.2	C	285 941	7.6	10.6	C	11 111	16.3	...	...	...

4. Vital statistics summary and expectation of life at birth: 1998-2002
Aperçu des statistiques de l'état civil et espérance de vie à la naissance: 1998-2002 (continued — suite)

(See notes at end of table. — Voir notes à la fin du tableau.)

Continent, country or area and year / Continent, pays ou zone et année	Live births - Naissances vivantes			Deaths - Décès			Rate of natural increase Taux d'accroiss-ement naturel	Infant deaths - Décès d'enfants de moins d'un an			Expectation of life at birth Espérance de vie à la naissance		Total fertility rate L'indice synthétiq-ue de fécondité
	Code[a]	Number Nombre	Crude birth rate Taux bruts de natalité	Code[a]	Number Nombre	Crude death rate Taux bruts de mortalité		Code[a]	Number Nombre	Rate (per 1000 births) Taux (par 1000 naiss-ances)	Male Masculin	Female Féminin	
AMERICA, SOUTH — AMERIQUE DU SUD													
Argentina - Argentine													
2002	C	694 684	18.3	C	291 190	7.7	10.6	C	11 703	16.8	...	...	...
Bolivia - Bolivie													
1998	...	...	...	U	71 618	...	...	U	16 942	...	...	...	...
1999	...	...	...	U	71 680	...	...	U	16 492	...	...	...	...
2000	U	264 941	...	U	71 742	...	...	U	16 042	...	...	...	...
Brazil - Brésil[6,8]													
1998	U	2 459 275	...	U	936 885	...	...	U	64 702	...	64.4	72.0	2.254
1999	U	2 657 613	...	U	943 524	...	...	U	58 767	...	...	...	2.226
2000	U	2 611 422	...	U	927 783	...	...	U	53 097	...	64.8	72.6	2.200
2001	U	2 509 354	...	U	931 017	...	...	U	47 171	...	...	...	2.180
2002	U	2 581 055	...	U	958 475	...	...	U	45 243	...	67.3	74.9	2.160
Chile - Chili													
1998	C	257 105	17.3	C	80 257	5.4	11.9	C	2 793	10.9	72.3	78.3	2.300
1999	C	250 674	16.7	C	81 984	5.5	11.2	C	2 654	10.6	72.4	78.4	2.200
2000	C	248 893	16.4	C	78 814	5.2	11.2	C	2 336	9.4	...	...	2.100
2001	C	246 116	16.0	C	81 873	5.3	10.7	C	2 159	8.8	^74.4	^80.4	2.000
2002	C	238 981	15.3	C	81 079	5.2	10.1	C	1 964	8.2	...	...	2.000
Colombia - Colombie[9]													
1998	U	720 984	...	U	175 363	...	...	U	14 178	...	...	...	2.760
1999	U	746 194	...	U	183 551	...	...	U	14 619	...	...	...	2.730
2000	U	752 834	...	U	187 432	...	...	U	15 367	...	^69.2	^75.3	...
2001	U	724 319	...	U	191 513	...	...	U	14 430	...	^69.4	^75.5	...
2002	U	678 388	...	U	187 943	...	...	U	12 096	...	^69.6	^75.7	...
Ecuador - Équateur[10]													
1998	U	199 079	...	U	54 357	...	...	U	5 186	...	...	...	...
1999	U	218 108	...	U	55 921	...	...	U	5 372	...	...	...	...
2000	U	202 257	...	U	56 420	...	...	U	5 190	...	^71.3	^77.2	2.020
2001	U	192 786	...	U	55 214	...	...	U	4 800	...	...	...	...
2002	U	183 792	...	U	55 549	...	...	U	4 530	...	...	...	...
Falkland Islands (Malvinas) - Îles Falkland (Malvinas)													
1998	+C	28	...	+C	12	...	...	...	...	...	...	...	...
1999	+C	33	...	+C	20	...	...	...	...	...	...	...	...
2000	+C	27	...	+C	11	...	...	...	...	...	...	...	...
French Guiana - Guyane française[1]													
1998	C	4 691	30.7	C	620	4.1	26.6	C	52	11.1	...	...	3.800
1999	C	4 898	30.9	C	658	4.2	26.8	C	63	12.9	...	...	3.900
2000	C	5 116	31.2	C	620	3.8	27.4	C	64	12.5	...	...	4.000
2001	C	5 114	30.1	C	668	3.9	26.2	C	70	13.7	...	...	3.900
2002	C	5 249	29.9	C	656	3.7	26.2	C	52	9.9	72.5	79.2	3.900
Guyana													
1998	...	...	...	+C	4 977	6.4	...	...	...	...	...	...	...
1999	...	...	...	+C	4 197	5.4	...	...	...	...	...	...	...
Paraguay													
2000	...	...	...	...	...	...	...	...	...	...	^68.6	^73.1	3.800
Peru - Pérou[3,8,11]													
1998	I	648 075	25.8	I	161 615	6.4	19.4	I	26 603	41.0	...	...	3.160
1999	I	642 874	25.2	I	162 457	6.4	18.8	I	25 098	39.0	...	...	3.090
2000	I	636 064	24.5	I	163 263	6.3	18.2	I	23 681	37.2	...	...	3.020
2001	I	630 947	23.9	I	164 296	6.2	17.7	I	22 455	35.6	...	...	2.960
2002	I	626 714	23.4	I	165 467	6.2	17.2	...	...	...	...	...	2.890

(See notes at end of table. — Voir notes à la fin du tableau.)

Continent, country or area and year / Continent, pays ou zone et année	Code[a]	Live births Naissances vivantes Number Nombre	Live births Crude birth rate Taux bruts de natalité	Code[a]	Deaths Décès Number Nombre	Deaths Crude death rate Taux bruts de mortalité	Rate of natural increase Taux d'accroiss-ement naturel	Code[a]	Infant deaths Décès d'enfants de moins d'un an Number Nombre	Infant deaths Rate (per 1000 births) Taux (par 1000 naissances)	Expectation of life at birth Espérance de vie à la naissance Male Masculin	Expectation of life at birth Female Féminin	Total fertility rate L'indice synthétique de fécondité
AMERICA, SOUTH — AMERIQUE DU SUD													
Suriname													
1998	C	10 221	22.6	C	2 814	6.2	16.4	C	163	15.9	...	...	...
1999	C	10 144	22.2	C	2 992	6.5	15.6	C	227	22.4	...	...	...
2000	C	9 804	21.1	C	3 090	6.7	14.5	C	156	15.9	...	...	...
Uruguay													
1998	+C	54 760	16.7	C	32 082	9.8	6.9	C	910	16.6	...	...	2.310
1999	+C	54 004	16.4	C	32 430	9.8	6.5	C	776	14.4	...	...	2.260
2000	+C	52 770	15.9	C	30 456	9.2	6.7	C	742	14.1	...	...	2.250
2001	+C	51 959	15.5	C	31 228	9.3	6.2	C	721	13.9	...	...	2.230
2002	+C	51 997	15.5	C	31 628	9.4	6.1	C	708	13.6	...	...	2.210
Venezuela[8]													
1998	C	501 808	21.4	C	98 624	4.2	17.2	C	9 871	19.7	...	...	2.930
1999	C	527 888	22.1	C	101 907	4.3	17.8	C	9 030	17.1	...	...	...
2000	C	544 416	22.4	C	103 255	4.2	18.1	C	8 524	15.7	...	...	...
2001	C	529 552	21.4	C	107 867	4.4	17.0	C	8 158	15.4	...	...	...
2002	C	492 678	19.5	C	105 388	4.2	15.4	C	7 645	15.5	...	...	...
ASIA — ASIE													
Armenia - Arménie[12]													
1998	C	39 366	10.4	C	23 210	6.1	4.3	C	580	14.7	70.8	78.0	1.290
1999	C	36 502	9.6	C	24 087	6.3	3.3	C	572	15.7	70.6	75.5	1.194
2000	C	34 276	9.0	C	24 025	6.3	2.7	C	540	15.8	70.6	75.5	1.100
2001	C	32 065	8.4	C	24 003	6.3	2.1	C	497	15.5	...	...	...
Azerbaijan - Azerbaïdjan[12]													
1998	+C	123 996	15.7	+C	46 299	5.9	9.8	+C	2 061	16.6	67.9	75.0	2.000
1999	+C	117 539	14.7	+C	46 295	5.8	8.9	+C	1 943	16.5	68.1	75.1	2.000
2000	+C	116 994	14.5	+C	46 701	5.8	8.7	+C	1 501	12.8	68.6	75.1	2.000
2001	+C	110 356	13.6	+C	45 284	5.6	8.0	+C	1 382	12.5	68.6	75.2	1.830
2002	+C	110 715	13.5	+C	46 522	5.7	7.9	+C	1 422	12.8	69.4	75.0	1.840
Bahrain - Bahreïn													
1998	+U	13 381	...	U	1 997	...	...	U	111	...	...	...	2.780
1999	+U	14 280	...	U	1 920	...	...	U	129	...	...	...	2.895
2000	+U	13 947	...	U	2 045	...	...	U	117	...	...	...	2.749
2001	U	13 468	...	U	1 979	...	...	U	117	...	73.2	76.2	2.576
2002	U	13 576	...	U	2 035	...	...	U	94	...	...	...	2.528
Brunei Darussalam - Brunéi Darussalam													
1998	+C	7 411	23.9	+C	928	3.0	20.9	+C	48	6.5	...	...	2.734
1999	+C	7 408	23.4	+C	905	2.9	20.5	+C	44	5.9	...	...	2.398
2000	+C	7 481	23.0	+C	965	3.0	20.1	+C	55	7.4	...	...	2.360
2001	+C	7 363	22.1	+C	1 014	3.0	19.1	+C	50	6.8	...	...	2.238
2002	+C	7 464	21.9	+C	1 041	3.1	18.8	+C	62	8.3	...	...	...
China - Chine[13,14]													
1998	I	19 910 000	16.0	...	8 070 000	...	...	...	...	...	...	...	...
1999	I	19 090 000	15.2	...	8 100 000	...	...	...	...	...	...	...	...
2000	...	...	14.0	...	...	6.4	7.6	...	...	...	69.6	73.3	...
2001	...	...	13.4	...	...	6.4	7.0	...	...	...	...	...	...
2002	...	...	12.9	...	...	6.4	6.4	...	...	...	...	...	...
China: Hong Kong SAR - Chine: Hong Kong RAS													
1998	C	52 977	8.1	C	32 847	5.0	3.1	C	167	3.2	77.2	82.6	0.990
1999	C	51 281	7.8	C	33 255	5.0	2.7	C	157	3.1	77.2	82.4	0.965
2000	C	54 134	8.1	C	33 758	5.1	3.1	C	162	3.0	77.0	82.2	1.024
2001	C	48 219	7.2	C	33 378	5.0	2.2	C	124	2.6	78.4	84.6	...

4. Vital statistics summary and expectation of life at birth: 1998-2002
Aperçu des statistiques de l'état civil et espérance de vie à la naissance: 1998-2002 (continued — suite)

(See notes at end of table. — Voir notes à la fin du tableau.)

Continent, country or area and year / Continent, pays ou zone et année	Code[a]	Live births - Naissances vivantes Number Nombre	Crude birth rate Taux bruts de natalité	Code[a]	Deaths - Décès Number Nombre	Crude death rate Taux bruts de mortalité	Rate of natural increase Taux d'accroiss-ement naturel	Code[a]	Infant deaths - Décès d'enfants de moins d'un an Number Nombre	Rate (per 1000 births) Taux (par 1000 naiss-ances)	Expectation of life at birth - Espérance de vie à la naissance Male Masculin	Female Féminin	Total fertility rate L'indice synthétiq-ue de fécondité
ASIA — ASIE													
China: Hong Kong SAR - Chine: Hong Kong RAS													
2002	C	48 209	7.1	C	34 267	5.0	2.1	C	110	2.3	...	...	...
China: Macao SAR - Chine: Macao RAS													
1998	C	4 434	10.5	C	1 356	3.2	7.3	C	27	...	...	...	...
1999	C	4 148	9.7	C	1 374	3.2	6.5	C	17	...	...	...	...
2000	C	3 849	8.9	C	1 338	3.1	5.8	C	11	...	...	...	...
2001	C	3 241	7.5	C	1 327	3.1	4.4	C	14	...	...	...	...
2002	C	3 162	7.2	C	1 415	3.2	4.0	C	11	...	...	...	...
Cyprus - Chypre[15]													
1998	C	8 879	11.6	C	5 432	7.1	4.5	C	62	7.0	^75.3	^80.4	1.760
1999	C	8 505	11.0	C	5 070	6.5	4.4	C	51	6.0	...	...	1.670
2000	C	8 447	10.8	C	5 355	6.9	4.0	C	47	5.6	...	...	1.640
2001	C	8 167	10.4	C	4 827	6.1	4.2	C	40	4.9	...	...	1.570
2002	C	7 883	9.9	C	5 168	6.5	3.4	C	37	4.7	...	...	1.491
Georgia - Géorgie[12]													
1998	C	46 800	8.6	C	39 400	7.2	1.4	C	710	15.2	...	...	1.160
1999	C	40 778	8.0	C	40 378	7.9	0.1	C	714	17.5	...	...	1.070
2000	C	40 392	8.0	C	41 320	8.2	-0.2	C	600	14.9	...	...	1.100
2001	C	40 416	8.2	C	39 339	8.0	0.2	C	478	11.8	...	...	...
India - Inde[16,17]													
1998	...	...	26.5	...	...	9.0	17.5	...	...	72.0	...	...	3.200
1999	...	...	26.0	...	...	8.7	17.3	...	...	70.0	...	...	3.200
2000	...	...	25.8	...	...	8.5	17.3	...	...	68.0	...	...	3.200
2001	...	...	25.4	...	...	8.4	17.0	...	...	66.0	...	...	...
2002	...	...	25.0	...	...	8.1	16.0	...	...	60.0	...	...	...
Indonesia - Indonésie													
1998	...	...	...	...	...	...	...	...	...	...	...	...	2.676
1999	...	...	...	...	...	...	...	...	...	...	...	...	2.593
2000	...	...	...	...	...	...	...	...	...	...	...	...	2.544
Iran (Islamic Republic of) - Iran (République islamique d')													
1998	C	1 185 639	19.2	...	...	...	...	C	...	...	...	...	...
1999	C	1 177 557	18.8	C	374 838	6.0	12.8	C	39 183	33.3	...	...	...
2000	C	1 095 165	17.2	...	...	...	...	...	...	...	...	...	...
2001	C	1 112 193	17.2	...	...	...	...	...	...	...	67.6	70.4	2.500
2002	C	1 122 104	17.1	...	...	...	...	...	...	...	...	...	...
Iraq[18]													
1998	U	519 216	...	U	160 039	...	...	...	...	...	...	...	...
1999	U	532 916	...	U	177 483	...	...	...	...	...	...	...	...
2000	U	471 886	...	U	179 928	...	...	...	...	...	...	...	...
Israel - Israël[19]													
1998	C	130 080	21.8	C	36 955	6.2	15.6	C	774	6.0	76.1	80.6	2.982
1999	C	131 936	21.5	C	37 291	6.1	15.5	C	771	5.8	...	...	2.941
2000	C	136 390	21.7	C	37 688	6.0	15.7	C	748	5.5	76.5	81.1	2.954
2001	C	136 638	21.2	C	37 179	5.8	15.4	C	699	5.1	...	...	2.887
2002	C	139 535	21.2	C	38 254	5.8	15.4	C	751	5.4	77.5	81.5	2.888
Japan - Japon[20]													
1998	C	1 203 147	9.5	C	936 484	7.4	2.1	C	4 380	3.6	77.2	84.0	1.384
1999	C	1 177 669	9.3	C	982 031	7.8	1.5	C	4 010	3.4	77.1	84.0	1.340
2000	C	1 190 547	9.4	C	961 653	7.6	1.8	C	3 830	3.2	77.6	84.6	...
2001	C	1 170 662	9.2	C	970 331	7.6	1.6	C	3 599	3.1	78.1	84.9	...
2002	C	1 153 855	9.1	C	982 379	7.7	1.3	C	3 497	3.0	78.3	85.2	1.319

85

(See notes at end of table. — Voir notes à la fin du tableau.)

Continent, country or area and year / Continent, pays ou zone et année	Code[a]	Live births / Naissances vivantes — Number Nombre	Crude birth rate Taux bruts de natalité	Code[a]	Deaths - Décès — Number Nombre	Crude death rate Taux bruts de mortalité	Rate of natural increase Taux d'accroiss-ement naturel	Code[a]	Infant deaths / Décès d'enfants de moins d'un an — Number Nombre	Rate (per 1000 births) Taux (par 1000 naiss-ances)	Expectation of life at birth / Espérance de vie à la naissance — Male Masculin	Female Féminin	Total fertility rate L'indice synthétiq-ue de fécondité
ASIA — ASIE													
Jordan - Jordanie[21]													
1998	C	133 714	28.1	C	13 552	2.8	25.3	...	...	...	...	...	...
1999	C	135 266	27.6	C	13 936	2.8	24.8	...	...	...	...	...	...
2000	C	126 016	25.0	C	13 339	2.6	22.4	...	...	...	68.8	71.1	...
2001	C	142 956	27.6	C	16 164	3.1	24.5	...	...	...	...	...	...
2002	C	146 077	27.4	C	17 220	3.2	24.2	...	...	...	...	...	...
Kazakhstan[12]													
1998	C	222 380	14.8	C	154 314	10.2	4.5	C	4 843	21.8	...	...	...
1999	C	217 578	14.6	C	147 416	9.9	4.7	C	4 444	20.4	...	...	...
2000	C	222 054	14.9	C	149 778	10.1	4.9	C	4 158	18.7	...	...	...
2001	C	221 487	14.9	C	147 876	10.0	5.0	C	4 238	19.1	...	...	...
2002	C	227 171	15.3	C	149 381	10.1	5.2	C	3 849	16.9	...	...	...
Korea (Republic of) - Corée (République de)[22]													
1998	C	640 126	13.8	C	245 597	5.3	8.5	C	1 460	2.3	...	...	1.465
1999	C	616 322	13.2	C	246 539	5.3	7.9	C	2 776	4.5	71.7	79.2	1.424
2000	C	636 780	13.5	C	247 346	5.3	8.3	C	2 885	4.5	...	...	1.470
2001	C	557 228	11.8	C	242 730	5.1	6.6	C	3 008	5.4	72.8	80.0	1.300
2002	C	494 625	10.4	C	246 515	5.2	5.2	C	2 545	5.1	...	...	...
Kuwait - Koweït													
1998	C	41 424	20.4	C	4 216	2.1	18.4	C	450	10.9	...	...	4.141
1999	C	41 135	19.5	C	4 187	2.0	17.5	C	386	9.4	...	...	4.161
2000	C	41 843	19.1	C	4 227	1.9	17.2	C	379	9.1	...	...	4.225
2001	C	41 342	18.2	C	4 364	1.9	16.3	C	420	10.2	...	...	4.042
2002	C	43 490	19.2	C	4 342	1.9	17.3	C	418	9.6	...	...	4.146
Kyrgyzstan - Kirghizistan[12]													
1998	C	104 183	21.7	C	34 596	7.2	14.5	C	2 708	26.0	63.1	71.2	2.804
1999	C	104 068	21.4	C	32 850	6.8	14.6	C	2 360	22.7	63.1	71.1	2.620
2000	C	96 770	19.7	C	34 111	6.9	12.7	C	2 225	23.0	64.9	72.4	2.409
2001	C	98 138	19.8	C	32 677	6.6	13.2	C	2 123	21.6	65.0	72.6	...
2002	C	101 012	20.2	C	35 235	7.1	13.2	C	2 128	21.1	64.4	72.1	2.465
Lao People's Democratic Republic - République démocratique populaire lao													
2000	...	...	...	...	...	...	...	...	...	...	...	...	4.900
Lebanon - Liban[18]													
1998	U	84 250	...	U	20 097	...	...	...	...	...	...	...	...
1999	U	85 516	...	U	19 133	...	...	...	...	...	...	...	...
2000	U	85 760	...	U	18 756	...	...	...	...	...	...	...	...
Malaysia - Malaisie													
1998	C	524 766	24.4	C	98 264	4.6	19.9	C	4 483	8.5	69.6	74.6	3.122
1999	C	521 870	23.9	C	111 738	5.1	18.8	C	4 660	8.9	...	...	3.020
2000	C	545 096	23.2	C	104 859	4.5	18.7	C	3 578	6.6	...	...	2.961
Maldives													
1998	C	5 687	21.3	C	1 130	4.2	17.0	C	115	20.2	70.6	71.8	...
1999	C	5 226	18.8	C	1 050	3.8	15.0	C	104	19.9	72.0	73.2	...
2000	C	5 314	19.6	C	1 031	3.8	15.8	C	113	21.3	...	...	...
2001	C	4 882	17.7	C	1 081	3.9	13.8	C	85	17.4	...	...	...
2002	C	4 991	17.8	C	1 109	4.0	13.8	C	88	17.6	...	...	...
Mongolia - Mongolie													
1998	C	49 256	21.0	C	15 799	6.8	14.3	C	1 741	35.3	...	...	2.300
1999	C	49 461	20.8	C	16 105	6.8	14.1	C	1 846	37.3	...	...	2.300
2000	C	48 721	20.2	C	15 472	6.4	13.8	C	1 596	32.8	...	...	2.200
2001	C	49 685	20.3	C	15 999	6.6	13.8	C	1 464	29.5	...	...	2.200
2002	C	46 922	19.0	C	15 857	6.4	12.5	C	1 390	29.6	...	...	2.100

4. Vital statistics summary and expectation of life at birth: 1998-2002
Aperçu des statistiques de l'état civil et espérance de vie à la naissance: 1998-2002 (continued — suite)

(See notes at end of table. — Voir notes à la fin du tableau.)

Continent, country or area and year / Continent, pays ou zone et année	Live births / Naissances vivantes			Deaths - Décès			Rate of natural increase / Taux d'accroiss-ement naturel	Infant deaths / Décès d'enfants de moins d'un an			Expectation of life at birth / Espérance de vie à la naissance		Total fertility rate / L'indice synthétiq-ue de fécondité
	Code[a]	Number Nombre	Crude birth rate Taux bruts de natalité	Code[a]	Number Nombre	Crude death rate Taux bruts de mortalité		Code[a]	Number Nombre	Rate (per 1000 births) Taux (par 1000 naiss-ances)	Male Masculin	Female Féminin	
ASIA — ASIE													
Nepal - Népal[23]													
2001	...	...	...	I	106 789	...	...	I	13 037	...	...	...	...
Occupied Palestinian Territory - Territoire palestinien occupé													
1998	U	99 841	...	U	6 205	...	...	U	1 038	...	...	...	...
1999	U	96 780	...	U	8 500	...	...	U	1 068	...	...	...	...
2000	U	98 026	...	U	8 701	...	...	U	1 037	...	...	...	5.930
2001	U	94 626	...	U	8 772	...	...	U	1 100	...	...	...	...
2002	U	93 488	...	U	9 216	...	...	U	1 043	...	70.4	73.6	...
Oman[24]													
1998	...	40 364	...	...	2 297	...	...	...	374	...	71.8	74.2	...
1999	...	39 922	...	...	2 440	...	...	...	386	...	72.3	74.3	...
2000	...	39 994	...	...	2 547	...	...	...	369	...	72.5	74.3	...
2001	...	39 297	...	...	2 550	...	...	...	335	...	72.4	75.3	4.700
2002	...	...	...	...	...	...	...	...	...	...	72.2	75.4	4.200
Pakistan[25,26]													
2000	...	...	...	...	...	...	...	...	...	...	...	...	4.300
2001	I	3 719 694	26.5	I	956 515	6.8	19.7	I	286 609	77.1	64.5	66.1	4.100
Philippines													
1998	C	1 632 859	22.3	C	352 992	4.8	17.5	C	28 196	17.3	...	...	2.800
1999	C	1 613 335	21.6	C	347 989	4.7	16.9	C	25 168	15.6	...	...	2.720
2000	C	1 766 440	23.1	C	366 931	4.8	18.3	C	27 714	15.7	...	...	2.965
2001	...	...	...	...	...	...	...	...	...	...	...	...	2.753
Qatar													
1998	C	10 781	19.8	C	1 157	2.1	17.7	C	141	13.1	...	...	...
1999	C	10 846	...	C	1 148	...	...	C	112	10.3	...	...	...
2000	C	11 250	19.4	C	1 173	2.0	17.4	C	132	11.7	...	...	...
2001	C	12 118	20.3	C	1 210	2.0	18.2	C	111	9.2	...	...	...
2002	C	12 200	...	C	1 220	...	...	...	...	...	...	...	...
Saudi Arabia - Arabie saoudite													
1999	...	509 352	...	...	68 521	...	...	...	11 344	...	...	...	...
2000	...	578 772	...	...	51 614	...	...	...	11 071	...	...	...	...
Singapore - Singapour[27]													
1998	C	43 664	11.1	+C	15 657	4.0	7.1	+C	183	4.2	75.4	79.5	1.473
1999	C	43 336	11.0	+C	15 516	3.9	7.0	+C	150	3.5	75.6	79.7	1.465
2000	C	46 997	11.7	+C	15 693	3.9	7.8	+C	137	2.9	76.0	80.0	1.598
2001	C	41 451	10.0	+C	15 367	3.7	6.3	+C	100	2.4	76.4	80.3	1.406
2002	C	40 760	9.8	+C	15 820	3.8	6.0		123	3.0	76.6	80.7	1.370
Sri Lanka													
1998	+C	329 148	17.5	+C	112 657	6.0	11.5	...	...	...	...	...	...
1999	+C	329 121	17.3	+C	114 392	6.0	11.3	...	...	...	...	...	...
2001	...	...	...	...	...	...	...	+C	4 323	...	...	...	...
2002	+C	363 549	19.1	+C	110 637	5.8	13.3	...	...	...	...	...	...
Syrian Arab Republic - République arabe syrienne[1,28,29]													
1998	C	505 008	32.4	U	57 893	...	...	...	...	...	...	...	...
1999	C	503 473	31.3	U	56 564	...	...	...	...	...	...	...	...
2000	C	505 484	31.0	U	57 759	...	...	...	...	...	...	...	...
2001	C	524 212	31.4	U	60 814	...	...	...	...	...	...	...	...
Tajikistan - Tadjikistan[12]													
1999	C	110 300	17.7	C	24 900	4.0	13.7	C	2 200	19.9	...	...	...
Thailand - Thaïlande													
1998	+U	897 495	...	+U	317 793	...	...	+U	4 062	...	...	...	...

4. Vital statistics summary and expectation of life at birth: 1998-2002
Aperçu des statistiques de l'état civil et espérance de vie à la naissance: 1998-2002 (continued — suite)

(See notes at end of table. — Voir notes à la fin du tableau.)

Continent, country or area and year / Continent, pays ou zone et année	Live births — Naissances vivantes Code[a]	Number Nombre	Crude birth rate Taux bruts de natalité	Deaths - Décès Code[a]	Number Nombre	Crude death rate Taux bruts de mortalité	Rate of natural increase Taux d'accroiss-ement naturel	Infant deaths — Décès d'enfants de moins d'un an Code[a]	Number Nombre	Rate (per 1000 births) Taux (par 1000 naiss-ances)	Expectation of life at birth — Espérance de vie à la naissance Male Masculin	Female Féminin	Total fertility rate L'indice synthétiq-ue de fécondité
ASIA — ASIE													
Thailand - Thaïlande													
1999	+U	772 604	...	+U	362 593	...	...	+U	5 003	...	...	...	...
2000	+U	773 009	...	+U	365 741	...	...	+U	4 822	...	...	...	...
2001	+U	790 425	...	+U	369 493	...	...	+U	5 105	...	...	...	...
2002	+U	782 911	...	+U	380 364	...	...	+U	5 105	...	...	...	...
Turkey - Turquie[30]													
1998	I	1 505 000	23.1	I	465 000	7.1	16.0	I	67 274	44.7	...	...	2.670
1999	I	1 501 000	22.6	I	471 000	7.1	15.5	I	64 993	43.3	...	...	2.620
2000	I	1 494 000	22.2	I	477 000	7.1	15.1	I	62 599	41.9	66.4	71.0	2.570
2001	I	1 486 000	21.7	I	485 000	7.1	14.6	I	60 332	40.6	...	...	2.520
2002	I	1 482 000	21.3	I	491 000	7.1	14.2	I	58 391	39.4	...	...	2.460
Turkmenistan - Turkménistan[12]													
1998	C	98 461	20.3	C	29 628	6.1	14.2	C	3 265	33.2	...	...	...
Uzbekistan - Ouzbékistan[12]													
1999	C	553 745	23.1	C	140 526	5.9	17.3	C	12 358	22.3	...	...	...
2000	C	527 580	21.4	C	135 598	5.5	15.9	C	10 091	19.1	...	...	...
2001	C	512 950	20.5	C	132 542	5.3	15.2	C	9 427	18.4	...	...	...
EUROPE													
Albania - Albanie													
1998	C	60 139	15.9	C	18 250	4.8	11.1	C	903	15.0	...	...	2.100
1999	...	...	...	...	...	...	...	...	...	...	...	...	...
Andorra - Andorre													
1998	C	781	11.8	C	235	3.6	8.3	C	5	...	...	...	...
1999	C	833	12.6	C	207	3.1	9.5	C	2	...	...	...	...
2000	C	747	11.3	C	259	3.9	7.4	C	2	...	...	...	...
2001	C	777	11.8	C	237	3.6	8.2	C	3	...	...	...	...
2002	C	749	11.3	C	218	3.3	8.0	...	...	...	...	...	...
Austria - Autriche													
1998	C	81 233	10.1	C	78 339	9.7	0.4	C	400	4.9	74.7	80.9	1.342
1999	C	78 138	9.7	C	78 200	9.7	0.0	C	341	4.4	75.1	81.0	1.315
2000	C	78 268	9.7	C	76 780	9.5	0.2	C	378	4.8	75.4	81.2	1.363
2001	C	75 458	9.4	C	74 767	9.3	0.1	C	365	4.8	75.9	81.7	1.333
2002	C	78 399	9.7	C	76 131	9.5	0.3	C	318	4.1	75.8	81.7	1.402
Belarus - Bélarus[12]													
1998	C	92 645	9.1	C	137 296	13.5	-4.4	C	1 041	11.2	62.7	74.4	1.266
1999	C	92 975	9.3	C	142 027	14.2	-4.9	C	1 064	11.4	62.2	73.9	1.300
2000	...	...	...	...	...	...	...	...	...	...	...	...	1.660
2001	...	...	...	...	...	...	...	...	...	...	...	...	1.650
2002	C	88 743	8.9	C	146 655	14.8	-5.8	C	695	7.8	62.3	74.1	1.222
Belgium - Belgique[31]													
1998	C	114 276	11.2	C	104 583	10.3	1.0	C	591	5.2	...	...	...
1999	C	113 469	11.1	C	104 904	10.3	0.8	C	556	4.9	74.9	81.4	1.613
2000	C	114 883	11.2	C	104 903	10.2	1.0	C	554	4.8	74.6	80.8	...
2001	C	114 014	11.1	C	103 447	10.1	1.0	C	518	4.5	...	...	...
2002	...	...	...	C	105 642	10.2	...	C	551	...	...	...	...
Bosnia and Herzegovina - Bosnie-Herzégovine													
1998	C	45 007	12.3	C	28 679	7.9	4.5	C	494	11.0	...	...	1.360
1999	...	...	...	...	...	...	...	...	...	...	...	...	...
Bulgaria - Bulgarie													
1998	C	65 360	7.9	C	118 193	14.3	-6.4	C	943	14.4	68.1	75.3	...
1999	C	72 291	8.8	C	111 786	13.6	-4.8	C	1 057	14.6	^68.5	^75.2	1.232

88

4. Vital statistics summary and expectation of life at birth: 1998-2002
Aperçu des statistiques de l'état civil et espérance de vie à la naissance: 1998-2002 (continued — suite)

(See notes at end of table. — Voir notes à la fin du tableau.)

Continent, country or area and year / Continent, pays ou zone et année	Code[a]	Live births Naissances vivantes Number Nombre	Crude birth rate Taux bruts de natalité	Code[a]	Deaths Décès Number Nombre	Crude death rate Taux bruts de mortalité	Rate of natural increase Taux d'accroiss-ement naturel	Code[a]	Infant deaths Décès d'enfants de moins d'un an Number Nombre	Rate (per 1000 births) Taux (par 1000 naiss-ances)	Expectation of life at birth Male Masculin	Female Féminin	Total fertility rate L'indice synthétique de fécondité
EUROPE													
Bulgaria - Bulgarie													
2000	C	73 679	9.0	C	115 087	14.1	-5.1	C	981	13.3	68.5	75.1	1.266
2001	C	68 180	8.6	C	112 368	14.2	-5.6	C	982	14.4	...	...	1.243
2002	C	66 499	8.5	C	112 617	14.3	-5.9	C	887	13.3	68.5	75.4	1.212
Channel Islands: Guernsey - Îles Anglo-Normandes: Guernesey													
1998	C	669	11.3	C	540	9.1	2.2	C	2	...	...	...	...
1999	C	672	11.2	C	529	8.8	2.4	C	2	...	...	...	...
2000	C	644	10.7	C	565	9.3	1.3	C	4	...	...	...	...
Croatia - Croatie													
1998	C	47 068	10.5	C	52 311	11.6	-1.2	C	388	8.2	...	...	1.450
1999	C	45 179	9.9	C	51 953	11.4	-1.5	C	350	7.7	...	...	1.380
2000	C	43 746	10.0	C	50 246	11.5	-1.5	C	324	7.4	...	...	1.390
2001	C	40 993	9.2	C	49 552	11.2	-1.9	C	315	7.7	...	...	1.380
2002	C	40 094	9.0	C	50 569	11.4	-2.4	C	282	7.0	...	...	1.340
Czech Republic - République tchèque													
1998	C	90 535	8.8	C	109 527	10.6	-1.8	C	472	5.2	^71.2	^77.9	1.150
1999	C	89 471	8.7	C	109 768	10.7	-2.0	C	413	4.6	71.4	78.1	1.131
2000	C	90 910	8.8	C	109 001	10.6	-1.8	C	373	4.1	71.6	78.3	1.144
2001	C	90 715	8.9	C	107 755	10.5	-1.7	C	360	4.0	72.1	78.5	1.146
2002	C	97 878	9.6	C	108 243	10.6	-1.0	C	385	3.9	72.1	78.5	1.171
Denmark - Danemark[32]													
1998	C	66 170	12.5	C	58 442	11.0	1.5	C	309	4.7	^74.0	^78.8	1.720
1999	C	66 232	12.4	C	59 156	11.1	1.3	C	281	4.2	74.2	79.0	1.733
2000	C	67 084	12.6	C	57 986	10.9	1.7	C	358	5.3	74.5	79.3	1.771
2001	C	65 458	12.2	C	58 338	10.9	1.3	C	320	4.9	74.6	79.2	1.747
2002	C	64 149	11.9	C	58 610	10.9	1.0	C	284	4.4	...	...	1.725
Estonia - Estonie[12]													
1998	C	12 170	8.4	C	19 440	13.4	-5.0	C	108	8.9	...	...	...
1999	C	12 545	8.7	C	18 455	12.8	-4.1	C	119	9.5	...	...	1.235
2000	C	13 089	9.6	C	18 403	13.4	-3.9	C	110	8.4	65.1	76.2	1.390
2001	C	12 632	9.3	C	18 516	13.6	-4.3	C	111	8.8	...	...	1.340
2002	C	13 001	9.6	C	18 355	13.5	-3.9	C	74	5.7	64.8	76.3	1.370
Finland - Finlande[33]													
1998	C	57 108	11.1	C	49 262	9.6	1.5	C	239	4.2	73.5	80.8	1.700
1999	C	57 574	11.1	C	49 345	9.6	1.6	C	208	3.6	73.8	81.0	1.735
2000	C	56 742	11.0	C	49 339	9.5	1.4	C	213	3.8	...	...	1.729
2001	C	56 189	10.8	C	48 550	9.4	1.5	C	181	3.2	74.6	81.5	1.726
2002	C	55 555	10.7	C	49 418	9.5	1.2	C	168	3.0	74.8	81.5	1.718
France[33,34]													
1998	C	738 080	12.6	C	534 005	9.1	3.5	C	3 399	4.6	74.8	82.4	1.764
1999	C	744 791	12.7	C	537 661	9.2	3.5	C	3 221	4.3	...	...	1.793
2000	C	774 782	13.2	C	536 300	9.1	4.0	C	3 417	4.4	...	...	1.880
2001	C	770 945	13.0	C	531 485	9.0	4.0	C	3 444	4.5	...	...	1.897
Germany - Allemagne													
1998	C	797 541	9.7	C	851 412	10.4	-0.7	C	3 667	4.6	74.8	80.8	...
1999	C	770 744	9.4	C	846 330	10.3	-0.9	C	3 496	4.5	74.7	80.7	1.360
2000	C	766 999	9.3	C	838 797	10.2	-0.9	C	3 362	4.4	...	...	1.360
2001	C	734 475	8.9	C	828 541	10.1	-1.1	C	3 163	4.3	...	...	1.349
2002	...	...	...	...	...	...	...	C	3 100	...	...	...	...
Gibraltar[35]													
1998	C	411	15.2	C	267	9.9	5.3	...	...	...	...	...	...
1999	C	381	14.0	C	277	10.2	3.8	...	...	...	...	...	...

89

4. Vital statistics summary and expectation of life at birth: 1998-2002
Aperçu des statistiques de l'état civil et espérance de vie à la naissance: 1998-2002 (continued — suite)

(See notes at end of table. — Voir notes à la fin du tableau.)

Continent, country or area and year / Continent, pays ou zone et année	Code[a]	Live births — Naissances vivantes Number Nombre	Crude birth rate Taux bruts de natalité	Code[a]	Deaths - Décès Number Nombre	Crude death rate Taux bruts de mortalité	Rate of natural increase Taux d'accroiss-ement naturel	Code[a]	Infant deaths — Décès d'enfants de moins d'un an Number Nombre	Rate (per 1000 births) Taux (par 1000 naiss-ances)	Expectation of life at birth — Espérance de vie à la naissance Male Masculin	Female Féminin	Total fertility rate L'indice synthétique de fécondité
EUROPE													
Gibraltar[35]													
2000	C	408	15.1	C	262	9.7	5.4	...	...	...	...	...	...
2001	C	399	14.1	C	249	8.8	5.3	...	...	...	...	...	...
2002	C	371	13.0	C	242	8.5	4.5	...	...	...	...	...	...
Greece - Grèce													
1998	C	100 894	9.6	C	102 668	9.8	-0.2	C	674	6.7	75.3	80.5	1.292
1999	C	116 038	11.0	C	103 304	9.8	1.2	C	619	5.3	...	...	1.300
2000	C	117 140	11.7	C	105 219	10.5	1.2	C	610	5.2	...	...	1.290
2001	C	102 282	10.2	C	102 559	10.2	0.0	C	522	5.1	...	...	1.290
2002	...	...	...	...	...	...	...	C	600	...	...	...	...
Holy See - Saint-Siège													
2000	C	1	...	C	10	...	...	C	-	...	...	...	...
Hungary - Hongrie													
1998	C	97 301	9.6	C	140 870	13.9	-4.3	C	944	9.7	66.1	75.2	1.326
1999	C	94 645	9.4	C	143 210	14.2	-4.8	C	798	8.4	66.3	75.1	1.285
2000	C	97 597	9.7	C	135 601	13.5	-3.8	C	900	9.2	67.1	75.6	1.330
2001	C	97 047	9.5	C	132 183	13.0	-3.4	C	789	8.1	68.2	76.5	1.313
2002	C	96 804	9.5	C	132 833	13.1	-3.5	C	693	7.2	68.3	76.6	1.305
Iceland - Islande													
1998	C	4 178	15.3	C	1 821	6.7	8.6	C	11	...	77.5	81.4	2.040
1999	C	4 100	14.8	C	1 901	6.9	7.9	C	10	...	77.8	81.5	1.989
2000	C	4 315	15.3	C	1 828	6.5	8.8	C	13	...	78.0	81.4	2.100
2001	C	4 091	14.4	C	1 725	6.1	8.3	C	11	...	78.4	82.6	1.950
2002	C	4 049	14.1	C	1 821	6.3	7.7	C	9	...	...	...	1.932
Ireland - Irlande[36]													
1998	+C	53 551	14.5	+C	31 437	8.5	6.0	+C	330	6.2	...	...	1.930
1999	+C	53 354	14.2	+C	31 683	8.5	5.8	+C	293	5.5	73.9	79.1	1.882
2000	+C	54 239	14.3	+C	31 115	8.2	6.1	+C	338	6.2	74.2	79.2	1.890
2001	+C	57 882	15.1	+C	29 812	7.8	7.3	+C	337	5.8	...	...	1.980
2002	+C	60 521	15.5	+C	29 381	7.5	7.9	+C	306	5.1	...	...	...
Isle of Man - Îles de Man													
1998	...	...	...	+C	893	12.1	...	+C	1	...	...	...	...
1999	+C	894	...	+C	983	...	...	+C	6	...	...	...	...
2000	+C	831	11.1	+C	897	12.0	-0.9	+C	5	...	...	...	...
2001	+C	863	11.3	+C	855	11.2	0.1	+C	-	...	...	...	...
2002	+C	903	11.7	+C	877	11.4	0.3	+C	3	...	...	...	...
Italy - Italie													
1998	C	515 439	9.0	C	574 231	10.0	-1.0	C	2 803	5.4	...	...	1.205
1999	C	523 463	9.1	C	571 356	9.9	-0.8	C	2 723	5.2	76.0	82.1	1.229
2000	C	543 039	9.4	C	560 241	9.7	-0.3	C	2 461	4.5	...	...	1.249
2001	C	535 282	9.2	C	555 247	9.6	-0.3	C	2 514	4.7	...	...	1.240
2002	C	537 070	9.3	C	556 006	9.7	-0.3	...	...	...	...	...	...
Latvia - Lettonie[12]													
1998	C	18 410	7.6	C	34 200	14.2	-6.6	C	276	15.0	64.1	75.5	1.093
1999	C	19 396	8.1	C	32 844	13.7	-5.6	C	219	11.3	64.9	76.2	1.162
2000	C	20 248	8.5	C	32 205	13.6	-5.0	C	210	10.4	64.9	76.0	1.237
2001	C	19 664	8.3	C	32 991	14.0	-5.7	C	217	11.0	65.2	76.6	1.207
2002	C	20 044	8.6	C	32 498	13.9	-5.3	C	197	9.8	65.4	76.8	1.232
Liechtenstein													
2001	...	...	...	C	220	6.6	...	...	...	...	...	...	...
2002	C	395	11.7	C	215	6.4	5.3	C	1	...	...	...	...
Lithuania - Lituanie[12]													
1998	C	37 019	10.4	C	40 757	11.5	-1.1	C	343	9.3	66.5	76.9	1.360
1999	C	36 415	10.3	C	40 003	11.4	-1.0	C	315	8.7	67.1	77.4	1.350
2000	C	34 149	9.8	C	38 919	11.1	-1.4	C	294	8.6	67.6	77.9	1.391
2001	C	31 546	9.1	C	40 399	11.6	-2.5	C	250	7.9	65.9	77.4	1.296

4. Vital statistics summary and expectation of life at birth: 1998-2002
Aperçu des statistiques de l'état civil et espérance de vie à la naissance: 1998-2002 (continued — suite)

(See notes at end of table. — Voir notes à la fin du tableau.)

Continent, country or area and year / Continent, pays ou zone et année	Code[a]	Live births - Naissances vivantes Number Nombre	Crude birth rate Taux bruts de natalité	Code[a]	Deaths - Décès Number Nombre	Crude death rate Taux bruts de mortalité	Rate of natural increase Taux d'accroiss-ement naturel	Code[a]	Infant deaths - Décès d'enfants de moins d'un an Number Nombre	Rate (per 1000 births) Taux (par 1000 naiss-ances)	Expectation of life at birth - Espérance de vie à la naissance Male Masculin	Female Féminin	Total fertility rate L'indice synthétiq-ue de fécondité
EUROPE													
Lithuania - Lituanie[12]													
2002	c	30 014	8.7	c	41 072	11.8	-3.2	c	238	7.9	66.2	77.6	1.236
Luxembourg													
1998	c	5 386	12.7	c	3 901	9.2	3.5	c	27	...	...	...	...
1999	c	5 582	13.0	c	3 793	8.8	4.2	c	26	...	74.7	81.2	1.734
2000	c	5 723	13.1	c	3 754	8.6	4.5	c	29	...	74.8	81.0	1.778
2001	c	5 459	12.4	c	3 719	8.4	3.9	c	32	5.9	...	...	1.654
2002	c	5 345	12.0	c	3 744	8.4	3.6	c	27	...	...	...	1.625
Malta - Malte[37,38]													
1998	c	4 488	11.6	c	3 044	7.9	3.7	c	24	...	74.4	80.1	...
1999	c	4 308	11.1	c	3 097	8.0	3.1	c	31	7.2	75.1	79.3	...
2000	c	4 255	10.9	c	2 957	7.6	3.3	c	26	...	...	...	...
2001	c	3 859	9.8	c	2 935	7.4	2.3	c	17	...	76.1	80.9	1.720
2002	c	3 805	9.6	c	3 031	7.6	1.9	c	23	...	75.8	80.5	1.460
Monaco													
1998	c	681	...	c	538	...	...	...	...	...	...	...	...
2000	c	760	22.8	c	547	16.4	6.4	...	...	...	...	...	...
Netherlands - Pays-Bas[39]													
1998	c	199 408	12.7	c	137 482	8.8	3.9	c	1 035	5.2	^75.1	^80.5	1.628
1999	c	200 445	12.7	c	140 487	8.9	3.8	c	1 048	5.2	75.3	80.5	1.650
2000	c	206 619	13.0	c	140 527	8.8	4.2	c	1 059	5.1	...	...	...
2001	c	202 603	12.6	c	140 377	8.7	3.9	c	1 088	5.4	75.8	80.7	1.710
2002	c	202 083	12.5	c	142 355	8.8	3.7	c	1 028	5.1	76.0	80.7	1.731
Norway - Norvège[40]													
1998	c	58 352	13.2	c	44 112	10.0	3.2	c	232	4.0	75.5	81.3	1.814
1999	c	59 298	13.3	c	45 170	10.1	3.2	c	232	3.9	75.6	81.1	1.840
2000	c	59 234	13.2	c	44 002	9.8	3.4	c	225	3.8	76.0	81.4	1.851
2001	c	56 696	12.6	c	43 981	9.7	2.8	c	223	3.9	76.2	81.5	1.784
2002	c	55 434	12.2	c	44 465	9.8	2.4	c	192	3.5	76.4	81.5	1.754
Poland - Pologne													
1998	c	395 619	10.2	c	375 354	9.7	0.5	c	3 771	9.5	68.9	77.3	1.430
1999	c	382 002	9.9	c	381 415	9.9	0.0	c	3 381	8.9	68.8	77.5	1.360
2000	c	378 700	9.8	c	368 028	9.5	0.3	c	3 068	8.1	69.7	77.9	1.340
2001	c	368 205	9.5	c	363 220	9.4	0.1	c	2 823	7.7	...	...	1.290
2002	c	353 765	9.2	c	359 486	9.4	-0.1	c	2 662	7.5	...	...	...
Portugal													
1998	c	113 510	11.4	c	106 382	10.7	0.7	c	683	6.0	...	...	...
1999	c	116 002	11.6	c	107 871	10.8	0.8	c	671	5.8	72.0	79.1	1.489
2000	c	118 551	11.8	c	105 804	10.6	1.3	c	662	5.6	72.7	79.7	1.520
2001	c	112 774	11.0	c	105 092	10.2	0.7	c	567	5.0	...	...	1.420
2002	c	114 383	11.0	c	106 258	10.2	0.8	c	574	5.0	...	...	...
Republic of Moldova - République de Moldova[12]													
1998	c	41 332	11.3	c	39 922	10.9	0.4	c	738	17.9	64.0	71.4	1.490
1999	c	38 501	10.6	c	41 315	11.3	-0.8	c	714	18.5	63.7	71.0	1.360
2000	c	36 939	10.2	c	41 224	11.3	-1.2	c	681	18.4	...	...	...
2001	c	36 448	10.0	c	40 075	11.0	-1.0	c	597	16.4	64.5	71.8	1.249
2002	c	35 705	9.9	c	41 852	11.6	-1.7	c	528	14.8	64.4	71.7	1.211
Romania - Roumanie													
1998	c	237 297	10.5	c	269 166	12.0	-1.4	c	4 868	20.5	67.0	74.2	1.316
1999	c	234 600	10.4	c	265 194	11.8	-1.4	c	4 360	18.6	67.7	74.8	1.300
2000	c	234 521	10.5	c	255 820	11.4	-0.9	c	4 370	18.6	67.7	74.6	1.305
2001	c	220 368	10.0	c	259 603	11.7	-1.8	c	4 057	18.4	...	...	1.232
2002	c	210 529	9.7	c	269 666	12.4	-2.7	c	3 648	17.3	67.6	74.9	1.254

4. Vital statistics summary and expectation of life at birth: 1998-2002
Aperçu des statistiques de l'état civil et espérance de vie à la naissance: 1998-2002 (continued — suite)

(See notes at end of table. — Voir notes à la fin du tableau.)

Continent, country or area and year — Continent, pays ou zone et année	Live births — Naissances vivantes			Deaths — Décès			Rate of natural increase — Taux d'accroiss-ement naturel	Infant deaths — Décès d'enfants de moins d'un an			Expectation of life at birth — Espérance de vie à la naissance		Total fertility rate — L'indice synthétiq-ue de fécondité
	Code[a]	Number Nombre	Crude birth rate Taux bruts de natalité	Code[a]	Number Nombre	Crude death rate Taux bruts de mortalité		Code[a]	Number Nombre	Rate (per 1000 births) Taux (par 1000 naiss-ances)	Male Masculin	Female Féminin	
EUROPE													
Russian Federation - Fédération de Russie[12]													
1998	C	1 283 292	8.8	C	1 988 744	13.6	-4.8	C	21 097	16.4	...	...	...
1999	C	1 214 689	8.3	C	2 144 316	14.7	-6.4	C	20 731	17.1	59.9	72.4	1.170
2000	C	1 266 800	8.7	C	2 225 332	15.3	-6.6	C	19 286	15.2	...	...	...
2001	C	1 311 604	9.1	C	2 251 814	15.6	-6.5	C	19 104	14.6	...	...	...
San Marino - Saint-Marin													
1998	+C	285	10.9	+C	190	7.3	3.6	+C	4	...	...	...	4.110
1999		303	11.5		198	7.5	4.0		1	...	...	...	4.375
2000	+C	290	10.8	+C	188	7.0	3.8	+C	-	...	77.4	84.0	4.185
Serbia and Montenegro - Serbie-et-Montenegro													
1998	C	128 461	12.1	C	113 312	10.7	1.4	C	1 791	13.9	...	...	1.693
1999	C	123 970	11.7	C	115 461	10.9	0.8	C	1 691	13.6	...	...	1.620
2000	C	125 868	11.8	C	118 078	11.1	0.7	C	1 668	13.3	70.1	75.0	1.640
2001	C	130 194	12.2	C	113 063	10.6	1.6	C	1 709	13.1	...	...	1.640
2002	...	...	...	...	...	...	...	C	1 635	...	...	...	...
Slovakia - Slovaquie													
1998	C	57 582	10.7	C	53 156	9.9	0.8	C	506	8.8	68.6	76.7	1.370
1999	C	56 223	10.4	C	52 402	9.7	0.7	C	467	8.3	69.0	77.0	1.330
2000	C	55 103	10.2	C	52 703	9.8	0.4	C	473	8.6	69.2	77.4	...
2001	C	51 136	9.5	C	51 980	9.7	-0.2	C	319	6.2	69.5	77.5	1.200
2002	C	50 841	9.5	C	51 532	9.6	-0.1	C	388	7.6	69.9	77.6	1.193
Slovenia - Slovénie													
1998	C	17 856	9.0	C	19 039	9.6	-0.6	C	93	5.2	^71.4	^78.8	1.234
1999	C	17 533	8.8	C	18 885	9.5	-0.7	C	79	4.5	^71.9	^79.1	1.210
2000	C	18 180	9.1	C	18 588	9.3	-0.2	C	89	4.9	...	...	1.260
2001	C	17 477	8.8	C	18 508	9.3	-0.5	C	74	4.2	72.1	79.6	1.211
2002	C	17 501	8.8	C	18 622	9.3	-0.6	C	67	3.8	...	...	1.212
Spain - Espagne													
1998	C	365 193	9.3	C	360 511	9.1	0.1	C	1 774	4.9	75.2	82.2	1.165
1999	C	380 130	9.6	C	371 102	9.4	0.2	C	1 700	4.5	...	...	1.200
2000	C	386 450	9.7	C	360 391	9.0	0.7	C	1 535	4.0	...	...	1.238
2001	C	407 135	10.1	C	351 147	8.7	1.4	C	1 394	3.4	...	...	1.242
Sweden - Suède													
1998	C	89 028	10.1	C	93 271	10.5	-0.5	C	316	3.5	76.9	81.9	1.510
1999	C	88 173	10.0	C	94 726	10.7	-0.7	C	297	3.4	77.1	81.9	1.497
2000	C	90 441	10.2	C	93 461	10.5	-0.3	C	309	3.4	...	...	1.574
2001	C	91 466	10.3	C	93 752	10.5	-0.3	C	334	3.7	77.6	82.1	1.570
2002	C	95 815	10.7	C	95 009	10.6	0.1	C	313	3.3	77.7	82.1	1.650
Switzerland - Suisse													
1998	C	78 949	11.1	C	62 568	8.8	2.3	C	376	4.8	^76.7	^82.6	1.776
1999	C	78 408	11.0	C	62 503	8.7	2.2	C	361	4.6	76.8	82.5	1.766
2000	C	78 458	10.9	C	62 528	8.7	2.2	C	386	4.9	76.9	82.6	1.496
2001	C	73 509	10.2	C	61 287	8.5	1.7	C	365	5.0	...	...	1.411
2002	C	72 372	9.9	C	61 768	8.5	1.5	C	326	4.5	...	...	...
The Former Yugoslav Rep. of Macedonia - L'ex-République yougoslave de Macédoine													
1998	C	29 244	14.6	C	16 870	8.4	6.2	C	476	16.3	^70.5	^74.8	...
1999	C	27 309	13.5	C	16 789	8.3	5.2	C	406	14.9	70.7	75.2	1.760
2000	C	29 308	14.5	C	17 253	8.5	6.0	C	346	11.8	...	...	1.760
2001	C	27 010	13.3	C	16 919	8.3	5.0	C	321	11.9	...	...	1.700
2002	C	27 761	13.6	C	17 962	8.8	4.8	C	283	10.2	...	...	...

(See notes at end of table. — Voir notes à la fin du tableau.)

Continent, country or area and year / Continent, pays ou zone et année	Live births - Naissances vivantes			Deaths - Décès			Rate of natural increase Taux d'accroiss-ement naturel	Infant deaths - Décès d'enfants de moins d'un an			Expectation of life at birth - Espérance de vie à la naissance		Total fertility rate L'indice synthétique de fécondité
	Code[a]	Number Nombre	Crude birth rate Taux bruts de natalité	Code[a]	Number Nombre	Crude death rate Taux bruts de mortalité		Code[a]	Number Nombre	Rate (per 1000 births) Taux (par 1000 naissances)	Male Masculin	Female Féminin	
EUROPE													
Ukraine[12]													
1998	C	419 238	8.3	C	719 954	14.3	-6.0	C	5 423	12.9	^63.0	^73.7	1.150
1999	...	...	...	C	739 170	14.8		C			...	...	
2000	C	385 126	7.7	C	758 082	15.2	-7.5	...	4 606	12.0	...	...	
2001	C	376 478	7.7	C	745 952	15.2	-7.5	C	4 283	11.4	...	...	
2002	C	390 688	8.1	C	754 911	15.6	-7.5	C	4 023	10.3	...	...	
United Kingdom - Royaume-Uni[41]													
1998	C	716 888	12.1	C	629 172	10.6	1.5	C	4 079	5.7	...	...	1.713
1999	C	699 976	11.8	C	632 062	10.6	1.1	C	4 045	5.8	75.0	79.8	1.686
2000	C	679 029	11.4	C	608 366	10.2	1.2	C	3 791	5.6	75.3	80.1	1.640
2001	C	669 123	11.2	C	602 268	10.1	1.1	C	3 664	5.5	...	...	1.630
2002	C	668 777	11.3	C	606 283	10.2	1.1	C	3 499	5.2	...	...	...
OCEANIA — OCEANIE													
American Samoa - Samoas américaines													
1998	C	1 688	30.3	C	243	4.4	25.9	C	27	...	...	...	...
1999	C	1 736	30.6	C	249	4.4	26.2	C	22	...	...	...	...
2000	C	1 730	30.0	C	224	3.9	26.1	C	11	...	...	...	...
Australia - Australie													
1998	+C	249 616	13.3	+C	127 202	6.8	6.5	+C	1 252	5.0	^76.6	^82.0	1.762
1999	+C	248 870	13.1	+C	128 102	6.8	6.4	+C	1 408	5.7	77.0	82.4	1.757
2000	+C	249 636	13.0	+C	128 291	6.7	6.3	+C	1 290	5.2	^77.4	^82.6	1.760
2001	+C	246 394	12.7	+C	128 544	6.6	6.1	+C	1 309	5.3	...	...	1.733
2002	+C	250 988	12.8	+C	133 707	6.8	6.0	+C	1 264	5.0	...	...	1.752
Cook Islands - Îles Cook													
1998	+C	386	22.2	+C	107	6.1	16.0	+C	8	...	...	...	...
1999	+C	346	21.1	+C	96	5.9	15.2	+C	5	...	...	...	...
2000	+C	309	17.3	+C	115	6.4	10.8	+C	6	...	...	...	...
2001	+C	313	17.2	+C	88	4.8	12.4	+C	4	...	...	...	...
2002	+C	224	12.2	+C	72	3.9	8.3	+C	2	...	...	...	...
Fiji - Fidji													
1998	+C	17 944	22.5	+C	5 241	6.6	15.9	+C	212	11.8	...	...	...
1999	+C	16 916	21.0	+C	3 603	4.5	16.5	+C	275	16.3	...	...	...
French Polynesia - Polynésie française													
1998	C	4 562	20.2	U	1 114	...	...	U	32	...	...	...	...
1999	C	4 580	20.1	U	1 003	...	...	U	31	...	...	...	...
2000	C	4 900	21.2	U	1 013	...	...	...	...	...	...	...	...
Guam[42]													
1998	C	4 322	28.9	C	651	4.3	24.5	C	34	7.9	...	...	...
1999	C	4 037	26.5	C	724	4.7	21.7	C	35	8.7	...	...	...
2000	C	3 790	24.5	C	667	4.3	20.2	C	23	...	...	...	...
2001	C	3 583	22.6	C	691	4.4	18.3	C	35	9.8	...	...	...
2002	C	3 222	20.0	C	658	4.1	15.9	C	20	...	...	...	...
Marshall Islands - Îles Marshall													
1998	+U	1 651	...	...	...	...	...	...	...	...	...	...	...
1999	+U	1 478	...	...	...	...	...	...	...	...	...	...	5.890
2001	+U	1 511	...	+U	271	...	...	+U	40	...	...	...	5.710
New Caledonia - Nouvelle-Calédonie													
1998	C	4 352	21.3	C	982	4.8	16.5	C	30	6.9	...	...	2.569
1999	C	4 316	20.8	C	1 095	5.3	15.5	C	27	...	69.8	75.8	2.523

(See notes at end of table. — Voir notes à la fin du tableau.)

Continent, country or area and year / Continent, pays ou zone et année	Code[a]	Live births / Naissances vivantes — Number / Nombre	Crude birth rate / Taux bruts de natalité	Code[a]	Deaths - Décès — Number / Nombre	Crude death rate / Taux bruts de mortalité	Rate of natural increase / Taux d'accroissement naturel	Code[a]	Infant deaths / Décès d'enfants de moins d'un an — Number / Nombre	Rate (per 1000 births) / Taux (par 1000 naissances)	Expectation of life at birth / Espérance de vie à la naissance — Male / Masculin	Female / Féminin	Total fertility rate / L'indice synthétique de fécondité
OCEANIA — OCEANIE													
New Caledonia - Nouvelle-Calédonie													
2000	C	4 566	21.6	C	1 077	5.1	16.5	C	21	...	...	...	...
2001	C	4 326	20.2	C	1 131	5.3	14.9	C	24	...	70.5	76.1	...
2002	C	4 194	19.3	C	1 121	5.2	14.1	C	29	...	...	...	...
New Zealand - Nouvelle-Zélande													
1998	+C	55 349	14.5	+C	26 206	6.9	7.6	+C	305	5.5	...	...	1.893
1999	+C	57 053	14.9	+C	28 122	7.3	7.5	+C	317	5.6	...	...	1.971
2000	+C	56 605	14.7	+C	26 660	6.9	7.8	+C	346	6.1	76.0	80.9	1.976
2001	+C	55 799	14.4	+C	27 825	7.2	7.2	+C	296	5.3	^76.7	^81.2	1.968
2002	+C	54 021	13.7	+C	28 065	7.1	6.6	+C	300	5.6	...	...	1.896
Niue - Nioué													
2002	...	*24*	...	...	*13*	...	...	...	-	...	...	...	...
Northern Mariana Islands - Îles Mariannes septentrionales													
1998	U	*1 421*	...	U	*180*	...	...	U	*15*	...	...	...	...
1999	U	*1 448*	...	U	*189*	...	...	U	*11*	...	...	...	...
Palau - Palaos													
1998	C	280	15.1	C	125	6.8	8.4	C	3	...	...	...	...
1999	C	250	13.2	C	131	6.9	6.3	C	5	...	...	...	...
Papua New Guinea - Papouasie-Nouvelle-Guinée													
2002	...	*175 824*	...	...	...	...	...	...	*1 078*	...	...	...	...
Samoa													
1998	...	...	...	U	*531*	...	...	U	*17*	...	...	...	...
Tonga													
1998	+C	2 737	27.6	+C	498	5.0	22.6	+C	29	...	69.8	71.8	4.048
1999	+C	2 599	26.0	+C	675	6.8	19.3	+C	48	18.5	...	...	3.523
2000	+C	2 471	24.6	+C	653	6.5	18.1	+C	28	...	...	...	3.677

GENERAL NOTES - NOTES GENERALES

Countries or areas not listed may be assumed to lack vital statistics of national scope. Crude birth, death and natural increase rates are computed per 1 000 mid-year population; infant mortality rates per 1 000 live births and total fertility rates are the sum of age-specific fertility rates per woman. For method of evaluation, and limitations of data, see Technical Notes for this table. For more precise information in terms of coverage, basis of tabulation, etc., see Tables 9, 15, 18 and 22. — Les pays et zones ne figurant pas au tableau n'ont vraisemblablement pas de statistiques de l'état civil de portée nationale. Les taux bruts de natalité, de mortalité et d'accroisement naturel sont calculés pour 1 000 personnes au milieu de l'année; les taux de mortalité infantile sont calculés pour 1 000 naissances vivantes et les indices synthétiques de fécondité sont la somme des taux de fécondité par âge par femme. Pour la méthode d'évaluation et les insuffisances des données, voir Notes techniques, pour ces tableaux. Pour plus de détails sur la portée, la base d'exploitation des données, etc., voir tableaux 9, 15, 18 et 22.

Italics: data from civil registers which are incomplete or of unknown completeness. — Italiques: données incomplètes ou dont le degré d'exactitude n'est pas connu provenant des registres de l'état civil.

FOOTNOTES - NOTES

^ The symbol '^' indicates that the figures for expectation of life at birth refer to more than one single year. For complete set of data on this topic, please see table 22. — Le symbole '^' indique que le chiffre pour l'expectation de vie a la naissance se réfère a une période d'années plutôt q'a un an seulement. Le tableau 22 présente l' l'information complète sur ce suject.

[a] 'Code' indicates the source of data, as follows:
C - Civil registration, estimated over 90% complete
U - Civil registration, estimated less than 90% complete
I - Other source, estimated reliable
+ - Indicates that events are counted when registered, not when they occurred.
... - Information not available

Le 'Code' indique la source des données, comme suit:
C - Registres de l'état civil considérés complets à 90 p. 100 au moins.
U - Registres de l'état civil qui ne sont pas considérés complets à 90 p. 100 au moins.
I - Autre source, considéré pas douteuses.
+ - Indique que les statistiques vitales sont comptées au moment de registration, pas au moment de l'évenement.
... - Information pas disponible.

[1] Excluding live-born infants who died before their birth was registered. - Non

compris les enfants nés vivants décédés avant l'enregistrement de leur naissance.

[2] For Algerian population only. - Pour la population algérienne seulement.

[3] Data refer to national projections. - Les données se referent aux projections nationales.

[4] For 1998, based on the results of the population census. Data for 1999 - 2002 refer to national projections - Pour 1998, d'après les résultats du recensement de la population.Les données pour 1999 - 2002 se referent aux projections nationales

[5] Data on births refer to the 1998 Population and Housing Census, adjusted for under-enumeration. - Les données sur les naissances referent au Recensement de la population et de l'habitat, ajustés pour compenser les lacunes de dénombrement.

[6] Data as reported by national statistical authorities; they may differ from data presented in other tables. - Les données comme elles ont été déclarées par l'institut national de la statistique; elles peuvent être différentes de ceux présentées dans autre tableaux.

[7] Including Canadian residents temporarily in the United States, but excluding United States residents temporarily in Canada. - Y compris les résidents canadiens se trouvant temporairement aux Etats-Unis, mais ne comprenant pas les résidents des Etats-Unis se trouvant temporairement au Canada.

[8] Excluding Indian jungle population. - Non compris les Indiens de la jungle.

[9] Data on live births and deaths are based on a civil registration system put in place in January 1998. - Les données sur les naissances et les décès sont basées sur un système d'enregistrement des faits d'état civil mis en place en janvier 1998.

[10] Excluding nomadic Indian tribes. - Non compris les tribus d'Indiens nomades.

[11] Including an upward adjustment for under-registration. - Y compris un ajustement pour sous-enregistrement.

[12] Excluding infants born alive with less than 28 weeks gestation, less than 1 000 grams in weight and 35 centimeters in length, who die within seven days of birth. - Non compris les enfants nés vivants avant 28 semaines de gestation, pesant moins de 1 000 grammes, mesurant moins de 35 centimètres et décédés dans les sept jours qui ont suivi leur naissance.

[13] For statistical purposes, the data for China do not include those for the Hong Kong Special Administrative Region (Hong Kong SAR), Macao Special Administrative Region (Macao SAR) and Taiwan province of China. - Pour la présentation des statistiques, les données pour Chine ne comprend pas la Région Administrative Spéciale de Hong Kong (Hong Kong RAS), la Région Administrative Spéciale de Macao (Macao RAS) et Taïwan province de Chine.

[14] Rates for 2000 - 2002 were obtained by the Sample Survey of Population Change 2002 in China. - Les taux pour 2000 - 2002 on été obtenus par la 2002 enquête de mouvement de la population par échantillon de la Chine.

[15] Data refer to government controlled areas. - Les données se raportent aux zones contrôlées par le Gouvernement.

[16] Including data for the Indian-held part of Jammu and Kashmir, the final status of which has not yet been determined. - Y compris les données pour la partie du Jammu et du Cachemire occupée par l'Inde dont le statut définitif n'a pas encore été déterminé.

[17] Rates were obtained by the Sample Registration System of India, a large demographic survey. - Les taux ont été obtenus par le Système de l'enregistrement par échantillon de l'Inde qui est au fait une large enquête démographique.

[18] Published by the United Nations Economic and Social Commission for Western Asia. - Publié par la Commission économique et sociale des Nations Unies pour l'Asie occidentale.

[19] Including data for East Jerusalem and Israeli residents in certain other territories under occupation by Israeli military forces since June 1967. - Y compris les données pour Jérusalem-Est et les résidents israéliens dans certains autres territoires occupés depuis 1967 par les forces armées israéliennes.

[20] Data refer to Japanese nationals in Japan only. - Les données se raportent aux nationaux japonais au Japon seulement.

[21] Excluding data for Jordanian territory under occupation since June 1967 by Israeli military forces. Excluding foreigners, including registered Palestinian refugees. - Non compris les données pour le territoire jordanien occupé depuis juin 1967 par les forces armées israéliennes. Non compris les étrangers, mais y compris les réfugiés de Palestine enregistrés.

[22] Excluding alien armed forces, civilian aliens employed by armed forces, and foreign diplomatic personnel and their dependants. - Non compris les militaires étrangers, les civils étrangers employés par les forces armées ni le personnel diplomatique étranger et les membres de leur famille les accompagnant.

[23] For 2001, data refer to last twelve months preceding census on June 2001. - - Pour 2001, les données se rapportent pour la dernière fois à douze mois précédant le recensement juin 2001.

[24] Data refer to the recorded events in Ministry of Health hospitals and health centres only. - Les données se rapportent aux faits d'état-civil enregistrés dans les hôpitaux et les dispensaires du Ministère de la santé seulement.

[25] Based on the results of the Population Growth Survey. - D'après les résultats de la 'Population Growth Survey.'

[26] Excluding data for the Pakistan-held part of Jammu and Kashmir, the final status of which has not yet been determined. - Non compris les données concernant la partie du Jammu et Cachemire occupée par le Pakistan dont le statut définitif n'a pas été déterminé.

[27] Excluding transients afloat and non-locally domiciled military and civilian services personnel and their dependants. - Non compris les personnes de passage þ bord de navires, ni les militaires et agents civils domiciliés hors du territoire et les membres de leur famille les accompagnant.

[28] Excluding nomad population and Palestinian refugees. - Non compris la population nomade et les réfugiés de Palestine.

[29] Including late registered deaths. - Y compris les décès enregistrés tardivement.

[30] Based on the results of the Population Demographic Survey. - D'après les résultats de la Population Demographic Survey.

[31] Including armed forces stationed outside the country, but excluding alien armed forces stationed in the area. - Y compris les militaires nationaux hors du pays, mais non compris les militaires étrangers en garnison sur le territoire.

[32] Excluding Faeroe Islands and Greenland. - Non compris les Iles Féroé et Gröenland.

[33] Including nationals temporarily outside the country. - Y compris les nationaux se trouvant temporairement hors du pays.

[34] Including armed forces stationed outside the country. - Y compris les militaires nationaux hors du pays.

[35] Excluding armed forces. - Non compris les militaires en garnison.

[36] Events registered within one year of occurrence. - Evénements enregistrés dans l'année qui suit l'événement.

[37] Rates computed on population including civilian nationals temporarily outside the country. - Les taux sont calculés sur la base d'un chiffre de population qui comprend les civils nationaux temporairement hors du pays.

[38] Live births to Maltese parents only. - Naissances vivantes aux parents maltais seulement.

[39] Including residents outside the country if listed in a Netherlands population register. - Y compris les résidents hors du pays, s'ils sont inscrits sur un registre de population néerlandais.

[40] Including residents temporarily outside the country. - Y compris les résidents se trouvant temporairement hors du pays.

[41] Data revised to exclude births in Northern Ireland to non-residents of Northern Ireland. - Données révisées non compris des naissances en Irlande du Nord aux non-résidents de l'Irlande du Nord.

[42] Including United States military personnel, their dependants and contract employees. - Y compris les militaires des Etats-Unis, les membres de leur famille les accompagnant et les agents contractuels des Etats-Unis.

Table 5

Table 5 presents national estimates of mid-year population for all available years between 1993 and 2002.

Description of variables: Mid-year estimates of the total population are those provided by national statistical offices. They refer to the *de facto* or *de jure* population on 1 July. In cases where the reference date is not mid-year (1 July) a footnote is appended. The data are presented in thousands, rounded by the Statistics Division.

Unless otherwise indicated, all estimates relate to the population within present geographical boundaries. Major exceptions to this principle are explained in footnotes.

Reliability of data: Reliable mid-year population estimates are those which are based on a complete census (or on a sample survey) and have been adjusted on a basis of a continuous population register or on the balance of births, deaths and migration. Reliable mid-year estimates appear in roman type. Mid-year estimates which are not calculated on this basis are considered less reliable and are shown in *italics*.

Limitations: Statistics on estimates of the mid-year total population are subject to the same qualifications as have been set forth for population statistics in general in section 3 of the Technical Notes.

International comparability of mid-year population estimates is also affected by the fact that some of these estimates refer to the *de jure*, and not the *de facto*, population. These are indicated in the column titled "Type". The difference between the *de facto* and the *de jure* population is discussed in section 3.1.1 of the Technical Notes.

Earlier data: Estimates of mid-year population have been shown in previous issues of the *Demographic Yearbook* . Information on the years and specific topics covered is presented in the Historical Index.

Tableau 5

Le tableau 5 présente des estimations nationales de la population en milieu d'année pour le plus grand nombre possible d'années entre 1993 et 2002.

Description des variables : Les estimations de la population totale en milieu d'année sont celles qui ont été communiquées par les services nationaux de statistique. Elles correspondent à la population de fait ou se réfèrent à la population de droit, au 1er juillet. Lorsque la date est différente, cela est signalé par une note. Sauf indication contraire, tous les chiffres sont exprimés en milliers. Les données ont été arrondies par la Division de statistique de l'ONU.

Sauf indication contraire, toutes les estimations se rapportent à la population présente sur le territoire actuel des pays ou zones considérés. Les principales exceptions à cette règle sont expliquées en note.

Fiabilité des données : Les estimations de la population en milieu d'année sont considérées sûres quand elles sont fondées sur un recensement complet (ou sur une enquête par sondage) qui a été ajusté en fonction des données provenant d'un registre permanent de population ou en fonction des naissances, décès et mouvements migratoires qui ont eu lieu pendant la période. Les estimations en milieu d'année sont considérées comme sûres et apparaissent en caractères romains. Les estimations en milieu d'année dont le calcul n'a pas été effectué sur cette base sont considérées comme moins sûres et apparaissent en italique.

Insuffisance des données : Les statistiques concernant les estimations de la population totale en milieu d'année appellent toutes les réserves qui ont été formulées à la section 3 des Notes techniques à propos des statistiques de la population en général.

Le fait que certaines des estimations concernant la population en milieu d'année se réfèrent à la population de droit et non à la population de fait influe sur la comparabilité internationale. Ces cas ont été signalés dans la colonne « Type ». La différence entre la population de fait et la population de droit est expliquée à la section 3.1.1 des Notes techniques.

Données publiées antérieurement : Des estimations de la population en milieu d'année ont été publiées dans des éditions antérieures de l'*Annuaire démographique*. Pour plus de précisions concernant les années et les sujets pour lesquels des données ont été publiées, se reporter à l'index.

(See notes at end of table. — Voir notes à la fin du tableau.)

Continent and country or area / Continent et pays ou zone	Ty-pe	Population estimates (in thousands) — Estimations (en milliers)									
		1993	1994	1995	1996	1997	1998	1999	2000	2001	2002
AFRICA — AFRIQUE											
Algeria - Algérie	DJ	26 894	27 496	28 060	28 566	29 045	29 507	29 965	30 416	30 879	31 357
Benin - Bénin	DF	5 075	5 242	5 412	5 594	5 639	5 816	5 990	6 169	6 417	...
Botswana	DF	1 391	1 425	1 459	1 496	1 533	1 572	1 611	1 653	...	...
Burkina Faso	DF	9 682	9 889	10 200	...	11 087	10 683	...	...	...	...
Burundi	DF	5 769	5 875	5 982	6 088	6 194	6 300	6 483	...	...	...
Cameroon - Cameroun	DF	...	...	13 277	...	14 298	14 439	...	...	...	...
Cape Verde - Cap-Vert	DF	...	...	386	396	407	417	428	435	445	453
Central African Republic - République centrafricaine	DF	...	2 998	...	...	3 245	...	...	...	...	...
Chad - Tchad	DF	6 098	6 214	...	...	...	...	...	...	8 322	...
Côte d'Ivoire	DF	13 175	13 695	14 230	14 781	...	15 367	...	16 398	16 939	...
Egypt - Égypte	DF	55 201	56 344	57 510	58 755	60 080	61 341	62 652	63 976	65 292	66 628
Ethiopia - Éthiopie	DF	53 236	...	54 649	56 372	58 117	59 882	61 672	63 495	65 374	67 220
Gabon	DF	1 015	1 040	1 066	1 093	1 120	1 148	1 177	1 206	1 237	...
Gambia - Gambie	DF	...	...	...	...	...	...	1 385	1 393	1 420	...
Ghana	DF	...	...	...	...	...	...	...	18 412	...	...
Kenya	DF	26 000	...	...	...	28 945	29 630	28 687	29 208	30 865	31 517
Lesotho	DF	...	...	...	...	2 012	2 055	2 100	2 144	...	...
Liberia - Libéria	DF	2 640	2 700	2 760	2 820	2 879	...	...	...	...	...
Libyan Arab Jamahiriya - Jamahiriya arabe libyenne[1]	DF	4 156	4 274	4 395	4 519	4 648	4 772	4 958	5 125	5 300	5 484
Malawi[2]	DF	9 135	9 461	9 788	10 114	10 441	...	10 153	10 475	10 816	11 175
Mali	DF	...	...	...	...	11 480	...	...	10 400	...	...
Mauritania - Mauritanie	DF	2 156	2 211	2 284	2 351	2 421	2 493	2 568	2 645	2 724	...
Mauritius - Maurice	DJ	1 097	1 113	1 122	1 134	1 148	1 160	1 175	1 187	1 200	1 210
Morocco - Maroc	DF	26 069	25 926	26 386	26 848	27 310	27 775	28 238	28 705	29 170	29 631
Mozambique[3]	DF	15 583	16 614	15 820	16 177	16 543	16 917	17 299	17 691	17 656	...
Namibia - Namibie	DF	...	...	...	...	...	...	...	1 817	...	...
Nigeria - Nigéria[2]	DF	...	...	99 210	...	...	...	...	115 224	118 801	122 444
Réunion	DF	632	...	...	669	686	698	710	722	735	748
Saint Helena ex. dep. - Sainte-Hélène sans dép.	DF	6	5	5	5	...	...	...	...	...	...
Sao Tome and Principe - Sao Tomé-et-Principe	DF	122	125	127	...	...	...	...	...	...	...
Senegal - Sénégal	DF	7 913	8 127	8 347	8 572	8 802	9 038	9 279	9 524	9 803	...
Seychelles	DF	72	74	75	76	77	79	80	81	81	81
Sierra Leone	DF	4 225	4 323	4 421	4 522	4 625	4 730	4 836	4 944	5 054	5 167
South Africa - Afrique du Sud[3]	DF	37 802	38 630	39 477	40 342	41 227	42 130	43 054	43 686	44 328	45 454
Sudan - Soudan	DF	25 588	26 289	27 008	27 747	28 507	29 266	30 046	31 081	31 627	32 468
Swaziland	DF	851	879	908	938	...	...	...	...	...	...
Togo	DF	...	3 928	...	...	...	...	...	...	...	...
Tunisia - Tunisie	DF	8 657	8 815	8 958	9 089	9 215	9 333	9 456	9 564	9 674	9 782
Uganda - Ouganda	DF	...	...	19 263	19 848	20 752	21 467	22 207	22 972	22 788	...
United Republic of Tanzania - République Unie de Tanzanie	DF	26 732	27 495	28 279	29 086	29 984	...	...	...	...	...
Zambia - Zambie	DF	8 458	8 764	9 112	9 454	9 780	10 096	10 407	9 337	10 089	10 409
Zimbabwe	DF	10 779	11 150	11 526	11 908	12 294	12 685	13 079	...	12 960	...
AMERICA, NORTH — AMERIQUE DU NORD											
Anguilla	DF	9	10	10	10	10	11	11	11	12	12
Antigua and Barbuda - Antigua-et-Barbuda	DF	66	66	68	69	...	...	...	...	...	...
Aruba	DJ	74	78	80	83	86	88	90	91	92	94
Bahamas	DF	269	274	279	284	288	293	298	303	309	...
Barbados - Barbade	DF	264	264	264	265	...	266	267	267	...	...
Belize	DF	205	211	216	222	230	238	243	250	257	265
Bermuda - Bermudes[4]	DJ	60	61	61	62	62	62	63	63	62	...
British Virgin Islands - Îles Vierges britanniques	DF	...	...	...	...	...	...	...	...	21	...

5. Estimates of mid-year population: 1993 - 2002
Estimations de la population au milieu de l'anneé: 1993 - 2002 (continued — suite)

(See notes at end of table. — Voir notes à la fin du tableau.)

Continent and country or area / Continent et pays ou zone	Type / Type	Population estimates (in thousands) — Estimations (en milliers)									
		1993	1994	1995	1996	1997	1998	1999	2000	2001	2002
AMERICA, NORTH — AMERIQUE DU NORD											
Canada[5,6,7]	DJ	28 682	28 999	29 302	29 611	29 907	30 157	30 404	30 689	31 021	31 373
Cayman Islands - Îles Caïmanes	DJ	31	31	33	34	36	38	39	40	41	40
Costa Rica	DJ	3 005	3 071	3 136	3 202	3 271	3 341	3 413	3 486	3 907	3 998
Cuba	DF	10 904	10 950	10 978	11 006	11 066	11 117	11 160	11 199	11 230	11 251
Dominica - Dominique	DF	72	72	73	72	72	72	72	72	71	70
Dominican Republic - République dominicaine	DF	7 620	7 769	7 705	7 833	7 966	8 105	8 325	8 396	8 528	...
El Salvador	DF	...	...	5 669	5 787	5 908	6 031	6 154	6 276	6 397	6 518
Greenland - Groenland	DJ	55	56	56	56	56	56	56	...	...	...
Grenada - Grenade[8]	DF	97	98	98	99	100	100	101	101	101	...
Guadeloupe[9]	DJ	396	400	405	409	414	419	424	428	432	437
Guatemala[3]	DF	9 466	9 717	9 976	10 243	10 517	10 799	11 088	11 385	11 683	11 987
Haiti - Haïti	DJ	6 903	7 041	7 180	7 336	7 492	7 647	7 803	7 959	8 132	...
Honduras	DF	5 319	5 460	5 606	5 755	5 908	6 057	6 211	6 369	6 530	6 695
Jamaica - Jamaïque	DF	2 444	2 473	2 503	2 527	2 553	2 572	2 590	2 605	2 621	...
Martinique	DJ	364	367	369	372	376	379	382	385	387	389
Mexico - Mexique	DJ	88 755	90 386	91 992	93 572	95 127	96 649	98 132	100 249	101 754	103 229
Montserrat	DF	...	...	...	...	...	...	...	5	...	...
Netherlands Antilles - Antilles néerlandaises[10]	DJ	194	198	202	205	208	208	205	...	...	...
Nicaragua	DJ	4 175	4 299	4 427	4 549	4 674	4 803	4 936	4 957	5 059	5 162
Panama	DF	2 535	2 583	2 631	2 674	2 719	2 764	2 809	2 856	2 897	3 060
Puerto Rico - Porto Rico[11,12]	DJ	3 600	3 627	3 655	3 685	3 716	3 748	3 782	3 818	3 840	3 859
Saint Kitts and Nevis - Saint-Kitts-et-Nevis	DF	44	43	44	42	41	40	42	40	46	...
Saint Lucia - Sainte-Lucie	DF	140	143	145	147	150	152	154	156	158	159
Saint Pierre and Miquelon - Saint Pierre-et-Miquelon	DF	7	7	7	7	...	...	...	...	...	...
Saint Vincent and the Grenadines - Saint Vincent-et-les Grenadines	DF	110	110	111	111	112	111	112	112	109	108
Trinidad and Tobago - Trinité-et-Tobago	DF	1 247	1 250	1 260	1 264	1 275	1 278	...	1 290	...	1 276
United States - États-Unis[13]	DJ	258 083	260 599	263 044	265 463	268 008	270 299	272 691	275 265	284 797	288 369
United States Virgin Islands - Îles Vierges américaines[11]	DJ	107	107	108	108	108	109	109	109	109	109
AMERICA, SOUTH — AMERIQUE DU SUD											
Argentina - Argentine	DF	33 869	34 318	34 768	35 220	35 672	36 125	36 578	37 032	37 487	37 944
Bolivia - Bolivie[3]	DF	7 065	7 237	7 414	7 588	7 767	7 950	8 137	8 329	8 274	...
Brazil - Brésil[14]	DF	151 572	153 726	155 822	157 872	159 636	161 790	165 371	167 724	172 386	174 633
Chile - Chili	DF	13 771	13 994	14 210	14 419	14 622	14 822	15 018	15 211	15 402	15 589
Colombia - Colombie	DF	33 951	37 849	38 542	39 296	40 064	40 827	41 589	42 321	43 071	43 834
Ecuador - Équateur[15]	DF	10 981	11 221	11 460	11 698	11 773	11 948	12 121	12 299	12 480	12 661
French Guiana - Guyane française	DJ	128	133	137	142	148	153	158	164	170	175
Guyana	DF	...	...	...	...	775	773	771	772	...	<773
Paraguay	DF	4 575	4 700	4 828	4 955	5 085	5 219	5 356	...	...	...
Peru - Pérou[3,16]	DF	23 009	23 421	23 837	24 258	24 681	25 104	25 525	25 939	26 347	26 749
Suriname	DF	422	428	434	440	446	452	458	464	470	476
Uruguay[3]	DF	3 171	3 193	3 217	3 241	3 263	3 284	3 303	3 322	3 342	3 361
Venezuela[3,16]	DF	20 910	21 377	21 844	22 502	22 959	23 413	23 867	24 311	24 766	25 220
ASIA — ASIE											
Afghanistan[17]	DF	...	...	...	...	...	...	...	...	...	20 298

(See notes at end of table. — Voir notes à la fin du tableau.)

Continent and country or area / Continent et pays ou zone	Type	Population estimates (in thousands) — Estimations (en milliers)									
		1993	1994	1995	1996	1997	1998	1999	2000	2001	2002
ASIA — ASIE											
Armenia - Arménie[18]	...	3 731	3 747	3 760	3 774	3 786	3 795	3 801	3 803	3 802	<3 213
Azerbaijan - Azerbaïdjan	DF	7 495	7 597	7 685	7 763	7 838	7 913	7 983	8 049	8 111	8 172
Bahrain - Bahreïn	DF	530	544	559	574	589	605	621	638	655	672
Bangladesh	DF	...	117 700	119 900	122 100	124 300	...	...	...	...	...
Bhutan - Bhoutan	DF	548	564	582	600	619	638	658	678	699	716
Brunei Darussalam - Brunéi Darussalam	DF	274	280	287	294	302	310	317	325	...	341
Cambodia - Cambodge[19]	DF	9 315	9 869	10 200	10 340	10 368	...	<12 351	<12 574	<12 803	<13 041
China - Chine[20,21]	DF	1 185 170	1 198 500	1 211 210	1 223 890	1 236 260	1 248 100	1 259 090	...	...	...
China: Hong Kong SAR - Chine: Hong Kong RAS[22]	...	5 901	6 035	6 156	6 436	6 489	6 544	6 606	6 665	6 725	6 787
China: Macao SAR - Chine: Macao RAS	DJ	384	397	409	415	417	422	427	431	434	439
Cyprus - Chypre[23,24]	DJ	720	731	742	751	759	767	774	782	789	797
Georgia - Géorgie	DF	5 440	5 426	5 417	5 420	5 431	5 441	5 101	5 023	<4 946	...
India - Inde[25]	DF	887 566	905 449	923 459	941 579	959 792	978 081	996 430	1 014 825	1 033 248	1 050 640
Indonesia - Indonésie	DF	187 590	190 676	...	198 320	201 353	204 392	207 440	...	208 437	211 063
Iran (Islamic Republic of) - Iran (République islamique d')	DJ	57 488	58 331	59 187	...	60 939	61 836	62 746	63 664	64 528	65 540
Iraq	DF	19 478	20 007	20 536	21 124	22 046	22 379	22 989	23 577	24 813	...
Israel - Israël[3,26]	DJ	5 261	5 399	5 545	5 685	5 829	5 971	6 125	6 289	6 439	6 570
Japan - Japon[27]	DF	124 829	125 178	125 472	125 757	126 057	126 400	126 631	126 843	127 130	127 401
Jordan - Jordanie[28]	DF	>3 993	...	>4 291	>4 444	>4 600	>4 756	>4 900	>5 039	>5 182	>5 329
Kazakhstan	DF	16 381	16 146	15 816	15 578	15 334	15 073	14 928	14 884	14 858	14 859
Korea (Republic of) - Corée (République de)[29]	DF	44 195	44 642	45 093	45 546	45 954	46 287	46 617	47 008	47 343	47 640
Kuwait - Koweït	DF	1 461	1 620	1 802	1 894	1 980	2 027	2 107	2 190	2 275	2 262
Kyrgyzstan - Kirghizistan	DF	4 543	4 540	4 590	4 657	4 725	4 797	4 865	4 915	4 955	4 993
Lao People's Democratic Republic - République démocratique populaire lao	DF	...	...	4 536	...	...	...	5 091	5 218	...	5 500
Malaysia - Malaisie	DF	19 564	20 112	20 689	21 169	20 996	21 475	21 852	23 495	...	...
Maldives	DF	238	246	...	251	259	267	278	271	276	281
Mongolia - Mongolie	DF	2 172	2 207	2 243	2 276	2 307	2 340	2 373	2 407	2 443	2 475
Myanmar	DF	43 116	43 922	...	...	46 402	...	...	...	...	...
Nepal - Népal	DJ	19 394	19 862	20 341	20 832	21 331	21 843	22 367	22 904	...	...
Occupied Palestinian Territory - Territoire palestinien occupé	DF	...	2 317	2 483	2 631	2 783	2 897	3 020	3 150	3 299	3 465
Oman	DF	2 000	2 050	2 131	2 214	2 256	2 288	2 325	2 401	2 478	...
Pakistan[30]	DF	116 470	119 390	122 360	125 380	128 420	131 510	134 510	137 510	140 470	144 852
Philippines	DJ	66 982	68 624	70 267	69 952	71 550	73 148	74 746	76 348	77 926	79 504
Qatar	DF	559	593	...	...	...	544	...	579	598	...
Saudi Arabia - Arabie saoudite	DF	17 329	17 720	18 123	18 537	18 963	19 402	19 895	20 847	...	22 000
Singapore - Singapour	DF	3 315	3 421	3 526	3 670	3 794	3 922	3 951	4 018	4 131	4 171
Sri Lanka	DF	17 646	17 891	18 136	18 315	18 552	18 774	19 043	19 359	18 700	19 007
Syrian Arab Republic - République arabe syrienne[31]	DF	13 393	13 844	14 153	14 619	15 100	15 597	16 110	16 320	16 720	17 130
Tajikistan - Tadjikistan	DF	5 638	5 745	5 836	5 919	...	6 103	6 237	6 170	6 293	6 433
Thailand - Thaïlande	DJ	58 010	58 713	59 401	60 003	60 602	61 156	61 564	61 770	...	63 482
Turkey - Turquie	DF	59 491	60 612	61 737	62 873	64 015	65 157	66 293	67 420	68 529	69 626
Turkmenistan - Turkménistan	DF	4 308	4 406	4 509	4 569	...	4 859	...	...	...	...
United Arab Emirates - Émirats arabes unis[32]	DF	...	...	2 314	2 443	2 624	2 776	2 938	...	...	...
Uzbekistan - Ouzbékistan	DF	21 852	22 282	22 690	23 130	23 560	24 051	23 954	24 650	24 964	25 368
Viet Nam	DF	71 026	72 510	73 962	75 355	74 346	75 526	76 597	77 686	...	79 727
Yemen - Yémen	DF	12 302	14 859	15 369	15 915	16 484	17 072	17 671	18 261	18 863	19 495

5. Estimates of mid-year population: 1993 - 2002
Estimations de la population au milieu de l'anneé: 1993 - 2002 (continued — suite)

(See notes at end of table. — Voir notes à la fin du tableau.)

Continent and country or area / Continent et pays ou zone	Type	Population estimates (in thousands) — Estimations (en milliers)									
		1993	1994	1995	1996	1997	1998	1999	2000	2001	2002
EUROPE											
Albania - Albanie	DF	3 485	3 547	3 609	3 650	3 731	3 791	...	...	...	...
Andorra - Andorre	DF	63	65	...	...	66	66	66	66	66	66
Austria - Autriche	DJ	7 991	8 030	8 047	8 059	8 072	8 078	8 092	8 109	8 030	8 053
Belarus - Bélarus	DF	10 356	10 308	10 281	10 250	10 220	10 191	10 035	10 002	9 973	9 925
Belgium - Belgique	DJ	10 084	10 116	10 137	10 157	10 181	10 203	10 226	10 251	10 287	10 333
Bosnia and Herzegovina - Bosnie-Herzégovine	DJ	4 434	4 459	4 180	4 174	3 738	3 653	...	...		3 828
Bulgaria - Bulgarie	DF	8 472	8 444	8 406	8 363	8 312	8 257	8 211	8 170	7 910	7 869
Channel Islands: Guernsey - Îles Anglo-Normandes: Guernesey	DF	58	58	59	59	59	59	60	60	...	...
Channel Islands: Jersey - Îles Anglo-Normandes: Jersey	DF	84	84	84		...	...	...	...	...	...
Croatia - Croatie	DJ	4 641	4 649	4 669	4 494	4 572	4 501	4 554	4 381	4 437	4 443
Czech Republic - République tchèque	DJ	10 331	10 336	10 331	10 315	10 304	10 295	10 283	10 273	10 224	10 201
Denmark - Danemark[33]	DJ	5 189	5 205	5 228	5 262	5 284	5 301	5 327	5 337	5 359	5 376
Estonia - Estonie	DF	1 517	1 499	1 484	1 469	1 458	1 450	1 442	1 370	1 364	1 359
Finland - Finlande	DJ	5 066	5 088	5 108	5 125	5 140	5 153	5 165	5 176	5 188	5 201
France[34]	DJ	57 467	57 659	57 844	58 026	58 610	58 398	58 623	58 893	59 192	59 486
Germany - Allemagne	DJ	81 187	81 422	81 661	81 896	82 061	82 029	82 057	82 183	82 350	82 488
Gibraltar[35]	DF	28	27	27	27	27	27	27	27	28	>29
Greece - Grèce[36]	DF	10 379	10 426	10 454	10 476	10 499	10 516	10 534	10 008	10 020	<10 969
Holy See - Saint-Siège[37]	DF	...	...	...	...	...	1	...	...	...	...
Hungary - Hongrie	DF	10 294	10 261	10 229	10 193	10 155	10 114	10 068	10 024	10 188	10 159
Iceland - Islande	DJ	264	266	267	269	271	274	277	281	285	288
Ireland - Irlande	DF	3 574	3 586	3 601	3 626	3 661	3 705	3 745	3 787	3 839	3 917
Isle of Man - Îles de Man	DJ	71	71	72	71	72	74		75	76	77
Italy - Italie	DJ	57 049	57 204	57 301	57 380	57 523	57 588	57 646	57 762	57 948	57 482
Latvia - Lettonie	DF	2 563	2 521	2 485	2 457	2 433	2 410	2 390	2 373	2 355	2 339
Liechtenstein	DF	>30	30	31	31	31	>32	>32	33	33	34
Lithuania - Lituanie	DJ	3 683	3 657	3 629	3 602	3 575	3 549	3 524	3 500	3 481	3 469
Luxembourg	DJ	397	403	409	414	419	425	430	436	442	446
Malta - Malte[38]	DJ	>373	>376	>378	>381	>384	>386	>389	>391	395	397
Monaco	DJ	...	...	...	...	32	...	33	33	...	...
Netherlands - Pays-Bas	DJ	15 290	15 383	15 459	15 531	15 611	15 707	15 812	15 908	16 046	16 149
Norway - Norvège[39]	DJ	4 312	4 325	4 359	4 381	4 405	4 431	4 462	4 491	4 514	4 538
Poland - Pologne[40]	DF	38 459	38 544	38 588	38 618	38 650	38 666	38 654	38 646	38 638	38 425
Portugal[41]	DF	9 881	9 902	9 916	9 927	9 946	9 968	9 989	10 008	10 296	10 368
Republic of Moldova - République de Moldova[42]	DJ	4 348	4 348	4 348	4 327	3 654	3 652	3 646	3 639	3 631	3 623
Romania - Roumanie	DJ	22 755	22 731	22 681	22 608	22 546	22 503	22 458	22 435	22 132	21 795
Russian Federation - Fédération de Russie	DF	148 146	147 968	147 774	147 739	147 105	146 539	145 943	<145 559	<143 954	...
San Marino - Saint-Marin	DF	24	25	25	25	26	26	26	27	...	...
Serbia and Montenegro - Serbie-et-Montenegro[43]	DJ	10 482	10 516	10 547	10 577	10 600	10 617	10 629	10 635	10 654	<10 662
Slovakia - Slovaquie	DJ	5 325	5 347	5 364	5 374	5 383	5 391	5 395	5 400	5 379	5 379
Slovenia - Slovénie	DJ	1 991	1 989	1 988	1 991	1 987	1 983	1 986	1 990	1 992	1 996
Spain - Espagne[44]	DJ	39 096	39 166	39 223	39 279	39 348	39 453	39 626	39 927	40 266	<40 851
Sweden - Suède	DJ	8 719	8 781	8 827	8 841	8 846	8 851	8 858	8 872	8 896	8 925
Switzerland - Suisse	DJ	6 938	6 994	7 041	7 072	7 089	7 110	7 144	7 184	7 233	7 290
The Former Yugoslav Rep. of Macedonia - L'ex-République yougoslave de Macédoine	...	...	...	1 963	1 975	1 997	2 008	2 017	2 024	2 035	<2 039
Ukraine	DF	52 244	52 114	51 728	51 334	50 894	50 500	50 106	49 711	<49 037	<48 402
United Kingdom - Royaume-Uni[45]	DF	58 198	58 401	58 612	58 807	59 014	59 237	59 501	59 756	59 756	59 232

(See notes at end of table. — Voir notes à la fin du tableau.)

Continent and country or area — Continent et pays ou zone	Type	Population estimates (in thousands) — Estimations (en milliers)									
		1993	1994	1995	1996	1997	1998	1999	2000	2001	2002
OCEANIA — OCEANIE											
American Samoa - Samoas américaines[11,46]	DJ	52	53	53	54	55	56	57	58	...	...
Australia - Australie[3]	DJ	17 667	17 855	18 072	18 311	18 518	18 711	18 926	19 153	19 413	19 641
Cook Islands - Îles Cook	DF	20	20	19	20	18	17	16	18	18	18
Fiji - Fidji	DF	771	784	796	775	...	797	806	...	...	...
French Polynesia - Polynésie française	DF	209	213	216	219	222	226	228	<231	...	...
Guam[11,12]	DJ	144	143	144	145	147	150	153	...	158	161
Kiribati	DF	...	...	78	...	83	...	...	...	...	...
Marshall Islands - Îles Marshall	DF	52	54	56	57	61	63	51	53	55	57
Micronesia, Federated States of - Micronésie, États Fédérés de La	DJ	...	104	107	110	110	112	113	119	117	120
Nauru	DF	10	10	10	11	11	11	11	12	12	...
New Caledonia - Nouvelle-Calédonie	DF	184	189	194	197	201	204	208	211	214	217
New Zealand - Nouvelle-Zélande	DJ	3 572	3 620	3 673	3 732	3 781	3 815	3 835	3 858	3 880	3 939
Niue - Nioué	DF	...	...	...	...	...	...	...	...	...	2
Northern Mariana Islands - Îles Mariannes septentrionales	DF	...	...	...	61	64	67	69	72	75	78
Palau - Palaos	DF	16	17	17	18	18	18	19	19	20	20
Papua New Guinea - Papouasie-Nouvelle-Guinée	DF	3 922	3 997	4 074	...	4 209	4 600	...	5 100	...	5 462
Samoa	DF	...	164	...	...	...	168	169	171	...	...
Tonga	DF	>97	>97	>98	...	>99	>99	>100	>100	>101	>101
Vanuatu	DF	158	162	166	170	174	...	...	...	...	...

GENERAL NOTES - NOTES GENERALES

For certain countries or areas, there is a discrepancy between the mid-year population estimates shown in this table and those shown in subsequent tables for the same year. Usually this discrepancy arises because the estimates for a given year are revised, although the remaining tabulations are not. Unless otherwise indicated, data are official estimates of population for 1 July, or averages of end-year estimates. For method of evaluation and limitations of data, see Technical Notes for the present table. — Pour quelques pays ou zones il y a une discordance entres les estimations au milieu de l'année présentées dans ce tableau et celles présentées dans des tableaux suivants pour la même année. Habituellement ces différences apparaissent lorsque les estimations pour une certaine année ont été révisées; alors que les autres tabulations ne l'ont pas été. Sauf indication contraire, les données sont des estimations officielles de population au 1er juillet ou des moyennes d'estimations de fin d'année. Pour la méthode d'évaluation et les insuffisances des données, voir Notes techniques, pour ce tableau.

Italics: estimates which are less reliable. — Italiques: estimations moins sûres.

FOOTNOTES - NOTES

< Data refer to 1 January — Données se raportent au 1 Janvier.
> Data refer to 31 December — Données se raportent au 31 Décembre.

DF Estimates of population de facto. — Population de fait
DJ Estimates of population de jure. — Population de droit

[1] Data refer to Libyan nationals only. - Les données se raportent aux nationaux libyens seulement.
[2] Data for estimates refer to national projections. - Les données se referent aux projections nationales.
[3] Mid-year estimates have been adjusted for underenumeration, at latest census. - Les estimations au milieu de l'année tiennent compte d'une ajustement destiné à compenser les lacunes du dénombrement lors du dernier recensement.
[4] Excluding the institutional population. - Non compris la population dans les institutions.
[5] For 2001 and 2002, final postcensal estimates. - Pour 2001 et 2002, évaluations postcensal finales.
[6] From 1996 to 2000, final intercensal estimates. - De 1996 à 2000, estimations inter censitaires finales.
[7] From 1993 to 1995, revised intercensal estimates adjusted for net undercoverage. - De 1993 à 1995, estimations inter censitaires corrigées pour tenir en compte du sous dénombrement net.
[8] Including Carriacou and other dependencies in the Grenadines. - Y compris Carriacou et les autres dépendances du groupe des îles Grenadines.
[9] Including dependencies: Marie-Galante, la Désirade, les Saintes, Petite-Terre, St. Barthélemy and French part of St. Martin. - Y compris les dépendances: Marie-Galante, la Désirade, les Saintes, Petite-Terre, Saint-Barthélemy et la partie française de Saint-Martin.
[10] Comprising Bonaire, Curaçao, Saba, St. Eustatius and Dutch part of St. Martin. - Comprend Bonaire, Curaçao, Saba, Saint-Eustache et la partie néederlandaise de Saint-Martin.
[11] Including armed forces stationed in the area. - Y compris les militaires en garnison sur le territoire.
[12] Definition of urban and rural distribution changed from the year 2000. - La définition des régions urbaines et rurales a changée depuis 2000.
[13] Excluding civilian citizens absent from country for extended periods of time. - Non compris les civils hors du pays pendant une période prolongée.
[14] Data include persons in remote areas, military personel outside the country, merchant seamen at sea, civilian seasonal workers outside the country, and other civilians outside the country, and exclude nomads, foreign military, civilian aliens temporarily in the country, transients on ships and Indian jungle population. - Y compris les personnes dans des régions éloignées, le personel militaire en dehors du pays, les marins marchands, les ouvriers saisonniers civils de couture en dehors du pays, et autres civils en dehors du pays, et non compris les nomades,

les militaires étrangers, les étrangers civils temporairement dans le pays, les transiteurs sur des bateaux et les Indiens de la jungle.

[15] Excluding nomadic Indian tribes. - Non compris les tribus d'Indiens nomades.

[16] Excluding Indian jungle population. - Non compris les Indiens de la jungle.

[17] Data refer to the settled population based on the 1979 Population Census; an estimated 1.5 million nomads are not included. - Les données se rapportent a la population stationnaire a la base de recensement de 1979; les nomades, estimées a 1.5 million, ne sont pas inclus.

[18] Data for 2001 and before refer to de facto population and after 2001 de jure population. - Les données pour 2001 et les années antérieures se rapportent sur la population de fait et après 2001 sur la population de droit.

[19] Excluding foreign diplomatic personnel and their dependants. - Non compris le personnel diplomatique étranger et les membres de leur famille les accompagnant.

[20] For statistical purposes, the data for China do not include those for the Hong Kong Special Administrative Region (Hong Kong SAR), Macao Special Administrative Region (Macao SAR) and Taiwan province of China. - Pour la présentation des statistiques, les données pour Chine ne comprend pas la Région Administrative Spéciale de Hong Kong (Hong Kong RAS), la Région Administrative Spéciale de Macao (Macao RAS) et Taïwan province de Chine.

[21] Estimated data on the basis of the annual National Sample Survey on Population Changes. - Les données ont été estimées sur la base de l'enquête annuelle "National Sample Survey on Population Changes".

[22] Data for 1996 and before refer to defacto population and after 1996 de jure population. - Les données concernent la population de fait pour les années antérieures à 1996 et la population de droit pour les années postérieures.

[23] Estimates of the number of Turkish Cypriots from 1974 onwards are the result of population projections based on the age and sex structure of the Turkish Cypriot community as at Census 1960 and with assumptions of fertility and mortality similar to the rest of the Cyprus population. With regard to the migration of Turkish Cypriots after 1974, migration assumptions are based on figures obtained from Turkish Cypriot sources. Settlers from Turkey are not included. - - Les estimations du nombre de Chypriotes turcs depuis 1974 résultent des projections de population préparées sur la base de la structure par sexe et age de la communauté chypriote turque au recensement de 1960, et avec des hypothèses de fécondité et de mortalité similaires à celles du reste de la population de Chypre. En ce qui concerne la migration des Chypriotes turcs après 1974, les hypothèses sont basées sur les données obtenues de sources chypriotes turques. Les occupants venus de Turquie ne sont pas inclus.

[24] Data for the period 1993-2002 have been revised on the basis of the Population Census of 2001. - Les données pour 1993 à 2002 ont été calculées sur la base du recensement de population de 2001.

[25] Including data for the Indian-held part of Jammu and Kashmir, the final status of which has not yet been determined. - Y compris les données pour la partie du Jammu et du Cachemire occupée par l'Inde dont le statut définitif n'a pas encore été déterminé.

[26] Including data for East Jerusalem and Israeli residents in certain other territories under occupation by Israeli military forces since June 1967. - Y compris les données pour Jérusalem-Est et les résidents israéliens dans certains autres territoires occupés depuis 1967 par les forces armées israéliennes.

[27] For 1993 and 1994, excluding diplomatic personnel outside the country and foreign military and civilian personnel and their dependants stationed in the area. - Pour 1993 et 1994, non compris le personnel diplomatique hors du pays ni les militaires et agents civils étrangers en poste sur le territoire et les membres de leur famille les accompagnant.

[28] Excluding data for Jordanian territory under occupation since June 1967 by Israeli military forces. Excluding foreigners, including registered Palestinian refugees. - Non compris les données pour le territoire jordanien occupé depuis juin 1967 par les forces armées israéliennes. Non compris les étrangers, mais y compris les réfugiés de Palestine enregistrés.

[29] For 1993 and 1994, excluding alien armed forces, civilian aliens employed by armed forces, foreign diplomatic personnel and their dependants and Korean diplomatic personnel and their dependants outside the country. - For 1993 et 1994, non compris les militaires étrangers, les civils étrangers employés par les forces armées, le personnel diplomatique étranger et les membres de leur famille les accompagnant et le personnel diplomatique coréen hors du pays et les membres de leurs familles les accompagnant.

[30] Excluding data for the Pakistan-held part of Jammu and Kashmir, the final status of which has not yet been determined. - Non compris les données concernant la partie du Jammu et Cachemire occupée par le Pakistan dont le statut définitif n'a pas été déterminé.

[31] Including Palestinian refugees. - Y compris les réfugiés de Palestine.

[32] Comprising 7 sheikdoms of Abu Dhabi, Dubai, Sharjah, Ajaman, Umm al Qaiwain, Ras al Khaimah and Fujairah, and the area lying within the modified Riyadh line as announced in October 1955. - Comprend les sept cheikhats de Abou Dhabi, Dabai, Ghârdja, Adjmân, Oumm-al-Quiwaïn, Ras al Khaîma et Foudjaïra, ainsi que la zone délimitée par la ligne de Riad modifiée comme il a été annoncé en octobre 1955.

[33] Excluding Faeroe Islands and Greenland. - Non compris les Iles Féroé et Gröenland.

[34] Excluding Overseas Departments, namely French Guiana, Guadeloupe, Martinique and Reunion, shown separately. De jure population but excluding diplomatic personnel outside the country and including members of alien armed forces not living in military camps and foreign diplomatic personnel not living in embassies or consulates. - Non compris les départements d'outre-mer, c'est-à-dire la Guyane française, la Guadeloupe, la Martinique et la Réunion, qui font l'objet de rubriques distinctes. Population de droit, non compris le personnel diplomatique hors du pays et y compris les militaires étrangers ne vivant pas dans des camps militaires et le personnel diplomatique étranger ne vivant pas dans les ambassades ou les consulats.

[35] Excluding armed forces. - Non compris les militaires en garnison.

[36] Mid-year population excludes armed forces stationed outside the country, but includes alien armed forces stationed in the area. - Les estimations au millieu de l'année non compris les militaires en garnison hors du pays, mais y compris les militaires étrangers en garnison sur le territoire.

[37] Data refer to the Vatican City State. - Les données se rapportent aux Etat du Saint-Siège.

[38] Including work and resident permit holders and foreigners residing in Malta. - Y compris les titulaires de permis de travail et de permis de séjour et les étrangers résidant à Malte.

[39] From 1997, including residents temporarily outside the country. - Après 1997, y compris les résidents se trouvant temporairement hors du pays.

[40] Excluding civilian aliens within country, but including civilian nationals temporarily outside country. - Non compris les civils étrangers dans le pays, mais y compris les civils nationaux temporairement hors du pays.

[41] Including the Azores and Madeira Islands. - Y compris les Açores et Madère.

[42] After 1998, data do not include information for Transnistria and the municipality of Bender. - Après 1998, les données ne tiennent pas compte de l'information sur la Transnistria et la municipalité de Bender.

[43] Beginning with 1998, estimates of Kosovo and Metohia computed on the basis of natural increases from year 1997. - A partir du 1998, les estimations pour le Kosovo et la Metohia ont été calculées sur la base des incréments naturelles depuis 1997.

[44] Including the Balearic and Canary Islands, and Alhucemas, Ceuta, Chafarinas, Melilla and Penon de Vélez de la Gomera. - Y compris les Baléares et les Canaries, Al Hoceima, Ceuta, les îles Zaffarines, Melilla et Penon de Vélez de la Gomera.

[45] For 1997 to 2000, data revised to exclude births in Northern Ireland to non-residents of Northern Ireland. - De 1997 à 2000, données révisées non compris des naissances en Irlande du Nord aux non-résidents de l'Irlande du Nord.

[46] Population estimates for the years 1991 to 1999 have been smoothed using the 1995 mid-decade household survey and the year 2000 census. - L'estimation de la population a été lissée pour les années entre 1991 et 1999 en utilisant l'enquête des ménages de 1995 et le recensement de l'année 2000.

Table 6

Table 6 presents urban and total population by sex for as many years as possible between 1993 and 2002.

Description of variables: Data are from nation-wide population censuses or are estimates, some of which are based on sample surveys of population carried out among all segments of the population. The results of censuses are identified by a code following the date in the stub; sample surveys are further identified by footnotes; other data are generally estimates, the characteristics of which (*de jure* or *de facto*) are also indicated with a code.

Estimates of urban population presented in this table have been limited to countries or areas for which estimates have been based on the results of a sample survey or have been constructed by the component method from the results of a population census or sample survey. Distributions that result from the estimated total population being distributed by urban/rural residence according to percentages in each group at the time of a census or sample survey have not been included in this table.

Urban is defined according to the national census definition. The definition for each country is set forth at the end of the technical notes to this table.

Percentage computation: Percentages urban are the number of persons residing in an area defined as "urban" per 100 total population. They are calculated by the United Nations Statistics Division.

Reliability of data: Estimates that are believed to be less reliable are set in *italics* rather than in roman type. Classification in terms of reliability is based on the method of construction of the total population estimate as shown in table 3 and discussed in the technical notes for that table.

Limitations: Statistics on urban population by sex are subject to the same qualifications as have been set forth for population statistics in general, as discussed in section 3 of the Technical Notes.

The basic limitations imposed by variations in the definition of the total population and in the degree of under-enumeration are perhaps more important in relation to urban/rural than to any other distributions. The classification by urban and rural is affected by variations in defining usual residence for purposes of sub-national tabulations. Likewise, the geographical differentials in the degree of under-enumeration in censuses affect the comparability of these categories throughout the table. The distinction between *de facto* and *de jure* population is also very important with respect to urban/rural distributions. The difference between the *de facto* and the *de jure* population is discussed at length in section 3.1.1 of the Technical Notes.

A most important and specific limitation, however, lies in the national differences in the definition of urban. Because the distinction between urban and rural areas is made in so many different ways, the definitions have been included at the end of this table. The definitions are necessarily brief and, where the classification as urban involves administrative civil divisions, they are often given in the terminology of the particular country or area. As a result of variations in terminology, it may appear that differences between countries or areas are greater than they actually are. On the other hand, similar or identical terms (for example, town, village, district) as used in different countries or areas may have quite different meanings.

It will be seen from an examination of the definitions that they fall roughly into three major types: (1) classification of localities as urban based on size; (2) classification of administrative centres of minor civil divisions as urban and the remainder of the division as rural; and (3) classification of minor civil divisions on a set of criteria, which may include type of local government, number of inhabitants or proportion of population engaged in agriculture.

The designation of areas as urban or rural is so closely bound to historical, political, cultural, and administrative considerations that the process of developing uniform definitions and procedures moves very slowly. Not only do the definitions differ from one country or area to the other, but, they may also no longer reflect the original intention for distinguishing urban from rural. The criteria once established on the basis of administrative subdivisions (as most of these are) become fixed and resistant to change. For this reason, comparisons of time-series data may be severely affected because the definitions used become outdated. Special care must be taken in comparing data from censuses with those from sample surveys because the definitions of urban used may differ.

Despite their shortcomings, however, statistics on urban and rural population are useful in describing the diversity within the population of a country or area.

The definition of urban/rural areas is based on both qualitative and quantitative criteria that may include any combination of the following: size of population, population density, distance between built-up areas, predominant type of economic activity, conformity to legal or administrative status and urban characteristics such as specific services and facilities[1]. Although statistics classified by urban/rural areas are widely available, no international standard definition appears to be possible at this tme since the meaning differs from one country or area to another. The urban/rural classification of population used here is reported according to the national definition, as indicated in a footnote to this table and described in detail in the technical notes for table 2 of the Historical Supplement[2].

Earlier data: Urban and total population by sex have been shown in previous issues of the Demographic Yearbook. For information on specific years covered, readers should consult the Historical Index.

DEFINITION OF "URBAN"

AFRICA

Botswana: Agglomeration of 5 000 or more inhabitants where 75 per cent of the economic activity is non-agricultural.
Burundi: Commune of Bujumbura.
Comoros: Administrative centres of prefectures and localities of 5 000 or more inhabitants.
Egypt: Governorates of Cairo, Alexandria, Port Said, Ismailia, Suez, frontier governorates and capitals of other governorates, as well as district capitals (Markaz).
Equatorial Guinea: District centres and localities with 300 dwellings and/or 1 500 inhabitants or more.
Ethiopia: Localities of 2 000 or more inhabitants.
Liberia: Localities of 2 000 or more inhabitants.
Malawi: All townships and town planning areas and all district centres.
Mauritius: Towns with proclaimed legal limits.
Senegal: Agglomerations of 10 000 or more inhabitants.
South Africa: Places with some form of local authority.
Sudan: Localities of administrative and/or commercial importance or with population of 5 000 or more inhabitants.
Swaziland: Localities proclaimed as urban.
Tunisia: Population living in communes.
United Republic of Tanzania: 16 gazetted townships.
Zambia: Localities of 5 000 or more inhabitants, the majority of whom all depend on non-agricultural activities.

AMERICA, NORTH

Canada: Places of 1 000 or more inhabitants, having a population density of 400 or more per square kilometre.
Costa Rica: Administrative centres of cantons.
Cuba: Population living In a nucleus of 2 000 or more inhabitants.
Dominican Republic: Administrative centres of municipalities and municipal districts, some of which include suburban zones of rural character.
El Salvador: Administrative centres of municipalities .
Greenland: Localities of 200 or more inhabitants.
Guatemala: Municipality of Guatemala Department and officially recognized centres of other departments and municipalities.
Haiti: Administrative centres of communes.
Honduras: Localities of 2 000 or more inhabitants, having essentially urban characteristics.
Mexico: Localities of 2 500 or more inhabitants.
Nicaragua: Administrative centres of municipalities and localities of 1 000 or more inhabitants with streets and electric light.
Panama: Localities of 1 500 or more inhabitants having essentially urban characteristics. Beginning 1970, localities of 1 500 or more inhabitants with such urban characteristics as streets, water supply systems, sewerage systems and electric light.
Puerto Rico: Agglomerations of 2 500 or more inhabitants, generally having population densities of 1 000 persons per square mile or more. Two types of urban areas: urbanized areas of 50 000 or more inhabitants and urban clusters of at least 2 500 and less than 50 000 inhabitants.
United States: Agglomerations of 2 500 or more inhabitants, generally having population densities of 1 000 persons per square mile or more. Two types of urban areas: urbanized areas of 50 000 or more inhabitants and urban clusters of at least 2 500 and less than 50 000 inhabitants.
U.S. Virgin Islands: Agglomerations of 2 500 or more inhabitants, generally having population densities of 1 000 persons per square mile or more. Two types of urban areas: urbanized areas of 50 000 or more inhabitants and urban clusters of at least 2 500 and less than 50 000 inhabitants. (As of Census 2000, no urbanized areas are identified in the U.S. Virgin Islands.)

AMERICA, SOUTH

Argentina: Populated centres with 2 000 or more inhabitants.
Bolivia: Localities of 2 000 or more inhabitants.
Brazil: Urban and suburban zones of administrative centres of municipalities and districts.
Chile: Populated centres which have definite urban characteristics such as certain public and municipal services.
Ecuador: Capitals of provinces and cantons.
Falkland Islands (Malvinas): Town of Stanley.
Paraguay: Cities, towns and administrative centres of departments and districts.
Peru: Populated centres with 100 or more dwellings.
Suriname: Paramaribo town.
Uruguay: Cities.
Venezuela: Centres with a population of 1 000 or more inhabitants.

ASIA

Armenia: Cities and urban-type localities, officially designated as such, usually according to the criteria of number of inhabitants and predominance of agricultural, or number of non-agricultural workers and their families.
Azerbaijan: Cities and urban-type localities, officially designated as such, usually according to the criteria of number of inhabitants and predominance of agricultural, or number of non-agricultural workers and their families.
Bahrain: Communes or villages of 2 500 or more inhabitants.
Cambodia: Towns.
China: Cities only refer to the cities proper of those designated by the State Council. In the case of cities with district establishment, the city proper refers to the whole administrative area of the district if its population density is 1 500 people per kilometre or higher; or the seat of the district government and other areas of streets under the administration of the district if the population density is less than 1 500 people per kilometre. In the case of cities without district establishment, the city proper refers to the seat of the city government and other areas of streets under the administration of the city. For the city district with the population density below 1 500 people per kilometre and the city without district establishment, if the urban construction of the district or city government seat has extended to some part of the neighboring designated town(s) or township(s), the city proper does include the whole administrative area of the town(s) or township(s).
Cyprus: Urban areas are those defined by local town plans.
Georgia: Cities and urban-type localities, officially designated as such, usually according to the criteria of number of inhabitants and predominance of agricultural, or number of non-agricultural workers and their families.
India: Towns (places with municipal corporation, municipal area committee, town committee, notified area committee or cantonment board); also, all places having 5 000 or more inhabitants, a density of not less than 1 000 persons per square mile or 400 per square kilometre, pronounced urban characteristics and at least three fourths of the adult male population employed in pursuits other than agriculture.
Indonesia: Places with urban characteristics.
Iran (Islamic Republic of): Every district with a municipality.
Israel: All settlements of more than 2 000 inhabitants, except those where at least one third of households, participating in the civilian labour force, earn their living from agriculture.
Japan: City (shi) having 50 000 or more inhabitants with 60 per cent or more of the houses located in the main built-up areas and 60 per cent or more of the population (including their dependants) engaged in manufacturing, trade or other urban type of business. Alternatively, a shi having urban facilities and conditions as defined by the prefectural order is considered as urban.
Kazakhstan: Cities and urban-type localities, officially designated as such, usually according to the criteria of number of inhabitants and predominance of agricultural, or number of non-agricultural workers and their families.
Korea, Republic of: Population living in cities irrespective of size of population.
Kyrgyzstan: Cities and urban-type localities, officially designated as such, usually according to the criteria of number of inhabitants and predominance of agricultural, or number of non-agricultural workers and their families.
Malaysia: Gazetted areas with population of 10 000 and more.
Maldives: Malé, the capital.
Mongolia: Capital and district centres.
Pakistan: Places with municipal corporation, town committee or cantonment.
Sri Lanka: Urban sector comprises of all municipal and urban council areas.
Syrian Arab Republic: Cities, Mohafaza centres and Mantika centres, and communities with 20 000 or more inhabitants.
Tajikistan: Cities and urban-type localities, officially designated as such, usually according to the criteria of number of inhabitants and predominance of agricultural, or number of non-agricultural workers and their families.
Thailand: Municipal areas.
Turkey: Population of the localities within the municipality limits of administrative centres of provinces and districts.

Turkmenistan: Cities and urban-type localities, officially designated as such, usually according to the criteria of number of inhabitants and predominance of agricultural, or number of non-agricultural workers and their families.

Uzbekistan: Cities and urban-type localities, officially designated as such, usually according to the criteria of number of inhabitants and predominance of agricultural, or number of non-agricultural workers and their families.

Viet Nam: Urban areas include inside urban districts of cities, urban quarters and towns. All other local administrative units (communes) belong to rural areas.

EUROPE

Albania: Towns and other industrial centres of more than 400 inhabitants.

Austria: Communes of more than 5 000 inhabitants.

Belarus: Cities and urban-type localities, officially designated as such, usually according to the criteria of number of inhabitants and predominance of agricultural, or number of non-agricultural workers and their families.

Bulgaria: Towns, that is, localities legally established as urban.

Czech Republic: Localities with 2 000 or more inhabitants.

Estonia: Cities and urban-type localities, officially designated as such, usually according to the criteria of number of inhabitants and predominance of agricultural, or number of non-agricultural workers and their families.

Finland: Urban communes. 1970: Localities.

France: Communes containing an agglomeration of more than 2 000 inhabitants living in contiguous houses or with not more than 200 metres between houses, also communes of which the major portion of the population is part of a multicommunal agglomeration of this nature.

Greece: Population of municipalities and communes in which the largest population centre has 10 000 or more inhabitants. Including also the population of the 18 urban agglomerations, as these were defined at the census of 1991, namely: Greater Athens, Thessaloniki, Patra, Iraklio, Volos, Chania, Irannina, Chalkida, Agrinio, Kalamata, Katerini, Kerkyra, Salamina, Chios, Egio, Rethymno, Ermoupolis, and Sparti.

Hungary: Budapest and all legally designated towns.

Iceland: Localities of 200 or more inhabitants.

Ireland: Cities and towns including suburbs of 1 500 or more inhabitants.

Latvia: Cities and urban-type localities, officially designated as such, usually according to the criteria of number of inhabitants and predominance of agricultural, or number of non-agricultural workers and their families.

Lithuania: Urban population refers to persons who live in cities and towns, i.e., the population areas with closely built permanent dwellings and with the resident population of more than 3 000 of which 2/3 of employees work in industry, social infrastructure and business. In a number of towns the population may be less than 3 000 since these areas had already the states of "town" before the law was enforced (July 1994)

Netherlands: Urban: Municipalities with a population of 2 000 and more inhabitants. Semi-urban: Municipalities with a population of less than 2 000 but with not more than 20 per cent of their economically active male population engaged in agriculture, and specific residential municipalities of commuters.

Norway: Localities of 200 or more inhabitants.

Poland: Towns and settlements of urban type, e.g. workers' settlements, fishermen's settlements, health resorts.

Portugal: Agglomeration of 10 000 or more inhabitants.

Republic of Moldova: Cities and urban-type localities, officially designated as such, usually according to the criteria of number of inhabitants and predominance of agricultural, or number of non-agricultural workers and their families.

Romania: Cities, municipalities and other towns.

Russian Federation: Cities and urban-type localities, officially designated as such, usually according to the criteria of number of inhabitants and predominance of agricultural, or number of non-agricultural workers and their families.

Slovakia: 138 cities with 5 000 inhabitants or more.

Spain: Localities of 2 000 or more inhabitants.

Switzerland: Communes of 10 000 or more inhabitants, including suburbs.

Ukraine: Cities and urban-type localities, officially designated as such, usually according to the criteria of number of inhabitants and predominance of agricultural, or number of non-agricultural workers and their families.

OCEANIA

American Samoa: Agglomerations of 2 500 or more inhabitants, generally having population densities of 1 000 persons per square mile or more. Two types of urban areas: urbanized areas of 50 000 or more inhabitants and urban clusters of at least 2 500 and less than 50 000 inhabitants. (As of Census 2000, no urbanized areas are identified in American Samoa.)

Guam: Agglomerations of 2 500 or more inhabitants, generally having population densities of 1 000 persons per square mile or more, referred to as "urban clusters".

New Caledonia: Nouméa and communes of Païta, Nouvel Dumbéa and Mont-Dore.

New Zealand: All cities, plus boroughs, town districts, townships and country towns with a population of 1 000 or more.

Northern Mariana Islands: Agglomerations of 2 500 or more inhabitants, generally having population densities of 1 000 persons per square mile or more. Two types of urban areas: urbanized areas of 50 000 or more inhabitants and urban clusters of at least 2 500 and less than 50 000 inhabitants.

Vanuatu: Luganville centre and Vila urban.

NOTES

[1] For further information, see *Social and Demographic Statistics: Classifications of Size and Type of Locality and Urban/Rural Areas*. E/CN.3/551, United Nations, New York, 1980.

[2] *Demographic Yearbook: Historical Supplement 1948-1997, CD-ROM Special Issue*, Sales No. E99.XIII.12, United Nations, 1997.

Tableau 6

Le tableau 6 présente des données sur la population urbaine et la population totale selon le sexe pour le plus grand nombre possible d'années entre 1993 et 2002.

Description des variables : Les données proviennent de recensements de la population ou sont des estimations fondées, dans certains cas, sur des enquêtes par sondage portant sur toutes les couches de la population. Le code qui figure dans la deuxième colonne du tableau indique comment les données ont été obtenues ; les enquêtes par sondage sont en outre signalées par une note en fin de tableau ; toutes les autres données sont en général des estimations et la colonne «Code» indique si elles portent sur la population de fait ou la population de droit.

Les estimations de la population urbaine qui figurent dans le tableau 6 ne concernent que les pays ou zones pour lesquels les estimations se fondent sur les résultats d'une enquête par sondage ou ont été établies par la méthode des composantes à partir des résultats d'un recensement de la population ou d'une enquête par sondage. Les répartitions selon le lieu de résidence (zone urbaine ou rurale) obtenues en appliquant à l'estimation de la population totale les pourcentages enregistrés pour chaque groupe lors d'un recensement ou d'une enquête par sondage n'ont pas été reproduites dans le tableau 6.

Le sens donné au terme « urbain » est conforme aux définitions utilisées dans les recensements nationaux. La définition pour chaque pays figure à la fin des présentes notes technique.

Calcul des pourcentages : Les pourcentages de la population urbaine sont calculés par la Division de statistique de l'Organisation des Nations Unies et représentent le nombre de personnes qui vivent dans des régions considérées comme urbaines pour 100 personnes de la population totale.

Fiabilité des données : Les estimations considérées comme moins sûres sont indiquées en italique plutôt qu'en caractères romains. Le classement du point de vue de la fiabilité est fondé sur la méthode utilisée pour établir l'estimation de la population totale qui figure au tableau 3 (voir les explications dans les notes techniques relatives à ce même tableau).

Insuffisance des données : Les statistiques de la population urbaine selon le sexe appellent toutes les réserves qui ont été formulées à la section 3 des Notes techniques à propos des statistiques de la population en général.

Les limitations fondamentales imposées par les variations de la définition de la population totale et par les lacunes du recensement se font peut-être sentir davantage dans la répartition de la population en population urbaine et population rurale que dans sa répartition suivant toute autre caractéristique. De fait, des différences dans la définition du lieu de résidence habituel utilisée pour l'exploitation des données à l'échelon sous-national influent sur la classification en population urbaine et en population rurale. De même, les différences de degré de sous-dénombrement suivant la zone, à l'occasion des recensements, ont une incidence sur la comparabilité de ces deux catégories dans l'ensemble du tableau. La distinction entre population de fait et population de droit est également très importante du point de vue de la répartition de la population en population urbaine et en population rurale. Cette distinction est expliquée en détail à la section 3.1.1 des Notes techniques.

Toutefois, la difficulté la plus importante tient au fait que les pays ou zones ne sont pas d'accord sur la définition du terme « urbain ». Les distinctions faites entre « zone urbaine » et « zone rurale » varient tellement que les définitions utilisées ont été reproduites à la fin des notes techniques du tableau 6. Les définitions sont forcément brèves et, lorsque le classement en « zone urbaine » repose sur des divisions administratives, on a souvent désigné celles-ci par le nom qu'elles portent dans la zone ou le pays considéré. Par suite des variations dans la terminologie, les différences entre pays ou zones peuvent sembler plus grandes qu'elles ne le sont réellement. Il se peut aussi que des termes similaires ou identiques, tels que ville, village ou district, aient des significations très différentes selon les pays ou zones.

On constatera, en examinant les définitions adoptées par les différents pays ou zones, qu'elles peuvent être ramenées à trois types principaux : 1) les localités dépassant certaines dimensions sont classées parmi les zones urbaines ; 2) les centres administratifs de petites circonscriptions administratives sont classées parmi les zones urbaines, le reste de la circonscription étant considéré comme zone rurale ; 3) les petites divisions administratives sont classées parmi les zones urbaines selon un critère déterminé, qui peut être soit le type d'administration locale, soit le nombre d'habitants, soit le pourcentage de la population exerçant une activité agricole.

La distinction entre régions urbaines et régions rurales est si étroitement liée à des considérations d'ordre historique, politique, culturel et administratif que l'on ne peut progresser que très lentement vers des définitions et des méthodes uniformes. Non seulement les définitions sont différentes d'une zone ou d'un pays à un autre, mais on n'y retrouve parfois même plus l'intention originale de distinguer les régions rurales des régions urbaines. Lorsque la classification est fondée, en particulier, sur le critère des circonscriptions administratives (comme la plupart le sont), elle a tendance à devenir rigide avec le temps et à décourager toute modification. Pour cette raison, la comparaison des données appartenant à des séries chronologiques risque d'être gravement faussée du fait que les définitions employées sont désormais périmées. Il faut être particulièrement prudent lorsque l'on compare des données issues de recensements avec des données provenant d'enquêtes par sondage, car il se peut que les définitions du terme « urbain » auxquelles ces données se réfèrent respectivement soient différentes.

Malgré leurs insuffisances, les statistiques sur la population urbaine et rurale permettent de mettre en évidence la diversité de la population d'un pays ou d'une zone.

La distinction entre « zone urbaine » et « zone rurale » repose sur une série de critères qualitatifs aussi bien que quantitatifs, notamment l'effectif de la population, la densité de peuplement, la distance entre îlots d'habitations, le type prédominant d'activité économique, le statut juridique ou administratif, et les caractéristiques d'une agglomération urbaine, c'est-à-dire l'existence de services publics et d'équipements collectifs[1]. Bien que les statistiques différenciant les zones urbaines des zones rurales soient très répandues, il ne paraît pas possible pour le moment d'adopter une classification internationale type de ces zones, vu la diversité des interprétations nationales. La classification de la population en population urbaine et population rurale retenue ici est celle qui correspond aux définitions nationales, comme signalé par une note à la fin du tableau 6 et dans les notes techniques relatives au tableau 2 du *Supplément historique*[2].

Données publiées antérieurement : Des statistiques concernant la population urbaine et la population totale selon le sexe ont été publiées dans des éditions antérieures de l'*Annuaire démographique*. Pour plus de précisions concernant les années pour lesquelles ces données ont été publiées, se reporter à l'index historique.

DÉFINITIONS DU TERME « URBAIN »

AFRIQUE

Afrique du Sud : Zones dotées d'une administration locale.
Botswana : Agglomération de 5 000 habitants et plus dont 75 p. 100 de l'activité économique n'est pas de type agricole.
Burundi : Commune de Bujumbura.
Comores : Chefs-lieux de préfectures et localités de 5 000 habitants et plus.
Égypte : Chefs-lieux des gouvernorats du Caire, d'Alexandrie, de Port Saïd, d'Ismaïlia, de Suez ; chefs-lieux des gouvernorats frontaliers, autres chefs-lieux de gouvernorat et chefs-lieux de district (Markaz).
Éthiopie : Localités de 2 000 habitants et plus.
Guinée équatoriale : Chefs-lieux de district et localités comprenant 300 habitations et/ou 1 500 habitants et plus.
Libéria : Localités de 2 000 habitants et plus.
Malawi : Toutes les villes et zones urbanisées et tous les chefs-lieux de district.
Maurice : Villes ayant des limites officiellement définies.
République-Unie de Tanzanie : 16 townships érigées en communes.
Sénégal : Agglomérations de 10 000 habitants et plus.
Soudan : Centres administratifs et/ou commerciaux ou localités ayant une population de 5 000 habitants et plus.
Swaziland : Localités déclarées urbaines.
Tunisie : Population vivant dans les communes.
Zambie : Localités de 5 000 habitants et plus dont l'activité économique prédominante n'est pas de type agricole.

AMÉRIQUE DU NORD

Canada : Agglomérations de 1 000 habitants ou plus ayant une densité de population d'au moins 400 habitants au kilomètre carré.

Costa Rica : Chefs-lieux de canton.

Cuba : Population vivant dans des agglomérations de 2 000 habitants ou plus.

El Salvador : Chefs-lieux de municipios.

États-Unis : Agglomérations de 2 500 habitants ou plus ayant généralement une densité de population d'au moins 1 000 habitants au mile carré. Deux types de zones urbaines : zones urbanisées de 50 000 habitants ou plus et groupements urbains comptant au moins 2 500 habitants mais moins de 50 000.

Groenland : Localités d'au moins 200 habitants.

Guatemala : Municipio du département de Guatemala et centres administratifs officiels d'autres départements et municipios.

Haïti : Chefs-lieux de communes.

Honduras : Localités d'au moins 2 000 habitants ayant des caractéristiques essentiellement urbaines.

Îles Vierges américaines : Agglomérations de 2 500 habitants ou plus ayant généralement une densité de population d'au moins 1 000 habitants au mile carré. Deux types de zones urbaines : zones urbanisées de 50 000 habitants ou plus et groupements urbains comptant au moins 2 500 habitants mais moins de 50 000. (D'après les résultats du recensement de 2000, les Îles Vierges américaines ne comptent aucune zone urbanisée.)

Mexique : Localités d'au moins 2 500 habitants.

Nicaragua : Chefs-lieux de municipios et agglomérations d'au moins 1 000 habitants dotées de rues et de l'éclairage électrique.

Panama : Localités d'au moins 1 500 habitants ayant des caractéristiques essentiellement urbaines. À partir de 1970, localités de 1 500 habitants et plus présentant des caractéristiques urbaines, telles que rues, éclairage électrique, systèmes d'approvisionnement en eau et réseaux d'égouts.

Porto Rico : Agglomérations de 2 500 habitants ou plus ayant généralement une densité de population d'au moins 1 000 habitants au mile carré. Deux types de zones urbaines : zones urbanisées de 50 000 habitants ou plus et groupements urbains comptant au moins 2 500 habitants mais moins de 50 000.

République dominicaine : Chefs-lieux de municipios et districts municipaux, dont certains comprennent des zones suburbaines ayant des caractéristiques rurales.

AMÉRIQUE DU SUD

Argentine : Centres comptant au moins 2 000 habitants.

Bolivie : Localités de 2 000 habitants et plus.

Brésil : Zones urbaines et suburbaines des chefs lieux de municipalités et de districts.

Chili : Centres de peuplement ayant des caractéristiques nettement urbaines (présence de certains services publics et municipaux).

Équateur : Capitales des provinces et chefs-lieux de canton.

Îles Falkland (Malvinas) : Ville de Stanley.

Paraguay : Grandes villes, villes et chefs-lieux des départements et des districts.

Pérou : Centres de peuplement comptant plus de 100 logements.

Suriname : Ville de Paramaribo.

Uruguay : Villes.

Venezuela : Centres de 1 000 habitants et plus.

ASIE

Arménie : Grandes villes et localités de type urbain, officiellement désignées comme telles, généralement sur la base du nombre d'habitants et de la prédominance des travailleurs agricoles ou non agricoles avec leur famille.

Azerbaïdjan : Grandes villes et localités de type urbain, officiellement désignées comme telles, généralement sur la base du nombre d'habitants et de la prédominance des travailleurs agricoles ou non agricoles avec leur famille.

Bahreïn : Communes ou villages comptant au moins 2 500 habitants.

Cambodge : Villes.

Chine : Villes désignées comme telles par le Conseil d'État. Dans le cas de villes ayant rang de district, la ville s'entend de l'ensemble de la zone administrative qui relève du district si sa densité est d'au moins 1 500 habitants au kilomètre carré ou du siège des autorités du district et d'autres zones ou rues qui relèvent du district si leur densité est inférieure à 1 500 habitants au kilomètre carré. Dans le cas des villes qui n'ont pas rang de district, la ville s'entend du siège des autorités de la commune et des autres zones ou rues qui relèvent des autorités de la commune. Dans le cas des villes ayant rang de district qui comptent moins de 1 500 habitants au kilomètre carré et des villes n'ayant pas rang de district, si l'urbanisation du siège du district ou du siège des autorités de la commune a empiété sur une partie de la ou des localités voisines, la ville inclut alors l'ensemble de la zone administrative desdites localités.

Chypre : Zones désignées comme urbaines dans les plans d'urbanisme locaux.

Géorgie : Grandes villes et localités de type urbain, officiellement désignées comme telles, généralement sur la base du nombre d'habitants et de la prédominance des travailleurs agricoles ou non agricoles avec leur famille.

Inde : Villes [localités dotées d'une charte municipale, d'un comité de zone municipale, d'un comité de zone déclarée urbaine ou d'un comité de zone de regroupement (cantonment)] ; également toutes les localités qui ont une population de 5 000 habitants au moins, une densité de population d'au moins 1 000 habitants au mile carré ou 400 au kilomètre carré, des caractéristiques urbaines prononcées et où les trois quarts au moins des adultes de sexe masculin ont une occupation non agricole.

Indonésie : Localités présentant des caractéristiques urbaines.

Iran (République islamique d') : Tous les districts comptant une municipalité.

Israël : Tous les lieux comptant au moins 2 000 habitants, à l'exception de ceux où le tiers au moins des chefs de ménage faisant partie de la population civile active vivent de l'agriculture.

Japon : Villes (shi), comptant au moins 50 000 habitants, où 60 p. 100 au moins des logements sont situés dans les principales zones bâties, et dont 60 p. 100 au moins de population (y compris les personnes à charge) exercent un métier dans l'industrie, le commerce et d'autres branches d'activités essentiellement urbaines. Tout shi possédant les équipements et présentant les caractéristiques définies comme urbaines par l'administration préfectorale est également considéré comme zone urbaine.

Kazakhstan : Grandes villes et localités de type urbain, officiellement désignées comme telles, généralement sur la base du nombre d'habitants et de la prédominance des travailleurs agricoles ou non agricoles avec leur famille.

Kirghizistan : Grandes villes et localités de type urbain, officiellement désignées comme telles, généralement sur la base du nombre d'habitants et de la prédominance des travailleurs agricoles ou non agricoles avec leur famille.

Malaisie : Zones déclarées « zones urbaines » et comptant au moins 10 000 habitants.

Maldives : Malé (capitale).

Mongolie : Capitale et chefs-lieux de district.

Ouzbékistan : Grandes villes et localités de type urbain, officiellement désignées comme telles, généralement sur la base du nombre d'habitants et de la prédominance des travailleurs agricoles ou non agricoles avec leur famille.

Pakistan : Localités dotées d'une charte municipale ou d'un comité municipal et regroupements (cantonments).

République arabe syrienne : Villes, chefs-lieux de district (Mohafaza) et chefs-lieux de sous district (Mantika), et communes d'au moins 20 000 habitants.

République de Corée : Population vivant dans des villes, quel qu'en soit le nombre d'habitants.

Sri Lanka : Secteur urbain composé de toutes les zones municipales et zones dotées d'un conseil urbain.

Tadjikistan : Grandes villes et localités de type urbain, officiellement désignées comme telles, généralement sur la base du nombre d'habitants et de la prédominance des travailleurs agricoles ou non agricoles avec leur famille.

Thaïlande : Zones municipales.

Turkménistan : Grandes villes et localités de type urbain, officiellement désignées comme telles, généralement sur la base du nombre d'habitants et de la prédominance des travailleurs agricoles ou non agricoles avec leur famille.

Turquie : Population des localités se trouvant dans les limites municipales des chefs-lieux des provinces et des districts.

Viet Nam : Zones urbaines comprises à l'intérieur des districts urbains des villes ainsi que des quartiers urbains et des localités. Toutes les autres unités administratives locales (communes) sont considérées comme zones rurales.

Yémen : Définition non communiquée.

EUROPE

Albanie : Villes et autres centres industriels de plus de 400 habitants.

Autriche : Communes de plus de 5 000 habitants.

Bélarus : Grandes villes et localités de type urbain, officiellement désignées comme telles, généralement sur la base du nombre d'habitants et de la prédominance des travailleurs agricoles ou non agricoles avec leur famille.

Bulgarie : Villes, c'est-à-dire localités reconnues comme urbaines.

Espagne : Localités de 2 000 habitants et plus.

Estonie : Grandes villes et localités de type urbain, officiellement désignées comme telles, généralement sur la base du nombre d'habitants et de la prédominance des travailleurs agricoles ou non agricoles avec leur famille.

Fédération de Russie : Grandes villes et localités de type urbain, officiellement désignées comme telles, généralement sur la base du nombre d'habitants et de la prédominance des travailleurs agricoles ou non agricoles avec leur famille.

Finlande : Communes urbaines. 1970 : Localités.

France : Communes comprenant une agglomération de plus de 2 000 habitants vivant dans des habitations contiguës ou qui ne sont pas distantes les unes des autres de plus de 200 mètres et communes où la majeure partie de la population vit dans une agglomération regroupant plusieurs communes de cette nature.

Grèce : Municipalités et communes de 10 000 habitants et plus pour l'agglomération. Y compris également 18 agglomérations urbaines, selon la définition qui en a été donnée lors du recensement de 1991, à savoir : Athènes et sa banlieue, Thessalonique, Patras, Héraklion, Volos, Chania, Ioannina, Chalkida, Agrinio, Kalamata, Katerini, Kerkyra, Salamine, Chios, Egio, Rethymno, Ermoupolis et Sparte.

Hongrie : Budapest et toutes les autres localités reconnues officiellement comme urbaines.

Irlande : Localités, y compris leur banlieues, comptant 1 500 habitants ou plus.

Islande : Localités de 200 habitants et plus.

Lettonie : Grandes villes et localités de type urbain, officiellement désignées comme telles, généralement sur la base du nombre d'habitants et de la prédominance des travailleurs agricoles ou non agricoles avec leur famille.

Lituanie : Par population urbaine, on entend les personnes qui vivent dans des villes ou des localités, à savoir les zones habitées comportant des logements permanents proches les uns des autres et dont la population est d'au moins 3 000 habitants, les deux tiers desquels sont employés dans le secteur industriel, l'infrastructure sociale ou le commerce. Un certain nombre de villes peuvent compter moins de 3 000 habitants dans la mesure où elles avaient acquis le statut de ville avant l'entrée en vigueur de la nouvelle loi en juillet 1994.

Norvège : Localités de 200 habitants et plus.

Pays Bas : Zones urbaines : municipalités comptant au moins 2000 habitants. Zones semi-urbaines : municipalités comptant moins de 2 000 habitants, mais où 20 p. 100 au maximum de la population active de sexe masculin pratiquent l'agriculture, et certaines municipalités de caractère résidentiel dont les habitants travaillent ailleurs.

Pologne : Villes et zones de type urbain, par exemple groupements de travailleurs ou de pêcheurs et stations climatiques.

Portugal : Agglomérations d'au moins 10 000 habitants.

République de Moldova : Grandes villes et localités de type urbain, officiellement désignées comme telles, généralement sur la base du nombre d'habitants et de la prédominance des travailleurs agricoles ou non agricoles avec leur famille.

République tchèque : Localités d'au moins 2 000 habitants.

Roumanie : Grandes villes, municipalités et autres villes.

Slovaquie : 138 localités comptant 5 000 habitants et plus.

Suisse : Communes de 10 000 habitants et plus, et leurs banlieues.

Ukraine : Grandes villes et localités de type urbain, officiellement désignées comme telles, généralement sur la base du nombre d'habitants et de la prédominance des travailleurs agricoles ou non agricoles avec leur famille.

OCÉANIE

Guam: Agglomérations de 2 500 habitants ou plus ayant généralement une densité de population d'au moins 1 000 habitants au mile carré et considérées comme étant des groupements urbains.

Îles Mariannes septentrionales : Agglomérations de 2 500 habitants ou plus ayant généralement une densité de population d'au moins 1 000 habitants au mile carré. Deux types de zones urbaines : zones urbanisées de 50 000 habitants ou plus et groupements urbains comptant au moins 2 500 habitants mais moins de 50 000.

Nouvelle-Calédonie: Nouméa et communes de Païta, Dumbéa et Mont-Dore.

Nouvelle-Zélande: Grandes villes, boroughs, chefs-lieux, municipalités et chefs-lieux de comté d'au moins 1 000 habitants.

Samoa américaines: Agglomérations de 2 500 habitants ou plus ayant généralement une densité de population d'au moins 1 000 habitants au mile carré. Deux types de zones urbaines : zones urbanisées de 50 000 habitants ou plus et groupements urbains comptant au moins 2 500 habitants mais moins de 50 000. (D'après les résultats du recensement de 2000, les Samoa américaines ne comptent aucune zone urbanisée.)

Vanuatu: Centre de Luganville et Port-Vila.

_____

NOTES

[1] Pour plus de précisions, voir *Social and Demographic Statistics: Classifications of Size and Type of Locality and Urban/Rural Areas*, E/CN.3/551, publication des Nations Unies, New York, 1980.
[2] *Annuaire démographique, Supplément historique, 1948-1997*, CD-ROM, publication des Nations Unies, numéro de vente : E/F.99.XIII.12, New York, 2000.

6. Urban and total population by sex: 1993 - 2002
Population urbaine et population totale selon le sexe: 1993 - 2002

(See notes at end of table. — Voir notes à la fin du tableau.)

Continent, country or area and date / Continent, pays ou zone et date	Code[1]	Both sexes - Les deux sexes			Male - Masculin			Female - Féminin		
		Total	Urban - Urbaine		Total	Urban - Urbaine		Total	Urban - Urbaine	
			Number Nombre	Percent P.100		Number Nombre	Percent P.100		Number Nombre	Percent P.100
AFRICA — AFRIQUE										
Benin - Bénin										
1 VII 1993	ESDF	5 074 561	1 832 946	36.1	2 467 604	891 792	36.1	2 606 957	941 154	36.1
1 VII 1994	ESDF	5 241 843	1 917 100	36.6	2 548 310	932 172	36.6	2 693 533	984 928	36.6
1 VII 1995	ESDF	5 412 160	2 003 213	37.0	2 633 479	974 914	37.0	2 778 681	1 028 299	37.0
1 VII 1996	ESDF	5 594 499	2 098 699	37.5	2 722 854	1 019 980	37.5	2 871 645	1 078 719	37.6
1 VII 1997	ESDF	5 638 987	2 177 515	38.6	...	...	...	...	...	...
1 VII 1998	ESDF	5 816 488	2 278 190	39.2	...	...	...	...	...	...
1 VII 1999	ESDF	5 990 396	2 383 244	39.8	...	...	...	...	...	...
1 VII 2000	ESDF	6 169 084	2 492 967	40.4	3 013 705	1 220 905	40.5	3 155 379	1 272 062	40.3
Botswana[2]										
1 VII 1994	ESDF	1 424 636	672 614	47.2	684 751	...	...	739 885	...	...
1 VII 1995	ESDF	1 458 828	696 282	47.7	701 603	...	...	757 225	...	...
1 VII 1996	ESDF	1 495 993	720 783	48.2	720 207	...	...	775 786	...	...
Burkina Faso										
1 VII 1993	ESDF	9 682 470	1 405 478	14.5	...	...	...	...	...	...
1 VII 1994	ESDF	9 888 789	1 469 006	14.9	4 582 412	732 887	16.0	5 306 377	736 119	13.9
1 VII 1995	ESDF	10 200 453	1 534 524	15.0	4 985 642	...	...	5 214 811	...	...
Burundi										
1 VII 1993	ESDF	5 769 144	402 856	7.0	2 805 797	214 398	7.6	2 963 347	188 458	6.4
1 VII 1994	ESDF	5 875 413	420 826	7.2	2 857 267	221 304	7.7	3 018 146	199 522	6.6
1 VII 1995	ESDF	5 981 682	437 417	7.3	2 908 737	227 568	7.8	3 072 945	209 849	6.8
1 VII 1996	ESDF	6 087 951	454 661	7.5	2 960 208	233 221	7.9	3 127 743	221 440	7.1
1 VII 1997	ESDF	6 194 220	473 284	7.6	3 011 678	240 554	8.0	3 182 542	232 730	7.3
1 VII 1998	ESDF	6 300 489	493 297	7.8	3 064 211	...	...	3 236 278	...	...
Cameroon - Cameroun										
1 VII 1997	ESDF	14 297 617	6 748 475	47.2	...	...	...	...	...	...
1 VII 1998	ESDF	14 439 000	6 960 000	48.2	...	...	...	...	...	...
Cape Verde - Cap-Vert										
16 VI 2000	CDFC	436 863	235 470	53.9	211 479	114 928	54.3	225 384	120 542	53.5
1 VII 2001	ESDF	444 683	242 484	54.5	215 288	118 351	55.0	229 395	124 133	54.1
1 VII 2002	ESDF	452 714	249 794	55.2	219 211	121 924	55.6	233 503	127 870	54.8
Côte d'Ivoire										
1 VII 1993	ESDF	13 175 000	6 008 000	45.6	6 718 000	3 063 000	45.6	6 457 000	2 944 000	45.6
Egypt - Égypte										
1 VII 1993	ESDF	55 200 568	24 127 060	43.7	28 285 012	12 362 808	43.7	26 915 556	11 764 252	43.7
1 VII 1994	ESDF	56 343 786	24 481 023	43.4	28 874 917	12 545 982	43.4	27 468 869	11 935 041	43.4
1 VII 1995	ESDF	57 509 998	24 840 066	43.2	29 428 956	12 711 132	43.2	28 081 042	12 128 934	43.2
1 VII 1996	ESDF	58 755 211	25 019 402	42.6	30 063 860	12 801 923	42.6	28 691 351	12 217 479	42.6
19 XI 1996	CDFC	59 312 914	25 286 335	42.6	30 351 390	12 957 775	42.7	28 961 524	12 328 560	42.6
1 VII 1997	ESDF	60 080 063	25 589 396	42.6	30 736 254	13 091 232	42.6	29 343 809	12 498 164	42.6
1 VII 1998	ESDF	61 340 882	26 123 481	42.6	31 379 023	13 363 507	42.6	29 961 859	12 759 974	42.6
1 VII 1999	ESDF	62 652 065	26 641 192	42.5	32 059 065	13 632 299	42.5	30 593 000	13 008 893	42.5
1 VII 2000	ESDF	63 976 000	27 204 000	42.5	32 695 000	...	...	31 281 000	...	...
Ethiopia - Éthiopie										
1 VII 1993	ESDF	53 236 400	7 789 100	14.6	...	...	...	...	...	...
11 X 1994	CDFC	53 477 265	7 323 207	13.7	26 910 698	3 534 805	13.1	26 566 567	3 788 402	14.3
1 VII 1995	ESDF	54 649 154	7 586 700	13.9	27 498 620	3 662 625	13.3	27 150 534	3 924 075	14.5
1 VII 1996	ESDF	56 372 000	7 950 000	14.1	28 344 000	3 885 000	13.7	28 028 000	4 065 000	14.5
1 VII 1997	ESDF	58 117 000	8 315 000	14.3	29 202 000	4 094 000	14.0	28 915 000	4 221 000	14.6
1 VII 1998	ESDF	59 882 000	8 691 000	14.5	30 071 000	4 299 000	14.3	29 811 000	4 392 000	14.7
1 VII 1999	ESDF	61 672 000	9 074 000	14.7	30 956 000	4 504 000	14.5	30 716 000	4 570 000	14.9
1 VII 2000	ESDF	63 494 702	9 472 971	14.9	...	...	...	...	...	...
1 VII 2001	ESDF	65 374 320	9 883 138	15.1	32 815 082	4 938 725	15.1	32 559 238	4 944 413	15.2
1 VII 2002	ESDF	67 220 000	10 307 000	15.3	33 707 000	5 134 000	15.2	33 513 000	5 173 000	15.4
Gabon										
31 VII 1993	CDFC	1 014 976	742 296	73.1	501 784	371 622	74.1	513 192	370 674	72.2
Ghana										
26 III 2000	CDFC	18 912 079	8 274 270	43.8	9 357 382	...	...	9 554 697	...	...

6. Urban and total population by sex: 1993 - 2002
Population urbaine et population totale selon le sexe: 1993 - 2002
(continued — suite)

(See notes at end of table. — Voir notes à la fin du tableau.)

Continent, country or area and date / Continent, pays ou zone et date	Code[1]	Both sexes - Les deux sexes			Male - Masculin			Female - Féminin		
		Total	Urban - Urbaine		Total	Urban - Urbaine		Total	Urban - Urbaine	
			Number Nombre	Percent P.100		Number Nombre	Percent P.100		Number Nombre	Percent P.100
AFRICA — AFRIQUE										
Kenya										
24 VIII 1999 *	CDFC	28 686 607	3 539 888	12.3	14 205 589	1 933 437	13.6	14 481 018	1 606 451	11.1
Lesotho[3]										
14 IV 1996	CDJC	1 960 069	312 444	15.9	964 346	...	...	995 723	...	...
1 VII 2001	SSDJ	2 157 537	288 895	13.4	1 065 484	131 861	12.4	1 092 053	157 034	14.4
Liberia - Libéria										
1 VII 1993	ESDF	2 640 062	1 156 282	43.8	...	...	...	...	...	...
1 VII 1994	ESDF	2 699 888	1 194 077	44.2	...	...	...	...	...	...
1 VII 1995	ESDF	2 759 714	1 231 872	44.6	...	...	...	...	...	...
1 VII 1996	ESDF	2 819 540	1 269 668	45.0	...	...	...	...	...	...
1 VII 1997	ESDF	2 879 366	1 307 463	45.4	...	...	...	...	...	...
Malawi[4]										
1 VII 1993	ESDF	9 134 976	1 576 500	17.3	...	...	...	...	...	...
1 VII 1994	ESDF	9 461 403	1 711 200	18.1	...	...	...	...	...	...
1 VII 1995	ESDF	9 787 831	1 845 900	18.9	...	...	...	...	...	...
1 VII 1996	ESDF	10 114 257	1 980 700	19.6	...	...	...	...	...	...
1 IX 1998	CDFC	9 933 868	1 435 436	14.4	4 867 563	742 839	15.3	5 066 305	692 597	13.7
Mauritius - Maurice										
1 VII 1993	ESDJ	1 097 374	478 329	43.6	...	...	...	...	...	...
1 VII 1994	ESDJ	1 112 846	483 602	43.5	...	...	...	...	...	...
1 VII 1995	ESDJ	1 122 457	486 294	43.3	...	...	...	...	...	...
1 VII 1996	ESDJ	1 133 996	489 793	43.2	...	...	...	...	...	...
1 VII 1997	ESDJ	1 148 284	494 446	43.1	...	...	...	...	...	...
1 VII 1998	ESDJ	1 160 421	498 138	42.9	...	...	...	...	...	...
1 VII 1999	ESDJ	1 175 267	502 958	42.8	...	...	...	...	...	...
1 VII 2000	ESDJ	1 186 873	506 357	42.7	588 212	249 678	42.4	598 661	256 679	42.9
2 VII 2000	CDJC	1 178 848	503 045	42.7	583 756	247 844	42.5	595 092	255 201	42.9
1 VII 2001	ESDJ	1 199 881	510 822	42.6	594 490	251 721	42.3	605 391	259 101	42.8
1 VII 2002	ESDJ	1 210 196	514 129	42.5	599 257	253 214	42.3	610 939	260 915	42.7
Morocco - Maroc										
1 VII 1993	ESDF	26 069 000	13 149 000	50.4	12 792 000	6 616 000	51.7	13 277 000	6 533 000	49.2
1 VII 1994	ESDF	25 926 000	13 270 000	51.2	...	...	...	...	...	...
2 IX 1994	CDFC	26 019 280	13 356 246	51.3	12 944 517	6 632 953	51.2	13 074 763	6 723 293	51.4
1 VII 1995	ESDF	26 386 000	13 684 000	51.9	...	...	...	...	...	...
1 VII 1996	ESDF	26 848 000	14 100 000	52.5	13 357 000	...	...	13 491 000	...	...
1 VII 1997	ESDF	27 310 000	14 524 000	53.2	13 588 000	7 173 000	52.8	13 722 000	7 351 000	53.6
1 VII 1998	ESDF	27 775 000	14 957 000	53.9	13 819 000	7 373 000	53.4	13 956 000	7 584 000	54.3
1 VII 1999	ESDF	28 238 000	15 401 000	54.5	14 049 000	7 580 000	54.0	14 189 000	7 821 000	55.1
1 VII 2000	ESDF	28 705 000	15 849 000	55.2	14 281 000	7 787 000	54.5	14 424 000	8 062 000	55.9
1 VII 2001	ESDF	29 170 000	16 307 000	55.9	14 512 000	8 000 000	55.1	14 658 000	8 307 000	56.7
1 VII 2002	ESDF	29 631 000	16 772 000	56.6	14 742 000	8 217 000	55.7	14 889 000	8 555 000	57.5
Mozambique[5]										
1 VIII 1997	CDFC	16 099 246	4 601 132	28.6	7 714 306	2 274 116	29.5	8 384 940	2 327 016	27.8
Saint Helena ex. dep. - Sainte-Hélène sans dép.										
8 III 1998	CDFC	5 157	884	17.1	2 612	452	17.3	2 545	432	17.0
Senegal - Sénégal										
1 VII 1993	ESDF	7 913 090	3 497 584	44.2	...	...	...	...	...	...
1 VII 1994	ESDF	8 127 374	3 324 304	40.9	...	...	...	...	...	...
1 VII 1995	ESDF	8 346 998	3 447 804	41.3	...	...	...	...	...	...
1 VII 1996	ESDF	8 572 004	3 575 365	41.7	...	...	...	...	...	...
1 VII 1997	ESDF	8 802 304	3 618 255	41.1	...	...	...	...	...	...
1 VIII 1998	ESDF	9 037 906	3 842 820	42.5	...	...	...	...	...	...
1 VII 1999	ESDF	9 278 617	3 982 772	42.9	...	...	...	...	...	...
Sierra Leone										
1 VII 1993	ESDF	4 225 415	1 465 850	34.7	...	...	...	...	...	...
1 VII 1994	ESDF	4 322 516	1 508 234	34.9	...	...	...	...	...	...
1 VII 1995	ESDF	4 421 481	1 551 087	35.1	...	...	...	...	...	...

6. Urban and total population by sex: 1993 - 2002
Population urbaine et population totale selon le sexe: 1993 - 2002
(continued — suite)

(See notes at end of table. — Voir notes à la fin du tableau.)

Continent, country or area and date / Continent, pays ou zone et date	Code[1]	Both sexes - Les deux sexes			Male - Masculin			Female - Féminin		
		Total	Urban - Urbaine		Total	Urban - Urbaine		Total	Urban - Urbaine	
			Number Nombre	Percent P.100		Number Nombre	Percent P.100		Number Nombre	Percent P.100
AFRICA — AFRIQUE										
Sierra Leone										
1 VII 1996	ESDF	4 522 314	1 594 408	35.3	...	...	...	...	...	...
1 VII 1997	ESDF	4 625 013	1 638 198	35.4	...	...	...	...	...	...
1 VII 1998	ESDF	4 729 579	1 682 456	35.6	...	...	...	...	...	...
1 VII 1999	ESDF	4 836 011	1 727 184	35.7	...	...	...	...	...	...
1 VII 2000	ESDF	4 944 310	1 772 379	35.8	...	...	...	...	...	...
1 VII 2001	ESDF	5 054 476	1 818 044	36.0	...	...	...	...	...	...
1 VII 2002	ESDF	5 166 508	1 864 177	36.1	...	...	...	...	...	...
Somalia - Somalie[6]										
1 VII 2002	SSDF	6 799 079	2 310 817	34.0	3 499 523	1 168 410	33.4	3 299 556	1 142 407	34.6
South Africa - Afrique du Sud[7,8]										
1 VII 1996	ESDF	40 342 300	21 659 400	53.7	19 394 900	10 604 600	54.7	20 947 400	11 054 800	52.8
10 X 1996	CDFC	40 583 573	21 781 807	53.7	19 520 887	10 667 927	54.6	21 062 686	11 113 880	52.8
1 VII 1997	ESDF	41 226 700	22 107 800	53.6	19 857 000	10 836 700	54.6	21 369 700	11 271 100	52.7
1 VII 1998	ESDF	42 130 500	22 565 300	53.6	20 330 100	11 073 800	54.5	21 800 400	11 491 500	52.7
1 VII 1999	ESDF	43 054 306	23 032 381	53.5	20 814 425	11 316 037	54.4	22 239 881	11 716 344	52.7
1 VII 2000	ESDF	43 685 699	23 125 194	52.9	21 016 530	11 273 108	53.6	22 669 169	11 852 086	52.3
Swaziland										
1 VII 1993	ESDF	850 628	206 203	24.2	...	...	...	...	...	...
1 VII 1994	ESDF	879 081	217 309	24.7	410 924	108 790	26.5	468 157	108 519	23.2
1 VII 1995	ESDF	908 119	225 074	24.8	...	...	...	...	...	...
1 VII 1996	ESDF	937 747	237 368	25.3	438 334	118 562	27.0	499 413	118 806	23.8
11 V 1997	CDFC	929 718	214 428	23.1	440 154	106 256	24.1	489 564	108 172	22.1
Tunisia - Tunisie										
20 IV 1994	CDFC	8 785 711	5 361 927	61.0	4 439 289	2 717 168	61.2	4 346 422	2 644 759	60.8
Uganda - Ouganda										
1 VII 1995	ESDF	19 262 626	2 587 105	13.4	9 504 221		...	9 758 406		...
1 VII 1996	ESDF	19 847 689	2 764 579	13.9	9 802 558		...	10 045 131		...
1 VII 1997	ESDF	20 752 400	2 732 878	13.2	...	...	...	...	...	...
1 VII 1998	ESDF	21 467 200	2 878 135	10.4	...	...	...	...	...	...
1 VII 1999	ESDF	22 206 600	3 026 742	13.6	...	...	...	...	...	...
1 VII 2000	ESDF	22 971 500	3 178 692	13.8	...	...	...	...	...	...
12 IX 2002	CDFC	24 748 977	3 028 811	12.2	12 124 761	...	...	12 624 216	...	...
Zambia - Zambie										
1 VII 1995	ESDF	9 112 045	3 499 309	38.4	...	...	...	...	...	...
1 VII 2000	ESDF	9 337 425	3 347 069	35.8	4 594 290	1 662 739	36.2	4 743 135	1 684 330	35.5
Zimbabwe										
18 VIII 1997	SSDF	11 789 274	3 826 580	32.5	5 647 090	1 906 476	33.8	6 142 184	1 920 104	31.3
AMERICA, NORTH — AMERIQUE DU NORD										
Belize										
1 VII 1993	ESDF	205 000	97 430	47.5	104 000	47 951	46.1	101 000	49 479	49.0
1 VII 1994	ESDF	211 000	106 975	50.7	104 000	52 000	50.0	107 000	54 975	51.4
1 VII 1995	ESDF	216 500	109 880	50.8	107 500	54 255	50.5	109 000	55 625	51.0
1 VII 1996	ESDF	222 000	113 640	51.2	111 000	54 440	49.0	111 000	59 200	53.3
1 VII 1997	ESDF	230 000	115 975	50.4	114 500	55 350	48.3	115 500	60 625	52.5
1 VII 1998	ESDF	238 500	120 110	50.4	118 500	57 095	48.2	120 000	63 015	52.5
1 VII 1999	ESDF	243 055	118 125	48.6	122 745	58 375	47.6	120 310	59 750	49.7
12 V 2000	CDFC	240 204	114 541	47.7	121 278	56 565	46.6	118 926	57 976	48.7
1 VII 2000	ESDF	249 800	121 455	48.6	126 080	59 985	47.6	123 720	61 470	49.7
1 VII 2001	ESDF	257 310	125 830	48.9	129 890	62 160	47.9	127 420	63 670	50.0
1 VII 2002	ESDF	265 200	130 500	49.2	133 900	64 400	48.1	131 300	66 100	50.3
Canada[9,10,11,12,13]										
1 VII 1993	ESDJ	28 681 676	22 115 303	77.1	...	...	...	...	...	...
1 VII 1994	ESDJ	28 999 006	22 433 823	77.4	...	...	...	...	...	...
1 VII 1995	ESDJ	29 302 091	22 742 313	77.6	...	...	...	...	...	...

6. Urban and total population by sex: 1993 - 2002
Population urbaine et population totale selon le sexe: 1993 - 2002
(continued — suite)

(See notes at end of table. — Voir notes à la fin du tableau.)

Continent, country or area and date / Continent, pays ou zone et date	Code[1]	Both sexes - Les deux sexes			Male - Masculin			Female - Féminin		
		Total	Urban - Urbaine		Total	Urban - Urbaine		Total	Urban - Urbaine	
			Number Nombre	Percent P.100		Number Nombre	Percent P.100		Number Nombre	Percent P.100
AMERICA, NORTH — AMERIQUE DU NORD										
Canada[9,10,11,12,13]										
14 V 1996	CDJC	28 846 760	22 461 210	77.9	14 170 030	10 902 295	76.9	14 676 735	11 558 910	78.8
1 VII 1996	ESDJ	29 610 757	23 056 084	77.9	...	...	...	...	...	...
1 VII 1997	ESDJ	29 907 172	23 397 908	78.2	...	...	...	...	...	...
1 VII 1998	ESDJ	30 157 082	23 704 015	78.6	...	...	...	...	...	...
1 VII 1999	ESDJ	30 403 878	24 008 123	79.0	15 101 937	...	...	15 397 282	...	...
1 VII 2000	ESDJ	30 689 035	24 343 062	79.3	15 234 321	...	...	15 535 348	...	...
15 V 2001	CDJC	30 007 095	23 908 105	79.7	14 706 850	11 594 915	78.8	15 300 245	12 313 190	80.5
1 VII 2001	ESDJ	31 021 251	24 716 136	79.7	15 316 459	...	...	15 704 792	...	...
Costa Rica										
1 VII 1993	ESDJ	3 004 577	1 324 667	44.1	...	...	...	...	...	...
1 VII 1994	ESDJ	3 070 918	1 352 375	44.0	...	...	...	...	...	...
1 VII 1995	ESDJ	3 136 020	1 369 421	43.7	...	...	...	...	...	...
1 VII 1996	ESDJ	3 202 440	1 392 892	43.5	...	...	...	...	...	...
1 VII 1997	ESDJ	3 270 700	1 419 407	43.4	...	...	...	...	...	...
1 VII 1998	ESDJ	3 340 909	1 440 272	43.1	...	...	...	...	...	...
1 VII 1999	ESDJ	3 412 613	1 576 288	46.2	...	...	...	...	...	...
26 VI 2000	CDJC	3 810 179	2 249 414	59.0	1 902 614	1 096 248	57.6	1 907 565	1 153 166	60.5
1 VII 2000	ESDJ	3 486 048	1 644 638	47.2	...	...	...	...	...	...
1 VII 2001	ESDJ	3 906 742	2 305 723	59.0	...	...	...	...	...	...
1 VII 2002	ESDJ	3 997 883	2 359 158	59.0	...	...	...	...	...	...
Cuba										
1 VII 1993	ESDF	10 904 466	8 111 613	74.4	5 482 360	4 001 875	73.0	5 422 106	4 109 738	75.8
1 VII 1994	ESDF	10 950 100	8 145 869	74.4	5 502 852	4 010 950	72.9	5 447 248	4 134 919	75.9
1 VII 1997	ESDF	11 065 878	8 295 762	75.0	5 541 552	4 069 554	73.4	5 524 326	4 226 208	76.5
1 VII 1998	ESDF	11 116 514	8 359 529	75.2	5 563 304	4 098 448	73.7	5 553 210	4 261 081	76.7
1 VII 1999	ESDF	11 159 991	8 395 944	75.2	5 580 344	4 112 359	73.7	5 579 647	4 283 585	76.8
1 VII 2000	ESDF	11 198 600	8 426 270	75.2	5 596 057	4 124 048	73.7	5 602 543	4 302 222	76.8
1 VII 2002	ESDF	11 250 979	8 466 744	75.3	5 624 025	4 142 468	73.7	5 626 954	4 324 276	76.8
Dominican Republic - République dominicaine										
1 VII 1993	ESDF	*7 620 395*	*4 615 596*	*60.6*	...	...	...	...	...	...
El Salvador										
1 VII 1995	ESDF	5 668 605	3 216 533	56.7	2 776 269	1 542 163	55.5	2 892 336	1 674 370	57.9
1 VII 1996	ESDF	5 787 093	3 305 082	57.1	2 835 313	1 585 186	55.9	2 951 780	1 719 896	58.3
1 VII 1997	ESDF	5 908 460	3 394 950	57.5	2 896 114	1 629 017	56.2	3 012 346	1 765 933	58.6
1 VII 1998	ESDF	6 031 326	3 485 465	57.8	2 957 835	1 673 250	56.6	3 073 491	1 812 215	59.0
1 VII 1999	ESDF	6 154 311	3 575 956	58.1	3 019 645	1 717 489	56.9	3 134 666	1 858 467	59.3
1 VII 2000	ESDF	6 276 037	3 665 747	58.4	3 080 704	1 761 327	57.2	3 195 333	1 904 420	59.6
1 VII 2001	ESDF	6 396 890	3 754 903	58.7	3 141 208	1 804 804	57.5	3 255 682	1 950 099	59.9
1 VII 2002	ESDF	6 517 798	3 843 878	59.0	3 201 720	1 848 194	57.7	3 316 078	1 995 684	60.2
Greenland - Groenland[14]										
1 VII 1993	ESDJ	55 117	44 289	80.4	29 549	23 577	79.8	25 719	20 896	81.2
1 VII 1994	ESDJ	55 576	44 902	80.8	29 665	23 767	80.1	25 911	21 135	81.6
1 VII 1995	ESDJ	55 798	45 228	81.1	29 762	23 930	80.4	26 036	21 298	81.8
1 VII 1996	ESDJ	55 917	45 330	81.1	29 828	23 993	80.4	26 089	21 337	81.8
1 VII 1997	ESDJ	56 323	45 420	80.6	29 871	24 042	80.5	26 452	21 377	80.8
1 VII 1998	ESDJ	56 076	45 489	81.1	29 904	24 092	80.6	26 172	21 397	81.8
1 VII 1999	ESDJ	56 087	45 523	81.2	29 941	24 189	80.8	26 146	21 334	81.6
1 VII 2000	CDJC	56 124	45 714	81.5	29 989	24 257	80.9	26 135	21 457	82.1
Haiti - Haïti										
1 VII 1993	ESDJ	*6 902 596*	*2 165 805*	*31.4*	...	...	...	...	...	...
1 VII 1994	ESDJ	*7 041 445*	*2 251 351*	*32.0*	...	...	...	...	...	...
1 VII 1995	ESDJ	*7 180 294*	*2 338 842*	*32.6*	...	...	...	...	...	...
1 VII 1996	ESDJ	*7 336 028*	*2 433 878*	*33.2*	...	...	...	...	...	...

6. Urban and total population by sex: 1993 - 2002
Population urbaine et population totale selon le sexe: 1993 - 2002
(continued — suite)

(See notes at end of table. — Voir notes à la fin du tableau.)

Continent, country or area and date / Continent, pays ou zone et date	Code[1]	Both sexes - Les deux sexes			Male - Masculin			Female - Féminin		
		Total	Urban - Urbaine		Total	Urban - Urbaine		Total	Urban - Urbaine	
			Number Nombre	Percent P.100		Number Nombre	Percent P.100		Number Nombre	Percent P.100
AMERICA, NORTH — AMERIQUE DU NORD										
Haiti - Haïti										
1 VII 1997	ESDJ	7 491 762	2 531 060	33.8	...	...	...	...	...	...
1 VII 1998	ESDJ	7 647 496	2 630 383	34.4	...	...	...	...	...	...
1 VII 1999	ESDJ	7 803 230	2 731 843	35.0	...	...	...	...	...	...
1 VII 2000	ESDJ	7 958 964	2 835 433	35.6	...	...	...	...	...	...
Honduras										
1 VII 1993	ESDF	5 318 527	2 215 083	41.6	...	...	...	...	...	...
1 VII 1994	ESDF	5 460 172	2 302 736	42.2	...	...	...	...	...	...
1 VII 1995	ESDF	5 605 581	2 393 858	42.7	...	...	...	...	...	...
1 VII 1996	ESDF	5 754 845	2 488 850	43.2	...	...	...	...	...	...
1 VII 1997	ESDF	5 908 069	2 587 337	43.8	...	...	...	...	...	...
1 VII 1998	ESDF	6 056 942	2 689 721	44.4	...	...	...	...	...	...
1 VII 1999	ESDF	6 211 412	2 796 156	45.0	...	...	...	...	...	...
1 VII 2000	ESDF	6 369 188	2 907 091	45.6	...	...	...	...	...	...
1 VII 2001	ESDF	6 530 331	3 022 150	46.3	...	...	...	...	...	...
1 VII 2002	ESDF	6 694 761	3 140 880	46.9	...	...	...	...	...	...
Jamaica - Jamaïque										
10 IX 2001	CDFC	2 607 633	1 355 334	52.0	1 283 547	646 426	50.4	1 324 085	708 929	53.5
Mexico - Mexique										
1 VII 1993	ESDJ	88 754 928	64 536 499	72.7	...	...	...	...	...	...
1 VII 1994	ESDJ	90 385 688	66 093 327	73.1	...	...	...	...	...	...
1 VII 1995	ESDJ	91 992 118	67 601 543	73.5	...	...	...	...	...	...
5 XI 1995	SSDJ	91 158 290	67 003 515	73.5	...	...	...	...	...	...
1 VII 1996	ESDJ	93 571 559	69 047 515	73.8	...	...	...	...	...	...
1 VII 1997	ESDJ	95 127 443	70 438 407	74.0	...	...	...	...	...	...
1 VII 1998	ESDJ	96 648 885	71 775 640	74.3	...	...	...	...	...	...
1 VII 1999	ESDJ	98 132 370	73 066 860	74.5	...	...	...	...	...	...
14 II 2000	CDJC	97 483 412	72 759 822	74.6	48 641 690	...	...	49 490 720	...	...
1 VII 2000	ESDJ	100 248 699	74 823 781	74.6	47 592 253	35 317 569	74.2	49 891 159	37 442 253	75.0
1 VII 2001	ESDJ	101 754 160	76 181 526	74.9	...	...	...	...	...	...
1 VII 2002	ESDJ	103 229 487	77 520 325	75.1	51 108 182	38 141 976	74.6	52 121 305	39 378 349	75.6
Nicaragua										
1 VII 1993	ESDJ	4 174 860	2 307 382	55.3	...	...	...	...	...	...
1 VII 1994	ESDJ	4 298 925	2 391 801	55.6	...	...	...	...	...	...
25 IV 1995	CDJC	4 357 099	2 370 810	54.4	2 147 105	...	...	2 209 994	...	...
1 VII 1995	ESDJ	4 426 677	2 479 178	56.0	2 199 918	1 192 131	54.2	2 226 759	1 287 047	57.8
1 VII 1996	ESDJ	4 548 755	2 535 091	55.7	2 261 141	1 221 317	54.0	2 287 614	1 313 774	57.4
1 VII 1997	ESDJ	4 674 199	2 621 328	56.1	2 324 066	1 264 550	54.4	2 350 133	1 356 778	57.7
1 VII 1998	ESDJ	4 803 102	2 710 381	56.4	2 388 742	1 309 236	54.8	2 414 360	1 401 145	58.0
1 VII 1999	ESDJ	4 935 559	2 802 340	56.8	2 455 217	1 355 417	55.2	2 480 342	1 446 923	58.3
1 VII 2000	ESDJ	4 956 964	2 835 184	57.2	2 474 984	1 361 335	55.0	2 481 980	1 473 849	59.4
1 VII 2001	ESDJ	5 058 642	2 911 746	57.6	2 526 353	1 399 561	55.4	2 532 289	1 512 185	59.7
1 VII 2002	ESDJ	5 162 274	2 990 342	57.9	2 578 680	1 438 771	55.8	2 583 594	1 551 571	60.1
Panama										
1 VII 1993	ESDF	2 535 012	1 381 542	54.5	1 282 633	673 074	52.5	1 252 379	708 468	56.6
1 VII 1994	ESDF	2 582 566	1 413 083	54.7	1 306 173	688 653	52.7	1 276 393	724 430	56.8
1 VII 1995	ESDF	2 631 013	1 444 622	54.9	1 330 145	704 231	52.9	1 300 868	740 391	56.9
1 VII 1996	ESDF	2 674 490	1 476 665	55.2	1 351 574	719 973	53.3	1 322 916	756 692	57.2
1 VII 1997	ESDF	2 718 686	1 508 703	55.5	1 373 349	735 709	53.6	1 345 337	772 994	57.5
1 VII 1998	ESDF	2 763 612	1 540 742	55.8	1 395 475	751 450	53.8	1 368 137	789 292	57.7
1 VII 1999	ESDF	2 809 280	1 572 780	56.0	1 417 957	767 186	54.1	1 391 323	805 594	57.9
1 VII 2000	ESDF	2 855 703	1 604 823	56.2	1 440 801	782 928	54.3	1 414 902	821 895	58.1
Puerto Rico - Porto Rico[15,16]										
1 IV 2000*	CDJC	3 808 610	3 594 948	94.4	1 833 577	1 723 589	94.0	1 975 033	1 871 359	94.8
1 VII 2000	ESDJ	3 817 633	3 604 039	94.4	1 837 619	...	...	1 980 014	...	...

6. Urban and total population by sex: 1993 - 2002
Population urbaine et population totale selon le sexe: 1993 - 2002
(continued — suite)

(See notes at end of table. — Voir notes à la fin du tableau.)

Continent, country or area and date / Continent, pays ou zone et date	Code[1]	Both sexes - Les deux sexes Total	Urban - Urbaine Number Nombre	Urban - Urbaine Percent P.100	Male - Masculin Total	Urban - Urbaine Number Nombre	Urban - Urbaine Percent P.100	Female - Féminin Total	Urban - Urbaine Number Nombre	Urban - Urbaine Percent P.100
AMERICA, NORTH — AMERIQUE DU NORD										
Saint Lucia - Sainte-Lucie[17]										
1 VII 1994	ESDF	142 689	42 193	29.6	69 327	20 500	29.6	73 362	21 693	29.6
1 VII 1995	ESDF	145 437	43 005	29.6	70 725	20 913	29.6	74 715	22 092	29.6
1 VII 1996	ESDF	147 047	43 486	29.6	71 760	21 219	29.6	75 302	22 267	29.6
1 VII 1997	ESDF	149 621	44 256	29.6	73 114	21 620	29.6	76 552	22 636	29.6
1 VII 1998	ESDF	151 972	44 932	29.6	74 320	21 976	29.6	77 632	22 956	29.6
22 V 2001	CDFC	157 164	43 316	27.6	76 741	20 711	27.0	80 423	22 605	28.1
Saint Vincent and the Grenadines - Saint Vincent-et-les Grenadines										
1 VII 1993	ESDF	109 653	47 890	43.7	...	...	...	...	...	...
1 VII 1994	ESDF	109 534	47 839	43.7	...	...	...	...	...	...
1 VII 1995	ESDF	110 724	48 353	43.7	...	...	...	...	...	...
1 VII 1996	ESDF	111 105	48 522	43.7	...	...	...	...	...	...
1 VII 1997	ESDF	111 655	48 761	43.7	55 713	...	...	55 942	...	...
1 VII 1998	ESDF	111 380	48 652	43.7	55 602	...	...	55 778	...	...
1 VII 2002	ESDF	107 854	48 535	45.0	54 434	...	...	53 420	...	...
United States - États-Unis[18]*										
1 IV 2000*	CDJC	281 421 906	222 360 539	79.0	138 053 563	108 375 797	78.5	143 368 343	113 984 742	79.5
AMERICA, SOUTH — AMERIQUE DU SUD										
Argentina - Argentine										
1 VII 1993	ESDF	33 869 405	29 723 071	87.8	...	...	...	17 481 914	...	...
1 VII 1994	ESDF	34 318 469	30 220 944	88.1	16 836 555	...	...	17 712 643	...	...
1 VII 1995	ESDF	34 768 458	30 715 258	88.3	17 055 814	14 889 186	87.3	17 943 728	15 826 072	89.3
1 VII 1996	ESDF	35 219 612	31 206 336	88.6	17 275 885	...	...	18 174 949	...	...
1 VII 1997	ESDF	35 671 894	31 697 444	88.9	17 496 945	...	...	18 406 194	...	...
1 VII 1998	ESDF	36 124 933	32 188 095	89.1	17 718 738	...	...	...	...	...
1 VII 1999	ESDF	36 578 358	32 677 810	89.3	...	...	...	...	...	...
18 XI 2001	CDFC	36 260 130	32 431 950	89.4	17 659 072	15 629 299	88.5	18 601 058	16 802 651	90.3
Bolivia - Bolivie[7]										
1 VII 1993	ESDF	7 065 211	4 063 965	57.5	...	...	...	...	...	...
1 VII 1994	ESDF	7 237 424	4 232 386	58.5	3 582 711	...	...	3 654 713	...	...
1 VII 1995	ESDF	7 413 834	4 406 129	59.4	3 680 139	2 139 324	58.1	3 733 695	2 266 805	60.7
1 VII 1996	ESDF	7 588 392	4 576 132	60.3	3 768 522	2 222 809	59.0	3 819 870	2 353 323	61.6
1 VII 1997	ESDF	7 767 059	4 751 190	61.2	3 859 028	2 308 866	59.8	3 908 031	2 442 324	62.5
1 VII 1998	ESDF	7 949 933	4 931 398	62.0	3 951 706	2 397 547	60.7	3 998 227	2 533 851	63.4
1 VII 1999	ESDF	8 137 113	5 116 850	62.9	4 046 609	2 488 906	61.5	4 090 504	2 627 944	64.2
1 VII 2000	ESDF	8 328 700	5 307 638	63.7	4 143 790	2 582 994	62.3	4 184 910	2 724 644	65.1
1 VII 2001	ESDF	8 274 325	5 165 882	62.4	...	...	...	...	...	...
5 IX 2001	CDFC	8 280 184	5 153 230	62.2	4 130 342	2 501 256	60.6	4 149 842	2 651 974	63.9
Brazil - Brésil[19]										
1 VIII 1996	CDJC	157 070 163	123 076 831	78.4	77 442 865	59 716 389	77.1	79 627 298	63 360 442	79.6
1 VIII 2000	CDJC	169 799 170	137 953 959	81.2	83 576 015	66 882 993	80.0	86 223 155	71 070 966	82.4
Chile - Chili										
1 VII 1993	ESDF	13 771 187	11 561 902	84.0	6 809 060	5 619 865	82.5	6 962 127	5 942 037	85.3
1 VII 1994	ESDF	13 994 355	11 785 639	84.2	6 921 150	5 732 505	82.8	7 073 205	6 053 134	85.6
1 VII 1995	ESDF	14 210 429	12 002 308	84.5	7 029 597	5 841 532	83.1	7 180 832	6 160 776	85.8
1 VII 1996	ESDF	14 418 864	12 213 883	84.7	7 134 144	5 948 050	83.4	7 284 720	6 265 833	86.0
1 VII 1997	ESDF	14 622 354	12 420 506	84.9	7 236 189	6 052 039	83.6	7 386 165	6 368 467	86.2
1 VII 1998	ESDF	14 821 714	12 623 059	85.2	7 336 118	6 153 975	83.9	7 485 596	6 469 084	86.4

6. Urban and total population by sex: 1993 - 2002
Population urbaine et population totale selon le sexe: 1993 - 2002
(continued — suite)

(See notes at end of table. — Voir notes à la fin du tableau.)

Continent, country or area and date / Continent, pays ou zone et date	Code[1]	Both sexes - Les deux sexes Total	Urban - Urbaine Number Nombre	Urban - Urbaine Percent P.100	Male - Masculin Total	Urban - Urbaine Number Nombre	Urban - Urbaine Percent P.100	Female - Féminin Total	Urban - Urbaine Number Nombre	Urban - Urbaine Percent P.100
AMERICA, SOUTH — AMERIQUE DU SUD										
Chile - Chili										
1 VII 1999	ESDF	15 017 760	12 822 261	85.4	7 434 317	6 254 136	84.1	7 583 443	6 568 125	86.6
1 VII 2000	ESDF	15 211 308	13 018 924	85.6	7 531 173	6 352 945	84.4	7 680 135	6 665 979	86.8
1 VII 2001	ESDF	15 401 952	13 216 121	85.8	7 626 482	6 451 736	84.6	7 775 470	6 764 385	87.0
24 IV 2002	CDFC	15 116 435	13 090 113	86.6	7 447 695	6 366 311	85.5	7 668 740	6 723 802	87.7
1 VII 2002	ESDF	15 589 147	13 409 844	86.0	7 719 986	6 548 696	84.8	7 869 161	6 861 148	87.2
Colombia - Colombie										
24 X 1993	CDFC	33 109 840	23 514 070	71.0	16 296 539	11 211 708	68.8	16 813 301	12 302 362	73.2
Ecuador - Équateur[20]										
1 VII 1993	ESDF	10 980 972	6 336 923	57.7						
1 VII 1994	ESDF	11 221 070	6 560 382	58.5	5 638 647	...	...	5 582 423	...	...
1 VII 1995	ESDF	11 460 117	6 784 855	59.2	5 758 141	...	...	5 701 976	...	...
1 VII 1996	ESDF	11 698 496	7 011 072	59.9	5 877 274	...	...	5 821 222	...	...
1 VII 1997	ESDF	11 772 866	6 953 116	59.1	5 914 625	3 433 722	58.1	5 858 242	3 519 394	60.1
1 VII 1998	ESDF	11 947 588	7 118 271	59.6	6 001 552	3 517 425	58.6	5 946 036	3 600 846	60.6
1 VII 1999	ESDF	12 120 984	7 282 105	60.1	6 087 690	3 600 349	59.1	6 033 294	3 681 756	61.0
1 VII 2000	ESDF	12 298 745	7 450 308	60.6	6 175 859	3 685 298	59.7	6 122 886	3 765 010	61.5
1 VII 2001	ESDF	12 479 924	7 633 850	61.2	6 265 558	3 778 158	60.3	6 214 366	3 855 692	62.0
25 XI 2001	CDFC	12 156 608	7 431 355	61.1	6 018 353	3 625 962	60.2	6 138 255	3 805 393	62.0
1 VII 2002	ESDF	12 660 727	7 817 018	61.7	6 354 906	3 870 667	60.9	6 305 821	3 946 351	62.6
Paraguay										
28 VIII 2002	CDFC	5 206 101	2 953 168	56.7	2 640 068	1 444 447	54.7	2 566 033	1 508 721	58.8
Peru - Pérou[7,21]										
11 VII 1993	CDFC	22 048 356	15 458 599	70.1	10 956 375	7 606 489	69.4	11 091 981	7 852 110	70.8
1 VII 1997	ESDF	24 681 045	17 640 917	71.5	12 419 397	8 849 804	71.3	12 261 648	8 791 113	71.7
1 VII 1998	ESDF	25 104 276	17 978 819	71.6	12 631 667	9 017 356	71.4	12 472 609	8 961 463	71.8
1 VII 1999	ESDF	25 524 613	18 312 557	71.7	12 843 267	9 182 458	71.5	12 682 346	9 130 099	72.0
1 VII 2000	ESDF	25 939 329	18 647 242	71.9	13 049 847	9 348 264	71.6	12 889 482	9 298 978	72.1
1 VII 2001	ESDF	26 346 840	18 980 589	72.0	13 253 619	9 513 198	71.8	13 093 221	9 467 391	72.3
1 VII 2002	ESDF	26 748 972	19 310 309	72.2	13 454 486	9 676 260	71.9	13 294 486	9 634 049	72.5
Uruguay[7]										
22 V 1996	CDFC	3 163 763	2 872 077	90.8	1 532 288	1 366 092	89.2	1 631 475	1 505 985	92.3
1 VII 1997	ESDF	3 263 451	3 000 598	91.9	1 582 607	1 431 934	90.5	1 680 844	1 568 664	93.3
1 VII 1998	ESDF	3 283 971	3 023 118	92.1	1 591 876	1 443 079	90.7	1 692 095	1 580 039	93.4
1 VII 1999	ESDF	3 302 843	3 044 240	92.2	1 600 369	1 453 569	90.8	1 702 474	1 590 671	93.4
1 VII 2000	ESDF	3 322 141	3 065 839	92.3	1 609 199	1 464 413	91.0	1 712 942	1 601 426	93.5
1 VII 2001	ESDF	3 341 521	3 087 636	92.4	1 618 140	1 475 418	91.2	1 723 381	1 612 218	93.5
1 VII 2002	ESDF	3 360 868	3 109 521	92.5	1 627 129	1 486 522	91.4	1 733 739	1 622 999	93.6
Venezuela[7,21]										
1 VII 1996	ESDF	22 501 988	19 710 481	87.6	11 333 607	9 818 511	86.6	11 168 381	9 891 970	88.6
1 VII 1997	ESDF	22 958 680	20 123 896	87.7	11 559 949	10 021 295	86.7	11 398 731	10 102 601	88.6
1 VII 1998	ESDF	23 412 742	20 534 451	87.7	11 784 967	10 222 629	86.7	11 627 775	10 311 822	88.7
1 VII 1999	ESDF	23 867 393	20 945 043	87.8	12 010 280	10 423 959	86.8	11 857 113	10 521 084	88.7
1 VII 2000	ESDF	24 310 896	21 345 288	87.8	12 229 953	10 620 092	86.8	12 080 943	10 725 196	88.8
1 VII 2001	ESDF	24 765 581	21 754 766	87.8	12 454 204	10 820 038	86.9	12 311 377	10 934 728	88.8
1 VII 2002	ESDF	25 219 910	22 163 339	87.9	12 678 275	11 021 146	86.9	12 541 635	11 142 193	88.8
ASIA — ASIE										
Afghanistan[22]										
1 VII 2002	ESDF	20 297 800	4 463 000	22.0	10 453 500	2 332 600	22.3	9 844 300	2 130 400	21.6
Armenia - Arménie[23,24]										
1 VII 1993	ESDF	3 731 300	2 534 300	67.9	1 807 100	1 208 500	66.9	1 924 200	1 325 800	68.9
1 VII 1994	ESDF	3 746 800	2 533 000	67.6	1 814 100	1 207 400	66.6	1 932 700	1 325 600	68.6
1 VII 1995	ESDF	3 759 950	2 534 250	67.4	1 820 165	1 207 260	66.3	1 939 785	1 326 990	68.4

6. Urban and total population by sex: 1993 - 2002
Population urbaine et population totale selon le sexe: 1993 - 2002
(continued — suite)

(See notes at end of table. — Voir notes à la fin du tableau.)

Continent, country or area and date / Continent, pays ou zone et date	Code[1]	Both sexes - Les deux sexes			Male - Masculin			Female - Féminin		
		Total	Urban - Urbaine		Total	Urban - Urbaine		Total	Urban - Urbaine	
			Number Nombre	Percent P.100		Number Nombre	Percent P.100		Number Nombre	Percent P.100
ASIA — ASIE										
Armenia - Arménie[23,24]										
1 VII 1996	ESDF	3 773 567	2 534 024	67.2	1 827 556	1 207 639	66.1	1 946 011	1 326 385	68.2
1 VII 1997	ESDF	3 785 982	2 534 076	66.9	1 835 093	1 208 745	65.9	1 950 889	1 325 331	67.9
1 VII 1998	ESDF	3 794 735	2 535 702	66.8	1 841 448	1 210 849	65.8	1 953 287	1 324 853	67.8
1 VII 1999	ESDF	3 800 817	2 535 846	66.7	1 846 592	1 212 207	65.6	1 954 225	1 323 639	67.7
1 VII 2000	ESDF	3 802 882	2 534 023	66.6	1 848 756	1 212 033	65.6	1 954 126	1 321 990	67.7
10 X 2001	CDJC	6 215 605	4 011 667	64.5	2 949 219	1 873 803	63.5	3 266 386	2 137 864	65.5
Azerbaijan - Azerbaïdjan										
1 VII 1993	ESDF	7 494 800	3 949 700	52.7	...	...	...	...	...	...
1 VII 1994	ESDF	7 596 600	3 988 300	52.5	3 728 600	1 969 100	52.8	3 868 000	2 021 700	52.3
1 VII 1995	ESDF	7 684 900	4 020 100	52.3	3 778 700	1 977 600	52.3	3 906 200	2 042 500	52.3
1 VII 1996	ESDF	7 763 000	4 046 200	52.1	3 824 000	1 988 900	52.0	3 939 000	2 057 300	52.2
1 VII 1997	ESDF	7 838 300	4 070 200	51.9	3 864 300	2 006 500	51.9	3 974 000	2 063 700	51.9
1 VII 1998	ESDF	7 913 000	4 072 600	51.5	3 882 100	1 993 500	51.4	4 030 900	2 079 100	51.6
27 I 1999*	CDJC	7 953 438	4 053 584	51.0	3 883 155	1 970 022	50.7	4 070 283	2 083 562	51.2
1 VII 1999	ESDF	7 982 800	4 074 600	51.0	3 899 600	1 981 300	50.8	4 083 200	2 093 300	51.3
1 VII 2000	ESDF	8 048 600	4 096 900	50.9	3 936 400	1 994 300	50.7	4 112 200	2 102 600	51.1
1 VII 2001	ESDF	8 111 200	4 118 800	50.8	3 971 600	2 006 800	50.5	4 139 600	2 112 000	51.0
1 VII 2002	ESDF	8 172 000	4 142 200	50.7	4 005 900	2 020 200	50.4	4 166 100	2 122 000	50.9
Bangladesh										
22 I 2001	CDFC	123 151 246	28 808 477	23.4	62 735 988	15 360 059	24.5	60 415 258	13 448 418	22.3
Brunei Darussalam - Brunéi Darussalam										
21 VIII 2001	CDFC	332 844	238 699	71.7	168 974	120 046	71.0	163 870	118 653	72.4
Cambodia - Cambodge[25,26,27]										
1 III 1996	SSDF	10 702 000	1 540 000	14.4	5 119 000	738 000	14.4	5 583 000	802 000	14.4
3 III 1998	CDFC	11 437 656	1 795 575	15.7	5 511 408	878 186	15.9	5 926 248	917 389	15.5
China - Chine[28,29,30]										
1 VII 1993	ESDF	1185170000	333 510 000	28.1	...	...	...	...	...	...
1 VII 1994	ESDF	1198500000	343 010 000	28.6	...	...	...	...	...	...
1 VII 1995	ESDF	1211210000	351 740 000	29.0	...	...	...	...	...	...
1 VII 1996	ESDF	1223890000	359 500 000	29.4	...	...	...	...	...	...
1 VII 1997	ESDF	1236260000	369 890 000	29.9	...	...	...	...	...	...
1 VII 1998	ESDF	1248100000	379 420 000	30.4	...	...	...	...	...	...
1 VII 1999	ESDF	1259090000	388 920 000	30.9	...	...	...	...	...	...
1 XI 2000	CDJC	1242612226	458 770 983	36.9	640 275 969	235 264 707	36.7	602 336 257	223 506 276	37.1
Cyprus - Chypre[31,32]										
1 X 2001	CDJC	689 565	474 450	68.8	338 497	231 128	68.3	351 068	243 322	69.3
Georgia - Géorgie										
1 VII 1993	ESDF	5 440 300	3 039 500	55.9	...	...	...	...	...	...
1 VII 1994	ESDF	5 425 600	3 022 600	55.7	...	...	...	...	...	...
1 VII 1995	ESDF	5 416 900	3 013 600	55.6	...	...	...	...	...	...
1 VII 1996	ESDF	5 419 800	3 013 400	55.6	...	...	...	...	...	...
1 VII 1997	ESDF	5 430 600	3 019 800	55.6	...	...	...	...	...	...
1 VII 1998	ESDF	5 441 100	3 028 500	55.7	...	...	...	...	...	...
1 VII 2000	ESDF	5 023 052	2 903 173	57.8	2 401 344	1 368 716	57.0	2 621 708	1 534 457	58.5
17 I 2002	CDJC	4 371 535	2 284 796	52.3	2 061 753	1 048 593	50.9	2 309 782	1 236 203	53.5
India - Inde[27,33,34]										
1 VII 1993	ESDF	887 566 373	232 337 942	26.2	...	...	...	...	...	...
1 VII 1994	ESDF	905 449 218	238 818 591	26.4	...	...	...	...	...	...
1 VII 1995	ESDF	923 459 258	245 399 484	26.6	...	...	...	...	...	...
1 VII 1996	ESDF	941 579 289	252 090 369	26.8	487 475 000	134 819 000	27.7	452 065 000	121 947 000	27.0
1 VII 1997	ESDF	959 792 170	258 905 376	27.0	495 212 000	138 345 000	27.9	460 008 000	125 610 000	27.3

6.   Urban and total population by sex: 1993 - 2002
Population urbaine et population totale selon le sexe: 1993 - 2002
(continued — suite)

(See notes at end of table. — Voir notes à la fin du tableau.)

Continent, country or area and date / Continent, pays ou zone et date	Code[1]	Both sexes - Les deux sexes Total	Urban - Urbaine Number Nombre	Percent P.100	Male - Masculin Total	Urban - Urbaine Number Nombre	Percent P.100	Female - Féminin Total	Urban - Urbaine Number Nombre	Percent P.100
ASIA — ASIE										
India - Inde[27,33,34]										
1 VII 1998	ESDF	978 081 151	265 864 270	27.2	503 002 000	141 939 000	28.2	467 931 000	129 333 000	27.6
1 VII 1999	ESDF	996 430 241	272 993 874	27.4	510 813 000	145 592 000	28.5	475 798 000	133 103 000	28.0
1 VII 2000	ESDF	1014824629	280 329 650	27.6	518 604 000	149 295 000	28.8	483 538 000	136 906 000	28.3
1 III 2001	CDFC	1028610328	286 119 689	27.8	532 156 772	150 554 098	28.3	496 453 556	135 565 591	27.3
1 VII 2001	ESDF	1033248000	287 857 000	27.9	534 319 000	153 031 000	28.6	498 932 000	140 738 000	28.2
1 VII 2002	ESDF	1050640000	301 479 000	28.7	534 085 000	156 817 000	29.4	498 919 000	144 662 000	29.0
Indonesia - Indonésie[27,35]										
1 VII 1993	ESDF	187 589 500	62 898 800	33.5	...	...	...	...	...	...
1 VII 1994	ESDF	190 676 050	65 856 300	34.5	...	...	...	...	...	...
31 X 1995	SSDF	194 754 808	69 937 110	35.9	96 929 931	34 722 443	35.8	97 824 877	35 214 667	36.0
1 VII 1996	ESDF	198 320 000	73 640 300	37.1	...	...	...	...	...	...
1 VII 1997	ESDF	201 353 100	76 914 000	38.2	100 206 800	...	...	101 146 300	...	...
1 VII 1998	ESDF	204 392 500	80 275 300	39.3	101 719 200	...	...	102 673 300	...	...
1 VII 1999	ESDF	207 439 900	83 718 400	40.4	103 234 400	...	...	104 202 700	...	...
30 VI 2000	CDFC	206 264 595	86 601 850	42.0	103 417 180	43 368 496	41.9	102 847 415	43 233 354	42.0
Iran (Islamic Republic of) - Iran (République islamique d')										
1 VII 1993	ESDJ	57 487 720	33 742 643	58.7	29 414 643	17 326 790	58.9	28 073 077	16 415 853	58.5
1 VII 1994	ESDJ	58 331 206	34 738 041	59.6	29 846 228	17 839 668	59.8	28 484 978	16 898 373	59.3
1 VII 1995	ESDJ	59 187 068	35 762 803	60.4	30 284 145	18 364 139	60.6	28 902 923	17 398 664	60.2
23 X 1996	CDJC	60 055 488	36 817 789	61.3	30 515 159	18 805 023	61.6	29 540 329	18 012 766	61.0
1 VII 1997	ESDJ	60 938 837	37 826 305	62.1	31 011 770	19 249 804	62.1	29 927 067	18 576 501	62.1
1 VII 1998	ESDJ	61 835 591	38 839 280	62.8	...	...	...	...	...	...
1 VII 1999	ESDJ	62 745 540	39 856 570	63.5	...	...	...	...	...	...
1 VII 2000	ESDJ	63 663 942	40 873 494	64.2	...	...	...	...	...	...
1 VII 2001	ESDJ	64 528 159	42 173 587	65.4	...	...	...	...	...	...
1 VII 2002	ESDJ	65 540 239	43 054 650	65.7	...	...	...	...	...	...
Iraq[36]										
16 X 1997	CDFC	19 184 543	12 945 776	67.5	9 530 570	6 466 325	67.8	9 647 973	6 479 451	67.2
Israel - Israël[7,37]										
1 VII 1993	ESDJ	5 261 400	4 723 500	89.8	2 609 400	2 333 200	89.4	2 652 000	2 390 300	90.1
1 VII 1994	ESDJ	5 399 300	4 843 700	89.7	2 675 800	2 390 900	89.4	2 723 500	2 453 000	90.1
1 VII 1995	ESDJ	5 544 900	4 970 500	89.6	2 746 500	2 452 000	89.3	2 798 400	2 518 200	90.0
4 XI 1995	CDJC	5 548 523	5 044 735	90.9	2 738 175	2 476 836	90.5	2 810 348	2 567 899	91.4
1 VII 1996	ESDJ	5 685 100	5 166 000	90.9	...	...	...	...	...	...
1 VII 1997	ESDJ	5 829 000	5 294 100	90.8	2 875 400	2 599 900	90.4	2 953 500	2 694 300	91.2
1 VII 1998	ESDJ	5 970 700	5 418 400	90.7	...	...	...	...	...	...
1 VII 1999	ESDJ	6 125 300	5 554 200	90.7	3 021 743	...	...	3 103 533	...	...
1 VII 2000	ESDJ	6 289 200	5 696 100	90.6	3 102 400	2 797 800	90.2	3 186 800	2 898 300	90.9
1 VII 2001	ESDJ	6 439 000	5 900 700	91.6	3 176 600	2 900 200	91.3	3 262 500	3 000 500	92.0
1 VII 2002	ESDJ	6 569 900	6 017 300	91.6	3 241 700	2 958 200	91.3	3 328 200	3 059 100	91.9
Japan - Japon[38]										
1 X 1995	CDFC	125 570 246	98 009 107	78.1	61 574 398	48 210 196	78.3	63 995 848	49 798 911	77.8
1 X 2000	CDFC	126 925 843	99 865 289	78.7	62 110 764	49 005 691	78.9	64 815 079	50 859 598	78.5
Jordan - Jordanie[39]										
10 XII 1994	CDFC	4 139 458	3 238 757	78.2	2 160 725	1 687 530	78.1	1 978 733	1 551 227	78.4
31 XII 1995	ESDF	4 291 000	3 355 510	78.2	...	...	...	...	...	...
31 XII 1996	ESDF	4 444 000	3 477 800	78.3	...	...	...	...	...	...
31 XII 1997	ESDF	4 600 000	3 620 200	78.7	2 404 400	...	...	2 195 600	...	...
31 XII 1998	ESDF	4 755 750	3 743 070	78.7	2 486 800	...	...	2 268 950	...	...
31 XII 1999	ESDF	4 900 000	3 856 300	78.7	2 562 200	...	...	2 337 800	...	...
31 XII 2000	ESDF	5 039 000	3 965 695	78.7	2 635 400	2 066 126	78.4	2 403 600	1 899 567	79.0
31 XII 2001	ESDF	5 182 000	4 078 235	78.7	2 710 235	...	...	2 471 765	...	...
31 XII 2002	ESDF	5 329 000	4 193 925	78.7	2 787 115	...	...	2 541 885	...	...

6. Urban and total population by sex: 1993 - 2002
Population urbaine et population totale selon le sexe: 1993 - 2002
(continued — suite)

(See notes at end of table. — Voir notes à la fin du tableau.)

Continent, country or area and date / Continent, pays ou zone et date	Code[1]	Both sexes - Les deux sexes			Male - Masculin			Female - Féminin		
		Total	Urban - Urbaine		Total	Urban - Urbaine		Total	Urban - Urbaine	
			Number Nombre	Percent P.100		Number Nombre	Percent P.100		Number Nombre	Percent P.100

ASIA — ASIE

Kazakhstan										
1 VII 1997	ESDF	15 334 405	8 567 329	55.9	7 393 786	4 014 495	54.3	7 940 619	4 552 834	57.3
1 VII 1998	ESDF	15 072 983	8 434 080	56.0	7 263 077	3 945 189	54.3	7 809 906	4 488 891	57.5
26 II 1999	CDJC	14 953 126	8 377 303	56.0	7 201 785	3 918 556	54.4	7 751 341	4 458 747	57.5
1 VII 1999	ESDF	14 928 373	8 366 509	56.0	7 190 238	3 914 043	54.4	7 738 135	4 452 466	57.5
1 VII 2000	ESDF	14 883 627	8 365 840	56.2	7 168 614	3 914 349	54.6	7 715 013	4 451 491	57.7
1 VII 2001	ESDF	14 858 335	8 381 924	56.4	7 156 582	3 922 817	54.8	7 701 753	4 459 107	57.9
1 VII 2002	ESDF	14 858 948	8 403 823	56.6	7 156 817	3 933 121	55.0	7 702 131	4 470 702	58.0
Korea (Dem. People's Republic of) - Corée (Rép. populaire dém. de)										
31 XII 1993	CDFC	21 213 378	12 501 217	58.9	10 329 699	5 951 077	57.6	10 883 679	6 550 140	60.2
Korea (Republic of) - Corée (République de)[27,40,41,42]										
1 XI 1995	CDFC	44 608 726	35 036 473	78.5	22 389 324	17 621 308	78.7	22 219 402	17 415 165	78.4
1 XI 2000	CDFC	46 136 101	36 755 144	79.7	23 158 582	18 484 139	79.8	22 977 519	18 271 005	79.5
Kyrgyzstan - Kirghizistan										
1 VII 1993	ESDF	4 542 600	1 671 800	36.8	...	...	...	...	...	...
1 VII 1994	ESDF	4 540 400	1 645 200	36.2	...	...	...	...	...	...
1 VII 1995	ESDF	4 589 900	1 646 300	35.9	...	...	...	...	...	...
1 VII 1996	ESDF	4 657 400	1 660 200	35.6	...	...	...	...	...	...
1 VII 1997	ESDF	4 724 900	1 675 900	35.5	...	...	...	...	...	...
1 VII 1998	ESDF	4 797 000	1 696 900	35.4	...	...	...	...	...	...
24 III 1999	CDJC	4 822 938	1 678 623	34.8	2 380 465	802 256	33.7	2 442 473	876 367	35.9
1 VII 1999	ESDF	4 864 600	1 717 100	35.3	...	...	...	...	...	...
1 VII 2000	ESDF	4 915 300	1 738 800	35.4	...	...	...	...	...	...
1 VII 2001	ESDF	4 954 800	1 760 600	35.5	...	...	...	...	...	...
1 VII 2002	ESDF	4 993 200	1 763 600	35.3	...	...	...	...	...	...
Lao People's Democratic Republic - République démocratique populaire lao[43]										
1 III 1995	CDFC	4 574 848	781 753	17.1	2 260 986	...	...	2 313 862	...	...
Malaysia - Malaisie[44,45]										
1 VII 1993	ESDF	19 563 728	10 354 587	52.9	9 956 183	...	...	9 607 545	...	...
1 VII 1994	ESDF	20 111 565	10 825 360	53.8	10 251 030	...	...	9 860 535	...	...
1 VII 1995	ESDF	20 689 344	11 317 218	54.7	10 563 895	...	...	10 125 449	...	...
5 VII 2000	CDJC	23 274 690	14 426 871	62.0	11 853 432	7 318 396	61.7	11 421 258	7 108 475	62.2
Maldives										
25 III 1995	CDFC	244 814	62 519	25.5	124 622	33 506	26.9	120 192	29 013	24.1
Mongolia - Mongolie[27]										
1 VII 1993	ESDF	2 171 898	1 167 973	53.8	...	...	...	...	...	...
1 VII 1994	ESDF	2 206 892	1 155 635	52.4	...	...	...	...	...	...
1 VII 1995	ESDF	2 242 998	1 156 249	51.5	...	...	...	...	...	...
1 VII 1996	ESDF	2 276 016	1 204 160	52.9	1 125 800	559 400	49.7	1 141 100	567 000	49.7
1 VII 1997	ESDF	2 307 484	1 215 080	52.7	1 145 568	565 300	49.3	1 161 916	573 400	49.3
1 VII 1998	ESDF	2 340 134	1 242 206	53.1	1 161 666	573 100	49.3	1 178 468	581 300	49.3
1 VII 1999	ESDF	2 373 493	1 344 516	56.6	1 177 981	686 000	58.2	1 195 512	696 100	58.2
5 I 2000	CDFC	2 373 493	1 344 516	56.6	1 177 981	657 081	55.8	1 195 512	687 435	57.5
1 VII 2000	ESDF	2 407 488	1 377 000	57.2	1 192 415	694 500	58.2	1 215 073	706 100	58.1
1 VII 2001	ESDF	2 442 544	1 397 100	57.2	1 209 728	...	...	1 232 816	...	...

6.   Urban and total population by sex: 1993 - 2002
Population urbaine et population totale selon le sexe: 1993 - 2002
(continued — suite)

(See notes at end of table. — Voir notes à la fin du tableau.)

Continent, country or area and date / Continent, pays ou zone et date	Code[1]	Both sexes - Les deux sexes			Male - Masculin			Female - Féminin		
		Total	Urban - Urbaine		Total	Urban - Urbaine		Total	Urban - Urbaine	
			Number Nombre	Percent P.100		Number Nombre	Percent P.100		Number Nombre	Percent P.100
ASIA — ASIE										
Mongolia - Mongolie[27]										
1 VII 2002	ESDF	2 475 381	1 421 000	57.4	1 228 059	...	...	1 247 322	...	...
Myanmar[46]										
1 VII 1994	ESDF	43 922 000	9 249 467	21.1	21 832 000	4 601 468	21.1	22 090 000	4 647 999	21.0
Nepal - Népal[47]										
1 VII 1996	ESDJ	20 831 644	2 207 967	10.6	10 393 913	1 138 641	11.0	10 437 731	1 069 326	10.2
Occupied Palestinian Territory - Territoire palestinien occupé[48,49]										
1 VII 1997	ESDF	2 783 084	1 987 886	71.4	1 404 481	...	...	1 378 603	...	...
1 VII 1998	ESDF	2 897 452	2 070 547	71.5	1 462 532	...	...	1 434 920	...	...
1 VII 1999	ESDF	3 019 704	2 157 773	71.5	1 524 649	...	...	1 495 055	...	...
1 VII 2000	ESDF	3 150 056	2 251 337	71.5	1 590 945	...	...	1 559 111	...	...
1 VII 2001	ESDF	3 298 951	2 357 971	71.5	1 666 805	...	...	1 632 146	...	...
1 VII 2002	ESDF	3 464 550	2 476 409	71.5	1 751 271	...	...	1 713 279	...	...
Pakistan[50]										
2 III 1998	CDFC	130 579 571	42 458 339	32.5	67 840 137	22 419 286	33.0	62 739 434	20 039 053	31.9
1 VII 1998	ESDF	131 510 000	42 910 000	32.6	68 290 000	22 100 000	32.4	63 220 000	20 810 000	32.9
Sri Lanka[51]										
17 VII 2001	CDFC	16 864 544	2 467 171	14.6	8 343 964	1 246 983	14.9	8 520 580	1 220 188	14.3
Syrian Arab Republic - République arabe syrienne[52]										
1 VII 1993	ESDF	13 393 000	6 815 000	50.9	6 842 000	3 547 000	51.8	6 551 000	3 268 000	49.9
1 VII 1994	ESDF	13 844 000	7 112 000	51.4	7 071 000	3 702 000	52.4	6 773 000	3 410 000	50.3
3 IX 1994	CDFC	13 782 315	6 864 525	40.8	7 048 906	3 540 051	50.2	6 733 409	3 324 474	49.4
1 VII 2001	ESDF	16 720 000	8 376 000	50.1	8 552 000	...	...	8 168 000	...	...
1 VII 2002	ESDF	17 130 000	8 599 000	50.2	8 763 000	4 439 000	50.7	8 367 000	4 324 000	51.7
Tajikistan - Tadjikistan										
1 VII 1993	ESDF	5 637 700	1 643 300	29.1	2 799 200	801 400	28.6	2 838 500	841 900	29.7
1 VII 1994	ESDF	5 744 700	1 631 300	28.4	...	...	...	...	...	...
Thailand - Thaïlande[53]										
1 IV 2000*	CDJC	60 617 200	18 833 700	31.1	29 850 100	9 085 400	30.4	30 767 100	9 748 300	31.7
1 VII 2002	ESDJ	63 482 287	20 731 494	32.7	31 623 509	10 072 055	31.8	31 858 778	10 659 439	33.5
Turkey - Turquie										
1 VII 1993	ESDF	59 491 000	36 309 672	61.0	...	...	...	...	...	...
1 VII 1994	ESDF	60 612 000	37 316 140	61.6	...	...	...	...	...	...
1 VII 1995	ESDF	61 737 000	38 336 473	62.1	...	...	...	...	...	...
1 VII 1996	ESDF	62 873 000	39 375 130	62.6	31 789 000	...	...	31 083 000	...	...
1 VII 1997	ESDF	64 015 000	40 429 122	63.2	32 358 000	...	...	31 657 000	...	...
1 VII 1998	ESDF	65 157 000	41 494 721	63.7	32 926 000	...	...	32 230 000	...	...
1 VII 1999	ESDF	66 293 000	42 567 640	64.2	33 492 000	...	...	32 801 000	...	...
1 VII 2000	ESDF	67 420 000	43 647 130	64.7	34 053 000	...	...	33 367 000	...	...
22 X 2000	CDFC	67 803 927	44 006 274	64.9	34 346 735	22 427 603	65.3	33 457 192	21 578 671	64.5
1 VII 2001	ESDF	68 529 000	44 725 884	65.3	34 605 000	...	...	33 925 000	...	...
1 VII 2002	ESDF	69 626 000	45 808 003	65.8	35 149 000	...	...	34 477 000	...	...
United Arab Emirates - Émirats arabes unis[54]										
17 XII 1995	CDFC	2 411 041	1 886 708	78.3	1 606 804	...	...	804 237	...	...
Uzbekistan - Ouzbékistan										
1 VII 1993	ESDF	21 852 500	8 559 300	39.2	10 824 400	4 199 900	38.8	11 028 100	4 359 400	39.5

6. Urban and total population by sex: 1993 - 2002
Population urbaine et population totale selon le sexe: 1993 - 2002
(continued — suite)

(See notes at end of table. — Voir notes à la fin du tableau.)

Continent, country or area and date / Continent, pays ou zone et date	Code[1]	Both sexes - Les deux sexes			Male - Masculin			Female - Féminin		
		Total	Urban - Urbaine		Total	Urban - Urbaine		Total	Urban - Urbaine	
			Number Nombre	Percent P.100		Number Nombre	Percent P.100		Number Nombre	Percent P.100
ASIA — ASIE										
Uzbekistan - Ouzbékistan										
1 VII 1994	ESDF	22 282 400	8 634 700	38.8	11 044 600	4 237 600	38.4	11 237 800	4 397 100	39.1
1 VII 1995	ESDF	22 689 700	8 711 900	38.4	11 255 900	4 278 100	38.0	11 433 800	4 433 800	38.8
1 VII 1996	ESDF	23 130 400	8 817 600	38.1	11 487 300	4 335 600	37.7	11 643 100	4 482 000	38.5
1 VII 1997	ESDF	23 560 400	8 931 400	37.9	11 710 400	4 394 700	37.5	11 850 000	4 536 700	38.3
1 VII 1998	ESDF	24 051 000	9 109 700	37.9	...	...	...	...	...	...
1 VII 1999	ESDF	23 953 922	9 037 904	37.7	11 913 994	4 450 641	37.4	12 039 928	4 587 263	38.1
1 VII 2000	ESDF	24 650 415	9 195 435	37.3	12 278 626	4 538 871	37.0	12 371 789	4 656 564	37.6
1 VII 2001	ESDF	24 964 433	9 256 101	37.1	12 442 510	4 573 055	36.8	12 521 923	4 683 046	37.4
Viet Nam										
1 VII 1993	ESDF	71 025 600	13 663 000	19.2	34 670 800	...	...	36 354 800	...	...
1 VII 1994	ESDF	72 509 500	14 139 200	19.5	35 386 400	...	...	37 123 100	...	...
1 VII 1995	ESDF	73 962 400	14 575 400	19.7	36 095 400	...	...	37 867 000	...	...
1 VII 1996	ESDF	75 355 200	15 231 500	20.2	36 773 300	...	...	38 581 900	...	...
1 IV 1999*	CDFC	76 324 753	17 916 983	23.5	37 519 754	...	...	38 804 999	...	...
1 VII 2002	ESDF	79 727 379	20 022 142	25.1	39 197 378	...	...	40 530 001	...	...
Yemen - Yémen										
1 VII 1993	ESDF	12 301 970	3 091 990	25.1	...	...	...	...	...	...
1 VII 1994	ESDF	14 859 000	3 487 000	23.5	7 411 000	...	...	7 448 000	...	...
16 XII 1994	CDFC	14 587 807	3 423 518	23.5	7 473 540	1 856 602	24.8	7 114 267	1 566 916	22.0
1 VII 1995	ESDF	15 369 000	3 699 000	24.1	7 668 000	...	...	7 701 000	...	...
1 VII 1996	ESDF	15 915 000	3 913 000	24.6	7 943 000	...	...	7 972 000	...	...
1 VII 1997	ESDF	16 484 000	4 130 000	25.1	8 229 000	...	...	8 255 000	...	...
1 VII 2000	ESDF	18 261 000	4 802 000	26.3	9 143 000	2 587 000	28.3	9 118 000	2 215 000	24.3
EUROPE										
Albania - Albanie										
1 IV 2001	CDFC	3 069 275	1 292 875	42.1	1 530 443	...	...	1 538 832	...	...
Austria - Autriche										
15 V 2001	CDJC	8 032 926	5 368 693	66.8	3 889 189	2 564 828	65.9	4 143 737	2 803 865	67.7
Belarus - Bélarus										
1 VII 1993	ESDF	10 356 500	7 049 700	68.1	4 867 600	3 313 400	68.1	5 488 900	3 736 300	68.1
1 VII 1994	ESDF	10 308 318	7 048 784	68.4	4 828 086	3 326 708	68.9	5 480 232	3 722 076	67.9
1 VII 1995	ESDF	10 280 805	7 066 181	68.7	4 799 416	3 319 964	69.2	5 481 389	3 746 217	68.3
1 VII 1996	ESDF	10 250 250	7 080 710	69.1	4 784 616	3 324 087	69.5	5 465 634	3 756 623	68.7
1 VII 1997	ESDF	10 219 982	7 106 247	69.5	4 769 223	3 332 777	69.9	5 450 759	3 773 470	69.2
1 VII 1998	ESDF	10 191 479	7 140 980	70.1	4 753 951	3 345 660	70.4	5 437 528	3 795 320	69.8
16 II 1999	CDJC	10 045 237	6 961 516	69.3	4 717 621	3 279 196	69.5	5 327 616	3 682 320	69.1
1 VII 1999	ESDF	10 035 210	6 971 628	69.5	4 711 689	3 282 317	69.7	5 323 521	3 689 311	69.3
1 VII 2002	ESDF	9 924 766	7 034 721	70.9	4 652 109	3 299 920	70.9	5 272 657	3 734 801	70.8
Bulgaria - Bulgarie										
1 VII 1993	ESDF	8 472 313	5 712 671	67.4	4 160 386	2 794 209	67.2	4 311 927	2 918 462	67.7
1 VII 1994	ESDF	8 443 591	5 718 212	67.7	4 140 802	2 792 807	67.4	4 302 789	2 925 405	68.0
1 VII 1995	ESDF	8 406 067	5 702 133	67.8	4 116 667	2 780 230	67.5	4 289 400	2 921 903	68.1
1 VII 1996	ESDF	8 362 826	5 661 482	67.7	...	...	...	...	...	...
1 VII 1997	ESDF	8 312 068	5 623 899	67.7	4 061 233	2 734 426	67.3	4 250 835	2 889 473	68.0
1 VII 1998	ESDF	8 256 786	5 603 501	67.9	4 029 518	...	...	4 227 268	...	...
1 VII 2000	ESDF	8 170 172	5 577 216	68.3	3 979 292	2 700 131	67.9	4 190 880	2 877 085	68.7
1 III 2001	CDFC	7 928 901	5 474 534	69.0	3 862 465	2 651 312	68.6	4 066 436	2 823 222	69.4
1 VII 2001	ESDF	7 910 430	5 477 604	69.2	3 852 034	2 652 367	68.9	4 058 397	2 825 237	69.6
1 VII 2002	ESDF	7 868 900	5 467 777	69.5	3 828 882	2 644 285	69.1	4 040 018	2 823 492	69.9
Croatia - Croatie										
31 III 2001	CDJC	4 437 460	2 471 328	55.7	2 135 900	1 171 950	54.9	2 301 560	1 299 378	56.5
Czech Republic - République tchèque										
1 VII 1993	ESDJ	10 330 607	7 719 966	74.7	5 016 950	...	...	5 313 657	...	...
1 VII 1994	ESDJ	10 336 162	7 722 404	74.7	5 021 408	...	...	5 314 754	...	...

126

6. Urban and total population by sex: 1993 - 2002
Population urbaine et population totale selon le sexe: 1993 - 2002
(continued — suite)

(See notes at end of table. — Voir notes à la fin du tableau.)

Continent, country or area and date / Continent, pays ou zone et date	Code[1]	Both sexes - Les deux sexes			Male - Masculin			Female - Féminin		
		Total	Urban - Urbaine		Total	Urban - Urbaine		Total	Urban - Urbaine	
			Number Nombre	Percent P.100		Number Nombre	Percent P.100		Number Nombre	Percent P.100
EUROPE										
Czech Republic - République tchèque										
1 VII 1995	ESDJ	10 330 759	7 715 655	74.7	5 020 163	...	...	5 310 596	...	...
1 VII 1996	ESDJ	10 315 353	7 701 911	74.7	5 014 667	...	...	5 300 686	...	...
1 VII 1997	ESDJ	10 303 642	7 692 120	74.7	5 010 531	...	...	5 293 111	...	...
1 VII 1998	ESDJ	10 294 943	7 675 220	74.6	5 007 480	...	...	5 287 463	...	...
1 VII 1999	ESDJ	10 282 784	7 659 954	74.5	5 002 823	...	...	5 279 961	...	...
1 VII 2000	ESDJ	10 272 503	7 641 415	74.4	4 999 326	3 694 433	73.9	5 273 177	3 946 982	74.9
1 III 2001	CDJC	10 230 060	7 564 200	73.9	4 982 071	3 657 775	73.4	5 247 989	3 906 425	74.4
1 VII 2001	ESDJ	10 224 192	7 559 732	73.9	4 978 951	3 655 116	73.4	5 245 241	3 904 616	74.4
1 VII 2002	ESDJ	10 200 774	7 536 154	73.9	4 964 598	3 640 572	73.3	5 236 176	3 895 582	74.4
Estonia - Estonie										
1 VII 1993	ESDF	1 516 728	1 068 133	70.4	708 438	492 432	69.5	808 290	575 701	71.2
1 VII 1994	ESDF	1 499 255	1 051 449	70.1	699 749	483 939	69.2	799 506	567 510	71.0
1 VII 1995	ESDF	1 483 942	1 037 099	69.9	691 934	476 322	68.8	792 008	560 777	70.8
1 VII 1996	ESDF	1 469 216	1 022 676	69.6	684 346	468 434	68.4	784 870	554 241	70.6
1 VII 1997	ESDF	1 457 987	1 011 012	69.3	678 674	462 004	68.1	779 313	549 008	70.4
1 VII 1998	ESDF	1 449 712	1 003 118	69.2	674 656	457 641	67.8	775 056	545 478	70.4
1 VII 1999	ESDF	1 442 389	997 188	69.1	671 130	454 363	67.7	771 259	542 825	70.4
31 III 2000	CDJC	1 370 052	923 211	67.4	631 851	415 515	65.8	738 201	507 696	68.8
1 VII 2000	ESDF	1 369 515	947 308	69.2	631 579	426 593	67.5	737 936	520 715	70.6
1 VII 2001	ESDF	1 364 101	943 944	69.2	629 020	424 985	67.6	735 081	518 959	70.6
1 VII 2002	ESDF	1 358 644	940 465	69.2	626 276	423 224	67.6	732 368	517 241	70.6
Finland - Finlande										
1 VII 1993	ESDJ	5 066 447	3 243 196	64.0	...	...	...	...	...	...
1 VII 1994	ESDJ	5 088 333	3 266 117	64.2	2 475 923	1 560 508	63.0	2 612 410	1 705 609	65.3
1 VII 1995	ESDJ	5 107 790	3 291 480	64.4	2 486 675	1 573 544	63.3	2 621 115	1 717 936	65.5
1 VII 1996	ESDJ	5 124 573	3 323 247	64.8	2 496 148	1 589 993	63.7	2 628 425	1 733 254	65.9
1 VII 1997	ESDJ	5 139 835	3 040 950	59.2	2 504 847	1 451 773	58.0	2 634 988	1 589 177	60.3
1 VII 1998	ESDJ	5 153 498	3 089 077	59.9	2 512 587	1 476 277	58.8	2 640 911	1 612 800	61.1
1 VII 1999	ESDJ	5 165 474	3 112 147	60.2	2 519 551	1 488 063	59.1	2 645 923	1 624 084	61.4
1 VII 2000	ESDJ	5 176 208	3 157 401	61.0	...	...	...	...	...	...
31 XII 2000	CDJC	5 181 115	3 167 668	61.1	2 529 341	1 516 812	60.0	2 651 774	1 650 856	62.3
1 VII 2001	ESDJ	5 188 008	3 179 283	61.3	2 533 469	1 523 008	60.1	2 654 539	1 656 275	62.4
1 VII 2002	ESDJ	5 200 598	3 217 447	61.9	2 541 257	1 543 243	60.7	2 659 342	1 674 204	63.0
Hungary - Hongrie										
1 VII 1993	ESDF	10 293 574	6 819 270	66.2	4 933 180	3 113 807	63.1	5 360 394	3 449 975	64.4
1 VII 1994	ESDF	10 261 323	6 749 527	65.8	4 913 327	3 085 533	62.8	5 347 996	3 435 370	64.2
1 VII 1995	ESDF	10 228 989	6 670 673	65.2	4 893 810	3 038 844	62.1	5 335 179	3 401 226	63.8
1 VII 1996	ESDF	10 193 371	6 636 078	65.1	4 873 597	3 037 842	62.3	5 319 774	3 405 105	64.0
1 VII 1997	ESDF	10 154 900	6 596 923	65.0	4 852 592	3 051 927	62.9	5 302 308	3 424 289	64.6
1 VII 1998	ESDF	10 113 574	6 553 655	64.8	4 829 734	3 028 148	62.7	5 283 840	3 403 554	64.4
1 VII 1999	ESDF	10 067 507	6 508 855	64.7	4 804 690	3 016 494	62.8	5 262 817	3 395 530	64.5
1 VII 2000	ESDF	10 024 222	6 461 457	64.5	4 781 700	3 038 795	63.6	5 242 522	3 422 662	65.3
1 II 2001	CDFC	10 198 315	6 572 880	64.5	4 850 650	3 091 857	63.7	5 347 665	3 481 023	65.1
1 VII 2001	ESDF	10 187 576	6 639 272	65.2	4 843 996	3 119 355	64.4	5 343 580	3 519 917	65.9
1 VII 2002	ESDF	10 158 608	6 601 834	65.0	4 827 718	3 098 867	64.2	5 330 890	3 502 968	65.7
Iceland - Islande										
1 VII 1993	ESDJ	263 783	240 824	91.3	132 308	120 006	90.7	131 475	120 818	91.9
1 VII 1994	ESDJ	266 006	243 261	91.4	133 332	121 133	90.9	132 519	121 952	92.0
1 VII 1995	ESDJ	267 380	245 027	91.6	134 038	122 044	91.1	133 342	122 983	92.2
1 VII 1996	ESDJ	268 927	246 983	91.8	134 779	123 025	91.3	134 148	123 958	92.4
1 VII 1997	ESDJ	270 915	249 293	92.0	135 779	124 196	91.5	135 136	125 097	92.6
1 VII 1998	ESDJ	273 794	252 356	92.2	137 092	125 634	91.6	136 702	126 722	92.7
1 VII 1999	ESDJ	277 184	255 910	92.3	138 783	127 433	91.8	138 401	128 477	92.8
1 VII 2000	ESDJ	281 154	259 661	92.4	140 718	129 258	91.9	140 436	130 403	92.9
1 VII 2001	ESDJ	285 054	263 409	92.4	142 660	131 217	92.0	142 308	132 192	92.9
1 VII 2002	ESDJ	287 559	266 010	92.5	143 860	132 371	92.0	143 699	133 639	93.0

6. Urban and total population by sex: 1993 - 2002
Population urbaine et population totale selon le sexe: 1993 - 2002
(continued — suite)

(See notes at end of table. — Voir notes à la fin du tableau.)

Continent, country or area and date / Continent, pays ou zone et date	Code[1]	Both sexes - Les deux sexes			Male - Masculin			Female - Féminin		
		Total	Urban - Urbaine		Total	Urban - Urbaine		Total	Urban - Urbaine	
			Number Nombre	Percent P.100		Number Nombre	Percent P.100		Number Nombre	Percent P.100
EUROPE										
Ireland - Irlande										
28 IV 1996	CDFC	3 626 087	2 107 991	58.1	1 800 232	1 018 779	56.6	1 825 855	1 089 212	59.7
1 VII 1996	ESDF	3 626 100	2 107 921	58.1	1 800 200	...	...	1 825 900	...	...
28 IV 2002	CDFC	3 917 203	2 334 300	59.6	1 946 164	1 133 500	58.2	1 971 039	1 200 800	60.9
1 VII 2002	ESDF	3 917 200	2 334 300	59.6	1 953 555	...	...	1 978 202	...	...
Italy - Italie										
1 VII 1997	ESDJ	57 522 971	17 459 276	30.4	...	...	...	...	...	...
1 VII 1998	ESDJ	57 587 985	17 419 059	30.2	27 959 131	...	...	29 628 854	...	...
1 VII 1999	ESDJ	57 646 255	17 348 485	30.1	27 985 491	...	...	29 660 764	...	...
1 VII 2000	ESDJ	57 761 956	17 329 002	30.0	...	...	...	...	...	...
Latvia - Lettonie										
1 VII 1993	ESDF	2 563 290	1 760 812	68.7	...	...	...	...	...	...
1 VII 1994	ESDF	2 520 742	1 734 300	68.8	1 181 408	807 576	68.4	1 366 291	953 832	69.8
1 VII 1995	ESDF	2 485 056	1 705 665	68.6	1 165 252	794 513	68.2	1 350 350	941 802	69.7
1 VII 1996	ESDF	2 457 222	1 685 462	68.6	1 153 326	785 853	68.1	1 337 439	933 233	69.8
1 VII 1997	ESDF	2 432 851	1 668 743	68.6	1 121 142	757 156	67.5	1 311 709	911 587	69.5
1 VII 1998	ESDF	2 410 019	1 651 759	68.5	1 110 461	747 636	67.3	1 299 558	904 123	69.6
1 VII 1999	ESDF	2 390 482	1 632 603	68.3	1 101 163	736 958	66.9	1 289 319	895 645	69.5
31 III 2000	CDJC	2 377 383	1 618 144	68.1	1 094 964	729 745	66.6	1 282 419	888 399	69.3
1 VII 2000	ESDF	2 372 985	1 614 159	68.0	1 092 871	727 722	66.6	1 280 114	886 437	69.2
1 VII 2001	ESDF	2 355 011	1 599 272	67.9	1 084 485	720 359	66.4	1 270 527	878 913	69.2
1 VII 2002	ESDF	2 338 624	1 586 220	67.8	1 076 587	713 616	66.3	1 262 037	872 604	69.1
Lithuania - Lituanie										
1 VII 1993	ESDJ	3 682 613	2 498 415	67.8	1 739 689	1 174 005	67.5	1 942 924	1 324 410	68.2
1 VII 1994	ESDJ	3 657 144	2 473 011	67.6	1 725 290	1 159 235	67.2	1 931 854	1 313 776	68.0
1 VII 1995	ESDJ	3 629 102	2 446 057	67.4	1 709 387	1 143 067	66.9	1 919 715	1 302 990	67.9
1 VII 1996	ESDJ	3 601 613	2 430 578	67.5	1 693 703	1 131 996	66.8	1 907 910	1 298 582	68.1
1 VII 1997	ESDJ	3 575 137	2 413 579	67.5	1 678 748	1 120 554	66.7	1 896 390	1 293 454	68.2
1 VII 1998	ESDJ	3 549 332	2 388 283	67.3	1 664 608	1 105 323	66.4	1 884 724	1 282 960	68.1
1 VII 1999	ESDJ	3 524 238	2 367 146	67.2	1 650 931	1 092 628	66.2	1 873 307	1 274 518	68.0
1 VII 2000	ESDJ	3 499 536	2 345 640	67.0	1 637 615	1 079 945	65.9	1 861 921	1 265 695	68.0
6 IV 2001	CDJC	3 483 972	2 332 098	66.9	1 629 148	1 071 986	65.8	1 854 824	1 260 112	67.9
1 VII 2001	ESDJ	3 481 292	2 330 184	66.9	1 627 704	1 070 901	65.8	1 853 588	1 259 283	67.9
1 VII 2002	ESDJ	3 469 070	2 321 713	66.9	1 620 891	1 065 912	65.8	1 848 179	1 255 801	67.9
Netherlands - Pays-Bas[55]										
1 VII 1993	ESDJ	15 290 348	9 257 818	60.5	...	...	...	...	...	...
1 VII 1994	ESDJ	15 382 830	9 316 457	60.6	7 606 682	4 563 873	60.0	7 776 149	4 752 580	61.1
1 VII 1995	ESDJ	15 458 995	9 419 243	60.9	7 644 888	4 616 362	60.4	7 814 107	4 802 881	61.5
1 VII 1996	ESDJ	15 530 509	9 467 677	61.0	7 679 546	4 640 765	60.4	7 850 963	4 826 912	61.5
1 VII 1997	ESDJ	15 610 640	9 672 080	62.0	7 718 434	4 742 775	61.4	7 892 206	4 929 305	62.5
1 VII 1998	ESDJ	15 707 209	9 755 109	62.1	7 766 673	4 785 293	61.6	7 940 536	4 969 818	62.6
1 I 2002	CDJC	16 105 285	10 447 684	64.9	7 971 967	5 137 422	64.4	8 133 318	5 310 262	65.3
Norway - Norvège[56]										
3 XI 2001	CDJC	4 520 947	3 458 699	76.5	2 240 281	1 694 153	75.6	2 280 666	1 764 546	77.4
Poland - Pologne[57]										
1 VII 1993	ESDF	38 459 031	23 747 649	61.7	18 726 070	11 293 109	60.3	19 732 961	12 299 224	62.3
1 VII 1994	ESDF	38 543 577	23 689 765	61.5	18 763 139	11 339 127	60.4	19 780 438	12 350 638	62.4
1 VII 1995	ESDF	38 587 596	23 873 641	61.9	18 779 284	11 423 370	60.8	19 808 312	12 450 271	62.9
1 VII 1996	ESDF	38 618 019	23 896 823	61.9	18 789 243	11 429 857	60.8	19 828 776	12 466 966	62.9
1 VII 1997	ESDF	38 649 914	23 927 869	61.9	18 800 457	11 439 693	60.8	19 849 457	12 488 176	62.9
1 VII 1998	ESDF	38 666 145	23 931 229	61.9	18 801 934	11 436 090	60.8	19 864 211	12 495 139	62.9
1 VII 1999	ESDF	38 653 625	23 908 265	61.9	18 788 696	11 417 385	60.8	19 864 929	12 490 880	62.9
1 VII 2000	ESDF	38 646 201	23 897 484	61.8	...	...	...	...	...	...

6. Urban and total population by sex: 1993 - 2002
Population urbaine et population totale selon le sexe: 1993 - 2002
(continued — suite)

(See notes at end of table. — Voir notes à la fin du tableau.)

Continent, country or area and date / Continent, pays ou zone et date	Code[1]	Both sexes - Les deux sexes			Male - Masculin			Female - Féminin		
		Total	Urban - Urbaine		Total	Urban - Urbaine		Total	Urban - Urbaine	
			Number Nombre	Percent P.100		Number Nombre	Percent P.100		Number Nombre	Percent P.100
EUROPE										
Republic of Moldova - République de Moldova[58]										
1 VII 1997	ESDJ	3 654 208	1 525 600	41.7	1 749 374	733 792	41.9	1 904 834	791 808	41.6
1 VII 1998	ESDJ	3 652 200	1 535 200	42.0	1 748 400	739 800	42.3	1 903 800	795 400	41.8
1 VII 1999	ESDJ	3 646 400	1 530 500	42.0	1 745 550	738 850	42.3	1 900 850	791 650	41.6
1 VII 2000	ESDJ	3 639 000	1 513 300	41.6	1 742 300	730 800	41.9	1 896 700	782 500	41.3
1 VII 2001	ESDJ	3 631 462	1 485 810	40.9	1 739 081	717 661	41.3	1 892 381	768 149	40.6
1 VII 2002	ESDJ	3 623 062	1 484 676	41.0	1 735 430	716 822	41.3	1 887 632	767 854	40.7
Romania - Roumanie										
1 VII 1993	ESDJ	22 755 260	12 406 204	54.5	11 176 390	6 032 330	54.0	11 578 870	6 373 874	55.0
1 VII 1994	ESDJ	22 730 622	12 427 612	54.7	11 156 807	6 037 065	54.1	11 573 815	6 390 547	55.2
1 VII 1995	ESDJ	22 680 951	12 457 195	54.9	11 123 977	6 047 572	54.4	11 556 974	6 409 623	55.5
1 VII 1996	ESDJ	22 607 620	12 411 174	54.9	11 080 933	6 016 714	54.3	11 526 687	6 394 460	55.5
1 VII 1997	ESDJ	22 545 925	12 404 690	55.0	11 041 414	6 007 827	54.4	11 504 511	6 396 863	55.6
1 VII 1998	ESDJ	22 502 803	12 347 886	54.9	11 012 110	5 971 134	54.2	11 490 693	6 376 752	55.5
1 VII 1999	ESDJ	22 458 022	12 302 729	54.8	10 984 529	...	...	11 473 493	...	...
1 VII 2000	ESDJ	22 435 205	12 244 598	54.6	10 968 854	5 907 848	53.9	11 466 351	6 336 750	55.3
1 VII 2001	ESDJ	22 131 970	12 243 748	55.3	10 813 775	5 903 537	54.6	11 318 195	6 340 211	56.0
1 VII 2002	ESDJ	21 794 793	11 608 735	53.3	10 642 538	5 579 042	52.4	11 152 255	6 029 693	54.1
Russian Federation - Fédération de Russie										
1 VII 1993	ESDF	148 145 900	108 234 100	73.1	...	...	...	...	...	...
1 VII 1994	ESDF	147 967 800	107 948 600	73.0	69 479 594	50 517 227	72.7	78 488 219	57 431 371	73.2
1 VII 1995	ESDF	147 773 657	107 779 133	72.9	69 387 481	50 405 185	72.6	78 386 176	57 373 948	73.2
1 VII 1999	ESDF	145 943 393	106 488 089	73.0	68 405 752	49 622 408	72.5	77 537 641	56 865 681	73.3
San Marino - Saint-Marin										
1 VII 1993	ESDF	24 360	22 031	90.4	12 118	10 945	90.3	12 242	11 086	90.6
1 VII 1994	ESDF	24 889	22 505	90.4	12 382	11 194	90.4	12 507	11 311	90.4
1 VII 1995	ESDF	24 988	22 339	89.4	12 375	11 063	89.4	12 613	11 276	89.4
1 VII 1997	ESDF	25 823	23 085	89.4	12 757	11 404	89.4	13 066	11 681	89.4
1 VII 2000	ESDF	26 941	22 738	84.4	13 185	11 787	89.4	13 756	10 951	79.6
Serbia and Montenegro - Serbie-et-Montene-gro[59]										
1 VII 1993	ESDJ	10 481 954	5 378 336	51.3	5 197 455	2 625 096	50.5	5 284 499	2 753 240	52.1
1 VII 1994	ESDJ	10 515 582	5 400 221	51.4	5 214 043	2 635 731	50.6	5 301 539	2 764 490	52.1
1 VII 1995	ESDJ	10 546 983	5 420 604	51.4	5 229 817	2 646 039	50.6	5 317 166	2 774 565	52.2
1 VII 1996	ESDJ	10 577 208	5 440 835	51.4	5 245 109	2 656 349	50.6	5 332 099	2 784 486	52.2
1 VII 1997	ESDJ	10 600 067	5 456 379	51.5	5 256 354	2 664 248	50.7	5 343 713	2 792 131	52.3
1 VII 1998	ESDJ	10 616 886	5 468 037	51.5	5 264 001	2 669 658	50.7	5 352 885	2 798 379	52.3
1 VII 1999	ESDJ	10 629 358	5 477 426	51.5	5 269 974	2 674 193	50.7	5 359 384	2 803 233	52.3
1 VII 2000	ESDJ	10 634 620	5 480 138	51.5	5 272 097	2 675 270	50.7	5 362 523	2 804 868	52.3
1 VII 2001	ESDJ	10 653 722	5 491 849	51.5	5 281 815	...	...	5 371 907	...	...
Slovakia - Slovaquie										
1 VII 1993	ESDJ	5 324 632	3 038 834	57.1	2 594 672	1 471 403	56.7	2 729 960	1 567 431	57.4
1 VII 1994	ESDJ	5 347 413	3 045 894	57.0	2 604 937	1 472 177	56.5	2 742 476	1 573 717	57.4
1 VII 1995	ESDJ	5 363 638	3 057 117	57.0	2 612 212	1 476 546	56.5	2 751 426	1 580 571	57.4
1 VII 1996	ESDJ	5 373 810	3 072 014	57.2	2 616 356	...	...	2 757 454	...	...
1 VII 1997	ESDJ	5 383 214	3 068 195	57.0	2 620 329	...	...	2 762 904	...	...
1 VII 1998	ESDJ	5 390 657	3 066 324	56.9	2 622 990	1 479 217	56.4	2 767 667	1 587 107	57.3
1 VII 1999	ESDJ	5 395 324	3 063 235	56.8	2 624 080	...	...	2 771 244	...	...
25 V 2001	CDJC	5 379 455	3 022 106	56.2	2 612 515	1 453 638	55.6	2 766 940	1 568 468	56.7

6. Urban and total population by sex: 1993 - 2002
Population urbaine et population totale selon le sexe: 1993 - 2002
(continued — suite)

(See notes at end of table. — Voir notes à la fin du tableau.)

Continent, country or area and date / Continent, pays ou zone et date	Code[1]	Both sexes - Les deux sexes			Male - Masculin			Female - Féminin		
		Total	Urban - Urbaine		Total	Urban - Urbaine		Total	Urban - Urbaine	
			Number Nombre	Percent P.100		Number Nombre	Percent P.100		Number Nombre	Percent P.100
EUROPE										
Slovakia - Slovaquie										
1 VII 2002	ESDJ	5 379 056	3 016 148	56.1	2 611 614	1 450 106	55.5	2 767 443	1 566 042	56.6
Slovenia - Slovénie										
1 VII 1993	ESDJ	1 990 623	1 002 422	50.4	965 175	478 022	49.5	1 025 448	524 400	51.1
1 VII 1994	ESDJ	1 988 850	997 916	50.2	964 113	475 551	49.3	1 024 737	522 365	51.0
1 VII 2002	ESDJ	1 995 718	975 163	48.9	976 111	462 513	47.4	1 019 607	512 650	50.3
Switzerland - Suisse										
1 VII 1993	ESDJ	6 938 265	4 719 177	68.0	3 388 890	...	...	3 549 375	...	...
1 VII 1994	ESDJ	6 993 795	4 745 834	67.9	3 416 116	...	...	3 577 679	...	...
1 VII 1995	ESDJ	7 040 687	4 768 417	67.7	3 438 605	2 304 085	67.0	3 602 082	2 464 332	68.4
1 VII 1996	ESDJ	7 071 851	4 783 434	67.6	3 453 232	2 311 082	66.9	3 618 619	2 472 352	68.3
1 VII 1997	ESDJ	7 088 906	4 789 234	67.6	3 461 432	2 314 317	66.9	3 627 474	2 474 917	68.2
1 VII 1998	ESDJ	7 110 002	4 799 607	67.5	3 471 966	2 320 098	66.8	3 638 036	2 479 509	68.2
1 VII 1999	ESDJ	7 143 991	4 823 202	67.5	3 489 699	2 333 007	66.9	3 654 292	2 490 195	68.1
1 VII 2000	ESDJ	7 184 250	4 854 390	67.6	3 510 203	2 349 347	66.9	3 674 047	2 505 043	68.2
5 XII 2000	CDJC	7 204 055	4 871 989	67.6	3 519 698	2 357 890	67.0	3 684 357	2 514 099	68.2
1 VII 2001	ESDJ	7 232 633	4 894 456	67.7	3 534 394	...	...	3 698 239	...	...
The Former Yugoslav Rep. of Macedonia - L'ex-République yougoslave de Macédoine										
20 VI 1994	CDJC	1 945 932	1 163 598	59.8	974 255	...	...	971 677	...	...
1 VII 1997	ESDF	1 996 869	1 189 442	59.6	999 595	590 300	59.1	997 274	599 142	60.1
Ukraine										
1 VII 1993	ESDF	52 244 100	35 471 000	67.9	...	...	...	...	...	...
1 VII 1994	ESDF	52 114 400	35 400 700	67.9	...	...	...	...	...	...
1 VII 1995	ESDF	51 728 400	35 118 800	67.9	...	...	...	...	...	...
1 VII 1996	ESDF	51 334 100	34 832 500	67.9	...	...	...	...	...	...
1 VII 1997	ESDF	50 893 500	34 521 800	67.8	...	...	...	...	...	...
1 VII 1998	ESDF	50 499 900	34 271 600	67.9	...	...	...	...	...	...
1 VII 1999	ESDF	50 105 600	34 017 400	67.9	...	...	...	...	...	...
1 VII 2000	ESDF	49 710 800	33 796 500	68.0	...	...	...	...	...	...
5 XII 2001	CDJC	48 457 102	32 574 371	67.2	22 441 344	15 056 675	67.1	26 015 758	17 517 696	67.3
OCEANIA — OCEANIE										
Cook Islands - Îles Cook										
1 XII 1996	CDFC	19 103	11 225	58.8	9 842	5 730	58.2	9 261	5 495	59.3
Fiji - Fidji										
25 VIII 1996	CDFC	775 077	359 495	46.4	393 931	180 119	45.7	381 146	179 376	47.1
Guam[15,16]										
1 VII 1993	ESDJ	143 825	54 873	38.2	...	...	...	...	...	...
1 VII 1994	ESDJ	143 157	54 618	38.2	...	...	...	...	...	...
1 VII 1995	ESDJ	144 190	55 012	38.2	...	...	...	...	...	...
1 VII 1996	ESDJ	145 324	55 445	38.2	...	...	...	...	...	...
1 VII 1997	ESDJ	146 799	56 008	38.2	...	...	...	...	...	...
1 VII 1998	ESDJ	149 724	57 124	38.2	...	...	...	...	...	...
1 VII 1999	ESDJ	152 590	58 217	38.2	...	...	...	...	...	...
1 IV 2000*	CDJC	154 805	144 129	93.1	79 181	...	...	75 624	...	...
1 VII 2001	ESDJ	158 330	147 411	93.1	...	...	...	...	...	...
1 VII 2002	ESDJ	161 057	149 950	93.1	...	...	...	...	...	...

6. Urban and total population by sex: 1993 - 2002
Population urbaine et population totale selon le sexe: 1993 - 2002
(continued — suite)

(See notes at end of table. — Voir notes à la fin du tableau.)

Continent, country or area and date / Continent, pays ou zone et date	Code[1]	Both sexes - Les deux sexes			Male - Masculin			Female - Féminin		
		Total	Urban - Urbaine		Total	Urban - Urbaine		Total	Urban - Urbaine	
			Number Nombre	Percent P.100		Number Nombre	Percent P.100		Number Nombre	Percent P.100
OCEANIA — OCEANIE										
New Caledonia - Nouvelle-Calédonie										
1 VII 1996	ESDF	*197 389*	*118 823*	*60.2*	*101 030*	...	...	*96 394*	...	...
New Zealand - Nouvelle-Zélande										
5 III 1996	CDJC	3 618 303	3 091 740	85.4	1 777 464	1 503 444	84.6	1 840 839	1 588 296	86.3
1 VII 1996	ESDJ	3 732 000	3 191 300	85.5	1 830 300	...	...	1 883 800	...	...
1 VII 1997	ESDJ	3 781 400	3 237 800	85.6	1 863 700	...	...	1 917 700	...	...
1 VII 1998	ESDJ	3 815 000	3 269 700	85.7	1 877 800	...	...	1 937 200	...	...
1 VII 1999	ESDJ	3 835 100	3 289 300	85.8	1 884 900	...	...	1 950 200	...	...
1 VII 2000	ESDJ	3 857 800	3 310 100	85.8	1 893 800	...	...	1 964 000	...	...
1 VII 2001	ESDJ	3 880 500	3 331 400	85.8	1 903 200	...	...	1 977 300	...	...
1 VII 2002	ESDJ	3 939 100	3 385 000	85.9	1 934 000	...	...	2 005 100	...	...
Palau - Palaos										
9 IX 1995	CDFC	17 225	12 299	71.4	9 213	...	...	8 012	...	...
15 IV 2000	CDFC	19 129	13 303	69.5	...	...	...	...	...	...
Tonga										
30 XI 1996	CDFC	97 784	22 400	22.9	49 615	...	...	48 168	...	...
Vanuatu										
16 XI 1999	CDJC	186 678	40 094	21.5	95 682	...	...	90 996	...	...

GENERAL NOTES - NOTES GENERALES

Percentages urban are the number of persons resident in areas defined as 'urban' per 100 Total Population. For some countries and areas the figures for male and female population do not add up to the total population or to the urban population; this is due to the fact that only statistics for total, urban and rural population were revised and sex distribution was not. For definition of 'urban', see end of Technical Notes for this table. For method of evaluation and limitations of data, see Technical Notes for this table. — Les pourcentages urbains représentent le nombre de personnes définies comme vivant dans des 'régions urbaines'. Pour certain pays ou zones les sommes des données pour la population masculine et la population féminine ne sont pas égaux à la population totale ou urbaine; c'est la conséquence d'une révision des données pour la population totale et urbaine qui n'était pas appliqué à la distribution par sexe. Pour la définitions des 'régions urbaines', se reporter à la fin des Notes Techniques pour ce tableau. Pour la méthode d'evaluation et les insuffisances des données, voir Notes techniques pour ce tableau.

Italics: estimates which are less reliable. — *Italiques:* estimations moins sûres.

FOOTNOTES - NOTES

* Provisional. — Données provisoires.

[1] 'Code' indicates the source of data, as follows:
CDFC - Census, de facto, complete tabulation
CDFS - Census, de facto, sample tabulation
CDJC - Census, de jure, complete tabulation
CDJS - Census, de jure, sample tabulation
SSDF - Sample survey, de facto
SSDJ - Sample survey, de jure
ESDF - Estimates, de facto
ESDJ - Estimates, de jure
Le 'Code' indique la source des données, comme suit:
CDFC - Recensement, population de fait, tabulation complète
CDFS - Recensement, population de fait, tabulation par sondage
CDJC - Recensement, population de droit, tabulation complète
CDJS - Recensement, population de droit, tabulation par sondage
SSDF - Enquête par sondage, population de fait
SSDJ - Enquête par sondage, population de droit
ESDF - Données estimatées, population de fait
ESDJ - Données estimatées, population de droit

[2] Series not strictly comparable due to differences of definitions of "urban". - - Les séries ne sont pas strictement comparables en raison de différences existant dans la définition des "regions urbaines".

[3] Data for urban and rural areas are not adjusted for under-enumeration, estimated around 5% for the total country. - Les données pour les zones urbaines et rurales n'ont pas été ajustées pour tenir en compte de la sous-estimation de 5% approximativement.

[4] Data for estimates refer to national projections. - Les données se referent aux projections nationales.

[5] Census results have been adjusted for underenumeration, estimated at 5.1 per cent. - Les résultats du recensement ont été ajustées pour compenser les lacunes du dénombrement, estimées à 5,1 p. 100.

[6] Based on results of a Socio Economic Survey. - Basé sur les résultats d'une enquête Socio-Economique.

[7] Mid-year estimates have been adjusted for underenumeration, at latest census. - Les estimations au millieu de l'année tiennent compte d'une ajustement destiné à compenser les lacunes du dénombrement lors du dernier recensement.

[8] Census result have been adjusted for underenumeration, estimated at 6.8 per cent. - Les résultat du recensement ont été ajustées pour compenser les lacunes du dénombrement, estimées à 6,8 p. 100.

[9] Because of rounding, totals are not in all cases the sum of the parts. - Les chiffres étant arrondis, les totaux ne correspondent pas toujours rigoureusement à la somme des chiffres partiels.

[10] Census data have not been adjusted for underenumeration. - Les données de recensement ne tiennent pas compte de d'une ajustement destiné à compenser les lacunes du dénombrement.

[11] For 2001, final postcensal estimates. - Pour 2001, évaluations postcensal finales.

[12] For 1996 to 2000, final intercensal estimates. - De 1996 à 2000, estimations inter censitaires finales.

[13] Revised intercensal estimates adjusted for net undercoverage. - Estimations inter censitaires corrigées pour tenir en compte du sous dénombrement net.

[14] Population statistics are based on administrative records. - La source de la statistique de la population sont des fichiers administratifs et pas un recensement de population basé sur un questionnaire.

[15] Including armed forces stationed in the area. - Y compris les militaires en garnison sur le territoire.

[16] Definition of urban and rural distribution changed from the year 2000. - La définition des régions urbaines et rurales a changée depuis 2000.

[17] Data refer to the total enumerated household population plus institutional population. - Les données se rapportent à la population totale recensée au sein des ménages et des institutions.

[18] Excluding civilian citizens absent from country for extended periods of time. - Non compris les civils hors du pays pendant une période prolongée.

[19] Data include persons in remote areas, military personel outside the country, merchant seamen at sea, civilian seasonal workers outside the country, and other civilians outside the country, and exclude nomads, foreign military, civilian aliens temporarily in the country, transients on ships and Indian jungle population. - Y compris les personnes dans des régions éloignées, le personel militaire en dehors du pays, les marins marchands, les ouvriers saisonniers civils de couture en dehors du pays, et autres civils en dehors du pays, et non compris les nomades, les militaires étrangers, les étrangers civils temporairement dans le pays, les transiteurs sur des bateaux et les Indiens de la jungle.

[20] Excluding nomadic Indian tribes. - Non compris les tribus d'Indiens nomades.

[21] Excluding Indian jungle population. - Non compris les Indiens de la jungle.

[22] Data refer to the settled population based on the 1979 Population Census; an estimated 1.5 million nomads are not included. - Les données se rapportent a la population stationnaire a la base de recensement de 1979; les nomades, estimées a 1.5 million, ne sont pas inclus.

[23] The methodology used for calculating the number of the de facto and de jure population in the 2001 census data differs as follows from the methodology used in previous censuses: the duration that defines a person as being 'temporary present' or 'temporary absent' is now 'under one year'. The previously applied definition was for '6 months'. - La méthode utilisée pour dénombrer la population présente et la population légale dans le contexte du recensement de 2001 diffère de celle qui a été appliquée lors des recensements antérieurs en ce que la durée considérée pour définir la 'présence temporaire' ou 'l'absence temporaire' était dorénavant fixée à 'moins d'un an' alors qu'elle était de '6 mois' auparavant.

[24] Data for 2001 and before refer to defacto population and after 2001 dejure population. - Les données pour 2001 et les années antérieures se rapportent sur la population de fait et après 2001 sur la population de droit.

[25] Excluding foreign diplomatic personnel and their dependants. - Non compris le personnel diplomatique étranger et les membres de leur famille les accompagnant.

[26] For 1996, based on results of a sample survey. - Pour 1996, d'après les résultats d'une enquête par sondage.

[27] Unrevised data. - Les données n'ont pas été révisées.

[28] For statistical purposes, the data for China do not include those for the Hong Kong Special Administrative Region (Hong Kong SAR), Macao Special Administrative Region (Macao SAR) and Taiwan province of China. - Pour la présentation des statistiques, les données pour Chine ne comprend pas la Région Administrative Spéciale de Hong Kong (Hong Kong RAS), la Région Administrative Spéciale de Macao (Macao RAS) et Taïwan province de Chine.

[29] For the civilian population of 31 provinces, municipalities and autonomous regions. - Pour la population civile seulement de 31 provinces, municipalités et régions autonomes.

[30] Estimated data on the basis of the annual National Sample Survey on Population Changes. - Les données ont été estimées sur la base de l'enquête annuelle "National Sample Survey on Population Changes".

[31] Data refer to government controlled areas. - Les données se raportent aux zones contrôlées par le Gouvernement.

[32] Estimates of the number of Turkish Cypriots from 1974 onwards are the result of population projections based on the age and sex structure of the Turkish Cypriot community as at Census 1960 and with assumptions of fertility and mortality similar to the rest of the Cyprus population. With regard to the migration of Turkish Cypriots after 1974, migration assumptions are based on figures obtained from Turkish Cypriot sources. Settlers from Turkey are not included. - - Les estimations du nombre de Chypriotes turcs depuis 1974 résultent des projections de population préparées sur la base de la structure par sexe et age de la communauté chypriote turque au recensement de 1960, et avec des hypothèses de fécondité et de mortalité similaires à celles du reste de la population de Chypre. En ce qui concerne la migration des Chypriotes turcs après 1974, les hypothèses sont basées sur les données obtenues de sources chypriotes turques. Les occupants venus de Turquie ne sont pas inclus.

[33] Including data for the Indian-held part of Jammu and Kashmir, the final status of which has not yet been determined. - Y compris les données pour la partie du Jammu et du Cachemire occupée par l'Inde dont le statut définitif n'a pas encore été déterminé.

[34] Census data exclude Mao-Maram, Paomata and Purul sub-divisions of Senapati district of Manipur. The population of Manipur including the estimated population of the three sub-divisions of Senapati district is 2,291,125 (Males 1,161,173 and females 1,129,952). - Les données de recensement non compris pas les subdivisions Mao-Maram Paomata et Purul du district de Senapati dans l'État du Manipur. Cet État compte 2 291 125 habitants (1 161 173 hommes et 1 129 952 femmes), y compris la population estimative des trois subdivisions du district de Senapati.

[35] For 2000, the figure includes an estimated population of 459 557 persons in urban and 1 857 659 persons in rural areas that were not directly enumerated, and a population of 566 403 persons in urban and 1 717 578 persons in rural areas that decline the participation. Also included are 421 399 non permanent residents (the homeless, the crew of ships carrying national flag, boat/floating house people, remote located tribesmen and refugees.) - Pour 2000, y compris la population estimée a 459 557 personnes dans les zones urbaines et de 1 857 659 personnes dans les zones rurales qui n'ont pas été énumérées directement, aussi que 566 403 personnes qui non pas répondu dans les zones urbaines et de 1 717 578 personnes dans les zones rurales. Y compris 421 399 résidants non permanents (les sans abri, l'équipage des bateaux portant le drapeau national, les habitants des embarcations ou des maisons flottantes, les habitants des tribus isolées et les réfugiés.)

[36] For the 1997 population census, data exclude population in three autonomous provinces in the north of the country. - Pour le recensement de 1997, la population des trois provinces autonomes dans le nord du pays est exclue.

[37] Including data for East Jerusalem and Israeli residents in certain other territories under occupation by Israeli military forces since June 1967. - Y compris les données pour Jérusalem-Est et les résidents israéliens dans certains autres territoires occupés depuis 1967 par les forces armées israéliennes.

[38] Excluding diplomatic personnel outside the country and foreign military and civilian personnel and their dependants stationed in the area. - Non compris le personnel diplomatique hors du pays ni les militaires et agents civils étrangers en poste sur le territoire et les membres de leur famille les accompagnant.

[39] Excluding data for Jordanian territory under occupation since June 1967 by Israeli military forces. Excluding foreigners, including registered Palestinian refugees. - Non compris les données pour le territoire jordanien occupé depuis juin 1967 par les forces armées israéliennes. Non compris les étrangers, mais y compris les réfugiés de Palestine enregistrés.

[40] Excluding alien armed forces, civilian aliens employed by armed forces, foreign diplomatic personnel and their dependants and Korean diplomatic personnel and their dependants outside the country. - Non compris les militaires étrangers, les civils étrangers employés par les forces armées, le personnel diplomatique étranger et les membres de leur famille les accompagnant et le personnel diplomatique coréen hors du pays et les membres de leurs familles les accompagnant.

[41] Census data exclude adjustment for underenumeration. - Les données de recensement n'ont pas été ajustées pour compenser les lacunes du dénombrement.

[42] Urban/Rural: Places with 50 000 or more inhabitants are usually considered urban in Korea. However, the census results are composed in the basis of the minor administrative divisions such as Dongs (mostly urban areas) and Eups or Myeons (rural areas) rather than urban or rural residences. In this report, urban refers to Dongs and rural refers ro Eups and Myeons. - Urbaine/rurale: les lieux avec 50,000 habitants ou plus sont habituellement considérés urbains en Corée. Cependant, les résultats du recensement ont été préparés sur la base des divisions administratives mineures comme les Dongs (principalement des zones urbaines), et les Eups ou Myeons (des zones rurales) plutôt que sur les résidences urbaines ou rurales. Dans ce rapport urbaine se rapporte aux Dongs et rural aux Eups et aux Myeons.

[43] For 1997, based on Lao expenditure and consumption survey 1997/98. - Les données se rapportent à l'Enquête sur la consommation et les dépenses des ménages du Laos du 1997/98.

[44] Excluding Malaysian citizens and permanent residents who were away or intended to be away from the country for more than six months. Excluding Malaysian military, naval and diplomatic personnel and their families outside the country, and tourists, businessman who intended to be in Malaysia for less than six months. - Non compris les citoyens malaisiens et les résidents permanents qui étaient ou qui ont prévu d'être hors du pays pour six mois ou plus. Non compris le personnel militaire Malaisien, le personnel naval ou diplomatique et leurs familles hors du pays, et les touristes et les hommes d'affaires qui avaient l'intention de rester en Malaisie moins de six mois.

[45] Census results have been adjusted for underenumeration. - Les résultats du recensement ont été ajustées pour compenser les lacunes du dénombrement

[46] Data for urban refer to 170 towns out of 254 towns. - Les données urbaines se rapportent à 170 des 254 villes.

[47] Data including estimated population from household listing from Village Development Committees and Wards which could not be enumerated at the time of census. - Les données incluent la population estimée par les listes des ménages des comités de développement des villages et des circonscriptions qui n'ont pas pu être énumérée au moment du recensement.

[48] Data for urban including population in refugee camps. - Les données pour la population urbaine comprennent la population dans des camps réfugiés.

[49] Total Population does not include Palestinian population living in those parts of Jerusalem governorate which were annexed by Israel in 1967, amounting to 210,209 persons. Likewise, the results does not include the estimates of not enumerated population based on the findings of the post enumeration study, i.e 83,805 persons. - Les données relatives à la population totale ne comprennent pas la population palestinienne -équivalent à 210 209 personnes - habitant dans les territoires du gouvernorat de Jérusalem qui ont été annexés par Israël en 1967. Egalement, les données ne tiennent pas compte des estimations de la

population calculée sur la base des résultats de l'enquête postcensitaire, équivalent à 83 805 personnes.

[50] Excluding data for the Pakistan-held part of Jammu and Kashmir, the final status of which has not yet been determined. - Non compris les données concernant la partie du Jammu et Cachemire occupée par le Pakistan dont le statut définitif n'a pas été déterminé.

[51] The Population and Housing Census 2001 did not cover the whole area of the country due to the security problems; the Census was complete in 18 districts only; in three districts it was not possible to conduct it; and in four districts it was partially conducted. - Le recensement de la population et de l'habitat en 2001 n'a pas couvert la totalité du pays pour des problèmes de sécurité ; le recensement a été complété seulement en 18 districts ; dans 3 districts ça n'a pas été possible de conduire le recensement et dans 4 districts il a été partiellement conduit.

[52] Including Palestinian refugees. - Y compris les réfugiés de Palestine.

[53] Data for "urban" refer to population in municipalities, data for "rural" refer to the population in non-municipal areas. - Les données pour la zone urbaine se rapportent a la population des municipalités, les données pour la zone rurale se rapportent a la population au dehors des municipalités.

[54] Comprising 7 sheikdoms of Abu Dhabi, Dubai, Sharjah, Ajaman, Umm al Qaiwain, Ras al Khaimah and Fujairah, and the area lying within the modified Riyadh line as announced in October 1955. - Comprend les sept cheikhats de Abou Dhabi, Dabai, Ghârdja, Adjmân, Oumm-al-Quiwaïn, Ras al Khaîma et Foudjaïra, ainsi que la zone délimitée par la ligne de Riad modifiée comme il a été annoncé en octobre 1955.

[55] Census result, based on compilation of continuous accounting and sample surveys. - Les résultat du recensement, d'après les résultats des dénombrements et enquêtes par sondage continue.

[56] Including residents temporarily outside the country. - Y compris les résidents se trouvant temporairement hors du pays.

[57] Excluding civilian aliens within country, but including civilian nationals temporarily outside country. - Non compris les civils étrangers dans le pays, mais y compris les civils nationaux temporairement hors du pays.

[58] Data do not include information for Transnistria and the municipality of Bender. - Les données ne tiennent pas compte de l'information sur la Transnistria et la municipalité de Bender.

[59] Beginning with 1998, estimates of Kosovo and Metohia computed on the basis of natural increases from year 1997. - A partir du 1998, les estimations pour le Kosovo et la Metohia ont été calculées sur la base des incréments naturelles depuis 1997.

Table 7

Table 7 presents population by age, sex and urban/rural residence for the latest available year.

Description of variables: Data in this table are either population census figures or estimates, some of which are based on sample surveys. Data refer to the de facto population unless otherwise noted.

The reference date of the census or estimate appears in the stub of the table. In general, the estimates refer to mid-year (1 July).

Age is defined as age at last birthday, that is, the difference between the date of birth and the reference date of the age distribution expressed in completed solar years. The age classification used in this table is the following: under 1 year, 1-4 years, 5-year groups through 95-99 years, and 100 years and over.

Statistics are presented for one year, the most recent available. However, if more complete disaggregation is available for earlier years, both are displayed.

The urban/rural classification of population by age and sex is that provided by each country or area; it is presumed to be based on the national census definitions of urban population that have been set forth at the end of the technical notes to table 6.

Estimates of population by age and sex presented in this table have been limited to countries or areas for which estimates have been based on the results of a sample survey or have been constructed by the component method from the results of a population census or sample survey. Estimations derived from distributing estimated total population according to percentages in each age-sex group at the time of a census or sample survey are not included in this table.

Reliability of data: Estimates which are believed to be less reliable are set in *italics* rather than in roman type. No attempt has been made to take account of age-reporting accuracy, the evaluation of which has been described in section 3.1.3 of the Technical Notes.

Limitations: Statistics on population by age and sex are subject to the same qualifications as have been set forth for population statistics in general and age distributions in particular, as discussed in sections 3 and 3.1.3, respectively, of the Technical Notes.

Comparability of population data classified by age and sex is limited by variations in the definition of total population, discussed in detail in section 3 of the Technical Notes, and by the accuracy of the original enumeration. Both factors are more important in relation to certain age groups than to others. For example, under-enumeration is known to be more prevalent among infants and young children than among older persons. Similarly, the exclusion from the total population of certain groups that tend to be of selected ages (such as the armed forces) can markedly affect the age structure and its comparability with that for other countries or areas. Consideration should be given to the implications of these basic limitations in using the data.

In addition to these general qualifications are the special problems of comparability that arise in relation to age statistics in particular. Age distributions of population are known to suffer from certain deficiencies that have their origin in irregularities in age reporting. Although some of the irregularities tend to be obscured or eliminated when data are tabulated in five-year age groups rather than by single years, precision still continues to be affected, though the degree of distortion is not always readily seen.

Another factor limiting comparability is the age classification employed by the various countries or areas. Age may be based on the year of birth rather than the age at last birthday, in other words, calculated using the day, month and year of birth. Distributions based only on the year of birth are footnoted when known.

The absence of frequencies in the unknown age group does not necessarily indicate completely accurate reporting and tabulation of the age item. The unknowns may have been eliminated by assigning ages to them before tabulation, or by proportionately distributing the unknown category across the age groups after tabulation.

As noted in connection with table 5, intercensal estimates of total population are usually revised to accord with the results of a census of population if inexplicable discontinuities appear to exist. Postcensal age-sex distributions, however, are less likely to be revised in this way. When it is known that a total population estimate for a given year has been revised and the corresponding age distribution has not been, the age distribution is shown as provisional. Distributions of this type should be used with caution when studying trends over a period of years, though their utility for studying age structure for the specified year is probably unimpaired.

The comparability of data by urban/rural residence is affected by the national definitions of urban and rural used in tabulating these data. When known, the definitions of urban used in national population censuses are presented at the end of the technical notes for table 6. As discussed in detail in the technical notes for table 6, these definitions vary considerably from one country or area to another.

Earlier data: Population by age, sex and urban/rural residence has been shown in previous issues of the *Demographic Yearbook*. For more information on specific topics, and years for which data are reported, readers should consult the Historical Index.

Tableau 7

Le tableau 7 présente les données les plus récentes dont on dispose sur la population selon l'âge, le sexe et le lieu de résidence (zone urbaine ou rurale).

Description des variables : Les données de ce tableau proviennent de recensements de la population ou correspondent à des estimations fondées, dans certains cas, sur des enquêtes par sondage. Sauf indication contraire, elles se rapportent à la population de fait.

La date du recensement ou de l'estimation figure dans la colonne de gauche du tableau. En général, les estimations se rapportent au milieu de l'année (1er juillet).

L'âge désigne l'âge au dernier anniversaire, c'est-à-dire la différence entre la date de naissance et la date de référence de la répartition par âge exprimée en années solaires révolues. La classification par âge utilisée dans ce tableau est la suivante : moins d'un an, 1 à 4 ans, groupes quinquennaux jusqu'à 95-99 ans et 100 ans et plus.

Les statistiques portent sur une année, qui correspond à celle pour laquelle on dispose des statistiques les plus récentes. Toutefois, si l'on dispose de répartitions plus complètes pour des années antérieures, les statistiques sont alors présentées pour les deux années.

La classification par zones urbaines et rurales de la population selon l'âge et le sexe est celle qui est communiquée par chaque pays ou zone ; on part du principe qu'elle repose sur les définitions de la population urbaine utilisées pour les recensements de la population nationaux telles qu'elles sont reproduites à la fin des notes techniques du tableau 6.

Les estimations de la population selon l'âge et le sexe qui figurent dans ce tableau ne concernent que les pays ou zones pour lesquels les estimations sont fondées sur les résultats d'une enquête par sondage ou ont été établies par la méthode des composantes à partir des résultats d'un recensement de la population ou d'une enquête par sondage. Les répartitions par âge et par sexe obtenues en appliquant à l'estimation de la population totale les pourcentages enregistrés pour les divers groupes d'âge pour chaque sexe lors d'un recensement ou d'une enquête par sondage n'ont pas été reproduites dans ce tableau.

Fiabilité des données : Les estimations considérées comme moins sûres sont indiquées en italique plutôt qu'en caractères romains. On n'a pas tenu compte des inexactitudes dans les déclarations d'âge, dont la méthode d'évaluation est exposée à la section 3.1.3 des Notes techniques.

Insuffisance des données : Les statistiques de la population selon l'âge et le sexe appellent les mêmes réserves que celles qui ont été formulées aux sections 3 et 3.1.3 des Notes techniques à propos des statistiques de la population en général et des répartitions par âge en particulier.

La comparabilité des statistiques de la population selon l'âge et le sexe pâtit du manque d'uniformité dans la définition de la population totale (voir la section 3 des Notes techniques) et des lacunes des dénombrements. L'influence de ces deux facteurs varie selon les groupes d'âge. Ainsi, le dénombrement des enfants de moins d'un an et des jeunes enfants comporte souvent plus de lacunes que celui des personnes plus âgées. De même, le fait que certains groupes de personnes appartenant souvent à des groupes d'âge déterminés, par exemple les militaires, ne soient pas pris en compte dans la population totale peut influer sensiblement sur la structure par âge et sur la comparabilité des données avec celles d'autres pays ou zones. Il conviendra de tenir compte de ces facteurs fondamentaux lorsque l'on utilisera les données du tableau.

Outre ces difficultés d'ordre général, la comparabilité pose des problèmes particuliers lorsqu'il s'agit des données par âge. On sait que les répartitions de la population selon l'âge présentent certaines imperfections dues à l'inexactitude des déclarations d'âge. Certaines de ces anomalies ont tendance à s'estomper ou à disparaître lorsque l'on classe les données par groupes d'âge quinquennaux et non par années d'âge, mais une certaine imprécision subsiste, même s'il n'est pas toujours facile de voir à quel point il y a distorsion.

Le degré de comparabilité dépend également de la classification par âge employée dans les divers pays ou zones. L'âge retenu peut être défini par date exacte (jour, mois et année) de naissance ou par celle du dernier anniversaire. Lorsqu'elles étaient connues, les répartitions établies seulement d'après l'année de la naissance ont été signalées en note à la fin du tableau.

Si aucun nombre ne figure dans la rangée réservée aux âges inconnus, cela ne signifie pas nécessairement que les déclarations d'âge et l'exploitation des données par âge aient été tout à fait exactes. C'est souvent une indication que l'on a attribué un âge aux personnes d'âge inconnu avant l'exploitation des données ou qu'elles ont été réparties proportionnellement entre les différents groupes après cette opération.

Comme on l'a indiqué à propos du tableau 5, les estimations intercensitaires de la population totale sont d'ordinaire rectifiées d'après les résultats des recensements de population si l'on constate des discontinuités inexplicables. Les données postcensitaires concernant la répartition de la population par âge et par sexe ont toutefois moins de chance d'être rectifiées de cette manière. Lorsque l'on savait qu'une estimation de la population totale pour une année donnée avait été rectifiée sans qu'il en soit de même pour la répartition par âge correspondante, cette dernière a été indiquée comme ayant un caractère provisoire. Les répartitions de ce type doivent être utilisées avec prudence lorsque l'on étudie les tendances sur un certain nombre d'années, quoique leur utilité pour l'étude de la structure par âge de la population pour l'année visée reste probablement entière.

La comparabilité des données selon le lieu de résidence (zone urbaine ou rurale) peut être limitée par les définitions nationales des termes «urbain» et « rural » utilisées pour la mise en tableaux de ces données. Les définitions du terme « urbain » utilisées pour les recensements nationaux de population ont été présentées à la fin des notes techniques du tableau 6 lorsqu'elles étaient connues. Comme on l'a précisé dans les notes techniques relatives au tableau 6, ces définitions varient considérablement d'un pays ou d'une zone à l'autre.

Données publiées antérieurement : Des statistiques concernant la population selon l'âge, le sexe et le lieu de résidence (zone urbaine ou rurale) ont été présentées dans des éditions antérieures de l'*Annuaire démographique*. Pour plus de précisions concernant les années et les sujets pour lesquels des données ont été publiées, se reporter à l'index historique.

7. Population by age, sex and urban/rural residence: latest available year, 1993 - 2002
Population selon l'âge, le sexe et la résidence, urbaine/rurale: dernière année disponible, 1993 - 2002

(See notes at end of table. — Voir notes à la fin du tableau.)

Continent, country or area, date and age (in years) / Continent, pays ou zone, date et âge (en années)	Code[1]	Total			Urban - Urbaine			Rural - Rurale		
		Both sexes Les deux sexes	Male Masculin	Female Féminin	Both sexes Les deux sexes	Male Masculin	Female Féminin	Both sexes Les deux sexes	Male Masculin	Female Féminin
AFRICA — AFRIQUE										
Algeria - Algérie										
1 VII 2000										
Total	ESDJ	30 356 983	15 342 862	15 014 119	...	...	...	...	...	...
0 - 1	ESDJ	560 642	285 634	275 008	...	...	...	...	...	...
1 - 4	ESDJ	2 961 940	1 512 548	1 449 392	...	...	...	...	...	...
5 - 9	ESDJ	3 526 386	1 802 732	1 723 653	...	...	...	...	...	...
10 - 14	ESDJ	3 790 666	1 930 669	1 859 999	...	...	...	...	...	...
15 - 19	ESDJ	3 707 672	1 889 972	1 817 699	...	...	...	...	...	...
20 - 24	ESDJ	3 182 663	1 612 810	1 569 853	...	...	...	...	...	...
25 - 29	ESDJ	2 677 989	1 347 962	1 330 027	...	...	...	...	...	...
30 - 34	ESDJ	2 284 987	1 147 847	1 137 138	...	...	...	...	...	...
35 - 39	ESDJ	1 844 892	929 666	915 226	...	...	...	...	...	...
40 - 44	ESDJ	1 492 587	749 189	743 399	...	...	...	...	...	...
45 - 49	ESDJ	1 233 670	625 710	607 959	...	...	...	...	...	...
50 - 54	ESDJ	885 103	440 371	444 732	...	...	...	...	...	...
55 - 59	ESDJ	706 062	345 808	360 253	...	...	...	...	...	...
60 - 64	ESDJ	650 309	317 028	333 281	...	...	...	...	...	...
65 - 69	ESDJ	548 675	267 561	281 115	...	...	...	...	...	...
70 - 74	ESDJ	383 322	188 651	194 672	...	...	...	...	...	...
75 - 79	ESDJ	232 192	114 795	117 396	...	...	...	...	...	...
80+	ESDJ	247 868	119 543	128 325	...	...	...	...	...	...
Benin - Bénin										
1 VII 2000										
Total	ESDF	6 169 084	3 013 705	3 155 379	2 492 967	1 220 905	1 272 062	3 676 117	1 792 800	1 883 317
0 - 4	ESDF	1 079 554	546 027	533 527	391 001	198 018	192 983	688 553	348 009	340 544
5 - 9	ESDF	897 767	449 283	448 484	328 285	162 197	166 088	569 482	287 086	282 396
10 - 14	ESDF	921 385	468 494	452 891	376 846	183 278	193 568	544 539	285 216	259 323
15 - 19	ESDF	757 852	395 867	361 985	329 941	172 182	157 759	427 911	223 685	204 226
20 - 24	ESDF	467 089	244 385	222 704	216 960	116 395	100 565	250 129	127 990	122 139
25 - 29	ESDF	387 118	179 632	207 486	171 245	82 819	88 426	215 873	96 813	119 060
30 - 34	ESDF	358 469	149 219	209 250	158 087	70 831	87 256	200 382	78 388	121 994
35 - 39	ESDF	325 169	137 686	187 483	139 841	62 837	77 004	185 328	74 849	110 479
40 - 44	ESDF	250 196	111 603	138 593	105 048	48 266	56 782	145 148	63 337	81 811
45 - 49	ESDF	200 864	90 725	110 139	81 818	37 658	44 160	119 046	53 067	65 979
50 - 54	ESDF	142 649	65 883	76 766	56 162	26 190	29 972	86 487	39 693	46 794
55 - 59	ESDF	111 888	51 260	60 628	44 354	20 390	23 964	67 534	30 870	36 664
60 - 64	ESDF	80 852	36 939	43 913	29 782	13 309	16 473	51 070	23 630	27 440
65 - 69	ESDF	58 328	26 402	31 926	21 850	9 392	12 458	36 478	17 010	19 468
70 - 74	ESDF	53 485	23 293	30 192	18 055	7 097	10 958	35 430	16 196	19 234
75 - 79	ESDF	29 333	13 747	15 586	9 931	4 171	5 760	19 402	9 576	9 826
80+	ESDF	47 086	23 260	23 826	13 761	5 875	7 886	33 325	17 385	15 940
1 VII 2001										
Total	ESDF	6 416 692	3 136 516	3 280 176	...	...	...	...	...	...
0 - 4	ESDF	1 114 233	563 594	550 639	...	...	...	...	...	...
5 - 9	ESDF	951 330	478 101	473 229	...	...	...	...	...	...
10 - 14	ESDF	881 265	444 239	437 026	...	...	...	...	...	...
15 - 19	ESDF	843 647	436 260	407 387	...	...	...	...	...	...
20 - 24	ESDF	510 694	270 545	240 149	...	...	...	...	...	...
25 - 29	ESDF	402 937	193 993	208 944	...	...	...	...	...	...
30 - 34	ESDF	354 910	149 768	205 142	...	...	...	...	...	...
35 - 39	ESDF	341 616	142 268	199 348	...	...	...	...	...	...
40 - 44	ESDF	260 713	115 027	145 686	...	...	...	...	...	...
45 - 49	ESDF	213 734	95 557	118 177	...	...	...	...	...	...
50 - 54	ESDF	153 520	70 293	83 227	...	...	...	...	...	...
55 - 59	ESDF	113 215	51 839	61 376	...	...	...	...	...	...
60 - 64	ESDF	91 038	41 028	50 010	...	...	...	...	...	...
65 - 69	ESDF	52 485	24 029	28 456	...	...	...	...	...	...
70 - 74	ESDF	57 896	24 995	32 901	...	...	...	...	...	...
75 - 79	ESDF	26 853	12 181	14 672	...	...	...	...	...	...
80+	ESDF	46 606	22 799	23 807	...	...	...	...	...	...

7. Population by age, sex and urban/rural residence: latest available year, 1993 - 2002
Population selon l'âge, le sexe et la résidence, urbaine/rurale: dernière année disponible, 1993 - 2002
(continued — suite)

(See notes at end of table. — Voir notes à la fin du tableau.)

Continent, country or area, date and age (in years) / Continent, pays ou zone, date et âge (en années)	Code[1]	Total			Urban - Urbaine			Rural - Rurale		
		Both sexes Les deux sexes	Male Masculin	Female Féminin	Both sexes Les deux sexes	Male Masculin	Female Féminin	Both sexes Les deux sexes	Male Masculin	Female Féminin
AFRICA — AFRIQUE										
Botswana										
17 VIII 2001										
Total	CDFC	1 680 863	813 488	867 375	...	...	...	...	...	...
0 - 1	CDFC	42 845	21 755	21 090	...	...	...	...	...	...
1 - 4	CDFC	152 800	76 879	75 921	...	...	...	...	...	...
5 - 9	CDFC	208 296	104 129	104 167	...	...	...	...	...	...
10 - 14	CDFC	209 968	104 610	105 358	...	...	...	...	...	...
15 - 19	CDFC	203 706	99 603	104 103	...	...	...	...	...	...
20 - 24	CDFC	170 614	80 148	90 466	...	...	...	...	...	...
25 - 29	CDFC	147 766	71 877	75 889	...	...	...	...	...	...
30 - 34	CDFC	113 755	54 997	58 758	...	...	...	...	...	...
35 - 39	CDFC	95 343	44 651	50 692	...	...	...	...	...	...
40 - 44	CDFC	76 373	35 236	41 137	...	...	...	...	...	...
45 - 49	CDFC	63 480	29 573	33 907	...	...	...	...	...	...
50 - 54	CDFC	45 100	21 585	23 515	...	...	...	...	...	...
55 - 59	CDFC	33 305	15 674	17 631	...	...	...	...	...	...
60 - 64	CDFC	28 615	13 378	15 237	...	...	...	...	...	...
65 - 69	CDFC	25 474	11 113	14 361	...	...	...	...	...	...
70 - 74	CDFC	21 130	8 891	12 239	...	...	...	...	...	...
75+	CDFC	36 640	14 411	22 229	...	...	...	...	...	...
Unk. - Inc.	CDFC	5 653	4 978	675	...	...	...	...	...	...
Burkina Faso										
10 XII 1996										
Total	CDFC	10 312 609	4 970 882	5 341 727	...	...	...	...	...	...
0 - 1	CDFC	346 453	173 583	172 870	...	...	...	...	...	...
1 - 4	CDFC	1 421 971	715 961	706 010	...	...	...	...	...	...
5 - 9	CDFC	1 798 242	913 006	885 236	...	...	...	...	...	...
10 - 14	CDFC	1 375 393	706 641	668 752	...	...	...	...	...	...
15 - 19	CDFC	1 082 487	534 025	548 462	...	...	...	...	...	...
20 - 24	CDFC	767 462	340 162	427 300	...	...	...	...	...	...
25 - 29	CDFC	666 645	285 292	381 353	...	...	...	...	...	...
30 - 34	CDFC	572 745	250 049	322 696	...	...	...	...	...	...
35 - 39	CDFC	467 470	205 558	261 912	...	...	...	...	...	...
40 - 44	CDFC	390 677	173 362	217 315	...	...	...	...	...	...
45 - 49	CDFC	311 624	145 091	166 533	...	...	...	...	...	...
50 - 54	CDFC	279 315	127 031	152 284	...	...	...	...	...	...
55 - 59	CDFC	208 700	102 910	105 790	...	...	...	...	...	...
60 - 64	CDFC	196 248	93 494	102 754	...	...	...	...	...	...
65 - 69	CDFC	132 659	66 895	65 764	...	...	...	...	...	...
70 - 74	CDFC	114 931	54 300	60 631	...	...	...	...	...	...
75 - 79	CDFC	62 654	31 623	31 031	...	...	...	...	...	...
80 - 84	CDFC	36 026	15 405	20 621	...	...	...	...	...	...
85 - 89	CDFC	14 151	6 253	7 898	...	...	...	...	...	...
90 - 94	CDFC	9 503	3 742	5 761	...	...	...	...	...	...
95+	CDFC	15 888	5 839	10 049	...	...	...	...	...	...
Unk. - Inc.	CDFC	41 365	20 660	20 705	...	...	...	...	...	...
Burundi										
1 VII 1993										
Total	ESDF	5 769 143	2 805 796	2 963 347	403 680	214 472	189 208	5 365 463	2 591 324	2 774 139
0 - 1	ESDF	224 612	112 804	111 808	12 371	6 101	6 270	212 241	106 703	105 538
1 - 4	ESDF	883 430	440 499	442 931	65 343	36 193	29 150	818 087	404 306	413 781
5 - 9	ESDF	897 159	445 841	451 318	62 896	34 079	28 817	834 263	411 762	422 501
10 - 14	ESDF	700 683	345 674	355 009	49 090	26 423	22 667	651 593	319 251	332 342
15 - 19	ESDF	575 666	281 702	293 964	40 303	21 533	18 770	535 364	260 169	275 195
20 - 24	ESDF	483 813	234 003	249 810	33 837	17 887	15 950	449 976	216 116	233 860
25 - 29	ESDF	408 301	196 125	212 176	28 539	14 992	13 547	379 761	181 134	198 627
30 - 34	ESDF	346 274	166 103	180 171	24 201	12 697	11 504	322 073	153 406	168 667
35 - 39	ESDF	284 561	135 801	148 760	19 877	10 380	9 497	264 682	125 421	139 261
40 - 44	ESDF	218 512	103 534	114 978	15 255	7 914	7 341	203 257	95 620	107 637
45 - 49	ESDF	173 824	81 368	92 456	12 123	6 220	5 903	161 701	75 148	86 553

139

7. Population by age, sex and urban/rural residence: latest available year, 1993 - 2002
Population selon l'âge, le sexe et la résidence, urbaine/rurale: dernière année disponible, 1993 - 2002
(continued — suite)

(See notes at end of table. — Voir notes à la fin du tableau.)

Continent, country or area, date and age (in years) / Continent, pays ou zone, date et âge (en années)	Code[1]	Total			Urban - Urbaine			Rural - Rurale		
		Both sexes Les deux sexes	Male Masculin	Female Féminin	Both sexes Les deux sexes	Male Masculin	Female Féminin	Both sexes Les deux sexes	Male Masculin	Female Féminin
AFRICA — AFRIQUE										
Burundi										
1 VII 1993										
50 - 54	ESDF	134 642	61 447	73 195	9 370	4 697	4 673	125 272	56 750	68 522
55 - 59	ESDF	108 961	49 101	59 860	7 577	3 753	3 824	101 386	45 348	56 038
60 - 64	ESDF	90 204	40 123	50 081	6 265	3 067	3 198	83 939	37 056	46 883
65 - 69	ESDF	73 426	32 828	40 598	5 101	2 509	2 592	68 325	30 319	38 006
70 - 74	ESDF	58 378	26 374	32 004	4 059	2 016	2 043	54 319	24 358	29 961
75 - 79	ESDF	45 623	21 325	24 298	3 181	1 630	1 551	42 442	19 694	22 748
80+	ESDF	61 074	31 144	29 930	4 292	2 381	1 911	56 782	28 763	28 019
Cape Verde - Cap-Vert										
1 VII 2002										
Total	ESDF	452 714	219 211	233 503	249 794	121 924	127 870	202 920	97 287	105 633
0 - 4	ESDF	57 723	29 376	28 347	29 161	14 864	14 297	28 562	14 512	14 050
5 - 9	ESDF	62 568	31 483	31 085	31 246	15 776	15 470	31 322	15 707	15 615
10 - 14	ESDF	64 920	32 484	32 436	33 856	16 756	17 100	31 064	15 728	15 336
15 - 19	ESDF	55 223	27 611	27 612	32 040	15 651	16 388	23 183	11 960	11 223
20 - 24	ESDF	40 592	20 401	20 191	25 361	12 708	12 653	15 230	7 692	7 538
25 - 29	ESDF	30 468	15 278	15 190	19 099	9 521	9 578	11 369	5 756	5 613
30 - 34	ESDF	27 551	13 461	14 090	16 697	8 342	8 355	10 853	5 119	5 734
35 - 39	ESDF	26 553	12 696	13 857	16 493	8 221	8 272	10 060	4 475	5 585
40 - 44	ESDF	21 657	9 863	11 794	13 068	6 389	6 679	8 588	3 474	5 114
45 - 49	ESDF	14 972	6 153	8 819	8 616	4 026	4 589	6 357	2 127	4 230
50 - 54	ESDF	8 177	3 258	4 919	4 754	2 100	2 653	3 423	1 158	2 265
55 - 59	ESDF	5 613	2 246	3 367	2 966	1 272	1 694	2 648	975	1 673
60 - 64	ESDF	8 519	3 283	5 236	3 979	1 560	2 419	4 540	1 723	2 817
65 - 69	ESDF	9 240	3 711	5 529	4 148	1 630	2 518	5 092	2 081	3 011
70 - 74	ESDF	7 767	3 337	4 430	3 317	1 288	2 029	4 450	2 049	2 401
75 - 79	ESDF	4 556	1 985	2 571	2 018	765	1 253	2 537	1 220	1 317
80+	ESDF	6 615	2 585	4 030	2 976	1 054	1 922	3 639	1 531	2 108
Chad - Tchad[2]										
8 IV 1993										
Total	CDJC	6 193 538	3 001 371	3 192 167	...	...	...	...	...	...
0 - 4	CDJC	1 125 473	565 539	559 934	...	...	...	...	...	...
5 - 9	CDJC	1 062 740	534 245	528 495	...	...	...	...	...	...
10 - 14	CDJC	777 185	400 917	376 268	...	...	...	...	...	...
15 - 19	CDJC	611 145	292 416	318 729	...	...	...	...	...	...
20 - 24	CDJC	453 417	204 657	248 760	...	...	...	...	...	...
25 - 29	CDJC	454 232	197 509	256 723	...	...	...	...	...	...
30 - 34	CDJC	354 363	163 792	190 571	...	...	...	...	...	...
35 - 39	CDJC	295 276	137 388	157 888	...	...	...	...	...	...
40 - 44	CDJC	257 420	117 788	139 632	...	...	...	...	...	...
45 - 49	CDJC	173 788	83 414	90 374	...	...	...	...	...	...
50 - 54	CDJC	176 935	81 489	95 446	...	...	...	...	...	...
55 - 59	CDJC	91 049	45 345	45 704	...	...	...	...	...	...
60 - 64	CDJC	127 259	60 027	67 232	...	...	...	...	...	...
65 - 69	CDJC	55 406	28 465	26 941	...	...	...	...	...	...
70 - 74	CDJC	74 940	36 932	38 008	...	...	...	...	...	...
75+	CDJC	78 654	41 237	37 417	...	...	...	...	...	...
Unk. - Inc.	CDJC	24 256	10 211	14 045	...	...	...	...	...	...
Egypt - Égypte										
19 XI 1996										
Total	CDFC	59 312 914	30 351 390	28 961 524	25 286 335	12 957 775	12 328 560	34 026 579	17 393 615	16 632 964
0 - 1	CDFC	560 622	288 082	272 540	238 653	122 073	116 580	321 969	166 009	155 960
1 - 4	CDFC	6 294 620	3 223 694	3 070 926	2 257 688	1 152 819	1 104 869	4 036 932	2 070 875	1 966 057
5 - 9	CDFC	7 626 252	3 939 121	3 687 131	2 852 218	1 464 520	1 387 698	4 774 034	2 474 601	2 299 433
10 - 14	CDFC	7 864 002	4 076 601	3 787 401	3 116 208	1 602 009	1 514 199	4 747 794	2 474 592	2 273 202
15 - 19	CDFC	6 901 611	3 602 857	3 298 754	2 930 311	1 510 230	1 420 081	3 971 300	2 092 627	1 878 673
20 - 24	CDFC	5 075 136	2 642 620	2 432 516	2 273 551	1 167 895	1 105 656	2 801 585	1 474 725	1 326 860
25 - 29	CDFC	4 370 522	2 105 063	2 265 459	1 916 234	933 765	982 469	2 454 288	1 171 298	1 282 990

7. Population by age, sex and urban/rural residence: latest available year, 1993 - 2002
Population selon l'âge, le sexe et la résidence, urbaine/rurale: dernière année disponible, 1993 - 2002
(continued — suite)

(See notes at end of table. — Voir notes à la fin du tableau.)

Continent, country or area, date and age (in years) / Continent, pays ou zone, date et âge (en années)	Code[1]	Total			Urban - Urbaine			Rural - Rurale		
		Both sexes Les deux sexes	Male Masculin	Female Féminin	Both sexes Les deux sexes	Male Masculin	Female Féminin	Both sexes Les deux sexes	Male Masculin	Female Féminin
AFRICA — AFRIQUE										
Egypt - Égypte										
19 XI 1996										
30 - 34	CDFC	3 979 720	1 993 212	1 986 508	1 847 108	917 762	929 346	2 132 612	1 075 450	1 057 162
35 - 39	CDFC	3 860 105	1 914 367	1 945 738	1 776 094	879 215	896 879	2 084 011	1 035 152	1 048 859
40 - 44	CDFC	3 173 226	1 616 449	1 556 777	1 573 960	810 931	763 029	1 599 266	805 518	793 748
45 - 49	CDFC	2 696 169	1 408 498	1 287 671	1 296 912	687 877	609 035	1 399 257	720 621	678 636
50 - 54	CDFC	2 022 136	994 936	1 027 200	984 817	503 584	481 233	1 037 319	491 352	545 967
55 - 59	CDFC	1 476 673	776 537	700 136	686 141	372 516	313 625	790 532	404 021	386 511
60 - 64	CDFC	1 398 994	706 189	692 805	665 441	349 766	315 675	733 553	356 423	377 130
65 - 69	CDFC	930 576	507 085	423 491	404 645	232 503	172 142	525 931	274 582	251 349
70 - 74	CDFC	617 669	315 767	301 902	269 065	144 153	124 912	348 604	171 614	176 990
75+	CDFC	464 858	240 302	224 556	197 282	106 154	91 128	267 576	134 148	133 428
Unk. - Inc.	CDFC	23	10	13	7	3	4	16	7	9
1 VII 2000										
Total	ESDF	63 976 000	32 695 000	31 281 000	...	...	...	...	...	...
0 - 4	ESDF	7 394 000	3 783 000	3 611 000	...	...	...	...	...	...
5 - 9	ESDF	8 225 000	4 245 000	3 980 000	...	...	...	...	...	...
10 - 14	ESDF	8 481 000	4 392 000	4 089 000	...	...	...	...	...	...
15 - 19	ESDF	7 445 000	3 882 000	3 563 000	...	...	...	...	...	...
20 - 24	ESDF	5 474 000	2 848 000	2 626 000	...	...	...	...	...	...
25 - 29	ESDF	4 714 000	2 266 000	2 448 000	...	...	...	...	...	...
30 - 34	ESDF	4 293 000	2 149 000	2 144 000	...	...	...	...	...	...
35 - 39	ESDF	4 164 000	2 064 000	2 100 000	...	...	...	...	...	...
40 - 44	ESDF	3 422 000	1 740 000	1 682 000	...	...	...	...	...	...
45 - 49	ESDF	2 909 000	1 516 000	1 393 000	...	...	...	...	...	...
50 - 54	ESDF	2 180 000	1 071 000	1 109 000	...	...	...	...	...	...
55 - 59	ESDF	1 593 000	835 000	758 000	...	...	...	...	...	...
60 - 64	ESDF	1 510 000	761 000	749 000	...	...	...	...	...	...
65 - 69	ESDF	1 003 000	546 000	457 000	...	...	...	...	...	...
70 - 74	ESDF	667 000	339 000	328 000	...	...	...	...	...	...
75+	ESDF	502 000	258 000	244 000	...	...	...	...	...	...
Ethiopia - Éthiopie										
1 VII 2002										
Total	ESDF	67 220 000	33 707 000	33 513 000	10 307 000	5 134 000	5 173 000	56 913 000	28 573 000	28 340 000
0 - 4	ESDF	11 613 528	5 858 730	5 754 798	1 295 225	675 800	619 426	10 318 302	5 182 930	5 135 372
5 - 9	ESDF	9 464 485	4 790 119	4 674 366	1 165 174	595 197	569 977	8 299 311	4 194 922	4 104 389
10 - 14	ESDF	8 134 907	4 131 454	4 003 453	1 180 977	584 705	596 272	6 953 930	3 546 749	3 407 181
15 - 19	ESDF	7 377 805	3 748 613	3 629 192	1 247 670	604 373	643 297	6 130 135	3 144 241	2 985 895
20 - 24	ESDF	6 378 061	3 230 355	3 147 705	1 186 998	579 032	607 966	5 191 062	2 651 323	2 539 739
25 - 29	ESDF	5 247 932	2 619 111	2 628 821	1 009 980	497 432	512 547	4 237 953	2 121 679	2 116 274
30 - 34	ESDF	4 259 586	2 088 116	2 171 470	809 268	405 560	403 708	3 450 318	1 682 556	1 767 762
35 - 39	ESDF	3 419 786	1 644 661	1 775 125	624 635	312 182	312 453	2 795 151	1 332 479	1 462 672
40 - 44	ESDF	2 752 267	1 309 273	1 442 994	466 806	232 349	234 457	2 285 461	1 076 924	1 208 537
45 - 49	ESDF	2 253 394	1 088 803	1 164 591	364 523	185 304	179 219	1 888 871	903 498	985 372
50 - 54	ESDF	1 829 663	902 219	927 444	284 003	144 121	139 882	1 545 660	758 098	787 562
55 - 59	ESDF	1 436 626	720 663	715 964	216 062	107 322	108 740	1 220 564	613 340	607 224
60 - 64	ESDF	1 098 600	559 503	539 097	164 553	78 729	85 824	934 047	480 774	453 273
65 - 69	ESDF	813 668	417 849	395 819	122 960	56 993	65 967	690 707	360 855	329 852
70 - 74	ESDF	555 964	288 146	267 817	81 805	37 057	44 748	474 159	251 090	223 069
75+	ESDF	583 730	309 385	274 344	86 361	37 844	48 517	497 369	271 542	225 827
Gabon										
31 VII 1993										
Total	CDFC	1 014 976	501 784	513 192	...	...	...	...	...	...
0 - 1	CDFC	35 791	17 875	17 916	...	...	...	...	...	...
1 - 4	CDFC	118 221	59 101	59 120	...	...	...	...	...	...
5 - 9	CDFC	140 487	70 051	70 436	...	...	...	...	...	...
10 - 14	CDFC	121 690	60 123	61 567	...	...	...	...	...	...
15 - 19	CDFC	100 800	48 841	51 959	...	...	...	...	...	...
20 - 24	CDFC	91 511	43 527	47 984	...	...	...	...	...	...
25 - 29	CDFC	81 750	40 475	41 275	...	...	...	...	...	...

7. Population by age, sex and urban/rural residence: latest available year, 1993 - 2002
Population selon l'âge, le sexe et la résidence, urbaine/rurale: dernière année disponible, 1993 - 2002
(continued — suite)

(See notes at end of table. — Voir notes à la fin du tableau.)

Continent, country or area, date and age (in years) / Continent, pays ou zone, date et âge (en années)	Code[1]	Total			Urban - Urbaine			Rural - Rurale		
		Both sexes Les deux sexes	Male Masculin	Female Féminin	Both sexes Les deux sexes	Male Masculin	Female Féminin	Both sexes Les deux sexes	Male Masculin	Female Féminin
AFRICA — AFRIQUE										
Gabon										
31 VII 1993										
30 - 34	CDFC	69 446	36 149	33 297	...	...	...	...	...	...
35 - 39	CDFC	52 254	28 364	23 890	...	...	...	...	...	...
40 - 44	CDFC	39 611	22 144	17 467	...	...	...	...	...	...
45 - 49	CDFC	32 206	16 706	15 500	...	...	...	...	...	...
50 - 54	CDFC	29 714	13 976	15 738	...	...	...	...	...	...
55 - 59	CDFC	29 442	13 384	16 058	...	...	...	...	...	...
60 - 64	CDFC	24 581	10 744	13 837	...	...	...	...	...	...
65 - 69	CDFC	18 091	7 882	10 209	...	...	...	...	...	...
70 - 74	CDFC	13 923	6 048	7 875	...	...	...	...	...	...
75 - 79	CDFC	8 081	3 637	4 444	...	...	...	...	...	...
80 - 84	CDFC	4 317	1 699	2 618	...	...	...	...	...	...
85 - 89	CDFC	1 813	633	1 180	...	...	...	...	...	...
90+	CDFC	1 247	425	822	...	...	...	...	...	...
Gambia - Gambie										
15 IV 1993										
Total	CDFC	1 038 145	519 950	518 195	385 400	198 926	186 474	652 745	321 024	331 721
0 - 1	CDFC	29 047	14 817	14 230	10 476	5 326	5 150	18 571	9 491	9 080
1 - 4	CDFC	139 170	69 882	69 288	44 667	22 298	22 369	94 503	47 584	46 919
5 - 9	CDFC	163 791	81 904	81 887	49 744	24 132	25 612	114 047	57 772	56 275
10 - 14	CDFC	122 653	61 472	61 181	42 335	19 916	22 419	80 318	41 556	38 762
15 - 19	CDFC	108 525	52 499	56 026	45 171	21 305	23 866	63 354	31 194	32 160
20 - 24	CDFC	91 368	44 742	46 626	43 209	22 716	20 493	48 159	22 026	26 133
25 - 29	CDFC	88 049	40 923	47 126	38 409	20 306	18 103	49 640	20 617	29 023
30 - 34	CDFC	65 266	30 510	34 756	27 235	14 738	12 497	38 031	15 772	22 259
35 - 39	CDFC	49 453	24 924	24 529	20 588	11 713	8 875	28 865	13 211	15 654
40 - 44	CDFC	41 696	21 142	20 554	15 419	9 033	6 386	26 277	12 109	14 168
45 - 49	CDFC	29 042	16 593	12 449	11 067	6 898	4 169	17 975	9 695	8 280
50 - 54	CDFC	26 197	14 320	11 877	8 558	5 069	3 489	17 639	9 251	8 388
55 - 59	CDFC	14 826	9 041	5 785	5 162	3 152	2 010	9 664	5 889	3 775
60 - 64	CDFC	18 165	9 754	8 411	5 218	2 793	2 425	12 947	6 961	5 986
65 - 69	CDFC	9 223	5 251	3 972	3 031	1 618	1 413	6 192	3 633	2 559
70 - 74	CDFC	9 678	4 981	4 697	2 577	1 234	1 343	7 101	3 747	3 354
75 - 79	CDFC	4 529	2 474	2 055	1 320	656	664	3 209	1 818	1 391
80 - 84	CDFC	4 959	2 334	2 625	1 241	521	720	3 718	1 813	1 905
85 - 89	CDFC	1 692	855	837	443	192	251	1 249	663	586
90 - 94	CDFC	1 351	628	723	292	96	196	1 059	532	527
95+	CDFC	2 062	964	1 098	521	211	310	1 541	753	788
Unk. - Inc.	CDFC	17 403	9 940	7 463	8 717	5 003	3 714	8 686	4 937	3 749
Ghana										
26 III 2000										
Total	CDFC	18 912 079	9 357 382	9 554 697	...	...	...	...	...	...
0 - 1	CDFC	525 258	262 041	263 217	...	...	...	...	...	...
1 - 4	CDFC	2 244 163	1 117 729	1 126 434	...	...	...	...	...	...
5 - 9	CDFC	2 775 206	1 390 652	1 384 554	...	...	...	...	...	...
10 - 14	CDFC	2 262 216	1 151 131	1 111 085	...	...	...	...	...	...
15 - 19	CDFC	1 883 753	961 162	922 591	...	...	...	...	...	...
20 - 24	CDFC	1 600 820	763 051	837 769	...	...	...	...	...	...
25 - 29	CDFC	1 487 299	695 494	791 805	...	...	...	...	...	...
30 - 34	CDFC	1 206 809	566 439	640 370	...	...	...	...	...	...
35 - 39	CDFC	1 029 765	490 864	538 901	...	...	...	...	...	...
40 - 44	CDFC	886 931	443 284	443 647	...	...	...	...	...	...
45 - 49	CDFC	720 357	377 315	343 042	...	...	...	...	...	...
50 - 54	CDFC	568 369	279 950	288 419	...	...	...	...	...	...
55 - 59	CDFC	355 842	182 843	172 999	...	...	...	...	...	...
60 - 64	CDFC	366 351	177 347	189 004	...	...	...	...	...	...
65 - 69	CDFC	258 709	129 090	129 619	...	...	...	...	...	...
70 - 74	CDFC	225 158	106 513	118 645	...	...	...	...	...	...
75 - 79	CDFC	144 830	74 268	70 562	...	...	...	...	...	...

7. Population by age, sex and urban/rural residence: latest available year, 1993 - 2002
Population selon l'âge, le sexe et la résidence, urbaine/rurale: dernière année disponible, 1993 - 2002
(continued — suite)

(See notes at end of table. — Voir notes à la fin du tableau.)

Continent, country or area, date and age (in years) / Continent, pays ou zone, date et âge (en années)	Code[1]	Total			Urban - Urbaine			Rural - Rurale		
		Both sexes Les deux sexes	Male Masculin	Female Féminin	Both sexes Les deux sexes	Male Masculin	Female Féminin	Both sexes Les deux sexes	Male Masculin	Female Féminin

AFRICA — AFRIQUE

Ghana
26 III 2000

80 - 84	CDFC	140 847	66 941	73 906	...	...	...	...	...	...
85+	CDFC	229 396	121 268	108 128	...	...	...	...	...	...

Lesotho
1 VII 2001

Total	SSDJ	2 157 537	1 065 484	1 092 053	288 895	131 861	157 034	1 868 642	933 623	935 019
0 - 1	SSDJ	45 867	24 441	21 426	5 590	3 177	2 413	40 277	21 264	19 013
1 - 4	SSDJ	184 467	92 420	92 047	21 097	10 832	10 265	163 370	81 588	81 782
5 - 9	SSDJ	250 417	127 720	122 697	27 655	13 408	14 247	222 762	114 312	108 450
10 - 14	SSDJ	280 429	141 486	138 943	29 492	14 094	15 398	250 937	127 392	123 545
15 - 19	SSDJ	286 404	145 591	140 813	35 686	14 075	21 611	250 719	131 517	119 202
20 - 24	SSDJ	225 779	116 163	109 616	35 176	14 235	20 941	190 603	101 928	88 675
25 - 29	SSDJ	159 700	79 705	79 995	30 051	12 477	17 574	129 648	67 227	62 421
30 - 34	SSDJ	114 507	56 175	58 332	23 915	11 542	12 373	90 592	44 633	45 959
35 - 39	SSDJ	110 264	55 375	54 889	21 547	11 162	10 385	88 717	44 213	44 504
40 - 44	SSDJ	93 645	43 925	49 720	15 044	7 468	7 576	78 602	36 457	42 145
45 - 49	SSDJ	81 488	41 152	40 336	11 468	5 651	5 817	70 019	35 501	34 518
50 - 54	SSDJ	77 212	33 959	43 253	9 388	3 592	5 796	67 824	30 367	37 457
55 - 59	SSDJ	56 352	28 197	28 155	5 927	2 782	3 145	50 425	25 415	25 010
60 - 64	SSDJ	48 107	21 105	27 002	4 770	1 866	2 904	43 337	19 239	24 098
65 - 69	SSDJ	49 001	21 165	27 836	4 284	1 949	2 335	44 717	19 216	25 501
70 - 74	SSDJ	29 628	11 671	17 957	1 801	843	958	27 828	10 829	16 999
75+	SSDJ	45 242	14 815	30 427	3 208	982	2 226	42 033	13 832	28 201
Unk. - Inc.	SSDJ	19 028	10 419	8 609	2 796	1 726	1 070	16 232	8 693	7 539

Madagascar
1 VIII 1993

Total	CDFC	12 238 914	6 088 116	6 150 798	2 800 229	1 368 566	1 431 663	9 438 685	4 719 550	4 719 135
0 - 4	CDFC	2 234 605	1 121 953	1 112 652	431 461	216 780	214 681	1 803 144	905 173	897 971
5 - 9	CDFC	1 704 664	962 106	842 438	355 350	178 468	176 882	1 349 214	683 657	665 557
10 - 14	CDFC	1 526 022	772 329	753 693	347 490	171 813	175 677	1 178 532	600 516	578 016
15 - 19	CDFC	1 372 659	673 803	698 856	332 039	158 937	173 102	1 040 620	514 866	525 754
20 - 24	CDFC	1 118 519	542 830	575 689	278 150	132 188	145 962	840 360	410 642	429 727
25 - 29	CDFC	903 176	437 855	465 321	226 337	106 973	119 364	676 839	330 882	345 957
30 - 34	CDFC	789 734	388 896	400 838	199 041	96 256	102 785	590 693	292 640	298 053
35 - 39	CDFC	631 357	318 808	312 549	165 839	81 648	84 191	465 518	237 160	228 358
40 - 44	CDFC	488 602	245 455	243 147	129 678	64 698	64 980	358 924	180 757	178 167
45 - 49	CDFC	332 625	161 173	171 452	84 046	41 312	42 734	248 579	119 861	128 718
50 - 54	CDFC	306 080	147 585	158 495	71 344	34 790	36 554	234 736	112 795	121 941
55 - 59	CDFC	248 217	120 897	127 320	56 738	27 082	29 656	191 479	93 815	97 664
60 - 64	CDFC	218 913	108 106	110 807	45 963	21 672	24 291	172 950	86 434	86 516
65 - 69	CDFC	147 867	75 705	72 162	31 530	15 004	16 526	116 337	60 701	55 636
70 - 74	CDFC	111 744	58 599	53 145	22 871	10 905	11 966	88 873	47 694	41 179
75 - 79	CDFC	54 183	28 062	26 121	11 951	5 521	6 430	42 232	22 541	19 691
80+	CDFC	50 047	23 935	26 112	10 401	4 519	5 882	39 646	19 416	20 230

Malawi
1 IX 1998

Total	CDFC	9 933 868	4 867 563	5 066 305	1 435 436	742 839	692 597	8 498 432	4 124 724	4 373 708
0 - 1	CDFC	368 325	182 508	185 817	49 018	24 549	24 469	319 307	157 959	161 348
1 - 4	CDFC	1 292 065	641 117	650 948	166 030	83 011	83 019	1 126 035	558 106	567 929
5 - 9	CDFC	1 440 370	714 830	725 540	183 924	90 095	93 829	1 256 446	624 735	631 711
10 - 14	CDFC	1 232 500	616 445	616 055	180 430	84 521	95 909	1 052 070	531 924	520 146
15 - 19	CDFC	1 087 936	527 865	560 071	179 240	88 044	91 196	908 696	439 821	468 875
20 - 24	CDFC	979 060	435 138	543 922	185 677	89 626	96 051	793 383	345 512	447 871
25 - 29	CDFC	792 465	393 913	398 552	152 217	85 808	66 409	640 248	308 105	332 143
30 - 34	CDFC	601 241	303 080	298 161	105 241	60 855	44 386	496 000	242 225	253 775
35 - 39	CDFC	484 827	239 043	245 784	75 067	42 734	32 333	409 760	196 309	213 451
40 - 44	CDFC	360 709	180 167	180 542	50 294	30 145	20 149	310 415	150 022	160 393
45 - 49	CDFC	332 756	166 258	166 498	38 650	23 268	15 382	294 106	142 990	151 116
50 - 54	CDFC	238 846	120 193	118 653	24 745	15 195	9 550	214 101	104 998	109 103

7. Population by age, sex and urban/rural residence: latest available year, 1993 - 2002
Population selon l'âge, le sexe et la résidence, urbaine/rurale: dernière année disponible, 1993 - 2002
(continued — suite)

(See notes at end of table. — Voir notes à la fin du tableau.)

Continent, country or area, date and age (in years) / Continent, pays ou zone, date et âge (en annèes)	Code[1]	Total			Urban - Urbaine			Rural - Rurale		
		Both sexes Les deux sexes	Male Masculin	Female Féminin	Both sexes Les deux sexes	Male Masculin	Female Féminin	Both sexes Les deux sexes	Male Masculin	Female Féminin
AFRICA — AFRIQUE										
Malawi										
1 IX 1998										
55 - 59	CDFC	175 226	89 909	85 317	14 921	9 171	5 750	160 305	80 738	79 567
60 - 64	CDFC	153 084	72 251	80 833	10 405	5 973	4 432	142 679	66 278	76 401
65 - 69	CDFC	139 320	65 655	73 665	7 818	4 226	3 592	131 502	61 429	70 073
70 - 74	CDFC	98 049	45 310	52 739	4 936	2 407	2 529	93 113	42 903	50 210
75 - 79	CDFC	65 485	32 151	33 334	2 936	1 489	1 447	62 549	30 662	31 887
80 - 84	CDFC	45 632	20 495	25 137	1 968	873	1 095	43 664	19 622	24 042
85 - 89	CDFC	25 214	11 540	13 674	1 042	463	579	24 172	11 077	13 095
90 - 94	CDFC	11 167	5 180	5 987	521	227	294	10 646	4 953	5 693
95+	CDFC	9 591	4 515	5 076	356	159	197	9 235	4 356	4 879
1 VII 2002										
Total	ESDF	*11 174 648*	*5 486 254*	*5 688 394*	...	...	...	...	...	...
0 - 4	ESDF	*2 248 173*	*1 126 236*	*1 121 937*	...	...	...	...	...	...
5 - 9	ESDF	*1 524 225*	*751 468*	*772 757*	...	...	...	...	...	...
10 - 14	ESDF	*1 368 161*	*680 165*	*687 996*	...	...	...	...	...	...
15 - 19	ESDF	*1 176 482*	*586 975*	*589 507*	...	...	...	...	...	...
20 - 24	ESDF	*1 043 485*	*495 436*	*548 049*	...	...	...	...	...	...
25 - 29	ESDF	*924 300*	*412 905*	*511 395*	...	...	...	...	...	...
30 - 34	ESDF	*730 558*	*368 097*	*362 461*	...	...	...	...	...	...
35 - 39	ESDF	*554 399*	*278 544*	*275 855*	...	...	...	...	...	...
40 - 44	ESDF	*440 271*	*216 675*	*223 596*	...	...	...	...	...	...
45 - 49	ESDF	*332 601*	*165 775*	*166 826*	...	...	...	...	...	...
50 - 54	ESDF	*300 533*	*149 241*	*151 292*	...	...	...	...	...	...
55+	ESDF	*531 460*	*254 737*	*276 723*	...	...	...	...	...	...
Mauritania - Mauritanie										
24 IV 1993										
Total	ESDF	*2 147 778*	*1 066 298*	*1 081 480*	...	...	...	...	...	...
0 - 4	ESDF	*390 397*	*196 530*	*193 867*	...	...	...	...	...	...
5 - 9	ESDF	*287 946*	*146 131*	*141 815*	...	...	...	...	...	...
10 - 14	ESDF	*294 024*	*152 069*	*141 955*	...	...	...	...	...	...
15 - 19	ESDF	*215 166*	*112 582*	*102 584*	...	...	...	...	...	...
20 - 24	ESDF	*185 066*	*90 442*	*94 624*	...	...	...	...	...	...
25 - 29	ESDF	*156 811*	*72 641*	*84 170*	...	...	...	...	...	...
30 - 34	ESDF	*140 238*	*64 843*	*75 395*	...	...	...	...	...	...
35 - 39	ESDF	*112 705*	*54 208*	*58 497*	...	...	...	...	...	...
40 - 44	ESDF	*85 646*	*42 337*	*43 309*	...	...	...	...	...	...
45 - 49	ESDF	*68 958*	*32 675*	*36 283*	...	...	...	...	...	...
50 - 54	ESDF	*51 822*	*25 394*	*26 428*	...	...	...	...	...	...
55 - 59	ESDF	*56 191*	*26 848*	*29 343*	...	...	...	...	...	...
60 - 64	ESDF	*27 591*	*14 406*	*13 185*	...	...	...	...	...	...
65 - 69	ESDF	*33 265*	*16 093*	*17 172*	...	...	...	...	...	...
70 - 74	ESDF	*16 779*	*8 307*	*8 472*	...	...	...	...	...	...
75+	ESDF	*25 173*	*10 792*	*14 381*	...	...	...	...	...	...
Mauritius - Maurice										
1 VII 2002										
Total	ESDJ	1 210 196	599 257	610 939	...	...	...	...	...	...
0 - 1	ESDJ	19 366	9 842	9 524	...	...	...	...	...	...
1 - 4	ESDJ	78 653	40 153	38 500	...	...	...	...	...	...
5 - 9	ESDJ	104 404	52 451	51 953	...	...	...	...	...	...
10 - 14	ESDJ	105 403	53 635	51 768	...	...	...	...	...	...
15 - 19	ESDJ	94 307	47 678	46 629	...	...	...	...	...	...
20 - 24	ESDJ	113 886	56 897	56 989	...	...	...	...	...	...
25 - 29	ESDJ	98 281	48 894	49 387	...	...	...	...	...	...
30 - 34	ESDJ	94 352	47 006	47 346	...	...	...	...	...	...
35 - 39	ESDJ	103 420	52 207	51 213	...	...	...	...	...	...
40 - 44	ESDJ	93 551	47 067	46 484	...	...	...	...	...	...
45 - 49	ESDJ	81 815	41 221	40 594	...	...	...	...	...	...
50 - 54	ESDJ	67 437	33 236	34 201	...	...	...	...	...	...

7. Population by age, sex and urban/rural residence: latest available year, 1993 - 2002
Population selon l'âge, le sexe et la résidence, urbaine/rurale: dernière année disponible, 1993 - 2002
(continued — suite)

(See notes at end of table. — Voir notes à la fin du tableau.)

Continent, country or area, date and age (in years) / Continent, pays ou zone, date et âge (en années)	Code[1]	Total			Urban - Urbaine			Rural - Rurale		
		Both sexes Les deux sexes	Male Masculin	Female Féminin	Both sexes Les deux sexes	Male Masculin	Female Féminin	Both sexes Les deux sexes	Male Masculin	Female Féminin
AFRICA — AFRIQUE										
Mauritius - Maurice										
1 VII 2002										
55 - 59	ESDJ	44 507	21 125	23 382	...	...	...	...	...	...
60 - 64	ESDJ	33 012	15 351	17 661	...	...	...	...	...	...
65 - 69	ESDJ	28 218	12 775	15 443	...	...	...	...	...	...
70 - 74	ESDJ	20 080	8 670	11 410	...	...	...	...	...	...
75 - 79	ESDJ	16 233	6 607	9 626	...	...	...	...	...	...
80 - 84	ESDJ	7 929	2 873	5 056	...	...	...	...	...	...
85+	ESDJ	5 342	1 569	3 773	...	...	...	...	...	...
Morocco - Maroc										
1 VII 2002										
Total	ESDF	29 631 000	14 742 000	14 889 000	12 859 000	6 525 000	6 334 000	16 772 000	8 217 000	8 555 000
0 - 4	ESDF	2 988 000	1 525 000	1 463 000	1 478 000	753 000	725 000	1 510 000	772 000	738 000
5 - 9	ESDF	2 968 000	1 511 000	1 457 000	1 519 000	777 000	742 000	1 449 000	734 000	715 000
10 - 14	ESDF	3 201 000	1 631 000	1 570 000	1 619 000	848 000	771 000	1 582 000	783 000	799 000
15 - 19	ESDF	3 236 000	1 641 000	1 595 000	1 572 000	830 000	742 000	1 664 000	811 000	853 000
20 - 24	ESDF	3 050 000	1 526 000	1 524 000	1 367 000	711 000	656 000	1 683 000	815 000	868 000
25 - 29	ESDF	2 692 000	1 329 000	1 363 000	1 083 000	551 000	532 000	1 609 000	778 000	831 000
30 - 34	ESDF	2 301 000	1 121 000	1 180 000	802 000	400 000	402 000	1 499 000	721 000	778 000
35 - 39	ESDF	1 956 000	926 000	1 030 000	641 000	313 000	328 000	1 315 000	613 000	702 000
40 - 44	ESDF	1 777 000	865 000	912 000	611 000	297 000	314 000	1 166 000	568 000	598 000
45 - 49	ESDF	1 427 000	732 000	695 000	498 000	247 000	251 000	929 000	485 000	444 000
50 - 54	ESDF	1 053 000	528 000	525 000	384 000	176 000	208 000	669 000	352 000	317 000
55 - 59	ESDF	759 000	351 000	408 000	304 000	138 000	166 000	455 000	213 000	242 000
60 - 64	ESDF	706 000	322 000	384 000	306 000	143 000	163 000	400 000	179 000	221 000
65 - 69	ESDF	583 000	282 000	301 000	247 000	122 000	125 000	336 000	160 000	176 000
70 - 74	ESDF	469 000	223 000	246 000	207 000	102 000	105 000	262 000	121 000	141 000
75+	ESDF	465 000	229 000	236 000	221 000	117 000	104 000	244 000	112 000	132 000
Mozambique										
1 VIII 1997										
Total	CDJC	15 278 334	7 320 948	7 957 386	4 454 859	2 201 292	2 253 567	10 823 475	5 119 656	5 703 819
0 - 1	CDJC	535 237	263 539	271 698	138 601	68 743	69 858	396 636	194 796	201 840
1 - 4	CDJC	2 206 319	1 089 667	1 116 652	558 601	277 008	281 593	1 647 718	812 659	835 059
5 - 9	CDJC	2 225 996	1 112 321	1 113 675	617 241	304 392	312 849	1 608 755	807 929	800 826
10 - 14	CDJC	1 825 665	947 236	878 429	600 911	301 921	298 990	1 224 754	645 315	579 439
15 - 19	CDJC	1 628 405	774 327	854 078	564 519	287 073	277 446	1 063 886	487 254	576 632
20 - 24	CDJC	1 464 727	637 113	827 614	461 071	217 269	243 802	1 003 656	419 844	583 812
25 - 29	CDJC	1 163 574	509 109	654 465	345 841	161 031	184 810	817 733	348 078	469 655
30 - 34	CDJC	887 710	410 148	477 562	284 119	137 905	146 214	603 591	272 243	331 348
35 - 39	CDJC	802 208	373 813	428 395	246 954	126 347	120 607	555 254	247 466	307 788
40 - 44	CDJC	573 193	270 046	303 147	173 329	90 578	82 751	399 864	179 468	220 396
45 - 49	CDJC	539 168	257 070	282 098	139 708	72 415	67 293	399 460	184 655	214 805
50 - 54	CDJC	390 962	178 902	212 060	95 508	48 098	47 410	295 454	130 804	164 650
55 - 59	CDJC	336 356	162 122	174 234	76 557	39 078	37 479	259 799	123 044	136 755
60 - 64	CDJC	239 431	114 335	125 096	57 172	27 663	29 509	182 259	86 672	95 587
65 - 69	CDJC	209 713	100 425	109 288	44 486	20 277	24 209	165 227	80 148	85 079
70 - 74	CDJC	98 014	47 407	50 607	21 390	9 542	11 848	76 624	37 865	38 759
75 - 79	CDJC	84 387	41 529	42 858	16 670	7 113	9 557	67 717	34 416	33 301
80 - 84	CDJC	32 631	15 305	17 326	6 162	2 542	3 620	26 469	12 763	13 706
85 - 89	CDJC	20 033	9 041	10 992	3 795	1 361	2 434	16 238	7 680	8 558
90 - 94	CDJC	7 179	3 537	3 642	1 114	430	684	6 065	3 107	2 958
95+	CDJC	7 426	3 956	3 470	1 110	506	604	6 316	3 450	2 866
1 VII 2000										
Total	ESDF	17 690 584	8 284 793	9 405 791	...	...	...	...	...	...
0 - 4	ESDF	3 139 293	1 514 640	1 624 653	...	...	...	...	...	...
5 - 9	ESDF	2 664 689	1 282 460	1 382 229	...	...	...	...	...	...
10 - 14	ESDF	2 208 552	1 059 016	1 149 536	...	...	...	...	...	...
15 - 19	ESDF	1 966 758	940 308	1 026 450	...	...	...	...	...	...
20 - 24	ESDF	1 540 328	743 941	796 387	...	...	...	...	...	...
25 - 29	ESDF	1 312 794	598 600	714 194	...	...	...	...	...	...

7. Population by age, sex and urban/rural residence: latest available year, 1993 - 2002
Population selon l'âge, le sexe et la résidence, urbaine/rurale: dernière année disponible, 1993 - 2002
(continued — suite)

(See notes at end of table. — Voir notes à la fin du tableau.)

Continent, country or area, date and age (in years) / Continent, pays ou zone, date et âge (en années)	Code[1]	Total			Urban - Urbaine			Rural - Rurale		
		Both sexes Les deux sexes	Male Masculin	Female Féminin	Both sexes Les deux sexes	Male Masculin	Female Féminin	Both sexes Les deux sexes	Male Masculin	Female Féminin
AFRICA — AFRIQUE										
Mozambique										
1 VII 2000										
30 - 34	ESDF	1 023 631	438 932	584 699	...	...	...	...	...	...
35 - 39	ESDF	858 865	372 869	485 996	...	...	...	...	...	...
40 - 44	ESDF	745 586	341 179	404 407	...	...	...	...	...	...
45 - 49	ESDF	621 564	286 675	334 889	...	...	...	...	...	...
50 - 54	ESDF	496 069	226 219	269 850	...	...	...	...	...	...
55 - 59	ESDF	388 778	173 800	214 978	...	...	...	...	...	...
60 - 64	ESDF	289 060	126 794	162 266	...	...	...	...	...	...
65 - 69	ESDF	201 364	86 207	115 157	...	...	...	...	...	...
70 - 74	ESDF	124 004	50 747	73 257	...	...	...	...	...	...
75 - 79	ESDF	66 792	26 277	40 515	...	...	...	...	...	...
80+	ESDF	42 457	16 129	26 328	...	...	...	...	...	...
Namibia - Namibie										
1 VII 2000										
Total	ESDF	1 816 600	886 900	929 600	...	...	...	...	...	...
0 - 1	ESDF	61 500	30 900	30 600	...	...	...	...	...	...
1 - 4	ESDF	221 700	110 300	111 400	...	...	...	...	...	...
5 - 9	ESDF	271 600	135 600	137 000	...	...	...	...	...	...
10 - 14	ESDF	201 300	99 900	101 400	...	...	...	...	...	...
15 - 19	ESDF	186 300	92 500	93 800	...	...	...	...	...	...
20 - 24	ESDF	171 600	84 700	86 900	...	...	...	...	...	...
25 - 29	ESDF	155 800	76 000	79 800	...	...	...	...	...	...
30 - 34	ESDF	121 700	58 600	63 200	...	...	...	...	...	...
35 - 39	ESDF	102 100	48 000	54 000	...	...	...	...	...	...
40 - 44	ESDF	78 300	36 700	41 700	...	...	...	...	...	...
45 - 49	ESDF	60 300	28 900	31 400	...	...	...	...	...	...
50 - 54	ESDF	48 800	23 600	25 300	...	...	...	...	...	...
55 - 59	ESDF	38 100	18 300	19 900	...	...	...	...	...	...
60 - 64	ESDF	30 900	14 700	16 300	...	...	...	...	...	...
65 - 69	ESDF	21 500	10 100	11 500	...	...	...	...	...	...
70 - 74	ESDF	19 400	7 900	11 500	...	...	...	...	...	...
75 - 79	ESDF	12 900	5 300	7 800	...	...	...	...	...	...
80 - 84	ESDF	8 500	3 400	4 900	...	...	...	...	...	...
85+	ESDF	3 700	1 500	2 200	...	...	...	...	...	...
Nigeria - Nigéria[3]										
1 VII 2000										
Total	ESDF	115 224 312	57 750 754	57 473 558	...	...	...	...	...	...
0 - 4	ESDF	20 294 315	10 329 530	9 964 785	...	...	...	...	...	...
5 - 9	ESDF	16 626 314	8 475 111	8 151 203	...	...	...	...	...	...
10 - 14	ESDF	14 049 846	7 040 493	7 009 353	...	...	...	...	...	...
15 - 19	ESDF	11 614 242	5 860 447	5 753 795	...	...	...	...	...	...
20 - 24	ESDF	10 607 152	5 337 280	5 269 872	...	...	...	...	...	...
25 - 29	ESDF	8 949 326	4 425 396	4 523 930	...	...	...	...	...	...
30 - 34	ESDF	7 163 277	3 354 804	3 808 473	...	...	...	...	...	...
35 - 39	ESDF	6 009 160	2 804 124	3 205 036	...	...	...	...	...	...
40 - 44	ESDF	5 162 668	2 499 916	2 662 752	...	...	...	...	...	...
45 - 49	ESDF	4 212 419	2 088 777	2 123 642	...	...	...	...	...	...
50 - 54	ESDF	3 164 357	1 636 220	1 528 137	...	...	...	...	...	...
55 - 59	ESDF	2 413 817	1 275 577	1 138 240	...	...	...	...	...	...
60 - 64	ESDF	1 715 811	921 096	794 715	...	...	...	...	...	...
65 - 69	ESDF	1 258 407	675 255	583 152	...	...	...	...	...	...
70 - 74	ESDF	928 888	480 324	448 564	...	...	...	...	...	...
75 - 79	ESDF	578 124	297 076	281 048	...	...	...	...	...	...
80+	ESDF	476 189	249 328	226 861	...	...	...	...	...	...
Réunion										
8 III 1999										
Total	CDJC	706 180	347 076	359 104	...	...	...	...	...	...
0 - 1	CDJC	2 352	1 173	1 179	...	...	...	...	...	...
1 - 4	CDJC	51 138	26 042	25 096	...	...	...	...	...	...

7. Population by age, sex and urban/rural residence: latest available year, 1993 - 2002
Population selon l'âge, le sexe et la résidence, urbaine/rurale: dernière année disponible, 1993 - 2002
(continued — suite)

(See notes at end of table. — Voir notes à la fin du tableau.)

Continent, country or area, date and age (in years) / Continent, pays ou zone, date et âge (en années)	Code[1]	Total Both sexes Les deux sexes	Male Masculin	Female Féminin	Urban - Urbaine Both sexes Les deux sexes	Male Masculin	Female Féminin	Rural - Rurale Both sexes Les deux sexes	Male Masculin	Female Féminin
AFRICA — AFRIQUE										
Réunion										
8 III 1999										
5 - 9	CDJC	68 635	34 964	33 671						
10 - 14	CDJC	68 706	34 799	33 907	...	...	...	...	...	...
15 - 19	CDJC	64 668	32 719	31 949	...	...	...	...	...	...
20 - 24	CDJC	54 528	26 932	27 596	...	...	...	...	...	...
25 - 29	CDJC	55 543	27 076	28 467	...	...	...	...	...	...
30 - 34	CDJC	63 513	30 903	32 610	...	...	...	...	...	...
35 - 39	CDJC	59 989	29 490	30 499	...	...	...	...	...	...
40 - 44	CDJC	48 666	24 039	24 627	...	...	...	...	...	...
45 - 49	CDJC	41 288	20 416	20 872	...	...	...	...	...	...
50 - 54	CDJC	30 843	15 496	15 347	...	...	...	...	...	...
55 - 59	CDJC	25 620	12 594	13 026	...	...	...	...	...	...
60 - 64	CDJC	21 632	10 232	11 400	...	...	...	...	...	...
65 - 69	CDJC	16 358	7 480	8 878	...	...	...	...	...	...
70 - 74	CDJC	13 097	5 737	7 360	...	...	...	...	...	...
75 - 79	CDJC	9 847	3 923	5 924	...	...	...	...	...	...
80 - 84	CDJC	5 252	1 775	3 477	...	...	...	...	...	...
85 - 89	CDJC	2 919	863	2 056	...	...	...	...	...	...
90 - 94	CDJC	1 187	316	871	...	...	...	...	...	...
95 - 99	CDJC	343	97	246	...	...	...	...	...	...
100+	CDJC	56	10	46	...	...	...	...	...	...
Saint Helena ex. dep. - Sainte-Hélène sans dép.										
8 III 1998										
Total	CDJC	4 913	2 481	2 432	...	...	...	...	...	...
0 - 1	CDJC	60	33	27	...	...	...	...	...	...
1 - 4	CDJC	252	139	113	...	...	...	...	...	...
5 - 9	CDJC	369	197	172	...	...	...	...	...	...
10 - 14	CDJC	368	199	169	...	...	...	...	...	...
15 - 19	CDJC	452	217	235	...	...	...	...	...	...
20 - 24	CDJC	300	154	146	...	...	...	...	...	...
25 - 29	CDJC	370	185	185	...	...	...	...	...	...
30 - 34	CDJC	329	150	179	...	...	...	...	...	...
35 - 39	CDJC	391	181	210	...	...	...	...	...	...
40 - 44	CDJC	336	181	155	...	...	...	...	...	...
45 - 49	CDJC	340	173	167	...	...	...	...	...	...
50 - 54	CDJC	346	200	146	...	...	...	...	...	...
55 - 59	CDJC	230	124	106	...	...	...	...	...	...
60 - 64	CDJC	202	127	75	...	...	...	...	...	...
65 - 69	CDJC	190	86	104	...	...	...	...	...	...
70 - 74	CDJC	143	51	92	...	...	...	...	...	...
75 - 79	CDJC	111	41	70	...	...	...	...	...	...
80 - 84	CDJC	69	25	44	...	...	...	...	...	...
85 - 89	CDJC	26	7	19	...	...	...	...	...	...
90 - 94	CDJC	18	7	11	...	...	...	...	...	...
95+	CDJC	1	-	1	...	...	...	...	...	...
Unk. - Inc.	CDJC	10	4	6	...	...	...	...	...	...
Saint Helena: Tristan da Cunha - Sainte-Hélène: Tristan da Cunha										
1 VII 1996										
Total	ESDF	286	137	149	...	...	...	...	...	...
0 - 1	ESDF	1	1	-	...	...	...	...	...	...
1 - 4	ESDF	10	7	3	...	...	...	...	...	...
5 - 9	ESDF	14	9	5	...	...	...	...	...	...
10 - 14	ESDF	17	9	8	...	...	...	...	...	...
15 - 19	ESDF	13	8	5	...	...	...	...	...	...

7. Population by age, sex and urban/rural residence: latest available year, 1993 - 2002
Population selon l'âge, le sexe et la résidence, urbaine/rurale: dernière année disponible, 1993 - 2002
(continued — suite)

(See notes at end of table. — Voir notes à la fin du tableau.)

Continent, country or area, date and age (in years) / Continent, pays ou zone, date et âge (en années)	Code[1]	Total			Urban - Urbaine			Rural - Rurale		
		Both sexes Les deux sexes	Male Masculin	Female Féminin	Both sexes Les deux sexes	Male Masculin	Female Féminin	Both sexes Les deux sexes	Male Masculin	Female Féminin
AFRICA — AFRIQUE										
Saint Helena: Tristan da Cunha - Sainte-Hélène: Tristan da Cunha										
1 VII 1996										
20 - 24	ESDF	17	3	14	...	...	...	...	...	...
25 - 29	ESDF	35	17	18	...	...	...	...	...	...
30 - 34	ESDF	12	6	6	...	...	...	...	...	...
35 - 39	ESDF	19	10	9	...	...	...	...	...	...
40 - 44	ESDF	14	4	10	...	...	...	...	...	...
45 - 49	ESDF	24	14	10	...	...	...	...	...	...
50 - 54	ESDF	18	8	10	...	...	...	...	...	...
55 - 59	ESDF	22	6	16	...	...	...	...	...	...
60 - 64	ESDF	18	11	7	...	...	...	...	...	...
65 - 69	ESDF	12	5	7	...	...	...	...	...	...
70 - 74	ESDF	22	12	10	...	...	...	...	...	...
75 - 79	ESDF	10	5	5	...	...	...	...	...	...
80 - 84	ESDF	6	1	5	...	...	...	...	...	...
85 - 89	ESDF	1	1	-	...	...	...	...	...	...
90+	ESDF	1	-	1	...	...	...	...	...	...
Senegal - Sénégal										
1 VII 1993										
Total	ESDJ	8 008 295	3 870 069	4 138 226	...	...	...	...	...	...
0 - 1	ESDJ	158 346	81 960	76 386	...	...	...	...	...	...
1 - 4	ESDJ	1 116 159	556 043	560 116	...	...	...	...	...	...
5 - 9	ESDJ	1 342 168	670 227	671 941	...	...	...	...	...	...
10 - 14	ESDJ	1 099 528	574 629	524 899	...	...	...	...	...	...
15 - 19	ESDJ	824 493	393 919	430 574	...	...	...	...	...	...
20 - 24	ESDJ	610 468	281 949	328 519	...	...	...	...	...	...
25 - 29	ESDJ	576 744	242 187	334 557	...	...	...	...	...	...
30 - 34	ESDJ	433 378	190 408	242 970	...	...	...	...	...	...
35 - 39	ESDJ	396 327	170 159	226 168	...	...	...	...	...	...
40 - 44	ESDJ	306 082	142 284	163 798	...	...	...	...	...	...
45 - 49	ESDJ	246 571	114 446	132 125	...	...	...	...	...	...
50 - 54	ESDJ	220 409	103 562	116 847	...	...	...	...	...	...
55 - 59	ESDJ	177 999	91 448	86 551	...	...	...	...	...	...
60 - 64	ESDJ	163 174	79 033	84 141	...	...	...	...	...	...
65 - 69	ESDJ	117 619	64 394	53 225	...	...	...	...	...	...
70 - 74	ESDJ	101 259	50 314	50 945	...	...	...	...	...	...
75 - 79	ESDJ	49 604	30 016	19 588	...	...	...	...	...	...
80 - 84	ESDJ	33 105	17 181	15 924	...	...	...	...	...	...
85 - 89	ESDJ	16 281	7 758	8 523	...	...	...	...	...	...
90+	ESDJ	18 581	8 152	10 429	...	...	...	...	...	...
Seychelles										
1 VII 1998										
Total	ESDF	78 846	39 359	39 487	...	...	...	...	...	...
0 - 4	ESDF	7 515	3 899	3 616	...	...	...	...	...	...
5 - 9	ESDF	7 262	3 688	3 574	...	...	...	...	...	...
10 - 14	ESDF	7 043	3 554	3 489	...	...	...	...	...	...
15 - 19	ESDF	7 206	3 664	3 542	...	...	...	...	...	...
20 - 24	ESDF	6 831	3 452	3 379	...	...	...	...	...	...
25 - 29	ESDF	7 067	3 536	3 531	...	...	...	...	...	...
30 - 34	ESDF	7 362	3 640	3 722	...	...	...	...	...	...
35 - 39	ESDF	6 705	3 477	3 228	...	...	...	...	...	...
40 - 44	ESDF	5 155	2 793	2 362	...	...	...	...	...	...
45 - 49	ESDF	3 376	1 788	1 588	...	...	...	...	...	...
50 - 54	ESDF	2 587	1 358	1 229	...	...	...	...	...	...
55 - 59	ESDF	2 746	1 339	1 407	...	...	...	...	...	...
60 - 64	ESDF	2 217	949	1 268	...	...	...	...	...	...
65 - 69	ESDF	1 954	827	1 127	...	...	...	...	...	...

7. Population by age, sex and urban/rural residence: latest available year, 1993 - 2002
Population selon l'âge, le sexe et la résidence, urbaine/rurale: dernière année disponible, 1993 - 2002
(continued — suite)

(See notes at end of table. — Voir notes à la fin du tableau.)

Continent, country or area, date and age (in years) / Continent, pays ou zone, date et âge (en années)	Code[1]	Total			Urban - Urbaine			Rural - Rurale		
		Both sexes Les deux sexes	Male Masculin	Female Féminin	Both sexes Les deux sexes	Male Masculin	Female Féminin	Both sexes Les deux sexes	Male Masculin	Female Féminin
AFRICA — AFRIQUE										
Seychelles										
1 VII 1998										
70 - 74	ESDF	1 555	655	900	...	...	...	...	...	...
75 - 79	ESDF	1 113	432	681	...	...	...	...	...	...
80+	ESDF	1 152	308	844	...	...	...	...	...	...
Somalia - Somalie										
1 VII 2002										
Total	SSDF	6 799 079	3 499 523	3 299 556	2 310 817	1 168 410	1 142 407	4 488 262	2 331 113	2 157 149
0 - 4	SSDF	1 235 105	634 959	600 146	408 646	206 987	201 659	826 459	427 972	398 487
5 - 9	SSDF	1 049 189	544 431	504 758	352 471	179 293	173 178	696 718	365 138	331 580
10 - 14	SSDF	870 180	455 323	414 857	297 807	151 845	145 962	572 373	303 478	268 895
15 - 19	SSDF	725 723	373 328	352 395	250 718	125 641	125 077	475 005	247 687	227 318
20 - 24	SSDF	581 690	280 786	300 904	202 030	95 671	106 359	379 660	185 115	194 545
25 - 29	SSDF	491 651	231 254	260 397	170 250	78 983	91 267	321 401	152 271	169 130
30 - 34	SSDF	428 269	198 101	230 168	146 024	67 081	78 943	282 245	131 020	151 225
35 - 39	SSDF	366 113	175 050	191 063	123 698	58 860	64 838	242 415	116 190	126 225
40 - 44	SSDF	311 989	164 941	147 048	104 080	54 778	49 302	207 909	110 163	97 746
45 - 49	SSDF	248 939	139 351	109 588	82 971	46 198	36 773	165 968	93 153	72 815
50 - 54	SSDF	174 517	105 972	68 545	58 869	35 355	23 514	115 648	70 617	45 031
55 - 59	SSDF	124 841	79 206	45 635	42 868	26 625	16 243	81 973	52 581	29 392
60 - 64	SSDF	80 530	51 293	29 237	28 988	17 492	11 496	51 542	33 801	17 741
65 - 69	SSDF	51 554	32 843	18 711	19 396	11 603	7 793	32 158	21 240	10 918
70 - 74	SSDF	28 997	17 795	11 202	11 675	6 878	4 797	17 322	10 917	6 405
75 - 79	SSDF	12 860	6 152	6 708	5 828	3 320	2 508	7 032	2 832	4 200
80+	SSDF	16 932	8 738	8 194	4 498	1 800	2 698	12 434	6 938	5 496
South Africa - Afrique du Sud[4]										
10 X 1996										
Total	CDFC	40 583 573	19 520 887	21 062 686	21 781 807	10 667 927	11 113 880	18 801 766	8 852 960	9 948 806
0 - 1	CDFC	856 238	426 858	429 380	407 569	204 037	203 532	448 669	222 821	225 848
1 - 4	CDFC	3 587 383	1 789 905	1 797 478	1 608 627	801 912	806 715	1 978 756	987 993	990 763
5 - 9	CDFC	4 668 721	2 333 562	2 335 159	2 038 226	1 016 905	1 021 321	2 630 495	1 316 657	1 313 838
10 - 14	CDFC	4 654 098	2 308 758	2 345 340	2 061 009	1 016 787	1 044 222	2 593 089	1 291 971	1 301 118
15 - 19	CDFC	4 180 717	2 050 214	2 130 503	1 995 798	978 031	1 017 767	2 184 919	1 072 183	1 112 736
20 - 24	CDFC	3 982 354	1 917 919	2 064 435	2 271 339	1 120 919	1 150 420	1 711 015	797 000	914 015
25 - 29	CDFC	3 455 728	1 663 064	1 792 664	2 186 820	1 088 452	1 098 368	1 268 908	574 612	694 296
30 - 34	CDFC	3 074 202	1 463 499	1 610 703	1 970 405	972 890	997 515	1 103 797	490 609	613 188
35 - 39	CDFC	2 653 756	1 284 957	1 368 799	1 709 987	847 993	861 994	943 769	436 964	506 805
40 - 44	CDFC	2 138 626	1 030 597	1 108 029	1 360 825	676 387	684 438	777 801	354 210	423 591
45 - 49	CDFC	1 677 526	813 816	863 710	1 050 144	525 516	524 628	627 382	288 300	339 082
50 - 54	CDFC	1 268 895	600 476	668 419	775 141	383 915	391 226	493 754	216 561	277 193
55 - 59	CDFC	1 069 936	483 678	586 258	621 620	294 100	327 520	448 316	189 578	258 738
60 - 64	CDFC	890 537	352 053	538 484	482 701	208 117	274 584	407 836	143 936	263 900
65 - 69	CDFC	758 886	304 013	454 873	374 423	160 695	213 728	384 463	143 318	241 145
70 - 74	CDFC	482 162	195 119	287 043	254 856	105 173	149 683	227 306	89 946	137 360
75 - 79	CDFC	377 427	141 844	235 583	184 420	70 699	113 721	193 007	71 145	121 862
80 - 84	CDFC	178 903	62 072	116 831	96 886	32 757	64 129	82 017	29 315	52 702
85+	CDFC	137 284	43 230	94 054	69 901	21 596	48 305	67 383	21 634	45 749
Unk. - Inc.	CDFC	490 194	255 253	234 941	261 110	141 046	120 064	229 084	114 207	114 877
Sudan - Soudan										
15 IV 1993										
Total	CDFC	24 941 000	12 519 000	12 422 000	...	...	...	...	...	...
0 - 4	CDFC	4 305 000	2 173 000	2 132 000	...	...	...	...	...	...
5 - 9	CDFC	3 786 000	1 911 000	1 875 000	...	...	...	...	...	...
10 - 14	CDFC	2 627 000	1 285 000	1 341 000	...	...	...	...	...	...
15 - 19	CDFC	2 445 000	1 247 000	1 199 000	...	...	...	...	...	...
20 - 24	CDFC	2 255 000	1 158 000	1 098 000	...	...	...	...	...	...
25 - 29	CDFC	2 026 000	1 028 000	997 000	...	...	...	...	...	...
30 - 34	CDFC	1 624 000	802 000	822 000	...	...	...	...	...	...
35 - 39	CDFC	1 359 000	658 000	700 000	...	...	...	...	...	...

7. **Population by age, sex and urban/rural residence: latest available year, 1993 - 2002**
Population selon l'âge, le sexe et la résidence, urbaine/rurale: dernière année disponible, 1993 - 2002
(continued — suite)

(See notes at end of table. — Voir notes à la fin du tableau.)

Continent, country or area, date and age (in years) / Continent, pays ou zone, date et âge (en années)	Code[1]	Total			Urban - Urbaine			Rural - Rurale		
		Both sexes Les deux sexes	Male Masculin	Female Féminin	Both sexes Les deux sexes	Male Masculin	Female Féminin	Both sexes Les deux sexes	Male Masculin	Female Féminin
AFRICA — AFRIQUE										
Sudan - Soudan										
15 IV 1993										
40 - 44	CDFC	1 109 000	526 000	582 000	...	...	...	...	...	...
45 - 49	CDFC	947 000	453 000	494 000	...	...	...	...	...	...
50 - 54	CDFC	766 000	377 000	388 000	...	...	...	...	...	...
55 - 59	CDFC	603 000	308 000	295 000	...	...	...	...	...	...
60 - 64	CDFC	433 000	229 000	205 000	...	...	...	...	...	...
65 - 69	CDFC	298 000	161 000	136 000	...	...	...	...	...	...
70 - 74	CDFC	195 000	109 000	85 000	...	...	...	...	...	...
75+	CDFC	163 000	94 000	73 000	...	...	...	...	...	...
Swaziland										
11 V 1997										
Total	CDFC	929 718	440 154	489 564	214 428	106 256	108 172	715 290	333 898	381 392
0 - 1	CDFC	24 405	12 049	12 356	5 123	2 519	2 604	19 282	9 530	9 752
1 - 4	CDFC	111 992	55 480	56 512	19 744	9 701	10 043	92 248	45 779	46 469
5 - 9	CDFC	139 245	68 976	70 269	22 232	10 663	11 569	117 013	58 313	58 700
10 - 14	CDFC	137 487	68 200	69 287	22 036	9 908	12 128	115 451	58 292	57 159
15 - 19	CDFC	112 356	54 775	57 581	24 504	10 716	13 788	87 852	44 059	43 793
20 - 24	CDFC	85 094	38 807	46 287	27 184	12 804	14 380	57 910	26 003	31 907
25 - 29	CDFC	68 043	30 147	37 896	24 731	12 610	12 121	43 312	17 537	25 775
30 - 34	CDFC	52 156	21 988	30 168	18 103	9 257	8 846	34 053	12 731	21 322
35 - 39	CDFC	45 802	19 645	26 157	15 043	7 841	7 202	30 759	11 804	18 955
40 - 44	CDFC	35 505	16 165	19 340	11 090	6 128	4 962	24 415	10 037	14 378
45 - 49	CDFC	30 371	14 461	15 910	8 627	5 068	3 559	21 744	9 393	12 351
50 - 54	CDFC	23 316	10 799	12 517	5 756	3 413	2 343	17 560	7 386	10 174
55 - 59	CDFC	17 920	8 758	9 162	3 759	2 275	1 484	14 161	6 483	7 678
60 - 64	CDFC	13 866	6 325	7 541	2 349	1 298	1 051	11 517	5 027	6 490
65 - 69	CDFC	10 152	4 645	5 507	1 340	710	630	8 812	3 935	4 877
70 - 74	CDFC	7 301	2 924	4 377	766	343	423	6 535	2 581	3 954
75 - 79	CDFC	5 269	2 175	3 094	527	256	271	4 742	1 919	2 823
80 - 84	CDFC	3 085	1 161	1 924	266	110	156	2 819	1 051	1 768
85 - 89	CDFC	1 765	707	1 058	145	64	81	1 620	643	977
90 - 94	CDFC	731	264	467	61	25	36	670	239	431
95+	CDFC	959	371	588	63	34	29	896	337	559
Unk. - Inc.	CDFC	2 898	1 332	1 566	979	513	466	1 919	819	1 100
Tunisia - Tunisie										
20 IV 1994										
Total	CDFC	8 785 711	4 439 289	4 346 422	5 361 927	2 717 168	2 644 759	3 423 784	1 722 121	1 701 663
0 - 1	CDFC	177 191	91 223	85 968	104 855	53 856	50 999	72 336	37 367	34 969
1 - 4	CDFC	791 125	405 657	385 468	447 380	229 089	218 291	343 745	176 568	167 177
5 - 9	CDFC	1 055 358	538 919	516 439	608 233	309 289	298 944	447 125	229 630	217 495
10 - 14	CDFC	1 034 646	530 178	504 468	605 460	307 625	297 835	429 186	222 553	206 633
15 - 19	CDFC	939 066	478 618	460 448	546 290	280 017	266 273	392 776	198 601	194 175
20 - 24	CDFC	818 718	412 463	406 255	497 919	254 409	243 510	320 799	158 054	162 745
25 - 29	CDFC	743 903	363 603	380 300	479 111	237 120	241 991	264 792	126 483	138 309
30 - 34	CDFC	656 615	326 172	330 443	443 690	223 004	220 686	212 925	103 168	109 757
35 - 39	CDFC	560 347	282 297	278 050	376 253	192 213	184 040	184 094	90 084	94 010
40 - 44	CDFC	437 893	219 789	218 104	291 220	150 579	140 641	146 673	69 210	77 463
45 - 49	CDFC	307 149	149 840	157 309	203 611	101 390	102 221	103 538	48 450	55 088
50 - 54	CDFC	270 357	133 005	137 352	169 597	84 240	85 357	100 760	48 765	51 995
55 - 59	CDFC	266 740	133 154	133 586	161 533	80 938	80 595	105 207	52 216	52 991
60 - 64	CDFC	251 363	127 279	124 084	150 315	75 525	74 790	101 048	51 754	49 294
65 - 69	CDFC	173 855	91 042	82 813	102 677	52 738	49 939	71 178	38 304	32 874
70 - 74	CDFC	137 177	69 561	67 616	79 962	38 819	41 143	57 215	30 742	26 473
75 - 79	CDFC	77 202	42 546	34 656	44 044	22 951	21 093	33 158	19 595	13 563
80 - 84	CDFC	58 593	30 245	28 348	33 199	15 977	17 222	25 394	14 268	11 126
85 - 89	CDFC	16 595	8 623	7 972	9 501	4 649	4 852	7 094	3 974	3 120
90 - 94	CDFC	9 663	4 194	5 469	5 746	2 255	3 491	3 917	1 939	1 978
95 - 99	CDFC	974	410	564	572	214	358	402	196	206
100+	CDFC	1 181	471	710	759	271	488	422	200	222

7. Population by age, sex and urban/rural residence: latest available year, 1993 - 2002
Population selon l'âge, le sexe et la résidence, urbaine/rurale: dernière année disponible, 1993 - 2002
(continued — suite)

(See notes at end of table. — Voir notes à la fin du tableau.)

Continent, country or area, date and age (in years) / Continent, pays ou zone, date et âge (en années)	Code[1]	Total			Urban - Urbaine			Rural - Rurale		
		Both sexes Les deux sexes	Male Masculin	Female Féminin	Both sexes Les deux sexes	Male Masculin	Female Féminin	Both sexes Les deux sexes	Male Masculin	Female Féminin
AFRICA — AFRIQUE										
Tunisia - Tunisie										
1 VII 1998										
Total	ESDF	9 333 300	4 709 000	4 624 300	...	...	...	...	...	...
0 - 4	ESDF	978 500	500 700	477 800	...	...	...	...	...	...
5 - 9	ESDF	1 015 200	519 500	495 700	...	...	...	...	...	...
10 - 14	ESDF	1 058 900	541 400	517 500	...	...	...	...	...	...
15 - 19	ESDF	1 006 100	514 400	491 700	...	...	...	...	...	...
20 - 24	ESDF	898 500	455 600	443 000	...	...	...	...	...	...
25 - 29	ESDF	795 900	395 900	399 900	...	...	...	...	...	...
30 - 34	ESDF	714 800	351 200	363 600	...	...	...	...	...	...
35 - 39	ESDF	621 900	310 300	311 600	...	...	...	...	...	...
40 - 44	ESDF	512 500	257 400	255 100	...	...	...	...	...	...
45 - 49	ESDF	384 400	190 800	193 700	...	...	...	...	...	...
50 - 54	ESDF	291 800	142 200	149 600	...	...	...	...	...	...
55 - 59	ESDF	266 800	131 200	135 600	...	...	...	...	...	...
60 - 64	ESDF	255 000	127 100	127 900	...	...	...	...	...	...
65 - 69	ESDF	208 200	105 500	102 700	...	...	...	...	...	...
70 - 74	ESDF	145 800	74 200	71 600	...	...	...	...	...	...
75 - 79	ESDF	94 700	48 500	46 200	...	...	...	...	...	...
80+	ESDF	84 100	43 000	41 000	...	...	...	...	...	...
Zambia - Zambie										
1 VII 2000										
Total	ESDF	9 337 425	4 594 290	4 743 135	3 347 069	1 662 739	1 684 330	5 990 356	2 931 551	3 058 805
0 - 1	ESDF	339 228	168 841	170 387	101 775	50 699	51 076	237 453	118 142	119 311
1 - 4	ESDF	1 317 492	656 948	660 544	420 759	209 814	210 945	896 733	447 134	449 599
5 - 9	ESDF	1 461 082	729 181	731 901	500 572	247 117	253 455	960 510	482 064	478 446
10 - 14	ESDF	1 205 646	601 279	604 367	428 831	206 305	222 526	776 815	394 974	381 841
15 - 19	ESDF	1 069 996	513 320	556 676	415 197	195 518	219 679	654 799	317 802	336 997
20 - 24	ESDF	908 672	416 083	492 589	376 695	174 331	202 364	531 977	241 752	290 225
25 - 29	ESDF	741 148	361 901	379 247	308 436	155 070	153 366	432 712	206 831	225 881
30 - 34	ESDF	557 873	282 439	275 434	225 707	119 524	106 183	332 166	162 915	169 251
35 - 39	ESDF	429 987	211 356	218 631	169 148	87 763	81 385	260 839	123 593	137 246
40 - 44	ESDF	325 776	161 179	164 597	125 995	66 050	59 945	199 781	95 129	104 652
45 - 49	ESDF	245 320	122 486	122 834	91 507	50 128	41 379	153 813	72 358	81 455
50 - 54	ESDF	203 612	97 850	105 762	65 547	37 513	28 034	138 065	60 337	77 728
55 - 59	ESDF	144 838	71 905	72 933	39 418	22 860	16 558	105 420	49 045	56 375
60 - 64	ESDF	131 475	62 678	68 797	29 438	15 308	14 130	102 037	47 370	54 667
65 - 69	ESDF	100 493	52 499	47 994	20 294	10 642	9 652	80 199	41 857	38 342
70 - 74	ESDF	68 935	37 066	31 869	12 763	6 634	6 129	56 172	30 432	25 740
75 - 79	ESDF	40 649	23 301	17 348	7 217	3 793	3 424	33 432	19 508	13 924
80 - 84	ESDF	24 242	13 311	10 931	4 418	2 206	2 212	19 824	11 105	8 719
85+	ESDF	20 961	10 667	10 294	3 352	1 464	1 888	17 609	9 203	8 406
25 X 2000										
Total	CDJC	9 885 591	4 946 298	4 939 293	...	...	...	...	...	...
0 - 1	CDJC	344 302	171 621	172 681	...	...	...	...	...	...
1 - 4	CDJC	1 350 718	674 381	676 337	...	...	...	...	...	...
5 - 9	CDJC	1 516 952	758 146	758 806	...	...	...	...	...	...
10 - 14	CDJC	1 266 462	633 357	633 105	...	...	...	...	...	...
15 - 19	CDJC	1 149 583	557 197	592 386	...	...	...	...	...	...
20 - 24	CDJC	977 269	458 727	518 542	...	...	...	...	...	...
25 - 29	CDJC	797 605	400 193	397 412	...	...	...	...	...	...
30 - 34	CDJC	601 213	314 108	287 105	...	...	...	...	...	...
35 - 39	CDJC	467 166	238 292	228 874	...	...	...	...	...	...
40 - 44	CDJC	354 338	182 745	171 593	...	...	...	...	...	...
45 - 49	CDJC	268 473	140 304	128 169	...	...	...	...	...	...
50 - 54	CDJC	221 088	111 862	109 226	...	...	...	...	...	...
55 - 59	CDJC	157 193	82 263	74 930	...	...	...	...	...	...
60 - 64	CDJC	143 213	72 222	70 991	...	...	...	...	...	...
65 - 69	CDJC	107 479	58 961	48 518	...	...	...	...	...	...
70 - 74	CDJC	72 942	40 941	32 001	...	...	...	...	...	...

7. Population by age, sex and urban/rural residence: latest available year, 1993 - 2002
Population selon l'âge, le sexe et la résidence, urbaine/rurale: dernière année disponible, 1993 - 2002
(continued — suite)

(See notes at end of table. — Voir notes à la fin du tableau.)

Continent, country or area, date and age (in years) / Continent, pays ou zone, date et âge (en années)	Code[1]	Total			Urban - Urbaine			Rural - Rurale		
		Both sexes Les deux sexes	Male Masculin	Female Féminin	Both sexes Les deux sexes	Male Masculin	Female Féminin	Both sexes Les deux sexes	Male Masculin	Female Féminin
AFRICA — AFRIQUE										
Zambia - Zambie										
25 X 2000										
75 - 79	CDJC	42 678	25 347	17 331	...	...	...	...	...	...
80 - 84	CDJC	25 241	14 287	10 954	...	...	...	...	...	...
85+	CDJC	21 676	11 344	10 332	...	...	...	...	...	...
Zimbabwe										
18 VIII 1997										
Total	SSDF	11 789 274	5 647 090	6 142 184	3 826 580	1 906 476	1 920 104	7 962 694	3 740 614	4 222 080
0 - 1	SSDF	328 913	161 914	166 999	104 258	50 698	53 560	224 655	111 216	113 439
1 - 4	SSDF	1 281 912	638 067	643 846	379 808	189 440	190 368	902 105	448 628	453 478
5 - 9	SSDF	1 646 115	797 775	848 341	417 356	197 224	220 132	1 228 760	600 552	628 209
10 - 14	SSDF	1 803 558	882 644	920 911	453 547	213 501	240 046	1 350 010	669 145	680 866
15 - 19	SSDF	1 484 654	730 379	754 274	463 901	204 411	259 491	1 020 754	525 969	494 786
20 - 24	SSDF	1 147 871	521 360	626 511	492 556	229 928	262 628	655 314	291 432	363 883
25 - 29	SSDF	888 600	427 729	460 872	415 758	223 500	192 258	472 843	204 232	268 611
30 - 34	SSDF	624 978	287 946	337 032	280 744	139 782	140 962	344 235	148 165	196 071
35 - 39	SSDF	583 724	254 357	329 366	241 206	124 241	116 966	342 519	130 119	212 399
40 - 44	SSDF	442 692	203 372	239 319	176 245	99 272	76 973	266 445	104 100	162 346
45 - 49	SSDF	366 842	179 562	187 280	131 674	80 556	51 118	235 167	99 008	136 159
50 - 54	SSDF	306 227	130 448	175 779	88 621	48 258	40 363	217 606	82 190	135 415
55 - 59	SSDF	248 868	121 506	127 362	64 434	38 289	26 144	184 435	83 217	101 218
60 - 64	SSDF	195 169	98 104	97 066	47 494	29 051	18 442	147 675	69 052	78 623
65 - 69	SSDF	179 884	93 671	86 213	32 095	19 553	12 542	147 788	74 117	73 670
70 - 74	SSDF	99 500	46 063	53 437	18 242	9 667	8 575	81 256	36 395	44 862
75+	SSDF	159 767	72 189	87 578	18 641	9 105	3 725	73 599	35 423	38 176
1 VII 1999										
Total	ESDF	*13 079 127*	*6 382 092*	*6 697 035*	...	...	...	...	...	...
0 - 4	ESDF	*2 310 243*	*1 139 151*	*1 171 092*	...	...	...	...	...	...
5 - 9	ESDF	*1 852 604*	*914 810*	*937 794*	...	...	...	...	...	...
10 - 14	ESDF	*1 546 743*	*769 315*	*777 428*	...	...	...	...	...	...
15 - 19	ESDF	*1 534 532*	*762 581*	*771 951*	...	...	...	...	...	...
20 - 24	ESDF	*1 314 285*	*651 638*	*662 647*	...	...	...	...	...	...
25 - 29	ESDF	*1 078 229*	*516 508*	*561 721*	...	...	...	...	...	...
30 - 34	ESDF	*790 666*	*370 892*	*419 774*	...	...	...	...	...	...
35 - 39	ESDF	*621 821*	*288 864*	*332 957*	...	...	...	...	...	...
40 - 44	ESDF	*521 774*	*241 733*	*280 041*	...	...	...	...	...	...
45 - 49	ESDF	*393 469*	*185 239*	*208 230*	...	...	...	...	...	...
50 - 54	ESDF	*290 602*	*142 943*	*147 659*	...	...	...	...	...	...
55 - 59	ESDF	*264 199*	*125 792*	*138 407*	...	...	...	...	...	...
60 - 64	ESDF	*190 673*	*92 081*	*98 592*	...	...	...	...	...	...
65 - 69	ESDF	*146 583*	*75 988*	*70 595*	...	...	...	...	...	...
70 - 74	ESDF	*95 959*	*47 899*	*48 060*	...	...	...	...	...	...
75+	ESDF	*126 745*	*56 658*	*70 087*	...	...	...	...	...	...
AMERICA, NORTH — AMERIQUE DU NORD										
Anguilla[5]										
9 V 2001										
Total	CDFC	11 430	5 628	5 802	...	...	...	...	...	...
0 - 1	CDFC	252	131	121	...	...	...	...	...	...
1 - 4	CDFC	821	394	427	...	...	...	...	...	...
5 - 9	CDFC	993	502	491	...	...	...	...	...	...
10 - 14	CDFC	1 136	563	573	...	...	...	...	...	...
15 - 19	CDFC	966	477	489	...	...	...	...	...	...
20 - 24	CDFC	788	375	413	...	...	...	...	...	...
25 - 29	CDFC	873	440	433	...	...	...	...	...	...
30 - 34	CDFC	999	494	505	...	...	...	...	...	...
35 - 39	CDFC	1 040	507	533	...	...	...	...	...	...
40 - 44	CDFC	881	429	452	...	...	...	...	...	...

7. Population by age, sex and urban/rural residence: latest available year, 1993 - 2002
Population selon l'âge, le sexe et la résidence, urbaine/rurale: dernière année disponible, 1993 - 2002
(continued — suite)

(See notes at end of table. — Voir notes à la fin du tableau.)

Continent, country or area, date and age (in years) / Continent, pays ou zone, date et âge (en années)	Code[1]	Total			Urban - Urbaine			Rural - Rurale		
		Both sexes Les deux sexes	Male Masculin	Female Féminin	Both sexes Les deux sexes	Male Masculin	Female Féminin	Both sexes Les deux sexes	Male Masculin	Female Féminin
AMERICA, NORTH — AMERIQUE DU NORD										
Anguilla[5]										
9 V 2001										
45 - 49	CDFC	714	364	350	...	...	...	...	...	...
50 - 54	CDFC	468	236	232	...	...	...	...	...	...
55 - 59	CDFC	323	166	157	...	...	...	...	...	...
60 - 64	CDFC	304	144	160	...	...	...	...	...	...
65 - 69	CDFC	288	159	129	...	...	...	...	...	...
70 - 74	CDFC	211	82	129	...	...	...	...	...	...
75 - 79	CDFC	155	65	90	...	...	...	...	...	...
80 - 84	CDFC	102	52	50	...	...	...	...	...	...
85 - 89	CDFC	79	31	48	...	...	...	...	...	...
90 - 94	CDFC	30	15	15	...	...	...	...	...	...
95+	CDFC	7	2	5	...	...	...	...	...	...
Antigua and Barbuda - Antigua-et-Barbuda										
1 VII 1996										
Total	ESDF	68 612	33 080	35 532	...	...	...	...	...	...
0 - 4	ESDF	6 259	3 193	3 066	...	...	...	...	...	...
5 - 9	ESDF	6 656	3 328	3 328	...	...	...	...	...	...
10 - 14	ESDF	6 625	3 283	3 342	...	...	...	...	...	...
15 - 19	ESDF	6 284	3 163	3 120	...	...	...	...	...	...
20 - 24	ESDF	5 687	2 842	2 845	...	...	...	...	...	...
25 - 29	ESDF	6 158	3 014	3 143	...	...	...	...	...	...
30 - 34	ESDF	5 959	2 823	3 136	...	...	...	...	...	...
35 - 39	ESDF	5 370	2 533	2 837	...	...	...	...	...	...
40 - 44	ESDF	4 246	1 980	2 266	...	...	...	...	...	...
45 - 49	ESDF	3 476	1 628	1 848	...	...	...	...	...	...
50 - 54	ESDF	2 630	1 259	1 372	...	...	...	...	...	...
55 - 59	ESDF	1 981	961	1 020	...	...	...	...	...	...
60 - 64	ESDF	1 758	804	953	...	...	...	...	...	...
65 - 69	ESDF	1 679	724	955	...	...	...	...	...	...
70 - 74	ESDF	1 511	652	859	...	...	...	...	...	...
75 - 79	ESDF	1 123	463	660	...	...	...	...	...	...
80+	ESDF	1 212	430	782	...	...	...	...	...	...
Aruba										
1 VII 2002										
Total	ESDJ	94 149	45 019	49 130	...	...	...	...	...	...
0 - 4	ESDJ	6 779	3 419	3 361	...	...	...	...	...	...
5 - 9	ESDJ	7 299	3 719	3 580	...	...	...	...	...	...
10 - 14	ESDJ	7 078	3 557	3 521	...	...	...	...	...	...
15 - 19	ESDJ	6 366	3 161	3 206	...	...	...	...	...	...
20 - 24	ESDJ	5 098	2 539	2 559	...	...	...	...	...	...
25 - 29	ESDJ	6 027	2 873	3 155	...	...	...	...	...	...
30 - 34	ESDJ	8 000	3 772	4 228	...	...	...	...	...	...
35 - 39	ESDJ	8 871	4 221	4 650	...	...	...	...	...	...
40 - 44	ESDJ	9 159	4 349	4 810	...	...	...	...	...	...
45 - 49	ESDJ	7 685	3 575	4 109	...	...	...	...	...	...
50 - 54	ESDJ	6 097	2 882	3 215	...	...	...	...	...	...
55 - 59	ESDJ	4 635	2 174	2 461	...	...	...	...	...	...
60 - 64	ESDJ	3 624	1 679	1 945	...	...	...	...	...	...
65 - 69	ESDJ	2 913	1 251	1 663	...	...	...	...	...	...
70 - 74	ESDJ	2 075	921	1 154	...	...	...	...	...	...
75 - 79	ESDJ	1 090	461	629	...	...	...	...	...	...
80 - 84	ESDJ	708	288	419	...	...	...	...	...	...
85 - 89	ESDJ	414	125	289	...	...	...	...	...	...
90 - 94	ESDJ	177	49	129	...	...	...	...	...	...
95+	ESDJ	54	6	48	...	...	...	...	...	...

7. Population by age, sex and urban/rural residence: latest available year, 1993 - 2002
Population selon l'âge, le sexe et la résidence, urbaine/rurale: dernière année disponible, 1993 - 2002
(continued — suite)

(See notes at end of table. — Voir notes à la fin du tableau.)

Continent, country or area, date and age (in years) / Continent, pays ou zone, date et âge (en annèes)	Code[1]	Total			Urban - Urbaine			Rural - Rurale		
		Both sexes Les deux sexes	Male Masculin	Female Féminin	Both sexes Les deux sexes	Male Masculin	Female Féminin	Both sexes Les deux sexes	Male Masculin	Female Féminin
AMERICA, NORTH — AMERIQUE DU NORD										
Bahamas										
1 V 2000										
Total	CDFC	303 611	147 715	155 896	...	...	...	...	...	...
0 - 1	CDFC	5 908	2 929	2 979	...	...	...	...	...	...
1 - 4	CDFC	23 212	11 737	11 475	...	...	...	...	...	...
5 - 9	CDFC	31 648	16 014	15 634	...	...	...	...	...	...
10 - 14	CDFC	28 561	14 149	14 412	...	...	...	...	...	...
15 - 19	CDFC	26 439	13 355	13 084	...	...	...	...	...	...
20 - 24	CDFC	24 772	12 140	12 632	...	...	...	...	...	...
25 - 29	CDFC	26 904	13 110	13 794	...	...	...	...	...	...
30 - 34	CDFC	26 117	12 601	13 516	...	...	...	...	...	...
35 - 39	CDFC	25 887	12 438	13 449	...	...	...	...	...	...
40 - 44	CDFC	21 014	9 971	11 043	...	...	...	...	...	...
45 - 49	CDFC	15 827	7 617	8 210	...	...	...	...	...	...
50 - 54	CDFC	11 978	5 749	6 229	...	...	...	...	...	...
55 - 59	CDFC	10 142	4 768	5 374	...	...	...	...	...	...
60 - 64	CDFC	8 011	3 750	4 261	...	...	...	...	...	...
65 - 69	CDFC	5 806	2 651	3 155	...	...	...	...	...	...
70 - 74	CDFC	4 072	1 689	2 383	...	...	...	...	...	...
75 - 79	CDFC	2 615	1 039	1 576	...	...	...	...	...	...
80 - 84	CDFC	1 919	714	1 205	...	...	...	...	...	...
85 - 89	CDFC	914	293	621	...	...	...	...	...	...
90+	CDFC	451	137	314	...	...	...	...	...	...
Unk. - Inc.	CDFC	1 414	864	550	...	...	...	...	...	...
Belize										
1 VII 1998										
Total	ESDF	238 500	118 500	120 000	...	...	...	...	...	...
0 - 4	ESDF	35 955	18 310	17 645	...	...	...	...	...	...
5 - 9	ESDF	33 205	16 840	16 365	...	...	...	...	...	...
10 - 14	ESDF	29 050	14 890	14 160	...	...	...	...	...	...
15 - 19	ESDF	28 235	14 095	14 140	...	...	...	...	...	...
20 - 24	ESDF	19 185	9 385	9 800	...	...	...	...	...	...
25 - 29	ESDF	15 810	7 185	8 625	...	...	...	...	...	...
30 - 34	ESDF	15 260	7 065	8 195	...	...	...	...	...	...
35 - 39	ESDF	14 120	6 715	7 405	...	...	...	...	...	...
40 - 44	ESDF	10 500	5 205	5 295	...	...	...	...	...	...
45 - 49	ESDF	8 350	4 275	4 075	...	...	...	...	...	...
50 - 54	ESDF	6 940	3 575	3 365	...	...	...	...	...	...
55 - 59	ESDF	5 725	2 950	2 775	...	...	...	...	...	...
60 - 64	ESDF	4 975	2 475	2 500	...	...	...	...	...	...
65 - 69	ESDF	3 985	1 910	2 075	...	...	...	...	...	...
70 - 74	ESDF	2 900	1 695	1 205	...	...	...	...	...	...
75 - 79	ESDF	1 805	825	980	...	...	...	...	...	...
80 - 84	ESDF	1 255	600	655	...	...	...	...	...	...
85+	ESDF	1 245	505	740	...	...	...	...	...	...
Bermuda - Bermudes[6]										
20 V 2000										
Total	CDJC	62 059	29 802	32 257	...	...	...	...	...	...
0 - 1	CDJC	823	404	419	...	...	...	...	...	...
1 - 4	CDJC	3 166	1 574	1 592	...	...	...	...	...	...
5 - 9	CDJC	4 031	2 016	2 015	...	...	...	...	...	...
10 - 14	CDJC	3 827	1 907	1 920	...	...	...	...	...	...
15 - 19	CDJC	3 542	1 776	1 766	...	...	...	...	...	...
20 - 24	CDJC	3 222	1 557	1 665	...	...	...	...	...	...
25 - 29	CDJC	4 661	2 250	2 411	...	...	...	...	...	...
30 - 34	CDJC	5 461	2 707	2 754	...	...	...	...	...	...
35 - 39	CDJC	6 228	3 071	3 157	...	...	...	...	...	...

7. Population by age, sex and urban/rural residence: latest available year, 1993 - 2002
Population selon l'âge, le sexe et la résidence, urbaine/rurale: dernière année disponible, 1993 - 2002
(continued — suite)

(See notes at end of table. — Voir notes à la fin du tableau.)

Continent, country or area, date and age (in years) / Continent, pays ou zone, date et âge (en années)	Code[1]	Total			Urban - Urbaine			Rural - Rurale		
		Both sexes Les deux sexes	Male Masculin	Female Féminin	Both sexes Les deux sexes	Male Masculin	Female Féminin	Both sexes Les deux sexes	Male Masculin	Female Féminin
AMERICA, NORTH — AMERIQUE DU NORD										
Bermuda - Bermudes[6]										
20 V 2000										
40 - 44	CDJC	5 618	2 706	2 912	...	...	...	...	...	...
45 - 49	CDJC	4 735	2 327	2 408	...	...	...	...	...	...
50 - 54	CDJC	4 146	1 994	2 152	...	...	...	...	...	...
55 - 59	CDJC	3 260	1 538	1 722	...	...	...	...	...	...
60 - 64	CDJC	2 617	1 229	1 388	...	...	...	...	...	...
65 - 69	CDJC	2 332	1 056	1 276	...	...	...	...	...	...
70 - 74	CDJC	1 845	794	1 051	...	...	...	...	...	...
75 - 79	CDJC	1 275	473	802	...	...	...	...	...	...
80 - 84	CDJC	713	249	464	...	...	...	...	...	...
85 - 89	CDJC	401	125	276	...	...	...	...	...	...
90 - 94	CDJC	122	43	79	...	...	...	...	...	...
95 - 99	CDJC	33	6	27	...	...	...	...	...	...
100+	CDJC	1	...	1	...	...	...	...	...	...
British Virgin Islands - Îles Vierges britanniques										
25 V 2001										
Total	CDJC	20 647	10 627	10 020	...	...	...	...	...	...
0 - 4	CDJC	1 787	913	874	...	...	...	...	...	...
5 - 9	CDJC	1 865	946	919	...	...	...	...	...	...
10 - 14	CDJC	1 768	880	888	...	...	...	...	...	...
15 - 19	CDJC	1 529	778	751	...	...	...	...	...	...
20 - 24	CDJC	1 465	752	713	...	...	...	...	...	...
25 - 29	CDJC	1 483	756	727	...	...	...	...	...	...
30 - 34	CDJC	1 826	913	913	...	...	...	...	...	...
35 - 39	CDJC	2 085	1 091	994	...	...	...	...	...	...
40 - 44	CDJC	1 910	991	919	...	...	...	...	...	...
45 - 49	CDJC	1 501	777	724	...	...	...	...	...	...
50 - 54	CDJC	1 128	614	514	...	...	...	...	...	...
55 - 59	CDJC	774	421	353	...	...	...	...	...	...
60 - 64	CDJC	523	267	256	...	...	...	...	...	...
65 - 69	CDJC	337	177	160	...	...	...	...	...	...
70 - 74	CDJC	282	145	137	...	...	...	...	...	...
75 - 79	CDJC	204	113	91	...	...	...	...	...	...
80+	CDJC	180	93	87	...	...	...	...	...	...
Canada										
1 VII 2002										
Total	ESDJ	31 413 990	15 552 644	15 861 346	...	...	...	...	...	...
0 - 1	ESDJ	326 349	167 470	158 879	...	...	...	...	...	...
1 - 4	ESDJ	1 378 964	705 368	673 596	...	...	...	...	...	...
5 - 9	ESDJ	1 994 619	1 023 040	971 579	...	...	...	...	...	...
10 - 14	ESDJ	2 108 813	1 081 375	1 027 438	...	...	...	...	...	...
15 - 19	ESDJ	2 095 589	1 076 030	1 019 559	...	...	...	...	...	...
20 - 24	ESDJ	2 144 749	1 094 105	1 050 644	...	...	...	...	...	...
25 - 29	ESDJ	2 138 932	1 083 359	1 055 573	...	...	...	...	...	...
30 - 34	ESDJ	2 274 591	1 147 675	1 126 916	...	...	...	...	...	...
35 - 39	ESDJ	2 595 256	1 309 077	1 286 179	...	...	...	...	...	...
40 - 44	ESDJ	2 687 093	1 345 859	1 341 234	...	...	...	...	...	...
45 - 49	ESDJ	2 458 713	1 226 112	1 232 601	...	...	...	...	...	...
50 - 54	ESDJ	2 137 920	1 064 855	1 073 065	...	...	...	...	...	...
55 - 59	ESDJ	1 744 680	862 993	881 687	...	...	...	...	...	...
60 - 64	ESDJ	1 338 526	654 141	684 385	...	...	...	...	...	...
65 - 69	ESDJ	1 139 015	547 310	591 705	...	...	...	...	...	...
70 - 74	ESDJ	1 025 560	473 380	552 180	...	...	...	...	...	...
75 - 79	ESDJ	822 689	345 527	477 162	...	...	...	...	...	...

7. Population by age, sex and urban/rural residence: latest available year, 1993 - 2002
Population selon l'âge, le sexe et la résidence, urbaine/rurale: dernière année disponible, 1993 - 2002
(continued — suite)

(See notes at end of table. — Voir notes à la fin du tableau.)

Continent, country or area, date and age (in years) / Continent, pays ou zone, date et âge (en années)	Code[1]	Total			Urban - Urbaine			Rural - Rurale		
		Both sexes Les deux sexes	Male Masculin	Female Féminin	Both sexes Les deux sexes	Male Masculin	Female Féminin	Both sexes Les deux sexes	Male Masculin	Female Féminin
AMERICA, NORTH — AMERIQUE DU NORD										
Canada										
1 VII 2002										
80 - 84	ESDJ	555 527	208 949	346 578	...	...	...	...	...	...
85 - 89	ESDJ	295 603	96 221	199 382	...	...	...	...	...	...
90+	ESDJ	150 802	39 798	111 004	...	...	...	...	...	...
Costa Rica										
1 VII 1998										
Total	ESDJ	3 340 909	1 662 735	1 678 174	1 440 272	693 376	746 896	1 900 637	969 359	931 278
0 - 4	ESDJ	330 080	171 391	158 689	123 359	61 585	61 774	206 721	109 806	96 915
5 - 9	ESDJ	367 842	185 671	182 171	138 355	72 631	65 724	229 487	113 040	116 447
10 - 14	ESDJ	376 707	192 290	184 417	142 370	70 194	72 176	234 337	122 096	112 241
15 - 19	ESDJ	338 969	175 655	163 314	143 411	71 428	71 983	195 558	104 227	91 331
20 - 24	ESDJ	281 060	140 235	140 825	133 999	67 538	66 461	147 061	72 697	74 364
25 - 29	ESDJ	254 773	128 366	126 407	111 689	56 116	55 573	143 084	72 250	70 834
30 - 39	ESDJ	495 595	237 298	258 297	208 495	100 113	108 382	287 100	137 185	149 915
40 - 49	ESDJ	367 004	179 883	187 121	172 826	77 748	95 078	194 178	102 135	92 043
50 - 59	ESDJ	233 207	112 649	120 558	114 478	51 086	63 392	118 729	61 563	57 166
60 - 69	ESDJ	157 077	73 739	83 338	80 933	35 025	45 908	76 144	38 714	37 430
70+	ESDJ	132 966	63 457	69 509	67 095	28 850	38 245	65 871	34 607	31 264
Unk. - Inc.	ESDJ	5 629	2 101	3 528	3 262	1 062	2 200	2 367	1 039	1 328
26 VI 2000										
Total	CDJC	3 810 179	1 902 614	1 907 565	...	...	...	...	...	...
0 - 4	CDJC	376 584	192 287	184 297	...	...	...	...	...	...
5 - 9	CDJC	411 204	210 443	200 761	...	...	...	...	...	...
10 - 14	CDJC	429 019	219 467	209 552	...	...	...	...	...	...
15 - 19	CDJC	392 063	198 561	193 502	...	...	...	...	...	...
20 - 24	CDJC	342 728	171 679	171 049	...	...	...	...	...	...
25 - 29	CDJC	295 752	146 407	149 345	...	...	...	...	...	...
30 - 34	CDJC	296 738	146 377	150 361	...	...	...	...	...	...
35 - 39	CDJC	288 790	141 138	147 652	...	...	...	...	...	...
40 - 44	CDJC	241 262	118 853	122 409	...	...	...	...	...	...
45 - 49	CDJC	183 629	90 323	93 306	...	...	...	...	...	...
50 - 54	CDJC	146 024	71 727	74 297	...	...	...	...	...	...
55 - 59	CDJC	104 912	51 519	53 393	...	...	...	...	...	...
60 - 64	CDJC	88 142	43 089	45 053	...	...	...	...	...	...
65 - 69	CDJC	71 650	34 555	37 095	...	...	...	...	...	...
70 - 74	CDJC	57 641	27 765	29 876	...	...	...	...	...	...
75+	CDJC	84 041	38 424	45 617	...	...	...	...	...	...
Cuba										
1 VII 2002										
Total	ESDF	11 250 979	5 624 025	5 626 954	8 466 744	4 142 468	4 324 276	2 784 235	1 481 557	1 302 678
0 - 1	ESDF	138 106	70 810	67 296	101 811	52 162	49 649	36 295	18 648	17 647
1 - 4	ESDF	596 431	307 397	289 034	437 572	225 219	212 353	158 859	82 178	76 681
5 - 9	ESDF	734 812	379 316	355 496	535 366	275 983	259 383	199 446	103 333	96 113
10 - 14	ESDF	884 888	454 517	430 371	651 785	333 369	318 416	233 103	121 148	111 955
15 - 19	ESDF	798 973	407 210	391 763	591 126	298 819	292 307	207 847	108 391	99 456
20 - 24	ESDF	674 575	343 179	331 396	489 776	246 088	243 688	184 799	97 091	87 708
25 - 29	ESDF	954 425	481 401	473 024	691 436	342 894	348 542	262 989	138 507	124 482
30 - 34	ESDF	1 082 275	543 232	539 043	795 815	390 622	405 193	286 460	152 610	133 850
35 - 39	ESDF	1 107 861	549 553	558 308	853 330	413 818	439 512	254 531	135 735	118 796
40 - 44	ESDF	772 515	381 557	390 958	594 670	286 695	307 975	177 845	94 862	82 983
45 - 49	ESDF	673 830	331 293	342 537	520 258	249 051	271 207	153 572	82 242	71 330
50 - 54	ESDF	642 146	315 158	326 988	501 833	240 338	261 495	140 313	74 820	65 493
55 - 59	ESDF	559 957	273 766	286 191	438 783	209 183	229 600	121 174	64 583	56 591
60 - 64	ESDF	469 741	233 483	236 258	363 960	174 924	189 036	105 781	58 559	47 222
65 - 74	ESDF	659 649	322 643	337 006	509 032	237 082	271 950	150 617	85 561	65 056
75 - 84	ESDF	371 107	173 426	197 681	289 583	126 486	163 097	81 524	46 940	34 584
85+	ESDF	129 688	56 084	73 604	100 608	39 735	60 873	29 080	16 349	12 731

7. Population by age, sex and urban/rural residence: latest available year, 1993 - 2002
Population selon l'âge, le sexe et la résidence, urbaine/rurale: dernière année disponible, 1993 - 2002
(continued — suite)

(See notes at end of table. — Voir notes à la fin du tableau.)

Continent, country or area, date and age (in years) Continent, pays ou zone, date et âge (en années)	Code[1]	Total			Urban - Urbaine			Rural - Rurale		
		Both sexes Les deux sexes	Male Masculin	Female Féminin	Both sexes Les deux sexes	Male Masculin	Female Féminin	Both sexes Les deux sexes	Male Masculin	Female Féminin

AMERICA, NORTH — AMERIQUE DU NORD

Dominica - Dominique
31 XII 1998

Total	ESDF	75 971	38 665	37 306	...	...	...	...	...	...
0 - 4	ESDF	8 085	4 115	3 970	...	...	...	...	...	...
5 - 9	ESDF	8 721	4 413	4 308	...	...	...	...	...	...
10 - 14	ESDF	8 549	4 307	4 242	...	...	...	...	...	...
15 - 19	ESDF	7 945	4 124	3 821	...	...	...	...	...	...
20 - 24	ESDF	7 263	3 682	3 581	...	...	...	...	...	...
25 - 29	ESDF	6 158	3 296	2 862	...	...	...	...	...	...
30 - 34	ESDF	5 285	2 861	2 424	...	...	...	...	...	...
35 - 39	ESDF	4 131	2 233	1 898	...	...	...	...	...	...
40 - 44	ESDF	3 146	1 639	1 507	...	...	...	...	...	...
45 - 49	ESDF	2 658	1 374	1 284	...	...	...	...	...	...
50 - 54	ESDF	2 242	1 094	1 148	...	...	...	...	...	...
55 - 59	ESDF	2 153	1 011	1 142	...	...	...	...	...	...
60 - 64	ESDF	2 331	1 063	1 268	...	...	...	...	...	...
65 - 69	ESDF	2 154	1 052	1 102	...	...	...	...	...	...
70 - 74	ESDF	1 837	867	970	...	...	...	...	...	...
75 - 79	ESDF	1 417	678	739	...	...	...	...	...	...
80 - 84	ESDF	916	466	450	...	...	...	...	...	...
85+	ESDF	653	252	401	...	...	...	...	...	...
Unk. - Inc.	ESDF	327	138	189	...	...	...	...	...	...

Dominican Republic - République dominicaine
1 VII 1995

Total	ESDF	7 915 321	4 023 015	3 892 306	4 881 102	2 411 347	2 469 755	3 034 219	1 611 668	1 422 551
0 - 4	ESDF	996 573	507 476	489 097	588 141	298 800	289 341	408 432	208 676	199 756
5 - 9	ESDF	967 749	492 012	475 737	584 911	295 943	288 968	382 838	196 069	186 769
10 - 14	ESDF	904 707	459 734	444 973	537 560	270 978	266 582	367 148	188 757	178 391
15 - 19	ESDF	801 256	407 795	393 461	455 435	225 757	229 678	345 821	182 038	163 783
20 - 24	ESDF	748 440	381 701	366 739	449 740	223 909	225 831	298 700	157 792	140 908
25 - 29	ESDF	711 809	363 168	348 641	450 014	221 671	228 343	261 795	141 497	120 298
30 - 34	ESDF	631 345	321 798	309 547	414 605	203 401	211 204	216 740	118 397	98 343
35 - 39	ESDF	511 345	260 956	250 389	334 141	162 580	171 561	177 204	98 376	78 828
40 - 44	ESDF	400 507	205 055	195 452	258 532	125 072	133 460	141 975	79 983	61 992
45 - 49	ESDF	319 318	163 488	155 830	205 582	99 004	106 578	113 736	64 484	49 252
50 - 54	ESDF	249 286	127 076	122 210	166 209	80 001	86 208	83 077	47 075	36 002
55 - 59	ESDF	204 709	103 490	101 219	138 491	66 113	72 378	66 218	37 377	28 841
60 - 64	ESDF	163 452	81 041	82 411	109 207	50 777	58 430	54 245	30 264	23 981
65 - 69	ESDF	133 491	66 557	66 934	87 565	41 569	45 996	45 926	24 988	20 938
70 - 74	ESDF	79 588	38 926	40 662	45 173	20 948	24 225	34 414	17 977	16 437
75+	ESDF	91 746	42 742	49 004	55 796	24 824	30 972	35 950	17 918	18 032

El Salvador
1 VII 2002

Total	ESDF	6 517 798	3 201 720	3 316 078	3 843 878	1 848 194	1 995 684	2 673 920	1 353 526	1 320 394
0 - 1	ESDF	162 605	83 142	79 463	85 402	43 691	41 711	77 203	39 451	37 752
1 - 4	ESDF	643 230	328 454	314 776	341 558	174 248	167 310	301 672	154 206	147 466
5 - 9	ESDF	770 293	392 384	377 909	437 374	221 826	215 548	332 919	170 558	162 361
10 - 14	ESDF	707 294	359 273	348 021	387 476	194 908	192 568	319 818	164 365	155 453
15 - 19	ESDF	656 323	332 404	323 919	354 915	176 391	178 524	301 408	156 013	145 395
20 - 24	ESDF	671 324	338 457	332 867	379 840	186 032	193 808	291 484	152 425	139 059
25 - 29	ESDF	616 797	307 030	309 767	369 631	178 166	191 465	247 166	128 864	118 302
30 - 34	ESDF	486 279	233 213	253 066	310 771	144 848	165 923	175 508	88 365	87 143
35 - 39	ESDF	367 365	168 679	198 686	247 404	111 843	135 561	119 961	56 836	63 125
40 - 44	ESDF	304 109	138 579	165 530	204 400	91 984	112 416	99 709	46 595	53 114
45 - 49	ESDF	259 953	120 804	139 149	168 811	77 090	91 721	91 142	43 714	47 428

7. Population by age, sex and urban/rural residence: latest available year, 1993 - 2002
Population selon l'âge, le sexe et la résidence, urbaine/rurale: dernière année disponible, 1993 - 2002
(continued — suite)

(See notes at end of table. — Voir notes à la fin du tableau.)

Continent, country or area, date and age (in years) / Continent, pays ou zone, date et âge (en années)	Code[1]	Total			Urban - Urbaine			Rural - Rurale		
		Both sexes Les deux sexes	Male Masculin	Female Féminin	Both sexes Les deux sexes	Male Masculin	Female Féminin	Both sexes Les deux sexes	Male Masculin	Female Féminin
AMERICA, NORTH — AMERIQUE DU NORD										
El Salvador										
1 VII 2002										
50 - 54	ESDF	220 810	104 221	116 589	139 617	64 773	74 844	81 193	39 448	41 745
55 - 59	ESDF	178 422	84 483	93 939	110 840	51 290	59 550	67 582	33 193	34 389
60 - 64	ESDF	143 443	67 314	76 129	88 479	40 145	48 334	54 964	27 169	27 795
65 - 69	ESDF	120 824	55 568	65 256	74 882	33 043	41 839	45 942	22 525	23 417
70 - 74	ESDF	94 211	42 005	52 206	59 576	25 536	34 040	34 635	16 469	18 166
75 - 79	ESDF	62 415	26 425	35 990	40 974	16 860	24 114	21 441	9 565	11 876
80+	ESDF	52 101	19 285	32 816	41 928	15 520	26 408	10 173	3 765	6 408
Greenland - Groenland										
1 VII 2000										
Total	ESDJ	56 184	30 029	26 210	45 821	24 310	21 511	10 364	5 697	4 667
0 - 1	ESDJ	843	421	422	654	325	329	190	96	94
1 - 4	ESDJ	3 966	2 022	1 944	3 097	1 603	1 497	869	420	450
5 - 9	ESDJ	5 339	2 713	2 627	4 203	2 156	2 047	1 137	558	580
10 - 14	ESDJ	5 007	2 518	2 491	4 023	2 024	1 999	984	494	492
15 - 19	ESDJ	3 982	2 064	1 921	3 313	1 684	1 629	670	380	292
20 - 24	ESDJ	3 387	1 748	1 641	2 804	1 421	1 383	584	327	258
25 - 29	ESDJ	3 432	1 854	1 579	2 745	1 485	1 263	688	370	319
30 - 34	ESDJ	5 669	3 034	2 635	4 671	2 465	2 207	1 000	570	430
35 - 39	ESDJ	5 933	3 180	2 754	4 936	2 610	2 326	998	570	429
40 - 44	ESDJ	4 775	2 723	2 052	3 975	2 238	1 737	801	488	315
45 - 49	ESDJ	3 704	2 114	1 590	3 088	1 746	1 343	617	368	249
50 - 54	ESDJ	2 949	1 796	1 154	2 465	1 483	983	485	315	172
55 - 59	ESDJ	2 667	1 573	1 094	2 202	1 285	918	466	291	177
60 - 64	ESDJ	1 715	964	752	1 360	759	601	355	205	152
65 - 69	ESDJ	1 291	651	641	1 041	530	512	251	123	129
70 - 74	ESDJ	878	398	481	711	318	396	168	83	85
75 - 79	ESDJ	392	165	227	316	127	190	77	40	37
80 - 84	ESDJ	190	65	126	160	55	106	31	13	20
85 - 89	ESDJ	70	18	54	59	16	46	11	4	9
90 - 94	ESDJ	20	5	16	18	4	15	3	1	2
95+	ESDJ	3	3	-	2	2	-	1	1	-
Grenada - Grenade										
1 VII 2000										
Total	ESDF	101 308	50 200	51 108	...	...	...	...	...	...
0 - 4	ESDF	10 412	5 292	5 120	...	...	...	...	...	...
5 - 9	ESDF	11 547	5 798	5 749	...	...	...	...	...	...
10 - 14	ESDF	13 546	6 837	6 709	...	...	...	...	...	...
15 - 19	ESDF	11 911	6 077	5 834	...	...	...	...	...	...
20 - 24	ESDF	9 267	4 686	4 581	...	...	...	...	...	...
25 - 29	ESDF	7 290	3 883	3 407	...	...	...	...	...	...
30 - 34	ESDF	5 977	2 999	2 978	...	...	...	...	...	...
35 - 39	ESDF	6 537	3 294	3 243	...	...	...	...	...	...
40 - 44	ESDF	5 364	2 628	2 736	...	...	...	...	...	...
45 - 49	ESDF	3 780	1 955	1 825	...	...	...	...	...	...
50 - 54	ESDF	2 904	1 371	1 533	...	...	...	...	...	...
55 - 59	ESDF	2 472	1 160	1 312	...	...	...	...	...	...
60 - 64	ESDF	2 383	1 078	1 305	...	...	...	...	...	...
65 - 69	ESDF	2 356	1 010	1 346	...	...	...	...	...	...
70+	ESDF	5 562	2 132	3 430	...	...	...	...	...	...
Guatemala										
1 VII 2001										
Total	ESDF	11 678 411	5 888 426	5 789 985	...	...	...	...	...	...
0 - 1	ESDF	387 025	197 549	189 476	...	...	...	...	...	...
1 - 4	ESDF	1 484 040	757 626	726 414	...	...	...	...	...	...
5 - 9	ESDF	1 689 604	862 809	826 795	...	...	...	...	...	...

7. Population by age, sex and urban/rural residence: latest available year, 1993 - 2002
Population selon l'âge, le sexe et la résidence, urbaine/rurale: dernière année disponible, 1993 - 2002
(continued — suite)

(See notes at end of table. — Voir notes à la fin du tableau.)

Continent, country or area, date and age (in years) / Continent, pays ou zone, date et âge (en années)	Code[1]	Total			Urban - Urbaine			Rural - Rurale		
		Both sexes Les deux sexes	Male Masculin	Female Féminin	Both sexes Les deux sexes	Male Masculin	Female Féminin	Both sexes Les deux sexes	Male Masculin	Female Féminin
AMERICA, NORTH — AMERIQUE DU NORD										
Guatemala										
1 VII 2001										
10 - 14	ESDF	1 495 114	763 539	731 575	...	...	...	...	...	...
15 - 19	ESDF	1 320 329	673 506	646 823	...	...	...	...	...	...
20 - 24	ESDF	1 110 418	562 982	547 436	...	...	...	...	...	...
25 - 29	ESDF	894 268	449 807	444 461	...	...	...	...	...	...
30 - 34	ESDF	708 522	351 762	356 760	...	...	...	...	...	...
35 - 39	ESDF	571 673	281 068	290 605	...	...	...	...	...	...
40 - 44	ESDF	462 850	226 817	236 033	...	...	...	...	...	...
45 - 49	ESDF	386 977	190 123	196 854	...	...	...	...	...	...
50 - 54	ESDF	306 124	150 654	155 470	...	...	...	...	...	...
55 - 59	ESDF	244 215	121 084	123 131	...	...	...	...	...	...
60 - 64	ESDF	201 985	100 065	101 920	...	...	...	...	...	...
65 - 69	ESDF	166 701	81 453	85 248	...	...	...	...	...	...
70 - 74	ESDF	122 040	58 725	63 315	...	...	...	...	...	...
75 - 79	ESDF	74 787	35 391	39 396	...	...	...	...	...	...
80+	ESDF	51 739	23 466	28 273	...	...	...	...	...	...
Haiti - Haïti										
1 VII 1999										
Total	ESDJ	7 803 232	3 834 240	3 968 992	2 731 843	1 234 809	1 497 034	5 071 389	2 599 431	2 471 958
0 - 1	ESDJ	242 106	122 835	119 271	68 885	36 499	32 386	173 221	86 336	86 885
1 - 4	ESDJ	913 669	462 018	451 651	252 773	130 783	121 990	660 896	331 235	329 661
5 - 9	ESDJ	1 034 513	521 302	513 211	321 389	154 420	166 969	713 124	366 882	346 242
10 - 14	ESDJ	925 920	466 007	459 913	363 812	161 340	202 472	562 108	304 667	257 441
15 - 19	ESDJ	810 881	407 544	403 337	375 052	156 361	218 691	435 829	251 183	184 646
20 - 24	ESDJ	696 906	347 026	349 880	337 696	153 000	184 696	359 210	194 026	165 184
25 - 29	ESDJ	612 995	301 403	311 592	272 739	124 048	148 691	340 256	177 355	162 901
30 - 34	ESDJ	526 616	255 640	270 976	198 846	88 085	110 761	327 770	167 555	160 215
35 - 39	ESDJ	452 327	216 102	236 225	135 215	57 299	77 916	317 112	158 803	158 309
40 - 44	ESDJ	370 430	173 392	197 038	106 911	42 010	64 901	263 519	131 382	132 137
45 - 49	ESDJ	306 075	141 518	164 557	71 946	29 912	42 034	234 129	111 606	122 523
50 - 54	ESDJ	247 324	114 254	133 070	70 080	31 126	38 954	177 244	83 128	94 116
55 - 59	ESDJ	201 858	93 663	108 195	51 060	22 494	28 566	150 798	71 169	79 629
60 - 64	ESDJ	161 143	74 625	86 518	40 580	18 949	21 631	120 563	55 676	64 887
65 - 69	ESDJ	122 392	56 450	65 942	28 310	12 719	15 591	94 082	43 731	50 351
70 - 74	ESDJ	84 796	38 744	46 052	18 717	7 726	10 991	66 079	31 018	35 061
75 - 79	ESDJ	52 884	23 831	29 053	11 309	5 008	6 301	41 575	18 823	22 752
80+	ESDJ	40 397	17 886	22 511	6 523	3 030	3 493	33 874	14 856	19 018
Jamaica - Jamaïque										
10 IX 2001										
Total	CDFC	2 607 630	1 283 546	1 324 085	1 353 240	645 375	707 866	1 254 390	638 171	616 219
0 - 4	CDFC	272 818	138 914	133 904	137 937	70 338	67 599	134 881	68 576	66 305
5 - 9	CDFC	294 872	149 653	145 219	144 692	72 949	71 743	150 180	76 704	73 476
10 - 14	CDFC	275 879	139 373	136 506	135 425	68 013	67 412	140 454	71 360	69 094
15 - 19	CDFC	251 975	126 463	125 512	128 832	63 204	65 628	123 143	63 259	59 884
20 - 24	CDFC	215 881	104 985	110 896	119 716	56 377	63 339	96 165	48 608	47 557
25 - 29	CDFC	206 938	99 112	107 826	116 613	53 649	62 964	90 325	45 463	44 862
30 - 34	CDFC	197 539	94 127	103 412	110 612	50 571	60 041	86 927	43 556	43 371
35 - 39	CDFC	184 933	87 626	97 307	102 673	46 388	56 285	82 260	41 238	41 022
40 - 44	CDFC	155 450	76 303	79 147	84 459	39 200	45 259	70 991	37 103	33 888
45 - 49	CDFC	113 672	55 856	57 816	62 001	28 839	33 162	51 671	27 017	24 654
50 - 54	CDFC	97 269	49 670	47 599	51 564	24 918	26 646	45 705	24 752	20 953
55 - 59	CDFC	75 636	38 646	36 990	38 078	18 436	19 642	37 558	20 210	17 348
60 - 64	CDFC	65 293	31 828	33 465	31 535	14 575	16 960	33 758	17 253	16 505
65 - 69	CDFC	59 870	28 901	30 969	27 817	12 697	15 120	32 053	16 204	15 849
70 - 74	CDFC	52 100	24 855	27 245	23 658	10 662	12 996	28 442	14 193	14 249
75 - 79	CDFC	38 587	17 711	20 876	16 928	7 129	9 799	21 659	10 582	11 077
80 - 84	CDFC	24 553	10 304	14 249	10 411	4 031	6 380	14 142	6 273	7 869

7. Population by age, sex and urban/rural residence: latest available year, 1993 - 2002
Population selon l'âge, le sexe et la résidence, urbaine/rurale: dernière année disponible, 1993 - 2002
(continued — suite)

(See notes at end of table. — Voir notes à la fin du tableau.)

Continent, country or area, date and age (in years) / Continent, pays ou zone, date et âge (en années)	Code[1]	Total			Urban - Urbaine			Rural - Rurale		
		Both sexes Les deux sexes	Male Masculin	Female Féminin	Both sexes Les deux sexes	Male Masculin	Female Féminin	Both sexes Les deux sexes	Male Masculin	Female Féminin
AMERICA, NORTH — AMERIQUE DU NORD										
Jamaica - Jamaïque										
10 IX 2001										
85+	CDFC	24 365	9 218	15 147	10 289	3 398	6 891	14 076	5 820	8 256
Mexico - Mexique										
14 II 2000										
Total	CDJC	97 483 412	47 592 253	49 891 159	72 759 822	35 317 569	37 442 253	24 723 590	12 274 684	12 448 906
0 - 1	CDJC	2 061 431	1 049 375	1 012 056	1 483 607	755 457	728 150	577 824	293 918	283 906
1 - 4	CDJC	8 573 726	4 351 931	4 221 795	6 105 143	3 102 158	3 002 985	2 468 583	1 249 773	1 218 810
5 - 9	CDJC	11 215 323	5 677 711	5 537 612	7 865 897	3 984 541	3 881 356	3 349 426	1 693 170	1 656 256
10 - 14	CDJC	10 736 493	5 435 737	5 300 756	7 487 732	3 782 974	3 704 758	3 248 761	1 652 763	1 595 998
15 - 19	CDJC	9 992 135	4 909 648	5 082 487	7 389 092	3 623 560	3 765 532	2 603 043	1 286 088	1 316 955
20 - 24	CDJC	9 071 134	4 303 600	4 767 534	7 019 039	3 337 619	3 681 420	2 052 095	965 981	1 086 114
25 - 29	CDJC	8 157 743	3 861 482	4 296 261	6 454 014	3 053 121	3 400 893	1 703 729	808 361	895 368
30 - 34	CDJC	7 136 523	3 383 356	3 753 167	5 666 844	2 677 805	2 989 039	1 469 679	705 551	764 128
35 - 39	CDJC	6 352 538	3 023 328	3 329 210	5 025 577	2 381 668	2 643 909	1 326 961	641 660	685 301
40 - 44	CDJC	5 194 833	2 494 771	2 700 062	4 115 978	1 964 652	2 151 326	1 078 855	530 119	548 736
45 - 49	CDJC	4 072 091	1 957 177	2 114 914	3 155 008	1 504 805	1 650 203	917 083	452 372	464 711
50 - 54	CDJC	3 357 953	1 624 033	1 733 920	2 572 644	1 229 440	1 343 204	785 309	394 593	390 716
55 - 59	CDJC	2 559 231	1 234 072	1 325 159	1 893 913	898 926	994 987	665 318	335 146	330 172
60 - 64	CDJC	2 198 146	1 045 404	1 152 742	1 592 246	735 836	856 410	605 900	309 568	296 332
65 - 69	CDJC	1 660 785	779 666	881 119	1 195 245	543 243	652 002	465 540	236 423	229 117
70 - 74	CDJC	1 245 674	589 106	656 568	889 049	402 401	486 648	356 625	186 705	169 920
75 - 79	CDJC	865 270	411 197	454 073	615 380	279 475	335 905	249 890	131 722	118 168
80 - 84	CDJC	483 876	217 330	266 546	340 470	144 998	195 472	143 406	72 332	71 074
85 - 89	CDJC	290 051	125 041	165 010	205 307	83 091	122 216	84 744	41 950	42 794
90 - 94	CDJC	122 006	50 843	71 163	84 105	32 603	51 502	37 901	18 240	19 661
95 - 99	CDJC	62 892	25 741	37 151	41 381	15 751	25 630	21 511	9 990	11 521
100+	CDJC	19 757	8 029	11 728	11 635	4 566	7 069	8 122	3 463	4 659
Unk. - Inc.	CDJC	2 053 801	1 033 675	1 020 126	1 550 516	778 879	771 637	503 285	254 796	248 489
Netherlands Antilles - Antilles néerlandaises										
29 I 2001										
Total	CDJC	175 653	82 521	93 132	...	...	...	...	...	...
0 - 1	CDJC	2 587	1 352	1 235	...	...	...	...	...	...
1 - 4	CDJC	10 336	5 235	5 101	...	...	...	...	...	...
5 - 9	CDJC	15 020	7 545	7 475	...	...	...	...	...	...
10 - 14	CDJC	14 573	7 349	7 224	...	...	...	...	...	...
15 - 19	CDJC	12 765	6 317	6 448	...	...	...	...	...	...
20 - 24	CDJC	8 431	4 147	4 284	...	...	...	...	...	...
25 - 29	CDJC	10 722	4 929	5 793	...	...	...	...	...	...
30 - 34	CDJC	13 421	6 135	7 286	...	...	...	...	...	...
35 - 39	CDJC	15 935	7 212	8 723	...	...	...	...	...	...
40 - 44	CDJC	15 358	6 985	8 373	...	...	...	...	...	...
45 - 49	CDJC	13 331	5 981	7 350	...	...	...	...	...	...
50 - 54	CDJC	11 359	5 325	6 034	...	...	...	...	...	...
55 - 59	CDJC	8 653	3 969	4 684	...	...	...	...	...	...
60 - 64	CDJC	6 937	3 171	3 766	...	...	...	...	...	...
65 - 69	CDJC	5 583	2 591	2 992	...	...	...	...	...	...
70 - 74	CDJC	4 078	1 792	2 286	...	...	...	...	...	...
75 - 79	CDJC	3 003	1 261	1 742	...	...	...	...	...	...
80 - 84	CDJC	2 010	759	1 251	...	...	...	...	...	...
85 - 89	CDJC	932	293	639	...	...	...	...	...	...
90 - 94	CDJC	473	141	332	...	...	...	...	...	...
95+	CDJC	146	32	114	...	...	...	...	...	...
Nicaragua										
1 VII 2000										
Total	ESDJ	5 071 670	2 523 542	2 548 128	2 897 293	1 403 141	1 494 152	2 174 377	1 120 400	1 053 977

7. Population by age, sex and urban/rural residence: latest available year, 1993 - 2002
Population selon l'âge, le sexe et la résidence, urbaine/rurale: dernière année disponible, 1993 - 2002
(continued — suite)

(See notes at end of table. — Voir notes à la fin du tableau.)

Continent, country or area, date and age (in years) / Continent, pays ou zone, date et âge (en années)	Code[1]	Total			Urban - Urbaine			Rural - Rurale		
		Both sexes Les deux sexes	Male Masculin	Female Féminin	Both sexes Les deux sexes	Male Masculin	Female Féminin	Both sexes Les deux sexes	Male Masculin	Female Féminin
AMERICA, NORTH — AMERIQUE DU NORD										
Nicaragua										
1 VII 2000										
0 - 4	ESDJ	801 055	408 066	392 989	415 325	212 904	202 421	385 730	195 162	190 568
5 - 9	ESDJ	730 885	371 680	359 205	393 844	200 271	193 573	337 041	171 409	165 632
10 - 14	ESDJ	629 819	319 734	310 085	350 185	175 868	174 317	279 634	143 866	135 768
15 - 19	ESDJ	602 356	304 085	298 271	340 251	167 250	173 001	262 105	136 835	125 270
20 - 24	ESDJ	482 531	240 909	241 622	277 409	132 917	144 492	205 122	107 992	97 130
25 - 29	ESDJ	398 727	196 347	202 380	242 869	115 174	127 695	155 858	81 173	74 685
30 - 34	ESDJ	322 729	157 017	165 711	206 092	96 966	109 126	116 636	60 051	56 585
35 - 39	ESDJ	264 515	127 961	136 553	166 298	77 637	88 661	98 216	50 324	47 892
40 - 44	ESDJ	215 410	103 959	111 451	133 403	62 101	71 302	82 007	41 858	40 149
45 - 49	ESDJ	173 111	83 521	89 590	103 070	47 405	55 665	70 041	36 116	33 925
50 - 54	ESDJ	124 207	59 916	64 290	73 390	32 989	40 401	50 816	26 927	23 889
55 - 59	ESDJ	94 762	45 306	49 456	56 034	24 690	31 344	38 728	20 616	18 112
60 - 64	ESDJ	77 002	36 388	40 614	45 973	19 943	26 030	31 029	16 445	14 584
65 - 69	ESDJ	59 388	27 292	32 097	35 718	14 971	20 747	23 671	12 321	11 350
70 - 74	ESDJ	44 784	19 903	24 882	26 895	10 666	16 229	17 890	9 237	8 653
75 - 79	ESDJ	29 641	13 017	16 624	17 911	6 949	10 962	11 730	6 068	5 662
80+	ESDJ	20 749	8 440	12 309	12 626	4 440	8 186	8 123	4 000	4 123
Panama										
1 VII 2000										
Total	ESDF	2 855 703	1 440 801	1 414 902	1 604 823	782 928	821 895	1 250 880	657 873	593 007
0 - 1	ESDF	59 949	30 595	29 354	30 248	15 460	14 788	29 701	15 135	14 566
1 - 4	ESDF	241 433	123 553	117 880	121 253	62 069	59 184	120 180	61 484	58 696
5 - 9	ESDF	300 852	153 986	146 866	150 849	77 061	73 786	150 003	76 925	73 079
10 - 14	ESDF	291 489	148 579	142 911	148 812	75 471	73 342	142 678	73 109	69 569
15 - 19	ESDF	271 684	137 805	133 878	146 537	73 631	72 906	125 147	64 174	60 974
20 - 24	ESDF	254 772	129 237	125 536	146 169	72 295	73 875	108 605	56 944	51 661
25 - 29	ESDF	250 152	125 922	124 230	150 336	71 923	78 413	99 816	53 999	45 817
30 - 34	ESDF	230 835	115 884	114 951	141 488	67 582	73 906	89 347	48 302	41 045
35 - 39	ESDF	203 446	101 421	102 025	126 268	59 890	66 378	77 178	41 531	35 647
40 - 44	ESDF	170 180	84 702	85 478	105 158	50 101	55 057	65 022	34 601	30 421
45 - 49	ESDF	140 684	70 369	70 315	86 739	41 477	45 262	53 945	28 892	25 053
50 - 54	ESDF	115 342	58 278	57 064	69 710	33 225	36 485	45 632	25 053	20 579
55 - 59	ESDF	93 684	47 379	46 305	53 771	25 760	28 011	39 913	21 619	18 294
60 - 64	ESDF	73 087	36 664	36 423	40 256	18 795	21 461	32 831	17 869	14 962
65 - 69	ESDF	55 236	27 712	27 524	30 061	13 914	16 147	25 175	13 798	11 377
70 - 74	ESDF	43 900	21 495	22 405	24 076	10 692	13 384	19 824	10 803	9 021
75 - 79	ESDF	30 250	14 158	16 092	17 010	7 216	9 794	13 240	6 942	6 298
80+	ESDF	28 727	13 063	15 664	16 083	6 367	9 716	12 644	6 696	5 948
Puerto Rico - Porto Rico[7]										
1 VII 2002										
Total	ESDJ	3 858 806	1 855 781	2 003 025	...	...	...	...	...	...
0 - 1	ESDJ	55 133	28 192	26 941	...	...	...	...	...	...
1 - 4	ESDJ	229 460	117 240	112 220	...	...	...	...	...	...
5 - 9	ESDJ	301 424	154 439	146 985	...	...	...	...	...	...
10 - 14	ESDJ	305 025	155 776	149 249	...	...	...	...	...	...
15 - 19	ESDJ	305 577	155 221	150 356	...	...	...	...	...	...
20 - 24	ESDJ	299 362	149 042	150 320	...	...	...	...	...	...
25 - 29	ESDJ	277 415	135 958	141 457	...	...	...	...	...	...
30 - 34	ESDJ	262 959	127 113	135 846	...	...	...	...	...	...
35 - 39	ESDJ	265 154	125 440	139 714	...	...	...	...	...	...
40 - 44	ESDJ	258 211	120 079	138 132	...	...	...	...	...	...
45 - 49	ESDJ	239 965	110 847	129 118	...	...	...	...	...	...
50 - 54	ESDJ	233 597	107 501	126 096	...	...	...	...	...	...
55 - 59	ESDJ	206 552	94 956	111 596	...	...	...	...	...	...
60 - 64	ESDJ	169 796	78 223	91 573	...	...	...	...	...	...

7. Population by age, sex and urban/rural residence: latest available year, 1993 - 2002
Population selon l'âge, le sexe et la résidence, urbaine/rurale: dernière année disponible, 1993 - 2002
(continued — suite)

(See notes at end of table. — Voir notes à la fin du tableau.)

Continent, country or area, date and age (in years) / Continent, pays ou zone, date et âge (en années)	Code[1]	Total			Urban - Urbaine			Rural - Rurale		
		Both sexes Les deux sexes	Male Masculin	Female Féminin	Both sexes Les deux sexes	Male Masculin	Female Féminin	Both sexes Les deux sexes	Male Masculin	Female Féminin
AMERICA, NORTH — AMERIQUE DU NORD										
Puerto Rico - Porto Rico[7]										
1 VII 2002										
65 - 69	ESDJ	141 869	64 595	77 274	...	...	...	...	...	...
70 - 74	ESDJ	112 416	49 870	62 546	...	...	...	...	...	...
75 - 79	ESDJ	85 137	36 568	48 569	...	...	...	...	...	...
80+	ESDJ	109 754	44 721	65 033	...	...	...	...	...	...
Saint Kitts and Nevis - Saint-Kitts-et-Nevis										
1 VII 2000										
Total	ESDF	40 410	20 400	20 010	...	...	...	...	...	...
0 - 4	ESDF	4 250	2 130	2 120	...	...	...	...	...	...
5 - 9	ESDF	4 100	2 140	1 960	...	...	...	...	...	...
10 - 14	ESDF	4 040	2 120	1 920	...	...	...	...	...	...
15 - 19	ESDF	3 870	2 000	1 870	...	...	...	...	...	...
20 - 24	ESDF	3 620	1 880	1 740	...	...	...	...	...	...
25 - 29	ESDF	3 240	1 640	1 600	...	...	...	...	...	...
30 - 34	ESDF	3 100	1 550	1 550	...	...	...	...	...	...
35 - 39	ESDF	2 910	1 430	1 480	...	...	...	...	...	...
40 - 44	ESDF	2 520	1 270	1 250	...	...	...	...	...	...
45 - 49	ESDF	1 880	900	980	...	...	...	...	...	...
50 - 54	ESDF	1 390	710	680	...	...	...	...	...	...
55 - 59	ESDF	1 100	560	540	...	...	...	...	...	...
60 - 64	ESDF	820	400	420	...	...	...	...	...	...
65 - 69	ESDF	840	410	430	...	...	...	...	...	...
70 - 74	ESDF	810	380	430	...	...	...	...	...	...
75 - 79	ESDF	700	330	370	...	...	...	...	...	...
80 - 84	ESDF	470	240	230	...	...	...	...	...	...
85+	ESDF	750	310	440	...	...	...	...	...	...
Saint Lucia - Sainte-Lucie										
1 VII 2002										
Total	ESDF	159 133	77 868	81 265	...	...	...	...	...	...
0 - 4	ESDF	13 903	6 839	7 064	...	...	...	...	...	...
5 - 9	ESDF	16 952	8 563	8 389	...	...	...	...	...	...
10 - 14	ESDF	17 481	8 742	8 739	...	...	...	...	...	...
15 - 19	ESDF	17 039	8 335	...	...	...	...	...	...	...
20 - 24	ESDF	14 084	6 949	7 135	...	...	...	...	...	...
25 - 29	ESDF	13 084	6 301	6 783	...	...	...	...	...	...
30 - 34	ESDF	11 903	5 767	6 136	...	...	...	...	...	...
35 - 39	ESDF	11 660	5 629	6 031	...	...	...	...	...	...
40 - 44	ESDF	9 834	4 807	5 027	...	...	...	...	...	...
45 - 49	ESDF	7 302	3 698	3 604	...	...	...	...	...	...
50 - 54	ESDF	5 693	2 864	2 864	...	...	...	...	...	...
55 - 59	ESDF	4 526	2 121	2 405	...	...	...	...	...	...
60 - 64	ESDF	3 953	1 880	2 073	...	...	...	...	...	...
65 - 69	ESDF	3 651	1 746	1 905	...	...	...	...	...	...
70 - 74	ESDF	2 792	1 351	1 441	...	...	...	...	...	...
75 - 79	ESDF	2 062	987	1 075	...	...	...	...	...	...
80+	ESDF	3 214	1 324	1 890	...	...	...	...	...	...
Saint Vincent and the Grenadines - Saint Vincent-et-les Grenadines										
1 VII 2000										
Total	ESDF	111 821	55 797	56 024	...	...	...	...	...	...
0 - 1	ESDF	2 149	1 104	1 045	...	...	...	...	...	...
1 - 4	ESDF	10 539	5 371	5 168	...	...	...	...	...	...

7. Population by age, sex and urban/rural residence: latest available year, 1993 - 2002
Population selon l'âge, le sexe et la résidence, urbaine/rurale: dernière année disponible, 1993 - 2002
(continued — suite)

(See notes at end of table. — Voir notes à la fin du tableau.)

Continent, country or area, date and age (in years) / Continent, pays ou zone, date et âge (en années)	Code[1]	Total			Urban - Urbaine			Rural - Rurale		
		Both sexes Les deux sexes	Male Masculin	Female Féminin	Both sexes Les deux sexes	Male Masculin	Female Féminin	Both sexes Les deux sexes	Male Masculin	Female Féminin
AMERICA, NORTH — AMERIQUE DU NORD										
Saint Vincent and the Grenadines - Saint Vincent-et-les Grenadines										
1 VII 2000										
5 - 9	ESDF	14 496	7 252	7 244	...	...	...	...	...	...
10 - 14	ESDF	14 402	7 307	7 095	...	...	...	...	...	...
15 - 19	ESDF	12 828	6 451	6 377	...	...	...	...	...	...
20 - 24	ESDF	10 224	5 244	4 980	...	...	...	...	...	...
25 - 29	ESDF	9 936	5 066	4 870	...	...	...	...	...	...
30 - 34	ESDF	8 063	4 164	3 899	...	...	...	...	...	...
35 - 39	ESDF	5 721	2 853	2 868	...	...	...	...	...	...
40 - 44	ESDF	4 254	2 182	2 072	...	...	...	...	...	...
45 - 49	ESDF	3 363	1 662	1 701	...	...	...	...	...	...
50 - 54	ESDF	3 115	1 516	1 599	...	...	...	...	...	...
55 - 59	ESDF	2 748	1 300	1 448	...	...	...	...	...	...
60 - 64	ESDF	2 702	1 283	1 419	...	...	...	...	...	...
65 - 69	ESDF	2 524	1 068	1 456	...	...	...	...	...	...
70 - 74	ESDF	1 948	862	1 086	...	...	...	...	...	...
75 - 79	ESDF	1 360	584	776	...	...	...	...	...	...
80 - 84	ESDF	827	316	511	...	...	...	...	...	...
85+	ESDF	622	212	410	...	...	...	...	...	...
Trinidad and Tobago - Trinité-et-Tobago										
1 VII 1997										
Total	ESDF	1 274 799	636 340	638 459	...	...	...	...	...	...
0 - 1	ESDF	15 980	7 952	8 028	...	...	...	...	...	...
1 - 4	ESDF	76 520	38 818	37 702	...	...	...	...	...	...
5 - 9	ESDF	118 002	60 461	57 541	...	...	...	...	...	...
10 - 14	ESDF	133 509	67 766	65 743	...	...	...	...	...	...
15 - 19	ESDF	125 488	64 788	60 700	...	...	...	...	...	...
20 - 24	ESDF	113 206	57 922	55 284	...	...	...	...	...	...
25 - 29	ESDF	104 999	53 530	51 469	...	...	...	...	...	...
30 - 34	ESDF	103 806	51 190	52 616	...	...	...	...	...	...
35 - 39	ESDF	101 070	49 871	51 199	...	...	...	...	...	...
40 - 44	ESDF	89 922	45 331	44 591	...	...	...	...	...	...
45 - 49	ESDF	73 655	36 002	37 653	...	...	...	...	...	...
50 - 54	ESDF	58 076	28 693	29 383	...	...	...	...	...	...
55 - 59	ESDF	44 179	20 927	23 252	...	...	...	...	...	...
60 - 64	ESDF	34 112	16 462	17 650	...	...	...	...	...	...
65 - 69	ESDF	27 875	13 198	14 677	...	...	...	...	...	...
70 - 74	ESDF	22 245	9 516	12 729	...	...	...	...	...	...
75 - 79	ESDF	17 300	7 325	9 975	...	...	...	...	...	...
80+	ESDF	14 855	6 588	8 267	...	...	...	...	...	...
United States - États-Unis[8]										
1 VII 2002										
Total	ESDJ	288 368 706	141 660 980	146 707 726	...	...	...	...	...	...
0 - 1	ESDJ	4 033 719	2 063 824	1 969 895	...	...	...	...	...	...
1 - 4	ESDJ	15 575 428	7 961 545	7 613 883	...	...	...	...	...	...
5 - 9	ESDJ	19 900 837	10 187 663	9 713 174	...	...	...	...	...	...
10 - 14	ESDJ	21 136 449	10 824 896	10 311 553	...	...	...	...	...	...
15 - 19	ESDJ	20 376 151	10 471 128	9 905 023	...	...	...	...	...	...
20 - 24	ESDJ	20 213 632	10 350 141	9 863 491	...	...	...	...	...	...
25 - 29	ESDJ	18 971 892	9 640 132	9 331 760	...	...	...	...	...	...
30 - 34	ESDJ	20 956 412	10 562 644	10 393 768	...	...	...	...	...	...
35 - 39	ESDJ	21 914 882	10 953 501	10 961 381	...	...	...	...	...	...
40 - 44	ESDJ	23 001 724	11 413 005	11 588 719	...	...	...	...	...	...

7. Population by age, sex and urban/rural residence: latest available year, 1993 - 2002
Population selon l'âge, le sexe et la résidence, urbaine/rurale: dernière année disponible, 1993 - 2002
(continued — suite)

(See notes at end of table. — Voir notes à la fin du tableau.)

Continent, country or area, date and age (in years) / Continent, pays ou zone, date et âge (en annèes)	Code[1]	Total			Urban - Urbaine			Rural - Rurale		
		Both sexes Les deux sexes	Male Masculin	Female Féminin	Both sexes Les deux sexes	Male Masculin	Female Féminin	Both sexes Les deux sexes	Male Masculin	Female Féminin
AMERICA, NORTH — AMERIQUE DU NORD										
United States - États-Unis[8]										
1 VII 2002										
45 - 49	ESDJ	21 302 064	10 491 757	10 810 307	...	...	...	...	...	...
50 - 54	ESDJ	18 781 873	9 184 564	9 597 309	...	...	...	...	...	...
55 - 59	ESDJ	14 990 542	7 260 459	7 730 083	...	...	...	...	...	...
60 - 64	ESDJ	11 611 184	5 523 852	6 087 332	...	...	...	...	...	...
65 - 69	ESDJ	9 580 927	4 439 389	5 141 538	...	...	...	...	...	...
70 - 74	ESDJ	8 693 288	3 861 616	4 831 672	...	...	...	...	...	...
75 - 79	ESDJ	7 420 394	3 071 419	4 348 975	...	...	...	...	...	...
80 - 84	ESDJ	5 314 239	2 009 637	3 304 602	...	...	...	...	...	...
85+	ESDJ	4 593 069	1 389 808	3 203 261	...	...	...	...	...	...
United States Virgin Islands - Îles Vierges américaines[7]										
1 IV 2000										
Total	CDJC	108 612	51 864	56 748	...	...	...	...	...	...
0 - 4	CDJC	8 553	...	...	...	...	...	...	...	...
5 - 9	CDJC	10 176	...	...	...	...	...	...	...	...
10 - 14	CDJC	9 676	...	...	...	...	...	...	...	...
15 - 19	CDJC	8 688	...	...	...	...	...	...	...	...
20 - 24	CDJC	5 916	...	...	...	...	...	...	...	...
25 - 34	CDJC	13 705	...	...	...	...	...	...	...	...
35 - 44	CDJC	15 746	...	...	...	...	...	...	...	...
45 - 54	CDJC	15 521	...	...	...	...	...	...	...	...
55 - 59	CDJC	6 757	...	...	...	...	...	...	...	...
60 - 64	CDJC	4 757	...	...	...	...	...	...	...	...
65 - 74	CDJC	5 845	...	...	...	...	...	...	...	...
75 - 84	CDJC	2 505	...	...	...	...	...	...	...	...
85+	CDJC	767	...	...	...	...	...	...	...	...
AMERICA, SOUTH — AMERIQUE DU SUD										
Argentina - Argentine[9]										
1 VII 1995										
Total	ESDF	34 768 457	16 976 701	17 609 936	30 556 905	14 820 662	15 736 243	4 029 732	2 156 039	1 873 693
0 - 4	ESDF	3 423 256	1 693 242	1 637 451	2 854 157	1 451 866	1 402 291	476 536	241 376	235 160
5 - 9	ESDF	3 339 853	1 692 161	1 638 391	2 860 036	1 452 476	1 407 560	470 516	239 685	230 831
10 - 14	ESDF	3 284 542	1 662 448	1 612 543	2 838 921	1 436 025	1 402 896	436 070	226 423	209 647
15 - 19	ESDF	3 349 962	1 683 418	1 646 642	2 943 654	1 473 952	1 469 702	386 406	209 466	176 940
20 - 24	ESDF	2 815 425	1 407 920	1 383 976	2 479 244	1 235 279	1 243 965	312 652	172 641	140 011
25 - 29	ESDF	2 470 850	1 234 773	1 220 298	2 182 440	1 085 594	1 096 846	272 631	149 179	123 452
30 - 34	ESDF	2 330 870	1 157 905	1 163 366	2 070 997	1 021 148	1 049 849	250 274	136 757	113 517
35 - 39	ESDF	2 198 005	1 072 637	1 118 988	1 960 731	946 918	1 013 813	230 894	125 719	105 175
40 - 44	ESDF	2 076 119	1 016 579	1 054 840	1 853 152	896 513	956 639	218 267	120 066	98 201
45 - 49	ESDF	1 851 125	923 726	943 144	1 669 726	813 793	855 933	197 144	109 933	87 211
50 - 54	ESDF	1 612 720	786 132	824 657	1 438 415	688 315	750 100	172 374	97 817	74 557
55 - 59	ESDF	1 431 429	683 301	746 669	1 280 730	598 896	681 834	149 240	84 405	64 835
60 - 64	ESDF	1 313 614	610 232	702 282	1 178 113	534 302	643 811	134 401	75 930	58 471
65 - 69	ESDF	1 173 708	527 186	645 792	1 055 243	462 065	593 178	117 735	65 121	52 614
70 - 74	ESDF	921 042	391 559	529 012	829 576	343 192	486 384	90 995	48 367	42 628
75 - 79	ESDF	637 312	249 995	386 978	574 790	219 340	355 450	62 183	30 655	31 528
80+	ESDF	538 624	183 487	354 907	486 980	160 988	325 992	51 414	22 499	28 915
1 VII 2000										
Total	ESDF	37 032 000	18 163 300	18 868 700	...	...	...	...	...	...
0 - 4	ESDF	3 498 600	1 778 300	1 720 300	...	...	...	...	...	...

7. Population by age, sex and urban/rural residence: latest available year, 1993 - 2002
Population selon l'âge, le sexe et la résidence, urbaine/rurale: dernière année disponible, 1993 - 2002
(continued — suite)

(See notes at end of table. — Voir notes à la fin du tableau.)

Continent, country or area, date and age (in years) / Continent, pays ou zone, date et âge (en années)	Code[1]	Total			Urban - Urbaine			Rural - Rurale		
		Both sexes Les deux sexes	Male Masculin	Female Féminin	Both sexes Les deux sexes	Male Masculin	Female Féminin	Both sexes Les deux sexes	Male Masculin	Female Féminin
AMERICA, SOUTH — AMERIQUE DU SUD										
Argentina - Argentine[9]										
1 VII 2000										
5 - 9	ESDF	3 421 800	1 738 300	1 683 500	...	...	...	...	...	...
10 - 14	ESDF	3 344 600	1 697 800	1 646 800	...	...	...	...	...	...
15 - 19	ESDF	3 297 000	1 671 400	1 625 600	...	...	...	...	...	...
20 - 24	ESDF	3 361 100	1 695 900	1 665 200	...	...	...	...	...	...
25 - 29	ESDF	2 817 300	1 417 400	1 399 900	...	...	...	...	...	...
30 - 34	ESDF	2 465 400	1 237 100	1 228 300	...	...	...	...	...	...
35 - 39	ESDF	2 319 100	1 154 200	1 164 900	...	...	...	...	...	...
40 - 44	ESDF	2 178 100	1 062 700	1 115 400	...	...	...	...	...	...
45 - 49	ESDF	2 043 100	996 900	1 046 200	...	...	...	...	...	...
50 - 54	ESDF	1 802 800	873 700	929 100	...	...	...	...	...	...
55 - 59	ESDF	1 546 100	741 500	804 600	...	...	...	...	...	...
60 - 64	ESDF	1 343 900	625 100	718 800	...	...	...	...	...	...
65 - 69	ESDF	1 197 600	535 400	662 200	...	...	...	...	...	...
70 - 74	ESDF	1 019 500	433 700	585 800	...	...	...	...	...	...
75 - 79	ESDF	737 200	290 900	446 300	...	...	...	...	...	...
80+	ESDF	638 800	213 000	425 800	...	...	...	...	...	...
Bolivia - Bolivie										
5 IX 2001										
Total	CDFC	8 274 325	4 123 850	4 150 475	5 165 230	2 517 106	2 648 124	3 109 095	1 606 744	1 502 351
0 - 9	CDFC	2 170 998	1 115 775	1 055 223	1 259 066	646 912	612 154	911 932	468 863	443 069
10 - 19	CDFC	1 899 973	962 123	937 850	1 221 503	602 995	618 508	678 470	359 128	319 342
20 - 29	CDFC	1 391 959	680 985	710 974	977 334	466 107	511 227	414 625	214 878	199 747
30 - 39	CDFC	992 121	482 454	509 667	659 816	309 209	350 607	332 305	173 245	159 060
40 - 49	CDFC	750 600	370 905	379 695	474 487	226 920	247 567	276 113	143 985	132 128
50 - 59	CDFC	489 310	243 269	246 041	281 057	135 671	145 386	208 253	107 598	100 655
60 - 69	CDFC	309 873	148 018	161 855	157 647	71 880	85 767	152 226	76 138	76 088
70 - 79	CDFC	195 678	88 986	106 692	97 984	42 787	55 197	97 694	46 199	51 495
80 - 89	CDFC	59 651	25 484	34 167	30 453	12 422	18 031	29 198	13 062	16 136
90+	CDFC	14 162	5 851	8 311	5 883	2 203	3 680	8 279	3 648	4 631
Brazil - Brésil[10]										
1 VIII 2000										
Total	CDJC	169 799 170	83 576 015	86 223 155	137 953 959	66 882 993	71 070 966	31 845 211	16 693 022	15 152 189
0 - 1	CDJC	3 213 310	1 635 916	1 577 394	2 518 464	1 282 941	1 235 523	694 846	352 975	341 871
1 - 4	CDJC	13 162 418	6 691 010	6 471 408	10 242 356	5 207 423	5 034 933	2 920 062	1 483 587	1 436 475
5 - 9	CDJC	16 542 327	8 402 353	8 139 974	12 821 519	6 500 814	6 320 705	3 720 808	1 901 539	1 819 269
10 - 14	CDJC	17 348 067	8 777 639	8 570 428	13 530 190	6 803 898	6 726 292	3 817 877	1 973 741	1 844 136
15 - 19	CDJC	17 939 815	9 019 130	8 920 685	14 403 539	7 132 822	7 270 717	3 536 276	1 886 308	1 649 968
20 - 24	CDJC	16 141 515	8 048 218	8 093 297	13 352 132	6 549 365	6 802 767	2 789 383	1 498 853	1 290 530
25 - 29	CDJC	13 849 665	6 814 328	7 035 337	11 570 969	5 606 425	5 964 544	2 278 696	1 207 903	1 070 793
30 - 34	CDJC	13 028 944	6 363 983	6 664 961	10 918 396	5 248 443	5 669 953	2 110 548	1 115 540	995 008
35 - 39	CDJC	12 261 529	5 955 875	6 305 654	10 326 271	4 929 130	5 397 141	1 935 258	1 026 745	908 513
40 - 44	CDJC	10 546 694	5 116 439	5 430 255	8 913 019	4 249 804	4 663 215	1 633 675	866 635	767 040
45 - 49	CDJC	8 721 541	4 216 418	4 505 123	7 309 621	3 472 375	3 837 246	1 411 920	744 043	667 877
50 - 54	CDJC	7 062 601	3 415 678	3 646 923	5 833 659	2 764 708	3 068 951	1 228 942	650 970	577 972
55 - 59	CDJC	5 444 715	2 585 244	2 859 471	4 387 995	2 032 135	2 355 860	1 056 720	553 109	503 611
60 - 64	CDJC	4 600 929	2 153 209	2 447 720	3 712 213	1 676 323	2 035 890	888 716	476 886	411 830
65 - 69	CDJC	3 581 106	1 639 325	1 941 781	2 916 899	1 284 812	1 632 087	664 207	354 513	309 694
70 - 74	CDJC	2 742 302	1 229 329	1 512 973	2 249 617	966 115	1 283 502	492 685	263 214	229 471
75 - 79	CDJC	1 779 587	780 571	999 016	1 456 665	610 767	845 898	322 922	169 804	153 118
80 - 84	CDJC	1 036 034	428 501	607 533	841 798	331 002	510 796	194 236	97 499	96 737
85 - 89	CDJC	534 871	208 088	326 783	436 121	160 379	275 742	98 750	47 709	51 041
90 - 94	CDJC	180 426	65 117	115 309	147 784	50 531	97 253	32 642	14 586	18 056
95 - 99	CDJC	56 198	19 221	36 977	45 682	14 899	30 783	10 516	4 322	6 194
100+	CDJC	24 576	10 423	14 153	19 050	7 882	11 168	5 526	2 541	2 985

7. Population by age, sex and urban/rural residence: latest available year, 1993 - 2002
Population selon l'âge, le sexe et la résidence, urbaine/rurale: dernière année disponible, 1993 - 2002
(continued — suite)

(See notes at end of table. — Voir notes à la fin du tableau.)

Continent, country or area, date and age (in years) / Continent, pays ou zone, date et âge (en années)	Code[1]	Total			Urban - Urbaine			Rural - Rurale		
		Both sexes Les deux sexes	Male Masculin	Female Féminin	Both sexes Les deux sexes	Male Masculin	Female Féminin	Both sexes Les deux sexes	Male Masculin	Female Féminin
AMERICA, SOUTH — AMERIQUE DU SUD										
Brazil - Brésil[10]										
1 VII 2002										
Total	ESDF	174 632 960	86 015 629	88 617 331	...	...	...	...	...	...
0 - 1	ESDF	3 340 323	1 704 422	1 635 901	...	...	...	...	...	...
1 - 4	ESDF	13 045 471	6 648 933	6 396 538	...	...	...	...	...	...
5 - 9	ESDF	16 081 473	8 193 394	7 888 079	...	...	...	...	...	...
10 - 14	ESDF	16 480 820	8 387 922	8 092 898	...	...	...	...	...	...
15 - 19	ESDF	17 220 881	8 723 183	8 497 698	...	...	...	...	...	...
20 - 24	ESDF	17 186 264	8 605 591	8 580 673	...	...	...	...	...	...
25 - 29	ESDF	15 250 118	7 525 474	7 724 644	...	...	...	...	...	...
30 - 34	ESDF	13 780 202	6 736 826	7 043 376	...	...	...	...	...	...
35 - 39	ESDF	13 175 677	6 405 278	6 770 399	...	...	...	...	...	...
40 - 44	ESDF	11 677 157	5 647 788	6 029 369	...	...	...	...	...	...
45 - 49	ESDF	9 708 152	4 683 401	5 024 751	...	...	...	...	...	...
50 - 54	ESDF	7 851 402	3 776 546	4 074 856	...	...	...	...	...	...
55 - 59	ESDF	5 965 408	2 844 829	3 120 579	...	...	...	...	...	...
60 - 64	ESDF	4 757 533	2 226 279	2 531 254	...	...	...	...	...	...
65 - 69	ESDF	3 631 037	1 650 929	1 980 108	...	...	...	...	...	...
70 - 74	ESDF	2 642 386	1 150 541	1 491 845	...	...	...	...	...	...
75 - 79	ESDF	1 650 775	675 394	975 381	...	...	...	...	...	...
80+	ESDF	1 187 881	428 899	758 982	...	...	...	...	...	...
Chile - Chili										
1 VII 2002										
Total	ESDF	15 589 147	7 719 986	7 869 161	13 409 844	6 548 696	6 861 148	2 179 303	1 171 290	1 008 013
0 - 1	ESDF	283 586	144 435	139 151	...	...	...	...	...	...
0 - 4	ESDF	...	...	...	1 218 495	619 863	598 632	207 872	106 365	101 507
1 - 4	ESDF	1 142 781	581 793	560 988	...	...	...	...	...	...
5 - 9	ESDF	1 450 763	738 300	712 463	1 244 398	631 543	612 855	206 365	106 757	99 608
10 - 14	ESDF	1 438 368	731 769	706 599	1 241 938	627 273	614 665	196 430	104 496	91 934
15 - 19	ESDF	1 335 806	678 910	656 896	1 160 752	582 813	577 939	175 054	96 097	78 957
20 - 24	ESDF	1 224 794	620 751	604 043	1 059 673	529 863	529 810	165 121	90 888	74 233
25 - 29	ESDF	1 197 860	604 016	593 844	1 035 012	513 759	521 253	162 848	90 257	72 591
30 - 34	ESDF	1 210 486	607 788	602 698	1 045 967	517 973	527 994	164 519	89 815	74 704
35 - 39	ESDF	1 208 093	603 395	604 698	1 045 661	516 003	529 658	162 432	87 392	75 040
40 - 44	ESDF	1 109 684	551 512	558 172	960 050	470 008	490 042	149 634	81 504	68 130
45 - 49	ESDF	931 098	460 110	470 988	802 723	389 676	413 047	128 375	70 434	57 941
50 - 54	ESDF	764 207	373 865	390 342	656 167	314 481	341 686	108 040	59 384	48 656
55 - 59	ESDF	633 555	304 812	328 743	542 582	254 750	287 832	90 973	50 062	40 911
60 - 64	ESDF	503 132	236 477	266 655	424 155	193 244	230 911	78 977	43 233	35 744
65 - 69	ESDF	401 346	181 766	219 580	338 531	147 882	190 649	62 815	33 884	28 931
70 - 74	ESDF	317 565	136 888	180 677	267 552	110 482	157 070	50 013	26 406	23 607
75 - 79	ESDF	221 430	88 995	132 435	185 450	70 614	114 836	35 980	18 381	17 599
80+	ESDF	214 593	74 404	140 189	180 738	58 469	122 269	33 855	15 935	17 920
Colombia - Colombie										
24 X 1993										
Total	CDFC	33 109 840	16 296 539	16 813 301	23 514 070	11 211 708	12 302 362	9 595 770	5 084 831	4 510 939
0 - 1	CDFC	655 167	335 257	319 910	428 832	218 599	210 233	226 335	116 658	109 677
1 - 4	CDFC	3 099 703	1 579 134	1 520 569	2 060 730	1 045 612	1 015 118	1 038 973	533 522	505 451
5 - 9	CDFC	3 816 670	1 943 375	1 873 295	2 533 072	1 280 393	1 252 679	1 283 598	662 982	620 616
10 - 14	CDFC	3 840 632	1 947 256	1 893 376	2 598 400	1 289 824	1 308 576	1 242 232	657 432	584 800
15 - 19	CDFC	3 301 436	1 614 187	1 687 249	2 316 196	1 077 176	1 239 020	985 240	537 011	448 229
20 - 24	CDFC	3 156 530	1 508 254	1 648 276	2 302 417	1 053 570	1 248 847	854 113	454 684	399 429
25 - 29	CDFC	2 977 533	1 420 298	1 557 235	2 242 535	1 032 450	1 210 085	734 998	387 848	347 150
30 - 34	CDFC	2 693 270	1 303 844	1 389 426	2 061 372	967 247	1 094 125	631 898	336 597	295 301
35 - 39	CDFC	2 219 750	1 060 353	1 159 397	1 666 555	769 837	896 718	553 195	290 516	262 679
40 - 44	CDFC	1 735 926	864 685	871 241	1 293 477	623 693	669 784	442 449	240 992	201 457
45 - 49	CDFC	1 323 815	650 119	673 696	959 787	456 546	503 241	364 028	193 573	170 455
50 - 54	CDFC	1 139 501	559 518	579 983	810 259	381 569	428 690	329 242	177 949	151 293

7. Population by age, sex and urban/rural residence: latest available year, 1993 - 2002
Population selon l'âge, le sexe et la résidence, urbaine/rurale: dernière année disponible, 1993 - 2002
(continued — suite)

(See notes at end of table. — Voir notes à la fin du tableau.)

Continent, country or area, date and age (in years) / Continent, pays ou zone, date et âge (en années)	Code[1]	Total			Urban - Urbaine			Rural - Rurale		
		Both sexes Les deux sexes	Male Masculin	Female Féminin	Both sexes Les deux sexes	Male Masculin	Female Féminin	Both sexes Les deux sexes	Male Masculin	Female Féminin
AMERICA, SOUTH — AMERIQUE DU SUD										
Colombia - Colombie										
24 X 1993										
55 - 59	CDFC	855 265	413 838	441 427	614 592	284 877	329 715	240 673	128 961	111 712
60 - 64	CDFC	798 234	388 860	409 374	560 005	257 531	302 474	238 229	131 329	106 900
65 - 69	CDFC	539 716	260 405	279 311	385 937	176 277	209 660	153 779	84 128	69 651
70 - 74	CDFC	417 485	201 401	216 084	292 756	131 927	160 829	124 729	69 474	55 255
75 - 79	CDFC	260 423	123 908	136 515	187 273	83 108	104 165	73 150	40 800	32 350
80 - 84	CDFC	161 961	73 107	88 854	115 289	48 381	66 908	46 672	24 726	21 946
85 - 89	CDFC	72 282	30 793	41 489	53 497	21 345	32 152	18 785	9 448	9 337
90+	CDFC	44 541	17 947	26 594	31 089	11 746	19 343	13 452	6 201	7 251
1 VII 2002										
Total	ESDF	43 834 119	21 666 433	22 167 686	...	...	...	...	...	...
0 - 1	ESDF	985 174	505 541	479 633	...	...	...	...	...	...
1 - 4	ESDF	3 804 989	1 939 715	1 865 274	...	...	...	...	...	...
5 - 9	ESDF	4 751 060	2 422 871	2 328 189	...	...	...	...	...	...
10 - 14	ESDF	4 517 872	2 300 530	2 217 342	...	...	...	...	...	...
15 - 19	ESDF	4 206 049	2 135 283	2 070 766	...	...	...	...	...	...
20 - 24	ESDF	4 006 790	2 018 553	1 988 237	...	...	...	...	...	...
25 - 29	ESDF	3 646 163	1 811 884	1 834 279	...	...	...	...	...	...
30 - 34	ESDF	3 486 025	1 708 054	1 777 971	...	...	...	...	...	...
35 - 39	ESDF	3 249 581	1 577 180	1 672 401	...	...	...	...	...	...
40 - 44	ESDF	2 745 467	1 319 731	1 425 736	...	...	...	...	...	...
45 - 49	ESDF	2 264 770	1 077 835	1 186 935	...	...	...	...	...	...
50 - 54	ESDF	1 782 883	845 592	937 291	...	...	...	...	...	...
55 - 59	ESDF	1 307 303	622 414	684 889	...	...	...	...	...	...
60 - 64	ESDF	972 211	457 952	514 259	...	...	...	...	...	...
65 - 69	ESDF	751 211	344 191	407 020	...	...	...	...	...	...
70 - 74	ESDF	565 516	251 949	313 567	...	...	...	...	...	...
75 - 79	ESDF	398 298	172 759	225 539	...	...	...	...	...	...
80+	ESDF	392 757	154 399	238 358	...	...	...	...	...	...
Ecuador - Équateur[11]										
25 XI 2001										
Total	CDFC	12 156 608	6 018 353	6 138 255	7 431 355	3 625 962	3 805 393	4 725 253	2 392 391	2 332 862
0 - 1	CDFC	237 209	120 000	117 209	132 634	67 302	65 332	104 575	52 698	51 877
1 - 4	CDFC	1 099 651	558 576	541 075	612 787	311 551	301 236	486 864	247 025	239 839
5 - 9	CDFC	1 362 121	689 123	672 998	771 344	389 609	381 735	590 777	299 514	291 263
10 - 14	CDFC	1 341 039	679 271	661 768	767 207	384 630	382 577	573 832	294 641	279 191
15 - 19	CDFC	1 240 531	617 087	623 444	754 865	368 673	386 192	485 666	248 414	237 252
20 - 24	CDFC	1 168 637	571 018	597 619	751 887	362 536	389 351	416 750	208 482	208 268
25 - 29	CDFC	947 395	457 309	490 086	619 497	295 689	323 808	327 898	161 620	166 278
30 - 34	CDFC	863 071	423 372	439 699	570 009	274 727	295 282	293 062	148 645	144 417
35 - 39	CDFC	774 543	374 505	400 038	513 318	243 762	269 556	261 225	130 743	130 482
40 - 44	CDFC	673 871	332 177	341 694	446 548	217 269	229 279	227 323	114 908	112 415
45 - 49	CDFC	538 983	264 970	274 013	349 836	169 592	180 244	189 147	95 378	93 769
50 - 54	CDFC	462 855	230 263	232 592	289 840	141 453	148 387	173 015	88 810	84 205
55 - 59	CDFC	339 411	168 060	171 351	205 081	99 313	105 768	134 330	68 747	65 583
60 - 64	CDFC	293 667	143 933	149 734	169 775	80 579	89 196	123 892	63 354	60 538
65 - 69	CDFC	244 031	117 495	126 536	141 921	65 770	76 151	102 110	51 725	50 385
70 - 74	CDFC	194 686	95 101	99 585	112 608	52 841	59 767	82 078	42 260	39 818
75 - 79	CDFC	142 949	69 055	73 894	82 944	38 340	44 604	60 005	30 715	29 290
80 - 84	CDFC	97 462	45 092	52 370	57 223	25 332	31 891	40 239	19 760	20 479
85 - 89	CDFC	63 167	28 985	34 182	38 910	17 333	21 577	24 257	11 652	12 605
90 - 94	CDFC	39 386	18 351	21 035	24 906	11 477	13 429	14 480	6 874	7 606
95+	CDFC	31 943	14 610	17 333	18 215	8 184	10 031	13 728	6 426	7 302

7. Population by age, sex and urban/rural residence: latest available year, 1993 - 2002
Population selon l'âge, le sexe et la résidence, urbaine/rurale: dernière année disponible, 1993 - 2002
(continued — suite)

(See notes at end of table. — Voir notes à la fin du tableau.)

Continent, country or area, date and age (in years) / Continent, pays ou zone, date et âge (en années)	Code[1]	Total			Urban - Urbaine			Rural - Rurale		
		Both sexes Les deux sexes	Male Masculin	Female Féminin	Both sexes Les deux sexes	Male Masculin	Female Féminin	Both sexes Les deux sexes	Male Masculin	Female Féminin
AMERICA, SOUTH — AMERIQUE DU SUD										
Falkland Islands (Malvinas) - Îles Falkland (Malvinas)										
8 IV 2001										
Total	CDFC	2 913	1 598	1 315	...	...	...	...	...	...
0 - 4	CDFC	137	70	67	...	...	...	...	...	...
5 - 9	CDFC	146	71	75	...	...	...	...	...	...
10 - 14	CDFC	155	87	68	...	...	...	...	...	...
15 - 19	CDFC	149	69	80	...	...	...	...	...	...
20 - 24	CDFC	223	111	112	...	...	...	...	...	...
25 - 29	CDFC	271	143	128	...	...	...	...	...	...
30 - 34	CDFC	292	173	119	...	...	...	...	...	...
35 - 39	CDFC	277	159	118	...	...	...	...	...	...
40 - 44	CDFC	250	124	126	...	...	...	...	...	...
45 - 49	CDFC	241	152	89	...	...	...	...	...	...
50 - 54	CDFC	233	139	94	...	...	...	...	...	...
55 - 59	CDFC	188	117	71	...	...	...	...	...	...
60 - 64	CDFC	110	68	42	...	...	...	...	...	...
65 - 69	CDFC	90	50	40	...	...	...	...	...	...
70 - 74	CDFC	64	26	38	...	...	...	...	...	...
75 - 79	CDFC	29	15	14	...	...	...	...	...	...
80+	CDFC	58	24	34	...	...	...	...	...	...
French Guiana - Guyane française										
8 III 1999										
Total	CDJC	156 790	78 963	77 827	...	...	...	...	...	...
0 - 1	CDJC	671	357	314	...	...	...	...	...	...
1 - 4	CDJC	16 739	8 537	8 202	...	...	...	...	...	...
5 - 9	CDJC	19 330	9 818	9 512	...	...	...	...	...	...
10 - 14	CDJC	16 533	8 410	8 123	...	...	...	...	...	...
15 - 19	CDJC	14 587	7 315	7 272	...	...	...	...	...	...
20 - 24	CDJC	10 862	5 667	5 195	...	...	...	...	...	...
25 - 29	CDJC	12 467	5 754	6 713	...	...	...	...	...	...
30 - 34	CDJC	13 130	6 384	6 746	...	...	...	...	...	...
35 - 39	CDJC	12 709	6 280	6 429	...	...	...	...	...	...
40 - 44	CDJC	10 736	5 433	5 303	...	...	...	...	...	...
45 - 49	CDJC	8 729	4 583	4 146	...	...	...	...	...	...
50 - 54	CDJC	6 557	3 517	3 040	...	...	...	...	...	...
55 - 59	CDJC	4 344	2 346	1 998	...	...	...	...	...	...
60 - 64	CDJC	2 971	1 529	1 442	...	...	...	...	...	...
65 - 69	CDJC	2 188	1 148	1 040	...	...	...	...	...	...
70 - 74	CDJC	1 597	783	814	...	...	...	...	...	...
75 - 79	CDJC	1 266	561	705	...	...	...	...	...	...
80 - 84	CDJC	726	301	425	...	...	...	...	...	...
85 - 89	CDJC	423	154	269	...	...	...	...	...	...
90 - 94	CDJC	152	53	99	...	...	...	...	...	...
95 - 99	CDJC	68	31	37	...	...	...	...	...	...
100+	CDJC	5	2	3	...	...	...	...	...	...
Paraguay										
1 VII 1994										
Total	ESDF	4 699 855	2 368 072	2 331 783	...	...	...	...	...	...
0 - 4	ESDF	715 014	364 150	350 864	...	...	...	...	...	...
5 - 9	ESDF	654 658	332 801	321 857	...	...	...	...	...	...
10 - 14	ESDF	586 281	297 813	288 468	...	...	...	...	...	...
15 - 19	ESDF	470 439	238 954	231 485	...	...	...	...	...	...
20 - 24	ESDF	411 468	208 846	202 622	...	...	...	...	...	...
25 - 29	ESDF	372 517	189 181	183 336	...	...	...	...	...	...
30 - 34	ESDF	329 185	166 900	162 285	...	...	...	...	...	...

7. Population by age, sex and urban/rural residence: latest available year, 1993 - 2002
Population selon l'âge, le sexe et la résidence, urbaine/rurale: dernière année disponible, 1993 - 2002
(continued — suite)

(See notes at end of table. — Voir notes à la fin du tableau.)

Continent, country or area, date and age (in years) / Continent, pays ou zone, date et âge (en années)	Code[1]	Total			Urban - Urbaine			Rural - Rurale		
		Both sexes Les deux sexes	Male Masculin	Female Féminin	Both sexes Les deux sexes	Male Masculin	Female Féminin	Both sexes Les deux sexes	Male Masculin	Female Féminin
AMERICA, SOUTH — AMERIQUE DU SUD										
Paraguay										
1 VII 1994										
35 - 39	ESDF	284 549	144 628	139 921	...	...	...	...	...	...
40 - 44	ESDF	246 627	126 630	119 997	...	...	...	...	...	...
45 - 49	ESDF	151 622	77 050	74 572	...	...	...	...	...	...
50 - 54	ESDF	128 128	64 973	63 155	...	...	...	...	...	...
55 - 59	ESDF	105 906	51 990	53 916	...	...	...	...	...	...
60 - 64	ESDF	76 980	34 849	42 131	...	...	...	...	...	...
65 - 69	ESDF	63 014	27 121	35 893	...	...	...	...	...	...
70 - 74	ESDF	45 379	19 310	26 069	...	...	...	...	...	...
75 - 79	ESDF	31 578	12 945	18 633	...	...	...	...	...	...
80+	ESDF	26 510	9 931	16 579	...	...	...	...	...	...
Peru - Pérou[12,13]										
1 VII 1998										
Total	ESDF	24 800 768	12 303 755	12 497 013	17 838 479	8 771 638	9 066 841	6 962 289	3 532 117	3 430 172
0 - 4	ESDF	2 900 190	1 476 026	1 424 164	1 855 712	945 850	909 862	1 044 478	530 176	514 302
5 - 9	ESDF	2 851 273	1 447 069	1 404 204	1 870 911	957 601	913 310	980 362	489 468	490 894
10 - 14	ESDF	2 781 819	1 409 773	1 372 046	1 904 255	966 710	937 545	877 564	443 063	434 501
15 - 19	ESDF	2 654 997	1 341 124	1 313 873	1 929 521	957 468	972 053	725 476	383 656	341 820
20 - 24	ESDF	2 446 999	1 225 205	1 221 794	1 865 335	917 815	947 520	581 664	307 390	274 274
25 - 29	ESDF	2 120 187	1 044 092	1 076 095	1 624 964	786 633	838 331	495 223	257 459	237 764
30 - 34	ESDF	1 830 822	888 261	942 561	1 411 958	673 764	738 194	418 864	214 497	204 367
35 - 39	ESDF	1 555 372	750 728	804 644	1 204 983	573 829	631 154	350 389	176 899	173 490
40 - 44	ESDF	1 289 468	624 829	664 639	999 183	480 094	519 089	290 285	144 735	145 550
45 - 49	ESDF	1 065 036	520 173	544 863	809 869	394 768	415 101	255 167	125 405	129 762
50 - 54	ESDF	858 806	420 725	438 081	634 806	311 616	323 190	224 000	109 109	114 891
55 - 59	ESDF	708 473	345 545	362 928	510 973	248 325	262 648	197 500	97 220	100 280
60 - 64	ESDF	580 760	284 358	304 402	415 491	198 352	217 139	173 269	86 006	87 263
65 - 69	ESDF	455 376	216 257	239 119	317 789	148 462	169 327	137 587	67 795	69 792
70 - 74	ESDF	319 388	147 990	171 398	222 130	100 692	121 438	97 258	47 298	49 960
75 - 79	ESDF	205 437	91 784	113 653	143 212	62 333	80 879	62 225	29 451	32 774
80+	ESDF	168 365	69 816	98 549	117 387	47 326	70 061	50 978	22 490	28 488
Suriname										
1 VII 2000										
Total	ESDF	435 797	218 677	217 120	...	...	...	...	...	...
0 - 4	ESDF	52 793	28 129	24 664	...	...	...	...	...	...
5 - 9	ESDF	44 683	23 928	20 755	...	...	...	...	...	...
10 - 14	ESDF	46 670	23 655	23 015	...	...	...	...	...	...
15 - 19	ESDF	46 248	22 544	23 704	...	...	...	...	...	...
20 - 24	ESDF	36 554	18 061	18 493	...	...	...	...	...	...
25 - 29	ESDF	33 413	16 508	16 905	...	...	...	...	...	...
30 - 34	ESDF	34 407	17 179	17 228	...	...	...	...	...	...
35 - 39	ESDF	32 015	16 568	15 447	...	...	...	...	...	...
40 - 44	ESDF	25 168	12 717	12 451	...	...	...	...	...	...
45 - 49	ESDF	19 825	9 247	10 578	...	...	...	...	...	...
50 - 54	ESDF	14 717	7 195	7 522	...	...	...	...	...	...
55 - 59	ESDF	12 436	5 511	6 925	...	...	...	...	...	...
60 - 64	ESDF	11 833	5 597	6 236	...	...	...	...	...	...
65 - 69	ESDF	10 669	5 056	5 613	...	...	...	...	...	...
70 - 74	ESDF	6 856	3 512	3 344	...	...	...	...	...	...
75 - 79	ESDF	4 165	1 843	2 322	...	...	...	...	...	...
80+	ESDF	3 345	1 427	1 918	...	...	...	...	...	...
Uruguay[13]										
1 VII 1999										
Total	ESDF	3 313 239	1 607 086	1 706 153	3 061 753	1 462 266	1 599 487	251 486	144 820	106 666
0 - 1	ESDF	56 956	29 095	27 861	52 963	27 056	25 907	3 993	2 039	1 954
1 - 4	ESDF	226 007	115 402	110 605	210 400	107 404	102 996	15 607	7 998	7 609
5 - 9	ESDF	276 500	141 239	135 261	257 983	131 787	126 196	18 517	9 452	9 065

7. Population by age, sex and urban/rural residence: latest available year, 1993 - 2002
Population selon l'âge, le sexe et la résidence, urbaine/rurale: dernière année disponible, 1993 - 2002
(continued — suite)

(See notes at end of table. — Voir notes à la fin du tableau.)

Continent, country or area, date and age (in years) Continent, pays ou zone, date et âge (en années)	Code[1]	Total			Urban - Urbaine			Rural - Rurale		
		Both sexes Les deux sexes	Male Masculin	Female Féminin	Both sexes Les deux sexes	Male Masculin	Female Féminin	Both sexes Les deux sexes	Male Masculin	Female Féminin
AMERICA, SOUTH — AMERIQUE DU SUD										
Uruguay[13]										
1 VII 1999										
10 - 14	ESDF	263 801	134 681	129 120	247 283	126 411	120 872	16 518	8 270	8 248
15 - 19	ESDF	257 829	131 364	126 465	241 024	122 444	118 580	16 805	8 920	7 885
20 - 24	ESDF	271 052	137 674	133 378	252 456	127 267	125 189	18 596	10 407	8 189
25 - 29	ESDF	247 250	125 054	122 196	229 771	114 406	115 365	17 479	10 648	6 831
30 - 34	ESDF	220 167	108 945	111 222	202 243	97 529	104 714	17 924	11 416	6 508
35 - 39	ESDF	218 260	106 409	111 851	201 856	96 634	105 222	16 404	9 775	6 629
40 - 44	ESDF	204 154	98 972	105 182	188 080	89 678	98 402	16 074	9 294	6 780
45 - 49	ESDF	182 137	88 501	93 636	166 094	79 074	87 020	16 043	9 427	6 616
50 - 54	ESDF	167 953	80 210	87 743	152 457	70 693	81 764	15 496	9 517	5 979
55 - 59	ESDF	153 608	72 387	81 221	139 810	63 743	76 067	13 798	8 644	5 154
60 - 64	ESDF	143 348	65 280	78 068	129 800	56 911	72 889	13 548	8 369	5 179
65 - 69	ESDF	137 944	61 510	76 434	125 241	53 486	71 755	12 703	8 024	4 679
70 - 74	ESDF	116 782	48 926	67 856	106 718	42 798	63 920	10 064	6 128	3 936
75 - 79	ESDF	83 309	32 483	50 826	76 788	28 698	48 090	6 521	3 785	2 736
80 - 84	ESDF	50 131	17 370	32 761	46 642	15 530	31 112	3 489	1 840	1 649
85+	ESDF	36 051	11 584	24 467	34 144	10 717	23 427	1 907	867	1 040
1 VII 2000										
Total	ESDF	3 322 141	1 609 199	1 712 942	...	...	...	...	...	...
0 - 1	ESDF	53 272	27 097	26 175	...	...	...	...	...	...
1 - 4	ESDF	223 611	113 764	109 847	...	...	...	...	...	...
5 - 9	ESDF	275 757	140 838	134 919	...	...	...	...	...	...
10 - 14	ESDF	270 998	137 785	133 213	...	...	...	...	...	...
15 - 19	ESDF	268 367	136 320	132 047	...	...	...	...	...	...
20 - 24	ESDF	252 458	127 174	125 284	...	...	...	...	...	...
25 - 29	ESDF	234 190	116 913	117 277	...	...	...	...	...	...
30 - 34	ESDF	226 990	112 334	114 656	...	...	...	...	...	...
35 - 39	ESDF	221 452	108 460	112 992	...	...	...	...	...	...
40 - 44	ESDF	205 578	100 259	105 319	...	...	...	...	...	...
45 - 49	ESDF	187 016	90 841	·96 175	...	...	...	...	...	...
50 - 54	ESDF	170 437	82 045	88 392	...	...	...	...	...	...
55 - 59	ESDF	152 548	72 515	80 033	...	...	...	...	...	...
60 - 64	ESDF	142 474	65 916	76 558	...	...	...	...	...	...
65 - 69	ESDF	134 895	60 173	74 722	...	...	...	...	...	...
70 - 74	ESDF	118 796	50 345	68 451	...	...	...	...	...	...
75 - 79	ESDF	84 643	33 635	51 008	...	...	...	...	...	...
80 - 84	ESDF	53 923	19 262	34 661	...	...	...	...	...	...
85 - 89	ESDF	29 259	9 192	20 067	...	...	...	...	...	...
90 - 94	ESDF	11 600	3 350	8 250	...	...	...	...	...	...
95+	ESDF	3 877	981	2 896	...	...	...	...	...	...
Venezuela[12]										
1 VII 2002										
Total	ESDF	25 219 910	12 678 275	12 541 635	22 163 339	11 021 146	11 142 193	3 056 571	1 657 129	1 399 442
0 - 1	ESDF	566 727	289 817	276 910	...	...	...	...	...	...
0 - 4	ESDF	...	...	...	2 365 585	1 212 601	1 152 984	431 255	216 828	214 427
1 - 4	ESDF	2 230 113	1 139 612	1 090 501	...	...	...	393 101	199 166	193 935
5 - 9	ESDF	2 731 128	1 394 224	1 336 904	2 338 027	1 195 058	1 142 969	357 133	185 976	171 157
10 - 14	ESDF	2 712 386	1 383 578	1 328 808	2 355 253	1 197 602	1 157 651	309 510	170 734	138 776
15 - 19	ESDF	2 568 391	1 306 597	1 261 794	2 258 881	1 135 863	1 123 018	261 795	146 592	115 203
20 - 24	ESDF	2 336 801	1 182 579	1 154 222	2 075 006	1 035 987	1 039 019	227 707	126 461	101 246
25 - 29	ESDF	2 055 341	1 034 449	1 020 892	1 827 634	907 988	919 646	195 961	109 069	86 892
30 - 34	ESDF	1 871 230	938 046	933 184	1 675 269	828 977	846 292	177 044	99 812	77 232
35 - 39	ESDF	1 744 170	872 099	872 071	1 567 126	772 287	794 839	148 161	84 520	63 641
40 - 44	ESDF	1 506 179	751 648	754 531	1 358 018	667 128	690 890	124 614	71 306	53 308
45 - 49	ESDF	1 266 420	631 252	635 168	1 141 806	559 946	581 860	109 479	62 717	46 762
50 - 54	ESDF	1 044 891	520 661	524 230	935 412	457 944	477 468	91 945	53 302	38 643
55 - 59	ESDF	800 903	396 302	404 601	708 958	343 000	365 958			

7. Population by age, sex and urban/rural residence: latest available year, 1993 - 2002
Population selon l'âge, le sexe et la résidence, urbaine/rurale: dernière année disponible, 1993 - 2002
(continued — suite)

(See notes at end of table. — Voir notes à la fin du tableau.)

Continent, country or area, date and age (in years) / Continent, pays ou zone, date et âge (en années)	Code[1]	Total			Urban - Urbaine			Rural - Rurale		
		Both sexes Les deux sexes	Male Masculin	Female Féminin	Both sexes Les deux sexes	Male Masculin	Female Féminin	Both sexes Les deux sexes	Male Masculin	Female Féminin
AMERICA, SOUTH — AMERIQUE DU SUD										
Venezuela[12]										
1 VII 2002										
60 - 64	ESDF	590 879	287 629	303 250	516 207	244 396	271 811	74 672	43 233	31 439
65 - 69	ESDF	450 395	214 998	235 397	391 277	180 798	210 479	59 118	34 200	24 918
70 - 74	ESDF	344 553	160 308	184 245	299 965	135 041	164 924	44 588	25 267	19 321
75 - 79	ESDF	232 921	104 448	128 473	203 220	87 769	115 451	29 701	16 679	13 022
80+	ESDF	166 482	70 028	96 454	145 695	58 761	86 934	20 787	11 267	9 520
ASIA — ASIE										
Armenia - Arménie										
1 VII 2000										
Total	ESDF	3 802 883	1 848 756	1 954 127	2 534 024	1 212 033	1 321 991	1 268 859	636 723	632 136
0 - 1	ESDF	34 891	18 906	15 985	21 590	11 614	9 976	13 301	7 292	6 009
1 - 4	ESDF	169 569	90 611	78 958	104 205	55 097	49 108	65 364	35 514	29 850
5 - 9	ESDF	312 705	161 455	151 250	188 935	97 424	91 511	123 770	64 031	59 739
10 - 14	ESDF	379 750	194 643	185 107	241 824	123 850	117 974	137 926	70 793	67 133
15 - 19	ESDF	369 535	188 966	180 569	247 129	126 344	120 785	122 406	62 622	59 784
20 - 24	ESDF	321 344	164 463	156 881	222 694	113 608	109 086	98 650	50 855	47 795
25 - 29	ESDF	286 588	145 710	140 878	191 905	97 913	93 992	94 683	47 797	46 886
30 - 34	ESDF	276 202	136 057	140 145	176 690	83 992	92 698	99 512	52 065	47 447
35 - 39	ESDF	316 118	149 145	166 973	205 547	92 740	112 807	110 571	56 405	54 166
40 - 44	ESDF	317 256	148 299	168 957	221 801	98 689	123 112	95 455	49 610	45 845
45 - 49	ESDF	235 188	108 547	126 641	172 439	76 613	95 826	62 749	31 934	30 815
50 - 54	ESDF	157 083	71 439	85 644	118 721	53 337	65 384	38 362	18 102	20 260
55 - 59	ESDF	107 984	48 437	59 547	78 600	35 358	43 242	29 384	13 079	16 305
60 - 64	ESDF	172 088	77 132	94 956	116 202	51 505	64 097	55 886	25 627	30 259
65 - 69	ESDF	128 212	57 050	71 162	80 146	34 801	45 345	48 066	22 249	25 817
70 - 74	ESDF	119 367	51 915	67 452	75 990	33 282	42 708	43 377	18 633	24 744
75 - 79	ESDF	51 263	18 907	32 356	35 135	13 333	21 802	16 128	5 574	10 554
80 - 84	ESDF	23 824	7 828	15 996	17 343	5 862	11 481	6 481	1 966	4 515
85+	ESDF	23 916	9 246	14 670	17 128	6 671	10 457	6 788	2 575	4 213
Azerbaijan - Azerbaïdjan										
1 I 2002										
Total	ESDF	8 141 400	3 988 800	...	4 130 100	2 013 400	...	4 011 300	1 975 400	...
0 - 1	ESDF	110 400	59 500	...	49 700	27 000	...	60 700	32 500	...
1 - 4	ESDF	463 600	246 200	...	199 400	107 100	...	264 200	139 100	...
5 - 9	ESDF	824 500	426 600	...	378 400	197 300	...	446 100	229 300	...
10 - 14	ESDF	931 000	477 100	...	462 900	237 600	...	468 100	239 500	...
15 - 19	ESDF	848 200	432 800	...	434 100	221 600	...	414 100	211 200	...
20 - 24	ESDF	703 000	348 500	...	361 400	179 300	...	341 600	169 200	...
25 - 29	ESDF	619 300	294 900	...	304 600	140 200	...	314 700	154 700	...
30 - 34	ESDF	650 200	307 400	...	319 600	146 600	...	330 600	160 800	...
35 - 39	ESDF	691 500	326 700	...	359 800	166 500	...	331 700	160 200	...
40 - 44	ESDF	652 800	316 600	...	361 900	175 700	...	290 900	140 900	...
45 - 49	ESDF	434 400	210 200	...	254 300	123 500	...	180 100	86 700	...
50 - 54	ESDF	293 800	142 200	...	177 800	87 000	...	116 000	55 200	...
55 - 59	ESDF	148 600	69 400	...	89 300	42 000	...	59 300	27 400	...
60 - 64	ESDF	258 900	117 500	...	135 200	62 100	...	123 700	55 400	...
65 - 69	ESDF	228 500	102 500	...	107 000	47 600	...	121 500	54 900	...
70 - 74	ESDF	151 400	66 900	...	72 300	31 000	...	79 100	35 900	...
75 - 79	ESDF	72 900	27 800	...	37 300	13 800	...	35 600	14 000	...
80 - 84	ESDF	30 500	9 100	...	14 200	4 500	...	16 300	4 600	...
85 - 89	ESDF	15 100	4 100	...	6 600	1 900	...	8 500	2 200	...
90 - 94	ESDF	7 300	1 700	...	2 600	700	...	4 700	1 000	...
95 - 99	ESDF	3 500	700	...	1 200	300	...	2 300	400	...
100+	ESDF	2 000	400	...	500	100	...	1 500	300	...

7. Population by age, sex and urban/rural residence: latest available year, 1993 - 2002
Population selon l'âge, le sexe et la résidence, urbaine/rurale: dernière année disponible, 1993 - 2002
(continued — suite)

(See notes at end of table. — Voir notes à la fin du tableau.)

Continent, country or area, date and age (in years) / Continent, pays ou zone, date et âge (en années)	Code[1]	Total			Urban - Urbaine			Rural - Rurale		
		Both sexes Les deux sexes	Male Masculin	Female Féminin	Both sexes Les deux sexes	Male Masculin	Female Féminin	Both sexes Les deux sexes	Male Masculin	Female Féminin
ASIA — ASIE										
Azerbaijan - Azerbaïdjan										
1 VII 2002										
Total	ESDF	8 172 000	4 005 900	4 166 100	4 142 200	2 020 200	2 122 000	4 029 800	1 985 700	2 044 100
0 - 1	ESDF	110 600	59 600	51 000	49 700	27 000	22 700	60 900	32 600	28 300
1 - 4	ESDF	455 700	242 700	213 000	196 500	105 700	90 800	259 200	137 000	122 200
5 - 9	ESDF	795 700	412 600	383 100	362 800	189 600	173 200	432 900	223 000	209 900
10 - 14	ESDF	930 100	476 900	453 200	459 800	236 200	223 600	470 300	240 700	229 600
15 - 19	ESDF	861 200	439 600	421 600	439 800	224 800	215 000	421 400	214 800	206 600
20 - 24	ESDF	715 700	356 200	359 500	368 700	183 500	185 200	347 000	172 700	174 300
25 - 29	ESDF	621 800	297 200	324 600	306 700	142 400	164 300	315 100	154 800	160 300
30 - 34	ESDF	647 800	306 100	341 700	318 200	145 600	172 600	329 600	160 500	169 100
35 - 39	ESDF	684 500	323 200	361 300	352 900	162 900	190 000	331 600	160 300	171 300
40 - 44	ESDF	665 700	321 800	343 900	367 500	177 600	189 900	298 200	144 200	154 000
45 - 49	ESDF	451 700	218 800	232 900	263 000	127 700	135 300	188 700	91 100	97 600
50 - 54	ESDF	306 200	147 900	158 300	184 900	90 300	94 600	121 300	57 600	63 700
55 - 59	ESDF	153 600	72 200	81 400	93 100	44 100	49 000	60 500	28 100	32 400
60 - 64	ESDF	247 400	112 000	135 400	130 200	59 600	70 600	117 200	52 400	64 800
65 - 69	ESDF	231 300	103 600	127 700	109 400	48 800	60 600	121 900	54 800	67 100
70 - 74	ESDF	158 300	69 800	88 500	74 800	32 000	42 800	83 500	37 800	45 700
75 - 79	ESDF	75 400	29 100	46 300	38 500	14 500	24 000	36 900	14 600	22 300
80 - 84	ESDF	32 100	9 800	22 300	15 000	4 800	10 200	17 100	5 000	12 100
85 - 89	ESDF	14 300	3 900	10 400	6 300	1 800	4 500	8 000	2 100	5 900
90 - 94	ESDF	7 700	1 800	5 900	2 800	800	2 000	4 900	1 000	3 900
95 - 99	ESDF	3 200	700	2 500	1 100	300	800	2 100	400	1 700
100+	ESDF	2 000	400	1 600	500	200	300	1 500	200	1 300
Bahrain - Bahreïn										
1 VII 2002										
Total	ESDF	672 123	386 220	285 903	...	...	...	...	...	...
0 - 4	ESDF	62 302	31 937	30 365	...	...	...	...	...	...
5 - 9	ESDF	64 116	32 463	31 652	...	...	...	...	...	...
10 - 14	ESDF	60 686	31 269	29 418	...	...	...	...	...	...
15 - 19	ESDF	52 588	27 156	25 433	...	...	...	...	...	...
20 - 24	ESDF	60 602	33 230	27 373	...	...	...	...	...	...
25 - 29	ESDF	71 767	44 331	27 436	...	...	...	...	...	...
30 - 34	ESDF	74 804	46 350	28 453	...	...	...	...	...	...
35 - 39	ESDF	67 664	41 323	26 342	...	...	...	...	...	...
40 - 44	ESDF	57 158	36 684	20 474	...	...	...	...	...	...
45 - 49	ESDF	39 065	25 884	13 181	...	...	...	...	...	...
50 - 54	ESDF	22 046	14 577	7 469	...	...	...	...	...	...
55 - 59	ESDF	12 655	7 375	5 280	...	...	...	...	...	...
60 - 64	ESDF	9 800	5 095	4 705	...	...	...	...	...	...
65 - 69	ESDF	6 600	3 252	3 348	...	...	...	...	...	...
70 - 74	ESDF	5 030	2 574	2 456	...	...	...	...	...	...
75 - 79	ESDF	2 746	1 419	1 326	...	...	...	...	...	...
80 - 84	ESDF	1 521	819	702	...	...	...	...	...	...
85 - 89	ESDF	616	311	305	...	...	...	...	...	...
90+	ESDF	356	171	184	...	...	...	...	...	...
Bhutan - Bhoutan										
31 XII 2001										
Total	ESDF	698 949	352 935	346 014	...	...	...	...	...	...
0 - 4	ESDF	107 990	54 115	53 875	...	...	...	...	...	...
5 - 9	ESDF	101 236	50 268	50 968	...	...	...	...	...	...
10 - 14	ESDF	84 687	42 889	41 798	...	...	...	...	...	...
15 - 19	ESDF	62 845	31 877	30 968	...	...	...	...	...	...
20 - 24	ESDF	55 493	27 570	27 923	...	...	...	...	...	...
25 - 29	ESDF	47 633	23 827	23 806	...	...	...	...	...	...
30 - 34	ESDF	42 745	21 569	21 176	...	...	...	...	...	...
35 - 39	ESDF	39 156	20 229	18 927	...	...	...	...	...	...

7. Population by age, sex and urban/rural residence: latest available year, 1993 - 2002
Population selon l'âge, le sexe et la résidence, urbaine/rurale: dernière année disponible, 1993 - 2002
(continued — suite)

(See notes at end of table. — Voir notes à la fin du tableau.)

Continent, country or area, date and age (in years) / Continent, pays ou zone, date et âge (en années)	Code[1]	Total			Urban - Urbaine			Rural - Rurale		
		Both sexes Les deux sexes	Male Masculin	Female Féminin	Both sexes Les deux sexes	Male Masculin	Female Féminin	Both sexes Les deux sexes	Male Masculin	Female Féminin
ASIA — ASIE										
Bhutan - Bhoutan										
31 XII 2001										
40 - 44	ESDF	33 001	17 015	15 986	...	...	...	...	...	...
45 - 49	ESDF	26 534	13 766	12 768	...	...	...	...	...	...
50 - 54	ESDF	25 170	12 955	12 215	...	...	...	...	...	...
55 - 59	ESDF	22 270	11 509	10 761	...	...	...	...	...	...
60 - 64	ESDF	20 451	10 555	9 896	...	...	...	...	...	...
65 - 69	ESDF	12 335	6 072	6 263	...	...	...	...	...	...
70 - 74	ESDF	8 388	4 201	4 187	...	...	...	...	...	...
75+	ESDF	9 015	4 518	4 497	...	...	...	...	...	...
Brunei Darussalam - Brunéi Darussalam										
21 VIII 2001										
Total	CDFC	332 844	168 974	163 870	238 699	120 046	118 653	94 145	48 928	45 217
0 - 14	CDFC	100 912	52 304	48 608	72 076	37 396	34 680	28 836	14 908	13 928
15 - 19	CDFC	27 963	14 014	13 949	20 019	10 085	9 934	7 944	3 929	4 015
20 - 24	CDFC	32 604	15 390	17 214	23 592	10 885	12 707	9 012	4 505	4 507
25 - 29	CDFC	35 773	17 884	17 889	25 856	12 573	13 283	9 917	5 311	4 606
30 - 34	CDFC	34 375	16 878	17 497	24 973	11 931	13 042	9 402	4 947	4 455
35 - 39	CDFC	28 764	14 581	14 183	21 112	10 461	10 651	7 652	4 120	3 532
40 - 44	CDFC	24 198	12 984	11 214	17 808	9 544	8 264	6 390	3 440	2 950
45 - 49	CDFC	17 149	9 150	7 999	12 402	6 637	5 765	4 747	2 513	2 234
50 - 54	CDFC	10 687	5 542	5 145	7 609	4 013	3 596	3 078	1 529	1 549
55 - 59	CDFC	6 140	3 249	2 891	4 153	2 197	1 956	1 987	1 052	935
60 - 64	CDFC	4 962	2 432	2 530	3 217	1 544	1 673	1 745	888	857
65 - 69	CDFC	3 757	1 768	1 989	2 366	1 102	1 264	1 391	666	725
70 - 74	CDFC	2 441	1 263	1 178	1 530	758	772	911	505	406
75 - 79	CDFC	1 582	793	789	1 027	492	535	555	301	254
80 - 84	CDFC	844	423	421	549	264	284	295	159	137
85 - 89	CDFC	397	188	209	252	98	154	145	90	55
90 - 94	CDFC	197	86	111	111	47	64	86	39	47
95 - 99	CDFC	66	33	33	33	14	19	33	19	14
100+	CDFC	33	12	21	15	5	10	18	7	11
Cambodia - Cambodge[14]										
3 III 1998										
Total	CDFC	11 437 656	5 511 408	5 926 248	1 795 575	878 186	917 389	9 642 081	4 633 222	5 008 859
0 - 1	CDFC	231 609	118 075	113 534	32 869	16 851	16 018	198 740	101 224	97 516
1 - 4	CDFC	1 235 183	629 217	605 966	160 680	82 377	78 303	1 074 503	546 840	527 663
5 - 9	CDFC	1 772 820	903 976	868 844	239 934	122 652	117 282	1 532 886	781 324	751 562
10 - 14	CDFC	1 658 196	851 139	807 057	246 998	126 217	120 781	1 411 198	724 922	686 276
15 - 19	CDFC	1 344 258	664 184	680 074	233 677	113 229	120 448	1 110 581	550 955	559 626
20 - 24	CDFC	745 687	354 100	391 587	128 884	63 561	65 323	616 803	290 539	326 264
25 - 29	CDFC	888 540	426 968	461 572	157 736	79 241	78 495	730 804	347 727	383 077
30 - 34	CDFC	782 682	370 090	412 592	137 139	69 093	68 046	645 543	300 997	344 546
35 - 39	CDFC	695 868	325 331	370 537	123 310	61 255	62 055	572 558	264 076	308 482
40 - 44	CDFC	497 067	199 722	297 345	92 433	40 499	51 934	404 634	159 223	245 411
45 - 49	CDFC	415 931	175 052	240 879	72 681	32 868	39 813	343 250	142 184	201 066
50 - 54	CDFC	312 463	132 413	180 050	50 505	22 227	28 278	261 958	110 186	151 772
55 - 59	CDFC	256 930	110 189	146 741	37 186	16 284	20 902	219 744	93 905	125 839
60 - 64	CDFC	204 994	86 602	118 392	28 433	11 627	16 806	176 561	74 975	101 586
65 - 69	CDFC	166 928	70 660	96 268	21 891	8 614	13 277	145 037	62 046	82 991
70 - 74	CDFC	112 213	46 769	65 444	14 851	5 535	9 316	97 362	41 234	56 128
75 - 79	CDFC	67 528	27 838	39 690	9 135	3 337	5 798	58 393	24 501	33 892
80 - 84	CDFC	30 652	12 159	18 493	4 288	1 515	2 773	26 364	10 644	15 720
85 - 89	CDFC	13 368	5 029	8 339	1 874	592	1 282	11 494	4 437	7 057
90 - 94	CDFC	2 867	1 026	1 841	453	157	296	2 414	869	1 545
95+	CDFC	1 872	869	1 003	618	455	163	1 254	414	840

7. Population by age, sex and urban/rural residence: latest available year, 1993 - 2002
Population selon l'âge, le sexe et la résidence, urbaine/rurale: dernière année disponible, 1993 - 2002
(continued — suite)

(See notes at end of table. — Voir notes à la fin du tableau.)

Continent, country or area, date and age (in years) / Continent, pays ou zone, date et âge (en années)	Code[1]	Total			Urban - Urbaine			Rural - Rurale		
		Both sexes Les deux sexes	Male Masculin	Female Féminin	Both sexes Les deux sexes	Male Masculin	Female Féminin	Both sexes Les deux sexes	Male Masculin	Female Féminin
ASIA — ASIE										
Cambodia - Cambodge[14]										
1 VII 2002										
Total	ESDF	13 473 352	6 540 309	6 933 010	...	...	...	...	...	...
0 - 4	ESDF	2 048 656	1 041 688	1 006 960	...	...	...	...	...	...
5 - 9	ESDF	1 860 083	943 041	917 043	...	...	...	...	...	...
10 - 14	ESDF	1 785 418	911 770	873 648	...	...	...	...	...	...
15 - 19	ESDF	1 642 844	838 947	803 896	...	...	...	...	...	...
20 - 24	ESDF	1 240 574	606 424	634 150	...	...	...	...	...	...
25 - 29	ESDF	729 709	344 711	384 997	...	...	...	...	...	...
30 - 34	ESDF	901 429	431 940	469 488	...	...	...	...	...	...
35 - 39	ESDF	767 668	361 749	405 919	...	...	...	...	...	...
40 - 44	ESDF	662 908	303 630	359 276	...	...	...	...	...	...
45 - 49	ESDF	469 834	185 373	284 459	...	...	...	...	...	...
50 - 54	ESDF	392 334	165 488	226 844	...	...	...	...	...	...
55 - 59	ESDF	289 564	121 856	167 705	...	...	...	...	...	...
60 - 64	ESDF	234 357	99 351	135 003	...	...	...	...	...	...
65 - 69	ESDF	178 601	74 186	104 411	...	...	...	...	...	...
70 - 74	ESDF	135 424	56 570	78 848	...	...	...	...	...	...
75+	ESDF	133 949	53 585	80 363	...	...	...	...	...	...
China - Chine[15]										
1 XI 2000										
Total	CDJC	1242612226	640 275 969	602 336 257	458 770 983	235 264 707	223 506 276	783 841 243	405 011 262	378 829 981
0 - 1	CDJC	13 793 799	7 460 206	6 333 593	4 449 020	2 376 585	2 072 435	9 344 779	5 083 621	4 261 158
1 - 4	CDJC	55 184 575	30 188 488	24 996 087	17 669 697	9 525 854	8 143 843	37 514 878	20 662 634	16 852 244
5 - 9	CDJC	90 152 587	48 303 208	41 849 379	26 588 363	14 180 433	12 407 930	63 564 224	34 122 775	29 441 449
10 - 14	CDJC	125 396 633	65 344 739	60 051 894	35 802 884	18 701 307	17 101 577	89 593 749	46 643 432	42 950 317
15 - 19	CDJC	103 031 165	52 878 170	50 152 995	42 231 585	21 086 911	21 144 674	60 799 580	31 791 259	29 008 321
20 - 24	CDJC	94 573 174	47 937 766	46 635 408	41 021 887	20 651 361	20 370 526	53 551 287	27 286 405	26 264 882
25 - 29	CDJC	117 602 265	60 230 758	57 371 507	48 788 516	24 820 721	23 967 795	68 813 749	35 410 037	33 403 712
30 - 34	CDJC	127 314 298	65 360 456	61 953 842	49 723 640	25 760 568	23 963 072	77 590 658	39 599 888	37 990 770
35 - 39	CDJC	109 147 295	56 141 391	53 005 904	44 518 164	23 269 889	21 248 275	64 629 131	32 871 502	31 757 629
40 - 44	CDJC	81 242 945	42 243 187	38 999 758	33 518 610	17 499 183	16 019 427	47 724 335	24 744 004	22 980 331
45 - 49	CDJC	85 521 045	43 939 603	41 581 442	31 708 706	16 245 324	15 463 382	53 812 339	27 694 279	26 118 060
50 - 54	CDJC	63 304 200	32 804 125	30 500 075	22 335 748	11 462 314	10 873 434	40 968 452	21 341 811	19 626 641
55 - 59	CDJC	46 370 375	24 061 506	22 308 869	16 004 389	8 077 159	7 927 230	30 365 986	15 984 347	14 381 639
60 - 64	CDJC	41 703 848	21 674 478	20 029 370	14 944 552	7 519 377	7 425 175	26 759 296	14 155 101	12 604 195
65 - 69	CDJC	34 780 460	17 549 348	17 231 112	12 174 470	6 128 605	6 045 865	22 605 990	11 420 743	11 185 247
70 - 74	CDJC	25 574 149	12 436 154	13 137 995	8 479 487	4 216 193	4 263 294	17 094 662	8 219 961	8 874 701
75 - 79	CDJC	15 928 330	7 175 811	8 752 519	5 000 134	2 291 543	2 708 591	10 928 196	4 884 268	6 043 928
80 - 84	CDJC	7 989 158	3 203 868	4 785 290	2 472 016	1 004 359	1 467 657	5 517 142	2 199 509	3 317 633
85 - 89	CDJC	3 030 698	1 056 941	1 973 757	994 079	347 550	646 529	2 036 619	709 391	1 327 228
90 - 94	CDJC	783 594	229 758	553 836	276 586	80 189	196 397	507 008	149 569	357 439
95 - 99	CDJC	169 756	51 373	118 383	62 255	17 827	44 428	107 501	33 546	73 955
100+	CDJC	17 877	4 635	13 242	6 195	1 455	4 740	11 682	3 180	8 502
China: Hong Kong SAR - Chine: Hong Kong RAS										
1 VII 2002										
Total	ESDJ	6 787 000	3 299 900	3 487 100	...	...	...	...	...	...
0 - 1	ESDJ	47 500	24 500	23 000	...	...	...	...	...	...
1 - 4	ESDJ	220 100	114 100	106 000	...	...	...	...	...	...
5 - 9	ESDJ	392 300	202 800	189 500	...	...	...	...	...	...
10 - 14	ESDJ	434 500	223 700	210 800	...	...	...	...	...	...
15 - 19	ESDJ	440 200	226 600	213 600	...	...	...	...	...	...
20 - 24	ESDJ	449 800	222 800	227 000	...	...	...	...	...	...
25 - 29	ESDJ	511 500	236 800	274 700	...	...	...	...	...	...
30 - 34	ESDJ	588 400	253 700	334 700	...	...	...	...	...	...
35 - 39	ESDJ	675 100	302 200	372 900	...	...	...	...	...	...

7. Population by age, sex and urban/rural residence: latest available year, 1993 - 2002
Population selon l'âge, le sexe et la résidence, urbaine/rurale: dernière année disponible, 1993 - 2002
(continued — suite)

(See notes at end of table. — Voir notes à la fin du tableau.)

Continent, country or area, date and age (in years) Continent, pays ou zone, date et âge (en années)	Code[1]	Total			Urban - Urbaine			Rural - Rurale		
		Both sexes Les deux sexes	Male Masculin	Female Féminin	Both sexes Les deux sexes	Male Masculin	Female Féminin	Both sexes Les deux sexes	Male Masculin	Female Féminin
ASIA — ASIE										
China: Hong Kong SAR - Chine: Hong Kong RAS										
1 VII 2002										
40 - 44	ESDJ	693 400	337 100	356 300	...	...	...	...	...	...
45 - 49	ESDJ	572 000	283 300	288 700	...	...	...	...	...	...
50 - 54	ESDJ	460 500	235 000	225 500	...	...	...	...	...	...
55 - 59	ESDJ	283 400	149 600	133 800	...	...	...	...	...	...
60 - 64	ESDJ	241 300	128 700	112 600	...	...	...	...	...	...
65 - 69	ESDJ	251 700	128 800	122 900	...	...	...	...	...	...
70 - 74	ESDJ	215 700	105 300	110 400	...	...	...	...	...	...
75 - 79	ESDJ	151 200	67 300	83 900	...	...	...	...	...	...
80 - 84	ESDJ	91 100	36 500	54 600	...	...	...	...	...	...
85+	ESDJ	67 300	21 100	46 200	...	...	...	...	...	...
China: Macao SAR - Chine: Macao RAS										
1 VII 2002										
Total	ESDJ	439 162	210 642	228 520	...	...	...	...	...	...
0 - 4	ESDJ	19 389	10 043	9 346	...	...	...	...	...	...
5 - 9	ESDJ	30 922	16 146	14 776	...	...	...	...	...	...
10 - 14	ESDJ	40 313	20 768	19 545	...	...	...	...	...	...
15 - 19	ESDJ	38 179	19 274	18 905	...	...	...	...	...	...
20 - 24	ESDJ	29 377	12 665	16 712	...	...	...	...	...	...
25 - 29	ESDJ	30 692	13 388	17 304	...	...	...	...	...	...
30 - 34	ESDJ	35 201	14 482	20 719	...	...	...	...	...	...
35 - 39	ESDJ	42 597	18 362	24 235	...	...	...	...	...	...
40 - 44	ESDJ	46 858	22 955	23 903	...	...	...	...	...	...
45 - 49	ESDJ	40 069	20 748	19 321	...	...	...	...	...	...
50 - 54	ESDJ	26 819	14 285	12 534	...	...	...	...	...	...
55 - 59	ESDJ	15 573	8 383	7 190	...	...	...	...	...	...
60 - 64	ESDJ	10 078	5 228	4 850	...	...	...	...	...	...
65 - 69	ESDJ	9 955	4 653	5 302	...	...	...	...	...	...
70 - 74	ESDJ	9 199	3 974	5 225	...	...	...	...	...	...
75+	ESDJ	13 941	5 288	8 653	...	...	...	...	...	...
Cyprus - Chypre[16]										
1 VII 2002										
Total	ESDJ	709 631	347 942	361 689	...	...	...	...	...	...
0 - 1	ESDJ	7 796	4 076	3 719	...	...	...	...	...	...
1 - 4	ESDJ	34 330	17 528	16 802	...	...	...	...	...	...
5 - 9	ESDJ	51 160	26 210	24 951	...	...	...	...	...	...
10 - 14	ESDJ	54 694	28 200	26 494	...	...	...	...	...	...
15 - 19	ESDJ	55 595	28 516	27 079	...	...	...	...	...	...
20 - 24	ESDJ	55 222	28 165	27 057	...	...	...	...	...	...
25 - 29	ESDJ	50 468	24 566	25 902	...	...	...	...	...	...
30 - 34	ESDJ	49 884	23 556	26 329	...	...	...	...	...	...
35 - 39	ESDJ	51 650	24 702	26 948	...	...	...	...	...	...
40 - 44	ESDJ	53 866	26 154	27 712	...	...	...	...	...	...
45 - 49	ESDJ	47 695	23 407	24 289	...	...	...	...	...	...
50 - 54	ESDJ	44 389	21 829	22 560	...	...	...	...	...	...
55 - 59	ESDJ	36 628	17 834	18 793	...	...	...	...	...	...
60 - 64	ESDJ	32 368	15 741	16 627	...	...	...	...	...	...
65 - 69	ESDJ	26 823	12 589	14 234	...	...	...	...	...	...
70 - 74	ESDJ	21 779	9 745	12 033	...	...	...	...	...	...
75 - 79	ESDJ	16 622	7 301	9 321	...	...	...	...	...	...
80+	ESDJ	18 661	7 822	10 839	...	...	...	...	...	...
Georgia - Géorgie										
1 VII 2000										
Total	ESDF	4 945 553	2 364 247	2 581 306	2 860 786	1 348 715	1 512 071	2 084 767	1 015 532	1 069 235
0 - 1	ESDF	42 247	22 938	19 309	26 206	14 152	12 054	16 041	8 786	7 255

7. Population by age, sex and urban/rural residence: latest available year, 1993 - 2002
Population selon l'âge, le sexe et la résidence, urbaine/rurale: dernière année disponible, 1993 - 2002
(continued — suite)

(See notes at end of table. — Voir notes à la fin du tableau.)

Continent, country or area, date and age (in years) / Continent, pays ou zone, date et âge (en années)	Code[1]	Total			Urban - Urbaine			Rural - Rurale		
		Both sexes Les deux sexes	Male Masculin	Female Féminin	Both sexes Les deux sexes	Male Masculin	Female Féminin	Both sexes Les deux sexes	Male Masculin	Female Féminin
ASIA — ASIE										
Georgia - Géorgie										
1 VII 2000										
1 - 4	ESDF	197 055	104 267	92 788	119 229	63 120	56 109	77 826	41 147	36 679
5 - 9	ESDF	361 619	185 741	175 878	208 452	107 038	101 414	153 167	78 703	74 464
10 - 14	ESDF	409 671	209 366	200 305	229 154	116 874	112 280	180 517	92 492	88 025
15 - 19	ESDF	388 789	198 066	190 723	222 064	113 224	108 840	166 725	84 842	81 883
20 - 24	ESDF	376 407	191 927	184 480	213 454	108 613	104 841	162 953	83 314	79 639
25 - 29	ESDF	350 129	181 759	168 370	213 415	110 488	102 927	136 714	71 271	65 443
30 - 34	ESDF	363 659	175 712	187 947	214 156	100 573	113 583	149 503	75 139	74 364
35 - 39	ESDF	403 179	191 543	211 636	241 215	109 394	131 821	161 964	82 149	79 815
40 - 44	ESDF	353 366	168 218	185 148	216 428	98 958	117 470	136 938	69 260	67 678
45 - 49	ESDF	305 841	143 921	161 920	193 528	88 504	105 024	112 313	55 417	56 896
50 - 54	ESDF	216 111	100 444	115 667	137 119	62 640	74 479	78 992	37 804	41 188
55 - 59	ESDF	225 223	99 437	125 786	130 629	56 530	74 099	94 594	42 907	51 687
60 - 64	ESDF	280 405	126 438	153 967	155 346	68 463	86 883	125 059	57 975	67 084
65 - 69	ESDF	242 085	102 877	139 208	123 373	51 091	72 282	118 712	51 786	66 926
70 - 74	ESDF	218 503	85 840	132 663	111 805	41 553	70 252	106 698	44 287	62 411
75 - 79	ESDF	113 417	34 835	78 582	56 587	16 900	39 687	56 830	17 935	38 895
80 - 84	ESDF	59 039	24 600	34 439	29 156	12 606	16 550	29 883	11 994	17 889
85 - 89	ESDF	27 302	11 583	15 719	13 332	5 601	7 731	13 970	5 982	7 988
90 - 94	ESDF	8 410	3 605	4 805	4 432	1 819	2 613	3 978	1 786	2 192
95 - 99	ESDF	2 730	1 020	1 710	1 510	527	983	1 220	493	727
100+	ESDF	366	110	256	196	47	149	170	63	107
India - Inde[17,18]										
1 III 2001										
Total	CDFC	1028610328	532 156 772	496 453 556	286 119 689	150 554 098	135 565 591	742 490 639	381 602 674	360 887 965
0 - 4	CDFC	110 447 164	57 119 612	53 327 552	25 338 754	13 262 414	12 076 340	85 108 410	43 857 198	41 251 212
5 - 9	CDFC	128 316 790	66 734 833	61 581 957	29 860 545	15 640 135	14 220 410	98 456 245	51 094 698	47 361 547
10 - 14	CDFC	124 846 858	65 632 877	59 213 981	32 464 536	17 030 132	15 434 404	92 382 322	48 602 745	43 779 577
15 - 19	CDFC	100 215 890	53 939 991	46 275 899	30 154 067	16 191 573	13 962 494	70 061 823	37 748 418	32 313 405
20 - 24	CDFC	89 764 132	46 321 150	43 442 982	28 365 228	15 193 668	13 171 560	61 398 904	31 127 482	30 271 422
25 - 29	CDFC	83 422 393	41 557 546	41 864 847	25 737 253	13 180 373	12 556 880	57 685 140	28 377 173	29 307 967
30 - 34	CDFC	74 274 044	37 361 916	36 912 128	22 445 165	11 673 137	10 772 028	51 828 879	25 688 779	26 140 100
35 - 39	CDFC	70 574 085	36 038 727	34 535 358	21 615 541	11 157 103	10 458 438	48 958 544	24 881 624	24 076 920
40 - 44	CDFC	55 738 297	29 878 715	25 859 582	17 173 126	9 458 276	7 714 850	38 565 171	20 420 439	18 144 732
45 - 49	CDFC	47 408 976	24 867 886	22 541 090	14 453 974	7 844 213	6 609 761	32 955 002	17 023 673	15 931 329
50 - 54	CDFC	36 587 559	19 851 608	16 735 951	10 809 961	6 038 917	4 771 044	25 777 598	13 812 691	11 964 907
55 - 59	CDFC	27 653 347	13 583 022	14 070 325	7 682 278	4 010 268	3 672 010	19 971 069	9 572 754	10 398 315
60 - 64	CDFC	27 516 779	13 586 347	13 930 432	6 864 810	3 439 621	3 425 189	20 651 969	10 146 726	10 505 243
65 - 69	CDFC	19 806 955	9 472 103	10 334 852	4 990 199	2 401 397	2 588 802	14 816 756	7 070 706	7 746 050
70 - 74	CDFC	14 708 644	7 527 688	7 180 956	3 579 168	1 780 696	1 798 472	11 129 476	5 746 992	5 382 484
75 - 79	CDFC	6 551 225	3 263 209	3 288 016	1 721 085	851 088	869 997	4 830 140	2 412 121	2 418 019
80+	CDFC	8 038 718	3 918 980	4 119 738	2 022 345	935 920	1 086 425	6 016 373	2 983 060	3 033 313
Unk. - Inc.	CDFC	2 738 472	1 500 562	1 237 910	841 654	465 167	376 487	1 896 818	1 035 395	861 423
1 VII 2001										
Total	ESDF	1017544000	526 356 000	491 187 000	...	...	...	...	...	...
0 - 4	ESDF	109 047 000	55 987 000	53 060 000	...	...	...	...	...	...
5 - 9	ESDF	116 737 000	59 531 000	57 206 000	...	...	...	...	...	...
10 - 14	ESDF	123 531 000	63 879 000	59 653 000	...	...	...	...	...	...
15 - 19	ESDF	109 619 000	57 958 000	51 661 000	...	...	...	...	...	...
20 - 24	ESDF	90 680 000	47 966 000	42 714 000	...	...	...	...	...	...
25 - 29	ESDF	81 887 000	41 598 000	40 289 000	...	...	...	...	...	...
30 - 34	ESDF	75 555 000	37 661 000	37 894 000	...	...	...	...	...	...
35 - 39	ESDF	65 743 000	33 527 000	32 215 000	...	...	...	...	...	...
40 - 44	ESDF	56 436 000	29 644 000	26 792 000	...	...	...	...	...	...
45 - 49	ESDF	46 993 000	24 945 000	22 047 000	...	...	...	...	...	...
50 - 54	ESDF	39 099 000	20 715 000	18 384 000	...	...	...	...	...	...
55 - 59	ESDF	31 287 000	16 558 000	14 729 000	...	...	...	...	...	...
60 - 64	ESDF	24 184 000	12 513 000	11 671 000	...	...	...	...	...	...

7. Population by age, sex and urban/rural residence: latest available year, 1993 - 2002
Population selon l'âge, le sexe et la résidence, urbaine/rurale: dernière année disponible, 1993 - 2002
(continued — suite)

(See notes at end of table. — Voir notes à la fin du tableau.)

Continent, country or area, date and age (in years) / Continent, pays ou zone, date et âge (en années)	Code[1]	Total — Both sexes Les deux sexes	Total — Male Masculin	Total — Female Féminin	Urban - Urbaine — Both sexes Les deux sexes	Urban - Urbaine — Male Masculin	Urban - Urbaine — Female Féminin	Rural - Rurale — Both sexes Les deux sexes	Rural - Rurale — Male Masculin	Rural - Rurale — Female Féminin
ASIA — ASIE										
India - Inde[17,18]										
1 VII 2001										
65 - 69	ESDF	19 438 000	9 871 000	9 567 000	...	...	...	...	...	...
70 - 74	ESDF	13 120 000	6 647 000	6 473 000	...	...	...	...	...	...
75 - 79	ESDF	8 352 000	4 317 000	4 035 000	...	...	...	...	...	...
80+	ESDF	5 837 000	3 040 000	2 798 000	...	...	...	...	...	...
Indonesia - Indonésie[19]										
30 VI 2000										
Total	CDFC	201 241 999	100 934 962	100 307 037	85 380 627	42 759 571	42 621 056	115 861 372	58 175 391	57 685 981
0 - 1	CDFC	3 492 259	1 799 525	1 692 734	1 529 180	790 207	738 973	1 963 079	1 009 318	953 761
1 - 4	CDFC	16 810 117	8 496 176	8 313 941	6 642 545	3 361 599	3 280 946	10 167 572	5 134 577	5 032 995
5 - 9	CDFC	20 494 091	10 433 865	10 060 226	7 962 806	4 034 352	3 928 454	12 531 285	6 399 513	6 131 772
10 - 14	CDFC	20 453 732	10 460 908	9 992 824	7 951 997	4 017 276	3 934 721	12 501 735	6 443 632	6 058 103
15 - 19	CDFC	21 149 517	10 649 348	10 500 169	9 501 797	4 656 022	4 845 775	11 647 720	5 993 326	5 654 394
20 - 24	CDFC	19 258 101	9 237 464	10 020 637	9 394 813	4 528 914	4 865 899	9 863 288	4 708 550	5 154 738
25 - 29	CDFC	18 640 937	9 130 504	9 510 433	8 720 487	4 321 110	4 399 377	9 920 450	4 809 394	5 111 056
30 - 34	CDFC	16 399 720	8 204 302	8 195 418	7 499 021	3 795 282	3 703 739	8 900 699	4 409 020	4 491 679
35 - 39	CDFC	14 904 226	7 432 840	7 471 386	6 430 999	3 230 371	3 200 628	8 473 227	4 202 469	4 270 758
40 - 44	CDFC	12 467 848	6 433 438	6 034 410	5 322 075	2 767 298	2 554 777	7 145 773	3 666 140	3 479 633
45 - 49	CDFC	9 656 005	5 087 252	4 568 753	4 015 532	2 137 790	1 877 742	5 640 473	2 949 462	2 691 011
50 - 54	CDFC	7 384 968	3 791 185	3 593 783	2 905 386	1 500 733	1 404 653	4 479 582	2 290 452	2 189 130
55 - 59	CDFC	5 678 664	2 883 226	2 795 438	2 235 074	1 145 432	1 089 642	3 443 590	1 737 794	1 705 796
60 - 64	CDFC	5 321 019	2 597 076	2 723 943	1 951 238	949 193	1 002 045	3 369 781	1 647 883	1 721 898
65 - 69	CDFC	3 564 926	1 666 191	1 898 735	1 310 805	600 348	710 457	2 254 121	1 065 843	1 188 278
70 - 74	CDFC	2 837 037	1 368 190	1 468 847	1 016 304	479 243	537 061	1 820 733	888 947	931 786
75+	CDFC	2 716 985	1 257 526	1 459 459	986 136	442 204	543 932	1 730 849	815 322	915 527
Unk. - Inc.	CDFC	11 847	5 946	5 901	4 432	2 197	2 235	7 415	3 749	3 666
Iran (Islamic Republic of) - Iran (République islamique d')										
23 X 1996										
Total	CDJC	60 055 488	30 515 159	29 540 329	36 817 789	18 805 023	18 012 766	23 026 293	11 604 972	11 421 321
0 - 1	CDJC	1 020 936	524 927	496 009	577 065	296 189	280 876	438 331	225 870	212 461
1 - 4	CDJC	5 142 088	2 639 181	2 502 907	2 849 490	1 460 895	1 388 595	2 265 600	1 164 225	1 101 375
5 - 9	CDJC	8 481 845	4 324 165	4 157 680	4 878 478	2 482 469	2 396 009	3 568 961	1 824 356	1 744 605
10 - 14	CDJC	9 080 676	4 622 473	4 458 203	5 519 239	2 815 729	2 703 510	3 532 506	1 792 962	1 739 544
15 - 19	CDJC	7 115 547	3 579 875	3 535 672	4 312 401	2 192 258	2 120 143	2 776 791	1 375 316	1 401 475
20 - 24	CDJC	5 221 982	2 566 453	2 655 529	3 154 588	1 552 571	1 602 017	2 049 270	1 005 536	1 043 734
25 - 29	CDJC	4 709 154	2 365 834	2 343 320	3 058 756	1 542 685	1 516 071	1 636 320	816 297	820 023
30 - 34	CDJC	3 980 066	2 012 720	1 967 346	2 709 279	1 379 337	1 329 942	1 260 670	628 651	632 019
35 - 39	CDJC	3 571 779	1 817 609	1 754 170	2 433 263	1 253 499	1 179 764	1 128 946	559 452	569 494
40 - 44	CDJC	2 812 086	1 431 062	1 381 024	1 907 112	999 736	907 376	896 847	427 395	469 452
45 - 49	CDJC	2 013 040	990 158	1 022 882	1 326 036	679 081	646 955	680 701	308 103	372 598
50 - 54	CDJC	1 529 078	768 621	760 457	978 343	508 898	469 445	545 616	257 191	288 425
55 - 59	CDJC	1 366 728	717 251	649 477	830 201	443 453	386 748	532 070	271 309	260 761
60 - 64	CDJC	1 382 946	753 502	629 444	783 511	426 040	357 471	593 925	324 115	269 810
65 - 69	CDJC	1 076 373	577 189	499 184	601 575	313 942	287 633	470 975	260 734	210 241
70 - 74	CDJC	846 509	463 018	383 491	479 380	253 061	226 319	364 876	208 499	156 377
75 - 79	CDJC	364 118	192 898	171 220	213 209	108 117	105 092	150 168	84 342	65 826
80 - 84	CDJC	146 470	74 081	72 389	86 330	41 073	45 257	59 770	32 783	26 987
85 - 89	CDJC	76 476	35 182	41 294	43 625	18 287	25 338	32 657	16 781	15 876
90 - 94	CDJC	44 780	19 977	24 803	25 563	10 855	14 708	19 067	9 050	10 017
95+	CDJC	40 455	20 103	20 352	21 018	10 022	10 996	19 224	9 963	9 261
Unk. - Inc.	CDJC	32 356	18 880	13 476	29 327	16 826	12 501	3 002	2 042	960
Iraq										
1 VII 2001										
Total	ESDF	24 813 365	12 424 655	12 388 710	16 786 216	8 435 417	8 350 799	8 027 149	3 989 238	4 037 911

7. Population by age, sex and urban/rural residence: latest available year, 1993 - 2002
Population selon l'âge, le sexe et la résidence, urbaine/rurale: dernière année disponible, 1993 - 2002
(continued — suite)

(See notes at end of table. — Voir notes à la fin du tableau.)

Continent, country or area, date and age (in years) / Continent, pays ou zone, date et âge (en années)	Code[1]	Total			Urban - Urbaine			Rural - Rurale		
		Both sexes Les deux sexes	Male Masculin	Female Féminin	Both sexes Les deux sexes	Male Masculin	Female Féminin	Both sexes Les deux sexes	Male Masculin	Female Féminin
ASIA — ASIE										
Iraq										
1 VII 2001										
0 - 4	ESDF	4 204 992	2 152 617	2 052 375	2 662 981	1 363 117	1 299 864	1 542 011	789 500	752 511
5 - 9	ESDF	3 530 274	1 792 771	1 737 503	2 271 485	1 152 236	1 119 249	1 258 789	640 535	618 254
10 - 14	ESDF	3 143 756	1 597 209	1 546 547	2 062 610	1 047 953	1 014 657	1 081 146	549 256	531 890
15 - 19	ESDF	2 704 919	1 372 868	1 332 051	1 814 193	921 904	892 289	890 726	450 964	439 762
20 - 24	ESDF	2 316 564	1 169 700	1 146 864	1 581 702	800 938	780 764	734 862	368 762	366 100
25 - 29	ESDF	1 952 402	977 701	974 701	1 359 271	684 350	674 921	593 131	293 351	299 780
30 - 34	ESDF	1 614 198	800 214	813 984	1 143 674	571 922	571 752	470 524	228 292	242 232
35 - 39	ESDF	1 279 987	623 408	656 579	927 093	458 110	468 983	352 894	165 298	187 596
40 - 44	ESDF	1 032 328	499 170	533 158	756 211	372 260	383 951	276 117	126 910	149 207
45 - 49	ESDF	807 388	388 977	418 411	595 650	293 047	302 603	211 738	95 930	115 808
50 - 54	ESDF	638 860	308 112	330 748	472 597	232 751	239 846	166 263	75 361	90 902
55 - 59	ESDF	491 447	239 599	251 848	362 238	179 763	182 475	129 209	59 836	69 373
60 - 64	ESDF	373 297	179 995	193 302	274 281	134 244	140 037	99 016	45 751	53 265
65 - 69	ESDF	267 876	125 726	142 150	195 763	92 766	102 997	72 113	32 960	39 153
70 - 74	ESDF	190 384	86 113	104 271	135 525	61 375	74 150	54 859	24 738	30 121
75 - 79	ESDF	125 816	53 516	72 300	84 924	35 403	49 521	40 892	18 113	22 779
80+	ESDF	138 877	56 959	81 918	86 018	33 278	52 740	52 859	23 681	29 178
Israel - Israël[9,20]										
1 VII 2002										
Total	ESDJ	6 569 900	3 241 700	3 328 200	6 017 300	2 958 200	3 059 100	552 600	283 500	269 100
0 - 1	ESDJ	137 500	70 400	67 000	125 000	64 100	60 900	12 400	6 300	6 100
1 - 4	ESDJ	537 000	275 800	261 200	487 700	250 600	237 100	49 300	25 200	24 100
5 - 9	ESDJ	615 300	315 700	299 600	555 800	285 000	270 800	59 500	30 700	28 800
10 - 14	ESDJ	575 100	294 500	280 600	518 900	265 200	253 700	56 200	29 300	26 900
15 - 19	ESDJ	563 400	288 800	274 600	505 800	257 600	248 200	57 600	31 200	26 400
20 - 24	ESDJ	538 900	273 100	265 800	494 800	249 800	245 000	44 100	23 300	20 800
25 - 29	ESDJ	531 000	268 000	263 000	490 700	247 300	243 400	40 300	20 700	19 600
30 - 34	ESDJ	455 800	228 100	227 800	419 500	209 900	209 600	36 400	18 200	18 200
35 - 39	ESDJ	393 100	194 400	198 800	358 000	176 700	181 300	35 200	17 700	17 500
40 - 44	ESDJ	382 500	186 000	196 500	349 100	169 000	180 100	33 400	17 000	16 400
45 - 49	ESDJ	373 600	180 500	193 200	342 700	164 500	178 200	31 000	16 000	15 000
50 - 54	ESDJ	356 500	171 600	184 900	329 100	157 300	171 800	27 400	14 300	13 100
55 - 59	ESDJ	255 500	122 900	132 500	236 100	113 000	123 100	19 300	9 900	9 400
60 - 64	ESDJ	207 400	96 500	110 900	194 400	89 800	104 600	13 000	6 700	6 300
65 - 69	ESDJ	191 300	86 400	104 900	180 200	80 900	99 300	11 100	5 500	5 600
70 - 74	ESDJ	165 300	71 700	93 600	156 300	67 600	88 700	9 000	4 100	4 900
75 - 79	ESDJ	142 100	57 200	84 900	134 300	53 800	80 500	7 800	3 400	4 400
80 - 84	ESDJ	83 500	35 200	48 200	78 500	33 000	45 500	4 900	2 200	2 700
85 - 89	ESDJ	43 400	16 400	26 900	40 200	15 200	25 000	3 100	1 200	1 900
90+	ESDJ	21 700	8 300	13 400	20 100	7 700	12 400	1 600	600	1 000
Japan - Japon[21]										
1 X 2000										
Total	CDFC	126 925 843	62 110 764	64 815 079	99 865 289	49 005 691	50 859 598	27 060 554	13 105 073	13 955 481
0 - 1	CDFC	1 171 652	600 466	571 186	946 482	485 130	461 352	225 170	115 336	109 834
1 - 4	CDFC	4 732 446	2 422 055	2 310 391	3 771 724	1 930 430	1 841 294	960 722	491 625	469 097
5 - 9	CDFC	6 021 789	3 083 431	2 938 358	4 686 566	2 399 688	2 286 878	1 335 223	683 743	651 480
10 - 14	CDFC	6 546 612	3 353 150	3 193 462	5 000 556	2 560 796	2 439 760	1 546 056	792 354	753 702
15 - 19	CDFC	7 488 165	3 833 984	3 654 181	5 878 320	3 010 056	2 868 264	1 609 845	823 928	785 917
20 - 24	CDFC	8 421 460	4 307 242	4 114 218	6 989 577	3 582 379	3 407 198	1 431 883	724 863	707 020
25 - 29	CDFC	9 790 309	4 965 277	4 825 032	8 149 612	4 131 227	4 018 385	1 640 697	834 050	806 647
30 - 34	CDFC	8 776 610	4 436 818	4 339 792	7 301 831	3 699 586	3 602 245	1 474 779	737 232	737 547
35 - 39	CDFC	8 114 865	4 096 286	4 018 579	6 578 179	3 330 783	3 247 396	1 536 686	765 503	771 183
40 - 44	CDFC	7 800 219	3 924 171	3 876 048	6 099 826	3 068 796	3 031 030	1 700 393	855 375	845 018
45 - 49	CDFC	8 916 008	4 467 772	4 448 236	6 895 939	3 440 338	3 455 601	2 020 069	1 027 434	992 635
50 - 54	CDFC	10 441 990	5 210 038	5 231 952	8 237 639	4 085 392	4 152 247	2 204 351	1 124 646	1 079 705
55 - 59	CDFC	8 734 172	4 290 239	4 443 933	6 965 529	3 418 751	3 546 778	1 768 643	871 488	897 155
60 - 64	CDFC	7 735 833	3 749 528	3 986 305	6 039 491	2 935 344	3 104 147	1 696 342	814 184	882 158

7. Population by age, sex and urban/rural residence: latest available year, 1993 - 2002
Population selon l'âge, le sexe et la résidence, urbaine/rurale: dernière année disponible, 1993 - 2002
(continued — suite)

(See notes at end of table. — Voir notes à la fin du tableau.)

Continent, country or area, date and age (in years) / Continent, pays ou zone, date et âge (en années)	Code[1]	Total			Urban - Urbaine			Rural - Rurale		
		Both sexes Les deux sexes	Male Masculin	Female Féminin	Both sexes Les deux sexes	Male Masculin	Female Féminin	Both sexes Les deux sexes	Male Masculin	Female Féminin
ASIA — ASIE										
Japan - Japon[21]										
1 X 2000										
65 - 69	CDFC	7 105 939	3 357 281	3 748 658	5 374 653	2 546 769	2 827 884	1 731 286	810 512	920 774
70 - 74	CDFC	5 900 576	2 670 270	3 230 306	4 304 854	1 951 802	2 353 052	1 595 722	718 468	877 254
75 - 79	CDFC	4 150 600	1 625 822	2 524 778	2 979 368	1 169 120	1 810 248	1 171 232	456 702	714 530
80 - 84	CDFC	2 614 689	915 268	1 699 421	1 864 830	652 632	1 212 198	749 859	262 636	487 223
85 - 89	CDFC	1 532 323	477 083	1 055 240	1 089 747	341 275	748 472	442 576	135 808	306 768
90 - 94	CDFC	570 281	149 295	420 986	401 755	105 381	296 374	168 526	43 914	124 612
95 - 99	CDFC	118 488	25 070	93 418	82 972	17 454	65 518	35 516	7 616	27 900
100+	CDFC	12 256	2 027	10 229	8 403	1 355	7 048	3 853	672	3 181
Unk. - Inc.	CDFC	228 561	148 191	80 370	217 436	141 207	76 229	11 125	6 984	4 141
1 X 2002										
Total	ESDF	127 435 000	62 252 000	65 183 000	...	...	...	...	...	...
0 - 1	ESDF	1 168 000	599 000	569 000	...	...	...	...	...	...
1 - 4	ESDF	4 707 000	2 413 000	2 293 000	...	...	...	...	...	...
5 - 9	ESDF	5 983 000	3 064 000	2 919 000	...	...	...	...	...	...
10 - 14	ESDF	6 244 000	3 200 000	3 044 000	...	...	...	...	...	...
15 - 19	ESDF	7 194 000	3 687 000	3 507 000	...	...	...	...	...	...
20 - 24	ESDF	8 012 000	4 102 000	3 910 000	...	...	...	...	...	...
25 - 29	ESDF	9 431 000	4 786 000	4 645 000	...	...	...	...	...	...
30 - 34	ESDF	9 492 000	4 794 000	4 699 000	...	...	...	...	...	...
35 - 39	ESDF	8 262 000	4 163 000	4 099 000	...	...	...	...	...	...
40 - 44	ESDF	7 797 000	3 921 000	3 876 000	...	...	...	...	...	...
45 - 49	ESDF	8 151 000	4 086 000	4 064 000	...	...	...	...	...	...
50 - 54	ESDF	10 608 000	5 287 000	5 321 000	...	...	...	...	...	...
55 - 59	ESDF	8 657 000	4 263 000	4 394 000	...	...	...	...	...	...
60 - 64	ESDF	8 102 000	3 930 000	4 171 000	...	...	...	...	...	...
65 - 69	ESDF	7 374 000	3 493 000	3 881 000	...	...	...	...	...	...
70 - 74	ESDF	6 211 000	2 828 000	3 382 000	...	...	...	...	...	...
75 - 79	ESDF	4 673 000	1 929 000	2 744 000	...	...	...	...	...	...
80 - 84	ESDF	2 856 000	982 000	1 873 000	...	...	...	...	...	...
85 - 89	ESDF	1 659 000	513 000	1 145 000	...	...	...	...	...	...
90+	ESDF	856 000	211 000	645 000	...	...	...	...	...	...
Jordan - Jordanie[22]										
10 XII 1994										
Total	CDFC	4 139 458	2 160 725	1 978 733	3 238 757	1 687 530	1 551 227	900 701	473 195	427 506
0 - 1	CDFC	123 963	63 377	60 586	95 860	49 143	46 717	28 103	14 234	13 869
1 - 4	CDFC	492 953	252 930	240 023	377 855	193 790	184 065	115 098	59 140	55 958
5 - 9	CDFC	566 406	289 767	276 639	432 615	220 987	211 628	133 791	68 780	65 011
10 - 14	CDFC	529 059	271 179	257 880	406 464	207 860	198 604	122 595	63 319	59 276
15 - 19	CDFC	483 548	251 160	232 388	374 507	194 129	180 378	109 041	57 031	52 010
20 - 24	CDFC	453 423	243 622	209 801	357 900	191 806	166 094	95 523	51 816	43 707
25 - 29	CDFC	378 952	209 365	169 587	302 167	166 150	136 017	76 785	43 215	33 570
30 - 34	CDFC	272 376	145 584	126 792	221 111	117 967	103 144	51 265	27 617	23 648
35 - 39	CDFC	188 510	98 364	90 146	152 152	79 303	72 849	36 358	19 061	17 297
40 - 44	CDFC	141 140	73 128	68 012	111 873	57 507	54 366	29 267	15 621	13 646
45 - 49	CDFC	127 400	63 161	64 239	103 397	51 162	52 235	24 003	11 999	12 004
50 - 54	CDFC	114 318	61 149	53 169	92 506	49 729	42 777	21 812	11 420	10 392
55 - 59	CDFC	91 621	48 299	43 322	73 611	38 940	34 671	18 010	9 359	8 651
60 - 64	CDFC	68 005	35 251	32 754	53 549	27 704	25 845	14 456	7 547	6 909
65 - 69	CDFC	42 232	22 799	19 433	33 797	18 037	15 760	8 435	4 762	3 673
70 - 74	CDFC	29 618	13 621	15 997	22 472	10 222	12 250	7 146	3 399	3 747
75 - 79	CDFC	14 497	7 507	6 990	11 050	5 615	5 435	3 447	1 892	1 555
80+	CDFC	17 786	8 328	9 458	13 145	5 835	7 310	4 641	2 493	2 148
Unk. - Inc.	CDFC	3 651	2 134	1 517	2 726	1 644	1 082	925	490	435
31 XII 2002										
Total	ESDF	5 329 000	2 787 115	2 541 885	...	...	...	...	...	...
0 - 1	ESDF	128 318	68 749	59 569	...	...	...	...	...	...
1 - 4	ESDF	516 490	268 490	248 000	...	...	...	...	...	...

7. Population by age, sex and urban/rural residence: latest available year, 1993 - 2002
Population selon l'âge, le sexe et la résidence, urbaine/rurale: dernière année disponible, 1993 - 2002
(continued — suite)

(See notes at end of table. — Voir notes à la fin du tableau.)

Continent, country or area, date and age (in years) / Continent, pays ou zone, date et âge (en années)	Code[1]	Total Both sexes Les deux sexes	Total Male Masculin	Total Female Féminin	Urban - Urbaine Both sexes Les deux sexes	Urban - Urbaine Male Masculin	Urban - Urbaine Female Féminin	Rural - Rurale Both sexes Les deux sexes	Rural - Rurale Male Masculin	Rural - Rurale Female Féminin
ASIA — ASIE										
Jordan - Jordanie[22]										
31 XII 2002										
5 - 9	ESDF	708 755	370 685	338 070	...	...	...	...	...	...
10 - 14	ESDF	660 795	345 600	315 195	...	...	...	...	...	...
15 - 19	ESDF	655 465	348 390	307 075	...	...	...	...	...	...
20 - 24	ESDF	572 870	320 520	252 350	...	...	...	...	...	...
25 - 29	ESDF	436 980	231 330	205 650	...	...	...	...	...	...
30 - 34	ESDF	373 030	183 950	189 080	...	...	...	...	...	...
35 - 39	ESDF	293 095	147 720	145 375	...	...	...	...	...	...
40 - 44	ESDF	213 160	103 125	110 035	...	...	...	...	...	...
45 - 49	ESDF	173 190	86 400	86 790	...	...	...	...	...	...
50 - 54	ESDF	151 875	72 465	79 410	...	...	...	...	...	...
55 - 59	ESDF	141 220	72 465	68 755	...	...	...	...	...	...
60 - 64	ESDF	117 240	66 890	50 350	...	...	...	...	...	...
65 - 69	ESDF	83 635	44 940	38 695	...	...	...	...	...	...
70 - 74	ESDF	51 885	28 110	23 775	...	...	...	...	...	...
75 - 79	ESDF	27 652	15 757	11 895	...	...	...	...	...	...
80 - 84	ESDF	12 825	6 540	6 285	...	...	...	...	...	...
85 - 89	ESDF	5 710	2 580	3 130	...	...	...	...	...	...
90 - 94	ESDF	3 035	1 675	1 360	...	...	...	...	...	...
95+	ESDF	1 471	732	739	...	...	...	...	...	...
Kazakhstan										
1 VII 1999										
Total	ESDF	14 926 945	7 190 822	7 736 123	8 345 487	3 899 728	4 445 759	6 581 458	3 291 094	3 290 364
0 - 1	ESDF	211 476	109 032	102 444	106 072	54 673	51 399	105 404	54 359	51 045
1 - 4	ESDF	942 069	480 483	461 586	450 352	228 274	222 078	491 717	252 209	239 508
5 - 9	ESDF	1 473 993	749 028	724 965	714 638	359 526	355 112	759 355	389 502	369 853
10 - 14	ESDF	1 604 524	806 408	798 116	807 352	402 630	404 722	797 172	403 778	393 394
15 - 19	ESDF	1 410 883	705 773	705 110	708 647	347 233	361 414	702 236	358 540	343 696
20 - 24	ESDF	1 297 244	643 622	653 622	713 214	335 201	378 013	584 030	308 421	275 609
25 - 29	ESDF	1 159 446	599 070	560 376	733 915	355 654	378 261	425 531	243 416	182 115
30 - 34	ESDF	1 062 048	532 510	529 538	643 431	313 951	329 480	418 617	218 559	200 058
35 - 39	ESDF	1 188 588	582 510	606 078	708 424	339 024	369 400	480 164	243 486	236 678
40 - 44	ESDF	1 050 684	507 944	542 740	642 428	303 479	338 949	408 256	204 465	203 791
45 - 49	ESDF	862 641	407 386	455 255	537 783	249 038	288 745	324 858	158 348	166 510
50 - 54	ESDF	569 824	264 005	305 819	356 757	161 784	194 973	213 067	102 221	110 846
55 - 59	ESDF	506 020	225 000	281 020	290 289	124 351	165 938	215 731	100 649	115 082
60 - 64	ESDF	583 940	252 751	331 189	341 540	141 312	200 228	242 400	111 439	130 961
65 - 69	ESDF	345 932	137 790	208 142	205 076	77 009	128 067	140 856	60 781	80 075
70 - 74	ESDF	336 102	112 166	223 936	203 819	65 078	138 741	132 283	47 088	85 195
75 - 79	ESDF	159 885	41 880	118 005	94 818	23 730	71 088	65 067	18 150	46 917
80 - 84	ESDF	84 296	19 271	65 025	48 436	10 711	37 725	35 860	8 560	27 300
85 - 89	ESDF	52 338	9 969	42 369	27 087	5 190	21 897	25 251	4 779	20 472
90 - 94	ESDF	19 680	3 219	16 461	8 815	1 404	7 411	10 865	1 815	9 050
95 - 99	ESDF	4 803	880	3 923	2 174	409	1 765	2 629	471	2 158
100+	ESDF	529	125	404	420	67	353	109	58	51
Korea (Dem. People's Republic of) - Corée (Rép. populaire dém. de)										
31 XII 1993										
Total	CDJC	20 522 351	9 677 663	10 844 688	12 501 217	5 951 077	6 550 140	8 021 134	3 726 586	4 294 548
0 - 1	CDJC	416 088	213 149	202 939	228 730	117 280	111 450	187 358	95 869	91 489
1 - 4	CDJC	1 672 420	858 805	813 615	955 496	490 788	464 708	716 924	368 017	348 907
5 - 9	CDJC	1 866 583	957 583	909 000	1 102 774	565 845	536 929	763 809	391 738	372 071
10 - 14	CDJC	1 767 112	904 764	862 348	1 081 711	554 589	527 122	685 401	350 175	335 226
15 - 19	CDJC	1 528 298	708 790	819 508	957 833	450 199	507 634	570 465	258 591	311 874
20 - 24	CDJC	1 862 989	765 479	1 097 510	1 158 144	493 090	665 054	704 845	272 389	432 456
25 - 29	CDJC	2 019 525	987 095	1 032 430	1 256 838	630 044	626 794	762 687	357 051	405 636

7. Population by age, sex and urban/rural residence: latest available year, 1993 - 2002
Population selon l'âge, le sexe et la résidence, urbaine/rurale: dernière année disponible, 1993 - 2002
(continued — suite)

(See notes at end of table. — Voir notes à la fin du tableau.)

Continent, country or area, date and age (in years) / Continent, pays ou zone, date et âge (en années)	Code[1]	Total			Urban - Urbaine			Rural - Rurale		
		Both sexes Les deux sexes	Male Masculin	Female Féminin	Both sexes Les deux sexes	Male Masculin	Female Féminin	Both sexes Les deux sexes	Male Masculin	Female Féminin
ASIA — ASIE										
Korea (Dem. People's Republic of) - Corée (Rép. populaire dém. de)										
31 XII 1993										
30 - 34	CDJC	1 607 929	791 117	816 812	1 002 111	498 143	503 968	605 818	292 974	312 844
35 - 39	CDJC	1 386 454	682 990	703 464	901 104	440 315	460 789	485 350	242 675	242 675
40 - 44	CDJC	990 787	482 309	508 478	638 616	306 319	332 297	352 171	175 990	176 181
45 - 49	CDJC	1 243 077	603 230	639 847	786 240	377 375	408 865	456 837	225 855	230 982
50 - 54	CDJC	1 208 802	582 990	625 812	754 557	361 150	393 407	454 245	221 840	232 405
55 - 59	CDJC	1 063 657	487 276	576 381	635 339	290 490	344 849	428 318	196 786	231 532
60 - 64	CDJC	748 594	301 764	446 830	437 753	187 062	250 691	310 841	114 702	196 139
65 - 69	CDJC	506 061	174 925	331 136	275 918	101 045	174 873	230 143	73 880	156 263
70 - 74	CDJC	339 533	102 975	236 558	177 353	53 214	124 139	162 180	49 761	112 419
75 - 79	CDJC	187 260	49 324	137 936	95 721	23 326	72 395	91 539	25 998	65 541
80 - 84	CDJC	81 332	19 005	62 327	41 691	8 893	32 798	39 641	10 112	29 529
85 - 89	CDJC	20 835	3 565	17 270	10 559	1 671	8 888	10 276	1 894	8 382
90 - 94	CDJC	4 100	485	3 615	2 145	217	1 928	1 955	268	1 687
95+	CDJC	818	40	778	530	20	510	288	20	268
Unk. - Inc.	CDJC	97	3	94	54	2	52	43	1	42
Korea (Republic of) - Corée (République de)[23]										
1 XI 1995										
Total	CDJC	44 553 710	22 357 352	22 196 358	34 991 964	17 595 723	17 396 241	9 561 746	4 761 629	4 800 117
0 - 1	CDJC	655 707	349 050	306 657	547 347	291 276	256 071	108 360	57 774	50 586
1 - 4	CDJC	2 771 702	1 472 300	1 299 402	2 287 750	1 215 282	1 072 468	483 952	257 018	226 934
5 - 9	CDJC	3 096 115	1 626 922	1 469 193	2 514 837	1 326 013	1 189 824	581 278	301 909	279 369
10 - 14	CDJC	3 711 980	1 913 801	1 798 179	2 956 665	1 533 376	1 423 289	755 315	380 425	374 890
15 - 19	CDJC	3 863 491	1 987 044	1 876 447	3 083 565	1 589 448	1 494 117	779 926	397 596	382 330
20 - 24	CDJC	4 304 378	2 237 940	2 066 438	3 509 790	1 758 084	1 751 706	794 588	479 856	314 732
25 - 29	CDJC	4 137 913	2 078 417	2 059 496	3 473 377	1 725 122	1 748 255	664 536	353 295	311 241
30 - 34	CDJC	4 230 239	2 146 351	2 083 888	3 517 693	1 774 770	1 742 923	712 546	371 581	340 965
35 - 39	CDJC	4 133 864	2 103 016	2 030 848	3 428 662	1 731 271	1 697 391	705 202	371 745	333 457
40 - 44	CDJC	3 071 101	1 579 850	1 491 251	2 519 966	1 295 738	1 224 228	551 135	284 112	267 023
45 - 49	CDJC	2 464 295	1 261 509	1 202 786	1 951 493	1 004 316	947 177	512 802	257 193	255 609
50 - 54	CDJC	2 063 768	1 028 887	1 034 881	1 516 333	774 968	741 365	547 435	253 919	293 516
55 - 59	CDJC	1 913 461	923 625	989 836	1 264 170	626 873	637 297	649 291	296 752	352 539
60 - 64	CDJC	1 495 082	673 719	821 363	905 622	413 690	491 932	589 460	260 029	329 431
65 - 69	CDJC	1 043 979	420 873	623 106	612 437	242 461	369 976	431 542	178 412	253 130
70 - 74	CDJC	762 544	293 696	468 848	437 794	159 518	278 276	324 750	134 178	190 572
75 - 79	CDJC	455 673	160 498	295 175	255 966	83 390	172 576	199 707	77 108	122 599
80 - 84	CDJC	246 191	71 267	174 924	137 645	36 561	101 084	108 546	34 706	73 840
85+	CDJC	131 818	28 370	103 448	70 675	14 468	56 207	61 143	13 902	47 241
Unk. - Inc.	CDJC	409	217	192	177	98	79	232	119	113
1 VII 2002										
Total	ESDF	47 639 618	23 983 838	23 655 780	...	...	...	...	...	...
0 - 1	ESDF	566 388	296 315	270 073	...	...	...	...	...	...
1 - 4	ESDF	2 481 974	1 300 984	1 180 990	...	...	...	...	...	...
5 - 9	ESDF	3 500 255	1 862 579	1 637 676	...	...	...	...	...	...
10 - 14	ESDF	3 243 956	1 722 259	1 521 697	...	...	...	...	...	...
15 - 19	ESDF	3 406 677	1 775 322	1 631 355	...	...	...	...	...	...
20 - 24	ESDF	4 012 443	2 067 228	1 945 215	...	...	...	...	...	...
25 - 29	ESDF	4 049 342	2 092 371	1 956 971	...	...	...	...	...	...
30 - 34	ESDF	4 392 130	2 235 791	2 156 339	...	...	...	...	...	...
35 - 39	ESDF	4 172 522	2 140 884	2 031 638	...	...	...	...	...	...
40 - 44	ESDF	4 252 553	2 155 291	2 097 262	...	...	...	...	...	...
45 - 49	ESDF	3 346 274	1 696 492	1 649 782	...	...	...	...	...	...
50 - 54	ESDF	2 497 147	1 256 640	1 240 507	...	...	...	...	...	...

7. Population by age, sex and urban/rural residence: latest available year, 1993 - 2002
Population selon l'âge, le sexe et la résidence, urbaine/rurale: dernière année disponible, 1993 - 2002
(continued — suite)

(See notes at end of table. — Voir notes à la fin du tableau.)

Continent, country or area, date and age (in years) / Continent, pays ou zone, date et âge (en années)	Code[1]	Total			Urban - Urbaine			Rural - Rurale		
		Both sexes Les deux sexes	Male Masculin	Female Féminin	Both sexes Les deux sexes	Male Masculin	Female Féminin	Both sexes Les deux sexes	Male Masculin	Female Féminin
ASIA — ASIE										
Korea (Republic of) - Corée (République de)[23]										
1 VII 2002										
55 - 59	ESDF	2 037 456	1 011 614	1 025 842	...	...	...	...	...	...
60 - 64	ESDF	1 908 047	897 293	1 010 754	...	...	...	...	...	...
65 - 69	ESDF	1 533 619	681 168	852 451	...	...	...	...	...	...
70 - 74	ESDF	1 028 596	399 779	628 817	...	...	...	...	...	...
75 - 79	ESDF	657 082	233 653	423 429	...	...	...	...	...	...
80 - 84	ESDF	350 790	110 492	240 298	...	...	...	...	...	...
85 - 89	ESDF	152 115	38 274	113 841	...	...	...	...	...	...
90 - 94	ESDF	42 459	8 363	34 096	...	...	...	...	...	...
95+	ESDF	7 793	1 046	6 747	...	...	...	...	...	...
Kuwait - Koweït										
1 VII 1998										
Total	ESDF	2 027 103	1 226 774	800 329	...	...	...	...	...	...
0 - 1	ESDF	38 759	19 737	19 022	...	...	...	...	...	...
1 - 4	ESDF	162 578	82 913	79 665	...	...	...	...	...	...
5 - 9	ESDF	178 527	91 301	87 226	...	...	...	...	...	...
10 - 14	ESDF	162 295	82 540	79 755	...	...	...	...	...	...
15 - 19	ESDF	135 096	69 853	65 243	...	...	...	...	...	...
20 - 24	ESDF	154 165	81 411	72 754	...	...	...	...	...	...
25 - 29	ESDF	245 307	156 663	88 644	...	...	...	...	...	...
30 - 34	ESDF	273 922	186 112	87 810	...	...	...	...	...	...
35 - 39	ESDF	228 935	152 744	76 191	...	...	...	...	...	...
40 - 44	ESDF	173 732	119 508	54 224	...	...	...	...	...	...
45 - 49	ESDF	110 552	77 575	32 977	...	...	...	...	...	...
50 - 54	ESDF	66 987	46 236	20 751	...	...	...	...	...	...
55 - 59	ESDF	41 362	27 964	13 398	...	...	...	...	...	...
60 - 64	ESDF	25 882	16 652	9 230	...	...	...	...	...	...
65 - 69	ESDF	13 541	7 701	5 840	...	...	...	...	...	...
70 - 74	ESDF	7 631	4 004	3 627	...	...	...	...	...	...
75 - 79	ESDF	4 060	1 998	2 062	...	...	...	...	...	...
80 - 84	ESDF	2 111	1 073	1 038	...	...	...	...	...	...
85+	ESDF	1 661	789	872	...	...	...	...	...	...
1 VII 2002										
Total	ESDF	2 261 956	1 355 300	906 656	...	...	...	...	...	...
0 - 14	ESDF	566 285	288 632	277 653	...	...	...	...	...	...
15 - 64	ESDF	1 658 601	1 047 074	611 527	...	...	...	...	...	...
65+	ESDF	37 070	19 594	17 476	...	...	...	...	...	...
Kyrgyzstan - Kirghizistan										
1 I 2002										
Total	ESDF	4 946 471	2 443 632	2 502 839	1 726 509	825 188	901 321	3 219 962	1 618 444	1 601 518
0 - 1	ESDF	96 418	49 329	47 089	27 778	14 130	13 648	68 640	35 199	33 441
1 - 4	ESDF	398 607	203 414	195 193	110 306	56 473	53 833	288 301	146 941	141 360
5 - 9	ESDF	573 205	290 583	282 622	159 243	80 406	78 837	413 962	210 177	203 785
10 - 14	ESDF	593 182	300 182	293 000	173 114	86 794	86 320	420 068	213 388	206 680
15 - 19	ESDF	539 876	271 601	268 275	163 598	80 456	83 142	376 278	191 145	185 133
20 - 24	ESDF	456 011	230 129	225 882	194 115	93 491	100 624	261 896	136 638	125 258
25 - 29	ESDF	402 293	202 468	199 825	156 484	75 767	80 717	245 809	126 701	119 108
30 - 34	ESDF	363 945	182 801	181 144	145 207	70 314	74 893	218 738	112 487	106 251
35 - 39	ESDF	337 355	166 989	170 366	131 248	63 278	67 970	206 107	103 711	102 396
40 - 44	ESDF	316 417	155 307	161 110	123 674	58 654	65 020	192 743	96 653	96 090
45 - 49	ESDF	229 563	110 860	118 703	91 499	42 735	48 764	138 064	68 125	69 939
50 - 54	ESDF	167 109	79 717	87 392	69 871	32 121	37 750	97 238	47 596	49 642
55 - 59	ESDF	77 265	36 559	40 706	32 013	14 377	17 636	45 252	22 182	23 070
60 - 64	ESDF	122 015	55 520	66 495	48 311	20 858	27 453	73 704	34 662	39 042
65 - 69	ESDF	97 244	42 818	54 426	35 191	14 363	20 828	62 053	28 455	33 598

7. Population by age, sex and urban/rural residence: latest available year, 1993 - 2002
Population selon l'âge, le sexe et la résidence, urbaine/rurale: dernière année disponible, 1993 - 2002
(continued — suite)

(See notes at end of table. — Voir notes à la fin du tableau.)

Continent, country or area, date and age (in years) / Continent, pays ou zone, date et âge (en années)	Code[1]	Total			Urban - Urbaine			Rural - Rurale		
		Both sexes Les deux sexes	Male Masculin	Female Féminin	Both sexes Les deux sexes	Male Masculin	Female Féminin	Both sexes Les deux sexes	Male Masculin	Female Féminin
ASIA — ASIE										
Kyrgyzstan - Kirghizistan										
1 I 2002										
70 - 74	ESDF	88 292	36 645	51 647	31 660	11 601	20 059	56 632	25 044	31 588
75 - 79	ESDF	50 557	18 461	32 096	19 507	5 844	13 663	31 050	12 617	18 433
80 - 84	ESDF	21 468	6 387	15 081	8 225	2 275	5 950	13 243	4 112	9 131
85 - 89	ESDF	9 333	2 364	6 969	3 688	827	2 861	5 645	1 537	4 108
90 - 94	ESDF	4 274	1 099	3 175	1 335	348	987	2 939	751	2 188
95 - 99	ESDF	1 335	297	1 038	324	65	259	1 011	232	779
100+	ESDF	707	102	605	118	11	107	589	91	498
Lao People's Democratic Republic - République démocratique populaire lao										
1 VII 2000										
Total	ESDF	5 218 300	2 579 000	2 639 300	...	...	...	...	...	...
0 - 4	ESDF	685 000	345 600	340 500	...	...	...	...	...	...
5 - 9	ESDF	807 100	407 400	398 500	...	...	...	...	...	...
10 - 14	ESDF	784 100	389 400	393 300	...	...	...	...	...	...
15 - 19	ESDF	550 600	276 000	274 500	...	...	...	...	...	...
20 - 24	ESDF	371 100	175 400	198 000	...	...	...	...	...	...
25 - 29	ESDF	357 800	165 100	192 700	...	...	...	...	...	...
30 - 34	ESDF	308 000	144 400	163 600	...	...	...	...	...	...
35 - 39	ESDF	326 900	159 900	166 300	...	...	...	...	...	...
40 - 44	ESDF	251 600	131 500	118 800	...	...	...	...	...	...
45 - 49	ESDF	205 100	110 900	95 000	...	...	...	...	...	...
50 - 54	ESDF	164 000	72 200	92 400	...	...	...	...	...	...
55 - 59	ESDF	124 700	61 900	63 300	...	...	...	...	...	...
60 - 64	ESDF	98 200	51 600	47 500	...	...	...	...	...	...
65 - 69	ESDF	73 500	36 100	37 000	...	...	...	...	...	...
70 - 74	ESDF	51 000	25 800	23 800	...	...	...	...	...	...
75+	ESDF	60 000	25 800	34 300	...	...	...	...	...	...
Malaysia - Malaisie										
5 VII 2000										
Total	CDJC	23 274 690	11 853 432	11 421 258	14 426 871	7 318 396	7 108 475	8 847 819	4 535 036	4 312 783
0 - 4	CDJC	2 612 744	1 347 633	1 265 111	1 574 757	812 456	762 301	1 037 987	535 177	502 810
5 - 9	CDJC	2 646 527	1 364 984	1 281 543	1 534 452	792 519	741 933	1 112 075	572 465	539 610
10 - 14	CDJC	2 491 777	1 276 348	1 215 429	1 383 003	709 140	673 863	1 108 774	567 208	541 566
15 - 19	CDJC	2 367 021	1 195 803	1 171 218	1 408 673	707 968	700 705	958 348	487 835	470 513
20 - 24	CDJC	2 087 173	1 050 916	1 036 257	1 436 911	708 607	728 304	650 262	342 309	307 953
25 - 29	CDJC	1 921 052	972 668	948 384	1 315 940	653 627	662 313	605 112	319 041	286 071
30 - 34	CDJC	1 800 196	915 814	884 382	1 207 148	606 473	600 675	593 048	309 341	283 707
35 - 39	CDJC	1 705 044	866 212	838 832	1 141 371	577 947	563 424	563 673	288 265	275 408
40 - 44	CDJC	1 487 498	764 706	722 792	976 771	504 183	472 588	510 727	260 523	250 204
45 - 49	CDJC	1 168 527	604 844	563 683	743 757	389 417	354 340	424 770	215 427	209 343
50 - 54	CDJC	918 868	480 261	438 607	562 704	298 115	264 589	356 164	182 146	174 018
55 - 59	CDJC	616 598	320 119	296 479	356 078	186 312	169 766	260 520	133 807	126 713
60 - 64	CDJC	551 027	274 216	276 811	306 351	153 941	152 410	244 676	120 275	124 401
65 - 69	CDJC	346 725	164 943	181 782	189 063	89 783	99 280	157 662	75 160	82 502
70 - 74	CDJC	264 119	125 883	138 236	138 716	64 354	74 362	125 403	61 529	63 874
75+	CDJC	289 794	128 082	161 712	151 176	63 554	87 622	138 618	64 528	74 090
Maldives										
25 III 1995										
Total	CDFC	244 814	124 622	120 192	62 519	33 506	29 013	182 295	91 116	91 179
0 - 1	CDFC	7 044	3 593	3 451	1 149	592	557	5 895	3 001	2 894
1 - 4	CDFC	29 928	15 520	14 408	4 978	2 603	2 375	24 950	12 917	12 033
5 - 9	CDFC	40 759	20 840	19 919	7 203	3 671	3 532	33 556	17 169	16 387
10 - 14	CDFC	35 870	18 286	17 584	8 441	4 256	4 185	27 429	14 030	13 399

7. Population by age, sex and urban/rural residence: latest available year, 1993 - 2002
Population selon l'âge, le sexe et la résidence, urbaine/rurale: dernière année disponible, 1993 - 2002
(continued — suite)

(See notes at end of table. — Voir notes à la fin du tableau.)

Continent, country or area, date and age (in years) / Continent, pays ou zone, date et âge (en années)	Code[1]	Total Both sexes Les deux sexes	Total Male Masculin	Total Female Féminin	Urban - Urbaine Both sexes Les deux sexes	Urban - Urbaine Male Masculin	Urban - Urbaine Female Féminin	Rural - Rurale Both sexes Les deux sexes	Rural - Rurale Male Masculin	Rural - Rurale Female Féminin
ASIA — ASIE										
Maldives										
25 III 1995										
15 - 19	CDFC	24 905	12 343	12 562	9 745	5 328	4 417	15 160	7 015	8 145
20 - 24	CDFC	21 021	9 944	11 077	7 339	4 075	3 264	13 682	5 869	7 813
25 - 29	CDFC	18 191	8 802	9 389	5 854	3 229	2 625	12 337	5 573	6 764
30 - 34	CDFC	15 364	7 579	7 785	4 656	2 526	2 130	10 708	5 053	5 655
35 - 39	CDFC	12 632	6 315	6 317	3 572	1 911	1 661	9 060	4 404	4 656
40 - 44	CDFC	6 922	3 625	3 297	2 061	1 216	845	4 861	2 409	2 452
45 - 49	CDFC	6 584	3 369	3 215	1 892	1 021	871	4 692	2 348	2 344
50 - 54	CDFC	6 247	3 205	3 042	1 643	885	758	4 604	2 320	2 284
55 - 59	CDFC	5 962	3 240	2 722	1 341	725	616	4 621	2 515	2 106
60 - 64	CDFC	5 294	3 010	2 284	1 061	563	498	4 233	2 447	1 786
65 - 69	CDFC	3 201	1 897	1 304	606	335	271	2 595	1 562	1 033
70 - 74	CDFC	2 101	1 279	822	387	222	165	1 714	1 057	657
75 - 79	CDFC	968	617	351	186	99	87	782	518	264
80 - 84	CDFC	695	394	301	102	44	58	593	350	243
85 - 89	CDFC	326	220	106	47	24	23	279	196	83
90 - 94	CDFC	163	86	77	27	12	15	136	74	62
95+	CDFC	94	67	27	17	9	8	77	58	19
Unk. - Inc.	CDFC	543	391	152	212	160	52	331	231	100
1 VII 2001										
Total	ESDF	275 975	140 100	135 875	...	...	...	...	...	...
0 - 4	ESDF	30 046	15 280	14 766	...	...	...	...	...	...
5 - 9	ESDF	36 928	18 839	18 089	...	...	...	...	...	...
10 - 14	ESDF	41 695	21 268	20 427	...	...	...	...	...	...
15 - 19	ESDF	35 609	17 848	17 761	...	...	...	...	...	...
20 - 24	ESDF	25 279	12 530	12 749	...	...	...	...	...	...
25 - 29	ESDF	20 695	10 127	10 568	...	...	...	...	...	...
30 - 34	ESDF	18 713	9 151	9 562	...	...	...	...	...	...
35 - 39	ESDF	16 377	8 146	8 231	...	...	...	...	...	...
40 - 44	ESDF	13 346	6 724	6 622	...	...	...	...	...	...
45 - 49	ESDF	8 304	4 395	3 909	...	...	...	...	...	...
50 - 54	ESDF	6 105	3 148	2 957	...	...	...	...	...	...
55 - 59	ESDF	5 909	3 066	2 843	...	...	...	...	...	...
60 - 64	ESDF	6 323	3 347	2 976	...	...	...	...	...	...
65 - 69	ESDF	4 963	2 792	2 171	...	...	...	...	...	...
70 - 74	ESDF	2 923	1 778	1 145	...	...	...	...	...	...
75+	ESDF	2 760	1 661	1 099	...	...	...	...	...	...
Mongolia - Mongolie										
5 I 2000										
Total	CDFC	2 373 493	1 177 981	1 195 512	1 344 516	657 081	687 435	1 028 977	520 900	508 077
0 - 1	CDFC	49 804	25 356	24 448	23 778	12 119	11 659	26 026	13 237	12 789
1 - 4	CDFC	196 219	99 126	97 093	91 687	46 096	45 591	104 532	53 030	51 502
5 - 9	CDFC	285 664	144 315	141 349	150 401	75 700	74 701	135 263	69 624	66 648
10 - 14	CDFC	317 434	159 294	158 140	179 974	89 670	90 304	137 460	69 624	67 836
15 - 19	CDFC	263 358	133 327	130 031	154 244	75 040	79 204	109 114	58 287	50 827
20 - 24	CDFC	235 751	118 023	117 728	135 694	66 010	69 684	100 057	52 013	48 044
25 - 29	CDFC	216 652	107 962	108 690	125 644	61 274	64 370	91 008	46 688	44 320
30 - 34	CDFC	187 872	92 473	95 399	113 537	54 332	59 205	74 335	38 141	36 194
35 - 39	CDFC	172 606	84 846	87 760	108 347	52 275	56 072	64 259	32 571	31 688
40 - 44	CDFC	127 220	62 619	64 601	79 563	38 840	40 723	47 657	23 779	23 878
45 - 49	CDFC	82 888	40 562	42 326	50 873	25 089	25 784	32 015	15 473	16 542
50 - 54	CDFC	57 835	27 707	30 128	35 016	17 094	17 922	22 819	10 613	12 206
55 - 59	CDFC	55 895	27 379	28 516	30 397	15 011	15 386	25 498	12 368	13 130
60 - 64	CDFC	42 292	20 778	21 514	21 889	10 658	11 231	20 403	10 120	10 283
65 - 69	CDFC	35 415	15 982	19 433	18 480	8 145	10 335	16 935	7 837	9 098
70 - 74	CDFC	20 239	8 766	11 473	10 946	4 579	6 367	9 293	4 187	5 106
75 - 79	CDFC	14 843	5 832	9 011	7 963	3 197	4 766	6 880	2 635	4 245
80 - 84	CDFC	7 036	2 329	4 707	3 777	1 281	2 496	3 259	1 048	2 211

7. Population by age, sex and urban/rural residence: latest available year, 1993 - 2002
Population selon l'âge, le sexe et la résidence, urbaine/rurale: dernière année disponible, 1993 - 2002
(continued — suite)

(See notes at end of table. — Voir notes à la fin du tableau.)

Continent, country or area, date and age (in years) / Continent, pays ou zone, date et âge (en annèes)	Code[1]	Total			Urban - Urbaine			Rural - Rurale		
		Both sexes Les deux sexes	Male Masculin	Female Féminin	Both sexes Les deux sexes	Male Masculin	Female Féminin	Both sexes Les deux sexes	Male Masculin	Female Féminin
ASIA — ASIE										
Mongolia - Mongolie										
5 I 2000										
85 - 89	CDFC	3 376	991	2 385	1 746	519	1 227	1 630	472	1 158
90 - 94	CDFC	869	257	612	441	125	316	428	132	296
95 - 99	CDFC	196	53	143	104	24	80	92	29	63
100+	CDFC	29	4	25	15	3	12	14	1	13
1 I 2001										
Total	ESDF	2 407 488	1 192 415	1 215 073	...	...	...	...	...	...
0 - 1	ESDF	42 354	21 422	20 932	...	...	...	...	...	...
1 - 4	ESDF	188 339	95 160	93 179	...	...	...	...	...	...
5 - 9	ESDF	267 992	135 329	132 663	...	...	...	...	...	...
10 - 14	ESDF	314 824	157 923	156 901	...	...	...	...	...	...
15 - 19	ESDF	276 626	138 551	138 075	...	...	...	...	...	...
20 - 24	ESDF	249 447	122 680	126 767	...	...	...	...	...	...
25 - 29	ESDF	219 824	108 963	110 861	...	...	...	...	...	...
30 - 34	ESDF	190 603	93 735	96 868	...	...	...	...	...	...
35 - 39	ESDF	172 606	85 266	87 340	...	...	...	...	...	...
40 - 44	ESDF	139 384	68 554	70 830	...	...	...	...	...	...
45 - 49	ESDF	90 233	44 648	45 585	...	...	...	...	...	...
50 - 54	ESDF	66 975	32 675	34 300	...	...	...	...	...	...
55 - 59	ESDF	57 203	28 099	29 104	...	...	...	...	...	...
60 - 64	ESDF	46 237	22 418	23 819	...	...	...	...	...	...
65 - 69	ESDF	35 173	16 382	18 791	...	...	...	...	...	...
70 - 74	ESDF	21 783	9 688	12 095	...	...	...	...	...	...
75 - 79	ESDF	15 268	6 473	8 795	...	...	...	...	...	...
80 - 84	ESDF	7 633	2 806	4 827	...	...	...	...	...	...
85 - 89	ESDF	3 685	1 222	2 463	...	...	...	...	...	...
90 - 94	ESDF	1 053	348	705	...	...	...	...	...	...
95 - 99	ESDF	204	65	139	...	...	...	...	...	...
100+	ESDF	42	8	34	...	...	...	...	...	...
Myanmar										
1 VII 1997										
Total	ESDF	46 402 000	23 039 000	23 363 000	...	...	...	...	...	...
0 - 4	ESDF	5 786 000	2 879 000	2 907 000	...	...	...	...	...	...
5 - 9	ESDF	4 959 000	2 558 000	2 401 000	...	...	...	...	...	...
10 - 14	ESDF	4 708 000	2 440 000	2 268 000	...	...	...	...	...	...
15 - 19	ESDF	4 593 000	2 343 000	2 250 000	...	...	...	...	...	...
20 - 24	ESDF	4 299 000	2 165 000	2 134 000	...	...	...	...	...	...
25 - 29	ESDF	3 952 000	1 961 000	1 991 000	...	...	...	...	...	...
30 - 34	ESDF	3 555 000	1 745 000	1 810 000	...	...	...	...	...	...
35 - 39	ESDF	3 060 000	1 496 000	1 564 000	...	...	...	...	...	...
40 - 44	ESDF	2 594 000	1 263 000	1 331 000	...	...	...	...	...	...
45 - 49	ESDF	2 131 000	1 035 000	1 096 000	...	...	...	...	...	...
50 - 54	ESDF	1 747 000	842 000	905 000	...	...	...	...	...	...
55 - 59	ESDF	1 466 000	695 000	771 000	...	...	...	...	...	...
60 - 64	ESDF	1 202 000	561 000	641 000	...	...	...	...	...	...
65+	ESDF	2 350 000	1 056 000	1 294 000	...	...	...	...	...	...
Nepal - Népal										
1 VII 1996										
Total	ESDJ	20 831 644	10 393 913	10 437 731	2 207 967	1 138 641	1 069 326	18 623 677	9 255 272	9 368 405
0 - 4	ESDJ	3 235 783	1 658 100	1 577 683	283 174	139 204	143 970	2 952 609	1 518 896	1 433 713
5 - 9	ESDJ	2 838 712	1 447 733	1 390 979	280 407	151 796	128 611	2 558 305	1 295 937	1 262 368
10 - 14	ESDJ	2 521 943	1 275 549	1 246 394	241 904	124 110	117 794	2 280 040	1 151 439	1 128 601
15 - 19	ESDJ	2 149 812	1 041 495	1 108 317	233 403	110 195	123 208	1 916 408	931 300	985 108
20 - 24	ESDJ	1 839 716	882 635	957 081	237 790	118 604	119 186	1 601 926	764 031	837 895
25 - 29	ESDJ	1 565 942	766 431	799 511	222 983	122 864	100 119	1 342 960	643 568	699 392
30 - 34	ESDJ	1 310 586	648 320	662 266	170 140	93 500	76 640	1 140 446	554 820	585 626
35 - 39	ESDJ	1 139 089	570 183	568 906	133 684	73 273	60 411	1 005 405	496 910	508 495
40 - 44	ESDJ	983 519	494 106	489 413	105 506	56 085	49 421	878 013	438 021	439 992

7. Population by age, sex and urban/rural residence: latest available year, 1993 - 2002
Population selon l'âge, le sexe et la résidence, urbaine/rurale: dernière année disponible, 1993 - 2002
(continued — suite)

(See notes at end of table. — Voir notes à la fin du tableau.)

Continent, country or area, date and age (in years) / Continent, pays ou zone, date et âge (en années)	Code[1]	Total			Urban - Urbaine			Rural - Rurale		
		Both sexes Les deux sexes	Male Masculin	Female Féminin	Both sexes Les deux sexes	Male Masculin	Female Féminin	Both sexes Les deux sexes	Male Masculin	Female Féminin
ASIA — ASIE										
Nepal - Népal										
1 VII 1996										
45 - 49	ESDJ	839 008	423 529	415 479	81 831	44 633	37 198	757 176	378 896	378 280
50 - 54	ESDJ	698 161	351 396	346 765	62 770	32 371	30 399	635 391	319 025	316 366
55 - 59	ESDJ	566 009	283 271	282 738	49 332	24 253	25 079	516 677	259 019	257 658
60 - 64	ESDJ	438 536	216 857	221 679	38 025	17 312	20 713	400 511	199 545	200 966
65 - 69	ESDJ	318 278	154 732	163 546	28 023	13 376	14 647	290 255	141 356	148 899
70 - 74	ESDJ	208 529	98 933	109 596	19 466	8 853	10 613	189 062	90 079	98 983
75 - 79	ESDJ	115 654	53 285	62 369	12 217	4 965	7 252	103 437	48 320	55 117
80+	ESDJ	62 367	27 358	35 009	7 312	3 247	4 065	55 056	24 110	30 946
22 VI 2001										
Total	CDJC	22 736 934	11 359 378	11 377 556	...	...	...	...	...	...
0 - 1	CDJC	494 813	252 519	242 294	...	...	...	...	...	...
1 - 4	CDJC	2 260 400	1 143 196	1 117 204	...	...	...	...	...	...
5 - 9	CDJC	3 211 442	1 633 087	1 578 355	...	...	...	...	...	...
10 - 14	CDJC	2 981 932	1 533 806	1 448 126	...	...	...	...	...	...
15 - 19	CDJC	2 389 002	1 185 826	1 203 176	...	...	...	...	...	...
20 - 24	CDJC	2 016 768	946 742	1 070 026	...	...	...	...	...	...
25 - 29	CDJC	1 725 478	821 014	904 464	...	...	...	...	...	...
30 - 34	CDJC	1 489 503	726 040	763 463	...	...	...	...	...	...
35 - 39	CDJC	1 310 653	651 351	659 302	...	...	...	...	...	...
40 - 44	CDJC	1 088 044	539 993	548 051	...	...	...	...	...	...
45 - 49	CDJC	923 373	469 695	453 678	...	...	...	...	...	...
50 - 54	CDJC	766 054	392 659	373 395	...	...	...	...	...	...
55 - 59	CDJC	602 093	318 610	283 483	...	...	...	...	...	...
60 - 64	CDJC	520 908	262 255	258 653	...	...	...	...	...	...
65 - 69	CDJC	387 223	196 053	191 170	...	...	...	...	...	...
70 - 74	CDJC	273 789	141 678	132 111	...	...	...	...	...	...
75 - 79	CDJC	165 764	82 335	83 429	...	...	...	...	...	...
80 - 84	CDJC	84 255	41 192	43 063	...	...	...	...	...	...
85 - 89	CDJC	27 947	13 630	14 317	...	...	...	...	...	...
90 - 94	CDJC	11 421	5 082	6 339	...	...	...	...	...	...
95 - 99	CDJC	6 072	2 615	3 457	...	...	...	...	...	...
Occupied Palestinian Territory - Territoire palestinien occupé										
1 VII 2002										
Total	ESDF	3 464 550	1 751 271	1 713 279	...	...	...	...	...	...
0 - 1	ESDF	132 618	67 470	65 148	...	...	...	...	...	...
1 - 4	ESDF	493 432	250 892	242 540	...	...	...	...	...	...
5 - 9	ESDF	533 531	271 366	262 165	...	...	...	...	...	...
10 - 14	ESDF	448 592	227 883	220 709	...	...	...	...	...	...
15 - 19	ESDF	363 072	185 670	177 402	...	...	...	...	...	...
20 - 24	ESDF	304 672	155 494	149 178	...	...	...	...	...	...
25 - 29	ESDF	257 839	131 126	126 713	...	...	...	...	...	...
30 - 34	ESDF	215 710	109 886	105 824	...	...	...	...	...	...
35 - 39	ESDF	179 733	92 817	86 916	...	...	...	...	...	...
40 - 44	ESDF	142 965	73 897	69 068	...	...	...	...	...	...
45 - 49	ESDF	99 653	51 008	48 645	...	...	...	...	...	...
50 - 54	ESDF	76 017	37 886	38 131	...	...	...	...	...	...
55 - 59	ESDF	58 528	26 997	31 531	...	...	...	...	...	...
60 - 64	ESDF	47 418	20 852	26 566	...	...	...	...	...	...
65 - 69	ESDF	42 015	18 188	23 827	...	...	...	...	...	...
70 - 74	ESDF	31 430	13 446	17 984	...	...	...	...	...	...
75 - 79	ESDF	20 229	8 626	11 603	...	...	...	...	...	...
80+	ESDF	17 096	7 767	9 329	...	...	...	...	...	...
Oman										
1 VII 2001										
Total	ESDF	2 477 687	1 451 041	1 026 646	...	...	...	...	...	...

7. Population by age, sex and urban/rural residence: latest available year, 1993 - 2002
Population selon l'âge, le sexe et la résidence, urbaine/rurale: dernière année disponible, 1993 - 2002
(continued — suite)

(See notes at end of table. — Voir notes à la fin du tableau.)

Continent, country or area, date and age (in years) / Continent, pays ou zone, date et âge (en années)	Code[1]	Total Both sexes Les deux sexes	Total Male Masculin	Total Female Féminin	Urban - Urbaine Both sexes Les deux sexes	Urban - Urbaine Male Masculin	Urban - Urbaine Female Féminin	Rural - Rurale Both sexes Les deux sexes	Rural - Rurale Male Masculin	Rural - Rurale Female Féminin
ASIA — ASIE										
Oman										
1 VII 2001										
0 - 4	ESDF	283 925	145 540	138 385	...	...	...	...	...	...
5 - 9	ESDF	284 169	145 183	138 986	...	...	...	...	...	...
10 - 14	ESDF	278 830	141 806	137 024	...	...	...	...	...	...
15 - 19	ESDF	249 899	127 830	122 069	...	...	...	...	...	...
20 - 24	ESDF	259 983	144 620	115 363	...	...	...	...	...	...
25 - 29	ESDF	278 408	181 730	96 678	...	...	...	...	...	...
30 - 34	ESDF	228 857	161 662	67 195	...	...	...	...	...	...
35 - 39	ESDF	190 508	137 555	52 953	...	...	...	...	...	...
40 - 44	ESDF	137 309	95 913	41 396	...	...	...	...	...	...
45 - 49	ESDF	89 330	58 590	30 740	...	...	...	...	...	...
50 - 54	ESDF	60 825	37 355	23 470	...	...	...	...	...	...
55 - 59	ESDF	42 732	23 974	18 758	...	...	...	...	...	...
60 - 64	ESDF	32 806	17 775	15 031	...	...	...	...	...	...
65 - 69	ESDF	23 695	12 606	11 089	...	...	...	...	...	...
70 - 74	ESDF	16 250	8 683	7 567	...	...	...	...	...	...
75+	ESDF	19 519	9 577	9 942	...	...	...	...	...	...
Unk. - Inc.	ESDF	642	642	...	...	...	...	...	...	...
Pakistan[24,25]										
2 III 1998										
Total	CDFC	127 441 708	66 204 793	61 236 915	42 375 208	22 374 052	20 001 156	85 066 500	43 830 741	41 235 759
0 - 4	CDFC	18 611 101	9 488 106	9 122 995	5 369 807	2 699 426	2 670 381	13 241 294	6 788 680	6 452 614
5 - 9	CDFC	19 944 265	10 376 230	9 568 035	5 860 782	2 975 132	2 885 650	14 083 483	7 401 098	6 682 385
10 - 14	CDFC	16 487 551	8 681 970	7 805 581	5 434 781	2 777 214	2 657 567	11 052 770	5 904 756	5 148 014
15 - 19	CDFC	13 193 775	6 780 579	6 413 196	4 720 114	2 404 205	2 315 909	8 473 661	4 376 374	4 097 287
20 - 24	CDFC	11 491 380	5 766 195	5 725 185	4 182 102	2 211 952	1 970 150	7 309 278	3 554 243	3 755 035
25 - 29	CDFC	9 565 376	4 964 363	4 601 013	3 579 238	2 022 092	1 557 146	5 986 138	2 942 271	3 043 867
30 - 34	CDFC	8 103 504	4 330 684	3 772 820	3 122 406	1 796 023	1 326 383	4 981 098	2 534 661	2 446 437
35 - 39	CDFC	6 144 394	3 278 330	2 866 064	2 373 755	1 336 906	1 036 849	3 770 639	1 941 424	1 829 215
40 - 44	CDFC	5 640 767	2 847 692	2 793 075	2 057 973	1 100 661	957 312	3 582 794	1 747 031	1 835 763
45 - 49	CDFC	4 494 396	2 294 132	2 200 264	1 528 816	815 066	713 750	2 965 580	1 479 066	1 486 514
50 - 54	CDFC	4 080 253	2 151 291	1 928 962	1 325 717	705 053	620 664	2 754 536	1 446 238	1 308 298
55 - 59	CDFC	2 698 411	1 448 731	1 249 680	861 236	471 026	390 210	1 837 175	977 705	859 470
60 - 64	CDFC	2 618 383	1 406 681	1 211 702	780 898	418 241	362 657	1 837 485	988 440	849 045
65 - 69	CDFC	1 509 437	828 153	681 284	447 364	243 412	203 952	1 062 073	584 741	477 332
70 - 74	CDFC	1 353 974	744 456	609 518	360 539	196 885	163 654	993 435	547 571	445 864
75+	CDFC	1 504 741	817 200	687 541	369 680	200 758	168 922	1 135 061	616 442	518 619
Philippines										
1 V 2000										
Total	CDJC	76 504 077	38 524 266	37 979 811	...	...	...	...	...	...
0 - 1	CDJC	1 917 431	986 506	930 925	...	...	...	...	...	...
1 - 4	CDJC	7 752 071	3 965 426	3 786 645	...	...	...	...	...	...
5 - 9	CDJC	9 694 781	4 962 013	4 732 768	...	...	...	...	...	...
10 - 14	CDJC	8 949 614	4 541 197	4 408 417	...	...	...	...	...	...
15 - 19	CDJC	8 017 298	4 017 830	3 999 468	...	...	...	...	...	...
20 - 24	CDJC	7 069 403	3 522 518	3 546 885	...	...	...	...	...	...
25 - 29	CDJC	6 071 089	3 053 616	3 017 473	...	...	...	...	...	...
30 - 34	CDJC	5 546 294	2 804 522	2 741 772	...	...	...	...	...	...
35 - 39	CDJC	4 901 023	2 496 821	2 404 202	...	...	...	...	...	...
40 - 44	CDJC	4 163 494	2 120 314	2 043 180	...	...	...	...	...	...
45 - 49	CDJC	3 330 054	1 696 712	1 633 342	...	...	...	...	...	...
50 - 54	CDJC	2 622 316	1 318 632	1 303 684	...	...	...	...	...	...
55 - 59	CDJC	1 903 649	943 133	960 516	...	...	...	...	...	...
60 - 64	CDJC	1 633 150	786 137	847 013	...	...	...	...	...	...
65 - 69	CDJC	1 138 842	533 468	605 374	...	...	...	...	...	...
70 - 74	CDJC	797 972	361 614	436 358	...	...	...	...	...	...
75 - 79	CDJC	505 356	218 622	286 734	...	...	...	...	...	...
80 - 84	CDJC	284 883	115 995	168 888	...	...	...	...	...	...

7. Population by age, sex and urban/rural residence: latest available year, 1993 - 2002
Population selon l'âge, le sexe et la résidence, urbaine/rurale: dernière année disponible, 1993 - 2002
(continued — suite)

(See notes at end of table. — Voir notes à la fin du tableau.)

Continent, country or area, date and age (in years) / Continent, pays ou zone, date et âge (en années)	Code[1]	Total			Urban - Urbaine			Rural - Rurale		
		Both sexes Les deux sexes	Male Masculin	Female Féminin	Both sexes Les deux sexes	Male Masculin	Female Féminin	Both sexes Les deux sexes	Male Masculin	Female Féminin
ASIA — ASIE										
Philippines										
1 V 2000										
85 - 89	CDJC	139 763	55 224	84 539	...	...	...	...	...	...
90 - 94	CDJC	44 423	15 289	29 134	...	...	...	...	...	...
95 - 99	CDJC	19 064	7 930	11 134	...	...	...	...	...	...
100+	CDJC	2 107	747	1 360	...	...	...	...	...	...
Saudi Arabia - Arabie saoudite										
1 VII 2000										
Total	ESDF	20 846 884	11 314 966	9 531 918	...	...	...	...	...	...
0 - 1	ESDF	573 951	295 855	278 096	...	...	...	...	...	...
1 - 4	ESDF	2 441 034	1 242 653	1 198 381	...	...	...	...	...	...
5 - 9	ESDF	2 944 818	1 495 405	1 449 413	...	...	...	...	...	...
10 - 14	ESDF	2 438 938	1 233 885	1 205 053	...	...	...	...	...	...
15 - 19	ESDF	1 982 212	996 045	986 167	...	...	...	...	...	...
20 - 24	ESDF	1 713 454	868 300	845 154	...	...	...	...	...	...
25 - 29	ESDF	1 792 333	1 036 646	755 687	...	...	...	...	...	...
30 - 34	ESDF	1 809 638	1 102 308	707 330	...	...	...	...	...	...
35 - 39	ESDF	1 521 432	925 466	595 966	...	...	...	...	...	...
40 - 44	ESDF	1 107 958	680 792	427 166	...	...	...	...	...	...
45 - 49	ESDF	750 196	451 535	298 661	...	...	...	...	...	...
50 - 54	ESDF	511 497	293 966	217 531	...	...	...	...	...	...
55 - 59	ESDF	368 594	199 305	169 289	...	...	...	...	...	...
60 - 64	ESDF	264 399	131 967	132 432	...	...	...	...	...	...
65 - 69	ESDF	210 292	124 778	85 514	...	...	...	...	...	...
70 - 74	ESDF	180 318	98 255	82 063	...	...	...	...	...	...
75 - 79	ESDF	97 011	58 465	38 546	...	...	...	...	...	...
80 - 84	ESDF	68 434	39 502	28 932	...	...	...	...	...	...
85+	ESDF	70 375	39 838	30 537	...	...	...	...	...	...
Singapore - Singapour[26]										
1 VII 2002										
Total	ESDJ	3 378 300	1 682 800	1 695 500	...	...	...	...	...	...
0 - 4	ESDJ	208 800	108 000	100 800	...	...	...	...	...	...
5 - 9	ESDJ	249 400	128 800	120 600	...	...	...	...	...	...
10 - 14	ESDJ	257 800	132 600	125 200	...	...	...	...	...	...
15 - 19	ESDJ	210 000	108 300	101 700	...	...	...	...	...	...
20 - 24	ESDJ	216 700	108 500	108 200	...	...	...	...	...	...
25 - 29	ESDJ	263 200	126 500	136 700	...	...	...	...	...	...
30 - 34	ESDJ	290 200	140 000	150 200	...	...	...	...	...	...
35 - 39	ESDJ	321 900	160 800	161 100	...	...	...	...	...	...
40 - 44	ESDJ	321 800	162 400	159 300	...	...	...	...	...	...
45 - 49	ESDJ	287 400	145 100	142 300	...	...	...	...	...	...
50 - 54	ESDJ	231 000	116 100	114 900	...	...	...	...	...	...
55 - 59	ESDJ	143 600	71 600	72 000	...	...	...	...	...	...
60 - 64	ESDJ	123 900	60 100	63 800	...	...	...	...	...	...
65 - 69	ESDJ	90 200	43 200	47 000	...	...	...	...	...	...
70 - 74	ESDJ	71 500	33 200	38 200	...	...	...	...	...	...
75 - 79	ESDJ	46 500	21 000	25 500	...	...	...	...	...	...
80+	ESDJ	44 600	16 400	28 100	...	...	...	...	...	...
Sri Lanka										
1 VII 1998										
Total	ESDF	18 774 000	9 570 000	9 204 000	...	...	...	...	...	...
0 - 4	ESDF	2 345 000	1 194 000	1 151 000	...	...	...	...	...	...
5 - 9	ESDF	2 128 000	1 082 000	1 046 000	...	...	...	...	...	...
10 - 14	ESDF	2 136 000	1 090 000	1 046 000	...	...	...	...	...	...
15 - 19	ESDF	2 028 000	1 028 000	1 000 000	...	...	...	...	...	...
20 - 24	ESDF	1 931 000	969 000	962 000	...	...	...	...	...	...
25 - 29	ESDF	1 612 000	807 000	805 000	...	...	...	...	...	...

7. Population by age, sex and urban/rural residence: latest available year, 1993 - 2002
Population selon l'âge, le sexe et la résidence, urbaine/rurale: dernière année disponible, 1993 - 2002
(continued — suite)

(See notes at end of table. — Voir notes à la fin du tableau.)

Continent, country or area, date and age (in years) / Continent, pays ou zone, date et âge (en années)	Code[1]	Total			Urban - Urbaine			Rural - Rurale		
		Both sexes Les deux sexes	Male Masculin	Female Féminin	Both sexes Les deux sexes	Male Masculin	Female Féminin	Both sexes Les deux sexes	Male Masculin	Female Féminin
ASIA — ASIE										
Sri Lanka										
1 VII 1998										
30 - 34	ESDF	1 424 000	721 000	703 000	...	...	...	...	...	...
35 - 39	ESDF	1 060 000	533 000	527 000	...	...	...	...	...	...
40 - 44	ESDF	883 000	455 000	428 000	...	...	...	...	...	...
45 - 49	ESDF	770 000	390 000	380 000	...	...	...	...	...	...
50 - 54	ESDF	682 000	360 000	322 000	...	...	...	...	...	...
55 - 59	ESDF	534 000	281 000	253 000	...	...	...	...	...	...
60 - 64	ESDF	431 000	232 000	199 000	...	...	...	...	...	...
65 - 69	ESDF	318 000	168 000	150 000	...	...	...	...	...	...
70+	ESDF	492 000	260 000	232 000	...	...	...	...	...	...
Syrian Arab Republic - République arabe syrienne[27]										
1 VII 2001										
Total	ESDF	16 720 000	8 552 000	8 168 000	8 376 000	4 319 000	4 057 000	8 344 000	4 233 000	4 111 000
0 - 1	ESDF	401 000	205 000	196 000	147 000	74 000	73 000	254 000	131 000	123 000
1 - 4	ESDF	1 705 000	880 000	825 000	791 000	410 000	381 000	914 000	470 000	444 000
5 - 9	ESDF	2 274 000	1 166 000	1 108 000	1 013 000	518 000	495 000	1 261 000	648 000	613 000
10 - 14	ESDF	2 382 000	1 213 000	1 169 000	1 093 000	553 000	540 000	1 289 000	660 000	629 000
15 - 19	ESDF	2 241 000	1 142 000	1 099 000	1 115 000	583 000	532 000	1 126 000	559 000	567 000
20 - 24	ESDF	1 572 000	792 000	780 000	834 000	436 000	398 000	738 000	356 000	382 000
25 - 29	ESDF	1 228 000	608 000	620 000	640 000	324 000	316 000	588 000	284 000	304 000
30 - 34	ESDF	1 006 000	500 000	506 000	552 000	276 000	276 000	454 000	224 000	230 000
35 - 39	ESDF	868 000	419 000	449 000	472 000	229 000	243 000	396 000	190 000	206 000
40 - 44	ESDF	731 000	360 000	371 000	406 000	199 000	207 000	325 000	161 000	164 000
45 - 49	ESDF	593 000	312 000	281 000	335 000	173 000	162 000	258 000	139 000	119 000
50 - 54	ESDF	540 000	279 000	261 000	306 000	160 000	146 000	234 000	119 000	115 000
55 - 59	ESDF	344 000	180 000	164 000	201 000	108 000	93 000	143 000	72 000	71 000
60 - 64	ESDF	318 000	175 000	143 000	180 000	99 000	81 000	138 000	76 000	62 000
65+	ESDF	517 000	321 000	196 000	291 000	177 000	114 000	226 000	144 000	82 000
Tajikistan - Tadjikistan										
1 VII 1993										
Total	ESDF	5 621 727	2 799 853	2 821 874	1 630 259	802 998	827 261	3 991 468	1 996 855	1 994 613
0 - 1	ESDF	184 774	94 831	89 943	40 106	20 635	19 471	144 668	74 196	70 472
1 - 4	ESDF	766 931	391 834	375 097	178 075	91 008	87 067	588 856	300 826	288 030
5 - 9	ESDF	850 331	430 324	420 007	216 453	109 526	106 927	633 878	320 798	313 080
10 - 14	ESDF	662 636	334 838	327 798	173 587	87 552	86 035	489 049	247 286	241 763
15 - 19	ESDF	556 944	280 895	276 049	154 090	78 932	75 158	402 854	201 963	200 891
20 - 24	ESDF	508 529	253 281	255 248	159 737	87 175	72 562	348 792	166 106	182 686
25 - 29	ESDF	442 462	214 034	228 428	128 423	62 552	65 871	314 039	151 482	162 557
30 - 34	ESDF	407 674	201 357	206 317	126 932	60 776	66 156	280 742	140 581	140 161
35 - 39	ESDF	288 358	142 831	145 527	101 141	48 758	52 383	187 217	94 073	93 144
40 - 44	ESDF	207 948	102 260	105 688	79 581	37 810	41 771	128 367	64 450	63 917
45 - 49	ESDF	117 936	61 378	56 558	45 662	22 419	23 243	72 274	38 959	33 315
50 - 54	ESDF	144 526	75 203	69 323	54 095	26 162	27 933	90 431	49 041	41 390
55 - 59	ESDF	141 142	69 598	71 544	51 033	23 940	27 093	90 109	45 658	44 451
60 - 64	ESDF	124 190	59 376	64 814	42 695	18 867	23 828	81 495	40 509	40 986
65 - 69	ESDF	91 521	41 320	50 201	33 770	13 001	20 769	57 751	28 319	29 432
70 - 74	ESDF	52 809	19 600	33 209	18 809	6 118	12 691	34 000	13 482	20 518
75 - 79	ESDF	31 647	11 305	20 342	12 670	3 774	8 896	18 977	7 531	11 446
80 - 84	ESDF	22 997	8 403	14 594	8 345	2 529	5 816	14 652	5 874	8 778
85 - 89	ESDF	11 267	4 426	6 841	3 458	992	2 466	7 809	3 434	4 375
90 - 94	ESDF	6 068	2 300	3 768	1 316	378	938	4 752	1 922	2 830
95 - 99	ESDF	711	327	384	198	74	124	513	253	260
100+	ESDF	326	132	194	83	20	63	243	112	131

7. Population by age, sex and urban/rural residence: latest available year, 1993 - 2002
Population selon l'âge, le sexe et la résidence, urbaine/rurale: dernière année disponible, 1993 - 2002
(continued — suite)

(See notes at end of table. — Voir notes à la fin du tableau.)

Continent, country or area, date and age (in years) / Continent, pays ou zone, date et âge (en années)	Code[1]	Total			Urban - Urbaine			Rural - Rurale		
		Both sexes Les deux sexes	Male Masculin	Female Féminin	Both sexes Les deux sexes	Male Masculin	Female Féminin	Both sexes Les deux sexes	Male Masculin	Female Féminin
ASIA — ASIE										
Thailand - Thaïlande										
1 VII 2002										
Total	ESDJ	63 482 287	31 623 509	31 858 778	20 731 494	10 072 055	10 659 439	42 750 793	21 551 454	21 199 339
1 - 4	ESDJ	5 120 027	2 598 894	2 521 133	1 511 818	759 380	752 438	3 608 209	1 839 514	1 768 695
5 - 9	ESDJ	5 274 505	2 668 992	2 605 513	1 511 013	755 466	755 547	3 763 492	1 913 526	1 849 966
10 - 14	ESDJ	5 385 639	2 724 988	2 660 651	1 602 403	793 632	808 771	3 783 236	1 931 356	1 851 880
15 - 19	ESDJ	5 574 029	2 825 669	2 748 360	1 790 997	880 104	910 893	3 783 032	1 945 565	1 837 467
20 - 24	ESDJ	5 763 091	2 925 567	2 837 524	1 960 757	960 965	999 792	3 802 334	1 964 602	1 837 732
25 - 29	ESDJ	5 716 021	2 909 450	2 806 571	2 023 745	985 662	1 038 083	3 692 276	1 923 788	1 768 488
30 - 34	ESDJ	5 419 519	2 749 748	2 669 771	1 953 228	953 584	999 644	3 466 291	1 796 164	1 670 127
35 - 39	ESDJ	4 998 304	2 495 630	2 502 674	1 770 599	863 412	907 187	3 227 705	1 632 218	1 595 487
40 - 44	ESDJ	4 566 841	2 264 011	2 302 830	1 577 302	768 102	809 200	2 989 539	1 495 909	1 493 630
45 - 49	ESDJ	4 014 693	1 978 140	2 036 553	1 347 651	651 525	696 126	2 667 042	1 326 615	1 340 427
50 - 54	ESDJ	3 171 357	1 548 338	1 623 019	1 036 000	497 272	538 728	2 135 357	1 051 066	1 084 291
55 - 59	ESDJ	2 484 371	1 194 773	1 289 598	783 686	371 332	412 354	1 700 685	823 441	877 244
60 - 64	ESDJ	2 076 583	976 768	1 099 815	652 935	302 531	350 404	1 423 648	674 237	749 411
65 - 69	ESDJ	1 675 416	776 509	898 907	520 678	237 393	283 285	1 154 738	539 116	615 622
70 - 74	ESDJ	1 109 922	504 276	605 646	329 248	144 969	184 279	780 674	359 307	421 367
75+	ESDJ	1 131 969	481 756	650 213	359 434	146 726	212 708	772 535	335 030	437 505
Turkey - Turquie										
1 VII 2002										
Total	ESDF	69 626 000	35 149 000	34 477 000	...	...	...	...	...	...
0 - 1	ESDF	1 473 000	752 000	721 000	...	...	...	...	...	...
1 - 4	ESDF	5 748 000	2 930 000	2 818 000	...	...	...	...	...	...
5 - 9	ESDF	6 940 000	3 530 000	3 409 000	...	...	...	...	...	...
10 - 14	ESDF	6 423 000	3 279 000	3 144 000	...	...	...	...	...	...
15 - 19	ESDF	6 457 000	3 306 000	3 151 000	...	...	...	...	...	...
20 - 24	ESDF	6 816 000	3 487 000	3 330 000	...	...	...	...	...	...
25 - 29	ESDF	6 571 000	3 352 000	3 219 000	...	...	...	...	...	...
30 - 34	ESDF	5 653 000	2 859 000	2 794 000	...	...	...	...	...	...
35 - 39	ESDF	4 821 000	2 427 000	2 394 000	...	...	...	...	...	...
40 - 44	ESDF	4 261 000	2 165 000	2 095 000	...	...	...	...	...	...
45 - 49	ESDF	3 651 000	1 862 000	1 789 000	...	...	...	...	...	...
50 - 54	ESDF	2 832 000	1 428 000	1 403 000	...	...	...	...	...	...
55 - 59	ESDF	2 214 000	1 096 000	1 118 000	...	...	...	...	...	...
60 - 64	ESDF	1 929 000	935 000	994 000	...	...	...	...	...	...
65 - 69	ESDF	1 599 000	756 000	843 000	...	...	...	...	...	...
70 - 74	ESDF	1 103 000	501 000	602 000	...	...	...	...	...	...
75+	ESDF	1 137 000	483 000	654 000	...	...	...	...	...	...
Turkmenistan - Turkménistan										
10 I 1995										
Total	CDFC	4 483 251	2 225 331	2 257 920	...	...	...	...	...	...
0 - 4	CDFC	674 693	344 429	330 264	...	...	...	...	...	...
5 - 9	CDFC	619 381	315 453	303 928	...	...	...	...	...	...
10 - 14	CDFC	516 995	263 071	253 924	...	...	...	...	...	...
15 - 19	CDFC	455 727	231 593	224 134	...	...	...	...	...	...
20 - 24	CDFC	414 632	204 256	210 376	...	...	...	...	...	...
25 - 29	CDFC	366 538	181 317	185 221	...	...	...	...	...	...
30 - 34	CDFC	351 856	173 927	177 929	...	...	...	...	...	...
35 - 39	CDFC	281 039	138 462	142 577	...	...	...	...	...	...
40 - 44	CDFC	204 313	99 575	104 738	...	...	...	...	...	...
45 - 49	CDFC	126 864	62 244	64 620	...	...	...	...	...	...
50 - 54	CDFC	97 136	48 330	48 806	...	...	...	...	...	...
55 - 59	CDFC	114 232	54 283	59 949	...	...	...	...	...	...
60 - 64	CDFC	91 473	43 379	48 094	...	...	...	...	...	...
65 - 69	CDFC	73 263	32 176	41 087	...	...	...	...	...	...
70 - 74	CDFC	43 818	15 709	28 109	...	...	...	...	...	...
75 - 79	CDFC	22 707	7 301	15 406	...	...	...	...	...	...

7. Population by age, sex and urban/rural residence: latest available year, 1993 - 2002
Population selon l'âge, le sexe et la résidence, urbaine/rurale: dernière année disponible, 1993 - 2002
(continued — suite)

(See notes at end of table. — Voir notes à la fin du tableau.)

Continent, country or area, date and age (in years) / Continent, pays ou zone, date et âge (en années)	Code[1]	Total			Urban - Urbaine			Rural - Rurale		
		Both sexes Les deux sexes	Male Masculin	Female Féminin	Both sexes Les deux sexes	Male Masculin	Female Féminin	Both sexes Les deux sexes	Male Masculin	Female Féminin
ASIA — ASIE										
Turkmenistan - Turkménistan										
10 I 1995										
80 - 84	CDFC	15 942	5 060	10 882	...	...	...	...	...	...
85 - 89	CDFC	5 813	1 782	4 031	...	...	...	...	...	...
90 - 94	CDFC	2 611	737	1 874	...	...	...	...	...	...
95 - 99	CDFC	639	179	460	...	...	...	...	...	...
100+	CDFC	722	274	448	...	...	...	...	...	...
Unk. - Inc.	CDFC	2 857	1 794	1 063	...	...	...	...	...	...
United Arab Emirates - Émirats arabes unis										
17 XII 1995										
Total	CDFC	2 411 041	1 606 804	804 237	...	...	...	...	...	...
0 - 4	CDFC	213 049	109 524	103 525	...	...	...	...	...	...
5 - 9	CDFC	219 291	112 984	106 307	...	...	...	...	...	...
10 - 14	CDFC	202 054	104 885	97 169	...	...	...	...	...	...
15 - 19	CDFC	158 909	83 438	75 471	...	...	...	...	...	...
20 - 24	CDFC	217 750	139 868	77 882	...	...	...	...	...	...
25 - 29	CDFC	326 513	238 104	88 409	...	...	...	...	...	...
30 - 34	CDFC	309 279	229 066	80 213	...	...	...	...	...	...
35 - 39	CDFC	288 701	219 961	68 740	...	...	...	...	...	...
40 - 44	CDFC	203 229	161 583	41 646	...	...	...	...	...	...
45 - 49	CDFC	132 016	106 166	25 850	...	...	...	...	...	...
50 - 54	CDFC	65 349	51 655	13 694	...	...	...	...	...	...
55 - 59	CDFC	33 390	25 046	8 344	...	...	...	...	...	...
60 - 64	CDFC	15 960	10 407	5 553	...	...	...	...	...	...
65 - 69	CDFC	11 089	6 492	4 597	...	...	...	...	...	...
70 - 74	CDFC	6 831	3 651	3 180	...	...	...	...	...	...
75 - 79	CDFC	3 109	1 649	1 460	...	...	...	...	...	...
80+	CDFC	4 357	2 194	2 163	...	...	...	...	...	...
Unk. - Inc.	CDFC	165	131	34	...	...	...	...	...	...
Uzbekistan - Ouzbékistan										
1 VII 2001										
Total	ESDF	24 964 433	12 442 510	12 521 923	9 256 101	4 573 055	4 683 046	15 708 332	7 869 455	7 838 877
0 - 1	ESDF	513 043	263 408	249 635	158 893	81 393	77 500	354 150	182 015	172 135
1 - 4	ESDF	2 219 863	1 138 212	1 081 651	693 448	355 999	337 449	1 526 415	782 213	744 202
5 - 9	ESDF	3 237 989	1 653 776	1 584 213	1 015 989	519 360	496 629	2 222 000	1 134 416	1 087 584
10 - 14	ESDF	3 203 022	1 627 673	1 575 349	1 049 577	533 870	515 707	2 153 445	1 093 803	1 059 642
15 - 19	ESDF	2 821 926	1 422 296	1 399 630	984 385	497 725	486 660	1 837 541	924 571	912 970
20 - 24	ESDF	2 296 834	1 157 998	1 138 836	841 326	425 348	415 978	1 455 508	732 650	722 858
25 - 29	ESDF	2 030 200	1 023 174	1 007 026	788 176	397 184	390 992	1 242 024	625 990	616 034
30 - 34	ESDF	1 749 557	861 368	888 189	726 099	372 846	353 253	1 023 458	488 522	534 936
35 - 39	ESDF	1 672 397	816 665	855 732	660 932	323 492	337 440	1 011 465	493 173	518 292
40 - 44	ESDF	1 479 057	728 780	750 277	612 755	297 460	315 295	866 302	431 320	434 982
45 - 49	ESDF	1 034 628	506 734	527 894	464 375	223 425	240 950	570 253	283 309	286 944
50 - 54	ESDF	696 648	337 634	359 014	340 008	161 069	178 939	356 640	176 565	180 075
55 - 59	ESDF	394 997	197 700	197 297	185 073	88 314	96 759	209 924	109 386	100 538
60 - 64	ESDF	553 697	265 428	288 269	254 409	115 715	138 694	299 288	149 713	149 575
65 - 69	ESDF	399 550	185 653	213 897	171 869	75 277	96 592	227 681	110 376	117 305
70 - 74	ESDF	325 230	143 466	181 764	146 702	57 100	89 602	178 528	86 366	92 162
75 - 79	ESDF	185 449	67 568	117 881	87 515	27 439	60 076	97 934	40 129	57 805
80 - 84	ESDF	78 794	23 459	55 335	39 138	10 729	28 409	39 656	12 730	26 926
85 - 89	ESDF	41 343	10 761	30 582	20 793	4 904	15 889	20 550	5 857	14 693
90 - 94	ESDF	19 195	6 220	12 975	9 150	2 774	6 376	10 045	3 446	6 599
95 - 99	ESDF	10 114	4 171	5 943	4 954	1 461	3 493	5 160	2 710	2 450
100+	ESDF	900	366	534	535	171	364	365	195	170

7. Population by age, sex and urban/rural residence: latest available year, 1993 - 2002
Population selon l'âge, le sexe et la résidence, urbaine/rurale: dernière année disponible, 1993 - 2002
(continued — suite)

(See notes at end of table. — Voir notes à la fin du tableau.)

Continent, country or area, date and age (in years) / Continent, pays ou zone, date et âge (en annèes)	Code[1]	Total			Urban - Urbaine			Rural - Rurale		
		Both sexes Les deux sexes	Male Masculin	Female Féminin	Both sexes Les deux sexes	Male Masculin	Female Féminin	Both sexes Les deux sexes	Male Masculin	Female Féminin
ASIA — ASIE										
Yemen - Yémen										
16 XII 1994										
Total	CDFC	14 587 807	7 473 540	7 114 267	3 423 518	1 856 602	1 566 916	11 164 289	5 616 938	5 547 351
0 - 1	CDFC	474 719	245 925	228 794	98 756	50 872	47 884	375 963	195 053	180 910
1 - 4	CDFC	1 920 253	969 884	950 369	372 120	189 919	182 201	1 548 133	779 965	768 168
5 - 9	CDFC	2 735 850	1 404 417	1 331 433	535 411	272 246	263 165	2 200 439	1 132 171	1 068 268
10 - 14	CDFC	2 202 884	1 186 231	1 016 653	492 788	260 979	231 809	1 710 096	925 252	784 844
15 - 19	CDFC	1 486 755	785 127	701 628	401 317	220 977	180 340	1 085 438	564 150	521 288
20 - 24	CDFC	990 006	514 157	475 849	316 136	185 604	130 532	673 870	328 553	345 317
25 - 29	CDFC	914 142	433 650	480 492	257 640	142 812	114 828	656 502	290 838	365 664
30 - 34	CDFC	780 524	370 666	409 858	219 905	123 317	96 588	560 619	247 349	313 270
35 - 39	CDFC	739 189	357 761	381 428	192 980	108 179	84 801	546 209	249 582	296 627
40 - 44	CDFC	534 930	267 057	267 873	134 608	77 669	56 939	400 322	189 388	210 934
45 - 49	CDFC	414 427	212 507	201 920	107 327	62 215	45 112	307 100	150 292	156 808
50 - 54	CDFC	383 799	193 636	190 163	88 698	49 044	39 654	295 101	144 592	150 509
55 - 59	CDFC	207 589	109 372	98 217	50 432	28 990	21 442	157 157	80 382	76 775
60 - 64	CDFC	284 731	149 934	134 797	57 530	31 440	26 090	227 201	118 494	108 707
65 - 69	CDFC	134 878	72 661	62 217	28 131	15 841	12 290	106 747	56 820	49 927
70 - 74	CDFC	171 999	89 830	82 169	30 560	15 868	14 692	141 439	73 962	67 477
75 - 79	CDFC	63 288	34 421	28 867	12 541	6 990	5 551	50 747	27 431	23 316
80 - 84	CDFC	80 755	40 421	40 334	13 648	6 582	7 066	67 107	33 839	33 268
85+	CDFC	66 040	35 095	30 945	12 457	6 596	5 861	53 583	28 499	25 084
Unk. - Inc.	CDFC	1 049	788	261	533	462	71	516	326	190
1 VII 1997										
Total	ESDF	*16 484 000*	*8 227 000*	*8 257 000*	...	...	...	...	...	...
0 - 1	ESDF	*712 000*	*363 000*	*349 000*	...	...	...	...	...	...
1 - 4	ESDF	*2 446 000*	*1 247 000*	*1 199 000*	...	...	...	...	...	...
5 - 9	ESDF	*2 384 000*	*1 213 000*	*1 171 000*	...	...	...	...	...	...
10 - 14	ESDF	*2 203 000*	*1 129 000*	*1 074 000*	...	...	...	...	...	...
15 - 19	ESDF	*2 024 000*	*1 047 000*	*977 000*	...	...	...	...	...	...
20 - 24	ESDF	*1 426 000*	*717 000*	*709 000*	...	...	...	...	...	...
25 - 29	ESDF	*957 000*	*456 000*	*501 000*	...	...	...	...	...	...
30 - 34	ESDF	*878 000*	*405 000*	*473 000*	...	...	...	...	...	...
35 - 39	ESDF	*821 000*	*377 000*	*444 000*	...	...	...	...	...	...
40 - 44	ESDF	*645 000*	*302 000*	*343 000*	...	...	...	...	...	...
45 - 49	ESDF	*495 000*	*240 000*	*255 000*	...	...	...	...	...	...
50 - 54	ESDF	*385 000*	*188 000*	*197 000*	...	...	...	...	...	...
55 - 59	ESDF	*297 000*	*146 000*	*151 000*	...	...	...	...	...	...
60 - 64	ESDF	*238 000*	*113 000*	*125 000*	...	...	...	...	...	...
65 - 69	ESDF	*198 000*	*99 000*	*99 000*	...	...	...	...	...	...
70 - 74	ESDF	*149 000*	*74 000*	*75 000*	...	...	...	...	...	...
75+	ESDF	*226 000*	*111 000*	*115 000*	...	...	...	...	...	...
EUROPE										
Andorra - Andorre										
31 XII 1994										
Total	ESDF	64 311	34 083	30 228	...	...	...	...	...	...
0 - 4	ESDF	3 314	1 725	1 589	...	...	...	...	...	...
5 - 9	ESDF	3 243	1 697	1 546	...	...	...	...	...	...
10 - 14	ESDF	3 513	1 795	1 718	...	...	...	...	...	...
15 - 19	ESDF	3 943	2 074	1 869	...	...	...	...	...	...
20 - 24	ESDF	5 312	2 726	2 586	...	...	...	...	...	...
25 - 29	ESDF	7 000	3 608	3 392	...	...	...	...	...	...
30 - 34	ESDF	7 131	3 822	3 309	...	...	...	...	...	...
35 - 39	ESDF	6 160	3 394	2 766	...	...	...	...	...	...
40 - 44	ESDF	5 058	2 840	2 218	...	...	...	...	...	...
45 - 49	ESDF	4 296	2 389	1 907	...	...	...	...	...	...
50 - 54	ESDF	3 441	1 845	1 596	...	...	...	...	...	...

7. Population by age, sex and urban/rural residence: latest available year, 1993 - 2002
Population selon l'âge, le sexe et la résidence, urbaine/rurale: dernière année disponible, 1993 - 2002
(continued — suite)

(See notes at end of table. — Voir notes à la fin du tableau.)

Continent, country or area, date and age (in years) / Continent, pays ou zone, date et âge (en années)	Code[1]	Total			Urban - Urbaine			Rural - Rurale		
		Both sexes Les deux sexes	Male Masculin	Female Féminin	Both sexes Les deux sexes	Male Masculin	Female Féminin	Both sexes Les deux sexes	Male Masculin	Female Féminin
EUROPE										
Andorra - Andorre										
31 XII 1994										
55 - 59	ESDF	2 659	1 417	1 242	...	...	...	...	...	...
60 - 64	ESDF	2 589	1 375	1 214	...	...	...	...	...	...
65 - 69	ESDF	2 267	1 181	1 086	...	...	...	...	...	...
70 - 74	ESDF	1 816	911	905	...	...	...	...	...	...
75 - 79	ESDF	1 095	565	530	...	...	...	...	...	...
80 - 84	ESDF	815	423	392	...	...	...	...	...	...
85+	ESDF	659	296	363	...	...	...	...	...	...
Austria - Autriche										
1 VII 2002										
Total	ESDJ	8 052 331	3 900 665	4 151 666	...	...	...	...	...	...
0 - 1	ESDJ	76 820	39 178	37 642	...	...	...	...	...	...
1 - 4	ESDJ	322 059	164 882	157 177	...	...	...	...	...	...
5 - 9	ESDJ	460 064	235 493	224 571	...	...	...	...	...	...
10 - 14	ESDJ	480 599	246 610	233 989	...	...	...	...	...	...
15 - 19	ESDJ	479 943	245 612	234 331	...	...	...	...	...	...
20 - 24	ESDJ	486 209	246 679	239 530	...	...	...	...	...	...
25 - 29	ESDJ	516 759	257 805	258 954	...	...	...	...	...	...
30 - 34	ESDJ	644 488	323 533	320 955	...	...	...	...	...	...
35 - 39	ESDJ	705 800	358 170	347 630	...	...	...	...	...	...
40 - 44	ESDJ	645 951	327 296	318 655	...	...	...	...	...	...
45 - 49	ESDJ	545 160	271 731	273 429	...	...	...	...	...	...
50 - 54	ESDJ	506 830	251 600	255 230	...	...	...	...	...	...
55 - 59	ESDJ	449 044	219 472	229 572	...	...	...	...	...	...
60 - 64	ESDJ	485 121	233 638	251 483	...	...	...	...	...	...
65 - 69	ESDJ	327 193	151 023	176 170	...	...	...	...	...	...
70 - 74	ESDJ	324 444	141 253	183 191	...	...	...	...	...	...
75 - 79	ESDJ	286 006	100 060	185 946	...	...	...	...	...	...
80 - 84	ESDJ	177 032	53 485	123 547	...	...	...	...	...	...
85 - 89	ESDJ	85 735	22 693	63 042	...	...	...	...	...	...
90 - 94	ESDJ	39 584	9 102	30 482	...	...	...	...	...	...
95+	ESDJ	7 490	1 350	6 140	...	...	...	...	...	...
Belarus - Bélarus										
1 VII 2002										
Total	ESDF	9 924 766	4 652 109	5 272 657	7 034 721	3 299 920	3 734 801	2 890 045	1 352 189	1 537 856
0 - 1	ESDF	89 652	46 205	43 447	65 624	33 848	31 776	24 028	12 357	11 671
1 - 4	ESDF	365 880	188 235	177 645	262 117	134 894	127 223	103 763	53 341	50 422
5 - 9	ESDF	520 852	267 278	253 574	360 973	185 523	175 450	159 879	81 755	78 124
10 - 14	ESDF	731 311	374 999	356 312	521 277	267 384	253 893	210 034	107 615	102 419
15 - 19	ESDF	840 611	428 802	411 809	646 529	325 640	320 889	194 082	103 162	90 920
20 - 24	ESDF	755 061	386 024	369 037	611 771	310 673	301 098	143 290	75 351	67 939
25 - 29	ESDF	696 577	349 736	346 841	537 369	266 542	270 827	159 208	83 194	76 014
30 - 34	ESDF	683 338	339 033	344 305	510 178	247 515	262 663	173 160	91 518	81 642
35 - 39	ESDF	739 186	364 501	374 685	551 439	262 898	288 541	187 747	101 603	86 144
40 - 44	ESDF	848 260	414 026	434 234	638 707	299 424	339 283	209 553	114 602	94 951
45 - 49	ESDF	737 814	352 374	385 440	561 912	258 198	303 714	175 902	94 176	81 726
50 - 54	ESDF	637 486	298 197	339 289	483 248	219 180	264 068	154 238	79 017	75 221
55 - 59	ESDF	382 057	171 670	210 387	267 209	119 927	147 282	114 848	51 743	63 105
60 - 64	ESDF	517 332	214 780	302 552	326 505	136 535	189 970	190 827	78 245	112 582
65 - 69	ESDF	466 403	180 131	286 272	248 889	96 425	152 464	217 514	83 706	133 808
70 - 74	ESDF	430 411	153 256	277 155	207 974	73 648	134 326	222 437	79 608	142 829
75 - 79	ESDF	287 307	79 262	208 045	140 455	40 179	100 276	146 852	39 083	107 769
80 - 84	ESDF	116 426	28 184	88 242	55 875	14 000	41 875	60 551	14 184	46 367
85 - 89	ESDF	52 557	10 690	41 867	24 738	5 289	19 449	27 819	5 401	22 418
90 - 94	ESDF	21 492	3 927	17 565	9 665	1 781	7 884	11 827	2 146	9 681
95 - 99	ESDF	4 034	686	3 348	1 900	338	1 562	2 134	348	1 786
100+	ESDF	719	113	606	367	79	288	352	34	318

7. Population by age, sex and urban/rural residence: latest available year, 1993 - 2002
Population selon l'âge, le sexe et la résidence, urbaine/rurale: dernière année disponible, 1993 - 2002
(continued — suite)

(See notes at end of table. — Voir notes à la fin du tableau.)

Continent, country or area, date and age (in years) / Continent, pays ou zone, date et âge (en années)	Code[1]	Total			Urban - Urbaine			Rural - Rurale		
		Both sexes Les deux sexes	Male Masculin	Female Féminin	Both sexes Les deux sexes	Male Masculin	Female Féminin	Both sexes Les deux sexes	Male Masculin	Female Féminin
EUROPE										
Belgium - Belgique										
1 VII 2002										
Total	ESDJ	10 332 785	5 054 587	5 278 198	...	...	...	...	...	...
0 - 4	ESDJ	574 226	293 284	280 942	...	...	...	...	...	...
5 - 9	ESDJ	598 547	305 867	292 681	...	...	...	...	...	...
10 - 14	ESDJ	631 200	322 917	308 283	...	...	...	...	...	...
15 - 19	ESDJ	604 184	308 734	295 450	...	...	...	...	...	...
20 - 24	ESDJ	644 075	325 237	318 838	...	...	...	...	...	...
25 - 29	ESDJ	658 953	332 955	325 998	...	...	...	...	...	...
30 - 34	ESDJ	742 236	375 926	366 310	...	...	...	...	...	...
35 - 39	ESDJ	805 694	408 876	396 818	...	...	...	...	...	...
40 - 44	ESDJ	797 683	402 870	394 814	...	...	...	...	...	...
45 - 49	ESDJ	741 591	373 368	368 223	...	...	...	...	...	...
50 - 54	ESDJ	690 598	347 428	343 171	...	...	...	...	...	...
55 - 59	ESDJ	594 066	295 821	298 245	...	...	...	...	...	...
60 - 64	ESDJ	495 345	240 238	255 108	...	...	...	...	...	...
65 - 69	ESDJ	496 236	232 722	263 514	...	...	...	...	...	...
70 - 74	ESDJ	470 880	207 685	263 196	...	...	...	...	...	...
75 - 79	ESDJ	383 587	154 466	229 121	...	...	...	...	...	...
80 - 84	ESDJ	229 370	81 226	148 144	...	...	...	...	...	...
85+	ESDJ	174 319	44 971	129 349	...	...	...	...	...	...
Bulgaria - Bulgarie										
1 VII 2002										
Total	ESDF	7 868 900	3 828 882	4 040 018	5 467 777	2 644 285	2 823 492	2 401 123	1 184 597	1 216 526
0 - 1	ESDF	65 733	33 945	31 788	47 059	24 297	22 762	18 674	9 648	9 026
1 - 4	ESDF	258 757	132 846	125 911	180 838	92 830	88 008	77 919	40 016	37 903
5 - 9	ESDF	355 525	182 345	173 180	244 714	125 495	119 219	110 811	56 850	53 961
10 - 14	ESDF	482 477	247 633	234 844	343 907	175 836	168 071	138 570	71 797	66 773
15 - 19	ESDF	531 954	272 822	259 132	404 936	206 597	198 339	127 018	66 225	60 793
20 - 24	ESDF	564 030	289 576	274 454	430 124	217 166	212 958	133 906	72 410	61 496
25 - 29	ESDF	583 110	297 588	285 522	444 103	224 440	219 663	139 007	73 148	65 859
30 - 34	ESDF	554 069	281 646	272 423	413 814	206 571	207 243	140 255	75 075	65 180
35 - 39	ESDF	512 093	257 963	254 130	380 556	187 251	193 305	131 537	70 712	60 825
40 - 44	ESDF	543 457	271 419	272 038	406 746	197 887	208 859	136 711	73 532	63 179
45 - 49	ESDF	562 466	277 205	285 261	419 770	202 260	217 510	142 696	74 945	67 751
50 - 54	ESDF	580 189	281 254	298 935	421 145	201 235	219 910	159 044	80 019	79 025
55 - 59	ESDF	506 857	240 498	266 359	340 597	161 820	178 777	166 260	78 678	87 582
60 - 64	ESDF	432 022	198 969	233 053	258 818	119 302	139 516	173 204	79 667	93 537
65 - 69	ESDF	446 998	199 818	247 180	249 640	108 861	140 779	197 358	90 957	106 401
70 - 74	ESDF	382 595	164 795	217 800	211 800	89 109	122 691	170 795	75 686	95 109
75 - 79	ESDF	296 027	119 694	176 333	158 743	62 971	95 772	137 284	56 723	80 561
80 - 84	ESDF	143 094	54 813	88 281	75 142	28 122	47 020	67 952	26 691	41 261
85 - 89	ESDF	48 837	17 835	31 002	25 499	8 988	16 511	23 338	8 847	14 491
90 - 94	ESDF	16 333	5 526	10 807	8 637	2 869	5 768	7 696	2 657	5 039
95 - 99	ESDF	2 086	642	1 444	1 092	350	742	994	292	702
100+	ESDF	191	50	141	97	28	69	94	22	72
Channel Islands: Guernsey - Îles Anglo-Normandes: Guernesey										
31 III 1996										
Total	CDFC	58 681	28 244	30 437	...	...	...	...	...	...
0 - 1	CDFC	599	300	299	...	...	...	...	...	...
1 - 4	CDFC	2 781	1 436	1 345	...	...	...	...	...	...
5 - 9	CDFC	3 624	1 813	1 811	...	...	...	...	...	...
10 - 14	CDFC	3 339	1 727	1 612	...	...	...	...	...	...
15 - 19	CDFC	3 351	1 682	1 669	...	...	...	...	...	...
20 - 24	CDFC	4 075	1 935	2 140	...	...	...	...	...	...
25 - 29	CDFC	4 659	2 202	2 457	...	...	...	...	...	...

7. **Population by age, sex and urban/rural residence: latest available year, 1993 - 2002**
Population selon l'âge, le sexe et la résidence, urbaine/rurale: dernière année disponible, 1993 - 2002
(continued — suite)

(See notes at end of table. — Voir notes à la fin du tableau.)

Continent, country or area, date and age (in years) / Continent, pays ou zone, date et âge (en années)	Code[1]	Total			Urban - Urbaine			Rural - Rurale		
		Both sexes Les deux sexes	Male Masculin	Female Féminin	Both sexes Les deux sexes	Male Masculin	Female Féminin	Both sexes Les deux sexes	Male Masculin	Female Féminin
EUROPE										
Channel Islands: Guernsey - Îles Anglo-Normandes: Guernesey										
31 III 1996										
30 - 34	CDFC	4 691	2 301	2 390	...	...	...	...	...	...
35 - 39	CDFC	4 342	2 125	2 217						
40 - 44	CDFC	4 044	2 057	1 987	...	...	...	...	...	...
45 - 49	CDFC	4 610	2 282	2 328	...	...	...	...	...	...
50 - 54	CDFC	3 309	1 669	1 640	...	...	...	...	...	...
55 - 59	CDFC	3 250	1 642	1 608	...	...	...	...	...	...
60 - 64	CDFC	2 798	1 360	1 438	...	...	...	...	...	...
65 - 69	CDFC	2 621	1 210	1 411						
70 - 74	CDFC	2 329	1 031	1 298	...	...	...	...	...	...
75 - 79	CDFC	1 810	727	1 083	...	...	...	...	...	...
80 - 84	CDFC	1 349	468	881						
85 - 89	CDFC	709	194	515	...	...	...	...	...	...
90 - 94	CDFC	316	74	242	...	...	...	...	...	...
95 - 99	CDFC	66	9	57	...	...	...	...	...	...
100+	CDFC	9	-	9	...	...	...	...	...	...
Channel Islands: Jersey - Îles Anglo-Normandes: Jersey										
10 III 1996										
Total	CDFC	85 150	41 394	43 756	...	...	...	...	...	...
0 - 1	CDFC	951	505	446	...	...	...	...	...	...
1 - 4	CDFC	3 942	2 037	1 905	...	...	...	...	...	...
5 - 9	CDFC	4 868	2 488	2 382	...	...	...	...	...	...
10 - 14	CDFC	4 356	2 231	2 125	...	...	...	...	...	...
15 - 19	CDFC	4 278	2 134	2 144	...	...	...	...	...	...
20 - 24	CDFC	5 637	2 706	2 931	...	...	...	...	...	...
25 - 29	CDFC	7 821	3 806	4 015	...	...	...	...	...	...
30 - 34	CDFC	8 074	3 961	4 113	...	...	...	...	...	...
35 - 39	CDFC	7 109	3 527	3 582	...	...	...	...	...	...
40 - 44	CDFC	6 269	3 103	3 166	...	...	...	...	...	...
45 - 49	CDFC	6 374	3 195	3 179	...	...	...	...	...	...
50 - 54	CDFC	4 876	2 419	2 457	...	...	...	...	...	...
55 - 59	CDFC	4 654	2 377	2 277	...	...	...	...	...	...
60 - 64	CDFC	3 981	2 003	1 978	...	...	...	...	...	...
65 - 69	CDFC	3 441	1 635	1 806	...	...	...	...	...	...
70 - 74	CDFC	2 994	1 360	1 634	...	...	...	...	...	...
75 - 79	CDFC	2 209	850	1 359	...	...	...	...	...	...
80 - 84	CDFC	1 833	654	1 179	...	...	...	...	...	...
85 - 89	CDFC	1 026	301	725	...	...	...	...	...	...
90 - 94	CDFC	378	85	293	...	...	...	...	...	...
95 - 99	CDFC	73	17	56	...	...	...	...	...	...
100+	CDFC	6	2	4	...	...	...	...	...	...
Croatia - Croatie										
1 VII 2002										
Total	ESDJ	4 442 900	2 138 400	2 304 500	...	...	...	...	...	...
0 - 1	ESDJ	40 300	20 700	19 600	...	...	...	...	...	...
1 - 4	ESDJ	185 500	94 900	90 600	...	...	...	...	...	...
5 - 9	ESDJ	251 600	128 800	122 800	...	...	...	...	...	...
10 - 14	ESDJ	265 600	135 900	129 700	...	...	...	...	...	...
15 - 19	ESDJ	294 400	150 300	144 100	...	...	...	...	...	...
20 - 24	ESDJ	309 700	158 000	151 700	...	...	...	...	...	...
25 - 29	ESDJ	298 400	150 600	147 800	...	...	...	...	...	...
30 - 34	ESDJ	292 800	146 800	146 000	...	...	...	...	...	...

7. Population by age, sex and urban/rural residence: latest available year, 1993 - 2002
Population selon l'âge, le sexe et la résidence, urbaine/rurale: dernière année disponible, 1993 - 2002
(continued — suite)

(See notes at end of table. — Voir notes à la fin du tableau.)

Continent, country or area, date and age (in years) / Continent, pays ou zone, date et âge (en annèes)	Code[1]	Total			Urban - Urbaine			Rural - Rurale		
		Both sexes Les deux sexes	Male Masculin	Female Féminin	Both sexes Les deux sexes	Male Masculin	Female Féminin	Both sexes Les deux sexes	Male Masculin	Female Féminin
EUROPE										
Croatia - Croatie										
1 VII 2002										
35 - 39	ESDJ	317 300	158 500	158 800	...	...	...	...	...	...
40 - 44	ESDJ	331 300	165 200	166 100	...	...	...	...	...	...
45 - 49	ESDJ	341 400	171 300	170 100	...	...	...	...	...	...
50 - 54	ESDJ	307 300	152 700	154 600	...	...	...	...	...	...
55 - 59	ESDJ	235 700	111 900	123 800	...	...	...	...	...	...
60 - 64	ESDJ	256 400	118 000	138 400	...	...	...	...	...	...
65 - 69	ESDJ	253 500	111 200	142 300	...	...	...	...	...	...
70 - 74	ESDJ	211 400	85 900	125 500	...	...	...	...	...	...
75+	ESDJ	250 300	77 700	172 600	...	...	...	...	...	...
Czech Republic - République tchèque										
31 XII 2002										
Total	ESDJ	10 203 269	4 966 706	5 236 563	7 532 064	3 638 599	3 893 465	2 671 205	1 328 107	1 343 098
0 - 1	ESDJ	92 811	47 715	45 096	68 298	35 087	33 211	24 513	12 628	11 885
1 - 4	ESDJ	357 965	184 099	173 866	258 895	133 155	125 740	99 070	50 944	48 126
5 - 9	ESDJ	501 720	257 301	244 419	359 042	183 748	175 294	142 678	73 553	69 125
10 - 14	ESDJ	637 270	326 424	310 846	465 332	237 949	227 383	171 938	88 475	83 463
15 - 19	ESDJ	665 282	340 702	324 580	488 971	250 462	238 509	176 311	90 240	86 071
20 - 24	ESDJ	773 754	394 817	378 937	570 141	289 828	280 313	203 613	104 989	98 624
25 - 29	ESDJ	906 497	461 655	444 842	672 165	339 712	332 453	234 332	121 943	112 389
30 - 34	ESDJ	723 525	368 755	354 770	536 989	270 527	266 462	186 536	98 228	88 308
35 - 39	ESDJ	699 943	356 387	343 556	524 251	263 948	260 303	175 692	92 439	83 253
40 - 44	ESDJ	634 824	320 911	313 913	470 542	234 824	235 718	164 282	86 087	78 195
45 - 49	ESDJ	759 640	379 452	380 188	564 439	277 800	286 639	195 201	101 652	93 549
50 - 54	ESDJ	795 040	391 958	403 082	589 654	286 418	303 236	205 386	105 540	99 846
55 - 59	ESDJ	722 800	348 398	374 402	543 921	258 266	285 655	178 879	90 132	88 747
60 - 64	ESDJ	514 236	239 711	274 525	383 571	177 600	205 971	130 665	62 111	68 554
65 - 69	ESDJ	413 708	182 867	230 841	303 278	133 489	169 789	110 430	49 378	61 052
70 - 74	ESDJ	404 994	165 908	239 086	295 676	120 836	174 840	109 318	45 072	64 246
75 - 79	ESDJ	322 056	116 285	205 771	235 359	84 959	150 400	86 697	31 326	55 371
80 - 84	ESDJ	179 025	57 452	121 573	130 511	41 616	88 895	48 514	15 836	32 678
85 - 89	ESDJ	65 344	18 192	47 152	47 362	12 975	34 387	17 982	5 217	12 765
90 - 94	ESDJ	28 784	6 932	21 852	20 748	4 863	15 885	8 036	2 069	5 967
95 - 99	ESDJ	3 813	750	3 063	2 745	515	2 230	1 068	235	833
100+	ESDJ	238	35	203	174	22	152	64	13	51
Denmark - Danemark[28]										
1 VII 2002										
Total	ESDJ	5 374 255	2 657 341	2 716 914	...	...	...	...	...	...
0 - 1	ESDJ	64 239	32 757	31 482	...	...	...	...	...	...
1 - 4	ESDJ	268 794	137 622	131 172	...	...	...	...	...	...
5 - 9	ESDJ	351 493	180 365	171 128	...	...	...	...	...	...
10 - 14	ESDJ	324 130	166 524	157 606	...	...	...	...	...	...
15 - 19	ESDJ	283 892	145 263	138 629	...	...	...	...	...	...
20 - 24	ESDJ	311 025	156 927	154 098	...	...	...	...	...	...
25 - 29	ESDJ	370 102	186 274	183 828	...	...	...	...	...	...
30 - 34	ESDJ	388 654	197 595	191 059	...	...	...	...	...	...
35 - 39	ESDJ	428 842	219 032	209 810	...	...	...	...	...	...
40 - 44	ESDJ	380 640	193 258	187 382	...	...	...	...	...	...
45 - 49	ESDJ	369 315	186 788	182 527	...	...	...	...	...	...
50 - 54	ESDJ	368 869	185 747	183 122	...	...	...	...	...	...
55 - 59	ESDJ	388 143	195 310	192 833	...	...	...	...	...	...
60 - 64	ESDJ	279 108	137 948	141 160	...	...	...	...	...	...
65 - 69	ESDJ	226 259	108 079	118 180	...	...	...	...	...	...
70 - 74	ESDJ	191 187	87 303	103 884	...	...	...	...	...	...
75 - 79	ESDJ	162 288	68 104	94 184	...	...	...	...	...	...
80 - 84	ESDJ	118 345	43 833	74 512	...	...	...	...	...	...

7. Population by age, sex and urban/rural residence: latest available year, 1993 - 2002
Population selon l'âge, le sexe et la résidence, urbaine/rurale: dernière année disponible, 1993 - 2002
(continued — suite)

(See notes at end of table. — Voir notes à la fin du tableau.)

Continent, country or area, date and age (in years) / Continent, pays ou zone, date et âge (en années)	Code[1]	Total			Urban - Urbaine			Rural - Rurale		
		Both sexes Les deux sexes	Male Masculin	Female Féminin	Both sexes Les deux sexes	Male Masculin	Female Féminin	Both sexes Les deux sexes	Male Masculin	Female Féminin
EUROPE										
Denmark - Danemark[28]										
1 VII 2002										
85 - 89	ESDJ	66 065	20 701	45 364	...	...	...	...	...	...
90 - 94	ESDJ	26 838	6 821	20 017	...	...	...	...	...	...
95 - 99	ESDJ	5 467	1 013	4 454	...	...	...	...	...	...
100+	ESDJ	560	77	483	...	...	...	...	...	...
Estonia - Estonie										
1 VII 2002										
Total	ESDF	1 358 644	626 276	732 368	940 465	423 224	517 241	418 179	203 052	215 127
0 - 1	ESDF	12 740	6 531	6 209	8 700	4 464	4 236	4 040	2 067	1 973
1 - 4	ESDF	49 024	25 341	23 683	32 847	16 984	15 863	16 177	8 357	7 820
5 - 9	ESDF	67 433	34 582	32 851	42 625	21 856	20 769	24 808	12 726	12 082
10 - 14	ESDF	100 098	51 355	48 743	64 339	32 967	31 372	35 759	18 388	17 371
15 - 19	ESDF	106 045	54 022	52 023	70 844	35 982	34 862	35 201	18 040	17 161
20 - 24	ESDF	97 446	49 730	47 716	72 257	35 536	36 721	25 189	14 194	10 995
25 - 29	ESDF	93 195	46 842	46 353	69 576	34 073	35 503	23 619	12 769	10 850
30 - 34	ESDF	92 972	45 936	47 036	65 889	31 993	33 896	27 083	13 943	13 140
35 - 39	ESDF	90 041	43 734	46 307	62 312	29 497	32 815	27 729	14 237	13 492
40 - 44	ESDF	99 233	47 302	51 931	69 162	31 678	37 484	30 071	15 624	14 447
45 - 49	ESDF	95 617	44 596	51 021	67 841	30 306	37 535	27 776	14 290	13 486
50 - 54	ESDF	90 783	41 319	49 464	64 454	28 106	36 348	26 329	13 213	13 116
55 - 59	ESDF	69 084	30 437	38 647	46 838	19 678	27 160	22 246	10 759	11 487
60 - 64	ESDF	81 637	34 123	47 514	56 712	22 714	33 998	24 925	11 409	13 516
65 - 69	ESDF	68 807	26 962	41 845	47 128	17 845	29 283	21 679	9 117	12 562
70 - 74	ESDF	62 624	22 332	40 292	43 899	15 373	28 526	18 725	6 959	11 766
75 - 79	ESDF	43 777	12 267	31 510	30 214	8 350	21 864	13 563	3 917	9 646
80 - 84	ESDF	21 370	5 214	16 156	14 132	3 498	10 634	7 238	1 716	5 522
85 - 89	ESDF	10 885	2 397	8 488	6 990	1 529	5 461	3 895	868	3 027
90 - 94	ESDF	4 514	852	3 662	2 798	495	2 303	1 716	357	1 359
95 - 99	ESDF	804	125	679	498	74	424	306	51	255
100+	ESDF	74	12	62	43	8	35	31	4	27
Unk. - Inc.	ESDF	441	265	176	367	218	149	74	47	27
Finland - Finlande										
1 VII 2002										
Total	ESDJ	5 200 598	2 541 257	2 659 342	3 217 448	1 543 244	1 674 204	1 983 151	998 013	985 138
0 - 1	ESDJ	55 653	28 519	27 134	35 855	18 429	17 426	19 798	10 090	9 708
1 - 4	ESDJ	229 341	117 198	112 144	142 198	72 539	69 659	87 144	44 659	42 485
5 - 9	ESDJ	318 120	162 133	155 988	189 934	96 638	93 296	128 186	65 495	62 692
10 - 14	ESDJ	326 185	166 561	159 624	188 154	95 803	92 351	138 031	70 759	67 273
15 - 19	ESDJ	326 175	166 770	159 406	193 208	96 035	97 173	132 968	70 735	62 233
20 - 24	ESDJ	326 431	166 777	159 654	238 198	116 861	121 337	88 233	49 916	38 317
25 - 29	ESDJ	315 838	161 944	153 894	231 800	117 865	113 936	84 038	44 079	39 959
30 - 34	ESDJ	328 358	167 406	160 952	222 870	113 438	109 432	105 488	53 968	51 520
35 - 39	ESDJ	374 998	191 004	183 994	240 656	121 304	119 353	134 342	69 700	64 642
40 - 44	ESDJ	377 350	191 375	185 975	231 250	115 323	115 927	146 100	76 052	70 048
45 - 49	ESDJ	395 797	199 639	196 158	238 901	116 689	122 213	156 896	82 950	73 946
50 - 54	ESDJ	417 603	210 719	206 884	252 895	122 784	130 111	164 708	87 935	76 773
55 - 59	ESDJ	344 741	171 734	173 007	212 000	102 318	109 682	132 741	69 416	63 325
60 - 64	ESDJ	271 045	130 585	140 460	159 125	73 966	85 159	111 920	56 619	55 301
65 - 69	ESDJ	226 701	104 838	121 863	128 010	56 738	71 272	98 692	48 100	50 592
70 - 74	ESDJ	212 475	90 708	121 768	117 871	47 756	70 115	94 605	42 952	51 653
75 - 79	ESDJ	167 916	62 203	105 713	91 766	32 144	59 622	76 150	30 059	46 091
80 - 84	ESDJ	105 573	31 932	73 642	58 117	16 727	41 390	47 457	15 205	32 252
85 - 89	ESDJ	55 809	14 076	41 733	30 920	7 267	23 653	24 889	6 809	18 081
90 - 94	ESDJ	20 666	4 484	16 183	11 573	2 284	9 289	9 094	2 200	6 894
95+	ESDJ	3 828	658	3 170	2 152	339	1 813	1 677	319	1 358

7. Population by age, sex and urban/rural residence: latest available year, 1993 - 2002
Population selon l'âge, le sexe et la résidence, urbaine/rurale: dernière année disponible, 1993 - 2002
(continued — suite)

(See notes at end of table. — Voir notes à la fin du tableau.)

Continent, country or area, date and age (in years) / Continent, pays ou zone, date et âge (en annèes)	Code[1]	Total			Urban - Urbaine			Rural - Rurale		
		Both sexes Les deux sexes	Male Masculin	Female Féminin	Both sexes Les deux sexes	Male Masculin	Female Féminin	Both sexes Les deux sexes	Male Masculin	Female Féminin
EUROPE										
France[29]										
1 VII 2002										
Total	ESDJ	59 486 121	28 902 304	30 583 817	...	...	...	...	...	...
0 - 4	ESDJ	3 728 126	1 908 054	1 820 072	...	...	...	...	...	...
5 - 9	ESDJ	3 579 121	1 832 983	1 746 139	...	...	...	...	...	...
10 - 14	ESDJ	3 808 532	1 949 161	1 859 372	...	...	...	...	...	...
15 - 19	ESDJ	3 867 566	1 973 320	1 894 246	...	...	...	...	...	...
20 - 24	ESDJ	3 873 306	1 959 164	1 914 143	...	...	...	...	...	...
25 - 29	ESDJ	3 874 350	1 944 281	1 930 069	...	...	...	...	...	...
30 - 34	ESDJ	4 251 043	2 122 638	2 128 405	...	...	...	...	...	...
35 - 39	ESDJ	4 350 839	2 158 553	2 192 286	...	...	...	...	...	...
40 - 44	ESDJ	4 264 537	2 102 953	2 161 584	...	...	...	...	...	...
45 - 49	ESDJ	4 174 156	2 055 579	2 118 578	...	...	...	...	...	...
50 - 54	ESDJ	4 202 086	2 085 429	2 116 657	...	...	...	...	...	...
55 - 59	ESDJ	3 246 088	1 609 634	1 636 455	...	...	...	...	...	...
60 - 64	ESDJ	2 589 233	1 256 198	1 333 035	...	...	...	...	...	...
65 - 69	ESDJ	2 627 321	1 218 146	1 409 176	...	...	...	...	...	...
70 - 74	ESDJ	2 492 984	1 088 570	1 404 414	...	...	...	...	...	...
75 - 79	ESDJ	2 093 431	841 589	1 251 842	...	...	...	...	...	...
80 - 84	ESDJ	1 329 514	486 334	843 180	...	...	...	...	...	...
85+	ESDJ	1 133 893	309 723	824 171	...	...	...	...	...	...
Germany - Allemagne										
1 VII 2002										
Total	ESDJ	82 488 495	40 309 778	42 178 717	...	...	...	...	...	...
0 - 4	ESDJ	3 848 753	1 976 178	1 872 575	...	...	...	...	...	...
5 - 9	ESDJ	4 011 500	2 058 417	1 953 084	...	...	...	...	...	...
10 - 14	ESDJ	4 656 960	2 389 730	2 267 230	...	...	...	...	...	...
15 - 19	ESDJ	4 657 032	2 389 574	2 267 458	...	...	...	...	...	...
20 - 24	ESDJ	4 797 570	2 438 375	2 359 195	...	...	...	...	...	...
25 - 29	ESDJ	4 713 526	2 403 994	2 309 533	...	...	...	...	...	...
30 - 34	ESDJ	6 247 553	3 208 576	3 038 977	...	...	...	...	...	...
35 - 39	ESDJ	7 248 219	3 733 490	3 514 729	...	...	...	...	...	...
40 - 44	ESDJ	6 685 035	3 417 600	3 267 436	...	...	...	...	...	...
45 - 49	ESDJ	5 841 512	2 953 617	2 887 895	...	...	...	...	...	...
50 - 54	ESDJ	5 326 238	2 672 722	2 653 516	...	...	...	...	...	...
55 - 59	ESDJ	4 467 742	2 228 774	2 238 969	...	...	...	...	...	...
60 - 64	ESDJ	5 734 587	2 814 226	2 920 361	...	...	...	...	...	...
65 - 69	ESDJ	4 507 592	2 137 219	2 370 373	...	...	...	...	...	...
70 - 74	ESDJ	3 592 497	1 587 787	2 004 710	...	...	...	...	...	...
75 - 79	ESDJ	2 847 777	1 006 119	1 841 659	...	...	...	...	...	...
80 - 84	ESDJ	1 808 519	535 314	1 273 206	...	...	...	...	...	...
85+	ESDJ	1 495 886	358 070	1 137 816	...	...	...	...	...	...
Greece - Grèce[30]										
1 VII 1998										
Total	ESDF	10 516 366	5 183 147	5 333 219	...	...	...	...	...	...
0 - 1	ESDF	100 841	51 955	48 886	...	...	...	...	...	...
1 - 4	ESDF	405 370	208 990	196 380	...	...	...	...	...	...
5 - 9	ESDF	529 098	272 273	256 825	...	...	...	...	...	...
10 - 14	ESDF	604 465	310 569	293 896	...	...	...	...	...	...
15 - 19	ESDF	728 568	374 505	354 063	...	...	...	...	...	...
20 - 24	ESDF	784 483	399 369	385 114	...	...	...	...	...	...
25 - 29	ESDF	808 127	409 297	398 830	...	...	...	...	...	...
30 - 34	ESDF	795 833	398 588	397 245	...	...	...	...	...	...
35 - 39	ESDF	750 348	373 325	377 023	...	...	...	...	...	...
40 - 44	ESDF	716 783	357 777	359 006	...	...	...	...	...	...
45 - 49	ESDF	676 343	339 070	337 273	...	...	...	...	...	...
50 - 54	ESDF	638 436	316 425	322 011	...	...	...	...	...	...
55 - 59	ESDF	588 076	286 255	301 821	...	...	...	...	...	...

7. Population by age, sex and urban/rural residence: latest available year, 1993 - 2002
Population selon l'âge, le sexe et la résidence, urbaine/rurale: dernière année disponible, 1993 - 2002
(continued — suite)

(See notes at end of table. — Voir notes à la fin du tableau.)

Continent, country or area, date and age (in years) / Continent, pays ou zone, date et âge (en années)	Code[1]	Total			Urban - Urbaine			Rural - Rurale		
		Both sexes Les deux sexes	Male Masculin	Female Féminin	Both sexes Les deux sexes	Male Masculin	Female Féminin	Both sexes Les deux sexes	Male Masculin	Female Féminin
EUROPE										
Greece - Grèce[30]										
1 VII 1998										
60 - 64	ESDF	630 119	301 195	328 924	...	...	...	...	...	...
65 - 69	ESDF	596 049	280 767	315 282	...	...	...	...	...	...
70 - 74	ESDF	482 754	217 301	265 453	...	...	...	...	...	...
75 - 79	ESDF	311 600	133 387	178 213	...	...	...	...	...	...
80 - 84	ESDF	192 538	78 670	113 868	...	...	...	...	...	...
85 - 89	ESDF	120 451	48 844	71 607	...	...	...	...	...	...
90 - 94	ESDF	41 144	17 938	23 206	...	...	...	...	...	...
95 - 99	ESDF	12 579	5 486	7 093	...	...	...	...	...	...
100+	ESDF	2 361	1 161	1 200	...	...	...	...	...	...
Hungary - Hongrie										
1 VII 2002										
Total	ESDF	10 158 608	4 827 718	5 330 890	6 601 834	3 098 867	3 502 968	3 556 774	1 728 852	1 827 922
0 - 1	ESDF	95 133	48 925	46 208	59 510	30 536	28 974	35 623	18 389	17 234
1 - 4	ESDF	383 303	196 308	186 995	233 520	119 295	114 225	149 783	77 013	72 770
5 - 9	ESDF	550 981	282 381	268 600	332 096	170 107	161 990	218 885	112 275	106 611
10 - 14	ESDF	617 485	315 870	301 615	379 817	193 853	185 964	237 668	122 017	115 651
15 - 19	ESDF	649 925	330 694	319 232	430 312	216 348	213 964	219 614	114 346	105 268
20 - 24	ESDF	764 788	391 926	372 862	515 448	260 675	254 773	249 341	131 251	118 090
25 - 29	ESDF	830 479	422 901	407 579	565 728	285 057	280 672	264 751	137 844	126 907
30 - 34	ESDF	718 088	364 290	353 798	475 883	239 653	236 230	242 205	124 637	117 568
35 - 39	ESDF	621 374	311 575	309 799	397 172	195 868	201 304	224 202	115 708	108 495
40 - 44	ESDF	657 990	323 695	334 295	413 848	197 719	216 130	244 142	125 977	118 165
45 - 49	ESDF	828 373	401 865	426 508	544 480	255 501	288 980	283 893	146 365	137 528
50 - 54	ESDF	728 122	345 619	382 503	484 045	223 451	260 594	244 077	122 168	121 909
55 - 59	ESDF	611 040	281 357	329 683	414 644	188 589	226 055	196 396	92 769	103 628
60 - 64	ESDF	545 951	236 423	309 528	355 483	153 617	201 866	190 468	82 807	107 662
65 - 69	ESDF	480 936	196 309	284 628	305 146	124 606	180 541	175 790	71 703	104 087
70 - 74	ESDF	434 187	167 849	266 338	276 390	107 749	168 641	157 797	60 101	97 697
75 - 79	ESDF	336 157	117 081	219 076	215 030	74 495	140 535	121 127	42 586	78 542
80 - 84	ESDF	189 067	60 051	129 016	123 886	39 264	84 622	65 181	20 787	44 394
85 - 89	ESDF	75 905	21 911	53 994	52 318	15 215	37 103	23 588	6 696	16 892
90+	ESDF	39 330	10 692	28 638	27 083	7 275	19 809	12 247	3 417	8 830
Iceland - Islande										
1 VII 2002										
Total	ESDJ	287 523	143 869	143 655	...	...	...	...	...	...
0 - 4	ESDJ	21 117	10 719	10 399	...	...	...	...	...	...
5 - 9	ESDJ	22 278	11 390	10 888	...	...	...	...	...	...
10 - 14	ESDJ	22 797	11 722	11 076	...	...	...	...	...	...
15 - 19	ESDJ	20 595	10 421	10 175	...	...	...	...	...	...
20 - 24	ESDJ	22 127	11 196	10 932	...	...	...	...	...	...
25 - 29	ESDJ	21 306	10 792	10 514	...	...	...	...	...	...
30 - 34	ESDJ	20 074	10 185	9 889	...	...	...	...	...	...
35 - 39	ESDJ	21 655	10 781	10 874	...	...	...	...	...	...
40 - 44	ESDJ	21 308	10 755	10 553	...	...	...	...	...	...
45 - 49	ESDJ	19 648	10 019	9 630	...	...	...	...	...	...
50 - 54	ESDJ	17 103	8 699	8 404	...	...	...	...	...	...
55 - 59	ESDJ	13 863	7 079	6 784	...	...	...	...	...	...
60 - 64	ESDJ	10 094	5 011	5 083	...	...	...	...	...	...
65 - 69	ESDJ	9 358	4 489	4 870	...	...	...	...	...	...
70 - 74	ESDJ	8 990	4 279	4 711	...	...	...	...	...	...
75 - 79	ESDJ	6 939	3 103	3 836	...	...	...	...	...	...
80 - 84	ESDJ	4 665	1 961	2 705	...	...	...	...	...	...
85+	ESDJ	3 609	1 273	2 336	...	...	...	...	...	...
Ireland - Irlande										
28 IV 2002										
Total	CDFC	3 917 200	1 946 200	1 971 000	2 334 300	1 133 500	1 200 800	1 582 900	812 600	770 300
0 - 1	CDFC	54 500	27 800	26 700	...	...	...	...	...	...

7. **Population by age, sex and urban/rural residence: latest available year, 1993 - 2002**
Population selon l'âge, le sexe et la résidence, urbaine/rurale: dernière année disponible, 1993 - 2002
(continued — suite)

(See notes at end of table. — Voir notes à la fin du tableau.)

Continent, country or area, date and age (in years) / Continent, pays ou zone, date et âge (en années)	Code[1]	Total			Urban - Urbaine			Rural - Rurale		
		Both sexes Les deux sexes	Male Masculin	Female Féminin	Both sexes Les deux sexes	Male Masculin	Female Féminin	Both sexes Les deux sexes	Male Masculin	Female Féminin
EUROPE										
Ireland - Irlande										
28 IV 2002										
0 - 4	CDFC	...	...	...	167 000	85 000	81 000	111 100	56 700	54 300
1 - 4	CDFC	223 100	114 200	108 900	...	...	...	...	...	...
5 - 9	CDFC	264 100	135 900	128 200	148 700	76 500	72 200	115 300	59 300	56 000
10 - 14	CDFC	285 700	146 100	139 600	156 500	79 800	76 700	129 200	66 300	62 900
15 - 19	CDFC	313 200	160 400	152 800	180 800	90 600	90 200	132 400	69 800	62 600
20 - 24	CDFC	328 300	165 300	163 000	229 300	110 600	118 700	99 000	54 700	44 300
25 - 29	CDFC	312 700	156 100	156 600	218 200	106 500	111 700	94 500	49 600	44 900
30 - 34	CDFC	304 700	152 400	152 300	198 500	98 200	100 300	106 100	54 100	52 000
35 - 39	CDFC	290 900	144 500	146 400	175 400	86 000	89 400	115 500	58 600	56 900
40 - 44	CDFC	272 000	135 300	136 700	156 600	76 600	80 000	115 400	58 700	56 700
45 - 49	CDFC	249 600	125 000	124 600	139 400	67 900	71 500	110 200	57 100	53 100
50 - 54	CDFC	230 800	116 600	114 200	128 100	62 600	65 500	102 700	53 900	48 800
55 - 59	CDFC	197 300	99 800	97 500	109 800	53 600	56 200	87 500	46 300	41 200
60 - 64	CDFC	154 300	77 600	76 700	87 900	42 500	45 400	66 300	35 000	31 300
65 - 69	CDFC	133 500	65 300	68 200	75 000	34 900	40 100	58 500	30 400	28 100
70 - 74	CDFC	112 100	51 700	60 400	62 000	26 800	35 200	50 100	25 000	25 100
75 - 79	CDFC	89 800	37 400	52 400	48 200	18 600	29 600	41 600	18 800	22 800
80 - 84	CDFC	58 900	22 300	36 600	31 000	10 600	20 400	27 900	11 700	16 200
85+	CDFC	41 700	12 500	29 200	22 100	5 800	16 300	19 600	6 700	12 900
1 VII 2002										
Total	ESDF	3 931 756	1 953 555	1 978 202	...	...	...	...	...	...
0 - 4	ESDF	279 807	143 174	136 634	...	...	...	...	...	...
5 - 9	ESDF	265 575	136 534	129 041	...	...	...	...	...	...
10 - 14	ESDF	284 574	145 753	138 821	...	...	...	...	...	...
15 - 19	ESDF	311 745	159 610	152 135	...	...	...	...	...	...
20 - 24	ESDF	329 831	165 804	164 028	...	...	...	...	...	...
25 - 29	ESDF	313 381	156 732	156 650	...	...	...	...	...	...
30 - 34	ESDF	305 938	153 155	152 783	...	...	...	...	...	...
35 - 39	ESDF	291 528	144 854	146 674	...	...	...	...	...	...
40 - 44	ESDF	273 745	136 101	137 644	...	...	...	...	...	...
45 - 49	ESDF	250 257	125 229	125 029	...	...	...	...	...	...
50 - 54	ESDF	232 018	117 064	114 954	...	...	...	...	...	...
55 - 59	ESDF	199 380	100 985	98 395	...	...	...	...	...	...
60 - 64	ESDF	156 246	78 498	77 749	...	...	...	...	...	...
65 - 69	ESDF	133 776	65 398	68 379	...	...	...	...	...	...
70 - 74	ESDF	112 645	52 151	60 495	...	...	...	...	...	...
75 - 79	ESDF	89 643	37 314	52 329	...	...	...	...	...	...
80 - 84	ESDF	59 691	22 569	37 123	...	...	...	...	...	...
85+	ESDF	41 979	12 636	29 343	...	...	...	...	...	...
Isle of Man - Îles de Man										
29 IV 2000										
Total	CDJC	76 315	37 372	38 943	...	...	...	...	...	...
0 - 1	CDJC	757	415	342	...	...	...	...	...	...
1 - 4	CDJC	3 469	1 814	1 655	...	...	...	...	...	...
5 - 9	CDJC	4 627	2 365	2 262	...	...	...	...	...	...
10 - 14	CDJC	4 759	2 426	2 333	...	...	...	...	...	...
15 - 19	CDJC	4 383	2 204	2 179	...	...	...	...	...	...
20 - 24	CDJC	4 248	2 153	2 095	...	...	...	...	...	...
25 - 29	CDJC	4 749	2 279	2 470	...	...	...	...	...	...
30 - 34	CDJC	5 634	2 807	2 827	...	...	...	...	...	...
35 - 39	CDJC	6 051	3 061	2 990	...	...	...	...	...	...
40 - 44	CDJC	5 571	2 736	2 835	...	...	...	...	...	...
45 - 49	CDJC	5 029	2 561	2 468	...	...	...	...	...	...
50 - 54	CDJC	5 714	2 916	2 798	...	...	...	...	...	...
55 - 59	CDJC	4 619	2 316	2 303	...	...	...	...	...	...
60 - 64	CDJC	3 947	1 980	1 967	...	...	...	...	...	...

7. Population by age, sex and urban/rural residence: latest available year, 1993 - 2002
Population selon l'âge, le sexe et la résidence, urbaine/rurale: dernière année disponible, 1993 - 2002
(continued — suite)

(See notes at end of table. — Voir notes à la fin du tableau.)

Continent, country or area, date and age (in years) / Continent, pays ou zone, date et âge (en années)	Code[1]	Total			Urban - Urbaine			Rural - Rurale		
		Both sexes Les deux sexes	Male Masculin	Female Féminin	Both sexes Les deux sexes	Male Masculin	Female Féminin	Both sexes Les deux sexes	Male Masculin	Female Féminin
EUROPE										
Isle of Man - Îles de Man										
29 IV 2000										
65 - 69	CDJC	3 359	1 633	1 726	...	...	...	...	...	...
70 - 74	CDJC	3 063	1 340	1 723	...	...	...	...	...	...
75 - 79	CDJC	2 733	1 128	1 605	...	...	...	...	...	...
80 - 84	CDJC	1 844	694	1 150	...	...	...	...	...	...
85 - 89	CDJC	1 131	389	742	...	...	...	...	...	...
90 - 94	CDJC	500	127	373	...	...	...	...	...	...
95 - 99	CDJC	117	26	91	...	...	...	...	...	...
100+	CDJC	11	2	9	...	...	...	...	...	...
Italy - Italie										
21 X 2001										
Total	CDJC	56 995 744	27 586 982	29 408 762	...	...	...	...	...	...
0 - 1	CDJC	530 966	272 400	258 566	...	...	...	...	...	...
1 - 4	CDJC	2 618 794	1 344 296	1 274 498	...	...	...	...	...	...
5 - 9	CDJC	2 679 104	1 375 399	1 303 705	...	...	...	...	...	...
10 - 14	CDJC	2 805 287	1 440 659	1 364 628	...	...	...	...	...	...
15 - 19	CDJC	2 963 629	1 517 900	1 445 729	...	...	...	...	...	...
20 - 24	CDJC	3 424 350	1 739 347	1 685 003	...	...	...	...	...	...
25 - 29	CDJC	4 246 776	2 138 204	2 108 572	...	...	...	...	...	...
30 - 34	CDJC	4 543 782	2 283 606	2 260 176	...	...	...	...	...	...
35 - 39	CDJC	4 623 588	2 313 969	2 309 619	...	...	...	...	...	...
40 - 44	CDJC	4 065 579	2 024 945	2 040 634	...	...	...	...	...	...
45 - 49	CDJC	3 739 570	1 850 242	1 889 328	...	...	...	...	...	...
50 - 54	CDJC	3 849 691	1 895 424	1 954 267	...	...	...	...	...	...
55 - 59	CDJC	3 324 773	1 620 147	1 704 626	...	...	...	...	...	...
60 - 64	CDJC	3 464 947	1 657 480	1 807 467	...	...	...	...	...	...
65 - 69	CDJC	3 079 948	1 426 778	1 653 170	...	...	...	...	...	...
70 - 74	CDJC	2 803 512	1 229 113	1 574 399	...	...	...	...	...	...
75 - 79	CDJC	2 286 776	913 342	1 373 434	...	...	...	...	...	...
80 - 84	CDJC	1 235 317	445 332	789 985	...	...	...	...	...	...
85 - 89	CDJC	841 951	267 981	573 970	...	...	...	...	...	...
90 - 94	CDJC	329 217	88 270	240 947	...	...	...	...	...	...
95 - 99	CDJC	62 840	13 468	49 372	...	...	...	...	...	...
100+	CDJC	6 313	1 080	5 233	...	...	...	...	...	...
Latvia - Lettonie										
1 VII 2002										
Total	ESDJ	2 338 624	1 076 587	1 262 037	1 586 220	713 616	872 604	752 404	362 971	389 433
0 - 1	ESDJ	19 843	10 114	9 729	12 743	6 481	6 262	7 100	3 633	3 467
1 - 4	ESDJ	75 986	38 841	37 145	47 476	24 298	23 178	28 510	14 543	13 967
5 - 9	ESDJ	112 912	57 866	55 046	68 595	35 104	33 491	44 317	22 762	21 555
10 - 14	ESDJ	172 819	88 306	84 513	107 772	54 998	52 774	65 047	33 308	31 739
15 - 19	ESDJ	185 794	94 586	91 208	122 552	61 844	60 708	63 242	32 742	30 500
20 - 24	ESDJ	163 261	83 032	80 229	111 182	55 733	55 449	52 079	27 299	24 780
25 - 29	ESDJ	160 781	81 341	79 440	110 713	54 787	55 926	50 068	26 554	23 514
30 - 34	ESDJ	161 156	80 119	81 037	110 675	53 612	57 063	50 481	26 507	23 974
35 - 39	ESDJ	162 509	79 734	82 775	110 420	52 323	58 097	52 089	27 411	24 678
40 - 44	ESDJ	178 535	86 228	92 307	123 710	57 411	66 299	54 825	28 817	26 008
45 - 49	ESDJ	159 133	74 815	84 318	113 474	51 104	62 370	45 659	23 711	21 948
50 - 54	ESDJ	148 488	67 754	80 734	107 237	46 791	60 446	41 251	20 963	20 288
55 - 59	ESDJ	123 983	54 327	69 656	86 847	36 721	50 126	37 136	17 606	19 530
60 - 64	ESDJ	146 704	61 193	85 511	102 555	41 588	60 967	44 149	19 605	24 544
65 - 69	ESDJ	119 427	46 026	73 401	81 540	30 787	50 753	37 887	15 239	22 648
70 - 74	ESDJ	107 312	38 112	69 200	74 333	26 304	48 029	32 979	11 808	21 171
75 - 79	ESDJ	76 261	19 585	56 676	52 967	13 884	39 083	23 294	5 701	17 593
80 - 84	ESDJ	36 399	8 806	27 593	24 133	6 008	18 125	12 266	2 798	9 468
85 - 89	ESDJ	17 966	3 924	14 042	11 489	2 664	8 825	6 477	1 260	5 217
90 - 94	ESDJ	7 743	1 568	6 175	4 804	989	3 815	2 939	579	2 360

7. Population by age, sex and urban/rural residence: latest available year, 1993 - 2002
Population selon l'âge, le sexe et la résidence, urbaine/rurale: dernière année disponible, 1993 - 2002
(continued — suite)

(See notes at end of table. — Voir notes à la fin du tableau.)

Continent, country or area, date and age (in years) / Continent, pays ou zone, date et âge (en années)	Code[1]	Total			Urban - Urbaine			Rural - Rurale		
		Both sexes Les deux sexes	Male Masculin	Female Féminin	Both sexes Les deux sexes	Male Masculin	Female Féminin	Both sexes Les deux sexes	Male Masculin	Female Féminin
EUROPE										
Latvia - Lettonie										
1 VII 2002										
95 - 99	ESDJ	1 474	288	1 186	921	174	747	553	114	439
100+	ESDJ	138	22	116	82	11	71	56	11	45
Liechtenstein										
1 VII 2002										
Total	ESDF	33 694	16 534	17 160	...	...	...	...	...	...
0 - 4	ESDF	1 998	1 013	985	...	...	...	...	...	...
5 - 9	ESDF	2 086	1 040	1 046	...	...	...	...	...	...
10 - 14	ESDF	2 101	1 095	1 006	...	...	...	...	...	...
15 - 19	ESDF	2 040	1 019	1 021	...	...	...	...	...	...
20 - 24	ESDF	2 110	1 067	1 044	...	...	...	...	...	...
25 - 29	ESDF	2 361	1 159	1 202	...	...	...	...	...	...
30 - 34	ESDF	2 885	1 440	1 445	...	...	...	...	...	...
35 - 39	ESDF	2 979	1 454	1 526	...	...	...	...	...	...
40 - 44	ESDF	2 898	1 415	1 483	...	...	...	...	...	...
45 - 49	ESDF	2 611	1 311	1 300	...	...	...	...	...	...
50 - 54	ESDF	2 395	1 232	1 164	...	...	...	...	...	...
55 - 59	ESDF	2 112	1 087	1 025	...	...	...	...	...	...
60 - 64	ESDF	1 543	763	780	...	...	...	...	...	...
65 - 69	ESDF	1 103	513	590	...	...	...	...	...	...
70 - 74	ESDF	841	373	468	...	...	...	...	...	...
75 - 79	ESDF	769	264	505	...	...	...	...	...	...
80 - 84	ESDF	508	186	322	...	...	...	...	...	...
85+	ESDF	359	107	253	...	...	...	...	...	...
Lithuania - Lituanie										
1 VII 2002										
Total	ESDJ	3 469 070	1 620 891	1 848 179	2 321 713	1 065 912	1 255 801	1 147 357	554 979	592 378
0 - 1	ESDJ	30 568	15 686	14 882	19 088	9 769	9 319	11 480	5 917	5 563
1 - 4	ESDJ	140 043	72 256	67 787	89 942	46 334	43 608	50 101	25 922	24 179
5 - 9	ESDJ	209 060	107 047	102 013	133 906	68 626	65 280	75 154	38 421	36 733
10 - 14	ESDJ	266 626	136 193	130 433	170 439	86 755	83 684	96 187	49 438	46 749
15 - 19	ESDJ	276 419	140 686	135 733	183 863	92 734	91 129	92 556	47 952	44 604
20 - 24	ESDJ	239 898	121 864	118 034	172 546	84 520	88 026	67 352	37 344	30 008
25 - 29	ESDJ	232 436	116 209	116 227	168 203	81 898	86 305	64 233	34 311	29 922
30 - 34	ESDJ	252 188	124 929	127 259	177 812	86 142	91 670	74 376	38 787	35 589
35 - 39	ESDJ	260 336	128 491	131 845	181 916	86 865	95 051	78 420	41 626	36 794
40 - 44	ESDJ	273 724	131 903	141 821	192 366	88 899	103 467	81 358	43 004	38 354
45 - 49	ESDJ	222 102	105 276	116 826	157 529	71 483	86 046	64 573	33 793	30 780
50 - 54	ESDJ	202 198	92 622	109 576	141 309	61 873	79 436	60 889	30 749	30 140
55 - 59	ESDJ	174 518	76 702	97 816	117 266	49 850	67 416	57 252	26 852	30 400
60 - 64	ESDJ	183 265	77 035	106 230	117 897	48 428	69 469	65 368	28 607	36 761
65 - 69	ESDJ	166 448	65 601	100 847	101 047	39 268	61 779	65 401	26 333	39 068
70 - 74	ESDJ	145 503	53 028	92 475	86 477	31 731	54 746	59 026	21 297	37 729
75 - 79	ESDJ	104 008	31 055	72 953	60 223	17 714	42 509	43 785	13 341	30 444
80 - 84	ESDJ	51 101	14 261	36 840	28 169	7 646	20 523	22 932	6 615	16 317
85 - 89	ESDJ	23 702	6 017	17 685	13 265	3 284	9 981	10 437	2 733	7 704
90 - 94	ESDJ	11 297	2 986	8 311	6 468	1 587	4 881	4 829	1 399	3 430
95 - 99	ESDJ	3 044	913	2 131	1 665	439	1 226	1 379	474	905
100+	ESDJ	586	131	455	317	67	250	269	64	205
Luxembourg										
1 VII 2002										
Total	ESDJ	446 175	219 917	226 258	...	...	...	...	...	...
0 - 1	ESDJ	5 375	2 752	2 623	...	...	...	...	...	...
1 - 4	ESDJ	22 700	11 668	11 032	...	...	...	...	...	...
5 - 9	ESDJ	28 936	14 816	14 120	...	...	...	...	...	...
10 - 14	ESDJ	27 193	13 903	13 290	...	...	...	...	...	...
15 - 19	ESDJ	25 024	12 792	12 232	...	...	...	...	...	...
20 - 24	ESDJ	25 962	13 105	12 857	...	...	...	...	...	...

7. Population by age, sex and urban/rural residence: latest available year, 1993 - 2002
Population selon l'âge, le sexe et la résidence, urbaine/rurale: dernière année disponible, 1993 - 2002
(continued — suite)

(See notes at end of table. — Voir notes à la fin du tableau.)

Continent, country or area, date and age (in years) / Continent, pays ou zone, date et âge (en années)	Code[1]	Total			Urban - Urbaine			Rural - Rurale		
		Both sexes Les deux sexes	Male Masculin	Female Féminin	Both sexes Les deux sexes	Male Masculin	Female Féminin	Both sexes Les deux sexes	Male Masculin	Female Féminin
EUROPE										
Luxembourg										
1 VII 2002										
25 - 29	ESDJ	30 450	15 208	15 242	...	...	...	...	...	...
30 - 34	ESDJ	37 264	18 631	18 633	...	...	...	...	...	...
35 - 39	ESDJ	39 697	20 190	19 507	...	...	...	...	...	...
40 - 44	ESDJ	36 431	18 551	17 880	...	...	...	...	...	...
45 - 49	ESDJ	32 341	16 340	16 001	...	...	...	...	...	...
50 - 54	ESDJ	28 245	14 604	13 641	...	...	...	...	...	...
55 - 59	ESDJ	23 540	12 033	11 507	...	...	...	...	...	...
60 - 64	ESDJ	20 613	10 021	10 592	...	...	...	...	...	...
65 - 69	ESDJ	18 347	8 648	9 699	...	...	...	...	...	...
70 - 74	ESDJ	17 789	8 022	9 767	...	...	...	...	...	...
75 - 79	ESDJ	12 685	4 691	7 994	...	...	...	...	...	...
80 - 84	ESDJ	7 515	2 383	5 132	...	...	...	...	...	...
85 - 89	ESDJ	4 123	1 157	2 966	...	...	...	...	...	...
90 - 94	ESDJ	1 630	342	1 288	...	...	...	...	...	...
95+	ESDJ	315	60	255	...	...	...	...	...	...
Malta - Malte[31]										
1 VII 2002										
Total	ESDF	397 296	196 836	200 460	...	...	...	...	...	...
0 - 1	ESDF	3 890	2 055	1 835	...	...	...	...	...	...
1 - 4	ESDF	17 137	8 698	8 439	...	...	...	...	...	...
5 - 9	ESDF	24 949	12 956	11 993	...	...	...	...	...	...
10 - 14	ESDF	28 403	14 528	13 875	...	...	...	...	...	...
15 - 19	ESDF	28 585	14 835	13 750	...	...	...	...	...	...
20 - 24	ESDF	30 050	15 394	14 656	...	...	...	...	...	...
25 - 29	ESDF	29 202	15 031	14 171	...	...	...	...	...	...
30 - 34	ESDF	25 069	12 832	12 237	...	...	...	...	...	...
35 - 39	ESDF	25 258	12 719	12 539	...	...	...	...	...	...
40 - 44	ESDF	29 719	14 922	14 797	...	...	...	...	...	...
45 - 49	ESDF	29 488	14 964	14 524	...	...	...	...	...	...
50 - 54	ESDF	29 734	14 857	14 877	...	...	...	...	...	...
55 - 59	ESDF	28 238	13 802	14 436	...	...	...	...	...	...
60 - 64	ESDF	16 611	7 864	8 747	...	...	...	...	...	...
65 - 69	ESDF	16 766	7 573	9 193	...	...	...	...	...	...
70 - 74	ESDF	13 327	5 635	7 692	...	...	...	...	...	...
75 - 79	ESDF	10 313	4 240	6 073	...	...	...	...	...	...
80 - 84	ESDF	6 540	2 584	3 956	...	...	...	...	...	...
85 - 89	ESDF	2 610	906	1 704	...	...	...	...	...	...
90+	ESDF	1 407	441	966	...	...	...	...	...	...
Monaco										
1 VII 2000										
Total	CDJC	32 017	15 544	16 473	...	...	...	...	...	...
0 - 14	CDJC	4 237	2 206	2 031	...	...	...	...	...	...
15 - 24	CDJC	2 634	1 367	1 267	...	...	...	...	...	...
25 - 44	CDJC	8 698	4 370	4 328	...	...	...	...	...	...
45 - 64	CDJC	9 250	4 552	4 698	...	...	...	...	...	...
65+	CDJC	7 181	3 042	4 139	...	...	...	...	...	...
Unk. - Inc.	CDJC	17	7	10	...	...	...	...	...	...
Netherlands - Pays-Bas										
1 I 2002										
Total	ESDJ	16 105 285	7 971 967	8 133 318	10 447 684	5 137 422	5 310 262	5 657 601	2 834 545	2 823 056
0 - 1	ESDJ	204 039	104 502	99 537	133 248	68 197	65 051	70 791	36 305	34 486
1 - 4	ESDJ	810 583	414 335	396 248	515 526	263 420	252 106	295 057	150 915	144 142
5 - 9	ESDJ	989 238	506 490	482 748	615 405	314 904	300 501	373 833	191 586	182 247
10 - 14	ESDJ	994 388	508 732	485 656	617 049	315 210	301 839	377 339	193 522	183 817
15 - 19	ESDJ	942 388	483 021	459 367	598 105	304 200	293 905	344 283	178 821	165 462
20 - 24	ESDJ	970 356	490 153	480 203	683 275	336 370	346 905	287 081	153 783	133 298

203

7. Population by age, sex and urban/rural residence: latest available year, 1993 - 2002
Population selon l'âge, le sexe et la résidence, urbaine/rurale: dernière année disponible, 1993 - 2002
(continued — suite)

(See notes at end of table. — Voir notes à la fin du tableau.)

Continent, country or area, date and age (in years) / Continent, pays ou zone, date et âge (en années)	Code[1]	Total			Urban - Urbaine			Rural - Rurale		
		Both sexes Les deux sexes	Male Masculin	Female Féminin	Both sexes Les deux sexes	Male Masculin	Female Féminin	Both sexes Les deux sexes	Male Masculin	Female Féminin
EUROPE										
Netherlands - Pays-Bas										
1 I 2002										
25 - 29	ESDJ	1 072 094	540 287	531 807	765 368	383 500	381 868	306 726	156 787	149 939
30 - 34	ESDJ	1 313 645	668 224	645 421	895 062	457 423	437 639	418 583	210 801	207 782
35 - 39	ESDJ	1 329 632	678 596	651 036	871 710	446 036	425 674	457 922	232 560	225 362
40 - 44	ESDJ	1 257 196	636 702	620 494	809 867	409 705	400 162	447 329	226 997	220 332
45 - 49	ESDJ	1 157 746	585 392	572 354	737 888	370 787	367 101	419 858	214 605	205 253
50 - 54	ESDJ	1 145 442	581 326	564 116	720 479	363 887	356 592	424 963	217 439	207 524
55 - 59	ESDJ	965 141	489 563	475 578	593 570	299 322	294 248	371 571	190 241	181 330
60 - 64	ESDJ	754 683	375 803	378 880	466 480	229 731	236 749	288 203	146 072	142 131
65 - 69	ESDJ	647 841	310 021	337 820	403 574	189 836	213 738	244 267	120 185	124 082
70 - 74	ESDJ	563 712	252 023	311 689	361 923	158 910	203 013	201 789	93 113	108 676
75 - 79	ESDJ	455 554	182 614	272 940	301 102	118 748	182 354	154 452	63 866	90 586
80 - 84	ESDJ	300 586	104 132	196 454	201 658	68 391	133 267	98 928	35 741	63 187
85 - 89	ESDJ	159 645	44 932	114 713	107 966	29 308	78 658	51 679	15 624	36 055
90 - 94	ESDJ	58 200	12 756	45 444	39 499	8 083	31 416	18 701	4 673	14 028
95 - 99	ESDJ	11 973	2 178	9 795	8 102	1 341	6 761	3 871	837	3 034
100+	ESDJ	1 203	185	1 018	828	113	715	375	72	303
Norway - Norvège[32]										
1 VII 2002										
Total	ESDJ	4 538 159	2 249 021	2 289 139	...	...	...	...	...	...
0 - 1	ESDJ	56 164	28 735	27 429	...	...	...	...	...	...
1 - 4	ESDJ	238 314	122 058	116 256	...	...	...	...	...	...
5 - 9	ESDJ	308 307	158 442	149 865	...	...	...	...	...	...
10 - 14	ESDJ	305 530	156 823	148 707	...	...	...	...	...	...
15 - 19	ESDJ	270 142	138 735	131 407	...	...	...	...	...	...
20 - 24	ESDJ	273 959	139 001	134 958	...	...	...	...	...	...
25 - 29	ESDJ	310 112	156 773	153 339	...	...	...	...	...	...
30 - 34	ESDJ	351 792	178 793	172 999	...	...	...	...	...	...
35 - 39	ESDJ	342 397	175 339	167 058	...	...	...	...	...	...
40 - 44	ESDJ	320 585	163 603	156 982	...	...	...	...	...	...
45 - 49	ESDJ	311 804	158 095	153 709	...	...	...	...	...	...
50 - 54	ESDJ	299 343	153 077	146 266	...	...	...	...	...	...
55 - 59	ESDJ	279 603	141 721	137 882	...	...	...	...	...	...
60 - 64	ESDJ	195 415	96 399	99 016	...	...	...	...	...	...
65 - 69	ESDJ	162 927	77 749	85 178	...	...	...	...	...	...
70 - 74	ESDJ	159 766	72 909	86 857	...	...	...	...	...	...
75 - 79	ESDJ	148 745	62 726	86 019	...	...	...	...	...	...
80 - 84	ESDJ	115 003	42 461	72 542	...	...	...	...	...	...
85 - 89	ESDJ	61 024	18 900	42 124	...	...	...	...	...	...
90 - 94	ESDJ	22 385	5 720	16 665	...	...	...	...	...	...
95 - 99	ESDJ	4 383	873	3 510	...	...	...	...	...	...
100+	ESDJ	460	89	371	...	...	...	...	...	...
Poland - Pologne[33]										
1 VII 1999										
Total	ESDF	38 653 625	18 788 696	19 864 929	23 908 265	11 417 385	12 490 880	14 745 360	7 371 311	7 374 049
0 - 1	ESDF	387 325	199 592	187 733	209 988	108 287	101 701	177 337	91 305	86 032
1 - 4	ESDF	1 691 030	868 884	822 146	918 097	472 039	446 058	772 933	396 845	376 088
5 - 9	ESDF	2 575 178	1 320 209	1 254 969	1 418 313	727 875	690 438	1 156 865	592 334	564 531
10 - 14	ESDF	3 057 596	1 564 305	1 493 291	1 795 759	918 726	877 033	1 261 837	645 579	616 258
15 - 19	ESDF	3 354 769	1 710 552	1 644 217	2 101 899	1 066 209	1 035 690	1 252 870	644 343	608 527
20 - 24	ESDF	3 140 940	1 598 940	1 542 000	1 995 021	1 001 458	993 563	1 145 919	597 482	548 437
25 - 29	ESDF	2 707 897	1 378 608	1 329 289	1 655 689	828 730	826 959	1 052 208	549 878	502 330
30 - 34	ESDF	2 430 207	1 236 424	1 193 783	1 468 385	723 489	744 896	961 822	512 935	448 887
35 - 39	ESDF	2 730 412	1 375 580	1 354 832	1 697 824	823 238	874 586	1 032 588	552 342	480 246
40 - 44	ESDF	3 233 372	1 615 737	1 617 635	2 141 900	1 028 239	1 113 661	1 091 472	587 498	503 974
45 - 49	ESDF	3 053 669	1 504 186	1 549 483	2 087 422	993 412	1 094 010	966 247	510 774	455 473
50 - 54	ESDF	2 291 423	1 107 929	1 183 494	1 565 775	741 882	823 893	725 648	366 047	359 601

7. Population by age, sex and urban/rural residence: latest available year, 1993 - 2002
Population selon l'âge, le sexe et la résidence, urbaine/rurale: dernière année disponible, 1993 - 2002
(continued — suite)

(See notes at end of table. — Voir notes à la fin du tableau.)

Continent, country or area, date and age (in years) / Continent, pays ou zone, date et âge (en années)	Code[1]	Total			Urban - Urbaine			Rural - Rurale		
		Both sexes Les deux sexes	Male Masculin	Female Féminin	Both sexes Les deux sexes	Male Masculin	Female Féminin	Both sexes Les deux sexes	Male Masculin	Female Féminin

EUROPE

Poland - Pologne[33]
1 VII 1999

55 - 59	ESDF	1 645 830	769 709	876 121	1 081 904	498 567	583 337	563 926	271 142	292 784
60 - 64	ESDF	1 733 364	778 568	954 796	1 089 723	480 729	608 994	643 641	297 839	345 802
65 - 69	ESDF	1 642 836	704 538	938 298	991 759	421 016	570 743	651 077	283 522	367 555
70 - 74	ESDF	1 346 060	519 579	826 481	779 395	297 863	481 532	566 665	221 716	344 949
75 - 79	ESDF	894 985	314 834	580 151	499 492	171 310	328 182	395 493	143 524	251 969
80 - 84	ESDF	385 259	122 127	263 132	209 779	62 572	147 207	175 480	59 555	115 925
85+	ESDF	351 473	98 395	253 078	200 141	51 744	148 397	151 332	46 651	104 681

1 VII 2002

Total	ESDF	38 425 492	18 633 769	19 791 724	...	...	...	...	...	...
0 - 4	ESDF	1 892 323	972 249	920 074	...	...	...	...	...	...
5 - 9	ESDF	2 267 141	1 160 932	1 106 209	...	...	...	...	...	...
10 - 14	ESDF	2 752 338	1 410 459	1 341 880	...	...	...	...	...	...
15 - 19	ESDF	3 276 779	1 672 115	1 604 664	...	...	...	...	...	...
20 - 24	ESDF	3 207 404	1 630 708	1 576 696	...	...	...	...	...	...
25 - 29	ESDF	2 947 618	1 496 687	1 450 931	...	...	...	...	...	...
30 - 34	ESDF	2 494 191	1 268 254	1 225 937	...	...	...	...	...	...
35 - 39	ESDF	2 462 879	1 243 540	1 219 339	...	...	...	...	...	...
40 - 44	ESDF	2 919 788	1 460 160	1 459 628	...	...	...	...	...	...
45 - 49	ESDF	3 142 498	1 549 952	1 592 546	...	...	...	...	...	...
50 - 54	ESDF	2 789 051	1 350 465	1 438 586	...	...	...	...	...	...
55 - 59	ESDF	1 788 268	840 344	947 924	...	...	...	...	...	...
60 - 64	ESDF	1 625 341	731 710	893 631	...	...	...	...	...	...
65 - 69	ESDF	1 587 314	679 654	907 661	...	...	...	...	...	...
70 - 74	ESDF	1 419 745	566 259	853 487	...	...	...	...	...	...
75 - 79	ESDF	1 017 765	350 204	667 562	...	...	...	...	...	...
80 - 84	ESDF	500 400	159 343	341 058	...	...	...	...	...	...
85+	ESDF	334 652	90 738	243 914	...	...	...	...	...	...

Portugal
1 VII 2002

Total	ESDJ	10 368 403	5 009 592	5 358 811	...	...	...	...	...	...
0 - 1	ESDJ	112 911	58 463	54 448	...	...	...	...	...	...
1 - 4	ESDJ	433 403	222 033	211 370	...	...	...	...	...	...
5 - 9	ESDJ	527 828	270 182	257 646	...	...	...	...	...	...
10 - 14	ESDJ	568 815	290 592	278 224	...	...	...	...	...	...
15 - 19	ESDJ	647 156	330 613	316 543	...	...	...	...	...	...
20 - 24	ESDJ	762 003	385 636	376 368	...	...	...	...	...	...
25 - 29	ESDJ	828 107	416 873	411 235	...	...	...	...	...	...
30 - 34	ESDJ	775 206	387 526	387 681	...	...	...	...	...	...
35 - 39	ESDJ	771 516	379 991	391 525	...	...	...	...	...	...
40 - 44	ESDJ	745 948	366 423	379 525	...	...	...	...	...	...
45 - 49	ESDJ	690 294	336 180	354 114	...	...	...	...	...	...
50 - 54	ESDJ	660 759	319 670	341 089	...	...	...	...	...	...
55 - 59	ESDJ	586 864	276 084	310 780	...	...	...	...	...	...
60 - 64	ESDJ	535 539	249 445	286 094	...	...	...	...	...	...
65 - 69	ESDJ	534 541	242 186	292 355	...	...	...	...	...	...
70 - 74	ESDJ	462 400	201 498	260 902	...	...	...	...	...	...
75 - 79	ESDJ	357 188	146 035	211 153	...	...	...	...	...	...
80 - 84	ESDJ	215 752	81 896	133 857	...	...	...	...	...	...
85+	ESDJ	152 177	48 271	103 906	...	...	...	...	...	...

Republic of Moldova - République de Moldova
1 VII 2002

Total	ESDJ	3 623 062	1 735 430	1 887 632	1 484 676	716 822	767 854	2 138 386	1 018 608	1 119 778
0 - 1	ESDJ	35 514	18 321	17 193	12 442	6 479	5 963	23 072	11 842	11 230
1 - 4	ESDJ	154 887	79 687	75 200	52 349	27 022	25 327	102 538	52 665	49 873
5 - 9	ESDJ	251 141	128 534	122 607	84 900	43 763	41 137	166 241	84 771	81 470

7. Population by age, sex and urban/rural residence: latest available year, 1993 - 2002
Population selon l'âge, le sexe et la résidence, urbaine/rurale: dernière année disponible, 1993 - 2002
(continued — suite)

(See notes at end of table. — Voir notes à la fin du tableau.)

Continent, country or area, date and age (in years) / Continent, pays ou zone, date et âge (en années)	Code[1]	Total			Urban - Urbaine			Rural - Rurale		
		Both sexes Les deux sexes	Male Masculin	Female Féminin	Both sexes Les deux sexes	Male Masculin	Female Féminin	Both sexes Les deux sexes	Male Masculin	Female Féminin
EUROPE										
Republic of Moldova - République de Moldova										
1 VII 2002										
10 - 14	ESDJ	327 471	166 835	160 636	125 200	63 947	61 253	202 271	102 888	99 383
15 - 19	ESDJ	364 950	184 990	179 960	140 519	71 578	68 941	224 431	113 412	111 019
20 - 24	ESDJ	317 257	160 273	156 984	126 161	64 977	61 184	191 096	95 296	95 800
25 - 29	ESDJ	289 180	145 122	144 058	121 335	58 913	62 422	167 845	86 209	81 636
30 - 34	ESDJ	222 590	110 620	111 970	118 894	62 514	56 380	103 696	48 106	55 590
35 - 39	ESDJ	240 925	115 111	125 814	111 312	52 787	58 525	129 613	62 324	67 289
40 - 44	ESDJ	293 715	139 871	153 844	135 089	63 029	72 060	158 626	76 842	81 784
45 - 49	ESDJ	265 279	125 837	139 442	122 671	57 021	65 650	142 608	68 816	73 792
50 - 54	ESDJ	236 781	110 108	126 673	108 739	51 238	57 501	128 042	58 870	69 172
55 - 59	ESDJ	119 608	52 265	67 343	51 360	23 907	27 453	68 248	28 358	39 890
60 - 64	ESDJ	152 471	65 258	87 213	59 243	26 676	32 567	93 228	38 582	54 646
65 - 69	ESDJ	128 903	53 297	75 606	43 662	18 641	25 021	85 241	34 656	50 585
70 - 74	ESDJ	106 197	40 965	65 232	33 042	12 713	20 329	73 155	28 252	44 903
75 - 79	ESDJ	69 199	23 480	45 719	22 814	7 395	15 419	46 385	16 085	30 300
80 - 84	ESDJ	32 249	10 882	21 367	9 446	2 841	6 605	22 803	8 041	14 762
85+	ESDJ	14 745	3 974	10 771	5 498	1 381	4 117	9 247	2 593	6 654
Romania - Roumanie										
1 VII 2002										
Total	ESDJ	21 794 793	10 642 538	11 152 255	11 608 735	5 579 042	6 029 693	10 186 058	5 063 496	5 122 562
0 - 1	ESDJ	208 769	107 843	100 926	96 048	49 555	46 493	112 721	58 288	54 433
1 - 4	ESDJ	885 444	454 200	431 244	391 062	200 881	190 181	494 382	253 319	241 063
5 - 9	ESDJ	1 138 448	582 996	555 452	519 080	265 926	253 154	619 368	317 070	302 298
10 - 14	ESDJ	1 546 637	789 605	757 032	820 913	417 831	403 082	725 724	371 774	353 950
15 - 19	ESDJ	1 646 667	843 651	803 016	943 191	478 560	464 631	703 476	365 091	338 385
20 - 24	ESDJ	1 752 646	895 967	856 679	1 019 609	511 621	507 988	733 037	384 346	348 691
25 - 29	ESDJ	1 733 618	887 293	846 325	950 006	471 101	478 905	783 612	416 192	367 420
30 - 34	ESDJ	1 953 607	989 501	964 106	1 110 055	530 233	579 822	843 552	459 268	384 284
35 - 39	ESDJ	1 219 037	614 594	604 443	723 336	338 328	385 008	495 701	276 266	219 435
40 - 44	ESDJ	1 427 621	711 550	716 071	900 782	421 476	479 306	526 839	290 074	236 765
45 - 49	ESDJ	1 603 366	787 916	815 450	1 033 035	498 313	534 722	570 331	289 603	280 728
50 - 54	ESDJ	1 433 857	694 720	739 137	835 315	410 403	424 912	598 542	284 317	314 225
55 - 59	ESDJ	1 061 665	503 241	558 424	530 835	254 439	276 396	530 830	248 802	282 028
60 - 64	ESDJ	1 122 390	511 587	610 803	508 819	233 544	275 275	613 571	278 043	335 528
65 - 69	ESDJ	1 085 893	480 016	605 877	450 185	197 501	252 684	635 708	282 515	353 193
70 - 74	ESDJ	900 956	383 576	517 380	358 978	149 651	209 327	541 978	233 925	308 053
75 - 79	ESDJ	630 292	250 273	380 019	241 732	92 256	149 476	388 560	158 017	230 543
80 - 84	ESDJ	279 105	98 341	180 764	108 354	35 624	72 730	170 751	62 717	108 034
85+	ESDJ	164 775	55 668	109 107	67 400	21 799	45 601	97 375	33 869	63 506
Russian Federation - Fédération de Russie										
1 VII 1999										
Total	ESDF	145 943 393	68 405 752	77 537 641	106 488 089	49 622 408	56 865 681	39 455 304	18 783 344	20 671 960
0 - 1	ESDF	1 247 988	641 652	606 336	857 488	441 150	416 338	390 500	200 502	189 998
1 - 4	ESDF	5 273 255	2 703 604	2 569 651	3 601 015	1 848 352	1 752 663	1 672 240	855 252	816 988
5 - 9	ESDF	8 624 225	4 423 897	4 200 328	5 853 019	3 003 247	2 849 772	2 771 206	1 420 650	1 350 556
10 - 14	ESDF	12 073 276	6 152 074	5 921 202	8 414 270	4 291 221	4 123 049	3 659 006	1 860 853	1 798 153
15 - 19	ESDF	11 640 353	5 903 004	5 737 349	8 427 541	4 235 850	4 191 691	3 212 812	1 667 154	1 545 658
20 - 24	ESDF	10 694 954	5 403 032	5 291 922	8 002 226	3 994 587	4 007 639	2 692 728	1 408 445	1 284 283
25 - 29	ESDF	10 132 910	5 223 463	4 909 447	7 823 180	4 033 537	3 789 643	2 309 730	1 189 926	1 119 804
30 - 34	ESDF	9 601 516	4 839 812	4 761 704	7 139 919	3 594 303	3 545 616	2 461 597	1 245 509	1 216 088
35 - 39	ESDF	12 142 415	6 036 862	6 105 553	8 979 325	4 386 590	4 592 735	3 163 090	1 650 272	1 512 818
40 - 44	ESDF	12 503 481	6 112 856	6 390 625	9 386 098	4 492 980	4 893 118	3 117 383	1 619 876	1 497 507
45 - 49	ESDF	11 209 888	5 366 036	5 843 852	8 637 306	4 051 810	4 585 496	2 572 582	1 314 226	1 258 356
50 - 54	ESDF	7 681 472	3 578 859	4 102 613	6 070 884	2 786 751	3 284 133	1 610 588	792 108	818 480
55 - 59	ESDF	6 440 897	2 807 088	3 633 809	4 772 163	2 063 501	2 708 662	1 668 734	743 587	925 147

7. Population by age, sex and urban/rural residence: latest available year, 1993 - 2002
Population selon l'âge, le sexe et la résidence, urbaine/rurale: dernière année disponible, 1993 - 2002
(continued — suite)

(See notes at end of table. — Voir notes à la fin du tableau.)

Continent, country or area, date and age (in years) Continent, pays ou zone, date et âge (en années)	Code[1]	Total			Urban - Urbaine			Rural - Rurale		
		Both sexes Les deux sexes	Male Masculin	Female Féminin	Both sexes Les deux sexes	Male Masculin	Female Féminin	Both sexes Les deux sexes	Male Masculin	Female Féminin
EUROPE										
Russian Federation - Fédération de Russie										
1 VII 1999										
60 - 64	ESDF	8 409 982	3 506 323	4 903 659	6 059 829	2 487 725	3 572 104	2 350 153	1 018 598	1 331 555
65 - 69	ESDF	6 341 925	2 423 364	3 918 561	4 335 136	1 620 168	2 714 968	2 006 789	803 196	1 203 593
70 - 74	ESDF	6 028 319	1 968 872	4 059 447	4 152 137	1 369 386	2 782 751	1 876 182	599 486	1 276 696
75 - 79	ESDF	2 941 515	713 392	2 228 123	2 034 447	501 317	1 533 130	907 068	212 075	694 993
80 - 84	ESDF	1 589 627	340 138	1 249 489	1 074 249	242 399	831 850	515 378	97 739	417 639
85 - 89	ESDF	1 000 845	192 218	808 627	642 772	132 578	510 194	358 073	59 640	298 433
90 - 94	ESDF	284 809	50 479	234 330	176 436	32 916	143 520	108 373	17 563	90 810
95 - 99	ESDF	66 543	14 515	52 028	40 569	9 526	31 043	25 974	4 989	20 985
100+	ESDF	13 198	4 212	8 986	8 080	2 514	5 566	5 118	1 698	3 420
1 I 2001										
Total	ESDF	143 954 391	67 287 019	76 667 372	...	...	...	...	...	...
0 - 1	ESDF	1 309 841	673 515	636 326	...	...	...	...	...	...
0 - 4	ESDF	4 996 000	2 566 260	2 429 740	...	...	...	...	...	...
5 - 9	ESDF	7 123 120	3 652 229	3 470 891	...	...	...	...	...	...
10 - 14	ESDF	10 825 129	5 532 869	5 292 260	...	...	...	...	...	...
15 - 19	ESDF	12 208 011	6 199 698	6 008 313	...	...	...	...	...	...
20 - 24	ESDF	10 901 116	5 494 678	5 406 438	...	...	...	...	...	...
25 - 29	ESDF	10 422 406	5 259 573	5 162 833	...	...	...	...	...	...
30 - 34	ESDF	9 534 224	4 879 484	4 654 740	...	...	...	...	...	...
35 - 30	ESDF	10 587 806	5 256 996	5 330 810	...	...	...	...	...	...
40 - 44	ESDF	12 594 636	6 146 961	6 447 675	...	...	...	...	...	...
45 - 49	ESDF	11 625 074	5 538 814	6 086 260	...	...	...	...	...	...
50 - 54	ESDF	9 832 545	4 553 051	5 279 494	...	...	...	...	...	...
55 - 59	ESDF	4 840 576	2 134 498	2 706 078	...	...	...	...	...	...
60 - 64	ESDF	8 624 902	3 525 417	5 099 485	...	...	...	...	...	...
65 - 69	ESDF	5 973 442	2 284 876	3 688 566	...	...	...	...	...	...
70 - 74	ESDF	5 966 463	2 033 884	3 932 579	...	...	...	...	...	...
75 - 79	ESDF	3 758 139	960 722	2 797 417	...	...	...	...	...	...
80 - 84	ESDF	1 533 539	338 265	1 195 274	...	...	...	...	...	...
85 - 89	ESDF	884 600	168 050	716 550	...	...	...	...	...	...
90 - 94	ESDF	299 404	59 221	240 183	...	...	...	...	...	...
95 - 99	ESDF	83 799	19 285	64 514	...	...	...	...	...	...
100+	ESDF	29 619	8 673	20 946	...	...	...	...	...	...
San Marino - Saint-Marin										
31 XII 2000										
Total	ESDF	26 941	13 185	13 756	...	...	...	...	...	...
0 - 1	ESDF	285	149	136	...	...	...	...	...	...
1 - 4	ESDF	1 187	627	560	...	...	...	...	...	...
5 - 9	ESDF	1 316	686	630	...	...	...	...	...	...
10 - 14	ESDF	1 230	635	595	...	...	...	...	...	...
15 - 19	ESDF	1 346	709	637	...	...	...	...	...	...
20 - 24	ESDF	1 601	803	798	...	...	...	...	...	...
25 - 29	ESDF	1 932	962	970	...	...	...	...	...	...
30 - 34	ESDF	2 422	1 154	1 268	...	...	...	...	...	...
35 - 39	ESDF	2 530	1 235	1 295	...	...	...	...	...	...
40 - 44	ESDF	2 109	1 063	1 046	...	...	...	...	...	...
45 - 49	ESDF	1 822	906	916	...	...	...	...	...	...
50 - 54	ESDF	1 848	913	935	...	...	...	...	...	...
55 - 59	ESDF	1 527	747	780	...	...	...	...	...	...
60 - 64	ESDF	1 443	717	726	...	...	...	...	...	...
65 - 69	ESDF	1 311	625	686	...	...	...	...	...	...
70 - 74	ESDF	1 085	501	584	...	...	...	...	...	...
75 - 79	ESDF	940	396	544	...	...	...	...	...	...
80 - 84	ESDF	537	211	326	...	...	...	...	...	...
85 - 89	ESDF	337	112	225	...	...	...	...	...	...

7. Population by age, sex and urban/rural residence: latest available year, 1993 - 2002
Population selon l'âge, le sexe et la résidence, urbaine/rurale: dernière année disponible, 1993 - 2002
(continued — suite)

(See notes at end of table. — Voir notes à la fin du tableau.)

Continent, country or area, date and age (in years) / Continent, pays ou zone, date et âge (en années)	Code[1]	Total			Urban - Urbaine			Rural - Rurale		
		Both sexes Les deux sexes	Male Masculin	Female Féminin	Both sexes Les deux sexes	Male Masculin	Female Féminin	Both sexes Les deux sexes	Male Masculin	Female Féminin

EUROPE

San Marino - Saint-Marin

31 XII 2000

90 - 94	ESDF	107	29	78	...	...	...	...	...	...
95 - 99	ESDF	24	5	19	...	...	...	...	...	...
100+	ESDF	2	-	2	...	...	...	...	...	...

Serbia and Montenegro - Serbie-et-Monteneg-ro[34]

1 VII 2000

Total	ESDJ	10 633 508	5 271 588	5 361 920	5 482 862	2 676 715	2 806 147	5 150 646	2 594 873	2 555 773
0 - 1	ESDJ	124 833	64 923	59 910	65 403	33 965	31 438	59 430	30 958	28 472
1 - 4	ESDJ	521 569	270 305	251 264	270 429	140 097	130 332	251 140	130 208	120 932
5 - 9	ESDJ	698 840	361 765	337 075	360 042	185 150	174 892	338 798	176 615	162 183
10 - 14	ESDJ	772 963	396 370	376 593	374 454	190 369	184 085	398 509	206 001	192 508
15 - 19	ESDJ	792 267	405 080	387 187	401 854	203 968	197 886	390 413	201 112	189 301
20 - 24	ESDJ	805 115	411 765	393 350	409 656	207 424	202 232	395 459	204 341	191 118
25 - 29	ESDJ	774 329	394 880	379 449	386 468	193 832	192 636	387 861	201 048	186 813
30 - 34	ESDJ	734 554	373 161	361 393	369 752	180 931	188 821	364 802	192 230	172 572
35 - 39	ESDJ	716 009	361 759	354 250	380 637	183 347	197 290	335 372	178 412	156 960
40 - 44	ESDJ	732 707	368 944	363 763	406 042	195 635	210 407	326 665	173 309	153 356
45 - 49	ESDJ	781 354	392 557	388 797	446 557	215 265	231 292	334 797	177 292	157 505
50 - 54	ESDJ	663 329	328 278	335 051	384 676	183 940	200 736	278 653	144 338	134 315
55 - 59	ESDJ	497 729	241 182	256 547	270 006	128 641	141 365	227 723	112 541	115 182
60 - 64	ESDJ	558 705	263 403	295 302	294 935	138 591	156 344	263 770	124 812	138 958
65 - 69	ESDJ	541 997	248 176	293 821	263 183	121 354	141 829	278 814	126 822	151 992
70 - 74	ESDJ	445 900	194 017	251 883	200 298	87 149	113 149	245 602	106 868	138 734
75 - 79	ESDJ	282 116	114 811	167 305	123 548	52 195	71 353	158 568	62 616	95 952
80 - 84	ESDJ	103 019	40 326	62 693	39 501	17 023	22 478	63 518	23 303	40 215
85 - 89	ESDJ	58 616	26 299	32 317	24 532	11 474	13 058	34 084	14 825	19 259
90 - 94	ESDJ	20 981	10 131	10 850	7 973	4 553	3 420	13 008	5 578	7 430
95 - 99	ESDJ	5 758	2 991	2 767	2 548	1 557	991	3 210	1 434	1 776
100+	ESDJ	818	465	353	368	255	113	450	210	240

1 VII 2001

Total	ESDF	10 653 722	5 281 815	5 371 907	...	...	...	...	...	...
0 - 4	ESDF	636 064	329 799	306 265	...	...	...	...	...	...
5 - 9	ESDF	686 736	355 934	330 802	...	...	...	...	...	...
10 - 14	ESDF	766 739	393 910	372 830	...	...	...	...	...	...
15 - 19	ESDF	789 491	403 522	385 969	...	...	...	...	...	...
20 - 24	ESDF	801 977	410 276	391 701	...	...	...	...	...	...
25 - 29	ESDF	785 525	400 410	385 115	...	...	...	...	...	...
30 - 34	ESDF	741 666	377 282	364 385	...	...	...	...	...	...
35 - 39	ESDF	711 767	359 922	351 845	...	...	...	...	...	...
40 - 44	ESDF	729 362	367 226	362 136	...	...	...	...	...	...
45 - 49	ESDF	779 585	391 401	388 185	...	...	...	...	...	...
50 - 54	ESDF	705 097	349 405	355 693	...	...	...	...	...	...
55 - 59	ESDF	486 652	235 918	250 734	...	...	...	...	...	...
60 - 64	ESDF	546 904	257 998	288 906	...	...	...	...	...	...
65 - 69	ESDF	535 432	244 854	290 578	...	...	...	...	...	...
70 - 74	ESDF	454 728	199 053	255 675	...	...	...	...	...	...
75 - 79	ESDF	290 924	117 907	173 017	...	...	...	...	...	...
80 - 84	ESDF	122 585	48 872	73 714	...	...	...	...	...	...
85+	ESDF	82 493	38 132	44 361	...	...	...	...	...	...

Slovakia - Slovaquie

1 VII 2002

Total	ESDJ	5 378 595	2 611 362	2 767 233	...	...	...	...	...	...
0 - 1	ESDJ	50 690	26 067	24 623	...	...	...	...	...	...
1 - 4	ESDJ	219 732	112 580	107 152	...	...	...	...	...	...

7. Population by age, sex and urban/rural residence: latest available year, 1993 - 2002
Population selon l'âge, le sexe et la résidence, urbaine/rurale: dernière année disponible, 1993 - 2002
(continued — suite)

(See notes at end of table. — Voir notes à la fin du tableau.)

Continent, country or area, date and age (in years) / Continent, pays ou zone, date et âge (en années)	Code[1]	Total			Urban - Urbaine			Rural - Rurale		
		Both sexes Les deux sexes	Male Masculin	Female Féminin	Both sexes Les deux sexes	Male Masculin	Female Féminin	Both sexes Les deux sexes	Male Masculin	Female Féminin
EUROPE										
Slovakia - Slovaquie										
1 VII 2002										
5 - 9	ESDJ	322 239	165 132	157 107	...	...	...	...	...	...
10 - 14	ESDJ	391 374	199 895	191 479	...	...	...	...	...	...
15 - 19	ESDJ	435 326	222 288	213 038	...	...	...	...	...	...
20 - 24	ESDJ	464 453	236 714	227 739	...	...	...	...	...	...
25 - 29	ESDJ	452 767	230 297	222 470	...	...	...	...	...	...
30 - 34	ESDJ	370 899	187 713	183 186	...	...	...	...	...	...
35 - 39	ESDJ	379 321	190 508	188 813	...	...	...	...	...	...
40 - 44	ESDJ	392 875	197 229	195 646	...	...	...	...	...	...
45 - 49	ESDJ	416 012	205 777	210 235	...	...	...	...	...	...
50 - 54	ESDJ	366 912	178 117	188 795	...	...	...	...	...	...
55 - 59	ESDJ	267 544	123 871	143 673	...	...	...	...	...	...
60 - 64	ESDJ	227 019	100 218	126 801	...	...	...	...	...	...
65 - 69	ESDJ	196 483	82 093	114 390	...	...	...	...	...	...
70 - 74	ESDJ	177 410	68 988	108 422	...	...	...	...	...	...
75 - 79	ESDJ	135 947	48 213	87 734	...	...	...	...	...	...
80 - 84	ESDJ	70 854	23 555	47 299	...	...	...	...	...	...
85 - 89	ESDJ	27 551	8 493	19 058	...	...	...	...	...	...
90 - 94	ESDJ	11 097	3 054	8 043	...	...	...	...	...	...
95 - 99	ESDJ	1 930	503	1 427	...	...	...	...	...	...
100+	ESDJ	160	57	103	...	...	...	...	...	...
Slovenia - Slovénie										
1 VII 2002										
Total	ESDJ	1 995 718	976 111	1 019 607	975 163	462 513	512 650	974 256	480 954	493 302
0 - 1	ESDJ	17 468	9 052	8 416	8 301	4 325	3 976	9 021	4 649	4 372
1 - 4	ESDJ	72 126	37 221	34 905	33 518	17 401	16 117	37 718	19 359	18 359
5 - 9	ESDJ	97 659	50 122	47 537	44 435	22 717	21 718	52 091	26 825	25 266
10 - 14	ESDJ	115 567	59 361	56 206	54 214	27 755	26 459	59 930	30 876	29 054
15 - 19	ESDJ	131 064	66 891	64 173	63 471	32 391	31 080	66 116	33 724	32 392
20 - 24	ESDJ	150 370	77 760	72 610	73 080	37 464	35 616	73 583	37 889	35 694
25 - 29	ESDJ	149 560	77 113	72 447	70 573	35 504	35 069	73 520	37 825	35 695
30 - 34	ESDJ	143 490	73 051	70 439	67 585	33 069	34 516	70 225	36 030	34 195
35 - 39	ESDJ	156 206	78 911	77 295	75 757	36 030	39 727	74 503	38 429	36 074
40 - 44	ESDJ	154 587	78 649	75 938	76 020	36 223	39 797	72 728	37 864	34 864
45 - 49	ESDJ	161 434	83 644	77 790	82 057	40 007	42 050	73 877	39 164	34 713
50 - 54	ESDJ	142 723	73 275	69 448	73 502	35 952	37 550	65 771	34 571	31 200
55 - 59	ESDJ	106 855	52 550	54 305	55 032	25 488	29 544	49 796	25 462	24 334
60 - 64	ESDJ	104 575	49 825	54 750	52 855	24 309	28 546	50 241	24 473	25 768
65 - 69	ESDJ	95 874	42 335	53 539	47 785	20 931	26 854	47 279	20 952	26 327
70 - 74	ESDJ	84 095	33 552	50 543	41 516	16 239	25 277	41 977	17 032	24 945
75 - 79	ESDJ	60 252	19 045	41 207	29 974	9 704	20 270	29 874	9 170	20 704
80 - 84	ESDJ	30 442	8 476	21 966	15 082	4 381	10 701	15 190	4 040	11 150
85 - 89	ESDJ	14 140	3 685	10 455	6 904	1 863	5 041	7 158	1 795	5 363
90 - 94	ESDJ	6 153	1 386	4 767	2 977	665	2 312	3 127	715	2 412
95 - 99	ESDJ	998	200	798	488	93	395	491	105	386
100+	ESDJ	80	7	73	37	2	35	40	5	35
Spain - Espagne										
1 VII 2001										
Total	ESDJ	40 265 502	19 709 429	20 556 073	...	...	...	...	...	...
0 - 4	ESDJ	1 902 858	979 921	922 937	...	...	...	...	...	...
5 - 9	ESDJ	1 927 628	994 121	933 507	...	...	...	...	...	...
10 - 14	ESDJ	2 056 138	1 056 798	999 340	...	...	...	...	...	...
15 - 19	ESDJ	2 454 000	1 258 136	1 195 865	...	...	...	...	...	...
20 - 24	ESDJ	3 109 192	1 588 556	1 520 636	...	...	...	...	...	...
25 - 29	ESDJ	3 449 474	1 759 656	1 689 818	...	...	...	...	...	...
30 - 34	ESDJ	3 375 823	1 718 359	1 657 465	...	...	...	...	...	...
35 - 39	ESDJ	3 217 265	1 621 882	1 595 383	...	...	...	...	...	...
40 - 44	ESDJ	2 921 760	1 459 858	1 461 903	...	...	...	...	...	...

7. Population by age, sex and urban/rural residence: latest available year, 1993 - 2002
Population selon l'âge, le sexe et la résidence, urbaine/rurale: dernière année disponible, 1993 - 2002
(continued — suite)

(See notes at end of table. — Voir notes à la fin du tableau.)

Continent, country or area, date and age (in years) / Continent, pays ou zone, date et âge (en années)	Code[1]	Total			Urban - Urbaine			Rural - Rurale		
		Both sexes Les deux sexes	Male Masculin	Female Féminin	Both sexes Les deux sexes	Male Masculin	Female Féminin	Both sexes Les deux sexes	Male Masculin	Female Féminin
EUROPE										
Spain - Espagne										
1 VII 2001										
45 - 49	ESDJ	2 552 551	1 269 686	1 282 865	...	...	...	...	...	...
50 - 54	ESDJ	2 404 106	1 185 309	1 218 797	...	...	...	...	...	...
55 - 59	ESDJ	2 173 917	1 059 892	1 114 026	...	...	...	...	...	...
60 - 64	ESDJ	1 874 949	892 133	982 816	...	...	...	...	...	...
65 - 69	ESDJ	2 042 372	945 204	1 097 168	...	...	...	...	...	...
70 - 74	ESDJ	1 824 273	808 936	1 015 337	...	...	...	...	...	...
75 - 79	ESDJ	1 422 655	585 838	836 818	...	...	...	...	...	...
80 - 84	ESDJ	884 919	321 079	563 840	...	...	...	...	...	...
85+	ESDJ	671 626	204 068	467 558	...	...	...	...	...	...
Sweden - Suède										
1 VII 2002										
Total	ESDJ	8 924 960	4 417 777	4 507 183	...	...	...	...	...	...
0 - 1	ESDJ	93 840	48 245	45 595	...	...	...	...	...	...
1 - 4	ESDJ	365 295	187 670	177 625	...	...	...	...	...	...
5 - 9	ESDJ	542 221	277 443	264 778	...	...	...	...	...	...
10 - 14	ESDJ	614 752	315 888	298 864	...	...	...	...	...	...
15 - 19	ESDJ	525 649	270 321	255 328	...	...	...	...	...	...
20 - 24	ESDJ	516 326	262 797	253 529	...	...	...	...	...	...
25 - 29	ESDJ	574 843	292 507	282 336	...	...	...	...	...	...
30 - 34	ESDJ	615 378	313 403	301 975	...	...	...	...	...	...
35 - 39	ESDJ	658 005	337 402	320 603	...	...	...	...	...	...
40 - 44	ESDJ	584 793	297 890	286 903	...	...	...	...	...	...
45 - 49	ESDJ	586 046	297 106	288 940	...	...	...	...	...	...
50 - 54	ESDJ	616 070	310 591	305 479	...	...	...	...	...	...
55 - 59	ESDJ	632 468	319 803	312 665	...	...	...	...	...	...
60 - 64	ESDJ	466 438	232 705	233 733	...	...	...	...	...	...
65 - 69	ESDJ	382 395	183 972	198 423	...	...	...	...	...	...
70 - 74	ESDJ	357 480	163 260	194 220	...	...	...	...	...	...
75 - 79	ESDJ	326 215	140 762	185 453	...	...	...	...	...	...
80 - 84	ESDJ	258 080	101 291	156 789	...	...	...	...	...	...
85 - 89	ESDJ	141 060	47 324	93 736	...	...	...	...	...	...
90 - 94	ESDJ	55 327	15 042	40 285	...	...	...	...	...	...
95 - 99	ESDJ	11 359	2 272	9 087	...	...	...	...	...	...
100+	ESDJ	1 088	166	922	...	...	...	...	...	...
Switzerland - Suisse										
1 VII 2002										
Total	ESDJ	7 289 542	3 563 894	3 725 648	...	...	...	...	...	...
0 - 4	ESDJ	387 260	199 070	188 190	...	...	...	...	...	...
5 - 9	ESDJ	415 300	213 737	201 563	...	...	...	...	...	...
10 - 14	ESDJ	438 178	225 748	212 431	...	...	...	...	...	...
15 - 19	ESDJ	422 763	217 314	205 449	...	...	...	...	...	...
20 - 24	ESDJ	427 452	215 670	211 783	...	...	...	...	...	...
25 - 29	ESDJ	461 444	228 033	233 411	...	...	...	...	...	...
30 - 34	ESDJ	558 388	275 460	282 928	...	...	...	...	...	...
35 - 39	ESDJ	629 595	316 592	313 003	...	...	...	...	...	...
40 - 44	ESDJ	580 086	293 126	286 961	...	...	...	...	...	...
45 - 49	ESDJ	517 467	260 551	256 916	...	...	...	...	...	...
50 - 54	ESDJ	490 317	245 727	244 590	...	...	...	...	...	...
55 - 59	ESDJ	463 239	231 626	231 613	...	...	...	...	...	...
60 - 64	ESDJ	367 993	178 726	189 268	...	...	...	...	...	...
65 - 69	ESDJ	318 200	148 399	169 801	...	...	...	...	...	...
70 - 74	ESDJ	278 134	121 531	156 603	...	...	...	...	...	...
75 - 79	ESDJ	230 857	92 644	138 213	...	...	...	...	...	...
80 - 84	ESDJ	161 174	59 107	102 067	...	...	...	...	...	...
85+	ESDJ	141 698	40 838	100 861	...	...	...	...	...	...

7. **Population by age, sex and urban/rural residence: latest available year, 1993 - 2002**
Population selon l'âge, le sexe et la résidence, urbaine/rurale: dernière année disponible, 1993 - 2002
(continued — suite)

(See notes at end of table. — Voir notes à la fin du tableau.)

Continent, country or area, date and age (in years) / Continent, pays ou zone, date et âge (en années)	Code[1]	Total			Urban - Urbaine			Rural - Rurale		
		Both sexes Les deux sexes	Male Masculin	Female Féminin	Both sexes Les deux sexes	Male Masculin	Female Féminin	Both sexes Les deux sexes	Male Masculin	Female Féminin
EUROPE										
The Former Yugoslav Rep. of Macedonia - L'ex-République yougoslave de Macédoine										
20 VI 1994										
Total	CDJC	1 935 034	968 931	966 103	1 156 297	574 461	581 836	778 737	394 470	384 267
0 - 1	CDJC	28 626	14 688	13 938	15 006	7 678	7 328	13 620	7 010	6 610
1 - 4	CDJC	122 661	63 281	59 380	65 521	33 772	31 749	57 140	29 509	27 631
5 - 9	CDJC	162 672	83 649	79 023	91 559	47 127	44 432	71 113	36 522	34 591
10 - 14	CDJC	166 993	85 716	81 277	97 231	49 572	47 659	69 762	36 144	33 618
15 - 19	CDJC	161 947	82 731	79 216	93 395	47 311	46 084	68 552	35 420	33 132
20 - 24	CDJC	152 720	77 984	74 736	87 496	44 132	43 364	65 224	33 852	31 372
25 - 29	CDJC	150 545	76 309	74 236	87 079	42 986	44 093	63 466	33 323	30 143
30 - 34	CDJC	147 733	74 873	72 860	89 325	44 130	45 195	58 408	30 743	27 665
35 - 39	CDJC	145 144	74 150	70 994	94 448	47 380	47 068	50 696	26 770	23 926
40 - 44	CDJC	136 590	68 684	67 906	94 134	47 158	46 976	42 456	21 526	20 930
45 - 49	CDJC	109 351	53 715	55 636	74 941	36 941	38 000	34 410	16 774	17 636
50 - 54	CDJC	99 300	48 653	50 647	64 263	31 747	32 516	35 037	16 906	18 131
55 - 59	CDJC	95 419	46 243	49 176	59 768	29 374	30 394	35 651	16 869	18 782
60 - 64	CDJC	88 511	42 203	46 308	52 236	24 720	27 516	36 275	17 483	18 792
65 - 69	CDJC	67 323	31 107	36 216	38 531	17 705	20 826	28 792	13 402	15 390
70 - 74	CDJC	50 502	22 826	27 676	27 771	12 443	15 328	22 731	10 383	12 348
75 - 79	CDJC	20 709	9 552	11 157	10 415	4 565	5 850	10 294	4 987	5 307
80 - 84	CDJC	17 372	8 030	9 342	8 587	3 792	4 795	8 785	4 238	4 547
85 - 89	CDJC	5 708	2 616	3 092	2 854	1 252	1 602	2 854	1 364	1 490
90 - 94	CDJC	1 651	671	980	844	343	501	807	328	479
95 - 99	CDJC	279	114	165	150	58	92	129	56	73
100+	CDJC	112	38	74	52	19	33	60	19	41
Unk. - Inc.	CDJC	3 166	1 098	2 068	691	256	435	2 475	842	1 633
1 VII 2001										
Total	ESDJ	2 034 882	1 017 927	1 016 955	...	...	...	...	...	...
0 - 1	ESDJ	24 831	12 824	12 007	...	...	...	...	...	...
1 - 4	ESDJ	105 372	54 690	50 682	...	...	...	...	...	...
5 - 9	ESDJ	152 547	78 857	73 690	...	...	...	...	...	...
10 - 14	ESDJ	160 555	82 945	77 610	...	...	...	...	...	...
15 - 19	ESDJ	166 643	85 345	81 298	...	...	...	...	...	...
20 - 24	ESDJ	164 855	84 322	80 533	...	...	...	...	...	...
25 - 29	ESDJ	158 317	80 672	77 645	...	...	...	...	...	...
30 - 34	ESDJ	150 961	76 692	74 269	...	...	...	...	...	...
35 - 39	ESDJ	149 349	75 608	73 741	...	...	...	...	...	...
40 - 44	ESDJ	147 070	74 651	72 419	...	...	...	...	...	...
45 - 49	ESDJ	140 529	71 060	69 469	...	...	...	...	...	...
50 - 54	ESDJ	120 305	58 700	61 605	...	...	...	...	...	...
55 - 59	ESDJ	94 110	45 413	48 697	...	...	...	...	...	...
60 - 64	ESDJ	88 702	42 208	46 494	...	...	...	...	...	...
65 - 69	ESDJ	83 540	38 832	44 708	...	...	...	...	...	...
70 - 74	ESDJ	60 472	26 999	33 473	...	...	...	...	...	...
75 - 79	ESDJ	39 060	16 628	22 432	...	...	...	...	...	...
80 - 84	ESDJ	15 792	6 713	9 079	...	...	...	...	...	...
85 - 89	ESDJ	6 661	2 815	3 846	...	...	...	...	...	...
90 - 94	ESDJ	2 070	835	1 235	...	...	...	...	...	...
95+	ESDJ	873	312	561	...	...	...	...	...	...
Unk. - Inc.	ESDJ	2 268	806	1 462	...	...	...	...	...	...
Ukraine										
1 I 2000										
Total	ESDF	49 456 088	22 978 364	26 477 724	33 505 862	15 617 268	17 888 594	15 950 226	7 361 096	8 589 130
0 - 1	ESDF	384 980	198 354	186 626	236 787	122 275	114 512	148 193	76 079	72 114

7. Population by age, sex and urban/rural residence: latest available year, 1993 - 2002
Population selon l'âge, le sexe et la résidence, urbaine/rurale: dernière année disponible, 1993 - 2002
(continued — suite)

(See notes at end of table. — Voir notes à la fin du tableau.)

Continent, country or area, date and age (in years) / Continent, pays ou zone, date et âge (en années)	Code[1]	Total			Urban - Urbaine			Rural - Rurale		
		Both sexes Les deux sexes	Male Masculin	Female Féminin	Both sexes Les deux sexes	Male Masculin	Female Féminin	Both sexes Les deux sexes	Male Masculin	Female Féminin
EUROPE										
Ukraine										
1 I 2000										
1 - 4	ESDF	1 788 699	919 015	869 684	1 111 882	571 821	540 061	676 817	347 194	329 623
5 - 9	ESDF	2 916 281	1 494 369	1 421 912	1 883 784	967 011	916 773	1 032 497	527 358	505 139
10 - 14	ESDF	3 735 293	1 902 893	1 832 400	2 512 646	1 280 784	1 231 862	1 222 647	622 109	600 538
15 - 19	ESDF	3 765 026	1 911 977	1 853 049	2 658 519	1 339 952	1 318 567	1 106 507	572 025	534 482
20 - 24	ESDF	3 591 292	1 819 369	1 771 923	2 558 515	1 283 993	1 274 522	1 032 777	535 376	497 401
25 - 29	ESDF	3 572 343	1 824 781	1 747 562	2 547 820	1 295 618	1 252 202	1 024 523	529 163	495 360
30 - 34	ESDF	3 237 966	1 613 622	1 624 344	2 251 564	1 099 648	1 151 916	986 402	513 974	472 428
35 - 39	ESDF	3 764 789	1 841 151	1 923 638	2 702 737	1 294 593	1 408 144	1 062 052	546 558	515 494
40 - 44	ESDF	3 778 496	1 815 712	1 962 784	2 757 518	1 297 091	1 460 427	1 020 978	518 621	502 357
45 - 49	ESDF	3 510 913	1 651 749	1 859 164	2 601 842	1 203 492	1 398 350	909 071	448 257	460 814
50 - 54	ESDF	2 751 783	1 255 818	1 495 965	2 023 520	918 093	1 105 427	728 263	337 725	390 538
55 - 59	ESDF	2 504 490	1 088 853	1 415 637	1 628 499	713 950	914 549	875 991	374 903	501 088
60 - 64	ESDF	3 324 060	1 400 640	1 923 420	2 151 452	909 188	1 242 264	1 172 608	491 452	681 156
65 - 69	ESDF	2 105 700	833 941	1 271 759	1 221 364	490 866	730 498	884 336	343 075	541 261
70 - 74	ESDF	2 288 411	786 754	1 501 657	1 348 209	479 513	868 696	940 202	307 241	632 961
75 - 79	ESDF	1 326 381	361 585	964 796	717 931	201 080	516 851	608 450	160 505	447 945
80 - 84	ESDF	580 522	141 516	439 006	322 726	85 139	237 587	257 796	56 377	201 419
85 - 89	ESDF	387 150	86 878	300 272	198 310	48 289	150 021	188 840	38 589	150 251
90 - 94	ESDF	117 445	23 065	94 380	57 130	11 590	45 540	60 315	11 475	48 840
95 - 99	ESDF	22 689	5 518	17 171	12 130	2 765	9 365	10 559	2 753	7 806
100+	ESDF	1 379	804	575	977	517	460	402	287	115
1 I 2001										
Total	ESDF	49 036 519	22 775 737	26 260 782	...	...	...	...	...	...
0 - 1	ESDF	381 239	197 071	184 168	...	...	...	...	...	...
1 - 4	ESDF	1 687 309	867 322	819 987	...	...	...	...	...	...
5 - 9	ESDF	2 743 948	1 406 999	1 336 949	...	...	...	...	...	...
10 - 14	ESDF	3 617 476	1 846 278	1 771 198	...	...	...	...	...	...
15 - 19	ESDF	3 787 495	1 921 596	1 865 899	...	...	...	...	...	...
20 - 24	ESDF	3 593 205	1 823 294	1 769 911	...	...	...	...	...	...
25 - 29	ESDF	3 610 466	1 840 033	1 770 433	...	...	...	...	...	...
30 - 34	ESDF	3 245 562	1 622 179	1 623 383	...	...	...	...	...	...
35 - 39	ESDF	3 591 935	1 756 452	1 835 483	...	...	...	...	...	...
40 - 44	ESDF	3 846 074	1 849 684	1 996 390	...	...	...	...	...	...
45 - 49	ESDF	3 491 859	1 641 602	1 850 257	...	...	...	...	...	...
50 - 54	ESDF	3 061 899	1 398 143	1 663 756	...	...	...	...	...	...
55 - 59	ESDF	2 173 474	942 392	1 231 082	...	...	...	...	...	...
60 - 64	ESDF	3 357 166	1 398 561	1 958 605	...	...	...	...	...	...
65 - 69	ESDF	2 047 769	821 034	1 226 735	...	...	...	...	...	...
70 - 74	ESDF	2 276 909	793 749	1 483 160	...	...	...	...	...	...
75 - 79	ESDF	1 430 314	393 268	1 037 046	...	...	...	...	...	...
80 - 84	ESDF	589 808	145 003	444 805	...	...	...	...	...	...
85 - 89	ESDF	372 258	78 363	293 895	...	...	...	...	...	...
90 - 94	ESDF	100 867	25 010	75 857	...	...	...	...	...	...
95 - 99	ESDF	25 971	6 572	19 399	...	...	...	...	...	...
100+	ESDF	3 516	1 132	2 384	...	...	...	...	...	...
United Kingdom - Royaume-Uni										
1 VII 1999										
Total	ESDF	59 500 915	29 298 873	30 202 042	...	...	...	...	...	...
0 - 4	ESDF	3 624 572	1 858 000	1 766 572	...	...	...	...	...	...
5 - 9	ESDF	3 906 613	2 001 191	1 905 422	...	...	...	...	...	...
10 - 14	ESDF	3 855 988	1 978 480	1 877 508	...	...	...	...	...	...
15 - 19	ESDF	3 682 658	1 890 892	1 791 766	...	...	...	...	...	...
20 - 24	ESDF	3 516 500	1 803 294	1 713 206	...	...	...	...	...	...
25 - 29	ESDF	4 261 094	2 189 108	2 071 986	...	...	...	...	...	...
30 - 34	ESDF	4 803 199	2 453 378	2 349 821	...	...	...	...	...	...
35 - 39	ESDF	4 707 589	2 395 827	2 311 762	...	...	...	...	...	...

7. Population by age, sex and urban/rural residence: latest available year, 1993 - 2002
Population selon l'âge, le sexe et la résidence, urbaine/rurale: dernière année disponible, 1993 - 2002
(continued — suite)

(See notes at end of table. — Voir notes à la fin du tableau.)

Continent, country or area, date and age (in years) / Continent, pays ou zone, date et âge (en années)	Code[1]	Total			Urban - Urbaine			Rural - Rurale		
		Both sexes Les deux sexes	Male Masculin	Female Féminin	Both sexes Les deux sexes	Male Masculin	Female Féminin	Both sexes Les deux sexes	Male Masculin	Female Féminin
EUROPE										
United Kingdom - Royaume-Uni										
1 VII 1999										
40 - 44	ESDF	4 038 253	2 029 357	2 008 896	...	...	...	...	...	...
45 - 49	ESDF	3 794 836	1 897 407	1 897 429	...	...	...	...	...	...
50 - 54	ESDF	3 999 336	1 992 852	2 006 484	...	...	...	...	...	...
55 - 59	ESDF	3 156 477	1 563 394	1 593 083	...	...	...	...	...	...
60 - 64	ESDF	2 860 674	1 400 454	1 460 220	...	...	...	...	...	...
65 - 69	ESDF	2 595 637	1 233 008	1 362 629	...	...	...	...	...	...
70 - 74	ESDF	2 333 352	1 050 881	1 282 471	...	...	...	...	...	...
75 - 79	ESDF	2 055 261	841 054	1 214 207	...	...	...	...	...	...
80 - 84	ESDF	1 166 572	414 014	752 558	...	...	...	...	...	...
85+	ESDF	1 142 304	306 282	836 022	...	...	...	...	...	...
OCEANIA — OCEANIE										
American Samoa - Samoas américaines[7]										
1 IV 2000										
Total	CDJC	57 291	29 264	28 027	...	...	...	...	...	...
0 - 4	CDJC	7 820	...	...	...	...	...	...	...	...
5 - 9	CDJC	7 788	...	...	...	...	...	...	...	...
10 - 14	CDJC	6 604	...	...	...	...	...	...	...	...
15 - 19	CDJC	5 223	...	...	...	...	...	...	...	...
20 - 24	CDJC	4 476	...	...	...	...	...	...	...	...
25 - 34	CDJC	8 707	...	...	...	...	...	...	...	...
35 - 44	CDJC	7 361	...	...	...	...	...	...	...	...
45 - 54	CDJC	4 733	...	...	...	...	...	...	...	...
55 - 59	CDJC	1 474	...	...	...	...	...	...	...	...
60 - 64	CDJC	1 204	...	...	...	...	...	...	...	...
65 - 74	CDJC	1 345	...	...	...	...	...	...	...	...
75 - 84	CDJC	465	...	...	...	...	...	...	...	...
85+	CDJC	91	...	...	...	...	...	...	...	...
Australia - Australie										
1 VII 2002										
Total	ESDJ	19 662 781	9 753 818	9 908 963	...	...	...	...	...	...
0 - 1	ESDJ	245 375	125 775	119 600	...	...	...	...	...	...
1 - 4	ESDJ	1 025 046	525 495	499 551	...	...	...	...	...	...
5 - 9	ESDJ	1 345 413	690 947	654 466	...	...	...	...	...	...
10 - 14	ESDJ	1 366 161	699 624	666 537	...	...	...	...	...	...
15 - 19	ESDJ	1 375 472	702 688	672 784	...	...	...	...	...	...
20 - 24	ESDJ	1 346 811	682 646	664 165	...	...	...	...	...	...
25 - 29	ESDJ	1 378 959	688 400	690 559	...	...	...	...	...	...
30 - 34	ESDJ	1 499 403	742 018	757 385	...	...	...	...	...	...
35 - 39	ESDJ	1 474 007	732 212	741 795	...	...	...	...	...	...
40 - 44	ESDJ	1 509 294	749 711	759 583	...	...	...	...	...	...
45 - 49	ESDJ	1 375 138	682 559	692 579	...	...	...	...	...	...
50 - 54	ESDJ	1 299 961	649 985	649 976	...	...	...	...	...	...
55 - 59	ESDJ	1 085 254	549 802	535 452	...	...	...	...	...	...
60 - 64	ESDJ	846 486	426 967	419 519	...	...	...	...	...	...
65 - 69	ESDJ	698 101	343 536	354 565	...	...	...	...	...	...
70 - 74	ESDJ	634 905	302 977	331 928	...	...	...	...	...	...
75 - 79	ESDJ	527 337	233 162	294 175	...	...	...	...	...	...
80 - 84	ESDJ	349 273	137 526	211 747	...	...	...	...	...	...
85 - 89	ESDJ	187 341	62 751	124 590	...	...	...	...	...	...
90 - 94	ESDJ	72 221	19 814	52 407	...	...	...	...	...	...
95 - 99	ESDJ	17 740	4 286	13 454	...	...	...	...	...	...
100+	ESDJ	3 083	937	2 146	...	...	...	...	...	...

7. Population by age, sex and urban/rural residence: latest available year, 1993 - 2002
Population selon l'âge, le sexe et la résidence, urbaine/rurale: dernière année disponible, 1993 - 2002
(continued — suite)

(See notes at end of table. — Voir notes à la fin du tableau.)

Continent, country or area, date and age (in years) / Continent, pays ou zone, date et âge (en années)	Code[1]	Total			Urban - Urbaine			Rural - Rurale		
		Both sexes Les deux sexes	Male Masculin	Female Féminin	Both sexes Les deux sexes	Male Masculin	Female Féminin	Both sexes Les deux sexes	Male Masculin	Female Féminin
OCEANIA — OCEANIE										
Cook Islands - Îles Cook										
1 XII 2001										
Total	CDFC	18 027	...	...	...	...	...	...	...	...
0 - 4	CDFC	1 722	...	...	...	...	...	...	...	...
5 - 9	CDFC	1 895	...	...	...	...	...	...	...	...
10 - 14	CDFC	1 798	...	...	...	...	...	...	...	...
15 - 19	CDFC	1 460	...	...	...	...	...	...	...	...
20 - 24	CDFC	1 227	...	...	...	...	...	...	...	...
25 - 29	CDFC	1 385	...	...	...	...	...	...	...	...
30 - 34	CDFC	1 431	...	...	...	...	...	...	...	...
35 - 39	CDFC	1 367	...	...	...	...	...	...	...	...
40 - 44	CDFC	1 194	...	...	...	...	...	...	...	...
45 - 49	CDFC	925	...	...	...	...	...	...	...	...
50 - 54	CDFC	906	...	...	...	...	...	...	...	...
55 - 59	CDFC	799	...	...	...	...	...	...	...	...
60 - 64	CDFC	730	...	...	...	...	...	...	...	...
65 - 69	CDFC	538	...	...	...	...	...	...	...	...
70 - 74	CDFC	324	...	...	...	...	...	...	...	...
75 - 79	CDFC	195	...	...	...	...	...	...	...	...
80+	CDFC	131	...	...	...	...	...	...	...	...
Fiji - Fidji										
25 VIII 1996										
Total	CDFC	775 077	393 931	381 146	359 495	180 119	179 376	415 582	213 812	201 770
0 - 1	CDFC	18 239	9 282	8 957	8 136	4 213	3 923	10 103	5 069	5 034
1 - 4	CDFC	75 975	39 281	36 694	32 702	16 877	15 825	43 273	22 404	20 869
5 - 9	CDFC	87 095	44 937	42 158	35 977	18 271	17 706	51 118	26 666	24 452
10 - 14	CDFC	92 855	47 709	45 146	40 497	20 644	19 853	52 358	27 065	25 293
15 - 19	CDFC	83 682	42 829	40 853	41 404	20 748	20 656	42 278	22 081	20 197
20 - 24	CDFC	66 955	34 444	32 511	35 678	17 936	17 742	31 277	16 508	14 769
25 - 29	CDFC	61 660	31 283	30 377	30 706	15 554	15 152	30 954	15 729	15 225
30 - 34	CDFC	60 841	30 727	30 114	28 905	14 318	14 587	31 936	16 409	15 527
35 - 39	CDFC	55 779	28 525	27 254	26 975	13 523	13 452	28 804	15 002	13 802
40 - 44	CDFC	44 180	22 341	21 839	21 863	10 765	11 098	22 317	11 576	10 741
45 - 49	CDFC	37 081	18 482	18 599	18 007	8 913	9 094	19 074	9 569	9 505
50 - 54	CDFC	28 683	14 286	14 397	13 300	6 567	6 733	15 383	7 719	7 664
55 - 59	CDFC	22 245	10 857	11 388	9 562	4 560	5 002	12 683	6 297	6 386
60 - 64	CDFC	15 459	7 605	7 854	6 389	3 039	3 350	9 070	4 566	4 504
65 - 69	CDFC	10 761	5 138	5 623	4 191	1 941	2 250	6 570	3 197	3 373
70 - 74	CDFC	6 357	3 054	3 303	2 473	1 129	1 344	3 884	1 925	1 959
75 - 79	CDFC	4 152	1 881	2 271	1 558	654	904	2 594	1 227	1 367
80 - 84	CDFC	1 938	843	1 095	782	339	443	1 156	504	652
85 - 89	CDFC	772	290	482	266	97	169	506	193	313
90 - 94	CDFC	265	100	165	82	23	59	183	77	106
95+	CDFC	103	37	66	42	8	34	61	29	32
French Polynesia - Polynésie française										
1 I 1999										
Total	ESDF	*227 525*	*117 738*	*109 787*	...	...	...	...	...	...
0 - 1	ESDF	*4 268*	*2 177*	*2 091*	...	...	...	...	...	...
1 - 4	ESDF	*18 470*	*9 604*	*8 866*	...	...	...	...	...	...
5 - 9	ESDF	*25 518*	*13 178*	*12 340*	...	...	...	...	...	...
10 - 14	ESDF	*25 533*	*13 055*	*12 478*	...	...	...	...	...	...
15 - 19	ESDF	*22 126*	*11 290*	*10 836*	...	...	...	...	...	...
20 - 24	ESDF	*19 077*	*9 884*	*9 193*	...	...	...	...	...	...
25 - 29	ESDF	*19 574*	*10 141*	*9 433*	...	...	...	...	...	...
30 - 34	ESDF	*19 667*	*10 179*	*9 488*	...	...	...	...	...	...
35 - 39	ESDF	*17 032*	*8 941*	*8 091*	...	...	...	...	...	...
40 - 44	ESDF	*14 421*	*7 640*	*6 781*	...	...	...	...	...	...

7. Population by age, sex and urban/rural residence: latest available year, 1993 - 2002
Population selon l'âge, le sexe et la résidence, urbaine/rurale: dernière année disponible, 1993 - 2002
(continued — suite)

(See notes at end of table. — Voir notes à la fin du tableau.)

Continent, country or area, date and age (in years) / Continent, pays ou zone, date et âge (en années)	Code[1]	Total Both sexes Les deux sexes	Total Male Masculin	Total Female Féminin	Urban - Urbaine Both sexes Les deux sexes	Urban - Urbaine Male Masculin	Urban - Urbaine Female Féminin	Rural - Rurale Both sexes Les deux sexes	Rural - Rurale Male Masculin	Rural - Rurale Female Féminin

OCEANIA — OCEANIE

French Polynesia - Polynésie française
1 I 1999

45 - 49	ESDF	11 037	5 830	5 207	...	...	...	...	...	...
50 - 54	ESDF	9 001	4 790	4 211	...	...	...	...	...	...
55 - 59	ESDF	7 202	3 845	3 357	...	...	...	...	...	...
60 - 64	ESDF	5 518	2 899	2 619	...	...	...	...	...	...
65 - 69	ESDF	3 998	2 042	1 956	...	...	...	...	...	...
70 - 74	ESDF	2 600	1 244	1 356	...	...	...	...	...	...
75 - 79	ESDF	1 365	585	780	...	...	...	...	...	...
80+	ESDF	1 118	414	704	...	...	...	...	...	...

Guam[7]
1 IV 2000

Total	CDJC	154 805	79 181	75 624	...	...	...	...	...	...
0 - 1	CDJC	3 535	1 862	1 673	...	...	...	...	...	...
1 - 4	CDJC	13 250	6 945	6 305	...	...	...	...	...	...
5 - 9	CDJC	16 090	8 270	7 820	...	...	...	...	...	...
10 - 14	CDJC	14 281	7 232	7 049	...	...	...	...	...	...
15 - 19	CDJC	12 379	6 273	6 106	...	...	...	...	...	...
20 - 24	CDJC	11 989	6 140	5 849	...	...	...	...	...	...
25 - 29	CDJC	12 944	6 584	6 360	...	...	...	...	...	...
30 - 34	CDJC	12 906	6 727	6 179	...	...	...	...	...	...
35 - 39	CDJC	12 751	6 692	6 059	...	...	...	...	...	...
40 - 44	CDJC	10 390	5 344	5 046	...	...	...	...	...	...
45 - 49	CDJC	9 042	4 608	4 434	...	...	...	...	...	...
50 - 54	CDJC	7 506	3 813	3 693	...	...	...	...	...	...
55 - 59	CDJC	4 993	2 548	2 445	...	...	...	...	...	...
60 - 64	CDJC	4 534	2 190	2 344	...	...	...	...	...	...
65 - 69	CDJC	3 399	1 628	1 771	...	...	...	...	...	...
70 - 74	CDJC	2 461	1 287	1 174	...	...	...	...	...	...
75 - 79	CDJC	1 384	681	703	...	...	...	...	...	...
80 - 84	CDJC	616	234	302	...	...	...	...	...	...
85 - 89	CDJC	248	83	165	...	...	...	...	...	...
90 - 94	CDJC	79	30	49	...	...	...	...	...	...
95 - 99	CDJC	22	9	13	...	...	...	...	...	...
100+	CDJC	6	1	5	...	...	...	...	...	...

Marshall Islands - Îles Marshall
1 VII 2001

Total	ESDF	54 584	27 960	26 624	...	...	...	...	...	...
0 - 4	ESDF	9 016	4 684	4 332	...	...	...	...	...	...
5 - 9	ESDF	6 653	3 391	3 262	...	...	...	...	...	...
10 - 14	ESDF	7 272	3 745	3 527	...	...	...	...	...	...
15 - 19	ESDF	6 998	3 576	3 422	...	...	...	...	...	...
20 - 24	ESDF	5 190	2 594	2 596	...	...	...	...	...	...
25 - 29	ESDF	3 982	1 991	1 991	...	...	...	...	...	...
30 - 34	ESDF	3 407	1 736	1 671	...	...	...	...	...	...
35 - 39	ESDF	2 996	1 538	1 458	...	...	...	...	...	...
40 - 44	ESDF	2 558	1 276	1 282	...	...	...	...	...	...
45 - 49	ESDF	2 174	1 155	1 019	...	...	...	...	...	...
50 - 54	ESDF	1 618	883	735	...	...	...	...	...	...
55 - 59	ESDF	957	514	443	...	...	...	...	...	...
60 - 64	ESDF	623	318	305	...	...	...	...	...	...
65 - 69	ESDF	478	236	242	...	...	...	...	...	...
70 - 74	ESDF	289	159	130	...	...	...	...	...	...
75+	ESDF	373	164	209	...	...	...	...	...	...

7. Population by age, sex and urban/rural residence: latest available year, 1993 - 2002
Population selon l'âge, le sexe et la résidence, urbaine/rurale: dernière année disponible, 1993 - 2002
(continued — suite)

(See notes at end of table. — Voir notes à la fin du tableau.)

Continent, country or area, date and age (in years) Continent, pays ou zone, date et âge (en années)	Code[1]	Total			Urban - Urbaine			Rural - Rurale		
		Both sexes Les deux sexes	Male Masculin	Female Féminin	Both sexes Les deux sexes	Male Masculin	Female Féminin	Both sexes Les deux sexes	Male Masculin	Female Féminin
OCEANIA — OCEANIE										
Micronesia, Federated States of - Micronésie, États Fédérés de La										
18 IX 1994										
Total	CDJC	105 506	53 923	51 583	...	...	...	...	...	...
0 - 4	CDJC	15 854	8 211	7 643	...	...	...	...	...	...
5 - 9	CDJC	15 330	8 051	7 279	...	...	...	...	...	...
10 - 14	CDJC	14 749	7 534	7 215	...	...	...	...	...	...
15 - 19	CDJC	12 251	6 431	5 820	...	...	...	...	...	...
20 - 24	CDJC	8 828	4 321	4 507	...	...	...	...	...	...
25 - 29	CDJC	7 063	3 496	3 567	...	...	...	...	...	...
30 - 34	CDJC	6 598	3 311	3 287	...	...	...	...	...	...
35 - 39	CDJC	6 079	3 077	3 002	...	...	...	...	...	...
40 - 44	CDJC	5 071	2 661	2 410	...	...	...	...	...	...
45 - 49	CDJC	3 579	1 930	1 649	...	...	...	...	...	...
50 - 54	CDJC	2 219	1 101	1 118	...	...	...	...	...	...
55 - 59	CDJC	2 105	1 033	1 072	...	...	...	...	...	...
60 - 64	CDJC	1 985	1 018	967	...	...	...	...	...	...
65 - 69	CDJC	1 395	668	727	...	...	...	...	...	...
70 - 74	CDJC	1 229	567	662	...	...	...	...	...	...
75 - 79	CDJC	581	274	307	...	...	...	...	...	...
80 - 84	CDJC	354	150	204	...	...	...	...	...	...
85+	CDJC	236	89	147	...	...	...	...	...	...
New Caledonia - Nouvelle-Calédonie										
16 IV 1996										
Total	CDFC	196 836	100 762	96 074	...	...	...	...	...	...
0 - 9	CDFC	41 383	21 463	19 920	...	...	...	...	...	...
10 - 19	CDFC	36 398	18 526	17 872	...	...	...	...	...	...
20 - 29	CDFC	36 027	18 335	17 692	...	...	...	...	...	...
30 - 39	CDFC	30 266	15 315	14 951	...	...	...	...	...	...
40 - 49	CDFC	22 393	11 752	10 641	...	...	...	...	...	...
50 - 59	CDFC	15 589	8 220	7 369	...	...	...	...	...	...
60 - 69	CDFC	9 022	4 592	4 430	...	...	...	...	...	...
70 - 79	CDFC	4 146	1 913	2 233	...	...	...	...	...	...
80 - 89	CDFC	1 443	593	850	...	...	...	...	...	...
90+	CDFC	169	53	116	...	...	...	...	...	...
New Zealand - Nouvelle-Zélande										
5 III 1996										
Total	CDJC	3 618 303	1 777 461	1 840 842	3 090 408	1 502 502	1 587 906	526 563	274 020	252 543
0 - 1	CDJC	54 747	28 293	26 454	46 440	24 021	22 422	8 301	4 272	4 032
1 - 4	CDJC	224 856	115 821	109 032	188 793	97 101	91 692	36 042	18 705	17 334
5 - 9	CDJC	288 294	147 723	140 571	238 686	122 124	116 559	49 566	25 560	23 997
10 - 14	CDJC	264 186	135 663	128 523	218 820	112 236	106 590	45 324	23 403	21 918
15 - 19	CDJC	262 980	133 575	129 405	228 459	114 618	113 835	34 419	18 885	15 537
20 - 24	CDJC	271 761	134 835	136 926	244 119	119 538	124 584	27 498	15 180	12 321
25 - 29	CDJC	273 303	132 453	140 850	240 270	115 875	124 386	32 931	16 491	16 437
30 - 34	CDJC	293 484	142 452	151 032	250 455	121 329	129 123	42 882	21 033	21 855
35 - 39	CDJC	285 216	139 293	145 923	238 338	115 833	122 502	46 737	23 352	23 385
40 - 44	CDJC	255 039	125 439	129 600	212 982	103 296	109 689	41 910	22 047	19 857
45 - 49	CDJC	241 191	120 249	120 942	201 657	99 564	102 093	39 396	20 592	18 807
50 - 54	CDJC	186 717	93 351	93 366	155 691	77 049	78 636	30 930	16 230	14 700
55 - 59	CDJC	158 601	78 783	79 818	132 129	64 716	67 407	26 400	14 004	12 393
60 - 64	CDJC	135 264	67 419	67 845	114 234	55 845	58 383	20 994	11 538	9 453
65 - 69	CDJC	132 972	65 184	67 788	115 509	55 380	60 129	17 430	9 783	7 644
70 - 74	CDJC	113 664	51 762	61 902	101 553	45 249	56 301	12 087	6 495	5 592
75 - 79	CDJC	82 287	33 561	48 726	74 937	29 880	45 060	7 332	3 675	3 663

7. Population by age, sex and urban/rural residence: latest available year, 1993 - 2002
Population selon l'âge, le sexe et la résidence, urbaine/rurale: dernière année disponible, 1993 - 2002
(continued — suite)

(See notes at end of table. — Voir notes à la fin du tableau.)

Continent, country or area, date and age (in years) / Continent, pays ou zone, date et âge (en années)	Code[1]	Total Both sexes Les deux sexes	Total Male Masculin	Total Female Féminin	Urban - Urbaine Both sexes Les deux sexes	Urban - Urbaine Male Masculin	Urban - Urbaine Female Féminin	Rural - Rurale Both sexes Les deux sexes	Rural - Rurale Male Masculin	Rural - Rurale Female Féminin
OCEANIA — OCEANIE										
New Zealand - Nouvelle-Zélande										
5 III 1996										
80 - 84	CDJC	55 281	20 412	34 869	51 240	18 540	32 700	4 041	1 869	2 169
85 - 89	CDJC	27 024	8 385	18 642	25 302	7 698	17 613	1 716	687	1 035
90 - 94	CDJC	9 225	2 382	6 840	8 712	2 205	6 504	513	177	336
95 - 99	CDJC	1 950	393	1 557	1 842	366	1 479	105	27	78
100+	CDJC	261	33	225	252	33	216	6	3	6
1 VII 2000										
Total	ESDJ	3 830 800	1 886 900	1 943 900	...	...	...	...	...	...
0 - 1	ESDJ	57 140	29 490	27 650	...	...	...	...	...	...
1 - 4	ESDJ	228 370	117 340	111 040	...	...	...	...	...	...
5 - 9	ESDJ	301 850	155 590	146 250	...	...	...	...	...	...
10 - 14	ESDJ	289 150	148 240	140 910	...	...	...	...	...	...
15 - 19	ESDJ	272 880	140 530	132 340	...	...	...	...	...	...
20 - 24	ESDJ	256 220	130 230	126 000	...	...	...	...	...	...
25 - 29	ESDJ	264 990	128 570	136 410	...	...	...	...	...	...
30 - 34	ESDJ	285 500	136 920	148 580	...	...	...	...	...	...
35 - 39	ESDJ	307 450	149 430	158 010	...	...	...	...	...	...
40 - 44	ESDJ	288 430	141 760	146 660	...	...	...	...	...	...
45 - 49	ESDJ	256 780	127 310	129 480	...	...	...	...	...	...
50 - 54	ESDJ	237 180	118 750	118 430	...	...	...	...	...	...
55 - 59	ESDJ	183 790	91 600	92 210	...	...	...	...	...	...
60 - 64	ESDJ	149 990	73 930	76 060	...	...	...	...	...	...
65 - 69	ESDJ	129 410	63 490	65 920	...	...	...	...	...	...
70 - 74	ESDJ	119 280	56 600	62 670	...	...	...	...	...	...
75 - 79	ESDJ	94 860	40 480	54 390	...	...	...	...	...	...
80 - 84	ESDJ	59 970	22 240	37 720	...	...	...	...	...	...
85 - 89	ESDJ	33 300	10 840	22 470	...	...	...	...	...	...
90+	ESDJ	14 260	3 550	10 710	...	...	...	...	...	...
Niue - Nioué										
17 VIII 1997										
Total	CDFC	2 088	1 053	1 035	...	...	...	...	...	...
0 - 4	CDFC	210	107	103	...	...	...	...	...	...
5 - 9	CDFC	229	124	105	...	...	...	...	...	...
10 - 14	CDFC	243	115	128	...	...	...	...	...	...
15 - 19	CDFC	195	105	90	...	...	...	...	...	...
20 - 24	CDFC	116	62	54	...	...	...	...	...	...
25 - 29	CDFC	126	66	60	...	...	...	...	...	...
30 - 34	CDFC	145	76	69	...	...	...	...	...	...
35 - 39	CDFC	122	68	54	...	...	...	...	...	...
40 - 44	CDFC	125	64	61	...	...	...	...	...	...
45 - 49	CDFC	94	40	54	...	...	...	...	...	...
50 - 54	CDFC	100	53	47	...	...	...	...	...	...
55 - 59	CDFC	109	52	57	...	...	...	...	...	...
60 - 64	CDFC	101	48	53	...	...	...	...	...	...
65 - 69	CDFC	51	23	28	...	...	...	...	...	...
70 - 74	CDFC	44	24	20	...	...	...	...	...	...
75+	CDFC	78	26	52	...	...	...	...	...	...
Northern Mariana Islands - Îles Mariannes septentrionales										
1 IV 2000										
Total	CDFC	69 221	31 984	37 237	...	...	...	...	...	...
0 - 4	CDFC	5 792	...	...	...	...	...	...	...	...
5 - 9	CDFC	5 420	...	...	...	...	...	...	...	...
10 - 14	CDFC	4 377	...	...	...	...	...	...	...	...
15 - 19	CDFC	3 943	...	...	...	...	...	...	...	...

7. Population by age, sex and urban/rural residence: latest available year, 1993 - 2002
Population selon l'âge, le sexe et la résidence, urbaine/rurale: dernière année disponible, 1993 - 2002
(continued — suite)

(See notes at end of table. — Voir notes à la fin du tableau.)

Continent, country or area, date and age (in years) / Continent, pays ou zone, date et âge (en années)	Code[1]	Total			Urban - Urbaine			Rural - Rurale		
		Both sexes Les deux sexes	Male Masculin	Female Féminin	Both sexes Les deux sexes	Male Masculin	Female Féminin	Both sexes Les deux sexes	Male Masculin	Female Féminin
OCEANIA — OCEANIE										
Northern Mariana Islands - Îles Mariannes septentrionales										
1 IV 2000										
20 - 24	CDFC	7 566	...	...	...	...	...	...	...	...
25 - 34	CDFC	20 181	...	...	...	...	...	...	...	...
35 - 44	CDFC	12 651	...	...	...	...	...	...	...	...
45 - 54	CDFC	6 208	...	...	...	...	...	...	...	...
55 - 59	CDFC	1 199	...	...	...	...	...	...	...	...
60 - 64	CDFC	837	...	...	...	...	...	...	...	...
65 - 74	CDFC	748	...	...	...	...	...	...	...	...
75 - 84	CDFC	233	...	...	...	...	...	...	...	...
85+	CDFC	66	...	...	...	...	...	...	...	...
Palau - Palaos										
9 IX 1995										
Total	CDFC	17 225	9 213	8 012	...	...	...	...	...	...
0 - 4	CDFC	1 762	916	846	...	...	...	...	...	...
5 - 9	CDFC	1 551	797	754	...	...	...	...	...	...
10 - 14	CDFC	1 527	798	729	...	...	...	...	...	...
15 - 19	CDFC	1 282	684	598	...	...	...	...	...	...
20 - 24	CDFC	1 427	723	704	...	...	...	...	...	...
25 - 29	CDFC	1 741	929	812	...	...	...	...	...	...
30 - 34	CDFC	1 717	1 005	712	...	...	...	...	...	...
35 - 39	CDFC	1 583	927	656	...	...	...	...	...	...
40 - 44	CDFC	1 261	727	534	...	...	...	...	...	...
45 - 49	CDFC	943	553	390	...	...	...	...	...	...
50 - 54	CDFC	603	329	274	...	...	...	...	...	...
55 - 59	CDFC	488	249	239	...	...	...	...	...	...
60 - 64	CDFC	361	174	187	...	...	...	...	...	...
65 - 69	CDFC	328	145	183	...	...	...	...	...	...
70 - 74	CDFC	278	122	156	...	...	...	...	...	...
75+	CDFC	373	135	238	...	...	...	...	...	...
15 IV 2000										
Total	CDFC	19 129	...	...	...	...	...	...	...	...
0 - 4	CDFC	1 308	...	...	...	...	...	...	...	...
5 - 9	CDFC	1 700	...	...	...	...	...	...	...	...
10 - 14	CDFC	1 555	...	...	...	...	...	...	...	...
15 - 19	CDFC	1 382	...	...	...	...	...	...	...	...
20 - 24	CDFC	1 342	...	...	...	...	...	...	...	...
25 - 29	CDFC	1 910	...	...	...	...	...	...	...	...
30 - 34	CDFC	2 169	...	...	...	...	...	...	...	...
35 - 39	CDFC	1 891	...	...	...	...	...	...	...	...
40 - 44	CDFC	1 651	...	...	...	...	...	...	...	...
45 - 49	CDFC	1 272	...	...	...	...	...	...	...	...
50 - 54	CDFC	886	...	...	...	...	...	...	...	...
55 - 59	CDFC	563	...	...	...	...	...	...	...	...
60 - 64	CDFC	463	...	...	...	...	...	...	...	...
65 - 69	CDFC	318	...	...	...	...	...	...	...	...
70 - 74	CDFC	274	...	...	...	...	...	...	...	...
75+	CDFC	445	...	...	...	...	...	...	...	...
Pitcairn										
31 XII 1993										
Total	ESDF	53	25	28	...	...	...	...	...	...
0 - 1	ESDF	1	1	-	...	...	...	...	...	...
1 - 4	ESDF	2	1	1	...	...	...	...	...	...
5 - 9	ESDF	6	3	3	...	...	...	...	...	...
10 - 14	ESDF	5	1	4	...	...	...	...	...	...
15 - 19	ESDF	4	3	1	...	...	...	...	...	...

7. Population by age, sex and urban/rural residence: latest available year, 1993 - 2002
Population selon l'âge, le sexe et la résidence, urbaine/rurale: dernière année disponible, 1993 - 2002
(continued — suite)

(See notes at end of table. — Voir notes à la fin du tableau.)

Continent, country or area, date and age (in years) / Continent, pays ou zone, date et âge (en années)	Code[1]	Total			Urban - Urbaine			Rural - Rurale		
		Both sexes Les deux sexes	Male Masculin	Female Féminin	Both sexes Les deux sexes	Male Masculin	Female Féminin	Both sexes Les deux sexes	Male Masculin	Female Féminin
OCEANIA — OCEANIE										
Pitcairn										
31 XII 1993										
20 - 24	ESDF	2	2	-	...	...	...	...	...	...
25 - 29	ESDF	-	-	-	...	...	...	...	...	...
30 - 34	ESDF	5	1	4	...	...	...	...	...	...
35 - 39	ESDF	8	6	2	...	...	...	...	...	...
40 - 44	ESDF	3	1	2	...	...	...	...	...	...
45 - 49	ESDF	1	-	1	...	...	...	...	...	...
50 - 54	ESDF	3	-	3	...	...	...	...	...	...
55 - 59	ESDF	2	1	1	...	...	...	...	...	...
60 - 64	ESDF	3	2	1	...	...	...	...	...	...
65 - 69	ESDF	4	1	3	...	...	...	...	...	...
70 - 74	ESDF	2	1	1	...	...	...	...	...	...
75 - 79	ESDF	1	1	-	...	...	...	...	...	...
80 - 84	ESDF	-	-	-	...	...	...	...	...	...
85+	ESDF	1	-	1	...	...	...	...	...	...
Tonga										
31 XII 2002										
Total	ESDF	*101 002*	*51 473*	*49 528*	...	...	...	...	...	...
0 - 4	ESDF	*12 179*	*6 295*	*5 884*	...	...	...	...	...	...
5 - 9	ESDF	*12 686*	*6 577*	*6 109*	...	...	...	...	...	...
10 - 14	ESDF	*11 795*	*6 303*	*5 492*	...	...	...	...	...	...
15 - 19	ESDF	*11 980*	*6 241*	*5 739*	...	...	...	...	...	...
20 - 24	ESDF	*9 942*	*5 111*	*4 831*	...	...	...	...	...	...
25 - 29	ESDF	*7 057*	*3 564*	*3 493*	...	...	...	...	...	...
30 - 34	ESDF	*6 284*	*3 207*	*3 077*	...	...	...	...	...	...
35 - 39	ESDF	*5 382*	*2 723*	*2 659*	...	...	...	...	...	...
40 - 44	ESDF	*4 541*	*2 186*	*2 355*	...	...	...	...	...	...
45 - 49	ESDF	*4 029*	*1 908*	*2 121*	...	...	...	...	...	...
50 - 54	ESDF	*3 397*	*1 572*	*1 825*	...	...	...	...	...	...
55 - 59	ESDF	*3 105*	*1 467*	*1 638*	...	...	...	...	...	...
60 - 64	ESDF	*2 775*	*1 393*	*1 382*	...	...	...	...	...	...
65 - 69	ESDF	*2 277*	*1 167*	*1 110*	...	...	...	...	...	...
70 - 74	ESDF	*1 668*	*840*	*828*	...	...	...	...	...	...
75+	ESDF	*1 904*	*919*	*985*	...	...	...	...	...	...

GENERAL NOTES - NOTES GENERALES

Unless otherwise specified, age is defined as age at last birthday (completed years). For definition of urban, see Technical notes for table 6. For method of evaluation and limitation of data, see Technical Notes for this table. — Sauf indication contraire, l'âge dernier anniversaire (années révolues). Pour la définitions de "zones urbaines", voir les Notes techniques relatives au tableau 6. Pour le méthode d'évaluation et les insuffissances des données, voire Notes techniques, pour ce tableau.

Italics: estimates which are less reliable. — *Italiques*: estimations moins sûres.

FOOTNOTES - NOTES

[1] 'Code' indicates the source of data, as follows:
CDFC - Census, de facto, complete tabulation
CDFS - Census, de facto, sample tabulation
CDJC - Census, de jure, complete tabulation
CDJS - Census, de jure, sample tabulation
SSDF - Sample survey, de facto
SSDJ - Sample survey, de jure
ESDF - Estimates, de facto

ESDJ - Estimates, de jure
Le 'Code' indique la source des données, comme suit:
CDFC - Recensement, population de fait, tabulation complète
CDFS - Recensement, population de fait, tabulation par sondage
CDJC - Recensement, population de droit, tabulation complète
CDJS - Recensement, population de droit, tabulation par sondage
SSDF - Enquête par sondage, population de fait
SSDJ - Enquête par sondage, population de droit
ESDF - Estimations, population de fait
ESDJ - Estimations, population de droit

[2] For 1993, data exclude adjustment for underenumeration, estimated at 1.4 per cent. - Pour 1993, les données n'ont pas été ajustées pour compenser les lacunes du dénombrement, estimées à 1,4 p. 100.

[3] Data for estimates refer to national projections. - Les données se referent aux projections nationales.

[4] Data have been adjusted for underenumeration estimated at 6.8 per cent. - Les données ont été ajustées pour compenser les lacunes du dénombrement estimées à 6,8 p. 100.

[5] Total population excludes persons who were not contacted at the time of the census. - La population non comprend pas les personnes qui n'ont pas été contactées à l'heure du recensement.

[6] Excluding the institutional population. - Non compris la population dans les institutions.

[7] Including armed forces stationed in the area. - Y compris les militaires en garnison sur le territoire.

8 De jure population, but excluding civilian citizens absent from country for an extended period of time. - Population de droit, mais non compris les civils hors du pays pendant une période prolongée.

9 Because of rounding, totals are not in all cases the sum of the parts. - Les chiffres étant arrondis, les totaux ne correspondent pas toujours rigoureusement à la somme des chiffres partiels.

10 Data include persons in remote areas, military personel outside the country, merchant seamen at sea, civilian seasonal workers outside the country, and other civilians outside the country, and exclude nomads, foreign military, civilian aliens temporarily in the country, transients on ships and Indian jungle population. - Y compris les personnes dans les régions éloignées, le personel militaire en dehors du pays, les marins marchands, les ouvriers saisonniers civils de couture en dehors du pays, et autres civils en dehors du pays, et non compris les nomades, les militaires étrangers, les étrangers civils temporairement dans le pays, les transiteurs sur des bateaux et les Indiens de la jungle.

11 Excluding nomadic Indian tribes. - Non compris les tribus d'Indiens nomades.

12 Excluding Indian jungle population. - Non compris les Indiens de la jungle.

13 Mid-year estimates have been adjusted for underenumeration, at latest census. - Les estimations au millieu de l'année tiennent compte d'une ajustement destiné à compenser les lacunes du dénombrement lors du dernier recensement.

14 Figures for male and female do not add up to the total, since only the figures for the total were adjusted for underenumeration. - Les données pour la population masculine et la population féminine ne s'ajoutent pas au total, parce-que elles n'ont pas été ajustées pour compenser les lacunes du dénombrement.

15 For statistical purposes, the data for China do not include those for the Hong Kong Special Administrative Region (Hong Kong SAR), Macao Special Administrative Region (Macao SAR) and Taiwan province of China. - Pour la présentation des statistiques, les données pour Chine ne comprend pas la Région Administrative Spéciale de Hong Kong (Hong Kong RAS), la Région Administrative Spéciale de Macao (Macao RAS) et Taïwan province de Chine.

16 Data refer to government controlled areas. - Les données se raportent aux zones contrôlées par le Gouvernement.

17 For the 2001 census, data exclude Mao-Maram, Paomata and Purul sub-divisions of Senapati district of Manipur. The population of Manipur including the estimated population of the three sub-divisions of Senapati district is 2,291,125 (Males 1,161,173 and females 1,129,952). - Pour le recensement de 2001, non compris les subdivisions Mao-Maram Paomata et Purul du district de Senapati dans l'État du Manipur. Cet État compte 2 291 125 habitants (1 161 173 hommes et 1 129 952 femmes), y compris la population estimative des trois subdivisions du district de Senapati.

18 Including data for the Indian-held part of Jammu and Kashmir, the final status of which has not yet been determined. - Y compris les données pour la partie du Jammu et du Cachemire occupée par l'Inde dont le statut définitif n'a pas encore été déterminé.

19 Data refer to only enumerated population with permanent residence. - Les données se rapportent à la population énumérée avec la résidence permanente.

20 Including data for East Jerusalem and Israeli residents in certain other territories under occupation by Israeli military forces since June 1967. - Y compris les données pour Jérusalem-Est et les résidents israéliens dans certains autres territoires occupés depuis 1967 par les forces armées israéliennes.

21 Excluding diplomatic personnel outside the country and foreign military and civilian personnel and their dependants stationed in the area. - Non compris le personnel diplomatique hors du pays ni les militaires et agents civils étrangers en poste sur le territoire et les membres de leur famille les accompagnant.

22 Excluding data for Jordanian territory under occupation since June 1967 by Israeli military forces. Excluding foreigners, including registered Palestinian refugees. - Non compris les données pour le territoire jordanien occupé depuis juin 1967 par les forces armées israéliennes. Non compris les étrangers, mais y compris les réfugiés de Palestine enregistrés.

23 Excluding alien armed forces, civilian aliens employed by armed forces, foreign diplomatic personnel and their dependants and Korean diplomatic personnel and their dependants outside the country. - Non compris les militaires étrangers, les civils étrangers employés par les forces armées, le personnel diplomatique étranger et les membres de leur famille les accompagnant et le personnel diplomatique coréen hors du pays et les membres de leurs familles les accompagnant.

24 Excluding the Federal Administrative tribal areas. - Non compris les zones tribales administrées par le gouvernement fédéral.

25 Excluding data for the Pakistan-held part of Jammu and Kashmir, the final status of which has not yet been determined. - Non compris les données concernant la partie du Jammu et Cachemire occupée par le Pakistan dont le statut définitif n'a pas été déterminé.

26 Excluding transients afloat and military and civilian services personnel and their dependants abroad. - Non compris les personnes de passage à bord de navires ni les militaires et agents civils et les membres de leur famille les accompagnant à l'étranger.

27 Including Palestinian refugees. - Y compris les réfugiés de Palestine.

28 Excluding Faeroe Islands and Greenland. - Non compris les Iles Féroé et Gröenland.

29 Excluding Overseas Departments, namely French Guiana, Guadeloupe, Martinique and Reunion, shown separately. De jure population but excluding diplomatic personnel outside the country and including members of alien armed forces not living in military camps and foreign diplomatic personnel not living in embassies or consulates. - Non compris les départements d'outre-mer, c'est-à-dire la Guyane française, la Guadeloupe, la Martinique et la Réunion, qui font l'objet de rubriques distinctes. Population de droit, non compris le personnel diplomatique hors du pays et y compris les militaires étrangers ne vivant pas dans des camps militaires et le personnel diplomatique étranger ne vivant pas dans les ambassades ou les consulats.

30 Mid-year population excludes armed forces stationed outside the country, but includes alien armed forces stationed in the area. - Les estimations au millieu de l'année non compris les militaires en garnison hors du pays, mais y compris les militaires étrangers en garnison sur le territoire.

31 Maltese population only. - Population Maltaise seulement.

32 Including residents temporarily outside the country. - Y compris les résidents se trouvant temporairement hors du pays.

33 Excluding civilian aliens within country, but including civilian nationals temporarily outside country. - Non compris les civils étrangers dans le pays, mais y compris les civils nationaux temporairement hors du pays.

34 Beginning with 1998, estimates of Kosovo and Metohia computed on the basis of natural increases from year 1997. - A partir du 1998, les estimations pour le Kosovo et la Metohia ont été calculées sur la base des incréments naturelles depuis 1997.

Table 8

Table 8 presents population of capital cities and cities of 100 000 or more inhabitants for the latest available year.

Description of variables: Since the way in which cities are delimited differs from one country or area to another, the table not only presents data for the so-called city proper, but also for the urban agglomeration, if available.

City proper is defined as a locality with legally fixed boundaries and an administratively recognized urban status, usually characterized by some form of local government.

Urban agglomeration has been defined as comprising the city or town proper and also the suburban fringe or densely settled territory lying outside of, but adjacent to, the city boundaries.

For some countries or areas, however, the data relate to entire administrative divisions known, for example, as shi or municipalities (municipios) which are composed of a populated centre and adjoining territory, some of which may contain other, often separate urban localities or may be distinctively rural in character. For this group of countries or areas the type of civil division is given in a footnote.

The surface area of the city or urban agglomeration is presented, when available.

City names are presented in the original language of the country or area in which the cities are located. In cases where the original names are not in the Roman alphabet, they have been Romanized. Cities are listed in English alphabetical order.

Capital cities are shown in the table regardless of their population size. The names of the capital cities are printed in capital letters. The designation of any specific city as a capital city is as reported by the country or area.

The table also covers cities whose urban agglomeration's population exceeds 100 000; that is, while the urban agglomeration should have a population of 100 000 or more to be included in the table, the city proper may be of a smaller population size.

The reference date of each population figure appears in the stub of the table. Estimates based on results of sample surveys and city censuses as well as those derived from other sources are noted in the "code" column.

Reliability of data: Specific information is generally not available on the reliability of the estimates of the population of cities or urban agglomerations presented in this table.

In the absence of such quality assessment, data from population censuses, sample surveys and city censuses are considered to be reliable and, therefore, set in roman type. Other estimates are considered to be reliable if they are based on a complete census (or a sample survey), and have been adjusted by a continuous population register or adjusted on the basis of the calculated balance of births, deaths, and migration.

Limitations: Statistics on the population of capital cities and cities of 100 000 or more inhabitants are subject to the same qualifications as have been set forth for population statistics in general as discussed in section 3 of the Technical Notes.

International comparability of data on city population is limited to a great extent by variations in national concepts and definitions. Although an effort is made to reduce the sources of non-comparability somewhat by presenting the data for both city proper and urban agglomeration, many serious problems of comparability remain.

Data presented in the "city proper" column for some countries represent an urban administrative area legally distinguished from surrounding rural territory, while for other countries these data represent a commune or an equally small administrative unit. In still other countries, the administrative units may be relatively extensive and thereby include considerable territories beyond the urban centre itself.

City data are also especially affected by whether the data refer to de facto or de jure population, as well as variations among countries in how each of these concepts is applied. With reference to the total population, the difference between the de facto and de jure population is discussed at length in section 3.1.1 of the Technical Notes.

Data on city populations based on intercensal estimates present additional problems: comparability is impaired by the different methods used in making the estimates and by the loss of precision in applying to selected segments of the population, methods best suited for the whole population. For example, it is far more difficult to apply the component method of estimating population growth to cities than it is to the entire country.

Births and deaths occurring in the cities do not all originate in the population present in or resident of that area. Therefore, the use of natural increase to estimate the probable size of the city population is a potential source of error. Internal migration is another component of population change that cannot be measured with accuracy in many areas. Because of these factors, estimates in this table may be less valuable in general and in particular limited for purposes of international comparison.

City data, even when set in roman type, are often not as reliable as estimates for the total population of the country or area. Furthermore, because the sources of these data include censuses (national or city), surveys and estimates, the years to which they refer vary widely. In addition, because city boundaries may alter over time, comparisons covering different years should be carried out with caution.

Earlier data: Population of capital cities and cities with a population of 100 000 or more have been shown in previous issues of the *Demographic Yearbook*. For more information on specific topics and years for which data are reported, readers should consult the Historical Index.

Tableau 8

Le tableau 8 présente les données les plus récentes dont on dispose sur la population des capitales et des villes de 100 000 habitants et plus.

Description des variables : Étant donné que les villes ne sont pas délimitées de la même manière dans tous les pays ou zones, on s'est efforcé de donner, dans ce tableau, des chiffres correspondant non seulement aux villes proprement dites, mais aussi, le cas échéant, aux agglomérations urbaines.

On entend par villes proprement dites les localités qui ont des limites juridiquement définies et sont administrativement considérées comme villes, ce qui se caractérise généralement par l'existence d'une autorité locale.

L'agglomération urbaine comprend, par définition, la ville proprement dite ainsi que la proche banlieue, c'est-à-dire la zone fortement peuplée qui est extérieure, mais contiguë aux limites de la ville.

En outre, dans certains pays ou zones, les données se rapportent à des divisions administratives entières, connues par exemple sous le nom de shi ou de municipios, qui comportent une agglomération et le territoire avoisinant, lequel peut englober d'autres agglomérations urbaines tout à fait distinctes ou être à caractère essentiellement rural. Pour ce groupe de pays ou zones, le type de division administrative est indiqué en note.

On trouvera à la fin du tableau la superficie de la ville ou agglomération urbaine chaque fois que possible.

Les noms des villes sont indiqués dans la langue du pays ou zone où ces villes sont situées. Les noms de villes qui ne sont pas à l'origine libellés en caractères latins ont été romanisés. Les villes sont énumérées dans l'ordre alphabétique anglais.

Les capitales figurent dans le tableau quel que soit le chiffre de leur population et leur nom a été imprimé en lettres majuscules. Ne sont indiquées comme capitales que les villes ainsi désignées par le pays ou zone intéressé.

En ce qui concerne les autres villes, le tableau indique celles dont la population est égale ou supérieure à 100 000 habitants. Ce chiffre limite s'applique à l'agglomération urbaine et non à la ville proprement dite, dont la population peut être moindre.

L'année à laquelle se réfère le chiffre correspondant à chaque population figure dans la colonne de gauche du tableau. La colonne « Code » permet de savoir si les estimations sont fondées sur les résultats d'enquêtes par sondage ou de recensements municipaux ou sont tirées d'autres sources.

Fiabilité des données : On ne possède généralement pas de renseignements précis sur la fiabilité des estimations de la population des villes ou agglomérations urbaines présentées dans ce tableau.

Les données provenant de recensements de la population, d'enquêtes par sondage ou de recensements municipaux sont jugées sûres et figurent par conséquent en caractères romains. D'autres estimations sont considérées comme sûres si elles sont fondées sur un recensement complet (ou une enquête par sondage) et ont été ajustées en fonction des données provenant d'un registre permanent de population ou en fonction de la balance, établie par le calcul des naissances, des décès et des migrations.

Insuffisance des données : Les statistiques portant sur la population des capitales et des villes de 100 000 habitants et plus appellent toutes les réserves qui ont été formulées à la section 3 des Notes techniques à propos des statistiques de la population en général.

La comparabilité internationale des données portant sur la population des villes est compromise dans une large mesure par la diversité des définitions nationales. Bien que l'on se soit efforcé de réduire les facteurs de non-comparabilité en présentant à la fois dans le tableau les données relatives aux villes proprement dites et celles concernant les agglomérations urbaines, de graves problèmes de comparabilité n'en subsistent pas moins.

Pour certains pays, les données figurant dans la colonne intitulée « Ville proprement dite » correspondent à une zone administrative urbaine juridiquement distincte du territoire rural environnant, tandis que pour d'autres pays ces données correspondent à une commune ou petite unité administrative analogue. Pour d'autres encore, les unités administratives en cause peuvent être relativement étendues et englober par conséquent un vaste territoire au-delà du centre urbain lui-même.

L'emploi de données se rapportant tantôt à la population de fait, tantôt à la population de droit, ainsi que les différences de traitement de ces deux notions d'un pays à l'autre influent particulièrement sur les statistiques urbaines. En ce qui concerne la population totale, la différence entre population de fait et population de droit est expliquée en détail à la section 3.1.1 des Notes techniques.

Les statistiques relatives à la population urbaine qui sont fondées sur des estimations intercensitaires posent encore plus de problèmes que les données issues de recensement. Leur comparabilité est compromise par la diversité des méthodes employées pour établir les estimations et par l'imprécision qui résulte de l'application de certaines méthodes à telles ou telles composantes de la population alors qu'elles sont conçues pour être appliquées à l'ensemble de la population. La méthode des composantes, par exemple, est beaucoup plus difficile à appliquer en vue de l'estimation de l'accroissement de la population lorsqu'il s'agit de villes que lorsqu'il s'agit d'un pays tout entier.

Les naissances et décès qui surviennent dans les villes ne correspondent pas tous à la population présente ou résidente. En conséquence, des erreurs peuvent se produire si l'on établit pour les villes des estimations fondées sur l'accroissement naturel de la population. Les migrations intérieures constituent un second élément d'estimation que, dans bien des régions, on ne peut pas toujours mesurer avec exactitude. Pour ces raisons, les estimations présentées dans ce tableau risquent dans l'ensemble d'être peu fiables et leur valeur est particulièrement limitée du point de vue des comparaisons internationales.

Même lorsqu'elles figurent en caractères romains, il arrive souvent que les statistiques urbaines ne soient pas aussi fiables que les estimations concernant la population totale de la zone ou du pays considéré. De surcroît, comme ces statistiques proviennent aussi bien de recensements (nationaux ou municipaux) que d'enquêtes ou d'estimations, les années auxquelles elles se rapportent sont extrêmement variables. Enfin, comme les limites urbaines varient parfois d'une époque à une autre, il y a lieu d'être prudent lorsque l'on compare des données se rapportant à des années différentes.

Données publiées antérieurement : Des statistiques concernant la population des capitales et des villes de 100 000 habitants ou plus ont été présentées dans des éditions antérieures de l'*Annuaire démographique*. Pour plus de précisions concernant les années et les sujets pour lesquels des données ont été publiées, se reporter à l'index.

8. Population of capital cities and cities of 100 000 and more inhabitants: latest available year
Population des capitales et des villes de 100 000 habitants et plus: dernière année disponible

(See notes at end of table. — Voir notes à la fin du tableau.)

Continent, country or area, date and city / Continent, pays ou zone, date et ville	Code[1]	City proper — Ville proprement dite Population				Urban agglomeration — Agglomération urbaine Population			
		Both sexes Les deux sexes	Male Masculin	Female Féminin	Surface area Superficie (km²)	Both sexes Les deux sexes	Male Masculin	Female Féminin	Surface area Superficie (km²)
AFRICA — AFRIQUE									
Algeria — Algérie									
25 VI 1998									
ALGER (EL DJAZAIR)	CDJC	1 569 897	...	...	...	...	...	...	...
Annaba	CDJC	352 523	...	...	...	...	...	...	...
Batna	CDJC	246 800	...	...	...	...	...	...	...
Béchar	CDJC	134 523	...	...	...	...	...	...	...
Bejaïa	CDJC	144 405	...	...	...	...	...	...	...
Biskra	CDJC	177 060	...	...	...	...	...	...	...
Blida (El Boulaïda)	CDJC	229 788	...	...	...	...	...	...	...
Bordj Bou Arreridj	CDJC	129 004	...	...	...	...	...	...	...
Bordj el Kiffan	CDJC	103 690	...	...	...	...	...	...	...
Chlef (Ech Cheliff)	CDJC	174 314	...	...	...	...	...	...	...
Constantine (Qacentina)	CDJC	465 021	...	...	...	...	...	...	...
El Djelfa	CDJC	158 679	...	...	...	...	...	...	...
El Eulma	CDJC	104 758	...	...	...	...	...	...	...
El Oued (El Wad)	CDJC	105 151	...	...	...	...	...	...	...
Ghardaïa	CDJC	127 959	...	...	...	...	...	...	...
Guelma	CDJC	108 682	...	...	...	...	...	...	...
Jijel	CDJC	106 306	...	...	...	...	...	...	...
Medea (Lemdiyya)	CDJC	128 427	...	...	...	...	...	...	...
Mostaganem	CDJC	125 911	...	...	...	...	...	...	...
M'Sila	CDJC	102 151	...	...	...	...	...	...	...
Oran (Wahran)	CDJC	705 335	...	...	...	...	...	...	...
Ouargla (Wargla)	CDJC	139 381	...	...	...	...	...	...	...
Relizane	CDJC	104 644	...	...	...	...	...	...	...
Saïda	CDJC	113 533	...	...	...	...	...	...	...
Sétif (Stif)	CDJC	214 842	...	...	...	...	...	...	...
Sidi-bel-Abbès	CDJC	183 931	...	...	...	...	...	...	...
Skikda	CDJC	153 531	...	...	...	...	...	...	...
Souk Ahras	CDJC	114 512	...	...	...	...	...	...	...
Tebessa	CDJC	154 335	...	...	...	...	...	...	...
Tiaert	CDJC	148 850	...	...	...	...	...	...	...
Tlemcen (Tilimsen)	CDJC	156 258	...	...	...	...	...	...	...
Tougourt	CDJC	114 183	...	...	...	...	...	...	...
Angola									
1 VII 1993									
Huambo	ESDF	...	...	...	...	400 000	...	...	...
LUANDA	ESDF	...	...	...	...	1 822 407	855 676	936 731	...
Benin — Bénin									
1 VII 2000									
Cotonou	ESDF	650 660	318 752	331 908	79	...	...	...	...
Parakou	ESDF	144 627	73 603	71 024	441	...	...	...	...
PORTO-NOVO	ESDF	232 756	113 737	119 019	50	...	...	...	...
Botswana									
17 VIII 2001									
Francistown	CDFC	83 023	...	...	79	113 315	...	...	...
GABORONE	CDFC	186 007	...	...	169	282 150	...	...	...
Burkina Faso									
10 XII 1996									
Bobo Dioulasso	CDFC	309 771	157 021	152 750	...	...	...	...	...
OUAGADOUGOU	CDFC	709 736	364 674	345 062	...	750 398	384 807	365 591	...
Burundi									
16 VIII 1990									
BUJUMBURA	CDFC	235 440	129 195	106 245	...	...	...	...	...
Cameroon — Cameroun									
1 VII 1998									
Bafoussam	ESDF	205 620	...	...	...	...	...	...	...
Bamenda	ESDF	252 083	...	...	...	...	...	...	...
Bertoua	ESDF	129 067	...	...	...	...	...	...	...
Douala	ESDF	1 382 900	...	...	...	...	...	...	...
Edéa	ESDF	101 200	...	...	...	...	...	...	...
Garoua	ESDF	293 081	...	...	...	...	...	...	...
Kousséri	ESDF	233 280	...	...	...	...	...	...	...
Kumba	ESDF	110 860	...	...	...	...	...	...	...
Loum	ESDF	115 781	...	...	...	...	...	...	...

8. Population of capital cities and cities of 100 000 and more inhabitants: latest available year
Population des capitales et des villes de 100 000 habitants et plus: dernière année disponible (continued — suite)

(See notes at end of table. — Voir notes à la fin du tableau.)

Continent, country or area, date and city / Continent, pays ou zone, date et ville	Code[1]	City proper — Ville proprement dite Population				Urban agglomeration — Agglomération urbaine Population			
		Both sexes Les deux sexes	Male Masculin	Female Féminin	Surface area Superficie (km²)	Both sexes Les deux sexes	Male Masculin	Female Féminin	Surface area Superficie (km²)
AFRICA — AFRIQUE									
Cameroon — Cameroun									
1 VII 1998									
Maroua	ESDF	*225 469*	...	...	...	...	...	...	...
Ngaoundéré	ESDF	*156 804*	...	...	...	...	...	...	...
Nkongsamba	ESDF	*104 908*	...	...	...	...	...	...	...
YAOUNDE	ESDF	*1 293 000*	...	...	...	...	...	...	...
Cape Verde — Cap-Vert									
1 VII 1990									
PRAIA	CDFC	61 644	...	...	...	...	...	...	...
Central African Republic — République centrafricaine									
8 XII 1988									
BANGUI	CDFC	451 690	...	...	...	...	...	...	...
Chad — Tchad									
8 IV 1993									
N'DJAMENA	CDFC	530 965	...	...	...	...	...	...	...
Comoros — Comores									
15 IX 1991									
MORONI	CDFC	30 365	...	...	...	...	...	...	...
Congo									
1 VII 1984									
BRAZZAVILLE	CDFC	596 200	...	...	...	...	...	...	...
Pointe-Noire	CDFC	298 014	...	...	...	...	...	...	...
Côte d'Ivoire									
1 III 1988									
Abidjan	CDFC	1 929 079	...	...	...	...	...	...	...
Bouake	CDFC	329 850	...	...	...	362 192	...	...	...
Daloa	CDFC	121 842	...	...	...	127 923	...	...	...
Korhogo	CDFC	109 445	...	...	...	112 888	...	...	...
YAMOUSSOUKRO	CDFC	106 786	...	...	...	126 191	...	...	...
Democratic Republic of the Congo — République démocratique du Congo									
1 VII 1984									
Boma	ESDF	*197 617*	...	...	...	...	...	...	...
Bukavu	ESDF	*167 950*	...	...	...	...	...	...	...
Kananga	ESDF	*298 693*	...	...	...	...	...	...	...
Kikwit	ESDF	*149 296*	...	...	...	...	...	...	...
KINSHASA	ESDF	*2 664 309*	...	...	...	...	...	...	...
Kisangani	ESDF	*317 581*	...	...	...	...	...	...	...
Kolwezi	ESDF	*416 122*	...	...	...	...	...	...	...
Likasi (Jadotville)	ESDF	*213 862*	...	...	...	...	...	...	...
Lubumbashi	ESDF	*564 830*	...	...	...	...	...	...	...
Matadi	ESDF	*138 798*	...	...	...	...	...	...	...
Mbandaka	ESDF	*137 291*	...	...	...	...	...	...	...
Mbuji-Mayi	ESDF	*486 235*	...	...	...	...	...	...	...
Djibouti									
1 VII 1995									
DJIBOUTI	ESDF	*383 000*	...	...	...	...	...	...	...
Egypt — Égypte									
19 XI 1996									
Alexandria	CDFC	3 339 076	1 707 477	1 631 599	...	...	...	...	...
Al Orizah	CDFC	100 482	53 081	47 401	...	...	...	...	...
Assyût	CDFC	343 662	182 151	161 511	...	...	...	...	...
Aswan	CDFC	219 541	111 640	107 901	...	...	...	...	...
Banha	CDFC	135 892	69 154	66 738	...	...	...	...	...
Beni-Suef	CDFC	171 734	87 105	84 629	...	...	...	...	...
CAIRO	CDFC	6 800 992	3 486 260	3 314 732	...	...	...	...	...
Damanhûr	CDFC	209 423	107 965	101 458	...	...	...	...	...
El-Mahalla El-Kubra	CDFC	394 924	199 100	195 824	...	...	...	...	...
Faiyûm	CDFC	260 830	134 462	126 368	...	...	...	...	...
Giza	CDFC	2 221 817	1 139 665	1 082 152	...	...	...	...	...
Imbaba	CDFC	523 265	266 793	256 472	...	...	...	...	...
Ismailia	CDFC	255 134	129 004	126 130	...	...	...	...	...
Kafr-El-Dwar	CDFC	101 056	51 491	49 565	...	...	...	...	...
Kena	CDFC	155 382	79 038	76 344	...	...	...	...	...

8. Population of capital cities and cities of 100 000 and more inhabitants: latest available year
Population des capitales et des villes de 100 000 habitants et plus: dernière année disponible (continued — suite)

(See notes at end of table. — Voir notes à la fin du tableau.)

Continent, country or area, date and city / Continent, pays ou zone, date et ville	Code[1]	City proper — Ville proprement dite Population				Urban agglomeration — Agglomération urbaine Population			
		Both sexes Les deux sexes	Male Masculin	Female Féminin	Surface area Superficie (km²)	Both sexes Les deux sexes	Male Masculin	Female Féminin	Surface area Superficie (km²)
AFRICA — AFRIQUE									
Egypt — Égypte									
19 XI 1996									
Luxer	CDFC	153 758	79 753	74 005	...	...	...	...	...
Mansûra	CDFC	369 409	187 622	181 787	...	...	...	...	...
Menia	CDFC	201 440	103 428	98 012	...	...	...	...	...
Port Said	CDFC	472 335	242 502	229 833	...	...	...	...	...
Shebin-El-Kom	CDFC	156 794	79 868	76 926	...	...	...	...	...
Shubra-El-Khema	CDFC	870 776	449 271	421 505	...	...	...	...	...
Sohag	CDFC	170 417	85 918	84 499	...	...	...	...	...
Suez	CDFC	417 527	214 133	203 394	...	...	...	...	...
Tanta	CDFC	372 893	188 594	184 299	...	...	...	...	...
Zagazig	CDFC	267 469	136 094	131 375	...	...	...	...	...
Equatorial Guinea — Guinée équatoriale									
1 VII 1983									
MALABO	CDFC	30 418	...	...	...	...	...	...	...
Eritrea — Érythrée									
1 VII 1990									
ASMARA	ESDF	358 100	...	...	...	...	...	...	...
Ethiopia — Ethiopie									
1 VII 2002									
ADDIS ABABA	ESDF	2 646 000	1 273 000	1 373 000	...	...	...	...	...
Awassa	ESDF	103 725	52 308	51 417	...	...	...	...	...
Bahir Dar	ESDF	140 084	72 736	67 348	...	...	...	...	...
Debre Zeit	ESDF	108 632	53 648	54 984	...	...	...	...	...
Dessie	ESDF	141 616	72 578	69 038	...	...	...	...	...
Dire Dawa	ESDF	237 012	118 880	118 132	...	...	...	...	...
Gondar	ESDF	163 097	82 229	80 868	...	...	...	...	...
Harar	ESDF	105 000	53 000	52 000	...	...	...	...	...
Jimma	ESDF	131 708	67 138	64 570	...	...	...	...	...
Mekele	ESDF	141 433	71 990	69 443	...	...	...	...	...
Nazareth	ESDF	189 362	94 822	94 540	...	...	...	...	...
Gabon									
1 VII 1993									
LIBREVILLE	CDFC	362 386	184 192	178 194	...	418 616	212 383	206 233	...
Gambia — Gambie									
1 VII 1993									
BANJUL[2]	CDFC	42 326	22 268	20 058	12	...	...	...	...
Ghana									
18 III 1984									
ACCRA[3]	CDFC	867 459	...	...	...	1 160 112	...	...	...
Kumasi	CDFC	376 246	...	...	...	489 586	...	...	...
Sekondi-Takoradi[4]	CDFC	93 400	...	...	...	178 257	...	...	...
Tamale	CDFC	135 952	...	...	...	167 778	...	...	...
Tema	CDFC	100 052	...	...	...	...	...	...	...
Guinea — Guinée									
1 XII 1996									
CONAKRY	CDFC	1 091 500	...	...	...	...	...	...	...
Kankan	CDFC	...	...	...	...	261 341	...	...	...
Kindia	CDFC	...	...	...	...	287 607	...	...	...
Labé	CDFC	...	...	...	...	249 515	...	...	...
Nzérékoré	CDFC	...	...	...	...	282 772	...	...	...
Guinea-Bissau — Guinée-Bissau									
1 XII 1991									
BISSAU	CDFC	197 600	...	...	...	...	...	...	...
Kenya									
24 VIII 1999									
Eldoret	CDFC	167 016	...	...	...	...	...	...	...
Kisumu	CDFC	322 734	...	...	...	...	...	...	...
Machakos	CDFC	144 109	...	...	...	...	...	...	...
Meru	CDFC	126 427	...	...	...	...	...	...	...
Mombasa	CDFC	665 018	...	...	...	...	...	...	...
NAIROBI	CDFC	2 143 254	...	...	...	...	...	...	...
Nakuru	CDFC	219 366	...	...	...	...	...	...	...

(See notes at end of table. — Voir notes à la fin du tableau.)

Continent, country or area, date and city / Continent, pays ou zone, date et ville	Code[1]	City proper — Ville proprement dite Population				Urban agglomeration — Agglomération urbaine Population			
		Both sexes Les deux sexes	Male Masculin	Female Féminin	Surface area Superficie (km²)	Both sexes Les deux sexes	Male Masculin	Female Féminin	Surface area Superficie (km²)
AFRICA — AFRIQUE									
Lesotho									
12 IV 1986									
MASERU	CDFC	109 382	...	...	...	...	...	...	...
Liberia — Libéria									
1 VII 1984									
MONROVIA	CDFC	421 053	...	...	...	...	...	...	...
Libyan Arab Jamahiriya — Jamahiriya arabe libyenne									
1 VII 1990									
Al Khums	ESDJ	*200 000*	...	...	...	...	...	...	...
BENGHAZI[5]	ESDJ	*800 000*	...	...	...	...	...	...	...
Misurata	ESDJ	*360 000*	...	...	...	...	...	...	...
Sebha	ESDJ	*150 000*	...	...	...	...	...	...	...
TRIPOLI[5]	ESDJ	*1 500 000*	...	...	...	...	...	...	...
Zuwarah	ESDJ	*280 000*	...	...	...	...	...	...	...
Madagascar									
1 VIII 1993									
ANTANANARIVO[6]	CDJC	710 236	346 073	364 163	72	...	...	...	...
Antsirabe	CDJC	126 062	62 288	63 774	112	...	...	...	...
Fianarantsoa	CDJC	109 260	52 757	56 504	85	...	...	...	...
Mahajanga	CDJC	106 780	52 711	54 068	14	...	...	...	...
Toamasina	CDJC	137 782	66 844	70 938	20	...	...	...	...
Malawi									
1 IX 1998									
Blantyre-Limbe	CDFC	502 053	...	...	220	...	...	...	...
LILONGWE	CDFC	440 471	...	...	328	...	...	...	...
Mali									
1 IV 1998									
BAMAKO	CDJC	1 016 167	520 688	495 479	252	...	...	...	...
Mauritania — Mauritanie									
1 XI 2000									
NOUAKCHOTT	CDFC	558 195	...	...	...	...	...	...	...
Mauritius — Maurice									
1 VII 2002									
Beau Bassin-Rose Hill	ESDJ	106 061	51 802	54 259	20	...	...	...	...
PORT LOUIS	ESDJ	146 876	72 924	73 952	46	...	...	...	...
Vacoas - Phoenix	ESDJ	102 604	50 723	51 881	54	...	...	...	...
Morocco — Maroc									
2 IX 1994									
Agadir	CDFC	155 244	...	...	...	...	...	...	...
Béni-Mellal	CDFC	140 212	...	...	...	...	...	...	...
Casablanca (Dar-el-Beida)	CDFC	2 765 931	...	...	...	...	...	...	...
El-Jadida	CDFC	119 083	...	...	...	...	...	...	...
Fès	CDFC	506 585	...	...	...	...	...	...	...
Kénitra	CDFC	292 627	...	...	...	...	...	...	...
Khouribga	CDFC	152 090	...	...	...	...	...	...	...
Ksar-el-Kebir	CDFC	107 065	...	...	...	...	...	...	...
Marrakech	CDFC	656 325	...	...	...	...	...	...	...
Meknès	CDFC	443 214	...	...	...	...	...	...	...
Mohammedia	CDFC	170 063	...	...	...	...	...	...	...
Nador	CDFC	112 450	...	...	...	...	...	...	...
Oujda	CDFC	351 878	...	...	...	...	...	...	...
RABAT[7]	CDFC	1 359 209	...	...	...	...	...	...	...
Safi	CDFC	262 276	...	...	...	...	...	...	...
Tanger	CDFC	497 147	...	...	...	...	...	...	...
Tétouan	CDFC	277 516	...	...	...	...	...	...	...
Mozambique									
1 VIII 1997									
Beira	CDFC	397 368	...	...	...	...	...	...	...
Chimoio	CDFC	171 056	...	...	...	...	...	...	...
MAPUTO	CDFC	966 837	...	...	...	1 391 499	...	...	...
Matola	CDFC	424 662	...	...	...	...	...	...	...
Mocuba	CDFC	124 650	...	...	...	...	...	...	...
Nacala	CDFC	158 248	...	...	...	...	...	...	...
Nampula	CDFC	303 346	...	...	...	...	...	...	...

(See notes at end of table. — Voir notes à la fin du tableau.)

Continent, country or area, date and city / Continent, pays ou zone, date et ville	Code[1]	City proper — Ville proprement dite Population				Urban agglomeration — Agglomeration urbaine Population			
		Both sexes Les deux sexes	Male Masculin	Female Féminin	Surface area Superficie (km²)	Both sexes Les deux sexes	Male Masculin	Female Féminin	Surface area Superficie (km²)
AFRICA — AFRIQUE									
Mozambique									
1 VIII 1997									
Quelimane	CDFC	150 116	...	...	...	...	...	...	...
Tete	CDFC	101 984	...	...	...	...	...	...	...
Namibia — Namibie									
1 VII 1991									
WINDHOEK	CDFC	147 056	...	...	...	...	...	...	...
Niger[8]									
1 VII 1988									
Maradi	CDJC	110 739	54 355	56 384	...	...	...	...	...
NIAMEY	CDJC	397 437	203 172	194 265	...	...	...	...	...
Zinder	CDJC	120 160	60 936	59 224	...	...	...	...	...
Nigeria — Nigéria									
26 XI 1991									
Aba	CDFC	500 183	...	...	...	...	...	...	...
Abeokuta	CDFC	352 735	...	...	...	...	...	...	...
ABUJA	CDFC	107 069	...	...	...	378 671	...	...	...
Ado-Ekiti	CDFC	156 122	...	...	...	...	...	...	...
Akure	CDFC	239 124	...	...	...	...	...	...	...
Awka	CDFC	104 682	...	...	...	...	...	...	...
Bauchi	CDFC	206 537	...	...	...	...	...	...	...
Benin City	CDFC	762 719	...	...	...	...	...	...	...
Bida	CDFC	111 245	...	...	...	...	...	...	...
Calabar	CDFC	310 839	...	...	...	...	...	...	...
Damaturu	CDFC	141 897	...	...	...	...	...	...	...
Ede	CDFC	142 363	...	...	...	...	...	...	...
Effon-Alaiye	CDFC	158 977	...	...	...	...	...	...	...
Enugu	CDFC	407 756	...	...	...	...	...	...	...
Gboko	CDFC	101 281	...	...	...	...	...	...	...
Gombe	CDFC	163 604	...	...	...	...	...	...	...
Gusau	CDFC	132 393	...	...	...	...	...	...	...
Ibadan	CDFC	1 835 300	...	...	...	...	...	...	...
Ife	CDFC	186 856	...	...	...	...	...	...	...
Ijebu-Ode	CDFC	124 313	...	...	...	...	...	...	...
Ikare	CDFC	103 843	...	...	...	...	...	...	...
Ikire	CDFC	111 435	...	...	...	...	...	...	...
Ikorodu	CDFC	184 674	...	...	...	...	...	...	...
Ikot Ekpene	CDFC	119 402	...	...	...	...	...	...	...
Ilawe-Ekiti	CDFC	104 049	...	...	...	...	...	...	...
Ilesha	CDFC	139 445	...	...	...	...	...	...	...
Ilorin	CDFC	532 089	...	...	...	...	...	...	...
Ise	CDFC	108 136	...	...	...	...	...	...	...
Iseyin	CDFC	170 936	...	...	...	...	...	...	...
Iwo	CDFC	125 645	...	...	...	...	...	...	...
Jimeta	CDFC	141 724	...	...	...	...	...	...	...
Jos	CDFC	510 300	...	...	...	...	...	...	...
Kaduna	CDFC	993 642	...	...	...	...	...	...	...
Kano	CDFC	2 166 554	...	...	...	...	...	...	...
Katsina	CDFC	259 315	...	...	...	...	...	...	...
Lagos	CDFC	5 195 247	...	...	...	...	...	...	...
Maiduguri	CDFC	618 278	...	...	...	...	...	...	...
Makurdi	CDFC	151 515	...	...	...	...	...	...	...
Minna	CDFC	189 191	...	...	...	...	...	...	...
Mubi	CDFC	128 900	...	...	...	...	...	...	...
Nnewi	CDFC	121 065	...	...	...	...	...	...	...
Ogbomosho	CDFC	433 030	...	...	...	...	...	...	...
Okene	CDFC	312 775	...	...	...	...	...	...	...
Okpogho	CDFC	105 127	...	...	...	...	...	...	...
Ondo	CDFC	146 051	...	...	...	...	...	...	...
Onitsha	CDFC	350 280	...	...	...	...	...	...	...
Oshogbo	CDFC	250 951	...	...	...	...	...	...	...
Owerri	CDFC	119 711	...	...	...	...	...	...	...
Owo	CDFC	157 181	...	...	...	...	...	...	...
Oyo	CDFC	369 894	...	...	...	...	...	...	...
Port Harcourt	CDFC	703 421	...	...	...	...	...	...	...

8. Population of capital cities and cities of 100 000 and more inhabitants: latest available year
Population des capitales et des villes de 100 000 habitants et plus: dernière année disponible (continued — suite)

(See notes at end of table. — Voir notes à la fin du tableau.)

Continent, country or area, date and city / Continent, pays ou zone, date et ville	Code[1]	City proper — Ville proprement dite Population				Urban agglomeration — Agglomération urbaine Population			
		Both sexes Les deux sexes	Male Masculin	Female Féminin	Surface area Superficie (km²)	Both sexes Les deux sexes	Male Masculin	Female Féminin	Surface area Superficie (km²)
AFRICA — AFRIQUE									
Nigeria — Nigéria									
26 XI 1991									
Sagamu	CDFC	127 513	...	...	...	...	...	...	...
Sango Otta	CDFC	103 332	...	...	...	...	...	...	...
Sapele	CDFC	109 576	...	...	...	...	...	...	...
Sokoto	CDFC	329 639	...	...	...	...	...	...	...
Suleja	CDFC	105 075	...	...	...	...	...	...	...
Ugep	CDFC	134 773	...	...	...	...	...	...	...
Umuahia	CDFC	147 167	...	...	...	...	...	...	...
Warri	CDFC	363 382	...	...	...	...	...	...	...
Zaria	CDFC	612 257	...	...	...	...	...	...	...
Réunion									
1 VII 2002									
SAINT-DENIS[9]	ESDF	134 042	63 922	70 120	143		...	...	...
Rwanda									
1 VII 1991									
KIGALI	CDJC	233 640	125 550	108 090	...	...	...	...	...
St. Helena ex. dep. — Sainte-Hélène sans dép.									
8 III 1998									
JAMESTOWN	CDFC	884	452	432	4	...	...	...	...
Sao Tome and Principe — Sao Tomé-et-Principe									
4 VIII 1991									
SAO TOME	CDJC	43 400	...	...	...	...	...	...	...
Senegal — Sénégal									
1 VII 1999									
DAKAR	ESDF	879 703	...	...	500	1 976 533	...	...	...
Kaolack	ESDF	227 915	...	...	...	...	...	...	...
Mbour	ESDF	135 619	...	...	...	...	...	...	...
Pikine-Guediawaye[10]	ESDF	1 096 830	...	...	...	...	...	...	...
Saint Louis	ESDF	147 961	...	...	...	...	...	...	...
Thiès	ESDF	256 113	...	...	...	...	...	...	...
Ziguinchor	ESDF	199 871	...	...	...	...	...	...	...
Seychelles									
29 VIII 1997									
VICTORIA	CDFC	...	...	...	...	24 701	...	...	...
Sierra Leone									
1 VII 1985									
FREETOWN	CDFC	469 776	...	...	...	...	...	...	...
Somalia — Somalie									
1 VII 2001									
MOGADISHU	ESDF	1 212 000	...	...	...	...	...	...	...
South Africa — Afrique du Sud									
10 X 1996									
Alexandra	CDFC	171 284	...	...	...	...	...	...	...
Benoni	CDFC	366 343	...	...	...	...	...	...	...
Bloemfontein	CDFC	350 504	...	...	...	...	...	...	...
Boksburg	CDFC	263 179	...	...	...	...	...	...	...
Botshabelo	CDFC	177 971	...	...	...	...	...	...	...
CAPE TOWN[11]	CDFC	987 007	...	...	...	...	...	...	...
Durban	CDFC	669 242	...	...	...	...	...	...	...
Germiston	CDFC	164 252	...	...	...	...	...	...	...
Johannesburg	CDFC	752 349	...	...	...	...	...	...	...
Kathlehong	CDFC	344 803	...	...	...	...	...	...	...
Kempton Park	CDFC	344 426	...	...	...	...	...	...	...
Khayelitsa	CDFC	314 239	...	...	...	...	...	...	...
Kimberley	CDFC	206 070	...	...	...	...	...	...	...
Mangaung	CDFC	176 525	...	...	...	...	...	...	...
Pietermaritzburg	CDFC	405 385	...	...	...	...	...	...	...
Port Elizabeth	CDFC	775 255	...	...	...	...	...	...	...
PRETORIA[11]	CDFC	692 348	340 363	351 985	...	...	...	...	...
Roodepoort	CDFC	279 340	...	...	...	...	...	...	...
Soweto	CDFC	904 165	...	...	...	...	...	...	...
Springs	CDFC	163 304	...	...	...	...	...	...	...

8. Population of capital cities and cities of 100 000 and more inhabitants: latest available year
Population des capitales et des villes de 100 000 habitants et plus: dernière année disponible (continued — suite)

(See notes at end of table. — Voir notes à la fin du tableau.)

Continent, country or area, date and city / Continent, pays ou zone, date et ville	Code[1]	City proper — Ville proprement dite Population				Urban agglomeration — Agglomération urbaine Population			
		Both sexes Les deux sexes	Male Masculin	Female Féminin	Surface area Superficie (km²)	Both sexes Les deux sexes	Male Masculin	Female Féminin	Surface area Superficie (km²)
AFRICA — AFRIQUE									
South Africa — Afrique du Sud									
10 X 1996									
Tembisa	CDFC	237 676	...	...	...	...	...	...	...
Umlazi	CDFC	339 715	...	...	...	...	...	...	...
Vereeniging	CDFC	379 638	...	...	...	...	...	...	...
Sudan — Soudan									
15 IV 1993									
Al-Fasher	CDFC	141 884	...	...	...	...	...	...	...
Al-Gadarif	CDFC	191 164	...	...	...	...	...	...	...
Al-Gezira	CDFC	211 362	...	...	...	...	...	...	...
Al-Obeid	CDFC	229 425	...	...	...	...	...	...	...
Juba	CDFC	114 980	...	...	...	...	...	...	...
Kassala	CDFC	234 622	...	...	...	...	...	...	...
KHARTOUM	CDFC	947 483	...	...	...	2 919 773	...	...	...
Khartoum North	CDFC	700 887	...	...	...	...	...	...	...
Kosti	CDFC	173 599	...	...	...	...	...	...	...
Nyala	CDFC	227 183	...	...	...	...	...	...	...
Omdurman	CDFC	1 271 403	...	...	...	...	...	...	...
Port Sudan	CDFC	308 195	...	...	...	...	...	...	...
Swaziland									
1 VII 1986									
MBABANE	CDFC	38 290	...	...	...	...	...	...	...
Togo									
1 VII 1990									
LOME	ESDF	450 000	...	...	...	...	...	...	...
Tunisia — Tunisie									
1 VII 1998									
Bizerte	ESDF	105 520	...	...	...	...	...	...	...
Gabes	ESDF	104 950	...	...	...	...	...	...	...
Kairouan	ESDF	110 280	...	...	...	...	...	...	...
Sfax	ESDF	248 800	...	...	...	...	...	...	...
TUNIS	ESDF	702 330	...	...	...	...	...	...	...
Uganda — Ouganda									
12 IX 2002									
Gulu	CDFC	113 144	...	...	...	...	...	...	...
KAMPALA	CDFC	1 208 544	588 433	620 111	...	...	...	...	...
United Republic of Tanzania — République Unie de Tanzanie									
28 VIII 1988									
Arusha	CDFC	134 708	69 875	64 833	...	...	...	...	...
Dar es Salaam	CDFC	1 360 850	715 925	644 925	...	...	...	...	...
DODOMA	CDFC	203 833	101 437	102 396	...	...	...	...	...
Mbeya	CDFC	152 844	74 259	78 585	...	...	...	...	...
Morogoro	CDFC	117 760	59 144	58 616	...	...	...	...	...
Mwanza	CDFC	223 013	113 779	109 234	...	...	...	...	...
Shinyanga	CDFC	100 724	50 117	50 607	...	...	...	...	...
Tanga	CDFC	187 455	96 259	91 196	...	...	...	...	...
Zanzibar	CDFC	157 634	77 787	79 847	...	...	...	...	...
Western Sahara — Sahara occidental									
1 VII 1999									
EL AAIUN	ESDF	169 000	...	...	...	...	...	...	...
Zambia — Zambie									
1 VII 2000									
Chingola	ESDF	164 964	82 643	82 321	1 678	...	...	...	...
Kabwe	ESDF	170 387	84 041	86 346	1 572	...	...	...	...
Kitwe	ESDF	362 423	180 865	181 558	777	...	...	...	...
Luanshya	ESDF	144 009	72 449	71 560	811	...	...	...	...
LUSAKA	ESDF	1 057 212	528 891	528 321	360	...	...	...	...
Mufulira	ESDF	137 272	68 253	69 019	1 637	...	...	...	...
Ndola	ESDF	371 221	185 043	186 178	1 103	...	...	...	...
Zimbabwe									
18 VIII 1992									
Bulawayo	CDFC	621 742	309 864	311 878	479	...	...	...	...
Chitungwiza	CDFC	274 912	137 890	137 022	...	...	...	...	...
Gweru	CDFC	128 037	64 472	63 565	...	...	...	...	...

8. Population of capital cities and cities of 100 000 and more inhabitants: latest available year
Population des capitales et des villes de 100 000 habitants et plus: dernière année disponible (continued — suite)

(See notes at end of table. — Voir notes à la fin du tableau.)

Continent, country or area, date and city Continent, pays ou zone, date et ville	Code[1]	City proper — Ville proprement dite Population				Urban agglomeration — Agglomération urbaine Population			
		Both sexes Les deux sexes	Male Masculin	Female Féminin	Surface area Superficie (km²)	Both sexes Les deux sexes	Male Masculin	Female Féminin	Surface area Superficie (km²)
AFRICA — AFRIQUE									
Zimbabwe									
18 VIII 1992									
HARARE	CDFC	1 189 103	623 345	565 758	872	...	...	...	...
Mutare	CDFC	131 367	68 413	62 954	...	...	...	...	...
AMERICA, NORTH — AMERIQUE DU NORD									
Anguilla									
9 V 2001									
THE VALLEY	CDJC	1 169	...	...	...	...	...	...	...
Antigua and Barbuda — Antigua-et-Barbuda									
1 VII 1991									
ST. JOHN	CDFC	22 342	...	...	...	...	...	...	...
Aruba									
6 X 1991									
ORANJESTAD	CDFC	20 045	9 441	10 604	...	...	...	...	...
Bahamas									
1 V 2000									
NASSAU	CDFC	...	...	...	...	210 832	...	...	...
Barbados — Barbade									
1 VII 1980									
BRIDGETOWN	CDFC	7 466	...	...	...	...	...	...	...
Belize									
1 VII 2000									
BELMOPAN	ESDF	*8 305*	*4 050*	*4 255*	...	...	...	...	...
Bermuda — Bermudes[12]									
20 V 2000									
HAMILTON	CDJC	969	508	461	0	...	...	...	...
British Virgin Islands — Iles Vierges britanniques									
1 VII 1992									
ROAD TOWN	ESDF	*3 500*	...	...	...	...	...	...	...
Canada[13]									
15 V 2001									
Abbotsford	CDJC	115 460	57 010	58 450	359	147 370	73 180	74 185	626
Barrie	CDJC	103 710	50 555	53 155	77	148 480	73 085	75 395	897
Brantford	CDJC	325 425	161 590	163 840	267	...	...	...	...
Burlington	CDJC	150 835	72 925	77 915	186	...	...	...	...
Burnaby	CDJC	193 955	94 820	99 130	90	...	...	...	...
Calgary	CDJC	878 865	438 025	440 845	702	951 395	474 715	476 680	5 083
Cambridge	CDJC	110 375	54 275	56 095	113	...	...	...	...
Cape Breton	CDJC	105 970	50 145	55 825	2 434	109 330	51 790	57 540	2 471
Chatham-Kent	CDJC	107 340	52 265	55 075	2 458	107 705	52 425	55 285	2 471
Coquitlam	CDJC	112 890	55 700	57 190	122	...	...	...	...
Edmonton	CDJC	666 100	327 560	338 545	684	937 840	464 255	473 580	9 419
Gatineau	CDJC	102 895	50 050	52 845	147	...	...	...	...
Guelph	CDJC	106 170	51 955	54 215	87	117 340	57 605	59 735	378
Halifax	CDJC	359 110	172 705	186 405	5 491	359 185	172 745	186 435	5 496
Hamilton	CDJC	490 270	239 525	250 745	1 117	662 400	322 935	339 465	1 372
Kingston	CDJC	114 195	55 590	58 605	450	146 840	72 060	74 780	1 907
Kitchener	CDJC	190 400	93 725	96 675	137	414 285	203 760	210 525	827
Laval	CDJC	343 005	166 535	176 465	247	...	...	...	...
London	CDJC	336 540	161 855	174 685	422	432 450	209 230	223 220	2 333
Longueuil	CDJC	128 015	61 080	66 935	44	...	...	...	...
Markham	CDJC	208 615	102 170	106 445	212	...	...	...	...
Mississauga	CDJC	612 925	302 190	310 730	288	...	...	...	...
Montréal	CDJC	1 039 535	502 440	537 095	186	3 426 350	1 657 635	1 768 720	4 047
Oakville	CDJC	144 740	70 520	74 220	139	...	...	...	...
Oshawa	CDJC	139 050	67 920	71 130	146	296 295	145 505	150 795	903
OTTAWA	CDJC	774 070	377 380	396 690	2 779	1 063 665	518 725	544 940	5 318
Québec	CDJC	169 080	79 645	89 430	93	682 755	328 585	354 170	3 154
Regina	CDJC	178 225	85 755	92 470	119	192 805	93 280	99 525	3 408
Richmond	CDJC	164 345	79 295	85 050	129	...	...	...	...

(See notes at end of table. — Voir notes à la fin du tableau.)

Continent, country or area, date and city / Continent, pays ou zone, date et ville	Code[1]	City proper — Ville proprement dite Population				Urban agglomeration — Agglomération urbaine Population			
		Both sexes Les deux sexes	Male Masculin	Female Féminin	Surface area Superficie (km²)	Both sexes Les deux sexes	Male Masculin	Female Féminin	Surface area Superficie (km²)
AMERICA, NORTH — AMERIQUE DU NORD									
Canada[13]									
15 V 2001									
Richmond Hill	CDJC	132 030	64 595	67 440	101	...	...	...	...
Saanich	CDJC	103 655	49 615	54 035	103	...	...	...	...
St. Catharines	CDJC	129 170	61 805	67 365	97	377 010	182 605	194 405	1 406
Saskatoon	CDJC	196 810	94 610	102 200	148	225 930	109 420	116 510	5 192
Sudbury	CDJC	155 220	75 340	79 880	3 354	155 605	75 525	80 080	3 536
Surrey	CDJC	347 825	172 110	175 720	317	...	...	...	...
Thunder Bay	CDJC	109 015	53 065	55 955	328	121 985	59 730	62 250	2 548
Toronto	CDJC	2 481 495	1 196 560	1 284 930	630	4 682 895	2 282 665	2 400 235	5 903
Trois-Rivières	CDJC	46 265	21 370	24 895	78	137 510	65 725	71 780	880
Vancouver	CDJC	545 670	267 705	277 965	115	1 986 965	972 725	1 014 235	2 879
Vaughan	CDJC	182 020	90 415	91 605	274	...	...	...	...
Victoria	CDJC	74 125	33 950	40 180	20	311 905	148 460	163 445	695
Windsor	CDJC	208 400	101 925	106 475	121	307 875	151 500	156 380	1 023
Winnipeg	CDJC	619 545	299 420	320 125	465	671 275	325 875	345 400	4 151
Cayman Islands — Iles Caïmanes									
1 X 1999									
GEORGE TOWN	CDFC	20 626	...	...	...	...	...	...	...
Costa Rica									
28 VI 2000									
Alajuela	CDJC	222 853	111 649	111 204	388	...	...	...	...
Cartago	CDJC	132 057	65 418	66 639	288	...	...	...	...
Heredia	CDJC	103 894	50 241	53 653	...	...	...	...	...
Puntarenas	CDJC	102 504	52 248	50 256	1 842	...	...	...	...
SAN JOSE[14]	CDJC	309 672	149 647	160 025	45	1 345 750	656 205	689 545	4 966
Cuba									
1 VII 2000									
Bayamo	ESDF	143 700	...	...	...	...	...	...	...
Camagüey	ESDF	308 288	...	...	...	...	...	...	...
Ciego de Avila	ESDF	103 350	...	...	...	...	...	...	...
Cienfuegos	ESDF	138 965	...	...	...	...	...	...	...
Guantánamo	ESDF	209 269	...	...	...	...	...	...	...
Holguín	ESDF	262 100	...	...	...	...	...	...	...
LA HABANA	ESDF	2 186 632	...	...	727	...	...	...	...
Las Tunas	ESDF	139 051	...	...	...	...	...	...	...
Matanzas	ESDF	125 466	...	...	...	...	...	...	...
Pinar del Río	ESDF	148 300	...	...	...	...	...	...	...
Sancti Spíritus	ESDF	105 568	...	...	...	...	...	...	...
Santa Clara	ESDF	210 568	...	...	...	...	...	...	...
Santiago de Cuba	ESDF	443 064	...	...	...	...	...	...	...
Dominica — Dominique									
1 VII 1991									
ROSEAU	CDFC	16 243	...	...	...	...	...	...	...
Dominican Republic — République dominicaine									
1 VII 2001									
San Pedro de Macoris	ESDF	266 629	...	...	...	...	...	...	...
Santiago de los Caballeros	ESDF	836 614	...	...	...	...	...	...	...
SANTO DOMINGO	ESDF	2 677 056	...	...	...	...	...	...	...
El Salvador[15]									
27 IX 1992									
Apopa	CDFC	109 179	52 651	56 528	52	...	...	...	...
Ciudad Delgado	CDFC	109 863	52 941	56 922	33	...	...	...	...
Mejicanos	CDFC	144 855	68 449	76 406	22	...	...	...	...
Nueva San Salvador	CDFC	113 698	52 528	61 170	112	...	...	...	...
SAN SALVADOR	CDFC	415 346	191 072	224 274	72	...	...	...	...
San Miguel	CDFC	191 116	91 065	100 051	594	...	...	...	...
Santa Ana	CDFC	210 970	101 015	109 955	400	...	...	...	...
Soyapango	CDFC	261 122	123 922	137 200	30	...	...	...	...
1 VII 2002									
Ahuachapan	ESDF	112 794	...	...	245	...	...	...	...
Apopa	ESDF	186 064	...	...	52	...	...	...	...

(See notes at end of table. — Voir notes à la fin du tableau.)

Continent, country or area, date and city / Continent, pays ou zone, date et ville	Code[1]	City proper — Ville proprement dite Population				Urban agglomeration — Agglomération urbaine Population			
		Both sexes Les deux sexes	Male Masculin	Female Féminin	Surface area Superficie (km²)	Both sexes Les deux sexes	Male Masculin	Female Féminin	Surface area Superficie (km²)
AMERICA, NORTH — AMERIQUE DU NORD									
El Salvador[15]									
1 VII 2002									
Ciudad Delgado	ESDF	160 684	...	...	33	...	...	...	...
Cuscatancingo	ESDF	101 276	...	...	5	...	...	...	...
Ilopango	ESDF	140 945	...	...	35	...	...	...	...
Mejicanos	ESDF	197 273	...	...	22	...	...	...	...
Nueva San Salvador	ESDF	169 514	...	...	112	...	...	...	...
SAN SALVADOR	ESDF	491 999	...	...	72	...	...	...	...
San Martin	ESDF	118 362	...	...	56	...	...	...	...
San Miguel	ESDF	252 151	...	...	594	...	...	...	...
Santa Ana	ESDF	257 253	...	...	400	...	...	...	...
Sonsonate	ESDF	101 217	...	...	233	...	...	...	...
Soyapango	ESDF	288 694	...	...	30	...	...	...	...
Greenland — Groenland									
1 VII 2000									
NUUK (GODTHAB)	ESDJ	13 552	7 265	6 287	...	...	...	...	...
Grenada — Grenade									
1 VII 1981									
ST. GEORGE'S	CDFC	4 788	...	...	...	...	...	...	...
Guadeloupe									
8 III 1999									
BASSE-TERRE	CDJC	12 377	5 687	6 690	...	44 747	21 252	23 495	...
Pointe-à-Pitre	CDJC	...	...	...	...	171 773	...	...	...
Guatemala									
1 VII 2001									
GUATEMALA	ESDF	1 022 001	491 891	530 110	228	...	...	...	...
Escuintla	ESDF	114 626	57 893	56 733	332	...	...	...	...
Mixco	ESDF	452 134	221 928	230 206	99	...	...	...	...
Quetzaltenango	ESDF	152 223	76 272	75 951	120	...	...	...	...
Villa Nueva	ESDF	390 329	192 238	198 091	114	...	...	...	...
Haiti — Haïti									
1 VII 1999									
Cap-Haitien	ESDJ	113 555	50 064	63 491	10	...	...	...	...
Carrefour	ESDJ	336 222	146 838	189 384	23	...	...	...	...
Delmas	ESDJ	284 079	124 774	159 305	26	...	...	...	...
PORT-AU-PRINCE	ESDJ	990 558	436 170	554 388	21	...	...	...	...
Honduras									
28 VII 2001									
Choloma	CDJC	126 402	59 834	66 568	...	...	...	...	...
La Ceiba	CDJC	126 721	60 313	66 408	...	...	...	...	...
San Pedro Sula	CDJC	483 384	230 662	252 722	...	...	...	...	...
TEGUCIGALPA	CDJC	819 867	385 110	434 757	...	...	...	...	...
Jamaica — Jamaïque									
1 VII 1991									
KINGSTON	CDFC	103 962	...	...	22	538 144	250 369	287 775	...
Martinique									
8 III 1999									
FORT-DE-FRANCE	CDJC	94 152	42 812	51 340	...	134 796	61 705	73 091	...
Mexico — Mexique[16,17]									
1 VII 2002									
Acapulco (de Juárez)	ESDJ	647 093	...	...	...	...	...	...	...
Aguascalientes	ESDJ	...	...	...	...	757 292	...	...	...
Benito Juárez	ESDJ	440 458	...	...	...	...	...	...	...
Campeche	ESDJ	205 935	...	...	...	...	...	...	...
Celaya	ESDJ	297 469	...	...	...	...	...	...	...
Chetumal	ESDJ	134 848	...	...	...	...	...	...	...
Chihuahua	ESDJ	...	...	...	...	738 695	...	...	...
Chilpacingo (de los Bravo)	ESDJ	148 826	...	...	...	...	...	...	...
Ciudad Acuña	ESDJ	117 744	...	...	...	...	...	...	...
Ciudad Del Carmen	ESDJ	136 011	...	...	...	...	...	...	...
Ciudad Juárez	ESDJ	1 295 248	...	...	...	...	...	...	...
Ciudad Obregón	ESDJ	269 205	...	...	...	...	...	...	...
Ciudad Victoria	ESDJ	273 460	...	...	...	...	...	...	...

8. Population of capital cities and cities of 100 000 and more inhabitants: latest available year
Population des capitales et des villes de 100 000 habitants et plus: dernière année disponible (continued — suite)

(See notes at end of table. — Voir notes à la fin du tableau.)

Continent, country or area, date and city / Continent, pays ou zone, date et ville	Code[1]	City proper — Ville proprement dite Population				Urban agglomeration — Agglomération urbaine Population			
		Both sexes Les deux sexes	Male Masculin	Female Féminin	Surface area Superficie (km²)	Both sexes Les deux sexes	Male Masculin	Female Féminin	Surface area Superficie (km²)
AMERICA, NORTH — AMERIQUE DU NORD									
Mexico — Mexique[16,17]									
1 VII 2002									
Coatzacoalcos	ESDJ	...	...	...	...	636 553	...	...	...
Colimas	ESDJ	...	...	...	...	218 430	...	...	...
Córdoba	ESDJ	111 537	...	...	...	231 995	...	...	...
Cuatlas	ESDJ	...	...	...	...	249 758	...	...	...
Cuernavaca	ESDJ	...	...	...	...	741 083	...	...	...
Culiacán Rosales	ESDJ	560 024	...	...	...	...	...	...	...
Durango (Victoria de Durango)	ESDJ	453 376	...	...	...	...	...	...	...
Ecatepec (de Morelos)	ESDJ	137 587	...	...	...	...	...	...	...
Ensenada	ESDJ	246 305	...	...	...	...	...	...	...
Guadalajara	ESDJ	...	...	...	...	3 863 855	...	...	...
Guaynas	ESDJ	...	...	...	...	193 556	...	...	...
Hermosillo	ESDJ	586 014	...	...	...	...	...	...	...
Iguala (de la Independencia)	ESDJ	109 221	...	...	...	...	...	...	...
Irapuato	ESDJ	341 806	...	...	...	...	...	...	...
La Paz	ESDJ	178 680	...	...	...	...	...	...	...
León (de los Aldama)	ESDJ	...	...	...	...	1 322 767	...	...	...
Los Mochis	ESDJ	208 039	...	...	...	...	...	...	...
Matamoros	ESDJ	413 194	...	...	...	...	...	...	...
Mazatlán	ESDJ	339 634	...	...	...	...	...	...	...
Mérida	ESDJ	...	...	...	...	885 769	...	...	...
Mexicali	ESDJ	606 002	...	...	...	...	...	...	...
MEXICO, CIUDAD DE	ESDJ	8 669 797	...	...	...	18 538 820	...	...	...
Monclova	ESDJ	...	...	...	...	329 743	...	...	...
Monterrey	ESDJ	...	...	...	...	3 436 078	...	...	...
Morelia	ESDJ	582 775	...	...	...	...	...	...	...
Nogales	ESDJ	168 371	...	...	...	...	...	...	...
Nuevo Laredo	ESDJ	330 126	...	...	...	...	...	...	...
Oaxaca de Juárez	ESDJ	...	...	...	...	440 072	...	...	...
Orizaba	ESDJ	...	...	...	...	317 371	...	...	...
Pachuca (de Soto)	CODJ	...	...	...	...	305 322	...	...	...
Poza Rica de Hidalgo	ESDJ	...	...	...	...	219 597	...	...	...
Puebla de Zaragoza	ESDJ	...	...	...	...	2 354 698	...	...	...
Puerto Vallarta	ESDJ	159 104	...	...	...	...	...	...	...
Querétaro	ESDJ	...	...	...	...	844 365	...	...	...
Reynosa	ESDJ	443 325	...	...	...	...	...	...	...
Salamanca	ESDJ	146 726	...	...	...	...	...	...	...
Saltillo	ESDJ	...	...	...	...	693 751	...	...	...
San Cristobal de las Casas	ESDJ	124 469	...	...	...	...	...	...	...
San Luis Potosí	ESDJ	...	...	...	...	897 637	...	...	...
San Luis Rio Colorado	ESDJ	135 944	...	...	...	...	...	...	...
Tampico	ESDJ	...	...	...	...	726 385	...	...	...
Tapachula (de Cordova y Ordoñez)	ESDJ	199 076	...	...	...	...	...	...	...
Tehuacán	ESDJ	216 858	...	...	...	...	...	...	...
Tepic	ESDJ	280 998	...	...	...	...	...	...	...
Tijuana	ESDJ	...	...	...	...	1 404 309	...	...	...
Tlalpan	ESDJ	...	...	...	...	207 445	...	...	...
Toluca (de Lerdo)	ESDJ	...	...	...	...	1 217 251	...	...	...
Torreón	ESDJ	...	...	...	...	1 086 073	...	...	...
Tuxtla Gutiérrez	ESDJ	469 994	...	...	...	...	...	...	...
Uruapan	ESDJ	239 274	...	...	...	...	...	...	...
Veracruz	ESDJ	...	...	...	...	616 165	...	...	...
Villahermosa	ESDJ	349 025	...	...	...	...	...	...	...
Xalapa-Enriquez	ESDJ	...	...	...	...	499 180	...	...	...
Zacatecas	ESDJ	...	...	...	...	246 267	...	...	...
Zamora de Hidalgo	ESDJ	...	...	...	...	228 924	...	...	...
Montserrat									
1 VII 1980									
PLYMOUTH	CDFC	1 478	...	...	...	...	...	...	...

8. Population of capital cities and cities of 100 000 and more inhabitants: latest available year
Population des capitales et des villes de 100 000 habitants et plus: dernière année disponible (continued — suite)

(See notes at end of table. — Voir notes à la fin du tableau.)

Continent, country or area, date and city Continent, pays ou zone, date et ville	Code[1]	City proper — Ville proprement dite Population				Urban agglomeration — Agglomération urbaine Population			
		Both sexes Les deux sexes	Male Masculin	Female Féminin	Surface area Superficie (km²)	Both sexes Les deux sexes	Male Masculin	Female Féminin	Surface area Superficie (km²)
AMERICA, NORTH — AMERIQUE DU NORD									
Netherlands Antilles — Antilles néerlandaises									
1 VII 1992									
WILLEMSTAD	CDJC	2 345	...	...	...	...	...	...	...
Nicaragua									
1 VII 2000									
Chinandega	ESDF	...	...	...	...	247 336	121 653	125 683	...
Granada	ESDF	...	...	...	...	115 315	56 191	59 124	...
Leon	ESDF	...	...	...	...	216 695	104 524	112 171	...
MANAGUA	ESDF	...	...	...	...	1 147 730	555 720	592 010	...
Masaya	ESDF	...	...	...	...	170 683	83 729	86 954	...
Panama									
1 VII 2000									
PANAMA[18]	ESDF	484 261	230 747	253 514	107	...	...	...	...
San Miguelito	ESDF	331 692	161 901	169 791	50	...	...	...	...
Puerto Rico — Porto Rico[19]									
1 VII 2002									
Arecibo	ESDJ	101 283	...	...	326	...	...	...	...
Bayamón	ESDJ	224 670	...	...	115	...	...	...	...
Caguas	ESDJ	141 693	...	...	152	...	...	...	...
Carolina	ESDJ	187 468	...	...	117	...	...	...	...
Guaynabo	ESDJ	101 280	...	...	70	...	...	...	...
Ponce[20]	ESDJ	186 112	...	...	297	...	...	...	...
SAN JUAN[21]	ESDJ	433 412	...	...	124	...	...	...	...
Saint Kitts-Nevis — Saint-Kitts-et-Nevis									
1 VII 1980									
BASSETERRE	CDFC	14 161	...	...	...	...	...	...	...
Saint Lucia — Sainte-Lucie									
22 V 2001									
CASTRIES	CDFC	11 092	5 238	5 854	...	...	...	...	...
Saint Pierre and Miquelon — Saint Pierre-et-Miquelon									
8 III 1999									
SAINT-PIERRE	CDFC	5 618	...	...	...	...	...	...	...
Saint Vincent and the Grenadines — Saint Vincent-et-les Grenadines									
12 V 1991									
KINGSTOWN	CDFC	15 466	...	...	...	...	...	...	...
Trinidad and Tobago — Trinité-et-Tobago									
1 VII 1996									
PORT-OF-SPAIN	ESDF	43 396	20 739	22 657	12	...	...	...	...
Turks and Caicos Islands — Iles Turques et Caïques									
1 VII 1990									
GRAND TURK	CDFC	3 691	...	...	...	...	...	...	...
United States — Etats-Unis[22,23]									
1 IV 2000									
Abilene (TX)	CDJC	115 930	58 529	57 401	...	...	...	...	...
Akron (OH)	CDJC	217 074	103 670	113 404	...	570 215	273 779	296 436	...
Albuquerque (NM)	CDJC	448 607	217 887	230 720	...	598 191	291 380	306 811	...
Alexandria (VA)[24]	CDJC	128 283	61 974	66 309	...	...	...	...	...
Allentown (PA)	CDJC	106 632	51 037	55 595	...	576 408	277 504	298 904	...
Amarillo (TX)	CDJC	173 627	83 370	90 257	...	179 312	88 361	90 951	...
Anaheim (CA)[25]	CDJC	328 014	164 058	163 956	...	...	...	...	...
Anchorage (AK)	CDJC	260 283	131 668	128 615	...	...	...	...	...
Ann Arbor (MI)	CDJC	114 024	56 352	57 672	...	283 904	140 009	143 895	...
Arlington (TX)[26]	CDJC	332 969	166 465	166 504	...	...	...	...	...
Arlington (VA)[24]	CDJC	189 453	95 443	94 010	...	...	...	...	...
Arvada (CO)[27]	CDJC	102 153	50 021	52 132	...	...	...	...	...
Athens (GA)	CDJC	101 489	49 532	51 957	...	106 482	51 880	54 602	...
Atlanta (GA)	CDJC	416 474	206 725	209 749	...	3 499 840	1 726 532	1 773 308	...

8. Population of capital cities and cities of 100 000 and more inhabitants: latest available year
Population des capitales et des villes de 100 000 habitants et plus: dernière année disponible (continued — suite)

(See notes at end of table. — Voir notes à la fin du tableau.)

Continent, country or area, date and city / Continent, pays ou zone, date et ville	Code[1]	City proper — Ville proprement dite Population				Urban agglomeration — Agglomération urbaine Population			
		Both sexes Les deux sexes	Male Masculin	Female Féminin	Surface area Superficie (km²)	Both sexes Les deux sexes	Male Masculin	Female Féminin	Surface area Superficie (km²)
AMERICA, NORTH — AMERIQUE DU NORD									
United States — Etats-Unis[22,23]									
1 IV 2000									
Augusta-Richmond (GA)	CDJC	199 775	96 375	103 400	...	335 630	161 488	174 142	...
Aurora (CO)[27]	CDJC	276 393	136 901	139 492	...	...	...	...	...
Aurora (IL)[28]	CDJC	142 990	72 020	70 970	...	...	...	...	...
Austin (TX)	CDJC	656 562	337 569	318 993	...	901 920	459 585	442 335	...
Bakersfield (CA)	CDJC	247 057	120 105	126 952	...	396 125	193 835	202 290	...
Baltimore (MD)	CDJC	651 154	303 687	347 467	...	2 076 354	992 299	1 084 055	...
Baton Rouge (LA)	CDJC	227 818	108 255	119 563	...	479 019	229 835	249 184	...
Beaumont (TX)	CDJC	113 866	54 142	59 724	...	139 304	66 185	73 119	...
Bellevue (WA)[29]	CDJC	109 569	54 347	55 222	...	...	...	...	...
Berkeley (CA)[30]	CDJC	102 743	50 456	52 287	...	...	...	...	...
Birmingham (AL)	CDJC	242 820	112 046	130 774	...	663 615	311 940	351 675	...
Boise City (ID)	CDJC	185 787	92 014	93 773	...	272 625	135 444	137 181	...
Boston (MA)	CDJC	589 141	283 588	305 553	...	4 032 484	1 943 524	2 088 960	...
Bridgeport (CT)	CDJC	139 529	66 554	72 975	...	888 890	427 957	460 933	...
Brownsville (TX)	CDJC	139 722	65 783	73 939	...	165 776	78 553	87 223	...
Buffalo (NY)	CDJC	292 648	137 443	155 205	...	976 703	462 511	514 192	...
Burbank (CA)[25]	CDJC	100 316	48 635	51 681	...	...	...	...	...
Cambridge (MA)[31]	CDJC	101 355	49 674	51 681	...	...	...	...	...
Cape Coral (FL)	CDJC	102 286	49 584	52 702	...	329 757	160 034	169 723	...
Carrollton (TX)[26]	CDJC	109 576	54 275	55 301	...	...	...	...	...
Cedar Rapids (IA)	CDJC	120 758	58 833	61 925	...	155 334	75 686	79 648	...
Chandler (AZ)[32]	CDJC	176 581	88 140	88 441	...	...	...	...	...
Charlotte (NC)	CDJC	540 828	264 978	275 850	...	758 927	372 894	386 033	...
Chattanooga (TN)	CDJC	155 554	73 370	82 184	...	343 509	163 502	180 007	...
Chesapeake (VA)[33]	CDJC	199 184	96 728	102 456	...	...	...	...	...
Chicago (IL)	CDJC	2 896 016	1 405 107	1 490 909	...	8 307 904	4 055 013	4 252 891	...
Chula Vista (CA)[34]	CDJC	173 556	84 237	89 319	...	...	...	...	...
Cincinnati (OH)	CDJC	331 285	156 357	174 928	...	1 503 262	725 248	778 014	...
Clarksville (TN)	CDJC	103 455	51 950	51 505	...	121 775	63 266	58 509	...
Clearwater (FL)[35]	CDJC	108 787	52 065	56 722	...	...	...	...	...
Cleveland (OH)	CDJC	478 403	226 550	251 853	...	1 786 647	849 505	937 142	...
Colorado Springs (CO)	CDJC	360 890	178 469	182 421	...	466 122	233 696	232 426	...
Columbia (SC)	CDJC	116 278	56 999	59 279	...	420 537	202 432	218 105	...
Columbus (GA)	CDJC	186 291	90 617	95 674	...	242 324	119 409	122 915	...
Columbus (OH)	CDJC	711 470	345 878	365 592	...	1 133 193	551 065	582 128	...
Concord (CA)	CDJC	121 780	60 147	61 633	...	552 624	270 187	282 437	...
Coral Springs (FL)[36]	CDJC	117 549	57 251	60 298	...	...	...	...	...
Corona (CA)[37]	CDJC	124 966	61 849	63 117	...	...	...	...	...
Corpus Christi (TX)	CDJC	277 454	135 572	141 882	...	293 925	143 704	150 221	...
Costa Mesa (CA)[25]	CDJC	108 724	55 694	53 030	...	...	...	...	...
Dallas (TX)	CDJC	1 188 580	598 991	589 589	...	4 145 659	2 063 116	2 082 543	...
Daly City (CA)[30]	CDJC	103 621	50 971	52 650	...	...	...	...	...
Dayton (OH)	CDJC	166 179	80 142	86 037	...	703 444	338 473	364 971	...
Denver (CO)	CDJC	554 636	280 207	274 429	...	1 984 887	991 426	993 461	...
Des Moines (IA)	CDJC	198 682	96 157	102 525	...	370 505	179 494	191 011	...
Detroit (MI)	CDJC	951 270	448 319	502 951	...	3 903 377	1 889 137	2 014 240	...
Downey (CA)[25]	CDJC	107 323	52 176	55 147	...	...	...	...	...
Durham (NC)	CDJC	187 035	89 884	97 151	...	287 796	137 048	150 748	...
El Monte (CA)[25]	CDJC	115 965	58 584	57 381	...	...	...	...	...
El Paso (TX)	CDJC	563 662	267 651	296 011	...	674 801	325 037	349 764	...
Elizabeth (NJ)[38]	CDJC	120 568	59 674	60 894	...	...	...	...	...
Erie (PA)	CDJC	103 717	49 355	54 362	...	194 804	93 306	101 498	...
Escondido (CA)[34]	CDJC	133 559	66 233	67 326	...	...	...	...	...
Eugene (OR)	CDJC	137 893	67 540	70 353	...	224 049	109 745	114 304	...
Evansville (IN)	CDJC	121 582	57 170	64 412	...	211 989	100 474	111 515	...
Fayetteville (NC)	CDJC	121 015	57 967	63 048	...	172 585	85 786	86 799	...
Flint (MI)	CDJC	124 943	58 704	66 239	...	365 096	173 954	191 142	...
Fontana (CA)[37]	CDJC	128 929	63 982	64 947	...	...	...	...	...
Fort Collins (CO)	CDJC	118 652	59 593	59 059	...	206 633	103 085	103 548	...
Fort Lauderdale (FL)[36]	CDJC	152 397	79 826	72 571	...	...	...	...	...
Fort Wayne (IN)	CDJC	205 727	99 659	106 068	...	287 759	140 309	147 450	...

8. Population of capital cities and cities of 100 000 and more inhabitants: latest available year
Population des capitales et des villes de 100 000 habitants et plus: dernière année disponible (continued — suite)

(See notes at end of table. — Voir notes à la fin du tableau.)

Continent, country or area, date and city / Continent, pays ou zone, date et ville	Code[1]	City proper — Ville proprement dite Population				Urban agglomeration — Agglomération urbaine Population			
		Both sexes Les deux sexes	Male Masculin	Female Féminin	Surface area Superficie (km²)	Both sexes Les deux sexes	Male Masculin	Female Féminin	Surface area Superficie (km²)
AMERICA, NORTH — AMERIQUE DU NORD									
United States — Etats-Unis[22,23]									
1 IV 2000									
Fort Worth (TX)[26]	CDJC	534 694	263 720	270 974	...	...	...	...	...
Fremont (CA)[30]	CDJC	203 413	102 273	101 140	...	...	...	...	...
Fresno (CA)	CDJC	427 652	210 107	217 545	...	554 923	271 889	283 034	...
Fullerton (CA)[25]	CDJC	126 003	62 276	63 727	...	...	...	...	...
Garden Grove (CA)[25]	CDJC	165 196	82 688	82 508	...	...	...	...	...
Garland (TX)[26]	CDJC	215 768	106 937	108 831	...	...	...	...	...
Gary (IN)[28]	CDJC	102 746	47 088	55 658	...	...	...	...	...
Gilbert (AZ)[32]	CDJC	109 697	54 531	55 166	...	...	...	...	...
Glendale (AZ)[32]	CDJC	218 812	109 168	109 644	...	...	...	...	...
Glendale (CA)[25]	CDJC	194 973	93 074	101 899	...	...	...	...	...
Grand Prairie (TX)[26]	CDJC	127 427	63 058	64 369	...	...	...	...	...
Grand Rapids (MI)	CDJC	197 800	96 761	101 039	...	539 080	263 464	275 616	...
Green Bay (WI)	CDJC	102 313	50 433	51 880	...	187 316	92 661	94 655	...
Greensboro (NC)	CDJC	223 891	105 573	118 318	...	267 884	127 184	140 700	...
Hampton (VA)[33]	CDJC	146 437	72 579	73 858	...	...	...	...	...
Hartford (CT)	CDJC	121 578	58 071	63 507	...	851 535	406 302	445 233	...
Hayward (CA)[30]	CDJC	140 030	69 490	70 540	...	...	...	...	...
Henderson (NV)[39]	CDJC	175 381	87 001	88 380	...	...	...	...	...
Hialeah (FL)[36]	CDJC	226 419	108 893	117 526	...	...	...	...	...
Hollywood (FL)[36]	CDJC	139 357	67 577	71 780	...	...	...	...	...
Honolulu (HI)	CDJC	371 657	182 628	189 029	...	718 182	359 930	358 252	...
Houston (TX)	CDJC	1 953 631	975 551	978 080	...	3 822 509	1 903 082	1 919 427	...
Huntington Beach (CA)[25]	CDJC	189 594	95 004	94 590	...	...	...	...	...
Huntsville (AL)	CDJC	158 216	76 174	82 042	...	213 253	104 854	108 399	...
Independence (MO)[40]	CDJC	113 288	54 173	59 115	...	...	...	...	...
Indianapolis (IN)	CDJC	791 926	383 035	408 891	...	1 218 919	592 172	626 747	...
Inglewood (CA)[25]	CDJC	112 580	53 423	59 157	...	...	...	...	...
Irvine (CA)[25]	CDJC	143 072	69 235	73 837	...	...	...	...	...
Irving (TX)[26]	CDJC	191 615	97 687	93 928	...	...	...	...	...
Jackson (MS)	CDJC	184 256	85 656	98 600	...	292 637	137 618	155 019	...
Jacksonville (FL)	CDJC	735 617	356 284	379 333	...	882 295	427 937	454 358	...
Jersey City (NJ)[38]	CDJC	240 055	117 144	122 911	...	...	...	...	...
Joliet (IL)[28]	CDJC	106 221	52 623	53 598	...	...	...	...	...
Kansas City (KS)[40]	CDJC	146 866	71 769	75 097	...	...	...	...	...
Kansas City (MO)	CDJC	441 545	213 141	228 404	...	1 361 744	659 663	702 081	...
Knoxville (TN)	CDJC	173 890	82 390	91 500	...	419 830	201 687	218 143	...
Lafayette (LA)	CDJC	110 257	53 158	57 099	...	178 079	86 129	91 950	...
Lakewood (CO)[27]	CDJC	144 126	71 141	72 985	...	...	...	...	...
Lancaster (CA)	CDJC	118 718	60 257	58 461	...	263 532	131 583	131 949	...
Lansing (MI)	CDJC	119 128	57 186	61 942	...	300 032	143 861	156 171	...
Laredo (TX)	CDJC	176 576	84 704	91 872	...	...	...	...	...
Las Vegas (NV)	CDJC	478 434	243 077	235 357	...	1 314 357	666 831	647 526	...
Lexington-Fayette (KY)	CDJC	260 512	127 905	132 607	...	...	...	...	...
Lincoln (NE)	CDJC	225 581	112 361	113 220	...	226 582	112 952	113 630	...
Little Rock (AR)	CDJC	183 133	86 322	96 811	...	360 331	171 576	188 755	...
Livonia (MI)[41]	CDJC	100 545	48 718	51 827	...	...	...	...	...
Long Beach (CA)[25]	CDJC	461 522	226 718	234 804	...	...	...	...	...
Los Angeles (CA)	CDJC	3 694 820	1 841 805	1 853 015	...	11 789 487	5 834 856	5 954 631	...
Louisville (KY)	CDJC	256 231	121 153	135 078	...	863 582	413 482	450 100	...
Lowell (MA)[31]	CDJC	105 167	51 807	53 360	...	...	...	...	...
Lubbock (TX)	CDJC	199 564	97 023	102 541	...	202 225	98 607	103 618	...
Madison (WI)	CDJC	208 054	102 248	105 806	...	329 533	161 918	167 615	...
Manchester (NH)	CDJC	107 006	52 394	54 612	...	143 549	70 246	73 303	...
McAllen (TX)	CDJC	106 414	50 438	55 976	...	523 144	253 443	269 701	...
Memphis (TN)	CDJC	650 100	307 643	342 457	...	972 091	464 365	507 726	...
Mesa (AZ)[32]	CDJC	396 375	196 378	199 997	...	...	...	...	...
Mesquite (TX)[26]	CDJC	124 523	59 987	64 536	...	...	...	...	...
Miami (FL)	CDJC	362 470	180 194	182 276	...	4 919 036	2 371 683	2 547 353	...
Milwaukee (WI)	CDJC	596 974	285 363	311 611	...	1 308 913	631 147	677 766	...
Minneapolis (MN)	CDJC	382 618	192 232	190 386	...	2 388 593	1 172 421	1 216 172	...
Mobile (AL)	CDJC	198 915	93 015	105 900	...	317 605	150 166	167 439	...

8. Population of capital cities and cities of 100 000 and more inhabitants: latest available year
Population des capitales et des villes de 100 000 habitants et plus: dernière année disponible (continued — suite)

(See notes at end of table. — Voir notes à la fin du tableau.)

Continent, country or area, date and city / Continent, pays ou zone, date et ville	Code[1]	City proper — Ville proprement dite Population				Urban agglomeration — Agglomération urbaine Population			
		Both sexes Les deux sexes	Male Masculin	Female Féminin	Surface area Superficie (km²)	Both sexes Les deux sexes	Male Masculin	Female Féminin	Surface area Superficie (km²)
AMERICA, NORTH — AMERIQUE DU NORD									
United States — Etats-Unis[22,23]									
1 IV 2000									
Modesto (CA)	CDJC	188 856	91 572	97 284	...	310 945	152 392	158 553	...
Montgomery (AL)	CDJC	201 568	94 573	106 995	...	...	...	...	...
Moreno Valley (CA)[37]	CDJC	142 381	69 645	72 736	...	...	...	...	...
Naperville (IL)[28]	CDJC	128 358	62 831	65 527	...	...	...	...	...
Nashville-Davidson (TN)	CDJC	569 891	275 865	294 026	...	749 935	363 237	386 698	...
New Haven (CT)	CDJC	123 626	59 185	64 441	...	531 314	255 062	276 252	...
New Orleans (LA)	CDJC	484 674	227 094	257 580	...	1 009 283	478 904	530 379	...
New York (NY)	CDJC	8 008 278	3 794 204	4 214 074	...	17 799 861	8 531 001	9 268 860	...
Newark (NJ)[38]	CDJC	273 546	132 701	140 845	...	...	...	...	...
Newport News (VA)[33]	CDJC	180 150	87 178	92 972	...	...	...	...	...
Norfolk (VA)[33]	CDJC	234 403	119 830	114 573	...	...	...	...	...
North Las Vegas (NV)[39]	CDJC	115 488	58 947	56 541	...	...	...	...	...
Norwalk (CA)[25]	CDJC	103 298	51 109	52 189	...	...	...	...	...
Oakland (CA)[30]	CDJC	399 484	192 757	206 727	...	...	...	...	...
Oceanside (CA)[34]	CDJC	161 029	79 719	81 310	...	...	...	...	...
Oklahoma City (OK)	CDJC	506 132	247 313	258 819	...	747 003	361 768	385 235	...
Omaha (NE)	CDJC	390 007	190 032	199 975	...	626 623	306 737	319 886	...
Ontario (CA)[25]	CDJC	158 007	79 225	78 782	...	...	...	...	...
Orange (CA)[25]	CDJC	128 821	64 665	64 156	...	...	...	...	...
Orlando (FL)	CDJC	185 951	90 080	95 871	...	1 157 431	569 693	587 738	...
Overland Park (KS)[40]	CDJC	149 080	72 170	76 910	...	...	...	...	...
Oxnard (CA)	CDJC	170 358	87 090	83 268	...	337 591	170 338	167 253	...
Palmdale (CA)[42]	CDJC	116 670	57 338	59 332	...	...	...	...	...
Pasadena (CA)[25]	CDJC	133 936	65 495	68 441	...	...	...	...	...
Pasadena (TX)[43]	CDJC	141 674	70 767	70 907	...	...	...	...	...
Paterson (NJ)[38]	CDJC	149 222	72 473	76 749	...	...	...	...	...
Pembroke Pines (FL)[36]	CDJC	137 427	64 044	73 383	...	...	...	...	...
Peoria (AZ)[32]	CDJC	108 364	52 058	56 306	...	...	...	...	...
Peoria (IL)	CDJC	112 936	53 471	59 465	...	247 172	118 965	128 207	...
Philadelphia (PA)	CDJC	1 517 550	705 107	812 443	...	5 149 079	2 458 575	2 690 504	...
Phoenix (AZ)	CDJC	1 321 045	671 760	649 285	...	2 907 049	1 451 459	1 455 590	...
Pittsburgh (PA)	CDJC	334 563	159 119	175 444	...	1 753 136	830 794	922 342	...
Plano (TX)[26]	CDJC	222 030	110 619	111 411	...	...	...	...	...
Pomona (CA)[25]	CDJC	149 473	75 630	73 843	...	...	...	...	...
Portland (OR)	CDJC	529 121	261 565	267 556	...	1 583 138	782 186	800 952	...
Portsmouth (VA)[33]	CDJC	100 565	48 583	51 982	...	...	...	...	...
Providence (RI)	CDJC	173 618	83 035	90 583	...	1 174 548	562 552	611 996	...
Provo (UT)	CDJC	105 166	50 572	54 594	...	303 680	149 740	153 940	...
Pueblo (CO)	CDJC	102 121	49 442	52 679	...	123 351	60 082	63 269	...
Raleigh (NC)	CDJC	276 093	136 648	139 445	...	541 527	268 248	273 279	...
Rancho Cucamonga (CA)[25]	CDJC	127 743	63 895	63 848	...	...	...	...	...
Reno (NV)	CDJC	180 480	92 254	88 226	...	303 689	153 751	149 938	...
Richmond (VA)	CDJC	197 790	92 068	105 722	...	818 836	388 082	430 754	...
Riverside (CA)	CDJC	255 166	125 705	129 461	...	1 506 816	744 245	762 571	...
Rochester (NY)	CDJC	219 773	105 083	114 690	...	694 396	333 601	360 795	...
Rockford (IL)	CDJC	150 115	72 384	77 731	...	270 414	132 078	138 336	...
Sacramento (CA)	CDJC	407 018	197 784	209 234	...	1 393 498	679 713	713 785	...
St. Louis (MO)	CDJC	348 189	163 567	184 622	...	2 077 662	989 609	1 088 053	...
St. Paul (MN)[44]	CDJC	287 151	138 863	148 288	...	...	...	...	...
St. Petersburg (FL)[35]	CDJC	248 232	118 411	129 821	...	...	...	...	...
Salem (OR)	CDJC	136 924	68 752	68 172	...	207 229	103 225	104 004	...
Salinas (CA)	CDJC	151 060	80 361	70 699	...	179 173	94 641	84 532	...
Salt Lake City (UT)	CDJC	181 743	92 045	89 698	...	887 650	447 308	440 342	...
San Antonio (TX)	CDJC	1 144 646	553 245	591 401	...	1 327 554	644 527	683 027	...
San Bernardino (CA)[37]	CDJC	185 401	91 150	94 251	...	...	...	...	...
San Buenaventura (CA)[45]	CDJC	100 916	49 654	51 262	...	...	...	...	...
San Diego (CA)	CDJC	1 223 400	616 884	606 516	...	2 674 436	1 340 333	1 334 103	...
San Francisco (CA)	CDJC	776 733	394 828	381 905	...	2 995 769	1 483 586	1 512 183	...
San Jose (CA)	CDJC	894 943	454 798	440 145	...	1 538 312	780 426	757 886	...
Santa Ana (CA)[25]	CDJC	337 977	175 219	162 758	...	...	...	...	...
Santa Clara (CA)[46]	CDJC	102 361	52 086	50 275	...	...	...	...	...

8. Population of capital cities and cities of 100 000 and more inhabitants: latest available year
Population des capitales et des villes de 100 000 habitants et plus: dernière année disponible (continued — suite)

(See notes at end of table. — Voir notes à la fin du tableau.)

Continent, country or area, date and city / Continent, pays ou zone, date et ville	Code[1]	City proper — Ville proprement dite Population				Urban agglomeration — Agglomération urbaine Population			
		Both sexes Les deux sexes	Male Masculin	Female Féminin	Surface area Superficie (km²)	Both sexes Les deux sexes	Male Masculin	Female Féminin	Surface area Superficie (km²)
AMERICA, NORTH — AMERIQUE DU NORD									
United States — Etats-Unis[22,23]									
1 IV 2000									
Santa Clarita (CA)	CDJC	151 088	74 764	76 324	...	170 481	84 389	86 092	...
Santa Rosa (CA)	CDJC	147 595	72 078	75 517	...	285 408	139 279	146 129	...
Savannah (GA)	CDJC	131 510	62 039	69 471	...	208 886	100 295	108 591	...
Scottsdale (AZ)[32]	CDJC	202 705	97 785	104 920	...	...	...	...	...
Seattle (WA)	CDJC	563 374	280 973	282 401	...	2 712 205	1 348 157	1 364 048	...
Shreveport (LA)	CDJC	200 145	93 333	106 812	...	275 213	129 928	145 285	...
Simi Valley (CA)	CDJC	111 351	55 098	56 253	...	112 345	55 613	56 732	...
Sioux Falls (SD)	CDJC	123 975	61 120	62 855	...	124 269	61 294	62 975	...
South Bend (IN)	CDJC	107 789	51 383	56 406	...	276 498	133 001	143 497	...
Spokane (WA)	CDJC	195 629	94 267	101 362	...	334 858	162 346	172 512	...
Springfield (IL)	CDJC	111 454	52 370	59 084	...	153 516	72 705	80 811	...
Springfield (MA)	CDJC	152 082	71 802	80 280	...	573 610	275 874	297 736	...
Springfield (MO)	CDJC	151 580	73 016	78 564	...	215 004	103 722	111 282	...
Stamford (CT)[47]	CDJC	117 083	56 622	60 461	...	...	...	...	...
Sterling Heights (MI)[41]	CDJC	124 471	60 970	63 501	...	...	...	...	...
Stockton (CA)	CDJC	243 771	118 751	125 020	...	313 392	154 676	158 716	...
Sunnyvale (CA)[46]	CDJC	131 760	67 783	63 977	...	...	...	...	...
Syracuse (NY)	CDJC	147 306	69 308	77 998	...	402 267	191 058	211 209	...
Tacoma (WA)[29]	CDJC	193 556	94 419	99 137	...	...	...	...	...
Tallahassee (FL)	CDJC	150 624	71 137	79 487	...	204 260	96 906	107 354	...
Tampa (FL)	CDJC	303 447	148 050	155 397	...	2 062 339	993 534	1 068 805	...
Tempe (AZ)[32]	CDJC	158 625	81 942	76 683	...	...	...	...	...
Thousand Oaks (CA)	CDJC	117 005	57 440	59 565	...	210 990	103 703	107 287	...
Toledo (OH)	CDJC	313 619	150 204	163 415	...	503 008	241 733	261 275	...
Topeka (KS)	CDJC	122 377	58 759	63 618	...	142 411	68 617	73 794	...
Torrance (CA)[25]	CDJC	137 946	67 087	70 859	...	...	...	...	...
Tucson (AZ)	CDJC	486 699	238 408	248 291	...	720 425	349 836	370 589	...
Tulsa (OK)	CDJC	393 049	189 937	203 112	...	558 329	270 413	287 916	...
Vallejo (CA)	CDJC	116 760	56 553	60 207	...	158 967	77 207	81 760	...
Vancouver (WA)[48]	CDJC	143 560	70 644	72 916	...	...	...	...	...
Virginia Beach (VA)	CDJC	425 257	210 524	214 733	...	1 394 439	686 732	707 707	...
Waco (TX)	CDJC	113 726	54 295	59 431	...	153 198	73 707	79 491	...
Warren (MI)[41]	CDJC	138 247	67 560	70 687	...	3 933 920	1 909 345	2 024 575	...
WASHINGTON (DC)	CDJC	572 059	269 366	302 693	...	189 026	90 406	98 620	...
Waterbury (CT)	CDJC	107 271	50 781	56 490	...	...	...	...	...
West Covina (CA)[25]	CDJC	105 080	51 019	54 061	...	...	...	...	...
West Valley City (UT)[49]	CDJC	108 896	55 078	53 818	...	...	...	...	...
Westminster (CO)[27]	CDJC	100 940	50 509	50 431	...	...	...	...	...
Wichita (KS)	CDJC	344 284	169 604	174 680	...	422 301	208 080	214 221	...
Wichita Falls (TX)	CDJC	104 197	53 657	50 540	...	...	...	...	...
Winston-Salem (NC)	CDJC	185 776	87 345	98 431	...	299 290	142 748	156 542	...
Worcester (MA)	CDJC	172 648	82 914	89 734	...	429 882	207 809	222 073	...
Yonkers (NY)[38]	CDJC	196 086	92 132	103 954	...	...	...	...	...
United States Virgin Islands — Iles Vierges américaines[19]									
1 IV 2000									
CHARLOTTE AMALIE	CDFC	11 004	...	...	...	18 914	...	...	...
AMERICA, SOUTH — AMERIQUE DU SUD									
Argentina — Argentine									
1 VII 1991									
Avellaneda	CDFC	344 024	...	...	...	...	...	...	...
Bahía Blanca	CDFC	260 096	...	...	...	...	...	...	...
BUENOS AIRES	CDFC	2 965 403	...	...	...	11 298 030	...	...	...
Catamarca	CDFC	109 882	...	...	...	132 626	...	...	...
Comodoro Rivadavia	CDFC	124 104	...	...	...	...	...	...	...
Concordia	CDFC	116 485	...	...	...	...	...	...	...
Córdoba	CDFC	1 157 507	...	...	...	1 208 554	...	...	...
Corrientes	CDFC	258 103	...	...	...	...	...	...	...

8. Population of capital cities and cities of 100 000 and more inhabitants: latest available year
Population des capitales et des villes de 100 000 habitants et plus: dernière année disponible (continued — suite)

(See notes at end of table. — Voir notes à la fin du tableau.)

Continent, country or area, date and city / Continent, pays ou zone, date et ville	Code[1]	City proper — Ville proprement dite Population				Urban agglomeration — Agglomération urbaine Population			
		Both sexes Les deux sexes	Male Masculin	Female Féminin	Surface area Superficie (km²)	Both sexes Les deux sexes	Male Masculin	Female Féminin	Surface area Superficie (km²)
AMERICA, SOUTH — AMERIQUE DU SUD									
Argentina — Argentine									
1 VII 1991									
Formosa	CDFC	147 636	...	...	...		...	...	...
General San Martín	CDFC	406 809	...	...	...	...	...	...	...
La Matanza	CDFC	1 120 088	...	...	...	...	...	...	...
Lanus	CDFC	468 561	...	...	...	...	...	...	...
La Plata	CDFC	521 936	...	...	...	642 979	...	...	...
Lomas de Zamora	CDFC	574 330	...	...	...		...	...	...
Mar del Plata	CDFC	512 880	...	...	...		...	...	...
Mendoza	CDFC	121 620	...	...	...	773 113	...	...	...
Morón	CDFC	643 553	...	...	...		...	...	...
Neuquén	CDFC	167 296	...	...	...	183 579	...	...	...
Paraná	CDFC	207 041	...	...	...	211 936	...	...	...
Posadas	CDFC	201 273	...	...	...	210 755	...	...	...
Quilmes	CDFC	511 234	...	...	...		...	...	...
Resistencia	CDFC	229 212	...	...	...	292 287	...	...	...
Río Cuarto	CDFC	134 355	...	...	...	138 853	...	...	...
Rosario	CDFC	907 718	...	...	...	1 118 905	...	...	...
Salta	CDFC	367 550	...	...	...	370 904	...	...	...
San Fernando	CDFC	141 063	...	...	...		...	...	...
San Isidro	CDFC	299 023	...	...	...		...	...	...
San Juan	CDFC	119 423	...	...	...	352 691	...	...	...
San Miguel de Tucumán	CDFC	470 809	...	...	...	622 324	...	...	...
San Nicolás	CDFC	119 302	...	...	...		...	...	...
San Salvador de Jujuy	CDFC	178 748	...	...	...	180 102	...	...	...
Santa Fé	CDFC	353 063	...	...	...	406 388	...	...	...
Santiago del Estero	CDFC	189 947	...	...	...	263 471	...	...	...
Vicente López	CDFC	289 505	...	...	...		...	...	...
Bolivia — Bolivie									
5 IX 2001									
Cochabamba	CDFC	778 422	374 428	403 994	...	...	...	...	...
El Alto	CDFC	694 740	340 497	354 252	...	...	...	...	...
LA PAZ[50]	CDFC	1 487 248	718 617	768 631	...	...	...	...	...
Oruro	CDFC	202 010	97 164	104 846	...	...	...	...	...
Potosí	CDFC	133 268	63 662	69 606	...	...	...	...	...
Santa Cruz	CDFC	1 114 095	545 303	568 792	...	...	...	...	...
SUCRE[50]	CDFC	194 888	92 142	102 746	...	...	...	...	...
Tarija	CDFC	135 651	65 027	70 624	...	...	...	...	...
Brazil — Brésil									
1 VII 2002									
Abaeteluba	ESDF	...	...	...	...	*125 055*	...	...	
Aguas Lindas de Goiás	ESDF	...	...	...	...	*132 076*	...	...	1 090
Alagoinhas	ESDF	...	...	...	...	*134 162*	...	...	...
Alvorada	ESDF	...	...	...	...	*196 882*	...	...	761
Americana	ESDF	...	...	...	...	*191 451*	...	...	...
Ananindeua	ESDF	...	...	...	...	*437 135*	...	...	...
Anápolis	ESDF	...	...	...	...	*298 155*	...	...	485
Angra dos Reis	ESDF	...	...	...	...	*129 621*	...	...	...
Aparecida de Goiania	ESDF	...	...	...	...	*385 037*	...	...	...
Apucarana	ESDF	...	...	...	...	*111 759*	...	...	556
Aracaju	ESDF	...	...	...	...	*479 767*	...	...	151
Araçatuba	ESDF	...	...	...	...	*174 399*	...	...	2 668
Araguaina	ESDF	...	...	...	...	*120 213*	...	...	...
Araguario	ESDF	...	...	...	...	*105 267*	...	...	...
Arapiraca	ESDF	...	...	...	...	*193 103*	...	...	...
Araraquara	ESDF	...	...	...	...	*189 634*	...	...	...
Araras	ESDF	...	...	...	...	*109 352*	...	...	...
Araucária	ESDF	...	...	...	...	*104 284*	...	...	...
Atibaia	ESDF	...	...	...	...	*118 990*	...	...	...
Bagé	ESDF	...	...	...	...	*118 016*	...	...	7 185
Barbacena	ESDF	...	...	...	...	*118 492*	...	...	...
Barueri	ESDF	...	...	...	...	*232 150*	...	...	...
Barra Mansa	ESDF	...	...	...	...	*173 003*	...	...	830

(See notes at end of table. — Voir notes à la fin du tableau.)

Continent, country or area, date and city / Continent, pays ou zone, date et ville	Code[1]	City proper — Ville proprement dite Population				Urban agglomeration — Agglomération urbaine Population			
		Both sexes Les deux sexes	Male Masculin	Female Féminin	Surface area Superficie (km²)	Both sexes Les deux sexes	Male Masculin	Female Féminin	Surface area Superficie (km²)
AMERICA, SOUTH — AMERIQUE DU SUD									
Brazil — Brésil									
1 VII 2002									
Barreiras	ESDF	...	...	...	...	123 609	...	...	...
Barretos	ESDF	...	...	...	...	106 531	...	...	...
Bauru	ESDF	...	...	...	...	332 993	...	...	702
Belém	ESDF	...	...	...	...	1 342 202	...	...	736
Belford Roxo	ESDF	...	...	...	...	457 201	...	...	...
Belo Horizonte	ESDF	...	...	...	...	2 305 812	...	...	335
Betim	ESDF	...	...	...	...	348 491	...	...	376
Birigui	ESDF	...	...	...	...	100 207	...	...	...
Blumenou	ESDF	...	...	...	...	277 144	...	...	509
Boa Vista	ESDF	...	...	...	...	221 027	...	...	...
Botucatu	ESDF	...	...	...	...	113 711	...	...	...
Bragança Paulista	ESDF	...	...	...	...	132 779	...	...	770
BRASILIA	ESDF	...	...	...	...	2 189 789	...	...	5 794
Cabo de Santo Agostinho	ESDF	...	...	...	...	160 968	...	...	...
Cabo Frio	ESDF	...	...	...	...	142 984	...	...	...
Cachoeirinha	ESDF	...	...	...	...	113 531	...	...	...
Cachoeiro de Itapemirim	ESDF	...	...	...	...	184 578	...	...	892
Camacari	ESDF	...	...	...	...	176 541	...	...	718
Camaragibe	ESDF	...	...	...	...	137 727	...	...	...
Cametá	ESDF	...	...	...	...	101 455	...	...	...
Campina Grande	ESDF	...	...	...	...	365 559	...	...	970
Campinas	ESDF	...	...	...	...	1 006 918	...	...	781
Campo Grande	ESDF	...	...	...	...	705 975	...	...	8 091
Campos dos Goytacazes	ESDF	...	...	...	...	416 441	...	...	4 536
Canoas	ESDF	...	...	...	...	317 442	...	...	...
Carapicuíba	ESDF	...	...	...	...	363 368	...	...	...
Cariacica	ESDF	...	...	...	...	339 612	...	...	279
Caruaru	ESDF	...	...	...	...	265 937	...	...	936
Cascavel	ESDF	...	...	...	...	261 505	...	...	2 074
Castanhal	ESDF	...	...	...	...	144 485	...	...	1 003
Catanduva	ESDF	...	...	...	...	110 489	...	...	...
Caucaia	ESDF	...	...	...	...	276 781	...	...	1 293
Caxias	ESDF	...	...	...	...	141 686	...	...	6 724
Caxias do Sul	ESDF	...	...	...	...	381 940	...	...	1 601
Chapecó	ESDF	...	...	...	...	157 927	...	...	...
Codo	ESDF	...	...	...	...	112 793	...	...	4 923
Colatina	ESDF	...	...	...	...	106 902	...	...	2 094
Colombo	ESDF	...	...	...	...	203 526	...	...	...
Conselheiro Lafaiete	ESDF	...	...	...	...	107 080	...	...	...
Contagem	ESDF	...	...	...	...	565 258	...	...	167
Coronel Fabriciano	ESDF	...	...	...	...	100 535	...	...	...
Cotia	ESDF	...	...	...	...	161 782	...	...	...
Crato	ESDF	...	...	...	...	108 998	...	...	...
Criciúma	ESDF	...	...	...	...	177 844	...	...	...
Cubatao	ESDF	...	...	...	...	113 599	...	...	...
Cuiabá	ESDF	...	...	...	...	508 156	...	...	3 922
Curitiba	ESDF	...	...	...	...	1 671 194	...	...	427
Diadema	ESDF	...	...	...	...	373 014	...	...	...
Divinópolis	ESDF	...	...	...	...	193 974	...	...	716
Dourados	ESDF	...	...	...	...	173 872	...	...	4 082
Duque de Caxias	ESDF	...	...	...	...	808 614	...	...	463
Embu	ESDF	...	...	...	...	223 581	...	...	...
Feira de Santana	ESDF	...	...	...	...	503 900	...	...	1 344
Ferraz de Vasconcelos	ESDF	...	...	...	...	156 613	...	...	...
Florianópolis	ESDF	...	...	...	...	369 102	...	...	440
Fortaleza	ESDF	...	...	...	...	2 256 233	...	...	336
Foz do Iguaçu	ESDF	...	...	...	...	279 620	...	...	596
Franca	ESDF	...	...	...	...	304 569	...	...	...
Francisco Morato	ESDF	...	...	...	...	149 096	...	...	...
Franco da Rocha	ESDF	...	...	...	...	115 080	...	...	...
Garanhuns	ESDF	...	...	...	...	122 188	...	...	456

(See notes at end of table. — Voir notes à la fin du tableau.)

Continent, country or area, date and city / Continent, pays ou zone, date et ville	Code[1]	City proper — Ville proprement dite Population				Urban agglomeration — Agglomération urbaine Population			
		Both sexes Les deux sexes	Male Masculin	Female Féminin	Surface area Superficie (km²)	Both sexes Les deux sexes	Male Masculin	Female Féminin	Surface area Superficie (km²)
AMERICA, SOUTH — AMERIQUE DU SUD									
Brazil — Brésil									
1 VII 2002									
Goiânia	ESDF	...	...	...	...	1 146 106	...	...	788
Governador Valadares	ESDF	...	...	...	...	252 247	...	...	2 447
Gravatai	ESDF	...	...	...	...	248 523	...	...	...
Guaratinguetá	ESDF	...	...	...	...	107 884	...	...	...
Guarapuava	ESDF	...	...	...	...	160 932	...	...	5 365
Guarujá	ESDF	...	...	...	...	281 634	...	...	...
Guarulhos	ESDF	...	...	...	...	1 160 468	...	...	...
Hortolandia	ESDF	...	...	...	...	173 060	...	...	...
Ibirité	ESDF	...	...	...	...	149 955	...	...	...
Ilhéus	ESDF	...	...	...	...	221 627	...	...	1 712
Imperatriz	ESDF	...	...	...	...	231 397	...	...	6 014
Indaiatuba	ESDF	...	...	...	...	161 252	...	...	...
Ipatinga	ESDF	...	...	...	...	222 485	...	...	231
Itabiraí	ESDF	...	...	...	...	102 239	...	...	...
Itaboraí	ESDF	...	...	...	...	201 443	...	...	569
Itabuna	ESDF	...	...	...	...	200 186	...	...	...
Itajaí	ESDF	...	...	...	...	156 077	...	...	...
Itapetininga	ESDF	...	...	...	...	132 869	...	...	2 035
Itapecerica da Serra	ESDF	...	...	...	...	143 253	...	...	...
Itapevi	ESDF	...	...	...	...	179 209	...	...	...
Itaquaquecetuba	ESDF	...	...	...	...	306 208	...	...	...
Itu	ESDF	...	...	...	...	144 008	...	...	640
Jaboatao dos Guarapes	ESDF	...	...	...	...	610 648	...	...	...
Jacareí	ESDF	...	...	...	...	199 739	...	...	...
Jandira	ESDF	...	...	...	...	100 775	...	...	...
Jaraguá do Sul	ESDF	...	...	...	...	118 199	...	...	...
Jaú	ESDF	...	...	...	...	117 645	...	...	...
Jequié	ESDF	...	...	...	...	147 951	...	...	3 113
Ji-Paraná	ESDF	...	...	...	...	109 573	...	...	...
Joao Pessoa	ESDF	...	...	...	...	628 838	...	...	...
Joinville	ESDF	...	...	...	...	461 576	...	...	1 080
Juazeiro	ESDF	...	...	...	...	188 676	...	...	5 615
Juàzeiro do Norte	ESDF	...	...	...	...	224 014	...	...	...
Juiz de Fora	ESDF	...	...	...	...	478 607	...	...	1 424
Jundiaí	ESDF	...	...	...	...	333 910	...	...	432
Lages	ESDF	...	...	...	...	162 060	...	...	5 287
Lauro de Freitas	ESDF	...	...	...	...	127 182	...	...	...
Limeira	ESDF	...	...	...	...	261 761	...	...	...
Linhares	ESDF	...	...	...	...	116 945	...	...	4 388
Londrina	ESDF	...	...	...	...	467 334	...	...	2 129
Luziânia	ESDF	...	...	...	...	160 330	...	...	4 653
Macae	ESDF	...	...	...	...	144 207	...	...	...
Macapá	ESDF	...	...	...	...	318 761	...	...	...
Maceió	ESDF	...	...	...	...	849 734	...	...	517
Magé	ESDF	...	...	...	...	218 821	...	...	744
Manaus	ESDF	...	...	...	...	1 527 314	...	...	11 349
Maraba	ESDF	...	...	...	...	181 683	...	...	14 320
Maracanau	ESDF	...	...	...	...	186 688	...	...	...
Marília	ESDF	...	...	...	...	208 492	...	...	1 194
Maringá	ESDF	...	...	...	...	303 551	...	...	490
Mauá	ESDF	...	...	...	...	384 461	...	...	...
Mesquita	ESDF	...	...	...	...	174 045	...	...	...
Moji das Cruzes	ESDF	...	...	...	...	347 821	...	...	749
Moji-Guaçu	ESDF	...	...	...	...	131 451	...	...	960
Montes Claros	ESDF	...	...	...	...	324 471	...	...	4 135
Mossoró	ESDF	...	...	...	...	220 487	...	...	2 108
Natal	ESDF	...	...	...	...	744 794	...	...	...
Nilópolis	ESDF	...	...	...	...	152 363	...	...	...
Niterói	ESDF	...	...	...	...	466 628	...	...	131
Nossa Senhora do Socorro	ESDF	...	...	...	...	151 427	...	...	...
Nova Friburgo	ESDF	...	...	...	...	175 370	...	...	930

243

8. Population of capital cities and cities of 100 000 and more inhabitants: latest available year
Population des capitales et des villes de 100 000 habitants et plus: dernière année disponible (continued — suite)

(See notes at end of table. — Voir notes à la fin du tableau.)

Continent, country or area, date and city / Continent, pays ou zone, date et ville	Code[1]	City proper — Ville proprement dite Population				Urban agglomeration — Agglomération urbaine Population			
		Both sexes Les deux sexes	Male Masculin	Female Féminin	Surface area Superficie (km²)	Both sexes Les deux sexes	Male Masculin	Female Féminin	Surface area Superficie (km²)
AMERICA, SOUTH — AMERIQUE DU SUD									
Brazil — Brésil									
1 VII 2002									
Nova Iguaçu	ESDF	...	...	...	...	792 208	...	...	795
Nôvo Hamburgo	ESDF	...	...	...	...	245 597	...	...	...
Olinda	ESDF	...	...	...	...	376 068	...	...	...
Osasco	ESDF	...	...	...	...	678 583	...	...	...
Palhoça	ESDF	...	...	...	...	113 312	...	...	...
Palmas	ESDF	...	...	...	...	172 176	...	...	...
Paranaguá	ESDF	...	...	...	...	135 923	...	...	1 015
Parnaíba	ESDF	...	...	...	...	137 030	...	...	1 053
Parnamirim	ESDF	...	...	...	...	143 598	...	...	...
Passo Fundo	ESDF	...	...	...	...	176 729	...	...	1 596
Passos	ESDF	...	...	...	...	101 089	...	...	...
Patos de Minas	ESDF	...	...	...	...	130 330	...	...	3 336
Paulista	ESDF	...	...	...	...	277 870	...	...	...
Pelotas	ESDF	...	...	...	...	331 372	...	...	1 924
Petrolina	ESDF	...	...	...	...	235 821	...	...	6 116
Petrópolis	ESDF	...	...	...	...	296 108	...	...	771
Pindamonhangaba	ESDF	...	...	...	...	133 408	...	...	719
Pinhais	ESDF	...	...	...	...	111 447	...	...	...
Piracicaba	ESDF	...	...	...	...	344 698	...	...	1 426
Poà	ESDF	...	...	...	...	101 808	...	...	...
Poços de Caldas	ESDF	...	...	...	...	143 484	...	...	533
Ponta Grossa	ESDF	...	...	...	...	286 685	...	...	2 212
Porto Alegre	ESDF	...	...	...	...	1 394 085	...	...	...
Porto Seguro	ESDF	...	...	...	...	114 531	...	...	...
Porto Velho	ESDF	...	...	...	...	353 961	...	...	...
Pouso Alegre	ESDF	...	...	...	...	114 459	...	...	...
Praia Grande	ESDF	...	...	...	...	215 174	...	...	...
Presidente Prudente	ESDF	...	...	...	...	196 488	...	...	554
Queimados	ESDF	...	...	...	...	129 131	...	...	...
Recife	ESDF	...	...	...	...	1 461 320	...	...	...
Resende	ESDF	...	...	...	...	110 876	...	...	...
Ribeirao das Neves	ESDF	...	...	...	...	278 574	...	...	...
Ribeirao Prêto	ESDF	...	...	...	...	527 733	...	...	...
Ribeirao Pires	ESDF	...	...	...	...	110 491	...	...	...
Rio Branco	ESDF	...	...	...	...	274 555	...	...	...
Rio Claro	ESDF	...	...	...	...	177 452	...	...	503
Rio de Janeiro	ESDF	...	...	...	...	5 974 081	...	...	1 256
Rio Grande	ESDF	...	...	...	...	190 894	...	...	2 825
Rio Verde	ESDF	...	...	...	...	124 753	...	...	9 136
Rondonópolis	ESDF	...	...	...	...	158 391	...	...	4 594
Sabára	ESDF	...	...	...	...	123 242	...	...	...
Salvador	ESDF	...	...	...	...	2 556 429	...	...	313
Santa Bárbara D'Oeste	ESDF	...	...	...	...	177 722	...	...	...
Santa Cruz do Sul	ESDF	...	...	...	...	112 705	...	...	...
Santa Luzia (Minas Gerais)	ESDF	...	...	...	...	199 406	...	...	...
Santa Maria	ESDF	...	...	...	...	254 640	...	...	3 279
Santa Rita	ESDF	...	...	...	...	122 446	...	...	...
Santarém	ESDF	...	...	...	...	268 180	...	...	...
Santo André	ESDF	...	...	...	...	659 294	...	...	...
Santos	ESDF	...	...	...	...	418 147	...	...	725
Sao Bernardo do Campo	ESDF	...	...	...	...	745 161	...	...	319
Sao Caetano do Sul	ESDF	...	...	...	...	137 276	...	...	...
Sao Carlo	ESDF	...	...	...	...	203 711	...	...	1 120
Sao Gonçalo	ESDF	...	...	...	...	925 402	...	...	...
Sao Joao de Meriti	ESDF	...	...	...	...	456 778	...	...	...
Sao José	ESDF	...	...	...	...	185 039	...	...	...
Sao José de Ribamar	ESDF	...	...	...	...	118 725	...	...	...
Sao José do Rio Prêto	ESDF	...	...	...	...	382 274	...	...	586
Sao José dos Campos	ESDF	...	...	...	...	569 177	...	...	1 186
Sao José dos Pinhais	ESDF	...	...	...	...	227 994	...	...	923
Sao Leopoldo	ESDF	...	...	...	...	201 446	...	...	...

(See notes at end of table. — Voir notes à la fin du tableau.)

Continent, country or area, date and city / Continent, pays ou zone, date et ville	Code[1]	City proper — Ville proprement dite Population				Urban agglomeration — Agglomération urbaine Population			
		Both sexes Les deux sexes	Male Masculin	Female Féminin	Surface area Superficie (km²)	Both sexes Les deux sexes	Male Masculin	Female Féminin	Surface area Superficie (km²)
AMERICA, SOUTH — AMERIQUE DU SUD									
Brazil — Brésil									
1 VII 2002									
Sao Luís	ESDF	...	...	...	...	923 526	...	...	822
Sao Paulo	ESDF	...	...	...	...	10 677 019	...	...	1 493
Sao Vicente	ESDF	...	...	...	...	314 312	...	...	...
Sapucaia do Sul	ESDF	...	...	...	...	128 255	...	...	...
Serra	ESDF	...	...	...	...	351 686	...	...	549
Sete Lagoas	ESDF	...	...	...	...	197 457	...	...	...
Simoes Filho	ESDF	...	...	...	...	100 702	...	...	...
Sobral	ESDF	...	...	...	...	163 836	...	...	1 646
Sorocaba	ESDF	...	...	...	...	528 729	...	...	...
Sumaré	ESDF	...	...	...	...	213 886	...	...	208
Susano	ESDF	...	...	...	...	250 208	...	...	...
Taboao da Serra	ESDF	...	...	...	...	209 215	...	...	...
Taubaté	ESDF	...	...	...	...	255 625	...	...	...
Teixeira de Freitas	ESDF	...	...	...	...	114 208	...	...	...
Teófilo Otoni	ESDF	...	...	...	...	128 634	...	...	...
Teresina	ESDF	...	...	...	...	751 464	...	...	1 356
Teresópolis	ESDF	...	...	...	...	143 433	...	...	768
Timon	ESDF	...	...	...	...	136 547	...	...	1 702
Toledo	ESDF	...	...	...	...	101 882	...	...	...
Uberaba	ESDF	...	...	...	...	265 823	...	...	4 524
Uberlândia	ESDF	...	...	...	...	542 541	...	...	4 040
Uruguaiana	ESDF	...	...	...	...	130 866	...	...	6 763
Valparaiso de Goiás	ESDF	...	...	...	...	106 970	...	...	...
Varginha	ESDF	...	...	...	...	115 460	...	...	...
Varzea Grande	ESDF	...	...	...	...	231 736	...	...	900
Varzea Paulista	ESDF	...	...	...	...	100 156	...	...	...
Viamao	ESDF	...	...	...	...	241 826	...	...	...
Vila Velha	ESDF	...	...	...	...	370 727	...	...	...
Vitória	ESDF	...	...	...	...	302 633	...	...	...
Vitória da Conquista	ESDF	...	...	...	...	274 016	...	...	3 743
Vitória de Santo Antao	ESDF	...	...	...	...	120 924	...	...	344
Volta Redonda	ESDF	...	...	...	...	248 766	...	...	...
Votorantim	ESDF	...	...	...	...	100 607	...	...	...
Chile — Chili									
1 VII 2002									
Antofagasta	ESDF	257 207	126 807	130 400	...	...	...	...	...
Arica	ESDF	189 743	94 142	95 601	...	...	...	...	...
Calama	ESDF	132 669	67 037	65 632	...	...	...	...	...
Chillán	ESDF	176 863	84 145	92 718	...	...	...	...	...
Concepción	ESDF	391 733	191 631	200 102	...	...	...	...	...
Copiapó	ESDF	127 504	64 719	62 785	...	...	...	...	...
Coquimbo	ESDF	141 796	69 022	72 774	...	...	...	...	...
Iquique	ESDF	175 677	89 698	85 979	...	...	...	...	...
La Serena	ESDF	135 526	65 476	70 050	...	...	...	...	...
Los Angeles	ESDF	121 649	59 268	62 381	...	...	...	...	...
Osorno	ESDF	135 204	65 076	70 128	...	...	...	...	...
Puente Alto	ESDF	458 906	224 970	233 936	...	...	...	...	...
Puerto Montt	ESDF	144 880	71 064	73 816	...	...	...	...	...
Punta Arenas	ESDF	126 586	65 204	61 382	...	...	...	...	...
Quilpué	ESDF	124 586	58 601	65 985	...	...	...	...	...
Rancagua	ESDF	221 881	107 635	114 246	...	...	...	...	...
San Bernardo	ESDF	262 623	131 378	131 245	...	...	...	...	...
SANTIAGO[51]	ESDF	4 886 629	2 350 058	2 536 571	...	...	...	...	...
Talca	ESDF	187 513	89 436	98 077	...	...	...	...	...
Talcahuano	ESDF	288 666	141 793	146 873	...	...	...	...	...
Temuco	ESDF	287 326	137 389	149 937	...	...	...	...	...
Valdivia	ESDF	128 533	62 578	65 955	...	...	...	...	...
Valparaíso	ESDF	285 389	139 970	145 419	...	...	...	...	...
Viña del Mar	ESDF	350 221	167 602	182 619	...	...	...	...	...

8. Population of capital cities and cities of 100 000 and more inhabitants: latest available year
Population des capitales et des villes de 100 000 habitants et plus: dernière année disponible (continued — suite)

(See notes at end of table. — Voir notes à la fin du tableau.)

Continent, country or area, date and city / Continent, pays ou zone, date et ville	Code[1]	City proper — Ville proprement dite Population				Urban agglomeration — Agglomération urbaine Population			
		Both sexes Les deux sexes	Male Masculin	Female Féminin	Surface area Superficie (km²)	Both sexes Les deux sexes	Male Masculin	Female Féminin	Surface area Superficie (km²)
AMERICA, SOUTH — AMERIQUE DU SUD									
Colombia — Colombie									
1 VII 2002									
Armenia	ESDF	305 551	...	...	115	...	...	...	...
Barrancabermeja	ESDF	202 167	...	...	1 274	...	...	...	...
Barranquilla	ESDF	1 305 334	...	...	166	...	...	...	...
Bello	ESDF	369 844	...	...	151	...	...	...	...
Bucaramanga	ESDF	549 263	...	...	154	...	...	...	...
Buenaventura	ESDF	271 401	...	...	6 785	...	...	...	...
Buga	ESDF	128 943	...	...	873	...	...	...	...
Cali	ESDF	2 264 256	...	...	552	...	...	...	...
Cartagena	ESDF	952 523	...	...	570	...	...	...	...
Cartago	ESDF	135 365	...	...	260	...	...	...	...
Ciénaga	ESDF	120 451	...	...	...	...	...	...	...
Cúcuta	ESDF	682 325	...	...	1 098	...	...	...	...
Dos Quebradas	ESDF	181 738	...	...	80	...	...	...	...
Duitama	ESDF	116 681	...	...	229	...	...	...	...
Envigado	ESDF	160 287	...	...	51	...	...	...	...
Florencia (Caquetá)	ESDF	138 500	...	...	2 292	...	...	...	...
Floridablanca	ESDF	243 568	...	...	101	...	...	...	...
Fusagasuga	ESDF	105 178	...	...	...	...	...	...	...
Girardot	ESDF	124 520	...	...	130	...	...	...	...
Girón	ESDF	111 406	...	...	...	...	...	...	...
Ibagué	ESDF	435 074	...	...	1 439	...	...	...	...
Itagüi	ESDF	260 406	...	...	17	...	...	...	...
Lorica	ESDF	122 521	...	...	...	...	...	...	...
Magangué	ESDF	160 187	...	...	...	...	...	...	...
Maicao	ESDF	127 156	...	...	2 229	...	...	...	...
Manizales	ESDF	372 278	...	...	477	...	...	...	...
Medellín	ESDF	2 026 789	...	...	387	...	...	...	...
Montería	ESDF	334 596	...	...	3 043	...	...	...	...
Neiva	ESDF	348 920	...	...	1 468	...	...	...	...
Palmira	ESDF	283 431	...	...	1 044	...	...	...	...
Pasto	ESDF	398 333	...	...	1 181	...	...	...	...
Popayán	ESDF	230 137	...	...	464	...	...	...	...
Pereira	ESDF	488 839	...	...	702	...	...	...	...
Sahagún	ESDF	128 933	...	...	...	...	...	...	...
SANTA FE DE BOGOTA	ESDF	6 712 247	...	...	1 605	...	...	...	...
Santa Marta	ESDF	410 309	...	...	2 369	...	...	...	...
Sincelejo	ESDF	248 356	...	...	292	...	...	...	...
Soacha	ESDF	297 192	...	...	187	...	...	...	...
Sogamoso	ESDF	154 785	...	...	214	...	...	...	...
Soledad	ESDF	320 115	...	...	67	...	...	...	...
Tuluá	ESDF	184 723	...	...	818	...	...	...	...
Tumaco	ESDF	159 182	...	...	...	...	...	...	...
Tunja	ESDF	122 832	...	...	118	...	...	...	...
Turbo	ESDF	118 752	...	...	...	...	...	...	...
Valledupar	ESDF	339 814	...	...	4 225	...	...	...	...
Villavicencio	ESDF	340 295	...	...	1 328	...	...	...	...
Ecuador — Equateur									
1 VII 2000									
Ambato	ESDF	174 261	...	...	27	...	...	...	...
Cuenca	ESDF	278 035	...	...	47	...	...	...	...
Esmeraldas	ESDF	125 914	...	...	8	...	...	...	...
Guayaquil	ESDF	2 117 553	...	...	193	...	...	...	...
Ibarra	ESDF	136 558	...	...	39	...	...	...	...
Loja	ESDF	127 200	...	...	21	...	...	...	...
Machala	ESDF	216 901	...	...	23	...	...	...	...
Manta	ESDF	168 642	...	...	38	...	...	...	...
Milagro	ESDF	126 433	...	...	17	...	...	...	...
Portoviejo	ESDF	180 641	...	...	38	...	...	...	...
Quevedo	ESDF	133 996	...	...	20	...	...	...	...
QUITO	ESDF	1 615 809	...	...	170	...	...	...	...
Riobamba	ESDF	126 101	...	...	24	...	...	...	...

(See notes at end of table. — Voir notes à la fin du tableau.)

Continent, country or area, date and city / Continent, pays ou zone, date et ville	Code[1]	City proper — Ville proprement dite Population				Urban agglomeration — Agglomération urbaine Population			
		Both sexes Les deux sexes	Male Masculin	Female Féminin	Surface area Superficie (km²)	Both sexes Les deux sexes	Male Masculin	Female Féminin	Surface area Superficie (km²)
AMERICA, SOUTH — AMERIQUE DU SUD									
Ecuador — Equateur									
1 VII 2000									
Santo Domingo de los Colorados	ESDF	211 732	...	...	43	...	...	...	...
Falkland Islands (Malvinas) — Iles Falkland (Malvinas)									
8 IV 2001									
STANLEY	CDFC	1 989	1 009	980	...	...	...	...	...
French Guiana — Guyane Française									
1 VII 1999									
CAYENNE[9]	CDFC	50 395	24 496	25 899	24	...	...	...	...
Guyana									
1 VII 2001									
GEORGETOWN	ESDF	...	...	...	...	280 000	...	...	...
Paraguay									
28 VIII 2002									
ASUNCION[52]	CDFC	513 399	...	...	117	1 620 483	...	...	...
Capiatá	CDFC	154 469	...	...	...	...	...	...	...
Ciudad del Este	CDFC	223 350	...	...	57	333 535	...	...	...
Fernando de la Mora	CDFC	114 332	...	...	...	...	...	...	...
Lambaré	CDFC	119 984	...	...	...	...	...	...	...
Luque	CDFC	170 433	...	...	...	...	...	...	...
San Lorenzo	CDFC	202 745	...	...	91	...	...	...	...
Peru — Pérou[53]									
I VII 2002									
Arequipa	ESDF	760 329	...	...	...	...	...	...	...
Ayacucho	ESDF	132 498	...	...	...	...	...	...	...
Cajamarca	ESDF	118 699	...	...	...	...	...	...	...
Callao	ESDF	707 108	...	...	...	...	...	...	...
Chiclayo	ESDF	491 292	...	...	...	...	...	...	...
Chimbote	ESDF	337 114	...	...	...	...	...	...	...
Cuzco	ESDF	301 342	...	...	...	...	...	...	...
Huancayo	ESDF	321 390	...	...	...	...	...	...	...
Huánuco	ESDF	157 024	...	...	...	...	...	...	...
Ica	ESDF	217 696	...	...	...	...	...	...	...
Iquitos	ESDF	362 531	...	...	...	...	...	...	...
Juliaca	ESDF	186 292	...	...	...	...	...	...	...
LIMA[54]	ESDF	6 958 428	...	...	...	...	...	...	...
Piura	ESDF	346 041	...	...	...	...	...	...	...
Pucallpa	ESDF	231 059	...	...	...	...	...	...	...
Sullana	ESDF	170 503	...	...	...	...	...	...	...
Tacna	ESDF	243 600	...	...	...	...	...	...	...
Trujillo	ESDF	611 007	...	...	...	...	...	...	...
Suriname									
1 VII 1995									
PARAMARIBO	ESDF	216 000	...	...	183	265 000	...	...	626
Uruguay									
1 VII 1996									
MONTEVIDEO	CDFC	1 303 182	605 658	697 524	530	...	...	...	...
Venezuela									
1 VII 1998									
Acarigua-Araure	ESDF	227 684	...	...	1 065	...	...	...	...
Barcelona	ESDF	301 595	...	...	463	...	...	...	...
Barcelona-Puerto La Cruz	ESDF	484 149	...	...	707	...	...	...	...
Barinas	ESDF	221 558	...	...	848	...	...	...	...
Barquisimeto	ESDF	810 809	...	...	2 645	...	...	...	...
Cabimas	ESDF	213 290	...	...	175	...	...	...	...
CARACAS[55]	ESDF	1 975 294	...	...	433	...	...	...	...
Carúpano	ESDF	116 107	...	...	203	...	...	...	...
Catia la Mar	ESDF	117 013	...	...	76	...	...	...	...
Ciudad Bolívar	ESDF	278 525	...	...	5 851	...	...	...	...
Ciudad Guayana	ESDF	641 998	...	...	1 612	...	...	...	...
Coro	ESDF	167 048	...	...	438	...	...	...	...
Cumaná	ESDF	265 621	...	...	405	...	...	...	...

8. Population of capital cities and cities of 100 000 and more inhabitants: latest available year
Population des capitales et des villes de 100 000 habitants et plus: dernière année disponible (continued — suite)

(See notes at end of table. — Voir notes à la fin du tableau.)

Continent, country or area, date and city Continent, pays ou zone, date et ville	Code[1]	City proper — Ville proprement dite Population				Urban agglomeration — Agglomération urbaine Population			
		Both sexes Les deux sexes	Male Masculin	Female Féminin	Surface area Superficie (km²)	Both sexes Les deux sexes	Male Masculin	Female Féminin	Surface area Superficie (km²)
AMERICA, SOUTH — AMERIQUE DU SUD									
Venezuela									
1 VII 1998									
Guarenas	ESDF	169 202	...	...	180	...	...	...	...
Los Teques	ESDF	176 292	...	...	98	...	...	...	...
Maracaibo	ESDF	1 706 547	...	...	604	...	...	...	...
Maracay	ESDF	458 761	...	...	169	...	...	...	...
Maturín	ESDF	262 167	...	...	...	...	...	...	...
Mérida	ESDF	272 437	...	...	482	...	...	...	...
Puerto Cabello	ESDF	176 347	...	...	309	...	...	...	...
Punto Fijo	ESDF	118 126	...	...	31	...	...	...	...
San Cristóbal	ESDF	272 374	...	...	248	...	...	...	...
San Fernando de Apure	ESDF	121 949	...	...	...	...	...	...	...
Turmero	ESDF	203 434	...	...	208	...	...	...	...
Valencia	ESDF	1 263 888	...	...	1 212	...	...	...	...
Valera	ESDF	121 090	...	...	55	...	...	...	...
ASIA — ASIE									
Afghanistan									
1 VII 1988									
Herat	ESDF	*177 300*	...	...	...	...	...	...	...
KABUL	ESDF	*1 424 400*	...	...	...	...	...	...	...
Kandahar (Quandahar)	ESDF	*225 500*	...	...	...	...	...	...	...
Mazar-i-Sharif	ESDF	*130 600*	...	...	...	...	...	...	...
Armenia — Arménie									
10 X 2001									
Gyumri (Leninakan)	CDJC	107 394	50 284	57 110	50	...	...	...	...
Vanadzor (Kirovakan)	CDJC	150 917	70 846	80 071	25	...	...	...	...
YEREVAN	CDJC	1 103 488	513 546	589 942	227	...	...	...	...
Azerbaijan — Azerbaïdjan									
1 VII 2002									
BAKU	ESDF	1 823 300	888 800	934 500	2 130	...	...	...	...
Ganja	ESDF	301 800	144 900	156 900	110	...	...	...	...
Sumgayit	ESDF	289 000	142 000	147 000	80	...	...	...	...
Bahrain — Bahreïn									
1 VII 1992									
MANAMA	ESDF	*140 401*	...	...	26	...	...	...	...
Bangladesh									
1 VII 1991									
Barisal	CDFC	...	...	...	...	163 481	...	...	...
Chittagong	CDFC	...	...	...	...	1 363 998	...	...	...
Comilla	CDFC	...	...	...	...	143 282	...	...	...
DHAKA	CDFC	...	...	...	...	3 397 187	...	...	...
Dinajpur	CDFC	...	...	...	...	126 189	...	...	...
Jamalpur	CDFC	...	...	...	...	101 242	...	...	...
Jessore	CDFC	...	...	...	...	160 198	...	...	...
Khulna	CDFC	...	...	...	...	545 849	...	...	...
Mymensingh	CDFC	...	...	...	...	185 517	...	...	...
Narayanganj	CDFC	...	...	...	...	268 952	...	...	...
Nawabganj	CDFC	...	...	...	...	121 205	...	...	...
Pabna	CDFC	...	...	...	...	104 479	...	...	...
Rajshahi	CDFC	...	...	...	...	299 671	...	...	...
Rangpur	CDFC	...	...	...	...	203 931	...	...	...
Saidpur	CDFC	...	...	...	...	102 030	...	...	...
Tangail	CDFC	...	...	...	...	104 387	...	...	...
Tongi	CDFC	...	...	...	...	154 175	...	...	...
Bhutan — Bhoutan									
1 VII 2001									
THIMPHU	ESDF	*32 000*	...	...	...	...	...	...	...
Brunei Darussalam — Brunéi Darussalam									
21 VIII 2001									
BANDAR SERI BEGAWAN	CDFC	27 285	13 639	13 646	...	...	...	...	...

(See notes at end of table. — Voir notes à la fin du tableau.)

Continent, country or area, date and city Continent, pays ou zone, date et ville	Code[1]	City proper — Ville proprement dite Population				Urban agglomeration — Agglomération urbaine Population			
		Both sexes Les deux sexes	Male Masculin	Female Féminin	Surface area Superficie (km²)	Both sexes Les deux sexes	Male Masculin	Female Féminin	Surface area Superficie (km²)
ASIA — ASIE									
Cambodia — Cambodge									
1 VII 2002									
Bat Dambang	ESDF	171 382	82 785	88 597	...	...	...	...	...
PHNOM PENH	ESDF	703 963	339 763	364 200	...	1 234 444	...	...	...
Seam Reab	ESDF	140 966	69 052	71 914	...	...	...	...	...
China — Chine									
1 VII 1999									
Chiayi	ESDF	264 286	133 270	131 016	...	...	...	...	...
Hsinchu	ESDF	359 087	183 682	175 405	...	...	...	...	...
Kaohsiung[56]	ESDF	1 468 586	744 243	724 343	...	...	...	...	...
Keelung	ESDF	383 272	196 952	186 320	...	...	...	...	...
Taichung	ESDF	930 175	461 069	469 106	...	...	...	...	...
Tainan	ESDF	725 445	366 061	359 384	...	...	...	...	...
Taipei[56]	ESDF	2 640 322	1 310 368	1 329 954	...	...	...	...	...
1 XI 2000									
Acheng	CDJC	638 894	327 774	311 120	...	...	...	...	...
Akesu	CDJC	561 822	295 811	266 011	...	...	...	...	...
Aletai	CDJC	178 510	91 207	87 303	...	...	...	...	...
Anda	CDJC	473 091	243 349	229 742	...	...	...	...	...
An'guo	CDJC	378 830	189 944	188 886	...	...	...	...	...
Ankang	CDJC	843 426	443 270	400 156	...	...	...	...	...
Anlu	CDJC	611 990	314 089	297 901	...	...	...	...	...
Anning	CDJC	295 173	161 481	133 692	...	...	...	...	...
Anqing	CDJC	582 751	293 884	288 867	...	...	...	...	...
Anqiu	CDJC	1 096 782	554 403	542 379	...	...	...	...	...
Anshan	CDJC	1 556 285	787 838	768 447	...	...	...	...	...
Anshun	CDJC	767 307	395 894	371 413	...	...	...	...	...
Anyang	CDJC	768 992	390 120	378 872	...	...	...	...	...
Atushi	CDJC	200 345	101 867	98 478	...	...	...	...	...
Baicheng	CDJC	484 979	244 453	240 526	...	...	...	...	...
Baise	CDJC	340 483	177 310	163 173	...	...	...	...	...
Baishan	CDJC	335 400	172 109	163 291	...	...	...	...	...
Baiyin	CDJC	460 982	243 672	217 310	...	...	...	...	...
Baoding	CDJC	902 496	455 625	446 871	...	...	...	...	...
Baoji	CDJC	600 377	308 493	291 884	...	...	...	...	...
Baoshan	CDJC	846 865	430 076	416 789	...	...	...	...	...
Baotou	CDJC	1 671 181	862 495	808 686	...	...	...	...	...
Bazhong	CDJC	1 185 862	616 323	569 539	...	...	...	...	...
Bazhou	CDJC	557 901	285 321	272 580	...	...	...	...	...
Beian	CDJC	442 474	226 743	215 731	...	...	...	...	...
Beihai	CDJC	558 635	290 544	268 091	...	...	...	...	...
BEIJING (PEKING)	CDJC	11 509 595	6 020 903	5 488 692	...	...	...	...	...
Beiliu	CDJC	1 049 035	557 967	491 068	...	...	...	...	...
Beining	CDJC	527 217	270 153	257 064	...	...	...	...	...
Beipiao	CDJC	573 836	291 584	282 252	...	...	...	...	...
Bengbu	CDJC	809 399	413 444	395 955	...	...	...	...	...
Benxi	CDJC	980 069	495 102	484 967	...	...	...	...	...
Bijie	CDJC	1 128 230	589 537	538 693	...	...	...	...	...
Binzhou	CDJC	600 883	299 952	300 931	...	...	...	...	...
Bole	CDJC	224 869	116 506	108 363	...	...	...	...	...
Botou	CDJC	550 888	280 209	270 679	...	...	...	...	...
Bozhou	CDJC	1 351 939	697 126	654 813	...	...	...	...	...
Cangzhou	CDJC	443 561	223 648	219 913	...	...	...	...	...
Cenxi	CDJC	731 623	384 212	347 411	...	...	...	...	...
Changchun	CDJC	3 225 557	1 647 216	1 578 341	...	...	...	...	...
Changde	CDJC	1 346 739	686 467	660 272	...	...	...	...	...
Changge	CDJC	646 306	332 022	314 284	...	...	...	...	...
Changji	CDJC	387 169	202 275	184 894	...	...	...	...	...
Changle	CDJC	689 815	358 963	330 852	...	...	...	...	...
Changning	CDJC	795 223	428 332	366 891	...	...	...	...	...
Changsha	CDJC	2 122 873	1 099 304	1 023 569	...	...	...	...	...
Changshu	CDJC	1 239 637	598 034	641 603	...	...	...	...	...
Changyi	CDJC	683 182	340 763	342 419	...	...	...	...	...
Changzhi	CDJC	648 981	332 246	316 735	...	...	...	...	...

(See notes at end of table. — Voir notes à la fin du tableau.)

Continent, country or area, date and city Continent, pays ou zone, date et ville	Code[1]	City proper — Ville proprement dite Population				Urban agglomeration — Agglomération urbaine Population			
		Both sexes Les deux sexes	Male Masculin	Female Féminin	Surface area Superficie (km²)	Both sexes Les deux sexes	Male Masculin	Female Féminin	Surface area Superficie (km²)
ASIA — ASIE									
China — Chine									
1 XI 2000									
Changzhou	CDJC	1 081 845	552 850	528 995	...	...	...	...	...
Chaohu	CDJC	778 864	396 961	381 903	...	...	...	...	...
Chaoyang (Guangdong)	CDJC	2 470 812	1 256 428	1 214 384	...	...	...	...	...
Chaoyang (Liaoning)	CDJC	475 038	238 128	236 910	...	...	...	...	...
Chaozhou	CDJC	363 582	181 260	182 322	...	...	...	...	...
Chengde	CDJC	437 251	221 221	216 030	...	...	...	...	...
Chengdu	CDJC	4 333 541	2 258 996	2 074 545	...	...	...	...	...
Chenghai	CDJC	860 003	428 157	431 846	...	...	...	...	...
Chenzhou	CDJC	655 014	340 799	314 215	...	...	...	...	...
Chibi	CDJC	510 926	267 233	243 693	...	...	...	...	...
Chifeng	CDJC	1 153 723	589 450	564 273	...	...	...	...	...
Chishui	CDJC	251 780	130 227	121 553	...	...	...	...	...
Chizhou	CDJC	555 489	280 395	275 094	...	...	...	...	...
Chongqing	CDJC	9 691 901	5 013 398	4 678 503	...	...	...	...	...
Chongzhou	CDJC	650 698	330 345	320 353	...	...	...	...	...
Chuxiong	CDJC	503 682	261 315	242 367	...	...	...	...	...
Chuzhou	CDJC	493 735	251 117	242 618	...	...	...	...	...
Cixi	CDJC	1 214 537	615 279	599 258	...	...	...	...	...
Conghua	CDJC	517 552	264 150	253 402	...	...	...	...	...
Daan	CDJC	430 512	219 682	210 830	...	...	...	...	...
Dafeng	CDJC	756 766	383 391	373 375	...	...	...	...	...
Dali	CDJC	521 169	262 564	258 605	...	...	...	...	...
Dalian	CDJC	3 245 191	1 641 485	1 603 706	...	...	...	...	...
Dandong	CDJC	780 414	389 277	391 137	...	...	...	...	...
Dangyang	CDJC	495 946	253 125	242 821	...	...	...	...	...
Danjiangkou	CDJC	501 126	262 922	238 204	...	...	...	...	...
Danyang	CDJC	877 232	442 296	434 936	...	...	...	...	...
Danzhou	CDJC	835 465	442 636	392 829	...	...	...	...	...
Daqing	CDJC	1 380 051	704 765	675 286	...	...	...	...	...
Dashiqiao	CDJC	714 670	370 713	343 957	...	...	...	...	...
Datong	CDJC	1 526 744	785 754	740 990	...	...	...	...	...
Daye	CDJC	873 859	460 417	413 442	...	...	...	...	...
Dazhou	CDJC	384 525	192 819	191 706	...	...	...	...	...
Dehui	CDJC	878 349	448 146	430 203	...	...	...	...	...
Dengfeng	CDJC	609 085	321 081	288 004	...	...	...	...	...
Dengta	CDJC	502 149	259 895	242 254	...	...	...	...	...
Dengzhou	CDJC	1 290 656	677 791	612 865	...	...	...	...	...
Dexing	CDJC	297 784	155 178	142 606	...	...	...	...	...
Deyang	CDJC	628 876	324 823	304 053	...	...	...	...	...
Dezhou	CDJC	552 445	277 994	274 451	...	...	...	...	...
Dingzhou	CDJC	1 107 903	559 214	548 689	...	...	...	...	...
Dongfang	CDJC	358 318	188 840	169 478	...	...	...	...	...
Donggang	CDJC	640 340	324 344	315 996	...	...	...	...	...
Dongguan	CDJC	6 445 777	3 035 742	3 410 035	...	...	...	...	...
Dongsheng	CDJC	252 566	129 512	123 054	...	...	...	...	...
Dongtai	CDJC	1 164 653	583 122	581 531	...	...	...	...	...
Dongxing	CDJC	108 131	58 939	49 192	...	...	...	...	...
Dongyang	CDJC	753 094	375 565	377 529	...	...	...	...	...
Dongying	CDJC	788 844	407 241	381 603	...	...	...	...	...
Dujiangyan	CDJC	621 980	314 845	307 135	...	...	...	...	...
Dunhua	CDJC	480 834	247 966	232 868	...	...	...	...	...
Dunhuang	CDJC	187 578	96 679	90 899	...	...	...	...	...
Duyun	CDJC	463 426	241 421	222 005	...	...	...	...	...
Enping	CDJC	464 898	240 765	224 133	...	...	...	...	...
Enshi	CDJC	755 725	397 284	358 441	...	...	...	...	...
Emeishan	CDJC	423 070	217 201	205 869	...	...	...	...	...
Ezhou	CDJC	1 023 285	533 940	489 345	...	...	...	...	...
Fangchenggang	CDJC	422 514	233 979	188 535	...	...	...	...	...
Feicheng	CDJC	948 602	476 032	472 570	...	...	...	...	...
Fengcheng (Jiangxi)	CDJC	1 216 412	644 029	572 383	...	...	...	...	...
Fengcheng (Liaoning)	CDJC	560 384	288 402	271 982	...	...	...	...	...
Fenghua	CDJC	471 558	239 252	232 306	...	...	...	...	...

8. Population of capital cities and cities of 100 000 and more inhabitants: latest available year
Population des capitales et des villes de 100 000 habitants et plus: dernière année disponible (continued — suite)

(See notes at end of table. — Voir notes à la fin du tableau.)

Continent, country or area, date and city / Continent, pays ou zone, date et ville	Code[1]	City proper — Ville proprement dite Population				Urban agglomeration — Agglomération urbaine Population			
		Both sexes Les deux sexes	Male Masculin	Female Féminin	Surface area Superficie (km²)	Both sexes Les deux sexes	Male Masculin	Female Féminin	Surface area Superficie (km²)
ASIA — ASIE									
China — Chine									
1 XI 2000									
Fengnan	CDJC	550 872	285 442	265 430	...	...	...	...	...
Fengzhen	CDJC	264 204	137 562	126 642					
Fenyang	CDJC	387 046	199 129	187 917	...	...	...	...	...
Foshan	CDJC	768 656	398 973	369 683	...	...	...	...	...
Fuan	CDJC	554 057	296 379	257 678					
Fuding	CDJC	521 070	276 419	244 651					
Fujin	CDJC	420 579	215 650	204 929	...	...	...	...	...
Fukang	CDJC	152 965	80 372	72 593	...	...	...	...	...
Fuqing	CDJC	1 174 540	597 890	576 650					
Fuquan	CDJC	292 720	155 972	136 748					
Fushun	CDJC	1 434 447	722 549	711 898	...	...	...	...	...
Fuxin	CDJC	627 855	311 912	315 943					
Fuyang (Anhui)	CDJC	628 633	324 172	304 461	...	...	...	...	...
Fuyang (Zhejiang)	CDJC	1 719 057	878 560	840 497	...	...	...	...	...
Fuzhou (Fujian)	CDJC	2 124 435	1 086 638	1 037 797	...	...	...	...	...
Fuzhou (Jiangxi)	CDJC	1 007 391	533 936	473 455	...	...	...	...	...
Gaizhou	CDJC	883 811	455 641	428 170	...	...	...	...	...
Ganzhou	CDJC	494 600	254 272	240 328					
Gaoan	CDJC	788 329	416 678	371 651	...	...	...	...	...
Gaobeidian	CDJC	538 582	268 027	270 555	...	...	...	...	...
Gaocheng	CDJC	758 269	380 317	377 952	...	...	...	...	...
Gaomi	CDJC	842 403	420 956	421 447					
Gaoming	CDJC	301 041	159 746	141 295					
Gaoping	CDJC	471 671	236 439	235 232	...	...	...	...	...
Gaoyao	CDJC	625 125	314 474	310 651					
Gaoyou	CDJC	797 752	392 863	404 889	...	...	...	...	...
Gaozhou	CDJC	1 219 132	639 497	579 635					
Geermu	CDJC	135 897	73 572	62 325	...	...	...	...	...
Gejiu	CDJC	453 311	243 377	209 934	...	...	...	...	...
Genhe	CDJC	157 337	80 485	76 852					
Gongyi	CDJC	777 202	395 784	381 418	...	...	...	...	...
Gongzhuling	CDJC	1 041 735	532 134	509 601	...	...	...	...	...
Guang'an	CDJC	1 093 103	561 454	531 649	...	...	...	...	...
Guanghan	CDJC	577 298	289 596	287 702	...	...	...	...	...
Guangshui	CDJC	885 936	458 607	427 329	...	...	...	...	...
Guangyuan	CDJC	905 057	467 422	437 635					
Guangzhou	CDJC	8 524 826	4 445 052	4 079 774	...	...	...	...	...
Guigang	CDJC	1 413 128	731 298	681 830	...	...	...	...	...
Guilin	CDJC	804 571	414 004	390 567	...	...	...	...	...
Guiping	CDJC	1 359 035	716 617	642 418	...	...	...	...	...
Guixi	CDJC	535 517	282 662	252 855	...	...	...	...	...
Guiyang	CDJC	2 985 105	1 568 544	1 416 561	...	...	...	...	...
Gujiao	CDJC	205 702	110 105	95 597	...	...	...	...	...
Haerbin	CDJC	3 481 504	1 759 609	1 721 895	...	...	...	...	...
Haicheng	CDJC	1 181 130	606 805	574 325	...	...	...	...	...
Haikou	CDJC	830 192	431 774	398 418	...	...	...	...	...
Hailaer	CDJC	262 184	132 849	129 335	...	...	...	...	...
Hailin	CDJC	435 677	222 525	213 152	...	...	...	...	...
Hailun	CDJC	720 008	368 751	351 257					
Haimen	CDJC	942 952	431 066	511 886	...	...	...	...	...
Haining	CDJC	666 080	331 349	334 731	...	...	...	...	...
Haiyang	CDJC	654 594	329 202	325 392	...	...	...	...	...
Hami	CDJC	388 714	201 005	187 709					
Hancheng	CDJC	387 041	201 881	185 160	...	...	...	...	...
Hanchuan	CDJC	1 057 396	552 093	505 303					
Handan	CDJC	1 329 734	693 882	635 852	...	...	...	...	...
Hangzhou	CDJC	2 451 319	1 301 103	1 150 216					
Hanzhong	CDJC	503 871	258 142	245 729	...	...	...	...	...
Hebi	CDJC	495 336	260 212	235 124	...	...	...	...	...
Hechi	CDJC	318 348	167 526	150 822	...	...	...	...	...
Hechuan	CDJC	1 420 520	732 503	688 017	...	...	...	...	...
Hefei	CDJC	1 659 075	879 749	779 326	...	...	...	...	...

(See notes at end of table. — Voir notes à la fin du tableau.)

Continent, country or area, date and city / Continent, pays ou zone, date et ville	Code[1]	City proper — Ville proprement dite Population				Urban agglomeration — Agglomération urbaine Population			
		Both sexes Les deux sexes	Male Masculin	Female Féminin	Surface area Superficie (km²)	Both sexes Les deux sexes	Male Masculin	Female Féminin	Surface area Superficie (km²)
ASIA — ASIE									
China — Chine									
1 XI 2000									
Hegang	CDJC	694 640	354 262	340 378	...	...	...	...	...
Heihe	CDJC	192 764	97 488	95 276	...	...	...	...	...
Hejian	CDJC	757 581	383 621	373 960	...	...	...	...	...
Hejin	CDJC	368 572	195 677	172 895	...	...	...	...	...
Helong	CDJC	215 266	110 051	105 215	...	...	...	...	...
Hengshui	CDJC	422 761	212 417	210 344	...	...	...	...	...
Hengyang	CDJC	879 051	450 222	428 829	...	...	...	...	...
Heshan (Guangdong)	CDJC	405 779	202 461	203 318	...	...	...	...	...
Heshan (Guangxi)	CDJC	131 249	69 205	62 044	...	...	...	...	...
Hetian	CDJC	186 127	94 034	92 093	...	...	...	...	...
Heyuan	CDJC	227 773	115 330	112 443	...	...	...	...	...
Heze	CDJC	1 280 031	656 790	623 241	...	...	...	...	...
Hezhou	CDJC	850 023	446 208	403 815	...	...	...	...	...
Honghu	CDJC	877 775	459 997	417 778	...	...	...	...	...
Hongjiang	CDJC	485 061	250 434	234 627	...	...	...	...	...
Houma	CDJC	225 123	113 997	111 126	...	...	...	...	...
Huadian	CDJC	444 415	228 624	215 791	...	...	...	...	...
Huaian	CDJC	1 200 679	619 541	581 138	...	...	...	...	...
Huaibei	CDJC	741 195	382 444	358 751	...	...	...	...	...
Huaihua	CDJC	346 522	178 221	168 301	...	...	...	...	...
Huainan	CDJC	1 357 228	701 205	656 023	...	...	...	...	...
Huaiyin	CDJC	555 052	282 186	272 866	...	...	...	...	...
Huanggang	CDJC	373 568	194 607	178 961	...	...	...	...	...
Huanghua	CDJC	483 273	251 128	232 145	...	...	...	...	...
Huangshan	CDJC	406 200	208 004	198 196	...	...	...	...	...
Huangshi (Hubei)	CDJC	653 722	334 712	319 010	...	...	...	...	...
Huayin	CDJC	242 488	125 006	117 482	...	...	...	...	...
Huaying	CDJC	352 257	183 962	168 295	...	...	...	...	...
Huazhou	CDJC	1 007 796	529 550	478 246	...	...	...	...	...
Huhehaote	CDJC	1 406 955	724 328	682 627	...	...	...	...	...
Huixian	CDJC	776 326	394 763	381 563	...	...	...	...	...
Huiyang	CDJC	862 822	429 006	433 816	...	...	...	...	...
Huizhou	CDJC	591 686	292 216	299 470	...	...	...	...	...
Hulin	CDJC	311 509	160 842	150 667	...	...	...	...	...
Huludao	CDJC	900 936	456 211	444 725	...	...	...	...	...
Hunchun	CDJC	211 091	108 873	102 218	...	...	...	...	...
Huozhou	CDJC	274 955	142 316	132 639	...	...	...	...	...
Huzhou	CDJC	1 145 414	573 421	571 993	...	...	...	...	...
Jiamusi	CDJC	859 944	433 369	426 575	...	...	...	...	...
Jian (Jiangxi)	CDJC	473 113	244 476	228 637	...	...	...	...	...
Jian (Jilin)	CDJC	239 849	124 475	115 374	...	...	...	...	...
Jiande	CDJC	473 062	242 606	230 456	...	...	...	...	...
Jiangdu	CDJC	1 053 023	512 151	540 872	...	...	...	...	...
Jiangjin	CDJC	1 322 890	686 106	636 784	...	...	...	...	...
Jiangmen	CDJC	536 317	271 693	264 624	...	...	...	...	...
Jiangshan	CDJC	473 222	241 301	231 921	...	...	...	...	...
Jiangyan	CDJC	861 321	419 333	441 988	...	...	...	...	...
Jiangyin	CDJC	1 315 472	665 719	649 753	...	...	...	...	...
Jiangyou	CDJC	849 761	436 112	413 649	...	...	...	...	...
Jian'ou	CDJC	478 651	249 624	229 027	...	...	...	...	...
Jianyang (Sichuan)	CDJC	1 412 523	728 353	684 170	...	...	...	...	...
Jianyang (Fujian)	CDJC	317 848	167 066	150 782	...	...	...	...	...
Jiaohe	CDJC	474 109	243 510	230 599	...	...	...	...	...
Jiaonan	CDJC	827 771	419 331	408 440	...	...	...	...	...
Jiaozhou	CDJC	783 478	388 207	395 271	...	...	...	...	...
Jiaozuo	CDJC	747 299	384 395	362 904	...	...	...	...	...
Jiaxing	CDJC	881 923	445 646	436 277	...	...	...	...	...
Jiayuguan	CDJC	159 541	85 959	73 582	...	...	...	...	...
Jieshou	CDJC	640 878	327 384	313 494	...	...	...	...	...
Jiexiu	CDJC	372 993	190 675	182 318	...	...	...	...	...
Jieyang	CDJC	633 570	324 831	308 739	...	...	...	...	...
Jilin	CDJC	1 953 134	984 762	968 372	...	...	...	...	...

8. Population of capital cities and cities of 100 000 and more inhabitants: latest available year
Population des capitales et des villes de 100 000 habitants et plus: dernière année disponible (continued — suite)

(See notes at end of table. — Voir notes à la fin du tableau.)

Continent, country or area, date and city Continent, pays ou zone, date et ville	Code[1]	City proper — Ville proprement dite Population				Urban agglomeration — Agglomération urbaine Population			
		Both sexes Les deux sexes	Male Masculin	Female Féminin	Surface area Superficie (km²)	Both sexes Les deux sexes	Male Masculin	Female Féminin	Surface area Superficie (km²)
ASIA — ASIE									
China — Chine									
1 XI 2000									
Jimo	CDJC	1 111 202	553 261	557 941	...	...	...	...	...
Ji'nan	CDJC	2 999 934	1 539 067	1 460 867	...	...	...	...	...
Jinchang	CDJC	204 902	106 725	98 177	...	...	...	...	...
Jincheng	CDJC	304 221	157 663	146 558	...	...	...	...	...
Jingdezhen	CDJC	444 720	228 747	215 973	...	...	...	...	...
Jinggangshan	CDJC	145 769	74 722	71 047	...	...	...	...	...
Jinghong	CDJC	443 672	229 846	213 826	...	...	...	...	...
Jingjiang	CDJC	639 665	316 885	322 780	...	...	...	...	...
Jingmen	CDJC	583 373	300 284	283 089	...	...	...	...	...
Jingzhou	CDJC	1 177 150	598 951	578 199	...	...	...	...	...
Jinhua	CDJC	424 859	216 773	208 086	...	...	...	...	...
Jining (Shandong)	CDJC	1 050 522	530 322	520 200	...	...	...	...	...
Jining (Inner Mongolia)	CDJC	272 448	136 913	135 535	...	...	...	...	...
Jinjiang	CDJC	1 479 259	772 066	707 193	...	...	...	...	...
Jinshi	CDJC	243 242	126 619	116 623	...	...	...	...	...
Jintan	CDJC	533 350	256 798	276 552	...	...	...	...	...
Jinzhong	CDJC	534 357	274 957	259 400	...	...	...	...	...
Jinzhou (Liaoning)	CDJC	861 991	430 777	431 214	...	...	...	...	...
Jinzhou (Hebei)	CDJC	520 942	265 012	255 930	...	...	...	...	...
Jishou	CDJC	294 297	151 422	142 875	...	...	...	...	...
Jiujiang	CDJC	551 329	280 126	271 203	...	...	...	...	...
Jiuquan	CDJC	346 258	177 943	168 315	...	...	...	...	...
Jiutai	CDJC	799 729	411 067	388 662	...	...	...	...	...
Jixi	CDJC	910 782	467 547	443 235	...	...	...	...	...
Jiyuan	CDJC	626 478	323 554	302 924	...	...	...	...	...
Jizhou	CDJC	373 825	187 005	186 820	...	...	...	...	...
Jurong	CDJC	594 316	302 713	291 603	...	...	...	...	...
Kaifeng	CDJC	796 171	398 133	398 038	...	...	...	...	...
Kaili	CDJC	433 236	230 692	202 544	...	...	...	...	...
Kaiping	CDJC	668 692	326 560	342 132	...	...	...	...	...
Kaiyuan (Liaoning)	CDJC	529 736	271 422	258 314	...	...	...	...	...
Kaiyuan (Yunnan)	CDJC	292 039	152 771	139 268	...	...	...	...	...
Kashi (Xinjiang)	CDJC	340 640	172 136	168 504	...	...	...	...	...
Kelamayi	CDJC	270 232	143 500	126 732	...	...	...	...	...
Kuerle	CDJC	381 943	199 344	182 599	...	...	...	...	...
Kuitun	CDJC	285 299	148 740	136 559	...	...	...	...	...
Kunming	CDJC	3 035 406	1 615 096	1 420 310	...	...	...	...	...
Kunshan	CDJC	750 074	377 433	372 641	...	...	...	...	...
Laiwu	CDJC	1 233 525	626 549	606 976	...	...	...	...	...
Laixi	CDJC	728 796	366 400	362 396	...	...	...	...	...
Laiyang	CDJC	897 681	453 293	444 388	...	...	...	...	...
Laizhou	CDJC	889 361	450 192	439 169	...	...	...	...	...
Langfang	CDJC	715 388	363 094	352 294	...	...	...	...	...
Langzhong	CDJC	787 809	400 390	387 419	...	...	...	...	...
Lanxi	CDJC	607 196	314 090	293 106	...	...	...	...	...
Lanzhou	CDJC	2 087 759	1 092 661	995 098	...	...	...	...	...
Laohekou	CDJC	509 468	257 204	252 264	...	...	...	...	...
Lasa	CDJC	223 001	117 004	105 997	...	...	...	...	...
Lechang	CDJC	423 444	223 788	199 656	...	...	...	...	...
Leiyang	CDJC	1 180 235	631 431	548 804	...	...	...	...	...
Leizhou	CDJC	1 268 298	674 213	594 085	...	...	...	...	...
Leling	CDJC	615 833	313 642	302 191	...	...	...	...	...
Lengshuijiang	CDJC	339 701	175 071	164 630	...	...	...	...	...
Leping	CDJC	729 639	381 937	347 702	...	...	...	...	...
Leqing	CDJC	1 162 765	605 494	557 271	...	...	...	...	...
Leshan	CDJC	1 120 158	567 028	553 130	...	...	...	...	...
Lianjiang	CDJC	1 205 764	642 214	563 550	...	...	...	...	...
Lianyuan	CDJC	996 893	521 941	474 952	...	...	...	...	...
Lianyungang	CDJC	687 242	354 350	332 892	...	...	...	...	...
Lianzhou	CDJC	409 360	212 292	197 068	...	...	...	...	...
Liaocheng	CDJC	950 319	474 976	475 343	...	...	...	...	...
Liaoyang	CDJC	728 492	365 833	362 659	...	...	...	...	...

(See notes at end of table. — Voir notes à la fin du tableau.)

Continent, country or area, date and city / Continent, pays ou zone, date et ville	Code[1]	City proper — Ville proprement dite Population				Urban agglomeration — Agglomération urbaine Population			
		Both sexes Les deux sexes	Male Masculin	Female Féminin	Surface area Superficie (km²)	Both sexes Les deux sexes	Male Masculin	Female Féminin	Surface area Superficie (km²)

ASIA — ASIE

China — Chine
1 XI 2000

Liaoyuan	CDJC	462 233	234 701	227 532	...	...	...	...	...
Lichuan	CDJC	786 984	417 988	368 996	...	...	...	...	...
Liling	CDJC	934 396	484 127	450 269	...	...	...	...	...
Lin'an	CDJC	514 238	261 852	252 386	...	...	...	...	...
Linfen	CDJC	724 403	367 377	357 026	...	...	...	...	...
Lingbao	CDJC	722 890	377 872	345 018	...	...	...	...	...
Linghai	CDJC	647 310	332 906	314 404	...	...	...	...	...
Lingwu	CDJC	249 890	128 364	121 526	...	...	...	...	...
Lingyuan	CDJC	620 121	324 554	295 567	...	...	...	...	...
Linhai	CDJC	948 618	479 625	468 993	...	...	...	...	...
Linhe	CDJC	510 965	260 835	250 130	...	...	...	...	...
Linjiang	CDJC	184 901	94 904	89 997	...	...	...	...	...
Linqing	CDJC	694 247	348 411	345 836	...	...	...	...	...
Linxia	CDJC	202 498	104 017	98 481	...	...	...	...	...
Linxiang	CDJC	448 452	235 723	212 729	...	...	...	...	...
Linyi	CDJC	1 938 510	988 940	949 570	...	...	...	...	...
Linzhou	CDJC	982 254	501 659	480 595	...	...	...	...	...
Lishi	CDJC	235 678	121 253	114 425	...	...	...	...	...
Lishui	CDJC	348 241	178 908	169 333	...	...	...	...	...
Liuan	CDJC	1 559 037	807 902	751 135	...	...	...	...	...
Liupanshui	CDJC	995 055	523 692	471 363	...	...	...	...	...
Liuyang	CDJC	1 307 572	680 610	626 962	...	...	...	...	...
Liuzhou	CDJC	1 220 392	634 909	585 483	...	...	...	...	...
Liyang	CDJC	740 871	375 694	365 177	...	...	...	...	...
Longhai	CDJC	816 318	415 936	400 382	...	...	...	...	...
Longjing	CDJC	261 551	132 150	129 401	...	...	...	...	...
Longkou	CDJC	671 335	337 507	333 828	...	...	...	...	...
Longquan	CDJC	250 398	131 534	118 864	...	...	...	...	...
Longyan	CDJC	543 731	298 481	245 250	...	...	...	...	...
Loudi	CDJC	398 577	205 172	193 405	...	...	...	...	...
Lucheng	CDJC	213 944	111 293	102 651	...	...	...	...	...
Lufeng	CDJC	1 164 767	600 959	563 808	...	...	...	...	...
Luoding	CDJC	866 190	449 131	417 059	...	...	...	...	...
Luohe	CDJC	304 105	150 273	153 832	...	...	...	...	...
Luoyang	CDJC	1 491 680	759 425	732 255	...	...	...	...	...
Luquan	CDJC	397 449	202 340	195 109	...	...	...	...	...
Luxi (Yunnan)	CDJC	337 406	172 038	165 368	...	...	...	...	...
Luzhou	CDJC	1 252 884	636 652	616 232	...	...	...	...	...
Maanshan	CDJC	567 576	292 994	274 582	...	...	...	...	...
Macheng	CDJC	1 129 047	595 391	533 656	...	...	...	...	...
Manzhouli	CDJC	181 112	92 853	88 259	...	...	...	...	...
Maoming	CDJC	644 301	335 713	308 588	...	...	...	...	...
Meihekou	CDJC	617 674	317 226	300 448	...	...	...	...	...
Meishan	CDJC	799 309	402 889	396 420	...	...	...	...	...
Meixian	CDJC	313 821	160 925	152 896	...	...	...	...	...
Meizhou	CDJC	354 302	178 658	175 644	...	...	...	...	...
Mianyang	CDJC	1 162 962	604 414	558 548	...	...	...	...	...
Mianzhu	CDJC	515 830	263 098	252 732	...	...	...	...	...
Miluo	CDJC	658 867	342 113	316 754	...	...	...	...	...
Mingguang	CDJC	569 585	290 126	279 459	...	...	...	...	...
Miquan	CDJC	180 952	95 368	85 584	...	...	...	...	...
Mishan	CDJC	438 277	224 565	213 712	...	...	...	...	...
Mudanjiang	CDJC	1 014 206	512 000	502 206	...	...	...	...	...
Muling	CDJC	310 096	158 623	151 473	...	...	...	...	...
Nan'an	CDJC	1 385 276	700 218	685 058	...	...	...	...	...
Nanchang	CDJC	1 844 253	952 504	891 749	...	...	...	...	...
Nanchong	CDJC	1 771 920	922 452	849 468	...	...	...	...	...
Nanchuan	CDJC	631 853	326 307	305 546	...	...	...	...	...
Nan'gong	CDJC	467 356	234 978	232 378	...	...	...	...	...
Nanhai	CDJC	2 133 741	1 111 731	1 022 010	...	...	...	...	...
Nanjing	CDJC	3 624 234	1 935 931	1 688 303	...	...	...	...	...
Nankang	CDJC	694 987	338 836	356 151	...	...	...	...	...

(See notes at end of table. — Voir notes à la fin du tableau.)

Continent, country or area, date and city / Continent, pays ou zone, date et ville	Code[1]	City proper — Ville proprement dite Population				Urban agglomeration — Agglomération urbaine Population			
		Both sexes Les deux sexes	Male Masculin	Female Féminin	Surface area Superficie (km²)	Both sexes Les deux sexes	Male Masculin	Female Féminin	Surface area Superficie (km²)
ASIA — ASIE									
China — Chine									
1 XI 2000									
Nanning	CDJC	1 766 701	924 916	841 785		...	...	...	...	...
Nanpin	CDJC	488 818	257 352	231 466		...	...	...	...
Nantong	CDJC	771 386	386 206	385 180		...	...	...	...
Nanxiong	CDJC	372 844	185 330	187 514		...	...	...	...
Nanyang	CDJC	1 584 715	814 822	769 893		...	...	...	...
Nehe	CDJC	672 295	343 873	328 422		...	...	...	...
Neijiang	CDJC	1 391 931	709 053	682 878		...	...	...	...
Ning'an	CDJC	437 328	223 201	214 127		...	...	...	...
Ningbo	CDJC	1 567 499	804 850	762 649		...	...	...	...
Ningde	CDJC	400 293	213 131	187 162		...	...	...	...
Ningguo	CDJC	381 842	199 915	181 927		...	...	...	...
Panjin	CDJC	602 541	309 377	293 164		...	...	...	...
Panshi	CDJC	530 470	273 219	257 251		...	...	...	...
Panzhihua	CDJC	690 739	363 585	327 154		...	...	...	...
Penglai	CDJC	500 408	252 726	247 682		...	...	...	...
Pengzhou	CDJC	770 749	389 697	381 052		...	...	...	...
Pingdingshan	CDJC	900 903	470 362	430 541		...	...	...	...
Pingdu	CDJC	1 321 975	670 685	651 290		...	...	...	...
Pinghu	CDJC	507 899	249 848	258 051		...	...	...	...
Pingliang	CDJC	454 996	236 426	218 570		...	...	...	...
Pingxiang (Jiangxi)	CDJC	783 445	402 198	381 247		...	...	...	...
Pingxiang (Guangxi)	CDJC	107 046	57 445	49 601		...	...	...	...
Pizhou	CDJC	1 539 922	791 332	748 590		...	...	...	...
Pulandian	CDJC	757 844	385 636	372 208		...	...	...	...
Puning	CDJC	1 856 402	954 242	902 160		...	...	...	...
Putian	CDJC	443 926	216 578	227 348		...	...	...	...
Puyang	CDJC	448 290	229 387	218 903		...	...	...	...
Qian'an	CDJC	632 704	323 330	309 374		...	...	...	...
Qianjiang	CDJC	992 438	506 290	486 148		...	...	...	...
Qidong	CDJC	1 057 073	495 819	561 254		...	...	...	...
Qingdao	CDJC	2 720 972	1 359 527	1 361 445		...	...	...	...
Qingtongxia	CDJC	248 640	129 121	119 519		...	...	...	...
Qingyuan	CDJC	506 680	258 819	247 861		...	...	...	...
Qingzhen	CDJC	471 305	248 079	223 226		...	...	...	...
Qingzhou	CDJC	894 468	450 090	444 378		...	...	...	...
Qinhuangdao	CDJC	817 487	411 355	406 132		...	...	...	...
Qinyang	CDJC	446 404	224 725	221 679		...	...	...	...
Qinzhou	CDJC	1 035 504	578 428	457 076		...	...	...	...
Qionghai	CDJC	449 845	236 560	213 285		...	...	...	...
Qionglai	CDJC	631 577	321 382	310 195		...	...	...	...
Qiongshan	CDJC	678 149	355 557	322 592		...	...	...	...
Qiqihaer	CDJC	1 540 089	776 191	763 898		...	...	...	...
Qitaihe	CDJC	486 704	254 500	232 204		...	...	...	...
Qixia	CDJC	651 357	331 148	320 209		...	...	...	...
Quanzhou	CDJC	1 192 286	616 826	575 460		...	...	...	...
Qufu	CDJC	625 313	317 685	307 628		...	...	...	...
Qujing	CDJC	648 956	333 756	315 200		...	...	...	...
Quzhou	CDJC	286 271	148 054	138 217		...	...	...	...
Renhuai	CDJC	520 759	270 091	250 668		...	...	...	...
Renqiu	CDJC	768 900	390 649	378 251		...	...	...	...
Rizhao	CDJC	1 148 190	576 050	572 140		...	...	...	...
Rongcheng	CDJC	732 147	368 156	363 991		...	...	...	...
Rugao	CDJC	1 362 533	659 720	702 813		...	...	...	...
Ruian	CDJC	1 207 788	627 593	580 195		...	...	...	...
Ruichang	CDJC	398 844	209 755	189 089		...	...	...	...
Ruijin	CDJC	535 499	280 328	255 171		...	...	...	...
Ruili	CDJC	155 210	80 532	74 678		...	...	...	...
Rushan	CDJC	580 326	291 047	289 279		...	...	...	...
Ruzhou	CDJC	923 245	474 090	449 155		...	...	...	...
Sanhe	CDJC	456 882	229 788	227 094		...	...	...	...
Sanmenxia	CDJC	288 746	149 846	138 900		...	...	...	...
Sanming	CDJC	337 105	178 031	159 074		...	...	...	...

8. Population of capital cities and cities of 100 000 and more inhabitants: latest available year
Population des capitales et des villes de 100 000 habitants et plus: dernière année disponible (continued — suite)

(See notes at end of table. — Voir notes à la fin du tableau.)

Continent, country or area, date and city / Continent, pays ou zone, date et ville	Code[1]	City proper — Ville proprement dite Population				Urban agglomeration — Agglomération urbaine Population			
		Both sexes Les deux sexes	Male Masculin	Female Féminin	Surface area Superficie (km²)	Both sexes Les deux sexes	Male Masculin	Female Féminin	Surface area Superficie (km²)
ASIA — ASIE									
China — Chine									
1 XI 2000									
Sanshui	CDJC	440 119	230 835	209 284		...	...	...	...
Sanya	CDJC	482 296	254 293	228 003		...	...	...	...
Shahe	CDJC	474 260	243 171	231 089		...	...	...	...
Shanghai	CDJC	14 348 535	7 414 274	6 934 261		...	...	...	...
Shangqiu	CDJC	1 428 983	729 319	699 664		...	...	...	...
Shangrao	CDJC	327 703	164 698	163 005		...	...	...	...
Shangyu	CDJC	722 523	354 917	367 606		...	...	...	...
Shangzhi	CDJC	582 764	298 966	283 798		...	...	...	...
Shangzhou	CDJC	530 883	279 160	251 723		...	...	...	...
Shantou	CDJC	1 270 112	636 189	633 923		...	...	...	...
Shanwei	CDJC	409 677	211 746	197 931		...	...	...	...
Shaoguan	CDJC	535 979	282 515	253 464		...	...	...	...
Shaowu	CDJC	288 401	151 117	137 284		...	...	...	...
Shaoxing	CDJC	633 118	310 860	322 258		...	...	...	...
Shaoyang	CDJC	607 868	309 563	298 305		...	...	...	...
Shengzhou	CDJC	671 221	345 614	325 607		...	...	...	...
Shenyang	CDJC	5 303 053	2 700 380	2 602 673		...	...	...	...
Shenzhen	CDJC	7 008 831	3 454 392	3 554 439		...	...	...	...
Shenzhou	CDJC	568 558	289 086	279 472		...	...	...	...
Shifang	CDJC	432 579	218 447	214 132		...	...	...	...
Shihezi	CDJC	590 115	305 253	284 862		...	...	...	...
Shijiazhuang	CDJC	1 969 975	1 005 476	964 499		...	...	...	...
Shishi	CDJC	498 786	264 700	234 086		...	...	...	...
Shishou	CDJC	602 649	310 486	292 163		...	...	...	...
Shiyan	CDJC	589 824	309 552	280 272		...	...	...	...
Shizuishan	CDJC	314 296	163 261	151 035		...	...	...	...
Shouguang	CDJC	1 081 991	548 020	533 971		...	...	...	...
Shuangcheng	CDJC	749 182	382 673	366 509		...	...	...	...
Shuangliao	CDJC	404 499	206 071	198 428		...	...	...	...
Shuangyashan	CDJC	487 294	248 542	238 752		...	...	...	...
Shulan	CDJC	660 065	340 293	319 772		...	...	...	...
Shunde	CDJC	1 694 152	893 580	800 572		...	...	...	...
Shuozhou	CDJC	563 896	290 621	273 275		...	...	...	...
Sihui	CDJC	409 804	209 936	199 868		...	...	...	...
Simao	CDJC	230 834	120 071	110 763		...	...	...	...
Siping	CDJC	492 841	247 416	245 425		...	...	...	...
Songyuan	CDJC	538 469	273 101	265 368		...	...	...	...
Songzi	CDJC	859 941	437 980	421 961		...	...	...	...
Suihua	CDJC	800 207	405 382	394 825		...	...	...	...
Suining	CDJC	1 355 388	696 590	658 798		...	...	...	...
Suizhou	CDJC	1 598 752	818 936	779 816		...	...	...	...
Suqian	CDJC	244 651	124 719	119 932		...	...	...	...
Suzhou (Anhui)	CDJC	1 601 181	819 067	782 114		...	...	...	...
Suzhou (Jiangsu)	CDJC	1 344 709	686 919	657 790		...	...	...	...
Tacheng	CDJC	149 210	76 056	73 154		...	...	...	...
Taian	CDJC	1 538 211	775 346	762 865		...	...	...	...
Taicang	CDJC	515 063	250 788	264 275		...	...	...	...
Taishan	CDJC	948 716	478 773	469 943		...	...	...	...
Taixing	CDJC	1 235 454	618 158	617 296		...	...	...	...
Taiyuan	CDJC	2 558 382	1 321 216	1 237 166		...	...	...	...
Taizhou (Zhejiang)	CDJC	1 491 963	766 497	725 466		...	...	...	...
Taizhou (Jiangsu)	CDJC	607 660	303 078	304 582		...	...	...	...
Tangshan	CDJC	1 711 311	863 091	848 220		...	...	...	...
Taonan	CDJC	441 096	224 878	216 218		...	...	...	...
Tengzhou	CDJC	1 548 817	811 999	736 818		...	...	...	...
Tianchang	CDJC	590 745	297 550	293 195		...	...	...	...
Tianjin	CDJC	7 499 181	3 825 069	3 674 112		...	...	...	...
Tianmen	CDJC	1 613 739	849 283	764 456		...	...	...	...
Tianshui	CDJC	1 146 986	594 508	552 478		...	...	...	...
Tiefa	CDJC	239 636	121 471	118 165		...	...	...	...
Tieli	CDJC	354 601	181 024	173 577		...	...	...	...
Tieling	CDJC	433 799	217 795	216 004		...	...	...	...

(See notes at end of table. — Voir notes à la fin du tableau.)

Continent, country or area, date and city / Continent, pays ou zone, date et ville	Code[1]	City proper — Ville proprement dite Population				Urban agglomeration — Agglomération urbaine Population			
		Both sexes Les deux sexes	Male Masculin	Female Féminin	Surface area Superficie (km²)	Both sexes Les deux sexes	Male Masculin	Female Féminin	Surface area Superficie (km²)
ASIA — ASIE									
China — Chine									
1 XI 2000									
Tongcheng	CDJC	660 772	321 098	339 674	...	...	...	...	...
Tongchuan	CDJC	404 257	211 294	192 963	...	...	...	...	...
Tonghua	CDJC	460 148	231 960	228 188	...	...	...	...	...
Tongjiang	CDJC	164 595	85 426	79 169	...	...	...	...	...
Tongliao	CDJC	793 913	400 930	392 983	...	...	...	...	...
Tongling	CDJC	362 477	188 130	174 347	...	...	...	...	...
Tongren	CDJC	308 583	163 632	144 951	...	...	...	...	...
Tongshi	CDJC	100 836	53 146	47 690	...	...	...	...	...
Tongxiang	CDJC	713 399	360 567	352 832	...	...	...	...	...
Tongzhou	CDJC	1 371 498	652 777	718 721	...	...	...	...	...
Tulufan	CDJC	251 652	129 183	122 469	...	...	...	...	...
Tumen	CDJC	132 368	67 067	65 301	...	...	...	...	...
Urumqi	CDJC	1 753 298	911 328	841 970	...	...	...	...	...
Wafangdian	CDJC	956 063	489 377	466 686	...	...	...	...	...
Wanning	CDJC	513 604	272 751	240 853	...	...	...	...	...
Wanyuan	CDJC	536 685	278 918	257 767	...	...	...	...	...
Weifang	CDJC	1 380 300	696 720	683 580	...	...	...	...	...
Weihai	CDJC	609 219	307 867	301 352	...	...	...	...	...
Weihui	CDJC	464 371	233 151	231 220	...	...	...	...	...
Weinan	CDJC	888 866	451 028	437 838	...	...	...	...	...
Wenchang	CDJC	509 271	260 432	248 839	...	...	...	...	...
Wendeng	CDJC	675 061	335 330	339 731	...	...	...	...	...
Wenling	CDJC	1 162 783	604 031	558 752	...	...	...	...	...
Wenzhou	CDJC	1 915 548	1 028 001	887 547	...	...	...	...	...
Wuan	CDJC	720 196	373 108	347 088	...	...	...	...	...
Wuchang	CDJC	888 782	454 587	434 195	...	...	...	...	...
Wuchuan	CDJC	822 482	429 336	393 146	...	...	...	...	...
Wudalianchi	CDJC	338 689	176 002	162 687	...	...	...	...	...
Wugang (Hunan)	CDJC	694 847	363 904	330 943	...	...	...	...	...
Wugang (Henan)	CDJC	313 089	164 347	148 742	...	...	...	...	...
Wuhai	CDJC	427 553	223 947	203 606	...	...	...	...	...
Wuhan	CDJC	8 312 700	4 306 729	4 005 971	...	...	...	...	...
Wuhu	CDJC	697 197	359 560	337 637	...	...	...	...	...
Wujiang	CDJC	857 104	426 423	430 681	...	...	...	...	...
Wujin	CDJC	1 420 204	719 200	701 004	...	...	...	...	...
Wulanhaote	CDJC	269 162	135 406	133 756	...	...	...	...	...
Wusu	CDJC	190 359	100 288	90 071	...	...	...	...	...
Wuwei	CDJC	946 506	488 872	457 634	...	...	...	...	...
Wuxi	CDJC	1 425 766	732 231	693 535	...	...	...	...	...
Wuxian	CDJC	1 128 429	557 717	570 712	...	...	...	...	...
Wuxue	CDJC	719 426	381 959	337 467	...	...	...	...	...
Wuyishan	CDJC	212 156	112 006	100 150	...	...	...	...	...
Wuzhong	CDJC	355 442	181 909	173 533	...	...	...	...	...
Wuzhou	CDJC	381 043	193 424	187 619	...	...	...	...	...
Xiamen	CDJC	2 053 070	1 061 697	991 373	...	...	...	...	...
Xi'an	CDJC	4 481 508	2 320 642	2 160 866	...	...	...	...	...
Xiangcheng	CDJC	1 052 468	546 760	505 708	...	...	...	...	...
Xiangfan	CDJC	871 388	443 899	427 489	...	...	...	...	...
Xiangtan	CDJC	707 783	363 619	344 164	...	...	...	...	...
Xiangxiang	CDJC	807 718	413 489	394 229	...	...	...	...	...
Xianning	CDJC	567 598	295 836	271 762	...	...	...	...	...
Xiantao	CDJC	1 474 078	774 487	699 591	...	...	...	...	...
Xianyang	CDJC	953 860	493 153	460 707	...	...	...	...	...
Xiaogan	CDJC	883 123	454 917	428 206	...	...	...	...	...
Xiaoshan	CDJC	1 233 348	613 229	620 119	...	...	...	...	...
Xiaoyi	CDJC	414 154	215 941	198 213	...	...	...	...	...
Xichang	CDJC	615 212	318 658	296 554	...	...	...	...	...
Xifeng	CDJC	317 669	163 228	154 441	...	...	...	...	...
Xilin'haote	CDJC	173 796	89 527	84 269	...	...	...	...	...
Xingcheng	CDJC	524 527	269 567	254 960	...	...	...	...	...
Xinghua	CDJC	1 441 659	745 856	695 803	...	...	...	...	...
Xingning	CDJC	871 507	436 749	434 758	...	...	...	...	...

(See notes at end of table. — Voir notes à la fin du tableau.)

Continent, country or area, date and city / Continent, pays ou zone, date et ville	Code[1]	City proper — Ville proprement dite Population				Urban agglomeration — Agglomération urbaine Population			
		Both sexes Les deux sexes	Male Masculin	Female Féminin	Surface area Superficie (km²)	Both sexes Les deux sexes	Male Masculin	Female Féminin	Surface area Superficie (km²)
ASIA — ASIE									
China — Chine									
1 XI 2000									
Xingping	CDJC	551 523	284 879	266 644	...	...	...	...	...
Xingtai	CDJC	536 282	272 661	263 621	...	...	...	...	...
Xingyang	CDJC	619 840	316 049	303 791	...	...	...	...	...
Xingyi	CDJC	719 605	375 079	344 526	...	...	...	...	...
Xinhui	CDJC	932 425	467 557	464 868	...	...	...	...	...
Xi'ning	CDJC	854 466	440 359	414 107	...	...	...	...	...
Xinji	CDJC	623 219	314 536	308 683	...	...	...	...	...
Xinle	CDJC	439 644	220 811	218 833	...	...	...	...	...
Xinmi	CDJC	779 014	406 291	372 723	...	...	...	...	...
Xinmin	CDJC	653 719	333 683	320 036	...	...	...	...	...
Xintai	CDJC	1 344 395	687 569	656 826	...	...	...	...	...
Xinxiang	CDJC	775 941	394 224	381 717	...	...	...	...	...
Xinyang	CDJC	1 255 750	644 031	611 719	...	...	...	...	...
Xinyi (Guangdong)	CDJC	907 978	464 088	443 890	...	...	...	...	...
Xinyi (Jiangsu)	CDJC	962 656	491 509	471 147	...	...	...	...	...
Xinyu	CDJC	778 391	408 940	369 451	...	...	...	...	...
Xinzheng	CDJC	609 173	315 462	293 711	...	...	...	...	...
Xinzhou	CDJC	496 608	251 708	244 900	...	...	...	...	...
Xishan	CDJC	1 181 073	599 540	581 533	...	...	...	...	...
Xuancheng	CDJC	822 707	428 470	394 237	...	...	...	...	...
Xuanwei	CDJC	1 292 825	691 846	600 979	...	...	...	...	...
Xuchang	CDJC	373 387	188 476	184 911	...	...	...	...	...
Xuzhou	CDJC	1 679 626	866 686	812 940	...	...	...	...	...
Yaan	CDJC	334 475	171 237	163 238	...	...	...	...	...
Yakeshi	CDJC	405 806	207 451	198 355	...	...	...	...	...
Yan'an	CDJC	403 868	209 240	194 628	...	...	...	...	...
Yancheng	CDJC	683 663	347 576	336 087	...	...	...	...	...
Yangchun	CDJC	840 581	440 930	399 651	...	...	...	...	...
Yangjiang	CDJC	538 069	276 769	261 300	...	...	...	...	...
Yangquan	CDJC	655 317	346 209	309 108	...	...	...	...	...
Yangzhong	CDJC	301 672	150 538	151 134	...	...	...	...	...
Yangzhou	CDJC	711 993	362 425	349 568	...	...	...	...	...
Yanji	CDJC	432 339	223 342	208 997	...	...	...	...	...
Yanshi	CDJC	816 026	414 890	401 136	...	...	...	...	...
Yantai	CDJC	1 724 404	871 452	852 952	...	...	...	...	...
Yibin	CDJC	809 099	419 397	389 702	...	...	...	...	...
Yichang	CDJC	712 738	371 510	341 228	...	...	...	...	...
Yicheng	CDJC	522 835	266 340	256 495	...	...	...	...	...
Yichun (Jiangxi)	CDJC	920 357	480 945	439 412	...	...	...	...	...
Yichun (Heilongjiang)	CDJC	814 016	413 071	400 945	...	...	...	...	...
Yidu	CDJC	385 779	196 716	189 063	...	...	...	...	...
Yima	CDJC	136 543	73 411	63 132	...	...	...	...	...
Yinchuan	CDJC	807 487	415 203	392 284	...	...	...	...	...
Yingcheng	CDJC	650 485	340 907	309 578	...	...	...	...	...
Yingde	CDJC	810 446	421 964	388 482	...	...	...	...	...
Yingkou	CDJC	698 059	353 751	344 308	...	...	...	...	...
Yingtan	CDJC	178 406	92 050	86 356	...	...	...	...	...
Yi'ning	CDJC	357 519	179 862	177 657	...	...	...	...	...
Yiwu	CDJC	912 670	461 103	451 567	...	...	...	...	...
Yixing	CDJC	1 164 275	592 095	572 180	...	...	...	...	...
Yiyang	CDJC	1 228 881	629 842	599 039	...	...	...	...	...
Yizheng	CDJC	610 356	311 144	299 212	...	...	...	...	...
Yizhou	CDJC	549 434	288 084	261 350	...	...	...	...	...
Yong'an	CDJC	334 852	180 109	154 743	...	...	...	...	...
Yongcheng	CDJC	1 264 607	654 047	610 560	...	...	...	...	...
Yongchuan	CDJC	984 730	507 848	476 882	...	...	...	...	...
Yongkang	CDJC	557 067	290 946	266 121	...	...	...	...	...
Yongji	CDJC	421 244	214 446	206 798	...	...	...	...	...
Yongzhou	CDJC	976 539	508 021	468 518	...	...	...	...	...
Yuanjiang	CDJC	700 236	363 730	336 506	...	...	...	...	...
Yuanping	CDJC	471 853	244 751	227 102	...	...	...	...	...
Yucheng	CDJC	494 301	248 103	246 198	...	...	...	...	...

8. Population of capital cities and cities of 100 000 and more inhabitants: latest available year
Population des capitales et des villes de 100 000 habitants et plus: dernière année disponible (continued — suite)

(See notes at end of table. — Voir notes à la fin du tableau.)

Continent, country or area, date and city / Continent, pays ou zone, date et ville	Code[1]	City proper — Ville proprement dite Population				Urban agglomeration — Agglomération urbaine Population			
		Both sexes Les deux sexes	Male Masculin	Female Féminin	Surface area Superficie (km²)	Both sexes Les deux sexes	Male Masculin	Female Féminin	Surface area Superficie (km²)
ASIA — ASIE									
China — Chine									
1 XI 2000									
Yueyang	CDJC	912 993	471 170	441 823	...	...	...	...	...
Yuhang	CDJC	817 715	419 877	397 838	...	...	...	...	...
Yulin (Shaanxi)	CDJC	451 337	232 951	218 386	...	...	...	...	...
Yulin (Guangxi)	CDJC	918 229	491 729	426 500	...	...	...	...	...
Yumen	CDJC	188 931	99 832	89 099	...	...	...	...	...
Yuncheng	CDJC	604 381	304 489	299 892	...	...	...	...	...
Yunfu	CDJC	261 636	136 789	124 847	...	...	...	...	...
Yunzhou	CDJC	598 387	303 581	294 806	...	...	...	...	...
Yushu	CDJC	1 155 670	592 213	563 457	...	...	...	...	...
Yuxi	CDJC	409 044	206 139	202 905	...	...	...	...	...
Yuyao	CDJC	852 719	429 835	422 884	...	...	...	...	...
Yuzhou	CDJC	1 122 669	587 728	534 941	...	...	...	...	...
Zaoyang	CDJC	1 054 374	538 588	515 786	...	...	...	...	...
Zaozhuang	CDJC	1 996 798	1 025 190	971 608	...	...	...	...	...
Zengcheng	CDJC	899 644	466 540	433 104	...	...	...	...	...
Zhalantun	CDJC	409 051	211 922	197 129	...	...	...	...	...
Zhangjiagang	CDJC	957 223	466 771	490 452	...	...	...	...	...
Zhangjiajie	CDJC	453 723	234 454	219 269	...	...	...	...	...
Zhangjiakou	CDJC	903 348	455 048	448 300	...	...	...	...	...
Zhangping	CDJC	264 757	140 779	123 978	...	...	...	...	...
Zhangqiu	CDJC	977 324	485 925	491 399	...	...	...	...	...
Zhangshu	CDJC	527 823	273 691	254 132	...	...	...	...	...
Zhangye	CDJC	486 688	248 469	238 219	...	...	...	...	...
Zhangzhou	CDJC	567 884	291 597	276 287	...	...	...	...	...
Zhanjiang	CDJC	1 350 665	707 187	643 478	...	...	...	...	...
Zhaodong	CDJC	832 657	424 694	407 963	...	...	...	...	...
Zhaoqing	CDJC	507 834	254 086	253 748	...	...	...	...	...
Zhaotong	CDJC	727 959	377 931	350 028	...	...	...	...	...
Zhaoyuan	CDJC	593 705	297 504	296 201	...	...	...	...	...
Zhengzhou	CDJC	2 589 387	1 347 037	1 242 350	...	...	...	...	...
Zhenjiang	CDJC	695 663	364 429	331 234	...	...	...	...	...
Zhijiang	CDJC	508 835	257 013	251 822	...	...	...	...	...
Zhongshan	CDJC	2 363 322	1 175 587	1 187 735	...	...	...	...	...
Zhongxiang	CDJC	1 021 998	516 758	505 240	...	...	...	...	...
Zhoukou	CDJC	323 738	162 443	161 295	...	...	...	...	...
Zhoushan	CDJC	715 685	362 426	353 259	...	...	...	...	...
Zhuanghe	CDJC	835 062	422 677	412 385	...	...	...	...	...
Zhucheng	CDJC	1 053 695	531 390	522 305	...	...	...	...	...
Zhuhai	CDJC	833 908	414 067	419 841	...	...	...	...	...
Zhuji	CDJC	1 070 675	535 820	534 855	...	...	...	...	...
Zhumadian	CDJC	338 036	170 485	167 551	...	...	...	...	...
Zhuozhou	CDJC	546 754	275 834	270 920	...	...	...	...	...
Zhuzhou	CDJC	879 996	454 057	425 939	...	...	...	...	...
Zibo	CDJC	2 817 479	1 429 838	1 387 641	...	...	...	...	...
Zigong	CDJC	1 051 384	532 479	518 905	...	...	...	...	...
Zixing	CDJC	351 581	181 632	169 949	...	...	...	...	...
Ziyang	CDJC	1 016 034	527 326	488 708	...	...	...	...	...
Zoucheng	CDJC	1 101 003	571 761	529 242	...	...	...	...	...
Zunhua	CDJC	683 662	348 121	335 541	...	...	...	...	...
Zunyi	CDJC	691 694	358 839	332 855	...	...	...	...	...
China - HongKong SAR — Chine - HongKong RAS									
14 III 2001									
HONG KONG	CDJC	6 708 389	3 285 344	3 423 045	1 099	...	...	...	...
China - Macao SAR — Chine - Macao RAS									
1 VII 2002									
MACAO	ESDJ	439 162	210 642	228 520	26	...	...	...	...
Cyprus — Chypre									
31 XII 2002									
LEFKOSIA[57]	ESDJ	...	...	...	...	208 900	...	...	...
Lemesos[58]	ESDJ	...	...	...	...	163 900	...	...	...

8. Population of capital cities and cities of 100 000 and more inhabitants: latest available year
Population des capitales et des villes de 100 000 habitants et plus: dernière année disponible (continued — suite)

(See notes at end of table. — Voir notes à la fin du tableau.)

Continent, country or area, date and city / Continent, pays ou zone, date et ville	Code[1]	City proper — Ville proprement dite Population				Urban agglomeration — Agglomération urbaine Population			
		Both sexes Les deux sexes	Male Masculin	Female Féminin	Surface area Superficie (km²)	Both sexes Les deux sexes	Male Masculin	Female Féminin	Surface area Superficie (km²)
ASIA — ASIE									
Georgia — Géorgie									
1 VII 1990									
Batumi	ESDF	137 000	...	...	...	...	...	...	...
Kutaisi	ESDF	236 000	...	...	...	...	...	...	...
Rustavi	ESDF	160 000	...	...	...	...	...	...	...
Sukhumi	ESDF	122 000	...	...	...	...	...	...	...
TBILISI	ESDF	1 268 000	...	...	...	...	...	...	...
India — Inde[59]									
1 III 2001									
Abohar	CDFC	124 303	66 434	57 869	23	...	...	...	...
Achalpur	CDFC	107 304	55 678	51 626	...	...	...	...	...
Adilabad	CDFC	108 233	55 023	53 210	...	128 196	64 883	63 313	...
Adityapur	CDFC	119 221	63 855	55 366	...	...	...	...	...
Adoni	CDFC	155 969	78 908	77 061	30	161 125	81 577	79 548	...
Agartala	CDFC	189 327	94 398	94 929	16	...	...	...	...
Agra	CDFC	1 259 979	674 902	585 077	121	1 321 410	708 622	612 788	141
Ahmedabad	CDFC	3 515 361	1 863 886	1 651 475	...	4 519 278	2 397 728	2 121 550	...
Ahmednagar	CDFC	307 455	159 409	148 046	18	347 396	184 604	162 792	30
Aizawl	CDFC	229 714	116 983	112 731	110	...	...	...	...
Ajmer	CDFC	485 197	253 854	231 343	242	490 138	256 379	233 759	...
Akola	CDFC	399 978	206 433	193 545	23	...	...	...	...
Alandur	CDFC	146 154	74 784	71 370	...	...	...	...	...
Alappuzha	CDFC	177 079	85 708	91 371	70	282 727	137 232	145 495	84
Aligarh	CDFC	667 732	357 152	310 580	34	...	...	...	...
Alipurduar	CDFC	...	...	...	...	114 069	58 527	55 542	26
Allahabad	CDFC	990 298	549 754	440 544	...	1 049 579	581 876	467 703	...
Alwal	CDFC	106 424	56 562	49 862	...	...	...	...	...
Alwar	CDFC	260 245	139 141	121 104	...	265 850	143 238	122 612	58
Ambala	CDFC	139 222	73 956	65 266	17	168 003	92 610	75 393	38
Ambala Sadar	CDFC	106 378	55 461	50 917	...	...	...	...	...
Ambarnath	CDFC	203 795	107 378	96 417	...	...	...	...	...
Ambattur	CDFC	302 492	156 237	146 255	...	...	...	...	...
Amravati	CDFC	549 370	283 789	265 581	122	...	...	...	...
Amritsar	CDFC	975 695	524 127	451 568	...	1 011 327	543 638	467 689	...
Amroha	CDFC	164 890	86 836	78 054	6	...	...	...	...
Anand	CDFC	130 462	68 032	62 430	...	218 064	115 183	102 881	...
Anantapur	CDFC	220 951	112 273	108 678	...	243 359	123 976	119 383	...
Anklesvar	CDFC	...	...	...	...	112 648	60 265	52 383	...
Arcot	CDFC	...	...	...	...	126 975	62 938	64 037	19
Arrah	CDFC	203 395	109 876	93 519	31	...	...	...	...
Asansol	CDFC	486 304	256 551	229 753	25	1 090 171	576 813	513 358	223
Ashoknagar Kalyangarh	CDFC	111 475	56 340	55 135	...	...	...	...	...
Aurangabad	CDFC	872 667	458 869	413 798	139	891 841	468 815	423 026	148
Avadi	CDFC	230 913	119 187	111 726	...	...	...	...	...
Azamgarh	CDFC	104 943	51 284	53 659	...	...	...	...	...
Bahadurgarh	CDFC	119 839	65 835	54 004	...	131 924	72 851	59 073	...
Baharampur	CDFC	160 168	81 795	78 373	17	170 343	87 038	83 305	19
Bahraich	CDFC	168 376	89 532	78 844	13	...	...	...	...
Baidyabati	CDFC	108 231	56 429	51 802	...	...	...	...	...
Baleshwar	CDFC	106 032	55 637	50 395	...	156 274	82 034	74 240	42
Ballia	CDFC	102 226	55 123	47 103	...	...	...	...	...
Bally	CDFC	261 575	149 810	111 765	12	...	...	...	...
Balurghat	CDFC	135 516	68 822	66 694	...	143 095	72 687	70 408	8
Banda	CDFC	134 822	72 663	62 159	...	139 387	75 172	64 215	...
Bangalore	CDFC	4 292 223	2 240 956	2 051 267	...	5 686 844	2 983 926	2 702 918	446
Bangaon	CDFC	102 115	52 489	49 626	...	...	...	...	...
Bankura	CDFC	128 811	66 333	62 478	19	...	...	...	...
Bansberia	CDFC	104 453	55 403	49 050	...	...	...	...	...
Baranagar	CDFC	250 615	132 701	117 914	7	...	...	...	...
Barasat	CDFC	231 515	118 367	113 148	...	...	...	...	...
Barddhaman	CDFC	285 871	148 824	137 047	23	...	...	...	...
Bareilly	CDFC	699 839	368 022	331 817	107	729 800	386 418	343 382	124
Baripada	CDFC	...	...	...	...	100 593	53 610	46 983	...
Barrackpur	CDFC	144 331	76 268	68 063	14	...	...	...	...

(See notes at end of table. — Voir notes à la fin du tableau.)

Continent, country or area, date and city Continent, pays ou zone, date et ville	Code[1]	City proper — Ville proprement dite Population				Urban agglomeration — Agglomération urbaine Population			
		Both sexes Les deux sexes	Male Masculin	Female Féminin	Surface area Superficie (km²)	Both sexes Les deux sexes	Male Masculin	Female Féminin	Surface area Superficie (km²)
ASIA — ASIE									
India — Inde[59]									
1 III 2001									
Barshi	CDFC	104 786	53 894	50 892	...	...	...	...	...
Basirhat	CDFC	113 120	57 876	55 244	22	...	...	...	...
Basti	CDFC	106 985	56 813	50 172	...	...	...	...	...
Batala	CDFC	126 646	67 026	59 620	...	147 753	78 342	69 411	...
Bathinda	CDFC	217 389	117 359	100 030	97	...	...	...	...
Beawar	CDFC	123 701	64 394	59 307	...	125 923	65 569	60 354	18
Begusarai	CDFC	...	...	...	...	107 203	57 349	49 854	...
Belgaum	CDFC	399 600	204 846	194 754	142	506 235	261 862	244 373	155
Bellary	CDFC	317 000	163 082	153 918	66	...	...	...	...
Bettiah	CDFC	116 692	61 803	54 889	...	...	...	...	...
Bhadravati	CDFC	160 392	81 260	79 132	...	...	...	...	...
Bhadreswar	CDFC	105 944	57 991	47 953	...	...	...	...	...
Bhagalpur	CDFC	340 349	182 704	157 645	30	349 709	187 627	162 082	31
Bhalswa Jahangir Pur	CDFC	151 427	83 289	68 138	...	...	...	...	...
Bharatpur	CDFC	204 456	109 809	94 647	41	205 104	110 148	94 956	51
Bharuch	CDFC	148 391	76 568	71 823	...	176 531	91 273	85 258	...
Bhatpara	CDFC	441 956	243 065	198 891	16	...	...	...	...
Bhavani	CDFC	...	...	...	...	104 285	52 804	51 481	...
Bhavnagar	CDFC	510 958	267 019	243 939	...	517 578	270 458	247 120	...
Bheemavaram	CDFC	137 327	69 487	67 840	26	141 975	71 938	70 037	...
Bhilai Nagar	CDFC	553 837	289 853	263 984	89	...	...	...	...
Bhilwara	CDFC	280 185	148 642	131 543	118	...	...	...	...
Bhind	CDFC	153 768	83 009	70 759	17	...	...	...	...
Bhiwandi	CDFC	598 703	367 858	230 845	26	621 390	382 493	238 897	28
Bhiwani	CDFC	169 424	91 726	77 698	28	...	...	...	...
Bhopal	CDFC	1 433 875	755 685	678 190	285	1 454 830	766 602	688 228	...
Dhubaneswar	CDFC	647 302	380 476	266 826	125	657 477	365 848	291 629	...
Bhusawal	CDFC	172 366	89 187	83 179	13	187 524	97 192	90 332	25
Bid	CDFC	138 091	71 790	66 301	8	...	...	...	...
Bidar	CDFC	172 298	89 715	82 583	...	173 678	90 449	83 229	47
Bidhan Nagar	CDFC	167 848	85 215	82 633	...	...	...	...	...
Bihar	CDFC	231 972	121 813	110 159	24	...	...	...	...
Bijapur	CDFC	245 946	126 554	119 392	...	253 307	130 237	123 070	75
Bikaner	CDFC	529 007	282 450	246 557	166	...	...	...	...
Bilaspur	CDFC	265 178	137 273	127 905	36	330 291	170 898	159 393	46
Birnagar	CDFC	...	...	...	...	115 104	59 179	55 925	...
Bokaro Steel City	CDFC	394 173	213 044	181 129	163	497 855	268 668	229 187	183
Bommanahalli	CDFC	201 220	108 040	93 180	...	...	...	...	...
Botad	CDFC	100 059	52 668	47 391	...	...	...	...	...
Brahmapur	CDFC	289 724	150 089	139 635	80	...	...	...	...
Budaun	CDFC	148 138	78 294	69 844	4	...	...	...	...
Bulandshahr	CDFC	176 256	93 066	83 190	12	...	...	...	...
Burhanpur	CDFC	194 360	100 031	94 329	13	...	...	...	...
Byatarayanapura	CDFC	180 931	94 683	86 248	...	...	...	...	...
Chakdaha	CDFC	...	...	...	...	101 278	51 321	49 957	...
Champdani	CDFC	103 232	57 874	45 358	...	...	...	...	...
Chandan Nagar	CDFC	162 166	84 222	77 944	10	...	...	...	...
Chandausi	CDFC	103 757	55 167	48 590	...	...	...	...	...
Chandigarh	CDFC	808 796	451 387	357 409	70	...	...	...	...
Chandrapur	CDFC	297 612	148 499	149 113	56	...	...	...	...
Chapra	CDFC	178 835	96 077	82 758	17	...	...	...	...
Chennai (Madras)	CDFC	4 216 268	2 161 605	2 054 663	174	6 424 624	3 294 328	3 130 296	612
Cherthala	CDFC	...	...	...	...	141 512	68 740	72 772	93
Chhatarpur	CDFC	...	...	...	...	109 021	58 393	50 628	...
Chhindwara	CDFC	122 309	63 583	58 726	...	153 635	79 889	73 746	...
Chikmagalur	CDFC	101 022	51 611	49 411	...	...	...	...	...
Chirala	CDFC	...	...	...	...	166 877	83 262	83 615	48
Chirkunda	CDFC	...	...	...	...	106 200	56 528	49 672	...
Chitradurga	CDFC	122 594	62 811	59 783	...	125 060	64 075	60 985	16
Chittoor	CDFC	152 966	77 044	75 922	33	...	...	...	...
Churu	CDFC	...	...	...	...	101 853	53 099	48 754	...
Coimbatore	CDFC	923 085	476 056	447 029	106	1 446 034	743 161	702 873	317

(See notes at end of table. — Voir notes à la fin du tableau.)

Continent, country or area, date and city / Continent, pays ou zone, date et ville	Code[1]	City proper — Ville proprement dite Population				Urban agglomeration — Agglomération urbaine Population			
		Both sexes Les deux sexes	Male Masculin	Female Féminin	Surface area Superficie (km²)	Both sexes Les deux sexes	Male Masculin	Female Féminin	Surface area Superficie (km²)
ASIA — ASIE									
India — Inde[59]									
1 III 2001									
Coonoor	CDFC	...	...	...	...	101 234	51 089	50 145	...
Cuddalore	CDFC	158 569	80 113	78 456	28	...	...	...	...
Cuddapah	CDFC	125 725	63 165	62 560	42	260 899	132 297	128 602	78
Cuttack	CDFC	535 139	286 192	248 947	122	587 637	314 435	273 202	153
Dallo Pura	CDFC	132 628	71 349	61 279	...	...	...	...	...
Damoh	CDFC	112 160	58 898	53 262	...	127 939	67 244	60 695	36
Darbhanga	CDFC	266 834	142 042	124 792	19	...	...	...	...
Darjiling	CDFC	107 530	53 325	54 205	...	109 163	54 131	55 032	...
Dasarahalli	CDFC	263 636	143 225	120 411	...	...	...	...	...
Davangere	CDFC	363 780	187 603	176 177	...	...	...	...	...
Dehradun	CDFC	447 808	236 852	210 956	37	527 859	279 653	248 206	86
Dehri	CDFC	119 007	63 552	55 455	...	...	...	...	...
Delhi[60]	CDFC	9 817 439	5 378 658	4 438 781	431	12 791 458	7 021 896	5 769 562	624
Delhi Cantonment	CDFC	124 452	75 700	48 752	...	...	...	...	...
Deoghar	CDFC	...	...	...	...	112 501	61 405	51 096	...
Deoli	CDFC	119 432	66 575	52 857	...	...	...	...	...
Deoria	CDFC	104 222	54 737	49 485	...	...	...	...	...
Dewas	CDFC	230 658	120 610	110 048	100	...	...	...	...
Dhanbad	CDFC	198 963	108 400	90 563	23	1 064 357	578 602	485 755	201
Dharmavaram	CDFC	103 400	52 799	50 601	...	...	...	...	...
Dhule	CDFC	341 473	177 631	163 842	46	...	...	...	...
Dibrugarh	CDFC	122 523	65 736	56 787	15	137 879	74 239	63 640	16
Dimapur	CDFC	107 382	61 595	45 787	...	...	...	...	...
Dinapur Nizamat	CDFC	130 339	69 024	61 315	...	...	...	...	...
Dindigul	CDFC	196 619	98 969	97 650	14	...	...	...	...
Dohad	CDFC	...	...	...	...	112 087	57 765	54 322	...
Dumdum	CDFC	101 319	52 868	48 451	...	...	...	...	...
Durg	CDFC	231 182	118 896	112 286	51	...	...	...	...
Durgapur	CDFC	492 996	263 426	229 570	154	...	...	...	...
Durg-Bhilai Nagar	CDFC	...	...	...	...	923 559	480 432	443 127	183
Eluru	CDFC	189 772	92 405	97 367	15	215 343	104 987	110 356	...
English Bazar	CDFC	161 448	82 932	78 516	...	224 392	115 454	108 938	19
Erode	CDFC	151 184	76 726	74 458	8	391 169	199 306	191 863	132
Etah	CDFC	107 098	56 960	50 138	...	...	...	...	...
Etawah	CDFC	211 460	112 833	98 627	9	...	...	...	...
Faizabad	CDFC	144 924	76 078	68 846	33	208 164	114 252	93 912	63
Faridabad	CDFC	1 054 981	580 548	474 433	178	...	...	...	...
Farrukhabad-cum-Fategarh	CDFC	227 876	120 783	107 093	17	242 558	129 608	112 950	21
Fatehpur	CDFC	151 757	79 836	71 921	57	...	...	...	...
Firozabad	CDFC	278 801	147 980	130 821	9	432 213	230 477	201 736	12
Gadag-Betgeri	CDFC	154 849	78 672	76 177	35	...	...	...	...
Gajuwaka	CDFC	258 944	133 461	125 483	...	...	...	...	...
Gandhinagar	CDFC	195 891	103 814	92 077	57	...	...	...	...
Ganganagar	CDFC	210 788	115 412	95 376	21	222 833	121 877	100 956	...
Gangawati	CDFC	...	...	...	...	101 397	51 253	50 144	...
Gaya	CDFC	383 197	203 252	179 945	29	394 185	209 926	184 259	32
Ghatlodiya	CDFC	106 259	56 040	50 219	...	...	...	...	...
Ghaziabad	CDFC	968 521	521 408	447 113	64	...	...	...	...
Ghazipur	CDFC	...	...	...	...	103 283	54 321	48 962	...
Giridih	CDFC	...	...	...	...	105 212	55 154	50 058	...
Godhra	CDFC	121 852	63 143	58 709	...	131 144	67 933	63 211	...
Gonda	CDFC	122 164	67 400	54 764	...	...	...	...	...
Gondiya	CDFC	120 878	61 435	59 443	18	...	...	...	...
Gorakhpur	CDFC	624 570	330 450	294 120	137	...	...	...	...
Gudivada	CDFC	112 245	55 439	56 806	13	...	...	...	...
Gudiyatham	CDFC	...	...	...	...	100 021	49 822	50 199	...
Gulbarga	CDFC	427 929	222 623	205 306	...	435 631	226 848	208 783	43
Guna	CDFC	137 132	72 462	64 670	46	...	...	...	...
Guntakul	CDFC	117 403	59 364	58 039	52	...	...	...	...
Guntur	CDFC	514 707	257 939	256 768	30	...	...	...	...
Gurgaon	CDFC	173 542	92 985	80 557	15	229 243	123 370	105 873	24
Guruvayur	CDFC	...	...	...	...	138 676	64 550	74 126	50

8. Population of capital cities and cities of 100 000 and more inhabitants: latest available year
Population des capitales et des villes de 100 000 habitants et plus: dernière année disponible (continued — suite)

(See notes at end of table. — Voir notes à la fin du tableau.)

Continent, country or area, date and city / Continent, pays ou zone, date et ville	Code[1]	City proper — Ville proprement dite Population				Urban agglomeration — Agglomération urbaine Population			
		Both sexes Les deux sexes	Male Masculin	Female Féminin	Surface area Superficie (km²)	Both sexes Les deux sexes	Male Masculin	Female Féminin	Surface area Superficie (km²)
ASIA — ASIE									
India — Inde[59]									
1 III 2001									
Guwahati	CDFC	808 021	441 347	366 674	217	814 575	445 649	368 926	...
Gwalior	CDFC	826 919	442 484	384 435	290	865 800	465 388	400 412	303
Habra	CDFC	127 695	65 263	62 432	18	239 170	121 603	117 567	37
Hajipur	CDFC	119 276	63 762	55 514	...	...	...	...	...
Haldia	CDFC	170 695	89 886	80 809	69	...	...	...	...
Haldwani-cum-Kathgodam	CDFC	129 140	68 826	60 314	11	159 020	84 611	74 409	...
Halisahar	CDFC	124 479	67 124	57 355	...	...	...	...	...
Hanumangarh	CDFC	129 654	69 583	60 071	...	...	...	...	...
Haora (Howrah)	CDFC	1 008 704	547 969	460 735	52	...	...	...	...
Hapur	CDFC	211 987	112 962	99 025	14	...	...	...	...
Hardoi	CDFC	112 474	59 877	52 597	...	...	...	...	...
Hardwar	CDFC	175 010	94 650	80 360	15	220 433	119 159	101 274	42
Hassan	CDFC	117 386	60 225	57 161	...	133 317	68 337	64 980	27
Hathras	CDFC	123 243	65 908	57 335	8	126 352	67 568	58 784	...
Hazaribag	CDFC	127 243	67 905	59 338	...	135 446	72 296	63 150	...
Hindupur	CDFC	125 056	64 159	60 897	38	...	...	...	...
Hisar	CDFC	256 810	140 240	116 570	45	263 070	143 816	119 254	49
Hoshiarpur	CDFC	148 243	78 946	69 297	28	...	...	...	...
Hospet	CDFC	163 284	83 430	79 854	28	...	...	...	...
Hubli-Dharwad	CDFC	786 018	403 270	382 748	191	...	...	...	...
Hugli-Chinsurah	CDFC	170 201	86 728	83 473	17	...	...	...	...
Hyderabad	CDFC	3 449 878	1 773 899	1 675 979	...	5 533 640	2 854 938	2 678 702	...
Ichalakaranji	CDFC	257 572	135 988	121 584	30	285 795	150 934	134 861	38
Imphal	CDFC	217 275	107 593	109 682	33	245 967	121 588	124 379	37
Indore	CDFC	1 597 441	839 843	757 598	...	1 639 044	861 758	777 286	165
Itarsi	CDFC	...	...	...	...	109 288	57 118	52 170	...
Jabalpur	CDFC	951 469	496 029	454 640	154	1 117 200	500 556	520 044	224
Jagadhri	CDFC	101 300	55 910	45 390	...	...	...	...	...
Jagdalpur	CDFC	...	...	...	...	103 216	53 048	50 168	...
Jaipur	CDFC	2 324 319	1 239 711	1 084 608	200	...	...	...	...
Jalandhar	CDFC	701 223	376 925	324 298	80	709 255	381 116	328 139	...
Jalgaon	CDFC	368 579	193 464	175 115	62	...	...	...	...
Jalna	CDFC	235 529	121 728	113 801	82	...	...	...	...
Jalpaiguri	CDFC	100 212	50 570	49 642	...	...	...	...	...
Jammu	CDFC	378 431	206 061	172 370	...	607 642	330 769	276 873	...
Jamnagar	CDFC	447 734	235 093	212 641	...	558 462	292 954	265 508	...
Jamshedpur	CDFC	570 349	300 081	270 268	60	1 101 804	580 336	521 468	160
Jamuria	CDFC	129 456	68 741	60 715	...	...	...	...	...
Jaunpur	CDFC	159 996	84 179	75 817	25	...	...	...	...
Jetpur Navagadh	CDFC	104 311	54 772	49 539	...	...	...	...	...
Jhansi	CDFC	383 248	203 003	180 245	48	463 281	246 495	216 786	83
Jhunjhunun	CDFC	100 476	52 814	47 662	...	...	...	...	...
Jind	CDFC	136 089	73 557	62 532	...	...	...	...	...
Jodhpur	CDFC	846 408	450 816	395 592	79	856 034	455 860	400 174	...
Jorhat	CDFC	...	...	...	60	135 091	71 837	63 254	69
Junagadh	CDFC	168 686	86 935	81 751	...	252 138	130 318	121 820	...
Kaithal	CDFC	117 226	63 090	54 136	...	...	...	...	...
Kakinada	CDFC	289 920	143 905	146 015	39	368 672	183 619	185 053	58
Kalol	CDFC	100 021	53 098	46 923	...	112 025	59 532	52 493	...
Kalyan	CDFC	1 193 266	633 395	559 871	225	...	...	...	...
Kamarhati	CDFC	314 334	168 633	145 701	11	...	...	...	...
Kamptee	CDFC	...	...	...	...	137 056	71 633	65 423	36
Kancheepuram	CDFC	152 984	77 058	75 926	12	188 349	94 942	93 407	40
Kanchrapara	CDFC	126 118	65 197	60 921	13	...	...	...	...
Kanhangad	CDFC	...	...	...	...	129 364	61 954	67 410	84
Kannur	CDFC	...	...	...	...	498 175	237 101	261 074	145
Kanpur	CDFC	2 532 138	1 354 581	1 177 557	267	2 690 486	1 440 140	1 250 346	299
Kapra	CDFC	159 176	82 914	76 262	...	...	...	...	...
Karaikkudi	CDFC	...	...	...	...	125 185	62 230	62 955	79
Karawal Nagar	CDFC	148 549	80 364	68 185	...	...	...	...	...
Karimnagar	CDFC	203 819	104 514	99 305	24	215 782	110 479	105 303	...
Karnal	CDFC	210 476	112 263	98 213	22	222 017	118 428	103 589	24

8. Population of capital cities and cities of 100 000 and more inhabitants: latest available year
Population des capitales et des villes de 100 000 habitants et plus: dernière année disponible (continued — suite)

(See notes at end of table. — Voir notes à la fin du tableau.)

Continent, country or area, date and city / Continent, pays ou zone, date et ville	Code[1]	City proper — Ville proprement dite Population				Urban agglomeration — Agglomération urbaine Population			
		Both sexes Les deux sexes	Male Masculin	Female Féminin	Surface area Superficie (km²)	Both sexes Les deux sexes	Male Masculin	Female Féminin	Surface area Superficie (km²)
ASIA — ASIE									
India — Inde[59]									
1 III 2001									
Karur	CDFC	...	...	...	...	153 123	77 130	75 993	19
Katihar	CDFC	175 169	93 567	81 602	25	190 862	102 126	88 736	...
Khammam	CDFC	158 022	80 072	77 950	...	196 763	100 255	96 508	26
Khandwa	CDFC	171 976	88 859	83 117	36	...	...	...	...
Khanna	CDFC	103 059	55 290	47 769	...	...	...	...	...
Kharagpur	CDFC	207 984	107 506	100 478	91	296 323	152 700	143 623	125
Khardaha	CDFC	116 252	61 254	54 998	...	...	...	...	...
Khargone	CDFC	...	...	...	...	103 980	54 236	49 744	...
Kirari Suleman Nagar	CDFC	153 874	84 908	68 966	...	...	...	...	...
Kishangarh	CDFC	116 156	61 025	55 131	...	...	...	...	...
Koch Bihar	CDFC	...	...	...	...	102 922	52 186	50 736	...
Kochi	CDFC	596 473	295 351	301 122	109	1 355 406	670 462	684 944	373
Kolar	CDFC	113 299	57 773	55 526	...	...	...	...	...
Kolhapur	CDFC	485 183	251 958	233 225	67	497 554	258 400	239 154	67
Kolkata (Calcutta)[61]	CDFC	4 580 544	2 506 029	2 074 515	185	13 216 546	7 072 114	6 144 432	897
Kollam	CDFC	361 441	177 586	183 855	41	379 975	186 842	193 133	68
Korba	CDFC	315 695	165 028	150 667	35	...	...	...	...
Kota	CDFC	695 899	369 897	326 002	221	704 731	374 570	330 161	...
Kothagudem	CDFC	...	...	...	...	105 265	52 377	52 888	35
Kottayam	CDFC	...	...	...	...	172 867	84 915	87 952	64
Kozhikode	CDFC	436 527	211 785	224 742	96	880 168	428 984	451 184	233
Krishnanagar	CDFC	139 070	70 512	68 558	16	148 645	75 381	73 264	...
Krishnarajapura	CDFC	187 453	98 107	89 346	...	...	...	...	...
Kukatpalle	CDFC	290 591	152 159	138 432	...	...	...	...	...
Kulti	CDFC	290 057	152 947	137 110	...	...	...	...	...
Kumbakonam	CDFC	140 021	69 607	70 414	13	160 827	80 012	80 815	15
Kurnool	CDFC	267 739	135 859	131 880	15	320 619	163 071	157 548	46
L.B. Nagar	CDFC	261 987	135 636	126 351	...	...	...	...	...
Lakhimpur	CDFC	120 566	64 804	55 762	...	...	...	...	...
Lalitpur	CDFC	111 810	58 901	52 909	...	...	...	...	...
Latur	CDFC	299 828	156 477	143 351	21	...	...	...	...
Loni	CDFC	120 659	64 976	55 683	...	...	...	...	...
Lucknow	CDFC	2 207 340	1 165 932	1 041 408	310	2 266 933	1 199 273	1 067 660	338
Ludhiana	CDFC	1 395 053	789 868	605 185	135	...	...	...	...
Machilipatnam	CDFC	183 370	91 400	91 970	27	...	...	...	...
Madanapalle	CDFC	...	...	...	...	107 262	54 507	52 755	...
Madhyamgram	CDFC	155 503	79 716	75 787	...	...	...	...	...
Madurai	CDFC	922 913	466 909	456 004	47	1 194 665	604 728	589 937	115
Mahadevapura	CDFC	135 597	72 803	62 794	...	...	...	...	...
Mahbubnagar	CDFC	130 849	67 019	63 830	14	139 483	71 508	67 975	...
Mahesana	CDFC	...	...	...	...	141 367	74 928	66 439	...
Maheshtala	CDFC	389 214	204 734	184 480	...	...	...	...	...
Mainpuri	CDFC	...	...	...	...	102 007	54 043	47 964	...
Malappuram	CDFC	...	...	...	...	170 364	83 669	86 695	111
Malegaon	CDFC	409 190	208 744	200 446	13	...	...	...	...
Malerkotla	CDFC	106 802	56 872	49 930	...	...	...	...	...
Malkajgiri	CDFC	175 000	90 000	85 000	...	...	...	...	...
Mancherial	CDFC	...	...	...	...	118 047	60 371	57 676	...
Mandsaur	CDFC	116 483	60 269	56 214	...	117 532	60 860	56 672	...
Mandya	CDFC	131 211	66 630	64 581	17	...	...	...	...
Mangalore	CDFC	398 745	200 234	198 511	75	538 560	269 176	269 384	155
Mango	CDFC	166 091	87 322	78 769	...	...	...	...	...
Mathura	CDFC	298 827	159 249	139 578	9	319 235	171 516	147 719	22
Maunath Bhanjan	CDFC	210 071	108 696	101 375	9	...	...	...	...
Medinipur	CDFC	153 349	78 365	74 984	15	...	...	...	...
Meerut	CDFC	1 074 229	571 074	503 155	142	1 167 399	624 904	542 495	178
Mira-Bhayandar	CDFC	520 301	286 458	233 843	...	...	...	...	...
Mirzapur-cum-Vindhyachal	CDFC	205 264	109 872	95 392	39	...	...	...	...
Modinagar	CDFC	112 918	60 260	52 658	10	139 642	74 570	65 072	17
Moga	CDFC	124 624	66 843	57 781	...	134 242	71 996	62 246	...
Moradabad	CDFC	641 240	340 217	301 023	34	...	...	...	...
Morena	CDFC	150 890	82 281	68 609	96	...	...	...	...

(See notes at end of table. — Voir notes à la fin du tableau.)

Continent, country or area, date and city / Continent, pays ou zone, date et ville	Code[1]	City proper — Ville proprement dite Population				Urban agglomeration — Agglomération urbaine Population			
		Both sexes Les deux sexes	Male Masculin	Female Féminin	Surface area Superficie (km²)	Both sexes Les deux sexes	Male Masculin	Female Féminin	Surface area Superficie (km²)
ASIA — ASIE									
India — Inde[59]									
1 III 2001									
Mormugoa	CDFC	...	...	...	...	104 689	55 927	48 762	...
Motihari	CDFC	101 506	54 629	46 877	...	109 250	59 517	49 733	...
Mughalsarai	CDFC	...	...	...	...	116 246	61 572	54 674	...
Mumbai (Bombay)	CDFC	11 914 398	6 577 902	5 336 496	466	16 368 084	8 979 172	7 388 912	1 041
Munger	CDFC	187 311	100 374	86 937	18	...	...	...	...
Murwara (Katni)	CDFC	186 738	97 666	89 072	107	...	...	...	...
Muzaffarnagar	CDFC	316 452	166 998	149 454	...	331 403	174 877	156 526	12
Muzaffarpur	CDFC	305 465	163 907	141 558	26	...	...	...	...
Mysore	CDFC	742 261	377 132	365 129	103	785 800	399 904	385 896	129
Nabadwip	CDFC	115 036	58 268	56 768	...	125 346	63 544	61 802	...
Nadiad	CDFC	192 799	100 452	92 347	...	196 679	102 469	94 210	...
Nagaon	CDFC	107 471	56 888	50 583	...	123 054	64 976	58 078	...
Nagercoil	CDFC	208 149	103 075	105 074	24	...	...	...	...
Nagpur	CDFC	2 051 320	1 058 692	992 628	217	2 122 965	1 097 723	1 025 242	229
Naihati	CDFC	215 432	113 706	101 726	4	...	...	...	...
Nala Sopara	CDFC	184 664	99 629	85 035	...	...	...	...	...
Nalgonda	CDFC	110 651	56 495	54 156	...	111 745	57 042	54 703	...
Nanded	CDFC	430 598	224 766	205 832	21	...	...	...	...
Nandyal	CDFC	151 771	76 914	74 857	15	156 216	79 145	77 071	...
Nangloi Jat	CDFC	150 371	82 358	68 013	...	...	...	...	...
Nashik	CDFC	1 076 967	579 638	497 329	259	1 152 048	619 962	532 086	322
Navghar-Manikpur	CDFC	116 700	61 806	54 894	...	...	...	...	...
Navi Mumbai (New Bombay)	CDFC	703 947	395 891	308 056	...	...	...	...	...
Navsari	CDFC	134 009	69 766	64 243	...	229 323	122 335	106 988	...
Neemuch	CDFC	107 496	56 509	50 987	...	112 691	59 250	53 441	...
Nellore	CDFC	378 947	191 283	187 664	48	404 922	204 269	200 653	...
NEW DELHI[62,63]	CDFC	294 783	161 596	133 187	...	...	...	...	...
Neyveli	CDFC	128 133	65 632	62 501	97	138 387	70 920	67 467	116
Nizamabad	CDFC	286 956	145 457	141 499	37	...	...	...	...
Noida	CDFC	293 908	162 306	131 602	90	...	...	...	...
North Barrackpur	CDFC	123 523	63 827	59 696	...	...	...	...	...
North Dumdum	CDFC	220 032	112 868	107 164	...	...	...	...	...
Ongole	CDFC	149 589	76 134	73 455	8	152 945	77 862	75 083	20
Orai	CDFC	139 444	74 974	64 470	...	...	...	...	...
Ozhukarai	CDFC	217 623	110 038	107 585	...	...	...	...	...
Palakkad	CDFC	130 736	64 293	66 443	30	197 281	96 790	100 491	59
Palanpur	CDFC	110 383	58 019	52 364	...	122 279	64 343	57 936	...
Pali	CDFC	187 571	99 258	88 313	84	...	...	...	...
Pallavaram	CDFC	143 984	73 152	70 832	...	...	...	...	...
Palwal	CDFC	100 528	53 577	46 951	...	...	...	...	...
Panchkula Urban Estate	CDFC	140 992	75 925	65 067	...	...	...	...	...
Panihati	CDFC	348 379	180 068	168 311	19	...	...	...	...
Panipat	CDFC	261 665	143 565	118 100	21	353 983	194 697	159 286	...
Panvel	CDFC	104 031	54 967	49 064	...	...	...	...	...
Parbhani	CDFC	259 170	133 892	125 278	58	...	...	...	...
Patan	CDFC	112 038	59 031	53 007	...	113 568	59 889	53 679	...
Pathankot	CDFC	159 559	87 505	72 054	...	168 275	91 998	76 277	...
Patiala	CDFC	302 870	162 465	140 405	...	323 309	173 412	149 897	...
Patna	CDFC	1 376 950	749 868	627 082	107	1 707 429	925 857	781 572	129
Phagwara	CDFC	...	...	...	...	102 111	55 224	46 887	...
Phusro	CDFC	...	...	...	...	174 367	93 656	80 711	84
Pilibhit	CDFC	124 082	65 824	58 258	10	...	...	...	...
Pimpri Chinchwad	CDFC	1 006 417	543 436	462 981	...	...	...	...	...
Pollachi	CDFC	...	...	...	...	127 993	64 417	63 576	43
Pondicherry	CDFC	220 749	109 386	111 363	20	505 715	253 336	252 379	67
Porbandar	CDFC	133 083	68 261	64 822	...	197 414	101 882	95 532	...
Port Blair	CDFC	100 186	55 507	44 679	...	...	...	...	...
Proddatur	CDFC	164 932	82 826	82 106	7	...	...	...	...
Pudukkottai	CDFC	108 947	54 537	54 410	...	...	...	...	...
Pune	CDFC	2 540 069	1 325 694	1 214 375	146	3 755 525	1 980 941	1 774 584	423
Puri	CDFC	157 610	82 229	75 381	17	...	...	...	...
Purnia	CDFC	171 235	92 573	78 662	45	196 757	106 051	90 706	60

(See notes at end of table. — Voir notes à la fin du tableau.)

Continent, country or area, date and city / Continent, pays ou zone, date et ville	Code[1]	City proper — Ville proprement dite Population				Urban agglomeration — Agglomération urbaine Population			
		Both sexes Les deux sexes	Male Masculin	Female Féminin	Surface area Superficie (km²)	Both sexes Les deux sexes	Male Masculin	Female Féminin	Surface area Superficie (km²)
ASIA — ASIE									
India — Inde[59]									
1 III 2001									
Puruliya	CDFC	113 766	59 171	54 595	...	...	...	...	...
Quthbullapur	CDFC	225 816	118 463	107 353	...	...	...	...	...
Rae Bareli	CDFC	169 285	88 961	80 324	50	...	...	...	...
Raichur	CDFC	205 634	105 714	99 920	...	...	...	...	...
Raiganj	CDFC	165 222	87 489	77 733	11	175 064	92 742	82 322	15
Raigarh	CDFC	110 987	57 465	53 522	...	115 740	59 916	55 824	...
Raipur	CDFC	605 131	314 369	290 762	...	699 264	364 034	335 230	64
Rajahmundry	CDFC	313 347	158 027	155 320	52	408 341	205 655	202 686	64
Rajapalayam	CDFC	121 982	61 080	60 902	11	...	...	...	...
Rajarhat Gopalpur	CDFC	271 781	140 179	131 602	...	...	...	...	...
Rajkot	CDFC	966 642	506 915	459 727	...	1 002 160	525 797	476 363	...
Rajnandgaon	CDFC	143 727	72 964	70 763	93	...	...	...	...
Rajpur Sonarpur	CDFC	336 390	173 591	162 799	...	...	...	...	...
Ramagundam	CDFC	235 540	120 307	115 233	28	236 623	120 871	115 752	...
Rampur	CDFC	281 549	146 621	134 928	20	...	...	...	...
Ranaghat	CDFC	...	...	...	...	145 172	73 804	71 368	25
Ranchi	CDFC	846 454	450 514	395 940	177	862 850	459 251	403 599	182
Raniganj	CDFC	122 891	65 360	57 531	...	...	...	...	...
Ratlam	CDFC	221 267	113 982	107 285	39	233 480	120 473	113 007	41
Raurkela	CDFC	224 601	121 028	103 573	133	484 292	258 466	225 826	157
Rewa	CDFC	183 232	98 476	84 756	55	...	...	...	...
Rewari	CDFC	100 946	54 111	46 835	...	...	...	...	...
Rishra	CDFC	113 259	62 602	50 657	...	...	...	...	...
Robertson Pet	CDFC	141 294	70 568	70 726	...	156 961	78 574	78 387	...
Rohtak	CDFC	286 773	154 153	132 620	28	294 537	158 299	136 238	...
Roorkee	CDFC	...	...	...	...	114 811	63 861	50 950	...
S.A.S. Nagar (Mohali)	CDFC	123 284	65 570	57 714	...	...	...	...	...
Sagar	CDFC	232 321	122 491	109 830	36	309 164	163 018	146 146	52
Saharanpur	CDFC	452 925	239 456	213 469	25	...	...	...	...
Saharasa	CDFC	124 015	67 010	57 005	...	...	...	...	...
Salem	CDFC	693 236	352 770	340 466	20	748 513	381 042	367 471	93
Sambalpur	CDFC	154 164	79 914	74 250	50	226 966	117 954	109 012	90
Sambhal	CDFC	182 930	97 264	85 666	16	...	...	...	...
Sangli-Miraj-Kupwad	CDFC	436 639	224 195	212 444	...	447 632	229 852	217 780	...
Santipur	CDFC	138 195	70 084	68 111	25	...	...	...	...
Sasaram	CDFC	131 042	69 665	61 377	...	...	...	...	...
Satara	CDFC	108 043	55 935	52 108	...	...	...	...	...
Satna	CDFC	225 468	120 203	105 265	...	229 323	122 335	106 988	...
Sawai Madhopur	CDFC	...	...	...	...	101 994	53 942	48 052	...
Secunderabad	CDFC	204 182	103 274	100 908	...	...	...	...	...
Serampore	CDFC	197 955	105 613	92 342	6	...	...	...	...
Serilingampalle	CDFC	150 525	75 462	75 063	...	...	...	...	...
Shahjahanpur	CDFC	297 932	162 796	135 136	13	323 166	176 910	146 256	23
Shillong	CDFC	132 876	66 129	66 747	10	267 881	134 416	133 465	25
Shimla	CDFC	142 161	80 772	61 389	32	144 578	82 424	62 154	35
Shimoga	CDFC	274 105	140 107	133 998	...	...	...	...	...
Shivapuri	CDFC	146 859	78 395	68 464	81	...	...	...	...
Sikar	CDFC	184 904	96 327	88 577	23	185 506	96 646	88 860	...
Silchar	CDFC	142 393	72 727	69 666	16	184 285	94 321	89 964	...
Siliguri	CDFC	470 275	249 942	220 333	16	...	...	...	...
Singrauli	CDFC	185 580	100 342	85 238	...	...	...	...	...
Sirsa	CDFC	160 129	85 802	74 327	19	...	...	...	...
Sitapur	CDFC	151 827	79 682	72 145	26	...	...	...	...
Sivakasi	CDFC	...	...	...	...	121 312	60 923	60 389	13
Siwan	CDFC	108 172	57 223	50 949	...	...	...	...	...
Solapur	CDFC	873 037	444 885	428 152	...	...	...	...	...
Sonipat	CDFC	216 213	117 654	98 559	28	225 151	122 488	102 663	...
South Dum Dum	CDFC	392 150	200 182	191 968	11	...	...	...	...
Srikakulam	CDFC	109 666	54 788	54 878	...	117 066	58 613	58 453	...
Srinagar	CDFC	894 940	481 750	413 190	...	971 357	523 017	448 340	...
Sultan Pur Majra	CDFC	163 716	88 313	75 403	...	...	...	...	...
Sultanpur	CDFC	100 085	53 163	46 922	...	...	...	...	...

8. Population of capital cities and cities of 100 000 and more inhabitants: latest available year
Population des capitales et des villes de 100 000 habitants et plus: dernière année disponible (continued — suite)

(See notes at end of table. — Voir notes à la fin du tableau.)

Continent, country or area, date and city Continent, pays ou zone, date et ville	Code[1]	City proper — Ville proprement dite Population				Urban agglomeration — Agglomération urbaine Population			
		Both sexes Les deux sexes	Male Masculin	Female Féminin	Surface area Superficie (km²)	Both sexes Les deux sexes	Male Masculin	Female Féminin	Surface area Superficie (km²)
ASIA — ASIE									
India — Inde[59]									
1 III 2001									
Surat	CDFC	2 433 787	1 372 307	1 061 480	...	2 811 466	1 597 093	1 214 373	...
Surendranagar Dudhrej	CDFC	156 417	81 430	74 987	...	...	...	...	...
Tadepalligudem	CDFC	102 303	50 476	51 827	...	...	...	...	...
Tambaram	CDFC	137 609	70 181	67 428	...	...	...	...	...
Tenali	CDFC	149 839	74 868	74 971	15	...	...	...	...
Thane	CDFC	1 261 517	674 660	586 857	144	...	...	...	...
Thanesar	CDFC	120 072	65 786	54 286	...	122 704	67 239	55 465	...
Thanjavur	CDFC	215 725	106 950	108 775	15	...	...	...	...
Thiruvananthapuram	CDFC	744 739	365 899	378 840	142	889 191	437 009	452 182	178
Thoothukkudi (Tuticorin)	CDFC	216 058	107 781	108 277	13	242 860	121 205	121 655	140
Thrissur	CDFC	317 474	154 188	163 286	...	330 067	160 386	169 681	88
Tinsukia	CDFC	...	...	...	...	108 102	59 515	48 587	...
Tiruchchirappalli	CDFC	746 062	373 541	372 521	23	847 131	424 541	422 590	166
Tirunelveli	CDFC	411 298	203 173	208 125	15	431 603	213 399	218 204	87
Tirupati	CDFC	227 657	117 786	109 871	16	302 678	154 845	147 833	20
Tiruppur	CDFC	346 551	180 629	165 922	44	542 787	282 872	259 915	91
Tiruvannamalai	CDFC	130 301	66 026	64 275	14	...	...	...	...
Tiruvottiyur	CDFC	211 768	108 938	102 830	...	...	...	...	...
Titagarh	CDFC	124 198	70 608	53 590	3	...	...	...	...
Tonk	CDFC	135 663	70 135	65 528	...	...	...	...	...
Tumkur	CDFC	248 592	129 215	119 377	...	...	...	...	...
Udaipur	CDFC	389 317	205 319	183 998	64	...	...	...	...
Udupi	CDFC	113 039	55 933	57 106	...	127 060	62 644	64 416	73
Ujjain	CDFC	429 933	223 745	206 188	...	430 669	224 223	206 446	92
Ulhasnagar	CDFC	472 943	251 610	221 333	22	...	...	...	...
Uluberia	CDFC	202 095	105 735	96 360	...	...	...	...	...
Unnao	CDFC	144 917	76 474	68 443	16	...	...	...	...
Uppal Kalan	CDFC	118 259	61 299	56 960	...	...	...	...	...
Uttarpara Kotrung	CDFC	150 204	78 661	71 543	...	...	...	...	...
Vadakara	CDFC	...	...	...	...	123 965	59 743	64 222	39
Vadodara	CDFC	1 306 035	684 130	621 905	...	1 492 398	783 237	709 161	...
Valsad	CDFC	...	...	...	...	145 650	75 322	70 328	...
Vaniyambadi	CDFC	...	...	...	...	103 841	51 668	52 173	...
Varanasi	CDFC	1 100 748	584 514	516 234	83	1 211 749	644 922	566 827	105
Vasai	CDFC	...	...	...	...	174 382	91 121	83 261	...
Vejalpur	CDFC	113 304	58 828	54 476	...	...	...	...	...
Vellore	CDFC	177 413	88 048	89 365	12	388 211	193 779	194 432	62
Veraval	CDFC	141 207	72 074	69 133	...	157 869	80 813	77 056	...
Vidisha	CDFC	125 457	66 579	58 878	...	...	...	...	...
Vijayawada	CDFC	825 436	436 366	389 070	...	1 011 152	531 084	480 068	105
Virar	CDFC	118 945	63 762	55 183	...	...	...	...	...
Visakhapatnam	CDFC	969 608	489 038	480 570	78	1 329 472	674 080	655 392	318
Vizianagarm	CDFC	174 324	86 111	88 213	21	195 462	96 771	98 691	30
Wadhwan	CDFC	...	...	...	...	219 828	114 217	105 611	...
Warangal	CDFC	528 570	267 820	260 750	57	577 190	292 709	284 481	67
Wardha	CDFC	111 070	57 447	53 623	8	...	...	...	...
Yamunanagar	CDFC	189 587	101 888	87 699	16	306 640	166 324	140 316	42
Yavatmal	CDFC	122 906	62 838	60 068	10	141 970	72 883	69 087	13
Indonesia — Indonésie									
30 VI 2000									
Ambon	CDFC	205 664	103 399	102 265	359	...	...	...	...
Balikpapan	CDFC	409 862	212 264	197 598	503	...	...	...	...
Banda Aceh	CDFC	215 542	110 298	105 244	61	...	...	...	...
Bandar Lampung	CDFC	743 127	374 517	368 610	193	...	...	...	...
Bandjarmasin	CDFC	530 908	263 987	266 921	72	...	...	...	...
Bandung	CDFC	2 138 066	1 074 862	1 063 204	1 670	...	...	...	...
Batam	CDFC	439 971	211 516	228 455	969	...	...	...	...
Bengkulu	CDFC	281 605	141 481	140 124	145	...	...	...	...
Binjai	CDFC	224 516	112 796	111 720	9	...	...	...	...
Bitung	CDFC	147 671	75 774	71 897	304	...	...	...	...
Blitar	CDFC	119 426	58 646	60 780	33	...	...	...	...
Bogor	CDFC	751 211	378 648	372 563	119	...	...	...	...

8. Population of capital cities and cities of 100 000 and more inhabitants: latest available year
Population des capitales et des villes de 100 000 habitants et plus: dernière année disponible (continued — suite)

(See notes at end of table. — Voir notes à la fin du tableau.)

Continent, country or area, date and city / Continent, pays ou zone, date et ville	Code[1]	City proper — Ville proprement dite Population				Urban agglomeration — Agglomération urbaine Population			
		Both sexes Les deux sexes	Male Masculin	Female Féminin	Surface area Superficie (km²)	Both sexes Les deux sexes	Male Masculin	Female Féminin	Surface area Superficie (km²)
ASIA — ASIE									
Indonesia — Indonésie									
30 VI 2000									
Cirebon	CDFC	272 597	135 602	136 995	37	...	...	...	...
Denpasar	CDFC	533 252	271 067	262 185	124	...	...	...	...
Gorontalo	CDFC	135 087	65 717	69 370	65	...	...	...	...
JAKARTA	CDFC	8 389 443	4 245 606	4 143 837	740	...	...	...	...
Jambi	CDFC	417 568	211 810	205 758	205	...	...	...	...
Jayapura	CDFC	166 201	89 196	77 005	740	...	...	...	...
Kediri	CDFC	244 705	121 813	122 892	63	...	...	...	...
Madiun	CDFC	164 048	78 503	85 545	34	...	...	...	...
Magelang	CDFC	117 715	57 626	60 089	18	...	...	...	...
Makasar (Ujung Pandang)	CDFC	1 101 933	543 169	558 764	199	...	...	...	...
Malang	CDFC	757 383	375 348	382 035	145	...	...	...	...
Manado	CDFC	382 451	192 164	190 287	157	...	...	...	...
Mataram	CDFC	317 374	156 606	160 768	61	...	...	...	...
Medan	CDFC	1 911 997	950 180	961 817	265	...	...	...	...
Mojokerto	CDFC	109 073	53 174	55 899	16	...	...	...	...
Padang	CDFC	716 283	352 871	363 412	694	...	...	...	...
Pekalongan	CDFC	262 678	130 364	132 314	45	...	...	...	...
Pakanbaru	CDFC	587 842	298 945	288 897	632	...	...	...	...
Palangkaraya	CDFC	160 572	81 843	78 729	2 400	...	...	...	...
Palembang	CDFC	1 458 664	722 818	735 846	369	...	...	...	...
Pangkal Pinang	CDFC	125 835	63 385	62 450	89	...	...	...	...
Pare Pare	CDFC	108 452	53 194	55 258	99	...	...	...	...
Pasuruan	CDFC	168 629	83 237	85 392	35	...	...	...	...
Pematang Siantar	CDFC	242 756	120 045	122 711	80	...	...	...	...
Pontianak	CDFC	473 360	238 249	235 111	108	...	...	...	...
Probolinggo	CDFC	191 674	94 300	97 374	57	...	...	...	...
Salatiga	CDFC	151 527	74 442	77 085	57	...	...	...	...
Samarinda	CDFC	523 119	266 857	256 262	781	...	...	...	...
Semarang	CDFC	1 427 207	700 940	726 267	374	...	...	...	...
Sukabumi	CDFC	252 688	126 753	125 935	48	...	...	...	...
Surabaya	CDFC	2 610 477	1 296 859	1 313 618	351	...	...	...	...
Surakarta	CDFC	491 272	238 458	252 814	44	...	...	...	...
Tangerang	CDFC	1 326 015	660 897	665 118	187	...	...	...	...
Tanjung Balai	CDFC	132 503	66 476	66 027	68	...	...	...	...
Tebing Tinggi	CDFC	125 211	61 990	63 221	32	...	...	...	...
Tegal	CDFC	237 250	118 125	119 125	35	...	...	...	...
Yogyakarta	CDFC	397 431	194 488	202 943	33	...	...	...	...
Iran (Islamic Republic of) — Iran (République islamique d')									
1 VII 1996									
Abadan	CDJC	206 073	104 252	101 821		...	...	...	...
Ahwaz	CDJC	804 980	410 328	394 652		...	...	...	...
Amol	CDJC	159 092	79 562	79 530		...	...	...	...
Andimeshk	CDJC	106 923	54 142	52 781		...	...	...	...
Arak	CDJC	380 755	193 112	187 643		...	...	...	...
Ardabil	CDJC	340 386	174 586	165 800		...	...	...	...
Babol	CDJC	158 346	79 703	78 643		...	...	...	...
Bandar-e-Abbas	CDJC	273 578	143 166	130 412		...	...	...	...
Birjand	CDJC	127 608	67 838	59 770		...	...	...	...
Bojnurd	CDJC	134 835	69 026	65 809		...	...	...	...
Borujerd	CDJC	217 804	109 196	108 608		...	...	...	...
Bukand	CDJC	120 020	61 001	59 019		...	...	...	...
Bushehr	CDJC	143 641	76 626	67 015		...	...	...	...
Dezful	CDJC	202 639	106 660	95 979		...	...	...	...
Esfahan	CDJC	1 266 072	651 270	614 802		...	...	...	...
Gonbad-e-Kavus	CDJC	111 253	55 601	55 652		...	...	...	...
Gorgan	CDJC	188 710	95 395	93 315		...	...	...	...
Hamadan	CDJC	401 281	205 007	196 274		...	...	...	...
Ilam	CDJC	126 346	64 551	61 795		...	...	...	...
Islam Shahr (Qasemabad)	CDJC	265 450	135 110	130 340		...	...	...	...
Karaj	CDJC	940 968	482 486	458 482		...	...	...	...
Kashan	CDJC	201 372	103 203	98 169		...	...	...	...

8. Population of capital cities and cities of 100 000 and more inhabitants: latest available year
Population des capitales et des villes de 100 000 habitants et plus: dernière année disponible (continued — suite)

(See notes at end of table. — Voir notes à la fin du tableau.)

Continent, country or area, date and city / Continent, pays ou zone, date et ville	Code[1]	City proper — Ville proprement dite Population				Urban agglomeration — Agglomération urbaine Population			
		Both sexes Les deux sexes	Male Masculin	Female Féminin	Surface area Superficie (km²)	Both sexes Les deux sexes	Male Masculin	Female Féminin	Surface area Superficie (km²)

ASIA — ASIE

Iran (Islamic Republic of) — Iran (République islamique d')
1 VII 1996

Kerman	CDJC	384 991	201 674	183 317	...	...	...	...	...
Kermanshah	CDJC	692 986	356 449	336 537	...	...	...	...	...
Khomeini shahr	CDJC	165 888	86 175	79 713	...	...	...	...	...
Khoramabad	CDJC	272 815	139 020	133 795	...	...	...	...	...
Khoramshahr	CDJC	105 636	53 541	52 095	...	...	...	...	...
Khoy	CDJC	148 944	75 429	73 515	...	...	...	...	...
Mahabad	CDJC	107 799	56 287	51 512	...	...	...	...	...
Malayer	CDJC	144 373	72 531	71 842	...	...	...	...	...
Marvadsht	CDJC	103 579	52 578	51 001	...	...	...	...	...
Maraqeh	CDJC	132 318	66 625	65 693	...	...	...	...	...
Mashhad	CDJC	1 887 405	957 345	930 060	...	...	...	...	...
Masjed Soleyman	CDJC	116 882	59 498	57 384	...	...	...	...	...
Najafabad	CDJC	178 498	90 601	87 897	...	...	...	...	...
Neyshabur	CDJC	158 847	79 568	79 279	...	...	...	...	...
Orumiyeh	CDJC	435 200	222 871	212 329	...	...	...	...	...
Qaem shahr	CDJC	143 286	71 491	71 795	...	...	...	...	...
Qazvin	CDJC	291 117	149 910	141 207	...	...	...	...	...
Qarchak	CDJC	142 690	73 326	69 364	...	...	...	...	...
Qods	CDJC	138 278	70 803	67 475	...	...	...	...	...
Qom	CDJC	777 677	397 638	380 039	...	...	...	...	...
Rasht	CDJC	417 748	209 495	208 253	...	...	...	...	...
Sabzewar	CDJC	170 738	86 789	83 949	...	...	...	...	...
Sanandaj	CDJC	277 808	144 326	133 482	...	...	...	...	...
Saqez	CDJC	115 394	58 652	56 742	...	...	...	...	...
Sari	CDJC	195 882	98 805	97 077	...	...	...	...	...
Shahr Kord	CDJC	100 477	50 995	49 402	...	...	...	...	...
Shahrud	CDJC	104 765	54 586	50 179	...	...	...	...	...
Shiraz	CDJC	1 053 025	541 307	511 718	...	...	...	...	...
Sirjan	CDJC	135 024	69 347	65 677	...	...	...	...	...
Tabriz	CDJC	1 191 043	609 813	581 230	...	...	...	...	...
TEHRAN	CDJC	6 758 845	3 468 946	3 289 899	...	...	...	...	...
Varamin	CDJC	107 233	54 492	52 741	...	...	...	...	...
Yazd	CDJC	326 776	168 834	157 942	...	...	...	...	...
Zabol	CDJC	100 887	51 074	49 813	...	...	...	...	...
Zahedan	CDJC	419 518	215 836	203 682	...	...	...	...	...
Zanjan	CDJC	286 295	146 150	140 145	...	...	...	...	...

Iraq
1 VII 1987

Adhamiyah	CDFC	464 151	...	...	...	...	...	...	...
Amara	CDFC	208 797	...	...	...	...	...	...	...
BAGHDAD[64]	CDFC	3 841 268	...	...	...	...	...	...	...
Basra	CDFC	406 296	...	...	...	...	...	...	...
Diwaniya	CDFC	196 519	...	...	...	...	...	...	...
Erbil	CDFC	485 968	...	...	...	...	...	...	...
Hilla	CDFC	268 834	...	...	...	...	...	...	...
Kadhimain	CDFC	521 444	...	...	...	...	...	...	...
Karradah Sharqiyah	CDFC	235 554	...	...	...	...	...	...	...
Kerbala	CDFC	296 705	...	...	...	...	...	...	...
Kirkuk	CDFC	418 624	...	...	...	...	...	...	...
Kut	CDFC	183 183	...	...	...	...	...	...	...
Majnoon	CDFC	244 545	...	...	...	...	...	...	...
Mosul	CDFC	664 221	...	...	...	...	...	...	...
Najaf	CDFC	309 010	...	...	...	...	...	...	...
Nasariya	CDFC	265 937	...	...	...	...	...	...	...
Ramadi	CDFC	192 556	...	...	...	...	...	...	...
Sulamaniya	CDFC	364 096	...	...	...	...	...	...	...

Israel — Israël
1 VII 2002

Ashdod	ESDJ	184 300	90 100	94 200	51	...	...	...	...
Ashqelon	ESDJ	102 400	49 900	52 500	53	...	...	...	...
Bat Yam	ESDJ	134 700	64 000	70 700	8	...	...	...	...

269

8. Population of capital cities and cities of 100 000 and more inhabitants: latest available year
Population des capitales et des villes de 100 000 habitants et plus: dernière année disponible (continued — suite)

(See notes at end of table. — Voir notes à la fin du tableau.)

Continent, country or area, date and city / Continent, pays ou zone, date et ville	Code[1]	City proper — Ville proprement dite Population				Urban agglomeration — Agglomération urbaine Population			
		Both sexes Les deux sexes	Male Masculin	Female Féminin	Surface area Superficie (km²)	Both sexes Les deux sexes	Male Masculin	Female Féminin	Surface area Superficie (km²)
ASIA — ASIE									
Israel — Israël									
1 VII 2002									
Be'er Sheva	ESDJ	179 700	87 400	92 300	53	...	...	...	...
Bene Beraq	ESDJ	138 900	69 400	69 500	7	...	...	...	...
Haifa	ESDJ	271 500	130 300	141 200	63	...	...	...	...
Holon	ESDJ	166 000	79 900	86 100	19	...	...	...	...
JERUSALEM[65,66]	ESDJ	675 200	335 200	340 000	125	...	...	...	...
Netanya	ESDJ	164 300	79 100	85 200	29	...	...	...	...
Petah Tiqwa	ESDJ	171 700	83 100	88 600	36	...	...	...	...
Ramat Gan	ESDJ	127 000	59 700	67 300	14	...	...	...	...
Rishon Leziyyon	ESDJ	209 700	102 200	107 600	51	...	...	...	...
Tel Aviv-Yafo	ESDJ	359 600	171 500	188 100	51	...	...	...	...
Japan — Japon[67,68,69]									
1 VII 2002									
Abiko	ESDF	129 096	64 233	64 863	43	...	...	...	...
Ageo	ESDF	215 126	107 706	107 420	46	...	...	...	...
Aizuwakamatsu	ESDF	117 538	56 103	61 435	315	...	...	...	...
Akashi	ESDF	292 280	142 678	149 602	49	...	...	...	...
Akishima	ESDF	108 302	54 718	53 584	17	...	...	...	...
Akita	ESDF	318 503	151 983	166 520	460	...	...	...	...
Amagasaki	ESDF	463 837	226 660	237 177	50	...	...	...	...
Anjo	ESDF	162 359	82 383	79 976	86	...	...	...	...
Aomori	ESDF	297 305	140 334	156 971	692	...	...	...	...
Asahikawa	ESDF	362 999	171 898	191 101	748	...	...	...	...
Asaka	ESDF	122 998	64 266	58 732	18	...	...	...	...
Ashikaga	ESDF	161 877	79 237	82 640	178	...	...	...	...
Atsugi	ESDF	220 720	115 194	105 526	94	...	...	...	...
Beppu	ESDF	126 658	57 113	69 545	125	...	...	...	...
Chiba	ESDF	902 326	454 309	448 017	272	...	...	...	...
Chigasaki	ESDF	223 835	110 676	113 159	36	...	...	...	...
Chofu	ESDF	208 522	105 653	102 869	22	...	...	...	...
Daito	ESDF	128 712	64 488	64 224	18	...	...	...	...
Ebetsu	ESDF	123 426	59 678	63 748	188	...	...	...	...
Ebina	ESDF	119 315	60 927	58 388	26	...	...	...	...
Fuchu	ESDF	234 072	122 597	111 475	29	...	...	...	...
Fuji	ESDF	236 323	117 384	118 939	214	...	...	...	...
Fujieda	ESDF	129 107	63 153	65 954	141	...	...	...	...
Fujimi	ESDF	104 149	52 381	51 768	20	...	...	...	...
Fujinomiya	ESDF	121 151	59 617	61 534	315	...	...	...	...
Fujisawa	ESDF	386 133	193 945	192 188	70	...	...	...	...
Fukaya	ESDF	103 647	51 727	51 920	69	...	...	...	...
Fukui	ESDF	252 456	123 061	129 395	341	...	...	...	...
Fukuoka	ESDF	1 365 888	657 976	707 912	339	...	...	...	...
Fukushima	ESDF	290 990	140 740	150 250	746	...	...	...	...
Fukuyama	ESDF	379 966	184 159	195 807	364	...	...	...	...
Funabashi	ESDF	558 675	284 618	274 057	86	...	...	...	...
Gifu	ESDF	403 853	191 508	212 345	195	...	...	...	...
Habikino	ESDF	120 346	57 651	62 695	26	...	...	...	...
Hachinohe	ESDF	241 944	116 826	125 118	214	...	...	...	...
Hachioji	ESDF	543 470	276 997	266 473	186	...	...	...	...
Hadano	ESDF	168 390	87 070	81 320	104	...	...	...	...
Hakodate	ESDF	286 617	132 198	154 419	347	...	...	...	...
Hamamatsu	ESDF	588 999	293 473	295 526	257	...	...	...	...
Handa	ESDF	112 457	55 673	56 784	47	...	...	...	...
Higashihiroshima	ESDF	126 513	64 915	61 598	288	...	...	...	...
Higashikurume	ESDF	113 451	56 244	57 207	13	...	...	...	...
Higashimurayama	ESDF	143 147	71 005	72 142	17	...	...	...	...
Higashiosaka	ESDF	514 093	253 315	260 778	62	...	...	...	...
Hikone	ESDF	108 545	53 480	55 065	98	...	...	...	...
Himeji	ESDF	479 571	230 968	248 603	276	...	...	...	...
Hino	ESDF	169 865	87 686	82 179	28	...	...	...	...
Hirakata	ESDF	403 805	195 525	208 280	65	...	...	...	...
Hiratsuka	ESDF	255 219	129 532	125 687	68	...	...	...	...
Hirosaki	ESDF	176 240	81 051	95 189	274	...	...	...	...

8. Population of capital cities and cities of 100 000 and more inhabitants: latest available year
Population des capitales et des villes de 100 000 habitants et plus: dernière année disponible (continued — suite)

(See notes at end of table. — Voir notes à la fin du tableau.)

Continent, country or area, date and city / Continent, pays ou zone, date et ville	Code[1]	City proper — Ville proprement dite Population				Urban agglomeration — Agglomération urbaine Population			
		Both sexes Les deux sexes	Male Masculin	Female Féminin	Surface area Superficie (km²)	Both sexes Les deux sexes	Male Masculin	Female Féminin	Surface area Superficie (km²)
ASIA — ASIE									
Japan — Japon[67,68,69]									
1 VII 2002									
Hiroshima	ESDF	1 133 320	550 247	583 073	742	...	...	...	...
Hitachi	ESDF	191 370	95 862	95 508	153	...	...	...	...
Hitachinaka	ESDF	152 231	76 723	75 508	99	...	...	...	...
Hofu	ESDF	118 627	57 104	61 523	189	...	...	...	...
Ibaraki	ESDF	260 973	128 833	132 140	77	...	...	...	...
Ichihara	ESDF	279 436	143 703	135 733	368	...	...	...	...
Ichikawa	ESDF	460 849	238 625	222 224	57	...	...	...	...
Ichinomiya	ESDF	276 765	135 367	141 398	82	...	...	...	...
Iida	ESDF	107 075	51 132	55 943	325	...	...	...	...
Ikeda	ESDF	101 196	49 484	51 712	22	...	...	...	...
Ikoma	ESDF	113 184	54 070	59 114	53	...	...	...	...
Imabari	ESDF	117 518	54 372	63 146	75	...	...	...	...
Inazawa	ESDF	100 744	50 195	50 549	48	...	...	...	...
Iruma	ESDF	149 773	74 528	75 245	45	...	...	...	...
Isehara	ESDF	100 259	51 419	48 840	56	...	...	...	...
Isesaki	ESDF	128 068	63 776	64 292	65	...	...	...	...
Ishinomaki	ESDF	118 776	57 397	61 379	137	...	...	...	...
Itami	ESDF	191 618	94 784	96 834	25	...	...	...	...
Iwaki	ESDF	358 962	174 920	184 042	1 231	...	...	...	...
Iwakuni	ESDF	104 856	50 020	54 836	221	...	...	...	...
Iwatsuki	ESDF	109 292	54 853	54 439	49	...	...	...	...
Izumi (Osaka)	ESDF	174 436	84 986	89 450	85	...	...	...	...
Joetsu	ESDF	134 876	65 734	69 142	...	...	...	...	...
Kadoma	ESDF	134 140	66 713	67 427	12	...	...	...	...
Kagoshima	ESDF	553 737	258 683	295 054	290	...	...	...	...
Kakamigahara	ESDF	133 004	65 218	67 786	80	...	...	...	...
Kakogawa	ESDF	266 352	130 503	135 849	139	...	...	...	...
Kamagaya	ESDF	102 941	51 267	51 674	21	...	...	...	...
Kamakura	ESDF	167 629	80 371	87 258	40	...	...	...	...
Kanazawa	ESDF	456 830	222 656	234 174	468	...	...	...	...
Kariya	ESDF	135 250	70 611	64 639	50	...	...	...	...
Kashihara	ESDF	125 619	60 439	65 180	40	...	...	...	...
Kashiwa	ESDF	331 233	165 689	165 544	73	...	...	...	...
Kasuga	ESDF	107 196	52 748	54 448	14	...	...	...	...
Kasugai	ESDF	291 774	145 991	145 783	93	...	...	...	...
Kasukabe	ESDF	204 039	101 844	102 195	38	...	...	...	...
Kawachinagano	ESDF	119 931	57 122	62 809	110	...	...	...	...
Kawagoe	ESDF	332 732	168 435	164 297	109	...	...	...	...
Kawaguchi	ESDF	469 166	239 625	229 541	56	...	...	...	...
Kawanishi	ESDF	155 702	74 424	81 278	53	...	...	...	...
Kawasaki	ESDF	1 279 701	664 038	615 663	143	...	...	...	...
Kiryu	ESDF	113 457	54 883	58 574	137	...	...	...	...
Kisarazu	ESDF	122 485	61 236	61 249	139	...	...	...	...
Kishiwada	ESDF	201 930	97 617	104 313	72	...	...	...	...
Kitakyushu[70]	ESDF	1 006 652	475 391	531 261	485	...	...	...	...
Kitami	ESDF	111 785	54 176	57 609	421	...	...	...	...
Kobe	ESDF	1 509 325	719 255	790 070	550	...	...	...	...
Kochi	ESDF	332 630	155 458	177 172	145	...	...	...	...
Kodaira	ESDF	181 895	91 085	90 810	20	...	...	...	...
Kofu	ESDF	195 381	96 200	99 181	172	...	...	...	...
Koganei	ESDF	112 931	57 391	55 540	11	...	...	...	...
Kokubunji	ESDF	114 655	57 939	56 716	11	...	...	...	...
Komaki	ESDF	145 095	73 578	71 517	63	...	...	...	...
Komatsu	ESDF	108 656	52 544	56 112	371	...	...	...	...
Koriyama	ESDF	337 075	167 025	170 050	757	...	...	...	...
Koshigaya	ESDF	312 036	156 685	155 351	60	...	...	...	...
Kumagaya	ESDF	156 705	78 800	77 905	85	...	...	...	...
Kumamoto	ESDF	667 285	316 530	350 755	267	...	...	...	...
Kurashiki	ESDF	432 917	209 041	223 876	299	...	...	...	...
Kure	ESDF	201 769	97 332	104 437	146	...	...	...	...
Kurume	ESDF	237 924	112 941	124 983	125	...	...	...	...
Kusatsu	ESDF	117 439	60 714	56 725	48	...	...	...	...

8. Population of capital cities and cities of 100 000 and more inhabitants: latest available year
Population des capitales et des villes de 100 000 habitants et plus: dernière année disponible (continued — suite)

(See notes at end of table. — Voir notes à la fin du tableau.)

Continent, country or area, date and city Continent, pays ou zone, date et ville	Code[1]	City proper — Ville proprement dite Population				Urban agglomeration — Agglomération urbaine Population			
		Both sexes Les deux sexes	Male Masculin	Female Féminin	Surface area Superficie (km²)	Both sexes Les deux sexes	Male Masculin	Female Féminin	Surface area Superficie (km²)
ASIA — ASIE									
Japan — Japon[67,68,69]									
1 VII 2002									
Kushiro	ESDF	191 151	91 677	99 474	222	...	...	...	...
Kuwana	ESDF	108 999	53 425	55 574	57	...	...	...	...
Kyoto	ESDF	1 467 290	702 379	764 911	610	...	...	...	...
Machida	ESDF	391 188	194 198	196 990	72	...	...	...	...
Maebashi	ESDF	284 377	138 776	145 601	147	...	...	...	...
Matsubara	ESDF	131 420	64 089	67 331	17	...	...	...	...
Matsudo	ESDF	470 111	236 693	233 418	61	...	...	...	...
Matsue	ESDF	152 613	73 954	78 659	221	...	...	...	...
Matsumoto	ESDF	209 526	103 741	105 785	266	...	...	...	...
Matsusaka	ESDF	124 788	60 185	64 603	210	...	...	...	...
Matsuyama	ESDF	475 890	224 353	251 537	289	...	...	...	...
Minoh	ESDF	124 909	60 400	64 509	48	...	...	...	...
Misato	ESDF	130 397	66 505	63 892	30	...	...	...	...
Mishima	ESDF	111 294	54 504	56 790	62	...	...	...	...
Mitaka	ESDF	174 038	87 316	86 722	17	...	...	...	...
Mito	ESDF	247 809	120 609	127 200	176	...	...	...	...
Miyakonojo	ESDF	132 190	62 218	69 972	306	...	...	...	...
Miyazaki	ESDF	306 988	144 017	162 971	287	...	...	...	...
Moriguchi	ESDF	150 164	73 617	76 547	13	...	...	...	...
Morioka	ESDF	288 142	138 017	150 125	489	...	...	...	...
Muroran	ESDF	102 746	49 609	53 137	81	...	...	...	...
Musashino	ESDF	136 382	66 259	70 123	11	...	...	...	...
Nagano	ESDF	361 428	175 986	185 442	404	...	...	...	...
Nagaoka	ESDF	194 215	95 371	98 844	262	...	...	...	...
Nagareyama	ESDF	151 659	75 201	76 458	35	...	...	...	...
Nagasaki	ESDF	420 327	194 627	225 700	241	...	...	...	...
Nagoya	ESDF	2 183 738	1 085 091	1 098 647	326	...	...	...	...
Naha	ESDF	304 507	146 543	157 964	39	...	...	...	...
Nara	ESDF	365 361	173 210	192 151	212	...	...	...	...
Narashino	ESDF	156 080	79 300	76 780	21	...	...	...	...
Neyagawa	ESDF	247 807	122 017	125 790	25	...	...	...	...
Niigata	ESDF	529 309	256 635	272 674	206	...	...	...	...
Niihama	ESDF	124 902	59 628	65 274	161	...	...	...	...
Niiza	ESDF	149 976	75 727	74 249	23	...	...	...	...
Nishio	ESDF	101 562	50 970	50 592	76	...	...	...	...
Nishinomiya	ESDF	450 063	214 557	235 506	99	...	...	...	...
Nishitokyo	ESDF	183 458	91 524	91 934	16	...	...	...	...
Nobeoka	ESDF	123 923	58 103	65 820	284	...	...	...	...
Noda	ESDF	120 305	60 339	59 966	74	...	...	...	...
Numazu	ESDF	207 128	102 401	104 727	152	...	...	...	...
Obihiro	ESDF	174 322	84 487	89 835	619	...	...	...	...
Odawara	ESDF	199 423	98 101	101 322	114	...	...	...	...
Ogaki	ESDF	150 287	72 967	77 320	80	...	...	...	...
Oita	ESDF	440 482	212 217	228 265	361	...	...	...	...
Okayama	ESDF	630 991	303 596	327 395	513	...	...	...	...
Okazaki	ESDF	342 006	171 159	170 847	227	...	...	...	...
Okinawa	ESDF	122 581	59 112	63 469	49	...	...	...	...
Omuta	ESDF	136 280	62 078	74 202	82	...	...	...	...
Osaka	ESDF	2 618 867	1 281 157	1 337 710	222	...	...	...	...
Ota	ESDF	149 630	75 615	74 015	98	...	...	...	...
Otaru	ESDF	149 100	68 363	80 737	243	...	...	...	...
Otsu	ESDF	293 712	142 751	150 961	302	...	...	...	...
Oume	ESDF	141 890	71 459	70 431	103	...	...	...	...
Oyama	ESDF	156 949	78 973	77 976	172	...	...	...	...
Saga	ESDF	167 156	79 260	87 896	104	...	...	...	...
Sagamihara	ESDF	614 148	312 062	302 086	90	...	...	...	...
Saitama	ESDF	1 044 842	527 169	517 673	168	...	...	...	...
Sakai	ESDF	793 405	383 840	409 565	137	...	...	...	...
Sakata	ESDF	100 750	48 322	52 428	176	...	...	...	...
Sakura	ESDF	171 826	84 382	87 444	104	...	...	...	...
Sanda	ESDF	113 350	55 197	58 153	210	...	...	...	...
Sapporo	ESDF	1 842 926	876 371	966 555	1 121	...	...	...	...

(See notes at end of table. — Voir notes à la fin du tableau.)

Continent, country or area, date and city / Continent, pays ou zone, date et ville	Code[1]	City proper — Ville proprement dite Population				Urban agglomeration — Agglomération urbaine Population			
		Both sexes Les deux sexes	Male Masculin	Female Féminin	Surface area Superficie (km²)	Both sexes Les deux sexes	Male Masculin	Female Féminin	Surface area Superficie (km²)
ASIA — ASIE									
Japan — Japon[67,68,69]									
1 VII 2002									
Sasebo	ESDF	240 899	113 308	127 591	248	...	...	...	...
Sayama	ESDF	161 208	81 668	79 540	49	...	...	...	...
Sendai	ESDF	1 018 150	499 234	518 916	784	...	...	...	...
Seto	ESDF	132 332	65 401	66 931	112	...	...	...	...
Shimizu	ESDF	234 894	114 858	120 036	228	...	...	...	...
Shimonoseki	ESDF	249 855	117 069	132 786	224	...	...	...	...
Shizuoka	ESDF	468 368	228 048	240 320	1 146	...	...	...	...
Soka	ESDF	228 897	117 475	111 422	27	...	...	...	...
Suita	ESDF	350 365	172 299	178 066	36	...	...	...	...
Suzuka	ESDF	189 083	94 004	95 079	195	...	...	...	...
Tachikawa	ESDF	166 729	83 699	83 030	24	...	...	...	...
Tajimi	ESDF	103 894	50 422	53 472	78	...	...	...	...
Takamatsu	ESDF	333 979	161 503	172 476	194	...	...	...	...
Takaoka	ESDF	170 840	81 882	88 958	151	...	...	...	...
Takarazuka	ESDF	216 365	101 985	114 380	102	...	...	...	...
Takasaki	ESDF	240 985	118 636	122 349	111	...	...	...	...
Takatsuki	ESDF	354 345	172 816	181 529	105	...	...	...	...
Tama	ESDF	145 508	73 494	72 014	21	...	...	...	...
Toda	ESDF	110 737	58 055	52 682	18	...	...	...	...
Tokai	ESDF	101 010	52 565	48 445	43	...	...	...	...
Tokorozawa	ESDF	334 099	167 570	166 529	72	...	...	...	...
Tokushima	ESDF	267 296	126 808	140 488	191	...	...	...	...
Tokuyama	ESDF	103 319	49 998	53 321	340	...	...	...	...
TOKYO[71]	ESDF	8 272 384	4 109 741	4 162 643	621	...	...	...	...
Tomakomai	ESDF	173 006	84 596	88 410	561	...	...	...	...
Tondabayashi	ESDF	126 500	60 572	65 928	40	...	...	...	...
Tottori	ESDF	151 428	74 064	77 364	237	...	...	...	...
Toyama	ESDF	325 497	157 720	167 777	209	...	...	...	...
Toyota	ESDF	356 136	187 961	168 175	290	...	...	...	...
Toyohashi	ESDF	368 113	182 857	185 256	261	...	...	...	...
Toyokawa	ESDF	118 281	58 678	59 603	65	...	...	...	...
Toyonaka	ESDF	389 467	188 881	200 586	36	...	...	...	...
Tsu	ESDF	163 729	79 520	84 209	102	...	...	...	...
Tsuchiura	ESDF	135 339	67 191	68 148	82	...	...	...	...
Tsukuba	ESDF	169 207	87 733	81 474	260	...	...	...	...
Ube	ESDF	173 338	82 926	90 412	210	...	...	...	...
Ueda	ESDF	125 592	61 898	63 694	177	...	...	...	...
Uji	ESDF	188 314	91 997	96 317	68	...	...	...	...
Urasoe	ESDF	103 389	50 731	52 658	19	...	...	...	...
Urayasu	ESDF	140 846	72 734	68 112	17	...	...	...	...
Utsunomiya	ESDF	446 568	223 099	223 469	312	...	...	...	...
Wakayama	ESDF	383 914	181 648	202 266	209	...	...	...	...
Yachiyo	ESDF	174 331	86 651	87 680	51	...	...	...	...
Yaizu	ESDF	119 634	58 222	61 412	46	...	...	...	...
Yamagata	ESDF	255 629	123 309	132 320	381	...	...	...	...
Yamaguchi	ESDF	141 792	67 759	74 033	357	...	...	...	...
Yamato	ESDF	216 530	110 075	106 455	27	...	...	...	...
Yao	ESDF	274 213	133 494	140 719	42	...	...	...	...
Yatsushiro	ESDF	105 394	49 311	56 083	147	...	...	...	...
Yokkaichi	ESDF	293 552	144 512	149 040	197	...	...	...	...
Yokohama	ESDF	3 491 159	1 765 389	1 725 770	437	...	...	...	...
Yokosuka	ESDF	430 575	216 859	213 716	101	...	...	...	...
Yonago	ESDF	139 746	66 491	73 255	106	...	...	...	...
Zama	ESDF	127 156	65 471	61 685	18	...	...	...	...
Jordan — Jordanie									
1 VII 2000									
AMMAN	ESDF	1 147 447	...	...	...	...	...	...	...
Irbid	ESDF	247 275	...	...	...	...	...	...	...
Russiefa	ESDF	218 211	...	...	...	...	...	...	...
Zarqa	ESDF	428 623	...	...	...	...	...	...	...

8. Population of capital cities and cities of 100 000 and more inhabitants: latest available year
Population des capitales et des villes de 100 000 habitants et plus: dernière année disponible (continued — suite)

(See notes at end of table. — Voir notes à la fin du tableau.)

Continent, country or area, date and city Continent, pays ou zone, date et ville	Code[1]	City proper — Ville proprement dite Population				Urban agglomeration — Agglomération urbaine Population			
		Both sexes Les deux sexes	Male Masculin	Female Féminin	Surface area Superficie (km²)	Both sexes Les deux sexes	Male Masculin	Female Féminin	Surface area Superficie (km²)
ASIA — ASIE									
Kazakhstan									
1 VII 2000									
Aktau	ESDF	142 600	...	...	...	157 900	...	...	706
Aktobe	ESDF	249 200	...	...	...	277 800	...	...	...
Almaty	ESDF	1 135 400	...	...	...	1 135 400	...	...	230
ASTANA	ESDF	322 400	...	...	...	322 400	...	...	252
Atirau	ESDF	142 700	...	...	...	194 600	...	...	...
Karaganda	ESDF	434 300	...	...	...	434 600	...	...	600
Koktshetau	ESDF	123 500	...	...	...	134 100	...	...	230
Kustanai	ESDF	216 700	...	...	...	216 700	...	...	...
Kyzylorda	ESDF	158 300	...	...	...	194 900	...	...	88
Pavlodar	ESDF	295 400	...	...	...	312 600	...	...	...
Petropavlovsk (Severo-Kazakhstanskaya oblast)	ESDF	201 500	...	...	...	202 400	...	...	155
Shimkent	ESDF	359 600	...	...	...	419 400	...	...	78
Taldykorgan	ESDF	97 200	...	...	...	117 100	...	...	59
Taraz	ESDF	329 200	...	...	...	329 200	...	...	...
Uralsk	ESDF	190 900	...	...	...	217 300	...	...	232
Ust-Kamenogorsk	ESDF	307 900	...	...	...	317 400	...	...	23
Korea (Dem. People's Republic of) — Corée (Rép. populaire dém. de)									
1 VII 1993									
Chongjin	CDFC	582 480	...	...	...	...	...	...	...
Haeju	CDFC	229 172	...	...	...	...	...	...	...
Hamhung	CDFC	709 730	...	...	...	...	...	...	...
Hyesan	CDFC	178 020	...	...	...	...	...	...	...
Kaesong	CDFC	334 433	...	...	...	...	...	...	...
Kanggye	CDFC	223 410	...	...	...	...	...	...	...
Nampho	CDFC	731 448	...	...	...	...	...	...	...
Phyongsong	CDFC	272 934	...	...	...	...	...	...	...
PYONGYANG	CDFC	2 741 260	...	...	...	...	...	...	...
Sariwon	CDFC	254 146	...	...	...	...	...	...	...
Sinuiji	CDFC	326 011	...	...	...	...	...	...	...
Wonsan	CDFC	300 148	...	...	...	...	...	...	...
Korea (Republic of) — Corée (République de)									
1 XI 2000									
Andong	CDFC	182 098	89 823	92 275	1 518	...	...	...	...
Asan	CDFC	180 763	90 812	89 951	...	...	...	...	...
Boryeong	CDFC	109 535	55 390	54 145	...	...	...	...	...
Bucheon (Puchon)	CDFC	761 389	384 935	376 454	53	...	...	...	...
Busan (Pusan)	CDFC	3 662 884	1 827 062	1 835 822	748	...	...	...	...
Changwon	CDFC	517 410	265 941	251 469	293	...	...	...	...
Cheonan	CDFC	417 835	212 874	204 961	637	...	...	...	...
Cheongju	CDFC	586 700	292 144	294 556	153	...	...	...	...
Chuncheon	CDFC	252 547	125 605	126 942	1 117	...	...	...	...
Chungju	CDFC	217 927	110 540	107 387	984	...	...	...	...
Daegu (Taegu)	CDFC	2 480 578	1 247 562	1 233 016	885	...	...	...	...
Daejeon (Taejon)	CDFC	1 368 207	690 600	677 607	539	...	...	...	...
Gangneung (Kangnung)	CDFC	228 232	113 826	114 406	1 039	...	...	...	...
Geoje	CDFC	168 022	87 169	80 853	...	...	...	...	...
Gimcheon	CDFC	147 855	73 629	74 226	...	...	...	...	...
Gimhae (Kimhae)	CDFC	331 979	167 255	164 724	463	...	...	...	...
Gimje	CDFC	102 589	50 067	52 522	...	...	...	...	...
Gongju	CDFC	130 376	64 537	65 839	...	...	...	...	...
Goyang	CDFC	763 971	381 072	382 899	...	...	...	...	...
Gumi (Kumi)	CDFC	341 550	173 253	168 297	127	...	...	...	...
Gunpo (Kunpo)	CDFC	263 760	133 013	130 747	36	...	...	...	...
Gunsan (Kunsan)	CDFC	272 715	138 537	134 178	388	...	...	...	...
Gwangju (Kwangchu)	CDFC	1 352 797	674 228	678 569	501	...	...	...	...
Gwangmyeong (Kwangmyong)	CDFC	334 089	167 115	166 974	38	...	...	...	...
Gwangyang	CDFC	132 639	67 629	65 010	...	...	...	...	...
Gyeongju (Kyongju)	CDFC	275 842	136 891	138 951	1 324	...	...	...	...
Gyeongsan	CDFC	228 206	114 162	114 044	...	...	...	...	...

8. Population of capital cities and cities of 100 000 and more inhabitants: latest available year
Population des capitales et des villes de 100 000 habitants et plus: dernière année disponible (continued — suite)

(See notes at end of table. — Voir notes à la fin du tableau.)

Continent, country or area, date and city / Continent, pays ou zone, date et ville	Code[1]	City proper — Ville proprement dite Population				Urban agglomeration — Agglomération urbaine Population			
		Both sexes Les deux sexes	Male Masculin	Female Féminin	Surface area Superficie (km²)	Both sexes Les deux sexes	Male Masculin	Female Féminin	Surface area Superficie (km²)
ASIA — ASIE									
Korea (Republic of) — Corée (République de)									
1 XI 2000									
Icheon	CDFC	179 719	88 460	91 259	...	...	...	...	...
Iksan (Iri)	CDFC	323 687	161 231	162 456	507	...	...	...	...
Incheon	CDFC	2 475 139	1 250 383	1 224 756	955	...	...	...	...
Jecheon (Chechon)	CDFC	143 710	72 855	70 855	882	...	...	...	...
Jeju (Cheju)	CDFC	279 996	138 932	141 064	255	...	...	...	...
Jeongeup	CDFC	129 152	62 902	66 250	...	...	...	...	...
Jeonju (Chonchu)	CDFC	616 468	306 661	309 807	206	...	...	...	...
Jinhae (Chinhae)	CDFC	127 578	64 317	63 261	...	...	...	...	...
Jinju (Chinju)	CDFC	339 791	168 576	171 215	712	...	...	...	...
Masan	CDFC	434 371	218 050	216 321	329	...	...	...	...
Miryang	CDFC	115 962	56 855	59 107	...	...	...	...	...
Mokpo	CDFC	250 480	125 922	124 558	46	...	...	...	...
Nonsan	CDFC	137 452	68 799	68 653	...	...	...	...	...
Pohang	CDFC	515 714	264 319	251 395	1 126	...	...	...	...
Sacheon	CDFC	111 078	55 285	55 793	...	...	...	...	...
Sangju	CDFC	116 493	57 152	59 341	...	...	...	...	...
Seongnam	CDFC	914 590	461 011	453 579	141	...	...	...	...
Seosan	CDFC	143 154	73 100	70 054	...	...	...	...	...
SEOUL	CDFC	9 895 217	4 966 993	4 928 224	605	...	...	...	...
Suncheon	CDFC	265 930	133 064	132 866	907	...	...	...	...
Suwon (Puwan)	CDFC	946 704	476 639	470 065	121	...	...	...	...
Tongyeong	CDFC	123 842	62 017	61 825	...	...	...	...	...
Uijeongbu (Eujeongbu)	CDFC	355 380	177 657	177 723	81	...	...	...	...
Ulsan	CDFC	1 014 428	522 062	492 366	1 055	...	...	...	...
Wonju	CDFC	268 352	134 901	133 451	865	...	...	...	...
Yangsan	CDFC	191 975	96 551	95 424	...	...	...	...	...
Yeongcheon	CDFC	111 302	55 176	56 216	...	...	...	...	...
Yeongju	CDFC	126 507	63 556	62 951	...	...	...	...	...
Yeosu	CDFC	303 233	152 836	150 397	45	...	...	...	...
Kuwait — Koweït									
20 IV 1995									
Jaleeb Al-Shuykh	CDFC	102 169	78 748	23 421	...	...	...	...	...
KUWAIT CITY	CDFC	28 747	23 601	5 146	...	...	...	...	...
Salmlya	CDFC	129 775	77 672	52 103	...	...	...	...	...
Kyrgyzstan — Kirghizistan									
1 I 2002									
BISHKEK	ESDF	781 800	374 700	407 100	127	...	...	...	...
Osh	ESDF	222 200	106 500	115 700	24	...	...	...	...
Lao People's Democratic Republic — République démocratique populaire lao									
1 III 1995									
VIENTIANE	CDFC	...	...	...	...	528 100	...	...	...
Lebanon — Liban									
15 XI 1970									
BEIRUT	SSDF	474 870	239 130	235 740	...	938 940	...	...	...
Tripoli	SSDF	127 611	...	...	...	...	...	...	...
Malaysia — Malaisie									
1 VII 1991									
Alor Setar	CDFC	124 412	...	...	...	164 444	...	...	...
George Town	CDFC	219 603	...	...	...	...	...	...	...
Ipoh	CDFC	382 853	...	...	...	468 841	...	...	...
Johore Bharu	CDFC	328 436	...	...	...	441 703	...	...	...
Klang	CDFC	243 355	...	...	...	368 379	...	...	...
Kota Bahru	CDFC	219 582	...	...	...	234 581	...	...	...
KUALA LUMPUR	CDFC	1 145 342	...	...	...	...	...	...	...
Kuala Terengganu	CDFC	228 119	...	...	...	...	...	...	...
Kuantan	CDFC	199 484	...	...	...	202 445	...	...	...
Petaling Jaya	CDFC	254 350	...	...	...	350 995	...	...	...
Seleyang Baru	CDFC	124 228	...	...	...	134 197	...	...	...
Seremban	CDFC	182 869	...	...	...	193 237	...	...	...

8. Population of capital cities and cities of 100 000 and more inhabitants: latest available year
Population des capitales et des villes de 100 000 habitants et plus: dernière année disponible (continued — suite)

(See notes at end of table. — Voir notes à la fin du tableau.)

Continent, country or area, date and city Continent, pays ou zone, date et ville	Code[1]	City proper — Ville proprement dite Population				Urban agglomeration — Agglomération urbaine Population			
		Both sexes Les deux sexes	Male Masculin	Female Féminin	Surface area Superficie (km²)	Both sexes Les deux sexes	Male Masculin	Female Féminin	Surface area Superficie (km²)
ASIA — ASIE									
Malaysia — Malaisie									
1 VII 1991									
Shah Alam	CDFC	102 019	...	...	...	117 027	...	...	...
Sungai Petani	CDFC	114 763	...	...	...	116 977	...	...	...
Taiping	CDFC	183 261	...	...	...	200 324	...	...	...
KOTA KINABALU	CDFC	76 120	...	...	...	160 184	...	...	...
Sandakan	CDFC	125 841	...	...	...	156 675	...	...	...
KUCHING	CDFC	148 059	...	...	...	277 905	...	...	...
Sibu	CDFC	126 381	...	...	...	133 479	...	...	...
Maldives									
31 III 2000									
MALE	CDFC	74 069	38 559	35 510	...	...	...	...	...
Mongolia — Mongolie									
1 I 2001									
ULAANBAATAR	ESDF	773 267	378 901	394 366	...	...	...	...	...
Myanmar									
1 VII 1983									
Bassein	CDFC	144 096	...	...	...	...	...	...	...
Mandalay	CDFC	532 949	...	...	...	...	...	...	...
Monywa	CDFC	106 843	...	...	...	...	...	...	...
Moulmein	CDFC	219 961	...	...	...	...	...	...	...
Pegu	CDFC	150 528	...	...	...	...	...	...	...
Sittwe	CDFC	107 621	...	...	...	...	...	...	...
Taunggyi	CDFC	108 231	...	...	...	...	...	...	...
YANGON	CDFC	2 513 023	...	...	...	...	...	...	...
Nepal — Népal									
22 VI 2001									
Biratnagar	CDJC	166 674	87 664	79 010	58	...	...	...	...
Birgunj	CDJC	112 484	60 956	51 528	21	...	...	...	...
KATHMANDU	CDJC	671 846	360 103	311 743	49	...	...	...	...
Lalitpur	CDJC	162 991	84 502	78 489	15	...	...	...	...
Pokhara	CDJC	156 312	79 563	76 749	55	...	...	...	...
Occupied Palestinian Territory — Territoire palestinien occupé									
1 VII 2002									
Gaza	ESDF	361 651	184 197	177 454	38	...	...	...	...
Hebron	ESDF	147 291	76 478	70 813	49	...	...	...	...
Khan Yunis	ESDF	110 677	56 397	54 280	...	...	...	...	...
Nablus	ESDF	121 344	61 745	59 599	26	...	...	...	...
Oman									
1 XII 1993									
MUSCAT	CDFC	40 856	...	...	...	...	...	...	...
Salalah	CDFC	131 802	...	...	...	...	...	...	...
Pakistan[72]									
1 VII 1998									
Abbotabad	CDFC	106 101	61 698	44 403	...	...	...	...	...
Bahawalnagar	CDFC	111 313	57 779	53 534	...	...	...	...	...
Bahawalpur	CDFC	408 395	222 228	186 167	...	...	...	...	...
Burewala	CDFC	152 097	78 726	73 371	...	...	...	...	...
Chiniot	CDFC	172 522	90 474	82 048	...	...	...	...	...
Chishtian	CDFC	102 287	52 427	49 860	...	...	...	...	...
Dadu	CDFC	102 550	53 508	49 042	...	...	...	...	...
Daska	CDFC	102 883	52 359	50 524	...	...	...	...	...
Dera Ghazi Khan	CDFC	190 542	98 738	91 804	...	...	...	...	...
Faisalabad (Lyallpur)	CDFC	2 008 861	1 053 085	955 776	...	...	...	...	...
Gojra	CDFC	117 872	60 598	57 294	...	...	...	...	...
Gujranwala	CDFC	1 132 509	588 512	543 997	...	...	...	...	...
Gujrat	CDFC	251 792	128 524	123 268	...	...	...	...	...
Hafizabad	CDFC	133 678	69 231	64 447	...	...	...	...	...
Hyderabad	CDFC	1 166 894	612 283	554 611	...	...	...	...	...
ISLAMABAD	CDFC	529 180	290 717	238 463	...	...	...	...	...
Jacobabad	CDFC	138 780	71 854	66 926	...	...	...	...	...
Jaranwala	CDFC	106 785	55 819	51 166	...	...	...	...	...
Jhang	CDFC	293 366	153 123	140 243	...	...	...	...	...

8. Population of capital cities and cities of 100 000 and more inhabitants: latest available year
Population des capitales et des villes de 100 000 habitants et plus: dernière année disponible (continued — suite)

(See notes at end of table. — Voir notes à la fin du tableau.)

Continent, country or area, date and city / Continent, pays ou zone, date et ville	Code[1]	City proper — Ville proprement dite Population				Urban agglomeration — Agglomération urbaine Population			
		Both sexes Les deux sexes	Male Masculin	Female Féminin	Surface area Superficie (km²)	Both sexes Les deux sexes	Male Masculin	Female Féminin	Surface area Superficie (km²)
ASIA — ASIE									
Pakistan[72]									
1 VII 1998									
Jhelum	CDFC	147 392	79 169	68 223	...	...	...	...	...
Kamoke	CDFC	152 288	78 848	73 440	...	...	...	...	...
Karachi	CDFC	9 339 023	5 029 900	4 309 123	...	...	...	...	...
Kasur	CDFC	245 321	129 553	115 768	...	...	...	...	...
Khairpur	CDFC	105 637	55 358	50 279	...	...	...	...	...
Khanewal	CDFC	133 986	69 145	64 841	...	...	...	...	...
Khanpur	CDFC	120 382	62 371	58 011	...	...	...	...	...
Kohat	CDFC	126 627	71 505	55 122	...	...	...	...	...
Lahore	CDFC	5 143 495	2 707 220	2 436 275	...	...	...	...	...
Larkana	CDFC	270 283	140 622	129 661	...	...	...	...	...
Mangora	CDFC	173 868	91 742	82 126	...	...	...	...	...
Mardan	CDFC	245 926	129 247	116 679	...	...	...	...	...
Mirpur Khas	CDFC	189 671	97 940	91 731	...	...	...	...	...
Multan	CDFC	1 197 384	637 911	559 473	...	...	...	...	...
Muridke	CDFC	111 951	58 210	53 741	...	...	...	...	...
Muzaffargharh	CDFC	123 404	66 556	56 848	...	...	...	...	...
Nawabshah	CDFC	189 244	98 116	91 128	...	...	...	...	...
Okara	CDFC	201 815	104 245	97 570	...	...	...	...	...
Pakpattan	CDFC	109 033	56 676	52 357	...	...	...	...	...
Peshawar	CDFC	982 816	521 901	460 915	...	...	...	...	...
Quetta	CDFC	565 137	307 759	257 378	...	...	...	...	...
Rahimyar Khan	CDFC	233 537	121 446	112 091	...	...	...	...	...
Rawalpindi	CDFC	1 409 768	750 530	659 238	...	...	...	...	...
Sadiqabad	CDFC	144 391	75 217	69 174	...	...	...	...	...
Sahiwal	CDFC	208 778	108 992	99 786	...	...	...	...	...
Sargodha	CDFC	458 440	239 837	218 603	...	...	...	...	...
Shakkarpur	CDFC	134 883	69 713	65 170	...	...	...	...	...
Sheikhu Pura	CDFC	280 263	146 739	133 524	...	...	...	...	...
Sialkote	CDFC	421 502	227 398	194 104	...	...	...	...	...
Sukkur	CDFC	335 551	175 679	159 872	...	...	...	...	...
Tandoadam	CDFC	104 907	54 670	50 237	...	...	...	...	...
Wah Cantonment	CDFC	108 801	104 200	94 661	...	...	...	...	...
Philippines									
1 V 2000									
Angeles	CDJC	267 788	132 972	134 816	60	...	...	...	...
Bacolod	CDJC	429 076	209 729	219 347	156	...	...	...	...
Baguio	CDJC	252 386	124 208	128 178	49	...	...	...	...
Batangas	CDJC	247 588	123 740	123 848	283	...	...	...	...
Butuan	CDJC	267 279	135 735	131 544	345	...	...	...	...
Cagayan de Oro	CDJC	461 877	228 524	233 353	373	...	...	...	...
Cebu	CDJC	718 821	351 640	367 181	281	...	...	...	...
Cotabato	CDJC	163 849	79 853	83 996	144	...	...	...	...
Dagupan	CDJC	130 328	64 468	65 860	37	...	...	...	...
Davao	CDJC	1 147 116	573 242	573 874	1 211	...	...	...	...
Digos	CDJC	125 171	63 107	62 064	...	...	...	...	...
Dumaguete	CDJC	102 265	49 378	52 887	...	...	...	...	...
General Santos	CDJC	411 822	207 496	204 326	402	...	...	...	...
Iligan	CDJC	285 061	141 641	143 420	673	...	...	...	...
Iloilo	CDJC	366 391	177 620	188 771	56	...	...	...	...
Kalookan (Caloocan)	CDJC	1 177 604	587 890	589 714	56	...	...	...	...
Kidapawan	CDJC	101 205	51 278	49 927	...	...	...	...	...
Koronadal	CDJC	133 786	67 493	66 293	...	...	...	...	...
Las Piñas	CDJC	472 780	229 776	243 004	...	...	...	...	...
Legasp	CDJC	157 010	78 141	78 869	154	...	...	...	...
Lucena City	CDJC	196 075	97 380	98 695	80	...	...	...	...
Makati	CDJC	471 379	226 422	244 957	...	...	...	...	...
Malabalay	CDJC	123 672	63 381	60 291	...	...	...	...	...
Mandaue	CDJC	259 728	128 501	131 227	12	...	...	...	...
Mandaluyong	CDJC	278 474	135 287	143 187	...	...	...	...	...
MANILA	CDJC	1 581 082	770 491	810 591	614	...	...	...	...
Marawi	CDJC	131 090	63 110	67 980	23	...	...	...	...
Marikina	CDJC	391 170	191 585	199 585	...	...	...	...	...

8. Population of capital cities and cities of 100 000 and more inhabitants: latest available year
Population des capitales et des villes de 100 000 habitants et plus: dernière année disponible (continued — suite)

(See notes at end of table. — Voir notes à la fin du tableau.)

Continent, country or area, date and city / Continent, pays ou zone, date et ville	Code[1]	City proper — Ville proprement dite Population				Urban agglomeration — Agglomération urbaine Population			
		Both sexes Les deux sexes	Male Masculin	Female Féminin	Surface area Superficie (km²)	Both sexes Les deux sexes	Male Masculin	Female Féminin	Surface area Superficie (km²)
ASIA — ASIE									
Philippines									
1 V 2000									
Muntinlupa	CDJC	379 310	187 381	191 929	47	...	...	...	...
Olongapo	CDJC	194 260	95 585	98 675	103	...	...	...	...
Pagadian	CDJC	142 585	71 009	71 576	332	...	...	...	...
Paranaque	CDJC	449 811	217 828	231 983	...	...	...	...	...
Pasay	CDJC	354 908	175 041	179 867	14	...	...	...	...
Pasig	CDJC	505 058	246 047	259 011	...	...	...	...	...
Puerto Princesa	CDJC	161 912	83 045	78 867	2	...	...	...	...
Quezon City	CDJC	2 173 831	1 064 780	1 109 051	166	...	...	...	...
Roxas	CDJC	126 352	62 542	63 810	95	...	...	...	...
San Fernando City	CDJC	102 082	50 792	51 290	...	...	...	...	...
Surigao	CDJC	118 534	59 253	59 281	225	...	...	...	...
Taguig	CDJC	467 375	233 712	233 663	...	...	...	...	...
Tagum	CDJC	179 531	90 004	89 527	...	...	...	...	...
Tarlac	CDJC	262 481	132 532	129 949	...	...	...	...	...
Valenzuela	CDJC	485 433	244 373	241 060	...	...	...	...	...
Zamboanga	CDJC	601 794	302 089	299 705	464	...	...,	...	...
Qatar									
1 III 1997									
Al-Rayyan	CDJC	169 774	110 588	59 186	893	...	...	...	...
DOHA	CDJC	264 009	171 791	92 218	159	...	...	...	...
Saudi Arabia — Arabie saoudite									
27 IX 1992									
Abha	CDFC	112 148	62 676	49 472	...	...	...	...	...
Ad-Dammam	CDFC	482 117	297 284	184 833	...	...	...	...	...
Al-Hufuf	CDFC	225 840	121 231	104 609	...	...	...	...	...
Al-Kharj	CDFC	148 687	83 339	65 348	...	...	...	...	...
Al-Khubar	CDFC	142 981	92 632	50 349	...	...	...	...	...
Al-Madinah	CDFC	609 318	333 229	276 089	...	...	...	...	...
Al-Mubarraz	CDFC	219 097	116 469	102 628	...	...	...	...	...
Ar'ar	CDFC	105 752	57 563	48 189	...	...	...	...	...
Ath-Thuqbah	CDFC	126 014	77 513	48 501	...	...	...	...	...
At-Ta'if	CDFC	408 129	217 879	190 250	...	...	...	...	...
Buraydah	CDFC	240 091	133 957	106 134	...	...	...	...	...
Hafar al-Batin	CDFC	138 401	73 863	64 538	...	...	...	...	...
Ha'il	CDFC	175 518	95 915	79 603	...	...	...	...	...
Jiddah	CDFC	2 021 095	1 196 740	824 355	...	...	...	...	...
Khamis Mushayt	CDFC	217 990	121 245	96 745	...	...	...	...	...
Makkah	CDFC	952 429	514 298	438 131	...	...	...	...	...
RIYADH	CDFC	2 723 222	1 594 407	1 128 819	...	...	...	...	...
Tabuk	CDFC	286 384	162 789	123 595	...	...	...	...	...
Singapore — Singapour									
1 VII 1999									
SINGAPORE	ESDF	3 894 000	...	...	...	...	...	...	...
Sri Lanka									
1 VII 1990									
COLOMBO	ESDF	615 000	...	...	...	...	...	...	...
Dehiwala-Mount Lavinia	ESDF	196 000	...	...	...	...	...	...	...
Jaffna	ESDF	129 000	...	...	...	...	...	...	...
Kandy	ESDF	104 000	...	...	...	...	...	...	...
Moratuwa	ESDF	170 000	...	...	...	...	...	...	...
Syrian Arab Republic — République arabe syrienne									
1 VII 2000									
Aleppo	ESDF	3 818 000	1 968 000	1 850 000	...	...	...	...	...
Al-Hasakeh	ESDF	1 295 000	657 000	638 000	...	...	...	...	...
Al-Kamishli	ESDF	467 120	229 542	237 578	...	...	...	...	...
Al-Rakka	ESDF	708 000	360 000	348 000	...	...	...	...	...
DAMASCUS	ESDF	1 675 000	865 000	810 000	...	...	...	...	...
Deir El-Zor	ESDF	803 000	404 000	399 000	...	...	...	...	...
Hama	ESDF	1 525 000	780 000	745 000	...	...	...	...	...
Homs	ESDF	1 365 000	698 000	667 000	...	...	...	...	...
Lattakia	ESDF	890 000	455 000	435 000	...	...	...	...	...

(See notes at end of table. — Voir notes à la fin du tableau.)

Continent, country or area, date and city / Continent, pays ou zone, date et ville	Code[1]	City proper — Ville proprement dite Population				Urban agglomeration — Agglomération urbaine Population			
		Both sexes Les deux sexes	Male Masculin	Female Féminin	Surface area Superficie (km²)	Both sexes Les deux sexes	Male Masculin	Female Féminin	Surface area Superficie (km²)
ASIA — ASIE									
Tajikistan — Tadjikistan									
1 VII 1993									
DUSHANBE	ESDJ	528 600	...	...	...	...	...	...	...
Thailand — Thaïlande[73]									
1 VII 2002									
BANGKOK	ESDJ	...	...	...	...	7 917 000	3 777 000	4 140 000	1 569
Buri Ram	ESDJ	...	...	...	...	209 422	103 236	106 186	10 323
Chachoengsao	ESDJ	...	...	...	...	136 757	66 900	69 857	5 351
Chaiyaphum	ESDJ	...	...	...	...	183 160	91 174	91 986	12 778
Chanthaburi	ESDJ	...	...	...	...	151 738	75 128	76 610	6 338
Chiang Mai	ESDJ	...	...	...	...	390 445	194 072	196 373	20 107
Chiang Rai	ESDJ	...	...	...	...	197 793	99 969	97 824	11 678
Chon Buri	ESDJ	...	...	...	...	556 545	275 351	281 194	4 363
Kalasin	ESDJ	...	...	...	...	191 744	96 148	95 596	6 947
Kanchanaburi	ESDJ	...	...	...	...	164 353	80 691	83 662	19 483
Khon Kaen	ESDJ	...	...	...	...	398 533	197 778	200 755	10 886
Lampang	ESDJ	...	...	...	...	226 503	112 418	114 085	12 534
Loei	ESDJ	...	...	...	...	101 540	51 723	49 817	11 425
Lop Buri	ESDJ	...	...	...	...	122 123	60 891	61 232	6 200
Lumphun	ESDJ	...	...	...	...	106 226	53 335	52 891	4 506
Maha Sarakham	ESDJ	...	...	...	...	120 926	58 649	62 277	5 292
Nakhon Pathom	ESDJ	...	...	...	...	243 813	117 596	126 217	2 168
Nakhon Ratchasima	ESDJ	...	...	...	...	566 104	276 925	289 179	20 494
Nakhon Sawan	ESDJ	...	...	...	...	236 163	113 951	122 212	9 598
Nakhon Si Thammarat	ESDJ	...	...	...	...	287 761	139 923	147 838	9 943
Narathiwat	ESDJ	...	...	...	...	166 081	83 082	82 999	4 475
Nong Bua Lam Phu	ESDJ	...	...	...	...	111 176	55 872	55 304	3 859
Nong Khai	ESDJ	...	...	...	...	185 556	93 325	92 231	7 332
Nonthaburi	ESDJ	...	...	...	...	564 835	273 604	291 231	622
Pathum Thani	ESDJ	...	...	...	...	280 365	136 072	144 293	1 526
Pattani	ESDJ	...	...	...	...	123 675	61 406	62 269	1 940
Phayao	ESDJ	...	...	...	...	111 195	56 311	54 884	6 335
Phetchabun	ESDJ	...	...	...	...	152 980	74 615	78 365	12 668
Phetchaburi	ESDJ	...	...	...	...	163 340	79 317	84 023	6 225
Phichit	ESDJ	...	...	...	...	120 795	57 339	63 456	4 531
Phitsanulok	ESDJ	...	...	...	...	158 628	76 015	82 613	10 816
Phra Nakhon Si Ayutthaya	ESDJ	...	...	...	...	243 518	116 101	127 417	2 557
Phrae	ESDJ	...	...	...	...	113 542	56 168	57 374	6 539
Prachuap Khiri Khan	ESDJ	...	...	...	...	163 070	79 845	83 225	6 368
Ratchaburi	ESDJ	...	...	...	...	250 650	120 854	129 796	5 197
Rayong	ESDJ	...	...	...	...	212 129	106 858	105 271	3 552
Roi Et	ESDJ	...	...	...	...	154 162	77 163	76 999	8 299
Sakon Nakhon	ESDJ	...	...	...	...	146 795	72 790	74 005	9 606
Samut Prakan	ESDJ	...	...	...	...	680 363	332 881	347 482	1 004
Samut Sakhon	ESDJ	...	...	...	...	190 595	91 375	99 220	872
Saraburi	ESDJ	...	...	...	...	209 274	104 501	104 773	3 577
Si Sa Ket	ESDJ	...	...	...	...	151 251	74 862	76 389	8 840
Songkhla	ESDJ	...	...	...	...	437 747	213 072	224 675	7 394
Sukhothai	ESDJ	...	...	...	...	116 026	55 681	60 345	6 596
Suphan Buri	ESDJ	...	...	...	...	154 249	73 024	81 225	5 358
Surat Thani	ESDJ	...	...	...	...	281 161	137 869	143 292	12 892
Surin	ESDJ	...	...	...	...	106 835	51 563	55 272	8 124
Trang	ESDJ	...	...	...	...	127 194	61 557	65 637	4 918
Ubon Ratchathani	ESDJ	...	...	...	...	274 120	135 579	138 541	15 745
Udon Thani	ESDJ	...	...	...	...	403 467	202 154	201 313	11 730
Yala	ESDJ	...	...	...	...	117 076	58 502	58 574	4 521
Timor-Leste									
1 VII 2001									
DILI	ESDF	56 000	...	...	...	...	...	...	...
Turkey — Turquie									
1 VII 2002									
Adana[74]	ESDF	...	...	...	...	1 166 011	...	...	...
Adiyaman	ESDF	194 224	...	...	...	...	...	...	...
Afyon	ESDF	134 088	...	...	...	...	...	...	...

8. Population of capital cities and cities of 100 000 and more inhabitants: latest available year
Population des capitales et des villes de 100 000 habitants et plus: dernière année disponible (continued — suite)

(See notes at end of table. — Voir notes à la fin du tableau.)

Continent, country or area, date and city / Continent, pays ou zone, date et ville	Code[1]	City proper — Ville proprement dite Population				Urban agglomeration — Agglomération urbaine Population			
		Both sexes Les deux sexes	Male Masculin	Female Féminin	Surface area Superficie (km²)	Both sexes Les deux sexes	Male Masculin	Female Féminin	Surface area Superficie (km²)
ASIA — ASIE									
Turkey — Turquie									
1 VII 2002									
Aksaray	ESDF	137 148	...	...	...	...	...	...	...
ANKARA[75]	ESDF	...	...	...	...	3 658 628	...	...	...
Antalya	ESDF	644 917	...	...	...	...	...	...	...
Aydin	ESDF	149 324	...	...	...	...	...	...	...
Balikesir	ESDF	222 939	...	...	...	...	...	...	...
Bandirma	ESDF	100 745	...	...	...	...	...	...	...
Bursa[76]	ESDF	...	...	...	...	1 263 015	...	...	...
Ceyhan	ESDF	112 571	...	...	...	...	...	...	...
Corlu	ESDF	155 635	...	...	...	...	...	...	...
Diyarbakir	ESDF	577 127	...	...	...	...	...	...	...
Erzincan	ESDF	109 114	...	...	...	...	...	...	...
Erzurum	ESDF	382 945	...	...	...	...	...	...	...
Eskisehir	ESDF	492 932	...	...	...	...	...	...	...
Gaziantep[77]	ESDF	...	...	...	...	898 923	...	...	...
Gebze	ESDF	271 753	...	...	...	...	...	...	...
Hatay	ESDF	147 886	...	...	...	...	...	...	...
Içel	ESDF	556 986	...	...	...	...	...	...	...
Inegol	ESDF	111 740	...	...	...	...	...	...	...
Iskenderun	ESDF	158 909	...	...	...	...	...	...	...
Isparta	ESDF	154 420	...	...	...	...	...	...	...
Istanbul[78]	ESDF	...	...	...	...	9 311 060	...	...	...
Izmir[79]	ESDF	...	...	...	...	2 231 687	...	...	...
Kahramanmaras	ESDF	344 060	...	...	...	...	...	...	...
Karaman	ESDF	110 556	...	...	...	...	...	...	...
Kayseri[80]	ESDF	...	...	...	...	555 005	...	...	...
Kirikkale	ESDF	207 046	...	...	...	...	...	...	...
Kiziltepe	ESDF	124 105	...	...	...	...	...	...	...
Kocaeli	ESDF	194 766	...	...	...	...	...	...	...
Konya[81]	ESDF	...	...	...	...	785 142	...	...	...
Kütahya	ESDF	172 467	...	...	...	...	...	...	...
Malatya	ESDF	400 822	...	...	...	...	...	...	...
Manisa	ESDF	224 237	...	...	...	...	...	...	...
Nazilli	ESDF	109 816	...	...	...	...	...	...	...
Ordu	ESDF	113 358	...	...	...	...	...	...	...
Osmaniye	ESDF	183 470	...	...	...	...	...	...	...
Sakarya	ESDF	283 716	...	...	...	...	...	...	...
Samsun	ESDF	372 438	...	...	...	...	...	...	...
Sanliurfa	ESDF	401 855	...	...	...	...	...	...	...
Siirt	ESDF	103 692	...	...	...	...	...	...	...
Sivas	ESDF	255 085	...	...	...	...	...	...	...
Siverek	ESDF	140 613	...	...	...	...	...	...	...
Tarsus	ESDF	220 385	...	...	...	...	...	...	...
Tekirdag	ESDF	111 067	...	...	...	...	...	...	...
Tokat	ESDF	118 456	...	...	...	...	...	...	...
Trabzon	ESDF	223 202	...	...	...	...	...	...	...
Turhal	ESDF	100 323	...	...	...	...	...	...	...
Usak	ESDF	142 469	...	...	...	...	...	...	...
Van	ESDF	309 242	...	...	...	...	...	...	...
Viransehir	ESDF	135 702	...	...	...	...	...	...	...
Zonguldak	ESDF	101 179	...	...	...	...	...	...	...
Turkmenistan — Turkménistan									
1 VII 1990									
ASHKHABAD	ESDF	407 000	...	...	...	...	...	...	...
Chardzhou	ESDF	164 000	...	...	...	...	...	...	...
Tashauz	ESDF	114 000	...	...	...	...	...	...	...
United Arab Emirates — Emirats Arabes Unis									
17 XII 1995									
ABU DHABI	CDFC	398 695	269 834	128 861	...	...	...	...	...
Ajman	CDFC	114 395	68 389	46 006	...	...	...	...	...
Al-Ayn	CDFC	225 970	144 693	81 277	...	...	...	...	...
Al-Sharjah	CDFC	320 095	204 729	115 366	...	...	...	...	...

(See notes at end of table. — Voir notes à la fin du tableau.)

Continent, country or area, date and city / Continent, pays ou zone, date et ville	Code[1]	City proper — Ville proprement dite Population				Urban agglomeration — Agglomération urbaine Population			
		Both sexes Les deux sexes	Male Masculin	Female Féminin	Surface area Superficie (km²)	Both sexes Les deux sexes	Male Masculin	Female Féminin	Surface area Superficie (km²)
ASIA — ASIE									
United Arab Emirates — Emirats Arabes Unis									
17 XII 1995									
Dubai	CDFC	669 181	463 479	205 702	...	...	...	...	...
1 VII 2002									
ABU DHABI	ESDF	527 000	359 000	168 000	...	...	...	...	...
Ajman	ESDF	205 000	122 000	83 000	...	...	...	...	...
Al-Ayn	ESDF	328 000	215 000	113 000	...	...	...	...	...
Al-Sharjah	ESDF	488 000	317 000	171 000	...	...	...	...	...
Dubai	ESDF	1 089 000	759 000	330 000	...	...	...	...	...
Uzbekistan — Ouzbékistan									
1 VII 2001									
Almalyk	ESDF	113 114	56 317	56 797	...	...	...	...	...
Andizhan	ESDF	338 366	165 159	173 207	...	...	...	...	...
Angren	ESDF	128 757	64 060	64 697	...	...	...	...	...
Bukhara	ESDF	237 361	118 613	118 748	...	...	...	...	...
Chirchik	ESDF	141 742	70 203	71 539	...	...	...	...	...
Banjzak	ESDF	131 512	68 441	63 071	...	...	...	...	...
Fergana	ESDF	183 037	87 142	95 895	...	...	...	...	...
Karshi	ESDF	204 690	104 159	100 531	...	...	...	...	...
Kokand	ESDF	197 450	95 872	101 578	...	...	...	...	...
Margilan	ESDF	149 646	73 899	75 747	...	...	...	...	...
Namangan	ESDF	391 297	197 962	193 335	...	...	...	...	...
Navoi	ESDF	138 082	70 577	67 505	...	...	...	...	...
Nukus	ESDF	212 012	103 918	108 094	...	...	...	...	...
Samarkand	ESDF	361 339	178 608	182 731	...	...	...	...	...
TASHKENT	ESDF	2 137 218	1 043 213	1 094 005	...	...	...	...	...
Termez	ESDF	116 467	60 031	56 436	...	...	...	...	...
Urgentch	ESDF	138 609	67 667	70 942	...	...	...	...	...
Viet Nam									
1 VII 1992									
Buonmathuot	ESDF	282 095	...	...	...	...	...	...	...
Campha	ESDF	209 086	...	...	...	...	...	...	...
Cantho	ESDF	215 587	...	...	...	...	...	...	...
Dalat	ESDF	106 409	...	...	...	...	...	...	...
Da Nang	ESDF	382 674	...	...	...	...	...	...	...
Haiphong	ESDF	783 133	...	...	22	...	...	...	...
HANOI	ESDF	1 073 760	...	...	46	...	...	...	...
Ho Chi Minh[82]	ESDF	3 015 743	...	...	140	...	...	...	...
Hon Gai	ESDF	127 484	...	...	...	...	...	...	...
Hué	ESDF	219 149	...	...	...	...	...	...	...
Longxuyen	ESDF	132 681	...	...	...	...	...	...	...
Mytho	ESDF	108 404	...	...	...	...	...	...	...
Namdinh	ESDF	171 699	...	...	...	...	...	...	...
Nhatrang	ESDF	221 331	...	...	...	...	...	...	...
Qui Nhon	ESDF	163 385	...	...	...	...	...	...	...
Rach Gia	ESDF	141 132	...	...	...	...	...	...	...
Thai Nguyen	ESDF	127 643	...	...	...	...	...	...	...
Vinh	ESDF	112 455	...	...	...	...	...	...	...
Vungtau	ESDF	145 145	...	...	...	...	...	...	...
Yemen — Yémen									
16 XII 1994									
Adan	CDFC	398 294	...	...	...	...	...	...	...
Al-Hudaydah (Hodeidah)	CDFC	298 452	...	...	...	...	...	...	...
Al-Mukalla	CDFC	122 359	...	...	...	...	...	...	...
Ibb	CDFC	103 312	...	...	...	...	...	...	...
SANA'A	CDFC	954 448	...	...	...	...	...	...	...
Ta'izz	CDFC	317 571	...	...	...	...	...	...	...
EUROPE									
Albania — Albanie									
1 VII 1990									
TIRANA	ESDF	244 153	...	...	...	...	...	...	...

8. Population of capital cities and cities of 100 000 and more inhabitants: latest available year
Population des capitales et des villes de 100 000 habitants et plus: dernière année disponible (continued — suite)

(See notes at end of table. — Voir notes à la fin du tableau.)

Continent, country or area, date and city / Continent, pays ou zone, date et ville	Code[1]	City proper — Ville proprement dite Population				Urban agglomeration — Agglomération urbaine Population			
		Both sexes Les deux sexes	Male Masculin	Female Féminin	Surface area Superficie (km²)	Both sexes Les deux sexes	Male Masculin	Female Féminin	Surface area Superficie (km²)
EUROPE									
Andorra — Andorre									
1 I 2002									
ANDORRA LA VELLA	ESDF	18 142	...	...	...	20 724	...	...	...
Austria — Autriche									
15 V 2001									
Bregenz	CDJC	...	...	...	...	180 987	88 830	92 157	150
Graz	CDJC	226 892	106 609	120 283	128	287 903	136 415	151 488	349
Innsbruck	CDJC	113 826	53 434	60 392	105	183 661	87 315	96 346	110
Klagenfurt	CDJC	90 257	41 482	48 775	120	100 513	46 440	54 073	187
Linz	CDJC	186 266	88 332	97 934	96	273 722	131 310	142 412	249
Salzburg	CDJC	144 817	67 464	77 353	66	212 666	100 360	112 306	259
WIEN	CDJC	1 562 482	738 168	824 314	415	1 838 225	870 893	967 332	1 161
Belarus — Bélarus									
1 VII 2000									
Baranovichi	ESDF	168 300	79 100	89 200	55	...	...	...	...
Bobruisk	ESDF	221 200	104 100	117 100	77	...	...	...	...
Borisov	ESDF	151 100	71 500	79 600	47	...	...	...	...
Brest	ESDF	288 900	134 300	154 600	74	...	...	...	...
Gomel	ESDF	...	...	...	...	487 400	223 200	264 200	117
Grodno	ESDF	304 100	142 000	162 100	93	...	...	...	...
Lida	ESDF	100 500	47 400	53 100	38	...	...	...	...
MINSK	ESDF	...	...	...	...	1 688 100	790 800	897 300	256
Mogilev	ESDF	358 400	167 500	190 900	99	...	...	...	...
Mozir	ESDF	110 200	53 400	56 800	36	...	...	...	...
Novopolotsk	ESDF	106 600	51 200	55 400	48	...	...	...	...
Orsha	ESDF	...	...	...	...	136 400	65 700	70 700	36
Pinsk	ESDF	131 000	61 900	69 100	42	...	...	...	...
Soligorsk	ESDF	101 400	48 100	53 300	8	...	...	...	...
Vitebsk	ESDF	...	...	...	...	348 700	158 000	190 700	89
Belgium — Belgique[83]									
1 VII 2000									
Antwerpen (Anvers)	ESDJ	445 570	216 319	229 251	205	...	...	...	...
Brugge	ESDJ	116 559	56 436	60 123	138	...	...	...	...
BRUXELLES (BRUSSEL)	ESDJ	964 405	461 065	503 340	161	...	...	...	...
Charleroi	ESDJ	200 233	96 214	104 019	102	...	...	...	...
Gent (Gand)	ESDJ	224 685	109 142	115 543	156	...	...	...	...
Liège (Luik)	ESDJ	184 550	89 176	95 374	69	...	...	...	...
Namur	ESDJ	105 248	50 251	54 997	176	...	...	...	...
Bosnia and Herzegovina — Bosnie-Herzégovine									
1 VII 1991									
Banja Luka	ESDJ	195 994	...	...	1 239	...	...	...	...
Doboj	ESDJ	102 624	...	...	697	...	...	...	...
Mostar	ESDJ	127 034	...	...	1 227	...	...	...	...
Prijedor	ESDJ	112 635	...	...	834	...	...	...	...
SARAJEVO	ESDJ	529 021	...	...	2 095	...	...	...	...
Tuzla	ESDJ	131 866	...	...	303	...	...	...	...
Zenica	ESDJ	145 837	...	...	505	...	...	...	...
Bulgaria — Bulgarie[84,85]									
1 VII 2002									
Bourgas	ESDF	192 699	93 372	99 327	...	194 778	94 390	100 388	481
Pleven	ESDF	120 433	58 559	61 874	...	125 174	60 910	64 264	817
Plovdiv	ESDF	340 299	162 522	177 777	...	340 299	162 522	177 777	74
Rousse	ESDF	160 633	77 552	83 081	...	160 633	77 552	83 081	437
Sliven	ESDF	99 547	48 170	51 377	...	101 699	49 259	52 440	1 354
SOFIA	ESDF	1 106 625	523 021	583 604	...	1 132 680	535 731	596 949	1 311
Stara Zagora	ESDF	143 999	70 463	73 536	...	143 999	70 463	73 536	1 005
Varna	ESDF	313 404	152 184	161 220	...	313 404	152 184	161 220	210
Channel Islands: Guernsey — Iles Anglo-Normandes: Guernesey									
29 IV 2001									
ST. PETER PORT	CDJC	16 488	...	...	...	...	...	...	...

8. Population of capital cities and cities of 100 000 and more inhabitants: latest available year
Population des capitales et des villes de 100 000 habitants et plus: dernière année disponible (continued — suite)

(See notes at end of table. — Voir notes à la fin du tableau.)

Continent, country or area, date and city Continent, pays ou zone, date et ville	Code[1]	City proper — Ville proprement dite Population				Urban agglomeration — Agglomération urbaine Population			
		Both sexes Les deux sexes	Male Masculin	Female Féminin	Surface area Superficie (km²)	Both sexes Les deux sexes	Male Masculin	Female Féminin	Surface area Superficie (km²)
EUROPE									
Channel Islands — Iles Anglo-Normandes: Jersey									
11 III 2001									
ST. HELIER	CDJC	28 310	13 669	14 641	9	...	...	...	...
Croatia — Croatie									
31 III 2001									
Rijeka	CDJC	143 800	68 382	75 418	...	...	...	...	...
Split	CDJC	175 140	83 720	91 420	...	...	...	...	...
ZAGREB	CDJC	691 724	321 507	370 217	1 405	...	...	...	...
Czech Republic — République tchéque									
1 VII 2002									
Brno	ESDJ	371 448	195 767	175 681	230	...	...	...	...
Olomouc	ESDJ	101 826	48 101	53 725	103	...	...	...	...
Ostrava	ESDJ	314 710	151 814	162 896	214	...	...	...	...
Plzen	ESDJ	164 065	78 837	85 228	125	...	...	...	...
PRAHA	ESDJ	1 158 800	549 419	609 381	496	...	...	...	...
TALLINN	ESDF	397 792	179 167	218 625	158	...	...	...	...
Tartu	ESDF	101 165	44 982	56 183	39	...	...	...	...
Denmark — Danemark									
1 VII 2001									
Ålborg	ESDJ	161 661	79 829	81 832	560	...	...	...	...
Århus	ESDJ	286 668	140 451	146 217	469	...	...	...	...
KØBENHAVN	ESDJ	499 148	244 025	255 123	123	...	...	...	...
Odense	ESDJ	183 691	89 341	94 350	364	...	...	...	...
Estonia — Estonie									
1 VII 2002									
TALLINN	ESDF	397 792	179 167	218 625	158	...	...	...	...
Tartu	ESDF	101 165	44 982	56 183	39	...	...	...	...
Faeroe Islands — Iles Féroé									
1 VII 1992									
THORSHAVN	ESDJ	14 671	...	...	63	16 218	...	...	79
Finland — Finlande									
1 VII 2002									
Espoo	ESDJ	219 217	106 958	112 259	312	...	...	...	...
HELSINKI	ESDJ	559 717	260 153	299 564	185	...	...	...	...
Oulu	ESDJ	123 931	60 159	63 773	328	...	...	...	...
Tampere	ESDJ	198 799	94 674	104 125	523	...	...	...	...
Turku	ESDJ	174 152	81 219	92 933	243	...	...	...	...
Vantaa	ESDJ	180 873	88 370	92 503	241	...	...	...	...
France[86,87]									
8 III 1999									
Aix-en-Provence	CDJC	134 280	62 220	72 060	186	...	...	...	...
Amiens	CDJC	135 406	63 513	71 893	49	...	...	...	...
Angers	CDJC	151 406	69 235	82 171	43	...	...	...	...
Besançon	CDJC	117 693	54 692	63 001	65	...	...	...	...
Bordeaux	CDJC	215 277	99 637	115 640	49	...	...	...	...
Boulogne-Billancourt	CDJC	106 384	49 840	56 544	6	...	...	...	...
Brest	CDJC	149 495	71 431	78 064	50	...	...	...	...
Caen	CDJC	114 079	52 605	61 474	26	...	...	...	...
Clermont-Ferrand	CDJC	136 968	63 702	73 266	43	...	...	...	...
Dijon	CDJC	150 144	69 331	80 813	40	...	...	...	...
Grenoble	CDJC	153 531	73 311	80 220	18	...	...	...	...
Le Havre	CDJC	190 806	90 882	99 924	47	...	...	...	...
Le Mans	CDJC	145 994	68 982	77 012	53	...	...	...	...
Lille[88]	CDJC	184 445	86 196	98 249	30	...	...	...	...
Limoges	CDJC	134 055	62 106	71 949	77	...	...	...	...
Lyon[89]	CDJC	444 852	206 422	238 430	48	...	...	...	...
Marseille	CDJC	796 525	376 082	420 443	241	...	...	...	...
Metz	CDJC	123 720	59 670	64 050	42	...	...	...	...
Montpellier	CDJC	225 748	103 437	122 311	57	...	...	...	...
Mulhouse	CDJC	110 129	53 963	56 166	22	...	...	...	...
Nantes	CDJC	270 474	126 599	143 875	65	...	...	...	...
Nancy	CDJC	103 533	47 345	56 188	15	...	...	...	...

8. Population of capital cities and cities of 100 000 and more inhabitants: latest available year
Population des capitales et des villes de 100 000 habitants et plus: dernière année disponible (continued — suite)

(See notes at end of table. — Voir notes à la fin du tableau.)

Continent, country or area, date and city / Continent, pays ou zone, date et ville	Code[1]	City proper — Ville proprement dite Population				Urban agglomeration — Agglomération urbaine Population			
		Both sexes Les deux sexes	Male Masculin	Female Féminin	Surface area Superficie (km²)	Both sexes Les deux sexes	Male Masculin	Female Féminin	Surface area Superficie (km²)
EUROPE									
France[86,87]									
8 III 1999									
Nice	CDJC	343 166	157 148	186 018	72	...	...	...	...
Nîmes	CDJC	133 391	62 451	70 940	162	...	...	...	...
Orléans	CDJC	113 077	53 728	59 349	27	...	...	...	...
PARIS	CDJC	2 125 017	995 844	1 129 173	105	...	...	...	...
Perpignan	CDJC	105 027	47 870	57 157	68	...	...	...	...
Reims	CDJC	187 183	88 707	98 476	47	...	...	...	...
Rennes	CDJC	206 221	95 224	110 997	50	...	...	...	...
Rouen	CDJC	106 356	49 432	56 924	21	...	...	...	...
Saint-Étienne	CDJC	180 393	84 135	96 258	80	...	...	...	...
Strasbourg[88]	CDJC	263 682	124 926	138 756	78	...	...	...	...
Toulon	CDJC	160 549	74 964	85 585	43	...	...	...	...
Toulouse	CDJC	390 174	185 107	205 067	118	...	...	...	...
Tours	CDJC	132 637	60 117	72 520	34	...	...	...	...
Villeurbanne	CDJC	124 451	59 519	64 932	15	...	...	...	...
Germany — Allemagne									
1 VII 1999									
Aachen	ESDJ	243 825	121 671	122 154	161	...	...	...	...
Augsburg	ESDJ	254 867	121 846	133 021	147	...	...	...	...
Bergisch Gladbach	ESDJ	106 150	50 723	55 427	83	...	...	...	...
BERLIN	ESDJ	3 386 667	1 644 575	1 742 092	891	...	...	...	...
Bielefeld	ESDJ	321 125	152 701	168 424	258	...	...	...	...
Bochum	ESDJ	392 830	190 433	202 397	145	...	...	...	...
Bonn	ESDJ	301 048	143 416	157 632	141	...	...	...	...
Bottrop	ESDJ	121 097	58 490	62 607	101	...	...	...	...
Braunschweig	ESDJ	246 322	119 350	126 972	192	...	...	...	...
Bremen	ESDJ	540 330	259 439	280 891	327	...	...	...	...
Bremerhaven	ESDJ	122 735	59 991	62 744	78	...	...	...	...
Chemnitz	ESDJ	263 222	125 123	138 099	176	...	...	...	...
Cottbus	ESDJ	110 894	53 712	57 182	150	...	...	...	...
Darmstadt	ESDJ	137 776	67 680	70 096	122	...	...	...	...
Dortmund	ESDJ	590 213	286 880	303 333	280	...	...	...	...
Dresden	ESDJ	476 668	229 565	247 103	237	...	...	...	...
Duisburg	ESDJ	519 793	252 735	267 058	233	...	...	...	...
Düsseldorf	ESDJ	568 855	268 630	300 225	217	...	...	...	...
Erfurt	ESDJ	201 267	96 937	104 330	269	...	...	...	...
Erlangen	ESDJ	100 750	48 939	51 811	77	...	...	...	...
Essen	ESDJ	599 515	286 350	313 165	210	...	...	...	...
Frankfurt am Main	ESDJ	643 821	314 431	329 390	248	...	...	...	...
Freiburg im Breisgau	ESDJ	202 455	96 025	106 430	153	...	...	...	...
Fürth	ESDJ	109 771	52 773	56 998	63	...	...	...	...
Gelsenkirchen	ESDJ	281 979	135 781	146 198	105	...	...	...	...
Gera	ESDJ	114 718	55 211	59 507	152	...	...	...	...
Göttingen	ESDJ	124 775	60 334	64 441	117	...	...	...	...
Hagen	ESDJ	205 201	98 338	106 863	160	...	...	...	...
Halle	ESDJ	254 360	121 314	133 046	135	...	...	...	...
Hamburg	ESDJ	1 704 735	824 686	880 049	755	...	...	...	...
Hamm	ESDJ	181 804	89 307	92 497	226	...	...	...	...
Hannover	ESDJ	514 718	245 017	269 701	204	...	...	...	...
Heidelberg	ESDJ	139 672	65 694	73 978	109	...	...	...	...
Heilbronn	ESDJ	119 526	58 400	61 126	100	...	...	...	...
Herne	ESDJ	175 661	85 577	90 084	51	...	...	...	...
Hildesheim	ESDJ	104 013	48 910	55 103	93	...	...	...	...
Ingolstadt	ESDJ	114 826	56 417	58 409	133	...	...	...	...
Kaiserslautern	ESDJ	100 025	49 247	50 778	140	...	...	...	...
Karlsruhe	ESDJ	277 204	134 775	142 429	173	...	...	...	...
Kassel	ESDJ	196 211	93 058	103 153	107	...	...	...	...
Kiel	ESDJ	233 795	113 274	120 521	117	...	...	...	...
Koblenz	ESDJ	108 003	51 340	56 663	105	...	...	...	...
Köln	ESDJ	962 507	466 543	495 964	405	...	...	...	...
Krefeld	ESDJ	241 769	117 087	124 682	138	...	...	...	...
Leipzig	ESDJ	489 532	235 789	253 743	176	...	...	...	...
Leverkusen	ESDJ	160 841	78 116	82 725	79	...	...	...	...

8. Population of capital cities and cities of 100 000 and more inhabitants: latest available year
Population des capitales et des villes de 100 000 habitants et plus: dernière année disponible (continued — suite)

(See notes at end of table. — Voir notes à la fin du tableau.)

Continent, country or area, date and city / Continent, pays ou zone, date et ville	Code[1]	City proper — Ville proprement dite Population				Urban agglomeration — Agglomération urbaine Population			
		Both sexes Les deux sexes	Male Masculin	Female Féminin	Surface area Superficie (km²)	Both sexes Les deux sexes	Male Masculin	Female Féminin	Surface area Superficie (km²)
EUROPE									
Germany — Allemagne									
1 VII 1999									
Lübeck	ESDJ	213 326	101 024	112 302	214	...	...	...	...
Lüdwigshafen am Rhein	ESDJ	163 771	81 257	82 514	78	...	...	...	...
Magdeburg	ESDJ	235 073	112 839	122 234	193	...	...	...	...
Mainz	ESDJ	183 134	89 093	94 041	98	...	...	...	...
Mannheim	ESDJ	307 730	151 145	156 585	145	...	...	...	...
Moers	ESDJ	106 837	51 824	55 013	68	...	...	...	...
Mönchengladbach	ESDJ	263 697	126 721	136 976	170	...	...	...	...
Mülheim an der Ruhr	ESDJ	173 895	82 677	91 218	91	...	...	...	...
München	ESDJ	1 194 560	571 363	623 197	311	...	...	...	...
Münster (Westf.)	ESDJ	264 670	123 825	140 845	303	...	...	...	...
Neuss	ESDJ	149 702	72 522	77 180	99	...	...	...	...
Nürnberg	ESDJ	486 628	233 415	253 213	186	...	...	...	...
Oberhausen	ESDJ	222 349	107 562	114 787	77	...	...	...	...
Offenbach am Main	ESDJ	116 627	57 539	59 088	45	...	...	...	...
Oldenburg	ESDJ	154 125	73 572	80 553	103	...	...	...	...
Osnabrück	ESDJ	164 539	77 981	86 558	120	...	...	...	...
Paderborn	ESDJ	137 647	67 010	70 637	179	...	...	...	...
Pforzheim	ESDJ	117 227	55 738	61 489	98	...	...	...	...
Potsdam	ESDJ	128 983	62 651	66 332	109	...	...	...	...
Recklinghausen	ESDJ	125 022	60 456	64 566	66	...	...	...	...
Regensburg	ESDJ	125 236	59 600	65 636	81	...	...	...	...
Remscheid	ESDJ	120 125	57 923	62 202	75	...	...	...	...
Reutlingen	ESDJ	110 343	53 564	56 779	87	...	...	...	...
Rostock	ESDJ	203 279	99 627	103 652	181	...	...	...	...
Saarbrücken	ESDJ	183 836	87 875	95 961	167	...	...	...	...
Salzgitter	ESDJ	112 934	54 808	58 126	224	...	...	...	...
Schwerin	ESDJ	102 878	49 428	53 450	130	...	...	...	...
Siegen	ESDJ	109 225	53 585	55 640	115	...	...	...	...
Solingen	ESDJ	165 583	79 712	85 871	89	...	...	...	...
Stuttgart	ESDJ	582 443	284 977	297 466	207	...	...	...	...
Ulm	ESDJ	116 103	56 511	59 592	119	...	...	...	...
Wiesbaden	ESDJ	268 716	129 032	139 684	204	...	...	...	...
Witten	ESDJ	103 384	49 545	53 839	72	...	...	...	...
Wolfsburg	E3DJ	121 954	59 761	62 193	204	...	...	...	...
Wuppertal	ESDJ	368 993	176 350	192 643	168	...	...	...	...
Würzburg	ESDJ	127 350	58 801	68 549	88	...	...	...	...
Zwickau	ESDJ	104 146	49 513	54 633	73	...	...	...	...
Gibraltar									
1 VII 1991									
GIBRALTAR	CDFC	28 074	...	...	...				
Greece — Grèce[90]									
18 III 2001									
ATHINAI	CDJC	789 166	374 900	414 266	39	...	...	...	...
Calithèa	CDJC	115 150	54 137	61 013	5	...	...	...	...
Iraclion	CDJC	135 761	66 956	68 805	52	...	...	...	...
Larissa	CDJC	131 095	64 000	67 095	88	...	...	...	...
Patrai	CDJC	168 530	82 981	85 549	57	...	...	...	...
Pésterion	CDJC	146 743	72 391	74 352	10	...	...	...	...
Pireas	CDJC	181 933	87 362	94 571	...	...	...	...	...
Thessaloniki	CDJC	385 406	180 122	205 284	...	...	...	...	...
Holy See — Saint-Siège[91]									
1 VII 1988									
VATICAN CITY	ESDF	766	...	...	...				
Hungary — Hongrie									
1 VII 2002									
BUDAPEST	ESDF	1 729 456	789 640	939 816	525	...	...	...	...
Debrecen	ESDF	206 223	96 019	110 204	462	...	...	...	...
Györ	ESDF	129 100	60 960	68 140	175	...	...	...	...
Kecskemét	ESDF	107 436	50 048	57 388	321	...	...	...	...
Miskolc	ESDF	181 345	84 346	96 999	237	...	...	...	...
Nyiregyhaza	ESDF	116 951	54 479	62 472	274	...	...	...	...
Pécs	ESDF	159 368	73 724	85 644	163	...	...	...	...

8. Population of capital cities and cities of 100 000 and more inhabitants: latest available year
Population des capitales et des villes de 100 000 habitants et plus: dernière année disponible (continued — suite)

(See notes at end of table. — Voir notes à la fin du tableau.)

Continent, country or area, date and city / Continent, pays ou zone, date et ville	Code[1]	City proper — Ville proprement dite Population				Urban agglomeration — Agglomération urbaine Population			
		Both sexes Les deux sexes	Male Masculin	Female Féminin	Surface area Superficie (km²)	Both sexes Les deux sexes	Male Masculin	Female Féminin	Surface area Superficie (km²)
EUROPE									
Hungary — Hongrie									
1 VII 2002									
Szeged	ESDF	163 280	75 286	87 994	281	...	...	...	...
Székesfehérvar	ESDF	103 365	49 014	54 351	171	...	...	...	...
Iceland — Islande									
1 VII 2000									
REYKJAVIK	ESDJ	110 903	54 420	56 483	100	173 710	85 609	88 101	...
Ireland — Irlande									
28 IV 2002									
Cork	CDFC	123 062	59 263	63 799	40	186 239	90 348	95 891	...
DUBLIN	CDFC	495 781	237 813	257 968	118	1 004 614	485 209	519 405	...
Isle of Man — Ile de Man									
30 IV 2001									
DOUGLAS	CDJC	25 347	12 460	12 887	...	...	...	...	...
Italy — Italie									
21 X 2001									
Ancona	CDJC	100 402	48 049	52 353	124	...	...	...	...
Bari	CDJC	312 452	150 311	162 141	116	...	...	...	...
Bergamo	CDJC	110 691	51 445	59 246	40	...	...	...	...
Bologna	CDJC	369 955	171 722	198 233	141	...	...	...	...
Brescia	CDJC	187 865	90 011	97 854	91	...	...	...	...
Cagliari	CDJC	158 351	73 952	84 399	86	...	...	...	...
Catania	CDJC	306 464	144 419	162 045	181	...	...	...	...
Ferrara	CDJC	130 461	60 975	69 486	404	...	...	...	...
Firenze	CDJC	352 227	164 356	187 871	102	...	...	...	...
Foggia	CDJC	146 072	71 029	75 043	508	...	...	...	...
Forli	CDJC	108 363	51 873	56 490	228	...	...	...	...
Genova	CDJC	603 560	282 002	321 558	244	...	...	...	...
Latina	CDJC	108 711	52 086	56 625	278	...	...	...	...
Livorno	CDJC	148 143	70 290	77 853	104	...	...	...	...
Messina	CDJC	236 621	112 995	123 626	211	...	...	...	...
Milano	CDJC	1 182 693	550 270	632 423	182	...	...	...	...
Modena	CDJC	175 442	83 953	91 489	183	...	...	...	...
Monza	CDJC	117 068	56 046	61 022	33	...	...	...	...
Napoli	CDJC	993 386	475 342	518 044	117	...	...	...	...
Novara	CDJC	101 921	48 280	53 641	103	...	...	...	...
Padova	CDJC	203 350	95 498	107 852	93	...	...	...	...
Palermo	CDJC	652 640	311 648	340 992	159	...	...	...	...
Parma	CDJC	156 172	73 799	82 373	261	...	...	...	...
Perugia	CDJC	148 575	70 622	77 953	450	...	...	...	...
Pescara	CDJC	115 197	54 469	60 728	34	...	...	...	...
Prato	CDJC	170 388	82 662	87 726	98	...	...	...	...
Ravenna	CDJC	138 204	67 075	71 129	653	...	...	...	...
Reggio di Calabria	CDJC	179 384	86 607	92 777	236	...	...	...	...
Reggio nell'Emilia	CDJC	141 383	68 047	73 336	232	...	...	...	...
Rimini	CDJC	128 301	61 699	66 602	135	...	...	...	...
ROMA	CDJC	2 459 776	1 155 247	1 304 529	1 285	...	...	...	...
Salerno	CDJC	144 078	69 044	75 034	59	...	...	...	...
Sassari	CDJC	112 959	53 958	59 001	546	...	...	...	...
Siracusa	CDJC	121 000	58 958	62 042	204	...	...	...	...
Taranto	CDJC	201 349	96 114	105 235	218	...	...	...	...
Terni	CDJC	103 964	49 276	54 688	212	...	...	...	...
Torino	CDJC	857 433	406 001	451 432	130	...	...	...	...
Trento	CDJC	104 844	50 136	54 708	158	...	...	...	...
Trieste	CDJC	209 520	97 325	112 195	85	...	...	...	...
Venezia	CDJC	266 181	125 846	140 335	413	...	...	...	...
Verona	CDJC	243 474	114 918	128 556	207	...	...	...	...
Vicenza	CDJC	106 069	50 174	55 895	81	...	...	...	...
Latvia — Lettonie									
31 III 2000									
Daugavpils	CDJC	115 265	52 175	63 090	73	...	...	...	...
RIGA	CDJC	764 329	341 430	422 899	307	...	...	...	...
1 VII 2001									
Daugavpils	ESDF	113 945	51 457	62 488	72	...	...	...	...

(See notes at end of table. — Voir notes à la fin du tableau.)

Continent, country or area, date and city / Continent, pays ou zone, date et ville	Code[1]	City proper — Ville proprement dite Population				Urban agglomeration — Agglomération urbaine Population			
		Both sexes Les deux sexes	Male Masculin	Female Féminin	Surface area Superficie (km²)	Both sexes Les deux sexes	Male Masculin	Female Féminin	Surface area Superficie (km²)
EUROPE									
Latvia — Lettonie									
1 VII 2001									
RIGA	ESDF	751 892	335 621	416 271	307	...	...	...	...
Liechtenstein									
30 VI 2001									
VADUZ	ESDF	4 911	2 313	2 598	17	...	...	...	...
Lithuania — Lituanie									
6 IV 2001									
Kaunas	CDJC	378 943	171 050	207 893	157	...	...	...	...
Klaipeda	CDJC	192 954	89 521	103 433	98	...	...	...	...
Panevezhis	CDJC	119 749	54 564	65 185	50	...	...	...	...
Shauliai	CDJC	133 883	61 205	72 678	81	...	...	...	...
VILNIUS	CDJC	542 287	247 097	295 190	393	...	...	...	...
1 VII 2002									
Kaunas	ESDJ	375 123	169 209	205 914	157	...	...	...	...
Klaipeda	ESDJ	192 061	89 002	103 059	98	...	...	...	...
Panevezhis	ESDJ	119 121	54 277	64 844	50	...	...	...	...
Shauliai	ESDJ	133 121	60 800	72 321	81	...	...	...	...
VILNIUS	ESDJ	541 682	246 666	295 016	394	...	...	...	...
Luxembourg									
1 VII 2002									
LUXEMBOURG-VILLE	ESDJ	78 329	...	...	51	...	...	...	...
Malta — Malte[92]									
1 VII 2001									
VALLETTA	ESDF	7 029	3 353	3 676	...	...	...	...	...
1 VII 2002									
VALLETTA	ESDF	7 173	3 419	3 754	...	...	...	...	...
Monaco									
1 VII 1999									
MONACO	ESDJ	33 208	...	...	...	...	...	...	...
Netherlands — Pays-Bas[93]									
1 I 2002									
Almere	CDJC	158 902	79 270	79 632	132	...	...	...	...
Amersfoort	CDJC	129 720	63 343	66 377	63	...	...	...	...
AMSTERDAM	CDJC	735 526	362 669	372 857	165	...	...	...	...
Apeldoorn	CDJC	154 859	76 045	78 814	340	...	...	...	...
Arnhem	CDJC	140 736	69 320	71 416	99	...	...	...	...
Breda	CDJC	163 427	79 541	83 886	127	...	...	...	...
Dordrecht	CDJC	120 222	59 140	61 082	81	...	...	...	...
Ede	CDJC	103 708	51 001	52 707	318	...	...	...	...
Eindhoven	CDJC	204 776	102 806	101 970	87	...	...	...	...
Emmen	CDJC	108 367	53 660	54 707	341	...	...	...	...
Enschede	CDJC	151 346	76 947	74 399	141	...	...	...	...
Groningen	CDJC	175 569	86 656	88 913	80	...	...	...	...
Haarlem	CDJC	147 831	71 714	76 117	29	...	...	...	...
Haarlemmermeer	CDJC	118 553	59 289	59 264	180	...	...	...	...
Leiden	CDJC	117 170	57 256	59 914	22	...	...	...	...
Maastricht	CDJC	122 005	58 638	63 367	57	...	...	...	...
Nijmegen	CDJC	154 616	74 512	80 104	54	...	...	...	...
Rotterdam	CDJC	598 660	293 952	304 708	209	...	...	...	...
s-Gravenhage	CDJC	457 726	223 661	234 065	83	...	...	...	...
s-Hertogenbosch	CDJC	131 697	64 882	66 815	85	...	...	...	...
Tilburg	CDJC	197 358	97 463	99 895	117	...	...	...	...
Utrecht	CDJC	260 625	125 701	134 924	96	...	...	...	...
Zaanstad	CDJC	137 669	67 808	69 861	75	...	...	...	...
Zoetermeer	CDJC	110 500	54 150	56 350	36	...	...	...	...
Zwolle	CDJC	109 000	52 989	56 011	113	...	...	...	...
Norway — Norvège									
1 VII 2002									
Bergen	ESDJ	234 359	115 156	119 201	445	...	...	...	...
OSLO	ESDJ	514 995	250 696	264 299	427	...	...	...	...
Stavanger	ESDJ	110 359	54 359	56 000	66	...	...	...	...
Trondheim	ESDJ	152 054	74 665	77 389	321	...	...	...	...

8. Population of capital cities and cities of 100 000 and more inhabitants: latest available year
Population des capitales et des villes de 100 000 habitants et plus: dernière année disponible (continued — suite)

(See notes at end of table. — Voir notes à la fin du tableau.)

Continent, country or area, date and city / Continent, pays ou zone, date et ville	Code[1]	City proper — Ville proprement dite Population				Urban agglomeration — Agglomération urbaine Population			
		Both sexes Les deux sexes	Male Masculin	Female Féminin	Surface area Superficie (km²)	Both sexes Les deux sexes	Male Masculin	Female Féminin	Surface area Superficie (km²)
EUROPE									
Poland — Pologne									
20 V 2002									
Bialystok	CDJC	291 383	137 279	154 104	94	...	...	...	...
Bielsko-Biala	CDJC	178 028	84 241	93 787	125	...	...	...	...
Bydgoszcz	CDJC	373 804	175 664	198 140	175	...	...	...	...
Bytom	CDJC	193 546	94 041	99 505	69	...	...	...	...
Chorzów	CDJC	117 430	56 157	61 273	34	...	...	...	...
Czestochowa	CDJC	251 436	118 763	132 673	160	...	...	...	...
Dabrowa Górnicza	CDJC	132 236	63 987	68 249	188	...	...	...	...
Elblag	CDJC	128 134	61 491	66 643	80	...	...	...	...
Gdansk	CDJC	461 334	219 494	241 840	262	...	...	...	...
Gdynia	CDJC	253 458	121 481	131 977	135	...	...	...	...
Gliwice	CDJC	203 814	98 825	104 989	134	...	...	...	...
Grudziadz	CDJC	100 376	47 715	52 661	59	...	...	...	...
Gorzów Wielkopolski	CDJC	125 914	60 149	65 765	86	...	...	...	...
Kalisz	CDJC	109 498	51 375	58 123	70	...	...	...	...
Katowice	CDJC	327 222	155 029	172 193	165	...	...	...	...
Kielce	CDJC	212 429	100 983	111 446	109	...	...	...	...
Koszalin	CDJC	108 709	51 891	56 818	83	...	...	...	...
Kraków	CDJC	758 544	355 550	402 994	327	...	...	...	...
Legnica	CDJC	107 100	50 843	56 257	56	...	...	...	...
Lódz	CDJC	789 318	360 420	428 898	294	...	...	...	...
Lublin	CDJC	357 110	165 545	191 565	147	...	...	...	...
Olsztyn	CDJC	173 102	80 341	92 761	88	...	...	...	...
Opole	CDJC	129 946	61 083	68 863	96	...	...	...	...
Plock	CDJC	128 361	61 667	66 694	88	...	...	...	...
Poznan	CDJC	578 886	269 899	308 987	261	...	...	...	...
Radom	CDJC	229 699	109 946	119 753	112	...	...	...	...
Ruda Slaska	CDJC	150 595	73 553	77 042	78	...	...	...	...
Rybnik	CDJC	142 731	70 109	72 622	148	...	...	...	...
Rzeszów	CDJC	160 376	75 763	84 613	54	...	...	...	...
Sosnowiec	CDJC	232 622	111 066	121 556	91	...	...	...	...
Szczecin	CDJC	415 399	198 264	217 135	301	...	...	...	...
Tarnów	CDJC	119 913	57 133	62 780	72	...	...	...	...
Torun	CDJC	211 243	98 451	112 792	116	...	...	...	...
Tychy	CDJC	132 816	64 860	67 956	82	...	...	...	...
Walbrzych	CDJC	130 268	61 526	68 742	85	...	...	...	...
WARSZAWA	CDJC	1 671 670	773 494	898 176	494	...	...	...	...
Wloclawek	CDJC	121 229	57 364	63 865	85	...	...	...	...
Wroclaw	CDJC	640 367	300 716	339 651	293	...	...	...	...
Zabrze	CDJC	195 293	94 636	100 657	80	...	...	...	...
Zielona Góra	CDJC	118 293	55 704	62 589	58	...	...	...	...
Portugal									
1 VII 2002									
LISBOA	ESDJ	554 366	253 179	301 187	85	...	...	...	...
Porto	ESDJ	253 562	115 241	138 321	40	...	...	...	...
Republic of Moldova — République de Moldova									
1 VII 2001									
Beltsy	ESDF	144 371	71 171	73 200	41	...	...	...	...
KISHINEV	ESDF	654 927	316 591	338 336	121	...	...	...	...
Romania — Roumanie									
18 III 2002									
Arad	CDJC	172 827	81 705	91 122	267	...	...	...	...
Bacau	CDJC	175 500	84 578	90 922	43	...	...	...	...
Baia Mare	CDJC	136 254	65 194	71 060	...	137 921	66 028	71 893	233
Botosani	CDJC	115 070	55 755	59 315	41	...	...	...	...
Braila	CDJC	216 292	103 801	112 491	33	...	...	...	...
Brasov	CDJC	284 246	136 807	147 439	...	284 596	136 981	147 615	267
BUCURESTI	CDJC	1 926 334	900 465	1 025 869	238	...	...	...	...
Buzau	CDJC	134 227	64 802	69 425	81	...	...	...	...
Cluj-Napoca	CDJC	317 953	150 341	167 612	180	...	...	...	...
Constanta	CDJC	306 288	147 270	159 018	...	310 471	149 324	161 147	125
Craiova	CDJC	291 443	140 857	150 586	...	302 601	146 491	156 110	81

(See notes at end of table. — Voir notes à la fin du tableau.)

Continent, country or area, date and city / Continent, pays ou zone, date et ville	Code[1]	City proper — Ville proprement dite Population				Urban agglomeration — Agglomération urbaine Population			
		Both sexes Les deux sexes	Male Masculin	Female Féminin	Surface area Superficie (km²)	Both sexes Les deux sexes	Male Masculin	Female Féminin	Surface area Superficie (km²)
EUROPE									
Romania — Roumanie									
18 III 2002									
Drobeta Turnu-Severin	CDJC	96 859	47 412	49 447	...	104 557	51 218	53 339	55
Focsani	CDJC	99 494	48 182	51 312	...	101 854	49 332	52 522	48
Galati	CDJC	298 861	145 968	152 893	246	...	...	...	...
Iasi	CDJC	320 888	151 812	169 076	94	...	...	...	...
Oradea	CDJC	206 614	98 438	108 176	111	...	...	...	...
Piatra Neamt	CDJC	102 694	48 701	53 993	...	104 914	49 818	55 096	77
Pitesti	CDJC	168 458	81 060	87 398	41	...	...	...	...
Ploiesti	CDJC	232 527	110 227	122 300	58	...	...	...	...
Rimnicu Vilcea	CDJC	97 186	46 802	50 384	...	107 726	51 955	55 771	90
Satu-Mare	CDJC	113 697	53 964	59 733	...	115 142	54 675	60 467	150
Sibiu	CDJC	154 841	73 097	81 744	...	154 892	73 124	81 768	122
Suceava	CDJC	105 865	50 684	55 181	52	...	...	...	...
Timisoara	CDJC	317 660	150 468	167 192	129	...	...	...	...
Tirgu-Mures	CDJC	128 612	61 083	67 529	...	150 041	71 631	78 410	49
Russian Federation — Fédération de Russie									
1 VII 1999									
Abakan	ESDF	168 047	77 027	91 020		...			
Achinsk	ESDF	121 419	57 161	64 258	...	122 800	...	...	...
Almetievsk	ESDF	141 764	68 085	73 679	...	151 850	...	...	...
Angarsk	ESDF	265 410	130 419	134 991	...	270 750	...	...	...
Arkhangelsk	ESDF	364 985	169 342	195 643	...	372 200	...	...	...
Armavir	ESDF	163 832	75 976	87 856	...	180 700	...	...	...
Arzamas	ESDF	110 465	51 174	59 291	...	...	...	...	...
Astrakhan	ESDF	482 402	224 336	258 066	...	...	...	...	...
Balakovo	ESDF	208 030	97 808	110 222	...	208 650	...	...	...
Balashlkha	ESDF	132 559	59 927	72 632	...	...	...	...	...
Barnaul	ESDF	579 900	269 949	310 951	...	647 600	...	...	...
Belgorod	ESDF	338 308	156 067	182 241	...	...	...	...	...
Berezniki	ESDF	182 900	92 307	90 593	...	185 150	...	...	...
Biisk	ESDF	224 493	103 772	120 721	...	236 250	...	...	...
Blagoveshchensk (Amurskaya oblast)	ESDF	220 102	106 277	113 825	...	223 500	...	...	...
Bratsk	ESDF	279 664	134 389	145 275	...	...	...	...	...
Bryansk	ESDF	455 158	213 605	241 553	...	477 450	...	...	...
Cheboksary	ESDF	459 156	216 659	242 497	...	471 650	...	...	...
Chelyabinsk	ESDF	1 084 208	501 602	582 606	...	1 111 100	...	...	...
Cherepovets	ESDF	323 545	153 635	169 910	...	...	...	...	...
Cherkessk	ESDF	121 032	56 199	64 833	...	...	...	...	...
Chita	ESDF	308 863	146 756	162 107	...	309 300	...	...	...
Dimitrovgrad	ESDF	136 605	65 234	71 371	...	...	...	...	...
Dzerzhinsk (Novgorodskaya oblast)	ESDF	278 246	129 783	148 463	...	289 100	...	...	...
Ekaterinburg	ESDF	1 267 393	578 680	688 713	...	1 313 750	...	...	...
Elektrostal	ESDF	147 159	67 416	79 743	...	...	...	...	...
Elets	ESDF	118 987	55 033	63 954	...	...	...	...	...
Elista	ESDF	102 189	47 480	54 709	...	106 150	...	...	...
Engels	ESDF	189 826	88 715	101 111	...	224 800	...	...	...
Glazov	ESDF	106 473	49 720	56 753	...	...	...	...	...
Ioshkap-Ola	ESDF	249 550	114 431	135 119	...	278 500	...	...	...
Irkutsk	ESDF	591 047	264 536	326 511	...	...	...	...	...
Ivanovo	ESDF	458 531	206 380	252 151	...	...	...	...	...
Izhevsk	ESDF	653 691	302 203	351 488	...	...	...	...	...
Kaliningrad (Kaliningradskaya oblast)	ESDF	425 089	204 456	220 633	...	...	...	...	...
Kaluga	ESDF	339 703	155 720	183 983	...	357 100	...	...	...
Kamensk-Uralsky	ESDF	190 352	88 328	102 024	...	192 000	...	...	...
Kamyshin	ESDF	125 901	58 968	66 933	...	...	...	...	...
Kansk	ESDF	108 063	51 654	56 409	...	...	...	...	...
Kazan	ESDF	1 091 656	499 838	591 818	...	1 092 150	...	...	...
Kemerovo	ESDF	492 240	222 475	269 765	...	532 200	...	...	...
Khabarovsk	ESDF	608 853	296 436	312 417	...	...	...	...	...

8. Population of capital cities and cities of 100 000 and more inhabitants: latest available year
Population des capitales et des villes de 100 000 habitants et plus: dernière année disponible (continued — suite)

(See notes at end of table. — Voir notes à la fin du tableau.)

Continent, country or area, date and city / Continent, pays ou zone, date et ville	Code[1]	City proper — Ville proprement dite Population				Urban agglomeration — Agglomération urbaine Population			
		Both sexes Les deux sexes	Male Masculin	Female Féminin	Surface area Superficie (km²)	Both sexes Les deux sexes	Male Masculin	Female Féminin	Surface area Superficie (km²)
EUROPE									
Russian Federation — Fédération de Russie									
1 VII 1999									
Khimki	ESDF	134 962	60 229	74 733	...	136 300	...	...	...
Kirov (Azerbaidzhanskaya SSR)	ESDF	465 628	213 653	251 975	...	508 150	...	...	...
Kiselevsk	ESDF	110 005	51 798	58 207	...	115 900	...	...	...
Kislovodsk	ESDF	112 481	51 301	61 180	...	117 100	...	...	...
Kolomna	ESDF	150 905	69 344	81 561	...	...	...	...	...
Komsomolsk-na-Amure	ESDF	294 268	140 015	154 253	...	...	...	...	...
Korolev	ESDF	133 789	60 577	73 212	...	161 600	...	...	...
Kostroma	ESDF	287 818	132 062	155 756	...	...	...	...	...
Kovrov	ESDF	161 298	73 154	88 144	...	...	...	...	...
Krasnodar	ESDF	639 917	298 694	341 223	...	757 150	...	...	...
Krasnoyarsk	ESDF	876 418	394 992	481 426	...	...	...	...	...
Kurgan	ESDF	364 211	168 153	196 058	...	...	...	...	...
Kursk	ESDF	440 208	200 923	239 285	...	...	...	...	...
Leninsk-Kuznetsky	ESDF	114 079	54 109	59 970	...	153 800	...	...	...
Lipetsk	ESDF	518 926	243 479	275 447	...	...	...	...	...
Lyubertsy	ESDF	164 210	73 397	90 813	...	...	...	...	...
Magadan	ESDF	121 330	59 226	62 104	...	130 450	...	...	...
Magnitogorsk	ESDF	426 866	199 646	227 220	...	427 300	...	...	...
Maikop	ESDF	166 860	75 470	91 390	...	178 550	...	...	...
Makhachkala	ESDF	330 942	163 560	167 382	...	378 650	...	...	...
Mezhdurechensk	ESDF	104 551	50 729	53 822	...	...	...	...	...
Miass	ESDF	165 811	77 932	87 879	...	179 400	...	...	...
Michurinsk	ESDF	118 610	53 026	65 584	...	...	...	...	...
MOSKVA	ESDF	8 297 056	3 724 694	4 572 362	...	8 537 700	...	...	...
Murmansk	ESDF	378 552	187 960	190 592	...	...	...	...	...
Murom	ESDF	140 993	65 615	75 378	...	...	...	...	...
Mytishchi	ESDF	156 631	69 397	87 234	...	...	...	...	...
Naberezhnye Tchelny	ESDF	521 282	250 577	270 705	...	524 400	...	...	...
Nakhodka	ESDF	158 559	80 172	78 387	...	188 150	...	...	...
Naltchik	ESDF	230 131	108 218	121 913	...	250 600	...	...	...
Neftekamsk	ESDF	117 352	55 296	62 056	...	124 650	...	...	...
Nevinnomyssk	ESDF	132 111	62 335	69 776	...	...	...	...	...
Nizhnekamsk	ESDF	224 426	105 993	118 433	...	...	...	...	...
Nizhenvartovsk	ESDF	238 071	118 840	119 231	...	...	...	...	...
Nizhny Tagil	ESDF	392 942	184 439	208 503	...	...	...	...	...
Nizhny Novgorod	ESDF	1 357 555	619 859	737 696	...	1 366 100	...	...	...
Noginsk	ESDF	117 446	52 784	64 662	...	...	...	...	...
Norilsk	ESDF	148 797	75 009	73 788	...	244 450	...	...	...
Novocheboksarsk	ESDF	124 628	58 624	66 004	...	124 900	...	...	...
Novocherkassk	ESDF	184 306	92 582	91 724	...	198 950	...	...	...
Novokuybishevsk	ESDF	115 758	51 706	64 052	...	117 900	...	...	...
Novokuznetsk	ESDF	564 353	262 313	302 040	...	579 250	...	...	...
Novomoskovsk (Tulskaya oblast)	ESDF	138 220	61 797	76 423	...	...	...	...	...
Novorossiysk	ESDF	204 652	97 198	107 454	...	248 850	...	...	...
Novoshakhtinsk	ESDF	101 566	48 083	53 483	...	118 450	...	...	...
Novosibirsk	ESDF	1 400 328	636 563	763 765	...	...	...	...	...
Novotroitsk	ESDF	109 681	53 577	56 104	...	117 400	...	...	...
Obninsk	ESDF	108 029	52 965	55 064	...	...	...	...	...
Odintsovo	ESDF	128 227	58 345	69 882	...	...	...	...	...
Oktyabrsky	ESDF	111 423	53 153	58 270	...	...	...	...	...
Omsk	ESDF	1 153 314	536 759	616 555	...	1 177 000	...	...	...
Orekhovo-Zuevo	ESDF	125 399	55 394	70 005	...	...	...	...	...
Orel	ESDF	341 854	155 373	186 481	...	...	...	...	...
Orenburg	ESDF	522 643	238 134	284 509	...	541 500	...	...	...
Orsk	ESDF	274 849	130 618	144 231	...	280 000	...	...	...
Penza	ESDF	528 140	243 904	284 236	...	528 500	...	...	...
Perm	ESDF	1 014 360	472 602	541 758	...	1 024 250	...	...	...
Pervouralsk	ESDF	135 588	64 826	70 762	...	163 850	...	...	...
Petropavlovsk-Kamchatsky	ESDF	198 424	102 034	96 390	...	209 650	...	...	...
Petrozavodsk	ESDF	282 401	130 133	152 268	...	282 650	...	...	...
Podolsk	ESDF	193 735	86 646	107 089	...	...	...	...	...

(See notes at end of table. — Voir notes à la fin du tableau.)

Continent, country or area, date and city / Continent, pays ou zone, date et ville	Code[1]	City proper — Ville proprement dite Population				Urban agglomeration — Agglomération urbaine Population			
		Both sexes Les deux sexes	Male Masculin	Female Féminin	Surface area Superficie (km²)	Both sexes Les deux sexes	Male Masculin	Female Féminin	Surface area Superficie (km²)
EUROPE									
Russian Federation — Fédération de Russie									
1 VII 1999									
Prokopyevsk	ESDF	236 174	111 692	124 482	...	236 350	...	...	...
Pskov	ESDF	201 846	91 042	110 804	...	...	...	...	...
Pyatigorsk	ESDF	128 257	56 836	71 421	...	184 600	...	...	...
Rostov-na-Donu	ESDF	1 003 482	461 383	542 099	...	...	...	...	...
Rubtsovsk	ESDF	163 252	77 811	85 441	...	...	...	...	...
Ryazan	ESDF	528 116	241 727	286 389	...	531 200	...	...	...
Rybinsk	ESDF	241 450	111 568	129 882	...	...	...	...	...
Salavat	ESDF	157 847	74 820	83 027	...	...	...	...	...
Samara (Samarskaya oblast)	ESDF	1 164 859	522 584	642 275	...	1 183 350	...	...	...
Saransk	ESDF	316 086	143 809	172 277	...	344 700	...	...	...
Sarapyul	ESDF	105 623	48 418	57 205	...	106 350	...	...	...
Saratov	ESDF	875 256	404 967	470 289	...	...	...	...	...
Sergiev Posad	ESDF	111 256	49 010	62 246	...	...	...	...	...
Serpukhov	ESDF	133 685	62 466	71 219	...	...	...	...	...
Severodvinsk	ESDF	235 799	120 852	114 947	...	238 250	...	...	...
Seversk	ESDF	119 146	56 316	62 830	...	...	...	...	...
Shakhty	ESDF	221 538	101 638	119 900	...	250 900	...	...	...
Shchelkovo	ESDF	104 847	46 819	58 028	...	...	...	...	...
Smolensk	ESDF	351 498	161 833	189 665	...	...	...	...	...
Sochi	ESDF	334 009	153 852	180 157	...	395 800	...	...	...
Solikamsk	ESDF	106 164	52 534	53 630	...	...	...	...	...
St. Petersburg	ESDF	4 678 102	2 110 381	2 567 721	...	...	...	...	...
Starsy Oskol	ESDF	212 182	100 715	111 467	...	...	...	...	...
Stavropol	ESDF	342 642	157 317	185 325	...	342 700	...	...	...
Sterlitamak	ESDF	264 729	125 804	138 925	...	...	...	...	...
Surgut	ESDF	277 781	138 507	139 274	...	...	...	...	...
Syktivkar	ESDF	229 870	108 010	121 069	...	240 000	...	...	...
Syzran	ESDF	186 367	83 947	102 420	...	...	...	...	...
Taganrog	ESDF	284 850	131 569	153 281	...	...	...	...	...
Tambov	ESDF	312 453	141 980	170 473	...	...	...	...	...
Tolyatti	ESDF	720 430	350 308	370 122	...	734 300	...	...	...
Tomsk	ESDF	481 462	231 737	249 725	...	...	...	...	...
Tula	ESDF	506 147	230 960	275 187	...	554 650	...	...	...
Tver	ESDF	450 795	208 622	242 173	...	455 150	...	...	...
Tyumen	ESDF	502 214	235 033	267 181	...	556 200	...	...	...
Ufa	ESDF	1 087 788	510 451	577 337	...	1 093 700	...	...	...
Uhta	ESDF	101 192	48 564	52 628	...	129 200	...	...	...
Ulan-Ude	ESDF	370 175	174 278	195 897	...	394 400	...	...	...
Ulyanovsk	ESDF	668 030	314 674	353 356	...	690 300	...	...	...
Usolie Sibirskoye	ESDF	103 831	51 374	52 457	...	...	...	...	...
Ussuriisk	ESDF	157 095	74 155	82 940	...	...	...	...	...
Ust-Ulimsk	ESDF	106 502	52 501	54 001	...	...	...	...	...
Uzno-Sakhalinsk	ESDF	176 515	83 990	92 525	...	184 500	...	...	...
Velikie Luky	ESDF	116 275	53 704	62 571	...	...	...	...	...
Velikiy Novgorod	ESDF	229 461	108 308	121 153	...	238 000	...	...	...
Vladikavkaz (Osetinskaya ASSR)	ESDF	308 810	142 412	166 398	...	322 500	...	...	...
Vladimir	ESDF	335 083	157 803	177 280	...	356 850	...	...	...
Vladivostok	ESDF	606 895	291 561	315 334	...	636 600	...	...	...
Volgodonsk	ESDF	179 712	88 832	90 880	...	187 000	...	...	...
Volgograd	ESDF	992 341	459 366	532 975	...	1 024 900	...	...	...
Vologda	ESDF	300 449	137 301	163 148	...	309 750	...	...	...
Volzhsky	ESDF	285 920	134 010	151 910	...	294 850	...	...	...
Voronezh	ESDF	903 224	416 952	486 272	...	978 100	...	...	...
Votkinsk	ESDF	102 102	47 727	54 375	...	...	...	...	...
Yakutsk	ESDF	196 417	93 210	103 207	...	228 350	...	...	...
Yaroslave	ESDF	614 095	278 692	335 403	...	...	...	...	...
Zelenodolsk	ESDF	101 300	45 749	55 551	...	...	...	...	...
Zelenograd	ESDF	207 501	97 718	109 783	...	...	...	...	...
Zlatoust	ESDF	197 928	91 663	106 265	...	200 350	...	...	...

(See notes at end of table. — Voir notes à la fin du tableau.)

Continent, country or area, date and city Continent, pays ou zone, date et ville	Code[1]	City proper — Ville proprement dite Population				Urban agglomeration — Agglomération urbaine Population			
		Both sexes Les deux sexes	Male Masculin	Female Féminin	Surface area Superficie (km²)	Both sexes Les deux sexes	Male Masculin	Female Féminin	Surface area Superficie (km²)
EUROPE									
San Marino — Saint-Marin									
31 XII 2000									
SAN MARINO	ESDF	2 822	1 341	1 481	7	4 508	2 174	2 334	...
Serbia and Montenegro — Serbie-et-Montenegro									
31 III 2002									
BEOGRAD	CDJC	1 119 642	522 451	597 191	...	1 576 124	747 854	828 270	3 224
Kragujevac	CDJC	146 373	71 005	75 368	...	175 802	85 630	90 172	835
Nis	CDJC	173 724	83 521	90 203	...	235 159	114 600	120 559	452
Novi Sad	CDJC	191 405	88 975	102 430	...	299 294	142 033	157 261	699
Slovakia — Slovaquie									
1 VII 2002									
BRATISLAVA	ESDJ	427 425	199 960	227 465	...	...	...	...	...
Kosice	ESDJ	235 832	112 642	123 190	...	...	...	...	...
Slovenia — Slovénie									
31 III 2002									
LJUBLJANA	CDJC	258 873	122 728	136 145	164	260 543	123 549	136 994	171
Maribor	CDJC	93 847	44 420	49 427	38	108 241	51 552	56 689	99
1 VII 2002									
LJUBLJANA	ESDJ	249 903	115 844	134 059	163	251 539	116 647	134 892	168
Spain — Espagne[94]									
1 VII 2000									
Alcalá de Henares	ESDJ	166 397	82 753	83 644	878	...	...	...	...
Alcorcón	ESDJ	144 636	71 408	73 228	337	...	...	...	...
Algeciras	ESDJ	104 087	51 166	52 921	851	...	...	...	...
Badalona	ESDJ	208 944	103 124	105 820	210	...	...	...	...
Cartagena	ESDJ	179 939	89 098	90 841	5 583	...	...	...	...
Elche	ESDJ	195 791	96 779	99 012	3 261	...	...	...	...
Fuenlabrada	ESDJ	173 788	87 695	86 093	387	...	...	...	...
Getafe	ESDJ	146 310	72 629	73 681	784	...	...	...	...
Gijón	ESDJ	267 426	126 994	140 432	1 816	...	...	...	...
Hospitalet de Llobregat	ESDJ	241 782	118 140	123 642	125	...	...	...	...
Jérez de la Frontera	ESDJ	183 677	89 617	94 060	14 118	...	...	...	...
Leganés	ESDJ	172 049	85 530	86 519	431	...	...	...	...
Marbella	ESDJ	105 910	52 263	53 647	...	...	...	...	...
Mataró	ESDJ	104 659	51 324	53 335	223	...	...	...	...
Móstoles	ESDJ	196 289	97 383	98 906	454	...	...	...	...
Sabadell	ESDJ	183 727	89 079	94 648	376	...	...	...	...
San Cristóbal de La Laguna	ESDJ	126 543	62 089	64 454	1 021	...	...	...	...
Santa Coloma de Gramanet	ESDJ	117 127	58 139	58 988	71	...	...	...	...
Terrassa	ESDJ	171 794	83 957	87 837	702	...	...	...	...
Vigo	ESDJ	285 526	135 413	150 113	1 091	...	...	...	...
1 VII 2001									
Albacete	ESDJ	149 434	73 118	76 316	12 431	...	...	...	...
Alicante	ESDJ	279 535	133 842	145 693	2 008	...	...	...	...
Almería	ESDJ	172 055	83 580	88 475	2 962	...	...	...	...
Badajoz	ESDJ	127 736	61 724	66 012	15 302	...	...	...	...
Barcelona	ESDJ	1 392 641	645 778	746 863	991	...	...	...	...
Bilbao	ESDJ	346 683	163 657	183 026	413	...	...	...	...
Burgos	ESDJ	161 520	77 752	83 768	1 084	...	...	...	...
Cádiz	ESDJ	132 872	63 267	69 605	112	...	...	...	...
Castellón de la Plana	ESDJ	139 009	67 626	71 383	1 075	...	...	...	...
Córdoba	ESDJ	303 874	145 870	158 004	12 533	...	...	...	...
Donostia - San Sebastián	ESDJ	177 831	83 418	94 413	615	...	...	...	...
Granada	ESDJ	231 577	107 066	124 511	882	...	...	...	...
Huelva	ESDJ	138 605	66 712	71 893	1 513	...	...	...	...
Jaén	ESDJ	106 449	51 274	55 175	4 243	...	...	...	...
La Coruña	ESDJ	235 847	109 402	126 445	376	...	...	...	...
Las Palmas de Gran Canaria	ESDJ	357 601	175 390	182 211	1 005	...	...	...	...
León	ESDJ	140 638	65 374	75 264	392	...	...	...	...
Lleida	ESDJ	110 770	53 629	57 141	2 120	...	...	...	...
Logroño	ESDJ	130 024	62 371	67 653	796	...	...	...	...
MADRID	ESDJ	2 912 705	1 353 349	1 559 356	6 058	...	...	...	...
Málaga	ESDJ	545 966	261 923	284 043	3 930	...	...	...	...

8. Population of capital cities and cities of 100 000 and more inhabitants: latest available year
Population des capitales et des villes de 100 000 habitants et plus: dernière année disponible (continued — suite)

(See notes at end of table. — Voir notes à la fin du tableau.)

Continent, country or area, date and city / Continent, pays ou zone, date et ville	Code[1]	City proper — Ville proprement dite Population				Urban agglomeration — Agglomération urbaine Population			
		Both sexes Les deux sexes	Male Masculin	Female Féminin	Surface area Superficie (km²)	Both sexes Les deux sexes	Male Masculin	Female Féminin	Surface area Superficie (km²)
EUROPE									
Spain — Espagne[94]									
1 VII 2001									
Murcia	ESDJ	353 943	171 763	182 180	8 865	...	...	...	...
Ourense	ESDJ	102 896	47 855	55 041	845	...	...	...	...
Oviedo	ESDJ	198 989	92 363	106 626	1 866	...	...	...	...
Palma de Mallorca	ESDJ	313 766	152 241	161 525	2 008	...	...	...	...
Pamplona	ESDJ	164 054	77 561	86 493	238	...	...	...	...
Salamanca	ESDJ	153 943	71 790	82 153	386	...	...	...	...
Santa Cruz de Tenerife	ESDJ	200 015	95 764	104 251	1 506	...	...	...	...
Santander	ESDJ	177 180	82 556	94 624	348	...	...	...	...
Sevilla	ESDJ	686 853	327 131	359 722	1 413	...	...	...	...
Tarragona	ESDJ	115 756	56 117	59 639	624	...	...	...	...
Valencia	ESDJ	745 216	354 340	390 876	1 346	...	...	...	...
Valladolid	ESDJ	309 116	147 960	161 156	1 975	...	...	...	...
Vitoria-Gasteiz	ESDJ	218 746	107 514	111 232	2 768	...	...	...	...
Zaragoza	ESDJ	593 204	284 834	308 370	10 631	...	...	...	...
Sweden — Suède									
1 VII 1999									
Göteborg	ESDJ	462 470	226 323	236 147	449	788 970	389 432	399 538	...
Helsingborg	ESDJ	116 870	56 377	60 493	346	...	...	...	...
Jönköping	ESDJ	116 344	56 809	59 535	1 485	...	...	...	...
Linköping	ESDJ	132 500	66 412	66 088	1 431	...	...	...	...
Malmö	ESDJ	257 574	123 610	133 964	154	518 506	252 814	265 692	...
Norrköping	ESDJ	122 212	60 089	62 123	1 491	...	...	...	...
Orebro	ESDJ	123 503	59 759	63 744	1 371	...	...	...	...
STOCKHOLM	ESDJ	743 703	356 604	387 099	187	1 643 366	800 874	842 492	...
Umeå	ESDJ	103 970	51 325	52 645	2 316	...	...	...	...
Uppsala	ESDJ	188 478	91 600	96 878	2 465	...	...	...	...
Västerås	ESDJ	125 433	62 033	63 400	956	...	...	...	...
Switzerland — Suisse									
5 XII 2000									
Baden-Brugg	CDFC	...	...	...	...	106 736	53 235	53 501	...
Bâle	CDFC	166 558	78 736	87 822	...	479 308	231 725	247 583	...
BERNE	CDFC	128 634	59 727	68 907	...	349 096	167 034	182 062	...
Genève	CDFC	177 964	83 449	94 515	...	471 314	225 597	245 717	...
Lausanne	CDFC	124 914	58 621	66 293	...	311 441	149 582	161 859	...
Lugano	CDFC	...	...	...	...	120 800	56 940	63 860	...
Luzern	CDFC	...	...	...	...	196 550	95 088	101 462	...
Olten-Zofingen	CDFC	...	...	...	...	101 909	50 122	51 787	...
St. Gallen	CDFC	...	...	...	...	146 385	71 430	74 955	...
Winterthur	CDFC	...	...	...	...	123 416	60 248	63 168	...
Zürich	CDFC	363 273	175 836	187 437	...	1 080 728	531 298	549 430	...
1 VII 2001									
Bâle	ESDJ	165 356	78 073	87 283	24	401 610	192 661	208 949	271
BERNE	ESDJ	122 427	56 721	65 706	52	320 058	152 617	167 441	410
Genève	ESDJ	175 403	82 201	93 202	16	467 040	223 324	243 716	436
Lausanne	ESDJ	115 208	53 701	61 507	41	290 881	139 072	151 809	275
Zürich	ESDJ	339 234	162 164	177 070	88	960 310	468 595	491 715	847
The Former Yougoslav Rep. of Macedonia — L'ex-République yougoslave de Macédoine									
31 X 2002									
SKOPLJE	CDJC	467 257	229 485	237 772	...	...	...	...	...
Ukraine									
5 XII 2001									
Alchevsk	CDFC	118 611	54 646	63 965	...	...	...	...	...
Berdyansk	CDFC	121 759	54 878	66 881	...	...	...	...	...
Bila Tserkva (Belaya Tserkov)	CDFC	196 023	92 100	103 923	...	...	...	...	...
Cherkasy	CDFC	292 761	135 539	157 222	...	...	...	...	...
Chernihiv	CDFC	299 038	139 444	159 594	...	...	...	...	...
Chernivtsy	CDFC	236 691	109 675	127 016	...	...	...	...	...
Dnieprodzerzhynsk	CDFC	254 869	115 539	139 330	...	...	...	...	...
Dnipropetrovsk	CDFC	1 053 951	482 903	571 048	...	...	...	...	...
Donetsk (Donestskaya oblast)	CDFC	1 007 440	451 820	555 620	...	...	...	...	...

(See notes at end of table. — Voir notes à la fin du tableau.)

Continent, country or area, date and city / Continent, pays ou zone, date et ville	Code[1]	City proper — Ville proprement dite Population				Urban agglomeration — Agglomération urbaine Population			
		Both sexes Les deux sexes	Male Masculin	Female Féminin	Surface area Superficie (km²)	Both sexes Les deux sexes	Male Masculin	Female Féminin	Surface area Superficie (km²)
EUROPE									
Ukraine									
5 XII 2001									
Enakievo (Yenakievo)	CDFC	104 266	46 894	57 372	...	...	...	...	...
Evpatoriya	CDFC	103 244	46 118	57 126	...	...	...	...	...
Horlivka	CDFC	289 872	131 508	158 364	...	...	...	...	...
Ivano-Frankivsk	CDFC	215 288	102 331	112 957	...	...	...	...	...
Kerch	CDFC	158 165	71 826	86 339	...	...	...	...	...
Kharkiv	CDFC	1 449 871	664 252	785 619	...	...	...	...	...
Kherson	CDFC	324 424	147 359	177 065	...	...	...	...	...
Khmelnytskiy (Hmilnyk)	CDFC	251 077	117 544	133 533	...	...	...	...	...
KYIV (KIEV)	CDFC	2 566 953	1 193 356	1 373 597	...	...	...	...	...
Kirovohrad	CDFC	250 629	114 460	136 169	...	...	...	...	...
Kramatorsk	CDFC	180 487	80 895	99 592	...	...	...	...	...
Kremenchuh	CDFC	232 960	107 642	125 318	...	...	...	...	...
Kryviy Rig	CDFC	666 812	304 784	362 028	...	...	...	...	...
Lysychansk	CDFC	114 905	52 218	62 687	...	...	...	...	...
Luhansk	CDFC	459 294	206 624	252 670	...	...	...	...	...
Lutsk	CDFC	205 585	93 911	111 674	...	...	...	...	...
Lviv	CDFC	725 202	341 779	383 423	...	...	...	...	...
Makyivka	CDFC	387 609	177 325	210 284	...	...	...	...	...
Mariupol	CDFC	488 462	224 232	264 230	...	...	...	...	...
Melitopol	CDFC	160 352	73 195	87 157	...	...	...	...	...
Mykolayiv (Nikolaevskaya oblast)	CDFC	509 102	232 823	276 279	...	...	...	...	...
Nikopol	CDFC	138 218	62 531	75 687	...	...	...	...	...
Odessa	CDFC	1 010 298	470 353	539 945	...	...	...	...	...
Pavlohrad	CDFC	119 672	56 077	63 595	...	...	...	...	...
Poltava	CDFC	310 755	143 567	167 188	...	...	...	...	...
Rivne	CDFC	245 323	113 525	131 798	...	...	...	...	...
Sevastopol	CDFC	340 190	154 896	185 294	...	...	...	...	...
Simpheropol	CDFC	338 038	150 159	187 879	...	...	...	...	...
Siverodonetsk	CDFC	120 225	54 272	65 953	...	...	...	...	...
Slovyansk	CDFC	122 575	54 068	68 507	...	...	...	...	...
Sumy	CDFC	292 139	133 927	158 212	...	...	...	...	...
Ternopil	CDFC	226 029	106 095	119 934	...	...	...	...	...
Uzhhorod	CDFC	115 568	54 078	61 490	...	...	...	...	...
Vinnytsya	CDFC	354 639	164 682	189 957	...	...	...	...	...
Zaporizhya	CDFC	810 620	369 432	441 188	...	...	...	...	...
Zhytomyr	CDFC	282 823	131 602	151 221	...	...	...	...	...
United Kingdom — Royaume-Uni[95]									
1 VII 1996									
Aberdeen	ESDF	217 260	106 198	111 062	186	...	...	...	...
Aberdeenshire	ESDF	227 430	113 042	114 388	6 318	...	...	...	...
Amber Valley	ESDF	115 224	57 285	57 939	265	...	...	...	...
Angus	ESDF	110 780	54 044	56 736	2 181	...	...	...	...
Arun	ESDF	137 978	65 564	72 414	221	...	...	...	...
Ashfield	ESDF	108 558	53 753	54 805	110	...	...	...	...
Aylesbury Vale	ESDF	154 927	77 051	77 876	903	...	...	...	...
Barking & Dagenham[96]	ESDF	153 715	75 092	78 623	34	...	...	...	...
Barnet[96]	ESDF	319 353	155 895	163 458	89	...	...	...	...
Barnsley	ESDF	227 213	111 642	115 571	328	...	...	...	...
Basildon	ESDF	163 280	80 407	82 873	110	...	...	...	...
Basingstoke & Deane	ESDF	147 914	73 469	74 445	634	...	...	...	...
Bassetlaw	ESDF	106 303	52 748	53 555	637	...	...	...	...
Bath & North East Somerset	ESDF	164 725	80 342	84 383	351	...	...	...	...
Bedford	ESDF	137 451	68 477	68 974	477	...	...	...	...
Belfast[97]	ESDF	297 300	...	...	110	...	...	...	...
Bexley[96]	ESDF	219 311	107 360	111 951	61	...	...	...	...
Birmingham	ESDF	1 020 589	504 342	516 247	265	...	...	...	...
Blackburn	ESDF	139 491	68 701	70 790	137	...	...	...	...
Blackpool	ESDF	152 459	73 875	78 584	35	...	...	...	...
Bolton	ESDF	265 449	130 861	134 588	140	...	...	...	...
Bournemouth	ESDF	160 749	76 297	84 452	46	...	...	...	...
Bracknell Forest	ESDF	110 092	55 725	54 367	109	...	...	...	...
Bradford	ESDF	483 422	238 407	245 015	366	...	...	...	...

8. Population of capital cities and cities of 100 000 and more inhabitants: latest available year
Population des capitales et des villes de 100 000 habitants et plus: dernière année disponible (continued — suite)

(See notes at end of table. — Voir notes à la fin du tableau.)

Continent, country or area, date and city — Continent, pays ou zone, date et ville	Code[1]	City proper — Ville proprement dite Population				Urban agglomeration — Agglomération urbaine Population			
		Both sexes Les deux sexes	Male Masculin	Female Féminin	Surface area Superficie (km²)	Both sexes Les deux sexes	Male Masculin	Female Féminin	Surface area Superficie (km²)
EUROPE									
United Kingdom — Royaume-Uni[95]									
1 VII 1996									
Braintree	ESDF	126 236	62 500	63 736	612	...	...	...	...
Breckland	ESDF	113 654	55 573	58 081	1 305	...	...	...	...
Brent[96]	ESDF	247 525	123 645	123 880	44	...	...	...	...
Bridgend	ESDF	130 080	63 056	67 024	246	...	...	...	...
Brighton	ESDF	156 124	76 842	79 282	58	...	...	...	...
Bristol	ESDF	399 633	198 167	201 466	110	...	...	...	...
Broadland	ESDF	113 896	55 984	57 912	552	...	...	...	...
Bromley[96]	ESDF	295 584	143 424	152 160	152	...	...	...	...
Broxtowe	ESDF	111 429	55 215	56 214	81	...	...	...	...
Bury	ESDF	181 873	90 104	91 769	99	...	...	...	...
Caerphilly	ESDF	169 125	83 049	86 076	278	...	...	...	...
Calderdale	ESDF	192 844	94 093	98 751	363	...	...	...	...
Cambridge	ESDF	116 701	58 498	58 203	41	...	...	...	...
Camden[96]	ESDF	189 119	92 370	96 749	22	...	...	...	...
Canterbury	ESDF	136 481	66 429	70 052	309	...	...	...	...
Cardiff[98]	ESDF	315 040	154 656	160 384	140	...	...	...	...
Carlisle	ESDF	103 102	50 308	52 794	1 040	...	...	...	...
Carmarthenshire	ESDF	169 108	82 270	86 838	2 395	...	...	...	...
Charnwood	ESDF	155 724	77 740	77 984	279	...	...	...	...
Chelmsford	ESDF	156 601	77 147	79 454	342	...	...	...	...
Cheltenham	ESDF	106 692	52 428	54 264	47	...	...	...	...
Cherwell	ESDF	132 687	65 387	67 300	589	...	...	...	...
Chester	ESDF	119 221	58 314	60 907	448	...	...	...	...
Chesterfield	ESDF	100 673	49 514	51 159	66	...	...	...	...
Chichester	ESDF	104 112	47 863	56 249	786	...	...	...	...
Colchester	ESDF	154 176	76 091	78 085	334	...	...	...	...
Conwy	ESDF	110 596	52 510	58 086	1 130	...	...	...	...
Coventry	ESDF	306 503	151 502	155 001	97	...	...	...	...
Crewe & Nantwich	ESDF	113 670	56 612	57 058	430	...	...	...	...
Croydon[96]	ESDF	333 787	163 998	169 789	87	...	...	...	...
Dacorum	ESDF	134 733	66 410	68 323	212	...	...	...	...
Darlington	ESDF	101 257	49 307	51 950	197	...	...	...	...
Derby	ESDF	233 708	115 901	117 807	78	...	...	...	...
Derry	ESDF	104 400	...	...	380	...	...	...	...
Doncaster	ESDF	291 804	143 806	147 998	581	...	...	...	...
Dover	ESDF	107 398	52 359	55 039	315	...	...	...	...
Dudley	ESDF	312 194	154 918	157 276	98	...	...	...	...
Dumfries & Galloway	ESDF	147 600	71 703	75 897	6 439	...	...	...	...
Dundee	ESDF	150 250	71 740	78 510	65	...	...	...	...
Ealing[96]	ESDF	297 033	148 140	148 893	55	...	...	...	...
East Ayrshire	ESDF	122 350	59 110	63 240	1 252	...	...	...	...
East Devon	ESDF	123 105	57 740	65 365	814	...	...	...	...
East Dunbartonshire	ESDF	110 750	54 125	56 625	172	...	...	...	...
East Hampshire	ESDF	110 761	53 872	56 889	515	...	...	...	...
East Hertfordshire	ESDF	123 553	61 771	61 782	477	...	...	...	...
East Lindsey	ESDF	123 058	59 401	63 657	1 760	...	...	...	...
East Riding of Yorkshire	ESDF	308 689	150 842	157 847	2 415	...	...	...	...
East Staffordshire	ESDF	100 421	49 951	50 470	390	...	...	...	...
Eastleigh	ESDF	111 732	55 310	56 422	80	...	...	...	...
Edinburgh[99]	ESDF	448 850	216 730	232 120	262	...	...	...	...
Elmbridge	ESDF	124 539	60 298	64 241	97	...	...	...	...
Enfield[96]	ESDF	262 613	129 236	133 377	81	...	...	...	...
Epping Forest	ESDF	119 512	58 424	61 088	340	...	...	...	...
Erewash	ESDF	106 818	53 033	53 785	109	...	...	...	...
Exeter	ESDF	107 729	53 152	54 577	47	...	...	...	...
Falkirk	ESDF	143 040	69 469	73 571	299	...	...	...	...
Fareham	ESDF	103 748	50 413	53 335	74	...	...	...	...
Fife	ESDF	349 300	169 204	180 096	1 323	...	...	...	...
Flintshire	ESDF	144 918	71 443	73 475	438	...	...	...	...
Gateshead	ESDF	200 968	98 242	102 726	143	...	...	...	...
Gedling	ESDF	112 194	54 985	57 209	120	...	...	...	...
Glasgow	ESDF	616 430	294 237	322 193	175	...	...	...	...

8. Population of capital cities and cities of 100 000 and more inhabitants: latest available year
Population des capitales et des villes de 100 000 habitants et plus: dernière année disponible (continued — suite)

(See notes at end of table. — Voir notes à la fin du tableau.)

Continent, country or area, date and city / Continent, pays ou zone, date et ville	Code[1]	City proper — Ville proprement dite Population				Urban agglomeration — Agglomération urbaine Population			
		Both sexes Les deux sexes	Male Masculin	Female Féminin	Surface area Superficie (km²)	Both sexes Les deux sexes	Male Masculin	Female Féminin	Surface area Superficie (km²)
EUROPE									
United Kingdom — Royaume-Uni[95]									
1 VII 1996									
Gloucester	ESDF	106 834	53 328	53 506	41	...	...	...	...
Greenwich[96]	ESDF	212 073	103 156	108 917	48	...	...	...	...
Guildford	ESDF	124 567	61 520	63 047	271	...	...	...	...
Gwynedd	ESDF	117 775	57 195	60 580	2 548	...	...	...	...
Hackney[96]	ESDF	193 843	95 559	98 284	20	...	...	...	...
Halton	ESDF	123 038	60 479	62 559	74	...	...	...	...
Hammersmith & Fulham[96]	ESDF	156 718	74 635	82 083	16	...	...	...	...
Haringey[96]	ESDF	216 111	107 188	108 923	30	...	...	...	...
Harrogate	ESDF	147 635	70 360	77 275	1 333	...	...	...	...
Harrow[96]	ESDF	210 670	103 517	107 153	51	...	...	...	...
Havant & Waterloo	ESDF	117 341	56 816	60 525	55	...	...	...	...
Havering[96]	ESDF	230 909	113 300	117 609	118	...	...	...	...
Highland	ESDF	208 700	102 383	106 317	25 784	...	...	...	...
Hillingdon[96]	ESDF	247 718	122 684	125 034	110	...	...	...	...
Horsham	ESDF	118 569	58 198	60 371	530	...	...	...	...
Hounslow[96]	ESDF	205 798	102 875	102 923	58	...	...	...	...
Huntingdonshire	ESDF	152 742	75 372	77 370	923	...	...	...	...
Ipswich	ESDF	113 642	55 641	58 001	39	...	...	...	...
Isle of Wight	ESDF	125 466	60 464	65 002	380	...	...	...	...
Islington[96]	ESDF	175 990	85 525	90 465	15	...	...	...	...
Kensington & Chelsea[96]	ESDF	159 039	77 469	81 570	12	...	...	...	...
Kings Lynn & West Norfolk	ESDF	131 214	64 551	66 663	1 429	...	...	...	...
Kingston-upon-Hull	ESDF	266 775	132 393	134 382	71	...	...	...	...
Kingston-upon-Thames[96]	ESDF	141 837	69 980	71 857	38	...	...	...	...
Kirklees	ESDF	388 807	191 176	197 631	410	...	...	...	...
Knowsley	ESDF	154 053	74 838	79 215	97	...	...	...	...
Lambeth[96]	ESDF	264 727	129 763	134 964	27	...	...	...	...
Lancaster	ESDF	136 948	66 569	70 379	576	...	...	...	...
Leeds	ESDF	726 939	359 351	367 588	562	...	...	...	...
Leicester	ESDF	294 830	146 359	148 471	73	...	...	...	...
Lewisham[96]	ESDF	241 495	116 451	125 044	35	...	...	...	...
Lisburn	ESDF	108 400	...	...	447	...	...	...	...
Liverpool	ESDF	467 995	228 398	239 597	113	...	...	...	...
LONDON[100]	ESDF	7 074 265	3 474 931	3 599 334	1 578	...	...	...	...
Luton	ESDF	181 468	91 012	90 456	43	...	...	...	...
Macclesfield	ESDF	152 604	74 565	78 039	525	...	...	...	...
Maidstone	ESDF	140 664	69 243	71 421	393	...	...	...	...
Manchester	ESDF	430 818	212 530	218 288	116	...	...	...	...
Mansfield	ESDF	101 355	50 288	51 067	77	...	...	...	...
Merton[96]	ESDF	182 291	89 704	92 587	38	...	...	...	...
Mid Bedfordshire	ESDF	118 945	58 957	59 988	503	...	...	...	...
Mid Sussex	ESDF	125 329	61 787	63 542	333	...	...	...	...
Middlesborough	ESDF	146 778	71 871	74 907	54	...	...	...	...
Milton Keynes	ESDF	197 131	98 274	98 857	309	...	...	...	...
Neath Port Talbot	ESDF	139 459	68 064	71 395	442	...	...	...	...
Newark & Sherwood	ESDF	104 464	51 558	52 906	651	...	...	...	...
Newbury	ESDF	143 727	71 390	72 337	704	...	...	...	...
Newcastle-under-Lyme	ESDF	122 314	60 137	62 177	211	...	...	...	...
Newcastle-upon-Tyne	ESDF	282 338	138 883	143 455	112	...	...	...	...
Newham[96]	ESDF	228 857	114 740	114 117	36	...	...	...	...
New Forest	ESDF	169 513	82 041	87 472	753	...	...	...	...
Newport	ESDF	136 789	66 839	69 950	190	...	...	...	...
North Ayrshire	ESDF	139 520	67 163	72 357	884	...	...	...	...
North East Lincolnshire	ESDF	158 503	77 615	80 888	192	...	...	...	...
North Hertfordshire	ESDF	114 941	56 925	58 016	375	...	...	...	...
North Lanarkshire	ESDF	325 940	158 347	167 593	474	...	...	...	...
North Lincolnshire	ESDF	152 767	75 457	77 310	838	...	...	...	...
North Somerset	ESDF	185 340	90 218	95 122	375	...	...	...	...
North Tyneside	ESDF	193 619	92 875	100 744	84	...	...	...	...
North Wiltshire	ESDF	121 747	60 947	60 800	768	...	...	...	...
Northampton	ESDF	192 382	94 840	97 542	81	...	...	...	...
Norwich	ESDF	126 221	61 878	64 343	39	...	...	...	...

8. Population of capital cities and cities of 100 000 and more inhabitants: latest available year
Population des capitales et des villes de 100 000 habitants et plus: dernière année disponible (continued — suite)

(See notes at end of table. — Voir notes à la fin du tableau.)

Continent, country or area, date and city / Continent, pays ou zone, date et ville	Code[1]	City proper — Ville proprement dite Population				Urban agglomeration — Agglomération urbaine Population			
		Both sexes Les deux sexes	Male Masculin	Female Féminin	Surface area Superficie (km²)	Both sexes Les deux sexes	Male Masculin	Female Féminin	Surface area Superficie (km²)
EUROPE									
United Kingdom — Royaume-Uni[95]									
1 VII 1996									
Nottingham	ESDF	283 969	140 237	143 732	75				
Nuneaton & Bedworth	ESDF	118 340	59 060	59 280	79	...	...	...	...
Oldham	ESDF	220 172	107 764	112 408	141	...	...	...	...
Oxford	ESDF	137 343	69 220	68 123	46	...	...	...	...
Pembrokeshire	ESDF	113 597	55 413	58 184	1 590	...	...	...	...
Perth & Kinross	ESDF	132 570	63 937	68 633	5 311	...	...	...	...
Peterborough	ESDF	158 674	79 264	79 410	333	...	...	...	...
Plymouth	ESDF	255 826	125 854	129 972	80	...	...	...	...
Poole	ESDF	139 226	67 391	71 835	65	...	...	...	...
Portsmouth	ESDF	190 370	97 010	93 360	40	...	...	...	...
Powys	ESDF	124 418	61 771	62 647	5 196	...	...	...	...
Preston	ESDF	134 818	67 195	67 623	142	...	...	...	...
Reading	ESDF	142 851	72 310	70 541	40	...	...	...	...
Redbridge[96]	ESDF	230 578	113 277	117 301	56	...	...	...	...
Redcar & Cleveland	ESDF	139 785	68 465	71 320	245	...	...	...	...
Reigate & Banstead	ESDF	119 307	58 576	60 731	129	...	...	...	...
Renfrewshire	ESDF	178 550	86 208	92 342	261	...	...	...	...
Rhondda, Cynon, Taff	ESDF	240 117	118 610	121 507	424	...	...	...	...
Richmond-upon-Thames[96]	ESDF	179 877	87 176	92 701	55	...	...	...	...
Rochdale	ESDF	207 563	101 884	105 679	160	...	...	...	...
Rochester-upon-Medway	ESDF	144 478	71 379	73 099	160	...	...	...	...
Rotherham	ESDF	255 342	126 360	128 982	283	...	...	...	...
Rushcliffe	ESDF	103 500	51 092	52 408	409	...	...	...	...
St. Albans	ESDF	130 267	64 373	65 894	161	...	...	...	...
St. Helens	ESDF	179 483	88 293	91 190	133	...	...	...	...
Salford	ESDF	229 179	113 589	115 590	97	...	...	...	...
Salisbury	ESDF	112 534	54 503	58 031	1 004	...	...	...	...
Sandwell	ESDF	292 196	143 434	148 762	86	...	...	...	...
Scarborough	ESDF	108 258	51 709	56 549	817	...	...	...	...
Scottish Borders	ESDF	106 100	51 101	54 999	4 734	...	...	...	...
Sedgemoor	ESDF	101 866	50 178	51 688	564	...	...	...	...
Sefton	ESDF	289 739	138 360	151 379	153	...	...	...	...
Sevenoaks	ESDF	110 476	53 984	56 492	368	...	...	...	...
Sheffield	ESDF	530 375	263 775	266 600	367	...	...	...	...
Slough	ESDF	110 462	54 664	55 798	27	...	...	...	...
Solihull	ESDF	203 922	99 688	104 234	179	...	...	...	...
South Ayrshire	ESDF	114 630	54 802	59 828	1 202	...	...	...	...
South Bedfordshire	ESDF	110 949	55 159	55 790	213	...	...	...	...
South Cambridgeshire	ESDF	128 422	63 498	64 924	902	...	...	...	...
South Gloucestershire	ESDF	235 129	117 579	117 550	497	...	...	...	...
South Lakeland	ESDF	100 889	48 658	52 231	1 554	...	...	...	...
South Lanarkshire	ESDF	307 450	148 701	158 749	1 771	...	...	...	...
South Kesteven	ESDF	119 951	58 374	61 577	943	...	...	...	...
South Norfolk	ESDF	105 778	52 113	53 665	908	...	...	...	...
South Oxfordshire	ESDF	124 637	61 467	63 170	679	...	...	...	...
South Ribble	ESDF	103 020	50 250	52 770	113	...	...	...	...
South Somerset	ESDF	150 710	73 645	77 065	959	...	...	...	...
South Staffordshire	ESDF	103 284	51 022	52 262	408	...	...	...	...
South Tyneside	ESDF	156 078	75 999	80 079	64	...	...	...	...
Southampton	ESDF	214 859	108 325	106 534	50	...	...	...	...
Southend-on-Sea	ESDF	172 266	82 911	89 355	42	...	...	...	...
Southwark[96]	ESDF	229 871	113 282	116 589	29	...	...	...	...
Stafford	ESDF	124 531	61 660	62 871	599	...	...	...	...
Stockport	ESDF	291 080	141 315	149 765	126	...	...	...	...
Stockton-on-Tees	ESDF	179 009	88 068	90 941	204	...	...	...	...
Stoke-on-Trent	ESDF	254 438	126 133	128 305	93	...	...	...	...
Stratford-on-Avon	ESDF	111 211	54 170	57 041	977	...	...	...	...
Stroud	ESDF	108 022	53 091	54 931	461	...	...	...	...
Suffolk Coastal	ESDF	118 681	58 278	60 403	892	...	...	...	...
Sunderland	ESDF	294 261	143 574	150 687	138	...	...	...	...
Sutton[96]	ESDF	175 527	85 353	90 174	43	...	...	...	...
Swale	ESDF	117 562	58 744	58 818	373	...	...	...	...

(See notes at end of table. — Voir notes à la fin du tableau.)

Continent, country or area, date and city — Continent, pays ou zone, date et ville	Code[1]	City proper — Ville proprement dite Population				Urban agglomeration — Agglomération urbaine Population			
		Both sexes Les deux sexes	Male Masculin	Female Féminin	Surface area Superficie (km²)	Both sexes Les deux sexes	Male Masculin	Female Féminin	Surface area Superficie (km²)

EUROPE

United Kingdom — Royaume-Uni[95]
1 VII 1996

Swansea	ESDF	230 180	112 876	117 304	378	...	...	...	...
Tameside	ESDF	220 722	109 005	111 717	103	...	...	...	...
Teignbridge	ESDF	116 743	56 289	60 454	674	...	...	...	...
Tendring	ESDF	132 265	62 860	69 405	337	...	...	...	...
Test Valley	ESDF	107 182	53 019	54 163	637	...	...	...	...
Thamesdown	ESDF	174 598	87 176	87 422	230	...	...	...	...
Thanet	ESDF	125 543	59 567	65 976	103	...	...	...	...
The Wrekin	ESDF	144 154	71 507	72 647	290	...	...	...	...
Thurrock	ESDF	132 283	65 807	66 476	164	...	...	...	...
Tonbridge & Malling	ESDF	104 991	52 141	52 850	240	...	...	...	...
Torbay	ESDF	123 413	57 936	65 477	63	...	...	...	...
Tower Hamlets[96]	ESDF	176 635	88 852	87 783	20	...	...	...	...
Trafford	ESDF	218 893	107 360	111 533	106	...	...	...	...
Tunbridge Wells	ESDF	102 616	49 544	53 072	332	...	...	...	...
Vale of Glamorgan	ESDF	119 358	58 142	61 216	335	...	...	...	...
Vale of White Horse	ESDF	112 545	56 987	55 558	579	...	...	...	...
Vale Royal	ESDF	115 233	56 748	58 485	380	...	...	...	...
Wakefield	ESDF	317 342	157 184	160 158	333	...	...	...	...
Walsall	ESDF	262 593	130 111	132 482	106	...	...	...	...
Waltham Forest[96]	ESDF	220 249	108 187	112 062	40	...	...	...	...
Wandsworth[96]	ESDF	266 169	129 106	137 063	35	...	...	...	...
Warrington	ESDF	189 012	93 732	95 280	176	...	...	...	...
Warwick	ESDF	122 506	60 228	62 278	282	...	...	...	...
Waveney	ESDF	107 731	52 025	55 706	370	...	...	...	...
Waverley	ESDF	114 133	55 348	58 785	345	...	...	...	...
Wealden	ESDF	138 030	65 888	72 142	836	...	...	...	...
West Lancashire	ESDF	109 763	54 031	55 732	338	...	...	...	...
West Lothian	ESDF	150 770	74 178	76 592	425	...	...	...	...
West Wiltshire	ESDF	108 889	53 732	55 157	517	...	...	...	...
Westminster[96]	ESDF	204 063	101 174	102 889	22	...	...	...	...
Wigan	ESDF	309 786	153 353	156 433	199	...	...	...	...
Winchester	ESDF	106 007	51 653	54 354	661	...	...	...	...
Windsor & Maidenhead	ESDF	141 548	70 387	71 161	198	...	...	...	...
Wirral	ESDF	329 179	157 640	171 539	159	...	...	...	...
Wokingham	ESDF	142 361	71 935	70 426	179	...	...	...	...
Wolverhampton	ESDF	244 453	120 455	123 998	69	...	...	...	...
Wrexham Maelor	ESDF	123 308	59 817	63 491	498	...	...	...	...
Wychavon	ESDF	108 009	52 849	55 160	664	...	...	...	...
Wycombe	ESDF	164 045	81 812	82 233	325	...	...	...	...
Wyre	ESDF	104 348	49 847	54 501	284	...	...	...	...
York	ESDF	175 095	85 359	89 736	271	...	...	...	...

OCEANIA — OCEANIE

American Samoa — Samoa américaines[19]
1 IV 2000

PAGO PAGO	CDFC	4 278	...	...	...	...	...	...	...

Australia — Australie[101]
1 VII 2002

Adelaide	ESDJ	...	...	...	...	1 113 765	545 897	567 868	1 827
Brisbane	ESDJ	...	...	...	...	1 690 541	834 649	855 892	4 673
Cairns	ESDJ	114 610	57 688	56 922	488	...	...	...	...
CANBERRA	ESDJ	321 134	158 495	162 639	806	321 512	158 697	162 815	2 349
Darwin	ESDJ	...	...	...	...	107 755	57 215	50 540	3 122
Geelong	ESDJ	161 232	78 661	82 571	388	...	...	...	...
Gold Coast	ESDJ	440 482	216 911	223 571	1 238	...	...	...	...
Greater Wollongong	ESDJ	271 833	135 886	135 947	1 089	...	...	...	...
Hobart	ESDJ	...	...	...	...	197 878	96 470	101 408	1 357
Melbourne	ESDJ	...	...	...	...	3 513 051	1 727 446	1 785 605	7 694
Newcastle	ESDJ	496 990	245 792	251 198	4 042	...	...	...	...
Perth	ESDJ	...	...	...	...	1 411 618	698 542	713 076	5 386

8. Population of capital cities and cities of 100 000 and more inhabitants: latest available year
Population des capitales et des villes de 100 000 habitants et plus: dernière année disponible (continued — suite)

(See notes at end of table. — Voir notes à la fin du tableau.)

Continent, country or area, date and city Continent, pays ou zone, date et ville	Code[1]	City proper — Ville proprement dite Population				Urban agglomeration — Agglomération urbaine Population			
		Both sexes Les deux sexes	Male Masculin	Female Féminin	Surface area Superficie (km²)	Both sexes Les deux sexes	Male Masculin	Female Féminin	Surface area Superficie (km²)
OCEANIA — OCEANIE									
Australia — Australie[101]									
1 VII 2002									
Sunshine Coast	ESDJ	192 094	93 628	98 466	457	...	...	...	...
Sydney	ESDJ	...	...	...	...	4 167 002	2 065 800	2 101 202	12 145
Townsville	ESDJ	137 507	69 659	67 848	454	...	...	...	...
Cook Islands — Iles Cook									
1 XII 2001									
RAROTONGA	CDFC	12 188	...	...	...	...	...	...	...
Fiji — Fidji									
31 VIII 1996									
SUVA	CDFC	77 366	38 518	38 848	...	167 975	83 910	84 065	...
French Polynesia — Polynésie française									
7 XI 2002									
PAPEETE	CDFC	26 181	...	...	...	124 864	...	...	...
Guam[19]									
1 IV 2000									
AGANA	CDJC	1 100	672	428	3	...	...	...	...
Kiribati									
7 XI 2000									
TARAWA	CDFC	...	...	...	...	36 717	...	...	...
Marshall Islands — Iles Marshall									
1 VI 1999									
MAJURO	CDFC	23 676	12 075	11 601	...	...	...	...	...
Micronesia, Federated States of — Micronésie, États fédérés de									
1 IV 2000									
PALIKIR	CDJC	6 227	...	...	...	...	...	...	...
Nauru									
17 IV 1992									
YAREN	CDFC	672	...	...	...	...	...	...	...
New Caledonia — Nouvelle-Calédonie									
16 IV 1996									
NOUMEA	CDFC	76 293	38 443	37 850	46	118 823	60 327	58 496	1 643
New Zealand — Nouvelle-Zélande[102,103,104]									
3 V 1991									
Auckland	CDJC	306 210	147 942	158 268	...	878 223	428 961	449 259	...
Christchurch	CDJC	289 071	139 839	149 232	...	303 411	147 099	156 315	...
Dunedin[105]	CDJC	114 504	55 146	59 355	...	107 523	51 570	55 953	...
Hamilton	CDJC	99 414	47 985	51 429	...	146 148	71 145	75 003	...
Manukau	CDJC	226 002	110 964	115 038	...	...	...	...	...
Napier-Hastings	CDJC	...	...	...	...	109 341	52 716	56 625	...
Northshore	CDJC	152 649	74 598	78 048	...	...	...	...	...
Waitakere	CDJC	137 001	67 776	69 222	...	...	...	...	...
WELLINGTON	CDJC	148 440	73 269	75 171	...	324 156	160 086	164 073	...
5 III 1996									
Auckland	CDJC	345 768	167 829	177 936	633	991 836	483 408	508 428	1 086
Christchurch	CDJC	309 027	149 637	159 390	452	325 251	157 728	167 523	608
Dunedin[105]	CDJC	118 143	56 721	61 422	3 342	110 790	52 959	57 831	255
Hamilton	CDJC	108 429	52 185	56 244	94	158 046	76 581	81 465	1 100
Manukau	CDJC	254 280	124 257	130 020	683	...	...	...	...
Napier-Hastings	CDJC	...	...	...	...	112 794	54 624	58 167	375
Northshore	CDJC	172 164	83 445	88 719	130	...	...	...	...
Waitakere	CDJC	155 565	76 515	79 047	367	...	...	...	...
WELLINGTON	CDJC	157 722	77 010	80 709	290	334 062	163 977	170 088	444
6 III 2001									
Auckland	CDJC	367 737	177 999	189 738	633	1 074 507	521 058	553 452	1 086
Christchurch	CDJC	316 224	152 238	163 989	452	334 104	161 082	173 022	608
Dunedin[105]	CDJC	114 342	54 567	59 775	3 342	107 088	50 853	56 238	255
Hamilton	CDJC	114 921	55 086	59 835	94	166 128	80 148	85 977	1 100
Manukau	CDJC	283 200	137 787	145 413	683	...	...	...	...
Napier-Hastings	CDJC	...	...	...	...	113 673	54 849	58 827	375
Northshore	CDJC	184 821	89 184	95 637	130	...	...	...	...

8. Population of capital cities and cities of 100 000 and more inhabitants: latest available year
Population des capitales et des villes de 100 000 habitants et plus: dernière année disponible (continued — suite)

(See notes at end of table. — Voir notes à la fin du tableau.)

Continent, country or area, date and city Continent, pays ou zone, date et ville	Code[1]	City proper — Ville proprement dite Population				Urban agglomeration — Agglomération urbaine Population			
		Both sexes Les deux sexes	Male Masculin	Female Féminin	Surface area Superficie (km²)	Both sexes Les deux sexes	Male Masculin	Female Féminin	Surface area Superficie (km²)
OCEANIA — OCEANIE									
New Zealand — Nouvelle-Zélande[102,103,104]									
6 III 2001									
Waitakere	CDJC	168 750	82 374	86 376	367	...	...	...	...
WELLINGTON	CDJC	163 824	79 251	84 573	290	339 747	165 588	174 159	444
1 VII 2002									
Auckland	ESDJ	401 500	...	...	633	1 162 500	...	...	1 086
Christchurch	ESDJ	332 000	...	...	452	350 700	...	...	608
Dunedin[105]	ESDJ	120 300	...	...	3 342	112 800	...	...	255
Hamilton	ESDJ	122 000	...	...	94	175 400	...	...	1 100
Manukau	ESDJ	307 300	...	...	683	...	...	...	...
Napier-Hastings	ESDJ	...	...	...	...	117 900	...	...	375
Northshore	ESDJ	198 900	...	...	130	...	...	...	...
Tauranga	ESDJ	95 600	...	...	168	100 600	...	...	178
Waitakere	ESDJ	180 700	...	...	367	...	...	...	...
WELLINGTON	ESDJ	174 600	...	...	290	358 100	...	...	444
Niue — Nioué									
13 IX 2001									
ALOFI	CDFC	615	...	...	...	...	...	...	...
Norfolk Island — Ile Norfolk									
1 VII 1997									
KINGSTON	ESDF	*800*	...	...	...	...	...	...	...
Northern Mariana Islands — Iles Mariannes du Nord									
1 IV 2000									
GARAPAN	CDFC	3 588	...	...	...	...	...	...	...
Palau — Palaos									
15 IV 2000									
KOROR	CDFC	10 600	...	...	...	...	...	...	...
Papua New Guinea — Papouasie-Nouvelle-Guinée									
9 VII 2000									
PORT MORESBY	CDFC	254 158	138 974	115 184	...	...	...	...	...
Pitcairn									
1 VII 1993									
ADAMSTOWN	CDFC	53	...	...	5	...	...	...	...
Samoa									
1 XI 2001									
APIA	CDFC	38 836	...	...	...	...	...	...	...
Solomon Islands — Iles Salomon									
21 XI 1999									
HONIARA	CDFC	49 107	...	...	...	...	...	...	...
Tonga									
1 VII 2000									
NUKU'ALOFA	ESDF	21 538	10 625	10 913	...	30 336	15 115	15 221	...
Tuvalu									
17 XI 1991									
FUNAFUTI	CDFC	3 839	...	...	...	...	...	...	...
Vanuatu									
16 XI 1999									
PORT VILA	CDFC	29 356	...	...	...	...	...	...	...
Wallis and Futuna Islands — Iles Wallis et Futuna									
3 X 1996									
META-UTU	CDFC	1 137	...	...	...	...	...	...	...

GENERAL NOTES - NOTES GENERALES

The capital city of each country is shown in capital letters. Figures in italics are estimates of questionable reliability. For definition of city proper and urban agglomeration, method of evaluation and limitations of data see Technical Notes for this table. — Le nom de la capitale de chaque pays est imprimé en majuscules. Les chiffres en italiques snot des estimations de quality duteous. Pour la definition de la vile procurement diet et de l'agglomération urbaine, et pour les méthodes d'évaluation et les insuffisances des données voir Notes techniques pour ce tableau.

FOOTNOTES - NOTES

[1] 'Code' indicates the source of data, as follows:
CDFC - Census, de facto, complete tabulation

CDFS - Census, de facto, sample tabulation
CDJC - Census, de jure, complete tabulation
CDJS - Census, de jure, sample tabulation
SSDF - Sample survey, de facto
SSDJ - Sample survey, de jure
ESDF - Estimates, de facto
ESDJ - Estimates, de jure
Le 'Code' indique la source des données, comme suit:
CDFC - Recensement, population de fait, tabulation complète
CDFS - Recensement, population de fait, tabulation par sondage
CDJC - Recensement, population de droit, tabulation complète
CDJS - Recensement, population de droit, tabulation par sondage
SSDF - Enquête par sondage, population de fait
SSDJ - Enquête par sondage, population de droit
ESDF - Données estimatées, population de fait
ESDJ - Données estimatées, population de droit

[2] Data for urban agglomeration includes Kombo St. Mary. — Les données relatives à l'agglomération urbaine se rapportent à Kombo St. Mary.

[3] Data for urban agglomeration refer to 'Accra-Tema Metropolitan area'. — Les données relatives à l'agglomération urbaine se rapportent à la 'zone métropolitaine d'Accra-Tema'.

[4] Data for urban agglomeration refer to the Sekondi-Takoradi Municipal Council. Including Sekondi (population 31 916) and Takoradi (population 61 484). — Les données concernant l'agglomération urbaine se rapportent au Conseil municipal de Sekondi-Takoradi. Y compris Sekondi (31 916 personnes) et Takoradi (61 484 personnes).

[5] Dual capitals. — Le pays a deux capitales.

[6] For the urban commune of Antananarivo. — Pour la commune urbaine de Antananarivo.

[7] Including Salé and Temara. — Y compris Salé et Temara.

[8] Data for cities proper refer to communes. — Les données pour les villes se réfèrent aux communes.

[9] For communes which may contain rural areas as well as urban centre. — Commune(s) pouvant comprendre un centre urbain et une zone rurale.

[10] Included in urban agglomeration of Dakar. — Comprise dans l'agglomération urbaine de Dakar.

[11] Pretoria is the administrative capital, Cape Town the legislative capital. — Pretoria est la capital administrative, Le Cap la capitale législative.

[12] Excluding persons residing in institutions. — Non compris les personnes dans les institutions.

[13] Due to random rounding technique figures for males and females do not add up to the total. — La somme des données pour hommes et femmes ne correspond pas au total grâce a la technique de l'arrondissement aléatoire.

[14] Data for urban agglomeration refer to 'metropolitan area', comprising central of San José (including San José city) cantones Curridabat, Escazu, Montes de Oca, Tibas and parts of cantones of Alajuelita, Desamparados, Goicoechea and Moravia. — Les données pour l'agglomération urbaine se rapportent à la 'zone métropolitaine' comprenant le canton central de San José (et la ville de San José), les cantons de Curridabat, Escazu, Montes de Oca et Tibas et certaines parties des cantons de Alajuelita, Desamparados, Goicoechea et Moravia.

[15] For municipalities which may contain an urban centre as well as a rural area. — Pour municipios qui peuvent comprendre un centre urbain et aussi une zone rurale.

[16] The definition of locality based on the 2000 Population census. - La localité est définie survant le recensement general de la population de 2000.

[17] Urban agglomeration (Metropolitan area) refers to 2 or more municipalities where there is only one urban concentration. - L'agglomération urbaine (zone métropolitaine) se rapporte à 2 municipalités ou plus où il y a seulement une concentration urbaine.

[18] Including municipalities of Bella Vista, Betania, Calidonia, Curundu, El Chorillo, Juan Diaz, Parque Lefevre, Pedregal, Pueblo Nuevo, Rio Abajo, San Felipe, San Francisco and Santa Ana. — Y compris les corregimientos de Bella Vista, Betania, Calidonia, Curundu, El Chorillo, Juan Diaz, Parque Lefevre, Pedregal, Pueblo Nuevo, Rio Abajo, San Felipe, San Francisco et Santa Ana.

[19] Including armed forces stationed in the area. — Y compris les militaires en garnison sur le territoire.

[20] Data for urban agglomeration refer to 'standard metropolitan area' comprised of municipality of Ponce, which includes Ponce proper. — Les données relatives à l'agglomération urbaine se rapportent à la 'zone métropolitaine officielle' qui comprend la municipalité de Ponce, comprenant Ponce proprement dite.

[21] Data for urban agglomeration refer to 'metropolitan statistical area', comprising municipalities of San Juan, Caguas, Carolina, Catano, Guaynabo, Rio Piedras and Trujillo Alto. — Les données concernant l'agglomération urbaine se rapportent à la 'zone métropolitaine statistique' qui comprend les municipios de San Juan, Caguas, Carolina, Catano, Guaynabo, Rio Piedras et Trujillo Alto.

[22] Excluding armed forces overseas and civilian citizens absent from country for extended period of time. — Non compris les militaires à l'étranger et les civils hors du pays pendant une période prolongée.

[23] City refers to a type of incorporated place in 49 states and the District of Columbia, that has an elected government and provides a range of government functions and services. Also included are Honolulu, Hawaii Census Designated Place (CDP), for which the Census Bureau reports data under agreement with the State of Hawaii (instead of the combined city and county of Honolulu), and Arlington, VA CDP (which is coextensive with Arlington County - an entirely urban county that provides the same levels of services and functions as a municipality. - Par ville, on entend un lieu doté de la personnalité morale dans 49 États et dans le district de Columbia, qui a un gouvernement élu et fournit tout un ensemble de fonctions et de services publics. Sont également inclus Honolulu, lieu chargé du recensement pour Hawaii, pour lequel le Census Bureau établit les données en accord avec l'État de Hawaii (au lieu de la ville et du comté d'Honolulu), et Arlington, lieu chargé du recensement pour la Virginie, qui est de même étendue que le comté d'Arlington, lequel est un comté entièrement urbain qui offre les mêmes niveaux de services et de fonctions qu'une municipalité.

[24] Included in urban agglomeration of Washington, DC--VA--MD. — Comprise dans l'agglomération urbaine de Washington, DC--VA--MD

[25] Included in urban agglomeration of Los Angeles--Long Beach--Santa Ana, CA. — Comprise dans l'agglomération urbaine de Los Angeles--Long Beach--Santa Ana, CA.

[26] Included in urban agglomeration of Dallas Fort Worth--Arlington, TX. — Comprise dans l'agglomération urbaine de Dallas--Fort Worth--Arlington, TX.

[27] Included in urban agglomeration of Denver--Aurora, CO. — Comprise dans l'agglomération urbaine de Denver--Aurora, CO.

[28] Included in urban agglomeration of Chicago, IL--IN. — Comprise dans l'agglomération urbaine de Chicago, IL--IN.

[29] Included in urban agglomeration of Seattle, WA. — Comprise dans l'agglomération urbaine de Seattle, WA.

[30] Included in urban agglomeration of San Francisco--Oakland, CA. — Comprise dans l'agglomération urbaine de San Francisco--Oakland, CA.

[31] Included in urban agglomeration of Boston, MA--NH--RI. — Comprise dans l'agglomération urbaine de Boston, MA--NH--RI.

[32] Included in urban agglomeration of Phoenix--Mesa, AZ. — Comprise dans l'agglomération urbaine de Phoenix--Mesa, AZ.

[33] Included in urban agglomeration of Virginia Beach, VA. — Comprise dans l'agglomération urbaine de Virginia Beach, VA.

[34] Included in urban agglomeration of San Diego, CA. — Comprise dans l'agglomération urbaine de San Diego, CA.

[35] Included in urban agglomeration of Tampa--St. Petersburg, FL. — Comprise dans l'agglomération urbaine de Tampa--St. Petersburg, FL.

[36] Included in urban agglomeration of Miami, FL. — Comprise dans l'agglomération urbaine de Miami, FL.

[37] Included in urban agglomeration of Riverside--San Bernardino, CA. — Comprise dans l'agglomération urbaine de Riverside--San Bernardino, CA.

[38] Included in urban agglomeration of New York--Newark, NY--NJ--CT. — Comprise dans l'agglomération urbaine de New York--Newark, NY--NJ--CT.

[39] Included in urban agglomeration of Las Vegas, NV. — Comprise dans l'agglomération urbaine de Las Vegas, NV.

[40] Included in urban agglomeration of Kansas City, MO KS. — Comprise dans l'agglomération urbaine de Kansas City, MO--KS.

[41] Included in urban agglomeration of Detroit, MI. — Comprise dans l'agglomération urbaine de Detroit, MI.

[42] Included in urban agglomeration of Lancaster--Palmdale, CA. — Comprise dans l'agglomération urbaine de Lancaster--Palmdale, CA.

[43] Included in urban agglomeration of Houston, TX. — Comprise dans l'agglomération urbaine de Houston, TX.

[44] Included in urban agglomeration of Minneapolis--St. Paul, MN. — Comprise dans l'agglomération urbaine de Minneapolis--St. Paul, MN.

[45] Included in urban agglomeration of Oxnard, CA. — Comprise dans l'agglomération urbaine de Oxnard, CA.

[46] Included in urban agglomeration of San Jose, CA. — Comprise dans l'agglomération urbaine de San Jose, CA.

[47] Included in urban agglomeration of Bridgeport--Stamford, CT--NY. — Comprise dans l'agglomération urbaine de Bridgeport--Stamford, CT--NY.

[48] Included in urban agglomeration of Portland, OR--WA. — Comprise dans l'agglomération urbaine de Portland, OR--WA.

[49] Included in urban agglomeration of Salt Lake City, UT. — Comprise dans l'agglomération urbaine de Salt Lake City, UT.

[50] La Paz is the actual capital and the seat of the Government but Sucre is the legal capital and the seat of the judiciary. — La Paz est la capitale effective et le siège du gouvernement, mais Sucre est la capitale constitutionnelle et la siège du pouvoir judiciaire.

[51] 'Metropolitan area' Gran Santiago. — 'Zone métropolitaine' Grand Santiago.

[52] Data for urban agglomeration refer to 'metropolitan area', comprising Asuncion proper and localities of Trinidad, Zeballos Cué, Campo Grande and Lamboré. — Les données pour l'agglomération urbaine se rapportent à la 'zone métropolitaine' comprenant la ville d'Asuncion proprement dite et les localités de Trinidad, Zeballos Cué, Campo Grande et Lamboré.

[53] City population refers to urban population of districts within the city. - La population des villes se rapporte à la population urbaine des districts compris dans la ville.

[54] Data for urban agglomeration refer to 'metropolitan area' Gran Lima. — Les données pour l'agglomération urbaine se rapportent à la 'zone métropolitaine' Grand Lima.

[55] Data for urban agglomeration refer to 'metropolitan area', comprising

Caracas proper (the urban parishes of Department of Libertador) and a part of district of Sucre in State of Miranda. — Les données pour l'agglomération urbaine se rapportent à la 'zone métropolitaine', comprenant la ville de Caracas proprement dite (paroisses urbaines du département du Libertador) et une partie du district de Sucre dans l'Etat de Miranda.

56 For municipalities which may contain rural area as well as urban centre. — Pour les municipalités qui peuvent comprendre un centre urbaine et une zone rurale.

57 Lefkosia urban agglomeration is composed of Lefkosia municipality, Agios Dometios, Egkomi, Strovolos, Aglangia, Lakatameia, Anthoupoli, Latsia and Geri. — L'agglomération urbaine de Lefkosia se comprend de la municipalité de Lefkosia et Agios Dometios, Egkomi, Strovolos, Aglangia, Lakatameia, Anthoupoli, Latsia et Geri.

58 Lemesos urban agglomeration is composed of Lemesos municipality, Mesa Geitonia, Agios Athanasios, Germasogeia, Pano Polemidia, Ypsonas, Kato Polemidia, and parts of Mouttagiaka, Agios Tychon, Parekklisia, Monagrouli, Moni, Pyrgos and Tserkezoi. — L'agglomération urbaine de Lemesos se comprend de la municipalité de Lemesos et Mesa Geitonia, Agios Athanasios, Germasogeia, Pano Polemidia, Ypsonas, Kato Polemidia, et certaines parties des Mouttagiaka, Agios Tychon, Parekklisia, Monagrouli, Moni, Pyrgos et Tserkezoi.

59 Including data for the India-held part of Jammu and Kashmir, the final status of which has not yet been determined. Excluding cities for Assam state. — Y compris les données concernant la partie de Jammu-et-Cachemire occupée par l'Inde, dont le statut définitif n'a pas encore été déterminé. Non compris les villes de l'état d'Assam.

60 Data for urban agglomeration includes New Delhi. — Les données pour l'agglomération urbaine y compris New Delhi.

61 Data for urban agglomeration include Bally, Baranagar, Barrackpur, Bhatpara, Calcutta Municipal Corporation, Chandan Nagar, Garden Reach, Houghly-Chinsura, Howrah, Jadarpur, Kamarhati, Naihati, Panihati, Serampore, South Dum Dum, South Suburban, and Titagarh. — Les données pour l'agglomération urbaine y compris Bally, Baranagar, Barrackpur, Bhatpara, Calcutta Municipal Corporation, Chandan Nagar, Garden Reach, Houghly Chinsura, Howrah, Jadarpur, Kamarhati, Naihati, Panihati, Serampopre, South Dum Dum, South Suburban et Titagarh.

62 Included in urban agglomeration of Delhi. — Comprise dans l'agglomération urbaine de Delhi.

63 Data refer to the New Delhi Municipal Council. — Les données se rapportent au New Delhi Municipal Council.

64 Including Karkh, Rassaiah, Adhamiya and Kadhimain Qadha Centres and Maamoon, Mansour and Karradah-Sharqiyah Nahlyas. — Y compris les cazas de Karkh, Adhamiya et Kadhimain ainsi que les nahiyas de Maamoon, Mansour et Karradah-Sharqiyah.

65 Designation and data provided by Israel. The position of the United Nations on the question of Jerusalem is contained in General Assembly resolution 181 (II) and subsequent resolutions of the General Assembly and the Security Council concerning this question. — Appelation de données fournies par Israel. La position des Nations Unies concernant la question de Jérusalem est décrite dans la resolution 181 (II) de l'Assemblée générale et résolutions ultérieures de l'Assemblée générale et du Conseil de sécurité sur cette question.

66 Including East Jerusalem. — Y compris Jérusalem-Est.

67 Excluding diplomatic personnel outside country and foreign military and civilian personnel and their dependants stationed in the area. — Non compris le personnel diplomatique hors du territoire, les militaires et agents civils étrangers en poste sur le territoire et les membres de leur famille les accompagnant.

68 Except for Tokyo, all data refer to shi, a minor division which may include some scattered or rural population as well as an urban centre. — Sauf pour Tokyo, toutes les données se rapportent à des shi, petites divisions administratives qui peuvent comprendre des peuplements dispersés ou ruraux en plus d'un centre urbain.

69 Data excluding Hokkaido region. — Non compris la region de Hokkaido.

70 Including Kokura, Moji, Tobata, Wakamatsu and Yahata (Yawata). — Y compris Kokura, Moji, Tobata, Wakamatsu et Yahata (Yawata).

71 Data for city proper refer to 23 wards (ku) of the old city. The urban agglomeration figures refer to Tokyo-to (Tokyo Prefecture), comprising the 23 wards plus 14 urban counties (shi), 18 towns (machi) and 8 villages (mura). The 'Tokyo Metropolitan Area' comprises the 23 wards of Tokyo-to plus 21 cities, 20 towns and 2 villages. The 'Keihin Metropolitan Area' (Tokyo-Yokohama Metropolitan Area) plus 9 cities (one of which is Yokohama City) and two towns, with a total population of 20 485 542 on 1 October 1965. — Les données concernant la ville proprement dite se rapportent aux 23 circonscriptions de la vieille ville. Les chiffres pour l'agglomération urbaine se rapportent à Tokyo-to (préfecture de Tokyo), comprenant les 23 circonscriptions plus 14 cantons urbains (Shi), 18 villes (machi) et 8 villages (mura). La 'zone métropolitaine de Tokyo' comprend les 23 circonscriptions de Tokyo-to plus 21 municipalités, 20 villes et 2 villages. La 'zone métropolitaine de Keihin' (zone métropolitaine de Tokyo-Yokohama) comprend la zone métropolitaine de Tokyo, plus 9 municipalités, dont l'une est Yokohama et 2 villes, elle comptait 20 485 542 habitants au 1er octobre 1965.

72 Excluding data for the Pakistan-held part of Jammu and Kashmir, the final status of which has not yet been determined, and for Junagardh, Manavadar, Gilgit and Baltistan. — Non compris les données pour la partie de Jammu-Cachemire occupée par le Pakistan dont le status definitif n'a pas encore été déterminé, et le Junagardh, le Manavadar, le Gilgit et le Baltistan.

73 Data for city proper refer to population in municipalities. - Les données concernant la ville proprement dite se rapportent a la population des municipalités.

74 Covers Seyhan and Yuregir districts in Adana. - Y compris la population des districts de Seyhan et de Yuregir.

75 Covers Altindag, Cankaya, Etimesgut, Golbasi, Kecioren, Mamak, Sincan, and Yenimahalle districts in Ankara. - Y compris la population des districts de Altindag, de Cankaya, de Etimesgut, de Golbasi, de Kecioren, de Mamak, de Sincan, et de Yenimahalle.

76 Covers Nilufer, Osmangazi and Yildirim districts in Bursa. - Y compris la population des districts de Nilufer, de Osmangazi et de Yildirim.

77 Covers Sahinbey and Sehitkamil districts in Gaziantep. - Y compris la population des districts de Sahinbey et de Sehitkamil.

78 Covers Adalar, Avcilar, Bagcilar, Bahcelievler, Bakirkoy, Bayrampasa, Besiktas, Beykoz, Beyoglu, Eminonu, Esenler, Eyup, Fatih, Gaziosmanpasa, Gungoren, Kadikoy, Kagithane, Kartal, Kucukcekmece, Maltepe, Pendik, Sariyer, Sisli, Sultanbeyli, Tuzla, Umraniye, Uskudar, Zentinburnu districts in Istanbul. - Y compris la population des districts de Adalar, de Avcilar, de Bagcilar, de Bahcelievler, de Bakirkoy, de Bayrampasa, de Besiktas, de Beykoz, de Beyoglu, de Eminonu, de Esenler, de Eyup, de Fatih, de Gaziosmanpasa, de Gungoren, de Kadikoy, de Kagithane, de Kartal, de Kucukcekmece, de Maltepe, de Pendik, de Sariyer, de Sisli, de Sultanbeyli, de Tuzla, de Umraniye, de Uskudar, et de Zentinburnu.

79 Covers Bolcova, Bornova, Buca, Cigli, Gaziemir, Guzelbahce, Karsiyaka, Konak and Narlidere districts in Izmir. - Y compris la population des districts de Bolcova, de Bornova, de Buca, de Cigli, de Gaziemir, de Guzelbahce, de Karsiyaka, de Konak et de Narlidere.

80 Covers Kocasinan and Melikgazi districts in Kayseri. - Y compris la population des districts de Kocasinan et de Melikgazi.

81 Covers Karatay, Meram and Selcuklu districts Konya. - Y compris la population des districts de Karatay, de Meram et de Selcuklu.

82 Including Cholon. — Y compris Cholon.

83 Data for cities proper refer to communes which may contain an urban centre and a rural area. — Les données concernant les villes proprement dites se rapportent à des communes qui peuvent comprendre un centre urbain et une zone rurale.

84 City is a settlement with a status of city according to the administrative-territorial division of the country at the end of the respective year. - La ville est une agglomération avec un statut de ville selon la division administratif-territoriale du pays à la fin de l'année respective.

85 Urban agglomeration refers to the urban part of the municipality with a proper city center. - L'agglomération urbaine se rapporte à la partie urbaine de la municipalité avec un centre de la ville.

86 Data for cities proper refer to communes which are centres for urban agglomeration. — Les données concernant les villes proprement dites se rapportent à des communes qui sont des centres d'agglomérations urbaines.

87 De jure population, but excluding diplomatic personnel outside the country and including foreign military personnel not living in embassies or consulates. — Population de droit, mais non compris le personnel diplomatique hors du pays et y compris le personnel diplomatique étranger qui ne vit pas dans les ambassades ou les consulats.

88 Data refer to French territory of this international agglomeration. — Les données se rapportent aux habitants de cette agglomération internationale qui vivent en territoire francais.

89 Including Villeurbanne. — Y compris Villeurbanne.

90 Including armed forces stationed outside the country but excluding alien armed forces stationed in the area. — Y compris les militaires en garnison hors du pays, mais non compris les militaires étrangers en garnison sur le territoire.

91 Data refer to the Vatican City State. — Les données se rapportent aux Etat du Saint-Siège.

92 Including civilian nationals temporarily outside the country. — Y compris les civils nationaux temporairement hors du pays.

93 Data for cities proper refer to administrative units (municipalities). — Les données concernant les villes proprement dites se rapportent à des unités administratives (municipalités).

94 2001 data refer to municipals with 100 000 + population and 2002 data refer to the capital of provinces. - Les données de 2001 font référence aux municipalités de plus de 100 000 habitants et celles de 2002 à la capitale des provinces.

95 For county districts, unitary authorities and London boroughs. — Pour les districts de province, autorités d'unité et cartiers de Londres.

96 Greater London Borough included in figure for 'Greater London' conurbation. — Le chiffre relatif à l'ensemble urbain du 'Grand Londres' comprend le Greater London Borough.

97 Capital of Northern Ireland. — Capitale de l'Irlande du Nord.

98 Capital of Wales for certain purposes. — Considérée à certains égards comme la capitale du pays de Galles.

99 Capital of Scotland. — Capitale de l'Ecosse.

100 'Greater London' conurbation as reconstituted in 1965 and comprising 32 new Greater London Boroughs. — Ensemble urbain du 'Grand Londres',

tel qu'il a été reconstitué en 1965, comprenant 32 nouveaux Greater London Boroughs.

[101] Data for urban agglomeration refer to metropolitan areas defined for census purposes and normally comprising city proper (municipality) and contiguous urban areas. — Les données relatives aux agglomérations urbaines se rapportent à la zone métropolitaine définie aux fins du recensement qui comprend généralement la ville proprement dite (municipalité) et la zone urbaine contigue.

[102] Excludes inland water and oceanic areas. - Exclut les eaux intérieures et les zones océaniques.

[103] A city is a territorial authority which is a distinct entity, is predominantly urban in character, has a minimum population of 50,000 and is a major centre of activity within its parent region. - Une ville est une collectivité territoriale qui constitue une entité distincte, est à prédominance urbaine, compte au moins 50 000 habitants et est un grand centre d'activité dans la région où elle est située.

[104] Urban agglomerations refer to main urban areas that are centres with populations of 30,000 or more. - Les agglomérations urbaines désignent les principales zones urbaines qui sont des centres de population comptant au moins 30 000 habitants.

[105] The Territorial Authority of Dunedin City (3341.53 sq km) includes a large hinterland of rural area. The Dunedin 'Urban Area' (255.13 sq km) is the area of Dunedin City that is urban. - La collectivité territoriale de Dunedin (3 341,53 kilomètres carrés) comprend de vastes étendues rurales. La 'zone urbaine' de Dunedin (255,13 kilomètres carrés) correspond à la zone urbanisée de la ville de Dunedin.

Table 9

Table 9 presents live births and live-birth rates by urban/rural residence for as many years as possible between 1998 and 2002.

Description of variables: Live birth is defined as the complete expulsion or extraction from its mother of a product of conception, irrespective of the duration of pregnancy, which after such separation, breathes or shows any other evidence of life such as beating of the heart, pulsation of the umbilical cord, or definite movements of voluntary muscles, whether or not the umbilical cord has been cut or the placenta is attached; each product of such a birth is considered live-born[1].

Statistics on the number of live births are obtained from civil registers unless otherwise noted. For those countries or areas where civil registration statistics on live births are considered reliable (estimated completeness of 90 per cent or more) the birth rates shown have been calculated on the basis of registered live births. However, for countries or areas where civil registration of live births is non-existent or considered unreliable (estimated completeness of less than 90 per cent or of unknown completeness), estimated rates provided by national statistical authorities are presented and are identified by the code "|" in the first column.

Rate computation: Crude live-birth rates are the annual number of live births per 1 000 mid-year population.

Rates by urban/rural residence are the annual number of live births, in the appropriate urban or rural category, per 1 000 corresponding mid-year population. Rates are calculated only for data considered complete, that is, coded with a "C". These rates have been calculated by the Statistics Division of the United Nations Department for Economic and Social Affairs.

Rates presented in this table are limited to those countries or areas having a minimum number of 30 live births in a given year.

In addition, some rates have been obtained from sample surveys, using different methods[2]; to distinguish them from civil registration data, estimated rates are identified by a footnote.

Reliability of data: Each country or area has been asked to indicate the estimated completeness of the live births recorded in its civil register. These national assessments are indicated by the quality codes (C) and (U) that appear in the first column of this table.

C indicates that the data are estimated to be virtually complete, that is, representing at least 90 per cent of the live births occurring each year, while U indicates that data are estimated to be incomplete, that is, representing less than 90 per cent of the live births occurring each year. A third code (...) indicates that no information was provided regarding completeness.

Data from civil registers which are reported as incomplete or of unknown completeness (coded U or ...) are considered unreliable. They appear in italics in this table and rates are not calculated for these data.

These quality codes apply only to data from civil registers. If data from other sources are presented, the symbol (|) is shown instead of the quality code. For more information about the quality of vital statistics data in general, and the information available on the basis of the completeness estimates in particular, see section 4.2 of the Technical Notes.

Limitations. Statistics on live births are subject to the same qualifications as have been set forth for vital statistics in general and birth statistics in particular as discussed in section 4 of the Technical Notes.

The reliability of data, an indication of which is described above, is an important factor in considering the limitations. In addition, some live births are tabulated by date of registration and not by date of occurrence; these have been indicated by a plus sign "+". Whenever the lag between the date of occurrence and date of registration is prolonged and, therefore, a large proportion of the live-birth registrations are delayed, birth statistics for any given year may be seriously affected.

Another factor that limits international comparability is the practice of some countries or areas not to include in live-birth statistics infants who were born alive but died before the registration of the birth or within the first 24 hours of life, thus underestimating the total number of life births. Statistics of this type are footnoted.

In addition, it should be noted that rates are affected also by the quality and limitations of the population estimates that are used in their computation. The problems of under-enumeration or over-enumeration and, to some extent, the differences in definition of total population have been discussed in section 3 of the Technical Notes dealing with population data in general, and specific information pertaining to individual countries or areas is given in the footnotes to table 3.

The rates estimated from the results of sample surveys are subject to possibilities of considerable error as a result of omissions in reporting of births, or as a result of erroneous reporting of births that occurred outside the reference period. However, rates estimated from sample surveys have the advantage of the availability of a built-in and strictly corresponding population base.

It should be emphasized that crude birth rates - like crude death, marriage and divorce rates - may be seriously affected by the age-sex structure of the populations to which they relate. Nevertheless, they do provide a simple measure of the level of and changes in natality.

The urban/rural classification of birth may refer to the residence of mother or the place of delivery, as the national practices vary and is provided by each country or area. In addition, the comparability of data by urban/rural residence is affected by the national definition of urban and rural used in tabulating these data. It is assumed, in the absence of specific information to the contrary, that the definitions of urban and rural used in connection with the national population census were also used in the compilation of the vital statistics for each country or area. However, it cannot be excluded that, for a given country or area, different definitions of urban and rural are used for the vital statistics data and the population census data respectively. When known, the definitions of urban used in national population census are presented at the end of the technical notes to table 6. As discussed in detail in the technical notes to table 6, these definitions vary considerably from one area or country to another. Urban/rural differentials in vital rates may also be affected by whether the vital events have been tabulated in terms of place of occurrence or place of usual residence. This problem is discussed in more detail in section 4.1.4.1 of the Technical notes.

Earlier data: Live births have been shown in each issue of the *Demographic Yearbook*. Data included in this table update the series covering a period of years as follows:

Issue	Years Covered
Special Edition on Natality, CD, 1999	
- Numbers	1980 - 1999
- Rates	1985 - 1999
Historical Supplement, CD, 1997	1948 – 1997
1992	1983 – 1992
1986	1967 – 1986
1981	1962 – 1981
Historical Supplement, 1979	1948 - 1977

For further information on years covered prior to 1948, readers should consult the Historical Index.

NOTES

[1] *Principles and Recommendations for a Vital Statistics System Revision 2*, Sales No. E. 01.XVII.10, United Nations, New York, 2001.
[2] *Manual X: Indirect Techniques for Demographic Estimation*, United Nations publication, Sales No. E.83.XIII.2, United Nations, New York, 1983.

Tableau 9

Le tableau 9 présente des données sur les naissances vivantes et les taux bruts de natalité selon le lieu de résidence (zone urbaine ou rurale) pour le plus grand nombre d'années possible entre 1998 et 2002.

Description des variables : La naissance vivante est l'expulsion ou l'extraction complète du corps de la mère, indépendamment de la durée de gestation, d'un produit de la conception qui, après cette séparation, respire ou manifeste tout autre signe de vie, tel que battement de cœur, pulsation du cordon ombilical ou contraction effective d'un muscle soumis à l'action de la volonté, que le cordon ombilical ait été coupé ou non et que le placenta soit ou non demeuré attaché ; tout produit d'une telle naissance est considéré comme « enfant né vivant »[1].

Sauf indication contraire, les statistiques relatives au nombre de naissances vivantes sont établies sur la base des registres de l'état civil. Pour les pays ou zones où les statistiques obtenues auprès des services de l'état civil sont jugées sûres (complétude estimée à 90 p. 100 ou plus), les taux de natalité indiqués ont été calculés par la Division de statistique de l'ONU d'après les naissances vivantes enregistrées. En revanche, pour les pays ou zones où les services de l'état civil n'enregistrent pas les naissances vivantes et ceux où l'enregistrement des naissances vivantes est de qualité douteuse (complétude estimée à moins de 90 p. 100 ou degré de complétude inconnu), on a présenté, autant que possible, des taux estimatifs nationaux signalés par le code '|'.

Calcul des taux : Les taux bruts de natalité représentent le nombre annuel de naissances vivantes pour 1 000 habitants au milieu de l'année.

Les taux selon le lieu de résidence (zone urbaine ou rurale) représentent le nombre annuel de naissances vivantes, classées selon la catégorie urbaine ou rurale appropriée pour 1 000 habitants au milieu de l'année. Les taux ont été calculés seulement pour les données considérées complètes, c'est-à-dire celles associées au code 'C'. Ces taux ont été calculés par la Division de statistique du Département des affaires économiques et sociales.

Les taux présentés dans ce tableau se rapportent seulement aux pays ou zones où l'on a enregistré un nombre minimal de 30 naissances vivantes au cours d'une année donnée.

Dans certains cas, les données ont été calculées à partir d'enquêtes par sondage, en utilisant différentes techniques indirectes d'estimation démographique[2]. Pour les distinguer des données qui proviennent des registres de l'état civil, les taux estimatifs ont été signalés par une note.

Fiabilité des données : Il a été demandé à chaque pays ou zone d'indiquer le degré estimatif de complétude des données sur les naissances vivantes figurant dans ses registres d'état civil. Ces évaluations nationales sont signalées par les codes de qualité 'C' et 'U' qui apparaissent dans la deuxième colonne du tableau.

La lettre 'C' indique que les données sont jugées à peu près complètes, c'est-à-dire qu'elles représentent au moins 90 p. 100 des naissances vivantes survenues chaque année ; la lettre 'U' signifie que les données sont jugées incomplètes, c'est-à-dire qu'elles représentent moins de 90 p. 100 des naissances vivantes survenues chaque année. Un troisième code, '...', indique qu'aucun renseignement n'a été communiqué quant à la complétude des données.

Les données provenant des registres de l'état civil qui sont déclarées incomplètes ou dont le degré de complétude n'est pas connu (code 'U' ou '...') sont jugées douteuses. Elles apparaissent en italique dans le tableau. Les taux pour ces données ne sont pas calculés.

Les codes de qualité ne s'appliquent qu'aux données provenant des registres de l'état civil. Si l'on présente des données autres que celles de l'état civil, le signe '|' est utilisé à la place du code de qualité. Pour plus de précisions sur la qualité des données reposant sur les statistiques de l'état civil en général et les estimations de complétude en particulier, voir la section 4.2 des Notes techniques.

Insuffisance des données : Les statistiques concernant les naissances vivantes appellent toutes les réserves qui ont été formulées à propos des statistiques de l'état civil en général et des statistiques des naissances en particulier (voir la section 4 des Notes techniques).

La fiabilité des données, au sujet de laquelle des indications ont été fournies plus haut, est un facteur important. Il faut également tenir compte du fait que, dans certains cas, les données relatives aux naissances vivantes sont exploitées selon la date de l'enregistrement et non selon la date de l'événement ; ces cas ont été signalés par le signe '+'. Chaque fois que le décalage entre l'événement et son enregistrement est grand et qu'une forte proportion des naissances vivantes fait l'objet d'un enregistrement tardif, les statistiques des naissances vivantes pour une année donnée peuvent être considérablement faussées.

Un autre facteur qui nuit à la comparabilité internationale est la pratique de certains pays ou zones qui consiste à ne pas inclure dans les statistiques des naissances vivantes les enfants nés vivants mais décédés avant l'enregistrement de leur naissance ou dans les 24 heures qui ont suivi la naissance, pratique qui conduit à sous-estimer le nombre total de naissances vivantes. Lorsque ce facteur a joué, cela a été signalé en note à la fin du tableau.

La qualité et les limitations des estimations concernant la population ont également une incidence sur le calcul des taux. Les problèmes liés au sur-dénombrement ou au sous-dénombrement et, dans une certaine mesure, aux différences dans la définition de la population totale ont été abordés à la section 3 des Notes techniques relative aux données sur la population en général et des précisions sur certains pays ou zones sont données dans les notes se rapportant au tableau 3.

Les taux estimatifs fondés sur les résultats d'enquêtes par sondage comportent des possibilités d'erreurs considérables dues soit à des omissions dans les déclarations, soit au fait que l'on a déclaré à tort des naissances survenues en réalité hors de la période considérée. Toutefois, les taux estimatifs fondés sur les résultats d'enquêtes par sondage présentent un gros avantage : le chiffre de population utilisé comme base est, par définition, rigoureusement correspondant.

Il faut souligner que les taux bruts de natalité, de même que les taux bruts de mortalité, de nuptialité et de divortialité, peuvent varier très sensiblement selon la structure par âge et par sexe de la population à laquelle ils se rapportent. Ils offrent néanmoins un moyen simple de mesurer le niveau et l'évolution de la natalité.

La classification des naissances selon le lieu de résidence (zone urbaine ou rurale) peut se rapporter au lieu de résidence de la mère ou au lieu d'occurrence et correspond à celle indiquée par chaque pays ou zone. En outre, la comparabilité des données selon le lieu de résidence (zone urbaine ou rurale) peut être limitée par les définitions nationales des termes « urbain » et « rural » utilisées pour la mise en tableaux de ces données. En l'absence d'indications contraires, on a supposé que les mêmes définitions avaient servi pour le recensement national de la population et pour l'établissement des statistiques de l'état civil pour chaque pays ou zone. Toutefois, il n'est pas exclu que, pour une zone ou un pays donné, des définitions différentes aient été retenues. Les définitions du terme « urbain » utilisées pour les recensements nationaux de population ont été présentées à la fin des notes techniques du tableau 6 lorsqu'elles étaient connues. Comme on l'a précisé dans les notes techniques relatives au tableau 6, ces définitions varient considérablement d'un pays ou d'une zone à l'autre. La différence entre ces taux pour les zones urbaines et rurales pourra aussi être faussée selon que les faits d'état civil auront été classés d'après le lieu de l'événement ou le lieu de résidence habituel. Ce problème est examiné plus en détail à la section 4.1.4.1 des Notes techniques.

Données publiées antérieurement : Les différentes éditions de l'*Annuaire démographique* contiennent des données sur les naissances vivantes. Les données qui figurent dans le tableau 9 actualisent les données qui portaient sur les périodes suivantes :

Éditions	Années considérées
Édition spéciale sur les statistiques de la natalité (CD-ROM), 1999	
- Nombre	1980 - 1999
- Taux	1985 - 1999
Supplément historique (CD-ROM), 1997	1948 – 1997

1992   1983 – 1992
1986   1967 – 1986
1981   1962 – 1981

Supplément rétrospectif, 1979   1948 - 1977

Pour plus de détails concernant les années antérieures à 1948, se reporter à l'index historique.

NOTES

[1] *Principes et recommandations pour un système de statistique de l'état civil, deuxième révision,* numéro de vente : F.01.XVII.10, publication des Nations Unies, New York, 2003.
[2] *Manuel X, techniques indirectes d'estimation démographique,* numéro de vente : F.83.XIII.2, publication des Nations Unies, New York, 1984.

9. Live births and crude birth rates, by urban/rural residence: 1998 - 2002
Naissances vivantes et taux bruts de natalité selon la résidence, urbaine/rurale: 1998 - 2002

(See notes at end of table. — Voir notes à la fin du tableau.)

Continent, country or area and urban/rural residence / Continent, pays ou zone et résidence urbaine/rurale	Code[a]	Number - Nombre					Rate - Taux				
		1998	1999	2000	2001	2002	1998	1999	2000	2001	2002
AFRICA — AFRIQUE											
Algeria - Algérie[1,2]											
Total	C	620 322	593 643	588 628	618 380	616 963	21.0	19.8	19.4	20.0	19.7
Benin - Bénin[3]											
Total	I	260 610	265 980	272 640	263 726	...	44.8	44.4	44.2	41.1	...
Botswana[3]											
Total	I	50 606	53 407	...	53 735	...	32.2	33.2	...	32.0	...
Burundi[3]											
Total	I	290 982	...	...	...	...	46.2	...	...	...	...
Cape Verde - Cap-Vert											
Total	C	*15 460	...	12 746	12 926	13 123	*37.1	...	29.3	29.1	29.0
Chad - Tchad											
Total	...	...	...	...	397 896	...	...	...	...	...	...
Côte d'Ivoire[3]											
Total	I	614 667	...	655 904	...	...	40.0	...	40.0	...	...
Egypt - Égypte											
Total	C	1 687 252	1 693 025	...	...	...	27.5	27.0	...	...	...
Urban-Urbaine	C	685 233	657 902	...	...	...	26.2	24.7	...	...	...
Rural-Rurale	C	1 002 019	1 035 123	...	...	...	28.5	28.7	...	...	...
Ethiopia - Éthiopie											
Total	...	...	2 186 023	...	...	...	...	...	...	...	...
Urban-Urbaine	...	...	171 698	...	...	...	...	...	...	...	...
Rural-Rurale	...	...	2 014 325	...	...	...	...	...	...	...	...
Libyan Arab Jamahiriya - Jamahiriya arabe libyenne											
Total	C	...	...	98 752	99 187	111 053	...	...	19.3	18.7	20.2
Malawi[3,4]											
Total	I	496 524	531 160	543 654	555 558	567 241	50.0	52.3	51.9	51.4	50.8
Mali											
Total	U	...	...	...	525 685	...	...	...	...	...	...
Mauritius - Maurice											
Total	+C	19 434	20 311	20 205	19 696	19 983	16.7	17.3	17.0	16.4	16.5
Urban-Urbaine	+C	7 886	8 140	7 994	7 768	7 930	15.8	16.2	15.8	15.2	15.4
Rural-Rurale	ιC	11 548	12 171	12 211	11 928	12 053	17.4	18.1	17.9	17.3	17.3
Morocco - Maroc[5]											
Total	C	540 907	529 383	...	...	...	19.5	18.7	...	...	...
Urban-Urbaine	C	256 491	256 501	...	...	...	17.1	16.7	...	...	...
Rural-Rurale	C	283 667	272 069	...	...	...	22.1	21.2	...	...	...
Mozambique[3]											
Total	I	...	...	...	753 252	...	...	...	...	42.7	...
Réunion[1]											
Total	C	13 538	14 153	14 842	14 541	...	19.4	19.9	20.6	19.8	...
Saint Helena ex. dep. - Sainte-Hélène sans dép.											
Total	C	59	52	56	36	...	11.4	...	...	...	...
Seychelles											
Total	+C	1 412	1 460	1 512	1 440	*1 481	17.9	18.2	18.6	17.7	*18.3
South Africa - Afrique du Sud											
Total	U	1 216 337	1 363 800	1 407 833	...	...	...	...	...	...	...
Tunisia - Tunisie											
Total	C	166 718	160 169	...	*163 300	...	17.9	16.9	...	*16.9	...
AMERICA, NORTH — AMERIQUE DU NORD											
Anguilla											
Total	+C	155	176	193	183	169	14.5	16.1	17.1	15.8	14.2
Antigua and Barbuda - Antigua-et-Barbuda											
Total	+C	1 366	1 329	1 528	...	...	...	...	...	...	...
Aruba[6]											
Total	+U	1 315	1 225	1 294	1 266	*1 374	...	...	...	...	...

9. Live births and crude birth rates, by urban/rural residence: 1998 - 2002
Naissances vivantes et taux bruts de natalité selon la résidence, urbaine/rurale: 1998 - 2002
(continued — suite)

(See notes at end of table. — Voir notes à la fin du tableau.)

Continent, country or area and urban/rural residence Continent, pays ou zone et résidence urbaine/rurale	Code[a]	Number - Nombre					Rate - Taux				
		1998	1999	2000	2001	2002	1998	1999	2000	2001	2002
AMERICA, NORTH — AMERIQUE DU NORD											
Bahamas[6]											
Total	U	*5 880*	*5 367*	*5 287*	*5 353*	...	...	...	...	...	...
Barbados - Barbade	+C										
Total	+C	...	...	3 762	...	...	...	...	7.3	...	...
Belize											
Total	U	*5 986*	*6 218*	**7 313*	**7 082*	**7 356*	...	...	...	...	...
Bermuda - Bermudes											
Total	C	825	828	838	831	830	13.2	13.2	13.3	13.4	...
British Virgin Islands - Îles Vierges britanniques											
Total	+C	...	...	...	*318	...	...	...	...	*15.4	...
Canada[7]											
Total	C	342 418	337 249	327 882	333 744	328 802	11.4	11.1	10.7	10.8	10.5
Cayman Islands - Îles Caïmanes											
Total	C	545	604	619	*622	...	14.5	15.5	15.4	*15.0	...
Costa Rica											
Total	C	76 982	78 526	78 178	76 401	71 144	23.0	23.0	22.4	19.6	17.8
Urban-Urbaine	C	...	35 326	34 958	...	...	...	22.4	21.3	...	...
Rural-Rurale	C	...	43 200	43 219	...	...	...	23.5	23.5	...	...
Cuba											
Total	C	151 080	150 785	143 528	*138 718	141 276	13.6	13.5	12.8	*12.4	12.6
Urban-Urbaine	C	109 024	109 028	104 521	...	...	13.0	13.0	12.4	...	...
Rural-Rurale	C	42 056	41 757	39 007	...	...	15.3	15.1	14.1	...	...
Dominica - Dominique											
Total	+C	1 230	1 291	1 199	1 213	1 081	17.1	18.0	16.8	17.1	15.4
Dominican Republic - République dominicaine											
Total	+U	*179 372*	*193 418*	*189 332*	...	...	...	...	...	...	...
El Salvador											
Total	C	158 350	153 636	150 176	138 354	129 363	26.3	25.0	23.9	21.6	19.8
Urban-Urbaine	C	102 332	100 458	92 959	83 478	77 779	29.4	28.1	25.4	22.2	20.2
Rural-Rurale	C	56 018	53 178	57 217	54 876	51 584	22.0	20.6	21.9	20.8	19.3
Greenland - Groenland											
Total	C	986	947	...	...	...	17.6	16.9	...	...	...
Urban-Urbaine	C	770	734	...	...	...	16.9	16.1	...	...	...
Rural-Rurale	C	216	213	...	...	...	20.4	20.2	...	...	...
Grenada - Grenade											
Total	+C	1 938	1 791	1 883	*1 899	...	19.4	17.8	18.6	*18.8	...
Guadeloupe											
Total	C	7 141	7 341	7 653	7 503	6 995	17.0	17.3	17.9	17.3	16.0
Guatemala											
Total	C	489 829	360 759	*426 346	403 532	...	45.4	32.5	*37.4	34.5	...
Urban-Urbaine	C	207 773	140 491	...	...	...	...	...	...	...	...
Rural-Rurale	C	282 056	220 268	...	...	...	...	...	...	...	...
Jamaica - Jamaïque											
Total	+C	56 937	56 911	*54 035	*55 270	...	22.1	22.0	*20.7	*21.1	...
Martinique											
Total	C	5 816	5 789	6 059	5 908	5 446	15.3	15.2	15.8	15.3	14.0
Mexico - Mexique[5]											
Total	+U	*2 668 428*	*2 769 089*	*2 798 339*	*2 767 610*	*2527732*	...	...	...	...	...
Urban-Urbaine	+U	*1 776 675*	*1 804 415*	*1 806 199*	*1 749 126*	...	...	...	...	...	...
Rural-Rurale	+U	*767 725*	*786 089*	*762 200*	*748 772*	...	...	...	...	...	...
Netherlands Antilles - Antilles néerlandaises											
Total	C	3 111	2 803	...	...	...	15.0	13.7	...	...	...
Nicaragua											
Total	+U	*111 154*	*123 446*	*126 873*	*108 299*	*120 846*	...	...	...	...	...
Urban-Urbaine	+U	*63 377*	*74 851*	*76 786*	*65 209*	*65 387*	...	...	...	...	...
Rural-Rurale	+U	*47 777*	*48 595*	*50 087*	*43 090*	*55 459*	...	...	...	...	...

9. Live births and crude birth rates, by urban/rural residence: 1998 - 2002
Naissances vivantes et taux bruts de natalité selon la résidence, urbaine/rurale: 1998 - 2002
(continued — suite)

(See notes at end of table. — Voir notes à la fin du tableau.)

Continent, country or area and urban/rural residence / Continent, pays ou zone et résidence urbaine/rurale	Code[a]	Number - Nombre					Rate - Taux				
		1998	1999	2000	2001	2002	1998	1999	2000	2001	2002
AMERICA, NORTH — AMERIQUE DU NORD											
Panama											
Total	C	62 351	64 248	64 839	63 900	61 671	22.6	22.9	22.7	22.1	20.2
Urban-Urbaine	C	31 751	32 724	32 510	...	...	20.6	20.8	20.3	...	...
Rural-Rurale	C	30 600	31 524	32 329	...	...	25.0	25.5	25.8	...	...
Puerto Rico - Porto Rico[5]											
Total	C	60 518	59 684	59 460	55 982	52 871	16.1	15.8	15.6	14.6	13.7
Urban-Urbaine	C	30 575	30 561	30 464	29 323	...	...	...	8.5	...	...
Rural-Rurale	C	29 931	29 096	28 967	26 635	...	...	...	135.6	...	...
Saint Kitts and Nevis - Saint-Kitts-et-Nevis											
Total	+C	865	864	838	*803	...	21.6	20.3	20.7	*17.4	...
Saint Lucia - Sainte-Lucie[6]											
Total	C	2 950	2 997	2 840	2 788	2 529	19.4	19.5	18.2	17.7	15.9
Urban-Urbaine	C	846	...	...	...	...	18.8	...	...	...	...
Rural-Rurale	C	2 014	...	...	...	...	18.8	...	...	...	...
Saint Vincent and the Grenadines - Saint Vincent-et-les Grenadines											
Total	+C	2 112	2 171	2 149	2 109	1 985	19.0	19.5	19.2	19.3	18.4
Trinidad and Tobago - Trinité-et-Tobago											
Total	C	...	...	...	...	*18 026	...	...	...	...	*14.1
Turks Caicos Islands - Îles Turques et Caïques											
Total	+C	272	292	290	...	...	...	...	...	...	...
United States - États-Unis											
Total	C	3 941 553	3 959 417	4 058 814	4 025 933	4 021 726	14.6	14.5	14.7	14.1	13.9
AMERICA, SOUTH — AMERIQUE DU SUD											
Argentina - Argentine											
Total	C	683 301	686 748	701 878	683 495	694 684	18.9	18.8	19.0	18.2	18.3
Bolivia - Bolivie											
Total	U	...	...	264 941	...	...	...	...	...	...	...
Brazil - Brésil[6,8]											
Total	U	2 459 275	2 657 613	2 611 422	2 509 354	2 581 055	...	...	...	...	...
Chile - Chili											
Total	C	257 105	250 674	248 893	246 116	238 981	17.3	16.7	16.4	16.0	15.3
Urban-Urbaine	C	224 097	218 607	218 395	216 015	213 171	17.8	17.0	16.8	16.3	15.9
Rural-Rurale	C	33 008	32 067	30 498	30 101	25 810	15.0	14.6	13.9	13.8	11.8
Colombia - Colombie[5,9]											
Total	U	720 984	746 194	752 834	724 319	*678 388	...	...	...	...	...
Urban-Urbaine	U	564 032	570 263	574 208	552 445	*523 650	...	...	...	...	...
Rural-Rurale	U	138 076	153 039	153 865	154 404	*142 356	...	...	...	...	...
Ecuador - Équateur[10]											
Total	U	199 079	218 108	202 257	192 786	183 792	...	...	...	...	...
Urban-Urbaine	U	142 383	162 276	151 570	148 551	143 377	...	...	...	...	...
Rural-Rurale	U	56 696	55 832	50 687	44 235	40 415	...	...	...	...	...
Falkland Islands (Malvinas) - Îles Falkland (Malvinas)											
Total	+C	28	33	27	...	...	...	...	...	...	...
French Guiana - Guyane française[1]											
Total	C	4 691	4 898	5 116	5 114	5 249	30.7	30.9	31.2	30.1	29.9
Peru - Pérou[3,8,11]											
Total	I	648 075	642 874	636 064	630 947	626 714	25.8	25.2	24.5	23.9	23.4
Suriname											
Total	C	10 221	10 144	9 804	...	...	22.6	22.2	21.1	...	...
Urban-Urbaine	C	6 848	6 875	6 018	...	...	...	...	...	...	...
Rural-Rurale	C	3 373	3 269	3 786	...	...	...	...	...	...	...

9. Live births and crude birth rates, by urban/rural residence: 1998 - 2002
Naissances vivantes et taux bruts de natalité selon la résidence, urbaine/rurale: 1998 - 2002
(continued — suite)

(See notes at end of table. — Voir notes à la fin du tableau.)

Continent, country or area and urban/rural residence / Continent, pays ou zone et résidence urbaine/rurale	Code[a]	Number - Nombre					Rate - Taux				
		1998	1999	2000	2001	2002	1998	1999	2000	2001	2002
AMERICA, SOUTH — AMERIQUE DU SUD											
Uruguay											
Total	+C	54 760	54 004	52 770	51 959	51 997	16.7	16.4	15.9	15.5	15.5
Venezuela[8]											
Total	C	501 808	527 888	544 416	529 552	492 678	21.4	22.1	22.4	21.4	19.5
ASIA — ASIE											
Armenia - Arménie[12]											
Total	C	39 366	36 502	34 276	32 065	...	10.4	9.6	9.0	8.4	...
Urban-Urbaine	C	24 535	22 458	21 390	...	...	9.7	8.9	8.4	...	...
Rural-Rurale	C	14 831	14 044	12 886	...	...	11.8	11.1	10.2	...	...
Azerbaijan - Azerbaïdjan[12]											
Total	+C	123 996	117 539	116 994	110 356	110 715	15.7	14.7	14.5	13.6	13.5
Urban-Urbaine	+C	53 217	50 083	49 631	49 676	49 733	13.1	12.3	12.1	12.1	12.0
Rural-Rurale	+C	70 779	67 456	67 363	60 680	60 982	18.4	17.3	17.0	15.2	15.1
Bahrain - Bahreïn[13]											
Total	+U	13 381	14 280	13 947	13 468	13 576	...	...	...	...	...
Brunei Darussalam - Brunéi Darussalam											
Total	+C	7 411	7 408	7 481	7 363	7 464	23.9	23.4	23.0	22.1	21.9
China - Chine[14]											
Total	I	19910000	19090000	...	...	...	16.0	15.2	...	...	...
China: Hong Kong SAR - Chine: Hong Kong RAS[15]											
Total	C	52 977	51 281	54 134	48 219	48 209	8.1	7.8	8.1	7.2	7.1
China: Macao SAR - Chine: Macao RAS											
Total	C	4 434	4 148	3 849	3 241	*3 162	10.5	9.7	8.9	7.5	*7.2
Cyprus - Chypre[5,16]											
Total	C	8 879	8 505	8 447	8 167	7 883	11.6	11.0	10.8	10.4	9.9
Urban-Urbaine	C	5 906	5 640	5 732	...	4 806	...	...	...	...	...
Rural-Rurale	C	2 839	2 789	2 648	...	2 637	...	...	...	...	...
Georgia - Géorgie[12]											
Total	C	46 800	40 778	40 392	40 416	...	8.6	8.0	8.0	8.2	...
Urban-Urbaine	C	28 000	25 862	25 520	25 078	...	9.2	...	8.8	...	...
Rural-Rurale	C	18 800	14 916	14 872	15 338	...	7.8	...	7.0	...	...
Iran (Islamic Republic of) - Iran (République islamique d')											
Total	C	1 185 639	1 177 557	1 095 165	1 112 193	1 122 104	19.2	18.8	17.2	17.2	17.1
Urban-Urbaine	C	738 225	744 839	709 638	724 072	734 332	19.0	18.7	17.4	17.2	17.1
Rural-Rurale	C	447 414	432 718	385 527	388 121	387 772	19.5	18.9	16.9	17.4	17.2
Iraq[17]											
Total	U	519 216	532 916	471 886	...	...	...	...	...	...	...
Israel - Israël[18]											
Total	C	130 080	131 936	136 390	136 638	139 535	21.8	21.5	21.7	21.2	21.2
Urban-Urbaine	C	116 527	118 003	121 700	124 640	126 795	21.5	21.2	21.4	21.1	21.1
Rural-Rurale	C	13 553	13 933	14 690	11 998	12 740	24.5	24.4	24.8	22.3	23.1
Japan - Japon[5,19]											
Total	C	1 203 147	1 177 669	1 190 547	1 170 662	1 153 855	9.5	9.3	9.4	9.2	9.1
Urban-Urbaine	C	970 682	951 533	962 392	947 755	939 091	...	...	...	...	...
Rural-Rurale	C	232 176	225 894	227 945	222 709	214 569	...	...	...	...	...
Jordan - Jordanie[20]											
Total	C	133 714	135 266	126 016	142 956	146 077	28.1	27.6	25.0	27.6	27.4
Kazakhstan[12]											
Total	C	222 380	217 578	222 054	221 487	227 171	14.8	14.6	14.9	14.9	15.3
Urban-Urbaine	C	112 002	110 167	114 505	115 316	122 151	13.3	13.2	13.7	13.8	14.5
Rural-Rurale	C	110 378	107 411	107 549	106 171	105 020	16.6	16.4	16.5	16.4	16.3
Korea (Republic of) - Corée (République de)[21]											
Total	C	640 126	616 322	636 780	557 228	494 625	13.8	13.2	13.5	11.8	10.4

9. Live births and crude birth rates, by urban/rural residence: 1998 - 2002
Naissances vivantes et taux bruts de natalité selon la résidence, urbaine/rurale: 1998 - 2002
(continued — suite)

(See notes at end of table. — Voir notes à la fin du tableau.)

Continent, country or area and urban/rural residence / Continent, pays ou zone et résidence urbaine/rurale	Code[a]	Number - Nombre					Rate - Taux				
		1998	1999	2000	2001	2002	1998	1999	2000	2001	2002
ASIA — ASIE											
Korea (Republic of) - Corée (République de)[21]											
Urban-Urbaine	C	523 452	500 744	519 767	453 431	404 409	...	...	...	...	...
Rural-Rurale	C	116 674	115 578	117 013	103 797	90 216	...	...	...	...	...
Kuwait - Koweït											
Total	C	41 424	41 135	41 843	41 342	43 490	20.4	19.5	19.1	18.2	19.2
Kyrgyzstan - Kirghizistan[12]											
Total	C	104 183	104 068	96 770	98 138	101 012	21.7	21.4	19.7	19.8	20.2
Urban-Urbaine	C	28 494	28 328	28 193	28 491	30 195	16.8	16.5	16.2	16.2	17.1
Rural-Rurale	C	75 689	75 740	68 577	69 647	70 817	24.4	24.1	21.6	21.8	21.9
Lebanon - Liban[17]											
Total	U	84 250	85 516	85 760	...	...	...	...	...	...	...
Malaysia - Malaisie											
Total	C	524 766	521 870	545 096	...	...	24.4	23.9	23.2	...	...
Maldives											
Total	C	5 687	5 226	5 314	4 882	*4 991	21.3	18.8	19.6	17.7	*17.8
Urban-Urbaine	C	1 467	1 489	1 567	1 636	*1 877	...	...	...	...	...
Rural-Rurale	C	4 220	3 737	3 747	3 246	*3 114	...	...	...	...	...
Mongolia - Mongolie											
Total	C	49 256	49 461	48 721	49 685	46 922	21.0	20.8	20.2	20.3	19.0
Urban-Urbaine	C	22 393	24 219	23 828	24 691	24 067	18.0	18.0	17.3	17.7	16.9
Rural-Rurale	C	26 863	25 242	24 893	24 994	22 855	24.5	24.5	24.2	23.9	21.7
Occupied Palestinian Territory - Territoire palestinien occupé											
Total	U	99 841	96 780	98 026	94 626	93 488	...	...	...	...	...
Oman[22]											
Total	...	40 364	39 922	39 994	39 297	...	...	...	...	...	...
Pakistan[23,24]											
Total	I	...	...	...	3 710 604	...	...	...	...	26.5	...
Urban-Urbaine	I	...	...	...	1 192 190	...	...	...	...	...	...
Rural-Rurale	I	...	...	...	2 527 504	...	...	...	...	...	...
Philippines											
Total	C	1 632 859	1 613 335	1 766 440	...	...	22.3	21.6	23.1	...	...
Qatar											
Total	C	10 781	10 846	*11 250	12 118	12 200	19.8	...	*19.4	20.3	...
Saudi Arabia - Arabie saoudite											
Total	...	...	509 352	578 772	...	...	...	...	...	...	...
Singapore - Singapour											
Total	C	43 664	43 336	46 997	41 451	40 760	11.1	11.0	11.7	10.0	9.8
Sri Lanka											
Total	+C	329 148	329 121	...	...	*363 549	17.5	17.3	...	...	*19.1
Syrian Arab Republic - République arabe syrienne[1,25]											
Total	C	505 008	503 473	505 484	524 212	...	32.4	31.3	31.0	31.4	...
Tajikistan - Tadjikistan[12]											
Total	C	...	*110 300	...	...	...	...	*17.7	...	...	...
Thailand - Thaïlande											
Total	+U	897 495	772 604	773 009	790 425	782 911	...	...	...	...	...
Urban-Urbaine	+U	...	116 268	119 794	...	...	...	...	...	...	...
Rural-Rurale	+U	...	656 336	653 215	...	...	...	...	...	...	...
Turkey - Turquie[26]											
Total	I	1 505 000	1 501 000	1 494 000	1 486 000	1 482 000	23.1	22.6	22.2	21.7	21.3
Turkmenistan - Turkménistan[12]											
Total	C	*98 461	...	...	...	...	*20.3	...	...	...	...
Uzbekistan - Ouzbékistan[12]											
Total	C	...	553 745	527 580	512 950	...	...	23.1	21.4	20.5	...
Urban-Urbaine	C	...	173 209	163 834	159 492	...	...	19.2	17.8	17.2	...
Rural-Rurale	C	...	380 536	363 746	353 458	...	...	25.5	23.5	22.5	...

9. Live births and crude birth rates, by urban/rural residence: 1998 - 2002
Naissances vivantes et taux bruts de natalité selon la résidence, urbaine/rurale: 1998 - 2002
(continued — suite)

(See notes at end of table. — Voir notes à la fin du tableau.)

Continent, country or area and urban/rural residence / Continent, pays ou zone et résidence urbaine/rurale	Code[a]	Number - Nombre					Rate - Taux				
		1998	1999	2000	2001	2002	1998	1999	2000	2001	2002
EUROPE											
Albania - Albanie	C						15.9	...	...	...	...
Total		60 139	...	...	...	...					
Andorra - Andorre	C						11.8	12.6	11.3	11.8	11.3
Total		781	833	747	777	749					
Austria - Autriche	C						10.1	9.7	9.7	9.4	9.7
Total		81 233	78 138	78 268	75 458	78 399					
Belarus - Bélarus[12]											
Total	C	92 645	92 975	...	...	88 743	9.1	9.3	...	...	8.9
Urban-Urbaine	C	64 856	66 380	...	...	65 091	9.1	9.5	...	...	9.3
Rural-Rurale	C	27 789	26 595	...	...	23 652	9.1	8.7	...	...	8.2
Belgium - Belgique[27]											
Total	C	114 276	113 469	114 883	*114 014	...	11.2	11.1	11.2	*11.1	...
Bosnia and Herzegovina - Bosnie-Herzégovine											
Total	C	45 007	...	...	...	...	12.3	...	...	...	...
Bulgaria - Bulgarie											
Total	C	65 360	72 291	73 679	68 180	66 499	7.9	8.8	9.0	8.6	8.5
Urban-Urbaine	C	...	...	52 789	48 567	47 779	...	...	9.5	8.9	8.7
Rural-Rurale	C	...	...	20 890	19 613	18 720	...	...	8.1	8.1	7.8
Channel Islands: Guernsey - Îles Anglo-Normandes: Guernesey											
Total	C	669	672	644	...	...	11.3	11.2	10.7	...	...
Croatia - Croatie											
Total	C	47 068	45 179	43 746	40 993	40 094	10.5	9.9	10.0	9.2	9.0
Urban-Urbaine	C	26 819	...	24 768	22 938	22 539	...	...	...	...	...
Rural-Rurale	C	20 249	...	18 978	18 055	17 555	...	...	...	...	...
Czech Republic - République tchèque											
Total	C	90 535	89 471	90 910	90 715	97 878	8.8	8.7	8.8	8.9	9.6
Urban-Urbaine	C	66 622	65 460	66 868	67 081	73 482	8.7	8.5	8.8	8.9	9.8
Rural-Rurale	C	23 913	24 011	24 042	23 634	24 396	9.1	9.2	9.1	8.9	9.2
Denmark - Danemark[28]											
Total	C	66 170	66 232	67 084	65 458	64 149	12.5	12.4	12.6	12.2	11.9
Estonia - Estonie[5,12]											
Total	C	12 170	12 545	13 089	12 632	13 001	8.4	8.7	9.6	9.3	9.6
Urban-Urbaine	C	...	...	8 684	...	8 840	...	...	9.2	...	9.4
Rural-Rurale	C	...	...	4 402	...	4 161	...	...	10.4	...	10.0
Finland - Finlande[29]											
Total	C	57 108	57 574	56 742	56 189	55 555	11.1	11.1	11.0	10.8	10.7
Urban-Urbaine	C	36 103	36 621	...	36 191	36 263	11.7	11.8	...	11.4	11.3
Rural-Rurale	C	21 005	20 953	...	19 998	19 292	10.2	10.2	...	10.0	9.7
France[30,31]											
Total	C	738 080	744 791	774 782	770 945	...	12.6	12.7	13.2	13.0	...
Urban-Urbaine	C	567 675	570 503	589 608	...	...	...	...	...	...	...
Rural-Rurale	C	168 952	172 966	183 787	...	...	...	...	...	...	...
Germany - Allemagne											
Total	C	797 541	770 744	766 999	734 475	...	9.7	9.4	9.3	8.9	...
Gibraltar[32]											
Total	C	411	381	408	399	371	15.2	14.0	15.1	14.1	13.0
Greece - Grèce											
Total	C	100 894	116 038	117 140	102 282	...	9.6	11.0	11.7	10.2	...
Urban-Urbaine	C	69 490	...	...	...	...	...	...	...	...	...
Rural-Rurale	C	31 404	...	...	...	...	...	...	...	...	...
Holy See - Saint-Siège											
Total	C	...	...	1	...	...	...	...	...	...	...
Hungary - Hongrie[5]											
Total	C	97 301	94 645	97 597	97 047	96 804	9.6	9.4	9.7	9.5	9.5
Urban-Urbaine	C	58 358	57 113	59 029	59 119	60 753	8.9	8.8	9.1	8.9	9.2
Rural-Rurale	C	38 341	36 836	37 781	37 019	35 248	10.8	10.4	10.6	10.4	9.9
Iceland - Islande											
Total	C	4 178	4 100	4 315	4 091	4 049	15.3	14.8	15.3	14.4	14.1

9. Live births and crude birth rates, by urban/rural residence: 1998 - 2002
Naissances vivantes et taux bruts de natalité selon la résidence, urbaine/rurale: 1998 - 2002
(continued — suite)

(See notes at end of table. — Voir notes à la fin du tableau.)

Continent, country or area and urban/rural residence / Continent, pays ou zone et résidence urbaine/rurale	Code[a]	Number - Nombre					Rate - Taux				
		1998	1999	2000	2001	2002	1998	1999	2000	2001	2002
EUROPE											
Iceland - Islande											
Urban-Urbaine	C	3 904	3 833	4 025	3 849	3 823	15.5	15.0	15.5	14.6	14.4
Rural-Rurale	C	274	267	290	242	226	12.8	12.6	13.5	11.2	10.5
Ireland - Irlande[33]											
Total	+C	53 551	53 354	54 239	57 882	60 521	14.5	14.2	14.3	15.1	15.5
Urban-Urbaine	+C	28 857	30 827	...	...	...	...	...	...	...	...
Rural-Rurale	+C	24 694	22 527	...	...	...	...	...	...	...	...
Isle of Man - Îles de Man											
Total	+C	...	894	831	863	903	...	...	11.1	11.3	11.7
Italy - Italie											
Total	C	515 439	523 463	543 039	535 282	*537 070	9.0	9.1	9.4	9.2	*9.3
Latvia - Lettonie[12]											
Total	C	18 410	19 396	20 248	19 664	20 044	7.6	8.1	8.5	8.3	8.6
Urban-Urbaine	C	11 328	12 072	12 737	12 531	12 938	6.9	7.4	7.9	7.8	8.2
Rural-Rurale	C	7 082	7 324	7 511	7 133	7 106	9.3	9.7	9.9	9.4	9.4
Liechtenstein											
Total	C	...	...	...	...	395	...	...	...	...	11.7
Lithuania - Lituanie[12]											
Total	C	37 019	36 415	34 149	31 546	30 014	10.4	10.3	9.8	9.1	8.7
Urban-Urbaine	C	23 066	...	21 008	19 672	18 697	9.7	...	9.0	8.4	8.1
Rural-Rurale	C	13 953	...	13 141	11 874	11 317	12.0	...	11.4	10.3	9.9
Luxembourg											
Total	C	5 386	5 582	5 723	5 459	5 345	12.7	13.0	13.1	12.4	12.0
Malta - Malte[34,35]											
Total	C	4 488	4 308	4 255	3 859	3 805	11.6	11.1	10.9	9.8	9.6
Monaco											
Total	C	681	...	760	...	...	...	...	22.8	...	...
Netherlands - Pays-Bas[36]											
Total	C	199 408	200 445	206 619	202 603	202 083	12.7	12.7	13.0	12.6	12.5
Urban-Urbaine	C	123 487	...	132 318	132 295	132 825	12.7	...	...	...	...
Rural-Rurale	C	75 921	...	74 301	70 308	69 258	12.8	...	...	...	...
Norway - Norvège											
Total	C	58 352	59 298	59 234	56 696	55 434	13.2	13.3	13.2	12.6	12.2
Poland - Pologne											
Total	C	395 619	382 002	378 700	368 205	353 765	10.2	9.9	9.8	9.5	9.2
Urban-Urbaine	C	214 074	208 173	...	...	...	8.9	8.7	...	...	...
Rural-Rurale	C	181 545	173 829	...	...	...	12.3	11.8	...	...	...
Portugal											
Total	C	113 510	116 002	118 551	112 774	114 383	11.4	11.6	11.8	11.0	11.0
Republic of Moldova - République de Moldova[12]											
Total	C	41 332	38 501	36 939	36 448	35 705	11.3	10.6	10.2	10.0	9.9
Urban-Urbaine	C	14 221	13 238	12 722	12 542	12 747	9.3	8.6	8.4	8.4	8.6
Rural-Rurale	C	27 111	25 263	24 217	23 906	22 958	12.8	11.9	11.4	11.1	10.7
Romania - Roumanie											
Total	C	237 297	234 600	234 521	220 368	210 529	10.5	10.4	10.5	10.0	9.7
Urban-Urbaine	C	110 186	...	108 254	102 432	98 190	8.9	...	8.8	8.4	8.5
Rural-Rurale	C	127 111	...	126 267	117 936	112 339	12.5	...	12.4	11.6	11.0
Russian Federation - Fédération de Russie[12]											
Total	C	1 283 292	1 214 689	1 266 800	1 311 604	...	8.8	8.3	8.7	9.1	...
Urban-Urbaine	C	...	842 640	...	...	...	...	7.9	...	...	...
Rural-Rurale	C	...	372 049	...	...	...	...	9.4	...	...	...
San Marino - Saint-Marin											
Total	+C	285	303	290	...	...	10.9	11.5	10.8	...	...
Urban-Urbaine	+C	...	...	259	...	...	...	...	11.4	...	...
Rural-Rurale	+C	...	...	31	...	...	...	...	7.4	...	...
Serbia and Montenegro - Serbie-et-Montenegro											
Total	C	128 461	123 970	125 868	130 194	...	12.1	11.7	11.8	12.2	...
Urban-Urbaine	C	66 885	64 489	66 409	...	...	12.2	11.8	12.1	...	...

9. Live births and crude birth rates, by urban/rural residence: 1998 - 2002
Naissances vivantes et taux bruts de natalité selon la résidence, urbaine/rurale: 1998 - 2002
(continued — suite)

(See notes at end of table. — Voir notes à la fin du tableau.)

Continent, country or area and urban/rural residence / Continent, pays ou zone et résidence urbaine/rurale	Code[a]	Number - Nombre					Rate - Taux				
		1998	1999	2000	2001	2002	1998	1999	2000	2001	2002
EUROPE											
Serbia and Montenegro - Serbie-et-Montenegro											
Rural-Rurale	C	61 576	59 481	59 459	...	...	12.0	11.5	11.5	...	...
Slovakia - Slovaquie											
Total	C	57 582	56 223	55 103	51 136	50 841	10.7	10.4	10.2	9.5	9.5
Urban-Urbaine	C	29 725	28 693	...	26 106	26 321	9.7	9.4	...	...	8.7
Rural-Rurale	C	27 857	27 530	...	25 030	24 520	12.0	11.8	...	...	10.4
Slovenia - Slovénie											
Total	C	17 856	17 533	18 180	17 477	17 501	9.0	8.8	9.1	8.8	8.8
Urban-Urbaine	C	...	8 017	8 306	8 039	8 400	...	...	...	...	8.6
Rural-Rurale	C	...	9 516	9 874	9 438	9 101	...	...	...	...	9.3
Spain - Espagne											
Total	C	365 193	380 130	*386 450	*407 135	...	9.3	9.6	*9.7	*10.1	...
Sweden - Suède											
Total	C	89 028	88 173	90 441	91 466	95 815	10.1	10.0	10.2	10.3	10.7
Switzerland - Suisse											
Total	C	78 949	78 408	78 458	73 509	72 372	11.1	11.0	10.9	10.2	9.9
Urban-Urbaine	C	51 684	51 771	52 393	49 292	...	10.8	10.7	10.8	10.1	...
Rural-Rurale	C	27 265	26 637	26 065	24 217	...	11.8	11.5	11.2	10.4	...
The Former Yugoslav Rep. of Macedonia - L'ex-République yougoslave de Macédoine											
Total	C	29 244	27 309	29 308	27 010	27 761	14.6	13.5	14.5	13.3	13.6
Urban-Urbaine	C	...	14 375	15 579	14 761	14 909	...	...	...	...	...
Rural-Rurale	C	...	12 934	13 729	12 249	12 852	...	...	...	...	...
Ukraine[12]											
Total	C	419 238	...	385 126	376 478	390 688	8.3	...	7.7	7.7	8.1
Urban-Urbaine	C	258 724	...	...	237 228	248 877	7.5	...	...	...	...
Rural-Rurale	C	160 514	...	...	139 250	141 811	9.9	...	...	...	...
United Kingdom - Royaume-Uni[37]											
Total	C	716 888	699 976	679 029	669 123	668 777	12.1	11.8	11.4	11.2	11.3
OCEANIA — OCEANIE											
American Samoa - Samoas américaines											
Total	C	1 688	1 736	1 730	...	...	30.3	30.6	30.0	...	...
Australia - Australie											
Total	+C	249 616	248 870	249 636	246 394	250 988	13.3	13.1	13.0	12.7	12.8
Cook Islands - Îles Cook											
Total	+C	386	346	309	313	224	22.2	21.1	17.3	17.2	12.2
Fiji - Fidji											
Total	+C	17 944	16 916	...	...	...	22.5	21.0	...	...	...
French Polynesia - Polynésie française											
Total	C	4 562	4 580	4 900	...	...	20.2	20.1	21.2	...	...
Guam[38]											
Total	C	4 322	4 037	3 790	3 583	3 222	28.9	26.5	...	22.6	20.0
Marshall Islands - Îles Marshall											
Total	+U	1 651	1 478	...	*1 511	...	...	...	...	...	...
New Caledonia - Nouvelle-Calédonie											
Total	C	4 352	4 316	4 566	4 326	4 194	21.3	20.8	21.6	20.2	19.3
New Zealand - Nouvelle-Zélande[5]											
Total	+C	55 349	57 053	56 605	55 799	54 021	14.5	14.9	14.7	14.4	13.7
Urban-Urbaine	+C	48 337	49 536	49 374	48 745	47 068	14.8	15.1	14.9	14.6	13.9
Rural-Rurale	+C	6 717	7 293	7 126	6 986	6 896	12.3	13.4	13.0	12.7	12.5
Niue - Nioué											
Total	...	...	...	...	...	24	...	...	...	...	...

9. Live births and crude birth rates, by urban/rural residence: 1998 - 2002
Naissances vivantes et taux bruts de natalité selon la résidence, urbaine/rurale: 1998 - 2002
(continued — suite)

(See notes at end of table. — Voir notes à la fin du tableau.)

Continent, country or area and urban/rural residence Continent, pays ou zone et résidence urbaine/rurale	Code[a]	Number - Nombre					Rate - Taux				
		1998	1999	2000	2001	2002	1998	1999	2000	2001	2002
OCEANIA — OCEANIE											
Northern Mariana Islands - Îles Mariannes septentrionales											
Total	U	*1 421*	*1 448*	...	...	...	...	...	...	...	...
Palau - Palaos											
Total	C	280	250	...	...	...	15.1	13.2	...	...	...
Papua New Guinea - Papouasie-Nouvelle-Guinée											
Total	...		...	...	...	175 824	...	...	...	...	...
Tonga											
Total	+C	2 737	2 599	2 471	...	...	27.6	26.0	24.6	...	...

GENERAL NOTES - NOTES GENERALES

For certain countries, there is a discrepancy between the total number of live births shown in this table and those shown in subsequent tables for the same year. Usually this discrepancy arises because the total number of births occurring in a given year is revised, although the remaining tabulations are not. Rates are the number of live births per 1 000 mid-year population. For definitions of 'urban', see end of Technical Notes for table 6. For method of evaluation and limitations of data, see Technical Notes for this table. — Pour quelques pays il y a une discordance entre le nombre total des naissances vivantes présenté dans ce tableau et ceux présentés pour la même année dans d'autres tableaux. Habituellement ces différences apparaissent lorsque le nombre total des naissances pour une certaine année a été révisé; alors que les autres tabulations ne l'ont pas été. Les taux représentent le nombre de naissances vivantes pour 1 000 personnes au milieu de l'année. Pour les définitions des 'régions urbaines', se reporter à la fin des Notes techniques du tableau 6. Pour la méthode d'évaluation et les limitations des données, voir Notes techniques pour ce tableau.

Italics: data from civil registers which are incomplete or of unknown completeness. — Italiques: données incomplètes ou dont le degré de complétude n'est pas connu provenant des registres de l'état civil.

FOOTNOTES - NOTES

* Provisional. — Données provisoires.
[a] 'Code' indicates the source of data, as follows:
C - Civil registration, estimated over 90% complete
U - Civil registration, estimated less than 90% complete
I - Other source, estimated reliable
+ - Data tabulated by date of registration rather than occurence.
... - Information not available

Le 'Code' indique la source des données, comme suit:
C - Registres de l'état civil considérés complèts à 90 p. 100 au moins.
U - Registres de l'état civil qui ne sont pas considérés complèts à 90 p. 100 au moins.
I - Autre source, considérée pas douteuses.
+ - Données exploitées selon la date de l'enregistrement et non la date de l'événement.
... - Information pas disponible.

[1] Excluding live-born infants who died before their birth was registered. - Non compris les enfants nés vivants décédés avant l'enregistrement de leur naissance.
[2] For Algerian population only. - Pour la population algérienne seulement.
[3] Data refer to national projections. - Les données se referent aux projections nationales.
[4] Data on births refer to the 1998 Population and Housing Census, adjusted for under-enumeration. - Les données sur les naissances referent au Recensement de la population et de l'habitat, ajustés pour compenser les lacunes de dénombrement.
[5] Figures for urban and rural areas do not add up to the total, since they do not include the category "Unknown residence". - La somme des données pour la residence urbaine et rurale n'est pas égale au total parce qu'elle n'inclue pas la catégorie "Residence inconnue".
[6] Data as reported by national statistical authorities; they may differ from data presented in other tables. - Les données comme elles ont été déclarées par l'institut national de la statistique; elles peuvent être différentes de ceux présentées dans autre tableaux.
[7] Including Canadian residents temporarily in the United States, but excluding United States residents temporarily in Canada. - Y compris les résidents canadiens se trouvant temporairement aux Etats-Unis, mais ne comprenant pas les résidents des Etats-Unis se trouvant temporairement au Canada.
[8] Excluding Indian jungle population. - Non compris les Indiens de la jungle.
[9] Data on live births and deaths are based on a civil registration system put in place in January 1998. - Les données sur les naissances et les décès sont basées sur un système d'enregistrement des faits d'état civil mis en place en janvier 1998.
[10] Excluding nomadic Indian tribes. - Non compris les tribus d'Indiens nomades.
[11] Including an upward adjustment for under-registration. - Y compris un ajustement pour sous-enregistrement.
[12] Excluding infants born alive with less than 28 weeks gestation, less than 1 000 grams in weight and 35 centimeters in length, who die within seven days of birth. - Non compris les enfants nés vivants avant 28 semaines de gestation, pesant moins de 1 000 grammes, mesurant moins de 35 centimètres et décédés dans les sept jours qui ont suivi leur naissance.
[13] For 1997 - 2001 by registration, starting from 2001 by occurence. - Pour 1997 - 2001 les données sont presentées selon la date d'enregistrement; pour 2001 et après les données sont présentées selon la date de l'événement.
[14] For statistical purposes, the data for China do not include those for the Hong Kong Special Administrative Region (Hong Kong SAR), Macao Special Administrative Region (Macao SAR) and Taiwan province of China. - Pour la présentation des statistiques, les données pour Chine ne comprend pas la Région Administrative Spéciale de Hong Kong (Hong Kong RAS), la Région Administrative Spéciale de Macao (Macao RAS) et Taïwan province de Chine.
[15] Unrevised data. - Les données n'ont pas été révisées.
[16] Data refer to government controlled areas. - Les données se raportent aux zones contrôlées par le Gouvernement.
[17] Published by the United Nations Economic and Social Commission for Western Asia. - Publié par la Commission économique et sociale des Nations Unies pour l'Asie occidentale.
[18] Including data for East Jerusalem and Israeli residents in certain other territories under occupation by Israeli military forces since June 1967. - Y compris les données pour Jérusalem-Est et les résidents israéliens dans certains autres territoires occupés depuis 1967 par les forces armées israéliennes.
[19] Data refer to Japanese nationals in Japan only. - Les données se raportent aux nationaux japonais au Japon seulement.
[20] Excluding data for Jordanian territory under occupation since June 1967 by Israeli military forces. Excluding foreigners, including registered Palestinian refugees. - Non compris les données pour le territoire jordanien occupé depuis juin 1967 par les forces armées israéliennes. Non compris les étrangers, mais y

compris les réfugiés de Palestine enregistrés.

[21] Excluding alien armed forces, civilian aliens employed by armed forces, and foreign diplomatic personnel and their dependants. - Non compris les militaires étrangers, les civils étrangers employés par les forces armées ni le personnel diplomatique étranger et les membres de leur famille les accompagnant.

[22] Data refer to the recorded events in Ministry of Health hospitals and health centres only. - Les données se rapportent aux faits d'état-civil enregistrés dans les hôpitaux et les dispensaires du Ministère de la santé seulement.

[23] Based on the results of the Population Growth Survey. - D'après les résultats de la 'Population Growth Survey.'

[24] Excluding data for the Pakistan-held part of Jammu and Kashmir, the final status of which has not yet been determined. - Non compris les données concernant la partie du Jammu et Cachemire occupée par le Pakistan dont le statut définitif n'a pas été déterminé.

[25] Excluding nomad population and Palestinian refugees. - Non compris la population nomade et les réfugiés de Palestine.

[26] Based on the results of the Population Demographic Survey. - D'après les résultats de la Population Demographic Survey.

[27] Including armed forces stationed outside the country, but excluding alien armed forces stationed in the area. - Y compris les militaires nationaux hors du pays, mais non compris les militaires étrangers en garnison sur le territoire.

[28] Excluding Faeroe Islands and Greenland. - Non compris les îles Féroé et Gröenland.

[29] Including nationals temporarily outside the country. - Y compris les nationaux se trouvant temporairement hors du pays.

[30] Including armed forces stationed outside the country. - Y compris les militaires nationaux hors du pays.

[31] Urban/rural figures, excluding nationals outside the country. - Les chiffres urbaine/rurale, non compris les nationaux hors du pays.

[32] Excluding armed forces. - Non compris les militaires en garnison.

[33] Events registered within one year of occurrence. - Evénements enregistrés dans l'année qui suit l'événement.

[34] Live births to Maltese parents only. - Naissances vivantes aux parents maltais seulement.

[35] Rates computed on population including civilian nationals temporarily outside the country. - Les taux sont calculés sur la base d'un chiffre de population qui comprend les civils nationaux temporairement hors du pays.

[36] Including residents outside the country if listed in a Netherlands population register. - Y compris les résidents hors du pays, s'ils sont inscrits sur un registre de population néerlandais.

[37] Data revised to exclude births in Northern Ireland to non-residents of Northern Ireland. - Données révisées non compris des naissances en Irlande du Nord aux non-résidents de l'Irlande du Nord.

[38] Including United States military personnel, their dependants and contract employees. - Y compris les militaires des Etats-Unis, les membres de leur famille les accompagnant et les agents contractuels des Etats-Unis.

Table 10

Table 10 presents live births by age of mother, sex of the child and urban/rural residence for the latest available year.

Description of variables: Age is defined as age at last birthday, that is, the difference between the date of birth and the date of the occurrence of the event, expressed in completed solar years. The age classification used in this table is the following: under 15 years, 5-year age groups through 45-49 years, and 50 years and over.

Reliability of data: Data from civil registers of live births which are reported as incomplete (less than 90 per cent completeness) or of unknown completeness are considered unreliable and are set in *italics* rather than in roman type. Table 9 and the technical notes for that table provide more detailed information on the completeness of live-birth registration. For more information about the quality of vital statistics data in general, see section 4.2 of the Technical Notes.

Limitations: Statistics on live births by age of mother are subject to the same qualifications as have been set forth for vital statistics in general and birth statistics in particular as discussed in section 4 of the Technical Notes.

The reliability of the data described above, is an important factor in considering the limitations. In addition, some live births are tabulated by date of registration and not by date of occurrence; these are indicated in the table by a plus sign "+". Whenever the lag between the date of occurrence and date of registration is prolonged and, therefore, a large proportion of the live-birth registrations are delayed, birth statistics for any given year may be seriously affected. For example, the age of the mother will almost always refer to the date of registration rather than to the date of birth of the child. Hence, in those countries or areas where registration of births is delayed, possibly for years, statistics on births by age of mother should be used with caution.

Another factor which limits international comparability is the practice of some countries or areas of not including in live-birth statistics infants who were born alive but died before the registration of the birth or within the first 24 hours of life, thus underestimating the total number of live births. Statistics of this type are footnoted.

Because these statistics are classified according to age, they are subject to the limitations with respect to accuracy of age reporting similar to those already discussed in connection with section 3.1.3 of the Technical Notes. The factors influencing the accuracy of reporting may be somewhat dissimilar in vital statistics (because of the differences in the method of taking a census and registering a birth) but, in general, the same errors can be observed. The absence of frequencies in the unknown age group does not necessarily indicate completely accurate reporting and tabulation of the age item. It is often an indication that the unknowns have been eliminated by assigning ages to them before tabulation, or by proportionate distribution after tabulation.

On the other hand, large frequencies in the unknown age category may indicate that a large proportion of the births are born outside of wedlock, the records for which tend to be incomplete in so far as characteristics of the parents are concerned.

Another limitation of age reporting may result from calculating age of mother at birth of child (or at time of registration) from year of birth rather than from day, month and year of birth. Information on this factor is given in footnotes when known.

In few countries, data by age refer to deliveries rather than to live births causing under-enumeration in the event of a multiple birth. This practice leads to lack of strict comparability, both among countries or areas relying on this practice and between data shown in this table and table 9.

The comparability of data by urban/rural residence is affected by the national definitions of urban and rural used in tabulating these data. It is assumed, in the absence of specific information to the contrary, that the definitions of urban and rural used in connection with the national population census were also used in the compilation of the vital statistics for each country or area. However, the possibility cannot be excluded that, for a given country or area, the same definitions of urban and rural are not used for both the vital statistics data and the population census data. When known, the definitions of urban used in national population censuses are presented at the end of table 6. As discussed in detail in the technical notes for table 6, these definitions vary considerably from one country or area to another.

Earlier data: Live births by age of mother have been shown for the latest available year in each issue of the Yearbook. Data included in this table update the series covering period of years as follows:

Issue	Years Covered
Special Edition on Natality, CD, 1999	1990 – 1998
Historical Supplement CD, 1997	1948 – 1997
1992	1983 – 1992
1986	1977 – 1988
1981	1972 – 1980
Historical Supplement, 1979	1948 - 1977

For further information on years covered prior to 1948, readers should consult the Historical Index.

Tableau 10

Le tableau 10 présente les données les plus récentes dont on dispose sur les naissances vivantes selon l'âge de la mère, le sexe de l'enfant et le lieu de résidence (zone urbaine ou rurale).

Description des variables : L'âge désigne l'âge au dernier anniversaire, c'est-à-dire la différence entre la date de naissance et la date de l'événement exprimée en années solaires révolues. La classification par âge utilisée dans ce tableau comprend les catégories suivantes : moins de 15 ans, groupes quinquennaux jusqu'à 45-49 ans, 50 ans et plus, et âge inconnu.

Fiabilité des données : Les données sur les naissances vivantes provenant des registres de l'état civil qui sont déclarées incomplètes (degré de complétude inférieur à 90 p. 100) ou dont le degré de complétude n'est pas connu sont jugées douteuses et apparaissent en italique et non en caractères romains. Le tableau 9 et les notes techniques qui s'y rapportent présentent des renseignements plus détaillés sur le degré de complétude de l'enregistrement des naissances vivantes. Pour plus de précisions sur la qualité des statistiques de l'état civil en général, voir la section 4.2 des Notes techniques.

Insuffisance des données : Les statistiques relatives aux naissances vivantes selon l'âge de la mère appellent toutes les réserves qui ont été formulées à propos des statistiques de l'état civil en général et des statistiques de naissances en particulier (voir la section 4 des Notes techniques).

La fiabilité des données, au sujet de laquelle des indications ont été données plus haut, est un facteur important. Il faut également tenir compte du fait que, dans certains cas, les données relatives aux naissances vivantes sont exploitées selon la date de l'enregistrement et non la date de l'événement ; ces cas ont été signalés dans le tableau par le signe '+'. Chaque fois que le décalage entre l'événement et son enregistrement est grand et qu'une forte proportion des naissances vivantes fait l'objet d'un enregistrement tardif, les statistiques des naissances vivantes pour une année donnée peuvent être considérablement faussées. Par exemple, l'âge de la mère représente presque toujours son âge à la date de l'enregistrement et non à la date de la naissance de l'enfant. Ainsi, dans les pays ou zones où l'enregistrement des naissances est tardif, le retard atteignant parfois plusieurs années, il faut utiliser avec prudence les statistiques concernant les naissances selon l'âge de la mère.

Un autre facteur qui nuit à la comparabilité internationale est la pratique de certains pays ou zones qui consiste à ne pas inclure dans les statistiques des naissances vivantes les enfants nés vivants mais décédés avant l'enregistrement de leur naissance ou dans les 24 heures qui ont suivi la naissance, pratique qui conduit à sous-estimer le nombre total de naissances vivantes. Quand pareil facteur a joué, cela a été signalé en note à la fin du tableau.

Étant donné que les statistiques du tableau 10 sont classées selon l'âge, elles appellent les mêmes réserves concernant l'exactitude des déclarations d'âge que celles formulées à la section 3.1.3 des Notes techniques. Dans le cas des statistiques de l'état civil, les facteurs qui interviennent à cet égard sont parfois différents, étant donné que le recensement de la population et l'enregistrement des naissances se font par des méthodes différentes, mais, d'une manière générale, les erreurs observées seront les mêmes. Si aucun nombre ne figure dans la rangée réservée aux âges inconnus, cela ne signifie pas nécessairement que les déclarations d'âge et l'exploitation des données par âge ont été tout à fait exactes. C'est souvent une indication que l'on a attribué un âge aux personnes d'âge inconnu avant l'exploitation des données ou qu'elles ont été réparties proportionnellement entre les différents groupes après cette opération.

À l'inverse, lorsque le nombre des personnes d'âge inconnu est important, cela peut signifier que la proportion de naissances parmi les mères célibataires est élevée, étant donné qu'en pareil cas l'acte de naissance ne contient pas tous les renseignements concernant les parents.

Les déclarations par âge peuvent comporter des distorsions, du fait que l'âge de la mère au moment de la naissance d'un enfant (ou de la déclaration de naissance) est donné par année de naissance et non par date exacte (jour, mois et année).

Dans quelques pays, la classification par âges se réfère aux accouchements, et non aux naissances vivantes, ce qui conduit à un sous-dénombrement en cas de naissances gémellaires. Cette pratique nuit à la comparabilité des données, à la fois entre pays ou zones qui recourent à cette méthode et entre les données présentées dans le tableau 10 et celles du tableau 9.

La comparabilité des données selon le lieu de résidence (zone urbaine ou rurale) peut être limitée par les définitions nationales des termes «urbain» et «rural» utilisées pour la mise en tableaux de ces données. En l'absence d'indications contraires, on a supposé que les mêmes définitions avaient servi pour le recensement national de la population et pour l'établissement des statistiques de l'état civil pour chaque pays ou zone. Toutefois, il n'est pas exclu que, pour une zone ou un pays donné, des définitions différentes aient été retenues. Les définitions du terme «urbain» utilisées pour les recensements nationaux de population ont été présentées à la fin des notes techniques du tableau 6 lorsqu'elles étaient connues. Comme on l'a précisé dans les notes techniques relatives au tableau 6, ces définitions varient considérablement d'un pays ou d'une zone à l'autre.

Données publiées antérieurement : Les différentes éditions de l'*Annuaire démographique* regroupent les dernières statistiques dont on disposait à l'époque sur les naissances vivantes selon l'âge de la mère. Les données qui figurent dans le tableau 10 actualisent les données qui portaient sur les périodes suivantes :

Éditions	Années considérées
Édition spéciale sur les statistiques de la natalité (CD-ROM), 1999	1990 – 1998
Supplément historique (CD-ROM), 1997	1948 – 1997
1992	1983 – 1992
1986	1977 – 1988
1981	1972 – 1980
Supplément rétrospectif, 1979	1948 – 1977

Pour plus de détails concernant les années antérieures à 1948, se reporter à l'index historique.

10. Live births by age of mother, sex of the child and urban/rural residence: latest available year, 1993 - 2002

Naissances vivantes selon l'âge de la mère, le sexe de l'enfant et la résidence, urbaine/rurale: dernière année disponible, 1993 - 2002

(See notes at end of table.— Voir notes à la fin du tableau.)

Continent, country or area, year and age (in years) / Continent, pays ou zone, année et âge (en années)	Code[a]	Total			Urban - Urbaine			Rural - Rurale		
		Both sexes - Les deux sexes	Male - Masculin	Female - Féminin	Both sexes - Les deux sexes	Male - Masculin	Female - Féminin	Both sexes - Les deux sexes	Male - Masculin	Female - Féminin
AFRICA — AFRIQUE										
Egypt - Égypte										
1999										
Total	C	1 693 025	870 195	822 830	657 902	338 638	319 264	1 035 123	531 557	503 566
0 - 19	C	58 512	29 955	28 557	20 778	10 785	9 993	37 734	19 170	18 564
20 - 24	C	449 584	231 642	217 942	169 931	87 629	82 302	279 653	144 013	135 640
25 - 29	C	491 555	252 991	238 564	187 184	96 644	90 540	304 371	156 347	148 024
30 - 34	C	309 972	159 186	150 786	124 244	63 653	60 591	185 728	95 533	90 195
35 - 39	C	163 663	83 988	79 675	61 243	31 423	29 820	102 420	52 565	49 855
40 - 44	C	38 298	19 828	18 470	13 614	7 005	6 609	24 684	12 823	11 861
45+	C	8 219	4 201	4 018	2 341	1 193	1 148	5 878	3 008	2 870
Unk.- Inc.	C	173 222	88 404	84 818	78 567	40 306	38 261	94 655	48 098	46 557
Libyan Arab Jamahiriya - Jamahiriya arabe libyenne										
2002										
Total	C	111 053	57 722	53 331	...	...	...	...	...	...
0 - 19	C	1 196	592	604	...	...	...	...	...	...
20 - 24	C	15 018	7 845	7 173	...	...	...	...	...	...
25 - 29	C	32 713	16 877	15 836	...	...	...	...	...	...
30 - 34	C	33 325	17 384	15 941	...	...	...	...	...	...
35 - 39	C	18 702	9 777	8 925	...	...	...	...	...	...
40 - 44	C	6 422	3 296	3 126	...	...	...	...	...	...
45+	C	676	364	312	...	...	...	...	...	...
Unk.- Inc.	C	3 001	1 587	1 414	...	...	...	...	...	...
Mauritius - Maurice										
2002										
Total	C	19 799	10 034	9 765	...	...	...	...	...	...
0 - 14	C	33	17	16	...	...	...	...	...	...
15 - 19	C	1 697	848	849	...	...	...	...	...	...
20 - 24	C	6 583	3 340	3 243	...	...	...	...	...	...
25 - 29	C	5 773	2 923	2 850	...	...	...	...	...	...
30 - 34	C	3 449	1 758	1 691	...	...	...	...	...	...
35 - 39	C	1 781	891	890	...	...	...	...	...	...
40 - 44	C	413	212	201	...	...	...	...	...	...
45 - 49	C	20	12	8	...	...	...	...	...	...
50+	C	1	-	1	...	...	...	...	...	...
Unk.- Inc.	C	49	33	16	...	...	...	...	...	...
Morocco - Maroc										
1999										
Total	C	529 383	270 719	258 664	256 501	131 296	125 205	272 069	138 979	133 090
0 - 14	C	494	274	220	188	104	84	303	167	136
15 - 19	C	48 067	24 686	23 381	18 485	9 474	9 011	29 529	15 182	14 347
20 - 24	C	125 963	64 787	61 176	55 702	28 748	26 954	70 091	35 952	34 139
25 - 29	C	134 263	68 787	65 476	67 453	34 607	32 846	66 585	34 060	32 525
30 - 34	C	116 005	59 164	56 841	62 250	31 782	30 468	53 558	27 260	26 298
35 - 39	C	74 432	37 762	36 670	39 356	19 988	19 368	34 957	17 710	17 247
40 - 44	C	24 443	12 351	12 092	11 339	5 732	5 607	13 071	6 606	6 465
45 - 49	C	4 555	2 327	2 228	1 431	712	719	3 118	1 612	1 506
50+	C	1 138	566	572	286	141	145	851	425	426
Unk.- Inc.	C	23	15	8	11	8	3	6	5	1
Réunion										
2001										
Total	C	14 541	7 356	7 185	...	...	...	...	...	...
0 - 19	C	1 303	644	659	...	...	...	...	...	...
20 - 24	C	3 284	1 687	1 597	...	...	...	...	...	...
25 - 29	C	3 835	1 892	1 943	...	...	...	...	...	...
30 - 34	C	3 545	1 806	1 739	...	...	...	...	...	...
35 - 39	C	2 054	1 062	992	...	...	...	...	...	...

10. Live births by age of mother, sex of the child and urban/rural residence: latest available year, 1993 - 2002
Naissances vivantes selon l'âge de la mère, le sexe de l'enfant et la résidence, urbaine/rurale: dernière année disponible, 1993 - 2002 (continued — suite)

(See notes at end of table.— Voir notes à la fin du tableau.)

Continent, country or area, year and age (in years) / Continent, pays ou zone, année et âge (en années)	Code[a]	Total			Urban - Urbaine			Rural - Rurale		
		Both sexes - Les deux sexes	Male - Masculin	Female - Féminin	Both sexes - Les deux sexes	Male - Masculin	Female - Féminin	Both sexes - Les deux sexes	Male - Masculin	Female - Féminin
AFRICA — AFRIQUE										
Réunion										
2001										
40+	C	520	265	255	...	...	...	...	...	...
Saint Helena ex. dep. - Sainte-Hélène sans dép.										
2000										
Total	C	56	32	24	...	...	...	...	...	...
15 - 19	C	7	3	4	...	...	...	...	...	...
20 - 24	C	16	10	6	...	...	...	...	...	...
25 - 29	C	12	5	7	...	...	...	...	...	...
30 - 34	C	13	9	4	...	...	...	...	...	...
35 - 39	C	7	4	3	...	...	...	...	...	...
40 - 44	C	1	1	-	...	...	...	...	...	...
Seychelles										
1993										
Total	+C	1 689	860	829	...	...	...	...	...	...
0 - 14	+C	3	2	1	...	...	...	...	...	...
15 - 19	+C	271	157	114	...	...	...	...	...	...
20 - 24	+C	522	254	268	...	...	...	...	...	...
25 - 29	+C	473	246	227	...	...	...	...	...	...
30 - 34	+C	275	137	138	...	...	...	...	...	...
35 - 39	+C	126	56	70	...	...	...	...	...	...
40 - 44	+C	16	7	9	...	...	...	...	...	...
45+	+C	3	1	2	...	...	...	...	...	...
South Africa - Afrique du Sud										
1999										
Total	U	*1 363 800*	...	...	...	...	...	...	...	...
15 - 19	U	*195 560*	...	...	...	...	...	...	...	...
20 - 24	U	*362 872*	...	...	...	...	...	...	...	...
25 - 29	U	*339 586*	...	...	...	...	...	...	...	...
30 - 34	U	*246 119*	...	...	...	...	...	...	...	...
35 - 39	U	*140 344*	...	...	...	...	...	...	...	...
40 - 44	U	*52 428*	...	...	...	...	...	...	...	...
45 - 49	U	*13 437*	...	...	...	...	...	...	...	...
50+	U	*4 439*	...	...	...	...	...	...	...	...
Unk.- Inc.	U	*9 015*	...	...	...	...	...	...	...	...
Swaziland[1]										
1997										
Total	I	31 087	...	...	6 915	...	...	24 172	...	...
15 - 19	I	4 192	...	...	897	...	...	3 295	...	...
20 - 24	I	8 927	...	...	2 107	...	...	6 820	...	...
25 - 29	I	7 537	...	...	1 895	...	...	5 642	...	...
30 - 34	I	4 893	...	...	1 021	...	...	3 872	...	...
35 - 39	I	3 413	...	...	664	...	...	2 749	...	...
40 - 44	I	1 247	...	...	194	...	...	1 053	...	...
45 - 49	I	564	...	...	78	...	...	486	...	...
50+	I	230	...	...	32	...	...	198	...	...
Unk.- Inc.	I	84	...	...	27	...	...	57	...	...
Tunisia - Tunisie										
1998										
Total	C	166 718	...	...	...	...	...	...	...	...
15 - 19	C	3 650	...	...	...	...	...	...	...	...
20 - 24	C	28 802	...	...	...	...	...	...	...	...
25 - 29	C	44 260	...	...	...	...	...	...	...	...
30 - 34	C	39 518	...	...	...	...	...	...	...	...
35 - 39	C	19 869	...	...	...	...	...	...	...	...
40 - 44	C	5 327	...	...	...	...	...	...	...	...

10. Live births by age of mother, sex of the child and urban/rural residence: latest available year, 1993 - 2002

Naissances vivantes selon l'âge de la mère, le sexe de l'enfant et la résidence, urbaine/rurale: dernière année disponible, 1993 - 2002 (continued — suite)

(See notes at end of table.— Voir notes à la fin du tableau.)

Continent, country or area, year and age (in years) Continent, pays ou zone, année et âge (en années)	Code[a]	Total			Urban - Urbaine			Rural - Rurale		
		Both sexes - Les deux sexes	Male - Masculin	Female - Féminin	Both sexes - Les deux sexes	Male - Masculin	Female - Féminin	Both sexes - Les deux sexes	Male - Masculin	Female - Féminin
AFRICA — AFRIQUE										
Tunisia - Tunisie										
1998										
45+	C	650	...	...	...	...	...	...	...	...
Unk.- Inc.	C	2 446	...	...	...	...	...	...	...	...
AMERICA, NORTH — AMERIQUE DU NORD										
Anguilla										
2002										
Total	+C	169	...	...	...	...	...	...	...	...
0 - 14	+C	1	...	...	...	...	...	...	...	...
15 - 19	+C	22	...	...	...	...	...	...	...	...
20 - 24	+C	42	...	...	...	...	...	...	...	...
25 - 29	+C	41	...	...	...	...	...	...	...	...
30 - 34	+C	40	...	...	...	...	...	...	...	...
35 - 39	+C	16	...	...	...	...	...	...	...	...
40+	+C	7	...	...	...	...	...	...	...	...
Antigua and Barbuda - Antigua-et-Barbuda										
1995										
Total	+C	1 347	...	...	...	...	...	...	...	...
0 - 14	+C	4	...	...	...	...	...	...	...	...
15 - 19	+C	209	...	...	...	...	...	...	...	...
20 - 24	+C	377	...	...	...	...	...	...	...	...
25 - 29	+C	350	...	...	...	...	...	...	...	...
30 - 34	+C	246	...	...	...	...	...	...	...	...
35 - 39	+C	128	...	...	...	...	...	...	...	...
40 - 44	+C	23	...	...	...	...	...	...	...	...
45+	+C	2	...	...	...	...	...	...	...	...
Unk.- Inc.	+C	8	...	...	...	...	...	...	...	...
Aruba										
2002										
Total	+U	1 315	...	...	...	...	...	...	...	...
15 - 19	+U	126	...	...	...	...	...	...	...	...
20 - 24	+U	309	...	...	...	...	...	...	...	...
25 - 29	+U	321	...	...	...	...	...	...	...	...
30 - 34	+U	327	...	...	...	...	...	...	...	...
35 - 39	+U	198	...	...	...	...	...	...	...	...
40 - 44	+U	29	...	...	...	...	...	...	...	...
45 - 49	+U	5	...	...	...	...	...	...	...	...
Bahamas										
2001										
Total	U	4 495	2 305	2 190	...	...	...	...	...	...
0 - 14	U	5	3	2	...	...	...	...	...	...
15 - 19	U	568	282	286	...	...	...	...	...	...
20 - 24	U	1 120	567	553	...	...	...	...	...	...
25 - 29	U	1 154	602	552	...	...	...	...	...	...
30 - 34	U	904	460	444	...	...	...	...	...	...
35 - 39	U	601	319	282	...	...	...	...	...	...
40 - 44	U	125	63	62	...	...	...	...	...	...
45 - 49	U	10	5	5	...	...	...	...	...	...
Unk.- Inc.	U	8	4	4	...	...	...	...	...	...
Belize										
2002										
Total	U	7 356	...	...	...	...	...	...	...	...
0 - 14	U	22	...	...	...	...	...	...	...	...
15 - 19	U	1 237	...	...	...	...	...	...	...	...
20 - 24	U	2 233	...	...	...	...	...	...	...	...

10. Live births by age of mother, sex of the child and urban/rural residence: latest available year, 1993 - 2002
Naissances vivantes selon l'âge de la mère, le sexe de l'enfant et la résidence, urbaine/rurale: dernière année disponible, 1993 - 2002 (continued — suite)

(See notes at end of table.— Voir notes à la fin du tableau.)

Continent, country or area, year and age (in years) / Continent, pays ou zone, année et âge (en années)	Code[a]	Total			Urban - Urbaine			Rural - Rurale		
		Both sexes - Les deux sexes	Male - Masculin	Female - Féminin	Both sexes - Les deux sexes	Male - Masculin	Female - Féminin	Both sexes - Les deux sexes	Male - Masculin	Female - Féminin
AMERICA, NORTH — AMERIQUE DU NORD										
Belize										
2002										
25 - 29	U	1 712	...	...	...	...	...	...	...	...
30 - 34	U	1 106	...	...	...	...	...	...	...	...
35 - 39	U	566	...	...	...	...	...	...	...	...
40 - 44	U	165	...	...	...	...	...	...	...	...
45+	U	17	...	...	...	...	...	...	...	...
Unk.- Inc.	U	298	...	...	...	...	...	...	...	...
Bermuda - Bermudes										
2002										
Total	C	830	...	...	...	...	...	...	...	...
15 - 19	C	57	...	...	...	...	...	...	...	...
20 - 24	C	130	...	...	...	...	...	...	...	...
25 - 29	C	197	...	...	...	...	...	...	...	...
30 - 34	C	261	...	...	...	...	...	...	...	...
35 - 39	C	146	...	...	...	...	...	...	...	...
40+	C	39	...	...	...	...	...	...	...	...
Canada[2]										
2001										
Total	C	333 744	171 153	162 591	...	...	...	...	...	...
0 - 14	C	116	67	49	...	...	...	...	...	...
15 - 19	C	16 456	8 511	7 945	...	...	...	...	...	...
20 - 24	C	58 186	26 962	28 494	...	...	...	...	...	...
25 - 29	C	102 453	52 677	49 776	...	...	...	...	...	...
30 - 34	C	101 460	52 039	49 421	...	...	...	...	...	...
35 - 39	C	46 704	23 913	22 791	...	...	...	...	...	...
40 - 44	C	8 043	4 094	3 949	...	...	...	...	...	...
45 - 49	C	299	146	153	...	...	...	...	...	...
50+	C	5	3	2	...	...	...	...	...	...
Unk.- Inc.	C	22	11	11	...	...	...	...	...	...
Cayman Islands - Îles Caïmanes										
1994										
Total	+C	531	246	285	...	...	...	...	...	...
0 - 14	+C	2	1	1	...	...	...	...	...	...
15 - 19	+C	62	31	31	...	...	...	...	...	...
20 - 24	+C	136	69	67	...	...	...	...	...	...
25 - 29	+C	139	55	84	...	...	...	...	...	...
30 - 34	+C	142	64	78	...	...	...	...	...	...
35 - 39	+C	37	20	17	...	...	...	...	...	...
40+	+C	13	6	7	...	...	...	...	...	...
Costa Rica										
2002										
Total	C	71 144	...	...	...	...	...	...	...	...
0 - 14	C	473	...	...	...	...	...	...	...	...
15 - 19	C	13 981	...	...	...	...	...	...	...	...
20 - 24	C	21 408	...	...	...	...	...	...	...	...
25 - 29	C	16 046	...	...	...	...	...	...	...	...
30 - 34	C	11 346	...	...	...	...	...	...	...	...
35 - 39	C	6 050	...	...	...	...	...	...	...	...
40 - 44	C	1 517	...	...	...	...	...	...	...	...
45+	C	103	...	...	...	...	...	...	...	...
Unk.- Inc.	C	220	...	...	...	...	...	...	...	...
Cuba										
2000										
Total	C	143 528	74 610	68 918	104 521	54 415	50 106	39 007	20 195	18 812
0 - 14	C	510	285	225	301	166	135	209	119	90

10. Live births by age of mother, sex of the child and urban/rural residence: latest available year, 1993 - 2002
Naissances vivantes selon l'âge de la mère, le sexe de l'enfant et la résidence, urbaine/rurale: dernière année disponible, 1993 - 2002 (continued — suite)

(See notes at end of table.— Voir notes à la fin du tableau.)

Continent, country or area, year and age (in years) / Continent, pays ou zone, année et âge (en années)	Code[a]	Total			Urban - Urbaine			Rural - Rurale		
		Both sexes - Les deux sexes	Male - Masculin	Female - Féminin	Both sexes - Les deux sexes	Male - Masculin	Female - Féminin	Both sexes - Les deux sexes	Male - Masculin	Female - Féminin
AMERICA, NORTH — AMERIQUE DU NORD										
Cuba										
2000										
15 - 19	C	18 235	9 556	8 679	11 352	5 976	5 376	6 883	3 580	3 303
20 - 24	C	35 317	18 449	16 868	24 907	13 035	11 872	10 410	5 414	4 996
25 - 29	C	45 965	23 902	22 063	34 159	17 766	16 393	11 806	6 136	5 670
30 - 34	C	30 253	15 561	14 692	23 367	12 082	11 285	6 886	3 479	3 407
35 - 39	C	11 750	6 068	5 682	9 310	4 808	4 502	2 440	1 260	1 180
40 - 44	C	1 343	706	637	1 004	516	488	339	190	149
45 - 49	C	63	33	30	42	23	19	21	10	11
50+	C	24	11	13	16	7	9	8	4	4
Unk.- Inc.	C	68	39	29	63	36	27	5	3	2
Dominican Republic - République dominicaine										
1999										
Total	+U	*193 418*	*99 127*	*94 291*	...	...	...	...	...	...
0 - 14	+U	*1 665*	*909*	*756*	...	...	...	...	...	...
15 - 19	+U	*23 353*	*11 880*	*11 473*	...	...	...	...	...	...
20 - 24	+U	*53 145*	*27 213*	*25 932*	...	...	...	...	...	...
25 - 29	+U	*51 520*	*26 568*	*24 952*	...	...	...	...	...	...
30 - 34	+U	*32 644*	*16 649*	*15 995*	...	...	...	...	...	...
35 - 39	+U	*15 335*	*7 867*	*7 468*	...	...	...	...	...	...
40 - 44	+U	*6 015*	*3 124*	*2 891*	...	...	...	...	...	...
45 - 49	+U	*2 624*	*1 388*	*1 236*	...	...	...	...	...	...
50+	+U	*2 558*	*1 238*	*1 320*	...	...	...	...	...	...
Unk.- Inc.	+U	*4 559*	*2 291*	*2 268*	...	...	...	...	...	...
El Salvador										
2002										
Total	C	129 363	66 851	62 512	77 779	40 176	37 603	51 584	26 675	24 909
0 - 14	C	1 186	581	605	621	299	322	565	282	283
15 - 19	C	25 542	13 279	12 263	14 502	7 535	6 967	11 040	5 744	5 296
20 - 24	C	40 401	21 083	19 318	24 898	13 025	11 873	15 503	8 058	7 445
25 - 29	C	31 654	16 280	15 374	19 858	10 244	9 614	11 796	6 036	5 760
30 - 34	C	18 046	9 178	8 868	11 235	5 673	5 562	6 811	3 505	3 306
35 - 39	C	9 049	4 701	4 348	5 043	2 602	2 441	4 006	2 099	1 907
40 - 44	C	2 998	1 480	1 518	1 391	672	719	1 607	808	799
45 - 49	C	304	168	136	118	63	55	186	105	81
50+	C	43	20	23	23	13	10	20	7	13
Unk.- Inc.	C	140	81	59	90	50	40	50	31	19
Greenland - Groenland										
1999										
Total	C	947	472	475	734	365	369	213	107	106
0 - 14	C	6	2	4	6	2	4	-	-	-
15 - 19	C	77	37	40	58	28	30	19	9	10
20 - 24	C	246	115	131	185	84	101	61	31	30
25 - 29	C	197	111	86	140	81	59	57	30	27
30 - 34	C	257	127	130	209	104	105	48	23	25
35 - 39	C	130	66	64	108	55	53	22	11	11
40 - 44	C	31	13	18	25	10	15	6	3	3
45 - 49	C	2	-	2	2	-	2	-	-	-
50+	C	1	1	-	1	1	-	-	-	-
Grenada - Grenade										
2000										
Total	+C	1 883	...	...	...	...	...	...	...	...
0 - 14	+C	9	...	...	...	...	...	...	...	...
15 - 19	+C	310	...	...	...	...	...	...	...	...

10. Live births by age of mother, sex of the child and urban/rural residence: latest available year, 1993 - 2002
Naissances vivantes selon l'âge de la mère, le sexe de l'enfant et la résidence, urbaine/rurale: dernière année disponible, 1993 - 2002 (continued — suite)

(See notes at end of table.— Voir notes à la fin du tableau.)

Continent, country or area, year and age (in years) / Continent, pays ou zone, année et âge (en années)	Code[a]	Total			Urban - Urbaine			Rural - Rurale		
		Both sexes - Les deux sexes	Male - Masculin	Female - Féminin	Both sexes - Les deux sexes	Male - Masculin	Female - Féminin	Both sexes - Les deux sexes	Male - Masculin	Female - Féminin
AMERICA, NORTH — AMERIQUE DU NORD										
Grenada - Grenade										
2000										
20 - 24	+C	490	...	...	...	...	...	...	...	...
25 - 29	+C	452	...	...	...	...	...	...	...	...
30 - 34	+C	339	...	...	...	...	...	...	...	...
35 - 39	+C	208	...	...	...	...	...	...	...	...
40 - 44	+C	73	...	...	...	...	...	...	...	...
45+	+C	2	...	...	...	...	...	...	...	...
Guadeloupe										
2002										
Total	C	6 995	3 551	3 444	...	...	...	...	...	...
0 - 14	C	13	8	5	...	...	...	...	...	...
15 - 19	C	409	190	219	...	...	...	...	...	...
20 - 24	C	1 114	561	553	...	...	...	...	...	...
25 - 29	C	1 976	1 022	954	...	...	...	...	...	...
30 - 34	C	1 880	928	952	...	...	...	...	...	...
35 - 39	C	1 252	653	599	...	...	...	...	...	...
40 - 44	C	332	178	154	...	...	...	...	...	...
45+	C	19	11	8	...	...	...	...	...	...
Guatemala										
1999										
Total	C	360 759	183 621	177 138	140 491	...	...	220 268	...	...
0 - 14	C	1 776	892	884	677	...	...	1 099	...	...
15 - 19	C	65 999	33 808	32 191	25 674	...	...	40 325	...	...
20 - 24	C	108 223	54 947	53 276	44 487	...	...	63 736	...	...
25 - 29	C	79 683	40 608	39 075	32 492	...	...	47 191	...	...
30 - 34	C	53 921	27 473	26 448	20 520	...	...	33 401	...	...
35 - 39	C	34 730	17 623	17 107	11 694	...	...	23 036	...	...
40 - 44	C	13 305	6 722	6 583	3 955	...	...	9 350	...	...
45 - 49	C	1 981	973	1 008	502	...	...	1 479	...	...
50+	C	557	288	269	119	...	...	438	...	...
Unk.- Inc.	C	584	287	297	371	...	...	213	...	...
Jamaica - Jamaïque										
1996										
Total	+C	54 164	...	...	...	...	...	...	...	...
0 - 14	+C	400	...	...	...	...	...	...	...	...
15 - 19	+C	10 760	...	...	...	...	...	...	...	...
20 - 24	+C	15 881	...	...	...	...	...	...	...	...
25 - 29	+C	12 949	...	...	...	...	...	...	...	...
30 - 34	+C	8 824	...	...	...	...	...	...	...	...
35 - 39	+C	4 277	...	...	...	...	...	...	...	...
40 - 44	+C	974	...	...	...	...	...	...	...	...
45+	+C	99	...	...	...	...	...	...	...	...
Martinique[3,4]										
2002										
Total	C	5 446	2 758	2 688	...	...	...	...	...	...
0 - 14	C	6	4	2	...	...	...	...	...	...
15 - 19	C	397	205	192	...	...	...	...	...	...
20 - 24	C	878	458	420	...	...	...	...	...	...
25 - 29	C	1 336	696	640	...	...	...	...	...	...
30 - 34	C	1 573	787	786	...	...	...	...	...	...
35 - 39	C	987	464	523	...	...	...	...	...	...
40 - 44	C	257	137	120	...	...	...	...	...	...
45+	C	12	7	5	...	...	...	...	...	...
Mexico - Mexique[5]										
2001										
Total	+U	2 767 610	1 390 066	1 377 544	1 749 126	...	...	748 772	...	...

328

10. Live births by age of mother, sex of the child and urban/rural residence: latest available year, 1993 - 2002
Naissances vivantes selon l'âge de la mère, le sexe de l'enfant et la résidence, urbaine/rurale: dernière année disponible, 1993 - 2002 (continued — suite)

(See notes at end of table.— Voir notes à la fin du tableau.)

Continent, country or area, year and age (in years) / Continent, pays ou zone, année et âge (en années)	Code[a]	Total Both sexes - Les deux sexes	Total Male - Masculin	Total Female - Féminin	Urban - Urbaine Both sexes - Les deux sexes	Urban - Urbaine Male - Masculin	Urban - Urbaine Female - Féminin	Rural - Rurale Both sexes - Les deux sexes	Rural - Rurale Male - Masculin	Rural - Rurale Female - Féminin
AMERICA, NORTH — AMERIQUE DU NORD										
Mexico - Mexique[5]										
2001										
0 - 14	+U	11 957	5 849	6 108	5 710	...	...	5 890	...	...
15 - 19	+U	427 057	216 654	210 403	280 505	...	...	137 276	...	...
20 - 24	+U	771 299	390 734	380 565	527 404	...	...	226 680	...	...
25 - 29	+U	669 560	339 399	330 161	477 010	...	...	175 740	...	...
30 - 34	+U	412 117	208 366	203 751	300 743	...	...	100 758	...	...
35 - 39	+U	191 541	96 588	94 953	126 531	...	...	60 366	...	...
40 - 44	+U	54 753	27 213	27 540	31 316	...	...	22 222	...	...
45 - 49	+U	8 213	4 048	4 165	3 895	...	...	4 157	...	...
50+	+U	2 611	1 234	1 377	1 155	...	...	1 380	...	...
Unk.- Inc.	+U	218 502	99 981	118 521	214 199	...	...	4 003	...	...
Nicaragua										
2002										
Total	+U	120 846	62 191	58 655	65 387	33 676	31 711	55 459	28 515	26 944
0 - 14	+U	1 030	522	508	538	273	265	492	249	243
15 - 19	+U	33 070	17 035	16 035	17 973	9 304	8 669	15 097	7 731	7 366
20 - 24	+U	40 075	20 693	19 382	22 040	11 347	10 693	18 035	9 346	8 689
25 - 29	+U	23 986	12 335	11 651	13 348	6 866	6 482	10 637	5 469	5 169
30 - 34	+U	13 091	6 817	6 274	7 159	3 748	3 411	5 932	3 069	2 863
35 - 39	+U	7 265	3 661	3 604	3 443	1 723	1 720	3 823	1 938	1 884
40 - 44	+U	1 966	957	1 009	793	374	419	1 173	583	590
45 - 49	+U	310	145	165	81	36	45	229	109	120
50+	+U	53	26	27	12	5	7	41	21	20
Panama										
1999										
Total	C	64 248	33 077	31 171	32 724	16 894	15 830	31 524	16 183	15 341
0 - 14	C	537	290	247	205	114	91	332	176	156
15 - 19	C	12 126	6 288	5 838	5 594	2 893	2 701	6 532	3 395	3 137
20 - 24	C	18 281	9 435	8 846	9 344	4 846	4 498	8 937	4 589	4 348
25 - 29	C	15 488	7 964	7 524	8 369	4 321	4 048	7 119	3 643	3 476
30 - 34	C	10 451	5 314	5 137	5 822	2 989	2 833	4 629	2 325	2 304
35 - 39	C	4 925	2 581	2 344	2 553	1 309	1 244	2 372	1 272	1 100
40 - 44	C	1 076	528	548	448	226	222	628	302	326
45 - 49	C	95	46	49	14	9	5	81	37	44
50+	C	23	9	14	1	...	1	22	9	13
Unk.- Inc.	C	1 246	622	624	374	187	187	872	435	437
2002										
Total	C	61 671	...	...	...	...	...	...	...	...
0 - 14	C	476	...	...	...	...	...	...	...	...
15 - 19	C	11 265	...	...	...	...	...	...	...	...
20 - 24	C	17 578	...	...	...	...	...	...	...	...
25 - 29	C	14 636	...	...	...	...	...	...	...	...
30 - 34	C	10 711	...	...	...	...	...	...	...	...
35 - 39	C	4 927	...	...	...	...	...	...	...	...
40 - 44	C	1 202	...	...	...	...	...	...	...	...
45 - 49	C	85	...	...	...	...	...	...	...	...
50+	C	22	...	...	...	...	...	...	...	...
Unk.- Inc.	C	769	...	...	...	...	...	...	...	...
Puerto Rico - Porto Rico[5]										
2000										
Total	C	59 460	30 593	28 867	30 464	15 589	14 875	28 967	14 991	13 976
0 - 14	C	272	155	117	115	62	53	156	93	63
15 - 19	C	11 118	5 735	5 383	4 972	2 552	2 420	6 140	3 181	2 959
20 - 24	C	19 423	10 005	9 418	9 360	4 804	4 556	10 057	5 197	4 860
25 - 29	C	15 152	7 806	7 346	8 167	4 169	3 998	6 983	3 637	3 346

10. Live births by age of mother, sex of the child and urban/rural residence: latest available year, 1993 - 2002
Naissances vivantes selon l'âge de la mère, le sexe de l'enfant et la résidence, urbaine/rurale: dernière année disponible, 1993 - 2002 (continued — suite)

(See notes at end of table.— Voir notes à la fin du tableau.)

Continent, country or area, year and age (in years) / Continent, pays ou zone, année et âge (en années)	Code[a]	Total			Urban - Urbaine			Rural - Rurale		
		Both sexes - Les deux sexes	Male - Masculin	Female - Féminin	Both sexes - Les deux sexes	Male - Masculin	Female - Féminin	Both sexes - Les deux sexes	Male - Masculin	Female - Féminin
AMERICA, NORTH — AMERIQUE DU NORD										
Puerto Rico - Porto Rico[5]										
2000										
30 - 34	C	8 902	4 515	4 387	5 123	2 586	2 537	3 779	1 929	1 850
35 - 39	C	3 762	1 974	1 788	2 243	1 176	1 067	1 518	797	721
40 - 44	C	748	362	386	437	218	219	311	144	167
45 - 49	C	29	14	15	18	7	11	10	7	3
Unk.- Inc.	C	54	27	27	29	15	14	13	6	7
2002										
Total	C	52 871	27 136	25 735	...	...	...	...	...	...
0 - 14	C	257	108	149	...	...	...	...	...	...
15 - 19	C	9 350	4 795	4 555	...	...	...	...	...	...
20 - 24	C	17 152	8 825	8 327	...	...	...	...	...	...
25 - 29	C	13 419	6 928	6 491	...	...	...	...	...	...
30 - 34	C	8 314	4 245	4 069	...	...	...	...	...	...
35 - 39	C	3 570	1 815	1 755	...	...	...	...	...	...
40 - 44	C	758	390	368	...	...	...	...	...	...
45 - 49	C	27	14	13	...	...	...	...	...	...
50+	C	1	-	1	...	...	...	...	...	...
Unk.- Inc.	C	23	16	7	...	...	...	...	...	...
Saint Kitts and Nevis - Saint-Kitts-et-Nevis										
2001										
Total	+C	803	...	...	...	...	...	...	...	...
10 - 14	+C	3	...	...	...	...	...	...	...	...
15 - 19	+C	164	...	...	...	...	...	...	...	...
20 - 24	+C	241	...	...	...	...	...	...	...	...
25 - 29	+C	166	...	...	...	...	...	...	...	...
30 - 34	+C	148	...	...	...	...	...	...	...	...
35 - 39	+C	67	...	...	...	...	...	...	...	...
40+	+C	14	...	...	...	...	...	...	...	...
Saint Lucia - Sainte-Lucie[6]										
2002										
Total	C	2 529	1 299	1 230	...	...	...	...	...	...
0 - 14	C	8	5	3	...	...	...	...	...	...
15 - 19	C	447	223	224	...	...	...	...	...	...
20 - 24	C	686	356	330	...	...	...	...	...	...
25 - 29	C	569	284	285	...	...	...	...	...	...
30 - 34	C	469	238	231	...	...	...	...	...	...
35 - 39	C	277	156	121	...	...	...	...	...	...
40 - 44	C	71	36	35	...	...	...	...	...	...
45 - 49	C	2	1	1	...	...	...	...	...	...
Saint Vincent and the Grenadines - Saint Vincent-et-les Grenadines[6]										
2002										
Total	+C	1 985	1 002	983	...	...	...	...	...	...
0 - 14	+C	13	1	12	...	...	...	...	...	...
15 - 19	+C	412	203	209	...	...	...	...	...	...
20 - 24	+C	551	301	250	...	...	...	...	...	...
25 - 29	+C	466	230	236	...	...	...	...	...	...
30 - 34	+C	319	147	172	...	...	...	...	...	...
35 - 39	+C	175	88	87	...	...	...	...	...	...
40 - 44	+C	37	26	11	...	...	...	...	...	...
45 - 49	+C	4	1	3	...	...	...	...	...	...

10. Live births by age of mother, sex of the child and urban/rural residence: latest available year, 1993 - 2002
Naissances vivantes selon l'âge de la mère, le sexe de l'enfant et la résidence, urbaine/rurale: dernière année disponible, 1993 - 2002 (continued — suite)

(See notes at end of table.— Voir notes à la fin du tableau.)

Continent, country or area, year and age (in years) / Continent, pays ou zone, année et âge (en années)	Code[a]	Total			Urban - Urbaine			Rural - Rurale		
		Both sexes - Les deux sexes	Male - Masculin	Female - Féminin	Both sexes - Les deux sexes	Male - Masculin	Female - Féminin	Both sexes - Les deux sexes	Male - Masculin	Female - Féminin
AMERICA, NORTH — AMERIQUE DU NORD										
Saint Vincent and the Grenadines - Saint Vincent-et-les Grenadines[6]										
2002										
Unk.- Inc.	+C	8	5	3	...	...	...	...	...	...
Trinidad and Tobago - Trinité-et-Tobago										
1997										
Total	C	18 452	9 343	9 109	...	...	...	...	...	...
0 - 14	C	37	20	17	...	...	...	...	...	...
15 - 19	C	2 588	1 323	1 265	...	...	...	...	...	...
20 - 24	C	5 353	2 721	2 632	...	...	...	...	...	...
25 - 29	C	4 519	2 297	2 222	...	...	...	...	...	...
30 - 34	C	3 678	1 877	1 801	...	...	...	...	...	...
35 - 39	C	1 804	879	925	...	...	...	...	...	...
40 - 44	C	417	198	219	...	...	...	...	...	...
45+	C	24	11	13	...	...	...	...	...	...
Unk.- Inc.	C	32	17	15	...	...	...	...	...	...
United States - États-Unis										
2002										
Total	C	4 021 726	...	...	...	...	...	...	...	...
0 - 14	C	7 315	...	...	...	...	...	...	...	...
15 - 19	C	425 493	...	...	...	...	...	...	...	...
20 - 24	C	1 022 106	...	...	...	...	...	...	...	...
25 - 29	C	1 060 391	...	...	...	...	...	...	...	...
30 - 34	C	951 219	...	...	...	...	...	...	...	...
35 - 39	C	453 927	...	...	...	...	...	...	...	...
40 - 44	C	95 788	...	...	...	...	...	...	...	...
45 - 49	C	5 224	...	...	...	...	...	...	...	...
50+	C	263	...	...	...	...	...	...	...	...
United States Virgin Islands - Îles Vierges américaines										
1993										
Total	C	2 529	1 290	1 239	...	...	...	...	...	...
0 - 14	C	18	7	11	...	...	...	...	...	...
15 - 19	C	404	201	203	...	...	...	...	...	...
20 - 24	C	733	377	356	...	...	...	...	...	...
25 - 29	C	612	319	293	...	...	...	...	...	...
30 - 34	C	462	232	230	...	...	...	...	...	...
35 - 39	C	227	123	104	...	...	...	...	...	...
40+	C	42	17	25	...	...	...	...	...	...
Unk.- Inc.	C	31	14	17	...	...	...	...	...	...
AMERICA, SOUTH — AMERIQUE DU SUD										
Argentina - Argentine										
2000										
Total	C	701 878	...	...	...	...	...	...	...	...
0 - 14	C	3 208	...	...	...	...	...	...	...	...
15 - 19	C	103 129	...	...	...	...	...	...	...	...
20 - 24	C	192 871	...	...	...	...	...	...	...	...
25 - 29	C	176 768	...	...	...	...	...	...	...	...
30 - 34	C	129 374	...	...	...	...	...	...	...	...

10. Live births by age of mother, sex of the child and urban/rural residence: latest available year, 1993 - 2002
Naissances vivantes selon l'âge de la mère, le sexe de l'enfant et la résidence, urbaine/rurale: dernière année disponible, 1993 - 2002 (continued — suite)

(See notes at end of table.— Voir notes à la fin du tableau.)

Continent, country or area, year and age (in years) Continent, pays ou zone, année et âge (en années)	Code[a]	Total			Urban - Urbaine			Rural - Rurale		
		Both sexes - Les deux sexes	Male - Masculin	Female - Féminin	Both sexes - Les deux sexes	Male - Masculin	Female - Féminin	Both sexes - Les deux sexes	Male - Masculin	Female - Féminin
AMERICA, SOUTH — AMERIQUE DU SUD										
Argentina - Argentine										
2000										
35 - 39	C	69 733	...	...	...	...	...	...	...	...
40 - 44	C	19 767	...	...	...	...	...	...	...	...
45 - 49	C	1 575	...	...	...	...	...	...	...	...
50+	C	163	...	...	...	...	...	...	...	...
Unk.- Inc.	C	5 290	...	...	...	...	...	...	...	...
Brazil - Brésil[6,7]										
2001										
Total	U	2 510 940	1 285 384	1 225 556	...	...	...	...	...	...
0 - 14	U	17 239	8 809	8 430	...	...	...	...	...	...
15 - 19	U	515 653	264 754	250 899	...	...	...	...	...	...
20 - 24	U	771 703	395 195	376 508	...	...	...	...	...	...
25 - 29	U	585 318	299 717	285 601	...	...	...	...	...	...
30 - 34	U	370 368	189 143	181 225	...	...	...	...	...	...
35 - 39	U	179 495	91 690	87 805	...	...	...	...	...	...
40 - 44	U	46 386	23 383	23 003	...	...	...	...	...	...
45 - 49	U	4 123	2 053	2 070	...	...	...	...	...	...
50+	U	367	191	176	...	...	...	...	...	...
Unk.- Inc.	U	20 288	10 449	9 839	...	...	...	...	...	...
Chile - Chili										
2002										
Total	C	238 981	121 975	117 006	...	...	...	...	...	...
0 - 14	C	1 118	563	555	...	...	...	...	...	...
15 - 19	C	36 500	18 701	17 799	...	...	...	...	...	...
20 - 24	C	55 414	28 196	27 218	...	...	...	...	...	...
25 - 29	C	58 775	29 923	28 852	...	...	...	...	...	...
30 - 34	C	49 575	25 480	24 095	...	...	...	...	...	...
35 - 39	C	29 450	14 932	14 518	...	...	...	...	...	...
40 - 44	C	7 821	4 017	3 804	...	...	...	...	...	...
45 - 49	C	326	162	164	...	...	...	...	...	...
50+	C	2	1	1	...	...	...	...	...	...
Colombia - Colombie[5]										
2002										
Total	U	678 388	347 990	330 398	523 650	268 359	255 291	142 356	73 192	69 164
0 - 14	U	5 457	2 776	2 681	3 604	1 846	1 758	1 697	853	844
15 - 19	U	144 129	74 098	70 031	106 418	54 667	51 751	34 956	18 028	16 928
20 - 24	U	201 035	103 261	97 774	155 033	79 426	75 607	42 713	22 087	20 626
25 - 29	U	147 145	75 435	71 710	116 606	59 719	56 887	28 136	14 431	13 705
30 - 34	U	103 280	53 144	50 136	82 903	42 745	40 158	18 756	9 545	9 211
35 - 39	U	56 005	28 493	27 512	44 392	22 577	21 815	10 732	5 493	5 239
40 - 44	U	14 539	7 355	7 184	10 714	5 396	5 318	3 580	1 824	1 756
45 - 49	U	1 143	576	567	749	380	369	371	188	183
50+	U	69	33	36	51	25	26	16	8	8
Unk.- Inc.	U	5 586	2 819	2 767	3 180	1 578	1 602	1 399	735	664
Ecuador - Équateur[8]										
2002										
Total	U	183 792	93 685	90 107	143 377	73 174	70 203	40 415	20 511	19 904
0 - 14	U	630	332	298	497	263	234	133	69	64
15 - 19	U	30 398	15 470	14 928	23 225	11 802	11 423	7 173	3 668	3 505
20 - 24	U	56 418	28 872	27 546	44 120	22 666	21 454	12 298	6 206	6 092
25 - 29	U	41 894	21 307	20 587	33 268	16 960	16 308	8 626	4 347	4 279
30 - 34	U	28 479	14 458	14 021	22 643	11 472	11 171	5 836	2 986	2 850
35 - 39	U	15 576	7 932	7 644	11 767	5 982	5 785	3 809	1 950	1 859
40 - 44	U	5 397	2 731	2 666	3 688	1 880	1 808	1 709	851	858
45 - 49	U	765	378	387	462	220	242	303	158	145
Unk.- Inc.	U	4 235	2 205	2 030	3 707	1 929	1 778	528	276	252

10. Live births by age of mother, sex of the child and urban/rural residence: latest available year, 1993 - 2002
Naissances vivantes selon l'âge de la mère, le sexe de l'enfant et la résidence, urbaine/rurale: dernière année disponible, 1993 - 2002 (continued — suite)

(See notes at end of table.— Voir notes à la fin du tableau.)

Continent, country or area, year and age (in years) / Continent, pays ou zone, année et âge (en années)	Code[a]	Total			Urban - Urbaine			Rural - Rurale		
		Both sexes - Les deux sexes	Male - Masculin	Female - Féminin	Both sexes - Les deux sexes	Male - Masculin	Female - Féminin	Both sexes - Les deux sexes	Male - Masculin	Female - Féminin
AMERICA, SOUTH — AMERIQUE DU SUD										
French Guiana - Guyane française[3]										
2002										
Total	C	5 249	2 648	2 601	...	...	...	...	...	...
0 - 14	C	64	32	32	...	...	...	...	...	...
15 - 19	C	830	419	411	...	...	...	...	...	...
20 - 24	C	1 162	578	584	...	...	...	...	...	...
25 - 29	C	1 291	664	627	...	...	...	...	...	...
30 - 34	C	1 061	531	530	...	...	...	...	...	...
35 - 39	C	664	333	331	...	...	...	...	...	...
40 - 44	C	165	87	78	...	...	...	...	...	...
45 - 49	C	12	4	8	...	...	...	...	...	...
Peru - Pérou[9]										
2002										
Total	+U	318 358	164 087	154 271	...	...	...	...	...	...
0 - 14	+U	886	456	430	...	...	...	...	...	...
15 - 19	+U	43 637	22 491	21 146	...	...	...	...	...	...
20 - 24	+U	85 841	44 456	41 385	...	...	...	...	...	...
25 - 29	+U	78 626	40 542	38 084	...	...	...	...	...	...
30 - 34	+U	58 143	29 859	28 284	...	...	...	...	...	...
35 - 39	+U	34 685	17 824	16 861	...	...	...	...	...	...
40 - 44	+U	11 610	6 007	5 603	...	...	...	...	...	...
45 - 49	+U	1 272	633	639	...	...	...	...	...	...
50+	+U	189	100	89	...	...	...	...	...	...
Unk.- Inc.	+U	3 460	1 719	1 750	...	...	...	...	...	...
Suriname										
2000										
Total	C	9 804	...	...	6 018	...	...	3 786	...	...
0 - 14	C	52	...	...	31	...	...	21	...	...
15 - 19	C	1 495	...	...	904	...	...	591	...	...
20 - 24	C	2 652	...	...	1 720	...	...	932	...	...
25 - 29	C	2 395	...	...	1 606	...	...	789	...	...
30 - 34	C	1 717	...	...	1 108	...	...	609	...	...
35 - 39	C	830	...	...	536	...	...	294	...	...
40 - 44	C	190	...	...	108	...	...	82	...	...
45+	C	18	...	...	1	...	...	17	...	...
Unk.- Inc.	C	455	...	...	4	...	...	451	...	...
Uruguay										
2002										
Total	+C	51 997	...	...	...	...	...	...	...	...
0 - 14	+C	207	...	...	...	...	...	...	...	...
15 - 19	+C	8 226	...	...	...	...	...	...	...	...
20 - 24	+C	13 117	...	...	...	...	...	...	...	...
25 - 29	+C	13 033	...	...	...	...	...	...	...	...
30 - 34	+C	9 954	...	...	...	...	...	...	...	...
35 - 39	+C	5 395	...	...	...	...	...	...	...	...
40 - 44	+C	1 473	...	...	...	...	...	...	...	...
45 - 49	+C	79	...	...	...	...	...	...	...	...
50+	+C	4	...	...	...	...	...	...	...	...
Unk.- Inc.	+C	508	...	...	...	...	...	...	...	...
Venezuela[7]										
2002										
Total	C	492 678	254 969	237 709	...	...	...	...	...	...
0 - 14	C	5 148	2 660	2 488	...	...	...	...	...	...
15 - 19	C	100 062	51 874	48 188	...	...	...	...	...	...
20 - 24	C	146 417	75 965	70 452	...	...	...	...	...	...
25 - 29	C	110 318	56 888	53 430	...	...	...	...	...	...

10. Live births by age of mother, sex of the child and urban/rural residence: latest available year, 1993 - 2002

Naissances vivantes selon l'âge de la mère, le sexe de l'enfant et la résidence, urbaine/rurale: dernière année disponible, 1993 - 2002 (continued — suite)

(See notes at end of table.— Voir notes à la fin du tableau.)

Continent, country or area, year and age (in years) / Continent, pays ou zone, année et âge (en années)	Code[a]	Total Both sexes - Les deux sexes	Total Male - Masculin	Total Female - Féminin	Urban - Urbaine Both sexes - Les deux sexes	Urban - Urbaine Male - Masculin	Urban - Urbaine Female - Féminin	Rural - Rurale Both sexes - Les deux sexes	Rural - Rurale Male - Masculin	Rural - Rurale Female - Féminin
AMERICA, SOUTH — AMERIQUE DU SUD										
Venezuela[7]										
2002										
30 - 34	C	73 522	38 081	35 441	...	...	...	...	...	...
35 - 39	C	36 756	18 951	17 805	...	...	...	...	...	...
40 - 44	C	10 443	5 408	5 035	...	...	...	...	...	...
45 - 49	C	1 376	685	691	...	...	...	...	...	...
50+	C	412	186	226	...	...	...	...	...	...
Unk.- Inc.	C	8 224	4 271	3 953	...	...	...	...	...	...
ASIA — ASIE										
Armenia - Arménie[10]										
2000										
Total	C	34 276	...	...	21 390	...	...	12 886	...	...
15 - 19	C	4 937	...	...	2 673	...	...	2 264	...	...
20 - 24	C	16 183	...	...	10 067	...	...	6 116	...	...
25 - 29	C	7 562	...	...	5 029	...	...	2 533	...	...
30 - 34	C	3 292	...	...	2 100	...	...	1 192	...	...
35 - 39	C	1 765	...	...	1 154	...	...	611	...	...
40 - 44	C	501	...	...	343	...	...	158	...	...
45 - 49	C	21	...	...	13	...	...	8	...	...
50+	C	15	...	...	11	...	...	4	...	...
Azerbaijan - Azerbaïdjan[10]										
2002										
Total	+C	110 715	59 742	50 973	49 733	26 985	22 748	60 982	32 757	28 225
15 - 19	+C	11 076	5 765	5 311	4 176	2 186	1 990	6 900	3 579	3 321
20 - 24	+C	44 244	23 283	20 961	19 468	10 287	9 181	24 776	12 996	11 780
25 - 29	+C	30 669	16 728	13 941	14 676	8 061	6 615	15 993	8 667	7 326
30 - 34	+C	15 768	8 840	6 928	7 283	4 057	3 226	8 485	4 783	3 702
35 - 39	+C	7 006	4 034	2 972	3 282	1 913	1 369	3 724	2 121	1 603
40 - 44	+C	1 849	1 038	811	800	457	343	1 049	581	468
45 - 49	+C	94	48	46	41	19	22	53	29	24
50+	+C	9	6	3	7	5	2	2	1	1
Bahrain - Bahreïn										
2002										
Total	U	13 576	6 953	6 623	...	...	...	...	...	...
15 - 19	U	349	185	164	...	...	...	...	...	...
20 - 24	U	2 645	1 359	1 286	...	...	...	...	...	...
25 - 29	U	4 147	2 098	2 049	...	...	...	...	...	...
30 - 34	U	3 413	1 779	1 634	...	...	...	...	...	...
35 - 39	U	2 299	1 175	1 124	...	...	...	...	...	...
40 - 44	U	655	322	333	...	...	...	...	...	...
45 - 49	U	51	27	24	...	...	...	...	...	...
50+	U	9	5	4	...	...	...	...	...	...
Unk.- Inc.	U	8	3	5	...	...	...	...	...	...
Brunei Darussalam - Brunéi Darussalam										
2002										
Total	+C	7 464	3 818	3 646	...	...	...	...	...	...
0 - 14	+C	7	4	3	...	...	...	...	...	...
15 - 19	+C	387	187	200	...	...	...	...	...	...
20 - 24	+C	1 585	819	766	...	...	...	...	...	...
25 - 29	+C	2 125	1 072	1 053	...	...	...	...	...	...
30 - 34	+C	1 967	994	973	...	...	...	...	...	...
35 - 39	+C	1 052	560	492	...	...	...	...	...	...
40 - 44	+C	317	169	148	...	...	...	...	...	...

10. Live births by age of mother, sex of the child and urban/rural residence: latest available year, 1993 - 2002

Naissances vivantes selon l'âge de la mère, le sexe de l'enfant et la résidence, urbaine/rurale: dernière année disponible, 1993 - 2002 (continued — suite)

(See notes at end of table.— Voir notes à la fin du tableau.)

Continent, country or area, year and age (in years) / Continent, pays ou zone, année et âge (en années)	Code[a]	Total			Urban - Urbaine			Rural - Rurale		
		Both sexes - Les deux sexes	Male - Masculin	Female - Féminin	Both sexes - Les deux sexes	Male - Masculin	Female - Féminin	Both sexes - Les deux sexes	Male - Masculin	Female - Féminin
ASIA — ASIE										
Brunei Darussalam - Brunéi Darussalam										
2002										
45 - 49	+C	21	12	9	...	...	...	...	...	...
Unk.- Inc.	+C	3	1	2	...	...	...	...	...	...
China: Hong Kong SAR - Chine: Hong Kong RAS[11]										
2001										
Total	C	48 219	25 160	23 058	...	...	...	...	...	...
0 - 14	C	14	8	6	...	...	...	...	...	...
15 - 19	C	872	454	418	...	...	...	...	...	...
20 - 24	C	5 988	3 076	2 912	...	...	...	...	...	...
25 - 29	C	13 637	7 094	6 542	...	...	...	...	...	...
30 - 34	C	16 772	8 789	7 983	...	...	...	...	...	...
35 - 39	C	9 420	4 923	4 497	...	...	...	...	...	...
40 - 44	C	1 419	767	652	...	...	...	...	...	...
45 - 49	C	45	17	28	...	...	...	...	...	...
50+	C	2	1	1	...	...	...	...	...	...
Unk.- Inc.	C	50	31	19	...	...	...	...	...	...
China: Macao SAR - Chine: Macao RAS										
2002										
Total	C	3 162	1 616	1 546	...	...	...	...	...	...
15 - 19	C	79	43	36	...	...	...	...	...	...
20 - 24	C	395	203	192	...	...	...	...	...	...
25 - 29	C	954	473	481	...	...	...	...	...	...
30 - 34	C	1 138	579	559	...	...	...	...	...	...
35 - 39	C	523	278	245	...	...	...	...	...	...
40 - 44	C	67	38	29	...	...	...	...	...	...
45 - 49	C	5	1	4	...	...	...	...	...	...
50+	C	1	1	-	...	...	...	...	...	...
Cyprus - Chypre[12,13,14]										
2002										
Total	C	7 443	3 891	3 552	4 806	2 496	2 310	2 637	1 395	1 242
15 - 19	C	170	104	66	91	57	34	79	47	32
20 - 24	C	1 341	696	645	731	381	350	610	315	295
25 - 29	C	2 372	1 262	1 110	1 521	813	708	851	449	402
30 - 34	C	1 827	913	914	1 224	599	625	603	314	289
35 - 39	C	742	399	343	504	265	239	238	134	104
40 - 44	C	157	87	70	109	60	49	48	27	21
45 - 49	C	10	6	4	8	5	3	2	1	1
50+	C	4	2	2	4	2	2	-	-	-
Unk.- Inc.	C	820	422	398	614	314	300	206	108	98
Georgia - Géorgie[10]										
2001										
Total	C	40 416	21 906	18 510	25 078	13 427	11 651	15 338	8 479	6 859
0 - 14	C	86	45	41	53	31	22	33	14	19
15 - 19	C	4 814	2 557	2 257	2 769	1 440	1 329	2 045	1 117	928
20 - 24	C	15 733	8 392	7 341	9 193	4 883	4 310	6 540	3 509	3 031
25 - 29	C	9 640	5 334	4 306	6 397	3 501	2 896	3 243	1 833	1 410
30 - 34	C	5 992	3 291	2 701	3 896	2 098	1 798	2 096	1 193	903
35 - 39	C	3 058	1 686	1 372	2 046	1 097	949	1 012	589	423
40 - 44	C	809	449	360	535	287	248	274	162	112
45 - 49	C	146	80	66	89	42	47	57	38	19
50+	C	38	17	21	26	11	15	12	6	6
Unk.- Inc.	C	100	55	45	74	37	37	26	18	8

10. Live births by age of mother, sex of the child and urban/rural residence: latest available year, 1993 - 2002

Naissances vivantes selon l'âge de la mère, le sexe de l'enfant et la résidence, urbaine/rurale: dernière année disponible, 1993 - 2002 (continued — suite)

(See notes at end of table.— Voir notes à la fin du tableau.)

Continent, country or area, year and age (in years) / Continent, pays ou zone, année et âge (en années)	Code[a]	Total			Urban - Urbaine			Rural - Rurale		
		Both sexes - Les deux sexes	Male - Masculin	Female - Féminin	Both sexes - Les deux sexes	Male - Masculin	Female - Féminin	Both sexes - Les deux sexes	Male - Masculin	Female - Féminin
ASIA — ASIE										
Iran (Islamic Republic of) - Iran (République islamique d')										
1994										
Total	U	1 304 255	...	...	657 275	...	...	646 980	...	...
0 - 14	U	2 059	...	...	1 647	...	...	412	...	...
15 - 19	U	150 317	...	...	70 834	...	...	79 483	...	...
20 - 24	U	411 003	...	...	216 621	...	...	194 382	...	...
25 - 29	U	338 933	...	...	177 085	...	...	161 848	...	...
30 - 34	U	212 503	...	...	102 545	...	...	109 958	...	...
35 - 39	U	126 843	...	...	66 304	...	...	60 539	...	...
40 - 44	U	45 713	...	...	17 297	...	...	28 416	...	...
45 - 49	U	12 355	...	...	2 883	...	...	9 472	...	...
50+	U	4 529	...	...	2 059	...	...	2 470	...	...
Iraq[15]										
2000										
Total	U	471 886	...	...	...	...	...	...	...	...
15 - 19	U	21 367	...	...	...	...	...	...	...	...
20 - 24	U	115 973	...	...	...	...	...	...	...	...
25 - 29	U	149 287	...	...	...	...	...	...	...	...
30 - 34	U	110 981	...	...	...	...	...	...	...	...
35 - 39	U	52 196	...	...	...	...	...	...	...	...
40 - 44	U	16 717	...	...	...	...	...	...	...	...
45+	U	5 365	...	...	...	...	...	...	...	...
Israel - Israël[16]										
2002										
Total	C	139 535	71 318	68 217	126 795	64 855	61 940	12 740	6 463	6 277
0 - 14	C	4	2	2	4	2	2	-	-	-
15 - 19	C	4 351	2 243	2 108	4 061	2 101	1 960	290	142	148
20 - 24	C	29 778	15 265	14 513	27 711	14 213	13 498	2 067	1 052	1 015
25 - 29	C	46 540	23 875	22 665	42 301	21 697	20 604	4 239	2 178	2 061
30 - 34	C	36 464	18 555	17 909	32 606	16 627	15 979	3 858	1 928	1 930
35 - 39	C	17 635	8 948	8 687	15 787	8 011	7 776	1 848	937	911
40 - 44	C	4 150	2 112	2 038	3 753	1 911	1 842	397	201	196
45 - 49	C	283	144	139	264	135	129	19	9	10
50+	C	25	12	13	23	10	13	2	2	-
Unk.- Inc.	C	305	162	143	285	148	137	20	14	6
Japan - Japon[5,17]										
2002										
Total	C	1 153 855	592 840	561 015	939 091	482 285	456 806	214 569	110 450	104 119
0 - 14	C	52	27	25	44	23	21	8	4	4
15 - 19	C	21 349	10 937	10 412	16 561	8 527	8 034	4 787	2 410	2 377
20 - 24	C	152 493	78 238	74 255	117 912	60 533	57 379	34 578	17 703	16 875
25 - 29	C	425 817	219 131	206 686	343 633	176 734	166 899	82 131	42 371	39 760
30 - 34	C	406 482	208 839	197 643	338 093	173 457	164 636	68 287	35 325	32 962
35 - 39	C	131 040	67 289	63 751	109 247	56 183	53 064	21 758	11 086	10 672
40 - 44	C	16 200	8 174	8 026	13 262	6 662	6 600	2 937	1 512	1 425
45 - 49	C	396	191	205	318	154	164	78	37	41
50+	C	10	6	4	8	6	2	2	-	99
Unk.- Inc.	C	16	8	8	13	6	7	3	2	1
Kazakhstan[10]										
2002										
Total	C	227 171	116 066	111 105	122 151	62 691	59 460	105 020	53 375	51 645
0 - 14	C	28	15	13	17	8	9	11	7	4
15 - 19	C	19 047	9 599	9 448	10 080	5 078	5 002	8 967	4 521	4 446
20 - 24	C	81 519	41 572	39 947	42 646	21 852	20 794	38 873	19 720	19 153
25 - 29	C	64 659	33 093	31 566	35 660	18 344	17 316	28 999	14 749	14 250
30 - 34	C	38 831	19 879	18 952	21 424	11 040	10 384	17 407	8 839	8 568

(See notes at end of table.— Voir notes à la fin du tableau.)

Continent, country or area, year and age (in years) / Continent, pays ou zone, année et âge (en années)	Code[a]	Total			Urban - Urbaine			Rural - Rurale		
		Both sexes - Les deux sexes	Male - Masculin	Female - Féminin	Both sexes - Les deux sexes	Male - Masculin	Female - Féminin	Both sexes - Les deux sexes	Male - Masculin	Female - Féminin
ASIA — ASIE										
Kazakhstan[10]										
2002										
35 - 39	C	18 314	9 455	8 859	9 718	5 028	4 690	8 596	4 427	4 169
40 - 44	C	4 090	2 113	1 977	2 123	1 090	1 033	1 967	1 023	944
45 - 49	C	170	77	93	84	39	45	86	38	48
50+	C	26	14	12	11	6	5	15	8	7
Unk.- Inc.	C	487	249	238	388	206	182	99	43	56
Korea (Dem. People's Republic of) - Corée (Rép. populaire dém. de)										
1993										
Total	U	420 576	215 444	205 132	230 111	117 944	112 167	190 465	97 500	92 965
0 - 24	U	54 774	27 978	26 796	27 672	14 130	13 542	27 102	13 848	13 254
25 - 29	U	268 774	137 297	131 477	149 546	76 348	73 198	119 228	60 949	58 279
30 - 34	U	82 021	42 255	39 766	45 049	23 258	21 791	36 972	18 997	17 975
35 - 39	U	12 617	6 557	6 060	6 683	3 538	3 145	5 934	3 019	2 915
40 - 44	U	1 679	917	762	811	456	355	868	461	407
45+	U	711	440	271	350	214	136	361	226	135
Korea (Republic of) - Corée (République de)[18]										
2002										
Total	C	494 625	259 123	235 502	...	...	...	...	...	...
0 - 14	C	54	24	30	...	...	...	...	...	...
15 - 19	C	4 323	2 474	1 849	...	...	...	...	...	...
20 - 24	C	52 150	27 094	25 056	...	...	...	...	...	...
25 - 29	C	227 172	117 622	109 550	...	...	...	...	...	...
30 - 34	C	170 489	90 306	80 183	...	...	...	...	...	...
35 - 39	C	34 265	18 364	15 901	...	...	...	...	...	...
40 - 44	C	5 177	2 732	2 445	...	...	...	...	...	...
45 - 49	C	353	165	188	...	...	...	...	...	...
50+	C	36	16	20	...	...	...	...	...	...
Unk.- Inc.	C	606	326	280	...	...	...	...	...	...
Kyrgyzstan - Kirghizistan[10]										
2002										
Total	C	101 012	51 506	49 506	30 195	15 315	14 880	70 817	36 191	34 626
0 - 14	C	1	1	-	1	1	-	-	-	-
15 - 19	C	8 301	4 283	4 018	2 179	1 139	1 040	6 122	3 144	2 978
20 - 24	C	36 386	18 410	17 976	10 329	5 220	5 109	26 057	13 190	12 867
25 - 29	C	27 611	14 118	13 493	8 685	4 409	4 276	18 926	9 709	9 217
30 - 34	C	17 031	8 664	8 367	5 358	2 687	2 671	11 673	5 977	5 696
35 - 39	C	8 578	4 423	4 155	2 619	1 315	1 304	5 959	3 108	2 851
40 - 44	C	2 495	1 270	1 225	727	375	352	1 768	895	873
45 - 49	C	283	149	134	85	50	35	198	99	99
50+	C	326	188	138	212	119	93	114	69	45
Malaysia: Peninsular Malaysia - Malaisie: Malaisie Péninsulaire[3]										
2000										
Total	C	442 502	227 833	214 669	288 681	148 872	139 809	153 821	78 961	74 860
0 - 14	C	89	47	42	41	24	17	48	23	25
15 - 19	C	10 816	5 444	5 372	6 023	3 011	3 012	4 793	2 433	2 360
20 - 24	C	76 980	39 595	37 385	46 425	23 962	22 463	30 555	15 633	14 922
25 - 29	C	145 378	74 917	70 461	97 627	50 283	47 344	47 751	24 634	23 117
30 - 34	C	120 993	62 746	58 247	83 106	43 051	40 055	37 887	19 695	18 192
35 - 39	C	66 180	33 916	32 264	43 270	22 313	20 957	22 910	11 603	11 307

10. Live births by age of mother, sex of the child and urban/rural residence: latest available year, 1993 - 2002

Naissances vivantes selon l'âge de la mère, le sexe de l'enfant et la résidence, urbaine/rurale: dernière année disponible, 1993 - 2002 (continued — suite)

(See notes at end of table.— Voir notes à la fin du tableau.)

Continent, country or area, year and age (in years) Continent, pays ou zone, année et âge (en années)	Code[a]	Total			Urban - Urbaine			Rural - Rurale		
		Both sexes - Les deux sexes	Male - Masculin	Female - Féminin	Both sexes - Les deux sexes	Male - Masculin	Female - Féminin	Both sexes - Les deux sexes	Male - Masculin	Female - Féminin
ASIA — ASIE										
Malaysia: Peninsular Malaysia - Malaisie: Malaisie Péninsulaire[3]										
2000										
40 - 44	C	19 668	9 960	9 708	10 850	5 536	5 314	8 818	4 424	4 394
45 - 49	C	1 628	809	819	761	390	371	867	419	448
50+	C	91	47	44	51	26	25	40	21	19
Unk.- Inc.	C	679	352	327	527	276	251	152	76	76
Maldives										
1999										
Total	C	5 225	2 641	2 584	1 489	753	736	3 736	1 888	1 848
0 - 14	C	2	2	-	-	-	-	2	2	-
15 - 19	C	587	286	301	157	74	83	430	212	218
20 - 24	C	1 581	830	751	479	245	234	1 102	585	517
25 - 29	C	1 364	672	692	421	202	219	943	470	473
30 - 34	C	972	479	493	264	137	127	708	342	366
35 - 39	C	547	271	276	130	67	63	417	204	213
40 - 44	C	147	89	58	29	23	6	118	66	52
45 - 49	C	24	11	13	8	4	4	16	7	9
50+	C	1	1	-	1	1	-	-	-	-
Mongolia - Mongolie										
2002										
Total	C	46 922	24 112	22 810	24 067	...	...	22 855	...	...
0 - 14	C	15	8	7	2	...	...	13	...	...
15 - 19	C	3 053	1 578	1 475	1 353	...	...	1 700	...	...
20 - 24	C	16 456	8 380	8 076	8 219	...	...	8 237	...	...
25 - 29	C	14 511	7 413	7 098	7 413	...	...	7 098	...	...
30 - 34	C	8 463	4 384	4 079	4 715	...	...	3 748	...	...
35 - 39	C	3 281	1 711	1 570	1 795	...	...	1 486	...	...
40 - 44	C	971	549	422	468	...	...	503	...	...
45 - 49	C	119	61	58	58	...	...	61	...	...
50+	C	53	28	25	44	...	...	9	...	...
Oman[15]										
1999										
Total	...	44 067	...	...	...	...	...	...	...	...
15 - 19	...	4 096	...	...	...	...	...	...	...	...
20 - 24	...	13 224	...	...	...	...	...	...	...	...
25 - 29	...	11 504	...	...	...	...	...	...	...	...
30 - 34	...	7 759	...	...	...	...	...	...	...	...
35 - 39	...	5 563	...	...	...	...	...	...	...	...
40 - 44	...	1 739	...	...	...	...	...	...	...	...
45+	...	182	...	...	...	...	...	...	...	...
Pakistan[19,20]										
2001										
Total	I	3 719 694	1 942 845	1 776 849	1 192 190	610 755	581 435	2 527 504	1 332 090	1 195 414
15 - 19	I	174 701	98 230	76 471	52 677	26 339	26 338	122 024	71 891	50 133
20 - 24	I	984 168	520 993	463 175	316 062	163 001	153 061	668 106	357 992	310 114
25 - 29	I	1 162 599	613 628	548 971	389 611	202 757	186 854	772 988	410 871	362 117
30 - 34	I	768 434	405 355	363 079	247 483	129 705	117 778	520 951	275 650	245 301
35 - 39	I	415 924	205 786	210 138	133 183	61 622	71 561	282 741	144 164	138 577
40 - 44	I	157 293	69 010	88 283	41 247	20 872	20 375	116 046	48 138	67 908
45 - 49	I	56 576	29 842	26 734	11 927	6 460	5 467	44 649	23 382	21 267
Philippines										
2000										
Total	C	1 766 440	918 243	848 197	...	...	...	...	...	...
0 - 14	C	755	391	364	...	...	...	...	...	...
15 - 19	C	125 270	64 743	60 527	...	...	...	...	...	...
20 - 24	C	492 745	256 359	236 386	...	...	...	...	...	...

10. Live births by age of mother, sex of the child and urban/rural residence: latest available year, 1993 - 2002
Naissances vivantes selon l'âge de la mère, le sexe de l'enfant et la résidence, urbaine/rurale: dernière année disponible, 1993 - 2002 (continued — suite)

(See notes at end of table.— Voir notes à la fin du tableau.)

Continent, country or area, year and age (in years) / Continent, pays ou zone, année et âge (en années)	Code[a]	Total			Urban - Urbaine			Rural - Rurale		
		Both sexes - Les deux sexes	Male - Masculin	Female - Féminin	Both sexes - Les deux sexes	Male - Masculin	Female - Féminin	Both sexes - Les deux sexes	Male - Masculin	Female - Féminin
ASIA — ASIE										
Philippines										
2000										
25 - 29	C	491 158	256 023	235 135	...	...	...	...	...	...
30 - 34	C	362 264	188 466	173 798	...	...	...	...	...	...
35 - 39	C	207 148	107 634	99 514	...	...	...	...	...	...
40 - 44	C	73 525	37 659	35 866	...	...	...	...	...	...
45 - 49	C	9 365	4 799	4 566	...	...	...	...	...	...
50+	C	762	398	364	...	...	...	...	...	...
Unk.- Inc.	C	3 448	1 771	1 677	...	...	...	...	...	...
Qatar										
2001										
Total	C	12 118	6 186	5 932	...	...	...	...	...	...
15 - 19	C	348	167	181	...	...	...	...	...	...
20 - 24	C	2 337	1 191	1 146	...	...	...	...	...	...
25 - 29	C	3 639	1 867	1 772	...	...	...	...	...	...
30 - 34	C	3 097	1 593	1 504	...	...	...	...	...	...
35 - 39	C	1 822	911	911	...	...	...	...	...	...
40 - 44	C	634	329	305	...	...	...	...	...	...
45 - 49	C	85	47	38	...	...	...	...	...	...
50+	C	12	6	6	...	...	...	...	...	...
Unk.- Inc.	C	144	75	69	...	...	...	...	...	...
Saudi Arabia - Arabie saoudite										
2000										
Total	...	578 772	296 617	282 155	...	...	...	...	...	...
0 - 19	...	27 317	15 093	12 224	...	...	...	...	...	...
20 - 24	...	109 111	54 997	54 114	...	...	...	...	...	...
25 - 29	...	148 705	71 437	77 268	...	...	...	...	...	...
30 - 34	...	129 008	70 830	58 178	...	...	...	...	...	...
35 - 39	...	106 755	54 235	52 520	...	...	...	...	...	...
40 - 44	...	48 231	25 075	23 156	...	...	...	...	...	...
45+	...	9 645	4 950	4 695	...	...	...	...	...	...
Singapore - Singapour[21]										
2002										
Total	C	40 757	20 977	19 780	...	...	...	...	...	...
0 - 14	C	14	6	8	...	...	...	...	...	...
15 - 19	C	828	438	390	...	...	...	...	...	...
20 - 24	C	3 892	2 035	1 857	...	...	...	...	...	...
25 - 29	C	13 088	6 698	6 390	...	...	...	...	...	...
30 - 34	C	15 327	7 885	7 442	...	...	...	...	...	...
35 - 39	C	6 567	3 412	3 155	...	...	...	...	...	...
40 - 44	C	994	480	514	...	...	...	...	...	...
45 - 49	C	47	23	24	...	...	...	...	...	...
Sri Lanka										
1996										
Total	+C	340 649	173 603	167 046	234 715	119 540	115 175	105 934	54 063	51 871
0 - 14	+C	139	73	66	109	59	50	30	14	16
15 - 19	+C	28 271	14 483	13 788	18 849	9 594	9 255	9 422	4 889	4 533
20 - 24	+C	83 244	42 548	40 696	54 727	27 881	26 846	28 517	14 667	13 850
25 - 29	+C	101 510	51 840	49 670	70 277	35 933	34 344	31 233	15 907	15 326
30 - 34	+C	76 096	38 601	37 495	55 159	27 969	27 190	20 937	10 632	10 305
35 - 39	+C	42 130	21 467	20 663	28 886	14 765	14 121	13 244	6 702	6 542
40 - 44	+C	8 378	4 168	4 210	6 143	3 076	3 067	2 235	1 092	1 143
45 - 49	+C	804	386	418	534	250	284	270	136	134
50+	+C	77	37	40	31	13	18	46	24	22

10. Live births by age of mother, sex of the child and urban/rural residence: latest available year, 1993 - 2002

Naissances vivantes selon l'âge de la mère, le sexe de l'enfant et la résidence, urbaine/rurale: dernière année disponible, 1993 - 2002 (continued — suite)

(See notes at end of table.— Voir notes à la fin du tableau.)

Continent, country or area, year and age (in years) / Continent, pays ou zone, année et âge (en années)	Code[a]	Total			Urban - Urbaine			Rural - Rurale		
		Both sexes - Les deux sexes	Male - Masculin	Female - Féminin	Both sexes - Les deux sexes	Male - Masculin	Female - Féminin	Both sexes - Les deux sexes	Male - Masculin	Female - Féminin
ASIA — ASIE										
Tajikistan - Tadjikistan[10]										
1994										
Total	C	162 152	...	...	38 006	...	...	124 146	...	...
0 - 19	C	15 886	...	...	3 832	...	...	12 054	...	...
20 - 24	C	59 943	...	...	14 476	...	...	45 467	...	...
25 - 29	C	43 322	...	...	10 202	...	...	33 120	...	...
30 - 34	C	28 073	...	...	6 393	...	...	21 680	...	...
35 - 39	C	11 323	...	...	2 351	...	...	8 972	...	...
40 - 44	C	2 936	...	...	494	...	...	2 442	...	...
45 - 49	C	282	...	...	45	...	...	237	...	...
50+	C	41	...	...	4	...	...	37	...	...
Unk.- Inc.	C	346	...	...	209	...	...	137	...	...
Thailand - Thaïlande										
2000										
Total	+U	773 009	397 523	375 486	...	...	...	...	...	...
0 - 14	+U	1 478	779	699	...	...	...	...	...	...
15 - 19	+U	86 675	44 787	41 888	...	...	...	...	...	...
20 - 24	+U	207 225	106 314	100 911	...	...	...	...	...	...
25 - 29	+U	218 767	112 516	106 251	...	...	...	...	...	...
30 - 34	+U	154 337	79 321	75 016	...	...	...	...	...	...
35 - 39	+U	68 568	35 298	33 270	...	...	...	...	...	...
40 - 44	+U	16 339	8 497	7 842	...	...	...	...	...	...
45 - 49	+U	1 850	932	918	...	...	...	...	...	...
50+	+U	421	212	209	...	...	...	...	...	...
Unk.- Inc.	+U	17 349	8 867	8 482	...	...	...	...	...	...
Turkey - Turquie[6,19]										
1997										
Total	I	1 377 000	...	...	...	...	...	...	...	...
0 - 14	I	-	...	...	...	...	...	...	...	...
15 - 19	I	165 000	...	...	...	...	...	...	...	...
20 - 24	I	531 000	...	...	...	...	...	...	...	...
25 - 29	I	387 000	...	...	...	...	...	...	...	...
30 - 34	I	182 000	...	...	...	...	...	...	...	...
35 - 39	I	79 000	...	...	...	...	...	...	...	...
40 - 44	I	28 000	...	...	...	...	...	...	...	...
45+	I	5 000	...	...	...	...	...	...	...	...
Uzbekistan - Ouzbékistan[10]										
2000										
Total	C	527 580	...	...	163 834	...	...	363 746	...	...
15 - 19	C	28 179	...	...	10 217	...	...	17 962	...	...
20 - 24	C	228 743	...	...	69 369	...	...	159 374	...	...
25 - 29	C	160 082	...	...	48 315	...	...	111 767	...	...
30 - 34	C	78 316	...	...	25 084	...	...	53 232	...	...
35 - 39	C	26 866	...	...	9 095	...	...	17 771	...	...
40 - 44	C	4 979	...	...	1 639	...	...	3 340	...	...
45 - 49	C	348	...	...	96	...	...	252	...	...
50+	C	67	...	...	19	...	...	48	...	...
EUROPE										
Austria - Autriche										
2002										
Total	C	78 399	...	...	...	...	...	...	...	...
12 - 14	C	12	...	...	...	...	...	...	...	...
15 - 19	C	3 244	...	...	...	...	...	...	...	...
20 - 24	C	14 631	...	...	...	...	...	...	...	...

10. Live births by age of mother, sex of the child and urban/rural residence: latest available year, 1993 - 2002

Naissances vivantes selon l'âge de la mère, le sexe de l'enfant et la résidence, urbaine/rurale: dernière année disponible, 1993 - 2002 (continued — suite)

(See notes at end of table.— Voir notes à la fin du tableau.)

Continent, country or area, year and age (in years) / Continent, pays ou zone, année et âge (en années)	Code[a]	Total			Urban - Urbaine			Rural - Rurale		
		Both sexes - Les deux sexes	Male - Masculin	Female - Féminin	Both sexes - Les deux sexes	Male - Masculin	Female - Féminin	Both sexes - Les deux sexes	Male - Masculin	Female - Féminin
EUROPE										
Austria - Autriche										
2002										
25 - 29	C	25 148	...	...	...	...	...	...	...	...
30 - 34	C	23 508	...	...	...	...	...	...	...	...
35 - 39	C	10 017	...	...	...	...	...	...	...	...
40 - 44	C	1 767	...	...	...	...	...	...	...	...
45 - 49	C	68	...	...	...	...	...	...	...	...
50+	C	4	...	...	...	...	...	...	...	...
Belarus - Bélarus[10]										
2002										
Total	C	88 743	45 652	43 091	65 091	33 500	31 591	23 652	12 152	11 500
0 - 14	C	19	11	8	9	5	4	10	6	4
15 - 19	C	9 637	5 022	4 615	6 288	3 269	3 019	3 349	1 753	1 596
20 - 24	C	35 627	18 249	17 378	26 183	13 407	12 776	9 444	4 842	4 602
25 - 29	C	25 322	13 089	12 233	19 068	9 870	9 198	6 254	3 219	3 035
30 - 34	C	12 749	6 546	6 203	9 652	4 956	4 696	3 097	1 590	1 507
35 - 39	C	4 365	2 195	2 170	3 158	1 596	1 562	1 207	599	608
40 - 44	C	907	481	426	643	353	290	264	128	136
45 - 49	C	43	19	24	28	12	16	15	7	8
50+	C	1	-	1	1	-	1	-	-	-
Unk.- Inc.	C	73	40	33	61	32	29	12	8	4
Bosnia and Herzegovina - Bosnie-Herzégovine										
1998										
Total	C	45 007	...	...	...	...	...	...	...	...
0 - 14	C	2	...	...	...	...	...	...	...	...
15 - 19	C	3 191	...	...	...	...	...	...	...	...
20 - 24	C	14 515	...	...	...	...	...	...	...	...
25 - 29	C	12 937	...	...	...	...	...	...	...	...
30 - 34	C	7 971	...	...	...	...	...	...	...	...
35 - 39	C	3 577	...	...	...	...	...	...	...	...
40 - 44	C	756	...	...	...	...	...	...	...	...
45 - 49	C	53	...	...	...	...	...	...	...	...
50+	C	4	...	...	...	...	...	...	...	...
Unk.- Inc.	C	2 001	...	...	...	...	...	...	...	...
Bulgaria - Bulgarie										
2002										
Total	C	66 499	34 497	32 002	47 779	24 713	23 066	18 720	9 784	8 936
0 - 14	C	315	168	147	204	110	94	111	58	53
15 - 19	C	10 448	5 430	5 018	6 094	3 167	2 927	4 354	2 263	2 091
20 - 24	C	22 571	11 719	10 852	15 302	7 883	7 419	7 269	3 836	3 433
25 - 29	C	20 888	10 849	10 039	16 324	8 482	7 842	4 564	2 367	2 197
30 - 34	C	9 271	4 761	4 510	7 491	3 845	3 646	1 780	916	864
35 - 39	C	2 500	1 302	1 198	1 975	1 019	956	525	283	242
40 - 44	C	462	243	219	349	184	165	113	59	54
45 - 49	C	16	9	7	14	8	6	2	1	1
50+	C	1	-	1	-	-	-	1	-	1
Unk.- Inc.	C	27	16	11	26	15	11	1	1	-
Channel Islands: Guernsey - Îles Anglo-Normandes: Guernesey										
2000										
Total	C	644	336	308	...	...	...	...	...	...
15 - 19	C	42	15	27	...	...	...	...	...	...
20 - 24	C	84	49	35	...	...	...	...	...	...
25 - 29	C	192	101	91	...	...	...	...	...	...

10. Live births by age of mother, sex of the child and urban/rural residence: latest available year, 1993 - 2002

Naissances vivantes selon l'âge de la mère, le sexe de l'enfant et la résidence, urbaine/rurale: dernière année disponible, 1993 - 2002 (continued — suite)

(See notes at end of table.— Voir notes à la fin du tableau.)

Continent, country or area, year and age (in years) / Continent, pays ou zone, année et âge (en années)	Code[a]	Total			Urban - Urbaine			Rural - Rurale		
		Both sexes - Les deux sexes	Male - Masculin	Female - Féminin	Both sexes - Les deux sexes	Male - Masculin	Female - Féminin	Both sexes - Les deux sexes	Male - Masculin	Female - Féminin
EUROPE										
Channel Islands: Guernsey - Îles Anglo-Normandes: Guernesey										
2000										
30 - 34	C	200	102	98	...	...	...	...	...	...
35 - 39	C	106	60	46	...	...	...	...	...	...
40 - 44	C	20	9	11	...	...	...	...	...	...
Channel Islands: Jersey - Îles Anglo-Normandes: Jersey										
1994										
Total	+C	1 142	589	553	...	...	...	...	...	...
0 - 14	+C	1	1	-	...	...	...	...	...	...
15 - 19	+C	31	17	14	...	...	...	...	...	...
20 - 24	+C	161	86	75	...	...	...	...	...	...
25 - 29	+C	390	201	189	...	...	...	...	...	...
30 - 34	+C	398	198	200	...	...	...	...	...	...
35 - 39	+C	140	77	63	...	...	...	...	...	...
40+	+C	21	9	12	...	...	...	...	...	...
Croatia - Croatie										
2002										
Total	C	40 094	20 584	19 510	22 539	11 578	10 961	17 555	9 006	8 549
0 - 14	C	11	6	5	3	3	-	8	3	5
15 - 19	C	2 138	1 088	1 050	783	385	398	1 355	703	652
20 - 24	C	10 539	5 378	5 161	4 886	2 533	2 353	5 653	2 845	2 808
25 - 29	C	13 997	7 232	6 765	8 235	4 270	3 965	5 762	2 962	2 800
30 - 34	C	8 951	4 638	4 313	5 790	2 960	2 830	3 161	1 678	1 483
35 - 39	C	3 606	1 820	1 786	2 294	1 160	1 134	1 312	660	652
40 - 44	C	766	386	380	488	243	245	278	143	135
45 - 49	C	33	17	16	19	10	9	14	7	7
Unk.- Inc.	C	53	19	34	41	14	27	12	5	7
Czech Republic - République tchèque										
2002										
Total	C	97 878	50 333	47 545	73 482	37 767	35 715	24 396	12 566	11 830
0 - 14	C	27	16	11	20	13	7	7	3	4
15 - 19	C	4 426	2 196	2 230	3 429	1 712	1 717	997	484	513
20 - 24	C	24 457	12 645	11 812	17 337	8 930	8 407	7 120	3 715	3 405
25 - 29	C	42 806	21 969	20 837	31 987	16 458	15 529	10 819	5 511	5 308
30 - 34	C	19 122	9 880	9 242	15 128	7 767	7 361	3 994	2 113	1 881
35 - 39	C	6 065	3 150	2 915	4 817	2 513	2 304	1 248	637	611
40 - 44	C	944	462	482	742	365	377	202	97	105
45 - 49	C	30	15	15	21	9	12	9	6	3
50+	C	1	-	1	1	-	1	-	-	-
Denmark - Danemark[22]										
2002										
Total	C	64 149	...	...	...	...	...	...	...	...
12 - 14	C	1	...	...	...	...	...	...	...	...
15 - 19	C	907	...	...	...	...	...	...	...	...
20 - 24	C	7 536	...	...	...	...	...	...	...	...
25 - 29	C	22 655	...	...	...	...	...	...	...	...
30 - 34	C	22 093	...	...	...	...	...	...	...	...
35 - 39	C	9 560	...	...	...	...	...	...	...	...
40 - 44	C	1 351	...	...	...	...	...	...	...	...
45 - 49	C	46	...	...	...	...	...	...	...	...

10. Live births by age of mother, sex of the child and urban/rural residence: latest available year, 1993 - 2002
Naissances vivantes selon l'âge de la mère, le sexe de l'enfant et la résidence, urbaine/rurale: dernière année disponible, 1993 - 2002 (continued — suite)

(See notes at end of table.— Voir notes à la fin du tableau.)

Continent, country or area, year and age (in years) / Continent, pays ou zone, année et âge (en années)	Code[a]	Total			Urban - Urbaine			Rural - Rurale		
		Both sexes - Les deux sexes	Male - Masculin	Female - Féminin	Both sexes - Les deux sexes	Male - Masculin	Female - Féminin	Both sexes - Les deux sexes	Male - Masculin	Female - Féminin
EUROPE										
Estonia - Estonie[10]										
2002										
Total	C	13 001	6 619	6 382	8 840	4 505	4 335	4 161	2 114	2 047
0 - 14	C	2	-	2	1	-	1	1	-	1
15 - 19	C	1 137	545	592	668	327	341	469	218	251
20 - 24	C	3 644	1 854	1 790	2 407	1 220	1 187	1 237	634	603
25 - 29	C	4 105	2 089	2 016	2 948	1 507	1 441	1 157	582	575
30 - 34	C	2 729	1 416	1 313	1 887	973	914	842	443	399
35 - 39	C	1 125	578	547	761	386	375	364	192	172
40 - 44	C	252	136	116	162	91	71	90	45	45
45 - 49	C	5	1	4	4	1	3	1	-	1
50+	C	1	-	1	1	-	1	-	-	-
Unk.- Inc.	C	1	-	1	1	-	1	-	-	-
Finland - Finlande[23]										
2002										
Total	C	55 555	28 563	26 992	36 263	18 681	17 582	19 292	9 882	9 410
0 - 14	C	3	2	1	2	1	1	1	1	...
15 - 19	C	1 781	931	850	1 151	597	554	630	334	296
20 - 24	C	9 129	4 683	4 446	6 032	3 123	2 909	3 097	1 560	1 537
25 - 29	C	17 318	8 933	8 385	11 415	5 860	5 555	5 903	3 073	2 830
30 - 34	C	16 560	8 556	8 004	10 840	5 572	5 268	5 720	2 984	2 736
35 - 39	C	8 817	4 464	4 353	5 634	2 887	2 747	3 183	1 577	1 606
40 - 44	C	1 830	937	893	1 133	608	525	697	329	368
45 - 49	C	117	57	60	56	33	23	61	24	37
France[4,24]										
2000										
Total	C	773 395	396 638	376 757	589 608	302 146	207 402	183 787	94 492	80 205
0 - 14	C	49	22	27	41	18	23	8	4	4
15 - 19	C	15 646	7 995	7 651	13 267	6 707	6 560	2 379	1 288	1 091
20 - 24	C	103 451	53 181	50 270	83 572	42 960	40 612	19 879	10 221	9 658
25 - 29	C	273 133	140 100	133 033	204 106	104 653	99 453	69 027	35 447	33 580
30 - 34	C	247 171	126 914	120 257	184 175	94 477	89 698	62 996	32 437	30 559
35 - 39	C	109 626	56 084	53 542	84 690	43 250	41 440	24 936	12 834	12 102
40 - 44	C	23 273	11 812	11 461	18 880	9 634	9 246	4 393	2 178	2 215
45 - 49	C	1 006	513	493	841	432	409	165	81	84
50+	C	40	17	23	36	15	21	4	2	2
2001										
Total	C	770 945	...	...	...	...	...	...	...	...
12 - 14	C	108	...	...	...	...	...	...	...	...
15 - 19	C	21 986	...	...	...	...	...	...	...	...
20 - 24	C	119 395	...	...	...	...	...	...	...	...
25 - 29	C	273 641	...	...	...	...	...	...	...	...
30 - 34	C	234 635	...	...	...	...	...	...	...	...
35 - 39	C	100 863	...	...	...	...	...	...	...	...
40 - 44	C	19 530	...	...	...	...	...	...	...	...
45 - 49	C	750	...	...	...	...	...	...	...	...
50+	C	37	...	...	...	...	...	...	...	...
Germany - Allemagne										
2001										
Total	C	734 475	377 586	356 889	...	...	...	...	...	...
0 - 14	C	210	119	91	...	...	...	...	...	...
15 - 19	C	29 158	14 862	14 296	...	...	...	...	...	...
20 - 24	C	126 140	64 752	61 388	...	...	...	...	...	...
25 - 29	C	209 534	107 864	101 670	...	...	...	...	...	...
30 - 34	C	244 724	125 823	118 901	...	...	...	...	...	...
35 - 39	C	108 187	55 677	52 510	...	...	...	...	...	...
40 - 44	C	15 948	8 198	7 750	...	...	...	...	...	...
45 - 49	C	537	275	262	...	...	...	...	...	...

10. Live births by age of mother, sex of the child and urban/rural residence: latest available year, 1993 - 2002

Naissances vivantes selon l'âge de la mère, le sexe de l'enfant et la résidence, urbaine/rurale: dernière année disponible, 1993 - 2002 (continued — suite)

(See notes at end of table.— Voir notes à la fin du tableau.)

Continent, country or area, year and age (in years) / Continent, pays ou zone, année et âge (en années)	Code[a]	Total			Urban - Urbaine			Rural - Rurale		
		Both sexes - Les deux sexes	Male - Masculin	Female - Féminin	Both sexes - Les deux sexes	Male - Masculin	Female - Féminin	Both sexes - Les deux sexes	Male - Masculin	Female - Féminin
EUROPE										
Germany - Allemagne										
2001										
50+	C	37	16	21	...	...	...	...	...	...
Gibraltar										
1997										
Total	C	427	...	...	...	...	...	...	...	...
0 - 14	C	-	...	...	...	...	...	...	...	...
15 - 19	C	18	...	...	...	...	...	...	...	...
20 - 24	C	93	...	...	...	...	...	...	...	...
25 - 29	C	143	...	...	...	...	...	...	...	...
30 - 34	C	117	...	...	...	...	...	...	...	...
35 - 39	C	51	...	...	...	...	...	...	...	...
40 - 44	C	4	...	...	...	...	...	...	...	...
45+	C	1	...	...	...	...	...	...	...	...
Greece - Grèce										
2001										
Total	C	102 282	...	...	...	...	...	...	...	...
0 - 14	C	74	...	...	...	...	...	...	...	...
15 - 19	C	3 724	...	...	...	...	...	...	...	...
20 - 24	C	17 859	...	...	...	...	...	...	...	...
25 - 29	C	34 421	...	...	...	...	...	...	...	...
30 - 34	C	31 656	...	...	...	...	...	...	...	...
35 - 39	C	12 123	...	...	...	...	...	...	...	...
40 - 44	C	2 169	...	...	...	...	...	...	...	...
45 - 49	C	186	...	...	...	...	...	...	...	...
50+	C	70	...	...	...	...	...	...	...	...
Hungary - Hongrie										
2002										
Total	C	96 001	49 297	46 704	60 753	31 129	29 624	35 248	18 168	17 080
0 - 14	C	88	50	38	39	20	19	49	30	19
15 - 19	C	6 737	3 477	3 260	3 294	1 718	1 576	3 443	1 759	1 684
20 - 24	C	22 355	11 488	10 867	12 344	6 347	5 997	10 011	5 141	4 870
25 - 29	C	37 457	19 169	18 288	24 831	12 720	12 111	12 626	6 449	6 177
30 - 34	C	21 120	10 894	10 226	14 786	7 517	7 269	6 334	3 377	2 957
35 - 39	C	6 830	3 511	3 319	4 546	2 339	2 207	2 284	1 172	1 112
40 - 44	C	1 356	678	678	873	446	427	483	232	251
45 - 49	C	58	30	28	40	22	18	18	8	10
50+	C	-	-	-	-	-	-	-	-	-
Iceland - Islande										
2002										
Total	C	4 049	2 067	1 982	3 823	1 950	1 873	226	117	109
15 - 19	C	188	99	89	176	95	81	12	4	8
20 - 24	C	824	434	390	784	411	373	40	23	17
25 - 29	C	1 269	658	611	1 209	626	583	60	32	28
30 - 34	C	1 064	516	548	991	478	513	73	38	35
35 - 39	C	591	296	295	556	279	277	35	17	18
40 - 44	C	106	59	47	100	56	44	6	3	3
45 - 49	C	7	5	2	7	5	2	-	-	-
Ireland - Irlande[25]										
2002										
Total	+C	60 521	...	...	...	...	...	...	...	...
12 - 14	+C	1	...	...	...	...	...	...	...	...
15 - 19	+C	2 971	...	...	...	...	...	...	...	...
20 - 24	+C	8 589	...	...	...	...	...	...	...	...
25 - 29	+C	14 572	...	...	...	...	...	...	...	...
30 - 34	+C	20 346	...	...	...	...	...	...	...	...
35 - 39	+C	11 633	...	...	...	...	...	...	...	...
40 - 44	+C	1 999	...	...	...	...	...	...	...	...

10. Live births by age of mother, sex of the child and urban/rural residence: latest available year, 1993 - 2002
Naissances vivantes selon l'âge de la mère, le sexe de l'enfant et la résidence, urbaine/rurale: dernière année disponible, 1993 - 2002 (continued — suite)

(See notes at end of table.— Voir notes à la fin du tableau.)

Continent, country or area, year and age (in years) / Continent, pays ou zone, année et âge (en années)	Code[a]	Total			Urban - Urbaine			Rural - Rurale		
		Both sexes - Les deux sexes	Male - Masculin	Female - Féminin	Both sexes - Les deux sexes	Male - Masculin	Female - Féminin	Both sexes - Les deux sexes	Male - Masculin	Female - Féminin
EUROPE										
Ireland - Irlande[25]										
2002										
45 - 49	+C	70	...	...	...	...	...	...	...	...
50+	+C	1	...	...	...	...	...	...	...	...
Italy - Italie										
2000										
Total	C	543 039	279 953	263 086	...	...	...	...	...	...
0 - 14	C	39	19	20	...	...	...	...	...	...
15 - 19	C	10 680	5 537	5 143	...	...	...	...	...	...
20 - 24	C	61 075	31 609	29 466	...	...	...	...	...	...
25 - 29	C	166 047	85 537	80 510	...	...	...	...	...	...
30 - 34	C	195 584	100 799	94 784	...	...	...	...	...	...
35 - 39	C	93 298	48 055	45 242	...	...	...	...	...	...
40 - 44	C	15 506	7 980	7 525	...	...	...	...	...	...
45 - 49	C	675	349	327	...	...	...	...	...	...
50+	C	137	68	69	...	...	...	...	...	...
Latvia - Lettonie[10]										
2002										
Total	C	20 044	10 273	9 771	12 938	6 627	6 311	7 106	3 646	3 460
0 - 14	C	1	1	-	1	1	-	-	-	-
15 - 19	C	1 456	768	688	802	410	392	654	358	296
20 - 24	C	5 821	2 985	2 836	3 509	1 820	1 689	2 312	1 165	1 147
25 - 29	C	6 381	3 271	3 110	4 288	2 169	2 119	2 093	1 102	991
30 - 34	C	4 147	2 119	2 028	2 858	1 491	1 367	1 289	628	661
35 - 39	C	1 746	889	857	1 176	579	597	570	310	260
40 - 44	C	455	227	228	282	148	134	173	79	94
45 - 49	C	30	9	21	17	5	12	13	4	9
50+	C	1	1	-	1	1	-	-	-	-
Unk.- Inc.	C	6	3	3	4	3	1	2	-	2
Liechtenstein										
2002										
Total	C	395	...	...	...	...	...	...	...	...
15 - 19	C	4	...	...	...	...	...	...	...	...
20 - 24	C	34	...	...	...	...	...	...	...	...
25 - 29	C	108	...	...	...	...	...	...	...	...
30 - 34	C	164	...	...	...	...	...	...	...	...
35 - 39	C	76	...	...	...	...	...	...	...	...
40 - 44	C	9	...	...	...	...	...	...	...	...
Lithuania - Lituanie[10]										
2002										
Total	C	30 014	15 490	14 524	18 697	9 638	9 059	11 317	5 852	5 465
0 - 14	C	6	4	2	3	2	1	3	2	1
15 - 19	C	2 786	1 412	1 374	1 457	743	714	1 329	669	660
20 - 24	C	9 388	4 853	4 535	5 507	2 831	2 676	3 881	2 022	1 859
25 - 29	C	9 285	4 760	4 525	6 195	3 172	3 023	3 090	1 588	1 502
30 - 34	C	5 706	2 935	2 771	3 775	1 947	1 828	1 931	988	943
35 - 39	C	2 226	1 184	1 042	1 393	738	655	833	446	387
40 - 44	C	588	328	260	350	196	154	238	132	106
45 - 49	C	21	10	11	9	5	4	12	5	7
Unk.- Inc.	C	8	4	4	8	4	4	-	-	-
Luxembourg										
2002										
Total	C	5 345	2 744	2 601	...	...	...	...	...	...
0 - 14	C	2	1	1	...	...	...	...	...	...
15 - 19	C	152	75	77	...	...	...	...	...	...
20 - 24	C	753	360	393	...	...	...	...	...	...
25 - 29	C	1 552	804	748	...	...	...	...	...	...
30 - 34	C	1 864	984	880	...	...	...	...	...	...

10. Live births by age of mother, sex of the child and urban/rural residence: latest available year, 1993 - 2002

Naissances vivantes selon l'âge de la mère, le sexe de l'enfant et la résidence, urbaine/rurale: dernière année disponible, 1993 - 2002 (continued — suite)

(See notes at end of table.— Voir notes à la fin du tableau.)

Continent, country or area, year and age (in years) / Continent, pays ou zone, année et âge (en années)	Code[a]	Total			Urban - Urbaine			Rural - Rurale		
		Both sexes - Les deux sexes	Male - Masculin	Female - Féminin	Both sexes - Les deux sexes	Male - Masculin	Female - Féminin	Both sexes - Les deux sexes	Male - Masculin	Female - Féminin
EUROPE										
Luxembourg										
2002										
35 - 39	C	881	450	431	...	...	...	...	...	...
40 - 44	C	135	67	68	...	...	...	...	...	...
45 - 49	C	4	2	2	...	...	...	...	...	...
Unk.- Inc.	C	2	1	1	...	...	...	...	...	...
Malta - Malte[26]										
2002										
Total	C	3 805	...	...	...	...	...	...	...	...
15 - 19	C	232	...	...	...	...	...	...	...	...
20 - 24	C	718	...	...	...	...	...	...	...	...
25 - 29	C	1 528	...	...	...	...	...	...	...	...
30 - 34	C	880	...	...	...	...	...	...	...	...
35 - 39	C	366	...	...	...	...	...	...	...	...
40 - 44	C	80	...	...	...	...	...	...	...	...
45 - 49	C	1	...	...	...	...	...	...	...	...
Netherlands - Pays-Bas[27]										
2002										
Total	C	202 083	103 734	98 349	132 825	68 325	64 500	69 258	35 409	33 849
0 - 14	C	17	10	7	16	9	7	1	1	-
15 - 19	C	2 632	1 358	1 274	2 141	1 100	1 041	491	258	233
20 - 24	C	17 667	9 018	8 649	13 355	6 840	6 515	4 312	2 178	2 134
25 - 29	C	51 907	26 519	25 388	33 612	17 205	16 407	18 295	9 314	8 981
30 - 34	C	86 077	44 322	41 755	54 218	28 014	26 204	31 859	16 308	15 551
35 - 39	C	37 859	19 477	18 382	25 198	12 977	12 221	12 661	6 500	6 161
40 - 44	C	5 701	2 910	2 791	4 118	2 092	2 026	1 583	818	765
45 - 49	C	213	116	97	162	86	76	51	30	21
50+	C	10	4	6	5	2	3	5	2	3
Norway - Norvège[4]										
2002										
Total	C	55 434	...	...	...	...	...	...	...	...
12 - 14	C	4	...	...	...	...	...	...	...	...
15 - 19	C	1 322	...	...	...	...	...	...	...	...
20 - 24	C	8 032	...	...	...	...	...	...	...	...
25 - 29	C	18 556	...	...	...	...	...	...	...	...
30 - 34	C	18 907	...	...	...	...	...	...	...	...
35 - 39	C	7 365	...	...	...	...	...	...	...	...
40 - 44	C	1 211	...	...	...	...	...	...	...	...
45 - 49	C	37	...	...	...	...	...	...	...	...
Poland - Pologne										
2002										
Total	C	353 765	...	...	...	...	...	...	...	...
12 - 14	C	51	...	...	...	...	...	...	...	...
15 - 19	C	24 280	...	...	...	...	...	...	...	...
20 - 24	C	106 462	...	...	...	...	...	...	...	...
25 - 29	C	127 101	...	...	...	...	...	...	...	...
30 - 34	C	63 009	...	...	...	...	...	...	...	...
35 - 39	C	25 795	...	...	...	...	...	...	...	...
40 - 44	C	6 743	...	...	...	...	...	...	...	...
45 - 49	C	321	...	...	...	...	...	...	...	...
50+	C	3	...	...	...	...	...	...	...	...
Portugal										
2002										
Total	C	114 383	...	...	...	...	...	...	...	...
12 - 14	C	92	...	...	...	...	...	...	...	...
15 - 19	C	6 638	...	...	...	...	...	...	...	...
20 - 24	C	20 544	...	...	...	...	...	...	...	...

10. Live births by age of mother, sex of the child and urban/rural residence: latest available year, 1993 - 2002

Naissances vivantes selon l'âge de la mère, le sexe de l'enfant et la résidence, urbaine/rurale: dernière année disponible, 1993 - 2002 (continued — suite)

(See notes at end of table.— Voir notes à la fin du tableau.)

Continent, country or area, year and age (in years) / Continent, pays ou zone, année et âge (en années)	Code[a]	Total			Urban - Urbaine			Rural - Rurale		
		Both sexes - Les deux sexes	Male - Masculin	Female - Féminin	Both sexes - Les deux sexes	Male - Masculin	Female - Féminin	Both sexes - Les deux sexes	Male - Masculin	Female - Féminin
EUROPE										
Portugal										
2002										
25 - 29	C	38 274	...	...	...	...	...	...	...	...
30 - 34	C	32 339	...	...	...	...	...	...	...	...
35 - 39	C	13 748	...	...	...	...	...	...	...	...
40 - 44	C	2 578	...	...	...	...	...	...	...	...
45 - 49	C	152	...	...	...	...	...	...	...	...
50+	C	8	...	...	...	...	...	...	...	...
Republic of Moldova - République de Moldova[10]										
2002										
Total	C	35 705	18 500	17 205	12 747	6 645	6 102	22 958	11 855	11 103
0 - 14	C	11	6	5	4	1	3	7	5	2
15 - 19	C	5 425	2 766	2 659	1 360	693	667	4 065	2 073	1 992
20 - 24	C	14 357	7 484	6 873	4 880	2 544	2 336	9 477	4 940	4 537
25 - 29	C	9 541	4 938	4 603	3 799	2 002	1 797	5 742	2 936	2 806
30 - 34	C	4 315	2 238	2 077	1 880	957	923	2 435	1 281	1 154
35 - 39	C	1 636	860	776	655	353	302	981	507	474
40 - 44	C	392	194	198	153	88	65	239	106	133
45 - 49	C	17	7	10	7	2	5	10	5	5
50+	C	3	2	1	2	1	1	1	1	5
Unk.- Inc.	C	8	5	3	7	4	3	1	1	-
Romania - Roumanie										
2002										
Total	C	210 529	108 295	102 234	98 190	50 533	47 657	112 339	57 762	54 577
0 - 14	C	531	250	281	194	93	101	337	157	180
15 - 19	C	26 246	13 455	12 791	8 387	4 301	4 086	17 859	9 154	8 705
20 - 24	C	69 836	35 971	33 865	28 471	14 786	13 685	41 365	21 185	20 180
25 - 29	C	65 635	33 703	31 932	34 094	17 494	16 600	31 541	16 209	15 332
30 - 34	C	36 891	19 072	17 819	21 099	10 808	10 291	15 792	8 264	7 528
35 - 39	C	9 089	4 642	4 447	4 886	2 497	2 389	4 203	2 145	2 058
40 - 44	C	2 137	1 107	1 030	996	517	479	1 141	590	551
45 - 49	C	161	93	68	62	37	25	99	56	43
50+	C	3	2	1	1	-	1	2	2	-
Russian Federation - Fédération de Russie[10]										
2000										
Total	C	1 266 800	...	...	...	...	...	...	...	...
15 - 19	C	162 997	...	...	...	...	...	...	...	...
20 - 24	C	505 997	...	...	...	...	...	...	...	...
25 - 29	C	343 148	...	...	...	...	...	...	...	...
30 - 34	C	167 240	...	...	...	...	...	...	...	...
35 - 39	C	69 327	...	...	...	...	...	...	...	...
40 - 44	C	15 251	...	...	...	...	...	...	...	...
45 - 49	C	719	...	...	...	...	...	...	...	...
50+	C	17	...	...	...	...	...	...	...	...
Unk.- Inc.	C	2 104	...	...	...	...	...	...	...	...
San Marino - Saint-Marin										
2000										
Total	+C	290	151	139	...	...	...	...	...	...
20 - 24	+C	18	13	5	...	...	...	...	...	...
25 - 29	+C	65	34	31	...	...	...	...	...	...
30 - 34	+C	142	74	68	...	...	...	...	...	...
35 - 39	+C	55	24	31	...	...	...	...	...	...
40 - 44	+C	9	6	3	...	...	...	...	...	...

10. Live births by age of mother, sex of the child and urban/rural residence: latest available year, 1993 - 2002
Naissances vivantes selon l'âge de la mère, le sexe de l'enfant et la résidence, urbaine/rurale: dernière année disponible, 1993 - 2002 (continued — suite)

(See notes at end of table.— Voir notes à la fin du tableau.)

Continent, country or area, year and age (in years) / Continent, pays ou zone, année et âge (en années)	Code[a]	Total			Urban - Urbaine			Rural - Rurale		
		Both sexes - Les deux sexes	Male - Masculin	Female - Féminin	Both sexes - Les deux sexes	Male - Masculin	Female - Féminin	Both sexes - Les deux sexes	Male - Masculin	Female - Féminin
EUROPE										
San Marino - Saint-Marin										
2000										
45 - 49	+C	1	-	1	...	...	...	...	...	...
Serbia and Montenegro - Serbie-et-Montenegro										
2000										
Total	C	125 868	65 403	60 465	66 409	34 508	31 901	59 459	30 895	28 564
0 - 14	C	68	40	28	41	22	19	27	18	9
15 - 19	C	9 602	5 008	4 594	4 220	2 197	2 023	5 382	2 811	2 571
20 - 24	C	41 126	21 243	19 883	19 694	10 193	9 501	21 432	11 050	10 382
25 - 29	C	40 983	21 134	19 849	22 176	11 481	10 695	18 807	9 653	9 154
30 - 34	C	22 422	11 884	10 538	13 213	6 933	6 280	9 209	4 951	4 258
35 - 39	C	8 611	4 491	4 120	5 313	2 741	2 572	3 298	1 750	1 548
40 - 44	C	1 778	918	860	1 082	578	504	696	340	356
45 - 49	C	160	87	73	78	39	39	82	48	34
50+	C	31	13	18	13	6	7	18	7	11
Unk.- Inc.	C	1 087	585	502	579	318	261	508	267	241
2001										
Total	C	130 194	...	...	...	...	...	...	...	...
12 - 14	C	71	...	...	...	...	...	...	...	...
15 - 19	C	9 612	...	...	...	...	...	...	...	...
20 - 24	C	41 056	...	...	...	...	...	...	...	...
25 - 29	C	43 367	...	...	...	...	...	...	...	...
30 - 34	C	23 951	...	...	...	...	...	...	...	...
35 - 39	C	9 041	...	...	...	...	...	...	...	...
40 - 44	C	1 814	...	...	...	...	...	...	...	...
45 - 49	C	139	...	...	...	...	...	...	...	...
50+	C	27	...	...	...	...	...	...	...	...
Slovakia - Slovaquie										
2002										
Total	C	50 841	26 015	24 826	26 321	13 449	12 872	24 520	12 566	11 954
0 - 14	C	37	13	24	22	7	15	15	6	9
15 - 19	C	4 543	2 284	2 259	1 890	916	974	2 653	1 368	1 285
20 - 24	C	15 619	8 039	7 580	7 214	3 661	3 553	8 405	4 378	4 027
25 - 29	C	18 557	9 472	9 085	10 207	5 275	4 932	8 350	4 197	4 153
30 - 34	C	8 434	4 350	4 084	4 910	2 529	2 381	3 524	1 821	1 703
35 - 39	C	3 050	1 556	1 494	1 733	887	846	1 317	669	648
40 - 44	C	577	291	286	330	167	163	247	124	123
45 - 49	C	24	10	14	15	7	8	9	3	6
Slovenia - Slovénie										
2002										
Total	C	17 501	9 025	8 476	8 400	4 392	4 008	9 101	4 633	4 468
0 - 14	C	4	3	1	2	2	-	2	1	1
15 - 19	C	383	195	188	157	80	77	226	115	111
20 - 24	C	3 367	1 751	1 616	1 350	707	643	2 017	1 044	973
25 - 29	C	7 055	3 663	3 392	3 250	1 716	1 534	3 805	1 947	1 858
30 - 34	C	4 740	2 421	2 319	2 545	1 340	1 205	2 195	1 081	1 114
35 - 39	C	1 688	854	834	950	473	477	738	381	357
40 - 44	C	257	136	121	142	73	69	115	63	52
45 - 49	C	7	2	5	4	1	3	3	1	2
Spain - Espagne										
1998										
Total	C	365 193	188 997	176 196	...	...	...	...	...	...
0 - 14	C	97	58	39	...	...	...	...	...	...
15 - 19	C	10 804	5 548	5 256	...	...	...	...	...	...
20 - 24	C	38 473	20 097	18 376	...	...	...	...	...	...

10. Live births by age of mother, sex of the child and urban/rural residence: latest available year, 1993 - 2002
Naissances vivantes selon l'âge de la mère, le sexe de l'enfant et la résidence, urbaine/rurale: dernière année disponible, 1993 - 2002 (continued — suite)

(See notes at end of table.— Voir notes à la fin du tableau.)

Continent, country or area, year and age (in years) / Continent, pays ou zone, année et âge (en années)	Code[a]	Total			Urban - Urbaine			Rural - Rurale		
		Both sexes - Les deux sexes	Male - Masculin	Female - Féminin	Both sexes - Les deux sexes	Male - Masculin	Female - Féminin	Both sexes - Les deux sexes	Male - Masculin	Female - Féminin
EUROPE										
Spain - Espagne										
1998										
25 - 29	C	110 492	57 257	53 235	...	...	...	...	...	...
30 - 34	C	142 219	73 558	68 661	...	...	...	...	...	...
35 - 39	C	55 084	28 401	26 683	...	...	...	...	...	...
40 - 44	C	7 721	3 934	3 787	...	...	...	...	...	...
45 - 49	C	294	139	155	...	...	...	...	...	...
50+	C	9	5	4	...	...	...	...	...	...
Sweden - Suède										
2002										
Total	C	95 815	...	...	...	...	...	...	...	...
12 - 14	C	5	...	...	...	...	...	...	...	...
15 - 19	C	1 691	...	...	...	...	...	...	...	...
20 - 24	C	12 081	...	...	...	...	...	...	...	...
25 - 29	C	30 818	...	...	...	...	...	...	...	...
30 - 34	C	33 423	...	...	...	...	...	...	...	...
35 - 39	C	15 151	...	...	...	...	...	...	...	...
40 - 44	C	2 545	...	...	...	...	...	...	...	...
45 - 49	C	96	...	...	...	...	...	...	...	...
50+	C	5	...	...	...	...	...	...	...	...
Switzerland - Suisse										
2001										
Total	C	73 509	37 739	35 770	49 292	25 221	24 071	24 217	12 518	11 699
0 - 14	C	2	2	-	2	2	-	-	-	-
15 - 19	C	1 144	588	556	825	427	398	319	161	158
20 - 24	C	8 919	4 578	4 341	6 131	3 098	3 033	2 788	1 480	1 308
25 - 29	C	22 003	11 362	10 641	14 119	7 276	6 843	7 884	4 086	3 798
30 - 34	C	27 327	14 025	13 302	18 207	9 356	8 851	9 120	4 669	4 451
35 - 39	C	12 187	6 193	5 994	8 587	4 347	4 240	3 600	1 846	1 754
40 - 44	C	1 856	947	909	1 367	683	684	489	264	225
45 - 49	C	60	37	23	43	25	18	17	12	5
50+	C	11	7	4	11	7	4	-	-	-
2002										
Total	C	72 372	...	...	...	...	...	...	...	...
12 - 14	C	1	...	...	...	...	...	...	...	...
15 - 19	C	1 105	...	...	...	...	...	...	...	...
20 - 24	C	8 680	...	...	...	...	...	...	...	...
25 - 29	C	21 080	...	...	...	...	...	...	...	...
30 - 34	C	26 795	...	...	...	...	...	...	...	...
35 - 39	C	12 656	...	...	...	...	...	...	...	...
40 - 44	C	1 963	...	...	...	...	...	...	...	...
45 - 49	C	83	...	...	...	...	...	...	...	...
50+	C	9	...	...	...	...	...	...	...	...
The Former Yugoslav Rep. of Macedonia - L'ex-République yougoslave de Macédoine										
2002										
Total	C	27 761	14 312	13 449	14 909	7 706	7 203	12 852	6 606	6 246
0 - 14	C	35	16	19	27	10	17	8	6	2
15 - 19	C	2 062	1 067	995	1 046	558	488	1 016	509	507
20 - 24	C	9 338	4 916	4 422	4 711	2 480	2 231	4 627	2 436	2 191
25 - 29	C	9 764	5 006	4 758	5 337	2 750	2 587	4 427	2 256	2 171
30 - 34	C	4 828	2 434	2 394	2 793	1 391	1 402	2 035	1 043	992
35 - 39	C	1 417	703	714	807	413	394	610	290	320
40 - 44	C	287	152	135	172	96	76	115	56	59
45 - 49	C	11	8	3	7	4	3	4	4	-

10. Live births by age of mother, sex of the child and urban/rural residence: latest available year, 1993 - 2002
Naissances vivantes selon l'âge de la mère, le sexe de l'enfant et la résidence, urbaine/rurale: dernière année disponible, 1993 - 2002 (continued — suite)

(See notes at end of table.— Voir notes à la fin du tableau.)

Continent, country or area, year and age (in years) / Continent, pays ou zone, année et âge (en années)	Code[a]	Total			Urban - Urbaine			Rural - Rurale		
		Both sexes - Les deux sexes	Male - Masculin	Female - Féminin	Both sexes - Les deux sexes	Male - Masculin	Female - Féminin	Both sexes - Les deux sexes	Male - Masculin	Female - Féminin
EUROPE										
The Former Yugoslav Rep. of Macedonia - L'ex-République yougoslave de Macédoine										
2002										
Unk.- Inc.	C	19	10	9	9	4	5	10	6	4
Ukraine[10]										
2001										
Total	C	376 478	...	...	237 228	...	...	139 250	...	...
0 - 14	C	149	...	...	69	...	...	80	...	...
15 - 19	C	54 859	...	...	29 509	...	...	25 350	...	...
20 - 24	C	156 246	...	...	98 007	...	...	58 239	...	...
25 - 29	C	99 608	...	...	65 776	...	...	33 832	...	...
30 - 34	C	44 502	...	...	30 090	...	...	14 412	...	...
35 - 39	C	16 019	...	...	10 413	...	...	5 606	...	...
40 - 44	C	3 683	...	...	2 181	...	...	1 502	...	...
45 - 49	C	165	...	...	90	...	...	75	...	...
50+	C	5	...	...	8	...	...	1	...	...
Unk.- Inc.	C	1 242	...	...	1 089	...	...	153	...	...
United Kingdom - Royaume-Uni										
2002										
Total	C	668 777	...	...	...	...	...	...	...	...
12 - 14	C	297	...	...	...	...	...	...	...	...
15 - 19	C	48 865	...	...	...	...	...	...	...	...
20 - 24	C	123 845	...	...	...	...	...	...	...	...
25 - 29	C	171 852	...	...	...	...	...	...	...	...
30 - 34	C	203 261	...	...	...	...	...	...	...	...
35 - 39	C	101 379	...	...	...	...	...	...	...	...
40 - 44	C	18 273	...	...	...	...	...	...	...	...
45 - 49	C	890	...	...	...	...	...	...	...	...
50+	C	78	...	...	...	...	...	...	...	...
OCEANIA — OCEANIE										
American Samoa - Samoas américaines										
1993										
Total	C	1 998	...	...	...	...	...	...	...	...
0 - 14	C	2	...	...	...	...	...	...	...	...
15 - 19	C	137	...	...	...	...	...	...	...	...
20 - 24	C	574	...	...	...	...	...	...	...	...
25 - 29	C	614	...	...	...	...	...	...	...	...
30 - 34	C	433	...	...	...	...	...	...	...	...
35 - 39	C	197	...	...	...	...	...	...	...	...
40+	C	41	...	...	...	...	...	...	...	...
Australia - Australie										
2002										
Total	+C	250 988	128 623	122 365	...	...	...	...	...	...
0 - 14	+C	95	50	45	...	...	...	...	...	...
15 - 19	+C	11 410	5 794	5 616	...	...	...	...	...	...
20 - 24	+C	36 782	18 726	18 056	...	...	...	...	...	...
25 - 29	+C	71 820	36 928	34 892	...	...	...	...	...	...
30 - 34	+C	84 052	43 160	40 892	...	...	...	...	...	...
35 - 39	+C	38 621	19 830	18 791	...	...	...	...	...	...
40 - 44	+C	7 362	3 720	3 642	...	...	...	...	...	...
45 - 49	+C	292	142	150	...	...	...	...	...	...

10. Live births by age of mother, sex of the child and urban/rural residence: latest available year, 1993 - 2002
Naissances vivantes selon l'âge de la mère, le sexe de l'enfant et la résidence, urbaine/rurale: dernière année disponible, 1993 - 2002 (continued — suite)

(See notes at end of table.— Voir notes à la fin du tableau.)

Continent, country or area, year and age (in years) / Continent, pays ou zone, année et âge (en années)	Code[a]	Total			Urban - Urbaine			Rural - Rurale		
		Both sexes - Les deux sexes	Male - Masculin	Female - Féminin	Both sexes - Les deux sexes	Male - Masculin	Female - Féminin	Both sexes - Les deux sexes	Male - Masculin	Female - Féminin
OCEANIA — OCEANIE										
Australia - Australie										
2002										
50+	+C	13	7	6	...	...	...	...	...	...
Unk.- Inc.	+C	541	266	275	...	...	...	...	...	...
Guam[28]										
2002										
Total	C	3 222	1 692	1 530	...	...	...	...	...	...
0 - 14	C	1	1	-	...	...	...	...	...	...
15 - 19	C	347	187	160	...	...	...	...	...	...
20 - 24	C	863	451	412	...	...	...	...	...	...
25 - 29	C	850	454	396	...	...	...	...	...	...
30 - 34	C	683	356	327	...	...	...	...	...	...
35 - 39	C	378	197	181	...	...	...	...	...	...
40 - 44	C	88	41	47	...	...	...	...	...	...
45 - 49	C	8	5	3	...	...	...	...	...	...
Unk.- Inc.	C	4	-	4	...	...	...	...	...	...
Marshall Islands - Îles Marshall[29]										
1999										
Total	+U	1 478	...	...	...	...	...	...	...	...
0 - 14	+U	3	...	...	...	...	...	...	...	...
15 - 19	+U	279	...	...	...	...	...	...	...	...
20 - 24	+U	482	...	...	...	...	...	...	...	...
25 - 29	+U	373	...	...	...	...	...	...	...	...
30 - 34	+U	211	...	...	...	...	...	...	...	...
35 - 39	+U	108	...	...	...	...	...	...	...	...
40 - 44	+U	19	...	...	...	...	...	...	...	...
50+	+U	1	...	...	...	...	...	...	...	...
New Caledonia - Nouvelle-Calédonie										
2001										
Total	C	4 326	...	...	...	...	...	...	...	...
15 - 19	C	246	...	...	...	...	...	...	...	...
20 - 24	C	1 068	...	...	...	...	...	...	...	...
25 - 29	C	1 397	...	...	...	...	...	...	...	...
30 - 34	C	990	...	...	...	...	...	...	...	...
35 - 39	C	501	...	...	...	...	...	...	...	...
40 - 44	C	123	...	...	...	...	...	...	...	...
45 - 49	C	1	...	...	...	...	...	...	...	...
New Zealand - Nouvelle-Zélande[5]										
2002										
Total	+C	54 021	27 577	26 444	47 068	24 079	22 989	6 896	3 466	3 430
0 - 14	+C	29	14	15	22	12	10	7	2	5
15 - 19	+C	3 593	1 834	1 759	3 224	1 635	1 589	363	194	169
20 - 24	+C	9 264	4 769	4 495	8 272	4 283	3 989	979	481	498
25 - 29	+C	13 747	6 992	6 755	11 932	6 055	5 877	1 800	928	872
30 - 34	+C	16 926	8 658	8 268	14 627	7 518	7 109	2 282	1 131	1 151
35 - 39	+C	8 655	4 413	4 242	7 432	3 811	3 621	1 217	598	619
40 - 44	+C	1 741	862	879	1 500	733	767	241	129	112
45 - 49	+C	65	34	31	58	31	27	7	3	4
50+	+C	1	1	-	1	1	-	-	-	-
Palau - Palaos										
1999										
Total	C	250	...	...	...	...	...	...	...	...
15 - 19	C	20	...	...	...	...	...	...	...	...
20 - 24	C	40	...	...	...	...	...	...	...	...
25 - 29	C	70	...	...	...	...	...	...	...	...

10. Live births by age of mother, sex of the child and urban/rural residence: latest available year, 1993 - 2002

Naissances vivantes selon l'âge de la mère, le sexe de l'enfant et la résidence, urbaine/rurale: dernière année disponible, 1993 - 2002 (continued — suite)

(See notes at end of table.— Voir notes à la fin du tableau.)

Continent, country or area, year and age (in years) / Continent, pays ou zone, année et âge (en années)	Code[a]	Total			Urban - Urbaine			Rural - Rurale		
		Both sexes - Les deux sexes	Male - Masculin	Female - Féminin	Both sexes - Les deux sexes	Male - Masculin	Female - Féminin	Both sexes - Les deux sexes	Male - Masculin	Female - Féminin
OCEANIA — OCEANIE										
Palau - Palaos										
1999										
30 - 34	C	77	...	...	...	...	...	...	...	...
35 - 39	C	33	...	...	...	...	...	...	...	...
40 - 44	C	10	...	...	...	...	...	...	...	...
Tonga										
2000										
Total	+C	2 471	...	...	...	...	...	...	...	...
0 - 14	+C	2	...	...	...	...	...	...	...	...
15 - 19	+C	101	...	...	...	...	...	...	...	...
20 - 24	+C	528	...	...	...	...	...	...	...	...
25 - 29	+C	695	...	...	...	...	...	...	...	...
30 - 34	+C	688	...	...	...	...	...	...	...	...
35 - 39	+C	314	...	...	...	...	...	...	...	...
40 - 44	+C	122	...	...	...	...	...	...	...	...
45 - 49	+C	14	...	...	...	...	...	...	...	...
Unk.- Inc.	+C	7	...	...	...	...	...	...	...	...

GENERAL NOTES - NOTES GENERALES

For definition of 'urban', see end of Technical Notes for table 6. For method of evaluation and limitations of data, see Technical Notes for this table. — Pour les définitions des 'régions urbaines', se reporter à la fin des Notes techniques du tableau 6. Pour la méthode d''evaluations et les limitations des données, voir Notes techniques, pour ce tableau.

Italics: data from civil registers which are incomplete or of unknown completeness. — *Italiques:* données incomplètes ou dont le degré d'exactitude n'est pas connu provenant des registres de l'état civil.

FOOTNOTES - NOTES

[a] 'Code' indicates the source of data, as follows:
C - Civil registration, estimated over 90% complete
U - Civil registration, estimated less than 90% complete
I - Other source, estimated reliable
+ - Data tabulated by date of registration rather than occurence.
... - Information not available

Le 'Code' indique la source des données, comme suit:
C - Registres de l'état civil considérés complèts à 90 p. 100 au moins.
U - Registres de l'état civil qui ne sont pas considérés complèts à 90 p. 100 au moins.
I - Autre source, considérée pas douteuses.
+ - Données exploitées selon la date de l'enregistrement et non la date de l'événement.
... - Information pas disponible.

[1] Data for 1997 refer to last twelve months preceding population and housing census of 1997. - Les données pour 1997 se réfèrent au douze mois précédant le recensement de population et de l'habitat de 1997.
[2] Including Canadian residents temporarily in the United States, but excluding United States residents temporarily in Canada. - Y compris les résidents canadiens se trouvant temporairement aux Etats-Unis, mais ne comprenant pas les résidents des Etats-Unis se trouvant temporairement au Canada.
[3] Excluding live-born infants who died before their birth was registered. - Non compris les enfants nés vivants décédés avant l'enregistrement de leur naissance.
[4] Age classification is based on year of birth of mother rather than the exact age of mother at birth of child. - Le classement selon l'âge est basé sur l'année de naissance de la mère et non sur l'age exacte de la mère au moment de naissance de l'enfant.
[5] Figures for urban and rural areas do not add up to the total, since they do not include the category "Unknown residence". - La somme des donées pour la residence urbaine et rurale n'est pas égale au total parce qu'elle n'inclue pas la catégorie "Residence inconnue".
[6] Data as reported by national statistical authorities; they may differ from data presented in other tables. - Les données comme elles ont été déclarées par l'institut national de la statistique; elles peuvent être différentes de ceux présentées dans autre tableaux.
[7] Excluding Indian jungle population. - Non compris les Indiens de la jungle.
[8] Excluding nomadic Indian tribes. - Non compris les tribus d'Indiens nomades.
[9] Data refer to registered live births only. - Les données concernent les naissances vivantes enregistrées seulement.
[10] Excluding infants born alive with less than 28 weeks gestation, less than 1 000 grams in weight and 35 centimeters in length, who die within seven days of birth. - Non compris les enfants nés vivants avant 28 semaines de gestation, pesant moins de 1 000 grammes, mesurant moins de 35 centimètres et décédés dans les sept jours qui ont suivi leur naissance.
[11] Including unknown sex. - Y compris le sexe inconnu.
[12] Data refer to government controlled areas. - Les données se raportent aux zones contrôlées par le Gouvernement.
[13] Excluding 440 live births of unknown residence. - Non compris 440 enfants nés vivants, dont on ignore la résidence.
[14] Data for urban and rural residence excluded 438 births of unknown residence. - Les données pour la résidence urbaine/rurale ne comprennent pas 438 naissances d'enfants dont on ignore la résidence.
[15] Published by the United Nations Economic and Social Commission for Western Asia. - Publié par la Commission économique et sociale des Nations Unies pour l'Asie occidentale.
[16] Beginning 1970, including data for East Jerusalem and Israeli residents in certain other territories under occupation by Israeli military forces since 1967. - A partir de 1970, y compris les données pour Jérusalem-Est et les résidents israéliens dans certains autres

territoires occupés depuis juin 1967 par les forces armées israéliennes.

[17] Data refer to Japanese nationals in Japan only. - Les données se raportent aux nationaux japonais au Japon seulement.

[18] Excluding alien armed forces, civilian aliens employed by armed forces, and foreign diplomatic personnel and their dependants. - Non compris les militaires étrangers, les civils étrangers employés par les forces armées ni le personnel diplomatique étranger et les membres de leur famille les accompagnant.

[19] Based on the results of the Population Growth Survey. - D'après les résultats de la 'Population Growth Survey.'

[20] Excluding data for the Pakistan-held part of Jammu and Kashmir, the final status of which has not yet been determined. - Non compris les données concernant la partie du Jammu et Cachemire occupée par le Pakistan dont le statut définitif n'a pas été déterminé.

[21] Excluding transients afloat and military and civilian services personnel and their dependants abroad. - Non compris les personnes de passage à bord de navires ni les militaires et agents civils et les membres de leur famille les accompagnant à l'étranger.

[22] Excluding Faeroe Islands and Greenland. - Non compris les îles Féroé et Gröenland.

[23] Including nationals temporarily outside the country. - Y compris les nationaux se trouvant temporairement hors du pays.

[24] Including armed forces stationed outside the country. - Y compris les militaires nationaux hors du pays.

[25] Births registered within one year of occurrence. - Naissances enregistrées dans l'année qui suit l'événement.

[26] Live births to Maltese parents only. - Naissances vivantes aux parents maltais seulement.

[27] Including residents outside the country if listed in a Netherlands population register. - Y compris les résidents hors du pays, s'ils sont inscrits sur un registre de population néerlandais.

[28] Including United States military personnel, their dependants and contract employees. - Y compris les militaires des Etats-Unis, les membres de leur famille les accompagnant et les agents contractuels des Etats-Unis.

[29] Excluding United States military personnel, their dependants and contract employees. - Non compris les militaires des Etats-Unis, les membres de leur famille les accompagnant et les agents contractuels des Etats-Unis.

Table 11

Table 11 presents live-birth rates by age of mother and urban/rural residence for the latest available year.

Description of variables: Age is defined as age at last birthday preceding the live birth, that is, the difference between the date of birth and the date of the occurrence of the event, expressed in completed solar years. The age classification used in this table is the following: under 20 years, 5-year age groups through 40-44 years, and 45 years or over.

Rate computation: Live-birth rates specific to age of mother are the annual number of births to women in each age group (as shown in table 10) per 1 000 female population in the same age group.

Birth rates by age of mother and urban/rural residence are the annual number of live births that occurred to a specific age-urban/rural group (as shown in table 10) per 1 000 females in the corresponding age-urban/rural group. These rates have been calculated by the Statistics Division of the United Nations.

Since relatively few births occur to women below 15 or above 50 years of age, birth rates for women under 20 years of age and for those 45 years of age or over are computed on the female population aged 15-19 and 45-49, respectively. Similarly, the rate for women of "All ages" is based on all live births irrespective of age of mother, and is computed on the female population aged 15-49 years. This rate for "All ages" is known as the general fertility rate.

Births to mothers of unknown age are distributed proportionately across the age groups, by the Statistics Division of the United Nations, in accordance with the distribution of births by age of mother prior to the calculation of the rates.

The population used in computing the rates is the estimated or enumerated distribution of females by age. First priority is given to an estimate for the mid-point of the same year (as shown in table 7), second priority to census returns of the year to which the births referred, and third priority to an estimate for some other point of time in the year.

Rates presented in this table are limited to those for countries or areas having at least a total of 100 live births in a given year.

Reliability of data: Rates are not computed if the data on live births from civil registers are reported as incomplete (less than 90 per cent completeness) or of unknown completeness. Table 9 and the technical notes for that table provides more detailed information on the completeness of live-birth registration. For more information about the quality of vital statistics data in general, and the information available on the basis of the completeness of estimates in particular, see section 4.2 of the Technical Notes.

Limitations: Rates shown in this table are subject to the same limitations that affect the corresponding frequencies and are set forth in the technical notes for table 10. These include differences in the completeness of registration, the treatment of infants who were born alive but died before the registration of the birth or within the first 24 hours of life, the method used to determine age of mother and the quality of the reported information relating to age of mother. In addition, some rates are based on births tabulated by date of registration and not by date of occurrence; these have been indicated by a plus sign "+".

The effect of including delayed registration on the distribution of births by age of mother may be noted in the age-specific fertility rates for women at older ages. In some cases, high age-specific rates for women aged 45 years and over may reflect age of mother at registration of birth and not fertility at these older ages.

The comparability of data by urban/rural residence is affected by the national definitions of urban and rural used in tabulating these data. It is assumed, in the absence of specific information to the contrary, that the definitions of urban and rural used in connection with the national population census were also used in the compilation of the vital statistics for each country or area. However, it is possible that, for a given country or area, the definitions of urban and rural used for both the vital statistics data and the population census data are not the same. When known, the definitions of urban used in national population censuses are presented at the end of the technical notes for table 6. As discussed in detail in the technical notes for table 6, these definitions vary considerably from one country or area to another.

In addition to problems of comparability, vital rates classified by urban/rural residence are also subject to certain special types of bias. If, when calculating vital rates, different definitions of urban are used in connection with the vital events and the population data and if this results in a net difference between the numerator and denominator of the rate in the population at risk, then the vital rates would be biased. Urban/rural differentials in vital rates may also be affected by whether the vital events have been tabulated in terms of place of occurrence or place of usual residence. This problem is discussed in more detail in section 4.1.4.1 of the Technical Notes.

Earlier data: Live-birth rates specific for age of mother have been shown for the latest available year in each issue of the Yearbook. Data included in this table update the series covering a period of years as follows:

Issue	Years Covered
Special Topic on Natality, CD, 1999	1990 – 1998
Historical Supplement CD, 1997	1948 – 1997
1992	1983 – 1992
1986	1977 – 1985
1981	1972 – 1980
Historical Supplement, 1979	1948 - 1977

Tableau 11

Le tableau 11 présente les taux des naissances vivantes selon l'âge de la mère et selon le lieu de résidence (zone urbaine ou rurale) correspondant aux données les plus récentes dont on dispose.

Description des variables : L'âge désigne l'âge au dernier anniversaire précédant la naissance, c'est-à-dire la différence entre la date de naissance et la date de l'événement, exprimée en années solaires révolues. La classification par âge utilisée dans le tableau 11 comprend les catégories suivantes : moins de 20 ans, groupes quinquennaux jusqu'à 40-44 ans, et 45 et plus.

Calcul des taux : Les taux des naissances vivantes selon l'âge de la mère représentent le nombre annuel de naissances dans chaque groupe d'âge (voir tableau 10) pour 1 000 femmes des mêmes groupes d'âge.

Les taux de natalité selon l'âge de la mère et le lieu de résidence (zone urbaine ou rurale) représentent le nombre annuel de naissances vivantes intervenues dans un groupe d'âge donné parmi la population urbaine ou rurale (comme il est indiqué au tableau 10) pour 1 000 femmes du groupe d'âge correspondant parmi la population urbaine ou rurale. Ces taux ont été calculés par la Division de statistique de l'ONU.

Étant donné que le nombre de naissances parmi les femmes de moins de 15 ans ou de plus de 50 ans est relativement peu élevé, les taux de natalité parmi les femmes âgées de moins de 20 ans et celles de 45 ans et plus ont été calculés sur la base des populations féminines âgées de 15 à 19 ans et de 45 à 49 ans, respectivement. De même, le taux pour les femmes de « tous âges » est fondé sur la totalité des naissances vivantes, indépendamment de l'âge de la mère et ce chiffre est rapporté à l'effectif de la population féminine âgée de 15 à 49 ans. Ce taux « tous âges » est le taux global de fécondité.

Les naissances pour lesquelles l'âge de la mère était inconnu ont été réparties par la Division de statistique de l'ONU, avant le calcul des taux, suivant les proportions observées pour celles où l'âge de la mère était connu.

Les chiffres de population utilisés pour le calcul des taux proviennent de dénombrements ou de répartitions estimatives de la population féminine selon l'âge. On a utilisé de préférence les estimations de la population au milieu de l'année considérée selon les chiffres du tableau 7 ; à défaut, on s'est contenté des données censitaires se rapportant à l'année des naissances et, si ces données manquaient également, d'estimations établies à un autre moment de l'année.

Les taux présentés dans ce tableau ne concernent que les pays ou zones où l'on a enregistré un total d'au moins 100 naissances vivantes dans une année donnée.

Fiabilité des données : On a choisi de ne pas faire figurer dans le tableau 11 des taux calculés à partir de données sur les naissances vivantes issues de registres de l'état civil qui sont déclarées incomplètes (degré de complétude inférieur à 90 p. 100) ou dont le degré de complétude n'est pas connu. Le tableau 9 et les notes techniques qui s'y rapportent présentent des renseignements plus détaillés sur le degré de complétude de l'enregistrement des naissances vivantes. Pour plus de précisions sur la qualité des données reposant sur les statistiques de l'état civil en général et les estimations de complétude en particulier, voir la section 4.2 des Notes techniques.

Insuffisance des données : Les taux du tableau 11 appellent les mêmes réserves que celles concernant les fréquences correspondantes (voir à ce sujet les notes techniques relatives au tableau 10). Leurs imperfections tiennent notamment au degré de complétude de l'enregistrement, au classement des enfants nés vivants décédés avant l'enregistrement de leur naissance ou dans les 24 heures qui ont suivi la naissance, à la méthode utilisée pour déterminer l'âge de la mère et à l'exactitude des renseignements concernant l'âge de la mère. En outre, dans certains cas, les données relatives aux naissances sont exploitées selon la date de l'enregistrement et non selon la date de l'événement ; ces cas ont été signalés par le signe '+'.

On peut se rendre compte, d'après les taux relatifs aux groupes d'âge les plus avancés, des conséquences que peut avoir l'inclusion, dans les statistiques des naissances selon l'âge de la mère, des naissances enregistrées tardivement. Dans certains cas, il se peut que des taux élevés pour le groupe d'âge 45 ans et plus ne traduisent pas le niveau de fécondité de ce groupe d'âge, mais l'âge de la mère au moment où la naissance a été enregistrée.

La comparabilité des données selon le lieu de résidence (zone urbaine ou rurale) peut être limitée par les définitions nationales des termes « urbain » et « rural » utilisées pour le classement de ces données. En l'absence d'indications contraires, on a supposé que les mêmes définitions avaient servi pour le recensement national de la population et pour l'établissement des statistiques de l'état civil pour chaque pays ou zone. Toutefois, il n'est pas exclu que, pour une zone ou un pays donné, des définitions différentes aient été retenues. Les définitions du terme «urbain» utilisées pour les recensements nationaux de population ont été présentées à la fin du tableau 6 lorsqu'elles étaient connues. Comme on l'a précisé dans les notes techniques relatives au tableau 6, ces définitions varient considérablement d'un pays ou d'une zone à l'autre.

Outre les problèmes de comparabilité, les taux démographiques classés selon le lieu de résidence (zone urbaine ou rurale) sont également sujets à des distorsions particulières. Si l'on utilise des définitions différentes du terme « urbain » pour classer les faits d'état civil et les données relatives à la population lors du calcul des taux et qu'il en résulte une différence nette entre le numérateur et le dénominateur pour le taux de la population exposée au risque, les taux démographiques s'en trouveront faussés. La différence entre ces taux pour les zones urbaines et rurales pourra aussi être faussée selon que les faits d'état civil auront été classés d'après le lieu de l'événement ou d'après le lieu de résidence habituel. Ce problème est examiné plus en détail à la section 4.1.4.1 des Notes techniques.

Données publiées antérieurement : Les différentes éditions de l'*Annuaire démographique* regroupent les statistiques les plus récentes dont on disposait à l'époque sur les taux de naissances vivantes selon l'âge de la mère. Les données qui figurent dans le tableau 11 actualisent les données qui portaient sur les périodes suivantes :

Éditions	Années considérées
Édition spéciale sur les statistiques de la natalité (CD-ROM), 1999	1990 – 1998
Supplément historique (CD-ROM), 1997	1948 – 1997
1992	1983 – 1992
1986	1977 – 1985
1981	1972 – 1980
Supplément rétrospectif, 1979	1948 - 1977

11. Live-birth rates by age of mother and urban/rural residence: latest available year, 1993 - 2002
Naissances vivantes, taux selon l'âge de la mère et la résidence, urbaine/rurale: dernière année disponible, 1993 - 2002

(See notes at end of table. — Voir notes à la fin du tableau.)

Continent, country or area, year and urban/rural residence / Continent, pays ou zone,année, et résidence urbaine/rurale	All ages Tous âges[1]	Age of mother (in years) - Age de la mère (en années)						
		-20[2]	20-24	25-29	30-34	35-39	40-44	45+[3]
AFRICA — AFRIQUE								
Egypt - Égypte								
1999								
Total	108.4	18.5	192.8	226.3	162.8	87.7	25.7	6.7
Mauritius - Maurice								
2002								
Total	58.5	37.2	115.8	117.2	73.0	34.9	8.9	♦0.5
Morocco - Maroc								
1999								
Total	68.6	30.8	88.6	105.2	109.5	74.3	32.1	9.2
Urban - Urbaine	56.1	22.6	70.2	87.4	90.4	61.3	23.6	4.7
Rural - Rurale	86.4	39.6	111.6	132.1	144.8	97.1	46.7	15.7
Swaziland[4]								
1997								
Total	133.2	73.0	193.4	199.4	162.6	130.8	64.7	50.0
Urban - Urbaine	106.6	65.3	147.1	157.0	115.9	92.6	39.2	31.0
Rural - Rurale	143.5	75.4	214.3	219.4	182.0	145.4	73.4	55.5
Tunisia - Tunisie								
1998								
Total	67.8	7.5	66.0	112.3	110.3	64.7	21.2	3.4
AMERICA, NORTH — AMERIQUE DU NORD								
Anguilla+								
2001								
Total	57.6	♦61.7	136.3	102.2	♦49.8	♦37.7	♦15.6	...
Bermuda - Bermudes								
2000								
Total	49.1	25.5	81.1	83.4	97.3	51.3	♦5.1	...
Canada[5]								
2001								
Total	43.0	16.6	59.8	106.4	95.2	36.6	6.2	0.3
Cuba								
2000								
Total	47.4	51.0	96.6	89.2	55.0	22.4	3.8	0.2
Urban - Urbaine	45.2	42.7	93.1	89.5	56.0	22.5	3.6	0.2
Rural - Rurale	54.4	74.7	106.1	88.4	51.8	22.2	4.5	♦0.4
El Salvador								
2002								
Total	75.1	82.6	121.5	102.3	71.4	45.6	18.1	2.5
Urban - Urbaine	72.7	84.8	128.6	103.8	67.8	37.2	12.4	1.5
Rural - Rurale	78.9	79.9	111.6	99.8	78.2	63.5	30.3	4.3
Greenland - Groenland								
1999								
Total	66.9	44.3	160.3	106.9	87.7	50.0	16.3	♦2.0
Urban - Urbaine	62.3	41.0	145.3	94.5	85.7	49.4	♦15.6	♦2.4
Rural - Rurale	90.3	♦60.9	232.8	157.9	97.4	♦53.4	♦20.6	♦0.0
Grenada - Grenade+								
2000								
Total	76.5	54.7	107.0	132.7	113.8	64.1	26.7	♦1.1
Guatemala								
1999								
Total	141.4	110.3	211.2	193.4	162.6	128.3	60.1	13.8
Jamaica - Jamaïque+								
1995								
Total	91.2	98.6	141.1	125.8	96.9	57.6	17.9	1.3
Panama								
1999								
Total	86.6	97.4	148.3	128.8	95.0	51.0	13.3	1.8
Urban - Urbaine	71.7	81.1	127.1	109.7	81.7	40.3	8.5	♦0.3
Rural - Rurale	110.6	117.3	179.0	161.1	118.7	70.7	22.0	4.4

11. Live-birth rates by age of mother and urban/rural residence: latest available year, 1993 - 2002
Naissances vivantes, taux selon l'âge de la mère et la résidence, urbaine/rurale: dernière année disponible, 1993 - 2002 (continued — suite)

(See notes at end of table. — Voir notes à la fin du tableau.)

Continent, country or area, year and urban/rural residence Continent, pays ou zone,année, et résidence urbaine/rurale	All ages Tous âges[1]	Age of mother (in years) - Age de la mère (en années)						
		-20[2]	20-24	25-29	30-34	35-39	40-44	45+[3]
AMERICA, NORTH — AMERIQUE DU NORD								
Panama 2000								
Total	85.7	95.8	148.7	128.2	94.8	50.8	14.2	1.8
Puerto Rico - Porto Rico 2000								
Total	60.5	74.0	128.0	109.5	65.2	26.7	5.5	♦0.2
Saint Kitts and Nevis - Saint-Kitts-et-Nevis+ 2000								
Total	80.0	86.6	140.2	123.1	80.0	57.4	♦20.0	♦1.0
Saint Lucia - Sainte-Lucie 2002								
Total	72.8	...	96.1	83.9	76.4	45.9	14.1	♦0.6
Saint Vincent and the Grenadines - Saint Vincent-et-les Grenadines+ 2000								
Total	80.3	73.0	128.5	100.1	80.0	72.8	16.5	♦0.6
Trinidad and Tobago - Trinité-et-Tobago 1997								
Total	52.2	43.3	97.0	88.0	70.0	35.3	9.4	♦0.6
United States - États-Unis 2002								
Total	55.2	43.7	103.6	113.6	91.5	41.4	8.3	0.5
AMERICA, SOUTH — AMERIQUE DU SUD								
Argentina - Argentine 2000								
Total	75.9	65.9	116.7	127.2	106.1	60.3	17.9	1.7
Chile - Chili 1999								
Total	63.4	64.9	99.8	106.4	84.0	48.5	13.1	0.7
French Guiana - Guyane française[6] 1999								
Total	117.2	119.2	206.7	198.3	140.7	83.7	24.9	♦4.6
Suriname 2000								
Total	85.4	68.3	150.1	148.2	104.3	56.2	16.0	♦1.8
Uruguay+ 2000								
Total	65.7	64.9	106.3	107.0	100.0	48.1	12.9	0.7
Venezuela[7] 2002								
Total	74.3	84.8	129.0	109.9	80.1	42.9	14.1	2.9
ASIA — ASIE								
Armenia - Arménie[8] 2000								
Total	31.7	27.3	103.2	53.7	23.5	10.6	3.0	0.3
Urban - Urbaine	28.6	22.1	92.3	53.5	22.7	10.2	2.8	♦0.3
Rural - Rurale	38.7	37.9	128.0	54.0	25.1	11.3	3.4	♦0.4
Azerbaijan - Azerbaïdjan+,[8] 2002								
Total	46.4	26.3	123.1	94.5	46.1	19.4	5.4	0.4

11. Live-birth rates by age of mother and urban/rural residence: latest available year, 1993 - 2002
Naissances vivantes, taux selon l'âge de la mère et la résidence, urbaine/rurale: dernière année disponible, 1993 - 2002 (continued — suite)

(See notes at end of table. — Voir notes à la fin du tableau.)

Continent, country or area, year and urban/rural residence / Continent, pays ou zone,année, et résidence urbaine/rurale	All ages Tous âges[1]	-20[2]	20-24	25-29	30-34	35-39	40-44	45+[3]
				Age of mother (in years) - Age de la mère (en années)				

ASIA — ASIE

Azerbaijan - Azerbaïdjan[+,8]
2002

Urban - Urbaine	39.7	19.4	105.1	89.3	42.2	17.3	4.2	0.4
Rural - Rurale	53.8	33.4	142.1	99.8	50.2	21.7	6.8	0.6

Brunei Darussalam - Brunéi Darussalam[+]
2001

Total	73.7	29.9	90.9	125.0	108.1	68.0	24.5	♦1.8

China: Hong Kong SAR - Chine: Hong Kong RAS[9]
2001

Total	23.5	4.1	24.8	48.1	51.2	25.4	4.1	0.2

China: Macao SAR - Chine: Macao RAS
2002

Total	22.4	4.2	23.6	55.1	54.9	21.6	2.8	♦0.3

Cyprus - Chypre[10]
2002

Total	40.2	7.0	55.0	101.7	77.0	30.6	6.3	♦0.6

Georgia - Géorgie[8]
2000

Total	31.3	30.9	82.5	59.5	30.2	12.9	3.9	0.7
Urban - Urbaine	32.5	31.6	86.7	64.2	34.2	14.4	4.4	0.8
Rural - Rurale	29.4	30.0	77.0	52.1	24.1	10.5	3.1	0.6

Israel - Israël[11]
2002

Total	86.1	15.9	112.3	177.3	160.4	88.9	21.2	1.6
Urban - Urbaine	85.3	16.4	113.4	174.2	155.9	87.3	20.9	1.6
Rural - Rurale	95.1	11.0	99.5	216.6	212.3	105.8	24.2	♦1.4

Japan - Japon[12]
2002

Total	40.1	6.1	39.0	91.7	86.5	32.0	4.2	0.1

Kazakhstan[8]
1999

Total	53.7	32.8	127.6	104.4	62.6	26.3	5.9	0.6
Urban - Urbaine	45.1	32.7	110.0	79.5	51.8	21.7	4.4	0.3
Rural - Rurale	66.8	32.9	151.7	156.1	80.3	33.5	8.4	1.0

Korea (Republic of) - Corée (République de)[13]
2002

Total	36.7	2.7	26.8	116.2	79.2	16.9	2.5	0.2

Kyrgyzstan - Kirghizistan[8]
2002

Total	76.2	30.9	161.1	138.2	94.0	50.4	15.5	5.1
Urban - Urbaine	57.9	26.2	102.6	107.6	71.5	38.5	11.2	6.1
Rural - Rurale	88.1	33.1	208.0	158.9	109.9	58.2	18.4	4.5

Maldives
1996

Total	119.8	54.4	190.9	176.5	137.7	114.2	40.0	♦6.8

Mongolia - Mongolie
2001

Total	73.5	29.3	137.4	134.9	85.1	45.3	12.6	3.6

Pakistan[14,15]
1997

Total	152.8	52.3	231.0	273.2	211.2	142.9	68.4	30.7
Urban - Urbaine	131.5	38.1	189.7	258.0	189.8	116.6	52.6	17.6
Rural - Rurale	163.6	59.6	251.9	281.1	222.0	156.3	75.9	36.8

Philippines
2000

Total	91.1	31.6	139.2	163.1	132.4	86.3	36.1	6.2

11. Live-birth rates by age of mother and urban/rural residence: latest available year, 1993 - 2002
Naissances vivantes, taux selon l'âge de la mère et la résidence, urbaine/rurale: dernière année disponible, 1993 - 2002 (continued — suite)

(See notes at end of table. — Voir notes à la fin du tableau.)

Continent, country or area, year and urban/rural residence / Continent, pays ou zone, année, et résidence urbaine/rurale	All ages Tous âges[1]	-20[2]	20-24	25-29	Age of mother (in years) - Age de la mère (en années) 30-34	35-39	40-44	45+[3]
ASIA — ASIE								
Singapore - Singapour[16]								
2002								
Total	42.5	8.3	36.0	95.7	102.0	40.8	6.2	0.3
Sri Lanka+								
1996								
Total	72.6	29.1	88.7	129.1	110.9	81.8	20.0	2.4
Tajikistan - Tadjikistan[8]								
1993								
Total	146.4	53.9	271.9	225.5	159.6	93.6	35.7	6.9
Urban - Urbaine	101.4	46.0	215.7	167.7	104.2	50.0	13.8	2.2
Rural - Rurale	166.8	56.9	294.3	248.9	185.7	118.1	50.0	10.2
Turkey - Turquie[14]								
1997								
Total	81.1	50.0	173.6	144.9	73.3	36.1	15.5	3.4
Uzbekistan - Ouzbékistan[8]								
2000								
Total	82.7	21.1	205.4	161.4	89.7	31.5	7.0	0.8
Urban - Urbaine	65.7	21.8	167.9	123.6	73.0	26.6	5.4	0.5
Rural - Rurale	93.6	20.7	227.5	185.9	100.6	34.7	8.2	1.1
EUROPE								
Austria - Autriche								
2002								
Total	39.3	13.8	61.1	97.1	73.2	28.8	5.5	0.3
Belarus - Bélarus[8]								
2002								
Total	33.3	23.5	96.6	73.1	37.1	11.7	2.1	0.1
Urban - Urbaine	31.2	19.6	87.0	70.6	36.8	11.0	1.9	♦0.1
Rural - Rurale	40.8	37.0	139.1	82.3	38.0	14.0	2.8	♦0.2
Bulgaria - Bulgarie								
2002								
Total	34.9	41.6	82.3	73.2	34.0	9.8	1.7	♦0.1
Urban - Urbaine	32.8	31.8	71.9	74.4	36.2	10.2	1.7	♦0.1
Rural - Rurale	42.1	73.4	118.2	69.3	27.3	8.6	1.8	0.0
Croatia - Croatie								
2002								
Total	37.0	14.9	69.6	94.8	61.4	22.7	4.6	0.2
Czech Republic - République tchèque								
2002								
Total	38.5	13.7	64.5	96.2	53.9	17.7	3.0	0.1
Urban - Urbaine	38.7	14.5	61.8	96.2	56.8	18.5	3.1	♦0.1
Rural - Rurale	38.1	11.7	72.2	96.3	45.2	15.0	2.6	♦0.1
Denmark - Danemark[17]								
2002								
Total	51.4	6.5	48.9	123.2	115.6	45.6	7.2	0.3
Estonia - Estonie[8]								
2002								
Total	38.0	21.9	76.4	88.6	58.0	24.3	4.9	♦0.1
Urban - Urbaine	35.5	19.2	65.6	83.0	55.7	23.2	4.3	♦0.1
Rural - Rurale	44.5	27.4	112.5	106.6	64.1	27.0	6.2	♦0.1
Finland - Finlande[18]								
2002								
Total	46.3	11.2	57.2	112.5	102.9	47.9	9.8	0.6
Urban - Urbaine	45.4	11.9	49.7	100.2	99.1	47.2	9.8	0.5
Rural - Rurale	48.1	10.1	80.8	147.7	111.0	49.2	10.0	0.8
France[19,20]								
2001								
Total	53.6	11.5	63.5	137.0	110.6	46.0	9.1	0.4

11. Live-birth rates by age of mother and urban/rural residence: latest available year, 1993 - 2002
Naissances vivantes, taux selon l'âge de la mère et la résidence, urbaine/rurale: dernière année disponible, 1993 - 2002 (continued — suite)

(See notes at end of table. — Voir notes à la fin du tableau.)

Continent, country or area, year and urban/rural residence / Continent, pays ou zone,année, et résidence urbaine/rurale	All ages Tous âges[1]	-20[2]	20-24	25-29	30-34	35-39	40-44	45+[3]
EUROPE								
Germany - Allemagne								
2001								
Total	37.4	13.0	54.6	88.5	76.8	30.8	5.0	0.2
Greece - Grèce								
1998								
Total	38.7	11.8	53.2	89.6	71.9	26.4	4.9	0.5
Hungary - Hongrie								
2002								
Total	38.0	21.4	60.0	91.9	59.7	22.0	4.1	0.1
Urban - Urbaine	35.9	15.6	48.5	88.5	62.6	22.6	4.0	0.1
Rural - Rurale	42.4	33.2	84.8	99.5	53.9	21.1	4.1	♦0.1
Iceland - Islande								
2000								
Total	60.1	23.2	87.6	128.7	113.4	51.1	10.5	♦0.4
Urban - Urbaine	59.7	23.5	89.2	128.3	110.0	48.3	10.3	♦0.3
Rural - Rurale	65.7	♦20.3	67.8	137.6	166.7	88.4	♦12.6	♦1.6
2002								
Total	55.8	18.5	75.4	120.7	107.6	54.3	10.0	♦0.7
Ireland - Irlande[+,21]								
2002								
Total	58.5	19.5	52.4	93.0	133.2	79.3	14.5	0.6
Italy - Italie								
2000								
Total	38.8	7.1	33.5	75.8	83.5	41.4	7.7	0.4
Latvia - Lettonie[8]								
2002								
Total	33.9	16.0	72.6	80.3	51.2	21.1	4.9	0.4
Urban - Urbaine	31.1	13.2	63.3	76.7	50.1	20.2	4.3	♦0.3
Rural - Rurale	40.5	21.4	93.3	89.0	53.8	23.1	6.7	♦0.6
Liechtenstein								
2002								
Total	43.8	♦3.9	32.6	89.9	113.5	49.8	♦6.1	...
Lithuania - Lituanie[8]								
2002								
Total	33.8	20.6	79.6	79.9	44.8	16.9	4.1	♦0.2
Urban - Urbaine	29.1	16.0	62.6	71.8	41.2	14.7	3.4	♦0.1
Rural - Rurale	46.0	29.9	129.3	103.3	54.3	22.6	6.2	♦0.4
Luxembourg								
2002								
Total	47.6	12.6	58.6	101.9	100.1	45.2	7.6	♦0.3
Malta - Malte[22]								
2002								
Total	39.4	16.9	49.0	107.8	71.9	29.2	5.4	♦0.1
Netherlands - Pays-Bas[23]								
2002								
Total	51.0	5.8	36.8	97.6	133.4	58.2	9.2	0.4
Urban - Urbaine	50.1	7.3	38.5	88.0	123.9	59.2	10.3	0.5
Rural - Rurale	53.0	3.0	32.3	122.0	153.3	56.2	7.2	0.3
Norway - Norvège[20]								
2002								
Total	51.8	10.1	59.5	121.0	109.3	44.1	7.7	0.2
Poland - Pologne								
2002								
Total	34.9	15.1	67.5	87.6	51.4	21.2	4.6	0.2
Portugal								
2002								
Total	43.7	21.0	54.6	93.1	83.4	35.1	6.8	0.5

11. Live-birth rates by age of mother and urban/rural residence: latest available year, 1993 - 2002
Naissances vivantes, taux selon l'âge de la mère et la résidence, urbaine/rurale: dernière année disponible, 1993 - 2002 (continued — suite)

(See notes at end of table. — Voir notes à la fin du tableau.)

Continent, country or area, year and urban/rural residence / Continent, pays ou zone, année, et résidence urbaine/rurale	Age of mother (in years) - Age de la mère (en années)							
	All ages Tous âges[1]	-20[2]	20-24	25-29	30-34	35-39	40-44	45+[3]
EUROPE								
Republic of Moldova - République de Moldova[8]								
2002								
Total	35.3	30.2	91.5	66.2	38.5	13.0	2.5	♦0.1
Urban - Urbaine	28.6	19.8	79.8	60.9	33.4	11.2	2.1	♦0.1
Rural - Rurale	40.5	36.7	98.9	70.3	43.8	14.6	2.9	♦0.1
Romania - Roumanie								
2002								
Total	37.6	33.3	81.5	77.6	38.3	15.0	3.0	0.2
Urban - Urbaine	28.6	18.5	56.0	71.2	36.4	12.7	2.1	0.1
Rural - Rurale	51.6	53.8	118.6	85.8	41.1	19.2	4.8	0.4
Russian Federation - Fédération de Russie[8]								
1999								
Total	31.1	29.3	92.6	64.9	32.5	11.2	2.2	0.1
Urban - Urbaine	28.5	25.2	85.6	60.4	30.7	10.1	1.8	0.1
Rural - Rurale	39.4	40.4	114.4	79.8	37.8	14.4	3.5	0.2
San Marino - Saint-Marin+								
2000								
Total	41.8	...	♦22.6	67.0	112.0	42.5	♦8.6	♦1.1
Serbia and Montenegro - Serbie-et-Montenegro								
2000								
Total	47.9	25.2	105.5	108.9	62.6	24.5	4.9	0.5
Urban - Urbaine	46.7	21.7	98.2	116.1	70.6	27.2	5.2	0.4
Rural - Rurale	49.2	28.8	113.1	101.5	53.8	21.2	4.6	0.6
2001								
Total	49.5	24.9	104.8	112.6	65.7	25.7	5.0	0.4
Slovakia - Slovaquie								
2002								
Total	35.3	21.5	68.6	83.4	46.0	16.2	2.9	♦0.1
Slovenia - Slovénie								
2002								
Total	34.3	6.0	46.4	97.4	67.3	21.8	3.4	♦0.1
Urban - Urbaine	32.6	5.1	37.9	92.7	73.7	23.9	3.6	♦0.1
Rural - Rurale	37.4	7.0	56.5	106.6	64.2	20.5	3.3	♦0.1
Spain - Espagne								
1998								
Total	35.8	8.0	24.0	68.6	90.1	37.1	5.8	0.2
Sweden - Suède								
2002								
Total	48.2	6.6	47.7	109.2	110.7	47.3	8.9	0.3
Switzerland - Suisse								
2002								
Total	40.4	5.4	41.0	90.3	94.7	40.4	6.8	0.4
The Former Yugoslav Rep. of Macedonia - L'ex-République yougoslave de Macédoine								
2001								
Total	51.0	27.1	114.7	122.1	60.5	18.5	3.0	♦0.2
Ukraine[8]								
2001								
Total	29.6	29.6	88.6	56.4	27.5	8.8	1.9	0.1
United Kingdom - Royaume-Uni[24,25]								
1999								
Total	49.5	30.7	72.4	98.9	88.9	39.5	7.6	0.4

11. Live-birth rates by age of mother and urban/rural residence: latest available year, 1993 - 2002
Naissances vivantes, taux selon l'âge de la mère et la résidence, urbaine/rurale: dernière année disponible, 1993 - 2002 (continued — suite)

(See notes at end of table. — Voir notes à la fin du tableau.)

Continent, pays ou zone,année, et résidence urbaine/rurale	All ages Tous âges[1]	-20[2]	20-24	25-29	30-34	35-39	40-44	45+[3]
OCEANIA — OCEANIE								
Australia - Australie[+]								
2002								
Total	50.4	17.1	55.5	104.2	111.2	52.2	9.7	0.4
New Caledonia - Nouvelle-Calédonie								
1994								
Total	89.5	33.9	140.3	182.3	130.0	60.8	16.4	♦1.1
New Zealand - Nouvelle-Zélande[+]								
2000								
Total	57.9	28.8	78.4	115.6	115.5	53.4	10.2	0.4
Tonga[+]								
1999								
Total	110.2	28.3	128.3	220.2	201.6	128.2	49.3	♦3.2

GENERAL NOTES - NOTES GENERALES

Rates are the number of live births by age of mother per 1 000 corresponding female population. For definitions of 'urban', see end of Technical Notes for table 6. For method of evaluation and limitations of data, see Technical Notes for this table. — Les taux représentent les nombres vivantes selon l'âge de la mère pour 1 000 femmes du même groupe d'âge. Pour les définitions des 'régions urbaines', se reporter à la fin des Notes techniques du tableau 6. Pour la méthode d'évaluation et les insuffisances des données, voir Notes techniques pour ce tableau.

FOOTNOTES - NOTES

♦ Rates based on 30 or fewer live births. — Taux basés sur 30 naissances vivantes ou moins.

[+] Data tabulated by date of registration rather than occurrence. — Données exploitées selon la date de l'enregistrement et non la date de l'événement.

[1] Rates computed on female population aged 15-49. — Taux calculés sur la base de la population féminine de 15 à 49 ans.

[2] Rates computed on female population aged 15-19. — Taux calculés sur la base de la population féminine de 15 à 19 ans.

[3] Rates computed on female population aged 45-49. — Taux calculés sur la base de la population féminine de 45 à 49 ans.

[4] Data for 1997 refer to last twelve months preceding population and housing census of 1997. - Les données pour 1997 se réfèrent au douze mois précédant le recensement de population et de l'habitat de 1997.

[5] Including Canadian residents temporarily in the United States, but excluding United States residents temporarily in Canada. - Y compris les résidents canadiens se trouvant temporairement aux Etats-Unis, mais ne comprenant pas les résidents des Etats-Unis se trouvant temporairement au Canada.

[6] Excluding live-born infants who died before their birth was registered. - Non compris les enfants nés vivants décédés avant l'enregistrement de leur naissance.

[7] Excluding Indian jungle population. - Non compris les Indiens de la jungle.

[8] Excluding infants born alive with less than 28 weeks gestation, less than 1 000 grams in weight and 35 centimeters in length, who die within seven days of birth. - Non compris les enfants nés vivants avant 28 semaines de gestation, pesant moins de 1 000 grammes, mesurant moins de 35 centimètres et décédés dans les sept jours qui ont suivi leur naissance.

[9] Including unknown sex. - Y compris le sexe inconnu.

[10] Data refer to government controlled areas. - Les données se raportent aux zones contrôlées par le Gouvernement.

[11] Beginning 1970, including data for East Jerusalem and Israeli residents in certain other territories under occupation by Israeli military forces since 1967. - A partir de 1970, y compris les données pour Jérusalem-Est et les résidents israéliens dans certains autres territoires occupés depuis juin 1967 par les forces armées israéliennes.

[12] Data refer to Japanese nationals in Japan only. - Les données se raportent aux nationaux japonais au Japon seulement.

[13] Excluding alien armed forces, civilian aliens employed by armed forces, and foreign diplomatic personnel and their dependants. - Non compris les militaires étrangers, les civils étrangers employés par les forces armées ni le personnel diplomatique étranger et les membres de leur famille les accompagnant.

[14] Based on the results of the Population Growth Survey. - D'après les résultats de la 'Population Growth Survey.'

[15] Excluding data for the Pakistan-held part of Jammu and Kashmir, the final status of which has not yet been determined. - Non compris les données concernant la partie du Jammu et Cachemire occupée par le Pakistan dont le statut définitif n'a pas été déterminé.

[16] Excluding transients afloat and non-locally domiciled military and civilian services personnel and their dependants. - Non compris les personnes de passage þ bord de navires, ni les militaires et agents civils domiciliés hors du territoire et les membres de leur famille les accompagnant.

[17] Excluding Faeroe Islands and Greenland. - Non compris les Iles Féroé et Gröenland.

[18] Including nationals temporarily outside the country. - Y compris les nationaux se trouvant temporairement hors du pays.

[19] Including armed forces stationed outside the country. - Y compris les militaires nationaux hors du pays.

[20] Age classification is based on year of birth of mother rather than the exact age of mother at birth of child. - Le classement selon l'âge est basé sur l'année de naissance de la mère et non sur l'age exacte de la mère au moment de naissance de l'enfant.

[21] Births registered within one year of occurrence. - Naissances enregistrées dans l'année qui suit l'événement.

[22] Live births to Maltese parents only. - Naissances vivantes aux parents maltais seulement.

[23] Including residents outside the country if listed in a Netherlands population register. - Y compris les résidents hors du pays, s'ils sont inscrits sur un registre de population néerlandais.

[24] Data revised to exclude births in Northern Ireland to non-residents of Northern Ireland. - Données révisées non compris des naissances en Irlande du Nord aux non-résidents de l'Irlande du Nord.

[25] Data tabulated by date of occurrence for England and Wales, and by date of registration for Northern Ireland and Scotland. - Données exploitées selon la date de l'événement pour l'Angleterre et le pays de Galles, et selon la date de l'enregistrement pour l'Irlande du Nord et l'Ecosse.

Table 11a presents life births by month of occurrence for as many years as possible between 1980 and 2002.

Description of variables: Live birth is defined as the complete expulsion or extraction from its mother of a product of conception, irrespective of the duration of pregnancy, which after such separation, breathes or shows any other evidence of life such as beating of the heart, pulsation of the umbilical cord, or definite movements of voluntary muscles, whether or not the umbilical cord has been cut or the placenta is attached; each product of such a birth is considered live-born[i].

Month of birth is the calendar month when birth occurred, rather than the month when the event was registered.

Statistics on the number of births are obtained from civil registers unless otherwise noted.

Reliability of data: Each country or area has been asked to indicate the estimated completeness of the deaths recorded in its civil register. These national assessments are indicated by the quality codes C and U that appear in the first column of this table.

C indicates that the data are estimated to be virtually complete, that is, representing at least 90 per cent of the live births occurring each year, while U indicates that data are estimated to be incomplete, that is, representing less than 90 per cent of the live births occurring each year. A third code (...) indicates that no information was provided regarding completeness.

Data from civil registers that are reported as incomplete or of unknown completeness (coded U or ...) are considered unreliable. They appear in italics in this table and rates are not calculated for these data.

These quality codes apply only to data from civil registers. If data from other sources are presented, the symbol (|) is shown instead of the quality code. For more information about the quality of vital statistics data in general, and the information available on the basis of the completeness estimates in particular, see section 4.2 of the Technical Notes.

Limitations: Statistics on births by month are subject to the same qualifications as have been set forth for vital statistics in general and birth statistics in particular as discussed in section 4 of the Technical Notes.

The reliability of the data is an important factor in considering the limitations. In addition, some births are tabulated by date of registration and not by date of occurrence; these have been indicated by a plus sign (+). Whenever the lag between the date of occurrence and date of registration is prolonged and, therefore, a large proportion of the birth registrations are delayed, birth statistics for any given year may be seriously affected.

Another factor that limits international comparability is the practice of some countries or areas not to include in live-birth statistics infants who were born alive but died before the registration of the birth or within the first 24 hours of life, thus underestimating the total number of life births. Statistics of this type are footnoted.

Earlier data: This is the first time data on births by month are published in the Demographic Yearbook.

NOTES

[i] *Principles and Recommendations for a Vital Statistics System Revision 2,* Sales No. E. 01.XVII.10, United Nations, New York, 2001.

Tableau 11a

Le tableau 11a présente des statistiques sur les naissances vivantes mois par mois pour le plus grand nombre d'années possible entre 1980 et 2002.

Description des variables : La naissance vivante est l'expulsion ou l'extraction complète du corps de la mère, indépendamment de la durée de gestation, d'un produit de la conception qui, après cette séparation, respire ou manifeste tout autre signe de vie, tel que battement de cœur, pulsation du cordon ombilical ou contraction effective d'un musde soumis à l'action de la volonté, que le cordon ombilical ait été coupé ou non et que le placenta soit ou non demeuré attaché ; tout produit d'une telle naissance est considéré comme « enfant né vivant[1] » .

Le mois de la naissance est le mois civil de la naissance effective et non de son enregistrement.

Sauf indication contraire, les statistiques concernant le nombre de naissances sont établies sur la base des données provenant des registres d'état civil.

Fiabilité des données : Il a été demandé à chaque pays ou zone d'indiquer le degré estimatif de complétude des données sur les naissances figurant dans ses registres d'état civil. Ces évaluations nationales sont désignées par les codes de qualité 'C' et 'U' qui apparaissent dans la deuxième colonne du tableau.

La lettre 'C' indique que les données sont jugées à peu près complètes, c'est à dire qu'elles représentent au moins 90 p. 100 des naissances vivantes survenues chaque année ; la lettre 'U' signale que les données sont jugées incomplètes, c'est à dire qu'elles représentent moins de 90 p. 100 des naissances vivantes survenues chaque année. Le code '...' indique qu'aucun renseignement n'a été communiqué quant à l'exhaustivité des données.

Les données issues des registres d'état civil qui sont déclarées incomplètes ou dont le degré d'exhaustivité n'est pas connu (code 'U' ou '...') sont jugées douteuses. Elles apparaissent en italique dans le présent tableau. Les taux pour ces données ne sont pas calculés.

Les codes de qualité ne s'appliquent qu'aux données provenant des registres de l'état civil. Si l'on présente des données autres que celles de l'état civil, le signe '|' est utilisé à la place du code de qualité. Pour plus de précisions sur la qualité des données reposant sur les statistiques de l'état civil en général et les estimations de complétude en particulier, voir la section 4.2 des Notes techniques.

Insuffisance des données : Les statistiques concernant les naissances vivantes mois par mois appellent toutes les réserves qui ont été formulées à propos des statistiques de l'état civil en général et des statistiques des naissances en particulier (voir la section 4 des Notes techniques).

La fiabilité des données est un facteur important. Il faut également tenir compte du fait que, dans certains cas, les données relatives aux naissances sont exploitées selon la date de l'enregistrement et non selon la date de l'événement ; ces cas ont été signalés par le signe '+'. Chaque fois que le décalage entre l'événement et son enregistrement est grand et qu'une forte proportion des naissances fait l'objet d'un enregistrement tardif, les statistiques des naissances vivantes pour une année donnée peuvent être considérablement faussées.

Un autre facteur qui nuit à la comparabilité internationale est la pratique de certains pays ou zones qui consiste à ne pas prendre en considération dans les statistiques des naissances vivantes les enfants nés vivants mais décédés avant l'enregistrement de leur naissance ou dans les 24 heures qui ont suivi la naissance, pratique qui conduit à sous-estimer le nombre total de naissances vivantes. Lorsque ce facteur a joué, cela a été signalé en note à la fin du tableau.

Données publiées antérieurement : C'est la première fois que des statistiques sur les naissances mois par mois sont publiées dans l'*Annuaire démographique*.

NOTE

[1] *Principes et recommandations pour un système de statistique de l'état civil, deuxième révision*, numéro de vente : F.01.XVII.10, publication des Nations Unies, New York, 2003.

11a. Live births by month of occurence: 1980 - 2002
Naissances vivantes selon le mois de naissance: 1980 - 2002

(See notes at end of table. — Voir notes à la fin du tableau.)

Continent, country or area / Continent, pays ou zone	Code[a]	Total	Jan	Feb	March	April	May	June	July	Aug	Sep	Oct	Nov	Dec
AFRICA — AFRIQUE														
Algeria - Algérie[1,2]														
1980	C	818 613	83 368	79 826	79 226	72 592	69 305	57 776	59 581	65 310	65 279	61 311	62 125	62 914
1981	C	835 100	82 333	77 915	83 017	77 038	72 365	61 967	63 209	67 599	61 945	60 596	62 098	65 018
1985	C	845 383	93 578	78 854	82 345	67 350	72 706	69 240	70 916	69 547	64 724	61 931	56 451	57 741
1986	C	766 186	82 496	70 265	69 622	62 917	64 430	63 123	56 663	58 640	58 924	60 857	60 250	57 999
1998	C	607 118	59 167	50 778	50 794	46 819	50 306	50 646	51 476	52 166	49 684	49 004	47 384	48 894
1999	C	593 643	55 704	47 505	49 160	45 366	49 173	50 254	53 224	54 723	47 414	47 119	44 724	49 277
2000	C	588 628	55 519	45 971	46 044	45 570	47 817	47 684	53 617	52 523	46 251	47 985	48 022	51 625
2001	C	618 380	55 930	46 091	47 938	46 425	50 570	52 460	57 651	53 880	51 583	50 917	51 008	53 927
2002	C	616 963	52 873	46 391	48 335	46 338	48 775	53 046	57 296	55 098	50 593	52 340	53 142	52 736
Cape Verde - Cap-Vert														
1980	C	9 650	845	878	854	829	830	763	630	829	870	903	784	635
1981	C	8 580	677	607	742	572	453	357	699	932	921	961	826	833
1982	C	11 066	977	874	941	903	879	813	835	881	1 018	1 043	888	1 014
1983	C	11 438	1 138	960	945	927	866	813	804	944	1 152	992	935	962
1984	C	11 696	1 058	951	1 003	954	985	837	949	938	1 058	1 002	984	977
1985	C	11 282	1 099	929	991	911	911	777	914	852	1 032	1 037	894	935
1990	C	9 669	1 065	825	853	738	650	463	689	750	757	1 004	952	923
Egypt - Égypte[3]														
1980	C	1569247	177 868	128 197	136 924	115 668	106 881	107 557	122 852	122 807	148 667	127 730	141 562	132 534
1981	C	1593698	199 252	139 687	145 733	116 343	107 610	104 400	106 138	135 422	140 197	128 766	142 050	128 100
1982	C	1601265	200 893	137 777	149 642	120 572	111 392	102 548	107 366	135 760	126 010	150 233	133 634	125 438
1983	C	1690000	192 000	140 000	161 000	151 000	103 000	94 000	113 000	141 000	138 000	153 000	133 000	171 000
1984	C	1797206	224 430	144 259	141 823	120 867	116 036	133 665	173 615	139 037	159 667	163 956	279 851	...
1985	C	1903022	254 154	105 989	149 121	103 184	131 687	125 593	201 714	165 739	190 242	169 635	305 964	...
1986	C	1907975	235 307	154 218	153 102	133 211	122 541	128 453	150 350	147 965	192 060	179 536	311 232	...
1987	C	1902604	239 690	151 142	166 473	139 593	114 029	143 124	143 885	146 043	184 673	167 736	157 467	148 749
1988	C	1912765	232 813	152 839	166 649	136 344	127 523	145 343	132 699	170 398	185 209	173 950	149 692	139 306
1989	C	1722934	211 882	139 834	142 655	115 594	114 326	118 818	134 280	149 922	173 755	154 108	142 716	125 044
1990	C	1686877	223 906	141 878	143 969	109 778	134 314	122 969	120 484	136 809	171 265	145 741	129 434	106 330
1991	C	1636551	225 132	114 426	129 463	113 646	133 148	116 245	140 996	138 105	170 061	147 973	119 013	88 343
1992	C	1496866	174 112	123 940	123 187	112 716	115 435	105 274	115 324	128 047	157 747	125 710	117 693	97 681
1993	C	1600549	177 091	131 583	122 336	131 789	112 898	112 535	126 390	145 830	177 837	131 708	130 123	100 429
1994	C	1610652	188 087	122 299	133 482	122 694	113 364	124 116	128 577	139 393	173 422	142 815	120 717	101 686
1995	C	1604835	203 563	120 931	137 901	122 209	115 329	115 671	127 541	136 517	180 803	133 622	119 466	91 282
1996	C	1662065	206 361	141 531	146 391	112 621	128 330	123 254	134 910	142 716	187 496	137 555	117 893	83 007
1997	C	1654695	189 351	138 306	142 992	118 416	125 138	124 073	138 303	144 987	181 005	122 592	128 484	101 048
1998	C	1687252	174 511	151 222	135 022	122 508	121 943	128 206	134 153	142 050	186 807	136 277	142 143	112 410
1999	C	1693025	199 053	145 822	136 976	133 071	117 243	116 851	138 094	151 506	181 176	132 567	134 070	106 596
Malawi[4]														
1982	I	281 888	21 351	19 296	21 570	22 672	21 855	25 677	23 103	24 688	27 789	30 694	18 611	23 086
Mali														
1987	C	95 482	326	1 339	8 728	8 935	9 702	8 628	8 585	9 948	10 835	10 578	10 063	7 815
Mauritius - Maurice														
1990	+C	22 369	1 752	1 693	2 010	1 879	1 962	1 837	1 916	1 918	1 904	1 936	1 795	1 767
1991	+C	22 182	1 715	1 706	1 922	1 836	2 011	1 872	1 966	1 918	1 861	1 797	1 766	1 812
1994	+C	21 704	1 674	1 627	1 838	1 771	1 924	1 925	1 855	1 939	2 024	1 830	1 581	1 716
1995	+C	20 604	1 668	1 653	1 859	1 760	1 799	1 709	1 701	1 639	1 786	1 704	1 599	1 727
1996	+C	20 498	1 660	1 523	1 852	1 684	1 890	1 723	1 826	1 832	1 734	1 542	1 581	1 651
1997	+C	19 852	1 565	1 603	1 692	1 546	1 814	1 685	1 725	1 749	1 719	1 622	1 460	1 672
1998	+C	19 270	1 510	1 485	1 714	1 740	1 810	1 576	1 783	1 687	1 586	1 523	1 353	1 503
1999	+C	20 399	1 588	1 589	1 781	1 802	1 875	1 647	1 797	1 862	1 695	1 581	1 514	1 668
2000	+C	20 237	1 495	1 521	1 664	1 700	1 838	1 789	1 730	1 774	1 716	1 678	1 576	1 756
2001	+C	19 504	1 668	1 427	1 768	1 699	1 781	1 615	1 729	1 625	1 572	1 581	1 452	1 587
2002	+C	19 799	1 574	1 542	1 701	1 807	1 798	1 578	1 729	1 688	1 629	1 636	1 541	1 576
Réunion[1]														
1980	C	12 272	1 022	1 002	1 083	1 035	1 118	1 065	1 043	1 010	1 028	983	925	958
1981	C	11 800	972	843	984	987	1 038	1 053	1 021	1 013	998	982	939	970
1982	C	11 951	1 001	877	1 046	1 012	1 049	1 005	989	1 062	983	1 009	903	1 015
1983	C	12 461	949	967	1 079	1 018	1 101	1 061	1 125	1 104	1 018	1 092	946	1 001
1984	C	13 116	1 132	1 037	1 083	1 049	1 160	1 129	1 145	1 067	1 079	1 117	1 072	1 046
1985	C	13 163	1 086	1 047	1 160	1 101	1 050	1 136	1 222	1 115	1 094	1 074	1 019	1 059

(See notes at end of table. — Voir notes à la fin du tableau.)

Continent, country or area / Continent, pays ou zone	C-o-d-e[a]	Total	Jan	Feb	March	April	May	June	July	Aug	Sep	Oct	Nov	Dec
AFRICA — AFRIQUE														
Réunion[1]														
1986	C	12 797	1 116	897	1 081	1 062	1 173	1 061	1 071	1 082	1 106	1 082	949	1 117
1988	C	13 559	1 016	957	1 202	1 142	1 175	1 155	1 214	1 163	1 216	1 123	1 085	1 111
1989	C	13 898	1 139	1 076	1 205	1 181	1 237	1 119	1 234	1 121	1 172	1 229	1 071	1 114
1990	C	13 911	1 181	1 108	1 216	1 142	1 226	1 146	1 108	1 108	1 140	1 227	1 161	1 148
1998	C	13 538	1 136	992	1 234	1 102	1 263	1 154	1 247	1 115	1 132	1 099	998	1 066
1999	C	14 153	1 301	1 238	1 201	1 185	931	1 188	1 266	1 166	1 182	1 148	1 147	1 200
2000	C	14 842	1 213	1 144	1 280	1 319	1 279	1 226	1 256	1 253	1 221	1 186	1 155	1 310
2001	C	14 541	1 272	1 163	1 246	1 323	1 300	1 230	1 291	1 215	1 174	1 149	1 044	1 134
Saint Helena ex. dep. - Sainte-Hélène sans dép.														
1981	C	129	18	5	6	7	10	16	9	10	13	7	17	11
1982	C	123	8	8	8	9	14	10	10	9	18	10	11	8
1983	C	99	14	7	10	9	9	8	8	6	9	5	6	8
1984	C	87	4	12	8	6	7	8	8	7	11	6	5	5
1985	C	83	12	10	5	5	5	7	7	8	11	8	3	2
1986	C	101	9	5	10	12	6	10	10	6	6	12	4	11
1989	C	89	9	5	9	10	7	6	9	9	7	6	7	5
1990	C	65	9	11	4	6	8	4	4	3	5	4	5	2
1991	C	72	8	2	4	10	6	5	7	5	4	9	4	8
1992	C	78	5	13	3	7	5	7	8	6	6	7	6	5
1993	C	69	11	4	7	7	9	7	5	5	-	4	4	6
1994	C	58	8	-	6	10	7	6	5	4	2	4	5	1
1995	C	72	7	9	5	2	2	8	5	8	9	7	6	4
1996	C	59	2	5	7	8	7	4	6	5	5	5	3	2
1997	C	64	5	6	9	5	4	4	11	3	4	2	7	4
1998	C	59	5	2	5	2	11	3	11	3	4	2	7	4
1999	C	52	6	5	4	7	2	5	2	4	6	2	3	6
2000	C	56	4	7	8	6	4	4	-	9	4	3	5	2
2001	C	36	3	3	5	2	3	4	2	6	-	3	4	1
Saint Helena: Ascension - Sainte-Hélène: Ascension														
1980	C	5	-	-	-	-	-	2	1	1	-	-	1	-
1981	C	15	-	1	2	-	1	1	3	1	-	1	2	3
Seychelles														
1980	+C	1 830	163	130	150	170	200	169	156	111	173	149	120	130
1981	+C	1 802	122	126	157	173	152	180	171	147	148	134	127	165
1982	+C	1 552	136	121	148	117	152	142	122	138	126	132	126	92
1983	+C	1 662	133	101	145	146	144	142	132	161	152	139	135	132
1984	+C	1 739	119	132	122	158	181	144	159	140	146	170	122	146
1985	+C	1 729	156	140	132	175	141	124	156	134	133	140	138	160
1986	+C	1 722	126	140	136	174	144	138	177	140	163	140	120	124
1987	+C	1 684	118	128	129	140	167	160	143	148	142	137	138	134
1988	+C	1 643	118	126	131	130	151	158	154	139	163	142	103	128
1989	+C	1 600	118	114	145	136	164	143	130	131	128	142	128	121
1990	+C	1 617	115	121	127	157	146	135	149	138	130	162	130	107
1991	+C	1 708	136	118	133	182	165	151	173	134	132	156	113	115
1992	+C	1 603	94	79	124	134	152	158	154	148	130	138	138	154
1993	+C	1 689	123	122	141	136	134	164	146	151	158	130	141	143
1995	+C	1 582	108	105	131	141	159	138	145	137	114	161	122	121
1996	+C	1 611	154	114	122	142	163	115	138	152	130	153	125	103
1997	+C	1 475	128	122	131	137	160	127	139	121	100	105	88	117
1998	+C	1 412	120	114	124	125	123	142	135	93	114	112	106	104
1999	+C	1 460	78	76	113	153	149	157	134	139	125	98	116	122
2000	+C	1 512	119	115	137	119	158	110	123	136	117	123	136	119
2001	+C	1 440	112	120	107	137	144	116	141	111	102	131	125	94
2002	+C	1 481	132	97	105	130	167	126	137	137	114	123	124	89
Tunisia - Tunisie														
1980	C	225 201	22 097	19 001	19 752	19 908	19 689	17 394	17 706	18 871	18 930	17 662	16 866	17 325
1981	C	225 671	20 460	18 636	20 812	22 387	21 136	18 840	18 472	19 312	17 017	15 910	16 246	16 443

11a. Live births by month of occurence: 1980 - 2002
Naissances vivantes selon le mois de naissance: 1980 - 2002 (continued — suite)

(See notes at end of table. — Voir notes à la fin du tableau.)

Continent, country or area Continent, pays ou zone	C-o-d-e[a]	Total	Jan	Feb	March	April	May	June	July	Aug	Sep	Oct	Nov	Dec
AFRICA — AFRIQUE														
Tunisia - Tunisie														
1982	C	221 027	21 228	19 003	21 003	19 417	19 672	18 635	18 236	18 866	17 053	16 708	15 591	15 615
1985	C	227 188	22 503	19 270	20 363	19 337	20 459	19 768	19 666	18 228	17 377	17 226	16 371	16 620
1986	C	234 736	22 561	19 271	20 401	18 721	20 842	21 477	21 356	20 030	18 416	17 954	16 848	16 859
1987	C	224 169	22 592	18 642	19 220	18 681	19 248	19 771	19 480	19 254	17 249	16 314	16 107	17 611
1988	C	215 069	23 408	19 551	18 691	17 326	19 225	16 854	18 461	18 017	16 628	16 873	15 525	14 510
1989	C	199 459	18 813	15 650	15 563	16 371	17 458	16 852	17 559	16 973	16 323	16 436	15 646	15 815
1990	C	205 315	19 721	16 360	17 054	17 415	17 976	17 218	18 421	18 015	16 879	16 231	14 893	15 132
1991	C	207 455	18 892	15 313	16 758	17 331	18 858	18 583	18 158	17 803	16 807	16 948	16 194	15 810
1992	C	211 649	19 642	16 151	18 343	17 839	18 844	18 815	19 243	18 475	16 875	16 373	15 374	15 675
1993	C	207 786	18 967	15 795	18 119	17 388	18 040	18 953	19 375	18 242	17 355	16 438	14 355	14 759
1994	C	200 223	17 520	16 150	16 903	15 926	17 845	17 782	18 538	17 730	16 527	15 627	14 652	15 023
1995	C	186 416	16 775	15 027	15 119	14 602	15 971	16 288	17 303	17 081	15 618	14 657	14 156	13 819
1997	C	173 757	16 331	13 736	13 560	13 544	15 281	16 400	16 720	15 969	14 064	13 227	12 563	12 362
1998	C	166 718	15 031	12 191	12 384	12 613	14 506	15 841	15 779	14 911	14 226	14 051	12 528	12 657
AMERICA, NORTH — AMERIQUE DU NORD														
Antigua and Barbuda - Antigua-et-Barbuda														
1980	+C	1 238	112	89	88	102	81	97	94	98	124	128	123	102
1981	+C	1 177	114	90	112	67	71	90	93	93	85	130	116	104
1982	+C	1 152	110	73	104	104	76	75	98	116	117	103	99	77
1983	+C	1 172	112	102	92	108	86	70	82	112	101	108	96	103
1984	+C	1 126	94	84	90	77	92	83	85	100	97	118	110	96
1985	+C	1 190	107	96	98	103	96	90	101	100	114	110	79	96
1986	+C	1 130	97	85	84	94	84	87	83	89	108	119	98	102
Bahamas														
1980	U	5 035	424	386	423	344	331	362	420	431	523	471	437	483
1981	U	5 251	454	259	410	363	367	374	443	521	507	522	457	474
1982	U	5 293	455	421	408	359	354	380	475	481	569	468	458	465
1983	U	5 280	501	362	377	354	393	400	415	463	541	491	486	476
1984	U	5 023	504	430	379	316	346	329	493	414	481	476	435	410
1985	U	5 439	484	417	449	387	389	417	488	489	499	512	471	433
1986	U	4 664	503	311	373	365	323	305	446	395	431	456	381	369
1987	U	4 331	383	368	337	301	323	306	369	365	370	443	366	400
1988	U	4 943	446	363	389	329	341	326	406	438	534	456	464	451
1989	U	4 971	434	317	384	359	365	367	421	483	523	497	407	414
1990	U	5 007	462	350	398	328	350	313	410	521	517	488	441	429
1991	U	5 124	475	382	350	350	343	399	446	451	565	484	430	449
1992	U	4 870	407	408	409	315	363	350	372	508	435	464	417	422
1993	U	6 674	671	535	501	375	456	480	526	668	718	632	574	538
1994	U	4 357	411	359	344	283	304	304	325	387	425	432	390	393
1995	U	6 253	569	455	496	437	455	452	505	594	599	630	552	509
1996	U	5 873	493	500	426	312	380	391	452	580	638	596	539	566
1997	U	6 022	579	465	433	381	449	375	470	510	632	599	531	521
1998	U	5 880	616	464	458	302	398	392	485	534	572	549	496	531
1999	U	5 367	421	375	297	342	415	323	480	545	454	438	605	671
2000	U	5 287	452	389	390	360	359	374	398	450	649	513	481	469
2001	U	5 353	493	380	450	353	382	364	447	567	523	501	443	450
Barbados - Barbade														
1982	+C	4 499	379	356	374	311	323	366	369	366	422	431	441	361
1983	+C	4 496	412	368	373	305	332	322	346	418	415	412	386	407
1984	+C	4 214	395	288	359	321	333	300	324	370	352	371	347	454
1985	+C	4 281	398	318	333	317	335	321	322	311	342	445	429	410
1986	+C	4 043	359	267	289	294	318	306	284	328	365	455	387	391
1987	+C	3 828	333	290	287	309	318	239	296	305	355	395	342	359
1988	+C	3 745	289	265	268	299	280	263	264	314	369	384	361	389
1989	+C	4 015	337	271	289	299	292	254	294	354	399	421	412	393
1990	+C	4 313	397	324	324	316	341	284	317	330	413	427	374	466
1991	+C	4 240	392	290	330	291	290	298	301	322	388	525	535	278

(See notes at end of table. — Voir notes à la fin du tableau.)

Continent, country or area / Continent, pays ou zone	Code[a]	Total	Jan	Feb	March	April	May	June	July	Aug	Sep	Oct	Nov	Dec
AMERICA, NORTH — AMERIQUE DU NORD														
Belize														
1997	U	5 738	605	494	479	517	492	459	474	510	635	528	349	196
Bermuda - Bermudes														
1984	C	840	73	58	63	86	73	46	78	65	88	73	57	80
1985	C	914	76	80	45	81	70	61	81	90	87	72	83	88
1986	C	889	81	64	65	66	70	69	77	65	95	91	59	87
1987	C	899	70	64	75	74	65	71	76	83	81	90	75	75
1988	C	935	79	80	81	57	80	77	75	81	95	84	75	75
1989	C	912	66	59	75	55	74	81	76	85	88	84	75	66
1990	C	895	77	69	70	59	58	59	91	78	94	88	77	81
1991	C	901	68	73	74	70	62	74	75	86	84	83	68	71
1995	C	839	73	63	80	66	69	57	65	86	76	77	67	60
1996	C	834	62	59	61	77	79	63	76	85	87	67	58	60
1997	C	849	66	52	82	65	69	81	74	62	86	73	59	80
1998	C	825	79	62	57	63	67	69	62	68	77	89	61	71
1999	C	828	62	61	75	51	68	65	48	93	82	82	71	70
2000	C	838	64	48	84	61	67	63	82	69	75	85	54	86
2001	C	831	66	73	65	58	66	62	70	76	67	78	71	79
British Virgin Islands - Îles Vierges britanniques														
1980	+C	261	25	20	15	16	19	17	26	21	23	22	27	30
1981	+C	231	29	11	20	23	11	21	18	13	25	20	23	17
1982	+C	235	24	19	15	21	15	12	14	22	26	25	20	22
1983	+C	281	32	20	18	16	18	24	26	25	22	21	31	28
1984	+C	225	22	19	11	11	21	18	19	23	17	27	15	22
1985	+C	248	15	16	15	32	20	18	26	20	20	26	20	20
1986	+C	213	24	18	18	15	17	15	16	17	17	15	17	24
1988	+C	237	23	21	13	25	20	12	14	15	23	18	33	20
Canada[5]														
1980	C	370 709	29 520	28 888	31 792	31 272	32 159	30 919	32 255	31 224	32 573	31 398	28 849	29 860
1981	C	370 330	29 431	27 892	32 537	31 979	32 104	31 516	32 713	31 532	31 500	30 336	28 933	29 863
1982	C	373 082	29 793	28 560	32 514	31 998	32 583	31 555	32 329	31 496	32 197	30 589	29 542	29 726
1983	C	373 689	29 278	28 101	32 893	31 989	33 286	32 071	32 063	31 022	31 591	30 662	29 666	30 267
1984	C	377 001	29 048	29 253	32 530	31 930	33 205	31 898	32 805	32 785	32 422	32 006	29 224	30 267
1985	C	375 027	29 704	27 972	32 409	32 438	33 469	31 693	32 981	31 891	32 297	31 517	29 178	29 478
1986	C	372 431	29 234	28 137	32 107	32 865	33 809	31 131	32 541	31 577	32 106	30 803	28 397	29 724
1987	C	369 441	28 962	27 696	32 609	32 702	33 247	32 223	32 353	30 664	31 128	29 504	28 739	29 616
1988	C	375 743	28 822	28 810	32 404	31 570	33 440	32 471	32 510	32 526	32 717	31 257	29 450	29 766
1989	C	391 925	30 351	28 904	33 723	33 196	34 694	34 011	34 140	34 027	33 615	32 423	31 071	31 770
1990	C	404 669	32 132	30 697	35 540	35 187	36 861	34 820	35 117	34 886	34 424	33 069	30 978	30 958
1992	C	398 642	31 974	31 557	34 949	35 250	36 082	33 814	35 239	32 944	33 648	32 120	30 072	30 993
1993	C	388 394	30 989	29 544	34 268	34 125	34 805	33 433	33 958	32 728	33 169	31 289	29 550	30 536
1994	C	385 112	30 265	29 195	34 093	33 183	34 526	33 667	33 690	32 951	32 592	30 883	29 802	30 265
1995	C	378 011	29 975	29 051	33 426	31 755	34 567	33 039	33 304	32 780	32 529	30 683	28 664	28 238
1996	C	366 200	29 410	28 811	31 792	31 802	33 119	31 316	32 460	31 296	30 884	29 866	27 290	28 154
1997	C	348 598	28 408	26 542	30 018	30 678	31 735	29 982	31 033	29 235	29 232	28 284	26 266	27 185
1999	C	337 249	26 956	25 642	29 292	28 546	30 000	29 329	30 175	28 395	29 202	27 209	25 668	26 835
2000	C	327 882	27 228	26 196	29 203	28 227	29 821	28 753	28 548	27 740	26 885	25 846	24 903	24 532
2001	C	333 744	26 769	25 392	29 189	28 820	29 907	28 576	29 089	28 794	28 240	27 636	25 811	25 521
Cayman Islands - Îles Caïmanes														
1981	C	348	28	21	29	19	20	19	36	29	43	38	38	28
1982	C	339	28	27	29	22	24	21	25	39	34	30	32	28
1983	C	387	34	31	31	23	31	24	26	29	42	35	44	37
1986	C	360	22	25	26	16	35	27	34	48	31	30	31	35
1987	C	359	32	35	31	24	18	23	29	31	35	32	33	36
1988	C	380	40	31	42	22	31	31	20	26	30	36	36	35
1989	C	438	39	25	30	29	30	33	32	38	46	47	51	38
1990	C	490	41	39	52	39	36	25	37	42	33	62	37	47
1991	C	500	43	30	34	30	35	26	40	59	61	53	40	49

11a. Live births by month of occurence: 1980 - 2002
Naissances vivantes selon le mois de naissance: 1980 - 2002 (continued — suite)

(See notes at end of table. — Voir notes à la fin du tableau.)

Continent, country or area / Continent, pays ou zone	Code / Code[a]	Total	Jan	Feb	March	April	May	June	July	Aug	Sep	Oct	Nov	Dec
AMERICA, NORTH — AMERIQUE DU NORD														
Cayman Islands - Îles Caïmanes														
1992	C	520	31	44	46	34	37	41	42	48	57	52	53	35
1993	C	527	32	46	38	37	55	50	37	52	35	56	48	41
1994	C	531	47	42	28	41	36	34	50	44	47	57	46	59
1995	C	484	39	39	33	21	48	34	43	48	49	44	41	45
Costa Rica														
1980	C	66 101	5 460	5 004	5 732	5 337	5 404	5 589	5 794	5 631	6 043	5 867	5 418	4 822
1981	C	67 715	5 675	5 190	5 957	5 723	5 758	6 441	5 681	5 931	6 419	6 302	5 736	2 902
1982	C	67 422	5 425	4 848	5 416	5 621	5 909	5 821	5 827	6 134	6 269	6 216	5 815	4 121
1987	C	80 326	7 124	6 201	6 684	6 382	6 413	6 152	6 496	6 696	7 038	7 337	6 815	6 988
1988	C	81 376	6 675	5 960	6 898	6 411	6 736	6 514	6 434	6 945	7 297	7 476	7 077	6 953
1989	C	83 460	7 078	6 089	6 847	6 803	6 788	6 724	6 663	7 087	7 489	7 486	7 482	6 924
1990	C	81 939	7 228	6 121	6 758	6 513	6 782	6 300	6 632	6 836	6 966	7 356	7 128	7 319
1991	C	81 100	7 202	5 952	6 717	6 639	6 554	6 308	6 325	6 750	7 096	7 095	7 153	7 309
1994	C	80 391	6 757	5 660	6 328	6 283	6 427	6 549	6 591	6 863	7 380	7 528	7 035	6 990
1995	C	80 306	6 949	5 783	6 499	6 454	6 586	6 381	6 651	6 940	7 177	7 318	6 828	6 740
1996	C	79 203	6 581	5 740	6 255	6 185	6 338	5 966	6 478	6 954	7 157	7 542	7 195	6 812
1997	C	78 018	6 642	5 824	6 323	6 164	6 500	6 181	6 179	6 322	6 978	7 272	6 772	6 861
1999	C	78 526	5 997	5 564	6 442	6 335	6 954	6 224	6 605	6 658	7 109	7 217	6 798	6 623
Cuba														
1980	C	136 900	12 047	10 541	10 815	9 720	9 994	9 857	10 541	11 773	12 732	13 553	12 869	12 458
1981	C	136 211	11 714	10 216	10 488	9 535	9 670	9 807	10 624	11 578	12 940	14 166	12 804	12 669
1982	C	159 759	12 348	10 640	10 871	10 196	10 779	11 266	13 194	15 468	17 134	16 490	15 552	15 821
1983	C	165 284	15 058	12 660	13 073	11 426	11 583	11 164	12 946	15 136	15 769	16 038	15 161	15 270
1984	C	166 281	14 601	13 229	12 577	10 694	11 302	11 712	13 071	15 284	15 449	16 800	15 790	15 772
1985	C	182 067	14 812	13 150	14 346	13 224	13 102	13 038	15 504	17 130	17 373	17 612	16 374	16 402
1986	C	166 049	15 544	12 832	12 395	11 899	12 316	11 872	13 685	15 357	16 439	15 889	14 041	13 780
1987	C	179 477	13 879	12 769	13 103	12 274	12 645	12 991	14 810	16 101	17 327	18 346	17 961	17 271
1988	C	187 911	16 600	14 925	14 272	12 288	12 169	12 373	14 521	17 170	18 701	18 838	18 237	17 817
1990	C	186 658	15 764	13 453	13 835	12 979	13 445	13 261	14 714	17 017	17 788	18 756	18 084	17 572
1991	C	173 896	16 472	13 122	12 986	12 112	12 140	11 875	13 054	15 780	17 387	17 437	15 997	15 534
1992	C	157 349	14 061	11 995	11 513	10 466	10 937	10 994	11 952	14 014	15 359	16 141	15 041	14 876
1993	C	152 238	14 103	12 522	12 517	11 030	12 116	11 877	12 415	12 532	13 210	13 704	12 742	13 470
1994	C	147 265	12 827	12 195	11 356	9 781	10 341	10 946	11 312	12 222	13 961	14 678	14 008	13 638
1995	C	147 170	12 522	10 587	10 856	9 966	10 632	10 422	11 231	12 885	13 785	14 792	14 587	14 905
1996	C	140 276	13 099	10 868	10 464	9 303	9 527	9 253	10 303	12 058	13 769	14 830	13 645	13 157
1997	C	152 681	13 001	11 294	11 305	9 743	10 759	10 687	12 063	13 581	15 822	15 719	14 356	14 351
1998	C	151 080	13 559	11 230	11 176	10 030	10 128	10 681	12 680	13 664	14 230	14 918	14 633	14 151
1999	C	150 785	13 164	11 310	10 225	9 476	10 243	10 573	11 555	13 858	15 142	15 305	14 793	15 141
2000	C	143 528	12 893	11 003	10 856	9 779	9 750	9 503	10 595	12 795	14 425	14 658	13 857	13 414
Dominican Republic - République dominicaine														
1980	+U	192 800	16 846	16 353	15 908	13 791	14 545	13 820	16 943	15 229	20 756	17 297	14 401	16 911
1981	+U	249 145	18 654	17 587	19 414	16 532	17 652	18 860	21 635	20 809	31 147	25 301	20 954	20 600
1997	+U	164 556	14 227	12 758	12 807	13 059	12 180	13 245	14 774	16 695	17 455	13 737	11 797	11 822
1998	+U	179 372	15 019	14 679	14 376	12 531	13 469	14 357	16 683	19 027	18 810	15 609	13 909	10 903
1999	+U	193 418	15 410	15 330	14 602	13 470	14 615	14 165	17 226	19 000	20 982	16 918	16 090	15 610
El Salvador														
1980	U	169 930	16 887	13 996	12 937	14 408	13 777	12 826	12 828	13 868	15 053	15 705	14 382	13 263
1981	U	163 305	16 476	12 983	13 397	12 041	13 091	12 193	12 534	13 534	14 559	14 460	14 679	13 358
1982	U	156 807	15 492	12 479	11 685	12 792	12 552	11 815	12 156	13 478	13 985	13 525	13 802	13 046
1983	U	144 193	14 004	11 650	11 113	11 607	11 754	10 889	11 372	12 132	12 966	12 937	12 195	11 574
1984	U	142 202	13 215	10 901	10 841	10 369	12 194	11 708	12 372	12 290	12 290	12 682	12 225	11 115
1985	U	140 784	13 595	10 942	10 191	10 877	11 850	7 280	14 872	11 764	12 069	11 364	13 483	12 497
1986	U	145 126	12 320	12 179	12 027	12 364	11 634	11 209	11 859	12 084	13 291	12 963	12 072	11 124
1987	U	148 397	13 815	11 855	12 892	12 259	11 891	11 738	11 526	11 991	12 963	13 238	12 503	11 726
1988	U	149 299	14 851	12 506	12 345	12 252	12 450	11 713	11 674	12 919	12 719	12 271	12 291	11 308
1989	U	151 893	13 408	12 672	12 650	11 805	12 375	11 597	12 083	12 905	14 179	13 597	12 078	12 544
1990	U	148 379	14 387	12 532	12 238	12 089	12 343	11 416	11 953	12 255	12 915	12 055	12 457	11 739

11a. Live births by month of occurence: 1980 - 2002
Naissances vivantes selon le mois de naissance: 1980 - 2002 (continued — suite)

(See notes at end of table. — Voir notes à la fin du tableau.)

Continent, country or area / Continent, pays ou zone	Code [a]	Total	Jan	Feb	March	April	May	June	July	Aug	Sep	Oct	Nov	Dec
AMERICA, NORTH — AMERIQUE DU NORD														
El Salvador														
1991	U	151 229	14 344	11 495	11 495	12 095	12 635	11 069	12 817	13 317	13 757	13 482	12 882	11 601
1992	U	154 014	15 214	12 850	11 776	11 228	12 567	11 317	12 722	12 827	13 997	13 627	12 834	13 055
1993	U	157 640	14 914	10 151	11 320	13 870	13 001	11 720	13 573	12 945	14 802	15 344	13 593	12 407
1994	U	160 772	13 796	11 223	13 105	13 311	14 188	13 726	12 202	12 511	16 894	11 597	15 802	12 417
1995	U	159 336	13 846	13 185	12 788	12 256	13 835	12 591	12 343	14 494	14 510	13 768	13 828	11 892
1996	C	163 007	10 506	13 143	12 359	11 939	13 796	12 107	14 370	13 365	14 090	14 746	13 933	18 653
1997	C	164 143	13 986	11 876	12 964	13 019	13 517	12 424	14 009	12 941	14 123	15 744	13 784	15 756
1998	C	158 350	13 716	11 810	12 549	12 185	12 567	12 252	13 172	13 090	14 721	14 878	13 759	13 651
1999	C	153 636	12 998	10 964	12 000	11 480	12 000	12 821	12 470	12 657	13 090	13 456	13 657	13 372	14 671
2000	C	150 176	12 132	11 790	12 367	11 383	12 769	11 664	12 169	12 992	13 439	14 245	12 525	12 701
2001	C	138 354	11 737	10 432	11 012	11 190	11 694	10 526	11 246	11 505	12 295	12 787	11 703	12 227
2002	C	129 363	10 633	9 961	10 116	10 417	10 628	10 767	10 764	11 398	11 742	11 768	10 175	10 994
Greenland - Groenland														
1980	C	1 028	91	71	96	100	91	62	93	83	90	99	78	74
1981	C	1 051	86	76	78	77	86	87	111	82	106	80	75	107
1982	C	1 066	81	91	86	79	90	95	99	103	89	76	96	81
1983	C	985	80	82	86	71	86	68	90	109	94	61	79	79
1984	C	1 054	74	105	87	93	85	89	92	80	93	93	88	75
1985	C	1 140	97	66	84	104	100	96	105	112	108	90	79	99
1986	C	1 070	83	73	105	95	88	103	102	96	79	71	84	91
1987	C	1 090	101	84	80	95	88	87	99	91	101	76	80	108
1989	C	1 210	90	105	89	107	113	92	101	135	100	95	93	90
1990	C	1 257	92	93	96	93	132	115	122	108	99	112	106	89
1992	C	1 237	90	108	118	89	113	92	118	104	109	103	101	92
1993	C	1 180	91	91	115	91	105	77	94	112	100	77	116	111
1994	C	1 156	84	97	96	110	83	112	114	78	102	98	86	96
1995	C	1 120	89	83	122	79	95	95	101	96	97	87	88	88
1996	C	1 066	82	86	97	85	110	83	101	80	104	87	67	84
1997	C	1 100	98	82	86	88	93	91	94	105	99	77	103	84
1998	C	986	85	101	82	72	74	77	80	83	73	85	79	95
1999	C	947	88	82	86	66	84	83	91	75	62	76	77	77
Guadeloupe														
1980	C	6 425	534	423	489	531	500	491	520	538	598	606	583	612
1982	C	6 643	624	501	564	454	532	520	519	553	591	608	590	587
1983	C	6 722	628	532	552	495	569	505	526	581	608	619	535	572
1984	C	6 671	602	541	498	482	540	451	537	563	618	655	592	592
1985	C	6 750	558	504	544	520	584	514	521	541	577	618	604	665
1986	C	6 374	563	477	503	485	487	417	528	575	581	612	576	570
1991	C	7 547	656	568	610	575	565	546	573	631	695	757	689	682
1997	C	7 554	667	559	539	593	552	522	596	673	734	739	705	675
1998	C	7 141	632	557	574	548	514	540	559	590	651	658	653	665
1999	C	7 341	616	518	530	529	515	498	634	623	667	745	731	735
2000	C	7 653	671	555	559	588	579	542	641	605	700	738	757	718
2001	C	7 503	751	527	570	532	569	538	630	614	713	754	644	661
2002	C	6 995	623	485	487	549	535	472	554	596	635	674	722	663
Guatemala														
1981	C	308 413	28 876	24 697	25 582	23 883	25 332	24 054	25 546	26 128	26 433	26 601	25 606	25 675
1982	C	312 047	28 518	22 851	23 881	23 314	24 596	24 228	26 522	26 272	27 128	27 504	29 111	28 122
1983	C	306 827	28 865	23 170	25 631	24 787	25 226	19 654	31 037	25 736	25 494	25 201	25 013	27 013
1984	C	312 094	29 058	25 458	24 971	23 314	25 957	24 170	26 420	25 778	26 478	27 278	25 235	27 977
1985	C	326 849	33 292	25 284	25 875	24 168	27 255	24 933	27 241	27 080	27 807	26 432	25 546	31 936
1986	C	319 321	30 870	27 170	23 488	28 045	26 293	24 281	28 244	24 981	27 607	28 525	25 815	24 002
1987	C	324 784	32 877	27 457	26 315	25 355	24 887	25 109	28 044	27 043	26 644	28 481	27 098	25 474
1988	C	341 382	30 168	30 073	27 275	27 683	28 556	26 458	27 654	30 657	28 683	28 032	29 468	26 675
1989	C	340 807	30 711	24 348	27 764	26 097	28 003	27 626	29 053	28 868	30 672	29 284	27 509	30 872
1990	C	347 207	32 695	27 031	28 310	27 527	30 130	29 288	29 207	29 207	29 452	29 823	26 035	28 502
1991	C	359 904	33 235	29 300	30 164	29 311	29 175	29 268	29 922	28 958	32 151	28 841	29 144	30 435
1992	C	363 648	33 357	28 061	28 462	28 422	29 847	29 181	31 073	31 784	31 541	31 139	30 071	30 710
1993	C	370 138	33 917	29 547	29 523	29 017	31 271	29 086	31 979	30 563	32 930	31 081	29 407	31 817

373

(See notes at end of table. — Voir notes à la fin du tableau.)

Continent, country or area / Continent, pays ou zone	C-o-d-e[a]	Total	Jan	Feb	March	April	May	June	July	Aug	Sep	Oct	Nov	Dec
AMERICA, NORTH — AMERIQUE DU NORD														
Guatemala														
1994	C	381 497	33 850	28 872	31 132	30 343	32 425	31 036	32 053	32 055	33 596	33 243	30 439	32 453
1995	C	371 091	34 202	29 128	30 396	29 332	32 057	30 012	30 734	29 958	32 961	30 918	29 756	31 637
1996	C	377 723	35 375	30 362	30 690	30 132	30 757	29 767	31 515	32 259	33 024	31 811	29 560	32 471
1997	C	387 862	34 776	29 359	31 656	30 708	32 474	31 259	32 215	31 866	33 800	33 216	31 173	35 360
1998	C	400 133	35 814	31 055	32 794	32 163	32 915	31 497	33 439	33 500	35 002	34 270	32 608	35 076
1999	C	409 034	35 750	31 136	33 469	31 676	33 690	32 844	34 259	34 466	36 283	35 018	33 794	36 649
Honduras														
1980	+U	155 908	14 821	12 462	12 721	12 075	13 371	12 803	13 314	12 234	12 734	12 856	13 243	13 274
1981	+U	161 020	14 826	12 638	14 662	12 857	13 084	13 086	12 787	12 473	13 074	13 586	13 696	14 251
1982	+U	161 653	13 462	12 951	13 881	12 234	13 106	13 273	13 079	13 842	13 288	13 695	14 086	14 756
1983	+U	158 419	14 839	12 730	12 436	12 900	13 353	12 604	12 442	13 728	12 744	13 200	13 844	13 599
Jamaica - Jamaïque[6]														
1982	+C	59 079	5 277	4 365	4 638	4 505	4 614	4 180	4 332	4 948	5 529	5 492	5 568	5 631
1983	+C	61 436	5 660	4 725	5 300	4 981	4 642	4 274	4 861	5 296	5 936	5 477	5 103	5 181
1987	+C	52 476	4 719	4 128	4 481	4 080	4 028	3 804	4 061	4 037	4 882	5 003	4 708	4 545
1991	+C	59 879	15 964	...	...	13 979	...	...	14 350	...	...	15 586	...	...
1992	+C	58 627	16 727	...	...	12 728	...	...	13 714	...	...	15 458	...	...
1993	+C	57 404	14 144	...	...	12 864	...	...	14 533	...	...	15 863	...	...
1994	+C	59 235	16 395	...	...	13 060	...	...	14 205	...	...	15 575	...	...
1995	+C	57 607	15 739	...	...	12 836	...	...	14 124	...	...	14 908	...	...
1997	+C	59 385	16 697	...	...	13 307	...	...	13 841	...	...	15 540	...	...
Martinique														
1980	C	5 392	509	355	430	425	442	387	447	417	485	486	510	499
1981	C	5 397	472	396	440	397	441	401	407	441	530	513	485	474
1982	C	5 376	440	410	450	418	412	394	369	424	492	548	506	513
1983	C	5 641	458	389	487	451	457	412	465	506	517	553	522	424
1984	C	5 705	507	425	458	441	492	425	440	463	472	537	545	500
1985	C	5 719	497	398	462	422	479	432	437	467	531	596	503	495
1986	C	5 961	503	429	458	460	471	441	471	470	588	606	540	524
1987	C	6 328	512	428	465	480	523	479	468	497	640	668	614	554
1988	C	6 386	550	476	539	468	503	432	460	501	579	658	606	614
1989	C	6 565	548	458	505	481	492	508	493	534	647	639	622	638
1990	C	6 437	630	463	548	510	493	444	489	507	591	608	575	579
1991	C	6 316	544	460	517	483	468	398	460	538	621	666	579	582
1992	C	6 305	565	453	512	483	478	446	487	533	596	581	595	576
1998	C	5 816	545	472	423	433	440	382	419	480	562	561	515	584
1999	C	5 789	502	418	455	402	419	384	465	482	542	539	583	598
2000	C	6 059	560	445	460	466	462	405	500	512	511	614	542	582
2001	C	5 908	519	446	518	434	461	410	480	474	532	561	535	538
2002	C	5 446	489	399	419	435	423	356	444	449	479	478	534	541
Mexico - Mexique														
1981	+U	2530662	215 579	194 904	210 190	199 061	208 777	205 444	212 754	221 634	218 698	217 968	207 486	215 477
1982	+U	2392849	203 676	186 183	202 775	192 137	202 598	198 233	203 878	214 746	207 098	200 117	186 990	192 250
1983	+U	2609088	220 921	198 149	214 838	207 821	216 327	213 516	219 019	234 830	224 503	221 737	213 875	221 110
1984	+U	2511894	206 446	188 706	204 586	200 146	210 887	209 908	216 380	229 110	217 851	216 174	201 278	208 116
1985	+U	2655571	227 659	213 329	214 558	204 707	313 127	196 243	216 314	238 808	215 316	227 504	200 231	187 775
1986	+U	2577045	237 397	207 229	196 689	228 814	201 363	197 909	218 754	235 884	214 033	228 385	201 468	209 120
1988	+U	2622031	217 358	233 166	218 593	214 623	225 696	207 168	196 632	242 982	217 279	232 997	218 814	196 723
1989	+U	2620262	225 431	211 201	195 060	213 944	225 188	212 766	216 679	243 549	218 327	236 107	224 346	197 664
1990	+U	2735312	238 559	220 313	224 378	216 132	234 630	209 961	227 504	265 769	231 355	270 093	207 165	189 453
1991	+U	2756447	242 594	232 561	209 591	276 443	230 402	203 758	228 003	248 301	235 169	239 681	210 753	199 191
1992	+U	2797397	222 545	226 620	232 061	225 871	221 374	226 679	248 248	254 787	245 406	237 327	239 911	216 568
1993	+U	2839686	234 713	233 785	261 009	227 254	229 297	225 987	230 154	251 125	236 390	243 811	243 058	223 103
1994	+U	2904389	241 101	216 223	238 917	224 327	238 880	238 481	247 598	270 004	256 784	252 083	235 480	243 253
1995	+U	2750444	228 084	204 183	224 289	213 195	226 295	224 159	234 035	257 444	244 416	239 396	223 510	230 617
1996	+U	2707718	223 462	200 029	217 044	209 995	219 439	215 048	231 197	258 000	242 350	239 278	221 848	229 154
1997	+U	2698425	230 340	220 239	209 952	285 225	216 287	202 578	213 082	230 357	225 371	231 339	218 194	215 461
1998	+U	2668428	218 708	196 177	212 867	204 512	214 572	214 278	229 501	259 781	236 925	234 750	220 128	225 592
1999	+U	2769089	227 531	214 831	236 721	270 162	222 033	204 213	213 556	254 687	233 870	226 095	244 031	221 359
2000	+U	2798339	240 182	232 619	243 803	251 557	236 623	222 576	215 551	255 232	230 724	254 973	221 774	192 715

(See notes at end of table. — Voir notes à la fin du tableau.)

Continent, country or area / Continent, pays ou zone	Code[a]	Total	Jan	Feb	March	April	May	June	July	Aug	Sep	Oct	Nov	Dec
AMERICA, NORTH — AMERIQUE DU NORD														
Mexico - Mexique														
2001	+U	2767610	244 857	214 777	225 503	280 048	245 654	213 801	217 735	246 065	224 671	242 235	219 972	192 292
Montserrat														
1983	+C	266	19	23	17	14	26	18	28	25	24	24	26	22
1984	+C	243	24	14	13	18	23	17	18	27	26	23	21	19
1985	+C	237	33	18	16	18	15	15	21	19	23	17	18	24
1986	+C	200	14	19	13	11	13	13	21	21	18	15	21	21
Nicaragua														
1985	+U	103 968	7 696	9 126	9 348	8 323	8 991	8 041	9 010	8 787	8 887	9 573	9 066	7 120
1986	+U	109 410	9 536	9 799	8 300	10 926	8 389	8 404	8 776	8 921	9 293	9 845	9 472	7 749
1987	+U	98 240	10 028	9 674	10 002	8 061	8 034	8 208	7 054	7 402	7 462	8 444	7 955	5 916
1995	+U	114 452	10 119	8 521	9 473	9 334	9 522	8 772	8 345	9 163	10 930	10 602	9 841	9 830
1996	+U	109 447	8 877	8 007	8 452	8 254	9 023	8 412	8 824	9 417	10 017	10 286	9 987	9 891
1997	+U	113 498	9 358	8 360	8 713	8 864	9 419	8 922	9 119	9 779	10 726	10 564	9 768	9 906
1998	+U	111 154	9 692	8 418	8 116	7 831	8 047	8 516	9 003	9 527	10 505	11 146	10 398	9 955
1999	+U	123 446	10 046	8 631	9 390	9 363	10 096	9 552	9 641	10 980	11 592	11 500	11 380	11 275
2000	+U	126 873	10 825	9 508	9 856	9 784	10 673	10 071	10 474	11 072	11 681	11 479	10 763	10 687
2001	+U	108 299	10 571	8 473	9 294	8 728	9 166	8 513	8 900	9 337	9 547	9 545	8 536	7 689
2002	+U	120 846	10 308	8 980	9 420	9 743	9 750	9 409	9 490	10 510	11 130	11 084	10 443	10 579
Panama														
1980	C	52 626	4 440	4 059	4 375	4 135	4 120	4 180	4 235	4 337	4 528	4 646	4 761	4 810
1981	C	53 873	4 732	4 058	4 311	4 198	4 598	4 084	4 430	4 533	4 706	4 948	4 740	4 535
1982	C	54 491	4 660	3 946	4 449	4 465	4 595	4 263	4 435	4 486	4 732	4 803	4 793	4 864
1983	C	55 222	4 875	4 278	4 508	4 420	4 654	4 298	4 746	4 752	4 816	4 836	4 623	4 416
1984	C	56 659	4 416	4 213	4 338	4 356	4 432	4 675	4 901	4 863	5 105	5 078	5 132	5 150
1985	C	58 038	5 210	4 468	4 914	4 759	4 811	4 478	4 589	4 738	4 866	5 267	4 948	4 990
1986	C	57 655	4 950	4 378	4 668	4 677	4 650	4 466	4 680	4 605	4 997	5 196	5 171	5 217
1987	C	58 392	4 825	4 876	4 851	4 874	4 891	4 917	4 896	4 874	4 833	4 838	4 834	4 883
1988	C	58 459	4 795	4 566	4 702	4 592	4 851	4 656	4 816	4 889	4 927	5 248	5 343	5 074
1989	C	59 069	5 147	4 332	5 010	4 838	4 932	4 402	4 628	4 883	5 233	5 292	5 252	5 120
1990	C	59 904	5 414	4 578	4 985	4 568	4 966	4 704	4 752	5 012	4 992	5 373	5 300	5 271
1991	C	60 080	5 351	4 697	4 896	4 831	4 998	4 482	4 895	4 881	5 246	5 401	5 252	5 150
1992	C	59 905	5 230	4 847	4 930	4 603	4 663	4 501	4 873	4 958	5 539	5 465	5 119	5 177
1993	C	59 191	5 148	4 610	4 971	4 906	5 024	4 479	4 593	4 676	5 057	5 206	5 218	5 303
1994	C	59 947	5 188	4 349	4 772	4 926	4 986	5 133	4 780	4 894	5 227	5 287	5 196	5 209
1995	C	61 939	5 225	4 464	4 825	4 790	5 035	4 765	4 831	5 205	5 512	5 932	5 663	5 692
1996	C	63 401	4 885	4 571	5 296	5 263	4 913	5 074	5 235	5 552	5 754	5 728	5 831	
1997	C	68 009	6 201	5 488	5 721	5 570	5 732	5 372	5 456	5 621	5 841	5 826	5 591	5 590
1998	C	62 351	5 907	4 884	5 321	4 841	4 599	4 827	4 956	5 080	5 451	5 689	5 448	5 348
1999	C	64 248	5 254	4 411	5 064	5 050	5 562	5 138	5 268	5 451	5 705	5 996	5 609	5 740
2002	C	61 671	5 585	4 542	5 037	4 935	4 836	4 877	5 053	5 558	5 289	5 314	5 368	5 277
Puerto Rico - Porto Rico														
1980	C	73 060	6 261	5 594	5 669	5 400	5 676	5 666	5 854	6 223	6 944	6 910	6 320	6 543
1981	C	71 365	6 033	5 082	5 481	5 460	5 618	5 477	5 950	6 225	6 803	6 668	6 300	6 268
1982	C	69 336	6 068	5 192	5 736	5 307	5 321	5 188	5 616	5 885	6 182	6 390	6 131	6 319
1983	C	65 742	5 716	5 105	5 309	5 014	5 257	5 113	5 336	5 803	6 131	5 946	6 131	6 319
1984	C	63 321	5 325	4 773	4 945	4 609	4 922	4 907	5 054	5 579	5 735	5 907	5 578	5 434
1985	C	63 629	5 554	4 872	5 119	4 900	5 016	4 738	5 122	5 542	5 825	5 878	5 749	5 816
1987	C	64 393	5 277	4 761	5 193	4 932	4 968	4 912	5 287	5 529	6 092	5 934	5 390	5 673
1988	C	64 081	5 152	4 679	5 163	4 824	4 890	4 906	5 070	5 530	6 020	6 162	5 782	5 818
1989	C	66 692	5 480	4 540	5 224	5 021	5 318	5 206	5 479	5 963	6 332	6 249	5 887	5 993
1990	C	66 555	5 829	4 954	5 368	5 008	5 160	5 133	5 366	5 869	5 902	6 092	5 991	5 883
1991	C	64 516	5 667	4 809	4 983	5 021	5 039	4 698	5 224	5 541	6 072	6 011	5 650	5 801
1992	C	64 481	5 480	4 851	4 986	4 805	4 772	4 882	5 249	5 648	6 231	6 163	5 578	5 838
1994	C	64 325	5 516	4 734	5 284	4 787	5 058	5 055	5 155	5 772	5 873	5 747	5 673	5 671
1996	C	63 259	5 390	4 952	4 897	4 521	4 858	4 813	5 182	5 601	5 929	5 816	5 452	5 848
1997	C	64 214	5 454	4 890	4 886	4 999	4 838	4 799	5 204	5 662	6 186	6 031	5 369	5 896
1998	C	60 518	5 278	4 697	4 980	4 709	4 623	4 716	4 843	5 317	5 396	5 527	5 091	5 341
1999	C	59 684	4 883	4 251	4 762	4 369	4 303	4 664	4 770	5 271	5 863	5 555	5 393	5 600
2000	C	59 460	5 011	4 454	4 818	4 276	4 597	4 529	4 684	5 265	5 584	5 515	5 434	5 293

11a. Live births by month of occurence: 1980 - 2002
Naissances vivantes selon le mois de naissance: 1980 - 2002 (continued — suite)

(See notes at end of table. — Voir notes à la fin du tableau.)

Continent, country or area / Continent, pays ou zone	C-o-d-e[a]	Total	Jan	Feb	March	April	May	June	July	Aug	Sep	Oct	Nov	Dec
AMERICA, NORTH — AMERIQUE DU NORD														
Puerto Rico - Porto Rico														
2002	C	52 871	4 641	3 983	4 055	4 181	4 178	3 993	4 237	4 763	4 721	4 876	4 583	4 660
Saint Kitts and Nevis - Saint-Kitts-et-Nevis[6]														
1983	+C	1 093	300	...	...	215	...	...	276	...	...	302	...	...
1984	+C	1 115	264	...	...	262	...	...	282	...	...	307	...	...
1985	+C	1 026	226	...	...	232	...	...	264	...	...	304	...	...
1986	+C	1 007	263	...	...	221	...	...	265	...	...	256	...	...
1988	+C	944	222	...	...	177	...	...	275	...	...	270	...	...
1989	+C	989	215	...	...	206	...	...	271	...	...	297	...	...
Saint Lucia - Sainte-Lucie														
1980	C	3 389	204	171	197	267	265	326	292	315	365	330	329	328
1981	C	3 860	339	261	313	274	297	291	299	330	398	372	338	348
1982	C	4 045	352	270	327	303	293	299	285	347	379	386	384	420
1983	C	4 069	419	333	321	323	285	316	302	360	359	350	356	345
1984	C	4 040	332	315	323	316	322	336	317	349	369	383	359	319
1985	C	4 223	422	336	367	330	344	295	289	337	407	372	339	385
1986	C	3 907	353	343	312	328	281	297	305	319	374	351	352	292
1994	C	3 684	331	232	270	266	239	250	291	312	402	361	426	304
1995	C	3 705	338	272	303	278	299	292	308	258	321	344	331	361
1996	C	3 299	289	261	236	259	231	214	282	272	316	269	319	351
1997	C	3 444	334	275	255	275	247	215	239	309	340	306	307	342
1998	C	2 950	257	200	237	233	222	217	229	223	283	282	278	289
1999	C	2 997	265	190	199	241	204	193	199	286	313	330	304	273
2000	C	2 904	284	230	251	193	184	170	215	247	265	302	297	266
2001	C	2 788	311	209	222	199	170	174	212	236	270	274	260	251
2002	C	2 529	251	187	235	205	182	155	171	210	200	225	250	258
Saint Pierre and Miquelon - Saint Pierre-et-Miquelon														
1980	C	90	7	3	8	10	8	9	7	8	9	9	7	5
1981	C	109	10	9	11	9	11	9	8	5	8	6	11	12
Saint Vincent and the Grenadines - Saint Vincent-et-les Grenadines														
1980	+C	3 075	271	251	255	239	234	220	228	240	288	303	276	270
1983	+C	3 295	337	248	287	256	226	218	259	265	311	283	283	322
1984	+C	2 831	269	209	234	222	255	181	188	239	241	263	267	263
1986	+C	2 708	224	219	254	203	189	178	213	218	224	280	247	259
1988	+C	2 537	224	165	207	222	196	185	180	199	236	227	229	267
1992	+C	2 686	259	219	220	167	213	172	196	240	268	246	252	234
1993	+C	2 687	229	192	211	192	193	188	195	208	234	294	274	277
1994	+C	2 549	200	174	189	189	208	175	168	227	236	259	267	257
1995	+C	2 614	267	200	210	175	178	194	188	198	234	245	265	260
1996	+C	2 338	202	163	179	165	159	138	191	205	229	247	247	213
1997	+C	2 311	219	173	181	185	132	148	162	195	211	240	243	222
1998	+C	2 112	199	176	163	151	162	128	143	136	200	211	208	235
1999	+C	2 171	185	162	144	143	129	154	146	183	226	230	253	216
2000	+C	2 149	182	157	146	173	129	127	149	140	230	230	248	238
2001	+C	2 109	179	158	177	160	149	130	151	160	213	232	168	232
2002	+C	1 985	195	165	173	147	139	135	137	164	152	192	202	184
Trinidad and Tobago - Trinité-et-Tobago														
1980	C	29 869	2 236	2 126	1 938	1 886	2 374	2 351	2 370	2 585	2 912	3 006	3 043	3 042
1981	C	32 177	2 867	2 305	2 563	2 453	2 572	2 307	2 495	2 708	2 983	3 023	3 049	2 852
1982	C	32 537	2 801	2 416	2 670	2 548	2 564	2 409	2 569	2 457	2 794	3 254	3 020	3 035
1983	C	33 208	2 931	2 434	2 702	2 529	2 581	2 363	2 623	2 823	3 109	3 124	3 144	2 845
1984	C	31 599	2 577	2 310	2 355	2 292	2 479	2 178	2 359	2 743	2 944	3 136	3 132	3 094

(See notes at end of table. — Voir notes à la fin du tableau.)

Continent, country or area / Continent, pays ou zone	C-o-d-e[a]	Total	Jan	Feb	March	April	May	June	July	Aug	Sep	Oct	Nov	Dec

AMERICA, NORTH — AMERIQUE DU NORD

Trinidad and Tobago - Trinité-et-Tobago

Year	Code	Total	Jan	Feb	March	April	May	June	July	Aug	Sep	Oct	Nov	Dec
1985	C	33 719	3 006	2 519	2 816	2 548	2 606	2 394	2 476	2 733	3 063	3 260	3 152	3 146
1986	C	31 886	2 918	2 379	2 639	2 406	2 473	2 343	2 569	2 640	2 937	2 989	2 856	2 737
1987	C	29 167	2 632	2 247	2 500	2 265	2 234	2 087	2 345	2 425	2 704	2 583	2 523	2 622
1988	C	26 983	2 328	2 032	2 220	2 104	2 034	1 944	2 066	2 206	2 345	2 506	2 566	2 632
1989	C	25 072	2 306	1 916	1 976	1 859	1 912	1 778	1 875	2 071	2 289	2 386	2 394	2 310
1990	C	23 960	2 243	1 939	1 930	1 823	1 811	1 689	1 839	1 901	2 182	2 287	2 192	2 124
1991	C	22 368	1 994	1 626	1 729	1 636	1 654	1 541	1 572	1 785	2 164	2 247	2 152	2 268
1992	C	23 064	2 060	1 806	1 824	1 755	1 712	1 582	1 780	1 969	2 167	2 154	2 097	2 158
1993	C	21 094	1 844	1 537	1 702	1 681	1 606	1 635	1 686	1 768	1 922	1 984	1 859	1 870
1994	C	19 682	1 673	1 306	1 441	1 466	1 471	1 451	1 530	1 707	1 862	1 967	1 942	1 866
1995	C	19 258	1 757	1 441	1 597	1 452	1 541	1 338	1 435	1 507	1 753	1 860	1 847	1 730
1997	C	18 452	1 758	1 421	1 481	1 325	1 273	1 217	1 315	1 489	1 644	1 807	1 862	1 860

Turks Caicos Islands - Îles Turques et Caïques

Year	Code	Total	Jan	Feb	March	April	May	June	July	Aug	Sep	Oct	Nov	Dec
1997	+C	287	29	19	22	20	23	23	19	20	33	36	23	20
1998	+C	272	18	16	12	15	18	22	28	26	35	26	20	34
1999	+C	292	18	28	23	22	28	16	20	30	27	26	22	32
2000	+C	290	29	17	26	18	24	14	15	26	27	31	35	28

United States - États-Unis

Year	Code	Total	Jan	Feb	March	April	May	June	July	Aug	Sep	Oct	Nov	Dec
1980	C	3612258	292 009	279 961	297 309	286 780	293 687	293 018	321 836	323 129	320 536	311 312	289 580	303 101
1981	C	3629238	294 632	273 234	301 691	285 578	296 323	297 935	326 182	329 870	319 971	309 106	290 843	303 873
1982	C	3704000	311 000	281 000	298 000	287 000	305 000	302 000	339 000	323 000	315 000	323 000	300 000	320 000
1983	C	3638933	297 750	276 981	310 928	293 920	303 224	303 957	317 969	323 960	314 468	305 777	290 944	299 055
1984	C	3669141	292 200	281 564	303 970	285 823	299 395	298 889	325 516	335 222	326 454	321 371	296 816	301 921
1985	C	3760561	304 073	281 261	310 679	301 777	317 596	308 477	333 484	336 575	331 283	322 997	301 551	310 808
1986	C	3756547	306 183	282 526	312 394	304 103	315 975	307 668	334 499	333 875	334 196	319 134	293 252	312 742
1987	C	3809394	305 069	283 477	317 462	307 700	319 784	321 024	336 381	331 351	334 068	326 392	306 040	320 282
1988	C	3909510	310 214	298 464	321 920	309 185	325 953	328 868	346 417	354 165	346 855	331 220	314 321	321 928
1989	C	4040958	320 422	308 391	339 912	318 779	336 320	330 973	356 716	366 579	357 344	344 161	325 543	335 818
1990	C	4179000	330 000	316 000	342 000	330 000	368 000	361 000	364 000	362 000	362 000	361 000	333 000	350 000
1991	C	4110907	335 172	309 130	344 079	335 626	353 131	334 265	362 913	366 786	356 016	348 934	323 635	341 220
1992	C	4084000	334 000	304 000	360 000	330 000	361 000	333 000	352 000	350 000	357 000	345 000	332 000	326 000
1993	C	4000240	323 073	304 656	342 187	327 042	335 989	335 349	352 554	350 898	348 013	332 937	316 379	331 163
1994	C	3952767	320 705	301 327	339 736	317 392	330 295	329 737	345 862	352 173	339 223	330 172	319 397	326 748
1995	C	3899589	316 013	295 094	328 503	309 119	334 543	329 805	340 873	350 737	339 103	330 012	310 817	314 970
1996	C	3891494	314 283	301 763	322 581	312 595	325 708	318 525	345 162	346 317	336 348	336 346	309 397	322 469
1997	C	3880894	317 211	291 541	321 212	314 230	330 331	321 867	346 506	339 122	333 600	328 657	307 282	329 335
1998	C	3941553	319 340	298 711	329 436	319 758	330 519	327 091	348 651	344 736	343 384	332 790	313 241	333 896
1999	C	3959417	319 182	297 568	332 939	316 889	328 526	332 201	349 812	351 371	349 409	332 980	315 289	333 251
2000	C	4058814	330 108	317 377	340 553	317 180	341 207	341 206	348 975	360 080	347 609	343 921	333 811	336 787
2001	C	4025933	335 198	303 534	338 684	323 613	344 017	331 085	351 047	361 802	342 564	344 074	323 746	326 569
2002	C	4021726	330 674	303 977	331 505	324 432	339 007	327 588	357 669	359 417	348 814	345 814	318 573	334 256

United States Virgin Islands - Îles Vierges américaines

Year	Code	Total	Jan	Feb	March	April	May	June	July	Aug	Sep	Oct	Nov	Dec
1981	C	2 450	212	180	188	194	186	175	167	200	252	261	222	213
1982	C	2 528	232	183	189	176	193	173	197	184	217	281	252	251
1983	C	2 600	239	193	202	205	187	199	200	196	240	253	237	249
1984	C	2 452	220	181	186	199	179	173	213	193	246	230	219	213
1985	C	2 402	225	178	181	166	175	170	212	191	215	230	236	223
1986	C	2 288	216	194	171	170	169	160	175	196	225	208	196	208
1987	C	2 375	183	180	193	192	166	170	161	183	253	243	217	234
1988	C	2 315	199	180	184	172	172	175	171	178	223	216	214	231
1989	C	2 418	223	181	183	179	196	196	210	199	246	199	183	223
1990	C	2 401	221	154	162	148	178	177	205	222	225	225	238	246
1993	C	2 529	211	181	193	195	181	205	191	222	251	238	228	233

11a. Live births by month of occurence: 1980 - 2002
Naissances vivantes selon le mois de naissance: 1980 - 2002 (continued — suite)

(See notes at end of table. — Voir notes à la fin du tableau.)

Continent, country or area / Continent, pays ou zone	C-o-d-e[a]	Total	Jan	Feb	March	April	May	June	July	Aug	Sep	Oct	Nov	Dec
AMERICA, SOUTH — AMERIQUE DU SUD														
Argentina - Argentine														
1980	C	697 461	62 263	58 138	59 903	56 362	56 376	57 219	59 409	57 586	57 547	57 222	54 774	56 977
1981	C	680 292	54 075	51 122	57 458	57 485	60 194	59 392	59 628	57 217	56 304	56 995	53 517	53 736
Brazil - Brésil[7]														
1980	U	2769502	255 468	236 101	264 862	253 796	258 422	241 606	240 327	232 562	226 692	225 942	195 991	137 733
1981	U	2865839	251 005	228 889	256 408	252 485	270 037	260 086	268 487	254 414	244 736	232 589	205 129	141 574
1982	U	2972992	276 178	252 067	284 935	272 825	280 563	265 171	267 144	253 622	243 995	235 713	201 627	139 152
1983	U	2710350	255 912	236 689	267 601	247 608	254 845	239 858	241 563	230 753	219 641	207 633	182 974	125 273
1984	U	2559038	242 884	225 811	248 478	236 996	245 818	225 676	227 242	218 683	209 139	195 994	170 558	111 759
1985	U	2619604	238 884	216 338	249 760	238 726	250 723	232 861	235 329	225 595	220 671	209 671	182 158	118 888
1986	U	2779253	259 854	241 398	272 345	264 522	265 350	249 681	249 404	236 207	228 065	213 989	179 013	119 425
1987	U	2660886	251 231	230 422	259 687	248 739	247 613	236 115	239 730	226 455	219 109	206 347	176 877	118 561
1988	U	2809657	264 531	248 654	284 379	264 273	269 657	254 143	248 162	238 551	227 525	206 369	178 745	124 668
1989	U	2581035	247 987	229 572	259 579	246 153	250 101	228 861	224 866	215 810	204 795	197 201	168 342	107 768
1990	U	2419927	232 304	208 128	239 746	226 831	231 869	216 627	220 628	210 339	195 116	184 476	158 749	95 114
1991	U	2333202	215 840	200 095	226 454	219 404	223 609	210 393	205 419	194 882	193 329	187 149	157 805	98 823
1992	U	2417470	234 167	227 704	242 525	230 551	231 236	216 743	214 544	200 812	189 294	173 717	154 247	101 930
1994	U	2472325	222 779	210 667	249 204	234 322	242 449	224 171	220 380	212 893	202 819	187 494	161 030	104 117
1995	U	2357337	229 124	208 453	240 243	226 441	234 408	219 036	209 642	197 864	184 839	168 826	148 983	89 478
1996	U	2412615	237 218	223 962	249 850	231 890	236 078	220 777	219 439	204 335	190 220	168 812	141 965	88 069
1998	U	2459275	242 834	223 071	252 803	237 303	237 919	220 409	219 678	203 678	199 488	177 437	150 496	94 159
Chile - Chili														
1980	C	234 662	20 527	18 200	19 498	19 071	19 694	19 936	20 092	19 447	20 707	20 548	18 845	18 097
1981	C	251 569	20 641	17 608	20 171	19 728	21 203	21 640	21 790	22 159	23 068	22 827	20 884	19 850
1982	C	256 503	22 373	19 658	21 972	21 313	21 433	21 856	21 605	22 161	22 827	22 078	20 166	19 061
1983	C	243 712	21 337	18 598	20 506	19 222	19 992	20 433	20 169	20 669	21 706	21 139	20 209	19 732
1984	C	251 765	21 243	19 281	20 171	18 936	20 143	20 272	21 280	22 207	22 625	23 041	21 630	20 936
1985	C	248 879	21 888	17 982	19 828	19 264	20 745	20 654	20 626	21 352	22 555	22 707	21 148	20 130
1986	C	259 347	21 999	19 148	20 786	20 923	21 450	21 447	21 528	22 160	23 550	23 466	21 398	21 492
1987	C	265 774	22 514	19 595	21 928	20 847	20 889	21 245	23 016	23 301	24 454	23 901	22 064	22 020
1988	C	281 752	23 794	21 758	23 245	21 276	22 345	23 179	23 900	24 263	25 823	25 081	23 769	23 319
1989	C	288 608	24 844	21 909	23 949	22 536	23 285	24 403	24 317	24 737	25 948	25 511	23 769	23 400
1990	C	292 146	25 470	22 871	24 728	23 314	23 823	23 773	24 505	24 907	25 384	25 963	24 167	23 241
1991	C	284 483	25 242	22 088	23 940	23 170	23 275	23 015	23 671	23 797	24 844	25 465	22 989	22 987
1992	C	279 098	24 856	22 101	23 049	21 965	22 809	22 894	23 322	22 930	24 774	24 483	22 987	22 928
1993	C	275 916	23 834	20 762	22 903	21 914	21 989	22 709	23 209	23 453	24 613	23 993	22 893	22 644
1994	C	273 766	22 795	20 299	22 784	21 711	22 439	22 917	23 427	23 942	24 384	23 789	22 717	22 562
1995	C	265 932	23 215	20 457	22 675	20 824	21 959	21 791	22 247	22 601	22 665	23 413	22 322	21 763
1996	C	264 793	23 178	20 221	21 521	20 914	21 654	21 387	22 128	22 277	23 497	23 833	22 261	21 922
1997	C	259 959	23 676	19 987	21 074	20 943	21 402	21 502	22 016	21 404	22 353	22 492	21 247	21 863
1998	C	257 105	22 657	19 489	21 381	20 962	20 727	20 361	21 174	21 392	23 066	22 791	21 461	21 644
1999	C	250 674	21 804	19 010	21 679	20 387	20 925	20 838	20 868	20 765	21 604	21 049	20 813	20 932
2000	C	248 893	20 909	19 313	20 536	19 532	20 316	20 214	20 420	21 166	21 886	22 090	21 181	21 330
2001	C	246 116	21 883	19 139	20 811	19 782	20 510	20 243	20 135	20 841	20 633	21 374	20 495	20 270
2002	C	238 981	21 451	18 199	19 532	18 836	19 787	19 433	20 032	20 292	20 615	21 065	19 597	20 142
Colombia - Colombie[8]														
1980	U	821 645	103 018	74 496	62 483	61 428	60 091	57 928	68 308	60 668	67 216	72 305	71 011	62 693
1981	U	839 255	100 026	80 118	66 575	59 357	56 805	57 707	69 882	63 486	68 832	72 609	79 575	64 283
1982	U	837 932	95 949	79 059	67 195	58 759	57 947	59 020	69 420	69 475	66 544	69 558	79 815	65 191
1983	U	829 348	95 559	74 597	61 865	58 182	61 827	59 810	64 523	67 046	67 431	70 897	81 684	65 927
1984	U	825 842	96 545	81 229	64 098	59 160	63 309	61 077	65 539	66 676	62 865	72 489	70 863	61 992
1985	U	835 922	100 394	79 960	67 576	62 318	62 307	56 332	71 089	65 389	65 853	69 432	68 874	66 398
1998	+U	720 984	57 818	50 780	58 869	57 541	60 588	59 531	62 194	62 478	65 875	62 672	60 666	61 972
1999	+U	746 194	61 431	54 569	63 605	61 114	62 060	60 688	63 003	63 729	67 199	64 823	62 311	61 662
2000	+U	752 834	61 327	57 617	61 341	58 651	61 630	60 845	63 740	65 751	68 734	66 452	63 254	63 492
2001	+U	724 319	60 773	54 079	61 592	57 699	60 230	57 990	60 670	61 402	64 519	63 366	60 938	61 061
2002	+U	678 388	56 172	50 295	56 609	55 121	55 268	53 596	56 725	57 717	60 238	60 469	58 613	57 565
Ecuador - Équateur[9]														
1988	U	211 392	21 546	19 277	21 019	20 696	21 451	19 817	19 504	19 070	17 679	15 490	11 833	4 010
1989	U	200 099	21 214	18 211	20 662	19 900	20 359	19 199	18 729	17 621	16 652	14 346	9 958	3 248
1992	U	198 468	21 346	19 531	20 442	19 858	20 389	18 863	18 684	17 440	15 939	13 540	9 464	2 972

11a. Live births by month of occurence: 1980 - 2002
Naissances vivantes selon le mois de naissance: 1980 - 2002 (continued — suite)

(See notes at end of table. — Voir notes à la fin du tableau.)

Continent, country or area / Continent, pays ou zone	C-o-d-e[a]	Total	Jan	Feb	March	April	May	June	July	Aug	Sep	Oct	Nov	Dec
AMERICA, SOUTH — AMERIQUE DU SUD														
Ecuador - Équateur[9]														
1993	U	198 722	21 303	18 599	21 101	21 052	21 363	20 038	19 338	17 646	15 376	12 424	8 215	2 267
1995	U	181 268	22 276	18 811	20 721	19 678	19 700	17 511	16 739	15 071	13 029	10 163	6 026	1 543
1996	U	182 242	21 439	19 332	20 418	19 573	19 840	17 880	17 133	15 341	13 358	10 290	6 174	1 464
1997	U	169 869	20 659	17 962	19 621	18 652	18 609	16 663	15 958	13 884	11 782	9 369	5 390	1 320
1998	U	199 079	21 459	18 125	19 277	18 437	19 371	20 117	20 585	19 138	16 530	13 587	9 962	2 491
1999	U	218 108	22 948	19 883	22 686	22 498	22 627	20 866	21 013	19 647	17 811	15 079	10 134	2 916
2000	U	202 257	23 814	21 002	22 303	21 214	21 448	18 992	18 137	16 298	14 670	13 079	9 048	2 252
2001	U	192 786	22 446	18 834	20 988	20 068	20 177	18 602	17 409	16 416	14 948	12 654	8 338	1 906
2002	U	183 792	21 104	18 447	20 567	19 931	19 392	17 469	16 969	15 250	13 832	11 311	7 654	1 866
French Guiana - Guyane française														
1980	C	1 933	148	138	161	176	153	157	148	147	170	169	164	202
1981	C	1 963	171	139	159	173	174	180	161	186	176	209	177	58
1982	C	2 379	200	165	220	182	188	211	169	207	197	205	218	201
1983	C	2 314	203	193	226	176	186	192	155	162	195	238	176	197
1984	C	2 319	171	175	189	165	194	169	211	206	194	197	199	227
1985	C	2 482	212	192	197	190	216	212	199	189	218	190	233	234
1986	C	2 392	204	169	207	196	198	184	184	142	183	250	203	242
1997	C	4 431	382	322	364	375	361	307	331	346	371	439	405	428
1998	C	4 691	438	361	409	377	349	341	395	345	403	457	406	410
1999	C	4 898	413	336	384	388	432	388	382	413	423	456	430	453
2000	C	5 116	452	350	460	400	445	391	391	393	459	438	474	463
2001	C	5 114	453	415	432	392	390	427	402	414	439	508	454	388
2002	C	5 249	506	396	449	417	430	381	434	445	456	492	435	408
Paraguay														
1981	U	30 466	3 542	3 313	3 580	3 273	3 094	2 733	2 493	2 115	1 769	1 632	1 537	1 385
1982	U	31 882	3 300	2 928	3 420	3 066	3 060	2 750	2 676	2 457	2 363	2 179	1 959	1 724
1983	U	32 660	3 392	3 024	3 376	2 780	2 728	2 590	2 681	2 834	2 556	2 318	2 243	2 138
1984	U	40 484	4 111	3 744	3 850	3 842	4 865	4 044	2 995	2 650	2 706	2 793	2 513	2 371
1985	U	39 969	3 626	3 258	3 795	3 715	4 006	3 693	3 630	3 392	3 274	2 836	2 371	2 273
1987	U	37 693	4 098	3 581	4 163	3 811	3 616	3 469	3 165	2 881	2 720	2 277	2 112	1 800
1988	U	37 460	3 751	3 706	4 075	3 559	3 547	3 447	3 125	2 894	2 743	2 473	2 117	2 023
1989	U	28 221	3 065	2 898	3 170	2 803	2 766	2 546	2 410	2 213	2 020	1 857	1 508	965
1990	U	12 231	1 925	1 807	1 842	1 590	1 450	1 274	1 091	648	337	170	68	29
1991	U	34 591	4 345	4 314	4 699	4 409	3 932	3 408	2 724	2 109	1 765	1 503	933	450
1992	U	37 649	4 579	4 472	4 526	4 192	3 920	3 374	3 306	2 897	2 445	1 853	1 370	715
Peru - Pérou[7,10,11]														
1980	I	466 411	39 074	37 102	40 573	38 947	39 605	37 137	40 169	38 620	40 599	39 805	37 046	37 331
1981	I	458 293	38 101	33 427	37 704	36 759	38 441	37 727	39 572	40 341	41 398	39 270	38 091	37 035
1982	I	526 999	45 427	41 960	45 955	43 839	43 779	42 419	44 263	44 551	45 627	44 826	42 779	41 145
1983	I	401 300	34 390	30 616	34 191	33 436	34 022	32 615	34 450	33 466	32 637	30 496	38 977	31 821
1984	I	362 657	28 223	26 057	30 014	29 107	30 833	31 475	32 449	32 223	32 583	32 337	30 648	26 408
1985	I	413 304	36 298	32 664	36 075	36 442	36 990	35 302	36 820	36 947	37 857	34 655	32 962	20 240
2001	I	343 744	31 295	28 180	30 929	31 052	30 475	29 155	29 601	29 112	29 413	28 014	25 856	20 662
2002	I	318 358	31 837	27 017	29 911	28 852	27 828	26 462	27 955	28 106	27 861	25 479	21 736	15 314
Suriname														
1989	C	10 214	940	785	827	860	821	735	755	777	904	940	944	926
1990	C	9 545	911	777	848	739	717	641	723	756	858	870	843	862
1991	C	9 104	846	636	715	705	747	679	685	656	794	869	906	866
1992	C	9 835	961	806	822	722	760	763	799	784	848	901	903	766
1993	C	9 398	883	677	810	756	797	695	699	706	815	892	892	776
1994	C	8 418	702	611	665	602	622	620	679	686	805	848	820	758
1995	C	8 717	746	696	723	608	604	622	643	717	804	779	939	836
1996	C	9 393	865	804	768	643	585	613	652	732	894	987	923	927
1998	C	10 221	970	933	891	756	807	738	763	813	964	976	803	807
1999	C	10 144	822	645	793	755	746	741	835	889	1 001	1 107	972	838
2000	C	9 804	905	760	789	741	740	739	697	751	832	954	944	952
2001	C	9 717	912	770	785	770	776	698	720	714	853	931	889	899
2002	C	10 188	1 017	837	825	752	760	772	755	804	914	923	900	929

(See notes at end of table. — Voir notes à la fin du tableau.)

Continent, country or area / Continent, pays ou zone	C-o-d-e[a]	Total	Jan	Feb	March	April	May	June	July	Aug	Sep	Oct	Nov	Dec
ASIA — ASIE														
Armenia - Arménie[12]														
1987	C	78 492	10 212	5 663	6 133	5 926	4 699	5 055	6 863	6 682	7 057	6 988	6 745	6 469
1988	C	74 707	6 967	6 214	6 117	5 468	5 841	5 915	6 288	7 583	6 034	6 509	5 987	5 784
1989	C	75 250	6 589	5 198	5 921	5 375	5 882	5 895	6 329	7 137	6 741	6 928	6 601	6 654
1990	C	79 882	7 694	6 524	6 414	5 710	5 777	6 146	7 352	7 211	6 943	6 954	6 661	6 496
1991	C	77 825	6 970	6 421	6 308	6 959	6 326	6 064	6 522	6 556	6 291	6 942	6 373	6 093
1992	C	70 581	6 698	6 316	6 714	5 722	5 853	5 796	6 162	6 241	5 988	5 718	5 131	4 242
1993	C	59 041	6 448	5 197	5 100	5 253	5 662	5 283	5 303	4 815	4 878	4 379	3 590	3 133
1994	C	51 143	4 246	3 984	4 607	4 147	4 171	4 711	4 074	4 342	4 311	4 456	4 099	3 995
1995	C	48 960	5 006	4 774	3 329	4 300	4 242	3 924	4 141	4 588	4 103	4 105	3 482	2 966
1996	C	48 134	4 372	4 236	4 261	4 081	4 090	3 796	4 099	4 065	3 859	3 984	3 786	3 505
1997	C	43 929	4 194	3 742	4 106	3 680	3 533	3 454	3 886	3 987	3 612	3 612	3 368	2 755
1998	C	39 366	3 701	3 315	3 562	3 352	3 276	3 071	3 396	3 344	3 334	3 252	2 952	2 811
1999	C	36 502	3 303	3 049	3 242	3 181	2 863	2 989	3 063	3 149	3 009	3 031	2 830	2 793
Azerbaijan - Azerbaïdjan[12]														
1992	C	181 364	15 322	16 172	15 689	14 874	13 409	13 297	16 136	15 906	17 077	14 977	13 319	15 186
1993	C	174 618	16 487	14 849	15 897	15 576	13 578	13 170	13 954	14 329	14 395	14 035	12 442	15 906
1994	C	159 761	12 982	12 574	14 189	14 646	12 637	12 286	13 827	14 103	12 723	12 804	13 090	13 900
1995	C	143 315	12 100	14 373	12 816	12 384	12 250	12 215	11 234	11 988	10 711	10 629	11 115	11 500
1996	C	129 247	12 671	11 420	10 078	11 754	9 899	10 690	10 001	10 716	9 564	10 169	9 886	12 399
1997	+C	132 052	10 278	14 594	16 938	10 760	9 229	8 262	9 659	11 054	10 308	10 475	9 473	11 022
1998	+C	123 996	12 911	10 212	10 304	8 963	9 499	9 964	11 096	11 960	10 625	9 887	8 816	9 759
1999	+C	117 539	8 948	11 721	11 340	9 863	9 390	8 574	8 074	10 028	9 248	8 786	9 603	11 964
2000	+C	116 994	10 838	13 171	10 221	9 157	8 636	8 239	8 011	8 456	8 954	9 598	9 851	11 862
2001	+C	110 356	10 716	10 674	10 238	9 357	8 524	8 002	7 751	7 709	7 807	8 400	9 004	12 174
2002	+C	110 715	9 824	10 147	9 635	9 527	9 322	8 317	8 236	7 701	7 791	8 096	9 794	12 325
Bahrain - Bahreïn														
1980	U	10 140	1 044	819	873	749	722	762	803	779	846	768	815	1 160
1981	U	10 300	839	722	950	847	862	676	773	742	927	838	913	1 211
1982	U	11 037	840	735	1 012	813	1 230	844	865	1 001	816	734	1 158	989
1983	U	11 431	1 103	824	981	862	937	882	802	1 034	794	909	1 157	1 146
1984	U	11 519	1 045	991	912	1 049	811	766	1 072	975	1 084	945	955	914
1985	U	12 314	1 549	989	931	961	1 014	851	1 049	1 008	925	1 063	1 023	951
1986	U	12 893	985	1 136	1 380	1 194	1 072	912	1 078	857	967	1 118	1 048	1 146
1987	U	12 699	1 066	1 013	942	990	907	1 009	975	1 127	1 143	1 220	1 102	1 205
1988	U	12 555	1 196	1 017	1 045	981	1 031	978	863	999	1 142	1 110	1 041	1 152
1989	U	13 611	1 412	1 092	1 021	1 029	1 090	796	1 168	1 175	1 218	1 131	1 322	1 157
1990	U	13 370	1 214	976	996	980	1 138	982	970	1 354	1 262	1 116	1 177	1 205
1991	U	13 229	1 346	1 109	1 017	968	1 099	845	1 263	1 076	1 105	1 129	1 006	1 266
1992	U	13 874	843	1 200	1 317	1 013	1 198	1 053	1 158	1 269	1 302	1 148	1 238	1 135
1993	U	14 191	1 252	1 109	1 131	1 159	1 102	1 054	1 193	1 239	1 312	1 231	1 208	1 201
1994	U	13 766	1 286	1 003	1 122	1 068	919	1 100	1 261	919	1 482	1 163	1 385	1 058
1995	U	13 481	1 401	1 027	992	1 019	1 011	1 072	1 154	1 175	1 069	1 192	1 100	1 269
1996	U	13 123	1 153	915	1 261	749	954	1 185	1 112	1 151	1 098	1 189	1 127	1 229
1997	+U	13 382	1 079	993	1 117	961	963	1 055	1 127	1 215	1 235	1 024	1 336	1 277
1998	+U	13 381	1 054	1 147	1 170	850	1 070	1 163	1 131	1 173	1 067	1 311	1 162	1 083
1999	+U	14 280	958	1 409	1 029	1 031	1 154	969	1 186	1 378	1 188	1 169	1 364	1 445
2000	+U	13 947	829	989	1 269	1 152	1 230	952	1 225	1 257	1 010	1 449	1 069	1 516
2001	U	13 468	1 283	1 231	927	1 070	950	1 230	1 232	1 078	1 163	1 189	1 123	992
2002	U	13 576	957	931	1 008	1 168	1 165	993	1 056	1 295	1 213	1 213	1 138	1 439
Brunei Darussalam - Brunéi Darussalam														
1980	+C	5 767	432	439	491	504	440	472	529	466	496	523	484	491
1981	+C	5 877	479	407	477	497	490	493	502	534	452	511	511	524
1982	+C	5 986	452	409	446	475	520	553	491	532	456	624	518	510
1983	+C	5 983	516	451	525	468	502	446	499	570	445	560	480	521
1984	+C	6 330	509	441	504	514	549	537	554	492	559	582	560	529
1985	+C	6 682	561	499	561	535	546	547	605	580	575	555	554	564
1986	+C	6 920	534	518	614	543	548	642	542	533	596	635	589	626
1987	+C	7 088	549	485	596	602	560	603	602	568	656	624	638	605
1988	+C	6 881	556	494	545	559	555	593	550	594	554	668	631	582

11a. Live births by month of occurence: 1980 - 2002
Naissances vivantes selon le mois de naissance: 1980 - 2002 (continued — suite)

(See notes at end of table. — Voir notes à la fin du tableau.)

Continent, country or area / Continent, pays ou zone	C-o-d-e[a]	Total	Jan	Feb	March	April	May	June	July	Aug	Sep	Oct	Nov	Dec
ASIA — ASIE														
Brunei Darussalam - Brunéi Darussalam														
1989	+C	6 926	531	552	578	542	576	535	559	585	587	668	615	598
1990	+C	7 011	590	576	590	504	605	561	593	588	579	602	600	623
1991	+C	7 106	519	558	578	603	564	546	636	599	609	647	607	640
1992	+C	7 290	600	562	602	562	546	604	591	617	613	670	633	690
1996	+C	7 633	633	561	620	591	637	579	690	624	660	689	656	693
1997	+C	7 459	629	541	623	582	567	612	653	584	641	661	693	673
1998	+C	7 411	581	599	652	599	604	572	621	631	659	680	599	614
1999	+C	7 408	554	520	599	636	555	640	591	695	689	625	648	656
2000	+C	7 481	665	616	640	591	626	635	615	678	537	668	622	588
China: Hong Kong SAR - Chine: Hong Kong RAS[13]														
1980	C	85 290	6 877	6 536	6 345	5 951	6 270	6 697	7 592	7 922	7 747	8 024	7 873	7 456
1981	C	86 751	7 135	5 962	6 502	6 082	6 363	6 817	7 678	8 284	8 068	8 369	7 790	7 701
1982	C	86 120	6 846	6 264	6 720	6 152	6 463	6 781	7 530	7 760	7 964	8 444	7 610	7 586
1983	C	83 293	6 936	6 179	6 524	5 871	6 047	6 422	7 337	7 489	7 648	7 848	7 733	7 259
1984	C	77 297	6 453	5 509	5 808	5 509	5 907	6 014	6 557	6 959	6 942	7 569	7 212	6 858
1985	C	76 126	6 395	5 498	5 731	5 438	5 824	6 120	6 557	6 740	6 712	7 356	7 107	6 648
1986	C	71 620	6 069	5 270	5 662	5 285	5 427	5 498	6 239	6 173	6 438	6 809	6 661	6 089
1987	C	69 958	5 704	5 160	5 502	5 163	5 441	5 550	5 990	6 246	6 153	6 882	6 254	5 913
1988	C	75 412	5 478	5 129	5 520	5 106	5 491	5 886	6 305	6 640	7 105	7 464	7 882	7 406
1989	C	69 621	6 590	4 983	5 325	4 943	5 228	5 480	5 722	6 189	6 250	6 529	6 315	6 067
1990	C	67 731	5 597	4 811	5 297	4 886	5 176	5 466	5 686	5 953	5 931	6 802	6 168	5 958
1991	C	68 281	5 454	4 979	5 130	4 919	5 169	5 235	5 833	5 949	6 166	6 583	6 839	6 025
1992	C	70 949	5 652	5 003	5 475	5 191	5 327	5 684	6 053	6 222	6 414	6 913	6 705	6 310
1993	C	70 451	5 957	5 024	5 475	5 144	5 444	5 635	5 993	6 348	6 209	6 933	6 142	6 147
1994	C	71 646	5 531	5 022	5 416	5 226	5 554	6 034	6 265	6 334	6 631	6 691	6 691	6 251
1995	C	68 637	5 788	5 008	5 513	5 056	5 332	5 497	5 504	5 742	6 085	6 711	6 373	6 028
1996	C	63 291	5 589	4 881	4 888	4 583	4 843	4 801	5 193	5 365	5 540	5 826	5 968	5 814
1997	C	59 250	5 377	4 883	5 027	4 772	4 947	4 812	4 717	4 880	5 004	5 157	5 068	4 916
1998	C	52 977	4 461	3 893	4 371	3 977	4 231	4 449	4 358	4 349	4 762	5 003	4 528	4 595
1999	C	51 281	4 569	3 768	4 148	3 840	3 959	4 183	4 358	4 422	4 609	4 323	4 559	4 543
2000	C	54 134	4 298	3 917	4 069	3 788	4 127	4 100	4 438	4 714	5 243	5 207	5 293	4 940
2001	C	48 219	4 535	3 734	3 921	3 626	3 714	3 784	3 892	4 127	4 220	4 516	4 036	4 114
China: Macao SAR - Chine: Macao RAS														
1981	C	4 207	307	264	278	249	279	307	403	415	423	485	393	404
1982	C	5 262	392	336	417	309	367	410	438	484	543	561	490	515
1984	C	6 666	546	442	447	449	518	552	575	585	622	704	562	664
1985	C	7 560	567	494	545	523	563	660	636	683	734	738	702	715
1986	C	7 477	630	530	547	535	583	587	657	675	690	694	684	665
1987	C	7 565	615	530	542	527	526	634	670	745	699	770	664	643
1988	C	7 913	600	543	585	505	569	599	674	706	736	780	813	803
1989	C	7 568	665	577	639	538	565	585	632	680	630	665	745	647
1991	C	6 832	599	470	510	504	499	574	574	643	571	655	656	577
1992	C	6 676	567	480	490	495	500	563	580	596	610	619	601	575
1993	C	6 267	502	454	495	433	524	527	527	571	575	613	553	493
1994	C	6 115	478	403	505	424	473	485	502	559	558	593	586	549
1995	C	5 876	460	432	466	423	484	500	470	531	524	585	527	474
1996	C	5 468	482	404	425	415	409	385	471	512	476	508	529	452
1997	C	5 031	484	404	376	406	400	390	419	416	408	508	450	370
1998	C	4 434	368	330	341	340	360	336	385	389	417	392	411	365
1999	C	4 148	328	285	335	335	357	321	381	391	405	355	356	299
2000	C	3 849	283	273	295	263	273	325	316	362	308	409	387	355
2001	C	3 241	322	256	250	243	261	244	252	273	261	345	261	273
2002	C	3 162	251	212	249	242	242	234	279	269	269	293	311	311
Cyprus - Chypre[14]														
1980	C	13 647	1 097	1 066	1 072	1 053	1 101	1 160	1 307	1 223	1 195	1 205	1 065	1 103
1981	C	13 272	1 079	1 043	1 075	971	1 077	1 159	1 240	1 178	1 197	1 154	987	1 112
1982	C	14 251	1 027	1 075	1 184	978	1 157	1 248	1 256	1 283	1 342	1 291	1 231	1 179

(See notes at end of table. — Voir notes à la fin du tableau.)

Continent, country or area / Continent, pays ou zone	Code[a]	Total	Jan	Feb	March	April	May	June	July	Aug	Sep	Oct	Nov	Dec
ASIA — ASIE														
Cyprus - Chypre[14]														
1983	C	13 400	1 129	1 044	1 034	1 037	1 081	1 114	1 204	1 268	1 219	1 132	1 076	1 062
1984	C	13 528	1 131	1 030	1 041	1 083	1 166	1 184	1 295	1 172	1 131	1 173	1 103	1 019
1985	C	12 992	1 040	897	1 020	1 007	1 158	1 095	1 290	1 100	1 178	1 179	1 027	1 001
1986	C	10 691	835	796	858	901	847	894	1 006	992	915	979	821	847
1987	C	10 337	765	767	870	823	821	887	922	901	916	950	879	836
1988	C	10 752	900	827	882	763	867	936	983	958	1 003	970	856	807
1989	C	10 273	859	787	801	722	828	882	935	929	923	904	864	839
1990	C	10 622	824	792	831	820	889	940	964	947	917	911	902	885
1991	C	10 442	912	744	846	778	823	872	931	892	929	934	914	867
1992	C	11 372	917	856	874	893	961	975	1 003	973	1 044	1 043	934	899
1993	C	10 514	903	818	856	805	848	839	896	870	957	950	885	887
1994	C	10 379	863	812	820	798	850	827	899	914	909	931	863	893
1995	C	9 869	786	744	780	779	833	778	858	894	952	879	830	756
1996	C	9 638	774	714	780	732	799	772	879	843	894	865	801	785
1997	C	9 275	846	700	774	680	736	767	838	823	793	753	792	773
1998	C	8 879	768	689	695	696	736	771	831	746	770	768	700	709
1999	C	8 505	677	600	735	597	606	721	809	760	796	833	690	681
2000	C	8 447	776	611	643	596	654	707	754	760	737	783	763	663
2001	C	8 167	708	608	648	560	625	692	786	724	747	769	689	611
2002	C	7 883	658	548	597	584	581	628	744	719	748	774	683	619
Georgia - Géorgie[12]														
1992	C	72 631	5 764	6 370	6 265	5 775	5 728	7 145	7 210	5 561	5 870	6 089	4 706	6 148
1994	C	57 311	5 527	5 053	5 286	4 985	5 127	4 729	4 809	4 692	4 632	4 753	4 020	3 698
1995	C	56 341	3 696	4 546	5 105	4 162	4 508	5 248	4 637	4 508	4 772	4 524	4 410	6 225
1996	C	53 669	3 278	4 631	4 527	4 587	4 458	3 909	4 553	4 192	3 927	4 520	4 634	6 453
1999	C	40 778	2 641	3 344	3 242	3 148	3 147	3 419	3 403	3 565	3 569	3 274	3 346	4 680
2000	C	40 392	3 188	3 571	3 536	3 246	3 271	3 287	3 325	3 623	3 419	3 229	2 917	3 780
2001	C	40 416	3 489	3 590	3 657	3 029	3 373	3 247	3 411	3 587	3 320	3 086	3 290	3 206
Iran (Islamic Republic of) - Iran (République islamique d')														
1983	U	2127942	164 950	165 874	146 040	153 738	155 190	146 318	141 424	158 105	176 107	179 261	269 852	271 083
1984	U	2067803	207 548	171 900	127 092	149 498	195 830	149 684	146 619	160 544	183 216	190 426	192 992	192 454
1986	U	2033285	187 579	163 813	134 236	114 947	170 358	124 670	157 461	164 375	181 832	242 392	213 799	177 823
Israel - Israël[15]														
1980	C	94 321	7 532	6 945	7 374	7 145	7 615	7 755	8 344	8 347	8 351	8 560	8 016	8 337
1981	C	93 308	7 622	6 781	7 510	7 139	7 296	7 657	8 539	8 058	7 997	8 344	8 165	8 200
1983	C	98 724	8 145	7 081	7 838	7 464	7 959	7 742	8 792	9 196	8 741	9 019	8 212	8 535
1984	C	98 478	8 223	7 445	7 793	7 539	8 082	8 068	8 874	8 933	8 635	8 656	8 075	8 155
1985	C	99 376	8 181	7 291	8 110	7 732	8 082	7 973	8 603	8 771	8 799	9 023	8 187	8 624
1986	C	99 341	8 547	7 424	7 854	7 718	7 657	7 597	8 939	8 956	8 934	8 922	8 410	8 383
1987	C	99 022	8 116	7 271	8 102	7 751	7 888	7 927	8 674	8 766	8 657	8 684	8 367	8 819
1988	C	100 454	8 807	7 606	8 048	7 495	7 646	7 920	8 969	9 252	8 801	9 058	8 249	8 603
1990	C	103 349	8 641	7 536	8 352	8 047	8 262	8 381	9 326	9 421	8 691	8 988	8 731	8 973
1991	C	105 725	9 176	7 745	8 693	8 305	8 454	8 803	8 865	9 487	9 201	8 984	8 750	9 262
1992	C	110 062	9 417	8 427	9 076	8 214	8 938	9 083	9 553	9 649	9 264	9 505	9 203	9 733
1993	C	112 330	9 627	8 575	9 348	8 909	8 906	8 457	9 779	10 169	9 797	9 846	9 308	9 609
1994	C	114 543	9 559	8 672	9 285	8 714	9 220	9 064	9 658	10 094	10 285	10 481	9 468	10 043
1995	C	116 886	9 789	8 817	9 406	9 036	9 416	8 906	9 494	10 707	10 637	10 553	9 986	10 139
1996	C	121 333	10 179	9 190	9 430	9 320	9 542	9 724	10 809	11 020	10 533	10 732	10 212	10 642
1997	C	124 478	10 496	9 284	9 959	9 444	9 756	10 080	11 380	11 293	10 875	10 591	10 388	10 932
1998	C	130 080	11 320	9 688	10 628	9 935	10 512	10 795	11 577	11 644	10 808	11 205	10 608	11 360
1999	C	131 936	10 951	9 742	10 796	10 032	9 919	10 107	11 562	12 015	11 793	11 643	11 360	12 016
2000	C	136 390	11 781	10 559	11 063	10 469	10 529	10 722	12 043	12 318	11 638	12 011	11 404	11 853
2001	C	136 638	11 848	10 134	10 889	10 114	10 696	10 715	11 944	12 595	12 167	12 063	11 726	11 747
2002	C	139 535	12 040	10 319	11 286	10 645	10 757	10 932	12 245	12 662	12 325	12 453	11 687	12 184
Japan - Japon[16]														
1980	C	1576889	135 848	125 070	129 692	128 240	134 367	128 227	138 952	138 266	136 886	133 342	120 455	127 544
1981	C	1529455	127 356	117 324	124 117	125 800	130 663	125 310	135 137	134 770	133 295	130 813	118 667	126 203
1982	C	1515392	125 918	114 176	119 541	118 768	127 009	126 734	137 024	138 478	133 150	128 288	118 708	127 598
1983	C	1508687	125 821	113 421	124 437	124 646	128 176	122 982	134 823	133 733	129 111	125 266	119 127	127 144

11a. Live births by month of occurence: 1980 - 2002
Naissances vivantes selon le mois de naissance: 1980 - 2002 (continued — suite)

(See notes at end of table. — Voir notes à la fin du tableau.)

Continent, country or area / Continent, pays ou zone	C-o-d-e[a]	Total	Jan	Feb	March	April	May	June	July	Aug	Sep	Oct	Nov	Dec
ASIA — ASIE														
Japan - Japon[16]														
1984	C	1489780	124 743	116 152	123 614	118 265	124 664	119 351	134 464	134 734	126 899	125 459	117 753	123 682
1985	C	1431577	120 404	110 470	115 172	114 977	120 997	116 341	130 375	126 433	122 563	123 053	111 961	118 831
1986	C	1382946	115 725	105 520	113 925	110 660	116 126	114 143	123 741	118 972	117 616	119 692	110 269	116 557
1987	C	1346658	113 130	101 619	112 072	109 459	116 004	112 886	121 525	117 306	113 287	112 275	105 854	111 241
1988	C	1314006	106 395	98 756	106 419	105 059	109 922	108 663	115 287	118 994	115 611	114 451	106 814	107 635
1989	C	1246802	105 421	94 305	103 074	101 035	106 984	101 018	108 412	109 357	103 748	104 883	101 612	106 953
1990	C	1221585	104 065	92 531	101 119	99 284	106 308	99 869	107 568	106 991	102 113	102 899	97 078	101 760
1991	C	1223245	101 310	91 477	99 731	98 175	104 204	100 529	107 970	106 426	104 097	106 709	98 662	103 955
1992	C	1208989	100 287	92 589	97 330	97 678	103 125	100 783	108 168	104 600	105 409	102 734	95 337	100 949
1994	C	1238328	101 150	92 036	101 124	100 103	105 206	102 382	109 896	109 101	105 906	105 981	101 019	104 424
1995	C	1187064	102 692	90 495	98 348	95 520	101 422	99 783	105 878	105 391	100 759	96 208	92 999	97 569
1996	C	1206555	98 837	92 664	96 686	97 939	104 037	99 621	107 672	104 832	103 442	104 634	96 903	99 288
1997	C	1191665	100 094	88 370	96 481	95 741	104 980	100 265	106 929	103 388	99 935	100 329	94 887	100 266
1998	C	1203147	99 928	89 559	98 303	98 225	102 052	101 074	108 093	105 304	104 695	101 428	94 007	100 479
1999	C	1177669	100 349	89 861	97 176	97 863	99 474	97 744	103 713	103 206	100 320	95 781	93 595	98 587
2000	C	1190547	101 351	93 683	98 985	94 902	100 134	95 465	102 806	103 706	103 131	100 752	96 407	99 225
2001	C	1170662	99 647	88 001	94 653	93 106	99 540	95 160	101 511	102 745	102 619	103 308	94 650	95 722
2002	C	1153855	98 407	88 750	95 563	93 832	98 589	93 373	102 331	100 775	99 261	97 586	90 400	94 988
Kazakhstan[12]														
1987	C	417 139	35 859	32 049	35 800	34 863	37 033	35 542	36 815	34 943	33 692	33 495	33 553	33 495
1988	C	407 116	34 010	33 129	35 854	34 471	35 259	35 014	37 076	35 059	33 626	32 649	30 666	30 303
1989	C	382 269	33 762	31 093	33 066	31 319	33 288	33 065	33 961	32 677	31 218	31 206	28 838	28 776
1990	C	363 335	32 127	29 965	31 097	30 017	31 741	30 222	32 815	29 326	29 489	29 664	27 803	29 069
1991	C	354 101	31 701	27 536	30 886	29 526	30 909	29 466	30 683	29 345	29 348	28 536	28 017	28 139
1992	C	338 475	29 760	27 243	29 044	28 273	29 796	30 716	29 212	28 735	27 697	26 891	25 567	25 529
1993	C	316 263	27 977	24 894	28 170	27 048	26 782	28 304	27 288	26 865	26 103	25 299	23 339	24 180
1994	C	306 509	28 836	25 214	27 717	25 009	28 251	27 723	26 425	26 219	25 446	24 590	20 362	20 709
1995	C	277 006	25 421	22 265	24 868	23 494	25 306	23 656	23 909	23 296	22 323	22 204	20 316	19 942
1996	C	253 175	21 128	21 326	21 730	21 669	22 432	21 394	22 366	20 846	19 931	20 741	19 952	19 660
1997	C	232 009	10 729	18 458	19 109	20 391	20 408	20 144	21 168	19 564	19 012	18 632	16 896	27 498
1998	C	222 380	9 719	17 660	18 526	18 941	18 020	19 285	20 979	18 650	18 759	18 756	17 298	25 787
1999	C	217 578	8 572	16 907	16 593	17 863	17 376	17 290	20 148	18 209	18 452	17 151	17 105	31 912
2000	C	222 054	10 622	18 791	17 650	17 427	17 228	18 817	18 528	18 149	17 461	17 576	17 603	32 202
2001	C	221 487	9 013	15 814	16 722	19 177	18 475	18 102	19 054	18 457	17 393	18 353	17 467	33 460
2002	C	227 171	7 761	11 553	13 857	22 432	19 798	18 829	21 387	19 254	18 798	19 849	19 646	34 007
Korea (Republic of) - Corée (République de)[17]														
1980	I	892 116	78 506	79 398	80 290	76 722	71 369	67 801	66 909	65 124	74 046	81 183	74 938	75 830
1981	I	858 557	87 380	92 659	69 649	65 396	68 193	63 918	67 053	68 241	67 498	68 661	69 605	70 304
1982	I	835 113	91 668	92 622	69 810	65 225	63 398	62 153	63 098	63 463	63 173	67 431	65 657	67 415
1983	I	746 375	84 129	86 241	59 582	55 109	55 965	53 323	55 951	56 877	57 540	61 499	61 257	58 902
1984	I	665 670	77 729	84 372	50 156	48 344	47 483	46 963	49 963	51 038	52 191	56 129	52 354	48 948
1985	I	652 064	72 680	74 959	48 137	45 101	47 080	46 093	49 941	52 110	51 425	57 118	54 093	53 327
1986	I	631 021	69 141	73 059	48 196	47 518	47 413	44 892	48 482	49 201	49 817	52 247	52 244	48 811
1987	I	619 931	66 552	72 196	45 983	47 331	47 138	45 303	46 642	48 266	50 197	53 322	50 164	46 837
1988	I	630 347	69 091	72 113	43 210	44 102	46 527	44 297	46 895	49 575	52 246	55 244	54 689	52 358
1989	I	637 416	66 877	74 182	44 791	45 830	48 032	45 146	48 045	50 018	52 964	53 675	52 834	55 022
1990	I	648 203	65 982	79 233	45 483	49 505	51 542	47 972	50 981	51 561	52 807	52 919	50 734	49 484
1991	I	708 390	71 222	71 813	53 706	53 912	54 202	50 634	55 103	55 975	58 485	62 242	59 920	61 176
1992	I	728 973	71 775	72 282	57 494	57 872	56 425	54 242	56 276	57 523	60 072	63 245	60 338	61 429
1993	I	716 637	69 722	69 898	62 832	59 006	56 369	53 786	55 903	56 650	57 924	58 800	57 585	58 162
1994	I	722 834	70 176	67 489	63 176	60 352	59 329	54 583	56 438	56 941	58 911	59 398	57 983	58 058
1995	I	716 993	67 199	65 930	65 386	55 213	55 711	53 535	54 454	57 296	60 055	61 577	59 185	61 452
1996	C	692 495	67 521	62 692	63 311	56 727	54 647	50 539	52 634	54 280	57 768	60 970	55 499	55 907
1997	C	675 227	63 335	58 134	62 153	56 946	55 299	50 935	53 348	53 221	55 414	57 107	53 819	55 516
1998	C	640 126	60 295	56 749	60 141	54 767	51 971	49 422	50 031	49 519	53 325	52 510	50 007	51 389
1999	C	616 322	58 320	53 054	57 215	52 117	50 188	46 465	48 425	48 130	50 695	51 762	50 083	49 868
2000	C	636 780	61 458	56 503	59 674	52 867	52 269	46 538	48 156	50 347	52 611	54 050	52 042	50 265
2001	C	557 228	56 770	49 788	54 398	48 181	46 609	41 651	42 186	43 584	45 394	44 560	42 416	41 691
2002	C	494 625	48 719	43 492	47 690	43 281	41 822	37 415	40 136	39 525	39 402	39 244	37 629	36 270

11a. Live births by month of occurence: 1980 - 2002
Naissances vivantes selon le mois de naissance: 1980 - 2002 (continued — suite)

(See notes at end of table. — Voir notes à la fin du tableau.)

Continent, country or area / Continent, pays ou zone	Code[a]	Total	Jan	Feb	March	April	May	June	July	Aug	Sep	Oct	Nov	Dec
ASIA — ASIE														
Kuwait - Koweït														
1980	C	51 090	4 470	3 835	4 047	3 967	4 204	3 956	4 390	4 164	4 317	4 600	4 513	4 627
1981	C	52 041	4 593	3 994	4 364	4 105	4 391	4 115	4 383	4 211	4 216	4 496	4 483	4 690
1982	C	54 257	4 728	3 976	4 487	4 334	4 433	4 332	4 408	4 549	4 488	4 848	4 757	4 917
1983	C	55 617	4 864	4 144	4 619	4 296	4 684	4 442	4 593	4 527	4 797	4 920	4 716	5 015
1984	C	56 776	4 945	4 434	4 316	4 571	4 669	4 621	4 897	4 852	4 701	4 985	4 783	5 002
1985	C	55 087	4 874	4 108	4 257	4 435	4 692	4 591	4 732	4 448	4 680	4 866	4 604	4 800
1986	C	53 845	4 724	3 876	4 590	4 229	4 494	4 360	4 665	4 468	4 549	4 796	4 534	4 560
1987	C	52 412	4 380	3 601	4 539	4 125	4 029	4 509	4 409	4 474	4 652	4 672	4 489	4 533
1991	C	20 609	1 137	1 052	1 235	764	1 324	1 475	2 278	2 291	2 598	1 859	2 029	2 567
1992	C	34 817	2 930	2 727	3 075	2 729	2 899	2 843	2 838	3 099	2 872	3 033	2 762	3 010
1993	C	37 379	3 195	2 616	3 051	2 990	3 068	3 001	3 263	3 285	3 278	3 464	3 192	2 976
1994	C	38 868	2 981	2 617	3 274	3 211	3 373	3 224	3 373	3 466	3 296	3 367	3 269	3 417
1995	C	41 169	3 403	2 903	3 315	3 225	3 506	3 382	3 535	3 615	3 533	3 647	3 439	3 666
1996	C	44 620	3 650	3 541	3 642	3 550	3 944	3 731	3 782	3 881	3 884	3 783	3 582	3 650
1997	C	42 817	3 605	3 207	3 647	3 299	3 607	3 625	3 715	3 670	3 660	3 633	3 669	3 480
1998	C	41 424	3 734	3 279	3 590	3 384	3 541	3 373	3 437	3 561	3 429	3 455	3 311	3 330
1999	C	41 135	3 619	3 261	3 371	3 389	3 422	3 216	3 440	3 509	3 392	3 643	3 471	3 402
2000	C	41 843	3 810	3 289	3 448	3 407	3 539	3 402	3 462	3 422	3 465	3 596	3 397	3 606
2001	C	41 342	3 687	3 043	3 414	3 279	3 406	3 413	3 596	3 504	3 352	3 678	3 364	3 606
2002	C	43 490	3 798	3 294	3 494	3 513	3 567	3 582	3 815	3 642	3 695	3 746	3 577	3 767
Kyrgyzstan - Kirghizistan[12]														
1980	C	107 278	9 790	8 386	9 615	9 410	9 295	8 999	9 798	8 874	8 259	8 470	8 181	8 201
1985	C	128 460	11 975	10 550	11 038	10 785	11 071	10 523	11 443	11 073	10 549	10 167	9 457	9 829
1986	C	133 728	12 083	10 554	11 449	11 051	11 537	11 106	11 520	11 395	11 230	10 734	10 568	10 501
1987	C	136 588	12 377	10 842	11 956	11 312	11 823	11 385	11 535	11 579	10 908	11 245	10 780	10 846
1988	C	133 710	10 854	11 466	11 797	11 104	11 273	11 052	11 074	11 688	10 819	10 806	10 441	11 336
1989	C	131 508	11 099	10 616	11 646	10 607	11 373	10 850	10 752	11 658	11 010	10 531	10 272	11 094
1990	C	128 810	11 963	10 328	11 074	10 828	11 144	10 720	10 901	11 087	10 822	10 412	9 653	9 878
1991	C	129 536	12 415	10 411	11 445	10 576	10 906	10 608	10 958	11 184	10 927	10 800	9 904	9 402
1992	C	128 352	12 058	10 717	11 725	10 566	11 448	10 633	11 035	10 626	10 418	10 334	9 620	9 172
1993	C	116 795	12 121	9 534	10 384	9 985	10 320	9 797	9 813	10 105	9 545	9 042	8 554	7 595
1994	C	110 113	12 274	9 815	9 928	9 629	9 969	9 084	8 662	9 141	8 758	8 516	7 347	6 990
1995	C	117 340	11 496	10 699	10 814	9 535	11 295	10 401	7 620	12 412	7 739	9 847	8 570	6 911
1996	C	108 007	10 323	9 014	9 311	9 390	8 864	9 168	8 791	9 074	8 986	8 998	8 430	7 658
1997	C	102 050	9 355	7 851	8 651	8 509	9 274	8 665	8 416	8 679	8 426	7 842	8 083	8 299
1998	C	104 183	9 884	8 338	9 021	8 655	9 085	9 080	8 142	9 038	8 994	7 739	7 827	8 380
1999	C	104 068	9 453	8 286	8 815	8 669	9 038	8 817	8 620	9 133	8 711	8 593	8 066	7 867
2000	C	96 770	8 994	7 631	8 401	7 891	8 333	8 413	7 896	8 526	8 151	7 585	7 475	7 474
2001	C	98 138	8 962	7 681	8 487	8 158	8 540	8 312	8 056	8 687	8 185	7 960	7 458	7 652
2002	C	101 012	9 305	7 821	8 617	8 334	8 860	8 572	8 628	8 813	8 386	7 963	7 703	8 010
Malaysia - Malaisie														
1990	C	497 522	41 316	38 575	41 608	40 916	41 850	40 693	42 422	43 525	43 102	45 167	41 240	37 108
1991	C	507 889	41 922	37 253	41 799	41 514	43 133	41 308	43 455	44 025	43 867	45 630	43 504	40 479
1992	C	524 349	44 383	40 169	44 443	40 929	42 909	42 227	43 928	47 237	46 342	46 869	43 246	41 667
1994	C	529 080	44 075	38 977	44 081	42 409	44 849	43 664	45 540	46 950	45 239	46 603	43 412	43 281
1995	C	534 646	44 125	40 802	44 262	42 622	45 514	44 602	45 725	47 896	45 981	46 387	44 048	42 682
1996	C	540 866	44 700	40 989	44 653	43 730	47 351	43 810	45 476	46 845	47 328	47 241	45 838	42 905
1997	C	540 515	44 494	39 537	44 906	42 745	45 134	43 594	45 752	45 953	47 593	48 573	47 734	44 500
1998	C	524 766	52 923	45 338	52 021	49 370	50 715	49 069	41 524	38 718	41 738	36 534	31 575	35 241
1999	C	521 870	37 534	33 512	39 661	46 236	45 460	50 411	45 592	44 399	45 567	44 121	44 881	44 496
2000	C	545 096	44 178	42 923	46 681	44 580	46 546	44 213	44 165	46 077	44 497	50 213	46 436	44 587
Maldives														
1980	C	6 822	523	474	586	570	630	622	575	474	532	659	631	546
1981	C	7 010	476	498	638	635	690	550	505	485	558	699	647	629
1982	C	7 248	563	498	712	676	627	605	491	570	672	658	647	529
1983	C	7 236	499	557	667	701	685	679	535	511	520	659	654	569
1984	C	8 193	556	592	647	767	757	722	581	584	748	782	781	676
1985	C	8 968	649	606	739	777	847	730	759	779	810	831	751	690
1986	C	8 615	696	666	843	730	871	606	642	753	676	710	687	735
1987	C	8 364	654	551	724	693	804	674	686	730	698	780	651	719

(See notes at end of table. — Voir notes à la fin du tableau.)

Continent, country or area / Continent, pays ou zone	C-o-d-e[a]	Total	Jan	Feb	March	April	May	June	July	Aug	Sep	Oct	Nov	Dec
ASIA — ASIE														
Maldives														
1988	C	8 237	650	614	740	772	745	609	628	662	632	766	713	706
1989	C	8 726	670	670	743	835	653	661	708	731	757	755	700	843
1990	C	8 639	860	693	762	768	668	643	665	677	689	721	734	759
1991	C	8 390	750	681	820	697	651	667	620	657	779	735	662	671
1992	C	8 139	657	550	739	618	694	671	632	696	677	741	760	704
1993	C	7 780	679	638	678	608	651	632	654	625	634	707	650	624
1994	C	7 382	601	596	618	568	658	624	574	594	623	644	659	623
1995	C	6 849	556	527	535	532	577	567	578	580	582	657	592	566
1996	C	6 772	596	545	490	543	593	580	547	559	565	659	592	503
1997	C	6 184	568	456	466	520	518	498	530	517	531	576	518	486
1998	C	5 687	497	368	496	490	494	489	473	500	465	515	449	451
1999	C	5 226	377	348	454	414	483	450	404	416	511	551	416	402
2000	C	5 314	401	364	485	456	454	407	415	447	443	587	413	442
2001	C	4 882	429	321	394	416	419	415	393	439	423	445	454	334
Mongolia - Mongolie														
1994	C	54 286	3 804	4 064	4 517	4 959	4 638	4 439	4 313	4 301	4 615	4 516	4 888	5 232
1995	C	54 099	4 256	4 677	4 722	4 913	4 577	4 419	4 316	4 273	4 336	4 304	4 537	4 769
1996	C	51 141	3 996	3 950	4 697	4 713	4 354	4 212	4 060	4 084	4 332	4 264	4 192	4 287
1997	C	48 834	3 826	3 659	3 770	4 437	4 228	4 202	4 040	3 932	4 156	3 730	4 195	4 659
1998	C	50 340	3 764	4 048	4 001	4 434	4 251	4 392	4 250	4 222	4 070	4 149	4 145	4 614
1999	C	51 094	4 036	4 066	4 202	4 577	4 370	4 448	4 227	4 439	4 142	3 963	4 362	4 262
2000	C	51 111	3 768	4 769	4 456	4 701	4 139	4 329	4 340	4 312	4 295	3 910	4 057	4 035
2001	C	48 449	3 751	3 781	4 011	4 305	4 129	4 321	4 162	4 188	4 326	3 860	3 828	3 787
2002	C	45 687	3 622	3 475	3 508	4 079	3 912	3 986	4 034	3 928	3 836	3 644	4 064	3 599
Occupied Palestinian Territory - Territoire palestinien occupé														
1996	U	101 937	8 883	8 609	8 457	7 711	8 022	7 957	8 664	8 692	8 166	8 365	8 829	9 582
1997	U	97 707	8 827	7 730	8 213	7 188	7 474	7 719	8 381	8 392	8 018	8 120	8 297	9 348
1998	U	99 841	8 929	7 971	8 355	7 585	8 123	8 031	8 463	8 522	8 260	8 377	8 137	9 088
1999	U	96 780	8 340	7 376	7 959	7 199	6 969	7 184	8 216	8 794	8 213	8 528	8 629	9 373
2000	U	98 026	9 122	7 760	7 730	7 412	7 477	7 583	8 522	8 379	7 841	8 232	8 495	9 473
2001	U	94 626	8 640	7 593	7 928	6 782	7 415	7 450	7 834	7 866	7 726	7 983	8 367	9 042
2002	U	93 488	8 894	7 480	7 861	6 897	6 970	6 909	7 799	7 923	7 991	8 354	8 278	8 132
Pakistan[18,19]														
1984	I	3044237	331 951	237 439	202 911	204 057	202 056	240 778	258 337	268 072	287 261	256 677	234 664	320 034
1985	I	3167156	300 411	246 129	258 948	217 161	233 912	251 111	259 166	279 740	322 293	239 090	259 714	299 481
1986	I	3255647	319 783	234 867	257 181	184 831	237 825	225 629	247 128	294 310	334 152	319 101	267 887	332 953
1987	I	3340319	340 024	257 507	224 310	224 562	239 258	287 612	252 080	309 563	297 385	290 672	289 837	327 509
1988	I	3194926	276 977	265 676	242 623	222 220	186 990	222 235	275 800	334 081	315 276	265 091	270 430	317 527
1989	I	3575959	281 113	248 501	234 392	217 719	200 010	277 787	277 593	395 734	370 345	359 729	314 813	398 223
1990	I	3608678	314 441	303 701	288 902	279 815	225 052	258 647	322 669	322 999	331 334	350 400	264 853	345 865
1991	I	3593303	297 902	269 938	287 979	252 474	205 945	295 656	319 040	326 738	347 427	342 262	328 690	319 252
1992	I	3628799	303 815	321 753	276 435	290 122	224 966	289 952	330 515	316 636	342 386	335 012	284 075	313 132
1993	I	3607157	344 707	338 734	310 484	236 432	204 084	294 318	273 489	293 894	330 248	347 062	270 595	363 110
1994	I	3497399	333 194	308 471	268 406	246 321	235 488	300 178	289 168	277 429	308 610	315 223	253 913	360 998
Philippines														
1980	U	1456860	123 696	110 326	117 340	113 196	118 353	111 162	118 882	121 228	131 795	133 601	127 194	130 087
1981	U	1461204	129 371	106 672	117 549	116 706	121 111	115 589	116 482	117 982	124 437	133 053	130 391	131 861
1982	U	1474491	124 992	108 047	121 087	120 213	121 454	113 627	119 570	122 730	132 855	131 923	128 389	129 604
1983	U	1506356	129 628	110 066	118 988	120 107	124 349	117 643	123 331	127 591	132 852	135 670	133 843	132 288
1984	U	1478205	129 305	112 544	117 368	114 933	122 802	114 852	120 688	123 671	134 651	133 827	127 705	125 859
1985	U	1437154	123 830	105 854	117 285	115 686	118 300	111 389	114 441	117 010	126 393	133 256	127 054	126 656
1986	U	1493995	124 777	106 162	117 862	120 608	123 463	115 965	119 402	123 868	132 246	137 332	134 271	138 039
1987	U	1582469	132 758	111 560	124 843	127 406	133 753	126 266	127 924	126 284	139 324	144 846	143 544	143 961
1988	U	1565372	135 824	118 329	126 327	122 845	127 431	122 809	126 102	129 081	139 293	139 669	136 119	141 543
1989	U	1565254	132 259	111 866	126 413	123 391	126 787	119 841	125 375	131 699	145 698	143 444	137 561	140 920
1990	U	1631069	137 329	116 473	129 193	127 604	134 620	127 040	129 890	136 863	150 893	151 095	143 309	146 760
1991	U	1643296	138 277	115 874	129 335	130 887	136 488	129 461	133 976	135 259	147 620	151 919	146 031	148 169
1992	U	1684395	143 226	123 359	132 768	128 879	135 411	127 275	134 198	143 422	156 966	158 850	149 375	150 666
1993	U	1680896	141 872	119 126	127 046	130 470	139 385	128 473	134 456	144 140	156 279	155 477	151 002	153 170

11a. Live births by month of occurence: 1980 - 2002
Naissances vivantes selon le mois de naissance: 1980 - 2002 (continued — suite)

(See notes at end of table. — Voir notes à la fin du tableau.)

Continent, country or area / Continent, pays ou zone	Code[a]	Total	Jan	Feb	March	April	May	June	July	Aug	Sep	Oct	Nov	Dec
ASIA — ASIE														
Philippines														
1994	U	1645557	143 732	120 147	123 480	123 233	135 825	131 338	135 578	137 378	147 397	151 944	146 922	147 491
1995	U	1645043	137 779	113 432	128 275	133 791	137 260	130 144	133 627	142 929	153 076	151 857	142 741	140 132
1996	U	1608476	143 187	120 337	120 866	121 302	131 880	126 804	130 556	133 605	147 649	152 373	141 801	138 100
1997	C	1653236	139 186	114 183	130 415	129 047	136 368	127 957	127 657	136 354	155 867	163 217	146 917	146 068
1998	C	1632859	145 765	122 242	130 213	126 696	131 633	127 988	132 225	139 306	152 067	151 509	137 318	135 897
1999	C	1613335	140 742	114 217	118 755	118 840	127 542	126 434	133 158	136 491	147 500	152 540	151 513	145 603
2000	C	1766440	146 083	128 383	142 041	143 383	150 362	140 459	141 948	147 348	158 456	161 055	154 475	152 447
Qatar														
1980	C	6 750	557	500	540	492	545	503	531	594	575	634	627	652
1981	C	7 192	647	540	597	472	576	551	580	630	620	628	655	696
1982	C	8 031	687	597	629	619	627	584	692	666	669	760	726	775
1983	C	8 261	697	662	656	635	700	622	638	701	718	763	712	757
1985	C	9 225	755	704	742	730	829	746	775	796	779	786	773	810
1986	C	9 942	830	669	838	740	817	823	876	860	838	892	905	854
1987	C	9 919	780	659	881	823	770	758	818	811	910	880	908	921
1988	C	10 842	861	795	875	848	860	948	892	897	888	1 045	963	970
1989	C	10 908	853	791	912	872	939	894	839	920	945	1 046	972	925
1990	C	11 022	907	820	943	926	960	863	947	914	967	942	932	901
1992	C	10 459	863	769	890	847	846	842	867	879	886	944	924	902
1993	C	10 822	924	778	879	897	954	879	926	919	913	922	907	924
1994	C	10 561	904	750	871	858	842	846	901	917	931	912	900	929
1999	C	10 846	966	843	862	870	914	869	966	919	886	910	887	954
2001	C	12 118	1 036	928	975	994	989	973	1 024	998	1 039	1 103	984	1 075
Singapore - Singapour														
1980	C	41 217	3 137	3 026	3 319	3 087	3 164	3 163	3 613	3 780	3 790	3 991	3 656	3 491
1981	C	42 250	3 258	2 984	3 244	3 200	3 456	3 499	3 535	3 659	3 722	4 150	3 875	3 668
1982	C	42 654	3 159	2 909	3 282	3 086	3 296	3 563	3 515	3 673	3 963	4 413	3 951	3 844
1983	C	40 585	3 286	2 977	3 179	3 087	3 381	3 392	3 426	3 451	3 645	3 754	3 596	3 411
1984	C	41 556	3 033	2 938	3 286	3 164	3 265	3 200	3 391	3 603	3 799	4 135	3 893	3 849
1985	C	42 484	3 425	3 070	3 344	3 284	3 473	3 355	3 593	3 651	3 714	4 059	3 907	3 609
1986	C	38 379	3 282	2 668	3 166	3 047	3 154	3 095	3 268	3 318	3 357	3 605	3 289	3 130
1987	C	43 889	2 819	2 786	3 229	3 427	3 278	3 783	4 159	3 680	3 885	4 352	4 158	4 333
1988	+C	52 957	3 431	3 501	4 070	3 834	4 181	4 233	4 441	4 643	5 243	5 478	5 180	4 722
1989	+C	47 669	3 990	3 411	3 899	3 588	3 783	3 719	3 783	4 026	4 301	4 485	4 347	4 337
1990	+C	51 142	3 740	3 586	3 958	3 717	4 138	4 006	4 196	4 403	4 668	5 263	4 876	4 591
1991	+C	49 114	4 070	3 570	3 919	3 718	4 083	3 759	4 058	4 148	4 375	4 590	4 355	4 469
1992	+C	49 402	3 945	3 667	4 027	3 713	3 860	3 868	4 131	4 152	4 498	4 765	4 394	4 382
1993	+C	50 225	3 723	3 723	4 079	3 805	4 094	4 115	4 287	4 336	4 456	4 746	4 384	4 477
1994	+C	49 602	4 112	3 538	4 146	3 953	3 968	4 057	3 993	4 176	4 244	4 515	4 469	4 431
1995	+C	48 635	3 752	3 678	3 982	3 758	4 051	3 995	4 094	4 153	4 224	4 413	4 253	4 282
1996	+C	48 577	3 982	3 517	4 002	3 838	4 029	3 756	3 953	4 068	4 187	4 396	4 539	4 310
1997	+C	47 333	3 963	3 328	3 646	3 665	3 793	3 712	3 932	3 884	4 290	4 638	4 287	4 195
1998	+C	43 664	3 750	3 337	3 701	3 593	3 721	3 555	3 590	3 787	3 665	3 933	3 500	3 532
1999	+C	43 336	3 448	3 082	3 738	3 603	3 794	3 466	3 556	3 647	3 727	3 689	3 810	3 776
2000	C	46 997	3 585	3 636	3 916	3 642	4 004	3 618	3 954	4 019	4 147	4 288	4 308	3 880
2001	C	41 451	3 654	3 222	3 410	3 455	3 563	3 354	3 357	3 484	3 383	3 680	3 499	3 390
2002	C	40 760	3 343	3 046	3 295	3 311	3 484	3 131	3 403	3 443	3 504	3 669	3 592	3 539
Sri Lanka[20]														
1980	+C	418 373	35 292	32 458	35 949	35 007	35 391	33 200	34 240	34 468	36 387	37 058	34 798	34 125
1981	+C	423 793	38 674	33 371	38 582	34 957	34 187	31 480	32 393	31 593	35 053	37 974	36 837	38 692
1982	+C	408 895	36 828	31 921	36 570	33 416	32 926	31 551	32 875	32 658	33 632	36 138	35 024	35 356
1983	+C	405 122	35 999	32 816	34 740	32 291	34 797	35 301	31 788	32 055	32 971	33 831	33 189	35 344
1984	+C	391 064	33 663	29 916	32 694	30 916	31 284	30 162	31 414	30 879	32 097	35 507	36 013	36 519
1985	+C	389 599	33 431	27 468	31 472	32 058	33 213	31 333	32 223	30 925	33 598	31 665	22 077	10 747
1986	+C	361 735	29 339	24 750	30 469	30 857	30 422	28 855	29 682	29 698	30 219	33 071	31 922	30 570
1987	+C	357 723	29 931	25 564	30 278	29 575	29 827	28 434	28 145	29 466	30 073	27 557	21 265	10 747
1988	+C	344 179	30 053	27 215	30 906	29 582	29 619	27 595	27 029	26 935	28 219	24 011	17 776	9 233
1989	+C	363 343	30 184	26 731	31 994	29 624	29 614	28 264	28 723	27 972	28 582	26 554	20 554	10 545
1991	+C	356 593	9 915	16 778	25 546	27 751	29 473	30 779	28 949	29 464	28 795	31 030	31 241	32 416
1995	+C	343 224	28 761	24 500	30 131	29 556	29 665	27 250	27 390	28 508	27 875	25 922	20 102	9 701

(See notes at end of table. — Voir notes à la fin du tableau.)

Continent, country or area / Continent, pays ou zone	Code[a]	Total	Jan	Feb	March	April	May	June	July	Aug	Sep	Oct	Nov	Dec
ASIA — ASIE														
Sri Lanka[20]														
1996	+C	340 649	28 406	27 172	27 631	25 883	28 646	29 808	28 519	28 517	27 899	29 594	30 294	28 280
Syrian Arab Republic - République arabe syrienne[1,21]														
1981	U	378 318	61 533	37 413	35 778	28 876	31 179	27 453	26 111	30 128	31 089	23 420	23 033	22 305
1982	U	424 399	71 332	37 146	39 894	34 408	38 328	33 782	30 257	34 525	26 456	31 257	25 113	21 901
1983	U	419 221	81 298	41 678	42 617	34 030	32 729	28 358	26 264	32 771	26 883	28 788	24 297	19 508
1984	U	433 898	87 985	44 973	40 683	34 297	32 479	27 917	33 028	32 401	28 994	27 703	22 072	21 366
1985	U	548 636	110 309	52 459	54 077	44 028	38 694	31 338	39 777	28 753	42 775	43 817	37 550	25 059
1986	U	429 418	86 025	38 806	36 739	34 707	31 132	29 471	35 801	30 448	34 321	28 074	24 100	19 794
1987	U	478 136	104 325	43 958	49 119	42 822	33 228	36 202	35 302	31 684	32 975	27 136	22 767	18 618
1988	U	435 795	99 206	40 892	37 229	34 070	29 732	28 051	22 354	35 625	36 245	29 437	23 877	19 077
1989	U	421 733	96 074	38 347	33 169	30 643	31 569	36 964	32 454	33 344	29 881	27 999	19 396	11 893
1990	U	359 390	106 820	32 013	28 064	23 202	33 534	25 355	23 491	24 380	22 698	16 976	12 999	9 858
1991	U	390 890	104 156	38 384	33 607	29 724	31 819	25 372	32 043	26 986	25 363	19 324	13 515	10 597
1992	U	404 948	115 337	39 568	34 425	29 790	32 042	26 253	29 766	28 662	26 313	19 366	13 436	9 990
1993	C	433 324	114 878	41 316	33 969	35 924	35 255	31 202	26 306	31 569	29 868	22 452	16 507	14 078
Tajikistan - Tadjikistan[12]														
1989	C	200 430	19 891	15 813	18 920	18 077	17 463	15 851	16 858	17 311	16 200	15 415	13 585	15 033
1990	C	205 813	18 567	17 088	19 453	19 385	18 305	16 658	16 811	17 258	16 184	15 245	14 584	16 244
1991	C	212 598	20 640	18 083	21 107	18 749	18 157	16 763	17 913	17 984	16 853	16 428	14 754	15 118
1992	C	179 534	19 764	18 509	20 842	18 201	17 478	15 774	15 377	14 468	11 818	9 723	8 431	9 086
1993	C	186 504	18 869	16 169	17 498	15 677	16 558	15 073	15 516	16 245	15 482	14 132	12 755	12 396
1994	C	162 152	17 801	15 944	16 542	15 017	15 211	13 622	12 989	12 217	11 857	10 580	9 910	10 462
Thailand - Thaïlande														
1980	+U	1077300	97 939	89 010	93 242	92 225	89 033	84 770	87 320	89 175	91 083	89 296	84 299	89 908
1981	+U	1062238	89 829	84 080	88 340	90 060	87 499	88 602	84 951	87 041	89 562	92 501	87 721	92 052
1982	+U	1075632	91 228	89 879	94 317	92 292	95 779	91 354	81 492	85 003	88 830	86 912	90 414	88 132
1983	+U	1055802	93 116	88 847	91 812	85 753	90 410	82 902	82 306	87 290	85 718	83 695	84 664	89 291
1984	+U	956 680	71 762	74 911	77 103	77 359	83 430	76 556	82 743	83 464	83 592	85 745	82 475	77 540
1985	+U	973 624	86 039	78 879	80 696	82 515	82 821	74 860	77 079	81 503	84 939	84 465	79 521	80 307
1986	+U	945 304	84 685	80 771	77 877	79 702	76 009	76 905	78 296	74 626	79 490	80 917	76 360	79 666
1987	+U	884 043	75 123	72 314	73 629	77 281	72 434	74 625	70 920	71 276	76 050	73 029	74 281	73 081
1988	+U	870 532	71 691	66 536	70 695	66 826	69 109	72 548	65 402	77 777	76 618	78 362	77 118	77 850
1991	+U	960 556	83 632	73 790	77 062	81 332	79 373	77 946	78 935	80 517	86 389	85 351	75 412	80 817
1992	+U	964 557	79 968	73 822	82 543	81 959	76 732	79 376	77 999	81 310	86 474	81 981	79 824	82 569
1994	+U	960 248	78 868	72 207	74 915	76 409	78 445	79 719	77 531	84 433	87 883	84 702	86 040	79 096
1997	+U	897 604	80 533	65 119	69 731	71 497	78 392	75 356	76 939	77 649	75 986	82 595	80 512	63 295
1998	+U	897 495	81 032	69 090	75 887	75 865	76 249	71 274	74 561	76 593	76 138	77 782	71 847	71 177
1999	+U	772 604	70 124	59 862	69 223	68 168	67 821	68 824	74 240	77 683	77 351	66 252	43 570	29 486
2000	+U	773 009	68 007	64 433	70 251	66 461	69 158	65 636	69 229	73 975	74 881	70 458	54 549	25 971
United Arab Emirates - Émirats arabes unis														
1980	...	34 774	3 007	2 566	2 701	2 601	2 700	2 661	3 091	3 031	3 072	3 117	2 904	3 323
EUROPE														
Albania - Albanie														
1981	C	72 180	5 211	5 636	7 161	7 151	7 216	7 004	6 905	6 144	5 685	5 427	4 115	4 525
1982	C	77 232	5 266	6 060	7 606	7 950	8 010	7 174	7 235	6 551	5 813	5 450	4 822	5 295
1983	C	73 762	5 119	5 846	7 009	7 036	7 419	6 745	6 793	6 715	5 799	5 685	4 586	5 010
1984	C	79 177	5 484	6 607	7 254	7 407	8 257	7 537	7 396	7 177	5 849	6 268	4 697	5 244
1985	C	77 535	5 336	5 399	7 288	7 900	8 403	7 509	7 398	6 839	6 204	5 680	4 749	4 830
1986	C	76 435	5 150	5 760	6 988	7 818	7 811	7 196	7 171	6 564	5 841	6 065	4 759	5 312
1987	C	79 696	6 042	6 250	7 364	7 887	7 825	7 752	7 496	6 812	6 301	6 042	4 787	5 138
1988	C	80 241	6 125	6 220	7 145	7 996	7 961	7 826	7 461	7 016	6 416	6 101	4 619	5 355
1989	C	78 862	5 735	5 886	7 166	7 119	7 773	7 402	7 447	7 271	6 421	5 722	5 158	5 762
1990	C	82 125	6 077	6 488	7 720	7 555	8 130	7 555	7 473	7 145	6 981	6 324	5 257	5 420
1991	C	77 361	6 790	6 843	7 610	7 772	7 774	7 023	7 128	6 347	5 625	5 153	4 416	4 880

11a. Live births by month of occurence: 1980 - 2002
Naissances vivantes selon le mois de naissance: 1980 - 2002 (continued — suite)

(See notes at end of table. — Voir notes à la fin du tableau.)

Continent, country or area / Continent, pays ou zone	Code[a]	Total	Jan	Feb	March	April	May	June	July	Aug	Sep	Oct	Nov	Dec
EUROPE														
Andorra - Andorre														
1992	C	729	48	45	67	53	77	61	72	60	72	63	53	58
1993	C	723	51	53	70	57	60	51	66	54	57	61	83	60
1994	C	704	56	51	62	54	65	70	49	46	70	68	64	49
1996	C	700	61	38	66	68	59	56	48	61	71	62	58	52
1997	C	730	57	46	73	64	56	77	81	48	52	60	49	67
1999	C	833	69	62	61	70	74	69	81	77	59	77	72	62
2000	C	747	69	56	59	69	73	78	59	68	47	70	52	47
2001	C	777	70	53	58	76	82	63	52	65	58	54	77	69
Austria - Autriche														
1980	C	90 872	7 481	7 094	7 628	7 499	7 796	7 362	7 802	7 543	7 859	7 717	7 535	7 556
1981	C	93 942	7 890	7 501	8 023	7 836	7 852	7 717	8 114	7 989	7 857	7 770	7 693	7 700
1982	C	94 840	8 142	7 407	8 114	7 915	7 974	7 842	8 224	8 134	8 000	7 845	7 553	7 690
1983	C	90 118	7 825	7 106	7 649	7 383	7 554	7 414	8 020	7 856	7 640	7 376	7 032	7 263
1984	C	89 234	7 424	7 296	7 590	7 146	7 585	7 501	7 996	7 614	7 427	7 262	7 321	7 072
1985	C	87 440	7 546	6 805	7 727	7 271	7 583	7 135	7 761	7 178	7 394	7 310	6 796	6 934
1986	C	86 964	7 468	6 820	7 412	7 390	7 300	7 089	7 608	7 460	7 516	7 150	6 660	7 091
1987	C	86 503	7 279	6 592	7 327	7 027	7 126	7 288	7 709	7 577	7 312	7 044	7 012	7 210
1988	C	88 052	7 442	7 251	7 585	6 956	7 649	7 046	7 480	7 655	7 584	7 171	7 048	7 185
1989	C	88 759	7 470	6 991	7 789	7 164	7 407	7 244	7 935	7 874	7 484	7 357	6 846	7 198
1990	C	90 454	7 612	6 886	7 787	7 231	7 526	7 319	8 053	7 855	7 784	7 738	7 285	7 378
1991	C	94 629	7 925	7 312	7 788	7 762	7 966	7 781	8 404	8 135	8 284	8 058	7 483	7 731
1992	C	95 302	7 932	7 560	8 034	7 508	7 869	7 846	8 544	8 300	8 337	7 916	7 505	7 951
1993	C	95 227	8 266	7 611	8 144	7 728	7 860	7 756	8 461	8 170	8 242	8 000	7 323	7 666
1994	C	92 415	7 798	7 466	7 921	7 686	7 942	7 866	8 003	7 950	7 664	7 341	7 174	7 604
1995	C	88 669	7 603	7 008	7 609	7 259	7 301	7 238	8 007	7 614	7 576	7 537	6 892	7 025
1996	C	88 809	7 436	7 130	7 510	7 173	7 337	7 357	7 755	7 462	7 472	7 455	7 114	7 608
1997	C	84 045	7 318	6 704	7 146	7 157	7 183	7 292	7 366	7 111	7 116	6 794	6 231	6 627
1998	C	81 233	6 860	6 266	6 813	6 771	6 972	6 597	7 257	7 104	7 026	6 714	6 537	6 316
1999	C	78 138	6 697	6 150	6 532	6 190	6 369	6 460	7 012	7 035	7 010	6 282	5 916	6 485
2000	C	78 268	6 587	6 384	6 799	6 327	6 668	6 419	6 755	6 685	6 827	6 433	6 101	6 283
2001	C	75 458	6 611	5 866	6 376	6 187	6 409	6 127	6 625	6 491	6 513	6 372	5 801	6 080
2002	C	78 399	6 594	6 110	6 724	6 313	6 500	6 373	6 927	6 573	6 944	6 671	6 244	6 426
Belarus - Bélarus[12]														
1980	C	154 432	12 536	11 788	12 760	13 672	14 254	13 375	14 033	13 380	12 281	12 239	12 128	11 986
1981	C	157 899	13 288	11 821	13 555	13 360	13 864	13 281	13 676	14 204	13 430	12 449	12 354	12 617
1982	C	159 364	13 093	12 483	13 248	13 177	14 183	13 232	13 568	13 176	12 810	12 705	13 436	14 253
1983	C	173 510	14 925	13 481	14 883	14 822	15 525	14 521	15 592	14 811	14 009	14 111	13 455	13 375
1985	C	165 034	14 241	12 859	14 420	14 664	14 996	14 172	14 906	14 413	13 130	13 091	12 139	12 003
1987	C	162 937	12 124	11 971	13 334	13 724	14 296	13 881	14 220	13 428	13 945	14 822	13 278	13 914
1988	C	163 193	13 944	13 409	14 353	14 279	15 196	14 243	14 715	13 997	12 875	12 580	11 860	11 742
1989	C	153 449	13 918	12 428	13 398	13 034	14 055	13 487	13 628	13 283	11 944	11 995	11 362	10 917
1990	C	142 167	11 818	11 146	12 255	11 447	13 384	12 299	12 548	12 506	10 658	12 152	11 067	10 887
1991	C	132 045	10 724	10 737	12 035	11 048	11 776	10 794	12 297	11 209	9 802	11 340	10 061	10 222
1992	C	127 971	10 632	10 189	10 808	10 019	10 842	11 474	11 551	10 705	10 444	10 545	9 956	10 806
1993	C	117 384	11 064	9 418	10 449	10 273	10 404	10 050	10 419	9 988	9 312	9 063	8 521	8 423
1994	C	110 599	10 363	9 082	10 342	10 066	9 951	9 796	9 904	9 307	8 492	8 285	7 638	7 373
1995	C	101 144	9 590	8 163	9 044	9 063	9 236	8 976	9 220	8 745	7 802	7 676	7 024	6 605
1996	C	95 798	9 173	7 823	8 485	8 646	8 627	8 212	8 568	8 090	7 171	7 393	6 878	6 732
1997	C	89 586	7 866	7 117	7 112	7 754	7 914	7 377	8 306	7 801	7 070	7 691	6 498	7 080
1998	C	92 645	8 851	7 173	7 926	7 776	8 184	8 022	8 416	7 886	7 719	7 500	6 807	6 385
1999	C	92 975	9 016	7 377	7 938	8 027	8 069	8 479	8 443	8 034	7 818	7 145	6 356	6 273
Belgium - Belgique[22]														
1980	C	124 398	10 282	9 780	10 484	10 570	10 744	10 431	10 820	10 366	10 472	10 697	9 630	10 122
1981	C	123 792	10 165	9 517	10 453	10 582	10 667	10 510	10 771	10 727	10 596	10 185	9 629	9 990
1982	C	120 231	9 835	9 246	10 504	10 417	10 438	10 191	10 446	10 109	10 182	9 921	9 328	9 614
1983	C	117 145	9 790	8 804	9 810	9 772	10 188	10 292	10 296	10 144	10 076	9 575	9 055	9 343
1984	C	115 715	9 600	9 169	9 845	9 253	10 016	9 874	10 231	10 082	9 469	10 125	9 025	9 026
1985	C	114 030	9 245	8 561	9 754	9 880	10 102	9 388	10 365	9 563	9 647	9 664	8 663	9 198
1986	C	117 114	9 370	8 956	9 918	9 830	10 216	10 121	10 192	10 012	9 901	9 944	9 014	9 640
1987	C	117 334	9 754	9 024	9 910	9 837	10 105	10 281	10 286	9 842	10 019	9 947	9 050	9 279
1988	C	119 456	9 453	9 550	10 704	9 997	10 475	10 125	10 238	10 283	9 953	9 622	9 390	9 666

(See notes at end of table. — Voir notes à la fin du tableau.)

Continent, country or area / Continent, pays ou zone	C-o-d-e[a]	Total	Jan	Feb	March	April	May	June	July	Aug	Sep	Oct	Nov	Dec
EUROPE														
Belgium - Belgique[22]														
1989	C	121 117	9 757	9 210	10 549	10 280	10 428	10 434	10 542	10 438	9 715	10 242	9 520	10 002
1990	C	123 726	10 115	9 588	10 519	10 289	10 594	10 375	10 900	10 695	10 040	10 767	9 780	10 064
1991	C	126 068	10 772	9 428	11 021	10 443	10 764	10 234	11 342	10 642	10 887	10 759	9 840	9 936
1992	C	124 774	10 776	10 360	10 731	10 370	10 402	10 448	11 095	10 552	10 614	10 218	9 370	9 838
1993	C	120 998	9 841	9 408	10 687	10 213	10 057	10 571	10 810	10 192	10 239	10 042	9 230	9 708
1994	C	116 449	9 472	9 018	10 169	9 566	10 231	10 241	10 249	9 761	9 721	9 661	9 004	9 356
1995	C	115 638	9 653	8 753	10 032	8 984	9 931	10 172	10 141	10 305	9 796	9 828	9 010	9 033
2001	C	114 014	9 732	8 574	9 721	9 557	9 985	9 423	10 024	9 909	9 241	9 720	9 022	9 106
2002	C	111 225	9 487	8 700	9 627	8 947	9 283	8 829	9 947	9 628	9 318	9 605	8 640	9 214
Bosnia and Herzegovina - Bosnie-Herzégovine														
1990	C	66 952	6 134	5 304	5 964	5 412	5 661	5 326	5 789	5 901	5 858	5 667	5 001	4 935
1991	C	64 769	5 958	5 173	5 535	5 303	5 585	5 331	5 571	5 724	5 743	5 568	4 482	4 796
1996	C	46 594	3 627	3 332	3 551	3 388	3 767	3 674	4 215	4 368	4 432	4 548	4 026	3 666
1997	C	48 397	4 590	3 867	4 169	3 983	4 293	4 048	4 133	4 214	4 149	3 870	3 561	3 520
1998	C	45 007	3 803	3 490	3 776	3 726	3 880	3 600	3 961	4 057	3 809	4 051	3 519	3 335
Bulgaria - Bulgarie														
1980	C	128 190	11 090	10 239	10 662	10 734	11 283	10 832	10 995	10 932	10 887	10 405	9 669	10 462
1981	C	124 372	10 729	9 806	10 674	10 329	11 059	10 844	11 180	10 603	10 598	9 762	9 239	9 549
1982	C	124 166	10 533	9 737	10 765	10 223	11 291	10 967	10 546	10 615	10 294	10 181	9 306	9 708
1983	C	122 993	10 115	9 350	10 544	9 974	10 704	10 207	10 735	11 125	10 503	10 288	9 481	9 967
1984	C	122 303	10 477	9 706	10 714	10 048	11 027	10 355	10 798	10 477	10 130	9 972	9 282	9 317
1985	C	118 955	9 525	8 830	9 589	9 788	10 447	9 650	10 899	10 916	10 265	10 109	8 895	10 042
1986	C	120 078	10 373	9 141	10 397	10 199	10 526	10 228	10 836	10 577	9 906	9 701	8 874	9 320
1987	C	116 672	9 744	8 597	9 853	9 724	10 282	10 047	10 773	10 197	9 473	9 555	8 888	9 539
1988	C	117 440	9 770	9 459	10 035	9 295	10 190	10 107	10 767	10 257	9 760	9 479	8 963	9 358
1989	C	112 289	9 729	8 991	9 651	9 074	9 715	9 762	10 077	9 699	9 071	9 137	8 487	8 896
1990	C	105 180	9 516	8 293	9 144	8 649	9 105	8 894	9 377	8 957	8 431	8 480	7 949	8 385
1992	C	89 134	7 006	7 224	7 777	7 499	7 985	7 900	7 814	7 834	7 467	7 101	6 654	6 873
1993	C	84 400	7 506	6 665	7 143	6 987	7 242	7 195	7 963	7 350	7 244	6 801	6 093	6 231
1994	C	79 442	6 723	6 366	6 850	6 752	7 000	6 910	7 088	7 038	6 643	6 254	5 773	6 045
1995	C	71 967	6 185	5 693	6 102	5 790	6 141	5 974	6 313	6 443	6 205	6 100	5 519	5 502
1997	C	64 125	5 701	5 091	5 665	5 500	6 056	5 769	5 838	5 693	5 260	4 819	4 300	4 433
1999	C	72 291	5 820	5 586	6 312	5 961	6 056	6 294	6 644	6 439	6 197	5 920	5 484	5 578
2000	C	73 679	6 436	6 024	6 371	5 883	6 259	6 209	6 664	6 529	6 248	5 716	5 253	6 087
2001	C	68 180	5 932	5 537	5 889	5 489	5 801	5 662	6 184	5 991	5 889	5 752	4 858	5 196
2002	C	66 499	5 415	5 008	5 650	5 331	5 520	5 472	5 896	5 904	5 905	5 684	5 229	5 485
Channel Islands: Guernsey - Îles Anglo-Normandes: Guernesey														
1983	C	659	62	48	56	32	76	61	53	69	57	56	45	44
1984	C	596	40	43	58	45	48	53	56	45	60	42	49	57
1985	C	642	46	52	66	54	60	42	67	49	60	51	46	49
1986	C	671	42	48	64	59	60	58	49	65	55	59	43	69
1988	C	680	48	54	83	53	56	56	57	54	52	53	55	59
1989	C	687	60	47	55	58	73	64	65	56	54	49	57	49
1990	C	754	63	61	59	64	71	57	67	73	65	66	56	52
1992	C	701	73	52	63	54	63	52	59	69	50	59	64	43
1993	C	681	58	32	69	58	57	52	65	52	68	59	66	45
1994	C	676	58	60	54	54	59	55	68	63	42	56	46	61
1995	C	624	37	51	62	49	50	58	50	44	52	79	58	34
1996	C	660	60	50	50	54	50	51	55	57	47	63	59	64
1997	C	672	56	57	53	47	56	46	58	67	58	57	49	68
1998	C	669	56	57	55	56	59	47	64	57	60	60	50	48
1999	C	672	46	41	65	55	61	58	60	60	68	57	50	51
2000	C	644	58	47	57	37	57	69	58	58	52	44	57	50

(See notes at end of table. — Voir notes à la fin du tableau.)

Continent, country or area / Continent, pays ou zone	Code[a]	Total	Jan	Feb	March	April	May	June	July	Aug	Sep	Oct	Nov	Dec
EUROPE														
Channel Islands: Jersey - Îles Anglo-Normandes: Jersey														
1980	+C	867	62	68	93	72	63	61	93	77	68	69	70	71
1981	+C	857	75	67	91	79	76	61	76	58	72	86	53	63
1982	+C	865	61	60	67	68	75	79	79	77	78	73	67	81
1983	+C	884	76	72	71	70	91	63	74	66	83	69	76	73
1984	+C	931	76	82	67	79	87	81	86	84	78	78	75	58
1985	+C	907	70	65	93	91	70	68	72	71	82	85	86	54
1986	+C	948	73	84	84	72	76	90	78	80	79	79	73	80
1987	+C	1 009	63	74	78	100	69	101	91	77	107	84	83	82
1988	+C	1 071	85	76	86	105	94	83	91	85	81	82	97	106
1989	+C	1 074	77	82	97	88	107	94	94	82	106	94	69	84
Croatia - Croatie[23]														
1988	C	58 525	5 004	4 777	5 114	4 627	5 128	4 853	4 938	5 088	5 109	4 821	4 433	4 633
1989	C	55 651	4 795	4 379	4 827	4 591	4 673	4 720	4 855	4 913	4 772	4 528	4 165	4 433
1990	C	55 409	4 710	4 155	4 765	4 467	4 597	4 482	4 985	4 898	4 797	4 738	4 355	4 460
1991	C	51 829	4 608	4 144	4 620	4 407	4 557	4 534	4 632	4 323	4 424	3 938	3 753	3 889
1992	C	46 970	4 040	3 760	3 730	3 448	3 655	3 494	3 796	3 801	4 253	4 365	4 273	4 355
1993	C	48 535	4 457	3 859	4 312	4 035	3 979	3 769	4 275	4 140	4 101	4 059	3 732	3 817
1994	C	48 584	4 000	3 583	3 994	4 113	4 011	4 065	4 207	4 296	4 311	4 036	3 839	4 129
1995	C	50 182	4 412	3 813	4 168	3 779	4 011	4 065	4 207	4 296	4 311	4 036	3 839	4 129
1996	C	53 811	4 450	4 092	4 447	4 020	4 405	4 561	4 766	4 753	4 747	4 711	4 515	4 344
1997	C	55 501	4 780	4 277	4 437	4 650	4 858	4 634	5 007	4 782	4 861	4 660	4 191	4 364
1998	C	47 068	3 923	3 635	3 986	3 798	4 095	3 836	4 213	4 006	4 172	3 985	3 669	3 750
1999	C	45 179	3 830	3 544	3 726	3 472	3 579	3 767	4 015	4 104	4 271	3 867	3 470	3 534
2000	C	43 746	3 827	3 550	3 589	3 417	3 600	3 429	3 864	3 739	3 896	3 737	3 548	3 550
2001	C	40 993	3 656	3 142	3 352	3 385	3 359	3 185	3 596	3 648	3 646	3 432	3 209	3 383
2002	C	40 094	3 548	3 199	3 401	3 218	3 230	3 140	3 419	3 481	3 659	3 482	3 100	3 217
Czech Republic - République tchèque														
1991	C	129 354	11 443	10 657	11 892	11 757	11 899	11 333	11 182	10 701	10 543	9 663	9 056	9 228
1992	C	121 705	10 011	9 638	10 975	10 553	10 992	10 772	10 884	10 324	10 109	9 419	8 768	9 260
1993	C	121 025	9 885	9 632	10 790	10 472	10 933	10 819	11 100	10 613	10 170	9 274	8 707	8 630
1994	C	106 579	9 162	8 770	10 149	10 050	10 213	9 543	9 373	8 460	8 087	7 691	7 494	7 587
1995	C	96 097	8 162	7 558	8 869	8 185	8 575	8 417	8 562	8 168	7 722	7 662	7 030	7 187
1996	C	90 446	7 613	7 273	7 979	7 901	8 340	7 983	8 216	7 389	7 069	6 947	6 827	6 909
1997	C	90 657	7 490	6 890	7 857	8 219	8 587	7 818	8 381	7 724	7 537	7 047	6 392	6 715
1998	C	92 535	7 066	8 758	7 856	8 143	8 149	8 069	8 493	7 785	7 511	7 112	6 789	6 804
1999	C	89 471	7 187	6 907	7 875	7 892	8 007	7 927	8 007	7 759	7 648	6 816	6 408	7 038
2000	C	90 910	7 557	7 142	8 025	7 983	8 391	7 837	7 906	7 797	7 269	7 177	6 946	6 880
2001	C	90 715	7 574	6 798	7 878	7 948	8 207	7 870	8 088	7 889	7 396	7 301	6 950	6 816
2002	C	92 786	7 432	7 184	8 166	8 145	8 417	7 834	8 122	8 073	7 717	7 498	6 968	7 230
Denmark - Danemark[24]														
1980	C	57 293	4 738	4 590	5 233	5 345	5 190	4 919	5 076	4 805	4 685	4 461	4 124	4 127
1981	C	53 089	4 200	4 087	4 595	4 765	4 745	4 725	4 790	4 545	4 616	4 155	3 870	3 996
1982	C	52 658	4 368	4 067	4 732	4 640	4 876	4 600	4 606	4 405	4 334	4 239	3 878	3 913
1983	C	50 822	3 863	3 864	4 597	4 577	4 363	4 521	4 474	4 493	4 342	4 188	3 816	3 724
1984	C	51 800	3 974	4 009	4 653	4 570	4 623	4 490	4 545	4 546	4 340	4 247	4 027	3 776
1985	C	53 749	4 060	3 952	4 662	4 929	4 834	4 604	4 826	4 754	4 631	4 422	4 037	4 038
1986	C	55 312	4 080	4 301	4 751	5 030	4 926	4 692	4 993	4 721	4 892	4 533	4 124	4 269
1987	C	56 221	4 367	4 058	4 940	4 998	5 000	5 112	5 100	4 927	4 660	4 438	4 279	4 342
1988	C	58 844	4 500	4 471	5 201	5 061	5 169	4 989	5 160	5 288	5 158	4 716	4 474	4 657
1989	C	61 351	4 707	4 651	5 293	5 300	5 578	5 237	5 486	5 423	5 275	4 846	4 721	4 834
1990	C	63 433	4 930	4 800	5 488	5 426	5 545	5 354	5 878	5 552	5 509	5 380	4 771	4 800
1991	C	64 358	5 146	4 914	5 444	5 641	5 768	5 488	5 818	5 620	5 388	5 130	4 955	5 046
1992	C	67 726	5 244	5 358	5 851	5 739	5 725	5 949	6 156	5 937	5 803	5 614	5 107	5 243
1993	C	67 369	5 539	5 165	5 940	5 783	5 690	5 842	6 110	5 893	5 828	5 414	4 962	5 203
1994	C	69 666	5 361	5 188	5 913	5 988	6 046	6 031	6 237	5 946	5 722	5 869	5 704	5 661
1995	C	69 771	5 708	5 435	6 161	5 931	5 849	5 914	6 292	6 300	5 858	5 731	5 404	5 188

(See notes at end of table. — Voir notes à la fin du tableau.)

Continent, country or area / Continent, pays ou zone	C-o-d-e[a]	Total	Jan	Feb	March	April	May	June	July	Aug	Sep	Oct	Nov	Dec
EUROPE														
Denmark - Danemark[24]														
1996	C	67 638	5 524	5 320	5 889	5 625	5 533	5 613	5 914	5 924	5 719	5 581	5 521	5 475
1997	C	67 636	5 554	5 346	5 741	5 733	5 943	5 875	6 181	6 032	5 764	5 554	4 827	5 086
1998	C	66 170	5 372	4 957	5 677	5 692	5 537	5 344	6 088	5 992	5 810	5 458	5 098	5 145
1999	C	66 220	5 316	4 977	5 783	5 686	5 815	5 704	5 946	5 897	5 754	5 297	5 019	5 026
2000	C	67 084	5 439	5 193	5 578	5 768	5 716	5 718	5 963	5 882	5 689	5 719	5 266	5 153
2001	C	65 458	5 577	4 980	5 603	5 362	5 827	5 559	5 861	5 847	5 429	5 462	5 095	4 856
2002	C	64 149	5 338	4 940	5 376	5 386	5 515	5 344	5 727	5 693	5 595	5 455	4 953	4 827
Estonia - Estonie[12]														
1989	C	24 292	1 990	1 946	2 244	2 060	2 108	2 067	2 063	2 083	1 993	1 928	1 851	1 959
1990	C	22 308	1 930	1 902	2 076	2 031	2 031	1 912	1 956	1 777	1 797	1 672	1 533	1 691
1991	C	19 320	1 791	1 564	1 794	1 841	1 726	1 612	1 666	1 603	1 495	1 426	1 428	1 374
1992	C	18 006	1 473	1 471	1 711	1 579	1 657	1 579	1 559	1 503	1 455	1 408	1 313	1 298
1993	C	15 170	1 344	1 351	1 438	1 414	1 405	1 305	1 270	1 170	1 184	1 144	993	1 152
1994	C	14 178	1 120	1 163	1 380	1 259	1 312	1 210	1 249	1 150	1 095	1 077	1 065	1 098
1995	C	13 560	1 119	1 065	1 263	1 178	1 197	1 183	1 209	1 160	1 127	999	1 064	996
1996	C	13 291	1 057	1 135	1 179	1 230	1 258	1 109	1 174	1 090	992	1 014	1 046	1 007
1997	C	12 626	1 069	981	1 128	1 053	1 176	1 130	1 139	1 030	1 066	996	936	922
1999	C	12 425	947	960	1 104	1 091	1 185	1 054	1 053	1 083	1 094	975	915	964
2000	C	13 067	1 131	1 022	1 176	1 116	1 188	1 176	1 121	1 099	1 026	1 025	965	1 022
2001	C	12 632	1 099	951	1 158	1 027	1 176	1 083	1 048	1 096	1 027	1 020	971	976
2002	C	13 001	1 100	994	1 162	1 115	1 143	1 094	1 134	1 092	1 095	1 033	1 002	1 037
Faeroe Islands - Îles Féroé														
1980	C	741	72	47	54	67	75	50	70	59	60	66	59	62
1981	C	753	73	55	72	65	61	63	59	58	59	62	60	66
1982	C	726	74	57	68	69	51	53	67	59	48	65	43	72
1983	C	669	41	55	57	53	57	61	58	55	69	61	57	45
1984	C	691	47	55	55	45	56	72	60	56	62	72	50	61
1985	C	738	59	45	58	62	68	68	75	57	71	66	68	51
1986	C	787	64	60	56	73	69	61	63	87	80	68	52	54
1987	C	777	61	57	58	83	62	64	49	75	73	65	67	63
1989	C	933	75	54	73	87	78	80	80	90	81	82	81	72
Finland - Finlande[25]														
1980	C	63 064	5 113	5 062	5 931	5 640	5 660	5 389	5 486	5 330	5 283	4 814	4 414	4 942
1981	C	63 469	5 114	4 833	5 739	5 780	5 508	5 411	5 429	5 377	5 501	4 954	4 778	5 045
1982	C	66 106	5 232	5 097	6 176	5 835	5 830	5 470	5 518	5 387	5 641	5 491	5 179	5 250
1983	C	66 892	5 427	5 126	6 135	5 945	5 915	5 713	5 729	5 634	5 599	5 327	5 150	5 192
1984	C	65 076	5 274	5 401	5 942	5 622	5 665	5 423	5 533	5 559	5 318	5 404	5 051	4 884
1985	C	62 796	5 359	4 723	5 806	5 679	5 504	5 259	5 362	5 236	5 255	4 928	4 603	5 082
1986	C	60 632	5 054	4 704	5 540	5 435	5 246	5 136	5 232	5 138	5 080	4 958	4 426	4 683
1987	C	59 827	4 803	4 456	5 447	5 384	5 172	5 171	5 314	5 047	4 940	4 783	4 590	4 720
1988	C	63 316	5 047	4 910	5 972	5 623	5 561	5 316	5 217	5 429	5 442	5 076	4 734	4 989
1990	C	65 549	5 353	5 058	5 958	5 528	5 792	5 595	5 674	5 617	5 590	5 312	5 129	4 943
1994	C	65 231	5 136	5 048	5 903	5 789	5 685	5 748	5 622	5 686	5 190	5 239	5 057	5 128
1995	C	63 067	5 266	5 075	5 754	5 606	5 563	5 419	5 545	5 327	5 159	4 895	4 751	4 707
1996	C	60 723	5 193	4 842	5 241	5 372	5 509	4 978	5 151	5 136	5 088	4 887	4 504	4 822
1997	C	59 329	5 135	4 586	5 169	5 276	5 237	5 138	5 388	5 114	4 876	4 672	4 247	4 491
1998	C	57 108	4 739	4 233	4 963	4 958	4 753	4 929	5 259	4 910	5 049	4 722	4 356	4 237
1999	C	57 574	4 646	4 452	5 123	4 907	5 078	4 997	5 217	4 953	4 908	4 552	4 210	4 531
2000	C	56 742	4 768	4 497	4 970	4 759	5 001	4 835	5 043	4 853	4 693	4 536	4 359	4 428
2001	C	56 189	4 805	4 407	4 870	4 842	4 800	4 877	4 813	4 862	4 735	4 644	4 313	4 221
2002	C	55 555	4 503	4 168	4 607	4 600	4 795	4 647	4 947	4 986	4 880	4 770	4 265	4 387
France[26]														
1980	C	800 376	63 538	60 354	67 017	68 442	73 984	67 896	71 028	67 362	65 719	67 243	62 887	64 906
1981	C	805 680	64 700	60 530	68 630	70 480	72 620	69 720	71 950	68 310	65 400	65 200	62 170	65 970
1982	C	797 223	64 717	60 701	69 193	69 541	72 406	68 944	70 847	67 083	65 181	64 998	61 178	62 434
1983	C	748 525	61 042	57 134	62 166	62 754	68 829	66 146	68 091	63 518	61 396	60 295	57 089	60 065
1984	C	759 939	60 189	58 353	63 252	61 144	66 841	65 570	68 678	64 674	62 899	64 887	61 239	62 213
1985	C	768 431	63 003	56 278	64 260	64 679	70 206	65 603	69 242	63 905	62 793	64 195	60 909	63 358
1986	C	778 468	63 920	58 689	65 629	65 781	70 208	66 807	67 734	65 760	64 206	65 099	60 307	64 328

(See notes at end of table. — Voir notes à la fin du tableau.)

Continent, country or area / Continent, pays ou zone	C-o-d-e[a]	Total	Jan	Feb	March	April	May	June	July	Aug	Sep	Oct	Nov	Dec
EUROPE														
France[26]														
1987	C	767 828	62 628	57 137	64 507	64 830	69 074	68 275	67 974	64 129	63 190	63 511	59 689	62 884
1988	C	771 268	62 358	59 563	65 930	63 550	68 600	64 456	66 600	66 037	64 609	64 432	61 714	63 419
1989	C	765 473	60 905	57 666	64 569	64 191	68 364	66 118	68 170	64 007	60 567	64 292	62 184	64 440
1991	C	759 056	62 758	57 319	62 463	62 560	65 687	64 174	68 810	64 545	63 655	64 147	60 402	62 536
1992	C	743 658	61 964	58 811	62 478	61 694	64 604	62 280	66 802	62 163	61 773	61 693	58 132	61 264
1993	C	711 610	58 502	53 452	58 950	58 898	60 138	61 634	64 789	60 699	59 787	59 102	56 417	59 242
1994	C	710 993	56 329	52 901	58 381	58 486	62 801	60 951	63 826	59 604	57 880	60 406	58 605	60 823
1995	C	729 609	58 573	53 474	60 020	57 521	62 061	63 217	65 736	62 474	61 638	63 788	59 746	61 361
1996	C	734 338	59 552	56 692	60 400	59 500	63 232	62 819	66 108	61 124	60 767	62 493	59 994	61 657
1997	C	726 768	60 206	55 141	59 007	61 726	63 004	61 616	65 170	60 381	59 341	61 058	58 508	61 610
1999	C	744 791	59 837	55 445	61 726	61 179	63 900	62 656	67 137	63 892	63 828	62 887	59 317	62 987
2000	C	774 782	63 559	60 149	64 315	62 469	67 324	63 940	67 916	66 778	64 297	65 720	63 262	65 053
2001	C	770 945	64 850	57 456	63 962	62 957	67 673	63 176	68 550	66 010	63 452	66 765	63 160	62 934
2002	C	762 700	64 000	57 900	63 600	61 700	65 700	62 600	67 800	65 400	64 200	66 500	60 200	63 100
Germany - Allemagne														
1991	C	830 019	74 004	66 326	71 220	68 278	70 444	68 764	74 019	72 095	72 030	65 906	62 980	63 953
1992	C	809 114	69 448	66 329	69 054	65 138	67 643	67 418	72 534	71 124	70 823	64 630	61 386	63 587
1993	C	798 447	69 610	63 234	68 782	64 947	65 542	67 217	71 983	70 550	69 915	64 842	60 173	61 652
1994	C	769 603	64 558	59 902	65 572	63 867	65 713	65 321	67 844	66 971	65 722	62 103	59 712	62 318
1995	C	765 221	63 792	59 078	64 265	58 170	61 697	65 065	69 423	68 629	67 345	65 766	61 000	60 991
1996	C	796 013	63 899	61 974	65 162	61 628	64 092	65 785	71 778	71 270	71 168	67 869	64 473	66 915
1997	C	812 173	70 346	64 683	65 929	67 408	69 023	69 531	73 624	70 862	70 455	66 226	60 189	63 897
1999	C	770 744	65 738	60 068	63 952	61 772	65 267	65 262	70 402	68 500	68 495	62 041	57 771	61 476
2001	C	734 475	63 906	55 518	60 892	58 822	63 234	61 365	66 373	65 577	63 156	61 158	57 174	57 300
2002	C	719 250	47 613	54 686	56 307	61 366	58 086	56 308	67 563	62 166	62 129	65 018	54 904	73 104
Gibraltar[27]														
1980	C	550	48	54	37	53	51	41	42	50	45	41	50	38
1981	C	511	54	40	38	43	28	46	43	31	46	46	39	57
1982	C	566	45	44	48	34	50	50	62	55	50	38	42	48
1983	C	510	41	32	30	45	47	42	58	38	52	37	42	46
1984	C	506	40	41	31	48	37	48	48	53	42	45	43	30
1985	C	498	31	25	53	39	44	34	57	44	43	41	36	51
1986	C	507	34	46	38	47	56	37	29	38	61	44	39	38
1987	C	531	40	41	44	46	46	39	42	44	54	50	44	41
1988	C	523	35	42	47	45	50	38	47	51	48	47	40	33
1990	C	531	38	46	50	53	52	40	44	48	35	41	43	41
1995	C	435	29	38	43	36	44	32	35	29	39	34	43	33
1996	C	445	36	40	36	37	44	38	32	34	34	35	40	39
1997	C	427	23	31	39	46	36	38	28	39	35	25	37	50
2002	C	375	36	26	29	37	25	29	29	28	38	26	34	38
Greece - Grèce														
1980	C	148 134	12 555	11 966	12 311	12 380	13 196	12 976	13 415	12 504	12 715	12 452	11 181	10 483
1981	C	140 953	12 697	11 223	12 451	11 731	12 063	12 602	12 591	11 975	11 698	11 248	10 425	10 249
1982	C	137 275	11 458	10 698	11 836	11 370	12 168	11 738	11 896	11 813	11 598	11 529	10 920	10 251
1983	C	132 608	11 398	10 273	11 549	11 355	12 023	11 538	12 136	11 627	10 800	10 890	9 661	9 358
1984	C	125 724	10 008	9 921	10 855	10 354	11 283	11 154	11 517	10 994	10 599	10 482	9 730	8 827
1985	C	116 481	9 603	8 657	10 247	9 801	10 970	9 638	10 457	9 923	9 969	9 833	8 925	8 458
1990	C	102 229	8 289	7 681	8 724	8 407	8 954	8 880	9 316	8 789	8 477	8 847	8 075	7 790
1991	C	102 620	8 748	7 607	8 420	8 125	9 068	9 044	8 985	8 861	8 759	8 842	8 359	7 802
1992	C	104 081	8 842	8 056	8 374	8 415	8 925	8 985	9 166	8 817	9 081	8 845	8 354	8 221
1993	C	101 799	8 398	7 631	8 495	8 159	8 572	8 629	9 266	8 961	8 820	8 769	8 329	7 770
1994	C	103 763	8 766	7 666	8 530	8 551	8 788	8 509	9 489	8 918	8 777	8 966	8 340	8 463
1995	C	101 495	8 218	7 728	8 311	8 072	8 616	8 169	9 130	8 918	9 193	9 021	8 103	8 016
1996	C	100 718	8 330	7 412	7 959	8 044	8 757	8 617	9 719	9 304	8 713	8 365	7 790	7 708
1997	C	102 038	8 834	7 463	8 159	8 100	8 751	8 616	9 890	8 899	8 635	8 701	7 995	7 995
1998	C	100 894	8 201	7 443	7 837	7 836	8 968	9 135	9 708	8 621	8 731	9 051	7 838	7 525
1999	C	100 643	8 146	7 476	8 078	7 532	7 938	8 568	9 813	9 078	9 082	9 028	8 013	7 891
2000	C	103 267	8 890	7 686	8 159	7 712	8 172	8 663	9 665	9 412	9 138	8 994	8 678	8 098
2001	C	102 282	8 484	7 497	8 475	7 936	8 455	8 458	9 429	9 072	9 023	9 279	8 444	7 730
Hungary - Hongrie														
1980	C	148 673	12 948	11 910	12 675	12 354	12 911	12 489	13 314	12 759	12 607	12 025	11 172	11 509

(See notes at end of table. — Voir notes à la fin du tableau.)

Continent, country or area / Continent, pays ou zone	C-o-d-e[a]	Total	Jan	Feb	March	April	May	June	July	Aug	Sep	Oct	Nov	Dec
EUROPE														
Hungary - Hongrie														
1981	C	142 890	11 900	11 477	12 739	12 067	12 631	12 518	12 980	12 066	11 660	11 198	10 432	11 222
1982	C	133 559	11 488	10 450	11 553	11 104	11 384	11 250	11 777	11 802	11 424	10 596	10 242	10 489
1983	C	127 258	10 636	9 987	11 206	10 314	10 740	10 569	11 556	11 360	11 003	10 314	9 569	10 004
1984	C	125 357	10 427	9 984	10 702	9 955	10 632	10 754	11 676	10 997	10 506	10 263	9 676	9 785
1985	C	130 200	10 457	9 737	11 140	10 522	11 223	10 681	11 864	11 454	11 514	10 898	10 369	10 341
1986	C	128 204	10 843	9 942	11 081	10 698	10 547	10 901	11 775	11 288	10 752	10 342	9 687	10 348
1987	C	125 840	10 601	9 512	10 563	10 446	10 509	10 827	11 478	11 009	10 619	10 102	9 981	10 193
1988	C	124 296	10 735	10 086	10 753	9 524	10 821	10 199	11 015	10 872	10 445	10 073	9 761	10 012
1989	C	123 304	10 317	9 917	10 613	10 020	10 371	10 463	11 310	10 832	10 272	9 868	9 380	9 941
1990	C	125 679	10 515	9 645	10 779	10 040	10 523	10 143	11 373	10 942	10 651	10 419	9 970	10 679
1991	C	127 207	10 759	9 942	11 032	10 461	11 057	10 681	11 385	10 801	10 650	10 290	9 965	10 184
1992	C	121 724	10 420	9 924	10 507	9 779	10 081	10 319	10 987	10 609	10 290	9 724	9 320	9 764
1994	C	115 598	10 238	9 285	10 105	9 617	9 548	9 717	9 965	9 980	9 844	9 021	8 740	9 538
1995	C	112 054	9 498	8 399	9 371	8 241	8 833	8 974	10 037	10 147	10 348	9 879	9 380	8 947
1996	C	105 272	9 112	8 497	9 080	8 512	8 738	8 752	9 608	9 178	8 705	8 429	8 202	8 459
1997	C	100 350	8 708	7 722	8 534	8 329	8 617	8 366	8 990	8 527	8 604	8 195	7 620	8 138
1998	C	97 301	8 167	7 481	8 424	8 060	8 390	8 219	8 938	8 230	8 218	7 854	7 580	7 740
1999	C	94 645	7 947	7 195	7 920	7 572	7 571	8 025	8 617	8 446	8 340	7 718	7 290	8 004
2000	C	97 597	8 161	7 761	8 091	7 547	8 008	8 063	8 533	8 523	8 156	8 233	8 183	8 338
2001	C	97 047	8 462	7 490	8 292	7 882	8 047	7 869	8 824	8 487	8 258	7 981	7 621	7 834
2002	C	96 804	8 266	7 370	8 101	7 661	7 772	7 832	8 613	8 207	8 670	8 461	7 699	8 152
Iceland - Islande														
1980	C	4 528	400	364	402	412	441	372	386	362	377	349	314	349
1982	C	4 337	359	348	377	377	383	377	389	363	361	336	323	344
1983	C	4 371	366	306	382	381	409	406	379	371	408	332	319	312
1984	C	4 113	330	361	362	369	301	340	404	372	343	348	303	280
1985	C	3 856	313	260	332	348	342	322	367	309	337	315	307	304
1986	C	3 881	323	291	313	306	340	351	334	353	332	325	311	302
1987	C	4 193	336	273	359	374	367	335	373	373	371	341	334	357
1988	C	4 673	351	338	419	405	445	417	422	408	397	379	354	338
1989	C	4 560	369	315	389	369	401	371	404	428	406	386	372	350
1990	C	4 768	386	348	410	370	461	403	431	440	415	397	371	336
1991	C	4 533	370	353	398	394	440	377	390	410	382	364	325	330
1992	C	4 609	409	348	385	381	382	401	410	419	391	373	354	356
1993	C	4 623	391	362	402	413	439	371	408	379	418	383	314	343
1995	C	4 280	335	357	341	359	386	365	390	363	351	368	344	321
1996	C	4 329	328	351	380	370	374	355	384	367	339	378	376	327
1997	C	4 151	366	298	362	342	383	342	360	365	363	330	307	333
1998	C	4 178	330	299	360	342	376	358	396	364	369	363	307	314
1999	C	4 100	372	312	346	320	344	321	353	380	357	331	335	329
2000	C	4 315	338	347	372	346	373	378	365	361	379	383	332	341
2001	C	4 091	351	306	307	349	336	330	371	398	371	352	349	271
2002	C	4 049	356	316	361	316	333	341	331	366	369	342	321	297
Ireland - Irlande[28]														
1980	+C	74 064	6 233	5 880	6 531	6 430	6 672	5 962	6 378	6 060	6 131	6 128	5 598	6 061
1981	+C	72 158	6 135	5 667	6 456	6 282	6 284	5 941	6 150	5 801	6 035	5 885	5 645	5 877
1982	+C	70 843	5 911	5 560	6 441	6 166	6 174	5 758	6 205	5 926	5 940	5 624	5 420	5 718
1983	+C	67 117	5 819	5 294	6 045	5 653	5 927	5 626	5 821	5 625	5 714	5 281	5 081	5 231
1984	+C	64 062	5 315	5 316	5 822	5 345	5 305	5 135	5 490	5 404	5 455	5 433	5 081	4 961
1985	+C	62 245	5 402	4 910	5 502	5 271	5 698	5 011	5 406	5 128	5 320	5 290	4 470	4 837
1986	+C	61 620	5 011	4 750	5 691	5 405	5 668	5 114	5 240	5 001	5 173	5 096	4 611	4 860
1987	+C	58 433	4 897	4 581	5 055	5 069	5 210	5 066	5 142	5 790	4 887	4 705	4 352	3 679
1988	+C	54 287	4 622	4 291	4 887	4 705	4 860	4 739	4 742	4 542	4 583	4 196	4 163	3 957
1989	+C	52 018	4 248	3 948	4 682	4 408	4 829	4 435	4 485	4 302	4 309	4 107	3 956	4 309
1990	+C	53 044	4 152	4 072	4 582	4 424	4 851	4 633	4 556	4 392	4 482	4 522	4 196	4 182
1991	+C	52 684	4 394	4 116	4 488	4 462	4 682	4 274	4 615	4 536	4 489	4 437	4 019	4 172
1992	+C	51 089	4 315	4 076	4 478	4 513	4 601	4 283	4 515	4 240	4 298	3 997	3 815	3 958
1993	+C	49 304	4 083	3 806	4 165	4 144	4 410	4 249	4 325	4 158	4 285	4 192	3 790	3 697
1994	+C	48 255	3 826	3 582	4 314	3 944	4 271	4 108	4 141	4 051	4 072	3 987	3 967	3 992
1995	+C	48 787	4 108	3 657	4 187	4 100	4 336	4 132	4 318	4 121	4 130	4 117	3 727	3 854
1996	+C	50 390	4 132	3 844	4 084	4 183	4 189	4 065	4 495	4 358	4 439	4 353	4 125	4 123

11a. Live births by month of occurence: 1980 - 2002
Naissances vivantes selon le mois de naissance: 1980 - 2002 (continued — suite)

(See notes at end of table. — Voir notes à la fin du tableau.)

Continent, country or area Continent, pays ou zone	Code[a]	Total	Jan	Feb	March	April	May	June	July	Aug	Sep	Oct	Nov	Dec
EUROPE														
Ireland - Irlande[28]														
1997	+C	52 775	4 451	3 997	4 387	4 346	4 478	4 447	4 682	4 603	4 606	4 300	4 073	4 405
1998	+C	53 551	4 341	3 991	4 592	4 650	4 555	4 511	4 837	4 504	4 787	4 467	4 005	4 311
1999	+C	53 354	4 408	4 037	4 568	4 486	4 571	4 647	4 640	4 471	4 628	4 339	4 135	4 424
2000	+C	54 789	4 467	4 267	4 584	4 460	4 677	4 589	4 745	4 652	4 680	4 656	4 566	4 446
2001	+C	57 882	5 861	4 289	4 635	4 686	5 226	4 391	5 021	5 535	4 132	5 557	5 151	3 398
2002	+C	60 521	5 916	4 401	4 655	5 181	5 494	4 572	5 350	5 329	4 914	5 641	5 034	4 034
Isle of Man - Îles de Man														
1980	+C	741	48	58	77	58	63	61	60	62	51	78	60	65
1981	+C	752	57	59	65	71	61	60	56	58	76	66	67	56
1982	+C	724	72	60	64	65	45	65	61	72	50	61	66	43
1983	+C	680	68	53	65	60	54	49	53	55	59	60	51	53
1984	+C	666	61	50	60	52	60	60	47	65	61	54	47	49
1985	+C	703	52	54	66	59	56	60	54	61	68	47	63	63
1986	+C	709	60	68	50	73	57	59	49	54	63	73	51	52
1987	+C	729	65	50	60	67	61	74	73	64	58	55	49	53
1988	+C	781	59	58	58	73	59	74	71	70	68	65	65	61
Italy - Italie[29]														
1980	C	640 401	52 886	48 441	54 757	51 726	57 290	56 152	58 799	55 133	54 584	53 564	48 936	48 133
1981	C	623 103	51 158	45 752	52 362	52 557	55 551	53 914	56 739	53 400	54 535	51 410	47 454	48 271
1982	C	619 097	50 443	45 802	50 406	50 760	56 257	53 522	56 240	53 923	53 002	51 783	48 820	48 139
1983	C	601 928	49 908	44 307	49 682	47 343	53 621	52 156	56 181	52 887	51 642	51 300	46 538	46 363
1984	C	587 871	47 921	44 455	49 445	46 577	50 335	51 560	54 820	52 932	50 673	50 174	45 013	43 966
1985	C	577 345	46 939	41 785	48 932	48 307	53 760	51 219	53 889	48 924	47 866	48 991	43 694	43 039
1988	C	569 698	46 618	43 272	47 821	44 539	49 480	46 877	50 618	50 025	51 429	49 014	45 071	44 934
1989	C	560 688	44 786	39 860	45 670	43 892	47 996	49 298	51 897	49 635	48 276	48 316	45 074	45 988
1990	C	569 255	46 054	40 908	47 236	45 365	50 147	48 598	53 320	50 807	48 207	48 274	44 718	45 621
1991	C	562 787	46 262	40 794	44 873	44 924	50 618	48 842	50 634	47 372	49 012	48 550	45 380	45 526
1992	C	567 841	47 088	43 314	47 019	45 020	48 192	47 881	51 857	48 996	49 438	48 334	45 094	45 608
1993	C	549 484	45 704	39 578	45 536	43 942	45 465	46 215	52 284	48 270	47 807	47 353	43 330	44 000
1994	C	533 050	43 859	38 767	44 163	43 948	47 419	45 082	47 703	45 599	45 976	44 419	42 382	43 733
1995	C	525 609	42 996	38 420	42 618	40 172	44 708	44 533	47 839	46 507	47 050	47 118	41 321	42 327
1996	C	525 640	42 645	39 315	42 758	40 910	45 116	44 680	48 922	46 096	45 585	45 331	41 007	43 275
1997	C	528 901	42 961	38 353	41 745	43 413	47 167	48 858	51 186	44 149	45 933	41 570	39 199	44 367
1998	C	515 439	41 732	37 342	41 508	41 828	45 053	43 048	45 865	44 114	47 268	45 092	40 577	42 012
1999	C	523 463	41 972	38 512	43 073	39 829	43 015	43 380	48 747	46 834	47 957	45 010	41 994	43 140
2000	C	543 039	44 926	40 573	43 761	43 342	47 415	44 595	48 994	47 388	47 821	47 148	44 182	42 894
2001	C	535 282	45 224	38 962	43 201	41 696	48 290	43 118	47 491	46 254	45 391	47 129	43 000	42 124
2002	C	535 538	44 329	38 999	42 384	42 626	45 699	42 820	48 423	46 391	48 388	49 127	42 543	43 809
Latvia - Lettonie[12]														
1989	C	38 922	3 232	3 061	3 532	3 350	3 652	3 332	3 383	3 343	3 116	3 114	2 807	3 000
1990	C	37 918	3 204	3 090	3 415	3 207	3 470	3 363	3 380	3 108	2 949	2 835	2 837	3 060
1991	C	34 633	2 898	2 820	3 302	3 127	3 212	3 066	2 982	2 850	2 717	2 644	2 415	2 600
1992	C	31 569	2 651	2 675	3 011	2 841	2 860	2 857	2 895	2 634	2 492	2 297	2 185	2 171
1993	C	26 759	2 422	2 200	2 443	2 442	2 449	2 254	2 218	2 152	2 104	1 907	1 982	2 186
1994	C	24 256	2 101	2 223	2 461	2 204	2 213	2 081	2 118	1 927	1 789	1 771	1 591	1 777
1995	C	21 595	1 863	1 771	2 049	1 924	1 916	1 857	1 908	1 837	1 781	1 612	1 496	1 581
1996	C	19 782	1 626	1 546	1 719	1 784	1 773	1 777	1 795	1 698	1 493	1 479	1 505	1 587
1997	C	18 830	1 654	1 401	1 640	1 768	1 713	1 678	1 698	1 523	1 524	1 494	1 263	1 474
1998	C	18 410	1 369	1 422	1 632	1 567	1 622	1 552	1 643	1 548	1 541	1 550	1 448	1 516
1999	C	19 396	1 488	1 473	1 707	1 691	1 684	1 718	1 748	1 673	1 660	1 474	1 481	1 599
2000	C	20 248	1 657	1 671	1 775	1 726	1 824	1 809	1 779	1 694	1 583	1 535	1 529	1 666
2001	C	19 664	1 705	1 508	1 769	1 573	1 835	1 734	1 746	1 675	1 551	1 562	1 485	1 521
2002	C	20 044	1 681	1 530	1 788	1 592	1 701	1 709	1 856	1 757	1 618	1 705	1 536	1 571
Liechtenstein														
1980	C	393	28	39	31	36	33	37	39	25	28	33	26	38
1981	C	369	27	25	26	34	36	32	35	26	31	36	29	32
1982	C	384	33	27	37	31	29	41	28	39	34	32	24	29
1983	C	348	36	33	29	25	29	30	35	34	30	18	29	20
1984	C	405	31	23	40	41	39	32	42	36	27	31	26	37
1985	C	373	26	21	44	22	32	30	36	33	30	32	29	38

(See notes at end of table. — Voir notes à la fin du tableau.)

Continent, country or area / Continent, pays ou zone	Code[a]	Total	Jan	Feb	March	April	May	June	July	Aug	Sep	Oct	Nov	Dec
EUROPE														
Liechtenstein														
1986	C	351	32	29	25	24	30	38	26	34	30	28	21	34
1987	C	365	38	22	26	34	27	33	32	27	25	37	36	28
1993	C	415	24	33	30	41	30	29	42	36	29	43	38	40
1994	C	358	29	23	28	40	28	22	29	39	35	30	31	24
1995	C	425	22	26	38	30	39	40	37	44	38	43	41	27
1996	C	405	32	33	27	33	44	41	30	36	32	27	31	39
1997	C	435	40	41	35	34	29	30	34	43	31	42	39	37
2002	C	395	34	37	34	34	37	27	33	48	36	29	16	30
Lithuania - Lituanie[12]														
1987	C	59 360	5 074	5 253	5 443	5 410	5 631	5 441	5 394	4 926	4 438	4 543	4 219	3 588
1988	C	56 727	4 592	5 940	5 244	5 181	5 362	4 905	5 044	4 745	4 305	4 322	3 774	3 313
1989	C	55 782	5 719	4 396	5 003	4 682	5 152	4 903	4 954	4 706	4 284	4 468	3 987	3 528
1990	C	56 868	5 676	4 486	5 119	5 039	5 296	4 877	4 949	4 717	4 533	4 412	4 010	3 754
1991	C	56 219	5 649	4 520	5 060	4 989	5 203	4 713	5 133	4 594	4 330	3 960	3 358	4 710
1992	C	53 617	4 774	4 366	4 736	4 610	4 777	4 790	4 960	4 605	4 224	3 970	3 135	4 670
1993	C	47 464	4 117	3 901	4 545	4 388	4 300	4 065	4 072	3 929	3 491	3 419	3 352	3 885
1994	C	42 376	3 477	3 257	3 994	3 935	4 019	3 822	3 830	3 417	3 416	3 044	2 945	3 220
1995	C	41 195	3 489	3 226	3 759	3 546	3 737	3 508	3 682	3 466	3 271	3 237	3 028	3 246
1996	C	39 066	3 122	3 158	3 258	3 546	3 713	3 414	3 677	3 282	2 964	3 014	2 900	3 018
1997	C	37 812	3 218	2 825	3 231	3 399	3 460	3 285	3 481	3 265	3 018	3 164	2 613	2 853
1998	C	37 019	2 940	2 791	3 332	3 322	3 370	3 281	3 432	3 209	3 022	2 842	2 760	2 718
1999	C	36 415	2 909	2 886	3 357	3 215	3 439	3 206	3 328	3 022	2 936	2 764	2 655	2 698
2000	C	34 149	2 867	2 813	3 116	3 016	3 102	2 968	3 045	2 870	2 709	2 504	2 519	2 620
2001	C	31 546	2 772	2 520	2 796	2 688	2 894	2 716	2 879	2 612	2 486	2 536	2 315	2 332
2002	C	30 014	2 536	2 341	2 684	2 484	2 629	2 437	2 719	2 647	2 570	2 450	2 208	2 309
Luxembourg														
1980	C	4 169	338	304	333	306	369	346	365	360	373	343	369	363
1981	C	4 414	388	390	376	323	417	365	401	375	359	372	313	335
1982	C	4 300	348	322	373	346	392	369	428	351	342	341	335	353
1983	C	4 186	347	294	348	315	402	355	387	409	352	330	280	357
1984	C	4 192	351	325	376	314	361	367	392	355	323	359	335	334
1985	C	4 104	364	331	357	328	355	332	372	344	294	368	323	336
1986	C	4 309	334	303	371	320	390	415	353	389	374	331	353	376
1987	C	4 238	361	341	330	352	367	360	389	332	369	376	321	340
1988	C	4 603	393	364	377	327	423	398	352	388	422	391	363	405
1989	C	4 665	353	369	416	409	387	383	413	410	374	400	372	379
1994	C	5 451	415	414	495	444	500	513	499	456	433	461	361	460
1995	C	5 421	431	406	492	425	490	486	479	433	460	416	429	474
1996	C	5 689	478	423	462	427	500	465	498	499	479	492	469	497
1998	C	5 386	460	414	479	465	479	470	478	423	448	470	385	415
1999	C	5 582	440	462	497	461	488	511	499	445	473	443	426	437
2000	C	5 723	503	472	497	446	501	493	530	501	424	459	416	481
2001	C	5 459	452	404	464	456	506	473	505	451	421	451	418	458
2002	C	5 345	449	422	460	462	436	423	500	437	448	433	414	461
Malta - Malte[30]														
1980	C	5 602	470	436	424	434	422	500	442	524	476	513	468	493
1981	C	5 292	458	405	450	423	432	460	449	436	486	522	437	334
1982	C	5 912	515	441	463	440	499	446	492	509	503	545	507	552
1983	C	5 651	474	402	483	424	459	422	483	495	517	551	449	492
1984	C	5 571	448	426	446	385	437	450	481	533	501	513	486	465
1985	C	5 430	469	422	436	429	470	447	497	466	505	430	415	444
1986	C	5 245	366	380	388	399	442	464	490	481	473	488	433	441
1987	C	5 314	450	387	407	431	417	459	433	487	466	465	445	467
1988	C	5 533	486	439	438	434	448	411	496	458	500	515	411	497
1990	C	5 368	405	417	423	433	455	457	490	490	496	433	398	471
1992	C	5 474	491	395	431	416	458	395	468	443	443	464	497	573
1993	C	5 147	408	376	432	412	436	398	462	444	452	471	426	430
1994	C	4 826	437	377	405	382	375	400	453	411	419	377	390	400
1995	C	4 613	393	344	376	373	386	378	428	331	415	434	362	393
1996	C	4 944	434	385	407	391	373	423	466	416	424	416	374	435
1997	C	4 835	394	368	396	383	352	437	488	395	410	400	396	416

(See notes at end of table. — Voir notes à la fin du tableau.)

Continent, country or area / Continent, pays ou zone	Code[a]	Total	Jan	Feb	March	April	May	June	July	Aug	Sep	Oct	Nov	Dec
EUROPE														
Malta - Malte[30]														
1998	C	4 488	393	358	344	332	357	362	391	380	419	415	360	377
1999	C	4 308	404	302	345	311	347	305	381	364	418	391	353	387
2000	C	4 255	381	338	350	327	320	312	374	385	350	356	369	393
2001	C	3 859	310	303	336	304	308	336	347	308	328	349	310	320
Netherlands - Pays-Bas[31]														
1980	C	181 294	14 585	13 544	14 978	15 349	15 606	14 954	16 182	15 832	15 694	15 479	14 342	14 749
1981	C	178 569	14 484	13 711	15 511	15 321	15 258	14 864	15 742	15 603	15 476	14 946	13 587	14 066
1982	C	172 071	14 246	13 198	14 901	14 574	14 556	14 448	15 038	14 597	14 755	14 391	13 543	13 824
1983	C	170 246	14 045	12 937	14 035	14 247	14 585	14 631	14 805	14 593	14 412	14 129	13 862	13 965
1984	C	174 436	14 693	13 876	14 986	14 334	14 892	14 617	15 302	14 950	14 704	14 737	13 994	13 351
1985	C	178 136	14 820	13 702	15 393	14 976	15 192	14 181	15 250	15 411	15 260	15 473	14 329	14 149
1986	C	184 513	15 248	14 283	15 993	16 090	16 111	15 397	15 521	15 785	15 761	15 422	14 187	14 715
1987	C	186 667	15 299	14 148	15 968	15 573	16 352	16 266	16 576	16 109	15 970	15 400	14 343	14 663
1988	C	186 647	15 529	14 849	16 542	15 509	16 402	14 974	15 593	16 093	16 028	15 254	14 760	15 114
1990	C	197 965	16 153	15 110	16 634	16 308	17 467	16 177	16 867	17 408	16 862	16 971	16 028	15 980
1991	C	198 665	16 768	15 402	16 957	16 215	16 797	16 110	17 315	17 239	17 325	16 966	15 899	15 672
1992	C	196 734	16 759	15 729	17 082	16 075	16 643	15 853	17 131	16 992	17 159	16 523	15 260	15 528
1993	C	195 748	16 236	14 972	16 171	15 918	16 578	16 549	17 171	17 518	17 182	16 503	15 294	15 656
1994	C	195 611	16 055	14 924	16 724	16 541	17 245	16 857	17 100	16 830	16 012	15 980	15 766	15 577
1995	C	190 513	16 436	14 824	16 205	14 906	16 167	16 124	16 698	16 491	16 222	16 508	15 199	14 733
1996	C	189 521	15 272	14 972	15 531	15 090	15 901	15 567	16 561	16 680	16 430	16 412	15 508	15 597
1998	C	199 408	16 398	15 179	16 508	16 139	16 337	16 138	17 805	17 543	18 137	17 222	16 008	15 994
1999	C	200 445	16 218	15 191	16 818	16 880	16 379	16 941	17 638	17 713	17 566	16 691	15 983	16 427
2000	C	206 619	17 068	16 606	17 445	16 625	17 513	16 773	17 694	18 315	17 736	17 155	16 996	16 693
2001	C	202 603	17 344	15 334	16 834	15 679	17 537	17 050	17 942	17 726	17 147	17 556	16 345	16 109
2002	C	202 083	17 019	15 448	16 792	15 995	16 800	16 116	18 011	17 959	17 586	17 831	16 011	16 515
Norway - Norvège														
1980	C	51 039	4 094	4 172	4 783	4 763	4 668	4 242	4 397	4 129	4 097	4 018	3 762	3 914
1981	C	50 708	4 152	4 116	4 873	4 697	4 417	4 225	4 318	4 234	4 249	3 980	3 695	3 752
1982	C	51 245	4 117	3 960	4 894	4 858	4 593	4 395	4 266	4 311	4 335	3 952	3 742	3 822
1983	C	49 937	3 990	3 914	4 667	4 540	4 359	4 320	4 315	4 188	4 192	3 861	3 694	3 897
1984	C	50 274	4 037	4 194	4 631	4 509	4 484	4 220	4 346	4 179	4 046	3 989	3 813	3 826
1985	C	51 134	4 232	3 990	4 762	4 728	4 553	4 210	4 414	4 232	4 054	4 026	3 878	4 055
1986	C	52 514	4 200	4 117	4 745	4 894	4 581	4 389	4 599	4 496	4 475	4 111	3 939	3 968
1987	C	54 027	4 196	4 117	4 807	4 856	4 779	4 635	4 820	4 526	4 541	4 329	4 121	4 300
1990	C	60 939	5 118	5 012	5 516	5 436	5 275	5 111	5 132	5 174	4 939	4 842	4 668	4 716
1991	C	60 808	5 137	4 926	5 524	5 489	5 439	5 057	5 266	4 991	5 135	4 767	4 398	4 679
1992	C	60 109	4 943	4 959	5 469	5 429	5 293	5 005	5 141	5 098	5 135	4 642	4 414	4 581
1993	C	59 678	4 907	4 577	5 312	5 406	5 322	5 094	5 278	4 996	4 980	4 814	4 434	4 558
1995	C	60 292	4 972	4 788	5 364	5 333	5 351	5 274	5 405	5 143	5 030	4 718	4 613	4 301
1996	C	60 927	4 975	4 875	5 408	5 409	5 387	5 074	5 343	5 054	4 939	4 975	4 762	4 726
1997	C	59 801	5 274	4 760	5 244	5 446	5 244	5 154	5 284	5 074	4 993	4 700	4 204	4 424
1998	C	58 352	4 742	4 614	5 185	5 317	5 021	4 974	5 319	5 068	5 091	4 641	4 232	4 148
1999	C	59 298	4 768	4 610	5 358	5 207	5 389	5 064	5 208	5 158	5 026	4 710	4 318	4 482
2000	C	59 234	4 838	4 988	5 326	5 185	5 421	4 937	5 201	5 118	4 885	4 575	4 280	4 480
2001	C	56 696	4 959	4 495	4 958	5 009	5 018	4 955	4 919	4 852	4 742	4 555	4 153	4 081
2002	C	55 434	4 664	4 415	4 777	4 757	4 831	4 663	5 072	4 795	4 613	4 579	4 143	4 125
Poland - Pologne														
1980	C	692 798	59 390	55 841	61 451	61 733	63 077	59 035	61 370	57 853	54 909	53 587	51 007	53 545
1981	C	678 696	55 918	53 644	61 987	59 231	59 385	57 842	59 937	55 716	54 599	52 648	52 333	55 456
1982	C	702 351	59 423	54 362	62 916	59 393	62 296	59 277	61 807	59 320	55 574	56 054	54 881	57 048
1983	C	720 756	62 057	57 966	66 258	62 079	62 909	60 881	64 683	60 716	58 626	56 485	54 437	53 659
1984	C	699 041	60 329	58 272	63 848	61 286	63 076	58 970	62 861	59 230	56 548	54 122	50 823	49 676
1985	C	677 576	59 158	54 020	62 701	59 262	60 217	56 544	60 438	57 038	55 363	52 484	49 219	51 132
1986	C	634 748	55 149	51 245	57 671	57 102	55 841	53 320	56 812	52 914	51 645	49 561	45 347	48 141
1987	C	605 492	51 219	47 374	52 453	51 044	52 527	53 736	55 893	52 030	48 107	46 193	45 379	49 537
1988	C	587 741	51 145	48 465	53 827	49 852	52 933	49 499	51 620	49 439	47 670	45 563	43 210	44 518
1989	C	562 530	49 279	45 750	49 541	47 441	49 132	48 274	50 132	47 755	46 400	45 252	41 549	42 025
1990	C	545 817	48 165	43 859	48 728	45 215	47 291	45 356	48 750	47 982	45 156	42 093	40 937	42 285
1991	C	545 954	48 950	42 895	48 907	45 862	47 692	45 987	48 722	46 093	44 926	42 680	39 763	43 477

(See notes at end of table. — Voir notes à la fin du tableau.)

Continent, country or area / Continent, pays ou zone	Code[a]	Total	Jan	Feb	March	April	May	June	July	Aug	Sep	Oct	Nov	Dec
EUROPE														
Poland - Pologne														
1992	C	513 616	43 783	41 840	45 841	43 148	43 323	43 809	46 381	43 577	42 501	40 266	37 985	41 162
1993	C	492 925	43 413	39 003	43 837	41 271	41 323	41 132	44 461	41 867	41 308	39 504	36 797	39 009
1994	C	481 285	41 819	38 105	43 508	41 829	42 089	40 335	41 598	39 382	38 847	36 504	34 157	43 112
1995	C	433 109	38 539	35 442	39 911	36 593	37 060	37 381	40 652	37 799	37 093	35 667	33 193	23 779
1996	C	428 203	36 549	34 188	37 423	36 727	37 758	36 288	39 502	37 138	35 814	33 810	31 732	31 274
1997	C	412 635	37 035	32 592	35 353	36 427	36 346	34 693	37 058	35 017	34 695	32 008	28 820	32 591
1998	C	395 619	33 539	30 686	35 029	33 643	34 213	32 986	36 406	34 124	34 253	30 839	29 270	30 631
1999	C	382 002	32 768	29 620	33 672	32 125	32 948	33 020	34 606	33 516	33 482	29 017	27 501	29 727
2000	C	378 348	33 946	30 960	32 838	31 267	32 905	32 355	33 530	32 932	32 626	30 034	27 495	27 460
2001	C	368 205	33 171	28 044	32 319	31 611	32 312	30 463	33 018	31 584	31 336	29 933	26 961	27 453
2002	C	353 765	30 903	27 414	31 233	29 566	29 981	29 043	32 030	31 007	30 828	29 279	26 253	26 228
Portugal														
1980	C	158 352	13 562	12 048	13 361	13 236	14 490	13 484	14 324	13 651	12 991	12 819	11 839	12 547
1981	C	152 102	12 681	11 340	12 701	12 622	13 660	12 839	13 308	12 874	12 925	12 664	12 272	12 216
1982	C	151 029	12 334	11 328	12 391	12 045	13 706	12 866	13 215	12 860	12 889	12 947	12 066	12 382
1983	C	144 327	12 099	10 862	12 192	11 926	13 014	12 301	12 693	12 334	11 882	12 032	11 370	11 622
1984	C	142 805	11 851	11 129	12 323	11 907	12 755	11 824	12 166	12 068	12 034	12 317	11 325	11 106
1985	C	130 492	11 037	9 937	11 016	10 668	12 043	11 173	11 311	10 937	11 061	11 019	10 007	10 283
1986	C	126 748	10 448	9 581	10 693	10 469	11 436	10 480	10 937	10 495	10 823	10 710	10 238	10 438
1987	C	123 218	10 614	9 388	10 168	10 318	10 939	10 686	10 714	10 524	10 684	10 175	9 407	9 601
1988	C	122 121	9 997	9 131	10 393	9 557	10 712	10 292	10 629	10 764	10 695	10 505	9 787	9 659
1989	C	118 560	9 721	8 747	9 834	9 712	10 687	9 756	10 151	9 919	10 159	10 376	9 695	9 803
1990	C	116 383	9 958	8 492	9 619	9 443	10 346	9 780	10 199	9 960	9 898	9 767	9 447	9 474
1991	C	116 415	9 779	8 428	9 682	9 331	10 410	9 616	10 011	9 969	10 373	10 146	9 262	9 408
1992	C	115 018	9 502	8 829	9 443	9 228	9 891	9 282	10 149	9 776	10 152	10 035	9 449	9 282
1993	C	114 030	9 590	8 422	9 795	9 338	10 026	9 466	10 194	9 637	9 799	9 718	9 058	8 987
1995	C	107 184	8 905	7 724	9 180	8 861	9 692	8 998	9 354	8 950	9 134	8 959	8 583	8 844
1996	C	110 363	9 038	8 379	9 171	8 925	9 619	8 742	9 355	9 163	9 484	9 753	9 424	9 310
1997	C	113 047	9 552	8 556	9 182	9 315	10 217	9 493	10 203	9 303	9 650	9 446	8 916	9 214
1999	C	116 002	9 534	8 241	9 621	9 371	9 906	9 428	10 108	10 108	10 000	10 344	9 701	9 831
2000	G	120 008	9 825	9 214	9 867	9 583	10 366	9 756	10 254	10 545	10 561	10 677	9 934	9 646
2001	C	112 774	10 133	8 582	9 545	9 129	10 212	9 055	9 790	9 683	9 528	9 549	8 827	8 741
2002	C	114 383	9 378	8 328	9 299	9 055	9 788	9 200	9 932	10 040	10 353	9 987	9 148	9 875
Republic of Moldova - République de Moldova[12]														
1987	C	91 762	7 926	7 390	8 261	8 050	8 281	7 989	8 308	7 643	6 788	7 037	7 000	7 089
1988	C	88 568	6 761	7 109	7 614	7 578	8 285	7 745	8 234	7 871	7 009	6 764	6 932	6 666
1989	C	82 221	6 685	6 701	7 050	6 682	7 214	7 022	7 170	7 546	6 436	6 849	6 427	6 439
1990	C	77 085	6 623	6 098	6 350	6 429	6 965	6 442	6 952	6 482	6 072	6 292	6 362	6 018
1991	C	72 020	6 195	5 984	6 205	6 032	6 507	5 761	6 684	5 955	5 705	6 112	5 585	5 295
1992	C	69 654	5 380	6 344	5 770	5 334	6 064	5 417	6 349	4 968	5 558	5 783	5 549	7 138
1995	C	56 411	5 459	4 778	5 081	4 760	4 921	4 652	4 928	5 022	4 656	4 540	3 993	3 612
1996	C	51 865	4 682	4 243	4 554	4 628	4 948	4 566	4 862	4 363	3 781	4 013	3 784	3 435
1998	C	41 332	3 065	3 287	3 544	3 282	3 582	3 477	3 865	3 206	3 453	3 437	3 410	3 724
1999	C	38 501	2 839	3 283	3 264	3 302	3 402	3 268	3 537	3 013	3 273	3 209	3 095	3 016
2000	C	36 939	2 493	3 368	3 137	2 630	3 056	3 264	3 212	3 202	3 118	2 818	3 504	3 137
2001	C	36 448	3 031	3 187	2 945	2 840	3 321	2 882	3 199	3 015	2 761	3 232	3 230	2 805
2002	C	35 705	2 985	3 054	2 912	2 806	2 896	2 730	3 076	2 893	2 955	3 323	3 186	2 889
Romania - Roumanie														
1986	C	376 896	28 866	26 053	29 849	29 717	29 361	29 190	33 793	36 026	36 835	34 696	31 385	31 125
1987	C	383 199	31 002	29 509	33 205	32 244	32 583	32 481	35 177	31 545	31 945	32 389	30 685	30 434
1988	C	380 043	32 367	30 631	32 145	29 248	32 633	32 525	34 455	33 141	33 631	31 593	28 947	28 727
1989	C	369 544	30 370	28 611	31 129	29 342	30 781	31 586	33 381	32 523	31 086	30 902	29 197	30 636
1990	C	314 746	30 155	28 745	31 820	29 946	30 695	28 735	26 556	22 213	21 085	22 138	21 220	21 438
1991	C	275 275	22 255	20 947	23 613	23 397	24 845	24 785	25 082	23 407	23 056	22 055	20 880	20 953
1992	C	260 393	22 868	21 877	23 317	21 613	22 865	23 502	23 925	22 940	20 997	19 894	18 315	18 280
1994	C	246 736	20 316	19 181	21 386	21 780	22 927	22 125	22 732	20 911	20 165	18 729	17 651	18 833
1995	C	236 640	19 369	18 317	20 077	19 427	20 388	20 097	21 437	20 812	20 161	19 712	18 627	18 216
1996	C	231 348	18 664	18 197	19 641	19 949	21 398	20 613	22 089	20 254	18 974	17 696	16 492	17 381
1997	C	236 891	18 859	17 519	19 450	19 763	21 095	20 923	22 066	20 717	20 150	19 905	17 967	18 477

11a. Live births by month of occurence: 1980 - 2002
Naissances vivantes selon le mois de naissance: 1980 - 2002 (continued — suite)

(See notes at end of table. — Voir notes à la fin du tableau.)

Continent, country or area / Continent, pays ou zone	C-o-d-e[a]	Total	Jan	Feb	March	April	May	June	July	Aug	Sep	Oct	Nov	Dec
EUROPE														
Romania - Roumanie														
1998	C	237 297	18 987	18 442	20 356	20 533	21 024	20 629	22 065	20 314	20 101	19 130	18 014	17 702
1999	C	234 600	19 623	18 228	20 318	19 337	19 902	21 255	22 139	20 592	20 175	18 662	16 664	17 705
2000	C	234 521	19 745	18 574	19 951	18 575	19 923	20 247	21 502	20 518	20 135	19 190	18 028	18 133
2001	C	220 368	18 317	16 920	18 987	18 089	18 707	18 546	20 644	19 065	19 215	18 178	16 986	16 714
2002	C	210 529	17 874	16 141	17 829	16 941	17 291	18 155	19 828	18 492	18 282	17 668	16 197	15 831
Russian Federation - Fédération de Russie[12,32]														
1992	C	1587644	147 709	134 529	143 820	134 967	140 401	142 066	140 220	131 461	122 006	121 441	115 253	113 771
1993	C	1378983	124 373	110 805	123 734	119 464	121 571	118 019	120 409	115 425	109 629	108 202	102 785	104 567
1994	C	1408159	123 473	112 083	126 858	121 018	122 555	122 787	124 084	120 990	113 858	110 409	104 991	105 018
1995	C	1363806	123 380	109 511	122 623	116 552	120 686	116 894	118 792	116 221	108 297	106 982	101 247	102 503
1999	C	1214689	109 603	99 798	106 860	104 833	103 795	108 167	108 539	102 398	96 133	93 426	87 968	93 132
2000	C	1266800	111 541	100 151	109 119	103 332	108 432	109 807	111 541	109 563	104 566	102 745	97 473	98 519
2001	C	1311604	106 570	100 761	109 879	103 402	115 946	107 628	117 069	119 612	102 906	116 681	105 304	102 838
San Marino - Saint-Marin														
1980	+C	239	19	26	17	21	16	25	20	22	19	20	14	20
1981	+C	217	11	12	16	16	19	29	17	25	21	21	15	15
1982	+C	237	20	14	18	16	19	20	24	25	21	25	15	20
1984	+C	223	21	21	10	18	14	17	18	27	12	31	13	21
1985	+C	207	17	18	11	20	19	18	15	18	23	25	13	10
1986	+C	179	18	13	1	19	11	10	19	17	16	16	15	24
1987	+C	220	18	16	17	14	14	20	22	18	20	17	21	23
1988	+C	242	21	19	22	16	16	20	17	22	19	27	13	30
1989	+C	231	18	14	17	12	28	20	17	20	26	20	19	20
1992	+C	237	19	21	29	13	21	17	21	19	18	14	26	19
1993	+C	244	20	12	24	23	10	20	21	17	36	12	23	26
1994	+C	268	14	17	19	19	21	20	29	33	27	16	19	34
1995	+C	244	22	15	21	19	13	21	26	17	19	30	18	23
1997	+C	287	26	23	12	27	27	32	33	31	22	16	20	18
2000	+C	290	19	28	23	27	29	23	16	23	36	20	24	22
Serbia and Montenegro - Serbie-et-Montenegro														
1990	C	155 022	13 068	11 687	13 536	13 474	15 023	13 508	13 149	12 987	13 543	12 650	10 892	11 505
1991	C	152 250	12 970	11 367	12 744	12 519	13 389	12 952	13 635	13 262	13 461	12 920	11 580	11 451
1992	C	140 819	12 030	11 245	11 599	11 142	12 023	11 932	12 148	12 279	12 576	12 278	11 012	10 555
1993	C	140 985	11 903	10 695	11 815	11 467	11 883	11 715	12 715	12 858	12 480	12 122	10 711	10 621
1994	C	137 629	11 512	10 309	11 383	11 201	11 942	11 391	11 897	12 476	12 360	11 841	10 598	10 719
1995	C	140 504	11 660	10 263	11 213	11 001	11 945	11 504	12 694	13 172	12 976	12 849	10 802	10 425
1996	C	137 683	11 484	10 802	11 588	11 194	11 962	11 670	12 432	12 256	12 026	11 606	10 016	10 647
1997	C	131 394	11 112	9 711	10 383	10 836	11 672	11 118	12 110	11 672	11 666	11 271	9 971	9 872
1998	C	128 461	10 517	9 457	10 300	10 309	11 160	10 855	11 693	11 476	11 722	11 310	9 926	9 736
1999	C	123 970	10 300	9 492	10 016	9 638	10 373	10 434	11 387	11 348	11 398	11 112	9 691	8 781
2000	C	125 868	9 547	8 813	10 070	10 098	10 645	10 742	11 701	11 808	11 225	10 966	10 206	10 047
2001	C	130 194	11 076	9 640	10 536	10 422	11 042	10 604	11 699	11 789	11 567	11 559	10 201	10 059
Slovakia - Slovaquie														
1988	C	83 242	6 744	6 590	7 521	6 995	7 467	7 196	7 448	7 343	6 987	6 395	6 214	6 342
1989	C	80 116	6 644	6 352	7 185	6 881	7 069	6 840	7 279	7 083	6 590	6 239	5 874	6 080
1990	C	79 989	6 801	6 130	6 822	6 674	6 766	6 703	7 084	6 929	6 813	6 651	6 284	6 332
1991	C	78 569	6 884	6 096	7 046	6 714	7 043	6 723	7 096	6 633	6 696	5 911	5 742	5 985
1992	C	74 640	6 201	5 848	6 456	6 145	6 477	6 569	6 997	6 561	6 346	5 836	5 409	5 795
1993	C	73 256	6 209	5 756	6 527	6 249	6 228	6 277	6 770	6 546	6 302	5 589	5 447	5 356
1994	C	66 370	5 782	5 337	6 111	5 769	6 013	5 813	5 903	5 579	5 329	4 980	4 795	4 959
1995	C	61 427	5 403	4 904	5 523	5 126	5 353	5 223	5 380	5 322	5 130	4 782	4 585	4 696
1998	C	57 582	4 518	4 288	4 889	4 996	5 062	4 776	5 175	4 971	5 270	4 703	4 256	4 678
1999	C	56 223	4 429	4 268	4 802	4 965	4 666	4 630	5 202	5 118	5 059	4 273	4 233	4 578
2000	C	55 151	4 781	4 470	4 848	4 581	4 911	4 677	4 958	4 961	4 736	4 302	3 847	4 079
2001	C	51 136	4 489	3 945	4 418	4 441	4 522	4 472	4 573	4 464	4 344	3 955	3 743	3 770
2002	C	50 841	4 218	3 807	4 462	4 365	4 407	4 155	4 539	4 275	4 416	4 170	3 845	4 182

(See notes at end of table. — Voir notes à la fin du tableau.)

Continent, country or area / Continent, pays ou zone	C-o-d-e[a]	Total	Jan	Feb	March	April	May	June	July	Aug	Sep	Oct	Nov	Dec
EUROPE														
Slovenia - Slovénie														
1988	C	25 209	2 207	2 010	2 261	2 155	2 153	2 061	2 104	2 185	2 126	2 066	1 806	2 075
1989	C	23 447	2 041	1 851	2 008	1 902	1 967	1 960	2 031	2 039	1 948	1 961	1 809	1 930
1990	C	22 368	1 867	1 707	1 922	1 889	1 875	1 764	1 972	1 949	1 863	1 961	1 755	1 844
1991	C	21 583	1 912	1 702	1 833	1 920	1 863	1 872	1 883	1 790	1 826	1 680	1 637	1 665
1992	C	19 982	1 773	1 583	1 604	1 570	1 604	1 599	1 805	1 728	1 675	1 657	1 600	1 784
1993	C	19 793	1 734	1 462	1 750	1 615	1 714	1 624	1 732	1 731	1 719	1 683	1 444	1 585
1994	C	19 463	1 663	1 532	1 703	1 637	1 669	1 549	1 694	1 668	1 628	1 508	1 544	1 668
1995	C	18 980	1 649	1 391	1 618	1 511	1 649	1 624	1 647	1 559	1 707	1 586	1 477	1 562
1996	C	18 788	1 572	1 395	1 566	1 567	1 619	1 587	1 714	1 567	1 585	1 566	1 507	1 543
1998	C	17 856	1 501	1 388	1 539	1 450	1 604	1 419	1 579	1 535	1 591	1 430	1 416	1 404
1999	C	17 533	1 449	1 310	1 564	1 417	1 446	1 461	1 570	1 571	1 555	1 467	1 297	1 426
2000	C	18 180	1 506	1 429	1 522	1 546	1 551	1 480	1 527	1 570	1 600	1 554	1 400	1 495
2001	C	17 477	1 547	1 297	1 478	1 409	1 536	1 396	1 553	1 438	1 486	1 468	1 381	1 488
2002	C	17 501	1 457	1 307	1 494	1 407	1 451	1 457	1 546	1 502	1 646	1 507	1 288	1 439
Spain - Espagne														
1980	C	571 018	48 642	44 822	48 217	47 860	50 140	47 379	49 741	48 274	48 524	47 950	43 323	46 146
1981	C	533 008	44 260	40 739	44 944	45 842	48 839	44 728	46 318	45 207	45 209	44 619	41 172	41 131
1982	C	515 706	42 472	39 145	43 587	43 797	46 998	43 133	44 357	42 804	43 470	43 131	41 044	41 768
1983	C	485 352	40 786	37 137	41 228	39 187	43 650	40 679	43 012	41 714	41 129	40 170	37 402	39 258
1984	C	465 709	38 250	37 031	39 813	37 500	41 283	39 118	39 204	39 031	39 136	40 213	37 747	37 383
1985	C	451 373	37 809	33 695	39 989	37 523	40 466	37 393	39 613	36 608	38 089	38 439	35 442	36 307
1987	C	421 098	35 833	31 749	35 738	35 911	36 596	34 743	35 481	36 126	36 935	34 925	32 914	34 147
1988	C	415 844	35 104	32 107	36 243	34 147	35 670	32 829	35 237	35 443	35 906	35 137	33 542	34 479
1991	C	395 989	33 534	30 431	33 441	32 695	33 861	31 811	33 599	32 990	34 580	34 229	32 071	32 747
1992	C	396 747	32 866	31 622	32 988	32 996	33 507	31 414	34 211	33 565	34 349	33 828	32 350	33 051
1993	C	385 786	32 870	29 386	34 073	31 902	33 307	31 815	33 422	32 256	33 335	32 528	30 208	30 684
1994	C	370 148	30 653	28 417	32 601	31 737	32 804	30 658	31 995	30 829	30 407	30 529	29 255	30 263
1995	C	363 469	30 304	27 142	30 976	29 917	31 392	30 140	31 955	30 651	30 775	31 103	29 238	29 876
1996	C	362 626	30 093	27 826	31 059	29 835	31 294	29 833	30 993	29 317	30 077	30 670	30 166	31 463
1997	C	369 035	31 210	28 562	30 692	31 650	32 585	30 229	32 667	29 893	30 624	30 889	29 366	30 668
1998	C	365 193	30 087	27 517	30 649	31 081	31 527	29 411	30 677	29 951	32 012	31 277	29 860	31 144
1999	C	380 130	31 002	28 445	31 951	31 060	32 332	30 432	33 033	32 034	33 310	32 058	31 237	33 236
2000	C	397 632	32 995	30 696	33 608	32 196	34 026	31 832	33 754	33 666	33 758	34 004	33 317	33 780
2001	C	400 859	34 181	29 851	33 364	32 582	35 384	32 599	34 636	34 638	34 005	36 006	33 828	32 785
Sweden - Suède														
1980	C	97 064	8 293	8 260	9 409	9 502	8 785	8 241	8 408	7 740	7 740	7 176	6 633	6 877
1981	C	94 065	7 971	7 795	8 947	8 971	8 577	8 016	8 104	7 837	7 772	7 023	6 401	6 651
1982	C	92 748	7 856	7 579	9 136	8 900	8 208	7 808	7 674	7 713	7 771	7 147	6 488	6 468
1983	C	91 780	7 615	7 565	8 862	8 598	8 336	8 046	7 629	7 679	7 494	7 024	6 394	6 538
1984	C	93 889	7 715	7 896	8 959	8 717	8 727	7 848	7 957	7 778	7 614	7 300	6 896	6 482
1985	C	98 463	8 103	8 005	9 503	9 264	9 107	8 337	8 452	8 258	7 952	7 537	6 878	7 067
1986	C	101 950	8 583	8 191	9 610	9 809	9 152	8 689	8 703	8 624	8 680	7 679	7 050	7 180
1987	C	104 699	8 429	8 441	9 966	9 750	9 554	9 189	9 208	8 650	8 574	7 844	7 428	7 666
1988	C	112 080	9 027	9 065	10 863	10 248	10 345	9 575	9 585	9 492	9 360	8 537	7 817	8 166
1989	C	116 023	9 431	9 300	10 838	10 242	10 614	9 864	10 210	9 888	9 442	9 106	8 520	8 568
1990	C	123 938	10 207	10 194	11 594	11 380	11 127	10 496	10 663	10 436	10 274	9 836	8 768	8 963
1992	C	122 848	10 845	10 406	11 738	11 369	10 905	10 671	10 539	10 187	10 094	9 162	8 395	8 537
1993	C	117 998	10 250	9 638	11 286	11 220	10 611	10 285	10 157	10 101	9 425	8 902	7 966	8 157
1994	C	112 257	9 296	9 511	10 900	10 694	10 241	9 975	9 607	9 285	8 383	8 317	7 914	8 134
1995	C	103 422	8 745	8 690	9 922	9 616	9 403	9 130	9 032	8 735	8 225	7 958	7 018	6 948
1996	C	95 297	8 001	7 963	8 774	8 939	8 455	8 066	8 551	8 116	7 613	7 360	6 693	6 766
1997	C	90 502	7 750	7 288	8 256	8 491	8 248	8 060	8 165	7 883	7 245	6 844	5 970	6 302
1998	C	89 028	7 274	7 227	7 937	8 155	8 074	7 522	8 129	7 930	7 463	6 893	6 186	6 238
1999	C	88 173	7 187	7 080	7 981	7 967	8 072	7 738	7 832	7 595	7 206	7 008	6 139	6 368
2000	C	90 441	7 306	7 441	8 001	7 931	8 186	7 815	8 000	7 768	7 490	7 267	6 770	6 466
2001	C	91 466	7 677	7 288	8 237	8 217	8 437	7 765	8 103	7 928	7 526	7 427	6 497	6 364
2002	C	95 815	7 807	7 483	8 448	8 799	8 745	8 088	8 317	8 274	8 038	8 058	6 898	6 860
Switzerland - Suisse														
1980	C	73 661	6 241	5 999	6 428	6 353	6 534	6 261	6 460	5 920	6 177	5 933	5 603	5 752
1981	C	73 747	6 140	5 829	6 463	6 438	6 549	6 320	6 269	6 180	6 287	5 888	5 567	5 817
1982	C	74 916	6 138	6 001	6 693	6 594	6 591	6 211	6 447	6 377	6 222	6 049	5 842	5 751

(See notes at end of table. — Voir notes à la fin du tableau.)

Continent, country or area / Continent, pays ou zone	Code[a]	Total	Jan	Feb	March	April	May	June	July	Aug	Sep	Oct	Nov	Dec
EUROPE														
Switzerland - Suisse														
1984	C	74 710	6 323	5 998	6 560	6 039	6 518	6 282	6 578	6 298	6 200	6 176	5 929	5 809
1985	C	74 684	6 326	5 774	6 801	6 452	6 564	6 148	6 568	6 199	6 288	6 196	5 698	5 670
1986	C	76 320	6 367	6 038	6 635	6 655	6 681	6 425	6 582	6 558	6 500	6 106	5 693	6 080
1987	C	76 505	6 228	5 780	6 518	6 609	6 617	6 643	6 698	6 326	6 578	6 261	6 015	6 232
1988	C	80 345	6 445	6 471	7 222	6 511	6 822	6 651	6 791	7 013	6 975	6 665	6 246	6 533
1989	C	81 180	6 577	6 100	7 039	6 751	7 113	6 962	7 219	6 900	6 759	6 503	6 517	6 740
1990	C	83 939	6 906	6 506	7 240	6 958	7 312	6 987	7 361	7 067	7 237	6 956	6 647	6 762
1992	C	86 910	7 336	7 037	7 556	7 397	7 451	7 195	7 640	7 176	7 498	7 068	6 669	6 887
1994	C	82 980	6 788	6 553	7 284	7 039	7 188	7 028	7 197	7 060	6 908	6 745	6 328	6 862
1995	C	82 203	6 859	6 377	7 107	6 585	7 045	6 878	7 293	6 988	7 148	6 997	6 343	6 583
1996	C	83 007	6 933	6 711	6 985	6 726	7 163	6 961	7 462	7 039	6 962	6 818	6 504	6 743
1998	C	78 949	6 705	6 056	6 670	6 764	6 764	6 687	6 531	6 978	6 841	6 750	6 498	6 254
1999	C	78 408	6 478	6 181	6 765	6 523	6 503	6 649	6 842	6 867	6 802	6 375	6 136	6 287
2000	C	78 458	6 731	6 329	6 778	6 538	6 651	6 456	6 678	6 725	6 739	6 263	6 265	6 305
2001	C	73 509	6 304	5 690	6 200	6 185	6 479	6 108	6 632	6 255	6 336	5 965	5 732	5 623
2002	C	72 372	5 973	5 590	6 092	6 066	6 030	5 932	6 347	6 351	6 285	6 210	5 738	5 758
The Former Yugoslav Rep. of Macedonia - L'ex-République yougoslave de Macédoine														
1989	C	35 927	3 077	2 827	3 015	2 962	2 849	2 976	3 111	3 084	3 144	3 127	2 922	2 833
1990	C	35 401	3 082	2 779	2 999	3 029	2 944	2 823	2 950	2 934	3 163	3 150	2 797	2 751
1991	C	34 830	3 051	2 617	2 967	2 871	2 958	2 982	3 019	3 045	3 170	3 010	2 625	2 515
1992	C	33 238	2 783	2 461	2 679	2 669	2 918	2 750	2 784	2 982	3 056	3 068	2 637	2 451
1993	C	32 855	3 067	2 127	2 464	2 575	2 859	2 597	2 401	2 968	2 975	2 986	2 918	2 918
1995	C	32 154	2 707	2 506	2 546	2 525	2 750	2 445	2 837	2 857	2 942	2 976	2 647	2 416
1997	C	29 478	2 466	2 208	2 290	2 445	2 620	2 588	2 643	2 615	2 613	2 451	2 223	2 316
1999	C	27 309	2 263	2 036	2 174	2 238	2 297	2 352	2 521	2 551	2 449	2 320	2 068	2 040
2000	C	29 308	2 232	2 258	2 359	2 402	2 576	2 531	2 649	2 581	2 625	2 495	2 207	2 393
2001	C	27 010	2 380	2 100	2 249	2 130	2 466	2 210	2 421	2 355	2 349	2 317	2 079	1 954
2002	C	27 761	2 181	1 941	2 193	2 126	2 298	2 365	2 595	2 555	2 519	2 477	2 274	2 237
Ukraine[12]														
1980	C	742 489	61 261	56 037	62 350	65 089	67 458	65 304	68 145	64 793	59 506	59 808	56 821	55 917
1981	C	733 183	62 402	56 265	62 167	62 322	65 884	65 298	66 895	63 006	58 389	57 685	56 422	56 448
1982	C	745 591	63 568	56 645	62 016	62 581	66 429	64 322	66 661	64 268	59 544	58 853	60 007	60 697
1983	C	807 111	66 732	60 181	70 474	69 789	72 202	69 146	74 149	71 430	65 217	64 941	61 392	61 458
1984	C	792 035	65 675	62 713	67 964	66 516	70 618	68 443	73 181	70 877	65 027	62 268	59 796	58 957
1985	C	762 775	65 048	58 587	66 074	65 716	68 319	65 623	70 072	68 000	61 733	61 240	56 733	55 630
1986	C	792 574	67 118	59 899	68 012	70 302	70 556	67 350	73 045	69 075	63 831	63 004	60 243	60 139
1989	C	690 981	60 481	55 496	59 276	57 783	60 264	60 765	62 432	60 836	54 128	55 007	51 473	53 040
1990	C	657 202	59 014	53 311	56 505	55 598	57 578	56 591	59 540	57 272	51 327	51 017	49 312	50 137
1991	C	630 813	55 941	50 055	54 788	53 599	56 293	55 044	57 161	54 087	50 764	49 623	46 619	46 839
1992	C	596 785	52 158	47 752	51 255	48 121	51 963	53 033	55 013	52 724	47 877	47 998	45 114	43 777
1993	C	557 467	50 784	45 068	48 493	47 743	48 536	48 050	51 702	48 034	44 924	43 511	40 349	40 268
1994	C	521 545	46 361	42 292	46 899	46 391	45 974	42 490	41 184	41 976	42 039	41 980	39 532	38 848
1995	C	492 861	38 867	41 518	42 789	37 331	44 307	42 490	41 184	41 976	42 039	41 980	39 532	38 848
1996	C	467 211	36 204	38 121	37 285	37 042	42 026	40 075	42 364	41 007	38 994	40 428	36 901	36 764
1998	C	419 238	32 894	33 645	33 962	35 711	36 089	35 736	38 811	34 397	36 339	36 179	31 891	33 584
2001	C	376 478	29 577	30 752	31 833	29 204	33 253	28 945	35 095	33 222	31 095	32 989	31 498	29 015
United Kingdom - Royaume-Uni[33]														
1982	C	719 155	59 281	54 837	62 571	60 249	61 175	58 734	62 385	61 363	62 109	61 180	57 322	57 949
1983	C	721 467	59 135	54 625	61 575	60 056	62 438	62 153	63 137	62 068	62 208	59 360	57 052	57 660
1984	C	729 617	59 060	56 137	60 868	57 357	61 479	65 605	61 861	66 742	65 130	64 836	59 297	57 568
1985	C	750 728	62 993	56 732	63 560	61 479	65 605	61 861	66 742	65 130	64 836	64 606	59 297	57 887
1986	C	754 982	61 868	56 554	63 991	63 823	66 261	63 612	65 042	64 806	64 668	64 285	58 102	61 970
1987	C	775 617	62 627	57 724	65 421	64 101	67 588	67 396	68 148	65 922	66 702	65 896	60 939	63 153
1988	C	787 556	65 319	62 908	69 253	65 639	68 365	69 373	68 416	70 786	69 203	67 551	61 112	62 434
1990	C	798 612	64 842	59 799	66 645	64 643	69 373	66 452	70 442	68 356	67 127	66 987	62 531	63 342
1991	C	792 506	67 462	61 129	65 943	64 740	67 995	66 452	70 442	68 356	67 127	66 987	62 531	63 342

(See notes at end of table. — Voir notes à la fin du tableau.)

Continent, country or area Continent, pays ou zone	C-o-d-e[a]	Total	Jan	Feb	March	April	May	June	July	Aug	Sep	Oct	Nov	Dec
EUROPE														
United Kingdom - Royaume-Uni[33]														
1992	C	781 017	66 664	62 497	66 632	65 355	66 762	66 577	69 192	66 226	66 121	64 186	60 405	60 400
1993	C	761 713	62 962	57 286	64 119	62 179	64 540	65 346	66 733	65 379	66 567	64 318	59 948	62 336
1994	C	750 671	63 019	57 423	65 461	62 564	65 287	64 697	64 416	62 963	63 346	62 759	59 209	59 527
1995	C	732 049	61 014	56 122	62 654	58 648	64 084	63 046	63 652	62 897	62 152	62 432	58 354	56 994
1996	C	733 375	60 565	56 760	60 142	57 145	60 685	60 375	64 932	63 137	63 714	63 633	60 761	61 526
1997	C	726 622	62 225	55 937	60 283	61 736	62 368	60 862	63 809	61 643	60 812	60 293	56 914	59 740
1998	C	716 888	60 496	54 939	60 563	59 271	59 416	60 162	63 616	61 110	62 389	60 774	56 397	57 755
1999	C	699 976	57 858	53 696	60 322	57 449	59 635	59 931	61 178	59 731	59 348	57 348	56 275	57 205
2000	C	679 029	57 446	53 017	57 703	54 551	58 466	56 192	58 761	58 422	56 640	57 427	55 807	54 597
2001	C	669 123	57 880	50 805	56 180	53 725	57 861	55 421	57 798	57 351	56 540	58 206	54 570	52 786
2002	C	668 777	55 829	50 471	54 665	54 089	57 084	53 991	58 474	57 364	57 962	59 004	54 487	55 357
OCEANIA — OCEANIE														
American Samoa - Samoas américaines														
1982	C	1 160	92	88	97	113	114	98	96	83	88	106	86	99
1984	C	1 368	95	105	126	109	119	116	126	122	112	111	112	115
1985	C	1 526	120	101	132	167	147	139	126	125	126	107	114	122
1986	C	1 517	116	110	134	135	124	150	139	129	117	123	111	129
1987	C	1 640	143	122	151	157	158	137	149	137	134	133	100	119
1988	C	1 625	112	112	174	156	142	150	151	151	125	111	126	115
1990	C	1 856	136	132	145	146	169	165	167	186	171	146	140	153
1991	C	1 817	146	128	156	152	183	137	160	161	162	151	133	148
1992	C	1 953	147	156	185	175	178	176	165	136	149	164	161	161
1993	C	1 998	158	147	203	198	183	162	178	175	153	139	157	145
Australia - Australie[34]														
1980	C	226 395	18 917	18 205	19 557	18 846	19 782	19 067	19 115	18 467	19 003	19 103	17 251	19 082
1981	C	237 565	19 465	18 532	20 983	20 309	20 644	19 710	20 149	20 020	20 293	20 001	18 080	19 379
1982	C	238 664	19 477	18 706	21 552	19 776	19 965	19 865	20 221	20 530	20 319	20 018	18 706	19 520
1983	C	242 903	19 882	19 351	22 173	20 455	20 843	20 111	20 680	20 643	20 677	20 309	18 603	19 176
1984	C	242 121	19 886	19 491	21 663	19 982	20 707	19 753	20 221	20 748	20 108	20 631	19 295	19 636
1985	C	243 887	20 669	18 986	21 421	20 385	21 041	19 514	20 615	20 813	20 524	21 112	19 439	19 368
1986	C	243 643	20 014	18 945	21 091	20 472	20 625	19 795	20 926	20 651	20 871	21 285	18 838	20 130
1987	C	243 805	19 998	19 123	21 735	20 511	20 660	20 077	21 051	20 400	21 052	20 351	19 148	19 699
1988	C	250 450	20 152	19 666	22 131	20 446	20 982	20 650	20 643	21 277	21 777	21 403	20 346	20 977
1989	C	253 694	20 418	19 349	21 523	20 175	21 759	21 247	21 501	22 045	22 013	22 080	20 787	20 797
1990	C	261 712	21 170	20 154	22 826	21 659	22 283	21 643	22 225	22 581	22 315	23 044	20 934	20 878
1991	C	257 159	21 607	19 958	22 302	21 821	22 124	21 207	21 856	21 906	21 525	21 986	19 895	20 972
1992	C	262 918	21 931	21 192	22 633	21 824	22 301	21 767	22 758	21 918	22 597	22 590	20 439	20 968
1993	C	260 018	21 459	20 129	22 851	21 616	21 992	21 752	22 070	21 790	22 358	22 079	20 396	21 526
1994	C	260 371	21 771	20 280	23 494	21 249	21 945	21 055	21 856	22 051	22 448	22 143	20 704	21 375
1995	C	257 856	21 670	20 313	23 041	20 980	22 400	21 511	21 919	22 212	21 862	21 753	20 224	19 971
1996	C	255 018	20 946	20 450	21 703	20 639	21 624	20 658	21 597	21 700	21 863	22 153	20 680	21 005
1997	C	251 805	21 365	19 400	21 417	20 651	21 461	20 761	21 765	21 155	21 684	22 160	19 666	20 320
1998	C	248 832	20 694	19 393	21 535	20 707	20 797	20 511	21 621	20 927	21 517	21 533	19 550	20 047
1999	C	250 074	20 998	19 691	22 159	20 795	20 925	20 873	21 281	21 252	21 672	20 806	19 445	20 177
2000	C	248 090	21 100	19 770	21 766	20 093	21 342	20 424	20 334	21 265	21 227	21 770	20 015	18 984
2001	C	242 859	19 916	19 016	21 343	20 040	20 678	19 888	20 573	21 222	20 930	20 978	19 263	19 012
2002	C	242 142	20 667	19 179	20 882	19 994	20 565	19 451	20 633	20 423	20 751	20 991	19 173	19 433
Christmas Islands - Îles Christmas														
1980	+C	39	3	3	1	3	3	1	7	5	4	4	2	3
Cook Islands - Îles Cook[6]														
1980	+C	492	102	...	...	134	...	...	138	...	...	118	...	...
1981	+C	461	128	...	...	129	...	...	108	...	...	96	...	...
1982	+C	434	112	...	...	122	...	...	104	...	...	96	...	...
1983	+C	414	35	33	35	28	32	34	34	40	40	30	38	35
1984	+C	408	37	36	28	32	48	44	31	34	38	33	24	23

(See notes at end of table. — Voir notes à la fin du tableau.)

Continent, country or area / Continent, pays ou zone	C-o-d-e[a]	Total	Jan	Feb	March	April	May	June	July	Aug	Sep	Oct	Nov	Dec
OCEANIA — OCEANIE														
Cook Islands - Îles Cook[6]														
1985	+C	423	29	36	37	38	43	30	32	46	33	46	25	28
1986	+C	430	45	31	48	29	27	36	29	46	45	32	31	31
1987	+C	408	24	24	42	33	28	39	29	48	38	44	27	32
1988	+C	430	41	35	36	44	44	39	29	29	38	24	31	40
Fiji - Fidji[35,36]														
1984	+C	19 502	1 542	1 655	1 853	1 786	1 807	1 759	1 718	1 683	1 504	1 367	1 385	1 443
1985	+C	19 464	1 341	1 375	1 646	1 719	1 781	1 614	1 604	1 542	1 294	1 199	1 120	1 174
1986	+C	11 691	1 165	1 219	1 507	1 441	1 354	1 277	1 143	978	825	529	201	52
1987	+C	19 445	1 476	1 589	1 858	1 800	1 894	1 837	1 829	1 691	1 473	1 415	1 279	1 304
French Polynesia - Polynésie française														
1985	C	5 413	436	401	483	497	475	416	455	413	471	480	440	446
1986	C	5 406	420	413	447	515	476	485	445	402	438	449	445	471
1987	C	5 409	445	424	480	462	488	432	504	476	461	454	387	396
1988	C	5 797	450	444	527	549	527	495	460	474	490	462	445	474
1989	C	5 507	501	444	497	483	498	432	460	449	456	441	401	445
1990	C	5 565	444	458	528	503	508	454	444	468	444	455	386	473
1991	C	5 391	437	416	479	473	478	463	444	431	458	450	422	440
1992	C	5 296	468	418	472	474	460	462	446	450	424	387	386	449
Guam[37]														
1980	C	3 003	250	248	262	222	235	224	246	248	259	279	248	282
1981	C	3 008	257	233	253	265	236	240	251	265	221	285	241	261
1982	C	2 992	248	228	243	220	241	245	255	243	274	250	270	275
1985	C	3 197	265	223	248	245	274	237	270	264	306	288	281	296
1986	C	3 309	265	253	261	276	254	250	276	311	280	300	290	293
1988	C	3 548	299	250	277	247	317	273	294	317	287	354	324	309
1989	C	3 565	291	277	287	267	287	275	324	327	323	305	294	308
1990	C	3 850	320	283	323	315	314	308	317	318	346	341	365	300
1991	C	3 921	335	298	283	319	308	296	326	345	323	365	344	379
1992	C	4 214	303	332	346	337	339	321	377	369	392	382	346	370
1997	C	4 318	355	356	338	338	352	384	379	373	373	345	350	375
New Caledonia - Nouvelle-Calédonie														
1982	C	3 819	344	310	355	340	350	324	334	283	294	313	280	292
1983	C	3 807	324	288	333	346	352	333	345	331	301	319	283	252
1984	C	3 772	249	285	328	346	400	349	321	341	303	325	258	267
1985	C	3 651	306	301	328	335	348	306	307	289	298	317	264	252
1986	C	3 969	305	284	400	364	387	379	346	324	317	303	265	295
1987	C	4 172	342	320	367	370	383	353	361	344	368	343	296	325
1988	C	4 091	334	308	346	359	335	389	334	337	377	326	304	342
1989	C	3 984	316	326	312	354	357	344	340	373	338	337	271	316
1990	C	4 419	369	353	394	410	386	364	360	408	370	346	352	307
1991	C	4 538	337	352	416	388	415	424	390	368	402	384	323	339
1992	C	4 460	356	357	404	395	367	351	403	358	379	374	379	337
1993	C	4 375	357	353	366	383	387	376	360	366	371	363	351	342
1994	C	4 296	331	358	374	370	414	368	349	358	361	357	297	359
1995	C	4 284	367	346	382	381	398	373	376	337	359	394	284	287
1996	C	4 445	337	336	408	419	416	363	374	391	356	389	332	324
1997	C	4 524	345	372	394	388	380	392	381	381	377	405	354	355
1998	C	4 393	351	385	394	393	406	405	375	346	339	336	311	352
1999	C	4 344	314	307	341	404	421	430	373	389	393	336	300	336
New Zealand - Nouvelle-Zélande[38,39]														
1980	+C	50 542	4 164	3 925	4 153	4 059	4 256	4 077	4 283	4 256	4 431	4 344	3 285	982
1981	+C	50 794	4 278	3 992	4 373	4 184	4 127	3 964	4 306	4 367	4 358	4 170	3 115	947
1982	+C	49 938	4 060	3 830	4 200	4 054	4 049	3 977	4 201	4 284	4 327	4 375	3 404	893
1983	+C	50 474	4 187	3 791	4 328	4 057	4 074	3 971	4 081	4 448	4 574	4 442	3 269	913
1984	+C	51 636	4 222	4 018	4 053	4 015	4 217	4 129	4 282	4 415	4 432	4 687	3 602	950
1985	+C	51 798	4 190	3 991	4 396	4 154	4 369	4 084	4 452	4 517	4 436	4 519	3 447	929

11a. Live births by month of occurence: 1980 - 2002
Naissances vivantes selon le mois de naissance: 1980 - 2002 (continued — suite)

(See notes at end of table. — Voir notes à la fin du tableau.)

Continent, country or area / Continent, pays ou zone	C-o-d-e[a]	Total	Jan	Feb	March	April	May	June	July	Aug	Sep	Oct	Nov	Dec
OCEANIA — OCEANIE														
New Zealand - Nouvelle-Zélande[38],[39]														
1986	+C	52 824	4 277	3 959	4 339	4 236	4 420	4 352	4 537	4 576	4 651	4 540	3 317	867
1987	+C	55 254	4 448	4 134	4 408	4 419	4 579	4 351	4 648	4 851	4 945	4 898	3 478	942
1988	+C	57 546	4 682	4 469	4 821	4 439	4 761	4 521	4 741	5 017	5 152	4 971	3 456	926
1989	+C	58 091	4 851	4 353	4 761	4 372	4 833	4 612	4 837	5 231	5 124	5 057	3 557	881
1990	+C	60 153	4 897	4 400	4 984	4 715	4 918	4 684	4 910	5 244	5 440	5 238	3 671	917
1991	+C	59 911	5 160	4 651	4 996	4 826	4 949	4 861	5 140	5 203	5 274	5 324	4 605	4 922
1992	+C	59 166	4 924	4 849	5 089	4 611	4 629	4 528	4 923	5 081	5 197	5 229	4 970	5 136
1993	+C	58 782	5 002	4 493	4 847	4 693	4 833	4 824	4 857	5 162	5 096	5 198	4 864	4 913
1994	+C	57 321	4 539	4 321	4 875	4 476	4 740	4 628	4 856	4 929	5 124	5 159	4 845	4 829
1995	+C	57 671	4 776	4 554	4 856	4 519	4 732	4 724	4 810	4 960	5 018	4 784	4 728	5 210
1996	+C	57 280	4 703	4 636	4 823	4 423	4 616	4 586	4 746	4 880	4 900	5 220	4 906	4 841
1997	+C	57 604	4 675	4 243	4 539	4 591	4 853	4 643	4 889	4 954	4 967	5 316	4 863	5 071
1998	+C	55 349	4 818	4 268	4 810	4 631	4 789	4 445	4 812	4 624	4 645	4 836	4 287	4 384
1999	+C	57 053	4 559	4 305	4 678	4 594	4 808	4 707	4 831	4 951	5 067	5 248	4 659	4 646
2000	+C	56 605	4 685	4 548	4 881	4 613	4 845	4 518	4 681	4 906	4 951	4 877	4 483	4 617
2001	+C	55 799	4 732	4 241	4 834	4 430	4 799	4 285	4 567	4 825	4 689	4 979	4 593	4 825
2002	+C	54 021	4 585	4 025	4 506	4 317	4 575	4 356	4 644	4 553	4 609	4 823	4 420	4 608
Niue - Nioué														
1982	...	100	11	7	7	9	6	15	11	5	13	6	5	5
1983	...	94	7	5	10	4	12	11	8	9	10	2	9	7
1984	...	69	3	8	5	10	4	8	4	4	10	2	4	7
1985	...	84	7	14	6	5	5	2	9	8	12	6	7	3
1986	...	48	2	3	5	3	4	3	5	5	5	7	5	1
1987	...	50	5	6	3	1	7	3	7	2	4	5	4	3
Norfolk Island - Île Norfolk														
1980	C	23	1	1	2	3	4	1	2	3	2	1	2	1
1981	C	20	1	1	1	3	4	1	2	2	2	1	1	1
1983	C	28	2	1	2	1	-	4	7	1	4	1	2	3
1984	C	20	2	3	-	1	5	2	1	-	3	-	2	1
1988	C	29	1	1	3	3	2	4	4	3	2	2	3	1
Northern Mariana Islands - Îles Mariannes septentrionales														
1985	U	698	72	45	56	54	59	57	44	62	55	68	64	62
1989	U	989	78	77	65	77	70	88	93	94	74	87	96	90
1994	U	1 426	117	136	103	109	102	104	124	120	132	150	126	103
1995	U	1 525	113	109	133	115	141	110	118	133	132	129	154	138
1996	U	1 467	135	120	109	105	110	129	125	139	135	107	119	134
1997	U	1 536	125	97	111	134	129	120	138	131	145	139	130	137
1998	U	1 421	124	93	123	100	105	107	101	134	130	155	117	132
1999	U	1 448	136	88	137	107	117	112	103	120	141	154	119	114
Palau - Palaos														
1982	U	3 066	330	275	272	272	263	267	227	232	230	269	225	204
Samoa														
1980	U	2 693	229	202	288	218	179	187	232	228	276	260	223	171
Tokelau - Tokélaou														
1981	...	44	3	1	5	1	4	8	2	7	2	5	4	2
1982	...	43	3	5	2	5	5	6	1	3	1	3	5	4
Tonga														
1993	+C	2 737	257	209	234	189	291	242	232	220	210	225	213	215
1994	+C	2 775	234	252	248	238	252	255	251	220	216	190	197	222
1995	+C	2 915	322	242	328	288	256	258	233	213	219	209	186	161
1996	+C	2 742	224	233	236	243	255	311	231	229	219	186	197	178
1997	+C	2 700	231	228	238	230	235	254	264	226	205	194	200	195
1998	+C	2 737	221	245	268	222	234	213	249	204	220	208	221	232
1999	+C	2 599	237	214	275	251	238	226	230	202	177	168	170	211
2000	+C	2 471	148	245	274	228	225	227	223	214	201	179	151	156

GENERAL NOTES - NOTES GENERALES

For certain countries, there is a discrepancy between the total number of live births shown in this table and those shown in other tables for the same year. Usually this discrepancy arises because the total number of births occurring in a given year is revised, although the remaining tabulations are not. For method of evaluation and limitations of data, see Technical Notes for this table. — Pour quelques pays il y a une discordance entre le nombre total des naissances vivantes présenté dans ce tableau et ceux présentés dans d'autres tableaux pour la même année. Habituellement ces différences apparaissent lorsque le nombre total des naissances pour une certaine année a été révisé; alors que les autres tabulations ne l'ont pas été. Pour la méthode d'évaluation et les insuffisances des données, voir Notes techniques, pour ce tableaux.

Italics: data from civil registers which are incomplete or of unknown completeness. — *Italiques:* données incomplètes ou dont le degré d'exactitude n'est pas connu, provenant des registres de l'état civil.

FOOTNOTES - NOTES

[a] 'Code' indicates the source of data, as follows:
C - Civil registration, estimated over 90% complete
U - Civil registration, estimated less than 90% complete
I - Other source, estimated reliable
+ - Data tabulated by date of registration rather than occurence.
... - Information not available

Le 'Code' indique la source des données, comme suit:
C - Registres de l'état civil considérés complèts à 90 p. 100 au moins.
U - Registres de l'état civil qui ne sont pas considérés complèts à 90 p. 100 au moins.
I - Autre source, considérée pas douteuses.
+ - Données exploitées selon la date de l'enregistrement et non la date de l'événement.
... - Information pas disponible.

[1] Excluding live-born infants who died before their birth was registered. - Non compris les enfants nés vivants décédés avant l'enregistrement de leur naissance.
[2] For Algerian population only. - Pour la population algérienne seulement.
[3] For 1985 - 1987: Data for November refer to "November - December". - Pour 1985 - 1987: Les données pour novembre se rapportent à "novembre - décembre".
[4] Data for estimates refer to national projections. - Les données se referent aux projections nationales.
[5] Including Canadian residents temporarily in the United States, but excluding United States residents temporarily in Canada. - Y compris les résidents canadiens se trouvant temporairement aux Etats-Unis, mais ne comprenant pas les résidents des Etats-Unis se trouvant temporairement au Canada.
[6] Data for January refer to "January - March"; data for April refer to "April - June"; data for July refer to "July - September"; data for October refer to "October - December". - Les données pour janvier se rapportent à "janvier - mars" ; les données pour avril se rapportent à "avril - juin" ; les données pour juillet se rapportent à "juillet - septembre" ; les données pour octobre se rapportent à "octobre - décembre".
[7] Excluding Indian jungle population. - Non compris les Indiens de la jungle.
[8] Data on live births and deaths are based on a civil registration system put in place in January 1998. - Les données sur les naissances et les décès sont basées sur un système d'enregistrement des faits d'état civil mis en place en janvier 1998.
[9] Excluding nomadic Indian tribes. - Non compris les tribus d'Indiens nomades.
[10] Including an upward adjustment for under-registration. - Y compris un ajustement pour sous-enregistrement.
[11] Data refer to registered live births only. - Les données concernent les naissances vivantes enregistrées seulement.
[12] Excluding infants born alive with less than 28 weeks gestation, less

than 1 000 grams in weight and 35 centimeters in length, who die within seven days of birth. - Non compris les enfants nés vivants avant 28 semaines de gestation, pesant moins de 1 000 grammes, mesurant moins de 35 centimètres et décédés dans les sept jours qui ont suivi leur naissance.
[13] Unrevised data. - Les données n'ont pas été révisées.
[14] Data refer to government controlled areas. - Les données se raportent aux zones contrôlées par le Gouvernement.
[15] Including data for East Jerusalem and Israeli residents in certain other territories under occupation by Israeli military forces since June 1967. - Y compris les données pour Jérusalem-Est et les résidents israéliens dans certains autres territoires occupés depuis 1967 par les forces armées israéliennes.
[16] Data refer to Japanese nationals in Japan only. - Les données se raportent aux nationaux japonais au Japon seulement.
[17] Excluding alien armed forces, civilian aliens employed by armed forces, and foreign diplomatic personnel and their dependants. - Non compris les militaires étrangers, les civils étrangers employés par les forces armées ni le personnel diplomatique étranger et les membres de leur famille les accompagnant.
[18] Based on the results of the Population Growth Survey. - D'après les résultats de la 'Population Growth Survey.'
[19] Excluding data for the Pakistan-held part of Jammu and Kashmir, the final status of which has not yet been determined. - Non compris les données concernant la partie du Jammu et Cachemire occupée par le Pakistan dont le statut définitif n'a pas été déterminé.
[20] Data as reported by national statistical authorities. Figures for the twelve months do not add up to the total. - Les données comme elles ont été déclarées par l'institut national de la statistique. La somme des données pour les douze mois ne correspond pas au total.
[21] Excluding nomad population and Palestinian refugees. - Non compris la population nomade et les réfugiés de Palestine.
[22] Including armed forces stationed outside the country, but excluding alien armed forces stationed in the area. - Y compris les militaires nationaux hors du pays, mais non compris les militaires étrangers en garnison sur le territoire.
[23] The total for 1995 includes 1116 births with month unknown. - Le total pour 1995 y compris 1116 naissances dont le mois est inconnu.
[24] Excluding Faeroe Islands and Greenland. - Non compris les Iles Féroé et Gröenland.
[25] Including nationals temporarily outside the country. - Y compris les nationaux se trouvant temporairement hors du pays.
[26] Including armed forces stationed outside the country. - Y compris les militaires nationaux hors du pays.
[27] Excluding armed forces. - Non compris les militaires en garnison.
[28] Events registered within one year of occurrence. - Evénements enregistrés dans l'année qui suit l'événement.
[29] The total for 2001 includes 3402 births with month unknown. - Le total pour 2001 y compris 3402 naissances dont le mois est inconnu.
[30] Live births to Maltese parents only. - Naissances vivantes aux parents maltais seulement.
[31] Including residents outside the country if listed in a Netherlands population register. - Y compris les résidents hors du pays, s'ils sont inscrits sur un registre de population néerlandais.
[32] The total for 2000 includes 11 births with month unknown. -
[33] Data revised to exclude births in Northern Ireland to non-residents of Northern Ireland. - Données révisées non compris des naissances en Irlande du Nord aux non-résidents de l'Irlande du Nord.
[34] Data are tabulated by year and month of occurrence on data registered to 31 December 2003. - Données exploitées selon la date de l'événement, registrées jusque le 31 Decembre 2003.
[35] Total for 1985: Including late registered births. - Pour 1985 : Y compris les naissances enregistrées tardivement.
[36] Data for 1986: Excluding late registered births. - Pour 1986: Non compris les naissances enregistrées tardivement.
[37] Including United States military personnel, their dependants and contract employees. - Y compris les militaires des Etats-Unis, les membres de leur famille les accompagnant et les agents contractuels des Etats-Unis.
[38] Data are tabulated by year and month of occurrence on data registered to 31 December of a given year. - Données exploitées selon la date de l'événement, registrées jusque le 31 Decembre.
[39] Data as reported by national statistical authorities. - Les données

comme elles ont été déclarées par l'institut national de la statistique.

Table 12

Table 12 presents late foetal deaths and late foetal-death ratios by urban/rural residence for as many years as possible between 1998 and 2002.

Description of variables: Late foetal deaths are foetal deaths[i] of 28 or more completed weeks of gestation. Foetal deaths of unknown gestational age are included with those 28 or more weeks.

Statistics on the number of late foetal deaths are obtained from civil registers unless otherwise noted.

The urban/rural classification of late foetal deaths is as provided by each country or area; it is presumed to be based on the national census definitions of urban population that have been set forth at the end of the technical notes for table 6.

Ratio computation: Late foetal-death ratios are the annual number of late foetal deaths per 1 000 live births (as shown in table 9) in the same year. The live-birth base was adopted because it is assumed to be more comparable from one country or area to another than the sum of live births and foetal deaths.

Ratios by urban/rural residence are the annual number of late foetal deaths, in the appropriate urban or rural category, per 1 000 corresponding live births (as shown in table 9). These ratios have been calculated by the Statistics Division of the United Nations.

Ratios presented in this table have been limited to those for countries or areas and urban/rural areas having at least a total of 30 late foetal deaths in a given year.

Reliability of data: Each country or area has been asked to indicate the estimated completeness of the late foetal deaths recorded in its civil register. These national assessments are indicated by the quality codes, C and U that appear in the first column of this table.

C indicates that the data are estimated to be virtually complete, that is, representing at least 90 per cent of the late foetal deaths occurring each year, while U indicates that data are estimated to be incomplete, that is, representing less than 90 per cent of the late foetal deaths occurring each year. The code ... indicates that no information was provided regarding completeness.

Data from civil registers which are reported as incomplete or of unknown completeness (coded U or ...) are considered unreliable. They appear in italics in this table. Ratios are not computed for data so coded.

For more information about the quality of vital statistics data in general, see section 4.2 of the Technical Notes.

Limitations: Statistics on late foetal deaths are subject to the same qualifications as have been set forth for vital statistics in general and foetal-death statistics in particular as discussed in section 4 of the Technical Notes.

The reliability of the data is a very important factor. Of all vital statistics , the registration of foetal deaths is probably the most incomplete.

Variation in the definition of foetal deaths, and in particular late foetal deaths, also limits international comparability. The criterion of 28 or more completed weeks of gestation to distinguish late foetal deaths is not universally used; some countries or areas use different durations of gestation or other criteria such as size of the foetus. In addition, the difficulty of accurately determining gestational age further reduces comparability. However, to promote comparability, late foetal deaths shown in this table are restricted to those of at least 28 or more completed weeks of gestation. Wherever this is not possible a footnote is provided.

Another factor introducing variation in the definition of late foetal deaths is the practice by some countries or areas of including in late foetal-death statistics infants who were born alive but died before the registration of the birth or within the first 24 hours of life, thus overestimating the total number of late foetal deaths. This has also the effect of inflating the late foetal-death ratios unduly by decreasing the birth denominator and increasing the foetal-death numerator. Statistics of this type are footnoted.

In addition, late foetal-death ratios are subject to the limitations of the data on live births with which they have been calculated. These have been set forth in the technical notes for table 9.

Regarding the computation of the ratios, it must be pointed out that when late foetal deaths and live births are both under registered, the resulting ratios may be of reasonable magnitude. For the countries or areas where live-birth registration is poorest, the late foetal-death ratios may be the largest, effectively masking the completeness of the base data. For this reason, possible variations in birth-registration completeness as well as the reported completeness of late foetal deaths must always be borne in mind in evaluating late foetal-death ratios.

In addition to the indirect effect of live-birth under-registration, late foetal-death ratios may be seriously affected by date-of-registration tabulation of live births. When the annual number of live births registered and reported fluctuates over a wide range due to changes in legislation or to special needs for proof of birth on the part of large segments of the population, then the late foetal-death ratios will also fluctuate, but inversely. Because of these effects, data for countries or areas known to tabulate live births by date of registration should be used with caution.

Finally, it may be noted that the counting of live-born infants as late foetal deaths, because they died before the registration of the birth or within the first 24 hours of life, has the effect of inflating the late foetal-death ratios unduly by decreasing the birth denominator and increasing the foetal-death numerator. This factor should not be overlooked in using data from this table.

The comparability of data by urban/rural residence is affected by the national definitions of urban and rural used in tabulating these data. It is assumed, in the absence of specific information to the contrary, that the definitions of urban and rural used in connection with the national population census were also used in the compilation of the vital statistics for each country or area. However, it cannot be excluded that, for a given country or area, different definitions of urban and rural are used for the vital statistics data and the population census data respectively. When known, the definitions of urban used in national population censuses are presented at the end of the technical notes for table 6. As discussed in detail in the technical notes for table 6, these definitions vary considerably from one country or area to another.

Urban/rural differentials in late foetal death ratios may also be affected by whether the late foetal deaths and live births have been tabulated in terms of place of occurrence or place of usual residence. This problem is discussed in more detail in section 4.1.4.1 of the Technical Notes.

Earlier data: Late foetal deaths and late foetal-death ratios have been shown in each issue of the Demographic Yearbook beginning with the 1951 issue. A special topic CD on natality published in 2001 presents the data for all available years from 1990 to 1998. For more information on specific topics, and years for which data are reported, readers should consult the Historical Index.

NOTES

[i] For definition, see section 4.1.1.3 of the Technical Notes.

Tableau 12

Le tableau 12 présente des données sur les morts fœtales tardives et les rapports de mortinatalité selon le lieu de résidence (zone urbaine ou rurale) pour le plus grand nombre d'années possible entre 1998 et 2002.

Description des variables : Par mort fœtale tardive, on entend le décès d'un fœtus[1] survenu après 28 semaines complètes de gestation au moins. Les morts fœtales pour lesquelles la durée de la période de gestation n'est pas connue sont comprises dans cette catégorie.

Sauf indication contraire, les statistiques du nombre de morts fœtales tardives sont établies sur la base des registres de l'état civil.

La classification des morts fœtales tardives selon le lieu de résidence (zone urbaine ou rurale) est celle qui a été communiquée par chaque pays ou zone ; on part du principe qu'elle repose sur les définitions de la population urbaine utilisées pour les recensements nationaux, telles qu'elles sont reproduites à la fin des notes techniques du tableau 6.

Calcul des rapports : Les rapports de mortinatalité représentent le nombre annuel de morts fœtales tardives pour 1 000 naissances vivantes (telles qu'elles sont présentées au tableau 9) survenues pendant la même année. On a pris pour base de calcul les naissances vivantes parce que l'on pense qu'elle sont plus facilement comparables d'un pays ou d'une zone à l'autre que la somme des naissances vivantes et des morts fœtales.

Les rapports selon le lieu de résidence (zone urbaine ou rurale) représentent le nombre annuel de morts fœtales tardives, classées selon la catégorie urbaine ou rurale appropriée pour 1 000 naissances vivantes (telles qu'elles sont présentées au tableau 9) survenues parmi la population correspondante. Ces rapports ont été calculés par la Division de statistique de l'ONU.

Les rapports présentés dans le tableau 12 ne concernent que les pays ou zones où l'on a enregistré un total d'au moins 1 000 morts fœtales tardives pendant une année donnée.

Fiabilité des données : Il a été demandé à chaque pays ou zone d'indiquer le degré estimatif de complétude des données sur les morts fœtales tardives figurant dans ses registres d'état civil. Ces évaluations nationales sont signalées par les codes de qualité 'C', 'U' et '...' qui apparaissent dans la deuxième colonne du tableau.

La lettre 'C' indique que les données sont jugées à peu près complètes, c'est-à-dire qu'elles représentent au moins 90 p. 100 des morts fœtales tardives survenues chaque année ; la lettre 'U' signifie que les données sont jugées incomplètes, c'est-à-dire qu'elles représentent moins de 90 p.100 des morts fœtales tardives survenues chaque année. Le code '...' indique qu'aucun renseignement n'a été communiqué quant à la complétude des données.

Les données provenant des registres de l'état civil qui sont déclarées incomplètes ou dont le degré de complétude n'est pas connu (code 'U' ou '...') sont jugées douteuses. Elles apparaissent en italique dans le tableau ; les rapports, dans ces cas, n'ont pas été calculés.

Pour plus de précisions sur la qualité des données reposant sur les statistiques de l'état civil en général, voir la section 4.2 des Notes techniques.

Insuffisance des données : Les statistiques des morts fœtales tardives appellent toutes les réserves qui ont été formulées à propos des statistiques de l'état civil en général et des statistiques concernant les morts fœtales en particulier (voir la section 4 des Notes techniques).

La fiabilité des données est un facteur très important. Les statistiques concernant les morts fœtales sont probablement les moins complètes de toutes les statistiques de l'état civil.

L'hétérogénéité des définitions de la mort fœtale et, en particulier, de la mort fœtale tardive nuit aussi à la comparabilité internationale des données. Le critère des 28 semaines complètes de gestation au moins n'est pas universellement utilisé ; certains pays ou zones retiennent des critères différents pour la durée de la période de gestation ou d'autres critères tels que la taille du fœtus. De surcroît, la comparabilité est rendue malaisée par le fait qu'il est difficile d'établir avec précision l'âge gestationnel. Pour faciliter les comparaisons, les morts fœtales tardives considérées ici sont exclusivement celles qui sont survenues au terme de 28 semaines de gestation au moins. Les exceptions sont signalées en note.

Un autre facteur d'hétérogénéité dans la définition de la mort fœtale tardive est la pratique de certains pays ou zones qui consiste à inclure dans les statistiques des morts fœtales tardives les enfants nés vivants mais décédés avant l'enregistrement de leur naissance ou dans les 24 heures qui ont suivi la naissance, pratique qui conduit à surestimer le nombre total des morts fœtales tardives. Cela donne aussi des rapports de mortinatalité exagérés parce que le dénominateur (nombre de naissances) se trouve alors diminué et le numérateur (morts fœtales) augmenté. Quand pareil facteur a joué, cela a été signalé en note.

Les rapports de mortinatalité appellent en outre toutes les réserves qui ont été formulées à propos des statistiques des naissances vivantes qui ont servi à leur calcul (voir à ce sujet les notes techniques relatives au tableau 9).

En ce qui concerne le calcul des rapports, il convient de noter que, si l'enregistrement des morts fœtales tardives et celui des naissances vivantes sont loin d'être exhaustifs, les rapports de mortinatalité peuvent être raisonnables. C'est parfois pour les pays ou zones où l'enregistrement des naissances vivantes laisse le plus à désirer que les rapports de mortinatalité sont les plus élevés, ce qui masque le caractère incomplet des données de base. Aussi, pour porter un jugement sur la qualité des rapports de mortinatalité, il ne faut jamais oublier que la complétude de l'enregistrement des naissances comme celle de l'enregistrement des morts fœtales tardives peuvent varier sensiblement.

Hormis les effets indirects des lacunes de l'enregistrement des naissances vivantes, il arrive que les rapports de mortinatalité soient considérablement faussés lorsque l'exploitation des données relatives aux naissances se fait d'après la date de l'enregistrement. Si le nombre des naissances vivantes enregistrées vient à varier notablement d'une année à l'autre par suite de modifications de la législation ou parce que de très nombreuses personnes ont besoin de se procurer une attestation de naissance, les rapports de mortinatalité varient également, mais en sens inverse. Il convient donc d'utiliser avec prudence le données des pays ou zones où les statistiques sont établies d'après la date de l'enregistrement.

Enfin, on notera que l'inclusion parmi les morts fœtales tardives des décès d'enfants nés vivants qui sont décédés avant l'enregistrement de leur naissance ou dans les 24 heures qui ont suivi la naissance conduit à des rapports de mortinatalité exagérés parce que le dénominateur (nombre de naissances) se trouve alors diminué et le numérateur (morts fœtales) augmenté. Il importe de ne pas négliger ce facteur lorsque l'on utilise les données du tableau 12.

La comparabilité des données selon le lieu de résidence (zone urbaine ou rurale) peut être limitée par les définitions nationales des termes «urbain» et «rural» utilisées pour la mise en tableaux de ces données. En l'absence d'indications contraires, on a supposé que les mêmes définitions avaient servi pour le recensement national de la population et pour l'établissement des statistiques de l'état civil pour chaque pays ou zone. Toutefois, il n'est pas exclu que, pour une zone ou un pays donné, des définitions différentes aient été retenues. Les définitions du terme «urbain» utilisées pour les recensements nationaux de population ont été présentées à la fin des notes techniques du tableau 6 lorsqu'elles étaient connues. Comme on l'a précisé dans les notes techniques relatives au tableau 6, ces définitions varient considérablement d'un pays ou d'une zone à l'autre.

La différence entre les rapports de mortinatalité pour les zones urbaines et rurales pourra aussi être faussée selon que les morts fœtales tardives et les naissances vivantes auront été classées d'après le lieu de l'événement ou le lieu de résidence habituel. Ce problème est examiné plus en détail à la section 4.1.4.1 des Notes techniques.

Données publiées antérieurement : Les éditions de l'*Annuaire démographique* parues à partir de 1951 contiennent des statistiques concernant les morts fœtales tardives et les rapports de mortinatalité. Un CD-ROM sur la natalité paru en 2001 présente les données pour toutes les années disponibles de 1990 à 1998. Pour plus de précisions concernant les années et les sujets pour lesquels des données ont été publiées, se reporter à l'index.

---

[1] Pour la définition, voir la section 4.1.1.3 des Notes techniques.

12. Late foetal deaths and late foetal death ratios, by urban/rural residence; 1998 - 2002
Morts foetales tardives et rapports de mortinatalité, selon la résidence, urbaine/rurale: 1998 - 2002

(See notes at end of table. — Voir notes à la fin du tableau.)

Continent, country or area and urban/rural residence / Continent, pays ou zone et résidence, urbaine/rurale	Code[1]	Number - Nombre					Ratio - Rapport				
		1998	1999	2000	2001	2002	1998	1999	2000	2001	2002
AFRICA — AFRIQUE											
Algeria - Algérie	+C										
Total		5 344	14 420	14 891	15 654	17 135	8.6	24.3	25.3	25.3	27.8
Egypt - Égypte[2]	+U										
Total	+U	*6 526*	*5 782*	...	...	...	...	...	...	...	...
Urban - Urbaine	+U	*5 361*	*4 630*	...	...	...	...	...	...	...	...
Rural - Rurale	+U	*1 165*	*1 152*	...	...	...	...	...	...	...	...
Mauritius - Maurice	+C										
Total	+C	227	226	266	244	203	11.7	11.1	13.2	12.4	10.2
Urban - Urbaine	+C	91	90	115	83	86	11.5	11.1	14.4	10.7	10.8
Rural - Rurale	+C	136	136	151	161	117	11.8	11.2	12.4	13.5	9.7
AMERICA, NORTH — AMERIQUE DU NORD											
Bermuda - Bermudes	C										
Total		...	2	...	...	...	...	...	...	...	...
Canada[3]	C										
Total		...	1 087	1 060	1 097	...	...	3.2	3.2	3.3	...
Costa Rica	C										
Total		...	...	528	510	...	...	...	6.8	6.7	...
Cuba	C										
Total	C	1 680	1 643	...	...	...	11.1	10.9	...	...	...
Urban - Urbaine	C	...	1 202	...	...	...	...	11.0	...	...	...
Rural - Rurale	C	...	441	...	...	...	...	10.6	...	...	...
El Salvador	C										
Total	C	664	621	766	706	617	4.2	4.0	5.1	5.1	4.8
Urban - Urbaine	C	538	491	557	611	550	5.3	4.9	6.0	7.3	7.1
Rural - Rurale	C	126	130	209	95	67	2.2	2.4	3.7	1.7	1.3
Greenland - Groenland	C										
Total	C	3	...	...	...	...	...	...	...	...	...
Urban - Urbaine	C	3	...	...	...	...	...	...	...	...	...
Rural - Rurale		-	...	...	...	...	...	...	...	...	...
Guadeloupe	C										
Total		...	101	90	77	118	...	13.8	11.8	10.3	16.9
Guatemala	C										
Total	C	6 531	6 253	...	...	...	13.3	17.3	...	...	...
Urban - Urbaine	C	4 091	4 124	...	...	...	19.7	29.4	...	...	...
Rural - Rurale		2 440	2 129	...	...	...	8.7	9.7	...	...	...
Martinique	C										
Total		51	42	62	60	89	8.8	7.3	10.2	10.2	16.3
Mexico - Mexique[4]	+C										
Total	+C	17 552	16 916	16 487	15 270	14 971	6.6	6.1	5.9	5.5	5.9
Urban - Urbaine	+C	...	...	12 347	...	...	...	...	6.8	...	...
Rural - Rurale		...	...	4 064	...	...	...	...	5.3	...	...
Panama[5]	U										
Total	U	*343*	*428*	...	*394*	...	...	...	...	...	...
Urban - Urbaine	U	*184*	*217*	...	...	...	...	...	...	...	...
Rural - Rurale		*159*	*211*	...	...	...	...	...	...	...	...
Puerto Rico - Porto Rico[4]	C										
Total	C	692	684	651	584	234	11.4	11.5	10.9	10.4	4.4
Urban - Urbaine	C	...	...	360	361	138	...	...	11.8	12.3	...
Rural - Rurale		...	...	290	220	90	...	...	10.0	8.3	...
Saint Lucia - Sainte-Lucie	...										
Total		*39*	*46*	*49*	...	...	...	...	...	...	...
Saint Vincent and the Grenadines - Saint Vincent-et-les Grenadines	+C										
Total		24	18	20	18	16	...	...	...	...	...
United States - États-Unis	C										
Total		14 043	12 968	13 016	12 794	...	3.6	3.3	3.2	3.2	...

12. Late foetal deaths and late foetal death ratios, by urban/rural residence; 1998 - 2002
Morts foetales tardives et rapports de mortinatalité, selon la résidence, urbaine/rurale: 1998 - 2002
(continued — suite)

(See notes at end of table. — Voir notes à la fin du tableau.)

Continent, country or area and urban/rural residence Continent, pays ou zone et résidence, urbaine/rurale	Code[1]	Number - Nombre					Ratio - Rapport				
		1998	1999	2000	2001	2002	1998	1999	2000	2001	2002
AMERICA, SOUTH —											
AMERIQUE DU SUD											
Argentina - Argentine											
Total	...	5 039	4 296	...	5 314	...	...	...	...	...	...
Brazil - Brésil[6]											
Total	...	...	19 849	19 298	18 341	...	...	...	...	...	...
Chile - Chili											
Total	C	1 161	1 080	1 116	1 278	1 197	4.5	4.3	4.5	5.2	5.0
Urban - Urbaine	C	954	915	672	1 095	1 044	4.3	4.2	3.1	5.1	4.9
Rural - Rurale	C	207	165	444	183	153	6.3	5.1	14.6	6.1	5.9
Colombia - Colombie[7,8]											
Total	...	14 009	14 613	14 220	17 891	14 615	...	...	...	...	...
Urban - Urbaine	...	11 978	10 278	9 663	12 795	10 083	...	...	...	...	...
Rural - Rurale	...	1 182	3 223	3 421	3 793	3 603	...	...	...	...	...
Ecuador - Équateur[9]											
Total	...	2 792	3 173	2 824	2 751	2 685	...	...	...	...	...
Urban - Urbaine	...	2 318	2 801	2 412	2 384	2 372	...	...	...	...	...
Rural - Rurale	...	474	372	412	367	313	...	...	...	...	...
French Guiana - Guyane française											
Total	C	54	61	61	51	72	11.5	12.5	11.9	10.0	13.7
Suriname											
Total	...	106	108	...	...	...	...	...	...	...	...
Uruguay											
Total	+C	441	535	436	...	...	8.1	9.9	8.3	...	...
Venezuela[6]											
Total	...	4 328	4 664	4 529	4 149	3 852	...	...	...	...	...
ASIA — ASIE											
Armenia - Arménie											
Total	C	283	292	289	289	...	7.2	8.0	8.4	8.4	...
Urban - Urbaine	C	239	234	215	...	...	9.7	10.4	10.1	...	...
Rural - Rurale	C	44	58	74	...	...	3.0	4.1	5.7	...	...
Azerbaijan - Azerbaïdjan											
Total	+C	561	425	418	425	443	4.5	3.6	3.6	3.9	4.0
Bahrain - Bahreïn											
Total	...	19	26	20	17	19	...	...	...	...	...
China: Hong Kong SAR - Chine: Hong Kong RAS											
Total	...	226	228	301	221	308	...	...	...	...	...
China: Macao SAR - Chine: Macao RAS											
Total	C	13	10	12	8	8	...	...	...	...	...
Georgia - Géorgie											
Total	C	...	794	693	...	...	...	19.5	17.2	...	...
Urban - Urbaine	C	...	790	690	...	...	...	30.5	27.0	...	...
Rural - Rurale	C	...	4	3	...	...	...	...	...	...	...
Israel - Israël[4,10,11]											
Total	C	...	557	573	...	...	...	4.2	4.2	...	...
Urban - Urbaine	C	...	506	507	...	...	...	4.3	4.2	...	...
Rural - Rurale	C	...	43	55	...	...	...	3.1	3.7	...	...
Japan - Japon[4,12]											
Total	C	3 296	3 139	3 050	2 882	2 851	2.7	2.7	2.6	2.5	2.5
Urban - Urbaine	C	2 606	2 509	2 424	2 345	2 288	2.7	2.6	2.5	2.5	2.4
Rural - Rurale	C	675	625	624	534	562	2.9	2.8	2.7	2.4	2.6
Kazakhstan											
Total	C	2 015	1 899	1 812	1 719	1 748	9.1	8.7	8.2	7.8	7.7
Urban - Urbaine	C	1 294	1 194	1 147	1 059	1 050	11.6	10.8	10.0	9.2	8.6
Rural - Rurale	C	721	705	665	660	698	6.5	6.6	6.2	6.2	6.6
Kuwait - Koweït											
Total	C	299	255	269	286	325	7.2	6.2	6.4	6.9	7.5

12. Late foetal deaths and late foetal death ratios, by urban/rural residence; 1998 - 2002
Morts foetales tardives et rapports de mortinatalité, selon la résidence, urbaine/rurale: 1998 - 2002
(continued — suite)

(See notes at end of table. — Voir notes à la fin du tableau.)

Continent, country or area and urban/rural residence / Continent, pays ou zone et résidence, urbaine/rurale	Code[1]	Number - Nombre					Ratio - Rapport				
		1998	1999	2000	2001	2002	1998	1999	2000	2001	2002
ASIA — ASIE											
Kyrgyzstan - Kirghizistan											
Total	C	654	660	608	617	759	6.3	6.3	6.3	6.3	7.5
Urban - Urbaine	C	...	...	361	335	395	...	...	12.8	11.8	13.1
Rural - Rurale	C	...	...	247	282	364	...	...	3.6	4.0	5.1
Malaysia - Malaisie[13]											
Total	...	2 042	...	...	...	...	...	...	...	...	...
Malaysia: Peninsular Malaysia - Malaisie: Malaisie Péninsulaire											
Total	...	1 910	...	2 003	...	...	...	...	...	...	...
Urban - Urbaine	...	981	...	...	...	...	...	...	...	...	...
Rural - Rurale	...	929	...	...	...	...	...	...	...	...	...
Oman[14]											
Total	...	429	425	388	365	...	...	...	...	...	...
Philippines											
Total	...	3 082	4 721	5 127	4 765	...	...	...	...	...	...
Qatar											
Total	...	...	77	...	...	...	...	...	...	...	...
Singapore - Singapour											
Total	+C	133	125	143	107	114	3.0	2.9	3.0	2.6	2.8
Uzbekistan - Ouzbékistan											
Total	C	...	3 600	3 062	2 902	...	...	...	6.5	5.8	5.7	...
Urban - Urbaine	C	...	1 441	1 148	1 138	...	...	...	8.3	7.0	7.1	...
Rural - Rurale	C	...	2 159	1 914	1 764	...	...	...	5.7	5.3	5.0	...
EUROPE											
Andorra - Andorre											
Total	C	...	...	...	1	...	...	...	...	...	...
Austria - Autriche											
Total	C	256	316	331	278	338	3.2	4.0	4.2	3.7	4.3
Belgium - Belgique[15]											
Total	C	513	556	554	583	...	4.5	4.9	4.8	5.1	...
Bulgaria - Bulgarie											
Total	C	...	540	555	500	539	...	7.5	7.5	7.3	8.1
Urban - Urbaine	C	...	...	365	246	323	...	...	6.9	5.1	6.8
Rural - Rurale	C	...	...	190	254	216	...	...	9.1	13.0	11.5
Channel Islands: Guernsey - Îles Anglo-Normandes: Guernesey											
Total	C	7	1	4	...	...	...	...	...	...	...
Croatia - Croatie											
Total	C	225	205	229	216	189	4.8	4.5	5.2	5.3	4.7
Urban - Urbaine	C	129	...	127	111	108	4.8	...	5.1	4.8	4.8
Rural - Rurale	C	96	...	102	105	81	4.7	...	5.4	5.8	4.6
Czech Republic - République tchèque											
Total	C	294	303	259	263	261	3.2	3.4	2.8	2.9	2.7
Urban - Urbaine	C	205	215	197	200	207	3.1	3.3	2.9	3.0	2.8
Rural - Rurale	C	89	88	62	63	54	3.7	3.7	2.6	2.7	2.2
Denmark - Danemark											
Total	C	...	...	248	277	...	...	...	3.7	4.2	...
Estonia - Estonie											
Total	C	...	82	67	63	74	...	6.5	5.1	5.0	5.7
Urban - Urbaine	C	...	...	41	42	45	...	...	4.7	...	5.1
Rural - Rurale	C	...	...	24	21	29	...	...	...	...	...
Finland - Finlande[16]											
Total	C	150	...	...	185	...	2.6	...	...	3.3	...
Urban - Urbaine	C	87	...	...	94	...	2.4	...	...	2.6	...
Rural - Rurale	C	63	...	...	91	...	3.0	...	...	4.6	...

12. Late foetal deaths and late foetal death ratios, by urban/rural residence; 1998 - 2002
Morts foetales tardives et rapports de mortinatalité, selon la résidence, urbaine/rurale: 1998 - 2002
(continued — suite)

(See notes at end of table. — Voir notes à la fin du tableau.)

Continent, country or area and urban/rural residence / Continent, pays ou zone et résidence, urbaine/rurale	Code[1]	Number - Nombre					Ratio - Rapport				
		1998	1999	2000	2001	2002	1998	1999	2000	2001	2002
EUROPE											
France[2,17]											
Total	C	3 685	3 442	...	...	...	5.0	4.6	...	...	...
Urban - Urbaine	C	2 869	2 674	...	...	...	5.1	4.7	...	...	...
Rural - Rurale	C	788	719	...	...	...	4.7	4.2	...	...	...
Germany - Allemagne											
Total	C	...	3 118	...	2 881	...	...	4.0	...	3.9	...
Greece - Grèce[18]											
Total	C	517	550	...	588	...	5.1	4.7	...	5.7	...
Urban - Urbaine	C	398	...	...	...	...	5.7	...	...	...	...
Rural - Rurale	C	199	...	...	...	...	6.3	...	...	...	...
Hungary - Hongrie[4]											
Total	C	556	471	538	550	523	5.7	5.0	5.5	5.7	5.4
Urban - Urbaine	C	296	241	313	304	315	5.1	4.2	5.3	5.1	5.2
Rural - Rurale	C	257	225	225	244	208	6.7	6.1	6.0	6.6	5.9
Iceland - Islande											
Total	C	9	19	15	10	7	...	...	...	...	...
Urban - Urbaine	C	7	...	13	9	7	...	...	...	...	...
Rural - Rurale	C	2	...	2	1	-	...	...	...	...	...
Ireland - Irlande											
Total	+C	...	311	...	...	...	...	5.8	...	...	...
Isle of Man - Îles de Man											
Total	+C	...	4	3	...	...	...	...	...	...	...
Latvia - Lettonie											
Total	C	179	165	158	138	176	9.7	8.5	7.8	7.0	8.8
Urban - Urbaine	C	115	93	99	88	108	10.2	7.7	7.8	7.0	8.3
Rural - Rurale	C	64	72	59	50	68	9.0	9.8	7.9	7.0	9.6
Lithuania - Lituanie											
Total	C	205	207	221	167	193	5.5	5.7	6.5	5.3	6.4
Urban - Urbaine	C	...	...	120	90	125	...	...	5.7	4.6	6.7
Rural - Rurale	C	...	...	101	77	68	...	...	7.7	6.5	6.0
Luxembourg											
Total	C	32	14	...	23	20	5.9	...	...	...	...
Netherlands - Pays-Bas[19]											
Total	C	970	944	...	...	945	4.9	4.7	...	...	4.7
Urban - Urbaine	C	...	...	...	...	617	...	...	...	...	4.6
Rural - Rurale	C	...	...	...	...	328	...	...	...	...	4.7
Norway - Norvège											
Total	C	247	241	225	241	197	4.2	4.1	3.8	4.3	3.6
Poland - Pologne											
Total	C	1 983	1 882	...	1 574	...	5.0	4.9	...	4.3	...
Urban - Urbaine	C	990	983	...	...	...	4.6	4.7	...	...	...
Rural - Rurale	C	993	899	...	...	...	5.5	5.2	...	...	...
Portugal											
Total	C	...	...	...	390	388	...	...	...	3.5	3.4
Romania - Roumanie											
Total	C	1 514	1 459	1 393	1 282	1 319	6.4	6.2	5.9	5.8	6.3
Urban - Urbaine	C	714	...	612	567	602	6.5	...	5.7	5.5	6.1
Rural - Rurale	C	800	...	781	715	717	6.3	...	6.2	6.1	6.4
Russian Federation - Fédération de Russie											
Total	C	...	8 864	...	...	...	...	7.3	...	...	...
Urban - Urbaine	C	...	6 472	...	...	...	...	7.7	...	...	...
Rural - Rurale	C	...	2 392	...	...	...	...	6.4	...	...	...
San Marino - Saint-Marin											
Total	+C	...	1	2	...	...	...	...	...	...	...
Urban - Urbaine	+C	...	...	2	...	...	...	...	...	...	...
Rural - Rurale	+C	...	...	-	...	...	...	...	...	...	...
Serbia and Montenegro - Serbie-et-Montenegro											
Total	C	786	722	715	741	...	6.1	5.8	5.7	5.7	...

413

12. Late foetal deaths and late foetal death ratios, by urban/rural residence; 1998 - 2002
Morts foetales tardives et rapports de mortinatalité, selon la résidence, urbaine/rurale: 1998 - 2002
(continued — suite)

(See notes at end of table. — Voir notes à la fin du tableau.)

Continent, country or area and urban/rural residence / Continent, pays ou zone et résidence, urbaine/rurale	Code[1]	Number - Nombre					Ratio - Rapport				
		1998	1999	2000	2001	2002	1998	1999	2000	2001	2002
EUROPE											
Slovakia - Slovaquie											
Total	C	281	259	...	207	194	4.9	4.6	...	4.0	3.8
Urban - Urbaine	C	141	117	...	100	95	4.7	4.1	...	3.8	3.6
Rural - Rurale	C	140	142	...	107	99	5.0	5.2	...	4.3	4.0
Slovenia - Slovénie											
Total	C	83	66	68	85	93	4.6	3.8	3.7	4.9	5.3
Urban - Urbaine	C	...	...	32	38	43	...	...	3.9	4.7	5.1
Rural - Rurale	C	...	...	36	46	50	...	...	3.6	4.9	5.5
Spain - Espagne											
Total	C	1 267	1 275	...	...	...	3.5	3.4	...	...	...
Sweden - Suède											
Total	C	303	321	355	349	352	3.4	3.6	3.9	3.8	3.7
Switzerland - Suisse											
Total	C	308	277	283	279	...	3.9	3.5	3.6	3.8	...
Urban - Urbaine	C	218	165	170	176	...	4.2	3.2	3.2	3.6	...
Rural - Rurale	C	90	112	113	103	...	3.3	4.2	4.3	4.3	...
The Former Yugoslav Rep. of Macedonia - L'ex-République yougoslave de Macédoine											
Total	C	...	...	266	284	291	...	...	9.1	10.5	10.5
Urban - Urbaine	C	...	...	150	182	187	...	...	9.6	12.3	12.5
Rural - Rurale	C	...	...	116	102	104	...	...	8.4	8.3	8.1
Ukraine											
Total	C	2 597	...	...	1 830	...	6.2	...	...	4.9	...
Urban - Urbaine	C	1 744	...	...	1 214	...	6.7	...	...	5.1	...
Rural - Rurale	C	853	...	...	616	...	5.3	...	...	4.4	...
United Kingdom - Royaume-Uni											
Total	C	3 890	3 723	3 594	...	...	5.4	5.3	5.3	...	...
OCEANIA — OCEANIE											
Australia - Australie											
Total	+C	858	770	802	751	714	3.4	3.1	3.2	3.0	2.8
New Caledonia - Nouvelle-Calédonie											
Total	+C	41	28	...	...	...	9.4	...	...	...	...
New Zealand - Nouvelle-Zélande											
Total	+C	...	172	168	157	167	...	3.0	3.0	2.8	3.1
Urban - Urbaine	+C	...	147	137	138	150	...	3.0	2.8	2.8	3.2
Rural - Rurale	+C	...	25	31	19	17	...	...	4.4	...	...

GENERAL NOTES - NOTES GENERALES

Late foetal deaths are deaths of foetuses of 28 or more completed weeks of gestation. Data include foetal deaths of unknown gestational age. Ratios are the number of late foetal deaths per 1 000 live births. Ratios are shown only for countries or areas having at least a total of 30 late foetal deaths in a given year. For definitions of 'urban', see end of Technical Notes for table 6. For method of evaluation and limitations of data, see Technical Notes for this table. — Les morts foetales tardives sont celles qui surviennent après 28 semaines complètes de gestation au moins. Les données comprennent les morts foetales survenues après une période de gestation de durée inconnue. Les rapports représentent le nombre de morts foetales tardives pour 1 000 naissances vivantes. Les rapports présentés ne se rapportent qu'aux pays ou zones ou l'on enregistré un total d'au moins 30 morts foetales tardives dans une année donnée. Pour les définitions des 'régions urbaines', se reporter à la fin des Notes techniques du tableau 6. Pour la méthode d'évaluation et les insuffisances des données, voir Notes techniques, pour ce tableau.

Italics: data from civil registers which are incomplete or of unknown completeness. — *Italiques:* données incomplètes ou dont le degré d'exactitude n'est pas connu, provenant des registres de l'état civil.

FOOTNOTES - NOTES

* Provisional. — Données provisoires.
+ Data tabulated by date of registration rather than occurence. — Données exploitées selon la date de l'enregistrement et non la date de l'événement.

[1] 'Code' indicates the source of data, as follows:
C - Civil registration, estimated over 90% complete
U - Civil registration, estimated less than 90% complete
I - Other source, estimated reliable
+ - Data tabulated by date of registration rather than occurence.
... - Information not available

Le 'Code' indique la source des données, comme suit:

C - Registres de l'état civil considérés complèts à 90 p. 100 au moins.
U - Registres de l'état civil qui ne sont pas considérés complèts à 90 p. 100 au moins.
I - Autre source, considérée pas douteuses.
+ - Données exploitées selon la date de l'enregistrement et non la date de l'événement.
... - Information pas disponible.

[2] Foetal deaths after at least 180 days (6 calendar months or 26 weeks) of gestation. - Morts foetales survenues après 180 jours (6 mois civils ou 26 semaines) au moins de gestation.

[3] Including Canadian residents temporarily in the United States, but excluding United States residents temporarily in Canada. - Y compris les résidents canadiens se trouvant temporairement aux Etats-Unis, mais ne comprenant pas les résidents des Etats-Unis se trouvant temporairement au Canada.

[4] Data for urban and rural areas exclude foetal deaths of unknown residence. - Les données urbaines/rurales ne comprennent pas les morts foetales tardives dont on ignore la résidence.

[5] Excluding tribal Indian population. - Non compris les Indiens vivant en tribus.

[6] Excluding Indian jungle population. - Non compris les Indiens de la jungle.

[7] Data refer to total foetal deaths. - Y compris toutes les morts foetales.

[8] Figures for urban and rural areas do not add up to the total, since they do not include the category 'Unknown residence'. - La somme des donées pour la residence urbaine et rurale n'est pas égale au total parce qu'elle n'inclue pas la catégorie 'Residence inconnue'.

[9] Excluding nomadic Indian tribes. - Non compris les tribus d'Indiens nomades.

[10] Including data for East Jerusalem and Israeli residents in certain other territories under occupation by Israeli military forces since June 1967. - Y compris les données pour Jérusalem-Est et les résidents israéliens dans certains autres territoires occupés depuis 1967 par les forces armées israéliennes.

[11] Data for 1999 and 2000 include 8 and 9 foetal deaths of unknown gestational age and weight over 1000 grams respectively. - Les données pour 1999 et 2000 comprennent huit et neuf décès intra-utérins, respectivement, pour lesquels l'âge gestationnel est inconnu et le poids est supérieur à 1 000 grammes.

[12] Data refer to Japanese nationals in Japan only. - Les données se raportent aux nationaux japonais au Japon seulement.

[13] Total was revised to include late registration. - Le total a été revisé avec les enregistrements tardives.

[14] Data refer to the recorded events in Ministry of Health hospitals and health centres only. - Les données se rapportent aux faits d'état-civil enregistrés dans les hôpitaux et les dispensaires du Ministère de la santé seulement.

[15] Including armed forces stationed outside the country, but excluding alien armed forces stationed in the area. - Y compris les militaires nationaux hors du pays, mais non compris les militaires étrangers en garnison sur le territoire.

[16] Including nationals temporarily outside the country. - Y compris les nationaux se trouvant temporairement hors du pays.

[17] Ratios computed on live births in the population including national armed forces outside the country. - Rapports calculés sur la base des naissances vivantes qui comprennent les militaires nationaux hors du pays.

[18] For urban/rural, foetal deaths after at least 150 days (5 calendar months or 20 weeks) of gestation. - Pour les chiffres urbaine/rurale, morts foetales survenues après 150 jours (5 mois civils ou 26 semaines) ou moins de gestation.

[19] Including residents outside the country if listed in a Netherlands population register. - Y compris les résidents hors du pays, s'ils sont inscrits sur un registre de population néerlandais.

Table 13

Table 13 presents legally induced abortions for as many years as possible between 1993 and 2002.

Description of variables: There are two major categories of abortion: spontaneous and induced. Induced abortions are those initiated by deliberate action undertaken with the intention of terminating pregnancy; all other abortions are considered as spontaneous.

The induction of abortion is subject to governmental regulation in most, if not all, countries or areas. This regulation varies from complete prohibition in some countries or areas to abortion on request, with services provided by governmental health authorities, in others. More generally, governments have attempted to define the conditions under which a pregnancy may lawfully be terminated and have established procedures for authorizing abortion in individual cases.

Legally induced abortions are further classified according to the legal grounds on which induced abortion may be performed. A code shown next to the country or area name indicates the grounds on which induced abortion is legal in that particular country or area, the meanings of which are shown below:

a) Continuation of pregnancy would involve risk to the life of the pregnant woman greater than if the pregnancy were terminated.

b) Continuation of pregnancy would involve greater risk of injury to the physical health of the pregnant woman than if the pregnancy were terminated.

c) Continuation of pregnancy would involve risk of injury to the mental health of the pregnant woman greater than if the pregnancy were terminated.

d) Continuation of pregnancy would involve risk of injury to mental or physical health of any existing children of the family greater than if the pregnancy were terminated.

e) There is a substantial risk that if the child were born it would experience such physical or mental abnormalities as to be seriously disabled.

f) Other.

Reliability of data: Unlike data on live births and foetal deaths, which are generally collected through systems of vital registration, data on abortion are collected from a variety of sources. Because of this, the quality specification, showing the completeness of civil registers, which is presented for other tables, does not appear here.

Limitations: With regard to the collection of information on abortions, a variety of sources are used, but hospital records are the most common source of information. This implies that most cases that have no contact with hospitals are missed. Data from other sources are probably also incomplete. The data in the present table are limited to legally induced abortions, which, by their nature, might be assumed to be more complete than data on all induced abortions.

Earlier data: Legally induced abortions have been shown previously in all issues of the *Demographic Yearbook* since the 1971 issue.

Tableau 13

Ce tableau présente des données relatives aux avortements provoqués légalement, pour le plus grand nombre d'années possible entre 1993 et 2002.

Description des variables : L'avortement peut être spontané ou provoqué. L'avortement provoqué est celui qui résulte de manœuvres délibérées, entreprises afin d'interrompre la grossesse ; tous les autres avortements sont considérés comme spontanés.

L'interruption délibérée de la grossesse fait l'objet d'une réglementation officielle dans la plupart des pays ou zones, sinon dans tous. Cette réglementation va de l'interdiction totale à l'autorisation de l'avortement sur demande, pratiqué par des services de santé publique. Le plus souvent, les gouvernements se sont efforcés de définir les circonstances dans lesquelles la grossesse peut être interrompue licitement et de fixer une procédure d'autorisation.

Les interruptions légales de grossesse sont également classées selon le motif d'autorisation. Un code, figurant en regard du pays ou de la zone, signale les motifs d'autorisation de l'avortement. La signification des différents codes est la suivante :

a) La non-interruption de la grossesse comporterait, pour la vie de la femme enceinte, un risque plus grave que celui de l'avortement ;

b) La non-interruption de la grossesse comporterait, pour la santé physique de la femme enceinte, un risque plus grave que celui de l'avortement ;

c) La non-interruption de la grossesse comporterait, pour la santé mentale de la femme, un risque plus grave que celui de l'avortement ;

d) La non-interruption de la grossesse comporterait, pour la santé mentale ou physique d'un enfant déjà né dans la famille, un risque plus grave que celui de l'avortement ;

e) L'enfant né à terme courrait un risque important de souffrir d'anomalies physiques ou mentales entraînant pour lui un grave handicap ;

f) Autres motifs.

Fiabilité des données : À la différence des données sur les naissances vivantes et les morts fœtales, qui proviennent généralement des registres d'état civil, les données sur l'avortement sont tirées de sources diverses. Aussi ne trouve-t-on pas ici une évaluation de la qualité des données semblable à celle qui indique, pour les autres tableaux, le degré d'exhaustivité des données de l'état civil.

Insuffisance des données : En ce qui concerne les renseignements sur l'avortement, un grand nombre de sources sont utilisées, les relevés hospitaliers restant cependant la source la plus commune. Il s'ensuit que la plupart des cas qui ne passent pas par les hôpitaux sont ignorés. Il faut aussi tenir compte du fait que les données provenant d'autres sources sont probablement incomplètes. Les données du tableau 13 se limitent aux avortements provoqués pour raisons légales dont on peut supposer, en raison de leur nature même, que les statistiques sont plus complètes que les données concernant l'ensemble des avortements provoqués.

Données publiées antérieurement : Des statistiques concernant les avortements provoqués pour raisons légales sont publiées dans l'*Annuaire démographique* depuis 1971.

13. Legally induced abortions: 1993 - 2002
Avortements provoqués légalement: 1993 - 2002

(See notes at end of table. — Voir notes à la fin du tableau.)

Continent and country or area / Continent et pays ou zone	Number — Nombre									
	1993	1994	1995	1996	1997	1998	1999	2000	2001	2002
AFRICA — AFRIQUE										
Réunion	...	...	...	4 567	4 729	4 652	4 522	4 404	...	...
South Africa - Afrique du Sud[1]	...	...	...	...	...	28 978	...	...	...	...
AMERICA, NORTH — AMERIQUE DU NORD										
Canada[a,b,c]	104 403	106 255	108 248	111 659	111 709	110 331	105 666	105 427	106 418	...
Cuba	86 906	89 421	83 963	...	80 097	75 109	80 037	76 293	...	...
Dominican Republic - République dominicaine	...	...	18 377	20 852	22 911	31 068	...	...	...	...
Greenland - Groenland	977	1 000	879	862	865	913	816	...	...	...
Panama[2]	...	...	...	...	...	...	...	11	...	...
Puerto Rico - Porto Rico	...	...	...	...	...	...	...	...	1 229	...
ASIA — ASIE										
Armenia - Arménie	27 907	30 571	30 726	31 323	25 266	18 286	14 403	11 769	10 419	...
Azerbaijan - Azerbaïdjan	33 951	33 280	28 610	28 375	25 182	24 914	20 878	17 501	18 332	16 606
Bahrain - Bahreïn	...	...	...	...	1 592	1 680	1 658	1 655	1 747	1 749
China: Hong Kong SAR - Chine: Hong Kong RAS	26 057	26 049	25 363	25 041	23 939	22 086	20 891	21 375	20 235	...
Georgia - Géorgie	45 131	48 953	43 549	...	...	...	...	...	...	...
Israel - Israël[3,4,a,b,c,e,f]	17 164	16 903	17 627	17 447	19 210	18 500	18 372	18 689	19 131	...
Japan - Japon[5,a,b,c,d,e]	386 807	364 350	343 024	338 867	337 799	333 220	337 314	341 164	341 588	329 326
Kazakhstan	206 877	260 200	224 100	193 462	156 222	148 799	137 808	...	...	...
Kyrgyzstan - Kirghizistan	52 724	49 325	27 111	...	31 598	28 090	25 790	22 044	23 390	18 690
Mongolia - Mongolie	...	...	...	15 588	12 870	...	...	...	...	...
Singapore - Singapour[a,b,c,d,e]	16 476	15 690	14 504	14 362	13 827	13 838	13 753	13 734	...	...
Tajikistan - Tadjikistan	40 078	35 709	...	...	...	...	...	...	...	...
Uzbekistan - Ouzbékistan	...	120 434	104 400	104 620	...	...	...	...	...	...
EUROPE										
Belarus - Bélarus	212 729	207 658	193 280	174 098	152 660	145 339	135 824	121 895	101 402	89 895
Belgium - Belgique	...	...	...	...	...	11 999	12 734	13 762	14 775	...
Bulgaria - Bulgarie	107 416	97 567	97 092	...	87 896	...	...	61 378	51 165	50 824
Channel Islands: Guernsey - Îles Anglo-Normandes: Guernesey	...	...	...	...	57	104	92	89	...	...
Channel Islands: Jersey - Îles Anglo-Normandes: Jersey	296	...	...	...	...	...	...	...	...	...
Croatia - Croatie	25 179	19 673	14 282	12 339	10 036	8 907	8 064	7 534	6 574	...
Czech Republic - République tchèque[a,b,c,e]	70 634	54 836	49 531	48 086	45 022	42 959	39 382	34 623	32 528	31 142
Denmark - Danemark[6,a,b,c,d,e]	18 607	17 598	17 720	18 135	17 152	16 592	16 271	15 681	15 315	14 967
Estonia - Estonie[a,b,c,d,e]	23 284	19 784	17 671	16 887	16 615	...	14 503	12 743	...	10 834
Finland - Finlande[a,b,c,e,f]	10 342	10 013	9 884	10 437	10 238	10 744	10 819	10 930	10 696	10 908
France[a,b,c,e]	157 886	152 963	146 433	...	163 985	...	...	...	...	...
Germany - Allemagne	111 236	103 586	97 937	...	130 890	...	130 471	134 609	134 964	130 387
Greece - Grèce[a,b,c,e,f]	12 289	12 608	...	12 542	...	...	...	...	...	...
Hungary - Hongrie[a,b,c,d,e,f]	75 258	74 491	76 957	76 600	74 564	68 971	65 981	59 249	56 404	56 075
Iceland - Islande[a,b,c,e,f]	827	775	807	854	921	...	945	947	996	926
Italy - Italie	145 229	135 956	134 137	138 925	140 166	138 354	138 708	...	...	126 164
Latvia - Lettonie[a,b,c,e]	31 348	26 795	25 933	24 227	21 768	19 964	18 031	17 240	15 647	14 685
Lithuania - Lituanie[7,a,e,f]	38 864	30 326	31 278	27 832	22 680	21 022	18 846	16 259	13 677	12 495
Netherlands - Pays-Bas[a,b,c,e,f]	19 804	20 811	20 932	22 441	...	24 141	...	...	...	...
Norway - Norvège[a,b,c,d,e,f]	14 909	...	13 672	...	...	14 028	14 251	14 635	13 867	13 557
Poland - Pologne[8,a,b,c,e,f]	1 208	874	559	491	3 171	312	151	138	123	...
Republic of Moldova - République de Moldova	...	...	44 252	46 010	...	31 293	27 908	20 395	16 028	15 739
Romania - Roumanie	585 761	530 191	502 840	456 221	347 126	259 888	...	257 865	198 086	247 608
Russian Federation - Fédération de Russie	3 243 957	2 481 493	2 766 362	...	...	...	...	...	...	...
Serbia and Montenegro - Serbie-et-Montenegro	119 254	98 942	96 854	83 577	64 099	58 739	...	...	...	...
Slovakia - Slovaquie	38 852	34 883	35 879	...	...	21 109	19 949	...	18 026	17 382

13. Legally induced abortions: 1993 - 2002
Avortements provoqués légalement: 1993 - 2002 (continued — suite)

(See notes at end of table. — Voir notes à la fin du tableau.)

Continent and country or area Continent et pays ou zone	Number — Nombre									
	1993	1994	1995	1996	1997	1998	1999	2000	2001	2002
EUROPE										
Slovenia - Slovénie	12 154	11 324	10 791	10 218	...	9 116	8 707	8 429	7 799	7 327
Spain - Espagne	...	47 832	...	51 002	46 902	53 847	58 399	63 756	...	...
Sweden - Suède	34 169	32 293	31 441	32 117	31 433	31 008	...	30 980	31 772	33 365
The Former Yugoslav Rep. of Macedonia - L'ex-République yougoslave de Macédoine	...	...	...	...	12 028	...	...	...	...	...
United Kingdom - Royaume-Uni[9,a,b,c,d,e,f]	173 686	169 964	167 297	189 473	191 855	199 887	195 394	197 366	197 913	...
OCEANIA — OCEANIE										
New Caledonia - Nouvelle-Calédonie	...	...	...	...	1 528	1 466	...	...	...	...
New Zealand - Nouvelle-Zélande	11 893	12 835	13 652	14 805	15 208	15 029	15 501	16 103	16 410	17 380

GENERAL NOTES - NOTES GENERALES

For method of evaluation and limitations of data, see Technical Notes, for this table. — Pour la méthode d'évaluation et les insuffisances des données, voir Notes techniques, pour ce tableau.

FOOTNOTES - NOTES

* Provisional. — Données provisoires.

a Continuation of pregnancy would involve risk to the life of the pregnant woman greater than if the pregnancy were terminated. — La prolongation de la grossesse exposerait la vie de la femme enceinte davantage que son interruption.

b Continuation of pregnancy would involve risk of injury to the physical health of the pregnant woman greater than if the pregnancy were terminated. — La prolongation de la grossesse couserait des complication pouvant affecter la santé physique de la femme enceinte davantage que son interruption.

c Continuation of pregnancy would involve risk of injury to the mental health of the pregnant woman greater than if the pregnancy were terminated. — La prolongation de la grossesse couserait des complications affectant les facultés mentales de la femme enceinte davantage que son interruption.

d Continuation of pregnancy would involve risk of injury to the mental or physical health of any existing children of the family greater than if the pregnancy were terminated. — La prolongation de la grossesse couserait des complications affectant les facultés mentales ou physiques des enfants vivants de cettee famille, davantage que son interruption.

e There is a substaintial risk that if the child were born it would suffer from such physical or mental abnormalities as to be seriously handicapped. — Il y aurait des risques majeurs pour l'enfant de naître avec des anomalies physiques ou mentales qui l'handicaperaient gravement.

f Other. — Autres.

1 Data refer to both 1997 and 1998. - Les données se rapportent à 1997 et à 1998.

2 Data refer to abortions granted for medical reasons by the Comision Multidisciplinaria Nacional de Aborto Terapéutico. - Les données se référént aux avortements autorisés pour des raisons médicales par la Comision Multidisciplinaria Nacional de Aborto Terapéutico.

3 Including data for East Jerusalem and Israeli residents in certain other territories under occupation by Israeli military forces since June 1967. - Y compris les données pour Jérusalem-Est et les résidents israéliens dans certains autres territoires occupés depuis 1967 par les forces armées Israéliennes.

4 Data refer to authorization to interrupt pregancy. - Les données se rapportent à l'autorisation d'interrompre le pregancy.

5 Data refer to Japanese nationals in Japan only. - Les données se raportent aux nationaux japonais au Japon seulement.

6 Excluding Faeroe Islands and Greenland. - Non compris les îles Féroé et Gröenland.

7 Data refer to requested abortions only and exclude a abortions due to therapeutic reasons. - Les données se rapportent seulement aux interruptions volontaires de grossesse et excluent les avortements effectués pour des rasions thérapeutiques.

8 Based on hospital and polyclinic records. - D'après les registres des hôpitaux et des polycliniques.

9 For residents only. - Pour les résidents seulement.

Table 14

Table 14 presents legally induced abortions by age and number of previous live births of women for the latest available year.

Description of variables: The technical notes for table 13 provide more detailed information on the classification of legally induced abortion.

Age is defined as age at last birthday, that is, the difference between the date of birth and the date of the occurrence of the event, expressed in complete solar years. The age classification used in this table is the following: under 15 years, 5-year age groups through 45-49 years and 50 years and over.

Except where otherwise indicated, eight categories are used in classifying the number of previous live births: 0 through 5, 6 or more live births, and, if required, number of live births unknown.

Reliability of data: Unlike data on live births and foetal deaths, which are generally collected through systems of vital registration, data on abortion are collected from a variety of sources. Because of this, the quality specification, showing the completeness of civil registers, which is presented for other tables, does not appear here.

Limitations: With regard to the collection of information on abortions, a variety of sources are used, but hospital records are the most common source of information. This implies that most cases that have no contact with hospitals are missed. Data from other sources are probably also incomplete. The data in the present table are limited to legally induced abortions, which, by their nature, might be assumed to be more complete than data on all induced abortions.

In addition, deficiencies in the reporting of age and number of previous live births of the woman, differences in the method used for obtaining the age of the woman, and the proportion of abortions for which age or previous live births of the woman are unknown must all be taken into account in using these data.

Earlier data: Legally induced abortions by age and previous live births of women have been shown previously in most issues of the *Demographic Yearbook* since the 1971 issue. For more information on specific topics and years for which data are reported, readers should consult the Index.

Tableau 14

Le tableau 14 présente les données les plus récentes dont on dispose sur les avortements provoqués pour des raisons légales, selon l'âge de la mère et le nombre de naissances vivantes précédentes.

Description des variables : Les notes techniques du tableau 13 contiennent une classification des avortements provoqués légalement.

L'âge considéré est l'âge au dernier anniversaire, c'est-à-dire la différence entre la date de naissance et la date de l'avortement, exprimée en années solaires révolues. La classification par âge utilisée dans le tableau 14 est la suivante : moins de 15 ans, groupes quinquennaux jusqu'à 45-49 ans, 50 ans et plus, et âge inconnu.

Sauf indication contraire, les naissances vivantes antérieures sont classées dans les huit catégories suivantes: 0 à 5 naissances vivantes, 6 naissances vivantes ou plus et, le cas échéant, nombre de naissances vivantes inconnu.

Fiabilité des données : À la différence des données sur les naissances vivantes et les morts fœtales, qui proviennent généralement des registres d'état civil, les données sur l'avortement sont tirées de sources diverses. Aussi ne trouve-t-on pas ici une évaluation de la qualité des données semblable à celle qui indique, pour les autres tableaux, le degré d'exhaustivité des données de l'état civil.

Insuffisance des données : En ce qui concerne les renseignements sur l'avortement, un grand nombre de sources sont utilisées, les relevés hospitaliers restant cependant la source la plus commune. Il s'ensuit que la plupart des cas qui ne passent pas par les hôpitaux sont ignorés. Il faut aussi tenir compte du fait que les données provenant d'autres sources sont probablement incomplètes. Les données du tableau 14 se limitent aux avortements provoqués pour raisons légales dont on peut supposer, en raison de leur nature même, que les statistiques sont plus complètes que les données concernant l'ensemble des avortements provoqués.

En outre, on doit tenir compte, lorsque l'on utilise ces données, des erreurs de déclaration de l'âge de la mère et du nombre des naissances vivantes précédentes, de l'hétérogénéité des méthodes de calcul de l'âge de la mère et de la proportion d'avortements pour lesquels l'âge de la mère ou le nombre des naissances vivantes ne sont pas connus.

Données publiées antérieurement : Depuis 1971, la plupart des éditions de l'*Annuaire démographique* contiennent des statistiques concernant les avortements provoqués pour raisons légales, selon l'âge de la mère et le nombre de naissances vivantes antérieures. Pour plus de précisions concernant les années et les sujets pour lesquels des données ont été publiées, se reporter à l'index.

14. Legally induced abortions by age and number of previous live births of women: latest available year, 1993 - 2002
Avortments provoqués légalement selon l'âge de la femme et selon le nombre des naissances vivantes précédentes: dernière année disponible, 1993 - 2002

(See notes at end of table. — Voir notes à la fin du tableau.)

Continent, country or area, year and age — Continent, pays ou zone, année et âge	Total	0	1	2	3	4	5	6+	Unknown Inconnu
AMERICA, NORTH — AMERIQUE DU NORD									
Canada									
1993									
Total	104 403	...	...	...	...	...	...	...	...
0 - 14	659	...	...	...	...	...	...	...	...
15 - 19	19 989	...	...	...	...	...	...	...	...
20 - 24	31 227	...	...	...	...	...	...	...	...
25 - 29	23 295	...	...	...	...	...	...	...	...
30 - 34	16 929	...	...	...	...	...	...	...	...
35 - 39	9 411	...	...	...	...	...	...	...	...
40+	2 892	...	...	...	...	...	...	...	...
Unknown	1	...	...	...	...	...	...	...	...
1994									
Total	106 255	...	...	...	...	...	...	...	...
0 - 14	560	...	...	...	...	...	...	...	...
15 - 19	20 978	...	...	...	...	...	...	...	...
20 - 24	31 372	...	...	...	...	...	...	...	...
25 - 29	23 643	...	...	...	...	...	...	...	...
30 - 34	16 681	...	...	...	...	...	...	...	...
35 - 39	10 033	...	...	...	...	...	...	...	...
40+	2 906	...	...	...	...	...	...	...	...
Unknown	82	...	...	...	...	...	...	...	...
1995									
Total	108 248	...	...	...	...	...	...	...	...
0 - 14	556	...	...	...	...	...	...	...	...
15 - 19	20 668	...	...	...	...	...	...	...	...
20 - 24	32 215	...	...	...	...	...	...	...	...
25 - 29	23 455	...	...	...	...	...	...	...	...
30 - 34	17 504	...	...	...	...	...	...	...	...
35 - 39	10 423	...	...	...	...	...	...	...	...
40+	3 220	...	...	...	...	...	...	...	...
Unknown	207	...	...	...	...	...	...	...	...
1996									
Total	111 659	...	...	...	...	...	...	...	...
0 - 14	544	...	...	...	...	...	...	...	...
15 - 19	21 574	...	...	...	...	...	...	...	...
20 - 24	33 207	...	...	...	...	...	...	...	...
25 - 29	24 087	...	...	...	...	...	...	...	...
30 - 34	17 862	...	...	...	...	...	...	...	...
35 - 39	10 821	...	...	...	...	...	...	...	...
40+	3 448	...	...	...	...	...	...	...	...
Unknown	116	...	...	...	...	...	...	...	...
1997									
Total	111 709	...	...	...	...	...	...	...	...
0 - 14	530	...	...	...	...	...	...	...	...
15 - 19	21 262	...	...	...	...	...	...	...	...
20 - 24	33 714	...	...	...	...	...	...	...	...
25 - 29	24 014	...	...	...	...	...	...	...	...
30 - 34	17 517	...	...	...	...	...	...	...	...
35 - 39	11 020	...	...	...	...	...	...	...	...
40+	3 598	...	...	...	...	...	...	...	...
Unknown	54	...	...	...	...	...	...	...	...
1998									
Total	110 331	...	...	...	...	...	...	...	...
0 - 14	483	...	...	...	...	...	...	...	...
15 - 19	21 591	...	...	...	...	...	...	...	...
20 - 24	33 422	...	...	...	...	...	...	...	...
25 - 29	22 956	...	...	...	...	...	...	...	...
30 - 34	16 959	...	...	...	...	...	...	...	...

14. Legally induced abortions by age and number of previous live births of women: latest available year, 1993 - 2002
Avortments provoqués légalement selon l'âge de la femme et selon le nombre des naissances vivantes précédentes: dernière année disponible, 1993 - 2002 (continued — suite)

(See notes at end of table. — Voir notes à la fin du tableau.)

| Continent, country or area, year and age / Continent, pays ou zone, année et âge | Total | \multicolumn{9}{c}{Number of previous live births - Nombre des naissances vivantes précédentes} |
		0	1	2	3	4	5	6+	Unknown Inconnu

AMERICA, NORTH — AMERIQUE DU NORD

	Total	0	1	2	3	4	5	6+	Unknown Inconnu
Canada									
1998									
35 - 39	11 269	...	...	...	...	...	...	...	...
40+	3 636	...	...	...	...	...	...	...	...
Unknown	15	...	...	...	...	...	...	...	...
1999									
Total	105 666	...	...	...	...	...	...	...	...
0 - 14	468	...	...	...	...	...	...	...	...
15 - 19	20 672	...	...	...	...	...	...	...	...
20 - 24	32 462	...	...	...	...	...	...	...	...
25 - 29	21 983	...	...	...	...	...	...	...	...
30 - 34	15 708	...	...	...	...	...	...	...	...
35 - 39	10 646	...	...	...	...	...	...	...	...
40+	3 726	...	...	...	...	...	...	...	...
Unknown	1	...	...	...	...	...	...	...	...
2000									
Total	105 427	...	...	...	...	...	...	...	...
0 - 14	389	...	...	...	...	...	...	...	...
15 - 19	20 475	...	...	...	...	...	...	...	...
20 - 24	32 623	...	...	...	...	...	...	...	...
25 - 29	21 735	...	...	...	...	...	...	...	...
30 - 34	15 790	...	...	...	...	...	...	...	...
35 - 39	10 631	...	...	...	...	...	...	...	...
40+	3 780	...	...	...	...	...	...	...	...
Unknown	4	...	...	...	...	...	...	...	...
2001									
Total	106 418	...	...	...	...	...	...	...	...
0 - 14	412	...	...	...	...	...	...	...	...
15 - 19	19 968	...	...	...	...	...	...	...	...
20 - 24	32 730	...	...	...	...	...	...	...	...
25 - 29	22 012	...	...	...	...	...	...	...	...
30 - 34	16 243	...	...	...	...	...	...	...	...
35 - 39	10 977	...	...	...	...	...	...	...	...
40+	4 043	...	...	...	...	...	...	...	...
Unknown	33	...	...	...	...	...	...	...	...
Panama[1]									
2000									
Total	11	7	3	-	-	-	-	1	-
15 - 19	2	2	-	-	-	-	-	-	-
20 - 24	4	3	1	-	-	-	-	-	-
25 - 29	2	1	1	-	-	-	-	-	-
30 - 34	2	-	1	-	-	-	-	1	-
35+	1	1	-	-	-	-	-	-	-

ASIA — ASIE

	Total	0	1	2	3	4	5	6+	Unknown Inconnu
Azerbaijan - Azerbaïdjan									
2002									
Total	16 606	...	...	...	...	...	...	...	...
15 - 19	868	...	...	...	...	...	...	...	...
20 - 24	4 362	...	...	...	...	...	...	...	...
25 - 29	4 747	...	...	...	...	...	...	...	...
30 - 34	3 935	...	...	...	...	...	...	...	...
35+	2 694	...	...	...	...	...	...	...	...
China: Hong Kong SAR - Chine: Hong Kong RAS[2]									
2001									
Total	20 235	10 924	3 861	4 390	1 060	...	...	...	...

14. Legally induced abortions by age and number of previous live births of women: latest available year, 1993 - 2002
Avortments provoqués légalement selon l'âge de la femme et selon le nombre des naissances vivantes précédentes: dernière année disponible, 1993 - 2002 (continued — suite)

(See notes at end of table. — Voir notes à la fin du tableau.)

Continent, country or area, year and age / Continent, pays ou zone, année et âge	Total	*Number of previous live births - Nombre des naissances vivantes précédentes*							Unknown Inconnu
		0	1	2	3	4	5	6+	
ASIA — ASIE									
China: Hong Kong SAR - Chine: Hong Kong RAS[2]									
2001									
0 - 14	26	26	-	-	-	...	...	...	...
15 - 19	1 812	1 741	65	6	-	...	...	...	...
20 - 24	4 771	4 213	433	108	17	...	...	...	...
25 - 29	4 369	2 873	911	494	91	...	...	...	...
30 - 34	3 809	1 352	1 021	1 206	230	...	...	...	...
35 - 39	3 629	561	1 005	1 659	404	...	...	...	...
40 - 44	1 657	153	393	831	280	...	...	...	...
45+	162	5	33	86	38	...	...	...	...
Georgia - Géorgie[3]									
1995									
Total	32 016	...	...	...	...	...	...	...	...
0 - 14	177	...	...	...	...	...	...	...	...
15 - 19	2 508	...	...	...	...	...	...	...	...
20 - 34	25 510	...	...	...	...	...	...	...	...
35+	3 821	...	...	...	...	...	...	...	...
Israel - Israël[4]									
2001									
Total	19 131	7 999	3 297	3 888	2 277	968	380	305	17
0 - 14	21	20	1	-	-	-	-	-	-
15 - 19	2 319	2 261	52	2	1	-	-	-	3
20 - 24	3 973	3 099	618	212	36	4	2	1	1
25 - 29	4 131	1 773	1 122	872	241	87	22	8	6
30 - 34	3 749	629	904	1 276	595	198	96	48	3
35 - 39	2 980	171	438	969	823	363	117	97	2
40 - 44	1 739	40	152	501	518	276	125	125	2
45 - 49	211	5	10	54	59	40	18	25	-
50+	6	-	-	2	3	-	-	1	-
Unknown	2	1	-	10	1	-	-	-	-
Japan - Japon[5]									
2001									
Total	341 588	...	...	...	...	...	...	...	...
0 - 19	46 511	...	...	...	...	...	...	...	...
20 - 24	82 540	...	...	...	...	...	...	...	...
25 - 29	72 621	...	...	...	...	...	...	...	...
30 - 34	63 153	...	...	...	...	...	...	...	...
35 - 39	51 391	...	...	...	...	...	...	...	...
40 - 44	23 085	...	...	...	...	...	...	...	...
45 - 49	2 139	...	...	...	...	...	...	...	...
50+	30	...	...	...	...	...	...	...	...
Unknown	118	...	...	...	...	...	...	...	...
2002									
Total	329 326	...	...	...	...	...	...	...	...
0 - 19	45 384	...	...	...	...	...	...	...	...
20 - 24	79 203	...	...	...	...	...	...	...	...
25 - 29	68 689	...	...	...	...	...	...	...	...
30 - 34	63 221	...	...	...	...	...	...	...	...
35 - 39	49 281	...	...	...	...	...	...	...	...
40 - 44	21 518	...	...	...	...	...	...	...	...
45 - 49	1 880	...	...	...	...	...	...	...	...
50+	36	...	...	...	...	...	...	...	...
Unknown	114	...	...	...	...	...	...	...	...
Kazakhstan									
1999									
Total	137 808	...	...	...	...	...	...	...	...
0 - 14	177	...	...	...	...	...	...	...	...
15 - 18	8 971	...	...	...	...	...	...	...	...

14. Legally induced abortions by age and number of previous live births of women: latest available year, 1993 - 2002
Avortments provoqués légalement selon l'âge de la femme et selon le nombre des naissances vivantes précédentes: dernière année disponible, 1993 - 2002 (continued — suite)

(See notes at end of table. — Voir notes à la fin du tableau.)

Continent, country or area, year and age — Continent, pays ou zone, année et âge	Total	Number of previous live births - Nombre des naissances vivantes précédentes								Unknown Inconnu
		0	1	2	3	4	5	6+	

ASIA — ASIE

Kazakhstan
1999
19 - 35	105 204	...	...	...	...	...	...	...	...
36+	23 456	...	...	...	...	...	...	...	...

Singapore - Singapour[6]
2000
Total	13 734	6 529	1 983	3 116	1 607	499	...	...	...
0 - 14	37	37	-	-	-	-	...	...	...
15 - 19	1 693	1 571	101	21	-	-	...	...	...
20 - 24	3 302	2 668	399	181	46	8	...	...	...
25 - 29	3 053	1 498	601	666	224	64	...	...	...
30 - 34	2 506	497	480	919	487	123	...	...	...
35 - 39	2 169	200	290	918	569	192	...	...	...
40 - 44	901	56	107	376	263	99	...	...	...
45+	73	2	5	35	18	13	...	...	...

EUROPE

Belarus - Bélarus
2002
Total	89 895	...	...	...	...	...	...	...	...
0 - 14	34	...	...	...	...	...	...	...	...
15 - 19	8 509	...	...	...	...	...	...	...	...
20 - 24	23 072	...	...	...	...	...	...	...	...
25 - 29	22 387	...	...	...	...	...	...	...	...
30 - 34	17 752	...	...	...	...	...	...	...	...
35 - 39	12 122	...	...	...	...	...	...	...	...
40 - 44	5 493	...	...	...	...	...	...	...	...
45+	526	...	...	...	...	...	...	...	...

Belgium - Belgique
2001
Total	14 775	...	...	...	...	...	...	...	...
0 - 14	75	...	...	...	...	...	...	...	...
15 - 19	2 133	...	...	...	...	...	...	...	...
20 - 24	3 761	...	...	...	...	...	...	...	...
25 - 29	3 332	...	...	...	...	...	...	...	...
30 - 34	2 822	...	...	...	...	...	...	...	...
35 - 39	1 936	...	...	...	...	...	...	...	...
40 - 44	656	...	...	...	...	...	...	...	...
45 - 49	54	...	...	...	...	...	...	...	...
Unknown	6	...	...	...	...	...	...	...	...

Bulgaria - Bulgarie
2002
Total	50 824	...	...	...	...	...	...	...	...
0 - 14	180	...	...	...	...	...	...	...	...
15 - 19	4 792	...	...	...	...	...	...	...	...
20 - 24	13 205	...	...	...	...	...	...	...	...
25 - 29	13 840	...	...	...	...	...	...	...	...
30 - 34	10 706	...	...	...	...	...	...	...	...
35 - 39	6 100	...	...	...	...	...	...	...	...
40 - 44	1 788	...	...	...	...	...	...	...	...
45 - 49	202	...	...	...	...	...	...	...	...
50+	11	...	...	...	...	...	...	...	...

Channel Islands: Guernsey - Îles Anglo-Normandes: Guernesey
2000
Total	89	46	21	11	9	1	1	-	-
0 - 14	1	1	-	-	-	-	-	-	-

14. Legally induced abortions by age and number of previous live births of women: latest available year, 1993 - 2002
Avortments provoqués légalement selon l'âge de la femme et selon le nombre des naissances vivantes précédentes: dernière année disponible, 1993 - 2002 (continued — suite)

(See notes at end of table. — Voir notes à la fin du tableau.)

Continent, country or area, year and age / Continent, pays ou zone, année et âge	Total	Number of previous live births - Nombre des naissances vivantes précédentes							Unknown Inconnu
		0	1	2	3	4	5	6+	

EUROPE

Channel Islands: Guernsey - Îles Anglo-Normandes: Guernesey

2000

15 - 19	12	11	1	-	-	-	-	-	-
20 - 24	30	17	13	-	-	-	-	-	-
25 - 29	18	11	3	3	1	-	-	-	-
30 - 34	15	4	3	4	2	1	1	-	-
35 - 39	10	1	1	4	4	-	-	-	-
40 - 44	3	1	-	-	2	-	-	-	-

Croatia - Croatie[7]

2000

Total	7 534	1 730	1 301	2 668	839	311	...	26	-
0 - 14	4	4	-	-	-	-	...	-	-
15 - 19	422	365	23	8	1	-	...	-	-
20 - 24	1 284	788	254	126	18	1	...	-	-
25 - 29	1 344	320	328	449	98	36	...	1	-
30 - 34	1 650	113	309	723	257	86	...	11	-
35 - 39	1 662	63	216	783	299	113	...	7	-
40 - 49	916	27	125	480	140	55	...	5	-
Unknown	252	50	46	99	26	20	...	2	-

2001

Total	6 574	...	...	...	...	...	...	...	...
0 - 14	6	...	...	...	...	...	...	...	...
15 - 19	447	...	...	...	...	...	...	...	...
20 - 24	1 123	...	...	...	...	...	...	...	...
25 - 29	1 297	...	...	...	...	...	...	...	...
30 - 34	1 470	...	...	...	...	...	...	...	...
35 - 39	1 447	...	...	...	...	...	...	...	...
40 - 44	617	...	...	...	...	...	...	...	...
45 - 49	68	...	...	...	...	...	...	...	...
50+	1	...	...	...	...	...	...	...	...
Unknown	98	...	...	...	...	...	...	...	...

Czech Republic - République tchèque

2001

Total	32 513	8 060	8 320	11 982	3 146	705	201	99	-
0 - 14	18	17	1	-	-	-	-	-	-
15 - 19	2 816	2 474	301	38	3	-	-	-	-
20 - 24	6 802	3 543	2 290	811	117	37	4	-	-
25 - 29	8 539	1 519	2 943	3 306	581	138	38	14	-
30 - 34	6 784	331	1 619	3 556	955	206	74	43	-
35 - 39	5 120	124	826	2 921	938	220	56	35	-
40 - 44	2 155	51	296	1 199	483	92	27	7	-
45 - 49	274	1	44	147	68	12	2	-	-
50+	5	-	-	4	1	-	-	-	-

2002

Total	31 142	...	...	...	...	...	...	...	...
0 - 14	33	...	...	...	...	...	...	...	...
15 - 19	2 782	...	...	...	...	...	...	...	...
20 - 24	6 420	...	...	...	...	...	...	...	...
25 - 29	7 989	...	...	...	...	...	...	...	...
30 - 34	6 663	...	...	...	...	...	...	...	...
35 - 39	4 996	...	...	...	...	...	...	...	...
40 - 44	2 006	...	...	...	...	...	...	...	...
45 - 49	247	...	...	...	...	...	...	...	...
50+	6	...	...	...	...	...	...	...	...

14. Legally induced abortions by age and number of previous live births of women: latest available year, 1993 - 2002
Avortments provoqués légalement selon l'âge de la femme et selon le nombre des naissances vivantes précédentes: dernière année disponible, 1993 - 2002 (continued — suite)

(See notes at end of table. — Voir notes à la fin du tableau.)

Continent, country or area, year and age / Continent, pays ou zone, année et âge	Total	0	1	2	3	4	5	6+	Unknown Inconnu
EUROPE									
Denmark - Danemark[8]									
2001									
Total	15 315	...	...	...	...	...	...	...	...
15 - 19	1 924	...	...	...	...	...	...	...	...
20 - 24	3 093	...	...	...	...	...	...	...	...
25 - 29	3 423	...	...	...	...	...	...	...	...
30 - 34	3 292	...	...	...	...	...	...	...	...
35 - 39	2 668	...	...	...	...	...	...	...	...
40 - 44	844	...	...	...	...	...	...	...	...
45 - 49	71	...	...	...	...	...	...	...	...
2002									
Total	14 967	...	...	...	...	...	...	...	...
15 - 19	1 912	...	...	...	...	...	...	...	...
20 - 24	3 097	...	...	...	...	...	...	...	...
25 - 29	3 149	...	...	...	...	...	...	...	...
30 - 34	3 154	...	...	...	...	...	...	...	...
35 - 39	2 749	...	...	...	...	...	...	...	...
40 - 44	837	...	...	...	...	...	...	...	...
45 - 49	69	...	...	...	...	...	...	...	...
Estonia - Estonie									
2002									
Total	10 834	2 758	3 948	2 958	813	248	64	30	15
0 - 14	18	17	1	-	-	-	-	-	-
15 - 19	1 414	1 196	200	15	1	-	-	-	2
20 - 24	2 656	1 093	1 275	241	40	4	2	-	1
25 - 29	2 404	333	1 213	681	127	33	8	3	6
30 - 34	2 055	80	667	961	262	62	18	2	3
35 - 39	1 524	26	430	693	242	93	19	19	2
40 - 44	711	13	157	334	128	56	16	6	1
45 - 49	51	-	5	32	13	-	1	-	-
Unknown	1	-	-	1	-	-	-	-	-
Finland - Finlande									
2002									
Total	10 908	5 714	1 906	2 009	909	271	70	29	-
0 - 14	90	90	-	-	-	-	-	-	-
15 - 19	2 486	2 354	121	11	-	-	-	-	-
20 - 24	2 628	1 816	560	206	43	3	-	-	-
25 - 29	1 927	775	478	473	154	40	5	2	-
30 - 34	1 722	403	373	573	273	79	18	3	-
35 - 39	1 402	211	259	518	279	93	26	16	-
40 - 44	611	62	108	218	145	53	18	7	-
45 - 49	40	2	6	10	15	3	3	1	-
Unknown	2	1	1	-	-	-	-	-	-
France									
1997									
Total	163 985	...	...	...	...	...	...	...	...
15 - 19	18 695	...	...	...	...	...	...	...	...
20 - 24	38 120	...	...	...	...	...	...	...	...
25 - 29	36 510	...	...	...	...	...	...	...	...
30 - 34	32 812	...	...	...	...	...	...	...	...
35 - 39	24 846	...	...	...	...	...	...	...	...
40 - 44	10 443	...	...	...	...	...	...	...	...
45 - 49	1 171	...	...	...	...	...	...	...	...
50+	42	...	...	...	...	...	...	...	...
Unknown	1 346	...	...	...	...	...	...	...	...
Germany - Allemagne									
2001									
Total	134 964	53 352	34 413	32 277	10 705	2 883	830	504	-
0 - 14	696	685	7	4	-	-	-	-	-

14. Legally induced abortions by age and number of previous live births of women: latest available year, 1993 - 2002
Avortments provoqués légalement selon l'âge de la femme et selon le nombre des naissances vivantes précédentes: dernière année disponible, 1993 - 2002 (continued — suite)

(See notes at end of table. — Voir notes à la fin du tableau.)

Continent, country or area, year and age / Continent, pays ou zone, année et âge	Total	Number of previous live births - Nombre des naissances vivantes précédentes							Unknown Inconnu
		0	1	2	3	4	5	6+	
EUROPE									
Germany - Allemagne									
2001									
15 - 19	16 453	14 835	1 440	150	27	-	-	1	-
20 - 24	30 120	18 444	8 012	2 942	592	110	13	7	-
25 - 29	27 897	9 651	8 917	6 854	1 844	487	106	38	-
30 - 34	29 053	6 036	8 539	9 979	3 242	853	262	142	-
35 - 39	22 091	2 879	5 658	8 745	3 391	955	278	185	-
40 - 44	8 025	779	1 732	3 315	1 481	443	155	120	-
45 - 49	629	43	108	288	128	35	16	11	-
2002									
Total	130 387	...	...	...	...	...	...	...	...
0 - 14	761	...	...	...	...	...	...	...	...
15 - 19	15 948	...	...	...	...	...	...	...	...
20 - 24	29 923	...	...	...	...	...	...	...	...
25 - 29	26 550	...	...	...	...	...	...	...	...
30 - 34	27 068	...	...	...	...	...	...	...	...
35 - 39	21 405	...	...	...	...	...	...	...	...
40 - 44	8 045	...	...	...	...	...	...	...	...
45 - 49	687	...	...	...	...	...	...	...	...
Greece - Grèce									
1996									
Total	12 542	...	...	...	...	...	...	...	...
0 - 14	17	...	...	...	...	...	...	...	...
15 - 19	468	...	...	...	...	...	...	...	...
20 - 29	5 460	...	...	...	...	...	...	...	...
30 - 39	5 313	...	...	...	...	...	...	...	...
40 - 49	1 007	...	...	...	...	...	...	...	...
50+	41	...	...	...	...	...	...	...	...
Unknown	236	...	...	...	...	...	...	...	...
Hungary - Hongrie									
2002									
Total	56 075	15 617	13 382	14 730	7 786	2 736	1 048	776	-
0 - 14	155	150	5	-	-	-	-	-	-
15 - 19	6 337	4 962	1 138	197	38	2	-	-	-
20 - 24	12 827	5 989	3 558	1 893	1 057	256	54	20	-
25 - 29	14 353	3 135	4 108	3 853	2 089	776	234	158	-
30 - 34	11 424	886	2 705	4 078	2 213	855	401	286	-
35 - 39	7 475	251	1 304	3 181	1 648	607	242	242	-
40 - 44	2 989	70	478	1 371	671	220	112	67	-
45 - 49	253	7	55	120	53	13	4	1	-
50+	12	4	3	3	2	-	-	-	-
Unknown	250	163	28	34	15	7	1	2	-
Iceland - Islande									
2000									
Total	947	...	...	...	...	...	...	...	...
0 - 14	3	...	...	...	...	...	...	...	...
15 - 19	189	...	...	...	...	...	...	...	...
20 - 24	275	...	...	...	...	...	...	...	...
25 - 29	192	...	...	...	...	...	...	...	...
30 - 34	139	...	...	...	...	...	...	...	...
35 - 39	102	...	...	...	...	...	...	...	...
40 - 44	43	...	...	...	...	...	...	...	...
45 - 49	4	...	...	...	...	...	...	...	...
Italy - Italie									
1999									
Total	138 708	54 644	27 589	35 614	11 636	2 683	703	349	10 980
0 - 14	223	186	4	1	-	-	-	-	64
15 - 19	11 160	9 284	766	115	19	1	-	1	1 948
20 - 24	28 139	19 122	4 723	2 026	316	54	9	4	3 770

14. Legally induced abortions by age and number of previous live births of women: latest available year, 1993 - 2002

Avortments provoqués légalement selon l'âge de la femme et selon le nombre des naissances vivantes précédentes: dernière année disponible, 1993 - 2002 (continued — suite)

(See notes at end of table. — Voir notes à la fin du tableau.)

Continent, country or area, year and age / Continent, pays ou zone, année et âge	Total	Number of previous live births - Nombre des naissances vivantes précédentes							Unknown Inconnu
		0	1	2	3	4	5	6+	
EUROPE									
Italy - Italie									
1999									
25 - 29	31 438	14 185	7 584	6 564	1 412	271	57	27	2 676
30 - 34	30 961	7 508	7 335	11 161	3 314	643	176	82	1 484
35 - 39	25 101	3 267	5 155	10 753	4 191	995	258	120	724
40 - 44	10 416	914	1 829	4 487	2 124	648	176	103	270
45 - 49	974	84	143	409	229	68	24	11	12
50+	39	5	9	13	7	-	2	-	6
Unknown	257	89	41	85	24	3	1	1	26
2002									
Total	126 164	...	...	...	...	...	...	...	...
0 - 14	229	...	...	...	...	...	...	...	...
15 - 19	10 136	...	...	...	...	...	...	...	...
20 - 24	25 226	...	...	...	...	...	...	...	...
25 - 29	28 856	...	...	...	...	...	...	...	...
30 - 34	28 148	...	...	...	...	...	...	...	...
35 - 39	23 000	...	...	...	...	...	...	...	...
40 - 44	9 347	...	...	...	...	...	...	...	...
45 - 49	879	...	...	...	...	...	...	...	...
50+	40	...	...	...	...	...	...	...	...
Unknown	303	...	...	...	...	...	...	...	...
Latvia - Lettonie									
2002									
Total	14 685	...	...	...	...	...	...	...	...
0 - 14	8	...	...	...	...	...	...	...	...
15 - 19	1 518	...	...	...	...	...	...	...	...
20 - 24	3 529	...	...	...	...	...	...	...	...
25 - 29	3 459	...	...	...	...	...	...	...	...
30 - 34	2 985	...	...	...	...	...	...	...	...
35 - 39	2 078	...	...	...	...	...	...	...	...
40 - 44	988	...	...	...	...	...	...	...	...
45 - 49	107	...	...	...	...	...	...	...	...
50+	13	...	...	...	...	...	...	...	...
Lithuania - Lituanie[9]									
2002									
Total	12 495	1 458	...	...	...	...	...	...	11 037
0 - 14	3	2	...	...	...	...	...	...	1
15 - 19	860	434	...	...	...	...	...	...	426
20 - 24	2 601	585	...	...	...	...	...	...	2 016
25 - 29	3 034	271	...	...	...	...	...	...	2 763
30 - 34	2 843	143	...	...	...	...	...	...	2 700
35 - 39	2 135	17	...	...	...	...	...	...	2 118
40 - 44	931	6	...	...	...	...	...	...	925
45 - 49	88	-	...	...	...	...	...	...	88
Norway - Norvège									
2002									
Total	13 557	...	...	...	...	...	...	...	...
0 - 14	43	...	...	...	...	...	...	...	...
15 - 19	2 187	...	...	...	...	...	...	...	...
20 - 24	3 629	...	...	...	...	...	...	...	...
25 - 29	2 929	...	...	...	...	...	...	...	...
30 - 34	2 499	...	...	...	...	...	...	...	...
35 - 39	1 638	...	...	...	...	...	...	...	...
40 - 44	572	...	...	...	...	...	...	...	...
45 - 49	59	...	...	...	...	...	...	...	...
Unknown	1	...	...	...	...	...	...	...	...

14. Legally induced abortions by age and number of previous live births of women: latest available year, 1993 - 2002
Avortments provoqués légalement selon l'âge de la femme et selon le nombre des naissances vivantes précédentes: dernière année disponible, 1993 - 2002 (continued — suite)

(See notes at end of table. — Voir notes à la fin du tableau.)

Continent, country or area, year and age / Continent, pays ou zone, année et âge	Total	Number of previous live births - Nombre des naissances vivantes précédentes							Unknown Inconnu
		0	1	2	3	4	5	6+	
EUROPE									
Republic of Moldova - République de Moldova									
2002									
Total	15 739	...	...	...	...	...	...	...	...
0 - 14	33	...	...	...	...	...	...	...	...
15 - 19	1 713	...	...	...	...	...	...	...	...
20 - 34	11 159	...	...	...	...	...	...	...	...
35+	2 834	...	...	...	...	...	...	...	...
Romania - Roumanie									
2002									
Total	247 608	...	...	...	...	...	...	...	...
0 - 14	870	...	...	...	...	...	...	...	...
15 - 19	19 058	...	...	...	...	...	...	...	...
20 - 24	57 534	...	...	...	...	...	...	...	...
25 - 29	66 168	...	...	...	...	...	...	...	...
30 - 34	60 604	...	...	...	...	...	...	...	...
35 - 39	31 554	...	...	...	...	...	...	...	...
40 - 44	10 547	...	...	...	...	...	...	...	...
45 - 49	1 249	...	...	...	...	...	...	...	...
50+	24	...	...	...	...	...	...	...	...
Russian Federation - Fédération de Russie[3]									
1995									
Total	2 255 797	...	...	...	...	...	...	...	...
0 - 14	2 217	...	...	...	...	...	...	...	...
15 - 19	233 166	...	...	...	...	...	...	...	...
20 - 34	1 551 440	...	...	...	...	...	...	...	...
35+	468 974	...	...	...	...	...	...	...	...
Serbia and Montenegro - Serbie-et-Montenegro[6]									
1998									
Total	58 739	6 941	10 691	31 998	7 022	2 085	...	...	2
0 - 14	10	...	...	...	...	...	...	...	...
15 - 19	9 725	...	...	...	...	...	...	...	...
20 - 24	28 223	...	...	...	...	...	...	...	...
25 - 29	19 649	...	...	...	...	...	...	...	...
30 - 34	1 121	...	...	...	...	...	...	...	...
35 - 39	4	...	...	...	...	...	...	...	...
40+	7	...	...	...	...	...	...	...	...
Slovakia - Slovaquie									
2002									
Total	17 382	4 539	4 204	5 786	1 905	606	201	141	-
0 - 14	10	10	-	-	-	-	-	-	-
15 - 19	1 622	1 346	222	44	10	-	-	-	-
20 - 24	3 762	1 868	1 184	553	113	34	9	1	-
25 - 29	4 489	915	1 433	1 549	395	120	50	27	-
30 - 34	3 555	241	777	1 692	569	181	55	40	-
35 - 39	2 716	114	454	1 340	525	186	59	38	-
40 - 44	1 140	38	125	562	271	84	27	33	-
45 - 49	86	6	9	45	22	1	1	2	-
50+	2	1	-	1	-	-	-	-	-
Slovenia - Slovénie									
2002									
Total	7 327	2 164	1 659	2 737	605	131	15	15	1
0 - 14	2	2	-	-	-	-	-	-	-
15 - 19	584	555	26	3	-	-	-	-	-
20 - 24	1 436	948	346	125	16	1	-	-	-
25 - 29	1 471	439	454	489	73	14	-	2	-
30 - 34	1 540	142	375	819	160	33	5	5	1

14. Legally induced abortions by age and number of previous live births of women: latest available year, 1993 - 2002
Avortments provoqués légalement selon l'âge de la femme et selon le nombre des naissances vivantes précédentes: dernière année disponible, 1993 - 2002 (continued — suite)

(See notes at end of table. — Voir notes à la fin du tableau.)

Continent, country or area, year and age / Continent, pays ou zone, année et âge	Total	Number of previous live births - Nombre des naissances vivantes précédentes							
		0	1	2	3	4	5	6+	Unknown Inconnu
EUROPE									
Slovenia - Slovénie									
2002									
35 - 39	1 527	59	317	852	235	51	6	7	-
40 - 44	694	13	129	406	110	31	4	1	-
45 - 49	65	5	9	39	11	1	-	-	-
50+	8	1	3	4	-	-	-	-	-
Spain - Espagne[10]									
1994									
Total	47 832	24 926	8 768	9 082	3 237	1 096	612	...	111
0 - 14	97	94	2	1	-	-	-	...	-
15 - 19	6 598	6 134	404	44	7	2	2	...	5
20 - 24	12 772	10 019	1 949	649	105	23	5	...	22
25 - 29	10 594	5 461	2 616	1 849	477	113	46	...	32
30 - 34	8 613	2 252	2 157	2 905	884	261	126	...	28
35 - 39	6 259	764	1 227	2 581	1 074	384	213	...	16
40 - 44	2 627	191	393	977	602	272	184	...	8
45+	272	11	20	76	88	41	36	...	-
Unknown	-	-	-	-	-	-	-	...	-
2000									
Total	63 756	...	...	...	...	...	...	...	...
0 - 14	157	...	...	...	...	...	...	...	...
15 - 19	9 047	...	...	...	...	...	...	...	...
20 - 24	18 370	...	...	...	...	...	...	...	...
25 - 29	14 090	...	...	...	...	...	...	...	...
30 - 34	10 979	...	...	...	...	...	...	...	...
35 - 39	7 810	...	...	...	...	...	...	...	...
40 - 44	3 035	...	...	...	...	...	...	...	...
45 - 49	268	...	...	...	...	...	...	...	...
Sweden - Suède[11]									
2002									
Total	33 365	16 730	5 271	6 757	2 859	875	250	130	493
0 - 14	263	258	-	-	-	-	-	-	5
15 - 19	6 240	5 888	191	7	3	-	-	-	151
20 - 24	7 614	5 781	1 253	386	56	2	-	1	135
25 - 29	6 416	2 978	1 504	1 369	384	71	18	5	87
30 - 34	5 895	1 221	1 208	2 207	872	260	55	17	55
35 - 39	4 973	473	826	2 030	1 075	374	99	56	40
40 - 44	1 771	116	268	696	414	149	68	43	17
45 - 49	187	10	21	62	55	19	10	8	2
50+	1	1	-	-	-	-	-	-	-
Unknown	5	4	-	-	-	-	-	-	1
United Kingdom - Royaume-Uni[12]									
2000									
Total	197 366	105 328	37 645	33 532	13 982	4 683	1 414	753	29
0 - 14	1 170	1 165	4	1	-	-	-	-	-
15 - 19	40 225	35 254	4 393	528	40	4	-	-	6
20 - 24	53 590	35 263	11 732	5 183	1 150	222	25	9	6
25 - 29	42 680	20 273	9 640	8 295	3 212	953	231	71	5
30 - 34	31 928	8 925	7 004	9 504	4 339	1 491	455	205	5
35 - 39	20 684	3 562	3 711	7 438	3 771	1 433	485	279	5
40 - 44	6 526	794	1 081	2 375	1 359	542	203	171	1
45 - 49	490	62	66	189	108	36	14	15	-
50+	25	4	4	9	2	2	1	3	-
Unknown	48	26	10	10	1	-	-	-	1
2001									
Total	197 913	...	...	...	...	...	...	...	...
0 - 14	1 157	...	...	...	...	...	...	...	...
15 - 19	40 387	...	...	...	...	...	...	...	...

14. Legally induced abortions by age and number of previous live births of women: latest available year, 1993 - 2002
Avortments provoqués légalement selon l'âge de la femme et selon le nombre des naissances vivantes précédentes: dernière année disponible, 1993 - 2002 (continued — suite)

(See notes at end of table. — Voir notes à la fin du tableau.)

Continent, country or area, year and age / Continent, pays ou zone, année et âge	Total	Number of previous live births - Nombre des naissances vivantes précédentes							Unknown Inconnu
		0	1	2	3	4	5	6+	
EUROPE									
United Kingdom - Royaume-Uni[12]									
2001									
20 - 24	54 878	...	...	...	...	...	...	...	...
25 - 29	41 126	...	...	...	...	...	...	...	...
30 - 34	31 921	...	...	...	...	...	...	...	...
35 - 39	21 096	...	...	...	...	...	...	...	...
40 - 44	6 833	...	...	...	...	...	...	...	...
45 - 49	513	...	...	...	...	...	...	...	...
Unknown	2	...	...	...	...	...	...	...	...
OCEANIA — OCEANIE									
New Zealand - Nouvelle-Zélande									
2000									
Total	16 410	7 682	3 148	3 111	1 469	640	227	133	-
0 - 14	66	66	...	-	-	-	-	-	-
15 - 19	3 240	2 839	340	55	6	-	-	-	-
20 - 24	4 728	2 699	1 096	675	211	39	7	1	-
25 - 29	3 450	1 213	798	822	394	164	43	16	-
30 - 34	2 555	569	532	762	385	198	68	41	-
35 - 39	1 730	239	290	563	345	169	74	50	-
40 - 44	593	54	84	216	122	63	32	22	-
45 - 49	48	3	8	18	6	7	3	3	-
2002									
Total	17 380	8 547	3 223	3 121	1 516	602	221	150	-
0 - 14	78	78	-	-	-	-	-	-	-
15 - 19	3 602	3 182	355	54	11	-	-	-	-
20 - 24	5 124	3 090	1 107	660	209	45	10	3	-
25 - 29	3 450	1 301	783	767	395	132	51	21	-
30 - 34	2 676	593	572	798	408	191	74	40	-
35 - 39	1 715	244	299	585	329	156	51	51	-
40 - 44	686	51	99	240	155	76	31	34	-
45+	49	8	8	17	9	2	4	1	-

GENERAL NOTES - NOTES GENERALES

For method of evaluation and limitations of data, see Technical Notes for this table. — Pour la méthode d'évaluation et les insuffisances des données, voir Notes techniques pour ce tableau.

FOOTNOTES - NOTES

[1] Data refer to abortions granted for medical reasons by the Comision Multidisciplinaria Nacional de Aborto Terapéutico. - Les données se réfèrent aux avortements autorisés pour des raisons médicales par la Comision Multidisciplinaria Nacional de Aborto Terapéutico.

[2] Column '3' including '4' and over. - Colonne '3' compris 4 plus.

[3] Data as reported by national statistical authorities; they may differ from data presented in other tables. - Les données comme elles ont été déclarées par l'institut national de la statistique; elles peuvent être différentes de ceux présentées dans autre tableaux.

[4] Including data for East Jerusalem and Israeli residents in certain other territories under occupation by Israeli military forces since June 1967. - Y compris les données pour Jérusalem-Est et les résidents israéliens dans certains autres territoires occupés depuis 1967 par les forces armées israéliennes.

[5] Data refer to Japanese nationals in Japan only. - Les données se raportent aux nationaux japonais au Japon seulement.

[6] Column '4' includes also data for '5+'. - Colonne '4' comprenne aussi les données pour '5+'.

[7] Column '4' includes data for both '4' and '5'. - Colonne '4' comprenne les données pour l'ensemble de '4' et '5'.

[8] Excluding Faeroe Islands and Greenland. - Non compris les Iles Féroé et Gröenland.

[9] Data refer to requested abortions only and exclude a abortions due to therapeutic reasons. - Les données se rapportent seulement aux interruptions volontaires de grossesse et excluent les avortements effectués pour des rasions thérapeutiques.

[10] Column '5' including '6' and over. - Colonne '5' compris 6 plus.

[11] Abortion by previous deliveries of mother rather than previous live births of mother. - Avortements selon les accouchements précédents de la mère plutôt que selon les naissances vivantes de la mère.

[12] For residents only. - Pour les résidents seulement.

Table 15

Table 15 presents infant deaths and infant mortality rates by urban/rural residence for as many years as possible between 1998 and 2002.

Description of variables: Infant deaths are deaths of live-born infants under one year of age.

Statistics on the number of infant deaths are obtained from civil registers unless otherwise noted. Infant mortality rates are, in most instances, calculated from data on registered infant deaths and registered live births for a country or area where civil registration is considered reliable (that is, with an estimated completeness of 90 per cent or more).

The urban/rural classification of infant deaths is that provided by each country or area; it is presumed to be based on the national census definitions of urban population that have been set forth at the end of the technical notes of table 6.

Rate computation: Infant mortality rates are the annual number of deaths of infants under one year of age per 1 000 live births (as shown in table 9) in the same year.

Rates by urban/rural residence are the annual number of infant deaths, in the appropriate urban or rural category, per 1 000 corresponding live births (as shown in table 9). These rates have been calculated by the Statistics Division of the United Nations.

Rates presented in this table have been limited to those for countries or areas having at least a total of 100 infant deaths in a given year and for which the quality code is represented by a C or a symbol |.

Reliability of data: Each country or area has been asked to indicate the estimated completeness of the infant deaths recorded in its civil register. These national assessments are indicated by the quality codes C, U and | that appear in the first column of this table.

C indicates that the data are estimated to be virtually complete, that is, representing at least 90 per cent of the infant deaths occurring each year, while U indicates that data are estimated to be incomplete that is, representing less than 90 per cent of the infant deaths occurring each year. The code I indicates that the source of data is not civil registration, but is still considered reliable. The code ... indicates that no information was provided regarding completeness.

Data from civil registers that are reported as incomplete or of unknown completeness (coded U or ...) are considered unreliable. They appear in italics in this table; rates are not computed for data so coded.

Limitations: Statistics on infant deaths are subject to the same qualifications as have been set forth for vital statistics in general and death statistics in particular as discussed in section 4 of the Technical Notes.

The reliability of the data, an indication of which is described above, is an important factor in considering the limitations. In addition, some infant deaths are tabulated by date of registration and not by date of occurrence; these have been indicated by a plus sign (+). Whenever the lag between the date of occurrence and date of registration is prolonged and, therefore, a large proportion of the infant-death registrations are delayed, infant-death statistics for any given year may be seriously affected.

Another factor that limits international comparability is the practice of some countries or areas not to include in infant-death statistics infants who were born alive but died before the registration of the birth or within the first 24 hours of life, thus underestimating the total number of infant deaths. Statistics of this type are footnoted.

The method of reckoning age at death for infants may also introduce non-comparability. If year alone, rather than completed minutes, hours, days and months elapsed since birth, is used to calculate age at time of death, many of the infants who died during the eleventh month of life and some of those who died at younger ages will be classified as having completed one year of age and thus be excluded. The effect would be to underestimate the number of infant deaths. Information on this factor is given in footnotes when known. Reckoning of infant age is further discussed in the technical notes for table 16.

In addition, infant mortality rates are subject to the limitations of the data on live births with which they have been calculated. These have been set forth in the technical notes for table 9.

Because the two components of the infant mortality rate, infant deaths in the numerator and live births in the denominator, are both obtained from systems of civil registration, the limitations which affect live-birth statistics are very similar to those which have been mentioned above in connection with the infant-death statistics. It is important to consider the reliability of the data (the completeness of registration) and the method of tabulation (by date of occurrence or by date of registration) of live-birth statistics as well as infant-death statistics, both of which are used to calculate infant mortality rates. The quality code and use of italics to indicate unreliable data presented in this table refer only to infant deaths. Similarly, the indication of the basis of tabulation (the use of the symbol (+) to indicate data tabulated by date of registration) presented in this table also refers only to infant deaths. Table 9 provides the corresponding information for live births.

If the registration of infant deaths is more complete than the registration of live births, then infant mortality rates would be biased upwards. If, however, the registration of live births is more complete than registration of infant deaths, infant mortality rates would be biased downwards. If both infant deaths and live births are tabulated by registration, it should be noted that deaths tend to be more promptly reported than births.

Infant mortality rates may be seriously affected by the practice of some countries or areas of not considering infants that were born alive but died before the registration of the birth or within the first 24 hours of life as live-birth and subsequently infant death. Although this practice results in both the number of infant deaths in the numerator and the number of live births in the denominator being underestimated, its impact is greater on the numerator of the infant mortality rate. As a result this practice causes infant mortality rates to be biased downwards.

Infant mortality rates will also be underestimated if the method of reckoning age at death results in an underestimation of the number of infant deaths. This point has been discussed above.

Because of all these factors care should be taken in comparing and rank ordering infant mortality rates.

With respect to the method of calculating infant mortality rates used in this table, it should be noted that no adjustment was made to take account of the fact that a proportion of the infant deaths that occur during a given year are deaths of infants that were born during the preceding year and hence are not taken from the universe of births used to compute the rates. However, unless the number of live births or infant deaths is changing rapidly, the error involved is insignificant.

Estimated rates based directly on the results of sample surveys are subject to considerable error as a result of omissions in reporting infant deaths or as a result of erroneous reporting of those infant deaths that occurred outside the period of reference. However, such rates do have the advantage of having a "built-in" and corresponding base.

The comparability of data by urban/rural residence is affected by the national definitions of urban and rural used in tabulating these data. It is assumed, in the absence of specific information to the contrary, that the definitions of urban and rural used in connection with the national population census were also used in the compilation of the vital statistics for each country or area. However, it cannot be excluded that, for a given country or area, different definitions of urban and rural are used for the vital statistics data and the population census data respectively. When known, the definitions of urban used in national population censuses are presented at the end of the technical notes for table 6. As discussed in detail in the technical notes for table 6, these definitions vary considerably from one country or area to another.

Urban/rural differentials in infant mortality rates may also be affected by whether the infant deaths and live births have been tabulated in terms of place of occurrence or place of usual residence. This problem is discussed in more detail in section 4.1.4.1 of the Technical Notes.

Earlier data: Infant deaths and infant mortality rates have been shown in previous issues of the *Demographic Yearbook*. For more information on specific topics and years for which data are reported, readers should consult the Historical Index.

Tableau 15

Le tableau 15 présente des données sur les décès d'enfants de moins d'un an et les taux de mortalité infantile selon le lieu de résidence (zone urbaine ou rurale) pour le plus grand nombre d'années possible entre 1998 et 2002.

Description des variables : Les chiffres se rapportent aux décès d'enfants de moins d'un an.

Sauf indication contraire, les statistiques concernant le nombre de décès d'enfants de moins d'un an sont établies à partir des registres de l'état civil. Dans la plupart des cas, les taux de mortalité infantile sont calculés à partir des données relatives aux décès enregistrés d'enfants de moins d'un an et aux naissances vivantes enregistrées dans un pays ou une zone lorsque les registres de l'état civil sont jugés fiables (exhaustivité estimée à 90 p. 100 ou plus).

La classification des décès d'enfants de moins d'un an selon le lieu de résidence (zone urbaine ou rurale) est celle qui a été communiquée par chaque pays ou zone ; on part du principe qu'elle repose sur les définitions de la population urbaine utilisées pour les recensements nationaux, telles qu'elles sont reproduites à la fin des notes techniques du tableau 6.

Calcul des taux : Les taux de mortalité infantile représentent le nombre annuel de décès d'enfants de moins d'un an pour 1 000 naissances vivantes (fréquences du tableau 9) survenues pendant la même année.

Les taux selon le lieu de résidence (zone urbaine ou rurale) représentent le nombre annuel de décès d'enfants de moins d'un an, classés selon la catégorie urbaine ou rurale appropriée pour 1 000 naissances vivantes survenues parmi la population correspondante (fréquences du tableau 9). Ces taux ont été calculés par la Division de statistique de l'ONU.

Les taux présentés dans ce tableau se rapportent seulement aux pays ou zones où l'on a enregistré au moins un total de 100 décès d'enfants de moins d'un an au cours d'une année donnée et pour lesquels le code de qualité est soit 'C', soit 'I'.

Fiabilité des données : Il a été demandé à chaque pays ou zone d'indiquer le degré estimatif de complétude des données sur les décès d'enfants de moins d'un an figurant dans ses registres d'état civil. Ces évaluations nationales sont signalées par les codes de qualité 'C', 'U' et 'I' qui apparaissent dans la deuxième colonne du tableau.

La lettre 'C' indique que les données sont jugées à peu près complètes, c'est-à-dire qu'elles représentent au moins 90 p. 100 des décès d'enfants de moins d'un an survenus chaque année ; la lettre 'U' signifie que les données sont jugées incomplètes, c'est-à-dire qu'elles représentent moins de 90 p.100 des décès d'enfants de moins d'un an survenus chaque année. Le symbole 'I' indique que la source des données n'est pas un registre de l'état civil, mais est quand même considérée fiable. Le code '...' dénote qu'aucun renseignement n'a été communiqué quant à la complétude des données.

Les données provenant des registres de l'état civil qui sont déclarées incomplètes ou dont le degré de complétude n'est pas connu (code 'U' ou '...') sont jugées douteuses. Elles apparaissent en italique dans le tableau ; les taux, dans ces cas là, n'ont pas été calculés.

Insuffisance des données : Les statistiques des décès d'enfants de moins d'un an appellent toutes les réserves qui ont été formulées à propos des statistiques de l'état civil en général et des statistiques concernant les décès en particulier (voir la section 4 des Notes techniques).

La fiabilité des données, au sujet de laquelle des indications ont été fournies plus haut, est un facteur important. Il faut également tenir compte du fait que, dans certains cas, les données relatives aux décès d'enfants de moins d'un an sont exploitées selon la date de l'enregistrement et non la date de l'événement ; ces cas ont été signalés par le signe '+'. Chaque fois que le décalage entre l'événement et son enregistrement est grand et qu'une forte proportion des décès d'enfants de moins d'un an fait l'objet d'un enregistrement tardif, les statistiques des décès d'enfants de moins d'un an pour une année donnée peuvent être considérablement faussées.

Un autre facteur qui nuit à la comparabilité internationale est la pratique de certains pays ou zones qui consiste à ne pas inclure dans les statistiques des décès d'enfants de moins d'un an les enfants nés vivants mais décédés avant l'enregistrement de leur naissance ou dans les 24 heures qui ont suivi la naissance, pratique qui conduit à sous-estimer le nombre total de décès d'enfants de moins d'un an. Quand pareil facteur a joué, cela a été signalé en note.

Les méthodes appliquées pour calculer l'âge au moment du décès peuvent également nuire à la comparabilité des données. Si l'on utilise à cet effet l'année seulement, et non pas les minutes, heures, jours et mois qui se sont écoulés depuis la naissance, de nombreux enfants décédés au cours du onzième mois qui a suivi leur naissance et certains enfants décédés encore plus jeunes seront classés comme décédés à un an révolu et donc exclus des données. Cette pratique conduit à sous-estimer le nombre de décès d'enfants de moins d'un an. Les renseignements dont on dispose sur ce facteur apparaissent en note à la fin du tableau. La question du calcul de l'âge au moment du décès est examinée plus en détail dans les notes techniques se rapportant au tableau 16.

Les taux de mortalité infantile appellent en outre toutes les réserves qui ont été formulées à propos des statistiques des naissances vivantes qui ont servi à leur calcul (voir à ce sujet les notes techniques relatives au tableau 9).

Les deux composantes du taux de mortalité infantile - décès d'enfants de moins d'un an au numérateur et naissances vivantes au dénominateur - étant obtenues à partir des registres de l'état civil, les statistiques des naissances vivantes appellent des réserves presque identiques à celles qui ont été formulées plus haut à propos des statistiques des décès d'enfants de moins d'un an. Il importe de prendre en considération la fiabilité des données (complétude de l'enregistrement) et le mode d'exploitation (selon la date de l'événement ou selon la date de l'enregistrement) dans le cas des statistiques des naissances vivantes tout comme dans le cas de celles des décès d'enfants de moins d'un an, puisque les unes et les autres servent au calcul des taux de mortalité infantile. Dans le tableau 15, le code de qualité et l'emploi de caractères italiques pour signaler les données moins sûres ne concernent que les décès d'enfants de moins d'un an. L'indication du mode d'exploitation des données (emploi du signe '+' pour signaler les données exploitées selon la date de l'enregistrement) ne porte là aussi que sur les décès d'enfants de moins d'un an. Le tableau 9 contient les renseignements correspondants pour les naissances vivantes.

Si l'enregistrement des décès d'enfants de moins d'un an est plus complet que l'enregistrement des naissances vivantes, les taux de mortalité infantile seront entachés d'une erreur par excès. En revanche, si l'enregistrement des naissances vivantes est plus complet que l'enregistrement des décès d'enfants de moins d'un an, les taux de mortalité infantile seront entachés d'une erreur par défaut. Si les décès d'enfants de moins d'un an et les naissances vivantes sont exploitées selon la date de l'enregistrement, il convient de ne pas perdre de vue que les décès sont, en règle générale, déclarés plus rapidement que les naissances.

Les taux de mortalité infantile peuvent être gravement faussés par la pratique de certains pays ou zones qui consiste à ne pas classer dans les naissances vivantes et ensuite dans les décès d'enfants de moins d'un an les enfants nés vivants mais décédés soit avant l'enregistrement de leur naissance, soit dans les 24 heures qui ont suivi la naissance. Cette pratique conduit à sous-estimer aussi bien le nombre des décès d'enfants de moins d'un an, qui constitue le numérateur, que le nombre des naissances vivantes, qui constitue le dénominateur, mais c'est pour le numérateur du taux de mortalité infantile que la distorsion est la plus marquée. Ce système a pour effet d'introduire une erreur par défaut dans les taux de mortalité infantile.

Les taux de mortalité infantile seront également sous-estimés si la méthode utilisée pour calculer l'âge au moment du décès conduit à sous-estimer le nombre de décès d'enfants de moins d'un an. Cette question a été examinée plus haut.

Tous ces facteurs sont importants et il faut donc en tenir compte lorsque l'on compare et classe les taux de mortalité infantile.

En ce qui concerne la méthode de calcul des taux de mortalité infantile utilisée dans le tableau, il convient de noter qu'il n'a pas été tenu compte du fait qu'une partie des décès survenus pendant une année donnée sont des décès d'enfants nés l'année précédente et ne correspondent donc pas à l'ensemble des naissances utilisé pour le calcul des taux. Toutefois, l'erreur n'est pas grave, à moins que le nombre des naissances vivantes ou des décès d'enfants de moins d'un an ne varie rapidement.

Les taux estimatifs fondés directement sur les résultats d'enquêtes par sondage comportent des possibilités d'erreurs considérables dues soit à des omissions dans les déclarations de décès d'enfants de moins d'un an, soit au fait que l'on a déclaré à tort des décès survenus en réalité hors de la période considérée. Ils présentent aussi un avantage puisque le chiffre des naissances vivantes utilisé comme base est connu par définition et rigoureusement correspondant.

La comparabilité des données selon le lieu de résidence (zone urbaine ou rurale) peut être limitée par les définitions nationales des termes «urbain» et «rural» utilisées pour la mise en tableaux de ces données. En l'absence d'indications contraires, on a supposé que les mêmes définitions avaient servi pour le recensement national de la population et pour l'établissement des statistiques de l'état civil pour chaque pays ou zone. Toutefois, il n'est pas exclu que, pour une zone ou un pays donné, des définitions différentes aient été retenues. Les définitions du terme «urbain» utilisées pour les recensements nationaux de population ont été présentées à la fin des notes techniques du tableau 6 lorsqu'elles étaient connues. Comme on l'a précisé dans les notes techniques relatives au tableau 6, ces définitions varient considérablement d'un pays ou d'une zone à l'autre.

La différence entre les taux de mortalité infantile pour les zones urbaines et rurales pourra aussi être faussée selon que les décès d'enfants de moins d'un an et les naissances vivantes auront été classés d'après le lieu de l'événement ou le lieu de résidence habituel. Ce problème est examiné plus en détail à la section 4.1.4.1 des Notes techniques.

Données publiées antérieurement : Des statistiques concernant les décès d'enfants de moins d'un an et les taux de mortalité infantile ont déjà été présentées dans des éditions antérieures de l'*Annuaire démographique*. Pour plus de précisions concernant les années et les sujets pour lesquels des données ont été publiées, se reporter à l'index historique.

15. Infant deaths and infant mortality rates, by urban/rural residence: 1998 - 2002
Décès d'enfants de moins d'un an et taux de mortalité infantile, selon la résidence, urbaine/rurale: 1998 - 2002

(See notes at end of table. — Voir notes à la fin du tableau.)

Continent, country or area and urban/rural residence / Continent, pays ou zone et résidence, urbaine/rurale	Code[1]	Number - Nombre					Rate - Taux				
		1998	1999	2000	2001	2002	1998	1999	2000	2001	2002
AFRICA — AFRIQUE											
Algeria - Algérie[2,3]											
Total	U	*33 093*	*21 798*	*20 291*	*21 622*	*19 850*	...	...	...	...	...
Benin - Bénin[4]											
Total	I	24 422	...	...	25 001	...	93.7	...	...	94.8	...
Urban-Urbaine	I	9 402	...	...	...	...	...	...	...	...	...
Rural-Rurale	I	15 020	...	...	...	...	...	...	...	...	...
Botswana[4]											
Total	I	...	...	...	1 576	...	...	...	...	29.3	...
Burundi[4]											
Total	I	45 684	...	...	...	...	157.0	...	...	...	...
Côte d'Ivoire[4]											
Total	I	44 045	...	47 000	...	...	71.7	...	71.7	...	...
Egypt - Égypte											
Total	C	49 168	49 765	...	...	...	29.1	29.4	...	...	...
Urban-Urbaine	C	18 083	19 265	...	...	...	26.4	29.3	...	...	...
Rural-Rurale	C	31 085	30 500	...	...	...	31.0	29.5	...	...	...
Ethiopia - Éthiopie											
Total	...	...	*232 660*	...	...	...	...	...	...	...	...
Libyan Arab Jamahiriya - Jamahiriya arabe libyenne											
Total	U	...	...	*2 155*	*2 568*	...	...	...	...	...	...
Malawi[5]											
Total	I	44 928	...	...	...	...	90.5	...	...	...	...
Mauritius - Maurice											
Total	+C	376	396	322	282	297	19.3	19.5	15.9	14.3	14.9
Urban-Urbaine	+C	145	149	127	114	102	18.4	18.3	15.9	14.7	12.9
Rural-Rurale	+C	231	247	195	168	195	20.0	20.3	16.0	14.1	16.2
Morocco - Maroc[6]											
Total	U	*9 061*	*8 885*	...	...	...	...	...	...	...	...
Urban-Urbaine	U	*3 160*	*2 867*	...	...	...	...	...	...	...	...
Rural-Rurale	U	*5 888*	*5 998*	...	...	...	...	...	...	...	...
Mozambique[4]											
Total	I	...	...	...	99 164	...	...	...	...	131.6	...
Réunion[2]											
Total	C	111	84	88	89	...	8.2	...	...	...	...
Saint Helena ex. dep. - Sainte-Hélène sans dép.											
Total	C	1	-	-	-	...	...	...	...	...	...
Seychelles											
Total	+C	12	15	15	19	*26	...	...	...	...	...
Tunisia - Tunisie											
Total	U	*3 098*	*4 200*	...	...	...	...	...	...	...	...
AMERICA, NORTH — AMERIQUE DU NORD											
Anguilla											
Total	+C	-	1	1	-	2	...	...	...	...	...
Aruba											
Total	+U	...	...	...	4	...	...	...	...	...	...
Bahamas											
Total	C	59	48	52	37	...	...	...	...	...	...
Barbados - Barbade											
Total	+C	...	...	63	...	...	...	...	...	...	...
Belize											
Total	U	*144*	*123*	*155*	*120*	*145*	...	...	...	...	...
Bermuda - Bermudes											
Total	C	-	2	-	3	-	...	...	...	...	...
British Virgin Islands - Îles Vierges britanniques											
Total	+C	...	...	1	...	...	...	...	...	...	...

15. Infant deaths and infant mortality rates, by urban/rural residence: 1998 - 2002
Décès d'enfants de moins d'un an et taux de mortalité infantile, selon la résidence, urbaine/rurale: 1998 - 2002
(continued — suite)

(See notes at end of table. — Voir notes à la fin du tableau.)

Continent, country or area and urban/rural residence / Continent, pays ou zone et résidence, urbaine/rurale	Code[1]	Number - Nombre					Rate - Taux				
		1998	1999	2000	2001	2002	1998	1999	2000	2001	2002
AMERICA, NORTH — AMERIQUE DU NORD											
Canada[7]											
Total	C	1 811	1 776	1 737	1 739	1 762	5.3	5.3	5.3	5.2	5.4
Costa Rica											
Total	C	970	925	798	827	793	12.6	11.8	10.2	10.8	11.1
Cuba[6]											
Total	C	1 070	977	1 039	861	922	7.1	6.5	7.2	6.2	6.5
Urban-Urbaine	C	800	747	...	...	...	7.3	6.9	...	...	...
Rural-Rurale	C	270	230	...	...	...	6.4	5.5	...	...	...
Dominica - Dominique											
Total	C	...	...	...	24	...	...	...	...	...	...
Dominican Republic - République dominicaine											
Total	+U	1 972	1 966	2 116	...	...	...	...	...	...	...
El Salvador											
Total	C	2 380	1 768	1 678	1 682	1 284	15.0	11.5	11.2	12.2	9.9
Urban-Urbaine	C	1 513	1 114	1 079	1 091	821	14.8	11.1	11.6	13.1	10.6
Rural-Rurale	C	867	654	599	591	463	15.5	12.3	10.5	10.8	9.0
Greenland - Groenland											
Total	C	25	16	...	...	...	...	...	...	...	...
Urban-Urbaine	C	25	16	...	...	...	...	...	...	...	...
Rural-Rurale	C	-	-	...	...	...	...	...	...	...	...
Grenada - Grenade											
Total	+C	37	29	27	33	...	...	...	...	...	...
Guadeloupe											
Total	C	65	55	57	49	45	...	...	...	...	...
Guatemala											
Total	C	15 414	13 161	13 247	...	...	31.5	36.5	31.1	...	...
Jamaica - Jamaïque											
Total	+C	480	...	...	...	...	8.4	...	...	...	...
Martinique											
Total	C	52	41	40	43	33	...	...	...	...	...
Mexico - Mexique[6]											
Total	C	42 183	40 283	38 621	35 911	...	15.8	14.5	13.8	13.0	...
Urban-Urbaine	C	30 818	29 940	29 135	27 056	...	17.3	16.6	16.1	15.5	...
Rural-Rurale	C	11 041	10 054	9 163	8 503	...	14.4	12.8	12.0	11.4	...
Nicaragua											
Total	+U	2 552	1 768	2 075	1 933	2 217	...	...	...	...	...
Urban-Urbaine	+U	1 503	1 004	1 140	1 114	1 309	...	...	...	...	...
Rural-Rurale	+U	1 049	764	935	819	908	...	...	...	...	...
Panama											
Total	U	1 047	1 005	1 081	1 053	...	...	...	...	...	...
Urban-Urbaine	U	483	490	...	...	...	...	...	...	...	...
Rural-Rurale	U	564	515	...	...	...	...	...	...	...	...
Puerto Rico - Porto Rico[6]											
Total	C	637	632	589	515	516	10.5	10.6	9.9	9.2	9.8
Urban-Urbaine	C	...	357	327	311	...	...	11.7	10.7	10.6	...
Rural-Rurale	C	...	274	262	204	...	...	9.4	9.0	7.7	...
Saint Kitts and Nevis - Saint-Kitts-et-Nevis											
Total	+C	24	...	...	...	...	...	...	...	...	...
Saint Lucia - Sainte-Lucie											
Total	C	48	42	38	37	36	...	...	...	...	...
Urban-Urbaine	C	14	...	...	...	...	...	...	...	...	...
Rural-Rurale	C	34	...	...	...	...	...	...	...	...	...
Saint Vincent and the Grenadines - Saint Vincent-et-les Grenadines											
Total	+C	47	47	35	39	36	...	...	...	...	...
United States - États-Unis											
Total	C	28 371	27 937	28 035	27 568	*27 977	7.2	7.1	6.9	6.8	*7.0

15. Infant deaths and infant mortality rates, by urban/rural residence: 1998 - 2002
Décès d'enfants de moins d'un an et taux de mortalité infantile, selon la résidence, urbaine/rurale: 1998 - 2002
(continued — suite)

(See notes at end of table. — Voir notes à la fin du tableau.)

Continent, country or area and urban/rural residence Continent, pays ou zone et résidence, urbaine/rurale	Code[1]	Number - Nombre					Rate - Taux				
		1998	1999	2000	2001	2002	1998	1999	2000	2001	2002
AMERICA, SOUTH — AMERIQUE DU SUD											
Argentina - Argentine											
Total	C	13 082	12 120	11 649	11 111	11 703	19.1	17.6	16.6	16.3	16.8
Bolivia - Bolivie											
Total	U	16 942	16 492	16 042	...		...	...	...	...	...
Brazil - Brésil[8]											
Total	U	64 702	58 767	53 097	47 171	45 243	...	...	...	...	...
Chile - Chili											
Total	C	2 793	2 654	2 336	2 159	1 964	10.9	10.6	9.4	8.8	8.2
Urban-Urbaine	C	2 345	2 252	1 991	1 855	1 715	10.5	10.3	9.1	8.6	8.0
Rural-Rurale	C	448	402	345	304	249	13.6	12.5	11.3	10.1	9.6
Colombia - Colombie[6,9]											
Total	U	14 178	14 619	15 367	14 430	*12 096	...	...	...	...	...
Urban-Urbaine	U	10 466	10 234	11 014	10 458	*8 538	...	...	...	...	...
Rural-Rurale	U	3 007	3 299	3 354	3 163	*2 839	...	...	...	...	...
Ecuador - Équateur[10]											
Total	U	5 186	5 372	5 480	4 800	4 530	...	...	...	...	...
Urban-Urbaine	U	3 740	3 885	4 020	3 544	3 420	...	...	...	...	...
Rural-Rurale	U	1 446	1 487	1 460	1 256	1 110	...	...	...	...	...
French Guiana - Guyane française											
Total	C	52	63	64	70	52	...	...	...	...	...
Peru - Pérou[4,8,11]											
Total	I	26 603	25 098	23 681	22 455	...	41.0	39.0	37.2	35.6	...
Suriname											
Total	C	163	227	156	...	...	15.9	22.4	15.9	...	...
Uruguay											
Total	C	910	776	742	721	708	16.6	14.4	14.1	13.9	13.6
Venezuela[8]											
Total	C	9 871	9 030	8 524	8 158	7 645	19.7	17.1	15.7	15.4	15.5
ASIA — ASIE											
Armenia - Arménie[12]											
Total	C	580	572	540	497	...	14.7	15.7	15.8	15.5	...
Urban-Urbaine	C	428	373	357	...	...	17.4	16.6	16.7	...	...
Rural-Rurale	C	152	199	183	...	...	10.2	14.2	14.2	...	...
Azerbaijan - Azerbaïdjan[12]											
Total	+C	2 061	1 943	1 501	1 382	1 422	16.6	16.5	12.8	12.5	12.8
Urban-Urbaine	+C	842	780	642	558	554	15.8	15.6	12.9	11.2	11.1
Rural-Rurale	+C	1 219	1 163	859	824	868	17.2	17.2	12.8	13.6	14.2
Bahrain - Bahreïn											
Total	U	111	129	117	117	94	...	...	...	...	...
Brunei Darussalam - Brunéi Darussalam											
Total	+C	48	44	55	50	62	...	...	...	...	...
China: Hong Kong SAR - Chine: Hong Kong RAS											
Total	C	167	157	162	124	*110	3.2	3.1	3.0	2.6	*2.3
China: Macao SAR - Chine: Macao RAS											
Total	C	27	17	11	14	*11	...	...	...	...	...
Cyprus - Chypre[13]											
Total	C	62	51	47	40	37	...	...	...	...	...
Georgia - Géorgie[12]											
Total	C	710	714	600	478	...	15.2	17.5	14.9	11.8	...
Urban-Urbaine	C	...	642	550	439	...	...	24.8	21.6	17.5	...
Rural-Rurale	C	...	72	50	39	...	...	4.8	3.4	2.5	...
India - Inde[14]											
Total	...	...	...	...	...	...	72.0	70.0	68.0	66.0	63.0
Urban-Urbaine	...	...	...	...	...	...	45.0	44.0	44.0	42.0	40.0

15. Infant deaths and infant mortality rates, by urban/rural residence: 1998 - 2002
Décès d'enfants de moins d'un an et taux de mortalité infantile, selon la résidence, urbaine/rurale: 1998 - 2002
(continued — suite)

(See notes at end of table. — Voir notes à la fin du tableau.)

Continent, country or area and urban/rural residence / Continent, pays ou zone et résidence, urbaine/rurale	Code[1]	Number - Nombre					Rate - Taux				
		1998	1999	2000	2001	2002	1998	1999	2000	2001	2002
ASIA — ASIE											
India - Inde[14]											
Rural-Rurale	...	...	...	...	...	...	77.0	75.0	74.0	72.0	69.0
Iran (Islamic Republic of) - Iran (République islamique d')											
Total	C	...	39 183	...	...	...	...	33.3	...	...	...
Israel - Israël[6,15]											
Total	C	774	771	*748	*699	*751	6.0	5.8	*5.5	*5.1	*5.4
Urban-Urbaine	C	681	678	*675	*632	*677	5.8	5.7	*5.5	*5.1	*5.3
Rural-Rurale	C	93	93	*73	*67	*73	6.9	6.7	*5.0	*5.6	*5.7
Japan - Japon[6,16]											
Total	C	4 380	4 010	3 830	3 599	3 497	3.6	3.4	3.2	3.1	3.0
Urban-Urbaine	C	3 491	3 144	3 075	2 896	2 815	3.6	3.3	3.2	3.1	3.0
Rural-Rurale	C	882	857	747	698	672	3.8	3.8	3.3	3.1	3.1
Kazakhstan[12]											
Total	C	4 843	4 444	4 158	4 238	3 849	21.8	20.4	18.7	19.1	16.9
Urban-Urbaine	C	2 701	2 458	2 310	2 370	2 202	24.1	22.3	20.2	20.6	18.0
Rural-Rurale	C	2 142	1 986	1 848	1 868	1 647	19.4	18.5	17.2	17.6	15.7
Korea (Republic of) - Corée (République de)[17]											
Total	C	1 460	2 776	2 885	3 008	2 545	2.3	4.5	4.5	5.4	5.1
Kuwait - Koweït											
Total	C	450	386	379	420	418	10.9	9.4	9.1	10.2	9.6
Kyrgyzstan - Kirghizistan[12]											
Total	C	2 708	2 360	2 225	2 123	2 128	26.0	22.7	23.0	21.6	21.1
Urban-Urbaine	C	821	756	836	785	852	28.8	26.7	29.7	27.6	28.2
Rural-Rurale	C	1 887	1 604	1 389	1 338	1 276	24.9	21.2	20.3	19.2	18.0
Malaysia - Malaisie											
Total	C	4 483	4 660	3 578	...	...	8.5	8.9	6.6	...	...
Maldives[18]											
Total	C	115	104	113	85	*88	20.2	19.9	21.3	17.4	*17.6
Urban-Urbaine	C	31	19	27	22	*28	21.1	12.8	17.2	13.4	*14.9
Rural-Rurale	C	84	85	86	63	*60	19.9	22.7	23.0	19.4	*19.3
Mongolia - Mongolie											
Total	C	1 741	1 846	1 596	1 464	1 390	35.3	37.3	32.8	29.5	29.6
Urban-Urbaine	C	936	903	808	710	626	41.8	37.3	33.9	28.8	26.0
Rural-Rurale	C	805	943	788	754	764	30.0	37.4	31.7	30.2	33.4
Nepal - Népal[19]											
Total	I	...	...	...	13 037	...	...	...	...	...	...
Occupied Palestinian Territory - Territoire palestinien occupé											
Total	U	*1 038*	*1 068*	*1 037*	*1 100*	*1 043*	...	...	...	...	...
Oman[20]											
Total	...	*374*	*386*	*369*	*335*		...	...	...	...	...
Pakistan[21,22]											
Total	I	...	...	...	286 609	...	...	...	...	...	...
Urban-Urbaine	I	...	...	...	82 185	...	...	...	...	77.1	...
Rural-Rurale	I	...	...	...	204 424	...	...	...	...	68.9	...
Philippines											
Total	C	28 196	25 168	27 714	...	...	17.3	15.6	15.7	80.9	...
Qatar											
Total	C	141	112	*132	111	...	13.1	10.3	*11.7	9.2	...
Saudi Arabia - Arabie saoudite											
Total	...	...	11 344	11 071	...	...	...	...	...	...	...
Singapore - Singapour											
Total	+C	183	150	137	100	123	4.2	3.5	2.9	2.4	3.0
Sri Lanka											
Total	+C	...	...	...	*4 323	...	...	...	...	...	...
Tajikistan - Tadjikistan[12]											
Total	C	...	*2 200	...	...	...	...	*19.9	...	...	...
Thailand - Thaïlande											
Total	+U	*4 062*	*5 003*	*4 822*	*5 105*	*5 105*	...	...	...	...	...

15. Infant deaths and infant mortality rates, by urban/rural residence: 1998 - 2002
Décès d'enfants de moins d'un an et taux de mortalité infantile, selon la résidence, urbaine/rurale: 1998 - 2002
(continued — suite)

(See notes at end of table. — Voir notes à la fin du tableau.)

Continent, country or area and urban/rural residence / Continent, pays ou zone et résidence, urbaine/rurale	Code[1]	Number - Nombre					Rate - Taux				
		1998	1999	2000	2001	2002	1998	1999	2000	2001	2002
ASIA — ASIE											
Thailand - Thaïlande											
Urban-Urbaine	+U	...	711	801	...	...	...	...	...	...	...
Rural-Rurale	+U	...	4 292	4 021	...	...	...	...	...	...	...
Turkey - Turquie[23]											
Total	I	67 274	64 993	62 599	60 332	58 391	44.7	43.3	41.9	40.6	39.4
Urban-Urbaine	I	17 704	15 870	15 543	14 947	...	...	...	...	...	...
Rural-Rurale	I	49 570	49 123	47 056	45 385	...	...	...	...	...	...
Turkmenistan - Turkménistan[12]											
Total	C	*3 265	...	...	...	...	*33.2	...	...	...	...
Uzbekistan - Ouzbékistan[12]											
Total	C	...	12 358	10 091	9 427	...	...	22.3	19.1	18.4	...
Urban-Urbaine	C	...	4 293	3 703	3 399	...	...	24.8	22.6	21.3	...
Rural-Rurale	C	...	8 065	6 388	6 028	...	...	21.2	17.6	17.1	...
EUROPE											
Albania - Albanie											
Total	C	903	...	...	...	...	15.0	...	...	...	...
Andorra - Andorre											
Total	C	5	2	2	3	...	...	...	...	...	...
Austria - Autriche											
Total	C	400	341	378	365	318	4.9	4.4	4.8	4.8	4.1
Urban-Urbaine	C	233	...	...	...	...	...	...	...	...	...
Rural-Rurale	C	167	...	...	...	...	...	...	...	...	...
Belarus - Bélarus[12]											
Total	C	1 041	1 064	...	...	695	11.2	11.4	...	...	7.8
Urban-Urbaine	C	644	651	...	...	454	9.9	9.8	...	...	7.0
Rural-Rurale	C	397	413	...	...	241	14.3	15.5	...	...	10.2
Belgium - Belgique[24]											
Total	C	591	556	554	518	551	5.2	4.9	4.8	4.5	...
Bosnia and Herzegovina - Bosnie-Herzégovine											
Total	C	494	...	...	...	...	11.0	...	...	...	...
Bulgaria - Bulgarie											
Total	C	943	1 057	981	982	887	14.4	14.6	13.3	14.4	13.3
Urban-Urbaine	C	...	...	657	625	571	...	...	12.4	12.9	12.0
Rural-Rurale	C	...	...	324	357	316	...	...	15.5	18.2	16.9
Channel Islands: Guernsey - Îles Anglo-Normandes: Guernesey											
Total	C	2	2	4	...	...	...	...	...	...	...
Croatia - Croatie											
Total	C	388	350	324	315	282	8.2	7.7	7.4	7.7	7.0
Urban-Urbaine	C	223	...	194	179	144	8.3	...	7.8	7.8	6.4
Rural-Rurale	C	165	...	130	136	138	8.1	...	6.9	7.5	7.9
Czech Republic - République tchèque											
Total	C	472	413	373	360	385	5.2	4.6	4.1	4.0	3.9
Urban-Urbaine	C	340	307	272	266	288	5.1	4.7	4.1	4.0	3.9
Rural-Rurale	C	132	106	101	94	97	5.5	4.4	4.2	4.0	4.0
Denmark - Danemark[25]											
Total	C	309	281	358	320	284	4.7	4.2	5.3	4.9	4.4
Estonia - Estonie[6,12]											
Total	C	108	119	110	111	74	8.9	9.5	8.4	8.8	5.7
Urban-Urbaine	C	...	...	73	81	53	...	...	8.4	...	6.0
Rural-Rurale	C	...	...	36	30	21	...	...	8.2	...	5.0
Finland - Finlande[26]											
Total	C	239	208	213	181	168	4.2	3.6	3.8	3.2	3.0
Urban-Urbaine	C	141	...	...	112	109	3.9	...	...	3.1	3.0
Rural-Rurale	C	98	...	...	69	59	4.7	...	...	3.5	3.1

15. Infant deaths and infant mortality rates, by urban/rural residence: 1998 - 2002
Décès d'enfants de moins d'un an et taux de mortalité infantile, selon la résidence, urbaine/rurale: 1998 - 2002
(continued — suite)

(See notes at end of table. — Voir notes à la fin du tableau.)

Continent, country or area and urban/rural residence / Continent, pays ou zone et résidence, urbaine/rurale	Code[1]	Number - Nombre					Rate - Taux				
		1998	1999	2000	2001	2002	1998	1999	2000	2001	2002
EUROPE											
France[27,28]											
Total	C	3 399	3 221	3 417	3 444	...	4.6	4.3	4.4	4.5	...
Urban-Urbaine	C	2 610	2 551	...	...	...	4.6	4.5	...	...	...
Rural-Rurale	C	752	644	...	...	...	4.5	3.7	...	...	...
Germany - Allemagne											
Total	C	3 667	3 496	3 362	3 163	3 100	4.6	4.5	4.4	4.3	...
Greece - Grèce											
Total	C	674	619	610	522	600	6.7	5.3	5.2	5.1	...
Urban-Urbaine	C	467	...	...	...	...	6.7	...	...	...	...
Rural-Rurale	C	207	...	...	...	...	6.6	...	...	...	...
Hungary - Hongrie[6]											
Total	C	944	798	900	789	693	9.7	8.4	9.2	8.1	7.2
Urban-Urbaine	C	537	480	532	471	421	9.2	8.4	9.0	8.0	6.9
Rural-Rurale	C	391	312	359	311	269	10.2	8.5	9.5	8.4	7.6
Iceland - Islande											
Total	C	11	10	13	11	9	...	...	...	...	...
Ireland - Irlande[6,29]											
Total	+C	330	293	338	337	306	6.2	5.5	6.2	5.8	5.1
Urban-Urbaine	+C	202	195	...	...	...	7.0	6.3	...	...	...
Rural-Rurale	+C	128	98	...	...	...	5.2	4.4	...	...	...
Isle of Man - Îles de Man											
Total	+C	1	6	5	-	3	...	...	...	...	...
Italy - Italie											
Total	C	2 803	2 723	2 461	2 514	...	5.4	5.2	4.5	4.7	...
Latvia - Lettonie[12]											
Total	C	276	219	210	217	197	15.0	11.3	10.4	11.0	9.8
Urban-Urbaine	C	157	144	124	139	105	13.9	11.9	9.7	11.1	8.1
Rural-Rurale	C	119	75	86	78	92	16.8	10.2	11.4	10.9	12.9
Liechtenstein											
Total	C	...	...	...	...	1	...	...	...	...	...
Lithuania - Lituanie[12]											
Total	C	343	315	294	250	238	9.3	8.7	8.6	7.9	7.9
Urban-Urbaine	C	188	174	172	148	128	8.2	...	8.2	7.5	6.8
Rural-Rurale	C	155	141	122	102	110	11.1	...	9.3	8.6	9.7
Luxembourg											
Total	C	27	26	29	32	27	...	...	...	...	...
Malta - Malte											
Total	C	24	31	26	17	23	...	...	...	...	...
Netherlands - Pays-Bas[30]											
Total	C	1 035	1 048	1 059	1 088	1 028	5.2	5.2	5.1	5.4	5.1
Norway - Norvège[31]											
Total	C	232	232	225	223	192	4.0	3.9	3.8	3.9	3.5
Poland - Pologne											
Total	C	3 771	3 381	3 068	2 823	2 662	9.5	8.9	8.1	7.7	7.5
Urban-Urbaine	C	2 062	1 908	...	...	...	9.6	9.2	...	...	...
Rural-Rurale	C	1 709	1 473	...	...	...	9.4	8.5	...	...	...
Portugal											
Total	C	683	671	662	567	574	6.0	5.8	5.6	5.0	5.0
Republic of Moldova - République de Moldova[12]											
Total	C	738	714	681	597	528	17.9	18.5	18.4	16.4	14.8
Urban-Urbaine	C	294	277	236	212	192	20.7	20.9	18.6	16.9	15.1
Rural-Rurale	C	444	437	445	385	336	16.4	17.3	18.4	16.1	14.6
Romania - Roumanie											
Total	C	4 868	4 360	4 370	4 057	3 648	20.5	18.6	18.6	18.4	17.3
Urban-Urbaine	C	1 907	...	1 744	1 594	1 426	17.3	...	16.1	15.6	14.5
Rural-Rurale	C	2 961	...	2 626	2 463	2 222	23.3	...	20.8	20.9	19.8
Russian Federation - Fédération de Russie[12]											
Total	C	21 097	20 731	19 286	19 104	...	16.4	17.1	15.2	14.6	...
Urban-Urbaine	C	...	13 657	...	...	...	...	16.2	...	...	...

443

15. Infant deaths and infant mortality rates, by urban/rural residence: 1998 - 2002
Décès d'enfants de moins d'un an et taux de mortalité infantile, selon la résidence, urbaine/rurale: 1998 - 2002
(continued — suite)

(See notes at end of table. — Voir notes à la fin du tableau.)

Continent, country or area and urban/rural residence Continent, pays ou zone et résidence, urbaine/rurale	Code[1]	Number - Nombre					Rate - Taux				
		1998	1999	2000	2001	2002	1998	1999	2000	2001	2002
EUROPE											
Russian Federation - Fédération de Russie[12]											
Rural-Rurale	C	...	7 074	...	...	...	...	19.0	...	...	...
San Marino - Saint-Marin											
Total	+C	4	1	-	...	...	...	...	...	...	...
Serbia and Montenegro - Serbie-et-Montenegro											
Total	C	1 791	1 691	1 668	1 709	1 635	13.9	13.6	13.3	13.1	...
Urban-Urbaine	C	1 016	939	962	...	...	15.2	14.6	14.5	...	...
Rural-Rurale	C	775	752	706	...	...	12.6	12.6	11.9	...	...
Slovakia - Slovaquie											
Total	C	506	467	473	319	388	8.8	8.3	8.6	6.2	7.6
Urban-Urbaine	C	234	235	...	147	191	7.9	8.2	...	5.6	7.3
Rural-Rurale	C	272	232	...	172	197	9.8	8.4	...	6.9	8.0
Slovenia - Slovénie											
Total	C	93	79	89	74	67	...	...	...	...	...
Urban-Urbaine	C	39	31	34	33	37	...	...	...	...	...
Rural-Rurale	C	54	48	55	41	30	...	...	...	...	...
Spain - Espagne											
Total	C	1 774	1 700	1 535	1 394	...	4.9	4.5	4.0	3.4	...
Sweden - Suède											
Total	C	316	297	309	334	313	3.5	3.4	3.4	3.7	3.3
Switzerland - Suisse											
Total	C	376	361	386	365	326	4.8	4.6	4.9	5.0	4.5
Urban-Urbaine	C	230	237	262	248	...	4.5	4.6	5.0	5.0	...
Rural-Rurale	C	146	124	124	117	...	5.4	4.7	4.8	4.8	...
The Former Yugoslav Rep. of Macedonia - L'ex-République yougoslave de Macédoine											
Total	C	476	406	346	321	283	16.3	14.9	11.8	11.9	10.2
Urban-Urbaine	C	...	201	185	182	157	...	14.0	11.9	12.3	10.5
Rural-Rurale	C	...	205	161	139	126	...	15.8	11.7	11.3	9.8
Ukraine[12]											
Total	C	5 423	...	4 606	4 283	*4 023	12.9	...	12.0	11.4	*10.3
Urban-Urbaine	C	3 361	...	...	2 690	...	13.0	...	...	11.3	...
Rural-Rurale	C	2 062	...	...	1 593	...	12.8	...	...	11.4	...
United Kingdom - Royaume-Uni											
Total	C	4 079	4 045	3 791	3 664	3 499	5.7	5.8	5.6	5.5	5.2
OCEANIA — OCEANIE											
American Samoa - Samoas américaines											
Total	C	27	22	11	...	...	...	...	...	...	...
Australia - Australie											
Total	+C	1 252	1 408	1 290	1 309	1 264	5.0	5.7	5.2	5.3	5.0
Cook Islands - Îles Cook											
Total	+C	8	5	6	4	2	...	...	...	...	...
Fiji - Fidji											
Total	+C	212	275	...	...	...	11.8	16.3	...	...	...
French Polynesia - Polynésie française											
Total	U	*32*	*31*	...	...	...	...	...	...	...	...
Guam[32]											
Total	C	34	35	23	35	20	...	...	...	...	...
Marshall Islands - Îles Marshall											
Total	+U	...	...	...	*40*	...	...	...	...	...	...
New Caledonia - Nouvelle-Calédonie											
Total	C	30	27	21	24	29	...	...	...	...	...

15. Infant deaths and infant mortality rates, by urban/rural residence: 1998 - 2002
Décès d'enfants de moins d'un an et taux de mortalité infantile, selon la résidence, urbaine/rurale: 1998 - 2002
(continued — suite)

(See notes at end of table. — Voir notes à la fin du tableau.)

Continent, country or area and urban/rural residence Continent, pays ou zone et résidence, urbaine/rurale	Code[1]	Number - Nombre					Rate - Taux				
		1998	1999	2000	2001	2002	1998	1999	2000	2001	2002
OCEANIA — OCEANIE											
New Zealand - Nouvelle-Zélande[6]											
Total	+C	305	317	346	296	300	5.5	5.6	6.1	5.3	5.6
Urban-Urbaine	+C	259	261	289	253	255	5.4	5.3	5.9	5.2	5.4
Rural-Rurale	+C	39	33	32	26	24	5.8	4.5	4.5	3.7	3.5
Northern Mariana Islands - Îles Mariannes septentrionales											
Total	U	*15*	*11*	...			...	...	...	...	...
Palau - Palaos											
Total	C	3	5	...			...	...	...	...	...
Papua New Guinea - Papouasie-Nouvelle-Guinée											
Total	...	...	...	...	...	1 078	...	...	...	...	...
Samoa											
Total	U	*17	...	...			...	...	...	...	...
Tonga											
Total	+C	29	48	28	...		...	...	...	...	...

GENERAL NOTES - NOTES GENERALES

Data exclude foetal deaths. For certain countries, there is a discrepancy between the total number of infant deaths shown in this table and those shown in subsequent tables for the same year. Usually this discrepancy arises because the total number of infant deaths occurring in a given year is revised, although the remaining tabulations are not. Rates are the number of deaths of infants under one year of age per 1 000 live births. Rates are shown only for countries or areas having at least a total of 100 infant deaths in a given year. For definitions of 'urban', see end of Technical Notes for table 6. For method of evaluation and limitations of data, see Technical Notes for this table. — Les données ne comprennent pas les morts foetales. Pour quelques pays il y a une discordance entre le nombre total des décès d'enfants vivantes présenté dans ce tableau et ceux présentés après pour la même année. Habituellement ces différences apparaissent lorsque le nombre total des décès d'enfants pour une certaine année a été révisé; alors que les autres tabulations ne l'ont pas été. Les taux représentent le nombre de décès d'enfants de moins d'un an pour 1 000 naissances vivantes. Les taux présentés ne se rapportent qu'aux pays ou zones où l'on a enregistré un total d'au moins 100 décès d'enfants de moins d'un an dans un année donnée. Pour les définitions des 'régions urbaines', se reporter à la fin des Notes techniques du tableau 6. Pour la méthode d'évaluation et les insuffisances des données, voir Notes techniques pour ce tableau.

Italics: data from civil registers which are incomplete or of unknown completeness. — *Italiques:* données incomplètes ou dont le degré d'exactitude n'est pas connu provenant des registres de l'état civil.

FOOTNOTES - NOTES

* Provisional. — Données provisoires.
[1] 'Code' indicates the source of data, as follows:
C - Civil registration, estimated over 90% complete
U - Civil registration, estimated less than 90% complete
I - Other source, estimated reliable
+ - Data tabulated by date of registration rather than occurence.
... - Information not available

Le 'Code' indique la source des données, comme suit:

C - Registres de l'état civil considérés complèts à 90 p. 100 au moins.
U - Registres de l'état civil qui ne sont pas considérés complèts à 90 p. 100 au moins.
I - Autre source, considérée pas douteuses.
+ - Données exploitées selon la date de l'enregistrement et non la date de l'événement.
... - Information pas disponible.

[2] Excluding live-born infants who died before their birth was registered. - Non compris les enfants nés vivants décédés avant l'enregistrement de leur naissance.
[3] For Algerian population only. - Pour la population algérienne seulement.
[4] Data for estimates refer to national projections. - Les données se referent aux projections nationales.
[5] For 1998, based on the results of the population census. - Pour 1998, d'après les résultats du recensement de la population.
[6] Figures for urban and rural areas do not add up to the total, since they do not include the category 'Unknown residence'. - La somme des donées pour la residence urbaine et rurale n'est pas égale au total parce qu'elle n'inclue pas la catégorie 'Residence inconnue'.
[7] Including Canadian residents temporarily in the United States, but excluding United States residents temporarily in Canada. - Y compris les résidents canadiens se trouvant temporairement aux Etats-Unis, mais ne comprenant pas les résidents des Etats-Unis se trouvant temporairement au Canada.
[8] Excluding Indian jungle population. - Non compris les Indiens de la jungle.
[9] Data on live births and deaths are based on a civil registration system put in place in January 1998. - Les données sur les naissances et les décès sont basées sur un système d'enregistrement des faits d'état civil mis en place en janvier 1998.
[10] Excluding nomadic Indian tribes. - Non compris les tribus d'Indiens nomades.
[11] Including an upward adjustment for under-registration. - Y compris un ajustement pour sous-enregistrement.
[12] Excluding infants born alive with less than 28 weeks gestation, less than 1 000 grams in weight and 35 centimeters in length, who die within seven days of birth. - Non compris les enfants nés vivants avant 28 semaines de gestation, pesant moins de 1 000 grammes, mesurant moins de 35 centimètres et décédés dans les sept jours qui ont suivi leur naissance.
[13] Data refer to government controlled areas. - Les données se raportent aux zones contrôlées par le Gouvernement.
[14] Rates were obtained by the Sample Registration System of India, a

large demographic survey. - Les taux ont été obtenus par le Système de l'enregistrement par échantillon de l'Inde qui est au fait une large enquête démographique.

[15] Including data for East Jerusalem and Israeli residents in certain other territories under occupation by Israeli military forces since June 1967. - Y compris les données pour Jérusalem-Est et les résidents israéliens dans certains autres territoires occupés depuis 1967 par les forces armées israéliennes.

[16] Data refer to Japanese nationals in Japan only. - Les données se rapportent aux nationaux japonais au Japon seulement.

[17] Excluding alien armed forces, civilian aliens employed by armed forces, and foreign diplomatic personnel and their dependants. - Non compris les militaires étrangers, les civils étrangers employés par les forces armées ni le personnel diplomatique étranger et les membres de leur famille les accompagnant.

[18] Including unknown sex. - Y compris le sexe inconnu.

[19] For 2001, data refer to last twelve months preceding census on June 2001. - Pour 2001, les données se rapportent pour la dernière fois à douze mois précédant le recensement juin 2001.

[20] Data refer to the recorded events in Ministry of Health hospitals and health centres only. - Les données se rapportent aux faits d'état-civil enregistrés dans les hôpitaux et les dispensaires du Ministère de la santé seulement.

[21] Based on the results of the Population Growth Survey. - D'après les résultats de la 'Population Growth Survey.'

[22] Excluding data for the Pakistan-held part of Jammu and Kashmir, the final status of which has not yet been determined. - Non compris les données concernant la partie du Jammu et Cachemire occupée par le Pakistan dont le statut définitif n'a pas été déterminé.

[23] Based on the results of the Population Demographic Survey. - - D'après les résultats de la Population Demographic Survey.

[24] Including armed forces stationed outside the country, but excluding alien armed forces stationed in the area. - Y compris les militaires nationaux hors du pays, mais non compris les militaires étrangers en garnison sur le territoire.

[25] Excluding Faeroe Islands and Greenland. - Non compris les Iles Féroé et Gröenland.

[26] Including nationals temporarily outside the country. - Y compris les nationaux se trouvant temporairement hors du pays.

[27] Including armed forces stationed outside the country. - Y compris les militaires nationaux hors du pays.

[28] Urban/rural figures, excluding nationals outside the country. - Les chiffres urbaine/rurale, non compris les nationaux hors du pays.

[29] Events registered within one year of occurrence. - Evénements enregistrés dans l'année qui suit l'événement.

[30] Including residents outside the country if listed in a Netherlands population register. - Y compris les résidents hors du pays, s'ils sont inscrits sur un registre de population néerlandais.

[31] Including residents temporarily outside the country. - Y compris les résidents se trouvant temporairement hors du pays.

[32] Including United States military personnel, their dependants and contract employees. - Y compris les militaires des Etats-Unis, les membres de leur famille les accompagnant et les agents contractuels des Etats-Unis.

Table 16

Table 16 presents infant deaths and infant mortality rates by age and sex for latest available year.

Description of variables: Age is defined as hours, days and months of life completed, based on the difference between the hour, day, month and year of birth and the hour, day, month and year of death. The age classification used in this table is the following: under 1 day, 1-6 days, 7-27 days and 28-364 days. For some countries or areas the statistics presented are for several years, and include those years for which data only recently become available and were therefore not published in pervious issues of the *Demographic Yearbook*.

Rate computation: Infant mortality rates are the annual number of deaths of infants under one year of age per 1 000 live births (as shown in table 9) in the same year.

Infant mortality rates by age and sex are the annual number of infant deaths that occurred in a specific age-sex group per 1 000 live births in the corresponding sex group (as shown in table 9). These rates have been calculated by the Statistics Division of the United Nations. The denominator for all these rates, regardless of age of infant at death, is the number of live births by sex.

Infant deaths of unknown age are included only in the rate for under one year of age. Deaths under the category of sex "unknown" are included in the rate for the total and, hence, these rates, shown in the first column of the table, should agree with the infant mortality rates shown in table 15. Discrepancies are explained in footnotes.

Rates presented in this table have been limited to those for countries or areas having at least a total of 1 000 deaths in a given year. Moreover, rates specific for individual sub-categories based on 30 or fewer infant deaths are identified by the symbol (?).

Reliability of data: Data from civil registers of infant deaths which are reported as incomplete (less than 90 percent completeness) or of unknown completeness are considered unreliable and are set in italics rather than in roman type. Rates on these data are not computed. Tables 9 and 15 and the technical notes for these tables provide more detailed information on the completeness of infant death registration. For more information about the quality of vital statistics data in general, and the information available on the basis of the completeness of estimates in particular, see section 4.2 of the Technical Notes.

Limitations: Statistics on infant deaths by age and sex are subject to the same qualifications as have been set forth for vital statistics in general and death statistics in particular as discussed in section 4 of the Technical Notes.

The reliability of the data, an indication of which is described above, is an important factor in considering the limitations. In addition, some infant deaths are tabulated by date of registration and not by date of occurrence; these have been indicated by a plus sign (+). Whenever the lag between the date of occurrence and date of registration is prolonged and, therefore, a large proportion of the infant-death registrations are delayed, infant-death statistics for any given year may be seriously affected.

Another factor that limits international comparability is the practice of some countries or areas of not including in infant-death statistics infants who were born alive but died before the registration of the birth or within the first 24 hours of life, thus underestimating the total number of infant deaths. Statistics of this type are footnoted. In this table in particular, this practice may contribute to the lack of comparability among deaths under one year, under 28 days, under one week and under one day.

Variation in the method of reckoning age at the time of death may also introduce non-comparability. Although it is to some degree a limiting factor throughout the age span, it is an especially important consideration with respect to deaths at ages under one day and under one week (early neonatal deaths) and under 28 days (neonatal deaths). As noted above, the recommended method of reckoning infant age at death is to calculate duration of life in minutes, hours and days, as appropriate. This gives age in completed units of time. In some countries or areas, however, infant age is calculated to the nearest day only, that is, age at death for an infant is the difference between the day, month and year of birth and the day, month and year of death. The result of this procedure is to classify as deaths at age one day, many deaths of infants that occurred before the infants had completed 24 hours of life. The under-one-day class is thus understated while the frequency in the 1-6-day age group is inflated.

447

A special limitation on comparability of neonatal (under 28 days) deaths is the variation in the classification of infant age used. It is evident from the footnotes that some countries or areas continue to report infant age in calendar, rather than lunar month (4-week or 28- day) periods. This failure to tabulate infant deaths under 4 weeks of age in terms of completed days introduces another source of variation between countries or areas. Deaths classified as occurring under one month usually connote deaths within any one calendar month; these frequencies are not strictly comparable with those referring to deaths within 4 weeks or 27 completed days.

In addition, infant mortality rates by age and sex are subject to the limitations of the data on live births with which they have been calculated. These have been set forth in the technical notes for table 9. These limitations have also been discussed in the technical notes for table 15.

In addition, it should be noted that infant mortality rates by age are affected by the problems related to the practice of excluding infants who were born alive but died before the registration of the birth or within the first 24 hours of life from both infant-death and live-birth statistics and the problems related to the reckoning of infant age at death. These factors, which have been described above, may affect certain age groups more than others. In so far as the numbers of infant deaths for the various age groups are underestimated or overestimated, the corresponding rates for the various age groups will also be underestimated or overestimated. The youngest age groups are more likely to be underestimated than other age groups; the youngest age group (under one day) is likely to be the most seriously affected.

Earlier data: Infant deaths and infant mortality rates by age and sex have been shown in previous issues of the *Demographic Yearbook*. For information on specific years covered, readers should consult the Historical Index.

Tableau 16

Le tableau 16 présente les données les plus récentes dont on dispose sur les décès d'enfants de moins d'un an et les taux de mortalité infantile selon l'âge et le sexe.

Description des variables : L'âge est exprimé en heures, jours et mois révolus et est calculé en retranchant la date de la naissance (heure, jour, mois et année) de celle du décès (heure, jour, mois et année). La classification par âge utilisée dans le tableau est la suivante : moins d'un jour, 1 à 6 jours, 7 à 27 jours et 28 à 364 jours. Pour certains pays et zones, les statistiques portent sur plusieurs années. Cela s'explique par le fait qu'elles ne sont disponibles que depuis peu et n'ont donc pas pu être publiées dans les éditions précédentes de l'*Annuaire démographique*.

Calcul des taux : Les taux de mortalité infantile selon l'âge et le sexe représentent le nombre annuel de décès d'enfants de moins d'un an selon l'âge et le sexe pour 1 000 naissances vivantes d'enfants du même sexe (fréquences du tableau 9) survenues au cours de l'année considérée.

Les taux de mortalité infantile selon l'âge et le sexe représentent le nombre annuel de décès d'enfants de moins d'un an intervenu dans un groupe d'âge donné parmi la population de sexe masculin ou féminin (fréquences du tableau 9) pour 1 000 naissances vivantes survenues parmi la population du même sexe. Ces taux ont été calculés par la Division de statistique de l'ONU.

Le dénominateur de tous ces taux, quel que soit l'âge de l'enfant au moment du décès, est le nombre de naissances vivantes selon le sexe.

Il n'est tenu compte des décès d'enfants d'âge « inconnu » que pour le calcul du taux relatif à l'ensemble des décès de moins d'un an. Étant donné que les décès d'enfants de sexe inconnu sont compris dans le numérateur des taux concernant le total qui figurent dans la deuxième colonne du tableau 16, les chiffres obtenus devraient concorder avec les taux de mortalité infantile du tableau 15. Les divergences sont expliquées en note.

Les taux présentés dans le tableau 16 ne concernent que les pays ou zones où l'on a enregistré un total d'au moins 1 000 décès au cours d'une année donnée. Les taux relatifs à des sous-catégories qui sont fondées sur un nombre égal ou inférieur à 30 décès d'enfants âgés de moins d'un an sont signalés par le signe '?.

Fiabilité des données : Les données relatives aux décès d'enfants de moins d'un an provenant de registres de l'état civil qui sont déclarées incomplètes (degré de complétude inférieur à 90 p.100) ou dont le degré de complétude n'est pas connu sont jugées douteuses et apparaissent en italique et non en caractères romains. Les taux à partir de ces données n'ont pas été calculés. Les tableaux 9 et 15 et les notes techniques se rapportant à ces tableaux comportent des renseignements plus détaillés sur le degré de complétude de l'enregistrement des décès d'enfants de moins d'un an. Pour plus de précisions sur la qualité des données reposant sur les statistiques de l'état civil en général et les estimations de complétude en particulier, voir la section 4.2 des Notes techniques.

Insuffisance des données : Les statistiques des décès d'enfants de moins d'un an selon l'âge et le sexe appellent toutes les réserves qui ont été formulées à propos des statistiques de l'état civil en général et des statistiques concernant les décès en particulier (voir la section 4 des Notes techniques).

La fiabilité des données, au sujet de laquelle des indications ont été fournies plus haut, est un facteur important. Il faut également tenir compte du fait que, dans certains cas, les données relatives aux décès d'enfants de moins d'un an sont exploitées selon la date de l'enregistrement et non la date de l'événement ; ces cas ont été signalés par le signe '+'. Chaque fois que le décalage entre l'événement et son enregistrement est grand et qu'une forte proportion des décès d'enfants de moins d'un an fait l'objet d'un enregistrement tardif, les statistiques des décès d'enfants de moins d'un an pour une année donnée peuvent être considérablement faussées.

Un autre facteur qui nuit à la comparabilité internationale est la pratique de certains pays ou zones qui consiste à ne pas inclure dans les statistiques des décès d'enfants de moins d'un an les enfants nés vivants mais décédés soit avant l'enregistrement de leur naissance, soit dans les 24 heures qui ont suivi la naissance, pratique qui conduit à sous-estimer le nombre total de décès d'enfants de moins d'un an. Quand pareil facteur a joué, cela a été signalé en note. Dans le tableau 16 en particulier, ce système peut limiter la comparabilité des données concernant les décès d'enfants de moins d'un an, de moins de 28 jours, de moins d'une semaine et de moins d'un jour.

Le manque d'uniformité des méthodes suivies pour calculer l'âge au moment du décès nuit également à la comparabilité des données. Ce facteur influe dans une certaine mesure sur les données relatives à la mortalité à tous les âges, mais il a des répercussions particulièrement marquées sur les statistiques des décès de moins d'un jour et de moins d'une semaine (mortalité néo-natale précoce) et de moins de 28 jours (mortalité néo-natale). Comme on l'a dit, l'âge d'un enfant de moins d'un an à son décès est calculé, selon la méthode recommandée, en évaluant la durée de vie en minutes, heures et jours, selon le cas. L'âge est ainsi exprimé en unités de temps révolues. Toutefois, dans certains pays ou zones, l'âge de ces enfants est ramené au jour le plus proche en retranchant la date de la naissance (jour, mois et année) de celle du décès (jour, mois et année). Il s'ensuit que de nombreux décès survenus dans les vingt-quatre heures qui suivent la naissance sont classés comme décès d'un jour. Dans ces conditions, les données concernant les décès de moins d'un jour sont entachées d'une erreur par défaut et celles qui se rapportent aux décès de 1 à 6 jours d'une erreur par excès.

La comparabilité des données relatives à la mortalité néo-natale (moins de 28 jours) est influencée par un facteur spécial : l'hétérogénéité de la classification par âge utilisée pour les enfants de moins d'un an. Les notes figurant à la fin des tableaux montrent que, dans un certain nombre de pays ou zones, on continue d'utiliser le mois civil au lieu du mois lunaire (4 semaines ou 28 jours).

Lorsque les données relatives aux décès de moins de 4 semaines ne sont pas exploitées sur la base de l'âge en jours révolus, il existe une nouvelle cause de non-comparabilité internationale. Les décès de moins d'un mois sont généralement ceux qui se produisent au cours d'un mois civil ; les taux calculés sur la base de ces données ne sont pas strictement comparables à ceux qui sont établis à partir des données concernant les décès survenus dans les 4 semaines ou 27 jours révolus qui suivent la naissance.

Les taux de mortalité infantile selon l'âge et le sexe appellent en outre toutes les réserves qui ont été formulées à propos des statistiques des naissances vivantes qui ont servi à leur calcul (voir à ce sujet les notes techniques relatives au tableau 9). Ces insuffisances ont également été examinées dans les notes techniques relatives au tableau 15.

Il convient de signaler aussi que les taux de mortalité infantile selon l'âge peuvent être gravement faussés par la pratique qui consiste à ne pas classer dans les naissances vivantes et ensuite dans les décès d'enfants de moins d'un an les enfants nés vivants mais décédés soit avant l'enregistrement de leur naissance, soit dans les 24 heures qui ont suivi la naissance, et par les problèmes que pose le calcul de l'âge de l'enfant au moment du décès. Ces facteurs, qui ont été décrits plus haut, peuvent fausser les statistiques concernant certains groupes d'âge plus que d'autres. Si le nombre des décès d'enfants de moins d'un an pour chaque groupe d'âge est sous-estimé ou surestimé, les taux correspondants pour chacun de ces groupes d'âge seront eux aussi sous-estimés ou surestimés. Les risques de sous-estimation sont plus grands pour les groupes les plus jeunes ; c'est pour le groupe d'âge le plus jeune de tous (moins d'un jour) que les données risquent de comporter les plus grosses erreurs.

Données publiées antérieurement : Des statistiques des décès d'enfants de moins d'un an et des taux de mortalité infantile selon l'âge et le sexe ont déjà été présentées dans des éditions antérieures de l'*Annuaire démographique*. Pour plus de précisions concernant les années pour lesquelles ces données ont été publiées, se reporter à l'index.

16. Infant deaths and infant mortality rates by age and sex: latest available year, 1993 - 2002
Décès d'enfants de moins d'un an et taux de mortalité infantile selon l'âge et le sexe: dernière année disponible, 1993 - 2002

(See notes at end of table. — Voir notes à la fin du tableau.)

Continent, country or area, year, age (in days) and urban/rural residence Continent, pays ou zone, année, âge (en jours) et résidence,urbaine/rurale	Number - Nombre			Rate - Taux		
	Both sexes Les deux sexes	Male Masculin	Female Féminin	Both sexes Les deux sexes	Male Masculin	Female Féminin
AFRICA — AFRIQUE						
Egypt - Égypte						
1999						
Total	49 765	26 263	23 502	29.4	30.2	28.6
Under 1 day - Moins d'un jour	7 992	4 418	3 574	4.7	5.1	4.3
1-6	8 352	5 127	3 225	4.9	5.9	3.9
7-27	6 028	3 488	2 540	3.6	4.0	3.1
28-364	27 393	13 230	14 163	16.2	15.2	17.2
Mauritius - Maurice+						
2001						
Total	282	165	117	...	...	...
Under 1 day - Moins d'un jour	65	44	21	...	...	...
1-6	94	49	45	...	...	...
7-27	50	29	21	...	...	...
28-364	73	43	30	...	...	...
2002						
Total	297	163	134	...	...	...
Under 1 day - Moins d'un jour	53	29	24	...	...	...
1-6	123	63	60	...	...	...
7-27	35	20	15	...	...	...
28-364	86	51	35	...	...	...
Morocco - Maroc						
1999						
Total	8 885	4 711	4 174	...	...	...
0-27	1 781	1 039	742	...	...	...
28-364	7 076	3 661	3 415	...	...	...
Saint Helena ex. dep. - Sainte-Hélène sans dép.						
1998						
Total	1	1	-	...	...	...
Under 1 day - Moins d'un jour	1	1	-	...	...	...
1-6	-	-	-	...	...	...
7-27	-	-	-	...	...	...
28-364	-	-	-	...	...	...
South Africa - Afrique du Sud						
1996						
Total	24 560	12 979	11 581	...	...	...
Under 1 day - Moins d'un jour	3 795	2 098	1 697	...	...	...
1-6	4 542	2 427	2 115	...	...	...
7-27	2 415	1 288	1 127	...	...	...
28-364	13 808	7 166	6 642	...	...	...
Tunisia - Tunisie						
1998						
Total	3 098	1 775	1 323	...	...	...
Under 1 day - Moins d'un jour	464	281	183	...	...	...
1-6	847	485	362	...	...	...
7-27	559	332	227	...	...	...
28-364	1 227	677	550	...	...	...
Unknown - Inconnu	1	-	1	...	...	...
AMERICA, NORTH — AMERIQUE DU NORD						
Antigua and Barbuda - Antigua-et-Barbuda+						
1995						
Total	23	12	11	...	...	...
Under 1 day - Moins d'un jour	6	3	3	...	...	...
1-6	10	5	5	...	...	...
7-27	3	2	1	...	...	...
28-364	4	2	2	...	...	...
Bahamas						
2000						
Total	52	...	...	...	...	...
0-6	11	...	...	...	...	...
7-27	10	...	...	...	...	...

16. Infant deaths and infant mortality rates by age and sex: latest available year, 1993 - 2002
Décès d'enfants de moins d'un an et taux de mortalité infantile selon l'âge et le sexe: dernière année disponible, 1993 - 2002 (continued — suite)

(See notes at end of table. — Voir notes à la fin du tableau.)

Continent, country or area, year, age (in days) and urban/rural residence / Continent, pays ou zone, année, âge (en jours) et résidence,urbaine/rurale	Number - Nombre			Rate - Taux		
	Both sexes Les deux sexes	Male Masculin	Female Féminin	Both sexes Les deux sexes	Male Masculin	Female Féminin
AMERICA, NORTH — AMERIQUE DU NORD						
Bahamas						
2000						
28-364	23	...	...	...	...	...
Unknown - Inconnu	8	...	...	...	...	...
2001						
Total	37	23	14	...	...	...
0-6	8	7	1	...	...	...
7-27	15	8	7	...	...	...
28-364	14	8	6	...	...	...
Belize						
1993						
Total	113	58	55	...	...	...
Under 1 day - Moins d'un jour	18	9	9	...	...	...
1-6	22	15	7	...	...	...
7-27	12	5	7	...	...	...
28-364	51	25	26	...	...	...
Unknown - Inconnu	10	4	6	...	...	...
Bermuda - Bermudes						
1996						
Total	3	1	2	...	...	...
Under 1 day - Moins d'un jour	1	1	-	...	...	...
1-6	1	-	1	...	...	...
7-27	-	-	-	...	...	...
28-364	1	-	1	...	...	...
Canada[1]						
2001						
Total	1 739	997	742	5.2	5.8	4.6
Under 1 day - Moins d'un jour	757	430	327	2.3	2.5	2.0
1-6	267	151	116	0.8	0.9	0.7
7-27	237	139	98	0.7	0.8	0.6
28-364	478	277	201	1.4	1.6	1.2
Cayman Islands - Îles Caïmanes						
1996						
Total	6	3	3	...	...	...
Under 1 day - Moins d'un jour	4	1	3	...	...	...
1-6	-	-	-	...	...	...
7-27	-	-	-	...	...	...
28-364	2	2	-	...	...	...
Costa Rica						
1999						
Total	925	535	390	...	...	...
Under 1 day - Moins d'un jour	254	148	106	...	...	...
1-6	245	134	111	...	...	...
7-27	136	79	57	...	...	...
28-364	290	174	116	...	...	...
Cuba						
1999						
Total	977	561	416	...	...	...
Under 1 day - Moins d'un jour	101	44	57	...	...	...
1-6	339	203	136	...	...	...
7-27	157	88	69	...	...	...
28-364	380	226	154	...	...	...
El Salvador						
1999						
Total	1 768	987	781	11.5	12.4	10.5
Under 1 day - Moins d'un jour	189	115	74	1.2	1.4	1.0
1-6	281	166	115	1.8	2.1	1.5
7-27	207	115	92	1.3	1.4	1.2
28-364	1 091	591	500	7.1	7.5	6.7

16. Infant deaths and infant mortality rates by age and sex: latest available year, 1993 - 2002
Décès d'enfants de moins d'un an et taux de mortalité infantile selon l'âge et le sexe: dernière année disponible, 1993 - 2002 (continued — suite)

(See notes at end of table. — Voir notes à la fin du tableau.)

Continent, country or area, year, age (in days) and urban/rural residence Continent, pays ou zone, année, âge (en jours) et résidence,urbaine/rurale	Number - Nombre			Rate - Taux		
	Both sexes Les deux sexes	Male Masculin	Female Féminin	Both sexes Les deux sexes	Male Masculin	Female Féminin
AMERICA, NORTH — AMERIQUE DU NORD						
Greenland - Groenland						
1999						
Total	16	11	5	...	...	...
Under 1 day - Moins d'un jour	7	6	1	...	...	...
1-6	4	3	1	...	...	...
7-27	1	1	-	...	...	...
28-364	4	1	3	...	...	...
Guadeloupe						
2000						
Total	58	33	25	...	...	...
Under 1 day - Moins d'un jour	13	8	5	...	...	...
1-6	13	10	3	...	...	...
7-27	13	5	8	...	...	...
28-364	19	10	9	...	...	...
Guatemala						
1999						
Total	13 161	7 349	5 812	36.5	40.0	32.8
Under 1 day - Moins d'un jour	999	570	429	2.8	3.1	2.4
1-6	2 180	1 286	894	6.0	7.0	5.0
7-27	1 741	949	792	4.8	5.2	4.5
28-364	8 241	4 544	3 697	22.8	24.7	20.9
Martinique						
2000						
Total	40	23	17	...	...	...
Under 1 day - Moins d'un jour	20	14	6	...	...	...
1-6	6	2	4	...	...	...
7-27	5	6	4	...	...	...
28-364	9	4	5	...	...	...
Mexico - Mexique[2]						
2000						
Total	38 621	21 793	16 769	13.8	15.6	12.0
Under 1 day - Moins d'un jour	8 190	4 628	3 527	2.9	3.3	2.5
1-6	18 686	10 840	7 830	6.7	7.7	5.6
7-27	6 273	3 551	2 717	2.2	2.5	1.9
28-364	14 413	7 954	6 450	5.2	5.7	4.6
Unknown - Inconnu	402	240	160	0.1	0.2	0.1
Nicaragua[+]						
2000						
Total	2 075	1 209	866	...	...	...
Under 1 day - Moins d'un jour	255	154	101	...	...	...
1-6	793	455	338	...	...	...
7-27	275	168	107	...	...	...
28-364	752	432	320	...	...	...
2001						
Total	1 933	1 114	819	...	...	...
Under 1 day - Moins d'un jour	278	175	103	...	...	...
1-6	762	473	289	...	...	...
7-27	258	135	123	...	...	...
28-364	635	331	304	...	...	...
2002						
Total	2 203	1 301	902	...	...	...
Under 1 day - Moins d'un jour	338	185	153	...	...	...
1-6	876	532	344	...	...	...
7-27	325	201	124	...	...	...
28-364	664	383	281	...	...	...
Panama						
1999						
Total	1 005	571	434	...	...	...
Under 1 day - Moins d'un jour	147	78	69	...	...	...
1-6	253	145	108	...	...	...
7-27	207	127	80	...	...	...

16. Infant deaths and infant mortality rates by age and sex: latest available year, 1993 - 2002
Décès d'enfants de moins d'un an et taux de mortalité infantile selon l'âge et le sexe: dernière année disponible, 1993 - 2002 (continued — suite)

(See notes at end of table. — Voir notes à la fin du tableau.)

Continent, country or area, year, age (in days) and urban/rural residence Continent, pays ou zone, année, âge (en jours) et résidence,urbaine/rurale	Number - Nombre			Rate - Taux		
	Both sexes Les deux sexes	Male Masculin	Female Féminin	Both sexes Les deux sexes	Male Masculin	Female Féminin
AMERICA, NORTH — AMERIQUE DU NORD						
Panama						
1999						
28-364	398	221	177	...	...	...
Urban - Urbaine						
Total	490	284	206	...	...	...
Under 1 day - Moins d'un jour	88	46	42	...	...	...
1-6	143	86	57	...	...	...
7-27	117	69	48	...	...	...
28-364	142	83	59	...	...	...
Rural - Rurale						
Total	515	287	228	...	...	...
Under 1 day - Moins d'un jour	59	32	27	...	...	...
1-6	110	59	51	...	...	...
7-27	90	58	32	...	...	...
28-364	256	138	118	...	...	...
Puerto Rico - Porto Rico						
2002						
Total	515	292	223	...	...	...
Under 1 day - Moins d'un jour	128	72	56	...	...	...
1-6	133	78	55	...	...	...
7-27	116	62	54	...	...	...
28-364	56	32	24	...	...	...
Saint Lucia - Sainte-Lucie						
2000						
Total	38	21	17	...	...	...
Under 1 day - Moins d'un jour	10	6	4	...	...	...
1-6	19	9	10	...	...	...
7-27	3	1	2	...	...	...
28-364	6	5	1	...	...	...
2001						
Total	37	16	21	...	...	...
Under 1 day - Moins d'un jour	12	3	9	...	...	...
1-6	14	8	6	...	...	...
7-27	4	3	1	...	...	...
28-364	7	2	5	...	...	...
2002						
Total	36	17	19	...	...	...
Under 1 day - Moins d'un jour	11	5	6	...	...	...
1-6	16	6	10	...	...	...
7-27	2	1	1	...	...	...
28-364	7	5	2	...	...	...
Saint Vincent and the Grenadines - Saint Vincent-et-les Grenadines+						
2000						
Total	35	24	11	...	...	...
Under 1 day - Moins d'un jour	13	9	4	...	...	...
1-6	7	4	3	...	...	...
7-27	2	2	-	...	...	...
28-364	13	9	4	...	...	...
Trinidad and Tobago - Trinité-et-Tobago						
1997						
Total	316	170	146	...	...	...
Under 1 day - Moins d'un jour	76	45	31	...	...	...
1-6	118	62	56	...	...	...
7-27	48	22	26	...	...	...
28-364	74	41	33	...	...	...
United States - États-Unis						
2001						
Total	27 568	15 477	12 091	6.8	7.5	6.1
Under 1 day - Moins d'un jour	5 781	3 852	1 929	1.4	1.9	1.0
1-6	3 713	2 139	1 574	0.9	1.0	0.8

16. Infant deaths and infant mortality rates by age and sex: latest available year, 1993 - 2002
Décès d'enfants de moins d'un an et taux de mortalité infantile selon l'âge et le sexe: dernière année disponible, 1993 - 2002 (continued — suite)

(See notes at end of table. — Voir notes à la fin du tableau.)

Continent, country or area, year, age (in days) and urban/rural residence Continent, pays ou zone, année, âge (en jours) et résidence,urbaine/rurale	Number - Nombre			Rate - Taux		
	Both sexes Les deux sexes	Male Masculin	Female Féminin	Both sexes Les deux sexes	Male Masculin	Female Féminin
AMERICA, NORTH — AMERIQUE DU NORD						
United States - États-Unis						
2001						
7-27	3 654	1 976	1 678	0.9	1.0	0.9
28-364	9 303	5 240	4 063	2.3	2.5	2.1
United States Virgin Islands - Îles Vierges américaines						
1993						
Total	31	18	13	...	...	...
Under 1 day - Moins d'un jour	19	11	8	...	...	...
1-6	6	4	2	...	...	...
7-27	4	1	3	...	...	...
28-364	2	2	-	...	...	...
AMERICA, SOUTH — AMERIQUE DU SUD						
Argentina - Argentine[2]						
1998						
Total	13 082	7 472	5 576	19.1	21.2	16.8
0-6	6 084	3 531	2 546	8.9	10.0	7.7
7-27	1 881	1 073	807	2.8	3.0	2.4
28-364	5 117	2 868	2 223	7.5	8.2	6.7
Brazil - Brésil[2,3]						
1999						
Total	58 767	33 417	25 243	...	...	...
Under 1 day - Moins d'un jour	13 180	7 602	5 564	...	...	...
1-6	15 885	9 263	6 614	...	...	...
7-27	8 020	4 432	10 647	...	...	...
28-364	21 682	11 977	11 195	...	...	...
Unknown - Inconnu	5 387	4 130	1 246	...	...	...
2000						
Total	53 097	29 997	22 949	...	...	...
Under 1 day - Moins d'un jour	12 440	7 123	5 292	...	...	...
1-6	13 811	8 151	5 642	...	...	...
7-27	7 505	4 115	3 375	...	...	...
28-364	19 341	10 608	8 640	...	...	...
Unknown - Inconnu	4 436	3 541	887	...	...	...
2001						
Total	47 171	26 335	20 567	...	...	...
Under 1 day - Moins d'un jour	11 381	6 321	4 991	...	...	...
1-6	12 139	6 997	5 101	...	...	...
7-27	6 912	3 858	3 032	...	...	...
28-364	16 739	9 159	7 443	...	...	...
Unknown - Inconnu	4 094	1 720	799	...	...	...
Chile - Chili						
2000						
Total	2 336	1 263	1 073	9.4	9.9	8.9
Under 1 day - Moins d'un jour	659	366	293	2.6	2.9	2.4
1-6	480	261	219	1.9	2.0	1.8
7-27	328	185	143	1.3	1.4	1.2
28-364	869	451	418	3.5	3.5	3.5
2001						
Total	2 159	1 187	972	8.8	9.5	8.0
Under 1 day - Moins d'un jour	576	335	241	2.3	2.7	2.0
1-6	383	215	168	1.6	1.7	1.4
7-27	331	183	148	1.3	1.5	1.2
28-364	869	454	415	3.5	3.6	3.4
2002						
Total	1 964	1 127	837	8.2	9.2	7.2
Under 1 day - Moins d'un jour	579	326	253	2.4	2.7	2.2
1-6	361	217	144	1.5	1.8	1.2
7-27	309	170	139	1.3	1.4	1.2

16. Infant deaths and infant mortality rates by age and sex: latest available year, 1993 - 2002
Décès d'enfants de moins d'un an et taux de mortalité infantile selon l'âge et le sexe: dernière année disponible, 1993 - 2002 (continued — suite)

(See notes at end of table. — Voir notes à la fin du tableau.)

Continent, country or area, year, age (in days) and urban/rural residence Continent, pays ou zone, année, âge (en jours) et résidence,urbaine/rurale	Number - Nombre			Rate - Taux		
	Both sexes Les deux sexes	Male Masculin	Female Féminin	Both sexes Les deux sexes	Male Masculin	Female Féminin
AMERICA, SOUTH — AMERIQUE DU SUD						
Chile - Chili						
2002						
28-364	715	414	301	3.0	3.4	2.6
Colombia - Colombie[2,4]						
2000						
Total	15 367	8 666	6 698	...	...	...
Under 1 day - Moins d'un jour	3 324	1 930	1 394	...	...	...
1-6	3 302	1 931	1 371	...	...	...
7-27	2 416	1 361	1 055	...	...	...
28-364	5 608	3 050	2 557	...	...	...
Unknown - Inconnu	717	394	321	...	...	...
2001						
Total	14 430	8 215	6 214	...	...	...
Under 1 day - Moins d'un jour	3 018	1 752	1 266	...	...	...
1-6	2 980	1 760	1 220	...	...	...
7-27	2 223	1 282	940	...	...	...
28-364	5 584	3 072	2 512	...	...	...
Unknown - Inconnu	625	349	276	...	...	...
2002						
Total	12 096	6 811	5 269	...	...	...
Under 1 day - Moins d'un jour	2 488	1 391	1 087	...	...	...
1-6	2 543	1 475	1 064	...	...	...
7-27	1 957	1 111	846	...	...	...
28-364	4 605	2 542	2 063	...	...	...
Unknown - Inconnu	503	292	209	...	...	...
Ecuador - Équateur[5]						
2000						
Total	5 480	2 974	2 506	...	...	...
Under 1 day - Moins d'un jour	879	492	387	...	...	...
1-6	1 057	614	443	...	...	...
7-27	724	388	336	...	...	...
28-364	2 820	1 480	1 340	...	...	...
2001						
Total	4 800	2 722	2 078	...	...	...
Under 1 day - Moins d'un jour	837	514	323	...	...	...
1-6	870	496	374	...	...	...
7-27	706	401	305	...	...	...
28-364	2 387	1 311	1 076	...	...	...
2002						
Total	4 530	2 544	1 986	...	...	...
Under 1 day - Moins d'un jour	821	467	354	...	...	...
1-6	891	534	357	...	...	...
7-27	581	318	263	...	...	...
28-364	2 237	1 225	1 012	...	...	...
French Guiana - Guyane française						
2000						
Total	64	35	29	...	...	...
Under 1 day - Moins d'un jour	9	5	4	...	...	...
1-6	22	10	12	...	...	...
7-27	7	6	1	...	...	...
28-364	26	14	12	...	...	...
Peru - Pérou[3,6]						
2000						
Total	7 453	4 083	3 370	11.7	...	...
Under 1 day - Moins d'un jour	1 364	789	575	2.1	...	...
1-6	2 828	805	609	4.4	...	...
7-27	1 268	1 416	560	2.0	...	...
28-364	3 407	1 781	1 626	5.4	...	...
Suriname						
1994						
Total	211	...	...	...	...	...

456

16. Infant deaths and infant mortality rates by age and sex: latest available year, 1993 - 2002
Décès d'enfants de moins d'un an et taux de mortalité infantile selon l'âge et le sexe: dernière année disponible, 1993 - 2002 (continued — suite)

(See notes at end of table. — Voir notes à la fin du tableau.)

Continent, country or area, year, age (in days) and urban/rural residence Continent, pays ou zone, année, âge (en jours) et résidence,urbaine/rurale	Number - Nombre			Rate - Taux		
	Both sexes Les deux sexes	Male Masculin	Female Féminin	Both sexes Les deux sexes	Male Masculin	Female Féminin
AMERICA, SOUTH — AMERIQUE DU SUD						
Suriname						
1994						
Under 1 day - Moins d'un jour	16	...	...	...	...	...
1-6	85	...	...	...	...	...
7-27	28	...	...	...	...	...
28-364	82	...	...	...	...	...
Uruguay[2]						
2000						
Total	742	434	304	...	...	...
Under 1 day - Moins d'un jour	152	87	61	...	...	...
1-6	124	74	50	...	...	...
7-27	142	90	52	...	...	...
28-364	324	183	141	...	...	...
Venezuela[3]						
2001						
Total	8 158	4 710	3 448	15.4	17.1	13.5
0-27	5 657	3 288	2 369	10.7	12.0	9.3
28-364	2 501	1 422	1 079	4.7	5.2	4.2
ASIA — ASIE						
Armenia - Arménie[7]						
2001						
Total	497	313	184	...	...	...
Under 1 day - Moins d'un jour	104	68	36	...	...	...
1-6	179	124	55	...	...	...
7-27	59	37	22	...	...	...
28-364	155	84	71	...	...	...
Azerbaijan - Azerbaïdjan+,[7]						
2001						
Total	1 382	769	613	12.5	12.9	12.1
Under 1 day - Moins d'un jour	94	57	37	0.9	1.0	0.7
1-6	197	127	70	1.8	2.1	1.4
7-27	33	21	12	0.3	♦0.4	♦0.2
28-364	1 058	564	494	9.6	9.5	9.7
2002						
Total	1 422	793	629	12.8	13.3	12.3
Under 1 day - Moins d'un jour	82	55	27	0.7	0.9	♦0.5
1-6	185	116	69	1.7	1.9	1.4
7-27	28	15	13	♦0.3	♦0.3	♦0.3
28-364	1 127	607	520	10.2	10.2	10.2
Bahrain - Bahreïn						
2000						
Total	117	68	49	...	...	...
0-6	43	25	18	...	...	...
7-27	27	16	11	...	...	...
28-364	47	27	20	...	...	...
2001						
Total	117	67	50	...	...	...
0-6	33	20	13	...	...	...
7-27	31	22	9	...	...	...
28-364	53	25	28	...	...	...
2002						
Total	94	48	46	...	...	...
0-6	29	14	15	...	...	...
7-27	22	9	13	...	...	...
28-364	43	25	18	...	...	...
China: Hong Kong SAR - Chine: Hong Kong RAS						
2000						
Total	162	90	72	...	...	...

16. Infant deaths and infant mortality rates by age and sex: latest available year, 1993 - 2002
Décès d'enfants de moins d'un an et taux de mortalité infantile selon l'âge et le sexe: dernière année disponible, 1993 - 2002 (continued — suite)

(See notes at end of table. — Voir notes à la fin du tableau.)

Continent, country or area, year, age (in days) and urban/rural residence / Continent, pays ou zone, année, âge (en jours) et résidence,urbaine/rurale	Number - Nombre			Rate - Taux		
	Both sexes Les deux sexes	Male Masculin	Female Féminin	Both sexes Les deux sexes	Male Masculin	Female Féminin
ASIA — ASIE						
China: Hong Kong SAR - Chine: Hong Kong RAS						
2000						
Under 1 day - Moins d'un jour	18	9	9	...	...	...
1-6	52	31	21	...	...	...
7-27	25	16	9	...	...	...
28-364	67	34	33	...	...	...
China: Macao SAR - Chine: Macao RAS						
2000						
Total	11	6	5	...	...	...
Under 1 day - Moins d'un jour	3	1	2	...	...	...
1-6	4	2	2	...	...	...
7-27	1	-	1	...	...	...
28-364	3	3	-	...	...	...
Georgia - Géorgie[7]						
2001						
Total	478	301	177	...	...	...
Under 1 day - Moins d'un jour	149	101	48	...	...	...
1-6	183	111	72	...	...	...
7-27	35	16	19	...	...	...
28-364	111	73	38	...	...	...
Israel - Israël[2,8]						
2000						
Total	748	436	309	...	...	...
Under 1 day - Moins d'un jour	162	93	68	...	...	...
1-6	182	115	66	...	...	...
7-27	136	68	68	...	...	...
28-364	268	160	107	...	...	...
2001						
Total	699	363	335	...	...	...
Under 1 day - Moins d'un jour	154	92	62	...	...	...
1-6	176	96	80	...	...	...
7-27	125	69	56	...	...	...
28-364	244	106	137	...	...	...
2002						
Total	751	402	347	...	...	...
Under 1 day - Moins d'un jour	197	116	80	...	...	...
1-6	190	101	89	...	...	...
7-27	121	62	59	...	...	...
28-364	243	123	119	...	...	...
Japan - Japon[9]						
2002						
Total	3 497	1 903	1 594	3.0	3.2	2.8
Under 1 day - Moins d'un jour	822	445	377	0.7	0.8	0.7
1-6	552	307	245	0.5	0.5	0.4
7-27	563	294	269	0.5	0.5	0.5
28-364	1 560	857	703	1.4	1.4	1.3
Kazakhstan[7]						
2000						
Total	4 158	2 448	1 710	18.7	21.5	15.8
Under 1 day - Moins d'un jour	375	210	165	1.7	1.8	1.5
1-6	1 421	877	544	6.4	7.7	5.0
7-27	529	330	199	2.4	2.9	1.8
28-364	1 833	1 031	802	8.3	9.1	7.4
Kuwait - Koweït						
2001						
Total	420	237	183	...	...	...
Under 1 day - Moins d'un jour	139	80	59	...	...	...
1-6	91	52	39	...	...	...
7-27	52	27	25	...	...	...
28-364	138	78	60	...	...	...

16. Infant deaths and infant mortality rates by age and sex: latest available year, 1993 - 2002
Décès d'enfants de moins d'un an et taux de mortalité infantile selon l'âge et le sexe: dernière année disponible, 1993 - 2002 (continued — suite)

(See notes at end of table. — Voir notes à la fin du tableau.)

Continent, country or area, year, age (in days) and urban/rural residence — Continent, pays ou zone, année, âge (en jours) et résidence,urbaine/rurale	Number - Nombre			Rate - Taux		
	Both sexes Les deux sexes	Male Masculin	Female Féminin	Both sexes Les deux sexes	Male Masculin	Female Féminin
ASIA — ASIE						
Kuwait - Koweït						
2002						
Total	418	225	193	...	...	...
Under 1 day - Moins d'un jour	114	72	42			
1-6	82	45	37	...	...	...
7-27	89	47	42	...	...	...
28-364	133	61	72	...	...	...
Kyrgyzstan - Kirghizistan[7]						
2002						
Total	2 128	1 288	840	21.1	25.0	17.0
Under 1 day - Moins d'un jour	274	157	117	2.7	3.0	2.4
1-6	628	396	232	6.2	7.7	4.7
7-27	229	130	99	2.3	2.5	2.0
28-364	997	605	392	9.9	11.7	7.9
Malaysia - Malaisie						
2000						
Total	3 578	2 026	1 552	6.6	7.2	5.9
Under 1 day - Moins d'un jour	115	69	46	0.2	0.2	0.2
1-6	1 353	777	576	2.5	2.8	2.2
7-27	584	319	265	1.1	1.1	1.0
28-364	1 526	861	665	2.8	3.1	2.5
Maldives						
1996						
Total	193	112	81	...	...	...
Under 1 day - Moins d'un jour	32	17	15	...	...	...
1-6	66	44	22	...	...	...
7-27	20	8	12	...	...	...
28-364	75	43	32	...	...	...
Myanmar[10]						
1994						
Urban - Urbaine						
Total	12 395	6 685	6 685	...	...	...
Under 1 day - Moins d'un jour	419	228	191	...	...	...
1-6	3 492	1 862	1 630	...	...	...
7-27	2 548	1 308	1 240	...	...	...
28-364	5 764	3 184	2 580	...	...	...
Unknown - Inconnu	172	103	69	...	...	...
Occupied Palestinian Territory - Territoire palestinien occupé						
2001						
Total	1 100	583	517	...	...	...
Under 1 day - Moins d'un jour	74	42	32	...	...	...
1-6	272	172	100	...	...	...
7-27	205	111	94	...	...	...
28-364	549	258	291	...	...	...
2002						
Total	1 043	554	489	...	...	...
Under 1 day - Moins d'un jour	68	43	25	...	...	...
1-6	278	151	127	...	...	...
7-27	219	118	101	...	...	...
28-364	478	242	236	...	...	...
Pakistan[11,12]						
2001						
Total	286 609	149 832	136 777	...	...	...
Under 1 day - Moins d'un jour	14 921	10 569	4 352	...	...	...
1-6	106 313	58 441	47 873	...	...	...
7-27	52 846	25 491	27 355	...	...	...
28-364	112 531	55 332	57 198	...	...	...
Philippines						
1998						
Total	28 196	16 655	11 541	17.3	19.5	14.8

16. Infant deaths and infant mortality rates by age and sex: latest available year, 1993 - 2002
Décès d'enfants de moins d'un an et taux de mortalité infantile selon l'âge et le sexe: dernière année disponible, 1993 - 2002 (continued — suite)

(See notes at end of table. — Voir notes à la fin du tableau.)

Continent, country or area, year, age (in days) and urban/rural residence Continent, pays ou zone, année, âge (en jours) et résidence,urbaine/rurale	Number - Nombre			Rate - Taux		
	Both sexes Les deux sexes	Male Masculin	Female Féminin	Both sexes Les deux sexes	Male Masculin	Female Féminin
ASIA — ASIE						
Philippines						
1998						
Under 1 day - Moins d'un jour	5 248	3 050	2 198	3.2	3.6	2.8
1-6	7 130	4 385	2 745	4.4	5.1	3.5
7-27	3 076	1 850	1 226	1.9	2.2	1.6
28-364	12 742	7 370	5 372	7.8	8.6	6.9
Qatar						
1999						
Total	112	58	54	...	...	...
1-6	55	26	29	...	...	...
7-27	19	11	8	...	...	...
28-364	38	21	17	...	...	...
Singapore - Singapour[+,2]						
2000						
Total	137	80	57	...	...	...
Under 1 day - Moins d'un jour	22	10	12	...	...	...
1-6	39	21	18	...	...	...
7-27	21	12	9	...	...	...
28-364	55	37	18	...	...	...
2001						
Total	100	57	43	...	...	...
Under 1 day - Moins d'un jour	10	7	3	...	...	...
1-6	29	20	9	...	...	...
7-27	16	8	8	...	...	...
28-364	45	22	23	...	...	...
2002						
Total	123	73	48	...	...	...
Under 1 day - Moins d'un jour	17	12	4	...	...	...
1-6	28	21	6	...	...	...
7-27	23	11	12	...	...	...
28-364	55	29	26	...	...	...
Sri Lanka[+]						
1996						
Total	5 879	3 271	2 608	17.3	18.8	15.6
Under 1 day - Moins d'un jour	1 630	899	731	4.8	5.2	4.4
1-6	1 818	1 072	746	5.3	6.2	4.5
7-27	952	526	426	2.8	3.0	2.6
28-364	1 479	774	705	4.3	4.5	4.2
Tajikistan - Tadjikistan[7]						
1994						
Total	6 880	3 896	2 984	42.4	46.4	38.2
Under 1 day - Moins d'un jour	251	153	98	1.5	1.8	1.3
1-6	1 006	617	389	6.2	7.3	5.0
7-27	526	293	233	3.2	3.5	3.0
28-364	5 099	2 827	2 272	31.4	33.6	29.1
Unknown - Inconnu	13	6	7	◆0.1	◆0.1	◆0.1
Thailand - Thaïlande[+]						
1999						
Total	*5 003*	*2 765*	*2 238*	...	...	...
Under 1 day - Moins d'un jour	*287*	*135*	*152*	...	...	...
1-6	*764*	*439*	*325*	...	...	...
7-27	*760*	*434*	*326*	...	...	...
28-364	*3 192*	*1 757*	*1 435*	...	...	...
Turkey - Turquie[13,14]						
1998						
Urban - Urbaine						
Total	17 704	10 181	7 523	...	...	...
1-6	8 532	5 683	3 702	...	...	...
7-27	2 236	1 272	968	...	...	...
28-364	5 707	3 151	2 575	...	...	...

16. Infant deaths and infant mortality rates by age and sex: latest available year, 1993 - 2002
Décès d'enfants de moins d'un an et taux de mortalité infantile selon l'âge et le sexe: dernière année disponible, 1993 - 2002 (continued — suite)

(See notes at end of table. — Voir notes à la fin du tableau.)

Continent, country or area, year, age (in days) and urban/rural residence Continent, pays ou zone, année, âge (en jours) et résidence, urbaine/rurale	Number - Nombre			Rate - Taux		
	Both sexes Les deux sexes	Male Masculin	Female Féminin	Both sexes Les deux sexes	Male Masculin	Female Féminin
ASIA — ASIE						
Turkey - Turquie[13,14]						
1999						
Urban - Urbaine						
Total	15 870	8 931	6 939	...	...	...
1-6	8 483	4 876	3 607	...	...	...
7-27	1 978	1 093	885	...	...	...
28-364	5 409	2 962	2 447	...	...	...
Uzbekistan - Ouzbékistan[7]						
2000						
Total	10 091	5 805	4 286	19.1	21.4	16.7
Under 1 day - Moins d'un jour	607	355	252	1.2	1.3	1.0
1-6	2 179	1 352	827	4.1	5.0	3.2
7-27	1 279	731	548	2.4	2.7	2.1
28-364	6 026	3 367	2 659	11.4	12.4	10.4
EUROPE						
Austria - Autriche						
2002						
Total	318	189	129	...	...	...
Under 1 day - Moins d'un jour	119	70	49	...	...	...
1-6	48	31	17	...	...	...
7-27	51	27	24	...	...	...
28-364	100	61	39	...	...	...
Belarus - Bélarus[7]						
2002						
Total	695	397	298	...	...	...
Under 1 day - Moins d'un jour	82	46	36	...	...	...
1-6	268	168	100	...	...	...
7-27	246	164	82	...	...	...
28-364	356	185	171	...	...	...
Belgium - Belgique[15]						
2000						
Total	554	305	249	...	...	...
Under 1 day - Moins d'un jour	91	46	45	...	...	...
1-6	153	85	68	...	...	...
7-27	90	56	34	...	...	...
28-364	220	118	102	...	...	...
Bulgaria - Bulgarie						
2002						
Total	887	495	392	...	...	...
Under 1 day - Moins d'un jour	126	71	55	...	...	...
1-6	178	105	73	...	...	...
7-27	182	98	84	...	...	...
28-364	401	221	180	...	...	...
Channel Islands: Guernsey - Îles Anglo-Normandes: Guernesey						
1995						
Total	2	...	...	...	...	...
Under 1 day - Moins d'un jour	-	...	...	...	...	...
1-6	-	...	...	...	...	...
7-27	1	...	...	...	...	...
28-364	1	...	...	...	...	...
Channel Islands: Jersey - Îles Anglo-Normandes: Jersey[+]						
1994						
Total	2	-	2	...	...	...
Under 1 day - Moins d'un jour	-	-	-	...	...	...
1-6	1	-	1	...	...	...
7-27	-	-	-	...	...	...
28-364	1	-	1	...	...	...

16. Infant deaths and infant mortality rates by age and sex: latest available year, 1993 - 2002
Décès d'enfants de moins d'un an et taux de mortalité infantile selon l'âge et le sexe: dernière année disponible, 1993 - 2002 (continued — suite)

(See notes at end of table. — Voir notes à la fin du tableau.)

Continent, country or area, year, age (in days) and urban/rural residence / Continent, pays ou zone, année, âge (en jours) et résidence,urbaine/rurale	Number - Nombre			Rate - Taux		
	Both sexes Les deux sexes	Male Masculin	Female Féminin	Both sexes Les deux sexes	Male Masculin	Female Féminin
EUROPE						
Channel Islands: Jersey - Îles Anglo-Normandes: Jersey[+]						
1994						
Unknown - Inconnu	-	-	-	...	...	...
Croatia - Croatie						
2002						
Total	282	159	123	...	...	...
Under 1 day - Moins d'un jour	83	48	35	...	...	...
1-6	78	47	31	...	...	...
7-27	38	23	15	...	...	...
28-364	83	41	42	...	...	...
Czech Republic - République tchèque						
2002						
Total	385	216	169	...	...	...
Under 1 day - Moins d'un jour	63	36	27	...	...	...
1-6	94	57	37	...	...	...
7-27	94	44	50	...	...	...
28-364	134	79	55	...	...	...
Denmark - Danemark[16]						
2002						
Total	284	159	125	...	...	...
Under 1 day - Moins d'un jour	92	55	37	...	...	...
1-6	85	43	42	...	...	...
7-27	40	27	13	...	...	...
28-364	67	34	33	...	...	...
Estonia - Estonie[7]						
2001						
Total	111	65	46	...	...	...
Under 1 day - Moins d'un jour	21	13	8	...	...	...
1-6	11	6	5	...	...	...
7-27	31	17	14	...	...	...
28-364	48	29	19	...	...	...
2002						
Total	74	46	28	...	...	...
Under 1 day - Moins d'un jour	17	9	8	...	...	...
1-6	14	11	3	...	...	...
7-27	16	11	5	...	...	...
28-364	27	15	12	...	...	...
Finland - Finlande[17]						
2002						
Total	168	91	77	...	...	...
Under 1 day - Moins d'un jour	60	33	27	...	...	...
1-6	36	23	13	...	...	...
7-27	25	11	14	...	...	...
28-364	47	24	23	...	...	...
France[18]						
1999						
Total	3 221	1 844	1 377	4.3	4.8	3.8
Under 1 day - Moins d'un jour	697	380	317	0.9	1.0	0.9
1-6	760	441	319	1.0	1.2	0.9
7-27	588	325	263	0.8	0.9	0.7
28-364	1 176	698	478	1.6	1.8	1.3
Germany - Allemagne						
2001						
Total	3 163	1 815	1 348	4.3	4.8	3.8
Under 1 day - Moins d'un jour	791	447	344	1.1	1.2	1.0
1-6	707	414	293	1.0	1.1	0.8
7-27	476	280	196	0.6	0.7	0.5
28-364	1 189	674	515	1.6	1.8	1.4

16. Infant deaths and infant mortality rates by age and sex: latest available year, 1993 - 2002
Décès d'enfants de moins d'un an et taux de mortalité infantile selon l'âge et le sexe: dernière année disponible, 1993 - 2002 (continued — suite)

(See notes at end of table. — Voir notes à la fin du tableau.)

Continent, country or area, year, age (in days) and urban/rural residence / Continent, pays ou zone, année, âge (en jours) et résidence,urbaine/rurale	Number - Nombre			Rate - Taux		
	Both sexes Les deux sexes	Male Masculin	Female Féminin	Both sexes Les deux sexes	Male Masculin	Female Féminin
EUROPE						
Greece - Grèce						
2001						
Total	522	...	...	...	...	...
0-6	235	...	...	...	...	...
7-27	129	...	...	...	...	...
28-364	158	...	...	...	...	...
Hungary - Hongrie						
2002						
Total	693	362	331	...	...	...
Under 1 day - Moins d'un jour	175	97	78	...	...	...
1-6	188	92	96	...	...	...
7-27	144	79	65	...	...	...
28-364	186	94	92	...	...	...
Iceland - Islande						
2002						
Total	9	7	2	...	...	...
Under 1 day - Moins d'un jour	2	2	-	...	...	...
1-6	2	1	1	...	...	...
7-27	1	1	-	...	...	...
28-364	4	3	1	...	...	...
Ireland - Irlande[+,19]						
2001						
Total	337	...	...	...	...	...
0-6	180	...	...	...	...	...
7-27	55	...	...	...	...	...
28-364	102	...	...	...	...	...
Isle of Man - Îles de Man[+]						
1996						
Total	2	1	1	...	...	...
Under 1 day - Moins d'un jour	1	-	1	...	...	...
1-6	1	1	-	...	...	...
7-27	-	-	-	...	...	...
28-364	-	-	-	...	...	...
Italy - Italie						
1997						
Total	2 973	1 638	1 335	5.6	5.9	5.2
Under 1 day - Moins d'un jour	842	449	393	1.6	1.6	1.5
1-6	822	471	351	1.5	1.7	1.4
7-27	598	329	269	1.1	1.2	1.0
28-364	711	389	322	1.3	1.4	1.2
Latvia - Lettonie[7]						
2002						
Total	197	111	86	...	...	...
Under 1 day - Moins d'un jour	20	13	7	...	...	...
1-6	58	30	28	...	...	...
7-27	37	20	17	...	...	...
28-364	82	48	34	...	...	...
Lithuania - Lituanie[7]						
2002						
Total	238	133	105	...	...	...
Under 1 day - Moins d'un jour	48	31	17	...	...	...
1-6	50	28	22	...	...	...
7-27	32	15	17	...	...	...
28-364	108	59	49	...	...	...
Luxembourg						
2002						
Total	27	15	12	...	...	...
Under 1 day - Moins d'un jour	6	5	1	...	...	...
1-6	6	3	3	...	...	...
7-27	7	4	3	...	...	...
28-364	8	3	5	...	...	...

16. Infant deaths and infant mortality rates by age and sex: latest available year, 1993 - 2002
Décès d'enfants de moins d'un an et taux de mortalité infantile selon l'âge et le sexe: dernière année disponible, 1993 - 2002 (continued — suite)

(See notes at end of table. — Voir notes à la fin du tableau.)

Continent, country or area, year, age (in days) and urban/rural residence Continent, pays ou zone, année, âge (en jours) et résidence,urbaine/rurale	Number - Nombre			Rate - Taux		
	Both sexes Les deux sexes	Male Masculin	Female Féminin	Both sexes Les deux sexes	Male Masculin	Female Féminin
EUROPE						
Malta - Malte						
2001						
Total	17	12	5	...	...	...
0-6	10	7	3	...	...	...
7-27	2	1	1	...	...	...
28-364	5	4	1	...	...	...
Netherlands - Pays-Bas[20]						
2001						
Total	1 088	615	473	5.4	5.9	4.8
Under 1 day - Moins d'un jour	332	200	132	1.6	1.9	1.3
1-6	284	155	129	1.4	1.5	1.3
7-27	168	86	82	0.8	0.8	0.8
28-364	304	174	130	1.5	1.7	1.3
Norway - Norvège[21]						
2002						
Total	192	94	98	...	...	...
Under 1 day - Moins d'un jour	45	20	25	...	...	...
1-6	49	21	28	...	...	...
7-27	42	23	19	...	...	...
28-364	14	7	7	...	...	...
Poland - Pologne						
2001						
Total	2 823	...	...	7.7	...	...
0-6	1 439	...	...	3.9	...	...
7-27	535	...	...	1.5	...	...
28-364	849	...	...	2.3	...	...
Portugal						
2002						
Total	574	316	258	...	...	...
Under 1 day - Moins d'un jour	157	85	72	...	...	...
1-6	140	73	67	...	...	...
7-27	94	53	41	...	...	...
28-364	183	105	78	...	...	...
Republic of Moldova - République de Moldova[7]						
2002						
Total	528	308	220	...	...	...
Under 1 day - Moins d'un jour	66	42	24	...	...	...
1-6	156	88	68	...	...	...
7-27	54	33	21	...	...	...
28-364	231	133	98	...	...	...
Unknown - Inconnu	21	12	9	...	...	...
Romania - Roumanie						
2002						
Total	3 648	2 055	1 593	17.3	19.0	15.6
Under 1 day - Moins d'un jour	252	133	119	1.2	1.2	1.2
1-6	947	569	378	4.5	5.3	3.7
7-27	573	309	264	2.7	2.9	2.6
28-364	1 876	1 044	832	8.9	9.6	8.1
Russian Federation - Fédération de Russie[7]						
2000						
Total	19 286	11 248	8 038	15.2	17.2	13.1
Under 1 day - Moins d'un jour	2 476	1 409	1 067	2.0	2.2	1.7
1-6	5 834	3 591	2 243	4.6	5.5	3.7
7-27	3 179	1 845	1 334	2.5	2.8	2.2
28-364	7 786	4 396	3 390	6.1	6.7	5.5
Unknown - Inconnu	11	7	4	0.0	0.0	0.0
San Marino - Saint-Marin[+]						
1999						
Total	1	1	-	...	...	...
Under 1 day - Moins d'un jour	1	1	-	...	...	...
1-6	-	-	-	...	...	...

16. Infant deaths and infant mortality rates by age and sex: latest available year, 1993 - 2002
Décès d'enfants de moins d'un an et taux de mortalité infantile selon l'âge et le sexe: dernière année disponible, 1993 - 2002 (continued — suite)

(See notes at end of table. — Voir notes à la fin du tableau.)

Continent, country or area, year, age (in days) and urban/rural residence Continent, pays ou zone, année, âge (en jours) et résidence,urbaine/rurale	Number - Nombre			Rate - Taux		
	Both sexes Les deux sexes	Male Masculin	Female Féminin	Both sexes Les deux sexes	Male Masculin	Female Féminin
EUROPE						
San Marino - Saint-Marin+						
1999						
7-27	-	-	-	...	...	...
28-364	-	-	-	...	...	...
Serbia and Montenegro - Serbie-et-Montenegro						
2000						
Total	1 668	993	675	13.3	15.2	11.2
Under 1 day - Moins d'un jour	316	199	117	2.5	3.0	1.9
1-6	571	351	220	4.5	5.4	3.6
7-27	221	132	89	1.8	2.0	1.5
28-364	560	311	249	4.4	4.8	4.1
2001						
Total	1 709	...	...	13.1	...	...
0-6	893	...	...	6.9	...	...
7-27	249	...	...	1.9	...	...
28-364	567	...	...	4.4	...	...
Slovakia - Slovaquie						
2002						
Total	388	189	199	...	...	...
Under 1 day - Moins d'un jour	73	38	35	...	...	...
1-6	97	41	56	...	...	...
7-27	68	30	38	...	...	...
28-364	150	80	70	...	...	...
Slovenia - Slovénie						
2002						
Total	67	44	23	...	...	...
Under 1 day - Moins d'un jour	21	16	5	...	...	...
1-6	22	12	10	...	...	...
7-27	11	7	4	...	...	...
28-364	13	9	3	...	...	...
Spain - Espagne						
1998						
Total	1 774	991	783	4.9	5.2	4.4
Under 1 day - Moins d'un jour	380	210	170	1.0	1.1	1.0
1-6	361	206	155	1.0	1.1	0.9
7-27	345	195	150	0.9	1.0	0.9
28-364	688	380	308	1.9	2.0	1.7
1999						
Total	1 700	...	...	4.5	...	...
0-6	703	...	...	1.8	...	...
7-27	368	...	...	1.0	...	...
28-364	629	...	...	1.7	...	...
Sweden - Suède						
2002						
Total	313	172	141	...	...	...
Under 1 day - Moins d'un jour	62	32	30	...	...	...
1-6	98	49	49	...	...	...
7-27	51	30	21	...	...	...
28-364	101	60	41	...	...	...
Switzerland - Suisse						
2001						
Total	365	209	156	...	...	...
Under 1 day - Moins d'un jour	127	72	55	...	...	...
1-6	102	53	49	...	...	...
7-27	33	21	12	...	...	...
28-364	101	61	40	...	...	...
The Former Yugoslav Rep. of Macedonia - L'ex-République yougoslave de Macédoine						
2002						
Total	283	147	136	...	...	...
Under 1 day - Moins d'un jour	89	45	44	...	...	...

16. Infant deaths and infant mortality rates by age and sex: latest available year, 1993 - 2002
Décès d'enfants de moins d'un an et taux de mortalité infantile selon l'âge et le sexe: dernière année disponible, 1993 - 2002 (continued — suite)

(See notes at end of table. — Voir notes à la fin du tableau.)

Continent, country or area, year, age (in days) and urban/rural residence — Continent, pays ou zone, année, âge (en jours) et résidence,urbaine/rurale	Number - Nombre			Rate - Taux		
	Both sexes Les deux sexes	Male Masculin	Female Féminin	Both sexes Les deux sexes	Male Masculin	Female Féminin
EUROPE						
The Former Yugoslav Rep. of Macedonia - L'ex-République yougoslave de Macédoine						
2002						
1-6	93	54	39	...	...	...
7-27	33	14	19	...	...	...
28-364	68	34	34	...	...	...
Ukraine[7]						
2001						
Total	4 283	2 488	1 795	11.4	12.8	9.8
Under 1 day - Moins d'un jour	368	219	149	1.0	1.1	0.8
1-6	1 252	743	509	3.3	3.8	2.8
7-27	684	403	281	1.8	2.1	1.5
28-364	1 976	1 122	854	5.2	5.8	4.7
Unknown - Inconnu	3	1	2	0.0	0.0	0.0
United Kingdom - Royaume-Uni						
2001						
Total	3 664	2 042	1 622	5.5	...	...
Under 1 day - Moins d'un jour	1 006	567	439	1.5	...	...
1-6	815	457	358	1.2	...	...
7-27	613	347	266	0.9	...	...
28-364	1 230	671	559	1.8	...	...
OCEANIA — OCEANIE						
Australia - Australie+						
2001						
Total	1 309	751	558	5.3	5.9	4.6
Under 1 day - Moins d'un jour	512	272	240	2.1	2.2	2.0
1-6	220	139	81	0.9	1.1	0.7
7-27	185	115	70	0.8	0.9	0.6
28-364	392	225	167	1.6	1.8	1.4
2002						
Total	1 264	699	565	5.0	5.4	4.6
Under 1 day - Moins d'un jour	459	256	203	1.8	2.0	1.7
1-6	472	240	232	1.9	1.9	1.9
7-27	326	180	146	1.3	1.4	1.2
28-364	406	233	173	1.6	1.8	1.4
New Caledonia - Nouvelle-Calédonie						
1999						
Total	27	12	15	...	...	...
Under 1 day - Moins d'un jour	5	2	3	...	...	...
1-6	5	2	3	...	...	...
7-27	3	1	2	...	...	...
28-364	14	7	7	...	...	...
New Zealand - Nouvelle-Zélande+						
2001						
Total	296	174	122	...	...	...
Under 1 day - Moins d'un jour	82	41	41	...	...	...
1-6	45	25	20	...	...	...
7-27	27	13	14	...	...	...
28-364	142	95	47	...	...	...
2002						
Total	300	155	145	...	...	...
Under 1 day - Moins d'un jour	100	55	45	...	...	...
1-6	55	27	28	...	...	...
7-27	34	17	17	...	...	...
28-364	111	56	55	...	...	...
Tonga+						
1997						
Total	20	...	...	...	...	...
Under 1 day - Moins d'un jour	4	...	...	...	...	...

16. Infant deaths and infant mortality rates by age and sex: latest available year, 1993 - 2002
Décès d'enfants de moins d'un an et taux de mortalité infantile selon l'âge et le sexe: dernière année disponible, 1993 - 2002 (continued — suite)

(See notes at end of table. — Voir notes à la fin du tableau.)

Continent, country or area, year, age (in days) and urban/rural residence / Continent, pays ou zone, année, âge (en jours) et résidence,urbaine/rurale	Number - Nombre			Rate - Taux		
	Both sexes Les deux sexes	Male Masculin	Female Féminin	Both sexes Les deux sexes	Male Masculin	Female Féminin
OCEANIA — OCEANIE						
Tonga+						
1997						
1-6	2	...	...	...	...	...
7-27	2	...	...	...	...	...
28-364	12	...	...	...	...	...

GENERAL NOTES - NOTES GENERALES

Data exclude foetal deaths. Rates are the number of deaths of infants of specified age by sex per 1 000 live births of same sex. Rates are shown only for countries having at least a total of 1 000 infant deaths in a given year. For definition of 'urban', see Technical Notes for table 6. For method of evaluation and limitations of data, see Technical Notes for this table. — Les données ne comprennent pas les morts foetales. Les taux représent le nombre de décès d'enfants d'âge et de sex données pour 1 000 naissances vivantes du même sexe. Les taux présentés ne se rapportent qu'aux pays ou zones où l'on a enregistré un total d'au moins 1 000 décès d'un an dans un année donnée. Pour les définitions des 'regions urbaines', se reporter à la fin des Notes techniques du tableau 6. Pour la méthode d'évaluation et les insuffisances des données voir, Notes techniques pour ce tableau.

Italics: data from civil registers which are incomplete or of unknown completeness. — *Italiques:* données incomplètes ou dont le degré d'exactitude n'est pas connu provenant des registres de l'état civil.

FOOTNOTES - NOTES

+ Data tabulated by date of registration rather than occurrence. — Données exploitées selon la date de l'enregistrement et non la date de l'événement.
♦ Rates based on 30 or fewer infant deaths. — Taux basés sur 30 décès d'enfants ou moins.

[1] Including Canadian residents temporarily in the United States, but excluding United States residents temporarily in Canada. - Y compris les résidents canadiens se trouvant temporairement aux Etats-Unis, mais ne comprenant pas les résidents des Etats-Unis se trouvant temporairement au Canada.
[2] The category "Both sexes" includes infant deaths of unknown sex. - La catégorie "Les deux sexes" comprenne les décès d'enfants de moins d'un an dont on ignore le sexe.
[3] Excluding Indian jungle population. - Non compris les Indiens de la jungle.
[4] Data on live births and deaths are based on a civil registration system put in place in January 1998. - Les données sur les naissances et les décès sont basées sur un système d'enregistrement des faits d'état civil mis en place en janvier 1998.

[5] Excluding nomadic Indian tribes. - Non compris les tribus d'Indiens nomades.
[6] Data refer to registered infant deaths only. - Les données se rapportent aux décès enregistrés d'enfants de moins de 1 an seulement.
[7] Excluding infants born alive with less than 28 weeks gestation, less than 1 000 grams in weight and 35 centimeters in length, who die within seven days of birth. - Non compris les enfants nés vivants avant 28 semaines de gestation, pesant moins de 1 000 grammes, mesurant moins de 35 centimètres et décédés dans les sept jours qui ont suivi leur naissance.
[8] Including data for East Jerusalem and Israeli residents in certain other territories under occupation by Israeli military forces since June 1967. - Y compris les données pour Jérusalem-Est et les résidents israéliens dans certains autres territoires occupés depuis 1967 par les forces armées israéliennes.
[9] Data refer to Japanese nationals in Japan only. - Les données se raportent aux nationaux japonais au Japon seulement.
[10] Data for urban refer to 170 towns out of 254 towns. - Les données urbaines se rapportent à 170 des 254 villes.
[11] Based on the results of the Population Growth Survey. - D'après les résultats de la 'Population Growth Survey.'
[12] Excluding data for the Pakistan-held part of Jammu and Kashmir, the final status of which has not yet been determined. - Non compris les données concernant la partie du Jammu et Cachemire occupée par le Pakistan dont le statut définitif n'a pas été déterminé.
[13] Based on the results of the Population Demographic Survey. - D'après les résultats de la Population Demographic Survey.
[14] Deaths in province and district centers. - Les décès aux centres des provinces et des zones seulement.
[15] Including armed forces stationed outside the country, but excluding alien armed forces stationed in the area. - Y compris les militaires nationaux hors du pays, mais non compris les militaires étrangers en garnison sur le territoire.
[16] Excluding Faeroe Islands and Greenland. - Non compris les Iles Féroé et Gröenland.
[17] Including nationals temporarily outside the country. - Y compris les nationaux se trouvant temporairement hors du pays.
[18] Including armed forces stationed outside the country. - Y compris les militaires nationaux hors du pays.
[19] Events registered within one year of occurrence. - Evénements enregistrés dans l'année qui suit l'événement.
[20] Including residents outside the country if listed in a Netherlands population register. - Y compris les résidents hors du pays, s'ils sont inscrits sur un registre de population néerlandais.
[21] Including residents temporarily outside the country. - Y compris les résidents se trouvant temporairement hors du pays.

Table 17

Table 17 presents maternal deaths and maternal mortality rates for as many years as possible between 1995 and 2002.

Description of variables: Maternal deaths are defined for the purposes of the Demographic Yearbook as those caused by deliveries and complications of pregnancy, childbirth and the puerperium, within 42 days of termination of pregnancy. They are usually defined as deaths coded "38-41" for ICD-9 Basic Tabulation List or as deaths coded "A34", "O00-O95", "O98-O99" for ICD-10, respectively. However, data for ICD-10 shown in this table include deaths due to "O96" and "O97" which refer to deaths from any obstetric cause occurring more than 42 days but less than one year after delivery and death from sequelae of direct obstetric causes occurring one year or more after delivery. For details on causes and corresponding ICD codes, see Technical Notes for Table 21.

For further information on the definition of maternal mortality from the tenth revisions of the *International Statistical Classification of Diseases and Related Health Problems*[1], see also section 4.3 of the Technical Notes.

Statistics on maternal death presented in this table are provided by the World Health Organisation. They are limited to countries or areas that meet the criterion that cause-of-death statistics are either classified by or convertible to the ninth or tenth revisions mentioned above. Data that are classified by the tenth revision are set in bold in the table.

Rate computation: Maternal mortality rates are the annual number of maternal deaths per 100 000 live births (table 9) in the same year. These rates have been calculated by the Statistics Division of the United Nations. Rates based on 30 or fewer maternal deaths are identified by the symbol (♦).

Reliability of data: In general the quality code for deaths shown in table 18 is used to determine whether data on deaths in other tables appear in roman or *italic* type. However, the reliability of data for the completeness of cause of death data is provided by the World Health Organisation it may differ from the reliability of data for the total number of deaths. Therefore, there are cases when the quality code in table 18 does not correspond with the typeface used in this table.

Countries and areas that have incomplete (less than 90 per cent completeness) or of unknown completeness of cause of deaths data coverage are considered unreliable and are set in italics rather than in roman type. Rates on these data are not computed.

In addition, when it is known that registration of cause of death does not cover certain areas of a country, rates are not computed. Those countries are Georgia, Republic of Moldova and Russian Federation, as indicated in the footnote 7, 19 and 20, respectively. All other footnotes pertaining to the inclusion or exclusion of certain population of a country refer only to the live births in the denominator.

Limitations: Statistics on maternal deaths are subject to the same qualifications that have been set forth for vital statistics in general and death statistics in particular as discussed in section 4 of the Technical Notes. The reliability of the data, an indication of which is described above, is an important factor in considering the limitations. In addition, maternal-death statistics are subject to all the qualifications relating to cause-of-death statistics. These have been set forth in section 4 of the Technical Notes.

Maternal mortality rates are subject to the limitations of the data on live births with which they have been calculated. These have been set forth in the technical notes for table 9.

The calculation of the maternal mortality rates based on the total number of live births approximates the risk of dying from complications of pregnancy, childbirth or puerperium. Ideally this rate should be based on the number of women exposed to the risk of pregnancy, in other words, the number of women conceiving. Since it is impossible to know how many women have conceived, the total number of live births is used in calculating this rate.

NOTES

[1] *International Statistical Classification of Diseases and Related Health Problems*, Tenth Revision, Volume 2, World Health Organization, Geneva, 1992.

Earlier data: Maternal deaths and maternal mortality rates have been shown in previous issues of the *Demographic Yearbook*. For information on specific years covered, the reader should consult the Index.

It should however be noted that in issues prior to 1975, maternal mortality rates were calculated using the female population rather than live births. Therefore, maternal mortality rates published since 1975 are not comparable to the earlier maternal death rates.

Tableau 17

Ce tableau présente des statistiques et des taux de mortalité liée à la maternité pour le plus grand nombre d'années possible entre 1995 et 2002.

Description des variables : Aux fins de *l'Annuaire démographique*, les décès liés à la maternité sont ceux entraînés par l'accouchement ou les complications de la grossesse, de l'accouchement et des suites de couches dans un délai de 42 jours après la terminaison de la grossesse. Ils sont généralement associés aux codes 38 à 41 dans le cas de la liste de base pour la mise en tableaux de la CIM-9 et aux codes A34, O00 à O95 et O98 et O99 dans le cas de la CIM-10. Les statistiques associées à des codes correspondant à la CIM-10 englobent des décès de type O96 et O97, qui désignent les décès liés à des causes obstétriques se produisant après 42 jours mais moins d'un an après l'accouchement et les décès entraînés par les séquelles de complications obstétriques directes qui se produisent un an ou plus après l'accouchement. Pour plus de précisions sur les causes des décès et les codes correspondants de la CIM, voir les notes techniques correspondant au tableau 21.

Pour plus de précisions concernant les définitions de la mortalité liée à la maternité dans la dixième révision de la *Classification statistique internationale des maladies et des problèmes de santé connexes*[1], se reporter également à la section 4.3 des Notes techniques.

Les statistiques de mortalité liée à la maternité présentées dans le tableau 17 émanent de l'Organisation mondiale de la santé. Elles ne se rapportent qu'aux pays ou zones qui répondent aux critères selon lesquels les statistiques relatives à la cause des décès sont conformes à la liste de la neuvième ou de la dixième révision de la CIM ou peuvent être aisément comparées aux catégories de cette liste. Les données conformes à la dixième révision sont indiquées en gras dans le tableau.

Calcul des taux : Les taux de mortalité liée à la maternité représentent le nombre annuel de décès dus à la maternité pour 100 000 naissances vivantes (fréquences du tableau 9) de la même année. Ces taux ont été calculés par la Division de statistique de l'ONU. Les taux fondés sur 30 décès liés à la maternité ou moins sont signalés par le signe '♦'.

Fiabilité des données : En général, les code de qualité associés aux données sur les décès indiqués au tableau 18 servent à déterminer si, dans les autres tableaux, les données relatives à la mortalité apparaissent en caractères romains ou italiques. Toutefois, les renseignements relatifs à la fiabilité des données concernant l'exhaustivité des données classées en fonction de la cause des décès émanent de l'Organisation mondiale de la santé et il est possible qu'ils ne correspondent pas avec le degré de fiabilité des données portant sur le nombre total des décès. Il y a donc des cas où les codes de qualité figurant dans le tableau 18 ne coïncident pas avec les caractères utilisés dans le présent tableau.

Les statistiques relatives aux pays et aux zones pour lesquels la couverture des données concernant les causes des décès est incomplète (degré de complétude inférieur à 90 p. 100) ou dont le degré de complétude n'est pas connu sont jugées douteuses et apparaissent en italique et non en caractères romains. Les taux correspondants ne sont pas calculés.

En outre, lorsque l'on sait que l'enregistrement des causes des décès ne couvre pas certaines zones d'un pays, les taux ne sont pas non plus calculés. Cela est le cas de la Géorgie, de la République de Moldova et de la Fédération de Russie, comme indiqué dans les notes 7, 19 et 20 respectivement. En ce qui concerne toutes les autres notes qui portent sur l'inclusion ou l'exclusion de certaines populations dans un pays, ce sont les naissances vivantes qui figurent au dénominateur.

Insuffisance des données : Les statistiques de la mortalité liée à la maternité appellent toutes les réserves qui ont été formulées à propos des statistiques de l'état civil en général et des statistiques relatives à la mortalité en particulier (voir la section 4 des Notes techniques). La fiabilité des données, au sujet de laquelle des indications ont été fournies plus haut, est un facteur important. En outre, les statistiques de la mortalité liée à la maternité appellent les mêmes réserves que celles exposées à la section 4 des Notes techniques en ce qui concerne les statistiques des causes de décès.

Les taux de mortalité liée à la maternité appellent également toutes les réserves formulées à propos des statistiques des naissances vivantes qui ont servi à leur calcul (voir à ce sujet les notes techniques relatives au tableau 9).

En prenant le nombre total des naissances vivantes comme base pour le calcul des taux de mortalité liée à la maternité, on obtient une mesure approximative de la probabilité de décès dus aux complications de la grossesse, de l'accouchement et des suites de couches. Idéalement, ces taux devraient être calculés sur la base du nombre de femmes exposées aux risques liés à la grossesse, c'est-à-dire sur la base du nombre de femmes qui conçoivent. Étant donné qu'il est impossible de connaître le nombre de femmes ayant conçu, c'est le nombre total de naissances vivantes que l'on utilise pour calculer ces taux.

Données publiées antérieurement : Des statistiques concernant les décès liés à la maternité (nombre de décès et taux) ont déjà été présentées dans des éditions antérieures de l'*Annuaire démographique*. Pour plus de précisions concernant les années pour lesquelles ces données ont été publiées, se reporter à l'index.

Il faut souligner que, avant 1975, les taux de mortalité liée à la maternité étaient calculés sur la base de la population féminine et non sur celle du nombre de naissances vivantes. Ils ne sont donc pas comparables à ceux qui figurent dans les éditions de l'*Annuaire démographique* parues après 1975.

NOTE

[1] *Classification statistique internationale des maladies et des problèmes de santé connexes*, dixième révision, volume 2. Genève, Organisation mondiale de la santé, 1992.

17. Maternal deaths and maternal death rates: 1995 - 2002
Mortalité liée à la maternité nombre de décès et taux: 1995 - 2002

(See notes at end of table. — Voir notes à la fin du tableau.)

Continent and country or area / Continent et pays ou zone	1995	1996	1997	1998	1999	2000	2001	2002
AFRICA — AFRIQUE								
Egypt - Égypte								
Number - Nombre	...	...	...	...	...	*492*	...	...
Mauritius - Maurice								
Number - Nombre	12	6	10	4	7	3	...	...
Rate — Taux	♦58.2	♦29.3	♦50.0	♦20.6	♦34.5	♦14.8	...	...
South Africa - Afrique du Sud								
Number - Nombre	*499*	*606*	...	...	...	...	...	...
AMERICA, NORTH — AMERIQUE DU NORD								
Anguilla								
Number - Nombre	-	...	...	...	...	-	...	...
Antigua and Barbuda - Antigua-et-Barbuda								
Number - Nombre	*2*	...	...	...	...	...	...	...
Bahamas								
Number - Nombre	*4*	-	-	*1*	*1*	*2*	...	...
Barbados - Barbade								
Number - Nombre	-	...	...	...	...	1	...	...
Rate — Taux		...	...	...	...	♦26.6	...	...
Belize								
Number - Nombre	1	-	3	9	3	5	...	...
Rate — Taux	♦15.1	-	♦40.8	♦150.4	♦48.2	♦68.4	...	...
Bermuda - Bermudes								
Number - Nombre	...	...	...	...	...	-	...	...
British Virgin Islands - Îles Vierges britanniques								
Number - Nombre	-	-	-	-	...	...	...	...
Canada[1]								
Number - Nombre	17	18	19	13	8	11	...	...
Rate — Taux	♦4.5	♦4.9	♦5.5	♦3.8	♦2.4	♦3.4	...	...
Cayman Islands - Îles Caïmanes								
Number - Nombre	-	-	-	-	-	1	...	...
Costa Rica								
Number - Nombre	*16*	*23*	*29*	*14*	*15*	*28*	*24*	*27*
Cuba								
Number - Nombre	70	51	59	59	66	58	57	...
Rate — Taux	47.6	36.4	38.6	39.1	43.8	40.4	41.1	...
Dominica - Dominique								
Number - Nombre	1	-	-	1	-	...	...	...
Rate — Taux	♦66.6	-	-	♦81.3		...	...	...
Dominican Republic - République dominicaine								
Number - Nombre	*77*	*43*	*74*	*64*	...	...	...	...
El Salvador								
Number - Nombre	*55*	*42*	*42*	*42*	*23*	...	...	...
Grenada - Grenade								
Number - Nombre	-	-	...	...	...	...	...	...
Guatemala								
Number - Nombre	*360*	*335*	*342*	*324*	*316*	...	...	...
Mexico - Mexique								
Number - Nombre	1 454	1 291	1 266	*1 430*	*1 411*	*1 325*	*1 268*	...
Rate — Taux	52.9	47.7	46.9	*53.6*	*51.0*	*47.3*	*45.8*	...
Nicaragua								
Number - Nombre	...	*123*	*127*	*113*	*138*	*97*	...	...
Panama								
Number - Nombre	...	*35*	*28*	*30*	*31*	*30*	...	...
Puerto Rico - Porto Rico								
Number - Nombre	*9*	*11*	*13*	*8*	*10*	*14*	...	...
Saint Kitts and Nevis - Saint-Kitts-et-Nevis								
Number - Nombre	1	...	...	...	...	...	...	...
Rate — Taux	♦125.5	...	...	...	...	...	...	...
Saint Lucia - Sainte-Lucie								
Number - Nombre	-	1	-	-	1	3	1	...
Rate — Taux	-	♦31.8	-	-	♦33.4	♦105.6	♦35.9	...

17. Maternal deaths and maternal death rates: 1995 - 2002
Mortalité liée à la maternité nombre de décès et taux: 1995 - 2002 (continued — suite)

(See notes at end of table. — Voir notes à la fin du tableau.)

Continent and country or area Continent et pays ou zone	1995	1996	1997	1998	1999	2000	2001	2002
AMERICA, NORTH — AMERIQUE DU NORD								
Saint Vincent and the Grenadines - Saint Vincent-et-les Grenadines								
Number - Nombre	4	2	1	-	1	...	...	...
Rate — Taux	♦153.0	♦85.5	♦43.3	-	♦46.1			
Trinidad and Tobago - Trinité-et-Tobago								
Number - Nombre	13	...	...	8	...	...	...	...
Rate — Taux	♦67.5	...	...	...	...	...	...	...
Turks Caicos Islands - Îles Turques et Caïques								
Number - Nombre	-	-	-	-	-	...	...	...
United States - États-Unis								
Number - Nombre	277	294	327	281	**406**	**404**	...	...
Rate — Taux	7.1	7.6	8.4	7.1	10.3	10.0	...	...
United States Virgin Islands - Îles Vierges américaines								
Number - Nombre	...	...	1	-	-	1	...	...
AMERICA, SOUTH — AMERIQUE DU SUD								
Argentina - Argentine								
Number - Nombre	290	317	**265**	**260**	287	245	309	...
Rate — Taux [2]	44.0	46.9	**38.3**	**38.1**	41.8	34.9	45.2	...
Brazil - Brésil [2]								
Number - Nombre	*1 632*	*1 465*	*1 791*	*1 937*	*1 823*	*1 648*	...	...
Chile - Chili								
Number - Nombre	86	63	61	55	60	49	45	...
Rate — Taux	30.7	23.8	**23.5**	**21.4**	23.9	19.7	18.3	...
Colombia - Colombie [3]								
Number - Nombre	*411*	*430*	*420*	*721*	*676*	...	...	...
Ecuador - Équateur [4]								
Number - Nombre	*170*	*194*	*162*	*153*	*209*	*232*	...	...
Guyana								
Number - Nombre	35	26	...	...	...	...	...	...
Paraguay								
Number - Nombre	*104*	*109*	*89*	*96*	*103*	*140*	...	...
Peru - Pérou [2,5]								
Number - Nombre	*301*	*337*	*246*	*279*	*261*	*263*	...	...
Uruguay								
Number - Nombre	14	11	**17**	**11**	6	9	...	...
Rate — Taux	♦24.7	♦18.7	♦**29.3**	♦**20.1**	♦11.1	♦17.1	...	...
Venezuela [2]								
Number - Nombre	...	297	308	256	313	327	...	...
Rate — Taux	...	59.6	59.6	51.0	59.3	60.1	...	...
ASIA — ASIE								
Armenia - Arménie [6]								
Number - Nombre	17	10	17	10	12	18	7	3
Rate — Taux	♦34.7	♦20.8	♦38.7	♦25.4	♦32.9	♦52.5	♦21.8	...
Azerbaijan - Azerbaïdjan [6]								
Number - Nombre	*53*	*56*	*41*	*51*	*51*	*44*	*27*	*22*
Bahrain - Bahreïn								
Number - Nombre	...	...	**2**	**2**	3	2	...	...
Rate — Taux	...	...	♦**14.9**	♦**14.9**	♦21.0	♦14.3	...	...
China: Hong Kong SAR - Chine: Hong Kong RAS								
Number - Nombre	5	2	1	1	1	3	...	...
Georgia - Géorgie [7]								
Number - Nombre	*17*	*9*	*13*	*15*	*9*	*4*	*4*	...
Israel - Israël [8]								
Number - Nombre	7	9	12	11	9	...	...	...
Rate — Taux	♦6.0	♦7.4	♦9.6	♦8.5	♦6.8	...	...	...

17. Maternal deaths and maternal death rates: 1995 - 2002
Mortalité liée à la maternité nombre de décès et taux: 1995 - 2002 (continued — suite)

(See notes at end of table. — Voir notes à la fin du tableau.)

Continent and country or area Continent et pays ou zone	1995	1996	1997	1998	1999	2000	2001	2002
ASIA — ASIE								
Japan - Japon[9]								
Number - Nombre	90	80	81	89	79	84	...	...
Rate — Taux	7.6	6.6	6.8	7.4	6.7	7.1	...	...
Kazakhstan[6]								
Number - Nombre	159	134	137	122	98	94	87	80
Korea (Republic of) - Corée (République de)[10]								
Number - Nombre	88	75	66	63	77	62	70	...
Kuwait - Koweït								
Number - Nombre	1	3	7	3	3	2	1	3
Kyrgyzstan - Kirghizistan[6]								
Number - Nombre	52	27	64	35	44	44	43	54
Philippines								
Number - Nombre	1 485	1 549	1 513	1 579	...	...	...	...
Qatar								
Number - Nombre	-	...	...	...	...	...	...	...
Singapore - Singapour								
Number - Nombre	2	2	1	5	2	8	4	...
Sri Lanka								
Number - Nombre	81	...	...	...	...	...	...	...
Tajikistan - Tadjikistan[6]								
Number - Nombre	95	58	38	...	45	36	40	...
Thailand - Thaïlande								
Number - Nombre	96	120	87	63	93	102	...	114
Turkmenistan - Turkménistan[6]								
Number - Nombre	63	49	21	16	...	...	...	...
Uzbekistan - Ouzbékistan[6]								
Number - Nombre	128	76	62	48	80	182		
EUROPE								
Albania - Albanie								
Number - Nombre	9	8	5	8	2	8	2	...
Austria - Autriche								
Number - Nombre	1	4	2	4	1	2	5	2
Rate — Taux	♦1.1	♦4.5	♦2.4	♦4.9	♦1.3	♦2.6	♦6.6	♦2.6
Belarus - Bélarus[6]								
Number - Nombre	14	21	23	26	19	20	13	...
Rate — Taux	♦13.8	♦21.9	♦25.7	♦28.1	♦20.4	...	...	...
Belgium - Belgique[11]								
Number - Nombre	11	6	10	...	...	...	...	...
Rate — Taux	♦9.5	♦5.3	♦8.6	...	...	...	...	...
Bulgaria - Bulgarie								
Number - Nombre	10	14	12	10	16	13	13	11
Rate — Taux	♦13.9	♦19.4	♦18.7	♦15.3	♦22.1	♦17.6	♦19.1	♦16.5
Croatia - Croatie								
Number - Nombre	6	1	6	3	5	3	1	4
Rate — Taux	♦12.0	♦1.9	♦10.8	♦6.4	♦11.1	♦6.9	♦2.4	♦10.0
Czech Republic - République tchèque								
Number - Nombre	2	5	2	5	6	5	3	3
Rate — Taux	♦2.1	♦5.5	♦2.2	♦5.5	♦6.7	♦5.5	♦3.3	♦3.1
Denmark - Danemark[12]								
Number - Nombre	7	4	5	2	4	-	...	...
Rate — Taux	♦10.0	♦5.9	♦7.4	♦3.0	♦6.0	-	...	...
Estonia - Estonie[6]								
Number - Nombre	7	-	2	2	2	5	1	1
Rate — Taux	♦51.6	-	♦15.8	♦16.4	♦15.9	♦38.2	♦7.9	♦7.7
Finland - Finlande[13]								
Number - Nombre	1	2	3	3	2	3	3	3
Rate — Taux	♦1.6	♦3.3	♦5.1	♦5.3	♦3.5	♦5.3	♦5.3	♦5.4
France[14]								
Number - Nombre	70	97	70	75	55	50	...	...
Rate — Taux	9.6	13.2	9.6	10.2	7.4	6.5	...	...

17. Maternal deaths and maternal death rates: 1995 - 2002
Mortalité liée à la maternité nombre de décès et taux: 1995 - 2002 (continued — suite)

(See notes at end of table. — Voir notes à la fin du tableau.)

Continent and country or area Continent et pays ou zone	1995	1996	1997	1998	1999	2000	2001	2002
EUROPE								
Germany - Allemagne								
Number - Nombre	41	51	49	44	37	43	27	...
Rate — Taux	5.4	6.4	6.0	5.5	4.8	5.6	♦3.7	...
Greece - Grèce								
Number - Nombre	-	4	-	7	6	-	4	...
Rate — Taux	-	♦4.0	-	♦6.9	♦5.2	-	♦3.9	...
Hungary - Hongrie								
Number - Nombre	17	12	21	6	4	10	5	8
Rate — Taux	♦15.2	♦11.4	♦20.9	♦6.2	♦4.2	♦10.2	♦5.2	♦8.3
Iceland - Islande								
Number - Nombre	-	-	-	-	-	-	1	...
Rate — Taux	-	-	-	-	-	-	♦24.4	...
Ireland - Irlande[15]								
Number - Nombre	-	3	3	2	1	1	3	...
Rate — Taux	-	♦6.0	♦5.7	♦3.7	♦1.9	♦1.8	♦5.2	...
Italy - Italie								
Number - Nombre	17	20	23	18	14	16	11	...
Rate — Taux	♦3.2	♦3.8	♦4.3	♦3.5	♦2.7	♦2.9	♦2.1	...
Latvia - Lettonie[6]								
Number - Nombre	5	4	8	9	8	5	5	1
Rate — Taux	♦23.2	♦20.2	♦42.5	♦48.9	♦41.2	♦24.7	♦25.4	♦5.0
Lithuania - Lituanie[6]								
Number - Nombre	7	5	6	5	5	3	4	6
Rate — Taux	♦17.0	♦12.8	♦15.9	♦13.5	♦13.7	♦8.8	♦12.7	♦20.0
Luxembourg								
Number - Nombre	1	-	-	1	-	1	-	-
Rate — Taux	♦18.4	-	-	♦18.6	-	♦17.5	-	-
Malta - Malte[16]								
Number - Nombre	1	1	-	1	1	-	2	-
Rate — Taux	♦21.7	♦20.2	-	♦22.3	♦23.2	-	♦51.8	-
Netherlands - Pays-Bas[17]								
Number - Nombre	14	23	15	23	19	18	...	...
Rate — Taux	♦7.3	♦12.1	♦7.8	♦11.5	♦9.5	♦8.7	...	...
Norway - Norvège[18]								
Number - Nombre	4	1	1	4	5	2	3	...
Rate — Taux	♦6.6	♦1.6	♦1.7	♦6.9	♦8.4	♦3.4	♦5.3	...
Poland - Pologne								
Number - Nombre	43	21	...	...	20	30	13	19
Rate — Taux	9.9	♦4.9	...	...	♦5.2	♦7.9	♦3.5	♦5.4
Portugal								
Number - Nombre	9	6	6	9	6	3	6	8
Rate — Taux	♦8.4	♦5.4	♦5.3	♦7.9	♦5.2	♦2.5	♦5.3	♦7.0
Republic of Moldova - République de Moldova[19]								
Number - Nombre	23	22	23	15	11	10	16	11
Romania - Roumanie								
Number - Nombre	113	95	98	96	98	75	75	47
Rate — Taux	47.8	41.1	41.4	40.5	41.8	32.0	34.0	22.3
Russian Federation - Fédération de Russie[20]								
Number - Nombre	727	636	633	565	537	503	479	469
San Marino - Saint-Marin								
Number - Nombre	-	-	-	-	-	-	...	...
Serbia and Montenegro - Serbie-et-Montenegro								
Number - Nombre	...	...	...	...	...	7	...	...
Rate — Taux	...	...	...	...	...	♦5.6	...	...
Slovakia - Slovaquie								
Number - Nombre	5	3	1	5	5	1	7	...
Rate — Taux	♦8.1	♦5.0	♦1.7	♦8.7	♦8.9	♦1.8	♦13.7	...
Slovenia - Slovénie								
Number - Nombre	1	3	2	-	2	2	3	-
Rate — Taux	♦5.3	♦16.0	♦11.0	-	♦11.4	♦11.0	♦17.2	-

17. Maternal deaths and maternal death rates: 1995 - 2002
Mortalité liée à la maternité nombre de décès et taux: 1995 - 2002 (continued — suite)

(See notes at end of table. — Voir notes à la fin du tableau.)

Continent and country or area Continent et pays ou zone	1995	1996	1997	1998	1999	2000	2001	2002
EUROPE								
Spain - Espagne								
Number - Nombre	11	11	8	10	14	14	17	...
Rate — Taux	◆3.0	◆3.0	◆2.2	◆2.7	◆3.7	◆3.6	◆4.2	...
Sweden - Suède								
Number - Nombre	4	5	3	7	1	4	3	...
Rate — Taux	◆3.9	◆5.3	◆3.3	◆7.9	◆1.1	◆4.4	◆3.3	...
Switzerland - Suisse								
Number - Nombre	7	3	3	3	6	5	1	...
Rate — Taux	◆8.5	◆3.6	◆3.7	◆3.8	◆7.7	◆6.4	◆1.4	...
The Former Yugoslav Rep. of Macedonia - L'ex-République yougoslave de Macédoine								
Number - Nombre	7	-	1	1	2	4	...	...
Rate — Taux	◆21.8	-	◆3.4	◆3.4	◆7.3	◆13.6	...	...
Ukraine[6]								
Number - Nombre	159	142	111	114	98	95	90	85
Rate — Taux	32.3	30.4	25.1	27.2	...	24.7	23.9	21.8
United Kingdom - Royaume-Uni[21]								
Number - Nombre	51	48	39	49	37	46	**50**	**40**
Rate — Taux	7.0	6.5	5.4	6.8	5.3	6.8	**7.5**	**6.0**
OCEANIA — OCEANIE								
Australia - Australie								
Number - Nombre	21	13	12	5	13	13	12	...
Rate — Taux	◆8.2	◆5.1	◆4.8	◆2.0	◆5.2	◆5.2	◆4.9	...
Fiji - Fidji								
Number - Nombre	...	...	...	...	*1*	...	...	...
New Zealand - Nouvelle-Zélande								
Number - Nombre	2	4	3	3	4	5	...	...
Rate — Taux	◆3.5	◆7.0	◆5.2	◆5.4	◆7.0	◆8.8	...	...

GENERAL NOTES - NOTES GENERALES

Rates are the number of maternal deaths per 100 000 live births. For method of evaluation and limitations of data, see Technical Notes for this table. — Les taux représentent le nombre de décès 'Affections périnatales' liés à la maternité per 100 000 naissances vivantes. Pour la méthode d'évaluation et les insuffisances des données, voir Notes techniques pour ce tableaux.

Data in bold refer to maternal deaths based on ICD-10 Classification, otherwise data refer to maternal deaths based on ICD-9 Classification. - Les données en typographie gras se rapportent aux décès maternelles basées sur la classification CIM-10, autrement les données se rapportent aux décès maternelles basées sur la classification CIM-9.

Maternal deaths are usually defined as deaths coded "38-41" for ICD-9 or as deaths coded "A34, O00-O99" for ICD-10, respectively. However, data coded according to ICD-10 shown in this table include deaths due to "O96" and "O97". For details see Technical Notes for this table.

Italics: data from civil registers that are incomplete or of unknown completeness. — *Italiques:* données incomplètes ou dont le degré d'exactitude n'est pas connu, provenant des registres de l'état civil.

FOOTNOTES - NOTES

◆ Rates based on 30 or fewer deaths. — Taux basés sur 30 décès ou moins.

[1] Including Canadian residents temporarily in the United States, but excluding United States residents temporarily in Canada. - Y compris les résidents canadiens se trouvant temporairement aux Etats-Unis, mais ne comprenant pas les résidents des Etats-Unis se trouvant temporairement au Canada.

[2] Excluding Indian jungle population. - Non compris les Indiens de la jungle.

[3] Data on live births and deaths are based on a civil registration system put in place in January 1998. - Les données sur les naissances et les décès sont basées sur un système d'enregistrement des faits d'état civil mis en place en janvier 1998.

[4] Excluding nomadic Indian tribes. - Non compris les tribus d'Indiens nomades.

[5] Denominator refer to national projections. - Le dénominateur se referent aux projections nationales.

[6] The denominator excluded infants born alive with less than 28 weeks gestation, less than 1 000 grams in weight and 35 centimeters in length, who die within seven days of birth. - Le dénominateur ne compris pas des enfants nés vivants avant 28 semaines de gestation, pesant moins de 1 000 grammes, mesurant moins de 35 centimètres et décédés dans les sept jours qui ont suivi leur naissance.

[7] Data on maternal deaths do not include those in the Abkhazia and South Osetia region; therefore rates are not computed. - Les données sur le mortalité liée a la maternité ne comprennent pas ceux de la région de Abkhazia et South Osetia, en conséquence, les taux n'ont pas étés calcules.

[8] Including data for East Jerusalem and Israeli residents in certain other territories under occupation by Israeli military forces since June 1967. - Y compris les données pour Jérusalem-Est et les résidents israéliens dans certains autres territoires occupés depuis 1967 par les forces armées israéliennes.

[9] Data refer to Japanese nationals in Japan only. - Les données se raportent aux nationaux japonais au Japon seulement.

[10] Excluding alien armed forces, civilian aliens employed by armed forces, and foreign diplomatic personnel and their dependants. - Non compris les militaires étrangers, les civils étrangers employés par les forces armées ni le personnel diplomatique étranger et les membres de leur famille les accompagnant.

476

11 Including armed forces stationed outside the country, but excluding alien armed forces stationed in the area. - Y compris les militaires nationaux hors du pays, mais non compris les militaires étrangers en garnison sur le territoire.

12 Excluding Faeroe Islands and Greenland. - Non compris les îles Féroé et Gröenland.

13 Including nationals temporarily outside the country. - Y compris les nationaux se trouvant temporairement hors du pays.

14 Including armed forces stationed outside the country. - Y compris les militaires nationaux hors du pays.

15 Denominator refers to live births registered within one year of occurrence. - Le dénominateur se referrer aux Evénements enregistrés dans l'année qui suit l'événement.

16 Denominator refers to live births to Maltese parents only. - Le dénominateur se referrer aux naissances vivantes aux parents maltais seulement.

17 Including residents outside the country if listed in a Netherlands population register. - Y compris les résidents hors du pays, s'ils sont inscrits sur un registre de population néerlandais.

18 Including residents temporarily outside the country. - Y compris les résidents se trouvant temporairement hors du pays.

19 Data on maternal deaths do not include those in the Transnistria region; therefore rates are not computed. - Les données sur le mortalité liée a la maternité ne comprennent pas ceux de la région de Transnistria,en conséquence, les taux n'ont pas étés calcules.

20 Data on maternal deaths do not include those in the Chechnya region; therefore rates are not computed. - Les données sur le mortalité liée a la maternité ne comprennent pas ceux de la région de Chechnya,en conséquence, les taux n'ont pas étés calcules.

21 Denominator excludes births in Northern Ireland to non-residents of Northern Ireland. - Le dénominateur n'inclure pas des naissances en Irlande du Nord aux non-résidents de l'Irlande du Nord.

477

Table 18

Table 18 presents deaths and crude death rates by urban/rural residence for as many years as possible between 1998 and 2002.

Description of variables: Death is defined as the permanent disappearance of all evidence of life at any time after live birth has taken place (post-natal cessation of vital functions without capability of resuscitation).

Statistics on the number of deaths are obtained from civil registers unless otherwise noted. For those countries or areas where civil registration statistics on deaths are considered reliable (estimated completeness of 90 per cent or more), the death rates shown have been calculated on the basis of registered deaths.

The urban/rural classification of deaths is that provided by each country or area; it is presumed to be based on the national census definitions of urban population that have been set forth at the end of the technical notes for table 6.

Rate computation: Crude death rates are the annual number of deaths per 1 000 mid-year population.

Rates by urban/rural residence are the annual number of deaths, in the appropriate urban or rural category, per 1 000 corresponding mid-year population. These rates are calculated by the Statistics Division of the United Nations.

Rates presented in this table are limited to those countries or areas with a minimum number of 30 deaths in a given year.

Reliability of data: Each country or area has been asked to indicate the estimated completeness of the infant deaths recorded in its civil register. These national assessments are indicated by the quality codes (C), (U) and (|) that appear in the first column of this table. C indicates that the data are estimated to be virtually complete, that is, representing at least 90 per cent of the deaths occurring each year, while U indicates that data are estimated to be incomplete that is, representing less than 90 per cent of the deaths occurring each year. The code (I) indicates that the source of data is different than civil registration, but still considered reliable and explained by footnote. The code (...) indicates that no information was provided regarding completeness.

Data from civil registers that are reported as incomplete or of unknown completeness (code U or ...) are considered unreliable. They appear in italics in this table; rates based on these data are not computed.

Limitations: Statistics on deaths are subject to the same qualifications as have been set forth for vital statistics in general and death statistics in particular as discussed in section 4 of the Technical Notes.

The reliability of the data, an indication of which is described above, is an important factor in considering the limitations. In addition, some deaths are tabulated by date of registration and not by date of occurrence; these have been indicated with a plus sign (+). Whenever the lag between the date of occurrence and date of registration is prolonged and, therefore, a large proportion of the death registrations are delayed, death statistics for any given year may be seriously affected. However, delays in the registration of deaths are less common and shorter than in the registration of live births.

International comparability in mortality statistics may also be affected by the exclusion of deaths of infants who were born alive but died before the registration of the birth or within the first 24 hours of life. Statistics of this type are footnoted.

In addition, it should be noted that rates are affected also by the quality and limitations of the population estimates that are used in their computation. The problems of under-enumeration or over-enumeration and, to some extent, the differences in definition of total population have been discussed in section 3 of the Technical Notes dealing with population data in general, and specific information pertaining to individual countries or areas is given in the footnotes to table 3.

Estimated rates based directly on the results of sample surveys are subject to considerable error as a result of omissions in reporting deaths or as a result of erroneous reporting of those that occurred outside the period of reference. However, such rates do have the advantage of having a "built-in" and corresponding base.

It should be emphasized that crude death rates -- like other crude rates, such as of birth, marriage and divorce -- may be seriously affected by the age-sex structure of the populations to which they relate. Nevertheless, they do provide a simple measure of the level and changes in mortality.

The comparability of data by urban/rural residence is affected by the national definitions of urban and rural used in tabulating these data. It is assumed, in the absence of specific information to the contrary, that the definitions of urban and rural used in connection with the national population census were also used in the compilation of the vital statistics for each country or area. However, it cannot be excluded that, for a given country or area, different definitions of urban and rural are used for the vital statistics data and the population census data respectively. When known, the definitions of urban used in national population censuses are presented at the end of the technical notes for table 6. As discussed in detail in the technical notes for table 6, these definitions vary considerably from one country or area to another.

In addition to problems of comparability, vital rates classified by urban/rural residence are also subject to certain types of bias. If, when calculating vital rates, different definitions of urban are used in connection with the vital events and the population data and if this results in a net difference between the numerator and denominator of the rate in the population at risk, then the vital rates would be biased. Urban/rural differentials in vital rates may also be affected by whether the vital events have been tabulated in terms of place of occurrence or place of usual residence. This problem is discussed in more detail in section 4.1.4.1 of the Technical Notes.

Earlier data: Deaths and crude death rates have been shown in each issue of the Demographic Yearbook. Data included in this table update the series covering a period of years as follows :

Issue	Years Covered
Historical Supplement CD, 1997	1948 – 1997
1992	1983 – 1992
1985	1976 – 1985
1980	1971 – 1980
Historical Supplement, 1979	1948 – 1977

Tableau 18

Le tableau 18 présente le nombre des décès et les taux bruts de mortalité selon le lieu de résidence (zone urbaine ou rurale) pour le plus grand nombre d'années possible entre 1998 et 2002.

Description des variables : Le décès est défini comme la disparition permanente de tout signe de vie à un moment quelconque postérieur à la naissance vivante (cessation des fonctions vitales après la naissance sans possibilité de réanimation).

Sauf indication contraire, les statistiques relatives au nombre de décès sont établies sur la base des registres d'état civil. Pour les pays ou zones où les données concernant l'enregistrement des décès par les services de l'état civil sont jugées sûres (complétude estimée à 90 p. 100 ou plus), les taux de mortalité ont été calculés d'après les décès enregistrés.

La répartition des décès entre zones urbaines et zones rurales est celle qui a été communiquée par chaque pays ou zone ; on part du principe qu'elle repose sur les définitions de la population urbaine utilisées pour les recensements nationaux, qui sont reproduites à la fin des notes techniques du tableau 6.

Calcul des taux : Les taux bruts de mortalité représentent le nombre annuel de décès pour 1 000 habitants en milieu d'année.

Les taux selon le lieu de résidence (zone urbaine ou rurale) représentent le nombre annuel de décès, classés selon la catégorie urbaine ou rurale appropriée, pour 1 000 habitants en milieu d'année. Ces taux ont été calculés par la Division de statistique de l'ONU.

Les taux présentés dans ce tableau se rapportent seulement aux pays ou zones où l'on a enregistré un nombre minimal de 30 décès au cours d'une année donnée.

Fiabilité des données : Il a été demandé à chaque pays ou zone d'indiquer le degré estimatif de complétude des données sur les décès d'enfants de moins d'un an figurant dans ses registres d'état civil. Ces évaluations nationales sont signalées par les codes de qualité 'C', 'U' et 'I' qui apparaissent dans la deuxième colonne du tableau.

La lettre 'C' indique que les données sont jugées à peu près complètes, c'est-à-dire qu'elles représentent au moins 90 p. 100 des décès d'enfants de moins d'un an survenus chaque année ; la lettre 'U' signifie que les données sont jugées incomplètes, c'est-à-dire qu'elles représentent moins de 90 p.100 des décès d'enfants de moins d'un an survenus chaque année. Le symbole 'I' indique que la source des données est fiable mais n'est pas un registre de l'état civil ; le symbole, dans ce cas, est accompagné par une note explicative. Le code '...' dénote qu'aucun renseignement n'a été communiqué quant à la complétude des données.

Les données provenant des registres de l'état civil qui sont déclarées incomplètes ou dont le degré de complétude n'est pas connu (code 'U' ou '...') sont jugées douteuses. Elles apparaissent en italique dans le présent tableau et les taux correspondants n'ont pas été calculés.

Insuffisance des données : Les statistiques relatives à la mortalité appellent les mêmes réserves que celles qui ont été formulées à propos des statistiques de l'état civil en général et des statistiques relatives aux décès en particulier (voir la section 4 des Notes techniques).

La fiabilité des données, au sujet de laquelle des indications ont été fournies plus haut, est un facteur important. Il faut également tenir compte du fait que, dans certains cas, les décès sont classés par date d'enregistrement et non par date d'occurrence ; ces cas ont été signalés par le signe '+'. Chaque fois que le décalage entre le décès et son enregistrement est grand et qu'une forte proportion des décès fait l'objet d'un enregistrement tardif, les statistiques relatives aux décès survenus pendant l'année peuvent être considérablement faussées.

En règle générale, toutefois, les décès sont enregistrés beaucoup plus rapidement que les naissances vivantes, et les retards prolongés sont rares.

Un autre facteur qui nuit à la comparabilité internationale est la pratique qui consiste à ne pas inclure dans les statistiques de la mortalité les enfants nés vivants mais décédés avant l'enregistrement de leur naissance ou dans les 24 heures qui ont suivi la naissance. Quand pareil facteur a joué, cela a été signalé en note à la fin du tableau.

Il convient de noter par ailleurs que l'exactitude des taux dépend également de la qualité et des limitations des estimations de la population qui sont utilisées pour leur calcul. Le problème des erreurs par excès ou par défaut commises lors du dénombrement et, dans une certaine mesure, le problème de l'hétérogénéité des définitions de la population totale ont été examinés à la section 3 des Notes techniques, relative à la population en général ; des indications concernant certains pays ou zones sont données en note à la fin du tableau 3.

Les taux estimatifs fondés directement sur les résultats d'enquêtes par sondage comportent des possibilités d'erreurs considérables dues soit à des omissions dans les déclarations des décès, soit au fait que l'on a déclaré à tort des décès survenus en réalité hors de la période considérée. Toutefois, ces taux présentent un avantage : le chiffre de population utilisé comme base est connu par définition et rigoureusement correspondant.

Il faut souligner que les taux bruts de mortalité, de même que les taux bruts de natalité, de nuptialité et de divortialité, peuvent varier très sensiblement selon la composition par âge et par sexe de la population à laquelle ils se rapportent. Ils offrent néanmoins un moyen simple de mesurer le niveau et l'évolution de la mortalité.

La comparabilité des données selon le lieu de résidence (zone urbaine ou rurale) peut être limitée par les définitions nationales des termes « urbain » et « rural » utilisées pour le classement de ces données. En l'absence d'indications contraires, on a supposé que les mêmes définitions avaient servi pour le recensement national de la population et pour l'établissement des statistiques de l'état civil pour chaque pays ou zone. Toutefois, il n'est pas exclu que, pour une zone ou un pays donné, des définitions différentes aient été retenues. Les définitions du terme «urbain» utilisées pour les recensements nationaux de population ont été présentées à la fin du tableau 6 lorsqu'elles étaient connues. Comme on l'a précisé dans les notes techniques relatives au tableau 6, ces définitions varient considérablement d'un pays ou d'une zone à l'autre.

Outre les problèmes de comparabilité, les taux démographiques classés selon le lieu de résidence « urbaine » ou « rurale » sont également sujets à des distorsions particulières. Si l'on utilise des définitions différentes du terme « urbain » pour classer les faits d'état civil et les données relatives à la population lors du calcul des taux et qu'il en résulte une différence nette entre le numérateur et le dénominateur pour le taux de la population exposée au risque, les taux démographiques s'en trouveront faussés. La différence entre ces taux pour les zones urbaines et rurales pourra aussi être faussée selon que les faits d'état civil auront été classés d'après le lieu où ils se sont produits ou d'après le lieu de résidence habituel. Ce problème est examiné plus en détail à la section 4.1.4.1 des Notes techniques.

Données publiées antérieurement : Les différentes éditions de l'*Annuaire démographique* contiennent des statistiques des décès et des taux bruts de mortalité. Les données qui figurent dans le tableau 18 actualisent les données qui portaient sur les périodes suivantes :

Éditions	Années considérées
Supplément historique (CD-ROM), 1997	1948 – 1997
1992	1983 – 1992
1985	1976 – 1985
1980	1971 – 1980
Supplément rétrospectif, 1979	1948 – 1977

18. Deaths and crude death rates, by urban/rural residence: 1998 - 2002
Décès et taux bruts de mortalité, selon la résidence, urbaine/rurale: 1998 - 2002

(See notes at end of table. — Voir notes à la fin du tableau.)

Continent, country or area, and urban/rural residence / Continent, pays ou zone et résidence, urbaine/rurale	Co-de[1]	Number - Nombre					Rate - Taux				
		1998	1999	2000	2001	2002	1998	1999	2000	2001	2002
AFRICA — AFRIQUE											
Algeria - Algérie[2,3]											
Total	U	_171 775_	_129 686_	_127 951_	_129 092_	_126 557_	...	...	...	...	...
Benin - Bénin[4]											
Total	I	72 130	71 680	71 540	83 417	...	12.4	12.0	11.6	13.0	...
Botswana[4]											
Total	I	16 244	16 352	...	16 570	...	10.3	10.2	...	9.9	...
Burundi[4]											
Total	I	115 693	...	...	...	...	18.4	...	...	...	...
Chad - Tchad											
Total	...	...	...	...	...	_138 025_	...	...	...	...	...
Côte d'Ivoire[4]											
Total	I	189 010	...	201 690	...	...	12.3	...	12.3	...	...
Egypt - Égypte											
Total	C	399 772	401 433	...	...	...	6.5	6.4	...	...	...
Urban - Urbaine	C	177 404	181 665	...	...	...	6.8	6.8	...	...	...
Rural - Rurale	C	222 368	219 768	...	...	...	6.3	6.1	...	...	...
Ethiopia - Éthiopie											
Total	...	...	_1 062 114_	...	...	...	...	...	...	...	...
Urban - Urbaine	...	...	_110 929_	...	...	...	...	...	...	...	...
Rural - Rurale	...	...	_951 185_	...	...	...	...	...	...	...	...
Libyan Arab Jamahiriya - Jamahiriya arabe libyenne											
Total	U	...	...	_17 367_	_18 334_	_19 362_	...	...	...	...	...
Malawi[4,5]											
Total	I	208 040	234 641	228 245	221 963	217 205	20.9	23.1	21.8	20.5	19.4
Urban - Urbaine	I	22 186	...	...	...	...	15.5	...	...	...	...
Rural - Rurale	I	185 854	...	...	...	...	21.9	...	...	...	...
Mauritius - Maurice											
Total	+C	7 839	7 944	7 982	7 983	8 310	6.8	6.8	6.7	6.7	6.9
Urban - Urbaine	+C	3 583	3 711	3 685	3 634	3 702	7.2	7.4	7.3	7.1	7.2
Rural - Rurale	+C	4 256	4 233	4 297	4 349	4 608	6.4	6.3	6.3	6.3	6.6
Morocco - Maroc[6]											
Total	U	_95 111_	_98 304_	...	...	...	...	...	...	...	...
Urban - Urbaine	U	_52 691_	_53 935_	...	...	...	...	...	...	...	...
Rural - Rurale	U	_42 163_	_44 121_	...	...	...	...	...	...	...	...
Mozambique[4]											
Total	I	...	...	...	331 162	...	...	...	...	18.8	...
Réunion[2]											
Total	C	3 731	3 825	*3 781	*3 740	...	5.3	5.4	*5.2	*5.1	...
Saint Helena ex. dep. - Sainte-Hélène sans dép.											
Total	C	39	45	53	41	...	...	...	...	...	...
Seychelles											
Total	+C	570	560	553	554	*647	7.2	7.0	6.8	6.8	*8.0
Tunisia - Tunisie											
Total	U	_42 571_	_54 400_	...	*_53 300_	...	...	...	...	...	...
AMERICA, NORTH — AMERIQUE DU NORD											
Anguilla											
Total	+C	62	58	73	50	52	5.8	5.3	6.5	4.3	4.4
Antigua and Barbuda - Antigua-et-Barbuda											
Total	+C	456	508	451	...	...	...	...	...	...	...
Aruba											
Total	+U	_505_	_554_	_531_	_477_	*_489_	...	...	...	...	...
Bahamas											
Total	C	1 725	1 567	1 625	1 609	...	5.9	5.3	5.4	5.2	...

18. Deaths and crude death rates, by urban/rural residence: 1998 - 2002
Décès et taux bruts de mortalité, selon la résidence, urbaine/rurale: 1998 - 2002 (continued — suite)

(See notes at end of table. — Voir notes à la fin du tableau.)

Continent, country or area, and urban/rural residence / Continent, pays ou zone et résidence, urbaine/rurale	Code[1]	Number - Nombre					Rate - Taux				
		1998	1999	2000	2001	2002	1998	1999	2000	2001	2002
AMERICA, NORTH — AMERIQUE DU NORD											
Barbados - Barbade											
Total	+C	...	...	2 367	...	...	...	...	8.8	...	...
Belize											
Total	U	*1 350*	*1 190*	*1 534*	*1 261*	*1 284*	...	...	...	...	...
Bermuda - Bermudes											
Total	C	505	427	473	442	404	8.1	6.8	7.5	7.1	...
British Virgin Islands - Îles Vierges britanniques											
Total	+C	...	...	...	*101	...	...	...	...	*4.9	...
Canada[7]											
Total	C	218 091	219 530	218 062	219 538	223 603	7.2	7.2	7.1	7.1	7.1
Cayman Islands - Îles Caïmanes											
Total	C	117	128	137	132	...	3.1	3.3	3.4	3.2	...
Costa Rica											
Total	C	14 708	15 052	14 944	15 609	15 004	4.4	4.4	4.3	4.0	3.8
Cuba[6]											
Total	C	77 565	79 499	76 463	79 395	73 882	7.0	7.1	6.8	7.1	6.6
Urban - Urbaine	C	63 354	64 362	...	...	...	7.6	7.7	...	...	...
Rural - Rurale	C	14 146	15 072	...	...	...	5.1	5.5	...	...	...
Dominica - Dominique											
Total	+C	595	631	503	510	...	8.3	8.8	7.0	7.2	...
Dominican Republic - République dominicaine											
Total	+U	*25 278*	*26 956*	*23 776*	...	...	...	...	...	...	...
El Salvador											
Total	C	29 919	28 056	28 154	29 559	27 458	5.0	4.6	4.5	4.6	4.2
Urban - Urbaine	C	20 533	18 770	19 276	20 921	19 595	5.9	5.2	5.3	5.6	5.1
Rural - Rurale	C	9 386	9 286	8 878	8 638	7 863	3.7	3.6	3.4	3.3	2.9
Greenland - Groenland											
Total	C	468	482	...	...	...	8.3	8.6	...	...	...
Urban - Urbaine	C	391	372	...	...	...	8.6	8.2	...	...	...
Rural - Rurale	C	77	110	...	...	...	7.3	10.4	...	...	...
Grenada - Grenade											
Total	+C	819	794	716	727	...	8.2	7.9	7.1	7.2	...
Guadeloupe											
Total	C	2 564	2 670	2 698	2 765	2 584	6.1	6.3	6.3	6.4	5.9
Guatemala											
Total	C	70 504	64 563	66 831	69 934	...	6.5	5.8	5.9	6.0	...
Jamaica - Jamaïque											
Total	+C	18 110	17 353	*16 338	*17 205	...	7.0	6.7	*6.3	*6.6	...
Martinique[2]											
Total	C	2 548	2 581	2 692	2 754	2 681	6.7	6.8	7.0	7.1	6.9
Mexico - Mexique[6]											
Total	C	444 665	443 950	437 667	443 127	...	4.6	4.5	4.4	4.4	...
Urban - Urbaine	C	329 170	332 434	333 980	336 551	...	4.6	4.5	4.5	4.4	...
Rural - Rurale	C	109 283	105 664	97 870	100 670	...	4.4	4.2	3.8	3.9	...
Netherlands Antilles - Antilles néerlandaises											
Total	C	1 282	1 321	...	...	...	6.2	6.4	...	...	...
Nicaragua											
Total	+U	*14 804*	*10 818*	*13 602*	*12 789*	*15 061*	...	...	...	...	...
Urban - Urbaine	+U	*9 487*	*7 173*	*8 851*	*8 240*	*9 801*	...	...	...	...	...
Rural - Rurale	+U	*5 317*	*3 645*	*4 751*	*4 549*	*5 260*	...	...	...	...	...
Panama											
Total	U	*11 824*	*11 938*	*11 841*	*12 442*	...	...	...	...	...	...
Urban - Urbaine	U	*6 664*	*7 108*	...	...	...	...	...	...	...	...

18. Deaths and crude death rates, by urban/rural residence: 1998 - 2002
Décès et taux bruts de mortalité, selon la résidence, urbaine/rurale: 1998 - 2002 (continued — suite)

(See notes at end of table. — Voir notes à la fin du tableau.)

Continent, country or area, and urban/rural residence / Continent, pays ou zone et résidence, urbaine/rurale	Code[1]	Number - Nombre					Rate - Taux				
		1998	1999	2000	2001	2002	1998	1999	2000	2001	2002
AMERICA, NORTH — AMERIQUE DU NORD											
Panama											
Rural - Rurale	U	5 160	4 830	...	...	...	...	...	...	...	...
Puerto Rico - Porto Rico[6]											
Total	C	29 990	29 145	28 550	28 794	28 098	8.0	7.7	7.5	7.5	7.3
Urban - Urbaine	C	15 843	15 595	15 516	15 406	15 026	...	...	...	...	...
Rural - Rurale	C	14 127	13 542	12 991	13 367	13 009	...	...	...	...	...
Saint Kitts and Nevis - Saint-Kitts-et-Nevis											
Total	+C	390	418	357	352	...	9.7	9.8	8.8	7.6	...
Saint Lucia - Sainte-Lucie[6]											
Total	C	976	981	941	998	957	6.4	6.4	6.0	6.3	6.0
Urban - Urbaine	C	287	...	...	...	...	6.4	...	...	...	...
Rural - Rurale	C	686	...	...	...	...	6.4	...	...	...	...
Saint Vincent and the Grenadines - Saint Vincent-et-les Grenadines											
Total	+C	830	833	700	765	770	7.5	7.5	6.3	7.0	7.1
Trinidad and Tobago - Trinité-et-Tobago											
Total	C	...	...	...	...	*9 670	...	...	...	...	*7.6
Turks Caicos Islands - Îles Turques et Caïques											
Total	+C	22	39	67	...	...	...	...	...	...	...
United States - États-Unis											
Total	C	2 337 256	2 391 399	2 403 351	2 416 425	*2447864	8.6	8.8	8.7	8.5	*8.5
AMERICA, SOUTH — AMERIQUE DU SUD											
Argentina - Argentine											
Total	C	280 180	289 543	277 148	285 941	291 190	7.8	7.9	7.5	7.6	7.7
Bolivia - Bolivie											
Total	U	71 618	71 680	71 742	...	...	...	...	...	...	...
Brazil - Brésil[8]											
Total	U	936 885	943 524	927 783	931 017	958 475	...	...	...	...	...
Chile - Chili											
Total	C	80 257	81 984	78 814	81 873	81 079	5.4	5.5	5.2	5.3	5.2
Urban - Urbaine	C	67 146	68 715	66 422	68 884	69 209	5.3	5.4	5.1	5.2	5.2
Rural - Rurale	C	13 111	13 269	12 392	12 989	11 870	6.0	6.0	5.7	5.9	5.4
Colombia - Colombie[6,9]											
Total	U	175 363	183 551	187 432	191 513	*187 943	...	...	...	...	...
Urban - Urbaine	U	131 784	135 788	138 935	143 333	*139 955	...	...	...	...	...
Rural - Rurale	U	33 780	36 772	38 316	38 610	*37 291	...	...	...	...	...
Ecuador - Équateur[10]											
Total	U	54 357	55 921	56 420	55 214	55 549	...	...	...	...	...
Urban - Urbaine	U	37 836	38 834	41 278	40 423	42 236	...	...	...	...	...
Rural - Rurale	U	16 521	17 087	15 142	14 791	13 313	...	...	...	...	...
Falkland Islands (Malvinas) - Îles Falkland (Malvinas)											
Total	+C	12	20	11	...	...	...	...	...	...	...

18. Deaths and crude death rates, by urban/rural residence: 1998 - 2002
Décès et taux bruts de mortalité, selon la résidence, urbaine/rurale: 1998 - 2002 (continued — suite)

(See notes at end of table. — Voir notes à la fin du tableau.)

Continent, country or area, and urban/rural residence / Continent, pays ou zone et résidence, urbaine/rurale	Co-de[1]	Number - Nombre					Rate - Taux				
		1998	1999	2000	2001	2002	1998	1999	2000	2001	2002
AMERICA, SOUTH — AMERIQUE DU SUD											
French Guiana - Guyane française[2]											
Total	C	620	658	620	668	656	4.1	4.2	3.8	3.9	3.7
Guyana											
Total	+C	4 977	4 197	...	...	...	6.4	5.4	...	...	...
Peru - Pérou[4,8,11]											
Total	I	161 615	162 457	163 263	164 296	165 467	6.4	6.4	6.3	6.2	6.2
Suriname											
Total	C	2 814	2 992	3 090	...	...	6.2	6.5	6.7	...	...
Urban - Urbaine	C	2 220	2 171	2 249	...	...	...	...	...	...	...
Rural - Rurale	C	594	821	841	...	...	...	...	...	...	...
Uruguay											
Total	C	32 082	32 430	30 456	31 228	31 628	9.8	9.8	9.2	9.3	9.4
Venezuela[8]											
Total	C	98 624	101 907	103 255	107 867	105 388	4.2	4.3	4.2	4.4	4.2
ASIA — ASIE											
Armenia - Arménie[12]											
Total	C	23 210	24 087	24 025	24 003	...	6.1	6.3	6.3	6.3	...
Urban - Urbaine	C	15 474	15 834	15 682	...	...	6.1	6.2	6.2	...	...
Rural - Rurale	C	7 736	8 253	8 343	...	...	6.1	6.5	6.6	...	...
Azerbaijan - Azerbaïdjan[12]											
Total	+C	46 299	46 295	46 701	45 284	46 522	5.9	5.8	5.8	5.6	5.7
Urban - Urbaine	+C	23 463	22 828	23 530	23 382	23 605	5.8	5.6	5.7	5.7	5.7
Rural - Rurale	+C	22 836	23 467	23 171	21 902	22 917	5.9	6.0	5.9	5.5	5.7
Bahrain - Bahreïn											
Total	U	1 997	1 920	2 045	1 979	2 035	...	...	...	...	...
Brunei Darussalam - Brunéi Darussalam											
Total	+C	928	905	965	1 014	1 041	3.0	2.9	3.0	3.0	3.1
China - Chine[13]											
Total	...	8 070 000	8 100 000	...	...	...	...	...	...	...	...
China: Hong Kong SAR - Chine: Hong Kong RAS											
Total	C	32 847	33 255	33 758	33 378	*34 267	5.0	5.0	5.1	5.0	*5.0
China: Macao SAR - Chine: Macao RAS											
Total	C	1 356	1 374	1 338	1 327	*1 415	3.2	3.2	3.1	3.1	*3.2
Cyprus - Chypre[14]											
Total	C	5 432	5 070	5 355	4 827	5 168	7.1	6.5	6.9	6.1	6.5
Georgia - Géorgie[12]											
Total	C	39 400	40 378	41 320	39 339	...	7.2	7.9	8.2	8.0	...
Urban - Urbaine	C	20 800	22 044	22 440	21 600	...	6.9	...	7.7	...	...
Rural - Rurale	C	18 600	18 334	18 880	17 739	...	7.7	...	8.9	...	...
Iran (Islamic Republic of) - Iran (République islamique d')											
Total	C	...	374 838	...	...	...	...	6.0	...	...	...
Iraq[15]											
Total	U	160 039	177 483	179 928	...	...	...	...	...	...	...
Israel - Israël[6,16]											
Total	C	36 955	37 291	*37 688	*37 179	*38 254	6.2	6.1	*6.0	*5.8	*5.8
Urban - Urbaine	C	34 449	34 836	*35 308	*34 748	*35 817	6.4	6.3	*6.2	*5.9	*6.0
Rural - Rurale	C	2 498	2 452	*2 377	*2 428	*2 435	4.5	4.3	*4.0	*4.5	*4.4
Japan - Japon[6,17]											
Total	C	936 484	982 031	961 653	970 331	982 379	7.4	7.8	7.6	7.6	7.7

18. Deaths and crude death rates, by urban/rural residence: 1998 - 2002
Décès et taux bruts de mortalité, selon la résidence, urbaine/rurale: 1998 - 2002 (continued — suite)

(See notes at end of table. — Voir notes à la fin du tableau.)

Continent, country or area, and urban/rural residence / Continent, pays ou zone et résidence, urbaine/rurale	Co-de[1]	Number - Nombre					Rate - Taux				
		1998	1999	2000	2001	2002	1998	1999	2000	2001	2002
ASIA — ASIE											
Japan - Japon[6,17]											
Urban - Urbaine	C	683 357	717 456	704 610	712 639	724 274	...	...	...	...	...
Rural - Rurale	C	250 890	262 171	254 767	255 462	256 004	...	...	...	...	...
Jordan - Jordanie[18]											
Total	C	13 552	13 936	13 339	16 164	17 220	2.8	2.8	2.6	3.1	3.2
Kazakhstan[12]											
Total	C	154 314	147 416	149 778	147 876	149 381	10.2	9.9	10.1	10.0	10.1
Urban - Urbaine	C	96 877	92 526	94 594	94 166	95 470	11.5	11.1	11.3	11.2	11.4
Rural - Rurale	C	57 437	54 890	55 184	53 710	53 911	8.7	8.4	8.5	8.3	8.4
Korea (Republic of) - Corée (République de)[19]											
Total	C	245 597	246 539	247 346	242 730	246 515	5.3	5.3	5.3	5.1	5.2
Urban - Urbaine	C	150 941	152 121	155 754	154 230	157 755	...	...	...	...	...
Rural - Rurale	C	94 656	94 418	91 592	88 500	88 760	...	...	...	...	...
Kuwait - Koweït											
Total	C	4 216	4 187	4 227	4 364	4 342	2.1	2.0	1.9	1.9	1.9
Kyrgyzstan - Kirghizistan[12]											
Total	C	34 596	32 850	34 111	32 677	35 235	7.2	6.8	6.9	6.6	7.1
Urban - Urbaine	C	13 179	12 628	13 595	12 783	13 583	7.8	7.4	7.8	7.3	7.7
Rural - Rurale	C	21 417	20 222	20 516	19 894	21 652	6.9	6.4	6.5	6.2	6.7
Lebanon - Liban[15]											
Total	U	*20 097*	*19 133*	*18 756*	...	...	...	...	...	...	...
Malaysia - Malaisie											
Total	C	98 264	111 738	104 859	...	...	4.6	5.1	4.5	...	...
Maldives											
Total	C	1 130	1 050	1 031	1 081	*1 109	4.2	3.8	3.8	3.9	*4.0
Urban - Urbaine	C	158	301	298	288	*347	...	...	...	...	...
Rural - Rurale	C	972	749	733	793	*762	...	...	...	...	...
Mongolia - Mongolie											
Total	C	15 799	16 105	15 472	15 999	15 857	6.8	6.8	6.4	6.6	6.4
Urban - Urbaine	C	8 779	8 726	8 888	9 215	8 981	7.1	6.5	6.5	6.6	6.3
Rural - Rurale	C	7 020	7 379	6 584	6 784	6 876	6.4	7.2	6.4	6.5	6.5
Nepal - Népal[20]											
Total	I	...	...	...	106 789	...	...	...	...	4.6	...
Occupied Palestinian Territory - Territoire palestinien occupé											
Total	U	*6 205*	*8 500*	*8 701*	*8 772*	*9 216*	...	...	...	...	...
Oman[21]											
Total	...	*2 297*	*2 440*	*2 547*	*2 550*	...	...	...	...	...	...
Pakistan[22,23]											
Total	I	...	...	...	956 515	...	...	...	...	6.8	...
Urban - Urbaine	I	...	...	...	302 482	...	...	...	...	...	...
Rural - Rurale	I	...	...	...	654 033	...	...	...	...	...	...
Philippines											
Total	C	352 992	347 989	366 931	...	...	4.8	4.7	4.8	...	...
Qatar											
Total	C	1 157	1 148	1 173	1 210	1 220	2.1	...	2.0	2.0	...
Saudi Arabia - Arabie saoudite											
Total	...	...	*68 521*	*51 614*	...	...	...	...	...	...	...
Singapore - Singapour[24]											
Total	+C	15 657	15 516	15 693	15 367	15 820	4.9	4.8	4.8	4.6	4.7
Sri Lanka											
Total	+C	*112 657	*114 392	...	...	*110 637	*6.0	*6.0	...	...	*5.8

18. Deaths and crude death rates, by urban/rural residence: 1998 - 2002
Décès et taux bruts de mortalité, selon la résidence, urbaine/rurale: 1998 - 2002 (continued — suite)

(See notes at end of table. — Voir notes à la fin du tableau.)

Continent, country or area, and urban/rural residence / Continent, pays ou zone et résidence, urbaine/rurale	Code[1]	Number - Nombre					Rate - Taux				
		1998	1999	2000	2001	2002	1998	1999	2000	2001	2002
ASIA — ASIE											
Syrian Arab Republic - République arabe syrienne[2,25,26]											
Total	U	57 893	56 564	57 759	60 814	...	...	...	...	...	...
Tajikistan - Tadjikistan[12]											
Total	C	...	*24 900	...	...	...	...	*4.0	...	...	...
Thailand - Thaïlande											
Total	+U	317 793	362 593	365 741	369 493	380 364	...	...	...	...	...
Urban - Urbaine	+U	...	36 796	37 257	...	...	...	...	...	...	...
Rural - Rurale	+U	...	325 797	328 484	...	...	...	...	...	...	...
Turkey - Turquie[27]											
Total	I	465 000	471 000	477 000	485 000	491 000	7.1	7.1	7.1	7.1	7.1
Urban - Urbaine	I	175 429	185 141	174 315	175 137	...	4.2	4.3	4.0	3.9	...
Rural - Rurale	I	289 571	285 859	302 685	309 863	...	12.2	12.0	12.7	13.0	...
Turkmenistan - Turkménistan[12]											
Total	C	29 628	...	...	...	...	6.1	...	...	...	...
Uzbekistan - Ouzbékistan[12]											
Total	C	...	140 526	135 598	132 542	...	...	5.9	5.5	5.3	...
Urban - Urbaine	C	...	61 167	61 130	59 743	...	...	6.8	6.6	6.5	...
Rural - Rurale	C	...	79 359	74 468	72 799	...	...	5.3	4.8	4.6	...
EUROPE											
Albania - Albanie											
Total	C	18 250	...	...	...	...	4.8	...	...	...	...
Andorra - Andorre											
Total	U	235	207	259	237	218	3.6	3.1	3.9	3.6	3.3
Austria - Autriche											
Total	C	78 339	78 200	76 780	74 767	76 131	9.7	9.7	9.5	9.3	9.5
Urban - Urbaine	C	46 639	46 752	...	...	...	...	...	...	...	...
Rural - Rurale	C	31 700	31 448	...	...	...	...	...	...	...	...
Belarus - Bélarus[12]											
Total	C	137 296	142 027	...	...	146 655	13.5	14.2	...	...	14.8
Urban - Urbaine	C	69 796	73 654	...	...	77 020	9.8	10.6	...	...	10.9
Rural - Rurale	C	67 500	68 373	...	...	69 635	22.1	22.3	...	...	24.1
Belgium - Belgique[28]											
Total	C	104 583	104 904	104 903	103 447	105 642	10.3	10.3	10.2	10.1	10.2
Bosnia and Herzegovina - Bosnie-Herzégovine											
Total	C	28 679	...	...	...	...	7.9	...	...	...	...
Bulgaria - Bulgarie											
Total	C	118 193	111 786	115 087	112 368	112 617	14.3	13.6	14.1	14.2	14.3
Urban - Urbaine	C	...	...	64 184	62 778	63 765	...	...	11.5	11.5	11.7
Rural - Rurale	C	...	...	50 903	49 590	48 852	...	...	19.6	20.4	20.3
Channel Islands: Guernsey - Îles Anglo-Normandes: Guernesey											
Total	C	540	529	*565	...	...	9.1	8.8	*9.3	...	...
Croatia - Croatie											
Total	C	52 311	51 953	50 246	49 552	50 569	11.6	11.4	11.5	11.2	11.4
Urban - Urbaine	C	26 302	...	25 130	24 838	24 984	...	...	...	...	...
Rural - Rurale	C	26 009	...	25 116	24 714	25 585	...	...	...	...	...
Czech Republic - République tchèque											
Total	C	109 527	109 768	109 001	107 755	108 243	10.6	10.7	10.6	10.5	10.6

18. Deaths and crude death rates, by urban/rural residence: 1998 - 2002
Décès et taux bruts de mortalité, selon la résidence, urbaine/rurale: 1998 - 2002 (continued — suite)

(See notes at end of table. — Voir notes à la fin du tableau.)

Continent, country or area, and urban/rural residence Continent, pays ou zone et résidence, urbaine/rurale	Code[1]	Number - Nombre					Rate - Taux				
		1998	1999	2000	2001	2002	1998	1999	2000	2001	2002
EUROPE											
Czech Republic - République tchèque											
Urban - Urbaine	C	78 326	78 518	78 276	77 649	78 023	10.2	10.3	10.2	10.3	10.4
Rural - Rurale	C	31 201	31 250	30 725	30 106	30 220	11.9	11.9	11.7	11.3	11.3
Denmark - Danemark[29]											
Total	C	58 442	59 156	57 986	58 338	58 610	11.0	11.1	10.9	10.9	10.9
Estonia - Estonie[6,12]											
Total	C	19 440	18 455	18 403	18 516	18 355	13.4	12.8	13.4	13.6	13.5
Urban - Urbaine	C	...	...	11 665	11 735	11 953	...	...	12.3	12.4	12.7
Rural - Rurale	C	...	...	6 518	6 624	6 276	...	...	15.4	15.8	15.0
Finland - Finlande[30]											
Total	C	49 262	49 345	49 339	48 550	49 418	9.6	9.6	9.5	9.4	9.5
Urban - Urbaine	C	26 784	...	...	26 928	27 591	8.7	...	...	8.5	8.6
Rural - Rurale	C	22 478	...	...	21 622	21 827	10.9	...	...	10.8	11.0
France[31,32]											
Total	C	534 005	537 661	536 300	531 485	...	9.1	9.2	9.1	9.0	...
Urban - Urbaine	C	376 390	378 644	...	...	...	...	...	...	...	...
Rural - Rurale	C	155 488	157 115	...	...	...	...	...	...	...	...
Germany - Allemagne											
Total	C	851 412	846 330	838 797	828 541	...	10.4	10.3	10.2	10.1	...
Gibraltar[33]											
Total	C	267	277	262	249	242	9.9	10.2	9.7	8.8	8.5
Greece - Grèce											
Total	C	102 668	103 304	105 219	102 559	...	9.8	9.8	10.5	10.2	...
Urban - Urbaine	C	55 464	...	...	...	...	...	...	...	...	...
Rural - Rurale	C	47 204	...	...	...	...	...	...	...	...	...
Holy See - Saint-Siège											
Total	C	...	...	10	...	...	...	...	...	...	...
Hungary - Hongrie[34]											
Total	C	140 870	143 210	135 601	132 183	132 833	13.9	14.2	13.5	13.0	13.1
Urban - Urbaine	C	85 084	86 726	82 209	81 673	83 112	13.0	13.3	12.7	12.3	12.6
Rural - Rurale	C	55 074	55 646	52 614	49 857	49 128	15.5	15.6	14.8	14.1	13.8
Iceland - Islande											
Total	C	1 821	1 901	1 828	1 725	1 821	6.7	6.9	6.5	6.1	6.3
Urban - Urbaine	C	1 633	1 729	1 683	1 555	1 658	6.5	6.8	6.5	5.9	6.2
Rural - Rurale	C	188	172	145	170	163	8.8	8.1	6.7	7.9	7.6
Ireland - Irlande[35]											
Total	+C	31 437	31 683	31 115	29 812	29 381	8.5	8.5	8.2	7.8	7.5
Urban - Urbaine	+C	17 397	17 288	...	...	...	...	...	...	...	...
Rural - Rurale	+C	14 040	14 395	...	...	...	...	...	...	...	...
Isle of Man - Îles de Man											
Total	+C	893	983	897	855	877	12.1	...	12.0	11.2	11.4
Italy - Italie											
Total	C	574 231	571 356	560 241	555 247	*556 006	10.0	9.9	9.7	9.6	*9.7
Latvia - Lettonie[12]											
Total	C	34 200	32 844	32 205	32 991	32 498	14.2	13.7	13.6	14.0	13.9
Urban - Urbaine	C	22 043	21 246	20 921	21 460	21 059	13.3	13.0	13.0	13.4	13.3
Rural - Rurale	C	12 157	11 598	11 284	11 531	11 439	16.0	15.3	14.9	15.3	15.2
Liechtenstein											
Total	C	...	...	...	220	215	...	...	...	6.6	6.4
Lithuania - Lituanie[12]											
Total	C	40 757	40 003	38 919	40 399	41 072	11.5	11.4	11.1	11.6	11.8
Urban - Urbaine	C	22 413	...	21 932	22 962	23 175	9.4	...	9.4	9.9	10.0
Rural - Rurale	C	18 344	...	16 987	17 437	17 897	15.8	...	14.7	15.1	15.6
Luxembourg											
Total	C	3 901	3 793	3 754	3 719	3 744	9.2	8.8	8.6	8.4	8.4
Malta - Malte[36]											
Total	C	3 044	3 097	2 957	2 935	3 031	7.9	8.0	7.6	7.4	7.6

18. Deaths and crude death rates, by urban/rural residence: 1998 - 2002
Décès et taux bruts de mortalité, selon la résidence, urbaine/rurale: 1998 - 2002 (continued — suite)

(See notes at end of table. — Voir notes à la fin du tableau.)

Continent, country or area, and urban/rural residence / Continent, pays ou zone et résidence, urbaine/rurale	Code[1]	Number - Nombre					Rate - Taux				
		1998	1999	2000	2001	2002	1998	1999	2000	2001	2002
EUROPE											
Monaco											
Total	C	538	...	547	...	...	...	...	16.4	...	...
Netherlands - Pays-Bas[37]											
Total	C	137 482	140 487	140 527	140 377	142 355	8.8	8.9	8.8	8.7	8.8
Urban - Urbaine	C	88 815	...	92 934	93 616	94 926	9.1	...	...	...	9.1
Rural - Rurale	C	48 667	...	47 593	46 761	47 429	8.2	...	...	...	8.4
Norway - Norvège[38]											
Total	C	44 112	45 170	44 002	43 981	44 465	10.0	10.1	9.8	9.7	9.8
Poland - Pologne											
Total	C	375 354	381 415	368 028	363 220	359 486	9.7	9.9	9.5	9.4	9.4
Urban - Urbaine	C	219 331	223 630	...	...	...	9.2	9.4	...	...	...
Rural - Rurale	C	156 023	157 785	...	...	...	10.6	10.7	...	...	...
Portugal											
Total	C	106 382	107 871	105 804	105 092	106 258	10.7	10.8	10.6	10.2	10.2
Republic of Moldova - République de Moldova[12]											
Total	C	39 922	41 315	41 224	40 075	41 852	10.9	11.3	11.3	11.0	11.6
Urban - Urbaine	C	13 180	13 512	13 266	12 844	13 229	8.6	8.8	8.8	8.6	8.9
Rural - Rurale	C	26 742	27 803	27 958	27 231	28 623	12.6	13.1	13.2	12.7	13.4
Romania - Roumanie											
Total	C	269 166	265 194	255 820	259 603	269 666	12.0	11.8	11.4	11.7	12.4
Urban - Urbaine	C	112 733	...	108 436	110 063	113 225	9.1	...	8.9	9.0	9.8
Rural - Rurale	C	156 433	...	147 384	149 540	156 441	15.4	...	14.5	14.7	15.4
Russian Federation - Fédération de Russie[12]											
Total	C	1 988 744	2 144 316	2 225 332	2 251 814	...	13.6	14.7	15.3	15.6	...
Urban - Urbaine	C	1 379 804	1 499 466	...	...	...	...	14.1	...	...	...
Rural - Rurale	C	608 940	644 850	...	...	...	...	16.3	...	...	...
San Marino - Saint-Marin											
Total	+C	190	198	188	...	...	7.3	7.5	7.0	...	...
Urban - Urbaine	+C	...	...	168	...	...	...	...	7.4	...	...
Rural - Rurale	+C	...	...	20	...	...	...	...	...	...	...
Serbia and Montenegro - Serbie-et-Montenegro											
Total	C	113 312	115 461	118 078	113 063		10.7	10.9	11.1	10.6	...
Urban - Urbaine	C	55 867	57 007	59 324	...	...	10.2	10.4	10.8	...	...
Rural - Rurale	C	57 445	58 454	58 754	...	...	11.2	11.3	11.4	...	...
Slovakia - Slovaquie											
Total	C	53 156	52 402	52 703	51 980	51 532	9.9	9.7	9.8	9.7	9.6
Urban - Urbaine	C	24 983	24 492	...	24 520	24 737	8.1	8.0	...	...	8.2
Rural - Rurale	C	28 173	27 910	...	27 460	26 795	12.1	12.0	...	...	11.3
Slovenia - Slovénie											
Total	C	19 039	18 885	18 588	18 508	18 622	9.6	9.5	9.3	9.3	9.3
Urban - Urbaine	C	8 429	8 409	8 345	8 277	8 640	...	...	...	...	8.9
Rural - Rurale	C	10 610	10 476	10 243	10 231	9 982	...	...	...	...	10.2
Spain - Espagne											
Total	C	360 511	371 102	360 391	*351 147	...	9.1	9.4	9.0	*8.7	...
Sweden - Suède											
Total	C	93 271	94 726	93 461	93 752	95 009	10.5	10.7	10.5	10.5	10.6
Switzerland - Suisse											
Total	C	62 568	62 503	62 528	61 287	61 768	8.8	8.7	8.7	8.5	8.5
Urban - Urbaine	C	42 928	42 693	42 868	42 157	...	8.9	8.9	8.8	8.6	...
Rural - Rurale	C	19 640	19 810	19 660	19 130	...	8.5	8.5	8.4	8.2	...

18. Deaths and crude death rates, by urban/rural residence: 1998 - 2002
Décès et taux bruts de mortalité, selon la résidence, urbaine/rurale: 1998 - 2002 (continued — suite)

(See notes at end of table. — Voir notes à la fin du tableau.)

Continent, country or area, and urban/rural residence / Continent, pays ou zone et résidence, urbaine/rurale	Code[1]	Number - Nombre					Rate - Taux				
		1998	1999	2000	2001	2002	1998	1999	2000	2001	2002
EUROPE											
The Former Yugoslav Rep. of Macedonia - L'ex-République yougoslave de Macédoine											
Total	C	16 870	16 789	17 253	16 919	17 962	8.4	8.3	8.5	8.3	8.8
Urban - Urbaine	C	...	9 539	10 013	9 939	10 452	...	...	...	...	...
Rural - Rurale	C	...	7 250	7 240	6 980	7 510	...	...	...	...	...
Ukraine[12]											
Total	C	719 954	739 170	758 082	745 952	754 911	14.3	14.8	15.2	15.2	15.6
Urban - Urbaine	C	425 521	...	...	450 329	454 406	12.4	...	...	...	...
Rural - Rurale	C	294 433	...	...	295 623	300 505	18.1	...	...	...	...
United Kingdom - Royaume-Uni											
Total	C	629 172	632 062	608 366	602 268	606 283	10.6	10.6	10.2	10.1	10.2
OCEANIA — OCEANIE											
American Samoa - Samoas américaines											
Total	C	243	249	224	...	...	4.4	4.4	3.9	...	...
Australia - Australie											
Total	+C	127 202	128 102	128 291	128 544	133 707	6.8	6.8	6.7	6.6	6.8
Cook Islands - Îles Cook											
Total	+C	107	96	115	88	72	6.1	5.9	6.4	4.8	3.9
Fiji - Fidji											
Total	+C	5 241	3 603	...	...	...	6.6	4.5	...	...	...
French Polynesia - Polynésie française											
Total	U	1 114	1 003	1 013	...	...	...	...	...	...	...
Guam[39]											
Total	C	651	724	667	691	658	4.3	4.7	4.3	4.4	4.1
Marshall Islands - Îles Marshall											
Total	+U	...	...	...	271	...	...	...	...	...	...
New Caledonia - Nouvelle-Calédonie											
Total	C	982	1 095	1 077	1 131	1 121	4.8	5.3	5.1	5.3	5.2
New Zealand - Nouvelle-Zélande											
Total	+C	26 206	28 122	26 660	27 825	28 065	6.9	7.3	6.9	7.2	7.1
Urban - Urbaine	+C	23 668	25 385	24 014	25 093	25 390	7.2	7.7	7.3	7.5	7.5
Rural - Rurale	+C	2 418	2 620	2 563	2 677	2 611	4.4	4.8	4.7	4.9	4.7
Niue - Nioué											
Total	...	...	...	...	...	13	...	...	...	...	...
Northern Mariana Islands - Îles Mariannes septentrionales											
Total	U	180	189	...	...	...	...	...	...	...	...
Palau - Palaos											
Total	C	125	131	...	...	...	6.8	6.9	...	...	...
Samoa											
Total	U	531	...	...	...	...	...	...	...	...	...
Tonga											
Total	+C	498	675	653	...	...	5.0	6.8	6.5	...	...

GENERAL NOTES - NOTES GENERALES

For certain countries, there is a discrepancy between the total number of deaths shown in this table and those shown in subsequent tables for the same year. Usually this discrepancy arises because the total number of deaths occurring in a given year is revised, although the remaining tabulations are not. Data exclude foetal deaths. Rates are the number of deaths per 1 000 mid-year population. For definitions of 'urban', see end of Technical Notes for table 6. For method of evaluation and limitations of data, see Technical Notes for this table. — Pour quelques pays il y a une discordance entre le nombre total des décès vivantes présenté dans ce tableau et ceux présentés après pour la même année. Habituellement ces différences apparaissent lorsque le nombre total des décès pour une certaine année a été révisé; alors que les autres tabulations ne l'ont pas été. Les données ne comprennent pas les morts foetales. Les taux représentent le nombre de décès pour 1 000 personnes au milieu de l'année. Pour les définitions des 'régions urbaines', se reporter à la fin des Notes techniques du tableau 6. Pour la méthode d'évaluation et les insuffisances des données, voir Notes techniques, pour ce tableaux.

Italics: data from civil registers which are incomplete or of unknown completeness. — *Italiques:* données incomplètes ou dont le degré d'exactitude n'est pas connu, provenant des registres de l'état civil.

FOOTNOTES - NOTES

[*] Provisional. — Données provisoires.
[1] 'Code' indicates the source of data, as follows:
C - Civil registration, estimated over 90% complete
U - Civil registration, estimated less than 90% complete
I - Other source, estimated reliable
+ - Data tabulated by date of registration rather than occurence.
... - Information not available

Le 'Code' indique la source des données, comme suit:
C - Registres de l'état civil considérés complets à 90 p. 100 au moins.
U - Registres de l'état civil qui ne sont pas considérés complets à 90 p. 100 au moins.
I - Autre source, considérée pas douteuses.
+ - Données exploitées selon la date de l'enregistrement et non la date de l'événement.
... - Information pas disponible.

[2] Excluding live-born infants who died before their birth was registered. - Non compris les enfants nés vivants décédés avant l'enregistrement de leur naissance.
[3] For Algerian population only. - Pour la population algérienne seulement.
[4] Data refer to national projections. - Les données se referent aux projections nationales.
[5] For 1998, based on the results of the population census. - Pour 1998, d'après les résultats du recensement de la population.
[6] Figures for urban and rural areas do not add up to the total, since they do not include the category 'Unknown residence'. - La somme des donées pour la residence urbaine et rurale n'est pas égale au total parce qu'elle n'inclue pas la catégorie 'Residence inconnue'.
[7] Including Canadian residents temporarily in the United States, but excluding United States residents temporarily in Canada. - Y compris les résidents canadiens se trouvant temporairement aux Etats-Unis, mais ne comprenant pas les résidents des Etats-Unis se trouvant temporairement au Canada.
[8] Excluding Indian jungle population. - Non compris les Indiens de la jungle.
[9] Data on live births and deaths are based on a civil registration system put in place in January 1998. - Les données sur les naissances et les décès sont basées sur un système d'enregistrement des faits d'état civil mis en place en janvier 1998.
[10] Excluding nomadic Indian tribes. - Non compris les tribus d'Indiens nomades.
[11] Including an upward adjustment for under-registration. - Y compris un ajustement pour sous-enregistrement.
[12] Excluding infants born alive with less than 28 weeks gestation, less than 1 000 grams in weight and 35 centimeters in length, who die within seven days of birth. - Non compris les enfants nés vivants avant 28 semaines de gestation, pesant moins de 1 000 grammes, mesurant moins de 35 centimètres et décédés dans les sept jours qui ont suivi leur naissance.
[13] For statistical purposes, the data for China do not include those for the Hong Kong Special Administrative Region (Hong Kong SAR), Macao Special Administrative Region (Macao SAR) and Taiwan province of China. - Pour la présentation des statistiques, les données pour Chine ne comprend pas la Région Administrative Spéciale de Hong Kong (Hong Kong RAS), la Région Administrative Spéciale de Macao (Macao RAS) et Taïwan province de Chine.
[14] Data refer to government controlled areas. - Les données se raportent aux zones contrôlées par le Gouvernement.

[15] Published by the United Nations Economic and Social Commission for Western Asia. - Publié par la Commission économique et sociale des Nations Unies pour l'Asie occidentale.
[16] Including data for East Jerusalem and Israeli residents in certain other territories under occupation by Israeli military forces since June 1967. - Y compris les données pour Jérusalem-Est et les résidents israéliens dans certains autres territoires occupés depuis 1967 par les forces armées israéliennes.
[17] For Japanese nationals in Japan only; however, rates computed on population including foreigners except foreign military and civilian personnel and their dependants stationed in the area. — Pour les nationaux japonais au Japon seulement; toutefois, les taux sont calculés sur la base d'une population comprenant les étrangers, mais ne comprenant ni les militaires et agents civils étrangers en poste sur le territoire ni les membres de leur famille les accompagnant.
[18] Excluding data for Jordanian territory under occupation since June 1967 by Israeli military forces. Excluding foreigners, including registered Palestinian refugees. - Non compris les données pour le territoire jordanien occupé depuis juin 1967 par les forces armées israéliennes. Non compris les étrangers, mais y compris les réfugiés de Palestine enregistrés.
[19] Excluding alien armed forces, civilian aliens employed by armed forces, and foreign diplomatic personnel and their dependants. - Non compris les militaires étrangers, les civils étrangers employés par les forces armées ni le personnel diplomatique étranger et les membres de leur famille les accompagnant.
[20] For 2001, data refer to last twelve months preceding census on June 2001. - Pour 2001, les données se rapportent pour la dernière fois à douze mois précédant le recensement juin 2001.
[21] Data refer to the recorded events in Ministry of Health hospitals and health centres only. - Les données se rapportent aux faits d'état-civil enregistrés dans les hôpitaux et les dispensaires du Ministère de la santé seulement.
[22] Excluding data for the Pakistan-held part of Jammu and Kashmir, the final status of which has not yet been determined. - Non compris les données concernant la partie du Jammu et Cachemire occupée par le Pakistan dont le statut définitif n'a pas été déterminé.
[23] Based on the results of the Population Growth Survey. - D'après les résultats de la 'Population Growth Survey.'
[24] Excluding transients afloat and non-locally domiciled military and civilian services personnel and their dependants. - Non compris les personnes de passage þ bord de navires, ni les militaires et agents civils domiciliés hors du territoire et les membres de leur famille les accompagnant.
[25] Excluding nomad population and Palestinian refugees. - Non compris la population nomade et les réfugiés de Palestine.
[26] Including late registered deaths. - Y compris les décès enregistrés tardivement.
[27] Based on the results of the Population Demographic Survey. - - D'après les résultats de la Population Demographic Survey.
[28] Including armed forces stationed outside the country, but excluding alien armed forces stationed in the area. - Y compris les militaires nationaux hors du pays, mais non compris les militaires étrangers en garnison sur le territoire.
[29] Excluding Faeroe Islands and Greenland. - Non compris les Iles Féroé et Gröenland.
[30] Including nationals temporarily outside the country. - Y compris les nationaux se trouvant temporairement hors du pays.
[31] Including armed forces stationed outside the country. - Y compris les militaires nationaux hors du pays.
[32] Data for urban/rural, excluding nationals outside the country. - Les données selon la résidence urbaine/rurale, non compris les nationaux hors du pays.
[33] Excluding armed forces. - Non compris les militaires en garnison.
[34] Data for urban/rural residence, for the de jure population. - Les données selon la résidence urbaine/rurale, pour la population de droit.
[35] Events registered within one year of occurrence. - Evénements enregistrés dans l'année qui suit l'événement.
[36] Rates computed on population including civilian nationals temporarily outside the country. - Les taux sont calculés sur la base d'un chiffre de population qui comprend les civils nationaux temporairement hors du pays.
[37] Including residents outside the country if listed in a Netherlands population register. - Y compris les résidents hors du pays, s'ils sont inscrits sur un registre de population néerlandais.
[38] Including residents temporarily outside the country. - Y compris les résidents se trouvant temporairement hors du pays.
[39] Including United States military personnel, their dependants and contract employees. - Y compris les militaires des Etats-Unis, les membres de leur famille les accompagnant et les agents contractuels des Etats-Unis.

Table 19

Table 19 presents deaths by age, sex and urban/rural residence for latest available year.

Description of variables: Age is defined as age at last birthday, that is, the difference between the date of birth and the date of the occurrence of the event, expressed in completed solar years. The age classification used in this table is the following: under 1 year, 1-4 years, 5-year age groups through 95-99 years, and 100 years or over.

The urban/rural classification of deaths is that provided by each country or area; it is presumed to be based on the national census definitions of urban population that have been set forth at the end of the technical notes for table 6.

Reliability of data: Data from civil registers of deaths that are reported as incomplete (less than 90 per cent completeness) or of unknown completeness are considered unreliable and are set in italics rather than in roman type. Table 18 and the technical notes for that table provide more detailed information on the completeness of death registration. For more information about the quality of vital statistics data in general, and the information available on the basis of the completeness estimates in particular, see section 4.2 of the Technical Notes.

Limitations: Statistics on deaths by age and sex are subject to the same qualifications as have been set forth for vital statistics in general and death statistics in particular as discussed in section 4 of the Technical Notes.

The reliability of the data is an important factor in considering the limitations. In addition, some deaths are tabulated by date of registration and not by date of occurrence; these have been indicated by a plus sign (+). Whenever the lag between the date of occurrence and date of registration is prolonged and, therefore, a large proportion of the death registrations are delayed, death statistics for any given year may be seriously affected. However, delays in the registration of deaths are less common and shorter than in the registration of live births.

International comparability in mortality statistics may also be affected by the exclusion of deaths of infants who were born alive but died before the registration of the birth or within the first 24 hours of life. Statistics of this type are footnoted.

Because these statistics are classified according to age, they are subject to the limitations with respect to accuracy of age reporting similar to those already discussed in connection with section 3.1.3 of the Technical Notes. The factors influencing the accuracy of reporting may be somewhat dissimilar in vital statistics (because of the differences in the method of taking a census and registering a death) but, in general, the same errors can be observed.

The absence of frequencies in the unknown age group does not necessarily indicate completely accurate reporting and tabulation of the age item. It is often an indication that the unknowns have been eliminated by assigning ages to them before tabulation, or by proportionate distribution after tabulation.

International comparability of statistics on deaths by age is also affected by the use of different methods to determine age at death. If age is obtained from an item that simply requests age at death in completed years or is derived from information on year of birth and death rather than from information on complete date (day, month and year) of birth and death, the number of deaths classified in the under-one-year age group will tend to be reduced and the number of deaths in the next age group will tend to be somewhat increased. A similar bias may affect other age groups but its impact is usually negligible. Information on this factor is given in the footnotes when known.

The comparability of data by urban/rural residence is affected by the national definitions of urban and rural used in tabulating these data. It is assumed, in the absence of specific information to the contrary, that the definitions of urban and rural used in connection with the national population census were also used in the compilation of the vital statistics for each country or area. However, it cannot be excluded that, for a given country or area, different definitions of urban and rural are used for the vital statistics data and the population census data respectively. When known, the definitions of urban used in national population censuses are presented at the end of the technical notes for table 6. As discussed in detail in the technical notes for table 6, these definitions vary considerably from one country or area to another.

Earlier data: Deaths by age and sex have been shown for the latest available year in each issue of the Yearbook since the 1955 issue. Data included in this table update the series covering a period of years as follows:

Issue	Years Covered
Historical Supplement CD, 1997	1948 – 1997
1996	1987 – 1995
1992	1983 – 1992
1985	1976 – 1984
1980	1971 – 1979
Historical Supplement, 1979	1948 - 1977

Data have been presented by urban/rural residence in each regular issue of the Yearbook since the 1967 issue.

Tableau 19

Le tableau 19 présente les données les plus récentes dont on dispose sur les décès selon l'âge, le sexe et le lieu de résidence (zone urbaine ou rurale).

Description des variables : L'âge considéré est l'âge au dernier anniversaire, c'est-à-dire la différence entre la date de naissance et la date du décès, exprimée en années solaires révolues. La classification par âge est la suivante : moins d'un an, 1 à 4 ans, groupes quinquennaux jusqu'à 95-99 ans et 100 ans et plus.

La classification des décès selon le lieu de résidence (zone urbaine ou rurale) est celle qui a été communiquée par chaque pays ou zone ; on part du principe qu'elle repose sur les définitions de la population urbaine utilisées pour les recensements nationaux, qui sont reproduites à la fin des notes techniques du tableau 6.

Fiabilité des données : Les données sur les décès issues des registres d'état civil qui sont déclarées incomplètes (degré d'exhaustivité inférieur à 90 p.100) ou dont le degré d'exhaustivité n'est pas connu sont jugées douteuses et apparaissent en italique et non en caractères romains. Le tableau 18 et les notes techniques s'y rapportant présentent des renseignements plus détaillés sur le degré d'exhaustivité de l'enregistrement des décès. Pour plus de précisions sur la qualité des statistiques de l'état civil en général et le degré de complétude en particulier, voir la section 4.2 des Notes techniques.

Insuffisance des données : Les statistiques des décès selon l'âge et le sexe appellent les mêmes réserves que les statistiques de l'état civil en général et les statistiques relatives à la mortalité en particulier (voir la section 4 des Notes techniques).

La fiabilité des données est un facteur important. Il faut également tenir compte du fait que, dans certains cas, les données relatives aux décès sont classées par date d'enregistrement et non par date d'occurrence ; ces cas ont été signalés par le signe '+'. Chaque fois que le décalage entre le décès et son enregistrement est grand et qu'une forte proportion des décès fait l'objet d'un enregistrement tardif, les statistiques des décès de l'année peuvent être considérablement faussées.

En règle générale, toutefois, les décès sont enregistrés beaucoup plus rapidement que les naissances vivantes, et les retards prolongés sont rares.

Un autre facteur qui nuit à la comparabilité internationale est la pratique de certains pays ou zones qui consiste à ne pas inclure dans les statistiques des décès les enfants nés vivants mais décédés avant l'enregistrement de leur naissance ou dans les 24 heures qui ont suivi la naissance, pratique qui conduit à sous-évaluer le nombre de décès à moins d'un an. Quand pareil facteur a joué, cela a été signalé en note à la fin du tableau.

Étant donné que les statistiques relatives à la mortalité sont classées selon l'âge, elles appellent les mêmes réserves concernant l'exactitude des déclarations d'âge que celles qui ont été formulées à la section 3.1.3 des Notes techniques. Dans le cas des données d'état civil, les facteurs qui interviennent à cet égard sont parfois un peu différents, du fait que le recensement et l'enregistrement des décès se font par des méthodes différentes, mais, d'une manière générale, les erreurs observées sont les mêmes.

Si aucun nombre ne figure dans la rangée réservée aux âges inconnus, cela ne signifie pas nécessairement que les déclarations d'âge et le classement par âge sont tout à fait exacts. C'est souvent une indication que l'on a attribué un âge aux personnes d'âge inconnu avant l'exploitation des données ou qu'elles ont été réparties proportionnellement entre les différents groupes après cette opération.

Le manque d'uniformité des méthodes suivies pour obtenir l'âge au moment du décès nuit également à la comparabilité internationale des données. Si l'âge est connu, soit d'après la réponse à une simple question sur l'âge du décès en années révolues, soit d'après l'année de la naissance et l'année du décès, et non d'après des renseignements concernant la date exacte (jour, mois et année) de la naissance et du décès, le nombre de décès classés dans la catégorie « moins d'un an » sera entaché d'une erreur par défaut et le chiffre figurant dans la catégorie suivante d'une erreur par excès.

Les données pour les autres groupes d'âge pourront être entachées d'une distorsion analogue, mais les répercussions seront généralement négligeables. Les imperfections, lorsqu'elles étaient connues, ont été signalées en note à la fin du tableau.

La comparabilité des données selon le lieu de résidence (zone urbaine ou rurale) peut être limitée par les définitions nationales des termes « urbain » et « rural » utilisées pour le classement de ces données. En l'absence d'indications contraires, on a supposé que les mêmes définitions avaient servi pour le recensement national de la population et pour l'établissement des statistiques de l'état civil pour chaque pays ou zone. Toutefois, il n'est pas exclu que, pour une zone ou un pays donné, des définitions différentes aient été retenues. Les définitions du terme «urbain » utilisées pour les recensements nationaux de population ont été présentées à la fin du tableau 6 lorsqu'elles étaient connues. Comme on l'a précisé dans les notes techniques relatives au tableau 6, ces définitions varient considérablement d'un pays ou d'une zone à l'autre.

Données publiées antérieurement : Les éditions de l'*Annuaire démographique* parues depuis 1955 présentent les statistiques les plus récentes dont on disposait à l'époque sur les décès selon l'âge et le sexe. Les données qui figurent dans le tableau 19 actualisent les données qui portaient sur les périodes suivantes :

Éditions	Années considérées
Supplément historique (CD-ROM), 1997	1948 – 1997
1996	1987 – 1995
1992	1983 – 1992
1985	1976 – 1984
1980	1971 – 1979
Supplément rétrospectif, 1979	1948 - 1977

Des données selon le lieu de résidence (zone urbaine ou rurale) ont été présentées dans toutes les éditions de l'*Annuaire* depuis celle de 1967, exception faite des éditions spéciales.

19. Deaths by age, sex and urban/rural residence: latest available year, 1993 - 2002
Décès selon l'âge, le sexe et la résidence, urbaine/rurale: dernière année disponible, 1993 - 2002

(See notes at end of table.— Voir notes à la fin du tableau.)

Continent, country or area, year and age (in years) / Continent, pays ou zone, année et âge (en années)	Code[1]	Total			Urban - Urbaine			Rural - Rurale		
		Both sexes - Les deux sexes	Male - Masculin	Female - Féminin	Both sexes - Les deux sexes	Male - Masculin	Female - Féminin	Both sexes - Les deux sexes	Male - Masculin	Female - Féminin
AFRICA — AFRIQUE										
Algeria - Algérie[2,3]										
1998										
Total	+U	131 708	73 352	58 356	...	...	...	...	...	...
0 - 1	+U	21 169	12 009	9 160	...	...	...	...	...	...
1 - 4	+U	4 475	2 378	2 097	...	...	...	...	...	...
5 - 9	+U	2 759	1 592	1 167	...	...	...	...	...	...
10 - 14	+U	2 272	1 373	899	...	...	...	...	...	...
15 - 19	+U	3 017	1 947	1 070	...	...	...	...	...	...
20 - 24	+U	3 425	2 335	1 090	...	...	...	...	...	...
25 - 29	+U	3 508	2 355	1 153	...	...	...	...	...	...
30 - 34	+U	3 216	1 958	1 258	...	...	...	...	...	...
35 - 39	+U	3 195	1 770	1 425	...	...	...	...	...	...
40 - 44	+U	3 468	1 959	1 509	...	...	...	...	...	...
45 - 49	+U	3 771	2 135	1 636	...	...	...	...	...	...
50 - 54	+U	3 777	2 184	1 593	...	...	...	...	...	...
55 - 59	+U	5 113	2 908	2 205	...	...	...	...	...	...
60 - 64	+U	7 616	4 227	3 389	...	...	...	...	...	...
65 - 69	+U	8 962	4 937	4 025	...	...	...	...	...	...
70 - 74	+U	10 320	5 732	4 588	...	...	...	...	...	...
75 - 79	+U	11 346	6 241	5 105	...	...	...	...	...	...
80+	+U	30 299	15 312	14 987	...	...	...	...	...	...
Botswana[4]										
2001										
Total	I	20 823	10 800	10 023	10 041	5 204	4 837	10 782	5 596	5 186
0 - 1	I	1 576	815	761	718	364	354	858	451	407
1 - 4	I	1 187	637	550	551	294	257	636	343	293
5 - 9	I	484	251	233	210	118	92	274	133	141
10 - 14	I	249	114	135	112	51	61	137	63	74
15 - 19	I	386	179	207	192	88	104	194	91	103
20 - 24	I	1 090	388	702	520	197	323	570	191	379
25 - 29	I	2 091	848	1 243	1 056	443	613	1 035	405	630
30 - 34	I	2 376	1 235	1 141	1 208	631	577	1 168	604	564
35 - 39	I	2 039	1 132	907	997	550	447	1 042	582	460
40 - 44	I	1 595	910	685	842	483	359	753	427	326
45 - 49	I	1 334	814	520	702	422	280	632	392	240
50 - 54	I	858	529	329	418	253	165	440	276	164
55 - 59	I	669	416	253	333	208	125	336	208	128
60 - 64	I	638	386	252	316	197	119	322	189	133
65 - 69	I	673	374	299	308	154	154	365	220	145
70 - 74	I	601	322	279	261	131	130	340	191	149
75 - 79	I	569	315	254	256	144	112	313	171	142
80+	I	1 634	740	894	762	329	433	872	411	461
Unknown - Inconnu	I	774	395	379	279	147	132	495	248	247
Egypt - Égypte										
1999										
Total	C	401 433	218 195	183 238	181 665	103 100	78 565	219 768	115 095	104 673
0 - 1	C	49 765	26 263	23 502	19 265	10 846	8 419	30 500	15 417	15 083
1 - 4	C	13 891	7 032	6 859	4 047	2 254	1 793	9 844	4 778	5 066
5 - 9	C	5 502	3 213	2 289	2 232	1 367	865	3 270	1 846	1 424
10 - 14	C	5 222	3 008	2 214	2 354	1 429	925	2 868	1 579	1 289
15 - 19	C	6 150	3 830	2 320	3 275	2 151	1 124	2 875	1 679	1 196
20 - 24	C	6 219	3 978	2 241	3 449	2 362	1 087	2 770	1 616	1 154
25 - 29	C	5 738	3 532	2 206	3 104	2 062	1 042	2 634	1 470	1 164
30 - 34	C	6 060	3 744	2 316	3 090	1 990	1 100	2 970	1 754	1 216
35 - 39	C	8 567	5 239	3 328	4 281	2 705	1 576	4 286	2 534	1 752
40 - 44	C	10 907	7 090	3 817	5 595	3 611	1 984	5 312	3 479	1 833
45 - 49	C	16 651	10 812	5 839	8 632	5 570	3 062	8 019	5 242	2 777
50 - 54	C	22 002	13 557	8 445	11 596	7 229	4 367	10 406	6 328	4 078
55 - 59	C	24 114	14 682	9 432	12 154	7 548	4 606	11 960	7 134	4 826
60 - 64	C	33 825	19 470	14 355	16 736	9 696	7 040	17 089	9 774	7 315
65 - 69	C	42 332	23 770	18 562	19 916	11 497	8 419	22 416	12 273	10 143
70 - 74	C	46 533	24 287	22 246	21 071	11 253	9 818	25 462	13 034	12 428

(See notes at end of table.— Voir notes à la fin du tableau.)

Continent, country or area, year and age (in years) / Continent, pays ou zone, année et âge (en années)	Code[1]	Total			Urban - Urbaine			Rural - Rurale		
		Both sexes - Les deux sexes	Male - Masculin	Female - Féminin	Both sexes - Les deux sexes	Male - Masculin	Female - Féminin	Both sexes - Les deux sexes	Male - Masculin	Female - Féminin
AFRICA — AFRIQUE										
Egypt - Égypte										
1999										
75+	C	97 955	44 688	53 267	40 868	19 530	21 338	57 087	25 158	31 920
Libyan Arab Jamahiriya - Jamahiriya arabe libyenne										
2002										
Total	U	19 362	11 278	8 084	...	...	...	...	...	...
0 - 1	U	2 194	1 190	1 004	...	...	...	...	...	...
1 - 4	U	891	546	345	...	...	...	...	...	...
5 - 9	U	267	142	125	...	...	...	...	...	...
10 - 19	U	670	432	238	...	...	...	...	...	...
20 - 29	U	1 100	824	276	...	...	...	...	...	...
30 - 39	U	1 287	820	467	...	...	...	...	...	...
40 - 49	U	1 118	621	497	...	...	...	...	...	...
50 - 59	U	1 492	860	632	...	...	...	...	...	...
60 - 69	U	2 936	1 754	1 182	...	...	...	...	...	...
70 - 79	U	3 812	2 254	1 558	...	...	...	...	...	...
80+	U	3 595	1 835	1 760	...	...	...	...	...	...
Madagascar[5]										
1993										
Total	I	92 151	48 531	43 620	17 421	9 526	7 895	74 730	39 005	35 725
0 - 1	I	14 019	7 565	6 454	2 388	1 332	1 056	11 631	6 233	5 398
1 - 4	I	21 817	11 524	10 293	3 518	1 895	1 623	18 299	9 629	8 670
5 - 9	I	5 795	3 115	2 680	840	459	381	4 955	2 656	2 299
10 - 14	I	3 761	2 002	1 759	574	303	271	3 187	1 699	1 488
15 - 19	I	3 921	1 816	2 105	640	310	330	3 281	1 506	1 775
20 - 24	I	4 112	1 901	2 211	793	381	412	3 319	1 520	1 799
25 - 29	I	3 233	1 494	1 739	685	359	326	2 548	1 135	1 413
30 - 34	I	3 601	1 610	1 991	710	363	347	2 891	1 247	1 644
35 - 39	I	2 904	1 415	1 489	687	365	322	2 217	1 050	1 167
40 - 44	I	3 253	1 664	1 589	709	397	312	2 544	1 267	1 277
45 - 49	I	2 126	1 169	957	517	293	224	1 609	876	733
50 - 54	I	3 133	1 733	1 400	704	428	276	2 429	1 305	1 124
55 - 59	I	2 046	1 225	821	536	336	200	1 510	889	621
60 - 64	I	3 918	2 162	1 756	847	515	332	3 071	1 647	1 424
65 - 69	I	2 496	1 400	1 096	602	342	260	1 894	1 058	836
70 - 74	I	3 996	2 326	1 670	880	518	362	3 116	1 808	1 308
75+	I	8 020	4 410	3 610	1 791	930	861	6 229	3 480	2 749
Malawi[6]										
1998										
Total	I	208 040	113 856	94 184	22 186	12 404	9 782	185 854	101 452	84 402
0 - 1	I	44 928	24 977	19 951	5 241	2 968	2 273	39 687	22 009	17 678
1 - 4	I	59 930	32 821	27 109	6 180	3 435	2 745	53 750	29 386	24 364
5 - 9	I	16 717	9 200	7 517	1 628	926	702	15 089	8 274	6 815
10 - 14	I	9 638	4 849	4 789	801	440	361	8 837	4 409	4 428
15 - 19	I	7 130	3 427	3 703	672	336	336	6 458	3 091	3 367
20 - 24	I	11 710	6 947	4 763	1 240	629	611	10 470	6 318	4 152
25 - 29	I	9 290	4 853	4 437	1 168	548	620	8 122	4 305	3 817
30 - 34	I	8 797	4 481	4 316	1 168	621	547	7 629	3 860	3 769
35 - 39	I	7 036	3 678	3 358	969	553	416	6 067	3 125	2 942
40 - 44	I	6 338	3 713	2 625	822	527	295	5 516	3 186	2 330
45 - 49	I	5 639	3 705	1 934	587	388	199	5 052	3 317	1 735
50 - 54	I	3 677	2 160	1 517	461	310	151	3 216	1 850	1 366
55 - 59	I	3 872	1 739	2 133	335	200	135	3 537	1 539	1 998
60 - 64	I	2 921	1 620	1 301	259	152	107	2 662	1 468	1 194
65 - 69	I	2 695	1 257	1 438	156	90	66	2 539	1 167	1 372
70 - 74	I	2 228	1 358	870	131	76	55	2 097	1 282	815
75 - 79	I	1 599	942	657	104	64	40	1 495	878	617
80 - 84	I	1 516	842	674	92	52	40	1 424	790	634
85+	I	2 379	1 287	1 092	172	89	83	2 207	1 198	1 009

Décès selon l'âge, le sexe et la résidence, urbaine/rurale: dernière année disponible, 1993 - 2002 (continued — suite)

(See notes at end of table.— Voir notes à la fin du tableau.)

Continent, country or area, year and age (in years) Continent, pays ou zone, année et âge (en années)	Code[1]	Total			Urban - Urbaine			Rural - Rurale		
		Both sexes - Les deux sexes	Male - Masculin	Female - Féminin	Both sexes - Les deux sexes	Male - Masculin	Female - Féminin	Both sexes - Les deux sexes	Male - Masculin	Female - Féminin
AFRICA — AFRIQUE										
Mauritius - Maurice										
2002										
Total	+C	8 310	4 671	3 639	...	...	...	...	...	...
0 - 1	+C	297	163	134	...	...	...	...	...	...
1 - 4	+C	49	22	27	...	...	...	...	...	...
5 - 9	+C	23	17	6	...	...	...	...	...	...
10 - 14	+C	32	18	14	...	...	...	...	...	...
15 - 19	+C	57	38	19	...	...	...	...	...	...
20 - 24	+C	101	68	33	...	...	...	...	...	...
25 - 29	+C	102	69	33	...	...	...	...	...	...
30 - 34	+C	118	71	47	...	...	...	...	...	...
35 - 39	+C	243	181	62	...	...	...	...	...	...
40 - 44	+C	339	238	101	...	...	...	...	...	...
45 - 49	+C	437	312	125	...	...	...	...	...	...
50 - 54	+C	592	415	177	...	...	...	...	...	...
55 - 59	+C	625	408	217	...	...	...	...	...	...
60 - 64	+C	722	408	314	...	...	...	...	...	...
65 - 69	+C	838	489	349	...	...	...	...	...	...
70 - 74	+C	903	507	396	...	...	...	...	...	...
75 - 79	+C	1 109	561	548	...	...	...	...	...	...
80 - 84	+C	819	372	447	...	...	...	...	...	...
85+	+C	898	310	588	...	...	...	...	...	...
Unknown - Inconnu	+C	6	4	2	...	...	...	...	...	...
Morocco - Maroc[7]										
1999										
Total	U	98 304	63 651	34 653	53 935	33 089	20 846	44 121	30 404	13 717
0 - 1	U	8 885	4 711	4 174	2 867	1 578	1 289	5 998	3 119	2 879
1 - 4	U	4 370	2 264	2 106	1 105	610	495	3 258	1 651	1 607
5 - 9	U	1 676	985	691	596	354	242	1 080	631	449
10 - 14	U	1 559	902	657	611	358	253	946	544	402
15 - 19	U	2 098	1 249	849	1 057	679	378	1 035	567	468
20 - 24	U	2 883	1 742	1 141	1 385	884	501	1 486	853	633
25 - 29	U	2 641	1 657	984	1 491	986	505	1 142	665	477
30 - 34	U	2 685	1 587	1 098	1 505	931	574	1 173	651	522
35 - 39	U	3 086	1 857	1 229	1 884	1 156	728	1 194	695	499
40 - 44	U	3 402	2 136	1 266	2 125	1 344	781	1 264	782	482
45 - 49	U	3 585	2 354	1 231	2 281	1 469	812	1 292	877	415
50 - 54	U	3 934	2 591	1 343	2 438	1 553	885	1 487	1 033	454
55 - 59	U	5 658	3 651	2 007	3 525	2 078	1 447	2 111	1 559	552
60 - 64	U	8 267	5 483	2 784	5 254	3 207	2 047	2 990	2 261	729
65 - 69	U	10 269	6 870	3 399	6 345	3 848	2 497	3 899	3 004	895
70 - 74	U	10 259	7 127	3 132	6 276	3 903	2 373	3 970	3 217	753
75 - 79	U	9 680	6 790	2 890	5 702	3 500	2 202	3 957	3 276	681
80+	U	13 205	9 627	3 578	7 381	4 613	2 768	5 798	4 996	802
Unknown - Inconnu	U	162	68	94	107	38	69	41	23	18
Mozambique[8]										
1997										
Total	I	385 754	206 737	179 017	70 750	39 060	31 690	315 004	167 677	147 327
0 - 1	I	99 947	54 065	45 882	16 506	9 132	7 374	83 441	44 933	38 508
1 - 4	I	123 644	66 656	56 988	16 230	8 766	7 464	107 414	57 890	49 524
5 - 9	I	31 778	17 034	14 744	4 267	2 367	1 900	27 511	14 667	12 844
10 - 14	I	14 914	8 144	6 770	2 407	1 337	1 070	12 507	6 807	5 700
15 - 19	I	12 169	5 896	6 273	2 624	1 379	1 245	9 545	4 517	5 028
20 - 24	I	10 633	4 883	5 750	2 691	1 328	1 363	7 942	3 555	4 387
25 - 29	I	9 556	4 643	4 913	2 606	1 378	1 228	6 950	3 265	3 685
30 - 34	I	8 691	4 610	4 081	2 490	1 454	1 036	6 201	3 156	3 045
35 - 39	I	8 180	4 411	3 769	2 340	1 350	990	5 840	3 061	2 779
40 - 44	I	7 276	4 092	3 184	2 158	1 289	869	5 118	2 803	2 315
45 - 49	I	7 208	4 194	3 014	2 130	1 307	823	5 078	2 887	2 191
50 - 54	I	7 386	4 227	3 159	2 191	1 299	892	5 195	2 928	2 267
55 - 59	I	5 300	3 090	2 210	1 484	890	594	3 816	2 200	1 616
60 - 64	I	7 853	4 380	3 473	2 309	1 293	1 016	5 544	3 087	2 457

(See notes at end of table.— Voir notes à la fin du tableau.)

Continent, country or area, year and age (in years) Continent, pays ou zone, année et âge (en années)	Code[1]	Total			Urban - Urbaine			Rural - Rurale		
		Both sexes - Les deux sexes	Male - Masculin	Female - Féminin	Both sexes - Les deux sexes	Male - Masculin	Female - Féminin	Both sexes - Les deux sexes	Male - Masculin	Female - Féminin
AFRICA — AFRIQUE										
Mozambique[8]										
1997										
65 - 69	I	5 348	2 962	2 386	1 608	911	697	3 740	2 051	1 689
70 - 74	I	5 008	2 897	2 111	1 536	855	681	3 472	2 042	1 430
75 - 79	I	3 440	1 918	1 522	1 054	589	465	2 386	1 329	1 057
80+	I	6 610	3 512	3 098	1 751	894	857	4 859	2 618	2 241
Unknown - Inconnu	I	10 813	5 123	5 690	2 368	1 242	1 126	8 445	3 881	4 564
Réunion[2]										
2001										
Total	C	3 829	2 196	1 633	...	...	...	...	...	...
0 - 1	C	103	59	44	...	...	...	...	...	...
1 - 4	C	21	14	7	...	...	...	...	...	...
5 - 9	C	14	9	5	...	...	...	...	...	...
10 - 14	C	14	8	6	...	...	...	...	...	...
15 - 19	C	37	25	12	...	...	...	...	...	...
20 - 24	C	41	32	9	...	...	...	...	...	...
25 - 29	C	59	47	12	...	...	...	...	...	...
30 - 34	C	75	55	20	...	...	...	...	...	...
35 - 39	C	127	92	35	...	...	...	...	...	...
40 - 44	C	142	97	45	...	...	...	...	...	...
45 - 49	C	211	150	61	...	...	...	...	...	...
50 - 54	C	218	161	57	...	...	...	...	...	...
55 - 59	C	252	177	75	...	...	...	...	...	...
60 - 64	C	310	212	98	...	...	...	...	...	...
65 - 69	C	326	205	121	...	...	...	...	...	...
70 - 74	C	386	217	169	...	...	...	...	...	...
75 - 79	C	470	265	205	...	...	...	...	...	...
80 - 84	C	411	184	227	...	...	...	...	...	...
85+	C	612	187	425	...	...	...	...	...	...
Saint Helena ex. dep. - Sainte-Hélène sans dép.										
1999										
Total	C	45	24	21	...	...	...	...	...	...
50 - 54	C	2	1	1	...	...	...	...	...	...
55 - 59	C	3	3	-	...	...	...	...	...	...
60 - 64	C	5	3	2	...	...	...	...	...	...
65 - 69	C	2	1	1	...	...	...	...	...	...
70 - 74	C	7	3	4	...	...	...	...	...	...
75 - 79	C	9	5	4	...	...	...	...	...	...
80 - 84	C	8	5	3	...	...	...	...	...	...
85 - 89	C	5	2	3	...	...	...	...	...	...
90 - 94	C	3	-	3	...	...	...	...	...	...
95+	C	1	1	-	...	...	...	...	...	...
Seychelles										
2001										
Total	+C	554	330	224	...	...	...	...	...	...
0 - 1	+C	19	8	11	...	...	...	...	...	...
1 - 4	+C	3	2	1	...	...	...	...	...	...
5 - 9	+C	1	-	1	...	...	...	...	...	...
10 - 14	+C	1	1	-	...	...	...	...	...	...
15 - 19	+C	2	1	1	...	...	...	...	...	...
20 - 24	+C	8	8	-	...	...	...	...	...	...
25 - 29	+C	10	10	-	...	...	...	...	...	...
30 - 34	+C	13	11	2	...	...	...	...	...	...
35 - 39	+C	17	11	6	...	...	...	...	...	...
40 - 44	+C	32	25	7	...	...	...	...	...	...
45 - 49	+C	27	21	6	...	...	...	...	...	...
50 - 54	+C	26	20	6	...	...	...	...	...	...
55 - 59	+C	28	22	6	...	...	...	...	...	...
60 - 64	+C	44	29	15	...	...	...	...	...	...
65 - 69	+C	59	33	26	...	...	...	...	...	...
70 - 74	+C	57	35	22	...	...	...	...	...	...

(See notes at end of table.— Voir notes à la fin du tableau.)

Continent, country or area, year and age (in years) / Continent, pays ou zone, année et âge (en années)	Code[1]	Total			Urban - Urbaine			Rural - Rurale		
		Both sexes - Les deux sexes	Male - Masculin	Female - Féminin	Both sexes - Les deux sexes	Male - Masculin	Female - Féminin	Both sexes - Les deux sexes	Male - Masculin	Female - Féminin
AFRICA — AFRIQUE										
Seychelles										
2001										
75 - 79	+C	61	35	26	...	...	...	...	...	...
80 - 84	+C	68	36	32	...	...	...	...	...	...
85+	+C	78	22	56	...	...	...	...	...	...
South Africa - Afrique du Sud										
1996										
Total	...	327 068	186 538	140 530	...	...	...	...	...	...
0 - 1	...	24 560	12 979	11 581	...	...	...	...	...	...
1 - 4	...	8 052	4 313	3 739	...	...	...	...	...	...
5 - 9	...	3 098	1 816	1 282	...	...	...	...	...	...
10 - 14	...	2 758	1 602	1 156	...	...	...	...	...	...
15 - 19	...	6 789	4 334	2 455	...	...	...	...	...	...
20 - 24	...	14 257	9 347	4 910	...	...	...	...	...	...
25 - 29	...	17 690	11 477	6 213	...	...	...	...	...	...
30 - 34	...	19 258	12 709	6 549	...	...	...	...	...	...
35 - 39	...	18 249	11 953	6 296	...	...	...	...	...	...
40 - 44	...	18 562	12 328	6 234	...	...	...	...	...	...
45 - 49	...	19 259	12 895	6 364	...	...	...	...	...	...
50 - 54	...	18 817	12 366	6 451	...	...	...	...	...	...
55 - 59	...	22 238	13 715	8 523	...	...	...	...	...	...
60 - 64	...	21 975	12 084	9 891	...	...	...	...	...	...
65 - 69	...	25 965	13 942	12 023	...	...	...	...	...	...
70 - 74	...	22 817	12 274	10 543	...	...	...	...	...	...
75 - 79	...	25 202	11 837	13 365	...	...	...	...	...	...
80 - 84	...	17 137	7 376	9 761	...	...	...	...	...	...
85+	...	19 193	6 443	12 750	...	...	...	...	...	...
Unknown - Inconnu	...	1 192	748	444	...	...	...	...	...	...
Sudan - Soudan[9,10]										
1993										
Total	I	321 692	178 232	143 008	97 928	55 191	42 589	223 764	123 041	100 419
0 - 1	I	60 018	34 270	25 640	16 252	9 136	7 097	43 766	25 134	18 543
1 - 4	I	75 955	40 561	35 388	18 659	9 935	8 718	57 296	30 626	26 670
5 - 9	I	21 952	12 148	9 803	4 355	2 443	1 911	17 597	9 705	7 892
10 - 14	I	8 959	5 347	3 612	2 197	1 187	1 009	6 762	4 160	2 603
15 - 19	I	9 321	5 143	4 177	2 863	1 723	1 139	6 458	3 420	3 038
20 - 24	I	9 023	4 740	4 280	3 214	1 956	1 255	5 809	2 784	3 025
25 - 29	I	8 659	4 304	4 352	3 143	1 829	1 311	5 516	2 475	3 041
30 - 34	I	7 733	3 883	3 850	2 553	1 462	1 091	5 180	2 421	2 759
35 - 39	I	7 747	4 062	3 682	3 069	1 784	1 281	4 678	2 278	2 401
40 - 44	I	7 820	4 597	3 223	3 138	1 864	1 274	4 682	2 733	1 949
45 - 49	I	8 269	5 085	3 183	3 308	1 993	1 314	4 961	3 092	1 869
50 - 54	I	10 811	6 339	4 437	4 369	2 513	1 856	6 442	3 826	2 581
55 - 59	I	5 952	3 498	2 453	2 561	1 543	1 018	3 391	1 955	1 435
60 - 64	I	14 151	8 041	6 106	5 332	3 155	2 173	8 819	4 886	3 933
65 - 69	I	9 508	5 609	3 899	3 679	2 157	1 522	5 829	3 452	2 377
70 - 74	I	15 918	9 200	6 716	5 755	3 262	2 491	10 163	5 938	4 225
75 - 79	I	8 179	4 778	3 391	3 106	1 744	1 362	5 073	3 034	2 029
80+	I	29 341	15 543	13 797	9 453	5 032	4 420	19 888	10 511	9 377
Unknown - Inconnu	I	2 376	1 084	1 019	922	473	347	1 454	611	672
Swaziland[8]										
1997										
Total	I	8 480	4 714	3 766	1 370	753	617	7 110	3 961	3 149
0 - 4	I	2 043	1 068	975	301	165	136	1 742	903	839
5 - 9	I	191	104	87	29	15	14	162	89	73
10 - 14	I	143	74	69	23	12	11	120	62	58
15 - 19	I	258	123	135	42	20	22	216	103	113
20 - 24	I	455	199	256	86	39	47	369	160	209
25 - 29	I	603	317	286	112	62	50	491	255	236
30 - 34	I	577	321	256	97	54	43	480	267	213
35 - 39	I	529	315	214	95	49	46	434	266	168
40 - 44	I	489	309	180	86	54	32	403	255	148

19. Deaths by age, sex and urban/rural residence: latest available year, 1993 - 2002
Décès selon l'âge, le sexe et la résidence, urbaine/rurale: dernière année disponible, 1993 - 2002 (continued — suite)

(See notes at end of table.— Voir notes à la fin du tableau.)

Continent, country or area, year and age (in years) Continent, pays ou zone, année et âge (en années)	Code[1]	Total			Urban - Urbaine			Rural - Rurale		
		Both sexes - Les deux sexes	Male - Masculin	Female - Féminin	Both sexes - Les deux sexes	Male - Masculin	Female - Féminin	Both sexes - Les deux sexes	Male - Masculin	Female - Féminin
AFRICA — AFRIQUE										
Swaziland[8]										
1997										
45 - 49	I	434	287	147	81	49	32	353	238	115
50 - 54	I	439	274	165	78	48	30	361	226	135
55 - 59	I	358	235	123	64	40	24	294	195	99
60 - 64	I	365	237	128	50	25	25	315	212	103
65 - 69	I	305	195	110	43	31	12	262	164	98
70 - 74	I	315	189	126	41	22	19	274	167	107
75+	I	745	341	404	97	41	56	648	300	348
Unknown - Inconnu	I	231	126	105	45	27	18	186	99	87
Tunisia - Tunisie										
1995										
Total	U	42 601	25 213	17 388	32 359	19 003	13 356	10 242	6 210	4 032
0 - 1	U	4 248	2 434	1 814	3 538	2 063	1 475	710	371	339
1 - 4	U	1 055	574	481	718	398	320	337	176	161
5 - 9	U	533	301	232	410	227	183	123	74	49
10 - 14	U	398	238	160	319	189	130	79	49	30
15 - 19	U	529	345	184	408	261	147	121	84	37
20 - 24	U	684	457	227	555	371	184	129	86	43
25 - 29	U	698	479	219	564	397	167	134	82	52
30 - 34	U	805	511	294	646	424	222	159	87	72
35 - 39	U	797	480	317	639	386	253	158	94	64
40 - 44	U	887	520	367	726	434	292	161	86	75
45 - 49	U	991	598	393	815	498	317	176	100	76
50 - 54	U	1 154	748	406	959	636	323	195	112	83
55 - 59	U	2 093	1 341	752	1 714	1 105	609	379	236	143
60 - 64	U	3 012	1 847	1 165	2 420	1 490	930	592	357	235
65 - 69	U	3 883	2 394	1 489	3 045	1 890	1 155	838	504	334
70 - 74	U	4 227	2 503	1 724	3 243	1 923	1 320	984	580	404
75 - 79	U	5 002	2 966	2 036	3 619	2 071	1 548	1 383	895	488
80 - 84	U	4 854	2 885	1 969	3 308	1 863	1 445	1 546	1 022	524
85+	U	4 815	2 501	2 314	3 303	1 585	1 718	1 512	916	596
Unknown - Inconnu	U	1 936	1 091	845	1 410	792	618	526	299	227
1998										
Total	U	42 571	25 319	17 252	...	...	...	...	...	...
0 - 1	U	3 098	1 775	1 323	...	...	...	...	...	...
1 - 4	U	2 096	1 196	900	...	...	...	...	...	...
5 - 9	U	412	252	160	...	...	...	...	...	...
10 - 14	U	382	236	146	...	...	...	...	...	...
15 - 19	U	578	408	170	...	...	...	...	...	...
20 - 24	U	653	459	194	...	...	...	...	...	...
25 - 29	U	612	425	187	...	...	...	...	...	...
30 - 34	U	801	528	273	...	...	...	...	...	...
35 - 39	U	812	519	293	...	...	...	...	...	...
40 - 44	U	998	631	367	...	...	...	...	...	...
45 - 49	U	1 161	737	424	...	...	...	...	...	...
50 - 54	U	1 267	805	462	...	...	...	...	...	...
55 - 59	U	1 833	1 152	681	...	...	...	...	...	...
60 - 64	U	2 920	1 843	1 077	...	...	...	...	...	...
65 - 69	U	4 337	2 673	1 664	...	...	...	...	...	...
70 - 74	U	4 918	2 943	1 975	...	...	...	...	...	...
75 - 79	U	5 201	2 930	2 271	...	...	...	...	...	...
80+	U	10 199	5 681	4 518	...	...	...	...	...	...
Unknown - Inconnu	U	293	126	167	...	...	...	...	...	...
AMERICA, NORTH — **AMERIQUE DU NORD**										
Anguilla										
1999										
Total	+C	58	22	36	...	...	...	...	...	...
1 - 9	+C	1	...	...	...	...	...	...	...	...

(See notes at end of table.— Voir notes à la fin du tableau.)

Continent, country or area, year and age (in years) / Continent, pays ou zone, année et âge (en années)	Code[1]	Total			Urban - Urbaine			Rural - Rurale		
		Both sexes - Les deux sexes	Male - Masculin	Female - Féminin	Both sexes - Les deux sexes	Male - Masculin	Female - Féminin	Both sexes - Les deux sexes	Male - Masculin	Female - Féminin
AMERICA, NORTH — AMERIQUE DU NORD										
Anguilla										
1999										
10 - 19	+C	3	...	...	...	...	...	...	...	...
30 - 39	+C	1	...	...	...	...	...	...	...	...
40 - 49	+C	3	...	...	...	...	...	...	...	...
50 - 59	+C	5	...	...	...	...	...	...	...	...
60 - 69	+C	7	...	...	...	...	...	...	...	...
70+	+C	38	...	...	...	...	...	...	...	...
Antigua and Barbuda - Antigua-et-Barbuda										
1995										
Total	+C	454	233	221	...	...	...	...	...	...
0 - 1	+C	23	11	12	...	...	...	...	...	...
1 - 4	+C	4	3	1	...	...	...	...	...	...
10 - 14	+C	1	1	-	...	...	...	...	...	...
15 - 19	+C	2	1	1	...	...	...	...	...	...
20 - 24	+C	5	2	3	...	...	...	...	...	...
25 - 29	+C	3	2	1	...	...	...	...	...	...
30 - 34	+C	8	6	2	...	...	...	...	...	...
35 - 39	+C	10	5	5	...	...	...	...	...	...
40 - 44	+C	12	5	7	...	...	...	...	...	...
45 - 49	+C	7	5	2	...	...	...	...	...	...
50 - 54	+C	22	14	8	...	...	...	...	...	...
55 - 59	+C	27	22	5	...	...	...	...	...	...
60 - 64	+C	31	21	10	...	...	...	...	...	...
65 - 69	+C	46	25	21	...	...	...	...	...	...
70 - 74	+C	47	25	22	...	...	...	...	...	...
75 - 79	+C	62	24	38	...	...	...	...	...	...
80 - 84	+C	62	28	34	...	...	...	...	...	...
85+	+C	79	31	48	...	...	...	...	...	...
Unknown - Inconnu	+C	3	2	1	...	...	...	...	...	...
Bahamas										
2001										
Total	C	1 609	879	730	...	...	...	...	...	...
0 - 1	C	37	23	14	...	...	...	...	...	...
1 - 4	C	14	6	8	...	...	...	...	...	...
5 - 9	C	7	5	2	...	...	...	...	...	...
10 - 14	C	7	3	4	...	...	...	...	...	...
15 - 19	C	22	17	5	...	...	...	...	...	...
20 - 24	C	25	17	8	...	...	...	...	...	...
25 - 29	C	62	40	22	...	...	...	...	...	...
30 - 34	C	86	55	31	...	...	...	...	...	...
35 - 39	C	97	58	39	...	...	...	...	...	...
40 - 44	C	118	78	40	...	...	...	...	...	...
45 - 49	C	106	64	42	...	...	...	...	...	...
50 - 54	C	91	53	38	...	...	...	...	...	...
55 - 59	C	108	63	45	...	...	...	...	...	...
60 - 64	C	111	71	40	...	...	...	...	...	...
65 - 69	C	145	80	65	...	...	...	...	...	...
70 - 74	C	126	64	62	...	...	...	...	...	...
75 - 79	C	120	60	60	...	...	...	...	...	...
80 - 84	C	141	72	69	...	...	...	...	...	...
85 - 89	C	108	37	71	...	...	...	...	...	...
90 - 94	C	52	7	45	...	...	...	...	...	...
95 - 99	C	19	6	13	...	...	...	...	...	...
100+	C	7	-	7	...	...	...	...	...	...
Belize										
2001										
Total	U	1 261	762	499	...	...	...	...	...	...
0 - 1	U	120	...	...	...	...	...	...	...	...

19. Deaths by age, sex and urban/rural residence: latest available year, 1993 - 2002
Décès selon l'âge, le sexe et la résidence, urbaine/rurale: dernière année disponible, 1993 - 2002 (continued — suite)

(See notes at end of table.— Voir notes à la fin du tableau.)

Continent, country or area, year and age (in years) / Continent, pays ou zone, année et âge (en années)	Code[1]	Total			Urban - Urbaine			Rural - Rurale		
		Both sexes - Les deux sexes	Male - Masculin	Female - Féminin	Both sexes - Les deux sexes	Male - Masculin	Female - Féminin	Both sexes - Les deux sexes	Male - Masculin	Female - Féminin
AMERICA, NORTH — AMERIQUE DU NORD										
Belize										
2001										
1 - 4	U	32	...	...	...	...	...	...	...	...
5 - 9	U	15	...	...	...	...	...	...	...	...
10 - 14	U	12	...	...	...	...	...	...	...	...
15 - 19	U	35	...	...	...	...	...	...	...	...
20 - 24	U	41	...	...	...	...	...	...	...	...
25 - 29	U	54	...	...	...	...	...	...	...	...
30 - 34	U	51	...	...	...	...	...	...	...	...
35 - 39	U	56	...	...	...	...	...	...	...	...
40 - 44	U	53	...	...	...	...	...	...	...	...
45 - 49	U	62	...	...	...	...	...	...	...	...
50 - 54	U	53	...	...	...	...	...	...	...	...
55 - 59	U	57	...	...	...	...	...	...	...	...
60 - 64	U	68	...	...	...	...	...	...	...	...
65 - 69	U	98	...	...	...	...	...	...	...	...
70 - 74	U	122	...	...	...	...	...	...	...	...
75 - 79	U	87	...	...	...	...	...	...	...	...
80+	U	239	...	...	...	...	...	...	...	...
Unknown - Inconnu	U	6	...	...	...	...	...	...	...	...
Bermuda - Bermudes										
2002										
Total	C	404	196	208	...	...	...	...	...	...
1 - 4	C	1	...	...	...	...	...	...	...	...
15 - 24	C	1	...	...	...	...	...	...	...	...
25 - 44	C	25	...	...	...	...	...	...	...	...
45 - 64	C	73	...	...	...	...	...	...	...	...
65 - 84	C	200	...	...	...	...	...	...	...	...
85+	C	104	...	...	...	...	...	...	...	...
Canada[11]										
2001										
Total	C	219 538	112 001	107 537	...	...	...	...	...	...
0 - 1	C	1 739	997	742	...	...	...	...	...	...
1 - 4	C	340	191	149	...	...	...	...	...	...
5 - 9	C	245	132	113	...	...	...	...	...	...
10 - 14	C	286	163	123	...	...	...	...	...	...
15 - 19	C	1 033	728	305	...	...	...	...	...	...
20 - 24	C	1 267	943	324	...	...	...	...	...	...
25 - 29	C	1 238	886	352	...	...	...	...	...	...
30 - 34	C	1 616	1 101	515	...	...	...	...	...	...
35 - 39	C	2 649	1 667	982	...	...	...	...	...	...
40 - 44	C	3 829	2 356	1 473	...	...	...	...	...	...
45 - 49	C	5 488	3 358	2 130	...	...	...	...	...	...
50 - 54	C	7 620	4 690	2 930	...	...	...	...	...	...
55 - 59	C	9 396	5 806	3 590	...	...	...	...	...	...
60 - 64	C	12 100	7 570	4 530	...	...	...	...	...	...
65 - 69	C	17 452	10 613	6 839	...	...	...	...	...	...
70 - 74	C	24 938	14 748	10 190	...	...	...	...	...	...
75 - 79	C	32 381	17 718	14 663	...	...	...	...	...	...
80 - 84	C	34 630	16 828	17 802	...	...	...	...	...	...
85 - 89	C	32 192	13 024	19 168	...	...	...	...	...	...
90+	C	29 096	8 481	20 615	...	...	...	...	...	...
Unknown - Inconnu	C	3	1	2	...	...	...	...	...	...
Cayman Islands - Îles Caïmanes										
1994										
Total	C	149	81	68	...	...	...	...	...	...
0 - 1	C	7	1	6	...	...	...	...	...	...
15 - 24	C	5	5	-	...	...	...	...	...	...
25 - 44	C	11	7	4	...	...	...	...	...	...

19. Deaths by age, sex and urban/rural residence: latest available year, 1993 - 2002
Décès selon l'âge, le sexe et la résidence, urbaine/rurale: dernière année disponible, 1993 - 2002 (continued — suite)

(See notes at end of table.— Voir notes à la fin du tableau.)

Continent, country or area, year and age (in years) / Continent, pays ou zone, année et âge (en années)	Code[1]	Total			Urban - Urbaine			Rural - Rurale		
		Both sexes - Les deux sexes	Male - Masculin	Female - Féminin	Both sexes - Les deux sexes	Male - Masculin	Female - Féminin	Both sexes - Les deux sexes	Male - Masculin	Female - Féminin
AMERICA, NORTH — AMERIQUE DU NORD										
Cayman Islands - Îles Caïmanes										
1994										
45 - 64	C	30	24	6	...	...	...	...	...	...
65+	C	96	44	52	...	...	...	...	...	...
Costa Rica										
2002										
Total	C	15 004	8 647	6 357	...	...	...	...	...	...
0 - 1	C	793	447	346	...	...	...	...	...	...
1 - 4	C	151	88	63	...	...	...	...	...	...
5 - 14	C	206	122	84	...	...	...	...	...	...
15 - 24	C	544	388	156	...	...	...	...	...	...
25 - 44	C	1 526	1 055	471	...	...	...	...	...	...
45 - 64	C	3 000	1 847	1 153	...	...	...	...	...	...
65+	C	8 708	4 635	4 073	...	...	...	...	...	...
Unknown - Inconnu	C	76	65	11	...	...	...	...	...	...
Cuba[7]										
1999										
Total	C	79 499	43 804	35 695	64 362	34 700	29 662	15 072	9 056	6 016
0 - 1	C	977	561	416	747	431	316	230	130	100
1 - 4	C	292	165	127	217	119	98	75	46	29
5 - 9	C	225	129	96	160	89	71	65	40	25
10 - 14	C	300	184	116	215	130	85	85	54	31
15 - 19	C	446	262	184	329	185	144	115	76	39
20 - 24	C	660	467	193	496	353	143	164	114	50
25 - 29	C	1 182	795	387	875	580	295	306	214	92
30 - 34	C	1 429	957	472	1 101	733	368	327	223	104
35 - 39	C	1 654	1 078	576	1 283	840	443	369	237	132
40 - 44	C	1 772	1 087	685	1 398	861	537	373	225	148
45 - 49	C	2 573	1 549	1 024	2 109	1 271	838	460	274	186
50 - 54	C	3 426	2 004	1 422	2 824	1 652	1 172	596	347	249
55 - 59	C	4 402	2 649	1 753	3 619	2 202	1 417	781	445	336
60 - 64	C	5 402	3 100	2 302	4 453	2 551	1 902	946	547	399
65 - 69	C	7 018	3 981	3 037	5 768	3 245	2 523	1 244	731	513
70 - 74	C	8 850	4 945	3 905	7 232	3 976	3 256	1 612	964	648
75 - 79	C	10 369	5 732	4 637	8 501	4 567	3 934	1 863	1 163	700
80 - 84	C	10 933	5 736	5 197	8 933	4 532	4 401	1 986	1 195	791
85+	C	17 579	8 415	9 164	14 096	6 379	7 717	3 473	2 029	1 444
Unknown - Inconnu	C	10	8	2	6	4	2	2	2	-
2001										
Total	C	79 395	43 048	36 347	...	...	...	...	...	...
0 - 4	C	1 109	619	490	...	...	...	...	...	...
5 - 9	C	191	125	66	...	...	...	...	...	...
10 - 14	C	234	143	91	...	...	...	...	...	...
15 - 19	C	440	297	143	...	...	...	...	...	...
20 - 24	C	556	384	172	...	...	...	...	...	...
25 - 29	C	930	634	296	...	...	...	...	...	...
30 - 34	C	1 198	771	427	...	...	...	...	...	...
35 - 39	C	1 616	1 013	603	...	...	...	...	...	...
40 - 44	C	1 642	962	680	...	...	...	...	...	...
45 - 49	C	2 477	1 486	991	...	...	...	...	...	...
50 - 54	C	3 444	2 011	1 433	...	...	...	...	...	...
55 - 59	C	4 539	2 669	1 870	...	...	...	...	...	...
60 - 64	C	5 742	3 320	2 422	...	...	...	...	...	...
65 - 69	C	7 028	3 938	3 090	...	...	...	...	...	...
70+	C	48 235	24 663	23 572	...	...	...	...	...	...
Unknown - Inconnu	C	14	13	1	...	...	...	...	...	...

(See notes at end of table.— Voir notes à la fin du tableau.)

Continent, country or area, year and age (in years) / Continent, pays ou zone, année et âge (en années)	Code[1]	Total			Urban - Urbaine			Rural - Rurale		
		Both sexes - Les deux sexes	Male - Masculin	Female - Féminin	Both sexes - Les deux sexes	Male - Masculin	Female - Féminin	Both sexes - Les deux sexes	Male - Masculin	Female - Féminin
AMERICA, NORTH — AMERIQUE DU NORD										
Dominican Republic - République dominicaine										
1999										
Total	+U	26 956	15 624	11 332	...	...	...	...	...	...
0 - 1	+U	2 250	1 218	1 032	...	...	...	...	...	...
1 - 4	+U	477	273	204	...	...	...	...	...	...
5 - 9	+U	276	143	133	...	...	...	...	...	...
10 - 14	+U	259	138	121	...	...	...	...	...	...
15 - 19	+U	495	330	165	...	...	...	...	...	...
20 - 24	+U	823	570	253	...	...	...	...	...	...
25 - 29	+U	945	600	345	...	...	...	...	...	...
30 - 34	+U	981	651	330	...	...	...	...	...	...
35 - 39	+U	955	619	336	...	...	...	...	...	...
40 - 44	+U	954	615	339	...	...	...	...	...	...
45 - 49	+U	994	600	394	...	...	...	...	...	...
50 - 54	+U	1 175	719	456	...	...	...	...	...	...
55 - 59	+U	1 246	765	481	...	...	...	...	...	...
60 - 64	+U	1 644	985	659	...	...	...	...	...	...
65 - 69	+U	2 065	1 192	873	...	...	...	...	...	...
70 - 74	+U	2 090	1 233	857	...	...	...	...	...	...
75 - 79	+U	2 050	1 185	865	...	...	...	...	...	...
80 - 84	+U	1 726	956	770	...	...	...	...	...	...
85+	+U	2 944	1 440	1 504	...	...	...	...	...	...
Unknown - Inconnu	+U	2 607	1 392	1 215	...	...	...	...	...	...
El Salvador										
2002										
Total	C	27 458	15 948	11 510	19 595	11 287	8 308	7 863	4 661	3 202
0 - 1	C	1 284	729	555	821	464	357	463	265	198
1 - 4	C	531	292	239	289	161	128	242	131	111
5 - 9	C	237	136	101	156	88	68	81	48	33
10 - 14	C	279	151	128	181	96	85	98	55	43
15 - 19	C	678	489	189	477	359	118	201	130	71
20 - 24	C	1 150	929	221	858	699	159	292	230	62
25 - 29	C	1 098	863	235	828	654	174	270	209	61
30 - 34	C	1 045	799	246	761	590	171	284	209	75
35 - 39	C	1 098	798	300	811	594	217	287	204	83
40 - 44	C	1 093	764	329	785	555	230	308	209	99
45 - 49	C	1 165	766	399	822	542	280	343	224	119
50 - 54	C	1 240	762	478	881	529	352	359	233	126
55 - 59	C	1 453	859	594	1 033	614	419	420	245	175
60 - 64	C	1 697	952	745	1 212	663	549	485	289	196
65 - 69	C	1 974	1 067	907	1 419	738	681	555	329	226
70 - 74	C	2 330	1 220	1 110	1 652	865	787	678	355	323
75 - 79	C	2 397	1 237	1 160	1 737	888	849	660	349	311
80 - 84	C	2 573	1 287	1 286	1 829	892	937	744	395	349
85+	C	3 989	1 744	2 245	2 939	1 225	1 714	1 050	519	531
Unknown - Inconnu	C	147	104	43	104	71	33	43	33	10
Greenland - Groenland										
1999										
Total	C	482	281	201	372	220	152	110	61	49
0 - 1	C	16	11	5	16	11	5	-	-	-
1 - 4	C	5	2	3	2	-	2	3	2	1
5 - 9	C	2	1	1	1	1	-	1	-	1
10 - 14	C	3	3	-	2	2	-	1	1	1
15 - 19	C	14	10	4	10	7	3	4	3	1
20 - 24	C	13	12	1	8	7	1	5	5	-
25 - 29	C	17	10	7	10	4	6	7	6	1
30 - 34	C	15	12	3	12	9	3	3	3	-
35 - 39	C	21	15	6	17	11	6	4	4	-
40 - 44	C	26	18	8	22	15	7	4	3	1

(See notes at end of table.— Voir notes à la fin du tableau.)

Continent, country or area, year and age (in years) / Continent, pays ou zone, année et âge (en années)	Code[1]	Total			Urban - Urbaine			Rural - Rurale		
		Both sexes - Les deux sexes	Male - Masculin	Female - Féminin	Both sexes - Les deux sexes	Male - Masculin	Female - Féminin	Both sexes - Les deux sexes	Male - Masculin	Female - Féminin
AMERICA, NORTH — AMERIQUE DU NORD										
Greenland - Groenland										
1999										
45 - 49	C	23	10	13	18	8	10	5	2	3
50 - 54	C	30	18	12	22	17	5	8	1	7
55 - 59	C	42	32	10	35	28	7	7	4	3
60 - 64	C	54	33	21	43	29	14	11	4	7
65 - 69	C	57	32	25	38	24	14	19	8	11
70 - 74	C	64	33	31	52	25	27	12	8	4
75 - 79	C	36	16	20	27	12	15	9	4	5
80 - 84	C	33	10	23	29	9	20	4	1	3
85+	C	11	3	8	8	1	7	3	2	1
Grenada - Grenade										
2000										
Total	+C	716	365	351	...	...	...	...	...	...
0 - 1	+C	27	10	17	...	...	...	...	...	...
1 - 4	+C	1	1	-	...	...	...	...	...	...
5 - 9	+C	1	1	-	...	...	...	...	...	...
10 - 14	+C	4	4	-	...	...	...	...	...	...
15 - 19	+C	8	2	6	...	...	...	...	...	...
20 - 24	+C	11	9	2	...	...	...	...	...	...
25 - 29	+C	17	13	4	...	...	...	...	...	...
30 - 34	+C	21	11	10	...	...	...	...	...	...
35 - 39	+C	17	7	10	...	...	...	...	...	...
40 - 44	+C	14	9	5	...	...	...	...	...	...
45 - 49	+C	21	13	8	...	...	...	...	...	...
50 - 54	+C	27	15	12	...	...	...	...	...	...
55 - 59	+C	24	17	7	...	...	...	...	...	...
60 - 64	+C	50	30	20	...	...	...	...	...	...
65 - 69	+C	61	35	26	...	...	...	...	...	...
70 - 74	+C	81	52	29	...	...	...	...	...	...
75 - 79	+C	96	50	46	...	...	...	...	...	...
80 - 84	+C	69	27	42	...	...	...	...	...	...
85 - 89	+C	84	34	50	...	...	...	...	...	...
90 - 94	+C	52	16	36	...	...	...	...	...	...
95 - 99	+C	24	8	16	...	...	...	...	...	...
100+	+C	6	1	5	...	...	...	...	...	...
Guadeloupe										
2000										
Total	C	2 698	1 444	1 254	...	...	...	...	...	...
0 - 1	C	57	32	25	...	...	...	...	...	...
1 - 4	C	12	9	3	...	...	...	...	...	...
5 - 9	C	9	4	5	...	...	...	...	...	...
10 - 14	C	7	6	1	...	...	...	...	...	...
15 - 19	C	11	9	2	...	...	...	...	...	...
20 - 24	C	40	30	10	...	...	...	...	...	...
25 - 29	C	49	33	16	...	...	...	...	...	...
30 - 34	C	42	32	10	...	...	...	...	...	...
35 - 39	C	64	47	17	...	...	...	...	...	...
40 - 44	C	84	50	34	...	...	...	...	...	...
45 - 49	C	98	73	25	...	...	...	...	...	...
50 - 54	C	116	89	27	...	...	...	...	...	...
55 - 59	C	101	68	33	...	...	...	...	...	...
60 - 64	C	140	96	44	...	...	...	...	...	...
65 - 69	C	211	124	87	...	...	...	...	...	...
70 - 74	C	266	149	117	...	...	...	...	...	...
75 - 79	C	346	187	159	...	...	...	...	...	...
80 - 84	C	355	166	189	...	...	...	...	...	...
85 - 89	C	348	151	197	...	...	...	...	...	...
90 - 94	C	225	59	166	...	...	...	...	...	...
95 - 99	C	89	24	65	...	...	...	...	...	...

19. Deaths by age, sex and urban/rural residence: latest available year, 1993 - 2002
Décès selon l'âge, le sexe et la résidence, urbaine/rurale: dernière année disponible, 1993 - 2002 (continued — suite)

(See notes at end of table.— Voir notes à la fin du tableau.)

Continent, country or area, year and age (in years) / Continent, pays ou zone, année et âge (en années)	Code[1]	Total			Urban - Urbaine			Rural - Rurale		
		Both sexes - Les deux sexes	Male - Masculin	Female - Féminin	Both sexes - Les deux sexes	Male - Masculin	Female - Féminin	Both sexes - Les deux sexes	Male - Masculin	Female - Féminin
AMERICA, NORTH — AMERIQUE DU NORD										
Guadeloupe										
2000										
100+	C	28	6	22	...	...	...	...	...	...
Guatemala										
1999										
Total	C	64 563	37 062	27 501	...	...	...	...	...	...
0 - 1	C	13 161	7 349	5 812	...	...	...	...	...	...
1 - 4	C	5 113	2 670	2 443	...	...	...	...	...	...
5 - 9	C	1 179	611	568	...	...	...	...	...	...
10 - 14	C	935	564	371	...	...	...	...	...	...
15 - 19	C	1 712	1 091	621	...	...	...	...	...	...
20 - 24	C	2 229	1 544	685	...	...	...	...	...	...
25 - 29	C	2 190	1 563	627	...	...	...	...	...	...
30 - 34	C	2 272	1 565	707	...	...	...	...	...	...
35 - 39	C	2 372	1 631	741	...	...	...	...	...	...
40 - 44	C	2 344	1 514	830	...	...	...	...	...	...
45 - 49	C	2 503	1 609	894	...	...	...	...	...	...
50 - 54	C	2 521	1 545	976	...	...	...	...	...	...
55 - 59	C	2 508	1 421	1 087	...	...	...	...	...	...
60 - 64	C	2 978	1 702	1 276	...	...	...	...	...	...
65 - 69	C	3 793	2 062	1 731	...	...	...	...	...	...
70 - 74	C	4 140	2 231	1 909	...	...	...	...	...	...
75 - 79	C	4 260	2 276	1 984	...	...	...	...	...	...
80 - 84	C	3 590	1 887	1 703	...	...	...	...	...	...
85 - 89	C	2 784	1 320	1 464	...	...	...	...	...	...
90 - 94	C	1 219	537	682	...	...	...	...	...	...
95+	C	541	213	328	...	...	...	...	...	...
Unknown - Inconnu	C	219	157	62	...	...	...	...	...	...
Martinique[2]										
2000										
Total	C	2 692	1 451	1 241	...	...	...	...	...	...
0 - 1	C	40	23	17	...	...	...	...	...	...
1 - 4	C	4	3	1	...	...	...	...	...	...
5 - 9	C	1	1	-	...	...	...	...	...	...
10 - 14	C	1	1	-	...	...	...	...	...	...
15 - 19	C	14	11	3	...	...	...	...	...	...
20 - 24	C	18	15	3	...	...	...	...	...	...
25 - 29	C	33	24	9	...	...	...	...	...	...
30 - 34	C	44	30	14	...	...	...	...	...	...
35 - 39	C	39	24	15	...	...	...	...	...	...
40 - 44	C	63	47	16	...	...	...	...	...	...
45 - 49	C	78	51	27	...	...	...	...	...	...
50 - 54	C	97	59	38	...	...	...	...	...	...
55 - 59	C	105	71	34	...	...	...	...	...	...
60 - 64	C	159	99	60	...	...	...	...	...	...
65 - 69	C	193	121	72	...	...	...	...	...	...
70 - 74	C	293	172	121	...	...	...	...	...	...
75 - 79	C	382	226	156	...	...	...	...	...	...
80 - 84	C	370	187	183	...	...	...	...	...	...
85 - 89	C	373	171	202	...	...	...	...	...	...
90 - 94	C	240	85	155	...	...	...	...	...	...
95 - 99	C	115	25	90	...	...	...	...	...	...
100+	C	30	5	25	...	...	...	...	...	...
Mexico - Mexique[7,9]										
2001										
Total	C	443 127	245 998	196 789	336 551	183 445	152 901	100 670	58 024	42 558
0 - 1	C	35 911	20 302	15 487	27 056	15 342	11 624	8 503	4 758	3 718
1 - 4	C	6 620	3 613	2 996	4 377	2 372	1 997	2 206	1 220	983
5 - 9	C	3 369	1 975	1 391	2 325	1 372	950	1 014	583	431
10 - 14	C	3 768	2 295	1 470	2 562	1 538	1 023	1 163	730	431

19. Deaths by age, sex and urban/rural residence: latest available year, 1993 - 2002
Décès selon l'âge, le sexe et la résidence, urbaine/rurale: dernière année disponible, 1993 - 2002 (continued — suite)

(See notes at end of table.— Voir notes à la fin du tableau.)

Continent, country or area, year and age (in years) Continent, pays ou zone, année et âge (en années)	Code[1]	Total			Urban - Urbaine			Rural - Rurale		
		Both sexes - Les deux sexes	Male - Masculin	Female - Féminin	Both sexes - Les deux sexes	Male - Masculin	Female - Féminin	Both sexes - Les deux sexes	Male - Masculin	Female - Féminin
AMERICA, NORTH — AMERIQUE DU NORD										
Mexico - Mexique[7,9]										
2001										
15 - 19	C	7 469	5 118	2 350	5 336	3 667	1 668	1 996	1 350	646
20 - 24	C	9 738	7 165	2 566	7 260	5 357	1 899	2 233	1 608	622
25 - 29	C	11 060	8 149	2 902	8 183	6 071	2 109	2 479	1 749	725
30 - 34	C	11 910	8 615	3 293	8 824	6 389	2 433	2 665	1 870	795
35 - 39	C	13 624	9 447	4 166	10 077	6 937	3 134	3 061	2 090	967
40 - 44	C	15 726	10 349	5 373	11 950	7 778	4 171	3 377	2 249	1 126
45 - 49	C	18 335	11 658	6 668	14 011	8 755	5 249	3 949	2 583	1 366
50 - 54	C	22 004	13 315	8 683	17 021	10 191	6 825	4 596	2 819	1 777
55 - 59	C	25 873	14 885	10 977	20 114	11 439	8 668	5 446	3 200	2 242
60 - 64	C	31 479	17 342	14 125	24 545	13 305	11 233	6 556	3 760	2 791
65 - 69	C	36 421	19 810	16 584	28 400	15 188	13 191	7 729	4 407	3 316
70 - 74	C	40 686	21 550	19 125	31 625	16 407	15 213	8 787	4 963	3 818
75 - 79	C	42 262	22 058	20 187	32 826	16 744	16 071	9 214	5 166	4 043
80 - 84	C	37 597	18 377	19 212	28 838	13 627	15 206	8 607	4 662	3 942
85+	C	67 102	28 504	38 574	50 264	20 384	29 867	16 639	8 018	8 611
Unknown - Inconnu	C	2 173	1 471	660	957	582	370	450	239	208
Nicaragua										
2002										
Total	+U	15 061	8 551	6 510	9 801	5 392	4 409	5 260	3 159	2 101
0 - 1	+U	2 217	1 309	908	1 168	692	476	1 049	617	432
1 - 4	+U	445	235	210	170	91	79	275	144	131
5 - 9	+U	183	97	86	74	42	32	109	55	54
10 - 14	+U	199	117	82	108	61	47	91	56	35
15 - 19	+U	411	251	160	228	147	81	183	104	79
20 - 24	+U	526	389	137	325	246	79	201	143	58
25 - 29	+U	469	344	125	259	195	64	210	149	61
30 - 34	+U	420	282	138	257	182	75	163	100	63
35 - 39	+U	531	325	206	333	214	119	198	111	87
40 - 44	+U	583	374	209	404	255	149	179	119	60
45 - 49	+U	652	404	248	457	268	189	195	136	59
50 - 54	+U	684	411	273	471	285	186	213	126	87
55 - 59	+U	724	424	300	485	276	209	239	148	91
60 - 64	+U	830	442	388	582	297	285	248	145	103
65 - 69	+U	1 037	597	440	758	418	340	279	179	100
70 - 74	+U	1 104	606	498	787	426	361	317	180	137
75 - 79	+U	1 123	605	518	808	413	395	315	192	123
80 - 84	+U	1 142	589	553	810	379	431	332	210	122
85 - 89	+U	871	389	482	637	261	376	234	128	106
90 - 94	+U	519	230	289	391	157	234	128	73	55
95+	+U	391	131	260	289	87	202	102	44	58
Panama										
1999										
Total	U	11 938	6 978	4 960	7 108	4 042	3 066	4 830	2 936	1 894
0 - 1	U	1 005	571	434	490	284	206	515	287	228
1 - 4	U	302	157	145	81	42	39	221	115	106
5 - 9	U	122	76	46	49	25	24	73	51	22
10 - 14	U	95	58	37	30	17	13	65	41	24
15 - 19	U	222	154	68	117	84	33	105	70	35
20 - 24	U	302	224	78	159	119	40	143	105	38
25 - 29	U	332	246	86	190	139	51	142	107	35
30 - 34	U	369	261	108	225	163	62	144	98	46
35 - 39	U	329	222	107	197	128	69	132	94	38
40 - 44	U	396	260	136	239	158	81	157	102	55
45 - 49	U	411	272	139	265	178	87	146	94	52
50 - 54	U	496	329	167	301	210	91	195	119	76
55 - 59	U	514	322	192	319	198	121	195	124	71
60 - 64	U	663	405	258	413	251	162	250	154	96
65 - 69	U	817	489	328	468	268	200	349	221	128

19. Deaths by age, sex and urban/rural residence: latest available year, 1993 - 2002
Décès selon l'âge, le sexe et la résidence, urbaine/rurale: dernière année disponible, 1993 - 2002 (continued — suite)

(See notes at end of table.— Voir notes à la fin du tableau.)

Continent, country or area, year and age (in years) / Continent, pays ou zone, année et âge (en années)	Code[1]	Total			Urban - Urbaine			Rural - Rurale		
		Both sexes - Les deux sexes	Male - Masculin	Female - Féminin	Both sexes - Les deux sexes	Male - Masculin	Female - Féminin	Both sexes - Les deux sexes	Male - Masculin	Female - Féminin
AMERICA, NORTH — AMERIQUE DU NORD										
Panama										
1999										
70 - 74	U	1 012	594	418	620	360	260	392	234	158
75 - 79	U	1 255	693	562	796	415	381	459	278	181
80 - 84	U	1 324	704	620	860	449	411	464	255	209
85 - 89	U	1 066	548	518	690	328	362	376	220	156
90 - 94	U	553	241	312	376	142	234	177	99	78
95 - 99	U	210	75	135	141	45	96	69	30	39
100+	U	49	24	25	38	17	21	11	7	4
Unknown - Inconnu	U	94	53	41	44	22	22	50	31	19
Puerto Rico - Porto Rico[7]										
2002										
Total	C	28 098	15 845	12 253	15 026	8 200	6 826	13 009	7 591	5 418
0 - 1	C	515	292	223	297	166	131	217	125	92
1 - 4	C	61	37	24	36	23	13	25	14	11
5 - 9	C	30	15	15	12	5	7	18	10	8
10 - 14	C	53	33	20	29	16	13	24	17	7
15 - 19	C	211	171	40	117	91	26	94	80	14
20 - 24	C	455	395	60	259	225	34	195	169	26
25 - 29	C	438	357	81	260	217	43	178	140	38
30 - 34	C	447	345	102	265	204	61	181	140	41
35 - 39	C	609	439	170	318	221	97	289	216	73
40 - 44	C	692	475	217	395	270	125	297	205	92
45 - 49	C	961	649	312	556	368	188	405	281	124
50 - 54	C	1 177	775	402	594	405	189	583	370	213
55 - 59	C	1 549	999	550	794	505	289	755	494	261
60 - 64	C	1 907	1 182	725	965	590	375	942	592	350
65 - 69	C	2 323	1 306	027	1 192	697	495	1 131	699	432
70 - 74	C	2 812	1 594	1 218	1 476	813	662	1 337	781	556
75 - 79	C	3 440	1 865	1 575	1 861	1 018	843	1 579	847	732
80 - 84	C	3 750	1 883	1 867	2 041	958	1 083	1 708	924	784
85+	C	6 597	2 883	3 714	3 548	1 398	2 150	3 048	1 485	1 563
Unknown - Inconnu	C	71	60	11	12	10	2	3	2	1
Saint Kitts and Nevis - Saint-Kitts-et-Nevis										
2001										
Total	+C	352	181	171	...	...	...	...	...	...
0 - 1	+C	10	3	7	...	...	...	...	...	...
1 - 4	+C	6	1	5	...	...	...	...	...	...
5 - 9	+C	3	3	-	...	...	...	...	...	...
10 - 14	+C	2	1	1	...	...	...	...	...	...
15 - 19	+C	2	1	1	...	...	...	...	...	...
20 - 24	+C	2	1	1	...	...	...	...	...	...
25 - 29	+C	6	4	2	...	...	...	...	...	...
30 - 34	+C	5	3	2	...	...	...	...	...	...
35 - 39	+C	8	6	2	...	...	...	...	...	...
40 - 44	+C	9	6	3	...	...	...	...	...	...
45 - 49	+C	22	16	6	...	...	...	...	...	...
50 - 54	+C	9	4	5	...	...	...	...	...	...
55 - 59	+C	12	8	4	...	...	...	...	...	...
60 - 64	+C	13	9	4	...	...	...	...	...	...
65 - 69	+C	19	9	10	...	...	...	...	...	...
70 - 74	+C	29	17	12	...	...	...	...	...	...
75 - 79	+C	63	31	32	...	...	...	...	...	...
80 - 84	+C	56	25	31	...	...	...	...	...	...
85+	+C	76	33	43	...	...	...	...	...	...
Saint Lucia - Sainte-Lucie										
2002										
Total	C	957	511	446	...	...	...	...	...	...
0 - 1	C	36	17	19	...	...	...	...	...	...

(See notes at end of table.— Voir notes à la fin du tableau.)

Continent, country or area, year and age (in years) / Continent, pays ou zone, année et âge (en années)	Code[1]	Total			Urban - Urbaine			Rural - Rurale		
		Both sexes - Les deux sexes	Male - Masculin	Female - Féminin	Both sexes - Les deux sexes	Male - Masculin	Female - Féminin	Both sexes - Les deux sexes	Male - Masculin	Female - Féminin
AMERICA, NORTH — AMERIQUE DU NORD										
Saint Lucia - Sainte-Lucie										
2002										
1 - 4	C	6	2	4	...	...	...	...	...	...
5 - 9	C	3	2	1	...	...	...	...	...	...
10 - 14	C	8	4	4	...	...	...	...	...	...
15 - 19	C	7	6	1	...	...	...	...	...	...
20 - 24	C	22	12	10	...	...	...	...	...	...
25 - 29	C	23	17	6	...	...	...	...	...	...
30 - 34	C	22	17	5	...	...	...	...	...	...
35 - 39	C	27	17	10	...	...	...	...	...	...
40 - 44	C	30	17	13	...	...	...	...	...	...
45 - 49	C	46	30	16	...	...	...	...	...	...
50 - 54	C	44	30	14	...	...	...	...	...	...
55 - 59	C	53	34	19	...	...	...	...	...	...
60 - 64	C	55	27	28	...	...	...	...	...	...
65 - 69	C	61	30	31	...	...	...	...	...	...
70 - 74	C	101	59	42	...	...	...	...	...	...
75 - 79	C	117	65	52	...	...	...	...	...	...
80 - 84	C	110	55	55	...	...	...	...	...	...
85+	C	168	65	103	...	...	...	...	...	...
Unknown - Inconnu	C	18	5	13	...	...	...	...	...	...
Saint Vincent and the Grenadines - Saint Vincent-et-les Grenadines										
2002										
Total	+C	770	377	393	...	...	...	...	...	...
0 - 1	+C	36	22	14	...	...	...	...	...	...
1 - 4	+C	4	1	3	...	...	...	...	...	...
5 - 9	+C	6	3	3	...	...	...	...	...	...
10 - 14	+C	7	4	3	...	...	...	...	...	...
15 - 19	+C	8	6	2	...	...	...	...	...	...
20 - 24	+C	16	11	5	...	...	...	...	...	...
25 - 29	+C	13	7	6	...	...	...	...	...	...
30 - 34	+C	23	12	11	...	...	...	...	...	...
35 - 39	+C	32	20	12	...	...	...	...	...	...
40 - 44	+C	19	15	4	...	...	...	...	...	...
45 - 49	+C	28	16	12	...	...	...	...	...	...
50 - 54	+C	41	23	18	...	...	...	...	...	...
55 - 59	+C	39	20	19	...	...	...	...	...	...
60 - 64	+C	49	23	26	...	...	...	...	...	...
65 - 69	+C	50	22	28	...	...	...	...	...	...
70 - 74	+C	74	43	31	...	...	...	...	...	...
75 - 79	+C	98	47	51	...	...	...	...	...	...
80 - 84	+C	90	35	55	...	...	...	...	...	...
85+	+C	132	46	86	...	...	...	...	...	...
Unknown - Inconnu	+C	5	1	4	...	...	...	...	...	...
Trinidad and Tobago - Trinité-et-Tobago										
1997										
Total	C	9 157	5 034	4 123	...	...	...	...	...	...
0 - 1	C	316	170	146	...	...	...	...	...	...
1 - 4	C	58	32	26	...	...	...	...	...	...
5 - 9	C	38	24	14	...	...	...	...	...	...
10 - 14	C	48	25	23	...	...	...	...	...	...
15 - 19	C	92	53	39	...	...	...	...	...	...
20 - 24	C	157	105	52	...	...	...	...	...	...
25 - 29	C	165	103	62	...	...	...	...	...	...
30 - 34	C	261	163	98	...	...	...	...	...	...
35 - 39	C	303	184	119	...	...	...	...	...	...
40 - 44	C	350	219	131	...	...	...	...	...	...

(See notes at end of table.— Voir notes à la fin du tableau.)

Continent, country or area, year and age (in years) / Continent, pays ou zone, année et âge (en années)	Code[1]	Total			Urban - Urbaine			Rural - Rurale		
		Both sexes - Les deux sexes	Male - Masculin	Female - Féminin	Both sexes - Les deux sexes	Male - Masculin	Female - Féminin	Both sexes - Les deux sexes	Male - Masculin	Female - Féminin
AMERICA, NORTH — AMERIQUE DU NORD										
Trinidad and Tobago - Trinité-et-Tobago										
1997										
45 - 49	C	399	236	163	...	...	...	...	...	...
50 - 54	C	480	296	184	...	...	...	...	...	...
55 - 59	C	600	347	253	...	...	...	...	...	...
60 - 64	C	755	398	357	...	...	...	...	...	...
65 - 69	C	883	475	408	...	...	...	...	...	...
70 - 74	C	995	577	418	...	...	...	...	...	...
75 - 79	C	1 083	606	477	...	...	...	...	...	...
80 - 84	C	971	510	461	...	...	...	...	...	...
85 - 89	C	727	326	401	...	...	...	...	...	...
90 - 94	C	323	134	189	...	...	...	...	...	...
95 - 99	C	126	45	81	...	...	...	...	...	...
100+	C	25	5	20	...	...	...	...	...	...
Unknown - Inconnu	C	2	1	1	...	...	...	...	...	...
United States - États-Unis										
2001										
Total	C	2 416 425	1 183 421	1 233 004	...	...	...	...	...	...
0 - 1	C	27 568	15 477	12 091	...	...	...	...	...	...
1 - 4	C	5 107	2 899	2 208	...	...	...	...	...	...
5 - 9	C	3 093	1 727	1 366	...	...	...	...	...	...
10 - 14	C	4 002	2 441	1 561	...	...	...	...	...	...
15 - 19	C	13 555	9 766	3 789	...	...	...	...	...	...
20 - 24	C	18 697	14 197	4 500	...	...	...	...	...	...
25 - 29	C	18 211	13 006	5 205	...	...	...	...	...	...
30 - 34	C	23 472	15 751	7 721	...	...	...	...	...	...
35 - 39	C	36 895	23 727	13 168	...	...	...	...	...	...
40 - 44	C	54 779	34 437	20 342	...	...	...	...	...	...
45 - 49	C	73 684	46 567	27 117	...	...	...	...	...	...
50 - 54	C	94 381	58 281	36 100	...	...	...	...	...	...
55 - 59	C	109 523	65 801	43 722	...	...	...	...	...	...
60 - 64	C	134 616	79 157	55 459	...	...	...	...	...	...
65 - 69	C	178 232	102 110	76 122	...	...	...	...	...	...
70 - 74	C	252 728	139 471	113 257	...	...	...	...	...	...
75 - 79	C	333 677	171 311	162 366	...	...	...	...	...	...
80 - 84	C	368 252	169 431	198 821	...	...	...	...	...	...
85 - 89	C	339 775	130 405	209 370	...	...	...	...	...	...
90 - 94	C	221 314	65 527	155 787	...	...	...	...	...	...
95 - 99	C	85 954	18 732	67 222	...	...	...	...	...	...
100+	C	18 488	2 869	15 619	...	...	...	...	...	...
Unknown - Inconnu	C	422	331	91	...	...	...	...	...	...
United States Virgin Islands - Îles Vierges américaines										
1993										
Total	C	569	328	241	...	...	...	...	...	...
0 - 1	C	31	18	13	...	...	...	...	...	...
1 - 4	C	3	2	1	...	...	...	...	...	...
5 - 9	C	2	1	1	...	...	...	...	...	...
10 - 14	C	4	4	-	...	...	...	...	...	...
15 - 19	C	8	5	3	...	...	...	...	...	...
20 - 24	C	11	9	2	...	...	...	...	...	...
25 - 29	C	13	8	5	...	...	...	...	...	...
30 - 34	C	22	16	6	...	...	...	...	...	...
35 - 39	C	19	15	4	...	...	...	...	...	...
40 - 44	C	20	14	6	...	...	...	...	...	...
45 - 49	C	28	20	8	...	...	...	...	...	...
50 - 54	C	41	24	17	...	...	...	...	...	...
55 - 59	C	37	25	12	...	...	...	...	...	...
60 - 64	C	39	29	10	...	...	...	...	...	...

19. Deaths by age, sex and urban/rural residence: latest available year, 1993 - 2002
Décès selon l'âge, le sexe et la résidence, urbaine/rurale: dernière année disponible, 1993 - 2002 (continued — suite)

(See notes at end of table.— Voir notes à la fin du tableau.)

Continent, country or area, year and age (in years) / Continent, pays ou zone, année et âge (en années)	Code[1]	Total			Urban - Urbaine			Rural - Rurale		
		Both sexes - Les deux sexes	Male - Masculin	Female - Féminin	Both sexes - Les deux sexes	Male - Masculin	Female - Féminin	Both sexes - Les deux sexes	Male - Masculin	Female - Féminin
AMERICA, NORTH — AMERIQUE DU NORD										
United States Virgin Islands - Îles Vierges américaines										
1993										
65 - 69	C	46	31	15	...	...	...	...	...	...
70 - 74	C	65	28	37	...	...	...	...	...	...
75 - 79	C	51	24	27	...	...	...	...	...	...
80 - 84	C	60	29	31	...	...	...	...	...	...
85+	C	68	25	43	...	...	...	...	...	...
Unknown - Inconnu	C	1	1	-	...	...	...	...	...	...
AMERICA, SOUTH — AMERIQUE DU SUD										
Argentina - Argentine[9]										
1998										
Total	C	280 180	153 747	126 319	...	...	...	...	...	...
0 - 1	C	13 082	7 472	5 576	...	...	...	...	...	...
1 - 4	C	2 285	1 287	996	...	...	...	...	...	...
5 - 9	C	1 002	604	395	...	...	...	...	...	...
10 - 14	C	1 045	627	418	...	...	...	...	...	...
15 - 19	C	2 639	1 814	823	...	...	...	...	...	...
20 - 24	C	3 225	2 344	879	...	...	...	...	...	...
25 - 29	C	3 300	2 340	959	...	...	...	...	...	...
30 - 34	C	3 479	2 349	1 129	...	...	...	...	...	...
35 - 39	C	4 053	2 609	1 442	...	...	...	...	...	...
40 - 44	C	5 719	3 703	2 013	...	...	...	...	...	...
45 - 49	C	8 581	5 504	3 076	...	...	...	...	...	...
50 - 54	C	11 692	7 710	3 976	...	...	...	...	...	...
55 - 59	C	15 084	10 079	5 002	...	...	...	...	...	...
60 - 64	C	19 791	13 010	6 773	...	...	...	...	...	...
65 - 69	C	27 471	17 604	9 862	...	...	...	...	...	...
70 - 74	C	33 324	20 030	13 287	...	...	...	...	...	...
75 - 79	C	36 600	19 638	16 957	...	...	...	...	...	...
80 - 84	C	36 107	16 553	19 552	...	...	...	...	...	...
85+	C	50 913	17 914	32 993	...	...	...	...	...	...
Unknown - Inconnu	C	788	556	211	...	...	...	...	...	...
Brazil - Brésil[12]										
2001										
Total	U	931 017	547 440	383 577	...	...	...	...	...	...
0 - 1	U	47 171	26 538	20 633	...	...	...	...	...	...
1 - 4	U	9 932	5 371	4 561	...	...	...	...	...	...
5 - 9	U	4 904	2 867	2 037	...	...	...	...	...	...
10 - 14	U	5 918	3 724	2 194	...	...	...	...	...	...
15 - 19	U	18 615	14 499	4 116	...	...	...	...	...	...
20 - 24	U	25 487	20 638	4 849	...	...	...	...	...	...
25 - 29	U	25 132	19 536	5 596	...	...	...	...	...	...
30 - 34	U	27 897	20 638	7 259	...	...	...	...	...	...
35 - 39	U	32 583	23 100	9 483	...	...	...	...	...	...
40 - 44	U	39 193	26 384	12 809	...	...	...	...	...	...
45 - 49	U	46 329	30 367	15 962	...	...	...	...	...	...
50 - 54	U	53 055	33 950	19 105	...	...	...	...	...	...
55 - 59	U	58 276	36 259	22 017	...	...	...	...	...	...
60 - 64	U	71 282	43 307	27 975	...	...	...	...	...	...
65 - 69	U	81 447	47 949	33 498	...	...	...	...	...	...
70 - 74	U	95 054	53 646	41 408	...	...	...	...	...	...
75 - 79	U	92 898	49 784	43 114	...	...	...	...	...	...
80 - 84	U	82 384	40 333	42 051	...	...	...	...	...	...
85 - 89	U	63 590	27 892	35 698	...	...	...	...	...	...
90 - 94	U	32 938	12 872	20 066	...	...	...	...	...	...
95 - 99	U	11 986	4 210	7 776	...	...	...	...	...	...

19. Deaths by age, sex and urban/rural residence: latest available year, 1993 - 2002
Décès selon l'âge, le sexe et la résidence, urbaine/rurale: dernière année disponible, 1993 - 2002 (continued — suite)

(See notes at end of table.— Voir notes à la fin du tableau.)

Continent, country or area, year and age (in years) / Continent, pays ou zone, année et âge (en années)	Code[1]	Total			Urban - Urbaine			Rural - Rurale		
		Both sexes - Les deux sexes	Male - Masculin	Female - Féminin	Both sexes - Les deux sexes	Male - Masculin	Female - Féminin	Both sexes - Les deux sexes	Male - Masculin	Female - Féminin
AMERICA, SOUTH — AMERIQUE DU SUD										
Brazil - Brésil[12]										
2001										
100+	U	852	285	567	...	...	...	...	...	...
Unknown - Inconnu	U	4 094	3 291	803	...	...	...	...	...	...
Chile - Chili										
2002										
Total	C	81 079	44 345	36 734	69 209	37 035	32 174	11 870	7 310	4 560
0 - 1	C	1 964	1 127	837	1 715	974	741	249	153	96
1 - 4	C	449	242	207	355	195	160	94	47	47
5 - 9	C	255	146	109	209	119	90	46	27	19
10 - 14	C	357	232	125	297	194	103	60	38	22
15 - 19	C	654	484	170	544	405	139	110	79	31
20 - 24	C	996	783	213	803	620	183	193	163	30
25 - 29	C	1 131	881	250	909	702	207	222	179	43
30 - 34	C	1 250	962	288	1 011	779	232	239	183	56
35 - 39	C	1 697	1 231	466	1 406	994	412	291	237	54
40 - 44	C	2 247	1 535	712	1 899	1 272	627	348	263	85
45 - 49	C	2 788	1 803	985	2 377	1 512	865	411	291	120
50 - 54	C	3 489	2 199	1 290	2 945	1 830	1 115	544	369	175
55 - 59	C	4 634	2 927	1 707	3 962	2 459	1 503	672	468	204
60 - 64	C	5 783	3 533	2 250	4 967	3 005	1 962	816	528	288
65 - 69	C	7 320	4 406	2 914	6 246	3 705	2 541	1 074	701	373
70 - 74	C	10 289	5 899	4 390	8 853	5 011	3 842	1 436	888	548
75 - 79	C	10 263	5 440	4 823	8 770	4 565	4 205	1 493	875	618
80 - 84	C	10 108	4 867	5 241	8 624	4 020	4 604	1 484	847	637
85 - 89	C	8 664	3 481	5 183	7 464	2 886	4 578	1 200	595	605
90 - 94	C	4 833	1 682	3 151	4 195	1 383	2 812	638	299	339
95 - 99	C	1 616	433	1 183	1 407	358	1 049	209	75	134
100+	C	292	52	240	251	47	204	41	5	36
Colombia - Colombie[7,9]										
2002										
Total	U	187 943	113 385	74 510	139 955	81 123	58 813	37 291	23 871	13 408
0 - 1	U	11 595	6 519	5 062	8 207	4 582	3 615	2 719	1 524	1 191
1 - 4	U	2 830	1 557	1 272	1 705	952	752	1 022	545	477
5 - 9	U	1 409	846	563	919	541	378	428	267	161
10 - 14	U	1 653	1 006	647	1 056	649	407	478	278	200
15 - 19	U	6 626	5 138	1 485	4 440	3 500	939	1 442	1 027	413
20 - 24	U	9 978	8 554	1 424	6 707	5 754	953	2 043	1 724	319
25 - 29	U	8 608	7 311	1 295	5 491	4 599	891	1 807	1 536	271
30 - 34	U	7 605	6 150	1 453	5 043	3 983	1 060	1 638	1 347	289
35 - 39	U	7 516	5 715	1 800	5 132	3 783	1 348	1 583	1 209	374
40 - 44	U	7 349	5 149	2 200	5 196	3 484	1 712	1 562	1 156	406
45 - 49	U	7 227	4 740	2 487	5 319	3 338	1 981	1 484	1 058	426
50 - 54	U	7 895	4 898	2 996	5 915	3 507	2 408	1 577	1 078	499
55 - 59	U	8 336	4 811	3 524	6 369	3 522	2 847	1 647	1 038	608
60 - 64	U	11 247	6 335	4 912	8 772	4 827	3 945	2 133	1 278	855
65 - 69	U	13 917	7 621	6 296	11 016	5 861	5 155	2 533	1 517	1 016
70 - 74	U	17 530	9 529	8 001	13 829	7 363	6 466	3 265	1 903	1 362
75 - 79	U	17 139	8 957	8 181	13 639	6 928	6 710	3 114	1 795	1 319
80 - 84	U	16 297	7 963	8 334	12 982	6 141	6 841	2 989	1 627	1 362
85 - 89	U	11 939	5 374	6 565	9 801	4 277	5 524	1 954	1 013	941
90 - 94	U	6 187	2 612	3 575	5 053	2 065	2 988	1 015	483	532
95 - 97	U	1 576	601	975	1 317	475	842	239	115	124
98+	U	1 104	372	732	915	309	606	163	54	109
Unknown - Inconnu	U	2 380	1 627	731	1 132	683	445	456	299	154
Ecuador - Équateur[13]										
2002										
Total	U	55 549	31 504	24 045	42 236	24 034	18 202	13 313	7 470	5 843
0 - 1	U	4 530	2 544	1 986	3 420	1 924	1 496	1 110	620	490
1 - 4	U	2 032	1 058	974	1 353	725	628	679	333	346

19. Deaths by age, sex and urban/rural residence: latest available year, 1993 - 2002
Décès selon l'âge, le sexe et la résidence, urbaine/rurale: dernière année disponible, 1993 - 2002 (continued — suite)

(See notes at end of table.— Voir notes à la fin du tableau.)

Continent, country or area, year and age (in years) / Continent, pays ou zone, année et âge (en années)	Code[1]	Total			Urban - Urbaine			Rural - Rurale		
		Both sexes - Les deux sexes	Male - Masculin	Female - Féminin	Both sexes - Les deux sexes	Male - Masculin	Female - Féminin	Both sexes - Les deux sexes	Male - Masculin	Female - Féminin
AMERICA, SOUTH — AMERIQUE DU SUD										
Ecuador - Équateur[13]										
2002										
5 - 14	U	1 457	814	643	1 004	546	458	453	268	185
15 - 49	U	12 573	8 540	4 033	9 833	6 769	3 064	2 740	1 771	969
50 - 64	U	8 240	4 903	3 337	6 438	3 823	2 615	1 802	1 080	722
65+	U	26 646	13 593	13 053	20 144	10 214	9 930	6 502	3 379	3 123
Unknown - Inconnu	U	71	52	19	44	33	11	27	19	8
French Guiana - Guyane française[2]										
2000										
Total	C	620	385	235	...	...	...	...	...	...
0 - 1	C	64	35	29	...	...	...	...	...	...
1 - 4	C	24	16	8	...	...	...	...	...	...
5 - 9	C	4	3	1	...	...	...	...	...	...
10 - 14	C	1	1	-	...	...	...	...	...	...
15 - 19	C	14	11	3	...	...	...	...	...	...
20 - 24	C	16	10	6	...	...	...	...	...	...
25 - 29	C	25	12	13	...	...	...	...	...	...
30 - 34	C	26	17	9	...	...	...	...	...	...
35 - 39	C	34	24	10	...	...	...	...	...	...
40 - 44	C	27	21	6	...	...	...	...	...	...
45 - 49	C	24	16	8	...	...	...	...	...	...
50 - 54	C	37	24	13	...	...	...	...	...	...
55 - 59	C	33	26	7	...	...	...	...	...	...
60 - 64	C	39	21	18	...	...	...	...	...	...
65 - 69	C	41	28	13	...	...	...	...	...	...
70 - 74	C	50	34	16	...	...	...	...	...	...
75 - 79	C	47	33	14	...	...	...	...	...	...
80 - 84	C	44	21	23	...	...	...	...	...	...
85 - 89	C	34	17	17	...	...	...	...	...	...
90 - 94	C	19	7	12	...	...	...	...	...	...
95 - 99	C	15	8	7	...	...	...	...	...	...
100+	C	2	-	2	...	...	...	...	...	...
Peru - Pérou[12,14]										
2001										
Total	+U	79 871	42 702	37 169	...	...	...	...	...	...
0 - 1	+U	6 559	3 632	2 927	...	...	...	...	...	...
1 - 4	+U	2 241	1 182	1 059	...	...	...	...	...	...
5 - 9	+U	997	582	415	...	...	...	...	...	...
10 - 14	+U	849	495	354	...	...	...	...	...	...
15 - 19	+U	1 491	883	608	...	...	...	...	...	...
20 - 24	+U	1 980	1 210	770	...	...	...	...	...	...
25 - 29	+U	2 107	1 372	735	...	...	...	...	...	...
30 - 34	+U	2 157	1 394	763	...	...	...	...	...	...
35 - 39	+U	2 371	1 457	914	...	...	...	...	...	...
40 - 44	+U	2 542	1 487	1 055	...	...	...	...	...	...
45 - 49	+U	2 817	1 561	1 256	...	...	...	...	...	...
50 - 54	+U	3 372	1 850	1 522	...	...	...	...	...	...
55 - 59	+U	3 626	2 016	1 610	...	...	...	...	...	...
60 - 64	+U	4 783	2 643	2 140	...	...	...	...	...	...
65 - 69	+U	5 827	3 220	2 607	...	...	...	...	...	...
70 - 74	+U	7 185	3 923	3 262	...	...	...	...	...	...
75 - 79	+U	7 690	4 157	3 533	...	...	...	...	...	...
80 - 84	+U	7 722	3 888	3 834	...	...	...	...	...	...
85 - 89	+U	6 464	2 971	3 493	...	...	...	...	...	...
90 - 94	+U	3 999	1 655	2 344	...	...	...	...	...	...
95+	+U	2 677	906	1 771	...	...	...	...	...	...
Unknown - Inconnu	+U	415	218	197	...	...	...	...	...	...

(See notes at end of table.— Voir notes à la fin du tableau.)

Continent, country or area, year and age (in years) / Continent, pays ou zone, année et âge (en années)	Code[1]	Total			Urban - Urbaine			Rural - Rurale		
		Both sexes - Les deux sexes	Male - Masculin	Female - Féminin	Both sexes - Les deux sexes	Male - Masculin	Female - Féminin	Both sexes - Les deux sexes	Male - Masculin	Female - Féminin
AMERICA, SOUTH — AMERIQUE DU SUD										
Suriname										
2000										
Total	C	3 090	1 756	1 334	2 249	...	...	841	...	...
0 - 1	C	156	83	73	117	...	...	39	...	...
1 - 4	C	73	36	37	44	...	...	29	...	...
5 - 9	C	19	13	6	11	...	...	8	...	...
10 - 14	C	23	16	7	17	...	...	6	...	...
15 - 19	C	54	33	21	29	...	...	25	...	...
20 - 24	C	68	50	18	42	...	...	26	...	...
25 - 29	C	97	57	40	72	...	...	25	...	...
30 - 34	C	118	75	43	83	...	...	35	...	...
35 - 39	C	132	89	43	95	...	...	37	...	...
40 - 44	C	128	86	42	98	...	...	30	...	...
45 - 49	C	161	92	69	134	...	...	27	...	...
50 - 54	C	170	103	67	130	...	...	40	...	...
55 - 59	C	191	111	80	137	...	...	54	...	...
60 - 64	C	264	148	116	196	...	...	68	...	...
65 - 69	C	320	186	134	238	...	...	82	...	...
70 - 74	C	312	177	135	217	...	...	95	...	...
75 - 79	C	303	172	131	218	...	...	85	...	...
80 - 84	C	211	100	111	165	...	...	46	...	...
85 - 89	C	162	76	86	104	...	...	58	...	...
90 - 94	C	80	39	41	60	...	...	20	...	...
95 - 99	C	44	12	32	38	...	...	6	...	...
100+	C	4	2	2	4	...	...	-	...	...
Uruguay[9]										
2002										
Total	C	31 628	16 796	14 819	...	...	...	...	...	...
0 - 1	C	708	401	304	...	...	...	...	...	...
1 - 4	C	104	69	35	...	...	...	...	...	...
5 - 9	C	63	31	32	...	...	...	...	...	...
10 - 14	C	07	42	25	...	...	...	...	...	...
15 - 19	C	182	139	43	...	...	...	...	...	...
20 - 24	C	249	199	50	...	...	...	...	...	...
25 - 29	C	260	196	64	...	...	...	...	...	...
30 - 34	C	301	200	101	...	...	...	...	...	...
35 - 39	C	339	218	120	...	...	...	...	...	...
40 - 44	C	494	273	221	...	...	...	...	...	...
45 - 49	C	754	467	287	...	...	...	...	...	...
50 - 54	C	1 108	724	384	...	...	...	...	...	...
55 - 59	C	1 501	990	511	...	...	...	...	...	...
60 - 64	C	2 095	1 422	673	...	...	...	...	...	...
65 - 69	C	2 842	1 818	1 024	...	...	...	...	...	...
70 - 74	C	3 938	2 395	1 542	...	...	...	...	...	...
75+	C	16 534	7 149	9 381	...	...	...	...	...	...
Unknown - Inconnu	C	89	63	22	...	...	...	...	...	...
Venezuela[12]										
2002										
Total	C	105 388	64 917	40 471	...	...	...	...	...	...
0 - 1	C	7 645	4 406	3 239	...	...	...	...	...	...
1 - 4	C	1 937	1 077	860	...	...	...	...	...	...
5 - 9	C	829	493	336	...	...	...	...	...	...
10 - 14	C	1 061	668	393	...	...	...	...	...	...
15 - 19	C	3 540	2 929	611	...	...	...	...	...	...
20 - 24	C	5 301	4 579	722	...	...	...	...	...	...
25 - 29	C	4 293	3 578	715	...	...	...	...	...	...
30 - 34	C	3 957	3 002	955	...	...	...	...	...	...
35 - 39	C	3 621	2 586	1 035	...	...	...	...	...	...
40 - 44	C	4 168	2 795	1 373	...	...	...	...	...	...
45 - 49	C	4 878	3 164	1 714	...	...	...	...	...	...

(See notes at end of table.— Voir notes à la fin du tableau.)

Continent, country or area, year and age (in years) / Continent, pays ou zone, année et âge (en années)	Code[1]	Total			Urban - Urbaine			Rural - Rurale		
		Both sexes - Les deux sexes	Male - Masculin	Female - Féminin	Both sexes - Les deux sexes	Male - Masculin	Female - Féminin	Both sexes - Les deux sexes	Male - Masculin	Female - Féminin
AMERICA, SOUTH — AMERIQUE DU SUD										
Venezuela[12]										
2002										
50 - 54	C	5 518	3 549	1 969	...	...	...	...	...	...
55 - 59	C	5 802	3 719	2 083	...	...	...	...	...	...
60 - 64	C	6 494	4 032	2 462	...	...	...	...	...	...
65 - 69	C	7 964	4 746	3 218	...	...	...	...	...	...
70 - 74	C	9 145	5 339	3 806	...	...	...	...	...	...
75 - 79	C	9 369	5 076	4 293	...	...	...	...	...	...
80 - 84	C	8 247	4 164	4 083	...	...	...	...	...	...
85 - 89	C	6 270	2 793	3 477	...	...	...	...	...	...
90 - 94	C	3 518	1 463	2 055	...	...	...	...	...	...
95 - 99	C	1 201	420	781	...	...	...	...	...	...
100+	C	364	133	231	...	...	...	...	...	...
Unknown - Inconnu	C	266	206	60	...	...	...	...	...	...
ASIA — ASIE										
Armenia - Arménie[15]										
2000										
Total	C	24 025	12 277	11 748	15 682	8 115	7 567	8 343	4 162	4 181
0 - 1	C	540	348	192	357	234	123	183	114	69
1 - 4	C	143	80	63	81	45	36	62	35	27
5 - 9	C	60	27	33	39	18	21	21	9	12
10 - 14	C	68	51	17	45	35	10	23	16	7
15 - 19	C	136	108	28	78	57	21	58	51	7
20 - 24	C	155	113	42	109	82	27	46	31	15
25 - 29	C	169	108	61	122	77	45	47	31	16
30 - 34	C	253	175	78	166	117	49	87	58	29
35 - 39	C	456	303	153	305	198	107	151	105	46
40 - 44	C	662	437	225	458	310	148	204	127	77
45 - 49	C	806	541	265	633	423	210	173	118	55
50 - 54	C	898	576	322	697	443	254	201	133	68
55 - 59	C	874	570	304	666	443	223	208	127	81
60 - 64	C	2 689	1 639	1 050	1 900	1 186	714	789	453	336
65 - 69	C	3 332	1 952	1 380	2 117	1 234	883	1 215	718	497
70 - 74	C	4 898	2 510	2 388	3 098	1 548	1 550	1 800	962	838
75 - 79	C	3 018	1 255	1 763	1 954	769	1 185	1 064	486	578
80 - 84	C	1 860	602	1 258	1 197	385	812	663	217	446
85+	C	3 008	882	2 126	1 660	511	1 149	1 348	371	977
2001										
Total	C	24 003	12 468	11 535	...	...	...	...	...	...
0 - 1	C	518	326	192	...	...	...	...	...	...
1 - 4	C	88	54	34	...	...	...	...	...	...
5 - 9	C	38	22	16	...	...	...	...	...	...
10 - 14	C	61	43	18	...	...	...	...	...	...
15 - 19	C	133	109	24	...	...	...	...	...	...
20 - 24	C	144	111	33	...	...	...	...	...	...
25 - 29	C	188	120	68	...	...	...	...	...	...
30 - 34	C	270	189	81	...	...	...	...	...	...
35 - 39	C	466	310	156	...	...	...	...	...	...
40 - 44	C	737	486	251	...	...	...	...	...	...
45 - 49	C	859	563	296	...	...	...	...	...	...
50 - 54	C	945	628	317	...	...	...	...	...	...
55 - 59	C	929	588	341	...	...	...	...	...	...
60 - 64	C	2 780	1 676	1 104	...	...	...	...	...	...
65 - 69	C	3 352	1 961	1 391	...	...	...	...	...	...
70 - 74	C	5 039	2 671	2 368	...	...	...	...	...	...
75 - 79	C	3 161	1 305	1 856	...	...	...	...	...	...
80 - 84	C	1 720	567	1 153	...	...	...	...	...	...
85 - 89	C	1 574	467	1 107	...	...	...	...	...	...

19. Deaths by age, sex and urban/rural residence: latest available year, 1993 - 2002
Décès selon l'âge, le sexe et la résidence, urbaine/rurale: dernière année disponible, 1993 - 2002 (continued — suite)

(See notes at end of table.— Voir notes à la fin du tableau.)

Continent, country or area, year and age (in years) / Continent, pays ou zone, année et âge (en années)	Code[1]	Total			Urban - Urbaine			Rural - Rurale		
		Both sexes - Les deux sexes	Male - Masculin	Female - Féminin	Both sexes - Les deux sexes	Male - Masculin	Female - Féminin	Both sexes - Les deux sexes	Male - Masculin	Female - Féminin
ASIA — ASIE										
Armenia - Arménie[15]										
2001										
90 - 94	C	766	212	554	...	...	...	...	...	...
95 - 99	C	176	46	130	...	...	...	...	...	...
100+	C	59	14	45	...	...	...	...	...	...
Azerbaijan - Azerbaïdjan[15]										
2002										
Total	+C	46 522	24 405	22 117	23 605	12 659	10 946	22 917	11 746	11 171
0 - 1	+C	1 422	793	629	554	318	236	868	475	393
1 - 4	+C	1 130	617	513	292	172	120	838	445	393
5 - 9	+C	463	249	214	202	115	87	261	134	127
10 - 14	+C	301	187	114	128	78	50	173	109	64
15 - 19	+C	458	299	159	220	152	68	238	147	91
20 - 24	+C	547	350	197	281	186	95	266	164	102
25 - 29	+C	685	446	239	346	228	118	339	218	121
30 - 34	+C	819	531	288	407	280	127	412	251	161
35 - 39	+C	1 177	794	383	669	457	212	508	337	171
40 - 44	+C	1 708	1 158	550	954	676	278	754	482	272
45 - 49	+C	1 877	1 268	609	1 156	807	349	721	461	260
50 - 54	+C	2 141	1 398	743	1 372	917	455	769	481	288
55 - 59	+C	1 656	1 046	610	1 052	671	381	604	375	229
60 - 64	+C	4 735	2 846	1 889	2 587	1 601	986	2 148	1 245	903
65 - 69	+C	7 071	4 003	3 068	3 535	1 968	1 567	3 536	2 035	1 501
70 - 74	+C	7 597	4 051	3 546	3 657	1 909	1 748	3 940	2 142	1 798
75 - 79	+C	5 081	2 219	2 862	2 808	1 146	1 662	2 273	1 073	1 200
80 - 84	+C	2 994	987	2 007	1 469	467	1 002	1 525	520	1 005
85 - 89	+C	2 111	596	1 515	1 038	287	751	1 073	309	764
90 - 94	+C	1 389	356	1 033	587	160	427	802	196	606
95 - 99	+C	575	113	462	179	43	136	396	70	326
100+	+C	585	98	487	112	21	91	473	77	396
Bahrain - Bahreïn										
2002										
Total	U	2 035	1 239	796	...	...	...	...	...	...
0 - 1	U	94	48	46	...	...	...	...	...	...
1 - 4	U	27	15	12	...	...	...	...	...	...
5 - 9	U	21	9	12	...	...	...	...	...	...
10 - 14	U	18	14	4	...	...	...	...	...	...
15 - 19	U	24	15	9	...	...	...	...	...	...
20 - 24	U	43	31	12	...	...	...	...	...	...
25 - 29	U	46	32	14	...	...	...	...	...	...
30 - 34	U	62	47	15	...	...	...	...	...	...
35 - 39	U	81	48	33	...	...	...	...	...	...
40 - 44	U	105	72	33	...	...	...	...	...	...
45 - 49	U	97	69	28	...	...	...	...	...	...
50 - 54	U	99	74	25	...	...	...	...	...	...
55 - 59	U	119	85	34	...	...	...	...	...	...
60 - 64	U	174	100	74	...	...	...	...	...	...
65 - 69	U	199	107	92	...	...	...	...	...	...
70 - 74	U	269	142	127	...	...	...	...	...	...
75+	U	557	331	226	...	...	...	...	...	...
Brunei Darussalam - Brunéi Darussalam										
2000										
Total	+C	965	553	412	...	...	...	...	...	...
0 - 1	+C	55	26	29	...	...	...	...	...	...
1 - 4	+C	22	15	7	...	...	...	...	...	...
5 - 9	+C	9	5	4	...	...	...	...	...	...
10 - 14	+C	11	6	5	...	...	...	...	...	...
15 - 19	+C	21	16	5	...	...	...	...	...	...
20 - 24	+C	25	15	10	...	...	...	...	...	...
25 - 29	+C	27	13	14	...	...	...	...	...	...

(See notes at end of table.— Voir notes à la fin du tableau.)

Continent, country or area, year and age (in years) / Continent, pays ou zone, année et âge (en années)	Code[1]	Total			Urban - Urbaine			Rural - Rurale		
		Both sexes - Les deux sexes	Male - Masculin	Female - Féminin	Both sexes - Les deux sexes	Male - Masculin	Female - Féminin	Both sexes - Les deux sexes	Male - Masculin	Female - Féminin
ASIA — ASIE										
Brunei Darussalam - Brunéi Darussalam										
2000										
30 - 34	+C	25	18	7	...	...	...	...	...	...
35 - 39	+C	33	24	9	...	...	...	...	...	...
40 - 44	+C	39	22	17	...	...	...	...	...	...
45 - 49	+C	29	19	10	...	...	...	...	...	...
50 - 54	+C	51	22	29	...	...	...	...	...	...
55 - 59	+C	63	42	21	...	...	...	...	...	...
60 - 64	+C	61	34	27	...	...	...	...	...	...
65 - 69	+C	108	57	51	...	...	...	...	...	...
70+	+C	386	219	167	...	...	...	...	...	...
China - Chine[16]										
1999										
Total	...	7 420 000	4 140 000	3 280 000	...	...	...	...	...	...
0 - 4	...	474 000	237 000	237 000	...	...	...	...	...	...
5 - 9	...	40 000	22 000	18 000	...	...	...	...	...	...
10 - 14	...	33 000	20 000	13 000	...	...	...	...	...	...
15 - 19	...	72 000	38 000	34 000	...	...	...	...	...	...
20 - 24	...	104 000	59 000	45 000	...	...	...	...	...	...
25 - 29	...	165 000	87 000	78 000	...	...	...	...	...	...
30 - 34	...	180 000	112 000	68 000	...	...	...	...	...	...
35 - 39	...	147 000	93 000	54 000	...	...	...	...	...	...
40 - 44	...	229 000	150 000	79 000	...	...	...	...	...	...
45 - 49	...	306 000	199 000	107 000	...	...	...	...	...	...
50 - 54	...	286 000	177 000	109 000	...	...	...	...	...	...
55 - 59	...	414 000	242 000	172 000	...	...	...	...	...	...
60 - 64	...	673 000	432 000	241 000	...	...	...	...	...	...
65 - 69	...	906 000	540 000	366 000	...	...	...	...	...	...
70 - 74	...	1 028 000	594 000	434 000	...	...	...	...	...	...
75 - 79	...	947 000	528 000	419 000	...	...	...	...	...	...
80 - 84	...	799 000	381 000	418 000	...	...	...	...	...	...
85 - 89	...	423 000	174 000	249 000	...	...	...	...	...	...
90+	...	193 000	54 000	139 000	...	...	...	...	...	...
China: Hong Kong SAR - Chine: Hong Kong RAS[9]										
2001										
Total	C	33 378	19 089	14 287	...	...	...	...	...	...
0 - 1	C	124	69	54	...	...	...	...	...	...
1 - 4	C	51	31	20	...	...	...	...	...	...
5 - 9	C	40	27	13	...	...	...	...	...	...
10 - 14	C	50	26	24	...	...	...	...	...	...
15 - 19	C	94	61	33	...	...	...	...	...	...
20 - 24	C	165	112	53	...	...	...	...	...	...
25 - 29	C	299	213	86	...	...	...	...	...	...
30 - 34	C	300	193	107	...	...	...	...	...	...
35 - 39	C	504	299	205	...	...	...	...	...	...
40 - 44	C	824	507	317	...	...	...	...	...	...
45 - 49	C	1 085	742	343	...	...	...	...	...	...
50 - 54	C	1 276	889	387	...	...	...	...	...	...
55 - 59	C	1 273	945	328	...	...	...	...	...	...
60 - 64	C	1 941	1 378	563	...	...	...	...	...	...
65 - 69	C	3 432	2 302	1 130	...	...	...	...	...	...
70 - 74	C	4 732	3 064	1 668	...	...	...	...	...	...
75 - 79	C	5 237	3 077	2 160	...	...	...	...	...	...
80 - 84	C	5 024	2 625	2 399	...	...	...	...	...	...
85+	C	6 903	2 512	4 391	...	...	...	...	...	...
Unknown - Inconnu	C	24	17	6	...	...	...	...	...	...

19. Deaths by age, sex and urban/rural residence: latest available year, 1993 - 2002
Décès selon l'âge, le sexe et la résidence, urbaine/rurale: dernière année disponible, 1993 - 2002 (continued — suite)

(See notes at end of table.— Voir notes à la fin du tableau.)

Continent, country or area, year and age (in years) / Continent, pays ou zone, année et âge (en années)	Code[1]	Total			Urban - Urbaine			Rural - Rurale		
		Both sexes - Les deux sexes	Male - Masculin	Female - Féminin	Both sexes - Les deux sexes	Male - Masculin	Female - Féminin	Both sexes - Les deux sexes	Male - Masculin	Female - Féminin
ASIA — ASIE										
China: Macao SAR - Chine: Macao RAS										
2001										
Total	C	1 327	730	597	...	...	...	...	...	...
0 - 1	C	14	9	5	...	...	...	...	...	...
1 - 4	C	3	2	1	...	...	...	...	...	...
5 - 9	C	1	-	1	...	...	...	...	...	...
10 - 14	C	4	2	2	...	...	...	...	...	...
15 - 19	C	8	5	3	...	...	...	...	...	...
20 - 24	C	9	4	5	...	...	...	...	...	...
25 - 29	C	16	8	8	...	...	...	...	...	...
30 - 34	C	26	17	9	...	...	...	...	...	...
35 - 39	C	37	23	14	...	...	...	...	...	...
40 - 44	C	45	29	16	...	...	...	...	...	...
45 - 49	C	65	42	23	...	...	...	...	...	...
50 - 54	C	62	41	21	...	...	...	...	...	...
55 - 59	C	48	35	13	...	...	...	...	...	...
60 - 64	C	59	41	18	...	...	...	...	...	...
65 - 69	C	109	71	38	...	...	...	...	...	...
70 - 74	C	177	112	65	...	...	...	...	...	...
75 - 79	C	204	113	91	...	...	...	...	...	...
80 - 84	C	195	92	103	...	...	...	...	...	...
85+	C	235	77	158	...	...	...	...	...	...
Unknown - Inconnu	C	10	7	3	...	...	...	...	...	...
Cyprus - Chypre[17]										
2002										
Total	C	5 168	2 752	2 416	...	...	...	...	...	...
0 - 1	C	37	19	18	...	...	...	...	...	...
1 - 4	C	18	7	11	...	...	...	...	...	...
5 - 9	C	16	10	6	...	...	...	...	...	...
10 - 14	C	9	5	4	...	...	...	...	...	...
15 - 19	C	32	26	6	...	...	...	...	...	...
20 - 24	C	48	32	16	...	...	...	...	...	...
25 - 29	C	40	27	13	...	...	...	...	...	...
30 - 34	C	42	30	12	...	...	...	...	...	...
35 - 39	C	43	27	16	...	...	...	...	...	...
40 - 44	C	50	39	11	...	...	...	...	...	...
45 - 49	C	84	57	27	...	...	...	...	...	...
50 - 54	C	123	68	55	...	...	...	...	...	...
55 - 59	C	206	144	62	...	...	...	...	...	...
60 - 64	C	236	147	89	...	...	...	...	...	...
65 - 69	C	400	252	148	...	...	...	...	...	...
70 - 74	C	558	336	222	...	...	...	...	...	...
75 - 79	C	812	425	387	...	...	...	...	...	...
80+	C	2 414	1 101	1 313	...	...	...	...	...	...
Georgia - Géorgie[15]										
2001										
Total	C	39 339	19 569	19 770	21 600	11 077	10 523	17 739	8 492	9 247
0 - 1	C	478	301	177	439	280	159	39	21	18
1 - 4	C	58	26	32	29	10	19	29	16	13
5 - 9	C	40	29	11	27	21	6	13	8	5
10 - 14	C	74	53	21	50	36	14	24	17	7
15 - 19	C	183	114	69	99	66	33	84	48	36
20 - 24	C	208	137	71	134	88	46	74	49	25
25 - 29	C	370	271	99	231	169	62	139	102	37
30 - 34	C	463	350	113	270	204	66	193	146	47
35 - 39	C	668	506	162	427	327	100	241	179	62
40 - 44	C	953	711	242	629	484	145	324	227	97
45 - 49	C	1 156	857	299	778	584	194	378	273	105
50 - 54	C	1 294	924	370	890	635	255	404	289	115
55 - 59	C	1 311	877	434	823	568	255	488	309	179

(See notes at end of table.— Voir notes à la fin du tableau.)

Continent, country or area, year and age (in years) / Continent, pays ou zone, année et âge (en années)	Code[1]	Total			Urban - Urbaine			Rural - Rurale		
		Both sexes - Les deux sexes	Male - Masculin	Female - Féminin	Both sexes - Les deux sexes	Male - Masculin	Female - Féminin	Both sexes - Les deux sexes	Male - Masculin	Female - Féminin
ASIA — ASIE										
Georgia - Géorgie[15]										
2001										
60 - 64	C	3 440	1 980	1 460	2 067	1 242	825	1 373	738	635
65 - 69	C	5 046	2 936	2 110	2 693	1 560	1 133	2 353	1 376	977
70 - 74	C	7 055	3 787	3 268	3 703	1 965	1 738	3 352	1 822	1 530
75 - 79	C	6 361	2 713	3 648	3 381	1 361	2 020	2 980	1 352	1 628
80 - 84	C	4 249	1 361	2 888	2 177	676	1 501	2 072	685	1 387
85 - 89	C	3 498	997	2 501	1 775	512	1 263	1 723	485	1 238
90 - 94	C	1 558	413	1 145	636	175	461	922	238	684
95 - 99	C	487	97	390	165	37	128	322	60	262
100+	C	301	75	226	93	25	68	208	50	158
Unknown - Inconnu	C	88	54	34	84	52	32	4	2	2
Israel - Israël[7,9,18]										
2002										
Total	C	38 254	19 295	18 956	35 816	18 086	17 729	2 435	1 208	1 225
0 - 1	C	751	402	347	677	361	315	73	41	31
1 - 4	C	165	93	72	145	80	65	19	13	6
5 - 9	C	91	49	42	78	43	35	13	6	7
10 - 14	C	83	45	38	71	39	32	12	6	6
15 - 19	C	269	195	74	242	181	61	27	14	13
20 - 24	C	421	331	90	368	290	78	52	40	12
25 - 29	C	331	259	72	301	239	62	30	20	10
30 - 34	C	307	221	86	282	204	78	25	17	8
35 - 39	C	369	254	115	350	241	109	19	13	6
40 - 44	C	584	378	206	540	350	190	44	28	16
45 - 49	C	785	474	311	735	448	287	50	26	24
50 - 54	C	1 183	740	443	1 121	702	419	62	38	24
55 - 59	C	1 332	797	535	1 249	755	494	83	42	41
60 - 64	C	1 840	1 095	745	1 734	1 037	697	106	58	48
65 - 69	C	2 799	1 633	1 166	2 660	1 551	1 109	139	82	57
70 - 74	C	4 303	2 340	1 963	4 098	2 225	1 873	205	115	90
75 - 79	C	5 964	2 869	3 095	5 641	2 711	2 930	323	158	165
80 - 84	C	5 860	2 713	3 147	5 516	2 546	2 970	344	167	177
85+	C	10 816	4 407	6 408	10 007	4 083	5 924	809	324	484
Unknown - Inconnu	C	1	-	1	1	-	1	-	-	-
Japan - Japon[19]										
2002										
Total	C	982 379	535 305	447 074	...	...	...	...	...	...
0 - 1	C	3 497	1 903	1 594	...	...	...	...	...	...
1 - 4	C	1 249	681	568	...	...	...	...	...	...
5 - 9	C	730	410	320	...	...	...	...	...	...
10 - 14	C	644	386	258	...	...	...	...	...	...
15 - 19	C	2 191	1 540	651	...	...	...	...	...	...
20 - 24	C	3 468	2 467	1 001	...	...	...	...	...	...
25 - 29	C	4 419	3 053	1 366	...	...	...	...	...	...
30 - 34	C	5 782	3 848	1 934	...	...	...	...	...	...
35 - 39	C	6 955	4 574	2 381	...	...	...	...	...	...
40 - 44	C	10 110	6 765	3 345	...	...	...	...	...	...
45 - 49	C	17 014	11 372	5 642	...	...	...	...	...	...
50 - 54	C	36 605	24 892	11 713	...	...	...	...	...	...
55 - 59	C	43 427	30 084	13 343	...	...	...	...	...	...
60 - 64	C	58 667	40 492	18 175	...	...	...	...	...	...
65 - 69	C	85 289	58 221	27 068	...	...	...	...	...	...
70 - 74	C	116 977	77 488	39 489	...	...	...	...	...	...
75 - 79	C	140 943	83 891	57 052	...	...	...	...	...	...
80 - 84	C	147 737	73 270	74 467	...	...	...	...	...	...
85 - 89	C	152 140	64 874	87 266	...	...	...	...	...	...
90 - 94	C	103 304	34 424	68 880	...	...	...	...	...	...
95 - 99	C	34 126	8 885	25 241	...	...	...	...	...	...
100+	C	6 444	1 227	5 217	...	...	...	...	...	...
Unknown - Inconnu	C	661	558	103	...	...	...	...	...	...

(See notes at end of table.— Voir notes à la fin du tableau.)

Continent, country or area, year and age (in years) / Continent, pays ou zone, année et âge (en années)	Code[1]	Total			Urban - Urbaine			Rural - Rurale		
		Both sexes - Les deux sexes	Male - Masculin	Female - Féminin	Both sexes - Les deux sexes	Male - Masculin	Female - Féminin	Both sexes - Les deux sexes	Male - Masculin	Female - Féminin
ASIA — ASIE										
Kazakhstan[15]										
2002										
Total	C	149 381	83 396	65 985	95 470	53 376	42 094	53 911	30 020	23 891
0 - 1	C	3 849	2 252	1 597	2 202	1 283	919	1 647	969	678
1 - 4	C	1 096	641	455	417	246	171	679	395	284
5 - 9	C	586	349	237	285	168	117	301	181	120
10 - 14	C	739	461	278	356	220	136	383	241	142
15 - 19	C	1 634	1 101	533	902	617	285	732	484	248
20 - 24	C	2 740	1 978	762	1 616	1 189	427	1 124	789	335
25 - 29	C	3 608	2 705	903	2 200	1 642	558	1 408	1 063	345
30 - 34	C	4 118	3 037	1 081	2 654	1 963	691	1 464	1 074	390
35 - 39	C	5 318	3 950	1 368	3 432	2 593	839	1 886	1 357	529
40 - 44	C	7 846	5 862	1 984	5 320	3 980	1 340	2 526	1 882	644
45 - 49	C	8 957	6 500	2 457	6 168	4 514	1 654	2 789	1 986	803
50 - 54	C	10 629	7 463	3 166	7 271	5 135	2 136	3 358	2 328	1 030
55 - 59	C	7 600	5 089	2 511	4 993	3 404	1 589	2 607	1 685	922
60 - 64	C	16 837	10 633	6 204	10 671	6 742	3 929	6 166	3 891	2 275
65 - 69	C	15 692	9 336	6 356	9 724	5 743	3 981	5 968	3 593	2 375
70 - 74	C	18 522	9 408	9 114	11 791	5 850	5 941	6 731	3 558	3 173
75 - 79	C	16 324	6 231	10 093	10 706	3 947	6 759	5 618	2 284	3 334
80 - 84	C	9 820	2 984	6 836	6 288	1 870	4 418	3 532	1 114	2 418
85 - 89	C	7 324	1 768	5 556	4 756	1 109	3 647	2 568	659	1 909
90 - 94	C	3 805	756	3 049	2 263	439	1 824	1 542	317	1 225
95 - 99	C	1 158	218	940	585	120	465	573	98	475
100+	C	427	57	370	163	20	143	264	37	227
Unknown - Inconnu	C	752	617	135	707	582	125	45	35	10
Korea (Dem. People's Republic of) - Corée (Rép. populaire dém. de)										
1993										
Total	...	115 609	62 046	53 563	64 067	...	...	51 542	...	...
0 - 4	...	11 202	5 978	5 224	5 212	...	...	5 990	...	...
5 - 9	...	1 065	636	429	562	...	...	503	...	...
10 - 14	...	532	322	210	310	...	...	222	...	...
15 - 19	...	730	399	331	432	...	...	298	...	...
20 - 24	...	1 245	596	649	773	...	...	472	...	...
25 - 29	...	1 776	1 084	692	1 083	...	...	693	...	...
30 - 34	...	1 626	1 048	578	985	...	...	641	...	...
35 - 39	...	1 564	1 057	507	993	...	...	571	...	...
40 - 44	...	1 866	1 316	550	1 211	...	...	655	...	...
45 - 49	...	3 452	2 428	1 024	2 213	...	...	1 239	...	...
50 - 54	...	5 575	3 963	1 612	3 509	...	...	2 066	...	...
55 - 59	...	9 785	7 027	2 758	5 945	...	...	3 840	...	...
60 - 64	...	13 900	9 369	4 531	8 441	...	...	5 459	...	...
65 - 69	...	14 526	8 547	5 979	8 245	...	...	6 281	...	...
70 - 74	...	16 149	7 955	8 194	8 521	...	...	7 628	...	...
75 - 79	...	14 977	5 769	9 208	7 628	...	...	7 349	...	...
80 - 84	...	10 461	3 397	7 064	5 401	...	...	5 060	...	...
85+	...	5 178	1 155	4 023	2 603	...	...	2 575	...	...
Korea (Republic of) - Corée (République de)[20]										
2002										
Total	C	246 515	135 510	111 005	...	...	...	...	...	...
0 - 1	C	2 545	1 416	1 129	...	...	...	...	...	...
1 - 4	C	1 080	608	472	...	...	...	...	...	...
5 - 9	C	802	481	321	...	...	...	...	...	...
10 - 14	C	566	343	223	...	...	...	...	...	...
15 - 19	C	1 229	831	398	...	...	...	...	...	...
20 - 24	C	2 006	1 322	684	...	...	...	...	...	...
25 - 29	C	2 527	1 725	802	...	...	...	...	...	...
30 - 34	C	3 902	2 674	1 228	...	...	...	...	...	...

19. Deaths by age, sex and urban/rural residence: latest available year, 1993 - 2002
Décès selon l'âge, le sexe et la résidence, urbaine/rurale: dernière année disponible, 1993 - 2002 (continued — suite)

(See notes at end of table.— Voir notes à la fin du tableau.)

Continent, country or area, year and age (in years) / Continent, pays ou zone, année et âge (en années)	Code[1]	Total			Urban - Urbaine			Rural - Rurale		
		Both sexes - Les deux sexes	Male - Masculin	Female - Féminin	Both sexes - Les deux sexes	Male - Masculin	Female - Féminin	Both sexes - Les deux sexes	Male - Masculin	Female - Féminin
ASIA — ASIE										
Korea (Republic of) - Corée (République de)[20]										
2002										
35 - 39	C	5 656	4 069	1 587	...	...	...	...	...	...
40 - 44	C	9 363	7 007	2 356	...	...	...	...	...	...
45 - 49	C	11 303	8 559	2 744	...	...	...	...	...	...
50 - 54	C	12 071	9 053	3 018	...	...	...	...	...	...
55 - 59	C	14 950	10 905	4 045	...	...	...	...	...	...
60 - 64	C	22 047	15 389	6 658	...	...	...	...	...	...
65 - 69	C	26 236	16 826	9 410	...	...	...	...	...	...
70 - 74	C	29 232	15 929	13 303	...	...	...	...	...	...
75 - 79	C	33 455	15 798	17 657	...	...	...	...	...	...
80 - 84	C	31 314	12 519	18 795	...	...	...	...	...	...
85 - 89	C	22 262	6 958	15 304	...	...	...	...	...	...
90 - 94	C	10 674	2 605	8 069	...	...	...	...	...	...
95+	C	3 273	487	2 786	...	...	...	...	...	...
Unknown - Inconnu	C	22	6	16	...	...	...	...	...	...
Kuwait - Koweït										
2002										
Total	C	4 342	2 755	1 587	...	...	...	...	...	...
0 - 1	C	418	225	193	...	...	...	...	...	...
1 - 4	C	74	43	31	...	...	...	...	...	...
5 - 9	C	56	33	23	...	...	...	...	...	...
10 - 14	C	48	28	20	...	...	...	...	...	...
15 - 19	C	76	61	15	...	...	...	...	...	...
20 - 24	C	135	103	32	...	...	...	...	...	...
25 - 29	C	150	120	30	...	...	...	...	...	...
30 - 34	C	163	123	40	...	...	...	...	...	...
35 - 39	C	163	130	33	...	...	...	...	...	...
40 - 44	C	247	197	50	...	...	...	...	...	...
45 - 49	C	239	165	74	...	...	...	...	...	...
50 - 54	C	266	181	85	...	...	...	...	...	...
55 - 59	C	280	186	94	...	...	...	...	...	...
60 - 64	C	365	221	144	...	...	...	...	...	...
65 - 69	C	348	222	126	...	...	...	...	...	...
70 - 74	C	392	227	165	...	...	...	...	...	...
75 - 79	C	309	170	139	...	...	...	...	...	...
80 - 84	C	250	132	118	...	...	...	...	...	...
85+	C	239	118	121	...	...	...	...	...	...
Unknown - Inconnu	C	124	70	54	...	...	...	...	...	...
Kyrgyzstan - Kirghizistan[15]										
2002										
Total	C	35 235	19 249	15 986	13 583	7 407	6 176	21 652	11 842	9 810
0 - 1	C	2 128	1 288	840	852	515	337	1 276	773	503
1 - 4	C	779	402	377	116	57	59	663	345	318
5 - 9	C	245	145	100	49	32	17	196	113	83
10 - 14	C	256	165	91	64	36	28	192	129	63
15 - 19	C	390	253	137	107	70	37	283	183	100
20 - 24	C	612	425	187	183	121	62	429	304	125
25 - 29	C	776	537	239	280	205	75	496	332	164
30 - 34	C	1 000	706	294	356	257	99	644	449	195
35 - 39	C	1 323	929	394	447	325	122	876	604	272
40 - 44	C	1 649	1 213	436	681	495	186	968	718	250
45 - 49	C	1 759	1 203	556	767	535	232	992	668	324
50 - 54	C	1 908	1 326	582	916	651	265	992	675	317
55 - 59	C	1 304	867	437	592	403	189	712	464	248
60 - 64	C	2 961	1 832	1 129	1 184	726	458	1 777	1 106	671
65 - 69	C	3 541	2 134	1 407	1 403	848	555	2 138	1 286	852
70 - 74	C	4 732	2 493	2 239	1 770	912	858	2 962	1 581	1 381
75 - 79	C	4 052	1 687	2 365	1 632	605	1 027	2 420	1 082	1 338
80 - 84	C	2 548	837	1 711	1 001	313	688	1 547	524	1 023

19. Deaths by age, sex and urban/rural residence: latest available year, 1993 - 2002
Décès selon l'âge, le sexe et la résidence, urbaine/rurale: dernière année disponible, 1993 - 2002 (continued — suite)

(See notes at end of table.— Voir notes à la fin du tableau.)

Continent, country or area, year and age (in years) / Continent, pays ou zone, année et âge (en années)	Code[1]	Total			Urban - Urbaine			Rural - Rurale		
		Both sexes - Les deux sexes	Male - Masculin	Female - Féminin	Both sexes - Les deux sexes	Male - Masculin	Female - Féminin	Both sexes - Les deux sexes	Male - Masculin	Female - Féminin
ASIA — ASIE										
Kyrgyzstan - Kirghizistan[15]										
2002										
85 - 89	C	1 659	457	1 202	707	187	520	952	270	682
90 - 94	C	958	239	719	351	79	272	607	160	447
95 - 99	C	336	57	279	76	15	61	260	42	218
100+	C	319	54	265	49	20	29	270	34	236
Malaysia - Malaisie[21]										
2000										
Total	C	104 859	60 793	44 066	53 723	31 170	22 553	35 457	20 347	15 110
0 - 1	C	3 578	2 026	1 552	1 678	953	725	1 265	721	544
1 - 4	C	1 282	694	588	555	301	254	540	294	246
5 - 9	C	836	500	336	336	194	142	343	214	129
10 - 14	C	961	597	364	402	256	146	377	242	135
15 - 19	C	1 966	1 480	486	984	748	236	741	562	179
20 - 24	C	2 229	1 677	552	1 072	799	273	813	623	190
25 - 29	C	2 281	1 746	535	1 166	909	257	768	600	168
30 - 34	C	2 669	2 000	669	1 418	1 085	333	863	651	212
35 - 39	C	3 249	2 337	912	1 772	1 325	447	968	681	287
40 - 44	C	4 078	2 793	1 285	2 274	1 621	653	1 191	790	401
45 - 49	C	4 728	3 090	1 638	2 636	1 793	843	1 327	827	500
50 - 54	C	6 106	3 901	2 205	3 273	2 130	1 143	1 912	1 212	700
55 - 59	C	7 070	4 485	2 585	3 719	2 401	1 318	2 179	1 358	821
60 - 64	C	9 943	6 103	3 840	5 144	3 158	1 986	3 396	2 094	1 302
65 - 69	C	11 029	6 257	4 772	5 618	3 198	2 420	3 640	2 020	1 620
70 - 74	C	12 160	6 622	5 538	6 047	3 269	2 778	4 384	2 339	2 045
75 - 79	C	11 807	5 874	5 933	5 761	2 765	2 996	4 315	2 125	2 190
80 - 84	C	9 179	4 272	4 907	4 662	2 083	2 579	3 263	1 508	1 755
85+	C	9 571	4 276	5 295	5 132	2 140	2 992	3 167	1 484	1 683
Unknown - Inconnu	C	137	63	74	74	42	32	5	2	3
Maldives										
2001										
Total	C	1 081	610	471	288	168	120	793	442	351
0 - 1	C	85	42	43	22	11	11	63	31	32
1 - 4	C	41	23	18	5	3	2	36	20	16
5 - 9	C	15	8	7	4	3	1	11	5	6
10 - 14	C	12	8	4	7	5	2	5	3	2
15 - 19	C	14	12	2	8	7	1	6	5	1
20 - 24	C	19	13	6	7	5	2	12	8	4
25 - 29	C	16	6	10	5	2	3	11	4	7
30 - 34	C	16	9	7	4	3	1	12	6	6
35 - 39	C	19	9	10	6	5	1	13	4	9
40 - 44	C	29	14	15	6	1	5	23	13	10
45 - 49	C	23	13	10	11	6	5	12	7	5
50 - 54	C	48	27	21	23	16	7	25	11	14
55 - 59	C	57	34	23	21	15	6	36	19	17
60 - 64	C	115	65	50	30	15	15	85	50	35
65 - 69	C	141	74	67	36	21	15	105	53	52
70+	C	427	253	174	93	50	43	334	203	131
Unknown - Inconnu	C	4	-	4	-	-	-	4	-	4
Mongolia - Mongolie										
2002										
Total	C	15 857	9 081	6 776	8 981	...	...	6 876	...	...
0 - 1	C	1 390	799	591	626	...	...	764	...	...
1 - 4	C	450	249	201	153	...	...	297	...	...
5 - 9	C	124	70	54	55	...	...	69	...	...
10 - 14	C	131	87	44	57	...	...	74	...	...
15 - 19	C	226	148	78	123	...	...	103	...	...
20 - 24	C	330	212	118	186	...	...	144	...	...
25 - 29	C	439	314	125	259	...	...	180	...	...
30 - 34	C	547	366	181	328	...	...	219	...	...
35 - 39	C	712	478	234	477	...	...	235	...	...

(See notes at end of table.— Voir notes à la fin du tableau.)

Continent, country or area, year and age (in years) Continent, pays ou zone, année et âge (en années)	Code[1]	Total			Urban - Urbaine			Rural - Rurale		
		Both sexes - Les deux sexes	Male - Masculin	Female - Féminin	Both sexes - Les deux sexes	Male - Masculin	Female - Féminin	Both sexes - Les deux sexes	Male - Masculin	Female - Féminin
ASIA — ASIE										
Mongolia - Mongolie										
2002										
40 - 44	C	899	569	330	585	...	...	314	...	...
45 - 49	C	896	598	298	559	...	...	337	...	...
50 - 54	C	1 001	600	401	645	...	...	356	...	...
55 - 59	C	1 020	591	429	587	...	...	433	...	...
60 - 64	C	1 472	891	581	818	...	...	654	...	...
65 - 69	C	1 542	929	613	853	...	...	689	...	...
70 - 74	C	1 545	831	714	860	...	...	685	...	...
75 - 79	C	1 216	598	618	716	...	...	500	...	...
80 - 84	C	963	431	532	570	...	...	393	...	...
85 - 89	C	609	204	405	344	...	...	265	...	...
90 - 94	C	258	88	170	136	...	...	122	...	...
95 - 99	C	62	21	41	34	...	...	28	...	...
100+	C	25	7	18	10	...	...	15	...	...
Myanmar[22,23]										
1994										
Total	U	...	...	...	80 421	...	...	86 579	...	...
0 - 1	U	...	...	...	12 168	...	...	13 177	...	...
1 - 4	U	...	...	...	6 543	...	...	7 399	...	...
5 - 14	U	...	...	...	5 333	...	...	5 118	...	...
15 - 24	U	...	...	...	4 812	...	...	4 978	...	...
25 - 34	U	...	...	...	5 288	...	...	6 030	...	...
35 - 44	U	...	...	...	6 202	...	...	5 701	...	...
45 - 54	U	...	...	...	8 173	...	...	6 927	...	...
55 - 64	U	...	...	...	10 256	...	...	10 187	...	...
65 - 74	U	...	...	...	10 633	...	...	12 403	...	...
75 - 84	U	...	...	...	7 846	...	...	10 713	...	...
85+	U	...	...	...	2 531	...	...	3 810	...	...
Unknown - Inconnu	U	...	...	...	636	...	...	136	...	...
Nepal - Népal[24]										
2001										
Total	I	106 789	59 544	47 245	...	...	...	...	...	...
0 - 1	I	13 037	6 956	6 081	...	...	...	...	...	...
1 - 4	I	9 790	5 590	4 200	...	...	...	...	...	...
5 - 9	I	3 320	1 726	1 594	...	...	...	...	...	...
10 - 14	I	2 304	1 332	972	...	...	...	...	...	...
15 - 19	I	2 523	1 293	1 230	...	...	...	...	...	...
20 - 24	I	2 747	1 449	1 298	...	...	...	...	...	...
25 - 29	I	2 688	1 429	1 259	...	...	...	...	...	...
30 - 34	I	2 474	1 303	1 172	...	...	...	...	...	...
35 - 39	I	2 839	1 594	1 244	...	...	...	...	...	...
40 - 44	I	2 970	1 828	1 142	...	...	...	...	...	...
45 - 49	I	3 553	2 027	1 526	...	...	...	...	...	...
50 - 54	I	4 662	2 771	1 891	...	...	...	...	...	...
55 - 59	I	6 115	3 612	2 503	...	...	...	...	...	...
60 - 64	I	8 337	4 710	3 626	...	...	...	...	...	...
65 - 69	I	8 667	4 764	3 903	...	...	...	...	...	...
70 - 74	I	9 606	5 512	4 093	...	...	...	...	...	...
75 - 79	I	8 113	4 657	3 456	...	...	...	...	...	...
80+	I	13 042	6 990	6 052	...	...	...	...	...	...
Occupied Palestinian Territory - Territoire palestinien occupé										
2002										
Total	U	9 216	5 432	3 784	...	...	...	...	...	...
0 - 1	U	1 043	554	489	...	...	...	...	...	...
1 - 4	U	284	156	128	...	...	...	...	...	...
5 - 9	U	179	109	70	...	...	...	...	...	...
10 - 14	U	144	88	56	...	...	...	...	...	...
15 - 19	U	290	247	43	...	...	...	...	...	...
20 - 24	U	339	300	39	...	...	...	...	...	...

(See notes at end of table.— Voir notes à la fin du tableau.)

Continent, country or area, year and age (in years) / Continent, pays ou zone, année et âge (en années)	Code[1]	Total			Urban - Urbaine			Rural - Rurale		
		Both sexes - Les deux sexes	Male - Masculin	Female - Féminin	Both sexes - Les deux sexes	Male - Masculin	Female - Féminin	Both sexes - Les deux sexes	Male - Masculin	Female - Féminin
ASIA — ASIE										
Occupied Palestinian Territory - Territoire palestinien occupé										
2002										
25 - 29	U	280	234	46	...	...	...	...	...	...
30 - 34	U	208	163	45	...	...	...	...	...	...
35 - 39	U	234	177	57	...	...	...	...	...	...
40 - 44	U	252	188	64	...	...	...	...	...	...
45 - 49	U	257	168	89	...	...	...	...	...	...
50 - 54	U	312	198	114	...	...	...	...	...	...
55 - 59	U	456	256	200	...	...	...	...	...	...
60 - 64	U	569	289	280	...	...	...	...	...	...
65 - 69	U	788	406	382	...	...	...	...	...	...
70 - 74	U	950	487	463	...	...	...	...	...	...
75 - 79	U	949	502	447	...	...	...	...	...	...
80 - 84	U	681	375	306	...	...	...	...	...	...
85 - 89	U	460	243	217	...	...	...	...	...	...
90 - 94	U	271	150	121	...	...	...	...	...	...
95 - 99	U	185	94	91	...	...	...	...	...	...
100+	U	85	48	37	...	...	...	...	...	...
Oman[25]										
2001										
Total	...	2 550	...	...	...	...	...	...	...	...
0 - 1	...	335	...	...	...	...	...	...	...	...
1 - 4	...	57	...	...	...	...	...	...	...	...
5 - 14	...	80	...	...	...	...	...	...	...	...
15 - 44	...	306	...	...	...	...	...	...	...	...
45+	...	1 772	...	...	...	...	...	...	...	...
Pakistan[26,27]										
2001										
Total	I	956 515	511 841	444 674	302 482	163 260	139 222	654 033	348 581	305 452
0 - 4	I	371 909	193 418	178 491	107 672	56 590	51 081	264 237	136 827	127 410
5 - 9	I	32 340	16 170	16 170	9 515	5 509	4 006	22 825	10 661	12 164
10 - 14	I	22 389	7 463	14 926	9 014	3 506	5 509	13 375	3 957	9 417
15 - 19	I	21 145	11 817	9 329	7 011	4 006	3 005	14 134	7 810	6 324
20 - 24	I	23 011	9 329	13 682	6 510	3 506	3 005	16 501	5 823	10 677
25 - 29	I	19 280	9 951	9 329	6 510	3 005	3 506	12 769	6 946	5 823
30 - 34	I	19 280	12 438	6 841	7 011	4 006	3 005	12 268	8 432	3 836
35 - 39	I	29 852	17 414	12 438	11 018	7 011	4 006	18 835	10 403	8 432
40 - 44	I	22 389	11 195	11 195	8 514	3 005	5 509	13 876	8 190	5 686
45 - 49	I	28 608	17 414	11 195	12 019	8 514	3 506	16 589	8 900	7 689
50 - 54	I	35 450	19 901	15 548	13 522	9 515	4 006	21 928	10 386	11 542
55 - 59	I	39 181	20 523	18 658	13 021	6 010	7 011	26 160	14 514	11 646
60 - 64	I	54 107	27 365	26 743	13 522	7 011	6 510	40 586	20 353	20 232
65 - 69	I	53 485	25 499	27 986	17 027	6 510	10 517	36 458	18 988	17 470
70+	I	184 089	111 946	72 143	60 597	35 557	25 040	123 492	76 389	47 103
Philippines										
2000										
Total	C	366 931	217 404	149 527	...	...	...	...	...	...
0 - 1	C	27 714	16 286	11 428	...	...	...	...	...	...
1 - 4	C	11 651	6 389	5 262	...	...	...	...	...	...
5 - 9	C	5 690	3 300	2 390	...	...	...	...	...	...
10 - 14	C	4 786	2 844	1 942	...	...	...	...	...	...
15 - 19	C	6 411	4 251	2 160	...	...	...	...	...	...
20 - 24	C	9 352	6 520	2 832	...	...	...	...	...	...
25 - 29	C	10 511	7 314	3 197	...	...	...	...	...	...
30 - 34	C	11 865	8 124	3 741	...	...	...	...	...	...
35 - 39	C	13 945	9 443	4 502	...	...	...	...	...	...
40 - 44	C	16 023	10 760	5 263	...	...	...	...	...	...
45 - 49	C	18 890	12 728	6 162	...	...	...	...	...	...
50 - 54	C	22 239	14 943	7 296	...	...	...	...	...	...
55 - 59	C	23 479	15 808	7 671	...	...	...	...	...	...

(See notes at end of table.— Voir notes à la fin du tableau.)

Continent, country or area, year and age (in years) Continent, pays ou zone, année et âge (en années)	Code[1]	Total			Urban - Urbaine			Rural - Rurale		
		Both sexes - Les deux sexes	Male - Masculin	Female - Féminin	Both sexes - Les deux sexes	Male - Masculin	Female - Féminin	Both sexes - Les deux sexes	Male - Masculin	Female - Féminin
ASIA — ASIE										
Philippines										
2000										
60 - 64	C	29 247	18 800	10 447	...	...	...	...	...	...
65 - 69	C	30 176	18 474	11 702	...	...	...	...	...	...
70 - 74	C	31 220	17 927	13 293	...	...	...	...	...	...
75 - 79	C	30 540	16 130	14 410	...	...	...	...	...	...
80 - 84	C	26 970	12 689	14 281	...	...	...	...	...	...
85 - 89	C	22 042	9 210	12 832	...	...	...	...	...	...
90 - 94	C	9 169	3 510	5 659	...	...	...	...	...	...
95+	C	4 499	1 648	2 851	...	...	...	...	...	...
Unknown - Inconnu	C	512	306	206	...	...	...	...	...	...
Qatar										
2001										
Total	C	1 210	831	379	...	...	...	...	...	...
0 - 1	C	111	58	53	...	...	...	...	...	...
1 - 4	C	26	17	9	...	...	...	...	...	...
5 - 9	C	23	13	10	...	...	...	...	...	...
10 - 14	C	12	6	6	...	...	...	...	...	...
15 - 19	C	27	23	4	...	...	...	...	...	...
20 - 24	C	40	38	2	...	...	...	...	...	...
25 - 29	C	31	26	5	...	...	...	...	...	...
30 - 34	C	60	51	9	...	...	...	...	...	...
35 - 39	C	64	51	13	...	...	...	...	...	...
40 - 44	C	65	48	17	...	...	...	...	...	...
45 - 49	C	87	71	16	...	...	...	...	...	...
50 - 54	C	82	66	16	...	...	...	...	...	...
55 - 59	C	79	57	22	...	...	...	...	...	...
60 - 64	C	93	65	28	...	...	...	...	...	...
65 - 69	C	119	69	50	...	...	...	...	...	...
70 - 74	C	100	59	41	...	...	...	...	...	...
75 - 79	C	75	48	27	...	...	...	...	...	...
80 - 84	C	62	30	32	...	...	...	...	...	...
85 - 89	C	23	15	8	...	...	...	...	...	...
90 - 94	C	17	10	7	...	...	...	...	...	...
95+	C	8	5	3	...	...	...	...	...	...
Unknown - Inconnu	C	6	5	1	...	...	...	...	...	...
Saudi Arabia - Arabie saoudite										
2000										
Total	...	51 614	28 632	22 982	...	...	...	...	...	...
0 - 1	...	11 071	5 818	5 253	...	...	...	...	...	...
1 - 4	...	1 903	525	1 378	...	...	...	...	...	...
5 - 9	...	1 173	1 173	-	...	...	...	...	...	...
10 - 14	...	1 092	980	112	...	...	...	...	...	...
15 - 19	...	1 098	1 060	38	...	...	...	...	...	...
20 - 24	...	813	813	-	...	...	...	...	...	...
25 - 29	...	1 361	1 361	-	...	...	...	...	...	...
30 - 34	...	693	476	217	...	...	...	...	...	...
35 - 39	...	646	441	205	...	...	...	...	...	...
40 - 44	...	2 547	1 528	1 019	...	...	...	...	...	...
45 - 49	...	1 011	747	264	...	...	...	...	...	...
50 - 54	...	1 919	1 025	894	...	...	...	...	...	...
55 - 59	...	3 695	1 751	1 944	...	...	...	...	...	...
60 - 64	...	3 068	1 663	1 405	...	...	...	...	...	...
65 - 69	...	2 858	1 570	1 288	...	...	...	...	...	...
70 - 74	...	4 431	1 962	2 469	...	...	...	...	...	...
75 - 79	...	2 651	1 186	1 465	...	...	...	...	...	...
80 - 84	...	1 536	851	685	...	...	...	...	...	...
85+	...	8 048	3 702	4 346	...	...	...	...	...	...
Singapore - Singapour[9,28]										
2002										
Total	+C	15 820	8 734	7 084	...	...	...	...	...	...

(See notes at end of table.— Voir notes à la fin du tableau.)

Continent, country or area, year and age (in years) / Continent, pays ou zone, année et âge (en années)	Code[1]	Total			Urban - Urbaine			Rural - Rurale		
		Both sexes - Les deux sexes	Male - Masculin	Female - Féminin	Both sexes - Les deux sexes	Male - Masculin	Female - Féminin	Both sexes - Les deux sexes	Male - Masculin	Female - Féminin
ASIA — ASIE										
Singapore - Singapour[9,28]										
2002										
0 - 1	+C	123	73	48	...	...	...	...	...	...
1 - 4	+C	34	20	14	...	...	...	...	...	...
5 - 9	+C	27	15	12	...	...	...	...	...	...
10 - 14	+C	32	20	12	...	...	...	...	...	...
15 - 19	+C	82	40	42	...	...	...	...	...	...
20 - 24	+C	155	100	55	...	...	...	...	...	...
25 - 29	+C	190	128	62	...	...	...	...	...	...
30 - 34	+C	223	149	74	...	...	...	...	...	...
35 - 39	+C	327	217	110	...	...	...	...	...	...
40 - 44	+C	446	310	136	...	...	...	...	...	...
45 - 49	+C	652	433	219	...	...	...	...	...	...
50 - 54	+C	866	532	334	...	...	...	...	...	...
55 - 59	+C	959	640	319	...	...	...	...	...	...
60 - 64	+C	1 355	841	514	...	...	...	...	...	...
65 - 69	+C	1 642	1 007	635	...	...	...	...	...	...
70 - 74	+C	2 052	1 150	902	...	...	...	...	...	...
75 - 79	+C	2 105	1 132	973	...	...	...	...	...	...
80 - 84	+C	1 914	914	1 000	...	...	...	...	...	...
85 - 89	+C	1 490	612	878	...	...	...	...	...	...
90 - 94	+C	806	297	509	...	...	...	...	...	...
95 - 99	+C	264	80	184	...	...	...	...	...	...
100+	+C	59	9	50	...	...	...	...	...	...
Unknown - Inconnu	+C	17	15	2	...	...	...	...	...	...
Sri Lanka										
1996										
Total	+C	122 161	79 784	42 377	60 131	39 546	20 585	62 030	40 238	21 792
0 - 1	+C	5 879	3 271	2 608	5 062	2 816	2 246	817	455	362
1 - 4	+C	1 237	667	570	805	432	373	432	235	197
5 - 9	+C	924	514	410	551	301	250	373	213	160
10 - 14	+C	990	550	440	562	292	270	428	258	170
15 - 19	+C	3 320	2 487	833	1 512	1 015	497	1 808	1 472	336
20 - 24	+C	6 180	5 241	939	2 828	2 279	549	3 352	2 962	390
25 - 29	+C	5 875	4 966	909	2 557	2 041	516	3 318	2 925	393
30 - 34	+C	4 712	3 875	837	2 177	1 673	504	2 535	2 202	333
35 - 39	+C	4 838	3 793	1 045	2 467	1 853	614	2 371	1 940	431
40 - 44	+C	4 607	3 585	1 022	2 650	2 048	602	1 957	1 537	420
45 - 49	+C	5 819	4 309	1 510	3 514	2 649	865	2 305	1 660	645
50 - 54	+C	6 387	4 511	1 876	3 883	2 806	1 077	2 504	1 705	799
55 - 59	+C	6 904	4 867	2 037	4 015	2 896	1 119	2 889	1 971	918
60 - 64	+C	8 431	5 529	2 902	4 598	3 143	1 455	3 833	2 386	1 447
65 - 69	+C	10 699	6 751	3 948	5 491	3 530	1 961	5 208	3 221	1 987
70 - 74	+C	12 549	7 424	5 125	5 884	3 538	2 346	6 665	3 886	2 779
75 - 79	+C	10 704	6 080	4 624	4 489	2 569	1 920	6 215	3 511	2 704
80 - 84	+C	10 071	5 404	4 667	3 609	1 950	1 659	6 462	3 454	3 008
85+	+C	12 035	5 960	6 075	3 477	1 715	1 762	8 558	4 245	4 313
Tajikistan - Tadjikistan[15]										
1994										
Total	C	39 943	21 339	18 604	13 068	7 083	5 985	26 875	14 256	12 619
0 - 1	C	6 880	3 896	2 984	1 930	1 136	794	4 950	2 760	2 190
1 - 4	C	5 267	2 742	2 525	745	402	343	4 522	2 340	2 182
5 - 9	C	753	416	337	145	88	57	608	328	280
10 - 14	C	522	315	207	120	82	38	402	233	169
15 - 19	C	671	440	231	204	142	62	467	298	169
20 - 24	C	902	574	328	302	203	99	600	371	229
25 - 29	C	984	626	358	310	220	90	674	406	268
30 - 34	C	1 106	668	438	381	260	121	725	408	317
35 - 39	C	983	594	389	378	264	114	605	330	275
40 - 44	C	1 035	646	389	489	327	162	546	319	227
45 - 49	C	890	546	344	405	271	134	485	275	210

19. Deaths by age, sex and urban/rural residence: latest available year, 1993 - 2002
Décès selon l'âge, le sexe et la résidence, urbaine/rurale: dernière année disponible, 1993 - 2002 (continued — suite)

(See notes at end of table.— Voir notes à la fin du tableau.)

Continent, country or area, year and age (in years) / Continent, pays ou zone, année et âge (en années)	Code[1]	Total			Urban - Urbaine			Rural - Rurale		
		Both sexes - Les deux sexes	Male - Masculin	Female - Féminin	Both sexes - Les deux sexes	Male - Masculin	Female - Féminin	Both sexes - Les deux sexes	Male - Masculin	Female - Féminin
ASIA — ASIE										
Tajikistan - Tadjikistan[15]										
1994										
50 - 54	C	1 219	795	424	556	383	173	663	412	251
55 - 59	C	2 154	1 283	871	934	612	322	1 220	671	549
60 - 64	C	2 783	1 541	1 242	1 009	578	431	1 774	963	811
65 - 69	C	3 108	1 695	1 413	1 232	660	572	1 876	1 035	841
70 - 74	C	2 803	1 254	1 549	1 038	438	600	1 765	816	949
75 - 79	C	2 264	983	1 281	917	351	566	1 347	632	715
80 - 84	C	2 380	1 013	1 367	1 013	344	669	1 367	669	698
85+	C	3 219	1 299	1 920	949	315	634	2 270	984	1 286
Unknown - Inconnu	C	20	13	7	11	7	4	9	6	3
Thailand - Thaïlande										
1999										
Total	+U	362 593	213 427	149 166	36 796	21 674	15 122	325 797	191 753	134 044
0 - 1	+U	5 003	2 765	2 238	711	359	352	4 292	2 406	1 886
1 - 4	+U	5 948	3 193	2 755	451	246	205	5 497	2 947	2 550
5 - 9	+U	3 040	1 804	1 236	184	106	78	2 856	1 698	1 158
10 - 14	+U	2 162	1 300	862	181	112	69	1 981	1 188	793
15 - 19	+U	6 504	4 861	1 643	553	408	145	5 951	4 453	1 498
20 - 24	+U	11 727	8 192	3 535	1 280	972	308	10 447	7 220	3 227
25 - 29	+U	22 108	16 139	5 969	1 860	1 447	413	20 248	14 692	5 556
30 - 34	+U	23 928	18 116	5 812	2 242	1 715	527	21 686	16 401	5 285
35 - 39	+U	20 640	15 414	5 226	2 120	1 607	513	18 520	13 807	4 713
40 - 44	+U	18 982	13 089	5 893	2 120	1 480	640	16 862	11 609	5 253
45 - 49	+U	18 489	12 071	6 418	2 107	1 380	727	16 382	10 691	5 691
50 - 54	+U	18 660	11 727	6 933	2 017	1 267	750	16 643	10 460	6 183
55 - 59	+U	21 563	13 072	8 491	2 322	1 419	903	19 241	11 653	7 588
60 - 64	+U	27 435	16 057	11 378	3 029	1 810	1 219	24 406	14 247	10 159
65 - 69	+U	31 442	17 504	13 938	3 299	1 895	1 404	28 143	15 609	12 534
70 - 74	+U	32 171	17 261	14 910	3 202	1 660	1 542	28 969	15 601	13 368
75 - 79	+U	30 537	15 485	15 052	2 971	1 449	1 522	27 566	14 036	13 530
80 - 84	+U	26 406	11 901	14 505	2 803	1 203	1 600	23 603	10 698	12 905
85+	+U	32 613	12 063	20 550	3 292	1 118	2 174	29 321	10 945	18 376
Unknown - Inconnu	+U	3 235	1 413	1 822	52	21	31	3 183	1 392	1 791
Uzbekistan - Ouzbékistan[15]										
2000										
Total	C	135 598	70 794	64 804	61 130	32 195	28 935	74 468	38 599	35 869
0 - 1	C	10 091	5 805	4 286	3 703	2 136	1 567	6 388	3 669	2 719
1 - 4	C	5 417	2 925	2 492	1 177	645	532	4 240	2 280	1 960
5 - 9	C	1 474	886	588	423	251	172	1 051	635	416
10 - 14	C	1 436	852	584	442	260	182	994	592	402
15 - 19	C	2 001	1 289	712	709	475	234	1 292	814	478
20 - 24	C	2 849	1 758	1 091	1 155	789	366	1 694	969	725
25 - 29	C	3 427	2 177	1 250	1 501	1 023	478	1 926	1 154	772
30 - 34	C	3 660	2 403	1 257	1 657	1 185	472	2 003	1 218	785
35 - 39	C	4 181	2 759	1 422	1 993	1 407	586	2 188	1 352	836
40 - 44	C	5 086	3 277	1 809	2 584	1 789	795	2 502	1 488	1 014
45 - 49	C	5 290	3 445	1 845	2 797	1 924	873	2 493	1 521	972
50 - 54	C	5 765	3 647	2 118	3 140	2 052	1 088	2 625	1 595	1 030
55 - 59	C	6 104	3 794	2 310	3 056	1 990	1 066	3 048	1 804	1 244
60 - 64	C	12 287	7 257	5 030	5 897	3 603	2 294	6 390	3 654	2 736
65 - 69	C	14 077	7 757	6 320	6 312	3 601	2 711	7 765	4 156	3 609
70 - 74	C	17 094	8 713	8 381	8 142	4 010	4 132	8 952	4 703	4 249
75 - 79	C	12 547	4 824	7 723	6 043	2 111	3 932	6 504	2 713	3 791
80 - 84	C	8 807	2 836	5 971	4 430	1 285	3 145	4 377	1 551	2 826
85 - 89	C	7 198	2 312	4 886	3 747	1 011	2 736	3 451	1 301	2 150
90 - 94	C	3 782	1 295	2 487	1 515	421	1 094	2 267	874	1 393
95 - 99	C	1 963	579	1 384	511	167	344	1 452	412	1 040
100+	C	1 062	204	858	196	60	136	866	144	722

19. Deaths by age, sex and urban/rural residence: latest available year, 1993 - 2002
Décès selon l'âge, le sexe et la résidence, urbaine/rurale: dernière année disponible, 1993 - 2002 (continued — suite)

(See notes at end of table.— Voir notes à la fin du tableau.)

Continent, country or area, year and age (in years) / Continent, pays ou zone, année et âge (en années)	Code[1]	Total			Urban - Urbaine			Rural - Rurale		
		Both sexes - Les deux sexes	Male - Masculin	Female - Féminin	Both sexes - Les deux sexes	Male - Masculin	Female - Féminin	Both sexes - Les deux sexes	Male - Masculin	Female - Féminin
EUROPE										
Andorra - Andorre										
1994										
Total	C	184	105	79	...	...	...	...	...	...
0 - 1	C	2	1	1	...	...	...	...	...	...
10 - 14	C	1	-	1	...	...	...	...	...	...
15 - 19	C	2	1	1	...	...	...	...	...	...
20 - 24	C	1	-	1	...	...	...	...	...	...
25 - 29	C	11	6	5	...	...	...	...	...	...
30 - 34	C	3	3	-	...	...	...	...	...	...
35 - 39	C	6	5	1	...	...	...	...	...	...
40 - 44	C	4	1	3	...	...	...	...	...	...
45 - 49	C	6	4	2	...	...	...	...	...	...
50 - 54	C	8	6	2	...	...	...	...	...	...
55 - 59	C	12	7	5	...	...	...	...	...	...
60 - 64	C	12	9	3	...	...	...	...	...	...
65 - 69	C	19	12	7	...	...	...	...	...	...
70 - 74	C	14	6	8	...	...	...	...	...	...
75 - 79	C	27	16	11	...	...	...	...	...	...
80 - 84	C	19	10	9	...	...	...	...	...	...
85+	C	37	18	19	...	...	...	...	...	...
Austria - Autriche										
1999										
Total	C	78 200	35 880	42 320	46 752	20 596	26 156	31 448	15 284	16 164
0 - 1	C	341	176	165	191	100	91	150	76	74
1 - 4	C	98	67	31	51	37	14	47	30	17
5 - 9	C	51	28	23	25	11	14	26	17	9
10 - 14	C	72	36	36	38	17	21	34	19	15
15 - 19	C	276	197	79	116	78	38	160	119	41
20 - 24	C	330	257	73	177	136	41	153	121	32
25 - 29	C	348	251	97	183	132	51	165	119	46
30 - 34	C	512	352	160	313	201	112	199	151	48
35 - 39	C	806	550	256	472	324	148	334	226	108
40 - 44	C	1 075	714	361	621	406	215	454	308	146
45 - 49	C	1 433	922	511	848	523	325	585	399	186
50 - 54	C	2 251	1 468	783	1 425	916	509	826	552	274
55 - 59	C	3 554	2 373	1 181	2 238	1 464	774	1 316	909	407
60 - 64	C	3 939	2 654	1 285	2 194	1 461	733	1 745	1 193	552
65 - 69	C	6 004	3 939	2 065	3 267	2 091	1 176	2 737	1 848	889
70 - 74	C	8 963	5 084	3 879	5 131	2 793	2 338	3 832	2 291	1 541
75 - 79	C	12 409	5 726	6 683	7 297	3 256	4 041	5 112	2 470	2 642
80 - 84	C	10 218	3 965	6 253	6 134	2 373	3 761	4 084	1 592	2 492
85+	C	25 520	7 121	18 399	16 031	4 277	11 754	9 489	2 844	6 645
2002										
Total	C	76 131	35 166	40 965	...	...	...	...	...	...
0 - 1	C	318	189	129	...	...	...	...	...	...
1 - 4	C	63	39	24	...	...	...	...	...	...
5 - 9	C	47	31	16	...	...	...	...	...	...
10 - 14	C	59	30	29	...	...	...	...	...	...
15 - 19	C	248	179	69	...	...	...	...	...	...
20 - 24	C	305	232	73	...	...	...	...	...	...
25 - 29	C	327	244	83	...	...	...	...	...	...
30 - 34	C	425	303	122	...	...	...	...	...	...
35 - 39	C	700	460	240	...	...	...	...	...	...
40 - 44	C	1 079	719	360	...	...	...	...	...	...
45 - 49	C	1 432	943	489	...	...	...	...	...	...
50 - 54	C	2 258	1 527	731	...	...	...	...	...	...
55 - 59	C	3 000	1 997	1 003	...	...	...	...	...	...
60 - 64	C	4 382	2 938	1 444	...	...	...	...	...	...
65 - 69	C	4 901	3 119	1 782	...	...	...	...	...	...
70 - 74	C	8 130	4 892	3 238	...	...	...	...	...	...
75 - 79	C	11 952	5 621	6 331	...	...	...	...	...	...

19. Deaths by age, sex and urban/rural residence: latest available year, 1993 - 2002
Décès selon l'âge, le sexe et la résidence, urbaine/rurale: dernière année disponible, 1993 - 2002 (continued — suite)

(See notes at end of table.— Voir notes à la fin du tableau.)

Continent, country or area, year and age (in years) / Continent, pays ou zone, année et âge (en années)	Code[1]	Total			Urban - Urbaine			Rural - Rurale		
		Both sexes - Les deux sexes	Male - Masculin	Female - Féminin	Both sexes - Les deux sexes	Male - Masculin	Female - Féminin	Both sexes - Les deux sexes	Male - Masculin	Female - Féminin
EUROPE										
Austria - Autriche										
2002										
80 - 84	C	12 484	4 905	7 579	...	...	...	...	...	...
85 - 89	C	12 053	3 824	8 229	...	...	...	...	...	...
90 - 94	C	9 109	2 416	6 693	...	...	...	...	...	...
95 - 99	C	2 549	521	2 028	...	...	...	...	...	...
100+	C	310	37	273	...	...	...	...	...	...
Belarus - Bélarus[15]										
2002										
Total	C	146 655	77 583	69 072	77 020	42 900	34 120	69 635	34 683	34 952
0 - 1	C	695	397	298	454	263	191	241	134	107
1 - 4	C	285	172	113	138	81	57	147	91	56
5 - 9	C	172	98	74	87	49	38	85	49	36
10 - 14	C	218	147	71	121	79	42	97	68	29
15 - 19	C	652	466	186	412	285	127	240	181	59
20 - 24	C	1 170	911	259	719	541	178	451	370	81
25 - 29	C	1 700	1 386	314	1 086	872	214	614	514	100
30 - 34	C	2 163	1 719	444	1 302	1 008	294	861	711	150
35 - 39	C	3 179	2 568	611	1 942	1 545	397	1 237	1 023	214
40 - 44	C	5 212	4 114	1 098	3 288	2 512	776	1 924	1 602	322
45 - 49	C	6 681	5 094	1 587	4 448	3 332	1 116	2 233	1 762	471
50 - 54	C	8 651	6 396	2 255	5 716	4 168	1 548	2 935	2 228	707
55 - 59	C	7 551	5 214	2 337	4 802	3 376	1 426	2 749	1 838	911
60 - 64	C	14 231	9 557	4 674	8 369	5 673	2 696	5 862	3 884	1 978
65 - 69	C	16 814	10 210	6 604	8 588	5 251	3 337	8 226	4 959	3 267
70 - 74	C	22 622	12 151	10 471	10 902	5 762	5 140	11 720	6 389	5 331
75 - 79	C	21 849	8 415	13 434	10 469	4 085	6 384	11 380	4 330	7 050
80 - 84	C	13 949	4 209	9 740	6 473	2 004	4 469	7 476	2 205	5 271
85 - 89	C	10 327	2 477	7 850	4 437	1 166	3 271	5 890	1 311	4 579
90 - 94	C	6 070	1 262	4 808	2 274	497	1 777	3 796	765	3 031
95 - 99	C	1 720	327	1 393	612	123	489	1 108	204	904
100+	C	460	66	394	123	22	101	337	44	293
Unknown - Inconnu	C	284	227	57	258	206	52	26	21	5
Belgium - Belgique[29]										
2002										
Total	C	105 642	52 436	53 206	...	...	...	...	...	...
0 - 1	C	492	288	204	...	...	...	...	...	...
1 - 4	C	127	74	53	...	...	...	...	...	...
5 - 9	C	87	53	34	...	...	...	...	...	...
10 - 14	C	88	46	42	...	...	...	...	...	...
15 - 19	C	282	200	82	...	...	...	...	...	...
20 - 24	C	450	348	102	...	...	...	...	...	...
25 - 29	C	498	361	137	...	...	...	...	...	...
30 - 34	C	595	406	189	...	...	...	...	...	...
35 - 39	C	921	610	311	...	...	...	...	...	...
40 - 44	C	1 400	905	495	...	...	...	...	...	...
45 - 49	C	2 239	1 462	777	...	...	...	...	...	...
50 - 54	C	3 232	2 062	1 170	...	...	...	...	...	...
55 - 59	C	4 095	2 683	1 412	...	...	...	...	...	...
60 - 64	C	5 057	3 291	1 766	...	...	...	...	...	...
65 - 69	C	7 919	5 125	2 794	...	...	...	...	...	...
70 - 74	C	12 038	7 409	4 629	...	...	...	...	...	...
75 - 79	C	17 080	9 516	7 564	...	...	...	...	...	...
80 - 84	C	17 439	8 112	9 327	...	...	...	...	...	...
85 - 89	C	15 974	5 672	10 302	...	...	...	...	...	...
90 - 94	C	11 457	3 021	8 436	...	...	...	...	...	...
95 - 99	C	3 645	718	2 927	...	...	...	...	...	...
100+	C	527	74	453	...	...	...	...	...	...

19. Deaths by age, sex and urban/rural residence: latest available year, 1993 - 2002
Décès selon l'âge, le sexe et la résidence, urbaine/rurale: dernière année disponible, 1993 - 2002 (continued — suite)

(See notes at end of table.— Voir notes à la fin du tableau.)

Continent, country or area, year and age (in years) / Continent, pays ou zone, année et âge (en années)	Code[1]	Total			Urban - Urbaine			Rural - Rurale		
		Both sexes - Les deux sexes	Male - Masculin	Female - Féminin	Both sexes - Les deux sexes	Male - Masculin	Female - Féminin	Both sexes - Les deux sexes	Male - Masculin	Female - Féminin
EUROPE										
Bosnia and Herzegovina - Bosnie-Herzégovine										
1998										
Total	C	28 679	15 303	13 376						
0 - 1	C	483	294	189	...	...	...	...	...	...
1 - 4	C	99	62	37	...	...	...	...	...	...
5 - 9	C	62	40	22	...	...	...	...	...	...
10 - 14	C	53	34	19	...	...	...	...	...	...
15 - 19	C	108	84	24	...	...	...	...	...	...
20 - 24	C	182	126	56	...	...	...	...	...	...
25 - 29	C	193	141	52	...	...	...	...	...	...
30 - 34	C	269	189	80	...	...	...	...	...	...
35 - 39	C	409	276	133	...	...	...	...	...	...
40 - 44	C	698	485	213	...	...	...	...	...	...
45 - 49	C	931	617	314	...	...	...	...	...	...
50 - 54	C	1 164	776	388	...	...	...	...	...	...
55 - 59	C	2 012	1 332	680	...	...	...	...	...	...
60 - 64	C	3 683	2 260	1 423	...	...	...	...	...	...
65 - 69	C	4 851	2 838	2 013	...	...	...	...	...	...
70 - 74	C	4 733	2 272	2 461	...	...	...	...	...	...
75 - 79	C	3 761	1 522	2 239	...	...	...	...	...	...
80 - 84	C	2 102	797	1 305	...	...	...	...	...	...
85+	C	2 782	1 102	1 680	...	...	...	...	...	...
Unknown - Inconnu	C	104	56	48	...	...	...	...	...	...
Bulgaria - Bulgarie										
2002										
Total	C	112 617	59 942	52 675	63 765	34 261	29 504	48 852	25 681	23 171
0 - 1	C	887	495	392	571	319	252	316	176	140
1 - 4	C	174	100	74	95	57	38	79	43	36
5 - 9	C	99	56	43	55	26	29	44	30	14
10 - 14	C	120	79	41	79	54	25	41	25	16
15 - 19	C	244	171	73	174	119	55	70	52	18
20 - 24	C	428	301	127	311	217	94	117	84	33
25 - 29	C	492	365	127	345	252	93	147	113	34
30 - 34	C	680	467	213	472	314	158	208	153	55
35 - 39	C	996	667	329	661	422	239	335	245	90
40 - 44	C	1 735	1 239	496	1 185	806	379	550	433	117
45 - 49	C	2 905	2 060	845	2 015	1 381	634	890	679	211
50 - 54	C	4 851	3 452	1 399	3 345	2 312	1 033	1 506	1 140	366
55 - 59	C	6 111	4 255	1 856	4 004	2 787	1 217	2 107	1 468	639
60 - 64	C	7 820	5 203	2 617	4 756	3 172	1 584	3 064	2 031	1 033
65 - 69	C	12 219	7 421	4 798	7 015	4 208	2 807	5 204	3 213	1 991
70 - 74	C	16 849	9 299	7 550	9 426	5 187	4 239	7 423	4 112	3 311
75 - 79	C	22 178	10 590	11 588	11 860	5 623	6 237	10 318	4 967	5 351
80 - 84	C	17 394	7 499	9 895	9 027	3 898	5 129	8 367	3 601	4 766
85 - 89	C	10 282	4 024	6 258	5 255	2 034	3 221	5 027	1 990	3 037
90 - 94	C	5 142	1 862	3 280	2 598	908	1 690	2 544	954	1 590
95 - 99	C	928	304	624	467	141	326	461	163	298
100+	C	83	33	50	49	24	25	34	9	25
Channel Islands: Guernsey - Îles Anglo-Normandes: Guernesey										
2000										
Total	C	565	264	301						
0 - 1	C	4	3	1	...	...	...	...	...	...
1 - 4	C	1	-	1	...	...	...	...	...	...
15 - 19	C	4	3	1	...	...	...	...	...	...
20 - 24	C	1	-	1	...	...	...	...	...	...
25 - 29	C	1	1	-	...	...	...	...	...	...
30 - 34	C	2	1	1	...	...	...	...	...	...
35 - 39	C	2	2	-	...	...	...	...	...	...

19. Deaths by age, sex and urban/rural residence: latest available year, 1993 - 2002
Décès selon l'âge, le sexe et la résidence, urbaine/rurale: dernière année disponible, 1993 - 2002 (continued — suite)

(See notes at end of table.— Voir notes à la fin du tableau.)

Continent, country or area, year and age (in years) / Continent, pays ou zone, année et âge (en années)	Code[1]	Total			Urban - Urbaine			Rural - Rurale		
		Both sexes - Les deux sexes	Male - Masculin	Female - Féminin	Both sexes - Les deux sexes	Male - Masculin	Female - Féminin	Both sexes - Les deux sexes	Male - Masculin	Female - Féminin
EUROPE										
Channel Islands: Guernsey - Îles Anglo-Normandes: Guernesey										
2000										
40 - 44	C	4	4	-	...	...	...	...	...	...
45 - 49	C	7	5	2	...	...	...	...	...	...
50 - 54	C	13	9	4	...	...	...	...	...	...
55 - 59	C	13	7	6	...	...	...	...	...	...
60 - 64	C	30	15	15	...	...	...	...	...	...
65 - 69	C	45	29	16	...	...	...	...	...	...
70 - 74	C	57	27	30	...	...	...	...	...	...
75 - 79	C	71	38	33	...	...	...	...	...	...
80 - 84	C	103	55	48	...	...	...	...	...	...
85 - 89	C	108	45	63	...	...	...	...	...	...
90 - 94	C	68	14	54	...	...	...	...	...	...
95 - 99	C	24	3	21	...	...	...	...	...	...
100+	C	5	2	3	...	...	...	...	...	...
Unknown - Inconnu	C	2	1	1	...	...	...	...	...	...
Channel Islands: Jersey - Îles Anglo-Normandes: Jersey										
1994										
Total	+C	803	368	435	...	...	...	...	...	...
0 - 1	+C	2	-	2	...	...	...	...	...	...
5 - 9	+C	3	2	1	...	...	...	...	...	...
15 - 19	+C	5	3	2	...	...	...	...	...	...
20 - 24	+C	1	-	1	...	...	...	...	...	...
25 - 29	+C	2	1	1	...	...	...	...	...	...
30 - 34	+C	5	4	1	...	...	...	...	...	...
35 - 39	+C	5	3	2	...	...	...	...	...	...
40 - 44	+C	9	7	2	...	...	...	...	...	...
45 - 49	+C	23	11	12	...	...	...	...	...	...
50 - 54	+C	17	8	9	...	...	...	...	...	...
55 - 59	+C	30	24	6	...	...	...	...	...	...
60 - 64	+C	48	36	12	...	...	...	...	...	...
65 - 69	+C	55	34	21	...	...	...	...	...	...
70 - 74	+C	101	47	54	...	...	...	...	...	...
75+	+C	497	188	309	...	...	...	...	...	...
Croatia - Croatie										
2002										
Total	C	50 569	25 731	24 838	24 984	12 648	12 336	25 585	13 083	12 502
0 - 1	C	282	159	123	144	81	63	138	78	60
1 - 4	C	54	33	21	29	15	14	25	18	7
5 - 9	C	36	22	14	19	14	5	17	8	9
10 - 14	C	28	20	8	14	11	3	14	9	5
15 - 19	C	146	107	39	85	64	21	61	43	18
20 - 24	C	250	191	59	130	101	29	120	90	30
25 - 29	C	207	167	40	120	94	26	87	73	14
30 - 34	C	254	189	65	130	92	38	124	97	27
35 - 39	C	408	286	122	203	140	63	205	146	59
40 - 44	C	742	536	206	355	238	117	387	298	89
45 - 49	C	1 342	963	379	677	442	235	665	521	144
50 - 54	C	1 945	1 418	527	1 054	736	318	891	682	209
55 - 59	C	2 234	1 549	685	1 200	802	398	1 034	747	287
60 - 64	C	3 794	2 623	1 171	1 924	1 306	618	1 870	1 317	553
65 - 69	C	6 136	3 855	2 281	3 072	1 899	1 173	3 064	1 956	1 108
70 - 74	C	8 229	4 658	3 571	3 932	2 213	1 719	4 297	2 445	1 852
75 - 79	C	8 974	3 852	5 122	4 399	1 875	2 524	4 575	1 977	2 598
80 - 84	C	7 090	2 625	4 465	3 375	1 300	2 075	3 715	1 325	2 390
85 - 89	C	4 774	1 499	3 275	2 338	744	1 594	2 436	755	1 681
90 - 94	C	2 975	818	2 157	1 446	405	1 041	1 529	413	1 116
95 - 99	C	601	136	465	302	65	237	299	71	228

(See notes at end of table.— Voir notes à la fin du tableau.)

Continent, country or area, year and age (in years) / Continent, pays ou zone, année et âge (en années)	Code[1]	Total			Urban - Urbaine			Rural - Rurale		
		Both sexes - Les deux sexes	Male - Masculin	Female - Féminin	Both sexes - Les deux sexes	Male - Masculin	Female - Féminin	Both sexes - Les deux sexes	Male - Masculin	Female - Féminin
EUROPE										
Croatia - Croatie										
2002										
100+	C	53	14	39	28	6	22	25	8	17
Unknown - Inconnu	C	15	11	4	8	5	3	7	6	1
Czech Republic - République tchèque										
2002										
Total	C	108 243	54 377	53 866	78 023	38 971	39 052	30 220	15 406	14 814
0 - 1	C	385	216	169	288	157	131	97	59	38
1 - 4	C	100	60	40	78	47	31	22	13	9
5 - 9	C	82	51	31	61	41	20	21	10	11
10 - 14	C	91	54	37	62	37	25	29	17	12
15 - 19	C	319	218	101	224	151	73	95	67	28
20 - 24	C	527	406	121	394	302	92	133	104	29
25 - 29	C	602	455	147	443	331	112	159	124	35
30 - 34	C	611	439	172	451	321	130	160	118	42
35 - 39	C	861	601	260	620	434	186	241	167	74
40 - 44	C	1 404	989	415	1 000	690	310	404	299	105
45 - 49	C	2 869	2 021	848	2 086	1 432	654	783	589	194
50 - 54	C	4 896	3 442	1 454	3 568	2 459	1 109	1 328	983	345
55 - 59	C	6 644	4 552	2 092	4 912	3 334	1 578	1 732	1 218	514
60 - 64	C	7 278	4 915	2 363	5 307	3 549	1 758	1 971	1 366	605
65 - 69	C	9 554	5 988	3 566	6 891	4 302	2 589	2 663	1 686	977
70 - 74	C	14 710	8 117	6 593	10 479	5 770	4 709	4 231	2 347	1 884
75 - 79	C	19 158	8 896	10 262	13 757	6 344	7 413	5 401	2 552	2 849
80 - 84	C	16 587	6 493	10 094	11 975	4 691	7 284	4 612	1 802	2 810
85 - 89	C	12 454	4 129	8 325	8 910	2 924	5 986	3 544	1 205	2 339
90 - 94	C	7 468	2 030	5 438	5 306	1 432	3 874	2 162	598	1 564
95 - 99	C	1 510	285	1 225	1 116	208	908	394	77	317
100+	C	133	20	113	95	15	80	38	5	33
Denmark - Danemark[30]										
2002										
Total	C	58 610	28 321	30 289	...	...	...	...	...	...
0 - 1	C	284	159	125	...	...	...	...	...	...
1 - 4	C	68	33	35	...	...	...	...	...	...
5 - 9	C	32	22	10	...	...	...	...	...	...
10 - 14	C	38	21	17	...	...	...	...	...	...
15 - 19	C	128	91	37	...	...	...	...	...	...
20 - 24	C	167	125	42	...	...	...	...	...	...
25 - 29	C	207	144	63	...	...	...	...	...	...
30 - 34	C	302	214	88	...	...	...	...	...	...
35 - 39	C	513	333	180	...	...	...	...	...	...
40 - 44	C	732	469	263	...	...	...	...	...	...
45 - 49	C	1 134	689	445	...	...	...	...	...	...
50 - 54	C	1 874	1 177	697	...	...	...	...	...	...
55 - 59	C	2 910	1 777	1 133	...	...	...	...	...	...
60 - 64	C	3 327	1 992	1 335	...	...	...	...	...	...
65 - 69	C	4 564	2 627	1 937	...	...	...	...	...	...
70 - 74	C	6 313	3 500	2 813	...	...	...	...	...	...
75 - 79	C	8 542	4 463	4 079	...	...	...	...	...	...
80 - 84	C	9 902	4 669	5 233	...	...	...	...	...	...
85 - 89	C	9 228	3 524	5 704	...	...	...	...	...	...
90 - 94	C	6 078	1 830	4 248	...	...	...	...	...	...
95 - 99	C	1 966	422	1 544	...	...	...	...	...	...
100+	C	301	40	261	...	...	...	...	...	...
Estonia - Estonie[7,15]										
2002										
Total	C	18 355	9 369	8 986	11 953	6 078	5 875	6 276	3 189	3 087
0 - 1	C	74	46	28	53	35	18	21	11	10
1 - 4	C	24	18	6	9	7	2	15	11	4
5 - 9	C	24	15	9	16	10	6	8	5	3

19. Deaths by age, sex and urban/rural residence: latest available year, 1993 - 2002
Décès selon l'âge, le sexe et la résidence, urbaine/rurale: dernière année disponible, 1993 - 2002 (continued — suite)

(See notes at end of table.— Voir notes à la fin du tableau.)

Continent, country or area, year and age (in years) / Continent, pays ou zone, année et âge (en années)	Code[1]	Total			Urban - Urbaine			Rural - Rurale		
		Both sexes - Les deux sexes	Male - Masculin	Female - Féminin	Both sexes - Les deux sexes	Male - Masculin	Female - Féminin	Both sexes - Les deux sexes	Male - Masculin	Female - Féminin
EUROPE										
Estonia - Estonie[7,15]										
2002										
10 - 14	C	19	13	6	12	8	4	7	5	2
15 - 19	C	95	78	17	71	57	14	22	19	3
20 - 24	C	172	143	29	127	106	21	44	36	8
25 - 29	C	162	139	23	114	98	16	47	40	7
30 - 34	C	225	179	46	156	118	38	69	61	8
35 - 39	C	293	235	58	205	161	44	85	72	13
40 - 44	C	518	377	141	374	270	104	135	101	34
45 - 49	C	773	575	198	550	408	142	212	158	54
50 - 54	C	997	716	281	678	474	204	309	236	73
55 - 59	C	980	679	301	614	425	189	355	245	110
60 - 64	C	1 616	1 117	499	1 074	717	357	538	396	142
65 - 69	C	1 885	1 220	665	1 214	773	441	667	443	224
70 - 74	C	2 536	1 376	1 160	1 724	923	801	811	452	359
75 - 79	C	2 524	994	1 530	1 673	647	1 026	849	346	503
80 - 84	C	2 100	665	1 435	1 288	396	892	812	269	543
85 - 89	C	1 748	436	1 312	1 071	273	798	677	163	514
90 - 94	C	1 159	215	944	708	124	584	450	91	359
95 - 99	C	304	58	246	174	30	144	130	28	102
100+	C	42	3	39	29	2	27	13	1	12
Unknown - Inconnu	C	85	72	13	19	16	3	...	...	...
Finland - Finlande[31]										
2002										
Total	C	49 418	23 992	25 426	27 591	13 001	14 590	21 827	10 991	10 836
0 - 1	C	168	91	77	109	60	49	59	31	28
1 - 4	C	37	24	13	18	12	6	19	12	7
5 - 9	C	41	21	20	27	12	15	14	9	5
10 - 14	C	37	25	12	17	11	6	20	14	6
15 - 19	C	152	109	43	85	61	24	67	48	19
20 - 24	C	243	187	56	164	118	46	79	69	10
25 - 29	C	210	168	42	148	116	32	62	52	10
30 - 34	C	320	225	95	210	144	66	110	81	29
35 - 39	C	499	356	143	322	223	99	177	133	44
40 - 44	C	761	526	235	484	330	154	277	196	81
45 - 49	C	1 224	842	382	760	515	245	464	327	137
50 - 54	C	1 962	1 361	601	1 185	790	395	777	571	206
55 - 59	C	2 255	1 560	695	1 338	900	438	917	660	257
60 - 64	C	2 649	1 819	830	1 548	1 022	526	1 101	797	304
65 - 69	C	3 459	2 306	1 153	1 982	1 270	712	1 477	1 036	441
70 - 74	C	5 549	3 416	2 133	3 023	1 772	1 251	2 526	1 644	882
75 - 79	C	7 411	3 841	3 570	3 955	1 947	2 008	3 456	1 894	1 562
80 - 84	C	8 158	3 278	4 880	4 386	1 719	2 667	3 772	1 559	2 213
85 - 89	C	7 832	2 348	5 484	4 244	1 237	3 007	3 588	1 111	2 477
90 - 94	C	4 990	1 195	3 795	2 770	602	2 168	2 220	593	1 627
95 - 99	C	1 303	268	1 035	730	128	602	573	140	433
100+	C	158	26	132	86	12	74	72	14	58
France[32,33,34]										
1999										
Total	C	535 759	273 616	262 143	378 644	190 271	188 373	157 115	83 345	73 770
0 - 1	C	3 195	1 828	1 367	2 551	1 453	1 098	644	375	269
1 - 4	C	692	395	297	513	292	221	179	103	76
5 - 9	C	469	255	214	337	179	158	132	76	56
10 - 14	C	574	341	233	403	244	159	171	97	74
15 - 19	C	1 964	1 434	530	1 288	923	365	676	511	165
20 - 24	C	2 775	2 088	687	1 972	1 472	500	803	616	187
25 - 29	C	3 220	2 355	865	2 383	1 728	655	837	627	210
30 - 34	C	3 948	2 757	1 191	3 008	2 081	927	940	676	264
35 - 39	C	5 848	3 932	1 916	4 375	2 927	1 448	1 473	1 005	468
40 - 44	C	9 431	6 426	3 005	6 995	4 728	2 267	2 436	1 698	738
45 - 49	C	14 202	9 849	4 353	10 572	7 311	3 261	3 630	2 538	1 092

19. Deaths by age, sex and urban/rural residence: latest available year, 1993 - 2002
Décès selon l'âge, le sexe et la résidence, urbaine/rurale: dernière année disponible, 1993 - 2002 (continued — suite)

(See notes at end of table.— Voir notes à la fin du tableau.)

Continent, country or area, year and age (in years) / Continent, pays ou zone, année et âge (en années)	Code[1]	Total			Urban - Urbaine			Rural - Rurale		
		Both sexes - Les deux sexes	Male - Masculin	Female - Féminin	Both sexes - Les deux sexes	Male - Masculin	Female - Féminin	Both sexes - Les deux sexes	Male - Masculin	Female - Féminin
EUROPE										
France[32,33,34]										
1999										
50 - 54	C	18 326	12 853	5 473	13 730	9 560	4 170	4 596	3 293	1 303
55 - 59	C	18 164	12 818	5 346	13 478	9 470	4 008	4 686	3 348	1 338
60 - 64	C	26 635	18 577	8 058	19 091	13 182	5 909	7 544	5 395	2 149
65 - 69	C	40 631	27 672	12 959	28 533	19 088	9 445	12 098	8 584	3 514
70 - 74	C	56 335	35 808	20 527	39 009	24 310	14 699	17 326	11 498	5 828
75 - 79	C	77 544	43 773	33 771	53 673	29 573	24 100	23 871	14 200	9 671
80 - 84	C	59 109	27 964	31 145	42 097	19 532	22 565	17 012	8 432	8 580
85 - 89	C	99 118	38 022	61 096	68 681	25 568	43 113	30 437	12 454	17 983
90 - 94	C	66 686	19 217	47 469	46 649	12 976	33 673	20 037	6 241	13 796
95 - 99	C	23 136	4 737	18 399	16 538	3 316	13 222	6 598	1 421	5 177
100+	C	3 757	515	3 242	2 768	358	2 410	989	157	832
2001										
Total	C	531 485	272 337	259 148	...	...	...	...	...	...
0 - 1	C	3 444	1 960	1 484	...	...	...	...	...	...
1 - 4	C	761	426	335	...	...	...	...	...	...
5 - 9	C	416	251	165	...	...	...	...	...	...
10 - 14	C	603	362	241	...	...	...	...	...	...
15 - 19	C	2 001	1 434	567	...	...	...	...	...	...
20 - 24	C	2 637	1 986	651	...	...	...	...	...	...
25 - 29	C	2 995	2 225	770	...	...	...	...	...	...
30 - 34	C	3 775	2 679	1 096	...	...	...	...	...	...
35 - 39	C	5 939	4 008	1 931	...	...	...	...	...	...
40 - 44	C	9 170	6 216	2 954	...	...	...	...	...	...
45 - 49	C	14 344	9 889	4 455	...	...	...	...	...	...
50 - 54	C	19 864	13 984	5 880	...	...	...	...	...	...
55 - 59	C	19 655	13 748	5 907	...	...	...	...	...	...
60 - 64	C	24 655	17 155	7 500	...	...	...	...	...	...
65 - 69	C	37 638	25 485	12 153	...	...	...	...	...	...
70 - 74	C	54 563	34 548	20 015	...	...	...	...	...	...
75 - 79	C	74 799	42 457	32 342	...	...	...	...	...	...
80 - 84	C	69 380	34 413	34 967	...	...	...	...	...	...
85 - 89	C	86 272	33 205	53 067	...	...	...	...	...	...
90 - 94	C	69 198	20 157	49 041	...	...	...	...	...	...
95 - 99	C	25 150	5 179	19 971	...	...	...	...	...	...
100+	C	4 226	570	3 656	...	...	...	...	...	...
Germany - Allemagne										
2001										
Total	C	828 541	383 887	444 654	...	...	...	...	...	...
0 - 1	C	3 163	1 815	1 348	...	...	...	...	...	...
1 - 4	C	801	455	346	...	...	...	...	...	...
5 - 9	C	444	252	192	...	...	...	...	...	...
10 - 14	C	646	384	262	...	...	...	...	...	...
15 - 19	C	1 976	1 376	600	...	...	...	...	...	...
20 - 24	C	2 669	2 015	654	...	...	...	...	...	...
25 - 29	C	2 553	1 844	709	...	...	...	...	...	...
30 - 34	C	4 230	3 019	1 211	...	...	...	...	...	...
35 - 39	C	7 675	5 102	2 573	...	...	...	...	...	...
40 - 44	C	11 494	7 670	3 824	...	...	...	...	...	...
45 - 49	C	16 969	11 243	5 726	...	...	...	...	...	...
50 - 54	C	22 784	14 954	7 830	...	...	...	...	...	...
55 - 59	C	32 202	21 681	10 521	...	...	...	...	...	...
60 - 64	C	58 746	39 638	19 108	...	...	...	...	...	...
65 - 69	C	69 968	45 547	24 421	...	...	...	...	...	...
70 - 74	C	96 744	57 929	38 815	...	...	...	...	...	...
75 - 79	C	121 815	56 388	65 427	...	...	...	...	...	...
80 - 84	C	113 918	43 624	70 294	...	...	...	...	...	...
85 - 89	C	138 325	41 777	96 548	...	...	...	...	...	...
90 - 94	C	92 504	21 761	70 743	...	...	...	...	...	...
95 - 99	C	25 663	4 956	20 707	...	...	...	...	...	...

(See notes at end of table.— Voir notes à la fin du tableau.)

Continent, country or area, year and age (in years) / Continent, pays ou zone, année et âge (en années)	Code[1]	Total			Urban - Urbaine			Rural - Rurale		
		Both sexes - Les deux sexes	Male - Masculin	Female - Féminin	Both sexes - Les deux sexes	Male - Masculin	Female - Féminin	Both sexes - Les deux sexes	Male - Masculin	Female - Féminin
EUROPE										
Germany - Allemagne										
2001										
100+	C	3 252	457	2 795	...	...	...	...	...	...
Greece - Grèce										
1998										
Total	C	102 668	53 637	49 031	55 464	29 024	26 440	47 204	24 613	22 591
0 - 1	C	674	371	303	467	266	201	207	105	102
1 - 4	C	119	59	60	70	33	37	49	26	23
5 - 9	C	76	44	32	45	28	17	31	16	15
10 - 14	C	92	54	38	59	33	26	33	21	12
15 - 19	C	383	277	106	244	174	70	139	103	36
20 - 24	C	587	458	129	390	302	88	197	156	41
25 - 29	C	643	478	165	417	309	108	226	169	57
30 - 34	C	677	485	192	447	310	137	230	175	55
35 - 39	C	786	539	247	491	340	151	295	199	96
40 - 44	C	1 199	820	379	803	543	260	396	277	119
45 - 49	C	1 737	1 185	552	1 138	765	373	599	420	179
50 - 54	C	2 539	1 755	784	1 611	1 097	514	928	658	270
55 - 59	C	3 316	2 314	1 002	2 000	1 381	619	1 316	933	383
60 - 64	C	5 887	3 973	1 914	3 416	2 271	1 145	2 471	1 702	769
65 - 69	C	9 308	6 022	3 286	5 233	3 341	1 892	4 075	2 681	1 394
70 - 74	C	13 092	7 558	5 534	7 488	4 257	3 231	5 604	3 301	2 303
75 - 79	C	14 266	7 351	6 915	7 953	4 044	3 909	6 313	3 307	3 006
80 - 84	C	17 672	7 962	9 710	9 237	4 132	5 105	8 435	3 830	4 605
85 - 89	C	17 513	7 299	10 214	8 544	3 427	5 117	8 969	3 872	5 097
90 - 94	C	8 948	3 517	5 431	3 994	1 470	2 524	4 954	2 047	2 907
95 - 99	C	2 728	980	1 748	1 249	452	797	1 479	528	951
100+	C	426	136	290	168	49	119	258	87	171
2001										
Total	C	102 559	53 853	48 706	...	...	...	...	...	...
0 - 1	C	522	307	215	...	...	...	...	...	...
1 - 4	C	72	41	31	...	...	...	...	...	...
5 - 9	C	74	42	32	...	...	...	...	...	...
10 - 14	C	102	65	37	...	...	...	...	...	...
15 - 19	C	333	251	82	...	...	...	...	...	...
20 - 24	C	640	518	122	...	...	...	...	...	...
25 - 29	C	593	471	122	...	...	...	...	...	...
30 - 34	C	686	502	184	...	...	...	...	...	...
35 - 39	C	728	499	229	...	...	...	...	...	...
40 - 44	C	1 143	800	343	...	...	...	...	...	...
45 - 49	C	1 710	1 206	504	...	...	...	...	...	...
50 - 54	C	2 616	1 845	771	...	...	...	...	...	...
55 - 59	C	3 259	2 292	967	...	...	...	...	...	...
60 - 64	C	5 424	3 694	1 730	...	...	...	...	...	...
65 - 69	C	8 762	5 685	3 077	...	...	...	...	...	...
70 - 74	C	13 288	7 844	5 444	...	...	...	...	...	...
75 - 79	C	15 750	8 240	7 510	...	...	...	...	...	...
80 - 84	C	16 541	7 383	9 158	...	...	...	...	...	...
85 - 89	C	17 057	7 194	9 863	...	...	...	...	...	...
90 - 94	C	9 686	3 767	5 919	...	...	...	...	...	...
95 - 99	C	3 001	1 058	1 943	...	...	...	...	...	...
100+	C	572	149	423	...	...	...	...	...	...
Hungary - Hongrie[35]										
2002										
Total	C	132 833	68 837	63 996	83 112	41 882	41 230	49 128	26 517	22 611
0 - 1	C	693	362	331	421	225	196	269	136	133
1 - 4	C	139	79	60	74	42	32	65	37	28
5 - 9	C	95	59	36	43	28	15	49	29	20
10 - 14	C	127	83	44	70	46	24	52	33	19
15 - 19	C	259	178	81	158	113	45	98	62	36
20 - 24	C	478	370	108	290	217	73	174	143	31

19. Deaths by age, sex and urban/rural residence: latest available year, 1993 - 2002
Décès selon l'âge, le sexe et la résidence, urbaine/rurale: dernière année disponible, 1993 - 2002 (continued — suite)

(See notes at end of table.— Voir notes à la fin du tableau.)

Continent, country or area, year and age (in years) / Continent, pays ou zone, année et âge (en années)	Code[1]	Total			Urban - Urbaine			Rural - Rurale		
		Both sexes - Les deux sexes	Male - Masculin	Female - Féminin	Both sexes - Les deux sexes	Male - Masculin	Female - Féminin	Both sexes - Les deux sexes	Male - Masculin	Female - Féminin
EUROPE										
Hungary - Hongrie[35]										
2002										
25 - 29	C	621	446	175	369	256	113	228	169	59
30 - 34	C	791	584	207	458	329	129	313	239	74
35 - 39	C	1 442	1 027	415	832	577	255	580	425	155
40 - 44	C	3 033	2 155	878	1 731	1 179	552	1 259	940	319
45 - 49	C	5 995	4 187	1 808	3 594	2 412	1 182	2 333	1 722	611
50 - 54	C	7 400	5 190	2 210	4 523	3 077	1 446	2 818	2 063	755
55 - 59	C	8 310	5 736	2 574	5 240	3 518	1 722	3 016	2 174	842
60 - 64	C	10 250	6 753	3 497	6 197	3 976	2 221	3 992	2 729	1 263
65 - 69	C	12 958	7 810	5 148	7 743	4 569	3 174	5 175	3 212	1 963
70 - 74	C	17 772	9 746	8 026	10 915	5 938	4 977	6 812	3 775	3 037
75 - 79	C	21 291	9 897	11 394	13 260	6 085	7 175	7 984	3 780	4 204
80 - 84	C	18 459	7 191	11 268	11 795	4 548	7 247	6 630	2 632	3 998
85 - 89	C	13 161	4 405	8 756	8 877	2 975	5 902	4 268	1 424	2 844
90 - 94	C	7 720	2 158	5 562	5 263	1 485	3 778	2 448	670	1 778
95 - 99	C	1 663	375	1 288	1 144	263	881	516	112	404
100+	C	162	34	128	114	24	90	48	10	38
Unknown - Inconnu	C	14	12	2	1	-	1	1	1	-
Iceland - Islande										
2002										
Total	C	1 821	935	886	1 658	849	809	163	86	77
0 - 1	C	9	7	2	9	7	2	-	-	-
1 - 4	C	6	3	3	6	3	3	-	-	-
5 - 9	C	6	1	5	4	-	4	2	1	1
10 - 14	C	3	1	2	2	1	1	1	-	1
15 - 19	C	1	1	-	1	1	-	-	-	-
20 - 24	C	11	6	5	10	6	4	1	-	1
25 - 29	C	19	14	5	19	14	5	-	-	-
30 - 34	C	12	7	5	12	7	5	-	-	-
35 - 39	C	20	10	10	17	10	7	3	-	3
40 - 44	C	28	15	13	28	15	13	-	-	-
45 - 49	C	35	22	13	33	21	12	2	1	1
50 - 54	C	53	30	23	48	27	21	5	3	2
55 - 59	C	71	47	24	65	42	23	6	5	1
60 - 64	C	83	46	37	78	42	36	5	4	1
65 - 69	C	109	68	41	105	65	40	4	3	1
70 - 74	C	199	122	77	186	113	73	13	9	4
75 - 79	C	252	155	97	236	143	93	16	12	4
80 - 84	C	347	169	178	304	144	160	43	25	18
85 - 89	C	297	124	173	268	112	156	29	12	17
90 - 94	C	178	61	117	161	54	107	17	7	10
95 - 99	C	68	22	46	54	19	35	14	3	11
100+	C	14	4	10	12	3	9	2	1	1
Ireland - Irlande[36]										
1999										
Total	+C	31 683	16 480	15 203	17 288	8 599	8 689	14 395	7 881	6 514
0 - 1	+C	293	160	133	195	108	87	98	52	46
1 - 4	+C	68	39	29	37	25	12	31	14	17
5 - 9	+C	41	28	13	20	14	6	21	14	7
10 - 14	+C	56	37	19	31	19	12	25	18	7
15 - 19	+C	171	123	48	90	64	26	81	59	22
20 - 24	+C	233	179	54	130	103	27	103	76	27
25 - 29	+C	196	149	47	109	83	26	87	66	21
30 - 34	+C	222	153	69	141	94	47	81	59	22
35 - 39	+C	279	174	105	178	111	67	101	63	38
40 - 44	+C	406	243	163	232	143	89	174	100	74
45 - 49	+C	637	392	245	409	249	160	228	143	85
50 - 54	+C	888	553	335	514	301	213	374	252	122
55 - 59	+C	1 226	777	449	747	460	287	479	317	162
60 - 64	+C	1 675	1 065	610	1 003	626	377	672	439	233

(See notes at end of table.— Voir notes à la fin du tableau.)

Continent, country or area, year and age (in years) / Continent, pays ou zone, année et âge (en années)	Code[1]	Total			Urban - Urbaine			Rural - Rurale		
		Both sexes - Les deux sexes	Male - Masculin	Female - Féminin	Both sexes - Les deux sexes	Male - Masculin	Female - Féminin	Both sexes - Les deux sexes	Male - Masculin	Female - Féminin
EUROPE										
Ireland - Irlande[36]										
1999										
65 - 69	+C	2 606	1 630	976	1 485	897	588	1 121	733	388
70 - 74	+C	3 961	2 375	1 586	2 224	1 300	924	1 737	1 075	662
75 - 79	+C	5 492	3 005	2 487	2 877	1 499	1 378	2 615	1 506	1 109
80 - 84	+C	5 601	2 666	2 935	2 823	1 221	1 602	2 778	1 445	1 333
85+	+C	7 632	2 732	4 900	4 043	1 282	2 761	3 589	1 450	2 139
2002										
Total	+C	29 381	15 240	14 141	...	...	...	...	...	...
0 - 1	+C	307	165	142	...	...	...	...	...	...
1 - 4	+C	64	32	32	...	...	...	...	...	...
5 - 9	+C	26	14	12	...	...	...	...	...	...
10 - 14	+C	42	26	16	...	...	...	...	...	...
15 - 19	+C	151	111	40	...	...	...	...	...	...
20 - 24	+C	213	162	51	...	...	...	...	...	...
25 - 29	+C	233	185	48	...	...	...	...	...	...
30 - 34	+C	246	168	78	...	...	...	...	...	...
35 - 39	+C	296	186	110	...	...	...	...	...	...
40 - 44	+C	402	251	151	...	...	...	...	...	...
45 - 49	+C	574	358	216	...	...	...	...	...	...
50 - 54	+C	941	595	346	...	...	...	...	...	...
55 - 59	+C	1 201	794	407	...	...	...	...	...	...
60 - 64	+C	1 556	1 022	534	...	...	...	...	...	...
65 - 69	+C	2 287	1 446	841	...	...	...	...	...	...
70 - 74	+C	3 362	1 999	1 363	...	...	...	...	...	...
75 - 79	+C	4 664	2 546	2 118	...	...	...	...	...	...
80 - 84	+C	5 309	2 524	2 785	...	...	...	...	...	...
85 - 89	+C	4 497	1 791	2 706	...	...	...	...	...	...
90 - 94	+C	2 299	718	1 581	...	...	...	...	...	...
95 - 99	+C	619	131	488	...	...	...	...	...	...
100+	+C	92	16	76	...	...	...	...	...	...
Isle of Man - Îles de Man										
1999										
Total	+C	983	471	512	...	...	...	...	...	...
0 - 1	+C	6	3	3	...	...	...	...	...	...
1 - 4	+C	3	3	-	...	...	...	...	...	...
5 - 9	+C	1	-	1	...	...	...	...	...	...
10 - 14	+C	2	1	1	...	...	...	...	...	...
15 - 19	+C	2	1	1	...	...	...	...	...	...
20 - 24	+C	1	1	-	...	...	...	...	...	...
25 - 29	+C	3	1	2	...	...	...	...	...	...
30 - 34	+C	6	4	2	...	...	...	...	...	...
35 - 39	+C	10	7	3	...	...	...	...	...	...
40 - 44	+C	6	5	1	...	...	...	...	...	...
45 - 49	+C	12	7	5	...	...	...	...	...	...
50 - 54	+C	16	6	10	...	...	...	...	...	...
55 - 59	+C	27	19	8	...	...	...	...	...	...
60 - 64	+C	42	23	19	...	...	...	...	...	...
65 - 69	+C	68	33	35	...	...	...	...	...	...
70 - 74	+C	96	60	36	...	...	...	...	...	...
75 - 79	+C	166	82	84	...	...	...	...	...	...
80 - 84	+C	184	85	99	...	...	...	...	...	...
85+	+C	332	130	202	...	...	...	...	...	...
Italy - Italie										
1998										
Total	C	574 231	290 473	283 758	...	...	...	...	...	...
0 - 1	C	2 803	1 524	1 279	...	...	...	...	...	...
1 - 4	C	450	255	195	...	...	...	...	...	...
5 - 9	C	359	202	157	...	...	...	...	...	...
10 - 14	C	494	308	186	...	...	...	...	...	...
15 - 19	C	1 470	1 071	399	...	...	...	...	...	...

19. Deaths by age, sex and urban/rural residence: latest available year, 1993 - 2002
Décès selon l'âge, le sexe et la résidence, urbaine/rurale: dernière année disponible, 1993 - 2002 (continued — suite)

(See notes at end of table.— Voir notes à la fin du tableau.)

Continent, country or area, year and age (in years) / Continent, pays ou zone, année et âge (en années)	Code[1]	Total			Urban - Urbaine			Rural - Rurale		
		Both sexes - Les deux sexes	Male - Masculin	Female - Féminin	Both sexes - Les deux sexes	Male - Masculin	Female - Féminin	Both sexes - Les deux sexes	Male - Masculin	Female - Féminin

EUROPE

Italy - Italie
1998

20 - 24	C	2 623	2 017	606	...	...	...	...	...	...
25 - 29	C	2 987	2 264	723	...	...	...	...	...	...
30 - 34	C	3 715	2 688	1 027	...	...	...	...	...	...
35 - 39	C	4 406	2 991	1 415	...	...	...	...	...	...
40 - 44	C	5 649	3 629	2 020	...	...	...	...	...	...
45 - 49	C	8 483	5 376	3 107	...	...	...	...	...	...
50 - 54	C	13 195	8 562	4 633	...	...	...	...	...	...
55 - 59	C	20 663	13 642	7 021	...	...	...	...	...	...
60 - 64	C	31 779	21 103	10 676	...	...	...	...	...	...
65 - 69	C	49 176	32 144	17 032	...	...	...	...	...	...
70 - 74	C	71 571	43 786	27 785	...	...	...	...	...	...
75 - 79	C	84 401	45 564	38 837	...	...	...	...	...	...
80 - 84	C	90 333	41 542	48 791	...	...	...	...	...	...
85+	C	179 674	61 805	117 869	...	...	...	...	...	...

Latvia - Lettonie[15]
2002

Total	C	32 498	16 423	16 075	21 059	10 645	10 414	11 439	5 778	5 661
0 - 1	C	197	111	86	105	58	47	92	53	39
1 - 4	C	54	31	23	26	18	8	28	13	15
5 - 9	C	55	34	21	33	21	12	22	13	9
10 - 14	C	37	22	15	22	13	9	15	9	6
15 - 19	C	134	89	45	85	55	30	49	34	15
20 - 24	C	238	196	42	156	121	35	82	75	7
25 - 29	C	269	233	36	169	149	20	100	84	16
30 - 34	C	417	335	82	281	221	60	136	114	22
35 - 39	C	558	430	128	370	288	82	188	142	46
40 - 44	C	883	671	212	585	444	141	298	227	71
45 - 49	C	1 194	885	309	825	604	221	369	281	88
50 - 54	C	1 644	1 187	457	1 106	769	337	538	418	120
55 - 59	C	1 901	1 306	595	1 282	865	417	619	441	178
60 - 64	C	3 028	2 069	959	1 961	1 302	659	1 067	767	300
65 - 69	C	3 431	2 126	1 305	2 226	1 358	868	1 205	768	437
70 - 74	C	4 341	2 380	1 961	2 828	1 537	1 291	1 513	843	670
75 - 79	C	4 643	1 788	2 855	3 079	1 202	1 877	1 564	586	978
80 - 84	C	3 908	1 231	2 677	2 477	782	1 695	1 431	449	982
85 - 89	C	2 885	723	2 162	1 808	471	1 337	1 077	252	825
90 - 94	C	2 058	445	1 613	1 233	282	951	825	163	662
95 - 99	C	542	116	426	347	75	272	195	41	154
100+	C	74	9	65	52	7	45	22	2	20
Unknown - Inconnu	C	7	6	1	3	3	-	4	3	1

Liechtenstein
2002

Total	C	215	109	106	...	...	...	...	...	...
0 - 1	C	1	1	1	...	...	...	...	...	...
1 - 4	C	4	4	4	...	...	...	...	...	...
5 - 9	C	5	5	5	...	...	...	...	...	...
10 - 14	C	5	5	5	...	...	...	...	...	...
15 - 19	C	5	5	5	...	...	...	...	...	...
20 - 24	C	5	5	5	...	...	...	...	...	...
25 - 29	C	5	5	5	...	...	...	...	...	...
30 - 34	C	5	5	5	...	...	...	...	...	...
35 - 39	C	5	5	5	...	...	...	...	...	...
40 - 44	C	5	5	5	...	...	...	...	...	...
45 - 49	C	5	5	5	...	...	...	...	...	...
50 - 54	C	5	5	5	...	...	...	...	...	...
55 - 59	C	5	5	5	...	...	...	...	...	...
60 - 64	C	5	5	5	...	...	...	...	...	...
65 - 69	C	5	5	5	...	...	...	...	...	...
70 - 74	C	5	5	5	...	...	...	...	...	...

(See notes at end of table.— Voir notes à la fin du tableau.)

Continent, country or area, year and age (in years) / Continent, pays ou zone, année et âge (en années)	Code[1]	Total			Urban - Urbaine			Rural - Rurale		
		Both sexes - Les deux sexes	Male - Masculin	Female - Féminin	Both sexes - Les deux sexes	Male - Masculin	Female - Féminin	Both sexes - Les deux sexes	Male - Masculin	Female - Féminin
EUROPE										
Liechtenstein										
2002										
75 - 79	C	5	5	5	...	...	...	...	...	...
80 - 84	C	5	5	5	...	...	...	...	...	...
85 - 89	C	5	5	5	...	...	...	...	...	...
90 - 94	C	5	5	5	...	...	...	...	...	...
95 - 99	C	5	5	5	...	...	...	...	...	...
100+	C	1	1	1	...	...	...	...	...	...
Lithuania - Lituanie[15]										
2002										
Total	C	41 072	21 816	19 256	23 175	12 252	10 923	17 897	9 564	8 333
0 - 1	C	238	133	105	128	78	50	110	55	55
1 - 4	C	74	47	27	45	27	18	29	20	9
5 - 9	C	57	38	19	26	18	8	31	20	11
10 - 14	C	71	43	28	43	23	20	28	20	8
15 - 19	C	238	183	55	129	95	34	109	88	21
20 - 24	C	353	300	53	187	158	29	166	142	24
25 - 29	C	429	339	90	229	173	56	200	166	34
30 - 34	C	564	442	122	319	232	87	245	210	35
35 - 39	C	850	673	177	518	407	111	332	266	66
40 - 44	C	1 293	1 014	279	777	596	181	516	418	98
45 - 49	C	1 545	1 145	400	979	704	275	566	441	125
50 - 54	C	2 085	1 520	565	1 337	941	396	748	579	169
55 - 59	C	2 386	1 676	710	1 468	997	471	918	679	239
60 - 64	C	3 435	2 331	1 104	2 033	1 378	655	1 402	953	449
65 - 69	C	4 210	2 657	1 553	2 475	1 512	963	1 735	1 145	590
70 - 74	C	5 491	2 956	2 535	3 136	1 681	1 455	2 355	1 275	1 080
75 - 79	C	5 774	2 480	3 294	3 165	1 311	1 854	2 609	1 169	1 440
80 - 84	C	4 647	1 725	2 922	2 493	908	1 585	2 154	817	1 337
85 - 89	C	3 784	1 066	2 718	1 949	546	1 403	1 835	520	1 315
90 - 94	C	2 590	737	1 853	1 289	336	953	1 301	401	900
95 - 99	C	799	267	532	375	111	264	424	156	268
100+	C	156	42	114	72	18	54	84	24	60
Unknown - Inconnu	C	3	2	1	3	2	1	-	-	-
Luxembourg										
2002										
Total	C	3 744	1 894	1 850	...	...	...	...	...	...
0 - 1	C	27	15	12	...	...	...	...	...	...
1 - 4	C	9	7	2	...	...	...	...	...	...
5 - 9	C	5	4	1	...	...	...	...	...	...
10 - 14	C	8	7	1	...	...	...	...	...	...
15 - 19	C	15	12	3	...	...	...	...	...	...
20 - 24	C	17	14	3	...	...	...	...	...	...
25 - 29	C	19	17	2	...	...	...	...	...	...
30 - 34	C	34	24	10	...	...	...	...	...	...
35 - 39	C	47	33	14	...	...	...	...	...	...
40 - 44	C	59	39	20	...	...	...	...	...	...
45 - 49	C	96	56	40	...	...	...	...	...	...
50 - 54	C	122	76	46	...	...	...	...	...	...
55 - 59	C	188	128	60	...	...	...	...	...	...
60 - 64	C	210	142	68	...	...	...	...	...	...
65 - 69	C	294	201	93	...	...	...	...	...	...
70 - 74	C	501	310	191	...	...	...	...	...	...
75 - 79	C	574	269	305	...	...	...	...	...	...
80 - 84	C	530	221	309	...	...	...	...	...	...
85 - 89	C	534	198	336	...	...	...	...	...	...
90 - 94	C	345	92	253	...	...	...	...	...	...
95 - 99	C	104	28	76	...	...	...	...	...	...
100+	C	6	1	5	...	...	...	...	...	...

19. Deaths by age, sex and urban/rural residence: latest available year, 1993 - 2002
Décès selon l'âge, le sexe et la résidence, urbaine/rurale: dernière année disponible, 1993 - 2002 (continued — suite)

(See notes at end of table.— Voir notes à la fin du tableau.)

Continent, country or area, year and age (in years) / Continent, pays ou zone, année et âge (en années)	Code[1]	Total			Urban - Urbaine			Rural - Rurale		
		Both sexes - Les deux sexes	Male - Masculin	Female - Féminin	Both sexes - Les deux sexes	Male - Masculin	Female - Féminin	Both sexes - Les deux sexes	Male - Masculin	Female - Féminin
EUROPE										
Malta - Malte										
2002										
Total	C	3 031	1 604	1 427	...	...	...	...	...	...
0 - 1	C	23	9	14	...	...	...	...	...	...
1 - 4	C	5	5	-	...	...	...	...	...	...
5 - 9	C	2	2	-	...	...	...	...	...	...
10 - 14	C	4	2	2	...	...	...	...	...	...
15 - 19	C	9	8	1	...	...	...	...	...	...
20 - 24	C	13	10	3	...	...	...	...	...	...
25 - 29	C	21	16	5	...	...	...	...	...	...
30 - 34	C	13	7	6	...	...	...	...	...	...
35 - 39	C	17	9	8	...	...	...	...	...	...
40 - 44	C	26	17	9	...	...	...	...	...	...
45 - 49	C	59	34	25	...	...	...	...	...	...
50 - 54	C	96	64	32	...	...	...	...	...	...
55 - 59	C	136	83	53	...	...	...	...	...	...
60 - 64	C	150	84	66	...	...	...	...	...	...
65 - 69	C	281	182	99	...	...	...	...	...	...
70 - 74	C	404	223	181	...	...	...	...	...	...
75 - 79	C	508	265	243	...	...	...	...	...	...
80 - 84	C	561	301	260	...	...	...	...	...	...
85 - 89	C	407	182	225	...	...	...	...	...	...
90+	C	296	101	195	...	...	...	...	...	...
Netherlands - Pays-Bas[37]										
2002										
Total	C	142 355	68 998	73 357	94 926	44 845	50 081	47 429	24 153	23 276
0 - 1	C	919	515	404	613	344	269	306	171	135
1 - 4	C	302	174	128	207	118	89	95	56	39
5 - 9	C	113	62	51	72	42	30	41	20	21
10 - 14	C	133	87	46	86	60	26	47	27	20
15 - 19	C	321	211	110	183	114	69	138	97	41
20 - 24	C	434	319	115	290	211	79	144	108	36
25 - 29	C	468	286	182	333	198	135	135	88	47
30 - 34	C	786	493	293	540	340	200	246	153	93
35 - 39	C	1 152	694	458	807	489	318	345	205	140
40 - 44	C	1 713	979	734	1 140	654	486	573	325	248
45 - 49	C	2 837	1 558	1 279	1 866	1 044	822	971	514	457
50 - 54	C	4 208	2 397	1 811	2 822	1 620	1 202	1 386	777	609
55 - 59	C	6 103	3 720	2 383	3 982	2 406	1 576	2 121	1 314	807
60 - 64	C	7 411	4 641	2 770	4 760	2 925	1 835	2 651	1 716	935
65 - 69	C	10 245	6 475	3 770	6 674	4 104	2 570	3 571	2 371	1 200
70 - 74	C	15 550	9 423	6 127	10 298	6 100	4 198	5 252	3 323	1 929
75 - 79	C	21 005	11 620	9 385	13 918	7 529	6 389	7 087	4 091	2 996
80 - 84	C	24 897	11 723	13 174	16 746	7 714	9 032	8 151	4 009	4 142
85 - 89	C	22 897	8 504	14 393	15 474	5 589	9 885	7 423	2 915	4 508
90 - 94	C	14 979	3 947	11 032	10 130	2 507	7 623	4 849	1 440	3 409
95 - 99	C	5 063	1 041	4 022	3 417	656	2 761	1 646	385	1 261
100+	C	819	129	690	568	81	487	251	48	203
Norway - Norvège[38]										
2002										
Total	C	44 465	21 643	22 822	...	...	...	...	...	...
0 - 1	C	192	94	98	...	...	...	...	...	...
1 - 4	C	68	35	33	...	...	...	...	...	...
5 - 9	C	46	31	15	...	...	...	...	...	...
10 - 14	C	45	22	23	...	...	...	...	...	...
15 - 19	C	126	90	36	...	...	...	...	...	...
20 - 24	C	188	140	48	...	...	...	...	...	...
25 - 29	C	225	171	54	...	...	...	...	...	...
30 - 34	C	287	207	80	...	...	...	...	...	...
35 - 39	C	347	244	103	...	...	...	...	...	...
40 - 44	C	434	278	156	...	...	...	...	...	...

19. Deaths by age, sex and urban/rural residence: latest available year, 1993 - 2002
Décès selon l'âge, le sexe et la résidence, urbaine/rurale: dernière année disponible, 1993 - 2002 (continued — suite)

(See notes at end of table.— Voir notes à la fin du tableau.)

Continent, country or area, year and age (in years) / Continent, pays ou zone, année et âge (en années)	Code[1]	Total			Urban - Urbaine			Rural - Rurale		
		Both sexes - Les deux sexes	Male - Masculin	Female - Féminin	Both sexes - Les deux sexes	Male - Masculin	Female - Féminin	Both sexes - Les deux sexes	Male - Masculin	Female - Féminin
EUROPE										
Norway - Norvège[38]										
2002										
45 - 49	C	638	397	241	...	...	...	...	...	...
50 - 54	C	1 086	671	415	...	...	...	...	...	...
55 - 59	C	1 618	976	642	...	...	...	...	...	...
60 - 64	C	1 791	1 108	683	...	...	...	...	...	...
65 - 69	C	2 493	1 579	914	...	...	...	...	...	...
70 - 74	C	4 040	2 438	1 602	...	...	...	...	...	...
75 - 79	C	6 581	3 676	2 905	...	...	...	...	...	...
80 - 84	C	8 773	4 206	4 567	...	...	...	...	...	...
85 - 89	C	8 413	3 281	5 132	...	...	...	...	...	...
90 - 94	C	5 241	1 603	3 638	...	...	...	...	...	...
95 - 99	C	1 595	355	1 240	...	...	...	...	...	...
100+	C	238	41	197	...	...	...	...	...	...
Poland - Pologne										
1999										
Total	C	381 415	204 062	177 353	223 630	117 836	105 794	157 785	86 226	71 559
0 - 1	C	3 381	1 904	1 477	1 908	1 069	839	1 473	835	638
1 - 4	C	639	369	270	300	171	129	339	198	141
5 - 9	C	502	313	189	242	154	88	260	159	101
10 - 14	C	630	416	214	351	233	118	279	183	96
15 - 19	C	1 967	1 459	508	1 120	835	285	847	624	223
20 - 24	C	2 647	2 125	522	1 497	1 172	325	1 150	953	197
25 - 29	C	2 595	2 068	527	1 472	1 134	338	1 123	934	189
30 - 34	C	3 180	2 514	666	1 771	1 352	419	1 409	1 162	247
35 - 39	C	5 736	4 350	1 386	3 425	2 501	924	2 311	1 849	462
40 - 44	C	11 423	8 471	2 952	7 244	5 137	2 107	4 179	3 334	845
45 - 49	C	16 801	12 280	4 521	11 155	7 944	3 211	5 646	4 336	1 310
50 - 54	C	18 667	13 357	5 310	12 597	8 754	3 843	6 070	4 603	1 467
55 - 59	C	20 034	14 118	5 916	13 084	9 042	4 042	6 950	5 076	1 874
60 - 64	C	30 987	21 132	9 855	19 476	12 948	6 528	11 511	8 184	3 327
65 - 69	C	44 095	28 094	16 001	26 824	16 777	10 047	17 271	11 317	5 954
70 - 74	C	53 604	29 407	24 197	31 402	16 725	14 677	22 202	12 682	9 520
75 - 79	C	56 025	26 013	30 012	31 170	14 055	17 115	24 855	11 958	12 897
80 - 84	C	39 322	15 123	24 199	20 942	7 537	13 405	18 380	7 586	10 794
85+	C	69 180	20 549	48 631	37 650	10 296	27 354	31 530	10 253	21 277
2002										
Total	C	359 486	191 668	167 818	...	...	...	...	...	...
0 - 1	C	2 662	1 490	1 172	...	...	...	...	...	...
1 - 4	C	470	273	197	...	...	...	...	...	...
5 - 9	C	403	236	167	...	...	...	...	...	...
10 - 14	C	576	361	215	...	...	...	...	...	...
15 - 19	C	1 695	1 237	458	...	...	...	...	...	...
20 - 24	C	2 362	1 898	464	...	...	...	...	...	...
25 - 29	C	2 404	1 957	447	...	...	...	...	...	...
30 - 34	C	2 851	2 238	613	...	...	...	...	...	...
35 - 39	C	4 301	3 238	1 063	...	...	...	...	...	...
40 - 44	C	8 747	6 526	2 221	...	...	...	...	...	...
45 - 49	C	15 149	10 995	4 154	...	...	...	...	...	...
50 - 54	C	21 110	14 974	6 136	...	...	...	...	...	...
55 - 59	C	19 263	13 348	5 915	...	...	...	...	...	...
60 - 64	C	25 772	17 769	8 003	...	...	...	...	...	...
65 - 69	C	36 935	23 691	13 244	...	...	...	...	...	...
70 - 74	C	50 614	28 999	21 615	...	...	...	...	...	...
75 - 79	C	56 954	26 454	30 500	...	...	...	...	...	...
80 - 84	C	44 637	17 697	26 940	...	...	...	...	...	...
85 - 89	C	35 067	11 188	23 879	...	...	...	...	...	...
90 - 94	C	21 702	5 840	15 862	...	...	...	...	...	...
95 - 99	C	5 211	1 147	4 064	...	...	...	...	...	...
100+	C	601	112	489	...	...	...	...	...	...

19. Deaths by age, sex and urban/rural residence: latest available year, 1993 - 2002
Décès selon l'âge, le sexe et la résidence, urbaine/rurale: dernière année disponible, 1993 - 2002 (continued — suite)

(See notes at end of table.— Voir notes à la fin du tableau.)

Continent, country or area, year and age (in years) / Continent, pays ou zone, année et âge (en années)	Code[1]	Total			Urban - Urbaine			Rural - Rurale		
		Both sexes - Les deux sexes	Male - Masculin	Female - Féminin	Both sexes - Les deux sexes	Male - Masculin	Female - Féminin	Both sexes - Les deux sexes	Male - Masculin	Female - Féminin
EUROPE										
Portugal[7]										
1993										
Total	C	106 384	55 896	50 488	31 845	16 235	15 610	55 333	29 382	25 951
0 - 1	C	996	580	416	325	189	136	484	290	194
1 - 4	C	317	183	134	74	37	37	179	108	71
5 - 9	C	199	129	70	50	35	15	111	68	43
10 - 14	C	229	141	88	50	28	22	135	86	49
15 - 19	C	721	551	170	187	146	41	390	307	83
20 - 24	C	950	760	190	293	226	67	468	379	89
25 - 29	C	1 025	780	245	367	279	88	455	362	93
30 - 34	C	1 126	831	295	392	302	90	493	351	142
35 - 39	C	1 307	929	378	385	285	100	641	452	189
40 - 44	C	1 687	1 131	556	571	385	186	761	506	255
45 - 49	C	2 196	1 421	775	710	462	248	1 018	657	361
50 - 54	C	3 041	1 991	1 050	1 010	685	325	1 437	908	529
55 - 59	C	4 795	3 212	1 583	1 570	1 063	507	2 305	1 533	772
60 - 64	C	7 053	4 704	2 349	2 305	1 496	809	3 449	2 306	1 143
65 - 69	C	10 171	6 440	3 731	3 120	1 946	1 174	5 122	3 292	1 830
70 - 74	C	12 751	7 405	5 346	3 756	2 127	1 629	6 634	3 910	2 724
75 - 79	C	16 405	8 513	7 892	4 797	2 406	2 391	8 791	4 661	4 130
80 - 84	C	19 263	8 690	10 573	5 419	2 209	3 210	10 514	4 932	5 582
85+	C	22 152	7 505	14 647	6 464	1 929	4 535	11 946	4 274	7 672
2002										
Total	C	106 258	55 377	50 881	...	...	...	...	...	...
0 - 1	C	574	316	258	...	...	...	...	...	...
1 - 4	C	168	99	69	...	...	...	...	...	...
5 - 9	C	104	59	45	...	...	...	...	...	...
10 - 14	C	140	83	57	...	...	...	...	...	...
15 - 19	C	340	253	87	...	...	...	...	...	...
20 - 24	C	587	443	144	...	...	...	...	...	...
25 - 29	C	813	622	191	...	...	...	...	...	...
30 - 34	C	986	737	249	...	...	...	...	...	...
35 - 39	C	1 351	1 001	350	...	...	...	...	...	...
40 - 44	C	1 874	1 342	532	...	...	...	...	...	...
45 - 49	C	2 383	1 649	734	...	...	...	...	...	...
50 - 54	C	3 019	2 049	970	...	...	...	...	...	...
55 - 59	C	3 807	2 539	1 268	...	...	...	...	...	...
60 - 64	C	5 324	3 484	1 840	...	...	...	...	...	...
65 - 69	C	8 469	5 515	2 954	...	...	...	...	...	...
70 - 74	C	12 396	7 415	4 981	...	...	...	...	...	...
75 - 79	C	17 242	9 284	7 958	...	...	...	...	...	...
80 - 84	C	18 087	8 443	9 644	...	...	...	...	...	...
85 - 89	C	16 479	6 435	10 044	...	...	...	...	...	...
90 - 94	C	9 387	2 983	6 404	...	...	...	...	...	...
95 - 99	C	2 397	568	1 829	...	...	...	...	...	...
100+	C	331	58	273	...	...	...	...	...	...
Republic of Moldova - République de Moldova[15]										
2002										
Total	C	41 852	21 462	20 390	13 229	7 136	6 093	28 623	14 326	14 297
0 - 1	C	528	308	220	192	110	82	336	198	138
1 - 4	C	121	67	54	32	18	14	89	49	40
5 - 9	C	94	63	31	25	14	11	69	49	20
10 - 14	C	136	91	45	40	32	8	96	59	37
15 - 19	C	241	174	67	89	70	19	152	104	48
20 - 24	C	319	244	75	118	86	32	201	158	43
25 - 29	C	420	313	107	167	123	44	253	190	63
30 - 34	C	499	381	118	209	166	43	290	215	75
35 - 39	C	792	558	234	288	212	76	504	346	158
40 - 44	C	1 531	1 106	425	576	411	165	955	695	260
45 - 49	C	2 094	1 415	679	833	577	256	1 261	838	423

19. Deaths by age, sex and urban/rural residence: latest available year, 1993 - 2002
Décès selon l'âge, le sexe et la résidence, urbaine/rurale: dernière année disponible, 1993 - 2002 (continued — suite)

(See notes at end of table.— Voir notes à la fin du tableau.)

Continent, country or area, year and age (in years) / Continent, pays ou zone, année et âge (en années)	Code[1]	Total			Urban - Urbaine			Rural - Rurale		
		Both sexes - Les deux sexes	Male - Masculin	Female - Féminin	Both sexes - Les deux sexes	Male - Masculin	Female - Féminin	Both sexes - Les deux sexes	Male - Masculin	Female - Féminin
EUROPE										
Republic of Moldova - République de Moldova[15]										
2002										
50 - 54	C	2 736	1 767	969	1 101	744	357	1 635	1 023	612
55 - 59	C	2 131	1 247	884	833	533	300	1 298	714	584
60 - 64	C	4 250	2 368	1 882	1 432	882	550	2 818	1 486	1 332
65 - 69	C	5 088	2 752	2 336	1 484	827	657	3 604	1 925	1 679
70 - 74	C	6 255	3 157	3 098	1 795	896	899	4 460	2 261	2 199
75 - 79	C	6 042	2 424	3 618	1 759	672	1 087	4 283	1 752	2 531
80 - 84	C	4 701	1 751	2 950	1 203	444	759	3 498	1 307	2 191
85 - 89	C	2 437	861	1 576	689	225	464	1 748	636	1 112
90 - 94	C	1 142	345	797	297	76	221	845	269	576
95 - 99	C	252	63	189	59	15	44	193	48	145
100+	C	43	7	36	8	3	5	35	4	31
Romania - Roumanie										
2002										
Total	C	269 666	144 480	125 186	113 225	61 599	51 626	156 441	82 881	73 560
0 - 1	C	3 648	2 055	1 593	1 426	822	604	2 222	1 233	989
1 - 4	C	731	430	301	251	140	111	480	290	190
5 - 9	C	436	261	175	158	91	67	278	170	108
10 - 14	C	787	473	314	343	209	134	444	264	180
15 - 19	C	820	559	261	407	261	146	413	298	115
20 - 24	C	1 291	956	335	638	449	189	653	507	146
25 - 29	C	1 598	1 157	441	723	498	225	875	659	216
30 - 34	C	2 687	1 961	726	1 245	871	374	1 442	1 090	352
35 - 39	C	2 936	2 167	769	1 429	998	431	1 507	1 169	338
40 - 44	C	5 926	4 283	1 643	3 167	2 194	973	2 759	2 089	670
45 - 49	C	10 450	7 436	3 014	6 057	4 204	1 853	4 393	3 232	1 161
50 - 54	C	13 595	9 426	4 169	7 600	5 273	2 327	5 995	4 153	1 842
55 - 59	C	14 060	9 522	4 538	7 096	4 806	2 290	6 964	4 716	2 248
60 - 64	C	22 254	14 407	7 847	10 199	6 662	3 537	12 055	7 745	4 310
65 - 69	C	31 404	19 094	12 310	13 178	7 995	5 183	18 226	11 099	7 127
70 - 74	C	40 064	22 042	18 022	16 157	8 864	7 293	23 907	13 178	10 729
75 - 79	C	46 302	21 905	24 397	17 199	7 918	9 281	29 103	13 987	15 116
80 - 84	C	32 110	12 654	19 456	11 640	4 385	7 255	20 470	8 269	12 201
85 - 89	C	23 909	8 532	15 377	8 764	3 069	5 695	15 145	5 463	9 682
90 - 94	C	12 227	4 324	7 903	4 595	1 573	3 022	7 632	2 751	4 881
95 - 99	C	2 224	772	1 452	870	288	582	1 354	484	870
100+	C	207	64	143	83	29	54	124	35	89
Russian Federation - Fédération de Russie[15]										
1999										
Total	C	2 144 316	1 112 521	1 031 795	1 499 466	784 807	714 659	644 850	327 714	317 136
0 - 1	C	20 731	12 020	8 711	13 657	7 957	5 700	7 074	4 063	3 011
1 - 4	C	5 426	3 067	2 359	3 012	1 718	1 294	2 414	1 349	1 065
5 - 9	C	4 283	2 670	1 613	2 618	1 644	974	1 665	1 026	639
10 - 14	C	5 576	3 735	1 841	3 557	2 351	1 206	2 019	1 384	635
15 - 19	C	16 521	11 887	4 634	11 388	8 151	3 237	5 133	3 736	1 397
20 - 24	C	30 186	24 232	5 954	21 784	17 425	4 359	8 402	6 807	1 595
25 - 29	C	33 206	26 956	6 250	24 118	19 439	4 679	9 088	7 517	1 571
30 - 34	C	39 103	31 288	7 815	27 817	22 073	5 744	11 286	9 215	2 071
35 - 39	C	63 709	50 202	13 507	45 331	35 381	9 950	18 378	14 821	3 557
40 - 44	C	90 077	69 801	20 276	65 129	49 976	15 153	24 948	19 825	5 123
45 - 49	C	114 294	86 262	28 032	85 130	63 862	21 268	29 164	22 400	6 764
50 - 54	C	108 325	79 033	29 292	82 867	60 266	22 601	25 458	18 767	6 691
55 - 59	C	126 338	87 584	38 754	91 064	63 150	27 914	35 274	24 434	10 840
60 - 64	C	222 581	147 332	75 249	155 408	102 181	53 227	67 173	45 151	22 022
65 - 69	C	240 433	141 540	98 893	161 847	93 691	68 156	78 586	47 849	30 737
70 - 74	C	317 672	153 065	164 607	220 871	105 889	114 982	96 801	47 176	49 625
75 - 79	C	219 975	71 623	148 352	154 016	49 779	104 237	65 959	21 844	44 115
80 - 84	C	195 030	50 551	144 479	135 378	36 207	99 171	59 652	14 344	45 308

19. Deaths by age, sex and urban/rural residence: latest available year, 1993 - 2002
Décès selon l'âge, le sexe et la résidence, urbaine/rurale: dernière année disponible, 1993 - 2002 (continued — suite)

(See notes at end of table.— Voir notes à la fin du tableau.)

Continent, country or area, year and age (in years) / Continent, pays ou zone, année et âge (en années)	Code[1]	Total			Urban - Urbaine			Rural - Rurale		
		Both sexes - Les deux sexes	Male - Masculin	Female - Féminin	Both sexes - Les deux sexes	Male - Masculin	Female - Féminin	Both sexes - Les deux sexes	Male - Masculin	Female - Féminin
EUROPE										
Russian Federation - Fédération de Russie[15]										
1999										
85+	C	281 686	52 314	229 372	186 014	36 793	149 221	95 672	15 521	80 151
Unknown - Inconnu	C	9 164	7 359	1 805	8 460	6 874	1 586	704	485	219
2000										
Total	C	2 225 332	1 179 775	1 045 557	...	...	...	...	...	...
0 - 1	C	21 700	11 484	10 216	...	...	...	...	...	...
1 - 4	C	5 082	2 878	2 204	...	...	...	...	...	...
5 - 9	C	3 736	2 376	1 360	...	...	...	...	...	...
10 - 14	C	5 222	3 459	1 763	...	...	...	...	...	...
15 - 19	C	17 735	12 977	4 758	...	...	...	...	...	...
20 - 24	C	33 137	27 019	6 118	...	...	...	...	...	...
25 - 29	C	37 812	30 982	6 830	...	...	...	...	...	...
30 - 34	C	41 445	33 234	8 211	...	...	...	...	...	...
35 - 39	C	65 534	51 922	13 612	...	...	...	...	...	...
40 - 44	C	98 178	76 630	21 548	...	...	...	...	...	...
45 - 49	C	125 318	95 309	30 009	...	...	...	...	...	...
50 - 54	C	135 611	99 617	35 994	...	...	...	...	...	...
55 - 59	C	112 695	78 134	34 561	...	...	...	...	...	...
60 - 64	C	242 826	161 400	81 426	...	...	...	...	...	...
65 - 69	C	230 628	136 427	94 201	...	...	...	...	...	...
70 - 74	C	332 916	165 859	167 057	...	...	...	...	...	...
75 - 79	C	243 518	80 826	162 692	...	...	...	...	...	...
80 - 84	C	181 619	47 893	133 726	...	...	...	...	...	...
85 - 89	C	186 998	38 061	148 937	...	...	...	...	...	...
90 - 94	C	76 265	12 108	64 157	...	...	...	...	...	...
95+	C	15 932	1 923	14 009	...	...	...	...	...	...
Unknown - Inconnu	C	11 425	9 257	2 168	...	...	...	...	...	...
San Marino - Saint-Marin										
2000										
Total	+C	188	105	83	...	...	...	...	...	...
15 - 19	+C	2	2	-	...	...	...	...	...	...
20 - 24	+C	2	2	-	...	...	...	...	...	...
25 - 29	+C	1	1	-	...	...	...	...	...	...
35 - 39	+C	6	4	2	...	...	...	...	...	...
45 - 49	+C	7	6	1	...	...	...	...	...	...
50 - 54	+C	5	3	2	...	...	...	...	...	...
55 - 59	+C	3	3	-	...	...	...	...	...	...
60 - 64	+C	11	6	5	...	...	...	...	...	...
65 - 69	+C	17	9	8	...	...	...	...	...	...
70 - 74	+C	17	12	5	...	...	...	...	...	...
75 - 79	+C	26	18	8	...	...	...	...	...	...
80 - 84	+C	32	15	17	...	...	...	...	...	...
85+	+C	59	24	35	...	...	...	...	...	...
Serbia and Montenegro - Serbie-et-Montenegro										
2000										
Total	C	118 078	61 656	56 422	59 324	30 965	28 359	58 754	30 691	28 063
0 - 1	C	1 668	993	675	962	571	391	706	422	284
1 - 4	C	318	174	144	154	83	71	164	91	73
5 - 9	C	157	99	58	53	31	22	104	68	36
10 - 14	C	187	110	77	91	52	39	96	58	38
15 - 19	C	358	247	111	189	129	60	169	118	51
20 - 24	C	564	407	157	332	248	84	232	159	73
25 - 29	C	564	403	161	308	224	84	256	179	77
30 - 34	C	717	450	267	402	243	159	315	207	108
35 - 39	C	1 103	729	374	624	398	226	479	331	148
40 - 44	C	1 959	1 331	628	1 162	768	394	797	563	234
45 - 49	C	3 660	2 418	1 242	2 214	1 431	783	1 446	987	459
50 - 54	C	4 932	3 324	1 608	3 015	2 002	1 013	1 917	1 322	595

19. Deaths by age, sex and urban/rural residence: latest available year, 1993 - 2002
Décès selon l'âge, le sexe et la résidence, urbaine/rurale: dernière année disponible, 1993 - 2002 (continued — suite)

(See notes at end of table.— Voir notes à la fin du tableau.)

Continent, country or area, year and age (in years) / Continent, pays ou zone, année et âge (en années)	Code[1]	Total			Urban - Urbaine			Rural - Rurale		
		Both sexes - Les deux sexes	Male - Masculin	Female - Féminin	Both sexes - Les deux sexes	Male - Masculin	Female - Féminin	Both sexes - Les deux sexes	Male - Masculin	Female - Féminin
EUROPE										
Serbia and Montenegro - Serbie-et-Montenegro										
2000										
55 - 59	C	6 066	3 918	2 148	3 456	2 185	1 271	2 610	1 733	877
60 - 64	C	10 562	6 547	4 015	5 838	3 574	2 264	4 724	2 973	1 751
65 - 69	C	16 955	9 984	6 971	8 696	5 085	3 611	8 259	4 899	3 360
70 - 74	C	21 041	10 931	10 110	10 311	5 302	5 009	10 730	5 629	5 101
75 - 79	C	21 185	9 399	11 786	10 002	4 379	5 623	11 183	5 020	6 163
80 - 84	C	10 787	4 382	6 405	4 741	1 835	2 906	6 046	2 547	3 499
85+	C	15 185	5 728	9 457	6 688	2 360	4 328	8 497	3 368	5 129
Unknown - Inconnu	C	110	82	28	86	65	21	24	17	7
2001										
Total	C	113 063	58 949	54 114	...	...	...	...	...	...
0 - 1	C	1 709	1 017	692	...	...	...	...	...	...
1 - 4	C	284	167	117	...	...	...	...	...	...
5 - 9	C	178	114	64	...	...	...	...	...	...
10 - 14	C	158	97	61	...	...	...	...	...	...
15 - 19	C	327	213	114	...	...	...	...	...	...
20 - 24	C	525	380	145	...	...	...	...	...	...
25 - 29	C	560	399	161	...	...	...	...	...	...
30 - 34	C	685	454	231	...	...	...	...	...	...
35 - 39	C	1 049	690	359	...	...	...	...	...	...
40 - 44	C	1 872	1 209	663	...	...	...	...	...	...
45 - 49	C	3 651	2 390	1 261	...	...	...	...	...	...
50 - 54	C	5 154	3 394	1 760	...	...	...	...	...	...
55 - 59	C	5 596	3 620	1 976	...	...	...	...	...	...
60 - 64	C	9 814	6 021	3 793	...	...	...	...	...	...
65 - 69	C	15 445	9 045	6 400	...	...	...	...	...	...
70 - 74	C	20 265	10 748	9 517	...	...	...	...	...	...
75 - 79	C	20 827	9 218	11 609	...	...	...	...	...	...
80 - 84	C	11 805	4 751	7 054	...	...	...	...	...	...
85 - 89	C	8 299	3 162	5 137	...	...	...	...	...	...
90 - 94	C	3 860	1 468	2 392	...	...	...	...	...	...
95 - 99	C	802	283	519	...	...	...	...	...	...
100+	C	102	33	69	...	...	...	...	...	...
Slovakia - Slovaquie										
2002										
Total	C	51 532	27 415	24 117	24 737	13 002	11 735	26 795	14 413	12 382
0 - 1	C	388	189	199	191	94	97	197	95	102
1 - 4	C	74	38	36	33	18	15	41	20	21
5 - 9	C	78	50	28	35	22	13	43	28	15
10 - 14	C	71	39	32	37	18	19	34	21	13
15 - 19	C	197	136	61	106	76	30	91	60	31
20 - 24	C	312	246	66	181	150	31	131	96	35
25 - 29	C	348	267	81	192	146	46	156	121	35
30 - 34	C	376	287	89	177	137	40	199	150	49
35 - 39	C	598	457	141	300	227	73	298	230	68
40 - 44	C	1 140	856	284	612	440	172	528	416	112
45 - 49	C	2 017	1 494	523	1 043	727	316	974	767	207
50 - 54	C	2 761	2 056	705	1 466	1 046	420	1 295	1 010	285
55 - 59	C	3 074	2 150	924	1 602	1 094	508	1 472	1 056	416
60 - 64	C	3 822	2 570	1 252	1 849	1 229	620	1 973	1 341	632
65 - 69	C	5 092	3 137	1 955	2 464	1 481	983	2 628	1 656	972
70 - 74	C	6 969	3 805	3 164	3 260	1 718	1 542	3 709	2 087	1 622
75 - 79	C	8 695	4 038	4 657	4 068	1 843	2 225	4 627	2 195	2 432
80 - 84	C	7 129	2 889	4 240	3 224	1 314	1 910	3 905	1 575	2 330
85 - 89	C	4 840	1 660	3 180	2 254	751	1 503	2 586	909	1 677
90 - 94	C	2 835	869	1 966	1 300	390	910	1 535	479	1 056
95 - 99	C	654	166	488	316	72	244	338	94	244
100+	C	62	16	46	27	9	18	35	7	28

19. Deaths by age, sex and urban/rural residence: latest available year, 1993 - 2002
Décès selon l'âge, le sexe et la résidence, urbaine/rurale: dernière année disponible, 1993 - 2002 (continued — suite)

(See notes at end of table.— Voir notes à la fin du tableau.)

Continent, country or area, year and age (in years) / Continent, pays ou zone, année et âge (en années)	Code[1]	Total			Urban - Urbaine			Rural - Rurale		
		Both sexes - Les deux sexes	Male - Masculin	Female - Féminin	Both sexes - Les deux sexes	Male - Masculin	Female - Féminin	Both sexes - Les deux sexes	Male - Masculin	Female - Féminin
EUROPE										
Slovenia - Slovénie										
2002										
Total	C	18 622	9 653	8 969	8 640	4 485	4 155	9 982	5 168	4 814
0 - 1	C	67	44	23	37	28	9	30	16	14
1 - 4	C	19	12	7	6	4	2	13	8	5
5 - 9	C	14	8	6	7	5	2	7	3	4
10 - 14	C	15	10	5	10	7	3	5	3	2
15 - 19	C	71	50	21	36	26	10	35	24	11
20 - 24	C	112	92	20	53	46	7	59	46	13
25 - 29	C	106	88	18	51	41	10	55	47	8
30 - 34	C	138	105	33	68	52	16	70	53	17
35 - 39	C	213	147	66	84	51	33	129	96	33
40 - 44	C	323	236	87	143	98	45	180	138	42
45 - 49	C	583	395	188	267	173	94	316	222	94
50 - 54	C	857	610	247	433	299	134	424	311	113
55 - 59	C	921	659	262	465	313	152	456	346	110
60 - 64	C	1 390	989	401	647	448	199	743	541	202
65 - 69	C	1 852	1 209	643	869	566	303	983	643	340
70 - 74	C	2 643	1 578	1 065	1 239	737	502	1 404	841	563
75 - 79	C	2 873	1 298	1 575	1 325	605	720	1 548	693	855
80 - 84	C	2 503	945	1 558	1 149	450	699	1 354	495	859
85 - 89	C	2 106	701	1 405	930	332	598	1 176	369	807
90 - 94	C	1 453	396	1 057	653	171	482	800	225	575
95 - 99	C	331	73	258	152	30	122	179	43	136
100+	C	32	8	24	16	3	13	16	5	11
Spain - Espagne										
2000										
Total	C	360 391	189 468	170 923	...	...	...	...	...	...
0 - 1	C	1 740	959	781	...	...	...	...	...	...
1 - 4	C	383	220	163	...	...	...	...	...	...
5 - 9	C	300	181	119	...	...	...	...	...	...
10 - 14	C	365	220	145	...	...	...	...	...	...
15 - 19	C	1 198	862	336	...	...	...	...	...	...
20 - 24	C	1 996	1 533	463	...	...	...	...	...	...
25 - 29	C	2 339	1 806	533	...	...	...	...	...	...
30 - 34	C	2 975	2 191	784	...	...	...	...	...	...
35 - 39	C	4 052	2 935	1 117	...	...	...	...	...	...
40 - 44	C	5 267	3 678	1 589	...	...	...	...	...	...
45 - 49	C	6 523	4 603	1 920	...	...	...	...	...	...
50 - 54	C	9 331	6 691	2 640	...	...	...	...	...	...
55 - 59	C	12 024	8 622	3 402	...	...	...	...	...	...
60 - 64	C	17 127	12 125	5 002	...	...	...	...	...	...
65 - 69	C	29 420	20 008	9 412	...	...	...	...	...	...
70 - 74	C	41 327	26 300	15 027	...	...	...	...	...	...
75 - 79	C	55 264	31 507	23 757	...	...	...	...	...	...
80 - 84	C	58 873	27 072	31 801	...	...	...	...	...	...
85 - 89	C	59 660	22 691	36 969	...	...	...	...	...	...
90 - 94	C	37 319	11 834	25 485	...	...	...	...	...	...
95 - 99	C	11 363	3 065	8 298	...	...	...	...	...	...
100+	C	1 545	365	1 180	...	...	...	...	...	...
Sweden - Suède										
2002										
Total	C	95 009	45 780	49 229	...	...	...	...	...	...
0 - 1	C	313	172	141	...	...	...	...	...	...
1 - 4	C	69	46	23	...	...	...	...	...	...
5 - 9	C	36	16	20	...	...	...	...	...	...
10 - 14	C	67	41	26	...	...	...	...	...	...
15 - 19	C	173	109	64	...	...	...	...	...	...
20 - 24	C	274	210	64	...	...	...	...	...	...
25 - 29	C	258	180	78	...	...	...	...	...	...
30 - 34	C	341	231	110	...	...	...	...	...	...

19. Deaths by age, sex and urban/rural residence: latest available year, 1993 - 2002
Décès selon l'âge, le sexe et la résidence, urbaine/rurale: dernière année disponible, 1993 - 2002 (continued — suite)

(See notes at end of table.— Voir notes à la fin du tableau.)

Continent, country or area, year and age (in years) / Continent, pays ou zone, année et âge (en années)	Code[1]	Total			Urban - Urbaine			Rural - Rurale		
		Both sexes - Les deux sexes	Male - Masculin	Female - Féminin	Both sexes - Les deux sexes	Male - Masculin	Female - Féminin	Both sexes - Les deux sexes	Male - Masculin	Female - Féminin
EUROPE										
Sweden - Suède										
2002										
35 - 39	C	477	308	169	...	...	...	...	...	...
40 - 44	C	708	458	250	...	...	...	...	...	...
45 - 49	C	1 143	675	468	...	...	...	...	...	...
50 - 54	C	1 973	1 214	759	...	...	...	...	...	...
55 - 59	C	3 411	2 067	1 344	...	...	...	...	...	...
60 - 64	C	3 876	2 412	1 464	...	...	...	...	...	...
65 - 69	C	5 370	3 279	2 091	...	...	...	...	...	...
70 - 74	C	8 390	4 934	3 456	...	...	...	...	...	...
75 - 79	C	13 237	7 375	5 862	...	...	...	...	...	...
80 - 84	C	18 669	9 208	9 461	...	...	...	...	...	...
85 - 89	C	18 840	7 730	11 110	...	...	...	...	...	...
90 - 94	C	12 735	4 057	8 678	...	...	...	...	...	...
95 - 99	C	4 091	963	3 128	...	...	...	...	...	...
100+	C	558	95	463	...	...	...	...	...	...
Switzerland - Suisse										
2001										
Total	C	61 287	29 915	31 372	42 157	19 952	22 205	19 130	9 963	9 167
0 - 1	C	365	209	156	248	145	103	117	64	53
1 - 4	C	90	52	38	52	26	26	38	26	12
5 - 9	C	41	23	18	26	16	10	15	7	8
10 - 14	C	59	36	23	32	14	18	27	22	5
15 - 19	C	177	128	49	92	61	31	85	67	18
20 - 24	C	245	192	53	167	126	41	78	66	12
25 - 29	C	269	185	84	185	121	64	84	64	20
30 - 34	C	408	277	131	302	201	101	106	76	30
35 - 39	C	579	377	202	393	254	139	186	123	63
40 - 44	C	757	491	266	533	337	196	224	154	70
45 - 49	C	1 104	722	382	752	476	276	352	246	106
50 - 54	C	1 651	1 064	587	1 158	731	427	493	333	160
55 - 59	C	2 331	1 475	856	1 670	1 024	646	661	451	210
60 - 64	C	2 832	1 829	1 003	1 966	1 237	729	866	592	274
65 - 69	C	4 096	2 642	1 454	2 800	1 760	1 040	1 296	882	414
70 - 74	C	5 724	3 518	2 206	3 902	2 327	1 575	1 822	1 191	631
75 - 79	C	8 189	4 517	3 672	5 544	2 991	2 553	2 645	1 526	1 119
80 - 84	C	9 968	4 819	5 149	6 718	3 157	3 561	3 250	1 662	1 588
85 - 89	C	11 270	4 298	6 972	7 684	2 851	4 833	3 586	1 447	2 139
90 - 94	C	8 207	2 428	5 779	5 818	1 658	4 160	2 389	770	1 619
95 - 99	C	2 554	582	1 972	1 834	404	1 430	720	178	542
100+	C	371	51	320	281	35	246	90	16	74
2002										
Total	C	61 768	29 729	32 039	...	...	...	...	...	...
0 - 1	C	326	181	145	...	...	...	...	...	...
1 - 4	C	75	44	31	...	...	...	...	...	...
5 - 9	C	45	24	21	...	...	...	...	...	...
10 - 14	C	44	29	15	...	...	...	...	...	...
15 - 19	C	159	107	52	...	...	...	...	...	...
20 - 24	C	258	182	76	...	...	...	...	...	...
25 - 29	C	284	212	72	...	...	...	...	...	...
30 - 34	C	369	254	115	...	...	...	...	...	...
35 - 39	C	545	370	175	...	...	...	...	...	...
40 - 44	C	776	480	296	...	...	...	...	...	...
45 - 49	C	1 122	691	431	...	...	...	...	...	...
50 - 54	C	1 601	1 008	593	...	...	...	...	...	...
55 - 59	C	2 348	1 508	840	...	...	...	...	...	...
60 - 64	C	2 929	1 887	1 042	...	...	...	...	...	...
65 - 69	C	3 817	2 424	1 393	...	...	...	...	...	...
70 - 74	C	5 816	3 542	2 274	...	...	...	...	...	...
75 - 79	C	8 029	4 414	3 615	...	...	...	...	...	...
80 - 84	C	10 354	4 941	5 413	...	...	...	...	...	...

19. Deaths by age, sex and urban/rural residence: latest available year, 1993 - 2002
Décès selon l'âge, le sexe et la résidence, urbaine/rurale: dernière année disponible, 1993 - 2002 (continued — suite)

(See notes at end of table.— Voir notes à la fin du tableau.)

Continent, country or area, year and age (in years) / Continent, pays ou zone, année et âge (en années)	Code[1]	Total			Urban - Urbaine			Rural - Rurale		
		Both sexes - Les deux sexes	Male - Masculin	Female - Féminin	Both sexes - Les deux sexes	Male - Masculin	Female - Féminin	Both sexes - Les deux sexes	Male - Masculin	Female - Féminin
EUROPE										
Switzerland - Suisse										
2002										
85 - 89	C	11 248	4 248	7 000	...	...	...	...	...	...
90 - 94	C	8 376	2 450	5 926	...	...	...	...	...	...
95 - 99	C	2 826	649	2 177	...	...	...	...	...	...
100+	C	421	84	337	...	...	...	...	...	...
The Former Yugoslav Rep. of Macedonia - L'ex-République yougoslave de Macédoine										
2002										
Total	C	17 962	9 891	8 071	10 452	5 799	4 653	7 510	4 092	3 418
0 - 1	C	283	147	136	157	78	79	126	69	57
1 - 4	C	45	19	26	23	8	15	22	11	11
5 - 9	C	41	27	14	14	10	4	27	17	10
10 - 14	C	38	25	13	19	12	7	19	13	6
15 - 19	C	86	57	29	45	30	15	41	27	14
20 - 24	C	115	83	32	73	54	19	42	29	13
25 - 29	C	101	84	17	61	50	11	40	34	6
30 - 34	C	140	97	43	82	58	24	58	39	19
35 - 39	C	207	144	63	121	84	37	86	60	26
40 - 44	C	347	221	126	218	129	89	129	92	37
45 - 49	C	594	410	184	400	283	117	194	127	67
50 - 54	C	809	559	250	565	383	182	244	176	68
55 - 59	C	946	638	308	624	422	202	322	216	106
60 - 64	C	1 450	916	534	901	572	329	549	344	205
65 - 69	C	2 404	1 422	982	1 494	878	616	910	544	366
70 - 74	C	2 833	1 522	1 311	1 652	879	773	1 181	643	538
75 - 79	C	3 127	1 507	1 620	1 800	863	937	1 327	644	683
80 - 84	C	2 348	1 086	1 262	1 220	562	668	1 128	524	604
85+	C	...	...	...	983	444	539	1 064	483	581
85 - 89	C	1 320	599	721	...	...	...	...	...	...
90 - 94	C	585	278	307	...	...	...	...	...	...
95 - 99	C	113	41	72	...	...	...	...	...	...
100+	C	29	9	20	...	...	...	...	...	...
Unknown - Inconnu	C	1	-	1	-	-	-	1	-	1
Ukraine[15]										
2001										
Total	C	745 952	378 143	367 809	450 329	236 933	213 396	295 623	141 210	154 413
0 - 1	C	4 283	2 488	1 795	2 690	1 544	1 146	1 593	944	649
1 - 4	C	1 451	840	611	690	404	286	761	436	325
5 - 9	C	1 034	652	382	601	380	221	433	272	161
10 - 14	C	1 300	858	442	793	527	266	507	331	176
15 - 19	C	3 433	2 435	998	2 193	1 533	660	1 240	902	338
20 - 24	C	6 247	4 891	1 356	4 218	3 257	961	2 029	1 634	395
25 - 29	C	8 697	6 813	1 884	6 016	4 651	1 365	2 681	2 162	519
30 - 34	C	10 838	8 424	2 414	7 402	5 618	1 784	3 436	2 806	630
35 - 39	C	16 077	12 604	3 473	10 943	8 463	2 480	5 134	4 141	993
40 - 44	C	24 526	18 976	5 550	16 869	12 883	3 986	7 657	6 093	1 564
45 - 49	C	32 093	24 240	7 853	22 259	16 655	5 604	9 834	7 585	2 249
50 - 54	C	39 924	28 814	11 110	28 005	20 074	7 931	11 919	8 740	3 179
55 - 59	C	36 906	25 106	11 800	23 826	16 267	7 559	13 080	8 839	4 241
60 - 64	C	82 734	53 832	28 902	52 508	34 114	18 394	30 226	19 718	10 508
65 - 69	C	71 796	42 458	29 338	43 133	25 525	17 608	28 663	16 933	11 730
70 - 74	C	114 616	58 287	56 329	68 074	34 819	33 255	46 542	23 468	23 074
75 - 79	C	109 002	39 760	69 242	61 689	22 535	39 154	47 313	17 225	30 088
80 - 84	C	71 800	20 640	51 160	40 009	11 992	28 017	31 791	8 648	23 143
85+	C	105 627	23 129	82 498	55 011	12 932	42 079	50 616	10 197	40 419
Unknown - Inconnu	C	3 568	2 896	672	3 400	2 760	640	168	136	32

19. Deaths by age, sex and urban/rural residence: latest available year, 1993 - 2002
Décès selon l'âge, le sexe et la résidence, urbaine/rurale: dernière année disponible, 1993 - 2002 (continued — suite)

(See notes at end of table.— Voir notes à la fin du tableau.)

Continent, country or area, year and age (in years) / Continent, pays ou zone, année et âge (en années)	Code[1]	Total			Urban - Urbaine			Rural - Rurale		
		Both sexes - Les deux sexes	Male - Masculin	Female - Féminin	Both sexes - Les deux sexes	Male - Masculin	Female - Féminin	Both sexes - Les deux sexes	Male - Masculin	Female - Féminin
EUROPE										
United Kingdom - Royaume-Uni										
2002										
Total	C	606 283	287 878	318 405	...	...	...	...	...	...
0 - 1	C	3 499	2 033	1 466	...	...	...	...	...	...
1 - 4	C	644	368	276	...	...	...	...	...	...
5 - 9	C	403	223	180	...	...	...	...	...	...
10 - 14	C	535	321	214	...	...	...	...	...	...
15 - 19	C	1 444	994	450	...	...	...	...	...	...
20 - 24	C	2 031	1 508	523	...	...	...	...	...	...
25 - 29	C	2 419	1 755	664	...	...	...	...	...	...
30 - 34	C	3 585	2 398	1 187	...	...	...	...	...	...
35 - 39	C	4 919	3 112	1 807	...	...	...	...	...	...
40 - 44	C	6 778	4 200	2 578	...	...	...	...	...	...
45 - 49	C	9 865	5 909	3 956	...	...	...	...	...	...
50 - 54	C	15 334	9 221	6 113	...	...	...	...	...	...
55 - 59	C	22 723	13 863	8 860	...	...	...	...	...	...
60 - 64	C	30 338	18 564	11 774	...	...	...	...	...	...
65 - 69	C	44 023	26 563	17 460	...	...	...	...	...	...
70 - 74	C	66 813	38 256	28 557	...	...	...	...	...	...
75 - 79	C	93 966	49 646	44 320	...	...	...	...	...	...
80 - 84	C	107 580	49 562	58 018	...	...	...	...	...	...
85 - 89	C	98 339	36 420	61 919	...	...	...	...	...	...
90 - 94	C	65 343	18 189	47 154	...	...	...	...	...	...
95 - 99	C	22 023	4 317	17 706	...	...	...	...	...	...
100+	C	3 677	455	3 222	...	...	...	...	...	...
OCEANIA — OCEANIE										
American Samoa - Samoas américaines										
1993										
Total	C	223	128	95	...	...	...	...	...	...
0 - 1	C	23	12	11	...	...	...	...	...	...
1 - 4	C	4	2	2	...	...	...	...	...	...
5 - 9	C	4	3	1	...	...	...	...	...	...
10 - 14	C	1	1	-	...	...	...	...	...	...
15 - 19	C	6	4	2	...	...	...	...	...	...
20 - 24	C	2	2	-	...	...	...	...	...	...
25 - 29	C	6	5	1	...	...	...	...	...	...
30 - 34	C	7	4	3	...	...	...	...	...	...
35 - 39	C	8	3	5	...	...	...	...	...	...
40 - 44	C	2	1	1	...	...	...	...	...	...
45 - 49	C	9	8	1	...	...	...	...	...	...
50 - 54	C	15	8	7	...	...	...	...	...	...
55 - 59	C	13	9	4	...	...	...	...	...	...
60 - 64	C	25	16	9	...	...	...	...	...	...
65 - 69	C	19	11	8	...	...	...	...	...	...
70 - 74	C	25	11	14	...	...	...	...	...	...
75 - 79	C	25	13	12	...	...	...	...	...	...
80 - 84	C	14	6	8	...	...	...	...	...	...
85+	C	15	9	6	...	...	...	...	...	...
Australia - Australie										
2002										
Total	+C	133 707	68 885	64 822	...	...	...	...	...	...
0 - 1	+C	1 264	699	565	...	...	...	...	...	...
1 - 4	+C	260	163	97	...	...	...	...	...	...
5 - 9	+C	172	99	73	...	...	...	...	...	...
10 - 14	+C	186	112	74	...	...	...	...	...	...
15 - 19	+C	625	439	186	...	...	...	...	...	...
20 - 24	+C	815	619	196	...	...	...	...	...	...

(See notes at end of table.— Voir notes à la fin du tableau.)

Continent, country or area, year and age (in years) / Continent, pays ou zone, année et âge (en années)	Code[1]	Total			Urban - Urbaine			Rural - Rurale		
		Both sexes - Les deux sexes	Male - Masculin	Female - Féminin	Both sexes - Les deux sexes	Male - Masculin	Female - Féminin	Both sexes - Les deux sexes	Male - Masculin	Female - Féminin
OCEANIA — OCEANIE										
Australia - Australie										
2002										
25 - 29	+C	980	721	259	...	...	...	...	...	...
30 - 34	+C	1 212	845	367	...	...	...	...	...	...
35 - 39	+C	1 440	943	497	...	...	...	...	...	...
40 - 44	+C	2 024	1 263	761	...	...	...	...	...	...
45 - 49	+C	2 859	1 794	1 065	...	...	...	...	...	...
50 - 54	+C	3 951	2 360	1 591	...	...	...	...	...	...
55 - 59	+C	5 192	3 190	2 002	...	...	...	...	...	...
60 - 64	+C	6 769	4 265	2 504	...	...	...	...	...	...
65 - 69	+C	9 083	5 679	3 404	...	...	...	...	...	...
70 - 74	+C	14 146	8 747	5 399	...	...	...	...	...	...
75 - 79	+C	19 893	11 391	8 502	...	...	...	...	...	...
80 - 84	+C	22 533	11 072	11 461	...	...	...	...	...	...
85 - 89	+C	21 625	8 915	12 710	...	...	...	...	...	...
90 - 94	+C	13 407	4 329	9 078	...	...	...	...	...	...
95 - 99	+C	4 367	1 058	3 309	...	...	...	...	...	...
100+	+C	821	131	690	...	...	...	...	...	...
Unknown - Inconnu	+C	83	51	32	...	...	...	...	...	...
Marshall Islands - Îles Marshall										
1997										
Total	+U	243	135	108	...	...	...	...	...	...
0 - 1	+U	49	17	32	...	...	...	...	...	...
1 - 4	+U	7	1	6	...	...	...	...	...	...
5 - 9	+U	2	1	1	...	...	...	...	...	...
10 - 14	+U	2	1	1	...	...	...	...	...	...
15 - 19	+U	8	6	2	...	...	...	...	...	...
20 - 24	+U	10	9	1	...	...	...	...	...	...
25 - 29	+U	9	6	3	...	...	...	...	...	...
30 - 34	+U	8	2	6	...	...	...	...	...	...
35 - 39	+U	6	5	1	...	...	...	...	...	...
40 - 44	+U	10	5	5	...	...	...	...	...	...
45 - 49	+U	18	12	6	...	...	...	...	...	...
50 - 54	+U	13	9	4	...	...	...	...	...	...
55 - 59	+U	17	10	7	...	...	...	...	...	...
60 - 64	+U	17	13	4	...	...	...	...	...	...
65 - 69	+U	19	12	7	...	...	...	...	...	...
70 - 74	+U	13	6	7	...	...	...	...	...	...
75+	+U	35	20	15	...	...	...	...	...	...
New Caledonia - Nouvelle-Calédonie										
2001										
Total	C	1 131	655	476	...	...	...	...	...	...
0 - 1	C	24	14	10	...	...	...	...	...	...
1 - 4	C	9	3	6	...	...	...	...	...	...
5 - 9	C	1	-	1	...	...	...	...	...	...
10 - 14	C	4	3	1	...	...	...	...	...	...
15 - 19	C	10	7	3	...	...	...	...	...	...
20 - 24	C	27	20	7	...	...	...	...	...	...
25 - 29	C	35	26	9	...	...	...	...	...	...
30 - 34	C	29	22	7	...	...	...	...	...	...
35 - 39	C	31	22	9	...	...	...	...	...	...
40 - 44	C	33	24	9	...	...	...	...	...	...
45 - 49	C	50	26	24	...	...	...	...	...	...
50 - 54	C	62	38	24	...	...	...	...	...	...
55 - 59	C	86	53	33	...	...	...	...	...	...
60 - 64	C	97	70	27	...	...	...	...	...	...
65 - 69	C	106	64	42	...	...	...	...	...	...
70 - 74	C	125	77	48	...	...	...	...	...	...
75 - 79	C	138	77	61	...	...	...	...	...	...
80 - 84	C	110	51	59	...	...	...	...	...	...

19. Deaths by age, sex and urban/rural residence: latest available year, 1993 - 2002
Décès selon l'âge, le sexe et la résidence, urbaine/rurale: dernière année disponible, 1993 - 2002 (continued — suite)

(See notes at end of table.— Voir notes à la fin du tableau.)

Continent, country or area, year and age (in years) / Continent, pays ou zone, année et âge (en années)	Code[1]	Total			Urban - Urbaine			Rural - Rurale		
		Both sexes - Les deux sexes	Male - Masculin	Female - Féminin	Both sexes - Les deux sexes	Male - Masculin	Female - Féminin	Both sexes - Les deux sexes	Male - Masculin	Female - Féminin
OCEANIA — OCEANIE										
New Caledonia - Nouvelle-Calédonie										
2001										
85 - 89	C	96	40	56	...	...	...	...	...	...
90 - 94	C	47	16	31	...	...	...	...	...	...
95+	C	11	2	9	...	...	...	...	...	...
New Zealand - Nouvelle-Zélande[7]										
2002										
Total	+C	28 065	14 023	14 042	25 390	12 378	13 012	2 611	1 609	1 002
0 - 1	+C	300	155	145	255	130	125	24	12	12
1 - 4	+C	80	45	35	64	37	27	16	8	8
5 - 9	+C	47	27	20	37	22	15	10	5	5
10 - 14	+C	54	35	19	44	29	15	10	6	4
15 - 19	+C	167	116	51	140	95	45	26	20	6
20 - 24	+C	192	136	56	168	122	46	23	14	9
25 - 29	+C	206	141	65	164	115	49	41	25	16
30 - 34	+C	250	156	94	222	133	89	27	22	5
35 - 39	+C	331	206	125	273	164	109	58	42	16
40 - 44	+C	445	268	177	369	219	150	71	45	26
45 - 49	+C	606	354	252	505	285	220	98	66	32
50 - 54	+C	856	512	344	735	439	296	119	71	48
55 - 59	+C	1 182	690	492	989	576	413	193	114	79
60 - 64	+C	1 559	926	633	1 339	791	548	218	133	85
65 - 69	+C	2 041	1 235	806	1 739	1 034	705	298	200	98
70 - 74	+C	3 072	1 814	1 258	2 751	1 596	1 155	317	217	100
75 - 79	+C	4 090	2 255	1 835	3 754	2 045	1 709	331	208	123
80 - 84	+C	4 458	2 153	2 305	4 138	1 965	2 173	314	185	129
85 - 89	+C	4 380	1 765	2 615	4 103	1 615	2 488	271	148	123
90 - 94	+C	2 669	794	1 875	2 563	740	1 823	105	54	51
95 - 99	+C	914	212	702	873	198	675	40	14	26
100+	+C	166	28	138	165	28	137	1	...	1
Northern Mariana Islands - Îles Mariannes septentrionales[39]										
1999										
Total	U	189	99	91	...	...	...	...	...	...
0 - 4	U	16	8	8	...	...	...	...	...	...
5 - 9	U	1	-	1	...	...	...	...	...	...
15 - 19	U	6	4	3	...	...	...	...	...	...
20 - 24	U	9	6	3	...	...	...	...	...	...
25 - 29	U	7	6	1	...	...	...	...	...	...
30 - 34	U	5	4	1	...	...	...	...	...	...
35 - 39	U	10	4	6	...	...	...	...	...	...
40 - 44	U	7	6	1	...	...	...	...	...	...
45 - 49	U	16	4	12	...	...	...	...	...	...
50 - 54	U	16	8	8	...	...	...	...	...	...
55 - 59	U	9	3	6	...	...	...	...	...	...
60 - 64	U	15	8	7	...	...	...	...	...	...
65 - 69	U	15	9	6	...	...	...	...	...	...
70 - 74	U	20	13	7	...	...	...	...	...	...
75 - 79	U	12	5	7	...	...	...	...	...	...
80 - 84	U	13	7	6	...	...	...	...	...	...
85+	U	12	4	8	...	...	...	...	...	...
Palau - Palaos										
1999										
Total	C	131	78	53	...	...	...	...	...	...
0 - 1	C	5	3	2	...	...	...	...	...	...
1 - 14	C	4	2	2	...	...	...	...	...	...
15 - 24	C	3	3	-	...	...	...	...	...	...
25 - 44	C	22	16	6	...	...	...	...	...	...
45 - 64	C	41	27	14	...	...	...	...	...	...

19. Deaths by age, sex and urban/rural residence: latest available year, 1993 - 2002
Décès selon l'âge, le sexe et la résidence, urbaine/rurale: dernière année disponible, 1993 - 2002 (continued — suite)

(See notes at end of table.— Voir notes à la fin du tableau.)

Continent, country or area, year and age (in years) / Continent, pays ou zone, année et âge (en années)	Code[1]	Total			Urban - Urbaine			Rural - Rurale		
		Both sexes - Les deux sexes	Male - Masculin	Female - Féminin	Both sexes - Les deux sexes	Male - Masculin	Female - Féminin	Both sexes - Les deux sexes	Male - Masculin	Female - Féminin
OCEANIA — OCEANIE										
Palau - Palaos										
1999										
65¡	C	56	27	29	...	...	...	...	...	...
Tonga										
2000										
Total	+C	653	334	319	...	...	...	...	...	...
0 - 1	+C	28	12	16	...	...	...	...	...	...
1 - 9	+C	23	10	13	...	...	...	...	...	...
10 - 19	+C	14	10	4	...	...	...	...	...	...
20 - 29	+C	21	10	11	...	...	...	...	...	...
30 - 39	+C	16	5	11	...	...	...	...	...	...
40 - 49	+C	33	20	13	...	...	...	...	...	...
50 - 59	+C	78	37	41	...	...	...	...	...	...
60 - 69	+C	116	67	49	...	...	...	...	...	...
70+	+C	299	151	148	...	...	...	...	...	...
Unknown - Inconnu	+C	25	12	13	...	...	...	...	...	...

GENERAL NOTES - NOTES GENERALES

Data exclude foetal deaths. For definition 'urban', see end of Technical Notes for table 6. For method of evaluation and limitations of data, see Technical Notes, for this table. — Les données ne comprennent pas les morts foetales. Pour les définitions des 'régions urbaines', se reporter à la fin des Notes techniques du tableau 6. Pour la méthode d'evaluations et les insuffisances des données, voir Notes techniques, pour ce tableau.

Italics: data from civil registers which are incomplete or of unknown completeness. — Italiques: données incomplètes ou dont le degré d'exactitude n'est pas connu provenant des registres de l'état civil.

FOOTNOTES - NOTES

* Provisional. — Données provisoires.
[1] 'Code' indicates the source of data, as follows:
C - Civil registration, estimated over 90% complete
U - Civil registration, estimated less than 90% complete
I - Other source, estimated reliable
+ - Data tabulated by date of registration rather than occurence.
... - Information not available

Le 'Code' indique la source des données, comme suit:
C - Registres de l'état civil considérés complèts à 90 p. 100 au moins.
U - Registres de l'état civil qui ne sont pas considérés complèts à 90 p. 100 au moins.
I - Autre source, considérée pas douteuses.
+ - Données exploitées selon la date de l'enregistrement et non la date de l'événement.
... - Information pas disponible.

[2] Excluding live-born infants who died before their birth was registered. - - Non compris les enfants nés vivants décédés avant l'enregistrement de leur naissance.
[3] For Algerian population only. - Pour la population algérienne seulement.
[4] For 2001, data refer to last twelve months preceding census on August 2001. - Pour 2001, les données se rapportent pour la dernière fois à douze mois précédant le recensement août 2001.
[5] For 1993, data refer to last twelve months preceding census on August 1993. - Pour 1993, les données se rapportent pour la dernière fois à douze mois précédant le recensement août 1993.
[6] Based on the results of the population census. - D'après les résultats du recensement de la population.

[7] Figures for urban and rural areas do not add up to the total, since they do not include the category 'Unknown residence'. - La somme des donées pour la residence urbaine et rurale n'est pas égale au total parce qu'elle n'inclue pas la catégorie 'Residence inconnue'.
[8] Data for 1997 refer to last twelve months preceding population and housing census of 1997. - Les données pour 1997 se réfèrent au douze mois précédant le recensement de population et de l'habitat de 1997.
[9] Data for male and female categories exclude deaths of unknown sex. - - Les données pour le sexe masculin et féminin ne comprennent pas les décès ou on ignore le sexe.
[10] For 1993, data refer to last twelve months preceding census on April 1993. - Pour 1993, les données se rapportent pour la dernière fois à douze mois précédant le recensement avril 1993.
[11] Including Canadian residents temporarily in the United States, but excluding United States residents temporarily in Canada. - Y compris les résidents canadiens se trouvant temporairement aux Etats-Unis, mais ne comprenant pas les résidents des Etats-Unis se trouvant temporairement au Canada.
[12] Excluding Indian jungle population. - Non compris les Indiens de la jungle.
[13] Excluding nomadic Indian tribes. - Non compris les tribus d'Indiens nomades.
[14] Data refer to registered deaths only. - Les données se rapportent aux décès enregistrés seulement.
[15] Excluding infants born alive with less than 28 weeks gestation, less than 1 000 grams in weight and 35 centimeters in length, who die within seven days of birth. - Non compris les enfants nés vivants avant 28 semaines de gestation, pesant moins de 1 000 grammes, mesurant moins de 35 centimètres et décédés dans les sept jours qui ont suivi leur naissance.
[16] For statistical purposes, the data for China do not include those for the Hong Kong Special Administrative Region (Hong Kong SAR), Macao Special Administrative Region (Macao SAR) and Taiwan province of China. - Pour la présentation des statistiques, les données pour Chine ne comprend pas la Région Administrative Spéciale de Hong Kong (Hong Kong RAS), la Région Administrative Spéciale de Macao (Macao RAS) et Taïwan province de Chine.
[17] Data refer to government controlled areas. - Les données se raportent aux zones contrôlées par le Gouvernement.
[18] Including data for East Jerusalem and Israeli residents in certain other territories under occupation by Israeli military forces since June 1967. - Y compris les données pour Jérusalem-Est et les résidents israéliens dans certains autres territoires occupés depuis 1967 par les forces armées israéliennes.
[19] Data refer to Japanese nationals in Japan only. - Les données se raportent aux nationaux japonais au Japon seulement.
[20] Excluding alien armed forces, civilian aliens employed by armed forces, and foreign diplomatic personnel and their dependants. - Non compris les militaires étrangers, les civils étrangers employés par les forces armées ni le

personnel diplomatique étranger et les membres de leur famille les accompagnant.

[21] Data for urban/rural refer to Peninsular Malaysia only. - Les données ventilées par lieu de résidence (urbain/rural) concernent la Malaisie péninsulaire seulement.

[22] Data for urban refer to 170 towns out of 254 towns. - Les données urbaines se rapportent à 170 des 254 villes.

[23] Data for rural refer to 62 townships out of 158 townships. - Les données rurales se rapportent à 62 des 158 municipalités.

[24] For 2001, data refer to last twelve months preceding census on June 2001. - Pour 2001, les données se rapportent pour la dernière fois à douze mois précédant le recensement juin 2001.

[25] Data refer to the recorded events in Ministry of Health hospitals and health centres only. - Les données se rapportent aux faits d'état-civil enregistrés dans les hôpitaux et les dispensaires du Ministère de la santé seulement.

[26] Excluding data for the Pakistan-held part of Jammu and Kashmir, the final status of which has not yet been determined. - Non compris les données concernant la partie du Jammu et Cachemire occupée par le Pakistan dont le statut définitif n'a pas été déterminé.

[27] Based on the results of the Population Growth Survey. - D'après les résultats de la 'Population Growth Survey.'

[28] Excluding transients afloat and non-locally domiciled military and civilian services personnel and their dependants. - Non compris les personnes de passage þ bord de navires, ni les militaires et agents civils domiciliés hors du territoire et les membres de leur famille les accompagnant.

[29] Including armed forces stationed outside the country, but excluding alien armed forces stationed in the area. - Y compris les militaires nationaux hors du pays, mais non compris les militaires étrangers en garnison sur le territoire.

[30] Excluding Faeroe Islands and Greenland. - Non compris les Iles Féroé et Gröenland.

[31] Including nationals temporarily outside the country. - Y compris les nationaux se trouvant temporairement hors du pays.

[32] Including armed forces stationed outside the country. - Y compris les militaires nationaux hors du pays.

[33] For ages five years and over, age classification based on year of birth rather than exact date of birth. - A partir de cinq ans, le classement selon l'âge est basé sur l'année de naissances et non sur la date exacte de naissance.

[34] Excluding nationals outside the country. - Non compris les nationaux hors du pays.

[35] Data for urban/rural residence, for the de jure population. - Les données selon la résidence urbaine/rurale, pour la population de droit.

[36] Events registered within one year of occurrence. - Evénements enregistrés dans l'année qui suit l'événement.

[37] Including residents outside the country if listed in a Netherlands population register. - Y compris les résidents hors du pays, s'ils sont inscrits sur un registre de population néerlandais.

[38] Including residents temporarily outside the country. - Y compris les résidents se trouvant temporairement hors du pays.

[39] Figures for male and female do not add up to total since they were compiled from different sources. - La somme des données par sexe n'est pas identique au total car les données pour les hommes et les femmes proviennent de sources différentes.

Table 20

Table 20 presents death rates by age, sex and urban/rural residence for the latest available year.

Description of variables: Age is defined as age at last birthday, that is, the difference between the date of birth and the date of the occurrence of the event, expressed in completed solar years. The age classification used in this table is the following: under 1 year, 1-4 years, 5-year age groups through 95-99, and 100 years or over.

The urban/rural classification of deaths is that provided by each country or area; it is presumed to be based on the national census definition of urban population that have been set forth at the end of the technical notes for table 6.

Rate computation: Death rates specific for age and sex are the annual number of deaths in each age-sex group (as shown in table 19) per 1 000 population in the same age-sex group.

Death rates by age, sex and urban/rural residence are the annual number of deaths that occurred in a specific age-sex-urban/rural group (as shown in table 19) per 1 000 population in the corresponding age-sex-urban/rural group. These rates are calculated by the Statistics Division of the United Nations.

Deaths at unknown age and the population of unknown age are excluded from age-specific rate calculations but are part of the death rate for all ages combined.

It should be noted that the death rates for infants under one year of age in this table differ from the infant mortality rates shown elsewhere, because the latter are computed per 1 000 live births rather than per 1 000 population.

The population used in computing the rates is estimated or enumerated distributions by age and sex. First priority was given to an estimate for the mid-point of the same year (as shown in table 7), second priority to census returns of the year to which the deaths referred and third priority to an estimate for some other point of time in the year.

Rates presented in this table have been limited to those for countries or areas having at least a total of 1 000 deaths in a given year. Moreover, rates specific for individual sub-categories that are based on 30 or fewer deaths are identified by the symbol (♦).

Reliability of data: Rates are not computed if data from civil registers of deaths are reported as incomplete (less than 90 per cent completeness) or of unknown completeness, and therefore deemed unreliable. Table 18 and the technical notes for that table provide more detailed information on the completeness of death registration. For more information about the quality of vital statistics, see section 4.2 of the Technical Notes.

Limitations: Rates shown in this table are subject to all the same limitations that affect the corresponding frequencies and are set forth in the technical notes for table 19.

These include differences in the completeness of registration, the treatment of infants who were born alive but died before the registration of their birth or within the first 24 hours of life, the method used to determine age at death and the quality of the reported information relating to age at death. In addition, some rates are based on deaths tabulated by date of registration and not by date of occurrence; these have been indicated with a plus sign (+).

The problem of obtaining precise correspondence between deaths (numerator) and population (denominator) as regards the inclusion or exclusion of armed forces, refugees, displaced persons and other special groups is particularly difficult where age-specific death rates are concerned. In cases where it was not possible to achieve strict correspondence, the differences in coverage are noted. Male rates in the age range 20 to 40 years may be especially affected by this non-correspondence, and care should be exercised in using these rates for comparative purposes. Even when deaths and population do correspond conceptually, comparability of the rates may be affected by abnormal conditions such as absence from the country or area of large numbers of young men in the military forces or working abroad as temporary workers. Death rates may appear high in the younger ages, simply because a large section of the able-bodied members of the age group, whose death rates under normal conditions might be less than the average for persons of their age, is not included.

Also, in a number of cases the rates shown here for all ages combined differ from crude death rates shown elsewhere, because in this table they are computed on the population for which an appropriate age-sex distribution was available, while the crude death rates shown elsewhere may utilize a different total population. The population by age and sex might refer to a census date within the year rather than to the mid-point, or it might be more or less inclusive as regards ethnic groups, armed forces and so forth. In a few instances, the difference is attributable to the fact that the rates in this table were computed on the mean population whereas the corresponding rates in other tables were computed on an estimate for 1 July.

The comparability of data by urban/rural residence is affected by the national definitions of urban and rural used in tabulating these data. It is assumed, in the absence of specific information to the contrary, that the definitions of urban and rural used in connection with the national population census were also used in the compilation of the vital statistics for each country or area. However, it cannot be excluded that, for a given country or area, different definitions of urban and rural are used for the vital statistics data and the population census data respectively. When known, the definitions of urban used in national population censuses are presented at the end of the technical notes for table 6. As discussed in detail in the technical notes for table 6, these definitions vary considerably from one country or area to another.

In addition to problems of comparability, vital rates classified by urban/rural residence are also subject to certain special types of bias. If, when calculating vital rates, different definitions of urban are used in connection with the vital events and the population data and if this results in a net difference between the numerator and denominator of the rate in the population at risk, then the vital rates would be biased. Urban/rural differentials in vital rates may also be affected by whether the vital events have been tabulated in terms of place of occurrence or place of usual residence. This problem is discussed in more detail in section 4.1.4.1 of the Technical Notes.

Earlier data: Death rates specific for age and sex have been shown for the latest available year in many of the issues of the Yearbook since the 1955 issue. Data included in this table update the series shown in the Yearbook and in the Special Supplements covering a period of years as follows:

Issue	Years Covered
Historical Supplement CD, 1997	1948 – 1997
1996	1987 - 1995
1992	1983 – 1992
1985	1976 – 1984
1980	1971 – 1979
Historical Supplement, 1979	1948 - 1977

Tableau 20

Le tableau 20 présente les taux de mortalité selon l'âge et le sexe et selon le lieu de résidence (zone urbaine ou rurale) correspondant à la dernière année pour laquelle on disposait de données.

Description des variables : L'âge considéré est l'âge au dernier anniversaire, c'est-à-dire la différence entre la date de naissance et la date du décès, exprimée en années solaires révolues. La classification par âge est la suivante : moins d'un an, 1 à 4 ans, groupes quinquennaux jusqu'à 95-99 ans et 100 ans et plus.

La classification des décès selon le lieu de résidence (zone urbaine ou rurale) est celle qui a été communiquée par chaque pays ou zone ; on part du principe qu'elle repose sur les définitions de la population urbaine utilisées pour les recensements nationaux, qui sont reproduites à la fin des notes techniques du tableau 6.

Calcul des taux : Les taux de mortalité selon l'âge et le sexe représentent le nombre annuel de décès survenus pour chaque sexe et chaque groupe d'âge (fréquences du tableau 19) pour 1 000 personnes du même groupe.

Les taux de mortalité selon l'âge, le sexe et le lieu de résidence (zone urbaine ou rurale) représentent le nombre annuel de décès survenus dans un groupe d'âge et de sexe donnés parmi la population urbaine ou rurale (fréquences du tableau 19) pour 1 000 personnes du même groupe parmi la population urbaine ou rurale. Ces taux ont été calculés par la Division de statistique de l'ONU.

On n'a pas tenu compte des décès à un âge inconnu ni de la population d'âge inconnu, sauf dans les taux de mortalité pour tous les âges combinés.

Il convient de noter que, dans ce tableau, les taux de mortalité des groupes de moins d'un an sont différents des taux de mortalité infantile qui figurent dans d'autres tableaux, ces derniers ayant été établis pour 1 000 naissances vivantes et non pour 1 000 habitants.

Les chiffres de population utilisés pour le calcul des taux proviennent de dénombrements ou de répartitions estimatives de la population selon l'âge et le sexe. On a utilisé de préférence les estimations de la population au milieu de l'année considérée selon les chiffres du tableau 7 ; à défaut, on s'est contenté des données censitaires se rapportant à l'année des décès et, si ces données manquaient également, d'estimations établies à un autre moment de l'année.

Les taux présentés dans le tableau 20 ne se rapportent qu'aux pays ou zones où l'on a enregistré un total d'au moins 1 000 décès pendant l'année. Les taux relatifs à des sous-catégories, qui sont fondés sur 30 décès ou moins, sont signalés par le signe '♦'.

Fiabilité des données : On a choisi de ne pas faire figurer dans le tableau 20 des taux calculés à partir de données sur les décès issues de registres d'état civil qui sont déclarées incomplètes (degré d'exhaustivité inférieur à 90 p. 100) ou dont le degré d'exhaustivité n'est pas connu. Le tableau 18 et les notes techniques s'y rapportant présentent des renseignements plus détaillés sur le degré d'exhaustivité de l'enregistrement des décès. Pour plus de précisions sur la qualité des statistiques de l'état civil, voir la section 4.2 des Notes techniques.

Insuffisance des données : Les taux présentés dans le tableau 20 appellent les mêmes réserves que celles formulées à propos des fréquences correspondantes (voir à ce sujet les notes techniques se rapportant au tableau 19).

Leurs imperfections tiennent notamment aux différences d'exhaustivité de l'enregistrement, au classement des enfants nés vivants mais décédés avant l'enregistrement de leur naissance ou dans les 24 heures qui ont suivi la naissance, à la méthode utilisée pour obtenir l'âge au moment du décès, et à la qualité des déclarations concernant l'âge au moment du décès. En outre, dans certains cas, les données relatives aux décès sont classées par date d'enregistrement et non par date de l'événement ; ces cas ont été signalés par le signe '+'.

S'agissant des taux de mortalité par âge, il est particulièrement difficile d'établir une correspondance exacte entre les décès (numérateur) et la population (dénominateur) du fait de l'inclusion ou de l'exclusion des militaires, des réfugiés, des personnes déplacées et d'autres groupes spéciaux. Dans les cas où il n'a pas été possible de parvenir à une correspondance exacte, des notes signalent les différences de portée des données de base. Les taux de mortalité pour le sexe masculin dans les groupes d'âge de 20 à 40 ans peuvent être tout particulièrement influencés par ce manque de correspondance, et il importe d'être prudent quand on les utilise dans des comparaisons. Il convient d'ajouter que, même lorsque population et décès correspondent, la comparabilité des taux peut être compromise par des conditions anormales telles que l'absence du pays ou de la zone d'un grand nombre de jeunes gens qui sont sous les drapeaux ou qui travaillent à l'étranger comme travailleurs temporaires. Il arrive ainsi que les taux de mortalité paraissent élevés parmi les groupes les plus jeunes simplement parce que l'on en a exclu un grand nombre d'individus en bonne santé pour lesquels le taux de mortalité pourrait être, dans des conditions normales, inférieur à la moyenne observée pour les personnes du même âge.

De même, les taux indiqués pour tous les âges combinés diffèrent dans plusieurs cas des taux bruts de mortalité qui figurent dans d'autres tableaux, parce qu'ils se rapportent à une population pour laquelle on disposait d'une répartition par âge et par sexe appropriée, tandis que les taux bruts de mortalité indiqués ailleurs peuvent avoir été calculés sur la base d'un chiffre de population totale différent. Ainsi, il est possible que les chiffres de population par âge et par sexe proviennent d'un recensement effectué dans le courant de l'année et non au milieu de l'année, et qu'ils se différencient des autres chiffres de population en excluant ou en incluant certains groupes ethniques, les militaires, etc. Quelquefois, la différence tient à ce que les taux du tableau 20 ont été calculés sur la base de la population moyenne, alors que les taux correspondants des autres tableaux reposent sur une estimation au 1er juillet. Les écarts de cet ordre sont insignifiants, mais il n'en a pas été tenu compte dans le tableau.

La comparabilité des données selon le lieu de résidence (zone urbaine ou rurale) peut être limitée par les définitions nationales des termes « urbain » et « rural » utilisées pour le classement de ces données. En l'absence d'indications contraires, on a supposé que les mêmes définitions avaient servi pour le recensement national de la population et pour l'établissement des statistiques de l'état civil pour chaque pays ou zone. Toutefois, il n'est pas exclu que, pour une zone ou un pays donné, des définitions différentes aient été retenues. Les définitions du terme « urbain » utilisées pour les recensements nationaux de population ont été présentées à la fin du tableau 6 lorsqu'elles étaient connues. Comme on l'a précisé dans les notes techniques relatives au tableau 6, ces définitions varient considérablement d'un pays ou d'une zone à l'autre.

Outre les problèmes de comparabilité, les taux démographiques classés selon le lieu de résidence (zone urbaine ou rurale) sont également sujets à des distorsions particulières. Si l'on utilise des définitions différentes du terme « urbain » pour classer les faits d'état civil et les données relatives à la population lors du calcul des taux et qu'il en résulte une différence nette entre le numérateur et le dénominateur pour le taux de la population exposée au risque, les taux démographiques s'en trouveront faussés. La différence entre ces taux pour les zones urbaines et rurales pourra aussi être faussée selon que les faits d'état civil auront été classés d'après le lieu où ils se sont produits ou d'après le lieu de résidence habituel.

Ce problème est examiné plus en détail à la section 4.1.4.1 des Notes techniques.

Données publiées antérieurement : Un certain nombre d'éditions de l'*Annuaire* parues depuis 1955 présentent les statistiques les plus récentes dont on disposait à l'époque sur les taux de mortalité selon l'âge et le sexe. Les données du tableau 20 actualisent celles qui figuraient dans les éditions de l'*Annuaire démographique* et dans les *Suppléments spéciaux* qui portaient sur les périodes suivantes :

Éditions	Années considérées
Supplément historique (CD-ROM), 1997	1948 – 1997
1996	1987 - 1995
1992	1983 – 1992
1985	1976 – 1984
1980	1971 – 1979
Supplément rétrospectif, 1979	1948 - 1977

20. Death rates specific for age, sex and urban/rural residence: latest available year, 1993 - 2002
Taux de mortalité selon l'âge, le sexe et la résidence, urbaine/rurale: dernière année disponible, 1993 - 2002

(See notes at end of table. — Voir notes à la fin du tableau.)

Continent, country or area, year and age (in years) / Continent, pays ou zone, année et âge (en années)	Total			Urban - Urbaine			Rural - Rurale		
	Both sexes Les deux sexes	Male Masculin	Female Féminin	Both sexes Les deux sexes	Male Masculin	Female Féminin	Both sexes Les deux sexes	Male Masculin	Female Féminin
AFRICA — AFRIQUE									
Botswana[1]									
2001									
Total	12.4	13.3	11.6	...	...	...	...	...	...
0-1	36.8	37.5	36.1	...	...	...	...	...	...
1-4	7.8	8.3	7.2	...	...	...	...	...	...
5-9	2.3	2.4	2.2	...	...	...	...	...	...
10-14	1.2	1.1	1.3	...	...	...	...	...	...
15-19	1.9	1.8	2.0	...	...	...	...	...	...
20-24	6.4	4.8	7.8	...	...	...	...	...	...
25-29	14.2	11.8	16.4	...	...	...	...	...	...
30-34	20.9	22.5	19.4	...	...	...	...	...	...
35-39	21.4	25.4	17.9	...	...	...	...	...	...
40-44	20.9	25.8	16.7	...	...	...	...	...	...
45-49	21.0	27.5	15.3	...	...	...	...	...	...
50-54	19.0	24.5	14.0	...	...	...	...	...	...
55-59	20.1	26.5	14.3	...	...	...	...	...	...
60-64	22.3	28.9	16.5	...	...	...	...	...	...
65-69	26.4	33.7	20.8	...	...	...	...	...	...
70-74	28.4	36.2	22.8	...	...	...	...	...	...
75+	15.5	21.9	11.4	...	...	...	...	...	...
Egypt - Égypte									
1996									
Total	6.3	6.6	5.9	6.9	7.7	6.2	6.0	6.0	6.0
0-1	26.6	26.4	26.7	79.3	85.2	73.1	89.3	83.7	95.2
1-4	2.6	2.5	2.7	2.3	2.4	2.2	3.0	2.8	3.2
5-9	0.8	0.9	0.8	0.9	1.1	0.8	0.8	0.9	0.8
10-14	0.7	0.8	0.6	0.8	1.0	0.6	0.6	0.7	0.6
15-19	1.1	1.2	0.9	1.2	1.5	0.9	0.8	0.8	0.7
20-24	1.0	1.2	0.8	1.5	1.9	1.0	0.8	0.9	0.8
25-29	1.2	1.4	1.1	1.7	2.2	1.3	1.0	1.1	0.9
30-34	1.6	2.0	1.3	2.0	2.6	1.4	1.4	1.7	1.2
35-39	2.4	2.8	1.9	2.4	3.0	1.9	1.9	2.3	1.6
40-44	3.6	4.6	2.5	3.7	4.7	2.7	3.1	4.0	2.1
45-49	5.9	7.4	4.3	6.2	7.5	4.8	4.9	6.1	3.7
50-54	8.8	10.6	7.0	10.3	12.3	8.2	8.4	10.5	6.5
55-59	13.7	17.2	10.4	17.9	20.5	14.9	14.2	16.9	11.4
60-64	24.8	29.8	20.3	25.6	28.4	22.6	22.1	25.4	18.9
65-69	39.1	46.9	32.1	45.9	46.3	45.3	38.9	40.6	37.0
70-74	64.0	72.5	56.8	72.7	73.2	72.0	66.6	69.0	64.3
75+	148.5	143.9	152.4	185.3	163.6	210.5	187.5	159.2	216.0
1999									
Total	6.4	6.8	6.0	...	...	...	...	...	...
0-1	34.3	35.4	33.2	...	...	...	...	...	...
1-4	2.4	2.4	2.4	...	...	...	...	...	...
5-9	0.7	0.8	0.6	...	...	...	...	...	...
10-14	0.6	0.7	0.6	...	...	...	...	...	...
15-19	0.8	1.0	0.7	...	...	...	...	...	...
20-24	1.2	1.4	0.9	...	...	...	...	...	...
25-29	1.2	1.6	0.9	...	...	...	...	...	...
30-34	1.4	1.8	1.1	...	...	...	...	...	...
35-39	2.1	2.6	1.6	...	...	...	...	...	...
40-44	3.3	4.2	2.3	...	...	...	...	...	...
45-49	5.8	7.3	4.3	...	...	...	...	...	...
50-54	10.3	12.9	7.8	...	...	...	...	...	...
55-59	15.5	17.9	12.7	...	...	...	...	...	...
60-64	22.9	26.1	19.6	...	...	...	...	...	...
65-69	43.1	44.4	41.5	...	...	...	...	...	...
70-74	71.3	72.7	69.7	...	...	...	...	...	...
75+	199.5	175.9	224.8	...	...	...	...	...	...

20. Death rates specific for age, sex and urban/rural residence: latest available year, 1993 - 2002
Taux de mortalité selon l'âge, le sexe et la résidence, urbaine/rurale: dernière année disponible, 1993 - 2002 (continued — suite)

(See notes at end of table. — Voir notes à la fin du tableau.)

Continent, country or area, year and age (in years) Continent, pays ou zone, année et âge (en années)	Total			Urban - Urbaine			Rural - Rurale		
	Both sexes Les deux sexes	Male Masculin	Female Féminin	Both sexes Les deux sexes	Male Masculin	Female Féminin	Both sexes Les deux sexes	Male Masculin	Female Féminin
AFRICA — AFRIQUE									
Madagascar[2]									
1993									
Total	7.5	8.0	7.1	6.2	7.0	5.5	7.9	8.3	7.6
0-4	16.0	17.0	15.1	13.7	14.9	12.5	16.6	17.5	15.7
5-9	3.4	3.6	3.2	2.4	2.6	2.2	3.7	3.9	3.5
10-14	2.5	2.6	2.3	1.7	1.8	1.5	2.7	2.8	2.6
15-19	2.9	2.7	3.0	1.9	2.0	1.9	3.2	2.9	3.4
20-24	3.7	3.5	3.8	2.9	2.9	2.8	3.9	3.7	4.2
25-29	3.6	3.4	3.7	3.0	3.4	2.7	3.8	3.4	4.1
30-34	4.6	4.1	5.0	3.6	3.8	3.4	4.9	4.3	5.5
35-39	4.6	4.4	4.8	4.1	4.5	3.8	4.8	4.4	5.1
40-44	6.7	6.8	6.5	5.5	6.1	4.8	7.1	7.0	7.2
45-49	6.4	7.3	5.6	6.2	7.1	5.2	6.5	7.3	5.7
50-54	10.2	11.7	8.8	9.9	12.3	7.6	10.3	11.6	9.2
55-59	8.2	10.1	6.4	9.4	12.4	6.7	7.9	9.5	6.4
60-64	17.9	20.0	15.8	18.4	23.8	13.7	17.8	19.1	16.5
65-69	16.9	18.5	15.2	19.1	22.8	15.7	16.3	17.4	15.0
70-74	35.8	39.7	31.4	38.5	47.5	30.3	35.1	37.9	31.8
75+	148.0	157.2	138.2	149.9	168.4	133.9	147.5	154.4	139.6
Malawi[3]									
1998									
Total	20.9	23.4	18.6	15.5	16.7	14.1	21.9	24.6	19.3
0-1	122.0	136.9	107.4	106.9	120.9	92.9	124.3	139.3	109.6
1-4	46.4	51.2	41.6	37.2	41.4	33.1	47.7	52.7	42.9
5-9	11.6	12.9	10.4	8.9	10.3	7.5	12.0	13.2	10.8
10-14	7.8	7.9	7.8	4.4	5.2	3.8	8.4	8.3	8.5
15-19	6.6	6.5	6.6	3.7	3.8	3.7	7.1	7.0	7.2
20-24	12.0	16.0	8.8	6.7	7.0	6.4	13.2	18.3	9.3
25-29	11.7	12.3	11.1	7.7	6.4	9.3	12.7	14.0	11.5
30-34	14.6	14.8	14.5	11.1	10.2	12.3	15.4	15.9	14.9
35-39	14.5	15.4	13.7	12.9	12.9	12.9	14.8	15.9	13.8
40-44	17.6	20.6	14.5	16.3	17.5	14.6	17.8	21.2	14.5
45-49	16.9	22.3	11.6	15.2	16.7	12.9	17.2	23.2	11.5
50-54	15.4	18.0	12.8	18.6	20.4	15.8	15.0	17.6	12.5
55-59	22.1	19.3	25.0	22.5	21.8	23.5	22.1	19.1	25.1
60-64	19.1	22.4	16.1	24.9	25.4	24.1	18.7	22.1	15.6
65-69	19.3	19.1	19.5	20.0	21.3	18.4	19.3	19.0	19.6
70-74	22.7	30.0	16.5	26.5	31.6	21.7	22.5	29.9	16.2
75-79	24.4	29.3	19.7	35.4	43.0	27.6	23.9	28.6	19.3
80-84	33.2	41.1	26.8	46.7	59.6	36.5	32.6	40.3	26.4
85+	51.7	60.6	44.1	89.6	104.8	77.6	50.1	58.8	42.6
Mauritius - Maurice[+]									
2002									
Total	6.9	7.8	6.0	...	...	...	...	...	...
0-1	15.3	16.6	14.1	...	...	...	...	...	...
1-4	0.6	♦0.5	♦0.7	...	...	...	...	...	...
5-9	♦0.2	♦0.3	♦0.1	...	...	...	...	...	...
10-14	0.3	♦0.3	♦0.3	...	...	...	...	...	...
15-19	0.6	0.8	♦0.4	...	...	...	...	...	...
20-24	0.9	1.2	0.6	...	...	...	...	...	...
25-29	1.0	1.4	0.7	...	...	...	...	...	...
30-34	1.3	1.5	1.0	...	...	...	...	...	...
35-39	2.3	3.5	1.2	...	...	...	...	...	...
40-44	3.6	5.1	2.2	...	...	...	...	...	...
45-49	5.3	7.6	3.1	...	...	...	...	...	...
50-54	8.8	12.5	5.2	...	...	...	...	...	...
55-59	14.0	19.3	9.3	...	...	...	...	...	...
60-64	21.9	26.6	17.8	...	...	...	...	...	...
65-69	29.7	38.3	22.6	...	...	...	...	...	...
70-74	45.0	58.5	34.7	...	...	...	...	...	...
75-79	68.3	84.9	56.9	...	...	...	...	...	...

20. Death rates specific for age, sex and urban/rural residence: latest available year, 1993 - 2002
Taux de mortalité selon l'âge, le sexe et la résidence, urbaine/rurale: dernière année disponible, 1993 - 2002 (continued — suite)

(See notes at end of table. — Voir notes à la fin du tableau.)

Continent, country or area, year and age (in years) / Continent, pays ou zone, année et âge (en années)	Total			Urban - Urbaine			Rural - Rurale		
	Both sexes Les deux sexes	Male Masculin	Female Féminin	Both sexes Les deux sexes	Male Masculin	Female Féminin	Both sexes Les deux sexes	Male Masculin	Female Féminin
AFRICA — AFRIQUE									
Mauritius - Maurice+									
2002									
80-84	103.3	129.5	88.4	...	...	...	...	...	...
85+	168.1	197.6	155.8	...	...	...	...	...	...
Mozambique⁴									
1997									
Total	23.3	26.4	20.5	...	...	...	...	...	...
0-4	73.8	81.5	66.5	...	...	...	...	...	...
5-9	13.2	14.5	12.0	...	...	...	...	...	...
10-14	7.0	7.9	6.2	...	...	...	...	...	...
15-19	6.8	6.8	6.8	...	...	...	...	...	...
20-24	7.3	7.1	7.4	...	...	...	...	...	...
25-29	8.1	8.8	7.6	...	...	...	...	...	...
30-34	9.2	11.3	7.6	...	...	...	...	...	...
35-39	9.9	11.6	8.4	...	...	...	...	...	...
40-44	10.3	12.3	8.5	...	...	...	...	...	...
45-49	12.4	15.4	9.8	...	...	...	...	...	...
50-54	15.9	19.6	12.6	...	...	...	...	...	...
55-59	14.6	18.8	11.1	...	...	...	...	...	...
60-64	29.0	36.2	23.2	...	...	...	...	...	...
65-69	28.7	36.7	22.6	...	...	...	...	...	...
70-74	43.4	60.5	31.3	...	...	...	...	...	...
75-79	55.6	77.6	41.0	...	...	...	...	...	...
80+	167.9	233.8	127.3	...	...	...	...	...	...
Réunion⁵									
1999									
Total	5.4	6.5	4.4	...	...	...	...	...	...
0-1	35.7	40.1	31.4	...	...	...	...	...	...
1-4	♦0.5	♦0.6	♦0.4	...	...	...	...	...	...
5-9	♦0.2	♦0.2	♦0.1	...	...	...	...	...	...
10-14	♦0.3	♦0.3	♦0.3	...	...	...	...	...	...
15-19	0.5	♦0.9	♦0.2	...	...	...	...	...	...
20-24	0.9	1.6	♦0.3	...	...	...	...	...	...
25-29	1.0	1.3	♦0.6	...	...	...	...	...	...
30-34	1.6	2.3	♦0.9	...	...	...	...	...	...
35-39	1.5	2.4	♦0.7	...	...	...	...	...	...
40-44	3.2	4.8	1.5	...	...	...	...	...	...
45-49	4.7	6.7	2.7	...	...	...	...	...	...
50-54	7.3	11.1	3.4	...	...	...	...	...	...
55-59	9.9	14.6	5.3	...	...	...	...	...	...
60-64	14.8	20.5	9.6	...	...	...	...	...	...
65-69	21.0	29.1	14.1	...	...	...	...	...	...
70-74	31.5	45.8	20.4	...	...	...	...	...	...
75-79	46.6	64.2	34.9	...	...	...	...	...	...
80-84	77.9	106.5	63.3	...	...	...	...	...	...
85-89	108.9	134.4	98.2	...	...	...	...	...	...
90-94	160.1	183.5	151.5	...	...	...	...	...	...
95-99	180.8	♦123.7	203.3	...	...	...	...	...	...
100+	♦321.4	♦400.0	♦304.3	...	...	...	...	...	...
Swaziland⁴									
1997									
Total	9.1	10.7	7.7	6.4	7.1	5.7	9.9	11.9	8.3
0-4	15.0	15.8	14.2	12.1	13.5	10.8	15.6	16.3	14.9
5-9	1.4	1.5	1.2	♦1.3	♦1.4	♦1.2	1.4	1.5	1.2
10-14	1.0	1.1	1.0	♦1.0	♦1.2	♦0.9	1.0	1.1	1.0
15-19	2.3	2.2	2.3	1.7	♦1.9	♦1.6	2.5	2.3	2.6
20-24	5.3	5.1	5.5	3.2	3.0	3.3	6.4	6.2	6.6
25-29	8.9	10.5	7.5	4.5	4.9	4.1	11.3	14.5	9.2
30-34	11.1	14.6	8.5	5.4	5.8	4.9	14.1	21.0	10.0
35-39	11.5	16.0	8.2	6.3	6.2	6.4	14.1	22.5	8.9
40-44	13.8	19.1	9.3	7.8	8.8	6.4	16.5	25.4	10.3

20. Death rates specific for age, sex and urban/rural residence: latest available year, 1993 - 2002
Taux de mortalité selon l'âge, le sexe et la résidence, urbaine/rurale: dernière année disponible, 1993 - 2002 (continued — suite)

(See notes at end of table. — Voir notes à la fin du tableau.)

Continent, country or area, year and age (in years) Continent, pays ou zone, année et âge (en années)	Total			Urban - Urbaine			Rural - Rurale		
	Both sexes Les deux sexes	Male Masculin	Female Féminin	Both sexes Les deux sexes	Male Masculin	Female Féminin	Both sexes Les deux sexes	Male Masculin	Female Féminin
AFRICA — AFRIQUE									
Swaziland[4]									
1997									
45-49	14.3	19.8	9.2	9.4	9.7	9.0	16.2	25.3	9.3
50-54	18.8	25.4	13.2	13.6	14.1	♦12.8	20.6	30.6	13.3
55-59	20.0	26.8	13.4	17.0	17.6	♦16.2	20.8	30.1	12.9
60-64	26.3	37.5	17.0	21.3	♦19.3	♦23.8	27.4	42.2	15.9
65-69	30.0	42.0	20.0	32.1	43.7	♦19.0	29.7	41.7	20.1
70-74	43.1	64.6	28.8	53.5	♦64.1	♦44.9	41.9	64.7	27.1
75+	68.7	79.2	61.7	97.1	90.1	102.9	65.8	77.9	58.0
AMERICA, NORTH — **AMERIQUE DU NORD**									
Canada[6]									
2001									
Total	7.3	7.6	7.0	...	...	...	...	...	...
0-1	5.5	6.1	4.8	...	...	...	...	...	...
1-4	0.2	0.3	0.2	...	...	...	...	...	...
5-9	0.1	0.1	0.1	...	...	...	...	...	...
10-14	0.1	0.2	0.1	...	...	...	...	...	...
15-19	0.5	0.7	0.3	...	...	...	...	...	...
20-24	0.6	1.0	0.3	...	...	...	...	...	...
25-29	0.7	0.9	0.4	...	...	...	...	...	...
30-34	0.8	1.1	0.5	...	...	...	...	...	...
35-39	1.1	1.3	0.8	...	...	...	...	...	...
40-44	1.5	1.9	1.1	...	...	...	...	...	...
45-49	2.4	2.9	1.8	...	...	...	...	...	...
50-54	3.7	4.5	2.8	...	...	...	...	...	...
55-59	5.9	7.4	4.5	...	...	...	...	...	...
60-64	9.5	12.2	6.9	...	...	...	...	...	...
65-69	15.4	19.5	11.6	...	...	...	...	...	...
70-74	24.7	31.9	18.6	...	...	...	...	...	...
75-79	39.8	52.3	30.9	...	...	...	...	...	...
80-84	67.1	87.4	55.0	...	...	...	...	...	...
85-89	114.2	142.4	100.7	...	...	...	...	...	...
90+	216.9	248.4	206.2	...	...	...	...	...	...
Costa Rica									
2000									
Total	3.9	4.5	3.3	...	...	...	...	...	...
0-4	2.5	2.8	2.2	...	...	...	...	...	...
5-9	0.2	0.2	♦0.1	...	...	...	...	...	...
10-14	0.3	0.3	0.2	...	...	...	...	...	...
15-19	0.6	0.9	0.4	...	...	...	...	...	...
20-24	0.8	1.2	0.5	...	...	...	...	...	...
25-29	1.1	1.5	0.6	...	...	...	...	...	...
30-34	1.1	1.6	0.6	...	...	...	...	...	...
35-39	1.4	1.9	0.8	...	...	...	...	...	...
40-44	2.1	3.0	1.3	...	...	...	...	...	...
45-49	3.0	3.9	2.1	...	...	...	...	...	...
50-54	4.1	5.0	3.2	...	...	...	...	...	...
55-59	7.1	9.1	5.1	...	...	...	...	...	...
60-64	11.1	13.5	8.7	...	...	...	...	...	...
65-69	16.7	20.3	13.3	...	...	...	...	...	...
70-74	26.5	32.1	21.4	...	...	...	...	...	...
75+	19.3	23.1	16.2	...	...	...	...	...	...
Cuba									
1999									
Total	7.1	7.8	6.4	7.7	8.4	6.9	5.5	6.2	4.6
0-1	6.5	7.3	5.7	6.9	7.7	6.0	5.5	6.0	4.9
1-4	0.5	0.5	0.4	0.5	0.5	0.5	0.5	0.6	♦0.4
5-9	0.3	0.3	0.2	0.3	0.3	0.2	0.3	0.3	♦0.2

20. Death rates specific for age, sex and urban/rural residence: latest available year, 1993 - 2002
Taux de mortalité selon l'âge, le sexe et la résidence, urbaine/rurale: dernière année disponible, 1993 - 2002 (continued — suite)

(See notes at end of table. — Voir notes à la fin du tableau.)

Continent, country or area, year and age (in years) / Continent, pays ou zone, année et âge (en années)	Total			Urban - Urbaine			Rural - Rurale		
	Both sexes Les deux sexes	Male Masculin	Female Féminin	Both sexes Les deux sexes	Male Masculin	Female Féminin	Both sexes Les deux sexes	Male Masculin	Female Féminin
AMERICA, NORTH — AMERIQUE DU NORD									
Cuba									
1999									
10-14	0.3	0.4	0.3	0.3	0.4	0.3	0.4	0.5	0.3
15-19	0.6	0.7	0.5	0.6	0.7	0.6	0.6	0.8	0.4
20-24	0.8	1.2	0.5	0.9	1.2	0.5	0.7	1.0	0.5
25-29	1.1	1.5	0.7	1.1	1.5	0.7	1.1	1.4	0.7
30-34	1.3	1.7	0.8	1.3	1.8	0.9	1.2	1.5	0.8
35-39	1.7	2.2	1.2	1.7	2.3	1.1	1.7	2.0	1.3
40-44	2.6	3.3	2.0	2.7	3.5	2.0	2.4	2.7	2.0
45-49	3.7	4.5	2.9	3.9	4.9	3.0	3.0	3.3	2.6
50-54	5.5	6.6	4.5	5.8	7.1	4.6	4.4	4.9	3.9
55-59	8.3	10.1	6.6	8.8	11.0	6.7	6.7	7.0	6.3
60-64	12.4	14.4	10.4	13.1	15.8	10.7	9.7	10.1	9.1
65-74	25.4	29.2	21.8	26.9	32.1	22.4	20.1	20.9	19.1
75-84	86.2	99.9	74.0	90.3	109.2	75.6	71.0	74.4	66.3
85+	146.9	160.1	136.6	152.3	171.6	139.4	128.1	131.7	123.4
2000									
Total	6.8	7.5	6.1	...	...	...	...	...	...
0-4	1.8	2.1	1.5	...	...	...	...	...	...
5-9	0.3	0.3	0.2	...	...	...	...	...	...
10-14	0.3	0.4	0.2	...	...	...	...	...	...
15-19	0.5	0.7	0.4	...	...	...	...	...	...
20-24	0.9	1.1	0.6	...	...	...	...	...	...
25-29	1.0	1.3	0.7	...	...	...	...	...	...
30-34	1.2	1.6	0.9	...	...	...	...	...	...
35-39	1.6	2.0	1.2	...	...	...	...	...	...
40-44	2.5	3.0	2.0	...	...	...	...	...	...
45-49	3.5	4.3	2.8	...	...	...	...	...	...
50-54	5.5	6.8	4.3	...	...	...	...	...	...
55-59	8.1	9.8	6.5	...	...	...	...	...	...
60-64	11.7	13.9	9.7	...	...	...	...	...	...
65+	46.9	51.7	42.6	...	...	...	...	...	...
El Salvador									
2002									
Total	4.2	5.0	3.5	5.1	6.1	4.2	2.9	3.4	2.4
0-1	7.9	8.8	7.0	9.6	10.6	8.6	6.0	6.7	5.2
1-4	0.8	0.9	0.8	0.8	0.9	0.8	0.8	0.8	0.8
5-9	0.3	0.3	0.3	0.4	0.4	0.3	0.2	0.3	0.2
10-14	0.4	0.4	0.4	0.5	0.5	0.4	0.3	0.3	0.3
15-19	1.0	1.5	0.6	1.3	2.0	0.7	0.7	0.8	0.5
20-24	1.7	2.7	0.7	2.3	3.8	0.8	1.0	1.5	0.4
25-29	1.8	2.8	0.8	2.2	3.7	0.9	1.1	1.6	0.5
30-34	2.1	3.4	1.0	2.4	4.1	1.0	1.6	2.4	0.9
35-39	3.0	4.7	1.5	3.3	5.3	1.6	2.4	3.6	1.3
40-44	3.6	5.5	2.0	3.8	6.0	2.0	3.1	4.5	1.9
45-49	4.5	6.3	2.9	4.9	7.0	3.1	3.8	5.1	2.5
50-54	5.6	7.3	4.1	6.3	8.2	4.7	4.4	5.9	3.0
55-59	8.1	10.2	6.3	9.3	12.0	7.0	6.2	7.4	5.1
60-64	11.8	14.1	9.8	13.7	16.5	11.4	8.8	10.6	7.1
65-69	16.3	19.2	13.9	18.9	22.3	16.3	12.1	14.6	9.7
70-74	24.7	29.0	21.3	27.7	33.9	23.1	19.6	21.6	17.8
75-79	38.4	46.8	32.2	42.4	52.7	35.2	30.8	36.5	26.2
80+	125.9	157.2	107.6	113.7	136.4	100.4	176.3	242.8	137.3
Guatemala									
1999									
Total	5.8	6.6	5.0	...	...	...	...	...	...
0-1	34.9	38.1	31.4	...	...	...	...	...	...
1-4	3.6	3.6	3.5	...	...	...	...	...	...
5-9	0.7	0.7	0.7	...	...	...	...	...	...

20. Death rates specific for age, sex and urban/rural residence: latest available year, 1993 - 2002
Taux de mortalité selon l'âge, le sexe et la résidence, urbaine/rurale: dernière année disponible, 1993 - 2002 (continued — suite)

(See notes at end of table. — Voir notes à la fin du tableau.)

Continent, country or area, year and age (in years) Continent, pays ou zone, année et âge (en années)	Total			Urban - Urbaine			Rural - Rurale		
	Both sexes Les deux sexes	Male Masculin	Female Féminin	Both sexes Les deux sexes	Male Masculin	Female Féminin	Both sexes Les deux sexes	Male Masculin	Female Féminin
AMERICA, NORTH — **AMERIQUE DU NORD**									
Guatemala									
1999									
10-14	0.7	0.8	0.5	...	...	...	...	...	...
15-19	1.4	1.7	1.0	...	...	...	...	...	...
20-24	2.1	2.9	1.3	...	...	...	...	...	...
25-29	2.6	3.8	1.5	...	...	...	...	...	...
30-34	3.4	4.8	2.1	...	...	...	...	...	...
35-39	4.4	6.2	2.7	...	...	...	...	...	...
40-44	5.4	7.1	3.7	...	...	...	...	...	...
45-49	6.9	9.0	4.9	...	...	...	...	...	...
50-54	8.8	10.9	6.8	...	...	...	...	...	...
55-59	10.8	12.2	9.3	...	...	...	...	...	...
60-64	15.2	17.5	12.9	...	...	...	...	...	...
65+	9.8	11.1	8.6	...	...	...	...	...	...
Mexico - Mexique									
2000									
Total	4.5	5.1	3.9	4.6	5.2	4.0	4.0	4.6	3.3
0-1	18.7	20.8	16.6	19.6	21.8	17.4	15.9	17.6	14.1
1-4	0.8	0.9	0.8	0.7	0.8	0.7	1.0	1.0	1.0
5-9	0.3	0.4	0.3	0.3	0.3	0.3	0.3	0.4	0.3
10-14	0.3	0.4	0.3	0.3	0.4	0.3	0.3	0.4	0.3
15-19	0.7	1.0	0.4	0.7	1.0	0.4	0.7	1.0	0.5
20-24	1.1	1.7	0.5	1.1	1.6	0.5	1.2	1.7	0.6
25-29	1.4	2.2	0.7	1.3	2.0	0.6	1.5	2.3	0.8
30-34	1.7	2.6	0.9	1.6	2.4	0.8	1.7	2.6	1.0
35-39	2.2	3.3	1.2	2.1	3.1	1.2	2.3	3.3	1.4
40-44	3.0	4.2	1.9	2.9	4.0	1.9	3.1	4.2	1.9
45-49	4.4	5.9	3.1	4.4	5.8	3.1	4.1	5.2	3.0
50-54	6.3	7.7	4.9	6.4	7.9	5.1	5.4	6.5	4.2
55-59	10.0	12.0	8.0	10.5	12.8	8.5	7.9	9.3	6.4
60-64	14.0	16.4	11.9	15.2	18.0	12.8	10.4	11.8	9.0
65-69	21.7	25.0	18.7	23.6	27.7	20.3	16.0	18.0	13.9
70-74	31.6	35.4	28.2	34.6	39.7	30.4	23.3	24.9	21.4
75-79	47.3	52.3	42.8	51.9	58.6	46.3	35.1	38.0	31.9
80-84	72.1	78.4	67.0	79.1	88.0	72.4	54.5	58.0	50.9
85+	133.2	135.2	131.8	144.7	149.5	141.5	106.1	107.4	104.9
Puerto Rico - Porto Rico									
2002									
Total	7.3	8.5	6.1	...	...	...	...	...	...
0-1	9.3	10.4	8.3	...	...	...	...	...	...
1-4	0.3	0.3	◆0.2	...	...	...	...	...	...
5-9	◆0.1	◆0.1	◆0.1	...	...	...	...	...	...
10-14	0.2	0.2	◆0.1	...	...	...	...	...	...
15-19	0.7	1.1	0.3	...	...	...	...	...	...
20-24	1.5	2.7	0.4	...	...	...	...	...	...
25-29	1.6	2.6	0.6	...	...	...	...	...	...
30-34	1.7	2.7	0.8	...	...	...	...	...	...
35-39	2.3	3.5	1.2	...	...	...	...	...	...
40-44	2.7	4.0	1.6	...	...	...	...	...	...
45-49	4.0	5.9	2.4	...	...	...	...	...	...
50-54	5.0	7.2	3.2	...	...	...	...	...	...
55-59	7.5	10.5	4.9	...	...	...	...	...	...
60-64	11.2	15.1	7.9	...	...	...	...	...	...
65-69	16.4	21.6	12.0	...	...	...	...	...	...
70-74	25.0	32.0	19.5	...	...	...	...	...	...
75-79	40.4	51.0	32.4	...	...	...	...	...	...
80+	94.3	106.6	85.8	...	...	...	...	...	...

20. Death rates specific for age, sex and urban/rural residence: latest available year, 1993 - 2002
Taux de mortalité selon l'âge, le sexe et la résidence, urbaine/rurale: dernière année disponible, 1993 - 2002 (continued — suite)

(See notes at end of table. — Voir notes à la fin du tableau.)

Continent, country or area, year and age (in years) / Continent, pays ou zone, année et âge (en années)	Total			Urban - Urbaine			Rural - Rurale		
	Both sexes Les deux sexes	Male Masculin	Female Féminin	Both sexes Les deux sexes	Male Masculin	Female Féminin	Both sexes Les deux sexes	Male Masculin	Female Féminin
AMERICA, NORTH — AMERIQUE DU NORD									
Trinidad and Tobago - Trinité-et-Tobago									
1997									
Total	7.2	7.9	6.5	...	...	...	...	...	...
0-1	19.8	21.4	18.2	...	...	...	...	...	...
1-4	0.8	0.8	◆0.7	...	...	...	...	...	...
5-9	0.3	◆0.4	◆0.2	...	...	...	...	...	...
10-14	0.4	◆0.4	◆0.3	...	...	...	...	...	...
15-19	0.7	0.8	0.6	...	...	...	...	...	...
20-24	1.4	1.8	0.9	...	...	...	...	...	...
25-29	1.6	1.9	1.2	...	...	...	...	...	...
30-34	2.5	3.2	1.9	...	...	...	...	...	...
35-39	3.0	3.7	2.3	...	...	...	...	...	...
40-44	3.9	4.8	2.9	...	...	...	...	...	...
45-49	5.4	6.6	4.3	...	...	...	...	...	...
50-54	8.3	10.3	6.3	...	...	...	...	...	...
55-59	13.6	16.6	10.9	...	...	...	...	...	...
60-64	22.1	24.2	20.2	...	...	...	...	...	...
65-69	31.7	36.0	27.8	...	...	...	...	...	...
70-74	44.7	60.6	32.8	...	...	...	...	...	...
75-79	62.6	82.7	47.8	...	...	...	...	...	...
80+	146.2	154.8	139.3	...	...	...	...	...	...
United States - États-Unis									
2000									
Total	8.7	8.8	8.7	...	...	...	...	...	...
0-4	1.8	1.9	1.6	...	...	...	...	...	...
5-9	0.2	0.2	0.1	...	...	...	...	...	...
10-14	0.2	0.3	0.2	...	...	...	...	...	...
15-19	0.7	0.9	0.4	...	...	...	...	...	...
20-24	1.0	1.4	0.5	...	...	...	...	...	...
25-29	1.0	1.4	0.6	...	...	...	...	...	...
30-34	1.2	1.6	0.8	...	...	...	...	...	...
35-39	1.6	2.1	1.2	...	...	...	...	...	...
40-44	2.4	3.0	1.7	...	...	...	...	...	...
45-49	3.6	4.6	2.5	...	...	...	...	...	...
50-54	5.2	6.6	3.9	...	...	...	...	...	...
55-59	8.0	10.1	6.1	...	...	...	...	...	...
60-64	12.6	15.6	9.8	...	...	...	...	...	...
65-69	19.3	24.0	15.2	...	...	...	...	...	...
70-74	29.6	37.0	23.8	...	...	...	...	...	...
75-79	45.5	55.9	38.1	...	...	...	...	...	...
80-84	73.8	89.4	64.3	...	...	...	...	...	...
85+	152.6	165.8	146.9	...	...	...	...	...	...
AMERICA, SOUTH — AMERIQUE DU SUD									
Argentina - Argentine									
1995									
Total	7.7	8.7	6.8	...	...	...	...	...	...
0-4	4.9	5.5	4.5	...	...	...	...	...	...
5-9	0.3	0.3	0.2	...	...	...	...	...	...
10-14	0.3	0.4	0.3	...	...	...	...	...	...
15-19	0.7	1.0	0.5	...	...	...	...	...	...
20-24	1.1	1.5	0.6	...	...	...	...	...	...
25-29	1.3	1.8	0.8	...	...	...	...	...	...
30-34	1.4	1.9	1.0	...	...	...	...	...	...
35-39	1.9	2.5	1.3	...	...	...	...	...	...
40-44	2.8	3.6	2.0	...	...	...	...	...	...

20. Death rates specific for age, sex and urban/rural residence: latest available year, 1993 - 2002
Taux de mortalité selon l'âge, le sexe et la résidence, urbaine/rurale: dernière année disponible, 1993 - 2002 (continued — suite)

(See notes at end of table. — Voir notes à la fin du tableau.)

Continent, country or area, year and age (in years) / Continent, pays ou zone, année et âge (en années)	Total			Urban - Urbaine			Rural - Rurale		
	Both sexes Les deux sexes	Male Masculin	Female Féminin	Both sexes Les deux sexes	Male Masculin	Female Féminin	Both sexes Les deux sexes	Male Masculin	Female Féminin
AMERICA, SOUTH — AMERIQUE DU SUD									
Argentina - Argentine									
1995									
45-49	4.5	5.8	3.1	...	...	...	...	...	...
50-54	6.9	9.3	4.5	...	...	...	...	...	...
55-59	10.3	14.4	6.3	...	...	...	...	...	...
60-64	15.6	22.4	9.4	...	...	...	...	...	...
65-69	23.0	32.5	14.9	...	...	...	...	...	...
70-74	35.0	48.3	24.5	...	...	...	...	...	...
75-79	52.8	70.3	40.7	...	...	...	...	...	...
80+	146.1	170.7	131.4	...	...	...	...	...	...
Chile - Chili									
2002									
Total	5.2	5.7	4.7	5.2	5.7	4.7	5.4	6.2	4.5
0-1	6.9	7.8	6.0	...	...	...	...	...	...
0-4	...	...	...	1.7	1.9	1.5	1.7	1.9	1.4
1-4	0.4	0.4	0.4	...	...	...	...	◆0.3	◆0.2
5-9	0.2	0.2	0.2	0.2	0.2	0.1	0.2	0.4	◆0.2
10-14	0.2	0.3	0.2	0.2	0.3	0.2	0.3	0.8	0.4
15-19	0.5	0.7	0.3	0.5	0.7	0.2	0.6	1.8	◆0.4
20-24	0.8	1.3	0.4	0.8	1.2	0.3	1.2	2.0	0.6
25-29	0.9	1.5	0.4	0.9	1.4	0.4	1.4	2.0	0.7
30-34	1.0	1.6	0.5	1.0	1.5	0.4	1.5	2.7	0.7
35-39	1.4	2.0	0.8	1.3	1.9	0.8	1.8	3.2	1.2
40-44	2.0	2.8	1.3	2.0	2.7	1.3	2.3	4.1	2.1
45-49	3.0	3.9	2.1	3.0	3.9	2.1	3.2	6.2	3.6
50-54	4.6	5.9	3.3	4.5	5.8	3.3	5.0	9.3	5.0
55-59	7.3	9.6	5.2	7.3	9.7	5.2	7.4	12.2	8.1
60-64	11.5	14.9	8.4	11.7	15.6	8.5	10.3	20.7	12.9
65-69	18.2	24.2	13.3	18.5	25.1	13.3	17.1	33.6	23.2
70-74	32.4	43.1	24.3	33.1	45.4	24.5	28.7	47.6	35.1
75-79	46.3	61.1	36.4	47.3	64.6	36.6	41.5	114.3	97.7
80+	118.9	141.3	107.0	121.4	148.7	108.3	105.5		
Suriname									
2000									
Total	7.1	8.0	6.1	...	...	...	...	...	...
0-4	4.3	4.2	4.5	...	...	...	...	...	...
5-9	◆0.4	◆0.5	◆0.3	...	...	...	...	...	...
10-14	◆0.5	◆0.7	◆0.3	...	...	...	...	...	...
15-19	1.2	1.5	◆0.9	...	...	...	...	...	...
20-24	1.9	2.8	◆1.0	...	...	...	...	...	...
25-29	2.9	3.5	2.4	...	...	...	...	...	...
30-34	3.4	4.4	2.5	...	...	...	...	...	...
35-39	4.1	5.4	2.8	...	...	...	...	...	...
40-44	5.1	6.8	3.4	...	...	...	...	...	...
45-49	8.1	9.9	6.5	...	...	...	...	...	...
50-54	11.6	14.3	8.9	...	...	...	...	...	...
55-59	15.4	20.1	11.6	...	...	...	...	...	...
60-64	22.3	26.4	18.6	...	...	...	...	...	...
65-69	30.0	36.8	23.9	...	...	...	...	...	...
70-74	45.5	50.4	40.4	...	...	...	...	...	...
75-79	72.7	93.3	56.4	...	...	...	...	...	...
80+	149.8	160.5	141.8	...	...	...	...	...	...
Uruguay									
2000									
Total	9.2	10.2	8.2	...	...	...	...	...	...
0-1	13.9	16.0	11.6	...	...	...	...	...	...
1-4	0.6	0.7	0.5	...	...	...	...	...	...
5-9	0.2	0.3	◆0.1	...	...	...	...	...	...
10-14	0.2	0.2	◆0.2	...	...	...	...	...	...

20. Death rates specific for age, sex and urban/rural residence: latest available year, 1993 - 2002
Taux de mortalité selon l'âge, le sexe et la résidence, urbaine/rurale: dernière année disponible, 1993 - 2002 (continued — suite)

(See notes at end of table. — Voir notes à la fin du tableau.)

Continent, country or area, year and age (in years) / Continent, pays ou zone, année et âge (en années)	Total			Urban - Urbaine			Rural - Rurale		
	Both sexes Les deux sexes	Male Masculin	Female Féminin	Both sexes Les deux sexes	Male Masculin	Female Féminin	Both sexes Les deux sexes	Male Masculin	Female Féminin
AMERICA, SOUTH — AMERIQUE DU SUD									
Uruguay									
2000									
15-19	0.6	0.9	0.4	...	...	...	...	...	...
20-24	1.1	1.7	0.5	...	...	...	...	...	...
25-29	1.0	1.5	0.6	...	...	...	...	...	...
30-34	1.2	1.6	0.7	...	...	...	...	...	...
35-39	1.7	2.3	1.0	...	...	...	...	...	...
40-44	2.5	2.9	2.1	...	...	...	...	...	...
45-49	4.1	5.4	2.9	...	...	...	...	...	...
50-54	6.5	8.9	4.2	...	...	...	...	...	...
55-59	10.1	14.2	6.4	...	...	...	...	...	...
60-64	14.5	21.2	8.7	...	...	...	...	...	...
65-69	22.4	32.7	14.1	...	...	...	...	...	...
70-74	31.6	45.5	21.3	...	...	...	...	...	...
75-79	50.6	68.9	38.5	...	...	...	...	...	...
80-84	77.6	101.2	64.5	...	...	...	...	...	...
85+	152.4	173.0	143.4	...	...	...	...	...	...
Venezuela[7]									
2002									
Total	4.2	5.1	3.2	...	...	...	...	...	...
0-1	13.5	15.2	11.7	...	...	...	...	...	...
1-4	0.9	0.9	0.8	...	...	...	...	...	...
5-9	0.3	0.4	0.3	...	...	...	...	...	...
10-14	0.4	0.5	0.3	...	...	...	...	...	...
15-19	1.4	2.2	0.5	...	...	...	...	...	...
20-24	2.3	3.9	0.6	...	...	...	...	...	...
25-29	2.1	3.5	0.7	...	...	...	...	...	...
30-34	2.1	3.2	1.0	...	...	...	...	...	...
35-39	2.1	3.0	1.2	...	...	...	...	...	...
40-44	2.8	3.7	1.8	...	...	...	...	...	...
45-49	3.9	5.0	2.7	...	...	...	...	...	...
50-54	5.3	6.8	3.8	...	...	...	...	...	...
55-59	7.2	9.4	5.1	...	...	...	...	...	...
60-64	11.0	14.0	8.1	...	...	...	...	...	...
65-69	17.7	22.1	13.7	...	...	...	...	...	...
70-74	26.5	33.3	20.7	...	...	...	...	...	...
75-79	40.2	48.6	33.4	...	...	...	...	...	...
80+	117.7	128.1	110.2	...	...	...	...	...	...
ASIA — ASIE									
Armenia - Arménie[8]									
2000									
Total	6.3	6.6	6.0	6.2	6.7	5.7	6.6	6.5	6.6
0-1	15.5	18.4	12.0	16.5	20.1	12.3	13.8	15.6	11.5
1-4	0.8	0.9	0.8	0.8	0.8	0.7	0.9	1.0	◆0.9
5-9	0.2	◆0.2	0.2	0.2	◆0.2	◆0.2	◆0.2	◆0.1	◆0.2
10-14	0.2	0.3	◆0.1	0.2	0.3	◆0.1	◆0.2	◆0.2	◆0.1
15-19	0.4	0.6	◆0.2	0.3	0.5	◆0.2	0.5	0.8	◆0.1
20-24	0.5	0.7	0.3	0.5	0.7	◆0.2	0.5	0.6	◆0.3
25-29	0.6	0.7	0.4	0.6	0.8	0.5	0.5	0.6	◆0.3
30-34	0.9	1.3	0.6	0.9	1.4	0.5	0.9	1.1	◆0.6
35-39	1.4	2.0	0.9	1.5	2.1	0.9	1.4	1.9	0.8
40-44	2.1	2.9	1.3	2.1	3.1	1.2	2.1	2.6	1.7
45-49	3.4	5.0	2.1	3.7	5.5	2.2	2.8	3.7	1.8
50-54	5.7	8.1	3.8	5.9	8.3	3.9	5.2	7.3	3.4
55-59	8.1	11.8	5.1	8.5	12.5	5.2	7.1	9.7	5.0
60-64	15.6	21.2	11.1	16.4	23.0	11.0	14.1	17.7	11.1
65-69	26.0	34.2	19.4	26.4	35.5	19.5	25.3	32.3	19.3

20. Death rates specific for age, sex and urban/rural residence: latest available year, 1993 - 2002
Taux de mortalité selon l'âge, le sexe et la résidence, urbaine/rurale: dernière année disponible, 1993 - 2002 (continued — suite)

(See notes at end of table. — Voir notes à la fin du tableau.)

Continent, country or area, year and age (in years) / Continent, pays ou zone, année et âge (en années)	Total			Urban - Urbaine			Rural - Rurale		
	Both sexes Les deux sexes	Male Masculin	Female Féminin	Both sexes Les deux sexes	Male Masculin	Female Féminin	Both sexes Les deux sexes	Male Masculin	Female Féminin
ASIA — ASIE									
Armenia - Arménie[8]									
2000									
70-74	41.0	48.3	35.4	40.8	46.5	36.3	41.5	51.6	33.9
75-79	58.9	66.4	54.5	55.6	57.7	54.4	66.0	87.2	54.8
80-84	78.1	76.9	78.6	69.0	65.7	70.7	102.3	110.4	98.8
85+	125.8	95.4	144.9	96.9	76.6	109.9	198.6	144.1	231.9
2001									
Total	7.5	8.1	6.9	...	...	...	...	...	...
0-1	14.9	17.5	11.9	...	...	...	...	...	...
1-4	0.5	0.6	0.5	...	...	...	...	...	...
5-9	0.1	◆0.2	◆0.1	...	...	...	...	...	...
10-14	0.2	0.3	◆0.1	...	...	...	...	...	...
15-19	0.4	0.7	◆0.2	...	...	...	...	...	...
20-24	0.5	0.8	0.2	...	...	...	...	...	...
25-29	0.8	1.1	0.6	...	...	...	...	...	...
30-34	1.3	1.9	0.8	...	...	...	...	...	...
35-39	1.9	2.7	1.2	...	...	...	...	...	...
40-44	2.7	3.7	1.7	...	...	...	...	...	...
45-49	4.1	5.7	2.6	...	...	...	...	...	...
50-54	6.1	8.8	3.8	...	...	...	...	...	...
55-59	11.6	16.4	7.7	...	...	...	...	...	...
60-64	18.9	25.8	13.4	...	...	...	...	...	...
65-69	28.2	37.2	21.1	...	...	...	...	...	...
70-74	47.1	58.2	38.7	...	...	...	...	...	...
75-79	57.4	67.5	51.9	...	...	...	...	...	...
80-84	99.4	116.5	92.7	...	...	...	...	...	...
85+	193.1	197.4	191.4	...	...	...	...	...	...
Azerbaijan - Azerbaïdjan[+,8]									
2002									
Total	5.7	6.1	5.3	5.7	6.3	5.2	5.7	5.9	5.5
0-1	12.9	13.3	12.3	11.1	11.8	10.4	14.3	14.6	13.9
1-4	2.5	2.5	2.4	1.5	1.6	1.3	3.2	3.2	3.2
5-9	0.6	0.6	0.6	0.6	0.6	0.5	0.6	0.6	0.6
10-14	0.3	0.4	0.3	0.3	0.3	0.2	0.4	0.5	0.3
15-19	0.5	0.7	0.4	0.5	0.7	0.3	0.6	0.7	0.4
20-24	0.8	1.0	0.5	0.8	1.0	0.5	0.8	0.9	0.6
25-29	1.1	1.5	0.7	1.1	1.6	0.7	1.1	1.4	0.8
30-34	1.3	1.7	0.8	1.3	1.9	0.7	1.2	1.6	1.0
35-39	1.7	2.5	1.1	1.9	2.8	1.1	1.5	2.1	1.0
40-44	2.6	3.6	1.6	2.6	3.8	1.5	2.5	3.3	1.8
45-49	4.2	5.8	2.6	4.4	6.3	2.6	3.8	5.1	2.7
50-54	7.0	9.5	4.7	7.4	10.2	4.8	6.3	8.4	4.5
55-59	10.8	14.5	7.5	11.3	15.2	7.8	10.0	13.3	7.1
60-64	19.1	25.4	14.0	19.9	26.9	14.0	18.3	23.8	13.9
65-69	30.6	38.6	24.0	32.3	40.3	25.9	29.0	37.1	22.4
70-74	48.0	58.0	40.1	48.9	59.7	40.8	47.2	56.7	39.3
75-79	67.4	76.3	61.8	72.9	79.0	69.2	61.6	73.5	53.8
80-84	93.3	100.7	90.0	97.9	97.3	98.2	89.2	104.0	83.1
85-89	147.6	152.8	145.7	164.8	159.4	166.9	134.1	147.1	129.5
90-94	180.4	197.8	175.1	209.6	200.0	213.5	163.7	196.0	155.4
95-99	179.7	161.4	184.8	162.7	143.3	170.0	188.6	175.0	191.8
100+	292.5	245.0	304.4	224.0	◆105.0	303.3	315.3	385.0	304.6
China: Hong Kong SAR - Chine: Hong Kong RAS									
2001									
Total	5.0	5.8	4.2	...	...	...	...	...	...
0-1	2.5	2.6	2.3	...	...	...	...	...	...
1-4	0.2	0.3	◆0.2	...	...	...	...	...	...
5-9	0.1	◆0.1	◆0.1	...	...	...	...	...	...
10-14	0.1	◆0.1	◆0.1	...	...	...	...	...	...

568

(See notes at end of table. — Voir notes à la fin du tableau.)

Continent, country or area, year and age (in years) Continent, pays ou zone, année et âge (en années)	Total			Urban - Urbaine			Rural - Rurale		
	Both sexes Les deux sexes	Male Masculin	Female Féminin	Both sexes Les deux sexes	Male Masculin	Female Féminin	Both sexes Les deux sexes	Male Masculin	Female Féminin
ASIA — ASIE									
China: Hong Kong SAR - Chine: Hong Kong RAS									
2001									
15-19	0.2	0.3	0.2	...	...	...	...	...	...
20-24	0.4	0.5	0.2	...	...	...	...	...	...
25-29	0.6	0.9	0.3	...	...	...	...	...	...
30-34	0.5	0.8	0.3	...	...	...	...	...	...
35-39	0.7	1.0	0.6	...	...	...	...	...	...
40-44	1.2	1.5	0.9	...	...	...	...	...	...
45-49	2.0	2.7	1.3	...	...	...	...	...	...
50-54	2.9	3.9	1.8	...	...	...	...	...	...
55-59	5.0	6.9	2.8	...	...	...	...	...	...
60-64	7.7	10.3	4.8	...	...	...	...	...	...
65-69	13.7	17.9	9.3	...	...	...	...	...	...
70-74	22.5	29.9	15.5	...	...	...	...	...	...
75-79	36.3	48.3	26.9	...	...	...	...	...	...
80-84	58.3	76.8	46.1	...	...	...	...	...	...
85+	110.3	128.2	102.1	...	...	...	...	...	...
China: Macao SAR - Chine: Macao RAS									
2001									
Total	3.0	3.5	2.6	...	...	...	...	...	...
0-1	♦4.3	♦5.3	♦3.2	...	...	...	...	...	...
1-4	♦0.2	♦0.2	♦0.1	...	...	...	...	...	...
5-9	-	-	♦0.1	...	...	...	...	...	...
10-14	♦0.1	♦0.1	♦0.1	...	...	...	...	...	...
15-19	♦0.2	♦0.3	♦0.2	...	...	...	...	...	...
20-24	♦0.3	♦0.3	♦0.3	...	...	...	...	...	...
25-29	♦0.5	♦0.6	♦0.4	...	...	...	...	...	...
30-34	♦0.7	♦1.2	♦0.4	...	...	...	...	...	...
35-39	0.8	♦1.2	♦0.6	...	...	...	...	...	...
40-44	1.0	♦1.3	♦0.7	...	...	...	...	...	...
45-49	1.7	2.2	♦1.3	...	...	...	...	...	...
50-54	2.5	3.0	♦1.8	...	...	...	...	...	...
55-59	3.5	4.8	♦2.0	...	...	...	...	...	...
60-64	6.0	8.0	♦3.7	...	...	...	...	...	...
65-69	11.0	15.7	7.1	...	...	...	...	...	...
70-74	19.7	29.2	12.6	...	...	...	...	...	...
75-79	32.2	45.6	23.6	...	...	...	...	...	...
80-84	50.7	62.8	43.3	...	...	...	...	...	...
85+	88.7	88.2	89.0	...	...	...	...	...	...
Cyprus - Chypre[9]									
2002									
Total	7.3	7.9	6.7	...	...	...	...	...	...
0-1	4.7	♦4.7	♦4.8	...	...	...	...	...	...
1-4	♦0.5	♦0.4	♦0.7	...	...	...	...	...	...
5-9	♦0.3	♦0.4	♦0.2	...	...	...	...	...	...
10-14	♦0.2	♦0.2	♦0.2	...	...	...	...	...	...
15-19	0.6	♦0.9	♦0.2	...	...	...	...	...	...
20-24	0.9	1.1	♦0.6	...	...	...	...	...	...
25-29	0.8	♦1.1	♦0.5	...	...	...	...	...	...
30-34	0.8	♦1.3	♦0.5	...	...	...	...	...	...
35-39	0.8	♦1.1	♦0.6	...	...	...	...	...	...
40-44	0.9	1.5	♦0.4	...	...	...	...	...	...
45-49	1.8	2.4	♦1.1	...	...	...	...	...	...
50-54	2.8	3.1	2.4	...	...	...	...	...	...
55-59	5.6	8.1	3.3	...	...	...	...	...	...
60-64	7.3	9.3	5.4	...	...	...	...	...	...
65-69	14.9	20.0	10.4	...	...	...	...	...	...
70-74	25.6	34.5	18.4	...	...	...	...	...	...

20. Death rates specific for age, sex and urban/rural residence: latest available year, 1993 - 2002
Taux de mortalité selon l'âge, le sexe et la résidence, urbaine/rurale: dernière année disponible, 1993 - 2002 (continued — suite)

(See notes at end of table. — Voir notes à la fin du tableau.)

Continent, country or area, year and age (in years) / Continent, pays ou zone, année et âge (en années)	Total			Urban - Urbaine			Rural - Rurale		
	Both sexes Les deux sexes	Male Masculin	Female Féminin	Both sexes Les deux sexes	Male Masculin	Female Féminin	Both sexes Les deux sexes	Male Masculin	Female Féminin
ASIA — ASIE									
Cyprus - Chypre[9]									
2002									
75-79	48.9	58.2	41.5	...	...	...	...	...	...
80+	129.4	140.8	121.1	...	...	...	...	...	...
Georgia - Géorgie[8]									
2000									
Total	8.4	8.6	8.1	7.8	8.4	7.3	9.1	8.8	9.3
0-1	14.2	15.9	12.2	21.0	23.7	17.8	3.1	♦3.2	♦3.0
1-4	0.4	0.4	♦0.3	0.4	♦0.4	♦0.3	♦0.3	♦0.4	♦0.3
5-9	0.1	♦0.2	♦0.1	♦0.1	♦0.2	♦0.1	♦0.1	♦0.1	♦0.1
10-14	0.1	0.2	♦0.1	0.1	♦0.2	♦0.1	♦0.1	♦0.1	♦0.1
15-19	0.4	0.4	0.3	0.3	0.4	♦0.2	0.4	0.5	0.4
20-24	0.6	0.9	0.3	0.7	1.1	0.3	0.5	0.7	♦0.4
25-29	1.0	1.4	0.4	1.0	1.6	0.4	0.9	1.2	0.6
30-34	1.2	1.9	0.6	1.3	2.1	0.6	1.1	1.7	0.6
35-39	1.8	2.8	0.9	1.9	3.1	0.9	1.6	2.3	0.9
40-44	2.6	4.2	1.2	2.7	4.6	1.2	2.5	3.7	1.2
45-49	3.8	6.0	1.8	4.1	6.7	2.0	3.1	4.8	1.4
50-54	5.6	8.5	3.1	6.0	9.3	3.2	4.9	7.2	2.9
55-59	6.8	10.2	4.1	7.5	11.8	4.3	5.7	8.1	3.7
60-64	13.4	17.9	9.7	14.2	20.2	9.5	12.3	15.2	9.9
65-69	21.6	30.3	15.2	22.2	32.1	15.2	21.0	28.5	15.1
70-74	35.2	46.6	27.8	36.5	50.2	28.4	33.8	43.3	27.1
75-79	54.1	68.8	47.5	55.5	67.5	50.4	52.6	70.1	44.6
80-84	77.9	57.6	92.5	79.6	54.3	99.0	76.3	61.1	86.5
85+	164.4	109.3	204.4	146.4	96.7	181.0	182.6	121.3	228.9
Israel - Israël[10]									
2002									
Total	5.8	6.0	5.7	6.0	6.1	5.8	4.4	4.3	4.6
0-1	5.5	5.7	5.2	5.4	5.6	5.2	5.9	6.5	5.1
1-4	0.3	0.3	0.3	0.3	0.3	0.3	♦0.4	♦0.5	♦0.2
5-9	0.1	0.2	0.1	0.1	0.2	0.1	♦0.2	♦0.2	♦0.2
10-14	0.1	0.2	0.1	0.1	0.1	0.1	♦0.2	♦0.2	♦0.2
15-19	0.5	0.7	0.3	0.5	0.7	0.2	♦0.5	♦0.4	♦0.5
20-24	0.8	1.2	0.3	0.7	1.2	0.3	1.2	1.7	♦0.6
25-29	0.6	1.0	0.3	0.6	1.0	0.3	♦0.7	♦1.0	♦0.5
30-34	0.7	1.0	0.4	0.7	1.0	0.4	♦0.7	♦0.9	♦0.4
35-39	0.9	1.3	0.6	1.0	1.4	0.6	♦0.5	♦0.7	♦0.3
40-44	1.5	2.0	1.0	1.5	2.1	1.1	1.3	♦1.6	♦1.0
45-49	2.1	2.6	1.6	2.1	2.7	1.6	1.6	♦1.6	♦1.6
50-54	3.3	4.3	2.4	3.4	4.5	2.4	2.3	2.7	♦1.8
55-59	5.2	6.5	4.0	5.3	6.7	4.0	4.3	4.2	4.4
60-64	8.9	11.3	6.7	8.9	11.5	6.7	8.2	8.7	7.6
65-69	14.6	18.9	11.1	14.8	19.2	11.2	12.5	14.9	10.2
70-74	26.0	32.6	21.0	26.2	32.9	21.1	22.8	28.0	18.4
75-79	42.0	50.2	36.5	42.0	50.4	36.4	41.4	46.5	37.5
80-84	70.2	77.1	65.3	70.3	77.2	65.3	70.2	75.9	65.6
85+	166.1	178.4	159.0	166.0	178.3	158.4	172.1	180.0	166.9
Japan - Japon[11]									
2002									
Total	7.7	8.6	6.9	...	...	...	...	...	...
0-1	3.0	3.2	2.8	...	...	...	...	...	...
1-4	0.3	0.3	0.2	...	...	...	...	...	...
5-9	0.1	0.1	0.1	...	...	...	...	...	...
10-14	0.1	0.1	0.1	...	...	...	...	...	...
15-19	0.3	0.4	0.2	...	...	...	...	...	...
20-24	0.4	0.6	0.3	...	...	...	...	...	...
25-29	0.5	0.6	0.3	...	...	...	...	...	...
30-34	0.6	0.8	0.4	...	...	...	...	...	...
35-39	0.8	1.1	0.6	...	...	...	...	...	...

20. Death rates specific for age, sex and urban/rural residence: latest available year, 1993 - 2002
Taux de mortalité selon l'âge, le sexe et la résidence, urbaine/rurale: dernière année disponible, 1993 - 2002 (continued — suite)

(See notes at end of table. — Voir notes à la fin du tableau.)

Continent, country or area, year and age (in years) Continent, pays ou zone, année et âge (en années)	Total			Urban - Urbaine			Rural - Rurale		
	Both sexes Les deux sexes	Male Masculin	Female Féminin	Both sexes Les deux sexes	Male Masculin	Female Féminin	Both sexes Les deux sexes	Male Masculin	Female Féminin
ASIA — ASIE									
Japan - Japon[11]									
2002									
40-44	1.3	1.7	0.9	...	...	...	...	...	...
45-49	2.1	2.8	1.4	...	...	...	...	...	...
50-54	3.5	4.7	2.2	...	...	...	...	...	...
55-59	5.0	7.1	3.0	...	...	...	...	...	...
60-64	7.2	10.3	4.4	...	...	...	...	...	...
65-69	11.6	16.7	7.0	...	...	...	...	...	...
70-74	18.8	27.4	11.7	...	...	...	...	...	...
75-79	30.2	43.5	20.8	...	...	...	...	...	...
80-84	51.7	74.6	39.8	...	...	...	...	...	...
85-89	91.7	126.5	76.2	...	...	...	...	...	...
90+	168.1	211.1	154.0	...	...	...	...	...	...
Kazakhstan[8]									
1999									
Total	9.8	11.1	8.6	10.9	12.8	9.3	8.3	9.0	7.6
0-1	20.9	23.8	17.8	23.0	26.5	19.2	18.9	21.2	16.4
1-4	1.6	1.7	1.5	1.2	1.3	1.1	1.9	1.9	1.8
5-9	0.5	0.6	0.4	0.5	0.5	0.4	0.5	0.6	0.4
10-14	0.5	0.6	0.4	0.5	0.6	0.3	0.5	0.6	0.4
15-19	1.2	1.6	0.7	1.2	1.8	0.7	1.1	1.5	0.8
20-24	2.2	3.3	1.1	2.4	3.9	1.0	2.0	2.7	1.1
25-29	3.1	4.4	1.6	2.9	4.6	1.4	3.3	4.1	2.1
30-34	3.7	5.4	1.9	3.8	5.8	1.9	3.5	4.8	2.1
35-39	4.7	7.0	2.5	5.1	7.9	2.4	4.2	5.7	2.6
40-44	6.4	9.6	3.4	7.0	10.9	3.5	5.5	7.7	3.3
45-49	9.2	13.7	5.1	9.8	15.2	5.3	8.1	11.5	4.9
50-54	13.2	19.8	7.4	14.2	22.1	7.6	11.4	16.2	6.9
55-59	19.8	29.0	12.5	21.5	32.9	13.0	17.6	24.1	11.9
60-64	29.0	42.7	18.5	30.5	47.1	18.7	26.9	37.1	18.3
65-69	41.9	62.7	28.1	44.2	69.6	28.9	38.6	54.1	26.9
70-74	57.3	82.1	44.9	61.1	89.9	47.6	51.4	71.4	40.4
75-79	80.2	110.1	69.6	85.6	119.0	74.5	72.4	98.6	62.3
80-84	123.2	162.2	111.7	138.2	180.3	126.3	103.0	139.6	91.5
85-89	170.7	220.9	158.9	205.7	255.7	193.8	133.2	183.1	121.6
90-94	191.0	256.3	178.2	243.4	310.5	230.7	148.5	214.3	135.2
95+	312.6	293.5	317.1	275.6	235.3	284.7	347.7	345.9	348.1
Korea (Republic of) - Corée (République de)[12]									
2002									
Total	5.2	5.7	4.7	...	...	...	...	...	...
0-1	4.5	4.8	4.2	...	...	...	...	...	...
1-4	0.4	0.5	0.4	...	...	...	...	...	...
5-9	0.2	0.3	0.2	...	...	...	...	...	...
10-14	0.2	0.2	0.1	...	...	...	...	...	...
15-19	0.4	0.5	0.2	...	...	...	...	...	...
20-24	0.5	0.6	0.4	...	...	...	...	...	...
25-29	0.6	0.8	0.4	...	...	...	...	...	...
30-34	0.9	1.2	0.6	...	...	...	...	...	...
35-39	1.4	1.9	0.8	...	...	...	...	...	...
40-44	2.2	3.3	1.1	...	...	...	...	...	...
45-49	3.4	5.0	1.7	...	...	...	...	...	...
50-54	4.8	7.2	2.4	...	...	...	...	...	...
55-59	7.3	10.8	3.9	...	...	...	...	...	...
60-64	11.6	17.2	6.6	...	...	...	...	...	...
65-69	17.1	24.7	11.0	...	...	...	...	...	...
70-74	28.4	39.8	21.2	...	...	...	...	...	...
75-79	50.9	67.6	41.7	...	...	...	...	...	...
80-84	89.3	113.3	78.2	...	...	...	...	...	...
85-89	146.3	181.8	134.4	...	...	...	...	...	...

20. Death rates specific for age, sex and urban/rural residence: latest available year, 1993 - 2002
Taux de mortalité selon l'âge, le sexe et la résidence, urbaine/rurale: dernière année disponible, 1993 - 2002 (continued — suite)

(See notes at end of table. — Voir notes à la fin du tableau.)

Continent, country or area, year and age (in years) / Continent, pays ou zone, année et âge (en années)	Total			Urban - Urbaine			Rural - Rurale		
	Both sexes Les deux sexes	Male Masculin	Female Féminin	Both sexes Les deux sexes	Male Masculin	Female Féminin	Both sexes Les deux sexes	Male Masculin	Female Féminin
ASIA — ASIE									
Korea (Republic of) - Corée (République de)[12]									
2002									
90-94	251.4	311.5	236.7	...	...	...	...	...	...
95+	420.0	465.6	412.9	...	...	...	...	...	...
Kuwait - Koweït									
1998									
Total	2.1	2.2	1.9	...	...	...	...	...	...
0-1	11.6	12.6	10.6	...	...	...	...	...	...
1-4	0.6	0.6	0.5	...	...	...	...	...	...
5-9	0.3	◆0.3	◆0.3	...	...	...	...	...	...
10-14	0.2	◆0.3	◆0.2	...	...	...	...	...	...
15-19	0.6	0.9	◆0.3	...	...	...	...	...	...
20-24	0.7	1.0	0.4	...	...	...	...	...	...
25-29	0.5	0.6	0.4	...	...	...	...	...	...
30-34	0.6	0.7	0.4	...	...	...	...	...	...
35-39	0.8	0.9	0.7	...	...	...	...	...	...
40-44	1.3	1.5	0.8	...	...	...	...	...	...
45-49	2.0	2.1	1.5	...	...	...	...	...	...
50-54	3.9	4.3	3.1	...	...	...	...	...	...
55-59	7.0	7.0	6.9	...	...	...	...	...	...
60-64	13.5	12.8	14.7	...	...	...	...	...	...
65-69	25.9	27.3	24.1	...	...	...	...	...	...
70-74	46.3	47.0	45.5	...	...	...	...	...	...
75-79	69.7	77.6	62.1	...	...	...	...	...	...
80-84	120.8	119.3	122.4	...	...	...	...	...	...
85+	172.8	181.2	165.1	...	...	...	...	...	...
Kyrgyzstan - Kirghizistan[8]									
2002									
Total	7.1	7.9	6.4	7.9	9.0	6.9	6.7	7.3	6.1
0-1	22.1	26.1	17.8	30.7	36.4	24.7	18.6	22.0	15.0
1-4	2.0	2.0	1.9	1.1	1.0	1.1	2.3	2.3	2.2
5-9	0.4	0.5	0.4	0.3	0.4	◆0.2	0.5	0.5	0.4
10-14	0.4	0.5	0.3	0.4	0.4	◆0.3	0.5	0.6	0.3
15-19	0.7	0.9	0.5	0.7	0.9	0.4	0.8	1.0	0.5
20-24	1.3	1.8	0.8	0.9	1.3	0.6	1.6	2.2	1.0
25-29	1.9	2.7	1.2	1.8	2.7	0.9	2.0	2.6	1.4
30-34	2.7	3.9	1.6	2.5	3.7	1.3	2.9	4.0	1.8
35-39	3.9	5.6	2.3	3.4	5.1	1.8	4.3	5.8	2.7
40-44	5.2	7.8	2.7	5.5	8.4	2.9	5.0	7.4	2.6
45-49	7.7	10.9	4.7	8.4	12.5	4.8	7.2	9.8	4.6
50-54	11.4	16.6	6.7	13.1	20.3	7.0	10.2	14.2	6.4
55-59	16.9	23.7	10.7	18.5	28.0	10.7	15.7	20.9	10.7
60-64	24.3	33.0	17.0	24.5	34.8	16.7	24.1	31.9	17.2
65-69	36.4	49.8	25.9	39.9	59.0	26.6	34.5	45.2	25.4
70-74	53.6	68.0	43.4	55.9	78.6	42.8	52.3	63.1	43.7
75-79	80.1	91.4	73.7	83.7	103.5	75.2	77.9	85.8	72.6
80-84	118.7	131.0	113.5	121.7	137.6	115.6	116.8	127.4	112.0
85-89	177.8	193.3	172.5	191.7	226.1	181.8	168.6	175.7	166.0
90-94	224.1	217.5	226.5	262.9	227.0	275.6	206.5	213.0	204.3
95+	320.8	278.2	331.1	282.8	460.5	245.9	331.2	235.3	355.5
Malaysia - Malaisie									
2000									
Total	4.7	5.4	4.0	...	...	...	...	...	...
0-4	1.8	2.0	1.7	...	...	...	...	...	...
5-9	0.3	0.4	0.3	...	...	...	...	...	...
10-14	0.4	0.5	0.3	...	...	...	...	...	...
15-19	0.9	1.3	0.4	...	...	...	...	...	...
20-24	1.1	1.7	0.6	...	...	...	...	...	...
25-29	1.3	1.9	0.6	...	...	...	...	...	...

20. Death rates specific for age, sex and urban/rural residence: latest available year, 1993 - 2002
Taux de mortalité selon l'âge, le sexe et la résidence, urbaine/rurale: dernière année disponible, 1993 - 2002 (continued — suite)

(See notes at end of table. — Voir notes à la fin du tableau.)

Continent, country or area, year and age (in years) — Continent, pays ou zone, année et âge (en années)	Total			Urban - Urbaine			Rural - Rurale		
	Both sexes Les deux sexes	Male Masculin	Female Féminin	Both sexes Les deux sexes	Male Masculin	Female Féminin	Both sexes Les deux sexes	Male Masculin	Female Féminin
ASIA — ASIE									
Malaysia - Malaisie									
2000									
30-34	1.6	2.4	0.8	...	...	...	...	...	...
35-39	2.0	2.9	1.1	...	...	...	...	...	...
40-44	3.0	4.0	1.9	...	...	...	...	...	...
45-49	4.1	5.3	2.9	...	...	...	...	...	...
50-54	7.0	8.8	5.2	...	...	...	...	...	...
55-59	10.9	13.6	8.1	...	...	...	...	...	...
60-64	18.5	22.7	14.3	...	...	...	...	...	...
65-69	28.9	34.7	23.7	...	...	...	...	...	...
70-74	47.8	55.4	41.1	...	...	...	...	...	...
75-79	75.0	85.0	67.2	...	...	...	...	...	...
80+	145.2	161.9	133.7	...	...	...	...	...	...
Maldives									
2001									
Total	3.9	4.4	3.5	...	...	...	...	...	...
0-4	4.2	4.3	4.1	...	...	...	...	...	...
5-9	◆0.4	◆0.4	◆0.4	...	...	...	...	...	...
10-14	◆0.3	◆0.4	◆0.2	...	...	...	...	...	...
15-19	◆0.4	◆0.7	◆0.1	...	...	...	...	...	...
20-24	◆0.8	◆1.0	◆0.5	...	...	...	...	...	...
25-29	◆0.8	◆0.6	0.9	...	...	...	...	...	...
30-34	◆0.9	◆1.0	◆0.7	...	...	...	...	...	...
35-39	◆1.2	◆1.1	◆1.2	...	...	...	...	...	...
40-44	◆2.2	◆2.1	◆2.3	...	...	...	...	...	...
45-49	◆2.8	◆3.0	◆2.6	...	...	...	...	...	...
50-54	7.9	◆8.6	◆7.1	...	...	...	...	...	...
55-59	9.6	11.1	◆8.1	...	...	...	...	...	...
60-64	18.2	19.4	16.8	...	...	...	...	...	...
65-69	28.4	26.5	30.9	...	...	...	...	...	...
70+	75.1	73.6	77.5	...	...	...	...	...	...
Mongolia - Mongolie									
2001									
Total	6.6	7.5	5.6	...	...	...	...	...	...
0-1	30.4	31.7	29.0	...	...	...	...	...	...
1-4	3.0	3.3	2.7	...	...	...	...	...	...
5-9	0.5	0.7	0.4	...	...	...	...	...	...
10-14	0.4	0.5	0.3	...	...	...	...	...	...
15-19	0.7	0.9	0.4	...	...	...	...	...	...
20-24	1.4	1.9	0.9	...	...	...	...	...	...
25-29	2.0	2.7	1.2	...	...	...	...	...	...
30-34	2.9	3.9	1.8	...	...	...	...	...	...
35-39	3.8	5.2	2.4	...	...	...	...	...	...
40-44	5.5	7.1	3.9	...	...	...	...	...	...
45-49	8.4	11.0	5.9	...	...	...	...	...	...
50-54	12.8	15.8	9.8	...	...	...	...	...	...
55-59	18.8	22.8	15.0	...	...	...	...	...	...
60-64	31.1	38.0	24.7	...	...	...	...	...	...
65-69	44.2	54.2	35.3	...	...	...	...	...	...
70+	78.1	97.0	64.8	...	...	...	...	...	...
Nepal - Népal[13]									
2001									
Total	4.7	5.2	4.2	...	...	...	...	...	...
0-1	26.3	27.5	25.1	...	...	...	...	...	...
1-4	4.3	4.9	3.8	...	...	...	...	...	...
5-9	1.0	1.1	1.0	...	...	...	...	...	...
10-14	0.8	0.9	0.7	...	...	...	...	...	...
15-19	1.1	1.1	1.0	...	...	...	...	...	...
20-24	1.4	1.5	1.2	...	...	...	...	...	...
25-29	1.6	1.7	1.4	...	...	...	...	...	...

20. Death rates specific for age, sex and urban/rural residence: latest available year, 1993 - 2002
Taux de mortalité selon l'âge, le sexe et la résidence, urbaine/rurale: dernière année disponible, 1993 - 2002 (continued — suite)

(See notes at end of table. — Voir notes à la fin du tableau.)

Continent, country or area, year and age (in years) Continent, pays ou zone, année et âge (en années)	Total			Urban - Urbaine			Rural - Rurale		
	Both sexes Les deux sexes	Male Masculin	Female Féminin	Both sexes Les deux sexes	Male Masculin	Female Féminin	Both sexes Les deux sexes	Male Masculin	Female Féminin
ASIA — ASIE									
Nepal - Népal[13]									
2001									
30-34	1.7	1.8	1.5	...	...	...	...	...	...
35-39	2.2	2.4	1.9	...	...	...	...	...	...
40-44	2.7	3.4	2.1	...	...	...	...	...	...
45-49	3.8	4.3	3.4	...	...	...	...	...	...
50-54	6.1	7.1	5.1	...	...	...	...	...	...
55-59	10.2	11.3	8.8	...	...	...	...	...	...
60-64	16.0	18.0	14.0	...	...	...	...	...	...
65-69	22.4	24.3	20.4	...	...	...	...	...	...
70-74	35.1	38.9	31.0	...	...	...	...	...	...
75-79	48.9	56.6	41.4	...	...	...	...	...	...
80+	154.8	169.7	140.5	...	...	...	...	...	...
Pakistan[14,15]									
2001									
Total	7.2	7.4	6.9	6.3	6.6	6.0	7.6	7.9	7.3
0-4	19.9	20.6	19.1	18.2	19.1	17.3	20.6	21.3	19.9
5-9	1.6	1.5	1.7	1.5	1.6	1.3	1.7	1.5	1.9
10-14	1.2	0.8	1.7	1.4	1.0	1.8	1.2	0.6	1.7
15-19	1.4	1.5	1.3	1.2	1.3	1.1	1.5	1.6	1.4
20-24	1.9	1.5	2.3	1.4	1.4	1.3	2.2	1.6	2.9
25-29	2.1	2.2	1.9	1.9	1.7	2.1	2.2	2.5	1.9
30-34	2.5	3.4	1.8	2.5	2.8	2.1	2.6	3.7	1.5
35-39	4.2	4.8	3.5	3.9	4.9	2.9	4.3	4.7	4.0
40-44	4.0	3.9	4.1	4.0	2.6	5.6	4.0	4.7	3.3
45-49	5.4	6.4	4.3	6.0	8.0	3.7	5.0	5.4	4.7
50-54	8.7	9.1	8.1	9.1	11.7	5.9	8.4	7.6	9.4
55-59	13.2	13.2	13.1	12.2	10.8	13.8	13.7	14.6	12.8
60-64	20.3	18.4	22.6	14.9	14.1	15.7	23.0	20.5	26.3
65-69	28.9	24.2	34.9	26.7	18.3	37.2	30.0	27.3	33.7
70+	70.5	73.4	66.5	71.0	71.5	70.3	70.2	74.2	64.6
Philippines									
2000									
Total	4.8	5.6	3.9	...	...	...	...	...	...
0-1	14.5	16.5	12.3	...	...	...	...	...	...
1-4	1.5	1.6	1.4	...	...	...	...	...	...
5-9	0.6	0.7	0.5	...	...	...	...	...	...
10-14	0.5	0.6	0.4	...	...	...	...	...	...
15-19	0.8	1.1	0.5	...	...	...	...	...	...
20-24	1.3	1.9	0.8	...	...	...	...	...	...
25-29	1.7	2.4	1.1	...	...	...	...	...	...
30-34	2.1	2.9	1.4	...	...	...	...	...	...
35-39	2.8	3.8	1.9	...	...	...	...	...	...
40-44	3.8	5.1	2.6	...	...	...	...	...	...
45-49	5.7	7.5	3.8	...	...	...	...	...	...
50-54	8.5	11.3	5.6	...	...	...	...	...	...
55-59	12.3	16.8	8.0	...	...	...	...	...	...
60-64	17.9	23.9	12.3	...	...	...	...	...	...
65-69	26.5	34.6	19.3	...	...	...	...	...	...
70-74	39.1	49.6	30.5	...	...	...	...	...	...
75-79	60.4	73.8	50.3	...	...	...	...	...	...
80-84	94.7	109.4	84.6	...	...	...	...	...	...
85-89	157.7	166.8	151.8	...	...	...	...	...	...
90-94	206.4	229.6	194.2	...	...	...	...	...	...
95+	212.5	189.9	228.2	...	...	...	...	...	...
Qatar									
1997									
Total	2.0	2.1	1.8	...	...	...	...	...	...
0-1	16.4	15.1	17.9	...	...	...	...	...	...
1-4	◆0.6	◆0.9	◆0.3	...	...	...	...	...	...

20. Death rates specific for age, sex and urban/rural residence: latest available year, 1993 - 2002
Taux de mortalité selon l'âge, le sexe et la résidence, urbaine/rurale: dernière année disponible, 1993 - 2002 (continued — suite)

(See notes at end of table. — Voir notes à la fin du tableau.)

Continent, country or area, year and age (in years) Continent, pays ou zone, année et âge (en années)	Total			Urban - Urbaine			Rural - Rurale		
	Both sexes Les deux sexes	Male Masculin	Female Féminin	Both sexes Les deux sexes	Male Masculin	Female Féminin	Both sexes Les deux sexes	Male Masculin	Female Féminin
ASIA — ASIE									
Qatar									
1997									
5-9	◆0.4	◆0.4	◆0.3	...	...	...	...	...	...
10-14	◆0.3	◆0.4	◆0.2	...	...	...	...	...	...
15-19	◆0.5	◆1.0	◆0.1	...	...	...	...	...	...
20-24	0.9	◆1.2	◆0.3	...	...	...	...	...	...
25-29	0.8	0.9	◆0.4	...	...	...	...	...	...
30-34	0.7	0.9	◆0.5	...	...	...	...	...	...
35-39	0.8	0.9	◆0.6	...	...	...	...	...	...
40-44	1.0	1.1	◆0.8	...	...	...	...	...	...
45-49	1.9	1.9	◆1.9	...	...	...	...	...	...
50-54	3.1	2.8	◆4.2	...	...	...	...	...	...
55-59	7.3	7.7	◆6.3	...	...	...	...	...	...
60-64	14.9	14.5	◆15.8	...	...	...	...	...	...
65-69	28.7	32.2	◆22.2	...	...	...	...	...	...
70-74	39.3	41.3	◆35.7	...	...	...	...	...	...
75-79	84.0	89.9	◆74.3	...	...	...	...	...	...
80+	133.1	126.4	142.9	...	...	...	...	...	...
Singapore - Singapour+,16									
2002									
Total	4.7	5.2	4.2	...	...	...	...	...	...
0-4	0.8	0.9	0.6	...	...	...	...	...	...
5-9	◆0.1	◆0.1	◆0.1	...	...	...	...	...	...
10-14	0.1	◆0.2	◆0.1	...	...	...	...	...	...
15-19	0.4	0.4	0.4	...	...	...	...	...	...
20-24	0.7	0.9	0.5	...	...	...	...	...	...
25-29	0.7	1.0	0.5	...	...	...	...	...	...
30-34	0.8	1.1	0.5	...	...	...	...	...	...
35-39	1.0	1.3	0.7	...	...	...	...	...	...
40-44	1.4	1.9	0.9	...	...	...	...	...	...
45-49	2.3	3.0	1.5	...	...	...	...	...	...
50-54	3.7	4.6	2.9	...	...	...	...	...	...
55-59	6.7	8.9	4.4	...	...	...	...	...	...
60-64	10.9	14.0	8.1	...	...	...	...	...	...
65-69	18.2	23.3	13.5	...	...	...	...	...	...
70-74	28.7	34.6	23.6	...	...	...	...	...	...
75-79	45.3	53.9	38.2	...	...	...	...	...	...
80+	101.6	116.6	93.3	...	...	...	...	...	...
Sri Lanka+									
1996									
Total	6.7	8.5	4.7	...	...	...	...	...	...
0-4	3.1	3.4	2.8	...	...	...	...	...	...
5-9	0.4	0.5	0.4	...	...	...	...	...	...
10-14	0.5	0.5	0.4	...	...	...	...	...	...
15-19	1.7	2.5	0.9	...	...	...	...	...	...
20-24	3.3	5.5	1.0	...	...	...	...	...	...
25-29	3.7	6.3	1.2	...	...	...	...	...	...
30-34	3.4	5.5	1.2	...	...	...	...	...	...
35-39	4.7	7.3	2.0	...	...	...	...	...	...
40-44	5.3	8.1	2.4	...	...	...	...	...	...
45-49	7.7	11.3	4.1	...	...	...	...	...	...
50-54	9.6	12.9	6.0	...	...	...	...	...	...
55-59	13.2	17.7	8.2	...	...	...	...	...	...
60-64	20.1	24.5	15.0	...	...	...	...	...	...
65-69	34.5	41.2	27.0	...	...	...	...	...	...
70-74	56.3	61.9	49.8	...	...	...	...	...	...
75-79	81.7	88.1	74.6	...	...	...	...	...	...
80+	176.8	177.6	176.1	...	...	...	...	...	...

20. Death rates specific for age, sex and urban/rural residence: latest available year, 1993 - 2002
Taux de mortalité selon l'âge, le sexe et la résidence, urbaine/rurale: dernière année disponible, 1993 - 2002 (continued — suite)

(See notes at end of table. — Voir notes à la fin du tableau.)

Continent, country or area, year and age (in years) Continent, pays ou zone, année et âge (en années)	Total			Urban - Urbaine			Rural - Rurale		
	Both sexes Les deux sexes	Male Masculin	Female Féminin	Both sexes Les deux sexes	Male Masculin	Female Féminin	Both sexes Les deux sexes	Male Masculin	Female Féminin
ASIA — ASIE									
Tajikistan - Tadjikistan[8]									
1993									
Total	8.8	10.6	6.9	9.2	11.1	7.4	8.6	10.4	6.7
0-1	47.0	52.2	41.4	54.6	62.9	45.8	44.8	49.2	40.2
1-4	8.7	9.0	8.5	5.5	5.7	5.2	9.7	10.0	9.4
5-9	1.0	1.1	0.8	0.7	0.9	0.5	1.0	1.1	0.9
10-14	0.8	0.9	0.6	0.6	0.8	0.4	0.8	1.0	0.6
15-19	1.4	2.1	0.8	1.4	2.1	0.6	1.5	2.0	0.9
20-24	3.0	4.7	1.4	2.8	4.0	1.2	3.1	5.0	1.4
25-29	4.8	8.3	1.6	4.7	8.6	1.1	4.8	8.1	1.8
30-34	5.8	9.4	2.3	5.9	10.3	1.9	5.8	9.1	2.5
35-39	6.8	10.7	3.0	6.3	10.8	2.2	7.1	10.7	3.4
40-44	7.9	12.2	3.8	7.3	11.5	3.5	8.3	12.6	4.0
45-49	10.3	15.1	5.1	9.5	14.4	4.7	10.8	15.5	5.4
50-54	13.2	18.5	7.4	12.5	18.7	6.8	13.6	18.4	7.9
55-59	17.3	23.8	10.9	17.6	25.8	10.3	17.1	22.7	11.3
60-64	24.8	33.2	17.1	26.2	36.8	17.9	24.1	31.5	16.7
65-69	34.3	43.1	27.1	36.7	51.0	27.8	32.9	39.4	26.6
70-74	47.0	59.8	39.4	50.5	66.0	43.0	45.1	57.0	37.2
75-79	71.8	89.9	61.7	79.8	104.7	69.2	66.4	82.5	55.9
80-84	105.7	125.7	94.2	128.0	148.3	119.2	93.0	115.9	77.7
85+	174.2	185.2	167.2	191.7	221.3	179.6	167.6	176.0	161.3
Uzbekistan - Ouzbékistan[8]									
2000									
Total	5.5	5.8	5.2	6.6	7.1	6.2	4.8	5.0	4.6
0-1	19.1	21.4	16.6	22.6	25.4	19.6	17.5	19.6	15.3
1-4	2.3	2.4	2.2	1.6	1.7	1.5	2.6	2.8	2.5
5-9	0.4	0.5	0.4	0.4	0.5	0.3	0.5	0.6	0.4
10-14	0.5	0.5	0.4	0.4	0.5	0.4	0.5	0.6	0.4
15-19	0.7	0.9	0.5	0.7	1.0	0.5	0.7	0.9	0.5
20-24	1.3	1.6	1.0	1.4	1.9	0.9	1.2	1.4	1.0
25-29	1.7	2.2	1.3	1.9	2.5	1.2	1.6	1.9	1.3
30-34	2.1	2.9	1.4	2.4	3.3	1.4	2.0	2.5	1.5
35-39	2.5	3.4	1.7	3.0	4.3	1.7	2.2	2.7	1.6
40-44	3.6	4.8	2.6	4.4	6.3	2.6	3.1	3.7	2.5
45-49	5.4	7.2	3.7	6.2	8.9	3.7	4.7	5.8	3.6
50-54	9.4	12.2	6.7	10.2	14.1	6.7	8.5	10.4	6.6
55-59	14.2	17.6	10.8	15.3	20.9	10.2	13.2	15.0	11.3
60-64	22.3	27.5	17.5	23.3	31.4	16.5	21.5	24.5	18.4
65-69	35.9	43.2	29.7	37.2	49.2	28.2	34.8	39.0	30.9
70-74	52.7	61.0	46.2	54.6	69.8	45.0	51.2	55.1	47.4
75-79	72.9	80.3	68.9	73.8	84.7	69.0	72.1	77.2	68.8
80-84	114.2	129.9	108.1	115.6	127.9	111.3	112.9	131.6	104.7
85-89	164.0	194.7	152.6	166.2	183.1	160.8	161.7	204.8	143.4
90-94	195.5	192.3	197.2	171.3	152.4	179.9	215.8	219.9	213.3
95+	316.6	202.4	394.2	156.3	168.0	151.3	460.7	220.9	700.6
EUROPE									
Austria - Autriche									
2002									
Total	9.5	9.0	9.9	...	...	...	...	...	...
0-1	4.1	4.8	3.4	...	...	...	...	...	...
1-4	0.2	0.2	◆0.2	...	...	...	...	...	...
5-9	0.1	0.1	◆0.1	...	...	...	...	...	...
10-14	0.1	◆0.1	◆0.1	...	...	...	...	...	...
15-19	0.5	0.7	0.3	...	...	...	...	...	...
20-24	0.6	0.9	0.3	...	...	...	...	...	...
25-29	0.6	0.9	0.3	...	...	...	...	...	...
30-34	0.7	0.9	0.4	...	...	...	...	...	...

20. Death rates specific for age, sex and urban/rural residence: latest available year, 1993 - 2002
Taux de mortalité selon l'âge, le sexe et la résidence, urbaine/rurale: dernière année disponible, 1993 - 2002 (continued — suite)

(See notes at end of table. — Voir notes à la fin du tableau.)

Continent, country or area, year and age (in years) / Continent, pays ou zone, année et âge (en années)	Total			Urban - Urbaine			Rural - Rurale		
	Both sexes Les deux sexes	Male Masculin	Female Féminin	Both sexes Les deux sexes	Male Masculin	Female Féminin	Both sexes Les deux sexes	Male Masculin	Female Féminin
EUROPE									
Austria - Autriche									
2002									
35-39	1.0	1.3	0.7	...	...	...	...	...	...
40-44	1.7	2.2	1.1	...	...	...	...	...	...
45-49	2.6	3.5	1.8	...	...	...	...	...	...
50-54	4.5	6.1	2.9	...	...	...	...	...	...
55-59	6.7	9.1	4.4	...	...	...	...	...	...
60-64	9.0	12.6	5.7	...	...	...	...	...	...
65-69	15.0	20.7	10.1	...	...	...	...	...	...
70-74	25.1	34.6	17.7	...	...	...	...	...	...
75-79	41.8	56.2	34.0	...	...	...	...	...	...
80-84	70.5	91.7	61.3	...	...	...	...	...	...
85-89	140.6	168.5	130.5	...	...	...	...	...	...
90-94	230.1	265.4	219.6	...	...	...	...	...	...
95+	381.7	413.3	374.8	...	...	...	...	...	...
Belarus - Bélarus[8]									
2002									
Total	14.8	16.7	13.1	10.9	13.0	9.1	24.1	25.6	22.7
0-1	7.8	8.6	6.9	6.9	7.8	6.0	10.0	10.8	9.2
1-4	0.8	0.9	0.6	0.5	0.6	0.4	1.4	1.7	1.1
5-9	0.3	0.4	0.3	0.2	0.3	0.2	0.5	0.6	0.5
10-14	0.3	0.4	0.2	0.2	0.3	0.2	0.5	0.6	◆0.3
15-19	0.8	1.1	0.5	0.6	0.9	0.4	1.2	1.8	0.6
20-24	1.5	2.4	0.7	1.2	1.7	0.6	3.1	4.9	1.2
25-29	2.4	4.0	0.9	2.0	3.3	0.8	3.9	6.2	1.3
30-34	3.2	5.1	1.3	2.6	4.1	1.1	5.0	7.8	1.8
35-39	4.3	7.0	1.6	3.5	5.9	1.4	6.6	10.1	2.5
40-44	6.1	9.9	2.5	5.1	8.4	2.3	9.2	14.0	3.4
45-49	9.1	14.5	4.1	7.9	12.9	3.7	12.7	18.7	5.8
50-54	13.6	21.4	6.6	11.8	19.0	5.9	19.0	28.2	9.4
55-59	19.8	30.4	11.1	18.0	28.2	9.7	23.9	35.5	14.4
60-64	27.5	44.5	15.4	25.6	41.5	14.2	30.7	49.6	17.6
65-69	36.1	56.7	23.1	34.5	54.5	21.9	37.8	59.2	24.4
70-74	52.6	79.3	37.8	52.4	78.2	38.3	52.7	80.3	37.3
75-79	76.0	106.2	64.6	74.5	101.7	63.7	77.5	110.8	65.4
80-84	119.8	149.3	110.4	115.8	143.1	106.7	123.5	155.5	113.7
85-89	196.5	231.7	187.5	179.4	220.5	168.2	211.7	242.7	204.3
90-94	282.4	321.4	273.7	235.3	279.1	225.4	321.0	356.5	313.1
95+	458.7	491.9	451.9	324.2	347.7	318.9	581.3	649.2	568.9
Belgium - Belgique[17]									
2002									
Total	10.2	10.4	10.1	...	...	...	...	...	...
0-4	1.1	1.2	0.9	...	...	...	...	...	...
5-9	0.1	0.2	0.1	...	...	...	...	...	...
10-14	0.1	0.1	0.1	...	...	...	...	...	...
15-19	0.5	0.6	0.3	...	...	...	...	...	...
20-24	0.7	1.1	0.3	...	...	...	...	...	...
25-29	0.8	1.1	0.4	...	...	...	...	...	...
30-34	0.8	1.1	0.5	...	...	...	...	...	...
35-39	1.1	1.5	0.8	...	...	...	...	...	...
40-44	1.8	2.2	1.3	...	...	...	...	...	...
45-49	3.0	3.9	2.1	...	...	...	...	...	...
50-54	4.7	5.9	3.4	...	...	...	...	...	...
55-59	6.9	9.1	4.7	...	...	...	...	...	...
60-64	10.2	13.7	6.9	...	...	...	...	...	...
65-69	16.0	22.0	10.6	...	...	...	...	...	...
70-74	25.6	35.7	17.6	...	...	...	...	...	...
75-79	44.5	61.6	33.0	...	...	...	...	...	...
80-84	76.0	99.9	63.0	...	...	...	...	...	...
85+	181.3	210.9	171.0	...	...	...	...	...	...

20. Death rates specific for age, sex and urban/rural residence: latest available year, 1993 - 2002
Taux de mortalité selon l'âge, le sexe et la résidence, urbaine/rurale: dernière année disponible, 1993 - 2002 (continued — suite)

(See notes at end of table. — Voir notes à la fin du tableau.)

Continent, country or area, year and age (in years) / Continent, pays ou zone, année et âge (en années)	Total			Urban - Urbaine			Rural - Rurale		
	Both sexes Les deux sexes	Male Masculin	Female Féminin	Both sexes Les deux sexes	Male Masculin	Female Féminin	Both sexes Les deux sexes	Male Masculin	Female Féminin
EUROPE									
Bulgaria - Bulgarie									
2002									
Total	14.3	15.7	13.0	11.7	13.0	10.4	20.3	21.7	19.0
0-1	13.5	14.6	12.3	12.1	13.1	11.1	16.9	18.2	15.5
1-4	0.7	0.8	0.6	0.5	0.6	0.4	1.0	1.1	0.9
5-9	0.3	0.3	0.2	0.2	♦0.2	♦0.2	0.4	♦0.5	♦0.3
10-14	0.2	0.3	0.2	0.2	0.3	♦0.1	0.3	♦0.3	♦0.2
15-19	0.5	0.6	0.3	0.4	0.6	0.3	0.6	0.8	♦0.3
20-24	0.8	1.0	0.5	0.7	1.0	0.4	0.9	1.2	0.5
25-29	0.8	1.2	0.4	0.8	1.1	0.4	1.1	1.5	0.5
30-34	1.2	1.7	0.8	1.1	1.5	0.8	1.5	2.0	0.8
35-39	1.9	2.6	1.3	1.7	2.3	1.2	2.5	3.5	1.5
40-44	3.2	4.6	1.8	2.9	4.1	1.8	4.0	5.9	1.9
45-49	5.2	7.4	3.0	4.8	6.8	2.9	6.2	9.1	3.1
50-54	8.4	12.3	4.7	7.9	11.5	4.7	9.5	14.2	4.6
55-59	12.1	17.7	7.0	11.8	17.2	6.8	12.7	18.7	7.3
60-64	18.1	26.1	11.2	18.4	26.6	11.4	17.7	25.5	11.0
65-69	27.3	37.1	19.4	28.1	38.7	19.9	26.4	35.3	18.7
70-74	44.0	56.4	34.7	44.5	58.2	34.6	43.5	54.3	34.8
75-79	74.9	88.5	65.7	74.7	89.3	65.1	75.2	87.6	66.4
80-84	121.6	136.8	112.1	120.1	138.6	109.1	123.1	134.9	115.5
85-89	210.5	225.6	201.9	206.1	226.3	195.1	215.4	224.9	209.6
90-94	314.8	337.0	303.5	300.8	316.5	293.0	330.6	359.1	315.5
95-99	444.9	473.5	432.1	427.7	402.9	439.4	463.8	558.2	424.5
100+	434.6	660.0	354.6	505.2	♦857.1	♦362.3	361.7	♦409.1	♦347.2
Croatia - Croatie									
2001									
Total	11.2	11.7	10.6	10.1	10.8	9.4	12.6	12.9	12.3
0-1	7.3	7.6	7.1	7.6	7.8	7.4	7.0	7.2	6.7
1-4	0.3	0.4	♦0.2	♦0.3	♦0.3	♦0.2	0.4	♦0.5	♦0.2
5-9	0.2	♦0.2	♦0.1	♦0.1	♦0.2	♦0.1	♦0.2	♦0.2	♦0.2
10-14	0.2	♦0.2	♦0.1	♦0.1	♦0.2	♦0.1	♦0.2	♦0.3	♦0.1
15-19	0.5	0.8	0.3	0.5	0.7	♦0.3	0.5	0.9	♦0.2
20-24	0.8	1.2	0.3	0.8	1.3	♦0.3	0.7	1.1	♦0.3
25-29	0.7	1.1	0.3	0.7	1.0	♦0.3	0.7	1.2	♦0.2
30-34	0.9	1.2	0.5	0.9	1.2	0.6	0.9	1.2	♦0.5
35-39	1.4	2.1	0.8	1.3	1.9	0.8	1.5	2.2	0.7
40-44	2.4	3.5	1.3	2.1	3.0	1.2	2.9	4.2	1.5
45-49	4.0	5.9	2.1	3.6	5.5	1.9	4.7	6.6	2.4
50-54	6.5	9.4	3.7	5.9	8.5	3.7	7.4	10.6	3.9
55-59	9.8	14.4	5.6	9.5	13.9	5.6	10.2	15.0	5.6
60-64	15.2	22.4	9.1	14.5	21.0	8.8	16.1	24.1	9.4
65-69	24.2	34.9	16.0	23.3	33.0	15.5	25.2	37.0	16.4
70-74	39.4	54.0	29.5	38.9	53.7	28.9	39.8	54.3	30.2
75-79	62.9	80.2	54.7	60.9	75.0	54.0	65.1	85.7	55.5
80-84	106.1	126.4	97.4	100.2	122.5	90.3	112.4	130.7	104.8
85-89	168.2	191.2	159.2	155.3	182.5	144.5	182.5	201.1	175.3
90-94	275.0	318.6	260.5	254.2	322.9	232.1	298.2	314.8	292.4
95+	406.9	427.2	401.1	360.6	396.4	351.1	459.9	448.1	463.6
2002									
Total	11.4	12.0	10.8	...	...	...	...	...	...
0-1	7.0	7.7	6.3	...	...	...	...	...	...
1-4	0.3	0.3	♦0.2	...	...	...	...	...	...
5-9	0.1	♦0.2	♦0.1	...	...	...	...	...	...
10-14	♦0.1	♦0.1	♦0.1	...	...	...	...	...	...
15-19	0.5	0.7	0.3	...	...	...	...	...	...
20-24	0.8	1.2	0.4	...	...	...	...	...	...
25-29	0.7	1.1	0.3	...	...	...	...	...	...
30-34	0.9	1.3	0.4	...	...	...	...	...	...
35-39	1.3	1.8	0.8	...	...	...	...	...	...

20. Death rates specific for age, sex and urban/rural residence: latest available year, 1993 - 2002
Taux de mortalité selon l'âge, le sexe et la résidence, urbaine/rurale: dernière année disponible, 1993 - 2002 (continued — suite)

(See notes at end of table. — Voir notes à la fin du tableau.)

Continent, country or area, year and age (in years) / Continent, pays ou zone, année et âge (en années)	Total			Urban - Urbaine			Rural - Rurale		
	Both sexes Les deux sexes	Male Masculin	Female Féminin	Both sexes Les deux sexes	Male Masculin	Female Féminin	Both sexes Les deux sexes	Male Masculin	Female Féminin
EUROPE									
Croatia - Croatie									
2002									
40-44	2.2	3.2	1.2	...	...	...	...	...	...
45-49	3.9	5.6	2.2	...	...	...	...	...	...
50-54	6.3	9.3	3.4	...	...	...	...	...	...
55-59	9.5	13.8	5.5	...	...	...	...	...	...
60-64	14.8	22.2	8.5	...	...	...	...	...	...
65-69	24.2	34.7	16.0	...	...	...	...	...	...
70-74	38.9	54.2	28.5	...	...	...	...	...	...
75+	97.8	115.1	89.9	...	...	...	...	...	...
Czech Republic - République tchèque									
2002									
Total	10.6	10.9	10.3	10.4	10.7	10.0	11.3	11.6	11.0
0-1	4.1	4.5	3.7	4.2	4.5	3.9	4.0	4.7	3.2
1-4	0.3	0.3	0.2	0.3	0.4	0.2	◆0.2	◆0.3	◆0.2
5-9	0.2	0.2	0.1	0.2	0.2	◆0.1	◆0.1	◆0.1	◆0.2
10-14	0.1	0.2	0.1	0.1	0.2	◆0.1	◆0.2	◆0.2	◆0.1
15-19	0.5	0.6	0.3	0.5	0.6	0.3	0.5	0.7	◆0.3
20-24	0.7	1.0	0.3	0.7	1.0	0.3	0.7	1.0	◆0.3
25-29	0.7	1.0	0.3	0.7	1.0	0.3	0.7	1.0	0.3
30-34	0.8	1.2	0.5	0.8	1.2	0.5	0.9	1.2	0.5
35-39	1.2	1.7	0.8	1.2	1.6	0.7	1.4	1.8	0.9
40-44	2.2	3.1	1.3	2.1	2.9	1.3	2.5	3.5	1.3
45-49	3.8	5.3	2.2	3.7	5.2	2.3	4.0	5.8	2.1
50-54	6.2	8.8	3.6	6.1	8.6	3.7	6.5	9.3	3.5
55-59	9.2	13.1	5.6	9.0	12.9	5.5	9.7	13.5	5.8
60-64	14.2	20.5	8.6	13.8	20.0	8.5	15.1	22.0	8.8
65-69	23.1	32.7	15.4	22.7	32.2	15.2	24.1	34.1	16.0
70-74	36.3	48.9	27.6	35.4	47.8	26.9	38.7	52.1	29.3
75-79	59.5	76.5	49.9	58.5	74.7	49.3	62.3	81.5	51.5
80-84	92.7	113.0	83.0	91.8	112.7	81.9	95.1	113.8	86.0
85-89	190.6	227.0	176.6	188.1	225.4	174.1	197.1	231.0	183.2
90-94	259.4	292.8	248.9	255.7	294.5	243.9	269.0	289.0	262.1
95-99	396.0	380.0	399.9	406.6	403.9	407.2	368.9	327.7	380.6
100+	558.8	◆571.4	556.7	546.0	◆681.8	526.3	593.8	◆384.6	647.1
Denmark - Danemark[18]									
2002									
Total	10.9	10.7	11.1	...	...	...	...	...	...
0-1	4.4	4.9	4.0	...	...	...	...	...	...
1-4	0.3	0.2	0.3	...	...	...	...	...	...
5-9	0.1	◆0.1	◆0.1	...	...	...	...	...	...
10-14	0.1	◆0.1	◆0.1	...	...	...	...	...	...
15-19	0.5	0.6	0.3	...	...	...	...	...	...
20-24	0.5	0.8	0.3	...	...	...	...	...	...
25-29	0.6	0.8	0.3	...	...	...	...	...	...
30-34	0.8	1.1	0.5	...	...	...	...	...	...
35-39	1.2	1.5	0.9	...	...	...	...	...	...
40-44	1.9	2.4	1.4	...	...	...	...	...	...
45-49	3.1	3.7	2.4	...	...	...	...	...	...
50-54	5.1	6.3	3.8	...	...	...	...	...	...
55-59	7.5	9.1	5.9	...	...	...	...	...	...
60-64	11.9	14.4	9.5	...	...	...	...	...	...
65-69	20.2	24.3	16.4	...	...	...	...	...	...
70-74	33.0	40.1	27.1	...	...	...	...	...	...
75-79	52.6	65.5	43.3	...	...	...	...	...	...
80-84	83.7	106.5	70.2	...	...	...	...	...	...
85-89	139.7	170.2	125.7	...	...	...	...	...	...
90-94	226.5	268.3	212.2	...	...	...	...	...	...
95-99	359.6	416.6	346.7	...	...	...	...	...	...

20. Death rates specific for age, sex and urban/rural residence: latest available year, 1993 - 2002
Taux de mortalité selon l'âge, le sexe et la résidence, urbaine/rurale: dernière année disponible, 1993 - 2002 (continued — suite)

(See notes at end of table. — Voir notes à la fin du tableau.)

Continent, country or area, year and age (in years) Continent, pays ou zone, année et âge (en années)	Total			Urban - Urbaine			Rural - Rurale		
	Both sexes Les deux sexes	Male Masculin	Female Féminin	Both sexes Les deux sexes	Male Masculin	Female Féminin	Both sexes Les deux sexes	Male Masculin	Female Féminin
EUROPE									
Denmark - Danemark[18]									
2002									
100+	537.5	519.5	540.4	...	...	...	...	...	...
Estonia - Estonie[8]									
2002									
Total	13.5	15.0	12.3	12.7	14.4	11.4	15.0	15.7	14.3
0-1	5.8	7.0	♦4.5	6.1	7.8	♦4.2	♦5.2	♦5.3	♦5.1
1-4	♦0.5	♦0.7	♦0.3	♦0.3	♦0.4	♦0.1	♦0.9	♦1.3	♦0.5
5-9	♦0.4	♦0.4	♦0.3	♦0.4	♦0.5	♦0.3	♦0.3	♦0.4	♦0.2
10-14	♦0.2	♦0.3	♦0.1	♦0.2	♦0.2	♦0.1	♦0.2	♦0.3	♦0.1
15-19	0.9	1.4	♦0.3	1.0	1.6	♦0.4	♦0.6	♦1.1	♦0.2
20-24	1.8	2.9	♦0.6	1.8	3.0	♦0.6	1.7	2.5	♦0.7
25-29	1.7	3.0	♦0.5	1.6	2.9	♦0.5	2.0	3.1	♦0.6
30-34	2.4	3.9	1.0	2.4	3.7	1.1	2.5	4.4	♦0.6
35-39	3.3	5.4	1.3	3.3	5.5	1.3	3.1	5.1	♦1.0
40-44	5.2	8.0	2.7	5.4	8.5	2.8	4.5	6.5	2.4
45-49	8.1	12.9	3.9	8.1	13.5	3.8	7.6	11.1	4.0
50-54	11.0	17.3	5.7	10.5	16.9	5.6	11.7	17.9	5.6
55-59	14.2	22.3	7.8	13.1	21.6	7.0	16.0	22.8	9.6
60-64	19.8	32.7	10.5	18.9	31.6	10.5	21.6	34.7	10.5
65-69	27.4	45.2	15.9	25.8	43.3	15.1	30.8	48.6	17.8
70-74	40.5	61.6	28.8	39.3	60.0	28.1	43.3	65.0	30.5
75-79	57.7	81.0	48.6	55.4	77.5	46.9	62.6	88.3	52.1
80-84	98.3	127.5	88.8	91.1	113.2	83.9	112.2	156.8	98.3
85-89	160.6	181.9	154.6	153.2	178.5	146.1	173.8	187.8	169.8
90-94	256.8	252.3	257.8	253.0	250.5	253.6	262.2	254.9	264.2
95+	394.1	445.3	384.6	375.2	390.2	372.5	424.3	♦527.3	404.3
Finland - Finlande[19]									
2002									
Total	9.5	9.4	9.6	8.6	8.4	8.7	11.0	11.0	11.0
0-1	3.0	3.2	2.8	3.0	3.3	2.8	3.0	3.1	♦2.9
1-4	0.2	♦0.2	♦0.1	♦0.1	♦0.2	♦0.1	♦0.2	♦0.3	♦0.2
5-9	0.1	♦0.1	♦0.1	♦0.1	♦0.1	♦0.2	♦0.1	♦0.1	♦0.1
10-14	0.1	♦0.2	♦0.1	♦0.1	♦0.1	♦0.1	♦0.1	♦0.2	♦0.1
15-19	0.5	0.7	0.3	0.4	0.6	♦0.2	0.5	0.7	♦0.3
20-24	0.7	1.1	0.4	0.7	1.0	0.4	0.9	1.4	♦0.3
25-29	0.7	1.0	0.3	0.6	1.0	0.3	0.7	1.2	♦0.3
30-34	1.0	1.3	0.6	0.9	1.3	0.6	1.0	1.5	♦0.6
35-39	1.3	1.9	0.8	1.3	1.8	0.8	1.3	1.9	0.7
40-44	2.0	2.7	1.3	2.1	2.9	1.3	1.9	2.6	1.2
45-49	3.1	4.2	1.9	3.2	4.4	2.0	3.0	3.9	1.9
50-54	4.7	6.5	2.9	4.7	6.4	3.0	4.7	6.5	2.7
55-59	6.5	9.1	4.0	6.3	8.8	4.0	6.9	9.5	4.1
60-64	9.8	13.9	5.9	9.7	13.8	6.2	9.8	14.1	5.5
65-69	15.3	22.0	9.5	15.5	22.4	10.0	15.0	21.5	8.7
70-74	26.1	37.7	17.5	25.6	37.1	17.8	26.7	38.3	17.1
75-79	44.1	61.7	33.8	43.1	60.6	33.7	45.4	63.0	33.9
80-84	77.3	102.7	66.3	75.5	102.8	64.4	79.5	102.5	68.6
85-89	140.3	166.8	131.4	137.3	170.2	127.1	144.2	163.2	137.0
90-94	241.5	266.5	234.5	239.4	263.6	233.4	244.1	269.5	236.0
95+	381.7	446.8	368.1	379.2	413.0	372.9	384.6	482.8	361.6
France[20,21,22]									
2001									
Total	9.0	9.5	8.5	...	...	...	...	...	...
0-4	1.1	1.3	1.0	...	...	...	...	...	...
5-9	0.1	0.1	0.1	...	...	...	...	...	...
10-14	0.2	0.2	0.1	...	...	...	...	...	...
15-19	0.5	0.7	0.3	...	...	...	...	...	...
20-24	0.7	1.0	0.3	...	...	...	...	...	...
25-29	0.7	1.1	0.4	...	...	...	...	...	...

20. Death rates specific for age, sex and urban/rural residence: latest available year, 1993 - 2002
Taux de mortalité selon l'âge, le sexe et la résidence, urbaine/rurale: dernière année disponible, 1993 - 2002 (continued — suite)

(See notes at end of table. — Voir notes à la fin du tableau.)

Continent, country or area, year and age (in years)	Total			Urban - Urbaine			Rural - Rurale		
Continent, pays ou zone, année et âge (en années)	Both sexes Les deux sexes	Male Masculin	Female Féminin	Both sexes Les deux sexes	Male Masculin	Female Féminin	Both sexes Les deux sexes	Male Masculin	Female Féminin
EUROPE									
France[20,21,22]									
2001									
30-34	0.9	1.3	0.5	...	...	...	...	...	...
35-39	1.4	1.9	0.9	...	...	...	...	...	...
40-44	2.2	3.0	1.4	...	...	...	...	...	...
45-49	3.4	4.8	2.1	...	...	...	...	...	...
50-54	4.7	6.7	2.8	...	...	...	...	...	...
55-59	6.6	9.3	4.0	...	...	...	...	...	...
60-64	9.4	13.5	5.5	...	...	...	...	...	...
65-69	14.1	20.7	8.5	...	...	...	...	...	...
70-74	22.0	32.1	14.3	...	...	...	...	...	...
75-79	35.7	50.6	25.8	...	...	...	...	...	...
80-84	60.4	82.1	47.9	...	...	...	...	...	...
85+	154.9	180.4	145.3	...	...	...	...	...	...
Germany - Allemagne									
2001									
Total	10.1	9.5	10.6	...	...	...	...	...	...
0-4	1.0	1.1	0.9	...	...	...	...	...	...
5-9	0.1	0.1	0.1	...	...	...	...	...	...
10-14	0.1	0.2	0.1	...	...	...	...	...	...
15-19	0.4	0.6	0.3	...	...	...	...	...	...
20-24	0.6	0.8	0.3	...	...	...	...	...	...
25-29	0.5	0.7	0.3	...	...	...	...	...	...
30-34	0.6	0.9	0.4	...	...	...	...	...	...
35-39	1.1	1.4	0.7	...	...	...	...	...	...
40-44	1.8	2.3	1.2	...	...	...	...	...	...
45-49	3.0	3.9	2.0	...	...	...	...	...	...
50-54	4.5	5.8	3.1	...	...	...	...	...	...
55-59	6.9	9.3	4.5	...	...	...	...	...	...
60-64	10.2	14.0	6.5	...	...	...	...	...	...
65-69	16.4	22.6	10.9	...	...	...	...	...	...
70-74	26.8	37.0	19.1	...	...	...	...	...	...
75-79	42.9	58.2	34.9	...	...	...	...	...	...
80-84	71.7	93.3	62.7	...	...	...	...	...	...
85+	164.8	182.7	159.1	...	...	...	...	...	...
Greece - Grèce									
1998									
Total	9.8	10.3	9.2	...	...	...	...	...	...
0-1	6.7	7.1	6.2	...	...	...	...	...	...
1-4	0.3	0.3	0.3	...	...	...	...	...	...
5-9	0.1	0.2	0.1	...	...	...	...	...	...
10-14	0.2	0.2	0.1	...	...	...	...	...	...
15-19	0.5	0.7	0.3	...	...	...	...	...	...
20-24	0.7	1.1	0.3	...	...	...	...	...	...
25-29	0.8	1.2	0.4	...	...	...	...	...	...
30-34	0.9	1.2	0.5	...	...	...	...	...	...
35-39	1.0	1.4	0.7	...	...	...	...	...	...
40-44	1.7	2.3	1.1	...	...	...	...	...	...
45-49	2.6	3.5	1.6	...	...	...	...	...	...
50-54	4.0	5.5	2.4	...	...	...	...	...	...
55-59	5.6	8.1	3.3	...	...	...	...	...	...
60-64	9.3	13.2	5.8	...	...	...	...	...	...
65-69	15.6	21.4	10.4	...	...	...	...	...	...
70-74	27.1	34.8	20.8	...	...	...	...	...	...
75-79	45.8	55.1	38.8	...	...	...	...	...	...
80-84	91.8	101.2	85.3	...	...	...	...	...	...
85-89	145.4	149.4	142.6	...	...	...	...	...	...
90-94	217.5	196.1	234.0	...	...	...	...	...	...
95-99	216.9	178.6	246.4	...	...	...	...	...	...
100+	180.4	117.1	241.7	...	...	...	...	...	...

20. Death rates specific for age, sex and urban/rural residence: latest available year, 1993 - 2002
Taux de mortalité selon l'âge, le sexe et la résidence, urbaine/rurale: dernière année disponible, 1993 - 2002 (continued — suite)

(See notes at end of table. — Voir notes à la fin du tableau.)

Continent, country or area, year and age (in years) / Continent, pays ou zone, année et âge (en années)	Total			Urban - Urbaine			Rural - Rurale		
	Both sexes Les deux sexes	Male Masculin	Female Féminin	Both sexes Les deux sexes	Male Masculin	Female Féminin	Both sexes Les deux sexes	Male Masculin	Female Féminin
EUROPE									
Hungary - Hongrie[23]									
2002									
Total	13.1	14.3	12.0	12.6	13.5	11.8	13.8	15.3	12.4
0-1	7.3	7.4	7.2	7.1	7.4	6.8	7.6	7.4	7.7
1-4	0.4	0.4	0.3	0.3	0.4	0.3	0.4	0.5	♦0.4
5-9	0.2	0.2	0.1	0.1	♦0.2	♦0.1	0.2	♦0.3	♦0.2
10-14	0.2	0.3	0.1	0.2	0.2	♦0.1	0.2	0.3	♦0.2
15-19	0.4	0.5	0.3	0.4	0.5	0.2	0.4	0.5	0.3
20-24	0.6	0.9	0.3	0.6	0.8	0.3	0.7	1.1	0.3
25-29	0.7	1.1	0.4	0.7	0.9	0.4	0.9	1.2	0.5
30-34	1.1	1.6	0.6	1.0	1.4	0.5	1.3	1.9	0.6
35-39	2.3	3.3	1.3	2.1	2.9	1.3	2.6	3.7	1.4
40-44	4.6	6.7	2.6	4.2	6.0	2.6	5.2	7.5	2.7
45-49	7.2	10.4	4.2	6.6	9.4	4.1	8.2	11.8	4.4
50-54	10.2	15.0	5.8	9.3	13.8	5.5	11.5	16.9	6.2
55-59	13.6	20.4	7.8	12.6	18.7	7.6	15.4	23.4	8.1
60-64	18.8	28.6	11.3	17.4	25.9	11.0	21.0	33.0	11.7
65-69	26.9	39.8	18.1	25.4	36.7	17.6	29.4	44.8	18.9
70-74	40.9	58.1	30.1	39.5	55.1	29.5	43.2	62.8	31.1
75-79	63.3	84.5	52.0	61.7	81.7	51.1	65.9	88.8	53.5
80-84	97.6	119.7	87.3	95.2	115.8	85.6	101.7	126.6	90.1
85-89	173.4	201.0	162.2	169.7	195.5	159.1	180.9	212.7	168.4
90+	242.7	240.1	243.7	240.8	243.6	239.7	245.9	231.8	251.4
Iceland - Islande									
2000									
Total	6.5	6.5	6.5	6.5	6.4	6.5	6.7	6.7	6.7
0-1	♦5.9	♦8.9	♦2.8	♦6.4	♦9.7	♦3.0	-	-	-
1-4	♦0.2	♦0.1	♦0.4	♦0.3	♦0.1	♦0.4	-	-	-
5-9	♦0.1	♦0.2	-	♦0.1	♦0.2	-	-	-	-
10-14	-	♦0.1	-	♦0.1	♦0.1	-	-	-	-
15-19	♦0.7	♦0.8	♦0.5	♦0.7	♦0.9	♦0.4	♦0.5	-	♦1.1
20-24	♦1.0	♦1.6	♦0.4	♦1.0	♦1.6	♦0.4	♦0.6	♦1.2	-
25-29	♦0.6	♦1.1	-	♦0.5	♦1.1	-	♦0.8	♦1.5	-
30-34	♦0.7	♦1.4	♦0.1	♦0.7	♦1.3	♦0.1	♦1.6	♦3.0	-
35-39	♦0.9	♦1.3	♦0.5	♦0.9	♦1.3	♦0.5	♦0.6	♦1.2	-
40-44	♦1.3	♦1.7	♦0.9	♦1.3	♦1.6	♦0.9	-	-	-
45-49	2.1	♦2.4	♦1.7	2.0	♦2.2	♦1.7	♦3.5	♦5.1	♦1.6
50-54	3.4	4.9	♦1.9	3.4	4.9	♦1.9	♦3.2	♦4.3	♦1.8
55-59	5.7	5.4	6.0	6.0	5.8	6.3	♦1.9	♦1.8	♦2.0
60-64	8.7	8.1	9.3	8.4	8.3	8.4	♦10.8	♦4.1	♦18.5
65-69	14.5	17.4	11.7	14.5	17.1	12.1	♦13.6	♦18.1	♦7.7
70-74	22.2	27.1	17.8	22.2	27.4	17.8	♦22.2	♦25.2	♦18.0
75-79	38.7	43.2	34.9	38.8	44.7	34.2	♦36.8	♦31.0	♦44.5
80-84	64.5	72.6	58.7	66.9	76.8	60.3	♦40.7	♦41.3	♦40.0
85+	150.4	159.0	145.7	153.3	164.2	147.5	123.7	♦125.0	♦122.7
2002									
Total	6.3	6.5	6.2	...	...	...	...	...	...
0-4	♦0.7	♦0.9	♦0.5	...	...	...	...	...	...
5-9	♦0.3	♦0.1	♦0.5	...	...	...	...	...	...
10-14	♦0.1	♦0.1	♦0.2	...	...	...	...	...	...
15-19	-	♦0.1	-	...	...	...	...	...	...
20-24	♦0.5	♦0.5	♦0.5	...	...	...	...	...	...
25-29	♦0.9	♦1.3	♦0.5	...	...	...	...	...	...
30-34	♦0.6	♦0.7	♦0.5	...	...	...	...	...	...
35-39	♦0.9	♦0.9	♦0.9	...	...	...	...	...	...
40-44	♦1.3	♦1.4	♦1.2	...	...	...	...	...	...
45-49	1.8	♦2.2	♦1.3	...	...	...	...	...	...
50-54	3.1	♦3.4	♦2.7	...	...	...	...	...	...
55-59	5.1	6.6	♦3.5	...	...	...	...	...	...
60-64	8.2	9.2	7.3	...	...	...	...	...	...

20. Death rates specific for age, sex and urban/rural residence: latest available year, 1993 - 2002
Taux de mortalité selon l'âge, le sexe et la résidence, urbaine/rurale: dernière année disponible, 1993 - 2002 (continued — suite)

(See notes at end of table. — Voir notes à la fin du tableau.)

Continent, country or area, year and age (in years) / Continent, pays ou zone, année et âge (en années)	Total			Urban - Urbaine			Rural - Rurale		
	Both sexes Les deux sexes	Male Masculin	Female Féminin	Both sexes Les deux sexes	Male Masculin	Female Féminin	Both sexes Les deux sexes	Male Masculin	Female Féminin
EUROPE									
Iceland - Islande									
2002									
65-69	11.6	15.1	8.4	...	...	...	...	...	...
70-74	22.1	28.5	16.3	...	...	...	...	...	...
75-79	36.3	50.0	25.3	...	...	...	...	...	...
80-84	74.4	86.2	65.8	...	...	...	...	...	...
85+	154.3	165.8	148.1	...	...	...	...	...	...
Ireland - Irlande+,24									
1996									
Total	8.8	9.2	8.3	8.1	8.4	7.8	9.7	10.4	9.0
0-1	5.7	6.2	5.2	6.1	6.6	5.5	5.2	5.6	4.9
1-4	0.3	0.3	0.3	0.3	◆0.3	◆0.3	0.4	◆0.4	◆0.4
5-9	0.1	◆0.2	◆0.1	◆0.1	◆0.2	◆0.1	◆0.1	◆0.2	-
10-14	0.2	0.2	◆0.1	0.2	◆0.2	◆0.1	◆0.2	◆0.2	◆0.1
15-19	0.5	0.6	0.3	0.4	0.5	◆0.2	0.6	0.8	◆0.4
20-24	0.8	1.3	0.3	0.6	1.0	◆0.2	1.3	1.9	◆0.5
25-29	0.8	1.2	0.4	0.7	1.1	◆0.3	1.0	1.5	◆0.6
30-34	0.8	1.1	0.5	0.8	1.1	0.5	0.8	1.2	◆0.5
35-39	1.0	1.4	0.6	1.0	1.3	0.7	1.1	1.5	0.6
40-44	1.6	2.0	1.2	1.5	2.0	1.1	1.7	2.0	1.4
45-49	2.5	3.0	1.9	2.8	3.5	2.1	2.1	2.5	1.6
50-54	4.6	5.5	3.6	4.6	5.7	3.5	4.5	5.2	3.7
55-59	7.4	9.5	5.3	8.1	10.7	5.6	6.5	8.0	4.8
60-64	13.2	17.1	9.3	14.0	18.6	9.8	12.2	15.3	8.7
65-69	23.1	30.9	16.1	24.1	32.9	17.0	21.9	28.8	14.8
70-74	38.2	49.6	29.0	40.6	54.6	30.8	35.5	45.0	26.8
75-79	63.2	81.2	50.3	66.1	89.6	52.0	60.3	74.4	48.3
80-84	106.1	135.0	90.0	103.0	140.5	85.2	108.8	131.3	92.0
85+	202.3	239.5	185.9	196.8	247.4	179.4	200.0	233.2	194.7
2002									
Total	7.5	7.8	7.1	...	...	...	...	...	...
0-4	1.3	1.4	1.3	...	...	...	...	...	...
5-9	◆0.1	◆0.1	◆0.1	...	...	...	...	...	...
10-14	0.1	◆0.2	◆0.1	...	...	...	...	...	...
15-19	0.5	0.7	0.3	...	...	...	...	...	...
20-24	0.6	1.0	0.3	...	...	...	...	...	...
25-29	0.7	1.2	0.3	...	...	...	...	...	...
30-34	0.8	1.1	0.5	...	...	...	...	...	...
35-39	1.0	1.3	0.7	...	...	...	...	...	...
40-44	1.5	1.8	1.1	...	...	...	...	...	...
45-49	2.3	2.9	1.7	...	...	...	...	...	...
50-54	4.1	5.1	3.0	...	...	...	...	...	...
55-59	6.0	7.9	4.1	...	...	...	...	...	...
60-64	10.0	13.0	6.9	...	...	...	...	...	...
65-69	17.1	22.1	12.3	...	...	...	...	...	...
70-74	29.8	38.3	22.5	...	...	...	...	...	...
75-79	52.0	68.2	40.5	...	...	...	...	...	...
80-84	88.9	111.8	75.0	...	...	...	...	...	...
85+	178.8	210.2	165.3	...	...	...	...	...	...
Italy - Italie									
1998									
Total	10.0	10.4	9.6	...	...	...	...	...	...
0-4	1.2	1.3	1.1	...	...	...	...	...	...
5-9	0.1	0.1	0.1	...	...	...	...	...	...
10-14	0.2	0.2	0.1	...	...	...	...	...	...
15-19	0.5	0.7	0.3	...	...	...	...	...	...
20-24	0.7	1.0	0.3	...	...	...	...	...	...
25-29	0.7	1.0	0.3	...	...	...	...	...	...
30-34	0.8	1.1	0.4	...	...	...	...	...	...
35-39	1.0	1.4	0.7	...	...	...	...	...	...

20. Death rates specific for age, sex and urban/rural residence: latest available year, 1993 - 2002
Taux de mortalité selon l'âge, le sexe et la résidence, urbaine/rurale: dernière année disponible, 1993 - 2002 (continued — suite)

(See notes at end of table. — Voir notes à la fin du tableau.)

Continent, country or area, year and age (in years) Continent, pays ou zone, année et âge (en années)	Total			Urban - Urbaine			Rural - Rurale		
	Both sexes Les deux sexes	Male Masculin	Female Féminin	Both sexes Les deux sexes	Male Masculin	Female Féminin	Both sexes Les deux sexes	Male Masculin	Female Féminin
EUROPE									
Italy - Italie									
1998									
40-44	1.4	1.8	1.0	...	...	...	...	...	...
45-49	2.2	2.8	1.6	...	...	...	...	...	...
50-54	3.6	4.7	2.5	...	...	...	...	...	...
55-59	5.8	7.9	3.9	...	...	...	...	...	...
60-64	9.5	13.3	6.1	...	...	...	...	...	...
65-69	15.8	22.6	10.1	...	...	...	...	...	...
70-74	26.3	37.5	17.9	...	...	...	...	...	...
75-79	42.7	59.2	32.1	...	...	...	...	...	...
80-84	76.9	100.5	64.1	...	...	...	...	...	...
85+	158.8	186.4	147.4	...	...	...	...	...	...
Latvia - Lettonie[8]									
2002									
Total	13.9	15.3	12.7	13.3	14.9	11.9	15.2	15.9	14.5
0-1	9.9	11.0	8.8	8.2	8.9	7.5	13.0	14.6	11.2
1-4	0.7	0.8	♦0.6	♦0.5	♦0.7	♦0.3	♦1.0	♦0.9	♦1.1
5-9	0.5	0.6	♦0.4	0.5	♦0.6	0.4	♦0.5	♦0.6	♦0.4
10-14	0.2	♦0.2	♦0.2	♦0.2	♦0.2	♦0.2	♦0.2	♦0.3	♦0.2
15-19	0.7	0.9	0.5	0.7	0.9	♦0.5	0.8	1.0	♦0.5
20-24	1.5	2.4	0.5	1.4	2.2	0.6	1.6	2.7	♦0.3
25-29	1.7	2.9	0.5	1.5	2.7	♦0.4	2.0	3.2	♦0.7
30-34	2.6	4.2	1.0	2.5	4.1	1.1	2.7	4.3	♦0.9
35-39	3.4	5.4	1.5	3.4	5.5	1.4	3.6	5.2	1.9
40-44	4.9	7.8	2.3	4.7	7.7	2.1	5.4	7.9	2.7
45-49	7.5	11.8	3.7	7.3	11.8	3.5	8.1	11.9	4.0
50-54	11.1	17.5	5.7	10.3	16.4	5.6	13.0	19.9	5.9
55-59	15.3	24.0	8.5	14.8	23.6	8.3	16.7	25.0	9.1
60-64	20.6	33.8	11.2	19.1	31.3	10.8	24.2	39.1	12.2
65-69	28.7	46.2	17.8	27.3	44.1	17.1	31.8	50.4	19.3
70-74	40.5	62.4	28.3	38.0	58.4	26.9	45.9	71.4	31.6
75-79	60.9	91.3	50.4	58.1	86.6	48.0	67.1	102.8	55.6
80-84	107.4	139.8	97.0	102.6	130.2	93.5	116.7	160.5	103.7
85-89	160.6	184.3	154.0	157.4	176.8	151.5	166.3	200.0	158.1
90-94	265.8	283.8	261.2	256.7	285.1	249.3	280.7	281.5	280.5
95-99	367.7	402.8	359.2	376.8	431.0	364.1	352.6	359.6	350.8
100+	536.2	♦409.1	560.3	634.1	♦636.4	633.8	♦392.9	♦181.8	♦444.4
Lithuania - Lituanie[8]									
2002									
Total	11.8	13.5	10.4	10.0	11.5	8.7	15.6	17.2	14.1
0-1	7.8	8.5	7.1	6.7	8.0	5.4	9.6	9.3	9.9
1-4	0.5	0.7	♦0.4	0.5	♦0.6	♦0.4	♦0.6	♦0.8	♦0.4
5-9	0.3	0.4	♦0.2	♦0.2	♦0.3	♦0.1	0.4	♦0.5	♦0.3
10-14	0.3	0.3	♦0.2	0.3	♦0.3	♦0.2	♦0.3	♦0.4	♦0.2
15-19	0.9	1.3	0.4	0.7	1.0	0.4	1.2	1.8	♦0.5
20-24	1.5	2.5	0.4	1.1	1.9	♦0.3	2.5	3.8	♦0.8
25-29	1.8	2.9	0.8	1.4	2.1	0.6	3.1	4.8	1.1
30-34	2.2	3.5	1.0	1.8	2.7	0.9	3.3	5.4	1.0
35-39	3.3	5.2	1.3	2.8	4.7	1.2	4.2	6.4	1.8
40-44	4.7	7.7	2.0	4.0	6.7	1.7	6.3	9.7	2.6
45-49	7.0	10.9	3.4	6.2	9.8	3.2	8.8	13.1	4.1
50-54	10.3	16.4	5.2	9.5	15.2	5.0	12.3	18.8	5.6
55-59	13.7	21.9	7.3	12.5	20.0	7.0	16.0	25.3	7.9
60-64	18.7	30.3	10.4	17.2	28.5	9.4	21.4	33.3	12.2
65-69	25.3	40.5	15.4	24.5	38.5	15.6	26.5	43.5	15.1
70-74	37.7	55.7	27.4	36.3	53.0	26.6	39.9	59.9	28.6
75-79	55.5	79.9	45.2	52.6	74.0	43.6	59.6	87.6	47.3
80-84	90.9	121.0	79.3	88.5	118.8	77.2	93.9	123.5	81.9
85-89	159.6	177.2	153.7	146.9	166.3	140.6	175.8	190.3	170.7
90-94	229.3	246.8	223.0	199.3	211.7	195.2	269.4	286.6	262.4

20. Death rates specific for age, sex and urban/rural residence: latest available year, 1993 - 2002
Taux de mortalité selon l'âge, le sexe et la résidence, urbaine/rurale: dernière année disponible, 1993 - 2002 (continued — suite)

(See notes at end of table. — Voir notes à la fin du tableau.)

Continent, country or area, year and age (in years) / Continent, pays ou zone, année et âge (en années)	Total			Urban - Urbaine			Rural - Rurale		
	Both sexes Les deux sexes	Male Masculin	Female Féminin	Both sexes Les deux sexes	Male Masculin	Female Féminin	Both sexes Les deux sexes	Male Masculin	Female Féminin
EUROPE									
Lithuania - Lituanie[8]									
2002									
95-99	262.5	292.4	249.6	225.2	252.8	215.3	307.5	329.1	296.1
100+	266.2	320.6	250.5	227.1	♦268.7	216.0	312.3	♦375.0	292.7
Luxembourg									
2002									
Total	8.4	8.6	8.2	...	...	...	...	...	...
0-1	♦5.0	♦5.5	♦4.6	...	...	...	...	...	...
1-4	♦0.4	♦0.6	♦0.2	...	...	...	...	...	...
5-9	♦0.2	♦0.3	♦0.1	...	...	...	...	...	...
10-14	♦0.3	♦0.5	♦0.1	...	...	...	...	...	...
15-19	♦0.6	♦0.9	♦0.2	...	...	...	...	...	...
20-24	♦0.7	♦1.1	♦0.2	...	...	...	...	...	...
25-29	♦0.6	♦1.1	♦0.1	...	...	...	...	...	...
30-34	0.9	♦1.3	♦0.5	...	...	...	...	...	...
35-39	1.2	1.6	♦0.7	...	...	...	...	...	...
40-44	1.6	2.1	♦1.1	...	...	...	...	...	...
45-49	3.0	3.4	2.5	...	...	...	...	...	...
50-54	4.3	5.2	3.4	...	...	...	...	...	...
55-59	8.0	10.6	5.2	...	...	...	...	...	...
60-64	10.2	14.2	6.4	...	...	...	...	...	...
65-69	16.0	23.2	9.6	...	...	...	...	...	...
70-74	28.2	38.6	19.6	...	...	...	...	...	...
75-79	45.3	57.3	38.2	...	...	...	...	...	...
80-84	70.5	92.7	60.2	...	...	...	...	...	...
85-89	129.5	171.1	113.3	...	...	...	...	...	...
90-94	211.7	269.0	196.4	...	...	...	...	...	...
95+	349.2	♦483.3	317.6	...	...	...	...	...	...
Malta - Malte									
2002									
Total	7.6	8.1	7.1	...	...	...	...	...	...
0-1	♦5.9	♦4.4	♦7.6	...	...	...	...	...	...
1-4	♦0.3	♦0.6	-	...	...	...	...	...	...
5-9	♦0.1	♦0.2	-	...	...	...	...	...	...
10-14	♦0.1	♦0.1	♦0.1	...	...	...	...	...	...
15-19	♦0.3	♦0.5	♦0.1	...	...	...	...	...	...
20-24	♦0.4	♦0.6	♦0.2	...	...	...	...	...	...
25-29	♦0.7	♦1.1	♦0.4	...	...	...	...	...	...
30-34	♦0.5	♦0.5	♦0.5	...	...	...	...	...	...
35-39	♦0.7	♦0.7	♦0.6	...	...	...	...	...	...
40-44	♦0.9	♦1.1	♦0.6	...	...	...	...	...	...
45-49	2.0	2.3	♦1.7	...	...	...	...	...	...
50-54	3.2	4.3	2.2	...	...	...	...	...	...
55-59	4.8	6.0	3.7	...	...	...	...	...	...
60-64	9.0	10.7	7.5	...	...	...	...	...	...
65-69	16.8	24.0	10.8	...	...	...	...	...	...
70-74	30.3	39.6	23.5	...	...	...	...	...	...
75-79	49.3	62.5	40.0	...	...	...	...	...	...
80-84	85.8	116.5	65.7	...	...	...	...	...	...
85-89	155.9	200.9	132.0	...	...	...	...	...	...
90+	210.4	229.0	201.9	...	...	...	...	...	...
Netherlands - Pays-Bas[25]									
2002									
Total	8.8	8.7	9.0	9.1	8.7	9.4	8.4	8.5	8.2
0-1	4.5	4.9	4.1	4.6	5.0	4.1	4.3	4.7	3.9
1-4	0.4	0.4	0.3	0.4	0.4	0.4	0.3	0.4	0.3
5-9	0.1	0.1	0.1	0.1	0.1	♦0.1	0.1	♦0.1	♦0.1
10-14	0.1	0.2	0.1	0.1	0.2	♦0.1	0.1	♦0.1	♦0.1
15-19	0.3	0.4	0.2	0.3	0.4	0.2	0.4	0.5	0.2
20-24	0.4	0.7	0.2	0.4	0.6	0.2	0.5	0.7	0.3

20. Death rates specific for age, sex and urban/rural residence: latest available year, 1993 - 2002
Taux de mortalité selon l'âge, le sexe et la résidence, urbaine/rurale: dernière année disponible, 1993 - 2002 (continued — suite)

(See notes at end of table. — Voir notes à la fin du tableau.)

Continent, country or area, year and age (in years) Continent, pays ou zone, année et âge (en années)	Total			Urban - Urbaine			Rural - Rurale		
	Both sexes Les deux sexes	Male Masculin	Female Féminin	Both sexes Les deux sexes	Male Masculin	Female Féminin	Both sexes Les deux sexes	Male Masculin	Female Féminin
EUROPE									
Netherlands - Pays-Bas[25]									
2002									
25-29	0.4	0.5	0.3	0.4	0.5	0.4	0.4	0.6	0.3
30-34	0.6	0.7	0.5	0.6	0.7	0.5	0.6	0.7	0.4
35-39	0.9	1.0	0.7	0.9	1.1	0.7	0.8	0.9	0.6
40-44	1.4	1.5	1.2	1.4	1.6	1.2	1.3	1.4	1.1
45-49	2.5	2.7	2.2	2.5	2.8	2.2	2.3	2.4	2.2
50-54	3.7	4.1	3.2	3.9	4.5	3.4	3.3	3.6	2.9
55-59	6.3	7.6	5.0	6.7	8.0	5.4	5.7	6.9	4.5
60-64	9.8	12.3	7.3	10.2	12.7	7.8	9.2	11.7	6.6
65-69	15.8	20.9	11.2	16.5	21.6	12.0	14.6	19.7	9.7
70-74	27.6	37.4	19.7	28.5	38.4	20.7	26.0	35.7	17.8
75-79	46.1	63.6	34.4	46.2	63.4	35.0	45.9	64.1	33.1
80-84	82.8	112.6	67.1	83.0	112.8	67.8	82.4	112.2	65.6
85-89	143.4	189.3	125.5	143.3	190.7	125.7	143.6	186.6	125.0
90-94	257.4	309.4	242.8	256.5	310.2	242.6	259.3	308.2	243.0
95-99	422.9	478.0	410.6	421.7	489.2	408.4	425.2	460.0	415.6
100+	680.8	697.3	677.8	686.0	716.8	681.1	669.3	666.7	670.0
Norway - Norvège[26]									
2002									
Total	9.8	9.6	10.0	...	...	...	...	...	...
0-1	3.4	3.3	3.6	...	...	...	...	...	...
1-4	0.3	0.3	0.3	...	...	...	...	...	...
5-9	0.1	0.2	♦0.1	...	...	...	...	...	...
10-14	0.1	♦0.1	♦0.2	...	...	...	...	...	...
15-19	0.5	0.6	0.3	...	...	...	...	...	...
20-24	0.7	1.0	0.4	...	...	...	...	...	...
25-29	0.7	1.1	0.4	...	...	...	...	...	...
30-34	0.8	1.2	0.5	...	...	...	...	...	...
35-39	1.0	1.4	0.6	...	...	...	...	...	...
40-44	1.4	1.7	1.0	...	...	...	...	...	...
45-49	2.0	2.5	1.6	...	...	...	...	...	...
50-54	3.6	4.4	2.8	...	...	...	...	...	...
55-59	5.8	6.9	4.7	...	...	...	...	...	...
60-64	9.2	11.5	6.9	...	...	...	...	...	...
65-69	15.3	20.3	10.7	...	...	...	...	...	...
70-74	25.3	33.4	18.4	...	...	...	...	...	...
75-79	44.2	58.6	33.8	...	...	...	...	...	...
80-84	76.3	99.1	63.0	...	...	...	...	...	...
85-89	137.9	173.6	121.8	...	...	...	...	...	...
90+	259.8	299.2	247.0	...	...	...	...	...	...
Poland - Pologne									
1999									
Total	9.9	10.9	8.9	9.4	10.3	8.5	10.7	11.7	9.7
0-1	8.7	9.5	7.9	9.1	9.9	8.2	8.3	9.1	7.4
1-4	0.4	0.4	0.3	0.3	0.4	0.3	0.4	0.5	0.4
5-9	0.2	0.2	0.2	0.2	0.2	0.1	0.2	0.3	0.2
10-14	0.2	0.3	0.1	0.2	0.3	0.1	0.2	0.3	0.2
15-19	0.6	0.9	0.3	0.5	0.8	0.3	0.7	1.0	0.4
20-24	0.8	1.3	0.3	0.8	1.2	0.3	1.0	1.6	0.4
25-29	1.0	1.5	0.4	0.9	1.4	0.4	1.1	1.7	0.4
30-34	1.3	2.0	0.6	1.2	1.9	0.6	1.5	2.3	0.6
35-39	2.1	3.2	1.0	2.0	3.0	1.1	2.2	3.3	1.0
40-44	3.5	5.2	1.8	3.4	5.0	1.9	3.8	5.7	1.7
45-49	5.5	8.2	2.9	5.3	8.0	2.9	5.8	8.5	2.9
50-54	8.1	12.1	4.5	8.0	11.8	4.7	8.4	12.6	4.1
55-59	12.2	18.3	6.8	12.1	18.1	6.9	12.3	18.7	6.4
60-64	17.9	27.1	10.3	17.9	26.9	10.7	17.9	27.5	9.6
65-69	26.8	39.9	17.1	27.0	39.8	17.6	26.5	39.9	16.2
70-74	39.8	56.6	29.3	40.3	56.1	30.5	39.2	57.2	27.6

20. Death rates specific for age, sex and urban/rural residence: latest available year, 1993 - 2002
Taux de mortalité selon l'âge, le sexe et la résidence, urbaine/rurale: dernière année disponible, 1993 - 2002 (continued — suite)

(See notes at end of table. — Voir notes à la fin du tableau.)

Continent, country or area, year and age (in years) / Continent, pays ou zone, année et âge (en années)	Total			Urban - Urbaine			Rural - Rurale		
	Both sexes Les deux sexes	Male Masculin	Female Féminin	Both sexes Les deux sexes	Male Masculin	Female Féminin	Both sexes Les deux sexes	Male Masculin	Female Féminin
EUROPE									
Poland - Pologne									
1999									
75-79	62.6	82.6	51.7	62.4	82.0	52.2	62.8	83.3	51.2
80-84	102.1	123.8	92.0	99.8	120.5	91.1	104.7	127.4	93.1
85+	196.8	208.8	192.2	188.1	199.0	184.3	208.3	219.8	203.3
2002									
Total	9.4	10.3	8.5	...	...	...	...	...	...
0-4	1.7	1.8	1.5	...	...	...	...	...	...
5-9	0.2	0.2	0.2	...	...	...	...	...	...
10-14	0.2	0.3	0.2	...	...	...	...	...	...
15-19	0.5	0.7	0.3	...	...	...	...	...	...
20-24	0.7	1.2	0.3	...	...	...	...	...	...
25-29	0.8	1.3	0.3	...	...	...	...	...	...
30-34	1.1	1.8	0.5	...	...	...	...	...	...
35-39	1.7	2.6	0.9	...	...	...	...	...	...
40-44	3.0	4.5	1.5	...	...	...	...	...	...
45-49	4.8	7.1	2.6	...	...	...	...	...	...
50-54	7.6	11.1	4.3	...	...	...	...	...	...
55-59	10.8	15.9	6.2	...	...	...	...	...	...
60-64	15.9	24.3	9.0	...	...	...	...	...	...
65-69	23.3	34.9	14.6	...	...	...	...	...	...
70-74	35.7	51.2	25.3	...	...	...	...	...	...
75-79	56.0	75.5	45.7	...	...	...	...	...	...
80-84	89.2	111.1	79.0	...	...	...	...	...	...
85+	187.0	201.5	181.6	...	...	...	...	...	...
Portugal									
2002									
Total	10.2	11.1	9.5	...	...	...	...	...	...
0-1	5.1	5.4	4.7	...	...	...	...	...	...
1-4	0.4	0.4	0.3	...	...	...	...	...	...
5-9	0.2	0.2	0.2	...	...	...	...	...	...
10-14	0.2	0.3	0.2	...	...	...	...	...	...
15-19	0.5	0.8	0.3	...	...	...	...	...	...
20-24	0.8	1.1	0.4	...	...	...	...	...	...
25-29	1.0	1.5	0.5	...	...	...	...	...	...
30-34	1.3	1.9	0.6	...	...	...	...	...	...
35-39	1.8	2.6	0.9	...	...	...	...	...	...
40-44	2.5	3.7	1.4	...	...	...	...	...	...
45-49	3.5	4.9	2.1	...	...	...	...	...	...
50-54	4.6	6.4	2.8	...	...	...	...	...	...
55-59	6.5	9.2	4.1	...	...	...	...	...	...
60-64	9.9	14.0	6.4	...	...	...	...	...	...
65-69	15.8	22.8	10.1	...	...	...	...	...	...
70-74	26.8	36.8	19.1	...	...	...	...	...	...
75-79	48.3	63.6	37.7	...	...	...	...	...	...
80-84	83.8	103.1	72.0	...	...	...	...	...	...
85+	187.9	208.1	178.5	...	...	...	...	...	...
Republic of Moldova - République de Moldova[8]									
2002									
Total	11.6	12.4	10.8	8.9	10.0	7.9	13.4	14.1	12.8
0-1	14.9	16.8	12.8	15.4	17.0	13.8	14.6	16.7	12.3
1-4	0.8	0.8	0.7	0.6	♦0.7	♦0.6	0.9	0.9	0.8
5-9	0.4	0.5	0.3	♦0.3	♦0.3	♦0.3	0.4	0.6	♦0.2
10-14	0.4	0.5	0.3	0.3	0.5	♦0.1	0.5	0.6	0.4
15-19	0.7	0.9	0.4	0.6	1.0	♦0.3	0.7	0.9	0.4
20-24	1.0	1.5	0.5	0.9	1.3	0.5	1.1	1.7	0.4
25-29	1.5	2.2	0.7	1.4	2.1	0.7	1.5	2.2	0.8
30-34	2.2	3.4	1.1	1.8	2.7	0.8	2.8	4.5	1.3
35-39	3.3	4.8	1.9	2.6	4.0	1.3	3.9	5.6	2.3

20. Death rates specific for age, sex and urban/rural residence: latest available year, 1993 - 2002
Taux de mortalité selon l'âge, le sexe et la résidence, urbaine/rurale: dernière année disponible, 1993 - 2002 (continued — suite)

(See notes at end of table. — Voir notes à la fin du tableau.)

Continent, country or area, year and age (in years) / Continent, pays ou zone, année et âge (en années)	Total			Urban - Urbaine			Rural - Rurale		
	Both sexes Les deux sexes	Male Masculin	Female Féminin	Both sexes Les deux sexes	Male Masculin	Female Féminin	Both sexes Les deux sexes	Male Masculin	Female Féminin
EUROPE									
Republic of Moldova - République de Moldova[8]									
2002									
40-44	5.2	7.9	2.8	4.3	6.5	2.3	6.0	9.0	3.2
45-49	7.9	11.2	4.9	6.8	10.1	3.9	8.8	12.2	5.7
50-54	11.6	16.0	7.6	10.1	14.5	6.2	12.8	17.4	8.8
55-59	17.8	23.9	13.1	16.2	22.3	10.9	19.0	25.2	14.6
60-64	27.9	36.3	21.6	24.2	33.1	16.9	30.2	38.5	24.4
65-69	39.5	51.6	30.9	34.0	44.4	26.3	42.3	55.5	33.2
70-74	58.9	77.1	47.5	54.3	70.5	44.2	61.0	80.0	49.0
75-79	87.3	103.2	79.1	77.1	90.9	70.5	92.3	108.9	83.5
80-84	145.8	160.9	138.1	127.4	156.3	114.9	153.4	162.5	148.4
85+	262.7	321.1	241.2	191.5	231.0	178.3	305.1	369.1	280.1
Romania - Roumanie									
2002									
Total	12.4	13.6	11.2	9.8	11.0	8.6	15.4	16.4	14.4
0-1	17.5	19.1	15.8	14.8	16.6	13.0	19.7	21.2	18.2
1-4	0.8	0.9	0.7	0.6	0.7	0.6	1.0	1.1	0.8
5-9	0.4	0.4	0.3	0.3	0.3	0.3	0.4	0.5	0.4
10-14	0.5	0.6	0.4	0.4	0.5	0.3	0.6	0.7	0.5
15-19	0.5	0.7	0.3	0.4	0.5	0.3	0.6	0.8	0.3
20-24	0.7	1.1	0.4	0.6	0.9	0.4	0.9	1.3	0.4
25-29	0.9	1.3	0.5	0.8	1.1	0.5	1.1	1.6	0.6
30-34	1.4	2.0	0.8	1.1	1.6	0.6	1.7	2.4	0.9
35-39	2.4	3.5	1.3	2.0	2.9	1.1	3.0	4.2	1.5
40-44	4.2	6.0	2.3	3.5	5.2	2.0	5.2	7.2	2.8
45-49	6.5	9.4	3.7	5.9	8.4	3.5	7.7	11.2	4.1
50-54	9.5	13.6	5.6	9.1	12.8	5.5	10.0	14.6	5.9
55-59	13.2	18.9	8.1	13.4	18.9	8.3	13.1	19.0	8.0
60-64	19.8	28.2	12.8	20.0	28.5	12.8	19.6	27.9	12.8
65-69	28.9	39.8	20.3	29.3	40.5	20.5	28.7	39.3	20.2
70-74	44.5	57.5	34.8	45.0	59.2	34.8	44.1	56.3	34.8
75-79	73.5	87.5	64.2	71.1	85.8	62.1	74.9	88.5	65.6
80-84	115.0	128.7	107.6	107.4	123.1	99.8	119.9	131.8	112.9
85+	234.1	246.0	228.0	212.3	227.5	205.1	249.1	257.8	244.4
Russian Federation - Fédération de Russie[8]									
1999									
Total	14.7	16.3	13.3	14.1	15.8	12.6	16.3	17.4	15.3
0-1	16.6	18.7	14.4	15.9	18.0	13.7	18.1	20.3	15.8
1-4	1.0	1.1	0.9	0.8	0.9	0.7	1.4	1.6	1.3
5-9	0.5	0.6	0.4	0.4	0.5	0.3	0.6	0.7	0.5
10-14	0.5	0.6	0.3	0.4	0.5	0.3	0.6	0.7	0.4
15-19	1.4	2.0	0.8	1.4	1.9	0.8	1.6	2.2	0.9
20-24	2.8	4.5	1.1	2.7	4.4	1.1	3.1	4.8	1.2
25-29	3.3	5.2	1.3	3.1	4.8	1.2	3.9	6.3	1.4
30-34	4.1	6.5	1.6	3.9	6.1	1.6	4.6	7.4	1.7
35-39	5.2	8.3	2.2	5.0	8.1	2.2	5.8	9.0	2.4
40-44	7.2	11.4	3.2	6.9	11.1	3.1	8.0	12.2	3.4
45-49	10.2	16.1	4.8	9.9	15.8	4.6	11.3	17.0	5.4
50-54	14.1	22.1	7.1	13.6	21.6	6.9	15.8	23.7	8.2
55-59	19.6	31.2	10.7	19.1	30.6	10.3	21.1	32.9	11.7
60-64	26.5	42.0	15.3	25.6	41.1	14.9	28.6	44.3	16.5
65-69	37.9	58.4	25.2	37.3	57.8	25.1	39.2	59.6	25.5
70-74	52.7	77.7	40.5	53.2	77.3	41.3	51.6	78.7	38.9
75-79	74.8	100.4	66.6	75.7	99.3	68.0	72.7	103.0	63.5
80-84	122.7	148.6	115.6	126.0	149.4	119.2	115.7	146.8	108.5
85+	206.3	200.1	207.8	214.3	207.2	216.2	192.3	185.0	193.8

20. Death rates specific for age, sex and urban/rural residence: latest available year, 1993 - 2002
Taux de mortalité selon l'âge, le sexe et la résidence, urbaine/rurale: dernière année disponible, 1993 - 2002 (continued — suite)

(See notes at end of table. — Voir notes à la fin du tableau.)

Continent, country or area, year and age (in years) Continent, pays ou zone, année et âge (en années)	Total			Urban - Urbaine			Rural - Rurale		
	Both sexes Les deux sexes	Male Masculin	Female Féminin	Both sexes Les deux sexes	Male Masculin	Female Féminin	Both sexes Les deux sexes	Male Masculin	Female Féminin
EUROPE									
Serbia and Montenegro - Serbie-et-Montenegro									
2000									
Total	11.1	11.7	10.5	10.8	11.6	10.1	11.4	11.8	11.0
0-1	13.4	15.3	11.3	14.7	16.8	12.4	11.9	13.6	10.0
1-4	0.6	0.6	0.6	0.6	0.6	0.5	0.7	0.7	0.6
5-9	0.2	0.3	0.2	0.1	0.2	♦0.1	0.3	0.4	0.2
10-14	0.2	0.3	0.2	0.2	0.3	0.2	0.2	0.3	0.2
15-19	0.5	0.6	0.3	0.5	0.6	0.3	0.4	0.6	0.3
20-24	0.7	1.0	0.4	0.8	1.2	0.4	0.6	0.8	0.4
25-29	0.7	1.0	0.4	0.8	1.2	0.4	0.7	0.9	0.4
30-34	1.0	1.2	0.7	1.1	1.3	0.8	0.9	1.1	0.6
35-39	1.5	2.0	1.1	1.6	2.2	1.1	1.4	1.9	0.9
40-44	2.7	3.6	1.7	2.9	3.9	1.9	2.4	3.2	1.5
45-49	4.7	6.2	3.2	5.0	6.6	3.4	4.3	5.6	2.9
50-54	7.4	10.1	4.8	7.8	10.9	5.0	6.9	9.2	4.4
55-59	12.2	16.2	8.4	12.8	17.0	9.0	11.5	15.4	7.6
60-64	18.9	24.9	13.6	19.8	25.8	14.5	17.9	23.8	12.6
65-69	31.3	40.2	23.7	33.0	41.9	25.5	29.6	38.6	22.1
70-74	47.2	56.3	40.1	51.5	60.8	44.3	43.7	52.7	36.8
75-79	75.1	81.9	70.4	81.0	83.9	78.8	70.5	80.2	64.2
80-84	104.7	108.7	102.2	120.0	107.8	129.3	95.2	109.3	87.0
85+	176.2	143.6	204.3	188.8	132.3	246.2	167.4	152.8	178.7
2001									
Total	10.6	11.2	10.1	...	...	...	...	...	...
0-4	3.1	3.6	2.6	...	...	...	...	...	...
5-9	0.3	0.3	0.2	...	...	...	...	...	...
10-14	0.2	0.2	0.2	...	...	...	...	...	...
15-19	0.4	0.5	0.3	...	...	...	...	...	...
20-24	0.7	0.9	0.4	...	...	...	...	...	...
25-29	0.7	1.0	0.4	...	...	...	...	...	...
30-34	0.9	1.2	0.6	...	...	...	...	...	...
35-39	1.5	1.9	1.0	...	...	...	...	...	...
40-44	2.6	3.3	1.8	...	...	...	...	...	...
45-49	4.7	6.1	3.2	...	...	...	...	...	...
50-54	7.3	9.7	4.9	...	...	...	...	...	...
55-59	11.5	15.3	7.9	...	...	...	...	...	...
60-64	17.9	23.3	13.1	...	...	...	...	...	...
65-69	28.8	36.9	22.0	...	...	...	...	...	...
70-74	44.6	54.0	37.2	...	...	...	...	...	...
75-79	71.6	78.2	67.1	...	...	...	...	...	...
80-84	96.3	97.2	95.7	...	...	...	...	...	...
85+	158.4	129.7	183.0	...	...	...	...	...	...
Slovakia - Slovaquie									
2001									
Total	9.7	10.6	8.8	8.1	8.9	7.4	11.6	12.8	10.6
0-1	6.1	6.9	5.3	5.6	6.0	5.1	6.6	7.7	5.4
1-4	0.4	0.5	0.3	0.4	♦0.4	♦0.4	0.4	0.7	♦0.2
5-9	0.2	0.3	♦0.1	0.2	♦0.3	♦0.1	0.2	♦0.3	♦0.1
10-14	0.2	0.3	♦0.1	0.2	0.3	♦0.1	0.2	♦0.3	♦0.2
15-19	0.4	0.6	0.3	0.4	0.5	0.3	0.5	0.6	0.3
20-24	0.6	0.9	0.2	0.5	0.8	♦0.2	0.7	1.1	♦0.3
25-29	0.8	1.2	0.4	0.8	1.1	0.4	0.9	1.4	0.4
30-34	1.1	1.7	0.5	1.0	1.5	0.5	1.3	1.9	0.6
35-39	1.7	2.5	0.8	1.4	2.1	0.9	2.0	3.0	0.8
40-44	2.9	4.3	1.6	2.4	3.5	1.5	3.7	5.4	1.8
45-49	4.9	7.2	2.7	4.3	6.1	2.7	5.9	8.8	2.7
50-54	7.7	11.5	4.1	6.8	10.2	3.7	9.0	13.5	4.6
55-59	11.6	17.6	6.6	10.5	15.5	6.3	13.1	20.1	6.9
60-64	18.3	28.3	10.4	16.8	25.2	10.2	19.8	31.6	10.5

20. Death rates specific for age, sex and urban/rural residence: latest available year, 1993 - 2002
Taux de mortalité selon l'âge, le sexe et la résidence, urbaine/rurale: dernière année disponible, 1993 - 2002 (continued — suite)

(See notes at end of table. — Voir notes à la fin du tableau.)

Continent, country or area, year and age (in years) / Continent, pays ou zone, année et âge (en années)	Total			Urban - Urbaine			Rural - Rurale		
	Both sexes Les deux sexes	Male Masculin	Female Féminin	Both sexes Les deux sexes	Male Masculin	Female Féminin	Both sexes Les deux sexes	Male Masculin	Female Féminin
EUROPE									
Slovakia - Slovaquie									
2001									
65-69	27.0	40.5	17.2	25.9	37.8	17.3	28.0	43.3	17.2
70-74	41.7	59.7	30.3	40.5	55.5	30.8	42.8	63.7	29.9
75-79	65.1	83.4	55.1	63.3	79.9	54.0	66.7	86.6	56.0
80-84	106.5	131.3	94.1	103.4	126.3	91.4	109.3	135.9	96.3
85-89	174.9	198.7	164.3	170.7	196.1	159.3	178.5	200.9	168.5
90-94	274.0	293.2	266.7	266.7	278.1	262.6	279.9	304.7	270.1
95-99	339.0	318.9	345.9	326.0	262.0	349.0	351.0	375.0	343.2
100+	259.6	♦125.0	330.9	275.9	♦90.9	♦388.9	♦239.1	♦178.6	♦265.6
2002									
Total	9.6	10.5	8.7	...	...	...	...	...	...
0-1	7.7	7.3	8.1	...	...	...	...	...	...
1-4	0.3	0.3	0.3	...	...	...	...	...	...
5-9	0.2	0.3	♦0.2	...	...	...	...	...	...
10-14	0.2	0.2	0.2	...	...	...	...	...	...
15-19	0.5	0.6	0.3	...	...	...	...	...	...
20-24	0.7	1.0	0.3	...	...	...	...	...	...
25-29	0.8	1.2	0.4	...	...	...	...	...	...
30-34	1.0	1.5	0.5	...	...	...	...	...	...
35-39	1.6	2.4	0.7	...	...	...	...	...	...
40-44	2.9	4.3	1.5	...	...	...	...	...	...
45-49	4.8	7.3	2.5	...	...	...	...	...	...
50-54	7.5	11.5	3.7	...	...	...	...	...	...
55-59	11.5	17.4	6.4	...	...	...	...	...	...
60-64	16.8	25.6	9.9	...	...	...	...	...	...
65-69	25.9	38.2	17.1	...	...	...	...	...	...
70-74	39.3	55.2	29.2	...	...	...	...	...	...
75-79	64.0	83.8	53.1	...	...	...	...	...	...
80-84	100.6	122.6	89.6	...	...	...	...	...	...
85-89	175.7	195.5	166.9	...	...	...	...	...	...
90-94	255.5	284.5	244.4	...	...	...	...	...	...
95-99	338.9	330.0	342.0	...	...	...	...	...	...
100+	387.5	♦280.7	446.6	...	...	...	...	...	...
Slovenia - Slovénie									
2002									
Total	9.3	9.9	8.8	8.9	9.7	8.1	10.2	10.7	9.8
0-1	3.8	4.9	♦2.7	4.5	♦6.5	♦2.3	♦3.3	♦3.4	♦3.2
1-4	♦0.3	♦0.3	♦0.2	♦0.2	♦0.2	♦0.1	♦0.3	♦0.4	♦0.3
5-9	♦0.1	♦0.2	♦0.1	♦0.2	♦0.2	♦0.1	♦0.1	♦0.1	♦0.2
10-14	♦0.1	♦0.2	♦0.1	♦0.2	♦0.3	♦0.1	♦0.1	♦0.1	♦0.1
15-19	0.5	0.7	♦0.3	0.6	♦0.8	♦0.3	0.5	♦0.7	♦0.3
20-24	0.7	1.2	♦0.3	0.7	1.2	♦0.2	0.8	1.2	♦0.4
25-29	0.7	1.1	♦0.2	0.7	1.2	♦0.3	0.7	1.2	♦0.2
30-34	1.0	1.4	0.5	1.0	1.6	♦0.5	1.0	1.5	♦0.5
35-39	1.4	1.9	0.9	1.1	1.4	0.8	1.7	2.5	0.9
40-44	2.1	3.0	1.1	1.9	2.7	1.1	2.5	3.6	1.2
45-49	3.6	4.7	2.4	3.3	4.3	2.2	4.3	5.7	2.7
50-54	6.0	8.3	3.6	5.9	8.3	3.6	6.4	9.0	3.6
55-59	8.6	12.5	4.8	8.4	12.3	5.1	9.2	13.6	4.5
60-64	13.3	19.8	7.3	12.2	18.4	7.0	14.8	22.1	7.8
65-69	19.3	28.6	12.0	18.2	27.0	11.3	20.8	30.7	12.9
70-74	31.4	47.0	21.1	29.8	45.4	19.9	33.4	49.4	22.6
75-79	47.7	68.2	38.2	44.2	62.3	35.5	51.8	75.6	41.3
80-84	82.2	111.5	70.9	76.2	102.7	65.3	89.1	122.5	77.0
85-89	148.9	190.2	134.4	134.7	178.2	118.6	164.3	205.6	150.5
90-94	236.1	285.7	221.7	219.3	257.1	208.5	255.8	314.7	238.4
95+	336.7	391.3	323.8	320.0	347.4	314.0	367.2	436.4	349.2

20. Death rates specific for age, sex and urban/rural residence: latest available year, 1993 - 2002
Taux de mortalité selon l'âge, le sexe et la résidence, urbaine/rurale: dernière année disponible, 1993 - 2002 (continued — suite)

(See notes at end of table. — Voir notes à la fin du tableau.)

Continent, country or area, year and age (in years) / Continent, pays ou zone, année et âge (en années)	Total			Urban - Urbaine			Rural - Rurale		
	Both sexes Les deux sexes	Male Masculin	Female Féminin	Both sexes Les deux sexes	Male Masculin	Female Féminin	Both sexes Les deux sexes	Male Masculin	Female Féminin
EUROPE									
Spain - Espagne									
2000									
Total	9.0	9.7	8.4	...	...	...	...	...	...
0-1	4.5	4.8	4.2	...	...	...	...	...	...
1-4	0.3	0.3	0.2	...	...	...	...	...	...
5-9	0.2	0.2	0.1	...	...	...	...	...	...
10-14	0.2	0.2	0.1	...	...	...	...	...	...
15-19	0.5	0.7	0.3	...	...	...	...	...	...
20-24	0.6	0.9	0.3	...	...	...	...	...	...
25-29	0.7	1.0	0.3	...	...	...	...	...	...
30-34	0.9	1.3	0.5	...	...	...	...	...	...
35-39	1.3	1.9	0.7	...	...	...	...	...	...
40-44	1.9	2.6	1.1	...	...	...	...	...	...
45-49	2.6	3.7	1.5	...	...	...	...	...	...
50-54	3.9	5.7	2.2	...	...	...	...	...	...
55-59	5.8	8.5	3.2	...	...	...	...	...	...
60-64	9.0	13.4	5.0	...	...	...	...	...	...
65-69	14.3	21.0	8.5	...	...	...	...	...	...
70-74	23.1	33.2	15.1	...	...	...	...	...	...
75-79	40.0	55.6	29.2	...	...	...	...	...	...
80-84	69.5	89.0	58.6	...	...	...	...	...	...
85-89	129.0	155.8	116.7	...	...	...	...	...	...
90-94	229.7	252.9	220.4	...	...	...	...	...	...
95+	448.6	441.9	451.1	...	...	...	...	...	...
Sweden - Suède									
2002									
Total	10.6	10.4	10.9	...	...	...	...	...	...
0-1	3.3	3.6	3.1	...	...	...	...	...	...
1-4	0.2	0.2	◆0.1	...	...	...	...	...	...
5-9	0.1	◆0.1	◆0.1	...	...	...	...	...	...
10-14	0.1	0.1	◆0.1	...	...	...	...	...	...
15-19	0.3	0.4	0.3	...	...	...	...	...	...
20-24	0.5	0.8	0.3	...	...	...	...	...	...
25-29	0.4	0.6	0.3	...	...	...	...	...	...
30-34	0.6	0.7	0.4	...	...	...	...	...	...
35-39	0.7	0.9	0.5	...	...	...	...	...	...
40-44	1.2	1.5	0.9	...	...	...	...	...	...
45-49	2.0	2.3	1.6	...	...	...	...	...	...
50-54	3.2	3.9	2.5	...	...	...	...	...	...
55-59	5.4	6.5	4.3	...	...	...	...	...	...
60-64	8.3	10.4	6.3	...	...	...	...	...	...
65-69	14.0	17.8	10.5	...	...	...	...	...	...
70-74	23.5	30.2	17.8	...	...	...	...	...	...
75-79	40.6	52.4	31.6	...	...	...	...	...	...
80-84	72.3	90.9	60.3	...	...	...	...	...	...
85-89	133.6	163.3	118.5	...	...	...	...	...	...
90-94	230.2	269.7	215.4	...	...	...	...	...	...
95-99	360.2	423.9	344.2	...	...	...	...	...	...
100+	512.9	572.3	502.2	...	...	...	...	...	...
Switzerland - Suisse									
2002									
Total	8.5	8.3	8.6	...	...	...	...	...	...
0-4	1.0	1.1	0.9	...	...	...	...	...	...
5-9	0.1	◆0.1	◆0.1	...	...	...	...	...	...
10-14	0.1	◆0.1	◆0.1	...	...	...	...	...	...
15-19	0.4	0.5	0.3	...	...	...	...	...	...
20-24	0.6	0.8	0.4	...	...	...	...	...	...
25-29	0.6	0.9	0.3	...	...	...	...	...	...
30-34	0.7	0.9	0.4	...	...	...	...	...	...
35-39	0.9	1.2	0.6	...	...	...	...	...	...

20. Death rates specific for age, sex and urban/rural residence: latest available year, 1993 - 2002
Taux de mortalité selon l'âge, le sexe et la résidence, urbaine/rurale: dernière année disponible, 1993 - 2002 (continued — suite)

(See notes at end of table. — Voir notes à la fin du tableau.)

Continent, country or area, year and age (in years) / Continent, pays ou zone, année et âge (en années)	Total			Urban - Urbaine			Rural - Rurale		
	Both sexes Les deux sexes	Male Masculin	Female Féminin	Both sexes Les deux sexes	Male Masculin	Female Féminin	Both sexes Les deux sexes	Male Masculin	Female Féminin
EUROPE									
Switzerland - Suisse									
2002									
40-44	1.3	1.6	1.0	...	...	...	...	...	...
45-49	2.2	2.7	1.7	...	...	...	...	...	...
50-54	3.3	4.1	2.4	...	...	...	...	...	...
55-59	5.1	6.5	3.6	...	...	...	...	...	...
60-64	8.0	10.6	5.5	...	...	...	...	...	...
65-69	12.0	16.3	8.2	...	...	...	...	...	...
70-74	20.9	29.1	14.5	...	...	...	...	...	...
75-79	34.8	47.6	26.2	...	...	...	...	...	...
80-84	64.2	83.6	53.0	...	...	...	...	...	...
85+	161.4	182.0	153.1	...	...	...	...	...	...
The Former Yugoslav Rep. of Macedonia - L'ex-République yougoslave de Macédoine									
2001									
Total	8.3	9.1	7.5	...	...	...	...	...	...
0-1	12.9	15.1	10.6	...	...	...	...	...	...
1-4	0.4	♦0.4	♦0.5	...	...	...	...	...	...
5-9	0.2	♦0.3	♦0.2	...	...	...	...	...	...
10-14	0.2	♦0.2	♦0.2	...	...	...	...	...	...
15-19	0.4	0.5	♦0.3	...	...	...	...	...	...
20-24	0.5	0.8	♦0.2	...	...	...	...	...	...
25-29	0.7	1.0	♦0.3	...	...	...	...	...	...
30-34	0.9	1.2	0.5	...	...	...	...	...	...
35-39	1.4	1.9	0.9	...	...	...	...	...	...
40-44	2.2	3.0	1.5	...	...	...	...	...	...
45-49	3.9	5.2	2.6	...	...	...	...	...	...
50-54	6.5	9.0	4.0	...	...	...	...	...	...
55-59	10.1	13.2	7.2	...	...	...	...	...	...
60-64	16.2	21.9	11.0	...	...	...	...	...	...
65-69	26.7	34.4	20.0	...	...	...	...	...	...
70-74	43.3	50.7	37.3	...	...	...	...	...	...
75-79	77.2	86.2	70.6	...	...	...	...	...	...
80-84	124.6	138.1	114.6	...	...	...	...	...	...
85-89	205.4	223.1	192.4	...	...	...	...	...	...
90-94	252.2	279.0	234.0	...	...	...	...	...	...
95+	134.0	153.8	123.0	...	...	...	...	...	...
Ukraine[8]									
1998									
Total	14.3	15.2	13.6	12.5	13.8	11.4	18.1	18.3	18.0
0-1	12.4	14.5	10.2	12.4	14.5	10.1	12.4	14.5	10.3
1-4	0.9	1.0	0.8	0.7	0.8	0.6	1.3	1.4	1.2
5-9	0.4	0.5	0.3	0.3	0.4	0.3	0.5	0.6	0.4
10-14	0.4	0.5	0.3	0.4	0.5	0.3	0.4	0.5	0.3
15-19	0.9	1.2	0.6	0.8	1.1	0.5	1.1	1.4	0.7
20-24	1.6	2.5	0.7	1.5	2.3	0.7	1.8	2.8	0.7
25-29	2.1	3.3	1.0	2.0	3.1	1.0	2.4	3.7	0.9
30-34	2.9	4.5	1.2	2.7	4.4	1.2	3.1	4.8	1.3
35-39	4.0	6.3	1.7	3.7	6.0	1.7	4.6	7.2	1.8
40-44	5.8	9.3	2.6	5.4	8.8	2.4	6.9	10.6	3.1
45-49	8.5	13.5	4.1	8.0	12.6	4.0	10.1	15.9	4.6
50-54	12.3	19.4	6.4	11.9	18.7	6.2	13.2	21.0	6.8
55-59	15.9	24.9	9.0	15.6	24.1	8.8	16.6	26.2	9.3
60-64	24.8	37.5	15.2	24.8	37.1	15.4	24.9	38.2	14.9
65-69	32.7	48.6	22.4	33.4	48.6	23.3	31.7	48.5	21.2
70-74	50.1	71.5	39.8	51.6	72.0	41.4	48.0	70.8	37.7
75-79	77.4	99.6	69.1	79.3	98.6	71.6	75.3	100.9	66.6
80-84	118.3	138.9	111.9	120.3	136.4	114.7	115.9	142.6	108.7
85-89	189.9	206.2	185.3	195.8	206.6	192.4	184.2	205.6	178.6

20. Death rates specific for age, sex and urban/rural residence: latest available year, 1993 - 2002
Taux de mortalité selon l'âge, le sexe et la résidence, urbaine/rurale: dernière année disponible, 1993 - 2002 (continued — suite)

(See notes at end of table. — Voir notes à la fin du tableau.)

Continent, country or area, year and age (in years) / Continent, pays ou zone, année et âge (en années)	Total			Urban - Urbaine			Rural - Rurale		
	Both sexes Les deux sexes	Male Masculin	Female Féminin	Both sexes Les deux sexes	Male Masculin	Female Féminin	Both sexes Les deux sexes	Male Masculin	Female Féminin
EUROPE									
Ukraine[8]									
1998									
90-94	271.9	270.4	272.3	265.5	269.3	264.5	278.2	271.6	280.0
95+	389.6	267.6	430.8	334.4	247.7	364.0	450.0	289.8	503.4
2001									
Total	15.2	16.6	14.0	...	...	...	...	...	...
0-1	11.2	12.6	9.7	...	...	...	...	...	...
1-4	0.9	1.0	0.7	...	...	...	...	...	...
5-9	0.4	0.5	0.3	...	...	...	...	...	...
10-14	0.4	0.5	0.2	...	...	...	...	...	...
15-19	0.9	1.3	0.5	...	...	...	...	...	...
20-24	1.7	2.7	0.8	...	...	...	...	...	...
25-29	2.4	3.7	1.1	...	...	...	...	...	...
30-34	3.3	5.2	1.5	...	...	...	...	...	...
35-39	4.5	7.2	1.9	...	...	...	...	...	...
40-44	6.4	10.3	2.8	...	...	...	...	...	...
45-49	9.2	14.8	4.2	...	...	...	...	...	...
50-54	13.0	20.6	6.7	...	...	...	...	...	...
55-59	17.0	26.6	9.6	...	...	...	...	...	...
60-64	24.6	38.5	14.8	...	...	...	...	...	...
65-69	35.1	51.7	23.9	...	...	...	...	...	...
70-74	50.3	73.4	38.0	...	...	...	...	...	...
75-79	76.2	101.1	66.8	...	...	...	...	...	...
80-84	121.7	142.3	115.0	...	...	...	...	...	...
85+	210.2	208.2	210.7	...	...	...	...	...	...
United Kingdom - Royaume-Uni									
1999									
Total	10.6	10.3	11.0	...	...	...	...	...	...
0-4	1.3	1.5	1.2	...	...	...	...	...	...
5-9	0.1	0.1	0.1	...	...	...	...	...	...
10-14	0.1	0.2	0.1	...	...	...	...	...	...
15-19	0.4	0.6	0.3	...	...	...	...	...	...
20-24	0.6	0.9	0.3	...	...	...	...	...	...
25-29	0.6	0.9	0.4	...	...	...	...	...	...
30-34	0.8	1.0	0.5	...	...	...	...	...	...
35-39	1.0	1.3	0.8	...	...	...	...	...	...
40-44	1.6	1.9	1.3	...	...	...	...	...	...
45-49	2.6	3.1	2.1	...	...	...	...	...	...
50-54	4.1	5.0	3.2	...	...	...	...	...	...
55-59	6.9	8.6	5.2	...	...	...	...	...	...
60-64	11.4	14.2	8.7	...	...	...	...	...	...
65-69	19.2	24.5	14.4	...	...	...	...	...	...
70-74	32.6	41.4	25.4	...	...	...	...	...	...
75-79	52.7	67.3	42.5	...	...	...	...	...	...
80-84	86.1	109.1	73.4	...	...	...	...	...	...
85+	165.9	190.0	157.1	...	...	...	...	...	...
OCEANIA — OCEANIE									
Australia - Australie[+]									
2002									
Total	6.8	7.1	6.5	...	...	...	...	...	...
0-1	5.2	5.6	4.7	...	...	...	...	...	...
1-4	0.3	0.3	0.2	...	...	...	...	...	...
5-9	0.1	0.1	0.1	...	...	...	...	...	...
10-14	0.1	0.2	0.1	...	...	...	...	...	...
15-19	0.5	0.6	0.3	...	...	...	...	...	...
20-24	0.6	0.9	0.3	...	...	...	...	...	...
25-29	0.7	1.0	0.4	...	...	...	...	...	...

(See notes at end of table. — Voir notes à la fin du tableau.)

Continent, country or area, year and age (in years) / Continent, pays ou zone, année et âge (en années)	Total			Urban - Urbaine			Rural - Rurale		
	Both sexes Les deux sexes	Male Masculin	Female Féminin	Both sexes Les deux sexes	Male Masculin	Female Féminin	Both sexes Les deux sexes	Male Masculin	Female Féminin
OCEANIA — OCEANIE									
Australia - Australie[+]									
2002									
30-34	0.8	1.1	0.5	...	...	...	...	...	...
35-39	1.0	1.3	0.7	...	...	...	...	...	...
40-44	1.3	1.7	1.0	...	...	...	...	...	...
45-49	2.1	2.6	1.5	...	...	...	...	...	...
50-54	3.0	3.6	2.4	...	...	...	...	...	...
55-59	4.8	5.8	3.7	...	...	...	...	...	...
60-64	8.0	10.0	6.0	...	...	...	...	...	...
65-69	13.0	16.5	9.6	...	...	...	...	...	...
70-74	22.3	28.9	16.3	...	...	...	...	...	...
75-79	37.7	48.9	28.9	...	...	...	...	...	...
80-84	64.5	80.5	54.1	...	...	...	...	...	...
85-89	115.4	142.1	102.0	...	...	...	...	...	...
90-94	185.6	218.5	173.2	...	...	...	...	...	...
95-99	246.2	246.9	245.9	...	...	...	...	...	...
100+	266.3	139.8	321.5	...	...	...	...	...	...
New Caledonia - Nouvelle-Calédonie									
1994									
Total	5.8	6.6	4.9	...	...	...	...	...	...
0-1	9.8	◆10.4	◆9.2	...	...	...	...	...	...
1-4	◆1.4	◆1.3	◆1.4	...	...	...	...	...	...
5-9	◆0.8	◆1.1	◆0.4	...	...	...	...	...	...
10-14	◆0.2	◆0.2	◆0.2	...	...	...	...	...	...
15-19	◆1.1	◆1.8	◆0.3	...	...	...	...	...	...
20-24	2.2	3.4	◆1.0	...	...	...	...	...	...
25-29	◆1.1	◆1.4	0.7	...	...	...	...	...	...
30-34	◆1.9	◆3.3	◆0.6	...	...	...	...	...	...
35-39	2.8	◆3.6	◆2.0	...	...	...	...	...	...
40-44	3.7	◆4.2	◆3.1	...	...	...	...	...	...
45-49	4.7	6.0	◆3.3	...	...	...	...	...	...
50-54	7.9	8.1	◆7.6	...	...	...	...	...	...
55-59	12.2	14.1	10.1	...	...	...	...	...	...
60-64	22.0	25.8	18.1	...	...	...	...	...	...
65-69	26.2	36.5	16.2	...	...	...	...	...	...
75-84	77.2	87.8	67.6	...	...	...	...	...	...
80+	108.8	118.7	101.9	...	...	...	...	...	...
New Zealand - Nouvelle-Zélande[+]									
1996									
Total	7.8	8.1	7.5	8.3	8.6	8.0	4.8	5.5	4.1
0-1	7.4	7.8	7.0	8.0	8.5	7.5	4.2	◆4.2	◆4.2
1-4	0.4	0.5	0.4	0.4	0.5	0.4	◆0.3	◆0.4	◆0.3
5-9	0.2	◆0.2	◆0.2	0.2	◆0.2	◆0.2	◆0.1	-	◆0.2
10-14	0.3	0.3	0.3	0.3	◆0.2	◆0.3	◆0.3	◆0.3	◆0.3
15-19	1.0	1.3	0.7	0.9	1.2	0.7	1.2	◆1.6	◆0.8
20-24	1.0	1.5	0.5	0.9	1.4	0.5	1.6	2.4	◆0.5
25-29	1.0	1.5	0.5	1.0	1.4	0.5	1.2	2.0	◆0.5
30-34	1.0	1.4	0.7	1.1	1.4	0.7	0.9	1.5	◆0.4
35-39	1.2	1.5	0.8	1.2	1.6	0.9	1.0	◆1.3	◆0.6
40-44	1.4	1.7	1.1	1.4	1.7	1.1	1.4	1.6	◆1.1
45-49	2.9	3.2	2.5	3.0	3.3	2.7	2.3	2.6	1.9
50-54	4.5	5.4	3.7	4.7	5.7	3.8	3.5	3.8	3.3
55-59	7.4	9.1	5.7	7.8	9.8	5.9	5.1	5.9	4.3
60-64	12.8	15.7	9.9	13.1	16.3	10.0	11.1	12.8	9.1
65-69	19.7	24.6	14.9	20.1	25.5	15.1	16.8	19.8	12.8
70-74	31.1	40.2	23.4	31.5	41.6	23.4	27.3	30.3	23.8
75-79	49.3	64.0	39.2	50.1	65.5	39.8	41.9	51.7	31.9
80-84	83.6	104.8	71.2	83.8	105.6	71.5	80.4	96.3	66.9

20. Death rates specific for age, sex and urban/rural residence: latest available year, 1993 - 2002
Taux de mortalité selon l'âge, le sexe et la résidence, urbaine/rurale: dernière année disponible, 1993 - 2002 (continued — suite)

(See notes at end of table. — Voir notes à la fin du tableau.)

Continent, country or area, year and age (in years) / Continent, pays ou zone, année et âge (en années)	Total			Urban - Urbaine			Rural - Rurale		
	Both sexes Les deux sexes	Male Masculin	Female Féminin	Both sexes Les deux sexes	Male Masculin	Female Féminin	Both sexes Les deux sexes	Male Masculin	Female Féminin
OCEANIA — OCEANIE									
New Zealand - Nouvelle-Zélande+									
1996									
85-89	137.4	175.8	120.1	137.3	175.8	120.4	139.3	176.1	114.0
90-94	223.3	272.5	206.3	224.6	277.6	206.8	198.8	209.0	193.5
95-99	345.1	346.1	344.9	348.5	349.7	347.5	295.2	◆296.3	◆294.9
100+	475.1	◆606.1	462.2	472.2	◆545.5	467.6	◆833.3	◆666.7	◆500.0
2000									
Total	7.0	7.3	6.6	...	...	...	...	...	...
0-1	6.1	6.4	5.6	...	...	...	...	...	...
1-4	0.4	0.4	0.3	...	...	...	...	...	...
5-9	0.2	◆0.1	◆0.2	...	...	...	...	...	...
10-14	0.2	0.3	◆0.1	...	...	...	...	...	...
15-19	0.6	0.9	0.4	...	...	...	...	...	...
20-24	0.7	1.1	0.3	...	...	...	...	...	...
25-29	0.9	1.3	0.5	...	...	...	...	...	...
30-34	0.9	1.4	0.5	...	...	...	...	...	...
35-39	1.0	1.3	0.7	...	...	...	...	...	...
40-44	1.5	1.9	1.2	...	...	...	...	...	...
45-49	2.4	2.8	1.9	...	...	...	...	...	...
50-54	3.7	4.2	3.1	...	...	...	...	...	...
55-59	6.2	7.2	5.2	...	...	...	...	...	...
60-64	9.7	11.6	8.0	...	...	...	...	...	...
65-69	16.7	21.0	12.5	...	...	...	...	...	...
70-74	25.9	33.0	19.5	...	...	...	...	...	...
75-79	42.6	56.9	32.0	...	...	...	...	...	...
80-84	69.7	91.4	56.9	...	...	...	...	...	...
85-89	116.1	144.0	102.5	...	...	...	...	...	...
90+	216.4	249.3	206.6	...	...	...	...	...	...

GENERAL NOTES - NOTES GENERALES

Data exclude foetal deaths. For definition 'urban', see end of Technical Notes for table 6. For method of evaluation and limitations of data, see Technical Notes, for this table. — Les données ne comprennent pas les morts foetales. Pour les définitions des 'régions urbaines', se reporter à la fin des Notes techniques du tableau 6. Pour la méthode d'evaluations et les insuffisances des données, voir Notes techniques, pour ce tableau.

Italics: data from civil registers which are incomplete or of unknown completeness. — Italiques: données incomplètes ou dont le degré d'exactitude n'est pas connu provenant des registres de l'état civil.

FOOTNOTES - NOTES

◆ Rates based on 30 or fewer deaths. — Taux basés sur 30 décès ou moins.

+ Data tabulated by year of registration rather than occurrence. — Données exploitées selon l'année de l'enregistrement et non l'année de l'événement.

[1] For 2001, data refer to last twelve months preceding census on August 2001. - Pour 2001, les données se rapportent pour la dernière fois à douze mois précédant le recensement août 2001.
[2] For 1993, data refer to last twelve months preceding census on August 1993. - Pour 1993, les données se rapportent pour la dernière fois à douze mois précédant le recensement août 1993.
[3] Based on the results of the population census. - D'après les résultats du recensement de la population.
[4] Data for 1997 refer to last twelve months preceding population and housing census of 1997. - Les données pour 1997 se réfèrent au douze mois précédant le recensement de population et de l'habitat de 1997.
[5] Excluding live-born infants who died before their birth was registered. - Non compris les enfants nés vivants décédés avant l'enregistrement de leur naissance.
[6] Including Canadian residents temporarily in the United States, but excluding United States residents temporarily in Canada. - Y compris les résidents canadiens se trouvant temporairement aux Etats-Unis, mais ne comprenant pas les résidents des Etats-Unis se trouvant temporairement au Canada.
[7] Excluding Indian jungle population. - Non compris les Indiens de la jungle.
[8] Excluding infants born alive with less than 28 weeks gestation, less than 1 000 grams in weight and 35 centimeters in length, who die within seven days of birth. - Non compris les enfants nés vivants avant 28 semaines de gestation, pesant moins de 1 000 grammes, mesurant moins de 35 centimètres et décédés dans les sept jours qui ont suivi leur naissance.
[9] Data refer to government controlled areas. - Les données se raportent aux zones contrôlées par le Gouvernement.
[10] Including data for East Jerusalem and Israeli residents in certain other territories under occupation by Israeli military forces since June 1967. - Y compris les données pour Jérusalem-Est et les résidents israéliens dans certains autres territoires occupés depuis 1967 par les forces armées israéliennes.
[11] For Japanese nationals in Japan only; however, rates computed on population including foreigners except foreign military and civilian personnel and their dependants stationed in the area. — Pour les nationaux japonais au Japon seulement; toutefois, les taux sont calculés sur la base d'une population comprenant les étrangers, mais

ne comprenant ni les militaires et agents civils étrangers en poste sur le territoire ni les membres de leur famille les accompagnant.

[12] Excluding alien armed forces, civilian aliens employed by armed forces, and foreign diplomatic personnel and their dependants. - Non compris les militaires étrangers, les civils étrangers employés par les forces armées ni le personnel diplomatique étranger et les membres de leur famille les accompagnant.

[13] For 2001, data refer to last twelve months preceding census on June 2001. - Pour 2001, les données se rapportent pour la dernière fois à douze mois précédant le recensement juin 2001.

[14] Excluding data for the Pakistan-held part of Jammu and Kashmir, the final status of which has not yet been determined. - Non compris les données concernant la partie du Jammu et Cachemire occupée par le Pakistan dont le statut définitif n'a pas été déterminé.

[15] Based on the results of the Population Growth Survey. - D'après les résultats de la 'Population Growth Survey.'

[16] Excluding transients afloat and non-locally domiciled military and civilian services personnel and their dependants. - Non compris les personnes de passage þ bord de navires, ni les militaires et agents civils domiciliés hors du territoire et les membres de leur famille les accompagnant.

[17] Including armed forces stationed outside the country, but excluding alien armed forces stationed in the area. - Y compris les militaires nationaux hors du pays, mais non compris les militaires étrangers en garnison sur le territoire.

[18] Excluding Faeroe Islands and Greenland. - Non compris les Iles Féroé et Gröenland.

[19] Including nationals temporarily outside the country. - Y compris les nationaux se trouvant temporairement hors du pays.

[20] Including armed forces stationed outside the country. - Y compris les militaires nationaux hors du pays.

[21] For ages five years and over, age classification based on year of birth rather than exact date of birth. - A partir de cinq ans, le classement selon l'âge est basé sur l'année de naissances et non sur la date exacte de naissance.

[22] Excluding nationals outside the country. - Non compris les nationaux hors du pays.

[23] Data for urban/rural residence, for the de jure population. - Les données selon la résidence urbaine/rurale, pour la population de droit.

[24] Events registered within one year of occurrence. - Evénements enregistrés dans l'année qui suit l'événement.

[25] Including residents outside the country if listed in a Netherlands population register. - Y compris les résidents hors du pays, s'ils sont inscrits sur un registre de population néerlandais.

[26] Including residents temporarily outside the country. - Y compris les résidents se trouvant temporairement hors du pays.

Table 21

Table 21 presents deaths and death rates by cause for as many years as possible between 1995 and 2002.

Description of variables: Causes of death are all those diseases, morbid conditions or injuries which either resulted in or contributed to death and the circumstances of the accident or violence which produced any such injuries.[1]

The underlying cause of death, rather than direct or intermediate antecedent cause, is the one recommended as the main cause for tabulation of mortality statistics. It is defined as (a) the disease or injury which initiated the train of events leading directly to death, or (b) the circumstances of the accident or violence which produced the fatal injury.[1] Causes and corresponding ICD codes are presented in table 21-1 in the technical notes.

Statistics on deaths by cause presented in this table are provided by the World Health Organisation. They are limited to countries or areas that meet the criterion that cause-of-death statistics are classified to the ninth or tenth revisions. Data that are classified by the tenth revision are set in bold in the table.

Rate computation: Rates are the annual number of deaths in each cause group reported for the year per 100 000 corresponding mid-year population.

For other cause groups, for which the population more nearly approximates the population at risk, are specified below: rates (for malignant neoplasm of female breast and malignant neoplasm of cervix uteri) are computed per 100 000 female population 15 years and over; rates (for hyperplasic of prostate) are computed per 100 000 male population 50 years and over; and rates (for direct and indirect obstetric causes), and (conditions originating in the perinatal period) are computed per 100 000 total live births in the same year.

As noted above, rates presented in this table have been limited to those countries or areas having a total of at least 1 000 deaths from all causes in a given year. In certain cases death rates by cause have not been calculated because the population data needed for the denominator are not available. This may arise in either of two situations. First, no data on population at risk are available. Second, cause-of-death statistics are available for only a limited portion of the country and it is not possible to identify births or population at risk for that limited geographic area. Moreover, rates based on 30 or fewer deaths shown in this table are identified by the symbol (♦).

Reliability of data: Countries and areas that have incomplete (less than 90 per cent completeness) or of unknown completeness of cause of deaths data coverage are considered unreliable and are set in italics rather than In roman type. Rates on these data are not computed.

In general the quality code for deaths shown in table 18 is used to determine whether data on deaths in other tables appear in roman or *italic* type. However, the reliability of data for the completeness of cause of death is provided by the World Health Organisation[2] and it may differ from the reliability of data for the total number of reported deaths. Therefore, there are cases when the quality code in table 18 does not correspond with the typeface used in this table.

In addition, when it is known that registration of cause of death does not cover certain areas of a country, rates are not computed. Those countries are Georgia, Republic of Moldova and Russian Federation, as indicated in the footnote 7, 19 and 20, respectively. All other footnotes pertaining to the inclusion or exclusion of certain population of a country refer only to the denominator.

Limitations: Statistics on deaths by cause are subject to the same qualifications as have been set forth for vital statistics in general and death statistics in particular as discussed in section 4 of the Technical Notes.

In considering cause-of-death statistics it is important to take account of the differences among countries or areas in the quality, availability, and efficiency of medical services, certification procedures, and coding practices. When a death is registered and reported for statistical purposes, the cause of death if available will be stated in the death registration form. This statement of cause may have several sources: (1) If the death has been followed by an autopsy, presumably the "true" cause will have been discovered; (2) If an autopsy is not performed but the decedent was treated prior to death by a medical attendant, the reported cause of death will reflect the opinion of that physician based on observation of the patient while he or she was alive; and (3) If, on the other hand, the decedent has died without medical attendance, the body may be examined (without autopsy) by a physician who, aided by the questioning of persons who saw the patient before death, may come to a decision as to the probable cause of death. These three possible sources of information on cause of death constitute in general five degrees of decreasing accuracy in reporting.

Serious difficulties of comparability may stem also from differences in the form of death certificate being used, an increasing tendency to enter more than one cause of death on the certificate and diversity in the principles by which the primary or underlying cause is selected for statistical use when more than one is entered.

Differences in terminology used to identify the same disease also result in lack of comparability in statistics. These differences may arise in the same language in various parts of one country or area, but they are particularly troublesome between different languages.

Coding problems, and problems in interpretation of rules, arise constantly in using the various revisions of the International Statistical Classification of Diseases and Related Health Problems. Lack of uniformity between countries or areas in these interpretations and in adapting rules to national needs results in a lack of comparability that can be observed in the statistics. It is particularly evident in causes that are coded differently according to the age of the decedent, such as pneumonia, diarrhoeal diseases and others. Changing interpretations and new rules can also introduce disparities into the time series for one country or area. Hence, large increases or decreases in deaths reported from specified diseases should be examined carefully for possible explanations in terms of coding practice, before they are accepted as changes in mortality.

Further limitations of statistics by cause of death result from the periodic revision of the International Classification of Diseases. Data might not be comparable among countries or areas if different revisions of the Classification were used. Similarly, comparison over time for one country or area is not appropriate if different revisions were applied in the country. For a detailed indication of the revision that countries have used when cause of deaths data are available, see table 21-2 in the technical notes.

In addition to the qualifications explained in footnotes, particular care must be taken in using distributions with relatively large numbers of deaths attributed to ill-defined causes. Large frequencies in this category may indicate that cause of death among whole segments of the population has been undiagnosed, and the distribution of known causes in such cases is likely to be quite unrepresentative of the situation as a whole.

The possibility of error being introduced by the exclusion of deaths of infants who were born alive but died before the registration of the birth or within the first 24 hours of life should not be overlooked. These infant deaths are incorrectly classified as late foetal deaths. In several countries or areas, tabulation procedures have been devised to separate these pseudo-late-foetal deaths from true late foetal deaths and to incorporate them into the total deaths, but even in these cases there is no way of knowing the cause of death. Such distributions are footnoted.

For a further detailed discussion of the development of statistics of causes of death and the problems involved, see chapter II of the Demographic Yearbook 1951.

Earlier data: Deaths and death rates by cause have been shown in previous issues of the Demographic Yearbook. For information on specific years covered, readers should consult the Index.

---

[1] *International Statistical Classification of Diseases and Related Health Problems*, Tenth Revision, Volume 2, World Health Organization, Geneva, 1992
[2] For more information on specific method used for countries, see "Mathers CD, Bernard C, Iburg KM, Inoue M, Ma Fat D, Shibuya K et al. *Global burden of disease in 2002: data sources, methods and results*. Geneva, World Health Organization, 2003 (GPE Discussion Paper No. 54).

Tableau 21

Le tableau 21 présente des données sur les décès et les taux de mortalité par cause pour le plus grand nombre d'années possible entre 1995 et 2002.

Description des variables : Les causes des décès sont toutes les maladies, états morbides ou traumatismes qui ont abouti ou contribué au décès et les circonstances de l'accident ou de la violence qui ont entraîné ces traumatismes[1].

La cause initiale de décès, plutôt que la cause directe du décès, est recommandée pour les statistiques de la mortalité. La cause initiale de décès est définie comme : a) la maladie ou le traumatisme qui a déclenché l'évolution morbide conduisant directement au décès ; b) les circonstances de l'accident ou de la violence qui ont entraîné le traumatisme mortel[1]. Les causes et les codes correspondants de la CIM sont présentés dans le tableau 21-1, dans les notes techniques.

Les statistiques sur les décès classés en fonction de la cause qui les a provoqués émanent de l'Organisation mondiale de la santé. Elles ne portent que sur les pays ou les zones dans lesquels les statistiques relatives à la cause des décès sont conformes à la liste de la neuvième ou de la dixième révision de la CIM. Les données conformes à la liste de la dixième révision sont indiquées en caractères gras dans le tableau.

Calcul des taux : Les taux représentent le nombre annuel de décès signalés dans chaque groupe, pour l'année, dans une population de 100 000 habitants en milieu d'année.

Les taux relatifs aux autres catégories de causes correspondent aux populations les plus semblables à la population exposée. Les taux correspondant aux catégories « tumeur maligne du sein chez la femme » et « tumeur maligne du col de l'utérus » sont calculés sur une population de 100 000 femmes de 15 ans ou plus. Les taux correspondant à la catégorie « tumeur maligne de la prostate » sont calculés sur une population de 100 000 personnes de sexe masculin âgées de 50 ans ou plus, et les taux pour les catégorie « décès maternels directs », « décès maternels indirects » et « affections dont l'origine se situe dans la période périnatale » sont calculés sur 100 000 naissances vivantes dans la même année.

Comme indiqué plus haut, les taux figurant dans ce tableau ne concernent que les pays ou zones où l'on a relevé au moins 1 000 décès, toutes causes confondues, dans l'année. Dans certains cas, on n'a pas calculé les taux de mortalité selon la cause car l'on ne disposait pas des informations sur la population qui étaient nécessaires pour déterminer le dénominateur. Cela peut se présenter dans deux cas. Dans le premier, on n'a pas d'informations sur la population exposée au risque. Dans le second, il n'existe de statistiques selon les causes de décès que pour une partie limitée du pays, et il est impossible de déterminer le nombre de naissances et la population exposée dans cette zone limitée. De plus, les taux calculés sur la base de 30 décès ou moins, qui sont indiqués dans le tableau, sont signalés par le signe '♦'.

Fiabilité des données : Les statistiques relatives aux pays et aux zones pour lesquels la couverture des données concernant les causes des décès est incomplète (exhaustivité inférieure à 90 p. 100) ou dont le degré d'exhaustivité n'est pas connu sont jugées douteuses et apparaissent en italique et non en caractères romains. Les taux correspondants ne sont pas calculés.

En général, les code de qualité associés aux données sur les décès indiqués au tableau 18 servent à déterminer si, dans les autres tableaux, les données relatives à la mortalité apparaissent en caractères romains ou italiques. Toutefois, les renseignements relatifs à la fiabilité des données concernant la complétude des statistiques par cause de décès émanent de l'Organisation mondiale de la santé[2] et il est possible qu'ils ne correspondent pas avec le degré de fiabilité des données portant sur le nombre total des décès. Il y a donc des cas où les codes de qualité figurant dans le tableau 18 ne coïncident pas avec les caractères utilisés dans le présent tableau.

En outre, lorsque l'on sait que l'enregistrement des causes des décès ne couvre pas certaines zones d'un pays, les taux ne sont pas calculés. Cela est le cas de la Géorgie, de la République de Moldova et de

---

[1] *Classification statistique internationale des maladies et des problèmes de santé connexes*, dixième révision, volume 2. Genève, Organisation mondiale de la santé, 1992.
[2] Pour plus de précisions sur la méthode utilisée par les pays, voir « Mathers C. D., Bernard C., Iburg K.M., Inoue M., Ma Fat D., Shibuya K. et al. *Global burden of disease in 2002: data sources, methods and results*. Genève, Organisation mondiale de la santé, 2003 (GPE Discussion Paper n° 54).

la Fédération de Russie, comme indiqué dans les notes 7, 19 et 20 respectivement. Les autres notes qui ont trait à l'inclusion ou à l'exclusion de certaines populations dans un pays ne portent que sur le dénominateur.

Insuffisance des données : Les statistiques des décès selon la cause appellent les mêmes réserves que celles qui ont été formulées à propos des statistiques de l'état civil en général et des statistiques relatives aux décès en particulier (voir la section 4 des Notes techniques).

Lorsque l'on étudie les statistiques des causes des décès, il importe de prendre en considération les disparités existant entre pays ou zones du point de vue de la qualité, de la disponibilité et de l'efficacité des services médicaux, ainsi que des méthodes d'établissement des certificats de décès et des procédés de codage. Lorsqu'un décès est enregistré et déclaré aux fins de statistiques, le bulletin établi doit mentionner la cause du décès si elle est connue. Or la déclaration de la cause peut émaner de plusieurs sources : 1) si le décès a été suivi d'une autopsie, il est probable qu'on en aura décelé la cause « véritable » ; 2) s'il n'y a pas eu d'autopsie mais que le défunt a reçu, avant sa mort, les soins d'un médecin, la déclaration de la cause du décès reflétera l'opinion de ce médecin fondée sur l'observation du malade alors qu'il vivait encore ; 3) si, au contraire, le défunt est mort sans avoir reçu de soins médicaux, il se peut qu'un médecin examine le corps (sans qu'il soit fait d'autopsie), auquel cas il pourra, en questionnant les personnes qui ont vu le défunt avant sa mort, se former une opinion sur la cause probable du décès. À ces trois sources de renseignements possibles correspondent généralement trois degrés décroissants d'exactitude des données.

La comparabilité est aussi parfois très difficile à assurer par suite des différences existant dans la forme des certificats de décès utilisés, de la tendance croissante à indiquer plus d'une cause de décès sur le certificat et de la diversité des principes régissant le choix de la cause principale ou initiale à retenir dans les statistiques quand le certificat indique plus d'une cause.

Les différences entre les termes utilisés pour désigner une même maladie compromettent aussi la comparabilité des statistiques. On en rencontre parfois d'une région à l'autre dans un même pays ou une même zone où toute la population parle la même langue, mais elles sont particulièrement gênantes lorsque plusieurs langues interviennent.

En outre, des problèmes de codage et d'interprétation des règles se posent constamment lorsque l'on utilise les diverses révisions de la *Classification statistique internationale des maladies et des problèmes de santé connexes*. Les pays ou zones n'interprètent pas ces règles de manière uniforme et ne les adaptent pas de la même façon à leurs besoins ; la comparabilité s'en ressent comme le montrent les statistiques. Cela est particulièrement vrai pour les causes comme la pneumonie et les maladies diarrhéiques et autres, qui sont codées différemment selon l'âge du défunt. Les changements d'interprétation et l'adoption de nouvelles règles peuvent aussi introduire des divergences dans les séries chronologiques d'un même pays ou d'une même zone. En conséquence, il convient d'examiner attentivement les cas où le nombre de décès attribués à des maladies déterminées s'accroît ou diminue fortement, pour s'assurer, avant de conclure à une évolution de la mortalité, que le changement n'est pas dû à la méthode de codage.

D'autres irrégularités statistiques résultent des révisions périodiques de la *Classification statistique internationale des maladies*. Il est possible que les données ne soient pas comparables d'un pays ou d'une zone à un autre si différentes révisions de la classification ont été utilisées. De même, il n'est pas possible de comparer les données dans le temps pour un même pays ou zone lorsque différentes révisions y ont été utilisées. Pour une description détaillée des révisions utilisées par les pays qui ont communiqué des données concernant les causes des décès, voir le tableau 21-2 dans les notes techniques.

Outre les réserves expliquées dans les notes, il faut interpréter avec circonspection les répartitions comportant un nombre relativement élevé de décès attribués à des causes mal définies. Si les chiffres donnés pour cette catégorie sont importants, c'est peut-être parce que les décès survenus parmi des pans entiers de la population n'ont fait l'objet d'aucun diagnostic ; en pareil cas, il est probable que la répartition des causes connues est loin de donner une vue exacte de la situation d'ensemble.

Il ne faut pas négliger non plus le risque d'erreur que peut présenter l'exclusion des enfants nés vivants mais décédés avant l'enregistrement de leur naissance ou dans les 24 heures qui ont suivi la naissance. Ces décès sont classés à tort dans les morts fœtales tardives. Dans plusieurs pays ou zones, les méthodes d'exploitation permettent de différencier ces pseudo-morts fœtales tardives des morts fœtales tardives véritables et de les ajouter au nombre total des décès, mais, là encore, il est impossible de connaître la cause du décès. Ces répartitions sont signalées en note.

Pour un exposé plus détaillé de l'évolution des statistiques des décès selon la cause et des problèmes qui se posent, voir le chapitre II de l'*Annuaire démographique 1951*.

Données publiées antérieurement : Des statistiques des décès selon la cause (nombre et taux) ont été publiées dans des éditions antérieures de l'*Annuaire*. Pour plus de précisions concernant les années pour lesquels des données ont été publiées, se reporter à l'index.

21. Death and death rates by cause: 1995 - 2002
Décès selon la cause, nombres et taux: 1995 - 2002

(See notes at end of table. — Voir notes à la fin du tableau.)

Cause of death — Cause de décès	Egypt — Égypte 2000 Number Nombre
TOTAL	382 138
Certain infectious and parasitic diseases — Certaines maladies infectieuses et parasitaires	
Total	20 517
Intestinal infectious diseases — Maladies infectieuses intestinales	12 402
Tuberculosis — Tuberculose	722
Tetanus — Tétanos	288
Diphtheria — Diphtérie	-
Whooping cough — Coqueluche	1
Meningococcal infection — Infection à méningocoques	34
Septicaemia — Septicémie	1 178
Acute poliomyelitis — Poliomyélite aiguë	8
Measles — Rougeole	17
Viral hepatitis — Hépatite virale	1 618
Human immunodeficiency virus [HIV] disease — Maladies dues au virus de l'immunodéficience humaine (VIH)	12
Malaria — Paludisme	7
Neoplasms — Tumeurs	18 838
Malignant neoplasms — Tumeurs malignes	
Total	16 316
Malignant neoplasm of lip, oral cavity and pharynx — Tumeur maligne de la lèvre, de la cavité buccale et du pharynx	255
Malignant neoplasm of oesophagus — Tumeur maligne de l'oesophage	207
Malignant neoplasm of stomach — Tumeur maligne de l'estomac	685
Malignant neoplasm of colon, rectosigmoid junction, rectum, anus and anal canal — Tumeur maligne du côlon, de la jonction recto-sigmoïdienne, du rectum, de l'anus et du canal anal	693
Malignant neoplasm of liver and intrahepatic bile ducts — Tumeur maligne du foie et des voies bilaires intrahépatiques	2 701
Malignant neoplasm of pancreas — Tumeur maligne du pancréas	615
Malignant neoplasm of trachea, bronchus and lung — Tumeur maligne de la trachée, des bronches et du poumon	1 364
Malignant neoplasm of female breast — Tumeur maligne du sein chez la femme	1 354
Malignant neoplasm of cervix uteri — Tumeur maligne du col de l'utérus	88
Malignant neoplasm of prostate — Tumeur maligne de la prostate	386
Malignant neoplasm of lymphoid, haematopoietic and related tissue — Tumeurs malignes primitives ou présumées primitives des tissus lymphoïde, hématopoïétique et apparentés	1 656
Disorders of the blood and blood-forming organs and certain disorders involving the immune mechanism — Maladies du sang et des organes hématopoïétiques et certains troubles du système immunitaire	
Total	2 261
Anaemias — Anémies	655
Endocrine, nutritional and metabolic diseases — Maladies endocriniennes, nutritionnelles et métaboliques	
Total	7 289
Diabetes mellitus — Diabète sucré	3 348
Malnutrition — Malnutrition	1 330
Mental and behavioural disorders — Troubles mentaux et du comportement	308
Diseases of the nervous system — Maladies du système nerveux	3 216
Diseases of the circulatory system — Maladies de l'appareil circulatoire	
Total	146 161
Acute rheumatic fever and chronic rheumatic heart diseases — Rhumatisme articularie aigu et cardiopathies rhumatismales chroniques	1 779
Hypertensive diseases — Maladies hypertensives	17 885
Ischaemic heart disease — Cardiopathie ischémique	9 694
Cerebrovascular disease — Maladie cérébrovasculaire	21 601
Diseases of arteries, arterioles and capillaries — Maladies des artères, artérioles et capillaires	16 354
Diseases of the respiratory system — Maladies de l'appareil respiratoire	
Total	31 427
Influenza — Grippe	103
Pneumonia — Pneumopathies	17 038
Chronic lower respiratory diseases — Maladies chroniques des voies respiratoires inférieures	6 741
Diseases of the digestive system — Maladies de l'appareil digestif	
Total	30 852
Gastric and duodenal ulcer — Ulcère de l'estomac et du duodénum	417

21. Death and death rates by cause: 1995 - 2002
Décès selon la cause, nombres et taux: 1995 - 2002 (continued — suite)

(See notes at end of table. — Voir notes à la fin du tableau.)

Mauritius - Maurice

Cause of death — Cause de décès	1995 Number Nombre	1995 Rate Taux	1996 Number Nombre	1996 Rate Taux	1997 Number Nombre	1997 Rate Taux	1998 Number Nombre	1998 Rate Taux
TOTAL	7 298	650.2	7 508	662.1	7 798	679.1	7 651	659.3
Certain infectious and parasitic diseases — Certaines maladies infectieuses et parasitaires								
Total	152	13.5	137	12.1	151	13.2	97	8.4
Intestinal infectious diseases — Maladies infectieuses intestinales	43	3.8	24	♦2.1	24	♦2.1	13	♦1.1
Tuberculosis — Tuberculose	12	♦1.1	8	♦0.7	23	♦2.0	9	♦0.8
Tetanus — Tétanos	-	-	2	♦0.2	1	♦0.1	-	-
Diphtheria — Diphtérie	-	-	-	-	-	-	-	-
Whooping cough — Coqueluche	-	-	-	-	-	-	-	-
Meningococcal infection — Infection à méningocoques	-	-	-	-	-	-	-	-
Septicaemia — Septicémie	93	8.3	97	8.6	101	8.8	72	6.2
Acute poliomyelitis — Poliomyélite aiguë	-	-	-	-	-	-	-	-
Measles — Rougeole	-	-	-	-	-	-	-	-
Viral hepatitis — Hépatite virale	2	♦0.2	-	-	2	♦0.2	-	-
Human immunodeficiency virus [HIV] disease — Maladies dues au virus de l'immunodéficience humaine (VIH)	...	...	...	...	...	...	-	-
Malaria — Paludisme	..	..	..	..	..	..	1	♦0.1
Neoplasms — Tumeurs	657	58.5	652	57.5	641	55.8	725	62.5
Malignant neoplasms — Tumeurs malignes								
Total	633	56.4	644	56.8	638	55.6	721	62.1
Malignant neoplasm of lip, oral cavity and pharynx — Tumeur maligne de la lèvre, de la cavité buccale et du pharynx	29	♦2.6	29	♦2.6	20	♦1.7	23	♦2.0
Malignant neoplasm of oesophagus — Tumeur maligne de l'oesophage	23	♦2.0	16	♦1.4	31	2.7	17	♦1.5
Malignant neoplasm of stomach — Tumeur maligne de l'estomac	69	6.1	62	5.5	67	5.8	82	7.1
Malignant neoplasm of colon, rectosigmoid junction, rectum, anus and anal canal — Tumeur maligne du côlon, de la jonction recto-sigmoïdienne, du rectum, de l'anus et du canal anal	49	4.4	34	3.0	46	4.0	41	3.5
Malignant neoplasm of liver and intrahepatic bile ducts — Tumeur maligne du foie et des voies bilaires intrahépatiques	1	♦0.1	-	-	-	-	1	♦0.1
Malignant neoplasm of pancreas — Tumeur maligne du pancréas	22	♦2.0	27	♦2.4	25	♦2.2	35	3.0
Malignant neoplasm of trachea, bronchus and lung — Tumeur maligne de la trachée, des bronches et du poumon	93	8.3	88	7.8	74	6.4	98	8.4
Malignant neoplasm of female breast — Tumeur maligne du sein chez la femme	50	▲12.3	40	▲9.8	49	▲11.6	47	▲10.9
Malignant neoplasm of cervix uteri — Tumeur maligne du col de l'utérus	22	♦ ▲5.4	26	♦ ▲6.3	11	♦ ▲2.6	15	♦ ▲3.5
Malignant neoplasm of prostate — Tumeur maligne de la prostate	21	♦ ▼26.5	32	▼39.7	22	♦ ▼26.6	34	▼39.9
Malignant neoplasm of lymphoid, haematopoietic and related tissue — Tumeurs malignes primitives ou présumées primitives des tissus lymphoïde, hématopoïétique et apparentés	34	3.0	42	3.7	41	3.6	45	3.9
Disorders of the blood and blood-forming organs and certain disorders involving the immune mechanism — Maladies du sang et des organes hématopoïétiques et certains troubles du système immunitaire								
Total	23	♦2.0	21	♦1.9	22	♦1.9	27	♦2.3
Anaemias — Anémies	20	♦1.8	18	♦1.6	20	♦1.7	21	♦1.8
Endocrine, nutritional and metabolic diseases — Maladies endocriniennes, nutritionnelles et métaboliques								
Total	287	25.6	302	26.6	303	26.4	358	30.9
Diabetes mellitus — Diabète sucré	253	22.5	283	25.0	287	25.0	332	28.6
Malnutrition — Malnutrition	7	♦0.6	4	♦0.4	1	♦0.1	6	♦0.5
Mental and behavioural disorders — Troubles mentaux et du comportement	83	7.4	72	6.3	71	6.2	45	3.9
Diseases of the nervous system — Maladies du système nerveux	60	5.3	65	5.7	54	4.7	72	6.2
Diseases of the circulatory system — Maladies de l'appareil circulatoire								
Total	3 145	280.2	3 302	291.2	3 666	319.3	3 745	322.7
Acute rheumatic fever and chronic rheumatic heart diseases — Rhumatisme articularie aigu et cardiopathies rhumatismales chroniques	7	♦0.6	7	♦0.6	2	♦0.2	6	♦0.5
Hypertensive diseases — Maladies hypertensives	161	14.3	136	12.0	152	13.2	231	19.9
Ischaemic heart disease — Cardiopathie ischémique	1 243	110.7	1 322	116.6	1 540	134.1	1 605	138.3
Cerebrovascular disease — Maladie cérébrovasculaire	1 001	89.2	1 035	91.3	1 145	99.7	1 070	92.2
Diseases of arteries, arterioles and capillaries — Maladies des artères, artérioles et capillaires	9	♦0.8	5	♦0.4	10	♦0.9	13	♦1.1
Diseases of the respiratory system — Maladies de l'appareil respiratoire								
Total	706	62.9	609	53.7	627	54.6	711	61.3
Influenza — Grippe	1	♦0.1	1	♦0.1	1	♦0.1	1	♦0.1
Pneumonia — Pneumopathies	284	25.3	219	19.3	245	21.3	229	19.7
Chronic lower respiratory diseases — Maladies chroniques des voies respiratoires inférieures	210	18.7	188	16.6	206	17.9	258	22.2
Diseases of the digestive system — Maladies de l'appareil digestif								
Total	395	35.2	381	33.6	392	34.1	389	33.5
Gastric and duodenal ulcer — Ulcère de l'estomac et du duodénum	27	♦2.4	24	♦2.1	25	♦2.2	28	♦2.4

21. Death and death rates by cause: 1995 - 2002
Décès selon la cause, nombres et taux: 1995 - 2002 (continued — suite)

(See notes at end of table. — Voir notes à la fin du tableau.)

Cause of death — Cause de décès	Mauritius - Maurice 1999 Number Nombre	Mauritius - Maurice 1999 Rate Taux	Mauritius - Maurice 2000 Number Nombre	Mauritius - Maurice 2000 Rate Taux	South Africa — Afrique du Sud 1995 Number Nombre	South Africa — Afrique du Sud 1996 Number Nombre	Anguilla 1995 Number Nombre	Anguilla 2000 Number Nombre
TOTAL	7 791	662.9	7 806	657.7	*239 298*	*290 833*	*54*	*72*
Certain infectious and parasitic diseases — Certaines maladies infectieuses et parasitaires								
Total	104	8.8	120	10.1	*29 601*	*37 491*	*2*	*3*
Intestinal infectious diseases — Maladies infectieuses intestinales	11	♦0.9	18	♦1.5	*6 681*	*7 883*	-	-
Tuberculosis — Tuberculose	14	♦1.2	6	♦0.5	*12 360*	*17 314*	-	-
Tetanus — Tétanos	-	-	1	♦0.1	*28*	*55*	-	-
Diphtheria — Diphtérie	-	-	-	-	*2*	*1*	-	-
Whooping cough — Coqueluche	-	-	-	-	*5*	*8*	-	-
Meningococcal infection — Infection à méningocoques	1	♦0.1	2	♦0.2	*47*	*82*	-	-
Septicaemia — Septicémie	77	6.6	87	7.3	*3 691*	*3 654*	*2*	*2*
Acute poliomyelitis — Poliomyélite aiguë	-	-	-	-	*2*	*3*	-	-
Measles — Rougeole	-	-	-	-	*69*	*96*	-	-
Viral hepatitis — Hépatite virale	-	-	2	♦0.2	*471*	*252*	-	-
Human immunodeficiency virus [HIV] disease — Maladies dues au virus de l'immunodéficience humaine (VIH)	-	-	-	-	*5 221*	*6 367*	*...*	*1*
Malaria — Paludisme	-	-	-	-	*127*	*519*	-	-
Neoplasms — Tumeurs	731	62.2	736	62.0	*23 506*	*26 782*	*4*	*9*
Malignant neoplasms — Tumeurs malignes								
Total	729	62.0	717	60.4	*23 170*	*26 292*	*4*	*9*
Malignant neoplasm of lip, oral cavity and pharynx — Tumeur maligne de la lèvre, de la cavité buccale et du pharynx	38	3.2	36	3.0	*751*	*831*	-	*2*
Malignant neoplasm of oesophagus — Tumeur maligne de l'oesophage	23	♦2.0	23	♦1.9	*2 795*	*3 301*	-	-
Malignant neoplasm of stomach — Tumeur maligne de l'estomac	65	5.5	79	6.7	*1 143*	*1 385*	*2*	*1*
Malignant neoplasm of colon, rectosigmoid junction, rectum, anus and anal canal — Tumeur maligne du côlon, de la jonction recto-sigmoïdienne, du rectum, de l'anus et du canal anal	60	5.1	43	3.6	*1 347*	*1 443*	*1*	-
Malignant neoplasm of liver and intrahepatic bile ducts — Tumeur maligne du foie et des voies bilaires intrahépatiques	3	♦0.3	6	♦0.5	*...*	*1 552*	-	-
Malignant neoplasm of pancreas — Tumeur maligne du pancréas	17	♦1.4	29	♦2.4	*753*	*882*	*...*	-
Malignant neoplasm of trachea, bronchus and lung — Tumeur maligne de la trachée, des bronches et du poumon	88	7.5	82	6.9	*3 830*	*4 131*	-	*1*
Malignant neoplasm of female breast — Tumeur maligne du sein chez la femme	61	▲13.9	62	▲13.7	*1 543*	*1 707*	-	-
Malignant neoplasm of cervix uteri — Tumeur maligne du col de l'utérus	23	♦ ▲5.3	20	♦ ▲4.4	*1 708*	*1 959*	-	*4*
Malignant neoplasm of prostate — Tumeur maligne de la prostate	41	▼46.6	26	♦ ▼26.4	*1 209*	*1 462*	-	-
Malignant neoplasm of lymphoid, haematopoietic and related tissue — Tumeurs malignes primitives ou présumées primitives des tissus lymphoïde, hématopoïétique et apparentés	41	3.5	51	4.3	*1 496*	*1 673*	*1*	-
Disorders of the blood and blood-forming organs and certain disorders involving the immune mechanism — Maladies du sang et des organes hématopoïétiques et certains troubles du système immunitaire								
Total	24	♦2.0	32	2.7	*733*	*1 019*	-	*1*
Anaemias — Anémies	20	♦1.7	26	♦2.2	*501*	*638*	-	*1*
Endocrine, nutritional and metabolic diseases — Maladies endocriniennes, nutritionnelles et métaboliques								
Total	405	34.5	393	33.1	*10 273*	*11 894*	*2*	*6*
Diabetes mellitus — Diabète sucré	370	31.5	359	30.2	*8 045*	*8 351*	-	*4*
Malnutrition — Malnutrition	8	♦0.7	3	♦0.3	*1 633*	*2 654*	-	*2*
Mental and behavioural disorders — Troubles mentaux et du comportement	49	4.2	44	3.7	*481*	*524*	*2*	-
Diseases of the nervous system — Maladies du système nerveux	85	7.2	99	8.3	*4 211*	*5 926*	-	*3*
Diseases of the circulatory system — Maladies de l'appareil circulatoire								
Total	3 712	315.8	3 894	328.1	*40 899*	*60 433*	*13*	*34*
Acute rheumatic fever and chronic rheumatic heart diseases — Rhumatisme articularie aigu et cardiopathies rhumatismales chroniques	1	♦0.1	6	♦0.5	*326*	*557*	-	-
Hypertensive diseases — Maladies hypertensives	191	16.3	193	16.3	*4 242*	*5 717*	*1*	*4*
Ischaemic heart disease — Cardiopathie ischémique	1 513	128.7	1 564	131.8	*10 136*	*12 189*	*1*	*7*
Cerebrovascular disease — Maladie cérébrovasculaire	1 120	95.3	1 263	106.4	*15 722*	*20 362*	*6*	*14*
Diseases of arteries, arterioles and capillaries — Maladies des artères, artérioles et capillaires	16	♦1.4	28	♦2.4	*1 228*	*1 223*	-	-
Diseases of the respiratory system — Maladies de l'appareil respiratoire								
Total	745	63.4	723	60.9	*21 524*	*27 019*	*4*	*3*
Influenza — Grippe	-	-	-	-	*230*	*347*	-	-
Pneumonia — Pneumopathies	245	20.8	230	19.4	*10 084*	*11 215*	*2*	*1*
Chronic lower respiratory diseases — Maladies chroniques des voies respiratoires inférieures	237	20.2	274	23.1	*8 498*	*11 192*	*...*	*1*
Diseases of the digestive system — Maladies de l'appareil digestif								
Total	403	34.3	424	35.7	*6 286*	*8 206*	*1*	-
Gastric and duodenal ulcer — Ulcère de l'estomac et du duodénum	30	♦2.6	22	♦1.9	*963*	*1 089*	-	-

604

(See notes at end of table. — Voir notes à la fin du tableau.)

Cause of death — Cause de décès	Antigua and Barbuda — Antigua-et-Barbuda	Bahamas						Barbados — Barbade
	1995	1996	1997	1998	1999	2000	1995
				Number Nombre				
TOTAL	455	1 604	1 503	1 670	1 776	1 575	1 625	2 500
Certain infectious and parasitic diseases — Certaines maladies infectieuses et parasitaires								
Total	7	37	34	23	27	302	279	72
Intestinal infectious diseases — Maladies infectieuses intestinales	1	3	1	3	2	5	2	6
Tuberculosis — Tuberculose	-	12	8	4	11	8	6	2
Tetanus — Tétanos	-	-	1	-	-	-	-	-
Diphtheria — Diphtérie	-	-	-	-	-	-	-	-
Whooping cough — Coqueluche	-	-	-	-	-	-	-	-
Meningococcal infection — Infection à méningocoques	-	-	-	1	1	-	-	-
Septicaemia — Septicémie	5	16	22	13	6	9	18	53
Acute poliomyelitis — Poliomyélite aiguë	-	-	-	-	-	-	-	-
Measles — Rougeole	-	-	-	-	-	-	-	-
Viral hepatitis — Hépatite virale	1	2	-	-	2	1	2	-
Human immunodeficiency virus [HIV] disease — Maladies dues au virus de l'immunodéficience humaine (VIH)	...	...	...	...	...	275	245	...
Malaria — Paludisme	-	-	-	-	1		1	-
Neoplasms — Tumeurs	66	238	199	251	272	246	224	436
Malignant neoplasms — Tumeurs malignes								
Total	65	238	198	251	266	239	218	429
Malignant neoplasm of lip, oral cavity and pharynx — Tumeur maligne de la lèvre, de la cavité buccale et du pharynx	1	7	5	12	12	8	5	7
Malignant neoplasm of oesophagus — Tumeur maligne de l'oesophage	-	12	6	9	9	4	3	17
Malignant neoplasm of stomach — Tumeur maligne de l'estomac	4	21	22	15	15	13	16	28
Malignant neoplasm of colon, rectosigmoid junction, rectum, anus and anal canal — Tumeur maligne du côlon, de la jonction recto-sigmoïdienne, du rectum, de l'anus et du canal anal	6	20	12	23	28	22	19	48
Malignant neoplasm of liver and intrahepatic bile ducts — Tumeur maligne du foie et des voies bilaires intrahépatiques	-	-	1	6	1	11	9	-
Malignant neoplasm of pancreas — Tumeur maligne du pancréas	...	...	...	...	...	7	9	...
Malignant neoplasm of trachea, bronchus and lung — Tumeur maligne de la trachée, des bronches et du poumon	6	29	23	21	26	22	20	25
Malignant neoplasm of female breast — Tumeur maligne du sein chez la femme	7	26	23	30	30	29	28	46
Malignant neoplasm of cervix uteri — Tumeur maligne du col de l'utérus	2	11	7	10	6	11	15	23
Malignant neoplasm of prostate — Tumeur maligne de la prostate	14	28	35	36	38	35	34	95
Malignant neoplasm of lymphoid, haematopoietic and related tissue — Tumeurs malignes primitives ou présumées primitives des tissus lymphoïde, hématopoïétique et apparentés	5	11	5	17	19	18	13	27
Disorders of the blood and blood-forming organs and certain disorders involving the immune mechanism — Maladies du sang et des organes hématopoïétiques et certains troubles du système immunitaire								
Total	5	5	14	13	6	10	11	16
Anaemias — Anémies	5	4	12	11	5	8	7	14
Endocrine, nutritional and metabolic diseases — Maladies endocriniennes, nutritionnelles et métaboliques								
Total	49	385	400	378	415	98	114	394
Diabetes mellitus — Diabète sucré	21	101	114	88	127	86	105	250
Malnutrition — Malnutrition	-	3	-	-	3	1	-	-
Mental and behavioural disorders — Troubles mentaux et du comportement	9	9	19	14	20	15	11	45
Diseases of the nervous system — Maladies du système nerveux	7	23	30	34	44	30	25	60
Diseases of the circulatory system — Maladies de l'appareil circulatoire								
Total	158	445	370	473	461	434	458	965
Acute rheumatic fever and chronic rheumatic heart diseases — Rhumatisme articularie aigu et cardiopathies rhumatismales chroniques	-	1	1	1	1	1	1	4
Hypertensive diseases — Maladies hypertensives	30	79	117	132	125	103	107	56
Ischaemic heart disease — Cardiopathie ischémique	27	127	77	114	124	166	181	214
Cerebrovascular disease — Maladie cérébrovasculaire	54	130	83	143	137	109	82	342
Diseases of arteries, arterioles and capillaries — Maladies des artères, artérioles et capillaires	10	26	18	16	15	7	15	95
Diseases of the respiratory system — Maladies de l'appareil respiratoire								
Total	13	137	97	108	127	83	80	147
Influenza — Grippe	-	1	-	1	-	1	-	1
Pneumonia — Pneumopathies	8	69	50	47	49	45	40	89
Chronic lower respiratory diseases — Maladies chroniques des voies respiratoires inférieures	...	...	...	...	...	14	18	...
Diseases of the digestive system — Maladies de l'appareil digestif								
Total	20	68	44	73	69	68	76	90
Gastric and duodenal ulcer — Ulcère de l'estomac et du duodénum	-	4	-	5	5	6	2	8

(See notes at end of table. — Voir notes à la fin du tableau.)

Cause of death — Cause de décès	Barbados — Barbade			Belize				
	1995	2000		1995	1996	1997		1998
	Rate Taux	Number Nombre	Rate Taux		Number Nombre	Number Nombre	Rate Taux	Number Nombre
TOTAL	946.3	2 429	908.1	931	887	1 175	510.9	1 350
Certain infectious and parasitic diseases — Certaines maladies infectieuses et parasitaires								
Total	27.3	143	53.5	51	64	84	36.5	116
Intestinal infectious diseases — Maladies infectieuses intestinales	♦2.3	5	♦1.9	13	11	15	♦6.5	24
Tuberculosis — Tuberculose	♦0.8	-	-	6	12	14	♦6.1	40
Tetanus — Tétanos	-	1	♦0.4	-	1	-	-	-
Diphtheria — Diphtérie	-	-	-	-	-	-	-	-
Whooping cough — Coqueluche	-	-	-	-	-	-	-	-
Meningococcal infection — Infection à méningocoques	-	-	-	-	-	-	-	-
Septicaemia — Septicémie	20.1	34	12.7	30	38	34	14.8	18
Acute poliomyelitis — Poliomyélite aiguë	-	-	-	-	-	-	-	-
Measles — Rougeole	-	-	-	-	-	-	-	-
Viral hepatitis — Hépatite virale	-	-	-	-	-	-	-	2
Human immunodeficiency virus [HIV] disease — Maladies dues au virus de l'immunodéficience humaine (VIH)	...	89	33.3	...	...	17	♦7.4	30
Malaria — Paludisme	-	2	♦0.7	2	-	1	♦0.4	-
Neoplasms — Tumeurs	165.0	461	172.3	84	70	136	59.1	189
Malignant neoplasms — Tumeurs malignes								
Total	162.4	460	172.0	82	69	131	57.0	182
Malignant neoplasm of lip, oral cavity and pharynx — Tumeur maligne de la lèvre, de la cavité buccale et du pharynx	♦2.6	14	♦5.2	4	1	2	♦0.9	4
Malignant neoplasm of oesophagus — Tumeur maligne de l'oesophage	♦6.4	13	♦4.9	2	2	3	♦1.3	3
Malignant neoplasm of stomach — Tumeur maligne de l'estomac	♦10.6	44	16.4	12	3	5	♦2.2	27
Malignant neoplasm of colon, rectosigmoid junction, rectum, anus and anal canal — Tumeur maligne du côlon, de la jonction recto-sigmoïdienne, du rectum, de l'anus et du canal anal	18.2	30	♦11.2	7	4	2	♦0.9	5
Malignant neoplasm of liver and intrahepatic bile ducts — Tumeur maligne du foie et des voies bilaires intrahépatiques	-	19	♦7.1	-	-	5	♦2.2	14
Malignant neoplasm of pancreas — Tumeur maligne du pancréas	...	19	♦7.1	...	...	6	♦2.6	19
Malignant neoplasm of trachea, bronchus and lung — Tumeur maligne de la trachée, des bronches et du poumon	♦9.5	19	♦7.1	10	11	14	♦6.1	13
Malignant neoplasm of female breast — Tumeur maligne du sein chez la femme	...	50	...	2	2	2	♦ ▲3.0	12
Malignant neoplasm of cervix uteri — Tumeur maligne du col de l'utérus	...	20	...	3	5	11	♦ ▲16.3	17
Malignant neoplasm of prostate — Tumeur maligne de la prostate	...	91	...	5	4	20	♦ ▼150.0	24
Malignant neoplasm of lymphoid, haematopoietic and related tissue — Tumeurs malignes primitives ou présumées primitives des tissus lymphoïde, hématopoïétique et apparentés	♦10.2	36	13.5	5	9	15	♦6.5	9
Disorders of the blood and blood-forming organs and certain disorders involving the immune mechanism — Maladies du sang et des organes hématopoïétiques et certains troubles du système immunitaire								
Total	♦6.1	23	♦8.6	5	6	14	♦6.1	7
Anaemias — Anémies	♦5.3	19	♦7.1	5	6	13	♦5.7	6
Endocrine, nutritional and metabolic diseases — Maladies endocriniennes, nutritionnelles et métaboliques								
Total	149.1	262	97.9	60	43	72	31.3	88
Diabetes mellitus — Diabète sucré	94.6	226	84.5	28	10	36	15.7	52
Malnutrition — Malnutrition	-	4	♦1.5	12	4	23	♦10.0	26
Mental and behavioural disorders — Troubles mentaux et du comportement	17.0	19	♦7.1	4	2	4	♦1.7	8
Diseases of the nervous system — Maladies du système nerveux	22.7	51	19.1	15	10	10	♦4.3	16
Diseases of the circulatory system — Maladies de l'appareil circulatoire								
Total	365.3	819	306.2	258	251	302	131.3	349
Acute rheumatic fever and chronic rheumatic heart diseases — Rhumatisme articularie aigu et cardiopathies rhumatismales chroniques	♦1.5	5	♦1.9	1	-	2	♦0.9	1
Hypertensive diseases — Maladies hypertensives	21.2	129	48.2	10	18	44	19.1	69
Ischaemic heart disease — Cardiopathie ischémique	81.0	182	68.0	79	64	95	41.3	79
Cerebrovascular disease — Maladie cérébrovasculaire	129.4	191	71.4	67	67	72	31.3	96
Diseases of arteries, arterioles and capillaries — Maladies des artères, artérioles et capillaires	36.0	49	18.3	1	11	5	♦2.2	28
Diseases of the respiratory system — Maladies de l'appareil respiratoire								
Total	55.6	174	65.0	103	89	132	57.4	116
Influenza — Grippe	♦0.4	-	-	-	-	-	-	-
Pneumonia — Pneumopathies	33.7	91	34.0	72	68	83	36.1	68
Chronic lower respiratory diseases — Maladies chroniques des voies respiratoires inférieures	...	21	♦7.9	...	...	15	♦6.5	18
Diseases of the digestive system — Maladies de l'appareil digestif								
Total	34.1	94	35.1	35	28	38	16.5	33
Gastric and duodenal ulcer — Ulcère de l'estomac et du duodénum	♦3.0	6	♦2.2	-	-	3	♦1.3	6

21. Death and death rates by cause: 1995 - 2002
Décès selon la cause, nombres et taux: 1995 - 2002 (continued — suite)

(See notes at end of table. — Voir notes à la fin du tableau.)

Columns: Belize (1998, 1999, 2000) · Bermuda — Bermudes · British Virgin Islands — Iles Vierges britanniques (1995, 1996)

Cause of death — Cause de décès	Belize 1998 Rate/Taux	Belize 1999 Number/Nombre	Belize 1999 Rate/Taux	Belize 2000 Number/Nombre	Belize 2000 Rate/Taux	Bermudes	BVI 1995 Number/Nombre	BVI 1996
TOTAL	566.0	1 189	489.2	1 534	614.1	500	87	77
Certain infectious and parasitic diseases — Certaines maladies infectieuses et parasitaires								
Total	48.6	90	37.0	84	33.6	9	2	4
Intestinal infectious diseases — Maladies infectieuses intestinales	♦10.1	12	♦4.9	13	♦5.2	-	-	1
Tuberculosis — Tuberculose	16.8	17	♦7.0	9	♦3.6	-	1	-
Tetanus — Tétanos	-	-	-	-	-	-	-	-
Diphtheria — Diphtérie	-	-	-	-	-	-	-	-
Whooping cough — Coqueluche	-	-	-	-	-	-	-	-
Meningococcal infection — Infection à méningocoques	-	-	-	2	♦0.8	-	-	-
Septicaemia — Septicémie	♦7.5	14	♦5.8	10	♦4.0	-	1	3
Acute poliomyelitis — Poliomyélite aiguë	-	-	-	-	-	-	-	-
Measles — Rougeole	-	-	-	-	-	-	-	-
Viral hepatitis — Hépatite virale	♦0.8	1	♦0.4	1	♦0.4	-	-	-
Human immunodeficiency virus [HIV] disease — Maladies dues au virus de l'immunodéficience humaine (VIH)	♦12.6	44	18.1	47	18.8	9	...	-
Malaria — Paludisme	-	-	-	-	-	-	-	-
Neoplasms — Tumeurs	79.2	162	66.7	137	54.8	142	14	13
Malignant neoplasms — Tumeurs malignes								
Total	76.3	157	64.6	137	54.8	138	14	13
Malignant neoplasm of lip, oral cavity and pharynx — Tumeur maligne de la lèvre, de la cavité buccale et du pharynx	♦1.7	2	♦0.8	-		7	1	-
Malignant neoplasm of oesophagus — Tumeur maligne de l'oesophage	♦1.3	7	♦2.9	3	♦1.2	4	-	-
Malignant neoplasm of stomach — Tumeur maligne de l'estomac	♦11.3	22	♦9.1	11	♦4.4	5	2	1
Malignant neoplasm of colon, rectosigmoid junction, rectum, anus and anal canal — Tumeur maligne du côlon, de la jonction recto-sigmoïdienne, du rectum, de l'anus et du canal anal	♦2.1	8	♦3.3	2	♦0.8	6	2	1
Malignant neoplasm of liver and intrahepatic bile ducts — Tumeur maligne du foie et des voies bilaires intrahépatiques	♦5.9	17	♦7.0	14	♦5.6	5	-	1
Malignant neoplasm of pancreas — Tumeur maligne du pancréas	♦8.0	6	♦2.5	12	♦4.8	11	...	-
Malignant neoplasm of trachea, bronchus and lung — Tumeur maligne de la trachée, des bronches et du poumon	♦5.5	15	♦6.2	14	♦5.6	27	2	-
Malignant neoplasm of female breast — Tumeur maligne du sein chez la femme	♦▲16.7	4		5	...	13	*	2
Malignant neoplasm of cervix uteri — Tumeur maligne du col de l'utérus	♦▲23.7	12	...	13	...	2	-	-
Malignant neoplasm of prostate — Tumeur maligne de la prostate	♦▼165.1	15	...	15	...	9	4	4
Malignant neoplasm of lymphoid, haematopoietic and related tissue — Tumeurs malignes primitives ou présumées primitives des tissus lymphoïde, hématopoïétique et apparentés	♦3.8	9	♦3.7	11	♦4.4	13	1	1
Disorders of the blood and blood-forming organs and certain disorders involving the immune mechanism — Maladies du sang et des organes hématopoïétiques et certains troubles du système immunitaire								
Total	♦2.9	10	♦4.1	8	♦3.2	1	-	-
Anaemias — Anémies	♦2.5	9	♦3.7	6	♦2.4	-	-	-
Endocrine, nutritional and metabolic diseases — Maladies endocriniennes, nutritionnelles et métaboliques								
Total	36.9	96	39.5	106	42.4	23	5	5
Diabetes mellitus — Diabète sucré	21.8	67	27.6	89	35.6	20	1	3
Malnutrition — Malnutrition	♦10.9	19	♦7.8	10	♦4.0	2	-	-
Mental and behavioural disorders — Troubles mentaux et du comportement	♦3.4	6	♦2.5	-		-	-	-
Diseases of the nervous system — Maladies du système nerveux	♦6.7	19	♦7.8	24	♦9.6	10	6	1
Diseases of the circulatory system — Maladies de l'appareil circulatoire								
Total	146.3	301	123.8	622	249.0	209	37	28
Acute rheumatic fever and chronic rheumatic heart diseases — Rhumatisme articularie aigu et cardiopathies rhumatismales chroniques	♦0.4	-		4	♦1.6	2	-	-
Hypertensive diseases — Maladies hypertensives	28.9	76	31.3	172	68.9	23	10	-
Ischaemic heart disease — Cardiopathie ischémique	33.1	53	21.8	110	44.0	103	10	13
Cerebrovascular disease — Maladie cérébrovasculaire	40.3	78	32.1	122	48.8	34	6	8
Diseases of arteries, arterioles and capillaries — Maladies des artères, artérioles et capillaires	♦11.7	11	♦4.5	14	♦5.6	17	4	-
Diseases of the respiratory system — Maladies de l'appareil respiratoire								
Total	48.6	107	44.0	125	50.0	42	5	4
Influenza — Grippe	-	-	-	-	-	-	-	-
Pneumonia — Pneumopathies	28.5	55	22.6	72	28.8	24	3	3
Chronic lower respiratory diseases — Maladies chroniques des voies respiratoires inférieures	♦7.5	27	♦11.1	32	12.8	10	...	-
Diseases of the digestive system — Maladies de l'appareil digestif								
Total	13.8	41	16.9	47	18.8	17	2	4
Gastric and duodenal ulcer — Ulcère de l'estomac et du duodénum	♦2.5	4	♦1.6	5	♦2.0	1	1	-

(See notes at end of table. — Voir notes à la fin du tableau.)

Cause of death — Cause de décès	British Virgin Islands — Iles Vierges britanniques		Canada[1]					
	1997	1998	1995		1996		1997	
	Number Nombre	Number Nombre	Number Nombre	Rate Taux	Number Nombre	Rate Taux	Number Nombre	Rate Taux
TOTAL	*94*	*85*	210 733	719.2	212 859	718.9	215 668	721.1
Certain infectious and parasitic diseases — Certaines maladies infectieuses et parasitaires								
Total	6	4	3 497	11.9	3 117	10.5	2 482	8.3
Intestinal infectious diseases — Maladies infectieuses intestinales	-	-	57	0.2	64	0.2	74	0.2
Tuberculosis — Tuberculose	-	-	117	0.4	115	0.4	114	0.4
Tetanus — Tétanos	-	-	1	0.0	-	-	1	0.0
Diphtheria — Diphtérie	-	-	-	-	-	-	1	0.0
Whooping cough — Coqueluche	-	-	3	0.0	4	0.0	-	-
Meningococcal infection — Infection à méningocoques	-	-	16	♦0.1	12	0.0	22	♦0.1
Septicaemia — Septicémie	5	3	902	3.1	957	3.2	969	3.2
Acute poliomyelitis — Poliomyélite aiguë	-	-	2	0.0	1	0.0	-	-
Measles — Rougeole	-	-	-	-	-	-	-	-
Viral hepatitis — Hépatite virale	-	-	232	0.8	233	0.8	225	0.8
Human immunodeficiency virus [HIV] disease — Maladies dues au virus de l'immunodéficience humaine (VIH)	1	1	1 764	6.0	1 306	4.4	626	2.1
Malaria — Paludisme	-	-	1	0.0	1	0.0	1	0.0
Neoplasms — Tumeurs	*24*	*19*	58 817	200.7	60 285	203.6	59 775	199.9
Malignant neoplasms — Tumeurs malignes								
Total	24	19	57 810	197.3	59 238	200.1	58 703	196.3
Malignant neoplasm of lip, oral cavity and pharynx — Tumeur maligne de la lèvre, de la cavité buccale et du pharynx	1	1	1 010	3.4	952	3.2	1 026	3.4
Malignant neoplasm of oesophagus — Tumeur maligne de l'oesophage	1	1	1 160	4.0	1 207	4.1	1 280	4.3
Malignant neoplasm of stomach — Tumeur maligne de l'estomac	2	1	2 078	7.1	2 077	7.0	1 963	6.6
Malignant neoplasm of colon, rectosigmoid junction, rectum, anus and anal canal — Tumeur maligne du côlon, de la jonction recto-sigmoïdienne, du rectum, de l'anus et du canal anal	5	-	6 191	21.1	6 158	20.8	6 102	20.4
Malignant neoplasm of liver and intrahepatic bile ducts — Tumeur maligne du foie et des voies bilaires intrahépatiques	-	-	403	1.4	419	1.4	449	1.5
Malignant neoplasm of pancreas — Tumeur maligne du pancréas	1	-	2 817	9.6	2 991	10.1	2 847	9.5
Malignant neoplasm of trachea, bronchus and lung — Tumeur maligne de la trachée, des bronches et du poumon	2	1	15 076	51.5	15 708	53.0	15 439	51.6
Malignant neoplasm of female breast — Tumeur maligne du sein chez la femme	1	4	4 923	▲41.0	5 074	▲42.1	4 946	▲40.4
Malignant neoplasm of cervix uteri — Tumeur maligne du col de l'utérus	-	-	400	▲3.3	442	▲3.7	417	▲3.4
Malignant neoplasm of prostate — Tumeur maligne de la prostate	4	7	3 761	▼106.1	3 588	▼99.8	3 622	▼97.5
Malignant neoplasm of lymphoid, haematopoietic and related tissue — Tumeurs malignes primitives ou présumées primitives des tissus lymphoïde, hématopoïétique et apparentés	1	1	5 239	17.9	5 460	18.4	5 415	18.1
Disorders of the blood and blood-forming organs and certain disorders involving the immune mechanism — Maladies du sang et des organes hématopoïétiques et certains troubles du système immunitaire								
Total	-	2	803	2.7	806	2.7	796	2.7
Anaemias — Anémies	-	2	483	1.6	512	1.7	474	1.6
Endocrine, nutritional and metabolic diseases — Maladies endocriniennes, nutritionnelles et métaboliques								
Total	2	4	7 042	24.0	6 939	23.4	7 328	24.5
Diabetes mellitus — Diabète sucré	2	4	5 496	18.8	5 450	18.4	5 699	19.1
Malnutrition — Malnutrition	-	-	168	0.6	199	0.7	204	0.7
Mental and behavioural disorders — Troubles mentaux et du comportement	2	2	5 093	17.4	5 304	17.9	5 855	19.6
Diseases of the nervous system — Maladies du système nerveux	-	6	6 227	21.3	6 355	21.5	6 550	21.9
Diseases of the circulatory system — Maladies de l'appareil circulatoire								
Total	41	27	79 116	270.0	79 436	268.3	79 457	265.7
Acute rheumatic fever and chronic rheumatic heart diseases — Rhumatisme articularie aigu et cardiopathies rhumatismales chroniques	-	-	556	1.9	528	1.8	499	1.7
Hypertensive diseases — Maladies hypertensives	3	3	1 409	4.8	1 424	4.8	1 344	4.5
Ischaemic heart disease — Cardiopathie ischémique	12	9	44 065	150.4	44 016	148.6	43 526	145.5
Cerebrovascular disease — Maladie cérébrovasculaire	13	7	15 537	53.0	15 592	52.7	16 051	53.7
Diseases of arteries, arterioles and capillaries — Maladies des artères, artérioles et capillaires	-	-	4 858	16.6	4 727	16.0	4 767	15.9
Diseases of the respiratory system — Maladies de l'appareil respiratoire								
Total	5	2	18 888	64.5	19 137	64.6	20 036	67.0
Influenza — Grippe	-	-	190	0.6	182	0.6	304	1.0
Pneumonia — Pneumopathies	2	-	7 192	24.5	7 291	24.6	7 728	25.8
Chronic lower respiratory diseases — Maladies chroniques des voies respiratoires inférieures	2	2	9 185	31.3	9 346	31.6	9 618	32.2
Diseases of the digestive system — Maladies de l'appareil digestif								
Total	6	3	7 616	26.0	7 462	25.2	7 630	25.5
Gastric and duodenal ulcer — Ulcère de l'estomac et du duodénum	-	-	560	1.9	479	1.6	451	1.5

(See notes at end of table. — Voir notes à la fin du tableau.)

Cause of death — Cause de décès	Canada[1]						Cayman Islands — Iles Caïmanes	
	1998		1999		2000		1995	1996
	Number Nombre	Rate Taux	Number Nombre	Rate Taux	Number Nombre	Rate Taux	Number Nombre	Number Nombre
TOTAL	218 091	723.2	219 530	722.0	**218 062**	**710.6**	*110*	*115*
Certain infectious and parasitic diseases — Certaines maladies infectieuses et parasitaires								
Total	2 568	8.5	2 583	8.5	**3 112**	**10.1**	*4*	*1*
Intestinal infectious diseases — Maladies infectieuses intestinales	108	0.4	129	0.4	**250**	**0.8**	-	-
Tuberculosis — Tuberculose	101	0.3	105	0.3	**81**	**0.3**	-	-
Tetanus — Tétanos	-	-	-	-	-		-	-
Diphtheria — Diphtérie	-	-	-	-	-		-	-
Whooping cough — Coqueluche	3	0.0	1	0.0	**2**	**0.0**	-	-
Meningococcal infection — Infection à méningocoques	10	0.0	23	✦0.1	**24**	**✦0.1**	-	-
Septicaemia — Septicémie	1 105	3.7	1 054	3.5	**1 358**	**4.4**	*4*	*1*
Acute poliomyelitis — Poliomyélite aiguë	-	-	-	-	-		-	-
Measles — Rougeole	-	-	-	-	**1**	**0.0**	-	-
Viral hepatitis — Hépatite virale	290	1.0	309	1.0	**138**	**0.4**	-	-
Human immunodeficiency virus [HIV] disease — Maladies dues au virus de l'immunodéficience humaine (VIH)	485	1.6	431	1.4	**511**	**1.7**	...	...
Malaria — Paludisme	2	0.0	2	0.0	**1**	**0.0**	-	-
Neoplasms — Tumeurs	61 727	204.7	62 769	206.5	**64 111**	**208.9**	*23*	*32*
Malignant neoplasms — Tumeurs malignes								
Total	60 597	200.9	61 650	202.8	**62 672**	**204.2**	*23*	*30*
Malignant neoplasm of lip, oral cavity and pharynx — Tumeur maligne de la lèvre, de la cavité buccale et du pharynx	1 022	3.4	1 005	3.3	**901**	**2.9**	-	*1*
Malignant neoplasm of oesophagus — Tumeur maligne de l'oesophage	1 287	4.3	1 324	4.4	**1 392**	**4.5**	-	-
Malignant neoplasm of stomach — Tumeur maligne de l'estomac	1 953	6.5	1 992	6.6	**1 988**	**6.5**	*1*	*2*
Malignant neoplasm of colon, rectosigmoid junction, rectum, anus and anal canal — Tumeur maligne du côlon, de la jonction recto-sigmoïdienne, du rectum, de l'anus et du canal anal	6 412	21.3	6 508	21.4	**6 643**	**21.6**	*2*	*4*
Malignant neoplasm of liver and intrahepatic bile ducts — Tumeur maligne du foie et des voies bilaires intrahépatiques	521	1.7	557	1.8	**1 291**	**4.2**	-	-
Malignant neoplasm of pancreas — Tumeur maligne du pancréas	3 006	10.0	3 054	10.0	**3 092**	**10.1**	...	...
Malignant neoplasm of trachea, bronchus and lung — Tumeur maligne de la trachée, des bronches et du poumon	16 265	50.9	10 710	55.0	**16 134**	**52.6**	*3*	*6*
Malignant neoplasm of female breast — Tumeur maligne du sein chez la femme	4 873	▲39.3	4 762	...	**4 857**	...	*5*	*4*
Malignant neoplasm of cervix uteri — Tumeur maligne du col de l'utérus	405	▲3.3	422	...	**398**	...	-	-
Malignant neoplasm of prostate — Tumeur maligne de la prostate	3 664	▼95.7	3 601	...	**3 718**	...	*3*	*3*
Malignant neoplasm of lymphoid, haematopoietic and related tissue — Tumeurs malignes primitives ou présumées primitives des tissus lymphoïde, hématopoïétique et apparenté	5 610	18.6	5 797	19.1	**5 823**	**19.0**	*2*	*1*
Disorders of the blood and blood-forming organs and certain disorders involving the immune mechanism — Maladies du sang et des organes hématopoïétiques et certains troubles du système immunitaire								
Total	831	2.8	743	2.4	**780**	**2.5**	*2*	*1*
Anaemias — Anémies	499	1.7	457	1.5	**446**	**1.5**	*1*	-
Endocrine, nutritional and metabolic diseases — Maladies endocriniennes, nutritionnelles et métaboliques								
Total	7 429	24.6	7 837	25.8	**8 558**	**27.9**	*7*	*5*
Diabetes mellitus — Diabète sucré	5 756	19.1	6 137	20.2	**6 714**	**21.9**	*5*	*3*
Malnutrition — Malnutrition	197	0.7	200	0.7	**180**	**0.6**	-	-
Mental and behavioural disorders — Troubles mentaux et du comportement	6 276	20.8	6 672	21.9	**5 991**	**19.5**	*1*	-
Diseases of the nervous system — Maladies du système nerveux	6 587	21.8	6 739	22.2	**9 522**	**31.0**	*2*	*2*
Diseases of the circulatory system — Maladies de l'appareil circulatoire								
Total	79 389	263.3	78 942	259.6	**76 426**	**249.0**	*33*	*43*
Acute rheumatic fever and chronic rheumatic heart diseases — Rhumatisme articulaire aigu et cardiopathies rhumatismales chroniques	469	1.6	523	1.7	**426**	**1.4**	*1*	-
Hypertensive diseases — Maladies hypertensives	1 441	4.8	1 525	5.0	**1 692**	**5.5**	*10*	*7*
Ischaemic heart disease — Cardiopathie ischémique	43 029	142.7	42 619	140.2	**42 417**	**138.2**	*13*	*21*
Cerebrovascular disease — Maladie cérébrovasculaire	15 634	51.8	15 409	50.7	**15 576**	**50.8**	*5*	*7*
Diseases of arteries, arterioles and capillaries — Maladies des artères, artérioles et capillaires	4 802	15.9	4 774	15.7	**4 366**	**14.2**	*1*	*3*
Diseases of the respiratory system — Maladies de l'appareil respiratoire								
Total	21 833	72.4	22 026	72.4	**17 744**	**57.8**	*7*	*9*
Influenza — Grippe	763	2.5	682	2.2	**567**	**1.8**	-	*1*
Pneumonia — Pneumopathies	8 339	27.7	8 329	27.4	**4 399**	**14.3**	*4*	*4*
Chronic lower respiratory diseases — Maladies chroniques des voies respiratoires inférieures	10 036	33.3	10 128	33.3	**9 811**	**32.0**	...	...
Diseases of the digestive system — Maladies de l'appareil digestif								
Total	8 027	26.6	7 896	26.0	**8 148**	**26.6**	*5*	*2*
Gastric and duodenal ulcer — Ulcère de l'estomac et du duodénum	472	1.6	483	1.6	**424**	**1.4**	-	-

21. Death and death rates by cause: 1995 - 2002
Décès selon la cause, nombres et taux: 1995 - 2002 (continued — suite)

(See notes at end of table. — Voir notes à la fin du tableau.)

Cause of death — Cause de décès	Cayman Islands — Iles Caïmanes				Costa Rica			
	1997	1998	1999	2000	1995	1996	1997	1998
				Number / Nombre				
TOTAL	125	117	128	137	14 062	13 993	14 260	14 708
Certain infectious and parasitic diseases — Certaines maladies infectieuses et parasitaires								
Total	4	1	6	-	379	344	506	441
Intestinal infectious diseases — Maladies infectieuses intestinales	-	-	-	-	136	130	123	112
Tuberculosis — Tuberculose	-	-	-	-	74	83	82	84
Tetanus — Tétanos	-	-	-	-	3	1	1	3
Diphtheria — Diphtérie	-	-	-	-	-	-	-	-
Whooping cough — Coqueluche	-	-	-	-	2	-	4	-
Meningococcal infection — Infection à méningocoques	-	-	-	-	6	9	6	3
Septicaemia — Septicémie	4	-	4	-	63	48	48	41
Acute poliomyelitis — Poliomyélite aiguë	-	-	-	-	-	-	-	-
Measles — Rougeole	-	-	-	-	-	-	-	-
Viral hepatitis — Hépatite virale	-	-	-	-	22	15	21	15
Human immunodeficiency virus [HIV] disease — Maladies dues au virus de l'immunodéficience humaine (VIH)	...	1	2	-	...	...	176	128
Malaria — Paludisme	-	-	-	-	-	4	-	1
Neoplasms — Tumeurs	22	26	30	41	2 819	2 902	2 856	2 997
Malignant neoplasms — Tumeurs malignes								
Total	22	26	29	40	2 767	2 841	2 792	2 936
Malignant neoplasm of lip, oral cavity and pharynx — Tumeur maligne de la lèvre, de la cavité buccale et du pharynx	-	1	-	1	41	40	37	46
Malignant neoplasm of oesophagus — Tumeur maligne de l'oesophage	-	-	1	2	52	52	50	47
Malignant neoplasm of stomach — Tumeur maligne de l'estomac	1	-	-	5	646	620	581	608
Malignant neoplasm of colon, rectosigmoid junction, rectum, anus and anal canal — Tumeur maligne du côlon, de la jonction recto-sigmoïdienne, du rectum, de l'anus et du canal anal	1	-	2	2	177	202	201	209
Malignant neoplasm of liver and intrahepatic bile ducts — Tumeur maligne du foie et des voies bilaires intrahépatiques	-	1	1	-	48	51	153	156
Malignant neoplasm of pancreas — Tumeur maligne du pancréas	...	1	1	2	...	...	124	128
Malignant neoplasm of trachea, bronchus and lung — Tumeur maligne de la trachée, des bronches et du poumon	6	6	7	9	204	248	231	201
Malignant neoplasm of female breast — Tumeur maligne du sein chez la femme	3	5	-	2	169	174	159	175
Malignant neoplasm of cervix uteri — Tumeur maligne du col de l'utérus	-	-	-	-	150	145	147	144
Malignant neoplasm of prostate — Tumeur maligne de la prostate	4	3	6	5	229	223	199	240
Malignant neoplasm of lymphoid, haematopoietic and related tissue — Tumeurs malignes primitives ou présumées primitives des tissus lymphoïde, hématopoïétique et apparentés	1	3	-	-	267	275	293	283
Disorders of the blood and blood-forming organs and certain disorders involving the immune mechanism — Maladies du sang et des organes hématopoïétiques et certains troubles du système immunitaire								
Total	-	-	1	-	49	45	68	60
Anaemias — Anémies	-	-	1	-	29	26	32	45
Endocrine, nutritional and metabolic diseases — Maladies endocriniennes, nutritionnelles et métaboliques								
Total	5	7	6	6	622	656	516	547
Diabetes mellitus — Diabète sucré	4	7	5	5	400	440	442	485
Malnutrition — Malnutrition	-	-	-	-	19	14	25	22
Mental and behavioural disorders — Troubles mentaux et du comportement	1	1	1	-	79	83	78	78
Diseases of the nervous system — Maladies du système nerveux	2	3	-	-	246	255	301	270
Diseases of the circulatory system — Maladies de l'appareil circulatoire								
Total	53	45	55	55	4 174	4 308	4 087	4 225
Acute rheumatic fever and chronic rheumatic heart diseases — Rhumatisme articularie aigu et cardiopathies rhumatismales chroniques	-	-	-	-	47	46	54	50
Hypertensive diseases — Maladies hypertensives	3	3	3	6	358	366	354	380
Ischaemic heart disease — Cardiopathie ischémique	26	21	24	23	2 006	2 098	1 990	2 024
Cerebrovascular disease — Maladie cérébrovasculaire	13	6	8	10	950	950	928	987
Diseases of arteries, arterioles and capillaries — Maladies des artères, artérioles et capillaires	3	1	4	3	126	137	119	138
Diseases of the respiratory system — Maladies de l'appareil respiratoire								
Total	11	14	10	10	1 539	1 487	1 568	1 723
Influenza — Grippe	1	-	-	-	-	-	-	1
Pneumonia — Pneumopathies	6	8	6	7	558	521	454	504
Chronic lower respiratory diseases — Maladies chroniques des voies respiratoires inférieures	...	2	2	-	...	...	805	870
Diseases of the digestive system — Maladies de l'appareil digestif								
Total	3	3	2	5	908	879	893	964
Gastric and duodenal ulcer — Ulcère de l'estomac et du duodénum	-	1	-	-	97	94	61	80

610

(See notes at end of table. — Voir notes à la fin du tableau.)

Cause of death — Cause de décès	Costa Rica				Cuba			
	1999	2000	2001	2002	1995		1996	
			Number Nombre			Rate Taux	Number Nombre	Rate Taux
TOTAL	15 052	14 944	15 609	15 004	77 937	709.9	79 662	723.8
Certain infectious and parasitic diseases — Certaines maladies infectieuses et parasitaires								
Total	441	417	441	390	1 406	12.8	1 171	10.6
Intestinal infectious diseases — Maladies infectieuses intestinales	101	103	110	99	707	6.4	617	5.6
Tuberculosis — Tuberculose	86	65	72	67	94	0.9	94	0.9
Tetanus — Tétanos	-	-	1	2	3	0.0	3	0.0
Diphtheria — Diphtérie	-	-	-	-	-	-	-	-
Whooping cough — Coqueluche	-	1	4	1	-	-	-	-
Meningococcal infection — Infection à méningocoques	2	1	3	1	20	◆0.2	18	◆0.2
Septicaemia — Septicémie	44	51	38	30	230	2.1	175	1.6
Acute poliomyelitis — Poliomyélite aiguë	-	-	-	-	-	-	-	-
Measles — Rougeole	-	-	-	-	-	-	-	-
Viral hepatitis — Hépatite virale	19	17	22	14	58	0.5	59	0.5
Human immunodeficiency virus [HIV] disease — Maladies dues au virus de l'immunodéficience humaine (VIH)	124	115	134	118	...	...	...	...
Malaria — Paludisme	2	1	-	1	...	-	...	...
Neoplasms — Tumeurs	3 128	3 093	3 416	3 213	15 016	136.8	15 536	141.2
Malignant neoplasms — Tumeurs malignes								
Total	3 051	3 012	3 327	3 118	14 623	133.2	15 123	137.4
Malignant neoplasm of lip, oral cavity and pharynx — Tumeur maligne de la lèvre, de la cavité buccale et du pharynx	50	54	61	49	433	3.9	450	4.1
Malignant neoplasm of oesophagus — Tumeur maligne de l'oesophage	44	46	47	41	387	3.5	380	3.5
Malignant neoplasm of stomach — Tumeur maligne de l'estomac	580	568	629	550	657	6.0	657	6.0
Malignant neoplasm of colon, rectosigmoid junction, rectum, anus and anal canal — Tumeur maligne du côlon, de la jonction recto-sigmoïdienne, du rectum, de l'anus et du canal anal	253	219	246	244	1 494	13.6	1 601	14.5
Malignant neoplasm of liver and intrahepatic bile ducts — Tumeur maligne du foie et des voies biliaires intrahépatiques	156	152	167	188	...	...	-	-
Malignant neoplasm of pancreas — Tumeur maligne du pancréas	145	124	161	142	...	...	...	...
Malignant neoplasm of trachea, bronchus and lung — Tumeur maligne de la trachée, des bronches et du poumon	250	255	249	223	3 187	29.0	3 350	30.4
Malignant neoplasm of female breast — Tumeur maligne du sein chez la femme	186	102	197	205	915	▲21.4	1 039	▲24.1
Malignant neoplasm of cervix uteri — Tumeur maligne du col de l'utérus	135	128	150	97	339	▲7.9	382	▲8.9
Malignant neoplasm of prostate — Tumeur maligne de la prostate	263	282	309	271	1 605	▼134.0	1 618	▼132.5
Malignant neoplasm of lymphoid, haematopoietic and related tissue — Tumeurs malignes primitives ou présumées primitives des tissus lymphoïde, hématopoïétique et apparentés	305	270	338	335	1 126	10.3	1 158	10.5
Disorders of the blood and blood-forming organs and certain disorders involving the immune mechanism — Maladies du sang et des organes hématopoïétiques et certains troubles du système immunitaire								
Total	67	47	57	54	295	2.7	273	2.5
Anaemias — Anémies	47	31	37	31	232	2.1	217	2.0
Endocrine, nutritional and metabolic diseases — Maladies endocriniennes, nutritionnelles et métaboliques								
Total	595	604	629	581	2 913	26.5	3 020	27.4
Diabetes mellitus — Diabète sucré	533	522	582	513	2 519	22.9	2 582	23.5
Malnutrition — Malnutrition	14	20	10	19	66	0.6	80	0.7
Mental and behavioural disorders — Troubles mentaux et du comportement	83	80	71	88	1 408	12.8	1 440	13.1
Diseases of the nervous system — Maladies du système nerveux	296	269	370	363	1 191	10.8	1 079	9.8
Diseases of the circulatory system — Maladies de l'appareil circulatoire								
Total	4 578	4 739	4 884	4 517	33 543	305.5	34 316	311.8
Acute rheumatic fever and chronic rheumatic heart diseases — Rhumatisme articulaire aigu et cardiopathies rhumatismales chroniques	45	51	34	39	172	1.6	171	1.6
Hypertensive diseases — Maladies hypertensives	435	513	521	478	1 022	9.3	976	8.9
Ischaemic heart disease — Cardiopathie ischémique	2 217	2 316	2 345	2 295	17 841	162.5	18 518	168.3
Cerebrovascular disease — Maladie cérébrovasculaire	996	1 089	1 111	947	7 764	70.7	7 950	72.2
Diseases of arteries, arterioles and capillaries — Maladies des artères, artérioles et capillaires	135	119	135	123	3 531	32.2	3 511	31.9
Diseases of the respiratory system — Maladies de l'appareil respiratoire								
Total	1 598	1 499	1 553	1 285	7 041	64.1	8 343	75.8
Influenza — Grippe	2	-	3	3	-	-	8	◆0.1
Pneumonia — Pneumopathies	460	410	396	342	3 639	33.1	4 441	40.4
Chronic lower respiratory diseases — Maladies chroniques des voies respiratoires inférieures	793	824	849	676	...	...	...	...
Diseases of the digestive system — Maladies de l'appareil digestif								
Total	1 015	1 018	1 008	1 078	2 739	24.9	2 786	25.3
Gastric and duodenal ulcer — Ulcère de l'estomac et du duodénum	81	71	70	62	409	3.7	466	4.2

(See notes at end of table. — Voir notes à la fin du tableau.)

Cuba

Cause of death — Cause de décès	1997		1998		1999		2000	
	Number Nombre	Rate Taux	Number Nombre	Rate Taux	Number Nombre	Rate Taux	Number Nombre	Rate Taux
TOTAL	77 316	698.7	77 565	697.7	79 499	712.4	76 463	682.8
Certain infectious and parasitic diseases — Certaines maladies infectieuses et parasitaires								
Total	1 062	9.6	888	8.0	828	7.4	745	6.7
Intestinal infectious diseases — Maladies infectieuses intestinales	521	4.7	480	4.3	416	3.7	264	2.4
Tuberculosis — Tuberculose	82	0.7	47	0.4	58	0.5	44	0.4
Tetanus — Tétanos	1	0.0	3	0.0	-	-	1	0.0
Diphtheria — Diphtérie	-	-	-	-	-	-	-	-
Whooping cough — Coqueluche	-	-	-	-	-	-	-	-
Meningococcal infection — Infection à méningocoques	11	♦0.1	7	♦0.1	21	♦0.2	8	♦0.1
Septicaemia — Septicémie	174	1.6	152	1.4	110	1.0	120	1.1
Acute poliomyelitis — Poliomyélite aiguë	-	-	-	-	-	-	-	-
Measles — Rougeole	-	-	-	-	-	-	-	-
Viral hepatitis — Hépatite virale	52	0.5	32	0.3	32	0.3	33	0.3
Human immunodeficiency virus [HIV] disease — Maladies dues au virus de l'immunodéficience humaine (VIH)	...	...	...	...	...	...	142	1.3
Malaria — Paludisme	-	-	1	0.0	-	-	-	-
Neoplasms — Tumeurs	15 552	140.5	16 063	144.5	16 791	150.5	16 806	150.1
Malignant neoplasms — Tumeurs malignes								
Total	15 201	137.4	15 695	141.2	16 421	147.1	16 426	146.7
Malignant neoplasm of lip, oral cavity and pharynx — Tumeur maligne de la lèvre, de la cavité buccale et du pharynx	447	4.0	476	4.3	537	4.8	492	4.4
Malignant neoplasm of oesophagus — Tumeur maligne de l'oesophage	381	3.4	407	3.7	403	3.6	393	3.5
Malignant neoplasm of stomach — Tumeur maligne de l'estomac	648	5.9	681	6.1	747	6.7	724	6.5
Malignant neoplasm of colon, rectosigmoid junction, rectum, anus and anal canal — Tumeur maligne du côlon, de la jonction recto-sigmoïdienne, du rectum, de l'anus et du canal anal	1 612	14.6	1 616	14.5	1 660	14.9	1 718	15.3
Malignant neoplasm of liver and intrahepatic bile ducts — Tumeur maligne du foie et des voies bilaires intrahépatiques	218	2.0	213	1.9	-	-	180	1.6
Malignant neoplasm of pancreas — Tumeur maligne du pancréas	...	...	...	...	...	...	610	5.4
Malignant neoplasm of trachea, bronchus and lung — Tumeur maligne de la trachée, des bronches et du poumon	3 439	31.1	3 532	31.8	3 556	31.9	3 699	33.0
Malignant neoplasm of female breast — Tumeur maligne du sein chez la femme	1 018	▲23.5	973	▲22.3	1 081	▲24.6	1 012	▲22.8
Malignant neoplasm of cervix uteri — Tumeur maligne du col de l'utérus	385	▲8.9	368	▲8.4	385	▲8.7	398	▲9.0
Malignant neoplasm of prostate — Tumeur maligne de la prostate	1 734	▼139.2	1 800	▼141.2	1 831	▼140.5	1 844	▼138.6
Malignant neoplasm of lymphoid, haematopoietic and related tissue — Tumeurs malignes primitives ou présumées primitives des tissus lymphoïde, hématopoïétique et apparentés	1 198	10.8	1 226	11.0	1 203	10.8	1 213	10.8
Disorders of the blood and blood-forming organs and certain disorders involving the immune mechanism — Maladies du sang et des organes hématopoïétiques et certains troubles du système immunitaire								
Total	239	2.2	235	2.1	225	2.0	215	1.9
Anaemias — Anémies	180	1.6	181	1.6	179	1.6	162	1.4
Endocrine, nutritional and metabolic diseases — Maladies endocriniennes, nutritionnelles et métaboliques								
Total	2 433	22.0	2 048	18.4	1 957	17.5	1 731	15.5
Diabetes mellitus — Diabète sucré	2 037	18.4	1 699	15.3	1 594	14.3	1 490	13.3
Malnutrition — Malnutrition	85	0.8	65	0.6	68	0.6	59	0.5
Mental and behavioural disorders — Troubles mentaux et du comportement	1 683	15.2	1 730	15.6	1 891	16.9	2 023	18.1
Diseases of the nervous system — Maladies du système nerveux	962	8.7	962	8.7	947	8.5	952	8.5
Diseases of the circulatory system — Maladies de l'appareil circulatoire								
Total	33 032	298.5	33 190	298.6	33 845	303.3	32 270	288.2
Acute rheumatic fever and chronic rheumatic heart diseases — Rhumatisme articulaire aigu et cardiopathies rhumatismales chroniques	212	1.9	228	2.1	234	2.1	222	2.0
Hypertensive diseases — Maladies hypertensives	1 041	9.4	1 058	9.5	1 247	11.2	1 317	11.8
Ischaemic heart disease — Cardiopathie ischémique	17 675	159.7	17 222	154.9	16 860	151.1	15 220	135.9
Cerebrovascular disease — Maladie cérébrovasculaire	7 648	69.1	7 884	70.9	8 343	74.8	8 143	72.7
Diseases of arteries, arterioles and capillaries — Maladies des artères, artérioles et capillaires	3 426	31.0	3 571	32.1	3 759	33.7	3 687	32.9
Diseases of the respiratory system — Maladies de l'appareil respiratoire								
Total	8 352	75.5	8 225	74.0	8 844	79.2	8 281	73.9
Influenza — Grippe	1	0.0	6	♦0.1	4	0.0	5	0.0
Pneumonia — Pneumopathies	4 963	44.8	4 830	43.4	5 267	47.2	5 042	45.0
Chronic lower respiratory diseases — Maladies chroniques des voies respiratoires inférieures	...	...	...	...	...	...	2 347	21.0
Diseases of the digestive system — Maladies de l'appareil digestif								
Total	2 697	24.4	2 869	25.8	3 062	27.4	3 015	26.9
Gastric and duodenal ulcer — Ulcère de l'estomac et du duodénum	390	3.5	471	4.2	463	4.1	491	4.4

21. Death and death rates by cause: 1995 - 2002
Décès selon la cause, nombres et taux: 1995 - 2002 (continued — suite)

(See notes at end of table. — Voir notes à la fin du tableau.)

Cause of death — Cause de décès	Cuba 2001 Number Nombre	Cuba 2001 Rate Taux	Dominica — Dominique 1995	1996	1997	1998	1999	Dominican Republic — République dominicaine 1995
TOTAL	79 395	707.0	584	607	513	595	618	23 090
Certain infectious and parasitic diseases — Certaines maladies infectieuses et parasitaires								
Total	773	6.9	13	18	13	7	14	1 413
Intestinal infectious diseases — Maladies infectieuses intestinales	266	2.4	-	2	2	1	-	582
Tuberculosis — Tuberculose	32	0.3	2	1	3	2	5	461
Tetanus — Tétanos	-	-	-	1	-	-	1	18
Diphtheria — Diphtérie	-	-	-	-	-	-	-	4
Whooping cough — Coqueluche	-	-	-	-	-	-	-	-
Meningococcal infection — Infection à méningocoques	6	✦0.1	-	-	-	-	-	13
Septicaemia — Septicémie	122	1.1	7	13	6	2	6	181
Acute poliomyelitis — Poliomyélite aiguë	-	-	-	-	-	-	-	-
Measles — Rougeole	-	-	-	-	-	-	-	3
Viral hepatitis — Hépatite virale	68	0.6	-	-	-	-	-	51
Human immunodeficiency virus [HIV] disease — Maladies dues au virus de l'immunodéficience humaine (VIH)	116	1.0	...	...	...	...	...	...
Malaria — Paludisme	-	-	-	-	-	-	-	7
Neoplasms — Tumeurs	17 244	153.5	91	99	85	113	120	2 350
Malignant neoplasms — Tumeurs malignes								
Total	16 823	149.8	88	97	81	110	118	2 229
Malignant neoplasm of lip, oral cavity and pharynx — Tumeur maligne de la lèvre, de la cavité buccale et du pharynx	501	4.5	4	-	2	6	5	110
Malignant neoplasm of oesophagus — Tumeur maligne de l'oesophage	423	3.8	2	2	1	1	4	32
Malignant neoplasm of stomach — Tumeur maligne de l'estomac	723	6.4	13	14	7	16	14	143
Malignant neoplasm of colon, rectosigmoid junction, rectum, anus and anal canal — Tumeur maligne du côlon, de la jonction recto-sigmoïdienne, du rectum, de l'anus et du canal anal	1 715	15.3	6	6	2	2	2	151
Malignant neoplasm of liver and intrahepatic bile ducts — Tumeur maligne du foie et des voies bilaires intrahépatiques	612	5.4	-	1	1	2	-	22
Malignant neoplasm of pancreas — Tumeur maligne du pancréas	660	5.9	...	...	...	...	...	...
Malignant neoplasm of trachea, bronchus and lung — Tumeur maligne de la trachée, des bronches et du poumon	3 741	33.3	4	1	9	4	5	219
Malignant neoplasm of female breast — Tumeur maligne du sein chez la femme	1 118	...	8	5	4	4	9	144
Malignant neoplasm of cervix uteri — Tumeur maligne du col de l'utérus	374	...	4	7	3	2	6	104
Malignant neoplasm of prostate — Tumeur maligne de la prostate	1 838	...	21	30	22	36	31	340
Malignant neoplasm of lymphoid, haematopoietic and related tissue — Tumeurs malignes primitives ou présumées primitives des tissus lymphoïde, hématopoïétique et apparentés	1 241	11.1	11	7	11	15	10	154
Disorders of the blood and blood-forming organs and certain disorders involving the immune mechanism — Maladies du sang et des organes hématopoïétiques et certains troubles du système immunitaire								
Total	205	1.8	6	9	11	8	6	197
Anaemias — Anémies	134	1.2	6	8	11	8	6	170
Endocrine, nutritional and metabolic diseases — Maladies endocriniennes, nutritionnelles et métaboliques								
Total	1 757	15.6	68	54	64	72	69	1 706
Diabetes mellitus — Diabète sucré	1 557	13.9	49	40	47	54	56	721
Malnutrition — Malnutrition	37	0.3	4	2	1	2	1	253
Mental and behavioural disorders — Troubles mentaux et du comportement	2 066	18.4	1	4	6	6	2	66
Diseases of the nervous system — Maladies du système nerveux	1 069	9.5	11	11	9	13	7	305
Diseases of the circulatory system — Maladies de l'appareil circulatoire								
Total	33 192	295.6	200	210	176	187	217	6 490
Acute rheumatic fever and chronic rheumatic heart diseases — Rhumatisme articulaire aigu et cardiopathies rhumatismales chroniques	196	1.7	1	2	-	2	-	33
Hypertensive diseases — Maladies hypertensives	1 535	13.7	97	106	74	94	109	797
Ischaemic heart disease — Cardiopathie ischémique	15 182	135.2	16	14	11	9	9	1 892
Cerebrovascular disease — Maladie cérébrovasculaire	8 070	71.9	28	26	19	14	20	1 678
Diseases of arteries, arterioles and capillaries — Maladies des artères, artérioles et capillaires	4 074	36.3	9	14	7	15	10	93
Diseases of the respiratory system — Maladies de l'appareil respiratoire								
Total	9 967	88.8	39	51	22	39	51	1 511
Influenza — Grippe	1	0.0	2	-	-	-	-	1
Pneumonia — Pneumopathies	6 912	61.5	20	25	17	18	30	712
Chronic lower respiratory diseases — Maladies chroniques des voies respiratoires inférieures	2 810	25.0	...	...	...	...	...	...
Diseases of the digestive system — Maladies de l'appareil digestif								
Total	2 961	26.4	16	14	10	23	20	1 207
Gastric and duodenal ulcer — Ulcère de l'estomac et du duodénum	455	4.1	1	-	-	1	4	103

21. Death and death rates by cause: 1995 - 2002
Décès selon la cause, nombres et taux: 1995 - 2002 (continued — suite)

(See notes at end of table. — Voir notes à la fin du tableau.)

Cause of death — Cause de décès	Dominican Republic — République dominicaine			El Salvador[2]				
	1996	1997	1998	1995	1996	1997	1998	1999
				Number Nombre				
TOTAL	*23 696*	*25 491*	*27 043*	*29 161*	*28 904*	*29 134*	*29 934*	*28 078*
Certain infectious and parasitic diseases — Certaines maladies infectieuses et parasitaires								
Total	*2 094*	*2 240*	*2 499*	*1 687*	*1 658*	*2 001*	*2 195*	*2 021*
Intestinal infectious diseases — Maladies infectieuses intestinales	*501*	*491*	*472*	*1 217*	*1 057*	*962*	*887*	*592*
Tuberculosis — Tuberculose	*427*	*414*	*469*	*128*	*144*	*141*	*127*	*128*
Tetanus — Tétanos	*19*	*30*	*30*	*17*	*12*	*14*	*15*	*7*
Diphtheria — Diphtérie	*7*	*5*	*6*	*-*	*-*	*-*	*2*	*-*
Whooping cough — Coqueluche	*2*	*-*	*3*	*3*	*4*	*-*	*-*	*-*
Meningococcal infection — Infection à méningocoques	*16*	*31*	*27*	*-*	*-*	*-*	*-*	*-*
Septicaemia — Septicémie	*234*	*285*	*320*	*231*	*380*	*529*	*810*	*890*
Acute poliomyelitis — Poliomyélite aiguë	*-*	*-*	*-*	*1*	*3*	*-*	*-*	*-*
Measles — Rougeole	*2*	*1*	*-*	*3*	*2*	*1*	*-*	*1*
Viral hepatitis — Hépatite virale	*81*	*85*	*100*	*1*	*-*	*14*	*1*	*-*
Human immunodeficiency virus [HIV] disease — Maladies dues au virus de l'immunodéficience humaine (VIH)	*706*	*809*	*907*	*...*	*...*	*258*	*327*	*375*
Malaria — Paludisme	*3*	*4*	*13*	*9*	*4*	*4*	*-*	*-*
Neoplasms — Tumeurs	*2 763*	*2 979*	*3 214*	*2 170*	*2 615*	*2 788*	*2 696*	*2 736*
Malignant neoplasms — Tumeurs malignes								
Total	*2 499*	*2 868*	*3 107*	*2 053*	*2 501*	*2 745*	*2 688*	*2 734*
Malignant neoplasm of lip, oral cavity and pharynx — Tumeur maligne de la lèvre, de la cavité buccale et du pharynx	*105*	*110*	*152*	*36*	*43*	*46*	*46*	*38*
Malignant neoplasm of oesophagus — Tumeur maligne de l'oesophage	*43*	*46*	*56*	*40*	*42*	*50*	*56*	*39*
Malignant neoplasm of stomach — Tumeur maligne de l'estomac	*164*	*216*	*225*	*372*	*428*	*478*	*438*	*457*
Malignant neoplasm of colon, rectosigmoid junction, rectum, anus and anal canal — Tumeur maligne du côlon, de la jonction recto-sigmoïdienne, du rectum, de l'anus et du canal anal	*134*	*159*	*168*	*49*	*67*	*82*	*85*	*99*
Malignant neoplasm of liver and intrahepatic bile ducts — Tumeur maligne du foie et des voies bilaires intrahépatiques	*205*	*231*	*263*	*1*	*1*	*163*	*176*	*161*
Malignant neoplasm of pancreas — Tumeur maligne du pancréas	*42*	*82*	*74*	*...*	*...*	*48*	*60*	*52*
Malignant neoplasm of trachea, bronchus and lung — Tumeur maligne de la trachée, des bronches et du poumon	*277*	*326*	*354*	*76*	*157*	*139*	*131*	*134*
Malignant neoplasm of female breast — Tumeur maligne du sein chez la femme	*141*	*130*	*195*	*38*	*65*	*61*	*82*	*106*
Malignant neoplasm of cervix uteri — Tumeur maligne du col de l'utérus	*131*	*131*	*127*	*152*	*187*	*159*	*287*	*286*
Malignant neoplasm of prostate — Tumeur maligne de la prostate	*368*	*468*	*477*	*61*	*112*	*122*	*192*	*164*
Malignant neoplasm of lymphoid, haematopoietic and related tissue — Tumeurs malignes primitives ou présumées primitives des tissus lymphoïde, hématopoïétique et apparentés	*196*	*220*	*221*	*141*	*166*	*160*	*172*	*157*
Disorders of the blood and blood-forming organs and certain disorders involving the immune mechanism — Maladies du sang et des organes hématopoïétiques et certains troubles du système immunitaire								
Total	*317*	*222*	*218*	*196*	*170*	*165*	*191*	*177*
Anaemias — Anémies	*284*	*186*	*192*	*144*	*138*	*129*	*164*	*162*
Endocrine, nutritional and metabolic diseases — Maladies endocriniennes, nutritionnelles et métaboliques								
Total	*1 281*	*1 227*	*1 302*	*1 129*	*1 282*	*1 126*	*1 293*	*1 202*
Diabetes mellitus — Diabète sucré	*873*	*936*	*1 030*	*526*	*684*	*728*	*770*	*757*
Malnutrition — Malnutrition	*209*	*182*	*149*	*110*	*123*	*159*	*177*	*254*
Mental and behavioural disorders — Troubles mentaux et du comportement	*88*	*74*	*66*	*1 169*	*893*	*1 034*	*1 057*	*830*
Diseases of the nervous system — Maladies du système nerveux	*381*	*406*	*383*	*436*	*384*	*783*	*793*	*754*
Diseases of the circulatory system — Maladies de l'appareil circulatoire								
Total	*7 125*	*7 622*	*8 392*	*5 412*	*6 096*	*3 813*	*4 120*	*5 436*
Acute rheumatic fever and chronic rheumatic heart diseases — Rhumatisme articulaire aigu et cardiopathies rhumatismales chroniques	*37*	*36*	*37*	*11*	*5*	*14*	*-*	*3*
Hypertensive diseases — Maladies hypertensives	*861*	*947*	*1 072*	*28*	*49*	*135*	*151*	*132*
Ischaemic heart disease — Cardiopathie ischémique	*2 252*	*2 506*	*2 735*	*1 532*	*1 795*	*1 610*	*1 769*	*2 736*
Cerebrovascular disease — Maladie cérébrovasculaire	*1 785*	*1 898*	*2 281*	*1 317*	*1 443*	*948*	*1 015*	*1 044*
Diseases of arteries, arterioles and capillaries — Maladies des artères, artérioles et capillaires	*91*	*131*	*110*	*26*	*22*	*24*	*14*	*5*
Diseases of the respiratory system — Maladies de l'appareil respiratoire								
Total	*1 114*	*1 495*	*1 553*	*2 166*	*2 296*	*2 624*	*2 787*	*2 491*
Influenza — Grippe	*5*	*7*	*1*	*12*	*2*	*1*	*1*	*1*
Pneumonia — Pneumopathies	*426*	*596*	*580*	*1 185*	*1 282*	*1 606*	*1 794*	*1 514*
Chronic lower respiratory diseases — Maladies chroniques des voies respiratoires inférieures	*286*	*407*	*477*	*...*	*...*	*551*	*530*	*527*
Diseases of the digestive system — Maladies de l'appareil digestif								
Total	*1 349*	*1 339*	*1 407*	*1 598*	*1 495*	*1 689*	*1 672*	*1 589*
Gastric and duodenal ulcer — Ulcère de l'estomac et du duodénum	*153*	*137*	*142*	*227*	*207*	*270*	*353*	*278*

21. Death and death rates by cause: 1995 - 2002
Décès selon la cause, nombres et taux: 1995 - 2002 (continued — suite)

(See notes at end of table. — Voir notes à la fin du tableau.)

Cause of death — Cause de décès	Grenada-Grenade[3] 1995	Grenada-Grenade[3] 1996	Guatemala 1995	Guatemala 1996	Guatemala 1997	Guatemala 1998	Guatemala 1999	Mexico — Mexique 1995
			Number Nombre					
TOTAL	741	641	65 159	60 618	67 691	70 504	64 563	430 101
Certain infectious and parasitic diseases — Certaines maladies infectieuses et parasitaires								
Total	42	18	8 532	7 791	8 431	9 202	6 573	20 026
Intestinal infectious diseases — Maladies infectieuses intestinales	-	4	6 037	5 559	5 923	6 563	4 507	9 585
Tuberculosis — Tuberculose	-	-	518	546	541	509	471	4 648
Tetanus — Tétanos	1	-	35	24	17	15	22	93
Diphtheria — Diphtérie	-	-	2	1	-	2	2	-
Whooping cough — Coqueluche	-	-	137	118	151	102	44	28
Meningococcal infection — Infection à méningocoques	-	-	3	1	2	2	1	12
Septicaemia — Septicémie	40	10	733	745	1 011	1 253	934	2 855
Acute poliomyelitis — Poliomyélite aiguë	-	-	-	-	-	-	-	-
Measles — Rougeole	-	-	26	11	30	41	16	-
Viral hepatitis — Hépatite virale	-	1	7	10	4	1	8	701
Human immunodeficiency virus [HIV] disease — Maladies dues au virus de l'immunodéficience humaine (VIH)	...	...	...	...	...	...	...	...
Malaria — Paludisme	-	-	98	75	71	104	123	-
Neoplasms — Tumeurs	99	123	4 192	3 775	4 494	4 815	5 000	50 022
Malignant neoplasms — Tumeurs malignes								
Total	99	123	4 163	3 751	4 466	4 798	4 984	48 218
Malignant neoplasm of lip, oral cavity and pharynx — Tumeur maligne de la lèvre, de la cavité buccale et du pharynx	4	8	93	59	87	71	86	682
Malignant neoplasm of oesophagus — Tumeur maligne de l'oesophage	6	6	58	45	84	71	64	738
Malignant neoplasm of stomach — Tumeur maligne de l'estomac	7	13	901	939	1 046	1 062	1 108	4 685
Malignant neoplasm of colon, rectosigmoid junction, rectum, anus and anal canal — Tumeur maligne du côlon, de la jonction recto-sigmoïdienne, du rectum, de l'anus et du canal anal	13	10	88	92	112	164	147	1 975
Malignant neoplasm of liver and intrahepatic bile ducts — Tumeur maligne du foie et des voies bilaires intrahépatiques	-	2	-	-	-	-	-	769
Malignant neoplasm of pancreas — Tumeur maligne du pancréas	...	...	...	...	...	...	...	...
Malignant neoplasm of trachea, bronchus and lung — Tumeur maligne de la trachée, des bronches et du poumon	8	7	210	166	292	257	312	5 969
Malignant neoplasm of female breast — Tumeur maligne du sein chez la femme	9	5	103	85	100	143	120	3 026
Malignant neoplasm of cervix uteri — Tumeur maligne du col de l'utérus	3	3	121	121	116	132	138	4 392
Malignant neoplasm of prostate — Tumeur maligne de la prostate	15	23	181	143	155	209	246	3 157
Malignant neoplasm of lymphoid, haematopoietic and related tissue — Tumeurs malignes primitives ou présumées primitives des tissus lymphoïde, hématopoïétique et apparentés	5	8	274	206	246	314	294	4 877
Disorders of the blood and blood-forming organs and certain disorders involving the immune mechanism — Maladies du sang et des organes hématopoïétiques et certains troubles du système immunitaire								
Total	4	5	510	489	426	445	417	5 039
Anaemias — Anémies	4	5	458	449	396	420	395	4 371
Endocrine, nutritional and metabolic diseases — Maladies endocriniennes, nutritionnelles et métaboliques								
Total	39	88	5 071	5 023	5 718	5 615	5 340	52 917
Diabetes mellitus — Diabète sucré	18	68	1 196	1 129	1 392	1 424	1 648	33 315
Malnutrition — Malnutrition	3	4	2 869	3 048	3 276	3 028	2 709	10 094
Mental and behavioural disorders — Troubles mentaux et du comportement	4	6	1 498	1 366	1 420	1 585	1 507	5 131
Diseases of the nervous system — Maladies du système nerveux	8	11	922	744	914	917	971	6 456
Diseases of the circulatory system — Maladies de l'appareil circulatoire								
Total	300	231	7 714	7 360	7 880	8 942	8 283	97 345
Acute rheumatic fever and chronic rheumatic heart diseases — Rhumatisme articulaire aigu et cardiopathies rhumatismales chroniques	-	1	18	19	12	17	11	1 431
Hypertensive diseases — Maladies hypertensives	11	78	686	659	710	842	764	8 763
Ischaemic heart disease — Cardiopathie ischémique	52	30	1 560	1 390	1 470	1 897	1 767	38 340
Cerebrovascular disease — Maladie cérébrovasculaire	114	47	1 723	1 623	1 842	1 954	1 852	23 398
Diseases of arteries, arterioles and capillaries — Maladies des artères, artérioles et capillaires	3	15	237	219	183	220	234	2 621
Diseases of the respiratory system — Maladies de l'appareil respiratoire								
Total	70	38	11 294	10 373	12 207	12 830	12 286	42 941
Influenza — Grippe	-	-	319	169	100	69	55	168
Pneumonia — Pneumopathies	53	24	9 088	8 412	10 169	10 948	10 344	19 543
Chronic lower respiratory diseases — Maladies chroniques des voies respiratoires inférieures	...	...	...	...	...	...	...	...
Diseases of the digestive system — Maladies de l'appareil digestif								
Total	20	18	3 479	3 184	3 452	3 781	3 717	38 343
Gastric and duodenal ulcer — Ulcère de l'estomac et du duodénum	-	1	500	488	575	565	616	3 354

21. Death and death rates by cause: 1995 - 2002
Décès selon la cause, nombres et taux: 1995 - 2002 (continued — suite)

(See notes at end of table. — Voir notes à la fin du tableau.)

Mexico — Mexique

Cause of death — Cause de décès	1995	1996		1997		1998		1999
	Rate Taux	Number Nombre	Rate Taux	Number Nombre	Rate Taux	Number Nombre	Rate Taux	Number Nombre
TOTAL	467.5	436 185	466.2	440 259	462.8	444 665	460.1	443 950
Certain infectious and parasitic diseases — Certaines maladies infectieuses et parasitaires								
Total	21.8	18 747	20.0	17 307	18.2	20 987	21.7	19 384
Intestinal infectious diseases — Maladies infectieuses intestinales	10.4	8 359	8.9	7 424	7.8	6 666	6.9	5 622
Tuberculosis — Tuberculose	5.1	4 495	4.8	4 190	4.4	4 036	4.2	3 670
Tetanus — Tétanos	0.1	107	0.1	88	0.1	110	0.1	89
Diphtheria — Diphtérie	-	-	-	-	-	-	-	-
Whooping cough — Coqueluche	0.0	20	0.0	35	0.0	9	0.0	9
Meningococcal infection — Infection à méningocoques	0.0	11	0.0	8	0.0	2	0.0	6
Septicaemia — Septicémie	3.1	2 938	3.1	2 780	2.9	3 183	3.3	3 085
Acute poliomyelitis — Poliomyélite aiguë	-	-	-	-	-	-	-	-
Measles — Rougeole	-	-	-	-	-	-	-	-
Viral hepatitis — Hépatite virale	0.8	787	0.8	863	0.9	860	0.9	927
Human immunodeficiency virus [HIV] disease — Maladies dues au virus de l'immunodéficience humaine (VIH)	...	...	...	...	...	4 099	4.2	4 204
Malaria — Paludisme	-	6	0.0	-	-	-	-	1
Neoplasms — Tumeurs	54.4	51 862	55.4	53 367	56.1	55 227	57.1	56 397
Malignant neoplasms — Tumeurs malignes								
Total	52.4	49 916	53.3	51 251	53.9	52 663	54.5	53 660
Malignant neoplasm of lip, oral cavity and pharynx — Tumeur maligne de la lèvre, de la cavité buccale et du pharynx	0.7	735	0.8	728	0.8	767	0.8	748
Malignant neoplasm of oesophagus — Tumeur maligne de l'oesophage	0.8	760	0.8	692	0.7	706	0.7	705
Malignant neoplasm of stomach — Tumeur maligne de l'estomac	5.1	4 925	5.3	4 797	5.0	4 696	4.9	4 974
Malignant neoplasm of colon, rectosigmoid junction, rectum, anus and anal canal — Tumeur maligne du côlon, de la jonction recto-sigmoïdienne, du rectum, de l'anus et du canal anal	2.1	2 143	2.3	2 270	2.4	2 386	2.5	2 495
Malignant neoplasm of liver and intrahepatic bile ducts — Tumeur maligne du foie et des voies bilaires intrahépatiques	0.8	815	0.9	959	1.0	3 927	4.1	3 817
Malignant neoplasm of pancreas — Tumeur maligne du pancréas	...	...	...	...	...	2 547	2.6	2 586
Malignant neoplasm of trachea, bronchus and lung — Tumeur maligne de la trachée, des bronches et du poumon	6.5	6 000	6.4	6 385	6.7	6 224	6.4	6 377
Malignant neoplasm of female breast — Tumeur maligne du sein chez la femme	▲10.1	3 106	...	3 220	...	3 380	...	3 425
Malignant neoplasm of cervix uteri — Tumeur maligne du col de l'utérus	▲14.7	4 526	...	4 534	...	4 545	...	4 590
Malignant neoplasm of prostate — Tumeur maligne de la prostate	▼61.9	3 247	...	3 421	...	3 542	...	3 766
Malignant neoplasm of lymphoid, haematopoietic and related tissue — Tumeurs malignes primitives ou présumées primitives des tissus lymphoïde, hématopoïétique et apparentés	5.3	5 169	5.5	5 461	5.7	5 734	5.9	5 630
Disorders of the blood and blood-forming organs and certain disorders involving the immune mechanism — Maladies du sang et des organes hématopoïétiques et certains troubles du système immunitaire								
Total	5.5	4 975	5.3	4 573	4.8	4 531	4.7	4 221
Anaemias — Anémies	4.8	4 221	4.5	3 921	4.1	3 890	4.0	3 581
Endocrine, nutritional and metabolic diseases — Maladies endocriniennes, nutritionnelles et métaboliques								
Total	57.5	54 731	58.5	55 443	58.3	56 775	58.7	59 647
Diabetes mellitus — Diabète sucré	36.2	34 861	37.3	36 025	37.9	41 831	43.3	45 632
Malnutrition — Malnutrition	11.0	10 199	10.9	10 103	10.6	10 431	10.8	9 736
Mental and behavioural disorders — Troubles mentaux et du comportement	5.6	5 025	5.4	5 414	5.7	5 646	5.8	5 214
Diseases of the nervous system — Maladies du système nerveux	7.0	6 864	7.3	6 749	7.1	7 654	7.9	7 325
Diseases of the circulatory system — Maladies de l'appareil circulatoire								
Total	105.8	100 098	107.0	102 107	107.3	99 701	103.2	98 625
Acute rheumatic fever and chronic rheumatic heart diseases — Rhumatisme articularie aigu et cardiopathies rhumatismales chroniques	1.6	1 385	1.5	1 231	1.3	1 407	1.5	1 434
Hypertensive diseases — Maladies hypertensives	9.5	8 815	9.4	9 354	9.8	9 098	9.4	9 371
Ischaemic heart disease — Cardiopathie ischémique	41.7	40 282	43.0	42 512	44.7	42 869	44.4	44 067
Cerebrovascular disease — Maladie cérébrovasculaire	25.4	24 343	26.0	24 688	26.0	25 045	25.9	25 831
Diseases of arteries, arterioles and capillaries — Maladies des artères, artérioles et capillaires	2.8	2 618	2.8	2 412	2.5	2 290	2.4	2 203
Diseases of the respiratory system — Maladies de l'appareil respiratoire								
Total	46.7	44 858	47.9	44 583	46.9	41 525	43.0	41 691
Influenza — Grippe	0.2	170	0.2	188	0.2	212	0.2	175
Pneumonia — Pneumopathies	21.2	20 404	21.8	19 678	20.7	14 814	15.3	13 892
Chronic lower respiratory diseases — Maladies chroniques des voies respiratoires inférieures	...	...	...	...	...	17 732	18.3	19 220
Diseases of the digestive system — Maladies de l'appareil digestif								
Total	41.7	38 669	41.3	40 451	42.5	41 719	43.2	41 690
Gastric and duodenal ulcer — Ulcère de l'estomac et du duodénum	3.6	3 279	3.5	3 339	3.5	3 014	3.1	2 954

(See notes at end of table. — Voir notes à la fin du tableau.)

Cause of death — Cause de décès	Mexico — Mexique					Nicaragua		
	1999	2000	2000	2001	2001	1996	1997	1998
	Rate Taux	Number Nombre	Rate Taux	Number Nombre	Rate Taux	Number Nombre	Number Nombre	
TOTAL	452.4	437 667	436.6	441 004	433.4	*13 801*	*13 916*	*14 754*
Certain infectious and parasitic diseases — Certaines maladies infectieuses et parasitaires								
Total	19.8	18 599	18.6	18 429	18.1	*1 277*	*1 239*	*1 255*
Intestinal infectious diseases — Maladies infectieuses intestinales	5.7	5 215	5.2	4 893	4.8	*823*	*729*	*734*
Tuberculosis — Tuberculose	3.7	3 231	3.2	3 208	3.2	*227*	*235*	*225*
Tetanus — Tétanos	0.1	70	0.1	63	0.1	*8*	*4*	*2*
Diphtheria — Diphtérie	-	-	-	-	-	-	-	-
Whooping cough — Coqueluche	0.0	5	0.0	11	0.0	-	*4*	-
Meningococcal infection — Infection à méningocoques	0.0	7	0.0	1	0.0	*7*	*21*	*28*
Septicaemia — Septicémie	3.1	3 175	3.2	3 350	3.3	*75*	*99*	*105*
Acute poliomyelitis — Poliomyélite aiguë	-	-	-	-	-	-	-	-
Measles — Rougeole	-	-	-	-	-	-	-	-
Viral hepatitis — Hépatite virale	0.9	982	1.0	1 056	1.0	*22*	*22*	*25*
Human immunodeficiency virus [HIV] disease — Maladies dues au virus de l'immunodéficience humaine (VIH)	4.3	4 218	4.2	4 316	4.2	...	*20*	*23*
Malaria — Paludisme	0.0	-	-	-	-	*35*	*17*	*28*
Neoplasms — Tumeurs	57.5	57 781	57.6	58 663	57.7	*1 340*	*1 366*	*1 457*
Malignant neoplasms — Tumeurs malignes								
Total	54.7	54 993	54.9	55 867	54.9	*1 329*	*1 350*	*1 444*
Malignant neoplasm of lip, oral cavity and pharynx — Tumeur maligne de la lèvre, de la cavité buccale et du pharynx	0.8	773	0.8	833	0.8	*19*	*27*	*21*
Malignant neoplasm of oesophagus — Tumeur maligne de l'oesophage	0.7	770	0.8	771	0.8	*20*	*12*	*17*
Malignant neoplasm of stomach — Tumeur maligne de l'estomac	5.1	5 009	5.0	4 984	4.9	*210*	*191*	*206*
Malignant neoplasm of colon, rectosigmoid junction, rectum, anus and anal canal — Tumeur maligne du côlon, de la jonction recto-sigmoïdienne, du rectum, de l'anus et du canal anal	2.5	2 622	2.6	2 720	2.7	*74*	*47*	*60*
Malignant neoplasm of liver and intrahepatic bile ducts — Tumeur maligne du foie et des voies bilaires intrahépatiques	3.9	4 186	4.2	4 200	4.1	*46*	*117*	*130*
Malignant neoplasm of pancreas — Tumeur maligne du pancréas	2.6	2 669	2.7	2 775	2.7	...	*39*	*42*
Malignant neoplasm of trachea, bronchus and lung — Tumeur maligne de la trachée, des bronches et du poumon	6.5	6 273	6.3	6 401	6.3	*91*	*92*	*86*
Malignant neoplasm of female breast — Tumeur maligne du sein chez la femme	...	3 468	...	3 574	...	*59*	*69*	*72*
Malignant neoplasm of cervix uteri — Tumeur maligne du col de l'utérus	...	4 620	...	4 501	...	*203*	*192*	*185*
Malignant neoplasm of prostate — Tumeur maligne de la prostate	...	3 852	...	4 015	...	*74*	*106*	*125*
Malignant neoplasm of lymphoid, haematopoietic and related tissue — Tumeurs malignes primitives ou présumées primitives des tissus lymphoïde, hématopoïétique et apparentés	5.7	5 911	5.9	5 786	5.7	*125*	*162*	*164*
Disorders of the blood and blood-forming organs and certain disorders involving the immune mechanism — Maladies du sang et des organes hématopoïétiques et certains troubles du système immunitaire								
Total	4.3	3 855	3.8	3 975	3.9	*60*	*79*	*80*
Anaemias — Anémies	3.6	3 137	3.1	3 306	3.2	*49*	*70*	*69*
Endocrine, nutritional and metabolic diseases — Maladies endocriniennes, nutritionnelles et métaboliques								
Total	60.8	59 802	59.7	62 869	61.8	*866*	*940*	*981*
Diabetes mellitus — Diabète sucré	46.5	46 614	46.5	49 833	49.0	*626*	*656*	*675*
Malnutrition — Malnutrition	9.9	8 865	8.8	8 613	8.5	*182*	*240*	*266*
Mental and behavioural disorders — Troubles mentaux et du comportement	5.3	5 004	5.0	4 943	4.9	*396*	*183*	*169*
Diseases of the nervous system — Maladies du système nerveux	7.5	7 444	7.4	7 347	7.2	*335*	*336*	*339*
Diseases of the circulatory system — Maladies de l'appareil circulatoire								
Total	100.5	97 650	97.4	99 189	97.5	*3 185*	*3 232*	*3 074*
Acute rheumatic fever and chronic rheumatic heart diseases — Rhumatisme articularie aigu et cardiopathies rhumatismales chroniques	1.5	1 309	1.3	1 237	1.2	*22*	*39*	*23*
Hypertensive diseases — Maladies hypertensives	9.5	9 778	9.8	10 170	10.0	*367*	*451*	*374*
Ischaemic heart disease — Cardiopathie ischémique	44.9	44 061	44.0	45 402	44.6	*1 063*	*1 087*	*1 173*
Cerebrovascular disease — Maladie cérébrovasculaire	26.3	25 431	25.4	25 647	25.2	*824*	*932*	*871*
Diseases of arteries, arterioles and capillaries — Maladies des artères, artérioles et capillaires	2.2	2 092	2.1	2 075	2.0	*38*	*24*	*22*
Diseases of the respiratory system — Maladies de l'appareil respiratoire								
Total	42.5	38 536	38.4	37 280	36.6	*1 002*	*958*	*1 035*
Influenza — Grippe	0.2	142	0.1	112	0.1	-	-	-
Pneumonia — Pneumopathies	14.2	12 237	12.2	11 244	11.1	*640*	*559*	*598*
Chronic lower respiratory diseases — Maladies chroniques des voies respiratoires inférieures	19.6	18 132	18.1	18 057	17.7	...	*317*	*366*
Diseases of the digestive system — Maladies de l'appareil digestif								
Total	42.5	42 200	42.1	42 716	42.0	*675*	*841*	*874*
Gastric and duodenal ulcer — Ulcère de l'estomac et du duodénum	3.0	2 769	2.8	2 676	2.6	*80*	*89*	*72*

(See notes at end of table. — Voir notes à la fin du tableau.)

Cause of death — Cause de décès	Nicaragua		Panama					Puerto Rico — Porto Rico
	1999	2000	1996	1997	1998	1999	2000	1995
				Number Nombre				
TOTAL	*13 771*	*13 602*	*11 197*	*12 219*	*11 862*	*11 972*	*11 867*	*30 196*
Certain infectious and parasitic diseases — Certaines maladies infectieuses et parasitaires								
Total	*975*	*763*	*381*	*387*	*914*	*880*	*912*	*885*
Intestinal infectious diseases — Maladies infectieuses intestinales	*414*	*320*	*92*	*98*	*132*	*99*	*119*	*6*
Tuberculosis — Tuberculose	*261*	*197*	*153*	*131*	*164*	*182*	*163*	*80*
Tetanus — Tétanos	*3*	*5*	*3*	*1*	*1*	*3*	*3*	*1*
Diphtheria — Diphtérie	*-*			*1*				
Whooping cough — Coqueluche	*-*	*2*	*1*	*4*	*11*	*2*	*-*	*-*
Meningococcal infection — Infection à méningocoques	*25*	*18*	*3*	*2*	*4*	*3*	*3*	*4*
Septicaemia — Septicémie	*107*	*107*	*60*	*81*	*108*	*77*	*71*	*595*
Acute poliomyelitis — Poliomyélite aiguë	*-*	*-*	*-*	*-*	*-*	*-*	*-*	*1*
Measles — Rougeole	*-*	*-*					*1*	*-*
Viral hepatitis — Hépatite virale	*19*	*18*	*23*	*23*	*19*	*5*	*17*	*17*
Human immunodeficiency virus [HIV] disease — Maladies dues au virus de l'immunodéficience humaine (VIH)	*20*	*26*	...	...	*421*	*462*	*484*	...
Malaria — Paludisme	*11*	*11*	*-*	*-*	*-*	*-*	*1*	
Neoplasms — Tumeurs	*1 449*	*1 582*	*1 612*	*1 620*	*1 765*	*1 779*	*1 931*	*4 607*
Malignant neoplasms — Tumeurs malignes								
Total	*1 434*	*1 570*	*1 563*	*1 579*	*1 659*	*1 697*	*1 847*	*4 510*
Malignant neoplasm of lip, oral cavity and pharynx — Tumeur maligne de la lèvre, de la cavité buccale et du pharynx	*15*	*21*	*35*	*32*	*31*	*39*	*58*	*171*
Malignant neoplasm of oesophagus — Tumeur maligne de l'oesophage	*22*	*13*	*14*	*7*	*20*	*30*	*21*	*188*
Malignant neoplasm of stomach — Tumeur maligne de l'estomac	*203*	*234*	*187*	*194*	*210*	*187*	*204*	*318*
Malignant neoplasm of colon, rectosigmoid junction, rectum, anus and anal canal — Tumeur maligne du côlon, de la jonction recto-sigmoïdienne, du rectum, de l'anus et du canal anal	*68*	*63*	*119*	*117*	*115*	*129*	*147*	*434*
Malignant neoplasm of liver and intrahepatic bile ducts — Tumeur maligne du foie et des voies bilaires intrahépatiques	*132*	*142*	*39*	*34*	*66*	*70*	*73*	*58*
Malignant neoplasm of pancreas — Tumeur maligne du pancréas	*50*	*47*	...	...	*58*	*62*	*77*	...
Malignant neoplasm of trachea, bronchus and lung — Tumeur maligne de la trachée, des bronches et du poumon	*102*	*130*	*174*	*163*	*181*	*180*	*183*	*584*
Malignant neoplasm of female breast — Tumeur maligne du sein chez la femme	*62*	*80*	*95*	*98*	*108*	*96*	*127*	*325*
Malignant neoplasm of cervix uteri — Tumeur maligne du col de l'utérus	*170*	*180*	*111*	*118*	*121*	*132*	*108*	*48*
Malignant neoplasm of prostate — Tumeur maligne de la prostate	*99*	*116*	*171*	*181*	*195*	*224*	*240*	*502*
Malignant neoplasm of lymphoid, haematopoietic and related tissue — Tumeurs malignes primitives ou présumées primitives des tissus lymphoïde, hématopoïétique et apparentés	*141*	*160*	*168*	*186*	*157*	*182*	*175*	*426*
Disorders of the blood and blood-forming organs and certain disorders involving the immune mechanism — Maladies du sang et des organes hématopoïétiques et certains troubles du système immunitaire								
Total	*63*	*60*	*94*	*118*	*118*	*93*	*100*	*315*
Anaemias — Anémies	*54*	*53*	*89*	*104*	*106*	*85*	*89*	*196*
Endocrine, nutritional and metabolic diseases — Maladies endocriniennes, nutritionnelles et métaboliques								
Total	*998*	*883*	*912*	*1 043*	*668*	*790*	*851*	*4 160*
Diabetes mellitus — Diabète sucré	*769*	*716*	*433*	*475*	*501*	*586*	*611*	*2 216*
Malnutrition — Malnutrition	*188*	*140*	*101*	*142*	*131*	*169*	*198*	*42*
Mental and behavioural disorders — Troubles mentaux et du comportement	*201*	*183*	*34*	*28*	*45*	*49*	*54*	*429*
Diseases of the nervous system — Maladies du système nerveux	*337*	*300*	*181*	*203*	*210*	*232*	*241*	*852*
Diseases of the circulatory system — Maladies de l'appareil circulatoire								
Total	*3 225*	*3 395*	*2 855*	*3 217*	*2 983*	*3 078*	*2 999*	*8 995*
Acute rheumatic fever and chronic rheumatic heart diseases — Rhumatisme articulaire aigu et cardiopathies rhumatismales chroniques	*40*	*41*	*38*	*56*	*32*	*34*	*24*	*20*
Hypertensive diseases — Maladies hypertensives	*309*	*426*	*136*	*177*	*151*	*166*	*184*	*1 469*
Ischaemic heart disease — Cardiopathie ischémique	*1 361*	*1 286*	*1 142*	*1 237*	*1 149*	*1 087*	*1 149*	*3 213*
Cerebrovascular disease — Maladie cérébrovasculaire	*898*	*972*	*1 063*	*1 227*	*1 142*	*1 193*	*1 120*	*1 474*
Diseases of arteries, arterioles and capillaries — Maladies des artères, artérioles et capillaires	*28*	*40*	*148*	*139*	*106*	*127*	*131*	*408*
Diseases of the respiratory system — Maladies de l'appareil respiratoire								
Total	*923*	*933*	*880*	*1 036*	*926*	*1 050*	*811*	*3 402*
Influenza — Grippe	*-*	*-*	*-*	*-*	*3*	*37*	*4*	*6*
Pneumonia — Pneumopathies	*463*	*508*	*292*	*392*	*301*	*319*	*260*	*1 346*
Chronic lower respiratory diseases — Maladies chroniques des voies respiratoires inférieures	*364*	*335*	...	...	*481*	*542*	*428*	...
Diseases of the digestive system — Maladies de l'appareil digestif								
Total	*859*	*843*	*423*	*420*	*426*	*409*	*427*	*1 642*
Gastric and duodenal ulcer — Ulcère de l'estomac et du duodénum	*67*	*57*	*41*	*43*	*27*	*44*	*33*	*59*

(See notes at end of table. — Voir notes à la fin du tableau.)

Cause of death — Cause de décès	Puerto Rico — Porto Rico					Saint Kitts-Nevis — Saint-Kitts-et-Nevis	Saint Lucia — Sainte-Lucie	
	1996	1997	1998	1999	2000	1995	1995	1996
				Number Nombre				
TOTAL	29 871	28 963	29 861	28 967	28 365	405	966	933
Certain infectious and parasitic diseases — Certaines maladies infectieuses et parasitaires								
Total	879	855	848	1 655	1 540	23	30	31
Intestinal infectious diseases — Maladies infectieuses intestinales	4	10	10	14	11	4	9	9
Tuberculosis — Tuberculose	56	51	39	30	17	1	8	5
Tetanus — Tétanos	2	2	-	2	1	-	-	2
Diphtheria — Diphtérie	-	-	-	-	-	-	-	-
Whooping cough — Coqueluche	-	-	-	-	2	-	-	-
Meningococcal infection — Infection à méningocoques	-	1	4	2	1	-	-	-
Septicaemia — Septicémie	634	618	617	746	716	18	7	7
Acute poliomyelitis — Poliomyélite aiguë	1	-	-	-	-	-	-	-
Measles — Rougeole	-	-	-	-	-	-	-	-
Viral hepatitis — Hépatite virale	35	54	73	65	50	-	1	1
Human immunodeficiency virus [HIV] disease — Maladies dues au virus de l'immunodéficience humaine (VIH)	...	...	...	683	626	...	...	3
Malaria — Paludisme	-	1	-	-	-	...	...	-
Neoplasms — Tumeurs	4 702	4 649	4 813	4 737	4 858	43	147	142
Malignant neoplasms — Tumeurs malignes								
Total	4 563	4 527	4 702	4 592	4 702	43	143	133
Malignant neoplasm of lip, oral cavity and pharynx — Tumeur maligne de la lèvre, de la cavité buccale et du pharynx	163	137	149	121	136	1	6	4
Malignant neoplasm of oesophagus — Tumeur maligne de l'oesophage	190	198	192	179	155	-	7	6
Malignant neoplasm of stomach — Tumeur maligne de l'estomac	266	321	313	282	277	5	22	14
Malignant neoplasm of colon, rectosigmoid junction, rectum, anus and anal canal — Tumeur maligne du côlon, de la jonction recto-sigmoïdienne, du rectum, de l'anus et du canal anal	436	481	488	503	518	4	2	5
Malignant neoplasm of liver and intrahepatic bile ducts — Tumeur maligne du foie et des voies biliaires intrahépatiques	55	65	53	236	262	-	-	2
Malignant neoplasm of pancreas — Tumeur maligne du pancréas	...	...	...	186	193	...	...	8
Malignant neoplasm of trachea, bronchus and lung — Tumeur maligne de la trachée, des bronches et du poumon	608	536	600	561	592	1	9	8
Malignant neoplasm of female breast — Tumeur maligne du sein chez la femme	349	306	346	345	338	4	9	10
Malignant neoplasm of cervix uteri — Tumeur maligne du col de l'utérus	36	60	60	50	54	2	6	9
Malignant neoplasm of prostate — Tumeur maligne de la prostate	535	571	553	486	524	9	17	15
Malignant neoplasm of lymphoid, haematopoietic and related tissue — Tumeurs malignes primitives ou présumées primitives des tissus lymphoïde, hématopoïétique et apparentés	416	442	481	441	461	4	18	7
Disorders of the blood and blood-forming organs and certain disorders involving the immune mechanism — Maladies du sang et des organes hématopoïétiques et certains troubles du système immunitaire								
Total	315	296	296	288	320	1	10	11
Anaemias — Anémies	186	181	170	162	188	1	10	9
Endocrine, nutritional and metabolic diseases — Maladies endocriniennes, nutritionnelles et métaboliques								
Total	4 099	3 591	3 628	2 931	2 897	26	123	106
Diabetes mellitus — Diabète sucré	2 091	2 169	2 411	2 392	2 346	14	102	87
Malnutrition — Malnutrition	48	32	54	58	69	4	8	3
Mental and behavioural disorders — Troubles mentaux et du comportement	419	329	403	342	344	3	15	8
Diseases of the nervous system — Maladies du système nerveux	881	903	1 007	1 089	1 225	8	20	28
Diseases of the circulatory system — Maladies de l'appareil circulatoire								
Total	8 988	9 097	9 426	8 865	8 314	192	329	331
Acute rheumatic fever and chronic rheumatic heart diseases — Rhumatisme articulaire aigu et cardiopathies rhumatismales chroniques	20	29	29	22	14	-	1	-
Hypertensive diseases — Maladies hypertensives	1 455	672	789	811	748	-	39	38
Ischaemic heart disease — Cardiopathie ischémique	3 291	4 204	4 324	4 193	4 063	46	48	36
Cerebrovascular disease — Maladie cérébrovasculaire	1 465	1 698	1 797	1 814	1 616	94	103	106
Diseases of arteries, arterioles and capillaries — Maladies des artères, artérioles et capillaires	439	248	202	215	197	3	7	10
Diseases of the respiratory system — Maladies de l'appareil respiratoire								
Total	3 104	2 974	3 292	3 072	2 832	36	43	56
Influenza — Grippe	2	2	1	2	-	1	-	-
Pneumonia — Pneumopathies	1 172	1 124	1 233	1 111	999	29	16	14
Chronic lower respiratory diseases — Maladies chroniques des voies respiratoires inférieures	...	...	...	1 294	1 172	...	...	25
Diseases of the digestive system — Maladies de l'appareil digestif								
Total	1 532	1 653	1 697	1 634	1 556	20	31	27
Gastric and duodenal ulcer — Ulcère de l'estomac et du duodénum	42	59	47	46	48	2	3	-

(See notes at end of table. — Voir notes à la fin du tableau.)

Cause of death — Cause de décès	Saint Lucia — Sainte-Lucie					Saint Vincent and the Grenadines — Saint Vincent-et-Grenadines		
	1997	1998	1999	2000	2001	1995	1996	1997
	Number Nombre							
TOTAL	972	965	956	818	929	760	777	743
Certain infectious and parasitic diseases — Certaines maladies infectieuses et parasitaires								
Total	29	33	48	22	30	44	24	14
Intestinal infectious diseases — Maladies infectieuses intestinales	7	5	2	3	2	6	3	3
Tuberculosis — Tuberculose	1	4	3	1	1	4	6	-
Tetanus — Tétanos	-	-	-	-	1	-	-	1
Diphtheria — Diphtérie	-	-	-	-	-	-	-	-
Whooping cough — Coqueluche	-	-	-	-	-	-	-	-
Meningococcal infection — Infection à méningocoques	-	-	-	-	-	-	-	-
Septicaemia — Septicémie	9	14	24	14	13	28	12	7
Acute poliomyelitis — Poliomyélite aiguë	-	-	-	-	-	-	-	-
Measles — Rougeole	-	-	-	-	-	-	-	-
Viral hepatitis — Hépatite virale	-	1	-	1	-	-	-	-
Human immunodeficiency virus [HIV] disease — Maladies dues au virus de l'immunodéficience humaine (VIH)	5	4	18	-	8	...	...	...
Malaria — Paludisme	-	-	-	-	-			
Neoplasms — Tumeurs	145	150	141	140	152	105	124	103
Malignant neoplasms — Tumeurs malignes								
Total	140	141	141	135	144	102	122	102
Malignant neoplasm of lip, oral cavity and pharynx — Tumeur maligne de la lèvre, de la cavité buccale et du pharynx	5	6	4	5	6	5	4	2
Malignant neoplasm of oesophagus — Tumeur maligne de l'oesophage	3	8	7	5	4	2	1	3
Malignant neoplasm of stomach — Tumeur maligne de l'estomac	13	16	10	12	16	11	9	9
Malignant neoplasm of colon, rectosigmoid junction, rectum, anus and anal canal — Tumeur maligne du côlon, de la jonction recto-sigmoïdienne, du rectum, de l'anus et du canal anal	5	9	9	5	10	2	10	7
Malignant neoplasm of liver and intrahepatic bile ducts — Tumeur maligne du foie et des voies bilaires intrahépatiques	4	3	2	7	5	1	-	-
Malignant neoplasm of pancreas — Tumeur maligne du pancréas	5	6	4	5	3	...	...	...
Malignant neoplasm of trachea, bronchus and lung — Tumeur maligne de la trachée, des bronches et du poumon	12	10	15	8	8	7	1	3
Malignant neoplasm of female breast — Tumeur maligne du sein chez la femme	14	9	12	14	11	16	14	13
Malignant neoplasm of cervix uteri — Tumeur maligne du col de l'utérus	7	14	12	9	7	8	12	5
Malignant neoplasm of prostate — Tumeur maligne de la prostate	29	24	25	24	32	10	28	18
Malignant neoplasm of lymphoid, haematopoietic and related tissue — Tumeurs malignes primitives ou présumées primitives des tissus lymphoïde, hématopoïétique et apparentés	13	11	9	13	11	12	6	9
Disorders of the blood and blood-forming organs and certain disorders involving the immune mechanism — Maladies du sang et des organes hématopoïétiques et certains troubles du système immunitaire								
Total	12	8	6	7	15	13	15	13
Anaemias — Anémies	9	7	6	5	10	11	12	11
Endocrine, nutritional and metabolic diseases — Maladies endocriniennes, nutritionnelles et métaboliques								
Total	97	99	77	96	141	101	134	99
Diabetes mellitus — Diabète sucré	75	85	68	87	125	76	80	55
Malnutrition — Malnutrition	7	3	-	1	4	13	19	9
Mental and behavioural disorders — Troubles mentaux et du comportement	9	7	-	5	3	4	3	5
Diseases of the nervous system — Maladies du système nerveux	25	24	13	11	22	13	9	16
Diseases of the circulatory system — Maladies de l'appareil circulatoire								
Total	356	345	353	254	274	268	253	286
Acute rheumatic fever and chronic rheumatic heart diseases — Rhumatisme articularie aigu et cardiopathies rhumatismales chroniques	1	1	-	2	-	6	2	1
Hypertensive diseases — Maladies hypertensives	37	32	9	27	27	70	77	58
Ischaemic heart disease — Cardiopathie ischémique	46	47	47	35	42	86	55	105
Cerebrovascular disease — Maladie cérébrovasculaire	121	117	123	87	121	67	69	78
Diseases of arteries, arterioles and capillaries — Maladies des artères, artérioles et capillaires	9	10	3	9	10	4	26	9
Diseases of the respiratory system — Maladies de l'appareil respiratoire								
Total	55	66	86	50	68	37	50	47
Influenza — Grippe	-	-	-	2	-	1	-	-
Pneumonia — Pneumopathies	22	18	44	15	34	23	28	26
Chronic lower respiratory diseases — Maladies chroniques des voies respiratoires inférieures	19	32	25	24	27	...	...	...
Diseases of the digestive system — Maladies de l'appareil digestif								
Total	42	39	23	32	28	30	26	33
Gastric and duodenal ulcer — Ulcère de l'estomac et du duodénum	3	2	-	2	1	4	2	2

21. Death and death rates by cause: 1995 - 2002
Décès selon la cause, nombres et taux: 1995 - 2002 (continued — suite)

(See notes at end of table. — Voir notes à la fin du tableau.)

Cause of death — Cause de décès	Saint Vincent and the Grenadines — Saint Vincent-et-Grenadines		Trinidad and Tobago — Trinité-et-Tobago				Turks Caicos Islands — Iles Turques et Caïques	
	1998	1999	1995		1998		1995	1996
	Number Nombre		Number Nombre	Rate Taux	Number Nombre	Rate Taux	Number Nombre	
TOTAL	831	833	9 042	717.6	9 636	754.2	80	71
Certain infectious and parasitic diseases — Certaines maladies infectieuses et parasitaires								
Total	11	12	177	14.0	171	13.4	2	9
Intestinal infectious diseases — Maladies infectieuses intestinales	-	-	46	3.7	15	♦1.2	1	1
Tuberculosis — Tuberculose	3	1	34	2.7	37	2.9	-	-
Tetanus — Tétanos	-	-	1	♦0.1	1	♦0.1	-	-
Diphtheria — Diphtérie	-	-	-	-	-	-	-	-
Whooping cough — Coqueluche	-	-	-	-	-	-	-	-
Meningococcal infection — Infection à méningocoques	-	-	2	♦0.2	4	♦0.3	-	-
Septicaemia — Septicémie	6	7	59	4.7	60	4.7	-	1
Acute poliomyelitis — Poliomyélite aiguë	-	-	-	-	-	-	-	-
Measles — Rougeole	-	-	-	-	-	-	-	-
Viral hepatitis — Hépatite virale	1	1	5	♦0.4	6	♦0.5	-	-
Human immunodeficiency virus [HIV] disease — Maladies dues au virus de l'immunodéficience humaine (VIH)	...	...	...	...	...	...	...	7
Malaria — Paludisme	-	-	-	-	-	-	-	-
Neoplasms — Tumeurs	116	155	1 266	100.5	1 268	99.2	8	5
Malignant neoplasms — Tumeurs malignes								
Total	114	149	1 227	97.4	1 216	95.2	8	5
Malignant neoplasm of lip, oral cavity and pharynx — Tumeur maligne de la lèvre, de la cavité buccale et du pharynx	5	7	19	♦1.5	41	3.2	-	-
Malignant neoplasm of oesophagus — Tumeur maligne de l'oesophage	2	3	19	♦1.5	30	♦2.3	-	-
Malignant neoplasm of stomach — Tumeur maligne de l'estomac	9	10	67	5.3	88	6.9	3	-
Malignant neoplasm of colon, rectosigmoid junction, rectum, anus and anal canal — Tumeur maligne du côlon, de la jonction recto-sigmoïdienne, du rectum, de l'anus et du canal anal	4	8	127	10.1	95	7.4	-	-
Malignant neoplasm of liver and intrahepatic bile ducts — Tumeur maligne du foie et des voies bilaires intrahépatiques	-	-	16	♦1.3	20	♦1.6	-	1
Malignant neoplasm of pancreas — Tumeur maligne du pancréas	...	...	...	...	...	...	...	-
Malignant neoplasm of trachea, bronchus and lung — Tumeur maligne de la trachée, des bronches et du poumon	11	8	92	7.3	108	8.6	-	-
Malignant neoplasm of female breast — Tumeur maligne du sein chez la femme	8	9	129	▲28.9	132	...	1	1
Malignant neoplasm of cervix uteri — Tumeur maligne du col de l'utérus	4	15	62	▲13.9	70	...	1	-
Malignant neoplasm of prostate — Tumeur maligne de la prostate	18	30	243	▼247.0	206	...	1	1
Malignant neoplasm of lymphoid, haematopoietic and related tissue — Tumeurs malignes primitives ou présumées primitives des tissus lymphoïde, hématopoïétique et apparentés	14	18	84	6.7	100	7.8	1	-
Disorders of the blood and blood-forming organs and certain disorders involving the immune mechanism — Maladies du sang et des organes hématopoïétiques et certains troubles du système immunitaire								
Total	9	15	70	5.6	73	5.7	-	1
Anaemias — Anémies	8	11	62	4.9	59	4.6	-	-
Endocrine, nutritional and metabolic diseases — Maladies endocriniennes, nutritionnelles et métaboliques								
Total	160	139	1 496	118.7	1 789	140.0	15	2
Diabetes mellitus — Diabète sucré	101	84	1 094	86.8	1 217	95.3	3	2
Malnutrition — Malnutrition	7	6	29	♦2.3	23	♦1.8	1	-
Mental and behavioural disorders — Troubles mentaux et du comportement	3	-	16	♦1.3	33	2.6	-	1
Diseases of the nervous system — Maladies du système nerveux	9	12	184	14.6	150	11.7	2	1
Diseases of the circulatory system — Maladies de l'appareil circulatoire								
Total	297	271	3 394	269.4	3 806	297.9	21	32
Acute rheumatic fever and chronic rheumatic heart diseases — Rhumatisme articulaire aigu et cardiopathies rhumatismales chroniques	1	2	28	♦2.2	20	♦1.6	-	-
Hypertensive diseases — Maladies hypertensives	54	54	370	29.4	405	31.7	1	1
Ischaemic heart disease — Cardiopathie ischémique	98	90	1 502	119.2	1 765	138.1	8	4
Cerebrovascular disease — Maladie cérébrovasculaire	101	78	1 055	83.7	1 080	84.5	6	9
Diseases of arteries, arterioles and capillaries — Maladies des artères, artérioles et capillaires	12	13	107	8.5	141	11.0	1	1
Diseases of the respiratory system — Maladies de l'appareil respiratoire								
Total	63	74	601	47.7	596	46.6	1	1
Influenza — Grippe	-	-	10	♦0.8	5	♦0.4	-	-
Pneumonia — Pneumopathies	45	54	300	23.8	334	26.1	1	-
Chronic lower respiratory diseases — Maladies chroniques des voies respiratoires inférieures	...	...	...	...	...	...	...	-
Diseases of the digestive system — Maladies de l'appareil digestif								
Total	30	26	316	25.1	332	26.0	4	-
Gastric and duodenal ulcer — Ulcère de l'estomac et du duodénum	5	3	75	6.0	54	4.2	-	-

21. Death and death rates by cause: 1995 - 2002
Décès selon la cause, nombres et taux: 1995 - 2002 (continued — suite)

(See notes at end of table. — Voir notes à la fin du tableau.)

Cause of death — Cause de décès	Turks Caicos Islands — Iles Turques et Caïques			United States — Etats-Unis				
	1997	1998	1999	1995		1996		1997
	Number Nombre				Rate Taux	Number Nombre	Rate Taux	Number Nombre
TOTAL	70	60	40	2 312 132	879.0	2 314 690	871.9	2 314 245
Certain infectious and parasitic diseases — Certaines maladies infectieuses et parasitaires								
Total	13	13	7	77 128	29.3	65 791	24.8	52 371
Intestinal infectious diseases — Maladies infectieuses intestinales	-	1	-	881	0.3	898	0.3	1 088
Tuberculosis — Tuberculose	1	-	-	1 336	0.5	1 202	0.5	1 166
Tetanus — Tétanos	-	-	-	5	0.0	1	0.0	4
Diphtheria — Diphtérie	-	-	-	1	0.0	-	-	-
Whooping cough — Coqueluche	-	-	-	6	0.0	4	0.0	6
Meningococcal infection — Infection à méningocoques	-	-	-	273	0.1	290	0.1	309
Septicaemia — Septicémie	1	-	-	20 965	8.0	21 423	8.1	22 396
Acute poliomyelitis — Poliomyélite aiguë	-	-	-	1	0.0	-	-	-
Measles — Rougeole	-	-	-	2	0.0	1	0.0	2
Viral hepatitis — Hépatite virale	3	-	-	3 400	1.3	3 780	1.4	4 057
Human immunodeficiency virus [HIV] disease — Maladies dues au virus de l'immunodéficience humaine (VIH)	7	11	7	43 115	16.4	31 130	11.7	16 516
Malaria — Paludisme	1	-	-	8	0.0	4	0.0	7
Neoplasms — Tumeurs	3	7	6	546 214	207.7	547 180	206.1	547 236
Malignant neoplasms — Tumeurs malignes								
Total	3	7	6	538 455	204.7	539 533	203.2	539 577
Malignant neoplasm of lip, oral cavity and pharynx — Tumeur maligne de la lèvre, de la cavité buccale et du pharynx	-	1	-	8 060	3.1	7 854	3.0	7 894
Malignant neoplasm of oesophagus — Tumeur maligne de l'oesophage	-	-	-	10 969	4.2	11 231	4.2	11 277
Malignant neoplasm of stomach — Tumeur maligne de l'estomac	-	-	-	13 645	5.2	13 336	5.0	13 062
Malignant neoplasm of colon, rectosigmoid junction, rectum, anus and anal canal — Tumeur maligne du côlon, de la jonction recto-sigmoïdienne, du rectum, de l'anus et du canal anal	1	-	-	57 333	21.8	56 497	21.3	56 503
Malignant neoplasm of liver and intrahepatic bile ducts — Tumeur maligne du foie et des voies bilaires intrahépatiques	-	1	-	5 010	1.9	5 203	2.0	5 541
Malignant neoplasm of pancreas — Tumeur maligne du pancréas	-	-	1	26 766	10.2	27 260	10.3	27 675
Malignant neoplasm of trachea, bronchus and lung — Tumeur maligne de la trachée, des bronches et du poumon	2	1	-	151 200	57.5	152 015	57.3	153 310
Malignant neoplasm of female breast — Tumeur maligne du sein chez la femme	-	1	2	43 844	▲41.3	43 091	▲40.2	41 943
Malignant neoplasm of cervix uteri — Tumeur maligne du col de l'utérus	-	-	-	4 503	▲4.2	4 542	▲4.2	4 499
Malignant neoplasm of prostate — Tumeur maligne de la prostate	-	3	1	34 475	▼113.6	34 123	▼110.7	32 891
Malignant neoplasm of lymphoid, haematopoietic and related tissue — Tumeurs malignes primitives ou présumées primitives des tissus lymphoïde, hématopoïétique et apparentés	-	-	-	54 367	20.7	54 930	20.7	55 835
Disorders of the blood and blood-forming organs and certain disorders involving the immune mechanism — Maladies du sang et des organes hématopoïétiques et certains troubles du système immunitaire								
Total	-	1	-	10 197	3.9	10 013	3.8	10 251
Anaemias — Anémies	-	1	-	4 556	1.7	4 332	1.6	4 471
Endocrine, nutritional and metabolic diseases — Maladies endocriniennes, nutritionnelles et métaboliques								
Total	10	4	3	79 620	30.3	82 767	31.2	84 967
Diabetes mellitus — Diabète sucré	6	4	3	59 254	22.5	61 767	23.3	62 636
Malnutrition — Malnutrition	1	-	-	3 447	1.3	3 531	1.3	3 744
Mental and behavioural disorders — Troubles mentaux et du comportement	-	-	-	40 718	15.5	44 010	16.6	47 481
Diseases of the nervous system — Maladies du système nerveux	-	-	-	51 161	19.4	53 734	20.2	56 140
Diseases of the circulatory system — Maladies de l'appareil circulatoire								
Total	21	15	13	955 591	363.3	954 407	359.5	948 412
Acute rheumatic fever and chronic rheumatic heart diseases — Rhumatisme articularie aigu et cardiopathies rhumatismales chroniques	-	-	-	5 147	2.0	5 006	1.9	5 014
Hypertensive diseases — Maladies hypertensives	1	-	1	39 981	15.2	41 634	15.7	42 565
Ischaemic heart disease — Cardiopathie ischémique	4	6	5	481 287	183.0	476 124	179.4	466 101
Cerebrovascular disease — Maladie cérébrovasculaire	4	4	5	157 991	60.1	159 942	60.3	159 791
Diseases of arteries, arterioles and capillaries — Maladies des artères, artérioles et capillaires	-	-	-	43 369	16.5	43 916	16.5	43 849
Diseases of the respiratory system — Maladies de l'appareil respiratoire								
Total	3	3	1	215 081	81.8	220 368	83.0	227 942
Influenza — Grippe	-	-	1	606	0.2	745	0.3	720
Pneumonia — Pneumopathies	2	2	-	82 317	31.3	82 982	31.3	85 729
Chronic lower respiratory diseases — Maladies chroniques des voies respiratoires inférieures	-	-	-	102 899	39.1	106 027	39.9	109 029
Diseases of the digestive system — Maladies de l'appareil digestif								
Total	5	3	1	76 861	29.2	77 429	29.2	79 069
Gastric and duodenal ulcer — Ulcère de l'estomac et du duodénum	-	-	-	5 464	2.1	5 105	1.9	5 115

(See notes at end of table. — Voir notes à la fin du tableau.)

Cause of death — Cause de décès	United States — Etats-Unis							US Virgin Islands — Iles Vierges américaines
	1997	1998		1999		2000		1997
	Rate Taux	Number Nombre	Rate Taux	Number Nombre	Rate Taux	Number Nombre	Rate Taux	Number Nombre
TOTAL	863.5	2 337 256	864.7	2 391 399	877.0	2 403 351	873.1	620
Certain infectious and parasitic diseases — Certaines maladies infectieuses et parasitaires								
Total	19.5	51 252	19.0	59 984	22.0	59 007	21.4	9
Intestinal infectious diseases — Maladies infectieuses intestinales	0.4	1 109	0.4	1 169	0.4	1 380	0.5	-
Tuberculosis — Tuberculose	0.4	1 112	0.4	930	0.3	776	0.3	1
Tetanus — Tétanos	0.0	7	0.0	7	0.0	5	0.0	-
Diphtheria — Diphtérie	-	1	0.0	1	0.0	-	-	-
Whooping cough — Coqueluche	0.0	5	0.0	7	0.0	12	0.0	-
Meningococcal infection — Infection à méningocoques	0.1	234	0.1	227	0.1	211	0.1	-
Septicaemia — Septicémie	8.4	23 731	8.8	30 680	11.3	31 224	11.3	8
Acute poliomyelitis — Poliomyélite aiguë	-		-		-		-	-
Measles — Rougeole	0.0	-	-	2	0.0	1	0.0	-
Viral hepatitis — Hépatite virale	1.5	4 796	1.8	4 853	1.8	5 357	1.9	-
Human immunodeficiency virus [HIV] disease — Maladies dues au virus de l'immunodéficience humaine (VIH)	6.2	13 426	5.0	14 802	5.4	14 478	5.3	...
Malaria — Paludisme	0.0	6	0.0	7	0.0	3	0.0	...
Neoplasms — Tumeurs	204.2	549 465	203.3	563 065	206.5	566 637	205.9	121
Malignant neoplasms — Tumeurs malignes								
Total	201.3	541 532	200.3	549 838	201.6	553 091	200.9	119
Malignant neoplasm of lip, oral cavity and pharynx — Tumeur maligne de la lèvre, de la cavité buccale et du pharynx	2.9	7 965	2.9	7 486	2.7	7 492	2.7	2
Malignant neoplasm of oesophagus — Tumeur maligne de l'oesophage	4.2	11 765	4.4	11 918	4.4	12 232	4.4	2
Malignant neoplasm of stomach — Tumeur maligne de l'estomac	4.9	12 959	4.8	12 711	4.7	12 645	4.6	3
Malignant neoplasm of colon, rectosigmoid junction, rectum, anus and anal canal — Tumeur maligne du côlon, de la jonction recto-sigmoïdienne, du rectum, de l'anus et du canal anal	21.1	56 785	21.0	57 155	21.0	57 477	20.9	16
Malignant neoplasm of liver and intrahepatic bile ducts — Tumeur maligne du foie et des voies biliaires intrahépatiques	2.1	5 682	2.1	12 382	4.5	12 916	4.7	-
Malignant neoplasm of pancreas — Tumeur maligne du pancréas	10.3	28 335	10.5	29 082	10.7	29 332	10.7	...
Malignant neoplasm of trachea, bronchus and lung — Tumeur maligne de la trachée, des bronches et du poumon	57.2	154 561	57.2	152 156	55.8	155 521	56.5	21
Malignant neoplasm of female breast — Tumeur maligne du sein chez la femme	▲38.7	41 737	▲38.0	41 144	▲37.1	41 872	▲37.3	11
Malignant neoplasm of cervix uteri — Tumeur maligne du col de l'utérus	▲4.2	4 340	▲4.0	4 205	▲3.8	4 200	▲3.7	2
Malignant neoplasm of prostate — Tumeur maligne de la prostate	▼103.5	32 203	▼98.6	31 729	▼94.8	31 078	▼90.6	21
Malignant neoplasm of lymphoid, haematopoietic and related tissue — Tumeurs malignes primitives ou présumées primitives des tissus lymphoïde, hématopoïétique et apparentés	20.8	55 538	20.5	56 318	20.7	56 518	20.5	10
Disorders of the blood and blood-forming organs and certain disorders involving the immune mechanism — Maladies du sang et des organes hématopoïétiques et certains troubles du système immunitaire								
Total	3.8	10 637	3.9	9 067	3.3	9 315	3.4	7
Anaemias — Anémies	1.7	4 544	1.7	4 503	1.7	4 494	1.6	3
Endocrine, nutritional and metabolic diseases — Maladies endocriniennes, nutritionnelles et métaboliques								
Total	31.7	88 158	32.6	92 872	34.1	94 345	34.3	59
Diabetes mellitus — Diabète sucré	23.4	64 751	24.0	68 399	25.1	69 301	25.2	37
Malnutrition — Malnutrition	1.4	3 881	1.4	3 985	1.5	3 926	1.4	-
Mental and behavioural disorders — Troubles mentaux et du comportement	17.7	52 819	19.5	42 128	15.4	46 015	16.7	15
Diseases of the nervous system — Maladies du système nerveux	20.9	57 658	21.3	84 077	30.8	91 014	33.1	14
Diseases of the circulatory system — Maladies de l'appareil circulatoire								
Total	353.9	944 962	349.6	954 337	350.0	941 524	342.0	219
Acute rheumatic fever and chronic rheumatic heart diseases — Rhumatisme articularie aigu et cardiopathies rhumatismales chroniques	1.9	4 792	1.8	3 676	1.3	3 582	1.3	-
Hypertensive diseases — Maladies hypertensives	15.9	44 005	16.4	42 997	15.8	44 619	16.2	13
Ischaemic heart disease — Cardiopathie ischémique	173.9	459 841	170.1	529 659	194.2	515 204	187.2	114
Cerebrovascular disease — Maladie cérébrovasculaire	59.6	158 448	58.6	167 366	61.4	167 661	60.9	51
Diseases of arteries, arterioles and capillaries — Maladies des artères, artérioles et capillaires	16.4	42 950	15.9	40 788	15.0	40 429	14.7	3
Diseases of the respiratory system — Maladies de l'appareil respiratoire								
Total	85.1	238 999	88.4	229 863	84.3	231 079	83.9	35
Influenza — Grippe	0.3	1 724	0.6	1 665	0.6	1 765	0.6	-
Pneumonia — Pneumopathies	32.0	90 147	33.4	62 065	22.8	63 548	23.1	16
Chronic lower respiratory diseases — Maladies chroniques des voies respiratoires inférieures	40.7	112 584	41.7	124 154	45.5	121 984	44.3	...
Diseases of the digestive system — Maladies de l'appareil digestif								
Total	29.5	79 357	29.4	82 876	30.4	84 015	30.5	21
Gastric and duodenal ulcer — Ulcère de l'estomac et du duodénum	1.9	4 695	1.7	4 567	1.7	4 504	1.6	-

21. Death and death rates by cause: 1995 - 2002
Décès selon la cause, nombres et taux: 1995 - 2002 (continued — suite)

(See notes at end of table. — Voir notes à la fin du tableau.)

Cause of death — Cause de décès	US Virgin Islands — Iles Vierges américaines			Argentina — Argentine				
	1998	1999	2000	1995		1996		1997
	Number Nombre			Number Nombre	Rate Taux	Number Nombre	Rate Taux	Number Nombre
TOTAL	615	659	641	266 171	765.6	266 216	755.9	270 910
Certain infectious and parasitic diseases — Certaines maladies infectieuses et parasitaires								
Total	18	28	19	9 449	27.2	9 894	28.1	12 431
Intestinal infectious diseases — Maladies infectieuses intestinales	1	-	-	656	1.9	630	1.8	687
Tuberculosis — Tuberculose	3	-	-	1 112	3.2	1 031	2.9	1 019
Tetanus — Tétanos	-	-	-	29	◆0.1	31	0.1	26
Diphtheria — Diphtérie	-	-	-	1	0.0	-	-	1
Whooping cough — Coqueluche	-	-	-	23	◆0.1	17	0.0	15
Meningococcal infection — Infection à méningocoques	-	-	-	49	0.1	63	0.2	88
Septicaemia — Septicémie	10	12	13	6 403	18.4	6 798	19.3	7 517
Acute poliomyelitis — Poliomyélite aiguë	-	-	-	-	-	1	0.0	-
Measles — Rougeole	2	2	1	143	0.4	162	0.5	184
Viral hepatitis — Hépatite virale	-	-	-	...	...	...	...	-
Human immunodeficiency virus [HIV] disease — Maladies dues au virus de l'immunodéficience humaine (VIH)	...	10	3	...	...	...	...	1 789
Malaria — Paludisme	...	-	-	4	0.0	3	0.0	2
Neoplasms — Tumeurs	123	121	134	50 363	144.9	52 897	150.2	53 380
Malignant neoplasms — Tumeurs malignes								
Total	122	117	132	48 847	140.5	51 324	145.7	51 555
Malignant neoplasm of lip, oral cavity and pharynx — Tumeur maligne de la lèvre, de la cavité buccale et du pharynx	2	3	2	755	2.2	850	2.4	746
Malignant neoplasm of oesophagus — Tumeur maligne de l'oesophage	6	2	1	1 807	5.2	1 896	5.4	1 862
Malignant neoplasm of stomach — Tumeur maligne de l'estomac	6	7	8	3 010	8.7	3 113	8.8	3 017
Malignant neoplasm of colon, rectosigmoid junction, rectum, anus and anal canal — Tumeur maligne du côlon, de la jonction recto-sigmoïdienne, du rectum, de l'anus et du canal anal	9	13	21	4 865	14.0	5 141	14.6	5 147
Malignant neoplasm of liver and intrahepatic bile ducts — Tumeur maligne du foie et des voies bilaires intrahépatiques	-	1	5	1 641	4.7	1 698	4.8	1 869
Malignant neoplasm of pancreas — Tumeur maligne du pancréas	...	4	6	...	...	...	...	2 974
Malignant neoplasm of trachea, bronchus and lung — Tumeur maligne de la trachée, des bronches et du poumon	14	7	21	8 003	23.0	8 209	23.3	8 167
Malignant neoplasm of female breast — Tumeur maligne du sein chez la femme	15	11	13	4 657	▲36.6	4 959	...	4 876
Malignant neoplasm of cervix uteri — Tumeur maligne du col de l'utérus	3	4	3	843	▲6.6	910	...	944
Malignant neoplasm of prostate — Tumeur maligne de la prostate	21	28	24	2 947	▼85.9	3 138	...	3 229
Malignant neoplasm of lymphoid, haematopoietic and related tissue — Tumeurs malignes primitives ou présumées primitives des tissus lymphoïde, hématopoïétique et apparentés	7	6	3	3 242	9.3	3 519	10.0	3 554
Disorders of the blood and blood-forming organs and certain disorders involving the immune mechanism — Maladies du sang et des organes hématopoïétiques et certains troubles du système immunitaire								
Total	6	2	3	987	2.8	1 019	2.9	938
Anaemias — Anémies	3	2	2	723	2.1	718	2.0	635
Endocrine, nutritional and metabolic diseases — Maladies endocriniennes, nutritionnelles et métaboliques								
Total	64	52	44	13 113	37.7	12 808	36.4	10 670
Diabetes mellitus — Diabète sucré	45	40	24	7 361	21.2	6 741	19.1	7 137
Malnutrition — Malnutrition	4	6	6	1 445	4.2	1 489	4.2	1 417
Mental and behavioural disorders — Troubles mentaux et du comportement	7	10	9	2 417	7.0	2 426	6.9	2 345
Diseases of the nervous system — Maladies du système nerveux	15	18	16	3 312	9.5	3 421	9.7	3 475
Diseases of the circulatory system — Maladies de l'appareil circulatoire								
Total	224	238	268	108 394	311.8	104 701	297.3	92 102
Acute rheumatic fever and chronic rheumatic heart diseases — Rhumatisme articularie aigu et cardiopathies rhumatismales chroniques	-	1	-	157	0.5	169	0.5	257
Hypertensive diseases — Maladies hypertensives	25	33	47	4 641	13.3	4 540	12.9	4 053
Ischaemic heart disease — Cardiopathie ischémique	115	125	121	20 944	60.2	20 437	58.0	20 341
Cerebrovascular disease — Maladie cérébrovasculaire	37	38	52	23 788	68.4	22 721	64.5	22 540
Diseases of arteries, arterioles and capillaries — Maladies des artères, artérioles et capillaires	6	6	2	5 630	16.2	5 072	14.4	4 876
Diseases of the respiratory system — Maladies de l'appareil respiratoire								
Total	31	30	21	22 595	65.0	22 816	64.8	28 384
Influenza — Grippe	-	-	-	43	0.1	23	◆0.1	24
Pneumonia — Pneumopathies	13	13	11	8 821	25.4	9 091	25.8	8 485
Chronic lower respiratory diseases — Maladies chroniques des voies respiratoires inférieures	...	7	7	...	...	...	...	4 810
Diseases of the digestive system — Maladies de l'appareil digestif								
Total	22	33	27	11 200	32.2	11 459	32.5	11 171
Gastric and duodenal ulcer — Ulcère de l'estomac et du duodénum	-	2	2	388	1.1	444	1.3	381

21. Death and death rates by cause: 1995 - 2002
Décès selon la cause, nombres et taux: 1995 - 2002 (continued — suite)

(See notes at end of table. — Voir notes à la fin du tableau.)

Argentina — Argentine

Cause of death — Cause de décès	1997 Rate Taux	1998 Number Nombre	1998 Rate Taux	1999 Number Nombre	1999 Rate Taux	2000 Number Nombre	2000 Rate Taux	2001 Number Nombre
TOTAL	759.4	280 180	775.6	289 543	791.6	277 148	748.4	285 941
Certain infectious and parasitic diseases — Certaines maladies infectieuses et parasitaires								
Total	34.8	12 648	35.0	12 675	34.7	13 004	35.1	13 827
Intestinal infectious diseases — Maladies infectieuses intestinales	1.9	557	1.5	525	1.4	427	1.2	430
Tuberculosis — Tuberculose	2.9	934	2.6	885	2.4	798	2.2	771
Tetanus — Tétanos	♦0.1	22	♦0.1	22	♦0.1	14	0.0	12
Diphtheria — Diphtérie	0.0	1	0.0	1	0.0	-	-	-
Whooping cough — Coqueluche	0.0	11	0.0	10	0.0	15	0.0	14
Meningococcal infection — Infection à méningocoques	0.2	63	0.2	56	0.2	43	0.1	38
Septicaemia — Septicémie	21.1	8 096	22.4	8 524	23.3	9 034	24.4	9 935
Acute poliomyelitis — Poliomyélite aiguë	-			-		-		-
Measles — Rougeole	-	64	0.2	2	0.0	-		-
Viral hepatitis — Hépatite virale	0.5	199	0.6	184	0.5	248	0.7	195
Human immunodeficiency virus [HIV] disease — Maladies dues au virus de l'immunodéficience humaine (VIH)	5.0	1 673	4.6	1 469	4.0	1 471	4.0	1 474
Malaria — Paludisme	0.0	2	0.0	-		-		-
Neoplasms — Tumeurs	149.6	54 845	151.8	55 253	151.1	55 490	149.8	55 769
Malignant neoplasms — Tumeurs malignes								
Total	144.5	52 845	146.3	53 206	145.5	53 342	144.0	53 533
Malignant neoplasm of lip, oral cavity and pharynx — Tumeur maligne de la lèvre, de la cavité buccale et du pharynx	2.1	793	2.2	831	2.3	817	2.2	832
Malignant neoplasm of oesophagus — Tumeur maligne de l'oesophage	5.2	1 881	5.2	1 914	5.2	1 980	5.3	1 922
Malignant neoplasm of stomach — Tumeur maligne de l'estomac	8.5	2 985	8.3	3 050	8.3	2 969	8.0	2 914
Malignant neoplasm of colon, rectosigmoid junction, rectum, anus and anal canal — Tumeur maligne du côlon, de la jonction recto-sigmoïdienne, du rectum, de l'anus et du canal anal	14.4	5 319	14.7	5 537	15.1	5 595	15.1	5 726
Malignant neoplasm of liver and intrahepatic bile ducts — Tumeur maligne du foie et des voies bilaires intrahépatiques	5.2	1 738	4.8	1 746	4.8	1 836	5.0	1 732
Malignant neoplasm of pancreas — Tumeur maligne du pancréas	8.3	2 966	8.2	3 096	8.5	3 171	8.6	3 115
Malignant neoplasm of trachea, bronchus and lung — Tumeur maligne de la trachée, des bronches et du poumon	22.0	0 478	23.5	8 606	23.5	8 409	22.7	8 169
Malignant neoplasm of female breast — Tumeur maligne du sein chez la femme		4 989	...	4 808	...	5 015	▲36.3	5 170
Malignant neoplasm of cervix uteri — Tumeur maligne du col de l'utérus	...	887	...	919	...	881	▲6.4	947
Malignant neoplasm of prostate — Tumeur maligne de la prostate	...	3 524	...	3 459	...	3 510	▼94.5	3 525
Malignant neoplasm of lymphoid, haematopoietic and related tissue — Tumeurs malignes primitives ou présumées primitives des tissus lymphoïde, hématopoïétique et apparentés	10.0	3 777	10.5	3 679	10.1	3 814	10.3	3 789
Disorders of the blood and blood-forming organs and certain disorders involving the immune mechanism — Maladies du sang et des organes hématopoïétiques et certains troubles du système immunitaire								
Total	2.6	1 018	2.8	1 075	2.9	1 030	2.8	1 018
Anaemias — Anémies	1.8	718	2.0	725	2.0	726	2.0	698
Endocrine, nutritional and metabolic diseases — Maladies endocriniennes, nutritionnelles et métaboliques								
Total	29.9	11 811	32.7	12 549	34.3	12 218	33.0	12 352
Diabetes mellitus — Diabète sucré	20.0	8 060	22.3	8 802	24.1	8 861	23.9	8 973
Malnutrition — Malnutrition	4.0	1 487	4.1	1 437	3.9	1 306	3.5	1 287
Mental and behavioural disorders — Troubles mentaux et du comportement	6.6	2 138	5.9	2 205	6.0	2 110	5.7	2 000
Diseases of the nervous system — Maladies du système nerveux	9.7	3 487	9.7	3 871	10.6	3 787	10.2	3 742
Diseases of the circulatory system — Maladies de l'appareil circulatoire								
Total	258.2	96 002	265.7	98 911	270.4	91 499	247.1	93 918
Acute rheumatic fever and chronic rheumatic heart diseases — Rhumatisme articulaire aigu et cardiopathies rhumatismales chroniques	0.7	283	0.8	297	0.8	246	0.7	233
Hypertensive diseases — Maladies hypertensives	11.4	4 358	12.1	4 622	12.6	4 365	11.8	4 527
Ischaemic heart disease — Cardiopathie ischémique	57.0	22 170	61.4	23 180	63.4	21 081	56.9	20 619
Cerebrovascular disease — Maladie cérébrovasculaire	63.2	23 642	65.4	23 195	63.4	22 397	60.5	22 654
Diseases of arteries, arterioles and capillaries — Maladies des artères, artérioles et capillaires	13.7	4 647	12.9	4 704	12.9	4 155	11.2	3 803
Diseases of the respiratory system — Maladies de l'appareil respiratoire								
Total	79.6	32 852	90.9	35 842	98.0	31 967	86.3	35 874
Influenza — Grippe	♦0.1	19	♦0.1	16	0.0	6	0.0	14
Pneumonia — Pneumopathies	23.8	9 786	27.1	11 258	30.8	9 786	26.4	11 557
Chronic lower respiratory diseases — Maladies chroniques des voies respiratoires inférieures	13.5	5 651	15.6	5 758	15.7	4 827	13.0	5 074
Diseases of the digestive system — Maladies de l'appareil digestif								
Total	31.3	11 275	31.2	11 338	31.0	11 015	29.7	11 474
Gastric and duodenal ulcer — Ulcère de l'estomac et du duodénum	1.1	386	1.1	438	1.2	383	1.0	400

21. Death and death rates by cause: 1995 - 2002
Décès selon la cause, nombres et taux: 1995 - 2002 (continued — suite)

(See notes at end of table. — Voir notes à la fin du tableau.)

Cause of death — Cause de décès	Argentina — Argentine	Brazil — Brésil						Chile — Chili
	2001	1995	1996	1997	1998	1999	2000	1995
	Rate Taux				Number Nombre			
TOTAL	762.8	890 258	908 882	903 516	929 023	938 658	946 391	78 531
Certain infectious and parasitic diseases — Certaines maladies infectieuses et parasitaires								
Total	36.9	38 486	52 396	47 861	48 635	46 440	44 465	2 083
Intestinal infectious diseases — Maladies infectieuses intestinales	1.1	11 667	9 360	7 545	8 858	7 437	6 130	273
Tuberculosis — Tuberculose	2.1	5 957	5 697	5 877	6 024	5 937	5 531	436
Tetanus — Tétanos	0.0	369	379	335	289	263	178	3
Diphtheria — Diphtérie	-	17	18	13	12	6	5	-
Whooping cough — Coqueluche	0.0	41	18	18	23	24	27	1
Meningococcal infection — Infection à méningocoques	0.1	983	1 016	914	799	718	650	38
Septicaemia — Septicémie	26.5	9 370	10 871	10 837	11 576	11 005	10 492	792
Acute poliomyelitis — Poliomyélite aiguë	-	-	-	-	-	-	-	-
Measles — Rougeole	-	7	7	41	3	2	-	-
Viral hepatitis — Hépatite virale	0.5	855	858	1 030	1 059	1 308	1 525	64
Human immunodeficiency virus [HIV] disease — Maladies dues au virus de l'immunodéficience humaine (VIH)	3.9	...	15 004	12 070	10 766	10 514	10 724	...
Malaria — Paludisme	-	350	224	151	170	203	243	-
Neoplasms — Tumeurs	148.8	98 876	103 302	106 947	110 716	115 640	120 471	17 010
Malignant neoplasms — Tumeurs malignes								
Total	142.8	96 317	101 802	105 928	109 682	114 196	119 045	16 429
Malignant neoplasm of lip, oral cavity and pharynx — Tumeur maligne de la lèvre, de la cavité buccale et du pharynx	2.2	3 660	3 976	4 010	4 130	4 493	4 642	192
Malignant neoplasm of oesophagus — Tumeur maligne de l'oesophage	5.1	4 527	4 929	4 932	5 016	5 156	5 307	634
Malignant neoplasm of stomach — Tumeur maligne de l'estomac	7.8	10 153	10 503	10 636	10 701	10 721	10 952	2 716
Malignant neoplasm of colon, rectosigmoid junction, rectum, anus and anal canal — Tumeur maligne du côlon, de la jonction recto-sigmoïdienne, du rectum, de l'anus et du canal anal	15.3	5 759	6 195	6 548	6 911	7 180	7 693	931
Malignant neoplasm of liver and intrahepatic bile ducts — Tumeur maligne du foie et des voies bilaires intrahépatiques	4.6	1 124	4 168	4 407	4 318	4 680	5 037	222
Malignant neoplasm of pancreas — Tumeur maligne du pancréas	8.3	...	3 625	3 784	3 933	4 251	4 406	...
Malignant neoplasm of trachea, bronchus and lung — Tumeur maligne de la trachée, des bronches et du poumon	21.8	12 243	12 590	13 341	13 568	14 123	14 712	1 698
Malignant neoplasm of female breast — Tumeur maligne du sein chez la femme	...	6 882	7 085	7 603	7 981	8 104	8 308	932
Malignant neoplasm of cervix uteri — Tumeur maligne du col de l'utérus	...	3 247	3 282	3 451	3 638	3 879	3 953	731
Malignant neoplasm of prostate — Tumeur maligne de la prostate	...	5 542	6 067	6 652	7 140	7 223	7 489	1 035
Malignant neoplasm of lymphoid, haematopoietic and related tissue — Tumeurs malignes primitives ou présumées primitives des tissus lymphoïde, hématopoïétique et apparentés	10.1	7 263	7 700	8 113	8 525	8 654	9 056	1 135
Disorders of the blood and blood-forming organs and certain disorders involving the immune mechanism — Maladies du sang et des organes hématopoïétiques et certains troubles du système immunitaire								
Total	2.7	3 197	3 807	3 932	4 160	4 656	4 796	238
Anaemias — Anémies	1.9	2 344	2 857	2 912	3 105	3 424	3 552	186
Endocrine, nutritional and metabolic diseases — Maladies endocriniennes, nutritionnelles et métaboliques								
Total	33.0	49 174	36 508	38 046	39 759	43 102	47 254	2 805
Diabetes mellitus — Diabète sucré	23.9	23 954	26 256	27 497	28 284	31 616	35 269	2 049
Malnutrition — Malnutrition	3.4	5 933	5 852	6 058	6 751	6 304	6 412	184
Mental and behavioural disorders — Troubles mentaux et du comportement	5.3	4 775	4 698	4 983	5 461	5 828	6 133	1 160
Diseases of the nervous system — Maladies du système nerveux	10.0	9 651	10 312	10 340	10 856	11 155	11 573	1 209
Diseases of the circulatory system — Maladies de l'appareil circulatoire								
Total	250.5	243 778	249 092	249 465	256 090	257 043	260 484	21 117
Acute rheumatic fever and chronic rheumatic heart diseases — Rhumatisme articulaire aigu et cardiopathies rhumatismales chroniques	0.6	1 665	1 792	1 924	1 901	1 900	2 077	321
Hypertensive diseases — Maladies hypertensives	12.1	17 796	19 498	19 527	20 858	22 093	23 711	1 541
Ischaemic heart disease — Cardiopathie ischémique	55.0	69 727	73 575	73 590	75 687	76 616	78 428	8 145
Cerebrovascular disease — Maladie cérébrovasculaire	60.4	81 357	80 890	82 062	83 370	83 437	84 667	6 797
Diseases of arteries, arterioles and capillaries — Maladies des artères, artérioles et capillaires	10.1	8 796	8 954	9 105	8 941	9 359	9 728	947
Diseases of the respiratory system — Maladies de l'appareil respiratoire								
Total	95.7	83 039	88 249	84 019	91 813	89 026	88 312	9 883
Influenza — Grippe	0.0	110	113	95	194	209	213	98
Pneumonia — Pneumopathies	30.8	36 256	33 811	29 917	32 251	29 954	29 335	6 931
Chronic lower respiratory diseases — Maladies chroniques des voies respiratoires inférieures	13.5	...	31 284	30 921	33 830	33 632	33 689	
Diseases of the digestive system — Maladies de l'appareil digestif								
Total	30.6	37 295	38 973	39 814	40 676	41 897	42 995	5 758
Gastric and duodenal ulcer — Ulcère de l'estomac et du duodénum	1.1	2 995	3 050	2 976	3 024	3 121	2 975	239

21. Death and death rates by cause: 1995 - 2002
Décès selon la cause, nombres et taux: 1995 - 2002 (continued — suite)

(See notes at end of table. — Voir notes à la fin du tableau.)

Chile — Chili

Cause of death — Cause de décès	1995 Rate Taux	1996 Number Nombre	1996 Rate Taux	1997 Number Nombre	1997 Rate Taux	1998 Number Nombre	1998 Rate Taux	1999 Number Nombre
TOTAL	552.6	79 123	548.7	78 472	536.7	80 257	541.5	81 984
Certain infectious and parasitic diseases — Certaines maladies infectieuses et parasitaires								
Total								
Intestinal infectious diseases — Maladies infectieuses intestinales	14.7	2 049	14.2	2 465	16.9	2 287	15.4	2 218
Tuberculosis — Tuberculose	1.9	250	1.7	244	1.7	236	1.6	237
Tetanus — Tétanos	3.1	443	3.1	387	2.6	357	2.4	351
Diphtheria — Diphtérie	0.0	9	♦0.1	3	0.0	3	0.0	2
Whooping cough — Coqueluche	-	-	-	-	-	-	-	-
Meningococcal infection — Infection à méningocoques	0.0	4	0.0	5	0.0	8	♦0.1	6
Septicaemia — Septicémie	0.3	32	0.2	36	0.2	36	0.2	39
Acute poliomyelitis — Poliomyélite aiguë	5.6	765	5.3	790	5.4	679	4.6	532
Measles — Rougeole	-	-	-	-	-	-	-	-
Viral hepatitis — Hépatite virale	0.5	76	0.5	76	0.5	88	0.6	86
Human immunodeficiency virus [HIV] disease — Maladies dues au virus de l'immunodéficience humaine (VIH)	...	...	...	410	2.8	383	2.6	474
Malaria — Paludisme	...	1	0.0	1	0.0	-	-	-
Neoplasms — Tumeurs	119.7	17 339	120.3	17 624	120.5	18 129	122.3	18 577
Malignant neoplasms — Tumeurs malignes								
Total	115.6	16 747	116.1	17 000	116.3	17 472	117.9	17 886
Malignant neoplasm of lip, oral cavity and pharynx — Tumeur maligne de la lèvre, de la cavité buccale et du pharynx	1.4	137	1.0	152	1.0	159	1.1	172
Malignant neoplasm of oesophagus — Tumeur maligne de l'oesophage	4.5	727	5.0	695	4.8	659	4.4	751
Malignant neoplasm of stomach — Tumeur maligne de l'estomac	19.1	2 632	18.3	2 979	20.4	2 891	19.5	3 038
Malignant neoplasm of colon, rectosigmoid junction, rectum, anus and anal canal — Tumeur maligne du côlon, de la jonction recto-sigmoïdienne, du rectum, de l'anus et du canal anal	6.6	985	6.8	1 043	7.1	1 005	6.8	1 114
Malignant neoplasm of liver and intrahepatic bile ducts — Tumeur maligne du foie et des voies bilaires intrahépatiques	1.6	219	1.5	691	4.7	749	5.1	659
Malignant neoplasm of pancreas — Tumeur maligne du pancréas	...	...	...	612	4.2	663	4.5	730
Malignant neoplasm of trachea, bronchus and lung — Tumeur maligne de la trachée, des bronches et du poumon	11.9	1 811	12.6	1 778	12.2	1 797	12.1	1 843
Malignant neoplasm of female breast — Tumeur maligne du sein chez la femme	▲18.2	962	▲18.4	885	▲16.7	982	▲18.2	973
Malignant neoplasm of cervix uteri — Tumeur maligne du col de l'utérus	▲14.3	733	▲14.1	733	▲13.8	728	▲13.5	727
Malignant neoplasm of prostate — Tumeur maligne de la prostate	▼93.0	1 153	▼100.1	1 126	▼94.6	1 218	▼99.2	1 224
Malignant neoplasm of lymphoid, haematopoietic and related tissue — Tumeurs malignes primitives ou présumées primitives des tissus lymphoïde, hématopoïétique et apparentés	8.0	1 184	8.2	1 190	8.1	1 261	8.5	1 343
Disorders of the blood and blood-forming organs and certain disorders involving the immune mechanism — Maladies du sang et des organes hématopoïétiques et certains troubles du système immunitaire								
Total	1.7	261	1.8	246	1.7	298	2.0	317
Anaemias — Anémies	1.3	206	1.4	181	1.2	222	1.5	221
Endocrine, nutritional and metabolic diseases — Maladies endocriniennes, nutritionnelles et métaboliques								
Total	19.7	3 197	22.2	2 567	17.6	3 129	21.1	3 294
Diabetes mellitus — Diabète sucré	14.4	2 278	15.8	2 079	14.2	2 235	15.1	2 381
Malnutrition — Malnutrition	1.3	243	1.7	214	1.5	575	3.9	611
Mental and behavioural disorders — Troubles mentaux et du comportement	8.2	1 492	10.3	1 584	10.8	869	5.9	488
Diseases of the nervous system — Maladies du système nerveux	8.5	1 150	8.0	1 136	7.8	1 219	8.2	1 082
Diseases of the circulatory system — Maladies de l'appareil circulatoire								
Total	148.6	21 471	148.9	20 719	141.7	22 036	148.7	22 728
Acute rheumatic fever and chronic rheumatic heart diseases — Rhumatisme articulaire aigu et cardiopathies rhumatismales chroniques	2.3	288	2.0	286	2.0	266	1.8	333
Hypertensive diseases — Maladies hypertensives	10.8	1 639	11.4	1 700	11.6	2 033	13.7	2 207
Ischaemic heart disease — Cardiopathie ischémique	57.3	7 962	55.2	7 720	52.8	7 970	53.8	7 955
Cerebrovascular disease — Maladie cérébrovasculaire	47.8	7 044	48.9	6 961	47.6	7 559	51.0	7 859
Diseases of arteries, arterioles and capillaries — Maladies des artères, artérioles et capillaires	6.7	929	6.4	836	5.7	982	6.6	1 026
Diseases of the respiratory system — Maladies de l'appareil respiratoire								
Total	69.5	9 799	68.0	9 986	68.3	10 222	69.0	11 467
Influenza — Grippe	0.7	126	0.9	84	0.6	87	0.6	135
Pneumonia — Pneumopathies	48.8	6 949	48.2	6 568	44.9	6 121	41.3	6 971
Chronic lower respiratory diseases — Maladies chroniques des voies respiratoires inférieures	...	...	...	1 683	11.5	2 337	15.8	2 544
Diseases of the digestive system — Maladies de l'appareil digestif								
Total	40.5	6 024	41.8	5 858	40.1	5 788	39.1	5 530
Gastric and duodenal ulcer — Ulcère de l'estomac et du duodénum	1.7	262	1.8	237	1.6	218	1.5	265

(See notes at end of table. — Voir notes à la fin du tableau.)

Cause of death — Cause de décès	Chile — Chili					Colombia — Colombie		
	1999	2000		2001		1995	1996	1997
	Rate Taux	Number Nombre	Rate Taux	Number Nombre	Rate Taux	Number Nombre		
TOTAL	545.9	78 814	518.1	81 871	531.6	169 896	173 506	170 532
Certain infectious and parasitic diseases — Certaines maladies infectieuses et parasitaires								
Total	14.8	2 030	13.3	1 999	13.0	5 503	5 056	7 309
Intestinal infectious diseases — Maladies infectieuses intestinales	1.6	237	1.6	225	1.5	1 906	1 653	1 895
Tuberculosis — Tuberculose	2.3	276	1.8	318	2.1	1 216	1 213	1 102
Tetanus — Tétanos	0.0	2	0.0	4	0.0	39	31	43
Diphtheria — Diphtérie	-	-	-	-	-	1		1
Whooping cough — Coqueluche	0.0	9	♦0.1	7	0.0	10	11	19
Meningococcal infection — Infection à méningocoques	0.3	38	0.2	49	0.3	43	39	28
Septicaemia — Septicémie	3.5	459	3.0	219	1.4	1 533	1 476	1 857
Acute poliomyelitis — Poliomyélite aiguë	-	-	-	-	-	2	1	1
Measles — Rougeole	-	-	-	-	-	173	111	164
Viral hepatitis — Hépatite virale	0.6	94	0.6	88	0.6			
Human immunodeficiency virus [HIV] disease — Maladies dues au virus de l'immunodéficience humaine (VIH)	3.2	458	3.0	552	3.6	...	...	1 467
Malaria — Paludisme	-	-	-	-	-	67	72	149
Neoplasms — Tumeurs	123.7	19 059	125.3	19 174	124.5	23 259	24 042	25 136
Malignant neoplasms — Tumeurs malignes								
Total	119.1	18 262	120.1	18 394	119.4	22 559	23 472	24 654
Malignant neoplasm of lip, oral cavity and pharynx — Tumeur maligne de la lèvre, de la cavité buccale et du pharynx	1.1	184	1.2	182	1.2	389	326	397
Malignant neoplasm of oesophagus — Tumeur maligne de l'oesophage	5.0	744	4.9	714	4.6	562	655	599
Malignant neoplasm of stomach — Tumeur maligne de l'estomac	20.2	3 022	19.9	2 932	19.0	3 882	3 919	3 903
Malignant neoplasm of colon, rectosigmoid junction, rectum, anus and anal canal — Tumeur maligne du côlon, de la jonction recto-sigmoïdienne, du rectum, de l'anus et du canal anal	7.4	1 195	7.9	1 252	8.1	1 261	1 363	1 434
Malignant neoplasm of liver and intrahepatic bile ducts — Tumeur maligne du foie et des voies bilaires intrahépatiques	4.4	633	4.2	620	4.0	447	531	1 316
Malignant neoplasm of pancreas — Tumeur maligne du pancréas	4.9	695	4.6	713	4.6	...	...	851
Malignant neoplasm of trachea, bronchus and lung — Tumeur maligne de la trachée, des bronches et du poumon	12.3	1 893	12.4	2 002	13.0	2 424	2 558	2 676
Malignant neoplasm of female breast — Tumeur maligne du sein chez la femme	▲17.8	1 027	▲18.5	1 024	▲18.1	1 184	1 206	1 316
Malignant neoplasm of cervix uteri — Tumeur maligne du col de l'utérus	▲13.3	683	▲12.3	674	▲11.9	1 386	1 511	1 446
Malignant neoplasm of prostate — Tumeur maligne de la prostate	▼96.8	1 284	▼98.7	1 285	▼95.2	1 372	1 587	1 578
Malignant neoplasm of lymphoid, haematopoietic and related tissue — Tumeurs malignes primitives ou présumées primitives des tissus lymphoïde, hématopoïétique et apparentés	8.9	1 346	8.8	1 415	9.2	1 988	2 078	2 161
Disorders of the blood and blood-forming organs and certain disorders involving the immune mechanism — Maladies du sang et des organes hématopoïétiques et certains troubles du système immunitaire								
Total	2.1	295	1.9	312	2.0	648	558	600
Anaemias — Anémies	1.5	199	1.3	223	1.4	437	384	384
Endocrine, nutritional and metabolic diseases — Maladies endocriniennes, nutritionnelles et métaboliques								
Total	21.9	3 310	21.8	3 651	23.7	7 488	8 309	6 834
Diabetes mellitus — Diabète sucré	15.9	2 501	16.4	2 951	19.2	4 365	4 687	5 208
Malnutrition — Malnutrition	4.1	501	3.3	416	2.7	1 180	1 490	1 227
Mental and behavioural disorders — Troubles mentaux et du comportement	3.2	1 332	8.8	2 206	14.3	87	36	34
Diseases of the nervous system — Maladies du système nerveux	7.2	1 430	9.4	1 896	12.3	1 784	1 725	1 973
Diseases of the circulatory system — Maladies de l'appareil circulatoire								
Total	151.3	21 956	144.3	22 665	147.2	48 748	51 110	47 804
Acute rheumatic fever and chronic rheumatic heart diseases — Rhumatisme articulaire aigu et cardiopathies rhumatismales chroniques	2.2	298	2.0	293	1.9	264	178	251
Hypertensive diseases — Maladies hypertensives	14.7	2 292	15.1	2 743	17.8	5 116	5 675	4 454
Ischaemic heart disease — Cardiopathie ischémique	53.0	7 676	50.5	7 812	50.7	19 539	20 861	20 161
Cerebrovascular disease — Maladie cérébrovasculaire	52.3	7 455	49.0	7 485	48.6	12 563	13 018	12 702
Diseases of arteries, arterioles and capillaries — Maladies des artères, artérioles et capillaires	6.8	803	5.3	719	4.7	1 572	1 460	1 590
Diseases of the respiratory system — Maladies de l'appareil respiratoire								
Total	76.4	8 287	54.5	8 531	55.4	14 353	15 021	15 112
Influenza — Grippe	0.9	33	0.2	56	0.4	4	10	10
Pneumonia — Pneumopathies	46.4	4 283	28.2	3 947	25.6	5 283	5 722	5 315
Chronic lower respiratory diseases — Maladies chroniques des voies respiratoires inférieures	16.9	2 248	14.8	2 787	18.1	...	...	7 285
Diseases of the digestive system — Maladies de l'appareil digestif								
Total	36.8	5 693	37.4	6 348	41.2	6 001	6 153	6 321
Gastric and duodenal ulcer — Ulcère de l'estomac et du duodénum	1.8	246	1.6	246	1.6	916	787	800

21. Death and death rates by cause: 1995 - 2002
Décès selon la cause, nombres et taux: 1995 - 2002 (continued — suite)

(See notes at end of table. — Voir notes à la fin du tableau.)

Cause of death — Cause de décès	Colombia — Colombie		Ecuador — Equateur[4]					
	1998	1999	1995	1996	1997	1998	1999	2000
					Number Nombre			
TOTAL	**175 363**	**183 553**	*50 867*	*52 300*	**52 089**	**54 357**	**55 921**	**56 420**
Certain infectious and parasitic diseases — Certaines maladies infectieuses et parasitaires								
Total	*7 387*	*6 810*	*3 406*	*3 044*	*3 437*	*3 535*	*3 312*	*3 384*
Intestinal infectious diseases — Maladies infectieuses intestinales	*2 392*	*1 652*	*1 390*	*1 354*	*1 060*	*986*	*793*	*875*
Tuberculosis — Tuberculose	*1 281*	*1 361*	*1 170*	*904*	*1 032*	*1 296*	*1 122*	*1 130*
Tetanus — Tétanos	*44*	*42*	*36*	*31*	*37*	*36*	*31*	*18*
Diphtheria — Diphtérie	*1*	*2*	*2*	-	-	*1*	*1*	*2*
Whooping cough — Coqueluche	*28*	*18*	*10*	*3*	*16*	*3*	*10*	*8*
Meningococcal infection — Infection à méningocoques	*26*	*21*	*7*	*4*	*3*	*3*	*1*	*1*
Septicaemia — Septicémie	*906*	*1 100*	*507*	*468*	*876*	*791*	*805*	*831*
Acute poliomyelitis — Poliomyélite aiguë	-	-	-	-	-	-	-	-
Measles — Rougeole	*3*	-	*14*	*6*	*2*	-	-	-
Viral hepatitis — Hépatite virale	*185*	*210*	*41*	*62*	*53*	*32*	*48*	*43*
Human immunodeficiency virus [HIV] disease — Maladies dues au virus de l'immunodéficience humaine (VIH)	*1 444*	*1 713*	...	...	*153*	*181*	*231*	*245*
Malaria — Paludisme	*227*	*88*	*64*	*42*	*55*	*78*	*89*	*66*
Neoplasms — Tumeurs	**25 314**	**26 931**	*6 002*	*6 301*	*6 499*	*6 606*	*6 823*	*6 930*
Malignant neoplasms — Tumeurs malignes								
Total	*24 896*	*26 426*	*5 821*	*6 075*	*6 349*	*6 450*	*6 660*	*6 701*
Malignant neoplasm of lip, oral cavity and pharynx — Tumeur maligne de la lèvre, de la cavité buccale et du pharynx	*385*	*431*	*57*	*61*	*71*	*58*	*85*	*76*
Malignant neoplasm of oesophagus — Tumeur maligne de l'oesophage	*603*	*639*	*51*	*53*	*99*	*94*	*87*	*99*
Malignant neoplasm of stomach — Tumeur maligne de l'estomac	*3 974*	*4 112*	*1 448*	*1 499*	*1 446*	*1 451*	*1 472*	*1 367*
Malignant neoplasm of colon, rectosigmoid junction, rectum, anus and anal canal — Tumeur maligne du côlon, de la jonction recto-sigmoïdienne, du rectum, de l'anus et du canal anal	*1 432*	*1 587*	*250*	*241*	*252*	*271*	*279*	*322*
Malignant neoplasm of liver and intrahepatic bile ducts — Tumeur maligne du foie et des voies bilaires intrahépatiques	*1 335*	*1 440*	*101*	*95*	*529*	*495*	*544*	*553*
Malignant neoplasm of pancreas — Tumeur maligne du pancréas	*876*	*852*	...	...	*180*	*215*	*241*	*247*
Malignant neoplasm of trachea, bronchus and lung — Tumeur maligne de la trachée, des bronches et du poumon	*2 605*	*2 877*	*428*	*406*	*438*	*456*	*437*	*460*
Malignant neoplasm of female breast — Tumeur maligne du sein chez la femme	*1 027*	*1 434*	*243*	*240*	*243*	*264*	*293*	*287*
Malignant neoplasm of cervix uteri — Tumeur maligne du col de l'utérus	*1 557*	*1 897*	*307*	*359*	*276*	*307*	*259*	*279*
Malignant neoplasm of prostate — Tumeur maligne de la prostate	*1 722*	*1 828*	*333*	*429*	*433*	*522*	*498*	*580*
Malignant neoplasm of lymphoid, haematopoietic and related tissue — Tumeurs malignes primitives ou présumées primitives des tissus lymphoïde, hématopoïétiqun et apparentés	*2 226*	*2 466*	*509*	*556*	*616*	*596*	*600*	*656*
Disorders of the blood and blood-forming organs and certain disorders involving the immune mechanism — Maladies du sang et des organes hématopoïétiques et certains troubles du système immunitaire								
Total	*716*	*721*	*363*	*351*	*540*	*754*	*665*	*655*
Anaemias — Anémies	*466*	*493*	*331*	*303*	*478*	*702*	*595*	*598*
Endocrine, nutritional and metabolic diseases — Maladies endocriniennes, nutritionnelles et métaboliques								
Total	*8 030*	*9 193*	*2 602*	*2 896*	*3 209*	*3 347*	*3 340*	*3 864*
Diabetes mellitus — Diabète sucré	*5 807*	*6 800*	*1 761*	*1 894*	*1 896*	*1 845*	*2 181*	*2 533*
Malnutrition — Malnutrition	*1 750*	*1 863*	*593*	*705*	*979*	*1 073*	*829*	*1 072*
Mental and behavioural disorders — Troubles mentaux et du comportement	*33*	*48*	*304*	*222*	*221*	*205*	*214*	*281*
Diseases of the nervous system — Maladies du système nerveux	*2 148*	*2 112*	*822*	*884*	*957*	*1 026*	*1 025*	*1 003*
Diseases of the circulatory system — Maladies de l'appareil circulatoire								
Total	*47 054*	*50 306*	*9 262*	*10 106*	*10 529*	*11 888*	*12 475*	*12 451*
Acute rheumatic fever and chronic rheumatic heart diseases — Rhumatisme articularie aigu et cardiopathies rhumatismales chroniques	*277*	*315*	*66*	*64*	*102*	*92*	*97*	*88*
Hypertensive diseases — Maladies hypertensives	*4 679*	*5 490*	*2 215*	*3 057*	*2 184*	*2 195*	*1 875*	*2 487*
Ischaemic heart disease — Cardiopathie ischémique	*20 244*	*21 908*	*1 330*	*1 519*	*1 944*	*2 268*	*2 463*	*2 324*
Cerebrovascular disease — Maladie cérébrovasculaire	*12 695*	*13 393*	*2 645*	*2 524*	*2 280*	*2 511*	*2 874*	*2 735*
Diseases of arteries, arterioles and capillaries — Maladies des artères, artérioles et capillaires	*1 486*	*1 476*	*172*	*211*	*254*	*295*	*345*	*342*
Diseases of the respiratory system — Maladies de l'appareil respiratoire								
Total	*15 802*	*17 160*	*5 269*	*4 960*	*4 760*	*4 569*	*4 988*	*4 577*
Influenza — Grippe	*25*	*32*	*49*	*49*	*48*	*26*	*35*	*27*
Pneumonia — Pneumopathies	*5 186*	*5 026*	*3 108*	*2 936*	*2 542*	*2 613*	*2 571*	*2 389*
Chronic lower respiratory diseases — Maladies chroniques des voies respiratoires inférieures	*7 900*	*9 452*	...	...	*807*	*803*	*902*	*852*
Diseases of the digestive system — Maladies de l'appareil digestif								
Total	*6 733*	*7 078*	*2 645*	*2 937*	*2 680*	*2 819*	*2 872*	*2 858*
Gastric and duodenal ulcer — Ulcère de l'estomac et du duodénum	*933*	*931*	*274*	*267*	*347*	*308*	*263*	*266*

(See notes at end of table. — Voir notes à la fin du tableau.)

Cause of death — Cause de décès	Guyana		Paraguay					
	1995	1996	1995	1996	1997	1998	1999	2000
				Number Nombre				
TOTAL	5 178	4 811	16 069	17 447	16 604	17 429	18 157	18 616
Certain infectious and parasitic diseases — Certaines maladies infectieuses et parasitaires								
Total	452	347	879	1 326	1 178	1 003	1 053	924
Intestinal infectious diseases — Maladies infectieuses intestinales	258	169	381	410	372	311	344	340
Tuberculosis — Tuberculose	42	61	150	176	177	151	168	141
Tetanus — Tétanos	1	-	13	19	26	16	12	17
Diphtheria — Diphtérie	-	-	-	-	-	-	-	-
Whooping cough — Coqueluche	-	1	-	4	4	2	2	1
Meningococcal infection — Infection à méningocoques	-	-	1	3	4	3	4	2
Septicaemia — Septicémie	71	50	291	610	489	415	416	272
Acute poliomyelitis — Poliomyélite aiguë	-	-	1	-	4	-	-	-
Measles — Rougeole	-	-	1	-	4	-	-	-
Viral hepatitis — Hépatite virale	5	15	4	4	5	6	3	4
Human immunodeficiency virus [HIV] disease — Maladies dues au virus de l'immunodéficience humaine (VIH)	...	...	...	40	29	42	47	80
Malaria — Paludisme	40	26	-	-	-	-	-	-
Neoplasms — Tumeurs	336	358	1 930	2 162	2 180	2 212	2 284	2 378
Malignant neoplasms — Tumeurs malignes								
Total	321	341	1 920	2 159	2 179	2 209	2 276	2 367
Malignant neoplasm of lip, oral cavity and pharynx — Tumeur maligne de la lèvre, de la cavité buccale et du pharynx	9	11	56	48	60	55	51	60
Malignant neoplasm of oesophagus — Tumeur maligne de l'oesophage	6	2	66	57	74	61	65	79
Malignant neoplasm of stomach — Tumeur maligne de l'estomac	34	33	198	204	221	244	204	232
Malignant neoplasm of colon, rectosigmoid junction, rectum, anus and anal canal — Tumeur maligne du côlon, de la jonction recto-sigmoïdienne, du rectum, de l'anus et du canal anal	22	28	93	93	99	113	114	99
Malignant neoplasm of liver and intrahepatic bile ducts — Tumeur maligne du foie et des voies bilaires intrahépatiques	1	8	5	66	77	76	60	67
Malignant neoplasm of pancreas — Tumeur maligne du pancréas	...	...	...	58	76	63	85	79
Malignant neoplasm of trachea, bronchus and lung — Tumeur maligne de la trachée, des bronches et du poumon	23	19	190	205	245	227	260	271
Malignant neoplasm of female breast — Tumeur maligne du sein chez la femme	23	30	123	157	143	158	161	163
Malignant neoplasm of cervix uteri — Tumeur maligne du col de l'utérus	25	35	120	113	114	100	99	142
Malignant neoplasm of prostate — Tumeur maligne de la prostate	45	34	124	167	143	178	175	172
Malignant neoplasm of lymphoid, haematopoietic and related tissue — Tumeurs malignes primitives ou présumées primitives des tissus lymphoïde, hématopoïétique et apparentés	21	23	180	204	183	176	186	239
Disorders of the blood and blood-forming organs and certain disorders involving the immune mechanism — Maladies du sang et des organes hématopoïétiques et certains troubles du système immunitaire								
Total	83	96	53	50	38	40	36	52
Anaemias — Anémies	79	89	39	46	26	34	22	34
Endocrine, nutritional and metabolic diseases — Maladies endocriniennes, nutritionnelles et métaboliques								
Total	542	667	741	797	802	916	859	1 148
Diabetes mellitus — Diabète sucré	216	255	630	675	650	687	687	873
Malnutrition — Malnutrition	64	52	46	61	52	128	81	159
Mental and behavioural disorders — Troubles mentaux et du comportement	18	17	102	86	64	72	41	61
Diseases of the nervous system — Maladies du système nerveux	85	82	225	200	177	195	179	236
Diseases of the circulatory system — Maladies de l'appareil circulatoire								
Total	1 858	1 599	5 537	5 546	3 900	4 520	4 527	4 424
Acute rheumatic fever and chronic rheumatic heart diseases — Rhumatisme articulaire aigu et cardiopathies rhumatismales chroniques	9	10	19	19	27	15	18	22
Hypertensive diseases — Maladies hypertensives	210	190	319	274	364	316	355	316
Ischaemic heart disease — Cardiopathie ischémique	528	476	1 573	1 555	970	1 299	1 227	1 118
Cerebrovascular disease — Maladie cérébrovasculaire	699	562	2 013	2 169	1 419	1 518	1 647	1 674
Diseases of arteries, arterioles and capillaries — Maladies des artères, artérioles et capillaires	35	34	101	114	78	106	105	90
Diseases of the respiratory system — Maladies de l'appareil respiratoire								
Total	373	336	1 115	1 470	1 192	1 416	1 374	1 325
Influenza — Grippe	10	6	1	1	1	-	-	3
Pneumonia — Pneumopathies	251	214	788	1 055	887	995	993	866
Chronic lower respiratory diseases — Maladies chroniques des voies respiratoires inférieures	...	...	...	162	141	190	146	160
Diseases of the digestive system — Maladies de l'appareil digestif								
Total	271	249	578	560	549	628	634	646
Gastric and duodenal ulcer — Ulcère de l'estomac et du duodénum	22	10	46	71	49	65	59	62

(See notes at end of table. — Voir notes à la fin du tableau.)

Cause of death — Cause de décès	Peru — Pérou						Uruguay	
	1995	1996	1997	1998	1999	2000	1995	1995
	Number / Nombre							Rate / Taux
TOTAL	91 485	92 674	89 790	91 469	86 539	84 393	31 700	985.4
Certain infectious and parasitic diseases — Certaines maladies infectieuses et parasitaires								
Total	6 593	6 230	5 628	6 373	5 890	6 309	510	15.9
Intestinal infectious diseases — Maladies infectieuses intestinales	1 883	1 801	1 533	1 927	885	862	98	3.0
Tuberculosis — Tuberculose	2 927	2 543	2 237	2 253	1 611	1 986	71	2.2
Tetanus — Tétanos	32	26	21	32	27	23	1	0.0
Diphtheria — Diphtérie	1	-	-	-	-	-		
Whooping cough — Coqueluche	2	-	-	-	2	-		
Meningococcal infection — Infection à méningocoques	2	1	1	2	5	8	1	0.0
Septicaemia — Septicémie	3	2	2	3	1	3	13	♦0.4
Acute poliomyelitis — Poliomyélite aiguë	1 268	1 382	1 446	1 663	1 861	1 887	243	7.6
Measles — Rougeole		-	-	-	-	-		
Viral hepatitis — Hépatite virale	3	4	-	-	-	1	-	-
Human immunodeficiency virus [HIV] disease — Maladies dues au virus de l'immunodéficience humaine (VIH)	137	152	124	129	129	155	7	♦0.2
Malaria — Paludisme	...	...	...	...	406	1 109	...	...
	51	33	28	60	45	23		
Neoplasms — Tumeurs	10 666	11 858	11 524	11 997	13 041	13 773	7 267	225.9
Malignant neoplasms — Tumeurs malignes								
Total	10 502	11 609	11 315	11 851	12 822	13 557	7 099	220.7
Malignant neoplasm of lip, oral cavity and pharynx — Tumeur maligne de la lèvre, de la cavité buccale et du pharynx	98	97	98	88	133	122	128	4.0
Malignant neoplasm of oesophagus — Tumeur maligne de l'oesophage	131	146	132	126	117	142	272	8.5
Malignant neoplasm of stomach — Tumeur maligne de l'estomac	1 831	2 132	2 120	2 152	2 302	2 431	481	15.0
Malignant neoplasm of colon, rectosigmoid junction, rectum, anus and anal canal — Tumeur maligne du côlon, de la jonction recto-sigmoïdienne, du rectum, de l'anus et du canal anal	489	523	539	582	645	632	804	25.0
Malignant neoplasm of liver and intrahepatic bile ducts — Tumeur maligne du foie et des voies bilaires intrahépatiques	208	272	216	206	887	950	28	♦0.9
Malignant neoplasm of pancreas — Tumeur maligne du pancréas	...	...	...	...	440	438	...	...
Malignant neoplasm of trachea, bronchus and lung — Tumeur maligne de la trachée, des bronches et du poumon	981	989	920	1 068	507	1 116	1 282	39.9
Malignant neoplasm of female breast — Tumeur maligne du sein chez la femme	571	618	592	630	664	686	606	...
Malignant neoplasm of cervix uteri — Tumeur maligne du col de l'utérus	634	711	639	674	752	824	89	...
Malignant neoplasm of prostate — Tumeur maligne de la prostate	644	728	729	788	875	934	518	...
Malignant neoplasm of lymphoid, haematopoietic and related tissue — Tumeurs malignes primitives ou présumées primitives des tissus lymphoïde, hématopoïétique et apparentés	1 016	1 092	1 141	1 075	1 242	1 347	456	14.2
Disorders of the blood and blood-forming organs and certain disorders involving the immune mechanism — Maladies du sang et des organes hématopoïétiques et certains troubles du système immunitaire								
Total	423	375	421	456	963	466	159	4.9
Anaemias — Anémies	347	311	365	390	352	389	114	3.5
Endocrine, nutritional and metabolic diseases — Maladies endocriniennes, nutritionnelles et métaboliques								
Total	4 071	4 495	4 387	4 073	3 047	3 565	1 005	31.2
Diabetes mellitus — Diabète sucré	1 452	1 474	1 406	1 315	1 676	1 757	643	20.0
Malnutrition — Malnutrition	1 645	1 847	1 770	1 420	1 080	1 511	61	1.9
Mental and behavioural disorders — Troubles mentaux et du comportement	382	397	302	475	208	105	796	24.7
Diseases of the nervous system — Maladies du système nerveux	1 294	1 397	1 341	1 395	1 548	1 487	587	18.2
Diseases of the circulatory system — Maladies de l'appareil circulatoire								
Total	12 598	12 591	11 454	12 929	12 132	13 903	11 412	354.8
Acute rheumatic fever and chronic rheumatic heart diseases — Rhumatisme articulaire aigu et cardiopathies rhumatismales chroniques	124	115	93	100	112	79	35	1.1
Hypertensive diseases — Maladies hypertensives	1 222	1 249	1 110	1 333	2 090	1 811	412	12.8
Ischaemic heart disease — Cardiopathie ischémique	3 293	3 034	2 723	3 002	1 793	3 449	3 357	104.4
Cerebrovascular disease — Maladie cérébrovasculaire	3 355	3 678	3 288	3 500	3 320	3 685	3 534	109.9
Diseases of arteries, arterioles and capillaries — Maladies des artères, artérioles et capillaires	920	819	763	812	906	729	734	22.8
Diseases of the respiratory system — Maladies de l'appareil respiratoire								
Total	11 914	11 379	11 327	13 661	12 826	11 764	2 806	87.2
Influenza — Grippe	10	12	6	3	31	13	20	♦0.6
Pneumonia — Pneumopathies	8 597	7 991	7 920	9 633	9 305	8 235	913	28.4
Chronic lower respiratory diseases — Maladies chroniques des voies respiratoires inférieures	...	...	...	...	899	957	...	...
Diseases of the digestive system — Maladies de l'appareil digestif								
Total	4 742	5 614	5 072	5 477	5 626	5 783	1 313	40.8
Gastric and duodenal ulcer — Ulcère de l'estomac et du duodénum	366	382	366	378	381	371	107	3.3

21. Death and death rates by cause: 1995 - 2002
Décès selon la cause, nombres et taux: 1995 - 2002 (continued — suite)

(See notes at end of table. — Voir notes à la fin du tableau.)

Uruguay

Cause of death — Cause de décès	1996		1997		1998		1999	
	Number Nombre	Rate Taux	Number Nombre	Rate Taux	Number Nombre	Rate Taux	Number Nombre	Rate Taux
TOTAL	31 110	959.8	30 454	933.2	31 917	971.9	32 431	981.9
Certain infectious and parasitic diseases — Certaines maladies infectieuses et parasitaires								
Total	554	17.1	620	19.0	629	19.2	676	20.5
Intestinal infectious diseases — Maladies infectieuses intestinales	95	2.9	101	3.1	77	2.3	97	2.9
Tuberculosis — Tuberculose	70	2.2	78	2.4	61	1.9	63	1.9
Tetanus — Tétanos	3	♦0.1	-	-	1	0.0	-	-
Diphtheria — Diphtérie	-	-	-	-	-	-	-	-
Whooping cough — Coqueluche	-	-	-	-	-	-	-	-
Meningococcal infection — Infection à méningocoques	21	♦0.6	9	♦0.3	5	♦0.2	10	♦0.3
Septicaemia — Septicémie	263	8.1	248	7.6	300	9.1	332	10.1
Acute poliomyelitis — Poliomyélite aiguë	-	-	-	-	-	-	-	-
Measles — Rougeole	-	-	-	-	-	-	-	-
Viral hepatitis — Hépatite virale	13	♦0.4	13	♦0.4	8	♦0.2	11	♦0.3
Human immunodeficiency virus [HIV] disease — Maladies dues au virus de l'immunodéficience humaine (VIH)	...	...	96	2.9	108	3.3	116	3.5
Malaria — Paludisme	-	-	-	-	-	-	1	0.0
Neoplasms — Tumeurs	7 355	226.9	7 551	231.4	7 506	228.6	7 344	222.4
Malignant neoplasms — Tumeurs malignes								
Total	7 197	222.0	7 369	225.8	7 315	222.7	7 143	216.3
Malignant neoplasm of lip, oral cavity and pharynx — Tumeur maligne de la lèvre, de la cavité buccale et du pharynx	124	3.8	139	4.3	131	4.0	114	3.5
Malignant neoplasm of oesophagus — Tumeur maligne de l'oesophage	267	8.2	294	9.0	272	8.3	299	9.1
Malignant neoplasm of stomach — Tumeur maligne de l'estomac	485	15.0	481	14.7	458	13.9	447	13.5
Malignant neoplasm of colon, rectosigmoid junction, rectum, anus and anal canal — Tumeur maligne du côlon, de la jonction recto-sigmoïdienne, du rectum, de l'anus et du canal anal	845	26.1	854	26.2	801	24.4	812	24.6
Malignant neoplasm of liver and intrahepatic bile ducts — Tumeur maligne du foie et des voies bilaires intrahépatiques	28	♦0.9	92	2.8	73	2.2	61	1.8
Malignant neoplasm of pancreas — Tumeur maligne du pancréas	...	...	365	11.2	367	11.2	381	11.5
Malignant neoplasm of trachea, bronchus and lung — Tumeur maligne de la trachée, des bronches et du poumon	1 153	35.6	1 212	37.1	1 190	36.2	1 124	34.0
Malignant neoplasm of female breast — Tumeur maligne du sein chez la femme	623	▲48.9	612	...	656	▲50.7	587	▲45.0
Malignant neoplasm of cervix uteri — Tumeur maligne du col de l'utérus	97	▲7.6	79	...	103	▲8.0	80	▲6.1
Malignant neoplasm of prostate — Tumeur maligne de la prostate	552	▼144.5	496	...	546	▼141.1	523	▼134.2
Malignant neoplasm of lymphoid, haematopoietic and related tissue — Tumeurs malignes primitives ou présumées primitives des tissus lymphoïde, hématopoïétique et apparentés	489	15.1	506	15.5	488	14.9	524	15.9
Disorders of the blood and blood-forming organs and certain disorders involving the immune mechanism — Maladies du sang et des organes hématopoïétiques et certains troubles du système immunitaire								
Total	134	4.1	148	4.5	122	3.7	162	4.9
Anaemias — Anémies	95	2.9	111	3.4	84	2.6	111	3.4
Endocrine, nutritional and metabolic diseases — Maladies endocriniennes, nutritionnelles et métaboliques								
Total	1 009	31.1	784	24.0	848	25.8	902	27.3
Diabetes mellitus — Diabète sucré	632	19.5	571	17.5	612	18.6	672	20.3
Malnutrition — Malnutrition	47	1.4	60	1.8	73	2.2	60	1.8
Mental and behavioural disorders — Troubles mentaux et du comportement	791	24.4	754	23.1	912	27.8	872	26.4
Diseases of the nervous system — Maladies du système nerveux	590	18.2	585	17.9	744	22.7	856	25.9
Diseases of the circulatory system — Maladies de l'appareil circulatoire								
Total	11 177	344.8	10 591	324.5	11 179	340.4	10 947	331.4
Acute rheumatic fever and chronic rheumatic heart diseases — Rhumatisme articulaire aigu et cardiopathies rhumatismales chroniques	29	♦0.9	30	♦0.9	26	♦0.8	36	1.1
Hypertensive diseases — Maladies hypertensives	386	11.9	393	12.0	447	13.6	439	13.3
Ischaemic heart disease — Cardiopathie ischémique	3 207	98.9	3 133	96.0	3 265	99.4	3 347	101.3
Cerebrovascular disease — Maladie cérébrovasculaire	3 610	111.4	3 514	107.7	3 617	110.1	3 652	110.6
Diseases of arteries, arterioles and capillaries — Maladies des artères, artérioles et capillaires	690	21.3	552	16.9	674	20.5	556	16.8
Diseases of the respiratory system — Maladies de l'appareil respiratoire								
Total	2 659	82.0	2 497	76.5	2 913	88.7	3 114	94.3
Influenza — Grippe	9	♦0.3	5	♦0.2	5	♦0.2	15	♦0.5
Pneumonia — Pneumopathies	909	28.0	900	27.6	1 033	31.5	1 137	34.4
Chronic lower respiratory diseases — Maladies chroniques des voies respiratoires inférieures	...	...	1 092	33.5	1 266	38.6	1 346	40.8
Diseases of the digestive system — Maladies de l'appareil digestif								
Total	1 197	36.9	1 327	40.7	1 287	39.2	1 266	38.3
Gastric and duodenal ulcer — Ulcère de l'estomac et du duodénum	83	2.6	73	2.2	72	2.2	62	1.9

(See notes at end of table. — Voir notes à la fin du tableau.)

Cause of death — Cause de décès	Uruguay		Venezuela[5]					
	2000		1996		1997		1998	
	Number Nombre	Rate Taux	Number Nombre	Rate Taux	Number Nombre	Rate Taux	Number Nombre	Rate Taux
TOTAL	30 455	916.7	100 045	444.6	98 011	426.9	100 963	431.2
Certain infectious and parasitic diseases — Certaines maladies infectieuses et parasitaires								
Total	644	19.4	7 324	32.5	6 766	29.5	6 731	28.7
Intestinal infectious diseases — Maladies infectieuses intestinales	89	2.7	3 384	15.0	2 630	11.5	2 593	11.1
Tuberculosis — Tuberculose	64	1.9	747	3.3	736	3.2	741	3.2
Tetanus — Tétanos	-	-	18	♦0.1	19	♦0.1	18	♦0.1
Diphtheria — Diphtérie	-	-	1	0.0				
Whooping cough — Coqueluche	-	-	30	♦0.1	36	0.2	33	0.1
Meningococcal infection — Infection à méningocoques	-	-	20	♦0.1	28	♦0.1	22	♦0.1
Septicaemia — Septicémie	277	8.3	618	2.7	663	2.9	639	2.7
Acute poliomyelitis — Poliomyélite aiguë	-	-	-	-	-		-	
Measles — Rougeole	-	-	-	-	-	-	-	-
Viral hepatitis — Hépatite virale	10	♦0.3	146	0.6	162	0.7	178	0.8
Human immunodeficiency virus [HIV] disease — Maladies dues au virus de l'immunodéficience humaine (VIH)	134	4.0	931	4.1	1 087	4.7	1 126	4.8
Malaria — Paludisme	-	-	68	0.3	56	0.2	62	0.3
Neoplasms — Tumeurs	7 517	226.3	14 376	63.9	14 800	64.5	15 040	64.2
Malignant neoplasms — Tumeurs malignes								
Total	7 317	220.2	13 632	60.6	14 024	61.1	14 163	60.5
Malignant neoplasm of lip, oral cavity and pharynx — Tumeur maligne de la lèvre, de la cavité buccale et du pharynx	137	4.1	244	1.1	274	1.2	269	1.1
Malignant neoplasm of oesophagus — Tumeur maligne de l'oesophage	295	8.9	243	1.1	213	0.9	245	1.0
Malignant neoplasm of stomach — Tumeur maligne de l'estomac	423	12.7	1 612	7.2	1 600	7.0	1 709	7.3
Malignant neoplasm of colon, rectosigmoid junction, rectum, anus and anal canal — Tumeur maligne du côlon, de la jonction recto-sigmoïdienne, du rectum, de l'anus et du canal anal	839	25.3	871	3.9	887	3.9	884	3.8
Malignant neoplasm of liver and intrahepatic bile ducts — Tumeur maligne du foie et des voies bilaires intrahépatiques	82	2.5	619	2.8	629	2.7	687	2.9
Malignant neoplasm of pancreas — Tumeur maligne du pancréas	394	11.9	503	2.2	517	2.3	506	2.2
Malignant neoplasm of trachea, bronchus and lung — Tumeur maligne de la trachée, des bronches et du poumon	1 171	35.2	1 782	7.9	1 976	8.6	1 958	8.4
Malignant neoplasm of female breast — Tumeur maligne du sein chez la femme	639	▲48.8	916	▲12.8	948	▲12.9	1 014	▲14.7
Malignant neoplasm of cervix uteri — Tumeur maligne du col de l'utérus	87	▲6.6	942	▲13.2	901	▲12.2	886	▲12.8
Malignant neoplasm of prostate — Tumeur maligne de la prostate	542	▼136.4	1 196	▼91.5	1 183	▼86.7	1 225	▼86.0
Malignant neoplasm of lymphoid, haematopoietic and related tissue — Tumeurs malignes primitives ou présumées primitives des tissus lymphoïde, hématopoïétique et apparentés	470	14.1	1 340	6.0	1 373	6.0	1 349	5.8
Disorders of the blood and blood-forming organs and certain disorders involving the immune mechanism — Maladies du sang et des organes hématopoïétiques et certains troubles du système immunitaire								
Total	166	5.0	483	2.1	397	1.7	426	1.8
Anaemias — Anémies	117	3.5	395	1.8	295	1.3	317	1.4
Endocrine, nutritional and metabolic diseases — Maladies endocriniennes, nutritionnelles et métaboliques								
Total	862	25.9	6 383	28.4	6 327	27.6	6 497	27.7
Diabetes mellitus — Diabète sucré	646	19.4	4 451	19.8	4 833	21.1	4 869	20.8
Malnutrition — Malnutrition	57	1.7	1 479	6.6	1 075	4.7	1 143	4.9
Mental and behavioural disorders — Troubles mentaux et du comportement	850	25.6	181	0.8	204	0.9	277	1.2
Diseases of the nervous system — Maladies du système nerveux	879	26.5	1 958	8.7	1 912	8.3	1 933	8.3
Diseases of the circulatory system — Maladies de l'appareil circulatoire								
Total	10 244	308.4	31 094	138.2	30 420	132.5	31 290	133.6
Acute rheumatic fever and chronic rheumatic heart diseases — Rhumatisme articularie aigu et cardiopathies rhumatismales chroniques	30	♦0.9	164	0.7	167	0.7	176	0.8
Hypertensive diseases — Maladies hypertensives	421	12.7	3 313	14.7	3 497	15.2	3 343	14.3
Ischaemic heart disease — Cardiopathie ischémique	2 976	89.6	14 526	64.6	14 247	62.1	15 061	64.3
Cerebrovascular disease — Maladie cérébrovasculaire	3 492	105.1	7 622	33.9	7 530	32.8	7 608	32.5
Diseases of arteries, arterioles and capillaries — Maladies des artères, artérioles et capillaires	559	16.8	762	3.4	683	3.0	643	2.7
Diseases of the respiratory system — Maladies de l'appareil respiratoire								
Total	2 462	74.1	6 770	30.1	6 740	29.4	7 444	31.8
Influenza — Grippe	2	♦0.1	53	0.2	71	0.3	57	0.2
Pneumonia — Pneumopathies	867	26.1	2 640	11.7	2 656	11.6	2 924	12.5
Chronic lower respiratory diseases — Maladies chroniques des voies respiratoires inférieures	1 051	31.6	2 402	10.7	2 401	10.5	2 759	11.8
Diseases of the digestive system — Maladies de l'appareil digestif								
Total	1 242	37.4	4 137	18.4	3 898	17.0	4 226	18.1
Gastric and duodenal ulcer — Ulcère de l'estomac et du duodénum	68	2.0	434	1.9	385	1.7	464	2.0

(See notes at end of table. — Voir notes à la fin du tableau.)

Cause of death — Cause de décès	Venezuela[5]				Armenia — Arménie[6]			
	1999		2000		1995		1996	
	Number Nombre	Rate Taux	Number Nombre	Rate Taux	Number Nombre	Rate Taux	Number Nombre	Rate Taux
TOTAL	104 625	438.4	105 948	435.8	24 842	660.7	24 935	660.8
Certain infectious and parasitic diseases — Certaines maladies infectieuses et parasitaires								
Total	6 317	26.5	5 973	24.6	354	9.4	318	8.4
Intestinal infectious diseases — Maladies infectieuses intestinales	2 106	8.8	1 784	7.3	151	4.0	108	2.9
Tuberculosis — Tuberculose	729	3.1	628	2.6	140	3.7	132	3.5
Tetanus — Tétanos	13	♦0.1	18	♦0.1	2	♦0.1	3	♦0.1
Diphtheria — Diphtérie	-	-	-	-	...	...	...	...
Whooping cough — Coqueluche	43	0.2	54	0.2	1	0.0	1	0.0
Meningococcal infection — Infection à méningocoques	41	0.2	17	♦0.1	1	0.0	5	♦0.1
Septicaemia — Septicémie	619	2.6	630	2.6	30	♦0.8	35	0.9
Acute poliomyelitis — Poliomyélite aiguë	-	-	-	-	...	...	...	...
Measles — Rougeole	-	-	-	-	-	-	3	♦0.1
Viral hepatitis — Hépatite virale	190	0.8	180	0.7	...	...	...	...
Human immunodeficiency virus [HIV] disease — Maladies dues au virus de l'immunodéficience humaine (VIH)	1 243	5.2	1 287	5.3	...	...	...	...
Malaria — Paludisme	24	♦0.1	24	♦0.1	-	-	1	0.0
Neoplasms — Tumeurs	15 778	66.1	16 210	66.7	3 454	91.9	3 682	97.6
Malignant neoplasms — Tumeurs malignes								
Total	14 897	62.4	15 211	62.6	3 384	90.0	3 663	97.1
Malignant neoplasm of lip, oral cavity and pharynx — Tumeur maligne de la lèvre, de la cavité buccale et du pharynx	279	1.2	259	1.1	56	1.5	72	1.9
Malignant neoplasm of oesophagus — Tumeur maligne de l'oesophage	215	0.9	219	0.9	42	1.1	44	1.2
Malignant neoplasm of stomach — Tumeur maligne de l'estomac	1 746	7.3	1 689	6.9	416	11.1	430	11.4
Malignant neoplasm of colon, rectosigmoid junction, rectum, anus and anal canal — Tumeur maligne du côlon, de la jonction recto-sigmoïdienne, du rectum, de l'anus et du canal anal	936	3.9	1 063	4.4	252	6.7	272	7.2
Malignant neoplasm of liver and intrahepatic bile ducts — Tumeur maligne du foie et des voies bilaires intrahépatiques	640	2.7	642	2.6	...	...	...	...
Malignant neoplasm of pancreas — Tumeur maligne du pancréas	533	2.2	556	2.3	...	...	...	...
Malignant neoplasm of trachea, bronchus and lung — Tumeur maligne de la trachée, des bronches et du poumon	2 101	8.8	2 106	8.7	705	18.8	728	19.3
Malignant neoplasm of female breast — Tumeur maligne du sein chez la femme	1 019	...	1 107	▲13.9	308	▲21.7	378	▲26.3
Malignant neoplasm of cervix uteri — Tumeur maligne du col de l'utérus	1 076	...	896	▲11.2	75	▲5.3	94	▲6.5
Malignant neoplasm of prostate — Tumeur maligne de la prostate	1 284	...	1 408	▼90.7	58	▼18.0	70	▼21.7
Malignant neoplasm of lymphoid, haematopoietic and related tissue — Tumeurs malignes primitives ou présumées primitives des tissus lymphoïde, hématopoïétique et apparentés	1 439	6.0	1 501	6.2	219	5.8	264	7.0
Disorders of the blood and blood-forming organs and certain disorders involving the immune mechanism — Maladies du sang et des organes hématopoïétiques et certains troubles du système immunitaire								
Total	365	1.5	365	1.5	14	♦0.4	19	♦0.5
Anaemias — Anémies	257	1.1	260	1.1	11	♦0.3	13	♦0.3
Endocrine, nutritional and metabolic diseases — Maladies endocriniennes, nutritionnelles et métaboliques								
Total	7 207	30.2	7 297	30.0	986	26.2	1 126	29.8
Diabetes mellitus — Diabète sucré	5 725	24.0	5 941	24.4	917	24.4	1 058	28.0
Malnutrition — Malnutrition	1 016	4.3	924	3.8	...	...	...	...
Mental and behavioural disorders — Troubles mentaux et du comportement	232	1.0	223	0.9	153	4.1	119	3.2
Diseases of the nervous system — Maladies du système nerveux	1 865	7.8	1 808	7.4	180	4.8	182	4.8
Diseases of the circulatory system — Maladies de l'appareil circulatoire								
Total	32 040	134.2	32 038	131.8	13 456	357.9	13 252	351.2
Acute rheumatic fever and chronic rheumatic heart diseases — Rhumatisme articularie aigu et cardiopathies rhumatismales chroniques	196	0.8	194	0.8	189	5.0	226	6.0
Hypertensive diseases — Maladies hypertensives	3 429	14.4	3 572	14.7	19	♦0.5	10	♦0.3
Ischaemic heart disease — Cardiopathie ischémique	15 162	63.5	15 702	64.6	8 698	231.3	8 543	226.4
Cerebrovascular disease — Maladie cérébrovasculaire	8 167	34.2	8 000	32.9	3 515	93.5	3 553	94.2
Diseases of arteries, arterioles and capillaries — Maladies des artères, artérioles et capillaires	722	3.0	669	2.8	122	3.2	153	4.1
Diseases of the respiratory system — Maladies de l'appareil respiratoire								
Total	7 344	30.8	6 316	26.0	1 600	42.6	1 703	45.1
Influenza — Grippe	62	0.3	23	♦0.1	17	♦0.5	17	♦0.5
Pneumonia — Pneumopathies	2 824	11.8	2 368	9.7	260	6.9	288	7.6
Chronic lower respiratory diseases — Maladies chroniques des voies respiratoires inférieures	3 004	12.6	2 634	10.8	...	...	...	...
Diseases of the digestive system — Maladies de l'appareil digestif								
Total	4 401	18.4	4 456	18.3	895	23.8	926	24.5
Gastric and duodenal ulcer — Ulcère de l'estomac et du duodénum	489	2.0	441	1.8	156	4.1	156	4.1

(See notes at end of table. — Voir notes à la fin du tableau.)

Armenia — Arménie[6]

Cause of death — Cause de décès	1997		1998		1999		2000	
	Number Nombre	Rate Taux	Number Nombre	Rate Taux	Number Nombre	Rate Taux	Number Nombre	Rate Taux
TOTAL	23 985	633.5	23 210	611.6	24 087	633.7	24 025	631.8
Certain infectious and parasitic diseases — Certaines maladies infectieuses et parasitaires								
Total	349	9.2	304	8.0	309	8.1	287	7.5
Intestinal infectious diseases — Maladies infectieuses intestinales	107	2.8	86	2.3	85	2.2	59	1.6
Tuberculosis — Tuberculose	159	4.2	148	3.9	161	4.2	157	4.1
Tetanus — Tétanos	1	0.0	2	◆0.1	-	-	1	0.0
Diphtheria — Diphtérie	...	...	...	...	...	...	...	...
Whooping cough — Coqueluche	-	-	-	-	-	-	-	-
Meningococcal infection — Infection à méningocoques	1	0.0	3	◆0.1	3	◆0.1	4	◆0.1
Septicaemia — Septicémie	45	1.2	31	0.8	32	0.8	32	0.8
Acute poliomyelitis — Poliomyélite aiguë	...	...	...	...	...	...	...	...
Measles — Rougeole	1	0.0	...	...	...	...	...	...
Viral hepatitis — Hépatite virale	...	...	-	-	-	-	-	-
Human immunodeficiency virus [HIV] disease — Maladies dues au virus de l'immunodéficience humaine (VIH)	...	...	...	...	...	...	...	...
Malaria — Paludisme	-	-	-	-	-	-	1	0.0
Neoplasms — Tumeurs	3 672	97.0	3 852	101.5	3 976	104.6	3 967	104.3
Malignant neoplasms — Tumeurs malignes								
Total	3 654	96.5	3 829	100.9	3 964	104.3	3 958	104.1
Malignant neoplasm of lip, oral cavity and pharynx — Tumeur maligne de la lèvre, de la cavité buccale et du pharynx	68	1.8	55	1.4	68	1.8	62	1.6
Malignant neoplasm of oesophagus — Tumeur maligne de l'oesophage	47	1.2	48	1.3	57	1.5	47	1.2
Malignant neoplasm of stomach — Tumeur maligne de l'estomac	408	10.8	424	11.2	392	10.3	395	10.4
Malignant neoplasm of colon, rectosigmoid junction, rectum, anus and anal canal — Tumeur maligne du côlon, de la jonction recto-sigmoïdienne, du rectum, de l'anus et du canal anal	286	7.6	275	7.2	297	7.8	318	8.4
Malignant neoplasm of liver and intrahepatic bile ducts — Tumeur maligne du foie et des voies bilaires intrahépatiques	...	...	...	...	...	...	...	...
Malignant neoplasm of pancreas — Tumeur maligne du pancréas	...	...	...	...	...	...	...	...
Malignant neoplasm of trachea, bronchus and lung — Tumeur maligne de la trachée, des bronches et du poumon	804	21.2	764	20.1	793	20.9	845	22.2
Malignant neoplasm of female breast — Tumeur maligne du sein chez la femme	367	▲25.2	410	▲27.8	432	▲28.8	444	▲29.2
Malignant neoplasm of cervix uteri — Tumeur maligne du col de l'utérus	91	▲6.2	101	▲6.8	114	▲7.6	86	▲5.6
Malignant neoplasm of prostate — Tumeur maligne de la prostate	79	▼24.3	87	▼26.3	84	▼25.0	94	▼27.5
Malignant neoplasm of lymphoid, haematopoietic and related tissue — Tumeurs malignes primitives ou présumées primitives des tissus lymphoïde, hématopoïétique et apparentés	226	6.0	248	6.5	227	6.0	267	7.0
Disorders of the blood and blood-forming organs and certain disorders involving the immune mechanism — Maladies du sang et des organes hématopoïétiques et certains troubles du système immunitaire								
Total	18	◆0.5	19	◆0.5	23	◆0.6	22	◆0.6
Anaemias — Anémies	7	◆0.2	6	◆0.2	10	◆0.3	11	◆0.3
Endocrine, nutritional and metabolic diseases — Maladies endocriniennes, nutritionnelles et métaboliques								
Total	1 236	32.6	1 267	33.4	1 262	33.2	1 324	34.8
Diabetes mellitus — Diabète sucré	1 184	31.3	1 206	31.8	1 198	31.5	1 266	33.3
Malnutrition — Malnutrition	...	...	...	...	...	...	...	...
Mental and behavioural disorders — Troubles mentaux et du comportement	102	2.7	80	2.1	83	2.2	65	1.7
Diseases of the nervous system — Maladies du système nerveux	169	4.5	180	4.7	155	4.1	170	4.5
Diseases of the circulatory system — Maladies de l'appareil circulatoire								
Total	12 745	336.6	12 333	325.0	13 065	343.7	13 198	347.1
Acute rheumatic fever and chronic rheumatic heart diseases — Rhumatisme articulaire aigu et cardiopathies rhumatismales chroniques	192	5.1	154	4.1	136	3.6	149	3.9
Hypertensive diseases — Maladies hypertensives	7	◆0.2	5	◆0.1	7	◆0.2	3	◆0.1
Ischaemic heart disease — Cardiopathie ischémique	8 490	224.2	8 367	220.5	8 838	232.5	8 745	230.0
Cerebrovascular disease — Maladie cérébrovasculaire	3 360	88.7	3 232	85.2	3 497	92.0	3 600	94.7
Diseases of arteries, arterioles and capillaries — Maladies des artères, artérioles et capillaires	142	3.8	146	3.8	148	3.9	172	4.5
Diseases of the respiratory system — Maladies de l'appareil respiratoire								
Total	1 472	38.9	1 223	32.2	1 457	38.3	1 416	37.2
Influenza — Grippe	6	◆0.2	3	◆0.1	15	◆0.4	5	◆0.1
Pneumonia — Pneumopathies	225	5.9	179	4.7	257	6.8	200	5.3
Chronic lower respiratory diseases — Maladies chroniques des voies respiratoires inférieures	...	...	...	...	...	...	...	...
Diseases of the digestive system — Maladies de l'appareil digestif								
Total	906	23.9	821	21.6	795	20.9	783	20.6
Gastric and duodenal ulcer — Ulcère de l'estomac et du duodénum	145	3.8	142	3.7	125	3.3	125	3.3

(See notes at end of table. — Voir notes à la fin du tableau.)

Cause of death — Cause de décès	Armenia — Arménie[6]				Azerbaijan — Azerbaïdjan[6]			
	2001		2002		1995	1996	1997	1998
	Number Nombre	Rate Taux	Number Nombre	Rate Taux	Number Nombre			
TOTAL	24 003	631.4	25 554	795.4	*50 828*	*48 242*	*46 961*	*46 299*
Certain infectious and parasitic diseases — Certaines maladies infectieuses et parasitaires								
Total	239	6.3	251	7.8	*2 279*	*1 933*	*1 894*	*1 726*
Intestinal infectious diseases — Maladies infectieuses intestinales	41	1.1	23	◆0.7	*680*	*515*	*502*	*394*
Tuberculosis — Tuberculose	145	3.8	167	5.2	*1 161*	*1 149*	*1 144*	*1 117*
Tetanus — Tétanos	2	◆0.1	2	◆0.1	*7*	*2*	*1*	*1*
Diphtheria — Diphtérie	...	...	-	-	*2*	*...*	*...*	*...*
Whooping cough — Coqueluche	-	-	-	-				
Meningococcal infection — Infection à méningocoques	3	◆0.1	-	-	*8*	*8*	*9*	*6*
Septicaemia — Septicémie	24	◆0.6	29	◆0.9	*125*	*90*	*98*	*84*
Acute poliomyelitis — Poliomyélite aiguë	...	...	-	...	*...*	*...*	*...*	*...*
Measles — Rougeole	-	-	-	-	*15*	*2*	*3*	*16*
Viral hepatitis — Hépatite virale	...	...	...	...	*...*	*...*	*...*	*...*
Human immunodeficiency virus [HIV] disease — Maladies dues au virus de l'immunodéficience humaine (VIH)	...	...	1	0.0	*...*	*...*	*...*	*...*
Malaria — Paludisme	-	-	-	-	*5*	*1*	*6*	*2*
Neoplasms — Tumeurs	4 136	108.8	4 242	132.0	*4 761*	*4 709*	*4 809*	*4 944*
Malignant neoplasms — Tumeurs malignes								
Total	4 128	108.6	4 233	131.8	*4 758*	*4 698*	*4 804*	*4 933*
Malignant neoplasm of lip, oral cavity and pharynx — Tumeur maligne de la lèvre, de la cavité buccale et du pharynx	80	2.1	57	1.8	*41*	*61*	*42*	*49*
Malignant neoplasm of oesophagus — Tumeur maligne de l'oesophage	48	1.3	44	1.4	*316*	*366*	*364*	*369*
Malignant neoplasm of stomach — Tumeur maligne de l'estomac	427	11.2	405	12.6	*984*	*969*	*955*	*970*
Malignant neoplasm of colon, rectosigmoid junction, rectum, anus and anal canal — Tumeur maligne du côlon, de la jonction recto-sigmoïdienne, du rectum, de l'anus et du canal anal	301	7.9	337	10.5	*313*	*304*	*251*	*243*
Malignant neoplasm of liver and intrahepatic bile ducts — Tumeur maligne du foie et des voies bilaires intrahépatiques	...	...	...	...	*...*	*...*	*...*	*...*
Malignant neoplasm of pancreas — Tumeur maligne du pancréas	...	...	...	...	*...*	*...*	*...*	*...*
Malignant neoplasm of trachea, bronchus and lung — Tumeur maligne de la trachée, des bronches et du poumon	875	23.0	880	27.4	*672*	*719*	*736*	*693*
Malignant neoplasm of female breast — Tumeur maligne du sein chez la femme	425	...	457	...	*297*	*274*	*318*	*356*
Malignant neoplasm of cervix uteri — Tumeur maligne du col de l'utérus	92	...	96	...	*59*	*53*	*76*	*70*
Malignant neoplasm of prostate — Tumeur maligne de la prostate	89	...	107	...	*124*	*90*	*97*	*90*
Malignant neoplasm of lymphoid, haematopoietic and related tissue — Tumeurs malignes primitives ou présumées primitives des tissus lymphoïde, hématopoïétique et apparentés	244	6.4	250	7.8	*406*	*368*	*419*	*419*
Disorders of the blood and blood-forming organs and certain disorders involving the immune mechanism — Maladies du sang et des organes hématopoïétiques et certains troubles du système immunitaire								
Total	17	◆0.4	11	◆0.3	*251*	*234*	*228*	*208*
Anaemias — Anémies	12	◆0.3	7	◆0.2	*118*	*58*	*45*	*29*
Endocrine, nutritional and metabolic diseases — Maladies endocriniennes, nutritionnelles et métaboliques								
Total	1 422	37.4	1 587	49.4	*907*	*931*	*1 017*	*1 103*
Diabetes mellitus — Diabète sucré	1 362	35.8	1 520	47.3	*825*	*844*	*925*	*1 025*
Malnutrition — Malnutrition	...	...	...	...	*...*	*...*	*...*	*...*
Mental and behavioural disorders — Troubles mentaux et du comportement	72	1.9	69	2.1	*249*	*176*	*180*	*204*
Diseases of the nervous system — Maladies du système nerveux	178	4.7	193	6.0	*867*	*913*	*959*	*903*
Diseases of the circulatory system — Maladies de l'appareil circulatoire								
Total	13 107	344.8	14 027	436.6	*25 767*	*24 765*	*24 153*	*24 681*
Acute rheumatic fever and chronic rheumatic heart diseases — Rhumatisme articulaire aigu et cardiopathies rhumatismales chroniques	133	3.5	147	4.6	*175*	*156*	*162*	*163*
Hypertensive diseases — Maladies hypertensives	-	-	44	1.4	*1 421*	*1 338*	*1 319*	*1 349*
Ischaemic heart disease — Cardiopathie ischémique	8 357	219.8	8 485	264.1	*17 167*	*16 558*	*16 334*	*16 601*
Cerebrovascular disease — Maladie cérébrovasculaire	3 837	100.9	4 373	136.1	*5 450*	*5 402*	*5 071*	*5 132*
Diseases of arteries, arterioles and capillaries — Maladies des artères, artérioles et capillaires	186	4.9	240	7.5	*10*	*10*	*5*	*6*
Diseases of the respiratory system — Maladies de l'appareil respiratoire								
Total	1 228	32.3	1 462	45.5	*6 527*	*5 742*	*5 321*	*4 630*
Influenza — Grippe	4	◆0.1	1	0.0	*43*	*11*	*12*	*4*
Pneumonia — Pneumopathies	179	4.7	198	6.2	*3 097*	*2 624*	*2 587*	*2 092*
Chronic lower respiratory diseases — Maladies chroniques des voies respiratoires inférieures	...	...	...	...	*...*	*...*	*...*	*...*
Diseases of the digestive system — Maladies de l'appareil digestif								
Total	900	23.7	1 009	31.4	*2 639*	*2 778*	*2 788*	*2 649*
Gastric and duodenal ulcer — Ulcère de l'estomac et du duodénum	137	3.6	141	4.4	*287*	*305*	*311*	*282*

(See notes at end of table. — Voir notes à la fin du tableau.)

Cause of death — Cause de décès	Azerbaijan — Azerbaïdjan[6]				Bahrain — Bahreïn			
	1999	2000	2001	2002	1997		1998	
			Number Nombre			Rate Taux	Number Nombre	Rate Taux
TOTAL	46 295	46 701	45 284	46 522	1 822	309.3	1 997	330.2
Certain infectious and parasitic diseases — Certaines maladies infectieuses et parasitaires								
Total	1 828	1 574	1 532	1 402	37	6.3	44	7.3
Intestinal infectious diseases — Maladies infectieuses intestinales	328	225	218	212	6	♦1.0	2	♦0.3
Tuberculosis — Tuberculose	1 279	1 184	1 107	1 019	5	♦0.8	10	♦1.7
Tetanus — Tétanos	2	2	5	1	-	-	-	-
Diphtheria — Diphtérie	...	...	4	2	-	-	-	-
Whooping cough — Coqueluche	1	-	-	-	-	-	-	-
Meningococcal infection — Infection à méningocoques	7	5	8	-	-	-	-	-
Septicaemia — Septicémie	97	60	59	62	14	♦2.4	17	♦2.8
Acute poliomyelitis — Poliomyélite aiguë	...	...	-	-	-	-	-	-
Measles — Rougeole	8	3	3	4	-	-	-	-
Viral hepatitis — Hépatite virale	...	...	32	29	-	-	-	-
Human immunodeficiency virus [HIV] disease — Maladies dues au virus de l'immunodéficience humaine (VIH)	...	...			11	♦1.9	12	♦2.0
Malaria — Paludisme	2	4	2	4	-	-	1	♦0.2
Neoplasms — Tumeurs	5 214	5 081	5 455	5 859	224	38.0	243	40.2
Malignant neoplasms — Tumeurs malignes								
Total	5 197	5 073	5 448	5 852	220	37.3	242	40.0
Malignant neoplasm of lip, oral cavity and pharynx — Tumeur maligne de la lèvre, de la cavité buccale et du pharynx	54	76	39	31	5	♦0.8	7	♦1.2
Malignant neoplasm of oesophagus — Tumeur maligne de l'oesophage	378	363	366	410	4	♦0.7	9	♦1.5
Malignant neoplasm of stomach — Tumeur maligne de l'estomac	1 018	946	964	1 088	21	♦3.6	10	♦1.7
Malignant neoplasm of colon, rectosigmoid junction, rectum, anus and anal canal — Tumeur maligne du côlon, de la jonction recto-sigmoïdienne, du rectum, de l'anus et du canal anal	284	280	272	322	21	♦3.6	17	♦2.8
Malignant neoplasm of liver and intrahepatic bile ducts — Tumeur maligne du foie et des voies bilaires intrahépatiques	...	...	397	420	8	♦1.4	12	♦2.0
Malignant neoplasm of pancreas — Tumeur maligne du pancréas	...	...	168	96	8	♦1.4	8	♦1.3
Malignant neoplasm of trachea, bronchus and lung — Tumeur maligne de la trachée, des bronches et du poumon	751	735	796	839	41	7.0	52	8.6
Malignant neoplasm of female breast — Tumeur maligne du sein chez la femme	374	318	375	410	17	♦ ▲10.3	21	♦ ▲12.2
Malignant neoplasm of cervix uteri — Tumeur maligne du col de l'utérus	65	77	66	48	1	♦ ▲0.6	1	♦ ▲0.6
Malignant neoplasm of prostate — Tumeur maligne de la prostate	92	88	184	200	4	♦ ▼13.4	9	♦ ▼29.0
Malignant neoplasm of lymphoid, haematopoietic and related tissue — Tumeurs malignes primitives ou présumées primitives des tissus lymphoïde, hématopoïétique et apparentés	441	485	...	...	25	♦4.2	38	6.3
Disorders of the blood and blood-forming organs and certain disorders involving the immune mechanism — Maladies du sang et des organes hématopoïétiques et certains troubles du système immunitaire								
Total	178	163	187	185	28	♦4.8	27	♦4.5
Anaemias — Anémies	30	25	121	83	23	♦3.9	24	♦4.0
Endocrine, nutritional and metabolic diseases — Maladies endocriniennes, nutritionnelles et métaboliques								
Total	1 080	1 082	1 323	1 372	139	23.6	143	23.6
Diabetes mellitus — Diabète sucré	1 015	1 031	1 278	1 313	117	19.9	114	18.8
Malnutrition — Malnutrition	...	...	7	9	1	♦0.2	1	♦0.2
Mental and behavioural disorders — Troubles mentaux et du comportement	123	115	79	82	7	♦1.2	9	♦1.5
Diseases of the nervous system — Maladies du système nerveux	880	793	922	805	25	♦4.2	31	5.1
Diseases of the circulatory system — Maladies de l'appareil circulatoire								
Total	25 181	26 205	25 267	26 505	622	105.6	552	91.3
Acute rheumatic fever and chronic rheumatic heart diseases — Rhumatisme articulaire aigu et cardiopathies rhumatismales chroniques	186	157	140	131	3	♦0.5	1	♦0.2
Hypertensive diseases — Maladies hypertensives	1 599	1 607	1 649	1 581	120	20.4	174	28.8
Ischaemic heart disease — Cardiopathie ischémique	16 745	17 247	16 564	17 721	318	54.0	201	33.2
Cerebrovascular disease — Maladie cérébrovasculaire	5 147	5 419	4 901	5 196	64	10.9	61	10.1
Diseases of arteries, arterioles and capillaries — Maladies des artères, artérioles et capillaires	4	2	...	...	3	♦0.5	1	♦0.2
Diseases of the respiratory system — Maladies de l'appareil respiratoire								
Total	4 352	4 207	3 519	3 196	76	12.9	99	16.4
Influenza — Grippe	7	4	2	1	-	-	-	-
Pneumonia — Pneumopathies	1 960	1 787	1 462	1 385	3	♦0.5	10	♦1.7
Chronic lower respiratory diseases — Maladies chroniques des voies respiratoires inférieures	...	...	930	897	39	6.6	53	8.8
Diseases of the digestive system — Maladies de l'appareil digestif								
Total	2 543	2 624	2 590	2 774	99	16.8	86	14.2
Gastric and duodenal ulcer — Ulcère de l'estomac et du duodénum	269	288	230	236	9	♦1.5	7	♦1.2

(See notes at end of table. — Voir notes à la fin du tableau.)

Cause of death — Cause de décès	Bahrain — Bahreïn 1999 Number Nombre	1999 Rate Taux	2000 Number Nombre	2000 Rate Taux	China - Hong Kong SAR — Chine - Hong-Kong RAS 1995 Number Nombre	1996 Number Nombre	1997 Number Nombre	1998 Number Nombre
TOTAL	1 920	309.2	2 033	318.9	30 892	32 045	32 076	32 675
Certain infectious and parasitic diseases — Certaines maladies infectieuses et parasitaires								
Total	53	8.5	86	13.5	1 060	1 037	943	797
Intestinal infectious diseases — Maladies infectieuses intestinales	6	♦1.0	4	♦0.6	13	12	10	5
Tuberculosis — Tuberculose	10	♦1.6	13	♦2.0	374	286	250	266
Tetanus — Tétanos	-	-	-	-	9	3	1	3
Diphtheria — Diphtérie	-	-	-	-	-	-	1	-
Whooping cough — Coqueluche	-	-	-	-	1	1	-	-
Meningococcal infection — Infection à méningocoques	-	-	-	-	-	-	-	-
Septicaemia — Septicémie	24	♦3.9	23	♦3.6	603	704	659	501
Acute poliomyelitis — Poliomyélite aiguë	-	-	-	-	-	-	-	-
Measles — Rougeole	-	-	-	-	-	-	-	-
Viral hepatitis — Hépatite virale	2	♦0.3	9	♦1.4	1	5	4	7
Human immunodeficiency virus [HIV] disease — Maladies dues au virus de l'immunodéficience humaine (VIH)	11	♦1.8	12	♦1.9	...	-	-	-
Malaria — Paludisme	-	-	-	-	1	2	-	-
Neoplasms — Tumeurs	229	36.9	246	38.6	9 793	10 215	10 435	10 773
Malignant neoplasms — Tumeurs malignes								
Total	222	35.7	235	36.9	9 680	10 134	10 373	10 691
Malignant neoplasm of lip, oral cavity and pharynx — Tumeur maligne de la lèvre, de la cavité buccale et du pharynx	7	♦1.1	7	♦1.1	539	537	565	597
Malignant neoplasm of oesophagus — Tumeur maligne de l'oesophage	5	♦0.8	4	♦0.6	367	369	397	354
Malignant neoplasm of stomach — Tumeur maligne de l'estomac	16	♦2.6	12	♦1.9	585	585	646	656
Malignant neoplasm of colon, rectosigmoid junction, rectum, anus and anal canal — Tumeur maligne du côlon, de la jonction recto-sigmoïdienne, du rectum, de l'anus et du canal anal	17	♦2.7	9	♦1.4	1 185	1 205	1 240	1 309
Malignant neoplasm of liver and intrahepatic bile ducts — Tumeur maligne du foie et des voies bilaires intrahépatiques	5	♦0.8	21	♦3.3	...	...	...	...
Malignant neoplasm of pancreas — Tumeur maligne du pancréas	10	♦1.6	9	♦1.4	262	297	270	290
Malignant neoplasm of trachea, bronchus and lung — Tumeur maligne de la trachée, des bronches et du poumon	44	7.1	41	6.4	2 835	2 966	2 968	3 091
Malignant neoplasm of female breast — Tumeur maligne du sein chez la femme	18	♦ ▲10.1	30	♦ ▲16.3	320	376	377	380
Malignant neoplasm of cervix uteri — Tumeur maligne du col de l'utérus	3	♦ ▲1.7	4	♦ ▲2.2	159	134	144	145
Malignant neoplasm of prostate — Tumeur maligne de la prostate	6	♦ ▼18.6	7	♦ ▼20.8	136	149	146	137
Malignant neoplasm of lymphoid, haematopoietic and related tissue — Tumeurs malignes primitives ou présumées primitives des tissus lymphoïde, hématopoïétique et apparentés	31	5.0	35	5.5	507	516	605	630
Disorders of the blood and blood-forming organs and certain disorders involving the immune mechanism — Maladies du sang et des organes hématopoïétiques et certains troubles du système immunitaire								
Total	23	♦3.7	19	♦3.0	84	63	62	46
Anaemias — Anémies	21	♦3.4	17	♦2.7	32	32	20	20
Endocrine, nutritional and metabolic diseases — Maladies endocriniennes, nutritionnelles et métaboliques								
Total	150	24.2	139	21.8	523	483	421	582
Diabetes mellitus — Diabète sucré	119	19.2	112	17.6	470	432	371	521
Malnutrition — Malnutrition	-	-	1	♦0.2	2	2	9	4
Mental and behavioural disorders — Troubles mentaux et du comportement	5	♦0.8	6	♦0.9	7	14	39	22
Diseases of the nervous system — Maladies du système nerveux	30	♦4.8	27	♦4.2	263	220	218	225
Diseases of the circulatory system — Maladies de l'appareil circulatoire								
Total	565	91.0	537	84.2	8 592	8 356	8 239	8 842
Acute rheumatic fever and chronic rheumatic heart diseases — Rhumatisme articulaire aigu et cardiopathies rhumatismales chroniques	3	♦0.5	4	♦0.6	145	145	144	178
Hypertensive diseases — Maladies hypertensives	189	30.4	161	25.3	631	615	567	530
Ischaemic heart disease — Cardiopathie ischémique	208	33.5	179	28.1	3 244	3 299	3 265	3 332
Cerebrovascular disease — Maladie cérébrovasculaire	53	8.5	87	13.6	3 310	3 102	3 026	3 297
Diseases of arteries, arterioles and capillaries — Maladies des artères, artérioles et capillaires	2	♦0.3	5	♦0.8	359	369	372	432
Diseases of the respiratory system — Maladies de l'appareil respiratoire								
Total	88	14.2	79	12.4	5 707	6 640	6 475	6 111
Influenza — Grippe	-	-	-	-	-	1	1	1
Pneumonia — Pneumopathies	6	♦1.0	6	♦0.9	3 266	3 980	4 100	3 691
Chronic lower respiratory diseases — Maladies chroniques des voies respiratoires inférieures	40	6.4	23	♦3.6	2 030	2 240	2 056	2 082
Diseases of the digestive system — Maladies de l'appareil digestif								
Total	74	11.9	72	11.3	1 354	1 390	1 378	1 370
Gastric and duodenal ulcer — Ulcère de l'estomac et du duodénum	10	♦1.6	11	♦1.7	173	204	170	149

(See notes at end of table. — Voir notes à la fin du tableau.)

Cause of death — Cause de décès	China - Hong Kong SAR — Chine - Hong-Kong RAS		Georgia — Géorgie[6,7]					
	1999	2000	1995	1996	1997	1998	1999	2000
			Number Nombre					
TOTAL	33 382	33 989	37 874	34 414	37 679	*39 404*	*40 378*	*41 285*
Certain infectious and parasitic diseases — Certaines maladies infectieuses et parasitaires								
Total	759	717	512	446	476	*381*	*397*	*389*
Intestinal infectious diseases — Maladies infectieuses intestinales	14	11	65	42	53	*54*	*36*	*32*
Tuberculosis — Tuberculose	293	272	328	291	336	*289*	*291*	*288*
Diphtheria — Diphtérie	1	2	2	3	1	*1*	*-*	*5*
Whooping cough — Coqueluche	-	-	...	...	...	*5*	*1*	*1*
Meningococcal infection — Infection à méningocoques	-	1	1	1	4	*3*	*-*	*1*
Septicaemia — Septicémie	412	387	75	66	67	*8*	*26*	*39*
Acute poliomyelitis — Poliomyélite aiguë	-	-	...	...	...	*-*	*-*	*-*
Measles — Rougeole	-	-	..	-	-	*-*	*-*	*-*
Viral hepatitis — Hépatite virale	2	4	...	...	...	*2*	*8*	*4*
Human immunodeficiency virus [HIV] disease — Maladies dues au virus de l'immunodéficience humaine (VIH)	-	-				*-*	*-*	*-*
Malaria — Paludisme	-	1	3	-	-	*-*	*-*	*1*
Neoplasms — Tumeurs	11 120	11 361	3 376	3 473	3 776	*4 334*	*4 422*	*4 516*
Malignant neoplasms — Tumeurs malignes								
Total	10 977	11 222	3 351	3 392	3 691	*4 268*	*4 301*	*4 391*
Malignant neoplasm of lip, oral cavity and pharynx — Tumeur maligne de la lèvre, de la cavité buccale et du pharynx	532	523	47	54	42	*105*	*150*	*91*
Malignant neoplasm of oesophagus — Tumeur maligne de l'oesophage	366	399	3	39	57	*67*	*57*	*65*
Malignant neoplasm of stomach — Tumeur maligne de l'estomac	699	652	375	406	418	*533*	*526*	*533*
Malignant neoplasm of colon, rectosigmoid junction, rectum, anus and anal canal — Tumeur maligne du côlon, de la jonction recto-sigmoïdienne, du rectum, de l'anus et du canal anal	1 329	1 351	249	252	222	*270*	*263*	*334*
Malignant neoplasm of liver and intrahepatic bile ducts — Tumeur maligne du foie et des voies bilaires intrahépatiques	...	...	...	...	...	*273*	*266*	*293*
Malignant neoplasm of pancreas — Tumeur maligne du pancréas	323	300	...	...	...	*131*	*135*	*135*
Malignant neoplasm of trachea, bronchus and lung — Tumeur maligne de la trachée, des bronches et du poumon	3 168	3 326	558	569	672	*739*	*769*	*827*
Malignant neoplasm of female breast — Tumeur maligne du sein chez la femme	395	397	411	395	433	*538*	*560*	*550*
Malignant neoplasm of cervix uteri — Tumeur maligne du col de l'utérus	159	128	182	140	110	*114*	*129*	*101*
Malignant neoplasm of prostate — Tumeur maligne de la prostate	219	187	61	74	76	*98*	*108*	*108*
Malignant neoplasm of lymphoid, haematopoietic and related tissue — Tumeurs malignes primitives ou présumées primitives des tissus lymphoïde, hématopoïétique et apparentés	619	643	192	205	234	*255*	*222*	*245*
Disorders of the blood and blood-forming organs and certain disorders involving the immune mechanism — Maladies du sang et des organes hématopoïétiques et certains troubles du système immunitaire								
Total	55	48	54	47	71	*37*	*30*	*20*
Anaemias — Anémies	24	20	50	36	44	*31*	*30*	*17*
Endocrine, nutritional and metabolic diseases — Maladies endocriniennes, nutritionnelles et métaboliques								
Total	779	875	569	450	478	*639*	*733*	*851*
Diabetes mellitus — Diabète sucré	725	830	567	448	469	*627*	*716*	*827*
Malnutrition — Malnutrition	-	1	...	...	...	*-*	*-*	*-*
Mental and behavioural disorders — Troubles mentaux et du comportement	45	87	44	48	47	*28*	*28*	*31*
Diseases of the nervous system — Maladies du système nerveux	266	271	84	259	316	*168*	*165*	*114*
Diseases of the circulatory system — Maladies de l'appareil circulatoire								
Total	9 157	9 549	27 248	23 966	26 484	*27 935*	*28 724*	*29 701*
Acute rheumatic fever and chronic rheumatic heart diseases — Rhumatisme articularie aigu et cardiopathies rhumatismales chroniques	164	171	159	101	116	*83*	*60*	*67*
Hypertensive diseases — Maladies hypertensives	642	735	5	175	345	*464*	*403*	*409*
Ischaemic heart disease — Cardiopathie ischémique	3 304	3 605	17 006	14 738	14 986	*15 119*	*14 927*	*16 207*
Cerebrovascular disease — Maladie cérébrovasculaire	3 491	3 553	8 916	7 532	8 892	*9 056*	*9 612*	*10 184*
Diseases of arteries, arterioles and capillaries — Maladies des artères, artérioles et capillaires	383	402	132	170	260	*338*	*212*	*491*
Diseases of the respiratory system — Maladies de l'appareil respiratoire								
Total	5 645	5 627	740	935	918	*923*	*827*	*1 088*
Influenza — Grippe	6	4	9	7	13	*3*	*9*	*7*
Pneumonia — Pneumopathies	2 977	3 041	285	319	266	*319*	*264*	*514*
Chronic lower respiratory diseases — Maladies chroniques des voies respiratoires inférieures	2 322	2 205	...	...	...	*367*	*426*	*385*
Diseases of the digestive system — Maladies de l'appareil digestif								
Total	1 342	1 433	1 436	1 406	1 385	*1 360*	*1 437*	*1 354*
Gastric and duodenal ulcer — Ulcère de l'estomac et du duodénum	131	149	166	147	125	*148*	*133*	*111*

(See notes at end of table. — Voir notes à la fin du tableau.)

Cause of death — Cause de décès	Georgia — Géorgie[6,7] 2001 Number Nombre	Israel — Israël[8] 1995 Number Nombre	1995 Rate Taux	1996 Number Nombre	1996 Rate Taux	1997 Number Nombre	1997 Rate Taux	1998 Number Nombre
TOTAL	*39 339*	35 348	637.5	34 658	609.6	36 106	619.4	*36 953*
Certain infectious and parasitic diseases — Certaines maladies infectieuses et parasitaires								
Total	*369*	584	10.5	661	11.6	696	11.9	747
Intestinal infectious diseases — Maladies infectieuses intestinales	*37*	32	0.6	14	♦0.2	12	♦0.2	49
Tuberculosis — Tuberculose	*255*	54	1.0	41	0.7	62	1.1	46
Tetanus — Tétanos	-	-	-	2	0.0	-	-	-
Diphtheria — Diphtérie	-	-	-	-	-	-	-	-
Whooping cough — Coqueluche	-	4	♦0.1	4	♦0.1	8	♦0.1	6
Meningococcal infection — Infection à méningocoques	-	4	♦0.1	4	♦0.1	8	♦0.1	6
Septicaemia — Septicémie	*55*	256	4.6	394	6.9	409	7.0	408
Acute poliomyelitis — Poliomyélite aiguë	-	-	-	-	-	-	-	-
Measles — Rougeole	-	-	-	-	-	-	-	-
Viral hepatitis — Hépatite virale	*8*	126	2.3	94	1.7	99	1.7	101
Human immunodeficiency virus [HIV] disease — Maladies dues au virus de l'immunodéficience humaine (VIH)	*1*	23	♦0.4	24	♦0.4	27	♦0.5	26
Malaria — Paludisme	-	-	-	1	0.0	-	-	-
Neoplasms — Tumeurs	*4 375*	8 519	153.6	8 708	153.2	8 656	148.5	9 189
Malignant neoplasms — Tumeurs malignes								
Total	*4 236*	8 053	145.2	8 396	147.7	8 306	142.5	8 868
Malignant neoplasm of lip, oral cavity and pharynx — Tumeur maligne de la lèvre, de la cavité buccale et du pharynx	*80*	74	1.3	68	1.2	78	1.3	94
Malignant neoplasm of oesophagus — Tumeur maligne de l'oesophage	*53*	92	1.7	112	2.0	89	1.5	82
Malignant neoplasm of stomach — Tumeur maligne de l'estomac	*490*	478	8.6	492	8.7	454	7.8	491
Malignant neoplasm of colon, rectosigmoid junction, rectum, anus and anal canal — Tumeur maligne du côlon, de la jonction recto-sigmoïdienne, du rectum, de l'anus et du canal anal	*396*	1 155	20.8	1 227	21.6	1 270	21.8	1 187
Malignant neoplasm of liver and intrahepatic bile ducts — Tumeur maligne du foie et des voies bilaires intrahépatiques	*291*	117	2.1	125	2.2	153	2.6	179
Malignant neoplasm of pancreas — Tumeur maligne du pancréas	*125*	453	8.2	452	8.0	434	7.4	488
Malignant neoplasm of trachea, bronchus and lung — Tumeur maligne de la trachée, des bronches et du poumon	*825*	1 167	21.0	1 115	19.6	1 163	20.0	1 174
Malignant neoplasm of female breast — Tumeur maligne du sein chez la femme	*535*	925	▲46.2	888	▲43.1	869	▲40.8	903
Malignant neoplasm of cervix uteri — Tumeur maligne du col de l'utérus	*138*	59	▲2.9	56	▲2.7	46	▲2.2	55
Malignant neoplasm of prostate — Tumeur maligne de la prostate	*90*	455	▼90.9	461	▼88.8	453	▼82.0	478
Malignant neoplasm of lymphoid, haematopoietic and related tissue — Tumeurs malignes primitives ou présumées primitives des tissus lymphoïde, hématopoïétique et apparentés	*192*	869	15.7	982	17.3	927	15.9	1 051
Disorders of the blood and blood-forming organs and certain disorders involving the immune mechanism — Maladies du sang et des organes hématopoïétiques et certains troubles du système immunitaire								
Total	*38*	138	2.5	163	2.9	190	3.3	200
Anaemias — Anémies	*34*	82	1.5	80	1.4	96	1.6	100
Endocrine, nutritional and metabolic diseases — Maladies endocriniennes, nutritionnelles et métaboliques								
Total	*681*	1 250	22.5	1 873	32.9	2 589	44.4	2 627
Diabetes mellitus — Diabète sucré	*676*	1 133	20.4	1 679	29.5	2 331	40.0	2 302
Malnutrition — Malnutrition	-	3	♦0.1	6	♦0.1	7	♦0.1	9
Mental and behavioural disorders — Troubles mentaux et du comportement	*22*	465	8.4	327	5.8	257	4.4	488
Diseases of the nervous system — Maladies du système nerveux	*76*	602	10.9	365	6.4	488	8.4	765
Diseases of the circulatory system — Maladies de l'appareil circulatoire								
Total	*28 337*	15 058	271.6	12 843	225.9	12 440	213.4	13 236
Acute rheumatic fever and chronic rheumatic heart diseases — Rhumatisme articulaire aigu et cardiopathies rhumatismales chroniques	*75*	49	0.9	100	1.8	142	2.4	218
Hypertensive diseases — Maladies hypertensives	*377*	801	14.4	643	11.3	658	11.3	728
Ischaemic heart disease — Cardiopathie ischémique	*15 676*	7 499	135.2	5 925	104.2	6 194	106.3	6 745
Cerebrovascular disease — Maladie cérébrovasculaire	*9 704*	3 099	55.9	3 742	65.8	2 905	49.8	2 660
Diseases of arteries, arterioles and capillaries — Maladies des artères, artérioles et capillaires	*729*	241	4.3	207	3.6	275	4.7	240
Diseases of the respiratory system — Maladies de l'appareil respiratoire								
Total	*940*	1 472	26.5	2 318	40.8	2 575	44.2	2 199
Influenza — Grippe	-	1	0.0	3	♦0.1	3	♦0.1	4
Pneumonia — Pneumopathies	*437*	365	6.6	717	12.6	887	15.2	710
Chronic lower respiratory diseases — Maladies chroniques des voies respiratoires inférieures	*362*	807	14.6	950	16.7	1 007	17.3	975
Diseases of the digestive system — Maladies de l'appareil digestif								
Total	*1 264*	1 251	22.6	1 186	20.9	1 241	21.3	1 112
Gastric and duodenal ulcer — Ulcère de l'estomac et du duodénum	*84*	120	2.2	124	2.2	168	2.9	93

(See notes at end of table. — Voir notes à la fin du tableau.)

	Israel — Israël[8]			Japan — Japon[9]				
Cause of death — Cause de décès	1998	1999		1995		1996		1997
	Rate Taux	Number Nombre	Rate Taux	Number Nombre	Rate Taux	Number Nombre	Rate Taux	Number Nombre
TOTAL	618.9	37 291	608.8	922 139	734.9	896 211	712.7	913 402
Certain infectious and parasitic diseases — Certaines maladies infectieuses et parasitaires								
Total	12.5	1 108	18.1	18 925	15.1	17 742	14.1	18 226
Intestinal infectious diseases — Maladies infectieuses intestinales	0.8	115	1.9	1 097	0.9	1 032	0.8	983
Tuberculosis — Tuberculose	0.8	31	0.5	3 178	2.5	2 858	2.3	2 742
Tetanus — Tétanos	-	-	-	14	0.0	16	0.0	16
Diphtheria — Diphtérie	-	-	-	-	-	-	-	-
Whooping cough — Coqueluche	-	-	-	5	0.0	5	0.0	2
Meningococcal infection — Infection à méningocoques	♦0.1	4	♦0.1	1	0.0	3	0.0	-
Septicaemia — Septicémie	6.8	675	11.0	4 905	3.9	4 912	3.9	5 318
Acute poliomyelitis — Poliomyélite aiguë	-	-	-	-	-	-	-	-
Measles — Rougeole	-	-	-	7	0.0	15	0.0	18
Viral hepatitis — Hépatite virale	1.7	131	2.1	5 029	4.0	4 696	3.7	4 843
Human immunodeficiency virus [HIV] disease — Maladies dues au virus de l'immunodéficience humaine (VIH)	♦0.4	20	♦0.3	56	0.0	76	0.1	75
Malaria — Paludisme		1	0.0	-	-	-	-	1
Neoplasms — Tumeurs	153.9	8 959	146.3	270 293	215.4	278 843	221.7	283 516
Malignant neoplasms — Tumeurs malignes								
Total	148.5	8 614	140.6	263 022	209.6	271 183	215.6	275 413
Malignant neoplasm of lip, oral cavity and pharynx — Tumeur maligne de la lèvre, de la cavité buccale et du pharynx	1.6	78	1.3	4 099	3.3	4 347	3.5	4 563
Malignant neoplasm of oesophagus — Tumeur maligne de l'oesophage	1.4	96	1.6	8 638	6.9	9 138	7.3	9 599
Malignant neoplasm of stomach — Tumeur maligne de l'estomac	8.2	463	7.6	50 076	39.9	50 165	39.9	49 739
Malignant neoplasm of colon, rectosigmoid junction, rectum, anus and anal canal — Tumeur maligne du côlon, de la jonction recto-sigmoïdienne, du rectum, de l'anus et du canal anal	19.9	1 199	19.6	31 502	25.1	32 819	26.1	33 413
Malignant neoplasm of liver and intrahepatic bile ducts — Tumeur maligne du foie et des voies bilaires intrahépatiques	3.0	216	3.5	31 707	25.3	32 175	25.6	32 359
Malignant neoplasm of pancreas — Tumeur maligne du pancréas	8.2	524	8.6	16 019	12.8	16 613	13.2	17 006
Malignant neoplasm of trachea, bronchus and lung — Tumeur maligne de la trachée, des bronches et du poumon	19.7	1 218	19.9	45 745	36.5	48 041	38.2	48 994
Malignant neoplasm of female breast — Tumeur maligne du sein chez la femme	▲41.3	918	▲40.9	7 763	...	7 900	▲14.5	8 393
Malignant neoplasm of cervix uteri — Tumeur maligne du col de l'utérus	▲2.5	48	▲2.1	2 268	...	2 219	▲4.1	2 241
Malignant neoplasm of prostate — Tumeur maligne de la prostate	▼83.3	423	▼71.1	5 399	...	6 009	▼30.5	6 251
Malignant neoplasm of lymphoid, haematopoietic and related tissue — Tumeurs malignes primitives ou présumées primitives des tissus lymphoïde, hématopoïétique et apparentés	17.6	994	16.2	15 479	12.3	16 035	12.8	16 338
Disorders of the blood and blood-forming organs and certain disorders involving the immune mechanism — Maladies du sang et des organes hématopoïétiques et certains troubles du système immunitaire								
Total	3.3	377	6.2	4 106	3.3	4 019	3.2	4 102
Anaemias — Anémies	1.7	244	4.0	1 652	1.3	1 749	1.4	1 808
Endocrine, nutritional and metabolic diseases — Maladies endocriniennes, nutritionnelles et métaboliques								
Total	44.0	2 822	46.1	19 360	15.4	17 152	13.6	16 692
Diabetes mellitus — Diabète sucré	38.6	2 245	36.7	14 225	11.3	12 838	10.2	12 370
Malnutrition — Malnutrition	♦0.2	22	♦0.4	1 037	0.8	919	0.7	936
Mental and behavioural disorders — Troubles mentaux et du comportement	8.2	807	13.2	3 762	3.0	3 299	2.6	3 220
Diseases of the nervous system — Maladies du système nerveux	12.8	1 019	16.6	8 625	6.9	8 385	6.7	8 692
Diseases of the circulatory system — Maladies de l'appareil circulatoire								
Total	221.7	11 637	190.0	304 824	242.9	296 610	235.9	297 055
Acute rheumatic fever and chronic rheumatic heart diseases — Rhumatisme articularie aigu et cardiopathies rhumatismales chroniques	3.7	179	2.9	2 811	2.2	2 568	2.0	2 488
Hypertensive diseases — Maladies hypertensives	12.2	738	12.0	8 222	6.6	7 245	5.8	6 884
Ischaemic heart disease — Cardiopathie ischémique	113.0	5 799	94.7	75 573	60.2	71 884	57.2	71 717
Cerebrovascular disease — Maladie cérébrovasculaire	44.6	2 273	37.1	146 552	116.8	140 366	111.6	138 697
Diseases of arteries, arterioles and capillaries — Maladies des artères, artérioles et capillaires	4.0	339	5.5	8 635	6.9	8 644	6.9	8 927
Diseases of the respiratory system — Maladies de l'appareil respiratoire								
Total	36.8	2 682	43.8	126 661	100.9	113 372	90.2	123 148
Influenza — Grippe	♦0.1	5	♦0.1	1 244	1.0	166	0.1	815
Pneumonia — Pneumopathies	11.9	637	10.4	79 629	63.5	70 971	56.4	78 904
Chronic lower respiratory diseases — Maladies chroniques des voies respiratoires inférieures	16.3	1 213	19.8	22 690	18.1	19 615	15.6	19 640
Diseases of the digestive system — Maladies de l'appareil digestif								
Total	18.6	1 285	21.0	38 726	30.9	37 437	29.8	37 463
Gastric and duodenal ulcer — Ulcère de l'estomac et du duodénum	1.6	78	1.3	4 314	3.4	3 918	3.1	3 876

(See notes at end of table. — Voir notes à la fin du tableau.)

	Japan — Japon[9]							Kazakhstan[6]
	1997	1998		1999		2000		1995
Cause of death — Cause de décès	Rate Taux	Number Nombre	Rate Taux	Number Nombre	Rate Taux	Number Nombre	Rate Taux	Number Nombre
TOTAL	724.6	936 484	740.9	982 031	775.5	961 653	758.1	168 884
Certain infectious and parasitic diseases — Certaines maladies infectieuses et parasitaires								
Total	14.5	18 845	14.9	20 281	16.0	19 858	15.7	6 784
Intestinal infectious diseases — Maladies infectieuses intestinales	0.8	1 047	0.8	1 177	0.9	1 212	1.0	1 316
Tuberculosis — Tuberculose	2.2	2 795	2.2	2 935	2.3	2 656	2.1	4 433
Tetanus — Tétanos	0.0	9	0.0	10	0.0	10	0.0	10
Diphtheria — Diphtérie	-	-	-	-	-	1	0.0	52
Whooping cough — Coqueluche	0.0	-	-	2	0.0	1	0.0	2
Meningococcal infection — Infection à méningocoques	-	2	0.0	1	0.0	3	0.0	115
Septicaemia — Septicémie	4.2	5 742	4.5	6 125	4.8	6 216	4.9	496
Acute poliomyelitis — Poliomyélite aiguë	-	-	-	-	-	-	-	12
Measles — Rougeole	0.0	25	0.0	29	0.0	18	0.0	...
Viral hepatitis — Hépatite virale	3.8	4 869	3.9	5 184	4.1	5 121	4.0	146
Human immunodeficiency virus [HIV] disease — Maladies dues au virus de l'immunodéficience humaine (VIH)	0.1	48	0.0	45	0.0	50	0.0	...
Malaria — Paludisme	0.0	4	0.0	6	0.0	1	0.0	...
Neoplasms — Tumeurs	224.9	292 447	231.4	299 323	236.4	304 489	240.1	22 207
Malignant neoplasms — Tumeurs malignes								
Total	218.5	283 921	224.6	290 556	229.5	295 484	233.0	22 093
Malignant neoplasm of lip, oral cavity and pharynx — Tumeur maligne de la lèvre, de la cavité buccale et du pharynx	3.6	4 770	3.8	4 846	3.8	5 066	4.0	690
Malignant neoplasm of oesophagus — Tumeur maligne de l'oesophage	7.6	9 705	7.7	9 991	7.9	10 256	8.1	1 982
Malignant neoplasm of stomach — Tumeur maligne de l'estomac	39.5	50 680	40.1	50 676	40.0	50 650	39.9	3 269
Malignant neoplasm of colon, rectosigmoid junction, rectum, anus and anal canal — Tumeur maligne du côlon, de la jonction recto-sigmoïdienne, du rectum, de l'anus et du canal anal	26.5	34 636	27.4	35 613	28.1	36 203	28.5	1 523
Malignant neoplasm of liver and intrahepatic bile ducts — Tumeur maligne du foie et des voies bilaires intrahépatiques	25.7	33 433	26.5	33 816	26.7	33 981	26.8	...
Malignant neoplasm of pancreas — Tumeur maligne du pancréas	13.5	17 643	14.0	18 654	14.7	19 094	15.1	...
Malignant neoplasm of trachea, bronchus and lung — Tumeur maligne de la trachée, des bronches et du poumon	38.9	50 871	40.2	52 177	41.2	53 724	42.4	4 604
Malignant neoplasm of female breast — Tumeur maligne du sein chez la femme	▲15.3	8 589	▲15.5	8 882	▲16.0	9 171	...	1 124
Malignant neoplasm of cervix uteri — Tumeur maligne du col de l'utérus	▲4.1	2 266	▲4.1	2 260	▲4.1	2 393	...	533
Malignant neoplasm of prostate — Tumeur maligne de la prostate	▼30.6	6 819	▼32.3	7 005	▼32.2	7 514	...	293
Malignant neoplasm of lymphoid, haematopoietic and related tissue — Tumeurs malignes primitives ou présumées primitives des tissus lymphoïde, hématopoïétique et apparentés	13.0	16 991	13.4	17 666	14.0	18 109	14.3	955
Disorders of the blood and blood-forming organs and certain disorders involving the immune mechanism — Maladies du sang et des organes hématopoïétiques et certains troubles du système immunitaire								
Total	3.3	4 154	3.3	4 198	3.3	4 057	3.2	164
Anaemias — Anémies	1.4	1 778	1.4	1 775	1.4	1 707	1.3	101
Endocrine, nutritional and metabolic diseases — Maladies endocriniennes, nutritionnelles et métaboliques								
Total	13.2	17 153	13.6	17 761	14.0	17 110	13.5	1 946
Diabetes mellitus — Diabète sucré	9.8	12 537	9.9	12 814	10.1	12 303	9.7	1 771
Malnutrition — Malnutrition	0.7	1 102	0.9	1 213	1.0	1 227	1.0	...
Mental and behavioural disorders — Troubles mentaux et du comportement	2.6	3 287	2.6	3 613	2.9	3 920	3.1	803
Diseases of the nervous system — Maladies du système nerveux	6.9	8 749	6.9	9 570	7.6	9 567	7.5	1 565
Diseases of the circulatory system — Maladies de l'appareil circulatoire								
Total	235.7	299 671	237.1	309 381	244.3	298 338	235.2	80 421
Acute rheumatic fever and chronic rheumatic heart diseases — Rhumatisme articularie aigu et cardiopathies rhumatismales chroniques	2.0	2 524	2.0	2 576	2.0	2 530	2.0	1 086
Hypertensive diseases — Maladies hypertensives	5.5	6 716	5.3	6 650	5.3	6 063	4.8	3 334
Ischaemic heart disease — Cardiopathie ischémique	56.9	71 678	56.7	73 927	58.4	70 183	55.3	42 117
Cerebrovascular disease — Maladie cérébrovasculaire	110.0	137 819	109.0	138 989	109.8	132 529	104.5	23 892
Diseases of arteries, arterioles and capillaries — Maladies des artères, artérioles et capillaires	7.1	9 550	7.6	10 136	8.0	10 401	8.2	3 771
Diseases of the respiratory system — Maladies de l'appareil respiratoire								
Total	97.7	124 551	98.5	144 320	114.0	134 501	106.0	15 644
Influenza — Grippe	0.6	528	0.4	1 382	1.1	575	0.5	171
Pneumonia — Pneumopathies	62.6	79 952	63.3	93 994	74.2	86 938	68.5	4 538
Chronic lower respiratory diseases — Maladies chroniques des voies respiratoires inférieures	15.6	19 084	15.1	20 593	16.3	19 155	15.1	7 769
Diseases of the digestive system — Maladies de l'appareil digestif								
Total	29.7	37 065	29.3	38 866	30.7	38 268	30.2	5 692
Gastric and duodenal ulcer — Ulcère de l'estomac et du duodénum	3.1	3 871	3.1	4 053	3.2	3 869	3.1	527

21. Death and death rates by cause: 1995 - 2002
Décès selon la cause, nombres et taux: 1995 - 2002 (continued — suite)

(See notes at end of table. — Voir notes à la fin du tableau.)

Cause of death — Cause de décès	Kazakhstan[6]							Korea, Republic of — Corée, République de
	1996	1997	1998	1999	2000	2001	2002	1995
	Number Nombre							
TOTAL	166 028	160 138	154 314	145 792	148 855	147 547	148 700	238 132
Certain infectious and parasitic diseases — Certaines maladies infectieuses et parasitaires								
Total	7 643	7 908	7 460	5 691	5 057	4 532	4 583	5 265
Intestinal infectious diseases — Maladies infectieuses intestinales	954	1 055	612	431	347	241	172	229
Tuberculosis — Tuberculose	5 697	5 934	6 015	4 531	3 899	3 612	3 748	3 929
Tetanus — Tétanos	9	3	5	3	3	3	...	12
Diphtheria — Diphtérie	32	23	7	1	2	2	2	-
Whooping cough — Coqueluche	2	3	2	1	3	1	1	-
Meningococcal infection — Infection à méningocoques	112	89	68	67	77	57	54	5
Septicaemia — Septicémie	471	457	366	325	377	346	319	669
Acute poliomyelitis — Poliomyélite aiguë	10	3	5	1	4	4	2	1
Measles — Rougeole	...	...	2	3	...	5	2	14
Viral hepatitis — Hépatite virale	186	198	187	167	180	123	135	197
Human immunodeficiency virus [HIV] disease — Maladies dues au virus de l'immunodéficience humaine (VIH)	...	...	...	...	...	...	...	13
Malaria — Paludisme	1	...	...	3	2	1	2	5
Neoplasms — Tumeurs	21 321	20 759	20 198	19 496	19 333	19 173	18 989	50 713
Malignant neoplasms — Tumeurs malignes								
Total	21 175	20 573	20 047	19 348	19 196	19 047	18 856	50 107
Malignant neoplasm of lip, oral cavity and pharynx — Tumeur maligne de la lèvre, de la cavité buccale et du pharynx	524	530	489	523	488	524	522	515
Malignant neoplasm of oesophagus — Tumeur maligne de l'oesophage	1 840	1 680	1 722	1 586	1 474	1 511	1 417	1 453
Malignant neoplasm of stomach — Tumeur maligne de l'estomac	3 163	2 991	2 834	2 793	2 716	2 642	2 594	11 997
Malignant neoplasm of colon, rectosigmoid junction, rectum, anus and anal canal — Tumeur maligne du côlon, de la jonction recto-sigmoïdienne, du rectum, de l'anus et du canal anal	1 523	1 640	1 491	1 508	1 515	1 521	1 461	2 648
Malignant neoplasm of liver and intrahepatic bile ducts — Tumeur maligne du foie et des voies bilaires intrahépatiques	...	...	...	...	...	...	...	9 963
Malignant neoplasm of pancreas — Tumeur maligne du pancréas	...	...	...	...	...	...	...	1 932
Malignant neoplasm of trachea, bronchus and lung — Tumeur maligne de la trachée, des bronches et du poumon	4 370	4 180	4 127	3 856	3 779	3 627	3 668	8 550
Malignant neoplasm of female breast — Tumeur maligne du sein chez la femme	1 231	1 276	1 240	1 283	1 324	1 289	1 317	905
Malignant neoplasm of cervix uteri — Tumeur maligne du col de l'utérus	600	571	546	554	581	539	522	544
Malignant neoplasm of prostate — Tumeur maligne de la prostate	291	283	270	274	297	286	325	269
Malignant neoplasm of lymphoid, haematopoietic and related tissue — Tumeurs malignes primitives ou présumées primitives des tissus lymphoïde, hématopoïétique et apparentés	921	867	945	892	898	910	931	2 596
Disorders of the blood and blood-forming organs and certain disorders involving the immune mechanism — Maladies du sang et des organes hématopoïétiques et certains troubles du système immunitaire								
Total	162	171	145	145	133	152	123	412
Anaemias — Anémies	108	124	109	101	98	110	83	275
Endocrine, nutritional and metabolic diseases — Maladies endocriniennes, nutritionnelles et métaboliques								
Total	1 951	1 977	1 610	1 679	1 449	1 485	1 618	8 466
Diabetes mellitus — Diabète sucré	1 729	1 724	1 432	1 532	1 315	1 311	1 473	7 789
Malnutrition — Malnutrition	...	...	...	...	...	...	...	181
Mental and behavioural disorders — Troubles mentaux et du comportement	821	1 048	725	579	480	510	569	5 148
Diseases of the nervous system — Maladies du système nerveux	1 488	1 578	1 433	1 356	1 361	1 461	1 285	2 230
Diseases of the circulatory system — Maladies de l'appareil circulatoire								
Total	79 013	76 336	75 150	73 049	74 422	73 549	75 447	62 718
Acute rheumatic fever and chronic rheumatic heart diseases — Rhumatisme articularie aigu et cardiopathies rhumatismales chroniques	1 027	954	880	796	747	726	681	206
Hypertensive diseases — Maladies hypertensives	3 897	3 548	2 973	3 103	3 162	4 382	4 699	8 276
Ischaemic heart disease — Cardiopathie ischémique	42 238	39 173	37 691	36 436	37 786	37 817	39 143	5 922
Cerebrovascular disease — Maladie cérébrovasculaire	22 884	22 645	23 043	21 694	22 389	20 421	20 241	36 061
Diseases of arteries, arterioles and capillaries — Maladies des artères, artérioles et capillaires	3 121	3 501	2 514	3 207	2 919	3 121	3 316	1 050
Diseases of the respiratory system — Maladies de l'appareil respiratoire								
Total	14 428	12 741	11 290	10 132	10 566	9 716	9 785	11 014
Influenza — Grippe	190	94	45	50	72	34	37	156
Pneumonia — Pneumopathies	4 004	3 667	3 135	2 672	2 981	2 946	2 908	1 909
Chronic lower respiratory diseases — Maladies chroniques des voies respiratoires inférieures	7 356	6 480	5 875	1 215	5 786	5 029	5 541	6 763
Diseases of the digestive system — Maladies de l'appareil digestif								
Total	5 917	5 891	5 545	5 315	5 631	6 025	6 275	17 734
Gastric and duodenal ulcer — Ulcère de l'estomac et du duodénum	571	603	566	152	525	557	486	817

(See notes at end of table. — Voir notes à la fin du tableau.)

Cause of death — Cause de décès	Korea, Republic of — Corée, République de						Kuwait — Koweït	
	1996	1997	1998	1999	2000	2001	1995	1996
	Number Nombre							
TOTAL	*236 234*	*238 714*	*240 267*	*243 948*	*244 874*	*240 876*	*3 781*	*3 812*
Certain infectious and parasitic diseases — Certaines maladies infectieuses et parasitaires								
Total	*4 921*	*4 966*	*6 072*	*5 534*	*6 200*	*5 781*	*107*	*99*
Intestinal infectious diseases — Maladies infectieuses intestinales	*174*	*189*	*198*	*177*	*271*	*205*	*2*	*-*
Tuberculosis — Tuberculose	*3 527*	*3 455*	*3 478*	*3 297*	*3 413*	*3 221*	*20*	*11*
Tetanus — Tétanos	*8*	*14*	*10*	*11*	*11*	*15*	*-*	*-*
Diphtheria — Diphtérie	*1*	*-*	*-*	*-*	*-*	*-*	*-*	*-*
Whooping cough — Coqueluche	*-*	*-*	*-*	*-*	*-*	*-*	*-*	*-*
Meningococcal infection — Infection à méningocoques	*6*	*2*	*2*	*2*	*4*	*3*	*2*	*2*
Septicaemia — Septicémie	*794*	*871*	*1 833*	*1 464*	*1 712*	*1 356*	*51*	*47*
Acute poliomyelitis — Poliomyélite aiguë	*-*	*2*	*-*	*-*	*-*	*-*	*-*	*-*
Measles — Rougeole	*3*	*5*	*2*	*3*	*14*	*16*	*-*	*-*
Viral hepatitis — Hépatite virale	*218*	*212*	*243*	*282*	*387*	*468*	*9*	*13*
Human immunodeficiency virus [HIV] disease — Maladies dues au virus de l'immunodéficience humaine (VIH)	*21*	*18*	*25*	*25*	*28*	*38*	*1*	*-*
Malaria — Paludisme	*5*	*2*	*3*	*2*	*6*	*7*	*-*	*-*
Neoplasms — Tumeurs	*51 218*	*53 096*	*51 449*	*55 005*	*59 020*	*60 086*	*410*	*410*
Malignant neoplasms — Tumeurs malignes								
Total	*50 402*	*52 187*	*50 731*	*54 090*	*58 042*	*59 119*	*374*	*386*
Malignant neoplasm of lip, oral cavity and pharynx — Tumeur maligne de la lèvre, de la cavité buccale et du pharynx	*545*	*516*	*482*	*506*	*1 056*	*729*	*6*	*7*
Malignant neoplasm of oesophagus — Tumeur maligne de l'oesophage	*1 381*	*1 501*	*1 380*	*1 426*	*1 511*	*1 433*	*4*	*11*
Malignant neoplasm of stomach — Tumeur maligne de l'estomac	*11 680*	*11 804*	*11 102*	*11 309*	*11 550*	*11 483*	*14*	*22*
Malignant neoplasm of colon, rectosigmoid junction, rectum, anus and anal canal — Tumeur maligne du côlon, de la jonction recto-sigmoïdienne, du rectum, de l'anus et du canal anal	*2 879*	*3 180*	*3 235*	*3 714*	*4 221*	*4 580*	*15*	*18*
Malignant neoplasm of liver and intrahepatic bile ducts — Tumeur maligne du foie et des voies bilaires intrahépatiques	*9 797*	*9 760*	*9 302*	*9 747*	*10 118*	*10 215*	*31*	*37*
Malignant neoplasm of pancreas — Tumeur maligne du pancréas	*1 997*	*2 317*	*2 214*	*2 535*	*2 720*	*2 845*	*19*	*12*
Malignant neoplasm of trachea, bronchus and lung — Tumeur maligne de la trachée, des bronches et du poumon	*8 893*	*9 567*	*9 583*	*10 417*	*11 606*	*11 971*	*54*	*59*
Malignant neoplasm of female breast — Tumeur maligne du sein chez la femme	*983*	*976*	*975*	*1 131*	*1 150*	*1 199*	*39*	*39*
Malignant neoplasm of cervix uteri — Tumeur maligne du col de l'utérus	*656*	*680*	*606*	*690*	*729*	*807*	*-*	*3*
Malignant neoplasm of prostate — Tumeur maligne de la prostate	*304*	*340*	*363*	*431*	*548*	*640*	*9*	*15*
Malignant neoplasm of lymphoid, haematopoietic and related tissue — Tumeurs malignes primitives ou présumées primitives des tissus lymphoïde, hématopoïétique et apparentés	*2 582*	*2 544*	*2 222*	*2 667*	*2 777*	*2 789*	*52*	*39*
Disorders of the blood and blood-forming organs and certain disorders involving the immune mechanism — Maladies du sang et des organes hématopoïétiques et certains troubles du système immunitaire								
Total	*397*	*380*	*501*	*473*	*481*	*457*	*21*	*13*
Anaemias — Anémies	*269*	*263*	*336*	*326*	*330*	*293*	*16*	*10*
Endocrine, nutritional and metabolic diseases — Maladies endocriniennes, nutritionnelles et métaboliques								
Total	*8 554*	*9 305*	*10 824*	*11 145*	*11 806*	*12 299*	*127*	*188*
Diabetes mellitus — Diabète sucré	*7 957*	*8 684*	*9 793*	*10 296*	*10 746*	*11 403*	*120*	*185*
Malnutrition — Malnutrition	*156*	*173*	*387*	*242*	*225*	*172*	*-*	*-*
Mental and behavioural disorders — Troubles mentaux et du comportement	*5 967*	*6 515*	*7 288*	*6 769*	*6 432*	*6 408*	*1*	*7*
Diseases of the nervous system — Maladies du système nerveux	*2 127*	*2 361*	*2 476*	*2 195*	*2 858*	*3 046*	*57*	*68*
Diseases of the circulatory system — Maladies de l'appareil circulatoire								
Total	*58 130*	*55 893*	*57 443*	*57 531*	*58 554*	*57 837*	*1 413*	*1 410*
Acute rheumatic fever and chronic rheumatic heart diseases — Rhumatisme articularie aigu et cardiopathies rhumatismales chroniques	*104*	*93*	*80*	*104*	*164*	*162*	*2*	*-*
Hypertensive diseases — Maladies hypertensives	*6 343*	*4 444*	*3 899*	*3 568*	*4 238*	*4 875*	*252*	*312*
Ischaemic heart disease — Cardiopathie ischémique	*5 934*	*6 340*	*7 573*	*8 727*	*10 219*	*10 504*	*716*	*646*
Cerebrovascular disease — Maladie cérébrovasculaire	*34 187*	*33 845*	*34 357*	*34 410*	*34 817*	*35 354*	*135*	*167*
Diseases of arteries, arterioles and capillaries — Maladies des artères, artérioles et capillaires	*847*	*763*	*708*	*725*	*764*	*876*	*72*	*61*
Diseases of the respiratory system — Maladies de l'appareil respiratoire								
Total	*10 613*	*11 228*	*12 440*	*13 011*	*16 105*	*15 680*	*208*	*189*
Influenza — Grippe	*87*	*140*	*114*	*151*	*171*	*134*	*-*	*-*
Pneumonia — Pneumopathies	*1 900*	*2 271*	*3 022*	*3 202*	*3 900*	*2 908*	*151*	*135*
Chronic lower respiratory diseases — Maladies chroniques des voies respiratoires inférieures	*6 412*	*6 281*	*5 904*	*6 465*	*7 967*	*9 112*	*36*	*41*
Diseases of the digestive system — Maladies de l'appareil digestif								
Total	*16 506*	*15 841*	*15 747*	*14 920*	*14 901*	*14 415*	*81*	*82*
Gastric and duodenal ulcer — Ulcère de l'estomac et du duodénum	*767*	*677*	*691*	*631*	*714*	*670*	*13*	*9*

(See notes at end of table. — Voir notes à la fin du tableau.)

Cause of death — Cause de décès	Kuwait — Koweït						Kyrgyzstan — Kirghizistan[6]	
	1997	1998	1999	2000	2001	2002	1995	1996
				Number Nombre				
TOTAL	4 017	4 215	4 186	4 227	4 364	4 342	36 916	34 562
Certain infectious and parasitic diseases — Certaines maladies infectieuses et parasitaires								
Total	97	141	129	98	91	118	1 547	1 363
Intestinal infectious diseases — Maladies infectieuses intestinales	-	5	2	6	4	3	616	432
Tuberculosis — Tuberculose	19	8	21	14	17	23	555	576
Diphtheria — Diphtérie	-	-	-	-	-	-	-	-
Whooping cough — Coqueluche	2	-	-	-	-	-	2	1
Meningococcal infection — Infection à méningocoques	-	-	-	-	-	-	77	113
Septicaemia — Septicémie	47	84	71	38	32	48	90	62
Acute poliomyelitis — Poliomyélite aiguë	-	-	-	-	-	-	...	...
Measles — Rougeole	-	-	-	-	-	-	1	1
Viral hepatitis — Hépatite virale	8	19	23	23	23	25	...	...
Human immunodeficiency virus [HIV] disease — Maladies dues au virus de l'immunodéficience humaine (VIH)	-	-	-	-	-	2	...	...
Malaria — Paludisme	-	-	-	-	-	1	...	...
Neoplasms — Tumeurs	426	461	466	519	531	552	2 860	2 867
Malignant neoplasms — Tumeurs malignes								
Total	411	443	447	498	509	529	2 826	2 818
Malignant neoplasm of lip, oral cavity and pharynx — Tumeur maligne de la lèvre, de la cavité buccale et du pharynx	3	8	10	10	9	10	76	65
Malignant neoplasm of oesophagus — Tumeur maligne de l'oesophage	10	11	8	13	7	11	165	220
Malignant neoplasm of stomach — Tumeur maligne de l'estomac	14	15	13	25	16	20	597	586
Malignant neoplasm of colon, rectosigmoid junction, rectum, anus and anal canal — Tumeur maligne du côlon, de la jonction recto-sigmoïdienne, du rectum, de l'anus et du canal anal	23	39	20	46	47	40	169	181
Malignant neoplasm of liver and intrahepatic bile ducts — Tumeur maligne du foie et des voies bilaires intrahépatiques	41	40	48	38	44	58	...	...
Malignant neoplasm of pancreas — Tumeur maligne du pancréas	18	18	19	25	21	17	...	...
Malignant neoplasm of trachea, bronchus and lung — Tumeur maligne de la trachée, des bronches et du poumon	70	67	56	70	58	61	437	413
Malignant neoplasm of female breast — Tumeur maligne du sein chez la femme	37	44	50	49	71	89	190	179
Malignant neoplasm of cervix uteri — Tumeur maligne du col de l'utérus	5	3	4	5	2	6	109	131
Malignant neoplasm of prostate — Tumeur maligne de la prostate	17	14	8	12	15	11	49	48
Malignant neoplasm of lymphoid, haematopoietic and related tissue — Tumeurs malignes primitives ou présumées primitives des tissus lymphoïde, hématopoïétique et apparentés	58	72	85	79	71	90	163	140
Disorders of the blood and blood-forming organs and certain disorders involving the immune mechanism — Maladies du sang et des organes hématopoïétiques et certains troubles du système immunitaire								
Total	10	7	20	20	23	22	59	85
Anaemias — Anémies	8	5	13	11	14	11	43	71
Endocrine, nutritional and metabolic diseases — Maladies endocriniennes, nutritionnelles et métaboliques								
Total	192	234	212	243	255	260	391	400
Diabetes mellitus — Diabète sucré	184	215	196	228	242	246	365	383
Malnutrition — Malnutrition	-	-	-	-	-	-	...	...
Mental and behavioural disorders — Troubles mentaux et du comportement	3	4	5	1	5	9	190	193
Diseases of the nervous system — Maladies du système nerveux	49	68	56	73	73	78	497	477
Diseases of the circulatory system — Maladies de l'appareil circulatoire								
Total	1 531	1 705	1 713	1 689	1 752	1 711	14 558	13 794
Acute rheumatic fever and chronic rheumatic heart diseases — Rhumatisme articulaire aigu et cardiopathies rhumatismales chroniques	-	9	12	3	4	11	288	214
Hypertensive diseases — Maladies hypertensives	344	395	429	450	462	490	314	263
Ischaemic heart disease — Cardiopathie ischémique	744	759	748	642	694	694	6 898	7 032
Cerebrovascular disease — Maladie cérébrovasculaire	152	175	159	200	201	171	5 930	5 459
Diseases of arteries, arterioles and capillaries — Maladies des artères, artérioles et capillaires	37	73	61	70	85	75	87	89
Diseases of the respiratory system — Maladies de l'appareil respiratoire								
Total	199	217	183	203	217	221	5 725	5 086
Influenza — Grippe	-	-	-	1	-	-	39	50
Pneumonia — Pneumopathies	141	154	139	126	141	127	1 821	1 485
Chronic lower respiratory diseases — Maladies chroniques des voies respiratoires inférieures	50	42	32	58	55	77	...	...
Diseases of the digestive system — Maladies de l'appareil digestif								
Total	86	78	104	103	110	111	1 733	1 668
Gastric and duodenal ulcer — Ulcère de l'estomac et du duodénum	5	4	5	7	8	9	130	156

21. Death and death rates by cause: 1995 - 2002
Décès selon la cause, nombres et taux: 1995 - 2002 (continued — suite)

(See notes at end of table. — Voir notes à la fin du tableau.)

Cause of death — Cause de décès	Kyrgyzstan — Kirghizistan[6]						Philippines	
	1997	1998	1999	2000	2001	2002	1995	1996
				Number Nombre				
TOTAL	34 540	34 596	32 851	34 113	32 677	35 235	324 737	344 363
Certain infectious and parasitic diseases — Certaines maladies infectieuses et parasitaires								
Total	1 845	1 827	1 688	1 665	1 678	1 414	43 730	46 823
Intestinal infectious diseases — Maladies infectieuses intestinales	708	647	532	368	305	245	5 552	6 203
Tuberculosis — Tuberculose	717	813	881	1 019	1 170	1 003	27 048	27 404
Tetanus — Tétanos	-	1	-	2	-	-	803	758
Diphtheria — Diphtérie	...	...	...	1	2	2	40	29
Whooping cough — Coqueluche	-	2	1	1	2	1	12	9
Meningococcal infection — Infection à méningocoques	52	26	18	29	13	17	159	167
Septicaemia — Septicémie	72	91	62	87	76	37	4 455	4 125
Acute poliomyelitis — Poliomyélite aiguë	...	...	...	-	-	-	15	40
Measles — Rougeole	3	5	1	-	-	-	1 121	2 448
Viral hepatitis — Hépatite virale	...	...	...	85	64	64	1 152	1 084
Human immunodeficiency virus [HIV] disease — Maladies dues au virus de l'immunodéficience humaine (VIH)	...	...	...	-	-	1	...	-
Malaria — Paludisme	-	2	-	-	-	-	643	536
Neoplasms — Tumeurs	2 911	2 985	2 990	3 019	2 941	3 061	28 459	30 299
Malignant neoplasms — Tumeurs malignes								
Total	2 861	2 932	2 927	2 964	2 878	2 998	28 214	30 037
Malignant neoplasm of lip, oral cavity and pharynx — Tumeur maligne de la lèvre, de la cavité buccale et du pharynx	67	64	81	83	100	99	1 641	1 727
Malignant neoplasm of oesophagus — Tumeur maligne de l'oesophage	118	184	153	140	130	137	400	329
Malignant neoplasm of stomach — Tumeur maligne de l'estomac	614	661	583	564	556	549	1 336	1 435
Malignant neoplasm of colon, rectosigmoid junction, rectum, anus and anal canal — Tumeur maligne du côlon, de la jonction recto-sigmoïdienne, du rectum, de l'anus et du canal anal	196	201	193	214	207	245	1 397	1 557
Malignant neoplasm of liver and intrahepatic bile ducts — Tumeur maligne du foie et des voies bilaires intrahépatiques	...	...	...	193	199	191	...	...
Malignant neoplasm of pancreas — Tumeur maligne du pancréas	...	...	...	117	125	103	603	621
Malignant neoplasm of trachea, bronchus and lung — Tumeur maligne de la trachée, des bronches et du poumon	429	411	410	400	400	438	4 753	5 300
Malignant neoplasm of female breast — Tumeur maligne du sein chez la femme	186	168	202	181	193	204	2 386	2 426
Malignant neoplasm of cervix uteri — Tumeur maligne du col de l'utérus	127	126	141	140	123	157	571	562
Malignant neoplasm of prostate — Tumeur maligne de la prostate	43	54	59	70	46	60	616	671
Malignant neoplasm of lymphoid, haematopoietic and related tissue — Tumeurs malignes primitives ou présumées primitives des tissus lymphoïde, hématopoïétique et apparentés	175	196	193	178	157	160	2 390	2 608
Disorders of the blood and blood-forming organs and certain disorders involving the immune mechanism — Maladies du sang et des organes hématopoïétiques et certains troubles du système immunitaire								
Total	79	94	83	78	64	59	2 656	2 801
Anaemias — Anémies	60	58	62	53	37	43	2 128	2 210
Endocrine, nutritional and metabolic diseases — Maladies endocriniennes, nutritionnelles et métaboliques								
Total	316	371	314	381	290	324	11 557	12 901
Diabetes mellitus — Diabète sucré	280	326	284	358	271	294	6 724	7 677
Malnutrition — Malnutrition	...	...	...	14	9	21	1 951	1 929
Mental and behavioural disorders — Troubles mentaux et du comportement	173	163	172	131	133	138	810	1 301
Diseases of the nervous system — Maladies du système nerveux	450	473	488	516	495	586	4 397	4 781
Diseases of the circulatory system — Maladies de l'appareil circulatoire								
Total	13 723	14 130	13 947	15 409	15 255	16 782	88 844	95 375
Acute rheumatic fever and chronic rheumatic heart diseases — Rhumatisme articularie aigu et cardiopathies rhumatismales chroniques	270	289	271	256	273	258	2 217	2 541
Hypertensive diseases — Maladies hypertensives	369	397	450	385	385	373	21 052	23 666
Ischaemic heart disease — Cardiopathie ischémique	6 992	7 175	6 854	7 632	7 630	8 670	27 718	29 176
Cerebrovascular disease — Maladie cérébrovasculaire	5 387	5 521	5 768	5 951	6 022	6 386	19 273	20 515
Diseases of arteries, arterioles and capillaries — Maladies des artères, artérioles et capillaires	74	62	75	222	113	80	2 956	2 854
Diseases of the respiratory system — Maladies de l'appareil respiratoire								
Total	5 270	5 207	4 608	4 427	3 723	4 146	52 310	53 703
Influenza — Grippe	35	27	17	288	40	24	313	340
Pneumonia — Pneumopathies	1 743	1 765	1 339	1 345	1 036	1 046	33 637	33 242
Chronic lower respiratory diseases — Maladies chroniques des voies respiratoires inférieures	...	...	...	2 401	2 208	2 695	11 309	12 482
Diseases of the digestive system — Maladies de l'appareil digestif								
Total	1 924	1 790	1 761	1 901	1 875	2 098	14 682	15 698
Gastric and duodenal ulcer — Ulcère de l'estomac et du duodénum	184	153	133	157	131	126	5 455	5 724

21. Death and death rates by cause: 1995 - 2002
Décès selon la cause, nombres et taux: 1995 - 2002 (continued — suite)

(See notes at end of table. — Voir notes à la fin du tableau.)

Cause of death — Cause de décès	Philippines		Qatar	Singapore — Singapour[10]				
	1997	1998	1995	1996	1997	1998	1999	
			Number Nombre					
TOTAL	339 400	352 992	*1 000*	*14 461*	*14 427*	*14 127*	*14 546*	*14 490*
Certain infectious and parasitic diseases — Certaines maladies infectieuses et parasitaires								
Total	43 097	48 013	34	342	326	286	336	283
Intestinal infectious diseases — Maladies infectieuses intestinales	4 484	6 325	-	25	27	20	20	25
Tuberculosis — Tuberculose	26 150	28 038	15	114	123	107	123	99
Tetanus — Tétanos	684	751	-	-	-	-	-	-
Diphtheria — Diphtérie	30	22	-	-	-	-	-	-
Whooping cough — Coqueluche	6	6	-	-	-	-	-	-
Meningococcal infection — Infection à méningocoques	168	137	-	-	1	2	-	1
Septicaemia — Septicémie	4 617	5 723	2	164	134	114	153	119
Acute poliomyelitis — Poliomyélite aiguë	-	-	-	-	-	-	-	-
Measles — Rougeole	1 449	697	-	-	-	-	-	-
Viral hepatitis — Hépatite virale	1 072	966	7	17	5	19	14	9
Human immunodeficiency virus [HIV] disease — Maladies dues au virus de l'immunodéficience humaine (VIH)	-	-	7	-	-	-	-	-
Malaria — Paludisme	514	561	-	1	1	2	4	-
Neoplasms — Tumeurs	30 393	32 055	120	3 739	3 817	3 975	3 914	3 997
Malignant neoplasms — Tumeurs malignes								
Total	29 653	31 571	120	3 720	3 772	3 930	3 876	3 964
Malignant neoplasm of lip, oral cavity and pharynx — Tumeur maligne de la lèvre, de la cavité buccale et du pharynx	1 671	1 733	1	239	242	236	190	201
Malignant neoplasm of oesophagus — Tumeur maligne de l'oesophage	323	391	5	94	103	95	93	81
Malignant neoplasm of stomach — Tumeur maligne de l'estomac	1 378	1 385	6	350	359	383	346	355
Malignant neoplasm of colon, rectosigmoid junction, rectum, anus and anal canal — Tumeur maligne du côlon, de la jonction recto-sigmoïdienne, du rectum, de l'anus et du canal anal	1 615	1 860	10	538	523	532	541	545
Malignant neoplasm of liver and intrahepatic bile ducts — Tumeur maligne du foie et des voies bilaires intrahépatiques	...	...	13	161	155	154	148	196
Malignant neoplasm of pancreas — Tumeur maligne du pancréas	685	698	7	105	132	129	138	119
Malignant neoplasm of trachea, bronchus and lung — Tumeur maligne de la trachée, des bronches et du poumon	5 038	5 504	10	833	853	891	956	938
Malignant neoplasm of female breast — Tumeur maligne du sein chez la femme	2 540	2 703	14	223	208	238	229	278
Malignant neoplasm of cervix uteri — Tumeur maligne du col de l'utérus	630	678	-	91	85	119	71	95
Malignant neoplasm of prostate — Tumeur maligne de la prostate	734	850	-	96	60	74	79	89
Malignant neoplasm of lymphoid, haematopoietic and related tissue — Tumeurs malignes primitives ou présumées primitives des tissus lymphoïde, hématopoïétique et apparentés	2 580	2 569	11	204	244	245	247	224
Disorders of the blood and blood-forming organs and certain disorders involving the immune mechanism — Maladies du sang et des organes hématopoïétiques et certains troubles du système immunitaire								
Total	2 704	2 625	6	34	35	39	31	48
Anaemias — Anémies	2 037	2 034	2	14	18	20	14	22
Endocrine, nutritional and metabolic diseases — Maladies endocriniennes, nutritionnelles et métaboliques								
Total	12 707	14 233	55	317	383	347	385	424
Diabetes mellitus — Diabète sucré	7 783	8 819	46	265	310	277	298	337
Malnutrition — Malnutrition	1 543	1 705	-	1	-	-	-	-
Mental and behavioural disorders — Troubles mentaux et du comportement	546	1 334	2	5	11	3	14	15
Diseases of the nervous system — Maladies du système nerveux	4 069	4 562	23	78	79	90	104	96
Diseases of the circulatory system — Maladies de l'appareil circulatoire								
Total	98 051	97 210	340	5 200	5 509	5 305	5 346	5 488
Acute rheumatic fever and chronic rheumatic heart diseases — Rhumatisme articulaire aigu et cardiopathies rhumatismales chroniques	2 283	2 277	8	37	34	28	31	34
Hypertensive diseases — Maladies hypertensives	24 453	24 560	26	353	349	340	267	340
Ischaemic heart disease — Cardiopathie ischémique	28 829	29 849	169	2 696	2 914	2 971	3 019	3 122
Cerebrovascular disease — Maladie cérébrovasculaire	21 020	19 218	85	1 620	1 731	1 573	1 556	1 556
Diseases of arteries, arterioles and capillaries — Maladies des artères, artérioles et capillaires	3 265	3 212	2	82	67	62	94	90
Diseases of the respiratory system — Maladies de l'appareil respiratoire								
Total	53 276	55 985	39	2 754	2 417	2 261	2 457	2 240
Influenza — Grippe	251	303	-	1	1	-	-	-
Pneumonia — Pneumopathies	32 030	33 549	8	1 915	1 604	1 467	1 684	1 551
Chronic lower respiratory diseases — Maladies chroniques des voies respiratoires inférieures	13 326	14 228	20	796	777	758	732	639
Diseases of the digestive system — Maladies de l'appareil digestif								
Total	16 169	16 289	31	379	388	333	392	386
Gastric and duodenal ulcer — Ulcère de l'estomac et du duodénum	5 430	5 274	3	93	87	73	71	95

(See notes at end of table. — Voir notes à la fin du tableau.)

Cause of death — Cause de décès	Singapore — Singapour[10] 2000	2001	Sri Lanka 1995	Tajikistan — Tadjikistan[6] 1996	1997	1999	2000
				Number Nombre			
TOTAL	14 715	14 449	104 707	34 274	31 792	28 289	25 368	25 899
Certain infectious and parasitic diseases — Certaines maladies infectieuses et parasitaires							
Total	257	264	3 445	3 732	3 423	2 940	1 913	1 829
Intestinal infectious diseases — Maladies infectieuses intestinales	17	18	708	2 401	2 302	1 977	1 167	913
Tuberculosis — Tuberculose	99	94	845	416	491	393	461	606
Tetanus — Tétanos	-	-	...	1	-	-	-	1
Diphtheria — Diphtérie	-	-	...	...	...	...	...	...
Whooping cough — Coqueluche	-	-	...	5	4	1	1	-
Meningococcal infection — Infection à méningocoques	5	4	...	41	33	20	10	9
Septicaemia — Septicémie	88	104	...	234	156	101	81	80
Acute poliomyelitis — Poliomyélite aiguë	-	-	...	...	...	...	...	...
Measles — Rougeole	-	-	...	4	1	11	1	1
Viral hepatitis — Hépatite virale	21	18	...	...	...	...	...	...
Human immunodeficiency virus [HIV] disease — Maladies dues au virus de l'immunodéficience humaine (VIH)	-	-	...	...	...	...	...	...
Malaria — Paludisme	2	1	...	-	50	89	13	15
Neoplasms — Tumeurs	4 101	4 175	5 710	1 629	1 521	1 415	1 711	1 695
Malignant neoplasms — Tumeurs malignes							
Total	4 063	4 136	5 624	1 598	1 501	1 402	1 691	1 677
Malignant neoplasm of lip, oral cavity and pharynx — Tumeur maligne de la lèvre, de la cavité buccale et du pharynx	213	218	443	42	30	27	26	30
Malignant neoplasm of oesophagus — Tumeur maligne de l'oesophage	107	96	...	131	170	154	151	152
Malignant neoplasm of stomach — Tumeur maligne de l'estomac	349	323	...	309	345	333	424	449
Malignant neoplasm of colon, rectosigmoid junction, rectum, anus and anal canal — Tumeur maligne du côlon, de la jonction recto-sigmoïdienne, du rectum, de l'anus et du canal anal	577	610	...	72	74	97	92	65
Malignant neoplasm of liver and intrahepatic bile ducts — Tumeur maligne du foie et des voies bilaires intrahépatiques	223	228	...	...	...	...	...	...
Malignant neoplasm of pancreas — Tumeur maligne du pancréas	143	183	...	...	...	...	...	...
Malignant neoplasm of trachea, bronchus and lung — Tumeur maligne de la trachée, des bronches et du poumon	898	947	...	133	122	139	138	116
Malignant neoplasm of female breast — Tumeur maligne du sein chez la femme	251	299	...	71	67	67	80	85
Malignant neoplasm of cervix uteri — Tumeur maligne du col de l'utérus	94	83	...	50	30	36	44	39
Malignant neoplasm of prostate — Tumeur maligne de la prostate	98	96	...	19	18	12	21	32
Malignant neoplasm of lymphoid, haematopoietic and related tissue — Tumeurs malignes primitives ou présumées primitives des tissus lymphoïde, hématopoïétique et apparentés	241	233	557	121	125	145	177	162
Disorders of the blood and blood-forming organs and certain disorders involving the immune mechanism — Maladies du sang et des organes hématopoïétiques et certains troubles du système immunitaire							
Total	52	45	563	251	679	418	183	159
Anaemias — Anémies	13	11	...	214	659	404	170	148
Endocrine, nutritional and metabolic diseases — Maladies endocriniennes, nutritionnelles et métaboliques							
Total	444	605	1 788	527	574	485	397	397
Diabetes mellitus — Diabète sucré	348	496	...	447	424	348	343	359
Malnutrition — Malnutrition	2	1	...	...	...	...	...	...
Mental and behavioural disorders — Troubles mentaux et du comportement	15	14	488	110	162	142	83	67
Diseases of the nervous system — Maladies du système nerveux	95	116	5 366	517	494	529	544	462
Diseases of the circulatory system — Maladies de l'appareil circulatoire							
Total	5 469	5 343	21 028	12 373	11 346	10 463	10 970	10 863
Acute rheumatic fever and chronic rheumatic heart diseases — Rhumatisme articulaire aigu et cardiopathies rhumatismales chroniques	32	32	98	226	216	199	231	202
Hypertensive diseases — Maladies hypertensives	330	367	2 362	2 011	2 293	2 597	2 766	2 639
Ischaemic heart disease — Cardiopathie ischémique	2 979	3 096	4 416	5 873	5 052	4 234	4 403	4 785
Cerebrovascular disease — Maladie cérébrovasculaire	1 572	1 368	3 425	2 394	1 701	1 308	1 315	1 331
Diseases of arteries, arterioles and capillaries — Maladies des artères, artérioles et capillaires	107	81	...	1 511	1 433	1 563	1 725	1 466
Diseases of the respiratory system — Maladies de l'appareil respiratoire							
Total	2 401	2 145	5 769	7 255	5 716	4 737	3 408	3 621
Influenza — Grippe	1	3	...	101	74	32	31	96
Pneumonia — Pneumopathies	1 713	1 474	...	2 671	2 263	2 152	1 666	1 716
Chronic lower respiratory diseases — Maladies chroniques des voies respiratoires inférieures	617	608	...	...	...	...	...	...
Diseases of the digestive system — Maladies de l'appareil digestif							
Total	292	282	3 490	1 279	1 232	1 168	1 147	1 170
Gastric and duodenal ulcer — Ulcère de l'estomac et du duodénum	51	58	...	209	196	227	197	194

(See notes at end of table. — Voir notes à la fin du tableau.)

Cause of death — Cause de décès	Tajikistan — Tadjikistan[6]	Thailand — Thaïlande						
	2001	1995	1996	1997	1998	1999	2000	2002
		Number Nombre						
TOTAL	26 737	324 842	342 643	298 084	310 512	362 607	365 583	380 364
Certain infectious and parasitic diseases — Certaines maladies infectieuses et parasitaires								
Total	1 929	17 567	17 908	16 531	18 106	25 472	31 956	44 831
Intestinal infectious diseases — Maladies infectieuses intestinales	919	1 388	1 560	1 066	1 133	1 212	1 360	1 359
Tuberculosis — Tuberculose	698	4 144	4 622	3 697	4 252	5 265	6 246	6 751
Tetanus — Tétanos	-	126	138	112	79	98	105	70
Diphtheria — Diphtérie	...	6	28	15	12	17	7	8
Whooping cough — Coqueluche	1	-	3	2	2	7	5	1
Meningococcal infection — Infection à méningocoques	25	1	2	1	2	2	-	4
Septicaemia — Septicémie	80	6 593	6 718	5 963	5 460	7 703	10 691	15 806
Acute poliomyelitis — Poliomyélite aiguë	...	5	38	22	45	41	42	22
Measles — Rougeole	-	8	7	6	12	7	9	4
Viral hepatitis — Hépatite virale	...	230	120	188	154	290	375	262
Human immunodeficiency virus [HIV] disease — Maladies dues au virus de l'immunodéficience humaine (VIH)	...	2 156	732	1 262	4 655	6 429	8 695	15 598
Malaria — Paludisme	11	856	776	745	576	740	625	361
Neoplasms — Tumeurs	1 829	30 195	30 172	26 237	29 812	36 091	39 480	45 834
Malignant neoplasms — Tumeurs malignes								
Total	1 792	29 891	29 631	26 060	29 629	35 703	39 238	45 825
Malignant neoplasm of lip, oral cavity and pharynx — Tumeur maligne de la lèvre, de la cavité buccale et du pharynx	43	470	651	404	574	675	762	1 124
Malignant neoplasm of oesophagus — Tumeur maligne de l'oesophage	178	216	210	188	154	282	389	729
Malignant neoplasm of stomach — Tumeur maligne de l'estomac	411	477	388	245	365	458	648	975
Malignant neoplasm of colon, rectosigmoid junction, rectum, anus and anal canal — Tumeur maligne du côlon, de la jonction recto-sigmoïdienne, du rectum, de l'anus et du canal anal	76	952	1 195	1 268	1 808	1 723	1 899	1 302
Malignant neoplasm of liver and intrahepatic bile ducts — Tumeur maligne du foie et des voies biliaires intrahépatiques	...	6 004	5 372	5 751	7 339	7 900	9 086	11 222
Malignant neoplasm of pancreas — Tumeur maligne du pancréas	...	132	148	89	202	523	479	579
Malignant neoplasm of trachea, bronchus and lung — Tumeur maligne de la trachée, des bronches et du poumon	120	2 772	2 913	2 936	3 500	4 220	5 486	6 877
Malignant neoplasm of female breast — Tumeur maligne du sein chez la femme	102	474	527	490	519	890	1 115	1 497
Malignant neoplasm of cervix uteri — Tumeur maligne du col de l'utérus	42	214	380	318	408	672	871	1 258
Malignant neoplasm of prostate — Tumeur maligne de la prostate	35	68	91	60	79	125	210	299
Malignant neoplasm of lymphoid, haematopoietic and related tissue — Tumeurs malignes primitives ou présumées primitives des tissus lymphoïde, hématopoïétique et apparentés	172	1 108	1 171	1 080	1 107	1 430	1 654	1 746
Disorders of the blood and blood-forming organs and certain disorders involving the immune mechanism — Maladies du sang et des organes hématopoïétiques et certains troubles du système immunitaire								
Total	201	4 125	7 611	8 696	8 013	9 886	9 180	3 361
Anaemias — Anémies	183	195	304	243	227	294	287	324
Endocrine, nutritional and metabolic diseases — Maladies endocriniennes, nutritionnelles et métaboliques								
Total	427	4 639	5 783	4 889	5 300	7 437	8 069	8 304
Diabetes mellitus — Diabète sucré	370	4 383	5 265	4 512	4 837	7 000	7 558	7 383
Malnutrition — Malnutrition	...	19	91	51	117	49	53	116
Mental and behavioural disorders — Troubles mentaux et du comportement	90	907	1 078	853	751	553	569	731
Diseases of the nervous system — Maladies du système nerveux	493	8 089	12 686	8 315	9 091	10 212	10 717	7 167
Diseases of the circulatory system — Maladies de l'appareil circulatoire								
Total	11 758	56 270	63 062	58 531	52 376	42 284	32 331	32 867
Acute rheumatic fever and chronic rheumatic heart diseases — Rhumatisme articularie aigu et cardiopathies rhumatismales chroniques	193	357	554	561	267	165	51	58
Hypertensive diseases — Maladies hypertensives	2 995	3 085	3 053	2 054	2 029	2 987	3 403	3 213
Ischaemic heart disease — Cardiopathie ischémique	5 147	1 572	2 784	1 870	2 199	4 849	6 251	9 011
Cerebrovascular disease — Maladie cérébrovasculaire	1 637	6 464	6 297	5 962	4 283	6 631	8 260	13 398
Diseases of arteries, arterioles and capillaries — Maladies des artères, artérioles et capillaires	1 218	206	380	344	324	414	605	696
Diseases of the respiratory system — Maladies de l'appareil respiratoire								
Total	3 682	22 493	19 753	19 807	22 637	20 599	21 101	25 251
Influenza — Grippe	45	84	146	197	148	110	128	73
Pneumonia — Pneumopathies	1 590	6 370	6 804	5 451	5 408	8 611	8 334	11 655
Chronic lower respiratory diseases — Maladies chroniques des voies respiratoires inférieures	...	2 786	3 972	2 221	2 572	4 329	4 618	5 831
Diseases of the digestive system — Maladies de l'appareil digestif								
Total	1 284	10 490	10 401	8 529	7 847	8 646	9 055	11 267
Gastric and duodenal ulcer — Ulcère de l'estomac et du duodénum	207	542	445	338	241	346	280	216

(See notes at end of table. — Voir notes à la fin du tableau.)

Cause of death — Cause de décès	Turkmenistan — Turkménistan[6]				Uzbekistan — Ouzbékistan[6]			
	1995	1996	1997	1998	1995	1996	1997	1998
	Number / Nombre							
TOTAL	31 404	32 266	30 301	29 696	145 425	144 829	137 331	140 526
Certain infectious and parasitic diseases — Certaines maladies infectieuses et parasitaires								
Total	3 192	2 966	2 640	2 222	7 793	6 805	6 160	5 406
Intestinal infectious diseases — Maladies infectieuses intestinales	1 964	1 737	1 365	986	3 472	2 437	1 835	1 049
Tuberculosis — Tuberculose	582	796	834	845	2 146	2 410	2 536	2 908
Tetanus — Tétanos	1	1	2	2	1	-	-	1
Diphtheria — Diphtérie	...	...	...	-	...	...	...	...
Whooping cough — Coqueluche	6	3	3	-	6	4	2	1
Meningococcal infection — Infection à méningocoques	56	41	35	32	53	31	32	47
Septicaemia — Septicémie	226	129	104	111	760	712	570	472
Acute poliomyelitis — Poliomyélite aiguë	...	...	...	...	...	...	...	...
Measles — Rougeole	4	8	6	11	9	6	5	15
Viral hepatitis — Hépatite virale	...	...	...	...	...	...	...	...
Human immunodeficiency virus [HIV] disease — Maladies dues au virus de l'immunodéficience humaine (VIH)	-	-	-	...	-	...	...	...
Malaria — Paludisme	-	-	-	-	-	-	-	2
Neoplasms — Tumeurs	2 175	2 297	2 118	2 008	10 126	9 904	9 426	9 585
Malignant neoplasms — Tumeurs malignes								
Total	2 113	2 239	2 076	1 970	9 977	9 799	9 333	9 496
Malignant neoplasm of lip, oral cavity and pharynx — Tumeur maligne de la lèvre, de la cavité buccale et du pharynx	93	62	87	88	433	418	375	406
Malignant neoplasm of oesophagus — Tumeur maligne de l'oesophage	403	386	356	309	1 296	1 165	1 066	1 035
Malignant neoplasm of stomach — Tumeur maligne de l'estomac	331	326	334	269	1 413	1 454	1 452	1 321
Malignant neoplasm of colon, rectosigmoid junction, rectum, anus and anal canal — Tumeur maligne du côlon, de la jonction recto-sigmoïdienne, du rectum, de l'anus et du canal anal	122	137	114	104	469	509	525	489
Malignant neoplasm of liver and intrahepatic bile ducts — Tumeur maligne du foie et des voies bilaires intrahépatiques	...	...	...	...	...	...	...	...
Malignant neoplasm of pancreas — Tumeur maligne du pancréas	...	...	...	...	...	...	...	...
Malignant neoplasm of trachea, bronchus and lung — Tumeur maligne de la trachée, des bronches et du poumon	224	259	248	197	1 228	1 149	1 176	1 127
Malignant neoplasm of female breast — Tumeur maligne du sein chez la femme	118	118	106	100	580	588	593	592
Malignant neoplasm of cervix uteri — Tumeur maligne du col de l'utérus	32	61	80	48	310	332	276	293
Malignant neoplasm of prostate — Tumeur maligne de la prostate	17	8	11	14	83	63	87	83
Malignant neoplasm of lymphoid, haematopoietic and related tissue — Tumeurs malignes primitives ou présumées primitives des tissus lymphoïde, hématopoïétique et apparentés	147	131	145	208	930	820	851	883
Disorders of the blood and blood-forming organs and certain disorders involving the immune mechanism — Maladies du sang et des organes hématopoïétiques et certains troubles du système immunitaire								
Total	61	104	110	107	540	664	596	505
Anaemias — Anémies	44	87	93	86	469	593	510	416
Endocrine, nutritional and metabolic diseases — Maladies endocriniennes, nutritionnelles et métaboliques								
Total	432	413	427	396	2 605	2 436	2 187	2 211
Diabetes mellitus — Diabète sucré	389	393	405	364	2 434	2 297	2 058	2 096
Malnutrition — Malnutrition	...	...	...	...	...	...	...	...
Mental and behavioural disorders — Troubles mentaux et du comportement	152	109	163	227	981	927	744	733
Diseases of the nervous system — Maladies du système nerveux	289	369	299	251	2 313	2 306	2 419	2 361
Diseases of the circulatory system — Maladies de l'appareil circulatoire								
Total	13 553	14 626	13 822	14 103	67 675	67 653	64 884	70 190
Acute rheumatic fever and chronic rheumatic heart diseases — Rhumatisme articulaire aigu et cardiopathies rhumatismales chroniques	162	175	168	156	1 426	1 408	1 254	1 331
Hypertensive diseases — Maladies hypertensives	2 072	2 624	3 311	3 246	4 777	5 278	5 404	6 459
Ischaemic heart disease — Cardiopathie ischémique	7 752	8 565	7 366	6 895	40 291	38 279	36 717	40 955
Cerebrovascular disease — Maladie cérébrovasculaire	2 482	2 017	1 297	1 376	18 041	17 570	16 292	15 669
Diseases of arteries, arterioles and capillaries — Maladies des artères, artérioles et capillaires	70	127	78	46	228	549	299	208
Diseases of the respiratory system — Maladies de l'appareil respiratoire								
Total	5 660	5 168	4 964	4 532	23 828	22 559	19 948	20 655
Influenza — Grippe	307	289	216	208	73	55	38	71
Pneumonia — Pneumopathies	2 268	2 026	2 197	2 031	7 820	7 986	7 276	7 387
Chronic lower respiratory diseases — Maladies chroniques des voies respiratoires inférieures	...	...	...	...	...	...	...	...
Diseases of the digestive system — Maladies de l'appareil digestif								
Total	1 259	1 415	1 555	1 443	7 336	7 881	7 973	7 341
Gastric and duodenal ulcer — Ulcère de l'estomac et du duodénum	77	98	92	114	603	669	726	647

(See notes at end of table. — Voir notes à la fin du tableau.)

Cause of death — Cause de décès	Uzbekistan — Ouzbékistan[6]		Albania — Albanie					
	1999	2000	1995	1996	1997	1998	1999	2000
				Number Nombre				
TOTAL	130 529	135 598	16 059	16 747	16 182	16 476	15 300	16 411
Certain infectious and parasitic diseases — Certaines maladies infectieuses et parasitaires								
Total	4 911	5 114	144	147	112	109	86	75
Intestinal infectious diseases — Maladies infectieuses intestinales	670	510	28	26	23	15	10	5
Tuberculosis — Tuberculose	2 979	3 352	16	34	19	21	17	16
Tetanus — Tétanos	1	-	3	5	-	1	1	1
Diphtheria — Diphtérie	...	...	3	-	-	1	1	-
Whooping cough — Coqueluche	3	1	-	1	2	-	-	-
Meningococcal infection — Infection à méningocoques	22	19	2	3	-	1	-	-
Septicaemia — Septicémie	485	528	19	20	21	19	14	5
Acute poliomyelitis — Poliomyélite aiguë	...	...	-	-	-	-	-	-
Measles — Rougeole	6	1	-	5	10	1	-	-
Viral hepatitis — Hépatite virale	...	...	17	6	13	5	10	6
Human immunodeficiency virus [HIV] disease — Maladies dues au virus de l'immunodéficience humaine (VIH)			-	-	1	-	-	-
Malaria — Paludisme	1	...	-	-	-	-	-	-
Neoplasms — Tumeurs	9 648	9 683	2 175	2 488	2 310	2 466	2 547	2 664
Malignant neoplasms — Tumeurs malignes								
Total	9 521	9 596	2 087	2 373	2 246	2 363	2 485	2 465
Malignant neoplasm of lip, oral cavity and pharynx — Tumeur maligne de la lèvre, de la cavité buccale et du pharynx	393	372	43	46	32	48	51	45
Malignant neoplasm of oesophagus — Tumeur maligne de l'oesophage	1 008	932	23	36	29	22	22	33
Malignant neoplasm of stomach — Tumeur maligne de l'estomac	1 247	1 327	282	344	313	345	351	364
Malignant neoplasm of colon, rectosigmoid junction, rectum, anus and anal canal — Tumeur maligne du côlon, de la jonction recto-sigmoïdienne, du rectum, de l'anus et du canal anal	485	461	82	81	73	89	86	78
Malignant neoplasm of liver and intrahepatic bile ducts — Tumeur maligne du foie et des voies biliaires intrahépatiques	...	...	68	67	57	78	79	85
Malignant neoplasm of pancreas — Tumeur maligne du pancréas	...	...		...	...	...	...	...
Malignant neoplasm of trachea, bronchus and lung — Tumeur maligne de la trachée, des bronches et du poumon	1 019	1 019	524	591	621	611	612	593
Malignant neoplasm of female breast — Tumeur maligne du sein chez la femme	668	696	86	95	84	98	130	127
Malignant neoplasm of cervix uteri — Tumeur maligne du col de l'utérus	334	269	7	18	17	10	8	19
Malignant neoplasm of prostate — Tumeur maligne de la prostate	85	119	82	112	91	112	143	153
Malignant neoplasm of lymphoid, haematopoietic and related tissue — Tumeurs malignes primitives ou présumées primitives des tissus lymphoïde, hématopoïétique et apparentés	926	870	132	138	141	156	176	155
Disorders of the blood and blood-forming organs and certain disorders involving the immune mechanism — Maladies du sang et des organes hématopoïétiques et certains troubles du système immunitaire								
Total	440	402	77	67	55	52	37	42
Anaemias — Anémies	341	296	44	40	33	38	24	28
Endocrine, nutritional and metabolic diseases — Maladies endocriniennes, nutritionnelles et métaboliques								
Total	2 110	2 453	161	179	181	138	129	150
Diabetes mellitus — Diabète sucré	2 017	2 355	78	90	99	91	86	121
Malnutrition — Malnutrition	...	...	64	54	59	32	35	11
Mental and behavioural disorders — Troubles mentaux et du comportement	691	512	65	62	62	87	63	65
Diseases of the nervous system — Maladies du système nerveux	2 309	2 586	477	501	382	439	293	363
Diseases of the circulatory system — Maladies de l'appareil circulatoire								
Total	66 084	71 387	6 721	7 367	6 728	7 440	6 890	7 841
Acute rheumatic fever and chronic rheumatic heart diseases — Rhumatisme articularie aigu et cardiopathies rhumatismales chroniques	1 268	1 267	51	25	33	35	35	29
Hypertensive diseases — Maladies hypertensives	6 482	6 893	243	268	241	270	167	307
Ischaemic heart disease — Cardiopathie ischémique	38 063	40 661	1 453	1 655	1 592	1 737	1 757	1 985
Cerebrovascular disease — Maladie cérébrovasculaire	14 772	17 190	2 264	2 622	2 572	2 832	2 783	2 843
Diseases of arteries, arterioles and capillaries — Maladies des artères, artérioles et capillaires	184	246	241	235	196	272	165	182
Diseases of the respiratory system — Maladies de l'appareil respiratoire								
Total	16 964	15 706	2 014	1 816	1 357	1 285	1 036	1 127
Influenza — Grippe	9	71	118	125	75	72	86	97
Pneumonia — Pneumopathies	5 796	5 170	1 323	1 131	836	752	555	555
Chronic lower respiratory diseases — Maladies chroniques des voies respiratoires inférieures	...	...	351	361	330	343	312	384
Diseases of the digestive system — Maladies de l'appareil digestif								
Total	7 318	7 564	540	481	382	377	339	342
Gastric and duodenal ulcer — Ulcère de l'estomac et du duodénum	602	645	41	32	29	34	14	27

(See notes at end of table. — Voir notes à la fin du tableau.)

Cause of death — Cause de décès	Albania — Albanie 2001 Number Nombre	Austria — Autriche 1995 Number Nombre	1995 Rate Taux	1996 Number Nombre	1996 Rate Taux	1997 Number Nombre	1997 Rate Taux	1998 Number Nombre
TOTAL	15 143	81 171	1008.8	80 790	1002.4	79 432	984.0	78 339
Certain infectious and parasitic diseases — Certaines maladies infectieuses et parasitaires								
Total	99	340	4.2	291	3.6	264	3.3	338
Intestinal infectious diseases — Maladies infectieuses intestinales	14	4	0.0	5	◆0.1	9	◆0.1	9
Tuberculosis — Tuberculose	14	75	0.9	79	1.0	79	1.0	91
Tetanus — Tétanos	-	-	-	-	-	-	-	-
Diphtheria — Diphtérie	-	-	-	-	-	-	-	-
Whooping cough — Coqueluche	-	10	◆0.1	13	◆0.2	7	◆0.1	10
Meningococcal infection — Infection à méningocoques	13	31	0.4	36	0.4	53	0.7	83
Septicaemia — Septicémie	-	-	-	-	-	-	-	-
Acute poliomyelitis — Poliomyélite aiguë	-	-	-	-	-	-	-	-
Measles — Rougeole	5	9	◆0.1	11	◆0.1	20	◆0.2	39
Viral hepatitis — Hépatite virale	-	171	2.1	116	1.4	59	0.7	64
Human immunodeficiency virus [HIV] disease — Maladies dues au virus de l'immunodéficience humaine (VIH)	-	1	0.0	1	0.0	3	0.0	2
Malaria — Paludisme								
Neoplasms — Tumeurs	2 398	19 592	243.5	19 251	238.9	19 287	238.9	19 062
Malignant neoplasms — Tumeurs malignes								
Total	2 146	19 154	238.0	18 819	233.5	18 845	233.5	18 656
Malignant neoplasm of lip, oral cavity and pharynx — Tumeur maligne de la lèvre, de la cavité buccale et du pharynx	45	427	5.3	410	5.1	375	4.6	443
Malignant neoplasm of oesophagus — Tumeur maligne de l'oesophage	29	249	3.1	265	3.3	262	3.2	284
Malignant neoplasm of stomach — Tumeur maligne de l'estomac	298	1 595	19.8	1 512	18.8	1 423	17.6	1 362
Malignant neoplasm of colon, rectosigmoid junction, rectum, anus and anal canal — Tumeur maligne du côlon, de la jonction recto-sigmoïdienne, du rectum, de l'anus et du canal anal	83	2 676	33.3	2 667	33.1	2 586	32.0	2 531
Malignant neoplasm of liver and intrahepatic bile ducts — Tumeur maligne du foie et des voies bilaires intrahépatiques	...	300	3.7	336	4.2	388	4.8	356
Malignant neoplasm of pancreas — Tumeur maligne du pancréas	87	1 191	14.8	1 152	14.3	1 196	14.8	1 148
Malignant neoplasm of trachea, bronchus and lung — Tumeur maligne de la trachée, des bronches et du poumon	510	3 156	39.2	3 241	40.2	3 264	40.4	3 323
Malignant neoplasm of female breast — Tumeur maligne du sein chez la femme	102	1 737	▲50.3	1 712	▲49.4	1 651	▲47.5	1 621
Malignant neoplasm of cervix uteri — Tumeur maligne du col de l'utérus	13	211	▲6.1	182	▲5.3	174	▲5.0	158
Malignant neoplasm of prostate — Tumeur maligne de la prostate	110	1 202	▼110.8	1 170	▼106.9	1 184	▼106.5	1 139
Malignant neoplasm of lymphoid, haematopoietic and related tissue — Tumeurs malignes primitives ou présumées primitives des tissus lymphoïde, hématopoïétique et apparentés	124	1 396	17.3	1 298	16.1	1 418	17.6	1 394
Disorders of the blood and blood-forming organs and certain disorders involving the immune mechanism — Maladies du sang et des organes hématopoïétiques et certains troubles du système immunitaire								
Total	54	108	1.3	87	1.1	82	1.0	79
Anaemias — Anémies	31	62	0.8	42	0.5	36	0.4	35
Endocrine, nutritional and metabolic diseases — Maladies endocriniennes, nutritionnelles et métaboliques								
Total	154	1 856	23.1	1 732	21.5	1 666	20.6	1 462
Diabetes mellitus — Diabète sucré	113	1 776	22.1	1 662	20.6	1 603	19.9	1 397
Malnutrition — Malnutrition	7	1	0.0	-	-	-	-	-
Mental and behavioural disorders — Troubles mentaux et du comportement	108	378	4.7	397	4.9	356	4.4	370
Diseases of the nervous system — Maladies du système nerveux	384	1 278	15.9	1 244	15.4	1 191	14.8	1 150
Diseases of the circulatory system — Maladies de l'appareil circulatoire								
Total	7 516	43 447	539.9	43 751	542.9	42 991	532.6	42 544
Acute rheumatic fever and chronic rheumatic heart diseases — Rhumatisme articulaire aigu et cardiopathies rhumatismales chroniques	30	219	2.7	180	2.2	184	2.3	163
Hypertensive diseases — Maladies hypertensives	308	1 271	15.8	1 346	16.7	1 372	17.0	1 273
Ischaemic heart disease — Cardiopathie ischémique	1 828	17 026	211.6	16 919	209.9	17 084	211.6	17 501
Cerebrovascular disease — Maladie cérébrovasculaire	2 692	9 857	122.5	10 354	128.5	10 045	124.4	9 629
Diseases of arteries, arterioles and capillaries — Maladies des artères, artérioles et capillaires	289	2 499	31.1	2 278	28.3	2 151	26.6	2 078
Diseases of the respiratory system — Maladies de l'appareil respiratoire								
Total	818	3 422	42.5	3 519	43.7	3 555	44.0	3 552
Influenza — Grippe	35	84	1.0	152	1.9	112	1.4	62
Pneumonia — Pneumopathies	401	986	12.3	1 156	14.3	1 228	15.2	1 282
Chronic lower respiratory diseases — Maladies chroniques des voies respiratoires inférieures	289	2 085	25.9	1 998	24.8	1 909	23.6	1 919
Diseases of the digestive system — Maladies de l'appareil digestif								
Total	333	3 832	47.6	3 727	46.2	3 495	43.3	3 478
Gastric and duodenal ulcer — Ulcère de l'estomac et du duodénum	15	398	4.9	378	4.7	321	4.0	283

21. Death and death rates by cause: 1995 - 2002
Décès selon la cause, nombres et taux: 1995 - 2002 (continued — suite)

(See notes at end of table. — Voir notes à la fin du tableau.)

Austria — Autriche

Cause of death — Cause de décès	1998 Rate Taux	1999 Number Nombre	1999 Rate Taux	2000 Number Nombre	2000 Rate Taux	2001 Number Nombre	2001 Rate Taux	2002 Number Nombre
TOTAL	969.7	78 200	966.4	76 780	946.9	74 767	931.1	76 131
Certain infectious and parasitic diseases — Certaines maladies infectieuses et parasitaires								
Total	4.2	342	4.2	308	3.8	297	3.7	490
Intestinal infectious diseases — Maladies infectieuses intestinales	♦0.1	8	♦0.1	6	♦0.1	7	♦0.1	19
Tuberculosis — Tuberculose	1.1	79	1.0	71	0.9	55	0.7	66
Tetanus — Tétanos	-	-	-	-	-	1	0.0	-
Diphtheria — Diphtérie	-	-	-	-	-	-	-	-
Whooping cough — Coqueluche	-	-	-	-	-	-	-	-
Meningococcal infection — Infection à méningocoques	♦0.1	7	♦0.1	8	♦0.1	9	♦0.1	7
Septicaemia — Septicémie	1.0	82	1.0	92	1.1	73	0.9	48
Acute poliomyelitis — Poliomyélite aiguë	-	-	-	2	0.0	-	-	-
Measles — Rougeole	-	-	-	-	-	1	0.0	1
Viral hepatitis — Hépatite virale	0.5	65	0.8	34	0.4	50	0.6	236
Human immunodeficiency virus [HIV] disease — Maladies dues au virus de l'immunodéficience humaine (VIH)	0.8	55	0.7	50	0.6	50	0.6	51
Malaria — Paludisme	0.0	3	0.0	-	-	2	0.0	1
Neoplasms — Tumeurs	236.0	19 076	235.7	19 112	235.7	18 906	235.4	19 106
Malignant neoplasms — Tumeurs malignes								
Total	230.9	18 710	231.2	18 749	231.2	18 487	230.2	18 623
Malignant neoplasm of lip, oral cavity and pharynx — Tumeur maligne de la lèvre, de la cavité buccale et du pharynx	5.5	457	5.6	479	5.9	461	5.7	473
Malignant neoplasm of oesophagus — Tumeur maligne de l'oesophage	3.5	298	3.7	266	3.3	310	3.9	319
Malignant neoplasm of stomach — Tumeur maligne de l'estomac	16.9	1 281	15.8	1 229	15.2	1 150	14.3	1 144
Malignant neoplasm of colon, rectosigmoid junction, rectum, anus and anal canal — Tumeur maligne du côlon, de la jonction recto-sigmoïdienne, du rectum, de l'anus et du canal anal	31.3	2 624	32.4	2 536	31.3	2 448	30.5	2 483
Malignant neoplasm of liver and intrahepatic bile ducts — Tumeur maligne du foie et des voies biliaires intrahépatiques	4.4	374	4.6	364	4.5	370	4.6	704
Malignant neoplasm of pancreas — Tumeur maligne du pancréas	14.2	1 223	15.1	1 264	15.6	1 237	15.4	1 244
Malignant neoplasm of trachea, bronchus and lung — Tumeur maligne de la trachée, des bronches et du poumon	41.1	3 247	40.1	3 269	40.3	3 195	39.8	3 419
Malignant neoplasm of female breast — Tumeur maligne du sein chez la femme	▲48.5	1 562	▲44.7	1 671	...	1 572	▲45.1	1 593
Malignant neoplasm of cervix uteri — Tumeur maligne du col de l'utérus	▲4.5	169	▲4.8	138	...	128	▲3.7	183
Malignant neoplasm of prostate — Tumeur maligne de la prostate	▼100.5	1 222	▼106.1	1 229	...	1 184	▼101.5	1 138
Malignant neoplasm of lymphoid, haematopoietic and related tissue — Tumeurs malignes primitives ou présumées primitives des tissus lymphoïde, hématopoïétique et apparentés	17.3	1 457	18.0	1 452	17.9	1 529	19.0	1 528
Disorders of the blood and blood-forming organs and certain disorders involving the immune mechanism — Maladies du sang et des organes hématopoïétiques et certains troubles du système immunitaire								
Total	1.0	84	1.0	70	0.9	102	1.3	95
Anaemias — Anémies	0.4	30	♦0.4	27	♦0.3	41	0.5	39
Endocrine, nutritional and metabolic diseases — Maladies endocriniennes, nutritionnelles et métaboliques								
Total	18.1	1 555	19.2	1 453	17.9	1 536	19.1	2 319
Diabetes mellitus — Diabète sucré	17.3	1 502	18.6	1 388	17.1	1 460	18.2	2 028
Malnutrition — Malnutrition	-	-	-	-	-	-	-	-
Mental and behavioural disorders — Troubles mentaux et du comportement	4.6	362	4.5	395	4.9	456	5.7	424
Diseases of the nervous system — Maladies du système nerveux	14.2	1 020	12.6	1 111	13.7	1 145	14.3	2 265
Diseases of the circulatory system — Maladies de l'appareil circulatoire								
Total	526.6	42 111	520.4	40 111	494.7	38 385	478.0	36 906
Acute rheumatic fever and chronic rheumatic heart diseases — Rhumatisme articularie aigu et cardiopathies rhumatismales chroniques	2.0	176	2.2	177	2.2	196	2.4	207
Hypertensive diseases — Maladies hypertensives	15.8	1 382	17.1	1 381	17.0	1 347	16.8	1 208
Ischaemic heart disease — Cardiopathie ischémique	216.6	17 154	212.0	16 242	200.3	15 647	194.9	16 355
Cerebrovascular disease — Maladie cérébrovasculaire	119.2	9 383	116.0	8 869	109.4	8 153	101.5	8 123
Diseases of arteries, arterioles and capillaries — Maladies des artères, artérioles et capillaires	25.7	1 939	24.0	2 042	25.2	2 055	25.6	2 210
Diseases of the respiratory system — Maladies de l'appareil respiratoire								
Total	44.0	4 041	49.9	4 087	50.4	3 914	48.7	4 090
Influenza — Grippe	0.8	144	1.8	145	1.8	59	0.7	18
Pneumonia — Pneumopathies	15.9	1 421	17.6	1 337	16.5	1 239	15.4	1 065
Chronic lower respiratory diseases — Maladies chroniques des voies respiratoires inférieures	23.8	2 119	26.2	2 195	27.1	2 238	27.9	2 587
Diseases of the digestive system — Maladies de l'appareil digestif								
Total	43.1	3 251	40.2	3 464	42.7	3 349	41.7	3 588
Gastric and duodenal ulcer — Ulcère de l'estomac et du duodénum	3.5	232	2.9	260	3.2	249	3.1	284

21. Death and death rates by cause: 1995 - 2002
Décès selon la cause, nombres et taux: 1995 - 2002 (continued — suite)

(See notes at end of table. — Voir notes à la fin du tableau.)

Cause of death — Cause de décès	Austria — Autriche 2002 Rate Taux	Belarus — Bélarus[6] 1995 Number Nombre	1995 Rate Taux	1996 Number Nombre	1996 Rate Taux	1997 Number Nombre	1997 Rate Taux	1998 Number Nombre
TOTAL	945.4	133 775	1301.2	142 943	1394.5	136 653	1337.1	137 296
Certain infectious and parasitic diseases — Certaines maladies infectieuses et parasitaires								
Total	6.1	929	9.0	899	8.8	897	8.8	951
Intestinal infectious diseases — Maladies infectieuses intestinales	◆0.2	53	0.5	50	0.5	34	0.3	38
Tuberculosis — Tuberculose	0.8	650	6.3	628	6.1	660	6.5	702
Tetanus — Tétanos	-	1	0.0	2	0.0	2	0.0	1
Diphtheria — Diphtérie	-	-	...	...	...	...	...	...
Whooping cough — Coqueluche	-	-	-	-	-	1	0.0	-
Meningococcal infection — Infection à méningocoques	◆0.1	49	0.5	32	0.3	44	0.4	35
Septicaemia — Septicémie	0.6	79	0.8	88	0.9	69	0.7	71
Acute poliomyelitis — Poliomyélite aiguë		...	...	...	...	...	...	...
Measles — Rougeole	0.0	-	-	-	-	-	-	-
Viral hepatitis — Hépatite virale	2.9	...	...	...	...	...	...	...
Human immunodeficiency virus [HIV] disease — Maladies dues au virus de l'immunodéficience humaine (VIH)	0.6	...	...	...	...	...	...	...
Malaria — Paludisme	0.0	-	-	1	0.0	-	-	...
Neoplasms — Tumeurs	237.3	19 599	190.6	19 126	186.6	19 607	191.8	19 726
Malignant neoplasms — Tumeurs malignes								
Total	231.3	19 432	189.0	18 956	184.9	19 453	190.3	19 556
Malignant neoplasm of lip, oral cavity and pharynx — Tumeur maligne de la lèvre, de la cavité buccale et du pharynx	5.9	605	5.9	560	5.5	611	6.0	599
Malignant neoplasm of oesophagus — Tumeur maligne de l'oesophage	4.0	375	3.6	331	3.2	345	3.4	345
Malignant neoplasm of stomach — Tumeur maligne de l'estomac	14.2	3 363	32.7	3 362	32.8	3 107	30.4	3 291
Malignant neoplasm of colon, rectosigmoid junction, rectum, anus and anal canal — Tumeur maligne du côlon, de la jonction recto-sigmoïdienne, du rectum, de l'anus et du canal anal	30.8	2 128	20.7	2 076	20.3	2 153	21.1	2 196
Malignant neoplasm of liver and intrahepatic bile ducts — Tumeur maligne du foie et des voies bilaires intrahépatiques	8.7	...	...	...	...	...	...	...
Malignant neoplasm of pancreas — Tumeur maligne du pancréas	15.4	...	...	...	...	...	...	...
Malignant neoplasm of trachea, bronchus and lung — Tumeur maligne de la trachée, des bronches et du poumon	42.5	3 974	38.7	3 898	38.0	4 023	39.4	3 897
Malignant neoplasm of female breast — Tumeur maligne du sein chez la femme	▲45.5	1 126	...	1 151	▲26.3	1 150	▲26.1	1 207
Malignant neoplasm of cervix uteri — Tumeur maligne du col de l'utérus	▲5.2	412	...	395	▲9.0	385	▲8.7	348
Malignant neoplasm of prostate — Tumeur maligne de la prostate	▼96.1	522	...	502	▼45.6	529	▼48.3	551
Malignant neoplasm of lymphoid, haematopoietic and related tissue — Tumeurs malignes primitives ou présumées primitives des tissus lymphoïde, hématopoïétique et apparentés	19.0	1 055	10.3	1 065	10.4	1 100	10.8	1 121
Disorders of the blood and blood-forming organs and certain disorders involving the immune mechanism — Maladies du sang et des organes hématopoïétiques et certains troubles du système immunitaire								
Total	1.2	92	0.9	57	0.6	75	0.7	66
Anaemias — Anémies	0.5	62	0.6	35	0.3	37	0.4	35
Endocrine, nutritional and metabolic diseases — Maladies endocriniennes, nutritionnelles et métaboliques								
Total	28.8	899	8.7	775	7.6	891	8.7	840
Diabetes mellitus — Diabète sucré	25.2	814	7.9	682	6.7	810	7.9	770
Malnutrition — Malnutrition	-	...	...	...	...	...	...	...
Mental and behavioural disorders — Troubles mentaux et du comportement	5.3	419	4.1	384	3.7	446	4.4	519
Diseases of the nervous system — Maladies du système nerveux	28.1	1 448	14.1	1 481	14.4	1 173	11.5	964
Diseases of the circulatory system — Maladies de l'appareil circulatoire								
Total	458.3	65 947	641.5	75 704	738.6	68 866	673.8	71 345
Acute rheumatic fever and chronic rheumatic heart diseases — Rhumatisme articulaire aigu et cardiopathies rhumatismales chroniques	2.6	740	7.2	734	7.2	692	6.8	694
Hypertensive diseases — Maladies hypertensives	15.0	674	6.6	636	6.2	637	6.2	694
Ischaemic heart disease — Cardiopathie ischémique	203.1	42 186	410.3	51 980	507.1	43 849	429.1	45 570
Cerebrovascular disease — Maladie cérébrovasculaire	100.9	17 656	171.7	17 969	175.3	19 106	186.9	19 972
Diseases of arteries, arterioles and capillaries — Maladies des artères, artérioles et capillaires	27.4	1 184	11.5	1 183	11.5	1 126	11.0	1 025
Diseases of the respiratory system — Maladies de l'appareil respiratoire								
Total	50.8	6 776	65.9	6 690	65.3	7 024	68.7	6 870
Influenza — Grippe	◆0.2	17	◆0.2	8	◆0.1	7	◆0.1	7
Pneumonia — Pneumopathies	13.2	870	8.5	849	8.3	1 038	10.2	1 071
Chronic lower respiratory diseases — Maladies chroniques des voies respiratoires inférieures	32.1	...	...	...	...	...	...	...
Diseases of the digestive system — Maladies de l'appareil digestif								
Total	44.6	2 649	25.8	2 562	25.0	2 810	27.5	2 799
Gastric and duodenal ulcer — Ulcère de l'estomac et du duodénum	3.5	362	3.5	334	3.3	401	3.9	395

21. Death and death rates by cause: 1995 - 2002
Décès selon la cause, nombres et taux: 1995 - 2002 (continued — suite)

(See notes at end of table. — Voir notes à la fin du tableau.)

	Belarus — Bélarus[6]							Belgium — Belgique[11]
	1998	1999		2000		2001		1995
Cause of death — Cause de décès	Rate Taux	Number Nombre	Rate Taux	Number Nombre	Rate Taux	Number Nombre	Rate Taux	Number Nombre
TOTAL	1347.2	142 025	1415.3	134 867	1348.4	140 299	1406.8	104 897
Certain infectious and parasitic diseases — Certaines maladies infectieuses et parasitaires								
Total	9.3	1 134	11.3	952	9.5	1 064	10.7	1 583
Intestinal infectious diseases — Maladies infectieuses intestinales	0.4	55	0.5	25	◆0.2	34	0.3	134
Tuberculosis — Tuberculose	6.9	877	8.7	726	7.3	827	8.3	98
Tetanus — Tétanos	0.0	2	0.0	-	-	3	0.0	4
Diphtheria — Diphtérie	...	...	...	...	...	...	...	-
Whooping cough — Coqueluche	-	...	-	...	...	-	...	-
Meningococcal infection — Infection à méningocoques	0.3	41	0.4	39	0.4	30	◆0.3	22
Septicaemia — Septicémie	0.7	73	0.7	64	0.6	75	0.8	750
Acute poliomyelitis — Poliomyélite aiguë	...	-	...	-	...	-	...	-
Measles — Rougeole	-	-	-	-	-	-	...	-
Viral hepatitis — Hépatite virale	...	...	...	...	...	...	...	111
Human immunodeficiency virus [HIV] disease — Maladies dues au virus de l'immunodéficience humaine (VIH)	...	...	...	...	...	...	...	221
Malaria — Paludisme	-	-	-	-	-	..	...	1
Neoplasms — Tumeurs	193.6	19 964	198.9	19 572	195.7	19 601	196.5	28 350
Malignant neoplasms — Tumeurs malignes								
Total	191.9	19 812	197.4	19 438	194.3	19 458	195.1	28 188
Malignant neoplasm of lip, oral cavity and pharynx — Tumeur maligne de la lèvre, de la cavité buccale et du pharynx	5.9	607	6.0	641	6.4	587	5.9	552
Malignant neoplasm of oesophagus — Tumeur maligne de l'oesophage	3.4	378	3.8	332	3.3	358	3.6	560
Malignant neoplasm of stomach — Tumeur maligne de l'estomac	32.3	3 253	32.4	3 128	31.3	2 966	29.7	1 183
Malignant neoplasm of colon, rectosigmoid junction, rectum, anus and anal canal — Tumeur maligne du côlon, de la jonction recto-sigmoïdienne, du rectum, de l'anus et du canal anal	21.5	2 262	22.5	2 241	22.4	2 304	23.1	3 198
Malignant neoplasm of liver and intrahepatic bile ducts — Tumeur maligne du foie et des voies biliaires intrahépatiques	...	...	...	...	...	...	...	404
Malignant neoplasm of pancreas — Tumeur maligne du pancréas	...	...	...	...	...	...	...	1 219
Malignant neoplasm of trachea, bronchus and lung — Tumeur maligne de la trachée, des bronches et du poumon	38.2	3 771	37.6	3 707	37.1	3 704	37.1	6 777
Malignant neoplasm of female breast — Tumeur maligne du sein chez la femme	▲27.2	1 319	▲29.6	1 291	▲29.4	1 272	...	2 565
Malignant neoplasm of cervix uteri — Tumeur maligne du col de l'utérus	▲7.8	378	▲8.5	349	▲7.9	348	...	205
Malignant neoplasm of prostate — Tumeur maligne de la prostate	▼50.2	602	▼54.6	570	▼50.8	638	...	1 846
Malignant neoplasm of lymphoid, haematopoietic and related tissue — Tumeurs malignes primitives ou présumées primitives des tissus lymphoïde, hématopoïétique et apparentés	11.0	1 127	11.2	1 221	12.2	1 163	11.7	2 058
Disorders of the blood and blood-forming organs and certain disorders involving the immune mechanism — Maladies du sang et des organes hématopoïétiques et certains troubles du système immunitaire								
Total	0.6	77	0.8	67	0.7	64	0.6	528
Anaemias — Anémies	0.3	48	0.5	46	0.5	39	0.4	235
Endocrine, nutritional and metabolic diseases — Maladies endocriniennes, nutritionnelles et métaboliques								
Total	8.2	848	8.5	749	7.5	753	7.6	2 331
Diabetes mellitus — Diabète sucré	7.6	760	7.6	673	6.7	662	6.6	1 655
Malnutrition — Malnutrition	...	...	...	...	...	...	...	45
Mental and behavioural disorders — Troubles mentaux et du comportement	5.1	574	5.7	467	4.7	614	6.2	2 054
Diseases of the nervous system — Maladies du système nerveux	9.5	997	9.9	875	8.7	852	8.5	2 998
Diseases of the circulatory system — Maladies de l'appareil circulatoire								
Total	700.0	75 304	750.4	72 401	723.9	76 736	769.4	39 075
Acute rheumatic fever and chronic rheumatic heart diseases — Rhumatisme articulaire aigu et cardiopathies rhumatismales chroniques	6.8	686	6.8	584	5.8	529	5.3	70
Hypertensive diseases — Maladies hypertensives	6.8	691	6.9	730	7.3	717	7.2	545
Ischaemic heart disease — Cardiopathie ischémique	447.1	49 436	492.6	47 494	474.9	50 659	508.0	12 322
Cerebrovascular disease — Maladie cérébrovasculaire	196.0	20 082	200.1	19 327	193.2	19 974	200.3	9 446
Diseases of arteries, arterioles and capillaries — Maladies des artères, artérioles et capillaires	10.1	1 071	10.7	986	9.9	1 077	10.8	2 280
Diseases of the respiratory system — Maladies de l'appareil respiratoire								
Total	67.4	7 244	72.2	6 686	66.8	6 515	65.3	10 151
Influenza — Grippe	◆0.1	15	◆0.1	5	0.0	2	0.0	164
Pneumonia — Pneumopathies	10.5	1 289	12.8	1 030	10.3	981	9.8	2 758
Chronic lower respiratory diseases — Maladies chroniques des voies respiratoires inférieures	...	...	...	...	...	...	...	5 191
Diseases of the digestive system — Maladies de l'appareil digestif								
Total	27.5	2 946	29.4	2 965	29.6	3 143	31.5	4 306
Gastric and duodenal ulcer — Ulcère de l'estomac et du duodénum	3.9	367	3.7	372	3.7	330	3.3	381

(See notes at end of table. — Voir notes à la fin du tableau.)

Cause of death — Cause de décès	Belgium — Belgique[11]					Bulgaria — Bulgarie		
	1995	1996		1997		1995		1996
	Rate Taux	Number Nombre	Rate Taux	Number Nombre	Rate Taux	Number Nombre	Rate Taux	Number Nombre
TOTAL	1034.8	104 370	1027.6	103 800	1019.5	114 670	1364.1	117 056
Certain infectious and parasitic diseases — Certaines maladies infectieuses et parasitaires								
Total	15.6	1 486	14.6	1 423	14.0	612	7.3	635
Intestinal infectious diseases — Maladies infectieuses intestinales	1.3	127	1.3	114	1.1	43	0.5	27
Tuberculosis — Tuberculose	1.0	108	1.1	82	0.8	332	3.9	340
Tetanus — Tétanos	0.0	2	0.0	1	0.0	5	◆0.1	5
Diphtheria — Diphtérie	-	-	-	-	-	-	-	-
Whooping cough — Coqueluche	-	-	-	-	-	-	-	-
Meningococcal infection — Infection à méningocoques	◆0.2	16	◆0.2	17	◆0.2	19	◆0.2	21
Septicaemia — Septicémie	7.4	675	6.6	744	7.3	81	1.0	89
Acute poliomyelitis — Poliomyélite aiguë	-	-	-	-	-	-	-	-
Measles — Rougeole	-	1	0.0	-	-	-	-	-
Viral hepatitis — Hépatite virale	1.1	111	1.1	101	1.0	48	0.6	50
Human immunodeficiency virus [HIV] disease — Maladies dues au virus de l'immunodéficience humaine (VIH)	2.2	183	1.8	88	0.9	...	...	...
Malaria — Paludisme	0.0	2	0.0	4	0.0	1	0.0	-
Neoplasms — Tumeurs	279.7	27 805	273.8	28 041	275.4	16 135	191.9	16 260
Malignant neoplasms — Tumeurs malignes								
Total	278.1	27 611	271.9	27 874	273.8	16 071	191.2	16 198
Malignant neoplasm of lip, oral cavity and pharynx — Tumeur maligne de la lèvre, de la cavité buccale et du pharynx	5.4	532	5.2	575	5.6	328	3.9	343
Malignant neoplasm of oesophagus — Tumeur maligne de l'oesophage	5.5	585	5.8	579	5.7	294	3.5	257
Malignant neoplasm of stomach — Tumeur maligne de l'estomac	11.7	1 148	11.3	1 143	11.2	1 883	22.4	1 868
Malignant neoplasm of colon, rectosigmoid junction, rectum, anus and anal canal — Tumeur maligne du côlon, de la jonction recto-sigmoïdienne, du rectum, de l'anus et du canal anal	31.5	3 187	31.4	3 159	31.0	2 047	24.4	2 300
Malignant neoplasm of liver and intrahepatic bile ducts — Tumeur maligne du foie et des voies bilaires intrahépatiques	4.0	...	...	442	4.3	...	...	...
Malignant neoplasm of pancreas — Tumeur maligne du pancréas	12.0	1 288	12.7	1 275	12.5	723	8.6	752
Malignant neoplasm of trachea, bronchus and lung — Tumeur maligne de la trachée, des bronches et du poumon	66.9	6 522	64.2	6 813	66.9	3 265	38.8	3 200
Malignant neoplasm of female breast — Tumeur maligne du sein chez la femme	▲59.7	2 494	...	2 416	...	1 169	▲32.8	1 190
Malignant neoplasm of cervix uteri — Tumeur maligne du col de l'utérus	▲4.8	178	...	224	...	334	▲9.4	318
Malignant neoplasm of prostate — Tumeur maligne de la prostate	▼126.8	1 796	...	1 924	...	631	▼49.6	680
Malignant neoplasm of lymphoid, haematopoietic and related tissue — Tumeurs malignes primitives ou présumées primitives des tissus lymphoïde, hématopoïétique et apparentés	20.3	2 075	20.4	2 125	20.9	838	10.0	782
Disorders of the blood and blood-forming organs and certain disorders involving the immune mechanism — Maladies du sang et des organes hématopoïétiques et certains troubles du système immunitaire								
Total	5.2	544	5.4	506	5.0	104	1.2	117
Anaemias — Anémies	2.3	238	2.3	224	2.2	61	0.7	83
Endocrine, nutritional and metabolic diseases — Maladies endocriniennes, nutritionnelles et métaboliques								
Total	23.0	2 288	22.5	2 322	22.8	2 290	27.2	2 234
Diabetes mellitus — Diabète sucré	16.3	1 612	15.9	1 697	16.7	2 237	26.6	2 173
Malnutrition — Malnutrition	0.4	54	0.5	53	0.5	-	-	17
Mental and behavioural disorders — Troubles mentaux et du comportement	20.3	2 063	20.3	2 464	24.2	310	3.7	280
Diseases of the nervous system — Maladies du système nerveux	29.6	3 070	30.2	3 415	33.5	672	8.0	704
Diseases of the circulatory system — Maladies de l'appareil circulatoire								
Total	385.5	39 172	385.7	37 952	372.8	72 934	867.6	75 175
Acute rheumatic fever and chronic rheumatic heart diseases — Rhumatisme articulaire aigu et cardiopathies rhumatismales chroniques	0.7	63	0.6	71	0.7	392	4.7	380
Hypertensive diseases — Maladies hypertensives	5.4	527	5.2	548	5.4	4 233	50.4	4 759
Ischaemic heart disease — Cardiopathie ischémique	121.6	12 235	120.5	11 979	117.7	23 504	279.6	22 387
Cerebrovascular disease — Maladie cérébrovasculaire	93.2	9 593	94.5	9 453	92.8	22 241	264.6	21 981
Diseases of arteries, arterioles and capillaries — Maladies des artères, artérioles et capillaires	22.5	2 224	21.9	2 069	20.3	9 209	109.6	9 378
Diseases of the respiratory system — Maladies de l'appareil respiratoire								
Total	100.1	10 769	106.0	10 671	104.8	5 280	62.8	5 521
Influenza — Grippe	1.6	243	2.4	277	2.7	11	◆0.1	58
Pneumonia — Pneumopathies	27.2	3 251	32.0	3 350	32.9	2 978	35.4	3 151
Chronic lower respiratory diseases — Maladies chroniques des voies respiratoires inférieures	51.2	5 226	51.5	4 973	48.8	1 769	21.0	1 746
Diseases of the digestive system — Maladies de l'appareil digestif								
Total	42.5	4 288	42.2	4 519	44.4	3 590	42.7	3 460
Gastric and duodenal ulcer — Ulcère de l'estomac et du duodénum	3.8	365	3.6	407	4.0	383	4.6	367

21. Death and death rates by cause: 1995 - 2002
Décès selon la cause, nombres et taux: 1995 - 2002 (continued — suite)

(See notes at end of table. — Voir notes à la fin du tableau.)

Bulgaria — Bulgarie

Cause of death — Cause de décès	1996 Rate Taux	1997 Number Nombre	1997 Rate Taux	1998 Number Nombre	1998 Rate Taux	1999 Number Nombre	1999 Rate Taux	2000 Number Nombre
TOTAL	1399.7	121 861	1466.1	118 190	1431.4	111 786	1361.5	115 087
Certain infectious and parasitic diseases — Certaines maladies infectieuses et parasitaires								
Total	7.6	737	8.9	775	9.4	685	8.3	724
Intestinal infectious diseases — Maladies infectieuses intestinales	◆0.3	49	0.6	36	0.4	18	◆0.2	42
Tuberculosis — Tuberculose	4.1	385	4.6	369	4.5	292	3.6	318
Tetanus — Tétanos	◆0.1	1	0.0	-	-	3	0.0	2
Diphtheria — Diphtérie	-	-	-	-	-	-	-	-
Whooping cough — Coqueluche	-	-	-	-	-	-	-	-
Meningococcal infection — Infection à méningocoques	◆0.3	30	◆0.4	19	◆0.2	28	◆0.3	24
Septicaemia — Septicémie	1.1	112	1.3	168	2.0	174	2.1	174
Acute poliomyelitis — Poliomyélite aiguë	-	-	-	-	-	-	-	-
Measles — Rougeole	-	-	-	-	-	-	-	-
Viral hepatitis — Hépatite virale	0.6	48	0.6	48	0.6	43	0.5	42
Human immunodeficiency virus [HIV] disease — Maladies dues au virus de l'immunodéficience humaine (VIH)	...	...	...	-	-	-	-	-
Malaria — Paludisme	-	1	0.0	-	-	1	0.0	1
Neoplasms — Tumeurs	194.4	16 037	192.9	15 768	191.0	15 956	194.3	15 343
Malignant neoplasms — Tumeurs malignes								
Total	193.7	15 991	192.4	15 723	190.4	15 902	193.7	15 285
Malignant neoplasm of lip, oral cavity and pharynx — Tumeur maligne de la lèvre, de la cavité buccale et du pharynx	4.1	334	4.0	378	4.6	333	4.1	289
Malignant neoplasm of oesophagus — Tumeur maligne de l'oesophage	3.1	277	3.3	242	2.9	222	2.7	174
Malignant neoplasm of stomach — Tumeur maligne de l'estomac	22.3	1 774	21.3	1 756	21.3	1 683	20.5	1 643
Malignant neoplasm of colon, rectosigmoid junction, rectum, anus and anal canal — Tumeur maligne du côlon, de la jonction recto-sigmoïdienne, du rectum, de l'anus et du canal anal	27.5	2 166	26.1	2 162	26.2	2 136	26.0	2 179
Malignant neoplasm of liver and intrahepatic bile ducts — Tumeur maligne du foie et des voies bilaires intrahépatiques	...	...	...	...	...	...	...	...
Malignant neoplasm of pancreas — Tumeur maligne du pancréas	9.0	740	8.9	777	9.4	784	9.5	777
Malignant neoplasm of trachea, bronchus and lung — Tumeur maligne de la trachée, des bronches et du poumon	38.3	0 052	30.7	2 955	35.8	3 066	37.3	2 909
Malignant neoplasm of female breast — Tumeur maligne du sein chez la femme	▲33.4	1 193	▲33.5	1 073	▲30.1	1 144	▲32.1	1 155
Malignant neoplasm of cervix uteri — Tumeur maligne du col de l'utérus	▲8.9	321	▲9.0	324	▲9.1	411	▲11.5	340
Malignant neoplasm of prostate — Tumeur maligne de la prostate	▼53.3	728	▼57.1	689	▼54.1	673	▼52.6	664
Malignant neoplasm of lymphoid, haematopoietic and related tissue — Tumeurs malignes primitives ou présumées primitives des tissus lymphoïde, hématopoïétique et apparentés	9.4	701	8.4	739	9.0	736	9.0	707
Disorders of the blood and blood-forming organs and certain disorders involving the immune mechanism — Maladies du sang et des organes hématopoïétiques et certains troubles du système immunitaire								
Total	1.4	169	2.0	154	1.9	151	1.8	156
Anaemias — Anémies	1.0	113	1.4	108	1.3	94	1.1	104
Endocrine, nutritional and metabolic diseases — Maladies endocriniennes, nutritionnelles et métaboliques								
Total	26.7	2 375	28.6	2 100	25.4	2 059	25.1	2 135
Diabetes mellitus — Diabète sucré	26.0	2 301	27.7	2 035	24.6	1 969	24.0	2 084
Malnutrition — Malnutrition	◆0.2	19	◆0.2	4	0.0	17	◆0.2	4
Mental and behavioural disorders — Troubles mentaux et du comportement	3.3	399	4.8	326	3.9	282	3.4	250
Diseases of the nervous system — Maladies du système nerveux	8.4	846	10.2	802	9.7	820	10.0	774
Diseases of the circulatory system — Maladies de l'appareil circulatoire								
Total	898.9	79 328	954.4	77 885	943.3	72 873	887.5	76 141
Acute rheumatic fever and chronic rheumatic heart diseases — Rhumatisme articulaire aigu et cardiopathies rhumatismales chroniques	4.5	305	3.7	233	2.8	189	2.3	260
Hypertensive diseases — Maladies hypertensives	56.9	5 138	61.8	3 950	47.8	3 939	48.0	4 248
Ischaemic heart disease — Cardiopathie ischémique	267.7	23 222	279.4	22 303	270.1	20 878	254.3	19 877
Cerebrovascular disease — Maladie cérébrovasculaire	262.8	21 968	264.3	22 090	267.5	20 874	254.2	21 711
Diseases of arteries, arterioles and capillaries — Maladies des artères, artérioles et capillaires	112.1	10 180	122.5	9 236	111.9	7 889	96.1	7 747
Diseases of the respiratory system — Maladies de l'appareil respiratoire								
Total	66.0	5 618	67.6	4 826	58.4	4 300	52.4	4 500
Influenza — Grippe	0.7	49	0.6	26	◆0.3	36	0.4	83
Pneumonia — Pneumopathies	37.7	3 093	37.2	2 444	29.6	2 185	26.6	2 182
Chronic lower respiratory diseases — Maladies chroniques des voies respiratoires inférieures	20.9	1 924	23.1	1 773	21.5	1 555	18.9	1 603
Diseases of the digestive system — Maladies de l'appareil digestif								
Total	41.4	3 410	41.0	3 206	38.8	2 865	34.9	2 974
Gastric and duodenal ulcer — Ulcère de l'estomac et du duodénum	4.4	376	4.5	286	3.5	244	3.0	222

(See notes at end of table. — Voir notes à la fin du tableau.)

Cause of death — Cause de décès	Bulgaria — Bulgarie					Croatia — Croatie		
	2000	2001		2002		1995		1996
	Rate Taux	Number Nombre	Rate Taux	Number Nombre	Rate Taux	Number Nombre	Rate Taux	Number Nombre
TOTAL	1408.6	112 368	1420.5	112 617	1431.2	50 536	1082.4	50 636
Certain infectious and parasitic diseases — Certaines maladies infectieuses et parasitaires								
Total	8.9	688	8.7	604	7.7	393	8.4	409
Intestinal infectious diseases — Maladies infectieuses intestinales	0.5	13	♦0.2	32	0.4	11	♦0.2	6
Tuberculosis — Tuberculose	3.9	285	3.6	283	3.6	224	4.8	224
Tetanus — Tétanos	0.0	1	0.0	2	0.0	2	0.0	5
Diphtheria — Diphtérie	-	-	-	-	-	-	-	1
Whooping cough — Coqueluche	-	-	-	-	-	-	-	2
Meningococcal infection — Infection à méningocoques	♦0.3	18	♦0.2	13	♦0.2	-	-	-
Septicaemia — Septicémie	2.1	183	2.3	157	2.0	119	2.5	134
Acute poliomyelitis — Poliomyélite aiguë	-	-	-	-	-	-	-	-
Measles — Rougeole	-	-	-	-	-	-	-	-
Viral hepatitis — Hépatite virale	0.5	65	0.8	41	0.5	3	♦0.1	9
Human immunodeficiency virus [HIV] disease — Maladies dues au virus de l'immunodéficience humaine (VIH)	-	-	-	-	-	7	♦0.1	9
Malaria — Paludisme	0.0	1	0.0	-	-	-	-	-
Neoplasms — Tumeurs	187.8	15 513	196.1	15 839	201.3	10 475	224.4	10 592
Malignant neoplasms — Tumeurs malignes								
Total	187.1	15 472	195.6	15 785	200.6	10 425	223.3	10 566
Malignant neoplasm of lip, oral cavity and pharynx — Tumeur maligne de la lèvre, de la cavité buccale et du pharynx	3.5	371	4.7	341	4.3	411	8.8	345
Malignant neoplasm of oesophagus — Tumeur maligne de l'oesophage	2.1	170	2.1	180	2.3	218	4.7	184
Malignant neoplasm of stomach — Tumeur maligne de l'estomac	20.1	1 576	19.9	1 674	21.3	1 029	22.0	1 014
Malignant neoplasm of colon, rectosigmoid junction, rectum, anus and anal canal — Tumeur maligne du côlon, de la jonction recto-sigmoïdienne, du rectum, de l'anus et du canal anal	26.7	2 189	27.7	2 188	27.8	1 171	25.1	1 255
Malignant neoplasm of liver and intrahepatic bile ducts — Tumeur maligne du foie et des voies bilaires intrahépatiques	...	...	...	...	...	386	8.3	358
Malignant neoplasm of pancreas — Tumeur maligne du pancréas	9.5	807	10.2	815	10.4	417	8.9	485
Malignant neoplasm of trachea, bronchus and lung — Tumeur maligne de la trachée, des bronches et du poumon	35.6	2 917	36.9	3 006	38.2	2 190	46.9	2 390
Malignant neoplasm of female breast — Tumeur maligne du sein chez la femme	▲32.4	1 069	▲30.8	1 087	▲31.3	768	▲38.1	706
Malignant neoplasm of cervix uteri — Tumeur maligne du col de l'utérus	▲9.5	363	▲10.4	366	▲10.5	113	▲5.6	104
Malignant neoplasm of prostate — Tumeur maligne de la prostate	▼51.6	722	▼56.3	750	▼58.4	354	▼55.5	432
Malignant neoplasm of lymphoid, haematopoietic and related tissue — Tumeurs malignes primitives ou présumées primitives des tissus lymphoïde, hématopoïétique et apparentés	8.7	671	8.5	646	8.2	633	13.6	531
Disorders of the blood and blood-forming organs and certain disorders involving the immune mechanism — Maladies du sang et des organes hématopoïétiques et certains troubles du système immunitaire								
Total	1.9	163	2.1	123	1.6	31	0.7	37
Anaemias — Anémies	1.3	112	1.4	96	1.2	23	♦0.5	21
Endocrine, nutritional and metabolic diseases — Maladies endocriniennes, nutritionnelles et métaboliques								
Total	26.1	2 009	25.4	2 039	25.9	1 103	23.6	1 186
Diabetes mellitus — Diabète sucré	25.5	1 960	24.8	1 968	25.0	1 072	23.0	1 160
Malnutrition — Malnutrition	0.0	5	♦0.1	8	♦0.1	-	-	-
Mental and behavioural disorders — Troubles mentaux et du comportement	3.1	228	2.9	185	2.4	534	11.4	510
Diseases of the nervous system — Maladies du système nerveux	9.5	892	11.3	776	9.9	389	8.3	374
Diseases of the circulatory system — Maladies de l'appareil circulatoire								
Total	931.9	74 756	945.0	76 312	969.8	25 340	542.8	25 515
Acute rheumatic fever and chronic rheumatic heart diseases — Rhumatisme articularie aigu et cardiopathies rhumatismales chroniques	3.2	228	2.9	173	2.2	32	0.7	37
Hypertensive diseases — Maladies hypertensives	52.0	4 509	57.0	4 761	60.5	851	18.2	858
Ischaemic heart disease — Cardiopathie ischémique	243.3	19 914	251.7	20 642	262.3	9 485	203.2	9 128
Cerebrovascular disease — Maladie cérébrovasculaire	265.7	20 952	264.9	21 844	277.6	8 366	179.2	8 822
Diseases of arteries, arterioles and capillaries — Maladies des artères, artérioles et capillaires	94.8	6 751	85.3	6 340	80.6	1 497	32.1	1 235
Diseases of the respiratory system — Maladies de l'appareil respiratoire								
Total	55.1	3 696	46.7	3 329	42.3	2 034	43.6	1 929
Influenza — Grippe	1.0	8	♦0.1	4	♦0.1	19	♦0.4	30
Pneumonia — Pneumopathies	26.7	1 668	21.1	1 545	19.6	829	17.8	819
Chronic lower respiratory diseases — Maladies chroniques des voies respiratoires inférieures	19.6	1 371	17.3	1 228	15.6	931	19.9	910
Diseases of the digestive system — Maladies de l'appareil digestif								
Total	36.4	2 942	37.2	2 865	36.4	2 344	50.2	2 430
Gastric and duodenal ulcer — Ulcère de l'estomac et du duodénum	2.7	207	2.6	184	2.3	257	5.5	246

21. Death and death rates by cause: 1995 - 2002
Décès selon la cause, nombres et taux: 1995 - 2002 (continued — suite)

(See notes at end of table. — Voir notes à la fin du tableau.)

Croatia — Croatie

Cause of death — Cause de décès	1996 Rate Taux	1997 Number Nombre	1997 Rate Taux	1998 Number Nombre	1998 Rate Taux	1999 Number Nombre	1999 Rate Taux	2000 Number Nombre
TOTAL	1126.9	51 964	1136.5	52 311	1162.2	51 953	1140.9	50 246
Certain infectious and parasitic diseases — Certaines maladies infectieuses et parasitaires								
Total	9.1	417	9.1	424	9.4	476	10.5	518
Intestinal infectious diseases — Maladies infectieuses intestinales	♦0.1	14	♦0.3	11	♦0.2	8	♦0.2	14
Tuberculosis — Tuberculose	5.0	192	4.2	187	4.2	214	4.7	169
Tetanus — Tétanos	♦0.1	2	0.0	3	♦0.1	4	♦0.1	6
Whooping cough — Coqueluche	-	-	-	-	-	-	-	-
Meningococcal infection — Infection à méningocoques	0.0	2	0.0					
Septicaemia — Septicémie	0.0	2	0.0	2	0.0	1	0.0	3
Acute poliomyelitis — Poliomyélite aiguë	3.0	164	3.6	176	3.9	194	4.3	286
Measles — Rougeole	-	-	-	-	-	-	-	1
Viral hepatitis — Hépatite virale	♦0.2	7	♦0.2	12	♦0.3	7	♦0.2	13
Human immunodeficiency virus [HIV] disease — Maladies dues au virus de l'immunodéficience humaine (VIH)	♦0.2	12	♦0.3	10	♦0.2	3	♦0.1	8
Malaria — Paludisme	-	1	0.0	-	-	-	-	-
Neoplasms — Tumeurs	235.7	11 079	242.3	11 455	254.5	11 580	254.3	11 728
Malignant neoplasms — Tumeurs malignes								
Total	235.1	11 046	241.6	11 412	253.5	11 540	253.4	11 683
Malignant neoplasm of lip, oral cavity and pharynx — Tumeur maligne de la lèvre, de la cavité buccale et du pharynx	7.7	401	8.8	350	7.8	381	8.4	390
Malignant neoplasm of oesophagus — Tumeur maligne de l'oesophage	4.1	241	5.3	210	4.7	201	4.4	213
Malignant neoplasm of stomach — Tumeur maligne de l'estomac	22.6	1 020	22.3	999	22.2	983	21.6	969
Malignant neoplasm of colon, rectosigmoid junction, rectum, anus and anal canal — Tumeur maligne du côlon, de la jonction recto-sigmoïdienne, du rectum, de l'anus et du canal anal	27.9	1 288	28.2	1 362	30.3	1 440	31.6	1 509
Malignant neoplasm of liver and intrahepatic bile ducts — Tumeur maligne du foie et des voies bilaires intrahépatiques	8.0	389	8.5	400	8.9	367	8.1	392
Malignant neoplasm of pancreas — Tumeur maligne du pancréas	10.8	428	9.4	506	11.2	534	11.7	513
Malignant neoplasm of trachea, bronchus and lung — Tumeur maligne de la trachée, des bronches et du poumon	53.2	2 451	53.6	2 569	57.1	2 495	54.8	2 478
Malignant neoplasm of female breast — Tumeur maligne du sein chez la femme	▲37.2	769	▲39.8	794	▲41.8	856	▲44.4	843
Malignant neoplasm of cervix uteri — Tumeur maligne du col de l'utérus	▲5.5	95	▲4.9	113	▲5.9	104	▲5.4	91
Malignant neoplasm of prostate — Tumeur maligne de la prostate	▼72.4	441	▼72.6	474	▼79.3	463	▼76.4	466
Malignant neoplasm of lymphoid, haematopoietic and related tissue — Tumeurs malignes primitives ou présumées primitives des tissus lymphoïde, hématopoïétique et apparentés	11.8	611	13.4	639	14.2	677	14.9	697
Disorders of the blood and blood-forming organs and certain disorders involving the immune mechanism — Maladies du sang et des organes hématopoïétiques et certains troubles du système immunitaire								
Total	0.8	42	0.9	43	1.0	36	0.8	43
Anaemias — Anémies	♦0.5	17	♦0.4	19	♦0.4	20	♦0.4	27
Endocrine, nutritional and metabolic diseases — Maladies endocriniennes, nutritionnelles et métaboliques								
Total	26.4	1 329	29.1	1 213	26.9	1 065	23.4	921
Diabetes mellitus — Diabète sucré	25.8	1 287	28.1	1 188	26.4	1 029	22.6	905
Malnutrition — Malnutrition	-	2	0.0	-	-	1	0.0	-
Mental and behavioural disorders — Troubles mentaux et du comportement	11.3	491	10.7	528	11.7	615	13.5	648
Diseases of the nervous system — Maladies du système nerveux	8.3	383	8.4	422	9.4	419	9.2	435
Diseases of the circulatory system — Maladies de l'appareil circulatoire								
Total	567.8	26 157	572.1	27 026	600.4	27 075	594.6	26 712
Acute rheumatic fever and chronic rheumatic heart diseases — Rhumatisme articularie aigu et cardiopathies rhumatismales chroniques	0.8	60	1.3	101	2.2	168	3.7	177
Hypertensive diseases — Maladies hypertensives	19.1	830	18.2	883	19.6	862	18.9	937
Ischaemic heart disease — Cardiopathie ischémique	203.1	9 471	207.1	9 515	211.4	8 994	197.5	9 341
Cerebrovascular disease — Maladie cérébrovasculaire	196.3	8 586	187.8	8 804	195.6	8 901	195.5	8 383
Diseases of arteries, arterioles and capillaries — Maladies des artères, artérioles et capillaires	27.5	1 437	31.4	1 380	30.7	1 343	29.5	1 288
Diseases of the respiratory system — Maladies de l'appareil respiratoire								
Total	42.9	2 224	48.6	2 184	48.5	2 538	55.7	2 043
Influenza — Grippe	♦0.7	68	1.5	57	1.3	160	3.5	36
Pneumonia — Pneumopathies	18.2	1 008	22.0	1 045	23.2	1 054	23.1	851
Chronic lower respiratory diseases — Maladies chroniques des voies respiratoires inférieures	20.3	914	20.0	907	20.2	1 141	25.1	1 023
Diseases of the digestive system — Maladies de l'appareil digestif								
Total	54.1	2 417	52.9	2 543	56.5	2 648	58.1	2 507
Gastric and duodenal ulcer — Ulcère de l'estomac et du duodénum	5.5	233	5.1	229	5.1	233	5.1	232

21. Death and death rates by cause: 1995 - 2002
Décès selon la cause, nombres et taux: 1995 - 2002 (continued — suite)

(See notes at end of table. — Voir notes à la fin du tableau.)

Cause of death — Cause de décès	Croatia — Croatie					Czech Republic — République Tchéque		
	2000	2001		2002		1995		1996
	Rate Taux	Number Nombre	Rate Taux	Number Nombre	Rate Taux	Number Nombre	Rate Taux	Number Nombre
TOTAL	1146.9	49 552	1116.7	50 569	1138.2	117 913	1141.4	112 782
Certain infectious and parasitic diseases — Certaines maladies infectieuses et parasitaires								
Total	11.8	517	11.7	558	12.6	245	2.4	251
Intestinal infectious diseases — Maladies infectieuses intestinales	♦0.3	9	♦0.2	10	♦0.2	11	♦0.1	9
Tuberculosis — Tuberculose	3.9	145	3.3	181	4.1	91	0.9	99
Tetanus — Tétanos	♦0.1	5	♦0.1	7	♦0.2	1	0.0	-
Diphtheria — Diphtérie	-	-	-	-	-	-	-	-
Whooping cough — Coqueluche	-	-	-	1	0.0	-	-	-
Meningococcal infection — Infection à méningocoques	♦0.1	1	0.0	5	♦0.1	14	♦0.1	20
Septicaemia — Septicémie	6.5	318	7.2	308	6.9	86	0.8	79
Acute poliomyelitis — Poliomyélite aiguë	0.0	-	-	-	-	-	-	-
Measles — Rougeole	-	-	-	-	-	-	-	-
Viral hepatitis — Hépatite virale	♦0.3	15	♦0.3	18	♦0.4	14	♦0.1	16
Human immunodeficiency virus [HIV] disease — Maladies dues au virus de l'immunodéficience humaine (VIH)	♦0.2	5	♦0.1	7	♦0.2	2	0.0	1
Malaria — Paludisme	-	-	-	-	-	-	-	1
Neoplasms — Tumeurs	267.7	11 779	265.4	12 157	273.6	28 631	277.1	27 879
Malignant neoplasms — Tumeurs malignes								
Total	266.7	11 725	264.2	12 077	271.8	28 462	275.5	27 742
Malignant neoplasm of lip, oral cavity and pharynx — Tumeur maligne de la lèvre, de la cavité buccale et du pharynx	8.9	354	8.0	364	8.2	536	5.2	586
Malignant neoplasm of oesophagus — Tumeur maligne de l'oesophage	4.9	216	4.9	218	4.9	388	3.8	394
Malignant neoplasm of stomach — Tumeur maligne de l'estomac	22.1	947	21.3	975	21.9	1 901	18.4	1 853
Malignant neoplasm of colon, rectosigmoid junction, rectum, anus and anal canal — Tumeur maligne du côlon, de la jonction recto-sigmoïdienne, du rectum, de l'anus et du canal anal	34.4	1 410	31.8	1 558	35.1	4 290	41.5	4 257
Malignant neoplasm of liver and intrahepatic bile ducts — Tumeur maligne du foie et des voies bilaires intrahépatiques	8.9	408	9.2	400	9.0	973	9.4	942
Malignant neoplasm of pancreas — Tumeur maligne du pancréas	11.7	545	12.3	540	12.2	1 502	14.5	1 488
Malignant neoplasm of trachea, bronchus and lung — Tumeur maligne de la trachée, des bronches et du poumon	56.6	2 616	59.0	2 598	58.5	5 795	56.1	5 588
Malignant neoplasm of female breast — Tumeur maligne du sein chez la femme	...	832	▲43.3	804	▲41.4	2 051	▲46.8	1 892
Malignant neoplasm of cervix uteri — Tumeur maligne du col de l'utérus	...	90	▲4.7	98	▲5.0	447	▲10.2	416
Malignant neoplasm of prostate — Tumeur maligne de la prostate	...	478	▼74.4	488	▼74.2	1 163	▼89.0	1 195
Malignant neoplasm of lymphoid, haematopoietic and related tissue — Tumeurs malignes primitives ou présumées primitives des tissus lymphoïde, hématopoïétique et apparentés	15.9	626	14.1	748	16.8	1 779	17.2	1 740
Disorders of the blood and blood-forming organs and certain disorders involving the immune mechanism — Maladies du sang et des organes hématopoïétiques et certains troubles du système immunitaire								
Total	1.0	37	0.8	45	1.0	116	1.1	120
Anaemias — Anémies	♦0.6	21	♦0.5	19	♦0.4	51	0.5	48
Endocrine, nutritional and metabolic diseases — Maladies endocriniennes, nutritionnelles et métaboliques								
Total	21.0	824	18.6	920	20.7	934	9.0	849
Diabetes mellitus — Diabète sucré	20.7	796	17.9	891	20.1	877	8.5	807
Malnutrition — Malnutrition	-	-	-	-	-	9	♦0.1	3
Mental and behavioural disorders — Troubles mentaux et du comportement	14.8	559	12.6	471	10.6	65	0.6	62
Diseases of the nervous system — Maladies du système nerveux	9.9	500	11.3	489	11.0	1 113	10.8	1 100
Diseases of the circulatory system — Maladies de l'appareil circulatoire								
Total	609.7	26 542	598.1	26 698	600.9	65 950	638.4	63 145
Acute rheumatic fever and chronic rheumatic heart diseases — Rhumatisme articularie aigu et cardiopathies rhumatismales chroniques	4.0	149	3.4	77	1.7	375	3.6	357
Hypertensive diseases — Maladies hypertensives	21.4	837	18.9	787	17.7	377	3.6	355
Ischaemic heart disease — Cardiopathie ischémique	213.2	8 871	199.9	8 829	198.7	30 442	294.7	27 845
Cerebrovascular disease — Maladie cérébrovasculaire	191.3	8 337	187.9	8 369	188.4	18 139	175.6	16 919
Diseases of arteries, arterioles and capillaries — Maladies des artères, artérioles et capillaires	29.4	1 382	31.1	1 184	26.6	11 483	111.2	11 431
Diseases of the respiratory system — Maladies de l'appareil respiratoire								
Total	46.6	1 939	43.7	2 105	47.4	5 073	49.1	4 673
Influenza — Grippe	0.8	3	♦0.1	11	♦0.2	130	1.3	43
Pneumonia — Pneumopathies	19.4	869	19.6	991	22.3	3 041	29.4	3 080
Chronic lower respiratory diseases — Maladies chroniques des voies respiratoires inférieures	23.4	923	20.8	874	19.7	1 435	13.9	1 171
Diseases of the digestive system — Maladies de l'appareil digestif								
Total	57.2	2 371	53.4	2 394	53.9	4 322	41.8	4 143
Gastric and duodenal ulcer — Ulcère de l'estomac et du duodénum	5.3	211	4.8	227	5.1	592	5.7	532

21. Death and death rates by cause: 1995 - 2002
Décès selon la cause, nombres et taux: 1995 - 2002 (continued — suite)

(See notes at end of table. — Voir notes à la fin du tableau.)

Czech Republic — République Tchéque

Cause of death — Cause de décès	1996 Rate Taux	1997 Number Nombre	1997 Rate Taux	1998 Number Nombre	1998 Rate Taux	1999 Number Nombre	1999 Rate Taux	2000 Number Nombre
TOTAL	1093.3	112 744	1094.2	109 527	1063.9	109 768	1067.5	109 001
Certain infectious and parasitic diseases — Certaines maladies infectieuses et parasitaires								
Total	2.4	229	2.2	266	2.6	265	2.6	268
Intestinal infectious diseases — Maladies infectieuses intestinales	♦0.1	21	♦0.2	16	♦0.2	10	♦0.1	9
Tuberculosis — Tuberculose	1.0	95	0.9	126	1.2	127	1.2	125
Diphtheria — Diphtérie	-	1	0.0	-	-	-	-	-
Whooping cough — Coqueluche	-	-	-	-	-	-	-	-
Meningococcal infection — Infection à méningocoques	♦0.2	13	♦0.1	14	♦0.1	7	♦0.1	9
Septicaemia — Septicémie	0.8	63	0.6	70	0.7	61	0.6	86
Acute poliomyelitis — Poliomyélite aiguë	-	-	-	-	-	-	-	-
Measles — Rougeole	-	-	-	-	-	-	-	-
Viral hepatitis — Hépatite virale	♦0.2	9	♦0.1	11	♦0.1	26	♦0.3	17
Human immunodeficiency virus [HIV] disease — Maladies dues au virus de l'immunodéficience humaine (VIH)	0.0	3	0.0	1	0.0	3	0.0	1
Malaria — Paludisme	0.0	-	-	1	0.0	-	-	-
Neoplasms — Tumeurs	270.3	28 008	271.8	28 015	272.1	28 185	274.1	28 705
Malignant neoplasms — Tumeurs malignes								
Total	268.9	27 836	270.2	27 866	270.7	28 038	272.7	28 539
Malignant neoplasm of lip, oral cavity and pharynx — Tumeur maligne de la lèvre, de la cavité buccale et du pharynx	5.7	563	5.5	559	5.4	585	5.7	590
Malignant neoplasm of oesophagus — Tumeur maligne de l'oesophage	3.8	411	4.0	419	4.1	390	3.8	407
Malignant neoplasm of stomach — Tumeur maligne de l'estomac	18.0	1 728	16.8	1 606	15.6	1 538	15.0	1 565
Malignant neoplasm of colon, rectosigmoid junction, rectum, anus and anal canal — Tumeur maligne du côlon, de la jonction recto-sigmoïdienne, du rectum, de l'anus et du canal anal	41.3	4 352	42.2	4 316	41.9	4 395	42.7	4 402
Malignant neoplasm of liver and intrahepatic bile ducts — Tumeur maligne du foie et des voies bilaires intrahépatiques	9.1	988	9.6	930	9.0	936	9.1	936
Malignant neoplasm of pancreas — Tumeur maligne du pancréas	14.4	1 540	14.9	1 512	14.7	1 457	14.2	1 566
Malignant neoplasm of trachea, bronchus and lung — Tumeur maligne de la trachée, des bronches et du poumon	54.2	5 561	54.0	5 433	52.8	5 620	54.7	5 726
Malignant neoplasm of female breast — Tumeur maligne du sein chez la femme	▲43.0	1 943	▲44.0	1 913	▲42.4	1 895	▲41.8	1 939
Malignant neoplasm of cervix uteri — Tumeur maligne du col de l'utérus	▲9.5	411	▲9.3	407	▲9.0	392	▲8.6	363
Malignant neoplasm of prostate — Tumeur maligne de la prostate	▼89.2	1 172	▼85.1	1 289	▼89.4	1 300	▼88.2	1 327
Malignant neoplasm of lymphoid, haematopoietic and related tissue — Tumeurs malignes primitives ou présumées primitives des tissus lymphoïde, hématopoïétique et apparentés	16.9	1 793	17.4	1 815	17.6	1 876	18.2	1 916
Disorders of the blood and blood-forming organs and certain disorders involving the immune mechanism — Maladies du sang et des organes hématopoïétiques et certains troubles du système immunitaire								
Total	1.2	116	1.1	89	0.9	92	0.9	94
Anaemias — Anémies	0.5	47	0.5	28	♦0.3	32	0.3	35
Endocrine, nutritional and metabolic diseases — Maladies endocriniennes, nutritionnelles et métaboliques								
Total	8.2	1 057	10.3	1 543	15.0	1 233	12.0	1 476
Diabetes mellitus — Diabète sucré	7.8	997	9.7	1 488	14.5	1 169	11.4	1 414
Malnutrition — Malnutrition	0.0	7	♦0.1	6	♦0.1	3	0.0	11
Mental and behavioural disorders — Troubles mentaux et du comportement	0.6	60	0.6	70	0.7	73	0.7	110
Diseases of the nervous system — Maladies du système nerveux	10.7	1 213	11.8	1 197	11.6	1 262	12.3	1 458
Diseases of the circulatory system — Maladies de l'appareil circulatoire								
Total	612.1	63 334	614.7	60 397	586.7	60 286	586.3	58 192
Acute rheumatic fever and chronic rheumatic heart diseases — Rhumatisme articularie aigu et cardiopathies rhumatismales chroniques	3.5	357	3.5	320	3.1	333	3.2	313
Hypertensive diseases — Maladies hypertensives	3.4	770	7.5	729	7.1	949	9.2	1 212
Ischaemic heart disease — Cardiopathie ischémique	269.9	26 126	253.6	24 040	233.5	24 521	238.5	23 384
Cerebrovascular disease — Maladie cérébrovasculaire	164.0	15 221	147.7	16 651	161.7	17 007	165.4	17 343
Diseases of arteries, arterioles and capillaries — Maladies des artères, artérioles et capillaires	110.8	15 283	148.3	12 830	124.6	11 841	115.2	10 943
Diseases of the respiratory system — Maladies de l'appareil respiratoire								
Total	45.3	4 313	41.9	4 105	39.9	4 659	45.3	4 959
Influenza — Grippe	0.4	44	0.4	39	0.4	98	1.0	123
Pneumonia — Pneumopathies	29.9	2 595	25.2	2 089	20.3	2 453	23.9	2 485
Chronic lower respiratory diseases — Maladies chroniques des voies respiratoires inférieures	11.4	1 319	12.8	1 563	15.2	1 655	16.1	1 876
Diseases of the digestive system — Maladies de l'appareil digestif								
Total	40.2	4 018	39.0	4 158	40.4	4 248	41.3	4 239
Gastric and duodenal ulcer — Ulcère de l'estomac et du duodénum	5.2	527	5.1	513	5.0	521	5.1	608

21. Death and death rates by cause: 1995 - 2002
Décès selon la cause, nombres et taux: 1995 - 2002 (continued — suite)

(See notes at end of table. — Voir notes à la fin du tableau.)

Cause of death — Cause de décès	Czech Republic — République Tchèque					Denmark — Danemark[12]		
	2000	2001		2002		1995		1996
	Rate Taux	Number Nombre	Rate Taux	Number Nombre	Rate Taux	Number Nombre	Rate Taux	Number Nombre
TOTAL	1061.1	107 755	1053.9	108 243	1061.1	62 815	1201.5	60 712
Certain infectious and parasitic diseases — Certaines maladies infectieuses et parasitaires								
Total	2.6	303	3.0	320	3.1	637	12.2	530
Intestinal infectious diseases — Maladies infectieuses intestinales	✝0.1	13	✝0.1	12	✝0.1	95	1.8	89
Tuberculosis — Tuberculose	1.2	94	0.9	82	0.8	23	✝0.4	40
Tetanus — Tétanos	-	2	0.0	2	0.0	1	0.0	-
Diphtheria — Diphtérie	-	-	-	-	-	1	0.0	-
Whooping cough — Coqueluche	-	-	-	-	-	-	-	-
Meningococcal infection — Infection à méningocoques	✝0.1	9	✝0.1	13	✝0.1	17	✝0.3	11
Septicaemia — Septicémie	0.8	125	1.2	175	1.7	127	2.4	125
Acute poliomyelitis — Poliomyélite aiguë	-	-	-	-	-	1	0.0	-
Measles — Rougeole	-	-	-	-	-	-	-	-
Viral hepatitis — Hépatite virale	✝0.2	17	✝0.2	14	✝0.1	5	✝0.1	14
Human immunodeficiency virus [HIV] disease — Maladies dues au virus de l'immunodéficience humaine (VIH)	0.0	3	0.0	-	-	255	4.9	162
Malaria — Paludisme	-	-	-	-	-	1	0.0	-
Neoplasms — Tumeurs	279.4	28 455	278.3	28 893	283.2	16 142	308.8	15 649
Malignant neoplasms — Tumeurs malignes								
Total	277.8	28 294	276.7	28 709	281.4	15 701	300.3	15 216
Malignant neoplasm of lip, oral cavity and pharynx — Tumeur maligne de la lèvre, de la cavité buccale et du pharynx	5.7	590	5.8	640	6.3	252	4.8	272
Malignant neoplasm of oesophagus — Tumeur maligne de l'oesophage	4.0	379	3.7	400	3.9	343	6.6	354
Malignant neoplasm of stomach — Tumeur maligne de l'estomac	15.2	1 466	14.3	1 482	14.5	479	9.2	500
Malignant neoplasm of colon, rectosigmoid junction, rectum, anus and anal canal — Tumeur maligne du côlon, de la jonction recto-sigmoïdienne, du rectum, de l'anus et du canal anal	42.9	4 381	42.8	4 453	43.7	2 068	39.6	2 061
Malignant neoplasm of liver and intrahepatic bile ducts — Tumeur maligne du foie et des voies biliaires intrahépatiques	9.1	938	9.2	953	9.3	301	5.8	269
Malignant neoplasm of pancreas — Tumeur maligne du pancréas	15.2	1 615	15.8	1 613	15.8	711	13.6	664
Malignant neoplasm of trachea, bronchus and lung — Tumeur maligne de la trachée, des bronches et du poumon	55.7	5 635	55.1	5 563	54.5	3 506	67.1	3 387
Malignant neoplasm of female breast — Tumeur maligne du sein chez la femme	▲43.5	1 893	▲42.5	1 965	▲44.0	1 476	▲66.9	1 365
Malignant neoplasm of cervix uteri — Tumeur maligne du col de l'utérus	▲8.1	388	▲8.7	399	▲8.9	177	▲8.0	173
Malignant neoplasm of prostate — Tumeur maligne de la prostate	▼90.1	1 341	▼90.3	1 400	▼91.6	1 050	▼137.6	1 045
Malignant neoplasm of lymphoid, haematopoietic and related tissue — Tumeurs malignes primitives ou présumées primitives des tissus lymphoïde, hématopoïétique et apparentés	18.7	1 918	18.8	1 824	17.9	1 178	22.5	1 042
Disorders of the blood and blood-forming organs and certain disorders involving the immune mechanism — Maladies du sang et des organes hématopoïétiques et certains troubles du système immunitaire								
Total	0.9	80	0.8	79	0.8	120	2.3	151
Anaemias — Anémies	0.3	26	✝0.3	29	✝0.3	80	1.5	93
Endocrine, nutritional and metabolic diseases — Maladies endocriniennes, nutritionnelles et métaboliques								
Total	14.4	1 263	12.4	1 334	13.1	1 034	19.8	901
Diabetes mellitus — Diabète sucré	13.8	1 207	11.8	1 276	12.5	795	15.2	629
Malnutrition — Malnutrition	✝0.1	3	0.0	7	✝0.1	4	✝0.1	9
Mental and behavioural disorders — Troubles mentaux et du comportement	1.1	114	1.1	111	1.1	935	17.9	786
Diseases of the nervous system — Maladies du système nerveux	14.2	1 671	16.3	1 814	17.8	890	17.0	805
Diseases of the circulatory system — Maladies de l'appareil circulatoire								
Total	566.5	57 404	561.5	57 152	560.3	24 926	476.8	22 540
Acute rheumatic fever and chronic rheumatic heart diseases — Rhumatisme articularie aigu et cardiopathies rhumatismales chroniques	3.0	295	2.9	229	2.2	80	1.5	32
Hypertensive diseases — Maladies hypertensives	11.8	1 204	11.8	1 218	11.9	344	6.6	312
Ischaemic heart disease — Cardiopathie ischémique	227.6	22 971	224.7	22 504	220.6	12 678	242.5	11 022
Cerebrovascular disease — Maladie cérébrovasculaire	168.8	16 845	164.8	16 536	162.1	5 543	106.0	5 464
Diseases of arteries, arterioles and capillaries — Maladies des artères, artérioles et capillaires	106.5	11 056	108.1	11 358	111.3	1 890	36.2	1 705
Diseases of the respiratory system — Maladies de l'appareil respiratoire								
Total	48.3	4 653	45.5	4 713	46.2	5 622	107.5	5 689
Influenza — Grippe	1.2	29	✝0.3	27	✝0.3	147	2.8	180
Pneumonia — Pneumopathies	24.2	2 318	22.7	2 374	23.3	1 948	37.3	2 104
Chronic lower respiratory diseases — Maladies chroniques des voies respiratoires inférieures	18.3	1 806	17.7	1 778	17.4	3 152	60.3	3 011
Diseases of the digestive system — Maladies de l'appareil digestif								
Total	41.3	4 418	43.2	4 435	43.5	2 828	54.1	2 428
Gastric and duodenal ulcer — Ulcère de l'estomac et du duodénum	5.9	583	5.7	577	5.7	651	12.5	571

21. Death and death rates by cause: 1995 - 2002
Décès selon la cause, nombres et taux: 1995 - 2002 (continued — suite)

(See notes at end of table. — Voir notes à la fin du tableau.)

Denmark — Danemark[12]

Cause of death — Cause de décès	1996 Rate Taux	1997 Number Nombre	1997 Rate Taux	1998 Number Nombre	1998 Rate Taux	1999 Number Nombre	1999 Rate Taux	2000 Number Nombre
TOTAL	1153.9	59 606	1128.0	58 079	1095.6	58 722	1102.3	57 044
Certain infectious and parasitic diseases — Certaines maladies infectieuses et parasitaires								
Total	10.1	376	7.1	351	6.6	465	8.7	374
Intestinal infectious diseases — Maladies infectieuses intestinales	1.7	71	1.3	59	1.1	77	1.4	65
Tuberculosis — Tuberculose	0.8	27	◆0.5	23	◆0.4	21	◆0.4	20
Tetanus — Tétanos	-	-	-	2	0.0	-	-	-
Diphtheria — Diphtérie	-	-	-	1	0.0	-	-	-
Whooping cough — Coqueluche	-	-	-	-	-	1	0.0	-
Meningococcal infection — Infection à méningocoques	◆0.2	8	◆0.2	5	◆0.1	10	◆0.2	12
Septicaemia — Septicémie	2.4	88	1.7	84	1.6	179	3.4	135
Acute poliomyelitis — Poliomyélite aiguë	-	-	-	-	-	-	-	-
Measles — Rougeole	-	-	-	-	-	-	-	-
Viral hepatitis — Hépatite virale	◆0.3	8	◆0.2	17	◆0.3	13	◆0.2	15
Human immunodeficiency virus [HIV] disease — Maladies dues au virus de l'immunodéficience humaine (VIH)	3.1	65	1.2	38	0.7	45	0.8	29
Malaria — Paludisme	-	3	◆0.1	1	0.0	-	-	1
Neoplasms — Tumeurs	297.4	15 814	299.3	15 730	296.7	15 956	299.5	15 966
Malignant neoplasms — Tumeurs malignes								
Total	289.2	15 254	288.7	15 184	286.4	15 444	289.9	15 478
Malignant neoplasm of lip, oral cavity and pharynx — Tumeur maligne de la lèvre, de la cavité buccale et du pharynx	5.2	265	5.0	271	5.1	262	4.9	308
Malignant neoplasm of oesophagus — Tumeur maligne de l'oesophage	6.7	347	6.6	366	6.9	396	7.4	412
Malignant neoplasm of stomach — Tumeur maligne de l'estomac	9.5	426	8.1	413	7.8	402	7.5	368
Malignant neoplasm of colon, rectosigmoid junction, rectum, anus and anal canal — Tumeur maligne du côlon, de la jonction recto-sigmoïdienne, du rectum, de l'anus et du canal anal	39.2	2 150	40.7	2 068	39.0	2 102	39.5	2 064
Malignant neoplasm of liver and intrahepatic bile ducts — Tumeur maligne du foie et des voies bilaires intrahépatiques	5.1	254	4.8	253	4.8	273	5.1	256
Malignant neoplasm of pancreas — Tumeur maligne du pancréas	12.6	664	12.6	771	14.5	791	14.8	795
Malignant neoplasm of trachea, bronchus and lung — Tumeur maligne de la trachée, des bronches et du poumon	64.4	3 427	64.9	3 267	61.6	3 376	63.4	3 430
Malignant neoplasm of female breast — Tumeur maligne du sein chez la femme	▲61.7	1 421	▲64.2	1 359	▲61.3	1 363	▲61.0	1 329
Malignant neoplasm of cervix uteri — Tumeur maligne du col de l'utérus	▲7.8	193	▲8.7	176	▲7.9	191	▲8.6	142
Malignant neoplasm of prostate — Tumeur maligne de la prostate	▼134.0	994	▼125.3	1 009	▼124.4	1 033	▼125.6	1 084
Malignant neoplasm of lymphoid, haematopoietic and related tissue — Tumeurs malignes primitives ou présumées primitives des tissus lymphoïde, hématopoïétique et apparentés	19.8	1 107	20.9	1 137	21.4	1 157	21.7	1 071
Disorders of the blood and blood-forming organs and certain disorders involving the immune mechanism — Maladies du sang et des organes hématopoïétiques et certains troubles du système immunitaire								
Total	2.9	151	2.9	181	3.4	190	3.6	197
Anaemias — Anémies	1.8	101	1.9	131	2.5	133	2.5	141
Endocrine, nutritional and metabolic diseases — Maladies endocriniennes, nutritionnelles et métaboliques								
Total	17.1	1 382	26.2	1 544	29.1	1 832	34.4	1 882
Diabetes mellitus — Diabète sucré	12.0	1 093	20.7	1 195	22.5	1 367	25.7	1 433
Malnutrition — Malnutrition	◆0.2	4	◆0.1	11	◆0.2	34	0.6	48
Mental and behavioural disorders — Troubles mentaux et du comportement	14.9	1 234	23.4	1 397	26.4	1 751	32.9	1 592
Diseases of the nervous system — Maladies du système nerveux	15.3	938	17.8	1 006	19.0	1 103	20.7	1 143
Diseases of the circulatory system — Maladies de l'appareil circulatoire								
Total	428.4	22 003	416.4	21 274	401.3	21 459	402.8	20 531
Acute rheumatic fever and chronic rheumatic heart diseases — Rhumatisme articularie aigu et cardiopathies rhumatismales chroniques	0.6	24	◆0.5	31	0.6	20	◆0.4	23
Hypertensive diseases — Maladies hypertensives	5.9	373	7.1	448	8.5	592	11.1	501
Ischaemic heart disease — Cardiopathie ischémique	209.5	10 764	203.7	10 029	189.2	9 906	185.9	9 111
Cerebrovascular disease — Maladie cérébrovasculaire	103.8	5 150	97.5	4 998	94.3	5 000	93.9	4 994
Diseases of arteries, arterioles and capillaries — Maladies des artères, artérioles et capillaires	32.4	1 773	33.6	1 684	31.8	1 597	30.0	1 643
Diseases of the respiratory system — Maladies de l'appareil respiratoire								
Total	108.1	5 429	102.7	5 284	99.7	5 626	105.6	5 222
Influenza — Grippe	3.4	62	1.2	44	0.8	114	2.1	55
Pneumonia — Pneumopathies	40.0	1 660	31.4	1 441	27.2	1 493	28.0	1 153
Chronic lower respiratory diseases — Maladies chroniques des voies respiratoires inférieures	57.2	3 360	63.6	3 502	66.1	3 651	68.5	3 663
Diseases of the digestive system — Maladies de l'appareil digestif								
Total	46.1	2 847	53.9	2 806	52.9	2 886	54.2	2 800
Gastric and duodenal ulcer — Ulcère de l'estomac et du duodénum	10.9	576	10.9	565	10.7	576	10.8	567

21. Death and death rates by cause: 1995 - 2002
Décès selon la cause, nombres et taux: 1995 - 2002 (continued — suite)

(See notes at end of table. — Voir notes à la fin du tableau.)

Cause of death — Cause de décès	Denmark — Danemark[12] 2000 Rate Taux	Estonia — Estonie[6] 1995 Number Nombre	1995 Rate Taux	1996 Number Nombre	1996 Rate Taux	1997 Number Nombre	1997 Rate Taux	1998 Number Nombre
TOTAL	1068.8	20 828	1403.6	19 020	1294.6	18 566	1273.4	19 446
Certain infectious and parasitic diseases — Certaines maladies infectieuses et parasitaires								
Total	7.0	203	13.7	178	12.1	180	12.3	180
Intestinal infectious diseases — Maladies infectieuses intestinales	1.2	7	♦0.5	4	♦0.3	3	♦0.2	6
Tuberculosis — Tuberculose	♦0.4	140	9.4	132	9.0	137	9.4	142
Tetanus — Tétanos	-	1	♦0.1	1	♦0.1	2	♦0.1	-
Diphtheria — Diphtérie	-	2	♦0.1	-	-	-	-	-
Whooping cough — Coqueluche	-	-	-	-	-	-	-	-
Meningococcal infection — Infection à méningocoques	♦0.2	5	♦0.3	3	♦0.2	4	♦0.3	1
Septicaemia — Septicémie	2.5	14	♦0.9	8	♦0.5	11	♦0.8	7
Acute poliomyelitis — Poliomyélite aiguë	-	-	-	-	-	-	-	-
Measles — Rougeole	-	-	-	-	-	-	-	-
Viral hepatitis — Hépatite virale	♦0.3	4	♦0.3	2	♦0.1	2	♦0.1	6
Human immunodeficiency virus [HIV] disease — Maladies dues au virus de l'immunodéficience humaine (VIH)	♦0.5	-	-	2	♦0.1	3	♦0.2	3
Malaria — Paludisme	0.0	1	♦0.1	-	-	-	-	-
Neoplasms — Tumeurs	299.1	3 310	223.1	3 298	224.5	3 357	230.2	3 445
Malignant neoplasms — Tumeurs malignes								
Total	290.0	3 280	221.0	3 284	223.5	3 329	228.3	3 407
Malignant neoplasm of lip, oral cavity and pharynx — Tumeur maligne de la lèvre, de la cavité buccale et du pharynx	5.8	108	7.3	105	7.1	90	6.2	101
Malignant neoplasm of oesophagus — Tumeur maligne de l'oesophage	7.7	48	3.2	72	4.9	55	3.8	49
Malignant neoplasm of stomach — Tumeur maligne de l'estomac	6.9	399	26.9	411	28.0	384	26.3	423
Malignant neoplasm of colon, rectosigmoid junction, rectum, anus and anal canal — Tumeur maligne du côlon, de la jonction recto-sigmoïdienne, du rectum, de l'anus et du canal anal	38.7	366	24.7	355	24.2	349	23.9	356
Malignant neoplasm of liver and intrahepatic bile ducts — Tumeur maligne du foie et des voies bilaires intrahépatiques	4.8	...	...	...	...	96	6.6	64
Malignant neoplasm of pancreas — Tumeur maligne du pancréas	14.9	173	11.7	148	10.1	155	10.6	180
Malignant neoplasm of trachea, bronchus and lung — Tumeur maligne de la trachée, des bronches et du poumon	64.3	713	48.0	674	45.9	710	48.7	702
Malignant neoplasm of female breast — Tumeur maligne du sein chez la femme	▲59.9	250	▲38.9	257	▲40.1	239	▲37.3	238
Malignant neoplasm of cervix uteri — Tumeur maligne du col de l'utérus	▲6.4	70	▲10.9	76	▲11.9	98	▲15.3	78
Malignant neoplasm of prostate — Tumeur maligne de la prostate	▼129.9	115	▼66.1	116	▼67.1	143	▼82.5	171
Malignant neoplasm of lymphoid, haematopoietic and related tissue — Tumeurs malignes primitives ou présumées primitives des tissus lymphoïde, hématopoïétique et apparentés	20.1	199	13.4	233	15.9	191	13.1	219
Disorders of the blood and blood-forming organs and certain disorders involving the immune mechanism — Maladies du sang et des organes hématopoïétiques et certains troubles du système immunitaire								
Total	3.7	27	♦1.8	25	♦1.7	10	♦0.7	19
Anaemias — Anémies	2.6	14	♦0.9	16	♦1.1	6	♦0.4	13
Endocrine, nutritional and metabolic diseases — Maladies endocriniennes, nutritionnelles et métaboliques								
Total	35.3	130	8.8	116	7.9	137	9.4	139
Diabetes mellitus — Diabète sucré	26.8	97	6.5	87	5.9	107	7.3	121
Malnutrition — Malnutrition	0.9	8	♦0.5	5	♦0.3	9	♦0.6	3
Mental and behavioural disorders — Troubles mentaux et du comportement	29.8	48	3.2	30	♦2.0	8	♦0.5	14
Diseases of the nervous system — Maladies du système nerveux	21.4	188	12.7	149	10.1	186	12.8	187
Diseases of the circulatory system — Maladies de l'appareil circulatoire								
Total	384.7	11 456	772.0	10 518	715.9	10 063	690.2	10 620
Acute rheumatic fever and chronic rheumatic heart diseases — Rhumatisme articulaire aigu et cardiopathies rhumatismales chroniques	♦0.4	86	5.8	92	6.3	100	6.9	100
Hypertensive diseases — Maladies hypertensives	9.4	258	17.4	212	14.4	242	16.6	249
Ischaemic heart disease — Cardiopathie ischémique	170.7	6 987	470.8	6 445	438.7	5 968	409.3	6 444
Cerebrovascular disease — Maladie cérébrovasculaire	93.6	3 474	234.1	3 173	216.0	3 057	209.7	3 111
Diseases of arteries, arterioles and capillaries — Maladies des artères, artérioles et capillaires	30.8	253	17.0	239	16.3	277	19.0	257
Diseases of the respiratory system — Maladies de l'appareil respiratoire								
Total	97.8	631	42.5	585	39.8	523	35.9	603
Influenza — Grippe	1.0	11	♦0.7	16	♦1.1	7	♦0.5	5
Pneumonia — Pneumopathies	21.6	302	20.4	302	20.6	250	17.1	309
Chronic lower respiratory diseases — Maladies chroniques des voies respiratoires inférieures	68.6	279	18.8	236	16.1	212	14.5	235
Diseases of the digestive system — Maladies de l'appareil digestif								
Total	52.5	535	36.1	513	34.9	567	38.9	643
Gastric and duodenal ulcer — Ulcère de l'estomac et du duodénum	10.6	81	5.5	91	6.2	78	5.3	92

21. Death and death rates by cause: 1995 - 2002
Décès selon la cause, nombres et taux: 1995 - 2002 (continued — suite)

(See notes at end of table. — Voir notes à la fin du tableau.)

Estonia — Estonie[6]

Cause of death — Cause de décès	1998 Rate Taux	1999 Number Nombre	1999 Rate Taux	2000 Number Nombre	2000 Rate Taux	2001 Number Nombre	2001 Rate Taux	2002 Number Nombre
TOTAL	1341.4	18 454	1279.4	18 403	1343.8	18 516	1357.4	18 355
Certain infectious and parasitic diseases — Certaines maladies infectieuses et parasitaires								
Total	12.4	180	12.5	147	10.7	145	10.6	123
Intestinal infectious diseases — Maladies infectieuses intestinales	♦0.4	8	♦0.6	3	♦0.2	1	♦0.1	5
Tuberculosis — Tuberculose	9.8	140	9.7	106	7.7	96	7.0	88
Tetanus — Tétanos	-	-	-	1	♦0.1	-	-	-
Diphtheria — Diphtérie	-	-	-	-	-	-	-	-
Whooping cough — Coqueluche	-	-	-	-	-	-	-	-
Meningococcal infection — Infection à méningocoques	♦0.1	3	♦0.2	2	♦0.1	2	♦0.1	-
Septicaemia — Septicémie	♦0.5	9	♦0.6	16	♦1.2	14	♦1.0	17
Acute poliomyelitis — Poliomyélite aiguë	-	-	-	-	-	-	-	-
Measles — Rougeole	-	-	-	-	-	-	-	-
Viral hepatitis — Hépatite virale	♦0.4	3	♦0.2	4	♦0.3	3	♦0.2	1
Human immunodeficiency virus [HIV] disease — Maladies dues au virus de l'immunodéficience humaine (VIH)	♦0.2	1	♦0.1	3	♦0.2	3	♦0.2	3
Malaria — Paludisme	-	-	-	-	-	-	-	-
Neoplasms — Tumeurs	237.6	3 277	227.2	3 389	247.5	3 331	244.2	3 453
Malignant neoplasms — Tumeurs malignes								
Total	235.0	3 243	224.8	3 365	245.7	3 301	242.0	3 426
Malignant neoplasm of lip, oral cavity and pharynx — Tumeur maligne de la lèvre, de la cavité buccale et du pharynx	7.0	86	6.0	99	7.2	119	8.7	107
Malignant neoplasm of oesophagus — Tumeur maligne de l'oesophage	3.4	51	3.5	43	3.1	52	3.8	46
Malignant neoplasm of stomach — Tumeur maligne de l'estomac	29.2	396	27.5	367	26.8	336	24.6	342
Malignant neoplasm of colon, rectosigmoid junction, rectum, anus and anal canal — Tumeur maligne du côlon, de la jonction recto-sigmoïdienne, du rectum, de l'anus et du canal anal	24.6	383	26.6	363	26.5	361	26.5	411
Malignant neoplasm of liver and intrahepatic bile ducts — Tumeur maligne du foie et des voies bilaires intrahépatiques	4.4	78	5.4	93	6.8	79	5.8	93
Malignant neoplasm of pancreas — Tumeur maligne du pancréas	12.4	169	11.7	170	12.4	184	13.5	180
Malignant neoplasm of trachea, bronchus and lung — Tumeur maligne de la trachée, des bronches et du poumon	40.4	652	45.2	687	50.2	678	49.7	686
Malignant neoplasm of female breast — Tumeur maligne du sein chez la femme	▲37.1	244	▲38.0	277	▲44.8	257	▲41.5	256
Malignant neoplasm of cervix uteri — Tumeur maligne du col de l'utérus	▲12.2	66	▲10.3	61	▲9.9	59	▲9.5	63
Malignant neoplasm of prostate — Tumeur maligne de la prostate	▼98.0	151	▼85.8	180	▼103.6	154	▼88.1	178
Malignant neoplasm of lymphoid, haematopoietic and related tissue — Tumeurs malignes primitives ou présumées primitives des tissus lymphoïde, hématopoïétique et apparentés	15.1	196	13.6	203	14.8	239	17.5	234
Disorders of the blood and blood-forming organs and certain disorders involving the immune mechanism — Maladies du sang et des organes hématopoïétiques et certains troubles du système immunitaire								
Total	♦1.3	17	♦1.2	12	♦0.9	15	♦1.1	11
Anaemias — Anémies	♦0.9	12	♦0.8	8	♦0.6	5	♦0.4	8
Endocrine, nutritional and metabolic diseases — Maladies endocriniennes, nutritionnelles et métaboliques								
Total	9.6	152	10.5	156	11.4	177	13.0	153
Diabetes mellitus — Diabète sucré	8.3	129	8.9	126	9.2	159	11.7	132
Malnutrition — Malnutrition	♦0.2	6	♦0.4	3	♦0.2	3	♦0.2	2
Mental and behavioural disorders — Troubles mentaux et du comportement	♦1.0	24	♦1.7	25	♦1.8	65	4.8	61
Diseases of the nervous system — Maladies du système nerveux	12.9	177	12.3	183	13.4	230	16.9	228
Diseases of the circulatory system — Maladies de l'appareil circulatoire								
Total	732.6	10 104	700.5	9 982	728.9	9 922	727.4	9 983
Acute rheumatic fever and chronic rheumatic heart diseases — Rhumatisme articulaire aigu et cardiopathies rhumatismales chroniques	6.9	77	5.3	64	4.7	68	5.0	57
Hypertensive diseases — Maladies hypertensives	17.2	293	20.3	332	24.2	345	25.3	440
Ischaemic heart disease — Cardiopathie ischémique	444.5	6 037	418.5	5 940	433.7	5 879	431.0	5 779
Cerebrovascular disease — Maladie cérébrovasculaire	214.6	2 969	205.8	2 904	212.0	2 816	206.4	2 815
Diseases of arteries, arterioles and capillaries — Maladies des artères, artérioles et capillaires	17.7	248	17.2	237	17.3	308	22.6	289
Diseases of the respiratory system — Maladies de l'appareil respiratoire								
Total	41.6	518	35.9	609	44.5	579	42.4	578
Influenza — Grippe	♦0.3	2	♦0.1	5	♦0.4	1	♦0.1	1
Pneumonia — Pneumopathies	21.3	238	16.5	303	22.1	321	23.5	305
Chronic lower respiratory diseases — Maladies chroniques des voies respiratoires inférieures	16.2	234	16.2	229	16.7	195	14.3	206
Diseases of the digestive system — Maladies de l'appareil digestif								
Total	44.4	575	39.9	636	46.4	664	48.7	673
Gastric and duodenal ulcer — Ulcère de l'estomac et du duodénum	6.3	70	4.9	82	6.0	72	5.3	86

21. Death and death rates by cause: 1995 - 2002
Décès selon la cause, nombres et taux: 1995 - 2002 (continued — suite)

(See notes at end of table. — Voir notes à la fin du tableau.)

Cause of death — Cause de décès	Estonia — Estonie[6] 2002 Rate Taux	Finland — Finlande[13] 1995 Number Nombre	1995 Rate Taux	1996 Number Nombre	1996 Rate Taux	1997 Number Nombre	1997 Rate Taux	1998 Number Nombre
TOTAL	1351.0	49 325	965.7	49 161	959.3	49 143	956.1	49 237
Certain infectious and parasitic diseases — Certaines maladies infectieuses et parasitaires								
Total	9.1	393	7.7	438	8.5	357	6.9	363
Intestinal infectious diseases — Maladies infectieuses intestinales	♦0.4	44	0.9	69	1.3	36	0.7	51
Tuberculosis — Tuberculose	6.5	92	1.8	109	2.1	77	1.5	59
Tetanus — Tétanos	-	-	-	1	0.0	-	-	-
Diphtheria — Diphtérie	-	1	0.0	1	0.0	-	-	1
Whooping cough — Coqueluche	-	6	♦0.1	6	♦0.1	1	0.0	5
Meningococcal infection — Infection à méningocoques	♦1.3	83	1.6	101	2.0	88	1.7	94
Septicaemia — Septicémie	-	-	-	1	0.0	-	-	-
Acute poliomyelitis — Poliomyélite aiguë	-	-	-	-	-	-	-	-
Measles — Rougeole	♦0.1	3	♦0.1	11	♦0.2	6	♦0.1	3
Viral hepatitis — Hépatite virale								
Human immunodeficiency virus [HIV] disease — Maladies dues au virus de l'immunodéficience humaine (VIH)	♦0.2	...	...	29	♦0.6	6	♦0.1	6
Malaria — Paludisme	-	1	0.0	-	-	-	-	2
Neoplasms — Tumeurs	254.2	10 308	201.8	10 309	201.2	10 415	202.6	10 503
Malignant neoplasms — Tumeurs malignes								
Total	252.2	10 042	196.6	10 061	196.3	10 155	197.6	10 250
Malignant neoplasm of lip, oral cavity and pharynx — Tumeur maligne de la lèvre, de la cavité buccale et du pharynx	7.9	142	2.8	150	2.9	140	2.7	124
Malignant neoplasm of oesophagus — Tumeur maligne de l'oesophage	3.4	216	4.2	187	3.6	193	3.8	174
Malignant neoplasm of stomach — Tumeur maligne de l'estomac	25.2	666	13.0	666	13.0	660	12.8	592
Malignant neoplasm of colon, rectosigmoid junction, rectum, anus and anal canal — Tumeur maligne du côlon, de la jonction recto-sigmoïdienne, du rectum, de l'anus et du canal anal	30.3	970	19.0	964	18.8	984	19.1	973
Malignant neoplasm of liver and intrahepatic bile ducts — Tumeur maligne du foie et des voies bilaires intrahépatiques	6.8	...	...	314	6.1	314	6.1	338
Malignant neoplasm of pancreas — Tumeur maligne du pancréas	13.2	656	12.8	690	13.5	734	14.3	755
Malignant neoplasm of trachea, bronchus and lung — Tumeur maligne de la trachée, des bronches et du poumon	50.5	1 880	36.8	1 879	36.7	1 843	35.9	1 927
Malignant neoplasm of female breast — Tumeur maligne du sein chez la femme	▲41.2	832	▲38.8	774	▲35.9	788	▲36.4	793
Malignant neoplasm of cervix uteri — Tumeur maligne du col de l'utérus	▲10.1	51	▲2.4	67	▲3.1	76	▲3.5	59
Malignant neoplasm of prostate — Tumeur maligne de la prostate	▼101.1	703	▼105.3	784	▼113.8	719	▼100.9	777
Malignant neoplasm of lymphoid, haematopoietic and related tissue — Tumeurs malignes primitives ou présumées primitives des tissus lymphoïde, hématopoïétique et apparentés	17.2	1 028	20.1	962	18.8	1 002	19.5	1 019
Disorders of the blood and blood-forming organs and certain disorders involving the immune mechanism — Maladies du sang et des organes hématopoïétiques et certains troubles du système immunitaire								
Total	♦0.8	41	0.8	60	1.2	56	1.1	58
Anaemias — Anémies	♦0.6	26	♦0.5	28	♦0.5	27	♦0.5	20
Endocrine, nutritional and metabolic diseases — Maladies endocriniennes, nutritionnelles et métaboliques								
Total	11.3	649	12.7	670	13.1	644	12.5	626
Diabetes mellitus — Diabète sucré	9.7	566	11.1	593	11.6	547	10.6	556
Malnutrition — Malnutrition	♦0.1	-	-	1	0.0	3	♦0.1	1
Mental and behavioural disorders — Troubles mentaux et du comportement	4.5	1 984	38.8	2 678	52.3	2 891	56.2	2 993
Diseases of the nervous system — Maladies du système nerveux	16.8	1 027	20.1	1 269	24.8	1 452	28.2	1 470
Diseases of the circulatory system — Maladies de l'appareil circulatoire								
Total	734.8	23 482	459.7	22 043	430.1	21 674	421.7	21 546
Acute rheumatic fever and chronic rheumatic heart diseases — Rhumatisme articularie aigu et cardiopathies rhumatismales chroniques	4.2	71	1.4	103	2.0	73	1.4	80
Hypertensive diseases — Maladies hypertensives	32.4	357	7.0	440	8.6	425	8.3	446
Ischaemic heart disease — Cardiopathie ischémique	425.4	13 670	267.6	12 969	253.1	12 611	245.4	12 822
Cerebrovascular disease — Maladie cérébrovasculaire	207.2	6 197	121.3	5 296	103.3	5 303	103.2	5 031
Diseases of arteries, arterioles and capillaries — Maladies des artères, artérioles et capillaires	21.3	947	18.5	1 005	19.6	978	19.0	953
Diseases of the respiratory system — Maladies de l'appareil respiratoire								
Total	42.5	3 762	73.7	4 214	82.2	3 999	77.8	4 098
Influenza — Grippe	♦0.1	47	0.9	187	3.6	68	1.3	139
Pneumonia — Pneumopathies	22.4	2 457	48.1	2 703	52.7	2 478	48.2	2 420
Chronic lower respiratory diseases — Maladies chroniques des voies respiratoires inférieures	15.2	1 043	20.4	1 106	21.6	1 174	22.8	1 281
Diseases of the digestive system — Maladies de l'appareil digestif								
Total	49.5	1 941	38.0	1 992	38.9	2 018	39.3	1 990
Gastric and duodenal ulcer — Ulcère de l'estomac et du duodénum	6.3	334	6.5	300	5.9	272	5.3	233

21. Death and death rates by cause: 1995 - 2002
Décès selon la cause, nombres et taux: 1995 - 2002 (continued — suite)

(See notes at end of table. — Voir notes à la fin du tableau.)

Finland — Finlande[13]

Cause of death — Cause de décès	1998 Rate Taux	1999 Number Nombre	1999 Rate Taux	2000 Number Nombre	2000 Rate Taux	2001 Number Nombre	2001 Rate Taux	2002 Number Nombre
TOTAL	955.4	49 368	955.7	49 316	952.7	48 504	934.9	49 389
Certain infectious and parasitic diseases — Certaines maladies infectieuses et parasitaires								
Total	7.0	395	7.6	393	7.6	365	7.0	381
Intestinal infectious diseases — Maladies infectieuses intestinales	1.0	44	0.9	32	0.6	32	0.6	60
Tuberculosis — Tuberculose	1.1	67	1.3	84	1.6	53	1.0	57
Tetanus — Tétanos	-	1	0.0	-	-	-	-	-
Diphtheria — Diphtérie	-	-	-	-	-	1	0.0	-
Whooping cough — Coqueluche	0.0	2	0.0	-	-	-	-	-
Meningococcal infection — Infection à méningocoques	♦0.1	13	♦0.3	6	♦0.1	6	♦0.1	7
Septicaemia — Septicémie	1.8	104	2.0	120	2.3	112	2.2	111
Acute poliomyelitis — Poliomyélite aiguë	-	-	-	-	-	-	-	-
Measles — Rougeole	-	-	-	-	-	-	-	-
Viral hepatitis — Hépatite virale	♦0.1	2	0.0	10	♦0.2	17	♦0.3	12
Human immunodeficiency virus [HIV] disease — Maladies dues au virus de l'immunodéficience humaine (VIH)	♦0.1	9	♦0.2	10	♦0.2	3	♦0.1	7
Malaria — Paludisme	0.0	-	-	-	-	-	-	-
Neoplasms — Tumeurs	203.8	10 445	202.2	10 492	202.7	10 608	204.5	10 522
Malignant neoplasms — Tumeurs malignes								
Total	198.9	10 188	197.2	10 234	197.7	10 326	199.0	10 221
Malignant neoplasm of lip, oral cavity and pharynx — Tumeur maligne de la lèvre, de la cavité buccale et du pharynx	2.4	149	2.9	149	2.9	153	2.9	135
Malignant neoplasm of oesophagus — Tumeur maligne de l'oesophage	3.4	206	4.0	176	3.4	202	3.9	191
Malignant neoplasm of stomach — Tumeur maligne de l'estomac	11.5	561	10.9	562	10.9	566	10.9	568
Malignant neoplasm of colon, rectosigmoid junction, rectum, anus and anal canal — Tumeur maligne du côlon, de la jonction recto-sigmoïdienne, du rectum, de l'anus et du canal anal	18.9	994	19.2	1 025	19.8	997	19.2	992
Malignant neoplasm of liver and intrahepatic bile ducts — Tumeur maligne du foie et des voies bilaires intrahépatiques	6.6	369	7.1	349	6.7	377	7.3	350
Malignant neoplasm of pancreas — Tumeur maligne du pancréas	14.7	695	13.5	721	13.9	747	14.4	755
Malignant neoplasm of trachea, bronchus and lung — Tumeur maligne de la trachée, des bronches et du poumon	37.4	1 811	35.1	1 846	35.7	1 894	36.5	1 852
Malignant neoplasm of female breast — Tumeur maligne du sein chez la femme	▲36.5	842	▲38.6	822	...	849	▲38.6	787
Malignant neoplasm of cervix uteri — Tumeur maligne du col de l'utérus	▲2.7	61	▲2.8	77	...	66	▲3.0	49
Malignant neoplasm of prostate — Tumeur maligne de la prostate	▼105.4	779	▼102.5	750	...	779	▼97.1	809
Malignant neoplasm of lymphoid, haematopoietic and related tissue — Tumeurs malignes primitives ou présumées primitives des tissus lymphoïde, hématopoïétique et apparentés	19.8	1 105	21.4	1 058	20.4	1 061	20.5	1 030
Disorders of the blood and blood-forming organs and certain disorders involving the immune mechanism — Maladies du sang et des organes hématopoïétiques et certains troubles du système immunitaire								
Total	1.1	67	1.3	49	0.9	64	1.2	61
Anaemias — Anémies	♦0.4	34	0.7	27	♦0.5	38	0.7	25
Endocrine, nutritional and metabolic diseases — Maladies endocriniennes, nutritionnelles et métaboliques								
Total	12.1	624	12.1	664	12.8	610	11.8	641
Diabetes mellitus — Diabète sucré	10.8	549	10.6	572	11.1	524	10.1	545
Malnutrition — Malnutrition	0.0	-	-	2	0.0	3	♦0.1	3
Mental and behavioural disorders — Troubles mentaux et du comportement	58.1	3 145	60.9	3 083	59.6	2 997	57.8	3 246
Diseases of the nervous system — Maladies du système nerveux	28.5	1 596	30.9	1 553	30.0	1 810	34.9	2 164
Diseases of the circulatory system — Maladies de l'appareil circulatoire								
Total	418.1	21 500	416.2	21 399	413.4	20 787	400.7	21 133
Acute rheumatic fever and chronic rheumatic heart diseases — Rhumatisme articularie aigu et cardiopathies rhumatismales chroniques	1.6	83	1.6	69	1.3	77	1.5	66
Hypertensive diseases — Maladies hypertensives	8.7	452	8.8	434	8.4	426	8.2	453
Ischaemic heart disease — Cardiopathie ischémique	248.8	12 981	251.3	12 900	249.2	12 433	239.6	12 730
Cerebrovascular disease — Maladie cérébrovasculaire	97.6	4 991	96.6	5 020	97.0	4 871	93.9	4 838
Diseases of arteries, arterioles and capillaries — Maladies des artères, artérioles et capillaires	18.5	896	17.3	919	17.8	854	16.5	938
Diseases of the respiratory system — Maladies de l'appareil respiratoire								
Total	79.5	4 178	80.9	4 293	82.9	3 839	74.0	3 865
Influenza — Grippe	2.7	159	3.1	155	3.0	26	♦0.5	29
Pneumonia — Pneumopathies	47.0	2 531	49.0	2 660	51.4	2 359	45.5	2 392
Chronic lower respiratory diseases — Maladies chroniques des voies respiratoires inférieures	24.9	1 200	23.2	1 202	23.2	1 194	23.0	1 170
Diseases of the digestive system — Maladies de l'appareil digestif								
Total	38.6	1 952	37.8	2 048	39.6	2 010	38.7	2 036
Gastric and duodenal ulcer — Ulcère de l'estomac et du duodénum	4.5	257	5.0	269	5.2	252	4.9	224

(See notes at end of table. — Voir notes à la fin du tableau.)

	Finland — Finlande[13]	France[14]						
	2002	1995		1996		1997		1998
Cause of death — Cause de décès	Rate Taux	Number Nombre	Rate Taux	Number Nombre	Rate Taux	Number Nombre	Rate Taux	Number Nombre
TOTAL	949.7	531 618	919.1	535 775	923.3	530 319	904.8	534 003
Certain infectious and parasitic diseases — Certaines maladies infectieuses et parasitaires								
Total	7.3	12 542	21.7	10 908	18.8	8 599	14.7	7 989
Intestinal infectious diseases — Maladies infectieuses intestinales	1.2	599	1.0	610	1.1	550	0.9	752
Tuberculosis — Tuberculose	1.1	758	1.3	693	1.2	692	1.2	725
Tetanus — Tétanos	-	17	0.0	16	0.0	18	0.0	7
Diphtheria — Diphtérie	-	-		-		-		-
Whooping cough — Coqueluche	-	4	0.0	2	0.0	7	0.0	2
Meningococcal infection — Infection à méningocoques	♦0.1	22	0.0	18	0.0	23	0.0	26
Septicaemia — Septicémie	2.1	1 921	3.3	1 837	3.2	1 778	3.0	1 402
Acute poliomyelitis — Poliomyélite aiguë	-	-		-		-		-
Measles — Rougeole	-	2	0.0	7	0.0	5	0.0	5
Viral hepatitis — Hépatite virale	♦0.2	424	0.7	335	0.6	270	0.5	233
Human immunodeficiency virus [HIV] disease — Maladies dues au virus de l'immunodéficience humaine (VIH)	♦0.1	4 733	8.2	3 490	6.0	1 287	2.2	1 013
Malaria — Paludisme	-	13	0.0	21	0.0	20	0.0	17
Neoplasms — Tumeurs	202.3	146 641	253.5	147 765	254.7	146 837	250.5	147 681
Malignant neoplasms — Tumeurs malignes								
Total	196.5	142 635	246.6	143 704	247.7	142 618	243.3	143 183
Malignant neoplasm of lip, oral cavity and pharynx — Tumeur maligne de la lèvre, de la cavité buccale et du pharynx	2.6	5 166	8.9	5 158	8.9	4 922	8.4	5 003
Malignant neoplasm of oesophagus — Tumeur maligne de l'oesophage	3.7	4 614	8.0	4 573	7.9	4 324	7.4	4 432
Malignant neoplasm of stomach — Tumeur maligne de l'estomac	10.9	5 886	10.2	5 794	10.0	5 599	9.6	5 516
Malignant neoplasm of colon, rectosigmoid junction, rectum, anus and anal canal — Tumeur maligne du côlon, de la jonction recto-sigmoïdienne, du rectum, de l'anus et du canal anal	19.1	16 168	28.0	16 050	27.7	16 134	27.5	16 183
Malignant neoplasm of liver and intrahepatic bile ducts — Tumeur maligne du foie et des voies bilaires intrahépatiques	6.7	4 155	7.2	4 755	8.2	4 771	8.1	4 827
Malignant neoplasm of pancreas — Tumeur maligne du pancréas	14.5	6 372	11.0	6 507	11.2	6 747	11.5	6 714
Malignant neoplasm of trachea, bronchus and lung — Tumeur maligne de la trachée, des bronches et du poumon	35.6	23 929	41.4	24 338	41.9	24 417	41.7	25 121
Malignant neoplasm of female breast — Tumeur maligne du sein chez la femme	▲35.7	10 789	▲44.6	11 014	▲45.2	10 831	▲44.2	10 811
Malignant neoplasm of cervix uteri — Tumeur maligne du col de l'utérus	▲2.2	766	▲3.2	675	▲2.8	746	▲3.0	782
Malignant neoplasm of prostate — Tumeur maligne de la prostate	▼98.4	9 263	▼120.8	9 383	▼121.1	9 345	▼117.9	9 239
Malignant neoplasm of lymphoid, haematopoietic and related tissue — Tumeurs malignes primitives ou présumées primitives des tissus lymphoïde, hématopoïétique et apparentés	19.8	11 448	19.8	11 286	19.4	11 510	19.6	11 558
Disorders of the blood and blood-forming organs and certain disorders involving the immune mechanism — Maladies du sang et des organes hématopoïétiques et certains troubles du système immunitaire								
Total	1.2	2 892	5.0	2 846	4.9	2 879	4.9	2 981
Anaemias — Anémies	♦0.5	1 841	3.2	1 888	3.3	1 892	3.2	2 002
Endocrine, nutritional and metabolic diseases — Maladies endocriniennes, nutritionnelles et métaboliques								
Total	12.3	13 886	24.0	13 965	24.1	14 053	24.0	16 070
Diabetes mellitus — Diabète sucré	10.5	6 437	11.1	6 622	11.4	6 770	11.6	8 962
Malnutrition — Malnutrition	♦0.1	2 321	4.0	2 399	4.1	2 428	4.1	2 311
Mental and behavioural disorders — Troubles mentaux et du comportement	62.4	13 259	22.9	13 277	22.9	13 670	23.3	14 568
Diseases of the nervous system — Maladies du système nerveux	41.6	12 441	21.5	12 901	22.2	13 624	23.2	15 461
Diseases of the circulatory system — Maladies de l'appareil circulatoire								
Total	406.4	171 652	296.7	173 269	298.6	169 724	289.6	166 297
Acute rheumatic fever and chronic rheumatic heart diseases — Rhumatisme articularie aigu et cardiopathies rhumatismales chroniques	1.3	1 059	1.8	960	1.7	955	1.6	1 160
Hypertensive diseases — Maladies hypertensives	8.7	6 324	10.9	6 437	11.1	6 421	11.0	7 867
Ischaemic heart disease — Cardiopathie ischémique	244.8	47 055	81.3	47 307	81.5	45 430	77.5	45 885
Cerebrovascular disease — Maladie cérébrovasculaire	93.0	43 553	75.3	43 494	75.0	42 473	72.5	40 374
Diseases of arteries, arterioles and capillaries — Maladies des artères, artérioles et capillaires	18.0	12 504	21.6	12 776	22.0	12 525	21.4	12 065
Diseases of the respiratory system — Maladies de l'appareil respiratoire								
Total	74.3	40 130	69.4	42 541	73.3	43 319	73.9	43 314
Influenza — Grippe	♦0.6	643	1.1	1 015	1.7	932	1.6	1 922
Pneumonia — Pneumopathies	46.0	15 831	27.4	16 821	29.0	17 506	29.9	16 047
Chronic lower respiratory diseases — Maladies chroniques des voies respiratoires inférieures	22.5	16 128	27.9	17 006	29.3	16 968	29.0	17 705
Diseases of the digestive system — Maladies de l'appareil digestif								
Total	39.1	26 136	45.2	26 453	45.6	26 144	44.6	26 194
Gastric and duodenal ulcer — Ulcère de l'estomac et du duodénum	4.3	1 583	2.7	1 507	2.6	1 447	2.5	1 502

(See notes at end of table. — Voir notes à la fin du tableau.)

	France[14]					Germany — Allemagne		
	1998	1999		2000		1995		1996
Cause of death — Cause de décès	Rate Taux	Number Nombre	Rate Taux	Number Nombre	Rate Taux	Number Nombre	Rate Taux	Number Nombre
TOTAL	914.4	537 459	916.8	530 850	901.4	884 588	1083.2	882 843
Certain infectious and parasitic diseases — Certaines maladies infectieuses et parasitaires								
Total	13.7	7 833	13.4	10 615	18.0	8 129	10.0	8 218
Intestinal infectious diseases — Maladies infectieuses intestinales	1.3	678	1.2	1 027	1.7	266	0.3	246
Tuberculosis — Tuberculose	1.2	695	1.2	633	1.1	709	0.9	691
Tetanus — Tétanos	0.0	10	0.0	13	0.0	2	0.0	1
Diphtheria — Diphtérie	-	-	-	-	-	2	0.0	1
Whooping cough — Coqueluche	0.0	6	0.0	10	0.0	-	-	-
Meningococcal infection — Infection à méningocoques	0.0	24	0.0	45	0.1	63	0.1	76
Septicaemia — Septicémie	2.4	1 441	2.5	3 858	6.6	2 820	3.5	3 003
Acute poliomyelitis — Poliomyélite aiguë	-	-	-	-	-	6	0.0	3
Measles — Rougeole	0.0	2	0.0	2	0.0	3	0.0	4
Viral hepatitis — Hépatite virale	0.4	220	0.4	900	1.5	283	0.3	383
Human immunodeficiency virus [HIV] disease — Maladies dues au virus de l'immunodéficience humaine (VIH)	1.7	978	1.7	1 012	1.7	2 045	2.5	1 583
Malaria — Paludisme	0.0	20	0.0	20	0.0	25	0.0	19
Neoplasms — Tumeurs	252.9	148 584	253.5	149 817	254.4	218 597	267.7	219 064
Malignant neoplasms — Tumeurs malignes								
Total	245.2	143 849	245.4	143 646	243.9	212 913	260.7	212 888
Malignant neoplasm of lip, oral cavity and pharynx — Tumeur maligne de la lèvre, de la cavité buccale et du pharynx	8.6	4 787	8.2	4 643	7.9	4 684	5.7	4 766
Malignant neoplasm of oesophagus — Tumeur maligne de l'oesophage	7.6	4 362	7.4	4 172	7.1	4 073	5.0	4 142
Malignant neoplasm of stomach — Tumeur maligne de l'estomac	9.4	5 366	9.2	5 168	8.8	15 389	18.8	15 244
Malignant neoplasm of colon, rectosigmoid junction, rectum, anus and anal canal — Tumeur maligne du côlon, de la jonction recto-sigmoïdienne, du rectum, de l'anus et du canal anal	27.7	16 558	28.2	15 950	27.1	30 321	37.1	30 460
Malignant neoplasm of liver and intrahepatic bile ducts — Tumeur maligne du foie et des voies bilaires intrahépatiques	8.3	4 895	8.4	6 619	11.2	2 902	3.6	2 984
Malignant neoplasm of pancreas — Tumeur maligne du pancréas	11.5	6 992	11.9	6 836	11.6	11 149	13.7	11 075
Malignant neoplasm of trachea, bronchus and lung — Tumeur maligne de la trachée, des bronches et du poumon	40.0	25 196	43.0	24 831	42.2	37 147	45.5	36 784
Malignant neoplasm of female breast — Tumeur maligne du sein chez la femme	▲43.7	11 281	▲45.5	10 950	▲43.9	18 674	▲52.6	18 878
Malignant neoplasm of cervix uteri — Tumeur maligne du col de l'utérus	▲3.2	764	▲3.1	689	▲2.8	2 207	▲6.2	2 154
Malignant neoplasm of prostate — Tumeur maligne de la prostate	▼112.4	9 476	▼114.0	9 080	▼106.8	11 868	▼96.7	11 916
Malignant neoplasm of lymphoid, haematopoietic and related tissue — Tumeurs malignes primitives ou présumées primitives des tissus lymphoïde, hématopoïétique et apparentés	19.8	11 731	20.0	12 458	21.2	15 168	18.6	15 427
Disorders of the blood and blood-forming organs and certain disorders involving the immune mechanism — Maladies du sang et des organes hématopoïétiques et certains troubles du système immunitaire								
Total	5.1	2 926	5.0	2 276	3.9	1 612	2.0	1 667
Anaemias — Anémies	3.4	1 974	3.4	1 217	2.1	903	1.1	933
Endocrine, nutritional and metabolic diseases — Maladies endocriniennes, nutritionnelles et métaboliques								
Total	27.5	17 257	29.4	19 008	32.3	26 323	32.2	27 049
Diabetes mellitus — Diabète sucré	15.3	9 796	16.7	10 816	18.4	23 328	28.6	23 940
Malnutrition — Malnutrition	4.0	2 300	3.9	2 524	4.3	153	0.2	116
Mental and behavioural disorders — Troubles mentaux et du comportement	24.9	15 894	27.1	17 320	29.4	11 383	13.9	11 765
Diseases of the nervous system — Maladies du système nerveux	26.5	16 798	28.7	20 042	34.0	14 643	17.9	15 935
Diseases of the circulatory system — Maladies de l'appareil circulatoire								
Total	284.8	164 919	281.3	161 913	274.9	429 407	525.8	425 884
Acute rheumatic fever and chronic rheumatic heart diseases — Rhumatisme articulaire aigu et cardiopathies rhumatismales chroniques	2.0	1 177	2.0	1 786	3.0	2 577	3.2	2 634
Hypertensive diseases — Maladies hypertensives	13.5	8 232	14.0	7 626	12.9	13 538	16.6	14 386
Ischaemic heart disease — Cardiopathie ischémique	78.6	45 070	76.9	45 330	77.0	183 736	225.0	181 305
Cerebrovascular disease — Maladie cérébrovasculaire	69.1	39 812	67.9	38 404	65.2	101 034	123.7	99 266
Diseases of arteries, arterioles and capillaries — Maladies des artères, artérioles et capillaires	20.7	11 990	20.5	11 093	18.8	26 761	32.8	26 410
Diseases of the respiratory system — Maladies de l'appareil respiratoire								
Total	74.2	43 841	74.8	35 666	60.6	53 898	66.0	53 843
Influenza — Grippe	3.3	1 486	2.5	1 561	2.7	425	0.5	422
Pneumonia — Pneumopathies	27.5	16 726	28.5	11 343	19.3	17 613	21.6	17 381
Chronic lower respiratory diseases — Maladies chroniques des voies respiratoires inférieures	30.3	17 918	30.6	9 494	16.1	29 988	36.7	29 730
Diseases of the digestive system — Maladies de l'appareil digestif								
Total	44.9	25 511	43.5	23 709	40.3	41 821	51.2	41 940
Gastric and duodenal ulcer — Ulcère de l'estomac et du duodénum	2.6	1 454	2.5	1 025	1.7	3 510	4.3	3 611

(See notes at end of table. — Voir notes à la fin du tableau.)

Germany — Allemagne

Cause of death — Cause de décès	1996 Rate Taux	1997 Number Nombre	1997 Rate Taux	1998 Number Nombre	1998 Rate Taux	1999 Number Nombre	1999 Rate Taux	2000 Number Nombre
TOTAL	1078.0	860 389	1048.5	852 382	1039.1	846 330	1031.4	838 797
Certain infectious and parasitic diseases — Certaines maladies infectieuses et parasitaires								
Total	10.0	7 697	9.4	7 801	9.5	9 122	11.1	10 129
Intestinal infectious diseases — Maladies infectieuses intestinales	0.3	263	0.3	317	0.4	305	0.4	325
Tuberculosis — Tuberculose	0.8	593	0.7	541	0.7	499	0.6	497
Tetanus — Tétanos	0.0	2	0.0	4	0.0	2	0.0	2
Diphtheria — Diphtérie	0.0	2	0.0	2	0.0	1	0.0	-
Whooping cough — Coqueluche	-	-	-	-	-	-	-	-
Meningococcal infection — Infection à méningocoques	0.1	74	0.1	68	0.1	80	0.1	65
Septicaemia — Septicémie	3.7	3 348	4.1	3 551	4.3	4 516	5.5	5 622
Acute poliomyelitis — Poliomyélite aiguë	0.0	4	0.0	3	0.0	-	-	-
Measles — Rougeole	0.0	-	-	2	0.0	4	0.0	2
Viral hepatitis — Hépatite virale	0.5	357	0.4	911	1.1	1 121	1.4	1 152
Human immunodeficiency virus [HIV] disease — Maladies dues au virus de l'immunodéficience humaine (VIH)	1.9	813	1.0	596	0.7	587	0.7	580
Malaria — Paludisme	0.0	15	0.0	21	0.0	18	0.0	8
Neoplasms — Tumeurs	267.5	215 722	262.9	218 445	266.3	216 264	263.6	216 419
Malignant neoplasms — Tumeurs malignes								
Total	260.0	210 053	256.0	212 748	259.4	210 837	256.9	210 738
Malignant neoplasm of lip, oral cavity and pharynx — Tumeur maligne de la lèvre, de la cavité buccale et du pharynx	5.8	4 778	5.8	4 965	6.1	4 941	6.0	4 645
Malignant neoplasm of oesophagus — Tumeur maligne de l'oesophage	5.1	4 157	5.1	3 966	4.8	4 139	5.0	4 125
Malignant neoplasm of stomach — Tumeur maligne de l'estomac	18.6	14 215	17.3	13 821	16.8	13 145	16.0	13 132
Malignant neoplasm of colon, rectosigmoid junction, rectum, anus and anal canal — Tumeur maligne du côlon, de la jonction recto-sigmoïdienne, du rectum, de l'anus et du canal anal	37.2	29 767	36.3	29 694	36.2	29 386	35.8	28 987
Malignant neoplasm of liver and intrahepatic bile ducts — Tumeur maligne du foie et des voies bilaires intrahépatiques	3.6	2 940	3.6	5 263	6.4	5 363	6.5	5 489
Malignant neoplasm of pancreas — Tumeur maligne du pancréas	13.5	11 317	13.8	11 634	14.2	12 134	14.8	12 116
Malignant neoplasm of trachea, bronchus and lung — Tumeur maligne de la trachée, des bronches et du poumon	44.9	37 240	45.4	37 971	46.3	37 648	45.9	38 990
Malignant neoplasm of female breast — Tumeur maligne du sein chez la femme	▲53.1	18 374	▲51.5	17 692	▲49.6	17 616	▲49.3	17 814
Malignant neoplasm of cervix uteri — Tumeur maligne du col de l'utérus	▲6.1	2 071	▲5.8	1 960	▲5.5	2 020	▲5.6	1 882
Malignant neoplasm of prostate — Tumeur maligne de la prostate	▼96.7	11 454	▼92.2	11 417	▼91.0	11 123	▼88.1	11 107
Malignant neoplasm of lymphoid, haematopoietic and related tissue — Tumeurs malignes primitives ou présumées primitives des tissus lymphoïde, hématopoïétique et apparentés	18.8	15 497	18.9	16 453	20.1	16 681	20.3	16 186
Disorders of the blood and blood-forming organs and certain disorders involving the immune mechanism — Maladies du sang et des organes hématopoïétiques et certains troubles du système immunitaire								
Total	2.0	1 744	2.1	1 605	2.0	1 658	2.0	1 815
Anaemias — Anémies	1.1	1 057	1.3	830	1.0	791	1.0	908
Endocrine, nutritional and metabolic diseases — Maladies endocriniennes, nutritionnelles et métaboliques								
Total	33.0	25 340	30.9	23 194	28.3	23 332	28.4	23 671
Diabetes mellitus — Diabète sucré	29.2	22 359	27.2	20 663	25.2	20 947	25.5	21 180
Malnutrition — Malnutrition	0.1	163	0.2	86	0.1	73	0.1	75
Mental and behavioural disorders — Troubles mentaux et du comportement	14.4	11 894	14.5	9 720	11.8	9 533	11.6	8 636
Diseases of the nervous system — Maladies du système nerveux	19.5	15 663	19.1	15 916	19.4	15 714	19.2	16 096
Diseases of the circulatory system — Maladies de l'appareil circulatoire								
Total	520.0	415 800	506.7	411 398	501.5	406 122	494.9	395 043
Acute rheumatic fever and chronic rheumatic heart diseases — Rhumatisme articulaire aigu et cardiopathies rhumatismales chroniques	3.2	2 449	3.0	2 448	3.0	2 408	2.9	2 265
Hypertensive diseases — Maladies hypertensives	17.6	15 066	18.4	15 065	18.4	16 753	20.4	18 775
Ischaemic heart disease — Cardiopathie ischémique	221.4	178 622	217.7	178 715	217.9	175 081	213.4	167 681
Cerebrovascular disease — Maladie cérébrovasculaire	121.2	93 627	114.1	90 191	110.0	85 755	104.5	80 786
Diseases of arteries, arterioles and capillaries — Maladies des artères, artérioles et capillaires	32.2	25 181	30.7	25 197	30.7	24 856	30.3	23 148
Diseases of the respiratory system — Maladies de l'appareil respiratoire								
Total	65.7	50 422	61.4	49 084	59.8	51 505	62.8	51 806
Influenza — Grippe	0.5	184	0.2	239	0.3	364	0.4	267
Pneumonia — Pneumopathies	21.2	17 324	21.1	17 262	21.0	18 603	22.7	18 490
Chronic lower respiratory diseases — Maladies chroniques des voies respiratoires inférieures	36.3	26 788	32.6	26 094	31.8	26 082	31.8	25 798
Diseases of the digestive system — Maladies de l'appareil digestif								
Total	51.2	40 799	49.7	40 510	49.4	40 154	48.9	40 712
Gastric and duodenal ulcer — Ulcère de l'estomac et du duodénum	4.4	3 335	4.1	3 352	4.1	3 292	4.0	3 219

(See notes at end of table. — Voir notes à la fin du tableau.)

Cause of death — Cause de décès	Germany — Allemagne			Greece — Grèce				
	2000	2001		1995		1996		1997
	Rate Taux	Number Nombre	Rate Taux	Number Nombre	Rate Taux	Number Nombre	Rate Taux	Number Nombre
TOTAL	1020.6	828 541	1006.1	100 158	958.1	100 740	961.6	99 738
Certain infectious and parasitic diseases — Certaines maladies infectieuses et parasitaires								
Total	12.3	10 373	12.6	681	6.5	710	6.8	682
Intestinal infectious diseases — Maladies infectieuses intestinales	0.4	368	0.4	-	-	2	0.0	2
Tuberculosis — Tuberculose	0.6	415	0.5	105	1.0	105	1.0	82
Tetanus — Tétanos	0.0	1	0.0	5	0.0	3	0.0	2
Diphtheria — Diphtérie	-	-	-	-	-	-	-	-
Whooping cough — Coqueluche	-	1	0.0	-	-	-	-	1
Meningococcal infection — Infection à méningocoques	0.1	69	0.1	2	0.0	8	♦0.1	17
Septicaemia — Septicémie	6.8	6 162	7.5	350	3.3	395	3.8	417
Acute poliomyelitis — Poliomyélite aiguë	-	-	-	1	0.0	-	-	-
Measles — Rougeole	0.0	1	0.0	-	-	2	0.0	-
Viral hepatitis — Hépatite virale	1.4	1 170	1.4	71	0.7	51	0.5	46
Human immunodeficiency virus [HIV] disease — Maladies dues au virus de l'immunodéficience humaine (VIH)	0.7	543	0.7	63	0.6	60	0.6	33
Malaria — Paludisme	0.0	8	0.0	1	0.0	1	0.0	-
Neoplasms — Tumeurs	263.3	213 058	258.7	22 030	210.7	22 354	213.4	22 601
Malignant neoplasms — Tumeurs malignes								
Total	256.4	207 619	252.1	22 020	210.6	22 350	213.3	22 591
Malignant neoplasm of lip, oral cavity and pharynx — Tumeur maligne de la lèvre, de la cavité buccale et du pharynx	5.7	4 853	5.9	217	2.1	259	2.5	237
Malignant neoplasm of oesophagus — Tumeur maligne de l'oesophage	5.0	4 296	5.2	193	1.8	166	1.6	206
Malignant neoplasm of stomach — Tumeur maligne de l'estomac	16.0	12 451	15.1	1 313	12.6	1 313	12.5	1 319
Malignant neoplasm of colon, rectosigmoid junction, rectum, anus and anal canal — Tumeur maligne du côlon, de la jonction recto-sigmoïdienne, du rectum, de l'anus et du canal anal	35.3	28 367	34.4	1 524	14.6	1 585	15.1	1 620
Malignant neoplasm of liver and intrahepatic bile ducts — Tumeur maligne du foie et des voies bilaires intrahépatiques	6.7	5 446	6.6	135	1.3	104	1.0	109
Malignant neoplasm of pancreas — Tumeur maligne du pancréas	14.7	12 438	15.1	1 005	9.6	1 001	9.6	1 052
Malignant neoplasm of trachea, bronchus and lung — Tumeur maligne de la trachée, des bronches et du poumon	47.4	38 569	46.8	5 157	49.3	5 308	50.7	5 316
Malignant neoplasm of female breast — Tumeur maligne du sein chez la femme	...	17 504	▲48.7	1 534	▲34.6	1 580	▲35.3	1 512
Malignant neoplasm of cervix uteri — Tumeur maligne du col de l'utérus	...	1 821	▲5.1	84	▲1.9	81	▲1.8	94
Malignant neoplasm of prostate — Tumeur maligne de la prostate	...	11 150	▼84.9	1 095	▼67.1	1 144	▼69.3	1 140
Malignant neoplasm of lymphoid, haematopoietic and related tissue — Tumeurs malignes primitives ou présumées primitives des tissus lymphoïde, hématopoïétique et apparentés	19.7	16 051	19.5	1 658	15.9	1 519	14.5	1 617
Disorders of the blood and blood-forming organs and certain disorders involving the immune mechanism — Maladies du sang et des organes hématopoïétiques et certains troubles du système immunitaire								
Total	2.2	1 901	2.3	196	1.9	175	1.7	173
Anaemias — Anémies	1.1	951	1.2	148	1.4	141	1.3	128
Endocrine, nutritional and metabolic diseases — Maladies endocriniennes, nutritionnelles et métaboliques								
Total	28.8	24 363	29.6	1 062	10.2	1 181	11.3	1 042
Diabetes mellitus — Diabète sucré	25.8	21 878	26.6	859	8.2	962	9.2	830
Malnutrition — Malnutrition	0.1	90	0.1	1	0.0	1	0.0	-
Mental and behavioural disorders — Troubles mentaux et du comportement	10.5	7 826	9.5	159	1.5	189	1.8	135
Diseases of the nervous system — Maladies du système nerveux	19.6	16 625	20.2	1 081	10.3	1 003	9.6	976
Diseases of the circulatory system — Maladies de l'appareil circulatoire								
Total	480.7	391 728	475.7	51 379	491.5	51 598	492.5	51 251
Acute rheumatic fever and chronic rheumatic heart diseases — Rhumatisme articulaire aigu et cardiopathies rhumatismales chroniques	2.8	2 309	2.8	69	0.7	18	♦0.2	18
Hypertensive diseases — Maladies hypertensives	22.8	20 805	25.3	1 046	10.0	1 284	12.3	1 150
Ischaemic heart disease — Cardiopathie ischémique	204.0	165 070	200.4	12 686	121.4	13 089	124.9	13 093
Cerebrovascular disease — Maladie cérébrovasculaire	98.3	78 691	95.6	19 024	182.0	18 106	172.8	18 363
Diseases of arteries, arterioles and capillaries — Maladies des artères, artérioles et capillaires	28.2	22 676	27.5	979	9.4	954	9.1	875
Diseases of the respiratory system — Maladies de l'appareil respiratoire								
Total	63.0	48 535	58.9	5 765	55.1	5 748	54.9	5 570
Influenza — Grippe	0.3	72	0.1	3	0.0	1	0.0	5
Pneumonia — Pneumopathies	22.5	17 540	21.3	682	6.5	707	6.7	824
Chronic lower respiratory diseases — Maladies chroniques des voies respiratoires inférieures	31.4	23 793	28.9	1 030	9.9	1 014	9.7	1 044
Diseases of the digestive system — Maladies de l'appareil digestif								
Total	49.5	40 918	49.7	2 538	24.3	2 546	24.3	2 433
Gastric and duodenal ulcer — Ulcère de l'estomac et du duodénum	3.9	3 247	3.9	225	2.2	234	2.2	249

21. Death and death rates by cause: 1995 - 2002
Décès selon la cause, nombres et taux: 1995 - 2002 (continued — suite)

(See notes at end of table. — Voir notes à la fin du tableau.)

Greece — Grèce

Cause of death — Cause de décès	1997 Rate Taux	1998 Number Nombre	1998 Rate Taux	1999 Number Nombre	1999 Rate Taux	2000 Number Nombre	2000 Rate Taux	2001 Number Nombre
TOTAL	950.0	102 668	976.3	103 304	980.7	105 219	1051.3	102 559
Certain infectious and parasitic diseases — Certaines maladies infectieuses et parasitaires								
Total	6.5	749	7.1	589	5.6	522	5.2	638
Intestinal infectious diseases — Maladies infectieuses intestinales	0.0	-		1	0.0	1	0.0	2
Tuberculosis — Tuberculose	0.8	78	0.7	89	0.8	83	0.8	105
Tetanus — Tétanos	0.0	7	♦0.1	3	0.0	5	0.0	-
Diphtheria — Diphtérie	-	-	-	-	-	-	-	-
Whooping cough — Coqueluche	0.0	-	-	-	-	-	-	1
Meningococcal infection — Infection à méningocoques	♦0.2	21	♦0.2	12	♦0.1	19	♦0.2	7
Septicaemia — Septicémie	4.0	447	4.3	349	3.3	282	2.8	377
Acute poliomyelitis — Poliomyélite aiguë	-	1	0.0	-	-	-	-	-
Measles — Rougeole	-	-	-	-	-	-	-	-
Viral hepatitis — Hépatite virale	0.4	74	0.7	47	0.4	53	0.5	61
Human immunodeficiency virus [HIV] disease — Maladies dues au virus de l'immunodéficience humaine (VIH)	0.3	37	0.4	32	0.3	29	♦0.3	17
Malaria — Paludisme	-	1	0.0	-	-	-	-	-
Neoplasms — Tumeurs	215.3	22 443	213.4	23 430	222.4	23 775	237.6	24 408
Malignant neoplasms — Tumeurs malignes								
Total	215.2	22 433	213.3	23 419	222.3	23 763	237.4	24 402
Malignant neoplasm of lip, oral cavity and pharynx — Tumeur maligne de la lèvre, de la cavité buccale et du pharynx	2.3	224	2.1	228	2.2	250	2.5	232
Malignant neoplasm of oesophagus — Tumeur maligne de l'oesophage	2.0	175	1.7	168	1.6	186	1.9	179
Malignant neoplasm of stomach — Tumeur maligne de l'estomac	12.6	1 327	12.6	1 335	12.7	1 333	13.3	1 423
Malignant neoplasm of colon, rectosigmoid junction, rectum, anus and anal canal — Tumeur maligne du côlon, de la jonction recto-sigmoïdienne, du rectum, de l'anus et du canal anal	15.4	1 694	16.1	2 115	20.1	1 824	18.2	1 928
Malignant neoplasm of liver and intrahepatic bile ducts — Tumeur maligne du foie et des voies bilaires intrahépatiques	1.0	149	1.4	190	1.8	175	1.7	184
Malignant neoplasm of pancreas — Tumeur maligne du pancréas	10.0	1 091	10.4	1 186	11.3	1 139	11.4	1 169
Malignant neoplasm of trachea, bronchus and lung — Tumeur maligne de la trachée, des bronches et du poumon	50.6	5 414	51.5	5 472	51.9	5 595	55.9	5 630
Malignant neoplasm of female breast — Tumeur maligne du sein chez la femme	▲33.5	1 440	▲31.7	1 531	...	1 603	...	1 720
Malignant neoplasm of cervix uteri — Tumeur maligne du col de l'utérus	▲2.1	108	▲2.4	130	...	108	...	80
Malignant neoplasm of prostate — Tumeur maligne de la prostate	▼68.3	1 208	▼71.6	1 244	...	1 253	...	1 337
Malignant neoplasm of lymphoid, haematopoietic and related tissue — Tumeurs malignes primitives ou présumées primitives des tissus lymphoïde, hématopoïétique et apparentés	15.4	1 565	14.9	1 720	16.3	1 831	18.3	1 930
Disorders of the blood and blood-forming organs and certain disorders involving the immune mechanism — Maladies du sang et des organes hématopoïétiques et certains troubles du système immunitaire								
Total	1.6	105	1.0	119	1.1	97	1.0	110
Anaemias — Anémies	1.2	83	0.8	95	0.9	77	0.8	87
Endocrine, nutritional and metabolic diseases — Maladies endocriniennes, nutritionnelles et métaboliques								
Total	9.9	849	8.1	1 010	9.6	1 076	10.8	985
Diabetes mellitus — Diabète sucré	7.9	668	6.4	824	7.8	839	8.4	700
Malnutrition — Malnutrition	-	-	-	-	-	-	-	-
Mental and behavioural disorders — Troubles mentaux et du comportement	1.3	87	0.8	69	0.7	84	0.8	132
Diseases of the nervous system — Maladies du système nerveux	9.3	986	9.4	1 017	9.7	1 347	13.5	1 241
Diseases of the circulatory system — Maladies de l'appareil circulatoire								
Total	488.2	52 776	501.8	52 028	493.9	52 283	522.4	51 513
Acute rheumatic fever and chronic rheumatic heart diseases — Rhumatisme articulaire aigu et cardiopathies rhumatismales chroniques	♦0.2	24	♦0.2	9	♦0.1	26	♦0.3	61
Hypertensive diseases — Maladies hypertensives	11.0	946	9.0	1 032	9.8	1 043	10.4	1 249
Ischaemic heart disease — Cardiopathie ischémique	124.7	12 276	116.7	12 743	121.0	12 910	129.0	13 114
Cerebrovascular disease — Maladie cérébrovasculaire	174.9	18 946	180.2	18 514	175.8	18 753	187.4	18 538
Diseases of arteries, arterioles and capillaries — Maladies des artères, artérioles et capillaires	8.3	911	8.7	944	9.0	923	9.2	986
Diseases of the respiratory system — Maladies de l'appareil respiratoire								
Total	53.1	6 850	65.1	7 230	68.6	7 995	79.9	7 021
Influenza — Grippe	0.0	8	♦0.1	13	♦0.1	19	♦0.2	-
Pneumonia — Pneumopathies	7.8	816	7.8	721	6.8	842	8.4	694
Chronic lower respiratory diseases — Maladies chroniques des voies respiratoires inférieures	9.9	1 049	10.0	1 305	12.4	1 461	14.6	1 547
Diseases of the digestive system — Maladies de l'appareil digestif								
Total	23.2	2 357	22.4	2 422	23.0	2 618	26.2	2 416
Gastric and duodenal ulcer — Ulcère de l'estomac et du duodénum	2.4	280	2.7	273	2.6	293	2.9	280

(See notes at end of table. — Voir notes à la fin du tableau.)

Cause of death — Cause de décès	Greece — Grèce	Hungary — Hongrie						
	2001	1995		1996		1997		1998
	Rate Taux	Number Nombre	Rate Taux	Number Nombre	Rate Taux	Number Nombre	Rate Taux	Number Nombre
TOTAL	1023.5	145 431	1421.8	143 130	1404.1	139 434	1373.1	140 870
Certain infectious and parasitic diseases — Certaines maladies infectieuses et parasitaires								
Total	6.4	819	8.0	785	7.7	731	7.2	717
Intestinal infectious diseases — Maladies infectieuses intestinales	0.0	21	♦0.2	16	♦0.2	28	♦0.3	18
Tuberculosis — Tuberculose	1.0	561	5.5	516	5.1	470	4.6	443
Tetanus — Tétanos	-	10	♦0.1	8	♦0.1	8	♦0.1	6
Diphtheria — Diphtérie	-	-	-	-	-	-	-	-
Whooping cough — Coqueluche	0.0	-	-	-	-	-	-	-
Meningococcal infection — Infection à méningocoques	♦0.1	4	0.0	10	♦0.1	4	0.0	4
Septicaemia — Septicémie	3.8	25	♦0.2	39	0.4	29	♦0.3	57
Acute poliomyelitis — Poliomyélite aiguë	-	-	-	-	-	-	-	-
Measles — Rougeole	-	-	-	1	0.0	-	-	-
Viral hepatitis — Hépatite virale	0.6	11	♦0.1	17	♦0.2	12	♦0.1	13
Human immunodeficiency virus [HIV] disease — Maladies dues au virus de l'immunodéficience humaine (VIH)	♦0.2	13	♦0.1	24	♦0.2	25	♦0.2	20
Malaria — Paludisme	-	1	0.0	-	-	-	-	2
Neoplasms — Tumeurs	243.6	33 265	325.2	33 876	332.3	33 837	333.2	33 951
Malignant neoplasms — Tumeurs malignes								
Total	243.5	32 941	322.0	33 475	328.4	33 458	329.5	33 547
Malignant neoplasm of lip, oral cavity and pharynx — Tumeur maligne de la lèvre, de la cavité buccale et du pharynx	2.3	1 419	13.9	1 485	14.6	1 529	15.1	1 624
Malignant neoplasm of oesophagus — Tumeur maligne de l'oesophage	1.8	696	6.8	682	6.7	698	6.9	733
Malignant neoplasm of stomach — Tumeur maligne de l'estomac	14.2	2 588	25.3	2 412	23.7	2 374	23.4	2 371
Malignant neoplasm of colon, rectosigmoid junction, rectum, anus and anal canal — Tumeur maligne du côlon, de la jonction recto-sigmoïdienne, du rectum, de l'anus et du canal anal	19.2	4 604	45.0	4 673	45.8	4 783	47.1	4 873
Malignant neoplasm of liver and intrahepatic bile ducts — Tumeur maligne du foie et des voies bilaires intrahépatiques	1.8	1 042	10.2	987	9.7	939	9.2	937
Malignant neoplasm of pancreas — Tumeur maligne du pancréas	11.7	1 533	15.0	1 575	15.5	1 596	15.7	1 585
Malignant neoplasm of trachea, bronchus and lung — Tumeur maligne de la trachée, des bronches et du poumon	56.2	7 551	73.8	7 858	77.1	7 763	76.4	7 898
Malignant neoplasm of female breast — Tumeur maligne du sein chez la femme	...	2 239	▲50.5	2 339	▲52.8	2 323	▲52.4	2 356
Malignant neoplasm of cervix uteri — Tumeur maligne du col de l'utérus	...	546	▲12.3	541	▲12.2	543	▲12.3	484
Malignant neoplasm of prostate — Tumeur maligne de la prostate	...	1 380	▼103.4	1 451	▼109.1	1 442	▼108.3	1 349
Malignant neoplasm of lymphoid, haematopoietic and related tissue — Tumeurs malignes primitives ou présumées primitives des tissus lymphoïde, hématopoïétique et apparentés	19.3	1 901	18.6	1 904	18.7	1 886	18.6	1 963
Disorders of the blood and blood-forming organs and certain disorders involving the immune mechanism — Maladies du sang et des organes hématopoïétiques et certains troubles du système immunitaire								
Total	1.1	166	1.6	149	1.5	112	1.1	155
Anaemias — Anémies	0.9	85	0.8	74	0.7	49	0.5	72
Endocrine, nutritional and metabolic diseases — Maladies endocriniennes, nutritionnelles et métaboliques								
Total	9.8	2 055	20.1	2 012	19.7	2 141	21.1	2 337
Diabetes mellitus — Diabète sucré	7.0	1 864	18.2	1 834	18.0	1 952	19.2	2 154
Malnutrition — Malnutrition	-	3	0.0	9	♦0.1	11	♦0.1	9
Mental and behavioural disorders — Troubles mentaux et du comportement	1.3	1 627	15.9	1 109	10.9	1 303	12.8	1 119
Diseases of the nervous system — Maladies du système nerveux	12.4	1 165	11.4	1 424	14.0	1 348	13.3	1 617
Diseases of the circulatory system — Maladies de l'appareil circulatoire								
Total	514.1	73 797	721.4	73 980	725.8	71 309	702.2	72 403
Acute rheumatic fever and chronic rheumatic heart diseases — Rhumatisme articulaire aigu et cardiopathies rhumatismales chroniques	0.6	657	6.4	669	6.6	536	5.3	505
Hypertensive diseases — Maladies hypertensives	12.5	4 560	44.6	4 130	40.5	4 252	41.9	4 972
Ischaemic heart disease — Cardiopathie ischémique	130.9	30 742	300.5	31 346	307.5	30 898	304.3	31 442
Cerebrovascular disease — Maladie cérébrovasculaire	185.0	20 013	195.6	20 158	197.8	18 884	186.0	19 205
Diseases of arteries, arterioles and capillaries — Maladies des artères, artérioles et capillaires	9.8	10 506	102.7	10 086	98.9	9 188	90.5	8 907
Diseases of the respiratory system — Maladies de l'appareil respiratoire								
Total	70.1	6 447	63.0	6 200	60.8	5 850	57.6	5 289
Influenza — Grippe	-	78	0.8	130	1.3	122	1.2	30
Pneumonia — Pneumopathies	6.9	930	9.1	1 072	10.5	1 197	11.8	995
Chronic lower respiratory diseases — Maladies chroniques des voies respiratoires inférieures	15.4	4 896	47.9	4 521	44.4	4 115	40.5	3 882
Diseases of the digestive system — Maladies de l'appareil digestif								
Total	24.1	11 822	115.6	10 023	98.3	9 936	97.8	10 488
Gastric and duodenal ulcer — Ulcère de l'estomac et du duodénum	2.8	1 015	9.9	1 013	9.9	939	9.2	949

21. Death and death rates by cause: 1995 - 2002
Décès selon la cause, nombres et taux: 1995 - 2002 (continued — suite)

(See notes at end of table. — Voir notes à la fin du tableau.)

Hungary — Hongrie

Cause of death — Cause de décès	1998 Rate Taux	1999 Number Nombre	1999 Rate Taux	2000 Number Nombre	2000 Rate Taux	2001 Number Nombre	2001 Rate Taux	2002 Number Nombre
TOTAL	1392.9	143 210	1422.5	135 601	1352.7	132 183	1297.5	132 833
Certain infectious and parasitic diseases — Certaines maladies infectieuses et parasitaires								
Total	7.1	748	7.4	659	6.6	611	6.0	576
Intestinal infectious diseases — Maladies infectieuses intestinales	◆0.2	12	◆0.1	24	◆0.2	13	◆0.1	23
Tuberculosis — Tuberculose	4.4	452	4.5	361	3.6	324	3.2	284
Tetanus — Tétanos	◆0.1	13	◆0.1	3	0.0	5	0.0	3
Diphtheria — Diphtérie	-	-	-	-	-	-	-	-
Whooping cough — Coqueluche	-	-	-	-	-	-	-	-
Meningococcal infection — Infection à méningocoques	0.0	11	◆0.1	13	◆0.1	12	◆0.1	5
Septicaemia — Septicémie	0.6	60	0.6	62	0.6	81	0.8	103
Acute poliomyelitis — Poliomyélite aiguë	-	-	-	-	-	-	-	-
Measles — Rougeole	-	-	-	-	-	-	-	-
Viral hepatitis — Hépatite virale	◆0.1	6	◆0.1	7	◆0.1	17	◆0.2	21
Human immunodeficiency virus [HIV] disease — Maladies dues au virus de l'immunodéficience humaine (VIH)	◆0.2	11	◆0.1	15	◆0.1	9	◆0.1	8
Malaria — Paludisme	0.0	-	-	-	-	1	0.0	-
Neoplasms — Tumeurs	335.7	34 255	340.3	33 679	336.0	33 758	331.4	33 537
Malignant neoplasms — Tumeurs malignes								
Total	331.7	33 821	335.9	33 280	332.0	33 319	327.1	33 013
Malignant neoplasm of lip, oral cavity and pharynx — Tumeur maligne de la lèvre, de la cavité buccale et du pharynx	16.1	1 618	16.1	1 688	16.8	1 737	17.1	1 717
Malignant neoplasm of oesophagus — Tumeur maligne de l'oesophage	7.2	723	7.2	722	7.2	675	6.6	675
Malignant neoplasm of stomach — Tumeur maligne de l'estomac	23.4	2 306	22.9	2 167	21.6	2 166	21.3	2 114
Malignant neoplasm of colon, rectosigmoid junction, rectum, anus and anal canal — Tumeur maligne du côlon, de la jonction recto-sigmoïdienne, du rectum, de l'anus et du canal anal	48.2	4 912	48.8	4 886	48.7	4 852	47.6	4 790
Malignant neoplasm of liver and intrahepatic bile ducts — Tumeur maligne du foie et des voies bilaires intrahépatiques	9.3	972	9.7	946	9.4	893	8.8	916
Malignant neoplasm of pancreas — Tumeur maligne du pancréas	15.7	1 562	15.5	1 546	15.4	1 561	15.3	1 670
Malignant neoplasm of trachea, bronchus and lung — Tumeur maligne de la trachée, des bronches et du poumon	78.1	7 883	78.3	7 824	78.1	7 902	77.6	7 939
Malignant neoplasm of female breast — Tumeur maligne du sein chez la femme	▲53.2	2 356	▲53.3	2 316	▲52.5	2 304	▲50.9	2 234
Malignant neoplasm of cervix uteri — Tumeur maligne du col de l'utérus	▲10.9	500	▲11.3	481	▲10.9	539	▲11.9	513
Malignant neoplasm of prostate — Tumeur maligne de la prostate	▼100.8	1 387	▼103.1	1 399	▼103.2	1 372	▼96.3	1 292
Malignant neoplasm of lymphoid, haematopoietic and related tissue — Tumeurs malignes primitives ou présumées primitives des tissus lymphoïde, hématopoïétique et apparentés	19.4	2 056	20.4	1 949	19.4	2 007	19.7	1 992
Disorders of the blood and blood-forming organs and certain disorders involving the immune mechanism — Maladies du sang et des organes hématopoïétiques et certains troubles du système immunitaire								
Total	1.5	129	1.3	139	1.4	123	1.2	138
Anaemias — Anémies	0.7	65	0.6	62	0.6	55	0.5	66
Endocrine, nutritional and metabolic diseases — Maladies endocriniennes, nutritionnelles et métaboliques								
Total	23.1	2 549	25.3	2 452	24.5	1 952	19.2	2 519
Diabetes mellitus — Diabète sucré	21.3	2 359	23.4	2 280	22.7	1 819	17.9	2 352
Malnutrition — Malnutrition	◆0.1	13	◆0.1	7	◆0.1	11	◆0.1	8
Mental and behavioural disorders — Troubles mentaux et du comportement	11.1	1 253	12.4	883	8.8	848	8.3	895
Diseases of the nervous system — Maladies du système nerveux	16.0	1 706	16.9	1 781	17.8	1 764	17.3	1 700
Diseases of the circulatory system — Maladies de l'appareil circulatoire								
Total	715.9	73 334	728.4	68 873	687.1	67 423	661.8	67 826
Acute rheumatic fever and chronic rheumatic heart diseases — Rhumatisme articularie aigu et cardiopathies rhumatismales chroniques	5.0	411	4.1	401	4.0	383	3.8	376
Hypertensive diseases — Maladies hypertensives	49.2	5 269	52.3	4 729	47.2	3 570	35.0	4 266
Ischaemic heart disease — Cardiopathie ischémique	310.9	31 489	312.8	29 799	297.3	29 962	294.1	29 674
Cerebrovascular disease — Maladie cérébrovasculaire	189.9	19 286	191.6	18 939	188.9	18 821	184.7	18 510
Diseases of arteries, arterioles and capillaries — Maladies des artères, artérioles et capillaires	88.1	9 475	94.1	8 303	82.8	7 759	76.2	8 200
Diseases of the respiratory system — Maladies de l'appareil respiratoire								
Total	52.3	6 208	61.7	5 168	51.6	4 334	42.5	4 701
Influenza — Grippe	◆0.3	104	1.0	45	0.4	15	◆0.1	8
Pneumonia — Pneumopathies	9.8	1 217	12.1	966	9.6	744	7.3	908
Chronic lower respiratory diseases — Maladies chroniques des voies respiratoires inférieures	38.4	4 490	44.6	3 844	38.3	3 222	31.6	3 419
Diseases of the digestive system — Maladies de l'appareil digestif								
Total	103.7	10 305	102.4	10 047	100.2	9 548	93.7	9 189
Gastric and duodenal ulcer — Ulcère de l'estomac et du duodénum	9.4	907	9.0	942	9.4	827	8.1	812

(See notes at end of table. — Voir notes à la fin du tableau.)

Cause of death — Cause de décès	Hungary — Hongrie	Iceland — Islande						
	2002	1995		1996		1997		1998
	Rate Taux	Number Nombre	Rate Taux	Number Nombre	Rate Taux	Number Nombre	Rate Taux	Number Nombre
TOTAL	1307.6	1 923	719.2	1 879	698.7	1 843	680.3	1 821
Certain infectious and parasitic diseases — Certaines maladies infectieuses et parasitaires								
Total	5.7	21	♦7.9	9	♦3.3	11	♦4.1	13
Intestinal infectious diseases — Maladies infectieuses intestinales	♦0.2	2	♦0.7	2	♦0.7	1	♦0.4	1
Tuberculosis — Tuberculose	2.8	2	♦0.7	-	-	-	-	-
Tetanus — Tétanos	0.0	-	-	-	-	-	-	-
Diphtheria — Diphtérie	-	-	-	-	-	-	-	-
Whooping cough — Coqueluche	-	-	-	-	-	-	-	-
Meningococcal infection — Infection à méningocoques	0.0	1	♦0.4	1	♦0.4	-	-	3
Septicaemia — Septicémie	1.0	7	♦2.6	3	♦1.1	3	♦1.1	3
Acute poliomyelitis — Poliomyélite aiguë	-	-	-	-	-	-	-	-
Measles — Rougeole	-	-	-	-	-	-	-	-
Viral hepatitis — Hépatite virale	♦0.2	-	-	-	-	1	♦0.4	1
Human immunodeficiency virus [HIV] disease — Maladies dues au virus de l'immunodéficience humaine (VIH)	♦0.1	3	♦1.1	1	♦0.4	1	♦0.4	-
Malaria — Paludisme	-	-	-	-	-	-	-	-
Neoplasms — Tumeurs	330.1	475	177.6	543	201.9	532	196.4	506
Malignant neoplasms — Tumeurs malignes								
Total	325.0	471	176.2	536	199.3	525	193.8	498
Malignant neoplasm of lip, oral cavity and pharynx — Tumeur maligne de la lèvre, de la cavité buccale et du pharynx	16.9	3	♦1.1	8	♦3.0	7	♦2.6	4
Malignant neoplasm of oesophagus — Tumeur maligne de l'oesophage	6.6	18	♦6.7	21	♦7.8	19	♦7.0	18
Malignant neoplasm of stomach — Tumeur maligne de l'estomac	20.8	29	♦10.8	32	11.9	42	15.5	26
Malignant neoplasm of colon, rectosigmoid junction, rectum, anus and anal canal — Tumeur maligne du côlon, de la jonction recto-sigmoïdienne, du rectum, de l'anus et du canal anal	47.2	48	18.0	50	18.6	56	20.7	56
Malignant neoplasm of liver and intrahepatic bile ducts — Tumeur maligne du foie et des voies bilaires intrahépatiques	9.0	3	♦1.1	13	♦4.8	9	♦3.3	11
Malignant neoplasm of pancreas — Tumeur maligne du pancréas	16.4	27	♦10.1	33	12.3	37	13.7	30
Malignant neoplasm of trachea, bronchus and lung — Tumeur maligne de la trachée, des bronches et du poumon	78.2	90	33.7	113	42.0	116	42.8	105
Malignant neoplasm of female breast — Tumeur maligne du sein chez la femme	▲49.3	64	▲63.0	28	♦ ▲27.3	44	▲42.5	43
Malignant neoplasm of cervix uteri — Tumeur maligne du col de l'utérus	▲11.3	4	♦ ▲3.9	4	♦ ▲3.9	5	♦ ▲4.8	7
Malignant neoplasm of prostate — Tumeur maligne de la prostate	▼89.9	30	♦ ▼100.5	59	▼193.3	42	▼134.6	43
Malignant neoplasm of lymphoid, haematopoietic and related tissue — Tumeurs malignes primitives ou présumées primitives des tissus lymphoïde, hématopoïétique et apparentés	19.6	41	15.3	49	18.2	41	15.1	43
Disorders of the blood and blood-forming organs and certain disorders involving the immune mechanism — Maladies du sang et des organes hématopoïétiques et certains troubles du système immunitaire								
Total	1.4	3	♦1.1	4	♦1.5	2	♦0.7	3
Anaemias — Anémies	0.6	1	♦0.4	2	♦0.7	1	♦0.4	1
Endocrine, nutritional and metabolic diseases — Maladies endocriniennes, nutritionnelles et métaboliques								
Total	24.8	15	♦5.6	29	♦10.8	22	♦8.1	30
Diabetes mellitus — Diabète sucré	23.2	10	♦3.7	22	♦8.2	15	♦5.5	25
Malnutrition — Malnutrition	♦0.1	-	-	-	-	-	-	1
Mental and behavioural disorders — Troubles mentaux et du comportement	8.8	4	♦1.5	11	♦4.1	42	15.5	75
Diseases of the nervous system — Maladies du système nerveux	16.7	52	19.4	63	23.4	68	25.1	75
Diseases of the circulatory system — Maladies de l'appareil circulatoire								
Total	667.7	824	308.2	774	287.8	758	279.8	740
Acute rheumatic fever and chronic rheumatic heart diseases — Rhumatisme articularie aigu et cardiopathies rhumatismales chroniques	3.7	7	♦2.6	-	-	3	♦1.1	5
Hypertensive diseases — Maladies hypertensives	42.0	14	♦5.2	11	♦4.1	20	♦7.4	22
Ischaemic heart disease — Cardiopathie ischémique	292.1	441	164.9	436	162.1	414	152.8	389
Cerebrovascular disease — Maladie cérébrovasculaire	182.2	219	81.9	193	71.8	179	66.1	187
Diseases of arteries, arterioles and capillaries — Maladies des artères, artérioles et capillaires	80.7	36	13.5	21	♦7.8	27	♦10.0	19
Diseases of the respiratory system — Maladies de l'appareil respiratoire								
Total	46.3	255	95.4	251	93.3	185	68.3	150
Influenza — Grippe	♦0.1	11	♦4.1	6	♦2.2	17	♦6.3	18
Pneumonia — Pneumopathies	8.9	162	60.6	147	54.7	94	34.7	47
Chronic lower respiratory diseases — Maladies chroniques des voies respiratoires inférieures	33.7	65	24.3	83	30.9	62	22.9	79
Diseases of the digestive system — Maladies de l'appareil digestif								
Total	90.5	43	16.1	39	14.5	45	16.6	51
Gastric and duodenal ulcer — Ulcère de l'estomac et du duodénum	8.0	4	♦1.5	2	♦0.7	9	♦3.3	9

21. Death and death rates by cause: 1995 - 2002
Décès selon la cause, nombres et taux: 1995 - 2002 (continued — suite)

(See notes at end of table. — Voir notes à la fin du tableau.)

	Iceland — Islande							Ireland — Irlande[15]
Cause of death — Cause de décès	1998	1999		2000		2001		1995
	Rate Taux	Number Nombre	Rate Taux	Number Nombre	Rate Taux	Number Nombre	Rate Taux	Number Nombre
TOTAL	665.1	1 901	685.8	1 828	650.2	1 725	605.1	32 259
Certain infectious and parasitic diseases — Certaines maladies infectieuses et parasitaires								
Total	♦4.7	18	♦6.5	22	♦7.8	17	♦6.0	223
Intestinal infectious diseases — Maladies infectieuses intestinales	♦0.4	3	♦1.1	3	♦1.1	-	-	17
Tuberculosis — Tuberculose	-	1	♦0.4	-	-	1	♦0.4	36
Tetanus — Tétanos	-	-	-	-	-	-	-	-
Diphtheria — Diphtérie	-	-	-	-	-	-	-	1
Whooping cough — Coqueluche	-	-	-	-	-	-	-	21
Meningococcal infection — Infection à méningocoques	♦1.1	1	♦0.4	3	♦1.1	1	♦0.4	21
Septicaemia — Septicémie	♦1.1	8	♦2.9	6	♦2.1	9	♦3.2	48
Acute poliomyelitis — Poliomyélite aiguë	-	-	-	-	-	-	-	1
Measles — Rougeole	-	-	-	-	-	-	-	5
Viral hepatitis — Hépatite virale	♦0.4	-	-	-	-	-	-	-
Human immunodeficiency virus [HIV] disease — Maladies dues au virus de l'immunodéficience humaine (VIH)	-	1	♦0.4	1	♦0.4	2	♦0.7	51
Malaria — Paludisme	-	-	-	-	-	-	-	-
Neoplasms — Tumeurs	184.8	531	191.6	500	177.8	492	172.6	7 553
Malignant neoplasms — Tumeurs malignes								
Total	181.9	527	190.1	495	176.1	485	170.1	7 519
Malignant neoplasm of lip, oral cavity and pharynx — Tumeur maligne de la lèvre, de la cavité buccale et du pharynx	♦1.5	6	♦2.2	3	♦1.1	10	♦3.5	144
Malignant neoplasm of oesophagus — Tumeur maligne de l'oesophage	♦6.6	8	♦2.9	12	♦4.3	12	♦4.2	289
Malignant neoplasm of stomach — Tumeur maligne de l'estomac	♦9.5	23	♦8.3	33	11.7	24	♦8.4	410
Malignant neoplasm of colon, rectosigmoid junction, rectum, anus and anal canal — Tumeur maligne du côlon, de la jonction recto-sigmoïdienne, du rectum, de l'anus et du canal anal	20.5	49	17.7	52	18.5	59	20.7	974
Malignant neoplasm of liver and intrahepatic bile ducts — Tumeur maligne du foie et des voies biliaires intrahépatiques	♦4.0	14	♦5.1	9	♦3.2	4	♦1.4	9
Malignant neoplasm of pancreas — Tumeur maligne du pancréas	♦11.0	46	16.6	25	♦8.9	25	♦8.8	348
Malignant neoplasm of trachea, bronchus and lung — Tumeur maligne de la trachée, des bronches et du poumon	38.4	112	40.4	107	38.1	106	37.2	1 574
Malignant neoplasm of female breast — Tumeur maligne du sein chez la femme	▲40.9	38	▲35.6	31	▲28.3	25	♦ ▲22.7	654
Malignant neoplasm of cervix uteri — Tumeur maligne du col de l'utérus	♦ ▲6.7	5	♦ ▲4.7	4	♦ ▲3.7	3	♦ ▲2.7	72
Malignant neoplasm of prostate — Tumeur maligne de la prostate	▼134.2	45	▼137.1	45	▼129.2	44	▼126.0	521
Malignant neoplasm of lymphoid, haematopoietic and related tissue — Tumeurs malignes primitives ou présumées primitives des tissus lymphoïde, hématopoïétique et apparentés	15.7	54	19.5	48	17.1	44	15.4	548
Disorders of the blood and blood-forming organs and certain disorders involving the immune mechanism — Maladies du sang et des organes hématopoïétiques et certains troubles du système immunitaire								
Total	♦1.1	-	-	4	♦1.4	2	♦0.7	140
Anaemias — Anémies	♦0.4	-	-	1	♦0.4	1	♦0.4	80
Endocrine, nutritional and metabolic diseases — Maladies endocriniennes, nutritionnelles et métaboliques								
Total	♦11.0	34	12.3	21	♦7.5	34	11.9	519
Diabetes mellitus — Diabète sucré	♦9.1	25	♦9.0	19	♦6.8	27	♦9.5	387
Malnutrition — Malnutrition	♦0.4	2	♦0.7	-	-	1	♦0.4	1
Mental and behavioural disorders — Troubles mentaux et du comportement	27.4	92	33.2	62	22.1	55	19.3	330
Diseases of the nervous system — Maladies du système nerveux	27.4	69	24.9	88	31.3	77	27.0	600
Diseases of the circulatory system — Maladies de l'appareil circulatoire								
Total	270.3	792	285.7	717	255.0	682	239.3	14 267
Acute rheumatic fever and chronic rheumatic heart diseases — Rhumatisme articulaire aigu et cardiopathies rhumatismales chroniques	♦1.8	1	♦0.4	4	♦1.4	3	♦1.1	58
Hypertensive diseases — Maladies hypertensives	♦8.0	15	♦5.4	17	♦6.0	12	♦4.2	210
Ischaemic heart disease — Cardiopathie ischémique	142.1	439	158.4	385	136.9	352	123.5	7 926
Cerebrovascular disease — Maladie cérébrovasculaire	68.3	185	66.7	177	63.0	180	63.1	2 892
Diseases of arteries, arterioles and capillaries — Maladies des artères, artérioles et capillaires	♦6.9	34	12.3	28	♦10.0	32	11.2	808
Diseases of the respiratory system — Maladies de l'appareil respiratoire								
Total	54.8	185	66.7	170	60.5	142	49.8	4 902
Influenza — Grippe	♦6.6	29	♦10.5	21	♦7.5	1	♦0.4	18
Pneumonia — Pneumopathies	17.2	62	22.4	58	20.6	60	21.0	2 343
Chronic lower respiratory diseases — Maladies chroniques des voies respiratoires inférieures	28.9	86	31.0	80	28.5	70	24.6	2 008
Diseases of the digestive system — Maladies de l'appareil digestif								
Total	18.6	36	13.0	51	18.1	47	16.5	895
Gastric and duodenal ulcer — Ulcère de l'estomac et du duodénum	♦3.3	8	♦2.9	5	♦1.8	7	♦2.5	179

21. Death and death rates by cause: 1995 - 2002
Décès selon la cause, nombres et taux: 1995 - 2002 (continued — suite)

(See notes at end of table. — Voir notes à la fin du tableau.)

Ireland — Irlande[15]

Cause of death — Cause de décès	1995 Rate Taux	1996 Number Nombre	1996 Rate Taux	1997 Number Nombre	1997 Rate Taux	1998 Number Nombre	1998 Rate Taux	1999 Number Nombre
TOTAL	895.8	31 723	874.9	31 581	862.7	31 563	851.9	32 608
Certain infectious and parasitic diseases — Certaines maladies infectieuses et parasitaires								
Total	6.2	186	5.1	199	5.4	215	5.8	223
Intestinal infectious diseases — Maladies infectieuses intestinales	♦0.5	15	♦0.4	10	♦0.3	1	0.0	13
Tuberculosis — Tuberculose	1.0	33	0.9	37	1.0	43	1.2	33
Tetanus — Tétanos	-	-	-	-	-	-	-	-
Diphtheria — Diphtérie	-	-	-	-	-	-	-	-
Whooping cough — Coqueluche	0.0	-	-	-	-	-	-	-
Meningococcal infection — Infection à méningocoques	♦0.6	13	♦0.4	21	♦0.6	15	♦0.4	12
Septicaemia — Septicémie	1.3	40	1.1	54	1.5	85	2.3	72
Acute poliomyelitis — Poliomyélite aiguë	-	-	-	-	-	-	-	-
Measles — Rougeole	0.0	-	-	2	♦0.1	-	-	1
Viral hepatitis — Hépatite virale	♦0.1	6	♦0.2	11	♦0.3	9	♦0.2	6
Human immunodeficiency virus [HIV] disease — Maladies dues au virus de l'immunodéficience humaine (VIH)	1.4	33	0.9	15	♦0.4	13	♦0.4	18
Malaria — Paludisme	-	-	-	-	-	-	-	-
Neoplasms — Tumeurs	209.7	7 439	205.2	7 569	206.8	7 554	203.9	7 651
Malignant neoplasms — Tumeurs malignes								
Total	208.8	7 389	203.8	7 486	204.5	7 480	201.9	7 541
Malignant neoplasm of lip, oral cavity and pharynx — Tumeur maligne de la lèvre, de la cavité buccale et du pharynx	4.0	142	3.9	140	3.8	133	3.6	138
Malignant neoplasm of oesophagus — Tumeur maligne de l'oesophage	8.0	303	8.4	311	8.5	293	7.9	304
Malignant neoplasm of stomach — Tumeur maligne de l'estomac	11.4	399	11.0	375	10.2	357	9.6	352
Malignant neoplasm of colon, rectosigmoid junction, rectum, anus and anal canal — Tumeur maligne du côlon, de la jonction recto-sigmoïdienne, du rectum, de l'anus et du canal anal	27.0	896	24.7	971	26.5	878	23.7	970
Malignant neoplasm of liver and intrahepatic bile ducts — Tumeur maligne du foie et des voies biliaires intrahépatiques	♦0.2	15	♦0.4	28	♦0.8	18	♦0.5	15
Malignant neoplasm of pancreas — Tumeur maligne du pancréas	9.7	336	9.3	364	9.9	374	10.1	370
Malignant neoplasm of trachea, bronchus and lung — Tumeur maligne de la trachée, des bronches et du poumon	43.7	1 469	40.5	1 389	37.9	1 523	41.1	1 440
Malignant neoplasm of female breast — Tumeur maligne du sein chez la femme	▲47.5	635	...	634	...	601	▲41.2	645
Malignant neoplasm of cervix uteri — Tumeur maligne du col de l'utérus	▲5.2	82	...	82	...	80	▲5.5	78
Malignant neoplasm of prostate — Tumeur maligne de la prostate	▼127.1	523	...	537	...	514	▼117.3	499
Malignant neoplasm of lymphoid, haematopoietic and related tissue — Tumeurs malignes primitives ou présumées primitives des tissus lymphoïde, hématopoïétique et apparentés	15.2	573	15.8	572	15.6	676	18.2	673
Disorders of the blood and blood-forming organs and certain disorders involving the immune mechanism — Maladies du sang et des organes hématopoïétiques et certains troubles du système immunitaire								
Total	3.9	135	3.7	107	2.9	104	2.8	102
Anaemias — Anémies	2.2	74	2.0	65	1.8	64	1.7	56
Endocrine, nutritional and metabolic diseases — Maladies endocriniennes, nutritionnelles et métaboliques								
Total	14.4	557	15.4	512	14.0	549	14.8	638
Diabetes mellitus — Diabète sucré	10.7	432	11.9	382	10.4	412	11.1	455
Malnutrition — Malnutrition	0.0	4	♦0.1	7	♦0.2	7	♦0.2	13
Mental and behavioural disorders — Troubles mentaux et du comportement	9.2	386	10.6	422	11.5	475	12.8	516
Diseases of the nervous system — Maladies du système nerveux	16.7	627	17.3	592	16.2	615	16.6	676
Diseases of the circulatory system — Maladies de l'appareil circulatoire								
Total	396.2	13 897	383.2	13 496	368.7	13 241	357.4	13 380
Acute rheumatic fever and chronic rheumatic heart diseases — Rhumatisme articularie aigu et cardiopathies rhumatismales chroniques	1.6	54	1.5	62	1.7	53	1.4	63
Hypertensive diseases — Maladies hypertensives	5.8	202	5.6	212	5.8	259	7.0	289
Ischaemic heart disease — Cardiopathie ischémique	220.1	7 601	209.6	7 314	199.8	7 240	195.4	7 059
Cerebrovascular disease — Maladie cérébrovasculaire	80.3	2 901	80.0	2 733	74.7	2 572	69.4	2 807
Diseases of arteries, arterioles and capillaries — Maladies des artères, artérioles et capillaires	22.4	741	20.4	747	20.4	725	19.6	773
Diseases of the respiratory system — Maladies de l'appareil respiratoire								
Total	136.1	4 717	130.1	4 855	132.6	4 834	130.5	5 391
Influenza — Grippe	♦0.5	17	♦0.5	21	♦0.6	18	♦0.5	23
Pneumonia — Pneumopathies	65.1	2 237	61.7	2 248	61.4	2 268	61.2	2 697
Chronic lower respiratory diseases — Maladies chroniques des voies respiratoires inférieures	55.8	1 887	52.0	1 997	54.6	1 943	52.4	1 943
Diseases of the digestive system — Maladies de l'appareil digestif								
Total	24.9	928	25.6	1 002	27.4	990	26.7	1 044
Gastric and duodenal ulcer — Ulcère de l'estomac et du duodénum	5.0	157	4.3	193	5.3	156	4.2	191

677

21. Death and death rates by cause: 1995 - 2002
Décès selon la cause, nombres et taux: 1995 - 2002 (continued — suite)

(See notes at end of table. — Voir notes à la fin du tableau.)

Cause of death — Cause de décès	Ireland — Irlande[15]					Italy — Italie		
	1999	2000		2001		1995		1996
	Rate Taux	Number Nombre	Rate Taux	Number Nombre	Rate Taux	Number Nombre	Rate Taux	Number Nombre
TOTAL	870.8	31 391	828.9	30 212	787.0	556 690	971.5	554 576
Certain infectious and parasitic diseases — Certaines maladies infectieuses et parasitaires								
Total	6.0	223	5.9	184	4.8	7 597	13.3	7 179
Intestinal infectious diseases — Maladies infectieuses intestinales	♦0.3	8	♦0.2	12	♦0.3	74	0.1	70
Tuberculosis — Tuberculose	0.9	36	1.0	27	♦0.7	647	1.1	609
Tetanus — Tétanos	-	-	-	-	-	37	0.1	28
Diphtheria — Diphtérie	-	-	-	-	-	-	-	-
Whooping cough — Coqueluche	-	-	-	2	♦0.1	1	0.0	1
Meningococcal infection — Infection à méningocoques	♦0.3	22	♦0.6	12	♦0.3	18	0.0	23
Septicaemia — Septicémie	1.9	75	2.0	67	1.7	601	1.0	621
Acute poliomyelitis — Poliomyélite aiguë	-	-	-	-	-	-	-	-
Measles — Rougeole	0.0	2	♦0.1	-	-	7	0.0	9
Viral hepatitis — Hépatite virale	♦0.2	15	♦0.4	14	♦0.4	622	1.1	681
Human immunodeficiency virus [HIV] disease — Maladies dues au virus de l'immunodéficience humaine (VIH)	♦0.5	-	-	-	-	4 821	8.4	4 466
Malaria — Paludisme	-	1	0.0	-	-	8	0.0	9
Neoplasms — Tumeurs	204.3	7 784	205.5	7 732	201.4	153 954	268.7	156 572
Malignant neoplasms — Tumeurs malignes								
Total	201.4	7 666	202.4	7 632	198.8	147 976	258.2	150 380
Malignant neoplasm of lip, oral cavity and pharynx — Tumeur maligne de la lèvre, de la cavité buccale et du pharynx	3.7	126	3.3	119	3.1	2 949	5.1	2 939
Malignant neoplasm of oesophagus — Tumeur maligne de l'oesophage	8.1	322	8.5	323	8.4	2 170	3.8	2 124
Malignant neoplasm of stomach — Tumeur maligne de l'estomac	9.4	352	9.3	336	8.8	12 454	21.7	12 452
Malignant neoplasm of colon, rectosigmoid junction, rectum, anus and anal canal — Tumeur maligne du côlon, de la jonction recto-sigmoïdienne, du rectum, de l'anus et du canal anal	25.9	904	23.9	923	24.0	15 750	27.5	16 226
Malignant neoplasm of liver and intrahepatic bile ducts — Tumeur maligne du foie et des voies bilaires intrahépatiques	♦0.4	25	♦0.7	27	♦0.7	4 738	8.3	5 248
Malignant neoplasm of pancreas — Tumeur maligne du pancréas	9.9	349	9.2	374	9.7	6 975	12.2	7 204
Malignant neoplasm of trachea, bronchus and lung — Tumeur maligne de la trachée, des bronches et du poumon	38.7	1 568	41.4	1 478	38.5	30 909	53.9	31 127
Malignant neoplasm of female breast — Tumeur maligne du sein chez la femme	▲43.5	668	▲44.4	671	▲43.5	11 328	▲44.7	11 597
Malignant neoplasm of cervix uteri — Tumeur maligne du col de l'utérus	▲5.3	65	▲4.3	67	▲4.3	459	▲1.8	436
Malignant neoplasm of prostate — Tumeur maligne de la prostate	▼111.4	541	▼118.3	544	▼115.1	6 603	▼74.6	6 890
Malignant neoplasm of lymphoid, haematopoietic and related tissue — Tumeurs malignes primitives ou présumées primitives des tissus lymphoïde, hématopoïétique et apparentés	18.0	687	18.1	665	17.3	11 883	20.7	11 998
Disorders of the blood and blood-forming organs and certain disorders involving the immune mechanism — Maladies du sang et des organes hématopoïétiques et certains troubles du système immunitaire								
Total	2.7	95	2.5	89	2.3	2 232	3.9	2 259
Anaemias — Anémies	1.5	57	1.5	50	1.3	1 493	2.6	1 581
Endocrine, nutritional and metabolic diseases — Maladies endocriniennes, nutritionnelles et métaboliques								
Total	17.0	582	15.4	577	15.0	20 073	35.0	21 065
Diabetes mellitus — Diabète sucré	12.2	412	10.9	398	10.4	17 471	30.5	18 483
Malnutrition — Malnutrition	♦0.3	7	♦0.2	11	♦0.3	124	0.2	110
Mental and behavioural disorders — Troubles mentaux et du comportement	13.8	498	13.2	466	12.1	7 451	13.0	7 675
Diseases of the nervous system — Maladies du système nerveux	18.1	653	17.2	700	18.2	11 590	20.2	11 659
Diseases of the circulatory system — Maladies de l'appareil circulatoire								
Total	357.3	12 666	334.5	11 886	309.6	243 108	424.3	240 072
Acute rheumatic fever and chronic rheumatic heart diseases — Rhumatisme articularie aigu et cardiopathies rhumatismales chroniques	1.7	53	1.4	48	1.3	2 281	4.0	2 218
Hypertensive diseases — Maladies hypertensives	7.7	266	7.0	239	6.2	16 745	29.2	17 357
Ischaemic heart disease — Cardiopathie ischémique	188.5	6 589	174.0	6 163	160.5	75 879	132.4	75 469
Cerebrovascular disease — Maladie cérébrovasculaire	75.0	2 738	72.3	2 584	67.3	69 348	121.0	67 495
Diseases of arteries, arterioles and capillaries — Maladies des artères, artérioles et capillaires	20.6	716	18.9	678	17.7	14 181	24.7	13 802
Diseases of the respiratory system — Maladies de l'appareil respiratoire								
Total	144.0	4 863	128.4	4 472	116.5	33 857	59.1	32 279
Influenza — Grippe	♦0.6	44	1.2	8	♦0.2	797	1.4	734
Pneumonia — Pneumopathies	72.0	2 474	65.3	2 240	58.3	6 860	12.0	6 666
Chronic lower respiratory diseases — Maladies chroniques des voies respiratoires inférieures	51.9	1 664	43.9	1 502	39.1	18 895	33.0	18 097
Diseases of the digestive system — Maladies de l'appareil digestif								
Total	27.9	1 050	27.7	1 047	27.3	26 912	47.0	26 161
Gastric and duodenal ulcer — Ulcère de l'estomac et du duodénum	5.1	170	4.5	140	3.6	2 091	3.6	2 019

21. Death and death rates by cause: 1995 - 2002
Décès selon la cause, nombres et taux: 1995 - 2002 (continued — suite)
(See notes at end of table. — Voir notes à la fin du tableau.)

Italy — Italie

Cause of death — Cause de décès	1996	1997		1998		1999		2000
	Rate Taux	Number Nombre	Rate Taux	Number Nombre	Rate Taux	Number Nombre	Rate Taux	Number Nombre
TOTAL	966.5	561 207	975.6	574 231	997.1	567 741	984.9	560 121
Certain infectious and parasitic diseases — Certaines maladies infectieuses et parasitaires								
Total	12.5	5 511	9.6	4 784	8.3	4 607	8.0	4 584
Intestinal infectious diseases — Maladies infectieuses intestinales	0.1	71	0.1	55	0.1	53	0.1	51
Tuberculosis — Tuberculose	1.1	597	1.0	558	1.0	517	0.9	460
Tetanus — Tétanos	0.0	31	0.1	41	0.1	30	♦0.1	42
Diphtheria — Diphtérie	-	-	-	-	-	-	-	-
Whooping cough — Coqueluche	0.0	-	-	2	0.0	-	-	-
Meningococcal infection — Infection à méningocoques	0.0	24	0.0	15	0.0	28	0.0	20
Septicaemia — Septicémie	1.1	707	1.2	884	1.5	947	1.6	1 019
Acute poliomyelitis — Poliomyélite aiguë	-	-	-	-	-	-	-	-
Measles — Rougeole	0.0	9	0.0	-	-	1	0.0	2
Viral hepatitis — Hépatite virale	1.2	1 087	1.9	1 349	2.3	1 413	2.5	1 448
Human immunodeficiency virus [HIV] disease — Maladies dues au virus de l'immunodéficience humaine (VIH)	7.8	2 334	4.1	1 287	2.2	1 013	1.8	975
Malaria — Paludisme	0.0	13	0.0	10	0.0	4	0.0	5
Neoplasms — Tumeurs	272.9	156 984	272.9	158 941	276.0	158 568	275.1	160 053
Malignant neoplasms — Tumeurs malignes								
Total	262.1	150 826	262.2	152 468	264.8	151 798	263.3	153 431
Malignant neoplasm of lip, oral cavity and pharynx — Tumeur maligne de la lèvre, de la cavité buccale et du pharynx	5.1	2 871	5.0	2 943	5.1	2 943	5.1	2 866
Malignant neoplasm of oesophagus — Tumeur maligne de l'oesophage	3.7	2 041	3.5	2 129	3.7	2 176	3.8	2 020
Malignant neoplasm of stomach — Tumeur maligne de l'estomac	21.7	11 827	20.6	11 729	20.4	11 388	19.8	11 278
Malignant neoplasm of colon, rectosigmoid junction, rectum, anus and anal canal — Tumeur maligne du côlon, de la jonction recto-sigmoïdienne, du rectum, de l'anus et du canal anal	28.3	16 126	28.0	16 688	29.0	16 408	28.5	16 646
Malignant neoplasm of liver and intrahepatic bile ducts — Tumeur maligne du foie et des voies bilaires intrahépatiques	9.1	4 772	8.3	4 422	7.7	5 584	9.7	5 490
Malignant neoplasm of pancreas — Tumeur maligne du pancréas	12.6	7 471	13.0	7 718	13.4	7 822	13.6	8 112
Malignant neoplasm of trachea, bronchus and lung — Tumeur maligne de la trachée, des bronches et du poumon	54.2	31 176	54.2	31 541	54.8	31 620	54.9	31 534
Malignant neoplasm of female breast — Tumeur maligne du sein chez la femme	...	11 339	...	11 031	▲43.2	11 093	▲43.3	11 354
Malignant neoplasm of cervix uteri — Tumeur maligne du col de l'utérus	...	441	...	430	▲1.7	402	▲1.6	359
Malignant neoplasm of prostate — Tumeur maligne de la prostate	...	6 992	...	7 109	▼77.1	7 084	▼75.7	6 941
Malignant neoplasm of lymphoid, haematopoietic and related tissue — Tumeurs malignes primitives ou présumées primitives des tissus lymphoïde, hématopoïétique et apparentés	20.9	12 462	21.7	12 609	21.9	12 721	22.1	13 006
Disorders of the blood and blood-forming organs and certain disorders involving the immune mechanism — Maladies du sang et des organes hématopoïétiques et certains troubles du système immunitaire								
Total	3.9	2 273	4.0	2 337	4.1	2 375	4.1	2 469
Anaemias — Anémies	2.8	1 571	2.7	1 626	2.8	1 598	2.8	1 688
Endocrine, nutritional and metabolic diseases — Maladies endocriniennes, nutritionnelles et métaboliques								
Total	36.7	20 186	35.1	20 355	35.3	20 844	36.2	20 345
Diabetes mellitus — Diabète sucré	32.2	17 641	30.7	17 798	30.9	18 212	31.6	17 648
Malnutrition — Malnutrition	0.2	115	0.2	137	0.2	133	0.2	126
Mental and behavioural disorders — Troubles mentaux et du comportement	13.4	8 578	14.9	9 329	16.2	9 324	16.2	9 553
Diseases of the nervous system — Maladies du système nerveux	20.3	12 208	21.2	12 785	22.2	12 976	22.5	13 288
Diseases of the circulatory system — Maladies de l'appareil circulatoire								
Total	418.4	243 839	423.9	252 946	439.2	246 195	427.1	240 430
Acute rheumatic fever and chronic rheumatic heart diseases — Rhumatisme articularie aigu et cardiopathies rhumatismales chroniques	3.9	2 351	4.1	1 881	3.3	1 789	3.1	1 681
Hypertensive diseases — Maladies hypertensives	30.2	18 522	32.2	19 754	34.3	20 383	35.4	21 041
Ischaemic heart disease — Cardiopathie ischémique	131.5	75 700	131.6	78 387	136.1	75 940	131.7	73 486
Cerebrovascular disease — Maladie cérébrovasculaire	117.6	69 207	120.3	71 278	123.8	68 343	118.6	67 345
Diseases of arteries, arterioles and capillaries — Maladies des artères, artérioles et capillaires	24.1	13 713	23.8	13 622	23.7	12 597	21.9	11 973
Diseases of the respiratory system — Maladies de l'appareil respiratoire								
Total	56.3	35 455	61.6	37 270	64.7	39 071	67.8	37 782
Influenza — Grippe	1.3	1 097	1.9	1 174	2.0	1 655	2.9	1 532
Pneumonia — Pneumopathies	11.6	7 776	13.5	9 028	15.7	8 921	15.5	9 068
Chronic lower respiratory diseases — Maladies chroniques des voies respiratoires inférieures	31.5	19 546	34.0	19 757	34.3	20 105	34.9	18 998
Diseases of the digestive system — Maladies de l'appareil digestif								
Total	45.6	26 083	45.3	26 525	46.1	25 684	44.6	25 039
Gastric and duodenal ulcer — Ulcère de l'estomac et du duodénum	3.5	1 978	3.4	2 006	3.5	1 912	3.3	1 805

21. Death and death rates by cause: 1995 - 2002
Décès selon la cause, nombres et taux: 1995 - 2002 (continued — suite)

(See notes at end of table. — Voir notes à la fin du tableau.)

Cause of death — Cause de décès	Italy — Italie			Latvia — Lettonie[6]				
	2000	2001		1995		1996		1997
	Rate Taux	Number Nombre	Rate Taux	Number Nombre	Rate Taux	Number Nombre	Rate Taux	Number Nombre
TOTAL	969.7	556 892	961.0	38 931	1566.6	**34 320**	1396.7	**33 533**
Certain infectious and parasitic diseases — Certaines maladies infectieuses et parasitaires								
Total	7.9	3 695	6.4	515	20.7	402	16.4	448
Intestinal infectious diseases — Maladies infectieuses intestinales	0.1	68	0.1	5	♦0.2	10	♦0.4	3
Tuberculosis — Tuberculose	0.8	415	0.7	338	13.6	269	10.9	305
Tetanus — Tétanos	0.1	21	0.0	-		1	0.0	2
Diphtheria — Diphtérie	-	-	-	...	...	4	♦0.2	3
Whooping cough — Coqueluche	-	-	-			-		-
Meningococcal infection — Infection à méningocoques	0.0	19	0.0	10	♦0.4	12	♦0.5	7
Septicaemia — Septicémie	1.8	1 147	2.0	18	♦0.7	16	♦0.7	24
Acute poliomyelitis — Poliomyélite aiguë	-	-	-	...	...	-		-
Measles — Rougeole	0.0	1	0.0	-		-		-
Viral hepatitis — Hépatite virale	2.5	1 499	2.6	...	...	6	♦0.2	8
Human immunodeficiency virus [HIV] disease — Maladies dues au virus de l'immunodéficience humaine (VIH)	1.7	-	-	...	...	-		-
Malaria — Paludisme	0.0	4	0.0			-		-
Neoplasms — Tumeurs	277.1	164 349	283.6	5 506	221.6	5 542	225.5	**5 500**
Malignant neoplasms — Tumeurs malignes								
Total	265.6	157 476	271.8	5 476	220.4	5 493	223.5	5 453
Malignant neoplasm of lip, oral cavity and pharynx — Tumeur maligne de la lèvre, de la cavité buccale et du pharynx	5.0	2 886	5.0	134	5.4	135	5.5	132
Malignant neoplasm of oesophagus — Tumeur maligne de l'oesophage	3.5	2 126	3.7	87	3.5	97	3.9	97
Malignant neoplasm of stomach — Tumeur maligne de l'estomac	19.5	11 036	19.0	721	29.0	652	26.5	664
Malignant neoplasm of colon, rectosigmoid junction, rectum, anus and anal canal — Tumeur maligne du côlon, de la jonction recto-sigmoïdienne, du rectum, de l'anus et du canal anal	28.8	16 898	29.2	590	23.7	647	26.3	663
Malignant neoplasm of liver and intrahepatic bile ducts — Tumeur maligne du foie et des voies bilaires intrahépatiques	9.5	5 165	8.9	...	...	117	4.8	119
Malignant neoplasm of pancreas — Tumeur maligne du pancréas	14.0	8 334	14.4	...	...	322	13.1	325
Malignant neoplasm of trachea, bronchus and lung — Tumeur maligne de la trachée, des bronches et du poumon	54.6	31 968	55.2	1 079	43.4	1 114	45.3	1 040
Malignant neoplasm of female breast — Tumeur maligne du sein chez la femme	▲44.3	11 525	▲44.8	394	▲35.9	402	▲36.8	382
Malignant neoplasm of cervix uteri — Tumeur maligne du col de l'utérus	▲1.4	398	▲1.5	94	▲8.6	95	▲8.7	93
Malignant neoplasm of prostate — Tumeur maligne de la prostate	▼73.7	7 119	▼74.6	189	▼62.4	216	▼72.2	206
Malignant neoplasm of lymphoid, haematopoietic and related tissue — Tumeurs malignes primitives ou présumées primitives des tissus lymphoïde, hématopoïétique et apparentés	22.5	13 166	22.7	328	13.2	339	13.8	318
Disorders of the blood and blood-forming organs and certain disorders involving the immune mechanism — Maladies du sang et des organes hématopoïétiques et certains troubles du système immunitaire								
Total	4.3	2 305	4.0	22	♦0.9	19	♦0.8	28
Anaemias — Anémies	2.9	1 606	2.8	4	♦0.2	11	♦0.4	15
Endocrine, nutritional and metabolic diseases — Maladies endocriniennes, nutritionnelles et métaboliques								
Total	35.2	21 508	37.1	313	12.6	281	11.4	286
Diabetes mellitus — Diabète sucré	30.6	17 833	30.8	276	11.1	248	10.1	245
Malnutrition — Malnutrition	0.2	133	0.2	...	...	3	♦0.1	6
Mental and behavioural disorders — Troubles mentaux et du comportement	16.5	9 967	17.2	424	17.1	318	12.9	228
Diseases of the nervous system — Maladies du système nerveux	23.0	13 945	24.1	247	9.9	262	10.7	276
Diseases of the circulatory system — Maladies de l'appareil circulatoire								
Total	416.2	235 289	406.0	21 741	874.9	19 059	775.6	18 622
Acute rheumatic fever and chronic rheumatic heart diseases — Rhumatisme articularie aigu et cardiopathies rhumatismales chroniques	2.9	1 542	2.7	207	8.3	178	7.2	163
Hypertensive diseases — Maladies hypertensives	36.4	21 020	36.3	73	2.9	63	2.6	56
Ischaemic heart disease — Cardiopathie ischémique	127.2	72 578	125.2	11 777	473.9	10 071	409.9	9 995
Cerebrovascular disease — Maladie cérébrovasculaire	116.6	65 329	112.7	7 330	295.0	6 817	277.4	6 946
Diseases of arteries, arterioles and capillaries — Maladies des artères, artérioles et capillaires	20.7	11 371	19.6	1 125	45.3	1 097	44.6	705
Diseases of the respiratory system — Maladies de l'appareil respiratoire								
Total	65.4	33 826	58.4	1 305	52.5	918	37.4	939
Influenza — Grippe	2.7	335	0.6	1	0.0	5	♦0.2	8
Pneumonia — Pneumopathies	15.7	8 377	14.5	573	23.1	341	13.9	299
Chronic lower respiratory diseases — Maladies chroniques des voies respiratoires inférieures	32.9	17 403	30.0	...	...	416	16.9	453
Diseases of the digestive system — Maladies de l'appareil digestif								
Total	43.3	25 073	43.3	1 077	43.3	953	38.8	946
Gastric and duodenal ulcer — Ulcère de l'estomac et du duodénum	3.1	1 719	3.0	149	6.0	154	6.3	164

(See notes at end of table. — Voir notes à la fin du tableau.)

Latvia — Lettonie[6]

Cause of death — Cause de décès	1997 Rate Taux	1998 Number Nombre	1998 Rate Taux	1999 Number Nombre	1999 Rate Taux	2000 Number Nombre	2000 Rate Taux	2001 Number Nombre
TOTAL	1378.3	34 200	1419.1	32 844	1373.9	32 205	1357.2	32 991
Certain infectious and parasitic diseases — Certaines maladies infectieuses et parasitaires								
Total	18.4	478	19.8	413	17.3	383	16.1	394
Intestinal infectious diseases — Maladies infectieuses intestinales	✝0.1	8	✝0.3	3	✝0.1	5	✝0.2	10
Tuberculosis — Tuberculose	12.5	328	13.6	306	12.8	288	12.1	263
Tetanus — Tétanos	✝0.1	1	0.0	2	✝0.1	1	0.0	-
Diphtheria — Diphtérie	✝0.1	13	✝0.5	9	✝0.4	11	✝0.5	9
Whooping cough — Coqueluche	-	-	-	-	-	-	-	-
Meningococcal infection — Infection à méningocoques	✝0.3	5	✝0.2	5	✝0.2	2	✝0.1	2
Septicaemia — Septicémie	✝1.0	18	✝0.7	12	✝0.5	25	✝1.1	29
Acute poliomyelitis — Poliomyélite aiguë	-	-	-	-	-	-	-	-
Measles — Rougeole	-	-	-	-	-	-	-	-
Viral hepatitis — Hépatite virale	✝0.3	12	✝0.5	1	0.0	7	✝0.3	5
Human immunodeficiency virus [HIV] disease — Maladies dues au virus de l'immunodéficience humaine (VIH)	-	2	✝0.1	2	✝0.1	3	✝0.1	7
Malaria — Paludisme	-	-	-	-	-	-	-	-
Neoplasms — Tumeurs	226.1	5 675	235.5	5 771	241.4	5 633	237.4	5 802
Malignant neoplasms — Tumeurs malignes								
Total	224.1	5 603	232.5	5 692	238.1	5 569	234.7	5 732
Malignant neoplasm of lip, oral cavity and pharynx — Tumeur maligne de la lèvre, de la cavité buccale et du pharynx	5.4	138	5.7	140	5.9	137	5.8	133
Malignant neoplasm of oesophagus — Tumeur maligne de l'oesophage	4.0	92	3.8	112	4.7	94	4.0	102
Malignant neoplasm of stomach — Tumeur maligne de l'estomac	27.3	630	26.1	635	26.6	585	24.7	607
Malignant neoplasm of colon, rectosigmoid junction, rectum, anus and anal canal — Tumeur maligne du côlon, de la jonction recto-sigmoïdienne, du rectum, de l'anus et du canal anal	27.3	637	26.4	660	27.6	603	25.4	614
Malignant neoplasm of liver and intrahepatic bile ducts — Tumeur maligne du foie et des voies bilaires intrahépatiques	4.9	122	5.1	109	4.6	129	5.4	123
Malignant neoplasm of pancreas — Tumeur maligne du pancréas	13.4	334	13.9	349	14.6	327	13.8	324
Malignant neoplasm of trachea, bronchus and lung — Tumeur maligne de la trachée, des bronches et du poumon	42.7	1 053	43.7	1 125	47.1	1 039	43.8	1 120
Malignant neoplasm of female breast — Tumeur maligne du sein chez la femme	▲35.1	398	▲36.6	421	▲38.6	413	▲38.3	409
Malignant neoplasm of cervix uteri — Tumeur maligne du col de l'utérus	▲8.5	105	▲9.6	98	▲9.0	117	▲10.9	110
Malignant neoplasm of prostate — Tumeur maligne de la prostate	▼69.2	184	▼61.8	226	▼75.6	233	▼77.2	264
Malignant neoplasm of lymphoid, haematopoietic and related tissue — Tumeurs malignes primitives ou présumées primitives des tissus lymphoïde, hématopoïétique et apparentés	13.1	345	14.3	307	12.8	377	15.9	342
Disorders of the blood and blood-forming organs and certain disorders involving the immune mechanism — Maladies du sang et des organes hématopoïétiques et certains troubles du système immunitaire								
Total	✝1.2	16	✝0.7	23	✝1.0	22	✝0.9	30
Anaemias — Anémies	✝0.6	5	✝0.2	11	✝0.5	12	✝0.5	16
Endocrine, nutritional and metabolic diseases — Maladies endocriniennes, nutritionnelles et métaboliques								
Total	11.8	303	12.6	289	12.1	258	10.9	312
Diabetes mellitus — Diabète sucré	10.1	267	11.1	268	11.2	235	9.9	287
Malnutrition — Malnutrition	✝0.2	2	✝0.1	1	0.0	2	✝0.1	3
Mental and behavioural disorders — Troubles mentaux et du comportement	9.4	236	9.8	256	10.7	207	8.7	252
Diseases of the nervous system — Maladies du système nerveux	11.3	309	12.8	239	10.0	255	10.7	346
Diseases of the circulatory system — Maladies de l'appareil circulatoire								
Total	765.4	18 992	788.0	18 134	758.6	17 866	752.9	18 438
Acute rheumatic fever and chronic rheumatic heart diseases — Rhumatisme articularie aigu et cardiopathies rhumatismales chroniques	6.7	170	7.1	143	6.0	124	5.2	111
Hypertensive diseases — Maladies hypertensives	2.3	60	2.5	57	2.4	74	3.1	89
Ischaemic heart disease — Cardiopathie ischémique	410.8	10 664	442.5	9 821	410.8	9 656	406.9	9 275
Cerebrovascular disease — Maladie cérébrovasculaire	285.5	6 764	280.7	6 671	279.1	6 414	270.3	6 772
Diseases of arteries, arterioles and capillaries — Maladies des artères, artérioles et capillaires	29.0	499	20.7	609	25.5	787	33.2	1 293
Diseases of the respiratory system — Maladies de l'appareil respiratoire								
Total	38.6	849	35.2	836	35.0	856	36.1	784
Influenza — Grippe	✝0.3	1	0.0	3	✝0.1	29	✝1.2	-
Pneumonia — Pneumopathies	12.3	305	12.7	322	13.5	361	15.2	354
Chronic lower respiratory diseases — Maladies chroniques des voies respiratoires inférieures	18.6	404	16.8	372	15.6	331	13.9	319
Diseases of the digestive system — Maladies de l'appareil digestif								
Total	38.9	1 033	42.9	941	39.4	1 000	42.1	1 061
Gastric and duodenal ulcer — Ulcère de l'estomac et du duodénum	6.7	148	6.1	124	5.2	156	6.6	149

21. Death and death rates by cause: 1995 - 2002
Décès selon la cause, nombres et taux: 1995 - 2002 (continued — suite)

(See notes at end of table. — Voir notes à la fin du tableau.)

Cause of death — Cause de décès	Latvia — Lettonie[6] 2001 Rate Taux	Latvia — Lettonie[6] 2002 Number Nombre	Latvia — Lettonie[6] 2002 Rate Taux	Lithuania — Lituanie[6] 1995 Number Nombre	Lithuania — Lituanie[6] 1995 Rate Taux	Lithuania — Lituanie[6] 1996 Number Nombre	Lithuania — Lituanie[6] 1996 Rate Taux	Lithuania — Lituanie[6] 1997 Number Nombre
TOTAL	1400.9	32 498	1389.6	45 306	1248.4	42 896	1191.0	41 143
Certain infectious and parasitic diseases — Certaines maladies infectieuses et parasitaires								
Total	16.7	309	13.2	611	16.8	537	14.9	515
Intestinal infectious diseases — Maladies infectieuses intestinales	♦0.4	6	♦0.3	18	♦0.5	17	♦0.5	10
Tuberculosis — Tuberculose	11.2	191	8.2	483	13.3	441	12.2	403
Tetanus — Tétanos	-	-	-	-	-	1	0.0	1
Diphtheria — Diphtérie	♦0.4	3	♦0.1	8	♦0.2	-	-	-
Whooping cough — Coqueluche	-	-	-	-	-	-	-	-
Meningococcal infection — Infection à méningocoques	♦0.1	3	♦0.1	10	♦0.3	12	♦0.3	12
Septicaemia — Septicémie	♦1.2	23	♦1.0	40	1.1	32	0.9	45
Acute poliomyelitis — Poliomyélite aiguë	-	-	-	-	-	-	-	-
Measles — Rougeole	-	-	-	-	-	-	-	-
Viral hepatitis — Hépatite virale	♦0.2	10	♦0.4	16	♦0.4	3	♦0.1	13
Human immunodeficiency virus [HIV] disease — Maladies dues au virus de l'immunodéficience humaine (VIH)	♦0.3	5	♦0.2	...	...	...	...	...
Malaria — Paludisme	-	-	-	-	-	-	-	-
Neoplasms — Tumeurs	246.4	5 729	245.0	7 613	209.8	7 578	210.4	7 464
Malignant neoplasms — Tumeurs malignes								
Total	243.4	5 666	242.3	7 549	208.0	7 517	208.7	7 401
Malignant neoplasm of lip, oral cavity and pharynx — Tumeur maligne de la lèvre, de la cavité buccale et du pharynx	5.6	136	5.8	220	6.1	212	5.9	215
Malignant neoplasm of oesophagus — Tumeur maligne de l'oesophage	4.3	89	3.8	121	3.3	144	4.0	127
Malignant neoplasm of stomach — Tumeur maligne de l'estomac	25.8	578	24.7	940	25.9	913	25.3	860
Malignant neoplasm of colon, rectosigmoid junction, rectum, anus and anal canal — Tumeur maligne du côlon, de la jonction recto-sigmoïdienne, du rectum, de l'anus et du canal anal	26.1	635	27.2	791	21.8	822	22.8	782
Malignant neoplasm of liver and intrahepatic bile ducts — Tumeur maligne du foie et des voies biliaires intrahépatiques	5.2	129	5.5	...	...	...	...	...
Malignant neoplasm of pancreas — Tumeur maligne du pancréas	13.8	335	14.3	410	11.3	388	10.8	401
Malignant neoplasm of trachea, bronchus and lung — Tumeur maligne de la trachée, des bronches et du poumon	47.6	1 068	45.7	1 503	41.4	1 447	40.2	1 420
Malignant neoplasm of female breast — Tumeur maligne du sein chez la femme	▲38.0	439	▲40.8	520	▲33.2	571	▲36.4	569
Malignant neoplasm of cervix uteri — Tumeur maligne du col de l'utérus	▲10.2	95	▲8.8	222	▲14.2	199	▲12.7	243
Malignant neoplasm of prostate — Tumeur maligne de la prostate	▼87.5	289	▼95.8	343	▼81.3	362	▼85.8	351
Malignant neoplasm of lymphoid, haematopoietic and related tissue — Tumeurs malignes primitives ou présumées primitives des tissus lymphoïde, hématopoïétique et apparentés	14.5	322	13.8	470	13.0	444	12.3	453
Disorders of the blood and blood-forming organs and certain disorders involving the immune mechanism — Maladies du sang et des organes hématopoïétiques et certains troubles du système immunitaire								
Total	♦1.3	25	♦1.1	33	0.9	35	1.0	47
Anaemias — Anémies	♦0.7	8	♦0.3	25	♦0.7	27	♦0.7	32
Endocrine, nutritional and metabolic diseases — Maladies endocriniennes, nutritionnelles et métaboliques								
Total	13.2	271	11.6	301	8.3	297	8.2	281
Diabetes mellitus — Diabète sucré	12.2	251	10.7	245	6.8	246	6.8	234
Malnutrition — Malnutrition	♦0.1	1	0.0	4	♦0.1	-	-	8
Mental and behavioural disorders — Troubles mentaux et du comportement	10.7	109	4.7	981	27.0	844	23.4	537
Diseases of the nervous system — Maladies du système nerveux	14.7	390	16.7	376	10.4	320	8.9	313
Diseases of the circulatory system — Maladies de l'appareil circulatoire								
Total	782.9	18 189	777.8	24 305	669.7	23 487	652.1	22 750
Acute rheumatic fever and chronic rheumatic heart diseases — Rhumatisme articularie aigu et cardiopathies rhumatismales chroniques	4.7	97	4.1	289	8.0	298	8.3	282
Hypertensive diseases — Maladies hypertensives	3.8	176	7.5	265	7.3	314	8.7	235
Ischaemic heart disease — Cardiopathie ischémique	393.8	8 925	381.6	16 278	448.5	15 518	430.9	15 261
Cerebrovascular disease — Maladie cérébrovasculaire	287.6	6 685	285.9	5 125	141.2	5 007	139.0	5 116
Diseases of arteries, arterioles and capillaries — Maladies des artères, artérioles et capillaires	54.9	1 364	58.3	1 618	44.6	1 572	43.6	1 001
Diseases of the respiratory system — Maladies de l'appareil respiratoire								
Total	33.3	851	36.4	1 834	50.5	1 693	47.0	1 593
Influenza — Grippe	-	5	♦0.2	6	♦0.2	9	♦0.2	10
Pneumonia — Pneumopathies	15.0	434	18.6	329	9.1	301	8.4	303
Chronic lower respiratory diseases — Maladies chroniques des voies respiratoires inférieures	13.5	338	14.5	1 384	38.1	1 272	35.3	1 179
Diseases of the digestive system — Maladies de l'appareil digestif								
Total	45.1	1 009	43.1	1 193	32.9	1 104	30.7	1 149
Gastric and duodenal ulcer — Ulcère de l'estomac et du duodénum	6.3	141	6.0	165	4.5	159	4.4	155

21. Death and death rates by cause: 1995 - 2002
Décès selon la cause, nombres et taux: 1995 - 2002 (continued — suite)

(See notes at end of table. — Voir notes à la fin du tableau.)

Lithuania — Lituanie[6]

Cause of death — Cause de décès	1997 Rate Taux	1998 Number Nombre	1998 Rate Taux	1999 Number Nombre	1999 Rate Taux	2000 Number Nombre	2000 Rate Taux	2001 Number Nombre
TOTAL	1150.8	40 757	1148.3	40 003	1135.1	38 919	1112.1	40 399
Certain infectious and parasitic diseases — Certaines maladies infectieuses et parasitaires								
Total	14.4	533	15.0	485	13.8	490	14.0	464
Intestinal infectious diseases — Maladies infectieuses intestinales	♦0.3	7	♦0.2	4	♦0.1	5	♦0.1	4
Tuberculosis — Tuberculose	11.3	428	12.1	371	10.5	361	10.3	350
Tetanus — Tétanos	0.0	-	-	7	♦0.2	-	-	2
Diphtheria — Diphtérie	-	-	-	1	0.0	-	-	-
Whooping cough — Coqueluche	-	-	-	-	-	-	-	1
Meningococcal infection — Infection à méningocoques	♦0.3	8	♦0.2	10	♦0.3	12	♦0.3	9
Septicaemia — Septicémie	1.3	32	0.9	54	1.5	67	1.9	47
Acute poliomyelitis — Poliomyélite aiguë	-	-	-	-	-	-	-	-
Measles — Rougeole	-	-	-	-	-	-	-	-
Viral hepatitis — Hépatite virale	♦0.4	12	♦0.3	13	♦0.4	12	♦0.3	12
Human immunodeficiency virus [HIV] disease — Maladies dues au virus de l'immunodéficience humaine (VIH)	...	2	♦0.1	1	0.0	6	♦0.2	5
Malaria — Paludisme	-	1	0.0	1	0.0	-	-	1
Neoplasms — Tumeurs	208.8	7 677	216.3	7 841	222.5	7 813	223.3	7 893
Malignant neoplasms — Tumeurs malignes								
Total	207.0	7 586	213.7	7 750	219.9	7 723	220.7	7 796
Malignant neoplasm of lip, oral cavity and pharynx — Tumeur maligne de la lèvre, de la cavité buccale et du pharynx	6.0	211	5.9	264	7.5	246	7.0	261
Malignant neoplasm of oesophagus — Tumeur maligne de l'oesophage	3.6	146	4.1	152	4.3	146	4.2	163
Malignant neoplasm of stomach — Tumeur maligne de l'estomac	24.1	840	23.7	855	24.3	848	24.2	803
Malignant neoplasm of colon, rectosigmoid junction, rectum, anus and anal canal — Tumeur maligne du côlon, de la jonction recto-sigmoïdienne, du rectum, de l'anus et du canal anal	21.9	855	24.1	807	22.9	827	23.6	844
Malignant neoplasm of liver and intrahepatic bile ducts — Tumeur maligne du foie et des voies bilaires intrahépatiques	...	159	4.5	160	4.5	133	3.8	132
Malignant neoplasm of pancreas — Tumeur maligne du pancréas	11.2	355	10.0	377	10.7	404	11.5	383
Malignant neoplasm of trachea, bronchus and lung — Tumeur maligne de la trachée, des bronches et du poumon	39.7	1 464	41.0	1 486	41.6	1 375	39.3	1 449
Malignant neoplasm of female breast — Tumeur maligne du sein chez la femme	▲36.1	533	▲33.7	520	▲32.7	549	▲34.3	546
Malignant neoplasm of cervix uteri — Tumeur maligne du col de l'utérus	▲15.4	226	▲14.3	226	▲14.2	251	▲15.7	229
Malignant neoplasm of prostate — Tumeur maligne de la prostate	▼82.9	365	▼85.9	389	▼91.0	413	▼95.7	428
Malignant neoplasm of lymphoid, haematopoietic and related tissue — Tumeurs malignes primitives ou présumées primitives des tissus lymphoïde, hématopoïétique et apparentés	12.7	481	13.6	526	14.9	483	13.8	507
Disorders of the blood and blood-forming organs and certain disorders involving the immune mechanism — Maladies du sang et des organes hématopoïétiques et certains troubles du système immunitaire								
Total	1.3	37	1.0	38	1.1	30	♦0.9	21
Anaemias — Anémies	0.9	19	♦0.5	24	♦0.7	17	♦0.5	12
Endocrine, nutritional and metabolic diseases — Maladies endocriniennes, nutritionnelles et métaboliques								
Total	7.9	278	7.8	286	8.1	274	7.8	314
Diabetes mellitus — Diabète sucré	6.5	246	6.9	250	7.1	241	6.9	266
Malnutrition — Malnutrition	♦0.2	1	0.0	4	♦0.1	2	♦0.1	5
Mental and behavioural disorders — Troubles mentaux et du comportement	15.0	288	8.1	128	3.6	114	3.3	95
Diseases of the nervous system — Maladies du système nerveux	8.8	328	9.2	335	9.5	322	9.2	341
Diseases of the circulatory system — Maladies de l'appareil circulatoire								
Total	636.3	22 288	627.9	21 903	621.5	20 930	598.1	21 869
Acute rheumatic fever and chronic rheumatic heart diseases — Rhumatisme articulaire aigu et cardiopathies rhumatismales chroniques	7.9	289	8.1	260	7.4	250	7.1	184
Hypertensive diseases — Maladies hypertensives	6.6	398	11.2	352	10.0	280	8.0	271
Ischaemic heart disease — Cardiopathie ischémique	426.9	14 031	395.3	13 323	378.0	12 613	360.4	13 922
Cerebrovascular disease — Maladie cérébrovasculaire	143.1	5 221	147.1	5 171	146.7	4 897	139.9	4 986
Diseases of arteries, arterioles and capillaries — Maladies des artères, artérioles et capillaires	28.0	1 081	30.5	1 207	34.2	950	27.1	1 075
Diseases of the respiratory system — Maladies de l'appareil respiratoire								
Total	44.6	1 673	47.1	1 525	43.3	1 560	44.6	1 473
Influenza — Grippe	♦0.3	7	♦0.2	10	♦0.3	18	♦0.5	1
Pneumonia — Pneumopathies	8.5	415	11.7	384	10.9	391	11.2	364
Chronic lower respiratory diseases — Maladies chroniques des voies respiratoires inférieures	33.0	1 146	32.3	1 045	29.7	1 050	30.0	1 013
Diseases of the digestive system — Maladies de l'appareil digestif								
Total	32.1	1 320	37.2	1 240	35.2	1 273	36.4	1 436
Gastric and duodenal ulcer — Ulcère de l'estomac et du duodénum	4.3	160	4.5	160	4.5	168	4.8	186

21. Death and death rates by cause: 1995 - 2002
Décès selon la cause, nombres et taux: 1995 - 2002 (continued — suite)

(See notes at end of table. — Voir notes à la fin du tableau.)

Cause of death — Cause de décès	Lithuania — Lituanie[6]			Luxembourg				
	2001	2002		1995		1996		1997
	Rate Taux	Number Nombre	Rate Taux	Number Nombre	Rate Taux	Number Nombre	Rate Taux	Number Nombre
TOTAL	1160.5	41 072	1183.9	3 700	905.5	3 839	926.8	3 766
Certain infectious and parasitic diseases — Certaines maladies infectieuses et parasitaires								
Total	13.3	474	13.7	19	♦4.6	16	♦3.9	22
Intestinal infectious diseases — Maladies infectieuses intestinales	♦0.1	8	♦0.2	3	♦0.7	6	♦1.4	1
Tuberculosis — Tuberculose	10.1	332	9.6	-	-	-	-	2
Tetanus — Tétanos	♦0.1	-	-	-	-	-	-	-
Diphtheria — Diphtérie	-	1	0.0	-	-	-	-	-
Whooping cough — Coqueluche	0.0	-	-	-	-	-	-	1
Meningococcal infection — Infection à méningocoques	♦0.3	7	♦0.2	-	-	2	♦0.5	2
Septicaemia — Septicémie	1.4	65	1.9	-	-	-	-	-
Acute poliomyelitis — Poliomyélite aiguë	-	-	-	-	-	-	-	-
Measles — Rougeole	♦0.3	16	♦0.5	1	♦0.2	-	-	2
Viral hepatitis — Hépatite virale								
Human immunodeficiency virus [HIV] disease — Maladies dues au virus de l'immunodéficience humaine (VIH)	♦0.1	5	♦0.1	...	...	...	...	-
Malaria — Paludisme	0.0	-	-	...				
Neoplasms — Tumeurs	226.7	7 974	229.9	1 022	250.1	978	236.1	974
Malignant neoplasms — Tumeurs malignes								
Total	223.9	7 870	226.9	1 019	249.4	978	236.1	969
Malignant neoplasm of lip, oral cavity and pharynx — Tumeur maligne de la lèvre, de la cavité buccale et du pharynx	7.5	277	8.0	28	♦6.9	31	7.5	22
Malignant neoplasm of oesophagus — Tumeur maligne de l'oesophage	4.7	143	4.1	28	♦6.9	28	♦6.8	19
Malignant neoplasm of stomach — Tumeur maligne de l'estomac	23.1	811	23.4	55	13.5	47	11.3	51
Malignant neoplasm of colon, rectosigmoid junction, rectum, anus and anal canal — Tumeur maligne du côlon, de la jonction recto-sigmoïdienne, du rectum, de l'anus et du canal anal	24.2	874	25.2	120	29.4	108	26.1	133
Malignant neoplasm of liver and intrahepatic bile ducts — Tumeur maligne du foie et des voies bilaires intrahépatiques	3.8	123	3.5	...	...	...	...	...
Malignant neoplasm of pancreas — Tumeur maligne du pancréas	11.0	442	12.7	47	11.5	39	9.4	44
Malignant neoplasm of trachea, bronchus and lung — Tumeur maligne de la trachée, des bronches et du poumon	41.6	1 414	40.8	213	52.1	201	48.5	214
Malignant neoplasm of female breast — Tumeur maligne du sein chez la femme	▲35.8	550	▲35.9	93	▲54.1	66	▲37.9	78
Malignant neoplasm of cervix uteri — Tumeur maligne du col de l'utérus	▲15.0	276	▲18.0	4	♦▲2.3	3	♦▲1.7	2
Malignant neoplasm of prostate — Tumeur maligne de la prostate	▼102.8	427	▼101.6	52	▼94.4	49	▼87.6	49
Malignant neoplasm of lymphoid, haematopoietic and related tissue — Tumeurs malignes primitives ou présumées primitives des tissus lymphoïde, hématopoïétique et apparentés	14.6	595	17.2	73	17.9	83	20.0	77
Disorders of the blood and blood-forming organs and certain disorders involving the immune mechanism — Maladies du sang et des organes hématopoïétiques et certains troubles du système immunitaire								
Total	♦0.6	35	1.0	12	♦2.9	10	♦2.4	20
Anaemias — Anémies	♦0.3	22	♦0.6	10	♦2.4	7	♦1.7	12
Endocrine, nutritional and metabolic diseases — Maladies endocriniennes, nutritionnelles et métaboliques								
Total	9.0	340	9.8	90	22.0	102	24.6	76
Diabetes mellitus — Diabète sucré	7.6	301	8.7	63	15.4	75	18.1	55
Malnutrition — Malnutrition	♦0.1	2	♦0.1	1	♦0.2	-	-	4
Mental and behavioural disorders — Troubles mentaux et du comportement	2.7	71	2.0	91	22.3	98	23.7	153
Diseases of the nervous system — Maladies du système nerveux	9.8	360	10.4	61	14.9	55	13.3	68
Diseases of the circulatory system — Maladies de l'appareil circulatoire								
Total	628.2	22 331	643.7	1 538	376.4	1 660	400.7	1 565
Acute rheumatic fever and chronic rheumatic heart diseases — Rhumatisme articularie aigu et cardiopathies rhumatismales chroniques	5.3	174	5.0	-	-	-	-	3
Hypertensive diseases — Maladies hypertensives	7.8	276	8.0	50	12.2	48	11.6	81
Ischaemic heart disease — Cardiopathie ischémique	399.9	13 988	403.2	470	115.0	531	128.2	500
Cerebrovascular disease — Maladie cérébrovasculaire	143.2	5 273	152.0	482	118.0	464	112.0	404
Diseases of arteries, arterioles and capillaries — Maladies des artères, artérioles et capillaires	30.9	1 304	37.6	70	17.1	90	21.7	88
Diseases of the respiratory system — Maladies de l'appareil respiratoire								
Total	42.3	1 613	46.5	252	61.7	263	63.5	269
Influenza — Grippe	0.0	3	♦0.1	3	♦0.7	-	-	1
Pneumonia — Pneumopathies	10.5	444	12.8	50	12.2	68	16.4	63
Chronic lower respiratory diseases — Maladies chroniques des voies respiratoires inférieures	29.1	1 079	31.1	154	37.7	135	32.6	132
Diseases of the digestive system — Maladies de l'appareil digestif								
Total	41.2	1 510	43.5	165	40.4	185	44.7	180
Gastric and duodenal ulcer — Ulcère de l'estomac et du duodénum	5.3	193	5.6	15	♦3.7	11	♦2.7	9

21. Death and death rates by cause: 1995 - 2002
Décès selon la cause, nombres et taux: 1995 - 2002 (continued — suite)

(See notes at end of table. — Voir notes à la fin du tableau.)

Luxembourg

Cause of death — Cause de décès	1997 Rate Taux	1998 Number Nombre	1998 Rate Taux	1999 Number Nombre	1999 Rate Taux	2000 Number Nombre	2000 Rate Taux	2001 Number Nombre
TOTAL	897.8	3 822	899.9	3 671	852.8	3 709	850.1	3 672
Certain infectious and parasitic diseases — Certaines maladies infectieuses et parasitaires								
Total	♦5.2	42	9.9	48	11.2	36	8.3	35
Intestinal infectious diseases — Maladies infectieuses intestinales	♦0.2	3	♦0.7	6	♦1.4	6	♦1.4	2
Tuberculosis — Tuberculose	♦0.5	5	♦1.2	2	♦0.5	1	♦0.2	2
Tetanus — Tétanos	-	-	-	-	-	-	-	-
Diphtheria — Diphtérie	-	-	-	-	-	-	-	-
Whooping cough — Coqueluche	-	-	-	-	-	-	-	-
Meningococcal infection — Infection à méningocoques	♦0.2	-	-	-	-	1	♦0.2	1
Septicaemia — Septicémie	♦0.5	4	♦0.9	-	-	1	♦0.2	2
Acute poliomyelitis — Poliomyélite aiguë	-	-	-	-	-	-	-	-
Measles — Rougeole	-	-	-	-	-	-	-	-
Viral hepatitis — Hépatite virale	♦0.5	4	♦0.9	5	♦1.2	2	♦0.5	4
Human immunodeficiency virus [HIV] disease — Maladies dues au virus de l'immunodéficience humaine (VIH)	-	5	♦1.2	4	♦0.9	3	♦0.7	1
Malaria — Paludisme	-	1	♦0.2	-	-	-	-	-
Neoplasms — Tumeurs	232.2	1 008	237.3	927	215.3	991	227.1	942
Malignant neoplasms — Tumeurs malignes								
Total	231.0	1 003	236.2	918	213.3	988	226.4	934
Malignant neoplasm of lip, oral cavity and pharynx — Tumeur maligne de la lèvre, de la cavité buccale et du pharynx	♦5.2	32	7.5	31	7.2	28	♦6.4	27
Malignant neoplasm of oesophagus — Tumeur maligne de l'oesophage	♦4.5	29	♦6.8	24	♦5.6	24	♦5.5	18
Malignant neoplasm of stomach — Tumeur maligne de l'estomac	12.2	43	10.1	44	10.2	33	7.6	34
Malignant neoplasm of colon, rectosigmoid junction, rectum, anus and anal canal — Tumeur maligne du côlon, de la jonction recto-sigmoïdienne, du rectum, de l'anus et du canal anal	31.7	137	32.3	114	26.5	118	27.0	114
Malignant neoplasm of liver and intrahepatic bile ducts — Tumeur maligne du foie et des voies bilaires intrahépatiques	...	29	♦6.8	24	♦5.6	26	♦6.0	27
Malignant neoplasm of pancreas — Tumeur maligne du pancréas	10.5	51	12.0	47	10.9	54	12.4	66
Malignant neoplasm of trachea, bronchus and lung — Tumeur maligne de la trachée, des bronches et du poumon	51.0	210	49.4	199	46.2	200	45.8	180
Malignant neoplasm of female breast — Tumeur maligne du sein chez la femme	...	66	▲37.1	68	▲37.8	82	...	86
Malignant neoplasm of cervix uteri — Tumeur maligne du col de l'utérus	...	6	♦ ▲3.4	9	♦ ▲5.0	5	...	6
Malignant neoplasm of prostate — Tumeur maligne de la prostate	...	49	▼83.9	50	▼83.7	60	...	47
Malignant neoplasm of lymphoid, haematopoietic and related tissue — Tumeurs malignes primitives ou présumées primitives des tissus lymphoïde, hématopoïétique et apparentés	18.4	93	21.9	67	15.6	81	18.6	72
Disorders of the blood and blood-forming organs and certain disorders involving the immune mechanism — Maladies du sang et des organes hématopoïétiques et certains troubles du système immunitaire								
Total	♦4.8	12	♦2.8	6	♦1.4	8	♦1.8	11
Anaemias — Anémies	♦2.9	5	♦1.2	4	♦0.9	6	♦1.4	8
Endocrine, nutritional and metabolic diseases — Maladies endocriniennes, nutritionnelles et métaboliques								
Total	18.1	50	11.8	57	13.2	63	14.4	66
Diabetes mellitus — Diabète sucré	13.1	35	8.2	40	9.3	53	12.1	54
Malnutrition — Malnutrition	♦1.0	-	-	-	-	1	♦0.2	1
Mental and behavioural disorders — Troubles mentaux et du comportement	36.5	73	17.2	58	13.5	92	21.1	103
Diseases of the nervous system — Maladies du système nerveux	16.2	120	28.3	112	26.0	109	25.0	109
Diseases of the circulatory system — Maladies de l'appareil circulatoire								
Total	373.1	1 562	367.8	1 489	345.9	1 441	330.3	1 443
Acute rheumatic fever and chronic rheumatic heart diseases — Rhumatisme articulaire aigu et cardiopathies rhumatismales chroniques	♦0.7	4	♦0.9	1	♦0.2	-	-	1
Hypertensive diseases — Maladies hypertensives	19.3	57	13.4	77	17.9	60	13.8	69
Ischaemic heart disease — Cardiopathie ischémique	119.2	491	115.6	436	101.3	466	106.8	434
Cerebrovascular disease — Maladie cérébrovasculaire	96.3	441	103.8	445	103.4	426	97.6	405
Diseases of arteries, arterioles and capillaries — Maladies des artères, artérioles et capillaires	21.0	79	18.6	78	18.1	59	13.5	70
Diseases of the respiratory system — Maladies de l'appareil respiratoire								
Total	64.1	314	73.9	351	81.5	288	66.0	286
Influenza — Grippe	♦0.2	7	♦1.6	11	♦2.6	5	♦1.1	-
Pneumonia — Pneumopathies	15.0	82	19.3	99	23.0	75	17.2	98
Chronic lower respiratory diseases — Maladies chroniques des voies respiratoires inférieures	31.5	112	26.4	143	33.2	134	30.7	130
Diseases of the digestive system — Maladies de l'appareil digestif								
Total	42.9	184	43.3	184	42.7	204	46.8	201
Gastric and duodenal ulcer — Ulcère de l'estomac et du duodénum	♦2.1	11	♦2.6	10	♦2.3	11	♦2.5	14

21. Death and death rates by cause: 1995 - 2002
Décès selon la cause, nombres et taux: 1995 - 2002 (continued — suite)

(See notes at end of table. — Voir notes à la fin du tableau.)

Cause of death — Cause de décès	Luxembourg			Malta — Malte[16]				
	2001	2002		1995		1996		1997
	Rate Taux	Number Nombre	Rate Taux	Number Nombre	Rate Taux	Number Nombre	Rate Taux	Number Nombre
TOTAL	831.2	3 696	828.4	2 708	715.6	2 765	725.0	2 888
Certain infectious and parasitic diseases — Certaines maladies infectieuses et parasitaires								
Total	7.9	56	12.6	23	♦6.1	22	♦5.8	19
Intestinal infectious diseases — Maladies infectieuses intestinales	♦0.5	7	♦1.6	2	♦0.5	4	♦1.0	2
Tuberculosis — Tuberculose	♦0.5	3	♦0.7	1	♦0.3	-	-	-
Tetanus — Tétanos	-	-	-	-	-	1	♦0.3	-
Diphtheria — Diphtérie	-	-	-	-	-	-	-	-
Whooping cough — Coqueluche	-	-	-	-	-	-	-	-
Meningococcal infection — Infection à méningocoques	♦0.2	-	-	2	♦0.5	-	-	2
Septicaemia — Septicémie	♦0.5	24	♦5.4	10	♦2.6	6	♦1.6	11
Acute poliomyelitis — Poliomyélite aiguë	-	-	-	-	-	-	-	-
Measles — Rougeole	-	-	-	-	-	-	-	-
Viral hepatitis — Hépatite virale	♦0.9	2	♦0.4	1	♦0.3	-	-	-
Human immunodeficiency virus [HIV] disease — Maladies dues au virus de l'immunodéficience humaine (VIH)	♦0.2	5	♦1.1	1	♦0.3	8	♦2.1	2
Malaria — Paludisme	-	-	-	-	-	-	-	-
Neoplasms — Tumeurs	213.2	918	205.7	731	193.2	726	190.3	696
Malignant neoplasms — Tumeurs malignes								
Total	211.4	916	205.3	717	189.5	704	184.6	682
Malignant neoplasm of lip, oral cavity and pharynx — Tumeur maligne de la lèvre, de la cavité buccale et du pharynx	♦6.1	30	♦6.7	12	♦3.2	20	♦5.2	8
Malignant neoplasm of oesophagus — Tumeur maligne de l'oesophage	♦4.1	23	♦5.2	13	♦3.4	13	♦3.4	12
Malignant neoplasm of stomach — Tumeur maligne de l'estomac	7.7	36	8.1	39	10.3	57	14.9	47
Malignant neoplasm of colon, rectosigmoid junction, rectum, anus and anal canal — Tumeur maligne du côlon, de la jonction recto-sigmoïdienne, du rectum, de l'anus et du canal anal	25.8	114	25.6	92	24.3	69	18.1	78
Malignant neoplasm of liver and intrahepatic bile ducts — Tumeur maligne du foie et des voies bilaires intrahépatiques	♦6.1	32	7.2	7	♦1.8	9	♦2.4	9
Malignant neoplasm of pancreas — Tumeur maligne du pancréas	14.9	65	14.6	43	11.4	32	8.4	46
Malignant neoplasm of trachea, bronchus and lung — Tumeur maligne de la trachée, des bronches et du poumon	40.7	182	40.8	116	30.7	144	37.8	116
Malignant neoplasm of female breast — Tumeur maligne du sein chez la femme	▲46.9	75	▲40.5	95	▲63.9	86	▲57.6	70
Malignant neoplasm of cervix uteri — Tumeur maligne du col de l'utérus	♦▲3.3	6	♦▲3.2	7	▲4.7	6	♦▲4.0	9
Malignant neoplasm of prostate — Tumeur maligne de la prostate	▼77.1	40	▼64.6	36	▼81.2	40	▼86.3	26
Malignant neoplasm of lymphoid, haematopoietic and related tissue — Tumeurs malignes primitives ou présumées primitives des tissus lymphoïde, hématopoïétique et apparentés	16.3	84	18.8	59	15.6	49	12.8	58
Disorders of the blood and blood-forming organs and certain disorders involving the immune mechanism — Maladies du sang et des organes hématopoïétiques et certains troubles du système immunitaire								
Total	♦2.5	14	♦3.1	14	♦3.7	4	♦1.0	6
Anaemias — Anémies	♦1.8	7	♦1.6	12	♦3.2	1	♦0.3	2
Endocrine, nutritional and metabolic diseases — Maladies endocriniennes, nutritionnelles et métaboliques								
Total	14.9	76	17.0	91	24.0	68	17.8	94
Diabetes mellitus — Diabète sucré	12.2	54	12.1	85	22.5	60	15.7	89
Malnutrition — Malnutrition	♦0.2	2	♦0.4	-	-	1	♦0.3	-
Mental and behavioural disorders — Troubles mentaux et du comportement	23.3	44	9.9	12	♦3.2	16	♦4.2	18
Diseases of the nervous system — Maladies du système nerveux	24.7	115	25.8	46	12.2	43	11.3	48
Diseases of the circulatory system — Maladies de l'appareil circulatoire								
Total	326.6	1 437	322.1	1 161	306.8	1 268	332.5	1 328
Acute rheumatic fever and chronic rheumatic heart diseases — Rhumatisme articulaire aigu et cardiopathies rhumatismales chroniques	♦0.2	-	-	-	-	3	♦0.8	8
Hypertensive diseases — Maladies hypertensives	15.6	52	11.7	10	♦2.6	9	♦2.4	21
Ischaemic heart disease — Cardiopathie ischémique	98.2	431	96.6	641	169.4	678	177.8	733
Cerebrovascular disease — Maladie cérébrovasculaire	91.7	414	92.8	297	78.5	337	88.4	293
Diseases of arteries, arterioles and capillaries — Maladies des artères, artérioles et capillaires	15.8	64	14.3	26	♦6.9	16	♦4.2	30
Diseases of the respiratory system — Maladies de l'appareil respiratoire								
Total	64.7	363	81.4	228	60.3	219	57.4	266
Influenza — Grippe	-	5	♦1.1	-	-	2	♦0.5	1
Pneumonia — Pneumopathies	22.2	137	30.7	64	16.9	75	19.7	80
Chronic lower respiratory diseases — Maladies chroniques des voies respiratoires inférieures	29.4	145	32.5	94	24.8	79	20.7	106
Diseases of the digestive system — Maladies de l'appareil digestif								
Total	45.5	164	36.8	98	25.9	108	28.3	98
Gastric and duodenal ulcer — Ulcère de l'estomac et du duodénum	♦3.2	9	♦2.0	17	♦4.5	11	♦2.9	12

(See notes at end of table. — Voir notes à la fin du tableau.)

Malta — Malte[16]

Cause of death — Cause de décès	1997 Rate Taux	1998 Number Nombre	1998 Rate Taux	1999 Number Nombre	1999 Rate Taux	2000 Number Nombre	2000 Rate Taux	2001 Number Nombre
TOTAL	751.7	3 044	787.8	3 097	796.6	2 973	759.6	2 935
Certain infectious and parasitic diseases — Certaines maladies infectieuses et parasitaires								
Total	◆4.9	25	◆6.5	27	◆6.9	24	◆6.1	12
Intestinal infectious diseases — Maladies infectieuses intestinales	◆0.5	-	-	1	◆0.3	1	◆0.3	-
Tuberculosis — Tuberculose	-	2	◆0.5	2	◆0.5	1	◆0.3	-
Tetanus — Tétanos	-	-	-	-	-	1	◆0.3	-
Diphtheria — Diphtérie	-	-	-	-	-	-	-	-
Whooping cough — Coqueluche	-	-	-	-	-	-	-	-
Meningococcal infection — Infection à méningocoques	◆0.5	4	◆1.0	4	◆1.0	3	◆0.8	1
Septicaemia — Septicémie	◆2.9	10	◆2.6	14	◆3.6	11	◆2.8	6
Acute poliomyelitis — Poliomyélite aiguë	-	-	-	-	-	-	-	-
Measles — Rougeole	-	-	-	-	-	-	-	-
Viral hepatitis — Hépatite virale	-	1	◆0.3	1	◆0.3	-	-	3
Human immunodeficiency virus [HIV] disease — Maladies dues au virus de l'immunodéficience humaine (VIH)	◆0.5	3	◆0.8	1	◆0.3	2	◆0.5	-
Malaria — Paludisme	-	-	-	-	-	-	-	-
Neoplasms — Tumeurs	181.2	722	186.9	718	184.7	722	184.5	723
Malignant neoplasms — Tumeurs malignes								
Total	177.5	707	183.0	712	183.1	709	181.1	707
Malignant neoplasm of lip, oral cavity and pharynx — Tumeur maligne de la lèvre, de la cavité buccale et du pharynx	◆2.1	16	◆4.1	22	◆5.7	12	◆3.1	12
Malignant neoplasm of oesophagus — Tumeur maligne de l'oesophage	◆3.1	14	◆3.6	10	◆2.6	5	◆1.3	11
Malignant neoplasm of stomach — Tumeur maligne de l'estomac	12.2	39	10.1	48	12.3	38	9.7	28
Malignant neoplasm of colon, rectosigmoid junction, rectum, anus and anal canal — Tumeur maligne du côlon, de la jonction recto-sigmoïdienne, du rectum, de l'anus et du canal anal	20.3	76	19.7	82	21.1	85	21.7	82
Malignant neoplasm of liver and intrahepatic bile ducts — Tumeur maligne du foie et des voies bilaires intrahépatiques	◆2.3	14	◆3.6	17	◆4.4	9	◆2.3	8
Malignant neoplasm of pancreas — Tumeur maligne du pancréas	12.0	43	11.1	47	12.1	43	11.0	47
Malignant neoplasm of trachea, bronchus and lung — Tumeur maligne de la trachée, des bronches et du poumon	30.2	104	26.9	116	29.8	121	30.9	136
Malignant neoplasm of female breast — Tumeur maligne du sein chez la femme	▲46.3	88	▲57.6	72	▲46.7	102	...	73
Malignant neoplasm of cervix uteri — Tumeur maligne du col de l'utérus	◆▲6.0	5	◆▲3.3	2	◆▲1.3	5	...	5
Malignant neoplasm of prostate — Tumeur maligne de la prostate	◆▼54.0	42	▼84.3	44	▼85.4	38	...	33
Malignant neoplasm of lymphoid, haematopoietic and related tissue — Tumeurs malignes primitives ou présumées primitives des tissus lymphoïde, hématopoïétique et apparentés	15.1	63	16.3	59	15.2	62	15.8	65
Disorders of the blood and blood-forming organs and certain disorders involving the immune mechanism — Maladies du sang et des organes hématopoïétiques et certains troubles du système immunitaire								
Total	◆1.6	2	◆0.5	4	◆1.0	2	◆0.5	3
Anaemias — Anémies	◆0.5	2	◆0.5	1	◆0.3	1	◆0.3	2
Endocrine, nutritional and metabolic diseases — Maladies endocriniennes, nutritionnelles et métaboliques								
Total	24.5	125	32.4	101	26.0	91	23.2	108
Diabetes mellitus — Diabète sucré	23.2	112	29.0	95	24.4	82	20.9	102
Malnutrition — Malnutrition	-	-	-	-	-	-	-	-
Mental and behavioural disorders — Troubles mentaux et du comportement	◆4.7	19	◆4.9	20	◆5.1	18	◆4.6	9
Diseases of the nervous system — Maladies du système nerveux	12.5	66	17.1	54	13.9	57	14.6	47
Diseases of the circulatory system — Maladies de l'appareil circulatoire								
Total	345.7	1 334	345.2	1 482	381.2	1 388	354.6	1 283
Acute rheumatic fever and chronic rheumatic heart diseases — Rhumatisme articularie aigu et cardiopathies rhumatismales chroniques	◆2.1	2	◆0.5	8	◆2.1	5	◆1.3	4
Hypertensive diseases — Maladies hypertensives	◆5.5	15	◆3.9	20	◆5.1	17	◆4.3	17
Ischaemic heart disease — Cardiopathie ischémique	190.8	683	176.8	764	196.5	730	186.5	718
Cerebrovascular disease — Maladie cérébrovasculaire	76.3	322	83.3	307	79.0	319	81.5	306
Diseases of arteries, arterioles and capillaries — Maladies des artères, artérioles et capillaires	◆7.8	29	◆7.5	26	◆6.7	44	11.2	34
Diseases of the respiratory system — Maladies de l'appareil respiratoire								
Total	69.2	301	77.9	306	78.7	291	74.3	361
Influenza — Grippe	◆0.3	-	-	2	◆0.5	6	◆1.5	2
Pneumonia — Pneumopathies	20.8	88	22.8	75	19.3	74	18.9	102
Chronic lower respiratory diseases — Maladies chroniques des voies respiratoires inférieures	27.6	114	29.5	117	30.1	96	24.5	62
Diseases of the digestive system — Maladies de l'appareil digestif								
Total	25.5	108	28.0	94	24.2	96	24.5	92
Gastric and duodenal ulcer — Ulcère de l'estomac et du duodénum	◆3.1	11	◆2.8	11	◆2.8	22	◆5.6	8

21. Death and death rates by cause: 1995 - 2002
Décès selon la cause, nombres et taux: 1995 - 2002 (continued — suite)

(See notes at end of table. — Voir notes à la fin du tableau.)

Cause of death — Cause de décès	Malta — Malte[16] 2001 Rate Taux	Malta — Malte[16] 2002 Number Nombre	Malta — Malte[16] 2002 Rate Taux	Netherlands — Pays-Bas[17] 1995 Number Nombre	Netherlands — Pays-Bas[17] 1995 Rate Taux	Netherlands — Pays-Bas[17] 1996 Number Nombre	Netherlands — Pays-Bas[17] 1996 Rate Taux	Netherlands — Pays-Bas[17] 1997 Number Nombre
TOTAL	743.7	3 031	762.9	135 675	877.6	137 561	885.7	135 783
Certain infectious and parasitic diseases — Certaines maladies infectieuses et parasitaires								
Total	♦3.0	18	♦4.5	1 612	10.4	1 601	10.3	1 452
Intestinal infectious diseases — Maladies infectieuses intestinales	-	-	-	36	0.2	64	0.4	30
Tuberculosis — Tuberculose	-	1	♦0.3	43	0.3	33	0.2	38
Tetanus — Tétanos	-	-	-	2	0.0	-	-	1
Diphtheria — Diphtérie	-	-	-	-	-	2	0.0	2
Whooping cough — Coqueluche	-	-	-	56	0.4	48	0.3	41
Meningococcal infection — Infection à méningocoques	♦0.3	2	♦0.5	577	3.7	629	4.1	676
Septicaemia — Septicémie	♦1.5	2	♦0.5	-	-	-	-	1
Acute poliomyelitis — Poliomyélite aiguë	-	-	-	-	-	-	-	-
Measles — Rougeole	-	-	-	-	-	-	-	-
Viral hepatitis — Hépatite virale	♦0.8	5	♦1.3	9	♦0.1	47	0.3	33
Human immunodeficiency virus [HIV] disease — Maladies dues au virus de l'immunodéficience humaine (VIH)	-	2	♦0.5	439	2.8	327	2.1	184
Malaria — Paludisme	-	-	-	2	0.0	1	0.0	2
Neoplasms — Tumeurs	183.2	740	186.3	37 339	241.5	38 271	246.4	38 087
Malignant neoplasms — Tumeurs malignes								
Total	179.2	723	182.0	36 489	236.0	37 220	239.7	37 133
Malignant neoplasm of lip, oral cavity and pharynx — Tumeur maligne de la lèvre, de la cavité buccale et du pharynx	♦3.0	6	♦1.5	452	2.9	461	3.0	459
Malignant neoplasm of oesophagus — Tumeur maligne de l'oesophage	♦2.8	13	♦3.3	1 017	6.6	1 070	6.9	1 025
Malignant neoplasm of stomach — Tumeur maligne de l'estomac	♦7.1	49	12.3	1 871	12.1	1 926	12.4	1 741
Malignant neoplasm of colon, rectosigmoid junction, rectum, anus and anal canal — Tumeur maligne du côlon, de la jonction recto-sigmoïdienne, du rectum, de l'anus et du canal anal	20.8	94	23.7	4 263	27.6	4 176	26.9	4 274
Malignant neoplasm of liver and intrahepatic bile ducts — Tumeur maligne du foie et des voies bilaires intrahépatiques	♦2.0	13	♦3.3	283	1.8	417	2.7	448
Malignant neoplasm of pancreas — Tumeur maligne du pancréas	11.9	55	13.8	1 668	10.8	1 729	11.1	1 741
Malignant neoplasm of trachea, bronchus and lung — Tumeur maligne de la trachée, des bronches et du poumon	34.5	135	34.0	8 651	56.0	8 571	55.2	8 619
Malignant neoplasm of female breast — Tumeur maligne du sein chez la femme	▲45.3	63	▲38.3	3 461	▲53.9	3 552	▲55.0	3 574
Malignant neoplasm of cervix uteri — Tumeur maligne du col de l'utérus	♦ ▲3.1	10	♦ ▲6.1	234	▲3.6	230	▲3.6	234
Malignant neoplasm of prostate — Tumeur maligne de la prostate	▼59.6	33	▼57.0	2 425	▼121.2	2 458	▼119.9	2 367
Malignant neoplasm of lymphoid, haematopoietic and related tissue — Tumeurs malignes primitives ou présumées primitives des tissus lymphoïde, hématopoïétique et apparentés	16.5	49	12.3	2 803	18.1	2 993	19.3	2 904
Disorders of the blood and blood-forming organs and certain disorders involving the immune mechanism — Maladies du sang et des organes hématopoïétiques et certains troubles du système immunitaire								
Total	♦0.8	3	♦0.8	638	4.1	362	2.3	363
Anaemias — Anémies	♦0.5	3	♦0.8	271	1.8	253	1.6	255
Endocrine, nutritional and metabolic diseases — Maladies endocriniennes, nutritionnelles et métaboliques								
Total	27.4	102	25.7	3 959	25.6	4 080	26.3	4 127
Diabetes mellitus — Diabète sucré	25.8	91	22.9	2 991	19.3	3 143	20.2	3 198
Malnutrition — Malnutrition	-	-	-	48	0.3	36	0.2	22
Mental and behavioural disorders — Troubles mentaux et du comportement	♦2.3	18	♦4.5	4 113	26.6	4 173	26.9	4 282
Diseases of the nervous system — Maladies du système nerveux	11.9	50	12.6	2 048	13.2	2 912	18.8	2 931
Diseases of the circulatory system — Maladies de l'appareil circulatoire								
Total	325.1	1 336	336.3	52 098	337.0	51 309	330.4	49 758
Acute rheumatic fever and chronic rheumatic heart diseases — Rhumatisme articulaire aigu et cardiopathies rhumatismales chroniques	♦1.0	8	♦2.0	202	1.3	82	0.5	21
Hypertensive diseases — Maladies hypertensives	♦4.3	21	♦5.3	779	5.0	803	5.2	788
Ischaemic heart disease — Cardiopathie ischémique	181.9	685	172.4	20 723	134.1	20 562	132.4	19 354
Cerebrovascular disease — Maladie cérébrovasculaire	77.5	328	82.6	12 409	80.3	12 232	78.8	12 146
Diseases of arteries, arterioles and capillaries — Maladies des artères, artérioles et capillaires	8.6	39	9.8	3 524	22.8	3 475	22.4	3 384
Diseases of the respiratory system — Maladies de l'appareil respiratoire								
Total	91.5	351	88.3	12 644	81.8	13 054	84.1	13 176
Influenza — Grippe	♦0.5	1	♦0.3	287	1.9	261	1.7	197
Pneumonia — Pneumopathies	25.8	111	27.9	5 211	33.7	5 526	35.6	5 731
Chronic lower respiratory diseases — Maladies chroniques des voies respiratoires inférieures	15.7	90	22.7	6 323	40.9	6 488	41.8	6 356
Diseases of the digestive system — Maladies de l'appareil digestif								
Total	23.3	106	26.7	5 044	32.6	5 157	33.2	5 011
Gastric and duodenal ulcer — Ulcère de l'estomac et du duodénum	♦2.0	10	♦2.5	417	2.7	423	2.7	386

21. Death and death rates by cause: 1995 - 2002
Décès selon la cause, nombres et taux: 1995 - 2002 (continued — suite)

(See notes at end of table. — Voir notes à la fin du tableau.)

Cause of death — Cause de décès	Netherlands — Pays-Bas[17]							Norway — Norvège[18]
	1997	1998		1999		2000		1995
	Rate Taux	Number Nombre	Rate Taux	Number Nombre	Rate Taux	Number Nombre	Rate Taux	Number Nombre
TOTAL	869.8	137 482	875.3	140 487	888.5	140 527	883.4	45 182
Certain infectious and parasitic diseases — Certaines maladies infectieuses et parasitaires								
Total	9.3	1 511	9.6	1 634	10.3	1 630	10.2	462
Intestinal infectious diseases — Maladies infectieuses intestinales	◆0.2	37	0.2	40	0.3	37	0.2	68
Tuberculosis — Tuberculose	0.2	29	◆0.2	42	0.3	.32	0.2	19
Tetanus — Tétanos	0.0	-		-		-		-
Diphtheria — Diphtérie		-		-		-		-
Whooping cough — Coqueluche	0.0	1	0.0	3	0.0	-		1
Meningococcal infection — Infection à méningocoques	0.3	52	0.3	48	0.3	42	0.3	15
Septicaemia — Septicémie	4.3	714	4.5	761	4.8	824	5.2	162
Acute poliomyelitis — Poliomyélite aiguë	0.0	-		-		-		-
Measles — Rougeole	-	1	0.0	2	0.0	-		-
Viral hepatitis — Hépatite virale	0.2	50	0.3	49	0.3	49	0.3	8
Human immunodeficiency virus [HIV] disease — Maladies dues au virus de l'immunodéficience humaine (VIH)	1.2	136	0.9	137	0.9	132	0.8	56
Malaria — Paludisme	0.0	3	0.0	2	0.0	1	0.0	-
Neoplasms — Tumeurs	244.0	38 361	244.2	39 129	247.5	38 805	243.9	10 652
Malignant neoplasms — Tumeurs malignes								
Total	237.9	37 372	237.9	38 146	241.2	37 746	237.3	10 371
Malignant neoplasm of lip, oral cavity and pharynx — Tumeur maligne de la lèvre, de la cavité buccale et du pharynx	2.9	477	3.0	519	3.3	533	3.4	152
Malignant neoplasm of oesophagus — Tumeur maligne de l'oesophage	6.6	1 034	6.6	1 154	7.3	1 225	7.7	142
Malignant neoplasm of stomach — Tumeur maligne de l'estomac	11.2	1 668	10.6	1 715	10.8	1 719	10.8	618
Malignant neoplasm of colon, rectosigmoid junction, rectum, anus and anal canal — Tumeur maligne du côlon, de la jonction recto-sigmoïdienne, du rectum, de l'anus et du canal anal	27.4	4 399	28.0	4 418	27.9	4 300	27.0	1 626
Malignant neoplasm of liver and intrahepatic bile ducts — Tumeur maligne du foie et des voies bilaires intrahépatiques	2.9	440	2.8	499	3.2	478	3.0	46
Malignant neoplasm of pancreas — Tumeur maligne du pancréas	11.2	1 698	10.8	1 776	11.2	1 767	11.1	569
Malignant neoplasm of trachea, bronchus and lung — Tumeur maligne de la trachée, des bronches et du poumon	55.2	8 646	55.0	8 725	55.2	8 559	53.8	1 009
Malignant neoplasm of female breast — Tumeur maligne du sein chez la femme	▲55.1	3 542	▲53.9	3 666	▲55.9	3 425	...	789
Malignant neoplasm of cervix uteri — Tumeur maligne du col de l'utérus	▲3.6	276	▲4.2	253	▲3.9	258	...	115
Malignant neoplasm of prostate — Tumeur maligne de la prostate	▼111.9	2 383	▼108.9	2 388	▼107.1	2 367	...	1 064
Malignant neoplasm of lymphoid, haematopoietic and related tissue — Tumeurs malignes primitives ou présumées primitives des tissus lymphoïde, hématopoïétique et apparentés	18.6	2 996	19.1	2 980	18.8	2 992	18.8	881
Disorders of the blood and blood-forming organs and certain disorders involving the immune mechanism — Maladies du sang et des organes hématopoïétiques et certains troubles du système immunitaire								
Total	2.3	386	2.5	397	2.5	367	2.3	100
Anaemias — Anémies	1.6	277	1.8	274	1.7	250	1.6	71
Endocrine, nutritional and metabolic diseases — Maladies endocriniennes, nutritionnelles et métaboliques								
Total	26.4	4 099	26.1	4 413	27.9	4 317	27.1	658
Diabetes mellitus — Diabète sucré	20.5	3 224	20.5	3 308	20.9	3 345	21.0	507
Malnutrition — Malnutrition	◆0.1	51	0.3	66	0.4	73	0.5	-
Mental and behavioural disorders — Troubles mentaux et du comportement	27.4	4 458	28.4	4 941	31.2	5 133	32.3	1 082
Diseases of the nervous system — Maladies du système nerveux	18.8	2 892	18.4	3 197	20.2	2 874	18.1	800
Diseases of the circulatory system — Maladies de l'appareil circulatoire								
Total	318.7	49 826	317.2	49 594	313.6	49 191	309.2	19 867
Acute rheumatic fever and chronic rheumatic heart diseases — Rhumatisme articularie aigu et cardiopathies rhumatismales chroniques	◆0.1	23	◆0.1	18	◆0.1	15	◆0.1	92
Hypertensive diseases — Maladies hypertensives	5.0	797	5.1	740	4.7	797	5.0	452
Ischaemic heart disease — Cardiopathie ischémique	124.0	19 113	121.7	18 304	115.8	17 443	109.6	9 647
Cerebrovascular disease — Maladie cérébrovasculaire	77.8	12 104	77.1	12 409	78.5	12 184	76.6	4 987
Diseases of arteries, arterioles and capillaries — Maladies des artères, artérioles et capillaires	21.7	3 348	21.3	3 430	21.7	3 434	21.6	1 106
Diseases of the respiratory system — Maladies de l'appareil respiratoire								
Total	84.4	14 013	89.2	14 369	90.9	14 677	92.3	4 930
Influenza — Grippe	1.3	246	1.6	261	1.7	369	2.3	98
Pneumonia — Pneumopathies	36.7	5 963	38.0	6 488	41.0	6 559	41.2	3 173
Chronic lower respiratory diseases — Maladies chroniques des voies respiratoires inférieures	40.7	6 974	44.4	6 740	42.6	6 753	42.5	1 468
Diseases of the digestive system — Maladies de l'appareil digestif								
Total	32.1	5 054	32.2	5 081	32.1	5 337	33.5	1 275
Gastric and duodenal ulcer — Ulcère de l'estomac et du duodénum	2.5	366	2.3	371	2.3	392	2.5	245

(See notes at end of table. — Voir notes à la fin du tableau.)

Norway — Norvège[18]

Cause of death — Cause de décès	1995	1996		1997		1998		1999
	Rate Taux	Number Nombre	Rate Taux	Number Nombre	Rate Taux	Number Nombre	Rate Taux	Number Nombre
TOTAL	1036.5	43 919	1002.4	44 646	1013.5	44 270	999.0	45 114
Certain infectious and parasitic diseases — Certaines maladies infectieuses et parasitaires								
Total	10.6	436	10.0	443	10.1	487	11.0	534
Intestinal infectious diseases — Maladies infectieuses intestinales	1.6	87	2.0	71	1.6	61	1.4	83
Tuberculosis — Tuberculose	◆0.4	13	◆0.3	14	◆0.3	13	◆0.3	9
Tetanus — Tétanos	-	1	0.0	-	-	-	-	-
Diphtheria — Diphtérie	-	-	-	-	-	-	-	-
Whooping cough — Coqueluche	0.0	-	-	1	0.0	-	-	1
Meningococcal infection — Infection à méningocoques	◆0.3	13	◆0.3	4	◆0.1	5	◆0.1	13
Septicaemia — Septicémie	3.7	153	3.5	170	3.9	213	4.8	237
Acute poliomyelitis — Poliomyélite aiguë	-	-	-	-	-	-	-	-
Measles — Rougeole	-	-	-	-	-	-	-	-
Viral hepatitis — Hépatite virale	◆0.2	4	◆0.1	13	◆0.3	14	◆0.3	20
Human immunodeficiency virus [HIV] disease — Maladies dues au virus de l'immunodéficience humaine (VIH)	1.3	49	1.1	23	◆0.5	27	◆0.6	12
Malaria — Paludisme								
Neoplasms — Tumeurs	244.4	10 960	250.2	10 948	248.5	10 552	238.1	10 684
Malignant neoplasms — Tumeurs malignes								
Total	237.9	10 643	242.9	10 649	241.7	10 340	233.3	10 413
Malignant neoplasm of lip, oral cavity and pharynx — Tumeur maligne de la lèvre, de la cavité buccale et du pharynx	3.5	153	3.5	158	3.6	160	3.6	155
Malignant neoplasm of oesophagus — Tumeur maligne de l'oesophage	3.3	125	2.9	151	3.4	145	3.3	160
Malignant neoplasm of stomach — Tumeur maligne de l'estomac	14.2	572	13.1	571	13.0	521	11.8	577
Malignant neoplasm of colon, rectosigmoid junction, rectum, anus and anal canal — Tumeur maligne du côlon, de la jonction recto-sigmoïdienne, du rectum, de l'anus et du canal anal	37.3	1 530	34.9	1 609	36.5	1 520	34.3	1 521
Malignant neoplasm of liver and intrahepatic bile ducts — Tumeur maligne du foie et des voies bilaires intrahépatiques	1.1	86	2.0	69	1.6	89	2.0	125
Malignant neoplasm of pancreas — Tumeur maligne du pancréas	13.1	585	13.4	572	13.0	547	12.3	563
Malignant neoplasm of trachea, bronchus and lung — Tumeur maligne de la trachée, des bronches et du poumon	36.9	1 668	38.1	1 736	39.4	1 685	38.0	1 707
Malignant neoplasm of female breast — Tumeur maligne du sein chez la femme	▲44.1	823	▲45.8	761	▲42.2	739	▲40.8	705
Malignant neoplasm of cervix uteri — Tumeur maligne du col de l'utérus	▲6.4	134	▲7.5	119	▲6.6	126	▲7.0	117
Malignant neoplasm of prostate — Tumeur maligne de la prostate	▼178.7	1 162	▼191.5	1 136	▼183.4	1 088	▼172.4	1 119
Malignant neoplasm of lymphoid, haematopoietic and related tissue — Tumeurs malignes primitives ou présumées primitives des tissus lymphoïde, hématopoïétique et apparentés	20.2	924	21.1	962	21.8	944	21.3	913
Disorders of the blood and blood-forming organs and certain disorders involving the immune mechanism — Maladies du sang et des organes hématopoïétiques et certains troubles du système immunitaire								
Total	2.3	107	2.4	123	2.8	92	2.1	86
Anaemias — Anémies	1.6	66	1.5	78	1.8	57	1.3	49
Endocrine, nutritional and metabolic diseases — Maladies endocriniennes, nutritionnelles et métaboliques								
Total	15.1	675	15.4	913	20.7	882	19.9	862
Diabetes mellitus — Diabète sucré	11.6	506	11.5	738	16.8	681	15.4	678
Malnutrition — Malnutrition								
Mental and behavioural disorders — Troubles mentaux et du comportement	24.8	1 121	25.6	1 108	25.2	1 140	25.7	1 136
Diseases of the nervous system — Maladies du système nerveux	18.4	889	20.3	1 028	23.3	1 005	22.7	1 065
Diseases of the circulatory system — Maladies de l'appareil circulatoire								
Total	455.8	19 498	445.0	19 521	443.1	19 305	435.6	19 240
Acute rheumatic fever and chronic rheumatic heart diseases — Rhumatisme articulaire aigu et cardiopathies rhumatismales chroniques	2.1	121	2.8	127	2.9	92	2.1	94
Hypertensive diseases — Maladies hypertensives	10.4	423	9.7	403	9.1	350	7.9	431
Ischaemic heart disease — Cardiopathie ischémique	221.3	8 991	205.2	9 106	206.7	8 821	199.1	8 744
Cerebrovascular disease — Maladie cérébrovasculaire	114.4	5 220	119.1	5 038	114.4	4 997	112.8	4 736
Diseases of arteries, arterioles and capillaries — Maladies des artères, artérioles et capillaires	25.4	1 063	24.3	993	22.5	1 036	23.4	1 087
Diseases of the respiratory system — Maladies de l'appareil respiratoire								
Total	113.1	3 933	89.8	4 010	91.0	3 929	88.7	4 374
Influenza — Grippe	2.2	47	1.1	107	2.4	140	3.2	200
Pneumonia — Pneumopathies	72.8	2 086	47.6	2 101	47.7	1 939	43.8	2 137
Chronic lower respiratory diseases — Maladies chroniques des voies respiratoires inférieures	33.7	1 548	35.3	1 568	35.6	1 590	35.9	1 778
Diseases of the digestive system — Maladies de l'appareil digestif								
Total	29.2	1 310	29.9	1 373	31.2	1 362	30.7	1 405
Gastric and duodenal ulcer — Ulcère de l'estomac et du duodénum	5.6	253	5.8	229	5.2	230	5.2	287

(See notes at end of table. — Voir notes à la fin du tableau.)

Cause of death — Cause de décès	Norway — Norvège[18] 1999 Rate Taux	2000 Number Nombre	2000 Rate Taux	2001 Number Nombre	2001 Rate Taux	Poland — Pologne 1995 Number Nombre	1995 Rate Taux	1996 Number Nombre
TOTAL	1011.1	44 018	980.1	43 977	974.3	386 084	1000.5	385 496
Certain infectious and parasitic diseases — Certaines maladies infectieuses et parasitaires								
Total	12.0	538	12.0	521	11.5	2 456	6.4	2 294
Intestinal infectious diseases — Maladies infectieuses intestinales	1.9	78	1.7	61	1.4	34	0.1	33
Tuberculosis — Tuberculose	♦0.2	10	♦0.2	16	♦0.4	1 130	2.9	1 024
Tetanus — Tétanos	-	-	-	1	0.0	19	0.0	15
Diphtheria — Diphtérie	-	-	-	-	-	-	-	-
Whooping cough — Coqueluche	0.0	-	-	-	-	1	0.0	1
Meningococcal infection — Infection à méningocoques	♦0.3	6	♦0.1	2	0.0	22	♦0.1	10
Septicaemia — Septicémie	5.3	234	5.2	247	5.5	570	1.5	553
Acute poliomyelitis — Poliomyélite aiguë	-	1	0.0	-	-	-	-	-
Measles — Rougeole	♦0.4	15	♦0.3	15	♦0.3	242	0.6	191
Viral hepatitis — Hépatite virale								
Human immunodeficiency virus [HIV] disease — Maladies dues au virus de l'immunodéficience humaine (VIH)	♦0.3	15	♦0.3	11	♦0.2	...	...	...
Malaria — Paludisme	-	2	0.0	1	0.0	1	0.0	2
Neoplasms — Tumeurs	239.4	10 712	238.5	10 808	239.4	79 183	205.2	79 858
Malignant neoplasms — Tumeurs malignes								
Total	233.4	10 447	232.6	10 563	234.0	78 094	202.4	78 657
Malignant neoplasm of lip, oral cavity and pharynx — Tumeur maligne de la lèvre, de la cavité buccale et du pharynx	3.5	140	3.1	173	3.8	1 760	4.6	1 673
Malignant neoplasm of oesophagus — Tumeur maligne de l'oesophage	3.6	145	3.2	138	3.1	1 314	3.4	1 347
Malignant neoplasm of stomach — Tumeur maligne de l'estomac	12.9	463	10.3	502	11.1	6 559	17.0	6 332
Malignant neoplasm of colon, rectosigmoid junction, rectum, anus and anal canal — Tumeur maligne du côlon, de la jonction recto-sigmoïdienne, du rectum, de l'anus et du canal anal	34.1	1 594	35.5	1 672	37.0	7 367	19.1	7 593
Malignant neoplasm of liver and intrahepatic bile ducts — Tumeur maligne du foie et des voies biliaires intrahépatiques	2.8	112	2.5	114	2.5	2 369	6.1	2 340
Malignant neoplasm of pancreas — Tumeur maligne du pancréas	12.6	571	12.7	618	13.7	3 446	8.9	3 451
Malignant neoplasm of trachea, bronchus and lung — Tumeur maligne de la trachée, des bronches et du poumon	38.3	1 773	39.5	1 812	40.1	19 036	49.3	18 889
Malignant neoplasm of female breast — Tumeur maligne du sein chez la femme	▲38.7	761	...	746	▲40.6	4 665	▲30.1	4 738
Malignant neoplasm of cervix uteri — Tumeur maligne du col de l'utérus	▲6.4	99	...	101	▲5.5	1 992	▲12.8	2 025
Malignant neoplasm of prostate — Tumeur maligne de la prostate	▼174.3	1 094	...	1 035	▼156.2	2 512	▼61.1	2 655
Malignant neoplasm of lymphoid, haematopoietic and related tissue — Tumeurs malignes primitives ou présumées primitives des tissus lymphoïde, hématopoïétique et apparentés	20.5	878	19.6	919	20.4	4 411	11.4	4 585
Disorders of the blood and blood-forming organs and certain disorders involving the immune mechanism — Maladies du sang et des organes hématopoïétiques et certains troubles du système immunitaire								
Total	1.9	85	1.9	129	2.9	678	1.8	693
Anaemias — Anémies	1.1	52	1.2	75	1.7	365	0.9	339
Endocrine, nutritional and metabolic diseases — Maladies endocriniennes, nutritionnelles et métaboliques								
Total	19.3	847	18.9	942	20.9	5 445	14.1	5 502
Diabetes mellitus — Diabète sucré	15.2	655	14.6	717	15.9	5 030	13.0	5 069
Malnutrition — Malnutrition	-	-	-	1	0.0	49	0.1	62
Mental and behavioural disorders — Troubles mentaux et du comportement	25.5	1 275	28.4	1 340	29.7	2 262	5.9	2 021
Diseases of the nervous system — Maladies du système nerveux	23.9	1 001	22.3	1 153	25.5	3 108	8.1	3 119
Diseases of the circulatory system — Maladies de l'appareil circulatoire								
Total	431.2	18 191	405.1	17 868	395.9	194 710	504.6	194 326
Acute rheumatic fever and chronic rheumatic heart diseases — Rhumatisme articulaire aigu et cardiopathies rhumatismales chroniques	2.1	98	2.2	94	2.1	2 428	6.3	2 458
Hypertensive diseases — Maladies hypertensives	9.7	346	7.7	398	8.8	7 298	18.9	7 360
Ischaemic heart disease — Cardiopathie ischémique	196.0	8 182	182.2	7 941	175.9	38 923	100.9	38 917
Cerebrovascular disease — Maladie cérébrovasculaire	106.1	4 481	99.8	4 262	94.4	29 035	75.2	30 205
Diseases of arteries, arterioles and capillaries — Maladies des artères, artérioles et capillaires	24.4	1 028	22.9	1 063	23.6	78 138	202.5	76 177
Diseases of the respiratory system — Maladies de l'appareil respiratoire								
Total	98.0	4 384	97.6	4 332	96.0	13 232	34.3	14 286
Influenza — Grippe	4.5	234	5.2	22	♦0.5	66	0.2	212
Pneumonia — Pneumopathies	47.9	2 148	47.8	2 346	52.0	5 454	14.1	6 316
Chronic lower respiratory diseases — Maladies chroniques des voies respiratoires inférieures	39.8	1 725	38.4	1 683	37.3	6 667	17.3	6 808
Diseases of the digestive system — Maladies de l'appareil digestif								
Total	31.5	1 420	31.6	1 370	30.4	12 729	33.0	12 521
Gastric and duodenal ulcer — Ulcère de l'estomac et du duodénum	6.4	261	5.8	263	5.8	1 455	3.8	1 463

(See notes at end of table. — Voir notes à la fin du tableau.)

Poland — Pologne

Cause of death — Cause de décès	1996 Rate Taux	1999 Number Nombre	1999 Rate Taux	2000 Number Nombre	2000 Rate Taux	2001 Number Nombre	2001 Rate Taux	2002 Number Nombre
TOTAL	998.2	381 415	986.8	368 028	952.3	363 220	940.1	359 486
Certain infectious and parasitic diseases — Certaines maladies infectieuses et parasitaires								
Total	5.9	2 283	5.9	2 430	6.3	2 313	6.0	2 387
Intestinal infectious diseases — Maladies infectieuses intestinales	0.1	47	0.1	39	0.1	43	0.1	50
Tuberculosis — Tuberculose	2.7	1 022	2.6	1 041	2.7	1 001	2.6	892
Tetanus — Tétanos	0.0	9	0.0	5	0.0	7	0.0	3
Diphtheria — Diphtérie	-	-	-	-	-	-	-	-
Whooping cough — Coqueluche	0.0							
Meningococcal infection — Infection à méningocoques	0.0	20	♦0.1	19	0.0	16	0.0	6
Septicaemia — Septicémie	1.4	611	1.6	760	2.0	746	1.9	892
Acute poliomyelitis — Poliomyélite aiguë	-	-	-	-	-	-	-	-
Measles — Rougeole	0.5	216	0.6	231	0.6	230	0.6	219
Viral hepatitis — Hépatite virale								
Human immunodeficiency virus [HIV] disease — Maladies dues au virus de l'immunodéficience humaine (VIH)	...	126	0.3	115	0.3	100	0.3	122
Malaria — Paludisme	0.0	1	0.0	1	0.0	-	-	1
Neoplasms — Tumeurs	206.8	83 536	216.1	86 272	223.2	88 234	228.4	89 771
Malignant neoplasms — Tumeurs malignes								
Total	203.7	81 595	211.1	84 556	218.8	86 431	223.7	87 731
Malignant neoplasm of lip, oral cavity and pharynx — Tumeur maligne de la lèvre, de la cavité buccale et du pharynx	4.3	1 685	4.4	1 690	4.4	1 767	4.6	1 762
Malignant neoplasm of oesophagus — Tumeur maligne de l'oesophage	3.5	1 264	3.3	1 382	3.6	1 387	3.6	1 513
Malignant neoplasm of stomach — Tumeur maligne de l'estomac	16.4	6 000	15.5	6 036	15.6	5 929	15.3	5 875
Malignant neoplasm of colon, rectosigmoid junction, rectum, anus and anal canal — Tumeur maligne du côlon, de la jonction recto-sigmoïdienne, du rectum, de l'anus et du canal anal	19.7	8 002	20.7	8 517	22.0	8 927	23.1	9 042
Malignant neoplasm of liver and intrahepatic bile ducts — Tumeur maligne du foie et des voies bilaires intrahépatiques	6.1	2 168	5.6	2 071	5.4	2 126	5.5	2 042
Malignant neoplasm of pancreas — Tumeur maligne du pancréas	8.9	3 524	9.1	3 764	9.7	3 720	9.6	3 809
Malignant neoplasm of trachea, bronchus and lung — Tumeur maligne de la trachée, des bronches et du poumon	48.9	19 234	49.8	20 002	51.8	20 627	53.4	21 254
Malignant neoplasm of female breast — Tumeur maligne du sein chez la femme	▲30.3	4 552	▲28.3	4 712	...	4 825	▲29.4	4 825
Malignant neoplasm of cervix uteri — Tumeur maligne du col de l'utérus	▲12.9	1 859	▲11.5	1 987	...	1 826	▲11.1	1 855
Malignant neoplasm of prostate — Tumeur maligne de la prostate	▼64.1	2 911	▼65.9	3 147	...	3 365	▼72.2	3 488
Malignant neoplasm of lymphoid, haematopoietic and related tissue — Tumeurs malignes primitives ou présumées primitives des tissus lymphoïde, hématopoïétique et apparentés	11.9	4 763	12.3	4 861	12.6	5 208	13.5	5 318
Disorders of the blood and blood-forming organs and certain disorders involving the immune mechanism — Maladies du sang et des organes hématopoïétiques et certains troubles du système immunitaire								
Total	1.8	598	1.5	549	1.4	572	1.5	584
Anaemias — Anémies	0.9	345	0.9	322	0.8	341	0.9	356
Endocrine, nutritional and metabolic diseases — Maladies endocriniennes, nutritionnelles et métaboliques								
Total	14.2	5 856	15.1	5 712	14.8	5 571	14.4	5 639
Diabetes mellitus — Diabète sucré	13.1	5 331	13.8	5 190	13.4	5 060	13.1	5 126
Malnutrition — Malnutrition	0.2	99	0.3	77	0.2	62	0.2	83
Mental and behavioural disorders — Troubles mentaux et du comportement	5.2	1 839	4.8	1 541	4.0	1 594	4.1	1 485
Diseases of the nervous system — Maladies du système nerveux	8.1	3 620	9.4	3 605	9.3	3 857	10.0	3 939
Diseases of the circulatory system — Maladies de l'appareil circulatoire								
Total	503.2	181 477	469.5	175 407	453.9	173 809	449.8	169 299
Acute rheumatic fever and chronic rheumatic heart diseases — Rhumatisme articulaire aigu et cardiopathies rhumatismales chroniques	6.4	1 382	3.6	1 311	3.4	1 240	3.2	1 192
Hypertensive diseases — Maladies hypertensives	19.1	4 956	12.8	4 695	12.1	4 409	11.4	4 314
Ischaemic heart disease — Cardiopathie ischémique	100.8	57 071	147.6	55 575	143.8	53 760	139.1	51 469
Cerebrovascular disease — Maladie cérébrovasculaire	78.2	42 183	109.1	41 443	107.2	42 071	108.9	41 033
Diseases of arteries, arterioles and capillaries — Maladies des artères, artérioles et capillaires	197.3	37 216	96.3	32 479	84.0	31 758	82.2	32 310
Diseases of the respiratory system — Maladies de l'appareil respiratoire								
Total	37.0	17 923	46.4	18 310	47.4	15 758	40.8	15 537
Influenza — Grippe	0.5	402	1.0	358	0.9	26	♦0.1	38
Pneumonia — Pneumopathies	16.4	8 202	21.2	8 630	22.3	7 060	18.3	6 806
Chronic lower respiratory diseases — Maladies chroniques des voies respiratoires inférieures	17.6	7 633	19.7	7 542	19.5	6 925	17.9	6 981
Diseases of the digestive system — Maladies de l'appareil digestif								
Total	32.4	14 556	37.7	14 653	37.9	14 556	37.7	14 772
Gastric and duodenal ulcer — Ulcère de l'estomac et du duodénum	3.8	1 482	3.8	1 524	3.9	1 484	3.8	1 499

(See notes at end of table. — Voir notes à la fin du tableau.)

Cause of death — Cause de décès	Poland — Pologne 2002 Rate Taux	Portugal 1995 Number Nombre	1995 Rate Taux	1996 Number Nombre	1996 Rate Taux	1997 Number Nombre	1997 Rate Taux	1998 Number Nombre
TOTAL	935.5	103 939	1048.1	107 259	1080.4	105 157	1057.3	106 574
Certain infectious and parasitic diseases — Certaines maladies infectieuses et parasitaires								
Total	6.2	1 959	19.8	2 247	22.6	2 194	22.1	2 219
Intestinal infectious diseases — Maladies infectieuses intestinales	0.1	9	♦0.1	20	♦0.2	15	♦0.2	15
Tuberculosis — Tuberculose	2.3	313	3.2	295	3.0	321	3.2	346
Tetanus — Tétanos	0.0	16	♦0.2	14	♦0.1	10	♦0.1	15
Diphtheria — Diphtérie	-	-	-	-	-	-	-	-
Whooping cough — Coqueluche	-	-	-	-	-	-	-	-
Meningococcal infection — Infection à méningocoques	0.0	10	♦0.1	15	♦0.2	14	♦0.1	9
Septicaemia — Septicémie	2.3	313	3.2	378	3.8	477	4.8	562
Acute poliomyelitis — Poliomyélite aiguë	-	-	-	-	-	-	-	-
Measles — Rougeole	-	4	0.0	7	♦0.1	2	0.0	3
Viral hepatitis — Hépatite virale	0.6	115	1.2	140	1.4	130	1.3	139
Human immunodeficiency virus [HIV] disease — Maladies dues au virus de l'immunodéficience humaine (VIH)	0.3	949	9.6	1 111	11.2	972	9.8	895
Malaria — Paludisme	0.0	7	♦0.1	8	♦0.1	3	0.0	7
Neoplasms — Tumeurs	233.6	20 439	206.1	20 833	209.9	20 922	210.4	21 325
Malignant neoplasms — Tumeurs malignes								
Total	228.3	20 007	201.8	20 331	204.8	20 474	205.9	20 860
Malignant neoplasm of lip, oral cavity and pharynx — Tumeur maligne de la lèvre, de la cavité buccale et du pharynx	4.6	483	4.9	506	5.1	572	5.8	535
Malignant neoplasm of oesophagus — Tumeur maligne de l'oesophage	3.9	457	4.6	482	4.9	480	4.8	493
Malignant neoplasm of stomach — Tumeur maligne de l'estomac	15.3	2 814	28.4	2 699	27.2	2 631	26.5	2 565
Malignant neoplasm of colon, rectosigmoid junction, rectum, anus and anal canal — Tumeur maligne du côlon, de la jonction recto-sigmoïdienne, du rectum, de l'anus et du canal anal	23.5	2 618	26.4	2 616	26.4	2 706	27.2	2 754
Malignant neoplasm of liver and intrahepatic bile ducts — Tumeur maligne du foie et des voies bilaires intrahépatiques	5.3	328	3.3	366	3.7	336	3.4	331
Malignant neoplasm of pancreas — Tumeur maligne du pancréas	9.9	827	8.3	798	8.0	893	9.0	871
Malignant neoplasm of trachea, bronchus and lung — Tumeur maligne de la trachée, des bronches et du poumon	55.3	2 573	25.9	2 621	26.4	2 648	26.6	2 843
Malignant neoplasm of female breast — Tumeur maligne du sein chez la femme	▲29.4	1 536	▲35.9	1 547	▲36.0	1 561	▲36.1	1 554
Malignant neoplasm of cervix uteri — Tumeur maligne du col de l'utérus	▲11.3	198	▲4.6	204	▲4.7	193	▲4.5	203
Malignant neoplasm of prostate — Tumeur maligne de la prostate	▼73.1	1 472	▼108.4	1 619	▼118.3	1 673	▼121.4	1 653
Malignant neoplasm of lymphoid, haematopoietic and related tissue — Tumeurs malignes primitives ou présumées primitives des tissus lymphoïde, hématopoïétique et apparentés	13.8	1 491	15.0	1 481	14.9	1 507	15.2	1 580
Disorders of the blood and blood-forming organs and certain disorders involving the immune mechanism — Maladies du sang et des organes hématopoïétiques et certains troubles du système immunitaire								
Total	1.5	261	2.6	211	2.1	223	2.2	254
Anaemias — Anémies	0.9	169	1.7	137	1.4	139	1.4	172
Endocrine, nutritional and metabolic diseases — Maladies endocriniennes, nutritionnelles et métaboliques								
Total	14.7	3 470	35.0	3 391	34.2	3 597	36.2	3 800
Diabetes mellitus — Diabète sucré	13.3	3 076	31.0	3 005	30.3	3 188	32.1	3 387
Malnutrition — Malnutrition	0.2	56	0.6	29	♦0.3	50	0.5	55
Mental and behavioural disorders — Troubles mentaux et du comportement	3.9	392	4.0	438	4.4	435	4.4	401
Diseases of the nervous system — Maladies du système nerveux	10.3	987	10.0	1 092	11.0	1 140	11.5	1 166
Diseases of the circulatory system — Maladies de l'appareil circulatoire								
Total	440.6	43 523	438.9	44 687	450.1	42 196	424.3	42 526
Acute rheumatic fever and chronic rheumatic heart diseases — Rhumatisme articularie aigu et cardiopathies rhumatismales chroniques	3.1	241	2.4	214	2.2	168	1.7	173
Hypertensive diseases — Maladies hypertensives	11.2	753	7.6	862	8.7	814	8.2	880
Ischaemic heart disease — Cardiopathie ischémique	133.9	9 085	91.6	9 355	94.2	9 184	92.3	9 394
Cerebrovascular disease — Maladie cérébrovasculaire	106.8	23 439	236.4	23 662	238.3	21 938	220.6	21 828
Diseases of arteries, arterioles and capillaries — Maladies des artères, artérioles et capillaires	84.1	2 547	25.7	2 403	24.2	2 370	23.8	2 248
Diseases of the respiratory system — Maladies de l'appareil respiratoire								
Total	40.4	7 955	80.2	8 570	86.3	9 120	91.7	9 458
Influenza — Grippe	0.1	93	0.9	83	0.8	86	0.9	112
Pneumonia — Pneumopathies	17.7	3 293	33.2	3 498	35.2	3 963	39.8	4 169
Chronic lower respiratory diseases — Maladies chroniques des voies respiratoires inférieures	18.2	2 581	26.0	2 898	29.2	2 696	27.1	2 641
Diseases of the digestive system — Maladies de l'appareil digestif								
Total	38.4	4 536	45.7	4 740	47.7	4 505	45.3	4 480
Gastric and duodenal ulcer — Ulcère de l'estomac et du duodénum	3.9	349	3.5	466	4.7	387	3.9	390

(See notes at end of table. — Voir notes à la fin du tableau.)

Portugal

Cause of death — Cause de décès	1998 Rate Taux	1999 Number Nombre	1999 Rate Taux	2000 Number Nombre	2000 Rate Taux	2001 Number Nombre	2001 Rate Taux	2002 Number Nombre
TOTAL	1069.1	108 268	1083.9	105 813	1057.2	105 582	1025.5	**106 690**
Certain infectious and parasitic diseases — Certaines maladies infectieuses et parasitaires								
Total	22.3	2 413	24.2	2 325	23.2	2 065	20.1	**2 041**
Intestinal infectious diseases — Maladies infectieuses intestinales	♦0.2	11	♦0.1	11	♦0.1	19	♦0.2	**21**
Tuberculosis — Tuberculose	3.5	289	2.9	260	2.6	242	2.4	**239**
Tetanus — Tétanos	♦0.2	7	♦0.1	4	0.0	4	0.0	**3**
Diphtheria — Diphtérie	-	-	-	-	-	-	-	**-**
Whooping cough — Coqueluche	-	-	-	-	-	-	-	**-**
Meningococcal infection — Infection à méningocoques	♦0.1	12	♦0.1	29	♦0.3	16	♦0.2	**32**
Septicaemia — Septicémie	5.6	770	7.7	747	7.5	413	4.0	**428**
Acute poliomyelitis — Poliomyélite aiguë	-	-	-	-	-	-	-	**-**
Measles — Rougeole	0.0	3	0.0	4	0.0	1	0.0	**-**
Viral hepatitis — Hépatite virale	1.4	124	1.2	122	1.2	78	0.8	**51**
Human immunodeficiency virus [HIV] disease — Maladies dues au virus de l'immunodéficience humaine (VIH)	9.0	980	9.8	951	9.5	1 026	10.0	**999**
Malaria — Paludisme	♦0.1	15	♦0.2	6	♦0.1	12	♦0.1	**5**
Neoplasms — Tumeurs	213.9	21 451	214.8	21 988	219.7	22 407	217.6	**22 788**
Malignant neoplasms — Tumeurs malignes								
Total	209.3	20 934	209.6	21 461	214.4	21 960	213.3	**22 273**
Malignant neoplasm of lip, oral cavity and pharynx — Tumeur maligne de la lèvre, de la cavité buccale et du pharynx	5.4	541	5.4	559	5.6	585	5.7	**607**
Malignant neoplasm of oesophagus — Tumeur maligne de l'oesophage	4.9	497	5.0	527	5.3	540	5.2	**543**
Malignant neoplasm of stomach — Tumeur maligne de l'estomac	25.7	2 647	26.5	2 617	26.1	2 578	25.0	**2 524**
Malignant neoplasm of colon, rectosigmoid junction, rectum, anus and anal canal — Tumeur maligne du côlon, de la jonction recto-sigmoïdienne, du rectum, de l'anus et du canal anal	27.6	2 913	29.2	2 863	28.6	3 178	30.9	**3 131**
Malignant neoplasm of liver and intrahepatic bile ducts — Tumeur maligne du foie et des voies bilaires intrahépatiques	3.3	359	3.6	342	3.4	...	...	**691**
Malignant neoplasm of pancreas — Tumeur maligne du pancréas	8.7	855	8.6	879	8.8	972	9.4	**949**
Malignant neoplasm of trachea, bronchus and lung — Tumeur maligne de la trachée, des bronches et du poumon	28.5	2 726	27.3	2 870	28.7	2 864	27.8	**3 035**
Malignant neoplasm of female breast — Tumeur maligne du sein chez la femme	▲35.8	1 498	▲34.3	1 524	...	1 653	▲36.5	**1 550**
Malignant neoplasm of cervix uteri — Tumeur maligne du col de l'utérus	▲4.7	199	▲4.6	227	...	270	▲6.0	**220**
Malignant neoplasm of prostate — Tumeur maligne de la prostate	▼118.8	1 700	▼120.9	1 805	...	1 650	▼106.9	**1 701**
Malignant neoplasm of lymphoid, haematopoietic and related tissue — Tumeurs malignes primitives ou présumées primitives des tissus lymphoïde, hématopoïétique et apparentés	15.9	1 564	15.7	1 630	16.3	1 663	16.2	**1 773**
Disorders of the blood and blood-forming organs and certain disorders involving the immune mechanism — Maladies du sang et des organes hématopoïétiques et certains troubles du système immunitaire								
Total	2.5	230	2.3	192	1.9	223	2.2	**224**
Anaemias — Anémies	1.7	144	1.4	120	1.2	148	1.4	**159**
Endocrine, nutritional and metabolic diseases — Maladies endocriniennes, nutritionnelles et métaboliques								
Total	38.1	3 820	38.2	3 604	36.0	4 404	42.8	**4 984**
Diabetes mellitus — Diabète sucré	34.0	3 385	33.9	3 138	31.4	3 962	38.5	**4 447**
Malnutrition — Malnutrition	0.6	62	0.6	60	0.6	50	0.5	**75**
Mental and behavioural disorders — Troubles mentaux et du comportement	4.0	397	4.0	349	3.5	463	4.5	**682**
Diseases of the nervous system — Maladies du système nerveux	11.7	1 442	14.4	1 501	15.0	1 770	17.2	**2 007**
Diseases of the circulatory system — Maladies de l'appareil circulatoire								
Total	426.6	41 998	420.5	40 994	409.6	40 743	395.7	**41 001**
Acute rheumatic fever and chronic rheumatic heart diseases — Rhumatisme articulaire aigu et cardiopathies rhumatismales chroniques	1.7	185	1.9	185	1.8	190	1.8	**218**
Hypertensive diseases — Maladies hypertensives	8.8	900	9.0	1 002	10.0	991	9.6	**1 139**
Ischaemic heart disease — Cardiopathie ischémique	94.2	9 195	92.1	9 018	90.1	9 077	88.2	**9 533**
Cerebrovascular disease — Maladie cérébrovasculaire	219.0	21 617	216.4	20 995	209.8	20 437	198.5	**19 562**
Diseases of arteries, arterioles and capillaries — Maladies des artères, artérioles et capillaires	22.6	2 103	21.1	2 088	20.9	2 069	20.1	**2 078**
Diseases of the respiratory system — Maladies de l'appareil respiratoire								
Total	94.9	11 254	112.7	10 279	102.7	8 976	87.2	**9 250**
Influenza — Grippe	1.1	175	1.8	58	0.6	14	♦0.1	**63**
Pneumonia — Pneumopathies	41.8	5 010	50.2	4 645	46.4	3 863	37.5	**3 538**
Chronic lower respiratory diseases — Maladies chroniques des voies respiratoires inférieures	26.5	2 951	29.5	2 622	26.2	2 462	23.9	**2 716**
Diseases of the digestive system — Maladies de l'appareil digestif								
Total	44.9	4 280	42.8	4 141	41.4	4 469	43.4	**4 579**
Gastric and duodenal ulcer — Ulcère de l'estomac et du duodénum	3.9	410	4.1	344	3.4	350	3.4	**372**

(See notes at end of table. — Voir notes à la fin du tableau.)

Cause of death — Cause de décès	Portugal	Republic of Moldova — République de Moldova[6,19]						
	2002	1995	1996	1997	1998	1999	2000	2001
	Rate Taux				Number Nombre			
TOTAL	1029.0	52 872	50 059	42 241	39 922	41 314	41 224	40 076
Certain infectious and parasitic diseases — Certaines maladies infectieuses et parasitaires								
Total	19.7	632	727	569	581	661	734	628
Intestinal infectious diseases — Maladies infectieuses intestinales	◆0.2	51	55	50	30	26	27	26
Tuberculosis — Tuberculose	2.3	428	530	408	436	536	608	536
Tetanus — Tétanos	0.0	1	1	-	-	-	1	1
Diphtheria — Diphtérie	-	24	8	2	1	-	-	-
Whooping cough — Coqueluche	-	-	-	1	-	-	-	-
Meningococcal infection — Infection à méningocoques	0.3	20	27	21	19	14	13	3
Septicaemia — Septicémie	4.1	15	20	18	16	19	14	12
Acute poliomyelitis — Poliomyélite aiguë	-	-	-	-	-	-	-	-
Measles — Rougeole	-	-	-	-	-	-	-	-
Viral hepatitis — Hépatite virale	0.5	43	27	28	34	25	29	20
Human immunodeficiency virus [HIV] disease — Maladies dues au virus de l'immunodéficience humaine (VIH)	9.6	...	1	5	8	4	11	7
Malaria — Paludisme	0.0		-	-	-	-	1	
Neoplasms — Tumeurs	219.8	5 832	5 803	4 783	4 820	4 644	4 605	4 718
Malignant neoplasms — Tumeurs malignes								
Total	214.8	5 785	5 747	4 716	4 738	4 583	4 547	4 655
Malignant neoplasm of lip, oral cavity and pharynx — Tumeur maligne de la lèvre, de la cavité buccale et du pharynx	5.9	275	298	235	246	258	220	228
Malignant neoplasm of oesophagus — Tumeur maligne de l'oesophage	5.2	86	79	63	84	66	61	73
Malignant neoplasm of stomach — Tumeur maligne de l'estomac	24.3	710	646	527	514	475	520	456
Malignant neoplasm of colon, rectosigmoid junction, rectum, anus and anal canal — Tumeur maligne du côlon, de la jonction recto-sigmoïdienne, du rectum, de l'anus et du canal anal	30.2	655	600	468	508	536	574	538
Malignant neoplasm of liver and intrahepatic bile ducts — Tumeur maligne du foie et des voies bilaires intrahépatiques	6.7	190	299	260	255	231	223	248
Malignant neoplasm of pancreas — Tumeur maligne du pancréas	9.2	256	266	236	244	215	236	209
Malignant neoplasm of trachea, bronchus and lung — Tumeur maligne de la trachée, des bronches et du poumon	29.3	1 030	1 045	919	816	756	728	815
Malignant neoplasm of female breast — Tumeur maligne du sein chez la femme	▲34.0	503	491	376	346	426	389	419
Malignant neoplasm of cervix uteri — Tumeur maligne du col de l'utérus	▲4.0	195	200	138	182	176	144	183
Malignant neoplasm of prostate — Tumeur maligne de la prostate	▼108.7	99	96	106	93	83	86	91
Malignant neoplasm of lymphoid, haematopoietic and related tissue — Tumeurs malignes primitives ou présumées primitives des tissus lymphoïde, hématopoïétique et apparentés	17.1	364	333	291	349	294	252	278
Disorders of the blood and blood-forming organs and certain disorders involving the immune mechanism — Maladies du sang et des organes hématopoïétiques et certains troubles du système immunitaire								
Total	2.2	30	34	29	20	22	31	19
Anaemias — Anémies	1.5	16	11	15	7	13	14	11
Endocrine, nutritional and metabolic diseases — Maladies endocriniennes, nutritionnelles et métaboliques								
Total	48.1	475	535	350	425	482	404	366
Diabetes mellitus — Diabète sucré	42.9	433	477	327	400	442	367	340
Malnutrition — Malnutrition	0.7	12	24	7	4	15	6	6
Mental and behavioural disorders — Troubles mentaux et du comportement	6.6	299	198	136	90	111	96	104
Diseases of the nervous system — Maladies du système nerveux	19.4	501	461	357	343	309	348	283
Diseases of the circulatory system — Maladies de l'appareil circulatoire								
Total	395.4	24 283	24 957	22 375	21 027	22 728	22 998	22 443
Acute rheumatic fever and chronic rheumatic heart diseases — Rhumatisme articularie aigu et cardiopathies rhumatismales chroniques	2.1	297	291	235	250	247	230	228
Hypertensive diseases — Maladies hypertensives	11.0	273	208	248	211	316	322	350
Ischaemic heart disease — Cardiopathie ischémique	91.9	15 615	16 488	14 151	13 752	15 405	15 483	15 007
Cerebrovascular disease — Maladie cérébrovasculaire	188.7	6 857	6 947	6 177	5 907	6 183	6 422	6 438
Diseases of arteries, arterioles and capillaries — Maladies des artères, artérioles et capillaires	20.0	448	397	345	327	273	264	154
Diseases of the respiratory system — Maladies de l'appareil respiratoire								
Total	89.2	3 313	3 052	2 665	2 405	2 595	2 527	2 345
Influenza — Grippe	0.6	6	10	2	-	5	7	1
Pneumonia — Pneumopathies	34.1	1 230	1 048	849	710	768	801	723
Chronic lower respiratory diseases — Maladies chroniques des voies respiratoires inférieures	26.2	1 798	1 734	1 603	1 512	1 683	1 586	1 486
Diseases of the digestive system — Maladies de l'appareil digestif								
Total	44.2	4 981	4 456	3 806	3 548	3 618	3 761	3 974
Gastric and duodenal ulcer — Ulcère de l'estomac et du duodénum	3.6	232	249	176	191	180	176	190

21. Death and death rates by cause: 1995 - 2002
Décès selon la cause, nombres et taux: 1995 - 2002 (continued — suite)

(See notes at end of table. — Voir notes à la fin du tableau.)

Cause of death — Cause de décès	Republic of Moldova — République de Moldova[6,-19] 2002 Number Nombre	Romania — Roumanie 1995 Number Nombre	Rate Taux	1996 Number Nombre	Rate Taux	1997 Number Nombre	Rate Taux	1998 Number Nombre
TOTAL	41 853	271 672	1197.8	286 158	1265.8	279 315	1238.9	269 166
Certain infectious and parasitic diseases — Certaines maladies infectieuses et parasitaires								
Total	678	3 662	16.1	3 872	17.1	4 002	17.8	3 697
Intestinal infectious diseases — Maladies infectieuses intestinales	17	184	0.8	216	1.0	165	0.7	183
Tuberculosis — Tuberculose	556	2 560	11.3	2 583	11.4	2 662	11.8	2 369
Tetanus — Tétanos	-	9	0.0	6	0.0	7	0.0	4
Diphtheria — Diphtérie	-	1	0.0	1	0.0	-	-	-
Whooping cough — Coqueluche	10	14	♦0.1	22	♦0.1	35	0.2	25
Meningococcal infection — Infection à méningocoques	7	-	-	-	-	-	-	-
Septicaemia — Septicémie	-	-	-	-	-	-	-	-
Acute poliomyelitis — Poliomyélite aiguë	2	2	0.0	2	0.0	24	♦0.1	6
Measles — Rougeole	14	81	0.4	73	0.3	56	0.2	57
Viral hepatitis — Hépatite virale	18	463	2.0	524	2.3	619	2.7	630
Human immunodeficiency virus [HIV] disease — Maladies dues au virus de l'immunodéficience humaine (VIH)	-	1	0.0	1	0.0	-	-	1
Malaria — Paludisme								
Neoplasms — Tumeurs	4 880	37 539	165.5	38 492	170.3	39 146	173.6	39 292
Malignant neoplasms — Tumeurs malignes								
Total	4 801	37 220	164.1	38 230	169.1	38 894	172.5	39 013
Malignant neoplasm of lip, oral cavity and pharynx — Tumeur maligne de la lèvre, de la cavité buccale et du pharynx	225	1 144	5.0	1 284	5.7	1 285	5.7	1 335
Malignant neoplasm of oesophagus — Tumeur maligne de l'oesophage	67	404	1.8	438	1.9	450	2.0	444
Malignant neoplasm of stomach — Tumeur maligne de l'estomac	486	3 968	17.5	3 914	17.3	3 954	17.5	3 704
Malignant neoplasm of colon, rectosigmoid junction, rectum, anus and anal canal — Tumeur maligne du côlon, de la jonction recto-sigmoïdienne, du rectum, de l'anus et du canal anal	588	3 267	14.4	3 376	14.9	3 466	15.4	3 563
Malignant neoplasm of liver and intrahepatic bile ducts — Tumeur maligne du foie et des voies bilaires intrahépatiques	312	2 011	8.9	1 941	8.6	2 070	9.2	2 071
Malignant neoplasm of pancreas — Tumeur maligne du pancréas	233	1 734	7.6	1 851	8.2	1 906	8.5	1 869
Malignant neoplasm of trachea, bronchus and lung — Tumeur maligne de la trachée, des bronches et du poumon	743	7 825	34.5	7 788	34.4	8 004	35.5	8 100
Malignant neoplasm of female breast — Tumeur maligne du sein chez la femme	434	2 696	▲29.0	2 682	▲28.8	2 682	▲28.6	2 791
Malignant neoplasm of cervix uteri — Tumeur maligne du col de l'utérus	164	1 595	▲17.2	1 741	▲18.7	1 762	▲18.8	1 817
Malignant neoplasm of prostate — Tumeur maligne de la prostate	95	1 267	▼43.7	1 452	▼50.3	1 372	▼47.6	1 421
Malignant neoplasm of lymphoid, haematopoietic and related tissue — Tumeurs malignes primitives ou présumées primitives des tissus lymphoïde, hématopoïétique et apparentés	267	1 955	8.6	2 064	9.1	2 037	9.0	1 963
Disorders of the blood and blood-forming organs and certain disorders involving the immune mechanism — Maladies du sang et des organes hématopoïétiques et certains troubles du système immunitaire								
Total	17	137	0.6	143	0.6	131	0.6	141
Anaemias — Anémies	7	78	0.3	77	0.3	80	0.4	8
Endocrine, nutritional and metabolic diseases — Maladies endocriniennes, nutritionnelles et métaboliques								
Total	358	1 979	8.7	1 917	8.5	1 963	8.7	1 92
Diabetes mellitus — Diabète sucré	336	1 852	8.2	1 823	8.1	1 864	8.3	1 83
Malnutrition — Malnutrition	5	88	0.4	62	0.3	63	0.3	5
Mental and behavioural disorders — Troubles mentaux et du comportement	139	2 062	9.1	2 080	9.2	2 404	10.7	1 78
Diseases of the nervous system — Maladies du système nerveux	369	1 991	8.8	2 048	9.1	2 048	9.1	1 91
Diseases of the circulatory system — Maladies de l'appareil circulatoire								
Total	23 719	166 954	736.1	177 681	785.9	171 694	761.5	166 20
Acute rheumatic fever and chronic rheumatic heart diseases — Rhumatisme articularie aigu et cardiopathies rhumatismales chroniques	246	1 192	5.3	1 235	5.5	1 167	5.2	1 05
Hypertensive diseases — Maladies hypertensives	383	13 913	61.3	14 974	66.2	14 026	62.2	13 41
Ischaemic heart disease — Cardiopathie ischémique	16 061	55 569	245.0	58 665	259.5	58 252	258.4	56 79
Cerebrovascular disease — Maladie cérébrovasculaire	6 599	55 144	243.1	57 575	254.7	57 010	252.9	55 47
Diseases of arteries, arterioles and capillaries — Maladies des artères, artérioles et capillaires	167	15 432	68.0	17 291	76.5	15 636	69.4	15 49
Diseases of the respiratory system — Maladies de l'appareil respiratoire								
Total	2 693	17 185	75.8	19 489	86.2	17 492	77.6	15 93
Influenza — Grippe	-	17	♦0.1	48	0.2	12	♦0.1	7 3
Pneumonia — Pneumopathies	748	8 286	36.5	9 532	42.2	8 488	37.6	7 3
Chronic lower respiratory diseases — Maladies chroniques des voies respiratoires inférieures	1 812	7 653	33.7	8 668	38.3	7 767	34.4	7 3
Diseases of the digestive system — Maladies de l'appareil digestif								
Total	3 984	15 474	68.2	16 215	71.7	17 031	75.5	16 12
Gastric and duodenal ulcer — Ulcère de l'estomac et du duodénum	187	865	3.8	865	3.8	857	3.8	8

(See notes at end of table. — Voir notes à la fin du tableau.)

Romania — Roumanie

Cause of death — Cause de décès	1998 Rate Taux	1999 Number Nombre	1999 Rate Taux	2000 Number Nombre	2000 Rate Taux	2001 Number Nombre	2001 Rate Taux	2002 Number Nombre
TOTAL	1196.1	265 194	1180.8	255 820	1140.3	259 603	1173.0	269 666
Certain infectious and parasitic diseases — Certaines maladies infectieuses et parasitaires								
Total	16.4	3 236	14.4	3 171	14.1	3 451	15.6	3 273
Intestinal infectious diseases — Maladies infectieuses intestinales	0.8	178	0.8	169	0.8	132	0.6	124
Tuberculosis — Tuberculose	10.5	2 152	9.6	2 130	9.5	2 387	10.8	2 339
Tetanus — Tétanos	0.0	4	0.0	1	0.0	7	0.0	8
Diphtheria — Diphtérie	-	-	-	1	0.0	1	0.0	-
Whooping cough — Coqueluche	♦0.1	49	0.2	24	♦0.1	41	0.2	34
Meningococcal infection — Infection à méningocoques	-	156	0.7	173	0.8	202	0.9	226
Septicaemia — Septicémie	-	-	-	2	0.0	-	-	-
Acute poliomyelitis — Poliomyélite aiguë	0.0	-	-	-	-	-	-	-
Measles — Rougeole	0.3	38	0.2	42	0.2	58	0.3	49
Viral hepatitis — Hépatite virale	2.8	484	2.2	486	2.2	494	2.2	365
Human immunodeficiency virus [HIV] disease — Maladies dues au virus de l'immunodéficience humaine (VIH)	0.0	2	0.0	1	0.0	-	-	1
Malaria — Paludisme								
Neoplasms — Tumeurs	174.6	39 677	176.7	41 290	184.0	42 750	193.2	43 191
Malignant neoplasms — Tumeurs malignes								
Total	173.4	39 357	175.2	40 969	182.6	42 466	191.9	42 939
Malignant neoplasm of lip, oral cavity and pharynx — Tumeur maligne de la lèvre, de la cavité buccale et du pharynx	5.9	1 367	6.1	1 488	6.6	1 635	7.4	1 735
Malignant neoplasm of oesophagus — Tumeur maligne de l'oesophage	2.0	502	2.2	504	2.2	510	2.3	553
Malignant neoplasm of stomach — Tumeur maligne de l'estomac	16.5	3 864	17.2	3 919	17.5	4 082	18.4	4 088
Malignant neoplasm of colon, rectosigmoid junction, rectum, anus and anal canal — Tumeur maligne du côlon, de la jonction recto-sigmoïdienne, du rectum, de l'anus et du canal anal	15.8	3 691	16.4	3 808	17.0	4 172	18.9	4 285
Malignant neoplasm of liver and intrahepatic bile ducts — Tumeur maligne du foie et des voies bilaires intrahépatiques	9.2	1 951	8.7	2 123	9.5	2 182	9.9	2 161
Malignant neoplasm of pancreas — Tumeur maligne du pancréas	8.3	2 001	8.9	2 004	8.9	2 191	9.9	2 129
Malignant neoplasm of trachea, bronchus and lung — Tumeur maligne de la trachée, des bronches et du poumon	36.0	7 951	35.4	8 507	37.9	8 606	38.9	8 587
Malignant neoplasm of female breast — Tumeur maligne du sein chez la femme	▲29.7	2 904	▲30.9	2 949	...	2 999	▲31.5	3 013
Malignant neoplasm of cervix uteri — Tumeur maligne du col de l'utérus	▲19.4	1 795	▲19.1	1 784	...	1 763	▲18.5	1 881
Malignant neoplasm of prostate — Tumeur maligne de la prostate	▼49.3	1 400	▼48.1	1 512	...	1 574	▼52.6	1 560
Malignant neoplasm of lymphoid, haematopoietic and related tissue — Tumeurs malignes primitives ou présumées primitives des tissus lymphoïde, hématopoïétique et apparentés	8.7	2 038	9.1	2 097	9.3	2 196	9.9	2 198
Disorders of the blood and blood-forming organs and certain disorders involving the immune mechanism — Maladies du sang et des organes hématopoïétiques et certains troubles du système immunitaire								
Total	0.6	155	0.7	133	0.6	121	0.5	135
Anaemias — Anémies	0.4	82	0.4	85	0.4	81	0.4	73
Endocrine, nutritional and metabolic diseases — Maladies endocriniennes, nutritionnelles et métaboliques								
Total	8.6	2 066	9.2	1 963	8.7	1 913	8.6	1 959
Diabetes mellitus — Diabète sucré	8.1	1 967	8.8	1 871	8.3	1 809	8.2	1 867
Malnutrition — Malnutrition	0.2	36	0.2	45	0.2	62	0.3	46
Mental and behavioural disorders — Troubles mentaux et du comportement	7.9	1 373	6.1	1 208	5.4	1 069	4.8	1 214
Diseases of the nervous system — Maladies du système nerveux	8.5	1 723	7.7	1 647	7.3	1 668	7.5	1 658
Diseases of the circulatory system — Maladies de l'appareil circulatoire								
Total	738.6	165 467	736.8	157 407	701.6	159 240	719.5	167 358
Acute rheumatic fever and chronic rheumatic heart diseases — Rhumatisme articularie aigu et cardiopathies rhumatismales chroniques	4.7	721	3.2	737	3.3	571	2.6	605
Hypertensive diseases — Maladies hypertensives	59.6	14 811	65.9	15 305	68.2	17 021	76.9	19 463
Ischaemic heart disease — Cardiopathie ischémique	252.4	57 635	256.6	54 427	242.6	54 868	247.9	56 509
Cerebrovascular disease — Maladie cérébrovasculaire	246.5	54 245	241.5	51 998	231.8	52 774	238.5	55 210
Diseases of arteries, arterioles and capillaries — Maladies des artères, artérioles et capillaires	68.9	15 206	67.7	15 154	67.5	15 595	70.5	16 826
Diseases of the respiratory system — Maladies de l'appareil respiratoire								
Total	70.8	16 715	74.4	14 822	66.1	14 088	63.7	15 325
Influenza — Grippe	0.0	99	0.4	45	0.2	29	♦0.1	28
Pneumonia — Pneumopathies	32.8	7 518	33.5	6 878	30.7	6 264	28.3	6 889
Chronic lower respiratory diseases — Maladies chroniques des voies respiratoires inférieures	32.9	7 465	33.2	6 532	29.1	6 413	29.0	7 024
Diseases of the digestive system — Maladies de l'appareil digestif								
Total	71.6	14 697	65.4	14 343	63.9	15 830	71.5	16 121
Gastric and duodenal ulcer — Ulcère de l'estomac et du duodénum	3.6	762	3.4	699	3.1	715	3.2	700

(See notes at end of table. — Voir notes à la fin du tableau.)

Cause of death — Cause de décès	Romania — Roumanie	Russian Federation — Fédération de Russie[6,20]						
	2002	1995	1996	1997	1998	1999	2000	2001
	Rate Taux				Number Nombre			
TOTAL	**1237.3**	2 203 811	2 082 249	2 015 779	1 988 744	**2 144 316**	**2 225 332**	**2 254 856**
Certain infectious and parasitic diseases — Certaines maladies infectieuses et parasitaires								
Total	15.0	30 499	31 236	30 099	27 796	**35 685**	**36 214**	**35 273**
Intestinal infectious diseases — Maladies infectieuses intestinales	0.6	2 092	1 427	1 078	1 075	**1 575**	**1 307**	**1 151**
Tuberculosis — Tuberculose	10.7	22 972	25 080	24 679	22 687	**29 254**	**29 800**	**28 850**
Tetanus — Tétanos	0.0	40	32	25	28	**18**	**15**	**20**
Diphtheria — Diphtérie	-	...	...	...	...	**33**	**30**	**45**
Whooping cough — Coqueluche	-	5	18	11	13	**5**	**12**	**7**
Meningococcal infection — Infection à méningocoques	0.2	786	680	562	521	**535**	**551**	**537**
Septicaemia — Septicémie	1.0	1 756	1 735	1 809	1 824	**1 731**	**1 888**	**1 873**
Acute poliomyelitis — Poliomyélite aiguë	-	...	...	...	...			
Measles — Rougeole	-	4	2	2	3	**1**	**-**	**1**
Viral hepatitis — Hépatite virale	0.2	...	...	...	...	**690**	**845**	**895**
Human immunodeficiency virus [HIV] disease — Maladies dues au virus de l'immunodéficience humaine (VIH)	1.7	...	...	...	...	**107**	**208**	**255**
Malaria — Paludisme	0.0	5	3	4	4	**2**	**6**	**8**
Neoplasms — Tumeurs	**198.2**	298 710	294 127	295 608	295 824	**298 505**	**297 943**	**294 063**
Malignant neoplasms — Tumeurs malignes								
Total	197.0	295 651	291 210	292 848	293 199	**295 665**	**295 325**	**291 540**
Malignant neoplasm of lip, oral cavity and pharynx — Tumeur maligne de la lèvre, de la cavité buccale et du pharynx	8.0	8 326	8 399	8 407	8 340	**9 023**	**8 980**	**8 748**
Malignant neoplasm of oesophagus — Tumeur maligne de l'oesophage	2.5	8 140	7 977	7 912	7 807	**7 459**	**7 234**	**7 244**
Malignant neoplasm of stomach — Tumeur maligne de l'estomac	18.8	49 309	47 524	46 268	45 731	**45 048**	**43 747**	**42 637**
Malignant neoplasm of colon, rectosigmoid junction, rectum, anus and anal canal — Tumeur maligne du côlon, de la jonction recto-sigmoïdienne, du rectum, de l'anus et du canal anal	19.7	31 472	31 714	32 149	32 975	**34 031**	**34 841**	**34 975**
Malignant neoplasm of liver and intrahepatic bile ducts — Tumeur maligne du foie et des voies bilaires intrahépatiques	9.9	...	...	...	...	**7 970**	**8 350**	**8 334**
Malignant neoplasm of pancreas — Tumeur maligne du pancréas	9.8	...	...	...	...	**11 647**	**13 018**	**13 394**
Malignant neoplasm of trachea, bronchus and lung — Tumeur maligne de la trachée, des bronches et du poumon	39.4	63 584	61 179	61 364	60 201	**59 301**	**58 872**	**57 018**
Malignant neoplasm of female breast — Tumeur maligne du sein chez la femme	▲32.4	19 141	19 597	20 423	20 925	**21 216**	**21 707**	**21 592**
Malignant neoplasm of cervix uteri — Tumeur maligne du col de l'utérus	▲20.2	6 148	6 097	6 142	6 078	**6 322**	**6 288**	**6 282**
Malignant neoplasm of prostate — Tumeur maligne de la prostate	▼52.4	5 281	5 583	6 001	6 305	**6 436**	**6 680**	**6 986**
Malignant neoplasm of lymphoid, haematopoietic and related tissue — Tumeurs malignes primitives ou présumées primitives des tissus lymphoïde, hématopoïétique et apparentés	10.1	14 173	14 024	14 030	14 265	...	...	...
Disorders of the blood and blood-forming organs and certain disorders involving the immune mechanism — Maladies du sang et des organes hématopoïétiques et certains troubles du système immunitaire								
Total	0.6	1 525	1 495	1 319	1 246	**1 541**	**1 521**	**1 367**
Anaemias — Anémies	0.3	1 064	1 050	881	861	**1 042**	**946**	**827**
Endocrine, nutritional and metabolic diseases — Maladies endocriniennes, nutritionnelles et métaboliques								
Total	9.0	16 463	15 605	14 846	14 773	**13 973**	**12 912**	**12 539**
Diabetes mellitus — Diabète sucré	8.6	14 926	14 190	13 453	13 451	**12 469**	**11 485**	**11 188**
Malnutrition — Malnutrition	0.2	...	...	...	...	**334**	**320**	**318**
Mental and behavioural disorders — Troubles mentaux et du comportement	5.6	14 968	10 357	7 464	6 665	**7 261**	**8 460**	**8 865**
Diseases of the nervous system — Maladies du système nerveux	7.6	16 703	15 327	13 396	12 977	**12 477**	**12 939**	**13 540**
Diseases of the circulatory system — Maladies de l'appareil circulatoire								
Total	767.9	1 163 511	1 113 714	1 100 340	1 094 095	**1 187 835**	**1 231 373**	**1 253 102**
Acute rheumatic fever and chronic rheumatic heart diseases — Rhumatisme articulaire aigu et cardiopathies rhumatismales chroniques	2.8	10 711	9 925	9 492	8 687	**8 739**	**8 410**	**7 748**
Hypertensive diseases — Maladies hypertensives	89.3	17 890	16 755	16 851	17 135	**27 414**	**26 493**	**26 636**
Ischaemic heart disease — Cardiopathie ischémique	259.3	554 605	526 537	515 285	512 104	**556 752**	**578 257**	**588 681**
Cerebrovascular disease — Maladie cérébrovasculaire	253.3	423 331	413 944	419 625	425 743	**446 634**	**463 638**	**475 163**
Diseases of arteries, arterioles and capillaries — Maladies des artères, artérioles et capillaires	77.2	84 990	77 294	75 715	70 735	...	...	...
Diseases of the respiratory system — Maladies de l'appareil respiratoire								
Total	70.3	108 780	99 427	93 325	83 506	**94 451**	**102 141**	**94 922**
Influenza — Grippe	⁺0.1	475	439	586	257	**546**	**513**	**197**
Pneumonia — Pneumopathies	31.6	29 539	25 150	21 976	20 732	**29 173**	**36 107**	**37 142**
Chronic lower respiratory diseases — Maladies chroniques des voies respiratoires inférieures	32.2	...	...	...	...	**55 542**	**56 885**	**49 586**
Diseases of the digestive system — Maladies de l'appareil digestif								
Total	74.0	67 825	61 896	57 499	55 667	**61 072**	**64 676**	**69 412**
Gastric and duodenal ulcer — Ulcère de l'estomac et du duodénum	3.2	8 515	8 227	8 366	8 408	**9 090**	**8 635**	**8 465**

(See notes at end of table. — Voir notes à la fin du tableau.)

Cause of death — Cause de décès	Russian Federation — Fédération de Russie[6,20] 2002	San Marino — Saint-Marin 1995	1996	1997	1998	1999	2000	Serbia and Montenegro — Serbie-et-Montenegro 2000
				Number Nombre				
TOTAL	2 332 272	186	173	178	190	198	188	118 078
Certain infectious and parasitic diseases — Certaines maladies infectieuses et parasitaires								
Total	36 931	-	-	-	-		-	827
Intestinal infectious diseases — Maladies infectieuses intestinales	966	-	-	-	-		-	133
Tuberculosis — Tuberculose	31 197	-	-	-	-		-	379
Tetanus — Tétanos	15	-	-	-	-		-	10
Diphtheria — Diphtérie	56	-	-	-	-		-	3
Whooping cough — Coqueluche	1	-	-	-	-		-	
Meningococcal infection — Infection à méningocoques	510	-	-	-	-		-	1
Septicaemia — Septicémie	1 497	-	-	-	-		-	161
Acute poliomyelitis — Poliomyélite aiguë	-	-	-	-	-		-	
Measles — Rougeole	-	-	-	-	-		-	3
Viral hepatitis — Hépatite virale	778	-	-	-	-		-	23
Human immunodeficiency virus [HIV] disease — Maladies dues au virus de l'immunodéficience humaine (VIH)	381	-	-	-	-		-	43
Malaria — Paludisme	3	-	-	-	-		-	1
Neoplasms — Tumeurs	292 953	67	55	51	50	55	65	20 160
Malignant neoplasms — Tumeurs malignes								
Total	290 316	67	54	50	49	55	65	19 956
Malignant neoplasm of lip, oral cavity and pharynx — Tumeur maligne de la lèvre, de la cavité buccale et du pharynx	8 929	-	1	1	1	2		466
Malignant neoplasm of oesophagus — Tumeur maligne de l'oesophage	6 902	1	1	-	-		1	271
Malignant neoplasm of stomach — Tumeur maligne de l'estomac	41 295	11	5	2	6	5	10	1 424
Malignant neoplasm of colon, rectosigmoid junction, rectum, anus and anal canal — Tumeur maligne du côlon, de la jonction recto-sigmoïdienne, du rectum, de l'anus et du canal anal	35 386	7	10	7	-	6	5	2 197
Malignant neoplasm of liver and intrahepatic bile ducts — Tumeur maligne du foie et des voies bilaires intrahépatiques	8 383	-	-	1	1	-	-	965
Malignant neoplasm of pancreas — Tumeur maligne du pancréas	13 762	4	4	3	2	2	3	859
Malignant neoplasm of trachea, bronchus and lung — Tumeur maligne de la trachée, des bronches et du poumon	56 245	10	6	10	9	14	13	4 558
Malignant neoplasm of female breast — Tumeur maligne du sein chez la femme	21 873	1	1	2	2	2	5	1 800
Malignant neoplasm of cervix uteri — Tumeur maligne du col de l'utérus	6 138	-	-	-	-	-	2	496
Malignant neoplasm of prostate — Tumeur maligne de la prostate	7 556	7	1	5	2	1	6	646
Malignant neoplasm of lymphoid, haematopoietic and related tissue — Tumeurs malignes primitives ou présumées primitives des tissus lymphoïde, hématopoïétique et apparentés	...	8	7	3	7	8	9	...
Disorders of the blood and blood-forming organs and certain disorders involving the immune mechanism — Maladies du sang et des organes hématopoïétiques et certains troubles du système immunitaire								
Total	1 355	-	-	-	-		-	93
Anaemias — Anémies	857	-	-	-	-		-	41
Endocrine, nutritional and metabolic diseases — Maladies endocriniennes, nutritionnelles et métaboliques								
Total	12 409	-	-	1	-		1	2 968
Diabetes mellitus — Diabète sucré	11 098	-	-	-	-		-	2 906
Malnutrition — Malnutrition	300	-	-	-	-		-	7
Mental and behavioural disorders — Troubles mentaux et du comportement	8 759	1	-	1	-		1	433
Diseases of the nervous system — Maladies du système nerveux	14 804	-	-	-	1		-	1 005
Diseases of the circulatory system — Maladies de l'appareil circulatoire								
Total	1 308 071	86	86	77	96	108	80	65 987
Acute rheumatic fever and chronic rheumatic heart diseases — Rhumatisme articulaire aigu et cardiopathies rhumatismales chroniques	7 215	-	-	-	-	1	-	213
Hypertensive diseases — Maladies hypertensives	30 882	-	-	-	-	3	2	1 509
Ischaemic heart disease — Cardiopathie ischémique	618 171	16	10	14	9	16	7	13 376
Cerebrovascular disease — Maladie cérébrovasculaire	485 841	9	15	17	14	18	16	19 260
Diseases of arteries, arterioles and capillaries — Maladies des artères, artérioles et capillaires	...	4	5	1	5		3	...
Diseases of the respiratory system — Maladies de l'appareil respiratoire								
Total	101 003	-	6	2	8	3	11	5 315
Influenza — Grippe	222	-	-	-	-		-	157
Pneumonia — Pneumopathies	42 386	-	4	1	5	3	8	1 077
Chronic lower respiratory diseases — Maladies chroniques des voies respiratoires inférieures	50 519	-	-	1	-		-	2 989
Diseases of the digestive system — Maladies de l'appareil digestif								
Total	75 514	3	3	6	4		4	3 300
Gastric and duodenal ulcer — Ulcère de l'estomac et du duodénum	7 872	-	-	-	-		-	572

699

(See notes at end of table. — Voir notes à la fin du tableau.)

Cause of death — Cause de décès	Serbia and Montenegro — Serbie-et-Montenegro 2000 Rate Taux	Slovakia — Slovaquie 1995 Number Nombre	1995 Rate Taux	1996 Number Nombre	1996 Rate Taux	1997 Number Nombre	1997 Rate Taux	1998 Number Nombre
TOTAL	1110.3	52 683	982.2	51 236	953.4	52 124	968.3	53 156
Certain infectious and parasitic diseases — Certaines maladies infectieuses et parasitaires								
Total	7.8	184	3.4	188	3.5	192	3.6	120
Intestinal infectious diseases — Maladies infectieuses intestinales	1.3	6	♦0.1	8	♦0.1	7	♦0.1	9
Tuberculosis — Tuberculose	3.6	84	1.6	77	1.4	59	1.1	46
Tetanus — Tétanos	♦0.1	-	-	1	0.0	-	-	-
Diphtheria — Diphtérie	0.0	-	-	-	-	-	-	-
Whooping cough — Coqueluche		-	-	-	-	-	-	-
Meningococcal infection — Infection à méningocoques	0.0	1	0.0	8	♦0.1	21	♦0.4	13
Septicaemia — Septicémie	1.5	77	1.4	79	1.5	80	1.5	27
Acute poliomyelitis — Poliomyélite aiguë		-	-	-	-	-	-	-
Measles — Rougeole	0.0	-	-	-	-	-	-	-
Viral hepatitis — Hépatite virale	♦0.2	3	♦0.1	2	0.0	3	♦0.1	10
Human immunodeficiency virus [HIV] disease — Maladies dues au virus de l'immunodéficience humaine (VIH)	0.4	1	0.0	2	0.0	1	0.0	3
Malaria — Paludisme	0.0	-	-	1	0.0	-	-	-
Neoplasms — Tumeurs	189.6	11 075	206.5	11 141	207.3	11 296	209.8	12 234
Malignant neoplasms — Tumeurs malignes								
Total	187.7	10 947	204.1	11 049	205.6	11 170	207.5	12 182
Malignant neoplasm of lip, oral cavity and pharynx — Tumeur maligne de la lèvre, de la cavité buccale et du pharynx	4.4	578	10.8	599	11.1	605	11.2	630
Malignant neoplasm of oesophagus — Tumeur maligne de l'oesophage	2.5	245	4.6	277	5.2	210	3.9	292
Malignant neoplasm of stomach — Tumeur maligne de l'estomac	13.4	860	16.0	842	15.7	837	15.5	893
Malignant neoplasm of colon, rectosigmoid junction, rectum, anus and anal canal — Tumeur maligne du côlon, de la jonction recto-sigmoïdienne, du rectum, de l'anus et du canal anal	20.7	1 333	24.9	1 520	28.3	1 572	29.2	1 768
Malignant neoplasm of liver and intrahepatic bile ducts — Tumeur maligne du foie et des voies bilaires intrahépatiques	9.1	357	6.7	369	6.9	332	6.2	411
Malignant neoplasm of pancreas — Tumeur maligne du pancréas	8.1	458	8.5	481	9.0	523	9.7	594
Malignant neoplasm of trachea, bronchus and lung — Tumeur maligne de la trachée, des bronches et du poumon	42.9	2 227	41.5	2 115	39.4	2 147	39.9	2 227
Malignant neoplasm of female breast — Tumeur maligne du sein chez la femme	▲36.9	684	...	690	...	737	▲33.5	764
Malignant neoplasm of cervix uteri — Tumeur maligne du col de l'utérus	▲11.4	187	...	192	...	176	▲8.0	208
Malignant neoplasm of prostate — Tumeur maligne de la prostate	▼43.9	416	...	447	...	459	▼80.3	522
Malignant neoplasm of lymphoid, haematopoietic and related tissue — Tumeurs malignes primitives ou présumées primitives des tissus lymphoïde, hématopoiétique et apparentés	...	693	12.9	666	12.4	667	12.4	763
Disorders of the blood and blood-forming organs and certain disorders involving the immune mechanism — Maladies du sang et des organes hématopoïétiques et certains troubles du système immunitaire								
Total	0.9	72	1.3	44	0.8	35	0.7	34
Anaemias — Anémies	0.4	49	0.9	30	♦0.6	22	♦0.4	6
Endocrine, nutritional and metabolic diseases — Maladies endocriniennes, nutritionnelles et métaboliques								
Total	27.9	733	13.7	645	12.0	653	12.1	785
Diabetes mellitus — Diabète sucré	27.3	668	12.5	590	11.0	613	11.4	739
Malnutrition — Malnutrition	♦0.1	15	♦0.3	7	♦0.1	6	♦0.1	8
Mental and behavioural disorders — Troubles mentaux et du comportement	4.1	39	0.7	21	♦0.4	32	0.6	29
Diseases of the nervous system — Maladies du système nerveux	9.5	237	4.4	212	3.9	268	5.0	434
Diseases of the circulatory system — Maladies de l'appareil circulatoire								
Total	620.5	28 920	539.2	27 845	518.2	28 486	529.2	29 668
Acute rheumatic fever and chronic rheumatic heart diseases — Rhumatisme articularie aigu et cardiopathies rhumatismales chroniques	2.0	78	1.5	85	1.6	69	1.3	82
Hypertensive diseases — Maladies hypertensives	14.2	1 382	25.8	1 152	21.4	1 339	24.9	1 710
Ischaemic heart disease — Cardiopathie ischémique	125.8	14 465	269.7	14 107	262.5	14 273	265.1	14 353
Cerebrovascular disease — Maladie cérébrovasculaire	181.1	5 368	100.1	4 949	92.1	4 979	92.5	5 229
Diseases of arteries, arterioles and capillaries — Maladies des artères, artérioles et capillaires	...	4 887	91.1	5 084	94.6	5 177	96.2	4 673
Diseases of the respiratory system — Maladies de l'appareil respiratoire								
Total	50.0	3 642	67.9	3 784	70.4	3 745	69.6	2 391
Influenza — Grippe	1.5	89	1.7	40	0.7	24	♦0.4	22
Pneumonia — Pneumopathies	10.1	2 666	49.7	2 924	54.4	3 115	57.9	1 191
Chronic lower respiratory diseases — Maladies chroniques des voies respiratoires inférieures	28.1	471	8.8	432	8.0	300	5.6	826
Diseases of the digestive system — Maladies de l'appareil digestif								
Total	31.0	2 257	42.1	2 153	40.1	2 191	40.7	2 470
Gastric and duodenal ulcer — Ulcère de l'estomac et du duodénum	5.4	210	3.9	248	4.6	238	4.4	253

21. Death and death rates by cause: 1995 - 2002
Décès selon la cause, nombres et taux: 1995 - 2002 (continued — suite)
(See notes at end of table. — Voir notes à la fin du tableau.)

Cause of death — Cause de décès	Slovakia — Slovaquie							Slovenia — Slovénie
	1998	1999		2000		2001		1995
	Rate Taux	Number Nombre	Rate Taux	Number Nombre	Rate Taux	Number Nombre	Rate Taux	Number Nombre
TOTAL	986.1	52 402	971.2	52 724	976.3	51 980	966.4	18 968
Certain infectious and parasitic diseases — Certaines maladies infectieuses et parasitaires								
Total	2.2	142	2.6	168	3.1	186	3.5	93
Intestinal infectious diseases — Maladies infectieuses intestinales	◆0.2	13	◆0.2	13	◆0.2	14	◆0.3	3
Tuberculosis — Tuberculose	0.9	50	0.9	54	1.0	55	1.0	31
Tetanus — Tétanos	-	-	-	-	-	-	-	1
Diphtheria — Diphtérie	-	-	-	-	-	-	-	
Whooping cough — Coqueluche	-	-	-	-	-	-	-	1
Meningococcal infection — Infection à méningocoques	◆0.2	8	◆0.1	7	◆0.1	6	◆0.1	1
Septicaemia — Septicémie	◆0.5	51	0.9	69	1.3	75	1.4	33
Acute poliomyelitis — Poliomyélite aiguë	-	-	-	-	-	-	-	
Measles — Rougeole	-	-	-	-	-	-	-	
Viral hepatitis — Hépatite virale	◆0.2	4	◆0.1	13	◆0.2	11	◆0.2	1
Human immunodeficiency virus [HIV] disease — Maladies dues au virus de l'immunodéficience humaine (VIH)	◆0.1			2	0.0	3	◆0.1	
Malaria — Paludisme	-	-	-	-		1	0.0	
Neoplasms — Tumeurs	226.9	11 935	221.2	11 930	220.9	11 870	220.7	4 646
Malignant neoplasms — Tumeurs malignes								
Total	226.0	11 898	220.5	11 871	219.8	11 815	219.7	4 573
Malignant neoplasm of lip, oral cavity and pharynx — Tumeur maligne de la lèvre, de la cavité buccale et du pharynx	11.7	556	10.3	557	10.3	612	11.4	143
Malignant neoplasm of oesophagus — Tumeur maligne de l'oesophage	5.4	297	5.5	253	4.7	269	5.0	93
Malignant neoplasm of stomach — Tumeur maligne de l'estomac	16.6	820	15.2	835	15.5	782	14.5	454
Malignant neoplasm of colon, rectosigmoid junction, rectum, anus and anal canal — Tumeur maligne du côlon, de la jonction recto-sigmoïdienne, du rectum, de l'anus et du canal anal	32.8	1 847	34.2	1 722	31.9	1 730	32.2	632
Malignant neoplasm of liver and intrahepatic bile ducts — Tumeur maligne du foie et des voies bilaires intrahépatiques	7.6	331	6.1	347	6.4	368	6.8	49
Malignant neoplasm of pancreas — Tumeur maligne du pancréas	11.0	523	9.7	576	10.7	593	11.0	179
Malignant neoplasm of trachea, bronchus and lung — Tumeur maligne de la trachée, des bronches et du poumon	41.3	2 168	40.2	2 249	41.6	2 106	39.2	955
Malignant neoplasm of female breast — Tumeur maligne du sein chez la femme	▲34.4	798	▲35.8	799	...	805	▲35.5	375
Malignant neoplasm of cervix uteri — Tumeur maligne du col de l'utérus	▲9.4	222	▲9.9	220	...	199	▲8.8	74
Malignant neoplasm of prostate — Tumeur maligne de la prostate	▼89.7	541	▼91.3	537	...	488	▼79.0	180
Malignant neoplasm of lymphoid, haematopoietic and related tissue — Tumeurs malignes primitives ou présumées primitives des tissus lymphoïde, hématopoiétique et apparentés	14.2	752	13.9	747	13.8	734	13.6	266
Disorders of the blood and blood-forming organs and certain disorders involving the immune mechanism — Maladies du sang et des organes hématopoïétiques et certains troubles du système immunitaire								
Total	0.6	32	0.6	56	1.0	66	1.2	38
Anaemias — Anémies	◆0.1	7	◆0.1	16	◆0.3	9	◆0.2	18
Endocrine, nutritional and metabolic diseases — Maladies endocriniennes, nutritionnelles et métaboliques								
Total	14.6	1 072	19.9	795	14.7	793	14.7	567
Diabetes mellitus — Diabète sucré	13.7	1 015	18.8	758	14.0	762	14.2	518
Malnutrition — Malnutrition	◆0.1	6	◆0.1	3	◆0.1	3	◆0.1	1
Mental and behavioural disorders — Troubles mentaux et du comportement	◆0.5	10	◆0.2	22	◆0.4	8	◆0.1	220
Diseases of the nervous system — Maladies du système nerveux	8.1	519	9.6	498	9.2	564	10.5	164
Diseases of the circulatory system — Maladies de l'appareil circulatoire								
Total	550.4	28 596	530.0	28 883	534.8	28 603	531.8	8 047
Acute rheumatic fever and chronic rheumatic heart diseases — Rhumatisme articulaire aigu et cardiopathies rhumatismales chroniques	1.5	135	2.5	120	2.2	135	2.5	82
Hypertensive diseases — Maladies hypertensives	31.7	2 758	51.1	3 382	62.6	3 442	64.0	421
Ischaemic heart disease — Cardiopathie ischémique	266.3	14 583	270.3	15 688	290.5	15 222	283.0	2 414
Cerebrovascular disease — Maladie cérébrovasculaire	97.0	4 646	86.1	4 677	86.6	4 692	87.2	2 407
Diseases of arteries, arterioles and capillaries — Maladies des artères, artérioles et capillaires	86.7	4 086	75.7	2 628	48.7	2 739	50.9	475
Diseases of the respiratory system — Maladies de l'appareil respiratoire								
Total	44.4	2 614	48.4	2 909	53.9	2 725	50.7	1 474
Influenza — Grippe	◆0.4	55	1.0	71	1.3	29	◆0.5	4
Pneumonia — Pneumopathies	22.1	1 282	23.8	1 587	29.4	1 535	28.5	679
Chronic lower respiratory diseases — Maladies chroniques des voies respiratoires inférieures	15.3	959	17.8	875	16.2	761	14.1	700
Diseases of the digestive system — Maladies de l'appareil digestif								
Total	45.8	2 634	48.8	2 623	48.6	2 599	48.3	1 117
Gastric and duodenal ulcer — Ulcère de l'estomac et du duodénum	4.7	260	4.8	268	5.0	253	4.7	115

(See notes at end of table. — Voir notes à la fin du tableau.)

Slovenia — Slovénie

Cause of death — Cause de décès	1995 Rate Taux	1996 Number Nombre	1996 Rate Taux	1997 Number Nombre	1997 Rate Taux	1998 Number Nombre	1998 Rate Taux	1999 Number Nombre
TOTAL	954.4	18 620	935.1	18 928	952.7	19 039	960.3	18 885
Certain infectious and parasitic diseases — Certaines maladies infectieuses et parasitaires								
Total	4.7	92	4.6	90	4.5	123	6.2	95
Intestinal infectious diseases — Maladies infectieuses intestinales	♦0.2	4	♦0.2	9	♦0.5	9	♦0.5	1
Tuberculosis — Tuberculose	1.6	28	♦1.4	27	♦1.4	23	♦1.2	27
Tetanus — Tétanos	♦0.1	1	♦0.1	2	♦0.1	-		-
Diphtheria — Diphtérie		-		-		-		-
Whooping cough — Coqueluche	♦0.1	-		-		-		-
Meningococcal infection — Infection à méningocoques	♦0.1	2	♦0.1	-		-		-
Septicaemia — Septicémie	1.7	38	1.9	24	♦1.2	64	3.2	43
Acute poliomyelitis — Poliomyélite aiguë		-		-		-		-
Measles — Rougeole		-		-		-		-
Viral hepatitis — Hépatite virale	♦0.1	4	♦0.2	6	♦0.3	5	♦0.3	5
Human immunodeficiency virus [HIV] disease — Maladies dues au virus de l'immunodéficience humaine (VIH)	♦0.1	1	♦0.1	2	♦0.1	10	♦0.5	6
Malaria — Paludisme	-	1	♦0.1	-		-		-
Neoplasms — Tumeurs	233.8	4 617	231.9	4 831	243.1	4 783	241.2	4 868
Malignant neoplasms — Tumeurs malignes								
Total	230.1	4 541	228.1	4 774	240.3	4 704	237.3	4 775
Malignant neoplasm of lip, oral cavity and pharynx — Tumeur maligne de la lèvre, de la cavité buccale et du pharynx	7.2	158	7.9	158	8.0	169	8.5	134
Malignant neoplasm of oesophagus — Tumeur maligne de l'oesophage	4.7	103	5.2	80	4.0	80	4.0	116
Malignant neoplasm of stomach — Tumeur maligne de l'estomac	22.8	385	19.3	450	22.6	414	20.9	405
Malignant neoplasm of colon, rectosigmoid junction, rectum, anus and anal canal — Tumeur maligne du côlon, de la jonction recto-sigmoïdienne, du rectum, de l'anus et du canal anal	31.8	597	30.0	623	31.4	602	30.4	628
Malignant neoplasm of liver and intrahepatic bile ducts — Tumeur maligne du foie et des voies bilaires intrahépatiques	2.5	70	3.5	129	6.5	124	6.3	130
Malignant neoplasm of pancreas — Tumeur maligne du pancréas	9.0	224	11.2	249	12.5	216	10.9	215
Malignant neoplasm of trachea, bronchus and lung — Tumeur maligne de la trachée, des bronches et du poumon	48.1	908	45.6	907	45.7	912	46.0	968
Malignant neoplasm of female breast — Tumeur maligne du sein chez la femme	▲44.5	355	▲41.8	347	...	373	▲43.7	394
Malignant neoplasm of cervix uteri — Tumeur maligne du col de l'utérus	▲8.8	59	▲6.9	63	...	54	▲6.3	52
Malignant neoplasm of prostate — Tumeur maligne de la prostate	▼77.3	203	▼82.5	249	...	245	▼95.9	234
Malignant neoplasm of lymphoid, haematopoietic and related tissue — Tumeurs malignes primitives ou présumées primitives des tissus lymphoïde, hématopoïétique et apparentés	13.4	273	13.7	290	14.6	278	14.0	277
Disorders of the blood and blood-forming organs and certain disorders involving the immune mechanism — Maladies du sang et des organes hématopoïétiques et certains troubles du système immunitaire								
Total	1.9	43	2.2	28	♦1.4	39	2.0	43
Anaemias — Anémies	♦0.9	18	♦0.9	17	♦0.9	18	♦0.9	24
Endocrine, nutritional and metabolic diseases — Maladies endocriniennes, nutritionnelles et métaboliques								
Total	28.5	453	22.8	744	37.4	489	24.7	427
Diabetes mellitus — Diabète sucré	26.1	416	20.9	706	35.5	440	22.2	399
Malnutrition — Malnutrition	♦0.1	-		1	♦0.1	2	♦0.1	1
Mental and behavioural disorders — Troubles mentaux et du comportement	11.1	204	10.2	205	10.3	253	12.8	196
Diseases of the nervous system — Maladies du système nerveux	8.3	150	7.5	182	9.2	232	11.7	210
Diseases of the circulatory system — Maladies de l'appareil circulatoire								
Total	404.9	7 899	396.7	7 525	378.7	7 887	397.8	7 667
Acute rheumatic fever and chronic rheumatic heart diseases — Rhumatisme articulaire aigu et cardiopathies rhumatismales chroniques	4.1	74	3.7	80	4.0	64	3.2	85
Hypertensive diseases — Maladies hypertensives	21.2	384	19.3	387	19.5	410	20.7	403
Ischaemic heart disease — Cardiopathie ischémique	121.5	2 376	119.3	2 722	137.0	2 786	140.5	2 627
Cerebrovascular disease — Maladie cérébrovasculaire	121.1	2 379	119.5	2 162	108.8	2 171	109.5	2 150
Diseases of arteries, arterioles and capillaries — Maladies des artères, artérioles et capillaires	23.9	456	22.9	369	18.6	499	25.2	422
Diseases of the respiratory system — Maladies de l'appareil respiratoire								
Total	74.2	1 357	68.2	1 602	80.6	1 532	77.3	1 563
Influenza — Grippe	♦0.2	-	-	8	♦0.4	1	♦0.1	12
Pneumonia — Pneumopathies	34.2	591	29.7	822	41.4	746	37.6	710
Chronic lower respiratory diseases — Maladies chroniques des voies respiratoires inférieures	35.2	669	33.6	641	32.3	647	32.6	718
Diseases of the digestive system — Maladies de l'appareil digestif								
Total	56.2	1 138	57.2	1 079	54.3	1 098	55.4	1 186
Gastric and duodenal ulcer — Ulcère de l'estomac et du duodénum	5.8	145	7.3	109	5.5	99	5.0	125

(See notes at end of table. — Voir notes à la fin du tableau.)

Cause of death — Cause de décès	Slovenia — Slovénie							Spain — Espagne
	1999	2000		2001		2002		1995
	Rate Taux	Number Nombre	Rate Taux	Number Nombre	Rate Taux	Number Nombre	Rate Taux	Number Nombre
TOTAL	951.1	18 588	933.9	18 508	929.1	18 701	937.1	346 227
Certain infectious and parasitic diseases — Certaines maladies infectieuses et parasitaires								
Total	4.8	101	5.1	124	6.2	106	5.3	10 138
Intestinal infectious diseases — Maladies infectieuses intestinales	✝0.1	5	✝0.3	5	✝0.3	9	✝0.5	243
Tuberculosis — Tuberculose	✝1.4	17	✝0.9	25	✝1.3	20	✝1.0	603
Tetanus — Tétanos	-	2	✝0.1	-	-	1	✝0.1	11
Diphtheria — Diphtérie	-	-	-	-	-	-	-	-
Whooping cough — Coqueluche	-	-	-	-	-	-	-	-
Meningococcal infection — Infection à méningocoques	-	1	✝0.1	2	✝0.1	2	✝0.1	49
Septicaemia — Septicémie	2.2	49	2.5	61	3.1	39	2.0	2 232
Acute poliomyelitis — Poliomyélite aiguë	-	-	-	-	-	-	-	1
Measles — Rougeole	-	-	-	-	-	-	-	2
Viral hepatitis — Hépatite virale	✝0.3	4	✝0.2	7	✝0.4	8	✝0.4	526
Human immunodeficiency virus [HIV] disease — Maladies dues au virus de l'immunodéficience humaine (VIH)	✝0.3	4	✝0.2	8	✝0.4	3	✝0.2	5 791
Malaria — Paludisme	-	-	-	-	-	-	-	8
Neoplasms — Tumeurs	245.2	4 824	242.4	4 889	245.4	5 063	253.7	89 493
Malignant neoplasms — Tumeurs malignes								
Total	240.5	4 752	238.8	4 813	241.6	4 978	249.4	86 904
Malignant neoplasm of lip, oral cavity and pharynx — Tumeur maligne de la lèvre, de la cavité buccale et du pharynx	6.7	127	6.4	179	9.0	147	7.4	2 181
Malignant neoplasm of oesophagus — Tumeur maligne de l'oesophage	5.8	77	3.9	82	4.1	108	5.4	1 791
Malignant neoplasm of stomach — Tumeur maligne de l'estomac	20.4	405	20.3	368	18.5	384	19.2	6 557
Malignant neoplasm of colon, rectosigmoid junction, rectum, anus and anal canal — Tumeur maligne du côlon, de la jonction recto-sigmoïdienne, du rectum, de l'anus et du canal anal	31.6	600	30.1	585	29.4	672	33.7	10 125
Malignant neoplasm of liver and intrahepatic bile ducts — Tumeur maligne du foie et des voies bilaires intrahépatiques	6.5	142	7.1	131	6.6	146	7.3	2 199
Malignant neoplasm of pancreas — Tumeur maligne du pancréas	10.8	234	11.8	246	12.3	247	12.4	3 372
Malignant neoplasm of trachea, bronchus and lung — Tumeur maligne de la trachée, des bronches et du poumon	48.8	931	46.8	948	47.6	948	47.5	16 510
Malignant neoplasm of female breast — Tumeur maligne du sein chez la femme	▲45.9	365	...	380	▲43.8	425	▲48.7	6 026
Malignant neoplasm of cervix uteri — Tumeur maligne du col de l'utérus	▲6.1	62	...	49	▲5.6	47	▲5.4	596
Malignant neoplasm of prostate — Tumeur maligne de la prostate	▼89.6	246	...	252	▼91.3	277	▼97.4	5 278
Malignant neoplasm of lymphoid, haematopoietic and related tissue — Tumeurs malignes primitives ou présumées primitives des tissus lymphoïde, hématopoïétique et apparentés	14.0	328	16.5	340	17.1	303	15.2	6 289
Disorders of the blood and blood-forming organs and certain disorders involving the immune mechanism — Maladies du sang et des organes hématopoïétiques et certains troubles du système immunitaire								
Total	2.2	39	2.0	21	✝1.1	33	1.7	1 541
Anaemias — Anémies	✝1.2	23	✝1.2	13	✝0.7	22	✝1.1	881
Endocrine, nutritional and metabolic diseases — Maladies endocriniennes, nutritionnelles et métaboliques								
Total	21.5	529	26.6	587	29.5	631	31.6	10 860
Diabetes mellitus — Diabète sucré	20.1	491	24.7	545	27.4	591	29.6	9 151
Malnutrition — Malnutrition	✝0.1	-	-	4	✝0.2	7	✝0.4	130
Mental and behavioural disorders — Troubles mentaux et du comportement	9.9	196	9.8	192	9.6	208	10.4	9 393
Diseases of the nervous system — Maladies du système nerveux	10.6	181	9.1	212	10.6	284	14.2	6 214
Diseases of the circulatory system — Maladies de l'appareil circulatoire								
Total	386.1	7 504	377.0	7 216	362.2	7 168	359.2	131 710
Acute rheumatic fever and chronic rheumatic heart diseases — Rhumatisme articulaire aigu et cardiopathies rhumatismales chroniques	4.3	81	4.1	85	4.3	83	4.2	1 599
Hypertensive diseases — Maladies hypertensives	20.3	438	22.0	385	19.3	467	23.4	4 212
Ischaemic heart disease — Cardiopathie ischémique	132.3	2 497	125.5	2 411	121.0	2 208	110.6	37 688
Cerebrovascular disease — Maladie cérébrovasculaire	108.3	2 039	102.4	1 947	97.7	2 008	100.6	39 973
Diseases of arteries, arterioles and capillaries — Maladies des artères, artérioles et capillaires	21.3	388	19.5	434	21.8	484	24.3	8 992
Diseases of the respiratory system — Maladies de l'appareil respiratoire								
Total	78.7	1 470	73.9	1 339	67.2	1 406	70.5	33 324
Influenza — Grippe	✝0.6	5	✝0.3	1	✝0.1	-	-	416
Pneumonia — Pneumopathies	35.8	703	35.3	541	27.2	646	32.4	7 103
Chronic lower respiratory diseases — Maladies chroniques des voies respiratoires inférieures	36.2	634	31.9	655	32.9	622	31.2	16 204
Diseases of the digestive system — Maladies de l'appareil digestif								
Total	59.7	1 220	61.3	1 266	63.6	1 224	61.3	18 352
Gastric and duodenal ulcer — Ulcère de l'estomac et du duodénum	6.3	128	6.4	137	6.9	126	6.3	1 082

21. Death and death rates by cause: 1995 - 2002
Décès selon la cause, nombres et taux: 1995 - 2002 (continued — suite)

(See notes at end of table. — Voir notes à la fin du tableau.)

Spain — Espagne

Cause of death — Cause de décès	1995 Rate Taux	1996 Number Nombre	1996 Rate Taux	1997 Number Nombre	1997 Rate Taux	1998 Number Nombre	1998 Rate Taux	1999 Number Nombre
TOTAL	882.7	351 449	894.8	349 521	888.3	360 511	913.8	371 102
Certain infectious and parasitic diseases — Certaines maladies infectieuses et parasitaires								
Total	25.8	10 114	25.7	7 262	18.5	6 353	16.1	6 520
Intestinal infectious diseases — Maladies infectieuses intestinales	0.6	213	0.5	217	0.6	250	0.6	267
Tuberculosis — Tuberculose	1.5	601	1.5	523	1.3	476	1.2	493
Tetanus — Tétanos	0.0	15	0.0	14	0.0	9	0.0	9
Diphtheria — Diphtérie	-	-	-	-	-	-	-	-
Whooping cough — Coqueluche	-	-	-	1	0.0	-	-	-
Meningococcal infection — Infection à méningocoques	0.1	131	0.3	101	0.3	60	0.2	90
Septicaemia — Septicémie	5.7	2 114	5.4	2 085	5.3	2 190	5.6	2 415
Acute poliomyelitis — Poliomyélite aiguë	0.0	-	-	-	-	-	-	-
Measles — Rougeole	0.0	-	-	-	-	-	-	1
Viral hepatitis — Hépatite virale	1.3	711	1.8	720	1.8	825	2.1	746
Human immunodeficiency virus [HIV] disease — Maladies dues au virus de l'immunodéficience humaine (VIH)	14.8	5 699	14.5	2 979	7.6	1 853	4.7	1 802
Malaria — Paludisme	0.0	3	0.0	8	0.0	12	0.0	12
Neoplasms — Tumeurs	228.2	89 204	227.1	90 930	231.1	92 327	234.0	94 566
Malignant neoplasms — Tumeurs malignes								
Total	221.6	86 699	220.7	88 268	224.3	89 665	227.3	91 145
Malignant neoplasm of lip, oral cavity and pharynx — Tumeur maligne de la lèvre, de la cavité buccale et du pharynx	5.6	2 073	5.3	2 268	5.8	2 205	5.6	2 172
Malignant neoplasm of oesophagus — Tumeur maligne de l'oesophage	4.6	1 822	4.6	1 762	4.5	1 797	4.6	1 753
Malignant neoplasm of stomach — Tumeur maligne de l'estomac	16.7	6 412	16.3	6 456	16.4	6 092	15.4	6 170
Malignant neoplasm of colon, rectosigmoid junction, rectum, anus and anal canal — Tumeur maligne du côlon, de la jonction recto-sigmoïdienne, du rectum, de l'anus et du canal anal	25.8	10 407	26.5	10 639	27.0	11 066	28.0	11 300
Malignant neoplasm of liver and intrahepatic bile ducts — Tumeur maligne du foie et des voies bilaires intrahépatiques	5.6	2 263	5.8	2 310	5.9	2 365	6.0	4 305
Malignant neoplasm of pancreas — Tumeur maligne du pancréas	8.6	3 468	8.8	3 635	9.2	3 623	9.2	3 827
Malignant neoplasm of trachea, bronchus and lung — Tumeur maligne de la trachée, des bronches et du poumon	42.1	16 270	41.4	16 607	42.2	17 215	43.6	17 428
Malignant neoplasm of female breast — Tumeur maligne du sein chez la femme	▲35.8	5 752	▲33.9	5 766	▲33.8	5 773	▲33.6	5 684
Malignant neoplasm of cervix uteri — Tumeur maligne du col de l'utérus	▲3.5	507	▲3.0	566	▲3.3	564	▲3.3	524
Malignant neoplasm of prostate — Tumeur maligne de la prostate	▼95.8	5 467	▼98.0	5 471	▼96.9	5 742	▼100.5	5 645
Malignant neoplasm of lymphoid, haematopoietic and related tissue — Tumeurs malignes primitives ou présumées primitives des tissus lymphoïde, hématopoïétique et apparentés	16.0	6 240	15.9	6 398	16.3	6 650	16.9	6 870
Disorders of the blood and blood-forming organs and certain disorders involving the immune mechanism — Maladies du sang et des organes hématopoïétiques et certains troubles du système immunitaire								
Total	3.9	1 593	4.1	1 674	4.3	1 826	4.6	1 124
Anaemias — Anémies	2.2	840	2.1	855	2.2	948	2.4	735
Endocrine, nutritional and metabolic diseases — Maladies endocriniennes, nutritionnelles et métaboliques								
Total	27.7	10 730	27.3	10 682	27.1	11 330	28.7	11 382
Diabetes mellitus — Diabète sucré	23.3	8 979	22.9	8 869	22.5	9 533	24.2	9 720
Malnutrition — Malnutrition	0.3	94	0.2	127	0.3	114	0.3	131
Mental and behavioural disorders — Troubles mentaux et du comportement	23.9	10 230	26.0	10 795	27.4	11 796	29.9	11 520
Diseases of the nervous system — Maladies du système nerveux	15.8	6 587	16.8	6 975	17.7	7 869	19.9	10 292
Diseases of the circulatory system — Maladies de l'appareil circulatoire								
Total	335.8	133 499	339.9	131 362	333.8	134 512	340.9	131 774
Acute rheumatic fever and chronic rheumatic heart diseases — Rhumatisme articulaire aigu et cardiopathies rhumatismales chroniques	4.1	1 633	4.2	1 719	4.4	1 757	4.5	1 787
Hypertensive diseases — Maladies hypertensives	10.7	4 443	11.3	4 528	11.5	5 112	13.0	4 911
Ischaemic heart disease — Cardiopathie ischémique	96.1	39 029	99.4	39 159	99.5	40 199	101.9	40 712
Cerebrovascular disease — Maladie cérébrovasculaire	101.9	38 868	99.0	37 881	96.3	38 121	96.6	38 730
Diseases of arteries, arterioles and capillaries — Maladies des artères, artérioles et capillaires	22.9	8 541	21.7	8 186	20.8	8 349	21.2	7 935
Diseases of the respiratory system — Maladies de l'appareil respiratoire								
Total	85.0	34 718	88.4	34 991	88.9	38 187	96.8	45 194
Influenza — Grippe	1.1	435	1.1	435	1.1	620	1.6	1 186
Pneumonia — Pneumopathies	18.1	7 144	18.2	7 337	18.6	7 871	20.0	8 302
Chronic lower respiratory diseases — Maladies chroniques des voies respiratoires inférieures	41.3	16 780	42.7	16 720	42.5	17 768	45.0	19 048
Diseases of the digestive system — Maladies de l'appareil digestif								
Total	46.8	18 861	48.0	18 476	47.0	18 922	48.0	18 972
Gastric and duodenal ulcer — Ulcère de l'estomac et du duodénum	2.8	1 077	2.7	995	2.5	978	2.5	921

21. Death and death rates by cause: 1995 - 2002
Décès selon la cause, nombres et taux: 1995 - 2002 (continued — suite)

(See notes at end of table. — Voir notes à la fin du tableau.)

Cause of death — Cause de décès	Spain — Espagne 1999 Rate/Taux	2000 Number/Nombre	2000 Rate/Taux	2001 Number/Nombre	2001 Rate/Taux	Sweden — Suède 1995 Number/Nombre	1995 Rate/Taux	1996 Number/Nombre
TOTAL	936.5	360 391	902.6	360 131	894.4	93 641	1060.9	93 815
Certain infectious and parasitic diseases — Certaines maladies infectieuses et parasitaires								
Total	16.5	6 278	15.7	6 554	16.3	849	9.6	843
Intestinal infectious diseases — Maladies infectieuses intestinales	0.7	320	0.8	316	0.8	37	0.4	40
Tuberculosis — Tuberculose	1.2	399	1.0	387	1.0	24	♦0.3	39
Tetanus — Tétanos	0.0	9	0.0	5	0.0	-	-	-
Diphtheria — Diphtérie	-	-	-	-	-	-	-	-
Whooping cough — Coqueluche	-	1	0.0	1	0.0	1	0.0	-
Meningococcal infection — Infection à méningocoques	0.2	84	0.2	51	0.1	10	♦0.1	9
Septicaemia — Septicémie	6.1	2 256	5.7	2 606	6.5	263	3.0	292
Acute poliomyelitis — Poliomyélite aiguë	-	-	-	-	-	-	-	-
Measles — Rougeole	0.0	1	0.0	2	0.0	-	-	-
Viral hepatitis — Hépatite virale	1.9	828	2.1	924	2.3	27	♦0.3	31
Human immunodeficiency virus [HIV] disease — Maladies dues au virus de l'immunodéficience humaine (VIH)	4.5	1 711	4.3	1 632	4.1	86	1.0	71
Malaria — Paludisme	0.0	6	0.0	9	0.0	2	0.0	-
Neoplasms — Tumeurs	238.6	95 072	238.1	97 714	242.7	21 369	242.1	21 482
Malignant neoplasms — Tumeurs malignes								
Total	230.0	91 846	230.0	94 363	234.4	20 705	234.6	20 757
Malignant neoplasm of lip, oral cavity and pharynx — Tumeur maligne de la lèvre, de la cavité buccale et du pharynx	5.5	2 186	5.5	2 186	5.4	244	2.8	244
Malignant neoplasm of oesophagus — Tumeur maligne de l'oesophage	4.4	1 790	4.5	1 788	4.4	297	3.4	347
Malignant neoplasm of stomach — Tumeur maligne de l'estomac	15.6	6 092	15.3	6 111	15.2	973	11.0	987
Malignant neoplasm of colon, rectosigmoid junction, rectum, anus and anal canal — Tumeur maligne du côlon, de la jonction recto-sigmoïdienne, du rectum, de l'anus et du canal anal	28.5	11 653	29.2	12 046	29.9	2 514	28.5	2 481
Malignant neoplasm of liver and intrahepatic bile ducts — Tumeur maligne du foie et des voies bilaires intrahépatiques	10.9	4 256	10.7	4 390	10.9	366	4.1	372
Malignant neoplasm of pancreas — Tumeur maligne du pancréas	9.7	4 000	10.0	4 216	10.5	1 383	15.7	1 438
Malignant neoplasm of trachea, bronchus and lung — Tumeur maligne de la trachée, des bronches et du poumon	44.0	17 363	43.5	18 214	45.2	2 895	32.8	2 900
Malignant neoplasm of female breast — Tumeur maligne du sein chez la femme	▲33.0	5 677	▲32.4	5 914	▲33.4	1 501	▲42.8	1 534
Malignant neoplasm of cervix uteri — Tumeur maligne du col de l'utérus	▲3.0	597	▲3.4	549	▲3.1	162	▲4.4	149
Malignant neoplasm of prostate — Tumeur maligne de la prostate	▼97.7	5 456	▼92.2	5 659	▼94.3	2 280	▼164.5	2 323
Malignant neoplasm of lymphoid, haematopoietic and related tissue — Tumeurs malignes primitives ou présumées primitives des tissus lymphoïde, hématopoïétique et apparentés	17.3	7 127	17.8	7 221	17.9	2 034	23.0	2 005
Disorders of the blood and blood-forming organs and certain disorders involving the immune mechanism — Maladies du sang et des organes hématopoïétiques et certains troubles du système immunitaire								
Total	2.8	1 210	3.0	1 118	2.8	354	4.0	337
Anaemias — Anémies	1.9	753	1.9	712	1.8	267	3.0	246
Endocrine, nutritional and metabolic diseases — Maladies endocriniennes, nutritionnelles et métaboliques								
Total	28.7	10 892	27.3	11 223	27.9	2 019	22.9	1 969
Diabetes mellitus — Diabète sucré	24.5	9 253	23.2	9 581	23.8	1 592	18.0	1 568
Malnutrition — Malnutrition	0.3	138	0.3	130	0.3	55	0.6	50
Mental and behavioural disorders — Troubles mentaux et du comportement	29.1	11 149	27.9	11 346	28.2	2 937	33.3	3 100
Diseases of the nervous system — Maladies du système nerveux	26.0	10 463	26.2	11 668	29.0	1 250	14.2	1 319
Diseases of the circulatory system — Maladies de l'appareil circulatoire								
Total	332.5	125 723	314.9	124 389	308.9	46 389	525.5	45 863
Acute rheumatic fever and chronic rheumatic heart diseases — Rhumatisme articulaire aigu et cardiopathies rhumatismales chroniques	4.5	1 800	4.5	1 677	4.2	192	2.2	163
Hypertensive diseases — Maladies hypertensives	12.4	5 055	12.7	5 224	13.0	675	7.6	680
Ischaemic heart disease — Cardiopathie ischémique	102.7	39 315	98.5	38 788	96.3	23 995	271.8	23 060
Cerebrovascular disease — Maladie cérébrovasculaire	97.7	36 596	91.7	36 567	90.8	9 948	112.7	10 114
Diseases of arteries, arterioles and capillaries — Maladies des artères, artérioles et capillaires	20.0	7 537	18.9	7 208	17.9	4 053	45.9	4 253
Diseases of the respiratory system — Maladies de l'appareil respiratoire								
Total	114.1	40 983	102.6	37 362	92.8	7 321	82.9	7 838
Influenza — Grippe	3.0	723	1.8	80	0.2	131	1.5	330
Pneumonia — Pneumopathies	21.0	7 590	19.0	7 092	17.6	4 141	46.9	4 415
Chronic lower respiratory diseases — Maladies chroniques des voies respiratoires inférieures	48.1	16 618	41.6	15 220	37.8	2 346	26.6	2 394
Diseases of the digestive system — Maladies de l'appareil digestif								
Total	47.9	18 419	46.1	18 407	45.7	2 986	33.8	2 935
Gastric and duodenal ulcer — Ulcère de l'estomac et du duodénum	2.3	753	1.9	710	1.8	550	6.2	464

21. Death and death rates by cause: 1995 - 2002
Décès selon la cause, nombres et taux: 1995 - 2002 (continued — suite)

(See notes at end of table. — Voir notes à la fin du tableau.)

Sweden — Suède

Cause of death — Cause de décès	1996 Rate Taux	1997 Number Nombre	1997 Rate Taux	1998 Number Nombre	1998 Rate Taux	1999 Number Nombre	1999 Rate Taux	2000 Number Nombre
TOTAL	1061.1	93 349	1055.3	93 628	1057.8	95 076	1073.4	93 516
Certain infectious and parasitic diseases — Certaines maladies infectieuses et parasitaires								
Total	9.5	861	9.7	941	10.6	1 082	12.2	1 007
Intestinal infectious diseases — Maladies infectieuses intestinales	0.5	36	0.4	45	0.5	47	0.5	52
Tuberculosis — Tuberculose	0.4	39	0.4	35	0.4	34	0.4	18
Tetanus — Tétanos	-	-	-	-	-	1	0.0	-
Diphtheria — Diphtérie	-	-	-	-	-	-	-	-
Whooping cough — Coqueluche		1	0.0	-	-	1	0.0	2
Meningococcal infection — Infection à méningocoques	♦0.1	4	0.0	5	♦0.1	2	0.0	7
Septicaemia — Septicémie	3.3	294	3.3	370	4.2	405	4.6	423
Acute poliomyelitis — Poliomyélite aiguë	-	-	-	-	-	-	-	1
Measles — Rougeole	-	-	-	-	-	-	-	-
Viral hepatitis — Hépatite virale	0.4	26	♦0.3	29	♦0.3	46	0.5	36
Human immunodeficiency virus [HIV] disease — Maladies dues au virus de l'immunodéficience humaine (VIH)	0.8	47	0.5	29	♦0.3	30	♦0.3	26
Malaria — Paludisme	-	1	0.0	-	-	2	0.0	-
Neoplasms — Tumeurs	243.0	22 068	249.5	21 971	248.2	21 969	248.0	22 004
Malignant neoplasms — Tumeurs malignes								
Total	234.8	21 365	241.5	21 075	238.1	21 109	238.3	21 153
Malignant neoplasm of lip, oral cavity and pharynx — Tumeur maligne de la lèvre, de la cavité buccale et du pharynx	2.8	241	2.7	272	3.1	274	3.1	266
Malignant neoplasm of oesophagus — Tumeur maligne de l'oesophage	3.9	373	4.2	349	3.9	349	3.9	354
Malignant neoplasm of stomach — Tumeur maligne de l'estomac	11.2	1 029	11.6	914	10.3	922	10.4	862
Malignant neoplasm of colon, rectosigmoid junction, rectum, anus and anal canal — Tumeur maligne du côlon, de la jonction recto-sigmoïdienne, du rectum, de l'anus et du canal anal	28.1	2 395	27.1	2 431	27.5	2 422	27.3	2 501
Malignant neoplasm of liver and intrahepatic bile ducts — Tumeur maligne du foie et des voies bilaires intrahépatiques	4.2	684	7.7	616	7.0	590	6.7	526
Malignant neoplasm of pancreas — Tumeur maligne du pancréas	16.3	1 381	15.6	1 370	15.5	1 329	15.0	1 451
Malignant neoplasm of trachea, bronchus and lung — Tumeur maligne de la trachée, des bronches et du poumon	32.8	2 962	33.5	2 919	33.0	2 999	33.9	2 986
Malignant neoplasm of female breast — Tumeur maligne du sein chez la femme	▲41.8	1 494	▲40.7	1 549	▲42.2	1 485	▲40.4	1 526
Malignant neoplasm of cervix uteri — Tumeur maligne du col de l'utérus	▲4.1	169	▲4.6	143	▲3.9	163	▲4.4	171
Malignant neoplasm of prostate — Tumeur maligne de la prostate	▼164.8	2 448	▼170.9	2 480	▼171.8	2 494	▼170.4	2 501
Malignant neoplasm of lymphoid, haematopoietic and related tissue — Tumeurs malignes primitives ou présumées primitives des tissus lymphoïde, hématopoïétique et apparentés	22.7	2 021	22.8	2 058	23.3	2 009	22.7	1 948
Disorders of the blood and blood-forming organs and certain disorders involving the immune mechanism — Maladies du sang et des organes hématopoïétiques et certains troubles du système immunitaire								
Total	3.8	201	2.3	212	2.4	258	2.9	252
Anaemias — Anémies	2.8	138	1.6	128	1.4	153	1.7	140
Endocrine, nutritional and metabolic diseases — Maladies endocriniennes, nutritionnelles et métaboliques								
Total	22.3	1 985	22.4	1 874	21.2	2 157	24.4	2 111
Diabetes mellitus — Diabète sucré	17.7	1 636	18.5	1 563	17.7	1 798	20.3	1 770
Malnutrition — Malnutrition	0.6	71	0.8	52	0.6	67	0.8	64
Mental and behavioural disorders — Troubles mentaux et du comportement	35.1	2 931	33.1	3 572	40.4	4 185	47.2	4 161
Diseases of the nervous system — Maladies du système nerveux	14.9	1 734	19.6	1 637	18.5	1 918	21.7	1 898
Diseases of the circulatory system — Maladies de l'appareil circulatoire								
Total	518.8	45 017	508.9	44 990	508.3	44 554	503.0	43 277
Acute rheumatic fever and chronic rheumatic heart diseases — Rhumatisme articulaire aigu et cardiopathies rhumatismales chroniques	1.8	172	1.9	164	1.9	173	2.0	150
Hypertensive diseases — Maladies hypertensives	7.7	740	8.4	629	7.1	715	8.1	724
Ischaemic heart disease — Cardiopathie ischémique	260.8	21 974	248.4	21 706	245.2	21 177	239.1	20 128
Cerebrovascular disease — Maladie cérébrovasculaire	114.4	10 402	117.6	10 480	118.4	10 313	116.4	10 193
Diseases of arteries, arterioles and capillaries — Maladies des artères, artérioles et capillaires	48.1	3 859	43.6	3 809	43.0	3 898	44.0	3 780
Diseases of the respiratory system — Maladies de l'appareil respiratoire								
Total	88.7	6 988	79.0	6 418	72.5	6 922	78.1	6 719
Influenza — Grippe	3.7	230	2.6	358	4.0	522	5.9	500
Pneumonia — Pneumopathies	49.9	3 633	41.1	2 828	32.0	3 016	34.0	2 909
Chronic lower respiratory diseases — Maladies chroniques des voies respiratoires inférieures	27.1	2 373	26.8	2 475	28.0	2 610	29.5	2 532
Diseases of the digestive system — Maladies de l'appareil digestif								
Total	33.2	2 802	31.7	2 931	33.1	2 935	33.1	2 914
Gastric and duodenal ulcer — Ulcère de l'estomac et du duodénum	5.2	439	5.0	457	5.2	468	5.3	440

(See notes at end of table. — Voir notes à la fin du tableau.)

Cause of death — Cause de décès	Sweden — Suède			Switzerland — Suisse				
	2000	2001		1995		1996		1997
	Rate Taux	Number Nombre	Rate Taux	Number Nombre	Rate Taux	Number Nombre	Rate Taux	Number Nombre
TOTAL	1054.0	93 808	1054.5	63 389	900.3	62 643	885.8	62 880
Certain infectious and parasitic diseases — Certaines maladies infectieuses et parasitaires								
Total	11.4	1 106	12.4	1 111	15.8	911	12.9	840
Intestinal infectious diseases — Maladies infectieuses intestinales	0.6	84	0.9	40	0.6	27	⁺0.4	29
Tuberculosis — Tuberculose	⁺0.2	27	⁺0.3	46	0.7	42	0.6	42
Tetanus — Tétanos	-	1	0.0	1	0.0	2	0.0	-
Diphtheria — Diphtérie	-	-	-	-	-	-	-	-
Whooping cough — Coqueluche	0.0	-	-	-	-	-	-	1
Meningococcal infection — Infection à méningocoques	⁺0.1	3	0.0	10	⁺0.1	9	⁺0.1	8
Septicaemia — Septicémie	4.8	424	4.8	140	2.0	141	2.0	245
Acute poliomyelitis — Poliomyélite aiguë	-	-	-	-	-	-	-	-
Measles — Rougeole	0.0	-	-	-	-	-	-	1
Viral hepatitis — Hépatite virale	0.4	37	0.4	28	⁺0.4	24	⁺0.3	25
Human immunodeficiency virus [HIV] disease — Maladies dues au virus de l'immunodéficience humaine (VIH)	⁺0.3	35	0.4	618	8.8	450	6.4	266
Malaria — Paludisme		4	0.0	3	0.0	3	0.0	4
Neoplasms — Tumeurs	248.0	22 509	253.0	15 816	224.6	15 635	221.1	15 598
Malignant neoplasms — Tumeurs malignes								
Total	238.4	21 615	243.0	15 323	217.6	15 105	213.6	15 156
Malignant neoplasm of lip, oral cavity and pharynx — Tumeur maligne de la lèvre, de la cavité buccale et du pharynx	3.0	281	3.2	305	4.3	334	4.7	347
Malignant neoplasm of oesophagus — Tumeur maligne de l'oesophage	4.0	391	4.4	356	5.1	337	4.8	353
Malignant neoplasm of stomach — Tumeur maligne de l'estomac	9.7	875	9.8	686	9.7	675	9.5	678
Malignant neoplasm of colon, rectosigmoid junction, rectum, anus and anal canal — Tumeur maligne du côlon, de la jonction recto-sigmoïdienne, du rectum, de l'anus et du canal anal	28.2	2 616	29.4	1 708	24.3	1 667	23.6	1 629
Malignant neoplasm of liver and intrahepatic bile ducts — Tumeur maligne du foie et des voies bilaires intrahépatiques	5.9	596	6.7	424	6.0	449	6.3	491
Malignant neoplasm of pancreas — Tumeur maligne du pancréas	16.4	1 420	16.0	820	11.6	800	11.3	838
Malignant neoplasm of trachea, bronchus and lung — Tumeur maligne de la trachée, des bronches et du poumon	33.7	3 150	35.4	2 554	36.3	2 557	36.2	2 579
Malignant neoplasm of female breast — Tumeur maligne du sein chez la femme	...	1 487	▲40.1	1 554	▲51.5	1 415	▲46.7	1 436
Malignant neoplasm of cervix uteri — Tumeur maligne du col de l'utérus	...	160	▲4.3	121	▲4.0	112	▲3.7	93
Malignant neoplasm of prostate — Tumeur maligne de la prostate	...	2 460	▼163.9	1 305	▼128.7	1 298	▼125.8	1 276
Malignant neoplasm of lymphoid, haematopoietic and related tissue — Tumeurs malignes primitives ou présumées primitives des tissus lymphoïde, hématopoïétique et apparentés	22.0	1 983	22.3	1 335	19.0	1 358	19.2	1 294
Disorders of the blood and blood-forming organs and certain disorders involving the immune mechanism — Maladies du sang et des organes hématopoïétiques et certains troubles du système immunitaire								
Total	2.8	247	2.8	144	2.0	151	2.1	150
Anaemias — Anémies	1.6	154	1.7	75	1.1	76	1.1	87
Endocrine, nutritional and metabolic diseases — Maladies endocriniennes, nutritionnelles et métaboliques								
Total	23.8	2 253	25.3	1 994	28.3	2 282	32.3	1 900
Diabetes mellitus — Diabète sucré	20.0	1 875	21.1	1 732	24.6	2 004	28.3	1 663
Malnutrition — Malnutrition	0.7	70	0.8	14	⁺0.2	12	⁺0.2	15
Mental and behavioural disorders — Troubles mentaux et du comportement	46.9	4 278	48.1	2 594	36.8	2 498	35.3	2 371
Diseases of the nervous system — Maladies du système nerveux	21.4	2 130	23.9	2 091	29.7	2 121	30.0	2 067
Diseases of the circulatory system — Maladies de l'appareil circulatoire								
Total	487.8	42 695	479.9	26 183	371.9	25 756	364.2	25 994
Acute rheumatic fever and chronic rheumatic heart diseases — Rhumatisme articularie aigu et cardiopathies rhumatismales chroniques	1.7	157	1.8	156	2.2	118	1.7	142
Hypertensive diseases — Maladies hypertensives	8.2	801	9.0	1 232	17.5	1 195	16.9	1 189
Ischaemic heart disease — Cardiopathie ischémique	226.9	19 922	223.9	11 208	159.2	11 063	156.4	11 127
Cerebrovascular disease — Maladie cérébrovasculaire	114.9	9 986	112.3	5 208	74.0	5 020	71.0	4 976
Diseases of arteries, arterioles and capillaries — Maladies des artères, artérioles et capillaires	42.6	3 684	41.4	1 738	24.7	1 711	24.2	1 790
Diseases of the respiratory system — Maladies de l'appareil respiratoire								
Total	75.7	6 080	68.3	3 803	54.0	3 768	53.3	4 477
Influenza — Grippe	5.6	68	0.8	164	2.3	216	3.1	323
Pneumonia — Pneumopathies	32.8	2 658	29.9	1 246	17.7	1 137	16.1	1 581
Chronic lower respiratory diseases — Maladies chroniques des voies respiratoires inférieures	28.5	2 584	29.0	1 873	26.6	1 933	27.3	2 009
Diseases of the digestive system — Maladies de l'appareil digestif								
Total	32.8	2 938	33.0	2 223	31.6	2 234	31.6	2 294
Gastric and duodenal ulcer — Ulcère de l'estomac et du duodénum	5.0	430	4.8	257	3.7	268	3.8	231

21. Death and death rates by cause: 1995 - 2002
Décès selon la cause, nombres et taux: 1995 - 2002 (continued — suite)

(See notes at end of table. — Voir notes à la fin du tableau.)

Switzerland — Suisse

Cause of death — Cause de décès	1997 Rate Taux	1998 Number Nombre	1998 Rate Taux	1999 Number Nombre	1999 Rate Taux	2000 Number Nombre	2000 Rate Taux	2001 Number Nombre
TOTAL	887.0	62 567	880.0	62 499	874.8	62 545	870.6	61 283
Certain infectious and parasitic diseases — Certaines maladies infectieuses et parasitaires								
Total	11.8	700	9.8	688	9.6	713	9.9	655
Intestinal infectious diseases — Maladies infectieuses intestinales	⁺0.4	24	⁺0.3	28	⁺0.4	26	⁺0.4	29
Tuberculosis — Tuberculose	0.6	31	0.4	27	⁺0.4	33	0.5	24
Tetanus — Tétanos	-	-	-	2	0.0	2	0.0	-
Diphtheria — Diphtérie	-	-	-	-	-	-	-	-
Whooping cough — Coqueluche	0.0	1	0.0	-	-	-	-	1
Meningococcal infection — Infection à méningocoques	⁺0.1	12	⁺0.2	14	⁺0.2	14	⁺0.2	16
Septicaemia — Septicémie	3.5	180	2.5	204	2.9	202	2.8	168
Acute poliomyelitis — Poliomyélite aiguë	-	-	-	-	-	-	-	-
Measles — Rougeole	0.0	-	-	-	-	-	-	-
Viral hepatitis — Hépatite virale	⁺0.4	23	⁺0.3	37	0.5	35	0.5	28
Human immunodeficiency virus [HIV] disease — Maladies dues au virus de l'immunodéficience humaine (VIH)	3.8	183	2.6	147	2.1	135	1.9	125
Malaria — Paludisme	⁺0.1	1	0.0	2	0.0	3	0.0	1
Neoplasms — Tumeurs	220.0	15 579	219.1	15 531	217.4	15 978	222.4	15 884
Malignant neoplasms — Tumeurs malignes								
Total	213.8	15 111	212.5	15 057	210.8	15 509	215.9	15 401
Malignant neoplasm of lip, oral cavity and pharynx — Tumeur maligne de la lèvre, de la cavité buccale et du pharynx	4.9	345	4.9	357	5.0	366	5.1	363
Malignant neoplasm of oesophagus — Tumeur maligne de l'oesophage	5.0	380	5.3	350	4.9	384	5.3	406
Malignant neoplasm of stomach — Tumeur maligne de l'estomac	9.6	646	9.1	623	8.7	575	8.0	602
Malignant neoplasm of colon, rectosigmoid junction, rectum, anus and anal canal — Tumeur maligne du côlon, de la jonction recto-sigmoïdienne, du rectum, de l'anus et du canal anal	23.0	1 661	23.4	1 604	22.5	1 720	23.9	1 687
Malignant neoplasm of liver and intrahepatic bile ducts — Tumeur maligne du foie et des voies bilaires intrahépatiques	6.9	460	6.5	461	6.5	501	7.0	508
Malignant neoplasm of pancreas — Tumeur maligne du pancréas	11.8	864	12.2	875	12.2	866	12.1	864
Malignant neoplasm of trachea, bronchus and lung — Tumeur maligne de la trachée, des bronches et du poumon	36.4	2 678	37.7	2 635	36.9	2 825	39.3	2 777
Malignant neoplasm of female breast — Tumeur maligne du sein chez la femme	...	1 344	▲44.1	1 258	▲41.0	1 337	...	1 333
Malignant neoplasm of cervix uteri — Tumeur maligne du col de l'utérus	...	101	▲3.3	87	▲2.8	85	...	89
Malignant neoplasm of prostate — Tumeur maligne de la prostate	...	1 267	▼118.7	1 361	▼125.3	1 307	...	1 318
Malignant neoplasm of lymphoid, haematopoietic and related tissue — Tumeurs malignes primitives ou présumées primitives des tissus lymphoïde, hématopoïétique et apparentés	18.3	1 349	19.0	1 327	18.6	1 338	18.6	1 405
Disorders of the blood and blood-forming organs and certain disorders involving the immune mechanism — Maladies du sang et des organes hématopoïétiques et certains troubles du système immunitaire								
Total	2.1	167	2.3	144	2.0	147	2.0	170
Anaemias — Anémies	1.2	83	1.2	83	1.2	90	1.3	96
Endocrine, nutritional and metabolic diseases — Maladies endocriniennes, nutritionnelles et métaboliques								
Total	26.8	1 936	27.2	1 873	26.2	1 804	25.1	1 856
Diabetes mellitus — Diabète sucré	23.5	1 695	23.8	1 619	22.7	1 558	21.7	1 603
Malnutrition — Malnutrition	⁺0.2	20	⁺0.3	18	⁺0.3	29	⁺0.4	26
Mental and behavioural disorders — Troubles mentaux et du comportement	33.4	2 371	33.3	2 339	32.7	2 312	32.2	2 520
Diseases of the nervous system — Maladies du système nerveux	29.2	2 235	31.4	2 304	32.3	2 290	31.9	2 525
Diseases of the circulatory system — Maladies de l'appareil circulatoire								
Total	366.7	25 443	357.8	25 449	356.2	24 910	346.7	24 148
Acute rheumatic fever and chronic rheumatic heart diseases — Rhumatisme articulaire aigu et cardiopathies rhumatismales chroniques	2.0	112	1.6	118	1.7	135	1.9	116
Hypertensive diseases — Maladies hypertensives	16.8	1 323	18.6	1 478	20.7	1 578	22.0	1 705
Ischaemic heart disease — Cardiopathie ischémique	157.0	11 257	158.3	10 916	152.8	10 706	149.0	10 188
Cerebrovascular disease — Maladie cérébrovasculaire	70.2	4 854	68.3	4 817	67.4	4 578	63.7	4 396
Diseases of arteries, arterioles and capillaries — Maladies des artères, artérioles et capillaires	25.3	1 582	22.3	1 571	22.0	1 473	20.5	1 466
Diseases of the respiratory system — Maladies de l'appareil respiratoire								
Total	63.2	4 558	64.1	4 725	66.1	4 625	64.4	3 734
Influenza — Grippe	4.6	362	5.1	286	4.0	287	4.0	32
Pneumonia — Pneumopathies	22.3	1 613	22.7	1 715	24.0	1 847	25.7	1 382
Chronic lower respiratory diseases — Maladies chroniques des voies respiratoires inférieures	28.3	1 994	28.0	2 112	29.6	1 873	26.1	1 717
Diseases of the digestive system — Maladies de l'appareil digestif								
Total	32.4	2 256	31.7	2 334	32.7	2 389	33.3	2 391
Gastric and duodenal ulcer — Ulcère de l'estomac et du duodénum	3.3	190	2.7	197	2.8	245	3.4	191

21. Death and death rates by cause: 1995 - 2002
Décès selon la cause, nombres et taux: 1995 - 2002 (continued — suite)

(See notes at end of table. — Voir notes à la fin du tableau.)

Cause of death — Cause de décès	Switzerland — Suisse 2001 Rate Taux	1995 Number Nombre	1995 Rate Taux	1996 Number Nombre	1996 Rate Taux	1997 Number Nombre	1997 Rate Taux	1998 Number Nombre
		The Former Yougoslav Rep. of Macedonia — L'ex-République yougoslave de Macédoine						
TOTAL	847.3	16 338	832.2	16 062	813.4	16 596	831.1	16 870
Certain infectious and parasitic diseases — Certaines maladies infectieuses et parasitaires								
Total	9.1	244	12.4	175	8.9	191	9.6	187
Intestinal infectious diseases — Maladies infectieuses intestinales	♦0.4	113	5.8	40	2.0	42	2.1	40
Tuberculosis — Tuberculose	♦0.3	89	4.5	111	5.6	113	5.7	98
Tetanus — Tétanos	-	1	♦0.1	2	♦0.1	1	♦0.1	-
Diphtheria — Diphtérie	-	-	-	-	-	-	-	-
Whooping cough — Coqueluche	0.0	-	-	-	-	-	-	-
Meningococcal infection — Infection à méningocoques	♦0.2	1	♦0.1	4	♦0.2	2	♦0.1	5
Septicaemia — Septicémie	2.3	21	♦1.1	7	♦0.4	11	♦0.6	12
Acute poliomyelitis — Poliomyélite aiguë	-	1	♦0.1	-	-	-	-	-
Measles — Rougeole	-	-	-	1	♦0.1	-	-	-
Viral hepatitis — Hépatite virale	♦0.4	1	♦0.1	2	♦0.1	5	♦0.3	11
Human immunodeficiency virus [HIV] disease — Maladies dues au virus de l'immunodéficience humaine (VIH)	1.7	...	...	...	...	-	-	-
Malaria — Paludisme	0.0	1	♦0.1	-	-	1	♦0.1	-
Neoplasms — Tumeurs	219.6	2 508	127.7	2 660	134.7	2 790	139.7	2 962
Malignant neoplasms — Tumeurs malignes								
Total	212.9	2 443	124.4	2 637	133.5	2 758	138.1	2 893
Malignant neoplasm of lip, oral cavity and pharynx — Tumeur maligne de la lèvre, de la cavité buccale et du pharynx	5.0	26	♦1.3	57	2.9	46	2.3	59
Malignant neoplasm of oesophagus — Tumeur maligne de l'oesophage	5.6	23	♦1.2	20	♦1.0	22	♦1.1	16
Malignant neoplasm of stomach — Tumeur maligne de l'estomac	8.3	355	18.1	375	19.0	372	18.6	409
Malignant neoplasm of colon, rectosigmoid junction, rectum, anus and anal canal — Tumeur maligne du côlon, de la jonction recto-sigmoïdienne, du rectum, de l'anus et du canal anal	23.3	206	10.5	225	11.4	244	12.2	251
Malignant neoplasm of liver and intrahepatic bile ducts — Tumeur maligne du foie et des voies bilaires intrahépatiques	7.0	...	...	...	...	...	...	...
Malignant neoplasm of pancreas — Tumeur maligne du pancréas	11.9	102	5.2	104	5.3	137	6.9	126
Malignant neoplasm of trachea, bronchus and lung — Tumeur maligne de la trachée, des bronches et du poumon	38.4	471	24.0	545	27.6	550	27.7	588
Malignant neoplasm of female breast — Tumeur maligne du sein chez la femme	▲43.1	198	...	188	...	222	▲29.0	200
Malignant neoplasm of cervix uteri — Tumeur maligne du col de l'utérus	▲2.9	30	...	48	...	39	▲5.1	42
Malignant neoplasm of prostate — Tumeur maligne de la prostate	▼119.9	66	...	78	...	91	▼41.2	104
Malignant neoplasm of lymphoid, haematopoietic and related tissue — Tumeurs malignes primitives ou présumées primitives des tissus lymphoïde, hématopoïétique et apparentés	19.4	130	6.6	126	6.4	131	6.6	146
Disorders of the blood and blood-forming organs and certain disorders involving the immune mechanism — Maladies du sang et des organes hématopoïétiques et certains troubles du système immunitaire								
Total	2.4	17	♦0.9	8	♦0.4	10	♦0.5	11
Anaemias — Anémies	1.3	7	♦0.4	6	♦0.3	7	♦0.4	8
Endocrine, nutritional and metabolic diseases — Maladies endocriniennes, nutritionnelles et métaboliques								
Total	25.7	365	18.6	467	23.6	487	24.4	455
Diabetes mellitus — Diabète sucré	22.2	351	17.9	456	23.1	481	24.1	445
Malnutrition — Malnutrition	♦0.4	2	♦0.1	3	♦0.2	2	♦0.1	1
Mental and behavioural disorders — Troubles mentaux et du comportement	34.8	29	♦1.5	30	♦1.5	21	♦1.1	21
Diseases of the nervous system — Maladies du système nerveux	34.9	99	5.0	74	3.7	79	4.0	135
Diseases of the circulatory system — Maladies de l'appareil circulatoire								
Total	333.9	9 005	458.7	8 877	449.5	9 242	462.8	9 296
Acute rheumatic fever and chronic rheumatic heart diseases — Rhumatisme articularie aigu et cardiopathies rhumatismales chroniques	1.6	29	♦1.5	24	♦1.2	31	1.6	47
Hypertensive diseases — Maladies hypertensives	23.6	396	20.2	435	22.0	416	20.8	363
Ischaemic heart disease — Cardiopathie ischémique	140.9	1 702	86.7	1 896	96.0	1 888	94.5	2 040
Cerebrovascular disease — Maladie cérébrovasculaire	60.8	2 862	145.8	2 957	149.7	3 226	161.6	3 098
Diseases of arteries, arterioles and capillaries — Maladies des artères, artérioles et capillaires	20.3	222	11.3	283	14.3	329	16.5	336
Diseases of the respiratory system — Maladies de l'appareil respiratoire								
Total	51.6	727	37.0	776	39.3	787	39.4	541
Influenza — Grippe	0.4	1	♦0.1	2	♦0.1	-	-	4
Pneumonia — Pneumopathies	19.1	191	9.7	127	6.4	175	8.8	97
Chronic lower respiratory diseases — Maladies chroniques des voies respiratoires inférieures	23.7	432	22.0	393	19.9	393	19.7	290
Diseases of the digestive system — Maladies de l'appareil digestif								
Total	33.1	348	17.7	311	15.7	347	17.4	369
Gastric and duodenal ulcer — Ulcère de l'estomac et du duodénum	2.6	42	2.1	67	3.4	61	3.1	50

(See notes at end of table. — Voir notes à la fin du tableau.)

Cause of death — Cause de décès	The Former Yougoslav Rep. of Macedonia — L'ex-République yougoslave de Macédoine					Ukraine[6]		
	1998	1999		2000		1995		1996
	Rate Taux	Number Nombre	Rate Taux	Number Nombre	Rate Taux	Number Nombre	Rate Taux	Number Nombre
TOTAL	840.3	16 789	832.3	17 253	852.4	792 615	1532.3	776 717
Certain infectious and parasitic diseases — Certaines maladies infectieuses et parasitaires								
Total	9.3	181	9.0	162	8.0	9 957	19.2	10 493
Intestinal infectious diseases — Maladies infectieuses intestinales	2.0	26	♦1.3	29	♦1.4	436	0.8	362
Tuberculosis — Tuberculose	4.9	107	5.3	92	4.5	7 371	14.2	8 233
Tetanus — Tétanos	-	2	♦0.1	-	-	49	0.1	38
Diphtheria — Diphtérie	-	-	-	-	-	...	...	...
Whooping cough — Coqueluche	-	-	-	-	-	5	0.0	4
Meningococcal infection — Infection à méningocoques	♦0.2	2	♦0.1	1	0.0	250	0.5	204
Septicaemia — Septicémie	♦0.6	16	♦0.8	13	♦0.6	605	1.2	588
Acute poliomyelitis — Poliomyélite aiguë	-	-	-	-	-	...	...	...
Measles — Rougeole	-	-	-	-	-	1	0.0	-
Viral hepatitis — Hépatite virale	♦0.5	4	♦0.2	8	♦0.4	...	...	...
Human immunodeficiency virus [HIV] disease — Maladies dues au virus de l'immunodéficience humaine (VIH)	-	-	-	-	-	...	...	...
Malaria — Paludisme	-	-	-	-	-	-	-	-
Neoplasms — Tumeurs	147.5	2 887	143.1	3 051	150.7	102 481	198.1	99 153
Malignant neoplasms — Tumeurs malignes								
Total	144.1	2 820	139.8	2 965	146.5	101 748	196.7	98 394
Malignant neoplasm of lip, oral cavity and pharynx — Tumeur maligne de la lèvre, de la cavité buccale et du pharynx	2.9	62	3.1	57	2.8	3 628	7.0	3 527
Malignant neoplasm of oesophagus — Tumeur maligne de l'oesophage	♦0.8	20	♦1.0	30	♦1.5	2 024	3.9	1 998
Malignant neoplasm of stomach — Tumeur maligne de l'estomac	20.4	318	15.8	359	17.7	13 908	26.9	13 364
Malignant neoplasm of colon, rectosigmoid junction, rectum, anus and anal canal — Tumeur maligne du côlon, de la jonction recto-sigmoïdienne, du rectum, de l'anus et du canal anal	12.5	235	11.7	301	14.9	11 320	21.9	11 048
Malignant neoplasm of liver and intrahepatic bile ducts — Tumeur maligne du foie et des voies bilaires intrahépatiques	...	...	...	...	...	...	...	...
Malignant neoplasm of pancreas — Tumeur maligne du pancréas	6.3	136	6.7	110	5.4	...	...	...
Malignant neoplasm of trachea, bronchus and lung — Tumeur maligne de la trachée, des bronches et du poumon	29.3	567	28.1	599	29.6	21 099	40.8	19 781
Malignant neoplasm of female breast — Tumeur maligne du sein chez la femme	▲27.0	220	▲28.1	239	...	7 682	▲34.3	7 558
Malignant neoplasm of cervix uteri — Tumeur maligne du col de l'utérus	▲5.4	41	▲5.2	56	...	2 572	▲11.5	2 483
Malignant neoplasm of prostate — Tumeur maligne de la prostate	▼46.2	111	▼48.3	105	...	2 174	▼35.2	2 171
Malignant neoplasm of lymphoid, haematopoietic and related tissue — Tumeurs malignes primitives ou présumées primitives des tissus lymphoïde, hématopoïétique et apparentés	7.3	158	7.8	132	6.5	5 575	10.8	5 172
Disorders of the blood and blood-forming organs and certain disorders involving the immune mechanism — Maladies du sang et des organes hématopoïétiques et certains troubles du système immunitaire								
Total	♦0.5	8	♦0.4	12	♦0.6	482	0.9	453
Anaemias — Anémies	♦0.4	5	♦0.2	8	♦0.4	319	0.6	288
Endocrine, nutritional and metabolic diseases — Maladies endocriniennes, nutritionnelles et métaboliques								
Total	22.7	461	22.9	538	26.6	5 166	10.0	4 951
Diabetes mellitus — Diabète sucré	22.2	451	22.4	534	26.4	4 501	8.7	4 262
Malnutrition — Malnutrition	0.0	2	♦0.1	1	0.0	...	...	...
Mental and behavioural disorders — Troubles mentaux et du comportement	♦1.0	25	♦1.2	32	1.6	4 386	8.5	4 054
Diseases of the nervous system — Maladies du système nerveux	6.7	109	5.4	133	6.6	5 775	11.2	5 421
Diseases of the circulatory system — Maladies de l'appareil circulatoire								
Total	463.1	9 289	460.5	9 670	477.8	450 401	870.7	446 824
Acute rheumatic fever and chronic rheumatic heart diseases — Rhumatisme articulaire aigu et cardiopathies rhumatismales chroniques	2.3	39	1.9	38	1.9	4 257	8.2	3 869
Hypertensive diseases — Maladies hypertensives	18.1	373	18.5	405	20.0	1 945	3.8	1 713
Ischaemic heart disease — Cardiopathie ischémique	101.6	1 976	98.0	1 947	96.2	270 134	522.2	272 885
Cerebrovascular disease — Maladie cérébrovasculaire	154.3	3 153	156.3	3 277	161.9	132 735	256.6	122 561
Diseases of arteries, arterioles and capillaries — Maladies des artères, artérioles et capillaires	16.7	337	16.7	393	19.4	27 813	53.8	32 250
Diseases of the respiratory system — Maladies de l'appareil respiratoire								
Total	26.9	588	29.2	622	30.7	46 121	89.2	43 991
Influenza — Grippe	♦0.2	2	♦0.1	4	♦0.2	82	0.2	71
Pneumonia — Pneumopathies	4.8	99	4.9	113	5.6	6 337	12.3	5 914
Chronic lower respiratory diseases — Maladies chroniques des voies respiratoires inférieures	14.4	343	17.0	375	18.5	...	...	...
Diseases of the digestive system — Maladies de l'appareil digestif								
Total	18.4	342	17.0	337	16.7	22 664	43.8	22 368
Gastric and duodenal ulcer — Ulcère de l'estomac et du duodénum	2.5	48	2.4	46	2.3	2 397	4.6	2 354

(See notes at end of table. — Voir notes à la fin du tableau.)

Ukraine[6]

Cause of death — Cause de décès	1996 Rate Taux	1997 Number Nombre	1997 Rate Taux	1998 Number Nombre	1998 Rate Taux	1999 Number Nombre	1999 Rate Taux	2000 Number Nombre
TOTAL	1513.1	754 151	1481.8	719 954	1425.7	739 170	1475.2	758 082
Certain infectious and parasitic diseases — Certaines maladies infectieuses et parasitaires								
Total	20.4	10 569	20.8	9 671	19.2	11 701	23.4	12 725
Intestinal infectious diseases — Maladies infectieuses intestinales	0.7	313	0.6	237	0.5	240	0.5	196
Tuberculosis — Tuberculose	16.0	8 651	17.0	8 024	15.9	9 914	19.8	10 976
Tetanus — Tétanos	0.1	26	♦0.1	21	0.0	34	0.1	20
Diphtheria — Diphtérie	...	...	...	...	...	...	...	...
Whooping cough — Coqueluche	0.0	3	0.0	2	0.0	1	0.0	4
Meningococcal infection — Infection à méningocoques	0.4	175	0.3	156	0.3	123	0.2	137
Septicaemia — Septicémie	1.1	459	0.9	407	0.8	471	0.9	569
Acute poliomyelitis — Poliomyélite aiguë	...	...	...	...	...	...	...	...
Measles — Rougeole	-	6	0.0	2	0.0	-	-	1
Viral hepatitis — Hépatite virale	...	...	...	...	...	...	...	...
Human immunodeficiency virus [HIV] disease — Maladies dues au virus de l'immunodéficience humaine (VIH)	...	...	...	...	...	...	...	...
Malaria — Paludisme	-	1	0.0	1	0.0	1	0.0	2
Neoplasms — Tumeurs	193.2	97 947	192.5	97 758	193.6	98 476	196.5	97 837
Malignant neoplasms — Tumeurs malignes								
Total	191.7	97 277	191.1	97 049	192.2	97 806	195.2	97 123
Malignant neoplasm of lip, oral cavity and pharynx — Tumeur maligne de la lèvre, de la cavité buccale et du pharynx	6.9	3 505	6.9	3 467	6.9	3 500	7.0	3 616
Malignant neoplasm of oesophagus — Tumeur maligne de l'oesophage	3.9	1 933	3.8	1 842	3.6	1 883	3.8	1 854
Malignant neoplasm of stomach — Tumeur maligne de l'estomac	26.0	13 016	25.6	12 901	25.5	12 644	25.2	12 434
Malignant neoplasm of colon, rectosigmoid junction, rectum, anus and anal canal — Tumeur maligne du côlon, de la jonction recto-sigmoïdienne, du rectum, de l'anus et du canal anal	21.5	10 953	21.5	11 152	22.1	11 669	23.3	11 563
Malignant neoplasm of liver and intrahepatic bile ducts — Tumeur maligne du foie et des voies bilaires intrahépatiques	...	...	...	...	...	...	...	...
Malignant neoplasm of pancreas — Tumeur maligne du pancréas	...	...	...	...	...	...	...	...
Malignant neoplasm of trachea, bronchus and lung — Tumeur maligne de la trachée, des bronches et du poumon	38.5	10 070	38.1	19 338	38.3	18 831	37.6	18 800
Malignant neoplasm of female breast — Tumeur maligne du sein chez la femme	...	7 554	▲34.0	7 712	▲34.8	7 929	▲35.0	7 998
Malignant neoplasm of cervix uteri — Tumeur maligne du col de l'utérus	...	2 471	▲11.1	2 528	▲11.4	2 443	▲11.0	2 443
Malignant neoplasm of prostate — Tumeur maligne de la prostate	...	2 289	▼38.3	2 339	▼39.4	2 480	▼41.8	2 537
Malignant neoplasm of lymphoid, haematopoietic and related tissue — Tumeurs malignes primitives ou présumées primitives des tissus lymphoïde, hématopoïétique et apparentés	10.1	5 159	10.1	5 067	10.0	5 323	10.6	5 181
Disorders of the blood and blood-forming organs and certain disorders involving the immune mechanism — Maladies du sang et des organes hématopoïétiques et certains troubles du système immunitaire								
Total	0.9	418	0.8	411	0.8	396	0.8	432
Anaemias — Anémies	0.6	298	0.6	265	0.5	238	0.5	261
Endocrine, nutritional and metabolic diseases — Maladies endocriniennes, nutritionnelles et métaboliques								
Total	9.6	4 296	8.4	4 209	8.3	4 221	8.4	4 465
Diabetes mellitus — Diabète sucré	8.3	3 633	7.1	3 479	6.9	3 427	6.8	3 474
Malnutrition — Malnutrition	...	...	...	...	...	...	...	...
Mental and behavioural disorders — Troubles mentaux et du comportement	7.9	3 330	6.5	2 480	4.9	2 509	5.0	2 713
Diseases of the nervous system — Maladies du système nerveux	10.6	5 357	10.5	4 586	9.1	4 856	9.7	5 138
Diseases of the circulatory system — Maladies de l'appareil circulatoire								
Total	870.4	446 369	877.1	433 990	859.4	448 948	896.0	463 876
Acute rheumatic fever and chronic rheumatic heart diseases — Rhumatisme articularie aigu et cardiopathies rhumatismales chroniques	7.5	3 416	6.7	3 149	6.2	3 041	6.1	3 089
Hypertensive diseases — Maladies hypertensives	3.3	1 805	3.5	2 106	4.2	1 316	2.6	1 094
Ischaemic heart disease — Cardiopathie ischémique	531.6	276 997	544.3	269 617	533.9	284 704	568.2	299 198
Cerebrovascular disease — Maladie cérébrovasculaire	238.8	119 774	235.3	115 403	228.5	115 575	230.7	116 026
Diseases of arteries, arterioles and capillaries — Maladies des artères, artérioles et capillaires	62.8	32 021	62.9	32 443	64.2	31 731	63.3	30 696
Diseases of the respiratory system — Maladies de l'appareil respiratoire								
Total	85.7	41 397	81.3	36 271	71.8	37 103	74.0	37 899
Influenza — Grippe	0.1	60	0.1	41	0.1	50	0.1	47
Pneumonia — Pneumopathies	11.5	5 552	10.9	4 657	9.2	5 595	11.2	7 040
Chronic lower respiratory diseases — Maladies chroniques des voies respiratoires inférieures	...	...	...	...	...	...	...	...
Diseases of the digestive system — Maladies de l'appareil digestif								
Total	43.6	21 478	42.2	19 872	39.4	20 682	41.3	22 208
Gastric and duodenal ulcer — Ulcère de l'estomac et du duodénum	4.6	2 216	4.4	2 129	4.2	2 019	4.0	2 077

21. Death and death rates by cause: 1995 - 2002
Décès selon la cause, nombres et taux: 1995 - 2002 (continued — suite)

(See notes at end of table. — Voir notes à la fin du tableau.)

Cause of death — Cause de décès	Ukraine[6] 2000 Rate Taux	2001 Number Nombre	2001 Rate Taux	2002 Number Nombre	2002 Rate Taux	United Kingdom — Royaume-Uni 1995 Number Nombre	1995 Rate Taux	1996 Number Nombre
TOTAL	1525.0	745 952	1521.2	754 911	1559.7	645 493	1101.3	636 007
Certain infectious and parasitic diseases — Certaines maladies infectieuses et parasitaires								
Total	25.6	13 548	27.6	12 868	26.6	4 166	7.1	4 188
Intestinal infectious diseases — Maladies infectieuses intestinales	0.4	128	0.3	107	0.2	295	0.5	362
Tuberculosis — Tuberculose	22.1	11 064	22.6	9 894	20.4	500	0.9	476
Tetanus — Tétanos	0.0	24	0.0	22	0.0	1	0.0	-
Diphtheria — Diphtérie	...	...	...	...	...	1	0.0	-
Whooping cough — Coqueluche	0.0	4	0.0	-	-	2	0.0	2
Meningococcal infection — Infection à méningocoques	0.3	137	0.3	132	0.3	215	0.4	252
Septicaemia — Septicémie	1.1	651	1.3	791	1.6	1 259	2.1	1 371
Acute poliomyelitis — Poliomyélite aiguë	...	...	...	...	...	1	0.0	1
Measles — Rougeole	0.0	11	0.0	3	0.0	2	0.0	-
Viral hepatitis — Hépatite virale	...	...	...	...	...	169	0.3	165
Human immunodeficiency virus [HIV] disease — Maladies dues au virus de l'immunodéficience humaine (VIH)	...	730	1.5	1 123	2.3	667	1.1	576
Malaria — Paludisme	0.0	1	0.0	2	0.0	4	0.0	12
Neoplasms — Tumeurs	196.8	95 639	195.0	95 064	196.4	160 353	273.6	158 593
Malignant neoplasms — Tumeurs malignes								
Total	195.4	94 858	193.4	94 314	194.9	157 876	269.4	156 253
Malignant neoplasm of lip, oral cavity and pharynx — Tumeur maligne de la lèvre, de la cavité buccale et du pharynx	7.3	3 480	7.1	3 621	7.5	1 928	3.3	1 956
Malignant neoplasm of oesophagus — Tumeur maligne de l'oesophage	3.7	1 742	3.6	1 645	3.4	6 664	11.4	6 700
Malignant neoplasm of stomach — Tumeur maligne de l'estomac	25.0	11 990	24.5	11 587	23.9	8 005	13.7	7 655
Malignant neoplasm of colon, rectosigmoid junction, rectum, anus and anal canal — Tumeur maligne du côlon, de la jonction recto-sigmoïdienne, du rectum, de l'anus et du canal anal	23.3	11 576	23.6	11 617	24.0	17 934	30.6	17 624
Malignant neoplasm of liver and intrahepatic bile ducts — Tumeur maligne du foie et des voies bilaires intrahépatiques	...	...	...	...	...	608	1.0	677
Malignant neoplasm of pancreas — Tumeur maligne du pancréas	...	...	...	...	...	6 520	11.1	6 563
Malignant neoplasm of trachea, bronchus and lung — Tumeur maligne de la trachée, des bronches et du poumon	37.8	17 852	36.4	17 454	36.1	36 600	62.4	35 751
Malignant neoplasm of female breast — Tumeur maligne du sein chez la femme	▲36.1	7 741	▲35.0	7 954	...	14 114	▲58.0	13 678
Malignant neoplasm of cervix uteri — Tumeur maligne du col de l'utérus	▲11.0	2 359	▲10.7	2 362	...	1 505	▲6.2	1 498
Malignant neoplasm of prostate — Tumeur maligne de la prostate	▼42.4	2 526	▼42.1	2 764	...	9 858	▼119.5	9 696
Malignant neoplasm of lymphoid, haematopoietic and related tissue — Tumeurs malignes primitives ou présumées primitives des tissus lymphoïde, hématopoïétique et apparentés	10.4	5 087	10.4	5 003	10.3	11 197	19.1	11 089
Disorders of the blood and blood-forming organs and certain disorders involving the immune mechanism — Maladies du sang et des organes hématopoïétiques et certains troubles du système immunitaire								
Total	0.9	415	0.8	396	0.8	2 089	3.6	2 192
Anaemias — Anémies	0.5	232	0.5	230	0.5	790	1.3	814
Endocrine, nutritional and metabolic diseases — Maladies endocriniennes, nutritionnelles et métaboliques								
Total	9.0	3 662	7.5	3 489	7.2	8 603	14.7	8 314
Diabetes mellitus — Diabète sucré	7.0	3 191	6.5	3 046	6.3	6 744	11.5	6 568
Malnutrition — Malnutrition	...	...	...	...	...	64	0.1	65
Mental and behavioural disorders — Troubles mentaux et du comportement	5.5	2 622	5.3	2 758	5.7	10 810	18.4	10 991
Diseases of the nervous system — Maladies du système nerveux	10.3	5 232	10.7	5 409	11.2	10 779	18.4	10 855
Diseases of the circulatory system — Maladies de l'appareil circulatoire								
Total	933.1	457 442	932.9	465 345	961.4	277 448	473.4	271 067
Acute rheumatic fever and chronic rheumatic heart diseases — Rhumatisme articularie aigu et cardiopathies rhumatismales chroniques	6.2	2 798	5.7	2 608	5.4	2 246	3.8	2 140
Hypertensive diseases — Maladies hypertensives	2.2	910	1.9	752	1.6	3 300	5.6	3 382
Ischaemic heart disease — Cardiopathie ischémique	601.9	296 514	604.7	304 931	630.0	152 930	260.9	147 556
Cerebrovascular disease — Maladie cérébrovasculaire	233.4	112 138	228.7	107 531	222.2	69 400	118.4	68 506
Diseases of arteries, arterioles and capillaries — Maladies des artères, artérioles et capillaires	61.7	30 471	62.1	33 380	69.0	17 089	29.2	17 151
Diseases of the respiratory system — Maladies de l'appareil respiratoire								
Total	76.2	33 471	68.3	31 825	65.8	101 659	173.4	99 269
Influenza — Grippe	0.1	16	0.0	9	0.0	293	0.5	230
Pneumonia — Pneumopathies	14.2	6 279	12.8	6 276	13.0	61 147	104.3	60 132
Chronic lower respiratory diseases — Maladies chroniques des voies respiratoires inférieures	...	...	...	...	...	31 722	54.1	30 277
Diseases of the digestive system — Maladies de l'appareil digestif								
Total	44.7	22 455	45.8	23 303	48.1	22 181	37.8	22 875
Gastric and duodenal ulcer — Ulcère de l'estomac et du duodénum	4.2	2 055	4.2	1 631	3.4	4 445	7.6	4 557

(See notes at end of table. — Voir notes à la fin du tableau.)

United Kingdom — Royaume-Uni

Cause of death — Cause de décès	1996 Rate Taux	1997 Number Nombre	1997 Rate Taux	1998 Number Nombre	1998 Rate Taux	1999 Number Nombre	1999 Rate Taux	2000 Number Nombre
TOTAL	1081.5	629 746	1067.1	629 172	1062.1	632 062	1062.3	608 366
Certain infectious and parasitic diseases — Certaines maladies infectieuses et parasitaires								
Total	7.1	3 994	6.8	3 959	6.7	4 166	7.0	4 321
Intestinal infectious diseases — Maladies infectieuses intestinales	0.6	403	0.7	452	0.8	510	0.9	603
Tuberculosis — Tuberculose	0.8	459	0.8	443	0.7	438	0.7	411
Tetanus — Tétanos	-	2	0.0	1	0.0	1	0.0	-
Diphtheria — Diphtérie	-	-	-	-	-	-	-	-
Whooping cough — Coqueluche	0.0	3	0.0	5	0.0	2	0.0	2
Meningococcal infection — Infection à méningocoques	0.4	258	0.4	236	0.4	235	0.4	226
Septicaemia — Septicémie	2.3	1 422	2.4	1 503	2.5	1 666	2.8	1 668
Acute poliomyelitis — Poliomyélite aiguë	0.0	1	0.0	-	-	1	0.0	-
Measles — Rougeole	-	3	0.0	3	0.0	3	0.0	1
Viral hepatitis — Hépatite virale	0.3	182	0.3	196	0.3	198	0.3	220
Human immunodeficiency virus [HIV] disease — Maladies dues au virus de l'immunodéficience humaine (VIH)	1.0	306	0.5	202	0.3	185	0.3	208
Malaria — Paludisme	0.0	12	0.0	9	0.0	14	0.0	17
Neoplasms — Tumeurs	269.7	156 344	264.9	156 989	265.0	154 803	260.2	153 698
Malignant neoplasms — Tumeurs malignes								
Total	265.7	154 122	261.2	154 731	261.2	152 476	256.3	151 186
Malignant neoplasm of lip, oral cavity and pharynx — Tumeur maligne de la lèvre, de la cavité buccale et du pharynx	3.3	1 994	3.4	2 000	3.4	1 982	3.3	1 914
Malignant neoplasm of oesophagus — Tumeur maligne de l'oesophage	11.4	6 733	11.4	6 836	11.5	6 977	11.7	6 919
Malignant neoplasm of stomach — Tumeur maligne de l'estomac	13.0	7 494	12.7	7 337	12.4	6 976	11.7	6 608
Malignant neoplasm of colon, rectosigmoid junction, rectum, anus and anal canal — Tumeur maligne du côlon, de la jonction recto-sigmoïdienne, du rectum, de l'anus et du canal anal	30.0	17 330	29.4	17 087	28.8	16 715	28.1	16 265
Malignant neoplasm of liver and intrahepatic bile ducts — Tumeur maligne du foie et des voies bilaires intrahépatiques	1.2	731	1.2	732	1.2	822	1.4	1 009
Malignant neoplasm of pancreas — Tumeur maligne du pancréas	11.2	6 499	11.0	6 562	11.1	6 672	11.2	6 897
Malignant neoplasm of trachea, bronchus and lung — Tumeur maligne de la trachée, des bronches et du poumon	60.8	34 851	59.1	34 958	59.0	34 235	57.5	33 769
Malignant neoplasm of female breast — Tumeur maligne du sein chez la femme	▲56.0	13 399	▲54.7	13 198	▲53.7	13 019	▲52.8	12 768
Malignant neoplasm of cervix uteri — Tumeur maligne du col de l'utérus	▲6.1	1 395	▲5.7	1 336	▲5.4	1 265	▲5.1	1 253
Malignant neoplasm of prostate — Tumeur maligne de la prostate	▼116.4	9 439	▼110.8	9 470	▼109.2	9 497	▼107.9	9 279
Malignant neoplasm of lymphoid, haematopoietic and related tissue — Tumeurs malignes primitives ou présumées primitives des tissus lymphoïde, hématopoïétique et apparentés	18.9	11 048	18.7	11 285	19.1	11 395	19.2	11 136
Disorders of the blood and blood-forming organs and certain disorders involving the immune mechanism — Maladies du sang et des organes hématopoïétiques et certains troubles du système immunitaire								
Total	3.7	2 230	3.8	2 188	3.7	2 087	3.5	1 934
Anaemias — Anémies	1.4	762	1.3	739	1.2	677	1.1	630
Endocrine, nutritional and metabolic diseases — Maladies endocriniennes, nutritionnelles et métaboliques								
Total	14.1	8 229	13.9	8 429	14.2	8 562	14.4	8 210
Diabetes mellitus — Diabète sucré	11.2	6 477	11.0	6 567	11.1	6 726	11.3	6 478
Malnutrition — Malnutrition	0.1	60	0.1	63	0.1	60	0.1	56
Mental and behavioural disorders — Troubles mentaux et du comportement	18.7	11 474	19.4	12 300	20.8	13 264	22.3	13 382
Diseases of the nervous system — Maladies du système nerveux	18.5	10 904	18.5	11 171	18.9	11 435	19.2	11 199
Diseases of the circulatory system — Maladies de l'appareil circulatoire								
Total	460.9	260 896	442.1	258 240	435.9	250 343	420.7	236 723
Acute rheumatic fever and chronic rheumatic heart diseases — Rhumatisme articularie aigu et cardiopathies rhumatismales chroniques	3.6	1 919	3.3	1 822	3.1	1 857	3.1	1 789
Hypertensive diseases — Maladies hypertensives	5.8	3 451	5.8	3 471	5.9	3 745	6.3	3 623
Ischaemic heart disease — Cardiopathie ischémique	250.9	140 213	237.6	138 114	233.2	132 025	221.9	124 067
Cerebrovascular disease — Maladie cérébrovasculaire	116.5	66 355	112.4	66 024	111.5	64 517	108.4	60 795
Diseases of arteries, arterioles and capillaries — Maladies des artères, artérioles et capillaires	29.2	16 397	27.8	16 482	27.8	16 007	26.9	15 794
Diseases of the respiratory system — Maladies de l'appareil respiratoire								
Total	168.8	103 097	174.7	100 854	170.3	109 807	184.5	102 056
Influenza — Grippe	0.4	438	0.7	144	0.2	652	1.1	679
Pneumonia — Pneumopathies	102.3	62 539	106.0	60 439	102.0	65 944	110.8	60 692
Chronic lower respiratory diseases — Maladies chroniques des voies respiratoires inférieures	51.5	30 677	52.0	30 484	51.5	32 155	54.0	29 264
Diseases of the digestive system — Maladies de l'appareil digestif								
Total	38.9	23 296	39.5	24 113	40.7	25 005	42.0	25 595
Gastric and duodenal ulcer — Ulcère de l'estomac et du duodénum	7.7	4 360	7.4	4 329	7.3	4 428	7.4	4 444

713

21. Death and death rates by cause: 1995 - 2002
Décès selon la cause, nombres et taux: 1995 - 2002 (continued — suite)

(See notes at end of table. — Voir notes à la fin du tableau.)

Cause of death — Cause de décès	United Kingdom — Royaume-Uni 2000 Rate Taux	2001 Number Nombre	2001 Rate Taux	2002 Number Nombre	2002 Rate Taux	Australia — Australie 1995 Number Nombre	1995 Rate Taux	1996 Number Nombre
TOTAL	1018.1	**602 268**	1007.9	**606 216**	1023.5	125 106	692.3	128 254
Certain infectious and parasitic diseases — Certaines maladies infectieuses et parasitaires								
Total	7.2	**4 928**	8.2	**5 115**	8.6	1 564	8.7	1 634
Intestinal infectious diseases — Maladies infectieuses intestinales	1.0	**849**	1.4	**954**	1.6	85	0.5	79
Tuberculosis — Tuberculose	0.7	**414**	0.7	**430**	0.7	26	♦0.1	37
Tetanus — Tétanos	-	**1**	0.0	-	-	2	0.0	-
Diphtheria — Diphtérie	-	**1**	0.0	-	-	-	-	-
Whooping cough — Coqueluche	0.0	**5**	0.0	**4**	0.0	-	-	2
Meningococcal infection — Infection à méningocoques	0.4	**217**	0.4	**135**	0.2	22	♦0.1	25
Septicaemia — Septicémie	2.8	**2 215**	3.7	**2 395**	4.0	505	2.8	600
Acute poliomyelitis — Poliomyélite aiguë	-	-	-	-	-	-	-	-
Measles — Rougeole	0.0	**1**	0.0	**1**	0.0	4	0.0	-
Viral hepatitis — Hépatite virale	0.4	**202**	0.3	**183**	0.3	129	0.7	110
Human immunodeficiency virus [HIV] disease — Maladies dues au virus de l'immunodéficience humaine (VIH)	0.3	**213**	0.4	**234**	0.4	502	2.8	489
Malaria — Paludisme	0.0	**13**	0.0	**11**	0.0	3	0.0	2
Neoplasms — Tumeurs	257.2	**158 415**	265.1	**159 332**	269.0	33 944	187.8	35 021
Malignant neoplasms — Tumeurs malignes								
Total	253.0	**154 733**	258.9	**155 481**	262.5	33 381	184.7	34 452
Malignant neoplasm of lip, oral cavity and pharynx — Tumeur maligne de la lèvre, de la cavité buccale et du pharynx	3.2	**1 978**	3.3	**1 985**	3.4	625	3.5	717
Malignant neoplasm of oesophagus — Tumeur maligne de l'oesophage	11.6	**7 014**	11.7	**7 256**	12.3	902	5.0	928
Malignant neoplasm of stomach — Tumeur maligne de l'estomac	11.1	**6 458**	10.8	**6 373**	10.8	1 258	7.0	1 225
Malignant neoplasm of colon, rectosigmoid junction, rectum, anus and anal canal — Tumeur maligne du côlon, de la jonction recto-sigmoïdienne, du rectum, de l'anus et du canal anal	27.2	**16 187**	27.1	**16 236**	27.4	4 423	24.5	4 606
Malignant neoplasm of liver and intrahepatic bile ducts — Tumeur maligne du foie et des voies bilaires intrahépatiques	1.7	**2 377**	4.0	**2 525**	4.3	362	2.0	364
Malignant neoplasm of pancreas — Tumeur maligne du pancréas	11.5	**6 782**	11.3	**6 898**	11.6	1 511	8.4	1 600
Malignant neoplasm of trachea, bronchus and lung — Tumeur maligne de la trachée, des bronches et du poumon	56.5	**33 425**	55.9	**33 647**	56.8	6 603	36.5	6 766
Malignant neoplasm of female breast — Tumeur maligne du sein chez la femme	...	**13 014**	...	**12 858**	...	2 598	▲36.2	2 620
Malignant neoplasm of cervix uteri — Tumeur maligne du col de l'utérus	...	**1 176**	...	**1 126**	...	328	▲4.6	301
Malignant neoplasm of prostate — Tumeur maligne de la prostate	...	**9 903**	...	**9 941**	...	2 532	▼115.6	2 644
Malignant neoplasm of lymphoid, haematopoietic and related tissue — Tumeurs malignes primitives ou présumées primitives des tissus lymphoïde, hématopoïétique et apparentés	18.6	**11 762**	19.7	**12 102**	20.4	3 236	17.9	3 350
Disorders of the blood and blood-forming organs and certain disorders involving the immune mechanism — Maladies du sang et des organes hématopoïétiques et certains troubles du système immunitaire								
Total	3.2	**1 162**	1.9	**1 238**	2.1	349	1.9	406
Anaemias — Anémies	1.1	**608**	1.0	**640**	1.1	178	1.0	212
Endocrine, nutritional and metabolic diseases — Maladies endocriniennes, nutritionnelles et métaboliques								
Total	13.7	**8 826**	14.8	**9 067**	15.3	3 544	19.6	3 905
Diabetes mellitus — Diabète sucré	10.8	**6 959**	11.6	**7 055**	11.9	2 671	14.8	2 970
Malnutrition — Malnutrition	0.1	**70**	0.1	**87**	0.1	64	0.4	71
Mental and behavioural disorders — Troubles mentaux et du comportement	22.4	**16 949**	28.4	**17 301**	29.2	3 101	17.2	3 557
Diseases of the nervous system — Maladies du système nerveux	18.7	**16 055**	26.9	**16 613**	28.0	2 932	16.2	3 055
Diseases of the circulatory system — Maladies de l'appareil circulatoire								
Total	396.2	**240 348**	402.2	**237 857**	401.6	52 697	291.6	53 720
Acute rheumatic fever and chronic rheumatic heart diseases — Rhumatisme articulaire aigu et cardiopathies rhumatismales chroniques	3.0	**1 520**	2.5	**1 358**	2.3	368	2.0	350
Hypertensive diseases — Maladies hypertensives	6.1	**3 705**	6.2	**3 836**	6.5	1 082	6.0	1 108
Ischaemic heart disease — Cardiopathie ischémique	207.6	**120 957**	202.4	**117 473**	198.3	29 188	161.5	29 492
Cerebrovascular disease — Maladie cérébrovasculaire	101.7	**66 669**	111.6	**67 363**	113.7	12 537	69.4	12 758
Diseases of arteries, arterioles and capillaries — Maladies des artères, artérioles et capillaires	26.4	**14 948**	25.0	**14 753**	24.9	2 972	16.4	2 913
Diseases of the respiratory system — Maladies de l'appareil respiratoire								
Total	170.8	**75 802**	126.9	**78 588**	132.7	9 348	51.7	10 382
Influenza — Grippe	1.1	**43**	0.1	**45**	0.1	86	0.5	165
Pneumonia — Pneumopathies	101.6	**35 034**	58.6	**36 048**	60.9	1 609	8.9	1 753
Chronic lower respiratory diseases — Maladies chroniques des voies respiratoires inférieures	49.0	**29 319**	49.1	**29 764**	50.2	6 316	34.9	6 968
Diseases of the digestive system — Maladies de l'appareil digestif								
Total	42.8	**27 005**	45.2	**27 859**	47.0	3 787	21.0	3 886
Gastric and duodenal ulcer — Ulcère de l'estomac et du duodénum	7.4	**4 186**	7.0	**4 158**	7.0	565	3.1	511

21. Death and death rates by cause: 1995 - 2002
Décès selon la cause, nombres et taux: 1995 - 2002 (continued — suite)

(See notes at end of table. — Voir notes à la fin du tableau.)

Australia — Australie

Cause of death — Cause de décès	1996 Rate / Taux	1997 Number / Nombre	1997 Rate / Taux	1998 Number / Nombre	1998 Rate / Taux	1999 Number / Nombre	1999 Rate / Taux	2000 Number / Nombre
TOTAL	700.4	128 695	695.0	127 358	680.6	128 079	676.7	128 784
Certain infectious and parasitic diseases — Certaines maladies infectieuses et parasitaires								
Total	8.9	1 448	7.8	1 463	7.8	1 590	8.4	1 658
Intestinal infectious diseases — Maladies infectieuses intestinales	0.4	51	0.3	29	♦0.2	42	0.2	35
Tuberculosis — Tuberculose	0.2	30	♦0.2	30	♦0.2	27	♦0.1	35
Tetanus — Tétanos	-	1	0.0	2	0.0	-		2
Diphtheria — Diphtérie	-	-		-		-		-
Whooping cough — Coqueluche	0.0	6	0.0	-		-		1
Meningococcal infection — Infection à méningocoques	♦0.1	25	♦0.1	35	0.2	40	0.2	30
Septicaemia — Septicémie	3.3	663	3.6	751	4.0	863	4.6	948
Acute poliomyelitis — Poliomyélite aiguë	-	-		-		-		-
Measles — Rougeole	-	-		-		-		-
Viral hepatitis — Hépatite virale	0.6	141	0.8	63	0.3	62	0.3	23
Human immunodeficiency virus [HIV] disease — Maladies dues au virus de l'immunodéficience humaine (VIH)	2.7	213	1.2	153	0.8	133	0.7	134
Malaria — Paludisme	0.0	1	0.0	-		2	0.0	3
Neoplasms — Tumeurs	191.3	34 860	188.3	35 675	190.7	35 880	189.6	36 567
Malignant neoplasms — Tumeurs malignes								
Total	188.2	34 290	185.2	35 010	187.1	35 079	185.3	35 825
Malignant neoplasm of lip, oral cavity and pharynx — Tumeur maligne de la lèvre, de la cavité buccale et du pharynx	3.9	631	3.4	645	3.4	660	3.5	670
Malignant neoplasm of oesophagus — Tumeur maligne de l'oesophage	5.1	944	5.1	976	5.2	939	5.0	971
Malignant neoplasm of stomach — Tumeur maligne de l'estomac	6.7	1 244	6.7	1 195	6.4	1 205	6.4	1 189
Malignant neoplasm of colon, rectosigmoid junction, rectum, anus and anal canal — Tumeur maligne du côlon, de la jonction recto-sigmoïdienne, du rectum, de l'anus et du canal anal	25.2	4 678	25.3	4 642	24.8	4 575	24.2	4 718
Malignant neoplasm of liver and intrahepatic bile ducts — Tumeur maligne du foie et des voies bilaires intrahépatiques	2.0	395	2.1	631	3.4	690	3.6	741
Malignant neoplasm of pancreas — Tumeur maligne du pancréas	8.7	1 603	8.7	1 618	8.6	1 708	9.0	1 748
Malignant neoplasm of trachea, bronchus and lung — Tumeur maligne de la trachée, des bronches et du poumon	37.0	6 683	36.1	6 762	36.1	6 769	35.8	6 911
Malignant neoplasm of female breast — Tumeur maligne du sein chez la femme	...	2 596	...	2 541	▲33.8	2 512	...	2 521
Malignant neoplasm of cervix uteri — Tumeur maligne du col de l'utérus	...	291	...	260	▲3.5	226	...	265
Malignant neoplasm of prostate — Tumeur maligne de la prostate	...	2 449	...	2 570	▼106.8	2 512	...	2 665
Malignant neoplasm of lymphoid, haematopoietic and related tissue — Tumeurs malignes primitives ou présumées primitives des tissus lymphoïde, hématopoïétique et apparentés	18.3	3 415	18.4	3 536	18.9	3 579	18.9	3 754
Disorders of the blood and blood-forming organs and certain disorders involving the immune mechanism — Maladies du sang et des organes hématopoïétiques et certains troubles du système immunitaire								
Total	2.2	396	2.1	432	2.3	455	2.4	406
Anaemias — Anémies	1.2	211	1.1	228	1.2	205	1.1	194
Endocrine, nutritional and metabolic diseases — Maladies endocriniennes, nutritionnelles et métaboliques								
Total	21.3	3 912	21.1	3 960	21.2	4 099	21.7	4 178
Diabetes mellitus — Diabète sucré	16.2	2 846	15.4	2 873	15.4	2 957	15.6	3 009
Malnutrition — Malnutrition	0.4	85	0.5	60	0.3	82	0.4	65
Mental and behavioural disorders — Troubles mentaux et du comportement	19.4	3 117	16.8	2 854	15.3	2 840	15.0	3 077
Diseases of the nervous system — Maladies du système nerveux	16.7	2 735	14.8	3 716	19.9	3 905	20.6	4 056
Diseases of the circulatory system — Maladies de l'appareil circulatoire								
Total	293.4	52 339	282.6	51 862	277.2	51 261	270.9	49 833
Acute rheumatic fever and chronic rheumatic heart diseases — Rhumatisme articulaire aigu et cardiopathies rhumatismales chroniques	1.9	343	1.9	219	1.2	265	1.4	259
Hypertensive diseases — Maladies hypertensives	6.1	1 115	6.0	1 229	6.6	1 167	6.2	1 207
Ischaemic heart disease — Cardiopathie ischémique	161.1	28 861	155.9	28 304	151.3	27 632	146.0	26 606
Cerebrovascular disease — Maladie cérébrovasculaire	69.7	12 054	65.1	12 295	65.7	12 262	64.8	12 346
Diseases of arteries, arterioles and capillaries — Maladies des artères, artérioles et capillaires	15.9	2 917	15.8	2 734	14.6	2 841	15.0	2 612
Diseases of the respiratory system — Maladies de l'appareil respiratoire								
Total	56.7	13 192	71.2	9 618	51.4	9 657	51.0	10 988
Influenza — Grippe	0.9	211	1.1	120	0.6	71	0.4	66
Pneumonia — Pneumopathies	9.6	4 791	25.9	1 897	10.1	1 873	9.9	2 873
Chronic lower respiratory diseases — Maladies chroniques des voies respiratoires inférieures	38.1	6 403	34.6	6 133	32.8	6 103	32.2	5 998
Diseases of the digestive system — Maladies de l'appareil digestif								
Total	21.2	3 947	21.3	4 007	21.4	4 215	22.3	4 145
Gastric and duodenal ulcer — Ulcère de l'estomac et du duodénum	2.8	472	2.5	453	2.4	449	2.4	471

(See notes at end of table. — Voir notes à la fin du tableau.)

Cause of death — Cause de décès	Australia — Australie 2000 Rate Taux	Australia — Australie 2001 Number Nombre	Australia — Australie 2001 Rate Taux	Fiji — Fidji 1999 Number Nombre	New Zealand — Nouvelle Zélande 1995 Number Nombre	New Zealand — Nouvelle Zélande 1995 Rate Taux	New Zealand — Nouvelle Zélande 1996 Number Nombre	New Zealand — Nouvelle Zélande 1996 Rate Taux
TOTAL	672.4	128 657	662.7	3 400	27 956	761.0	28 379	760.4
Certain infectious and parasitic diseases — Certaines maladies infectieuses et parasitaires								
Total	8.7	1 699	8.8	254	208	5.7	208	5.6
Intestinal infectious diseases — Maladies infectieuses intestinales	0.2	42	0.2	10	8	♦0.2	12	♦0.3
Tuberculosis — Tuberculose	0.2	44	0.2	17	21	♦0.6	13	♦0.3
Tetanus — Tétanos	0.0	1	0.0	-	1	0.0	-	-
Diphtheria — Diphtérie		-		-	-	-	1	0.0
Whooping cough — Coqueluche	0.0	2	0.0	-	-	-	-	-
Meningococcal infection — Infection à méningocoques	♦0.2	41	0.2	1	17	♦0.5	17	♦0.5
Septicaemia — Septicémie	4.9	990	5.1	226	51	1.4	49	1.3
Acute poliomyelitis — Poliomyélite aiguë	-	-	-	-	1	0.0	-	-
Measles — Rougeole	♦0.1	27	♦0.1	-	10	♦0.3	19	♦0.5
Viral hepatitis — Hépatite virale								
Human immunodeficiency virus [HIV] disease — Maladies dues au virus de l'immunodéficience humaine (VIH)	0.7	120	0.6	-	57	1.6	38	1.0
Malaria — Paludisme	0.0	2	0.0	-	-	-	-	-
Neoplasms — Tumeurs	190.9	37 459	193.0	229	7 527	204.9	7 602	203.7
Malignant neoplasms — Tumeurs malignes								
Total	187.0	36 709	189.1	229	7 416	201.9	7 457	199.8
Malignant neoplasm of lip, oral cavity and pharynx — Tumeur maligne de la lèvre, de la cavité buccale et du pharynx	3.5	693	3.6	-	109	3.0	113	3.0
Malignant neoplasm of oesophagus — Tumeur maligne de l'oesophage	5.1	1 039	5.4	-	223	6.1	192	5.1
Malignant neoplasm of stomach — Tumeur maligne de l'estomac	6.2	1 209	6.2	23	263	7.2	297	8.0
Malignant neoplasm of colon, rectosigmoid junction, rectum, anus and anal canal — Tumeur maligne du côlon, de la jonction recto-sigmoïdienne, du rectum, de l'anus et du canal anal	24.6	4 754	24.5	23	1 119	30.5	1 133	30.4
Malignant neoplasm of liver and intrahepatic bile ducts — Tumeur maligne du foie et des voies bilaires intrahépatiques	3.9	777	4.0	-	80	2.2	72	1.9
Malignant neoplasm of pancreas — Tumeur maligne du pancréas	9.1	1 811	9.3	-	286	7.8	297	8.0
Malignant neoplasm of trachea, bronchus and lung — Tumeur maligne de la trachée, des bronches et du poumon	36.1	7 041	36.3	29	1 404	38.2	1 402	37.6
Malignant neoplasm of female breast — Tumeur maligne du sein chez la femme	▲32.7	2 594	▲33.2	59	639	...	683	...
Malignant neoplasm of cervix uteri — Tumeur maligne du col de l'utérus	▲3.4	271	▲3.5	60	96	...	83	...
Malignant neoplasm of prostate — Tumeur maligne de la prostate	▼104.6	2 718	▼103.7	-	554	...	502	...
Malignant neoplasm of lymphoid, haematopoietic and related tissue — Tumeurs malignes primitives ou présumées primitives des tissus lymphoïde, hématopoïétique et apparentés	19.6	3 628	18.7	35	617	16.8	670	18.0
Disorders of the blood and blood-forming organs and certain disorders involving the immune mechanism — Maladies du sang et des organes hématopoïétiques et certains troubles du système immunitaire								
Total	2.1	410	2.1	14	65	1.8	66	1.8
Anaemias — Anémies	1.0	183	0.9	14	33	0.9	39	1.0
Endocrine, nutritional and metabolic diseases — Maladies endocriniennes, nutritionnelles et métaboliques								
Total	21.8	4 333	22.3	191	712	19.4	834	22.3
Diabetes mellitus — Diabète sucré	15.7	3 093	15.9	185	509	13.9	597	16.0
Malnutrition — Malnutrition	0.3	79	0.4	6	13	♦0.4	13	♦0.3
Mental and behavioural disorders — Troubles mentaux et du comportement	16.1	2 696	13.9	-	471	12.8	555	14.9
Diseases of the nervous system — Maladies du système nerveux	21.2	4 221	21.7	4	494	13.4	451	12.1
Diseases of the circulatory system — Maladies de l'appareil circulatoire								
Total	260.2	49 534	255.2	1 052	11 755	320.0	11 786	315.8
Acute rheumatic fever and chronic rheumatic heart diseases — Rhumatisme articularie aigu et cardiopathies rhumatismales chroniques	1.4	253	1.3	29	129	3.5	130	3.5
Hypertensive diseases — Maladies hypertensives	6.3	1 224	6.3	140	247	6.7	289	7.7
Ischaemic heart disease — Cardiopathie ischémique	138.9	26 304	135.5	421	6 697	182.3	6 634	177.8
Cerebrovascular disease — Maladie cérébrovasculaire	64.5	12 201	62.8	461	2 716	73.9	2 659	71.2
Diseases of arteries, arterioles and capillaries — Maladies des artères, artérioles et capillaires	13.6	2 632	13.6	1	672	18.3	654	17.5
Diseases of the respiratory system — Maladies de l'appareil respiratoire								
Total	57.4	10 622	54.7	255	3 023	82.3	3 211	86.0
Influenza — Grippe	0.3	32	0.2	-	30	♦0.8	94	2.5
Pneumonia — Pneumopathies	15.0	2 685	13.8	158	1 169	31.8	1 092	29.3
Chronic lower respiratory diseases — Maladies chroniques des voies respiratoires inférieures	31.3	5 913	30.5	97	1 589	43.3	1 789	47.9
Diseases of the digestive system — Maladies de l'appareil digestif								
Total	21.6	4 053	20.9	114	765	20.8	776	20.8
Gastric and duodenal ulcer — Ulcère de l'estomac et du duodénum	2.5	442	2.3	11	165	4.5	141	3.8

(See notes at end of table. — Voir notes à la fin du tableau.)

New Zealand — Nouvelle Zélande

Cause of death — Cause de décès	1997		1998		1999		2000	
	Number Nombre	Rate Taux	Number Nombre	Rate Taux	Number Nombre	Rate Taux	Number Nombre	Rate Taux
TOTAL	27 611	730.2	26 457	693.5	28 224	735.9	26 718	692.6
Certain infectious and parasitic diseases — Certaines maladies infectieuses et parasitaires								
Total	209	5.5	159	4.2	158	4.1	173	4.5
Intestinal infectious diseases — Maladies infectieuses intestinales	24	♦0.6	6	♦0.2	12	♦0.3	20	♦0.5
Tuberculosis — Tuberculose	6	♦0.2	18	♦0.5	11	♦0.3	12	♦0.3
Tetanus — Tétanos	-	-	-	-	-	-	-	-
Diphtheria — Diphtérie	-	-	-	-	-	-	-	-
Whooping cough — Coqueluche	-	-	-	-	-	-	1	0.0
Meningococcal infection — Infection à méningocoques	25	♦0.7	17	♦0.4	19	♦0.5	15	♦0.4
Septicaemia — Septicémie	50	1.3	26	♦0.7	22	♦0.6	40	1.0
Acute poliomyelitis — Poliomyélite aiguë	-	-	-	-	-	-	-	-
Measles — Rougeole	-	-	-	-	-	-	-	-
Viral hepatitis — Hépatite virale	13	♦0.3	19	♦0.5	25	♦0.7	21	♦0.5
Human immunodeficiency virus [HIV] disease — Maladies dues au virus de l'immunodéficience humaine (VIH)	34	0.9	14	♦0.4	21	♦0.5	22	♦0.6
Malaria — Paludisme	1	0.0	-	-	-	-	-	-
Neoplasms — Tumeurs	7 423	196.3	7 736	202.8	7 837	204.3	7 771	201.4
Malignant neoplasms — Tumeurs malignes								
Total	7 282	192.6	7 581	198.7	7 674	200.1	7 620	197.5
Malignant neoplasm of lip, oral cavity and pharynx — Tumeur maligne de la lèvre, de la cavité buccale et du pharynx	92	2.4	90	2.4	114	3.0	133	3.4
Malignant neoplasm of oesophagus — Tumeur maligne de l'oesophage	212	5.6	162	4.2	172	4.5	187	4.8
Malignant neoplasm of stomach — Tumeur maligne de l'estomac	268	7.1	303	7.9	334	8.7	309	8.0
Malignant neoplasm of colon, rectosigmoid junction, rectum, anus and anal canal — Tumeur maligne du côlon, de la jonction recto-sigmoïdienne, du rectum, de l'anus et du canal anal	1 089	28.8	1 122	29.4	1 137	29.6	1 134	29.4
Malignant neoplasm of liver and intrahepatic bile ducts — Tumeur maligne du foie et des voies biliaires intrahépatiques	86	2.3	79	2.1	76	2.0	143	3.7
Malignant neoplasm of pancreas — Tumeur maligne du pancréas	284	7.5	344	9.0	298	7.8	312	8.1
Malignant neoplasm of trachea, bronchus and lung — Tumeur maligne de la trachée, des bronches et du poumon	1 412	37.3	1 381	36.2	1 443	37.6	1 406	36.4
Malignant neoplasm of female breast — Tumeur maligne du sein chez la femme	620	...	628	▲41.7	647	▲42.9	622	▲41.0
Malignant neoplasm of cervix uteri — Tumeur maligne du col de l'utérus	73	...	77	▲5.1	71	▲4.7	66	▲4.3
Malignant neoplasm of prostate — Tumeur maligne de la prostate	525	...	524	▼114.2	552	▼117.6	594	▼123.4
Malignant neoplasm of lymphoid, haematopoietic and related tissue — Tumeurs malignes primitives ou présumées primitives des tissus lymphoïde, hématopoïétique et apparentés	701	18.5	740	19.4	743	19.4	675	17.5
Disorders of the blood and blood-forming organs and certain disorders involving the immune mechanism — Maladies du sang et des organes hématopoïétiques et certains troubles du système immunitaire								
Total	56	1.5	67	1.8	75	2.0	46	1.2
Anaemias — Anémies	28	♦0.7	32	0.8	34	0.9	22	♦0.6
Endocrine, nutritional and metabolic diseases — Maladies endocriniennes, nutritionnelles et métaboliques								
Total	889	23.5	1 000	26.2	993	25.9	1 007	26.1
Diabetes mellitus — Diabète sucré	633	16.7	730	19.1	740	19.3	802	20.8
Malnutrition — Malnutrition	14	♦0.4	8	♦0.2	7	♦0.2	5	♦0.1
Mental and behavioural disorders — Troubles mentaux et du comportement	631	16.7	802	21.0	862	22.5	541	14.0
Diseases of the nervous system — Maladies du système nerveux	467	12.3	477	12.5	491	12.8	798	20.7
Diseases of the circulatory system — Maladies de l'appareil circulatoire								
Total	11 423	302.1	10 863	284.7	11 695	304.9	10 920	283.1
Acute rheumatic fever and chronic rheumatic heart diseases — Rhumatisme articulaire aigu et cardiopathies rhumatismales chroniques	135	3.6	139	3.6	149	3.9	172	4.5
Hypertensive diseases — Maladies hypertensives	262	6.9	284	7.4	232	6.0	218	5.7
Ischaemic heart disease — Cardiopathie ischémique	6 370	168.5	6 204	162.6	6 571	171.3	5 973	154.8
Cerebrovascular disease — Maladie cérébrovasculaire	2 565	67.8	2 491	65.3	2 835	73.9	2 668	69.2
Diseases of arteries, arterioles and capillaries — Maladies des artères, artérioles et capillaires	648	17.1	534	14.0	600	15.6	552	14.3
Diseases of the respiratory system — Maladies de l'appareil respiratoire								
Total	2 910	77.0	2 148	56.3	2 730	71.2	2 053	53.2
Influenza — Grippe	16	♦0.4	7	♦0.2	27	♦0.7	2	♦0.1
Pneumonia — Pneumopathies	972	25.7	415	10.9	623	16.2	345	8.9
Chronic lower respiratory diseases — Maladies chroniques des voies respiratoires inférieures	1 717	45.4	1 603	42.0	1 918	50.0	1 560	40.4
Diseases of the digestive system — Maladies de l'appareil digestif								
Total	734	19.4	623	16.3	688	17.9	721	18.7
Gastric and duodenal ulcer — Ulcère de l'estomac et du duodénum	126	3.3	109	2.9	96	2.5	108	2.8

21. Death and death rates by cause: 1995 - 2002
Décès selon la cause, nombres et taux: 1995 - 2002
(continued — suite)

(See notes at end of table. — Voir notes à la fin du tableau.)

Cause of death — Cause de décès	Egypt — Égypte
	2000
	Number Nombre
Diseases of the digestive system — Maladies de l'appareil digestif	
Diseases of the liver — Maladies du foie	28 011
Diseases of the musculoskeletal system and connective tissue — Maladies du système ostéo-articulaire, des muscles et du tissu conjonctif	168
Diseases of the genitourinary system — Maladies de l'appareil génito-urinaire	
Total	9 997
Disorders of kidney and ureter — Affections du rein et de l'uretère	9 696
Hyperplasia of prostate — Hyperplasie de la prostate	162
Pregnancy, childbirth and the puerperium — Grossesse, accouchement et puerpéralité	
Total	492
Pregnancy with abortive outcome — Grossesse se terminant par un avortement	5
Other direct obstetric causes — Autres décès maternels directs	480
Indirect obstetric causes — Décès maternels indirects	3
Certain conditions originating in the perinatal period — Certaines affections dont l'origine se situe dans la période périnatale	5 876
Congenital malformations, deformations and chromosomal abnormalities — Malformations congénitales et anomalies chromosomiques	6 218
Symptoms, signs and abnormal clinical and laboratory findings, not elsewhere classified — Symptômes, signes et résultats anormaux d'examens cliniques et de laboratoire, non classés ailleurs	81 441
All other diseases — Toutes autres maladies	368
External causes — Causes externes	
Total	16 709
Accidents — Accidents	
Total	8 899
Transport accidents — Accidents de transport	5 355
Falls — Chutes	574
Accidental drowning and submersion — Noyade et submersion accidentelles	1 591
Exposure to smoke, fire and flames — Exposition à la fumée, au feu et aux flammes	209
Accidental poisoning by and exposure to noxious substances — Intoxication accidentelle par des substances nocives et exposition à ces substances	106
Intentional self-harm — Lésions auto-infligées	49
Assault — Agresssions	50
All other external causes — Toutes autres causes externes	7 711

21. Death and death rates by cause: 1995 - 2002
Décès selon la cause, nombres et taux: 1995 - 2002 (continued — suite)

(See notes at end of table. — Voir notes à la fin du tableau.)

Mauritius - Maurice

Cause of death — Cause de décès	1995		1996		1997		1998	
	Number Nombre	Rate Taux	Number Nombre	Rate Taux	Number Nombre	Rate Taux	Number Nombre	Rate Taux
Diseases of the digestive system — Maladies de l'appareil digestif								
Diseases of the liver — Maladies du foie	187	16.7	222	19.6	201	17.5	178	15.3
Diseases of the musculoskeletal system and connective tissue — Maladies du système ostéo-articularie, des muscles et du tissu conjonctif	4	♦0.4	10	♦0.9	6	♦0.5	5	♦0.4
Diseases of the genitourinary system — Maladies de l'appareil génito-urinaire								
Total	332	29.6	434	38.3	379	33.0	260	22.4
Disorders of kidney and ureter — Affections du rein et de l'uretère	325	29.0	429	37.8	374	32.6	254	21.9
Hyperplasia of prostate — Hyperplasie de la prostate	2	♦ ▼2.5	-	-	1	♦ ▼1.2	-	-
Pregnancy, childbirth and the puerperium — Grossesse, accouchement et puerpéralité								
Total	12	♦ ●58.2	6	♦ ●29.3	10	♦ ●50.0	4	♦ ●20.6
Pregnancy with abortive outcome — Grossesse se terminant par un avortement	1	♦ ●4.9	1	♦ ●4.9	5	♦ ●25.0	1	♦ ●5.1
Other direct obstetric causes — Autres décès maternels directs	9	♦ ●43.7	4	♦ ●19.5	5	♦ ●25.0	3	♦ ●15.4
Indirect obstetric causes — Décès maternels indirects	2	♦ ●9.7	1	♦ ●4.9	-	-	-	-
Certain conditions originating in the perinatal period — Certaines affections dont l'origine se situe dans la période périnatale	261	●1266.7	321	●1566.0	293	●1464.1	258	●1327.6
Congenital malformations, deformations and chromosomal abnormalities — Malformations congénitales et anomalies chromosomiques	80	●388.3	58	●283.0	36	●179.9	64	●329.3
Symptoms, signs and abnormal clinical and laboratory findings, not elsewhere classified — Symptômes, signes et résultats anormaux d'examens cliniques et de laboratoire, non classés ailleurs	547	48.7	610	53.8	677	59.0	395	34.0
All other diseases — Toutes autres maladies	3	♦0.3	3	♦0.3	1	♦0.1	4	♦0.3
External causes — Causes externes								
Total	551	49.1	525	46.3	469	40.8	492	42.4
Accidents — Accidents								
Total	387	34.5	341	30.1	326	28.4	309	26.6
Transport accidents — Accidents de transport	194	17.3	147	13.0	145	12.6	157	13.5
Falls — Chutes	13	♦1.2	18	♦1.6	22	♦1.9	32	2.8
Accidental drowning and submersion — Noyade et submersion accidentelles	53	4.7	60	5.3	47	4.1	38	3.3
Exposure to smoke, fire and flames — Exposition à la fumée, au feu et aux flammes	54	4.8	48	4.2	59	5.1	33	2.8
Accidental poisoning by and exposure to noxious substances — Intoxication accidentelle par des substances nocives et exposition à ces substances	3	♦0.3	1	♦0.1	-	-	1	♦0.1
Intentional self-harm — Lésions auto-infligées	147	13.1	153	13.5	122	10.6	155	13.4
Assault — Agressions	15	♦1.3	30	♦2.6	20	♦1.7	28	♦2.4
All other external causes — Toutes autres causes externes	2	♦0.2	1	♦0.1	1	♦0.1	-	-

21. Death and death rates by cause: 1995 - 2002
Décès selon la cause, nombres et taux: 1995 - 2002 (continued — suite)

(See notes at end of table. — Voir notes à la fin du tableau.)

	Mauritius - Maurice				South Africa — Afrique du Sud		Anguilla	
	1999		2000		1995	1996	1995	2000
Cause of death — Cause de décès	Number Nombre	Rate Taux	Number Nombre	Rate Taux	Number Nombre			
Diseases of the digestive system — Maladies de l'appareil digestif								
Diseases of the liver — Maladies du foie	183	15.6	170	14.3	2 011	4 414	-	-
Diseases of the musculoskeletal system and connective tissue — Maladies du système ostéo-articularie, des muscles et du tissu conjonctif	11	♦0.9	14	♦1.2	96	166	-	-
Diseases of the genitourinary system — Maladies de l'appareil génito-urinaire								
Total	291	24.8	255	21.5	3 632	4 691	2	4
Disorders of kidney and ureter — Affections du rein et de l'uretère	286	24.3	248	20.9	3 399	4 326	2	4
Hyperplasia of prostate — Hyperplasie de la prostate	-	-	1	♦ ▼1.0	32	89	-	-
Pregnancy, childbirth and the puerperium — Grossesse, accouchement et puerpéralité								
Total	7	♦ *34.5	3	♦ *14.8	499	606	-	-
Pregnancy with abortive outcome — Grossesse se terminant par un avortement	1	♦ *4.9	-	-	107	123	-	-
Other direct obstetric causes — Autres décès maternels directs	6	♦ *29.5	3	♦ *14.8	352	419	-	-
Indirect obstetric causes — Décès maternels indirects	-	-	-	-	40	64		
Certain conditions originating in the perinatal period — Certaines affections dont l'origine se situe dans la période périnatale	230	*1132.4	204	*1009.7	8 226	10 005	3	1
Congenital malformations, deformations and chromosomal abnormalities — Malformations congénitales et anomalies chromosomiques	74	*364.3	73	*361.3	1 350	1 525	-	
Symptoms, signs and abnormal clinical and laboratory findings, not elsewhere classified — Symptômes, signes et résultats anormaux d'examens cliniques et de laboratoire, non classés ailleurs	366	31.1	295	24.9	40 766	41 541	21	4
All other diseases — Toutes autres maladies	4	♦0.3	6	♦0.5	95	46	-	-
External causes — Causes externes								
Total	550	46.8	491	41.4	47 120	52 959	-	4
Accidents — Accidents								
Total	337	28.7	318	26.8	...	...	-	3
Transport accidents — Accidents de transport	189	16.1	181	15.3	...	...	-	2
Falls — Chutes	29	♦2.5	28	♦2.4	...	...	-	1
Accidental drowning and submersion — Noyade et submersion accidentelles	31	2.6	36	3.0	...	...	-	-
Exposure to smoke, fire and flames — Exposition à la fumée, au feu et aux flammes ..	38	3.2	33	2.8	...	...	-	-
Accidental poisoning by and exposure to noxious substances — Intoxication accidentelle par des substances nocives et exposition à ces substances	6	♦0.5	-	-	...	...	-	-
Intentional self-harm — Lésions auto-infligées	174	14.8	137	11.5	...	...	-	1
Assault — Agresssions	33	2.8	32	2.7	...	...	-	-
All other external causes — Toutes autres causes externes	6	♦0.5	4	♦0.3	...	...	-	-

21. Death and death rates by cause: 1995 - 2002
Décès selon la cause, nombres et taux: 1995 - 2002 (continued — suite)

(See notes at end of table. — Voir notes à la fin du tableau.)

Cause of death — Cause de décès	Antigua and Barbuda — Antigua-et-Barbuda	Bahamas						Barbados — Barbade
	1995	1995	1996	1997	1998	1999	2000	1995
		Number — Nombre						
Diseases of the digestive system — Maladies de l'appareil digestif								
Diseases of the liver — Maladies du foie	8	35	16	34	33	28	47	34
Diseases of the musculoskeletal system and connective tissue — Maladies du système ostéo-articularie, des muscles et du tissu conjonctif	1	10	5	8	13	20	13	8
Diseases of the genitourinary system — Maladies de l'appareil génito-urinaire								
Total	13	19	24	23	42	37	36	45
Disorders of kidney and ureter — Affections du rein et de l'uretère	13	14	16	16	16	34	28	31
Hyperplasia of prostate — Hyperplasie de la prostate	-	2	1	2	-	-	-	2
Pregnancy, childbirth and the puerperium — Grossesse, accouchement et puerpéralité								
Total	2	4	-	-	1	1	2	-
Pregnancy with abortive outcome — Grossesse se terminant par un avortement	-	2	-	-	-	-	-	-
Other direct obstetric causes — Autres décès maternels directs	2	2	-	-	1	1	1	-
Indirect obstetric causes — Décès maternels indirects	-	-	-	-	-	-	1	-
Certain conditions originating in the perinatal period — Certaines affections dont l'origine se situe dans la période périnatale	18	55	68	47	40	25	29	29
Congenital malformations, deformations and chromosomal abnormalities — Malformations congénitales et anomalies chromosomiques	4	21	12	26	13	4	13	13
Symptoms, signs and abnormal clinical and laboratory findings, not elsewhere classified — Symptômes, signes et résultats anormaux d'examens cliniques et de laboratoire, non classés ailleurs	61	27	57	23	26	19	24	65
All other diseases — Toutes autres maladies	7	10	9	10	17	9	13	20
External causes — Causes externes								
Total	15	111	121	166	183	174	217	95
Accidents — Accidents								
Total	8	50	50	101	113	104	118	58
Transport accidents — Accidents de transport	2	20	31	49	67	51	75	27
Falls — Chutes	-	7	2	4	6	8	1	12
Accidental drowning and submersion — Noyade et submersion accidentelles	2	14	7	17	26	19	16	15
Exposure to smoke, fire and flames — Exposition à la fumée, au feu et aux flammes	1	6	5	13	10	10	5	2
Accidental poisoning by and exposure to noxious substances — Intoxication accidentelle par des substances nocives et exposition à ces substances	-	-	-	1	1	3	1	-
Intentional self-harm — Lésions auto-infligées	-	3	3	2	3	6	11	17
Assault — Agresssions	7	42	41	47	49	54	63	17
All other external causes — Toutes autres causes externes	-	16	27	16	18	10	25	3

21. Death and death rates by cause: 1995 - 2002
Décès selon la cause, nombres et taux: 1995 - 2002 (continued — suite)

(See notes at end of table. — Voir notes à la fin du tableau.)

Cause of death — Cause de décès	Barbados — Barbade 1995 Rate Taux	Barbados 2000 Number Nombre	Barbados 2000 Rate Taux	Belize 1995 Number Nombre	Belize 1996 Number Nombre	Belize 1997 Number Nombre	Belize 1997 Rate Taux	Belize 1998 Number Nombre
Diseases of the digestive system — Maladies de l'appareil digestif								
Diseases of the liver — Maladies du foie	12.9	40	15.0	6	7	22	♦9.6	14
Diseases of the musculoskeletal system and connective tissue — Maladies du système ostéo-articulaire, des muscles et du tissu conjonctif	♦3.0	10	♦3.7	-	-	-	-	1
Diseases of the genitourinary system — Maladies de l'appareil génito-urinaire								
Total	17.0	79	29.5	23	15	37	16.1	33
Disorders of kidney and ureter — Affections du rein et de l'uretère	11.7	58	21.7	19	12	34	14.8	28
Hyperplasia of prostate — Hyperplasie de la prostate	...	1	...	-	1	1	♦▼7.5	2
Pregnancy, childbirth and the puerperium — Grossesse, accouchement et puerpéralité								
Total	-	1	♦ *26.6	1	-	3	♦ *40.8	9
Pregnancy with abortive outcome — Grossesse se terminant par un avortement	-	-	-	1	-	-	-	-
Other direct obstetric causes — Autres décès maternels directs	-	-	-	-	-	3	♦ *40.8	9
Indirect obstetric causes — Décès maternels indirects	-	1	♦ *26.6	-	-	-	-	-
Certain conditions originating in the perinatal period — Certaines affections dont l'origine se situe dans la période périnatale	♦ *835.0	41	*1089.8	42	40	83	*1129.6	71
Congenital malformations, deformations and chromosomal abnormalities — Malformations congénitales et anomalies chromosomiques	♦ *374.3	8	♦ *212.7	6	7	18	♦ *245.0	19
Symptoms, signs and abnormal clinical and laboratory findings, not elsewhere classified — Symptômes, signes et résultats anormaux d'examens cliniques et de laboratoire, non classés ailleurs	24.6	82	30.7	120	133	106	46.1	70
All other diseases — Toutes autres maladies	♦7.6	60	22.4	1	4	1	♦0.4	4
External causes — Causes externes								
Total	36.0	101	37.8	123	125	135	58.7	221
Accidents — Accidents								
Total	22.0	54	20.2	100	104	112	48.7	158
Transport accidents — Accidents de transport	♦10.2	36	13.5	48	40	82	35.7	101
Falls — Chutes	♦4.5	1	♦0.4	-	1	-	-	6
Accidental drowning and submersion — Noyade et submersion accidentelles	♦5.7	11	♦4.1	16	23	-	-	35
Exposure to smoke, fire and flames — Exposition à la fumée, au feu et aux flammes ..	♦0.8	1	♦0.4	-	-	-	-	-
Accidental poisoning by and exposure to noxious substances — Intoxication accidentelle par des substances nocives et exposition à ces substances	-	-	-	7	12	-	-	-
Intentional self-harm — Lésions auto-infligées	♦6.4	10	♦3.7	14	8	1	♦0.4	12
Assault — Agressions	♦6.4	28	♦10.5	-	-	18	♦7.8	49
All other external causes — Toutes autres causes externes	♦1.1	9	♦3.4	9	13	4	♦1.7	2

(See notes at end of table. — Voir notes à la fin du tableau.)

Cause of death — Cause de décès	Belize					Bermuda — Bermudes	British Virgin Islands — Iles Vierges britanniques	
	1998	1999		2000		1995	1995	1996
	Rate Taux	Number Nombre	Rate Taux	Number Nombre	Rate Taux	Number Nombre	Number Nombre	
Diseases of the digestive system — Maladies de l'appareil digestif								
Diseases of the liver — Maladies du foie	♦5.9	20	♦8.2	30	♦12.0	5	1	3
Diseases of the musculoskeletal system and connective tissue — Maladies du système ostéo-articulaire, des muscles et du tissu conjonctif	♦0.4	1	♦0.4	1	♦0.4	4	-	1
Diseases of the genitourinary system — Maladies de l'appareil génito-urinaire								
Total	13.8	31	12.8	29	♦11.6	12	2	1
Disorders of kidney and ureter — Affections du rein et de l'uretère	♦11.7	27	♦11.1	20	♦8.0	11	1	1
Hyperplasia of prostate — Hyperplasie de la prostate	♦ ▼13.8	-	-	-	-	-	-	
Pregnancy, childbirth and the puerperium — Grossesse, accouchement et puerpéralité								
Total	♦ *150.4	3	♦ *48.2	5	♦ *68.4	-	-	-
Pregnancy with abortive outcome — Grossesse se terminant par un avortement	-	-	-	-	-	-	-	-
Other direct obstetric causes — Autres décès maternels directs	♦ *150.4	3	♦ *48.2	5	♦ *68.4	-	-	-
Indirect obstetric causes — Décès maternels indirects	-	-	-	-	-	-	-	-
Certain conditions originating in the perinatal period — Certaines affections dont l'origine se situe dans la période périnatale	*1186.1	60	*964.9	72	*984.5	3	6	3
Congenital malformations, deformations and chromosomal abnormalities — Malformations congénitales et anomalies chromosomiques	♦ *317.4	18	♦ *289.5	28	♦ *382.9	-		1
Symptoms, signs and abnormal clinical and laboratory findings, not elsewhere classified — Symptômes, signes et résultats anormaux d'examens cliniques et de laboratoire, non classés ailleurs	29.4	54	22.2	32	12.8	2	1	1
All other diseases — Toutes autres maladies	♦1.7	2	♦0.8	4	♦1.6	1	1	-
External causes — Causes externes								
Total	92.7	188	77.3	210	84.1	25	6	11
Accidents — Accidents								
Total	66.2	129	53.1	130	52.0	23	4	9
Transport accidents — Accidents de transport	42.3	76	31.3	71	28.4	11	2	1
Falls — Chutes	♦2.5	7	♦2.9	8	♦3.2	-	-	1
Accidental drowning and submersion — Noyade et submersion accidentelles	14.7	18	♦7.4	25	*10.0	2	1	3
Exposure to smoke, fire and flames — Exposition à la fumée, au feu et aux flammes	-	6	♦2.5	3	♦1.2	-	-	-
Accidental poisoning by and exposure to noxious substances — Intoxication accidentelle par des substances nocives et exposition à ces substances	-			4	♦1.6	3	-	-
Intentional self-harm — Lésions auto-infligées	♦5.0	18	♦7.4	18	♦7.2	1	-	-
Assault — Agressions	20.5	40	16.5	57	22.8	-	2	2
All other external causes — Toutes autres causes externes	♦0.8	1	♦0.4	5	♦2.0	1	-	

21. Death and death rates by cause: 1995 - 2002
Décès selon la cause, nombres et taux: 1995 - 2002 (continued — suite)

(See notes at end of table. — Voir notes à la fin du tableau.)

Cause of death — Cause de décès	British Virgin Islands — Iles Vierges britanniques		Canada[1]					
	1997	1998	1995		1996		1997	
	Number Nombre	Number Nombre	Number Nombre	Rate Taux	Number Nombre	Rate Taux	Number Nombre	Rate Taux
Diseases of the digestive system — Maladies de l'appareil digestif								
Diseases of the liver — Maladies du foie	3	-	2 235	7.6	2 115	7.1	2 030	6.8
Diseases of the musculoskeletal system and connective tissue — Maladies du système ostéo-articularie, des muscles et du tissu conjonctif	-	-	948	3.2	966	3.3	1 032	3.5
Diseases of the genitourinary system — Maladies de l'appareil génito-urinaire								
Total	1	-	3 472	11.8	3 614	12.2	3 616	12.1
Disorders of kidney and ureter — Affections du rein et de l'uretère	1	-	2 725	9.3	2 812	9.5	2 746	9.2
Hyperplasia of prostate — Hyperplasie de la prostate	-	-	58	▼1.6	44	▼1.2	54	▼1.5
Pregnancy, childbirth and the puerperium — Grossesse, accouchement et puerpéralité								
Total	-	-	17	♦ *4.5	18	♦ *4.9	19	♦ *5.5
Pregnancy with abortive outcome — Grossesse se terminant par un avortement	-	-	1	♦ *0.3	3	♦ *0.8	4	♦ *1.1
Other direct obstetric causes — Autres décès maternels directs	-	-	15	♦ *4.0	15	♦ *4.1	14	♦ *4.0
Indirect obstetric causes — Décès maternels indirects	-	-	1	♦ *0.3	-	-	1	♦ *0.3
Certain conditions originating in the perinatal period — Certaines affections dont l'origine se situe dans la période périnatale	1	3	994	*263.0	982	*268.2	895	*256.7
Congenital malformations, deformations and chromosomal abnormalities — Malformations congénitales et anomalies chromosomiques	-	-	1 137	*300.8	1 066	*291.1	955	*274.0
Symptoms, signs and abnormal clinical and laboratory findings, not elsewhere classified — Symptômes, signes et résultats anormaux d'examens cliniques et de laboratoire, non classés ailleurs	1	3	3 257	11.1	3 661	12.4	5 946	19.9
All other diseases — Toutes autres maladies	-	-	246	0.8	252	0.9	247	0.8
External causes — Causes externes								
Total	4	10	13 563	46.3	13 459	45.5	13 049	43.6
Accidents — Accidents								
Total	3	10	8 820	30.1	8 660	29.2	8 626	28.8
Transport accidents — Accidents de transport	2	-	3 488	11.9	3 257	11.0	3 288	11.0
Falls — Chutes	-	-	2 432	8.3	2 684	9.1	2 622	8.8
Accidental drowning and submersion — Noyade et submersion accidentelles	1	9	360	1.2	344	1.2	283	0.9
Exposure to smoke, fire and flames — Exposition à la fumée, au feu et aux flammes ..	-	-	283	1.0	279	0.9	272	0.9
Accidental poisoning by and exposure to noxious substances — Intoxication accidentelle par des substances nocives et exposition à ces substances	-	-	744	2.5	692	2.3	703	2.4
Intentional self-harm — Lésions auto-infligées	1	-	3 970	13.5	3 941	13.3	3 681	12.3
Assault — Agresssions	-	-	489	1.7	511	1.7	431	1.4
All other external causes — Toutes autres causes externes	-	-	284	1.0	347	1.2	311	1.0

21. Death and death rates by cause: 1995 - 2002
Décès selon la cause, nombres et taux: 1995 - 2002 (continued — suite)

(See notes at end of table. — Voir notes à la fin du tableau.)

Cause of death — Cause de décès	Canada[1]						Cayman Islands — Iles Caïmanes	
	1998		1999		2000		1995	1996
	Number Nombre	Rate Taux	Number Nombre	Rate Taux	Number Nombre	Rate Taux	Number Nombre	
Diseases of the digestive system — Maladies de l'appareil digestif								
Diseases of the liver — Maladies du foie	2 166	7.2	2 091	6.9	2 673	8.7	2	1
Diseases of the musculoskeletal system and connective tissue — Maladies du système ostéo-articularie, des muscles et du tissu conjonctif	933	3.1	1 060	3.5	1 394	4.5	-	-
Diseases of the genitourinary system — Maladies de l'appareil génito-urinaire								
Total	3 887	12.9	3 974	13.1	4 137	13.5	7	1
Disorders of kidney and ureter — Affections du rein et de l'uretère	2 999	9.9	3 048	10.0	3 369	11.0	6	1
Hyperplasia of prostate — Hyperplasie de la prostate	51	▼1.3	44	...	51	...	-	-
Pregnancy, childbirth and the puerperium — Grossesse, accouchement et puerpéralité								
Total	13	♦ *3.8	8	♦ *2.4	11	♦ *3.4	-	-
Pregnancy with abortive outcome — Grossesse se terminant par un avortement	1	♦ *0.3	-	-	1	♦ *0.3	-	-
Other direct obstetric causes — Autres décès maternels directs	11	♦ *3.2	6	♦ *1.8	6	♦ *1.8	-	-
Indirect obstetric causes — Décès maternels indirects	1	♦ *0.3	2	♦ *0.6	2	♦ *0.6	-	-
Certain conditions originating in the perinatal period — Certaines affections dont l'origine se situe dans la période périnatale	812	*237.1	816	*242.0	898	*273.9	1	1
Congenital malformations, deformations and chromosomal abnormalities — Malformations congénitales et anomalies chromosomiques	974	*284.4	966	*286.4	920	*280.6	4	2
Symptoms, signs and abnormal clinical and laboratory findings, not elsewhere classified — Symptômes, signes et résultats anormaux d'examens cliniques et de laboratoire, non classés ailleurs	3 276	10.9	2 222	7.3	2 737	8.9	3	1
All other diseases — Toutes autres maladies	266	0.9	281	0.9	323	1.1	-	-
External causes — Causes externes								
Total	13 262	44.0	13 996	46.0	13 249	43.2	11	15
Accidents — Accidents								
Total	8 758	29.0	9 092	29.9	8 486	27.7	7	14
Transport accidents — Accidents de transport	3 104	10.6	3 300	10.9	3 120	10.2	7	5
Falls — Chutes	2 620	8.7	2 866	9.4	1 562	5.1	-	1
Accidental drowning and submersion — Noyade et submersion accidentelles	309	1.0	321	1.1	287	0.9	-	6
Exposure to smoke, fire and flames — Exposition à la fumée, au feu et aux flammes ..	245	0.8	285	0.9	242	0.8	-	-
Accidental poisoning by and exposure to noxious substances — Intoxication accidentelle par des substances nocives et exposition à ces substances	966	3.2	986	3.2	960	3.1	-	-
Intentional self-harm — Lésions auto-infligées	3 699	12.3	4 074	13.4	3 605	11.7	1	-
Assault — Agresssions	467	1.5	462	1.5	463	1.5	2	1
All other external causes — Toutes autres causes externes	338	1.1	368	1.2	695	2.3	1	-

(See notes at end of table. — Voir notes à la fin du tableau.)

Cause of death — Cause de décès	Cayman Islands — Iles Caïmanes				Costa Rica			
	1997	1998	1999	2000	1995	1996	1997	1998
				Number Nombre				
Diseases of the digestive system — Maladies de l'appareil digestif	-	1	-	2	400	354	397	448
Diseases of the liver — Maladies du foie								
Diseases of the musculoskeletal system and connective tissue — Maladies du système ostéo-articularie, des muscles et du tissu conjonctif	-	-	-	-	45	67	85	73
Diseases of the genitourinary system — Maladies de l'appareil génito-urinaire								
Total	2	2	1	1	290	313	341	382
Disorders of kidney and ureter — Affections du rein et de l'uretère	1	1	1	1	229	248	267	312
Hyperplasia of prostate — Hyperplasie de la prostate	-	-	-	-	6	11	12	4
Pregnancy, childbirth and the puerperium — Grossesse, accouchement et puerpéralité								
Total	-	-	-	1	16	23	29	14
Pregnancy with abortive outcome — Grossesse se terminant par un avortement	-	-	-	-	2	4	5	3
Other direct obstetric causes — Autres décès maternels directs	-	-	-	1	12	15	21	10
Indirect obstetric causes — Décès maternels indirects	-	-	-	-	2	4	3	1
Certain conditions originating in the perinatal period — Certaines affections dont l'origine se situe dans la période périnatale	7	4	-	-	521	450	508	460
Congenital malformations, deformations and chromosomal abnormalities — Malformations congénitales et anomalies chromosomiques	-	-	-	-	351	307	411	314
Symptoms, signs and abnormal clinical and laboratory findings, not elsewhere classified — Symptômes, signes et résultats anormaux d'examens cliniques et de laboratoire, non classés ailleurs	1	1	2	4	296	243	320	401
All other diseases — Toutes autres maladies	-	1	-	-	62	61	57	49
External causes — Causes externes								
Total	14	9	14	14	1 666	1 570	1 636	1 710
Accidents — Accidents								
Total	11	7	10	9	1 156	1 043	1 063	1 099
Transport accidents — Accidents de transport	4	1	6	4	544	441	583	628
Falls — Chutes	-	1	-	-	211	180	68	75
Accidental drowning and submersion — Noyade et submersion accidentelles	4	3	1	2	172	187	128	160
Exposure to smoke, fire and flames — Exposition à la fumée, au feu et aux flammes	1	-	1	-	12	17	16	10
Accidental poisoning by and exposure to noxious substances — Intoxication accidentelle par des substances nocives et exposition à ces substances	-	-	-	-	16	10	23	8
Intentional self-harm — Lésions auto-infligées	-	-	1	-	211	210	188	223
Assault — Agresssions	1	-	-	4	179	195	205	214
All other external causes — Toutes autres causes externes	2	1	3	1	120	122	180	174

(See notes at end of table. — Voir notes à la fin du tableau.)

Cause of death — Cause de décès	Costa Rica				Cuba			
	1999	2000	2001	2002	1995		1996	
			Number Nombre			Rate Taux	Number Nombre	Rate Taux
Diseases of the digestive system — Maladies de l'appareil digestif								
Diseases of the liver — Maladies du foie	463	455	435	510	900	8.2	924	8.4
Diseases of the musculoskeletal system and connective tissue — Maladies du système ostéo-articulaire, des muscles et du tissu conjonctif	100	99	93	95	309	2.8	328	3.0
Diseases of the genitourinary system — Maladies de l'appareil génito-urinaire								
Total	327	342	332	331	919	8.4	860	7.8
Disorders of kidney and ureter — Affections du rein et de l'uretère	264	271	266	271	646	5.9	567	5.2
Hyperplasia of prostate — Hyperplasie de la prostate	8	6	8	4	113	▼9.4	96	▼7.9
Pregnancy, childbirth and the puerperium — Grossesse, accouchement et puerpéralité								
Total	15	28	24	27	70	*47.6	51	*36.4
Pregnancy with abortive outcome — Grossesse se terminant par un avortement	1	3	2	-	9	♦ *6.1	8	♦ *5.7
Other direct obstetric causes — Autres décès maternels directs	11	20	15	20	39	*26.5	26	♦ *18.5
Indirect obstetric causes — Décès maternels indirects	3	5	7	6	22	♦ *14.9	17	♦ *12.1
Certain conditions originating in the perinatal period — Certaines affections dont l'origine se situe dans la période périnatale	471	387	411	404	578	*392.7	451	*321.5
Congenital malformations, deformations and chromosomal abnormalities — Malformations congénitales et anomalies chromosomiques	318	305	321	292	645	*438.3	634	*452.0
Symptoms, signs and abnormal clinical and laboratory findings, not elsewhere classified — Symptômes, signes et résultats anormaux d'examens cliniques et de laboratoire, non classés ailleurs	161	147	180	392	330	3.0	376	3.4
All other diseases — Toutes autres maladies	61	53	51	43	252	2.3	260	2.4
External causes — Causes externes								
Total	1 798	1 817	1 768	1 851	9 282	84.5	8 738	79.4
Accidents — Accidents								
Total	1 171	1 190	1 170	1 183	5 847	53.3	5 673	51.5
Transport accidents — Accidents de transport	671	696	676	677	2 320	21.1	2 168	19.7
Falls — Chutes	66	65	72	82	1 929	17.6	2 024	18.4
Accidental drowning and submersion — Noyade et submersion accidentelles	161	125	143	153	359	3.3	297	2.7
Exposure to smoke, fire and flames — Exposition à la fumée, au feu et aux flammes	14	36	6	7	157	1.4	129	1.2
Accidental poisoning by and exposure to noxious substances — Intoxication accidentelle par des substances nocives et exposition à ces substances	10	10	10	14	73	0.7	73	0.7
Intentional self-harm — Lésions auto-infligées	233	242	206	281	2 223	20.2	2 015	18.3
Assault — Agressions	236	241	243	236	852	7.8	732	6.7
All other external causes — Toutes autres causes externes	158	144	149	151	360	3.3	318	2.9

(See notes at end of table. — Voir notes à la fin du tableau.)

Cuba

Cause of death — Cause de décès	1997		1998		1999		2000	
	Number Nombre	Rate Taux	Number Nombre	Rate Taux	Number Nombre	Rate Taux	Number Nombre	Rate Taux
Diseases of the digestive system — Maladies de l'appareil digestif								
Diseases of the liver — Maladies du foie	937	8.5	980	8.8	1 127	10.1	988	8.8
Diseases of the musculoskeletal system and connective tissue — Maladies du système ostéo-articularie, des muscles et du tissu conjonctif	334	3.0	362	3.3	350	3.1	332	3.0
Diseases of the genitourinary system — Maladies de l'appareil génito-urinaire								
Total	779	7.0	854	7.7	801	7.2	701	6.3
Disorders of kidney and ureter — Affections du rein et de l'uretère	526	4.8	545	4.9	503	4.5	455	4.1
Hyperplasia of prostate — Hyperplasie de la prostate	77	▼6.2	95	▼7.5	93	▼7.1	76	▼5.7
Pregnancy, childbirth and the puerperium — Grossesse, accouchement et puerpéralité								
Total	59	●38.6	59	●39.1	66	●43.8	58	●40.4
Pregnancy with abortive outcome — Grossesse se terminant par un avortement	9	♦ ●5.9	7	♦ ●4.6	4	♦ ●2.7	9	♦ ●6.3
Other direct obstetric causes — Autres décès maternels directs	24	♦ ●15.7	34	●22.5	42	●27.9	38	●26.5
Indirect obstetric causes — Décès maternels indirects	26	♦ ●17.0	18	♦ ●11.9	20	♦ ●13.3	11	♦ ●7.7
Certain conditions originating in the perinatal period — Certaines affections dont l'origine se situe dans la période périnatale	440	●288.2	469	●310.4	462	●306.4	452	●314.9
Congenital malformations, deformations and chromosomal abnormalities — Malformations congénitales et anomalies chromosomiques	614	●402.1	612	●405.1	594	●393.9	565	●393.7
Symptoms, signs and abnormal clinical and laboratory findings, not elsewhere classified — Symptômes, signes et résultats anormaux d'examens cliniques et de laboratoire, non classés ailleurs	305	2.8	320	2.9	437	3.9	497	4.4
All other diseases — Toutes autres maladies	226	2.0	237	2.1	201	1.8	165	1.5
External causes — Causes externes								
Total	8 547	77.2	8 442	75.9	8 198	73.5	7 655	68.4
Accidents — Accidents								
Total	5 476	49.5	5 297	47.6	5 226	46.8	4 955	44.2
Transport accidents — Accidents de transport	2 134	19.3	1 987	17.9	1 724	15.4	1 704	15.2
Falls — Chutes	1 824	16.5	1 816	16.3	1 914	17.2	1 767	15.8
Accidental drowning and submersion — Noyade et submersion accidentelles	313	2.8	353	3.2	285	2.6	272	2.4
Exposure to smoke, fire and flames — Exposition à la fumée, au feu et aux flammes ..	114	1.0	111	1.0	102	0.9	85	0.8
Accidental poisoning by and exposure to noxious substances — Intoxication accidentelle par des substances nocives et exposition à ces substances	77	0.7	60	0.5	72	0.6	29	♦0.3
Intentional self-harm — Lésions auto-infligées	2 029	18.3	2 056	18.5	2 051	18.4	1 845	16.5
Assault — Agresssions	747	6.8	818	7.4	609	5.5	587	5.2
All other external causes — Toutes autres causes externes	295	2.7	271	2.4	312	2.8	268	2.4

(See notes at end of table. — Voir notes à la fin du tableau.)

Cause of death — Cause de décès	Cuba		Dominica — Dominique					Dominican Republic — République dominicaine
	2001		1995	1996	1997	1998	1999	1995
	Number Nombre	Rate Taux				Number Nombre		
Diseases of the digestive system — Maladies de l'appareil digestif								
Diseases of the liver — Maladies du foie	1 074	9.6	7	6	6	15	12	708
Diseases of the musculoskeletal system and connective tissue — Maladies du système ostéo-articularie, des muscles et du tissu conjonctif	370	3.3	1	-	1	2	1	29
Diseases of the genitourinary system — Maladies de l'appareil génito-urinaire								
Total	690	6.1	16	11	12	8	10	290
Disorders of kidney and ureter — Affections du rein et de l'uretère	519	4.6	12	6	10	5	7	209
Hyperplasia of prostate — Hyperplasie de la prostate	63	...	-	1	-	-	1	37
Pregnancy, childbirth and the puerperium — Grossesse, accouchement et puerpéralité								
Total	57	*41.1	1	-	-	1	-	77
Pregnancy with abortive outcome — Grossesse se terminant par un avortement	11	♦ *7.9	-	-	-	-	-	13
Other direct obstetric causes — Autres décès maternels directs	30	♦ *21.6	1	-	-	1	-	56
Indirect obstetric causes — Décès maternels indirects	6	♦ *4.3	-	-	-	-	-	8
Certain conditions originating in the perinatal period — Certaines affections dont l'origine se situe dans la période périnatale	409	*294.8	14	14	13	11	20	1 273
Congenital malformations, deformations and chromosomal abnormalities — Malformations congénitales et anomalies chromosomiques	512	*369.1	2	7	9	6	8	327
Symptoms, signs and abnormal clinical and laboratory findings, not elsewhere classified — Symptômes, signes et résultats anormaux d'examens cliniques et de laboratoire, non classés ailleurs	611	5.4	67	76	52	53	41	3 407
All other diseases — Toutes autres maladies	190	1.7	3	4	2	2	2	35
External causes — Causes externes								
Total	7 322	65.2	35	25	28	44	30	2 407
Accidents — Accidents								
Total	4 352	38.8	22	15	17	27	16	1 287
Transport accidents — Accidents de transport	1 601	14.3	13	7	10	18	10	048
Falls — Chutes	1 807	16.1	3	1	2	3	1	36
Accidental drowning and submersion — Noyade et submersion accidentelles	287	2.6	4	2	2	2	3	30
Exposure to smoke, fire and flames — Exposition à la fumée, au feu et aux flammes	88	0.8	-	-	1	2	-	5
Accidental poisoning by and exposure to noxious substances — Intoxication accidentelle par des substances nocives et exposition à ces substances	38	0.3	-	-	-	1	1	15
Intentional self-harm — Lésions auto-infligées	1 653	14.7	2	-	1	-	8	137
Assault — Agresssions	605	5.4	4	-	4	1	5	360
All other external causes — Toutes autres causes externes	712	6.3	7	10	6	16	1	623

(See notes at end of table. — Voir notes à la fin du tableau.)

Cause of death — Cause de décès	Dominican Republic — République dominicaine			El Salvador[2]				
	1996	1997	1998	1995	1996	1997	1998	1999
				Number Nombre				
Diseases of the digestive system — Maladies de l'appareil digestif	912	927	974	401	405	849	887	852
Diseases of the liver — Maladies du foie								
Diseases of the musculoskeletal system and connective tissue — Maladies du système ostéo-articularie, des muscles et du tissu conjonctif	39	50	48	173	148	157	118	127
Diseases of the genitourinary system — Maladies de l'appareil génito-urinaire								
Total	320	304	344	765	909	1 033	1 092	1 235
Disorders of kidney and ureter — Affections du rein et de l'uretère	271	262	282	658	842	968	1 053	1 215
Hyperplasia of prostate — Hyperplasie de la prostate	22	21	29	8	5	6	5	3
Pregnancy, childbirth and the puerperium — Grossesse, accouchement et puerpéralité								
Total	43	74	64	55	42	42	42	23
Pregnancy with abortive outcome — Grossesse se terminant par un avortement	6	6	9	7	2	2	7	1
Other direct obstetric causes — Autres décès maternels directs	28	64	48	48	40	38	35	22
Indirect obstetric causes — Décès maternels indirects	9	4	8	-	-	2	-	-
Certain conditions originating in the perinatal period — Certaines affections dont l'origine se situe dans la période périnatale	1 032	1 309	1 287	1 361	1 265	831	761	586
Congenital malformations, deformations and chromosomal abnormalities — Malformations congénitales et anomalies chromosomiques	262	302	296	363	453	294	280	397
Symptoms, signs and abnormal clinical and laboratory findings, not elsewhere classified — Symptômes, signes et résultats anormaux d'examens cliniques et de laboratoire, non classés ailleurs	2 889	2 701	2 517	4 414	3 525	5 538	5 344	3 383
All other diseases — Toutes autres maladies	36	25	22	244	172	130	57	22
External causes — Causes externes								
Total	2 558	3 113	3 418	5 823	5 501	5 086	5 436	5 069
Accidents — Accidents								
Total	1 576	1 919	1 910	2 655	2 420	2 241	2 312	2 251
Transport accidents — Accidents de transport	966	1 208	1 298	1 318	1 401	1 426	1 524	1 662
Falls — Chutes	18	22	11	202	225	207	229	145
Accidental drowning and submersion — Noyade et submersion accidentelles	10	30	21	339	324	295	378	283
Exposure to smoke, fire and flames — Exposition à la fumée, au feu et aux flammes	54	72	42	44	39	26	28	36
Accidental poisoning by and exposure to noxious substances — Intoxication accidentelle par des substances nocives et exposition à ces substances	12	8	13	213	159	92	16	12
Intentional self-harm — Lésions auto-infligées	122	156	154	631	546	577	512	515
Assault — Agresssions	392	529	633	2 534	2 535	2 197	2 606	2 300
All other external causes — Toutes autres causes externes	468	509	721	3	-	71	6	3

(See notes at end of table. — Voir notes à la fin du tableau.)

Cause of death — Cause de décès	Grenada-Grenade[3]		Guatemala					Mexico — Mexique
	1995	1996	1995	1996	1997	1998	1999	1995
			Number Nombre					
Diseases of the digestive system — Maladies de l'appareil digestif								
Diseases of the liver — Maladies du foie	2	9	1 634	1 412	1 516	1 697	1 664	21 242
Diseases of the musculoskeletal system and connective tissue — Maladies du système ostéo-articularie, des muscles et du tissu conjonctif	7	7	201	149	164	158	150	2 106
Diseases of the genitourinary system — Maladies de l'appareil génito-urinaire								
Total	33	13	817	737	811	928	934	12 950
Disorders of kidney and ureter — Affections du rein et de l'uretère	32	8	623	593	647	760	799	10 740
Hyperplasia of prostate — Hyperplasie de la prostate	-	2	28	20	35	27	32	418
Pregnancy, childbirth and the puerperium — Grossesse, accouchement et puerpéralité								
Total	-	-	360	335	342	324	316	1 454
Pregnancy with abortive outcome — Grossesse se terminant par un avortement	-	-	20	25	21	18	15	117
Other direct obstetric causes — Autres décès maternels directs	-	-	339	310	321	305	300	1 265
Indirect obstetric causes — Décès maternels indirects	-	-	1	-	-	1	1	72
Certain conditions originating in the perinatal period — Certaines affections dont l'origine se situe dans la période périnatale	18	16	4 962	4 552	5 029	4 726	4 445	20 479
Congenital malformations, deformations and chromosomal abnormalities — Malformations congénitales et anomalies chromosomiques	2	3	647	500	558	533	509	9 641
Symptoms, signs and abnormal clinical and laboratory findings, not elsewhere classified — Symptômes, signes et résultats anormaux d'examens cliniques et de laboratoire, non classés ailleurs	67	18	6 560	6 501	7 028	6 774	6 031	7 199
All other diseases — Toutes autres maladies	-	3	188	153	168	108	142	1 197
External causes — Causes externes								
Total	28	43	8 204	7 580	8 640	8 799	7 939	56 855
Accidents — Accidents								
Total	27	20	1 987	1 821	2 298	2 708	2 459	35 539
Transport accidents — Accidents de transport	9	1	508	439	526	503	311	14 326
Falls — Chutes	-	6	251	254	272	391	279	4 429
Accidental drowning and submersion — Noyade et submersion accidentelles	7	8	88	65	86	81	116	2 993
Exposure to smoke, fire and flames — Exposition à la fumée, au feu et aux flammes	-	1	41	50	15	22	14	683
Accidental poisoning by and exposure to noxious substances — Intoxication accidentelle par des substances nocives et exposition à ces substances	6	3	37	32	32	23	27	1 115
Intentional self-harm — Lésions auto-infligées	1	1	211	158	179	201	234	2 892
Assault — Agresssions	-	3	1 970	2 163	3 002	2 806	1 978	15 596
All other external causes — Toutes autres causes externes	-	19	4 036	3 338	3 161	3 086	3 268	2 828

21. Death and death rates by cause: 1995 - 2002
Décès selon la cause, nombres et taux: 1995 - 2002 (continued — suite)

(See notes at end of table. — Voir notes à la fin du tableau.)

Mexico — Mexique

Cause of death — Cause de décès	1995 Rate Taux	1996 Number Nombre	1996 Rate Taux	1997 Number Nombre	1997 Rate Taux	1998 Number Nombre	1998 Rate Taux	1999 Number Nombre
Diseases of the digestive system — Maladies de l'appareil digestif								
Diseases of the liver — Maladies du foie	23.1	21 751	23.2	22 861	24.0	27 206	28.1	27 038
Diseases of the musculoskeletal system and connective tissue — Maladies du système ostéo-articulaire, des muscles et du tissu conjonctif	2.3	2 346	2.5	2 228	2.3	3 099	3.2	3 115
Diseases of the genitourinary system — Maladies de l'appareil génito-urinaire								
Total	14.1	13 093	14.0	13 087	13.8	11 635	12.0	11 196
Disorders of kidney and ureter — Affections du rein et de l'uretère	11.7	10 881	11.6	10 836	11.4	9 752	10.1	9 485
Hyperplasia of prostate — Hyperplasie de la prostate	▼8.2	448	...	450	...	529	...	503
Pregnancy, childbirth and the puerperium — Grossesse, accouchement et puerpéralité								
Total	•52.9	1 291	•47.7	1 266	•46.9	1 430	•53.6	1 411
Pregnancy with abortive outcome — Grossesse se terminant par un avortement	•4.3	87	•3.2	107	•4.0	110	•4.1	93
Other direct obstetric causes — Autres décès maternels directs	•46.0	1 149	•42.4	1 114	•41.3	1 154	•43.2	1 137
Indirect obstetric causes — Décès maternels indirects	•2.6	55	•2.0	45	•1.7	151	•5.7	161
Certain conditions originating in the perinatal period — Certaines affections dont l'origine se situe dans la période périnatale	•744.6	19 681	•726.8	19 802	•733.8	19 851	•743.9	19 245
Congenital malformations, deformations and chromosomal abnormalities — Malformations congénitales et anomalies chromosomiques	•350.5	9 441	•348.7	9 548	•353.8	10 070	•377.4	9 673
Symptoms, signs and abnormal clinical and laboratory findings, not elsewhere classified — Symptômes, signes et résultats anormaux d'examens cliniques et de laboratoire, non classés ailleurs	7.8	7 440	8.0	7 036	7.4	7 547	7.8	9 457
All other diseases — Toutes autres maladies	1.3	1 268	1.4	1 342	1.4	1 118	1.2	998
External causes — Causes externes								
Total	61.8	55 796	59.6	55 956	58.8	55 975	57.9	54 523
Accidents — Accidents								
Total	38.6	35 062	37.5	35 852	37.7	35 012	36.2	35 202
Transport accidents — Accidents de transport	15.6	14 981	16.0	15 324	16.1	14 790	15.3	14 702
Falls — Chutes	4.8	4 334	4.6	4 272	4.5	2 177	2.3	2 291
Accidental drowning and submersion — Noyade et submersion accidentelles	3.3	2 799	3.0	2 815	3.0	2 930	3.0	2 839
Exposure to smoke, fire and flames — Exposition à la fumée, au feu et aux flammes	0.7	745	0.8	701	0.7	779	0.8	710
Accidental poisoning by and exposure to noxious substances — Intoxication accidentelle par des substances nocives et exposition à ces substances	1.2	1 022	1.1	1 112	1.2	1 083	1.1	1 011
Intentional self-harm — Lésions auto-infligées	3.1	3 018	3.2	3 369	3.5	3 341	3.5	3 339
Assault — Agresssions	17.0	14 493	15.5	13 542	14.2	13 642	14.1	12 238
All other external causes — Toutes autres causes externes	3.1	3 223	3.4	3 193	3.4	3 980	4.1	3 744

21. Death and death rates by cause: 1995 - 2002
Décès selon la cause, nombres et taux: 1995 - 2002 (continued — suite)

(See notes at end of table. — Voir notes à la fin du tableau.)

Cause of death — Cause de décès	Mexico — Mexique					Nicaragua		
	1999	2000		2001		1996	1997	1998
	Rate Taux	Number Nombre	Rate Taux	Number Nombre	Rate Taux		Number Nombre	
Diseases of the digestive system — Maladies de l'appareil digestif								
Diseases of the liver — Maladies du foie	27.6	27 425	27.4	27 786	27.3	326	494	575
Diseases of the musculoskeletal system and connective tissue — Maladies du système ostéo-articularie, des muscles et du tissu conjonctif	3.2	2 722	2.7	2 741	2.7	68	72	76
Diseases of the genitourinary system — Maladies de l'appareil génito-urinaire								
Total	11.4	11 954	11.9	12 736	12.5	528	577	531
Disorders of kidney and ureter — Affections du rein et de l'uretère	9.7	10 227	10.2	10 920	10.7	459	534	473
Hyperplasia of prostate — Hyperplasie de la prostate	...	497	...	563	...	42	21	32
Pregnancy, childbirth and the puerperium — Grossesse, accouchement et puerpéralité								
Total	*51.0	1 325	*47.3	1 268	*45.8	123	127	113
Pregnancy with abortive outcome — Grossesse se terminant par un avortement	*3.4	89	*3.2	68	*2.5	9	7	8
Other direct obstetric causes — Autres décès maternels directs	*41.1	1 077	*38.5	1 075	*38.8	105	107	85
Indirect obstetric causes — Décès maternels indirects	*5.8	141	*5.0	107	*3.9	9	13	19
Certain conditions originating in the perinatal period — Certaines affections dont l'origine se situe dans la période périnatale	*695.0	19 372	*692.3	18 142	*655.5	1 067	1 101	1 139
Congenital malformations, deformations and chromosomal abnormalities — Malformations congénitales et anomalies chromosomiques	*349.3	9 538	*340.8	9 116	*329.4	322	349	372
Symptoms, signs and abnormal clinical and laboratory findings, not elsewhere classified — Symptômes, signes et résultats anormaux d'examens cliniques et de laboratoire, non classés ailleurs	9.6	8 633	8.6	9 173	9.0	532	514	528
All other diseases — Toutes autres maladies	1.0	1 038	1.0	947	0.9	59	31	33
External causes — Causes externes								
Total	55.6	52 102	52.0	51 130	50.2	1 966	1 971	2 696
Accidents — Accidents								
Total	35.9	34 894	34.8	34 304	33.7	884	857	1 631
Transport accidents — Accidents de transport	15.0	14 704	14.7	14 332	14.1	343	381	399
Falls — Chutes	2.3	2 248	2.2	2 302	2.3	80	15	21
Accidental drowning and submersion — Noyade et submersion accidentelles	2.9	2 677	2.7	2 427	2.4	72	85	89
Exposure to smoke, fire and flames — Exposition à la fumée, au feu et aux flammes	0.7	681	0.7	626	0.6	6	10	16
Accidental poisoning by and exposure to noxious substances — Intoxication accidentelle par des substances nocives et exposition à ces substances	1.0	994	1.0	947	0.9	6	8	9
Intentional self-harm — Lésions auto-infligées	3.4	3 475	3.5	3 784	3.7	230	274	301
Assault — Agresssions	12.5	10 726	10.7	10 148	10.0	285	286	259
All other external causes — Toutes autres causes externes	3.8	3 007	3.0	2 894	2.8	567	554	505

(See notes at end of table. — Voir notes à la fin du tableau.)

Cause of death — Cause de décès	Nicaragua		Panama					Puerto Rico — Porto Rico
	1999	2000	1996	1997	1998	1999	2000	1995
			Number Nombre					
Diseases of the digestive system — Maladies de l'appareil digestif								
Diseases of the liver — Maladies du foie	550	483	148	164	213	169	191	719
Diseases of the musculoskeletal system and connective tissue — Maladies du système ostéo-articularie, des muscles et du tissu conjonctif	62	58	41	35	33	32	46	85
Diseases of the genitourinary system — Maladies de l'appareil génito-urinaire								
Total	496	593	244	242	287	234	246	823
Disorders of kidney and ureter — Affections du rein et de l'uretère	455	563	187	198	237	195	208	453
Hyperplasia of prostate — Hyperplasie de la prostate	27	12	13	13	17	11	13	4
Pregnancy, childbirth and the puerperium — Grossesse, accouchement et puerpéralité								
Total	138	97	35	28	30	31	30	9
Pregnancy with abortive outcome — Grossesse se terminant par un avortement	7	4	4	7	5	5	5	2
Other direct obstetric causes — Autres décès maternels directs	100	80	21	18	18	20	21	6
Indirect obstetric causes — Décès maternels indirects	31	14	10	3	7	6	4	1
Certain conditions originating in the perinatal period — Certaines affections dont l'origine se situe dans la période périnatale	1 066	1 125	455	478	434	460	436	476
Congenital malformations, deformations and chromosomal abnormalities — Malformations congénitales et anomalies chromosomiques	395	351	299	344	339	294	352	232
Symptoms, signs and abnormal clinical and laboratory findings, not elsewhere classified — Symptômes, signes et résultats anormaux d'examens cliniques et de laboratoire, non classés ailleurs	498	530	1 341	1 401	1 191	1 081	1 050	248
All other diseases — Toutes autres maladies	6	12	35	71	17	36	34	122
External causes — Causes externes								
Total	2 078	1 890	1 375	1 548	1 476	1 444	1 347	2 914
Accidents — Accidents								
Total	1 295	1 007	891	1 009	963	969	832	1 530
Transport accidents — Accidents de transport	527	485	416	540	567	549	432	660
Falls — Chutes	26	11	126	120	72	60	80	229
Accidental drowning and submersion — Noyade et submersion accidentelles	157	122	158	141	125	154	142	65
Exposure to smoke, fire and flames — Exposition à la fumée, au feu et aux flammes	15	16	7	9	11	10	15	27
Accidental poisoning by and exposure to noxious substances — Intoxication accidentelle par des substances nocives et exposition à ces substances	52	27	16	15	15	12	11	333
Intentional self-harm — Lésions auto-infligées	318	363	113	145	148	143	144	291
Assault — Agresssions	313	338	211	293	250	244	288	929
All other external causes — Toutes autres causes externes	152	182	160	101	115	88	83	164

21. Death and death rates by cause: 1995 - 2002
Décès selon la cause, nombres et taux: 1995 - 2002 (continued — suite)

(See notes at end of table. — Voir notes à la fin du tableau.)

Cause of death — Cause de décès	Puerto Rico — Porto Rico					Saint Kitts-Nevis — Saint-Kitts-et-Nevis	Saint Lucia — Sainte-Lucie	
	1996	1997	1998	1999	2000	1995	1995	1996
	Number Nombre							
Diseases of the digestive system — Maladies de l'appareil digestif								
Diseases of the liver — Maladies du foie	670	847	829	938	901	9	18	18
Diseases of the musculoskeletal system and connective tissue — Maladies du système ostéo-articulaire, des muscles et du tissu conjonctif	118	103	122	164	150	-	2	2
Diseases of the genitourinary system — Maladies de l'appareil génito-urinaire								
Total	911	914	907	1 010	966	9	19	20
Disorders of kidney and ureter — Affections du rein et de l'uretère	510	527	532	839	795	9	13	17
Hyperplasia of prostate — Hyperplasie de la prostate	5	2	3	3	8	-	2	1
Pregnancy, childbirth and the puerperium — Grossesse, accouchement et puerpéralité								
Total	11	13	8	10	14	1	-	1
Pregnancy with abortive outcome — Grossesse se terminant par un avortement	2	1	1	2	1	-	-	-
Other direct obstetric causes — Autres décès maternels directs	9	12	7	8	9	1	-	1
Indirect obstetric causes — Décès maternels indirects	-	-	-	-	4	-	-	-
Certain conditions originating in the perinatal period — Certaines affections dont l'origine se situe dans la période périnatale	414	411	364	363	345	8	41	22
Congenital malformations, deformations and chromosomal abnormalities — Malformations congénitales et anomalies chromosomiques	202	216	183	167	172	5	7	9
Symptoms, signs and abnormal clinical and laboratory findings, not elsewhere classified — Symptômes, signes et résultats anormaux d'examens cliniques et de laboratoire, non classés ailleurs	243	171	200	135	286	9	73	63
All other diseases — Toutes autres maladies	125	136	169	178	159	3	3	8
External causes — Causes externes								
Total	2 928	2 652	2 498	2 327	2 387	18	73	68
Accidents — Accidents								
Total	1 524	1 493	1 364	1 307	1 332	12	47	46
Transport accidents — Accidents de transport	676	636	573	585	599	6	23	25
Falls — Chutes	289	186	195	167	142	2	3	1
Accidental drowning and submersion — Noyade et submersion accidentelles	67	71	74	59	44	3	7	7
Exposure to smoke, fire and flames — Exposition à la fumée, au feu et aux flammes	21	38	21	11	19	1	1	2
Accidental poisoning by and exposure to noxious substances — Intoxication accidentelle par des substances nocives et exposition à ces substances	230	309	265	229	306	-	-	1
Intentional self-harm — Lésions auto-infligées	331	273	321	289	306	-	10	7
Assault — Agressions	928	877	804	664	677	6	16	12
All other external causes — Toutes autres causes externes	145	9	9	67	73	-	-	3

21. Death and death rates by cause: 1995 - 2002
Décès selon la cause, nombres et taux: 1995 - 2002 (continued — suite)

(See notes at end of table. — Voir notes à la fin du tableau.)

Cause of death — Cause de décès	Saint Lucia — Sainte-Lucie					Saint Vincent and the Grenadines — Saint Vincent-et-Grenadines		
	1997	1998	1999	2000	2001	1995	1996	1997
				Number Nombre				
Diseases of the digestive system — Maladies de l'appareil digestif								
Diseases of the liver — Maladies du foie	25	25	20	19	20	12	7	9
Diseases of the musculoskeletal system and connective tissue — Maladies du système ostéo-articularie, des muscles et du tissu conjonctif	4	4	-	2	6	-	-	6
Diseases of the genitourinary system — Maladies de l'appareil génito-urinaire								
Total	12	14	17	7	17	9	11	11
Disorders of kidney and ureter — Affections du rein et de l'uretère	8	11	17	5	13	8	8	10
Hyperplasia of prostate — Hyperplasie de la prostate	1	1	-	1	1	1	1	-
Pregnancy, childbirth and the puerperium — Grossesse, accouchement et puerpéralité								
Total	-	-	1	3	1	4	2	1
Pregnancy with abortive outcome — Grossesse se terminant par un avortement	-	-	-	-	-	2	-	-
Other direct obstetric causes — Autres décès maternels directs	-	-	1	3	1	2	-	-
Indirect obstetric causes — Décès maternels indirects	-	-	-	-	-	-	2	1
Certain conditions originating in the perinatal period — Certaines affections dont l'origine se situe dans la période périnatale	26	10	47	25	31	34	26	30
Congenital malformations, deformations and chromosomal abnormalities — Malformations congénitales et anomalies chromosomiques	11	12	-	12	4	9	9	13
Symptoms, signs and abnormal clinical and laboratory findings, not elsewhere classified — Symptômes, signes et résultats anormaux d'examens cliniques et de laboratoire, non classés ailleurs	52	56	103	47	53	29	18	14
All other diseases — Toutes autres maladies	12	10	-	8	5	1	12	10
External causes — Causes externes								
Total	85	88	41	97	79	59	61	42
Accidents — Accidents								
Total	61	65	15	53	46	27	24	30
Transport accidents — Accidents de transport	26	23	14	27	23	9	7	10
Falls — Chutes	1	-	-	-	1	-	5	3
Accidental drowning and submersion — Noyade et submersion accidentelles	11	14	-	15	5	12	8	12
Exposure to smoke, fire and flames — Exposition à la fumée, au feu et aux flammes	5	1	-	1	6	-	2	2
Accidental poisoning by and exposure to noxious substances — Intoxication accidentelle par des substances nocives et exposition à ces substances	1	2	-	-	-	-	-	-
Intentional self-harm — Lésions auto-infligées	9	8	8	14	7	7	8	3
Assault — Agresssions	13	14	16	28	26	14	9	4
All other external causes — Toutes autres causes externes	2	1	2	2	-	11	20	5

21. Death and death rates by cause: 1995 - 2002
Décès selon la cause, nombres et taux: 1995 - 2002 (continued — suite)

(See notes at end of table. — Voir notes à la fin du tableau.)

Cause of death — Cause de décès	Saint Vincent and the Grenadines — Saint Vincent-et-Grenadines		Trinidad and Tobago — Trinité-et-Tobago				Turks Caicos Islands — Iles Turques et Caïques	
	1998	1999	1995		1998		1995	1996
	Number Nombre	Number Nombre	Number Nombre	Rate Taux	Number Nombre	Rate Taux	Number Nombre	Number Nombre
Diseases of the digestive system — Maladies de l'appareil digestif								
Diseases of the liver — Maladies du foie	14	9	57	4.5	102	8.0	1	-
Diseases of the musculoskeletal system and connective tissue — Maladies du système ostéo-articularie, des muscles et du tissu conjonctif	1	1	57	4.5	55	4.3	-	-
Diseases of the genitourinary system — Maladies de l'appareil génito-urinaire								
Total	16	11	237	18.8	192	15.0	-	-
Disorders of kidney and ureter — Affections du rein et de l'uretère	8	7	164	13.0	122	9.5	-	-
Hyperplasia of prostate — Hyperplasie de la prostate	2	1	32	▼32.5	27	...	-	-
Pregnancy, childbirth and the puerperium — Grossesse, accouchement et puerpéralité								
Total	-	1	13	◆ ●67.5	8	...	-	-
Pregnancy with abortive outcome — Grossesse se terminant par un avortement	-	-	4	◆ ●20.8	1	...	-	-
Other direct obstetric causes — Autres décès maternels directs	-	-	8	◆ ●41.5	7	...	-	-
Indirect obstetric causes — Décès maternels indirects	-	1	1	◆ ●5.2	-	-	-	-
Certain conditions originating in the perinatal period — Certaines affections dont l'origine se situe dans la période périnatale	29	30	251	●1303.4	215	...	6	1
Congenital malformations, deformations and chromosomal abnormalities — Malformations congénitales et anomalies chromosomiques	4	14	55	●285.6	100	...	1	1
Symptoms, signs and abnormal clinical and laboratory findings, not elsewhere classified — Symptômes, signes et résultats anormaux d'examens cliniques et de laboratoire, non classés ailleurs	13	14	211	16.7	188	14.7	7	11
All other diseases — Toutes autres maladies	5	12	54	4.3	37	2.9	-	-
External causes — Causes externes								
Total	65	46	644	51.1	623	48.8	13	5
Accidents — Accidents								
Total	33	26	283	22.5	312	24.4	11	3
Transport accidents — Accidents de transport	6	5	113	9.0	151	11.8	4	-
Falls — Chutes	9	4	69	5.5	41	3.2	2	1
Accidental drowning and submersion — Noyade et submersion accidentelles	10	12	45	3.6	56	4.4	3	-
Exposure to smoke, fire and flames — Exposition à la fumée, au feu et aux flammes	4	3	14	◆1.1	8	◆0.6	-	1
Accidental poisoning by and exposure to noxious substances — Intoxication accidentelle par des substances nocives et exposition à ces substances	-	-	8	◆0.6	4	◆0.3	-	-
Intentional self-harm — Lésions auto-infligées	10	6	184	14.6	171	13.4	1	-
Assault — Agresssions	20	12	136	10.8	109	8.5	1	1
All other external causes — Toutes autres causes externes	2	2	41	3.3	31	2.4	-	1

21. Death and death rates by cause: 1995 - 2002
Décès selon la cause, nombres et taux: 1995 - 2002 (continued — suite)

(See notes at end of table. — Voir notes à la fin du tableau.)

Cause of death — Cause de décès	Turks Caicos Islands — Iles Turques et Caïques			United States — Etats-Unis				
	1997	1998	1999	1995		1996		1997
		Number Nombre			Rate Taux	Number Nombre	Rate Taux	Number Nombre
Diseases of the digestive system — Maladies de l'appareil digestif								
Diseases of the liver — Maladies du foie	2	-	-	25 222	9.6	25 047	9.4	25 175
Diseases of the musculoskeletal system and connective tissue — Maladies du système ostéo-articularie, des muscles et du tissu conjonctif	-	-	-	9 164	3.5	9 508	3.6	10 035
Diseases of the genitourinary system — Maladies de l'appareil génito-urinaire								
Total	1	1	-	43 356	16.5	44 538	16.8	46 353
Disorders of kidney and ureter — Affections du rein et de l'uretère	1	1	-	24 594	9.3	25 200	9.5	26 162
Hyperplasia of prostate — Hyperplasie de la prostate	-	-	-	406	▼1.3	457	▼1.5	420
Pregnancy, childbirth and the puerperium — Grossesse, accouchement et puerpéralité								
Total	-	-	-	277	*7.1	294	*7.6	327
Pregnancy with abortive outcome — Grossesse se terminant par un avortement	-	-	-	28	♦ *0.7	39	*1.0	41
Other direct obstetric causes — Autres décès maternels directs	-	-	-	230	*5.9	237	*6.1	278
Indirect obstetric causes — Décès maternels indirects	-	-	-	19	♦ *0.5	18	♦ *0.5	8
Certain conditions originating in the perinatal period — Certaines affections dont l'origine se situe dans la période périnatale	1	-	1	13 471	*345.4	13 069	*335.8	13 091
Congenital malformations, deformations and chromosomal abnormalities — Malformations congénitales et anomalies chromosomiques	-	-	1	11 891	*304.9	11 836	*304.2	11 912
Symptoms, signs and abnormal clinical and laboratory findings, not elsewhere classified — Symptômes, signes et résultats anormaux d'examens cliniques et de laboratoire, non classés ailleurs	3	5	2	27 283	10.4	26 190	9.9	25 753
All other diseases — Toutes autres maladies	-	-	-	3 310	1.3	3 258	1.2	3 214
External causes — Causes externes								
Total	10	8	4	150 809	57.3	150 298	56.6	149 691
Accidents — Accidents								
Total	5	6	4	93 320	35.5	94 948	35.8	95 644
Transport accidents — Accidents de transport	1	6	3	45 805	17.4	46 224	17.4	45 798
Falls — Chutes	-	-	1	13 986	5.3	14 986	5.6	15 447
Accidental drowning and submersion — Noyade et submersion accidentelles	2	-	-	3 790	1.4	3 488	1.3	3 561
Exposure to smoke, fire and flames — Exposition à la fumée, au feu et aux flammes ..	1	-	-	3 761	1.4	3 741	1.4	3 490
Accidental poisoning by and exposure to noxious substances — Intoxication accidentelle par des substances nocives et exposition à ces substances	-	-	-	9 072	3.4	9 510	3.6	10 163
Intentional self-harm — Lésions auto-infligées	1	1	-	31 284	11.9	30 903	11.6	30 535
Assault — Agresssions	2	-	-	22 552	8.6	20 634	7.8	19 491
All other external causes — Toutes autres causes externes	2	1	-	3 653	1.4	3 813	1.4	4 021

(See notes at end of table. — Voir notes à la fin du tableau.)

Cause of death — Cause de décès	United States — Etats-Unis							US Virgin Islands — Iles Vierges américaines
	1997	1998		1999		2000		1997
	Rate Taux	Number Nombre	Rate Taux	Number Nombre	Rate Taux	Number Nombre	Rate Taux	Number Nombre
Diseases of the digestive system — Maladies de l'appareil digestif								
Diseases of the liver — Maladies du foie	9.4	25 192	9.3	33 619	12.3	33 853	12.3	9
Diseases of the musculoskeletal system and connective tissue — Maladies du système ostéo-articularie, des muscles et du tissu conjonctif	3.7	10 166	3.8	13 347	4.9	13 764	5.0	2
Diseases of the genitourinary system — Maladies de l'appareil génito-urinaire								
Total	17.3	48 377	17.9	53 127	19.5	54 560	19.8	10
Disorders of kidney and ureter — Affections du rein et de l'uretère	9.8	27 010	10.0	37 642	13.8	39 370	14.3	4
Hyperplasia of prostate — Hyperplasie de la prostate	▼1.3	410	▼1.3	430	▼1.3	433	▼1.3	1
Pregnancy, childbirth and the puerperium — Grossesse, accouchement et puerpéralité								
Total	*8.4	281	*7.1	406	*10.3	404	*10.0	1
Pregnancy with abortive outcome — Grossesse se terminant par un avortement	*1.1	32	*0.8	31	*0.8	37	*0.9	-
Other direct obstetric causes — Autres décès maternels directs	*7.2	229	*5.8	313	*7.9	304	*7.5	1
Indirect obstetric causes — Décès maternels indirects	♦ *0.2	20	♦ *0.5	47	*1.2	55	*1.4	-
Certain conditions originating in the perinatal period — Certaines affections dont l'origine se situe dans la période périnatale	*337.3	13 428	*340.7	14 259	*360.1	14 069	*346.6	17
Congenital malformations, deformations and chromosomal abnormalities — Malformations congénitales et anomalies chromosomiques	*306.9	11 934	*302.8	10 393	*262.5	10 578	*260.6	9
Symptoms, signs and abnormal clinical and laboratory findings, not elsewhere classified — Symptômes, signes et résultats anormaux d'examens cliniques et de laboratoire, non classés ailleurs	9.6	25 992	9.6	26 674	9.8	31 878	11.6	7
All other diseases — Toutes autres maladies	1.2	3 326	1.2	3 815	1.4	3 879	1.4	4
External causes — Causes externes								
Total	55.9	150 445	55.7	151 109	55.4	151 268	55.0	70
Accidents — Accidents								
Total	35.7	97 835	36.2	96 486	35.4	96 563	35.1	38
Transport accidents — Accidents de transport	17.1	45 774	16.9	45 927	16.8	46 259	16.8	11
Falls — Chutes	5.8	16 274	6.0	13 162	4.8	13 322	4.8	3
Accidental drowning and submersion — Noyade et submersion accidentelles	1.3	3 964	1.5	3 529	1.3	3 482	1.3	12
Exposure to smoke, fire and flames — Exposition à la fumée, au feu et aux flammes ..	1.3	3 255	1.2	3 348	1.2	3 377	1.2	1
Accidental poisoning by and exposure to noxious substances — Intoxication accidentelle par des substances nocives et exposition à ces substances	3.8	10 801	4.0	12 186	4.5	12 757	4.6	3
Intentional self-harm — Lésions auto-infligées	11.4	30 575	11.3	29 180	10.7	29 319	10.7	3
Assault — Agressions	7.3	17 893	6.6	16 749	6.1	16 590	6.0	30
All other external causes — Toutes autres causes externes	1.6	4 142	1.5	8 694	3.2	8 796	3.2	1

21. Death and death rates by cause: 1995 - 2002
Décès selon la cause, nombres et taux: 1995 - 2002 (continued — suite)

(See notes at end of table. — Voir notes à la fin du tableau.)

Cause of death — Cause de décès	US Virgin Islands — Iles Vierges américaines			Argentina — Argentine				
	1998	1999	2000	1995		1996		1997
	Number Nombre				Rate Taux	Number Nombre	Rate Taux	Number Nombre
Diseases of the digestive system — Maladies de l'appareil digestif								
Diseases of the liver — Maladies du foie	9	21	13	2 857	8.2	2 942	8.4	4 568
Diseases of the musculoskeletal system and connective tissue — Maladies du système ostéo-articularie, des muscles et du tissu conjonctif	1	3	2	465	1.3	568	1.6	654
Diseases of the genitourinary system — Maladies de l'appareil génito-urinaire								
Total	10	15	13	5 910	17.0	6 048	17.2	5 787
Disorders of kidney and ureter — Affections du rein et de l'uretère	5	11	9	5 052	14.5	5 180	14.7	5 034
Hyperplasia of prostate — Hyperplasie de la prostate	1	1	-	57	▼1.7	57	...	39
Pregnancy, childbirth and the puerperium — Grossesse, accouchement et puerpéralité								
Total	-	-	1	290	*44.0	317	*46.9	265
Pregnancy with abortive outcome — Grossesse se terminant par un avortement	-	-	-	94	*14.3	115	*17.0	82
Other direct obstetric causes — Autres décès maternels directs	-	-	1	191	*29.0	184	*27.2	167
Indirect obstetric causes — Décès maternels indirects	-	-	-	5	♦ *0.8	17	♦ *2.5	16
Certain conditions originating in the perinatal period — Certaines affections dont l'origine se situe dans la période périnatale	9	13	11	7 104	*1078.4	6 746	*998.8	6 285
Congenital malformations, deformations and chromosomal abnormalities — Malformations congénitales et anomalies chromosomiques	6	6	5	3 028	*459.7	3 081	*456.1	2 949
Symptoms, signs and abnormal clinical and laboratory findings, not elsewhere classified — Symptômes, signes et résultats anormaux d'examens cliniques et de laboratoire, non classés ailleurs	6	9	7	9 621	27.7	9 410	26.7	17 081
All other diseases — Toutes autres maladies	4	7	2	180	0.5	225	0.6	204
External causes — Causes externes								
Total	69	74	59	17 743	51.0	18 380	52.2	19 015
Accidents — Accidents								
Total	37	40	28	9 612	27.6	9 682	27.5	10 056
Transport accidents — Accidents de transport	22	13	15	4 138	11.9	4 152	11.8	4 118
Falls — Chutes	5	2	2	813	2.3	941	2.7	573
Accidental drowning and submersion — Noyade et submersion accidentelles	3	9	3	612	1.8	708	2.0	710
Exposure to smoke, fire and flames — Exposition à la fumée, au feu et aux flammes	-	1	2	294	0.8	316	0.9	429
Accidental poisoning by and exposure to noxious substances — Intoxication accidentelle par des substances nocives et exposition à ces substances	1	-	1	214	0.6	223	0.6	334
Intentional self-harm — Lésions auto-infligées	6	6	5	2 215	6.4	2 245	6.4	2 215
Assault — Agresssions	25	27	23	1 441	4.1	1 611	4.6	1 661
All other external causes — Toutes autres causes externes	1	1	3	4 475	12.9	4 842	13.7	5 083

21. Death and death rates by cause: 1995 - 2002
Décès selon la cause, nombres et taux: 1995 - 2002 (continued — suite)

(See notes at end of table. — Voir notes à la fin du tableau.)

Argentina — Argentine

Cause of death — Cause de décès	1997 Rate Taux	1998 Number Nombre	1998 Rate Taux	1999 Number Nombre	1999 Rate Taux	2000 Number Nombre	2000 Rate Taux	2001 Number Nombre
Diseases of the digestive system — Maladies de l'appareil digestif								
Diseases of the liver — Maladies du foie	12.8	4 573	12.7	4 415	12.1	4 199	11.3	4 356
Diseases of the musculoskeletal system and connective tissue — Maladies du système ostéo-articulaire, des muscles et du tissu conjonctif	1.8	541	1.5	601	1.6	575	1.6	536
Diseases of the genitourinary system — Maladies de l'appareil génito-urinaire								
Total	16.2	6 566	18.2	6 757	18.5	6 972	18.8	7 113
Disorders of kidney and ureter — Affections du rein et de l'uretère	14.1	5 677	15.7	5 777	15.8	6 031	16.3	6 127
Hyperplasia of prostate — Hyperplasie de la prostate	...	47	...	49	...	53	▼1.4	42
Pregnancy, childbirth and the puerperium — Grossesse, accouchement et puerpéralité								
Total	*38.3	260	*38.1	287	*41.8	245	*34.9	309
Pregnancy with abortive outcome — Grossesse se terminant par un avortement	*11.8	86	*12.6	87	*12.7	71	*10.1	92
Other direct obstetric causes — Autres décès maternels directs	*24.1	146	*21.4	175	*25.5	149	*21.2	157
Indirect obstetric causes — Décès maternels indirects	♦ *2.3	28	♦ *4.1	20	♦ *2.9	25	♦ *3.6	48
Certain conditions originating in the perinatal period — Certaines affections dont l'origine se situe dans la période périnatale	*907.8	6 380	*933.7	6 107	*889.3	5 948	*847.4	5 572
Congenital malformations, deformations and chromosomal abnormalities — Malformations congénitales et anomalies chromosomiques	*425.9	2 968	*434.4	2 910	*423.7	2 901	*413.3	2 887
Symptoms, signs and abnormal clinical and laboratory findings, not elsewhere classified — Symptômes, signes et résultats anormaux d'examens cliniques et de laboratoire, non classés ailleurs	47.9	17 290	47.9	18 969	51.9	18 466	49.9	18 837
All other diseases — Toutes autres maladies	0.6	391	1.1	467	1.3	507	1.4	583
External causes — Causes externes								
Total	53.3	19 594	54.2	19 671	53.8	19 355	52.3	19 895
Accidents — Accidents								
Total	28.2	11 006	30.5	10 902	29.8	10 479	28.3	9 927
Transport accidents — Accidents de transport	11.5	4 782	13.2	4 651	12.7	4 119	11.1	4 221
Falls — Chutes	1.0	577	1.6	557	1.5	326	0.9	315
Accidental drowning and submersion — Noyade et submersion accidentelles	2.0	785	2.2	760	2.1	718	1.9	774
Exposure to smoke, fire and flames — Exposition à la fumée, au feu et aux flammes	1.2	390	1.1	490	1.3	379	1.0	391
Accidental poisoning by and exposure to noxious substances — Intoxication accidentelle par des substances nocives et exposition à ces substances	0.9	183	0.5	224	0.6	207	0.6	175
Intentional self-harm — Lésions auto-infligées	6.2	2 358	6.5	2 431	6.6	2 783	7.5	3 142
Assault — Agresssions	4.7	1 703	4.7	1 928	5.3	2 149	5.8	2 600
All other external causes — Toutes autres causes externes	14.2	4 527	12.5	4 410	12.1	3 944	10.7	4 226

(See notes at end of table. — Voir notes à la fin du tableau.)

Cause of death — Cause de décès	Argentina — Argentine 2001 Rate Taux	Brazil — Brésil 1995	1996	1997	1998 Number Nombre	1999	2000	Chile — Chili 1995
Diseases of the digestive system — Maladies de l'appareil digestif								
Diseases of the liver — Maladies du foie	11.6	14 470	18 562	19 038	19 459	19 884	20 508	3 336
Diseases of the musculoskeletal system and connective tissue — Maladies du système ostéo-articularie, des muscles et du tissu conjonctif	1.4	1 629	2 120	2 086	2 068	2 317	2 474	310
Diseases of the genitourinary system — Maladies de l'appareil génito-urinaire								
Total	19.0	12 511	12 771	12 630	12 858	12 859	13 364	1 690
Disorders of kidney and ureter — Affections du rein et de l'uretère	16.3	9 624	10 105	9 807	9 912	9 745	9 872	1 086
Hyperplasia of prostate — Hyperplasie de la prostate	...	275	291	318	330	358	397	97
Pregnancy, childbirth and the puerperium — Grossesse, accouchement et puerpéralité								
Total	*45.2	1 632	1 465	1 791	1 937	1 823	1 648	86
Pregnancy with abortive outcome — Grossesse se terminant par un avortement	*13.5	198	146	163	115	147	128	20
Other direct obstetric causes — Autres décès maternels directs	*23.0	1 249	1 077	1 163	1 233	1 271	1 220	54
Indirect obstetric causes — Décès maternels indirects	*7.0	185	241	448	574	370	267	12
Certain conditions originating in the perinatal period — Certaines affections dont l'origine se situe dans la période périnatale	*815.2	37 352	36 885	37 273	35 824	36 577	36 181	1 026
Congenital malformations, deformations and chromosomal abnormalities — Malformations congénitales et anomalies chromosomiques	*422.4	9 036	9 066	9 468	9 252	9 397	9 730	1 167
Symptoms, signs and abnormal clinical and laboratory findings, not elsewhere classified — Symptômes, signes et résultats anormaux d'examens cliniques et de laboratoire, non classés ailleurs	50.2	143 987	136 485	132 687	138 321	141 396	135 479	4 008
All other diseases — Toutes autres maladies	1.6	1 197	1 433	1 472	1 582	1 587	1 795	145
External causes — Causes externes								
Total	53.1	114 643	119 008	119 452	117 468	116 778	118 285	8 836
Accidents — Accidents								
Total	26.5	60 802	62 581	61 842	54 364	55 272	52 786	4 605
Transport accidents — Accidents de transport	11.3	33 092	35 505	35 731	30 961	30 101	29 621	1 704
Falls — Chutes	0.8	5 401	4 343	4 598	4 821	4 728	4 253	385
Accidental drowning and submersion — Noyade et submersion accidentelles	2.1	7 003	6 924	7 126	6 541	6 037	6 154	421
Exposure to smoke, fire and flames — Exposition à la fumée, au feu et aux flammes ..	1.0	1 349	1 285	1 316	1 245	1 058	1 014	339
Accidental poisoning by and exposure to noxious substances — Intoxication accidentelle par des substances nocives et exposition à ces substances	0.5	429	317	314	378	302	267	47
Intentional self-harm — Lésions auto-infligées	8.4	6 584	6 738	6 919	6 978	6 530	6 779	930
Assault — Agresssions	6.9	37 076	38 853	40 468	41 873	42 870	45 311	464
All other external causes — Toutes autres causes externes	11.3	10 181	10 836	10 223	14 253	12 106	13 409	2 837

(See notes at end of table. — Voir notes à la fin du tableau.)

Chile — Chili

Cause of death — Cause de décès	1995 Rate Taux	1996 Number Nombre	1996 Rate Taux	1997 Number Nombre	1997 Rate Taux	1998 Number Nombre	1998 Rate Taux	1999 Number Nombre
Diseases of the digestive system — Maladies de l'appareil digestif								
Diseases of the liver — Maladies du foie	23.5	3 589	24.9	**3 651**	**25.0**	**3 611**	**24.4**	**3 320**
Diseases of the musculoskeletal system and connective tissue — Maladies du système ostéo-articulaire, des muscles et du tissu conjonctif	2.2	269	1.9	**299**	**2.0**	**338**	**2.3**	**342**
Diseases of the genitourinary system — Maladies de l'appareil génito-urinaire								
Total	11.9	1 742	12.1	**1 703**	**11.6**	**1 812**	**12.2**	**1 932**
Disorders of kidney and ureter — Affections du rein et de l'uretère	7.6	1 119	7.8	**1 163**	**8.0**	**1 243**	**8.4**	**1 253**
Hyperplasia of prostate — Hyperplasie de la prostate	▼8.7	64	▼5.6	**61**	**▼5.1**	**64**	**▼5.2**	**62**
Pregnancy, childbirth and the puerperium — Grossesse, accouchement et puerpéralité								
Total	*30.7	63	*23.8	**61**	***23.5**	**55**	***21.4**	**60**
Pregnancy with abortive outcome — Grossesse se terminant par un avortement	♦ *7.1	14	♦ *5.3	**12**	**♦ *4.6**	**14**	**♦ *5.4**	**5**
Other direct obstetric causes — Autres décès maternels directs	*19.3	37	*14.0	**41**	***15.8**	**35**	***13.6**	**40**
Indirect obstetric causes — Décès maternels indirects	♦ *4.3	12	♦ *4.5	**8**	**♦ *3.1**	**6**	**♦ *2.3**	**15**
Certain conditions originating in the perinatal period — Certaines affections dont l'origine se situe dans la période périnatale	*366.5	1 036	*391.2	**995**	***382.8**	**948**	***368.7**	**932**
Congenital malformations, deformations and chromosomal abnormalities — Malformations congénitales et anomalies chromosomiques	*416.9	1 128	*426.0	**1 057**	***406.6**	**1 148**	***446.5**	**1 060**
Symptoms, signs and abnormal clinical and laboratory findings, not elsewhere classified — Symptômes, signes et résultats anormaux d'examens cliniques et de laboratoire, non classés ailleurs	28.2	3 545	24.6	**3 733**	**25.5**	**3 523**	**23.8**	**3 714**
All other diseases — Toutes autres maladies	1.0	149	1.0	**159**	**1.1**	**331**	**2.2**	**591**
External causes — Causes externes								
Total	62.2	8 409	58.3	**8 280**	**56.6**	**8 125**	**54.8**	**7 652**
Accidents — Accidents								
Total	32.4	4 308	29.9	**4 301**	**29.4**	**3 973**	**26.8**	**3 605**
Transport accidents — Accidents de transport	12.0	1 784	12.4	**1 873**	**12.8**	**1 968**	**13.3**	**1 654**
Falls — Chutes	2.7	483	3.3	**123**	**0.8**	**106**	**0.7**	**113**
Accidental drowning and submersion — Noyade et submersion accidentelles	3.0	360	2.6	**407**	**2.8**	**359**	**2.4**	**365**
Exposure to smoke, fire and flames — Exposition à la fumée, au feu et aux flammes	2.4	313	2.2	**249**	**1.7**	**130**	**0.9**	**136**
Accidental poisoning by and exposure to noxious substances — Intoxication accidentelle par des substances nocives et exposition à ces substances	0.3	55	0.4	**39**	**0.3**	**23**	**♦0.2**	**39**
Intentional self-harm — Lésions auto-infligées	6.5	917	6.4	**910**	**6.2**	**1 031**	**7.0**	**1 041**
Assault — Agresssions	3.3	437	3.0	**378**	**2.6**	**421**	**2.8**	**445**
All other external causes — Toutes autres causes externes	20.0	2 747	19.1	**2 691**	**18.4**	**2 700**	**18.2**	**2 561**

(See notes at end of table. — Voir notes à la fin du tableau.)

Cause of death — Cause de décès	Chile — Chili					Colombia — Colombie		
	1999	2000		2001		1995	1996	1997
	Rate Taux	Number Nombre	Rate Taux	Number Nombre	Rate Taux	Number Nombre		
Diseases of the digestive system — Maladies de l'appareil digestif								
Diseases of the liver — Maladies du foie	22.1	3 504	23.0	3 954	25.7	1 387	1 470	1 862
Diseases of the musculoskeletal system and connective tissue — Maladies du système ostéo-articularie, des muscles et du tissu conjonctif	2.3	381	2.5	427	2.8	441	334	419
Diseases of the genitourinary system — Maladies de l'appareil génito-urinaire								
Total	12.9	1 847	12.1	2 100	13.6	2 552	2 591	2 609
Disorders of kidney and ureter — Affections du rein et de l'uretère	8.3	1 185	7.8	1 395	9.1	2 335	2 373	2 209
Hyperplasia of prostate — Hyperplasie de la prostate	▼4.9	61	▼4.7	72	▼5.3	30	28	47
Pregnancy, childbirth and the puerperium — Grossesse, accouchement et puerpéralité								
Total	*23.9	49	*19.7	45	*18.3	411	430	420
Pregnancy with abortive outcome — Grossesse se terminant par un avortement	♦ *2.0	13	♦ *5.2	4	♦ *1.6	64	72	40
Other direct obstetric causes — Autres décès maternels directs	*16.0	28	♦ *11.2	30	♦ *12.2	335	351	339
Indirect obstetric causes — Décès maternels indirects	♦ *6.0	8	♦ *3.2	11	♦ *4.5	12	7	40
Certain conditions originating in the perinatal period — Certaines affections dont l'origine se situe dans la période périnatale	*371.8	926	*372.0	855	*347.4	4 875	4 719	5 488
Congenital malformations, deformations and chromosomal abnormalities — Malformations congénitales et anomalies chromosomiques	*422.9	975	*391.7	908	*368.9	2 318	2 091	1 971
Symptoms, signs and abnormal clinical and laboratory findings, not elsewhere classified — Symptômes, signes et résultats anormaux d'examens cliniques et de laboratoire, non classés ailleurs	24.7	3 103	20.4	2 872	18.6	9 775	8 877	7 299
All other diseases — Toutes autres maladies	3.9	387	2.5	259	1.7	121	147	211
External causes — Causes externes								
Total	51.0	7 754	51.0	7 623	49.5	41 532	42 307	40 992
Accidents — Accidents								
Total	24.0	4 567	30.0	4 777	31.0	14 023	13 308	12 475
Transport accidents — Accidents de transport	11.0	2 197	14.4	2 061	13.4	7 159	6 803	7 187
Falls — Chutes	0.8	305	2.0	297	1.9	1 425	1 349	689
Accidental drowning and submersion — Noyade et submersion accidentelles	2.6	470	3.1	528	3.4	1 322	1 275	1 137
Exposure to smoke, fire and flames — Exposition à la fumée, au feu et aux flammes ..	0.9	256	1.7	314	2.0	357	251	220
Accidental poisoning by and exposure to noxious substances — Intoxication accidentelle par des substances nocives et exposition à ces substances	0.3	152	1.0	130	0.8	258	237	164
Intentional self-harm — Lésions auto-infligées	6.9	1 473	9.7	1 625	10.6	1 172	1 229	1 260
Assault — Agresssions	3.0	793	5.2	839	5.4	23 443	24 849	22 693
All other external causes — Toutes autres causes externes	17.1	921	6.1	382	2.5	2 894	2 921	4 564

(See notes at end of table. — Voir notes à la fin du tableau.)

Cause of death — Cause de décès	Colombia — Colombie		Ecuador — Equateur[4]					
	1998	1999	1995	1996	1997	1998	1999	2000
				Number Nombre				
Diseases of the digestive system — Maladies de l'appareil digestif								
Diseases of the liver — Maladies du foie	1 938	2 076	1 132	1 246	1 385	1 453	1 457	1 435
Diseases of the musculoskeletal system and connective tissue — Maladies du système ostéo-articularie, des muscles et du tissu conjonctif	655	858	212	248	96	107	97	114
Diseases of the genitourinary system — Maladies de l'appareil génito-urinaire								
Total	2 849	2 998	1 202	1 352	1 584	1 677	1 644	1 647
Disorders of kidney and ureter — Affections du rein et de l'uretère	2 346	2 395	1 097	1 249	1 513	1 605	1 578	1 583
Hyperplasia of prostate — Hyperplasie de la prostate	87	91	49	62	42	48	45	44
Pregnancy, childbirth and the puerperium — Grossesse, accouchement et puerpéralité								
Total	721	676	170	194	162	153	209	232
Pregnancy with abortive outcome — Grossesse se terminant par un avortement	63	46	12	11	17	12	16	20
Other direct obstetric causes — Autres décès maternels directs	499	454	155	182	145	138	189	203
Indirect obstetric causes — Décès maternels indirects	108	166	3	1	-	2	3	9
Certain conditions originating in the perinatal period — Certaines affections dont l'origine se situe dans la période périnatale	7 367	8 057	2 509	2 689	2 104	2 134	2 250	2 250
Congenital malformations, deformations and chromosomal abnormalities — Malformations congénitales et anomalies chromosomiques	2 243	2 547	513	492	547	506	580	613
Symptoms, signs and abnormal clinical and laboratory findings, not elsewhere classified — Symptômes, signes et résultats anormaux d'examens cliniques et de laboratoire, non classés ailleurs	5 174	3 628	8 083	7 941	7 177	7 064	7 680	7 419
All other diseases — Toutes autres maladies	307	466	37	33	22	38	31	30
External causes — Causes externes								
Total	42 753	43 931	7 466	7 652	7 565	7 929	7 716	8 112
Accidents — Accidents								
Total	13 172	12 954	4 964	5 045	4 787	5 040	4 444	4 495
Transport accidents — Accidents de transport	8 565	7 683	1 844	1 748	2 041	2 132	1 826	2 050
Falls — Chutes	1 018	1 037	371	446	367	401	434	319
Accidental drowning and submersion — Noyade et submersion accidentelles	1 301	1 245	521	468	549	560	420	306
Exposure to smoke, fire and flames — Exposition à la fumée, au feu et aux flammes	200	191	152	167	137	118	110	133
Accidental poisoning by and exposure to noxious substances — Intoxication accidentelle par des substances nocives et exposition à ces substances	150	118	128	299	196	242	226	194
Intentional self-harm — Lésions auto-infligées	2 112	2 163	547	593	581	549	616	538
Assault — Agresssions	24 669	25 832	1 531	1 632	1 475	1 835	1 834	2 086
All other external causes — Toutes autres causes externes	2 800	2 982	424	382	722	505	822	993

(See notes at end of table. — Voir notes à la fin du tableau.)

Cause of death — Cause de décès	Guyana		Paraguay					
	1995	1996	1995	1996	1997	1998	1999	2000
			Number Nombre					
Diseases of the digestive system — Maladies de l'appareil digestif								
Diseases of the liver — Maladies du foie	119	123	161	234	227	275	248	246
Diseases of the musculoskeletal system and connective tissue — Maladies du système ostéo-articularie, des muscles et du tissu conjonctif	18	12	54	18	25	44	27	50
Diseases of the genitourinary system — Maladies de l'appareil génito-urinaire								
Total	76	71	284	329	256	310	274	306
Disorders of kidney and ureter — Affections du rein et de l'uretère	52	40	216	298	218	261	222	244
Hyperplasia of prostate — Hyperplasie de la prostate	11	12	8	1	7	6	-	4
Pregnancy, childbirth and the puerperium — Grossesse, accouchement et puerpéralité								
Total	35	26	104	109	89	96	103	140
Pregnancy with abortive outcome — Grossesse se terminant par un avortement	9	7	30	34	25	16	23	35
Other direct obstetric causes — Autres décès maternels directs	26	17	69	70	64	73	77	100
Indirect obstetric causes — Décès maternels indirects	-	2	5	5	1	7	3	5
Certain conditions originating in the perinatal period — Certaines affections dont l'origine se situe dans la période périnatale	299	208	623	848	801	796	864	825
Congenital malformations, deformations and chromosomal abnormalities — Malformations congénitales et anomalies chromosomiques	69	62	248	246	239	208	212	235
Symptoms, signs and abnormal clinical and laboratory findings, not elsewhere classified — Symptômes, signes et résultats anormaux d'examens cliniques et de laboratoire, non classés ailleurs	94	117	1 649	1 765	3 168	3 065	3 641	3 803
All other diseases — Toutes autres maladies	14	21	5	6	1	1	3	24
External causes — Causes externes								
Total	555	543	1 942	1 929	1 945	1 907	2 046	2 039
Accidents — Accidents								
Total	243	202	1 092	1 061	1 114	1 014	1 130	998
Transport accidents — Accidents de transport	55	39	471	458	514	441	496	409
Falls — Chutes	54	47	39	17	23	20	28	28
Accidental drowning and submersion — Noyade et submersion accidentelles	19	14	89	109	117	151	172	95
Exposure to smoke, fire and flames — Exposition à la fumée, au feu et aux flammes	2	5	33	35	35	18	28	56
Accidental poisoning by and exposure to noxious substances — Intoxication accidentelle par des substances nocives et exposition à ces substances	3	-	26	23	17	21	20	13
Intentional self-harm — Lésions auto-infligées	103	62	120	99	126	138	161	154
Assault — Agresssions	53	32	515	605	514	546	535	672
All other external causes — Toutes autres causes externes	156	247	215	164	191	209	220	215

21. Death and death rates by cause: 1995 - 2002
Décès selon la cause, nombres et taux: 1995 - 2002 (continued — suite)

(See notes at end of table. — Voir notes à la fin du tableau.)

Cause of death — Cause de décès	Peru — Pérou						Uruguay	
	1995	1996	1997	1998	1999	2000	1995	
				Number Nombre				Rate Taux
Diseases of the digestive system — Maladies de l'appareil digestif								
Diseases of the liver — Maladies du foie	2 036	2 421	2 196	2 496	2 777	3 002	351	10.9
Diseases of the musculoskeletal system and connective tissue — Maladies du système ostéo-articularie, des muscles et du tissu conjonctif	260	281	332	260	1 507	311	107	3.3
Diseases of the genitourinary system — Maladies de l'appareil génito-urinaire								
Total	2 718	2 944	2 751	2 975	3 138	3 186	526	16.4
Disorders of kidney and ureter — Affections du rein et de l'uretère	1 991	2 117	1 977	2 186	2 511	2 573	317	9.9
Hyperplasia of prostate — Hyperplasie de la prostate	128	120	89	91	27	80	25	...
Pregnancy, childbirth and the puerperium — Grossesse, accouchement et puerpéralité								
Total	301	337	246	279	261	263	14	♦ *24.7
Pregnancy with abortive outcome — Grossesse se terminant par un avortement	51	45	30	34	39	30	5	♦ *8.8
Other direct obstetric causes — Autres décès maternels directs	245	284	214	242	221	227	7	♦ *12.3
Indirect obstetric causes — Décès maternels indirects	5	8	2	3	1	6	2	♦ *3.5
Certain conditions originating in the perinatal period — Certaines affections dont l'origine se situe dans la période périnatale	3 182	3 592	3 198	2 602	2 571	2 558	479	*844.9
Congenital malformations, deformations and chromosomal abnormalities — Malformations congénitales et anomalies chromosomiques	874	940	840	787	1 086	1 093	277	*488.6
Symptoms, signs and abnormal clinical and laboratory findings, not elsewhere classified — Symptômes, signes et résultats anormaux d'examens cliniques et de laboratoire, non classés ailleurs	22 516	20 423	21 461	18 004	13 081	10 425	2 147	66.7
All other diseases — Toutes autres maladies	229	234	225	244	288	434	132	4.1
External causes — Causes externes								
Total	8 722	9 587	9 281	9 482	9 326	8 968	2 155	67.0
Accidents — Accidents								
Total	5 247	5 837	4 878	5 644	5 956	7 063	1 574	48.9
Transport accidents — Accidents de transport	1 943	1 995	1 882	2 262	1 910	1 989	456	14.2
Falls — Chutes	213	139	131	150	55	62	207	6.4
Accidental drowning and submersion — Noyade et submersion accidentelles	524	685	570	551	433	656	135	4.2
Exposure to smoke, fire and flames — Exposition à la fumée, au feu et aux flammes	121	146	126	93	153	153	48	1.5
Accidental poisoning by and exposure to noxious substances — Intoxication accidentelle par des substances nocives et exposition à ces substances	39	39	47	57	158	93	28	♦0.9
Intentional self-harm — Lésions auto-infligées	368	381	292	323	241	228	429	13.3
Assault — Agresssions	796	641	582	761	347	450	151	4.7
All other external causes — Toutes autres causes externes	2 311	2 728	3 529	2 754	2 782	1 227	1	0.0

(See notes at end of table. — Voir notes à la fin du tableau.)

Uruguay

Cause of death — Cause de décès	1996		1997		1998		1999	
	Number Nombre	Rate Taux	Number Nombre	Rate Taux	Number Nombre	Rate Taux	Number Nombre	Rate Taux
Diseases of the digestive system — Maladies de l'appareil digestif Diseases of the liver — Maladies du foie	329	10.1	434	13.3	387	11.8	400	12.1
Diseases of the musculoskeletal system and connective tissue — Maladies du système ostéo-articularie, des muscles et du tissu conjonctif	94	2.9	109	3.3	121	3.7	149	4.5
Diseases of the genitourinary system — Maladies de l'appareil génito-urinaire Total	511	15.8	497	15.2	544	16.6	555	16.8
Disorders of kidney and ureter — Affections du rein et de l'uretère	308	9.5	316	9.7	355	10.8	381	11.5
Hyperplasia of prostate — Hyperplasie de la prostate	25	♦ ▼6.5	11	...	18	♦ ▼4.7	17	♦ ▼4.4
Pregnancy, childbirth and the puerperium — Grossesse, accouchement et puerpéralité Total	11	♦ *18.7	17	♦ *29.3	11	♦ *20.1	6	♦ *11.1
Pregnancy with abortive outcome — Grossesse se terminant par un avortement	4	♦ *6.8	4	♦ *6.9	3	♦ *5.5	1	♦ *1.9
Other direct obstetric causes — Autres décès maternels directs	7	♦ *11.9	11	♦ *19.0	6	♦ *11.0	5	♦ *9.3
Indirect obstetric causes — Décès maternels indirects	-	-	2	♦ *3.4	2	♦ *3.7	-	-
Certain conditions originating in the perinatal period — Certaines affections dont l'origine se situe dans la période périnatale	413	*701.6	396	*682.4	372	*679.3	375	*694.4
Congenital malformations, deformations and chromosomal abnormalities — Malformations congénitales et anomalies chromosomiques	278	*472.3	287	*494.6	252	*460.2	223	*412.9
Symptoms, signs and abnormal clinical and laboratory findings, not elsewhere classified — Symptômes, signes et résultats anormaux d'examens cliniques et de laboratoire, non classés ailleurs	2 049	63.2	1 986	60.9	2 113	64.3	2 723	82.4
All other diseases — Toutes autres maladies	122	3.8	140	4.3	135	4.1	164	5.0
External causes — Causes externes Total	2 154	66.5	2 156	66.1	2 226	67.8	2 087	63.2
Accidents — Accidents Total	1 610	49.7	1 501	46.0	1 466	44.6	1 426	43.2
Transport accidents — Accidents de transport	433	13.4	536	16.4	492	15.0	472	14.3
Falls — Chutes	168	5.2	38	1.2	30	♦0.9	25	♦0.8
Accidental drowning and submersion — Noyade et submersion accidentelles	142	4.4	117	3.6	126	3.8	102	3.1
Exposure to smoke, fire and flames — Exposition à la fumée, au feu et aux flammes ..	87	2.7	68	2.1	43	1.3	75	2.3
Accidental poisoning by and exposure to noxious substances — Intoxication accidentelle par des substances nocives et exposition à ces substances	33	1.0	41	1.3	31	0.9	24	♦0.7
Intentional self-harm — Lésions auto-infligées	400	12.3	462	14.2	525	16.0	456	13.8
Assault — Agresssions	144	4.4	158	4.8	191	5.8	178	5.4
All other external causes — Toutes autres causes externes	-	-	35	1.1	44	1.3	27	♦0.8

(See notes at end of table. — Voir notes à la fin du tableau.)

Cause of death — Cause de décès	Uruguay		Venezuela[5]					
	2000		1996		1997		1998	
	Number Nombre	Rate Taux	Number Nombre	Rate Taux	Number Nombre	Rate Taux	Number Nombre	Rate Taux
Diseases of the digestive system — Maladies de l'appareil digestif								
Diseases of the liver — Maladies du foie	383	11.5	1 830	8.1	1 801	7.8	1 954	8.3
Diseases of the musculoskeletal system and connective tissue — Maladies du système ostéo-articularie, des muscles et du tissu conjonctif	126	3.8	534	2.4	480	2.1	500	2.1
Diseases of the genitourinary system — Maladies de l'appareil génito-urinaire								
Total	496	14.9	1 802	8.0	1 930	8.4	1 764	7.5
Disorders of kidney and ureter — Affections du rein et de l'uretère	331	10.0	1 501	6.7	1 563	6.8	1 447	6.2
Hyperplasia of prostate — Hyperplasie de la prostate	11	♦▼2.8	86	▼6.6	93	▼6.8	81	▼5.7
Pregnancy, childbirth and the puerperium — Grossesse, accouchement et puerpéralité								
Total	9	♦*17.1	297	*59.6	308	*59.6	256	*51.0
Pregnancy with abortive outcome — Grossesse se terminant par un avortement	-		46	*9.2	47	*9.1	53	*10.6
Other direct obstetric causes — Autres décès maternels directs	8	♦*15.2	231	*46.4	233	*45.1	175	*34.9
Indirect obstetric causes — Décès maternels indirects	1	♦*1.9	19	♦*3.8	28	♦*5.4	25	♦*5.0
Certain conditions originating in the perinatal period — Certaines affections dont l'origine se situe dans la période périnatale	327	*619.7	5 646	*1133.8	5 503	*1065.2	5 244	*1045.0
Congenital malformations, deformations and chromosomal abnormalities — Malformations congénitales et anomalies chromosomiques	216	*409.3	1 919	*385.4	1 911	*369.9	1 856	*369.9
Symptoms, signs and abnormal clinical and laboratory findings, not elsewhere classified — Symptômes, signes et résultats anormaux d'examens cliniques et de laboratoire, non classés ailleurs	2 245	67.6	1 764	7.8	1 923	8.4	1 783	7.6
All other diseases — Toutes autres maladies	138	4.2	280	1.2	272	1.2	252	1.1
External causes — Causes externes								
Total	2 027	61.0	15 097	67.1	14 220	61.9	15 444	66.0
Accidents — Accidents								
Total	1 220	37.0	7 189	31.9	7 070	30.8	7 784	33.2
Transport accidents — Accidents de transport	363	10.9	4 221	18.8	4 115	17.9	4 823	20.6
Falls — Chutes	28	*0.8	542	2.4	479	2.1	578	2.5
Accidental drowning and submersion — Noyade et submersion accidentelles	125	3.8	645	2.9	580	2.5	625	2.7
Exposure to smoke, fire and flames — Exposition à la fumée, au feu et aux flammes ..	47	1.4	56	0.2	73	0.3	120	0.5
Accidental poisoning by and exposure to noxious substances — Intoxication accidentelle par des substances nocives et exposition à ces substances	34	1.0	108	0.5	91	0.4	77	0.3
Intentional self-harm — Lésions auto-infligées	565	17.0	1 008	4.5	1 076	4.7	1 144	4.9
Assault — Agresssions	185	5.6	3 329	14.8	2 863	12.5	2 817	12.0
All other external causes — Toutes autres causes externes	48	1.4	3 571	15.9	3 211	14.0	3 699	15.8

(See notes at end of table. — Voir notes à la fin du tableau.)

Cause of death — Cause de décès	Venezuela[5]				Armenia — Arménie[6]			
	1999		2000		1995		1996	
	Number Nombre	Rate Taux	Number Nombre	Rate Taux	Number Nombre	Rate Taux	Number Nombre	Rate Taux
Diseases of the digestive system — Maladies de l'appareil digestif								
Diseases of the liver — Maladies du foie	2 013	8.4	2 118	8.7	...	...	...	...
Diseases of the musculoskeletal system and connective tissue — Maladies du système ostéo-articulaire, des muscles et du tissu conjonctif	480	2.0	494	2.0	33	0.9	32	0.8
Diseases of the genitourinary system — Maladies de l'appareil génito-urinaire								
Total	1 913	8.0	1 705	7.0	412	11.0	427	11.3
Disorders of kidney and ureter — Affections du rein et de l'uretère	1 606	6.7	1 423	5.9	333	8.9	350	9.3
Hyperplasia of prostate — Hyperplasie de la prostate	78	...	92	▼5.9	51	▼15.8	46	▼14.3
Pregnancy, childbirth and the puerperium — Grossesse, accouchement et puerpéralité								
Total	313	*59.3	327	*60.1	17	♦ *34.7	10	♦ *20.8
Pregnancy with abortive outcome — Grossesse se terminant par un avortement	43	*8.1	41	*7.5	3	♦ *6.1	2	♦ *4.2
Other direct obstetric causes — Autres décès maternels directs	249	*47.2	243	*44.6	...	...	...	...
Indirect obstetric causes — Décès maternels indirects	21	♦ *4.0	42	*7.7	...	...	...	...
Certain conditions originating in the perinatal period — Certaines affections dont l'origine se situe dans la période périnatale	5 310	*1005.9	5 279	*969.7	259	*529.0	348	*723.0
Congenital malformations, deformations and chromosomal abnormalities — Malformations congénitales et anomalies chromosomiques	1 996	*378.1	2 036	*374.0	142	*290.0	124	*257.6
Symptoms, signs and abnormal clinical and laboratory findings, not elsewhere classified — Symptômes, signes et résultats anormaux d'examens cliniques et de laboratoire, non classés ailleurs	1 411	5.9	1 227	5.0	1 171	31.1	1 107	29.3
All other diseases — Toutes autres maladies	164	0.7	126	0.5	10	♦0.3	7	♦0.2
External causes — Causes externes								
Total	17 489	73.3	20 068	82.5	1 706	45.4	1 553	41.2
Accidents — Accidents								
Total	7 826	32.8	7 933	32.6	1 146	30.5	890	23.6
Transport accidents — Accidents de transport	4 752	19.9	5 231	21.5	249	6.6	245	6.5
Falls — Chutes	568	2.4	676	2.8	60	1.6	22	♦0.6
Accidental drowning and submersion — Noyade et submersion accidentelles	600	2.5	573	2.4	68	1.8	39	1.0
Exposure to smoke, fire and flames — Exposition à la fumée, au feu et aux flammes ..	68	0.3	81	0.3	67	1.8	23	♦0.6
Accidental poisoning by and exposure to noxious substances — Intoxication accidentelle par des substances nocives et exposition à ces substances	73	0.3	86	0.4	81	2.2	49	1.3
Intentional self-harm — Lésions auto-infligées	1 245	5.2	1 264	5.2	130	3.5	87	2.3
Assault — Agresssions	4 017	16.8	6 369	26.2	164	4.4	114	3.0
All other external causes — Toutes autres causes externes	4 401	18.4	4 502	18.5	266	7.1	462	12.2

21. Death and death rates by cause: 1995 - 2002
Décès selon la cause, nombres et taux: 1995 - 2002 (continued — suite)

(See notes at end of table. — Voir notes à la fin du tableau.)

Armenia — Arménie[6]

Cause of death — Cause de décès	1997		1998		1999		2000	
	Number Nombre	Rate Taux	Number Nombre	Rate Taux	Number Nombre	Rate Taux	Number Nombre	Rate Taux
Diseases of the digestive system — Maladies de l'appareil digestif								
Diseases of the liver — Maladies du foie	...	...	...	...	...	...	...	...
Diseases of the musculoskeletal system and connective tissue — Maladies du système ostéo-articularie, des muscles et du tissu conjonctif	25	◆0.7	46	1.2	50	1.3	47	1.2
Diseases of the genitourinary system — Maladies de l'appareil génito-urinaire								
Total	430	11.4	344	9.1	386	10.2	383	10.1
Disorders of kidney and ureter — Affections du rein et de l'uretère	347	9.2	277	7.3	314	8.3	307	8.1
Hyperplasia of prostate — Hyperplasie de la prostate	46	▼14.1	42	▼12.7	43	▼12.8	31	▼9.1
Pregnancy, childbirth and the puerperium — Grossesse, accouchement et puerpéralité								
Total	17	◆ ●38.7	10	◆ ●25.4	12	◆ ●32.9	18	◆ ●52.5
Pregnancy with abortive outcome — Grossesse se terminant par un avortement	2	◆ ●4.6	2	◆ ●5.1	4	◆ ●11.0	4	◆ ●11.7
Other direct obstetric causes — Autres décès maternels directs	...	...	...	...	...	...	...	...
Indirect obstetric causes — Décès maternels indirects	...	...	...	...	...	...	...	...
Certain conditions originating in the perinatal period — Certaines affections dont l'origine se situe dans la période périnatale	303	●689.7	277	●703.7	231	●632.8	211	●615.6
Congenital malformations, deformations and chromosomal abnormalities — Malformations congénitales et anomalies chromosomiques	151	●343.7	156	●396.3	168	●460.2	191	●557.2
Symptoms, signs and abnormal clinical and laboratory findings, not elsewhere classified — Symptômes, signes et résultats anormaux d'examens cliniques et de laboratoire, non classés ailleurs	951	25.1	965	25.4	996	26.2	833	21.9
All other diseases — Toutes autres maladies	5	◆0.1	9	◆0.2	5	◆0.1	8	◆0.2
External causes — Causes externes								
Total	1 434	37.9	1 324	34.9	1 114	29.3	1 102	29.0
Accidents — Accidents								
Total	816	21.6	756	19.9	609	16.0	621	16.3
Transport accidents — Accidents de transport	224	5.9	216	5.7	177	4.7	211	5.5
Falls — Chutes	29	◆0.8	18	◆0.5	26	◆0.7	25	◆0.7
Accidental drowning and submersion — Noyade et submersion accidentelles	45	1.2	42	1.1	39	1.0	56	1.5
Exposure to smoke, fire and flames — Exposition à la fumée, au feu et aux flammes	36	1.0	31	0.8	10	◆0.3	13	◆0.3
Accidental poisoning by and exposure to noxious substances — Intoxication accidentelle par des substances nocives et exposition à ces substances	59	1.6	54	1.4	55	1.4	53	1.4
Intentional self-harm — Lésions auto-infligées	77	2.0	66	1.7	67	1.8	61	1.6
Assault — Agresssions	97	2.6	96	2.5	98	2.6	88	2.3
All other external causes — Toutes autres causes externes	444	11.7	406	10.7	340	8.9	332	8.7

(See notes at end of table. — Voir notes à la fin du tableau.)

Cause of death — Cause de décès	Armenia — Arménie[6]				Azerbaijan — Azerbaïdjan[6]			
	2001		2002		1995	1996	1997	1998
	Number Nombre	Rate Taux	Number Nombre	Rate Taux	Number Nombre			
Diseases of the digestive system — Maladies de l'appareil digestif								
Diseases of the liver — Maladies du foie	...	...	...	...	...	...	...	...
Diseases of the musculoskeletal system and connective tissue — Maladies du système ostéo-articularie, des muscles et du tissu conjonctif	60	1.6	79	2.5	52	82	53	97
Diseases of the genitourinary system — Maladies de l'appareil génito-urinaire								
Total	390	10.3	392	12.2	778	847	813	798
Disorders of kidney and ureter — Affections du rein et de l'uretère	297	7.8	287	8.9	697	672	638	623
Hyperplasia of prostate — Hyperplasie de la prostate	55	...	70	...	9	84	70	87
Pregnancy, childbirth and the puerperium — Grossesse, accouchement et puerpéralité								
Total	7	♦ ●21.8	3	...	53	56	41	51
Pregnancy with abortive outcome — Grossesse se terminant par un avortement	1	♦ ●3.1	1	...	2	3	2	7
Other direct obstetric causes — Autres décès maternels directs	...	...	...	...	...	...	...	...
Indirect obstetric causes — Décès maternels indirects	...	...	...	...	...	...	...	...
Certain conditions originating in the perinatal period — Certaines affections dont l'origine se situe dans la période périnatale	228	●711.1	210	...	550	435	425	394
Congenital malformations, deformations and chromosomal abnormalities — Malformations congénitales et anomalies chromosomiques	158	●492.7	158	...	309	197	181	178
Symptoms, signs and abnormal clinical and laboratory findings, not elsewhere classified — Symptômes, signes et résultats anormaux d'examens cliniques et de laboratoire, non classés ailleurs	753	19.8	779	24.2	1 311	1 585	1 449	1 245
All other diseases — Toutes autres maladies	7	♦0.2	11	♦0.3	4	3	-	1
External causes — Causes externes								
Total	1 101	29.0	1 071	33.3	3 524	2 856	2 650	2 487
Accidents — Accidents								
Total	613	16.1	582	18.1	2 356	1 964	1 790	1 811
Transport accidents — Accidents de transport	204	5.4	189	5.9	662	516	392	407
Falls — Chutes	26	♦0.7	22	♦0.7	35	37	41	60
Accidental drowning and submersion — Noyade et submersion accidentelles	42	1.1	39	1.2	230	237	240	233
Exposure to smoke, fire and flames — Exposition à la fumée, au feu et aux flammes	30	♦0.8	10	♦0.3	308	300	336	301
Accidental poisoning by and exposure to noxious substances — Intoxication accidentelle par des substances nocives et exposition à ces substances	44	1.2	70	2.2	355	186	145	129
Intentional self-harm — Lésions auto-infligées	60	1.6	74	2.3	49	69	107	56
Assault — Agresssions	67	1.8	70	2.2	665	541	459	444
All other external causes — Toutes autres causes externes	361	9.5	345	10.7	454	282	294	176

21. Death and death rates by cause: 1995 - 2002
Décès selon la cause, nombres et taux: 1995 - 2002 (continued — suite)

(See notes at end of table. — Voir notes à la fin du tableau.)

Cause of death — Cause de décès	Azerbaijan — Azerbaïdjan[6]				Bahrain — Bahreïn			
	1999	2000	2001	2002	1997		1998	
			Number Nombre			Rate Taux	Number Nombre	Rate Taux
Diseases of the digestive system — Maladies de l'appareil digestif								
Diseases of the liver — Maladies du foie	...	...	2 045	2 166	29	♦4.9	27	♦4.5
Diseases of the musculoskeletal system and connective tissue — Maladies du système ostéo-articulaire, des muscles et du tissu conjonctif	66	55	79	59	1	♦0.2	1	♦0.2
Diseases of the genitourinary system — Maladies de l'appareil génito-urinaire								
Total	911	909	790	725	74	12.6	77	12.7
Disorders of kidney and ureter — Affections du rein et de l'uretère	747	816	...	...	68	11.5	68	11.2
Hyperplasia of prostate — Hyperplasie de la prostate	81	56	...	...	-	-	-	-
Pregnancy, childbirth and the puerperium — Grossesse, accouchement et puerpéralité								
Total	51	44	27	22	2	♦ ♦14.9	2	♦ ♦14.9
Pregnancy with abortive outcome — Grossesse se terminant par un avortement	6	5	7	2	-	-	-	-
Other direct obstetric causes — Autres décès maternels directs	...	...	18	18	2	♦ ♦14.9	1	♦ ♦7.5
Indirect obstetric causes — Décès maternels indirects	...	...	-	-	-	-	1	♦ ♦7.5
Certain conditions originating in the perinatal period — Certaines affections dont l'origine se situe dans la période périnatale	426	345	290	268	46	♦343.7	52	♦388.6
Congenital malformations, deformations and chromosomal abnormalities — Malformations congénitales et anomalies chromosomiques	166	129	151	148	56	♦418.5	48	♦358.7
Symptoms, signs and abnormal clinical and laboratory findings, not elsewhere classified — Symptômes, signes et résultats anormaux d'examens cliniques et de laboratoire, non classés ailleurs	1 100	1 278	1 082	1 233	193	32.8	367	60.7
All other diseases — Toutes autres maladies	1	-	13	18	26	♦4.4	34	5.6
External causes — Causes externes								
Total	2 195	2 097	1 978	1 869	167	28.3	181	29.9
Accidents — Accidents								
Total	1 540	1 601	...	...	98	16.6	86	14.2
Transport accidents — Accidents de transport	339	455	382	389	74	12.6	69	11.4
Falls — Chutes	49	47	24	31	11	♦1.9	7	♦1.2
Accidental drowning and submersion — Noyade et submersion accidentelles	183	156	38	238	10	♦1.7	10	♦1.7
Exposure to smoke, fire and flames — Exposition à la fumée, au feu et aux flammes	217	195	338	290	-	-	-	-
Accidental poisoning by and exposure to noxious substances — Intoxication accidentelle par des substances nocives et exposition à ces substances	112	106	87	104	-	-	-	-
Intentional self-harm — Lésions auto-infligées	54	62	317	92	-	-	-	-
Assault — Agresssions	375	247	210	215	3	♦0.5	2	♦0.3
All other external causes — Toutes autres causes externes	228	187	...	...	66	11.2	93	15.4

(See notes at end of table. — Voir notes à la fin du tableau.)

Cause of death — Cause de décès	Bahrain — Bahreïn				China - Hong Kong SAR — Chine - Hong-Kong RAS			
	1999		2000		1995	1996	1997	1998
	Number Nombre	Rate Taux	Number Nombre	Rate Taux	Number Nombre			
Diseases of the digestive system — Maladies de l'appareil digestif								
Diseases of the liver — Maladies du foie	31	5.0	28	♦4.4	493	447	436	418
Diseases of the musculoskeletal system and connective tissue — Maladies du système ostéo-articularie, des muscles et du tissu conjonctif	4	♦0.6	3	♦0.5	65	49	58	71
Diseases of the genitourinary system — Maladies de l'appareil génito-urinaire								
Total	56	9.0	53	8.3	1 141	1 213	1 273	1 383
Disorders of kidney and ureter — Affections du rein et de l'uretère	49	7.9	46	7.2	894	978	1 026	1 098
Hyperplasia of prostate — Hyperplasie de la prostate	-	-	2	♦ ▼6.0	2	-	5	1
Pregnancy, childbirth and the puerperium — Grossesse, accouchement et puerpéralité								
Total	3	♦ *21.0	2	♦ *14.3	5	2	1	1
Pregnancy with abortive outcome — Grossesse se terminant par un avortement	-	-	1	♦ *7.2	1	-	-	-
Other direct obstetric causes — Autres décès maternels directs	1	♦ *7.0	-	-	4	2	1	1
Indirect obstetric causes — Décès maternels indirects	2	♦ *14.0	1	♦ *7.2	-	-	-	-
Certain conditions originating in the perinatal period — Certaines affections dont l'origine se situe dans la période périnatale	58	*406.2	46	*329.8	128	126	77	66
Congenital malformations, deformations and chromosomal abnormalities — Malformations congénitales et anomalies chromosomiques	67	*469.2	50	*358.5	151	110	128	84
Symptoms, signs and abnormal clinical and laboratory findings, not elsewhere classified — Symptômes, signes et résultats anormaux d'examens cliniques et de laboratoire, non classés ailleurs	325	52.3	319	50.0	403	424	350	345
All other diseases — Toutes autres maladies	31	5.0	39	6.1	26	33	71	47
External causes — Causes externes								
Total	159	25.6	310	48.6	1 590	1 670	1 908	1 910
Accidents — Accidents								
Total	37	6.0	223	35.0	755	724	1 016	864
Transport accidents — Accidents de transport	16	♦2.6	202	31.7	294	253	293	232
Falls — Chutes	3	♦0.5	12	♦1.9	161	124	228	156
Accidental drowning and submersion — Noyade et submersion accidentelles	17	♦2.7	9	♦1.4	38	45	50	42
Exposure to smoke, fire and flames — Exposition à la fumée, au feu et aux flammes ..	-	-	-	-	8	17	50	44
Accidental poisoning by and exposure to noxious substances — Intoxication accidentelle par des substances nocives et exposition à ces substances	-	-	-	-	151	176	252	271
Intentional self-harm — Lésions auto-infligées	17	♦2.7	29	♦4.5	724	788	642	847
Assault — Agresssions	2	♦0.3	9	♦1.4	77	63	75	66
All other external causes — Toutes autres causes externes	103	16.6	49	7.7	34	95	175	133

(See notes at end of table. — Voir notes à la fin du tableau.)

Cause of death — Cause de décès	China - Hong Kong SAR — Chine - Hong-Kong RAS		Georgia — Géorgie[6,7]					
	1999	2000	1995	1996	1997	1998	1999	2000
					Number Nombre			
Diseases of the digestive system — Maladies de l'appareil digestif								
Diseases of the liver — Maladies du foie	399	487	...	...	...	1 063	1 179	1 130
Diseases of the musculoskeletal system and connective tissue — Maladies du système ostéo-articularie, des muscles et du tissu conjonctif	67	92	1	8	2	13	11	11
Diseases of the genitourinary system — Maladies de l'appareil génito-urinaire								
Total	1 529	1 479	384	322	339	298	339	151
Disorders of kidney and ureter — Affections du rein et de l'uretère	1 197	1 189	379	287	297	273	309	131
Hyperplasia of prostate — Hyperplasie de la prostate	4	3	-	13	14	1	2	-
Pregnancy, childbirth and the puerperium — Grossesse, accouchement et puerpéralité								
Total	1	3	17	9	13	15	9	4
Pregnancy with abortive outcome — Grossesse se terminant par un avortement	-	1	1	1	2	2	-	1
Other direct obstetric causes — Autres décès maternels directs	1	2	...	...	...	9	8	3
Indirect obstetric causes — Décès maternels indirects	-	-	...	...	...	1	-	-
Certain conditions originating in the perinatal period — Certaines affections dont l'origine se situe dans la période périnatale	52	50	364	524	582	473	477	390
Congenital malformations, deformations and chromosomal abnormalities — Malformations congénitales et anomalies chromosomiques	92	99	78	82	82	34	33	16
Symptoms, signs and abnormal clinical and laboratory findings, not elsewhere classified — Symptômes, signes et résultats anormaux d'examens cliniques et de laboratoire, non classés ailleurs	399	357	865	895	1 238	1 212	1 160	1 409
All other diseases — Toutes autres maladies	21	35	1	4	7	10	15	3
External causes — Causes externes								
Total	2 053	1 906	2 101	1 540	1 465	1 544	1 571	1 237
Accidents — Accidents								
Total	806	709	1 300	960	795	700	720	545
Transport accidents — Accidents de transport	268	195	343	336	299	232	272	235
Falls — Chutes	192	150	38	39	27	41	23	12
Accidental drowning and submersion — Noyade et submersion accidentelles	32	34	115	98	82	71	62	51
Exposure to smoke, fire and flames — Exposition à la fumée, au feu et aux flammes ..	13	22	127	79	72	91	90	68
Accidental poisoning by and exposure to noxious substances — Intoxication accidentelle par des substances nocives et exposition à ces substances	239	198	150	74	83	48	50	36
Intentional self-harm — Lésions auto-infligées	972	890	138	162	176	148	189	131
Assault — Agressions	67	58	1	19	76	175	160	146
All other external causes — Toutes autres causes externes	218	249	563	399	418	521	502	415

(See notes at end of table. — Voir notes à la fin du tableau.)

Cause of death — Cause de décès	Georgia — Géorgie[6,7] 2001 Number Nombre	Israel — Israël[8] 1995 Number Nombre	1995 Rate Taux	1996 Number Nombre	1996 Rate Taux	1997 Number Nombre	1997 Rate Taux	1998 Number Nombre
Diseases of the digestive system — Maladies de l'appareil digestif								
Diseases of the liver — Maladies du foie	1 061	312	5.6	307	5.4	246	4.2	336
Diseases of the musculoskeletal system and connective tissue — Maladies du système ostéo-articularie, des muscles et du tissu conjonctif	4	116	2.1	117	2.1	101	1.7	145
Diseases of the genitourinary system — Maladies de l'appareil génito-urinaire								
Total	270	898	16.2	1 242	21.8	1 468	25.2	1 109
Disorders of kidney and ureter — Affections du rein et de l'uretère	235	605	10.9	665	♦ ▼11.7	918	15.7	814
Hyperplasia of prostate — Hyperplasie de la prostate	5	24	♦ ▼4.8	12	♦ ▼2.3	4	♦ ▼0.7	21
Pregnancy, childbirth and the puerperium — Grossesse, accouchement et puerpéralité								
Total	4	7	♦ *6.0	9	♦ *7.4	12	♦ *9.6	11
Pregnancy with abortive outcome — Grossesse se terminant par un avortement	-	1	♦ *0.9	2	♦ *1.6	1	♦ *0.8	3
Other direct obstetric causes — Autres décès maternels directs	3	4	♦ *3.4	7	♦ *5.8	11	*8.8	7
Indirect obstetric causes — Décès maternels indirects	1	2	♦ *1.7	-	-	-	-	1
Certain conditions originating in the perinatal period — Certaines affections dont l'origine se situe dans la période périnatale	331	379	*324.2	353	*290.9	319	*256.3	360
Congenital malformations, deformations and chromosomal abnormalities — Malformations congénitales et anomalies chromosomiques	15	312	*266.9	296	*244.0	315	*253.1	267
Symptoms, signs and abnormal clinical and laboratory findings, not elsewhere classified — Symptômes, signes et résultats anormaux d'examens cliniques et de laboratoire, non classés ailleurs	1 343	2 227	40.2	2 041	35.9	2 751	47.2	2 310
All other diseases — Toutes autres maladies	5	133	2.4	187	3.3	151	2.6	169
External causes — Causes externes								
Total	1 265	1 937	34.9	1 969	34.6	1 857	31.9	2 019
Accidents — Accidents								
Total	623	1 335	24.1	1 198	21.1	1 005	17.2	1 118
Transport accidents — Accidents de transport	355	591	10.7	517	9.1	532	9.1	578
Falls — Chutes	22	405	7.3	138	2.4	139	2.4	57
Accidental drowning and submersion — Noyade et submersion accidentelles	45	50	0.9	1	0.0	5	♦0.1	10
Exposure to smoke, fire and flames — Exposition à la fumée, au feu et aux flammes ..	65	32	0.6	6	♦0.1	17	♦0.3	17
Accidental poisoning by and exposure to noxious substances — Intoxication accidentelle par des substances nocives et exposition à ces substances	25	2	0.0	-	-	4	♦0.1	7
Intentional self-harm — Lésions auto-infligées	100	360	6.5	306	5.4	379	6.5	317
Assault — Agresssions	178	78	1.4	56	1.0	30	♦0.5	29
All other external causes — Toutes autres causes externes	364	164	3.0	409	7.2	443	7.6	555

(See notes at end of table. — Voir notes à la fin du tableau.)

Cause of death — Cause de décès	Israel — Israël[8] 1998 Rate Taux	Israel — Israël[8] 1999 Number Nombre	Israel — Israël[8] 1999 Rate Taux	Japan — Japon[9] 1995 Number Nombre	Japan — Japon[9] 1995 Rate Taux	Japan — Japon[9] 1996 Number Nombre	Japan — Japon[9] 1996 Rate Taux	Japan — Japon[9] 1997 Number Nombre
Diseases of the digestive system — Maladies de l'appareil digestif								
Diseases of the liver — Maladies du foie	5.6	366	6.0	17 018	13.6	16 517	13.1	16 599
Diseases of the musculoskeletal system and connective tissue — Maladies du système ostéo-articularie, des muscles et du tissu conjonctif	2.4	242	4.0	4 070	3.2	4 073	3.2	4 095
Diseases of the genitourinary system — Maladies de l'appareil génito-urinaire								
Total	18.6	1 379	22.5	21 381	17.0	20 899	16.6	21 280
Disorders of kidney and ureter — Affections du rein et de l'uretère	13.6	957	15.6	19 850	15.8	19 400	15.4	19 764
Hyperplasia of prostate — Hyperplasie de la prostate	♦ ▼3.7	30	♦ ▼5.0	221	...	172	▼0.9	177
Pregnancy, childbirth and the puerperium — Grossesse, accouchement et puerpéralité								
Total	♦ *8.5	9	♦ *6.8	90	*7.6	80	*6.6	81
Pregnancy with abortive outcome — Grossesse se terminant par un avortement	♦ *2.3	1	♦ *0.8	2	♦ *0.2	3	♦ *0.2	3
Other direct obstetric causes — Autres décès maternels directs	♦ *5.4	8	♦ *6.1	65	*5.5	51	*4.2	46
Indirect obstetric causes — Décès maternels indirects	♦ *0.8	-	-	18	♦ *1.5	18	♦ *1.5	29
Certain conditions originating in the perinatal period — Certaines affections dont l'origine se situe dans la période périnatale	*276.8	349	*264.5	1 547	*130.3	1 425	*118.1	1 288
Congenital malformations, deformations and chromosomal abnormalities — Malformations congénitales et anomalies chromosomiques	*205.3	262	*198.6	3 285	*276.7	2 935	*243.3	2 785
Symptoms, signs and abnormal clinical and laboratory findings, not elsewhere classified — Symptômes, signes et résultats anormaux d'examens cliniques et de laboratoire, non classés ailleurs	38.7	1 917	31.3	25 720	20.5	24 768	19.7	25 369
All other diseases — Toutes autres maladies	2.8	282	4.6	887	0.7	843	0.7	853
External causes — Causes externes								
Total	33.8	2 155	35.2	69 877	55.7	64 329	51.2	65 537
Accidents — Accidents								
Total	18.7	1 281	20.9	45 323	36.1	39 184	31.2	38 886
Transport accidents — Accidents de transport	9.7	531	8.7	15 147	12.1	14 343	11.4	13 981
Falls — Chutes	1.0	105	1.7	5 911	4.7	5 910	4.7	5 872
Accidental drowning and submersion — Noyade et submersion accidentelle	♦0.2	42	0.7	5 588	4.5	5 648	4.5	5 659
Exposure to smoke, fire and flames — Exposition à la fumée, au feu et aux flammes	♦0.3	25	♦0.4	1 383	1.1	1 420	1.1	1 444
Accidental poisoning by and exposure to noxious substances — Intoxication accidentelle par des substances nocives et exposition à ces substances	♦0.1	16	♦0.3	568	0.5	699	0.6	608
Intentional self-harm — Lésions auto-infligées	5.3	368	6.0	21 420	17.1	22 138	17.6	23 494
Assault — Agressions	♦0.5	127	2.1	727	0.6	680	0.5	718
All other external causes — Toutes autres causes externes	9.3	379	6.2	2 407	1.9	2 327	1.9	2 439

21. Death and death rates by cause: 1995 - 2002
Décès selon la cause, nombres et taux: 1995 - 2002 (continued — suite)

(See notes at end of table. — Voir notes à la fin du tableau.)

Cause of death — Cause de décès	Japan — Japon[9] 1997 Rate Taux	1998 Number Nombre	1998 Rate Taux	1999 Number Nombre	1999 Rate Taux	2000 Number Nombre	2000 Rate Taux	Kazakhstan[6] 1995 Number Nombre
Diseases of the digestive system — Maladies de l'appareil digestif								
Diseases of the liver — Maladies du foie	13.2	16 133	12.8	16 585	13.1	16 079	12.7	3 002
Diseases of the musculoskeletal system and connective tissue — Maladies du système ostéo-articulaire, des muscles et du tissu conjonctif	3.2	4 145	3.3	4 295	3.4	4 419	3.5	203
Diseases of the genitourinary system — Maladies de l'appareil génito-urinaire								
Total	16.9	21 306	16.9	22 617	17.9	21 977	17.3	2 232
Disorders of kidney and ureter — Affections du rein et de l'uretère	15.7	19 774	15.6	20 904	16.5	20 328	16.0	1 961
Hyperplasia of prostate — Hyperplasie de la prostate	▼0.9	153	▼0.7	140	▼0.6	108	...	110
Pregnancy, childbirth and the puerperium — Grossesse, accouchement et puerpéralité								
Total	*6.8	89	*7.4	79	*6.7	84	*7.1	159
Pregnancy with abortive outcome — Grossesse se terminant par un avortement	♦ *0.3	5	♦ *0.4	1	♦ *0.1	5	♦ *0.4	30
Other direct obstetric causes — Autres décès maternels directs	*3.9	59	*4.9	54	*4.6	58	*4.9	129
Indirect obstetric causes — Décès maternels indirects	♦ *2.4	22	♦ *1.8	17	♦ *1.4	15	♦ *1.3	...
Certain conditions originating in the perinatal period — Certaines affections dont l'origine se situe dans la période périnatale	*108.1	1 262	*104.9	1 206	*102.4	1 125	*94.5	2 119
Congenital malformations, deformations and chromosomal abnormalities — Malformations congénitales et anomalies chromosomiques	*233.7	2 885	*239.8	2 673	*227.0	2 702	*227.0	1 414
Symptoms, signs and abnormal clinical and laboratory findings, not elsewhere classified — Symptômes, signes et résultats anormaux d'examens cliniques et de laboratoire, non classés ailleurs	20.1	25 643	20.3	27 659	21.8	26 548	20.9	4 096
All other diseases — Toutes autres maladies	0.7	882	0.7	947	0.7	885	0.7	165
External causes — Causes externes								
Total	52.0	74 350	58.8	75 242	59.4	73 805	58.2	23 270
Accidents — Accidents								
Total	30.8	38 925	30.8	40 079	31.7	39 484	31.1	9 870
Transport accidents — Accidents de transport	11.1	13 464	10.7	13 111	10.4	12 857	10.1	2 930
Falls — Chutes	4.7	6 143	4.9	6 318	5.0	6 245	4.9	634
Accidental drowning and submersion — Noyade et submersion accidentelles	4.5	5 607	4.4	5 943	4.7	5 978	4.7	1 519
Exposure to smoke, fire and flames — Exposition à la fumée, au feu et aux flammes	1.1	1 339	1.1	1 463	1.2	1 416	1.1	715
Accidental poisoning by and exposure to noxious substances — Intoxication accidentelle par des substances nocives et exposition à ces substances	0.5	559	0.4	707	0.6	605	0.5	2 927
Intentional self-harm — Lésions auto-infligées	18.6	31 755	25.1	31 413	24.8	30 251	23.8	4 728
Assault — Agresssions	0.6	808	0.6	788	0.6	768	0.6	3 214
All other external causes — Toutes autres causes externes	1.9	2 862	2.3	2 962	2.3	3 302	2.6	5 458

(See notes at end of table. — Voir notes à la fin du tableau.)

Cause of death — Cause de décès	Kazakhstan[6]							Korea, Republic of — Corée, République de
	1996	1997	1998	1999	2000	2001	2002	1995
					Number Nombre			
Diseases of the digestive system — Maladies de l'appareil digestif								
Diseases of the liver — Maladies du foie	3 362	3 234	3 113	2 901	3 210	3 482	3 703	13 323
Diseases of the musculoskeletal system and connective tissue — Maladies du système ostéo-articularie, des muscles et du tissu conjonctif	179	156	170	164	114	164	148	2 058
Diseases of the genitourinary system — Maladies de l'appareil génito-urinaire								
Total	2 235	1 964	2 052	2 049	1 969	1 934	1 874	2 211
Disorders of kidney and ureter — Affections du rein et de l'uretère	1 926	1 733	1 797	1 467	1 681	1 723	1 645	1 992
Hyperplasia of prostate — Hyperplasie de la prostate	126	103	104	116	116	68	68	38
Pregnancy, childbirth and the puerperium — Grossesse, accouchement et puerpéralité								
Total	134	137	122	98	94	87	80	88
Pregnancy with abortive outcome — Grossesse se terminant par un avortement	32	38	19	22	12	8	5	5
Other direct obstetric causes — Autres décès maternels directs	102	99	103	76	82	79	75	81
Indirect obstetric causes — Décès maternels indirects	...	...	...	...	...	...	...	2
Certain conditions originating in the perinatal period — Certaines affections dont l'origine se situe dans la période périnatale	2 054	1 814	1 639	1 475	1 379	1 416	1 372	248
Congenital malformations, deformations and chromosomal abnormalities — Malformations congénitales et anomalies chromosomiques	1 106	1 176	1 073	1 036	1 050	1 112	1 043	992
Symptoms, signs and abnormal clinical and laboratory findings, not elsewhere classified — Symptômes, signes et résultats anormaux d'examens cliniques et de laboratoire, non classés ailleurs	4 264	4 675	4 703	5 664	4 775	4 495	4 687	34 482
All other diseases — Toutes autres maladies	144	127	100	114	121	122	129	221
External causes — Causes externes								
Total	23 168	21 680	20 899	17 750	20 921	21 614	20 693	34 132
Accidents — Accidents								
Total	9 634	8 948	8 982	9 547	11 747	12 295	11 845	27 585
Transport accidents — Accidents de transport	2 622	2 321	2 136	1 959	1 981	2 208	2 102	17 497
Falls — Chutes	506	467	444	456	438	383	326	2 400
Accidental drowning and submersion — Noyade et submersion accidentelles	1 471	1 315	1 535	1 078	1 286	1 249	1 461	1 774
Exposure to smoke, fire and flames — Exposition à la fumée, au feu et aux flammes	677	671	588	509	550	544	401	849
Accidental poisoning by and exposure to noxious substances — Intoxication accidentelle par des substances nocives et exposition à ces substances	3 346	3 156	3 215	4 526	6 474	6 959	6 490	1 330
Intentional self-harm — Lésions auto-infligées	4 796	4 666	4 330	4 004	4 451	4 404	4 271	4 840
Assault — Agresssions	2 986	2 818	2 724	2 448	2 475	2 306	1 962	824
All other external causes — Toutes autres causes externes	5 752	5 248	4 863	1 751	2 248	2 609	2 615	883

(See notes at end of table. — Voir notes à la fin du tableau.)

Cause of death — Cause de décès	Korea, Republic of — Corée, République de						Kuwait — Koweït	
	1996	1997	1998	1999	2000	2001	1995	1996
					Number Nombre			
Diseases of the digestive system — Maladies de l'appareil digestif								
Diseases of the liver — Maladies du foie	12 521	12 017	11 497	11 080	10 874	10 654	42	43
Diseases of the musculoskeletal system and connective tissue — Maladies du système ostéo-articularie, des muscles et du tissu conjonctif	2 024	1 892	2 452	2 561	2 130	2 115	-	1
Diseases of the genitourinary system — Maladies de l'appareil génito-urinaire	2 199	2 467	2 837	2 918	3 136	3 285	100	73
Total	1 979	2 247	2 554	2 605	2 803	2 932	93	73
Disorders of kidney and ureter — Affections du rein et de l'uretère	49	44	72	52	60	111	-	-
Hyperplasia of prostate — Hyperplasie de la prostate								
Pregnancy, childbirth and the puerperium — Grossesse, accouchement et puerpéralité								
Total	75	66	63	77	62	70	1	3
Pregnancy with abortive outcome — Grossesse se terminant par un avortement	5	5	4	5	1	7	-	-
Other direct obstetric causes — Autres décès maternels directs	67	61	59	67	56	61	-	3
Indirect obstetric causes — Décès maternels indirects	3	-	-	4	4	1	1	-
Certain conditions originating in the perinatal period — Certaines affections dont l'origine se situe dans la période périnatale	256	245	219	1 138	1 318	1 699	74	109
Congenital malformations, deformations and chromosomal abnormalities — Malformations congénitales et anomalies chromosomiques	956	852	598	925	930	948	148	215
Symptoms, signs and abnormal clinical and laboratory findings, not elsewhere classified — Symptômes, signes et résultats anormaux d'examens cliniques et de laboratoire, non classés ailleurs	37 734	40 934	37 489	39 414	31 669	27 561	456	365
All other diseases — Toutes autres maladies	189	214	358	385	398	453	3	5
External causes — Causes externes								
Total	34 368	32 459	32 011	29 947	28 874	28 736	574	575
Accidents — Accidents								
Total	26 663	24 270	20 906	20 312	19 357	18 094	454	471
Transport accidents — Accidents de transport	17 543	15 414	11 957	12 387	12 073	10 033	324	333
Falls — Chutes	2 342	2 406	2 292	2 618	2 740	2 768	42	43
Accidental drowning and submersion — Noyade et submersion accidentelles	1 817	1 674	1 838	1 586	1 634	1 307	29	21
Exposure to smoke, fire and flames — Exposition à la fumée, au feu et aux flammes	806	786	596	659	599	609	-	-
Accidental poisoning by and exposure to noxious substances — Intoxication accidentelle par des substances nocives et exposition à ces substances	1 108	1 070	1 135	853	404	401	12	39
Intentional self-harm — Lésions auto-infligées	5 856	6 022	8 569	7 075	6 460	6 933	26	31
Assault — Agresssions	882	985	988	790	819	760	16	31
All other external causes — Toutes autres causes externes	967	1 182	1 548	1 770	2 238	2 949	78	42

(See notes at end of table. — Voir notes à la fin du tableau.)

Cause of death — Cause de décès	Kuwait — Koweït						Kyrgyzstan — Kirghizistan[6]	
	1997	1998	1999	2000	2001	2002	1995	1996
				Number Nombre				
Diseases of the digestive system — Maladies de l'appareil digestif								
Diseases of the liver — Maladies du foie	49	49	59	48	58	56	...	...
Diseases of the musculoskeletal system and connective tissue — Maladies du système ostéo-articularie, des muscles et du tissu conjonctif	1	3	-	1	4	2	35	30
Diseases of the genitourinary system — Maladies de l'appareil génito-urinaire								
Total	72	74	74	86	60	72	564	603
Disorders of kidney and ureter — Affections du rein et de l'uretère	72	73	71	85	59	70	490	530
Hyperplasia of prostate — Hyperplasie de la prostate	-	1	2	1	1	-	23	32
Pregnancy, childbirth and the puerperium — Grossesse, accouchement et puerpéralité								
Total	7	3	3	2	1	3	52	27
Pregnancy with abortive outcome — Grossesse se terminant par un avortement	-	1	1	1	-	-	8	2
Other direct obstetric causes — Autres décès maternels directs	6	2	2	1	1	3	...	...
Indirect obstetric causes — Décès maternels indirects	1	-	-	-	-	-	...	...
Certain conditions originating in the perinatal period — Certaines affections dont l'origine se situe dans la période périnatale	97	164	136	160	164	173	794	625
Congenital malformations, deformations and chromosomal abnormalities — Malformations congénitales et anomalies chromosomiques	243	247	234	201	239	231	266	314
Symptoms, signs and abnormal clinical and laboratory findings, not elsewhere classified — Symptômes, signes et résultats anormaux d'examens cliniques et de laboratoire, non classés ailleurs	369	164	184	165	178	128	3 274	3 175
All other diseases — Toutes autres maladies	5	4	3	4	3	7	19	17
External causes — Causes externes								
Total	630	641	664	659	658	644	4 352	3 838
Accidents — Accidents								
Total	550	542	513	549	528	531	2 832	2 456
Transport accidents — Accidents de transport	374	348	380	382	363	071	555	556
Falls — Chutes	36	49	42	41	44	42	68	121
Accidental drowning and submersion — Noyade et submersion accidentelles	24	17	22	17	18	20	395	365
Exposure to smoke, fire and flames — Exposition à la fumée, au feu et aux flammes	-	22	-	37	20	23	118	90
Accidental poisoning by and exposure to noxious substances — Intoxication accidentelle par des substances nocives et exposition à ces substances	53	47	9	8	13	18	744	551
Intentional self-harm — Lésions auto-infligées	33	35	47	35	34	48	607	482
Assault — Agresssions	24	28	39	25	39	26	545	500
All other external causes — Toutes autres causes externes	23	36	65	50	57	39	368	400

(See notes at end of table. — Voir notes à la fin du tableau.)

Cause of death — Cause de décès	Kyrgyzstan — Kirghizistan[6]						Philippines	
	1997	1998	1999	2000	2001	2002	1995	1996
				Number Nombre				
Diseases of the digestive system — Maladies de l'appareil digestif								
Diseases of the liver — Maladies du foie	...	...	...	*1 468*	*1 482*	*1 721*	*3 511*	*3 867*
Diseases of the musculoskeletal system and connective tissue — Maladies du système ostéo-articularie, des muscles et du tissu conjonctif	*40*	*36*	*45*	*34*	*52*	*79*	*744*	*937*
Diseases of the genitourinary system — Maladies de l'appareil génito-urinaire								
Total	*561*	*535*	*680*	*601*	*632*	*747*	*8 513*	*9 848*
Disorders of kidney and ureter — Affections du rein et de l'uretère	*480*	*460*	*615*	*583*	*609*	*730*	*7 093*	*7 994*
Hyperplasia of prostate — Hyperplasie de la prostate	*19*	*16*	*18*	*10*	*16*	*16*	*99*	*239*
Pregnancy, childbirth and the puerperium — Grossesse, accouchement et puerpéralité								
Total	*64*	*35*	*44*	*44*	*43*	*54*	*1 485*	*1 549*
Pregnancy with abortive outcome — Grossesse se terminant par un avortement	*10*	*3*	*2*	*6*	*4*	*5*	*164*	*167*
Other direct obstetric causes — Autres décès maternels directs	...	...	...	*32*	*30*	*33*	*1 280*	*1 315*
Indirect obstetric causes — Décès maternels indirects	...	...	...	*3*	*7*	*15*	*40*	*67*
Certain conditions originating in the perinatal period — Certaines affections dont l'origine se situe dans la période périnatale	*598*	*594*	*611*	*737*	*810*	*990*	*14 026*	*14 638*
Congenital malformations, deformations and chromosomal abnormalities — Malformations congénitales et anomalies chromosomiques	*250*	*280*	*271*	*287*	*321*	*327*	*4 002*	*4 297*
Symptoms, signs and abnormal clinical and laboratory findings, not elsewhere classified — Symptômes, signes et résultats anormaux d'examens cliniques et de laboratoire, non classés ailleurs	*2 628*	*2 383*	*1 562*	*1 429*	*1 077*	*960*	*18 608*	*17 802*
All other diseases — Toutes autres maladies	*18*	*14*	*20*	*20*	*27*	*23*	*916*	*1 233*
External causes — Causes externes								
Total	*3 690*	*3 679*	*3 567*	*3 434*	*3 261*	*3 447*	*28 998*	*30 377*
Accidents — Accidents								
Total	*2 418*	*2 420*	*2 219*	*2 026*	*2 000*	*2 148*	...	...
Transport accidents — Accidents de transport	*530*	*490*	*433*	*417*	*513*	*635*	...	...
Falls — Chutes	*96*	*104*	*101*	*117*	*147*	*133*	...	...
Accidental drowning and submersion — Noyade et submersion accidentelles	*394*	*355*	*322*	*342*	*315*	*326*	...	...
Exposure to smoke, fire and flames — Exposition à la fumée, au feu et aux flammes ..	*94*	*82*	*52*	*45*	*47*	*70*	...	...
Accidental poisoning by and exposure to noxious substances — Intoxication accidentelle par des substances nocives et exposition à ces substances	*498*	*530*	*481*	*495*	*488*	*416*	...	...
Intentional self-harm — Lésions auto-infligées	*496*	*512*	*559*	*512*	*562*	*568*	...	...
Assault — Agresssions	*395*	*351*	*341*	*387*	*331*	*334*	...	...
All other external causes — Toutes autres causes externes	*381*	*396*	*448*	*509*	*368*	*397*	...	*30 377*

(See notes at end of table. — Voir notes à la fin du tableau.)

Cause of death — Cause de décès	Philippines		Qatar	Singapore — Singapour[10]			
	1997	1998	1995	1996	1997	1998	1999
				Number Nombre			
Diseases of the digestive system — Maladies de l'appareil digestif							
Diseases of the liver — Maladies du foie	4 098	4 237	15	139	149	130	132	138
Diseases of the musculoskeletal system and connective tissue — Maladies du système ostéo-articularie, des muscles et du tissu conjonctif	1 053	985	-	37	55	66	50	50
Diseases of the genitourinary system — Maladies de l'appareil génito-urinaire							
Total	9 595	9 793	24	467	426	386	481	454
Disorders of kidney and ureter — Affections du rein et de l'uretère	7 907	8 062	22	197	176	155	182	179
Hyperplasia of prostate — Hyperplasie de la prostate	177	180	-	1	3		1	3
Pregnancy, childbirth and the puerperium — Grossesse, accouchement et puerpéralité							
Total	1 513	1 579	-	2	2	1	5	2
Pregnancy with abortive outcome — Grossesse se terminant par un avortement	151	144	-	-	1	-	1	-
Other direct obstetric causes — Autres décès maternels directs	1 290	1 364	-	2	1	1	3	2
Indirect obstetric causes — Décès maternels indirects	72	71	-	-	-	-	-	-
Certain conditions originating in the perinatal period — Certaines affections dont l'origine se situe dans la période périnatale	14 179	13 782	50	42	59	56	60	46
Congenital malformations, deformations and chromosomal abnormalities — Malformations congénitales et anomalies chromosomiques	4 970	4 505	48	147	109	94	97	90
Symptoms, signs and abnormal clinical and laboratory findings, not elsewhere classified — Symptômes, signes et résultats anormaux d'examens cliniques et de laboratoire, non classés ailleurs	16 552	19 023	60	53	33	21	40	48
All other diseases — Toutes autres maladies	1 151	1 145	-	29	23	16	42	35
External causes — Causes externes							
Total	29 375	29 874	168	836	755	848	792	788
Accidents — Accidents							
Total	10 679	11 156	-	325	316	388	295	305
Transport accidents — Accidents de transport	5 409	5 521	-	183	180	220	170	157
Falls — Chutes	1 061	1 058	-	89	70	100	68	101
Accidental drowning and submersion — Noyade et submersion accidentelles	2 129	2 317	-	7	18	17	11	13
Exposure to smoke, fire and flames — Exposition à la fumée, au feu et aux flammes	66	72	-	3	3	3	3	2
Accidental poisoning by and exposure to noxious substances — Intoxication accidentelle par des substances nocives et exposition à ces substances	129	179	-	5	5	11	8	5
Intentional self-harm — Lésions auto-infligées	817	885	-	364	230	303	328	277
Assault — Agresssions	10 885	11 240	-	27	16	27	24	31
All other external causes — Toutes autres causes externes	6 994	6 593	168	120	184	130	145	175

21. Death and death rates by cause: 1995 - 2002
Décès selon la cause, nombres et taux: 1995 - 2002 (continued — suite)

(See notes at end of table. — Voir notes à la fin du tableau.)

Cause of death — Cause de décès	Singapore — Singapour[10] 2000	2001	Sri Lanka 1995	1996	1997	1999	2000
				Number Nombre			
Diseases of the digestive system — Maladies de l'appareil digestif							
Diseases of the liver — Maladies du foie	99	103	...	...	...	...	...
Diseases of the musculoskeletal system and connective tissue — Maladies du système ostéo-articulaire, des muscles et du tissu conjonctif	47	36	434	46	28	31	23
Diseases of the genitourinary system — Maladies de l'appareil génito-urinaire							
Total	473	472	1 544	797	659	633	734
Disorders of kidney and ureter — Affections du rein et de l'uretère	211	255	...	727	613	584	709
Hyperplasia of prostate — Hyperplasie de la prostate	2	9	...	17	8	15	6
Pregnancy, childbirth and the puerperium — Grossesse, accouchement et puerpéralité							
Total	8	4	81	95	58	38	45
Pregnancy with abortive outcome — Grossesse se terminant par un avortement	1	1	14	6	2	3	1
Other direct obstetric causes — Autres décès maternels directs	7	2	66	...	...	...	...
Indirect obstetric causes — Décès maternels indirects	-	1	1	...	...	...	...
Certain conditions originating in the perinatal period — Certaines affections dont l'origine se situe dans la période périnatale	40	20	3 956	938	1 055	853	700
Congenital malformations, deformations and chromosomal abnormalities — Malformations congénitales et anomalies chromosomiques	75	72	459	193	274	252	167
Symptoms, signs and abnormal clinical and laboratory findings, not elsewhere classified — Symptômes, signes et résultats anormaux d'examens cliniques et de laboratoire, non classés ailleurs	67	36	32 289	2 021	1 942	2 087	1 622
All other diseases — Toutes autres maladies	34	28	102	20	13	17	10
External causes — Causes externes							
Total	845	792	18 195	2 491	2 616	2 081	1 711
Accidents — Accidents							
Total	318	322	5 831	1 816	1 575	1 459	1 268
Transport accidents — Accidents de transport	174	166	1 737	316	242	190	180
Falls — Chutes	99	107	500	77	54	43	41
Accidental drowning and submersion — Noyade et submersion accidentelles	9	12	...	249	276	194	207
Exposure to smoke, fire and flames — Exposition à la fumée, au feu et aux flammes ..	3	5	247	92	88	110	54
Accidental poisoning by and exposure to noxious substances — Intoxication accidentelle par des substances nocives et exposition à ces substances	4	4	69	113	110	98	108
Intentional self-harm — Lésions auto-infligées	309	305	5 515	199	164	141	175
Assault — Agresssions	35	25	5 291	354	650	385	226
All other external causes — Toutes autres causes externes	183	140	1 558	122	227	96	42

(See notes at end of table. — Voir notes à la fin du tableau.)

Cause of death — Cause de décès	Tajikistan — Tadjikistan[6]	Thailand — Thaïlande						
	2001	1995	1996	1997	1998	1999	2000	2002
					Number Nombre			
Diseases of the digestive system — Maladies de l'appareil digestif								
Diseases of the liver — Maladies du foie	...	7 236	6 951	5 892	5 281	5 879	6 110	7 278
Diseases of the musculoskeletal system and connective tissue — Maladies du système ostéo-articulaire, des muscles et du tissu conjonctif	23	271	356	320	313	378	471	623
Diseases of the genitourinary system — Maladies de l'appareil génito-urinaire								
Total	718	6 684	5 060	5 191	6 115	6 977	9 430	10 979
Disorders of kidney and ureter — Affections du rein et de l'uretère	687	6 527	4 869	5 085	5 981	6 745	9 091	10 587
Hyperplasia of prostate — Hyperplasie de la prostate	4	7	12	9	8	15	25	32
Pregnancy, childbirth and the puerperium — Grossesse, accouchement et puerpéralité								
Total	40	96	120	87	63	93	102	114
Pregnancy with abortive outcome — Grossesse se terminant par un avortement	1	5	23	18	10	15	17	21
Other direct obstetric causes — Autres décès maternels directs	...	91	97	68	53	75	80	92
Indirect obstetric causes — Décès maternels indirects	...	-	-	1	-	3	5	1
Certain conditions originating in the perinatal period — Certaines affections dont l'origine se situe dans la période périnatale	471	1 448	541	855	594	2 275	989	1 273
Congenital malformations, deformations and chromosomal abnormalities — Malformations congénitales et anomalies chromosomiques	268	2 091	524	260	1 641	807	907	1 156
Symptoms, signs and abnormal clinical and laboratory findings, not elsewhere classified — Symptômes, signes et résultats anormaux d'examens cliniques et de laboratoire, non classés ailleurs	1 882	114 598	121 648	103 739	116 981	151 140	149 567	143 060
All other diseases — Toutes autres maladies	11	587	643	295	460	656	785	743
External causes — Causes externes								
Total	1 631	44 292	45 297	34 949	30 412	39 101	40 874	42 803
Accidents — Accidents								
Total	1 272	36 106	34 473	26 616	17 057	21 247	23 508	24 083
Transport accidents — Accidents de transport	209	16 782	16 792	12 962	7 986	11 624	13 194	13 438
Falls — Chutes	54	311	485	380	819	609	557	849
Accidental drowning and submersion — Noyade et submersion accidentelles	219	3 969	3 593	895	2 913	3 057	3 863	4 218
Exposure to smoke, fire and flames — Exposition à la fumée, au feu et aux flammes	53	193	248	223	135	187	212	220
Accidental poisoning by and exposure to noxious substances — Intoxication accidentelle par des substances nocives et exposition à ces substances	99	292	299	169	173	184	98	112
Intentional self-harm — Lésions auto-infligées	163	4 291	4 529	4 183	4 964	5 290	5 189	4 905
Assault — Agresssions	156	3 564	3 714	3 383	3 708	3 966	3 442	3 332
All other external causes — Toutes autres causes externes	40	331	2 581	767	4 683	8 590	8 735	10 483

(See notes at end of table. — Voir notes à la fin du tableau.)

Cause of death — Cause de décès	Turkmenistan — Turkménistan[6]				Uzbekistan — Ouzbékistan[6]			
	1995	1996	1997	1998	1995	1996	1997	1998
				Number Nombre				
Diseases of the digestive system — Maladies de l'appareil digestif								
Diseases of the liver — Maladies du foie	...	...	...	...	...	...	...	...
Diseases of the musculoskeletal system and connective tissue — Maladies du système ostéo-articularie, des muscles et du tissu conjonctif	24	7	21	16	166	155	144	179
Diseases of the genitourinary system — Maladies de l'appareil génito-urinaire								
Total	332	365	353	312	2 568	2 636	2 553	2 735
Disorders of kidney and ureter — Affections du rein et de l'uretère	279	319	304	258	2 330	2 373	2 355	2 564
Hyperplasia of prostate — Hyperplasie de la prostate	25	15	4	12	76	77	83	53
Pregnancy, childbirth and the puerperium — Grossesse, accouchement et puerpéralité								
Total	63	49	21	16	128	76	62	48
Pregnancy with abortive outcome — Grossesse se terminant par un avortement	5	5	6	1	10	6	3	3
Other direct obstetric causes — Autres décès maternels directs	...	...	...	...	...	...	...	...
Indirect obstetric causes — Décès maternels indirects	...	...	...	...	...	...	...	...
Certain conditions originating in the perinatal period — Certaines affections dont l'origine se situe dans la période périnatale	771	819	637	569	3 948	3 500	3 533	3 172
Congenital malformations, deformations and chromosomal abnormalities — Malformations congénitales et anomalies chromosomiques	328	257	198	191	1 158	1 100	1 054	924
Symptoms, signs and abnormal clinical and laboratory findings, not elsewhere classified — Symptômes, signes et résultats anormaux d'examens cliniques et de laboratoire, non classés ailleurs	878	1 029	637	718	3 788	4 660	4 501	3 526
All other diseases — Toutes autres maladies	23	14	15	7	99	92	114	97
External causes — Causes externes								
Total	2 212	2 259	2 321	2 578	10 373	11 475	11 033	10 858
Accidents — Accidents								
Total	1 725	1 682	1 714	1 797	7 300	7 767	7 367	7 542
Transport accidents — Accidents de transport	355	361	371	399	1 864	2 141	1 987	1 892
Falls — Chutes	34	62	71	58	322	468	415	323
Accidental drowning and submersion — Noyade et submersion accidentelles	405	428	392	413	1 424	1 522	1 576	1 713
Exposure to smoke, fire and flames — Exposition à la fumée, au feu et aux flammes	245	252	275	317	458	669	639	492
Accidental poisoning by and exposure to noxious substances — Intoxication accidentelle par des substances nocives et exposition à ces substances	80	87	91	116	409	528	454	482
Intentional self-harm — Lésions auto-infligées	244	283	333	406	1 486	1 701	1 554	1 620
Assault — Agresssions	162	257	236	333	1 041	1 050	836	790
All other external causes — Toutes autres causes externes	81	37	38	42	546	957	1 276	906

(See notes at end of table. — Voir notes à la fin du tableau.)

Cause of death — Cause de décès	Uzbekistan — Ouzbékistan[6]		Albania — Albanie					
	1999	2000	1995	1996	1997	1998	1999	2000
			Number Nombre					
Diseases of the digestive system — Maladies de l'appareil digestif								
Diseases of the liver — Maladies du foie	...	...	1	1	-	3	-	-
Diseases of the musculoskeletal system and connective tissue — Maladies du système ostéo-articulaire, des muscles et du tissu conjonctif	152	167	28	25	29	38	24	26
Diseases of the genitourinary system — Maladies de l'appareil génito-urinaire								
Total	2 650	2 532	323	265	269	261	248	284
Disorders of kidney and ureter — Affections du rein et de l'uretère	2 474	2 399	268	222	240	232	217	248
Hyperplasia of prostate — Hyperplasie de la prostate	65	55	28	21	13	15	15	18
Pregnancy, childbirth and the puerperium — Grossesse, accouchement et puerpéralité								
Total	80	182	9	8	5	8	2	8
Pregnancy with abortive outcome — Grossesse se terminant par un avortement	2	5	1	5	-	2	-	2
Other direct obstetric causes — Autres décès maternels directs	...	...	8	3	5	6	2	6
Indirect obstetric causes — Décès maternels indirects	...	...	-	-	-	-	-	-
Certain conditions originating in the perinatal period — Certaines affections dont l'origine se situe dans la période périnatale	3 317	3 326	245	224	191	191	271	240
Congenital malformations, deformations and chromosomal abnormalities — Malformations congénitales et anomalies chromosomiques	862	1 032	140	126	134	121	103	76
Symptoms, signs and abnormal clinical and laboratory findings, not elsewhere classified — Symptômes, signes et résultats anormaux d'examens cliniques et de laboratoire, non classés ailleurs	2 454	2 166	1 525	1 569	1 381	1 620	1 492	1 679
All other diseases — Toutes autres maladies	105	106	23	15	8	17	6	13
External causes — Causes externes								
Total	10 434	10 680	1 392	1 407	2 596	1 827	1 734	1 416
Accidents — Accidents								
Total	7 234	7 252	1 015	1 008	1 051	964	1 033	1 219
Transport accidents — Accidents de transport	2 179	2 152	238	211	183	278	192	73
Falls — Chutes	316	271	72	45	45	46	61	19
Accidental drowning and submersion — Noyade et submersion accidentelles	1 446	1 179	151	146	113	125	111	36
Exposure to smoke, fire and flames — Exposition à la fumée, au feu et aux flammes ..	377	391	23	19	19	12	14	6
Accidental poisoning by and exposure to noxious substances — Intoxication accidentelle par des substances nocives et exposition à ces substances	383	543	82	67	28	60	35	28
Intentional self-harm — Lésions auto-infligées	1 795	1 919	91	92	176	165	154	57
Assault — Agresssions	700	771	259	272	1 334	660	532	131
All other external causes — Toutes autres causes externes	705	738	27	35	35	38	16	9

21. Death and death rates by cause: 1995 - 2002
Décès selon la cause, nombres et taux: 1995 - 2002 (continued — suite)

(See notes at end of table. — Voir notes à la fin du tableau.)

Cause of death — Cause de décès	Albania — Albanie 2001	Austria — Autriche 1995		1996		1997		1998
	Number Nombre	Number Nombre	Rate Taux	Number Nombre	Rate Taux	Number Nombre	Rate Taux	Number Nombre
Diseases of the digestive system — Maladies de l'appareil digestif								
Diseases of the liver — Maladies du foie	-	2 101	26.1	2 095	26.0	1 958	24.3	1 906
Diseases of the musculoskeletal system and connective tissue — Maladies du système ostéo-articularie, des muscles et du tissu conjonctif	33	150	1.9	136	1.7	131	1.6	125
Diseases of the genitourinary system — Maladies de l'appareil génito-urinaire								
Total	327	778	9.7	767	9.5	776	9.6	734
Disorders of kidney and ureter — Affections du rein et de l'uretère	273	659	8.2	651	8.1	672	8.3	647
Hyperplasia of prostate — Hyperplasie de la prostate	21	19	◆ ▼1.8	20	◆ ▼1.8	12	◆ ▼1.1	13
Pregnancy, childbirth and the puerperium — Grossesse, accouchement et puerpéralité								
Total	2	1	◆ *1.1	4	◆ *4.5	2	◆ *2.4	4
Pregnancy with abortive outcome — Grossesse se terminant par un avortement	-	-	-	1	◆ *1.1	1	◆ *1.2	1
Other direct obstetric causes — Autres décès maternels directs	2	1	◆ *1.1	3	◆ *3.4	1	◆ *1.2	3
Indirect obstetric causes — Décès maternels indirects	-	-	-	-	-	-	-	-
Certain conditions originating in the perinatal period — Certaines affections dont l'origine se situe dans la période périnatale	181	220	*248.1	214	*241.0	184	*218.9	181
Congenital malformations, deformations and chromosomal abnormalities — Malformations congénitales et anomalies chromosomiques	61	238	*268.4	240	*270.2	214	*254.6	230
Symptoms, signs and abnormal clinical and laboratory findings, not elsewhere classified — Symptômes, signes et résultats anormaux d'examens cliniques et de laboratoire, non classés ailleurs	1 366	604	7.5	646	8.0	772	9.6	789
All other diseases — Toutes autres maladies	28	31	0.4	33	0.4	38	0.5	31
External causes — Causes externes								
Total	1 281	4 896	60.8	4 751	58.9	4 428	54.9	4 210
Accidents — Accidents								
Total	902	2 969	36.9	2 804	34.8	2 709	33.6	2 498
Transport accidents — Accidents de transport	328	1 178	14.6	1 014	12.6	1 086	13.5	917
Falls — Chutes	36	999	12.4	1 075	13.3	963	11.9	973
Accidental drowning and submersion — Noyade et submersion accidentelles	80	112	1.4	87	1.1	99	1.2	77
Exposure to smoke, fire and flames — Exposition à la fumée, au feu et aux flammes	13	57	0.7	50	0.6	72	0.9	52
Accidental poisoning by and exposure to noxious substances — Intoxication accidentelle par des substances nocives et exposition à ces substances	89	160	2.0	158	2.0	112	1.4	91
Intentional self-harm — Lésions auto-infligées	119	1 788	22.2	1 779	22.1	1 592	19.7	1 559
Assault — Agresssions	220	84	1.0	96	1.2	69	0.9	91
All other external causes — Toutes autres causes externes	40	55	0.7	72	0.9	58	0.7	62

21. Death and death rates by cause: 1995 - 2002
Décès selon la cause, nombres et taux: 1995 - 2002 (continued — suite)

(See notes at end of table. — Voir notes à la fin du tableau.)

Austria — Autriche

Cause of death — Cause de décès	1998	1999		2000		2001		2002
	Rate Taux	Number Nombre	Rate Taux	Number Nombre	Rate Taux	Number Nombre	Rate Taux	Number Nombre
Diseases of the digestive system — Maladies de l'appareil digestif								
Diseases of the liver — Maladies du foie	23.6	1 746	21.6	1 813	22.4	1 765	22.0	1 808
Diseases of the musculoskeletal system and connective tissue — Maladies du système ostéo-articularie, des muscles et du tissu conjonctif	1.5	116	1.4	125	1.5	117	1.5	229
Diseases of the genitourinary system — Maladies de l'appareil génito-urinaire								
Total	9.1	745	9.2	862	10.6	974	12.1	1 008
Disorders of kidney and ureter — Affections du rein et de l'uretère	8.0	651	8.0	753	9.3	847	10.5	908
Hyperplasia of prostate — Hyperplasie de la prostate	♦ ▼1.1	10	♦ ▼0.9	4	...	10	♦ ▼0.9	4
Pregnancy, childbirth and the puerperium — Grossesse, accouchement et puerpéralité								
Total	♦ *4.9	1	♦ *1.3	2	♦ *2.6	5	♦ *6.6	2
Pregnancy with abortive outcome — Grossesse se terminant par un avortement	♦ *1.2	1	♦ *1.3	-	-	-	-	-
Other direct obstetric causes — Autres décès maternels directs	♦ *3.7	-	-	2	♦ *2.6	5	♦ *6.6	1
Indirect obstetric causes — Décès maternels indirects	-	-	-	-	-	-	-	-
Certain conditions originating in the perinatal period — Certaines affections dont l'origine se situe dans la période périnatale	*222.8	145	*185.6	165	*210.8	191	*253.1	180
Congenital malformations, deformations and chromosomal abnormalities — Malformations congénitales et anomalies chromosomiques	*283.1	209	*267.5	207	*264.5	180	*238.5	203
Symptoms, signs and abnormal clinical and laboratory findings, not elsewhere classified — Symptômes, signes et résultats anormaux d'examens cliniques et de laboratoire, non classés ailleurs	9.8	759	9.4	880	10.9	954	11.9	860
All other diseases — Toutes autres maladies	0.4	24	♦0.3	29	♦0.4	29	♦0.4	49
External causes — Causes externes								
Total	52.1	4 359	53.9	4 399	54.3	4 227	52.6	4 317
Accidents — Accidents								
Total	30.9	2 686	33.2	2 673	33.0	2 598	32.4	2 383
Transport accidents — Accidents de transport	11.4	1 020	12.6	927	11.4	925	11.5	938
Falls — Chutes	12.0	968	12.0	987	12.2	969	12.1	976
Accidental drowning and submersion — Noyade et submersion accidentelles	1.0	80	1.0	90	1.1	82	1.0	89
Exposure to smoke, fire and flames — Exposition à la fumée, au feu et aux flammes	0.6	50	0.6	153	1.9	52	0.6	39
Accidental poisoning by and exposure to noxious substances — Intoxication accidentelle par des substances nocives et exposition à ces substances	1.1	105	1.3	122	1.5	92	1.1	55
Intentional self-harm — Lésions auto-infligées	19.3	1 555	10.2	1 588	19.6	1 489	18.5	1 551
Assault — Agressions	1.1	68	0.8	75	0.9	77	1.0	69
All other external causes — Toutes autres causes externes	0.8	50	0.6	63	0.8	63	0.8	314

21. Death and death rates by cause: 1995 - 2002
Décès selon la cause, nombres et taux: 1995 - 2002 (continued — suite)

(See notes at end of table. — Voir notes à la fin du tableau.)

Cause of death — Cause de décès	Austria — Autriche 2002 Rate Taux	Belarus — Bélarus[6] 1995 Number Nombre	1995 Rate Taux	1996 Number Nombre	1996 Rate Taux	1997 Number Nombre	1997 Rate Taux	1998 Number Nombre
Diseases of the digestive system — Maladies de l'appareil digestif								
Diseases of the liver — Maladies du foie	22.5	...	...	...	...	...	...	...
Diseases of the musculoskeletal system and connective tissue — Maladies du système ostéo-articularie, des muscles et du tissu conjonctif	2.8	197	1.9	173	1.7	152	1.5	167
Diseases of the genitourinary system — Maladies de l'appareil génito-urinaire								
Total	12.5	1 270	12.4	1 159	11.3	1 338	13.1	1 209
Disorders of kidney and ureter — Affections du rein et de l'uretère	11.3	938	9.1	899	8.8	1 020	10.0	935
Hyperplasia of prostate — Hyperplasie de la prostate	◆ ▼0.3	166	...	137	▼12.4	154	▼14.0	122
Pregnancy, childbirth and the puerperium — Grossesse, accouchement et puerpéralité								
Total	◆ *2.6	14	◆ *13.8	21	◆ *21.9	23	◆ *25.7	26
Pregnancy with abortive outcome — Grossesse se terminant par un avortement	-	4	◆ *4.0	9	◆ *9.4	4	◆ *4.5	8
Other direct obstetric causes — Autres décès maternels directs	◆ *1.3	...	...	...	...	...	...	...
Indirect obstetric causes — Décès maternels indirects	-	...	...	...	...	...	...	...
Certain conditions originating in the perinatal period — Certaines affections dont l'origine se situe dans la période périnatale	*229.6	512	*506.2	444	*463.5	335	*373.9	329
Congenital malformations, deformations and chromosomal abnormalities — Malformations congénitales et anomalies chromosomiques	*258.9	590	*583.3	602	*628.4	580	*647.4	603
Symptoms, signs and abnormal clinical and laboratory findings, not elsewhere classified — Symptômes, signes et résultats anormaux d'examens cliniques et de laboratoire, non classés ailleurs	10.7	17 311	168.4	17 327	169.0	16 600	162.4	13 947
All other diseases — Toutes autres maladies	0.6	57	0.6	55	0.5	48	0.5	36
External causes — Causes externes								
Total	53.6	15 066	146.5	15 484	151.1	15 788	154.5	16 899
Accidents — Accidents								
Total	29.6	9 199	89.5	9 206	89.8	9 301	91.0	10 149
Transport accidents — Accidents de transport	11.6	2 214	21.5	2 168	21.2	2 131	20.9	2 307
Falls — Chutes	12.1	771	7.5	742	7.2	673	6.6	688
Accidental drowning and submersion — Noyade et submersion accidentelles	1.1	1 163	11.3	876	8.5	1 074	10.5	1 202
Exposure to smoke, fire and flames — Exposition à la fumée, au feu et aux flammes	0.5	474	4.6	527	5.1	534	5.2	556
Accidental poisoning by and exposure to noxious substances — Intoxication accidentelle par des substances nocives et exposition à ces substances	0.7	2 801	27.2	3 080	30.0	2 969	29.1	3 348
Intentional self-harm — Lésions auto-infligées	19.3	3 206	31.2	3 632	35.4	3 541	34.6	3 566
Assault — Agresssions	0.9	1 215	11.8	1 128	11.0	1 215	11.9	1 236
All other external causes — Toutes autres causes externes	3.9	1 446	14.1	1 518	14.8	1 731	16.9	1 948

21. Death and death rates by cause: 1995 - 2002
Décès selon la cause, nombres et taux: 1995 - 2002 (continued — suite)

(See notes at end of table. — Voir notes à la fin du tableau.)

Cause of death — Cause de décès	Belarus — Bélarus[6] 1998 Rate Taux	1999 Number Nombre	1999 Rate Taux	2000 Number Nombre	2000 Rate Taux	2001 Number Nombre	2001 Rate Taux	Belgium — Belgique[11] 1995 Number Nombre
Diseases of the digestive system — Maladies de l'appareil digestif								
Diseases of the liver — Maladies du foie	...	...	...	...	...	...	...	1 216
Diseases of the musculoskeletal system and connective tissue — Maladies du système ostéo-articulaire, des muscles et du tissu conjonctif	1.6	151	1.5	175	1.7	175	1.8	708
Diseases of the genitourinary system — Maladies de l'appareil génito-urinaire								
Total	11.9	1 240	12.4	1 116	11.2	1 141	11.4	1 621
Disorders of kidney and ureter — Affections du rein et de l'uretère	9.2	958	9.5	900	9.0	886	8.9	1 266
Hyperplasia of prostate — Hyperplasie de la prostate	▼11.1	126	▼11.4	108	▼9.6	112	...	29
Pregnancy, childbirth and the puerperium — Grossesse, accouchement et puerpéralité								
Total	♦ *28.1	19	♦ *20.4	20	...	13	...	11
Pregnancy with abortive outcome — Grossesse se terminant par un avortement	♦ *8.6	4	♦ *4.3	4	...	3	...	3
Other direct obstetric causes — Autres décès maternels directs	...	...	...	...	...	...	...	7
Indirect obstetric causes — Décès maternels indirects	...	...	...	...	...	...	...	1
Certain conditions originating in the perinatal period — Certaines affections dont l'origine se situe dans la période périnatale	*355.1	334	*359.2	280	...	255	...	264
Congenital malformations, deformations and chromosomal abnormalities — Malformations congénitales et anomalies chromosomiques	*650.9	607	*652.9	462	...	483	...	301
Symptoms, signs and abnormal clinical and laboratory findings, not elsewhere classified — Symptômes, signes et résultats anormaux d'examens cliniques et de laboratoire, non classés ailleurs	136.8	13 423	133.8	12 198	122.0	12 198	122.3	3 637
All other diseases — Toutes autres maladies	0.4	63	0.6	69	0.7	53	0.5	485
External causes — Causes externes								
Total	165.8	17 100	170.4	15 813	158.1	16 639	166.8	6 494
Accidents — Accidents								
Total	99.6	10 434	104.0	9 227	92.3	10 192	102.2	3 920
Transport accidents — Accidents de transport	22.6	2 109	21.0	1 894	18.9	1 888	18.9	1 652
Falls — Chutes	6.8	743	7.4	611	6.1	618	6.2	1 252
Accidental drowning and submersion — Noyade et submersion accidentelles	11.8	1 622	16.2	999	10.0	1 471	14.7	114
Exposure to smoke, fire and flames — Exposition à la fumée, au feu et aux flammes	5.5	625	6.2	651	6.5	693	6.9	110
Accidental poisoning by and exposure to noxious substances — Intoxication accidentelle par des substances nocives et exposition à ces substances	32.9	3 130	31.2	3 035	30.3	3 334	33.4	198
Intentional self-harm — Lésions auto-infligées	35.0	3 408	34.0	3 491	34.9	3 314	33.2	2 155
Assault — Agresssions	12.1	1 123	11.2	1 139	11.4	1 120	11.2	169
All other external causes — Toutes autres causes externes	19.1	2 135	21.3	1 956	10.6	2 013	20.2	250

21. Death and death rates by cause: 1995 - 2002
Décès selon la cause, nombres et taux: 1995 - 2002 (continued — suite)

(See notes at end of table. — Voir notes à la fin du tableau.)

Cause of death — Cause de décès	Belgium — Belgique[11]					Bulgaria — Bulgarie		
	1995	1996		1997		1995		1996
	Rate Taux	Number Nombre	Rate Taux	Number Nombre	Rate Taux	Number Nombre	Rate Taux	Number Nombre
Diseases of the digestive system — Maladies de l'appareil digestif								
Diseases of the liver — Maladies du foie	12.0	1 224	12.1	1 345	13.2	1 918	22.8	1 799
Diseases of the musculoskeletal system and connective tissue — Maladies du système ostéo-articularie, des muscles et du tissu conjonctif	7.0	612	6.0	647	6.4	40	0.5	84
Diseases of the genitourinary system — Maladies de l'appareil génito-urinaire								
Total	16.0	1 660	16.3	1 504	14.8	1 371	16.3	1 381
Disorders of kidney and ureter — Affections du rein et de l'uretère	12.5	1 350	13.3	1 193	11.7	1 224	14.6	1 225
Hyperplasia of prostate — Hyperplasie de la prostate	◆ ▼2.0	36	...	21	...	41	▼3.2	44
Pregnancy, childbirth and the puerperium — Grossesse, accouchement et puerpéralité								
Total	◆ ●9.5	6	◆ ●5.3	10	◆ ●8.6	10	◆ ●13.9	14
Pregnancy with abortive outcome — Grossesse se terminant par un avortement	◆ ●2.6	1	◆ ●0.9	2	◆ ●1.7	3	◆ ●4.2	4
Other direct obstetric causes — Autres décès maternels directs	◆ ●6.1	5	◆ ●4.4	8	◆ ●6.9	7	◆ ●9.7	10
Indirect obstetric causes — Décès maternels indirects	◆ ●0.9	-		-		-		-
Certain conditions originating in the perinatal period — Certaines affections dont l'origine se situe dans la période périnatale	●228.8	242	●211.9	263	●227.0	363	●504.4	346
Congenital malformations, deformations and chromosomal abnormalities — Malformations congénitales et anomalies chromosomiques	●260.9	277	●242.5	302	●260.7	363	●504.4	407
Symptoms, signs and abnormal clinical and laboratory findings, not elsewhere classified — Symptômes, signes et résultats anormaux d'examens cliniques et de laboratoire, non classés ailleurs	35.9	3 340	32.9	3 042	29.9	5 032	59.9	5 057
All other diseases — Toutes autres maladies	4.8	449	4.4	427	4.2	30	◆0.4	26
External causes — Causes externes								
Total	64.1	6 299	62.0	6 292	61.8	5 534	65.8	5 355
Accidents — Accidents								
Total	38.7	3 809	37.5	3 776	37.1	3 532	42.0	3 242
Transport accidents — Accidents de transport	16.3	1 530	15.1	1 513	14.9	1 300	15.5	1 060
Falls — Chutes	12.4	1 321	13.0	1 293	12.7	526	6.3	410
Accidental drowning and submersion — Noyade et submersion accidentelles	1.1	79	0.8	65	0.6	245	2.9	248
Exposure to smoke, fire and flames — Exposition à la fumée, au feu et aux flammes	1.1	106	1.0	106	1.0	116	1.4	140
Accidental poisoning by and exposure to noxious substances — Intoxication accidentelle par des substances nocives et exposition à ces substances	2.0	182	1.8	174	1.7	310	3.7	299
Intentional self-harm — Lésions auto-infligées	21.3	2 013	19.8	2 146	21.1	1 433	17.0	1 526
Assault — Agresssions	1.7	202	2.0	177	1.7	398	4.7	422
All other external causes — Toutes autres causes externes	2.5	275	2.7	193	1.9	171	2.0	165

(See notes at end of table. — Voir notes à la fin du tableau.)

Bulgaria — Bulgarie

Cause of death — Cause de décès	1996 Rate Taux	1997 Number Nombre	1997 Rate Taux	1998 Number Nombre	1998 Rate Taux	1999 Number Nombre	1999 Rate Taux	2000 Number Nombre
Diseases of the digestive system — Maladies de l'appareil digestif								
Diseases of the liver — Maladies du foie	21.5	1 735	20.9	1 712	20.7	1 509	18.4	1 557
Diseases of the musculoskeletal system and connective tissue — Maladies du système ostéo-articularie, des muscles et du tissu conjonctif	1.0	51	0.6	53	0.6	48	0.6	51
Diseases of the genitourinary system — Maladies de l'appareil génito-urinaire								
Total	16.5	1 292	15.5	1 192	14.4	1 054	12.8	1 068
Disorders of kidney and ureter — Affections du rein et de l'uretère	14.6	1 101	13.2	1 047	12.7	930	11.3	942
Hyperplasia of prostate — Hyperplasie de la prostate	▼3.5	65	▼5.1	31	▼2.4	27	◆ ▼2.1	17
Pregnancy, childbirth and the puerperium — Grossesse, accouchement et puerpéralité								
Total	◆ ●19.4	12	◆ ●18.7	10	◆ ●15.3	16	◆ ●22.1	13
Pregnancy with abortive outcome — Grossesse se terminant par un avortement	◆ ●5.5	2	◆ ●3.1	1	◆ ●1.5	5	◆ ●6.9	2
Other direct obstetric causes — Autres décès maternels directs	◆ ●13.9	10	◆ ●15.6	9	◆ ●13.8	11	◆ ●15.2	11
Indirect obstetric causes — Décès maternels indirects	-	-	-	-	-	-	-	-
Certain conditions originating in the perinatal period — Certaines affections dont l'origine se situe dans la période périnatale	●479.3	340	●530.2	313	●478.9	348	●481.4	323
Congenital malformations, deformations and chromosomal abnormalities — Malformations congénitales et anomalies chromosomiques	●563.8	340	●530.2	278	●425.3	320	●442.7	274
Symptoms, signs and abnormal clinical and laboratory findings, not elsewhere classified — Symptômes, signes et résultats anormaux d'examens cliniques et de laboratoire, non classés ailleurs	60.5	5 825	70.1	5 500	66.6	5 376	65.5	5 678
All other diseases — Toutes autres maladies	◆0.3	33	0.4	18	◆0.2	38	0.5	30
External causes — Causes externes								
Total	64.0	5 049	60.7	4 984	60.4	4 595	56.0	4 653
Accidents — Accidents								
Total	38.8	3 033	36.5	2 927	35.4	2 875	35.0	2 792
Transport accidents — Accidents de transport	12.7	988	11.9	1 024	12.4	1 061	12.9	1 032
Falls — Chutes	4.9	395	4.8	383	4.6	354	4.3	363
Accidental drowning and submersion — Noyade et submersion accidentelles	3.0	218	2.6	273	3.3	251	3.1	204
Exposure to smoke, fire and flames — Exposition à la fumée, au feu et aux flammes	1.7	122	1.5	111	1.3	97	1.2	94
Accidental poisoning by and exposure to noxious substances — Intoxication accidentelle par des substances nocives et exposition à ces substances	3.6	266	3.2	241	2.9	231	2.8	239
Intentional self-harm — Lésions auto-infligées	18.2	1 465	17.6	1 503	18.2	1 307	15.9	1 383
Assault — Agressions	5.0	371	4.5	317	3.8	238	2.9	290
All other external causes — Toutes autres causes externes	2.0	180	2.2	237	2.9	175	2.1	188

(See notes at end of table. — Voir notes à la fin du tableau.)

Cause of death — Cause de décès	Bulgaria — Bulgarie					Croatia — Croatie		
	2000	2001		2002		1995		1996
	Rate Taux	Number Nombre	Rate Taux	Number Nombre	Rate Taux	Number Nombre	Rate Taux	Number Nombre
Diseases of the digestive system — Maladies de l'appareil digestif								
Diseases of the liver — Maladies du foie	19.1	1 560	19.7	1 463	18.6	**1 426**	**30.5**	1 424
Diseases of the musculoskeletal system and connective tissue — Maladies du système ostéo-articularie, des muscles et du tissu conjonctif	0.6	36	0.5	39	0.5	**60**	**1.3**	56
Diseases of the genitourinary system — Maladies de l'appareil génito-urinaire								
Total	13.1	1 029	13.0	900	11.4	587	12.6	574
Disorders of kidney and ureter — Affections du rein et de l'uretère	11.5	916	11.6	787	10.0	525	11.2	531
Hyperplasia of prostate — Hyperplasie de la prostate	◆ ▼1.3	21	◆ ▼1.6	20	◆ ▼1.6	35	▼5.5	16
Pregnancy, childbirth and the puerperium — Grossesse, accouchement et puerpéralité								
Total	◆ ●17.6	13	◆ ●19.1	11	◆ ●16.5	6	◆ ●12.0	1
Pregnancy with abortive outcome — Grossesse se terminant par un avortement	◆ ●2.7	2	◆ ●2.9	2	◆ ●3.0	-	-	-
Other direct obstetric causes — Autres décès maternels directs	◆ ●14.9	11	◆ ●16.1	9	◆ ●13.5	6	◆ ●12.0	1
Indirect obstetric causes — Décès maternels indirects	-	-	-	-	-	-	-	-
Certain conditions originating in the perinatal period — Certaines affections dont l'origine se situe dans la période périnatale	●438.4	288	●422.4	265	●398.5	239	●476.3	217
Congenital malformations, deformations and chromosomal abnormalities — Malformations congénitales et anomalies chromosomiques	●371.9	273	●400.4	234	●351.9	188	●374.6	166
Symptoms, signs and abnormal clinical and laboratory findings, not elsewhere classified — Symptômes, signes et résultats anormaux d'examens cliniques et de laboratoire, non classés ailleurs	69.5	5 439	68.8	4 827	61.3	2 962	63.4	3 334
All other diseases — Toutes autres maladies	◆0.4	32	0.4	26	◆0.3	4	◆0.1	11
External causes — Causes externes								
Total	57.0	4 371	55.3	4 243	53.9	3 847	82.4	3 295
Accidents — Accidents								
Total	34.2	2 616	33.1	2 516	32.0	2 112	45.2	1 956
Transport accidents — Accidents de transport	12.6	1 079	13.6	976	12.4	751	16.1	628
Falls — Chutes	4.4	337	4.3	281	3.6	429	9.2	501
Accidental drowning and submersion — Noyade et submersion accidentelles	2.5	151	1.9	185	2.4	110	2.4	108
Exposure to smoke, fire and flames — Exposition à la fumée, au feu et aux flammes ..	1.2	119	1.5	113	1.4	53	1.1	64
Accidental poisoning by and exposure to noxious substances — Intoxication accidentelle par des substances nocives et exposition à ces substances	2.9	207	2.6	187	2.4	76	1.6	87
Intentional self-harm — Lésions auto-infligées	16.9	1 314	16.6	1 317	16.7	930	19.9	1 002
Assault — Agresssions	3.5	244	3.1	225	2.9	158	3.4	133
All other external causes — Toutes autres causes externes	2.3	197	2.5	185	2.4	647	13.9	204

(See notes at end of table. — Voir notes à la fin du tableau.)

Croatia — Croatie

Cause of death — Cause de décès	1996 Rate Taux	1997 Number Nombre	1997 Rate Taux	1998 Number Nombre	1998 Rate Taux	1999 Number Nombre	1999 Rate Taux	2000 Number Nombre
Diseases of the digestive system — Maladies de l'appareil digestif								
Diseases of the liver — Maladies du foie	31.7	1 385	30.3	1 531	34.0	1 597	35.1	1 465
Diseases of the musculoskeletal system and connective tissue — Maladies du système ostéo-articulaire, des muscles et du tissu conjonctif	1.2	45	1.0	40	0.9	45	1.0	55
Diseases of the genitourinary system — Maladies de l'appareil génito-urinaire								
Total	12.8	596	13.0	578	12.8	634	13.9	574
Disorders of kidney and ureter — Affections du rein et de l'uretère	11.8	519	11.4	518	11.5	563	12.4	490
Hyperplasia of prostate — Hyperplasie de la prostate	♦ ▼2.7	27	♦ ▼4.4	9	♦ ▼1.5	13	♦ ▼2.1	17
Pregnancy, childbirth and the puerperium — Grossesse, accouchement et puerpéralité								
Total	♦ *1.9	6	♦ *10.8	3	♦ *6.4	5	♦ *11.1	3
Pregnancy with abortive outcome — Grossesse se terminant par un avortement	-	-	-	-	-	-	-	-
Other direct obstetric causes — Autres décès maternels directs	♦ *1.9	4	♦ *7.2	2	♦ *4.2	4	♦ *8.9	3
Indirect obstetric causes — Décès maternels indirects	-	1	♦ *1.8	1	♦ *2.1	1	♦ *2.2	-
Certain conditions originating in the perinatal period — Certaines affections dont l'origine se situe dans la période périnatale	*403.3	258	*464.9	212	*450.4	193	*427.2	182
Congenital malformations, deformations and chromosomal abnormalities — Malformations congénitales et anomalies chromosomiques	*308.5	161	*290.1	156	*331.4	146	*323.2	127
Symptoms, signs and abnormal clinical and laboratory findings, not elsewhere classified — Symptômes, signes et résultats anormaux d'examens cliniques et de laboratoire, non classés ailleurs	74.2	3 229	70.6	2 306	51.2	1 532	33.6	840
All other diseases — Toutes autres maladies	♦0.2	11	♦0.2	5	♦0.1	7	♦0.2	5
External causes — Causes externes								
Total	73.3	3 119	68.2	3 173	70.5	2 939	64.5	2 905
Accidents — Accidents								
Total	43.5	1 965	43.0	1 903	42.3	1 772	38.9	1 792
Transport accidents — Accidents de transport	14.0	661	14.5	669	14.9	682	15.0	717
Falls — Chutes	11.1	540	11.8	576	12.8	572	12.6	560
Accidental drowning and submersion — Noyade et submersion accidentelles	2.4	113	2.5	128	2.8	110	2.4	111
Exposure to smoke, fire and flames — Exposition à la fumée, au feu et aux flammes ..	1.4	42	0.9	67	1.5	49	1.1	64
Accidental poisoning by and exposure to noxious substances — Intoxication accidentelle par des substances nocives et exposition à ces substances	1.9	67	1.5	66	1.5	56	1.2	57
Intentional self-harm — Lésions auto-infligées	22.3	949	20.8	1 029	22.9	989	21.7	926
Assault — Agressions	3.0	124	2.7	146	3.2	128	2.8	113
All other external causes — Toutes autres causes externes	4.5	81	1.8	95	2.1	50	1.1	74

(See notes at end of table. — Voir notes à la fin du tableau.)

Cause of death — Cause de décès	Croatia — Croatie					Czech Republic — République Tchéque		
	2000	2001		2002		1995		1996
	Rate Taux	Number Nombre	Rate Taux	Number Nombre	Rate Taux	Number Nombre	Rate Taux	Number Nombre
Diseases of the digestive system — Maladies de l'appareil digestif Diseases of the liver — Maladies du foie	33.4	1 416	31.9	1 391	31.3	1 980	19.2	1 889
Diseases of the musculoskeletal system and connective tissue — Maladies du système ostéo-articularie, des muscles et du tissu conjonctif	1.3	46	1.0	45	1.0	60	0.6	36
Diseases of the genitourinary system — Maladies de l'appareil génito-urinaire Total	13.1	492	11.1	598	13.5	1 581	15.3	1 621
Disorders of kidney and ureter — Affections du rein et de l'uretère	11.2	437	9.8	510	11.5	1 444	14.0	1 497
Hyperplasia of prostate — Hyperplasie de la prostate	...	4	♦ ▼0.6	11	♦ ▼1.7	61	▼4.7	44
Pregnancy, childbirth and the puerperium — Grossesse, accouchement et puerpéralité Total	♦ *6.9	1	♦ *2.4	4	♦ *10.0	2	♦ *2.1	5
Pregnancy with abortive outcome — Grossesse se terminant par un avortement	-	-	-	-	-	1	♦ *1.0	-
Other direct obstetric causes — Autres décès maternels directs	♦ *6.9	1	♦ *2.4	4	♦ *10.0	1	♦ *1.0	5
Indirect obstetric causes — Décès maternels indirects	-	-	-	-	-	-	-	-
Certain conditions originating in the perinatal period — Certaines affections dont l'origine se situe dans la période périnatale	*416.0	173	*422.0	163	*406.5	400	*416.2	308
Congenital malformations, deformations and chromosomal abnormalities — Malformations congénitales et anomalies chromosomiques	*290.3	150	*365.9	126	*314.3	257	*267.4	193
Symptoms, signs and abnormal clinical and laboratory findings, not elsewhere classified — Symptômes, signes et résultats anormaux d'examens cliniques et de laboratoire, non classés ailleurs	19.2	871	19.6	1 076	24.2	617	6.0	575
All other diseases — Toutes autres maladies	♦0.1	9	♦0.2	13	♦0.3	37	0.4	22
External causes — Causes externes Total	66.3	2 742	61.8	2 707	60.9	8 510	82.4	7 800
Accidents — Accidents Total	40.9	1 729	39.0	1 725	38.8	6 214	60.2	5 686
Transport accidents — Accidents de transport	16.4	673	15.2	639	14.4	1 667	16.1	1 528
Falls — Chutes	12.8	539	12.1	618	13.9	2 796	27.1	2 423
Accidental drowning and submersion — Noyade et submersion accidentelles	2.5	112	2.5	89	2.0	289	2.8	231
Exposure to smoke, fire and flames — Exposition à la fumée, au feu et aux flammes ..	1.5	61	1.4	54	1.2	80	0.8	73
Accidental poisoning by and exposure to noxious substances — Intoxication accidentelle par des substances nocives et exposition à ces substances	1.3	82	1.8	42	0.9	320	3.1	309
Intentional self-harm — Lésions auto-infligées	21.1	882	19.9	875	19.7	1 733	16.8	1 568
Assault — Agresssions	2.6	87	2.0	67	1.5	185	1.8	175
All other external causes — Toutes autres causes externes	1.7	44	1.0	40	0.9	378	3.7	371

(See notes at end of table. — Voir notes à la fin du tableau.)

Czech Republic — République Tchéque

Cause of death — Cause de décès	1996 Rate Taux	1997 Number Nombre	1997 Rate Taux	1998 Number Nombre	1998 Rate Taux	1999 Number Nombre	1999 Rate Taux	2000 Number Nombre
Diseases of the digestive system — Maladies de l'appareil digestif								
Diseases of the liver — Maladies du foie	18.3	1 930	18.7	2 070	20.1	2 015	19.6	1 993
Diseases of the musculoskeletal system and connective tissue — Maladies du système ostéo-articularie, des muscles et du tissu conjonctif	0.3	38	0.4	33	0.3	39	0.4	40
Diseases of the genitourinary system — Maladies de l'appareil génito-urinaire								
Total	15.7	1 365	13.2	1 406	13.7	1 447	14.1	1 466
Disorders of kidney and ureter — Affections du rein et de l'uretère	14.5	1 249	12.1	1 295	12.6	1 345	13.1	1 336
Hyperplasia of prostate — Hyperplasie de la prostate	▼3.3	51	▼3.7	44	▼3.1	30	◆ ▼2.0	42
Pregnancy, childbirth and the puerperium — Grossesse, accouchement et puerpéralité								
Total	◆ *5.5	2	◆ *2.2	5	◆ *5.5	6	◆ *6.7	5
Pregnancy with abortive outcome — Grossesse se terminant par un avortement	-	-	-	-	-	1	◆ *1.1	3
Other direct obstetric causes — Autres décès maternels directs	◆ *5.5	2	◆ *2.2	5	◆ *5.5	5	◆ *5.6	2
Indirect obstetric causes — Décès maternels indirects	-	-	-	-	-	-	-	-
Certain conditions originating in the perinatal period — Certaines affections dont l'origine se situe dans la période périnatale	*340.5	302	*333.1	237	*261.8	205	*229.1	220
Congenital malformations, deformations and chromosomal abnormalities — Malformations congénitales et anomalies chromosomiques	*213.4	182	*200.8	184	*203.2	155	*173.2	111
Symptoms, signs and abnormal clinical and laboratory findings, not elsewhere classified — Symptômes, signes et résultats anormaux d'examens cliniques et de laboratoire, non classés ailleurs	5.6	642	6.2	807	7.8	679	6.6	573
All other diseases — Toutes autres maladies	◆0.2	11	◆0.1	2	0.0	9	◆0.1	15
External causes — Causes externes								
Total	75.6	7 854	76.2	7 013	68.1	6 925	67.3	7 070
Accidents — Accidents								
Total	55.1	5 575	54.1	4 949	48.1	4 874	47.4	4 933
Transport accidents — Accidents de transport	14.8	1 584	15.4	1 428	13.9	1 568	15.2	1 572
Falls — Chutes	23.5	2 168	21.0	1 999	19.4	1 892	18.4	1 957
Accidental drowning and submersion — Noyade et submersion accidentelles	2.2	265	2.6	223	2.2	233	2.3	219
Exposure to smoke, fire and flames — Exposition à la fumée, au feu et aux flammes	0.7	70	0.7	80	0.8	64	0.6	64
Accidental poisoning by and exposure to noxious substances — Intoxication accidentelle par des substances nocives et exposition à ces substances	3.0	331	3.2	303	2.9	294	2.9	303
Intentional self-harm — Lésions auto-infligées	15.2	1 666	16.2	1 613	15.7	1 610	15.7	1 649
Assault — Agressions	1.7	168	1.6	168	1.6	151	1.5	154
All other external causes — Toutes autres causes externes	3.6	445	4.3	283	2.7	290	2.8	334

(See notes at end of table. — Voir notes à la fin du tableau.)

Cause of death — Cause de décès	Czech Republic — République Tchéque					Denmark — Danemark[12]		
	2000	2001		2002		1995		1996
	Rate Taux	Number Nombre	Rate Taux	Number Nombre	Rate Taux	Number Nombre	Rate Taux	Number Nombre
Diseases of the digestive system — Maladies de l'appareil digestif								
Diseases of the liver — Maladies du foie	19.4	2 051	20.1	2 084	20.4	924	17.7	765
Diseases of the musculoskeletal system and connective tissue — Maladies du système ostéo-articularie, des muscles et du tissu conjonctif	0.4	42	0.4	32	0.3	221	4.2	211
Diseases of the genitourinary system — Maladies de l'appareil génito-urinaire								
Total	14.3	1 420	13.9	1 410	13.8	665	12.7	600
Disorders of kidney and ureter — Affections du rein et de i'uretère	13.0	1 297	12.7	1 318	12.9	482	9.2	421
Hyperplasia of prostate — Hyperplasie de la prostate	▼2.9	31	▼2.1	20	♦ ▼1.3	46	▼6.0	42
Pregnancy, childbirth and the puerperium — Grossesse, accouchement et puerpéralité								
Total	♦ *5.5	3	♦ *3.3	3	♦ *3.1	7	♦ *10.0	4
Pregnancy with abortive outcome — Grossesse se terminant par un avortement	♦ *3.3	1	♦ *1.1	1	♦ *1.0	-		-
Other direct obstetric causes — Autres décès maternels directs	♦ *2.2	2	♦ *2.2	2	♦ *2.0	7	♦ *10.0	4
Indirect obstetric causes — Décès maternels indirects	-	-		-		-		-
Certain conditions originating in the perinatal period — Certaines affections dont l'origine se situe dans la période périnatale	*242.0	183	*201.7	217	*221.7	176	*252.3	170
Congenital malformations, deformations and chromosomal abnormalities — Malformations congénitales et anomalies chromosomiques	*122.1	142	*156.5	118	*120.6	233	*333.9	261
Symptoms, signs and abnormal clinical and laboratory findings, not elsewhere classified — Symptômes, signes et résultats anormaux d'examens cliniques et de laboratoire, non classés ailleurs	5.6	675	6.6	765	7.5	4 702	89.9	6 568
All other diseases — Toutes autres maladies	♦0.1	19	♦0.2	9	♦0.1	53	1.0	48
External causes — Causes externes								
Total	68.8	6 910	67.6	6 838	67.0	3 624	69.3	3 371
Accidents — Accidents								
Total	48.0	4 823	47.2	4 821	47.3	2 437	46.6	2 231
Transport accidents — Accidents de transport	15.3	1 484	14.5	1 490	14.6	639	12.2	555
Falls — Chutes	19.1	1 892	18.5	1 817	17.8	1 316	25.2	1 239
Accidental drowning and submersion — Noyade et submersion accidentelles	2.1	215	2.1	235	2.3	38	0.7	38
Exposure to smoke, fire and flames — Exposition à la fumée, au feu et aux flammes	0.6	62	0.6	56	0.5	83	1.6	73
Accidental poisoning by and exposure to noxious substances — Intoxication accidentelle par des substances nocives et exposition à ces substances	2.9	328	3.2	300	2.9	218	4.2	162
Intentional self-harm — Lésions auto-infligées	16.1	1 623	15.9	1 534	15.0	922	17.6	892
Assault — Agresssions	1.5	135	1.3	134	1.3	62	1.2	59
All other external causes — Toutes autres causes externes	3.3	329	3.2	349	3.4	203	3.9	189

(See notes at end of table. — Voir notes à la fin du tableau.)

Denmark — Danemark[12]

Cause of death — Cause de décès	1996	1997		1998		1999		2000
	Rate Taux	Number Nombre	Rate Taux	Number Nombre	Rate Taux	Number Nombre	Rate Taux	Number Nombre
Diseases of the digestive system — Maladies de l'appareil digestif								
Diseases of the liver — Maladies du foie	14.5	937	17.7	867	16.4	900	16.9	873
Diseases of the musculoskeletal system and connective tissue — Maladies du système ostéo-articulaire, des muscles et du tissu conjonctif	4.0	323	6.1	369	7.0	398	7.5	317
Diseases of the genitourinary system — Maladies de l'appareil génito-urinaire								
Total	11.4	634	12.0	674	12.7	702	13.2	667
Disorders of kidney and ureter — Affections du rein et de l'uretère	8.0	434	8.2	448	8.5	456	8.6	444
Hyperplasia of prostate — Hyperplasie de la prostate	▼5.4	46	▼5.8	66	▼8.1	69	▼8.4	44
Pregnancy, childbirth and the puerperium — Grossesse, accouchement et puerpéralité								
Total	♦ *5.9	5	♦ *7.4	2	♦ *3.0	4	♦ *6.0	-
Pregnancy with abortive outcome — Grossesse se terminant par un avortement	-	1	♦ *1.5	-	-	-	-	-
Other direct obstetric causes — Autres décès maternels directs	♦ *5.9	4	♦ *5.9	2	♦ *3.0	4	♦ *6.0	-
Indirect obstetric causes — Décès maternels indirects	-	-	-	-	-	-	-	-
Certain conditions originating in the perinatal period — Certaines affections dont l'origine se situe dans la période périnatale	*251.3	169	*249.9	139	*210.1	125	*188.7	163
Congenital malformations, deformations and chromosomal abnormalities — Malformations congénitales et anomalies chromosomiques	*385.9	224	*331.2	219	*331.0	212	*320.1	220
Symptoms, signs and abnormal clinical and laboratory findings, not elsewhere classified — Symptômes, signes et résultats anormaux d'examens cliniques et de laboratoire, non classés ailleurs	124.8	4 492	85.0	3 612	68.1	2 506	47.0	2 554
All other diseases — Toutes autres maladies	0.9	48	0.9	79	1.5	66	1.2	60
External causes — Causes externes								
Total	64.1	3 537	66.9	3 412	64.4	3 441	64.6	3 356
Accidents — Accidents								
Total	42.4	2 397	45.4	2 328	43.9	2 415	45.3	2 339
Transport accidents — Accidents de transport	10.5	521	9.9	541	10.2	534	10.0	513
Falls — Chutes	23.5	1 439	27.2	1 398	26.4	1 446	27.1	582
Accidental drowning and submersion — Noyade et submersion accidentelles	0.7	42	0.8	34	0.6	50	0.9	37
Exposure to smoke, fire and flames — Exposition à la fumée, au feu et aux flammes	1.4	68	1.3	56	1.1	64	1.2	66
Accidental poisoning by and exposure to noxious substances — Intoxication accidentelle par des substances nocives et exposition à ces substances	3.1	165	3.1	136	2.6	168	3.2	186
Intentional self-harm — Lésions auto-infligées	17.0	817	15.5	763	14.4	762	14.3	727
Assault — Agressions	1.1	64	1.2	51	1.0	58	1.1	67
All other external causes — Toutes autres causes externes	3.6	259	4.9	270	5.1	206	3.9	223

(See notes at end of table. — Voir notes à la fin du tableau.)

Cause of death — Cause de décès	Denmark — Danemark[12] 2000 Rate Taux	Estonia — Estonie[6] 1995 Number Nombre	1995 Rate Taux	1996 Number Nombre	1996 Rate Taux	1997 Number Nombre	1997 Rate Taux	1998 Number Nombre
Diseases of the digestive system — Maladies de l'appareil digestif								
Diseases of the liver — Maladies du foie	16.4	208	14.0	161	11.0	226	15.5	282
Diseases of the musculoskeletal system and connective tissue — Maladies du système ostéo-articularie, des muscles et du tissu conjonctif	5.9	55	3.7	51	3.5	49	3.4	58
Diseases of the genitourinary system — Maladies de l'appareil génito-urinaire								
Total	12.5	208	14.0	199	13.5	206	14.1	228
Disorders of kidney and ureter — Affections du rein et de l'uretère	8.3	156	10.5	161	11.0	180	12.3	204
Hyperplasia of prostate — Hyperplasie de la prostate	▼5.3	28	♦ ▼16.1	20	♦ ▼11.6	21	♦ ▼12.1	20
Pregnancy, childbirth and the puerperium — Grossesse, accouchement et puerpéralité								
Total	-	7	♦ *51.6	-	-	2	♦ *15.8	2
Pregnancy with abortive outcome — Grossesse se terminant par un avortement	-	1	♦ *7.4	-	-	-	-	2
Other direct obstetric causes — Autres décès maternels directs	-	5	♦ *36.9	-	-	2	♦ *15.8	-
Indirect obstetric causes — Décès maternels indirects	-	1	♦ *7.4	-	-	-	-	-
Certain conditions originating in the perinatal period — Certaines affections dont l'origine se situe dans la période périnatale	*243.0	112	*826.0	70	*526.7	61	*483.1	45
Congenital malformations, deformations and chromosomal abnormalities — Malformations congénitales et anomalies chromosomiques	*327.9	63	*464.6	57	*428.9	55	*435.6	64
Symptoms, signs and abnormal clinical and laboratory findings, not elsewhere classified — Symptômes, signes et résultats anormaux d'examens cliniques et de laboratoire, non classés ailleurs	47.9	916	61.7	886	60.3	826	56.7	833
All other diseases — Toutes autres maladies	1.1	31	2.1	19	♦1.3	23	♦1.6	15
External causes — Causes externes								
Total	62.9	2 908	196.0	2 326	158.3	2 313	158.6	2 351
Accidents — Accidents								
Total	43.8	1 844	124.3	1 391	94.7	1 417	97.2	1 469
Transport accidents — Accidents de transport	9.6	411	27.7	273	18.6	343	23.5	341
Falls — Chutes	10.9	216	14.6	196	13.3	187	12.8	192
Accidental drowning and submersion — Noyade et submersion accidentelles	0.7	204	13.7	102	6.9	165	11.3	97
Exposure to smoke, fire and flames — Exposition à la fumée, au feu et aux flammes	1.2	228	15.4	195	13.3	157	10.8	183
Accidental poisoning by and exposure to noxious substances — Intoxication accidentelle par des substances nocives et exposition à ces substances	3.5	406	27.4	323	22.0	290	19.9	327
Intentional self-harm — Lésions auto-infligées	13.6	595	40.1	551	37.5	525	36.0	482
Assault — Agressions	1.3	328	22.1	293	19.9	237	16.3	265
All other external causes — Toutes autres causes externes	4.2	141	9.5	91	6.2	134	9.2	135

(See notes at end of table. — Voir notes à la fin du tableau.)

Estonia — Estonie[6]

Cause of death — Cause de décès	1998 Rate Taux	1999 Number Nombre	1999 Rate Taux	2000 Number Nombre	2000 Rate Taux	2001 Number Nombre	2001 Rate Taux	2002 Number Nombre
Diseases of the digestive system — Maladies de l'appareil digestif								
Diseases of the liver — Maladies du foie	19.5	244	16.9	285	20.8	332	24.3	330
Diseases of the musculoskeletal system and connective tissue — Maladies du système ostéo-articularie, des muscles et du tissu conjonctif	4.0	48	3.3	45	3.3	61	4.5	77
Diseases of the genitourinary system — Maladies de l'appareil génito-urinaire								
Total	15.7	169	11.7	176	12.9	151	11.1	143
Disorders of kidney and ureter — Affections du rein et de l'uretère	14.1	158	11.0	158	11.5	132	9.7	130
Hyperplasia of prostate — Hyperplasie de la prostate	◆ ▼11.5	9	◆ ▼5.1	17	◆ ▼9.8	15	◆ ▼8.6	9
Pregnancy, childbirth and the puerperium — Grossesse, accouchement et puerpéralité								
Total	◆ *16.4	2	◆ *15.9	5	◆ *38.2	1	◆ *7.9	1
Pregnancy with abortive outcome — Grossesse se terminant par un avortement	◆ *16.4	-	-	2	*15.3	1	◆ *7.9	-
Other direct obstetric causes — Autres décès maternels directs	-	2	◆ *15.9	3	*22.9	-	-	1
Indirect obstetric causes — Décès maternels indirects	-	-	-	-	-	-	-	-
Certain conditions originating in the perinatal period — Certaines affections dont l'origine se situe dans la période périnatale	*369.8	57	*454.4	51	*389.6	50	*395.8	30
Congenital malformations, deformations and chromosomal abnormalities — Malformations congénitales et anomalies chromosomiques	*525.9	64	*510.2	54	*412.6	49	*387.9	42
Symptoms, signs and abnormal clinical and laboratory findings, not elsewhere classified — Symptômes, signes et résultats anormaux d'examens cliniques et de laboratoire, non classés ailleurs	57.5	821	56.9	822	60.0	729	53.4	771
All other diseases — Toutes autres maladies	◆1.0	18	◆1.2	19	◆1.4	17	◆1.2	19
External causes — Causes externes								
Total	162.2	2 251	156.1	2 092	152.8	2 330	170.8	2 009
Accidents — Accidents								
Total	101.3	1 413	98.0	1 355	98.9	1 595	116.9	1 385
Transport accidents — Accidents de transport	23.5	278	19.3	262	18.4	237	17.4	247
Falls — Chutes	13.2	190	13.2	134	9.8	139	10.2	141
Accidental drowning and submersion — Noyade et submersion accidentelles	8.7	164	11.4	77	5.6	135	9.9	91
Exposure to smoke, fire and flames — Exposition à la fumée, au feu et aux flammes	12.5	148	10.3	151	11.0	168	12.3	152
Accidental poisoning by and exposure to noxious substances — Intoxication accidentelle par des substances nocives et exposition à ces substances	22.6	311	21.6	352	25.7	418	30.6	307
Intentional self-harm — Lésions auto-infligées	33.2	469	32.5	377	27.5	401	29.4	371
Assault — Agresssions	18.3	227	15.7	190	13.9	207	15.2	159
All other external causes — Toutes autres causes externes	9.3	142	9.8	170	12.4	127	9.3	94

21. Death and death rates by cause: 1995 - 2002
Décès selon la cause, nombres et taux: 1995 - 2002 (continued — suite)

(See notes at end of table. — Voir notes à la fin du tableau.)

Cause of death — Cause de décès	Estonia — Estonie[6]	Finland — Finlande[13]						
	2002	1995		1996		1997		1998
	Rate Taux	Number Nombre	Rate Taux	Number Nombre	Rate Taux	Number Nombre	Rate Taux	Number Nombre
Diseases of the digestive system — Maladies de l'appareil digestif								
Diseases of the liver — Maladies du foie	24.3	541	10.6	639	12.5	675	13.1	665
Diseases of the musculoskeletal system and connective tissue — Maladies du système ostéo-articularie, des muscles et du tissu conjonctif	5.7	260	5.1	279	5.4	284	5.5	302
Diseases of the genitourinary system — Maladies de l'appareil génito-urinaire								
Total	10.5	585	11.5	565	11.0	573	11.1	504
Disorders of kidney and ureter — Affections du rein et de l'uretère	9.6	404	7.9	408	8.0	408	7.9	387
Hyperplasia of prostate — Hyperplasie de la prostate	♦ ▼5.1	34	▼5.1	38	▼5.5	33	▼4.6	34
Pregnancy, childbirth and the puerperium — Grossesse, accouchement et puerpéralité								
Total	♦ *7.7	1	♦ *1.6	2	♦ *3.3	3	♦ *5.1	3
	-	-	-					-
Pregnancy with abortive outcome — Grossesse se terminant par un avortement								
Other direct obstetric causes — Autres décès maternels directs	♦ *7.7	1	♦ *1.6	2	♦ *3.3	3	♦ *5.1	2
Indirect obstetric causes — Décès maternels indirects	-	-						1
Certain conditions originating in the perinatal period — Certaines affections dont l'origine se situe dans la période périnatale	♦ *230.8	110	*174.4	117	*192.7	94	*158.4	99
Congenital malformations, deformations and chromosomal abnormalities — Malformations congénitales et anomalies chromosomiques	*323.1	196	*310.8	187	*308.0	193	*325.3	192
Symptoms, signs and abnormal clinical and laboratory findings, not elsewhere classified — Symptômes, signes et résultats anormaux d'examens cliniques et de laboratoire, non classés ailleurs	56.7	190	3.7	186	3.6	190	3.7	192
All other diseases — Toutes autres maladies	♦1.4	18	♦0.4	25	♦0.5	20	♦0.4	21
External causes — Causes externes								
Total	147.9	4 378	85.7	4 127	80.5	4 280	83.3	4 277
Accidents — Accidents								
Total	101.9	2 644	51.8	2 528	49.3	2 675	52.0	2 782
Transport accidents — Accidents de transport	18.2	580	11.4	503	9.8	561	10.9	551
Falls — Chutes	10.4	912	17.9	953	18.6	1 031	20.1	1 190
Accidental drowning and submersion — Noyade et submersion accidentelles	6.7	105	2.1	118	2.3	189	3.7	122
Exposure to smoke, fire and flames — Exposition à la fumée, au feu et aux flammes	11.2	81	1.6	80	1.6	91	1.8	79
Accidental poisoning by and exposure to noxious substances — Intoxication accidentelle par des substances nocives et exposition à ces substances	22.6	602	11.8	624	12.2	523	10.2	560
Intentional self-harm — Lésions auto-infligées	27.3	1 388	27.2	1 247	24.3	1 321	25.7	1 226
Assault — Agresssions	11.7	150	2.9	169	3.3	139	2.7	124
All other external causes — Toutes autres causes externes	6.9	196	3.8	183	3.6	145	2.8	145

(See notes at end of table. — Voir notes à la fin du tableau.)

Finland — Finlande[13]

Cause of death — Cause de décès	1998 Rate Taux	1999 Number Nombre	1999 Rate Taux	2000 Number Nombre	2000 Rate Taux	2001 Number Nombre	2001 Rate Taux	2002 Number Nombre
Diseases of the digestive system — Maladies de l'appareil digestif								
Diseases of the liver — Maladies du foie	12.9	632	12.2	692	13.4	724	14.0	804
Diseases of the musculoskeletal system and connective tissue — Maladies du système ostéo-articularie, des muscles et du tissu conjonctif	5.9	295	5.7	285	5.5	276	5.3	285
Diseases of the genitourinary system — Maladies de l'appareil génito-urinaire								
Total	9.8	503	9.7	442	8.5	481	9.3	470
Disorders of kidney and ureter — Affections du rein et de l'uretère	7.5	366	7.1	341	6.6	367	7.1	345
Hyperplasia of prostate — Hyperplasie de la prostate	▼4.6	28	◆ ▼3.7	25	...	26	◆ ▼3.2	27
Pregnancy, childbirth and the puerperium — Grossesse, accouchement et puerpéralité								
Total	◆ *5.3	2	◆ *3.5	3	◆ *5.3	3	◆ *5.3	3
Pregnancy with abortive outcome — Grossesse se terminant par un avortement	-	-	-	1	◆ *1.8	-	-	-
Other direct obstetric causes — Autres décès maternels directs	◆ *3.5	2	◆ *3.5	2	◆ *3.5	3	◆ *5.3	3
Indirect obstetric causes — Décès maternels indirects	◆ *1.8	-	-	-	-	-	-	-
Certain conditions originating in the perinatal period — Certaines affections dont l'origine se situe dans la période périnatale	*173.4	87	*151.1	85	*149.8	77	*137.0	76
Congenital malformations, deformations and chromosomal abnormalities — Malformations congénitales et anomalies chromosomiques	*336.2	186	*323.1	190	*334.8	169	*300.8	152
Symptoms, signs and abnormal clinical and laboratory findings, not elsewhere classified — Symptômes, signes et résultats anormaux d'examens cliniques et de laboratoire, non classés ailleurs	3.7	196	3.8	178	3.4	212	4.1	257
All other diseases — Toutes autres maladies	◆0.4	19	◆0.4	31	0.6	30	◆0.6	20
External causes — Causes externes								
Total	83.0	4 178	80.9	4 128	79.7	4 166	80.3	4 077
Accidents — Accidents								
Total	54.0	2 652	51.3	2 620	50.6	2 644	51.0	2 684
Transport accidents — Accidents de transport	10.7	544	10.5	501	9.7	541	10.4	531
Falls — Chutes	23.1	1 014	19.6	1 053	20.3	1 038	20.0	1 122
Accidental drowning and submersion — Noyade et submersion accidentelles	2.4	194	3.8	141	2.7	143	2.8	163
Exposure to smoke, fire and flames — Exposition à la fumée, au feu et aux flammes	1.5	74	1.4	75	1.4	52	1.0	66
Accidental poisoning by and exposure to noxious substances — Intoxication accidentelle par des substances nocives et exposition à ces substances	10.9	545	10.8	556	10.7	581	11.2	516
Intentional self-harm — Lésions auto-infligées	23.8	1 204	23.3	1 163	22.5	1 203	23.2	1 093
Assault — Agresssions	2.4	143	2.8	136	2.6	154	3.0	133
All other external causes — Toutes autres causes externes	2.8	179	3.5	209	4.0	165	3.2	167

(See notes at end of table. — Voir notes à la fin du tableau.)

Cause of death — Cause de décès	Finland — Finlande[13]	France[14]						
	2002	1995		1996		1997		1998
	Rate Taux	Number Nombre	Rate Taux	Number Nombre	Rate Taux	Number Nombre	Rate Taux	Number Nombre
Diseases of the digestive system — Maladies de l'appareil digestif								
Diseases of the liver — Maladies du foie	15.5	9 380	16.2	9 636	16.6	9 581	16.3	9 590
Diseases of the musculoskeletal system and connective tissue — Maladies du système ostéo-articularie, des muscles et du tissu conjonctif	5.5	2 642	4.6	2 605	4.5	2 577	4.4	2 856
Diseases of the genitourinary system — Maladies de l'appareil génito-urinaire	9.0	7 370	12.7	7 296	12.6	7 301	12.5	7 361
Total								
Disorders of kidney and ureter — Affections du rein et de l'uretère	6.6	5 259	9.1	5 293	9.1	5 244	8.9	5 185
Hyperplasia of prostate — Hyperplasie de la prostate	♦ ▼3.3	182	▼2.4	140	▼1.8	151	▼1.9	175
Pregnancy, childbirth and the puerperium — Grossesse, accouchement et puerpéralité								
Total	♦ *5.4	70	*9.6	97	*13.2	70	*9.6	75
Pregnancy with abortive outcome — Grossesse se terminant par un avortement	-	2	♦ *0.3	2	♦ *0.3	5	♦ *0.7	6
Other direct obstetric causes — Autres décès maternels directs	♦ *5.4	59	*8.1	78	*10.6	55	*7.6	53
Indirect obstetric causes — Décès maternels indirects		9	♦ *1.2	17	♦ *2.3	10	♦ *1.4	16
Certain conditions originating in the perinatal period — Certaines affections dont l'origine se situe dans la période périnatale	*136.8	1 308	*179.3	1 323	*180.2	1 441	*198.3	1 262
Congenital malformations, deformations and chromosomal abnormalities — Malformations congénitales et anomalies chromosomiques	*273.6	1 558	*213.5	1 559	*212.3	1 519	*209.0	1 458
Symptoms, signs and abnormal clinical and laboratory findings, not elsewhere classified — Symptômes, signes et résultats anormaux d'examens cliniques et de laboratoire, non classés ailleurs	4.9	31 663	54.7	32 690	56.3	32 494	55.4	33 778
All other diseases — Toutes autres maladies	♦0.4	2 590	4.5	2 548	4.4	2 680	4.6	2 550
External causes — Causes externes								
Total	78.4	44 838	77.5	43 732	75.4	43 388	74.0	44 108
Accidents — Accidents								
Total	51.6	29 955	51.8	29 668	51.1	29 605	50.5	31 058
Transport accidents — Accidents de transport	10.2	8 371	14.5	8 031	13.8	7 904	13.5	8 459
Falls — Chutes	21.6	9 808	17.0	9 645	16.6	9 556	16.3	10 210
Accidental drowning and submersion — Noyade et submersion accidentelles	3.1	605	1.0	615	1.1	566	1.0	541
Exposure to smoke, fire and flames — Exposition à la fumée, au feu et aux flammes	1.3	466	0.8	516	0.9	423	0.7	465
Accidental poisoning by and exposure to noxious substances — Intoxication accidentelle par des substances nocives et exposition à ces substances	9.9	419	0.7	430	0.7	547	0.9	728
Intentional self-harm — Lésions auto-infligées	21.0	11 819	20.4	11 279	19.4	11 139	19.0	10 534
Assault — Agresssions	2.6	624	1.1	595	1.0	551	0.9	436
All other external causes — Toutes autres causes externes	3.2	2 440	4.2	2 190	3.8	2 093	3.6	2 080

21. Death and death rates by cause: 1995 - 2002
Décès selon la cause, nombres et taux: 1995 - 2002 (continued — suite)

(See notes at end of table. — Voir notes à la fin du tableau.)

Cause of death — Cause de décès	France[14]					Germany — Allemagne		
	1998	1999		2000		1995		1996
	Rate Taux	Number Nombre	Rate Taux	Number Nombre	Rate Taux	Number Nombre	Rate Taux	Number Nombre
Diseases of the digestive system — Maladies de l'appareil digestif								
Diseases of the liver — Maladies du foie	16.4	9 254	15.8	9 438	16.0	19 445	23.8	19 202
Diseases of the musculoskeletal system and connective tissue — Maladies du système ostéo-articularie, des muscles et du tissu conjonctif	4.9	2 072	5.1	3 837	6.5	2 260	2.8	2 201
Diseases of the genitourinary system — Maladies de l'appareil génito-urinaire								
Total	12.6	7 776	13.3	7 261	12.3	9 876	12.1	9 539
Disorders of kidney and ureter — Affections du rein et de l'uretère	8.9	5 481	9.3	5 470	9.3	7 838	9.6	7 532
Hyperplasia of prostate — Hyperplasie de la prostate	▼2.1	177	▼2.1	215	▼2.5	246	▼2.0	234
Pregnancy, childbirth and the puerperium — Grossesse, accouchement et puerpéralité								
Total	•10.2	55	•7.4	50	•6.5	41	•5.4	51
Pregnancy with abortive outcome — Grossesse se terminant par un avortement	♦ •0.8	5	♦ •0.7	2	♦ •0.3	6	♦ •0.8	5
Other direct obstetric causes — Autres décès maternels directs	•7.2	43	•5.8	39	•5.0	31	•4.1	42
Indirect obstetric causes — Décès maternels indirects	♦ •2.2	7	♦ •0.9	7	♦ •0.9	4	♦ •0.5	4
Certain conditions originating in the perinatal period — Certaines affections dont l'origine se situe dans la période périnatale	•171.0	1 362	•182.9	1 422	•183.5	1 736	•226.9	1 625
Congenital malformations, deformations and chromosomal abnormalities — Malformations congénitales et anomalies chromosomiques	•197.5	1 501	•201.5	1 708	•220.4	1 990	•260.1	2 006
Symptoms, signs and abnormal clinical and laboratory findings, not elsewhere classified — Symptômes, signes et résultats anormaux d'examens cliniques et de laboratoire, non classés ailleurs	57.8	33 886	57.8	32 519	55.2	22 756	27.9	22 854
All other diseases — Toutes autres maladies	4.4	2 561	4.4	2 251	3.8	749	0.9	686
External causes — Causes externes								
Total	75.5	43 783	74.7	41 436	70.4	39 367	48.2	38 516
Accidents — Accidents								
Total	53.2	31 188	53.2	28 572	48.5	23 818	29.2	23 549
Transport accidents — Accidents de transport	14.5	8 122	13.9	7 662	13.0	9 574	11.7	8 944
Falls — Chutes	17.5	10 520	17.9	5 292	9.0	10 052	12.3	10 237
Accidental drowning and submersion — Noyade et submersion accidentelles	0.9	547	0.9	1 125	1.9	680	0.8	509
Exposure to smoke, fire and flames — Exposition à la fumée, au feu et aux flammes	0.8	460	0.8	443	0.8	614	0.8	714
Accidental poisoning by and exposure to noxious substances — Intoxication accidentelle par des substances nocives et exposition à ces substances	1.2	758	1.3	1 088	1.8	238	0.3	259
Intentional self-harm — Lésions auto-infligées	18.0	10 268	17.5	10 837	18.4	12 888	15.8	12 225
Assault — Agresssions	0.7	419	0.7	503	0.9	926	1.1	885
All other external causes — Toutes autres causes externes	3.6	1 908	3.3	1 524	2.6	1 735	2.1	1 857

(See notes at end of table. — Voir notes à la fin du tableau.)

Germany — Allemagne

Cause of death — Cause de décès	1996	1997		1998		1999		2000
	Rate Taux	Number Nombre	Rate Taux	Number Nombre	Rate Taux	Number Nombre	Rate Taux	Number Nombre
Diseases of the digestive system — Maladies de l'appareil digestif								
Diseases of the liver — Maladies du foie	23.4	18 617	22.7	18 563	22.6	18 295	22.3	18 428
Diseases of the musculoskeletal system and connective tissue — Maladies du système ostéo-articulaire, des muscles et du tissu conjonctif	2.7	2 063	2.5	1 846	2.3	1 800	2.2	1 832
Diseases of the genitourinary system — Maladies de l'appareil génito-urinaire								
Total	11.6	9 066	11.0	10 735	13.1	10 749	13.1	10 719
Disorders of kidney and ureter — Affections du rein et de l'uretère	9.2	6 926	8.4	8 562	10.4	8 546	10.4	8 601
Hyperplasia of prostate — Hyperplasie de la prostate	▼1.9	199	▼1.6	149	▼1.2	119	▼0.9	104
Pregnancy, childbirth and the puerperium — Grossesse, accouchement et puerpéralité								
Total	*6.4	49	*6.0	44	*5.5	37	*4.8	43
Pregnancy with abortive outcome — Grossesse se terminant par un avortement	◆ *0.6	3	◆ *0.4	1	◆ *0.1	2	◆ *0.3	2
Other direct obstetric causes — Autres décès maternels directs	*5.3	40	*4.9	39	*4.9	31	*4.0	35
Indirect obstetric causes — Décès maternels indirects	◆ *0.5	6	◆ *0.7	4	◆ *0.5	4	◆ *0.5	6
Certain conditions originating in the perinatal period — Certaines affections dont l'origine se situe dans la période périnatale	*204.1	1 623	*199.8	1 600	*200.6	1 625	*210.8	1 474
Congenital malformations, deformations and chromosomal abnormalities — Malformations congénitales et anomalies chromosomiques	*252.0	2 059	*253.5	1 822	*228.5	1 610	*208.9	1 643
Symptoms, signs and abnormal clinical and laboratory findings, not elsewhere classified — Symptômes, signes et résultats anormaux d'examens cliniques et de laboratoire, non classés ailleurs	27.9	23 058	28.1	23 589	28.8	22 579	27.5	23 789
All other diseases — Toutes autres maladies	0.8	589	0.7	488	0.6	463	0.6	447
External causes — Causes externes								
Total	47.0	36 801	44.8	34 585	42.2	34 063	41.5	34 523
Accidents — Accidents								
Total	28.8	21 963	26.8	19 128	23.3	19 117	23.3	19 680
Transport accidents — Accidents de transport	10.9	8 730	10.6	7 965	9.7	7 986	9.7	7 747
Falls — Chutes	12.5	8 904	10.9	7 229	8.8	7 302	8.9	7 404
Accidental drowning and submersion — Noyade et submersion accidentelles	0.6	602	0.7	477	0.6	597	0.7	507
Exposure to smoke, fire and flames — Exposition à la fumée, au feu et aux flammes	0.9	583	0.7	522	0.6	506	0.6	475
Accidental poisoning by and exposure to noxious substances — Intoxication accidentelle par des substances nocives et exposition à ces substances	0.3	280	0.3	269	0.3	225	0.3	590
Intentional self-harm — Lésions auto-infligées	14.9	12 256	14.9	11 648	14.2	11 157	13.6	11 065
Assault — Agresssions	1.1	752	0.9	708	0.9	719	0.9	602
All other external causes — Toutes autres causes externes	2.3	1 830	2.2	3 101	3.8	3 070	3.7	3 176

21. Death and death rates by cause: 1995 - 2002
Décès selon la cause, nombres et taux: 1995 - 2002 (continued — suite)

(See notes at end of table. — Voir notes à la fin du tableau.)

Cause of death — Cause de décès	Germany — Allemagne			Greece — Grèce				
	2000	2001		1995		1996		1997
	Rate Taux	Number Nombre	Rate Taux	Number Nombre	Rate Taux	Number Nombre	Rate Taux	Number Nombre
Diseases of the digestive system — Maladies de l'appareil digestif								
Diseases of the liver — Maladies du foie	22.4	18 140	22.0	678	6.5	609	5.8	598
Diseases of the musculoskeletal system and connective tissue — Maladies du système ostéo-articularie, des muscles et du tissu conjonctif	2.2	1 908	2.3	100	1.0	119	1.1	131
Diseases of the genitourinary system — Maladies de l'appareil génito-urinaire								
Total	13.0	11 221	13.6	1 427	13.7	1 709	16.3	1 585
Disorders of kidney and ureter — Affections du rein et de l'uretère	10.5	8 908	10.8	1 330	12.7	1 624	15.5	1 501
Hyperplasia of prostate — Hyperplasie de la prostate	...	116	▼0.9	-	-	-	-	1
Pregnancy, childbirth and the puerperium — Grossesse, accouchement et puerpéralité								
Total	*5.6	27	♦ *3.7	-	-	4	♦ *4.0	-
Pregnancy with abortive outcome — Grossesse se terminant par un avortement	♦ *0.3	3	♦ *0.4	-	-	-	-	-
Other direct obstetric causes — Autres décès maternels directs	*4.6	22	♦ *3.0	-	-	2	♦ *2.0	-
Indirect obstetric causes — Décès maternels indirects	♦ *0.8	1	♦ *0.1	-	-	2	♦ *2.0	-
Certain conditions originating in the perinatal period — Certaines affections dont l'origine se situe dans la période périnatale	*192.2	1 484	*202.0	411	*404.9	357	*354.5	327
Congenital malformations, deformations and chromosomal abnormalities — Malformations congénitales et anomalies chromosomiques	*214.2	1 612	*219.5	389	*383.3	374	*371.3	323
Symptoms, signs and abnormal clinical and laboratory findings, not elsewhere classified — Symptômes, signes et résultats anormaux d'examens cliniques et de laboratoire, non classés ailleurs	28.9	22 333	27.1	8 329	79.7	8 138	77.7	8 027
All other diseases — Toutes autres maladies	0.5	428	0.5	62	0.6	53	0.5	60
External causes — Causes externes								
Total	42.0	34 201	41.5	4 549	43.5	4 482	42.8	4 422
Accidents — Accidents								
Total	23.9	19 373	23.5	4 039	38.6	3 957	37.8	3 881
Transport accidents — Accidents de transport	9.4	7 181	8.7	2 450	23.4	2 613	24.3	2 408
Falls — Chutes	9.0	7 099	8.6	487	4.7	345	3.3	370
Accidental drowning and submersion — Noyade et submersion accidentelles	0.6	455	0.6	342	3.3	372	3.6	315
Exposure to smoke, fire and flames — Exposition à la fumée, au feu et aux flammes	0.6	478	0.6	120	1.1	110	1.1	128
Accidental poisoning by and exposure to noxious substances — Intoxication accidentelle par des substances nocives et exposition à ces substances	0.7	1 040	1.3	247	2.4	262	2.5	298
Intentional self-harm — Lésions auto-infligées	13.5	11 156	13.5	370	3.5	356	3.4	374
Assault — Agressions	0.7	564	0.7	139	1.3	166	1.6	167
All other external causes — Toutes autres causes externes	3.9	3 108	3.8	1	0.0	3	0.0	-

(See notes at end of table. — Voir notes à la fin du tableau.)

Greece — Grèce

Cause of death — Cause de décès	1997 Rate Taux	1998 Number Nombre	1998 Rate Taux	1999 Number Nombre	1999 Rate Taux	2000 Number Nombre	2000 Rate Taux	2001 Number Nombre
Diseases of the digestive system — Maladies de l'appareil digestif								
Diseases of the liver — Maladies du foie	5.7	604	5.7	646	6.1	700	7.0	692
Diseases of the musculoskeletal system and connective tissue — Maladies du système ostéo-articularie, des muscles et du tissu conjonctif	1.2	205	1.9	289	2.7	289	2.9	360
Diseases of the genitourinary system — Maladies de l'appareil génito-urinaire								
Total	15.1	1 202	11.4	1 411	13.4	1 607	16.1	1 536
Disorders of kidney and ureter — Affections du rein et de l'uretère	14.3	1 131	10.8	1 329	12.6	1 538	15.4	1 455
Hyperplasia of prostate — Hyperplasie de la prostate	♦ ▼0.1	-	-	1	...	1	...	1
Pregnancy, childbirth and the puerperium — Grossesse, accouchement et puerpéralité								
Total	-	7	♦ ●6.9	6	♦ ●5.2	-	-	4
Pregnancy with abortive outcome — Grossesse se terminant par un avortement	-	-	-	-	-	-	-	-
Other direct obstetric causes — Autres décès maternels directs	-	6	♦ ●5.9	5	♦ ●4.3	-	-	3
Indirect obstetric causes — Décès maternels indirects	-	1	♦ ●1.0	1	♦ ●0.9	-	-	-
Certain conditions originating in the perinatal period — Certaines affections dont l'origine se situe dans la période périnatale	●320.5	307	●304.3	305	●262.8	293	●250.1	237
Congenital malformations, deformations and chromosomal abnormalities — Malformations congénitales et anomalies chromosomiques	●316.5	355	●351.9	299	●257.7	267	●227.9	265
Symptoms, signs and abnormal clinical and laboratory findings, not elsewhere classified — Symptômes, signes et résultats anormaux d'examens cliniques et de laboratoire, non classés ailleurs	76.5	8 785	83.5	8 570	81.4	8 434	84.3	7 261
All other diseases — Toutes autres maladies	0.6	29	♦0.3	39	0.4	35	0.3	32
External causes — Causes externes								
Total	42.1	4 576	43.5	4 471	42.4	4 497	44.9	4 400
Accidents — Accidents								
Total	37.0	4 029	38.3	3 959	37.6	3 989	39.9	3 951
Transport accidents — Accidents de transport	22.9	2 351	22.4	2 256	21.4	2 288	22.9	2 035
Falls — Chutes	3.6	420	4.0	469	4.5	492	4.9	577
Accidental drowning and submersion — Noyade et submersion accidentelles	3.0	360	3.4	368	3.5	341	3.4	318
Exposure to smoke, fire and flames — Exposition à la fumée, au feu et aux flammes ..	1.2	115	1.1	95	0.9	118	1.2	135
Accidental poisoning by and exposure to noxious substances — Intoxication accidentelle par des substances nocives et exposition à ces substances	2.8	280	2.7	268	2.5	365	3.6	457
Intentional self-harm — Lésions auto-infligées	3.6	403	3.8	381	3.6	382	3.8	334
Assault — Agresssions	1.6	144	1.4	130	1.2	125	1.2	115
All other external causes — Toutes autres causes externes	-	-	-	1	0.0	1	0.0	

(See notes at end of table. — Voir notes à la fin du tableau.)

Cause of death — Cause de décès	Greece — Grèce 2001	Hungary — Hongrie 1995		1996		1997		1998
	Rate Taux	Number Nombre	Rate Taux	Number Nombre	Rate Taux	Number Nombre	Rate Taux	Number Nombre
Diseases of the digestive system — Maladies de l'appareil digestif								
Diseases of the liver — Maladies du foie	6.9	8 496	83.1	6 834	67.0	6 810	67.1	7 333
Diseases of the musculoskeletal system and connective tissue — Maladies du système ostéo-articularie, des muscles et du tissu conjonctif	3.6	332	3.2	297	2.9	337	3.3	311
Diseases of the genitourinary system — Maladies de l'appareil génito-urinaire								
Total	15.3	1 081	10.6	˙1 152	11.3	1 000	9.8	973
Disorders of kidney and ureter — Affections du rein et de l'uretère	14.5	765	7.5	996	9.8	844	8.3	830
Hyperplasia of prostate — Hyperplasie de la prostate	...	100	▼7.5	94	▼7.1	73	▼5.5	72
Pregnancy, childbirth and the puerperium — Grossesse, accouchement et puerpéralité								
Total	◆ *3.9	17	◆ *15.2	12	◆ *11.4	21	◆ *20.9	6
Pregnancy with abortive outcome — Grossesse se terminant par un avortement	-	3	◆ *2.7	2	◆ *1.9	4	◆ *4.0	2
Other direct obstetric causes — Autres décès maternels directs	◆ *2.9	14	◆ *12.5	9	◆ *8.5	16	◆ *15.9	4
Indirect obstetric causes — Décès maternels indirects	-	-	-	1	◆ *0.9	1	◆ *1.0	-
Certain conditions originating in the perinatal period — Certaines affections dont l'origine se situe dans la période périnatale	*231.7	690	*615.8	674	*640.2	608	*605.9	554
Congenital malformations, deformations and chromosomal abnormalities — Malformations congénitales et anomalies chromosomiques	*259.1	498	*444.4	482	*457.9	430	*428.5	446
Symptoms, signs and abnormal clinical and laboratory findings, not elsewhere classified — Symptômes, signes et résultats anormaux d'examens cliniques et de laboratoire, non classés ailleurs	72.5	193	1.9	129	1.3	129	1.3	158
All other diseases — Toutes autres maladies	0.3	50	0.5	27	◆0.3	33	0.3	32
External causes — Causes externes								
Total	43.9	11 407	111.5	10 799	105.9	10 309	101.5	10 314
Accidents — Accidents								
Total	39.4	7 596	74.3	6 879	67.5	6 554	64.5	6 550
Transport accidents — Accidents de transport	20.3	1 987	19.4	1 664	16.3	1 724	17.0	1 724
Falls — Chutes	5.8	3 800	37.1	3 536	34.7	3 405	33.5	3 326
Accidental drowning and submersion — Noyade et submersion accidentelles	3.2	259	2.5	249	2.4	216	2.1	301
Exposure to smoke, fire and flames — Exposition à la fumée, au feu et aux flammes	1.3	241	2.4	230	2.3	233	2.3	188
Accidental poisoning by and exposure to noxious substances — Intoxication accidentelle par des substances nocives et exposition à ces substances	4.6	238	2.3	209	2.1	163	1.6	167
Intentional self-harm — Lésions auto-infligées	3.3	3 369	32.9	3 438	33.7	3 214	31.6	3 247
Assault — Agresssions	1.1	360	3.5	325	3.2	344	3.4	326
All other external causes — Toutes autres causes externes	-	82	0.8	157	1.5	197	1.9	191

(See notes at end of table. — Voir notes à la fin du tableau.)

Hungary — Hongrie

Cause of death — Cause de décès	1998 Rate Taux	1999 Number Nombre	1999 Rate Taux	2000 Number Nombre	2000 Rate Taux	2001 Number Nombre	2001 Rate Taux	2002 Number Nombre
Diseases of the digestive system — Maladies de l'appareil digestif								
Diseases of the liver — Maladies du foie	72.5	7 279	72.3	6 883	68.7	6 457	63.4	6 137
Diseases of the musculoskeletal system and connective tissue — Maladies du système ostéo-articularie, des muscles et du tissu conjonctif	3.1	280	2.8	306	3.1	311	3.1	318
Diseases of the genitourinary system — Maladies de l'appareil génito-urinaire								
Total	9.6	1 075	10.7	970	9.7	1 023	10.0	988
Disorders of kidney and ureter — Affections du rein et de l'uretère	8.2	926	9.2	836	8.3	868	8.5	881
Hyperplasia of prostate — Hyperplasie de la prostate	▼5.4	71	▼5.3	71	▼5.2	82	▼5.8	56
Pregnancy, childbirth and the puerperium — Grossesse, accouchement et puerpéralité								
Total	♦ *6.2	4	♦ *4.2	10	♦ *10.2	5	♦ *5.2	8
Pregnancy with abortive outcome — Grossesse se terminant par un avortement	♦ *2.1	1	♦ *1.1	-		1	♦ *1.0	1
Other direct obstetric causes — Autres décès maternels directs	♦ *4.1	3	♦ *3.2	10	♦ *10.2	4	♦ *4.1	7
Indirect obstetric causes — Décès maternels indirects	-	-	-	-		-		-
Certain conditions originating in the perinatal period — Certaines affections dont l'origine se situe dans la période périnatale	*569.4	476	*502.9	534	*547.1	472	*486.4	428
Congenital malformations, deformations and chromosomal abnormalities — Malformations congénitales et anomalies chromosomiques	*458.4	377	*398.3	368	*377.1	361	*372.0	324
Symptoms, signs and abnormal clinical and laboratory findings, not elsewhere classified — Symptômes, signes et résultats anormaux d'examens cliniques et de laboratoire, non classés ailleurs	1.6	194	1.9	159	1.6	163	1.6	140
All other diseases — Toutes autres maladies	0.3	14	♦0.1	32	0.3	32	0.3	33
External causes — Causes externes								
Total	102.0	10 303	102.3	9 541	95.2	9 455	92.8	9 513
Accidents — Accidents								
Total	64.8	6 505	64.6	5 860	58.5	6 009	59.0	6 210
Transport accidents — Accidents de transport	17.0	1 618	16.1	1 519	15.2	1 555	15.3	1 748
Falls — Chutes	32.9	3 314	32.9	3 067	30.6	3 087	30.3	3 174
Accidental drowning and submersion — Noyade et submersion accidentelles	3.0	259	2.6	231	2.3	186	1.8	214
Exposure to smoke, fire and flames — Exposition à la fumée, au feu et aux flammes	1.9	172	1.7	180	1.8	213	2.1	179
Accidental poisoning by and exposure to noxious substances — Intoxication accidentelle par des substances nocives et exposition à ces substances	1.7	164	1.6	122	1.2	161	1.6	117
Intentional self-harm — Lésions auto-infligées	32.1	3 328	33.1	3 269	32.6	2 979	29.2	2 843
Assault — Agresssions	3.2	291	2.9	258	2.6	248	2.4	240
All other external causes — Toutes autres causes externes	1.9	179	1.8	154	1.5	219	2.1	220

(See notes at end of table. — Voir notes à la fin du tableau.)

	Hungary — Hongrie	Iceland — Islande						
Cause of death — Cause de décès	2002	1995		1996		1997		1998
	Rate Taux	Number Nombre	Rate Taux	Number Nombre	Rate Taux	Number Nombre	Rate Taux	Number Nombre
Diseases of the digestive system — Maladies de l'appareil digestif								
Diseases of the liver — Maladies du foie	60.4	4	♦1.5	5	♦1.9	4	♦1.5	5
Diseases of the musculoskeletal system and connective tissue — Maladies du système ostéo-articularie, des muscles et du tissu conjonctif	3.1	5	♦1.9	5	♦1.9	7	♦2.6	4
Diseases of the genitourinary system — Maladies de l'appareil génito-urinaire								
Total	9.7	27	♦10.1	26	♦9.7	24	♦8.9	22
Disorders of kidney and ureter — Affections du rein et de l'uretère	8.7	16	♦6.0	20	♦7.4	14	♦5.2	14
Hyperplasia of prostate — Hyperplasie de la prostate	▼3.9	2	♦ ▼6.7	-	-	-	-	1
Pregnancy, childbirth and the puerperium — Grossesse, accouchement et puerpéralité								
Total	♦ ●8.3	-	-	-	-	-	-	-
Pregnancy with abortive outcome — Grossesse se terminant par un avortement	♦ ●1.0	-	-	-	-	-	-	-
Other direct obstetric causes — Autres décès maternels directs	♦ ●7.2	-	-	-	-	-	-	-
Indirect obstetric causes — Décès maternels indirects		-	-	-	-	-	-	-
Certain conditions originating in the perinatal period — Certaines affections dont l'origine se situe dans la période périnatale	●442.1	14	♦ ●327.1	10	♦ ●231.0	13	♦ ●313.2	7
Congenital malformations, deformations and chromosomal abnormalities — Malformations congénitales et anomalies chromosomiques	●334.7	22	♦ ●514.0	11	♦ ●254.1	7	♦ ●168.6	11
Symptoms, signs and abnormal clinical and laboratory findings, not elsewhere classified — Symptômes, signes et résultats anormaux d'examens cliniques et de laboratoire, non classés ailleurs	1.4	11	♦4.1	12	♦4.5	23	♦8.5	17
All other diseases — Toutes autres maladies	0.3	1	♦0.4	-	-	-	-	1
External causes — Causes externes								
Total	93.6	151	56.5	92	34.2	104	38.4	116
Accidents — Accidents								
Total	61.1	116	43.4	54	20.1	55	20.3	79
Transport accidents — Accidents de transport	17.2	38	14.2	17	♦6.3	26	♦9.0	31
Falls — Chutes	31.2	15	♦5.6	17	♦6.3	7	♦2.6	21
Accidental drowning and submersion — Noyade et submersion accidentelles	2.1	7	♦2.6	6	♦2.2	4	♦1.5	2
Exposure to smoke, fire and flames — Exposition à la fumée, au feu et aux flammes	1.8	2	♦0.7	2	♦0.7	4	♦1.5	1
Accidental poisoning by and exposure to noxious substances — Intoxication accidentelle par des substances nocives et exposition à ces substances	1.2	7	♦2.6	5	♦1.9	5	♦1.8	18
Intentional self-harm — Lésions auto-infligées	28.0	27	♦10.1	33	12.3	33	12.2	30
Assault — Agresssions	2.4	-		1	♦0.4	3	♦1.1	-
All other external causes — Toutes autres causes externes	2.2	8	♦3.0	4	♦1.5	13	♦4.8	7

21. Death and death rates by cause: 1995 - 2002
Décès selon la cause, nombres et taux: 1995 - 2002 (continued — suite)

(See notes at end of table. — Voir notes à la fin du tableau.)

Cause of death — Cause de décès	Iceland — Islande							Ireland — Irlande[15]
	1998	1999		2000		2001		1995
	Rate Taux	Number Nombre	Rate Taux	Number Nombre	Rate Taux	Number Nombre	Rate Taux	Number Nombre
Diseases of the digestive system — Maladies de l'appareil digestif								
Diseases of the liver — Maladies du foie	♦1.8	8	♦2.9	5	♦1.8	4	♦1.4	101
Diseases of the musculoskeletal system and connective tissue — Maladies du système ostéo-articulaire, des muscles et du tissu conjonctif	♦1.5	6	♦2.2	5	♦1.8	7	♦2.5	180
Diseases of the genitourinary system — Maladies de l'appareil génito-urinaire								
Total	♦8.0	27	♦9.7	24	♦8.5	16	♦5.6	613
Disorders of kidney and ureter — Affections du rein et de l'uretère	♦5.1	18	♦6.5	14	♦5.0	9	♦3.2	434
Hyperplasia of prostate — Hyperplasie de la prostate	♦ ▼3.1	-	-	1	♦ ▼2.9	-	-	20
Pregnancy, childbirth and the puerperium — Grossesse, accouchement et puerpéralité								
Total	-	-	-	-	-	1	♦ ●24.4	-
Pregnancy with abortive outcome — Grossesse se terminant par un avortement	-	-	-	-	-	1	♦ ●24.4	-
Other direct obstetric causes — Autres décès maternels directs	-	-	-	-	-			-
Indirect obstetric causes — Décès maternels indirects	-	-	-	-	-			
Certain conditions originating in the perinatal period — Certaines affections dont l'origine se situe dans la période périnatale	♦ ●167.5	5	♦ ●122.0	10	♦ ●231.7	8	♦ ●195.6	132
Congenital malformations, deformations and chromosomal abnormalities — Malformations congénitales et anomalies chromosomiques	♦ ●263.3	6	♦ ●146.3	5	♦ ●115.9	4	♦ ●97.8	181
Symptoms, signs and abnormal clinical and laboratory findings, not elsewhere classified — Symptômes, signes et résultats anormaux d'examens cliniques et de laboratoire, non classés ailleurs	♦6.2	14	♦5.1	16	♦5.7	10	♦3.5	217
All other diseases — Toutes autres maladies	♦0.4	1	♦0.4	-	-	-	-	89
External causes — Causes externes								
Total	42.4	85	30.7	133	47.3	131	46.0	1 418
Accidents — Accidents								
Total	28.9	43	15.5	71	25.3	87	30.5	978
Transport accidents — Accidents de transport	11.3	24	♦8.7	38	13.5	38	13.3	442
Falls — Chutes	♦7.7	12	♦4.3	18	♦6.4	24	♦8.4	247
Accidental drowning and submersion — Noyade et submersion accidentelles	♦0.7	1	♦0.4	4	♦1.4	1	♦0.4	79
Exposure to smoke, fire and flames — Exposition à la fumée, au feu et aux flammes	♦0.4	-	-	1	♦0.4	1	♦0.4	54
Accidental poisoning by and exposure to noxious substances — Intoxication accidentelle par des substances nocives et exposition à ces substances	♦6.6	2	♦0.7	4	♦1.4	14	♦4.9	60
Intentional self-harm — Lésions auto-infligées	♦11.0	31	11.2	50	17.8	36	12.6	403
Assault — Agresssions	-	2	♦0.7	6	♦2.1	2	♦0.7	27
All other external causes — Toutes autres causes externes	♦2.6	9	♦3.2	6	♦2.1	6	♦2.1	10

21. Death and death rates by cause: 1995 - 2002
Décès selon la cause, nombres et taux: 1995 - 2002 (continued — suite)

(See notes at end of table. — Voir notes à la fin du tableau.)

Ireland — Irlande[15]

Cause of death — Cause de décès	1995 Rate Taux	1996 Number Nombre	1996 Rate Taux	1997 Number Nombre	1997 Rate Taux	1998 Number Nombre	1998 Rate Taux	1999 Number Nombre
Diseases of the digestive system — Maladies de l'appareil digestif								
Diseases of the liver — Maladies du foie	2.8	109	3.0	148	4.0	161	4.3	164
Diseases of the musculoskeletal system and connective tissue — Maladies du système ostéo-articularie, des muscles et du tissu conjonctif	5.0	175	4.8	181	4.9	185	5.0	177
Diseases of the genitourinary system — Maladies de l'appareil génito-urinaire								
Total	17.0	638	17.6	562	15.4	584	15.8	572
Disorders of kidney and ureter — Affections du rein et de l'uretère	12.1	459	12.7	387	10.6	402	10.9	404
Hyperplasia of prostate — Hyperplasie de la prostate	♦▼4.9	13	...	14	...	11	♦▼2.5	12
Pregnancy, childbirth and the puerperium — Grossesse, accouchement et puerpéralité								
Total	-	3	♦*6.0	3	♦*5.7	2	♦*3.7	1
Pregnancy with abortive outcome — Grossesse se terminant par un avortement	-			1	♦*1.9	-		-
Other direct obstetric causes — Autres décès maternels directs	-	3	♦*6.0	2	♦*3.8	2	♦*3.7	1
Indirect obstetric causes — Décès maternels indirects	-	-		-		-		-
Certain conditions originating in the perinatal period — Certaines affections dont l'origine se situe dans la période périnatale	*270.6	125	*248.1	123	*233.1	122	*227.8	129
Congenital malformations, deformations and chromosomal abnormalities — Malformations congénitales et anomalies chromosomiques	*371.0	157	*311.6	177	*335.4	202	*377.2	199
Symptoms, signs and abnormal clinical and laboratory findings, not elsewhere classified — Symptômes, signes et résultats anormaux d'examens cliniques et de laboratoire, non classés ailleurs	6.0	230	6.3	230	6.3	194	5.2	207
All other diseases — Toutes autres maladies	2.5	79	2.2	66	1.8	83	2.2	99
External causes — Causes externes								
Total	39.4	1 444	39.8	1 485	40.6	1 614	43.6	1 603
Accidents — Accidents								
Total	27.2	991	27.3	965	26.4	1 042	28.1	1 087
Transport accidents — Accidents de transport	12.3	451	12.4	450	12.3	463	12.5	434
Falls — Chutes	6.9	234	6.5	292	8.0	335	9.0	374
Accidental drowning and submersion — Noyade et submersion accidentelles	2.2	66	1.8	42	1.1	61	1.6	56
Exposure to smoke, fire and flames — Exposition à la fumée, au feu et aux flammes	1.5	72	2.0	58	1.6	49	1.3	68
Accidental poisoning by and exposure to noxious substances — Intoxication accidentelle par des substances nocives et exposition à ces substances	1.7	76	2.1	55	1.5	26	♦0.7	41
Intentional self-harm — Lésions auto-infligées	11.2	408	11.3	466	12.7	498	13.4	424
Assault — Agressions	♦0.7	33	0.9	30	♦0.8	41	1.1	37
All other external causes — Toutes autres causes externes	♦0.3	12	♦0.3	24	♦0.7	33	0.9	55

21. Death and death rates by cause: 1995 - 2002
Décès selon la cause, nombres et taux: 1995 - 2002 (continued — suite)

(See notes at end of table. — Voir notes à la fin du tableau.)

Cause of death — Cause de décès	Ireland — Irlande[15]					Italy — Italie		
	1999	2000		2001		1995		1996
	Rate Taux	Number Nombre	Rate Taux	Number Nombre	Rate Taux	Number Nombre	Rate Taux	Number Nombre
Diseases of the digestive system — Maladies de l'appareil digestif								
Diseases of the liver — Maladies du foie	4.4	150	4.0	204	5.3	13 350	23.3	12 743
Diseases of the musculoskeletal system and connective tissue — Maladies du système ostéo-articularie, des muscles et du tissu conjonctif	4.7	159	4.2	159	4.1	2 005	3.5	2 106
Diseases of the genitourinary system — Maladies de l'appareil génito-urinaire								
Total	15.3	605	16.0	588	15.3	7 121	12.4	7 311
Disorders of kidney and ureter — Affections du rein et de l'uretère	10.8	397	10.5	382	10.0	4 745	8.3	4 901
Hyperplasia of prostate — Hyperplasie de la prostate	♦ ▼2.7	5	♦ ▼1.1	13	♦ ▼2.8	334	▼3.8	271
Pregnancy, childbirth and the puerperium — Grossesse, accouchement et puerpéralité								
Total	♦ •1.9	1	♦ •1.8	3	♦ •5.2	17	♦ •3.2	20
Pregnancy with abortive outcome — Grossesse se terminant par un avortement	-	-	-	1	♦ •1.7	-	-	1
Other direct obstetric causes — Autres décès maternels directs	♦ •1.9	1	♦ •1.8	2	♦ •3.5	17	♦ •3.2	18
Indirect obstetric causes — Décès maternels indirects	-		-	-	-	-		1
Certain conditions originating in the perinatal period — Certaines affections dont l'origine se situe dans la période périnatale	•241.8	125	•230.5	124	•214.2	1 858	•353.5	1 811
Congenital malformations, deformations and chromosomal abnormalities — Malformations congénitales et anomalies chromosomiques	•373.0	200	•368.7	192	•331.7	1 673	•318.3	1 626
Symptoms, signs and abnormal clinical and laboratory findings, not elsewhere classified — Symptômes, signes et résultats anormaux d'examens cliniques et de laboratoire, non classés ailleurs	5.5	219	5.8	250	6.5	8 438	14.7	7 986
All other diseases — Toutes autres maladies	2.6	90	2.4	95	2.5	750	1.3	759
External causes — Causes externes								
Total	42.8	1 578	41.7	1 648	42.9	28 054	49.0	28 036
Accidents — Accidents								
Total	29.0	1 022	27.0	1 058	27.6	22 251	38.8	21 911
Transport accidents — Accidents de transport	11.6	427	11.3	407	10.6	8 312	14.5	7 761
Falls — Chutes	10.0	347	9.2	376	9.8	10 122	17.7	10 746
Accidental drowning and submersion — Noyade et submersion accidentelles	1.5	58	1.5	63	1.6	457	0.8	422
Exposure to smoke, fire and flames — Exposition à la fumée, au feu et aux flammes	1.8	47	1.2	54	1.4	364	0.6	340
Accidental poisoning by and exposure to noxious substances — Intoxication accidentelle par des substances nocives et exposition à ces substances	1.1	34	0.9	50	1.3	432	0.8	398
Intentional self-harm — Lésions auto-infligées	11.3	463	12.2	488	12.7	4 569	8.0	4 689
Assault — Agresssions	1.0	38	1.0	40	1.0	861	1.5	834
All other external causes — Toutes autres causes externes	1.5	55	1.5	62	1.6	373	0.7	602

(See notes at end of table. — Voir notes à la fin du tableau.)

Italy — Italie

Cause of death — Cause de décès	1996	1997		1998		1999		2000
	Rate Taux	Number Nombre	Rate Taux	Number Nombre	Rate Taux	Number Nombre	Rate Taux	Number Nombre
Diseases of the digestive system — Maladies de l'appareil digestif								
Diseases of the liver — Maladies du foie	22.2	12 441	21.6	11 980	20.8	11 499	19.9	11 297
Diseases of the musculoskeletal system and connective tissue — Maladies du système ostéo-articularie, des muscles et du tissu conjonctif	3.7	2 113	3.7	2 008	3.5	2 009	3.5	2 032
Diseases of the genitourinary system — Maladies de l'appareil génito-urinaire								
Total	12.7	7 567	13.2	8 216	14.3	7 727	13.4	7 672
Disorders of kidney and ureter — Affections du rein et de l'uretère	8.5	5 136	8.9	5 652	9.8	5 221	9.1	5 216
Hyperplasia of prostate — Hyperplasie de la prostate	...	256	...	288	▼3.1	249	▼2.7	203
Pregnancy, childbirth and the puerperium — Grossesse, accouchement et puerpéralité								
Total	♦ *3.8	23	♦ *4.3	18	♦ *3.5	14	♦ *2.7	16
Pregnancy with abortive outcome — Grossesse se terminant par un avortement	♦ *0.2	2	♦ *0.4	4	♦ *0.8	-		2
Other direct obstetric causes — Autres décès maternels directs	♦ *3.4	20	♦ *3.7	13	♦ *2.5	14	♦ *2.7	14
Indirect obstetric causes — Décès maternels indirects	♦ *0.2	1	♦ *0.2	1	♦ *0.2	-		-
Certain conditions originating in the perinatal period — Certaines affections dont l'origine se situe dans la période périnatale	*344.5	1 693	*316.8	1 545	*299.7	1 558	*297.6	1 328
Congenital malformations, deformations and chromosomal abnormalities — Malformations congénitales et anomalies chromosomiques	*309.3	1 506	*281.8	1 581	*306.7	1 489	*284.5	1 410
Symptoms, signs and abnormal clinical and laboratory findings, not elsewhere classified — Symptômes, signes et résultats anormaux d'examens cliniques et de laboratoire, non classés ailleurs	13.9	8 004	13.9	6 964	12.1	7 502	13.0	7 219
All other diseases — Toutes autres maladies	1.3	772	1.3	827	1.4	736	1.3	801
External causes — Causes externes								
Total	48.9	28 412	49.4	27 800	48.3	27 062	46.9	26 100
Accidents — Accidents								
Total	38.2	21 889	38.1	21 525	37.4	21 350	37.0	20 541
Transport accidents — Accidents de transport	13.5	8 059	14.0	8 286	14.4	7 948	13.8	7 530
Falls — Chutes	18.7	10 529	18.3	9 786	17.0	9 998	17.3	9 756
Accidental drowning and submersion — Noyade et submersion accidentelles	0.7	435	0.8	362	0.6	361	0.6	443
Exposure to smoke, fire and flames — Exposition à la fumée, au feu et aux flammes ..	0.6	379	0.7	347	0.6	334	0.6	329
Accidental poisoning by and exposure to noxious substances — Intoxication accidentelle par des substances nocives et exposition à ces substances	0.7	315	0.5	305	0.5	322	0.6	277
Intentional self-harm — Lésions auto-infligées	8.2	4 694	8.2	4 504	7.8	4 115	7.1	4 108
Assault — Agresssions	1.5	720	1.3	732	1.3	705	1.2	599
All other external causes — Toutes autres causes externes	1.0	1 109	1.9	1 039	1.8	892	1.5	852

(See notes at end of table. — Voir notes à la fin du tableau.)

Cause of death — Cause de décès	Italy — Italie			Latvia — Lettonie[6]				
	2000	2001		1995		1996		1997
	Rate Taux	Number Nombre	Rate Taux	Number Nombre	Rate Taux	Number Nombre	Rate Taux	Number Nombre
Diseases of the digestive system — Maladies de l'appareil digestif								
Diseases of the liver — Maladies du foie	19.6	11 268	19.4	...	...	362	14.7	329
Diseases of the musculoskeletal system and connective tissue — Maladies du système ostéo-articulaire, des muscles et du tissu conjonctif	3.5	1 996	3.4	68	2.7	84	3.4	83
Diseases of the genitourinary system — Maladies de l'appareil génito-urinaire								
Total	13.3	7 926	13.7	462	18.6	470	19.1	463
Disorders of kidney and ureter — Affections du rein et de l'uretère	9.0	5 421	9.4	314	12.6	393	16.0	362
Hyperplasia of prostate — Hyperplasie de la prostate	▼2.2	201	▼2.1	82	▼27.1	67	▼22.4	91
Pregnancy, childbirth and the puerperium — Grossesse, accouchement et puerpéralité								
Total	◆ ●2.9	11	◆ ●2.1	5	◆ ●23.2	4	◆ ●20.2	8
Pregnancy with abortive outcome — Grossesse se terminant par un avortement	◆ ●0.4	1	◆ ●0.2	1	◆ ●4.6	1	◆ ●5.1	2
Other direct obstetric causes — Autres décès maternels directs	◆ ●2.6	10	◆ ●1.9	...	...	3	◆ ●15.2	5
Indirect obstetric causes — Décès maternels indirects	-	-	-	...	...	-	-	1
Certain conditions originating in the perinatal period — Certaines affections dont l'origine se situe dans la période périnatale	●244.5	1 369	●255.8	208	●963.2	170	●859.4	141
Congenital malformations, deformations and chromosomal abnormalities — Malformations congénitales et anomalies chromosomiques	●259.6	1 466	●273.9	172	●796.5	146	●738.0	161
Symptoms, signs and abnormal clinical and laboratory findings, not elsewhere classified — Symptômes, signes et résultats anormaux d'examens cliniques et de laboratoire, non classés ailleurs	12.5	6 671	11.5	1 640	66.0	1 773	72.2	1 505
All other diseases — Toutes autres maladies	1.4	769	1.3	32	1.3	32	1.3	15
External causes — Causes externes								
Total	45.2	26 727	46.1	5 194	209.0	3 887	158.2	3 884
Accidents — Accidents								
Total	35.6	21 289	36.7	3 170	127.6	2 346	95.5	2 301
Transport accidents — Accidents de transport	13.0	7 665	13.2	852	34.3	691	28.1	645
Falls — Chutes	16.9	10 427	18.0	476	19.2	360	14.7	334
Accidental drowning and submersion — Noyade et submersion accidentelles	0.8	385	0.7	454	18.3	245	10.0	320
Exposure to smoke, fire and flames — Exposition à la fumée, au feu et aux flammes	0.6	285	0.5	343	13.8	271	11.0	154
Accidental poisoning by and exposure to noxious substances — Intoxication accidentelle par des substances nocives et exposition à ces substances	0.5	311	0.5	370	14.9	238	9.7	267
Intentional self-harm — Lésions auto-infligées	7.1	4 030	7.0	1 024	41.2	922	37.5	886
Assault — Agresssions	1.0	551	1.0	457	18.4	382	15.5	394
All other external causes — Toutes autres causes externes	1.5	857	1.5	543	21.9	237	9.6	303

(See notes at end of table. — Voir notes à la fin du tableau.)

Latvia — Lettonie[6]

Cause of death — Cause de décès	1997	1998		1999		2000		2001
	Rate Taux	Number Nombre	Rate Taux	Number Nombre	Rate Taux	Number Nombre	Rate Taux	Number Nombre
Diseases of the digestive system — Maladies de l'appareil digestif								
Diseases of the liver — Maladies du foie	13.5	389	16.1	347	14.5	361	15.2	427
Diseases of the musculoskeletal system and connective tissue — Maladies du système ostéo-articularie, des muscles et du tissu conjonctif	3.4	79	3.3	61	2.6	83	3.5	67
Diseases of the genitourinary system — Maladies de l'appareil génito-urinaire								
Total	19.0	435	18.0	397	16.6	362	15.3	336
Disorders of kidney and ureter — Affections du rein et de l'uretère	14.9	373	15.5	340	14.2	321	13.5	294
Hyperplasia of prostate — Hyperplasie de la prostate	▼30.6	53	▼17.8	50	▼16.7	32	▼10.6	33
Pregnancy, childbirth and the puerperium — Grossesse, accouchement et puerpéralité								
Total	♦ *42.5	9	♦ *48.9	8	♦ *41.2	5	♦ *24.7	5
Pregnancy with abortive outcome — Grossesse se terminant par un avortement	♦ *10.6	1	♦ *5.4	2	♦ *10.3	1	♦ *4.9	2
Other direct obstetric causes — Autres décès maternels directs	♦ *26.6	3	♦ *16.3	6	♦ *30.9	3	♦ *14.8	3
Indirect obstetric causes — Décès maternels indirects	♦ *5.3	4	♦ *21.7	-	-	1	♦ *4.9	-
Certain conditions originating in the perinatal period — Certaines affections dont l'origine se situe dans la période périnatale	*748.8	127	*689.8	118	*608.4	98	*484.0	90
Congenital malformations, deformations and chromosomal abnormalities — Malformations congénitales et anomalies chromosomiques	*855.0	169	*918.0	115	*592.9	125	*617.3	121
Symptoms, signs and abnormal clinical and laboratory findings, not elsewhere classified — Symptômes, signes et résultats anormaux d'examens cliniques et de laboratoire, non classés ailleurs	61.9	1 501	62.3	1 276	53.4	1 233	52.0	1 223
All other diseases — Toutes autres maladies	♦0.6	27	♦1.1	38	1.6	46	1.9	27
External causes — Causes externes								
Total	159.6	3 962	164.4	3 929	164.4	3 773	159.0	3 703
Accidents — Accidents								
Total	94.6	2 549	105.8	2 613	109.3	2 461	103.7	2 504
Transport accidents — Accidents de transport	26.5	750	31.2	736	30.8	699	29.5	628
Falls — Chutes	13.7	325	13.5	337	14.1	365	15.4	425
Accidental drowning and submersion — Noyade et submersion accidentelles	13.2	288	12.0	345	14.4	235	9.9	315
Exposure to smoke, fire and flames — Exposition à la fumée, au feu et aux flammes	6.3	204	8.5	274	11.5	214	9.0	204
Accidental poisoning by and exposure to noxious substances — Intoxication accidentelle par des substances noolves et exposition à ces substances	11.0	386	16.0	342	14.3	419	17.7	362
Intentional self-harm — Lésions auto-infligées	36.4	839	34.8	764	32.0	770	32.4	708
Assault — Agresssions	16.2	316	13.1	308	12.9	297	12.5	290
All other external causes — Toutes autres causes externes	12.5	258	10.7	244	10.2	245	10.3	201

21. Death and death rates by cause: 1995 - 2002
Décès selon la cause, nombres et taux: 1995 - 2002 (continued — suite)

(See notes at end of table. — Voir notes à la fin du tableau.)

	Latvia — Lettonie[6]			Lithuania — Lituanie[6]				
	2001	2002		1995		1996		1997
Cause of death — Cause de décès	Rate Taux	Number Nombre	Rate Taux	Number Nombre	Rate Taux	Number Nombre	Rate Taux	Number Nombre
Diseases of the digestive system — Maladies de l'appareil digestif Diseases of the liver — Maladies du foie	18.1	403	17.2	488	13.4	449	12.5	471
Diseases of the musculoskeletal system and connective tissue — Maladies du système ostéo-articularie, des muscles et du tissu conjonctif	2.8	83	3.5	86	2.4	73	2.0	86
Diseases of the genitourinary system — Maladies de l'appareil génito-urinaire Total	14.3	347	14.8	477	13.1	407	11.3	379
Disorders of kidney and ureter — Affections du rein et de l'uretère	12.5	301	12.9	341	9.4	297	8.2	265
Hyperplasia of prostate — Hyperplasie de la prostate	▼10.9	41	▼13.6	72	▼17.1	44	▼10.4	59
Pregnancy, childbirth and the puerperium — Grossesse, accouchement et puerpéralité Total	♦ *25.4	1	♦ *5.0	7	♦ *17.0	5	♦ *12.8	6
Pregnancy with abortive outcome — Grossesse se terminant par un avortement	♦ *10.2	-	-	1	♦ *2.4	2	♦ *5.1	-
Other direct obstetric causes — Autres décès maternels directs	♦ *15.3	1	♦ *5.0	6	♦ *14.6	3	♦ *7.7	6
Indirect obstetric causes — Décès maternels indirects		-	-	-		-		-
Certain conditions originating in the perinatal period — Certaines affections dont l'origine se situe dans la période périnatale	*457.7	75	*374.2	218	*529.2	152	*389.1	145
Congenital malformations, deformations and chromosomal abnormalities — Malformations congénitales et anomalies chromosomiques	*615.3	116	*578.7	272	*660.3	206	*527.3	207
Symptoms, signs and abnormal clinical and laboratory findings, not elsewhere classified — Symptômes, signes et résultats anormaux d'examens cliniques et de laboratoire, non classés ailleurs	51.9	1 294	55.3	432	11.9	287	8.0	204
All other diseases — Toutes autres maladies	♦1.1	34	1.5	28	♦0.8	23	♦0.6	24
External causes — Causes externes Total	157.2	3 666	156.8	6 539	180.2	5 848	162.4	5 443
Accidents — Accidents Total	106.3	2 450	104.8	4 169	114.9	3 528	98.0	3 220
Transport accidents — Accidents de transport	26.7	601	25.7	891	24.6	858	23.8	903
Falls — Chutes	18.0	393	16.8	592	16.3	469	13.0	389
Accidental drowning and submersion — Noyade et submersion accidentelles	13.4	269	11.5	597	16.5	393	10.9	456
Exposure to smoke, fire and flames — Exposition à la fumée, au feu et aux flammes	8.7	241	10.3	261	7.2	238	6.6	130
Accidental poisoning by and exposure to noxious substances — Intoxication accidentelle par des substances nocives et exposition à ces substances	15.4	331	14.2	1 019	28.1	857	23.8	700
Intentional self-harm — Lésions auto-infligées	30.1	670	28.6	1 694	46.7	1 723	47.8	1 632
Assault — Agresssions	12.3	266	11.4	434	12.0	344	9.6	336
All other external causes — Toutes autres causes externes	8.5	280	12.0	242	6.7	253	7.0	255

21. Death and death rates by cause: 1995 - 2002
Décès selon la cause, nombres et taux: 1995 - 2002 (continued — suite)

(See notes at end of table. — Voir notes à la fin du tableau.)

Lithuania — Lituanie[6]

Cause of death — Cause de décès	1997	1998		1999		2000		2001
	Rate Taux	Number Nombre	Rate Taux	Number Nombre	Rate Taux	Number Nombre	Rate Taux	Number Nombre
Diseases of the digestive system — Maladies de l'appareil digestif								
Diseases of the liver — Maladies du foie	13.2	640	18.0	577	16.4	608	17.4	742
Diseases of the musculoskeletal system and connective tissue — Maladies du système ostéo-articulaire, des muscles et du tissu conjonctif	2.4	85	2.4	85	2.4	79	2.3	87
Diseases of the genitourinary system — Maladies de l'appareil génito-urinaire								
Total	10.6	340	9.6	332	9.4	337	9.6	290
Disorders of kidney and ureter — Affections du rein et de l'uretère	7.4	298	8.4	289	8.2	296	8.5	241
Hyperplasia of prostate — Hyperplasie de la prostate	▼13.9	39	▼9.2	37	▼8.7	29	◆ ▼6.7	38
Pregnancy, childbirth and the puerperium — Grossesse, accouchement et puerpéralité								
Total	◆ *15.9	5	◆ *13.5	5	◆ *13.7	3	◆ *8.8	4
Pregnancy with abortive outcome — Grossesse se terminant par un avortement	-	2	◆ *5.4	1	◆ *2.7	1	◆ *2.9	1
Other direct obstetric causes — Autres décès maternels directs	◆ *15.9	3	◆ *8.1	4	◆ *11.0	2	◆ *5.9	3
Indirect obstetric causes — Décès maternels indirects		-		-		-		-
Certain conditions originating in the perinatal period — Certaines affections dont l'origine se situe dans la période périnatale	*383.5	117	*316.1	102	*280.1	94	*275.3	72
Congenital malformations, deformations and chromosomal abnormalities — Malformations congénitales et anomalies chromosomiques	*547.4	195	*526.8	167	*458.6	183	*535.9	160
Symptoms, signs and abnormal clinical and laboratory findings, not elsewhere classified — Symptômes, signes et résultats anormaux d'examens cliniques et de laboratoire, non classés ailleurs	5.7	222	6.3	244	6.9	300	8.6	345
All other diseases — Toutes autres maladies	◆0.7	13	◆0.4	19	◆0.5	15	◆0.4	37
External causes — Causes externes								
Total	152.2	5 358	151.0	5 268	149.5	5 102	145.8	5 498
Accidents — Accidents								
Total	90.1	3 216	90.6	3 111	88.3	2 752	78.6	3 236
Transport accidents — Accidents de transport	25.3	1 002	28.2	903	25.6	769	22.0	847
Falls — Chutes	10.9	418	11.8	432	12.3	420	12.0	469
Accidental drowning and submersion — Noyade et submersion accidentelles	12.8	405	11.4	526	14.9	362	10.3	454
Exposure to smoke, fire and flames — Exposition à la fumée, au feu et aux flammes	3.6	169	4.8	120	3.4	151	4.3	164
Accidental poisoning by and exposure to noxious substances — Intoxication accidentelle par des substances nocives et exposition à ces substances	19.6	627	17.7	529	15.0	580	16.6	664
Intentional self-harm — Lésions auto-infligées	45.6	1 554	43.8	1 552	44.0	1 631	46.6	1 535
Assault — Agresssions	9.4	303	8.5	297	8.4	345	9.9	356
All other external causes — Toutes autres causes externes	7.1	285	8.0	308	8.7	374	10.7	371

(See notes at end of table. — Voir notes à la fin du tableau.)

	Lithuania — Lituanie[6]			Luxembourg				
	2001	2002		1995		1996		1997
Cause of death — Cause de décès	Rate Taux	Number Nombre	Rate Taux	Number Nombre	Rate Taux	Number Nombre	Rate Taux	Number Nombre
Diseases of the digestive system — Maladies de l'appareil digestif								
Diseases of the liver — Maladies du foie	21.3	761	21.9	63	15.4	82	19.8	67
Diseases of the musculoskeletal system and connective tissue — Maladies du système ostéo-articularie, des muscles et du tissu conjonctif	2.5	92	2.7	12	*2.9	5	*1.2	8
Diseases of the genitourinary system — Maladies de l'appareil génito-urinaire								
Total	8.3	307	8.8	43	10.5	40	9.7	41
Disorders of kidney and ureter — Affections du rein et de l'uretère	6.9	268	7.7	39	9.5	37	8.9	40
Hyperplasia of prostate — Hyperplasie de la prostate	▼9.1	31	▼7.4	-	-	-	-	-
Pregnancy, childbirth and the puerperium — Grossesse, accouchement et puerpéralité								
Total	♦ *12.7	6	♦ *20.0	1	♦ *18.4	-	-	-
Pregnancy with abortive outcome — Grossesse se terminant par un avortement	♦ *3.2	3	♦ *10.0	-	-	-	-	-
Other direct obstetric causes — Autres décès maternels directs	♦ *9.5	3	♦ *10.0	1	♦ *18.4	-	-	-
Indirect obstetric causes — Décès maternels indirects	-	-	-	-	-	-	-	-
Certain conditions originating in the perinatal period — Certaines affections dont l'origine se situe dans la période périnatale	*228.2	70	*233.2	5	♦ *92.2	11	♦ *193.4	11
Congenital malformations, deformations and chromosomal abnormalities — Malformations congénitales et anomalies chromosomiques	*507.2'	162	*539.7	14	♦ *258.3	11	♦ *193.4	5
Symptoms, signs and abnormal clinical and laboratory findings, not elsewhere classified — Symptômes, signes et résultats anormaux d'examens cliniques et de laboratoire, non classés ailleurs	9.9	397	11.4	132	32.3	161	38.9	146
All other diseases — Toutes autres maladies	1.1	50	1.4	1	*0.2	1	*0.2	3
External causes — Causes externes								
Total	157.9	5 280	152.2	242	59.2	243	58.7	225
Accidents — Accidents								
Total	93.0	3 148	90.7	172	42.1	165	39.8	135
Transport accidents — Accidents de transport	24.3	828	23.9	69	16.9	74	17.9	59
Falls — Chutes	13.5	484	14.0	48	11.7	45	10.9	37
Accidental drowning and submersion — Noyade et submersion accidentelles	13.0	410	11.8	3	*0.7	2	*0.5	3
Exposure to smoke, fire and flames — Exposition à la fumée, au feu et aux flammes	4.7	136	3.9	2	*0.5	3	*0.7	2
Accidental poisoning by and exposure to noxious substances — Intoxication accidentelle par des substances nocives et exposition à ces substances	19.1	622	17.9	26	*6.4	17	*4.1	13
Intentional self-harm — Lésions auto-infligées	44.1	1 551	44.7	63	15.4	72	17.4	81
Assault — Agresssions	10.2	248	7.1	3	*0.7	4	*1.0	3
All other external causes — Toutes autres causes externes	10.7	333	9.6	4	*1.0	2	*0.5	6

21. Death and death rates by cause: 1995 - 2002
Décès selon la cause, nombres et taux: 1995 - 2002 (continued — suite)

(See notes at end of table. — Voir notes à la fin du tableau.)

Luxembourg

Cause of death — Cause de décès	1997 Rate Taux	1998 Number Nombre	1998 Rate Taux	1999 Number Nombre	1999 Rate Taux	2000 Number Nombre	2000 Rate Taux	2001 Number Nombre
Diseases of the digestive system — Maladies de l'appareil digestif								
Diseases of the liver — Maladies du foie	16.0	80	18.8	89	20.7	88	20.2	82
Diseases of the musculoskeletal system and connective tissue — Maladies du système ostéo-articularie, des muscles et du tissu conjonctif	◆1.9	14	◆3.3	19	◆4.4	9	◆2.1	10
Diseases of the genitourinary system — Maladies de l'appareil génito-urinaire								
Total	9.8	47	11.1	41	9.5	36	8.3	26
Disorders of kidney and ureter — Affections du rein et de l'uretère	9.5	43	10.1	38	8.8	31	7.1	21
Hyperplasia of prostate — Hyperplasie de la prostate	-	-	-	-	-	1	...	-
Pregnancy, childbirth and the puerperium — Grossesse, accouchement et puerpéralité								
Total	-	1	◆ *18.6	-	-	1	◆ *17.5	-
Pregnancy with abortive outcome — Grossesse se terminant par un avortement	-	-	-	-	-	-	-	-
Other direct obstetric causes — Autres décès maternels directs	-	1	◆ *18.6	-	-	1	◆ *17.5	-
Indirect obstetric causes — Décès maternels indirects	-	-	-	-	-	-	-	-
Certain conditions originating in the perinatal period — Certaines affections dont l'origine se situe dans la période périnatale	◆ *199.9	15	◆ *278.5	12	◆ *215.0	11	◆ *192.2	13
Congenital malformations, deformations and chromosomal abnormalities — Malformations congénitales et anomalies chromosomiques	◆ *90.9	4	◆ *74.3	7	◆ *125.4	2	◆ *34.9	8
Symptoms, signs and abnormal clinical and laboratory findings, not elsewhere classified — Symptômes, signes et résultats anormaux d'examens cliniques et de laboratoire, non classés ailleurs	34.8	114	26.8	104	24.2	111	25.4	124
All other diseases — Toutes autres maladies	◆0.7	7	◆1.6	9	◆2.1	14	◆3.2	7
External causes — Causes externes								
Total	53.6	255	60.0	247	57.4	293	67.2	288
Accidents — Accidents								
Total	32.2	172	40.5	156	36.2	208	47.7	201
Transport accidents — Accidents de transport	14.1	57	13.4	57	13.2	83	19.0	76
Falls — Chutes	8.8	38	8.9	36	8.4	42	9.6	36
Accidental drowning and submersion — Noyade et submersion accidentelles	◆0.7	3	◆0.7	1	◆0.2	-	-	5
Exposure to smoke, fire and flames — Exposition à la fumée, au feu et aux flammes	◆0.5	-	-	3	◆0.7	6	◆1.4	5
Accidental poisoning by and exposure to noxious substances — Intoxication accidentelle par des substances nocives et exposition à ces substances	◆3.1	20	◆4.7	16	◆3.7	29	◆6.6	24
Intentional self-harm — Lésions auto-infligées	19.3	65	15.3	76	17.7	63	14.4	76
Assault — Agresssions	◆0.7	4	◆0.9	4	◆0.9	7	◆1.6	9
All other external causes — Toutes autres causes externes	◆1.4	14	◆3.3	11	◆2.6	15	◆3.4	2

21. Death and death rates by cause: 1995 - 2002
Décès selon la cause, nombres et taux: 1995 - 2002 (continued — suite)

(See notes at end of table. — Voir notes à la fin du tableau.)

Cause of death — Cause de décès	Luxembourg			Malta — Malte[16]				
	2001	2002		1995		1996		1997
	Rate Taux	Number Nombre	Rate Taux	Number Nombre	Rate Taux	Number Nombre	Rate Taux	Number Nombre
Diseases of the digestive system — Maladies de l'appareil digestif								
Diseases of the liver — Maladies du foie	18.6	82	18.4	21	♦5.5	34	8.9	24
Diseases of the musculoskeletal system and connective tissue — Maladies du système ostéo-articularie, des muscles et du tissu conjonctif	♦2.3	20	♦4.5	7	♦1.8	7	♦1.8	8
Diseases of the genitourinary system — Maladies de l'appareil génito-urinaire								
Total	♦5.9	23	♦5.2	85	22.5	77	20.2	75
Disorders of kidney and ureter — Affections du rein et de l'uretère	♦4.8	17	♦3.8	74	19.6	63	16.5	57
Hyperplasia of prostate — Hyperplasie de la prostate	-	-	-	5	♦ ▼11.3	2	♦ ▼4.3	2
Pregnancy, childbirth and the puerperium — Grossesse, accouchement et puerpéralité								
Total	-	-	-	1	♦ *21.7	1	♦ *20.2	-
Pregnancy with abortive outcome — Grossesse se terminant par un avortement	-	-	-	-	-	-	-	-
Other direct obstetric causes — Autres décès maternels directs	-	-	-	1	♦ *21.7	1	♦ *20.2	-
Indirect obstetric causes — Décès maternels indirects	-	-	-	-	-	-	-	-
Certain conditions originating in the perinatal period — Certaines affections dont l'origine se situe dans la période périnatale	♦ *238.1	13	♦ *243.2	24	♦ *520.3	38	*768.6	15
Congenital malformations, deformations and chromosomal abnormalities — Malformations congénitales et anomalies chromosomiques	♦ *146.5	7	♦ *131.0	18	♦ *390.2	13	♦ *262.9	22
Symptoms, signs and abnormal clinical and laboratory findings, not elsewhere classified — Symptômes, signes et résultats anormaux d'examens cliniques et de laboratoire, non classés ailleurs	28.1	139	31.2	28	♦7.4	23	♦6.0	26
All other diseases — Toutes autres maladies	♦1.6	6	♦1.3	46	12.2	49	12.8	62
External causes — Causes externes								
Total	65.2	301	67.5	95	25.1	83	21.8	107
Accidents — Accidents								
Total	45.5	199	44.6	69	18.2	60	15.7	90
Transport accidents — Accidents de transport	17.2	87	19.5	24	♦6.3	16	♦4.2	23
Falls — Chutes	8.1	45	10.1	25	♦6.6	28	♦7.3	40
Accidental drowning and submersion — Noyade et submersion accidentelles	♦1.1	3	♦0.7	2	♦0.5	4	♦1.0	7
Exposure to smoke, fire and flames — Exposition à la fumée, au feu et aux flammes ..	♦1.1	2	♦0.4	-	-	2	♦0.5	1
Accidental poisoning by and exposure to noxious substances — Intoxication accidentelle par des substances nocives et exposition à ces substances	♦5.4	14	♦3.1	1	♦0.3	2	♦0.5	8
Intentional self-harm — Lésions auto-infligées	17.2	86	19.3	17	♦4.5	10	♦2.6	15
Assault — Agresssions	♦2.0	8	♦1.8	3	♦0.8	5	♦1.3	2
All other external causes — Toutes autres causes externes	♦0.5	8	♦1.8	6	♦1.6	8	♦2.1	-

(See notes at end of table. — Voir notes à la fin du tableau.)

Malta — Malte[16]

Cause of death — Cause de décès	1997 Rate Taux	1998 Number Nombre	1998 Rate Taux	1999 Number Nombre	1999 Rate Taux	2000 Number Nombre	2000 Rate Taux	2001 Number Nombre
Diseases of the digestive system — Maladies de l'appareil digestif								
Diseases of the liver — Maladies du foie	♦6.2	30	♦7.8	38	9.8	22	♦5.6	25
Diseases of the musculoskeletal system and connective tissue — Maladies du système ostéo-articularie, des muscles et du tissu conjonctif	♦2.1	9	♦2.3	13	♦3.3	13	♦3.3	4
Diseases of the genitourinary system — Maladies de l'appareil génito-urinaire								
Total	19.5	82	21.2	52	13.4	58	14.8	68
Disorders of kidney and ureter — Affections du rein et de l'uretère	14.8	72	18.6	46	11.8	54	13.8	59
Hyperplasia of prostate — Hyperplasie de la prostate	♦▼4.2	1	♦▼2.0	2	♦▼3.9	-	-	1
Pregnancy, childbirth and the puerperium — Grossesse, accouchement et puerpéralité								
Total	-	1	♦*22.3	1	♦*23.2	-	-	2
Pregnancy with abortive outcome — Grossesse se terminant par un avortement	-	-	-	-	-	-	-	-
Other direct obstetric causes — Autres décès maternels directs	-	1	♦*22.3	1	♦*23.2	-	-	2
Indirect obstetric causes — Décès maternels indirects	-	-	-	-	-	-	-	-
Certain conditions originating in the perinatal period — Certaines affections dont l'origine se situe dans la période périnatale	♦*310.2	13	♦*289.7	20	♦*464.3	18	♦*423.0	9
Congenital malformations, deformations and chromosomal abnormalities — Malformations congénitales et anomalies chromosomiques	♦*455.0	16	♦*356.5	10	♦*232.1	8	♦*188.0	12
Symptoms, signs and abnormal clinical and laboratory findings, not elsewhere classified — Symptômes, signes et résultats anormaux d'examens cliniques et de laboratoire, non classés ailleurs	♦6.8	30	♦7.8	30	♦7.7	23	♦5.9	18
All other diseases — Toutes autres maladies	16.1	89	23.0	54	13.9	59	15.1	52
External causes — Causes externes								
Total	27.9	102	26.4	111	28.6	105	26.8	132
Accidents — Accidents								
Total	23.4	83	21.5	74	19.0	76	19.4	91
Transport accidents — Accidents de transport	♦6.0	15	♦3.9	14	♦3.6	17	♦4.3	20
Falls — Chutes	10.4	44	11.4	31	8.0	27	♦6.9	49
Accidental drowning and submersion — Noyade et submersion accidentelles	♦1.8	3	♦0.8	4	♦1.0	12	♦3.1	7
Exposure to smoke, fire and flames — Exposition à la fumée, au feu et aux flammes	♦0.3	1	♦0.3	1	♦0.3	1	♦0.3	1
Accidental poisoning by and exposure to noxious substances — Intoxication accidentelle par des substances nocives et exposition à ces substances	♦2.1	6	♦1.6	7	♦1.8	5	♦1.3	5
Intentional self-harm — Lésions auto-infligées	♦3.9	12	♦3.1	27	♦6.9	23	♦5.9	30
Assault — Agressions	♦0.5	7	♦1.8	9	♦2.3	4	♦1.0	9
All other external causes — Toutes autres causes externes	-	-	-	1	♦0.3	2	♦0.5	2

(See notes at end of table. — Voir notes à la fin du tableau.)

Cause of death — Cause de décès	Malta — Malte[16]			Netherlands — Pays-Bas[17]				
	2001	2002		1995		1996		1997
	Rate Taux	Number Nombre	Rate Taux	Number Nombre	Rate Taux	Number Nombre	Rate Taux	Number Nombre
Diseases of the digestive system — Maladies de l'appareil digestif								
Diseases of the liver — Maladies du foie	♦6.3	23	♦5.8	782	5.1	879	5.7	923
Diseases of the musculoskeletal system and connective tissue — Maladies du système ostéo-articularie, des muscles et du tissu conjonctif	♦1.0	15	♦3.8	774	5.0	894	5.8	856
Diseases of the genitourinary system — Maladies de l'appareil génito-urinaire								
Total	17.2	55	13.8	2 649	17.1	2 657	17.1	2 580
Disorders of kidney and ureter — Affections du rein et de l'uretère	15.0	39	9.8	1 309	8.5	1 505	9.7	1 396
Hyperplasia of prostate — Hyperplasie de la prostate	♦ ▼1.8	-	-	92	▼4.6	81	▼4.0	65
Pregnancy, childbirth and the puerperium — Grossesse, accouchement et puerpéralité								
Total	♦ •51.8	-	-	14	♦ •7.3	23	♦ •12.1	15
Pregnancy with abortive outcome — Grossesse se terminant par un avortement		-	-	2	♦ •1.0	1	♦ •0.5	-
Other direct obstetric causes — Autres décès maternels directs	♦ •51.8	-	-	12	♦ •6.3	20	♦ •10.6	12
Indirect obstetric causes — Décès maternels indirects	-	-	-	-	-	2	♦ •1.1	3
Certain conditions originating in the perinatal period — Certaines affections dont l'origine se situe dans la période périnatale	♦ •233.2	9	♦ •236.5	503	•264.0	520	•274.4	417
Congenital malformations, deformations and chromosomal abnormalities — Malformations congénitales et anomalies chromosomiques	♦ •311.0	19	♦ •499.3	635	•333.3	629	•331.9	657
Symptoms, signs and abnormal clinical and laboratory findings, not elsewhere classified — Symptômes, signes et résultats anormaux d'examens cliniques et de laboratoire, non classés ailleurs	♦4.6	31	7.8	5 879	38.0	6 095	39.2	6 427
All other diseases — Toutes autres maladies	13.2	53	13.3	553	3.6	507	3.3	495
External causes — Causes externes								
Total	33.4	125	31.5	5 173	33.5	5 317	34.2	5 149
Accidents — Accidents								
Total	23.1	91	22.9	3 400	22.0	3 372	21.7	3 237
Transport accidents — Accidents de transport	♦5.1	17	♦4.3	1 292	8.4	1 314	8.5	1 196
Falls — Chutes	12.4	51	12.8	1 542	10.0	576	3.7	603
Accidental drowning and submersion — Noyade et submersion accidentelles	♦1.8	6	♦1.5	91	0.6	71	0.5	94
Exposure to smoke, fire and flames — Exposition à la fumée, au feu et aux flammes ..	♦0.3	2	♦0.5	59	0.4	80	0.5	62
Accidental poisoning by and exposure to noxious substances — Intoxication accidentelle par des substances nocives et exposition à ces substances	♦1.3	11	♦2.8	49	0.3	86	0.6	102
Intentional self-harm — Lésions auto-infligées	♦7.6	19	♦4.8	1 511	9.8	1 577	10.2	1 570
Assault — Agresssions	♦2.3	5	♦1.3	193	1.2	211	1.4	208
All other external causes — Toutes autres causes externes	♦0.5	10	♦2.5	69	0.4	157	1.0	134

(See notes at end of table. — Voir notes à la fin du tableau.)

Cause of death — Cause de décès	Netherlands — Pays-Bas[17]							Norway — Norvège[18]
	1997	1998	1998	1999	1999	2000	2000	1995
	Rate Taux	Number Nombre	Rate Taux	Number Nombre	Rate Taux	Number Nombre	Rate Taux	Number Nombre
Diseases of the digestive system — Maladies de l'appareil digestif								
Diseases of the liver — Maladies du foie	5.9	913	5.8	909	5.7	985	6.2	204
Diseases of the musculoskeletal system and connective tissue — Maladies du système ostéo-articularie, des muscles et du tissu conjonctif	6.5	821	5.2	913	5.8	812	5.1	254
Diseases of the genitourinary system — Maladies de l'appareil génito-urinaire								
Total	16.5	2 553	16.3	2 739	17.3	2 809	17.7	656
Disorders of kidney and ureter — Affections du rein et de l'uretère	8.9	1 385	8.8	1 420	9.0	1 469	9.2	358
Hyperplasia of prostate — Hyperplasie de la prostate	▼3.1	58	▼2.7	74	▼3.3	73	...	49
Pregnancy, childbirth and the puerperium — Grossesse, accouchement et puerpéralité								
Total	♦ *7.8	23	♦ *11.5	19	♦ *9.5	18	♦ *8.7	4
Pregnancy with abortive outcome — Grossesse se terminant par un avortement	-	2	♦ *1.0	2	♦ *1.0	-	-	1
Other direct obstetric causes — Autres décès maternels directs	♦ *6.2	14	♦ *7.0	15	♦ *7.5	12	♦ *5.8	3
Indirect obstetric causes — Décès maternels indirects	♦ *1.6	7	♦ *3.5	2	♦ *1.0	5	♦ *2.4	-
Certain conditions originating in the perinatal period — Certaines affections dont l'origine se situe dans la période périnatale	*216.7	502	*251.7	471	*235.0	531	*257.0	111
Congenital malformations, deformations and chromosomal abnormalities — Malformations congénitales et anomalies chromosomiques	*341.4	638	*319.9	609	*303.8	601	*290.9	142
Symptoms, signs and abnormal clinical and laboratory findings, not elsewhere classified — Symptômes, signes et résultats anormaux d'examens cliniques et de laboratoire, non classés ailleurs	41.2	6 933	44.1	7 226	45.7	7 744	48.7	1 877
All other diseases — Toutes autres maladies	3.2	498	3.2	566	3.6	512	3.2	38
External causes — Causes externes								
Total	33.0	4 914	31.3	5 189	32.8	5 169	32.5	2 274
Accidents — Accidents								
Total	20.7	3 059	19.5	3 336	21.1	3 345	21.0	1 663
Transport accidents — Accidents de transport	7.7	1 090	6.9	1 154	7.3	1 123	7.1	416
Falls — Chutes	3.9	599	3.8	681	4.3	735	4.6	896
Accidental drowning and submersion — Noyade et submersion accidentelles	0.6	83	0.5	91	0.6	107	0.7	72
Exposure to smoke, fire and flames — Exposition à la fumée, au feu et aux flammes ..	0.4	71	0.5	66	0.4	66	0.4	57
Accidental poisoning by and exposure to noxious substances — Intoxication accidentelle par des substances nocives et exposition à ces substances	0.7	72	0.5	95	0.6	123	0.8	80
Intentional self-harm — Lésions auto-infligées	10.1	1 519	9.7	1 517	9.6	1 500	9.4	548
Assault — Agresssions	1.3	176	1.1	203	1.3	180	1.1	45
All other external causes — Toutes autres causes externes	0.9	160	1.0	133	0.8	144	0.9	18

(See notes at end of table. — Voir notes à la fin du tableau.)

Norway — Norvège[18]

Cause of death — Cause de décès	1995 Rate Taux	1996 Number Nombre	1996 Rate Taux	1997 Number Nombre	1997 Rate Taux	1998 Number Nombre	1998 Rate Taux	1999 Number Nombre
Diseases of the digestive system — Maladies de l'appareil digestif								
Diseases of the liver — Maladies du foie	4.7	269	6.1	265	6.0	289	6.5	257
Diseases of the musculoskeletal system and connective tissue — Maladies du système ostéo-articulaire, des muscles et du tissu conjonctif	5.8	300	6.8	291	6.6	296	6.7	283
Diseases of the genitourinary system — Maladies de l'appareil génito-urinaire								
Total	15.0	571	13.0	549	12.5	620	14.0	654
Disorders of kidney and ureter — Affections du rein et de l'uretère	8.2	359	8.2	363	8.2	406	9.2	429
Hyperplasia of prostate — Hyperplasie de la prostate	▼8.2	44	▼7.3	43	▼6.9	29	◆ ▼4.6	32
Pregnancy, childbirth and the puerperium — Grossesse, accouchement et puerpéralité								
Total	◆ *6.6	1	◆ *1.6	1	◆ *1.7	4	◆ *6.9	5
Pregnancy with abortive outcome — Grossesse se terminant par un avortement	◆ *1.7	-	-	-	-	1	◆ *1.7	-
Other direct obstetric causes — Autres décès maternels directs	◆ *5.0	1	◆ *1.6	1	◆ *1.7	3	◆ *5.1	5
Indirect obstetric causes — Décès maternels indirects		-	-	-	-	-	-	-
Certain conditions originating in the perinatal period — Certaines affections dont l'origine se situe dans la période périnatale	*184.1	111	*182.2	117	*195.6	112	*191.9	95
Congenital malformations, deformations and chromosomal abnormalities — Malformations congénitales et anomalies chromosomiques	*235.5	163	*267.5	188	*314.4	166	*284.5	164
Symptoms, signs and abnormal clinical and laboratory findings, not elsewhere classified — Symptômes, signes et résultats anormaux d'examens cliniques et de laboratoire, non classés ailleurs	43.1	1 544	35.2	1 643	37.3	1 939	43.8	1 976
All other diseases — Toutes autres maladies	0.9	41	0.9	55	1.2	55	1.2	70
External causes — Causes externes								
Total	52.2	2 259	51.6	2 335	53.0	2 324	52.4	2 481
Accidents — Accidents								
Total	38.1	1 624	37.1	1 678	38.1	1 678	37.9	1 782
Transport accidents — Accidents de transport	9.5	362	8.3	395	9.0	452	10.2	401
Falls — Chutes	20.6	863	19.7	894	20.3	838	18.9	960
Accidental drowning and submersion — Noyade et submersion accidentelles	1.7	64	1.5	69	1.6	64	1.4	78
Exposure to smoke, fire and flames — Exposition à la fumée, au feu et aux flammes ..	1.3	67	1.5	63	1.4	52	1.2	54
Accidental poisoning by and exposure to noxious substances — Intoxication accidentelle par des substances nocives et exposition à ces substances	1.8	72	1.6	63	1.4	66	1.5	66
Intentional self-harm — Lésions auto-infligées	12.6	516	11.8	533	12.1	547	12.3	583
Assault — Agressions	1.0	47	1.1	41	0.9	43	1.0	38
All other external causes — Toutes autres causes externes	◆0.4	72	1.6	83	1.9	56	1.3	78

21. Death and death rates by cause: 1995 - 2002
Décès selon la cause, nombres et taux: 1995 - 2002 (continued — suite)

(See notes at end of table. — Voir notes à la fin du tableau.)

Cause of death — Cause de décès	Norway — Norvège[18] 1999 Rate Taux	Norway — Norvège[18] 2000 Number Nombre	Norway — Norvège[18] 2000 Rate Taux	Norway — Norvège[18] 2001 Number Nombre	Norway — Norvège[18] 2001 Rate Taux	Poland — Pologne 1995 Number Nombre	Poland — Pologne 1995 Rate Taux	Poland — Pologne 1996 Number Nombre
Diseases of the digestive system — Maladies de l'appareil digestif								
Diseases of the liver — Maladies du foie	5.8	262	5.8	231	5.1	4 895	12.7	4 720
Diseases of the musculoskeletal system and connective tissue — Maladies du système ostéo-articulaire, des muscles et du tissu conjonctif	6.3	258	5.7	254	5.6	934	2.4	894
Diseases of the genitourinary system — Maladies de l'appareil génito-urinaire								
Total	14.7	621	13.8	675	15.0	4 035	10.5	3 913
Disorders of kidney and ureter — Affections du rein et de l'uretère	9.6	406	9.0	463	10.3	3 642	9.4	3 548
Hyperplasia of prostate — Hyperplasie de la prostate	▼5.0	27	...	25	◆ ▼3.8	145	▼3.5	137
Pregnancy, childbirth and the puerperium — Grossesse, accouchement et puerpéralité								
Total	◆ *8.4	2	◆ *3.4	3	◆ *5.3	43	*9.9	21
Pregnancy with abortive outcome — Grossesse se terminant par un avortement	-	1	◆ *1.7	-	-	14	◆ *3.2	4
Other direct obstetric causes — Autres décès maternels directs	◆ *8.4	1	◆ *1.7	3	◆ *5.3	26	◆ *6.0	16
Indirect obstetric causes — Décès maternels indirects	-	-	-	-	-	3	◆ *0.7	1
Certain conditions originating in the perinatal period — Certaines affections dont l'origine se situe dans la période périnatale	*160.2	99	*167.1	108	*190.5	3 164	*730.5	2 724
Congenital malformations, deformations and chromosomal abnormalities — Malformations congénitales et anomalies chromosomiques	*276.6	142	*239.7	157	*276.9	2 161	*499.0	2 069
Symptoms, signs and abnormal clinical and laboratory findings, not elsewhere classified — Symptômes, signes et résultats anormaux d'examens cliniques et de laboratoire, non classés ailleurs	44.3	1 996	44.4	1 942	43.0	32 994	85.5	33 872
All other diseases — Toutes autres maladies	1.6	79	1.8	86	1.9	182	0.5	161
External causes — Causes externes								
Total	55.6	2 368	52.7	2 289	50.7	28 768	74.6	27 222
Accidents — Accidents								
Total	39.9	1 710	38.1	1 659	36.8	20 031	51.9	18 647
Transport accidents — Accidents de transport	9.0	428	9.5	330	7.3	8 025	20.8	7 424
Falls — Chutes	21.5	880	19.6	882	19.5	4 805	12.5	4 699
Accidental drowning and submersion — Noyade et submersion accidentelles	1.7	68	1.5	72	1.6	1 571	4.1	1 012
Exposure to smoke, fire and flames — Exposition à la fumée, au feu et aux flammes	1.2	56	1.2	55	1.2	561	1.5	592
Accidental poisoning by and exposure to noxious substances — Intoxication accidentelle par des substances nocives et exposition à ces substances	1.5	64	1.4	99	2.2	2 450	6.3	2 270
Intentional self-harm — Lésions auto-infligées	13.1	540	12.0	547	12.1	5 499	14.3	5 446
Assault — Agresssions	0.9	53	1.2	33	0.7	1 088	2.8	1 016
All other external causes — Toutes autres causes externes	1.7	65	1.4	50	1.1	2 150	5.6	2 113

21. Death and death rates by cause: 1995 - 2002
Décès selon la cause, nombres et taux: 1995 - 2002 (continued — suite)

(See notes at end of table. — Voir notes à la fin du tableau.)

Poland — Pologne

Cause of death — Cause de décès	1996 Rate Taux	1999 Number Nombre	1999 Rate Taux	2000 Number Nombre	2000 Rate Taux	2001 Number Nombre	2001 Rate Taux	2002 Number Nombre
Diseases of the digestive system — Maladies de l'appareil digestif								
Diseases of the liver — Maladies du foie	12.2	6 093	15.8	5 815	15.0	5 555	14.4	5 494
Diseases of the musculoskeletal system and connective tissue — Maladies du système ostéo-articularie, des muscles et du tissu conjonctif	2.3	600	1.6	593	1.5	565	1.5	516
Diseases of the genitourinary system — Maladies de l'appareil génito-urinaire								
Total	10.1	4 135	10.7	4 137	10.7	4 062	10.5	4 000
Disorders of kidney and ureter — Affections du rein et de l'uretère	9.2	3 936	10.2	3 946	10.2	3 892	10.1	3 838
Hyperplasia of prostate — Hyperplasie de la prostate	▼3.3	117	▼2.6	98	...	71	▼1.5	56
Pregnancy, childbirth and the puerperium — Grossesse, accouchement et puerpéralité								
Total	♦ *4.9	20	♦ *5.2	30	♦ *7.9	13	♦ *3.5	19
Pregnancy with abortive outcome — Grossesse se terminant par un avortement	♦ *0.9	1	♦ *0.3	6	♦ *1.6	1	♦ *0.3	3
Other direct obstetric causes — Autres décès maternels directs	♦ *3.7	16	♦ *4.2	24	♦ *6.3	10	♦ *2.7	15
Indirect obstetric causes — Décès maternels indirects	♦ *0.2	1	♦ *0.3	-	-	1	♦ *0.3	1
Certain conditions originating in the perinatal period — Certaines affections dont l'origine se situe dans la période périnatale	*636.1	1 669	*436.9	1 462	*386.1	1 414	*384.0	1 362
Congenital malformations, deformations and chromosomal abnormalities — Malformations congénitales et anomalies chromosomiques	*483.2	1 542	*403.7	1 438	*379.7	1 292	*350.9	1 194
Symptoms, signs and abnormal clinical and laboratory findings, not elsewhere classified — Symptômes, signes et résultats anormaux d'examens cliniques et de laboratoire, non classés ailleurs	87.7	34 367	88.9	26 060	67.4	24 524	63.5	23 557
All other diseases — Toutes autres maladies	0.4	46	0.1	66	0.2	43	0.1	37
External causes — Causes externes								
Total	70.5	27 348	70.8	25 763	66.7	25 043	64.8	25 388
Accidents — Accidents								
Total	48.3	17 956	46.5	16 506	42.7	15 787	40.9	15 988
Transport accidents — Accidents de transport	19.2	7 529	19.5	7 103	18.4	6 295	16.3	6 500
Falls — Chutes	12.2	4 503	11.6	4 094	10.6	3 928	10.2	3 717
Accidental drowning and submersion — Noyade et submersion accidentelles	2.6	1 333	3.4	944	2.4	1 085	2.8	1 148
Exposure to smoke, fire and flames — Exposition à la fumée, au feu et aux flammes	1.5	437	1.1	418	1.1	397	1.0	435
Accidental poisoning by and exposure to noxious substances — Intoxication accidentelle par des substances nocives et exposition à ces substances	5.9	1 519	3.9	1 549	4.0	1 638	4.2	1 599
Intentional self-harm — Lésions auto-infligées	14.1	5 778	14.9	5 841	15.1	5 855	15.2	5 924
Assault — Agresssions	2.6	900	2.3	800	2.1	664	1.7	680
All other external causes — Toutes autres causes externes	5.5	2 714	7.0	2 616	6.8	2 737	7.1	2 796

21. Death and death rates by cause: 1995 - 2002
Décès selon la cause, nombres et taux: 1995 - 2002 (continued — suite)

(See notes at end of table. — Voir notes à la fin du tableau.)

Cause of death — Cause de décès	Poland — Pologne 2002 Rate Taux	Portugal 1995 Number Nombre	1995 Rate Taux	1996 Number Nombre	1996 Rate Taux	1997 Number Nombre	1997 Rate Taux	1998 Number Nombre
Diseases of the digestive system — Maladies de l'appareil digestif								
Diseases of the liver — Maladies du foie	14.3	2 250	22.7	2 356	23.7	2 170	21.8	2 075
Diseases of the musculoskeletal system and connective tissue — Maladies du système ostéo-articularie, des muscles et du tissu conjonctif	1.3	228	2.3	238	2.4	204	2.1	183
Diseases of the genitourinary system — Maladies de l'appareil génito-urinaire								
Total	10.4	1 546	15.6	1 516	15.3	1 403	14.1	1 510
Disorders of kidney and ureter — Affections du rein et de l'uretère	10.0	1 420	14.3	1 397	14.1	1 269	12.8	1 323
Hyperplasia of prostate — Hyperplasie de la prostate	▼1.2	16	♦ ▼1.2	22	♦ ▼1.6	12	♦ ▼0.9	14
Pregnancy, childbirth and the puerperium — Grossesse, accouchement et puerpéralité								
Total	♦ *5.4	9	♦ *8.4	6	♦ *5.4	6	♦ *5.3	9
Pregnancy with abortive outcome — Grossesse se terminant par un avortement	♦ *0.8	3	♦ *2.8	2	♦ *1.8	1	♦ *0.9	2
Other direct obstetric causes — Autres décès maternels directs	♦ *4.2	6	♦ *5.6	4	♦ *3.6	5	♦ *4.4	7
Indirect obstetric causes — Décès maternels indirects	♦ *0.3	-	-	-	-	-	-	-
Certain conditions originating in the perinatal period — Certaines affections dont l'origine se situe dans la période périnatale	*385.0	347	*323.7	304	*275.5	276	*244.1	224
Congenital malformations, deformations and chromosomal abnormalities — Malformations congénitales et anomalies chromosomiques	*337.5	325	*303.2	316	*286.3	306	*270.7	321
Symptoms, signs and abnormal clinical and laboratory findings, not elsewhere classified — Symptômes, signes et résultats anormaux d'examens cliniques et de laboratoire, non classés ailleurs	61.3	11 887	119.9	12 701	127.9	12 905	129.8	13 180
All other diseases — Toutes autres maladies	0.1	146	1.5	174	1.8	192	1.9	245
External causes — Causes externes								
Total	66.1	5 929	59.8	5 795	58.4	5 533	55.6	5 273
Accidents — Accidents								
Total	41.6	4 018	40.5	3 688	37.1	3 412	34.3	3 291
Transport accidents — Accidents de transport	16.9	2 582	26.0	2 356	23.7	2 126	21.4	2 012
Falls — Chutes	9.7	608	6.1	553	5.6	536	5.4	554
Accidental drowning and submersion — Noyade et submersion accidentelles	3.0	65	0.7	58	0.6	42	0.4	30
Exposure to smoke, fire and flames — Exposition à la fumée, au feu et aux flammes	1.1	92	0.9	112	1.1	99	1.0	71
Accidental poisoning by and exposure to noxious substances — Intoxication accidentelle par des substances nocives et exposition à ces substances	4.2	166	1.7	124	1.2	100	1.0	105
Intentional self-harm — Lésions auto-infligées	15.4	809	8.2	653	6.6	628	6.3	556
Assault — Agresssions	1.8	172	1.7	131	1.3	125	1.3	131
All other external causes — Toutes autres causes externes	7.3	930	9.4	1 323	13.3	1 368	13.8	1 295

21. Death and death rates by cause: 1995 - 2002
Décès selon la cause, nombres et taux: 1995 - 2002 (continued — suite)

(See notes at end of table. — Voir notes à la fin du tableau.)

Portugal

Cause of death — Cause de décès	1998	1999		2000		2001		2002
	Rate Taux	Number Nombre	Rate Taux	Number Nombre	Rate Taux	Number Nombre	Rate Taux	Number Nombre
Diseases of the digestive system — Maladies de l'appareil digestif								
Diseases of the liver — Maladies du foie	20.8	1 923	19.3	1 822	18.2	1 964	19.1	**2 256**
Diseases of the musculoskeletal system and connective tissue — Maladies du système ostéo-articularie, des muscles et du tissu conjonctif	1.8	197	2.0	210	2.1	238	2.3	**262**
Diseases of the genitourinary system — Maladies de l'appareil génito-urinaire								
Total	15.1	1 573	15.7	1 579	15.8	1 842	17.9	**2 090**
Disorders of kidney and ureter — Affections du rein et de l'uretère	13.3	1 364	13.7	1 375	13.7	1 574	15.3	**1 784**
Hyperplasia of prostate — Hyperplasie de la prostate	♦ ▼1.0	22	♦ ▼1.6	11	...	18	♦ ▼1.2	**21**
Pregnancy, childbirth and the puerperium — Grossesse, accouchement et puerpéralité								
Total	♦ *7.9	6	♦ *5.2	3	♦ *2.5	6	♦ *5.3	**8**
Pregnancy with abortive outcome — Grossesse se terminant par un avortement	♦ *1.8	2	♦ *1.7	-	-	3	♦ *2.7	**2**
Other direct obstetric causes — Autres décès maternels directs	♦ *6.2	4	♦ *3.4	3	♦ *2.5	3	♦ *2.7	**5**
Indirect obstetric causes — Décès maternels indirects	-	-	-	-	-	-	-	**1**
Certain conditions originating in the perinatal period — Certaines affections dont l'origine se situe dans la période périnatale	*197.3	244	*210.3	253	*213.4	230	*203.9	**329**
Congenital malformations, deformations and chromosomal abnormalities — Malformations congénitales et anomalies chromosomiques	*282.8	286	*246.5	255	*215.1	252	*223.5	**261**
Symptoms, signs and abnormal clinical and laboratory findings, not elsewhere classified — Symptômes, signes et résultats anormaux d'examens cliniques et de laboratoire, non classés ailleurs	132.2	13 378	133.9	13 151	131.4	11 984	116.4	**10 046**
All other diseases — Toutes autres maladies	2.5	277	2.8	220	2.2	342	3.3	**397**
External causes — Causes externes								
Total	52.9	5 022	50.3	4 769	47.6	5 168	50.2	**5 741**
Accidents — Accidents								
Total	33.0	2 889	28.9	2 648	26.5	3 422	33.2	**4 002**
Transport accidents — Accidents de transport	20.2	1 734	17.4	1 450	14.5	1 947	18.9	**2 220**
Falls — Chutes	5.6	458	4.6	501	5.0	654	6.4	**624**
Accidental drowning and submersion — Noyade et submersion accidentelles	♦0.3	29	♦0.3	26	♦0.3	46	0.4	**172**
Exposure to smoke, fire and flames — Exposition à la fumée, au feu et aux flammes	0.7	90	0.9	86	0.9	87	0.8	**77**
Accidental poisoning by and exposure to noxious substances — Intoxication accidentelle par des substances nocives et exposition à ces substances	1.1	88	0.9	66	0.7	90	0.9	**77**
Intentional self-harm — Lésions auto-infligées	5.6	545	5.5	524	5.2	761	7.4	**1 212**
Assault — Agresssions	1.3	118	1.2	97	1.0	134	1.3	**182**
All other external causes — Toutes autres causes externes	13.0	1 470	14.7	1 500	15.0	851	8.3	**345**

(See notes at end of table. — Voir notes à la fin du tableau.)

Cause of death — Cause de décès	Portugal	Republic of Moldova — République de Moldova[6,19]						
	2002	1995	1996	1997	1998	1999	2000	2001
	Rate Taux				Number Nombre			
Diseases of the digestive system — Maladies de l'appareil digestif								
Diseases of the liver — Maladies du foie	21.8	3 937	3 442	2 991	2 699	2 916	3 049	3 244
Diseases of the musculoskeletal system and connective tissue — Maladies du système ostéo-articulaire, des muscles et du tissu conjonctif	2.5	68	50	33	53	40	62	47
Diseases of the genitourinary system — Maladies de l'appareil génito-urinaire								
Total	20.2	428	412	327	317	334	352	318
Disorders of kidney and ureter — Affections du rein et de l'uretère	17.2	316	346	281	272	290	301	267
♦ ▼Hyperplasia of prostate — Hyperplasie de la prostate	1.3	63	60	37	38	39	39	40
Pregnancy, childbirth and the puerperium — Grossesse, accouchement et puerpéralité								
♦ *Total	7.0	23	22	23	15	11	10	16
♦ *Pregnancy with abortive outcome — Grossesse se terminant par un avortement	1.7	6	6	5	5	1	-	3
♦ *Other direct obstetric causes — Autres décès maternels directs	4.4	8	10	10	6	7	8	11
♦ *Indirect obstetric causes — Décès maternels indirects	0.9	9	6	8	4	3	2	2
Certain conditions originating in the perinatal period — Certaines affections dont l'origine se situe dans la période périnatale	*287.6	442	352	276	251	226	236	185
Congenital malformations, deformations and chromosomal abnormalities — Malformations congénitales et anomalies chromosomiques	*228.2	355	324	274	255	248	237	228
Symptoms, signs and abnormal clinical and laboratory findings, not elsewhere classified — Symptômes, signes et résultats anormaux d'examens cliniques et de laboratoire, non classés ailleurs	96.9	6 207	3 951	2 317	2 125	1 766	1 396	781
All other diseases — Toutes autres maladies	3.8	69	34	45	37	38	47	49
External causes — Causes externes								
Total	55.4	4 934	4 691	3 876	3 610	3 481	3 380	3 572
Accidents — Accidents								
Total	38.6	3 093	2 965	2 498	2 282	2 078	2 031	2 256
Transport accidents — Accidents de transport	21.4	826	733	602	574	476	485	570
Falls — Chutes	6.0	253	252	186	174	153	194	155
Accidental drowning and submersion — Noyade et submersion accidentelles	1.7	323	354	233	301	274	214	276
Exposure to smoke, fire and flames — Exposition à la fumée, au feu et aux flammes ..	0.7	199	180	170	138	88	93	88
Accidental poisoning by and exposure to noxious substances — Intoxication accidentelle par des substances nocives et exposition à ces substances	0.7	555	480	462	401	347	350	396
Intentional self-harm — Lésions auto-infligées	11.7	802	777	626	575	579	544	622
Assault — Agresssions	1.8	719	589	479	414	410	432	407
All other external causes — Toutes autres causes externes	3.3	320	360	273	339	414	373	287

(See notes at end of table. — Voir notes à la fin du tableau.)

Cause of death — Cause de décès	Republic of Moldova — République de Moldova[6,-19] 2002 Number Nombre	Romania — Roumanie 1995 Number Nombre	1995 Rate Taux	1996 Number Nombre	1996 Rate Taux	1997 Number Nombre	1997 Rate Taux	1998 Number Nombre
Diseases of the digestive system — Maladies de l'appareil digestif Diseases of the liver — Maladies du foie	*3 158*	11 423	50.4	12 226	54.1	12 995	57.6	12 328
Diseases of the musculoskeletal system and connective tissue — Maladies du système ostéo-articularie, des muscles et du tissu conjonctif	*57*	88	0.4	47	0.2	59	0.3	53
Diseases of the genitourinary system — Maladies de l'appareil génito-urinaire Total	*294*	2 929	12.9	2 894	12.8	2 664	11.8	2 585
Disorders of kidney and ureter — Affections du rein et de l'uretère	*265*	2 212	9.8	2 257	10.0	2 059	9.1	2 101
Hyperplasia of prostate — Hyperplasie de la prostate	*23*	602	▼20.8	552	▼19.1	524	▼18.2	420
Pregnancy, childbirth and the puerperium — Grossesse, accouchement et puerpéralité Total	*11*	113	●47.8	95	●41.1	98	●41.4	96
Pregnancy with abortive outcome — Grossesse se terminant par un avortement	*2*	59	●24.9	51	●22.0	50	●21.1	43
Other direct obstetric causes — Autres décès maternels directs	*5*	54	●22.8	44	●19.0	48	●20.3	53
Indirect obstetric causes — Décès maternels indirects	*4*	-	-	-	-	-	-	-
Certain conditions originating in the perinatal period — Certaines affections dont l'origine se situe dans la période périnatale	*155*	1 452	●613.6	1 342	●580.1	1 391	●587.2	1 529
Congenital malformations, deformations and chromosomal abnormalities — Malformations congénitales et anomalies chromosomiques	*227*	1 136	●480.1	1 207	●521.7	1 382	●583.4	1 229
Symptoms, signs and abnormal clinical and laboratory findings, not elsewhere classified — Symptômes, signes et résultats anormaux d'examens cliniques et de laboratoire, non classés ailleurs	*681*	1 018	4.5	751	3.3	397	1.8	315
All other diseases — Toutes autres maladies	*27*	114	0.5	94	0.4	97	0.4	97
External causes — Causes externes Total	*3 564*	17 839	78.7	17 791	78.7	17 316	76.8	16 237
Accidents — Accidents Total	*2 281*	14 012	61.8	14 047	62.1	13 554	60.1	12 610
Transport accidents — Accidents de transport	*542*	4 752	21.0	4 817	21.3	4 503	20.0	4 182
Falls — Chutes	*181*	1 973	8.7	1 843	8.2	1 867	8.3	1 710
Accidental drowning and submersion — Noyade et submersion accidentelles	*248*	1 639	7.2	1 515	6.7	2 510	11.1	2 405
Exposure to smoke, fire and flames — Exposition à la fumée, au feu et aux flammes	*97*	792	3.5	801	3.5	785	3.5	623
Accidental poisoning by and exposure to noxious substances — Intoxication accidentelle par des substances nocives et exposition à ces substances	*474*	1 649	7.3	1 726	7.6	1 597	7.1	1 455
Intentional self-harm — Lésions auto-infligées	*583*	2 793	12.3	2 828	12.5	2 859	12.7	2 838
Assault — Agresssions	*374*	941	4.1	851	3.8	861	3.8	754
All other external causes — Toutes autres causes externes	*326*	93	0.4	65	0.3	42	0.2	35

21. Death and death rates by cause: 1995 - 2002
Décès selon la cause, nombres et taux: 1995 - 2002 (continued — suite)

(See notes at end of table. — Voir notes à la fin du tableau.)

Romania — Roumanie

Cause of death — Cause de décès	1998 Rate Taux	1999 Number Nombre	1999 Rate Taux	2000 Number Nombre	2000 Rate Taux	2001 Number Nombre	2001 Rate Taux	2002 Number Nombre
Diseases of the digestive system — Maladies de l'appareil digestif								
Diseases of the liver — Maladies du foie	54.8	10 843	48.3	10 582	47.2	11 776	53.2	12 055
Diseases of the musculoskeletal system and connective tissue — Maladies du système ostéo-articularie, des muscles et du tissu conjonctif	0.2	72	0.3	63	0.3	52	0.2	42
Diseases of the genitourinary system — Maladies de l'appareil génito-urinaire								
Total	11.5	2 597	11.6	2 386	10.6	2 326	10.5	2 380
Disorders of kidney and ureter — Affections du rein et de l'uretère	9.3	2 123	9.5	2 043	9.1	2 043	9.2	2 093
Hyperplasia of prostate — Hyperplasie de la prostate	▼14.6	444	▼15.3	318	...	252	▼8.4	265
Pregnancy, childbirth and the puerperium — Grossesse, accouchement et puerpéralité								
Total	*40.5	98	*41.8	75	*32.0	75	*34.0	47
Pregnancy with abortive outcome — Grossesse se terminant par un avortement	*18.1	44	*18.8	36	*15.4	37	*16.8	20
Other direct obstetric causes — Autres décès maternels directs	*22.3	54	*23.0	40	*17.1	38	*17.2	27
Indirect obstetric causes — Décès maternels indirects	-	-	-	-	-	-	-	-
Certain conditions originating in the perinatal period — Certaines affections dont l'origine se situe dans la période périnatale	*644.3	1 392	*593.4	1 450	*618.3	1 324	*600.8	1 055
Congenital malformations, deformations and chromosomal abnormalities — Malformations congénitales et anomalies chromosomiques	*517.9	1 064	*453.5	1 054	*449.4	1 086	*492.8	1 095
Symptoms, signs and abnormal clinical and laboratory findings, not elsewhere classified — Symptômes, signes et résultats anormaux d'examens cliniques et de laboratoire, non classés ailleurs	1.4	327	1.5	320	1.4	283	1.3	233
All other diseases — Toutes autres maladies	0.4	68	0.3	76	0.3	57	0.3	71
External causes — Causes externes								
Total	72.2	14 467	64.4	14 412	64.2	14 270	64.5	14 509
Accidents — Accidents								
Total	56.0	10 695	47.6	10 418	46.4	10 465	47.3	10 383
Transport accidents — Accidents de transport	18.6	3 531	15.7	3 627	16.2	3 671	16.6	3 479
Falls — Chutes	7.6	1 593	7.1	1 576	7.0	1 535	6.9	1 627
Accidental drowning and submersion — Noyade et submersion accidentelles	10.7	1 364	6.1	1 271	5.7	1 254	5.7	1 181
Exposure to smoke, fire and flames — Exposition à la fumée, au feu et aux flammes	2.8	430	1.9	484	2.2	479	2.2	432
Accidental poisoning by and exposure to noxious substances — Intoxication accidentelle par des substances nocives et exposition à ces substances	6.5	1 223	5.4	1 190	5.3	1 221	5.5	1 114
Intentional self-harm — Lésions auto-infligées	12.6	2 736	12.2	2 836	12.6	2 720	12.3	3 067
Assault — Agresssions	3.4	803	3.6	813	3.6	782	3.5	804
All other external causes — Toutes autres causes externes	0.2	233	1.0	345	1.5	303	1.4	255

(See notes at end of table. — Voir notes à la fin du tableau.)

Cause of death — Cause de décès	Romania — Roumanie	Russian Federation — Fédération de Russie[6,20]						
	2002	1995	1996	1997	1998	1999	2000	2001
	Rate Taux				Number Nombre			
Diseases of the digestive system — Maladies de l'appareil digestif								
Diseases of the liver — Maladies du foie	55.3	...	...	...	...	25 893	29 235	33 546
Diseases of the musculoskeletal system and connective tissue — Maladies du système ostéo-articularie, des muscles et du tissu conjonctif	0.2	2 397	2 292	2 113	2 019	2 357	2 505	2 325
Diseases of the genitourinary system — Maladies de l'appareil génito-urinaire								
Total	10.9	18 184	16 706	15 711	14 857	15 464	14 990	13 899
Disorders of kidney and ureter — Affections du rein et de l'uretère	9.6	13 719	12 798	11 961	11 254	...	...	...
Hyperplasia of prostate — Hyperplasie de la prostate	▼8.9	2 245	1 858	1 700	1 542			
Pregnancy, childbirth and the puerperium — Grossesse, accouchement et puerpéralité								
Total	*22.3	727	636	633	565	537	503	479
Pregnancy with abortive outcome — Grossesse se terminant par un avortement	♦ *9.5	169	148	154	129	178	155	125
Other direct obstetric causes — Autres décès maternels directs	♦ *12.8	...	...	...	...	299	281	288
Indirect obstetric causes — Décès maternels indirects		...	...	...	...	38	53	60
Certain conditions originating in the perinatal period — Certaines affections dont l'origine se situe dans la période périnatale	*501.1	10 771	9 894	9 181	8 945	8 709	8 517	8 660
Congenital malformations, deformations and chromosomal abnormalities — Malformations congénitales et anomalies chromosomiques	*520.1	8 666	8 055	7 934	7 568	7 619	7 150	7 256
Symptoms, signs and abnormal clinical and laboratory findings, not elsewhere classified — Symptômes, signes et résultats anormaux d'examens cliniques et de laboratoire, non classés ailleurs	1.1	93 792	92 594	89 880	86 890	94 906	102 932	105 594
All other diseases — Toutes autres maladies	0.3	1 783	1 664	1 503	1 398	1 768	1 840	1 926
External causes — Causes externes								
Total	66.6	348 507	307 224	274 928	273 953	300 156	318 716	331 634
Accidents — Accidents								
Total	47.6	192 135	165 985	145 391	146 855	...	...	...
Transport accidents — Accidents de transport	16.0	38 630	33 696	31 516	33 673	38 218	39 565	40 722
Falls — Chutes	7.5	9 264	7 740	7 055	6 520	9 847	13 099	14 443
Accidental drowning and submersion — Noyade et submersion accidentelles	5.4	20 458	16 157	14 533	16 403	17 062	16 017	17 695
Exposure to smoke, fire and flames — Exposition à la fumée, au feu et aux flammes	2.0	8 758	9 100	7 717	7 675	9 939	10 633	11 652
Accidental poisoning by and exposure to noxious substances — Intoxication accidentelle par des substances nocives et exposition à ces substances	5.1	60 853	52 408	44 901	44 002	48 219	59 500	61 690
Intentional self-harm — Lésions auto-infligées	14.1	60 953	57 812	55 031	51 770	57 276	56 934	57 284
Assault — Agressions	3.7	45 257	39 083	34 995	33 553	38 225	41 090	42 921
All other external causes — Toutes autres causes externes	1.2	50 162	44 344	39 511	41 775	...	...	...

21. Death and death rates by cause: 1995 - 2002
Décès selon la cause, nombres et taux: 1995 - 2002 (continued — suite)

(See notes at end of table. — Voir notes à la fin du tableau.)

Cause of death — Cause de décès	Russian Federation — Fédération de Russie[6,20] 2002	San Marino — Saint-Marin 1995	1996	1997	1998	1999	2000	Serbia and Montenegro — Serbie-et-Montenegro 2000
					Number Nombre			
Diseases of the digestive system — Maladies de l'appareil digestif								
Diseases of the liver — Maladies du foie	39 601	1	2	5	2	-	4	1 203
Diseases of the musculoskeletal system and connective tissue — Maladies du système ostéo-articularie, des muscles et du tissu conjonctif	2 210	-	-	-	-	-	-	111
Diseases of the genitourinary system — Maladies de l'appareil génito-urinaire								
Total	13 485	-	-	3	1	-	-	1 792
Disorders of kidney and ureter — Affections du rein et de l'uretère	...	-	-	1	-	-	-	...
Hyperplasia of prostate — Hyperplasie de la prostate	...	-	-	-	-	-	-	...
Pregnancy, childbirth and the puerperium — Grossesse, accouchement et puerpéralité								
Total	469	-	-	-	-	-	-	
Pregnancy with abortive outcome — Grossesse se terminant par un avortement	121	-	-	-	-	-	-	7
Other direct obstetric causes — Autres décès maternels directs	284	-	-	-	-	-	-	1
Indirect obstetric causes — Décès maternels indirects	59	-	-	-	-	-	-	6
Certain conditions originating in the perinatal period — Certaines affections dont l'origine se situe dans la période périnatale	8 512	3	1	-	-	1	-	1 006
Congenital malformations, deformations and chromosomal abnormalities — Malformations congénitales et anomalies chromosomiques	6 921	-	2	-	1	-	-	361
Symptoms, signs and abnormal clinical and laboratory findings, not elsewhere classified — Symptômes, signes et résultats anormaux d'examens cliniques et de laboratoire, non classés ailleurs	107 600	16	12	23	22	22	21	10 022
All other diseases — Toutes autres maladies	1 980	-	-	-	-	-	-	47
External causes — Causes externes								
Total	339 296	10	8	14	7	9	5	4 644
Accidents — Accidents								
Total	...	7	6	6	3	7	3	...
Transport accidents — Accidents de transport	41 751	5	5	4	3	6	2	...
Falls — Chutes	14 014	2	1	-	-	-	-	...
Accidental drowning and submersion — Noyade et submersion accidentelles	16 833	-	-	-	-	-	1	...
Exposure to smoke, fire and flames — Exposition à la fumée, au feu et aux flammes	12 568	-	-	-	-	1	-	...
Accidental poisoning by and exposure to noxious substances — Intoxication accidentelle par des substances nocives et exposition à ces substances	64 359	-	-	-	-	-	-	...
Intentional self-harm — Lésions auto-infligées	55 330	3	2	8	4	2	1	...
Assault — Agresssions	44 252	-	-	-	-	-	-	...
All other external causes — Toutes autres causes externes	...	-	-	-	-	-	1	...

(See notes at end of table. — Voir notes à la fin du tableau.)

Cause of death — Cause de décès	Serbia and Montenegro — Serbie-et-Montenegro 2000 Rate Taux	Slovakia — Slovaquie 1995 Number Nombre	1995 Rate Taux	1996 Number Nombre	1996 Rate Taux	1997 Number Nombre	1997 Rate Taux	1998 Number Nombre
Diseases of the digestive system — Maladies de l'appareil digestif Diseases of the liver — Maladies du foie	11.3	1 402	26.1	1 246	23.2	1 351	25.1	1 538
Diseases of the musculoskeletal system and connective tissue — Maladies du système ostéo-articularie, des muscles et du tissu conjonctif	1.0	10	◆0.2	5	◆0.1	10	◆0.2	62
Diseases of the genitourinary system — Maladies de l'appareil génito-urinaire Total	16.9	821	15.3	753	14.0	716	13.3	734
Disorders of kidney and ureter — Affections du rein et de l'uretère	...	774	14.4	709	13.2	693	12.9	707
Hyperplasia of prostate — Hyperplasie de la prostate	...	23	...	16	...	11	◆ ▼1.9	13
Pregnancy, childbirth and the puerperium — Grossesse, accouchement et puerpéralité Total	◆ *5.6	5	◆ *8.1	3	◆ *5.0	1	◆ *1.7	5
Pregnancy with abortive outcome — Grossesse se terminant par un avortement	◆ *0.8	2	◆ *3.3	-	-	-	-	1
Other direct obstetric causes — Autres décès maternels directs	◆ *4.8	3	◆ *4.9	3	◆ *5.0	1	◆ *1.7	3
Indirect obstetric causes — Décès maternels indirects		-		-		-		-
Certain conditions originating in the perinatal period — Certaines affections dont l'origine se situe dans la période périnatale	*799.3	361	*587.7	328	*545.5	233	*392.9	247
Congenital malformations, deformations and chromosomal abnormalities — Malformations congénitales et anomalies chromosomiques	*286.8	222	*361.4	171	*284.4	155	*261.3	162
Symptoms, signs and abnormal clinical and laboratory findings, not elsewhere classified — Symptômes, signes et résultats anormaux d'examens cliniques et de laboratoire, non classés ailleurs	94.2	451	8.4	397	7.4	411	7.6	430
All other diseases — Toutes autres maladies	0.4	9	◆0.2	13	◆0.2	6	◆0.1	2
External causes — Causes externes Total	43.7	3 645	68.0	3 533	65.7	3 694	68.6	3 349
Accidents — Accidents Total	...	2 649	49.4	2 602	48.4	2 726	50.6	2 380
Transport accidents — Accidents de transport	...	922	17.2	841	15.6	1 022	19.0	1 075
Falls — Chutes	...	955	17.8	944	17.6	948	17.6	488
Accidental drowning and submersion — Noyade et submersion accidentelles	...	154	2.9	153	2.8	144	2.7	172
Exposure to smoke, fire and flames — Exposition à la fumée, au feu et aux flammes	...	47	0.9	54	1.0	41	0.8	57
Accidental poisoning by and exposure to noxious substances — Intoxication accidentelle par des substances nocives et exposition à ces substances	...	175	3.3	164	3.1	189	3.5	140
Intentional self-harm — Lésions auto-infligées	...	735	13.7	672	12.5	630	11.7	673
Assault — Agresssions	...	114	2.1	108	2.0	138	2.6	115
All other external causes — Toutes autres causes externes	...	147	2.7	151	2.8	200	3.7	181

21. Death and death rates by cause: 1995 - 2002
Décès selon la cause, nombres et taux: 1995 - 2002 (continued — suite)

(See notes at end of table. — Voir notes à la fin du tableau.)

Cause of death — Cause de décès	Slovakia — Slovaquie							Slovenia — Slovénie
	1998	1999		2000		2001		1995
	Rate Taux	Number Nombre	Rate Taux	Number Nombre	Rate Taux	Number Nombre	Rate Taux	Number Nombre
Diseases of the digestive system — Maladies de l'appareil digestif								
Diseases of the liver — Maladies du foie	28.5	1 576	29.2	1 496	27.7	1 500	27.9	692
Diseases of the musculoskeletal system and connective tissue — Maladies du système ostéo-articularie, des muscles et du tissu conjonctif	1.2	53	1.0	65	1.2	49	0.9	39
Diseases of the genitourinary system — Maladies de l'appareil génito-urinaire								
Total	13.6	782	14.5	671	12.4	703	13.1	215
Disorders of kidney and ureter — Affections du rein et de l'uretère	13.1	723	13.4	632	11.7	666	12.4	179
Hyperplasia of prostate — Hyperplasie de la prostate	♦ ▼2.2	29	♦ ▼4.9	17	...	20	♦ ▼3.2	14
Pregnancy, childbirth and the puerperium — Grossesse, accouchement et puerpéralité								
Total	♦ *8.7	5	♦ *8.9	1	♦ *1.8	7	♦ *13.7	1
Pregnancy with abortive outcome — Grossesse se terminant par un avortement	♦ *1.7	-	-	-	-	-	-	-
Other direct obstetric causes — Autres décès maternels directs	♦ *5.2	5	♦ *8.9	1	♦ *1.8	6	♦ *11.7	1
Indirect obstetric causes — Décès maternels indirects		-	-	-	-	-	-	-
Certain conditions originating in the perinatal period — Certaines affections dont l'origine se situe dans la période périnatale	*429.0	221	*393.1	216	*392.0	138	*269.9	38
Congenital malformations, deformations and chromosomal abnormalities — Malformations congénitales et anomalies chromosomiques	*281.3	171	*304.1	179	*324.8	147	*287.5	74
Symptoms, signs and abnormal clinical and laboratory findings, not elsewhere classified — Symptômes, signes et résultats anormaux d'examens cliniques et de laboratoire, non classés ailleurs	8.0	520	9.6	592	11.0	480	8.9	498
All other diseases — Toutes autres maladies	0.0	2	0.0	2	0.0	3	♦0.1	10
External causes — Causes externes								
Total	62.1	3 094	57.3	3 114	57.7	3 039	56.5	1 727
Accidents — Accidents								
Total	44.2	2 093	38.8	2 087	38.6	1 996	37.1	1 004
Transport accidents — Accidents de transport	19.9	887	16.4	849	15.7	830	15.4	430
Falls — Chutes	9.1	479	8.9	473	8.8	433	8.1	410
Accidental drowning and submersion — Noyade et submersion accidentelles	3.2	141	2.6	158	2.9	153	2.8	23
Exposure to smoke, fire and flames — Exposition à la fumée, au feu et aux flammes	1.1	44	0.8	54	1.0	28	♦0.5	13
Accidental poisoning by and exposure to noxious substances — Intoxication accidentelle par des substances nocives et exposition à ces substances	2.6	152	2.8	157	2.9	150	2.8	44
Intentional self harm — Lésions auto-infligées	12.5	692	12.8	729	13.5	692	12.9	564
Assault — Agresssions	2.1	132	2.4	118	2.2	111	2.1	47
All other external causes — Toutes autres causes externes	3.4	177	3.3	180	3.3	240	4.5	22

(See notes at end of table. — Voir notes à la fin du tableau.)

Slovenia — Slovénie

Cause of death — Cause de décès	1995	1996		1997		1998		1999
	Rate Taux	Number Nombre	Rate Taux	Number Nombre	Rate Taux	Number Nombre	Rate Taux	Number Nombre
Diseases of the digestive system — Maladies de l'appareil digestif								
Diseases of the liver — Maladies du foie	34.8	653	32.8	617	31.1	644	32.5	682
Diseases of the musculoskeletal system and connective tissue — Maladies du système ostéo-articularie, des muscles et du tissu conjonctif	2.0	20	♦1.0	39	2.0	42	2.1	37
Diseases of the genitourinary system — Maladies de l'appareil génito-urinaire								
Total	10.8	179	9.0	225	11.3	192	9.7	175
Disorders of kidney and ureter — Affections du rein et de l'uretère	9.0	157	7.9	188	9.5	154	7.8	146
Hyperplasia of prostate — Hyperplasie de la prostate	♦ ▼5.7	5	♦ ▼2.0	7	...	4	♦ ▼1.6	3
Pregnancy, childbirth and the puerperium — Grossesse, accouchement et puerpéralité								
Total	♦ *5.3	3	♦ *16.0	2	♦ *11.0	-	-	2
Pregnancy with abortive outcome — Grossesse se terminant par un avortement		-				-	-	
Other direct obstetric causes — Autres décès maternels directs	♦ *5.3	2	♦ *10.6	2	♦ *11.0	-	-	1
Indirect obstetric causes — Décès maternels indirects	-	1	♦ *5.3			-	-	1
Certain conditions originating in the perinatal period — Certaines affections dont l'origine se situe dans la période périnatale	*200.2	40	*212.9	39	*214.7	37	*207.2	34
Congenital malformations, deformations and chromosomal abnormalities — Malformations congénitales et anomalies chromosomiques	*389.9	71	*377.9	67	*368.8	66	*369.6	58
Symptoms, signs and abnormal clinical and laboratory findings, not elsewhere classified — Symptômes, signes et résultats anormaux d'examens cliniques et de laboratoire, non classés ailleurs	25.1	539	27.1	500	25.2	604	30.5	652
All other diseases — Toutes autres maladies	♦0.5	3	♦0.2	10	♦0.5	13	♦0.7	14
External causes — Causes externes								
Total	86.9	1 812	91.0	1 760	88.6	1 649	83.2	1 658
Accidents — Accidents								
Total	55.0	1 126	56.5	988	49.7	876	44.2	864
Transport accidents — Accidents de transport	21.6	398	20.0	379	19.1	342	17.3	354
Falls — Chutes	20.6	401	20.1	426	21.4	346	17.5	328
Accidental drowning and submersion — Noyade et submersion accidentelies	♦1.2	38	1.9	21	♦1.1	45	2.3	30
Exposure to smoke, fire and flames — Exposition à la fumée, au feu et aux flammes	♦0.7	23	♦1.2	16	♦0.8	9	♦0.5	6
Accidental poisoning by and exposure to noxious substances — Intoxication accidentelle par des substances nocives et exposition à ces substances	2.2	44	2.2	31	1.6	37	1.9	36
Intentional self-harm — Lésions auto-infligées	28.4	607	30.5	593	29.8	612	30.9	590
Assault — Agresssions	2.4	42	2.1	46	2.3	20	♦1.0	30
All other external causes — Toutes autres causes externes	♦1.1	37	1.9	133	6.7	141	7.1	174

(See notes at end of table. — Voir notes à la fin du tableau.)

Cause of death — Cause de décès	Slovenia — Slovénie							Spain — Espagne
	1999	2000		2001		2002		1995
	Rate Taux	Number Nombre	Rate Taux	Number Nombre	Rate Taux	Number Nombre	Rate Taux	Number Nombre
Diseases of the digestive system — Maladies de l'appareil digestif								
Diseases of the liver — Maladies du foie	34.3	723	36.3	749	37.6	680	34.1	6 897
Diseases of the musculoskeletal system and connective tissue — Maladies du système ostéo-articularie, des muscles et du tissu conjonctif	1.9	37	1.9	32	1.6	52	2.6	2 835
Diseases of the genitourinary system — Maladies de l'appareil génito-urinaire								
Total	8.8	183	9.2	207	10.4	188	9.4	6 907
Disorders of kidney and ureter — Affections du rein et de l'uretère	7.4	152	7.6	157	7.9	155	7.8	5 404
Hyperplasia of prostate — Hyperplasie de la prostate	♦ ▼1.1	2	...	5	♦ ▼1.8	2	♦ ▼0.7	154
Pregnancy, childbirth and the puerperium — Grossesse, accouchement et puerpéralité								
Total	♦ *11.4	2	♦ *11.0	3	♦ *17.2	-	-	11
Pregnancy with abortive outcome — Grossesse se terminant par un avortement	-	-	-	-	-	-	-	1
Other direct obstetric causes — Autres décès maternels directs	♦ *5.7	1	♦ *5.5	3	♦ *17.2	-	-	10
Indirect obstetric causes — Décès maternels indirects	♦ *5.7	1	♦ *5.5	-	-	-	-	-
Certain conditions originating in the perinatal period — Certaines affections dont l'origine se situe dans la période périnatale	*193.9	45	*247.5	36	*206.0	32	*182.8	868
Congenital malformations, deformations and chromosomal abnormalities — Malformations congénitales et anomalies chromosomiques	*330.8	49	*269.5	51	*291.8	56	*320.0	1 175
Symptoms, signs and abnormal clinical and laboratory findings, not elsewhere classified — Symptômes, signes et résultats anormaux d'examens cliniques et de laboratoire, non classés ailleurs	32.8	647	32.5	745	37.4	742	37.2	6 477
All other diseases — Toutes autres maladies	♦0.7	18	♦0.9	23	♦1.2	19	♦1.0	604
External causes — Causes externes								
Total	83.5	1 543	77.5	1 565	78.6	1 489	74.6	16 325
Accidents — Accidents								
Total	43.5	800	40.2	841	42.2	770	38.6	12 700
Transport accidents — Accidents de transport	17.8	331	16.6	318	16.0	297	14.9	6 013
Falls — Chutes	16.5	338	17.0	342	17.2	297	14.0	1 487
Accidental drowning and submersion — Noyade et submersion accidentelles	♦1.5	26	♦1.3	30	♦1.5	36	1.8	614
Exposure to smoke, fire and flames — Exposition à la fumée, au feu et aux flammes	*0.3	8	♦0.4	16	♦0.8	12	♦0.6	169
Accidental poisoning by and exposure to noxious substances — Intoxication accidentelle par des substances nocives et exposition à ces substances	1.8	24	♦1.2	38	1.9	32	1.6	1 062
Intentional self-harm — Lésions auto-infligées	29.7	588	29.5	581	29.2	540	27.1	3 157
Assault — Agresssions	♦1.5	22	♦1.1	16	♦0.8	28	♦1.4	353
All other external causes — Toutes autres causes externes	8.8	133	6.7	127	6.4	151	7.6	106

(See notes at end of table. — Voir notes à la fin du tableau.)

Spain — Espagne

Cause of death — Cause de décès	1995	1996		1997		1998		1999
	Rate Taux	Number Nombre	Rate Taux	Number Nombre	Rate Taux	Number Nombre	Rate Taux	Number Nombre
Diseases of the digestive system — Maladies de l'appareil digestif								
Diseases of the liver — Maladies du foie	17.6	6 774	17.2	6 423	16.3	6 246	15.8	7 110
Diseases of the musculoskeletal system and connective tissue — Maladies du système ostéo-articulaire, des muscles et du tissu conjonctif	7.2	2 815	7.2	2 832	7.2	2 940	7.5	3 208
Diseases of the genitourinary system — Maladies de l'appareil génito-urinaire								
Total	17.6	7 076	18.0	7 357	18.7	7 789	19.7	7 713
Disorders of kidney and ureter — Affections du rein et de l'uretère	13.8	5 509	14.0	5 514	14.0	5 773	14.6	5 953
Hyperplasia of prostate — Hyperplasie de la prostate	▼2.8	164	▼2.9	140	▼2.5	134	▼2.3	129
Pregnancy, childbirth and the puerperium — Grossesse, accouchement et puerpéralité								
Total	♦ ●3.0	11	♦ ●3.0	8	♦ ●2.2	10	♦ ●2.7	14
Pregnancy with abortive outcome — Grossesse se terminant par un avortement	♦ ●0.3	2	♦ ●0.6	-	-	-	-	2
Other direct obstetric causes — Autres décès maternels directs	♦ ●2.8	8	♦ ●2.2	7	♦ ●1.9	9	♦ ●2.5	12
Indirect obstetric causes — Décès maternels indirects	-	1	♦ ●0.3	1	♦ ●0.3	1	♦ ●0.3	-
Certain conditions originating in the perinatal period — Certaines affections dont l'origine se situe dans la période périnatale	●238.8	869	●239.6	802	●217.3	779	●213.3	788
Congenital malformations, deformations and chromosomal abnormalities — Malformations congénitales et anomalies chromosomiques	●323.3	1 217	●335.6	1 191	●322.7	1 136	●311.1	1 142
Symptoms, signs and abnormal clinical and laboratory findings, not elsewhere classified — Symptômes, signes et résultats anormaux d'examens cliniques et de laboratoire, non classés ailleurs	16.5	6 916	17.6	6 921	17.6	6 950	17.6	9 561
All other diseases — Toutes autres maladies	1.5	685	1.7	770	2.0	922	2.3	921
External causes — Causes externes								
Total	41.6	16 324	41.6	16 493	41.9	16 863	42.7	16 411
Accidents — Accidents								
Total	32.4	12 541	31.9	12 653	32.2	13 112	33.2	12 219
Transport accidents — Accidents de transport	15.3	5 914	15.1	6 085	15.5	6 463	16.4	6 419
Falls — Chutes	3.8	1 724	4.4	1 753	4.5	1 784	4.5	1 455
Accidental drowning and submersion — Noyade et submersion accidentelles	1.6	649	1.7	608	1.5	619	1.6	529
Exposure to smoke, fire and flames — Exposition à la fumée, au feu et aux flammes	0.4	194	0.5	209	0.5	198	0.5	220
Accidental poisoning by and exposure to noxious substances — Intoxication accidentelle par des substances nocives et exposition à ces substances	2.7	1 088	2.8	1 068	2.7	1 034	2.6	935
Intentional self-harm — Lésions auto-infligées	8.0	3 320	8.5	3 373	8.6	3 261	8.3	3 218
Assault — Agressions	0.9	343	0.9	342	0.9	355	0.9	347
All other external causes — Toutes autres causes externes	0.3	120	0.3	125	0.3	135	0.3	627

(See notes at end of table. — Voir notes à la fin du tableau.)

Cause of death — Cause de décès	Spain — Espagne					Sweden — Suède		
	1999	2000		2001		1995		1996
	Rate Taux	Number Nombre	Rate Taux	Number Nombre	Rate Taux	Number Nombre	Rate Taux	Number Nombre
Diseases of the digestive system — Maladies de l'appareil digestif								
Diseases of the liver — Maladies du foie	17.9	6 797	17.0	6 733	16.7	589	6.7	501
Diseases of the musculoskeletal system and connective tissue — Maladies du système ostéo-articularie, des muscles et du tissu conjonctif	8.1	3 158	7.9	3 352	8.3	411	4.7	413
Diseases of the genitourinary system — Maladies de l'appareil génito-urinaire								
Total	19.5	7 918	19.8	8 278	20.6	1 254	14.2	1 243
Disorders of kidney and ureter — Affections du rein et de l'uretère	15.0	6 051	15.2	6 164	15.3	647	7.3	695
Hyperplasia of prostate — Hyperplasie de la prostate	▼2.2	124	▼2.1	116	▼1.9	68	▼4.9	39
Pregnancy, childbirth and the puerperium — Grossesse, accouchement et puerpéralité								
Total	◆ *3.7	14	◆ *3.6	17	◆ *4.2	4	◆ *3.9	5
Pregnancy with abortive outcome — Grossesse se terminant par un avortement	◆ *0.5	1	◆ *0.3	4	◆ *1.0	1	◆ *1.0	-
Other direct obstetric causes — Autres décès maternels directs	◆ *3.2	13	◆ *3.4	11	◆ *2.7	3	◆ *2.9	4
Indirect obstetric causes — Décès maternels indirects	-	-	-	2	◆ *0.5	-	-	1
Certain conditions originating in the perinatal period — Certaines affections dont l'origine se situe dans la période périnatale	*207.3	859	*222.3	894	*219.6	170	*164.5	139
Congenital malformations, deformations and chromosomal abnormalities — Malformations congénitales et anomalies chromosomiques	*300.4	1 112	*287.7	955	*234.6	294	*284.5	272
Symptoms, signs and abnormal clinical and laboratory findings, not elsewhere classified — Symptômes, signes et résultats anormaux d'examens cliniques et de laboratoire, non classés ailleurs	24.1	9 643	24.2	9 863	24.5	1 554	17.6	1 671
All other diseases — Toutes autres maladies	2.3	957	2.4	992	2.5	159	1.8	183
External causes — Causes externes								
Total	41.4	16 541	41.4	15 999	39.7	4 321	49.0	4 203
Accidents — Accidents								
Total	30.8	12 252	30.7	11 811	29.3	2 422	27.4	2 429
Transport accidents — Accidents de transport	16.2	6 480	16.2	6 096	15.1	603	6.8	573
Falls — Chutes	3.7	1 503	3.8	1 485	3.7	1 081	12.2	1 131
Accidental drowning and submersion — Noyade et submersion accidentelles	1.3	588	1.5	575	1.4	105	1.2	83
Exposure to smoke, fire and flames — Exposition à la fumée, au feu et aux flammes	0.6	206	0.5	211	0.5	71	0.8	95
Accidental poisoning by and exposure to noxious substances — Intoxication accidentelle par des substances nocives et exposition à ces substances	2.4	878	2.2	863	2.1	126	1.4	129
Intentional self-harm — Lésions auto-infligées	8.1	3 393	8.5	3 189	7.9	1 348	15.3	1 253
Assault — Agresssions	0.9	411	1.0	418	1.0	85	1.0	110
All other external causes — Toutes autres causes externes	1.6	485	1.2	581	1.4	466	5.3	411

21. Death and death rates by cause: 1995 - 2002
Décès selon la cause, nombres et taux: 1995 - 2002 (continued — suite)

(See notes at end of table. — Voir notes à la fin du tableau.)

Sweden — Suède

Cause of death — Cause de décès	1996 Rate Taux	1997 Number Nombre	1997 Rate Taux	1998 Number Nombre	1998 Rate Taux	1999 Number Nombre	1999 Rate Taux	2000 Number Nombre
Diseases of the digestive system — Maladies de l'appareil digestif								
Diseases of the liver — Maladies du foie	5.7	569	6.4	651	7.4	635	7.2	633
Diseases of the musculoskeletal system and connective tissue — Maladies du système ostéo-articulaire, des muscles et du tissu conjonctif	4.7	462	5.2	505	5.7	564	6.4	489
Diseases of the genitourinary system — Maladies de l'appareil génito-urinaire	14.1	1 275	14.4	1 358	15.3	1 370	15.5	1 323
Total								
Disorders of kidney and ureter — Affections du rein et de l'uretère	7.9	772	8.7	797	9.0	799	9.0	776
Hyperplasia of prostate — Hyperplasie de la prostate	▼2.8	61	▼4.3	61	▼4.2	47	▼3.2	49
Pregnancy, childbirth and the puerperium — Grossesse, accouchement et puerpéralité	◆ *5.3	3	◆ *3.3	7	◆ *7.9	1	◆ *1.1	4
Total								
Pregnancy with abortive outcome — Grossesse se terminant par un avortement	-	1	◆ *1.1	1	◆ *1.1	-	-	-
Other direct obstetric causes — Autres décès maternels directs	◆ *4.2	2	◆ *2.2	4	◆ *4.5	1	◆ *1.1	3
Indirect obstetric causes — Décès maternels indirects	◆ *1.1	-	-	1	◆ *1.1	-	-	-
Certain conditions originating in the perinatal period — Certaines affections dont l'origine se situe dans la période périnatale	*146.1	136	*150.5	134	*150.5	121	*137.2	124
Congenital malformations, deformations and chromosomal abnormalities — Malformations congénitales et anomalies chromosomiques	*285.8	279	*308.7	260	*292.0	246	*279.0	285
Symptoms, signs and abnormal clinical and laboratory findings, not elsewhere classified — Symptômes, signes et résultats anormaux d'examens cliniques et de laboratoire, non classés ailleurs	18.9	2 058	23.3	2 338	26.4	2 357	26.6	2 537
All other diseases — Toutes autres maladies	2.1	174	2.0	133	1.5	147	1.7	144
External causes — Causes externes	47.5	4 375	49.5	4 347	49.1	4 290	48.4	4 267
Total								
Accidents — Accidents	27.5	2 595	29.3	2 508	28.3	2 503	28.3	2 606
Total								
Transport accidents — Accidents de transport	6.5	599	6.8	564	6.4	563	6.4	617
Falls — Chutes	12.8	588	6.6	480	5.4	501	5.7	486
Accidental drowning and submersion — Noyade et submersion accidentelles	0.9	126	1.4	111	1.3	104	1.2	115
Exposure to smoke, fire and flames — Exposition à la fumée, au feu et aux flammes	1.1	92	1.0	138	1.6	74	0.8	90
Accidental poisoning by and exposure to noxious substances — Intoxication accidentelle par des substances nocives et exposition à ces substances	1.5	103	1.2	129	1.5	149	1.7	221
Intentional self-harm — Lésions auto-infligées	14.2	1 200	13.6	1 229	13.9	1 219	13.8	1 130
Assault — Agresssions	1.2	94	1.1	98	1.1	108	1.2	90
All other external causes — Toutes autres causes externes	4.6	486	5.5	512	5.8	460	5.2	441

(See notes at end of table. — Voir notes à la fin du tableau.)

Cause of death — Cause de décès	Sweden — Suède			Switzerland — Suisse				
	2000	2001		1995		1996		1997
	Rate Taux	Number Nombre	Rate Taux	Number Nombre	Rate Taux	Number Nombre	Rate Taux	Number Nombre
Diseases of the digestive system — Maladies de l'appareil digestif								
Diseases of the liver — Maladies du foie	7.1	679	7.6	745	10.6	741	10.5	766
Diseases of the musculoskeletal system and connective tissue — Maladies du système ostéo-articularie, des muscles et du tissu conjonctif	5.5	485	5.5	481	6.8	478	6.8	426
Diseases of the genitourinary system — Maladies de l'appareil génito-urinaire								
Total	14.9	1 430	16.1	704	10.0	620	8.8	634
Disorders of kidney and ureter — Affections du rein et de l'uretère	8.7	813	9.1	468	6.6	416	5.9	411
Hyperplasia of prostate — Hyperplasie de la prostate	...	43	▼2.9	53	▼5.2	36	▼3.5	47
Pregnancy, childbirth and the puerperium — Grossesse, accouchement et puerpéralité								
Total	♦ *4.4	3	♦ *3.3	7	♦ *8.5	3	♦ *3.6	3
Pregnancy with abortive outcome — Grossesse se terminant par un avortement		-	-	2	♦ *2.4	1	♦ *1.2	-
Other direct obstetric causes — Autres décès maternels directs	♦ *3.3	2	♦ *2.2	5	♦ *6.1	2	♦ *2.4	3
Indirect obstetric causes — Décès maternels indirects	-	1	♦ *1.1	-	-	-	-	-
Certain conditions originating in the perinatal period — Certaines affections dont l'origine se situe dans la période périnatale	*137.1	154	*168.4	170	*206.8	178	*214.4	171
Congenital malformations, deformations and chromosomal abnormalities — Malformations congénitales et anomalies chromosomiques	*315.1	245	*267.9	294	*357.7	299	*360.2	288
Symptoms, signs and abnormal clinical and laboratory findings, not elsewhere classified — Symptômes, signes et résultats anormaux d'examens cliniques et de laboratoire, non classés ailleurs	28.6	2 433	27.3	1 907	27.1	1 970	27.9	2 008
All other diseases — Toutes autres maladies	1.6	163	1.8	60	0.9	71	1.0	76
External causes — Causes externes								
Total	48.1	4 659	52.4	3 807	54.1	3 668	51.9	3 583
Accidents — Accidents								
Total	29.4	2 861	32.2	2 150	30.5	2 064	29.2	2 067
Transport accidents — Accidents de transport	7.0	637	7.2	742	10.5	638	9.0	629
Falls — Chutes	5.5	543	6.1	923	13.1	969	13.7	1 010
Accidental drowning and submersion — Noyade et submersion accidentelles	1.3	122	1.4	65	0.9	56	0.8	75
Exposure to smoke, fire and flames — Exposition à la fumée, au feu et aux flammes	1.0	101	1.1	20	♦0.3	36	0.5	49
Accidental poisoning by and exposure to noxious substances — Intoxication accidentelle par des substances nocives et exposition à ces substances	2.5	306	3.4	54	0.8	25	♦0.4	23
Intentional self-harm — Lésions auto-infligées	12.7	1 196	13.4	1 419	20.2	1 431	20.2	1 341
Assault — Agresssions	1.0	86	1.0	68	1.0	77	1.1	100
All other external causes — Toutes autres causes externes	5.0	516	5.8	170	2.4	96	1.4	75

21. Death and death rates by cause: 1995 - 2002
Décès selon la cause, nombres et taux: 1995 - 2002 (continued — suite)

(See notes at end of table. — Voir notes à la fin du tableau.)

Switzerland — Suisse

Cause of death — Cause de décès	1997 Rate Taux	1998 Number Nombre	1998 Rate Taux	1999 Number Nombre	1999 Rate Taux	2000 Number Nombre	2000 Rate Taux	2001 Number Nombre
Diseases of the digestive system — Maladies de l'appareil digestif Diseases of the liver — Maladies du foie	10.8	735	10.3	753	10.5	678	9.4	718
Diseases of the musculoskeletal system and connective tissue — Maladies du système ostéo-articularie, des muscles et du tissu conjonctif	6.0	475	6.7	469	6.6	451	6.3	493
Diseases of the genitourinary system — Maladies de l'appareil génito-urinaire Total	8.9	641	9.0	618	8.7	636	8.9	621
Disorders of kidney and ureter — Affections du rein et de l'uretère	5.8	410	5.8	411	5.8	401	5.6	381
Hyperplasia of prostate — Hyperplasie de la prostate	...	35	▼3.3	31	▼2.9	34	...	33
Pregnancy, childbirth and the puerperium — Grossesse, accouchement et puerpéralité Total	♦ *3.7	3	♦ *3.8	6	♦ *7.7	5	♦ *6.4	1
Pregnancy with abortive outcome — Grossesse se terminant par un avortement	-	1	♦ *1.3	1	♦ *1.3	-	-	-
Other direct obstetric causes — Autres décès maternels directs	♦ *3.7	2	♦ *2.5	5	♦ *6.4	4	♦ *5.1	1
Indirect obstetric causes — Décès maternels indirects	-	-	-	-	-	1	♦ *1.3	-
Certain conditions originating in the perinatal period — Certaines affections dont l'origine se situe dans la période périnatale	*212.2	163	*206.5	153	*195.1	174	*221.8	179
Congenital malformations, deformations and chromosomal abnormalities — Malformations congénitales et anomalies chromosomiques	*357.4	272	*344.5	263	*335.4	273	*348.0	246
Symptoms, signs and abnormal clinical and laboratory findings, not elsewhere classified — Symptômes, signes et résultats anormaux d'examens cliniques et de laboratoire, non classés ailleurs	28.3	2 115	29.7	2 021	28.3	2 003	27.9	2 072
All other diseases — Toutes autres maladies	1.1	92	1.3	108	1.5	91	1.3	107
External causes — Causes externes Total	50.5	3 561	50.1	3 474	48.6	3 744	52.1	3 681
Accidents — Accidents Total	29.2	2 036	28.6	2 011	28.1	2 194	30.5	2 137
Transport accidents — Accidents de transport	8.9	606	8.5	572	8.0	630	8.8	553
Falls — Chutes	14.2	987	13.9	992	13.9	1 093	15.2	1 071
Accidental drowning and submersion — Noyade et submersion accidentelles	1.1	61	0.9	64	0.9	53	0.7	82
Exposure to smoke, fire and flames — Exposition à la fumée, au feu et aux flammes	0.7	36	0.5	32	0.4	36	0.5	36
Accidental poisoning by and exposure to noxious substances — Intoxication accidentelle par des substances nocives et exposition à ces substances	*0.3	23	*0.3	14	*0.2	31	0.4	43
Intentional self-harm — Lésions auto-infligées	18.9	1 371	19.3	1 296	18.1	1 378	19.2	1 336
Assault — Agresssions	1.4	59	0.8	71	1.0	57	0.8	82
All other external causes — Toutes autres causes externes	1.1	95	1.3	96	1.3	115	1.6	126

(See notes at end of table. — Voir notes à la fin du tableau.)

Cause of death — Cause de décès	Switzerland — Suisse	The Former Yougoslav Rep. of Macedonia — L'ex-République yougoslave de Macédoine						
	2001	1995		1996		1997		1998
	Rate Taux	Number Nombre	Rate Taux	Number Nombre	Rate Taux	Number Nombre	Rate Taux	Number Nombre
Diseases of the digestive system — Maladies de l'appareil digestif								
Diseases of the liver — Maladies du foie	9.9	146	7.4	129	6.5	156	7.8	151
Diseases of the musculoskeletal system and connective tissue — Maladies du système ostéo-articularie, des muscles et du tissu conjonctif	6.8	8	◆0.4	-	-	5	◆0.3	8
Diseases of the genitourinary system — Maladies de l'appareil génito-urinaire								
Total	8.6	226	11.5	233	11.8	210	10.5	234
Disorders of kidney and ureter — Affections du rein et de l'uretère	5.3	211	10.7	215	10.9	202	10.1	209
Hyperplasia of prostate — Hyperplasie de la prostate	▼3.0	12	...	14	...	7	◆ ▼3.2	22
Pregnancy, childbirth and the puerperium — Grossesse, accouchement et puerpéralité								
Total	◆ *1.4	7	◆ *21.8	-	-	1	◆ *3.4	1
Pregnancy with abortive outcome — Grossesse se terminant par un avortement	-	2	◆ *6.2	-	-	-	-	-
Other direct obstetric causes — Autres décès maternels directs	◆ *1.4	5	◆ *15.6	-	-	1	◆ *3.4	1
Indirect obstetric causes — Décès maternels indirects	-	-	-	-	-	-	-	-
Certain conditions originating in the perinatal period — Certaines affections dont l'origine se situe dans la période périnatale	*243.5	339	*1054.3	262	*834.3	241	*817.6	255
Congenital malformations, deformations and chromosomal abnormalities — Malformations congénitales et anomalies chromosomiques	*334.7	82	*255.0	74	*235.6	69	*234.1	80
Symptoms, signs and abnormal clinical and laboratory findings, not elsewhere classified — Symptômes, signes et résultats anormaux d'examens cliniques et de laboratoire, non classés ailleurs	28.6	1 777	90.5	1 495	75.7	1 468	73.5	1 605
All other diseases — Toutes autres maladies	1.5	3	◆0.2	2	◆0.1	-	-	2
External causes — Causes externes								
Total	50.9	554	28.2	618	31.3	648	32.5	708
Accidents — Accidents								
Total	29.5	356	18.1	421	21.3	448	22.3	507
Transport accidents — Accidents de transport	7.6	104	5.3	158	8.0	150	7.5	150
Falls — Chutes	14.8	17	◆0.0	21	◆1.1	31	1.6	56
Accidental drowning and submersion — Noyade et submersion accidentelles	1.1	18	◆0.9	17	◆0.9	27	◆1.4	21
Exposure to smoke, fire and flames — Exposition à la fumée, au feu et aux flammes	0.5	7	◆0.4	5	◆0.3	6	◆0.3	9
Accidental poisoning by and exposure to noxious substances — Intoxication accidentelle par des substances nocives et exposition à des substances	0.6	5	◆0.3	6	◆0.3	5	◆0.3	25
Intentional self-harm — Lésions auto-infligées	18.5	131	6.7	146	7.4	155	7.8	153
Assault — Agresssions	1.1	32	1.6	48	2.4	47	2.4	45
All other external causes — Toutes autres causes externes	1.7	35	1.8	3	◆0.2	-	-	3

21. Death and death rates by cause: 1995 - 2002
Décès selon la cause, nombres et taux: 1995 - 2002 (continued — suite)

(See notes at end of table. — Voir notes à la fin du tableau.)

Cause of death — Cause de décès	The Former Yougoslav Rep. of Macedonia — L'ex-République yougoslave de Macédoine					Ukraine[6]		
	1998	1999		2000		1995		1996
	Rate Taux	Number Nombre	Rate Taux	Number Nombre	Rate Taux	Number Nombre	Rate Taux	Number Nombre
Diseases of the digestive system — Maladies de l'appareil digestif								
Diseases of the liver — Maladies du foie	7.5	133	6.6	132	6.5	...	...	...
Diseases of the musculoskeletal system and connective tissue — Maladies du système ostéo-articularie, des muscles et du tissu conjonctif	◆0.4	5	◆0.2	2	◆0.1	924	1.8	801
Diseases of the genitourinary system — Maladies de l'appareil génito-urinaire								
Total	11.7	248	12.3	246	12.2	6 129	11.8	5 751
Disorders of kidney and ureter — Affections du rein et de l'uretère	10.4	221	11.0	223	11.0	4 404	8.5	4 208
Hyperplasia of prostate — Hyperplasie de la prostate	◆ ▼9.8	25	◆ ▼10.9	20	...	817	▼13.2	702
Pregnancy, childbirth and the puerperium — Grossesse, accouchement et puerpéralité								
Total	◆ *3.4	2	◆ *7.3	4	◆ *13.6	159	*32.3	142
Pregnancy with abortive outcome — Grossesse se terminant par un avortement	-	-	-	-	-	39	*7.9	33
Other direct obstetric causes — Autres décès maternels directs	◆ *3.4	2	◆ *7.3	4	◆ *13.6	...	...	...
Indirect obstetric causes — Décès maternels indirects	-	-	-	-	-	...	...	...
Certain conditions originating in the perinatal period — Certaines affections dont l'origine se situe dans la période périnatale	*872.0	234	*856.9	208	*709.7	2 391	*485.1	2 372
Congenital malformations, deformations and chromosomal abnormalities — Malformations congénitales et anomalies chromosomiques	*273.6	78	*285.6	66	*225.2	3 242	*657.8	3 128
Symptoms, signs and abnormal clinical and laboratory findings, not elsewhere classified — Symptômes, signes et résultats anormaux d'examens cliniques et de laboratoire, non classés ailleurs	79.9	1 556	77.1	1 440	71.1	48 929	94.6	45 740
All other diseases — Toutes autres maladies	◆0.1	1	0.0	2	◆0.1	711	1.4	723
External causes — Causes externes								
Total	35.3	775	38.4	728	36.0	82 697	159.9	80 352
Accidents — Accidents								
Total	25.3	550	27.3	517	25.5	47 248	91.3	45 471
Transport accidents — Accidents de transport	7.5	122	6.0	115	5.7	9 906	19.2	8 394
Falls — Chutes	2.8	47	2.3	59	2.9	3 148	6.1	2 835
Accidental drowning and submersion — Noyade et submersion accidentelles	◆1.0	26	◆1.3	23	◆1.1	5 244	10.1	4 695
Exposure to smoke, fire and flames — Exposition à la fumée, au feu et aux flammes	◆0.4	9	◆0.4	11	◆0.5	1 580	3.1	1 765
Accidental poisoning by and exposure to noxious substances — Intoxication accidentelle par des substances nocives et exposition à ces substances	◆1.2	24	◆1.2	15	◆0.7	15 463	29.9	15 644
Intentional self-harm — Lésions auto-infligées	7.6	170	8.4	150	7.4	14 587	28.2	15 258
Assault — Agresssions	2.2	53	2.6	61	3.0	7 655	14.8	7 646
All other external causes — Toutes autres causes externes	◆0.1	2	◆0.1	-	-	13 207	25.5	11 977

(See notes at end of table. — Voir notes à la fin du tableau.)

Ukraine[6]

Cause of death — Cause de décès	1996 Rate Taux	1997 Number Nombre	1997 Rate Taux	1998 Number Nombre	1998 Rate Taux	1999 Number Nombre	1999 Rate Taux	2000 Number Nombre
Diseases of the digestive system — Maladies de l'appareil digestif								
Diseases of the liver — Maladies du foie	...	...	...	...	...	...	...	...
Diseases of the musculoskeletal system and connective tissue — Maladies du système ostéo-articulaire, des muscles et du tissu conjonctif	1.6	765	1.5	741	1.5	763	1.5	794
Diseases of the genitourinary system — Maladies de l'appareil génito-urinaire								
Total	11.2	5 204	10.2	4 812	9.5	4 999	10.0	4 665
Disorders of kidney and ureter — Affections du rein et de l'uretère	8.2	3 826	7.5	3 602	7.1	3 638	7.3	3 393
Hyperplasia of prostate — Hyperplasie de la prostate	...	593	▼9.9	530	▼8.9	522	▼8.8	486
Pregnancy, childbirth and the puerperium — Grossesse, accouchement et puerpéralité								
Total	*30.4	111	*25.1	114	*27.2	98	...	95
Pregnancy with abortive outcome — Grossesse se terminant par un avortement	*7.1	20	◆ *4.5	24	◆ *5.7	21	...	19
Other direct obstetric causes — Autres décès maternels directs	...	...	...	...	...	...	...	...
Indirect obstetric causes — Décès maternels indirects	...	...	...	...	...	...	...	...
Certain conditions originating in the perinatal period — Certaines affections dont l'origine se situe dans la période périnatale	*507.7	2 318	*523.7	2 044	*487.6	1 903	...	1 785
Congenital malformations, deformations and chromosomal abnormalities — Malformations congénitales et anomalies chromosomiques	*669.5	2 964	*669.7	2 479	*591.3	2 420	...	2 412
Symptoms, signs and abnormal clinical and laboratory findings, not elsewhere classified — Symptômes, signes et résultats anormaux d'examens cliniques et de laboratoire, non classés ailleurs	89.1	36 328	71.4	30 031	59.5	28 220	56.3	26 838
All other diseases — Toutes autres maladies	1.4	616	1.2	573	1.1	636	1.3	625
External causes — Causes externes								
Total	156.5	74 684	146.7	69 912	138.4	71 239	142.2	73 575
Accidents — Accidents								
Total	88.6	42 430	83.4	38 594	76.4	39 296	78.4	41 128
Transport accidents — Accidents de transport	16.4	7 552	14.8	6 996	13.9	6 674	13.3	7 197
Falls — Chutes	5.5	2 432	4.8	2 231	4.4	2 204	4.6	2 593
Accidental drowning and submersion — Noyade et submersion accidentelles	9.1	4 523	8.9	5 155	10.2	5 192	10.4	4 267
Exposure to smoke, fire and flames — Exposition à la fumée, au feu et aux flammes	3.4	1 697	3.3	1 459	2.9	1 705	3.4	1 842
Accidental poisoning by and exposure to noxious substances — Intoxication accidentelle par des substances nocives et exposition à ces substances	30.5	14 797	29.1	12 676	25.1	12 901	25.7	13 993
Intentional self-harm — Lésions auto-infligées	29.7	14 978	29.4	14 860	29.4	14 452	28.8	14 558
Assault — Agressions	14.9	6 585	12.9	6 109	12.1	6 260	12.5	6 458
All other external causes — Toutes autres causes externes	23.3	10 691	21.0	10 349	20.5	11 231	22.4	11 431

21. Death and death rates by cause: 1995 - 2002
Décès selon la cause, nombres et taux: 1995 - 2002 (continued — suite)

(See notes at end of table. — Voir notes à la fin du tableau.)

Cause of death — Cause de décès	Ukraine[6]					United Kingdom — Royaume-Uni		
	2000	2001		2002		1995		1996
	Rate Taux	Number Nombre	Rate Taux	Number Nombre	Rate Taux	Number Nombre	Rate Taux	Number Nombre
Diseases of the digestive system — Maladies de l'appareil digestif	...	...	...	...	...	4 290	7.3	4 599
Diseases of the liver — Maladies du foie	...	...	...	...	...			
Diseases of the musculoskeletal system and connective tissue — Maladies du système ostéo-articularie, des muscles et du tissu conjonctif	1.6	857	1.7	776	1.6	3 992	6.8	3 805
Diseases of the genitourinary system — Maladies de l'appareil génito-urinaire								
Total	9.4	4 423	9.0	4 266	8.8	8 317	14.2	7 860
Disorders of kidney and ureter — Affections du rein et de l'uretère	6.8	3 259	6.6	3 112	6.4	4 627	7.9	4 336
Hyperplasia of prostate — Hyperplasie de la prostate	▼8.1	415	▼6.9	357	...	295	▼3.6	249
Pregnancy, childbirth and the puerperium — Grossesse, accouchement et puerpéralité								
Total	*24.7	90	*23.9	85	*21.8	51	*7.0	48
Pregnancy with abortive outcome — Grossesse se terminant par un avortement	♦ *4.9	19	♦ *5.0	11	♦ *2.8	8	♦ *1.1	4
Other direct obstetric causes — Autres décès maternels directs	...	...	...	...	...	37	*5.1	38
Indirect obstetric causes — Décès maternels indirects	...	...	...	...	...	6	♦ *0.8	6
Certain conditions originating in the perinatal period — Certaines affections dont l'origine se situe dans la période périnatale	*463.5	1 689	*448.6	1 571	*402.1	2 391	*326.6	2 367
Congenital malformations, deformations and chromosomal abnormalities — Malformations congénitales et anomalies chromosomiques	*626.3	2 125	*564.4	2 182	*558.5	2 026	*276.8	1 950
Symptoms, signs and abnormal clinical and laboratory findings, not elsewhere classified — Symptômes, signes et résultats anormaux d'examens cliniques et de laboratoire, non classés ailleurs	54.0	26 317	53.7	28 563	59.0	10 269	17.5	11 260
All other diseases — Toutes autres maladies	1.3	647	1.3	700	1.4	1 243	2.1	1 208
External causes — Causes externes								
Total	148.0	75 318	153.6	76 311	157.7	19 116	32.6	19 165
Accidents — Accidents								
Total	82.7	44 870	91.5	46 474	96.0	12 027	20.5	12 437
Transport accidents — Accidents de transport	14.5	8 853	18.1	9 444	19.5	3 875	6.6	3 864
Falls — Chutes	5.2	2 814	5.7	3 155	6.5	4 369	7.5	4 409
Accidental drowning and submersion — Noyade et submersion accidentelles	8.6	5 108	10.4	4 447	9.2	289	0.5	250
Exposure to smoke, fire and flames — Exposition à la fumée, au feu et aux flammes	3.7	2 036	4.2	2 409	5.0	537	0.9	557
Accidental poisoning by and exposure to noxious substances — Intoxication accidentelle par des substances nocives et exposition à ces substances	28.1	14 493	29.6	15 097	31.2	990	1.7	1 147
Intentional self-harm — Lésions auto-infligées	29.3	13 244	27.0	12 543	25.9	4 315	7.4	4 165
Assault — Agresssions	13.0	6 175	12.6	5 709	11.8	571	1.0	493
All other external causes — Toutes autres causes externes	23.0	11 029	22.5	11 585	23.9	2 203	3.8	2 070

21. Death and death rates by cause: 1995 - 2002
Décès selon la cause, nombres et taux: 1995 - 2002 (continued — suite)

(See notes at end of table. — Voir notes à la fin du tableau.)

United Kingdom — Royaume-Uni

Cause of death — Cause de décès	1996	1997		1998		1999		2000
	Rate Taux	Number Nombre	Rate Taux	Number Nombre	Rate Taux	Number Nombre	Rate Taux	Number Nombre
Diseases of the digestive system — Maladies de l'appareil digestif								
Diseases of the liver — Maladies du foie	7.8	4 942	8.4	5 404	9.1	5 706	9.6	5 972
Diseases of the musculoskeletal system and connective tissue — Maladies du système ostéo-articularie, des muscles et du tissu conjonctif	6.5	3 873	6.6	3 883	6.6	3 904	6.6	3 853
Diseases of the genitourinary system — Maladies de l'appareil génito-urinaire								
Total	13.4	7 919	13.4	8 117	13.7	8 497	14.3	8 421
Disorders of kidney and ureter — Affections du rein et de l'uretère	7.4	4 187	7.1	4 166	7.0	4 147	7.0	4 106
Hyperplasia of prostate — Hyperplasie de la prostate	▼3.0	260	▼3.1	219	▼2.5	220	▼2.5	200
Pregnancy, childbirth and the puerperium — Grossesse, accouchement et puerpéralité								
Total	*6.5	39	*5.4	49	*6.8	37	*5.3	46
Pregnancy with abortive outcome — Grossesse se terminant par un avortement	♦ *0.5	2	♦ *0.3	7	♦ *1.0	5	♦ *0.7	8
Other direct obstetric causes — Autres décès maternels directs	*5.2	25	*3.4	30	*4.2	25	*3.6	28
Indirect obstetric causes — Décès maternels indirects	♦ *0.8	12	♦ 1.7	12	♦ *1.7	7	♦ *1.0	10
Certain conditions originating in the perinatal period — Certaines affections dont l'origine se situe dans la période périnatale	*322.8	2 211	*304.3	2 158	*301.0	2 123	*303.3	2 007
Congenital malformations, deformations and chromosomal abnormalities — Malformations congénitales et anomalies chromosomiques	*265.9	1 957	*269.3	1 875	*261.5	1 834	*262.0	1 762
Symptoms, signs and abnormal clinical and laboratory findings, not elsewhere classified — Symptômes, signes et résultats anormaux d'examens cliniques et de laboratoire, non classés ailleurs	19.1	12 833	21.7	14 461	24.4	15 288	25.7	14 227
All other diseases — Toutes autres maladies	2.1	1 164	2.0	1 227	2.1	1 309	2.2	1 402
External causes — Causes externes								
Total	32.6	19 286	32.7	19 159	32.3	19 598	32.9	19 530
Accidents — Accidents								
Total	21.1	12 533	21.2	12 168	20.5	12 545	21.1	12 492
Transport accidents — Accidents de transport	6.6	3 899	6.6	3 635	6.1	3 628	6.1	3 521
Falls — Chutes	7.5	4 642	7.9	4 605	7.0	4 867	8.2	5 087
Accidental drowning and submersion — Noyade et submersion accidentelles	0.4	244	0.4	241	0.4	256	0.4	210
Exposure to smoke, fire and flames — Exposition à la fumée, au feu et aux flammes	0.9	524	0.9	470	0.8	441	0.7	434
Accidental poisoning by and exposure to noxious substances — Intoxication accidentelle par des substances nocives et exposition à ces substances	2.0	1 126	1.9	1 119	1.9	1 098	1.8	1 123
Intentional self-harm — Lésions auto-infligées	7.1	4 143	7.0	4 389	7.4	4 448	7.5	4 290
Assault — Agresssions	0.8	401	0.7	415	0.7	440	0.7	529
All other external causes — Toutes autres causes externes	3.5	2 200	3.7	2 187	3.7	2 165	3.6	2 219

21. Death and death rates by cause: 1995 - 2002
Décès selon la cause, nombres et taux: 1995 - 2002 (continued — suite)

(See notes at end of table. — Voir notes à la fin du tableau.)

Cause of death — Cause de décès	United Kingdom — Royaume-Uni					Australia — Australie		
	2000	2001		2002		1995		1996
	Rate Taux	Number Nombre	Rate Taux	Number Nombre	Rate Taux	Number Nombre	Rate Taux	Number Nombre
Diseases of the digestive system — Maladies de l'appareil digestif								
Diseases of the liver — Maladies du foie	10.0	7 516	12.6	7 858	13.3	986	5.5	1 072
Diseases of the musculoskeletal system and connective tissue — Maladies du système ostéo-articulaire, des muscles et du tissu conjonctif	6.4	5 039	8.4	5 121	8.6	724	4.0	783
Diseases of the genitourinary system — Maladies de l'appareil génito-urinaire								
Total	14.1	8 930	14.9	9 798	16.5	2 069	11.4	2 246
Disorders of kidney and ureter — Affections du rein et de l'uretère	6.9	4 680	7.8	4 945	8.3	1 650	9.1	1 832
Hyperplasia of prostate — Hyperplasie de la prostate	...	170	...	180	...	61	▼2.8	42
Pregnancy, childbirth and the puerperium — Grossesse, accouchement et puerpéralité								
Total	*6.8	50	*7.5	40	*6.0	21	♦ *8.2	13
Pregnancy with abortive outcome — Grossesse se terminant par un avortement	♦ *1.2	4	♦ *0.6	4	♦ *0.6	3	♦ *1.2	1
Other direct obstetric causes — Autres décès maternels directs	♦ *4.1	27	♦ *4.0	28	♦ *4.2	14	♦ *5.5	12
Indirect obstetric causes — Décès maternels indirects	♦ *1.5	19	♦ *2.8	8	♦ *1.2	4	♦ *1.6	-
Certain conditions originating in the perinatal period — Certaines affections dont l'origine se situe dans la période périnatale	*295.6	1 959	*292.8	1 927	*288.1	613	*239.3	668
Congenital malformations, deformations and chromosomal abnormalities — Malformations congénitales et anomalies chromosomiques	*259.5	2 025	*302.6	1 950	*291.6	659	*257.2	650
Symptoms, signs and abnormal clinical and laboratory findings, not elsewhere classified — Symptômes, signes et résultats anormaux d'examens cliniques et de laboratoire, non classés ailleurs	23.8	13 780	23.1	13 555	22.9	2 476	13.7	538
All other diseases — Toutes autres maladies	2.3	1 449	2.4	1 655	2.8	263	1.5	194
External causes — Causes externes								
Total	32.7	19 546	32.7	19 200	32.4	7 015	38.8	7 596
Accidents — Accidents								
Total	20.9	12 352	20.7	12 027	20.3	4 436	24.5	4 703
Transport accidents — Accidents de transport	5.9	3 514	5.9	3 440	5.8	2 139	11.8	2 203
Falls — Chutes	8.5	3 296	5.5	3 237	5.5	968	5.4	1 090
Accidental drowning and submersion — Noyade et submersion accidentelles	0.4	216	0.4	224	0.4	227	1.3	249
Exposure to smoke, fire and flames — Exposition à la fumée, au feu et aux flammes	0.7	452	0.8	423	0.7	119	0.7	133
Accidental poisoning by and exposure to noxious substances — Intoxication accidentelle par des substances nocives et exposition à ces substances	1.9	1 100	1.8	881	1.5	379	2.1	342
Intentional self-harm — Lésions auto-infligées	7.2	4 013	6.7	4 066	6.9	2 170	12.0	2 426
Assault — Agressions	0.9	501	0.8	513	0.9	298	1.6	323
All other external causes — Toutes autres causes externes	3.7	2 680	4.5	2 594	4.4	111	0.6	144

21. Death and death rates by cause: 1995 - 2002
Décès selon la cause, nombres et taux: 1995 - 2002 (continued — suite)

(See notes at end of table. — Voir notes à la fin du tableau.)

Australia — Australie

Cause of death — Cause de décès	1996 Rate Taux	1997 Number Nombre	1997 Rate Taux	1998 Number Nombre	1998 Rate Taux	1999 Number Nombre	1999 Rate Taux	2000 Number Nombre
Diseases of the digestive system — Maladies de l'appareil digestif								
Diseases of the liver — Maladies du foie	5.9	1 039	5.6	1 247	6.7	1 249	6.6	1 172
Diseases of the musculoskeletal system and connective tissue — Maladies du système ostéo-articularie, des muscles et du tissu conjonctif	4.3	651	3.5	758	4.1	863	4.6	856
Diseases of the genitourinary system — Maladies de l'appareil génito-urinaire								
Total	12.3	2 450	13.2	2 720	14.5	2 759	14.6	2 671
Disorders of kidney and ureter — Affections du rein et de l'uretère	10.0	1 703	9.2	2 058	11.0	2 108	11.1	2 024
Hyperplasia of prostate — Hyperplasie de la prostate	...	47	...	40	▼1.7	33	...	38
Pregnancy, childbirth and the puerperium — Grossesse, accouchement et puerpéralité								
Total	♦ *5.1	12	♦ *4.8	5	♦ *2.0	13	♦ *5.2	13
Pregnancy with abortive outcome — Grossesse se terminant par un avortement	♦ *0.4	-	-	1	♦ *0.4	-	-	1
Other direct obstetric causes — Autres décès maternels directs	♦ *4.7	11	♦ *4.4	3	♦ *1.2	12	♦ *4.8	11
Indirect obstetric causes — Décès maternels indirects	-	1	♦ *0.4	1	♦ *0.4	1	♦ *0.4	1
Certain conditions originating in the perinatal period — Certaines affections dont l'origine se situe dans la période périnatale	*263.2	629	*249.8	588	*235.6	642	*258.0	647
Congenital malformations, deformations and chromosomal abnormalities — Malformations congénitales et anomalies chromosomiques	*256.1	754	*299.4	620	*248.4	706	*283.7	622
Symptoms, signs and abnormal clinical and laboratory findings, not elsewhere classified — Symptômes, signes et résultats anormaux d'examens cliniques et de laboratoire, non classés ailleurs	2.9	497	2.7	610	3.3	605	3.2	641
All other diseases — Toutes autres maladies	1.1	214	1.2	272	1.5	305	1.6	253
External causes — Causes externes								
Total	41.5	7 542	40.7	8 198	43.8	8 284	43.8	8 173
Accidents — Accidents								
Total	25.7	4 453	24.0	4 892	26.1	5 224	27.6	5 191
Transport accidents — Accidents de transport	12.0	1 946	10.5	1 996	10.7	1 995	10.5	2 027
Falls — Chutes	6.0	1 110	6.0	472	2.5	518	2.7	577
Accidental drowning and submersion — Noyade et submersion accidentelles	1.4	283	1.4	249	1.3	265	1.4	239
Exposure to smoke, fire and flames — Exposition à la fumée, au feu et aux flammes	0.7	101	0.5	114	0.6	91	0.5	98
Accidental poisoning by and exposure to noxious substances — Intoxication accidentelle par des substances nocives et exposition à ces substances	1.9	366	2.0	694	3.7	1 069	5.6	836
Intentional self-harm — Lésions auto-infligées	13.2	2 646	14.3	2 633	14.1	2 488	13.1	2 388
Assault — Agresssions	1.8	317	1.7	295	1.6	294	1.6	303
All other external causes — Toutes autres causes externes	0.8	126	0.7	378	2.0	278	1.5	291

21. Death and death rates by cause: 1995 - 2002
Décès selon la cause, nombres et taux: 1995 - 2002 (continued — suite)

(See notes at end of table. — Voir notes à la fin du tableau.)

Cause of death — Cause de décès	Australia — Australie			Fiji — Fidji	New Zealand — Nouvelle Zélande			
	2000	2001		1999	1995		1996	
	Rate Taux	Number Nombre	Rate Taux	Number Nombre	Number Nombre	Rate Taux	Number Nombre	Rate Taux
Diseases of the digestive system — Maladies de l'appareil digestif								
Diseases of the liver — Maladies du foie	6.1	1 170	6.0	17	113	3.1	115	3.1
Diseases of the musculoskeletal system and connective tissue — Maladies du système ostéo-articularie, des muscles et du tissu conjonctif	4.5	897	4.6	-	143	3.9	160	4.3
Diseases of the genitourinary system — Maladies de l'appareil génito-urinaire								
Total	13.9	2 846	14.7	163	433	11.8	435	11.7
Disorders of kidney and ureter — Affections du rein et de l'uretère	10.6	2 093	10.8	162	305	8.3	304	8.1
Hyperplasia of prostate — Hyperplasie de la prostate	▼1.5	38	▼1.4	1	11	...	14	...
Pregnancy, childbirth and the puerperium — Grossesse, accouchement et puerpéralité								
Total	♦ *5.2	12	♦ *4.9	1	2	♦ *3.5	4	♦ *7.0
Pregnancy with abortive outcome — Grossesse se terminant par un avortement	♦ *0.4	-	-	-	-	-	-	-
Other direct obstetric causes — Autres décès maternels directs	♦ *4.4	12	♦ *4.9	1	2	♦ *3.5	4	♦ *7.0
Indirect obstetric causes — Décès maternels indirects	♦ *0.4	-	-	-	-	-	-	-
Certain conditions originating in the perinatal period — Certaines affections dont l'origine se situe dans la période périnatale	*259.2	657	*266.6	109	119	*206.3	149	*260.1
Congenital malformations, deformations and chromosomal abnormalities — Malformations congénitales et anomalies chromosomiques	*249.2	601	*243.9	25	181	*313.8	181	*316.0
Symptoms, signs and abnormal clinical and laboratory findings, not elsewhere classified — Symptômes, signes et résultats anormaux d'examens cliniques et de laboratoire, non classés ailleurs	3.3	528	2.7	837	183	5.0	165	4.4
All other diseases — Toutes autres maladies	1.3	281	1.4	-	67	1.8	59	1.6
External causes — Causes externes								
Total	42.7	7 808	40.2	152	1 808	49.2	1 737	46.5
Accidents — Accidents								
Total	27.1	4 773	24.6	-	1 192	32.4	1 103	29.6
Transport accidents — Accidents de transport	10.6	2 008	10.3	-	680	18.5	606	16.2
Falls — Chutes	3.0	630	3.2	...	257	7.0	267	7.2
Accidental drowning and submersion — Noyade et submersion accidentelles	1.2	242	1.2	...	70	1.9	60	1.6
Exposure to smoke, fire and flames — Exposition à la fumée, au feu et aux flammes ..	0.5	58	0.3	...	35	1.0	35	0.9
Accidental poisoning by and exposure to noxious substances — Intoxication accidentelle par des substances nocives et exposition à ces substances	4.4	605	3.1	...	23	♦0.6	26	♦0.7
Intentional self-harm — Lésions auto-infligées	12.5	2 456	12.7	...	545	14.8	540	14.5
Assault — Agresssions	1.6	304	1.6	...	45	1.2	68	1.8
All other external causes — Toutes autres causes externes	1.5	275	1.4	...	26	♦0.7	26	♦0.7

21. Death and death rates by cause: 1995 - 2002
Décès selon la cause, nombres et taux: 1995 - 2002 (continued — suite)

(See notes at end of table. — Voir notes à la fin du tableau.)

New Zealand — Nouvelle Zélande

Cause of death — Cause de décès	1997		1998		1999		2000	
	Number Nombre	Rate Taux	Number Nombre	Rate Taux	Number Nombre	Rate Taux	Number Nombre	Rate Taux
Diseases of the digestive system — Maladies de l'appareil digestif								
Diseases of the liver — Maladies du foie	126	3.3	111	2.9	143	3.7	129	3.3
Diseases of the musculoskeletal system and connective tissue — Maladies du système ostéo-articulaire, des muscles et du tissu conjonctif	151	4.0	196	5.1	190	5.0	213	5.5
Diseases of the genitourinary system — Maladies de l'appareil génito-urinaire								
Total	419	11.1	284	7.4	357	9.3	340	8.8
Disorders of kidney and ureter — Affections du rein et de l'uretère	296	7.8	223	5.8	268	7.0	279	7.2
Hyperplasia of prostate — Hyperplasie de la prostate	9	...	6	♦ ▼1.3	13	♦ ▼2.8	14	♦ ▼2.9
Pregnancy, childbirth and the puerperium — Grossesse, accouchement et puerpéralité								
Total	3	♦ *5.2	3	♦ *5.4	4	♦ *7.0	5	♦ *8.8
Pregnancy with abortive outcome — Grossesse se terminant par un avortement	-	-	-	-	-		2	♦ *3.5
Other direct obstetric causes — Autres décès maternels directs	2	♦ *3.5	1	♦ *1.8	3	♦ *5.3	-	-
Indirect obstetric causes — Décès maternels indirects	1	♦ *1.7	2	♦ *3.6	1	♦ *1.8	3	♦ *5.3
Certain conditions originating in the perinatal period — Certaines affections dont l'origine se situe dans la période périnatale	134	*232.1	109	*196.9	120	*210.3	152	*268.5
Congenital malformations, deformations and chromosomal abnormalities — Malformations congénitales et anomalies chromosomiques	191	*330.8	189	*341.5	176	*308.5	191	*337.4
Symptoms, signs and abnormal clinical and laboratory findings, not elsewhere classified — Symptômes, signes et résultats anormaux d'examens cliniques et de laboratoire, non classés ailleurs	129	3.4	100	2.6	124	3.2	118	3.1
All other diseases — Toutes autres maladies	59	1.6	31	0.8	29	♦0.8	55	1.4
External causes — Causes externes								
Total	1 783	47.2	1 671	43.8	1 695	44.2	1 614	41.8
Accidents — Accidents								
Total	1 131	29.9	1 020	26.7	1 104	28.8	1 019	26.4
Transport accidents — Accidents de transport	617	16.3	592	15.5	598	15.6	573	14.9
Falls — Chutes	243	6.4	199	5.2	269	7.0	251	6.5
Accidental drowning and submersion — Noyade et submersion accidentelles	72	1.9	74	1.9	72	1.9	58	1.5
Exposure to smoke, fire and flames — Exposition à la fumée, au feu et aux flammes ..	33	0.9	20	♦0.5	22	♦0.6	19	♦0.5
Accidental poisoning by and exposure to noxious substances — Intoxication accidentelle par des substances nocives et exposition à ces substances	25	♦0.7	11	♦0.3	9	♦0.2	31	0.8
Intentional self harm — Lésions auto infligées	562	14.9	574	15.0	516	13.5	458	11.9
Assault — Agressions	60	1.8	57	1.5	51	1.3	55	1.4
All other external causes — Toutes autres causes externes	22	♦0.6	20	♦0.5	24	♦0.6	82	2.1

GENERAL NOTES - NOTES GENERALES

Data exclude foetal deaths. Cause of death is classified according to the Tenth Revision. Rates are the number of deaths from each cause per 100 000 population except for the rates for 'Maternal conditions', 'Perinatal period conditions', 'Breast cancer', 'Cervix, uteri cancer', and 'Prostate cancer' where, as specified in footnotes, the base has been changed in order to relate the deaths more closely to the population actually at risk. For method of evaluation and limitations of data, see Technical Notes for this table. — Il n'est pas tenu compte des mortes foetales. Les causes de décès sont dérivé de la Dixième Révision. Les taux représentent le nombre de décès attribuables à chaque cause pour 100 000 personnes dans la population totale. Font exception à cette règle les taux pour les catégories 'Affections maternelles', 'Affections périnatales', 'Sein', 'Col de l'utérus' et 'Prostate', où comme il est indique dans les notes, on a changé la base pour mieux relier les décès à la population effectivement exposée au risque. Pour la méthode d'évaluation et les insuffisances des données, voir Notes techniques pour ce tableaux.

Data in bold refer to deaths by cause based on ICD-10 Classification, otherwise data refer to deaths by cause based on ICD-9 Classification. - Les données en typographie gras se rapportent aux Décès selon la cause basées sur la classification CIM-10, autrement les données se rapportent aux Décès selon la cause basées sur la classification CIM-9.

Italics: data from civil registers which are incomplete or of unknown completeness. — Italiques: données incomplètes ou dont le degré d'exactitude n'est pas connu provenant des registres de l'état civil.

FOOTNOTES - NOTES

♦ Rates based on 30 or fewer deaths. — Taux basés sur 30 décès ou moins.
* Per 100 000 live-born. — Pour 100 000 enfants nés vivants.
▲ Per 100 000 females of 15 years and over. — Pour 100 000 personnes du sexe féminin âgées de 15 ans et plus.
▼ Per 100 000 males of 50 years and over. — Pour 100 000 personnes du sexe masculin âgées de 50 ans et plus.

[1] Including Canadian residents temporarily in the United States, but excluding United States residents temporarily in Canada. — Y compris les résidents canadiens se trouvant temporairement aux Etats-Unis, mais non compris les résidents des Etats-Unis se trouvant temporairement au Canada.
[2] Including deaths of foreigners temporarily in the country. — Y compris les décès étrangers temporairement dans le pays.
[3] Including Carriacou and other dependencies in the Grenadines. - Y compris Carriacou et les autres dépendances du groupe des îles Grenadines.
[4] Excluding nomadic Indian tribes. — Non compris les tribus d'Indiens nomades.
[5] Excluding Indian jungle population. — Non compris les Indiens de la jungle.
[6] Excluding infants born alive after less than 28 weeks of gestation, less than 1 000 grammes in weight and 35 centimetres in length, who die within seven days of birth. — Non compris les enfants nés vivants après moins de 28 semaines de gestation, pesant moins de 1 000 grammes, mesurant moins de 35 centimètres et décédés dans les sept jours qui ont suivi leur naissance.
[7] Data on cause of deaths do not include those in the Abkhazia and South Osetia region; therefore rates are not computed. - Les données sur la cause des décès ne comprennent pas ceux de la région de Abkhazia et South Osetia, en

[8] Including data for East Jerusalem and Israeli residents in certain other territories under occupation by Israeli military forces since June 1967. — Y compris les données pour Jérusalem-Est et les résidents israéliens dans certains autres territoires occupés depuis 1967 par les forces.

[9] For Japanese nationals in Japan only. — Pour les nationaux japonais au Japon seulement.

[10] Excluding transients afloat and non-locally domiciled military and civilian services personnel and their dependents. — Non compris les personnes de passage à bord de navires, les militaires et agents civils domiciliés hors du territoire et les membres de leur.

[11] Including armed forces stationed outside the country, but excluding alien armed forces stationed in the area. — Y compris les militaires nationaux hors du pays, mais non compris les militaires étrangers en garnison sur le territoire.

[12] Excluding Faeroe Islands and Greenland. — Non compris les îles Féroé et le Gröenland.

[13] Including nationals temporarily outside the country. — Y compris les nationaux temporairement hors du pays.

[14] Including armed forces outside the country. — Y compris les militaires en garnison hors du pays.

[15] Deaths registered within one year of occurrence. — Décès enregistrés dans l'année que suit l'événement.

[16] Rates computed on population including civilian nationals temporarily outside the country. — Les taux calculés sur la base d'un chiffre de population qui comprend les civils nationaux temporairemen hors du pays.

[17] Including residents outside the country if listed in a Netherlands population register. — Y compris les résidents hors du pays, s'ils sont inscrits sur un registre de population néerlandais.

[18] Including residents temporarily outside the country. — Y compris les résidents temporairement hors du pays.

[19] Data on cause of deaths do not include those in the Transnistria region; therefore rates are not computed. - Les données sur la cause des décès ne comprennent pas ceux de la région de Transnistria,en conséquence, les taux n'ont pas étés calcules.

[20] Data on cause of deaths do not include those in the Chechnya region; therefore rates are not computed. - Les données sur la cause des décès ne comprennent pas ceux de la région de Chechnya,en conséquence, les taux n'ont pas étés calcules.

Table 22

Table 22 presents expectation of life at specified ages for each sex for the latest available year.

Description of variables: Expectation of life, e_x is defined as the average number of years of life remaining to persons reaching age x if they continued to be subject to the mortality conditions of the period indicated in the table.

Male and female expectations are shown separately for selected ages beginning at birth (age 0) and proceeding with ages 5, 10, 15, 20, 25, 30, 35, 40, 45, 50, 55, 60, 65, 70, 75, 85, 90, 95 and 100 years.

The table shows life expectancy derived from an abridged or full life table as reported by the country or area.

Data are shown with one decimal regardless of the number of digits provided in the original computation.

Life table computation: From the demographic point of view, a life table is regarded as a theoretical model of a population that is continuously replenished by births and depleted by deaths. The model gives a complete picture of the mortality experience of a population based on the assumption that the theoretical cohort is subject, throughout its existence, to the age-specific mortality rates observed at a particular time. Thus levels of mortality prevailing at the time a life table is constructed are assumed to remain unchanged into the future until all members of the cohort have died.

Reliability of data: The values shown in this table come from official life tables. It is assumed that, if necessary, the basic data (population and deaths classified by age and sex) have been adjusted for deficiencies before their use in constructing the life tables.

Limitations: Expectation-of-life values are subject to the same qualifications as have been set forth for population statistics in general and death statistics in particular, as discussed in sections 3 and 4, respectively, of the Technical Notes. They must be interpreted strictly using the underlying assumption that surviving cohorts are subjected to the same age-specific mortality rates of the period to which the life table refers.

Earlier data: Expectation of life at specified ages for each sex has been shown in previous issues of the *Demographic Yearbook*. Data included in this table update the series covering a period of years as follows:

Issue	Years Covered
Historical Supplement CD, 1997	1948 – 1997
Special Issue on Population Ageing and the Situation of Elderly Persons, 1991	1950 – 1990
Historical Supplement, 1979	1948 – 1977
1948	1896 – 1947

Tableau 22

Le tableau 22 présente les espérances de vie à des âges déterminés, pour chaque sexe, qui correspondent à la dernière année pour laquelle on dispose de données.

Description des variables : L'espérance de vie, e_x, se définit comme le nombre moyen d'années restant à vivre aux hommes et aux femmes qui ont atteint les âges indiqués, à supposer qu'ils continuent de connaître les mêmes conditions de mortalité observées pendant la période sur laquelle porte le tableau.

Les chiffres sont présentés séparément pour chaque sexe à partir de la naissance (âge 0) et pour les âges suivants : 5,10, 15, 20, 25, 30, 35, 40, 45, 50, 55, 60, 65, 70, 75, 80, 85, 90, 95 et 100 ans.

Dans le tableau figurent les espérances de vie calculées selon les tables de mortalité abrégées ou complètes communiquées par les pays et les zones.

Les données sont arrondies à la première décimale, indépendamment du nombre de décimales qui figurent dans le calcul initial.

Calcul des tables de mortalité : Du point de vue démographique, les tables de mortalité sont considérées comme des modèles théoriques représentant une population constamment reconstituée par les naissances et réduite par les décès. Ces modèles donnent un aperçu complet de la mortalité d'une population et reposent sur l'hypothèse que chaque cohorte théoriquement distinguée connaît, pendant toute son existence, le taux de mortalité par âge observé à un moment donné. Les mortalités correspondant à l'époque à laquelle sont calculées les tables de mortalité sont ainsi censées demeurer inchangées dans l'avenir jusqu'au décès de tous les membres de la cohorte.

Fiabilité des donnés : Étant donné que les chiffres figurant dans ce tableau proviennent de tables officielles de mortalité, elles sont toutes présumées sûres. En ce qui concerne les chiffres extraits de tables officielles de mortalité, on part du principe que les données de base (effectif de la population et nombre de décès selon l'âge et le sexe) ont été ajustées, en tant que de besoin, avant de servir à l'établissement de la table de mortalité.

Insuffisance des données : Les espérances de vie appellent les mêmes réserves que celles qui ont été formulées à propos des statistiques de la population en général et des statistiques de mortalité en particulier (voir les sections 3 et 4 des Notes techniques). Lorsque l'on interprète les données, il ne faut jamais perdre de vue que, par hypothèse, les cohortes de survivants sont soumises, pour chaque âge, aux conditions de mortalité de la période visée par la table de mortalité.

Données publiées antérieurement : Les espérances de vie à des âges déterminés pour chaque sexe figuraient déjà dans des éditions antérieures de l'*Annuaire démographique*. Les données présentées dans le tableau 22 actualisent les données qui portaient sur les périodes suivantes :

Éditions	Années considérées
Supplément historique (CD-ROM), 1997	1948 – 1997
Édition spéciale sur le vieillissement de la population et la situation des personnes âgées, 1991	1950 – 1990
Supplément rétrospectif, 1979	1948 – 1977
1948	1896 – 1947

22. Expectation of life at specified ages for each sex: latest available year, 1993 - 2002
Espérance de vie à un âge donné pour chaque sexe: dernière année disponible, 1993 - 2002

(See notes at end of table. — Voir notes à la fin du tableau.)

Continent, country or area and date / Continent, pays ou zone et date	0	5	10	15	20	25	30	35	40	45	50	55	60	65	70	75	80	85	90	95	100
AFRICA — AFRIQUE																					
Algeria - Algérie[1]																					
2000																					
Male	72.5	70.6	65.8	61.0	56.3	51.6	46.9	42.2	37.6	33.0	28.5	24.1	19.9	16.1	12.4	9.0	5.9	...	...	...	...
Female	74.2	72.1	67.3	62.5	57.7	52.9	48.1	43.3	38.6	34.0	29.5	25.1	20.7	16.6	12.8	9.3	6.1	...	...	...	...
Botswana[2]																					
1999																					
Male	65.7	...	...	...	...	...	...	...	...	...	...	...	...	...	...	...	...	...	...	...	...
Female	69.0	...	...	...	...	...	...	...	...	...	...	...	...	...	...	...	...	...	...	...	...
Egypt - Égypte																					
2001																					
Male	65.6	64.7	59.9	55.1	50.4	45.6	40.9	36.2	31.6	27.2	22.9	18.9	15.4	12.1	9.2	6.8	5.2	4.0	...	...	...
Female	67.4	66.8	62.0	57.2	52.3	47.5	42.7	37.9	33.1	28.4	23.9	19.5	15.5	11.7	8.6	5.7	4.0	2.8	...	...	...
Ethiopia - Éthiopie																					
1994																					
Male	49.8	55.2	51.2	46.8	42.7	38.9	35.0	31.1	27.4	23.7	20.2	16.9	13.8	11.0	8.6	6.5	5.0	...	...	...	...
Female	51.8	56.9	53.0	48.8	44.8	40.9	37.1	33.4	29.6	25.9	22.1	18.6	15.2	12.1	9.4	7.1	5.4	...	...	...	...
Lesotho																					
2001																					
Male	48.7	...	...	...	...	...	...	...	...	...	...	...	...	...	...	...	...	...	...	...	...
Female	56.3	...	...	...	...	...	...	...	...	...	...	...	...	...	...	...	...	...	...	...	...
Malawi[3]																					
1992 - 1997																					
Male	43.5	52.1	49.5	45.7	41.9	38.4	34.8	31.2	27.6	24.0	20.6	17.3	14.1	11.2	8.6	6.3	4.4	...	...	...	...
Female	46.8	54.5	52.0	48.2	44.4	40.6	36.9	33.2	29.6	25.9	22.2	18.6	15.1	11.9	9.2	6.8	4.6	...	...	...	...
2002																					
Male	42.8	...	...	...	...	...	...	...	...	...	...	...	...	...	...	...	...	...	...	...	...
Female	45.5	...	...	...	...	...	...	...	...	...	...	...	...	...	...	...	...	...	...	...	...
Mauritius - Maurice																					
1999 - 2001																					
Male	68.2	64.6	59.7	54.8	50.0	45.3	40.6	36.0	31.6	27.3	23.3	19.6	16.1	13.2	10.6	8.4	6.5	5.0	...	...	...
Female	75.3	71.4	66.5	61.6	56.7	51.8	47.1	42.3	37.5	32.9	28.4	24.2	20.3	16.6	13.3	10.5	8.1	6.2	...	...	...
2002 - 2004																					
Male	68.4	64.7	59.8	54.9	50.1	45.4	40.7	36.0	31.6	27.3	23.3	19.6	16.2	13.2	10.6	8.5	6.5	5.2	...	...	...
Female	75.3	71.4	66.5	61.5	56.7	51.8	47.0	42.2	37.4	32.8	28.3	24.0	20.1	16.6	13.3	10.5	8.1	6.1	...	...	...
Réunion																					
2001																					
Male	71.0	...	...	...	...	...	...	...	...	...	...	...	...	...	...	...	...	...	...	...	...
Female	79.4	...	...	...	...	...	...	...	...	...	...	...	...	...	...	...	...	...	...	...	...
Swaziland[4]																					
1997																					
Male	58.0	...	...	...	...	...	...	...	...	...	...	...	...	...	...	...	...	...	...	...	...
Female	63.0	...	...	...	...	...	...	...	...	...	...	...	...	...	...	...	...	...	...	...	...
Tunisia - Tunisie																					
1995																					
Male	69.6	67.5	62.7	57.9	53.1	48.4	43.8	39.2	34.6	30.1	25.8	21.6	17.7	14.1	10.8	7.9	5.2	3.5	...	...	...
Female	73.1	70.7	65.9	61.0	56.2	51.3	46.5	41.7	37.0	32.4	27.8	23.3	19.1	15.0	11.3	7.8	4.8	2.9	...	...	...
AMERICA, NORTH — AMERIQUE DU NORD																					
Aruba																					
2000																					
Male	70.0	65.4	60.5	55.6	50.9	46.7	42.3	37.7	33.0	28.5	24.2	20.1	16.3	13.1	10.4	8.1	5.7	3.9	...	...	...
Female	76.0	71.9	67.0	62.0	57.2	52.5	47.7	43.0	38.3	33.6	28.9	24.4	20.5	16.7	13.1	10.4	7.5	5.5	...	...	...
Canada																					
2000																					
Male	77.0	72.6	67.6	62.7	57.9	53.1	48.3	43.5	38.8	34.1	29.6	25.2	21.0	17.1	13.6	10.5	7.9	5.8	4.4	...	...
Female	82.2	77.6	72.7	67.7	62.8	57.9	53.0	48.1	43.3	38.5	33.8	29.3	24.9	20.6	16.7	13.1	9.8	7.1	5.1	...	...
Costa Rica																					
1990 - 1995																					
Male	72.9	69.5	64.6	59.8	54.9	50.3	45.6	40.8	36.2	31.6	27.1	22.8	18.8	15.1	11.8	9.1	6.9	...	...	...	...

22. Expectation of life at specified ages for each sex: latest available year, 1993 - 2002
Espérance de vie à un âge donné pour chaque sexe: dernière année disponible, 1993 - 2002 (continued — suite)

(See notes at end of table. — Voir notes à la fin du tableau.)

Continent, country or area and date / Continent, pays ou zone et date	0	5	10	15	20	25	30	35	40	45	50	55	60	65	70	75	80	85	90	95	100
AMERICA, NORTH — AMERIQUE DU NORD																					
Costa Rica																					
1990 - 1995																					
Female	77.6	73.9	69.0	64.1	59.2	54.3	49.4	44.6	39.9	35.2	30.6	26.2	21.9	17.9	14.1	10.7	7.8	...	...	...	...
Cuba																					
1998																					
Male	74.2	69.9	65.0	60.2	55.4	50.7	46.0	41.4	36.8	32.4	28.0	23.9	20.0	16.3	13.0	10.0	7.4	5.2	...	...	...
Female	78.2	73.8	68.9	64.0	59.1	54.3	49.5	44.7	40.0	35.3	30.8	26.4	22.2	18.3	14.6	11.3	8.3	5.7	...	...	...
Dominican Republic - République dominicaine																					
1995 - 2000																					
Male	69.8	67.7	62.9	58.1	53.4	48.8	44.2	39.7	35.2	30.8	26.5	22.4	18.5	15.0	11.8	9.1	7.1	...	...	...	...
Female	73.1	71.2	66.4	61.6	56.8	52.0	47.3	42.7	38.1	33.5	29.1	24.8	20.7	16.9	13.3	10.3	7.9	...	...	...	...
El Salvador																					
1995 - 2000																					
Male	66.5	64.6	59.9	55.1	50.5	46.2	42.0	37.8	33.8	29.7	25.8	22.0	18.3	14.9	11.7	8.9	6.6	...	...	...	...
Female	72.5	70.3	65.5	60.7	56.0	51.4	46.8	42.3	37.9	33.6	29.3	25.2	21.2	17.4	13.9	10.8	8.1	...	...	...	...
2000 - 2005																					
Male	67.7	...	...	...	...	...	...	...	...	...	...	...	...	...	...	...	...	...	...	...	...
Female	73.7	...	...	...	...	...	...	...	...	...	...	...	...	...	...	...	...	...	...	...	...
Greenland - Groenland																					
1995 - 1999																					
Male	62.7	59.4	54.6	50.0	46.2	42.6	38.8	34.5	30.2	26.0	21.6	17.6	14.0	10.9	8.1	6.1	4.8	...	...	...	...
Female	68.0	64.9	60.0	55.2	50.6	46.0	41.3	36.6	32.1	27.7	23.3	19.3	15.7	12.4	9.5	7.1	5.3	...	...	...	...
Guadeloupe																					
2002																					
Male	74.6	70.2	65.3	60.4	55.7	51.2	46.8	42.2	37.7	33.2	29.0	24.8	20.9	17.3	13.8	10.6	7.9	5.1	2.0	0.5	...
Female	81.5	77.0	72.1	67.1	62.1	57.3	52.4	47.6	42.9	38.2	33.5	28.8	24.4	20.3	16.4	12.7	9.0	5.7	2.3	0.5	...
Guatemala																					
1995 - 2000																					
Male	61.4	60.6	56.0	51.2	46.8	42.7	38.8	34.9	31.2	27.4	23.7	20.1	16.8	13.6	10.7	8.2	6.1	...	...	...	...
Female	67.2	66.2	62.6	56.9	52.2	47.7	43.3	38.9	34.6	30.4	26.3	22.3	18.6	15.2	12.0	9.2	6.9	...	...	...	...
Martinique																					
2002																					
Male	75.4	71.0	66.0	61.1	56.3	51.7	47.1	42.5	37.9	33.4	28.9	24.7	20.4	16.5	13.0	10.0	7.5	4.8	2.0	0.5	...
Female	82.2	77.7	72.8	67.9	62.9	58.0	53.0	48.1	43.3	38.6	34.0	29.3	24.8	20.3	16.3	12.3	8.9	5.5	2.3	0.5	...
Nicaragua																					
2000 - 2005																					
Male	67.2	65.3	60.6	55.7	51.2	46.8	42.4	38.2	34.0	29.9	25.9	22.1	18.5	15.2	12.1	9.4	6.9	...	...	...	...
Female	71.9	69.5	64.8	60.0	55.3	50.6	45.9	41.3	36.8	32.4	28.1	24.0	20.2	16.6	13.3	10.3	7.5	...	...	...	...
Panama[5]																					
2000																					
Male	72.2	69.2	64.4	59.5	54.8	50.2	45.6	41.0	36.4	31.9	27.5	23.3	19.3	15.6	12.4	9.5	7.1	...	...	...	...
Female	76.8	73.7	68.9	64.0	59.2	54.3	49.5	44.8	40.1	35.4	30.9	26.4	22.2	18.1	14.3	10.9	7.9	...	...	...	...
Puerto Rico - Porto Rico																					
1997 - 1999																					
Male	71.4	71.2	67.3	62.4	57.5	52.8	48.3	43.9	39.5	35.3	31.2	27.3	23.5	19.9	16.4	13.3	10.4	8.1	6.3	5.2	4.9
Female	79.3	79.2	75.2	70.3	65.4	60.4	55.6	50.8	46.0	41.3	36.7	32.1	27.7	23.4	19.4	15.8	12.4	9.5	7.2	5.7	5.0
Saint Kitts and Nevis - Saint-Kitts-et-Nevis																					
1998																					
Male	68.2	65.0	60.1	55.3	50.5	45.8	41.1	36.5	32.7	28.5	24.3	20.6	16.6	13.3	11.0	9.1	6.6	4.7	3.4	2.2	0.4
Female	70.7	67.5	62.5	57.6	52.7	48.0	43.4	38.8	34.4	29.8	25.4	21.2	17.6	14.2	11.3	8.9	6.3	4.6	3.3	2.2	0.4

(See notes at end of table. — Voir notes à la fin du tableau.)

Continent, country or area and date / Continent, pays ou zone et date	Age (in years) - Age (en années)																				
	0	5	10	15	20	25	30	35	40	45	50	55	60	65	70	75	80	85	90	95	100
AMERICA, NORTH — AMERIQUE DU NORD																					
Saint Lucia - Sainte-Lucie 2002																					
Male	72.0	68.0	63.2	58.3	53.6	49.2	44.7	40.2	35.8	31.5	27.4	23.7	20.4	16.9	13.6	11.3	9.3	7.2	...	...	...
Female	76.7	73.0	68.1	63.2	58.3	53.5	48.6	43.8	39.0	34.5	30.2	26.0	21.9	18.5	15.0	12.1	9.9	6.9	...	...	...
United States - États-Unis 2001																					
Male	74.4	70.1	65.2	60.2	55.5	50.9	46.2	41.5	37.0	32.5	28.2	24.0	20.1	16.4	13.1	10.2	7.7	5.7	4.2	3.2	2.5
Female	79.8	75.4	70.4	65.5	60.6	55.7	50.9	46.0	41.3	36.6	32.1	27.7	22.6	19.4	15.7	12.4	9.4	6.9	5.0	3.7	2.8
AMERICA, SOUTH — AMERIQUE DU SUD																					
Bolivia - Bolivie 1995 - 2000																					
Male	59.8	60.8	56.7	52.2	48.0	43.7	39.5	35.3	31.2	27.1	23.2	19.5	15.9	12.7	9.8	7.5	5.9	...	...	...	...
Female	63.2	63.8	59.7	55.2	50.8	46.5	42.1	37.8	33.6	29.4	25.3	21.4	17.6	14.0	10.8	8.3	6.5	...	...	...	...
Brazil - Brésil[6] 2002																					
Male	67.3	65.0	60.2	55.3	50.8	46.6	42.3	38.1	34.0	29.9	26.1	22.4	19.0	15.8	13.0	10.6	8.8	...	...	...	...
Female	74.9	72.2	67.3	62.4	57.6	52.8	48.1	43.4	38.8	34.3	30.0	25.9	21.9	18.3	15.0	12.0	9.6	...	...	...	...
Chile - Chili 2001 - 2002																					
Male	74.4	70.3	65.4	60.4	55.7	51.0	46.4	41.8	37.2	32.6	28.2	24.1	20.1	16.5	13.3	10.5	8.1	6.2	4.8	4.5	8.5
Female	80.4	76.2	71.2	66.3	61.4	56.5	51.6	46.8	41.9	37.2	32.5	28.0	23.7	19.7	15.9	12.5	9.5	7.1	5.2	3.9	2.9
Colombia - Colombie 2001 - 2006																					
Male	69.4	66.9	62.0	57.1	52.6	48.4	44.1	39.8	35.4	31.0	26.8	22.6	18.8	15.3	12.2	9.6	7.5	...	...	...	...
Female	75.5	72.8	67.9	63.0	58.2	53.4	48.7	43.9	39.2	34.6	30.1	25.8	21.7	17.9	14.5	11.5	9.2	...	...	...	...
2002 - 2007																					
Male	69.6	67.0	62.2	57.3	52.8	48.5	44.2	39.8	35.5	31.1	26.8	22.7	18.8	15.3	12.2	9.6	7.5	...	...	...	...
Female	75.7	72.9	68.0	63.2	58.3	53.6	48.8	44.0	39.3	34.7	30.2	25.8	21.8	17.9	14.5	11.5	9.2	...	...	...	...
Ecuador - Équateur[7] 2000 - 2005																					
Male	71.3	68.8	64.1	59.3	54.8	50.5	46.3	42.0	37.8	33.6	29.6	25.5	21.6	17.9	14.4	11.2	8.1	...	...	...	...
Female	77.2	74.2	69.4	64.5	59.8	55.1	50.4	45.7	41.1	36.6	32.2	27.8	23.7	19.6	15.8	12.2	8.8	...	...	...	...
French Guiana - Guyane française 2002																					
Male	72.5	68.7	63.8	58.9	54.2	49.7	45.0	40.7	36.3	32.1	27.9	23.8	19.8	16.4	12.8	9.7	7.3	4.8	2.0	0.5	...
Female	79.2	75.3	70.6	65.7	60.8	55.9	51.1	46.4	41.8	37.1	32.7	28.1	23.8	19.8	15.6	12.1	8.4	4.9	2.3	0.5	...
Paraguay 1990 - 1995																					
Male	66.3	65.5	60.8	56.0	51.3	46.7	42.1	37.5	32.9	28.5	24.2	20.2	16.5	13.2	10.2	7.7	5.6	...	...	...	...
Female	70.8	69.3	64.5	59.7	54.9	50.1	45.4	40.7	36.0	31.5	27.0	22.8	18.7	14.9	11.5	8.5	6.2	...	...	...	...
2000 - 2005																					
Male	68.6	...	...	...	...	...	...	...	...	...	...	...	...	...	...	...	...	...	...	...	...
Female	73.1	...	...	...	...	...	...	...	...	...	...	...	...	...	...	...	...	...	...	...	...
Peru - Pérou[6] 1995 - 2000																					
Male	65.9	65.9	61.4	56.6	52.0	47.4	42.9	38.5	34.1	29.8	25.6	21.7	18.1	14.7	11.7	9.2	7.0	...	...	...	...
Female	70.8	70.2	65.6	60.7	55.9	51.2	46.5	41.9	37.3	32.9	28.5	24.3	20.3	16.5	13.3	10.4	7.8	...	...	...	...
Uruguay 1995 - 1996																					
Male	69.6	66.4	61.4	56.6	51.9	47.2	42.6	38.0	33.4	28.9	24.6	20.7	17.1	14.0	11.1	8.7	6.6	5.0	3.7	3.0	...
Female	77.6	74.0	69.0	64.1	59.3	54.4	49.6	44.8	40.1	35.5	31.0	26.6	22.4	18.4	14.7	11.4	8.4	6.2	4.6	4.0	...

22. Expectation of life at specified ages for each sex: latest available year, 1993 - 2002
Espérance de vie à un âge donné pour chaque sexe: dernière année disponible, 1993 - 2002 (continued — suite)

(See notes at end of table. — Voir notes à la fin du tableau.)

Continent, country or area and date / Continent, pays ou zone et date	Age (in years) - Age (en années)																				
	0	5	10	15	20	25	30	35	40	45	50	55	60	65	70	75	80	85	90	95	100
AMERICA, SOUTH — AMERIQUE DU SUD																					
Venezuela[6] 1995 - 2000																					
Male	68.6	66.6	61.8	56.9	52.3	47.8	43.3	38.8	34.3	29.9	25.6	21.6	17.9	14.5	11.4	8.6	5.9	...	...	...	...
Female	74.4	72.1	67.2	63.3	57.4	52.6	47.8	43.1	38.4	33.7	29.2	24.9	20.8	16.9	13.3	9.9	6.9	...	...	...	...
ASIA — ASIE																					
Armenia - Arménie 2000																					
Male	70.6	67.0	62.1	57.2	52.4	47.6	42.8	38.1	33.4	29.0	23.9	20.6	16.8	13.5	10.5	7.8	5.0	1.0	...	...	...
Female	75.5	71.7	66.8	61.8	56.9	52.0	47.1	42.2	37.4	32.6	28.0	23.4	19.1	15.1	11.4	8.0	5.0	1.0	...	...	...
Azerbaijan - Azerbaïdjan 2002																					
Male	69.4	66.3	61.5	56.6	51.8	47.0	42.4	37.7	33.2	28.7	24.5	20.5	16.8	13.9	11.3	9.2	7.2	5.2	4.3	3.5	0.9
Female	75.0	71.2	66.5	61.5	56.6	51.8	47.0	42.2	37.4	32.6	28.0	23.6	19.4	15.7	12.4	9.6	7.1	5.2	3.7	3.1	0.9
Bahrain - Bahreïn 2001																					
Male	73.2	...	64.4	59.5	54.7	49.9	45.2	40.4	35.6	30.9	26.4	22.0	17.8	14.1	11.3	9.5	...	...	...	...	...
Female	76.2	...	67.1	62.1	57.2	52.3	47.4	42.5	37.7	32.9	28.2	23.7	19.6	15.9	12.9	10.9	...	...	...	...	...
Bangladesh 1994																					
Male	58.6	61.4	57.3	53.0	48.6	44.0	40.1	34.8	30.8	26.0	22.0	18.6	15.1	12.1	9.0	6.4	4.6	...	...	...	...
Female	58.2	60.4	56.6	51.4	47.1	42.6	38.4	34.1	30.0	26.2	22.3	18.5	15.0	11.9	8.6	5.9	4.0	...	...	...	...
Bhutan - Bhoutan[8] 1994																					
Male	66.0	...	...	...	...	...	...	...	...	...	...	...	...	...	...	...	...	...	...	...	...
Female	66.2	...	...	...	...	...	...	...	...	...	...	...	...	...	...	...	...	...	...	...	...
China - Chine[9] 2000																					
Male	69.6	...	...	...	...	...	...	...	...	...	...	...	...	...	...	...	...	...	...	...	...
Female	73.3	...	...	...	...	...	...	...	...	...	...	...	...	...	...	...	...	...	...	...	...
China: Hong Kong SAR - Chine: Hong Kong RAS 2001																					
Male	78.4	73.7	68.7	63.8	58.8	54.0	49.2	44.4	39.6	34.9	30.3	25.9	21.7	17.7	14.1	11.0	8.4	6.3	4.6	3.3	2.3
Female	84.6	79.9	74.9	70.0	65.0	60.1	55.2	50.3	45.4	40.6	35.8	31.1	26.5	22.1	18.0	14.3	11.0	8.3	6.0	4.2	2.9
China: Macao SAR - Chine: Macao RAS 1993 - 1996																					
Male	75.1	70.8	65.8	61.0	56.1	51.3	46.6	41.8	37.1	32.4	27.8	23.3	19.2	15.3	11.9	8.9	6.3	4.5	3.1	...	...
Female	80.0	75.6	70.7	65.7	60.8	55.9	51.0	46.2	41.3	36.5	31.8	27.2	22.7	18.6	14.7	11.3	8.4	6.0	4.2	...	...
Cyprus - Chypre[10] 1998 - 1999																					
Male	75.3	70.9	65.9	61.0	56.3	51.7	47.0	42.3	37.6	32.9	28.3	23.9	19.8	16.0	12.5	9.5	7.1	...	...	...	...
Female	80.4	76.0	71.0	66.1	61.2	56.3	51.4	46.7	41.8	37.0	32.3	27.7	23.2	18.9	15.1	11.6	8.8	...	...	...	...
India - Inde[11] 1993 - 1997																					
Male	60.4	62.2	57.8	53.1	48.5	44.0	39.5	35.1	30.7	26.5	22.5	18.9	15.5	12.6	10.1	...	...	...	...	...	...
Female	61.8	64.6	60.4	55.8	51.3	47.0	42.7	38.2	33.8	29.4	25.1	21.2	17.5	14.2	11.4	...	...	...	...	...	...
Indonesia - Indonésie 1990 - 1995																					
Male	61.0	...	...	...	...	...	...	...	...	...	...	...	...	...	...	...	...	...	...	...	...
Female	64.5	...	...	...	...	...	...	...	...	...	...	...	...	...	...	...	...	...	...	...	...

22. Expectation of life at specified ages for each sex: latest available year, 1993 - 2002
Espérance de vie à un âge donné pour chaque sexe: dernière année disponible, 1993 - 2002 (continued — suite)

(See notes at end of table. — Voir notes à la fin du tableau.)

Continent, country or area and date / Continent, pays ou zone et date	0	5	10	15	20	25	30	35	40	45	50	55	60	65	70	75	80	85	90	95	100
ASIA — ASIE																					
Iran (Islamic Republic of) - Iran (République islamique d')																					
2001																					
Male	67.6	...	...	...	...	...	...	...	...	...	...	...	...	...	...	...	...	...	...	...	...
Female	70.4	...	...	...	...	...	...	...	...	...	...	...	...	...	...	...	...	...	...	...	...
Israel - Israël[12]																					
2000																					
Male	76.5	72.1	67.2	62.2	57.4	52.7	47.9	43.1	38.4	33.8	29.3	24.9	20.7	16.8	13.4	10.4	7.8	5.7	4.3	3.3	2.1
Female	81.1	76.5	71.6	66.6	61.7	56.8	51.8	47.0	42.1	37.3	32.6	28.0	23.5	19.3	15.4	11.9	8.9	6.7	5.1	4.0	2.4
2002																					
Male	77.5	73.1	68.1	63.2	58.4	53.7	49.0	44.2	39.5	34.8	30.3	25.9	21.6	17.8	14.2	11.3	8.8	6.9	3.9	3.1	3.3
Female	81.5	77.0	72.1	67.1	62.2	57.3	52.4	47.5	42.6	37.8	33.1	28.5	24.0	19.7	15.7	12.2	9.1	6.6	4.2	3.4	3.2
Japan - Japon[13]																					
2001																					
Male	78.1	73.4	68.5	63.5	58.6	53.8	49.0	44.2	39.4	34.8	30.2	25.9	21.7	17.8	14.2	11.0	8.1	5.9	4.2	3.0	2.2
Female	84.9	80.3	75.3	70.3	65.4	60.5	55.6	50.7	45.8	41.0	36.3	31.7	27.1	22.7	18.4	14.4	10.8	7.8	5.4	3.8	2.7
2002																					
Male	78.3	73.7	68.7	63.8	58.9	54.0	49.2	44.4	39.6	35.0	30.4	26.1	21.9	18.0	14.3	11.1	8.2	6.0	4.3	3.1	2.3
Female	85.2	80.6	75.6	70.6	65.7	60.8	55.9	51.0	46.1	41.3	36.6	32.0	27.4	23.0	18.7	14.7	11.0	7.9	5.6	3.9	2.7
Jordan - Jordanie[14]																					
2001																					
Male	68.8	...	...	...	...	...	...	...	...	...	...	...	...	...	...	...	...	...	...	...	...
Female	71.1	...	...	...	...	...	...	...	...	...	...	...	...	...	...	...	...	...	...	...	...
Kazakhstan																					
1997																					
Male	59.0	56.3	51.4	46.6	42.0	37.7	33.5	29.5	25.6	22.0	18.6	15.7	13.0	10.8	8.7	6.9	5.4	4.2	3.2	2.4	1.8
Female	70.2	67.2	62.3	57.4	52.6	48.0	43.3	38.7	34.2	29.8	25.6	21.8	18.0	14.7	11.7	9.0	6.8	5.0	3.6	2.6	1.8
Korea (Dem. People's Republic of) - Corée (Rép. populaire dém. du)																					
1990 - 1995																					
Male	67.7	...	...	...	...	...	...	...	...	...	...	...	...	...	...	...	...	...	...	...	...
Female	73.9	...	...	...	...	...	...	...	...	...	...	...	...	...	...	...	...	...	...	...	...
Korea (Republic of) - Corée (République de)[15]																					
2001																					
Male	72.8	68.4	63.5	58.6	53.7	48.9	44.1	39.4	34.7	30.3	26.0	22.0	18.1	14.6	11.4	8.6	6.4	4.8	3.5	2.6	2.0
Female	80.0	75.6	70.7	65.7	60.8	55.9	51.0	46.2	41.3	36.6	31.9	27.2	22.7	18.4	14.4	10.9	7.9	5.7	4.2	3.2	2.6
Kuwait - Koweït																					
1992 - 1993																					
Male	71.8	67.9	63.0	58.2	53.6	48.9	44.2	39.4	34.7	30.0	25.6	21.4	17.3	14.1	10.8	7.8	4.4	2.5	...	...	...
Female	73.3	69.2	64.3	59.4	54.5	49.6	44.7	39.8	35.0	30.2	25.5	21.1	16.8	13.3	10.0	7.4	4.3	2.6	...	...	...
Kyrgyzstan - Kirghizistan																					
2001																					
Male	65.0	62.4	57.6	52.7	47.9	43.3	38.8	34.5	30.3	26.3	22.5	18.9	15.8	12.8	10.3	7.6	5.1	3.0	1.6	0.7	...
Female	72.6	69.7	64.8	59.9	55.0	50.2	45.4	40.7	36.1	31.5	27.1	22.8	18.9	15.1	11.7	8.4	5.5	3.2	1.7	0.8	>0
2002																					
Male	64.4	61.5	56.7	51.8	47.0	42.4	37.9	33.6	29.4	25.5	21.6	18.2	15.0	12.2	9.9	7.5	5.3	3.5	2.2	1.2	0.6
Female	72.1	68.9	64.0	59.1	54.2	49.4	44.7	40.0	35.4	30.9	26.5	22.2	18.3	14.6	11.2	8.1	5.6	3.6	2.1	1.2	0.6
Malaysia - Malaisie																					
1998																					
Male	69.6	65.6	60.8	55.9	51.3	46.7	42.2	37.6	33.1	28.6	24.3	20.2	16.5	13.1	10.2	7.7	5.6	...	...	...	...
Female	74.6	70.5	65.6	60.8	55.9	51.0	46.2	41.4	36.6	31.9	27.4	23.0	18.8	15.0	11.7	8.8	6.4	...	...	...	...
Maldives																					
1998																					
Male	70.6	67.8	63.0	58.2	53.4	48.6	43.8	39.0	34.4	29.7	25.5	21.4	18.0	14.7	11.6	8.8	6.0	...	...	...	...

22. Expectation of life at specified ages for each sex: latest available year, 1993 - 2002
Espérance de vie à un âge donné pour chaque sexe: dernière année disponible, 1993 - 2002 (continued — suite)

(See notes at end of table. — Voir notes à la fin du tableau.)

Continent, pays ou zone et date	0	5	10	15	20	25	30	35	40	45	50	55	60	65	70	75	80	85	90	95	100
ASIA — ASIE																					
Maldives																					
1998																					
Female	71.8	68.9	64.1	59.2	54.4	49.6	44.8	40.1	35.5	30.9	26.6	22.4	18.6	15.4	12.3	9.4	6.3	...	...	...	...
1999																					
Male	72.0	68.8	64.0	59.2	54.3	49.5	44.7	40.0	35.3	30.6	26.2	22.2	18.8	15.7	12.7	9.6	6.4	...	...	...	...
Female	73.2	69.8	65.0	60.2	55.3	50.5	45.7	40.9	36.3	31.7	27.3	23.1	19.3	16.2	13.0	9.9	6.6	...	...	...	...
Occupied Palestinian Territory - Territoire palestinien occupé																					
2001																					
Male	70.4	67.5	62.7	57.8	53.1	48.4	43.6	38.9	34.2	29.6	25.2	21.1	17.2	13.8	10.7	8.1	6.1	...	...	...	...
Female	73.6	70.3	65.4	60.5	55.7	50.9	46.1	41.3	36.6	32.0	27.5	23.2	19.0	15.2	11.7	8.8	6.4	...	...	...	...
Oman																					
2002																					
Male	72.2	...	...	...	...	...	...	...	...	...	...	...	...	...	...	...	...	...	...	...	...
Female	75.4	...	...	...	...	...	...	...	...	...	...	...	...	...	...	...	...	...	...	...	...
Pakistan[16]																					
2001																					
Male	64.5	66.2	61.6	56.9	52.2	47.6	43.2	38.8	34.6	30.4	26.3	22.4	18.8	15.4	12.4	9.9	7.9	5.8	...	...	...
Female	66.1	67.7	63.3	58.8	54.2	49.8	45.2	40.6	36.3	32.0	27.6	23.7	20.1	17.2	14.4	11.3	9.1	6.6	...	...	...
Singapore - Singapour[17]																					
2001																					
Male	76.4	71.7	66.7	61.8	56.9	52.1	47.2	42.4	37.6	32.9	28.3	23.9	19.8	16.0	12.6	9.5	6.8	4.5	...	...	...
Female	80.3	75.6	70.6	65.7	60.8	55.8	50.9	46.0	41.2	36.3	31.6	27.0	22.6	18.3	14.4	10.9	7.7	4.7	...	...	...
2002																					
Male	76.6	71.9	67.0	62.0	57.1	52.3	47.5	42.6	37.8	33.1	28.5	24.1	20.0	16.1	12.8	9.7	6.9	4.5	...	...	...
Female	80.7	75.9	70.9	66.0	61.0	56.1	51.2	46.3	41.4	36.6	31.8	27.2	22.8	18.5	14.6	10.9	7.7	4.7	...	...	...
Turkey - Turquie[18]																					
2000																					
Male	66.4	...	...	...	...	...	...	...	...	...	...	...	...	...	...	...	...	...	...	...	...
Female	71.0	...	...	...	...	...	...	...	...	...	...	...	...	...	...	...	...	...	...	...	...
EUROPE																					
Austria - Autriche																					
2002																					
Male	75.8	71.2	66.3	61.3	56.5	51.8	47.0	42.2	37.5	32.8	28.4	24.2	20.2	16.3	12.8	9.8	7.1	5.0	3.4	2.4	...
Female	81.7	77.0	72.0	67.1	62.2	57.3	52.4	47.4	42.6	37.8	33.1	28.6	24.2	19.8	15.7	11.9	8.6	5.9	3.9	2.7	...
Belarus - Bélarus																					
2002																					
Male	62.3	58.0	53.1	48.2	43.4	38.9	34.7	30.5	26.5	22.7	19.2	16.1	13.4	11.0	8.9	7.0	5.4	4.0	2.9	2.0	1.4
Female	74.1	69.8	64.9	60.0	55.1	50.3	45.5	40.8	36.1	31.6	27.1	23.0	19.1	15.5	12.0	9.0	6.5	4.6	3.2	2.2	1.4
Belgium - Belgique[19]																					
2000																					
Male	74.6	70.1	65.1	60.2	55.4	50.7	46.0	41.3	36.6	32.0	27.5	23.3	19.3	15.5	12.1	9.1	6.7	4.7	3.2	2.1	...
Female	80.8	76.3	71.3	66.3	61.4	56.6	51.7	46.8	42.0	37.3	32.7	28.2	23.8	19.5	15.4	11.7	8.4	5.8	3.7	2.3	...
Bulgaria - Bulgarie																					
2002																					
Male	68.5	64.8	59.9	55.0	50.2	45.5	40.8	36.1	31.5	27.2	23.2	19.5	16.0	13.0	10.2	7.8	5.8	3.6	3.0	2.2	0.5
Female	75.4	71.6	66.7	61.7	56.8	52.0	47.1	42.3	37.5	32.9	28.4	24.0	19.7	15.7	12.1	8.9	6.4	4.0	3.2	2.3	0.5
Czech Republic - République tchèque																					
2002																					
Male	72.1	67.5	62.6	57.6	52.8	48.0	43.3	38.5	33.8	29.3	25.0	21.0	17.3	13.9	10.9	8.3	6.0	4.2	2.9	1.9	1.2
Female	78.5	73.9	68.9	64.0	59.1	54.2	49.3	44.4	39.5	34.8	30.1	25.6	21.3	17.2	13.3	9.9	6.9	4.6	2.9	1.8	1.0

22. Expectation of life at specified ages for each sex: latest available year, 1993 - 2002
Espérance de vie à un âge donné pour chaque sexe: dernière année disponible, 1993 - 2002 (continued — suite)

(See notes at end of table. — Voir notes à la fin du tableau.)

Continent, country or area and date / Continent, pays ou zone et date	0	5	10	15	20	25	30	35	40	45	50	55	60	65	70	75	80	85	90	95	100
EUROPE																					
Denmark - Danemark[20]																					
2001																					
Male	74.6	70.1	65.2	60.2	55.4	50.6	45.8	41.0	36.3	31.7	27.3	23.1	19.0	15.3	12.0	9.1	6.7	4.9	3.4	2.4	1.8
Female	79.2	74.7	69.7	64.8	59.8	54.9	50.0	45.1	40.3	35.6	31.0	26.5	22.3	18.2	14.6	11.3	8.5	6.0	4.1	2.8	1.9
Estonia - Estonie																					
2002																					
Male	64.8	60.5	55.7	50.8	46.0	41.6	37.1	32.7	28.6	24.8	21.4	18.2	15.3	12.6	10.2	8.1	6.2	4.6	3.5	2.5	1.8
Female	76.3	72.1	67.2	62.3	57.4	52.5	47.7	42.9	38.2	33.6	29.3	25.2	21.3	17.2	13.6	10.3	7.4	5.3	3.3	2.1	1.3
Finland - Finlande[21]																					
2002																					
Male	74.8	70.2	65.2	60.2	55.4	50.7	46.0	41.3	36.6	32.1	27.7	23.5	19.5	15.8	12.3	9.3	6.8	4.9	3.4	2.2	1.2
Female	81.5	76.8	71.8	66.9	62.0	57.1	52.1	47.3	42.5	37.7	33.0	28.5	24.0	19.7	15.5	11.7	8.3	5.7	3.8	2.6	1.6
France[21]																					
1998																					
Male	74.8	70.2	65.3	60.4	55.5	50.8	46.1	41.4	36.8	32.4	28.1	24.0	20.0	16.4	13.0	10.0	7.4	5.3	3.7	2.5	...
Female	82.4	77.8	72.8	67.9	63.0	58.1	53.2	48.4	43.6	38.8	34.2	29.7	25.2	20.9	16.7	12.9	9.4	6.5	4.3	2.7	...
Germany - Allemagne																					
1999																					
Male	74.7	70.2	65.2	60.3	55.5	50.7	45.9	41.1	36.4	31.9	27.4	23.2	19.2	15.5	12.2	9.3	6.8	4.9	3.4	2.3	...
Female	80.7	76.1	71.2	66.2	61.3	56.4	51.5	46.6	41.8	37.0	32.4	27.8	23.4	19.2	15.2	11.5	8.3	5.7	3.8	2.4	...
Greece - Grèce																					
1998																					
Male	75.3	70.9	66.0	61.1	56.3	51.6	46.9	42.1	37.4	32.8	28.4	24.1	20.0	16.2	12.8	9.8	7.3	5.6	4.3	3.1	2.1
Female	80.5	76.1	71.2	66.2	61.3	56.4	51.5	46.6	41.8	37.0	32.3	27.6	23.1	18.7	14.6	10.9	7.8	5.7	4.2	3.0	2.1
Hungary - Hongrie																					
2002																					
Male	68.3	63.9	58.9	54.0	49.2	44.4	39.6	34.9	30.4	26.3	22.6	19.2	16.0	13.0	10.4	8.0	6.0	4.2	2.5	1.4	0.6
Female	76.6	72.2	67.2	62.3	57.4	52.4	47.6	42.7	38.0	33.4	29.1	24.9	20.7	16.8	13.1	9.8	7.0	4.6	2.8	1.5	0.6
Iceland - Islande																					
2001																					
Male	78.4	73.7	68.7	63.8	58.9	54.2	49.5	44.6	39.8	35.1	30.4	25.9	21.7	17.5	13.7	10.5	7.7	5.6	3.8	2.8	...
Female	82.6	77.8	72.9	68.0	63.0	58.1	53.2	48.4	43.5	38.7	34.0	29.4	24.9	20.7	16.5	12.8	9.2	6.5	4.6	3.2	...
Ireland - Irlande																					
2000																					
Male	74.2	69.8	64.8	59.9	55.1	50.4	45.6	40.8	36.1	31.4	26.8	22.5	18.3	14.6	11.2	8.4	6.2	4.5	3.0	2.0	...
Female	79.2	74.6	69.7	64.7	59.8	54.9	50.0	45.1	40.3	35.5	30.8	26.3	21.9	17.7	13.9	10.4	7.5	5.2	3.4	2.1	...
Isle of Man - Îles de Man																					
1996																					
Male	73.7	68.7	65.7	58.7	53.7	49.2	44.8	40.3	35.9	31.3	26.7	22.4	18.4	15.2	12.1	9.4	7.5	5.6	...	...	...
Female	79.8	75.0	70.0	65.0	60.0	55.0	50.0	45.0	40.1	35.2	30.6	26.0	21.9	18.3	14.4	11.3	8.6	6.1	...	...	...
Italy - Italie																					
1999																					
Male	76.0	71.5	71.5	66.5	61.6	56.8	52.0	47.3	42.5	37.8	33.1	28.5	24.2	20.0	16.2	12.7	9.7	7.1	5.2	3.7	2.6
Female	82.1	77.6	77.6	72.7	67.7	62.8	57.9	53.0	48.1	43.2	38.4	33.7	29.1	24.6	20.2	16.1	12.3	8.9	6.4	4.3	2.9
Latvia - Lettonie																					
2002																					
Male	65.4	61.4	56.5	51.6	46.7	42.1	37.6	33.4	29.4	25.6	21.9	18.4	15.1	12.1	9.3	7.0	5.1	3.6	2.5	...	...
Female	76.8	72.8	67.9	63.0	58.1	53.3	48.5	43.7	39.0	35.4	30.0	25.8	21.8	18.1	14.7	11.7	9.1	7.0	5.2	...	...
Lithuania - Lituanie																					
2002																					
Male	66.2	61.9	57.0	52.1	47.4	43.0	38.6	34.2	30.1	26.2	22.5	19.2	16.1	13.3	10.8	8.5	6.5	5.0	3.9	3.3	3.1
Female	77.6	73.2	68.3	63.4	58.5	53.6	48.8	44.0	39.3	34.7	30.2	26.0	21.8	17.8	14.1	10.8	7.9	5.6	4.3	4.0	4.0
Luxembourg																					
2000																					
Male	74.8	70.4	65.4	60.5	55.7	51.0	46.3	41.6	36.9	32.3	27.8	23.6	19.5	15.8	12.5	9.5	7.0	5.0	3.4	2.1	1.5
Female	81.0	76.5	71.5	66.6	61.6	56.7	51.9	47.0	42.2	37.4	32.8	28.2	23.8	19.7	15.8	12.2	9.1	6.5	4.3	2.6	1.5

(See notes at end of table. — Voir notes à la fin du tableau.)

Continent, country or area and date / Continent, pays ou zone et date	Age (in years) - Age (en années)																				
	0	5	10	15	20	25	30	35	40	45	50	55	60	65	70	75	80	85	90	95	100
EUROPE																					
Malta - Malte																					
2002																					
Male	75.8	71.3	66.4	61.4	56.6	51.7	47.0	42.1	37.3	32.5	27.8	23.4	19.1	15.0	11.7	8.8	6.2	4.5	...	...	...
Female	80.5	75.8	71.1	66.2	61.2	56.2	51.3	46.5	41.6	36.7	32.0	27.6	23.2	19.0	14.9	11.5	8.6	6.1	...	...	...
Netherlands - Pays-Bas[22]																					
2002																					
Male	76.0	71.0	66.0	61.1	56.3	51.4	46.6	41.7	37.0	32.2	27.7	23.3	19.1	15.2	11.8	8.8	6.4	4.6	3.3	2.4	...
Female	80.7	75.6	70.7	65.7	60.8	55.9	51.0	46.1	41.2	36.5	31.9	27.4	23.1	18.9	14.9	11.3	8.2	5.6	3.8	2.6	...
Norway - Norvège[23]																					
2002																					
Male	76.4	71.8	66.8	61.9	57.1	52.4	47.6	42.9	38.2	33.5	28.9	24.4	20.2	16.3	12.7	9.6	6.9	4.9	3.4	2.6	...
Female	81.5	76.9	71.9	67.0	62.1	57.2	52.3	47.4	42.5	37.7	33.0	28.4	24.1	19.8	15.8	12.0	8.7	6.0	4.1	2.8	...
Poland - Pologne																					
2000																					
Male	69.7	65.4	60.5	55.6	50.8	46.0	41.3	36.7	32.2	27.9	23.9	20.1	16.7	13.6	10.9	8.5	6.5	4.8	3.6	2.6	...
Female	77.9	73.6	68.6	63.7	58.7	53.8	48.9	44.1	39.2	34.6	30.0	25.6	21.4	17.3	13.6	10.2	7.4	5.1	3.4	2.1	...
Portugal																					
2000																					
Male	72.7	68.3	63.4	58.5	53.7	49.1	44.5	39.9	35.4	31.0	26.7	22.5	18.5	14.7	11.4	8.3	5.8	3.6	2.4	1.4	...
Female	79.7	75.2	70.3	65.3	60.4	55.5	50.6	45.8	41.0	36.3	31.6	27.1	22.6	18.3	14.2	10.5	7.2	4.5	2.8	1.6	...
Republic of Moldova - République de Moldova																					
2001																					
Male	64.5	61.0	56.2	51.4	46.6	42.0	37.4	32.9	28.7	24.8	21.1	17.6	14.5	11.8	9.3	7.3	5.4	3.8	2.4	2.1	0.3
Female	71.8	68.2	63.3	58.4	53.5	48.6	43.8	39.0	34.3	29.8	25.4	21.3	17.6	14.2	11.0	8.3	6.1	4.4	2.9	2.2	>0
2002																					
Male	64.4	60.8	55.9	51.1	46.3	41.6	37.1	32.7	28.4	24.4	20.7	17.2	14.1	11.4	9.0	7.1	5.2	3.7	2.5	2.4	...
Female	71.7	67.9	63.0	58.1	53.2	48.3	43.5	38.7	34.0	29.5	25.2	21.0	17.3	14.0	10.9	8.2	5.9	4.4	2.7	2.2	...
Romania - Roumanie																					
2002																					
Male	67.6	64.2	59.4	54.6	49.8	45.0	40.3	35.7	31.2	27.1	23.2	19.6	16.3	13.3	10.6	8.2	6.2	4.7	3.5	2.7	2.0
Female	74.9	71.4	66.5	61.6	56.7	51.8	46.9	42.1	37.4	32.8	28.3	24.0	19.9	16.0	12.4	9.3	6.8	4.9	3.6	2.6	2.0
Russian Federation - Fédération de Russie																					
1999																					
Male	59.9	56.4	51.5	46.7	42.2	38.0	34.0	30.0	26.2	22.6	19.3	16.3	13.5	11.1	9.0	7.3	5.8	4.7	3.8	3.2	3.5
Female	72.4	68.7	63.8	59.0	54.2	49.5	44.8	40.1	35.5	31.0	26.7	22.6	18.6	15.0	11.8	9.0	6.8	5.0	3.7	2.9	3.1
San Marino - Saint-Marin																					
2000																					
Male	77.4	73.0	68.0	63.1	58.5	53.8	49.1	44.3	39.5	34.7	30.0	25.6	21.4	17.2	13.5	10.5	7.7	5.7	3.8	2.3	0.5
Female	84.0	79.6	74.6	69.6	64.7	59.7	54.8	49.9	45.0	40.2	35.4	30.7	26.0	21.6	17.1	13.1	9.2	6.3	4.2	2.7	0.5
Serbia and Montenegro - Serbie-et-Montenegro																					
2000																					
Male	70.1	66.3	61.4	56.5	51.7	46.9	42.1	37.4	32.7	28.2	24.1	20.2	16.6	13.5	10.9	8.7	6.9	5.4	4.1	3.1	...
Female	75.0	71.0	66.1	61.1	56.2	51.3	46.4	41.6	36.8	32.1	27.6	23.2	19.1	15.2	11.8	8.8	6.5	4.5	3.1	2.0	...
Slovakia - Slovaquie																					
2001																					
Male	69.5	65.1	60.1	55.2	50.3	45.4	40.6	35.8	31.1	26.5	22.1	18.0	14.1	10.7	7.7	5.2	3.2	2.0	3.2	2.2	0.8
Female	77.5	73.0	68.0	63.1	58.1	53.2	48.2	43.3	38.5	33.6	28.9	24.3	19.8	15.5	11.5	7.8	4.7	2.0	2.9	1.8	0.7

22. Expectation of life at specified ages for each sex: latest available year, 1993 - 2002
Espérance de vie à un âge donné pour chaque sexe: dernière année disponible, 1993 - 2002 (continued — suite)

(See notes at end of table. — Voir notes à la fin du tableau.)

Continent, country or area and date / Continent, pays ou zone et date	0	5	10	15	20	25	30	35	40	45	50	55	60	65	70	75	80	85	90	95	100
EUROPE																					
Slovakia - Slovaquie 2002																					
Male	69.9	65.5	60.4	55.5	50.6	45.7	40.9	36.1	31.4	26.8	22.4	18.3	14.5	11.0	8.0	5.3	3.2	2.0	3.1	2.1	0.8
Female	77.6	73.4	68.3	63.4	58.4	53.5	48.6	43.7	38.8	33.9	29.2	24.5	20.0	15.7	11.7	8.0	4.9	2.0	3.0	1.8	0.7
Slovenia - Slovénie 2001																					
Male	72.1	67.6	62.6	57.7	52.9	48.2	43.5	38.8	34.1	29.6	25.4	21.4	17.7	14.2	11.2	8.6	6.4	4.3	...	...	...
Female	79.6	74.9	70.0	65.0	60.1	55.2	50.3	45.4	40.5	35.8	31.2	26.8	22.4	18.2	14.3	10.7	7.4	4.6	...	...	...
Spain - Espagne 1998																					
Male	75.2	70.7	65.8	60.8	56.0	51.3	46.5	41.8	37.2	32.7	28.2	24.0	19.9	16.1	12.7	9.6	7.0	4.9	3.4	2.0	0.5
Female	82.2	77.6	72.6	67.7	62.8	57.9	53.0	48.1	43.2	38.5	33.8	29.1	24.5	20.1	15.8	11.9	8.5	5.7	3.6	2.0	0.5
Sweden - Suède 2002																					
Male	77.7	73.1	68.1	63.1	58.3	53.5	48.6	43.8	39.0	34.3	29.6	25.2	20.9	16.9	13.2	10.0	7.2	5.0	3.4	2.5	...
Female	82.1	77.4	72.4	67.5	62.5	57.6	52.7	47.8	42.9	38.1	33.4	28.8	24.3	20.0	16.0	12.2	8.8	6.1	4.1	2.9	...
Switzerland - Suisse 2000																					
Male	76.9	72.4	67.5	62.5	57.7	53.0	48.2	43.5	38.7	34.0	29.5	25.1	20.9	16.9	13.3	10.1	7.4	5.2	3.5	2.3	...
Female	82.6	78.0	73.0	68.1	63.1	58.2	53.3	48.4	43.6	38.8	34.1	29.4	25.0	20.7	16.5	12.6	9.1	6.2	4.0	2.4	...
The Former Yugoslav Rep. of Macedonia - L'ex-République yougoslave de Macédoine 1999																					
Male	70.7	67.0	62.1	57.2	52.3	47.5	42.8	38.0	33.3	28.8	24.4	20.4	16.7	13.2	10.3	7.6	5.6	4.0	3.5	3.4	0.2
Female	75.2	71.4	66.5	61.6	56.6	51.7	46.8	42.0	37.2	32.4	27.9	23.4	19.2	15.2	11.6	8.6	6.2	4.5	3.8	3.4	0.2
Ukraine 1998 1999																					
Male	63.0	59.2	54.3	49.4	44.7	40.3	35.9	31.7	27.7	23.9	20.4	17.2	14.3	11.7	9.4	7.4	5.6	4.0	2.7	1.6	0.9
Female	73.7	69.8	64.9	60.0	55.1	50.3	45.5	40.8	36.2	31.6	27.2	23.0	19.0	15.3	11.8	8.9	6.4	4.6	3.5	2.6	2.0
United Kingdom - Royaume-Uni 2000																					
Male	75.3	70.9	65.9	61.0	56.1	51.4	46.6	41.9	37.1	32.5	27.9	23.6	19.5	15.7	12.2	9.4	7.0	5.0	3.7	2.6	2.0
Female	80.1	75.6	70.6	65.7	60.8	55.8	51.0	46.1	41.2	36.5	31.8	27.3	23.0	18.8	15.0	11.5	8.6	6.1	4.2	3.0	2.2
OCEANIA — OCEANIE																					
Australia - Australie 1999																					
Male	77.0	72.6	67.6	62.7	57.9	53.2	48.5	43.8	39.1	34.5	29.9	25.4	21.2	17.2	13.6	10.4	7.8	5.6	...	...	...
Female	82.4	77.9	72.9	68.0	63.1	58.2	53.3	48.4	43.6	38.8	34.1	29.5	25.0	20.7	16.6	12.9	9.5	6.8	...	...	...
2000 - 2002																					
Male	77.4	72.9	68.0	63.0	58.2	53.5	48.8	44.1	39.4	34.7	30.1	25.6	21.4	17.4	13.7	10.5	7.8	5.6	4.1	3.2	2.5
Female	82.6	78.0	73.1	68.1	63.2	58.3	53.4	48.6	43.7	38.9	34.2	29.6	25.2	20.8	16.7	13.0	9.6	6.8	4.8	3.6	2.9
New Caledonia - Nouvelle-Calédonie 2001																					
Male	70.5	66.1	61.1	56.2	51.4	46.9	42.6	38.1	33.6	29.1	24.7	...	16.7	...	10.2	...	5.7	...	...	...	...
Female	76.1	71.6	66.7	61.7	56.8	52.0	47.3	42.4	37.6	32.9	28.5	...	20.3	...	12.4	...	6.7	...	...	...	...
New Zealand - Nouvelle-Zélande 2000																					
Male	76.0	71.6	66.6	61.7	57.0	52.3	47.6	42.9	38.2	33.5	28.9	24.5	20.3	16.5	13.0	9.9	7.4	5.3	3.7	...	...
Female	80.9	76.4	71.5	66.5	61.7	56.8	51.9	47.1	42.2	37.5	32.8	28.3	23.9	19.8	16.0	12.4	9.2	6.5	4.6	...	...

22. Expectation of life at specified ages for each sex: latest available year, 1993 - 2002
Espérance de vie à un âge donné pour chaque sexe: dernière année disponible, 1993 - 2002 (continued — suite)

(See notes at end of table. — Voir notes à la fin du tableau.)

Continent, country or area and date / Continent, pays ou zone et date	Age (in years) - Age (en années)																				
	0	5	10	15	20	25	30	35	40	45	50	55	60	65	70	75	80	85	90	95	100
OCEANIA — OCEANIE																					
New Zealand - Nouvelle-Zélande																					
2000 - 2002																					
Male	76.3	71.9	67.0	62.0	57.3	52.6	47.9	43.2	38.5	33.8	29.2	24.8	20.6	16.7	13.1	10.0	7.4	5.2	3.6	2.6	1.9
Female	81.1	76.6	71.7	66.8	61.9	57.0	52.1	47.3	42.4	37.6	33.0	28.4	24.1	20.0	16.0	12.4	9.2	6.5	4.4	3.0	2.1
2001 - 2003																					
Male	76.7	72.2	67.3	62.4	57.6	52.9	48.2	43.5	38.8	34.1	29.5	25.1	20.8	16.9	13.4	10.2	7.5	5.3	3.8	...	...
Female	81.2	76.7	71.8	66.8	62.0	57.1	52.2	47.3	42.5	37.7	33.1	28.5	24.1	20.0	16.1	12.4	9.2	6.5	4.5	...	...
Tonga																					
1998																					
Male	69.8	66.5	61.6	56.7	52.0	47.2	42.5	37.8	33.1	28.5	24.1	20.0	16.2	13.0	10.4	7.2	5.5	...	...	...	...
Female	71.8	68.3	63.4	58.6	53.7	48.9	44.2	39.4	34.8	30.2	25.8	21.6	17.7	14.1	11.2	7.8	5.9	...	...	...	...

GENERAL NOTES - NOTES GENERALES

Average number of years of life remaining to persons surviving to exact age specified, if subject to mortality conditions of the period indicated. For limitations of data, see Technical Notes for this table. — Nombre moyen d'années restant à vivre aux personnes ayant atteint l'âge donné si elles sont soumises aux conditions de mortalité de la période indiquée. Pour les insuffisances des données, voir Notes techniques pour ce tableau.

FOOTNOTES - NOTES

[1] For Algerian population only. - Pour la population algérienne seulement.

[2] Data refer to national projections. - Les données se referent aux projections nationales.

[3] Projections based on the 1998 Malawi Population and Housing Census. - Les projections sont basées sur les résultats du recensement de la population et de l'habitat de Malawi de 1998.

[4] Data for 1997 refer to last twelve months preceding population and housing census of 1997. - Les données pour 1997 se réfèrent au douze mois précédant le recensement de population et de l'habitat de 1997.

[5] Excluding tribal Indian population. - Non compris les Indiens vivant en tribus.

[6] Excluding Indian jungle population. - Non compris les Indiens de la jungle.

[7] Excluding nomadic Indian tribes. - Non compris les tribus d'Indiens nomades.

[8] Based on 1994 national health survey. - Basé sur l'enquête par sondage de santé pour 1994.

[9] For statistical purposes, the data for China do not include those for the Hong Kong Special Administrative Region (Hong Kong SAR), Macao Special Administrative Region (Macao SAR) and Taiwan province of China. - Pour la présentation des statistiques, les données pour Chine ne comprend pas la Région Administrative Spéciale de Hong Kong (Hong Kong RAS), la Région Administrative Spéciale de Macao (Macao RAS) et Taïwan province de Chine.

[10] Data refer to government controlled areas. - Les données se raportent aux zones contrôlées par le Gouvernement.

[11] Including data for the Indian-held part of Jammu and Kashmir, the final status of which has not yet been determined. - Y compris les données pour la partie du Jammu et du Cachemire occupée par l'Inde dont le statut définitif n'a pas encore été déterminé.

[12] Including data for East Jerusalem and Israeli residents in certain other territories under occupation by Israeli military forces since June 1967. - Y compris les données pour Jérusalem-Est et les résidents israéliens dans certains autres territoires occupés depuis 1967 par les forces armées israéliennes.

[13] Data refer to Japanese nationals in Japan only. - Les données se raportent aux nationaux japonais au Japon seulement.

[14] Excluding data for Jordanian territory under occupation since June 1967 by Israeli military forces. Excluding foreigners, including registered Palestinian refugees. - Non compris les données pour le territoire jordanien occupé depuis juin 1967 par les forces armées israéliennes. Non compris les étrangers, mais y compris les réfugiés de Palestine enregistrés.

[15] Excluding alien armed forces stationed in the area. - Non compris les militaires étrangers en garnison sur le territoire.

[16] Excluding data for the Pakistan-held part of Jammu and Kashmir, the final status of which has not yet been determined. - Non compris les données concernant la partie du Jammu et Cachemire occupée par le Pakistan dont le statut définitif n'a pas été déterminé.

[17] Excluding transients afloat and non-locally domiciled military and civilian services personnel and their dependants. - Non compris les personnes de passage þ bord de navires, ni les militaires et agents civils domiciliés hors du territoire et les membres de leur famille les accompagnant.

[18] Based on the results of the Population Demographic Survey. - D'après les résultats de la Population Demographic Survey.

[19] Including armed forces stationed outside the country, but excluding alien armed forces stationed in the area. - Y compris les militaires nationaux hors du pays, mais non compris les militaires étrangers en garnison sur le territoire.

[20] Excluding Faeroe Islands and Greenland. - Non compris les îles Féroé et Gröenland.

[21] Including nationals temporarily outside the country. - Y compris les nationaux se trouvant temporairement hors du pays.

[22] Including residents outside the country if listed in a Netherlands population register. - Y compris les résidents hors du pays, s'ils sont inscrits sur un registre de population néerlandais.

[23] Including residents temporarily outside the country. - Y compris les résidents se trouvant temporairement hors du pays.

>0 Value too small to display.

Table 23

Table 23 presents number of marriages and crude marriage rates by urban/rural residence for as many years as possible between 1998 and 2002.

Description of variables: Marriage is defined as the act, ceremony or process by which the legal relationship of husband and wife is constituted. The legality of the union may be established by civil, religious or other means as recognized by the laws of each country. [i]

Marriage statistics in this table, therefore, include both first marriages and remarriages after divorce, widowhood or annulment. They do not, unless otherwise noted, include resumption of marriage ties after legal separation. These statistics refer to the number of marriages performed, and not to the number of persons marrying.

Statistics shown are obtained from civil registers of marriage. Exceptions, such as data from church registers, are identified in the footnotes.

The urban/rural classification of marriages is that provided by each country or area; it is presumed to be based on the national census definitions of urban population which have been set forth at the end of the technical notes for table 6.

Rate computation: Crude marriage rates are the annual number of marriages per 1 000 mid-year population. Rates by urban/rural residence are the annual number of marriages, in the appropriate urban or rural category, per 1 000 corresponding mid-year population. These rates are calculated by the Statistics Division of the United Nations. Rates presented in this table have been limited to those for countries or areas having at least a total of 30 marriages in a given year.

Reliability of data: Each country or area has been asked to indicate the estimated completeness of the number of marriages recorded in its civil register. These national assessments are indicated by the quality codes C and U that appear in the first column of this table.

C indicates that the data are estimated to be virtually complete, that is, representing at least 90 per cent of the marriages occurring each year, while U indicates that data are estimated to be incomplete, that is, representing less than 90 per cent of the marriages occurring each year. The code ... indicates that no information was provided regarding completeness.

Data from civil registers which are reported as incomplete or of unknown completeness (coded U or ...) are considered unreliable. They appear in italics in this table; rates are not computed for these data.

These quality codes apply only to data from civil registers. For more information about the quality of vital statistics data in general, see section 4.2 of the Technical Notes.

Limitations: Statistics on marriages are subject to the same qualifications that have been set forth for vital statistics in general and marriage statistics in particular as discussed in section 4 of the Technical Notes.

The fact that marriage is a legal event, unlike birth and death that are biological events, has implications for international comparability of data. Marriage has been defined, for statistical purposes, in terms of the laws of individual countries or areas. These laws vary throughout the world. In addition, comparability is further limited because some countries or areas compile statistics only for civil marriages although religious marriages may also be legally recognized; in other countries or areas, the only available records are church registers and, therefore, the statistics may not reflect marriages that are civil marriages only.

Because in many countries or areas marriage is a civil legal contract which, to establish its legality, must be celebrated before a civil officer, it follows that for these countries or areas registration would tend to be almost automatic at the time of, or immediately following, the marriage ceremony. This factor should be kept in mind when considering the reliability of data, described above. For this reason the practice of tabulating data by date of registration does not generally pose serious problems of comparability as it does in the case of birth and death statistics.

As indicators of family formation, the statistics on the number of marriages presented in this table are bound to be deficient to the extent that they do not include either customary unions, which are not registered even though they are considered legal and binding under customary law, or consensual unions (also known as extra-legal or de facto unions). In general, lower marriage rates over a period of years are an indication of higher incidence of customary or consensual unions.

In addition, rates are affected also by the quality and limitations of the population estimates that are used in their computation. The problems of under-enumeration or over-enumeration and, to some extent, the differences in definition of total population have been discussed in section 3 of the Technical Notes dealing with population data in general, and specific information pertaining to individual countries or areas is given in the footnotes to table 3.

Strict correspondence between the numerator of the rate and the denominator is not always obtained; for example, marriages among civilian and military segments of the population may be related to civilian population. The effect of this may be to increase the rates, but, in most cases, this effect is negligible.

It should be emphasized that crude marriage rates like crude birth, death and divorce rates, may be seriously affected by the age-sex-marital structure of the population to which they relate. Crude marriage rates do, however, provide a simple measure of the level and changes in marriage.

The comparability of data by urban/rural residence is affected by the national definitions of urban and rural used in tabulating these data. It is assumed, in the absence of specific information to the contrary, that the definitions of urban and rural used in connection with the national population census were also used in the compilation of the vital statistics for each country or area. However, it cannot be excluded that, for a given country or area, different definitions of urban and rural are used for the vital statistics data and the population census data respectively. When known, the definitions of urban in national population censuses are presented at the end of the technical notes for table 6. As discussed in detail in the notes, these definitions vary considerably from one country or area to another.

In addition to problems of comparability, marriage rates classified by urban/rural residence are also subject to certain special types of bias. If, when calculating marriage rates, different definitions of urban are used in connection with the vital events and the population data, and if this results in a net difference between the numerator and denominator of the rate in the population at risk, then the marriage rates would be biased. Urban/rural differentials in marriage rates may also be affected by whether the vital events have been tabulated in terms of place of occurrence or place of usual residence. This problem is discussed in more detail in section 4.1.4.1. of the Technical Notes.

Earlier data: Marriages and crude marriage rates have been shown in each issue of the *Demographic Yearbook*. For more information on specific topics, and years for which data are reported, readers should consult the Historical Index.

NOTES

[i] *Principles and Recommendations for a Vital Statistics System Revision 2*, Sales No. E. 01.XVII.10, United Nations, New York, 2001

Tableau 23

Le tableau 23 présente des données sur les mariages et les taux bruts de nuptialité selon le lieu de résidence (zone urbaine ou rurale) pour le plus grand nombre possible d'années entre 1998 et 2002.

Description des variables : Le mariage désigne l'acte, la cérémonie ou la procédure qui établit un rapport légal entre mari et femme. L'union peut être rendue légale par une procédure civile ou religieuse, ou par toute autre procédure, conformément à la législation du pays[1].

Les statistiques de la nuptialité présentées dans ce tableau comprennent donc les premiers mariages et les remariages faisant suite à un divorce, un veuvage ou une annulation. Toutefois, sauf indication contraire, elles ne comprennent pas les unions reconstituées après une séparation légale. Ces statistiques se rapportent au nombre de mariages célébrés, non au nombre de personnes qui se marient.

Les statistiques présentées reposent sur l'enregistrement des mariages par les services de l'état civil. Les exceptions (données provenant des registres des églises, par exemple) font l'objet d'une note à la fin du tableau.

La classification des mariages selon le lieu de résidence (zone urbaine ou rurale) est celle qui a été communiquée par chaque pays ou zone ; on part du principe qu'elle repose sur les définitions de la population urbaine utilisées pour les recensements nationaux telles qu'elles sont reproduites à la fin des notes techniques se rapportant au tableau 6.

Calcul des taux : Les taux bruts de nuptialité représentent le nombre annuel de mariages pour 1 000 habitants au milieu de l'année. Les taux selon le lieu de résidence (zone urbaine ou rurale) représentent le nombre annuel de mariages, classés selon la catégorie urbaine ou rurale appropriée, pour 1 000 habitants au milieu de l'année. Ces taux ont été calculés par la Division de statistique de l'ONU. Les taux du tableau 23 ne se rapportent qu'aux pays ou zones où l'on a enregistré un total d'au moins 30 mariages pendant une année donnée.

Fiabilité des données : Il a été demandé à chaque pays ou zone d'indiquer le degré estimatif de complétude des données sur les mariages figurant dans ses registres d'état civil. Ces évaluations nationales sont signalées par les codes de qualité 'C' et 'U' qui apparaissent dans la deuxième colonne du tableau.

La lettre 'C' indique que les données sont jugées à peu près complètes, c'est-à-dire qu'elles représentent au moins 90 p. 100 des mariages survenus chaque année ; la lettre 'U' signale que les données sont jugées incomplètes, c'est-à-dire qu'elles représentent moins de 90 p. 100 des mariages survenus chaque année. Le code '...' indique qu'aucun renseignement n'a été communiqué quant à la complétude des données.

Les données issues des registres de l'état civil qui sont déclarées incomplètes ou dont le degré de complétude n'est pas connu (code 'U' ou '...') sont jugées douteuses. Elles apparaissent en italique dans le tableau et les taux correspondants n'ont pas été calculés.

Les codes de qualité ne s'appliquent qu'aux données provenant des registres de l'état civil. Pour plus de précisions sur la qualité des données reposant sur les statistiques de l'état civil en général, voir la section 4.2 des Notes techniques.

Insuffisance des données : Les statistiques relatives aux mariages appellent les mêmes réserves que celles qui ont été formulées à propos des statistiques de l'état civil en général et des statistiques concernant la nuptialité en particulier (voir la section 4 des Notes techniques).

Le fait que le mariage soit un acte juridique, à la différence de la naissance et du décès, qui sont des faits biologiques, a des répercussions sur la comparabilité internationale des données. Aux fins de la statistique, le mariage est défini par la législation de chaque pays ou zone. Cette législation varie d'un pays à l'autre. La comparabilité est limitée en outre du fait que certains pays ou zones ne réunissent des statistiques que pour les mariages civils, bien que les mariages religieux y soient également reconnus par la loi ; dans d'autres, les seuls relevés disponibles sont les registres des églises et, en conséquence, les statistiques peuvent ne pas rendre compte des mariages exclusivement civils.

Étant donné que, dans de nombreux pays ou zones, le mariage est un contrat juridique civil qui, pour être légal, doit être conclu devant un officier d'état civil, il s'ensuit que dans ces pays ou zones l'enregistrement se fait à peu près systématiquement au moment de la cérémonie ou immédiatement après. Il faut tenir compte de cet élément lorsque l'on évalue la fiabilité des données, dont il est question plus haut. C'est pourquoi la pratique consistant à exploiter les données selon la date de l'enregistrement ne pose généralement pas les graves problèmes de comparabilité auxquels on se heurte dans le cas des statistiques concernant les naissances et les décès.

Les statistiques relatives au nombre des mariages présentées dans ce tableau donnent une idée forcément trompeuse de la formation des familles, dans la mesure où elles ne tiennent compte ni des mariages coutumiers, qui ne sont pas enregistrés bien qu'ils soient considérés comme légaux et créateurs d'obligations en vertu du droit coutumier, ni des unions consensuelles (appelées également unions non légalisées ou unions de fait). En général, une diminution du taux de nuptialité pendant un certain nombre d'années indique une augmentation des mariages coutumiers ou des unions consensuelles.

L'exactitude des taux dépend également de la qualité et des insuffisances des estimations de population qui sont utilisées pour leur calcul. Le problème des erreurs par excès ou par défaut commises lors du dénombrement et, dans une certaine mesure, le problème de l'hétérogénéité des définitions de la population totale ont été examinés à la section 3 des Notes techniques relative à la population en général ; des indications concernant les différents pays ou zones sont données en note à la fin du tableau 3.

Il n'a pas toujours été possible d'obtenir une correspondance rigoureuse entre le numérateur et le dénominateur pour le calcul des taux. Par exemple, les mariages parmi la population civile et les militaires sont parfois rapportés à la population civile. Cela peut avoir pour effet d'accroître les taux, mais, dans la plupart des cas, il est probable que la différence sera négligeable.

Il faut souligner que les taux bruts de nuptialité, de même que les taux bruts de natalité, de mortalité et de divortialité, peuvent varier sensiblement selon la structure par âge et par sexe de la population à laquelle ils se rapportent. Les taux bruts de nuptialité offrent néanmoins un moyen simple de mesurer la fréquence et l'évolution des mariages.

La comparabilité des données selon le lieu de résidence (zone urbaine ou rurale) peut être limitée par les définitions nationales des termes « urbain » et « rural » utilisées pour le classement de ces données. En l'absence d'indications contraires, on a supposé que les mêmes définitions avaient servi pour le recensement national de la population et pour l'établissement des statistiques de l'état civil pour chaque pays ou zone. Toutefois, il n'est pas exclu que, pour une zone ou un pays donné, des définitions différentes aient été retenues. Les définitions du terme «urbain» utilisées pour les recensements nationaux de population ont été présentées à la fin des notes techniques du tableau 6 lorsqu'elles étaient connues. Comme on l'a précisé dans les notes techniques relatives au tableau 6, ces définitions varient considérablement d'un pays ou d'une zone à l'autre.

Outre les problèmes de comparabilité, les taux de nuptialité classés selon le lieu de résidence (zone urbaine ou rurale) sont également sujets à des distorsions particulières. Si l'on utilise des définitions différentes du terme « urbain » pour classer les faits d'état civil et les données relatives à la population lors du calcul des taux et qu'il en résulte une différence nette entre le numérateur et le dénominateur pour le taux de la population exposée au risque, les taux de nuptialité s'en trouveront faussés. La différence entre ces taux pour les zones urbaines et rurales pourra aussi être faussée selon que les faits d'état civil auront été classés d'après le lieu où ils se sont produits ou d'après le lieu de résidence habituel. Ce problème est examiné plus en détail à la section 4.1.4.1 des Notes techniques.

Données publiées antérieurement : Les différentes éditions de l'Annuaire démographique regroupent des données sur le nombre des mariages. Pour plus de précisions concernant les années et les sujets pour lesquels des données ont été publiées, se reporter à l'index historique.

NOTE

[1] Principes et recommandations pour un système de statistiques de l'état civil, deuxième révision, numéro de vente : F.01.XVII.10, publication des Nations Unies, New York, 2003.

23. Marriages and crude marriage rates, by urban/rural residence: 1998 - 2002
Mariages et taux bruts de nuptialité, selon la résidence, urbaine/rurale: 1998 - 2002

(See notes at end of table. — Voir notes à la fin du tableau.)

Continent, country or area and urban/rural residence / Continent, pays ou zone et résidence, urbaine/rurale	Code[1]	Marriages - Mariages					Rate - Taux				
		1998	1999	2000	2001	2002	1998	1999	2000	2001	2002
AFRICA — AFRIQUE											
Algeria - Algérie[2]											
Total	...	158 298	163 126	177 548	194 273	218 620	...	...	...	...	...
Djibouti											
Total	...	3 255	3 808	...	...	...	...	...	...	...	...
Egypt - Égypte[3]											
Total	+...	503 651	525 412	...	...	...	...	...	...	...	...
Urban-Urbaine	+...	183 976	191 224	...	...	...	...	...	...	...	...
Rural-Rurale	+...	319 675	334 188	...	...	...	...	...	...	...	...
Ethiopia - Éthiopie											
Total	...	...	630 290	...	...	...	...	...	...	...	...
Urban-Urbaine	...	...	24 093	...	...	...	...	...	...	...	...
Rural-Rurale	...	...	606 197	...	...	...	...	...	...	...	...
Libyan Arab Jamahiriya - Jamahiriya arabe libyenne[4]											
Total	U	19 051	19 348	27 655	28 661	33 323	...	...	...	...	...
Mauritius - Maurice											
Total	+C	10 898	11 295	10 963	10 635	10 484	9.4	9.6	9.2	8.9	8.7
Urban-Urbaine	+C	3 740	3 537	3 542	3 423	...	7.5	7.0	7.0	6.7	...
Rural-Rurale	+C	7 158	7 758	7 421	7 212	...	10.8	11.5	10.9	10.5	...
Réunion											
Total	C	3 343	3 446	3 444	*3 334	...	4.8	4.9	4.8	*4.5	...
Saint Helena ex. dep. - Sainte-Hélène sans dép.											
Total	C	29	25	17	20	...	...	...	...	...	...
Seychelles											
Total	+C	718	883	949	790	*865	9.1	11.0	11.7	9.7	*10.7
South Africa - Afrique du Sud											
Total	...	146 741	...	...	...	...	...	...	...	...	...
Tunisia - Tunisie											
Total	...	56 081	60 082	...	61 800	...	...	...	...	...	...
AMERICA, NORTH — AMERIQUE DU NORD											
Anguilla[5]											
Total	C	72	73	68	51	53	6.8	6.7	6.0	4.4	4.4
Aruba											
Total	C	564	578	616	546	649	6.4	6.4	6.8	5.9	6.9
Bahamas											
Total	C	1 684	2 204	2 366	1 787	...	5.7	7.4	7.8	5.8	...
Barbados - Barbade											
Total	C	...	...	*3 516	...	...	...	...	*13.1	...	...
Belize											
Total	+C	1 510	1 517	1 546	1 558	1 622	6.3	6.2	6.2	6.1	6.1
Bermuda - Bermudes											
Total	C	1 033	1 093	1 023	923	937	16.6	17.4	16.2	14.9	...
Canada											
Total	C	152 821	155 742	157 395	146 618	*147 634	5.1	5.1	5.1	4.7	*4.7
Cayman Islands - Îles Caïmanes											
Total	+C	300	375	...	...	...	8.0	9.6	...	...	...
Costa Rica											
Total	C	24 831	25 613	24 436	*23 790	...	7.4	7.5	7.0	*6.1	...
Cuba											
Total	C	64 900	57 252	57 001	54 345	56 876	5.8	5.1	5.1	4.8	5.1
Urban-Urbaine	C	59 009	51 645	51 762	...	...	7.1	6.2	6.1	...	...
Rural-Rurale	C	5 891	5 607	5 239	...	...	2.1	2.0	1.9	...	...
Dominica - Dominique											
Total	+C	336	*339	...	...	...	4.7	*4.7	...	...	...
Dominican Republic - République dominicaine											
Total	+C	28 723	*36 446	*33 904	*24 470	...	3.5	*4.4	*4.0	*2.9	...

23. Marriages and crude marriage rates, by urban/rural residence: 1998 - 2002
Mariages et taux bruts de nuptialité, selon la résidence, urbaine/rurale: 1998 - 2002 (continued — suite)

(See notes at end of table. — Voir notes à la fin du tableau.)

Continent, country or area and urban/rural residence / Continent, pays ou zone et résidence, urbaine/rurale	Code[1]	Marriages - Mariages					Rate - Taux				
		1998	1999	2000	2001	2002	1998	1999	2000	2001	2002
AMERICA, NORTH — AMERIQUE DU NORD											
El Salvador											
Total	+C	25 923	34 306	28 231	29 216	25 998	4.3	5.6	4.5	4.6	4.0
Urban-Urbaine	+C	21 219	27 071	22 525	23 668	22 102	6.1	7.6	6.1	6.3	5.7
Rural-Rurale	+C	4 704	7 235	5 706	5 548	3 896	1.8	2.8	2.2	2.1	1.5
Grenada - Grenade											
Total	+C	563	570	616	*509	...	5.6	5.7	6.1	*5.0	...
Guadeloupe											
Total	C	1 959	1 892	1 935	1 929	1 809	4.7	4.5	4.5	4.5	4.1
Guatemala											
Total	C	52 952	60 922	...	...	...	4.9	5.5	...	...	...
Jamaica - Jamaïque											
Total	+C	24 131	26 871	...	...	...	9.4	10.4	...	...	...
Martinique											
Total	C	1 501	1 591	1 591	1 572	1 524	4.0	4.2	4.1	4.1	3.9
Mexico - Mexique[6]											
Total	+C	704 456	743 856	707 442	665 434	570 060	7.3	7.6	7.1	6.5	5.5
Urban-Urbaine	+C	521 176	...	...	...	...	7.3	...	...	...	...
Rural-Rurale	+C	163 414	...	...	...	...	6.6	...	...	...	...
Netherlands Antilles - Antilles néerlandaises											
Total	C	1 276	956	...	...	...	6.1	4.7	...	...	...
Nicaragua											
Total	+C	20 816	28 005	24 268	21 140	21 039	4.3	5.7	4.9	4.2	4.1
Panama[7]											
Total	C	10 415	10 388	10 430	9 767	*9 392	3.8	3.7	3.7	3.4	*3.1
Urban-Urbaine	C	7 209	7 506	7 499	7 416	*7 687	4.7	4.8	4.7	...	...
Rural-Rurale	C	3 206	2 882	2 931	2 351	*1 705	2.6	2.3	2.3	...	...
Puerto Rico - Porto Rico											
Total	C	26 760	27 255	25 980	28 598	25 645	7.1	7.2	6.8	7.4	6.6
Saint Kitts and Nevis - Saint-Kitts-et-Nevis											
Total	+...	315	...	...	...	...	...	...	...	...	...
Saint Lucia - Sainte-Lucie											
Total	C	626	732	655	513	472	4.1	4.8	4.2	3.2	3.0
Saint Vincent and the Grenadines - Saint Vincent-et-les Grenadines											
Total	+C	521	630	673	506	509	4.7	5.6	6.0	4.6	4.7
Turks Caicos Islands - Îles Turques et Caïques											
Total	+...	274	388	348	...	...	...	...	...	...	...
United States - États-Unis											
Total	C	2 244 000	2 358 000	2 329 000	2 345 000	*2 254 000	8.3	8.6	8.5	8.2	*7.8
AMERICA, SOUTH — AMERIQUE DU SUD											
Argentina - Argentine											
Total	C	145 281	147 649	141 027	130 533	122 343	4.0	4.0	3.8	3.5	3.2
Brazil - Brésil[8]											
Total	U	698 614	788 744	732 721	710 121	...	...	...	...	...	...
Chile - Chili											
Total	+C	73 456	69 765	66 607	64 088	60 971	5.0	4.6	4.4	4.2	3.9
Urban-Urbaine	+C	64 073	60 636	58 502	56 258	54 404	5.1	4.7	4.5	4.3	4.1
Rural-Rurale	+C	9 383	9 129	8 105	7 830	6 567	4.3	4.2	3.7	3.6	3.0
Ecuador - Équateur[9]											
Total	U	69 867	77 593	74 875	67 741	66 208	...	...	...	...	...
French Guiana - Guyane française											
Total	C	510	548	518	547	522	3.3	3.5	3.2	3.2	3.0

23. Marriages and crude marriage rates, by urban/rural residence: 1998 - 2002
Mariages et taux bruts de nuptialité, selon la résidence, urbaine/rurale: 1998 - 2002 (continued — suite)

(See notes at end of table. — Voir notes à la fin du tableau.)

Continent, country or area and urban/rural residence Continent, pays ou zone et résidence, urbaine/rurale	Code[1]	Marriages - Mariages					Rate - Taux				
		1998	1999	2000	2001	2002	1998	1999	2000	2001	2002
AMERICA, SOUTH — AMERIQUE DU SUD											
Peru - Pérou											
Total	+C	60 730	...	...	...	...	2.4	...	...	...	...
Suriname											
Total	C	1 982	2 257	2 267	...	...	4.4	4.9	4.9	...	...
Uruguay											
Total	C	16 176	15 488	13 888	13 988	14 073	4.9	4.7	4.2	4.2	4.2
Venezuela[8]											
Total	C	86 152	90 220	91 088	81 516	73 163	3.7	3.8	3.7	3.3	2.9
ASIA — ASIE											
Armenia - Arménie											
Total	C	11 365	12 459	10 986	12 302	...	3.0	3.3	2.9	3.2	...
Urban-Urbaine	C	7 666	8 560	7 626	...	...	3.0	3.4	3.0	...	...
Rural-Rurale	C	3 699	3 899	3 360	...	...	2.9	3.1	2.6	...	...
Azerbaijan - Azerbaïdjan											
Total	+C	40 851	37 382	39 611	41 861	41 661	5.2	4.7	4.9	5.2	5.1
Urban-Urbaine	+C	20 322	18 799	19 994	22 927	22 438	5.0	4.6	4.9	5.6	5.4
Rural-Rurale	+C	20 529	18 583	19 617	18 934	19 223	5.3	4.8	5.0	4.7	4.8
Bahrain - Bahreïn											
Total	...	3 677	3 673	3 963	4 504	4 909	...	...	...	...	...
Brunei Darussalam - Brunéi Darussalam											
Total	...	2 039	2 318	2 184	2 091	2 288	...	...	...	...	...
China - Chine											
Total	+C	8 918 000	...	...	...	...	7.1	...	...	...	...
China: Hong Kong SAR - Chine: Hong Kong RAS											
Total	C	31 673	31 287	30 879	32 825	*32 070	4.8	4.7	4.6	4.9	*4.7
China: Macao SAR - Chine: Macao RAS											
Total	+C	1 451	1 367	1 222	1 222	*1 209	3.4	3.2	2.8	2.8	*2.8
Cyprus - Chypre[10]											
Total	C	7 738	9 080	9 282	10 574	10 284	10.1	11.7	11.9	13.4	12.9
Urban-Urbaine	C	...	...	...	...	6 641	...	...	...	...	...
Rural-Rurale	C	...	...	...	...	3 643	...	...	...	...	...
Georgia - Géorgie											
Total	C	15 300	13 845	12 870	13 336	...	2.8	2.7	2.6	2.7	...
Urban-Urbaine	C	...	...	7 977	8 027	...	...	...	2.7	...	...
Rural-Rurale	C	...	...	4 893	5 309	...	...	...	2.3	...	...
Iran (Islamic Republic of) - Iran (République islamique d')											
Total	C	531 490	611 073	646 498	640 710	650 960	8.6	9.7	10.2	9.9	9.9
Urban-Urbaine	C	412 565	476 284	499 143	495 629	513 772	10.6	11.9	12.2	11.8	11.9
Rural-Rurale	C	118 925	134 789	147 355	145 081	137 188	5.2	5.9	6.5	6.5	6.1
Iraq[11]											
Total	C	136 149	148 963	171 134	...	...	6.1	6.5	7.3	...	...
Israel - Israël[12]											
Total	C	40 137	40 236	38 894	38 924	39 718	6.7	6.6	6.2	6.0	6.0
Japan - Japon[13]											
Total	+C	784 595	762 028	798 138	799 999	757 331	6.2	6.0	6.3	6.3	5.9
Urban-Urbaine	+C	650 738	630 726	661 245	663 506	629 906	...	...	...	...	...
Rural-Rurale	+C	133 857	131 302	136 893	136 493	127 425	...	...	...	...	...
Jordan - Jordanie[14]											
Total	+C	39 376	39 443	45 618	49 794	46 873	8.3	8.0	9.1	9.6	8.8
Kazakhstan											
Total	C	96 048	85 872	90 873	92 852	98 986	6.4	5.8	6.1	6.2	6.7
Urban-Urbaine	C	54 801	50 178	52 006	54 395	58 529	6.5	6.0	6.2	6.5	7.0
Rural-Rurale	C	41 247	35 694	38 867	38 457	40 457	6.2	5.4	6.0	5.9	6.3

(See notes at end of table. — Voir notes à la fin du tableau.)

Continent, country or area and urban/rural residence / Continent, pays ou zone et résidence, urbaine/rurale	Code[1]	Marriages - Mariages					Rate - Taux				
		1998	1999	2000	2001	2002	1998	1999	2000	2001	2002
ASIA — ASIE											
Korea (Republic of) - Corée (République de)											
Total	+C	375 616	362 673	334 030	320 063	306 573	8.1	7.8	7.1	6.8	6.4
Urban-Urbaine	+C	304 318	294 612	273 040	261 575	252 808	...	...	...	...	...
Rural-Rurale	+C	71 298	68 061	60 990	58 488	53 765	...	...	...	...	...
Kuwait - Koweït											
Total	C	10 335	10 847	10 785	11 830	11 973	5.1	5.1	4.9	5.2	5.3
Kyrgyzstan - Kirghizistan											
Total	C	25 726	26 033	24 294	27 455	31 240	5.4	5.4	4.9	5.5	6.3
Urban-Urbaine	C	7 932	7 926	7 528	8 258	9 065	4.7	4.6	4.3	4.7	5.1
Rural-Rurale	C	17 794	18 107	16 766	19 197	22 175	5.7	5.8	5.3	6.0	6.9
Lebanon - Liban[11]											
Total	C	31 219	30 477	32 586	...	...	...	...	...	...	...
Mongolia - Mongolie											
Total	C	13 908	13 722	12 601	12 393	13 514	5.9	5.8	5.2	5.1	5.5
Urban-Urbaine	C	7 446	7 383	6 096	6 091	7 206	6.0	5.5	4.4	4.4	5.1
Rural-Rurale	C	6 462	6 339	6 505	6 302	6 308	5.9	6.2	6.3	6.0	6.0
Occupied Palestinian Territory - Territoire palestinien occupé											
Total	U	*24 400*	*24 874*	*23 890*	*24 635*	*22 611*	...	...	...	...	...
Philippines											
Total	U	*549 265*	*551 445*	*577 387*	*559 162*	...	...	...	...	...	...
Qatar											
Total	U	*1 851*	*1 905*	*2 096*	*2 194*	...	...	...	...	...	...
Saudi Arabia - Arabie saoudite											
Total	...	*70 169*	*74 938*	*79 595*	*81 576*	*90 982*	...	...	...	...	...
Singapore - Singapour[15,16,17]											
Total	C	23 106	25 648	22 561	22 280	23 198	5.9	6.5	5.6	5.4	5.6
Sri Lanka											
Total	+U	*169 813*	*169 634*	*186 548*	*186 698*	*190 618*	...	...	...	...	...
Syrian Arab Republic - République arabe syrienne[18]											
Total	+U	*130 835*	*136 157*	*139 843*	*153 842*	*174 449*	...	...	...	...	...
Tajikistan - Tadjikistan											
Total	C	...	*21 600	...	...	...	...	*3.5	...	...	...
Thailand - Thaïlande											
Total	C	...	*354 198	...	...	...	...	*5.8	...	...	...
Turkey - Turquie[19]											
Total	+U	*485 035*	*475 613*	*461 417*	*453 213*	...	...	...	...	...	...
Urban-Urbaine	+U	*302 739*	*294 248*	*301 280*	...	...	...	...	...	...	...
Rural-Rurale	+U	*182 296*	*181 365*	*160 137*	...	...	...	...	...	...	...
Turkmenistan - Turkménistan											
Total	C	*26 361	...	...	...	...	*5.4	...	...	...	...
Uzbekistan - Ouzbékistan											
Total	C	...	170 525	168 908	170 101	...	...	7.1	6.9	6.8	...
Urban-Urbaine	C	...	64 685	65 104	64 302	...	...	7.2	7.1	6.9	...
Rural-Rurale	C	...	105 840	103 804	105 799	...	...	7.1	6.7	6.7	...
Viet Nam											
Total	C	...	...	...	...	*964 701	...	...	...	...	*12.1
Urban-Urbaine	C	...	...	...	...	*254 281	...	...	...	...	*12.7
Rural-Rurale	C	...	...	...	...	*710 420	...	...	...	...	*11.9
EUROPE											
Albania - Albanie											
Total	C	27 887	...	...	...	...	7.4	...	...	...	...
Andorra - Andorre											
Total	C	208	178	226	213	186	3.2	2.7	3.4	3.2	2.8

23. Marriages and crude marriage rates, by urban/rural residence: 1998 - 2002
Mariages et taux bruts de nuptialité, selon la résidence, urbaine/rurale: 1998 - 2002 (continued — suite)

(See notes at end of table. — Voir notes à la fin du tableau.)

Continent, country or area and urban/rural residence / Continent, pays ou zone et résidence, urbaine/rurale	Code[1]	Marriages - Mariages					Rate - Taux				
		1998	1999	2000	2001	2002	1998	1999	2000	2001	2002
EUROPE											
Austria - Autriche[20]											
Total	C	39 143	39 485	39 228	34 213	36 570	4.8	4.9	4.8	4.3	4.5
Belarus - Bélarus											
Total	C	71 354	72 994	...	...	66 652	7.0	7.3	...	...	6.7
Urban-Urbaine	C	55 256	57 648	...	...	53 838	7.7	8.3	...	...	7.7
Rural-Rurale	C	16 098	15 346	...	...	12 814	5.3	5.0	...	...	4.4
Belgium - Belgique[21]											
Total	C	44 393	44 171	45 123	42 110	40 434	4.4	4.3	4.4	4.1	3.9
Bosnia and Herzegovina - Bosnie-Herzégovine											
Total	C	22 398	...	*21 216	...	...	6.1	...	...	...	...
Bulgaria - Bulgarie[22]											
Total	C	35 582	35 540	35 164	31 974	29 218	4.3	4.3	4.3	4.0	3.7
Urban-Urbaine	C	...	...	26 576	24 466	23 085	...	...	4.8	4.5	4.2
Rural-Rurale	C	...	...	8 588	7 508	6 133	...	...	3.3	3.1	2.6
Channel Islands: Guernsey - Îles Anglo-Normandes: Guernesey											
Total	C	356	385	343	...	...	6.0	6.4	5.7	...	...
Croatia - Croatie											
Total	C	24 243	23 778	22 017	22 076	22 806	5.4	5.2	5.0	5.0	5.1
Urban-Urbaine	C	14 241	...	12 439	12 380	12 918	...	...	...	...	...
Rural-Rurale	C	10 002	...	9 578	9 696	9 888	...	...	...	...	...
Czech Republic - République tchèque											
Total	C	55 027	53 523	55 321	52 374	52 732	5.3	5.2	5.4	5.1	5.2
Urban-Urbaine	C	41 476	40 370	41 763	39 666	40 014	5.4	5.3	5.5	5.2	5.3
Rural-Rurale	C	13 551	13 153	13 558	12 708	12 718	5.2	5.0	5.2	4.8	4.8
Denmark - Danemark[23]											
Total	C	34 733	35 439	38 388	36 567	37 210	6.6	6.7	7.2	6.8	6.9
Estonia - Estonie[24]											
Total	C	5 416	5 590	5 485	5 647	5 853	3.7	3.9	4.0	4.1	4.3
Urban-Urbaine	C	...	...	3 929	...	4 020	...	...	4.1	...	4.3
Rural-Rurale	C	...	...	1 304	...	1 491	...	...	3.1	...	3.6
Finland - Finlande[25]											
Total	C	24 023	24 271	26 150	24 830	26 069	4.7	4.7	5.1	4.8	5.2
Urban-Urbaine	C	16 992	...	...	17 843	19 398	5.5	...	...	5.6	6.0
Rural-Rurale	C	7 031	...	...	6 987	7 571	3.4	...	...	3.5	3.8
France[6,26]											
Total	C	271 361	286 191	297 922	288 255	280 600	4.6	4.9	5.1	4.9	4.7
Urban-Urbaine	C	212 630	222 831	...	...	...	...	...	...	...	...
Rural-Rurale	C	53 755	59 000	...	...	...	...	...	...	...	...
Germany - Allemagne											
Total	C	416 281	430 674	418 550	389 591	391 967	5.1	5.2	5.1	4.7	4.8
Gibraltar[27]											
Total	C	141	161	149	164	166	5.2	5.9	5.5	5.8	5.8
Greece - Grèce											
Total	C	55 489	61 165	61 848	58 491	...	5.3	5.8	6.2	5.8	...
Urban-Urbaine	C	38 197	...	...	...	...	...	...	...	...	...
Rural-Rurale	C	17 292	...	...	...	...	...	...	...	...	...
Hungary - Hongrie[6]											
Total	C	44 915	45 465	48 110	43 583	46 008	4.4	4.5	4.8	4.3	4.5
Urban-Urbaine	C	28 957	29 345	31 314	28 876	31 207	4.4	4.5	4.8	4.3	4.7
Rural-Rurale	C	15 117	15 138	15 890	13 769	13 912	4.2	4.3	4.5	3.9	3.9
Iceland - Islande[28]											
Total	C	1 529	1 560	1 777	1 484	1 619	5.6	5.6	6.3	5.2	5.6
Urban-Urbaine	C	1 415	1 471	1 668	1 406	1 550	5.6	5.7	6.4	5.3	5.8
Rural-Rurale	C	114	89	109	78	69	5.3	4.2	5.1	3.6	3.2
Ireland - Irlande											
Total	+C	16 783	18 526	19 168	*19 246	...	4.5	4.9	5.1	*5.0	...
Isle of Man - Îles de Man											
Total	C	435	377	417	392	430	5.9	...	5.6	5.1	5.6

23. Marriages and crude marriage rates, by urban/rural residence: 1998 - 2002
Mariages et taux bruts de nuptialité, selon la résidence, urbaine/rurale: 1998 - 2002 (continued — suite)

(See notes at end of table. — Voir notes à la fin du tableau.)

Continent, country or area and urban/rural residence / Continent, pays ou zone et résidence, urbaine/rurale	Code[1]	Marriages - Mariages					Rate - Taux				
		1998	1999	2000	2001	2002	1998	1999	2000	2001	2002
EUROPE											
Italy - Italie	C										
Total		280 034	280 330	284 410	280 488	265 635	4.9	4.9	4.9	4.8	4.6
Latvia - Lettonie	C										
Total		9 641	9 399	9 211	9 258	9 738	4.0	3.9	3.9	3.9	4.2
Urban-Urbaine	C	7 096	6 955	...	6 755	7 115	4.3	4.3	...	4.2	4.5
Rural-Rurale	C	2 545	2 444	...	2 503	2 623	3.4	3.2	...	3.3	3.5
Liechtenstein	C										
Total		...	...	...	...	173	...	...	...	...	5.1
Lithuania - Lituanie	C										
Total		18 486	17 868	16 906	15 764	16 151	5.2	5.1	4.8	4.5	4.7
Urban-Urbaine	C	12 423	12 150	11 705	11 036	11 637	5.2	5.1	5.0	4.7	5.0
Rural-Rurale	C	6 063	5 718	5 201	4 728	4 514	5.2	4.9	4.5	4.1	3.9
Luxembourg[28]	C										
Total		2 040	2 090	2 148	1 983	2 022	4.8	4.9	4.9	4.5	4.5
Malta - Malte[29]	C										
Total		2 376	2 409	2 545	2 194	2 240	6.1	6.2	6.5	5.6	5.6
Monaco	C										
Total		192	...	*160	...	...	...	...	*4.8	...	...
Netherlands - Pays-Bas[6,30,31]	C										
Total		86 956	89 428	88 074	79 677	85 808	5.5	5.7	5.5	5.0	5.3
Urban-Urbaine	C	...	...	48 058	45 261	47 645	...	...	...	...	...
Rural-Rurale	C	...	...	31 380	36 830	38 163	...	...	...	...	...
Norway - Norvège[32]	C										
Total		22 349	23 456	25 356	22 967	24 069	5.0	5.3	5.6	5.1	5.3
Poland - Pologne	C										
Total		209 430	219 398	211 150	195 122	191 935	5.4	5.7	5.5	5.0	5.0
Urban-Urbaine	C	125 194	131 990	...	...	...	5.2	5.5	...	...	...
Rural-Rurale	C	84 236	87 408	...	...	...	5.7	5.9	...	...	...
Portugal	C										
Total		66 575	68 710	63 752	58 390	56 457	6.7	6.9	6.4	5.7	5.4
Republic of Moldova - République de Moldova	C										
Total		21 814	23 524	21 684	21 065	21 685	6.0	6.5	6.0	5.8	6.0
Urban-Urbaine	C	9 479	9 886	9 514	9 727	10 194	6.2	6.5	6.3	6.5	6.9
Rural-Rurale	C	12 335	13 638	12 170	11 338	11 491	5.8	6.4	5.7	5.3	5.4
Romania - Roumanie	C										
Total		145 303	140 014	135 808	129 930	129 018	6.5	6.2	6.1	5.9	5.9
Urban-Urbaine	C	82 912	...	79 128	77 231	76 547	6.7	...	6.5	6.3	6.6
Rural-Rurale	C	62 391	...	56 680	52 699	52 471	6.1	...	5.6	5.2	5.2
Russian Federation - Fédération de Russie	C										
Total		848 691	911 162	1 266 800	*1 001 589	...	5.8	6.2	8.7	*7.0	...
San Marino - Saint-Marin	C										
Total		214	231	193	...	...	8.2	8.8	7.2	...	...
Serbia and Montenegro - Serbie-et-Montenegro	C										
Total		54 822	53 034	58 318	57 165	...	5.2	5.0	5.5	5.4	...
Urban-Urbaine	C	30 465	29 921	33 251	...	...	5.6	5.5	6.1	...	...
Rural-Rurale	C	24 357	23 113	25 067	...	...	4.7	4.5	4.9	...	...
Slovakia - Slovaquie	C										
Total		27 494	27 340	25 903	23 795	25 062	5.1	5.1	4.8	4.4	4.7
Urban-Urbaine	C	15 106	14 320	...	13 591	14 346	4.9	4.7	...	...	4.8
Rural-Rurale	C	12 388	13 020	...	10 204	10 716	5.3	5.6	...	...	4.5
Slovenia - Slovénie	C										
Total		7 528	7 716	7 201	6 935	7 064	3.8	3.9	3.6	3.5	3.5
Urban-Urbaine	C	3 764	...	3 571	3 569	3 768	...	...	...	...	3.9
Rural-Rurale	C	3 764	...	3 630	3 366	3 296	...	...	...	...	3.4
Spain - Espagne	C										
Total		207 041	208 129	216 451	206 254	...	5.2	5.3	5.4	5.1	...
Sweden - Suède	C										
Total		31 598	35 682	39 895	35 778	38 012	3.6	4.0	4.5	4.0	4.3

23. Marriages and crude marriage rates, by urban/rural residence: 1998 - 2002
Mariages et taux bruts de nuptialité, selon la résidence, urbaine/rurale: 1998 - 2002 (continued — suite)

(See notes at end of table. — Voir notes à la fin du tableau.)

Continent, country or area and urban/rural residence / Continent, pays ou zone et résidence, urbaine/rurale	Code[1]	Marriages - Mariages					Rate - Taux				
		1998	1999	2000	2001	2002	1998	1999	2000	2001	2002
EUROPE											
Switzerland - Suisse											
Total	C	38 683	40 646	39 758	35 987	40 213	5.4	5.7	5.5	5.0	5.5
Urban-Urbaine	C	26 952	28 427	28 031	25 668	...	5.6	5.9	5.8	5.2	...
Rural-Rurale	C	11 731	12 219	11 727	10 319	...	5.1	5.3	5.0	4.4	...
Tho Former Yugoslav Rep. of Macedonia - L'ex-République yougoslave de Macédoine											
Total	C	13 993	14 172	14 255	13 267	14 522	7.0	7.0	7.0	6.5	7.1
Urban-Urbaine	C	...	...	7 530	7 584	7 905	...	...	...	...	...
Rural-Rurale	C	...	...	6 725	5 683	6 617	...	...	...	...	...
Ukraine											
Total	C	310 504	...	...	309 602	317 228	6.1	...	...	6.3	6.6
Urban-Urbaine	C	219 172	...	...	223 638	231 532	6.4	...	...	...	...
Rural-Rurale	C	91 332	...	...	85 964	85 696	5.6	...	...	...	...
United Kingdom - Royaume-Uni											
Total	C	304 797	301 083	305 912	...	...	5.1	5.1	5.1	...	...
OCEANIA — OCEANIE											
Australia - Australie											
Total	+C	110 598	114 316	113 429	103 130	105 435	5.9	6.0	5.9	5.3	5.4
Cook Islands - Îles Cook											
Total	+C	259	387	715	578	604	14.9	23.6	39.9	31.8	32.8
Fiji - Fidji											
Total	+C	8 058	...	...	...	...	10.1	...	...	...	...
Guam[33]											
Total	C	1 328	1 456	1 499	1 418	1 288	8.9	9.5	9.7	9.0	8.0
New Caledonia - Nouvelle-Calédonie											
Total	C	1 005	943	995	925	905	4.9	4.5	4.7	4.3	4.2
New Zealand - Nouvelle-Zélande											
Total	+C	20 135	21 085	20 655	19 972	20 690	5.3	5.5	5.4	5.1	5.3
Niue - Nioué											
Total	...	10	15	12	8	15	...	...	...	...	...
Samoa											
Total	...	935	...	...	...	...	...	...	...	...	...
Tonga											
Total	+C	736	770	747	...	...	7.4	7.7	7.4	...	...

GENERAL NOTES - NOTES GENERALES

For certain countries, there is a discrepancy between the total number of marriages shown in this table and those shown in subsequent tables for the same year. Usually this discrepancy arises because the total number of marriages that occur in a given year is revised, although the remaining tabulations are not. Rates are the number of legal (recognized) marriages performed and registered per 1 000 mid-year population. Rates are shown only for countries or areas having a total of at least 30 marriages in a given year. For definitions of 'urban', see end of Technical Notes for table 6. For method of evaluation and limitations of data, see Technical Notes for this table. — Pour quelques pays il y a une discordance entre le nombre total des mariages présenté dans ce tableau et ceux présentés pour la même année. Habituellement ces différences apparaissent lorsque le nombre total des mariages pour une certaine année a été révisé; alors que les autres tabulations ne l'ont pas été. Les taux représentent le nombre de mariages qui ont été célébrés et reconnus par la loi pour 1 000 personnes au milieu de l'année. Les taux présentés ne se rapportent qu'aux pays où zones où l'on a enregistré un total d'au moins 30 mariages dans une année donnée. Pour les définitions des 'régions urbaines', se reporter à la fin des Notes techniques du tableau 6. Pour la méthode d'évaluation et les insuffisances des données, voir Notes techniques, pour ce tableau.

Italics: data from civil registers which are incomplete or of unknown completeness. — Italiques: données incomplètes ou dont le degré d'exactitude n'est pas connu, provenant des registres de l'état civil.

FOOTNOTES - NOTES

* Provisional. — Données provisoires.

[1] 'Code' indicates the source of data, as follows:
C - Civil registration, estimated over 90% complete
U - Civil registration, estimated less than 90% complete
+ - Data tabulated by date of registration rather than occurence.
... - Information not available

Le 'Code' indique la source des données, comme suit:
C - Registres de l'état civil considérés complets à 90 p. 100 au moins.
U - Registres de l'état civil qui ne sont pas considérés complets à 90 p. 100 au moins.
+ - Données exploitées selon la date de l'enregistrement et non la date de

l'événement.

... - Information pas disponible.

2 For Algerian population only. - Pour la population algérienne seulement.

3 Including marriages resumed after 'revocable divorce' (among Moslem population), which approximates legal separation. - Y compris les unions reconstituées après un 'divorce révocable' (parmi la population musulmane), qui est à peu près l'équivalent d'une séparation légale.

4 Data refer to Libyan nationals only. - Les données se raportent aux nationaux libyens seulement.

5 Data exclude visitors. - Les données non compris des visiteurs.

6 The difference between 'Total' and the sum of 'urban' and 'rural' is due to the cases of unknown place of residence or residence abroad. - La différence entre le 'Total' et la somme des données selon la résidence urbaine/rurale se rapporte à la situation ou on ignore la résidence ou si la résidence est à l'étranger.

7 Excluding tribal Indian population. - Non compris les Indiens vivant en tribus.

8 Excluding Indian jungle population. - Non compris les Indiens de la jungle.

9 Excluding nomadic Indian tribes. - Non compris les tribus d'Indiens nomades.

10 Data refer to government controlled areas. - Les données se raportent aux zones contrôlées par le Gouvernement.

11 Published by the United Nations Economic and Social Commission for Western Asia. - Publié par la Commission économique et sociale des Nations Unies pour l'Asie occidentale.

12 Including data for East Jerusalem and Israeli residents in certain other territories under occupation by Israeli military forces since June 1967. - Y compris les données pour Jérusalem-Est et les résidents israéliens dans certains autres territoires occupés depuis 1967 par les forces armées israéliennes.

13 For Japanese nationals in Japan only; however, rates computed using total population. - Pour les nationaux japonais au Japon seulement; toutefois, les taux sont calculés sur la base de la population totale.

14 Excluding data for Jordanian territory under occupation since June 1967 by Israeli military forces. Excluding foreigners, including registered Palestinian refugees. - Non compris les données pour le territoire jordanien occupé depuis juin 1967 par les forces armées israéliennes. Non compris les étrangers, mais y compris les réfugiés de Palestine enregistrés.

15 Registration of Kandyan marriages is complete; registration of Moslem and general marriages is incomplete. - Tous les mariages des Kandyens sont enregistrés; l'enregistrement des mariages musulmans et des autres mariages est incomplet.

16 Rates computed on population excluding transients afloat and non-locally domiciled military and civilian services personnel and their dependants. - Taux calculés sur la base d'un chiffre de population qui ne comprend pas les personnes de passage à bord de navires, ni les militaires et agents civils domiciliés hors du territoire et les membres de leur famille les accompagnant.

17 Figures exclude marriages previously officiated outside Singapore or under religious and customary rites. - Les figures excluent les mariages célébrés précédemment au dehors de Singapoure ou sous les rites réligieuse ou accoutumés.

18 Excluding nomads. - Non compris les nomades.

19 Data refer to provincial capitals and district centres only. - Les données se rapportent aux capitales des provinces et les chefs-lieux de districts seulement.

20 Excluding aliens temporarily in the area. - Non compris les étrangers se trouvant temporairement le territoire.

21 Including armed forces stationed outside the country, but excluding alien armed forces in the area unless marriage performed by local foreign authority. - Y compris les militaires nationaux hors du pays et les militaires étrangers en garnison sur le territoire, sauf si le mariage a été célébré pour l'autorité locale.

22 Including Bulgarian nationals outside the country, but excluding aliens in the area. - Y compris les nationaux bulgares à l'étranger, mais non compris les étrangers sur le territoire.

23 Excluding Faeroe Islands and Greenland. - Non compris les Iles Féroé et Gröenland.

24 Urban and rural distribution of marriages and divorces is displayed by place of residence of groom/husband. The difference between 'Total' and the sum of urban and rural is due to the unknown place of residence of grooms/husbands and to grooms/husbands living outside Estonia. - Les mariages et divorces sont classés par rapport à la résidence urbaine/rurale de l'époux. La somme des mariages et divorces par résidence urbaine/rurale est différente du 'total' car elle ne tient pas compte ni des résidences inconnues de l'époux ni des mariages et divorces d'époux vivant à l'étranger.

25 Marriages in which the bride was resident in Finland only. - Mariages où l'épouse a la résidence en Finlande seulement.

26 Including armed forces stationed outside the country. - Y compris les militaires nationaux hors du pays.

27 Rates computed on population excluding armed forces. - Taux calculés sur la base d'un chiffre de population qui ne comprend pas les militaires.

28 Data refer to de jure population. - Les données se raportent a la population de droit

29 Rates computed on population including civilian nationals temporarily outside the country. - Les taux sont calculés sur la base d'un chiffre de population qui comprend les civils nationaux temporairement hors du pays.

30 Including residents outside the country if listed in a Netherlands population register. - Y compris les résidents hors du pays, s'ils sont inscrits sur un registre de population néerlandais.

31 For 2002, including same sex marriages. - Pour 2002, y compris les mariages entre personnes du même sexe.

32 Marriages in which the groom was resident in Norway only. - Mariages où l'époux a la résidence en Norvège seulement.

33 Including United States military personnel, their dependants and contract employees. - Y compris les militaires des Etats-Unis, les membres de leur famille les accompagnant et les agents contractuels des Etats-Unis.

Table 24

Table 24 presents the marriages by age of groom and age of bride for as many years as possible between 1998 and 2002.

Description of variables: Marriage is defined as the act, ceremony or process by which the legal relationship of husband and wife is constituted. The legality of the union may be established by civil, religious or other means as recognized by the laws of each country. [i]

Marriage statistics in this table, therefore, include both first marriages and remarriages after divorce, widowhood or annulment. They do not, unless otherwise noted, include resumption of marriage ties after legal separation. These statistics refer to the number of marriages performed, and not to the number of persons marrying.

Age is defined as age at last birthday, that is, the difference between the date of birth and the date of the occurrence of the event, expressed in completed solar years. The age classification used in this table is the following: under 15 years, 5-year age groups through 70-74, and 75 years and over. The same classification is used for both grooms and brides.

To aid in the interpretation of data this table also provides information on the legal minimum age for marriage for grooms and the corresponding age for brides. Information is not available for all countries and, even for those for which data are at hand, it is sometimes not clear what "minimum age for marriage" refers to. In some cases, it appears to refer to the "age below which marriage is not valid without consent of parents or other specified persons"; in others, it appears to refer to the "age below which valid marriage cannot be performed, irrespective of consent". Beginning in 1986, the countries or areas providing data on marriages by age of bride and groom have been requested to specify "the minimum legal age at which marriage with parental consent can occur". The minimum age shown in this table primarily refers to this. When available the "age below which valid marriage cannot be performed, irrespective of consent" is noted in footnotes.

Reliability of data: Data from civil registers of marriages that are reported as incomplete (less than 90 per cent completeness) or of unknown completeness are considered unreliable and are set in *italics* rather than in roman type. Table 23 and the technical notes for that table provide more detailed information on the completeness of marriage registration. For more information about the quality of vital statistics data in general, see section 4.2 of the Technical Notes.

Limitations: Statistics on marriages by age of groom and age of bride are subject to the same qualifications as have been set forth for vital statistics in general and marriage statistics in particular as discussed in Section 4 of the Technical Notes.

The fact that marriage is a legal event, unlike birth and death that are biological events, has implications for international comparability of data. Marriage has been defined, for statistical purposes, in terms of the laws of individual countries or areas. These laws vary throughout the world. In addition, comparability is further limited because some countries or areas compile statistics only for civil marriages although religious marriages may also be legally recognized; in other countries or areas, the only available records are church registers and, therefore, the statistics may not reflect to marriages that are civil marriages only.

Because in many countries or areas marriage is a civil legal contract which, to establish its legality, must be celebrated before a civil officer, it follows that for these countries or areas registration would tend to be almost automatic at the time of, or immediately following, the marriage ceremony. This factor should be kept in mind when considering the reliability of data, described above. For this reason the practice of tabulating data by date of registration does not generally pose serious problems of comparability as it does in the case of birth and death statistics.

Because these statistics are classified according to age, they are subject to the limitations with respect to accuracy of age reporting similar to those already discussed in connection with Section 3.1.3 of the Technical Notes. It is probable that biases are less pronounced in marriage statistics, because information is obtained from the persons concerned and since marriage is a legal act, the participants are likely to give correct information. However, in some countries or areas, there appears to be an abnormal concentration of marriages at the legal minimum age for marriage and at the age at which valid marriage may be contracted without parental consent, indicating perhaps an overstatement in some cases to comply with the law.

Aside from the possibility of age misreporting, it should be noted that marriage patterns at younger ages, that is, for ages up to 24 years, are influenced to a large extent by laws regarding the minimum age for marriage. Information on legal minimum age for both grooms and brides is included in this table.

Factors that may influence age reporting, particularly at older ages include an inclination to understate the age of the bride in order that it may be equal to or less than that of the groom.

The absence of frequencies in the unknown age group does not necessarily indicate completely accurate reporting and tabulation of the age item. It is sometimes an indication that the unknowns have been eliminated by assigning ages to them before tabulation, or by proportionate distribution after tabulation.

Another age-reporting factor, that must be kept in mind in using these data is the variation that may result from calculating age at marriage from year of birth rather than from day, month and year of birth. Information on this factor is given in footnotes when known.

Earlier data: Marriages by age of groom and age of bride have been shown for the latest available year in most issues of the *Demographic Yearbook*. In addition, issues, including those featuring marriage and divorce statistics, have presented data covering a period of years. For information on the specific topics and the years covered, readers should consult the Historical Index.

NOTES

[i] *Principles and Recommendations for a Vital Statistics System Revision 2*, Sales No. E. 01.XVII.10, United Nations, New York, 2001

Tableau 24

Le tableau 24 présente des statistiques concernant les mariages classés selon l'âge de l'époux et selon l'âge de l'épouse pour le plus grand nombre possible d'années entre 1998 et 2002.

Description des variables : Le mariage désigne l'acte, la cérémonie ou la procédure qui établit un rapport légal entre mari et femme. L'union peut être rendue légale par une procédure civile ou religieuse, ou par toute autre procédure, conformément à la législation du pays[1].

Les statistiques de la nuptialité présentées dans ce tableau comprennent donc les premiers mariages et les remariages faisant suite à un divorce, un veuvage ou une annulation. Toutefois, sauf indication contraire, elles ne comprennent pas les unions reconstituées après une séparation légale. Ces statistiques se rapportent au nombre de mariages célébrés, non au nombre de personnes qui se marient.

L'âge désigne l'âge au dernier anniversaire, c'est-à-dire la différence entre la date de naissance et la date de l'événement, exprimée en années solaires révolues. Le classement par âge utilisé dans le tableau 24 comprend les groupes suivants : moins de 15 ans, groupes quinquennaux jusqu'à 70-74 ans, 75 ans et plus. On a adopté la même classification pour les deux sexes.

Pour faciliter l'interprétation des données, on a également indiqué l'âge minimal légal de nubilité pour le sexe masculin et pour le sexe féminin. On ne dispose pas à ce sujet de données pour tous les pays et, même lorsque l'on en possède, on ne sait pas toujours ce qu'il faut entendre par « âge minimum du mariage ». Dans certains cas, il semble qu'il s'agisse de « l'âge au-dessous duquel le mariage n'est pas valide sans le consentement des parents ou d'autres personnes autorisées »; dans d'autres, ce serait « l'âge au-dessous duquel le mariage ne peut pas être valide, même avec le consentement des personnes responsables ». À partir de 1986, il a été demandé aux pays ou zones qui communiquent des données sur les mariages selon l'âge de l'épouse et de l'époux de préciser l'âge de nubilité, à savoir « l'âge minimum auquel le mariage peut avoir lieu avec le consentement des parents ». Les âges minimaux cités dans le tableau correspondent principalement à cette notion. Lorsque les statistiques portent sur « l'âge au-dessous duquel le mariage ne peut pas être valide, même avec le consentement des personnes responsables », cela est indiqué en note.

Fiabilité des données : Les données sur les mariages issues des registres de l'état civil qui sont déclarées incomplètes (degré de complétude inférieur à 90 p. 100) ou dont le degré de complétude n'est pas connu sont jugées douteuses et apparaissent en itallque et non en caractères romains. Le tableau 23 et les notes techniques s'y rapportant présentent des renseignements plus détaillés sur le degré de complétude de l'enregistrement des mariages. Pour plus de précisions sur la qualité des données reposant sur les statistiques de l'état civil en général, voir la section 4.2 des notes techniques.

Insuffisance des données : Les statistiques des mariages selon l'âge de l'époux et selon l'âge de l'épouse appellent les mêmes réserves que celles formulées à propos des statistiques de l'état civil en général et des statistiques de la nuptialité en particulier (voir la section 4 des Notes techniques).

Le fait que le mariage soit un acte juridique, à la différence de la naissance et du décès, qui sont des faits biologiques, a des répercussions sur la comparabilité internationale des données. Aux fins de la statistique, le mariage est défini par la législation de chaque pays ou zone. Cette législation varie d'un pays à l'autre. La comparabilité est limitée en outre du fait que certains pays et zones ne réunissent des statistiques que pour les mariages civils, bien que les mariages religieux y soient également reconnus par la loi ; dans d'autres, les seuls relevés disponibles sont les registres des églises et, en conséquence, les statistiques peuvent ne pas rendre compte des mariages exclusivement civils.

Le mariage étant, dans de nombreux pays ou zones, un contrat juridique civil qui, pour être légal, doit être conclu devant un officier d'état civil, il s'ensuit que, dans ces pays ou zones, l'enregistrement se fait à peu près systématiquement au moment de la cérémonie ou immédiatement après. Il faut tenir compte de cet élément lorsque l'on évalue la fiabilité des données, dont il est question plus haut. C'est pourquoi la pratique consistant à exploiter les données selon la date de l'enregistrement ne pose généralement pas les graves problèmes de comparabilité auxquels on se heurte dans le cas des statistiques des naissances et des décès.

Étant donné que ces statistiques sont classées selon l'âge, elles appellent les mêmes réserves concernant l'exactitude des déclarations d'âge que celles dont il a déjà été question à la section 3.1.3 des Notes techniques. Il est probable que les statistiques de la nuptialité sont moins faussées par ce genre d'erreur, car les renseignements sont donnés par les intéressés eux-mêmes, et, comme le mariage est un acte juridique, il y a toutes chances que leurs déclarations soient exactes. Toutefois, dans certains pays ou zones, il semble y avoir une concentration anormale de mariages à l'âge minimal légal de nubilité ainsi qu'à l'âge auquel le mariage peut être valablement contracté sans le consentement des parents, ce qui peut indiquer que certains déclarants se vieillissent pour se conformer à la loi.

Outre la possibilité d'erreurs dans les déclarations d'âge, il convient de noter que la législation fixant l'âge minimal de nubilité influe notablement sur les caractéristiques de la nuptialité pour les premiers âges, c'est-à-dire jusqu'à 24 ans. Le tableau 24 indique l'âge minimal légal de nubilité pour les époux et les épouses.

Parmi les facteurs pouvant exercer une influence sur les déclarations d'âge, en particulier celles qui sont faites par des personnes plus âgées, il faut citer la tendance à diminuer l'âge de l'épouse de façon qu'il soit égal ou inférieur à celui de l'époux.

Si aucun nombre ne figure dans la rangée réservée aux âges inconnus, cela ne signifie pas nécessairement que les déclarations d'âge et l'exploitation des données par âge aient été tout à fait exactes. C'est parfois une indication que l'on a attribué un âge aux personnes d'âge inconnu avant l'exploitation des données ou qu'elles ont été réparties proportionnellement entre les différents groupes après cette opération.

Il importe de ne pas oublier non plus, lorsque l'on utilisera ces données, que l'on calcule parfois l'âge des conjoints au moment du mariage sur la base de l'année de naissance seulement et non d'après la date exacte (jour, mois et année) de naissance. Des renseignements à ce sujet sont donnés en note chaque fois que possible.

Donnés publiées antérieurement : On trouve dans la plupart des éditions de l'*Annuaire démographique* des statistiques concernant les mariages selon l'âge de l'époux et selon l'âge de l'épouse qui ont été établies à partir des données les plus récentes dont on disposait à l'époque. En outre, certaines éditions, y compris celles qui étaient plus particulièrement consacrées aux statistiques de la nuptialité et de la divortialité, présentaient des séries chronologiques. Pour plus de précisions concernant les années et les sujets pour lesquels des données ont été publiées, se reporter à l'index historique.

NOTE

[1] *Principes et recommandations pour un système de statistiques de l'état civil, deuxième révision,* numéro de vente F.01.XVII.10, publication des Nations Unies, New York, 2003.

24. Marriages by age of bridegroom and by age of bride: 1998 - 2002
Mariages selon l'âge de l'époux et selon l'âge de l'épouse: 1998 - 2002

(See notes at end of table. — Voir notes à la fin du tableau.)

Continent, country or area and age / Continent, pays ou zone et âge	1998 Groom Epoux	1998 Bride Epouse	1999 Groom Epoux	1999 Bride Epouse	2000 Groom Epoux	2000 Bride Epouse	2001 Groom Epoux	2001 Bride Epouse	2002 Groom Epoux	2002 Bride Epouse
AFRICA — AFRIQUE										
Egypt - Égypte+,1										
Groom — Epoux 18 ⊗										
Bride — Epouse 16 ⊗										
All ages - Tous âges	503 651	503 651	525 412	525 412	...	...	...	...	...	...
0-19	15 724	63 838	14 982	64 422	...	...	...	...	...	...
20-24	106 970	141 655	115 939	152 234	...	...	...	...	...	...
25-29	183 211	137 177	192 784	143 382	...	...	...	...	...	...
30-34	110 462	130 581	111 874	134 280	...	...	...	...	...	...
35-39	40 594	14 116	42 038	14 515	...	...	...	...	...	...
40-44	16 337	7 259	16 707	7 500	...	...	...	...	...	...
45-49	11 067	4 424	11 422	4 447	...	...	...	...	...	...
50-54	6 152	2 044	6 527	2 185	...	...	...	...	...	...
55-59	4 412	1 029	4 296	987	...	...	...	...	...	...
60-64	3 471	584	3 514	617	...	...	...	...	...	...
65-69	2 545	354	2 549	333	...	...	...	...	...	...
70-74	1 546	241	1 555	178	...	...	...	...	...	...
75+	1 021	345	1 045	329	...	...	...	...	...	...
Unknown - Inconnu	139	4	180	3	...	...	...	...	...	...
Mauritius - Maurice+										
Groom — Epoux 16 ⊗										
Bride — Epouse 16 ⊗										
All ages - Tous âges	10 898	10 898	11 295	11 295	10 635	10 635	...	...	10 484	10 484
0-14	-	-	-	-	-	1	...	...	-	-
15-19	198	2 522	172	2 442	167	1 819	...	...	134	1 666
20-24	2 268	4 110	2 402	4 356	2 131	4 025	...	...	2 130	4 078
25-29	3 741	1 927	3 879	2 009	3 587	2 152	...	...	3 599	2 162
30-34	2 435	1 111	2 405	1 142	2 206	1 184	...	...	2 109	1 156
35-39	1 068	593	1 115	673	1 148	675	...	...	1 129	687
40-44	517	298	573	318	548	352	...	...	579	338
45-49	306	194	342	195	345	227	...	...	357	210
50-54	145	76	174	98	246	108	...	...	201	97
55-59	103	32	115	25	119	50	...	...	123	46
60-64	56	18	54	19	58	22	...	...	59	27
65-69	24	5	39	11	35	9	...	...	41	11
70-74	19	8	13	3	23	7	...	...	15	3
75+	18	4	12	4	22	4	...	...	8	3
Unknown - Inconnu	-	-	-	-	-	-	...	...	8	3
Réunion										
All ages - Tous âges	...	...	3 446	3 446	...	...	...	...	...	...
15-19	...	...	...	214	...	...	...	...	...	...
18-19	...	...	19	...	...	...	...	...	...	...
20-24	...	...	461	985	...	...	...	...	...	...
25-29	...	...	1 113	954	...	...	...	...	...	...
30-34	...	...	835	629	...	...	...	...	...	...
35-39	...	...	409	315	...	...	...	...	...	...
40-44	...	...	237	146	...	...	...	...	...	...
45-49	...	...	142	93	...	...	...	...	...	...
50-54	...	...	94	49	...	...	...	...	...	...
55-59	...	...	49	26	...	...	...	...	...	...
60+	...	...	87	35	...	...	...	...	...	...
Seychelles+										
All ages - Tous âges	718	718	...	...	...	...	790	790	...	...
15-19	4	26	...	...	...	...	7	26	...	...
20-24	73	121	...	...	...	...	66	136	...	...
25-29	177	208	...	...	...	...	149	198	...	...
30-34	188	176	...	...	...	...	210	196	...	...
35-39	120	100	...	...	...	...	156	103	...	...
40-44	65	33	...	...	...	...	92	62	...	...
45-49	23	24	...	...	...	...	43	35	...	...
50-54	30	11	...	...	...	...	27	19	...	...
55+	38	19	...	...	...	...	40	15	...	...
South Africa - Afrique du Sud										
All ages - Tous âges	146 741	146 741	...	...	...	...	...	...	...	...
0-19	262	2 971	...	...	...	...	...	...	...	...

24. Marriages by age of bridegroom and by age of bride: 1998 - 2002
Mariages selon l'âge de l'époux et selon l'âge de l'épouse: 1998 - 2002 (continued — suite)

(See notes at end of table. — Voir notes à la fin du tableau.)

Continent, country or area and age / Continent, pays ou zone et âge	1998 Groom Epoux	1998 Bride Epouse	1999 Groom Epoux	1999 Bride Epouse	2000 Groom Epoux	2000 Bride Epouse	2001 Groom Epoux	2001 Bride Epouse	2002 Groom Epoux	2002 Bride Epouse
AFRICA — AFRIQUE										
South Africa - Afrique du Sud										
20-24	13 300	31 036	...	...	...	...	...	...	...	...
25-29	35 387	42 166	...	...	...	...	...	...	...	...
30-34	32 840	27 640	...	...	...	...	...	...	...	...
35-39	22 694	16 720	...	...	...	...	...	...	...	...
40-44	14 501	9 922	...	...	...	...	...	...	...	...
45-49	9 810	6 274	...	...	...	...	...	...	...	...
50-54	6 075	3 563	...	...	...	...	...	...	...	...
55-59	4 400	2 436	...	...	...	...	...	...	...	...
60-64	2 760	1 693	...	...	...	...	...	...	...	...
65-69	2 174	1 049	...	...	...	...	...	...	...	...
70-74	1 297	442	...	...	...	...	...	...	...	...
75+	1 241	829	...	...	...	...	...	...	...	...
Tunisia - Tunisie										
Groom — Epoux 20 ⊗										
Bride — Epouse 17 ⊗										
All ages - Tous âges	56 081	56 081	...	...	...	...	...	...	...	...
15-19	-	7 411	...	...	...	...	...	...	...	...
20-24	5 960	21 217	...	...	...	...	...	...	...	...
25-29	18 259	15 689	...	...	...	...	...	...	...	...
30-34	19 332	6 496	...	...	...	...	...	...	...	...
35-39	6 628	2 515	...	...	...	...	...	...	...	...
40-44	2 162	1 159	...	...	...	...	...	...	...	...
45+	...	918	...	...	...	...	...	...	...	...
45-49	961	...	...	...	...	...	...	...	...	...
50-54	507	...	...	...	...	...	...	...	...	...
55+	1 798	...	...	...	...	...	...	...	...	...
Unknown - Inconnu	474	676	...	...	...	...	...	...	...	...
AMERICA, NORTH — AMERIQUE DU NORD										
Bahamas										
Groom — Epoux 15 ⊗										
Bride — Epouse 15 ⊗										
All ages - Tous âges	...	...	...	...	...	...	1 787	1 787	...	...
15-19	...	...	...	...	...	...	11	82	...	...
20-24	...	...	...	...	...	...	254	430	...	...
25-29	...	...	...	...	...	...	490	474	...	...
30-34	...	...	...	...	...	...	406	333	...	...
35-39	...	...	...	...	...	...	247	197	...	...
40-44	...	...	...	...	...	...	120	132	...	...
45-49	...	...	...	...	...	...	97	61	...	...
50-54	...	...	...	...	...	...	64	41	...	...
55-59	...	...	...	...	...	...	36	12	...	...
60+	...	...	...	...	...	...	51	14	...	...
Unknown - Inconnu	...	...	...	...	...	...	11	11	...	...
Belize⁺										
All ages - Tous âges	1 374	1 374	...	...	...	...	...	...	...	...
0-14	-	13	...	...	...	...	...	...	...	...
15-19	97	329	...	...	...	...	...	...	...	...
20-24	443	434	...	...	...	...	...	...	...	...
25-29	332	273	...	...	...	...	...	...	...	...
30-34	198	142	...	...	...	...	...	...	...	...
35-39	99	64	...	...	...	...	...	...	...	...
40-44	62	31	...	...	...	...	...	...	...	...
45-49	41	35	...	...	...	...	...	...	...	...
50-54	25	13	...	...	...	...	...	...	...	...
55-59	21	14	...	...	...	...	...	...	...	...
60+	43	15	...	...	...	...	...	...	...	...
Unknown - Inconnu	13	11	...	...	...	...	...	...	...	...
Bermuda - Bermudes										
All ages - Tous âges	1 033	1 033	...	...	...	...	...	...	937	937
0-19	...	...	...	...	...	...	...	...	2	8

24. Marriages by age of bridegroom and by age of bride: 1998 - 2002
Mariages selon l'âge de l'époux et selon l'âge de l'épouse: 1998 - 2002 (continued — suite)

(See notes at end of table. — Voir notes à la fin du tableau.)

Continent, country or area and age / Continent, pays ou zone et âge	1998 Groom Epoux	1998 Bride Epouse	1999 Groom Epoux	1999 Bride Epouse	2000 Groom Epoux	2000 Bride Epouse	2001 Groom Epoux	2001 Bride Epouse	2002 Groom Epoux	2002 Bride Epouse
AMERICA, NORTH — AMERIQUE DU NORD										
Bermuda - Bermudes										
15-19	1	5	...	...	...	...	...	...	...	...
20-24	72	110	...	...	...	...	...	...	...	...
20-29	...	...	...	...	...	...	...	...	206	302
25-29	222	298	...	...	...	...	...	...	...	...
30-34	261	251	...	...	...	...	...	...	...	...
30-39	...	...	...	...	...	...	...	...	423	397
35-39	159	153	...	...	...	...	...	...	...	...
40-44	126	104	...	...	...	...	...	...	...	...
40-49	...	...	...	...	...	...	...	...	165	146
45-49	77	56	...	...	...	...	...	...	...	...
50-54	57	34	...	...	...	...	...	...	...	...
50-59	...	...	...	...	...	...	...	...	97	65
55-59	28	13	...	...	...	...	...	...	...	...
60-64	16	5	...	...	...	...	...	...	...	...
60+	...	...	...	...	...	...	...	...	44	19
65-69	11	2	...	...	...	...	...	...	...	...
70-74	2	-	...	...	...	...	...	...	...	...
75+	1	2	...	...	...	...	...	...	...	...
Canada										
Groom — Epoux 16 ⊗										
Bride — Epouse 16 ⊗										
All ages - Tous âges	...	...	...	...	...	...	146 618	146 618	...	...
15-19	...	...	...	...	...	...	976	3 674	...	...
20-24	...	...	...	...	...	...	19 912	32 479	...	...
25-29	...	...	...	...	...	...	43 787	45 073	...	...
30-34	...	...	...	...	...	...	30 309	25 056	...	...
35-39	...	...	...	...	...	...	18 172	14 550	...	...
40-44	...	...	...	...	...	...	11 308	9 481	...	...
45-49	...	...	...	...	...	...	7 580	6 728	...	...
50-54	...	...	...	...	...	...	5 670	4 345	...	...
55-59	...	...	...	...	...	...	3 466	2 295	...	...
60-64	...	...	...	...	...	...	2 053	1 190	...	...
65-69	...	...	...	...	...	...	1 386	791	...	...
70-74	...	...	...	...	...	...	965	501	...	...
75+	...	...	...	...	...	...	970	426	...	...
Unknown - Inconnu	...	...	...	...	...	...	64	29	...	...
Costa Rica										
Groom — Epoux 15 ⊗										
Bride — Epouse 15 ⊗										
All ages - Tous âges	...	...	...	...	24 436	24 436	23 790	23 790	...	...
0-14	...	...	...	...	-	155	-	81	...	...
15-19	...	...	...	...	1 419	5 209	1 328	4 907	...	...
20-24	...	...	...	...	7 094	7 722	6 934	7 629	...	...
25-29	...	...	...	...	6 413	4 852	6 101	4 669	...	...
30-34	...	...	...	...	3 797	2 525	3 667	2 444	...	...
35-39	...	...	...	...	2 046	1 394	2 015	1 394	...	...
40-44	...	...	...	...	1 209	870	1 184	923	...	...
45-49	...	...	...	...	763	547	807	530	...	...
50-54	...	...	...	...	478	294	444	294	...	...
55-59	...	...	...	...	270	179	300	162	...	...
60-64	...	...	...	...	207	94	227	105	...	...
65+	...	...	...	...	333	117	562	127	...	...
Unknown - Inconnu	...	...	...	...	407	478	441	525	...	...
Cuba										
Groom — Epoux 16 ⊗										
Bride — Epouse 14 ⊗										
All ages - Tous âges	64 900	64 900	57 252	57 252	57 001	57 001	...	...	...	...
0-14	4	324	2	318	5	282	...	...	...	...
15-19	1 860	8 423	1 608	7 629	1 509	7 141	...	...	...	...
20-24	12 826	16 434	10 239	13 212	9 384	12 143	...	...	...	...
25-29	16 446	14 719	13 724	12 174	13 332	11 956	...	...	...	...

(See notes at end of table. — Voir notes à la fin du tableau.)

Continent, country or area and age / Continent, pays ou zone et âge	1998 Groom Epoux	1998 Bride Epouse	1999 Groom Epoux	1999 Bride Epouse	2000 Groom Epoux	2000 Bride Epouse	2001 Groom Epoux	2001 Bride Epouse	2002 Groom Epoux	2002 Bride Epouse
AMERICA, NORTH — AMERIQUE DU NORD										
Cuba										
Groom — Epoux 16 ⊗										
Bride — Epouse 14 ⊗										
30-34	12 519	10 099	10 420	8 552	10 127	8 527	...	...	...	...
35-39	7 532	5 870	6 955	5 802	7 587	6 409	...	...	...	...
40-44	4 033	3 165	4 021	3 080	4 158	3 398	...	...	...	...
45-49	3 126	2 233	3 100	2 379	3 139	2 566	...	...	...	...
50-54	2 236	1 559	2 367	1 653	2 515	1 861	...	...	...	...
55-59	1 611	837	1 738	1 040	1 918	1 159	...	...	...	...
60-64	1 060	520	1 250	648	1 362	721	...	...	...	...
65-69	660	282	785	320	798	360	...	...	...	...
70-74	435	196	484	213	539	222	...	...	...	...
75+	472	177	507	176	572	202	...	...	...	...
Unknown - Inconnu	80	62	52	56	56	54	...	...	...	...
El Salvador+										
Groom — Epoux 16 ⊗										
Bride — Epouse 14 ⊗										
All ages - Tous âges	25 937	25 937	34 346	34 346	28 275	28 275	29 287	29 287	26 077	26 077
0-14	-	66	-	105	-	80		85	-	42
15-19	1 469	4 622	1 717	5 613	1 366	4 343	1 272	4 262	1 026	3 446
20-24	7 707	8 502	9 792	10 981	7 831	8 997	7 999	9 207	6 609	7 790
25-29	6 536	5 530	8 849	7 383	6 999	6 005	7 211	6 369	6 601	6 012
30-34	3 756	2 771	5 099	4 126	4 287	3 327	4 547	3 628	4 048	3 247
35-39	2 167	1 707	3 001	2 344	2 544	2 034	2 712	2 113	2 539	2 040
40-44	1 333	1 014	1 918	1 384	1 583	1 273	1 742	1 322	1 626	1 302
45-49	965	693	1 293	972	1 126	890	1 225	935	1 043	820
50-54	632	407	897	625	838	526	806	570	845	588
55-59	493	257	660	325	581	361	599	358	612	331
60-64	351	168	456	239	471	207	512	206	478	231
65+	526	196	664	249	649	232	662	232	650	228
Unknown - Inconnu	2	4	...	...	...	...	...	...	...	...
Grenada - Grenade+										
All ages - Tous âges	563	563	570	570	616	616	...	...	...	...
15-19	-	8	2	10	2	16	...	...	...	...
20-24	23	82	34	92	44	91	...	...	...	...
25-29	146	162	131	160	132	163	...	...	...	...
30-34	148	132	143	114	149	122	...	...	...	...
35-39	93	80	102	88	112	93	...	...	...	...
40-44	50	38	51	37	70	58	...	...	...	...
45-49	38	26	40	23	50	38	...	...	...	...
50-54	29	14	20	21	18	13	...	...	...	...
55-59	10	4	18	5	14	9	...	...	...	...
60-64	11	6	13	9	13	8	...	...	...	...
65+	13	9	13	8	11	4	...	...	...	...
Unknown - Inconnu	2	2	-	3	1	1	...	...	...	...
Guadeloupe										
All ages - Tous âges	...	...	...	...	...	...	...	...	1 809	1 809
15-19	...	...	...	...	...	...	...	...	-	35
20-24	...	...	...	...	...	...	...	...	91	223
25-29	...	...	...	...	...	...	...	...	377	523
30-34	...	...	...	...	...	...	...	...	503	401
35-39	...	...	...	...	...	...	...	...	369	255
40-44	...	...	...	...	...	...	...	...	204	165
45-49	...	...	...	...	...	...	...	...	99	89
50-54	...	...	...	...	...	...	...	...	68	45
55-59	...	...	...	...	...	...	...	...	44	29
60-64	...	...	...	...	...	...	...	...	19	23
65-69	...	...	...	...	...	...	...	...	34	10
70-74	...	...	...	...	...	...	...	...	1	11

(See notes at end of table. — Voir notes à la fin du tableau.)

Continent, country or area and age / Continent, pays ou zone et âge	1998		1999		2000		2001		2002	
	Groom Epoux	Bride Epouse	Groom Epoux	Bride Epouse	Groom Epoux	Bride Epouse	Groom Epoux	Bride Epouse	Groom Epoux	Bride Epouse
AMERICA, NORTH — AMERIQUE DU NORD										
Guatemala										
Groom — Epoux 16 [⊗]										
Bride — Epouse 14 [⊗]										
All ages - Tous âges	51 709	51 709	...	...	...	...	...	...	...	...
0-14	22	1 258	...	...	...	...	...	...	...	...
15-19	9 346	19 924	...	...	...	...	...	...	...	...
20-24	19 495	14 881	...	...	...	...	...	...	...	...
25-29	9 416	6 226	...	...	...	...	...	...	...	...
30-34	4 573	3 102	...	...	...	...	...	...	...	...
35-39	2 693	2 012	...	...	...	...	...	...	...	...
40-44	1 737	1 372	...	...	...	...	...	...	...	...
45-49	1 240	977	...	...	...	...	...	...	...	...
50-54	912	649	...	...	...	...	...	...	...	...
55-59	699	467	...	...	...	...	...	...	...	...
60-64	586	337	...	...	...	...	...	...	...	...
65-69	429	204	...	...	...	...	...	...	...	...
70-74	248	115	...	...	...	...	...	...	...	...
75+	204	76	...	...	...	...	...	...	...	...
Unknown - Inconnu	109	109	...	...	...	...	...	...	...	...
Martinique										
All ages - Tous âges	...	...	...	...	...	...	...	...	1 524	1 524
15-19	...	...	...	...	...	...	...	...	1	6
20-24	...	...	...	...	...	...	...	...	42	140
25-29	...	...	...	...	...	...	...	...	321	432
30-34	...	...	...	...	...	...	...	...	366	340
35-39	...	...	...	...	...	...	...	...	281	236
40-44	...	...	...	...	...	...	...	...	176	142
45-49	...	...	...	...	...	...	...	...	95	88
50-54	...	...	...	...	...	...	...	...	92	65
55-59	...	...	...	...	...	...	...	...	55	25
60-64	...	...	...	...	...	...	...	...	41	26
65-69	...	...	...	...	...	...	...	...	23	13
70+	...	...	...	...	...	...	...	...	31	11
Mexico - Mexique [1]										
Groom — Epoux 17 [⊗]										
Bride — Epouse 15 [⊗]										
All ages - Tous âges	704 456	704 456	743 856	743 856	707 422	707 422	...	...	...	...
0-14	571	9 100	432	9 005	684	8 345	...	...	...	...
15-19	97 762	216 809	100 317	221 571	95 878	208 090	...	...	...	...
20-24	275 221	255 541	279 710	262 171	257 844	243 353	...	...	...	...
25-29	182 025	130 411	194 658	142 456	186 990	140 046	...	...	...	...
30-34	72 583	45 423	79 061	51 580	77 951	51 131	...	...	...	...
35-39	31 232	19 848	35 831	23 587	34 904	23 276	...	...	...	...
40-44	15 557	10 383	18 654	12 724	18 056	12 392	...	...	...	...
45-49	8 826	6 094	10 605	7 475	11 030	7 740	...	...	...	...
50+	20 679	10 847	24 588	13 287	24 085	13 049	...	...	...	...
Panama [2]										
Groom — Epoux 16 [⊗]										
Bride — Epouse 14 [⊗]										
All ages - Tous âges	10 415	10 415	10 388	10 388	...	...	...	...	...	...
0-14	-	32	-	20	...	...	...	...	...	...
15-19	170	873	192	832	...	...	...	...	...	...
20-24	1 832	2 775	1 828	2 626	...	...	...	...	...	...
25-29	3 017	2 793	3 000	2 904	...	...	...	...	...	...
30-34	1 970	1 511	2 015	1 551	...	...	...	...	...	...
35-39	1 075	805	1 146	817	...	...	...	...	...	...
40-44	614	516	...	...	...	...	...	...	...	...
40-49	...	...	1 099	866	...	...	...	...	...	...
45-49	468	340	...	...	...	...	...	...	...	...
50-54	357	228	...	...	...	...	...	...	...	...
50-59	...	...	520	383	...	...	...	...	...	...
55-59	259	173	...	...	...	...	...	...	...	...

24. Marriages by age of bridegroom and by age of bride: 1998 - 2002
Mariages selon l'âge de l'époux et selon l'âge de l'épouse: 1998 - 2002 (continued — suite)

(See notes at end of table. — Voir notes à la fin du tableau.)

Continent, country or area and age / Continent, pays ou zone et âge	1998 Groom Epoux	1998 Bride Epouse	1999 Groom Epoux	1999 Bride Epouse	2000 Groom Epoux	2000 Bride Epouse	2001 Groom Epoux	2001 Bride Epouse	2002 Groom Epoux	2002 Bride Epouse
AMERICA, NORTH — AMERIQUE DU NORD										
Panama[2]										
Groom — Epoux 16 ⊗										
Bride — Epouse 14 ⊗										
60-64	252	102	...	...	...	...	...	...	...	...
60-69	...	...	316	131	...	...	...	...	...	...
65-69	108	68	...	...	...	...	...	...	...	...
70+	...	...	129	34	...	...	...	...	...	...
70-74	77	37	...	...	...	...	...	...	...	...
75+	89	22	...	...	...	...	...	...	...	...
Unknown - Inconnu	127	140	143	224	...	...	...	...	...	...
Puerto Rico - Porto Rico										
Groom — Epoux 16 ⊗										
Bride — Epouse 14 ⊗										
All ages - Tous âges	26 760	26 760	27 255	27 255	25 980	25 980	...	...	25 645	25 645
0-14	-	144	-	133	-	117	...	...	-	74
15-19	2 209	4 862	2 115	4 721	1 921	4 281	...	...	1 445	3 401
20-24	8 285	8 464	8 298	8 420	7 705	8 016	...	...	6 861	7 500
25-29	6 477	5 380	6 538	5 547	6 190	5 378	...	...	6 209	5 508
30-34	3 189	2 764	3 370	2 929	3 298	2 759	...	...	3 590	3 073
35-39	2 014	1 753	2 090	1 897	2 044	1 771	...	...	2 162	1 987
40-44	1 346	1 115	1 416	1 247	1 360	1 245	...	...	1 545	1 383
45-49	976	838	988	851	1 022	874	...	...	1 158	1 022
50-54	700	567	808	600	812	621	...	...	860	672
55+	1 563	872	1 632	910	1 628	917	...	...	1 815	1 025
Unknown - Inconnu	1	1	-	-	-	1	...	...	-	-
Saint Kitts and Nevis - Saint-Kitts-et-Nevis+										
All ages - Tous âges	315	315	...	...	...	...	...	...	...	...
15-19	3	5	...	...	...	...	...	...	...	...
20-24	28	44	...	...	...	...	...	...	...	...
25-29	72	84	...	...	...	...	...	...	...	...
30-34	62	76	...	...	...	...	...	...	...	...
35-39	57	47	...	...	...	...	...	...	...	...
40-44	36	28	...	...	...	...	...	...	...	...
45-49	21	13	...	...	...	...	...	...	...	...
50-54	19	8	...	...	...	...	...	...	...	...
55-59	6	3	...	...	...	...	...	...	...	...
60-64	2	...	...	...	...	...	...	...	...	...
65+	4	3	...	...	...	...	...	...	...	...
Unknown - Inconnu	5	4	...	...	...	...	...	...	...	...
Saint Lucia - Sainte-Lucie										
All ages - Tous âges	509	509	...	...	...	...	...	...	472	472
0-14	-	-	...	...	...	...	...	...	-	-
15-19	3	12	...	...	...	...	...	...	1	12
20-24	55	100	...	...	...	...	...	...	34	74
25-29	134	149	...	...	...	...	...	...	104	121
30-34	109	102	...	...	...	...	...	...	107	90
35-39	91	63	...	...	...	...	...	...	74	76
40-44	46	32	...	...	...	...	...	...	58	44
45-49	19	19	...	...	...	...	...	...	30	20
50-54	20	8	...	...	...	...	...	...	21	12
55-59	7	9	...	...	...	...	...	...	13	12
60-64	9	6	...	...	...	...	...	...	8	5
65+	16	7	...	...	...	...	...	...	22	6
Unknown - Inconnu	-	2	...	...	...	...	...	...	-	-

24. Marriages by age of bridegroom and by age of bride: 1998 - 2002
Mariages selon l'âge de l'époux et selon l'âge de l'épouse: 1998 - 2002 (continued — suite)

(See notes at end of table. — Voir notes à la fin du tableau.)

Continent, country or area and age / Continent, pays ou zone et âge	1998		1999		2000		2001		2002	
	Groom Epoux	Bride Epouse	Groom Epoux	Bride Epouse	Groom Epoux	Bride Epouse	Groom Epoux	Bride Epouse	Groom Epoux	Bride Epouse
AMERICA, SOUTH — AMERIQUE DU SUD										
Brazil - Brésil[3]										
Groom — Epoux 14 ⊗										
Bride — Epouse 12 ⊗										
All ages - Tous âges	698 614	698 614	788 744	788 744	732 721	732 721	710 121	710 121	...	...
0-14	8	2 021	33	2 029	44	1 685	68	1 270	...	...
15-19	41 022	193 967	42 959	204 117	38 702	181 666	29 709	150 034	...	...
20-24	246 436	239 035	265 970	264 658	242 980	245 478	219 990	238 056	...	...
25-29	206 529	136 968	229 418	158 292	212 531	149 788	208 510	154 755	...	...
30-34	100 957	61 355	117 125	73 913	109 911	70 890	114 045	75 584	...	...
35-39	43 271	27 860	54 337	36 382	52 524	35 456	55 806	38 510	...	...
40-44	20 264	14 510	26 571	18 968	25 876	18 483	28 223	20 246	...	...
45-49	11 748	8 682	15 655	11 660	14 766	10 978	16 104	12 624	...	...
50-54	7 742	5 386	10 198	7 099	9 851	6 960	11 121	7 971	...	...
55-59	5 981	3 621	7 738	4 768	7 190	4 281	7 659	4 688	...	...
60-64	4 703	2 044	6 125	2 746	5 824	2 630	6 132	2 803	...	...
65+	9 266	2 369	11 521	2 931	11 035	2 756	12 294	3 051	...	...
Unknown - Inconnu	687	793	1 094	1 181	1 487	1 670	460	529	...	...
Chile - Chili+										
Groom — Epoux 14 ⊗										
Bride — Epouse 12 ⊗										
All ages - Tous âges	73 456	73 456	69 765	69 765	...	...	...	...	60 971	60 971
0-14	1	210	2	178	...	...	...	...	-	91
15-19	3 076	12 042	2 687	10 607	...	...	...	...	1 757	7 169
20-24	22 874	26 043	20 200	23 817	...	...	...	...	14 876	19 574
25-29	24 867	19 772	24 430	19 675	...	...	...	...	21 636	18 399
30-34	11 977	7 832	11 648	7 712	...	...	...	...	11 669	7 767
35-39	4 784	3 468	4 748	3 493	...	...	...	...	4 797	3 365
40-44	2 100	1 558	2 165	1 670	...	...	...	...	2 209	1 806
45-49	1 037	898	1 067	905	...	...	...	...	1 151	972
50-54	703	573	743	603	...	...	...	...	758	671
55-59	557	384	547	414	...	...	...	...	550	441
60-64	437	288	443	291	...	...	...	...	442	297
65-69	417	210	417	184	...	...	...	...	375	193
70-74	289	90	288	118	...	...	...	...	318	138
75+	337	88	380	98	...	...	...	...	433	88
Ecuador - Équateur[4]										
Groom — Epoux 14 ⊗										
Bride — Epouse 12 ⊗										
All ages - Tous âges	69 867	69 867	...	...	...	...	...	...	66 208	66 208
0-14	30	884	...	...	...	...	...	...	41	676
15-19	8 421	20 577	...	...	...	...	...	...	7 701	18 148
20-24	25 480	24 604	...	...	...	...	...	...	23 466	23 091
25-29	17 426	12 250	...	...	...	...	...	...	16 284	12 147
30-34	8 620	5 578	...	...	...	...	...	...	8 059	5 285
35-39	4 176	2 636	...	...	...	...	...	...	4 162	2 903
40-44	2 218	1 426	...	...	...	...	...	...	2 314	1 592
45-49	1 239	820	...	...	...	...	...	...	1 523	999
50-54	790	438	...	...	...	...	...	...	942	563
55-59	507	248	...	...	...	...	...	...	605	333
60-64	334	168	...	...	...	...	...	...	409	178
65-69	263	120	...	...	...	...	...	...	263	141
70+	360	106	...	...	...	...	...	...	439	152
Unknown - Inconnu	3	12	...	...	...	...	...	...	...	...
French Guiana - Guyane française										
All ages - Tous âges	...	...	...	...	...	...	...	...	522	522
15-19	...	...	...	...	...	...	...	...	3	22
20-24	...	...	...	...	...	...	...	...	39	101
25-29	...	...	...	...	...	...	...	...	101	118
30-34	...	...	...	...	...	...	...	...	113	97
35-39	...	...	...	...	...	...	...	...	90	68
40-44	...	...	...	...	...	...	...	...	55	54

24. Marriages by age of bridegroom and by age of bride: 1998 - 2002
Mariages selon l'âge de l'époux et selon l'âge de l'épouse: 1998 - 2002 (continued — suite)

(See notes at end of table. — Voir notes à la fin du tableau.)

Continent, country or area and age Continent, pays ou zone et âge	1998 Groom Epoux	1998 Bride Epouse	1999 Groom Epoux	1999 Bride Epouse	2000 Groom Epoux	2000 Bride Epouse	2001 Groom Epoux	2001 Bride Epouse	2002 Groom Epoux	2002 Bride Epouse
AMERICA, SOUTH — AMERIQUE DU SUD										
French Guiana - Guyane française										
45-49	...	...	...	...	...	...	...	...	50	24
50-54	...	...	...	...	...	...	...	...	28	15
55-59	...	...	...	...	...	...	...	...	15	16
60-64	...	...	...	...	...	...	...	...	14	3
65-69	...	...	...	...	...	...	...	...	7	3
70-74	...	...	...	...	...	...	...	...	7	1
Suriname										
All ages - Tous âges	1 982	1 982	2 257	2 257	2 267	2 267	...	...	...	...
0-14	-	1	-	11	-	2	...	...	...	...
15-19	40	387	32	415	34	378	...	...	...	...
20-24	406	588	441	635	409	586	...	...	...	...
25-29	627	409	642	455	618	459	...	...	...	...
30-34	316	245	412	286	386	327	...	...	...	...
35-39	233	152	246	190	269	207	...	...	...	...
40-44	127	66	150	113	181	130	...	...	...	...
45-49	71	54	118	78	141	63	...	...	...	...
50-54	63	34	75	35	77	55	...	...	...	...
55+	99	46	141	39	152	60	...	...	...	...
Uruguay										
Groom — Epoux 14 ⊗										
Bride — Epouse 12 ⊗										
All ages - Tous âges	...	...	...	...	13 888	13 888	...	...	...	...
0-19	...	...	...	...	360	1 536	...	...	...	...
20-24	...	...	...	...	2 856	3 752	...	...	...	...
25-29	...	...	...	...	4 292	3 940	...	...	...	...
30-34	...	...	...	...	2 524	1 860	...	...	...	...
35-39	...	...	...	...	1 260	920	...	...	...	...
40-49	...	...	...	...	1 144	932	...	...	...	...
50+	...	...	...	...	1 444	940	...	...	...	...
Unknown - Inconnu	...	...	...	...	8	8	...	...	...	...
Venezuela[3]										
Groom — Epoux 21 ⊗										
Bride — Epouse 18 ⊗										
All ages - Tous âges	86 152	86 152	...	...	91 088	91 088	81 516	81 516	73 163	73 163
0-14	19	1 382	...	...	54	1 061	38	886	38	673
15-19	7 654	21 245	...	...	6 282	18 749	4 977	15 993	4 233	13 452
20-24	27 401	27 210	...	...	26 750	28 925	23 441	25 634	20 114	22 819
25-29	23 004	18 039	...	...	25 569	20 833	22 958	18 632	21 009	17 730
30-34	12 529	8 612	...	...	14 152	10 016	13 084	9 450	12 435	8 786
35-39	6 507	4 298	...	...	7 488	5 160	6 904	4 827	6 253	4 277
40-44	3 537	2 252	...	...	4 195	2 781	3 992	2 655	3 569	2 344
45-49	2 206	1 396	...	...	2 618	1 617	2 491	1 585	2 168	1 380
50-54	1 226	690	...	...	1 597	862	1 449	833	1 292	789
55-59	727	354	...	...	844	440	786	406	750	368
60+	1 342	674	...	...	1 539	644	1 396	615	1 302	545
ASIA — ASIE										
Armenia - Arménie										
Groom — Epoux 18 ⊗										
Bride — Epouse 17 ⊗										
All ages - Tous âges	11 365	11 365	12 459	12 459	10 986	10 986	...	...	...	...
15-19	243	3 177	202	3 088	104	1 865	...	...	...	...
20-24	4 020	5 635	4 460	6 548	3 603	6 349	...	...	...	...
25-29	4 077	1 413	4 528	1 625	4 342	1 709	...	...	...	...
30-34	1 697	423	1 845	473	1 607	404	...	...	...	...
35-39	634	298	710	264	624	222	...	...	...	...
40-44	255	181	257	199	272	177	...	...	...	...
45-49	135	93	130	114	137	112	...	...	...	...
50-54	61	48	99	60	83	63	...	...	...	...

24. Marriages by age of bridegroom and by age of bride: 1998 - 2002
Mariages selon l'âge de l'époux et selon l'âge de l'épouse: 1998 - 2002 (continued — suite)

(See notes at end of table. — Voir notes à la fin du tableau.)

Continent, country or area and age / Continent, pays ou zone et âge	1998 Groom Epoux	1998 Bride Epouse	1999 Groom Epoux	1999 Bride Epouse	2000 Groom Epoux	2000 Bride Epouse	2001 Groom Epoux	2001 Bride Epouse	2002 Groom Epoux	2002 Bride Epouse
ASIA — ASIE										
Armenia - Arménie										
Groom — Epoux 18 ⊗										
Bride — Epouse 17 ⊗										
55-59	79	28	67	29	43	21	...	...	...	...
60+	164	69	161	59	171	64	...	...	...	...
Azerbaijan - Azerbaïdjan+										
All ages - Tous âges	40 851	40 851	37 382	37 382	39 611	39 611	41 861	41 861	41 661	41 661
0-17	38	3 410	22	2 649	11	2 473	15	2 348	12	2 140
18-19	1 222	8 553	802	7 417	539	7 331	470	7 661	405	7 024
20-24	11 624	17 474	10 172	16 523	10 393	18 010	11 123	19 299	10 507	19 338
25-29	16 272	6 270	15 015	5 977	16 361	6 741	17 230	7 334	17 081	7 779
30-34	7 158	2 495	6 986	2 339	7 721	2 399	8 162	2 656	8 425	2 627
35-39	2 112	1 337	2 144	1 260	2 245	1 378	2 525	1 306	2 706	1 312
40-44	818	701	766	674	907	728	952	727	1 023	805
45-49	396	284	387	252	413	283	404	281	461	324
50-54	255	129	235	108	284	119	276	112	299	142
55-59	285	78	199	47	155	43	136	54	146	64
60+	671	120	654	136	582	106	568	83	596	106
Bahrain — Bahreïn										
Groom — Epoux 15 ⊗										
All ages - Tous âges	...	...	3 673	3 673	...	...	...	...	4 909	4 909
0-14	...	...	-	32	...	...	...	...	-	23
15-19	...	...	99	897	...	...	...	...	78	972
20-24	...	...	1 176	1 509	...	...	...	...	1 476	2 191
25-29	...	...	1 198	603	...	...	...	...	1 809	968
30-34	...	...	543	340	...	...	...	...	724	366
35-39	...	...	278	165	...	...	...	...	355	214
40-44	...	...	162	86	...	...	...	...	194	115
45-49	...	...	83	28	...	...	...	...	112	41
50+	...	...	133	12	...	...	...	...	158	17
Unknown - Inconnu	...	...	1	1	...	...	...	...	3	2
Brunei Darussalam - Brunéi Darussalam										
All ages - Tous âges	...	...	...	...	2 184	2 184	...	...	...	...
0-14	...	...	...	...	11	15	...	...	...	...
15-19	...	...	...	...	125	412	...	...	...	...
20-24	...	...	...	...	688	834	...	...	...	...
25-29	...	...	...	...	733	551	...	...	...	...
30-34	...	...	...	...	313	192	...	...	...	...
35-39	...	...	...	...	137	87	...	...	...	...
40-44	...	...	...	...	70	48	...	...	...	...
45-49	...	...	...	...	44	22	...	...	...	...
50-54	...	...	...	...	31	13	...	...	...	...
55-59	...	...	...	...	10	5	...	...	...	...
60-64	...	...	...	...	10	5	...	...	...	...
65-69	...	...	...	...	7	-	...	...	...	...
70+	...	...	...	...	5	-	...	...	...	...
China: Hong Kong SAR - Chine: Hong Kong RAS										
Groom — Epoux 16 ⊗										
Bride — Epouse 12 ⊗										
All ages - Tous âges	31 673	31 673	31 287	31 287	30 879	30 879	32 825	32 825	...	...
15-19	295	1 103	250	1 061	232	966	208	947	...	...
20-24	3 828	8 084	3 519	7 578	3 091	6 728	3 169	7 164	...	...
25-29	10 215	12 350	10 078	12 379	9 997	12 566	10 373	13 143	...	...
30-34	8 404	5 814	8 242	5 965	8 027	6 101	8 546	6 773	...	...
35-39	4 411	2 267	4 534	2 328	4 609	2 489	4 891	2 664	...	...
40-44	1 912	867	2 029	802	2 047	923	2 300	1 027	...	...
45-49	934	415	903	374	1 077	439	1 256	486	...	...
50-54	486	217	506	223	593	206	721	211	...	...
55-59	309	135	308	150	333	116	377	99	...	...
60-64	311	177	324	165	299	121	330	110	...	...

(See notes at end of table. — Voir notes à la fin du tableau.)

Continent, country or area and age / Continent, pays ou zone et âge	1998 Groom Epoux	1998 Bride Epouse	1999 Groom Epoux	1999 Bride Epouse	2000 Groom Epoux	2000 Bride Epouse	2001 Groom Epoux	2001 Bride Epouse	2002 Groom Epoux	2002 Bride Epouse
ASIA — ASIE										
China: Hong Kong SAR - Chine: Hong Kong RAS										
Groom — Epoux 16 ⊗										
Bride — Epouse 12 ⊗										
65-69	266	130	264	146	257	117	281	104	...	...
70-74	161	79	194	87	185	71	208	61	...	...
75+	141	35	136	29	132	36	165	36	...	...
China: Macao SAR - Chine: Macao RAS⁺										
All ages - Tous âges	1 451	1 451	1 367	1 367	1 222	1 222	...	...	1 209	1 209
15-19	11	45	11	54	7	43	...	...	9	45
20-24	162	327	140	267	142	223	...	...	126	247
25-29	477	618	484	613	411	509	...	...	388	462
30-34	390	263	357	224	271	227	...	...	290	243
35-39	228	91	200	110	175	102	...	...	165	88
40-44	82	58	73	43	99	54	...	...	79	54
45-49	42	16	28	18	42	20	...	...	77	34
50-54	19	14	26	10	24	11	...	...	30	16
55-59	14	5	8	4	13	9	...	...	14	8
60-64	5	7	13	10	9	8	...	...	8	1
65-69	8	5	8	9	11	10	...	...	8	6
70+	...	...	...	...	...	...	...	...	15	5
70-74	10	2	12	4	13	6	...	...	...	...
75+	3	-	7	1	5	-	...	...	...	...
Cyprus - Chypre⁵										
Groom — Epoux •										
Bride — Epouse •										
All ages - Tous âges	7 738	7 738	9 080	9 080	9 282	9 282	...	...	10 284	10 284
15-19	66	572	69	630	84	572	...	...	73	477
20-24	1 476	2 494	1 632	2 883	1 479	2 627	...	...	1 497	2 742
25-29	2 582	2 380	3 150	2 844	3 087	2 974	...	...	3 187	3 306
30-34	1 643	1 075	1 924	1 328	2 091	1 505	...	...	2 467	1 845
35-39	829	516	1 013	637	1 033	696	...	...	1 275	833
40-44	403	283	477	324	541	390	...	...	658	457
45-49	277	156	316	194	372	250	...	...	395	273
50-54	172	126	221	139	260	148	...	...	281	180
55-59	90	51	109	48	133	62	...	...	183	80
60+	169	54	166	53	194	50	...	...	226	48
Unknown - Inconnu	31	31	3	-	8	8	...	...	42	43
Georgia - Géorgie										
All ages - Tous âges	...	...	...	...	12 870	12 870	...	...	...	...
0-15	...	...	...	...	3	233	...	...	...	...
16-19	...	...	...	...	747	2 582	...	...	...	...
20-24	...	...	...	...	4 055	5 200	...	...	...	...
25-29	...	...	...	...	3 459	2 505	...	...	...	...
30-34	...	...	...	...	2 152	1 059	...	...	...	...
35-39	...	...	...	...	1 141	580	...	...	...	...
40-44	...	...	...	...	551	291	...	...	...	...
45-49	...	...	...	...	272	165	...	...	...	...
50-54	...	...	...	...	173	99	...	...	...	...
55-59	...	...	...	...	71	41	...	...	...	...
60+	...	...	...	...	241	108	...	...	...	...
Unknown - Inconnu	...	...	...	...	5	7	...	...	...	...
Israel - Israël⁶										
Groom — Epoux ≡										
Bride — Epouse 17 ⊗										
All ages - Tous âges	40 137	40 137	40 236	40 236	...	...	38 924	38 924	39 718	39 718
0-19	1 241	7 463	1 305	7 337	...	...	1 284	7 014	1 347	7 271
20-24	12 572	17 704	12 066	17 335	...	...	11 008	15 716	10 977	15 596
25-29	16 667	10 499	16 469	10 556	...	...	16 273	11 135	16 533	11 497
30-34	5 575	2 420	5 873	2 542	...	...	6 106	2 870	6 572	3 177
35-39	1 956	933	1 994	960	...	...	1 940	956	1 998	979
40-44	853	473	895	480	...	...	897	463	926	477

24. Marriages by age of bridegroom and by age of bride: 1998 - 2002
Mariages selon l'âge de l'époux et selon l'âge de l'épouse: 1998 - 2002 (continued — suite)

(See notes at end of table. — Voir notes à la fin du tableau.)

Continent, country or area and age / Continent, pays ou zone et âge	1998 Groom Epoux	1998 Bride Epouse	1999 Groom Epoux	1999 Bride Epouse	2000 Groom Epoux	2000 Bride Epouse	2001 Groom Epoux	2001 Bride Epouse	2002 Groom Epoux	2002 Bride Epouse
ASIA — ASIE										
Israel - Israël[6]										
Groom — Epoux =										
Bride — Epouse 17 ⊗										
45-49	438	241	502	299	...	...	542	291	479	268
50-54	268	137	306	139	...	...	295	217	313	189
55-59	162	90	188	85	...	...	185	73	188	84
60-64	120	51	139	65	...	...	144	71	144	58
65-69	109	53	101	58	...	...	108	46	108	38
70-74	72	29	96	38	...	...	71	20	63	30
75+	73	12	80	19	...	...	71	20	58	14
Unknown - Inconnu	31	32	222	323	...	...	-	32	12	40
Japan - Japon[+,7,8,9]										
Groom — Epoux 18 ⊗										
Bride — Epouse 16 ⊗										
All ages - Tous âges	709 087	709 087	685 626	685 626	708 159	708 159	709 864	709 864	671 602	671 602
0-19	9 972	20 181	9 836	20 075	10 772	21 607	10 894	22 216	9 946	20 818
20-24	130 922	204 356	120 702	184 703	119 706	179 410	113 415	169 807	102 377	151 931
25-29	301 426	326 866	290 946	318 464	296 363	326 418	290 929	322 253	268 111	298 966
30-34	151 013	98 603	148 177	102 291	155 381	113 693	163 873	124 696	163 467	127 802
35-39	57 959	28 917	57 572	30 029	62 382	34 542	63 731	37 556	63 537	38 848
40-44	23 274	10 759	23 290	10 785	24 912	11 800	25 989	12 848	25 743	13 138
45-49	15 363	8 685	14 587	7 907	15 031	7 858	15 241	7 573	14 130	7 187
50-54	8 739	5 519	9 394	5 760	11 179	6 564	12 530	6 750	11 232	6 376
55-59	5 274	2 968	5 576	3 150	6 221	3 430	6 457	3 214	6 109	3 361
60-64	2 721	1 326	2 889	1 462	3 229	1 669	3 545	1 700	3 660	1 842
65-69	1 403	582	1 471	631	1 608	743	1 831	778	1 780	789
70-74	594	214	712	251	828	286	876	289	866	367
75+	418	102	468	114	541	137	547	184	639	177
Unknown - Inconnu	9	9	6	4	6	2	6	-	5	-
Jordan - Jordanie[+,10]										
Groom — Epoux 18 ⊗										
Bride — Epouse 16 ⊗										
All ages - Tous âges	...	...	39 443	39 443	...	...	...	...	...	...
0-14	...	...	5	36	...	...	...	...	...	...
15-19	...	...	1 095	12 991	...	...	...	...	...	...
20-24	...	...	10 920	15 789	...	...	...	...	...	...
25-29	...	...	15 384	6 517	...	...	...	...	...	...
30-34	...	...	6 781	2 414	...	...	...	...	...	...
35-39	...	...	2 378	990	...	...	...	...	...	...
40-44	...	...	1 017	414	...	...	...	...	...	...
45-49	...	...	621	163	...	...	...	...	...	...
50+	...	...	...	129	...	...	...	...	...	...
50-54	...	...	361	...	...	...	...	...	...	...
55-59	...	...	345	...	...	...	...	...	...	...
60-64	...	...	231	...	...	...	...	...	...	...
65+	...	...	305	...	...	...	...	...	...	...
Kazakhstan										
Groom — Epoux 18 ⊗										
Bride — Epouse 17 ⊗										
All ages - Tous âges	96 048	96 048	85 872	85 872	...	...	...	...	...	...
0-14	-	1	1	1	...	...	...	...	...	...
15-19	5 424	22 697	4 214	18 629	...	...	...	...	...	...
20-24	40 346	43 521	36 288	40 975	...	...	...	...	...	...
25-29	27 195	14 577	25 026	13 429	...	...	...	...	...	...
30-34	9 857	5 602	9 047	4 960	...	...	...	...	...	...
35-39	5 098	3 623	4 372	2 849	...	...	...	...	...	...
40-44	2 573	1 898	2 391	1 641	...	...	...	...	...	...
45-49	1 824	1 455	1 409	1 136	...	...	...	...	...	...
50-54	942	733	854	751	...	...	...	...	...	...
55-59	906	743	590	467	...	...	...	...	...	...
60+	1 876	1 182	1 660	1 015	...	...	...	...	...	...
Unknown - Inconnu	7	16	20	19	...	...	...	...	...	...

24. Marriages by age of bridegroom and by age of bride: 1998 - 2002
Mariages selon l'âge de l'époux et selon l'âge de l'épouse: 1998 - 2002 (continued — suite)

(See notes at end of table. — Voir notes à la fin du tableau.)

Continent, country or area and age	1998		1999		2000		2001		2002	
Continent, pays ou zone et âge	Groom Epoux	Bride Epouse	Groom Epoux	Bride Epouse	Groom Epoux	Bride Epouse	Groom Epoux	Bride Epouse	Groom Epoux	Bride Epouse
ASIA — ASIE										
Korea (Republic of) - Corée (République de)[+]										
Groom — Epoux 18 ⊗										
Bride — Epouse 16 ⊗										
All ages - Tous âges	306 853	306 853	362 673	362 673	334 030	334 030	320 063	320 063	...	...
0-14	-	3	11	83	1	65	6	41	...	...
15-19	663	4 119	2 340	9 301	2 096	8 255	1 899	6 895	...	...
20-24	23 830	94 903	28 989	99 688	25 062	86 319	21 914	74 009	...	...
25-29	169 404	157 722	182 337	178 029	163 203	164 887	147 192	158 129	...	...
30-34	74 165	25 718	91 889	36 928	89 551	38 294	91 070	41 655	...	...
35-39	19 329	11 601	26 929	18 206	25 481	16 924	26 123	17 687	...	...
40-44	8 354	6 594	13 272	10 602	12 791	10 131	14 404	11 577	...	...
45-49	4 452	3 081	6 835	4 960	6 731	4 921	7 615	5 579	...	...
50-54	2 817	1 609	4 332	2 566	4 155	2 303	4 611	2 523	...	...
55+	3 720	1 423	5 590	2 247	4 959	1 931	5 223	1 963	...	...
Unknown - Inconnu	119	80	149	63	-	-	6	5	...	...
Kuwait - Koweït										
All ages - Tous âges	...	...	...	...	10 785	10 785	...	...	...	...
15-19	...	...	...	...	416	2 832	...	...	...	...
20-24	...	...	...	...	3 806	3 941	...	...	...	...
25-29	...	...	...	...	3 096	1 931	...	...	...	...
30-34	...	...	...	...	1 596	1 021	...	...	...	...
35-44	...	...	...	...	1 320	894	...	...	...	...
45+	...	...	...	...	551	166	...	...	...	...
Kyrgyzstan - Kirghizistan										
Groom — Epoux 18 ⊗										
Bride — Epouse 18 ⊗										
All ages - Tous âges	25 726	25 726	26 033	26 033	24 294	24 294	27 455	27 455	31 240	31 240
15-19	999	7 709	833	7 010	760	6 417	830	6 666	768	6 953
20-24	11 759	12 276	11 019	12 585	9 966	11 863	10 746	13 596	11 206	15 498
25-29	8 355	3 124	8 950	3 565	8 587	3 353	9 753	4 050	11 657	5 106
30-34	2 227	1 100	2 603	1 144	2 543	1 149	3 196	1 407	4 294	1 728
35-39	944	592	1 033	682	963	585	1 179	646	1 422	793
40-44	518	328	522	384	560	349	669	403	727	452
45-49	284	212	351	241	265	188	358	273	401	268
50-54	150	107	204	158	209	146	251	171	262	170
55-59	161	100	150	66	93	65	91	57	107	70
60-64	139	77	167	111	150	94	163	96	166	95
65-69	77	38	94	43	86	37	90	44	101	48
70-74	65	39	72	28	77	31	73	30	57	39
75+	45	19	32	15	35	17	56	16	72	20
Unknown - Inconnu	3	5	3	1	-	-	-	-	-	-
Mongolia - Mongolie										
All ages - Tous âges	...	...	13 722	13 722	12 601	12 601	12 393	12 393	...	...
18-19	...	...	780	1 506	417	1 323	473	1 177	...	...
20-24	...	...	5 771	6 778	5 173	5 989	4 917	5 813	...	...
25-29	...	...	4 477	3 567	4 342	3 433	4 135	3 335	...	...
30-34	...	...	1 634	1 165	1 689	1 212	1 580	1 196	...	...
35-39	...	...	644	411	611	434	839	620	...	...
40-44	...	...	244	176	208	211	302	175	...	...
45-49	...	...	94	72	85	47	78	54	...	...
50+	...	...	78	47	76	42	69	23	...	...
Occupied Palestinian Territory - Territoire palestinien occupé										
All ages - Tous âges	24 400	24 400	24 874	24 874	23 890	23 890	24 635	24 635	22 611	22 611
0-14	-	346	5	743	1	682	3	926	3	810
15-19	2 629	14 310	2 363	13 817	2 332	13 163	2 396	13 168	2 093	11 893
20-24	10 485	6 399	10 705	6 816	9 961	6 641	10 255	6 963	9 505	6 640
25-29	7 000	1 915	7 280	1 965	7 190	1 991	7 426	2 046	6 982	1 930
30-34	2 116	776	2 234	818	2 207	757	2 222	804	1 942	685
35-39	774	393	850	426	799	401	841	481	769	381
40-44	399	173	400	175	443	165	427	145	413	183
45-49	267	52	293	69	264	54	304	60	270	58

24. Marriages by age of bridegroom and by age of bride: 1998 - 2002
Mariages selon l'âge de l'époux et selon l'âge de l'épouse: 1998 - 2002 (continued — suite)

(See notes at end of table. — Voir notes à la fin du tableau.)

Continent, country or area and age / Continent, pays ou zone et âge	1998 Groom Epoux	1998 Bride Epouse	1999 Groom Epoux	1999 Bride Epouse	2000 Groom Epoux	2000 Bride Epouse	2001 Groom Epoux	2001 Bride Epouse	2002 Groom Epoux	2002 Bride Epouse
ASIA — ASIE										
Occupied Palestinian Territory - Territoire palestinien occupé										
50-54	200	18	216	19	206	22	235	30	200	20
55+	530	16	526	23	...	...	...	...	...	...
55-59	...	...	...	...	176	10	191	7	132	7
60-64	...	...	...	...	119	3	126	3	107	1
65-69	...	...	...	...	91	1	104	1	97	3
70-74	...	...	...	...	55	-	57	1	63	-
75+	...	...	...	...	45	-	48	-	35	-
Unknown - Inconnu	-	2	2	3	1	-	-	-	-	-
Philippines										
All ages - Tous âges	549 265	549 265	551 445	551 445	577 387	577 387	...	...	...	...
0-19	23 982	86 200	23 275	85 779	23 069	85 632	...	...	...	...
20-24	176 179	212 909	178 891	216 999	185 502	227 738	...	...	...	...
25-29	179 105	139 749	176 196	136 689	182 176	142 420	...	...	...	...
30-34	84 409	56 587	85 613	56 920	91 555	61 519	...	...	...	...
35-39	38 033	25 738	38 969	26 063	41 495	28 141	...	...	...	...
40-44	18 937	12 666	19 244	12 768	21 624	14 513	...	...	...	...
45-49	10 832	6 542	11 047	7 083	12 541	7 795	...	...	...	...
50+	17 542	8 607	17 936	8 803	19 176	9 365	...	...	...	...
Unknown - Inconnu	246	267	274	341	249	264	...	...	...	...
Qatar										
All ages - Tous âges	...	...	1 905	1 905	...	...	2 194	2 194	...	...
0-14	...	...	...	...	...	...	...	9	...	...
0-19	...	...	54	382	...	...	34	...	...	...
15-19	...	...	...	...	...	...	...	374	...	...
20-24	...	...	514	815	...	...	563	970	...	...
25-29	...	...	726	419	...	...	858	494	...	...
30-34	...	...	315	179	...	...	420	173	...	...
35-39	...	...	162	67	...	...	145	101	...	...
40-44	...	...	51	30	...	...	81	56	...	...
45-49	...	...	38	5	...	...	46	9	...	...
50-54	...	...	12	5	...	...	22	7	...	...
55-59	...	...	14	3	...	...	9	1	...	...
60-64	...	...	11	-	...	...	10	-	...	...
65-69	...	...	4	-	...	...	2	-	...	...
70-74	...	...	3	-	...	...	3	-	...	...
75+	...	...	1	-	...	...	-	-	...	...
Unknown - Inconnu	...	...	-	-	...	...	1	-	...	...
Singapore - Singapour[11,12,13]										
Groom — Epoux 18 ⊗										
Bride — Epouse 18 ⊗										
All ages - Tous âges	23 106	23 106	25 648	25 648	22 561	22 561	22 280	22 280	23 198	23 198
0-14	-	1	-	-	-	-	1	-	-	-
15-19	136	934	160	879	188	883	194	821	157	747
20-24	2 978	7 366	3 163	7 828	2 577	6 486	2 464	6 450	2 371	6 399
25-29	9 813	9 453	11 146	10 910	9 504	9 648	9 235	9 420	9 830	10 270
30-34	5 321	3 105	5 725	3 428	5 144	3 125	5 185	3 223	5 595	3 470
35-39	2 558	1 295	2 787	1 465	2 563	1 330	2 535	1 342	2 629	1 243
40-44	1 237	555	1 383	657	1 367	645	1 352	587	1 297	592
45-49	528	256	668	303	641	270	669	260	693	295
50-54	251	93	325	110	295	109	341	107	306	112
55-59	160	25	143	38	132	33	145	35	175	51
60+	124	23	148	30	150	32	159	35	145	19
Turkey - Turquie+,[14]										
Groom — Epoux 17 ⊗										
Bride — Epouse 15 ⊗										
All ages - Tous âges	485 035	485 035	475 613	475 613	461 417	461 417	...	...	...	...
0-14	-	1 283	-	1 044	-	794	...	...	...	...
15-19	25 768	144 015	23 958	134 599	20 557	122 116	...	...	...	...
20-24	181 810	209 339	166 893	202 235	159 922	199 168	...	...	...	...
25-29	182 760	81 863	190 673	89 314	188 516	91 997	...	...	...	...
30-34	54 082	25 967	53 441	25 684	52 057	25 011	...	...	...	...

875

24. Marriages by age of bridegroom and by age of bride: 1998 - 2002
Mariages selon l'âge de l'époux et selon l'âge de l'épouse: 1998 - 2002 (continued — suite)

(See notes at end of table. — Voir notes à la fin du tableau.)

Continent, country or area and age / Continent, pays ou zone et âge	1998 Groom Epoux	1998 Bride Epouse	1999 Groom Epoux	1999 Bride Epouse	2000 Groom Epoux	2000 Bride Epouse	2001 Groom Epoux	2001 Bride Epouse	2002 Groom Epoux	2002 Bride Epouse
ASIA — ASIE										
Turkey - Turquie[+,14]										
Groom — Epoux 17 ⊗										
Bride — Epouse 15 ⊗										
35-39	17 640	10 783	18 481	11 481	18 300	10 859	...	...	...	...
40-44	8 027	5 063	7 733	4 833	7 738	4 853	...	...	...	...
45-49	4 634	2 580	4 406	2 680	4 309	2 708	...	...	...	...
50-54	3 303	1 407	2 737	1 384	2 932	1 591	...	...	...	...
55-59	2 615	1 122	2 165	939	2 117	886	...	...	...	...
60+	4 396	1 613	5 126	1 420	4 969	1 434	...	...	...	...
Uzbekistan - Ouzbékistan										
Groom — Epoux 17 ⊗										
Bride — Epouse 17 ⊗										
All ages - Tous âges	...	...	170 525	170 525	168 908	168 908	...	...	...	...
0-17	...	...	183	10 847	158	9 606	...	...	...	...
18-19	...	...	12 058	61 917	8 625	52 422	...	...	...	...
20-24	...	...	106 637	77 044	102 113	84 289	...	...	...	...
25-29	...	...	36 733	12 092	41 332	13 386	...	...	...	...
30-34	...	...	7 074	4 026	8 139	4 351	...	...	...	...
35-39	...	...	3 114	2 077	3 369	2 103	...	...	...	...
40-44	...	...	1 645	932	1 911	1 134	...	...	...	...
45-49	...	...	1 101	556	1 118	626	...	...	...	...
50-54	...	...	536	363	684	440	...	...	...	...
55-59	...	...	581	278	454	194	...	...	...	...
60+	...	...	863	393	1 005	354	...	...	...	...
Unknown - Inconnu	...	...	-	-	-	3	...	...	...	...
EUROPE										
Austria - Autriche[15]										
Groom — Epoux 18 ⊗										
Bride — Epouse 16 ⊗										
All ages - Tous âges	39 143	39 143	39 485	39 485	39 228	39 228	34 213	34 213	36 570	36 570
15-19	363	1 540	398	1 469	360	1 507	389	1 334	449	1 420
20-24	4 861	9 458	4 597	8 840	4 386	8 227	3 852	7 261	4 020	7 565
25-29	12 642	13 008	11 600	12 528	11 118	12 369	9 019	10 063	9 182	10 528
30-34	10 069	7 473	10 388	7 857	10 346	8 071	8 795	7 063	9 343	7 368
35-39	4 772	3 409	5 239	3 870	5 579	4 103	5 118	3 740	5 662	4 290
40-44	2 314	1 839	2 628	2 068	2 872	2 248	2 704	2 151	3 143	2 423
45-49	1 405	1 063	1 534	1 284	1 610	1 234	1 527	1 233	1 767	1 369
50-54	1 185	721	1 238	795	1 191	785	1 148	740	1 213	830
55-59	901	423	1 014	524	951	424	823	365	859	490
60-64	276	108	414	127	446	157	478	165	581	190
65-69	145	67	194	70	176	55	169	46	160	48
70-74	128	19	127	34	100	30	94	30	101	28
75+	82	15	114	19	93	18	97	22	...	...
75-79	...	...	...	...	...	...	...	...	55	13
80-84	...	...	...	...	...	...	...	...	27	7
85-89	...	...	...	...	...	...	...	...	5	-
90-94	...	...	...	...	...	...	...	...	2	1
95+	...	...	...	...	...	...	...	...	1	-
Belarus - Bélarus										
Groom — Epoux 18 ⊗										
Bride — Epouse 18 ⊗										
All ages - Tous âges	71 354	71 354	72 994	72 994	...	...	...	...	66 652	66 652
0-17	194	2 352	207	2 234	...	...	...	...	174	1 473
18-19	2 849	13 482	2 821	13 130	...	...	...	...	2 205	10 378
20-24	32 853	30 106	32 986	31 399	...	...	...	...	28 696	29 986
25-29	16 415	10 810	17 337	11 159	...	...	...	...	17 032	10 687
30-34	7 084	5 192	7 097	5 164	...	...	...	...	6 658	4 851
35-39	4 419	3 383	4 611	3 527	...	...	...	...	3 779	2 901
40-44	2 652	2 122	2 837	2 325	...	...	...	...	2 820	2 205
45-49	1 732	1 474	1 768	1 496	...	...	...	...	1 853	1 572
50-54	923	815	1 114	942	...	...	...	...	1 317	1 074

24. Marriages by age of bridegroom and by age of bride: 1998 - 2002
Mariages selon l'âge de l'époux et selon l'âge de l'épouse: 1998 - 2002 (continued — suite)

(See notes at end of table. — Voir notes à la fin du tableau.)

Continent, country or area and age / Continent, pays ou zone et âge	1998 Groom Epoux	1998 Bride Epouse	1999 Groom Epoux	1999 Bride Epouse	2000 Groom Epoux	2000 Bride Epouse	2001 Groom Epoux	2001 Bride Epouse	2002 Groom Epoux	2002 Bride Epouse
EUROPE										
Belarus - Bélarus										
Groom — Epoux 18 ⊗										
Bride — Epouse 18 ⊗										
55-59	781	619	694	560	...	...	...	...	638	502
60+	1 452	999	1 522	1 058	...	...	...	...	1 480	1 023
Belgium - Belgique[16]										
Groom — Epoux 18 ⊗										
Bride — Epouse 15 ⊗										
All ages - Tous âges	...	...	...	...	45 123	45 123	...	...	...	...
15-19	...	...	...	...	217	1 410	...	...	...	...
20-24	...	...	...	...	6 944	13 112	...	...	...	...
25-29	...	...	...	...	16 216	14 485	...	...	...	...
30-34	...	...	...	...	8 374	6 169	...	...	...	...
35-39	...	...	...	...	4 795	3 702	...	...	...	...
40-44	...	...	...	...	2 963	2 556	...	...	...	...
45-49	...	...	...	...	2 138	1 805	...	...	...	...
50-54	...	...	...	...	1 599	1 065	...	...	...	...
55-59	...	...	...	...	831	437	...	...	...	...
60-64	...	...	...	...	494	195	...	...	...	...
65-69	...	...	...	...	255	106	...	...	...	...
70-74	...	...	...	...	159	45	...	...	...	...
75+	...	...	...	...	138	36	...	...	...	...
Bulgaria - Bulgarie[17]										
Groom — Epoux 18 ⊗										
Bride — Epouse 18 ⊗										
All ages - Tous âges	...	...	...	...	35 164	35 164	31 974	31 974	29 218	29 218
15-19	...	...	...	...	...	...	...	...	401	3 579
16-17	...	...	...	...	15	745	...	...		
16-19	...	...	...	...	...	...	473	3 523	...	...
18-19	...	...	...	...	518	4 312	...	...		
20-24	...	...	...	...	9 941	14 706	8 292	13 287	7 033	11 713
25-29	...	...	...	...	12 931	8 896	12 363	8 848	11 817	8 854
30-34	...	...	...	...	5 431	2 733	5 387	2 654	5 347	2 624
35-39	...	...	...	...	2 330	1 296	2 128	1 068	1 944	957
40-44	...	...	...	...	1 286	835	1 147	690	1 013	569
45-49	...	...	...	...	929	595	748	469	584	359
50-54	...	...	...	...	603	383	528	360	419	266
55-59	...	...	...	...	330	212	320	194	263	139
60-64	...	...	...	...	297	173	209	134	149	72
65-69	...	...	...	...	229	129	180	87	107	52
70-74	...	...	...	...	176	100	98	33	73	17
75+	...	...	...	...	148	49	101	31	68	17
Croatia - Croatie										
Groom — Epoux 16 ⊗										
Bride — Epouse 16 ⊗										
All ages - Tous âges	24 243	24 243	...	...	22 017	22 017	22 076	22 076	22 806	22 806
15-19	239	3 006	...	...	205	2 438	224	2 456	211	2 263
20-24	6 357	9 737	...	...	5 289	8 667	5 251	8 414	5 160	8 661
25-29	9 101	6 528	...	...	8 475	6 355	8 529	6 558	8 789	6 895
30-34	4 421	2 417	...	...	4 150	2 205	4 117	2 230	4 394	2 446
35-39	1 698	984	...	...	1 717	906	1 677	907	1 838	933
40-44	808	526	...	...	774	492	781	478	835	523
45-49	543	351	...	...	465	346	459	329	505	400
50-54	278	195	...	...	278	217	309	265	361	276
55-59	225	172	...	...	190	135	196	170	190	154
60-64	198	117	...	...	154	108	157	136	168	119
65-69	152	88	...	...	137	76	145	79	139	71
70-74	87	36	...	...	103	41	127	28	103	37
75+	83	21	...	...	72	10	94	14	104	16
Unknown - Inconnu	53	65	...	...	8	21	10	12	9	12

24. Marriages by age of bridegroom and by age of bride: 1998 - 2002
Mariages selon l'âge de l'époux et selon l'âge de l'épouse: 1998 - 2002 (continued — suite)

(See notes at end of table. — Voir notes à la fin du tableau.)

Continent, country or area and age / Continent, pays ou zone et âge	1998 Groom Epoux	1998 Bride Epouse	1999 Groom Epoux	1999 Bride Epouse	2000 Groom Epoux	2000 Bride Epouse	2001 Groom Epoux	2001 Bride Epouse	2002 Groom Epoux	2002 Bride Epouse
EUROPE										
Czech Republic - République tchèque										
Groom — Epoux 16 ⊗										
Bride — Epouse 16 ⊗										
All ages - Tous âges	55 027	55 027	53 523	53 523	55 321	55 321	52 374	52 374	52 732	52 732
15-19	1 200	5 269	913	4 037	701	3 014	482	2 404	414	1 960
20-24	19 031	26 628	16 183	24 214	14 462	23 523	11 569	19 971	9 629	17 782
25-29	16 787	11 568	17 987	13 484	20 368	16 164	20 343	17 486	21 160	19 285
30-34	6 911	3 930	7 041	4 061	7 732	4 497	8 195	4 717	8 941	5 495
35-39	3 328	2 099	3 443	2 125	3 834	2 375	4 053	2 356	4 389	2 573
40-44	2 494	1 901	2 355	1 810	2 356	1 845	2 234	1 699	2 436	1 707
45-49	2 061	1 662	2 038	1 713	2 220	1 786	1 973	1 662	2 058	1 720
50-54	1 466	1 123	1 675	1 162	1 668	1 145	1 651	1 144	1 669	1 165
55-59	784	424	901	474	1 014	563	929	560	1 081	638
60-64	388	212	430	212	443	206	444	189	457	229
65-69	281	122	285	125	266	116	227	85	237	95
70-74	157	61	142	67	142	55	129	61	153	53
75+	139	28	130	39	115	32	145	40	...	...
75-79	...	...	...	...	...	...	...	...	75	22
80-84	...	...	...	...	...	...	...	...	26	5
85-89	...	...	...	...	...	...	...	...	3	1
90-94	...	...	...	...	...	...	...	...	3	2
95+	...	...	...	...	...	...	...	...	1	-
Denmark - Danemark[18]										
Groom — Epoux 18 ⊗										
Bride — Epouse 15 ⊗										
All ages - Tous âges	34 733	34 733	...	...	38 388	38 388	...	...	37 210	37 210
0-14	-	1	...	...	-	-	...	...	-	2
15-19	106	467	...	...	203	753	...	...	207	845
20-24	1 907	4 178	...	...	2 195	4 458	...	...	2 026	3 941
25-29	9 138	10 712	...	...	9 821	12 002	...	...	9 034	11 196
30-34	8 593	7 321	...	...	9 214	7 922	...	...	8 844	7 788
35-39	5 051	3 932	...	...	5 988	4 593	...	...	6 143	4 639
40-44	3 008	2 446	...	...	3 326	2 749	...	...	3 389	2 761
45-49	2 102	1 652	...	...	2 360	1 810	...	...	2 317	1 910
50-54	1 723	1 231	...	...	1 825	1 363	...	...	1 745	1 294
55-59	964	555	...	...	1 203	732	...	...	1 367	793
60-64	466	282	...	...	582	328	...	...	603	384
65-69	228	144	...	...	272	171	...	...	309	180
70-74	128	77	...	...	131	72	...	...	142	72
75+	115	61	...	...	117	54	...	...	...	...
75-79	...	...	...	...	...	...	...	...	62	42
80-84	...	...	...	...	...	...	...	...	38	12
85-89	...	...	...	...	...	...	...	...	3	7
90-94	...	...	...	...	...	...	...	...	2	-
Unknown - Inconnu	1 204	1 674	...	...	1 151	1 381	...	...	979	1 344
Estonia - Estonie										
Groom — Epoux 18 ⊗										
Bride — Epouse 18 ⊗										
All ages - Tous âges	...	...	...	...	5 485	5 485	...	...	5 853	5 853
15-19	...	...	...	...	110	492	...	...	78	414
20-24	...	...	...	...	1 293	1 773	...	...	1 151	1 751
25-29	...	...	...	...	1 569	1 327	...	...	1 762	1 604
30-34	...	...	...	...	898	672	...	...	1 132	864
35-39	...	...	...	...	472	375	...	...	590	414
40-44	...	...	...	...	382	264	...	...	388	274
45-49	...	...	...	...	255	233	...	...	292	237
50-54	...	...	...	...	191	155	...	...	197	151
55-59	...	...	...	...	116	67	...	...	114	65
60-64	...	...	...	...	88	66	...	...	86	43
65-69	...	...	...	...	53	34	...	...	30	21
70-74	...	...	...	...	39	19	...	...	20	11
75+	...	...	...	...	19	8	...	...	...	...

24. Marriages by age of bridegroom and by age of bride: 1998 - 2002
Mariages selon l'âge de l'époux et selon l'âge de l'épouse: 1998 - 2002 (continued — suite)

(See notes at end of table. — Voir notes à la fin du tableau.)

Continent, country or area and age / Continent, pays ou zone et âge	1998 Groom Epoux	1998 Bride Epouse	1999 Groom Epoux	1999 Bride Epouse	2000 Groom Epoux	2000 Bride Epouse	2001 Groom Epoux	2001 Bride Epouse	2002 Groom Epoux	2002 Bride Epouse
EUROPE										
Estonia - Estonie										
Groom — Epoux 18⊗										
Bride — Epouse 18⊗										
75-79	...	...	...	...	...	...	...	...	9	3
80-84	...	...	...	...	...	...	...	...	3	1
90-94	...	...	...	...	...	...	...	...	1	-
Finland - Finlande[19]										
Groom — Epoux 18⊗										
Bride — Epouse 18⊗										
All ages - Tous âges	24 023	24 023	...	...	...	...	24 830	24 830	26 969	26 969
15-19	251	815	...	...	...	...	275	813	237	779
20-24	3 348	5 443	...	...	...	...	3 130	5 100	3 144	5 047
25-29	7 233	7 334	...	...	...	...	7 088	7 340	7 646	8 262
30-34	5 591	4 459	...	...	...	...	5 382	4 518	5 852	4 756
35-39	2 926	2 329	...	...	...	...	3 356	2 614	3 635	2 956
40-44	1 708	1 422	...	...	...	...	2 027	1 673	2 263	1 851
45-49	1 310	1 091	...	...	...	...	1 437	1 308	1 738	1 597
50-54	822	644	...	...	...	...	1 027	791	1 172	876
55-59	410	270	...	...	...	...	548	361	676	469
60-64	213	106	...	...	...	...	298	178	340	209
65-69	115	58	...	...	...	...	136	71	116	89
70-74	48	31	...	...	...	...	72	38	95	42
75+	48	21	...	...	...	...	54	25	...	...
75-79	...	...	...	...	...	...	...	...	29	23
80-84	...	...	...	...	...	...	...	...	21	11
85-89	...	...	...	...	...	...	...	...	4	2
90-94	...	...	...	...	...	...	...	...	1	-
France[20,21]										
Groom — Epoux 18⊗										
Bride — Epouse 18⊗										
All ages - Tous âges	...	...	286 191	286 191	...	...	...	...	...	...
0-14	...	...	-	3	...	...	...	...	...	...
15-19	...	...	407	3 509	...	...	...	...	...	...
20-24	...	...	22 455	53 482	...	...	...	...	...	...
25-29	...	...	106 040	110 711	...	...	...	...	...	...
30-34	...	...	67 503	51 868	...	...	...	...	...	...
35-39	...	...	35 368	27 928	...	...	...	...	...	...
40-44	...	...	20 575	16 302	...	...	...	...	...	...
45-49	...	...	13 420	10 429	...	...	...	...	...	...
50-54	...	...	9 861	6 818	...	...	...	...	...	...
55-59	...	...	4 689	2 633	...	...	...	...	...	...
60-64	...	...	2 722	1 210	...	...	...	...	...	...
65-69	...	...	1 473	691	...	...	...	...	...	...
70-74	...	...	828	344	...	...	...	...	...	...
75+	...	...	850	263	...	...	...	...	...	...
Greece - Grèce										
Groom — Epoux 18⊗										
Bride — Epouse 18⊗										
All ages - Tous âges	55 489	55 489	...	...	...	...	...	...	...	...
0-14	5	83	...	...	...	...	...	...	...	...
15-19	461	3 826	...	...	...	...	...	...	...	...
20-24	6 025	16 261	...	...	...	...	...	...	...	...
25-29	19 640	20 016	...	...	...	...	...	...	...	...
30-34	16 082	8 834	...	...	...	...	...	...	...	...
35-39	6 466	3 123	...	...	...	...	...	...	...	...
40-44	2 830	1 437	...	...	...	...	...	...	...	...
45-49	1 423	751	...	...	...	...	...	...	...	...
50-54	900	553	...	...	...	...	...	...	...	...
55-59	527	262	...	...	...	...	...	...	...	...
60-64	434	193	...	...	...	...	...	...	...	...
65-69	322	94	...	...	...	...	...	...	...	...
70-74	208	44	...	...	...	...	...	...	...	...
75+	166	12	...	...	...	...	...	...	...	...

(See notes at end of table. — Voir notes à la fin du tableau.)

Continent, country or area and age / Continent, pays ou zone et âge	1998		1999		2000		2001		2002	
	Groom Epoux	Bride Epouse	Groom Epoux	Bride Epouse	Groom Epoux	Bride Epouse	Groom Epoux	Bride Epouse	Groom Epoux	Bride Epouse
EUROPE										
Hungary - Hongrie										
Groom — Epoux 16 ⊗										
Bride — Epouse 16 ⊗										
All ages - Tous âges	44 915	44 915	45 465	45 465	48 110	48 110	43 583	43 583	46 008	46 008
15-19	1 072	5 239	887	4 495	769	3 821	667	2 978	559	2 631
20-24	15 570	20 750	14 143	19 910	12 651	19 345	9 409	15 230	8 253	14 639
25-29	14 582	10 204	15 301	11 426	17 853	14 203	16 383	14 216	18 422	16 561
30-34	5 577	3 202	6 408	3 793	7 662	4 746	7 629	4 959	8 770	5 708
35-39	2 420	1 590	2 690	1 772	2 906	1 922	3 158	2 074	3 437	2 177
40-44	1 956	1 417	1 969	1 434	2 040	1 335	2 028	1 337	1 975	1 361
45-49	1 372	1 121	1 521	1 171	1 633	1 254	1 663	1 236	1 763	1 260
50-54	958	700	977	689	1 046	723	1 089	769	1 161	869
55-59	588	345	658	375	657	365	663	392	718	402
60-64	305	162	371	191	357	202	371	216	416	197
65-69	251	94	242	116	228	111	233	102	233	111
70-74	117	64	161	59	168	57	153	49	163	59
75+	147	27	137	34	140	26	137	25	...	...
75-79	...	...	...	...	...	...	...	...	71	24
80-84	...	...	...	...	...	...	...	...	48	8
85-89	...	...	...	...	...	...	...	...	15	-
90-94	...	...	...	...	...	...	...	...	3	1
95-99	...	...	...	...	...	...	...	...	1	-
Iceland - Islande[22]										
Groom — Epoux 18 ⊗										
Bride — Epouse 18 ⊗										
All ages - Tous âges	1 529	1 529	1 560	1 560	1 777	1 777	...	...	1 619	1 619
15-19	4	23	4	31	5	30	...	...	3	28
20-24	115	216	115	226	117	259	...	...	118	224
25-29	420	503	433	501	477	590	...	...	433	495
30-34	385	356	388	330	459	361	...	...	399	363
35-39	277	224	260	223	300	244	...	...	259	220
40-44	132	92	140	112	167	136	...	...	161	133
45-49	84	46	109	68	108	79	...	...	102	70
50-54	53	33	56	37	77	37	...	...	56	36
55-59	30	21	27	20	29	23	...	...	49	28
60-64	12	6	14	2	18	13	...	...	15	13
65-69	11	4	4	5	14	3	...	...	14	6
70-74	2	2	6	4	3	1	...	...	4	1
75+	4	3	4	-	2	1	...	...	...	2
75-79	...	...	...	...	...	...	...	...	3	...
80-84	...	...	...	...	...	...	...	...	1	...
85+	...	...	...	...	...	...	...	...	2	...
Unknown - Inconnu	...	...	-	1	1	-	...	...	...	...
Isle of Man - Îles de Man										
All ages - Tous âges	...	...	403	403	...	...	...	...	...	...
15-19	...	...	1	7	...	...	...	...	...	...
20-24	...	...	37	64	...	...	...	...	...	...
25-29	...	...	99	119	...	...	...	...	...	...
30-34	...	...	103	79	...	...	...	...	...	...
35-39	...	...	59	47	...	...	...	...	...	...
40-44	...	...	30	34	...	...	...	...	...	...
45-49	...	...	22	23	...	...	...	...	...	...
50-54	...	...	21	16	...	...	...	...	...	...
55-59	...	...	12	5	...	...	...	...	...	...
60-64	...	...	8	3	...	...	...	...	...	...
65-69	...	...	2	5	...	...	...	...	...	...
70-74	...	...	6	1	...	...	...	...	...	...
75+	...	...	3	-	...	...	...	...	...	...
Italy - Italie										
Groom — Epoux 16 ⊗										
Bride — Epouse 16 ⊗										
All ages - Tous âges	280 034	280 034	280 330	280 330	...	...	...	...	...	...
15-19	1 129	10 034	1 180	9 520	...	...	...	...	...	...

(See notes at end of table. — Voir notes à la fin du tableau.)

Continent, country or area and age / Continent, pays ou zone et âge	1998		1999		2000		2001		2002	
	Groom Epoux	Bride Epouse	Groom Epoux	Bride Epouse	Groom Epoux	Bride Epouse	Groom Epoux	Bride Epouse	Groom Epoux	Bride Epouse

EUROPE

Italy - Italie
Groom — Epoux 16 ⊗
Bride — Epouse 16 ⊗

20-24	28 085	73 550	26 384	68 763	...	...	...	...	...	...
25-29	111 893	116 597	107 180	115 570	...	...	...	...	...	...
30-34	85 912	51 639	87 563	54 787	...	...	...	...	...	...
35-39	28 209	15 179	31 034	17 270	...	...	...	...	...	...
40-44	10 535	5 744	11 210	6 277	...	...	...	...	...	...
45-49	5 289	3 021	5 606	3 317	...	...	...	...	...	...
50-54	3 350	1 948	3 758	2 192	...	...	...	...	...	...
55-59	2 161	1 110	2 514	1 239	...	...	...	...	...	...
60-64	1 464	625	1 656	703	...	...	...	...	...	...
65-69	949	315	1 021	371	...	...	...	...	...	...
70-74	569	183	655	215	...	...	...	...	...	...
75+	489	89	569	106	...	...	...	...	...	...

Latvia - Lettonie
Groom — Epoux 18 ⊗
Bride — Epouse 18 ⊗

All ages - Tous âges	9 641	9 641	9 399	9 399	9 211	9 211	9 258	9 258	9 738	9 738
15-19	287	1 025	222	859	217	787	174	719	158	655
20-24	3 016	3 546	2 758	3 503	2 588	3 351	2 585	3 407	2 465	3 366
25-29	2 642	2 082	2 673	2 114	2 719	2 171	2 843	2 326	3 044	2 618
30-34	1 148	941	1 215	940	1 272	1 049	1 387	1 069	1 664	1 286
35-39	718	595	743	572	679	541	689	558	743	593
40-44	467	400	526	401	520	394	504	394	509	380
45-49	369	294	317	285	342	279	327	275	362	302
50-54	269	244	269	251	301	237	268	210	277	207
55-59	236	195	210	165	177	134	161	103	154	120
60-64	202	160	184	166	148	136	149	103	138	111
65-69	149	86	142	71	119	58	66	47	97	55
70-74	83	54	82	50	79	53	67	32	63	31
75+	55	19	58	22	50	21	38	15	...	...
75-79	...	...	...	...	...	...	...	...	43	12
80-84		...	...	...	...	...	...	...	13	2
85+	...	...	...	...	...	...	...	...	8	-

Lithuania - Lituanie
Groom — Epoux 18 ⊗
Bride — Epouse 18 ⊗

All ages - Tous âges	18 486	18 486	...	...	16 906	16 906	15 764	15 764	16 151	16 151
0-14	...	...	...	...	-	1	-	2	-	1
15-19	961	3 624	...	...	667	2 455	459	1 976	391	1 786
20-24	7 820	8 137	...	...	6 251	7 279	5 460	6 759	5 352	6 901
25-29	4 998	3 105	...	...	4 750	3 466	4 694	3 472	5 011	3 754
30-34	1 749	1 267	...	...	2 035	1 405	1 991	1 396	2 110	1 478
35-39	966	792	...	...	1 064	765	1 060	744	1 119	768
40-44	580	491	...	...	689	525	682	470	758	533
45-49	410	350	...	...	447	363	455	350	433	340
50-54	283	255	...	...	328	253	335	254	332	245
55-59	249	170	...	...	226	167	247	134	222	150
60-64	204	140	...	...	203	110	147	96	212	94
65-69	137	98	...	...	116	72	117	58	98	61
70-74	65	34	...	...	70	31	61	38	49	29
75+	64	17	...	...	60	14	56	15	...	...
75-79	...	...	...	...	...	...	...	...	64	11

Luxembourg[22]
Groom — Epoux 18 ⊗
Bride — Epouse 15 ⊗

All ages - Tous âges	...	...	...	...	...	...	1 983	1 983	2 022	2 022
15-19	...	...	...	...	...	...	6	59	7	62
20-24	...	...	...	...	...	...	206	346	191	389
25-29	...	...	...	...	...	...	521	660	562	592
30-34	...	...	...	...	...	...	541	452	521	479
35-39	...	...	...	...	...	...	284	203	302	229

(See notes at end of table. — Voir notes à la fin du tableau.)

Continent, country or area and age / Continent, pays ou zone et âge	1998 Groom Epoux	1998 Bride Epouse	1999 Groom Epoux	1999 Bride Epouse	2000 Groom Epoux	2000 Bride Epouse	2001 Groom Epoux	2001 Bride Epouse	2002 Groom Epoux	2002 Bride Epouse
EUROPE										
Luxembourg[22]										
Groom — Epoux 18⊗										
Bride — Epouse 15⊗										
40-44	...	...	...	...	...	...	161	115	183	124
45-49	...	...	...	...	...	...	130	81	120	75
50-54	...	...	...	...	...	...	69	39	65	39
55-59	...	...	...	...	...	...	36	13	28	18
60-64	...	...	...	...	...	...	11	10	19	7
65-69	...	...	...	...	...	...	10	2	14	4
70-74	...	...	...	...	...	...	5	1	5	2
75+	...	...	...	...	...	...	3	1	...	...
75-79	...	...	...	...	...	...	...	...	3	-
80-84	...	...	...	...	...	...	...	...	2	1
85-89	...	...	...	...	...	...	...	...	1	1
Malta - Malte										
Groom — Epoux 16⊗										
Bride — Epouse 16⊗										
All ages - Tous âges	...	...	...	...	2 545	2 545	...	...	2 240	2 240
16-19	...	...	...	...	41	169	...	...	22	120
20-24	...	...	...	...	724	1 230	...	...	478	193
25-29	...	...	...	...	1 123	776	...	...	1 007	766
30-34	...	...	...	...	379	210	...	...	381	223
35-39	...	...	...	...	132	67	...	...	169	116
40-44	...	...	...	...	61	43	...	...	83	42
45-49	...	...	...	...	30	27	...	...	36	32
50-54	...	...	...	...	28	10	...	...	29	10
55-59	...	...	...	...	15	5	...	...	15	15
60-64	...	...	...	...	5	2	...	...	11	3
65+	...	...	...	...	7	6	...	...	9	6
Netherlands - Pays-Bas[23]										
Groom — Epoux 18⊗										
Bride — Epouse 18⊗										
All ages - Tous âges	86 956	86 956	...	...	88 074	88 074	79 677	79 677	83 970	83 970
0-19	415	2 588	...	...	492	2 788	321	2 073	320	2 192
20-24	7 669	16 798	...	...	7 607	16 663	6 351	13 982	6 629	14 193
25-29	29 921	33 076	...	...	26 834	30 821	21 217	25 922	20 914	26 550
30-34	23 779	17 176	...	...	25 122	18 739	24 441	18 785	25 985	20 328
35-39	10 336	7 052	...	...	11 759	7 911	11 410	7 840	12 769	8 907
40-44	5 050	3 740	...	...	5 805	4 195	5 789	4 280	6 414	4 669
45-49	3 398	2 732	...	...	3 681	2 855	3 523	2 759	3 782	2 836
50-54	2 818	1 931	...	...	3 011	2 115	2 736	1 983	2 866	2 053
55-59	1 540	908	...	...	1 657	1 027	1 744	1 031	1 995	1 166
60-64	1 029	507	...	...	1 113	529	1 001	513	1 170	567
65+	1 001	448	...	...	993	431	...	...	...	...
65-69	...	...	...	...	...	...	606	297	638	317
70-74	...	...	...	...	...	...	305	122	295	116
75+	...	...	...	...	...	...	233	90	...	...
75-79	...	...	...	...	...	...	...	...	124	53
80-84	...	...	...	...	...	...	...	...	53	18
85-89	...	...	...	...	...	...	...	...	15	5
95-99	...	...	...	...	...	...	...	...	1	-
Norway - Norvège[21,24]										
Groom — Epoux 16⊗										
Bride — Epouse 16⊗										
All ages - Tous âges	23 354	23 354	23 456	23 456	25 356	25 356	22 967	22 967	...	...
15-19	133	605	90	516	110	501	114	551	...	...
20-24	2 138	4 300	1 796	4 004	1 800	4 101	1 641	3 706	...	...
25-29	7 210	8 456	6 754	8 145	7 010	8 666	5 932	7 459	...	...
30-34	6 041	4 860	6 105	5 014	6 845	5 696	6 114	5 149	...	...
35-39	3 155	2 184	3 414	2 504	3 827	2 793	3 565	2 622	...	...
40-44	1 818	1 309	1 953	1 385	2 115	1 526	2 028	1 413	...	...
45-49	1 229	812	1 331	893	1 466	993	1 417	1 025	...	...
50-54	870	477	1 024	570	1 121	661	1 087	574	...	...

(See notes at end of table. — Voir notes à la fin du tableau.)

Continent, country or area and age / Continent, pays ou zone et âge	1998 Groom Epoux	1998 Bride Epouse	1999 Groom Epoux	1999 Bride Epouse	2000 Groom Epoux	2000 Bride Epouse	2001 Groom Epoux	2001 Bride Epouse	2002 Groom Epoux	2002 Bride Epouse
EUROPE										
Norway - Norvège[21,24]										
Groom — Epoux 16 ⊗										
Bride — Epouse 16 ⊗										
55-59	390	211	547	255	583	265	578	282	...	...
60-64	213	73	244	84	281	82	309	97	...	...
65-69	83	38	106	44	111	37	99	52	...	...
70-74	44	14	57	20	45	20	42	22	...	...
75+	30	15	35	21	42	14	41	15	...	...
Unknown - Inconnu	-	-	-	1	-	1	...	...	...	...
Poland - Pologne										
Groom — Epoux 18 ⊗										
Bride — Epouse 16 ⊗										
All ages - Tous âges	209 430	209 430	219 398	219 398	...	...	...	...	...	...
15-19	5 007	29 046	6 746	29 583	...	...	...	...	...	...
20-24	94 680	114 776	95 243	118 358	...	...	...	...	...	...
25-29	65 977	37 654	71 636	42 483	...	...	...	...	...	...
30-34	17 933	9 119	19 143	9 708	...	...	...	...	...	...
35-39	8 086	4 972	8 100	4 762	...	...	...	...	...	...
40-44	5 119	4 100	5 206	4 094	...	...	...	...	...	...
45-49	3 657	3 390	3 815	3 416	...	...	...	...	...	...
50-54	2 429	2 195	2 639	2 530	...	...	...	...	...	...
55-59	1 688	1 524	1 677	1 492	...	...	...	...	...	...
60-64	1 617	1 231	1 693	1 410	...	...	...	...	...	...
65-69	1 461	886	1 532	928	...	...	...	...	...	...
70-74	1 006	381	1 081	438	...	...	...	...	...	...
75+	770	156	887	196	...	...	...	...	...	...
Portugal										
Groom — Epoux 16 ⊗										
Bride — Epouse 16 ⊗										
All ages - Tous âges	...	...	...	...	...	...	58 390	58 390	56 457	56 457
0-16	...	...	...	...	...	...	24	492	10	396
17-19	...	...	...	...	...	...	1 256	5 234	1 058	4 520
20-24	...	...	...	...	...	...	15 079	19 551	13 087	17 580
25-29	...	...	...	...	...	...	23 394	20 079	23 541	20 663
30-34	...	...	...	...	...	...	9 488	6 519	9 979	7 007
35-39	...	...	...	...	...	...	3 495	2 559	3 469	2 610
40-44	...	...	...	...	...	...	1 797	1 378	1 770	1 362
45-49	...	...	...	...	...	...	1 140	956	1 093	842
50-54	...	...	...	...	...	...	806	591	740	612
55-59	...	...	...	...	...	...	609	400	580	352
60-64	...	...	...	...	...	...	437	282	406	240
65-69	...	...	...	...	...	...	399	175	329	146
70-74	...	...	...	...	...	...	235	108	175	79
75+	...	...	...	...	...	...	231	66	...	...
75-79	...	...	...	...	...	...	...	...	...	...
80-84	...	...	...	...	...	...	...	...	129	38
85-89	...	...	...	...	...	...	...	...	60	9
90-94	...	...	...	...	...	...	...	...	28	-
95+	...	...	...	...	...	...	...	...	2	1
									1	-
Republic of Moldova - République de Moldova[25]										
Groom — Epoux 18 ⊗										
Bride — Epouse 16 ⊗										
All ages - Tous âges	16 644	16 644	18 221	18 221	16 554	16 554	16 076	16 076	16 663	16 663
0-15	-	77	-	67	-	53	-	28	-	13
16-19	1 093	6 777	1 058	7 170	1 026	6 118	838	5 572	863	5 183
20-24	10 457	7 956	11 199	8 883	9 669	8 302	9 176	8 344	9 145	8 961
25-29	3 903	1 331	4 639	1 553	4 480	1 500	4 676	1 619	5 148	1 915
30-34	772	242	849	281	844	285	887	267	984	299
35-39	222	101	245	94	251	76	251	80	233	85
40-44	61	41	71	41	76	33	90	38	93	40
45-49	31	23	42	29	29	29	26	13	28	20
50-54	13	11	22	11	13	11	19	9	27	11

24. Marriages by age of bridegroom and by age of bride: 1998 - 2002
Mariages selon l'âge de l'époux et selon l'âge de l'épouse: 1998 - 2002 (continued — suite)

(See notes at end of table. — Voir notes à la fin du tableau.)

Continent, country or area and age / Continent, pays ou zone et âge	1998 Groom Epoux	1998 Bride Epouse	1999 Groom Epoux	1999 Bride Epouse	2000 Groom Epoux	2000 Bride Epouse	2001 Groom Epoux	2001 Bride Epouse	2002 Groom Epoux	2002 Bride Epouse
EUROPE										
Republic of Moldova - République de Moldova[25]										
Groom — Epoux 18 ⊗										
Bride — Epouse 16 ⊗										
55-59	14	17	10	7	16	8	8	9	5	6
60-64	15	13	14	18	13	12	14	10	11	12
65-69	15	8	12	16	16	18	9	13	9	8
70-74	16	18	16	24	20	40	7	15	12	30
75+	27	22	39	19	101	69	72	56	105	80
Unknown - Inconnu	5	7	5	8	-	-	3	3	-	-
Romania - Roumanie										
Groom — Epoux 18 ⊗										
Bride — Epouse 16 ⊗										
All ages - Tous âges	145 303	145 303	...	...	135 808	135 808	129 930	129 930	129 018	129 018
15-19	2 882	31 639	...	...	1 993	24 646	1 604	21 434	1 566	20 325
20-24	57 734	65 116	...	...	47 311	60 585	41 940	56 394	38 798	54 046
25-29	48 513	26 965	...	...	47 973	27 792	47 305	28 671	48 987	30 400
30-34	16 601	9 693	...	...	19 580	11 571	20 085	12 196	20 420	12 549
35-39	7 003	3 916	...	...	6 494	3 692	6 179	3 485	6 734	4 102
40-44	4 937	3 051	...	...	4 530	2 865	4 561	2 781	4 345	2 556
45-49	3 111	2 277	...	...	3 156	2 015	3 191	2 168	3 259	2 179
50-54	1 590	1 080	...	...	1 831	1 204	1 990	1 273	2 016	1 368
55-59	1 095	684	...	...	1 029	619	1 143	616	1 051	645
60-64	...	...	...	...	943	409	...	...	...	...
60+	1 837	882	...	...	...	...	1 932	912	1 842	848
65-69	...	...	...	...	485	257	...	...	...	...
70-74	...	...	...	...	288	107	...	...	...	...
75+	...	...	...	...	195	46	...	...	...	...
Russian Federation - Fédération de Russie										
Groom — Epoux 18 ⊗										
Bride — Epouse 18 ⊗										
All ages - Tous âges	848 691	848 691	911 162	911 162	...	...	...	...	...	...
0-17	4 851	37 016	3 773	32 945	...	...	...	...	...	...
18-24	406 962	493 365	425 864	530 779	...	...	...	...	...	...
25-34	264 497	178 447	297 276	202 142	...	...	...	...	...	...
35+	172 250	139 743	184 148	145 226	...	...	...	...	...	...
Unknown - Inconnu	131	120	101	70	...	...	...	...	...	...
San Marino - Saint-Marin										
All ages - Tous âges	...	...	...	...	193	193	...	...	...	...
15-19	...	...	...	...	1	2	...	...	...	...
20-24	...	...	...	...	14	41	...	...	...	...
25-29	...	...	...	...	70	90	...	...	...	...
30-34	...	...	...	...	59	34	...	...	...	...
35-39	...	...	...	...	20	15	...	...	...	...
40-44	...	...	...	...	14	5	...	...	...	...
45-49	...	...	...	...	4	2	...	...	...	...
50-54	...	...	...	...	3	3	...	...	...	...
55-59	...	...	...	...	1	1	...	...	...	...
60-64	...	...	...	...	3	-	...	...	...	...
65-69	...	...	...	...	1	-	...	...	...	...
70-74	...	...	...	...	1	-	...	...	...	...
75+	...	...	...	...	1	-	...	...	...	...
Unknown - Inconnu	...	...	...	...	1	-	...	...	...	...
Serbia and Montenegro - Serbie-et-Montenegro										
Groom — Epoux 18 ⊗										
Bride — Epouse 18 ⊗										
All ages - Tous âges	54 822	54 822	...	...	58 318	58 318	...	...	...	...
15-19	1 029	8 503	...	...	1 060	8 356	...	...	...	...
20-24	15 220	22 122	...	...	14 740	22 784	...	...	...	...
25-29	18 977	13 170	...	...	20 743	14 859	...	...	...	...
30-34	9 305	4 753	...	...	10 463	5 389	...	...	...	...

(See notes at end of table. — Voir notes à la fin du tableau.)

Continent, country or area and age / Continent, pays ou zone et âge	1998		1999		2000		2001		2002	
	Groom Epoux	Bride Epouse	Groom Epoux	Bride Epouse	Groom Epoux	Bride Epouse	Groom Epoux	Bride Epouse	Groom Epoux	Bride Epouse
EUROPE										
Serbia and Montenegro - Serbie-et-Montenegro										
Groom — Epoux 18 ⊗										
Bride — Epouse 18 ⊗										
35-39	4 097	2 145	...	...	4 332	2 288	...	...	...	...
40-44	1 981	1 269	...	...	2 176	1 411	...	...	...	...
45-49	1 242	993	...	...	1 417	1 112	...	...	...	...
50-54	741	564	...	...	929	759	...	...	...	...
55-59	525	431	...	...	586	402	...	...	...	...
60-64	541	285	...	...	528	314	...	...	...	...
65-69	436	208	...	...	456	215	...	...	...	...
70-74	297	136	...	...	320	113	...	...	...	...
75+	293	117	...	...	291	114	...	...	...	...
Unknown - Inconnu	138	126	...	...	277	202	...	...	...	...
Slovakia - Slovaquie										
Groom — Epoux 16 ⊗										
Bride — Epouse 16 ⊗										
All ages - Tous âges	27 494	27 494	27 340	27 340	...	...	23 795	23 795	25 062	25 062
15-19	1 084	5 043	933	4 368	...	...	614	2 830	565	2 606
20-24	12 280	14 269	11 285	14 035	...	...	7 949	11 251	7 258	10 975
25-29	8 333	5 023	9 013	5 580	...	...	9 078	6 331	10 020	7 577
30-34	2 687	1 382	2 776	1 487	...	...	2 950	1 545	3 510	1 872
35-39	1 287	656	1 317	712	...	...	1 282	666	1 521	759
40-44	686	455	762	431	...	...	668	438	783	472
45-49	462	340	517	366	...	...	469	368	559	381
50-54	294	178	328	191	...	...	343	179	357	218
55-59	161	64	176	81	...	...	171	87	198	104
60-64	93	48	86	49	...	...	124	51	131	52
65-69	61	21	79	22	...	...	81	35	83	32
70-74	34	11	39	15	...	...	38	11	36	8
75+	32	4	29	3	...	...	28	3	...	...
75-79	...	...	...	...	...	...	...	...	30	4
80-84	...	...	...	...	...	...	...	...	9	2
85-89	...	...	...	...	...	...	...	...	1	-
90-94	...	...	...	...	...	...	...	...	1	
Slovenia - Slovénie										
Groom — Epoux 18 ⊗										
Bride — Epouse 18 ⊗										
All ages - Tous âges	7 528	7 528	7 716	7 716	7 201	7 201	6 935	6 935	7 064	7 064
0-14	...	...	-	1	...	...	-	1	-	1
15-19	42	308	42	334	32	226	34	225	29	189
20-24	1 316	2 777	1 318	2 656	1 076	2 279	976	1 988	865	1 874
25-29	3 080	2 686	3 092	2 768	2 894	2 820	2 770	2 799	2 666	2 790
30-34	1 681	910	1 693	995	1 724	976	1 646	997	1 756	1 162
35-39	588	357	695	384	633	392	683	380	793	422
40-44	327	172	314	216	316	171	281	194	354	249
45-49	168	141	184	166	205	165	200	127	227	159
50-54	119	73	140	85	118	71	129	97	136	111
55-59	74	41	80	44	70	42	78	53	87	47
60-64	48	35	51	29	46	33	42	33	59	29
65-69	40	12	52	23	40	16	38	25	39	18
70-74	21	9	22	10	33	8	30	11	24	5
75+	24	7	33	5	14	2	28	5	...	...
75-79	...	...	...	...	...	...	...	...	18	7
80-84	...	...	...	...	...	...	...	...	9	1
85-89	...	...	...	...	...	...	...	...	1	-
90-94	...	...	...	...	...	...	...	...	1	
Spain - Espagne										
Groom — Epoux 14 ⊗										
Bride — Epouse 12 ⊗										
All ages - Tous âges	207 041	207 041	...	...	...	...	...	...	...	...
0-14	...	19	...	...	...	...	...	...	...	...
15-19	1 518	6 302	...	...	...	...	...	...	...	...

24. Marriages by age of bridegroom and by age of bride: 1998 - 2002
Mariages selon l'âge de l'époux et selon l'âge de l'épouse: 1998 - 2002 (continued — suite)

(See notes at end of table. — Voir notes à la fin du tableau.)

Continent, country or area and age / Continent, pays ou zone et âge	1998		1999		2000		2001		2002	
	Groom Epoux	Bride Epouse	Groom Epoux	Bride Epouse	Groom Epoux	Bride Epouse	Groom Epoux	Bride Epouse	Groom Epoux	Bride Epouse
EUROPE										
Spain - Espagne										
Groom — Epoux 14⊗										
Bride — Epouse 12⊗										
20-24	24 432	48 589	...	...	...	...	...	...	...	...
25-29	92 989	96 350	...	...	...	...	...	...	...	...
30-34	56 526	36 434	...	...	...	...	...	...	...	...
35-39	16 291	10 420	...	...	...	...	...	...	...	...
40-44	6 169	4 074	...	...	...	...	...	...	...	...
45-49	3 361	2 059	...	...	...	...	...	...	...	...
50-54	2 109	1 224	...	...	...	...	...	...	...	...
55-59	1 243	678	...	...	...	...	...	...	...	...
60-64	952	409	...	...	...	...	...	...	...	...
65-69	651	215	...	...	...	...	...	...	...	...
70-74	368	156	...	...	...	...	...	...	...	...
75+	432	112	...	...	...	...	...	...	...	...
Sweden - Suède										
Groom — Epoux 18⊗										
Bride — Epouse 18⊗										
All ages - Tous âges	29 585	29 585	...	...	...	...	33 077	33 077	38 012	38 012
0-19	72	369	...	...	...	...	70	359	421	328
15-19	...	...	...	...	...	...	1 519	3 118	2 268	3 120
20-24	1 655	3 520	...	...	...	...	7 699	10 240	8 061	10 264
25-29	7 671	9 712	...	...	...	...	9 267	8 314	10 300	8 760
30-34	8 356	7 089	...	...	...	...	5 595	4 468	6 524	5 023
35-39	4 254	3 304	...	...	...	...	3 050	2 345	3 596	2 645
40-44	2 527	1 962	...	...	...	...	2 095	1 763	2 393	1 902
45-49	1 871	1 588	...	...	...	...	1 694	1 309	1 892	1 443
50-54	1 550	1 205	...	...	...	...	1 183	698	1 474	868
55-59	871	499	...	...	...	...	514	250	603	300
60-64	420	170	...	...	...	...	186	113	239	131
65-69	168	85	...	...	...	...	111	58	132	55
70-74	81	47	...	...	...	...	94	42	...	...
75+	89	35	...	...	...	...	...	...	67	34
75-79	...	...	...	...	...	...	...	...	32	13
80-84	...	...	...	...	...	...	...	...	10	2
85-89	...	...	...	...	...	...	...	...	-	1
90-94	...	...	...	...	...	...	...	...	-	3 123
Unknown - Inconnu	...	...	...	...	...	...	...	...		
Switzerland - Suisse										
Groom — Epoux 18⊗										
Bride — Epouse 17⊗										
All ages - Tous âges	38 683	38 683	...	...	39 758	39 758	35 987	35 987	...	...
0-14	-	1	...	...	-	3	-	1	...	...
15-19	169	982	...	...	229	1 112	189	950	...	...
20-24	3 505	7 702	...	...	3 628	7 357	3 040	6 486	...	...
25-29	11 674	13 508	...	...	10 574	13 047	8 939	11 398	...	...
30-34	10 799	8 430	...	...	10 962	9 051	10 100	8 476	...	...
35-39	5 126	3 592	...	...	5 756	4 059	5 641	4 035	...	...
40-44	2 547	1 764	...	...	3 071	2 039	2 905	1 883	...	...
45-49	1 723	1 249	...	...	1 962	1 413	1 812	1 208	...	...
50-54	1 440	838	...	...	1 605	938	1 425	851	...	...
55-59	868	370	...	...	1 045	470	1 041	457	...	...
60-64	442	150	...	...	501	158	479	149	...	...
65-69	204	47	...	...	218	59	230	47	...	...
70-74	94	30	...	...	97	31	102	26	...	...
75+	92	20	...	...	110	21	84	20	...	...
The Former Yugoslav Rep. of Macedonia - L'ex-République yougoslave de Macédoine										
Groom — Epoux 18⊗										
Bride — Epouse 18⊗										
All ages - Tous âges	...	...	14 172	14 172	14 255	14 255	13 267	13 267	14 522	14 522
15-19	...	...	539	3 314	551	3 151	458	2 759	472	2 869

24. Marriages by age of bridegroom and by age of bride: 1998 - 2002
Mariages selon l'âge de l'époux et selon l'âge de l'épouse: 1998 - 2002 (continued — suite)

(See notes at end of table. — Voir notes à la fin du tableau.)

Continent, country or area and age / Continent, pays ou zone et âge	1998 Groom Epoux	1998 Bride Epouse	1999 Groom Epoux	1999 Bride Epouse	2000 Groom Epoux	2000 Bride Epouse	2001 Groom Epoux	2001 Bride Epouse	2002 Groom Epoux	2002 Bride Epouse
EUROPE										
The Former Yugoslav Rep. of Macedonia - L'ex-République yougoslave de Macédoine										
Groom — Epoux 18⊗										
Bride — Epouse 18⊗										
20-24	...	...	5 258	6 292	5 059	6 241	4 397	5 719	4 955	6 398
25-29	...	...	5 214	3 057	5 205	3 166	5 109	3 152	5 516	3 459
30-34	...	...	1 877	772	2 032	848	1 946	869	2 111	908
35-39	...	...	666	331	715	376	674	319	774	380
40-44	...	...	274	153	307	179	270	172	296	194
45-49	...	...	117	99	131	107	153	114	134	137
50-54	...	...	74	47	75	65	84	71	89	74
55-59	...	...	44	35	56	29	45	23	37	29
60-64	...	...	39	20	47	19	42	33	40	30
65-69	...	...	33	12	29	14	33	16	46	20
70-74	...	...	17	6	24	6	32	6	29	5
75+	...	...	20	5	24	5	24	4	23	19
Unknown - Inconnu	...	...	-	29	-	49	-	10	-	-
Ukraine										
Groom — Epoux 18⊗										
Bride — Epouse 17⊗										
All ages - Tous âges	310 504	310 504	...	...	...	...	309 602	309 602	...	...
0-15	17	1 163	...	...	...	...	14	807	...	...
16-19	17 979	88 821	...	...	...	...	13 624	71 888	...	...
20-24	140 318	115 474	...	...	...	...	127 627	124 256	...	...
25-29	65 934	38 437	...	...	...	...	76 809	45 768	...	...
30-34	26 992	18 959	...	...	...	...	31 069	20 755	...	...
35-39	17 758	13 437	...	...	...	...	17 747	12 487	...	...
40-44	11 415	9 756	...	...	...	...	12 662	9 876	...	...
45-49	8 797	7 999	...	...	...	...	8 662	7 514	...	...
50-54	5 176	4 688	...	...	...	...	6 798	5 820	...	...
55-59	5 140	4 389	...	...	...	...	3 486	2 811	...	...
60+	10 978	7 381	...	...	...	...	11 104	7 620	...	...
United Kingdom - Royaume-Uni										
Groom — Epoux 16⊗										
Bride — Epouse 16⊗										
All ages - Tous âges	304 796	304 796	301 083	301 083	305 912	305 912	...	...	...	...
15-19	3 187	9 225	2 528	9 250	2 390	8 870	...	...	...	...
20-24	38 737	58 185	32 096	57 182	31 096	55 646	...	...	...	...
25-29	94 917	96 960	90 412	94 703	85 870	92 753	...	...	...	...
30-34	69 690	60 754	72 129	60 446	73 809	62 478	...	...	...	...
35-39	37 860	31 592	40 244	31 981	43 653	34 891	...	...	...	...
40-44	20 428	17 679	21 870	18 155	24 366	19 806	...	...	...	...
45-49	14 345	12 550	14 753	12 176	15 919	13 230	...	...	...	...
50-54	11 173	8 758	11 828	8 646	12 872	9 391	...	...	...	...
55-59	5 912	3 895	6 463	3 781	6 939	4 121	...	...	...	...
60-64	3 739	2 453	3 822	2 302	4 075	2 321	...	...	...	...
65-69	2 276	1 382	2 406	1 249	2 410	1 247	...	...	...	...
70-74	1 341	775	1 312	670	1 319	683	...	...	...	...
75+	1 191	588	1 220	542	1 194	475	...	...	...	...
OCEANIA — OCEANIE										
Australia - Australie+										
Groom — Epoux 16⊗										
Bride — Epouse 16⊗										
All ages - Tous âges	...	...	114 316	114 316	113 429	113 429	103 130	103 130	105 435	105 435
15-19	...	...	756	3 291	702	3 221	609	2 778	573	2 654
20-24	...	...	17 966	29 220	16 752	27 332	14 440	23 853	14 190	23 369
25-29	...	...	38 122	38 375	37 293	37 723	33 091	33 938	31 875	33 425
30-34	...	...	23 233	18 584	23 818	19 438	22 390	18 845	24 136	20 546
35-39	...	...	13 155	9 787	12 923	9 953	12 067	9 038	12 518	9 671
40-44	...	...	7 145	5 720	7 562	5 901	7 136	5 462	7 554	5 807

24. Marriages by age of bridegroom and by age of bride: 1998 - 2002
Mariages selon l'âge de l'époux et selon l'âge de l'épouse: 1998 - 2002 (continued — suite)

(See notes at end of table. — Voir notes à la fin du tableau.)

Continent, country or area and age / Continent, pays ou zone et âge	1998		1999		2000		2001		2002	
	Groom Epoux	Bride Epouse	Groom Epoux	Bride Epouse	Groom Epoux	Bride Epouse	Groom Epoux	Bride Epouse	Groom Epoux	Bride Epouse
OCEANIA — OCEANIE										
Australia - Australie+										
Groom — Epoux 16⊗										
Bride — Epoux 16⊗										
45-49	...	...	5 076	4 026	5 080	4 194	4 693	3 881	5 062	4 124
50-54	...	...	3 708	2 469	3 944	2 727	3 680	2 535	3 853	2 734
55-59	...	...	2 096	1 227	2 242	1 347	2 115	1 262	2 522	1 439
60-64	...	...	1 231	677	1 341	725	1 224	688	1 289	718
65-69	...	...	770	424	787	424	741	393	817	422
70-74	...	...	560	309	513	257	447	241	511	296
75+	...	...	498	207	472	187	497	216	...	...
75-79	...	...	...	...	...	...	...	...	326	153
80-84	...	...	...	...	...	...	...	...	159	59
85-89	...	...	...	...	...	...	...	...	41	14
90-94	...	...	...	...	...	...	...	...	8	4
New Caledonia - Nouvelle-Calédonie										
All ages - Tous âges	...	...	943	943	...	...	...	...	...	...
0-19	...	...	4	27	...	...	...	...	...	...
20-24	...	...	78	230	...	...	...	...	...	...
25-29	...	...	300	289	...	...	...	...	...	...
30-34	...	...	213	182	...	...	...	...	...	...
35-39	...	...	142	104	...	...	...	...	...	...
40-49	...	...	136	79	...	...	...	...	...	...
50-59	...	...	52	27	...	...	...	...	...	...
60+	...	...	18	5	...	...	...	...	...	...
New Zealand - Nouvelle-Zélande+										
Groom — Epoux 16⊗										
Bride — Epoux 16⊗									...	
All ages - Tous âges	20 135	20 135	21 085	21 085	...	...	...	...	20 690	20 690
15-19	182	644	199	665	...	...	...	...	225	639
20-24	3 022	4 677	3 033	4 692	...	...	...	...	2 776	4 178
25-29	5 951	6 254	6 200	6 585	...	...	...	...	5 417	5 849
30-34	4 295	3 580	4 539	3 820	...	...	...	...	4 583	4 199
35-39	2 531	1 958	2 637	2 095	...	...	...	...	2 651	2 256
40-44	1 377	1 135	1 580	1 291	...	...	...	...	1 760	1 377
45-49	1 026	843	1 019	821	...	...	...	...	1 182	929
50-54	713	505	783	542	...	...	...	...	845	614
55-59	430	233	465	255	...	...	...	...	539	283
60-64	226	118	261	141	...	...	...	...	307	169
65-69	177	79	168	91	...	...	...	...	182	91
70-74	114	65	106	42	...	...	...	...	119	50
75+	91	44	95	45	...	...	...	...	104	56
Tonga+										
All ages - Tous âges	736	736	...	...	747	747	...	...	...	...
15-19	52	139	...	...	62	169	...	...	...	...
20-24	234	290	...	...	257	278	...	...	...	...
25-29	241	171	...	...	217	163	...	...	...	...
30-34	106	70	...	...	106	82	...	...	...	...
35-39	42	30	...	...	36	27	...	...	...	...
40-44	25	20	...	...	28	9	...	...	...	...
45-49	11	9	...	...	12	10	...	...	...	...
50+	25	7	...	...	29	9	...	...	...	...

GENERAL NOTES - NOTES GENERALES

Data refer to legal (recognized) marriages performed and registered. For method of evaluation and limitations of data, see Technical Notes, for this table. — Les données représentent le nombre de mariages qui ont été célébrés et reconnus par la loi. Pour la méthode d'évaluation et les insuffisances des données, voir Notes techniques pour ce tableau.

Italics: data from civil registers which are incomplete or of unknown completeness. — *Italiques:* données incomplètes ou dont le degré d'exactitude n'est pas connu, provenant des registres de l'état civil.

FOOTNOTES - NOTES

* Provisional. — Données provisoires.

+ Data tabulated by date of registration rather than occurrence. — Données exploitées selon la date de l'enregistrement et non la date de l'événement.

⊗ Age below which marriage is unlawful or invalid without dispensation by competent authority. — Age en-dessous duquel le mariage est illégal ou nul sans une dispense de l'autorité compétente.

• Varies among major civil divisions, or ethnic or religious groups. — Varie selon les grandes divisions administratives ou selon les groups ethniques ou religieux.

1 Including marriages resumed after 'revocable divorce' (among Moslem population), which approximates legal separation. - Y compris les unions reconstituées après un 'divorce révocable' (parmi la population musulmane), qui est à peu près l'équivalent d'une séparation légale.

2 Excluding tribal Indian population. - Non compris les Indiens vivant en tribus.

3 Excluding Indian jungle population. - Non compris les Indiens de la jungle.

4 Excluding nomadic Indian tribes. - Non compris les tribus d'Indiens nomades.

5 Data refer to government controlled areas. - Les données se raportent aux zones contrôlées par le Gouvernement.

6 Including data for East Jerusalem and Israeli residents in certain other territories under occupation by Israeli military forces since June 1967. - Y compris les données pour Jérusalem-Est et les résidents israéliens dans certains autres territoires occupés depuis 1967 par les forces armées israéliennes.

7 Data refer to Japanese nationals in Japan only; and to grooms and brides married for the first time whose marriages occurred and were registered in the same year. - Les données se raportent aux nationaux japonais au Japon seulement; et aux époux et épouses mariés pour la première fois, dont le mariage a été célébré et enregistré la même année.

8 Minimum age of men with parental consent 18 years and without parental consent 20 years. - L'âge minimum pour les hommes est de 18 ans avec le consentement parental et de 20 ans sans ce consentement.

9 Minimum age of women with parental consent 16 years and without parental consent 20 years. - L'âge minimum pour les femmes est de 16 ans avec le consentement parental et de 20 ans sans ce consentement.

10 Excluding data for Jordanian territory under occupation since June 1967 by Israeli military forces. Excluding foreigners, including registered Palestinian refugees. - Non compris les données pour le territoire jordanien occupé depuis juin 1967 par les forces armées israéliennes. Non compris les étrangers, mais y compris les réfugiés de Palestine enregistrés.

11 Registration of Kandyan marriages is complete; registration of Moslem and general marriages is incomplete. - Tous les mariages des Kandyens sont enregistrés; l'enregistrement des mariages musulmans et des autres mariages est incomplet.

12 Figures exclude marriages previously officiated outside Singapore or under religious and customary rites. - Les figures excluent les mariages célébrés précédemment au dehors de Singapoure ou sous les rites réligieuse ou accoutumés.

13 Minimum age of marriage for men and women with parental consent is 16 years in case of Muslim marriage and 18 for civil marriage. Without parental consent, that age is 21 for both Muslim and civil marriages. - L'âge minimum du mariage pour les hommes et les femmes avec le consentement parental est de 16 ans en cas de mariage musulman et de 18 ans pour le mariage civil. Sans consentement parental, cet âge est 21 pour les mariages musulmans et civils.

14 Data refer to provincial capitals and district centres only. - Les données se rapportent aux capitales des provinces et les chefs-lieux de districts seulement.

15 Excluding aliens temporarily in the area. - Non compris les étrangers se trouvant temporairement le territoire.

16 Including armed forces stationed outside the country, but excluding alien armed forces in the area unless marriage performed by local foreign authority. - Y compris les militaires nationaux hors du pays et les militaires étrangers en garnison sur le territoire, sauf si le mariage a été célébré pour l'autorité locale.

17 Including Bulgarian nationals outside the country, but excluding aliens in the area. - Y compris les nationaux bulgares à l'étranger, mais non compris les étrangers sur le territoire.

18 Excluding Faeroe Islands and Greenland. - Non compris les Iles Féroé et Gröenland.

19 Marriages in which the bride was resident in Finland only. - Mariages où l'épouse a la résidence en Finlande seulement.

20 Including armed forces stationed outside the country. - Y compris les militaires nationaux hors du pays.

21 Age classification based on year of birth rather than exact date of birth. - Le classement selon l'âge est basé sur l'année de naissances et non sur la date exacte de naissance.

22 Data refer to de jure population. - Les données se raportent a la population de droit.

23 Including residents outside the country if listed in a Netherlands population register. - Y compris les résidents hors du pays, s'ils sont inscrits sur un registre de population néerlandais.

24 Marriages in which the groom was resident in Norway only. - Mariages où l'époux a la résidence en Norvège seulement.

25 Beginning with year 1998 data refer to first marriages only. - Après 1998 des données se rapportent aux premiers mariages seulement. Including residents outside the country. - Y compris les résidents hors du pays.

Table 25

Table 25 presents number of divorces and crude divorce rates for as many years as possible between 1998 and 2002.

Description of variables: Divorce is defined as a final legal dissolution of a marriage, that is, that separation of husband and wife which confers on the parties the right to remarriage under civil, religious and/or other provisions, according to the laws of each country.

Unless otherwise noted, divorce statistics exclude legal separations that do not allow remarriage. These statistics refer to the number of divorces granted, and not to the number of persons divorcing.

Divorce statistics are obtained from court records and/or civil registers according to national practice. The actual compilation of these statistics may be the responsibility of the civil registrar, the national statistical office or other government offices.

The urban/rural classification of divorces is that provided by each country or area; it is presumed to be based on the national census definitions of urban population which have been set forth at the end of the technical notes for table 6.

Rate computation: Crude divorce rates by urban/rural residence are the annual number of divorces per 1 000 mid-year population. Rates presented in this table have been limited to those countries or areas having at least a total of 30 divorces in a given year. These rates have been calculated by the Statistics Division of the United Nations.

Reliability of data: Each country or area has been asked to indicate the estimated completeness of the divorces recorded in its civil register. These national assessments are indicated by the quality codes C and U that appear in the first column of this table.

C indicates that the data are estimated to be virtually complete, that is, representing at least 90 per cent of the divorces that occur each year, while U indicates that data are estimated to be incomplete, that is, representing less than 90 per cent of the divorces occurring each year. The code ... indicates that no information was provided regarding completeness.

Data from civil registers which are reported as incomplete or of unknown completeness (coded U or ...) are considered unreliable. They appear in *italics* in this table and the rates were not computed on data so coded. These quality codes apply only to data from civil registers. For more information about the quality of vital statistics data in general, see section 4.2 of the Technical Notes.

Limitations: Statistics on divorces are subject to the same qualifications as have been set forth for vital statistics in general and divorce statistics in particular as discussed in section 4 of the Technical Notes.

Divorce, like marriage, is a legal event, and this has implications for international comparability of data. Divorce has been defined, for statistical purposes, in terms of the laws of individual countries or areas. The laws pertaining to divorce vary considerably from one country or area to another. This variation in the legal provision for divorce also affects the incidence of divorce, which is relatively low in countries or areas where divorce decrees are difficult to obtain.

Since divorces are granted by courts and statistics on divorce refer to the actual divorce decree, effective as of the date of the decree, marked year-to-year fluctuations may reflect court delays and clearances rather than trends in the incidence of divorce. The comparability of divorce statistics may also be affected by tabulation procedures. In some countries or areas annulments and/or legal separations may be included. This practice is more common for countries or areas in which the number of divorces is small. Information on this practice is given in the footnotes when known.

Because the registration of a divorce in many countries or areas is the responsibility solely of the court or the authority which granted it, and since the registration recording such cases is part of the records of the court proceedings, it follows that divorces are likely to be registered soon after the decree is granted. For this reason the practice of tabulating data by date of registration does not generally pose serious problems of comparability as it does in the case of birth and death statistics.

As noted briefly above, the incidence of divorce is affected by the relative ease or difficulty of obtaining a divorce according to the laws of individual countries or areas. The incidence of divorce is also affected by the ability of individuals to meet financial and other costs of the court procedures. Connected with this aspect is the influence of certain religious faiths on the incidence of divorce. For all these reasons, divorce statistics are not strictly comparable as measures of family dissolution by legal means. Furthermore, family dissolution by other than legal means, such as separation, is not measured in statistics for divorce.

For certain countries or areas there is or was no legal provision for divorce in the sense used here, and therefore no data for these countries or areas appear in this table.

In addition, it should be noted that rates are affected also by the quality and limitations of the population estimates that are used in their computation. The problems of under-enumeration or over-enumeration, and to some extent, the differences in definition of total population, have been discussed in section 3 of the Technical Notes dealing with population data in general, and specific information pertaining to individual countries or areas is given in the footnotes to table 3.

As will be seen from the footnotes, strict correspondence between the numerator of the rate and the denominator is not always obtained; for example, divorces among civilian plus military segments of the population may be related to civilian population only. The effect of this may be to increase the rates but, in most cases, the effect is negligible.

As mentioned above, data for some countries or areas may include annulments and/or legal separations. This practice affects the comparability of the crude divorce rates. For example, inclusion of annulments in the numerator of the rates produces a negligible effect on the rates, but inclusion of legal separations may have a measurable effect on the level.

It should be emphasized that crude divorce rates like crude birth, death and marriage rates may be seriously affected by age-sex structure of the populations to which they relate. Like crude marriage rates, they are also affected by the existing distribution of the population by marital status. Nevertheless, crude divorce rates provide a simple measure of the level and changes in divorce.

The comparability of data by urban/rural residence is affected by the national definitions of urban and rural used in tabulating these data. It is assumed, in the absence of specific information to the contrary, that the definitions of urban and rural used in connection with the national population census were also used in the compilation of the vital statistics for each country or area. However, it cannot be excluded that, for a given country or area, different definitions of urban and rural are used for the vital statistics data and the population census data respectively. When known, the definitions of urban in national population censuses are presented at the end of the technical notes for table 6. As discussed in detail in the notes, these definitions vary considerably from one country or area to another.

In addition to problems of comparability, divorce rates classified by urban/rural residence are also subject to certain special types of bias. If, when calculating divorce rates, different definitions of urban are used in connection with the vital events and the population data, and if this results in a net difference between the numerator and denominator of the rate in the population at risk, then the divorce rates would be biased. Urban/rural differentials in divorce rates may also be affected by whether the vital events have been tabulated in terms of place of occurrence or place of usual residence. This problem is discussed in more detail in section 4.1.4.1. of the Technical Notes.

Earlier data: Divorces have been shown in previous issues of the Demographic Yearbook. The earliest data, which were for 1935, appeared in the 1951 issue. For more information on specific topics and years for which data are reported, readers should consult the Historical Index.

NOTES

[i] For definition, please see section 4.1.1.4 of the Technical Notes.

Tableau 25

Le tableau 25 présente des statistiques concernant les divorces et les taux bruts de divortialité pour le plus grand nombre d'années possible entre 1998 et 2002.

Description des variables : Le divorce est la dissolution légale et définitive des liens du mariage, c'est-à-dire la séparation de l'époux et de l'épouse qui confère aux parties le droit de se remarier civilement ou religieusement, ou selon toute autre procédure, conformément à la législation du pays[1].

Sauf indication contraire, les statistiques de la divortialité n'englobent pas les séparations légales qui excluent un remariage. Ces statistiques se rapportent aux jugements de divorce prononcés, non aux personnes divorcées.

Les statistiques de la divortialité proviennent, selon la pratique suivie par chaque pays, des actes des tribunaux et/ou des registres de l'état civil. L'officier d'état civil, les services nationaux de statistique ou d'autres services gouvernementaux peuvent être chargés d'établir ces statistiques.

La classification des divorces selon le lieu de résidence (zone urbaine ou rurale) est celle qui a été communiquée par chaque pays ou zone ; on part du principe qu'elle repose sur les définitions de la population urbaine utilisées pour les recensements nationaux, qui sont reproduites à la fin des notes techniques du tableau 6.

Calcul des taux : Les taux bruts de divortialité selon le lieu de résidence (zone urbaine ou rurale) représentent le nombre annuel de divorces enregistrés pour 1 000 habitants au milieu de l'année. Les taux du tableau 25 ne se rapportent qu'aux pays ou zones où l'on a enregistré un total d'au moins 30 divorces pendant une année donnée. Ces taux ont été calculés par la Division de statistique de l'ONU.

Fiabilité des données : Il a été demandé à chaque pays ou zone d'indiquer le degré estimatif de complétude des données sur les divorces figurant dans ses registres d'état civil. Ces évaluations nationales sont désignées par les codes de qualité 'C' et 'U' qui apparaissent dans la deuxième colonne du tableau.

La lettre 'C' indique que les données sont jugées à peu près complètes, c'est-à-dire qu'elles représentent au moins 90 p. 100 des divorces survenus chaque année ; la lettre 'U' signale que les données sont jugées incomplètes, c'est-à-dire qu'elles représentent moins de 90 p. 100 des divorces survenus chaque année. Le code '...' indique qu'aucun renseignement n'a été communiqué quant à la complétude des données.

Les données issues des registres de l'état civil qui sont déclarées incomplètes ou dont le degré de complétude n'est pas connu (code 'U' ou '...') sont jugées douteuses. Elles apparaissent en italique dans le tableau et les taux correspondants n'ont pas été calculés. Les codes de qualité ne s'appliquent qu'aux données extraites des registres de l'état civil. Pour plus de précisions sur la qualité des données reposant sur les statistiques de l'état civil en général, voir la section 4.2 des Notes techniques.

Insuffisance des données : Les statistiques des divorces appellent les mêmes réserves que celles formulées à propos des statistiques de l'état civil en général et des statistiques de divortialité en particulier (voir la section 4 des Notes techniques).

Le divorce est, comme le mariage, un acte juridique, et ce fait influe sur la comparabilité internationale des données. Aux fins de la statistique, le divorce est défini par la législation de chaque pays ou zone. La législation sur le divorce varie considérablement d'un pays ou d'une zone à l'autre, ce qui influe aussi sur la fréquence des divorces, laquelle est relativement faible dans les pays ou zones où le jugement de divorce est difficile à obtenir.

Du fait que les divorces sont prononcés par les tribunaux et que les statistiques de la divortialité se rapportent aux jugements de divorce proprement dits, qui prennent effet à la date où ces jugements sont rendus, il se peut que des fluctuations annuelles accusées traduisent le rythme plus ou moins rapide auquel les affaires sont jugées plutôt que l'évolution de la fréquence des divorces. Les méthodes d'exploitation des données peuvent aussi influer sur la comparabilité des statistiques de la divortialité. Dans certains pays ou zones, ces statistiques peuvent comprendre les annulations et/ou les séparations légales. C'est notamment le cas dans les pays ou zones où les divorces sont peu nombreux. Lorsqu'ils sont connus, des renseignements à ce propos sont donnés en note à la fin du tableau.

Étant donné que dans de nombreux pays ou zones, le tribunal ou l'autorité qui a prononcé le divorce est seul habilité à enregistrer cet acte, et, comme l'acte d'enregistrement figure alors sur les registres du tribunal, l'enregistrement suit généralement de peu le jugement. C'est pourquoi la pratique consistant à exploiter les données selon la date de l'enregistrement ne pose généralement pas les graves problèmes de comparabilité auxquels on se heurte dans le cas des statistiques des naissances et des décès.

Comme on l'a brièvement mentionné ci-dessus, la fréquence des divorces est fonction notamment de la facilité relative avec laquelle la législation de chaque pays ou zone permet d'obtenir le divorce. Elle dépend également de la capacité des intéressés à supporter les frais de procédure. Il faut aussi citer l'influence de certaines religions sur la fréquence des divorces. Pour toutes ces raisons, les statistiques de divortialité ne sont pas rigoureusement comparables et ne permettent pas de mesurer exactement la fréquence des dissolutions légales des mariages. De plus, elles ne rendent pas compte des cas de dissolution extrajudiciaire du mariage, comme la séparation.

Dans certains pays ou zones, il n'existe ou il n'existait pas de législation sur le divorce selon l'acception retenue aux fins du tableau 25, si bien que l'on ne dispose pas de données les concernant.

De surcroît, il convient de noter que l'exactitude des taux dépend également de la qualité et des insuffisances des estimations de population qui sont utilisées pour leur calcul. Le problème des erreurs par excès ou par défaut commises lors du dénombrement et, dans une certaine mesure, le problème de l'hétérogénéité des définitions de la population totale ont été examinés à la section 3 des Notes techniques, relative à la population en général ; des explications concernant les différents pays ou zones sont données en note à la fin du tableau 3.

Comme on le verra dans les notes, il n'a pas toujours été possible d'obtenir une correspondance rigoureuse entre le numérateur et le dénominateur pour le calcul des taux. Par exemple, les divorces parmi la population civile et les militaires sont parfois rapportés à la population civile seulement. Cela peut avoir pour effet d'accroître les taux, mais, dans la plupart des cas, il est probable que la différence sera négligeable.

Comme indiqué plus haut, les données concernant certains pays ou zones peuvent comprendre les annulations et/ou les séparations légales. Cette pratique influe sur la comparabilité des taux bruts de divortialité. Par exemple, l'inclusion des annulations dans le numérateur a une influence négligeable, mais l'inclusion des séparations légales peut avoir un effet appréciable.

Il faut souligner que les taux bruts de divortialité, de même que les taux bruts de natalité, de mortalité et de nuptialité, peuvent varier sensiblement selon la structure par âge et par sexe. Comme les taux bruts de nuptialité, ils peuvent également varier en raison de la répartition de la population selon l'état matrimonial. Les taux bruts de divortialité offrent néanmoins un moyen simple de mesurer la fréquence et l'évolution des divorces.

La comparabilité des données selon le lieu de résidence (zone urbaine ou rurale) peut être limitée par les définitions nationales des termes «urbain» et «rural» utilisées pour la mise en tableaux de ces données. En l'absence d'indications contraires, on a supposé que les mêmes définitions avaient servi pour le recensement national de la population et pour l'établissement des statistiques de l'état civil pour chaque pays ou zone. Toutefois, il n'est pas exclu que, pour une zone ou un pays donné, des définitions différentes aient été retenues. Les définitions du terme «urbain» utilisées pour les recensements nationaux de population ont été présentées à la fin des notes techniques du tableau 6 lorsqu'elles étaient connues. Comme on l'a précisé dans les notes techniques relatives au tableau 6, ces définitions varient considérablement d'un pays ou d'une zone à l'autre.

Outre les problèmes de comparabilité, les taux de divortialité classés selon le lieu de résidence (zone urbaine ou rurale) sont également sujets à des distorsions particulières. Si l'on utilise des définitions différentes du terme « urbain » pour classer les faits d'état civil et les données relatives à la population lors du calcul des taux et qu'il en résulte une différence nette entre le numérateur et le dénominateur pour le taux de la population exposée au risque, les taux de divortialité s'en trouveront faussés. La différence entre ces taux pour les zones urbaines et rurales pourra aussi être faussée selon que les faits d'état civil auront été classés d'après le lieu de l'événement ou d'après le lieu de résidence habituel. Ce problème est examiné plus en détail à la section 4.1.4.1 des Notes techniques.

Données publiées antérieurement : Des statistiques concernant les divorces ont déjà été présentées dans des éditions antérieures de l'*Annuaire démographique*. Les plus anciennes, qui portaient sur 1935, ont été publiées dans l'édition de 1951. Pour plus de précisions concernant les années et les sujets pour lesquels des données ont été publiées, se reporter à l'index historique.

NOTE

[1] Pour la définition, voir la section 4.1.1.4 des Notes techniques.

25. Divorces and crude divorce rates by urban/rural residence: 1998 - 2002
Divorces et taux bruts de divortialité selon la résidence, urbaine/rurale: 1998 - 2002

(See notes at end of table. — Voir notes à la fin du tableau.)

Continent and country or area and urban/rural residence / Continent et pays ou zone et résidence urbaine/rurale	Code[1]	Divorces					Rate - Taux				
		1998	1999	2000	2001	2002	1998	1999	2000	2001	2002
AFRICA — AFRIQUE											
Côte d'Ivoire											
Total	...	52 083	...	...	...	...	...	...	...	...	...
Djibouti											
Total	C	1 327	1 207	...	...	...	...	...	...	...	...
Egypt - Égypte[2]											
Total	U	71 792	73 414	...	...	...	...	...	...	...	...
Urban	U	38 872	39 829	...	...	...	...	...	...	...	...
Rural	U	32 920	33 585	...	...	...	...	...	...	...	...
Ethiopia - Éthiopie											
Total	...	...	161 390	...	...	...	...	...	...	...	...
Urban	...	...	3 770	...	...	...	...	...	...	...	...
Rural	...	...	157 620	...	...	...	...	...	...	...	...
Libyan Arab Jamahiriya - Jamahiriya arabe libyenne[3]											
Total	C	1 279	1 095	1 444	1 662	1 740	0.27	0.22	0.28	0.31	0.32
Mauritius - Maurice											
Total	+C	1 012	1 150	1 191	1 512	1 291	0.87	0.98	1.00	1.26	1.07
Réunion											
Total	C	1 121	1 057	934	*904	...	1.61	1.49	1.29	*1.23	...
Saint Helena ex. dep. - Sainte-Hélène sans dép.											
Total	C	5	-	9	-	...	...	...	...	...	...
Seychelles											
Total	+C	79	102	88	109	*112	1.00	1.27	1.08	1.34	*1.39
South Africa - Afrique du Sud											
Total	...	35 792	...	...	...	...	...	...	...	...	...
Tunisia - Tunisie											
Total	...	...	8 915	...	...	...	...	...	...	...	...
AMERICA, NORTH — AMERIQUE DU NORD											
Anguilla											
Total	+C	...	...	10	2	8	...	...	...	...	...
Aruba											
Total	C	331	292	329	332	403	3.74	3.26	3.63	3.61	5.27
Bahamas[4]											
Total	C	340	452	503	...	...	1.16	1.52	1.66	...	...
Belize											
Total	+C	35	72	43	36	45	0.15	0.30	0.17	0.14	0.17
Bermuda - Bermudes											
Total	C	182	223	260	150	230	2.92	3.56	4.13	2.42	...
Canada											
Total	C	69 088	70 910	71 144	...	...	2.29	2.33	2.32	...	...
Cayman Islands - Îles Caïmanes											
Total	C	76	64	...	...	...	2.03	1.64	...	...	...
Costa Rica											
Total	C	7 188	...	...	...	...	2.15	...	...	...	...
Cuba											
Total	C	39 798	40 068	37 937	37 260	35 590	3.58	3.59	3.39	3.32	3.16
Dominica - Dominique											
Total	...	71	61	...	...	...	...	...	...	...	...
Dominican Republic - République dominicaine											
Total	C	7 813	9 639	...	8 358	...	0.96	1.16	...	0.98	...
El Salvador											
Total	C	2 931	3 146	3 430	2 662	4 253	0.49	0.51	0.55	0.42	0.65
Grenada - Grenade											
Total	C	127	120	102	*114	...	1.27	1.19	1.01	*1.13	...
Guadeloupe											
Total	C	641	861	695	904	...	1.53	2.03	1.62	2.09	...

25. Divorces and crude divorce rates by urban/rural residence: 1998 - 2002
Divorces et taux bruts de divortialité selon la résidence, urbaine/rurale: 1998 - 2002 (continued — suite)

(See notes at end of table. — Voir notes à la fin du tableau.)

Continent and country or area and urban/rural residence / Continent et pays ou zone et résidence urbaine/rurale	Code[1]	Divorces					Rate - Taux				
		1998	1999	2000	2001	2002	1998	1999	2000	2001	2002
AMERICA, NORTH — AMERIQUE DU NORD											
Guatemala											
Total	...	*1 275*	*1 373*	...	...	...	...	...	...	...	...
Jamaica - Jamaïque											
Total	C	1 420	1 131	...	...	...	0.55	0.44	...	...	...
Martinique											
Total	C	354	670	553	*453	...	0.93	1.75	1.44	*1.17	...
Mexico - Mexique[5]											
Total	+C	45 889	49 271	52 358	*57 370	...	0.47	0.50	0.52	*0.56	...
Urban	+C	40 995	...	...	...	...	0.57	...	...	...	...
Rural	+C	2 249	...	...	...	...	0.09	...	...	...	...
Netherlands Antilles - Antilles néerlandaises											
Total	+C	547	532	...	...	...	2.63	2.59	...	...	...
Nicaragua[6]											
Total	C	2 775	2 903	...	...	...	0.58	0.59	...	...	...
Panama[6]											
Total	C	2 126	2 135	2 189	2 309	*2 224	0.77	0.76	0.77	0.80	*0.73
Urban	C	1 749	1 838	1 856	1 987	*1 944	1.14	1.17	1.16	...	...
Rural	C	377	297	333	322	*233	0.31	0.24	0.27	...	...
Puerto Rico - Porto Rico											
Total	C	14 636	15 550	17 829	13 870	14 578	3.90	4.11	4.67	3.61	3.78
Saint Lucia - Sainte-Lucie											
Total	C	59	63	49	76	40	0.39	0.41	0.31	0.48	0.25
Saint Vincent and the Grenadines - Saint Vincent-et-les Grenadines											
Total	C	64	64	57	61	46	0.57	0.57	0.51	0.56	0.43
United States - États-Unis[7]											
Total	...	*1 135 000*	...	...	...	...	...	...	...	...	...
AMERICA, SOUTH — AMERIQUE DU SUD											
Brazil - Brésil[8]											
Total	...	...	*121 333*	*121 417*	*122 791*	...	...	...	...	...	...
Chile - Chili											
Total	...	*6 269*	...	...	...	...	...	...	...	...	...
Ecuador - Équateur[9]											
Total	+...	*8 907*	*8 968*	*10 796*	*11 068*	*10 987*	...	...	...	...	...
French Guiana - Guyane française											
Total	C	145	142	147	120	...	0.95	0.90	0.90	0.71	...
Suriname											
Total	C	357	384	392	...	...	0.79	0.84	0.85	...	...
Uruguay											
Total	+C	6 598	7 002	6 822	7 409	6 761	2.01	2.12	2.05	2.22	2.01
Venezuela[8]											
Total	...	*21 334*	*20 544*	*19 062*	*16 939*	*16 627*	...	...	...	...	...
ASIA — ASIE											
Armenia - Arménie											
Total	C	1 612	1 253	1 343	1 776	...	0.42	0.33	0.35	0.47	...
Urban	C	1 417	1 091	1 166	...	...	0.56	0.43	0.46	...	...
Rural	C	195	162	177	...	...	0.15	0.13	0.14	...	...
Azerbaijan - Azerbaïdjan											
Total	+C	5 657	5 013	5 478	5 382	5 738	0.71	0.63	0.68	0.66	0.70
Urban	+C	4 659	4 028	4 332	4 341	4 726	1.14	0.99	1.06	1.05	1.14
Rural	+C	998	985	1 146	1 041	1 012	0.26	0.25	0.29	0.26	0.25
Bahrain - Bahreïn											
Total	...	*790*	*834*	*769*	*801*	*838*	...	...	...	...	...

25. Divorces and crude divorce rates by urban/rural residence: 1998 - 2002
Divorces et taux bruts de divortialité selon la résidence, urbaine/rurale: 1998 - 2002 (continued — suite)

(See notes at end of table. — Voir notes à la fin du tableau.)

Continent and country or area and urban/rural residence / Continent et pays ou zone et résidence urbaine/rurale	Code[1]	Divorces					Rate - Taux				
		1998	1999	2000	2001	2002	1998	1999	2000	2001	2002
ASIA — ASIE											
Brunei Darussalam - Brunéi Darussalam											
Total	...	376	389	369	332	328	...	...	...	...	...
China - Chine											
Total	+C	1 191 000	...	...	...	...	0.95	...	...	...	...
China: Hong Kong SAR - Chine: Hong Kong RAS											
Total	...	13 129	13 408	13 247	13 425		...	...	...	...	...
China: Macao SAR - Chine: Macao RAS											
Total	C	260	283	369	348	*385	0.62	0.66	0.86	0.80	*0.88
Cyprus - Chypre[5,10]											
Total	C	852	1 193	1 182	1 197	1 320	1.11	1.54	1.51	1.52	1.66
Urban	C	662	929	898	...	1 023	...	...	...	...	...
Rural	C	144	172	234	...	247	...	...	...	...	...
Georgia - Géorgie											
Total	C	1 800	1 622	1 854	1 987	...	0.33	0.32	0.37	0.40	...
Urban	C	...	...	1 820	1 964	...	...	...	0.63	...	...
Rural	C	...	...	34	23	...	...	...	0.02	...	...
Iran (Islamic Republic of) - Iran (République islamique d')											
Total	C	42 391	51 044	53 797	60 559	67 256	0.69	0.81	0.85	0.94	1.03
Urban	C	37 626	45 274	47 936	54 603	61 074	0.97	1.14	1.17	1.29	1.42
Rural	C	4 765	5 770	5 861	5 956	6 182	0.21	0.25	0.26	0.27	0.27
Israel - Israël[11]											
Total	C	9 886	10 683	10 723	11 164	10 939	1.66	1.74	1.70	1.73	1.67
Japan - Japon[12]											
Total	+C	243 183	250 529	264 246	285 911	289 836	1.92	1.98	2.08	2.25	2.27
Urban	+C	202 537	208 522	218 935	235 968	238 811	...	...	...	...	...
Rural	+C	40 646	42 007	45 311	49 943	51 025	...	...	...	...	...
Jordan - Jordanie[13]											
Total	+C	7 671	7 885	8 241	9 017	9 032	1.61	1.61	1.64	1.74	1.69
Kazakhstan											
Total	C	35 460	25 583	27 391	29 599	31 236	2.35	1.71	1.84	1.99	2.10
Urban	C	28 662	21 226	22 753	24 227	25 563	3.40	2.54	2.72	2.80	3.04
Rural	C	6 798	4 357	4 638	5 372	5 673	1.02	0.66	0.71	0.83	0.88
Korea (Republic of) - Corée (République de)[14]											
Total	+C	116 727	118 014	119 982	135 014	145 324	2.52	2.53	2.55	2.85	3.05
Urban	+C	97 328	97 577	98 864	110 825	119 788	...	...	...	...	...
Rural	+C	19 399	20 437	21 118	24 189	25 536	...	...	...	...	...
Kuwait - Koweït											
Total	C	3 428	3 412	3 649	3 851	3 891	1.69	1.62	1.67	1.69	1.72
Kyrgyzstan - Kirghizistan											
Total	C	6 216	6 287	5 348	5 861	6 104	1.30	1.29	1.09	1.18	1.22
Urban	C	3 918	3 914	3 392	3 756	3 780	2.31	2.28	1.95	2.13	2.14
Rural	C	2 298	2 373	1 956	2 105	2 324	0.74	0.75	0.62	0.66	0.72
Lebanon - Liban[15]											
Total	+C	3 925	2 292	4 220	...	...	...	...	...	...	...
Mongolia - Mongolie											
Total	C	917	941	815	650	688	0.39	0.40	0.34	0.27	0.28
Urban	C	805	836	748	577	583	0.65	0.62	0.54	0.41	0.41
Rural	C	112	105	67	73	105	0.10	0.10	0.07	0.07	0.10
Occupied Palestinian Territory - Territoire palestinien occupé											
Total	U	3 465	3 761	3 546	3 687	3 045	...	...	...	...	...
Qatar											
Total	U	458	496	615	566	...	...	...	...	...	...
Saudi Arabia - Arabie saoudite											
Total	...	15 169	17 528	18 583	16 425	18 765	...	...	...	...	...

25. Divorces and crude divorce rates by urban/rural residence: 1998 - 2002
Divorces et taux bruts de divortialité selon la résidence, urbaine/rurale: 1998 - 2002 (continued — suite)

(See notes at end of table. — Voir notes à la fin du tableau.)

Continent and country or area and urban/rural residence / Continent et pays ou zone et résidence urbaine/rurale	Code[1]	Divorces					Rate - Taux				
		1998	1999	2000	2001	2002	1998	1999	2000	2001	2002
ASIA — ASIE											
Singapore - Singapour											
Total	+C	5 389	5 084	4 943	4 838	5 538	0.76	0.71	0.68	0.65	0.73
Syrian Arab Republic - République arabe syrienne[16]											
Total	U	11 363	12 453	11 863	13 077	14 314	...	...	...	...	...
Turkey - Turquie											
Total	U	32 167	31 540	34 862	...	...	...	...	...	...	...
Urban	U	28 022	27 405	29 891	...	...	...	...	...	...	...
Rural	U	4 145	4 135	4 971	...	...	...	...	...	...	...
Turkmenistan - Turkménistan											
Total	C	5 346	...	...	...	...	1.10	...	...	...	...
Uzbekistan - Ouzbékistan											
Total	C	...	14 608	19 903	15 646	...	...	0.61	0.81	0.63	...
Urban	C	...	10 503	12 169	...	...	...	1.16	1.32	...	...
Rural	C	...	4 105	7 734	...	...	...	0.28	0.50	...	...
Viet Nam											
Total	C	...	...	...	...	*39 829	...	...	...	...	*0.50
Urban	C	...	...	...	...	*14 542	...	...	...	...	*0.73
Rural	C	...	...	...	...	*25 287	...	...	...	...	*0.42
EUROPE											
Austria - Autriche[17]											
Total	C	17 884	18 512	19 552	20 582	19 639	2.21	2.29	2.41	2.56	2.44
Belarus - Bélarus											
Total	C	47 127	47 254	43 512	...	37 386	4.62	4.71	4.35	...	3.77
Urban	C	38 560	38 823	...	...	31 066	5.40	5.57	...	...	4.42
Rural	C	8 567	8 431	...	...	6 320	2.81	2.75	...	...	2.19
Belgium - Belgique[18]											
Total	C	26 503	26 423	27 002	29 314	30 628	2.60	2.58	2.63	2.85	2.96
Bosnia and Herzegovina - Bosnie-Herzégovine											
Total	C	1 964	...	1 436	...	...	0.54	...	...	...	...
Bulgaria - Bulgarie[19,20]											
Total	C	10 390	9 781	10 578	10 275	10 203	1.26	1.19	1.29	1.30	1.30
Urban	C	...	...	9 021	8 765	8 613	...	...	1.62	1.60	1.58
Rural	C	...	...	1 554	1 503	1 584	...	...	0.60	0.62	0.66
Channel Islands: Guernsey - Îles Anglo-Normandes: Guernesey											
Total	C	143	142	173	...	...	2.42	2.36	2.86	...	...
Croatia - Croatie											
Total	C	3 962	3 721	4 419	4 670	4 496	0.88	0.82	1.01	1.05	1.01
Urban	C	2 966	...	3 255	3 445	3 241	...	...	...	...	...
Rural	C	996	...	1 164	1 225	1 255	...	...	...	...	...
Czech Republic - République tchèque											
Total	C	32 363	23 657	29 704	31 586	31 758	3.14	2.30	2.89	3.09	3.11
Urban	C	26 843	19 376	24 454	26 044	26 070	3.50	2.53	3.20	3.45	3.46
Rural	C	5 520	4 281	5 250	5 542	5 688	2.11	1.63	2.00	2.08	2.13
Denmark - Danemark[21]											
Total	C	13 164	13 537	14 381	14 597	15 304	2.48	2.54	2.69	2.72	2.85
Estonia - Estonie[22]											
Total	C	4 491	4 561	4 230	4 312	4 074	3.10	3.16	3.09	3.16	3.00
Urban	C	...	...	3 169	...	3 030	...	...	3.35	...	3.22
Rural	C	...	...	935	...	907	...	...	2.21	...	2.17
Finland - Finlande[23]											
Total	C	13 848	14 030	13 913	13 568	13 336	2.69	2.72	2.69	2.62	2.56
Urban	C	9 830	...	...	9 624	9 561	3.18	...	...	3.03	2.97
Rural	C	4 018	...	...	3 944	3 775	1.95	...	...	1.96	1.90
France[24]											
Total	C	116 515	116 813	114 005	112 631	...	2.00	1.99	1.94	1.90	...

(See notes at end of table. — Voir notes à la fin du tableau.)

Continent and country or area and urban/rural residence — Continent et pays ou zone et résidence urbaine/rurale	Code[1]	Divorces					Rate - Taux				
		1998	1999	2000	2001	2002	1998	1999	2000	2001	2002
EUROPE											
Germany - Allemagne											
Total	C	...	190 590	194 408	197 498	...	...	2.32	2.37	2.40	...
Greece - Grèce											
Total	C	9 500	9 620	11 119	*9 500	...	0.90	0.91	1.11	*0.95	...
Hungary - Hongrie[5]											
Total	C	25 763	25 605	23 968	24 391	25 506	2.55	2.54	2.39	2.39	2.51
Urban	C	18 649	18 457	17 265	17 547	18 528	2.85	2.84	2.67	2.64	2.81
Rural	C	6 955	6 990	6 564	6 653	6 797	1.95	1.96	1.84	1.87	1.91
Iceland - Islande[25]											
Total	C	484	473	545	551	524	1.77	1.71	1.94	1.93	1.82
Urban	C	463	440	519	522	500	1.83	1.72	2.00	1.98	1.88
Rural	C	21	33	26	29	24	...	1.55	...	...	...
Ireland - Irlande											
Total	...	...	...	2 623	...	...	...	...	...	...	...
Isle of Man - Îles de Man											
Total	+C	372	388	394	353	402	5.04	...	5.26	4.62	5.21
Italy - Italie											
Total	C	33 540	34 341	37 573	40 051	...	0.58	0.60	0.65	0.69	...
Latvia - Lettonie											
Total	C	6 211	6 010	6 134	5 740	5 952	2.58	2.51	2.58	2.44	2.55
Urban	C	4 940	4 824	...	4 639	4 769	2.99	2.95	...	2.90	3.01
Rural	C	1 271	1 186	...	1 101	1 183	1.68	1.56	...	1.46	1.57
Lithuania - Lituanie											
Total	C	11 752	11 390	10 882	11 024	10 579	3.31	3.23	3.11	3.17	3.05
Urban	C	7 789	8 806	8 503	8 598	8 398	3.26	3.72	3.63	3.69	3.62
Rural	C	3 963	2 584	2 379	2 426	2 181	3.41	2.23	2.06	2.11	1.90
Luxembourg											
Total	C	1 017	1 043	1 030	1 028	1 092	2.39	2.42	2.36	2.33	2.45
Monaco											
Total	C	62	...	82	...	...	...	...	2.46	...	...
Netherlands - Pays-Bas[20]											
Total	C	32 459	33 571	34 650	37 104	33 179	2.07	2.12	2.18	2.31	2.05
Urban	C	...	...	24 507	...	23 582	...	...	...	...	...
Rural	C	...	...	9 708	...	9 597	...	...	...	...	...
Norway - Norvège											
Total	C	9 346	9 124	10 053	10 308	10 450	2.11	2.04	2.24	2.28	2.30
Poland - Pologne[5]											
Total	C	45 230	42 020	42 770	45 308	45 414	1.17	1.09	1.11	1.17	1.18
Urban	C	37 571	35 523	...	...	...	1.57	1.49	...	...	...
Rural	C	6 888	6 425	...	...	...	0.47	0.44	...	...	...
Portugal											
Total	C	...	17 676	19 104	18 851	*27 708	...	1.77	1.91	1.83	*2.67
Republic of Moldova - République de Moldova											
Total	C	10 156	8 913	9 707	10 808	12 698	2.78	2.44	2.67	2.98	3.50
Urban	C	7 555	6 526	6 652	7 309	8 947	4.92	4.26	4.40	4.92	6.03
Rural	C	2 601	2 387	3 055	3 499	3 751	1.23	1.13	1.44	1.63	1.75
Romania - Roumanie											
Total	C	39 985	34 408	30 725	31 135	31 790	1.78	1.53	1.37	1.41	1.46
Urban	C	28 702	...	22 486	22 362	22 675	2.32	...	1.84	1.83	1.95
Rural	C	11 283	...	8 239	8 773	9 115	1.11	...	0.81	0.86	0.89
Russian Federation - Fédération de Russie											
Total	C	501 654	532 533	627 703	*763 493	...	3.42	3.65	4.31	*5.30	...
San Marino - Saint-Marin											
Total	+C	36	51	38	...	...	1.38	1.93	1.41	...	...
Serbia and Montenegro - Serbie-et-Montenegro											
Total	C	7 874	7 211	8 520	8 511	...	0.74	0.68	0.80	0.80	...
Urban	C	5 384	4 999	5 817	...	...	0.98	0.91	1.06	...	...
Rural	C	2 490	2 212	2 703	...	...	0.48	0.43	0.52	...	...

25. Divorces and crude divorce rates by urban/rural residence: 1998 - 2002
Divorces et taux bruts de divortialité selon la résidence, urbaine/rurale: 1998 - 2002 (continued — suite)

(See notes at end of table. — Voir notes à la fin du tableau.)

Continent and country or area and urban/rural residence / Continent et pays ou zone et résidence urbaine/rurale	Code[1]	Divorces					Rate - Taux				
		1998	1999	2000	2001	2002	1998	1999	2000	2001	2002
EUROPE											
Slovakia - Slovaquie											
Total	C	9 312	9 664	9 273	9 817	10 960	1.73	1.79	1.72	1.83	2.04
Urban	C	7 086	7 150	...	7 172	7 782	2.31	2.33	...	...	2.58
Rural	C	2 226	2 514	...	2 645	3 178	0.96	1.08	...	...	1.35
Slovenia - Slovénie											
Total	C	2 074	2 074	2 125	2 274	2 457	1.05	1.04	1.07	1.14	1.23
Urban	C	1 037	...	1 392	1 433	1 533	...	...	...	...	1.57
Rural	C	1 037	...	733	841	924	...	...	...	...	0.95
Spain - Espagne											
Total	C	36 072	36 900	38 973	...	...	0.91	0.93	0.98	...	...
Sweden - Suède											
Total	C	20 761	21 000	21 502	21 022	21 322	2.35	2.37	2.42	2.36	2.39
Switzerland - Suisse[20]											
Total	C	17 868	20 768	10 511	15 778	...	2.51	2.91	1.46	2.18	...
Urban	C	13 341	15 513	7 841	11 707	...	2.78	3.22	1.62	2.39	...
Rural	C	4 527	5 296	2 670	4 071	...	1.96	2.28	1.15	1.74	...
The Former Yugoslav Rep. of Macedonia - L'ex-République yougoslave de Macédoine											
Total	C	...	1 045	1 325	1 448	1 310	...	0.52	0.65	0.71	0.64
Ukraine											
Total	C	179 688	...	...	181 334	183 538	3.56	...	...	3.70	3.79
Urban	C	148 720	...	...	147 877	145 457	4.34	...	...	...	...
Rural	C	30 968	...	...	33 457	38 081	1.91	...	...	...	...
United Kingdom - Royaume-Uni											
Total	C	159 688	158 418	154 273	...	...	2.70	2.66	2.58	...	...
OCEANIA — OCEANIE											
Australia - Australie											
Total	C	51 370	52 566	49 906	55 330	...	2.75	2.78	2.61	2.85	...
New Caledonia - Nouvelle-Calédonie											
Total	C	196	161	159	230	219	0.96	0.78	0.75	1.07	1.01
New Zealand - Nouvelle-Zélande											
Total	+C	10 067	9 931	9 699	9 683	10 292	2.64	2.59	2.51	2.50	2.61
Niue - Nioué											
Total	...	...	...	...	...	...	...	...	...	...	...
Tonga[26]											
Total	+C	86	91	113	...	...	0.87	0.91	1.13	...	...

GENERAL NOTES - NOTES GENERALES

Data exclude annulments and legal separations unless otherwise specified. Rates are the number of final divorce decrees granted under civil law per 1 000 mid-year population. Rates are shown only for countries or areas having at least a total of 100 divorces in a given year. For method of evaluation and limitations of data, see Technical Notes for this table. — Sauf indications contraires, il n'est pas tenu compte des annulations et des séparations légales. Les taux représentent le nombre de jugements de divorce définitifs prononcés par les tribunaux pour 1 000 personnes au milieu de l'année. Les taux présentés ne se rapportent qu'aux pays ou zones où l'on a enregistré un total d'au moins 100 divorces dans une année donnée. Pour la méthode d'évaluation et les insuffisances des données, voir Notes techniques pour ce tableau.

Italics: data from civil registers which are incomplete or of unknown completeness. — *Italiques:* données incomplètes ou dont le degré d'exactitude n'est pas connu, provenant des registres de l'état civil.

FOOTNOTES - NOTES

* Provisional. — Données provisoires.
+ Data tabulated by date of registration rather than occurrence. — Données exploitées selon la date de l'enregistrement et non la date de l'événement.

[1] 'Code' indicates the source of data, as follows:
C - Civil registration, estimated over 90% complete
U - Civil registration, estimated less than 90% complete
+ - Data tabulated by date of registration rather than occurence.
... - Information not available

Le 'Code' indique la source des données, comme suit:
C - Registres de l'état civil considérés complèts à 90 p. 100 au moins.
U - Registres de l'état civil qui ne sont pas considérés complèts à 90 p. 100 au moins.
+ - Données exploitées selon la date de l'enregistrement et non la date de l'événement.
... - Information pas disponible.

[2] Including 'revocable divorces' (among Moslem population), which approximate legal separations. - Y compris les 'divorces révocables' (parmi la population musulmane), qui sont à peu prè-s l'équivalent des séparations légales.

[3] Data refer to Libyan nationals only. - Les données se raportent aux nationaux libyens seulement.

[4] Petitions for divorce entered in court. - Demandes de divorce en instance devant les tribunaux.

[5] Figures for urban and rural areas do not add up to the total, since they do not include the category 'Unknown residence'. - La somme des donées pour la residence urbaine et rurale n'est pas égale au total parce qu'elle n'inclue pas la catégorie 'Residence inconnue'.

[6] Excluding tribal Indian population. - Non compris les Indiens vivant en tribus.

[7] Estimates based on divorces and annulments reported by varying number of states from year to year. - Estimations fondées sur les chiffres (divorces et annulations) communiqués par un nombre variable d'Etats d'une année a l'autre.

[8] Excluding Indian jungle population. - Non compris les Indiens de la jungle.

[9] Excluding nomadic Indian tribes. - Non compris les tribus d'Indiens nomades.

[10] Data refer to government controlled areas. - Les données se raportent aux zones contrôlées par le Gouvernement.

[11] Including data for East Jerusalem and Israeli residents in certain other territories under occupation by Israeli military forces since June 1967. - Y compris les données pour Jérusalem-Est et les résidents israéliens dans certains autres territoires occupés depuis 1967 par les forces armées israéliennes.

[12] Data refer to Japanese nationals in Japan only. - Les données se raportent aux nationaux japonais au Japon seulement.

[13] Excluding data for Jordanian territory under occupation since June 1967 by Israeli military forces. Excluding foreigners, including registered Palestinian refugees. - Non compris les données pour le territoire jordanien occupé depuis juin 1967 par les forces armées israéliennes. Non compris les étrangers, mais y compris les réfugiés de Palestine enregistrés.

[14] Excluding alien armed forces, civilian aliens employed by armed forces, and foreign diplomatic personnel and their dependants. - Non compris les militaires étrangers, les civils étrangers employés par les forces armées ni le personnel diplomatique étranger et les membres de leur famille les accompagnant.

[15] Published by the United Nations Economic and Social Commission for Western Asia. - Publié par la Commission économique et sociale des Nations Unies pour l'Asie occidentale.

[16] Excluding nomads. - Non compris les nomades.

[17] Excluding aliens temporarily in the area. - Non compris les étrangers se trouvant temporairement le territoire.

[18] Including divorces among armed forces stationed outside the country and alien armed forces in the area. - Y compris les divorces de militaires nationaux hors du pays et les militaires étrangers en garnison sur le territoire.

[19] Including Bulgarian nationals outside the country, but excluding foreigners in the country. - Y compris les nationaux bulgares à l'étranger, mais non compris les étrangers sur le territoire.

[20] Data for urban and rural areas were not revised, as opposed to data for the whole. - Les données selon la résidence urbaine/rurale n'ont pas été révisées, ce qui a été le cas avec les données pour l'ensemble du pays.

[21] Excluding Faeroe Islands and Greenland. - Non compris les Iles Féroé et Gröenland.

[22] Urban and rural distribution of marriages and divorces is displayed by place of residence of groom/husband. The difference between 'Total' and the sum of urban and rural is due to the unknown place of residence of grooms/husbands and to grooms/husbands living outside Estonia. - Les mariages et divorces sont classés par rapport à la résidence urbaine/rurale de l'époux. La somme des mariages et divorces par résidence urbaine/rurale est différente du 'total' car elle ne tient pas compte ni des résidences inconnues de l'époux ni des mariages et divorces d'époux vivant à l'étranger.

[23] Including nationals temporarily outside the country. - Y compris les nationaux se trouvant temporairement hors du pays.

[24] Rates computed on population including armed forces stationed outside the country, but excluding alien armed forces living in military camps within the country. - Taux calculés sur la base de la population qui comprend les militaires nationaux hors du pays, mais pas les militaires étrangers en garnison sur le territoire.

[25] Data refer to de jure population. - Les données se raportent a la population de droit.

[26] Including annulments. - Y compris les annulations.

Annex I: United Nations Projections - Annual interpolated mid-year population, estimates 1993-2002
Annexe I: Projections de la population - Population au milieu de l'année interpolée, estimations 1993 - 2002

(See notes at end of table. — Voir notes à la fin du tableau.)

Continent and country or area / Continent et pays ou zone	Population estimates (in thousands) - Estimations (en milliers)[1]									
	1993	1994	1995	1996	1997	1998	1999	2000	2001	2002
AFRICA — AFRIQUE										
Algeria - Algérie	27 159	27 736	28 271	28 756	29 200	29 617	30 033	30 463	30 914	31 383
Angola	11 573	11 936	12 280	12 597	12 897	13 191	13 501	13 841	14 215	14 619
Benin - Bénin	5 784	5 995	6 201	6 398	6 591	6 783	6 983	7 197	7 425	7 667
Botswana	1 543	1 580	1 616	1 650	1 682	1 711	1 736	1 754	1 766	1 771
Burkina Faso	9 299	9 563	9 832	10 103	10 378	10 662	10 965	11 292	11 645	12 022
Burundi	6 005	6 089	6 159	6 215	6 260	6 308	6 379	6 486	6 633	6 818
Cameroon - Cameroun	12 647	12 977	13 302	13 623	13 937	14 247	14 553	14 856	15 157	15 455
Cape Verde - Cap-Vert	382	392	401	411	420	430	440	451	461	472
Central African Republic - République centrafricaine	3 246	3 331	3 414	3 494	3 572	3 645	3 714	3 777	3 835	3 887
Chad - Tchad	6 624	6 825	7 034	7 248	7 469	7 701	7 948	8 216	8 505	8 814
Comoros - Comores	573	590	607	625	643	661	680	699	718	738
Congo	2 733	2 822	2 916	3 014	3 116	3 222	3 329	3 438	3 547	3 657
Côte d'Ivoire	13 922	14 339	14 755	15 174	15 591	15 999	16 383	16 735	17 051	17 336
Democratic Republic of the Congo - République démocratique du Congo	42 220	43 686	44 999	46 123	47 097	48 003	48 959	50 052	51 308	52 706
Djibouti	591	597	609	626	647	670	693	715	733	750
Egypt - Égypte	59 005	60 101	61 225	62 379	63 562	64 774	66 016	67 285	68 585	69 913
Equatorial Guinea - Guinée équatoriale	379	388	398	408	418	428	438	449	459	470
Eritrea - Érythrée	3 064	3 070	3 097	3 148	3 220	3 313	3 426	3 557	3 707	3 875
Ethiopia - Éthiopie	56 398	58 220	60 007	61 748	63 452	65 133	66 818	68 525	70 259	72 015
Gabon	1 053	1 086	1 119	1 151	1 183	1 215	1 245	1 272	1 297	1 320
Gambia - Gambie	1 041	1 078	1 115	1 154	1 194	1 234	1 275	1 316	1 357	1 397
Ghana	16 827	17 280	17 725	18 160	18 586	19 009	19 434	19 867	20 309	20 758
Guinea - Guinée	7 009	7 280	7 525	7 738	7 925	8 095	8 261	8 434	8 617	8 807
Guinea-Bissau - Guinée-Bissau	1 117	1 154	1 189	1 224	1 258	1 292	1 328	1 366	1 406	1 449
Kenya	25 737	26 491	27 226	27 942	28 643	29 331	30 011	30 689	31 364	32 040
Lesotho	1 652	1 672	1 692	1 714	1 735	1 756	1 774	1 788	1 796	1 800
Liberia - Libéria	2 048	2 067	2 141	2 283	2 480	2 704	2 909	3 065	3 161	3 206
Libyan Arab Jamahiriya - Jamahiriya arabe libyenne	4 619	4 713	4 808	4 904	5 001	5 101	5 203	5 306	5 412	5 519
Madagascar	13 142	13 536	13 946	14 371	14 812	15 266	15 727	16 195	16 667	17 144
Malawi	9 891	9 971	10 111	10 322	10 590	10 897	11 212	11 512	11 796	12 070
Mali	9 617	9 878	10 147	10 424	10 710	11 007	11 318	11 647	11 994	12 358
Mauritania - Mauritanie	2 184	2 241	2 300	2 362	2 428	2 496	2 569	2 645	2 724	2 807
Mauritius - Maurice[2]	1 096	1 111	1 125	1 138	1 150	1 162	1 174	1 186	1 198	1 210
Morocco - Maroc	26 098	26 553	27 004	27 452	27 898	28 343	28 787	29 231	29 675	30 120
Mozambique	14 772	15 333	15 854	16 321	16 747	17 143	17 526	17 911	18 296	18 676
Namibia - Namibie	1 552	1 601	1 652	1 703	1 755	1 806	1 853	1 894	1 930	1 960
Niger	9 306	9 609	9 929	10 268	10 624	10 997	11 384	11 782	12 193	12 617
Nigeria - Nigéria	98 491	101 196	103 914	106 639	109 371	112 109	114 854	117 608	120 368	123 134
Réunion	639	652	664	676	688	700	712	724	737	749
Rwanda	5 892	5 530	5 439	5 674	6 180	6 845	7 500	8 025	8 383	8 614
Saint Helena - Sainte-Hélène[3]	5	5	5	5	5	5	5	5	5	5
Sao Tome and Principe - Sao Tomé-et-Principe	123	125	128	130	132	134	137	140	143	146
Senegal - Sénégal	8 657	8 886	9 120	9 357	9 598	9 843	10 091	10 343	10 598	10 856
Seychelles	74	75	75	76	76	76	77	77	78	78
Sierra Leone	4 124	4 123	4 137	4 167	4 212	4 279	4 376	4 509	4 683	4 892
Somalia - Somalie	6 412	6 332	6 312	6 359	6 466	6 623	6 809	7 012	7 228	7 461
South Africa - Afrique du Sud	39 888	40 923	41 894	42 787	43 607	44 350	45 017	45 610	46 126	46 561
Sudan - Soudan	27 971	28 657	29 352	30 058	30 778	31 499	32 210	32 902	33 568	34 213
Swaziland	923	938	953	969	985	1 000	1 013	1 023	1 030	1 033
Togo	4 270	4 382	4 512	4 663	4 832	5 011	5 191	5 364	5 527	5 684
Tunisia - Tunisie	8 695	8 840	8 977	9 105	9 227	9 342	9 453	9 563	9 673	9 781
Uganda - Ouganda	19 628	20 257	20 892	21 533	22 183	22 853	23 558	24 309	25 111	25 965
United Republic of Tanzania - République Unie de Tanzanie	29 079	30 029	30 930	31 771	32 560	33 309	34 038	34 763	35 486	36 205

Annex I: United Nations Projections - Annual interpolated mid-year population, estimates 1993-2002
Annexe I: Projections de la population - Population au milieu de l'année interpolée, estimations 1993 - 2002
(continued — suite)

(See notes at end of table. — Voir notes à la fin du tableau.)

Continent and country or area Continent et pays ou zone	Population estimates (in thousands) - Estimations (en milliers)[1]									
	1993	1994	1995	1996	1997	1998	1999	2000	2001	2002
AFRICA — AFRIQUE										
Western Sahara - Sahara occidental	243	251	259	268	276	284	292	300	307	313
Zambia - Zambie	9 091	9 325	9 559	9 795	10 030	10 262	10 487	10 702	10 906	11 102
Zimbabwe	11 378	11 609	11 820	12 012	12 185	12 339	12 476	12 595	12 698	12 786
AMERICA, NORTH — **AMERIQUE DU NORD**										
Anguilla	10	10	10	11	11	11	11	11	11	12
Antigua and Barbuda - Antigua-et-Barbuda	67	68	70	71	72	74	75	76	78	79
Aruba	77	81	84	87	88	90	91	92	94	95
Bahamas	269	274	279	284	288	293	297	301	306	310
Barbados - Barbade	260	261	262	263	264	265	265	266	267	268
Belize	202	208	214	220	225	231	237	242	248	253
Bermuda - Bermudes	61	61	61	62	62	62	63	63	63	63
British Virgin Islands - Îles Vierges britanniques	18	18	18	19	19	20	20	21	21	21
Canada	28 702	29 007	29 302	29 586	29 858	30 127	30 401	30 689	30 993	31 312
Cayman Islands - Îles Caïmanes	30	31	33	34	36	37	38	40	41	42
Costa Rica	3 309	3 390	3 475	3 563	3 655	3 748	3 840	3 929	4 014	4 097
Cuba	10 750	10 809	10 867	10 924	10 980	11 033	11 082	11 125	11 161	11 193
Dominica - Dominique	74	74	75	76	76	77	77	78	78	78
Dominican Republic - République dominicaine	7 442	7 557	7 672	7 788	7 905	8 024	8 143	8 265	8 388	8 514
El Salvador	5 429	5 548	5 669	5 790	5 912	6 035	6 158	6 280	6 402	6 523
Greenland - Groenland	56	56	56	56	56	56	56	56	56	56
Grenada - Grenade	98	99	99	100	100	101	101	102	102	102
Guadeloupe	403	406	409	413	417	421	426	430	434	438
Guatemala	9 527	9 747	9 970	10 197	10 428	10 665	10 910	11 166	11 434	11 711
Haiti - Haïti	7 194	7 291	7 391	7 496	7 603	7 713	7 826	7 939	8 053	8 170
Honduras	5 314	5 469	5 625	5 783	5 944	6 105	6 265	6 424	6 582	6 738
Jamaica - Jamaïque	2 435	2 460	2 484	2 507	2 528	2 548	2 567	2 585	2 600	2 614
Martinique	370	373	375	378	380	382	384	386	388	390
Mexico - Mexique	89 276	90 915	92 523	94 096	95 636	97 144	98 627	100 088	101 528	102 946
Montserrat	11	11	10	9	8	6	5	4	3	4
Netherlands Antilles - Antilles néerlandaises	190	189	187	184	182	179	177	176	176	177
Nicaragua	4 268	4 374	4 477	4 576	4 671	4 766	4 861	4 959	5 059	5 162
Panama	2 564	2 617	2 670	2 725	2 781	2 837	2 893	2 950	3 006	3 063
Puerto Rico - Porto Rico	3 630	3 664	3 696	3 727	3 756	3 783	3 809	3 835	3 860	3 885
Saint Kitts and Nevis - Saint-Kitts-et-Nevis	40	40	40	40	40	40	40	40	41	41
Saint Lucia - Sainte-Lucie	144	146	148	149	151	152	153	154	156	157
Saint Pierre and Miquelon - Saint Pierre-et-Miquelon	6	6	6	6	6	6	6	6	6	6
Saint Vincent and the Grenadines - Saint Vincent-et-les Grenadines	112	112	113	114	114	115	115	116	117	117
Trinidad and Tobago - Trinité-et-Tobago	1 242	1 251	1 259	1 266	1 271	1 276	1 280	1 285	1 289	1 293
Turks Caicos Islands - Îles Turques et Caïques	14	15	15	16	17	17	18	19	21	22
United States - États-Unis	263 839	266 711	269 603	272 511	275 434	278 358	281 269	284 154	287 004	289 821
United States Virgin Islands - Îles Vierges américaines	105	106	107	108	109	110	110	111	111	112
AMERICA, SOUTH — **AMERIQUE DU SUD**										
Argentina - Argentine	33 948	34 396	34 835	35 266	35 689	36 102	36 504	36 896	37 274	37 642
Bolivia - Bolivie	7 149	7 315	7 482	7 648	7 813	7 980	8 147	8 317	8 488	8 661
Brazil - Brésil	156 614	158 978	161 376	163 819	166 301	168 812	171 335	173 858	176 377	178 895

Annex I: United Nations Projections - Annual interpolated mid-year population, estimates 1993-2002
Annexe I: Projections de la population - Population au milieu de l'année interpolée, estimations 1993 - 2002
(continued — suite)

(See notes at end of table. — Voir notes à la fin du tableau.)

Continent and country or area Continent et pays ou zone	Population estimates (in thousands) - Estimations (en milliers)[1]									
	1993	1994	1995	1996	1997	1998	1999	2000	2001	2002
AMERICA, SOUTH — **AMERIQUE DU SUD**										
Chile - Chili	13 916	14 161	14 395	14 617	14 828	15 029	15 223	15 412	15 596	15 776
Colombia - Colombie	37 096	37 819	38 542	39 262	39 981	40 697	41 410	42 120	42 826	43 528
Ecuador - Équateur	10 968	11 188	11 396	11 592	11 777	11 954	12 129	12 306	12 486	12 668
Falkland Islands (Malvinas) - Îles Falkland (Malvinas)	2	2	2	3	3	3	3	3	3	3
French Guiana - Guyane française	130	134	139	143	149	154	159	164	169	174
Guyana	728	730	732	734	737	739	741	744	746	747
Paraguay	4 584	4 705	4 829	4 954	5 080	5 208	5 338	5 470	5 604	5 740
Peru - Pérou	23 009	23 421	23 837	24 259	24 685	25 112	25 536	25 952	26 361	26 763
Suriname	409	412	415	418	422	426	430	434	437	441
Uruguay	3 171	3 195	3 218	3 242	3 267	3 292	3 317	3 342	3 366	3 391
Venezuela	21 153	21 620	22 087	22 554	23 020	23 486	23 952	24 418	24 884	25 350
ASIA — ASIE										
Afghanistan	18 231	19 566	20 669	21 471	22 031	22 476	22 999	23 735	24 724	25 912
Armenia - Arménie	3 372	3 293	3 227	3 178	3 143	3 119	3 100	3 082	3 065	3 050
Azerbaijan - Azerbaïdjan	7 575	7 689	7 791	7 880	7 957	8 024	8 085	8 143	8 198	8 250
Bahrain - Bahreïn	547	566	584	603	622	640	657	672	685	696
Bangladesh	111 428	113 946	116 455	118 946	121 426	123 905	126 398	128 916	131 461	134 029
Bhutan - Bhoutan	1 694	1 710	1 733	1 765	1 803	1 847	1 893	1 938	1 982	2 026
Brunei Darussalam - Brunéi Darussalam	280	287	295	303	310	318	326	333	341	349
Cambodia - Cambodge	10 738	11 059	11 368	11 662	11 943	12 215	12 481	12 744	13 007	13 268
China - Chine[4]	1 195 702	1 207 601	1 219 331	1 230 978	1 242 413	1 253 510	1 264 075	1 273 979	1 283 202	1 291 841
China - Hong Kong SAR - Chine - Hong Kong RAS[5]	5 980	6 085	6 187	6 283	6 375	6 464	6 551	6 637	6 721	6 803
China - Macao SAR - Chine - Macao RAS[6]	399	406	413	420	426	433	439	444	448	451
Cyprus - Chypre	709	720	731	742	753	765	776	786	797	807
Timor-Leste	827	846	848	830	797	758	730	722	738	775
Georgia - Géorgie	5 230	5 126	5 033	4 954	4 886	4 828	4 774	4 720	4 666	4 614
India - Inde	901 005	918 292	935 572	952 828	970 041	987 177	1 004 200	1 021 084	1 037 809	1 054 373
Indonesia - Indonésie	190 067	192 875	195 649	198 388	201 094	203 783	206 472	209 174	211 893	214 622
Iran (Islamic Republic of) - Iran (République islamique d')	60 333	61 359	62 324	63 239	64 105	64 918	65 671	66 365	66 998	67 587
Iraq	20 309	20 967	21 632	22 301	22 977	23 662	24 360	25 075	25 806	26 550
Israel - Israël	5 015	5 200	5 374	5 533	5 680	5 818	5 951	6 084	6 216	6 346
Japan - Japon	124 756	125 121	125 472	125 812	126 142	126 458	126 756	127 034	127 290	127 525
Jordan - Jordanie	3 876	4 094	4 288	4 453	4 594	4 718	4 841	4 972	5 113	5 261
Kazakhstan	16 224	16 048	15 866	15 682	15 495	15 317	15 161	15 033	14 942	14 885
Korea (Dem. People's Republic of) - Corée (Rép. populaire dém. de)	20 448	20 689	20 918	21 134	21 336	21 525	21 700	21 862	22 011	22 147
Korea (Republic of) - Corée (République de)	44 162	44 592	45 007	45 405	45 788	46 149	46 481	46 779	47 040	47 265
Kuwait - Koweït	1 845	1 739	1 696	1 727	1 820	1 955	2 099	2 230	2 340	2 438
Kyrgyzstan - Kirghizistan	4 507	4 542	4 588	4 648	4 720	4 799	4 878	4 952	5 020	5 084
Lao People's Democratic Republic - République démocratique populaire lao	4 460	4 572	4 686	4 801	4 917	5 036	5 156	5 279	5 404	5 531
Lebanon - Liban	2 989	3 091	3 177	3 243	3 292	3 330	3 364	3 398	3 434	3 469
Malaysia - Malaisie	19 323	19 839	20 362	20 892	21 427	21 961	22 486	22 997	23 492	23 971
Maldives	237	244	252	259	267	275	282	290	298	306
Mongolia - Mongolie	2 334	2 363	2 389	2 413	2 434	2 454	2 474	2 497	2 523	2 552
Myanmar	43 024	43 775	44 500	45 193	45 857	46 496	47 117	47 724	48 319	48 900
Nepal - Népal	20 614	21 145	21 682	22 226	22 776	23 329	23 881	24 431	24 975	25 515
Oman	2 046	2 113	2 177	2 239	2 299	2 354	2 402	2 442	2 471	2 493
Pakistan	120 294	123 105	126 075	129 247	132 581	135 998	139 381	142 648	145 772	148 791
Philippines	65 450	66 921	68 396	69 871	71 346	72 820	74 293	75 766	77 237	78 705

Annex I: United Nations Projections - Annual interpolated mid-year population, estimates 1993-2002
Annexe I: Projections de la population - Population au milieu de l'année interpolée, estimations 1993 - 2002
(continued — suite)

(See notes at end of table. — Voir notes à la fin du tableau.)

Continent and country or area Continent et pays ou zone	Population estimates (in thousands) - Estimations (en milliers)[1]									
	1993	1994	1995	1996	1997	1998	1999	2000	2001	2002
ASIA — ASIE										
Qatar	505	515	526	536	547	560	579	606	642	686
Saudi Arabia - Arabie saoudite	17 797	18 222	18 682	19 187	19 728	20 299	20 888	21 484	22 088	22 704
Singapore - Singapour	3 275	3 374	3 478	3 588	3 703	3 817	3 923	4 017	4 097	4 163
Sri Lanka	18 463	18 669	18 872	19 074	19 272	19 467	19 659	19 848	20 033	20 215
Syrian Arab Republic - République arabe syrienne	13 987	14 367	14 755	15 151	15 556	15 968	16 387	16 813	17 245	17 683
Tajikistan - Tadjikistan	5 606	5 688	5 770	5 851	5 932	6 011	6 087	6 159	6 227	6 293
Thailand - Thaïlande	56 920	57 642	58 336	59 001	59 638	60 252	60 851	61 438	62 017	62 586
Turkey - Turquie	60 443	61 522	62 620	63 742	64 883	66 026	67 149	68 234	69 275	70 277
Turkmenistan - Turkménistan	3 997	4 101	4 193	4 270	4 334	4 390	4 445	4 502	4 564	4 630
United Arab Emirates - Émirats arabes unis	2 188	2 307	2 435	2 569	2 709	2 863	3 040	3 247	3 488	3 756
Uzbekistan - Ouzbékistan	22 005	22 478	22 918	23 320	23 688	24 034	24 375	24 724	25 083	25 452
Viet Nam	70 516	71 878	73 163	74 362	75 481	76 548	77 602	78 671	79 765	80 877
Occupied Palestinian Territory - Territoire palestinien occupé	2 416	2 511	2 610	2 713	2 820	2 930	3 040	3 150	3 259	3 367
Yemen - Yémen	13 948	14 600	15 219	15 796	16 339	16 863	17 390	17 937	18 506	19 094
EUROPE										
Albania - Albanie	3 220	3 173	3 133	3 104	3 083	3 070	3 063	3 062	3 066	3 078
Andorra - Andorre	60	62	64	65	66	66	66	66	66	66
Austria - Autriche	7 933	7 998	8 047	8 076	8 088	8 090	8 090	8 096	8 110	8 128
Belarus - Bélarus	10 288	10 273	10 249	10 217	10 177	10 131	10 081	10 029	9 975	9 921
Belgium - Belgique	10 066	10 101	10 137	10 172	10 207	10 241	10 274	10 304	10 331	10 356
Bosnia and Herzegovina - Bosnie-Herzégovine	3 726	3 531	3 420	3 412	3 489	3 618	3 750	3 847	3 900	3 921
Bulgaria - Bulgarie	8 463	8 377	8 297	8 225	8 162	8 105	8 051	7 997	7 942	7 888
Channel Islands - Îles Anglo-Normandes	143	144	144	144	145	146	146	147	147	148
Croatia - Croatie	4 630	4 660	4 669	4 654	4 618	4 572	4 531	4 505	4 498	4 506
Czech Republic - République tchèque	10 327	10 331	10 331	10 324	10 312	10 297	10 281	10 267	10 256	10 246
Denmark - Danemark	5 187	5 207	5 228	5 250	5 273	5 295	5 318	5 340	5 360	5 379
Estonia - Estonie	1 509	1 476	1 447	1 424	1 405	1 390	1 378	1 367	1 357	1 348
Faeroe Islands - Îles Féroé	45	45	44	44	44	45	45	46	46	46
Finland - Finlande	5 061	5 086	5 108	5 125	5 140	5 152	5 164	5 177	5 191	5 205
France	57 649	57 937	58 203	58 441	58 655	58 857	59 061	59 278	59 511	59 756
Germany - Allemagne	80 885	81 312	81 661	81 917	82 086	82 191	82 268	82 344	82 427	82 507
Gibraltar	27	27	27	27	27	28	28	28	28	28
Greece - Grèce	10 454	10 561	10 657	10 741	10 813	10 875	10 928	10 975	11 015	11 048
Holy See - Saint-Siège[7]	1	1	1	1	1	1	1	1	1	1
Hungary - Hongrie	10 337	10 336	10 329	10 316	10 297	10 275	10 250	10 226	10 201	10 176
Iceland - Islande	262	265	267	270	273	276	279	281	284	287
Ireland - Irlande	3 557	3 582	3 609	3 638	3 670	3 706	3 749	3 801	3 863	3 933
Isle of Man - Îles de Man	71	72	72	73	74	75	76	77	77	77
Italy - Italie	57 054	57 184	57 301	57 401	57 486	57 562	57 637	57 715	57 797	57 880
Latvia - Lettonie	2 599	2 544	2 498	2 461	2 432	2 410	2 391	2 373	2 357	2 343
Liechtenstein	30	31	31	31	32	32	32	33	33	34
Lithuania - Lituanie	3 675	3 653	3 628	3 602	3 575	3 548	3 522	3 500	3 481	3 467
Luxembourg	393	399	405	411	417	423	429	435	441	447
Malta - Malte	371	374	378	381	384	387	389	392	394	396
Monaco	31	31	32	32	32	33	33	33	34	34
Netherlands - Pays-Bas	15 259	15 361	15 459	15 553	15 642	15 728	15 813	15 898	15 982	16 066
Norway - Norvège	4 308	4 333	4 359	4 387	4 416	4 446	4 475	4 502	4 528	4 552
Poland - Pologne	38 454	38 535	38 595	38 635	38 656	38 663	38 660	38 649	38 633	38 612
Portugal	9 993	10 009	10 030	10 058	10 092	10 132	10 177	10 225	10 277	10 331
Republic of Moldova - République de Moldova	4 362	4 351	4 339	4 327	4 314	4 302	4 289	4 275	4 260	4 246
Romania - Roumanie	22 956	22 816	22 681	22 555	22 435	22 323	22 217	22 117	22 025	21 942

Annex I: United Nations Projections - Annual interpolated mid-year population, estimates 1993-2002
Annexe I: Projections de la population - Population au milieu de l'année interpolée, estimations 1993 - 2002
(continued — suite)

(See notes at end of table. — Voir notes à la fin du tableau.)

Continent and country or area / Continent et pays ou zone	Population estimates (in thousands) - Estimations (en milliers)[1]									
	1993	1994	1995	1996	1997	1998	1999	2000	2001	2002
EUROPE										
Russian Federation - Fédération de Russie	148 673	148 440	148 189	147 947	147 691	147 398	147 030	146 560	145 985	145 327
San Marino - Saint-Marin	25	25	26	26	26	26	27	27	27	27
Serbia and Montenegro - Serbie-et-Montenegro	10 418	10 494	10 548	10 577	10 583	10 574	10 559	10 545	10 534	10 525
Slovakia - Slovaquie	5 326	5 347	5 364	5 377	5 386	5 393	5 397	5 400	5 402	5 402
Slovenia - Slovénie	1 952	1 959	1 964	1 967	1 968	1 968	1 967	1 967	1 967	1 967
Spain - Espagne	39 692	39 808	39 921	40 021	40 117	40 238	40 430	40 717	41 117	41 610
Sweden - Suède	8 737	8 789	8 827	8 850	8 859	8 861	8 865	8 877	8 901	8 933
Switzerland - Suisse	6 943	6 972	7 003	7 037	7 072	7 107	7 139	7 167	7 191	7 210
The Former Yugoslav Rep. of Macedonia - L'ex-République yougoslave de Macédoine	1 944	1 954	1 963	1 973	1 983	1 993	2 002	2 010	2 016	2 022
Ukraine	51 921	51 776	51 531	51 180	50 733	50 215	49 667	49 116	48 573	48 036
United Kingdom - Royaume-Uni	57 292	57 479	57 670	57 865	58 064	58 264	58 466	58 670	58 874	59 080
OCEANIA — OCEANIE										
American Samoa - Samoas américaines	51	52	53	54	55	56	57	58	59	60
Australia - Australie[8]	17 518	17 726	17 941	18 162	18 388	18 618	18 846	19 071	19 293	19 512
Cook Islands - Îles Cook	19	20	20	20	20	19	19	19	19	18
Fiji - Fidji	748	758	768	777	786	794	803	811	819	826
French Polynesia - Polynésie française	208	212	216	220	224	228	232	236	240	244
Guam	141	143	146	148	149	151	153	155	158	161
Kiribati	77	79	80	82	84	86	88	90	92	94
Marshall Islands - Îles Marshall	50	51	51	51	51	51	51	52	53	55
Micronesia, Federated States of - Micronésie, États Fédérés de La	104	106	107	108	108	108	107	107	107	108
Nauru	10	10	11	11	11	12	12	12	13	13
New Caledonia - Nouvelle-Calédonie	184	189	193	198	202	206	211	215	220	224
New Zealand - Nouvelle-Zélande	3 562	3 613	3 658	3 695	3 727	3 755	3 784	3 818	3 857	3 901
Niue - Nioué	2	2	2	2	2	2	2	2	2	2
Northern Mariana Islands - Îles Mariannes septentrionales	52	55	57	60	62	65	67	70	72	74
Palau - Palaos	16	17	17	18	18	19	19	19	20	20
Papua New Guinea - Papouasie-Nouvelle-Guinée	4 448	4 567	4 687	4 809	4 931	5 055	5 177	5 299	5 419	5 538
Pitcairn	-	-	-	-	-	-	-	-	-	-
Samoa	165	167	168	170	172	174	176	177	179	181
Solomon Islands - Îles Salomon	344	354	364	374	385	396	407	419	430	442
Tokelau - Tokélaou	1	1	1	1	1	1	1	1	1	1
Tonga	96	96	97	98	98	99	100	100	101	101
Tuvalu	10	10	10	10	10	10	10	10	10	10
Vanuatu	163	168	172	176	180	184	188	191	195	199
Wallis and Futuna Islands - Îles Wallis et Futuna	14	14	14	14	15	15	15	15	15	15

FOOTNOTES - NOTES

[1] For 1993-2002 all data refer to annual interpolated estimates of mid-year population. Both the estimates and the projections are produced by the Population Division of the Department for Economic and Social Affairs of the UN Secretariat and published in *World Population Prospects* - *The 2004 Revision*, United Nations publication, ST/ESA/SER.A/244, Volume I, New York, 2005. --- Les données pour 1993-2002 sont des estimations de population au milieu de l'année interpolée et ceux pour 2001 sont des projections de la population au milieu de l'année de variante moyenne. Toutes ces données sont produites par la Division pour la population de Département des affaires économiques et sociales du

Secrétariat de l'Organisation des Nations Unies et ont été publiées dans *World Population Prospects - The 2004 Revision,* United Nations publication, ST/ESA/SER.A/244, Volume I, New York, 2005.

[2] Including Agalega, Rodrigues and Saint Brandon. — Y compris Agalega, Rodrigues et Saint Brandon.

[3] Including Ascension and Tristan da Cunha. — Y compris Ascension et Tristan da Cunha.

[4] For statistical purposes, the data for China do not include Hong Kong and Macao Special Administrative Regions (SAR) of China. — A des fins statistiques, les données pour la Chine ne comprennent pas les Régions Administratives Spéciales (SAR) de Hong Kong et Macao.

[5] As of 1 July 1997, Hong Kong became a Special Administrative Region (SAR) of China. — A partir du 1 juillet 1997, Hong Kong est devenue une Région Administrative Spéciale (SAR) de la Chine.

[6] As of 20 December 1999, Macao became a Special Administrative Region (SAR) of China. — A partir du 20 décembre 1999, Macao est devenue une Région Administrative Spéciale (SAR) de la Chine.

[7] Refers to the Vatican City State. — Ce rapport à l'état du Vatican.

[8] Including Christmas Island, Cocos (Keeling) Islands and Norfolk Island. — Y compris Christmas Island, Cocos (Keeling) Islands et Norfolk Island.

Annex II: United Nations Medium Variant Population Projections - Vital statistics summary and expectation of life at birth: 2000 - 2005

Annexe II: Projections de la population de variante moyenne de l'ONU - Aperçu des statistiques de l'état civil et espérance de vie à la naissance: 2000 - 2005

(See notes at end of table. — Voir notes à la fin du tableau.)

Continent, country or area Continent, pays ou zone	Crude birth rate — Taux bruts de natalité[1]	Crude death rate — Taux bruts de mortalité[1]	Infant mortality rate — Décès d'enfants de moins d'un an[1]	Expectation of life at birth — Espérance de vie à la naissance[1]		Total fertility rate— Indice synthétique de fécondité[1]	Natural increase — Accroissement naturel[1]
				Male — Masculin	Female — Féminin		
AFRICA — AFRIQUE							
Algeria - Algérie	20.8	5.0	37.4	69.7	72.2	2.53	1.57
Angola	48.5	22.3	138.8	39.2	42.2	6.75	2.63
Benin - Bénin	42.1	12.9	105.1	53.0	54.5	5.87	2.92
Botswana	26.9	25.0	51.0	36.0	37.1	3.20	0.19
Burkina Faso	47.1	17.2	121.4	46.7	48.1	6.67	3.00
Burundi	43.7	18.9	105.9	42.5	44.4	6.80	2.48
Cameroon - Cameroun	35.9	17.2	94.3	45.1	46.5	4.65	1.86
Cape Verde - Cap-Vert	30.9	5.3	29.8	66.8	73.0	3.77	2.56
Central African Republic - République centrafricaine	37.8	22.1	98.2	38.5	40.3	4.96	1.56
Chad - Tchad	48.2	20.1	116.0	42.5	44.8	6.65	2.81
Comoros - Comores	36.5	7.4	57.7	60.9	65.1	4.89	2.91
Congo	44.1	13.2	72.3	50.6	53.1	6.29	3.09
Côte d'Ivoire	37.5	17.0	118.3	45.2	46.8	5.06	2.05
Democratic Republic of the Congo - République démocratique du Congo	49.5	20.4	118.5	42.1	44.1	6.70	2.91
Djibouti	36.2	12.7	93.2	51.4	53.9	5.09	2.34
Egypt - Égypte	26.3	6.0	36.7	67.5	71.8	3.29	2.04
Equatorial Guinea - Guinée équatoriale	42.9	20.0	102.0	42.8	44.2	5.89	2.30
Eritrea - Érythrée	39.9	11.6	64.6	51.5	55.4	5.53	2.84
Ethiopia - Éthiopie	41.1	16.3	99.5	46.5	48.6	5.87	2.48
Gabon	31.6	12.5	57.9	53.8	55.4	4.02	1.91
Gambia - Gambie	36.0	12.0	77.0	54.0	56.9	4.75	2.40
Ghana	32.1	10.8	62.3	56.2	57.2	4.39	2.13
Guinea - Guinée	42.2	13.8	105.5	53.2	54.0	5.92	2.84
Guinea-Bissau - Guinée-Bissau	49.8	20.0	119.7	43.1	46.2	7.10	2.97
Kenya	38.8	15.5	67.8	47.9	46.2	5.00	2.33
Lesotho	28.5	23.6	66.5	34.9	38.1	3.65	0.48
Liberia - Libéria	49.8	20.7	141.9	41.4	43.5	6.80	2.91
Libyan Arab Jamahiriya - Jamahiriya arabe libyenne	23.3	4.0	19.2	71.4	76.1	3.03	1.93
Madagascar	39.7	12.0	78.8	54.0	56.7	5.40	2.77
Malawi	44.6	21.8	110.8	39.7	39.6	6.10	2.28
Mali	49.7	17.8	133.5	47.1	48.4	6.92	3.19
Mauritania - Mauritanie	41.8	14.2	96.7	50.9	54.1	5.79	2.76
Mauritius - Maurice[2]	16.4	6.7	15.0	68.7	75.6	1.97	0.97
Morocco - Maroc	23.3	5.8	38.1	67.4	71.7	2.76	1.74
Mozambique	40.4	20.2	100.9	41.0	42.8	5.51	2.02
Namibia - Namibie	29.1	14.6	43.8	47.7	49.4	3.95	1.45
Niger	55.1	21.2	152.7	44.2	44.3	7.91	3.40
Nigeria - Nigéria	42.0	19.4	114.4	43.1	43.5	5.85	2.26
Réunion	20.1	5.4	7.7	71.3	79.6	2.49	1.48
Rwanda	41.0	18.3	115.5	41.9	45.3	5.70	2.27
Sao Tome and Principe - Sao Tomé-et-Principe	34.2	8.8	82.4	61.9	63.8	4.06	2.55
Senegal - Sénégal	37.4	11.7	83.5	54.4	56.8	5.05	2.57
Sierra Leone	46.7	23.7	165.1	39.3	42.0	6.50	2.31
Somalia - Somalie	45.8	18.4	126.1	45.0	47.3	6.43	2.75
South Africa - Afrique du Sud	23.8	16.2	42.7	47.1	51.0	2.80	0.76
Sudan - Soudan	33.5	11.2	72.2	54.9	57.9	4.45	2.23
Swaziland	29.6	26.7	73.1	32.5	33.4	3.95	0.30
Togo	39.5	12.3	92.5	52.3	56.2	5.37	2.73
Tunisia - Tunisie	16.8	5.4	22.2	71.1	75.3	2.00	1.14
Uganda - Ouganda	50.2	16.1	81.2	46.5	47.1	7.10	3.41
United Republic of Tanzania - République Unie de Tanzanie	38.1	16.7	104.4	45.6	46.4	5.04	2.14
Western Sahara - Sahara occidental	27.5	7.7	53.3	62.2	65.7	3.90	1.99
Zambia - Zambie	41.3	22.8	95.1	37.9	36.9	5.65	1.84
Zimbabwe	30.0	22.7	62.3	37.5	36.9	3.56	0.73

Annex II: United Nations Medium Variant Population Projections - Vital statistics summary and expectation of life at birth: 2000 - 2005
Annexe II: Projections de la population de variante moyenne de l'ONU - Aperçu des statistiques de l'état civil et espérance de vie à la naissance: 2000 - 2005

(continued — suite)

(See notes at end of table. — Voir notes à la fin du tableau.)

Continent, country or area Continent, pays ou zone	Crude birth rate — Taux bruts de natalité[1]	Crude death rate — Taux bruts de mortalité[1]	Infant mortality rate — Décès d'enfants de moins d'un an[1]	Expectation of life at birth — Espérance de vie à la naissance[1]		Total fertilty rate— Indice synthétique de fécondité[1]	Natural increase — Accroissement naturel[1]
				Male — Masculin	Female — Féminin		
AMERICA, NORTH — AMERIQUE DU NORD							
Bahamas	19.8	7.2	13.8	66.2	72.7	2.30	1.26
Barbados - Barbade	12.2	8.7	10.8	71.1	78.3	1.50	0.35
Belize	27.3	5.1	30.5	69.5	74.5	3.20	2.22
Canada	10.5	7.2	5.1	77.3	82.4	1.51	0.34
Costa Rica	19.1	3.9	10.5	75.8	80.6	2.28	1.52
Cuba	12.4	7.0	6.1	75.3	79.1	1.61	0.54
Dominican Republic - République dominicaine	24.5	6.5	34.6	63.7	70.9	2.73	1.79
El Salvador	25.3	5.8	26.4	67.7	73.7	2.88	1.94
Guadeloupe	16.3	6.1	7.3	74.9	81.7	2.06	1.02
Guatemala	35.8	6.6	38.9	63.4	70.8	4.60	2.92
Haiti - Haïti	30.4	13.6	61.6	50.6	52.3	3.98	1.69
Honduras	29.9	6.2	31.9	65.6	69.7	3.72	2.38
Jamaica - Jamaïque	20.3	7.6	14.9	68.9	72.5	2.44	1.27
Martinique	14.3	7.2	7.1	75.5	81.6	1.98	0.71
Mexico - Mexique	21.7	4.5	20.5	72.4	77.4	2.40	1.73
Netherlands Antilles - Antilles néerlandaises	14.8	7.0	13.2	72.9	79.1	2.12	0.78
Nicaragua	29.1	5.0	30.1	67.2	71.9	3.30	2.41
Panama	22.7	5.0	20.6	72.3	77.4	2.70	1.77
Puerto Rico - Porto Rico	14.4	8.1	9.9	71.6	80.5	1.92	0.63
Saint Lucia - Sainte-Lucie	18.8	7.0	14.9	70.8	73.9	2.24	1.18
Saint Vincent and the Grenadines - Saint Vincent-et-les Grenadines	20.5	6.8	25.6	68.2	73.8	2.27	1.38
Trinidad and Tobago - Trinité-et-Tobago	14.2	7.9	13.7	00.9	73.0	1.61	0.63
United States - États-Unis	14.0	8.4	6.9	74.6	80.0	2.04	0.57
United States Virgin Islands - Îles Vierges américaines	14.6	5.7	9.5	74.6	82.6	2.22	0.88
AMERICA, SOUTH — AMERIQUE DU SUD							
Argentina - Argentine	18.0	7.7	15.0	70.6	78.1	2.35	1.03
Bolivia - Bolivie	30.2	8.2	55.6	61.8	66.0	3.96	2.21
Brazil - Brésil	20.7	6.6	27.4	66.4	74.4	2.35	1.41
Chile - Chili	15.7	5.0	8.0	74.8	80.8	2.00	1.08
Colombia - Colombie	22.2	5.4	25.6	69.2	75.3	2.62	1.68
Ecuador - Équateur	23.3	4.9	24.9	71.3	77.2	2.82	1.84
French Guiana - Guyane française	25.0	3.7	14.1	72.5	78.4	3.41	2.13
Guyana	21.9	9.1	49.1	59.8	65.9	2.29	1.27
Paraguay	29.6	5.0	37.0	68.6	73.1	3.87	2.45
Peru - Pérou	23.3	6.1	33.4	67.3	72.4	2.86	1.72
Suriname	21.3	7.1	25.6	65.8	72.5	2.60	1.41
Uruguay	16.8	9.1	13.1	71.6	78.9	2.30	0.77
Venezuela	22.9	4.9	17.5	69.9	75.8	2.72	1.79
ASIA — ASIE							
Afghanistan	49.3	19.6	149.0	45.8	46.3	7.48	2.98
Armenia - Arménie	11.1	8.8	30.2	67.9	74.6	1.33	0.23
Azerbaijan - Azerbaïdjan	15.8	7.0	75.5	63.2	70.5	1.85	0.89
Bahrain - Bahreïn	18.8	3.2	13.8	72.9	75.8	2.47	1.56
Bangladesh	27.6	8.0	58.8	61.8	63.4	3.25	1.96
Bhutan - Bhoutan	30.6	8.7	55.7	61.5	63.9	4.40	2.19
Brunei Darussalam - Brunéi Darussalam ...	23.6	2.8	6.1	74.2	78.9	2.50	2.08
Cambodia - Cambodge	30.8	10.8	94.8	52.1	59.6	4.14	1.99
China - Chine[3]	13.6	6.8	34.7	69.8	73.3	1.70	0.68

Annex II: United Nations Medium Variant Population Projections - Vital statistics summary and expectation of life at birth: 2000 - 2005

Annexe II: Projections de la population de variante moyenne de l'ONU - Aperçu des statistiques de l'état civil et espérance de vie à la naissance: 2000 - 2005

(continued — suite)

(See notes at end of table. — Voir notes à la fin du tableau.)

Continent, country or area Continent, pays ou zone	Crude birth rate — Taux bruts de natalité[1]	Crude death rate — Taux bruts de mortalité[1]	Infant mortality rate — Décès d'enfants de moins d'un an[1]	Expectation of life at birth — Espérance de vie à la naissance[1]		Total fertility rate— Indice synthétique de fécondité[1]	Natural increase — Accroissement naturel[1]
				Male — Masculin	Female — Féminin		
ASIA — ASIE							
China - Hong Kong SAR - Chine - Hong Kong RAS[4]	8.3	5.3	3.8	78.6	84.6	0.94	0.30
China - Macao SAR - Chine - Macao RAS[5]	7.3	4.3	7.7	77.8	82.0	0.84	0.29
Cyprus - Chypre	12.1	7.2	6.2	76.0	81.0	1.63	0.49
Timor-Leste	47.4	12.6	93.7	54.1	56.3	7.79	3.47
Georgia - Géorgie	11.2	11.1	40.5	66.5	74.3	1.48	0.01
India - Inde	24.6	8.8	67.6	61.7	64.7	3.07	1.58
Indonesia - Indonésie	21.0	7.5	42.7	64.6	68.6	2.37	1.35
Iran (Islamic Republic of) - Iran (République islamique d')	18.6	5.3	33.7	68.8	71.7	2.12	1.33
Iraq	35.7	9.7	94.3	57.3	60.4	4.83	2.59
Israel - Israël	20.7	5.7	5.1	77.5	81.6	2.85	1.51
Japan - Japon	9.2	8.0	3.2	78.3	85.3	1.33	0.12
Jordan - Jordanie	27.8	4.2	23.3	69.8	72.8	3.53	2.36
Kazakhstan	16.1	10.8	61.2	57.8	68.9	1.95	0.52
Korea (Dem. People's Republic of) - Corée (Rép. populaire dém. de)	16.4	10.7	45.7	60.1	66.1	2.00	0.56
Korea (Republic of) - Corée (République de)	10.3	5.5	3.8	73.2	80.5	1.23	0.47
Kuwait - Koweït	19.5	1.8	10.3	75.1	79.4	2.38	1.77
Kyrgyzstan - Kirghizistan	22.6	7.5	55.1	62.6	71.1	2.71	1.51
Lao People's Democratic Republic - République démocratique populaire lao	35.9	12.6	88.0	53.3	55.8	4.83	2.33
Lebanon - Liban	19.0	6.7	22.5	69.7	74.0	2.32	1.23
Malaysia - Malaisie	22.9	4.6	10.1	70.8	75.5	2.93	1.82
Maldives	31.5	6.3	42.6	66.9	65.8	4.33	2.52
Mongolia - Mongolie	22.8	7.3	58.2	61.9	65.9	2.45	1.55
Myanmar	20.8	9.7	74.7	57.4	62.9	2.46	1.11
Nepal - Népal	30.4	8.7	64.4	60.9	61.7	3.71	2.17
Oman	25.6	2.8	15.6	72.7	75.6	3.78	2.28
Pakistan	31.1	8.3	78.6	62.7	63.1	4.27	2.28
Philippines	25.7	5.1	28.1	68.1	72.4	3.22	2.06
Qatar	19.1	3.2	11.6	71.1	75.9	3.03	1.59
Saudi Arabia - Arabie saoudite	28.5	3.9	22.5	69.9	73.8	4.09	2.47
Singapore - Singapour	10.1	4.9	3.0	76.7	80.5	1.35	0.52
Sri Lanka	16.4	6.0	17.2	71.3	76.7	1.97	1.04
Syrian Arab Republic - République arabe syrienne	28.7	3.5	18.2	71.4	74.9	3.47	2.52
Tajikistan - Tadjikistan	29.5	7.6	89.2	61.0	66.3	3.81	2.19
Thailand - Thaïlande	16.3	7.3	19.6	66.0	73.7	1.93	0.91
Turkey - Turquie	21.4	6.6	41.6	66.3	70.9	2.46	1.47
Turkmenistan - Turkménistan	22.9	8.3	78.3	58.2	66.7	2.76	1.46
United Arab Emirates - Émirats arabes unis	16.3	1.3	8.9	76.3	80.6	2.53	1.49
Uzbekistan - Ouzbékistan	23.7	6.8	58.0	63.3	69.7	2.74	1.69
Viet Nam	20.2	6.1	29.9	68.4	72.4	2.32	1.42
Occupied Palestinian Territory - Territoire palestinien occupé	38.8	4.2	20.9	70.8	73.9	5.57	3.46
Yemen - Yémen	41.0	8.7	69.0	59.1	61.7	6.20	3.23
EUROPE							
Albania - Albanie	17.2	6.4	25.0	70.9	76.7	2.29	1.08
Austria - Autriche	9.4	9.6	4.6	75.9	81.7	1.39	...
Belarus - Bélarus	9.2	14.5	14.9	62.4	74.0	1.24	...
Belgium - Belgique	10.9	10.0	4.2	75.7	81.9	1.66	0.09
Bosnia and Herzegovina - Bosnie-Herzégovine	9.7	8.6	13.5	71.3	76.7	1.32	0.10

(continued — suite)

(See notes at end of table. — Voir notes à la fin du tableau.)

Continent, country or area — Continent, pays ou zone	Crude birth rate — Taux bruts de natalité[1]	Crude death rate — Taux bruts de mortalité[1]	Infant mortality rate — Décès d'enfants de moins d'un an[1]	Expectation of life at birth — Espérance de vie à la naissance[1]		Total fertility rate— Indice synthétique de fécondité[1]	Natural increase — Accroissement naturel[1]
				Male — Masculin	Female — Féminin		
EUROPE							
Bulgaria - Bulgarie	8.7	14.3	13.2	68.8	75.6	1.24	...
Channel Islands - Îles Anglo-Normandes	10.3	9.9	5.5	75.9	80.8	1.40	0.04
Croatia - Croatie	9.1	11.5	6.9	71.3	78.4	1.35	...
Czech Republic - République tchèque	8.9	10.8	5.6	72.2	78.7	1.17	...
Denmark - Danemark	11.9	10.8	4.8	74.8	79.4	1.75	0.11
Estonia - Estonie	9.7	13.7	9.8	65.4	76.9	1.37	...
Finland - Finlande	10.7	9.5	3.9	75.0	81.7	1.72	0.12
France	12.5	9.4	4.5	75.8	83.0	1.87	0.31
Germany - Allemagne	8.5	10.3	4.5	75.6	81.4	1.32	...
Greece - Grèce	9.3	9.9	6.5	75.6	80.8	1.25	...
Hungary - Hongrie	9.5	13.0	8.3	68.4	76.7	1.30	...
Iceland - Islande	14.4	6.3	3.2	78.7	82.5	1.97	0.80
Ireland - Irlande	15.3	7.6	5.5	75.1	80.3	1.94	0.77
Italy - Italie	9.2	10.0	5.2	76.8	83.0	1.28	...
Latvia - Lettonie	8.8	13.4	10.2	65.6	76.9	1.26	...
Lithuania - Lituanie	9.0	11.8	9.1	66.5	77.8	1.28	...
Luxembourg	12.6	8.2	5.4	75.1	81.4	1.73	0.45
Malta - Malte	10.1	7.9	7.1	75.8	80.7	1.50	0.22
Netherlands - Pays-Bas	12.1	9.0	4.5	75.6	81.0	1.72	0.31
Norway - Norvège	12.2	9.6	3.8	76.7	81.8	1.79	0.26
Poland - Pologne	9.5	9.7	8.8	70.2	78.4	1.26	...
Portugal	10.9	10.5	5.6	73.8	80.5	1.47	0.04
Republic of Moldova - République de Moldova	10.1	11.5	25.8	63.7	71.1	1.23	...
Romania - Roumanie	9.9	12.2	18.1	67.7	75.0	1.26	...
Russian Federation - Fédération de Russie	10.1	15.3	16.9	59.1	72.2	1.33	...
Serbia and Montenegro - Serbie-et-Montenegro	11.8	10.7	13.0	70.9	75.6	1.65	0.11
Slovakia - Slovaquie	9.5	9.7	7.8	70.0	77.9	1.20	...
Slovenia - Slovénie	8.8	9.8	5.5	72.6	79.9	1.22	...
Spain - Espagne	10.4	8.8	4.6	75.8	83.1	1.27	0.15
Sweden - Suède	10.6	10.4	3.3	77.8	82.3	1.64	0.02
Switzerland - Suisse	9.7	8.5	4.4	77.6	83.1	1.41	0.12
The Former Yugoslav Rep. of Macedonia - l'ex-République yougoslave de Macédoine	11.8	8.4	16.0	71.2	76.2	1.53	0.34
Ukraine	8.2	16.3	15.6	60.1	72.5	1.12	...
United Kingdom - Royaume-Uni	11.4	10.3	5.3	75.9	80.6	1.66	0.11
OCEANIA — OCEANIE							
Australia - Australie[6]	12.7	6.7	4.9	77.6	82.8	1.75	0.60
Fiji - Fidji	23.6	6.2	21.8	65.7	70.0	2.92	1.73
French Polynesia - Polynésie française	19.3	4.8	8.8	70.6	75.8	2.39	1.45
Guam	22.3	4.7	9.8	72.4	77.0	2.95	1.75
Micronesia, Federated States of - Micronésie, États Fédérés de La	30.9	6.2	38.0	66.9	68.2	4.35	2.46
New Caledonia - Nouvelle-Calédonie	19.2	4.9	6.6	72.6	77.8	2.43	1.43
New Zealand - Nouvelle-Zélande	14.0	7.3	5.4	76.7	81.3	1.96	0.67
Papua New Guinea - Papouasie-Nouvelle-Guinée	31.7	10.7	70.6	54.7	55.8	4.10	2.10
Samoa	29.4	5.7	25.7	67.1	73.5	4.42	2.37
Solomon Islands - Îles Salomon	33.6	7.2	34.3	61.6	62.9	4.33	2.63
Tonga	24.2	5.9	21.0	70.9	73.4	3.54	1.83
Vanuatu	31.4	5.7	34.3	66.8	70.4	4.15	2.57

FOOTNOTES - NOTES

[1] All data are medium variant projections, produced by the Population Division of the Department for Economic and Social Affairs of the UN Secretariat and published in *World Population Prospects - The 2004 Revision*, United Nations

publication, ST/ESA/SER.A/244, Volume I, New York, 2005. — Toutes ces données sont des projections de la population au milieu de l'année de variante moyenne; elles sont produites par la Division pour la population de Département des affaires économiques et sociales du Secrétariat de l'Organisation des Nations Unies et ont été publiées dans *World Population Prospects - The 2004 Revision*, United Nations publication, ST/ESA/SER.A/244, Volume I, New York, 2005.

[2] Including Agalega, Rodrigues and Saint Brandon. — Y compris Agalega, Rodrigues et Saint Brandon.

[3] For statistical purposes, the data for China do not include Hong Kong and Macao Special Administrative Regions (SAR) of China. — A des fins statistiques, les données pour la Chine ne comprennent pas les Régions Administratives Spéciales (SAR) de Hong Kong et Macao.

[4] As of 1 July 1997, Hong Kong became a Special Administrative Region (SAR) of China. — A partir du 1 juillet 1997, Hong Kong est devenue une Région Administrative Spéciale (SAR) de la Chine.

[5] As of 20 December 1999, Macao became a Special Administrative Region (SAR) of China. — A partir du 20 décembre 1999, Macao est devenue une Région Administrative Spéciale (SAR) de la Chine.

[6] Including Christmas Island, Cocos (Keeling) Islands and Norfolk Island. — Y compris Christmas Island, Cocos (Keeling) Islands et Norfolk Island.

ABORIGINES

    See INDIGENOUS PEOPLES

ABORTION

    defined ... 8, 416

    grounds for, in different countries ... 416

    types, spontaneous and induced ... 416

ABORTIONS, LEGALLY INDUCED, NUMBER OF

    collection of data ... 420

    tabulation of

        Legally induced abortions ... Table 13

        Legally induced abortions by age and number of previous live births of woman ...

            Table 14

AFGHANISTAN ... 46; Tables 3, 5, 6, 8

AFRICA (MAJOR AREA) ... 46; Tables 1, 2

AGE

    at last birthday ... 5, 134, 492

    ending with zero or certain other digits ... 6

    errors in data, causes of ... 5–6

    misreporting and misrepresentations of ... 5

    reckoning of, English vs. Chinese systems ... 14n7

    reliability of data ... 5–6

    tabulation by

        abortions

            Legally induced abortions by age and number of previous live births of woman

                ... Table 14

        birth rate and births

            Live birth rates specific for age of mother, by urban/rural residence ... Table 11

            Live births by age of mother, sex and urban/rural residence ... Table 10

        death rate and deaths

            Death rates specific for age, sex and urban/rural residence ... Table 20

            Deaths by age, sex and urban/rural residence ... Table 19

            Infant deaths and infant mortality rates by age and sex ... Table 16

        expectation of life

            Expectation of life at specified ages for each sex ... Table 22

        marriages

            Marriages by age of groom and age of bride ... Table 24

        population

            Estimates of population and its percentage distribution, by age and sex and

                sex ratio for all ages for the world, major areas and regions ... Table 2

BIRTH, AT

tabulation by

Vital statistics summary and expectation of life at birth ... Table 4

BIRTH, LIVE

defined ... 8, 74, 304

sources of data ... 9

BIRTH RATE

defined ... 74

method of calculating series ... 45, 304, 354

tabulation of

Live birth rates specific for age of mother, by urban/rural residence ... Table 11

Live births and crude live-birth rates, by urban/rural residence ... Table 9

Population, rate of increase, birth and death rates, surface area and density for the world, major areas and regions ... Table 1

Vital statistics summary and expectation of life at birth ... Table 4; Annex II

BIRTHS, LIVE, NUMBER OF

method of calculating series ... 319

registration of, delayed ... 10, 319, 354, 366, 407, 433

sources of data ... 7

tabulation of

cause

Death and death rates by cause ... Table 21

summary

Vital statistics summary and expectation of life at birth ... Table 4

urban/rural residence

Deaths and crude death rates, by urban/rural residence ... Table 18

Deaths by age, sex and urban/rural residence ... Table 19

See also FOETAL DEATHS, LATE; INFANT DEATHS; MATERNAL DEATHS

DE FACTO POPULATION ... 4, 9, 56

DE JURE POPULATION ... 4

DEMOGRAPHIC ANALYSIS

used to assess vital statistics ... 11

DEMOGRAPHIC YEARBOOK

history and contents of ... 1

new table in ... 366

DENMARK ... 11, 12, 46; Tables 3, 4, 5, 7, 8, 9, 10, 11, 11a, 12, 13, 14, 15, 16, 17, 18, 19, 20, 21, 22, 23, 24, 25

DENOMINATOR

accuracy of, in computing rates ... 12

correspondence of population with that of numerator ... 555

DIVORCE

defined ... 8, 9, 890

DIVORCE RATE

method of calculating series ... 890

tabulation of

Divorces and crude divorce rates ... Table 25

DIVORCES, NUMBER OF

registration of ... 10, 890

statistics on ... 7

tabulation of

Divorces and crude divorce rates ... Table 25

DJIBOUTI ... 46; Tables 3, 8, 23, 25

DOMINICA ... 47; Tables 3, 4, 5, 7, 8, 9, 15, 17, 18, 21, 23, 25

DOMINICAN REPUBLIC ... 47; Tables 3, 4, 5, 6, 7, 8, 9, 10, 11a, 13, 15, 17, 18, 19, 21, 22, 23, 25

PLACE OF OCCURRENCE ... 9

PLACE OF USUAL RESIDENCE ... 9

POLAND ... 11, 12, 46; Tables 3, 4, 5, 6, 7, 8, 9, 10, 11, 11a, 12, 13, 15, 16, 17, 18, 19, 20, 21, 22, 23, 24, 25

POLYNESIA (MAJOR REGION) ... 47; Tables 1, 2

POPULATION

    defined ... 56

    statistics on ... 4–7

    tabulation of ... Tables 5–8

        age

            Estimates of population and its percentage distribution, by age and sex and sex ratio for all ages for the world, major areas and regions ... Table 2

            Population by age, sex and urban/rural residence ... Table 7

        cities

            Population of capital cities and cities of 100,000 and more inhabitants ... Table 8

        estimates

            Estimates of population and its percentage distribution, by age and sex and sex ratio for all ages for the world, major areas and regions ... Table 2

            Estimations of mid-year population ... Table 5; Annex I

        sex

            Estimates of population and its percentage distribution, by age and sex and sex ratio for all ages for the world, major areas and regions ... Table 2

            Population by age, sex and urban/rural residence ... Table 7

            Population by sex, rate of population increase, surface area and density ... Table 3

        urban/rural residence

            Population by age, sex and urban/rural residence ... Table 7

            Urban and total population by sex ... Tables 5, 6

        world

            Population, rate of increase, birth and death rates, surface area and density for the world, major areas and regions ... Table 1

POPULATION DENSITY

    defined ... 56

    method of calculating series ... 45

    tabulation of

        Population, rate of increase, birth and death rates, surface area and density for the world, major areas and regions ... Table 1

Index des thèmes traités dans la présente édition de l'*Annuaire démographique*

table nouveau ... 367

ANTIGUA-ET-BARBUDA ... 49; tableaux 3, 4, 5, 7, 8, 9, 10, 11a, 16, 17, 18, 19, 21

ANTILLES NÉERLANDAISES ... 49; tableaux 3, 4, 5, 7, 8, 9, 18, 23, 25

ARABIE SAOUDITE ... 50; tableaux 3, 4, 5, 7, 8, 9, 10, 15, 18, 19, 23, 25

ARGENTINE ... 28, 49; tableaux 3, 4, 5, 6, 7, 8, 9, 10, 11, 11a, 12, 15, 16, 17, 18, 19, 20, 21, 23

ARMÉNIE ... 18, 50; tableaux 3, 4, 5, 6, 7, 8, 9, 10, 11, 11a, 12, 13, 15, 16, 17, 18, 19, 20, 21, 22, 23, 24, 25

ARUBA ... 49; tableaux 3, 4, 5, 7, 8, 9, 10, 15, 18, 22, 23, 25

ASCENSION

>   *Voir* SAINT HELENA

ASIE (GRANDE ZONE) ... 50; tableaux 1, 2

ASIE CENTRALE ET DU SUD (RÉGION) ... 50; tableaux 1, 2

ASIE DU SUD-EST (RÉGION) ... 50; tableaux 1, 2

ASIE OCCIDENTALE (RÉGION) ... 50; tableaux 1, 2

ASIE ORIENTALE (RÉGION) ... 50; tableaux 1, 2

AUSTRALIE ... 28, 50; tableaux 3, 4, 5, 7, 8, 9, 10, 11, 11a, 12, 15, 16, 17, 18, 19, 20, 21, 22, 23, 24, 25

AUSTRALIE ET NOUVELLE-ZÉLANDE (RÉGION) ... 50; tableaux 1, 2

AUTRICHE ... 50; tableaux 3, 4, 5, 6, 7, 8, 9, 10, 11, 11a, 12, 15, 16, 17, 18, 19, 20, 21, 22, 23, 24, 25

AVORTEMENT

>   définition ... 24, 417

>   motifs d'autorisation, selon les pays ... 417

>   types ... 417

AVORTEMENTS LÉGAUX

>   collecte des données ... 421

>   exploitation des données

>>   avortements provoqués légalement ... tableau 13

>>   avortements provoqués légalement selon l'âge de la femme et selon le nombre de naissances vivantes précédentes ... tableau 14

AZERBAÏDJAN ... 18, 50; tableaux 3, 4, 5, 6, 7, 8, 9, 10, 11, 11a, 12, 13, 14, 15, 16, 17, 18, 19, 20, 21, 22, 23, 24, 25

BAHAMAS ... 28, 49; tableaux 3, 4, 5, 7, 8, 9, 10, 11a, 15, 16, 17, 18, 19, 21, 23, 24, 25

BAHREÏN ... 50; tableaux 3, 4, 5, 7, 8, 9, 10, 11a, 12, 13, 15, 16, 17, 18, 19, 21, 22, 23, 24, 25

Index des thèmes traités dans la présente édition de l'*Annuaire démographique*

Index des thèmes traités dans la présente édition de l'*Annuaire démographique*

Index des thèmes traités dans la présente édition de l'*Annuaire démographique*

Index des thèmes traités dans la présente édition de l'*Annuaire démographique*

exploitation des données

morts foetales tardives et rapports de mortinatalité selon le lieu de résidence

(zone urbaine ou rurale) ... tableau 12

MOZAMBIQUE ... 49; tableaux 3, 4, 5, 6, 7, 8, 9, 15, 18, 19, 20

MYANMAR ... 50; tableaux 3, 5, 6, 7, 8, 16, 19

NAISSANCE

exploitation des données

aperçu des statistiques de l'état civil et espérance de vie à la naissance ...

tableau 4

NAISSANCE VIVANTE

calcul ... 321

définition ... 24, 76, 306

enregistrement tardif ... 26, 321, 356, 367, 409, 435

exploitation des données

avortements provoqués légalement selon l'âge de la femme et selon le nombre

des naissances vivantes précédentes ... tableau 14

naissances vivantes et taux bruts de natalité selon le lieu de résidence (zone

urbaine ou rurale) ... tableau 9

naissances vivantes selon l'âge de la mère, le sexe de l'enfant et le lieu de

résidence (zone urbaine ou rurale) ... tableau 10

par mois d'occurrence ... tableau 11a

sources de données ... 23, 25

NAMIBIE ... 49; tableaux 3, 5, 7, 8

NATALITÉ

exploitation des données ... tableaux 9–11a

NAURU ... 50; tableaux 3, 5, 8

NÉPAL ... 50; tableaux 3, 4, 5, 6, 7, 8, 15, 18, 19, 20

NICARAGUA ... 49; tableaux 3, 4, 5, 6, 7, 8, 9, 10, 11a, 15, 16, 17, 18, 19, 21, 22, 23, 25

NIGER ... 49; tableaux 3, 8

NIGÉRIA ... 49; tableaux 3, 5, 7, 8

NIOUÉ ... 50; tableaux 3, 4, 5, 7, 8, 9, 11a, 18, 23, 25

NORVÈGE ... 28, 50; tableaux 3, 4, 5, 6, 7, 8, 9, 10, 11, 11a, 12, 13, 14, 15, 16, 17, 18,

19, 20, 21, 22, 23, 24, 25

NOUVELLE-CALÉDONIE ... 50; tableaux 3, 4, 5, 6, 7, 8, 9, 10, 11, 11a, 12, 13, 15, 16,

18, 19, 20, 22, 23, 24, 25

Index des thèmes traités dans la présente édition de l'*Annuaire démographique*

Index
Historical index
(See notes at end of index)

Subject-matter	Year of issue	Time coverage	Subject-matter	Year of issue	Time coverage
	1998	1994-98		1969	1963-68
	1999	1995-99		1975	1966-74
	1999CD[iv]	1980-99		1981	1972-80
	2000	1996-00		1986	1977-85
	2001	1997-01		1999CD[iv]	1990-98
	2002	1998-02	- by age of mother and sex	1965-1968	Latest
- by age of father	1949/50	1942-49		1969	1963-68
	1954	1936-53		1970-1974	Latest
	1959	1949-58		1975	1966-74
	1965	1955-64		1976-1978	Latest
	1969	1963-68		1978HS[ii]	1948-77
	1975	1966-74		1979-1980	Latest
	1981	1972-80		1981	1972-80
	1999CD[iv]	1990-98		1982-1985	Latest
- by age of mother	1948	1936-47		1986	1977-85
	1949/50	1936-49		1987-1991	Latest
	1954	1936-53		1992	1983-92
	1955-1956	Latest		1993-1997	Latest
	1958	Latest		1997HS[iii]	1948-96
	1959	1949-58		1998-99	Latest
	1960-1964	Latest		1999CD[iv]	1990-98
	1965	1955-64		2000-2002	Latest
	1966-1968	Latest	- by age of mother and urban/rural residence (see: by urban/rural residence, below)		
	1969	1963-68			
	1970-1974	Latest			
	1975	1966-74			
	1976-1978	Latest	- by birth order	1948	1936-47
	1978HS[ii]	1948-77		1949/50	1936-49
	1979-1980	Latest		1954	1936-53
	1981	1972-80		1955	Latest
	1982-1985	Latest		1959	1949-58
	1986	1977-85		1965	1955-64
	1987-1991	Latest		1969	1963-68
	1992	1983-92		1975	1966-74
	1993-1997	Latest		1981	1972-80
	1997HS[iii] [3]	1948-96		1986	1977-85
	1998-99	Latest		1999CD[iv]	1990-98
	1999CD[iv]	1990-98	- by birth weight	1975	Latest
	2000-2002	Latest		1981	1972-80
- by age of mother and birth order	1949/50	1936-47		1986	1977-85
	1954	Latest		1999CD[iv]	1990-98
	1959	1949-58	- by gestational age	1975	Latest
	1965	1955-64		1981	1972-80

Subject-matter	Year of issue	Time coverage	Subject-matter	Year of issue	Time coverage
	1986	1977-85		1973	1969-73
	1999CD[iv]	1990-98		1974	1970-74
				1975	1956-75
- by legitimacy status	1959	1949-58		1976	1972-76
	1965	1955-64		1977	1973-77
	1969	1963-68		1978	1974-78
	1975	1966-74		1979	1975-79
	1981	1972-80		1980	1976-80
	1986	1977-85		1981	1962-81
	1999CD[iv]	1990-98		1982	1978-82
- by month	2002	1980-02		1983	1979-83
				1984	1980-84
- by occupation of father	1965	Latest		1985	1981-85
	1969	Latest		1986	1967-86
				1987	1983-87
- by sex	1959	1949-58		1988	1984-88
	1965	1955-64		1989	1985-89
	1967-1968	Latest		1990	1986-90
	1969	1963-68		1991	1987-91
	1970-1974	Latest		1992	1983-92
	1975	1956-75		1993	1989-93
	1976-1980	Latest		1994	1990-94
	1981	1962-81		1995	1991-95
	1982-1985	Latest		1996	1992-96
	1986	1967-86		1997	1993-97
	1987-1991	Latest		1998	1994-98
	1992	1983-92		1999	1995-99
	1993-1999	Latest		1999CD[iv]	1980-99
	1999CD[iv]	1990-98		2000	1996-00
	2000-2002	Latest		2001	1997-01
				2002	1998-02
- by plurality	1965	Latest	- by urban/rural residence and age of mother	1965	Latest
	1969	Latest		1969-1974	Latest
	1975	Latest		1975	1966-74
	1981	1972-80		1976-1980	Latest
	1986	1977-85		1981	1972-80
	1999CD[iv]	1990-98		1982-1985	Latest
- by urban/rural residence	1965	Latest		1986	1977-85
	1967	Latest		1987-1991	Latest
	1968	1964-68		1992	1983-92
	1969	1964-68		1993-1997	Latest
	1970	1966-70		1997HS[iii]	1948-96
	1971	1967-71		1998-1999	Latest
	1972	1968-72		1999CD[iv]	1990-98
				2000-2002	Latest
			- illegitimate	1959	1949-58
				1965	1955-64

Subject-matter	Year of issue	Time coverage	Subject-matter	Year of issue	Time coverage
	1969	1963-68			1934-51
	1975	1966-74		1953	1920-39[v]
	1981	1972-80			1940-52
	1986	1977-85		1954	1920-39[v]
	1999CD[iv]	1990-98			1939-53
- legitimate	1948	1936-47		1955	1920-34[v]
	1949/50	1936-49			1946-54
	1954	1936-53		1956	1947-55
	1959	1949-58		1957	1948-56
	1965	1955-64		1958	1948-57
	1969	1963-68		1959	1920-54[v]
	1975	1966-74			1953-58
	1981	1972-80		1960	1950-59
	1986	1977-85		1961	1945-59[v]
	1999CD[iv]	1990-98			1952-61
- legitimate, by age of father	1959	1949-58		1962	1945-54[v]
	1965	1955-64			1952-62
	1969	1963-68		1963	1945-59[v]
	1975	1966-74			1954-63
	1981	1972-80		1964	1960-64
	1986	1977-85		1965	1920-64[v]
- legitimate, by age of mother	1954	1936-53			1950-65
	1959	1949-58		1966	1950-64[v]
	1965	1955-64			1957-66
	1969	1963-68		1967	1963-67
	1975	1966-74		1968	1964-68
	1981	1972-80		1969	1925-69[v]
	1986	1977-85			1954-69
- legitimate, by duration of marriage	1948	1936-47		1970	1966-70
	1949/50	1936-49		1971	1967-71
	1954	1936-53		1972	1968-72
	1959	1949-58		1973	1969-73
	1965	1955-64		1974	1970-74
	1969	1963-68		1975	1956-75
	1975	1966-74		1976	1972-76
	1981	1972-80		1977	1973-77
	1986	1977-85		1978	1974-78
	1999CD[iv]	1990-98		1978HS[ii]	1948-78
Birth rates	1948	1932-47		1979	1975-79
	1949/50	1932-49		1980	1976-80
	1951	1905-30[v]		1981	1962-81
		1930-50		1982	1978-82
	1952	1920-34[v]		1983	1979-83
				1984	1980-84
				1985	1981-85
				1986	1967-86
				1987	1983-87
				1988	1984-88
				1989	1985-89
				1990	1986-90
				1991	1987-91
				1992	1983-92
				1993	1989-93
				1994	1990-94

Subject-matter	Year of issue	Time coverage
	1995	1991-95
	1996	1992-96
	1997	1993-97
	1997HS[iii]	1948-97
	1998	1994-98
	1999	1995-99
	1999CD[iv]	1985-99
	2000	1996-00
	2001	1997-01
	2002	1998-02
- by age of father	1949/50	1942-49
	1954	1936-53
	1959	1949-58
	1965	1955-64
	1969	1963-68
	1975	1966-74
	1981	1972-80
	1986	1977-85
	1999CD[iv]	1990-98
- by age of mother	1948	1936-47
	1949/50	1936-49
	1951	1936-50
	1952	1936-50
	1953	1936-52
	1954	1936-53
	1955-1956	Latest
	1959	1949-58
	1965	1955-64
	1969	1963-68
	1975	1966-74
	1976-1978	Latest
	1978HS[ii]	1948-77
	1979-1980	Latest
	1981	1972-80
	1982-1985	Latest
	1986	1977-85
	1987-1991	Latest
	1992	1983-92
	1993-1997	Latest
	1997HS[iii]	1948-96
	1998-1999	Latest
	1999CD[iv]	1990-98
	2000-2002	Latest
- by age of mother and birth order	1954	1948 and 1951

Subject-matter	Year of issue	Time coverage
	1959	1949-58
	1965	1955-64
	1969	1963-68
	1975	1966-74
	1981	1972-80
	1986	1977-85
	1999CD[iv]	1990-98
- by age of mother and urban/rural residence (see: by urban/rural residence, below)		
- by birth order	1951	1936-49
	1952	1936-50
	1953	1936-52
	1954	1936-53
	1955	Latest
	1959	1949-58
	1965	1955-64
	1969	1963-68
	1975	1966-74
	1981	1972-80
	1986	1977-85
	1999CD[iv]	1990-98
- by urban/rural residence	1965	Latest
	1967	Latest
	1968	1964-68
	1969	1964-68
	1970	1966-70
	1971	1967-71
	1972	1968-72
	1973	1969-73
	1974	1970-74
	1975	1956-75
	1976	1972-76
	1977	1973-77
	1978	1974-78
	1979	1975-79
	1980	1976-80
	1981	1962-81
	1982	1978-82
	1983	1979-83
	1984	1980-84
	1985	1981-85
	1986	1967-86
	1987	1983-87
	1988	1984-88
	1989	1985-89

Subject-matter	Year of issue	Time coverage	Subject-matter	Year of issue	Time coverage
	1962	1953-62		1978HS[ii]	1948-77
	1963	1954-63		1980	1971-79
	1964	1960-64		1981-1984	Latest
	1966	1947-66		1985	1976-84
	1967	1963-67		1986-1991	Latest
	1968	1964-68		1992	1983-92
	1969	1965-69		1993-1995	Latest
	1970	1966-70		1996	1987-95
	1971	1967-71		1997	Latest
	1972	1968-72		1997HS[iii]	1948-96
	1973	1969-73		1998-2002	Latest
	1974	1965-74	- by age and sex and urban/rural residence		
	1975	1971-75		1967-1973	Latest
	1976	1972-76		1974	1965-73
	1977	1973-77		1975-1979	Latest
	1978	1974-78		1980	1971-79
	1978HS[ii]	1948-78		1981-1984	Latest
	1979	1975-79		1985	1976-84
	1980	1971-80		1986-1991	Latest
	1981	1977-81		1992	1983-92
	1982	1978-82		1993-1995	Latest
	1983	1979-83		1996	1987-95
	1984	1980-84		1997	Latest
	1985	1976-85		1997HS[iii]	1948-96
	1986	1982-86		1998-2002	Latest
	1987	1983-87			
	1988	1984-88	- by cause	1951	1947-50
	1989	1985-89		1952	1947-51[vi]
	1990	1986-90		1953	Latest
	1991	1987-91		1954	1945-53
	1992	1983-92		1955-1956	Latest
	1993	1989-93		1957	1952-56
	1994	1990-94		1958-1960	Latest
	1995	1991-95		1961	1955-60
	1996	1987-96		1962-1965	Latest
	1997	1993-97		1966	1960-65
	1997HS[iii]	1948-97		1967-1973	Latest
	1998	1994-98		1974	1965-73
	1999	1995-99		1975-1979	Latest
	2000	1996-00		1980	1971-79
	2001	1997-01		1981-1984	Latest
	2002	1998-02		1985	1976-84
				1986-1991	Latest
- by age and sex	1948	1936-47		1991PA[vii]	1960-90
	1951	1936-50		1992-1995	Latest
	1955-1956	Latest		1996	1987-95
	1957	1948-56		1997-2000	Latest
	1958-1960	Latest		2002	1985-02
	1961	1955-60			
	1962-1965	Latest	- by cause, age and sex	1951	Latest
	1966	1961-65		1952	Latest
	1967-1973	Latest		1957	Latest
	1974	1965-73		1961	Latest
	1975-1979	Latest			

Subject-matter	Year of issue	Time coverage	Subject-matter	Year of issue	Time coverage
	1979	1974-78		1965	5-Latest
	1980	1971-79		1966	1956-65
	1981	1972-80		1967-1968	Latest
	1982	1977-81		1969	1963-68
	1983	1978-82		1974	1965-73
	1984	1979-83		1975	1966-74
	1985	1975-84		1980	1971-79
	1986	1977-85		1981	1972-80
	1987	1982-86		1985	1976-84
	1988	1983-87		1986	1977-85
	1989	1984-88	- by urban/rural residence		
	1990	1985-89		1971	1966-70
	1991	1986-90		1972	1967-71
	1992	1987-91		1973	1968-72
	1993	1988-92		1974	1965-73
	1994	1989-93		1975	1966-74
	1995	1990-94		1976	1971-75
	1996	1987-95		1977	1972-76
	1997	1992-96		1978	1973-77
	1998	1993-97		1979	1974-78
	1999	1994-98		1980	1971-79
	1999CD[iv]	1990-98		1981	1972-80
	2000	1995-99		1982	1977-81
	2001	1997-01		1983	1978-82
	2002	1998-02		1984	1979-83
				1985	1975-84
- by age of mother	1954	1936-53		1986	1977-85
	1959	1949-58		1987	1982-86
	1965	1955-64		1988	1983-87
	1969	1963-68		1989	1984-88
	1975	1966-74		1990	1985-89
	1981	1972-80		1991	1986-90
	1986	1977-85		1992	1987-91
	1996	1987-95		1993	1988-92
	1999CD[iv]	1990-98		1994	1989-93
- by age of mother and birth order	1954	Latest		1995	1990-94
	1959	1949-58		1996	1987-95
	1965	3-Latest		1997	1992-96
	1969	1963-68		1998	1993-97
	1975	1966-74		1999	1994-98
	1981	1972-80		1999CD[iv]	1990-98
	1986	1977-85		2000	1995-99
	1999CD[iv]	1990-98		2001	1997-01
- by period of gestation				2002	1998-02
	1957	1950-56	- illegitimate	1961	1952-60
	1959	1949-58		1965	5-Latest
	1961	1952-60			
			- legitimate	1959	1949-58
				1965	1955-64
				1969	1963-68

Index
Historical index
(See notes at end of index)

Subject-matter	Year of issue	Time coverage
	1975	1966-74
	1981	1972-80
	1986	1977-85
- legitimate by age of mother	1959	1949-58
	1965	1955-64
	1969	1963-68
	1975	1966-74
	1981	1972-80
	1986	1977-85

G

Gestational age of foetal deaths (see: Foetal deaths)

Gross reproduction rates (see: Reproduction rates)

H

Homeless (see: Population)

Households

Subject-matter	Year of issue	Time coverage
- average size of	1962	1955-62
	1963	1955-63[vi]
	1968	Latest
	1971	1962-71
	1973	1965-73[vi]
	1976	Latest
	1982	Latest
	1987	1975-86
	1990	1980-89
- by age, sex of householder, size and urban/rural residence	1987	1975-86
- by family type and urban/rural residence	1987	1975-86
- by marital status of householder and urban/rural residence	1987	1975-86
	1995	1985-95
- by relationship to householder and urban/rural residence	1987	1975-86
	1995	1985-95
- by size	1955	1945-54
	1962	1955-62
	1963	1955-63[vi]
	1971	1962-71

Subject-matter	Year of issue	Time coverage
	1973	1965-73[vi]
	1976	Latest
	1982	Latest
	1987	1975-86
	1990	1980-89
	1995	1985-95
- and number of persons 60+	1991PA[vii]	Latest
- by urban/rural residence	1968	Latest
	1971	1962-71
	1973	1965-73[vi]
	1976	Latest
	1982	Latest
	1987	1975-86
	1990	1980-89
	1995	1985-95
- headship rates by age and sex of householder and urban/rural residence	1987	1975-86
	1995	1985-95
- number of	1955	1945-54
	1962	1955-62
	1963	1955-63[vi]
	1968	Latest
	1971	1962-71
	1973	1965-73[vi]
	1976	Latest
	1982	Latest
	1987	1975-86
	1990	1980-89
	1995	1985-95
- and number of persons 60+	1991PA[vii]	Latest
- number of family nuclei by size of	1973	1965-73
	1976	Latest
	1982	Latest
	1987	1975-86
	1990	1980-90
- population by relationship	1987	1975-86
	1991PA[vii]	Latest
- by sex and persons 60+	1991PA[vii]	Latest
- population in each type of	1955	1945-54
	1962	1955-62
	1963	1955-63[vi]
	1968	Latest
	1971	1962-71
	1973	1965-73[vi]
	1976	Latest
	1982	Latest

Subject-matter	Year of issue	Time coverage	Subject-matter	Year of issue	Time coverage
	1987	1975-86		1965	5-Latest
	1990	1980-89		1969	1963-68
	1995	1985-95		1975	1966-74
				1981	1972-80
				1986	1977-85

I

Subject-matter	Year of issue	Time coverage	Subject-matter	Year of issue	Time coverage
Illegitimacy rates and ratios			**Illiteracy rates(see: Population)**		
- of births	1959	1949-58			
	1965	1955-64	**Immigrants (see: Migration)**		
	1969	1963-68			
	1975	1966-74	Infant deaths............................	1948	1932-47
	1981	1972-80		1949/50	1934-49
	1986	1977-85		1951	1935-50
	1999CD^{iv}	1990-98		1952	1936-51
- of foetal deaths, late				1953	1950-52
	1961	1952-60		1954	1946-53
	1965	5-Latest		1955	1946-54
	1969	1963-68		1956	1947-55
	1975	1966-74		1957	1948-56
	1981	1972-80		1958	1948-57
	1986	1977-85		1959	1949-58
				1960	1950-59
Illegitimate (see also: Births and Foetal deaths, late)				1961	1952-61
				1962	1953-62
- birth(s)	1959	1949-58		1963	1954-63
	1965	1955-64		1964	1960-64
	1969	1963-68		1965	1961-65
	1975	1966-74		1966	1947-66
	1981	1972-80		1967	1963-67
	1986	1977-85		1968	1964-68
	1999CD^{iv}	1990-98		1969	1965-69
				1970	1966-70
- birth ratios	1959	1949-58		1971	1967-71
	1965	1955-64		1972	1968-72
	1969	1963-68		1973	1969-73
	1975	1966-74		1974	1965-74
	1981	1972-80		1975	1971-75
	1986	1977-85		1976	1972-76
	1999CD^{iv}	1990-98		1977	1973-77
				1978	1974-78
- foetal death(s),	1961	1952-60		1978HS^{ii}	1948-78
	1965	5-Latest		1979	1975-79
	1969	1963-68		1980	1971-80
	1975	1966-74		1981	1977-81
	1981	1972-80		1982	1978-82
	1986	1977-85		1983	1979-83
- foetal death ratios, late	1961	1952-60		1984	1980-84
				1985	1976-85
				1986	1982-86
				1987	1983-87
				1988	1984-88
				1989	1985-89
				1990	1986-90
				1991	1987-91
				1992	1983-92

Subject-matter	Year of issue	Time coverage
	1993	1989-93
	1994	1990-94
	1995	1991-95
	1996	1987-96
	1997	1993-97
	1997HS[iii]	1948-97
	1998	1994-98
	1999	1995-99
	2000	1996-00
	2001	1997-01
	2002	1998-02
- by age and sex	1948	1936-47
	1951	1936-49
	1957	1948-56
	1961	1952-60
	1962-1965	Latest
	1966	1956-65
	1967-1973	Latest
	1974	1965-73
	1975-1979	Latest
	1980	1971-79
	1981-1984	Latest
	1985	1976-84
	1986-1991	Latest
	1992	1983-92
	1993-1995	Latest
	1996	1987-95
	1997-2002	Latest
- by age and sex and urban/rural residence	1967-1973	Latest
	1974	1965-73
	1975-1979	Latest
	1980	1971-79
	1981-1984	Latest
	1985	1976-84
	1986-1991	Latest
	1992	1983-92
	1993-1995	Latest
	1996	1987-95
	1997-1999	Latest
- by month	1967	1962-66
	1974	1965-73
	1980	1971-79
	1985	1976-84
- by urban/rural residence	1967	Latest
	1968	1964-68
	1969	1965-69
	1970	1966-70
	1971	1967-71
	1972	1968-72
	1973	1969-73

Subject-matter	Year of issue	Time coverage
	1974	1965-74
	1975	1971-75
	1976	1972-76
	1977	1973-77
	1978	1974-78
	1979	1975-79
	1980	1971-80
	1981	1977-81
	1982	1978-82
	1983	1979-83
	1984	1980-84
	1985	1976-85
	1986	1982-86
	1987	1983-87
	1988	1984-88
	1989	1985-89
	1990	1986-90
	1991	1987-91
	1992	1983-92
	1993	1989-93
	1994	1990-94
	1995	1991-95
	1996	1987-96
	1997	1993-97
	1998	1994-98
	1999	1995-99
	2000	1996-00
	2001	1997-01
	2002	1998-02
Infant mortality rates..............	1948	1932-47
	1949/50	1932-49
	1951	1930-50
	1952	1920-34[v]
		1934-51
	1953	1920-39[v]
		1940-52
	1954	1920-39[v]
		1946-53
	1955	1920-34[v]
		1946-54
	1956	1947-55
	1957	1948-56
	1958	1948-57
	1959	1949-58
	1960	1950-59
	1961	1945-59[v]
		1952-61
	1962	1945-54[v]
		1952-62
	1963	1945-59[v]
	1963	1954-63
	1964	1960-64
	1965	1961-65

Subject-matter	Year of issue	Time coverage	Subject-matter	Year of issue	Time coverage
	1966	1962-66		1990	1980-89
	1967	1963-67	- by urban/rural residence		
	1968	1920-64ᵛ		1968	Latest
		1953-68		1969	1965-69
	1969	1965-69		1970	1966-70
	1970	1966-70		1971	1967-71
	1971	1967-71		1972	1968-72
	1972	1968-72		1973	1969-73
	1973	1969-73		1974	1970-74
	1974	1970-74		1975	1971-75
	1975	1971-75		1976	1957-76
	1976	1957-76		1977	1973-77
	1977	1973-77		1978	1974-78
	1978	1974-78		1979	1975-79
	1979	1975-79		1980	1976-80
	1980	1976-80		1981	1977-81
	1981	1977-81		1982	1963-82
	1982	1963-82		1983	1979-83
	1983	1979-83		1984	1980-84
	1984	1980-84		1985	1981-85
	1985	1981-85		1986	1982-86
	1986	1982-86		1987	1983-87
	1987	1983-87		1988	1984-88
	1988	1984-88		1989	1985-89
	1989	1985-89		1990	1971-90
	1990	1971-90		1991	1987-91
	1991	1987-91		1992	1988-92
	1992	1988-92		1993	1989-93
	1993	1989-93		1994	1990-94
	1994	1990-94		1995	1991-95
	1995	1991-95		1996	1992-96
	1996	1992-96		1997	1993-97
	1997	1993-97		1998	1994-98
	1998	1994-98		1999	1995-99
	1999	1995-99		2000	1996-00
	2000	1996-00		2001	1997-01
	2001	1997-01		2002	1998-02
	2002	1998-02			
- by age and sex	1948	1936-46	**Marriage rates, first** -by detailed age of groom and bride	1982	1972-81
	1949/50	1936-49		1990	1980-89
	1953	1936-51			
	1954	1936-52	**Married population by age and sex (see: Population by marital status)**		
	1958	1935-56			
	1968	1955-67			
	1976	1966-75	**Maternal death**	1951	1947-50
	1982	1972-81		1952	1947-51
	1987	1975-86		1953	Latest
	1990	1980-89		1954	1945-53
- by sex among marriageable population				1955-1956	Latest
	1958	1935-56		1957	1952-56
	1968	1935-67		1958-1960	Latest
	1976	1966-75		1961	1955-60
	1982	1972-81			

Subject-matter	Year of issue	Time coverage	Subject-matter	Year of issue	Time coverage
	1962-1965	Latest		1979	1969-78
	1966	1960-65		1980	1971-79
	1967-1973	Latest		1981	1972-80
	1974	1965-73		1982	1972-81
	1975-1979	Latest		1983	1973-82
	1980	1971-79		1984	1974-83
	1981	1972-80		1985	1975-84
	1982	1972-81		1986	1976-85
	1983	1973-82		1987	1977-86
	1984	1974-83		1988	1978-87
	1985	1975-84		1989	1979-88
	1986	1976-85		1990	1980-89
	1987	1977-86		1991	1981-90
	1988	1978-87		1992	1982-91
	1989	1979-88		1993	1983-92
	1990	1980-89		1994	1984-93
	1991	1981-90		1995	1985-94
	1992	1982-91		1996	1986-95
	1993	1983-92		1997	1987-96
	1994	1984-93		1998	1988-97
	1995	1985-94		1999	1989-98
	1996	1986-95		2000	1991-00
	1997	1987-96		2001	1991-00
	1998	1988-97		2002	1985-02
	1999	1989-98			
	2000	1991-00	**Migration (international):**		
	2001	1991-00	- arrivals	1970	1963-69
	2002	1985-02		1972	1965-71
				1974	1967-73
- by age	1951	Latest		1976	1969-75
	1952	Latest[vi]		1977	1967-76
	1957	Latest		1985	1975-84
	1961	Latest		1989	1979-88
	1967	Latest		1996	1986-95
	1974	Latest		1972	1965-71
	1980	Latest		1974	1967-73
	1985	Latest		1976	1969-75
			- arrivals, by major categories	1949/50	1945-49
Maternal mortality rates	1951	1947-50		1951	1946-50
	1952	1947-51		1952	1947-51
	1953	Latest		1954	1948-53
	1954	1945-53		1957	1951-56
	1955-1956	Latest		1959	1953-58
	1957	1952-62		1962	1956-61
	1958-1960	Latest		1966	1960-65
	1961	1955-60		1968	1966-67
	1962-1965	Latest		1977	1967-76
	1966	1960-65		1985	1975-84
	1967-1973	Latest		1989	1979-88
	1974	1965-73		1996	1986-95
	1975	1966-74			
	1976	1966-75	- continental and inter-continental	1948	1936-47
	1977	1967-76		1977	1967-76
	1978	1968-77			

Mortality [see: Death(s), Death rates, infant deaths, infant mortality rates, Foetal death(s), Foetal death ratios, Life tables, Maternal deaths, Maternal mortality rates, Neonatal deaths, Neo-natal mortality rates, Perinatal mortality, Post-neo-natal deaths, Post-neo-natal mortality rates]

N

Natality (see: Births and Birthrates)

Subject-matter	Year of issue	Time coverage	Subject-matter	Year of issue	Time coverage
	1973	1965-73	- by households, number and size (see also: Households)		
	1974-1978	Latest		1955	1945-54
	1978HS[ii]	1948-77		1962	1955-62
	1979-1991	Latest		1963	1955-63[vi]
	1991PA[vii]	1950-90		1968	Latest
	1992-1997	Latest		1971	1962-71
	1997HS[iii]	1948-97		1973	1965-73[vi]
	1998-2002	Latest		1976	Latest
estimated	1948-	1945 and		1982	Latest
	1949/50	Latest[vi]		1987	1975-86
	1951-1959	Latest		1990	1980-89
	1960	1940-60		1995	1985-95
	1961-1969	Latest	- by language and sex		
	1970	1950-70		1956	1945-55
	1971-1997	Latest		1963	1955-63
	1997HS[iii]	1948-97		1964	1955-64[vi]
	1998-2002	Latest		1971	1962-71
percentage distribution	1948-	1945 and		1973	1965-73[vi]
	1949/50	Latest[vi]		1979	1970-79[vi]
	1951-1952	Latest		1983	1974-83
- by country or area of birth and sex (see also: foreign-born, below)				1988	1980-88[vi]
	1956	1945-55		1993	1985-93
	1963	1955-63	- by level of education, age and sex		
	1964	1955-64[vi]		1956	1945-55
	1971	1962-71		1963	1955-63
	1973	1965-73[vi]		1964	1955-64[vi]
- by country or area of birth and sex and age (see also: foreign-born, below)				1971	1962-71
	1977	Latest		1973	1965-73[vi]
	1983	1974-83		1979	1970-79[vi]
	1989	1980-88[vi]		1983	1974-83
- by citizenship				1988	1980-88[vi]
	1956	1945-55		1993	1985-93
	1963	1955-63	- by literacy, age and sex (see also: illiteracy, below)		
	1964	1955-64[vi]		1948	Latest
	1971	1962-71		1955	1945-54
	1973	1965-73[vi]		1963	1955-63
- by citizenship, sex and age				1964	1955-64[vi]
	1977	Latest		1971	1962-71
	1983	1974-83	- by literacy, age and sex and urban/rural residence		
	1989	Latest		1973	1965-73[vi]
- by ethnic composition and sex				1979	1970-79[vi]
	1956	1945-55		1983	1974-83
	1963	1955-63		1988	1980-88[vi]
	1964	1955-64[vi]		1993	1985-93
	1971	1962-71	- by localities of: 100000+ inhabitants		
	1973	1965-73[vi]		1948	Latest
	1979	1970-79[vi]		1952	Latest
	1983	1974-83		1955	1945-54
	1993	1985-93		1960	1920-61
				1962	1955-62

Subject-matter	Year of issue	Time coverage	Subject-matter	Year of issue	Time coverage
by occupation, age and sex and urban/rural residence				1949/50	Latest
				1955	1945-54
				1964	1955-64
				1972	1962-72
	1973	1965-73[vi]	by status, industry, and sex and urban/rural residence		
	1979	1970-79[vi]			
	1984	1974-84			
	1988	1980-88[vi]		1973	1965-73[vi]
	1994	1985-94		1979	1970-79[vi]
by occupation, status and sex				1984	1974-84
				1988	1980-88[vi]
				1994	1985-94
	1956	1945-55	by status, occupation and sex		
	1964	1955-64		1956	1945-55
	1972	1962-72		1964	1955-64
by occupation, status and sex and urban/rural residence				1972	1962-72
			by status, occupation and sex and urban/rural residence		
	1973	1965-73[vi]		1973	1965-73[vi]
	1979	1970-7vi[vi]		1979	1970-79[vi]
	1984	1974-84		1984	1974-84
	1988	1980-88[vi]		1988	1980-88[vi]
	1994	1985-94		1994	1985-94
by sex	1948	Latest	female, by marital status and age		
	1949/50	1926-48			
	1955	1945-54			
	1956	1945-55		1956	1945-55
	1960	1920-60		1964	1955-64
	1963	1955-63		1968	Latest
	1964	1955-64		1972	1962-72
	1970	1950-70	female, by marital status and age and urban/rural residence		
	1972	1962-72			
	1973	1965-73[vi]			
	1979	1970-79[vi]			
	1984	1974-84		1973	1965-73[vi]
	1994	1985-94		1979	1970-79[vi]
by status, age and sex				1984	1974-84
	1956	1945-55		1988	1980-88[vi]
	1964	1955-64		1994	1985-94
	1972	1962-72	foreign-born by occupation, age and sex (see also: country of birth above)		
by status, age and sex and urban/rural residence					
				1984	1974-84
	1973	1965-73[vi]			1980-88
	1979	1970-79[vi]		1994	1985-94
	1984	1974-84	foreign-born by occupation and sex (see also: country of birth above)		
	1988	1980-88[vi]			
	1994	1985-94			
by status, industry and sex	1948	Latest		1977	Latest

Subject-matter	Year of issue	Time coverage	Subject-matter	Year of issue	Time coverage
unemployed, by age and sex	1949/50	1946-49	in households by age, sex of householder, size and relationship to householder and urban/rural residence		
- economically inactive by sub-groups and sex	1956	1945-54			
	1964	1955-64			
	1972	1962-72			
	1973	1965-73[vi]			
	1979	1970-79[vi]		1987	1975-86
	1984	1974-84[vi]		1995	1991-95
	1988	1980-88[vi]	institutional, by age, sex and urban/rural residence		
	1994	1985-94			
- Elderly					
- by economic, socio-demographic and urban/rural	1991PA[vii]	1950-90		1987	1875-86
				1995	1991-95
-female:			-growth rates:		
by age and duration of marriage	1968	Latest	average annual for countries or areas		
by number of children born alive and age	1949/50	Latest		1957	1953-56
	1954	1930-53		1958	1953-57
	1955	1945-54		1959	1953-58
	1959	1949-58		1960	1953-59
	1963	1955-63		1961	1953-60
	1965	1955-65		1962	1958-61
	1969	Latest		1963	1958-62
	1971	1962-71		1964	1958-63
	1973	1965-73[vi]		1965	1958-64
	1975	1965-74		1966	1958-66
	1978HS[ii]	1948-77		1967	1963-67
	1981	1972-80		1968	1963-68
	1986	1977-85		1969	1963-69
	1997HS[iii]	1948-96		1970	1963-70
by number of children living and age				1971	1963-71
				1972	1963-72
	1949/50	Latest		1973	1970-73
	1954	1930-53		1974	1970-74
	1955	1945-54		1975	1970-75
	1959	1949-58		1976	1970-76
	1963	1955-63		1977	1970-77
	1965	1955-65		1978	1975-78
	1968-1969	Latest		1979	1975-79
	1971	1962-71		1980	1975-80
	1973	1965-73[vi]		1981	1975-81
	1975	1965-74		1982	1975-82
	1978HS[ii]	1948-77		1983	1980-83
	1981	1972-80		1984	1980-84
	1986	1977-85		1985	1980-85
	1997HS[iii]	1948-96		1986	1980-86
				1987	1980-87
				1988	1985-88
				1989	1985-89

Subject-matter	Year of issue	Time coverage	Subject-matter	Year of issue	Time coverage
	1990	1985-90		1980-1983	1975-80
	1991	1985-91		1984-1986	1980-85
	1992	1985-92		1987-1992	1985-90
	1993	1990-93		1993-1997	1990-95
	1994	1990-94		1998-2000	1995-00
	1995	1990-95		2001-2002	2000-05
	1996	1990-96	- Homeless by age and sex		
	1997	1990-97		1991PA[vii]	Latest
	1998	1993-98	- illiteracy rates by sex		
	1999	1995-99		1948	Latest
	2000	1995-00		1955	1945-54
	2001-2002	2000-05		1960	1920-60
average annual for the world, macro-regions (continents) and regions				1963	1955-63[vi]
				1964	1955-64[vi]
				1970	1950-70
			- illiteracy rates by sex and urban/rural residence		
	1957	1950-56		1973	1965-73
	1958	1950-57		1979	1970-79[vi]
	1959	1950-58		1983	1974-83
	1960	1950-59		1988	1980-88[vi]
	1961	1950-60		1993	1985-93
	1962	1950-61	- illiterate, by sex	1948	Latest
	1963	1958-62		1955	1945-54
		1960-62		1960	1920-60
	1964	1958-63		1963	1955-63
		1960-63		1964	1955-64
	1965	1958-64		1970	1950-70
		1960-64	- illiterate, by sex and age	1948	Latest
	1966	1958-66		1955	1945-54
		1960-66		1963	1955-63
	1967	1960-67		1964	1955-64[vi]
		1963-67		1970	1950-70
	1968	1960-68	- illiterate, by sex and age and urban/rural residence		
		1963-68		1973	1965-73
	1969	1960-69		1979	1970-79[vi]
		1963-69		1983	1974-83
	1970	1963-70		1988	1980-88[vi]
		1965-70		1993	1985-93
	1971	1963-71	- illiterate, by sex and urban/rural residence		
		1965-71		1973	1965-73
	1972	1963-72		1979	1970-79[vi]
		1965-72		1983	1974-83
	1973	1965-73		1988	1980-88[vi]
		1970-73		1993	1985-93
	1974	1965-74	- in collective living quarters and homeless		
		1970-74		1991PA[vii]	Latest
	1975	1965-75			
		1970-75	- in households (see: by household		
	1976	1965-76			
		1970-76			
	1977	1965-77			
		1970-77			
	1978-1979	1970-75			

Index
Historical index
(See notes at end of index)

Subject-matter	Year of issue	Time coverage	Subject-matter	Year of issue	Time coverage
	1963	Latest		1994	1985-94
	1964	1955-64		1995	1986-95
	1965-1978	Latest		1996	1987-96
	1978HS[ii]	1948-78		1997	1988-97
	1979-1997	Latest		1997HS[iii]	1948-97
	1997HS[iii]	1948-97		1998	1989-98
	1998-2002	Latest		1999	1990-99
				2000	1991-00
estimated	1948	1932-47		2001	1992-01
	1949/50	1932-49		2002	1993-02
	1951	1930-50			
	1952	1920-51	- of major regions	1949/50	1920-49
	1953	1920-53		1951	1950
	1954	1920-54		1952	1920-51
	1955	1920-55		1953	1920-52
	1956	1920-56		1954	1920-53
	1957	1940-57		1955	1920-54
	1958	1939-58		1956	1920-55
	1959	1940-59		1957	1920-56
	1960	1920-60		1958	1920-57
	1961	1941-61		1959	1920-58
	1962	1942-62		1960	1920-59
	1963	1943-63		1961	1920-60
	1964	1955-64		1962	1920-61
	1965	1946-65		1963	1930-62
	1966	1947-66		1964	1930-63
	1967	1958-67		1965	1930-65
	1968	1959-68		1966	1930-66
	1969	1960-69		1967	1930-67
	1970	1950-70		1968	1930-68
	1971	1962-71		1969	1930-69
	1972	1963-72		1970	1950-70
	1973	1964-73		1971	1950-71
	1974	1965-74		1972	1950-72
	1975	1966-75		1973	1950-73
	1976	1967-76		1974	1950-74
	1977	1968-77		1975	1950-75
	1978	1969-78		1976	1950-76
	1978HS[ii]	1948-78		1977	1950-77
	1979	1970-79		1978	1950-78
	1980	1971-80		1979	1950-79
	1981	1972-81		1980	1950-80
	1982	1973-82		1981	1950-81
	1983	1974-83		1982	1950-82
	1984	1975-84		1983	1950-83
	1985	1976-85		1984	1950-84
	1986	1977-86		1985	1950-85
	1987	1978-87		1986	1950-86
	1988	1979-88		1987	1950-87
	1989	1980-89		1988	1950-88
	1990	1981-90		1989	1950-89
	1991	1982-91		1990	1950-90
	1992	1983-92		1991	1950-91
	1993	1984-93		1992	1950-92

Subject-matter	Year of issue	Time coverage	Subject-matter	Year of issue	Time coverage
	1993	1950-93		1995	1950-95
	1994	1950-94		1996	1950-96
	1995	1950-95		1997	1950-97
	1996	1950-96		1998-1999	1950-00
	1997	1950-97		2000	1950-00
	1998-1999	1950-00		2001	1950-01
	2000	1950-00		2002	1950-02
	2001	1950-01			
	2002	1950-02	- of the world	1949/50	1920-49
				1951	1950
- of regions	1949/50	1920-49		1952	1920-51
	1952	1920-51		1953	1920-52
	1953	1920-52		1954	1920-53
	1954	1920-53		1955	1920-54
	1955	1920-54		1956	1920-55
	1956	1920-55		1957	1920-56
	1957	1920-56		1958	1920-57
	1958	1920-57		1959	1920-58
	1959	1920-58		1960	1920-59
	1960	1920-59		1961	1920-60
	1961	1920-60		1962	1920-61
	1962	1920-61		1963	1930-62
	1963	1930-62		1964	1930-63
	1964	1930-63		1965	1930-65
	1965	1930-65		1966	1930-66
	1966	1930-66		1967	1930-67
	1967	1930-67		1968	1930-68
	1968	1930-68		1969	1930-69
	1969	1930-69		1970	1950-70
	1970	1950-70		1971	1950-71
	1971	1950-71		1972	1950-72
	1972	1950-72		1973	1950-73
	1973	1950-73		1974	1950-74
	1974	1950-74		1975	1950-75
	1975	1950-75		1976	1950-76
	1976	1950-76		1977	1950-77
	1977	1950-77		1978	1950-78
	1978	1950-78		1979	1950-79
	1979	1950-79		1980	1950-80
	1980	1950-80		1981	1950-81
	1981	1950-81		1982	1950-82
	1982	1950-82		1983	1950-83
	1983	1950-83		1984	1950-84
	1984	1950-84		1985	1950-85
	1985	1950-85		1986	1950-86
	1986	1950-86		1987	1950-87
	1987	1950-87		1988	1950-88
	1988	1950-88		1989	1950-89
	1989	1950-89		1990	1950-90
	1990	1950-90		1991	1950-91
	1991	1950-91		1992	1950-92
	1992	1950-92		1993	1950-93
	1993	1950-93		1994	1950-94
	1994	1950-94		1995	1950-95

R

Rates (see under following subject-matter headings: Annulments, Births, Deaths, Divorces, Fertility, Illiteracy, Infant Mortality, Intercensal, Life Tables, Literacy Marriages, Maternal mortality, Natural increase, Neo-natal mortality, Population growth, Post-neo-natal mortality, Reproduction)

Ratios (see under following

Index
Historical index
(See notes at end of index)

Subject-matter	Year of issue	Time coverage	Subject-matter	Year of issue	Time coverage
	1953	1850		1956	1945-55
		-1953		1963	1955-63
- Historical				1964	1955-64[vi]
Supplement	1978HS[ii]	1948-78		1971	1962-71
	1997HS[iii]	1948-97		1973	1965-73[vi]
- Marriage and				1979	1970-79[vi]
Divorce	1958	1930-57		1983	1974-83
	1968	1920-68		1988	1980-88[vi]
	1976	1957-76		1993	1985-93
	1982	1963-82	Ethnic		
	1990	1971-90	characteristics	1956	1945-55
- Migration				1963	1955-63
(international)	1977	1958-76		1964	1955-64[vi]
	1989	1975-88		1971	1962-71
				1973	1965-73[vi]
- Mortality	1951	1905-50		1979	1970-79[vi]
	1957	1930-56		1983	1974-83
	1961	1945-61		1988	1980-88[vi]
	1966	1920-66		1993	1985-93
	1967	1900-67	Fertility		
	1974	1965-74	characteristics	1940/50	1900-50
	1980	1971-80		1954	1900-53
	1985	1976-85		1955	1945-54
	1992	1983-92		1959	1935-59
	1996	1987-96		1963	1955-63
				1965	1955-65
- Natality	1949/50	1932-49		1969	Latest
	1954	1920-53		1971	1962-71
	1959	1920-58		1973	1965-73[vi]
	1965	1920-65		1975	1965-75
	1969	1925-69		1981	1972-81
	1975	1956-75		1986	1977-86
	1981	1962-81		1992	1983-92
	1986	1967-86	Geographic		
	1992	1983-92	characteristics	1952	1900-51
	1999CD[iv]	1980-99		1955	1945-54
- Nuptiality (see:				1962	1955-62
Marriage and				1964	1955-64[vi]
Divorce, above)				1971	1962-71
				1973	1965-73[vi]
- Population Ageing				1979	1970-79[vi]
and the Situation of				1983	1974-83
Elderly Persons	1991PA[vii]	1950-90		1988	1980-88[vi]
				1993	1985-93
- Population			Household		
Census:			characteristics	1955	1945-54
Economic				1962	1955-62
characteristics	1956	1945-55		1963	1955-63[vi]
	1964	1955-64		1971	1962-71
	1972	1962-72		1973	1965-73[vi]
	1973	1965-73[vi]		1976	1966-75
	1979	1970-79[vi]		1983	1974-83
	1984	1974-84		1987	1975-86
	1988	1980-88[vi]		1995	1985-95
	1994	1985-94			
Educational			Personal		
characteristics	1955	1945-54	characteristics	1955	1945-54

Subject-matter	Year of issue	Time coverage	Subject-matter	Year of issue	Time coverage
	1962	1955-62	**Urban/rural deaths** (see: Deaths)		
	1971	1962-71			
	1973	1965-73[vi]	**Urban/rural infant deaths** (see: Infant deaths)		
	1979	1970-79[vi]			
	1983	1974-83			
	1988	1980-88[vi]	**Urban/rural population** (see: Population: urban/rural residence)		
	1993	1985-93			
-Population trends	1960	1920-60			
	1970	1950-70	**Urban/rural population by average size of households** (see: Households)		

Urban/rural births
(see: Births)

APPENDIX

Special text of each Demographic Yearbook:

Divorce:
'Uses of Marriage and Divorce Statistics', 1958.

Marriage:
'Uses of Marriage and Divorce Statistics', 1958.

Households:
'Concepts and definitions of households, householder and institutional population', 1987.

Migration:
'Statistics of International Migration', 1977.

Mortality:
'Recent Mortality Trends', 1951.
'Development of Statistics of Causes of Death', 1951.
'Factors in Declining Mortality', 1957.
'Notes on Methods of Evaluating the Reliability of Conventional Mortality Statistics', 1961.
'Recent Trends of Mortality', 1966.
'Mortality Trends among Elderly Persons', 1991PA[vii].

Natality:
'Graphic Presentation of Trends in Fertility', 1959.
'Recent Trends in Birth Rates', 1965.
'Recent Changes in World Fertility', 1969.

Population
'World Population Trends, 1920-1949', 1949/50.
'Urban Trends and Characteristics', 1952.
'Background to the1950 Censuses of Population', 1955.
'The World Demographic Situation', 1956.
'How Well Do We Know the Present Size and Trend of the World's Population?', 1960.
'Notes on Availability of National Population Census Data and Methods of Estimating their Reliability', 1962.
'Availability and Adequacy of Selected Data Obtained from Population Censuses Taken 1955-1963', 1963.
'Availability of Selected Population Census Statistics: 1955-1964', 1964.
'Statistical Concepts and Definitions of Urban and Rural Population', 1967.
'Statistical Concepts and Definitions of Household', 1968.
'How Well Do We Know the Present Size and Trend of the World's Population?', 1970.
'United Nations Recommendations on Topics to be Investigated in a Population Census
Compared with Country Practice in National Censuses taken 1965-1971', 1971.
'Statistical Definitions of Urban Population and their Use in Applied Demography', 1972.
'Dates of National Population and Housing Census carried out during the decade1965-1974', 1974.
'Dates of National Population and/or Housing Censuses taken or anticipated during the decade 1975-1984', 1979.
'Dates of National Population and/or Housing Censuses taken during the decade1965-1974 and
taken or anticipated during the decade 1975-1984', 1983.
'Dates of National Population and/or Housing Censuses taken during the decade1975-1984 and taken or anticipated
during the decade 1985-1994', 1988 and 1993.
'Statistics Concerning the Economically Active Population: An Overview', 1984.
'Disability', 1991PA[vii].
'Population Ageing', 1991PA[vii].
'Special Needs for the Study of Population Ageing and Elderly Persons', 1991PA[vii].

General Notes

This cumulative index covers the contents of each of the 52 issues of the Demographic Yearbook. 'Year of issue' stands for the particular issue in which the indicated subject-matter appears. Unless otherwise specified, 'Time coverage' designates the years for which annual statistics are shown in the Demographic Yearbook referred to in 'Year of issue' column. 'Latest' or '2-Latest' indicates that data are for latest available year(s) only.

[i] Only titles not available for preceding bibliography.

[ii] Historical Supplement to the 30th DYB published in a separate volume in year 1979.

[iii] Historical Supplement to the 49th DYB published in a separate volume (CD-ROM) in year 2000.

[iv] Supplement to the 51st DYB focusing on natality published in a separate volume (CD-ROM) in year 2002.

[v] Five-year average rates.

[vi] Only data not available for preceding issue.

[vii] Population ageing published in separate volume.

Index
Index historique (suite)
(Voir notes à la fin de l'index)

Sujet	Année de l'édition	Période considérée

A

Accroissement intercensitaire de la population, taux d' ....

	Année de l'édition	Période considérée
	1948	1900-48
	1949/50	1900-50
	1951	1900-51
	1952	1850-1952
	1953	1850-1953
	1955	1850-1954
	1960	1900-61
	1962	1900-62
	1964	1955-64
	1970	1900-70
	1978 SR [i]	1948-78
	1997 SR [ii]	1948-97

Accroissement naturel, taux d' ....

	1958-1978	Dernière
	1978 SR [i]	1948-78
	1979-1997	Dernière
	1997 SR [ii]	1948-97
	1998	1995-98
	1999	1996-99
	2000	1995-00
	2001	2000-05
	2002	2000-05

Activité économique (voir: Population active)

Age (voir la rubrique appropriée par sujet, p.ex. Immigrants: Mortalité, taux de: Naissances: Population: etc.)

Analphabètes (voir:Population)

Alphabétisme selon le sexe, taux d' ....

	1948	Dernière
	1955	1945-54
	1960	1920-60
	1963	1955-63
	1964	1955-64 [iii]
	1970	1950-70
	1971	1962-71
	1973	1965-73[3]
	1979	1970-79 [iii]
	1983	1974-83
	1988	1980-88 [iii]
	1993	1985-93 [iii]

Alphabétisme selon le sexe et l'âge, taux d' ....

	1948	Dernière
	1955	1945-54
	1971	1962-71
	1973	1965-73 [iii]
	1979	1970-79 [iii]
	1983	1974-83
	1988	1980-88 [iii]

Sujet	Année de l'édition	Période considérée

Alphabètes (voir: Population)

Annulations

	1958	1948-57
	1968	1958-67
	1976	1966-75

Annulations, taux ....

	1958	1948-57
	1968	1958-67
	1976	1966-75

Avortements, légaux ....

	1971	Dernière
	1972	1964-72
	1973	1965-73
	1974	1965-74
	1975	1965-74
	1976	1965-75
	1977	1967-76
	1978	1968-77
	1979	1969-78
	1980	1971-79
	1981	1972-80
	1982	1973-81
	1983	1974-82
	1984	1975-83
	1985	1976-84
	1986	1977-85
	1987	1978-86
	1988	1979-87
	1989	1980-88
	1990	1981-89
	1992	1983-91
	1993	1984-92
	1994	1985-93
	1995	1986-94
	1996	1987-95
	1997	1988-96
	1998	1989-97
	1999	1990-98
	2000	1991-99
	2001	1993-01
	2002	1993-02

-selon l'âge de la mère et le nombre des naissances vivantes antèrieures de la mère

	1971-1975	Dernière
	1977-1981	Dernière
	1983-2002	Dernière

B

Bibliographie ....

	1948	1930-48
	1949/50	1930-50
	1951-1952	1930-51 [iv]
	1953	1900-53
	1954	1900-54 [iv]
	1955	1900-55 [iv]

C

Cause de décès (voir: Décès)

Index
Index historique (suite)
(Voir notes à la fin de l'index)

Index
Index historique (suite)
(Voir notes à la fin de l'index)

Index
Index historique (suite)
(Voir notes à la fin de l'index)

Index
Index historique (suite)
(Voir notes à la fin de l'index)

Index
Index historique (suite)
(Voir notes à la fin de l'index)

Index
Index historique (suite)
(Voir notes à la fin de l'index)

Sujet	Année de l'édition	Période considérée	Sujet	Année de l'édition	Période considérée
	1986	1977-85		1979	1975-79
-naissances	1959	1949-58		1980	1976-80
	1965	1955-64		1981	1977-81
	1969	1963-68		1982	1963-82
	1975	1966-74		1983	1979-83
	1981	1972-80		1984	1980-84
	1986	1977-85		1985	1981-85
	1999CD vii	1990-98		1986	1982-86
-naissances, rapports de	1959	1949-58		1987	1983-87
	1965	1955-64		1988	1984-88
	1969	1963-68		1989	1985-89
	1975	1966-74		1990	1971-90
	1981	1972-80		1991	1987-91
	1986	1977-85		1992	1988-92
	1999CD vii	1990-98		1993	1989-93
				1994	1990-94
Immigrants (voir: Migration internationale)				1995	1991-95
				1996	1992-96
Instruction, degré d' (voir: Population)				1997	1993-97
				1998	1994-98
				1999	1995-99
L				2000	1996-00
				2001	1997-01
				2002	1998-02
Langue et sexe (voir: Population)			-selon l'âge de l'épouse		
				1948	1936-47
Localités (voir: Population)				1949/50	1936-49
				1958	1948-57
M				1959-1967	Dernière
				1968	1958-67
				1969-1975	Dernière
				1976	1966-75
Mariages	1948	1932-47		1977-1981	Dernière
	1949/50	1934-49		1982	1972-81
	1951	1935-50		1983-1986	Dernière
	1952	1936-51		1987	1975-86
	1953	1950-52		1988-1989	Dernière
	1954	1946-53		1990	1980-89
	1955	1946-54		1991-1997	Dernière
	1956	1947-55		1998	1993-97
	1957	1948-56		1999	1994-98
	1958	1940-57		2000	1995-99
	1959	1949-58		2001	1997-01
	1960	1950-59		2002	1998-02
	1961	1952-61	-selon l'âge de l'épouse et l'âge de l'époux	1958	1948-57
	1962	1953-62		1968	Dernière
	1963	1954-63		1976	Dernière
	1964	1960-64		1982	Dernière
	1965	1956-65		1990	Dernière
	1966	1962-66	-selon l'âge de l'épouse et l'état matrimonial antérieur	1958	1948-57
	1967	1963-67		1968	Dernière
	1968	1949-68		1976	Dernière
	1969	1965-69		1982	Dernière
	1970	1966-70		1990	Dernière
	1971	1967-71	-selon l'âge de l'époux	1948	1936-47
	1972	1968-72		1949/50	1936-49
	1973	1969-73		1958	1948-57
	1974	1970-74		1959-1967	Dernière
	1975	1971-75		1968	1958-67
	1976	1957-76		1969-1975	Dernière
	1977	1973-77			
	1978	1974-78			

Index
Index historique (suite)
(Voir notes à la fin de l'index)

Sujet	Année de l'édition	Période considérée
	1976	1966-75
	1977-1981	Dernière
	1982	1972-81
	1983-1986	Dernière
	1987	1975-86
	1988-1989	Dernière
	1990	1980-89
	1991-1997	Dernière
	1998	1993-97
	1999	1994-98
	2000	1995-99
	2001	1997-01
	2002	1998-02
-selon l'âge de l'époux et l'âge de l'épouse	1958	1948-57
	1968	Dernière
	1976	Dernière
	1982	Dernière
	1990	Dernière
-selon l'âge de l'époux et l'état matrimonial Antérieur	1958	1946-57
	1968	Dernière
	1976	Dernière
	1982	Dernière
	1990	Dernière
-selon l'état matrimonial antérieur de l'épouse: et l'âge	1958	1946-57
	1968	Dernière
	1976	Dernière
	1982	Dernière
	1990	Dernière
-selon l'état matrimonial antérieur de l'épouse (suite): et l'état matrimonial antérieur de l'époux	1949/50	Dernière
	1958	1948-57
	1968	1958-67
	1976	1966-75
	1982	1972-81
	1990	1980-89
-selon l'état matrimonial antérieur de l'époux et l'âge	1958	1946-57
	1968	Dernière
	1976	Dernière
	1982	Dernière
	1990	Dernière
et l'état matrimonial antérieur de l'épouse	1949/50	Dernière
	1958	1948-57
	1968	1958-67
	1976	1966-75
	1982	1972-81
	1990	1980-89
-selon la résidence (urbaine/rurale)	1968	Dernière
	1969	1965-69
	1970	1966-70
	1971	1967-71
	1972	1968-72
	1973	1969-73

Sujet	Année de l'édition	Période considérée
	1974	1970-74
	1975	1971-75
	1976	1957-76
	1977	1973-77
	1978	1974-78
	1979	1975-79
	1980	1976-80
	1981	1977-81
	1982	1963-82
	1983	1979-83
	1984	1980-84
	1985	1981-85
	1986	1982-86
	1987	1983-87
	1988	1984-88
	1989	1985-89
	1990	1971-90
	1991	1987-91
	1992	1988-92
	1993	1989-93
	1994	1990-94
	1995	1991-95
	1996	1992-96
	1997	1993-97
	1998	1994-98
	1999	1995-99
	2000	1996-00
	2001	1997-01
	2002	1998-02
-selon le mois	1968	1963-67
Mariages, premiers:		
-classification détaillé selon l'âge de l'épouse et de l'époux	1976	Dernière
	1982	1972-81
	1990	1980-89
Mariages, taux de (voir: Nuptialité, taux de)		
Ménages:		
-dimension moyenne des	1962	1955-62
	1963	1955-63 [iii]
	1968	Dernière
	1971	1962-71
	1973	1965-73 [iii]
	1976	Dernière
	1982	Dernière
	1987	1975-86
	1990	1980-89
	1995	1985-95
-le lien avec le chef de ménage et la résidence urbaine/rurale	1987	1975-86
	1995	1985-95
-nombre de	1955	1945-54
	1962	1955-62
	1963	1955-63 [iii]
	1968	Dernière
	1971	1962-71
	1973	1965-73 [iii]

Index
Index historique (suite)
(Voir notes à la fin de l'index)

Index
Index historique (suite)
(Voir notes à la fin de l'index)

Index
Index historique (suite)
(Voir notes à la fin de l'index)

Index
Index historique (suite)
(Voir notes à la fin de l'index)

Sujet	Année de l'édition	Période considérée	Sujet	Année de l'édition	Période considérée
	1951	1935-50	résidence (urbaine/rurale)		
	1952	1936-51		1974	1965-73
	1953	1950-52		1975-1979	Dernière
	1954	1946-53		1980	1971-79
	1955	1946-54		1981-1984	Dernière
	1956	1947-55		1985	1976-84
	1957	1948-56		1986-1991	Dernière
	1958	1948-57		1992	1983-92
	1959	1949-58		1993-1995	Dernière
	1960	1950-59		1996	1987-95
	1961	1952-61		1998-2002	Dernière
	1962	1953-62	-selon la résidence	1967	Dernière
	1963	1954-63	(urbaine/rurale)	1968	1964-68
	1964	1960-64		1969	1965-69
	1965	1961-65		1970	1966-70
	1966	1947-66		1971	1967-71
	1967	1963-67		1972	1968-72
	1968	1964-68		1973	1969-73
	1969	1965-69		1974	1965-74
	1970	1966-70		1975	1971-75
	1971	1967-71		1976	1972-76
	1972	1968-72		1977	1973-77
	1973	1969-73		1978	1974-78
	1974	1965-74		1979	1975-79
	1975	1971-75		1980	1971-80
	1976	1972-76		1981	1977-81
	1977	1973-77		1982	1978-82
	1978	1974-78		1983	1979-83
	1978SR [i]	1948-78		1984	1980-84
	1979	1975-79		1985	1976-85
	1980	1971-80		1986	1982-86
	1981	1977-81		1987	1983-87
	1982	1978-82		1988	1984-88
	1983	1979-83		1989	1985-89
	1984	1980-84		1990	1986-90
	1985	1976-85		1991	1987-91
	1986	1982-86		1992	1983-92
	1987	1983-87		1993	1989-93
	1988	1984-88		1994	1990-94
	1989	1985-89		1995	1991-95
	1990	1986-90		1996	1987-96
	1991	1987-91		1997	1993-97
	1992	1983-92		1998	1994-98
	1993	1989-93		1999	1995-99
	1994	1990-94		2000	1996-00
	1995	1991-95		2001	1997-01
	1996	1987-96		2002	1998-02
	1997	1993-97	-selon le mois	1967	1962-66
	1997SR [ii]	1948-97		1974	1965-73
	1998	1994-98		1980	1971-79
	1999	1995-99		1985	1976-84
	2000	1996-00			
	2001	1997-01	**Mortalité infantile, taux de**	1948	1932-47
	2002	1998-02		1949/50	1932-49
-selon l'âge et le sexe	1948	1936-47		1951	1930-50
	1951	1936-49		1952	1920-34 [vi]
	1957	1948-56			1934-51
	1961	1952-60		1953	1920-39 [vi]
	1962-1965	Dernière			1940-52
	1966	1961-65		1954	1920-39 [vi]
	1967	1962-66			1946-53
-selon l'âge et le sexe et la	1968-1973	Dernière		1955	1920-34 [vi]

Index
Index historique (suite)
(Voir notes à la fin de l'index)

Sujet	Année de l'édition	Période considérée
		1946-54
	1956	1947-55
	1957	1948-56
	1958	1948-57
	1959	1949-58
	1960	1950-59
	1961	1945-59 [vi]
		1952-61
	1962	1945-59 [vi]
		1952-62
	1963	1945-59 [vi]
		1954-63
	1964	1960-64
	1965	1961-65
	1966	1920-64 [vi]
		1951-66
	1967	1963-67
	1968	1964-68
	1969	1965-69
	1970	1966-70
	1971	1967-71
	1972	1968-72
	1973	1969-73
	1974	1965-74
	1975	1971-75
	1976	1972-76
	1977	1973-77
	1978	1974-78
	1978SR [i]	1948-78
	1979	1975-79
	1980	1971-80
	1981	1977-81
	1982	1978-82
	1983	1979-83
	1984	1980-84
	1985	1976-85
	1986	1982-86
	1987	1983-87
	1988	1984-88
	1989	1985-89
	1990	1986-90
	1991	1987-91
	1992	1983-92
	1993	1989-93
	1994	1990-94
	1995	1991-95
	1996	1987-96
	1997	1993-97
	1997SR [ii]	1948-97
	1998	1994-98
	1999	1995-99
	2000	1996-00
	2001	1997-01
	2002	1998-02
-selon l'âge et le sexe	1948	1936-47
	1951	1936-49
	1957	1948-56
	1961	1952-60
	1966	1956-65
-selon l'âge et le sexe et la résidence (urbaine/rurale)	1971-1973	Dernière
	1974	1965-73

Sujet	Année de l'édition	Période considérée
	1975-1979	Dernière
	1980	1971-79
	1981-1984	Dernière
	1985	1976-84
	1986-1991	Dernière
	1992	1983-92
	1993-1995	Dernière
	1996	1987-95
	1997-2002	Dernière
-selon la résidence (urbaine/rurale)		
	1967	Dernière
	1968	1964-68
	1969	1965-69
	1970	1966-70
	1971	1967-71
	1972	1968-72
	1973	1969-73
	1974	1965-74
	1975	1971-75
	1976	1972-76
	1977	1973-77
	1978	1974-78
	1979	1975-79
	1980	1971-80
	1981	1977-81
	1982	1978-82
	1983	1979-83
	1984	1980-84
	1985	1976-85
	1986	1982-86
	1987	1983-87
	1988	1984-88
	1989	1985-89
	1990	1986-90
	1991	1987-91
	1992	1983-92
	1993	1989-93
	1994	1990-94
	1995	1991-95
	1996	1987-96
	1997	1993-97
	1998	1994-98
	1999	1995-99
	2000	1996-00
	2001	1997-01
	2002	1998-02
Mortalité liée à la maternité, taux de	1958	Dernière
	1975	1966-74
	1976	1966-75
	1977	1967-76
	1978	1968-77
	1979	1969-78
	1980	1971-79
	1981	1972-80
	1982	1972-81
	1983	1973-82
	1984	1974-83
	1985	1975-84
	1986	1976-85
	1987	1977-86

Index
Index historique (suite)
(Voir notes à la fin de l'index)

Index
Index historique (suite)
(Voir notes à la fin de l'index)

Index
Index historique (suite)
(Voir notes à la fin de l'index)

Index
Index historique (suite)
(Voir notes à la fin de l'index)

Index
Index historique (suite)
(Voir notes à la fin de l'index)

Sujet	Année de l'édition	Période considérée
l'âge et le sexe		
	1967	Dernière
	1974	Dernière
	1980	Dernière
	1985	Dernière
	1996	Dernière
-selon la profession, l'âge et le sexe	1957	Dernière
-selon la profession et l'âge (sexe masculin)	1961	Dernière
	1967	Dernière
-selon la résidence (urbaine/rurale)	1967	Dernière
	1968	1964-68
	1969	1965-69
	1970	1966-70
	1971	1967-71
	1972	1968-72
	1973	1969-73
	1974	1965-74
	1975	1971-75
	1976	1972-76
	1977	1973-77
	1978	1974-78
	1979	1975-79
	1980	1971-80
	1981	1977-81
	1982	1978-82
	1983	1979-83
	1984	1980-84
	1985	1976-85
	1986	1982-86
	1987	1983-87
	1988	1984-88
	1989	1985-89
	1990	1986-90
	1991	1987-91
	1992	1983-92
	1993	1989-93
	1994	1990-94
	1995	1991-95
	1996	1987-96
	1997	1993-97
	1998	1994-98
	1999	1995-99
	2000	1996-00
	2001	1997-01
	2002	1998-02
Mort-nés (voir: Morts fœtales tardives)		
Morts fœtales:		
-selon la période de gestation	1957	1950-56
	1959	1949-58
	1961	1952-60
	1965	5-Dernières
	1966	1956-65
	1967-1968	Dernière
	1969	1963-68
	1974	1965-73

Sujet	Année de l'édition	Période considérée
	1975	1966-74
	1980	1971-79
	1981	1972-80
	1985	1976-84
	1986	1977-85
	1996	1987-95
	1999CD [vii]	1990-98
Morts fœtales tardives	1951	1935-50
	1952	1936-51
	1953	1936-52
	1954	1938-53
	1955	1946-54
	1956	1947-55
	1957	1948-56
	1958	1948-57
	1959	1949-58
	1960	1950-59
	1961	1952-60
	1962	1953-61
	1963	1953-62
	1964	1959-63
	1965	1955-64
	1966	1947-65
	1967	1962-66
	1968	1963-67
	1969	1959-68
	1970	1965-69
	1971	1966-70
	1972	1967-71
	1973	1968-72
	1974	1965-73
	1975	1966-74
	1976	1971-75
	1977	1972-76
	1978	1973-77
	1979	1974-78
	1980	1971-79
	1981	1972-80
	1982	1977-81
	1983	1978-82
	1984	1979-83
	1985	1975-84
	1986	1977-85
	1987	1982-86
	1988	1983-87
	1989	1984-88
	1990	1985-89
	1991	1986-90
	1992	1987-91
	1993	1988-92
	1994	1989-93
	1995	1990-94
	1996	1987-95
	1997	1992-96
	1998	1993-97
	1999	1994-98
	1999CD [vii]	1990-98
	2000	1995-99
	2001	1997-01
	2002	1998-02
-illégitimes	1961	1952-60

Index
Index historique (suite)
(Voir notes à la fin de l'index)

Index
Index historique (suite)
(Voir notes à la fin de l'index)

Index
Index historique (suite)
(Voir notes à la fin de l'index)

Index
Index historique (suite)
(Voir notes à la fin de l'index)

Index
Index historique (suite)
(Voir notes à la fin de l'index)

Index
Index historique (suite)
(Voir notes à la fin de l'index)

Index
Index historique (suite)
(Voir notes à la fin de l'index)

Index
Index historique (suite)
(Voir notes à la fin de l'index)

Index
Index historique (suite)
(Voir notes à la fin de l'index)

Index
Index historique (suite)
(Voir notes à la fin de l'index)

Index
Index historique (suite)
(Voir notes à la fin de l'index)

Index
Index historique (suite)
(Voir notes à la fin de l'index)

Index
Index historique (suite)
(Voir notes à la fin de l'index)

Index
Index historique (suite)
(Voir notes à la fin de l'index)

Sujet	Année de l'édition	Période considérée
	1990	1980-89
	1997SR [ii]	1948-96
répartition en pourcentage	1948	Dernière
-selon le type de ménage et la résidence urbaine/rurale	1987	1975-86
	1995	1985-95
-selon l'importance des localités:		
de 100 000 habitants et plus	1948	Dernière
	1952	Dernière
	1955	1945-54
	1960	1920-61
	1962	1955-62
	1963	1955-63 [iii]
	1970	1950-70
	1971	1962-71
	1973	1965-73 [iii]
	1979	1970-79 [iii]
	1983	1974-83
	1988	1980-88 [iii]
	1993	1985-93
de 20 000 habitants et plus	1948	Dernière
	1952	Dernière
	1955	1945-54
	1960	1920-61
	1962	1955-62
	1963	1955-63 [iii]
	1970	1950-70
	1971	1962-71
	1973	1965-73 [iii]
	1979	1970-79 [iii]
	1983	1974-83
	1988	1980-88 [iii]
	1993	1985-93
-selon l'importance des localités et le sexe	1948	Dernière
	1952	Dernière
	1955	1945-54
	1962	1955-62
	1963	1955-63 [iii]
	1971	1962-71
	1973	1965-73 [iii]
	1979	1970-79 [iii]
	1983	1974-83
	1988	1980-88 [iii]
	1993	1985-93
-selon la langue et le sexe	1956	1945-55
	1963	1955-63
	1964	1955-64 [iii]
	1971	1962-71
	1973	1965-73 [iii]
	1979	1970-79 [iii]
	1983	1974-83
	1988	1980-88 [iii]
	1993	1985-93
-selon le niveau d'instruction, l'âge et le sexe	1956	1945-55
	1963	1955-63
	1964	1955-64 [iii]
	1971	1962-71

Sujet	Année de l'édition	Période considérée
	1973	1965-73 [iii]
	1979	1970-79 [iii]
	1983	1974-83
	1988	1980-88 [iii]
	1993	1985-93
-selon le pays ou zone de naissance et le sexe	1956	1945-55
	1963	1955-63
	1964	1955-64 [iii]
	1971	1962-71
	1973	1965-73 [iii]
-selon le pays ou zone de naissance et le sexe et l'âge	1977	Dernière
	1983	1974-83
	1989	1980-88
-selon la nationalité juridique et le sexe	1956	1945-55
	1963	1955-63
	1964	1955-64 [iii]
	1971	1962-71
	1973	1965-73 [iii]
-selon la nationalité juridique et le sexe et l'âge	1977	Dernière
	1983	1974-83
	1989	1980-88
-selon les principales divisions administratives (voir: des principales divisions administratives, ci-dessus)		
-selon la religion et le sexe	1956	1945-55
	1963	1955-63
	1964	1955-64 [iii]
	1971	1962-71
	1973	1965-73 [iii]
	1979	1970-79 [iii]
	1983	1974-83
	1988	1980-88 [iii]
	1993	1985-93
-selon la résidence (urbaine/rurale) (voir: urbaine/rurale (résidence), ci-dessous)		
-selon le sexe (voir: également: par année d'âge et par sexe, et aussi par groupes d'âge et par sexe, ci-dessus):		
dénombrée	1948-1952	Dernière
	1953	1950-52
	1954-1959	Dernière
	1960	1900-61
	1961	Dernière
	1962	1900-62
	1963	1955-63
	1964	1955-64
	1965-1969	Dernière
	1970	1950-70
	1971	1962-71
	1972	Dernière
	1973	1965-73
	1974-1978	Dernière

Index
Index historique (suite)
(Voir notes à la fin de l'index)

Sujet	Année de l'édition	Période considérée
	1978SR [i]	1948-78
	1979-1982	Dernière
	1983	1974-83
	1984-1991	Dernière
	1991 VP [v]	1950-90
	1992-1997	Dernière
	1997SR [ii]	1948-97
	1998-2002	Dernière
estimée	1948-	
	1949/50	1945 et Dernière
	1951-1954	Dernière [iii]
	1955-1959	Dernière
	1960	1940-60
	1961-1969	Dernière
	1970	1950-70
	1971	1962-71
	1972	Dernière
	1973	1965-73
	1974-1997	Dernière
	1997SR [ii]	1948-97
	1998-2002	Dernière
-urbaine/rurale (résidence)	1968	1964-68
	1969	1965-69
	1970	1950-70
	1971	1962-71
	1972	1968-72
	1973	1965-73
	1974	1966-74
	1975	1967-75
	1976	1967-76
	1977	1968-77
	1978	1969-78
	1979	1970-79
	1980	1971-80
	1981	1972-81
	1982	1973-82
	1983	1974-83
	1984	1975-84
	1985	1976-85
	1986	1977-86
	1987	1978-87
	1988	1979-88
	1989	1980-89
	1990	1981-90
	1991	1982-91
	1992	1983-92
	1993	1984-93
	1994	1985-94
	1995	1986-95
	1996	1987-96
	1997	1988-97
	1998	1989-98
	1999	1990-99
	2000	1991-00
	2001	1992-01
	2002	1993-02
féminine: selon le nombre total d'enfants nés vivants et l'âge	1971	1962-71
	1973	1965-73 [iii]
	1975	1965-74

Sujet	Année de l'édition	Période considérée
	1978SR [i]	1948-77
	1981	1972-80
	1986	1977-85
	1997SR [ii]	1948-96
féminine: selon le nombre total d'enfants vivants et l'âge	1971	1962-71
	1973	1965-73 [iii]
	1975	1965-74
	1978SR [i]	1948-77
	1981	1972-80
	1986	1977-85
	1997SR [ii]	1948-96
fréquentant l'école selon l'âge et le sexe	1971	1962-71
	1973	1965-73 [iii]
	1979	1970-79 [iii]
	1983	1974-83
	1988	1980-88 [iii]
	1988	1980-88 [iii]
	1993	1985-93
par année d'âge et par sexe	1971	1962-71
	1973	1965-73 [iii]
	1979	1970-79 [iii]
	1983	1974-83
	1993	1985-93
selon la situation familiale selon l'âge et le sexe: dénombrée	1991 VP [v]	Dernière
	1963	1955-63
	1964	1955-64 [iii]
	1967	Dernière
	1970	1950-70
	1971	1962-71
	1972	Dernière
	1973	1965-73
	1974-1978	Dernière
	1978SR [i]	1948-77
	1979-1991	Dernière
	1991VP [v]	1950-90
	1992-1997	Dernière
	1997SR [ii]	1948-97
	1998-2002	Dernière
selon l'âge et le sexe: estimée	1963	Dernière
	1967	Dernière
	1970	1950-70
	1971-1997	Dernière
	1997SR [ii]	1948-97
	1998-1999	Dernière
selon l'alphabétisme, l'âge et le sexe	1971	1962-71
	1973	1965-73 [iii]
	1979	1970-79 [iii]
	1983	1974-83
	1988	1980-88 [iii]
	1993	1985-93
selon la composition ethnique et le sexe	1971	1962-71
	1973	1965-73 [iii]
	1979	1970-79 [iii]
	1983	1974-83

Index
Index historique (suite)
(Voir notes à la fin de l'index)

Sujet	Année de l'édition	Période considérée	Sujet	Année de l'édition	Période considérée
	1988	1980-88 [iii]		1973	1965-73
	1993	1985-93		1974	1966-74
	1971	1962-71		1975	1967-75
selon l'état matrimonial, l'âge et le sexe	1971	1962-71		1976	1967-76
	1973	1965-73 [iii]		1977	1968-77
selon la langue et le sexe	1971	1962-71		1978	1969-78
	1973	1965-73 [iii]		1979	1970-79
	1979	1970-79 [iii]		1980	1971-80
	1983	1974-83		1981	1972-81
	1988	1980-88 [iii]		1982	1973-82
	1993	1985-93		1983	1974-83
selon la nationalité juridique et le sexe	1971	1962-71		1984	1975-84
	1973	1965-73 [iii]		1985	1976-85
selon la nationalité juridique et le sexe et l'âge	1977	Dernière		1986	1977-86
	1983	1974-83		1987	1978-87
	1989	1980-88		1988	1979-88
selon le niveau d'instruction, l'âge et le sexe	1971	1962-71		1989	1980-89
	1973	1965-73 [iii]		1990	1981-90
	1979	1970-79 [iii]		1991	1982-91
	1983	1974-83		1992	1983-92
	1988	1980-88 [iii]		1993	1984-93
	1993	1985-93		1994	1985-94
selon le pays ou zone de naissance et le sexe	1971	1962-71		1995	1986-95
	1973	1965-73 [iii]		1996	1987-96
selon le pays ou zone de naissance et le sexe et l'âge	1977	Dernière		1997	1988-97
	1983	1974-83		1998	1989-98
	1989	1980-88		1999	1990-99
selon les principales divisions administratives	1971	1962-71		2000	1991-00
	1973	1965-73 [iii]		2001	1992-01
	1979	1970-79 [iii]		2002	1993-02
	1983	1974-83	pourcentage	1948	Dernière
	1988	1980-88 [iii]		1952	1900-51
	1993	1985-93		1955	1945-54
selon la religion et le sexe	1971	1962-71		1960	1920-60
	1973	1965-73 [iii]		1962	1955-62
	1979	1970-79 [iii]		1970	1950-70
	1983	1974-83		1971	1962-71
	1988	1980-88 [iii]		1973	1965-73
	1993	1985-93		1974	1966-74
selon le sexe: nombres	1948	Dernière		1975	1967-75
	1952	1900-51		1976	1967-76
	1955	1945-54		1977	1968-77
	1960	1920-60		1978	1969-78
	1962	1955-62		1979	1970-79
	1963	1955-63		1980	1971-80
	1964	1955-64 [iii]		1981	1972-81
	1967	Dernière		1982	1973-82
	1970	1950-70		1983	1974-83
	1971	1962-71		1984	1975-84
	1972	Dernière		1985	1976-85
				1986	1977-86
				1987	1978-87
				1988	1979-88
				1989	1980-89
				1990	1981-90
				1991	1982-91
				1992	1983-92
				1993	1984-93
				1994	1985-94
				1995	1986-95
				1996	1987-96
				1997	1988-97

Index
Index historique (suite)
(Voir notes à la fin de l'index)

Index
Index historique (suite)
(Voir notes à la fin de l'index)

Index
Index historique (suite)
(Voir notes à la fin de l'index)

Sujet	Année de l'édition	Période considérée	Sujet	Année de l'édition	Période considérée
Ménages)					
Urbaine/rurale (mortalité infantile) (voir: Mortalité infantile)			**V**		
Urbaine/rurale(naissances) (voir: Naissances)			**Vieillissement** (voir: Population)		
Urbaine/rurale(population)			**Villes** (voir: Population)		

Index
Index historique (suite)
(Voir notes à la fin de l'index)

APPENDICE

Texte spécial de chaque Annuaire démographique

Divorce:

"Application des statistiques de la nuptialité et de la divortialité", 1958.

Mariage:

"Application des statistiques de la nuptialité et de la divortialité", 1958.

Ménages:

"Concepts et définitions des ménages, du chef de ménage et de la population des collectivités", 1987.

Migration:

"'Statistiques des migrations internationales",1977.

Mortalité:

"Tendances récentes de la mortalité", 1951.
"Développement des statistiques des causes de décès",1951.
"Les facteurs du fléchissement de la mortalité",1957.
"Notes sur les méthodes d'évaluation de la fiabilité des statistiques classiques de la mortalité",1961.
"Mortalité: Tendances récentes",1966.
"Tendances de la mortalité chez les personnes âgées",1991VP [v].

Natalité:

"Présentation graphiques des tendances de la fécondité",1959.

"Taux de natalité: Tendances récentes",1965.

Population:

"Tendances démo-graphiques mondiales,1920-1949",1949/50.
"Mouvements d'urbanisation et ses caractéristiques",1952.
"Les recensements de population de 1950",1955.
"Situation démographique mondiale",1956.
"Ce que nous savons de l'état et de l'évolution de la population mondiale",1960.
"Notes sur les statistiques disponibles des recensements nationaux de population et méthodes d'évaluation de leur exactitude",1962.
"Disponibilité et qualité de certaines données statistiques fondées sur les recensements de population effectués entre 1955 et 1963",1963.
"Disponibilité de certaines statistiques fondées sur les recensements de population: 1955-1964",1964.
"Définitions et concepts statistiques de la population urbaine et de la population rurale",1967.
"Application des statistiques de la nuptialité et de la divortialité",1958.
"Ce que nous savons de l'état et de l'évolution de la population mondiale",1970.
"Recommandations de l'Organisation des Nations Unies quant aux sujets sur lesquels doit porter un recensement de population, en regard de la pratique adoptée par les différents pays dans les recensements nationaux effectués de 1965 à 1971",1971.
"Les définitions statistiques de la population urbaine et leurs usages en démographie appliquée",1972.
"Evolution récente de la fécondité dans le monde",1969.
"Dates des recensements nationaux de la population et de l'habitation effectués au cours de la décennie 1965-1974", 1974.
"Dates des recensements nationaux de la population et de l'habitation effectués ou prévus, au cours de la décennie 1975-1984",1979.
"Dates des recensements nationaux de la population et/ou de l'habitation effectués au cours de la décennie 1965-1974 et effectués ou prévus au cours de la décennie1975-1984",1983.
"Définitions et concepts statistiques du ménage",1968.
"Dates des recensements nationaux de la population et/ou de l'habitation effectués au cours de la décennie 1975-1984 et effectués ou prévus au cours de la décennie1985-1994", 1988, 1993.
"Statistiques concernant la population active: un aperçu",1984.

Index
Index historique (suite)
(Voir notes à la fin de l'index)

"'Etude du vieillissement et de la situation des personnes âgées: Besoins particuliers",1991VP [v].
"Les incapacités", 1991VP [v].
"Le vieillissement", 1991VP [v].

Notes générales

Cet index alphabétique donne la liste des sujets traités dans chacune de 51 éditions de l'Annuaire démographique. La colonne "Année de l'édition" indique l'édition spécifique dans laquelle le sujet a été traité. Sauf indication contraire, la colonne "Période considérée" désigne les années pour lesquelles les statistiques annuelles apparaissant dans l'Annuaire démographique sont indiquées sous la colonne "Année de l'édition". La rubrique "Dernière" ou " 2-Dernières" indique que les données représentent la ou les dernières années disponibles seulement.

---

[i] Le Supplément rétrospectif du 30ème Annuaire Démographique fait l'objet d'un tirage spécial publié en 1979.

[ii] Le Supplément rétrospectif du 49ème Annuaire Démographique fait l'objet d'un tirage spécial (CD-ROM) publié en 2000

[iii] Données non disponibles dans l'édition précédente seulement.

[iv] Titres non disponibles dans la bibliographie précédente seulement.

[v] Taux moyens pour 5 ans.

[vi] Vieillissement de la population.

[vii] Le Supplément du 51 Annuaire Démographique, ayant comme suject la natalité, fait l'objet d'un tirage spécial (CD-ROM) publié en 2002.